Oxford Dictionary of
National Biography

Volume 14

Oxford Dictionary of National Biography

IN ASSOCIATION WITH

The British Academy

From the earliest times to the year 2000

Edited by
H. C. G. Matthew
and
Brian Harrison

Volume 14
Cranfield–Dalwood

OXFORD
UNIVERSITY PRESS

OXFORD

UNIVERSITY PRESS

Great Clarendon Street, Oxford OX2 6DP

Oxford University Press is a department of the University of Oxford.
It furthers the University's objective of excellence in research, scholarship,
and education by publishing worldwide in

Oxford New York

Auckland Bangkok Buenos Aires Cape Town
Chennai Dar es Salaam Delhi Hong Kong Istanbul Karachi
Kolkata Kuala Lumpur Madrid Melbourne Mexico City Mumbai Nairobi
São Paulo Shanghai Taipei Tokyo Toronto

Oxford is a registered trade mark of Oxford University Press
in the UK and in certain other countries

Published in the United States
by Oxford University Press Inc., New York

© Oxford University Press 2004

Illustrations © individual copyright holders as listed in
'Picture credits', and reproduced with permission

Database right Oxford University Press (maker)

First published 2004

All rights reserved. No part of this material may be reproduced,
stored in a retrieval system, or transmitted, in any form or by any means,
without the prior permission in writing of Oxford University Press,
or as expressly permitted by law, or under terms agreed with the appropriate
reprographics rights organization. Enquiries concerning reproduction
outside the scope of the above should be sent to the Rights Department,
Oxford University Press, at the address above

You must not circulate this book in any other binding or cover
and you must impose this same condition on any acquirer

British Library Cataloguing in Publication Data
Data available

Library of Congress Cataloging in Publication Data
Data available: for details see volume 1, p. iv

ISBN 0-19-861364-4 (this volume)
ISBN 0-19-861411-X (set of sixty volumes)

Text captured by Alliance Phototypesetters, Pondicherry
Illustrations reproduced and archived by
Alliance Graphics Ltd, UK
Typeset in OUP Swift by Interactive Sciences Limited, Gloucester
Printed in Great Britain on acid-free paper by
Butler and Tanner Ltd,
Frome, Somerset

LIST OF ABBREVIATIONS

1 *General abbreviations*

AB	bachelor of arts		BCnL	bachelor of canon law
ABC	Australian Broadcasting Corporation		BCom	bachelor of commerce
ABC TV	ABC Television		BD	bachelor of divinity
act.	active		BEd	bachelor of education
A$	Australian dollar		BEng	bachelor of engineering
AD	*anno domini*		bk *pl.* bks	book(s)
AFC	Air Force Cross		BL	bachelor of law / letters / literature
AIDS	acquired immune deficiency syndrome		BLitt	bachelor of letters
AK	Alaska		BM	bachelor of medicine
AL	Alabama		BMus	bachelor of music
A level	advanced level [examination]		BP	before present
ALS	associate of the Linnean Society		BP	British Petroleum
AM	master of arts		Bros.	Brothers
AMICE	associate member of the Institution of Civil Engineers		BS	(1) bachelor of science; (2) bachelor of surgery; (3) British standard
ANZAC	Australian and New Zealand Army Corps		BSc	bachelor of science
appx *pl.* appxs	appendix(es)		BSc (Econ.)	bachelor of science (economics)
AR	Arkansas		BSc (Eng.)	bachelor of science (engineering)
ARA	associate of the Royal Academy		bt	baronet
ARCA	associate of the Royal College of Art		BTh	bachelor of theology
ARCM	associate of the Royal College of Music		*bur.*	buried
ARCO	associate of the Royal College of Organists		C.	command [identifier for published parliamentary papers]
ARIBA	associate of the Royal Institute of British Architects		*c.*	*circa*
ARP	air-raid precautions		c.	*capitulum pl. capitula*: chapter(s)
ARRC	associate of the Royal Red Cross		CA	California
ARSA	associate of the Royal Scottish Academy		Cantab.	Cantabrigiensis
art.	article / item		cap.	*capitulum pl. capitula*: chapter(s)
ASC	Army Service Corps		CB	companion of the Bath
Asch	Austrian Schilling		CBE	commander of the Order of the British Empire
ASDIC	Antisubmarine Detection Investigation Committee		CBS	Columbia Broadcasting System
ATS	Auxiliary Territorial Service		cc	cubic centimetres
ATV	Associated Television		C$	Canadian dollar
Aug	August		CD	compact disc
AZ	Arizona		Cd	command [identifier for published parliamentary papers]
b.	born		CE	Common (*or* Christian) Era
BA	bachelor of arts		cent.	century
BA (Admin.)	bachelor of arts (administration)		cf.	compare
BAFTA	British Academy of Film and Television Arts		CH	Companion of Honour
BAO	bachelor of arts in obstetrics		chap.	chapter
bap.	baptized		ChB	bachelor of surgery
BBC	British Broadcasting Corporation / Company		CI	Imperial Order of the Crown of India
BC	before Christ		CIA	Central Intelligence Agency
BCE	before the common (*or* Christian) era		CID	Criminal Investigation Department
BCE	bachelor of civil engineering		CIE	companion of the Order of the Indian Empire
BCG	bacillus of Calmette and Guérin [inoculation against tuberculosis]		Cie	Compagnie
BCh	bachelor of surgery		CLit	companion of literature
BChir	bachelor of surgery		CM	master of surgery
BCL	bachelor of civil law		cm	centimetre(s)

Cmd	command [identifier for published parliamentary papers]
CMG	companion of the Order of St Michael and St George
Cmnd	command [identifier for published parliamentary papers]
CO	Colorado
Co.	company
co.	county
col. *pl.* cols.	column(s)
Corp.	corporation
CSE	certificate of secondary education
CSI	companion of the Order of the Star of India
CT	Connecticut
CVO	commander of the Royal Victorian Order
cwt	hundredweight
$	(American) dollar
d.	(1) penny (pence); (2) died
DBE	dame commander of the Order of the British Empire
DCH	diploma in child health
DCh	doctor of surgery
DCL	doctor of civil law
DCnL	doctor of canon law
DCVO	dame commander of the Royal Victorian Order
DD	doctor of divinity
DE	Delaware
Dec	December
dem.	demolished
DEng	doctor of engineering
des.	destroyed
DFC	Distinguished Flying Cross
DipEd	diploma in education
DipPsych	diploma in psychiatry
diss.	dissertation
DL	deputy lieutenant
DLitt	doctor of letters
DLittCelt	doctor of Celtic letters
DM	(1) Deutschmark; (2) doctor of medicine; (3) doctor of musical arts
DMus	doctor of music
DNA	dioxyribonucleic acid
doc.	document
DOL	doctor of oriental learning
DPH	diploma in public health
DPhil	doctor of philosophy
DPM	diploma in psychological medicine
DSC	Distinguished Service Cross
DSc	doctor of science
DSc (Econ.)	doctor of science (economics)
DSc (Eng.)	doctor of science (engineering)
DSM	Distinguished Service Medal
DSO	companion of the Distinguished Service Order
DSocSc	doctor of social science
DTech	doctor of technology
DTh	doctor of theology
DTM	diploma in tropical medicine
DTMH	diploma in tropical medicine and hygiene
DU	doctor of the university
DUniv	doctor of the university
dwt	pennyweight
EC	European Community
ed. *pl.* eds.	edited / edited by / editor(s)
Edin.	Edinburgh

edn	edition
EEC	European Economic Community
EFTA	European Free Trade Association
EICS	East India Company Service
EMI	Electrical and Musical Industries (Ltd)
Eng.	English
enl.	enlarged
ENSA	Entertainments National Service Association
ep. *pl.* epp.	*epistola(e)*
ESP	extra-sensory perception
esp.	especially
esq.	esquire
est.	estimate / estimated
EU	European Union
ex	sold by (*lit.* out of)
excl.	excludes / excluding
exh.	exhibited
exh. cat.	exhibition catalogue
f. *pl.* ff.	following [pages]
FA	Football Association
FACP	fellow of the American College of Physicians
facs.	facsimile
FANY	First Aid Nursing Yeomanry
FBA	fellow of the British Academy
FBI	Federation of British Industries
FCS	fellow of the Chemical Society
Feb	February
FEng	fellow of the Fellowship of Engineering
FFCM	fellow of the Faculty of Community Medicine
FGS	fellow of the Geological Society
fig.	figure
FIMechE	fellow of the Institution of Mechanical Engineers
FL	Florida
fl.	*floruit*
FLS	fellow of the Linnean Society
FM	frequency modulation
fol. *pl.* fols.	folio(s)
Fr	French francs
Fr.	French
FRAeS	fellow of the Royal Aeronautical Society
FRAI	fellow of the Royal Anthropological Institute
FRAM	fellow of the Royal Academy of Music
FRAS	(1) fellow of the Royal Asiatic Society; (2) fellow of the Royal Astronomical Society
FRCM	fellow of the Royal College of Music
FRCO	fellow of the Royal College of Organists
FRCOG	fellow of the Royal College of Obstetricians and Gynaecologists
FRCP(C)	fellow of the Royal College of Physicians of Canada
FRCP (Edin.)	fellow of the Royal College of Physicians of Edinburgh
FRCP (Lond.)	fellow of the Royal College of Physicians of London
FRCPath	fellow of the Royal College of Pathologists
FRCPsych	fellow of the Royal College of Psychiatrists
FRCS	fellow of the Royal College of Surgeons
FRGS	fellow of the Royal Geographical Society
FRIBA	fellow of the Royal Institute of British Architects
FRICS	fellow of the Royal Institute of Chartered Surveyors
FRS	fellow of the Royal Society
FRSA	fellow of the Royal Society of Arts

FRSCM	fellow of the Royal School of Church Music
FRSE	fellow of the Royal Society of Edinburgh
FRSL	fellow of the Royal Society of Literature
FSA	fellow of the Society of Antiquaries
ft	foot *pl.* feet
FTCL	fellow of Trinity College of Music, London
ft-lb per min.	foot-pounds per minute [unit of horsepower]
FZS	fellow of the Zoological Society
GA	Georgia
GBE	knight or dame grand cross of the Order of the British Empire
GCB	knight grand cross of the Order of the Bath
GCE	general certificate of education
GCH	knight grand cross of the Royal Guelphic Order
GCHQ	government communications headquarters
GCIE	knight grand commander of the Order of the Indian Empire
GCMG	knight or dame grand cross of the Order of St Michael and St George
GCSE	general certificate of secondary education
GCSI	knight grand commander of the Order of the Star of India
GCStJ	bailiff or dame grand cross of the order of St John of Jerusalem
GCVO	knight or dame grand cross of the Royal Victorian Order
GEC	General Electric Company
Ger.	German
GI	government (*or* general) issue
GMT	Greenwich mean time
GP	general practitioner
GPU	[Soviet special police unit]
GSO	general staff officer
Heb.	Hebrew
HEICS	Honourable East India Company Service
HI	Hawaii
HIV	human immunodeficiency virus
HK$	Hong Kong dollar
HM	his / her majesty('s)
HMAS	his / her majesty's Australian ship
HMNZS	his / her majesty's New Zealand ship
HMS	his / her majesty's ship
HMSO	His / Her Majesty's Stationery Office
HMV	His Master's Voice
Hon.	Honourable
hp	horsepower
hr	hour(s)
HRH	his / her royal highness
HTV	Harlech Television
IA	Iowa
ibid.	*ibidem*: in the same place
ICI	Imperial Chemical Industries (Ltd)
ID	Idaho
IL	Illinois
illus.	illustration
illustr.	illustrated
IN	Indiana
in.	inch(es)
Inc.	Incorporated
incl.	includes / including
IOU	I owe you
IQ	intelligence quotient
Ir£	Irish pound
IRA	Irish Republican Army

ISO	companion of the Imperial Service Order
It.	Italian
ITA	Independent Television Authority
ITV	Independent Television
Jan	January
JP	justice of the peace
jun.	junior
KB	knight of the Order of the Bath
KBE	knight commander of the Order of the British Empire
KC	king's counsel
kcal	kilocalorie
KCB	knight commander of the Order of the Bath
KCH	knight commander of the Royal Guelphic Order
KCIE	knight commander of the Order of the Indian Empire
KCMG	knight commander of the Order of St Michael and St George
KCSI	knight commander of the Order of the Star of India
KCVO	knight commander of the Royal Victorian Order
keV	kilo-electron-volt
KG	knight of the Order of the Garter
KGB	[Soviet committee of state security]
KH	knight of the Royal Guelphic Order
KLM	Koninklijke Luchtvaart Maatschappij (Royal Dutch Air Lines)
km	kilometre(s)
KP	knight of the Order of St Patrick
KS	Kansas
KT	knight of the Order of the Thistle
kt	knight
KY	Kentucky
£	pound(s) sterling
£E	Egyptian pound
L	lira *pl.* lire
l. *pl.* ll.	line(s)
LA	Lousiana
LAA	light anti-aircraft
LAH	licentiate of the Apothecaries' Hall, Dublin
Lat.	Latin
lb	pound(s), unit of weight
LDS	licence in dental surgery
lit.	literally
LittB	bachelor of letters
LittD	doctor of letters
LKQCPI	licentiate of the King and Queen's College of Physicians, Ireland
LLA	lady literate in arts
LLB	bachelor of laws
LLD	doctor of laws
LLM	master of laws
LM	licentiate in midwifery
LP	long-playing record
LRAM	licentiate of the Royal Academy of Music
LRCP	licentiate of the Royal College of Physicians
LRCPS (Glasgow)	licentiate of the Royal College of Physicians and Surgeons of Glasgow
LRCS	licentiate of the Royal College of Surgeons
LSA	licentiate of the Society of Apothecaries
LSD	lysergic acid diethylamide
LVO	lieutenant of the Royal Victorian Order
M. *pl.* MM.	Monsieur *pl.* Messieurs
m	metre(s)

m. *pl.* mm.	membrane(s)		ND	North Dakota
MA	(1) Massachusetts; (2) master of arts		n.d.	no date
MAI	master of engineering		NE	Nebraska
MB	bachelor of medicine		*nem. con.*	*nemine contradicente*: unanimously
MBA	master of business administration		new ser.	new series
MBE	member of the Order of the British Empire		NH	New Hampshire
MC	Military Cross		NHS	National Health Service
MCC	Marylebone Cricket Club		NJ	New Jersey
MCh	master of surgery		NKVD	[Soviet people's commissariat for internal affairs]
MChir	master of surgery		NM	New Mexico
MCom	master of commerce		nm	nanometre(s)
MD	(1) doctor of medicine; (2) Maryland		no. *pl.* nos.	number(s)
MDMA	methylenedioxymethamphetamine		Nov	November
ME	Maine		n.p.	no place [of publication]
MEd	master of education		NS	new style
MEng	master of engineering		NV	Nevada
MEP	member of the European parliament		NY	New York
MG	Morris Garages		NZBS	New Zealand Broadcasting Service
MGM	Metro-Goldwyn-Mayer		OBE	officer of the Order of the British Empire
Mgr	Monsignor		obit.	obituary
MI	(1) Michigan; (2) military intelligence		Oct	October
MI1c	[secret intelligence department]		OCTU	officer cadets training unit
MI5	[military intelligence department]		OECD	Organization for Economic Co-operation and Development
MI6	[secret intelligence department]		OEEC	Organization for European Economic Co-operation
MI9	[secret escape service]			
MICE	member of the Institution of Civil Engineers		OFM	order of Friars Minor [Franciscans]
MIEE	member of the Institution of Electrical Engineers		OFMCap	Ordine Frati Minori Cappucini: member of the Capuchin order
min.	minute(s)		OH	Ohio
Mk	mark		OK	Oklahoma
ML	(1) licentiate of medicine; (2) master of laws		O level	ordinary level [examination]
MLitt	master of letters		OM	Order of Merit
Mlle	Mademoiselle		OP	order of Preachers [Dominicans]
mm	millimetre(s)		op. *pl.* opp.	opus *pl.* opera
Mme	Madame		OPEC	Organization of Petroleum Exporting Countries
MN	Minnesota		OR	Oregon
MO	Missouri		orig.	original
MOH	medical officer of health		OS	old style
MP	member of parliament		OSB	Order of St Benedict
m.p.h.	miles per hour		OTC	Officers' Training Corps
MPhil	master of philosophy		OWS	Old Watercolour Society
MRCP	member of the Royal College of Physicians		Oxon.	Oxoniensis
MRCS	member of the Royal College of Surgeons		p. *pl.* pp.	page(s)
MRCVS	member of the Royal College of Veterinary Surgeons		PA	Pennsylvania
MRIA	member of the Royal Irish Academy		p.a.	per annum
MS	(1) master of science; (2) Mississippi		para.	paragraph
MS *pl.* MSS	manuscript(s)		PAYE	pay as you earn
MSc	master of science		pbk *pl.* pbks	paperback(s)
MSc (Econ.)	master of science (economics)		*per.*	[during the] period
MT	Montana		PhD	doctor of philosophy
MusB	bachelor of music		pl.	(1) plate(s); (2) plural
MusBac	bachelor of music		priv. coll.	private collection
MusD	doctor of music		pt *pl.* pts	part(s)
MV	motor vessel		pubd	published
MVO	member of the Royal Victorian Order		PVC	polyvinyl chloride
n. *pl.* nn.	note(s)		q. *pl.* qq.	(1) question(s); (2) quire(s)
NAAFI	Navy, Army, and Air Force Institutes		QC	queen's counsel
NASA	National Aeronautics and Space Administration		R	rand
NATO	North Atlantic Treaty Organization		R.	Rex / Regina
NBC	National Broadcasting Corporation		*r*	recto
NC	North Carolina		*r.*	reigned / ruled
NCO	non-commissioned officer		RA	Royal Academy / Royal Academician

RAC	Royal Automobile Club		Skr	Swedish krona
RAF	Royal Air Force		Span.	Spanish
RAFVR	Royal Air Force Volunteer Reserve		SPCK	Society for Promoting Christian Knowledge
RAM	[member of the] Royal Academy of Music		SS	(1) Santissimi; (2) Schutzstaffel; (3) steam ship
RAMC	Royal Army Medical Corps		STB	bachelor of theology
RCA	Royal College of Art		STD	doctor of theology
RCNC	Royal Corps of Naval Constructors		STM	master of theology
RCOG	Royal College of Obstetricians and Gynaecologists		STP	doctor of theology
RDI	royal designer for industry		*supp.*	supposedly
RE	Royal Engineers		suppl. *pl.* suppls.	supplement(s)
repr. *pl.* reprs.	reprint(s) / reprinted		s.v.	*sub verbo* / *sub voce*: under the word / heading
repro.	reproduced		SY	steam yacht
rev.	revised / revised by / reviser / revision		TA	Territorial Army
Revd	Reverend		TASS	[Soviet news agency]
RHA	Royal Hibernian Academy		TB	tuberculosis (*lit.* tubercle bacillus)
RI	(1) Rhode Island; (2) Royal Institute of Painters in Water-Colours		TD	(1) *teachtaí dála* (member of the Dáil); (2) territorial decoration
RIBA	Royal Institute of British Architects		TN	Tennessee
RIN	Royal Indian Navy		TNT	trinitrotoluene
RM	Reichsmark		trans.	translated / translated by / translation / translator
RMS	Royal Mail steamer			
RN	Royal Navy		TT	tourist trophy
RNA	ribonucleic acid		TUC	Trades Union Congress
RNAS	Royal Naval Air Service		TX	Texas
RNR	Royal Naval Reserve		U-boat	*Unterseeboot*: submarine
RNVR	Royal Naval Volunteer Reserve		Ufa	Universum-Film AG
RO	Record Office		UMIST	University of Manchester Institute of Science and Technology
r.p.m.	revolutions per minute			
RRS	royal research ship		UN	United Nations
Rs	rupees		UNESCO	United Nations Educational, Scientific, and Cultural Organization
RSA	(1) Royal Scottish Academician; (2) Royal Society of Arts		UNICEF	United Nations International Children's Emergency Fund
RSPCA	Royal Society for the Prevention of Cruelty to Animals			
			unpubd	unpublished
Rt Hon.	Right Honourable		USS	United States ship
Rt Revd	Right Reverend		UT	Utah
RUC	Royal Ulster Constabulary		*v*	verso
Russ.	Russian		v.	versus
RWS	Royal Watercolour Society		VA	Virginia
S4C	Sianel Pedwar Cymru		VAD	Voluntary Aid Detachment
s.	shilling(s)		VC	Victoria Cross
s.a.	*sub anno*: under the year		VE-day	victory in Europe day
SABC	South African Broadcasting Corporation		Ven.	Venerable
SAS	Special Air Service		VJ-day	victory over Japan day
SC	South Carolina		vol. *pl.* vols.	volume(s)
ScD	doctor of science		VT	Vermont
S$	Singapore dollar		WA	Washington [state]
SD	South Dakota		WAAC	Women's Auxiliary Army Corps
sec.	second(s)		WAAF	Women's Auxiliary Air Force
sel.	selected		WEA	Workers' Educational Association
sen.	senior		WHO	World Health Organization
Sept	September		WI	Wisconsin
ser.	series		WRAF	Women's Royal Air Force
SHAPE	supreme headquarters allied powers, Europe		WRNS	Women's Royal Naval Service
SIDRO	Société Internationale d'Énergie Hydro-Électrique		WV	West Virginia
			WVS	Women's Voluntary Service
sig. *pl.* sigs.	signature(s)		WY	Wyoming
sing.	singular		¥	yen
SIS	Secret Intelligence Service		YMCA	Young Men's Christian Association
SJ	Society of Jesus		YWCA	Young Women's Christian Association

2 *Institution abbreviations*

All Souls Oxf.	All Souls College, Oxford
AM Oxf.	Ashmolean Museum, Oxford
Balliol Oxf.	Balliol College, Oxford
BBC WAC	BBC Written Archives Centre, Reading
Beds. & Luton ARS	Bedfordshire and Luton Archives and Record Service, Bedford
Berks. RO	Berkshire Record Office, Reading
BFI	British Film Institute, London
BFI NFTVA	British Film Institute, London, National Film and Television Archive
BGS	British Geological Survey, Keyworth, Nottingham
Birm. CA	Birmingham Central Library, Birmingham City Archives
Birm. CL	Birmingham Central Library
BL	British Library, London
BL NSA	British Library, London, National Sound Archive
BL OIOC	British Library, London, Oriental and India Office Collections
BLPES	London School of Economics and Political Science, British Library of Political and Economic Science
BM	British Museum, London
Bodl. Oxf.	Bodleian Library, Oxford
Bodl. RH	Bodleian Library of Commonwealth and African Studies at Rhodes House, Oxford
Borth. Inst.	Borthwick Institute of Historical Research, University of York
Boston PL	Boston Public Library, Massachusetts
Bristol RO	Bristol Record Office
Bucks. RLSS	Buckinghamshire Records and Local Studies Service, Aylesbury
CAC Cam.	Churchill College, Cambridge, Churchill Archives Centre
Cambs. AS	Cambridgeshire Archive Service
CCC Cam.	Corpus Christi College, Cambridge
CCC Oxf.	Corpus Christi College, Oxford
Ches. & Chester ALSS	Cheshire and Chester Archives and Local Studies Service
Christ Church Oxf.	Christ Church, Oxford
Christies	Christies, London
City Westm. AC	City of Westminster Archives Centre, London
CKS	Centre for Kentish Studies, Maidstone
CLRO	Corporation of London Records Office
Coll. Arms	College of Arms, London
Col. U.	Columbia University, New York
Cornwall RO	Cornwall Record Office, Truro
Courtauld Inst.	Courtauld Institute of Art, London
CUL	Cambridge University Library
Cumbria AS	Cumbria Archive Service
Derbys. RO	Derbyshire Record Office, Matlock
Devon RO	Devon Record Office, Exeter
Dorset RO	Dorset Record Office, Dorchester
Duke U.	Duke University, Durham, North Carolina
Duke U., Perkins L.	Duke University, Durham, North Carolina, William R. Perkins Library
Durham Cath. CL	Durham Cathedral, chapter library
Durham RO	Durham Record Office
DWL	Dr Williams's Library, London
Essex RO	Essex Record Office
E. Sussex RO	East Sussex Record Office, Lewes
Eton	Eton College, Berkshire
FM Cam.	Fitzwilliam Museum, Cambridge
Folger	Folger Shakespeare Library, Washington, DC
Garr. Club	Garrick Club, London
Girton Cam.	Girton College, Cambridge
GL	Guildhall Library, London
Glos. RO	Gloucestershire Record Office, Gloucester
Gon. & Caius Cam.	Gonville and Caius College, Cambridge
Gov. Art Coll.	Government Art Collection
GS Lond.	Geological Society of London
Hants. RO	Hampshire Record Office, Winchester
Harris Man. Oxf.	Harris Manchester College, Oxford
Harvard TC	Harvard Theatre Collection, Harvard University, Cambridge, Massachusetts, Nathan Marsh Pusey Library
Harvard U.	Harvard University, Cambridge, Massachusetts
Harvard U., Houghton L.	Harvard University, Cambridge, Massachusetts, Houghton Library
Herefs. RO	Herefordshire Record Office, Hereford
Herts. ALS	Hertfordshire Archives and Local Studies, Hertford
Hist. Soc. Penn.	Historical Society of Pennsylvania, Philadelphia
HLRO	House of Lords Record Office, London
Hult. Arch.	Hulton Archive, London and New York
Hunt. L.	Huntington Library, San Marino, California
ICL	Imperial College, London
Inst. CE	Institution of Civil Engineers, London
Inst. EE	Institution of Electrical Engineers, London
IWM	Imperial War Museum, London
IWM FVA	Imperial War Museum, London, Film and Video Archive
IWM SA	Imperial War Museum, London, Sound Archive
JRL	John Rylands University Library of Manchester
King's AC Cam.	King's College Archives Centre, Cambridge
King's Cam.	King's College, Cambridge
King's Lond.	King's College, London
King's Lond., Liddell Hart C.	King's College, London, Liddell Hart Centre for Military Archives
Lancs. RO	Lancashire Record Office, Preston
L. Cong.	Library of Congress, Washington, DC
Leics. RO	Leicestershire, Leicester, and Rutland Record Office, Leicester
Lincs. Arch.	Lincolnshire Archives, Lincoln
Linn. Soc.	Linnean Society of London
LMA	London Metropolitan Archives
LPL	Lambeth Palace, London
Lpool RO	Liverpool Record Office and Local Studies Service
LUL	London University Library
Magd. Cam.	Magdalene College, Cambridge
Magd. Oxf.	Magdalen College, Oxford
Man. City Gall.	Manchester City Galleries
Man. CL	Manchester Central Library
Mass. Hist. Soc.	Massachusetts Historical Society, Boston
Merton Oxf.	Merton College, Oxford
MHS Oxf.	Museum of the History of Science, Oxford
Mitchell L., Glas.	Mitchell Library, Glasgow
Mitchell L., NSW	State Library of New South Wales, Sydney, Mitchell Library
Morgan L.	Pierpont Morgan Library, New York
NA Canada	National Archives of Canada, Ottawa
NA Ire.	National Archives of Ireland, Dublin
NAM	National Army Museum, London
NA Scot.	National Archives of Scotland, Edinburgh
News Int. RO	News International Record Office, London
NG Ire.	National Gallery of Ireland, Dublin

NG Scot.	National Gallery of Scotland, Edinburgh
NHM	Natural History Museum, London
NL Aus.	National Library of Australia, Canberra
NL Ire.	National Library of Ireland, Dublin
NL NZ	National Library of New Zealand, Wellington
NL NZ, Turnbull L.	National Library of New Zealand, Wellington, Alexander Turnbull Library
NL Scot.	National Library of Scotland, Edinburgh
NL Wales	National Library of Wales, Aberystwyth
NMG Wales	National Museum and Gallery of Wales, Cardiff
NMM	National Maritime Museum, London
Norfolk RO	Norfolk Record Office, Norwich
Northants. RO	Northamptonshire Record Office, Northampton
Northumbd RO	Northumberland Record Office
Notts. Arch.	Nottinghamshire Archives, Nottingham
NPG	National Portrait Gallery, London
NRA	National Archives, London, Historical Manuscripts Commission, National Register of Archives
Nuffield Oxf.	Nuffield College, Oxford
N. Yorks. CRO	North Yorkshire County Record Office, Northallerton
NYPL	New York Public Library
Oxf. UA	Oxford University Archives
Oxf. U. Mus. NH	Oxford University Museum of Natural History
Oxon. RO	Oxfordshire Record Office, Oxford
Pembroke Cam.	Pembroke College, Cambridge
PRO	National Archives, London, Public Record Office
PRO NIre.	Public Record Office for Northern Ireland, Belfast
Pusey Oxf.	Pusey House, Oxford
RA	Royal Academy of Arts, London
Ransom HRC	Harry Ransom Humanities Research Center, University of Texas, Austin
RAS	Royal Astronomical Society, London
RBG Kew	Royal Botanic Gardens, Kew, London
RCP Lond.	Royal College of Physicians of London
RCS Eng.	Royal College of Surgeons of England, London
RGS	Royal Geographical Society, London
RIBA	Royal Institute of British Architects, London
RIBA BAL	Royal Institute of British Architects, London, British Architectural Library
Royal Arch.	Royal Archives, Windsor Castle, Berkshire [by gracious permission of her majesty the queen]
Royal Irish Acad.	Royal Irish Academy, Dublin
Royal Scot. Acad.	Royal Scottish Academy, Edinburgh
RS	Royal Society, London
RSA	Royal Society of Arts, London
RS Friends, Lond.	Religious Society of Friends, London
St Ant. Oxf.	St Antony's College, Oxford
St John Cam.	St John's College, Cambridge
S. Antiquaries, Lond.	Society of Antiquaries of London
Sci. Mus.	Science Museum, London
Scot. NPG	Scottish National Portrait Gallery, Edinburgh
Scott Polar RI	University of Cambridge, Scott Polar Research Institute
Sheff. Arch.	Sheffield Archives
Shrops. RRC	Shropshire Records and Research Centre, Shrewsbury
SOAS	School of Oriental and African Studies, London
Som. ARS	Somerset Archive and Record Service, Taunton
Staffs. RO	Staffordshire Record Office, Stafford

Suffolk RO	Suffolk Record Office
Surrey HC	Surrey History Centre, Woking
TCD	Trinity College, Dublin
Trinity Cam.	Trinity College, Cambridge
U. Aberdeen	University of Aberdeen
U. Birm.	University of Birmingham
U. Birm. L.	University of Birmingham Library
U. Cal.	University of California
U. Cam.	University of Cambridge
UCL	University College, London
U. Durham	University of Durham
U. Durham L.	University of Durham Library
U. Edin.	University of Edinburgh
U. Edin., New Coll.	University of Edinburgh, New College
U. Edin., New Coll. L.	University of Edinburgh, New College Library
U. Edin. L.	University of Edinburgh Library
U. Glas.	University of Glasgow
U. Glas. L.	University of Glasgow Library
U. Hull	University of Hull
U. Hull, Brynmor Jones L.	University of Hull, Brynmor Jones Library
U. Leeds	University of Leeds
U. Leeds, Brotherton L.	University of Leeds, Brotherton Library
U. Lond.	University of London
U. Lpool	University of Liverpool
U. Lpool L.	University of Liverpool Library
U. Mich.	University of Michigan, Ann Arbor
U. Mich., Clements L.	University of Michigan, Ann Arbor, William L. Clements Library
U. Newcastle	University of Newcastle upon Tyne
U. Newcastle, Robinson L.	University of Newcastle upon Tyne, Robinson Library
U. Nott.	University of Nottingham
U. Nott. L.	University of Nottingham Library
U. Oxf.	University of Oxford
U. Reading	University of Reading
U. Reading L.	University of Reading Library
U. St Andr.	University of St Andrews
U. St Andr. L.	University of St Andrews Library
U. Southampton	University of Southampton
U. Southampton L.	University of Southampton Library
U. Sussex	University of Sussex, Brighton
U. Texas	University of Texas, Austin
U. Wales	University of Wales
U. Warwick Mod. RC	University of Warwick, Coventry, Modern Records Centre
V&A	Victoria and Albert Museum, London
V&A NAL	Victoria and Albert Museum, London, National Art Library
Warks. CRO	Warwickshire County Record Office, Warwick
Wellcome L.	Wellcome Library for the History and Understanding of Medicine, London
Westm. DA	Westminster Diocesan Archives, London
Wilts. & Swindon RO	Wiltshire and Swindon Record Office, Trowbridge
Worcs. RO	Worcestershire Record Office, Worcester
W. Sussex RO	West Sussex Record Office, Chichester
W. Yorks. AS	West Yorkshire Archive Service
Yale U.	Yale University, New Haven, Connecticut
Yale U., Beinecke L.	Yale University, New Haven, Connecticut, Beinecke Rare Book and Manuscript Library
Yale U. CBA	Yale University, New Haven, Connecticut, Yale Center for British Art

3 Bibliographic abbreviations

Adams, *Drama* W. D. Adams, *A dictionary of the drama*, 1: *A–G* (1904); 2: *H–Z* (1956) [vol. 2 microfilm only]

AFM J O'Donovan, ed. and trans., *Annala rioghachta Eireann / Annals of the kingdom of Ireland by the four masters*, 7 vols. (1848–51); 2nd edn (1856); 3rd edn (1990)

Allibone, *Dict.* S. A. Allibone, *A critical dictionary of English literature and British and American authors*, 3 vols. (1859–71); suppl. by J. F. Kirk, 2 vols. (1891)

ANB J. A. Garraty and M. C. Carnes, eds., *American national biography*, 24 vols. (1999)

Anderson, *Scot. nat.* W. Anderson, *The Scottish nation, or, The surnames, families, literature, honours, and biographical history of the people of Scotland*, 3 vols. (1859–63)

Ann. mon. H. R. Luard, ed., *Annales monastici*, 5 vols., Rolls Series, 36 (1864–9)

Ann. Ulster S. Mac Airt and G. Mac Niocaill, eds., *Annals of Ulster (to AD 1131)* (1983)

APC *Acts of the privy council of England*, new ser., 46 vols. (1890–1964)

APS *The acts of the parliaments of Scotland*, 12 vols. in 13 (1814–75)

Arber, *Regs. Stationers* F. Arber, ed., *A transcript of the registers of the Company of Stationers of London, 1554–1640 AD*, 5 vols. (1875–94)

ArchR *Architectural Review*

ASC D. Whitelock, D. C. Douglas, and S. I. Tucker, ed. and trans., *The Anglo-Saxon Chronicle: a revised translation* (1961)

AS chart. P. H. Sawyer, *Anglo-Saxon charters: an annotated list and bibliography*, Royal Historical Society Guides and Handbooks (1968)

AusDB D. Pike and others, eds., *Australian dictionary of biography*, 16 vols. (1966–2002)

Baker, *Serjeants* J. H. Baker, *The order of serjeants at law*, SeldS, suppl. ser., 5 (1984)

Bale, *Cat.* J. Bale, *Scriptorum illustrium Maioris Brytannie, quam nunc Angliam et Scotiam vocant: catalogus*, 2 vols. in 1 (Basel, 1557–9); facs. edn (1971)

Bale, *Index* J. Bale, *Index Britanniae scriptorum*, ed. R. L. Poole and M. Bateson (1902); facs. edn (1990)

BBCS *Bulletin of the Board of Celtic Studies*

BDMBR J. O. Baylen and N. J. Gossman, eds., *Biographical dictionary of modern British radicals*, 3 vols. in 4 (1979–88)

Bede, *Hist. eccl.* *Bede's Ecclesiastical history of the English people*, ed. and trans. B. Colgrave and R. A. B. Mynors, OMT (1969); repr. (1991)

Bénézit, *Dict.* E. Bénézit, *Dictionnaire critique et documentaire des peintres, sculpteurs, dessinateurs et graveurs*, 3 vols. (Paris, 1911–23); new edn, 8 vols. (1948–66); 3rd edn (1966); 3rd edn, rev. and enl., 10 vols. (1976); 4th edn, 14 vols. (1999)

BIHR *Bulletin of the Institute of Historical Research*

Birch, *Seals* W. de Birch, *Catalogue of seals in the department of manuscripts in the British Museum*, 6 vols. (1887–1900)

Bishop Burnet's History *Bishop Burnet's History of his own time*, ed. M. J. Routh, 2nd edn, 6 vols. (1833)

Blackwood *Blackwood's [Edinburgh] Magazine*, 328 vols. (1817–1980)

Blain, Clements & Grundy, *Feminist comp.* V. Blain, P. Clements, and I. Grundy, eds., *The feminist companion to literature in English* (1990)

BL cat. *The British Library general catalogue of printed books* [in 360 vols. with suppls., also CD-ROM and online]

BMJ *British Medical Journal*

Boase & Courtney, *Bibl. Corn.* G. C. Boase and W. P. Courtney, *Bibliotheca Cornubiensis: a catalogue of the writings … of Cornishmen*, 3 vols. (1874–82)

Boase, *Mod. Eng. biog.* F. Boase, *Modern English biography: containing many thousand concise memoirs of persons who have died since the year 1850*, 6 vols. (privately printed, Truro, 1892–1921); repr. (1965)

Boswell, *Life* *Boswell's Life of Johnson: together with Journal of a tour to the Hebrides and Johnson's Diary of a journey into north Wales*, ed. G. B. Hill, enl. edn, rev. L. F. Powell, 6 vols. (1934–50); 2nd edn (1964); repr. (1971)

Brown & Stratton, *Brit. mus.* J. D. Brown and S. S. Stratton, *British musical biography* (1897)

Bryan, *Painters* M. Bryan, *A biographical and critical dictionary of painters and engravers*, 2 vols. (1816); new edn, ed. G. Stanley (1849); new edn, ed. R. E. Graves and W. Armstrong, 2 vols. (1886–9); [4th edn], ed. G. C. Williamson, 5 vols. (1903–5) [various reprs.]

Burke, *Gen. GB* J. Burke, *A genealogical and heraldic history of the commoners of Great Britain and Ireland*, 4 vols. (1833–8); new edn as *A genealogical and heraldic dictionary of the landed gentry of Great Britain and Ireland*, 3 vols. [1843–9] [many later edns]

Burke, *Gen. Ire.* J. B. Burke, *A genealogical and heraldic history of the landed gentry of Ireland* (1899); 2nd edn (1904); 3rd edn (1912); 4th edn (1958); 5th edn as *Burke's Irish family records* (1976)

Burke, *Peerage* J. Burke, *A general [later edns A genealogical] and heraldic dictionary of the peerage and baronetage of the United Kingdom [later edns the British empire]* (1829–)

Burney, *Hist. mus.* C. Burney, *A general history of music, from the earliest ages to the present period*, 4 vols. (1776–89)

Burtchaell & Sadleir, *Alum. Dubl.* G. D. Burtchaell and T. U. Sadleir, *Alumni Dublinenses: a register of the students, graduates, and provosts of Trinity College* (1924); [2nd edn], with suppl., in 2 pts (1935)

Calamy rev. A. G. Matthews, *Calamy revised* (1934); repr. (1988)

CCI *Calendar of confirmations and inventories granted and given up in the several commissariots of Scotland* (1876–)

CClR *Calendar of the close rolls preserved in the Public Record Office*, 47 vols. (1892–1963)

CDS J. Bain, ed., *Calendar of documents relating to Scotland*, 4 vols., PRO (1881–8); suppl. vol. 5, ed. G. G. Simpson and J. D. Galbraith [1986]

CEPR letters W. H. Bliss, C. Johnson, and J. Twemlow, eds., *Calendar of entries in the papal registers relating to Great Britain and Ireland: papal letters* (1893–)

CGPLA *Calendars of the grants of probate and letters of administration* [in 4 ser.: England & Wales, Northern Ireland, Ireland, and Éire]

Chambers, *Scots.* R. Chambers, ed., *A biographical dictionary of eminent Scotsmen*, 4 vols. (1832–5)

Chancery records chancery records pubd by the PRO

Chancery records (RC) chancery records pubd by the Record Commissions

CIPM	*Calendar of inquisitions post mortem*, [20 vols.], PRO (1904–); also *Henry VII*, 3 vols. (1898–1955)
Clarendon, *Hist. rebellion*	E. Hyde, earl of Clarendon, *The history of the rebellion and civil wars in England*, 6 vols. (1888); repr. (1958) and (1992)
Cobbett, *Parl. hist.*	W. Cobbett and J. Wright, eds., *Cobbett's Parliamentary history of England*, 36 vols. (1806–1820)
Colvin, *Archs.*	H. Colvin, *A biographical dictionary of British architects, 1600–1840*, 3rd edn (1995)
Cooper, *Ath. Cantab.*	C. H. Cooper and T. Cooper, *Athenae Cantabrigienses*, 3 vols. (1858–1913); repr. (1967)
CPR	*Calendar of the patent rolls preserved in the Public Record Office* (1891–)
Crockford	*Crockford's Clerical Directory*
CS	Camden Society
CSP	*Calendar of state papers* [in 11 ser.: domestic, Scotland, Scottish series, Ireland, colonial, Commonwealth, foreign, Spain [at Simancas], Rome, Milan, and Venice]
CYS	Canterbury and York Society
DAB	*Dictionary of American biography*, 21 vols. (1928–36), repr. in 11 vols. (1964); 10 suppls. (1944–96)
DBB	D. J. Jeremy, ed., *Dictionary of business biography*, 5 vols. (1984–6)
DCB	G. W. Brown and others, *Dictionary of Canadian biography*, [14 vols.] (1966–)
Debrett's Peerage	*Debrett's Peerage* (1803–) [sometimes *Debrett's Illustrated peerage*]
Desmond, *Botanists*	R. Desmond, *Dictionary of British and Irish botanists and horticulturists* (1977); rev. edn (1994)
Dir. Brit. archs.	A. Felstead, J. Franklin, and L. Pinfield, eds., *Directory of British architects, 1834–1900* (1993); 2nd edn, ed. A. Brodie and others, 2 vols. (2001)
DLB	J. M. Bellamy and J. Saville, eds., *Dictionary of labour biography*, [10 vols.] (1972–)
DLitB	Dictionary of Literary Biography
DNB	*Dictionary of national biography*, 63 vols. (1885–1900), suppl., 3 vols. (1901); repr. in 22 vols. (1908–9); 10 further suppls. (1912–96); *Missing persons* (1993)
DNZB	W. H. Oliver and C. Orange, eds., *The dictionary of New Zealand biography*, 5 vols. (1990–2000)
DSAB	W. J. de Kock and others, eds., *Dictionary of South African biography*, 5 vols. (1968–87)
DSB	C. C. Gillispie and F. L. Holmes, eds., *Dictionary of scientific biography*, 16 vols. (1970–80); repr. in 8 vols. (1981); 2 vol. suppl. (1990)
DSBB	A. Slaven and S. Checkland, eds., *Dictionary of Scottish business biography, 1860–1960*, 2 vols. (1986–90)
DSCHT	N. M. de S. Cameron and others, eds., *Dictionary of Scottish church history and theology* (1993)
Dugdale, *Monasticon*	W. Dugdale, *Monasticon Anglicanum*, 3 vols. (1655–72); 2nd edn, 3 vols. (1661–82); new edn, ed. J. Caley, J. Ellis, and B. Bandinel, 6 vols. in 8 pts (1817–30); repr. (1846) and (1970)

DWB	J. E. Lloyd and others, eds., *Dictionary of Welsh biography down to 1940* (1959) [Eng. trans. of *Y bywgraffiadur Cymreig hyd 1940*, 2nd edn (1954)]
EdinR	*Edinburgh Review, or, Critical Journal*
EETS	Early English Text Society
Emden, *Cam.*	A. B. Emden, *A biographical register of the University of Cambridge to 1500* (1963)
Emden, *Oxf.*	A. B. Emden, *A biographical register of the University of Oxford to AD 1500*, 3 vols. (1957–9); also *A biographical register of the University of Oxford, AD 1501 to 1540* (1974)
EngHR	*English Historical Review*
Engraved Brit. ports.	F. M. O'Donoghue and H. M. Hake, *Catalogue of engraved British portraits preserved in the department of prints and drawings in the British Museum*, 6 vols. (1908–25)
ER	The English Reports, 178 vols. (1900–32)
ESTC	*English short title catalogue, 1475–1800* [CD-ROM and online]
Evelyn, *Diary*	*The diary of John Evelyn*, ed. E. S. De Beer, 6 vols. (1955); repr. (2000)
Farington, *Diary*	*The diary of Joseph Farington*, ed. K. Garlick and others, 17 vols. (1978–98)
Fasti Angl. (Hardy)	J. Le Neve, *Fasti ecclesiae Anglicanae*, ed. T. D. Hardy, 3 vols. (1854)
Fasti Angl., 1066–1300	[J. Le Neve], *Fasti ecclesiae Anglicanae, 1066–1300*, ed. D. E. Greenway and J. S. Barrow, [8 vols.] (1968–)
Fasti Angl., 1300–1541	[J. Le Neve], *Fasti ecclesiae Anglicanae, 1300–1541*, 12 vols. (1962–7)
Fasti Angl., 1541–1857	[J. Le Neve], *Fasti ecclesiae Anglicanae, 1541–1857*, ed. J. M. Horn, D. M. Smith, and D. S. Bailey, [9 vols.] (1969–)
Fasti Scot.	H. Scott, *Fasti ecclesiae Scoticanae*, 3 vols. in 6 (1871); new edn, [11 vols.] (1915–)
FO List	*Foreign Office List*
Fortescue, *Brit. army*	J. W. Fortescue, *A history of the British army*, 13 vols. (1899–1930)
Foss, *Judges*	E. Foss, *The judges of England*, 9 vols. (1848–64); repr. (1966)
Foster, *Alum. Oxon.*	J. Foster, ed., *Alumni Oxonienses: the members of the University of Oxford, 1715–1886*, 4 vols. (1887–8); later edn (1891); also *Alumni Oxonienses … 1500–1714*, 4 vols. (1891–2); 8 vol. repr. (1968) and (2000)
Fuller, *Worthies*	T. Fuller, *The history of the worthies of England*, 4 pts (1662); new edn, 2 vols., ed. J. Nichols (1811); new edn, 3 vols., ed. P. A. Nuttall (1840); repr. (1965)
GEC, *Baronetage*	G. E. Cokayne, *Complete baronetage*, 6 vols. (1900–09); repr. (1983) [microprint]
GEC, *Peerage*	G. E. C. [G. E. Cokayne], *The complete peerage of England, Scotland, Ireland, Great Britain, and the United Kingdom*, 8 vols. (1887–98); new edn, ed. V. Gibbs and others, 14 vols. in 15 (1910–98); microprint repr. (1982) and (1987)
Genest, *Eng. stage*	J. Genest, *Some account of the English stage from the Restoration in 1660 to 1830*, 10 vols. (1832); repr. [New York, 1965]
Gillow, *Lit. biog. hist.*	J. Gillow, *A literary and biographical history or bibliographical dictionary of the English Catholics, from the breach with Rome, in 1534, to the present time*, 5 vols. [1885–1902]; repr. (1961); repr. with preface by C. Gillow (1999)
Gir. Camb. opera	*Giraldi Cambrensis opera*, ed. J. S. Brewer, J. F. Dimock, and G. F. Warner, 8 vols., Rolls Series, 21 (1861–91)
GJ	*Geographical Journal*

Gladstone, *Diaries* — *The Gladstone diaries: with cabinet minutes and prime-ministerial correspondence*, ed. M. R. D. Foot and H. C. G. Matthew, 14 vols. (1968–94)

GM — *Gentleman's Magazine*

Graves, *Artists* — A. Graves, ed., *A dictionary of artists who have exhibited works in the principal London exhibitions of oil paintings from 1760 to 1880* (1884); new edn (1895); 3rd edn (1901); facs. edn (1969); repr. [1970], (1973), and (1984)

Graves, *Brit. Inst.* — A. Graves, *The British Institution, 1806–1867: a complete dictionary of contributors and their work from the foundation of the institution* (1875); facs. edn (1908); repr. (1969)

Graves, *RA exhibitors* — A. Graves, *The Royal Academy of Arts: a complete dictionary of contributors and their work from its foundation in 1769 to 1904*, 8 vols. (1905–6); repr. in 4 vols. (1970) and (1972)

Graves, *Soc. Artists* — A. Graves, *The Society of Artists of Great Britain, 1760–1791, the Free Society of Artists, 1761–1783: a complete dictionary* (1907); facs. edn (1969)

Greaves & Zaller, *BDBR* — R. L. Greaves and R. Zaller, eds., *Biographical dictionary of British radicals in the seventeenth century*, 3 vols. (1982–4)

Grove, *Dict. mus.* — G. Grove, ed., *A dictionary of music and musicians*, 5 vols. (1878–90); 2nd edn, ed. J. A. Fuller Maitland (1904–10); 3rd edn, ed. H. C. Colles (1927); 4th edn with suppl. (1940); 5th edn, ed. E. Blom, 9 vols. (1954); suppl. (1961) [see also *New Grove*]

Hall, *Dramatic ports.* — L. A. Hall, *Catalogue of dramatic portraits in the theatre collection of the Harvard College library*, 4 vols. (1930–34)

Hansard — *Hansard's parliamentary debates*, ser. 1–5 (1803–)

Highfill, Burnim & Langhans, *BDA* — P. H. Highfill, K. A. Burnim, and E. A. Langhans, *A biographical dictionary of actors, actresses, musicians, dancers, managers, and other stage personnel in London, 1660–1800*, 16 vols. (1973–93)

Hist. U. Oxf. — T. H. Aston, ed., *The history of the University of Oxford*, 8 vols. (1984–2000) [1: *The early Oxford schools*, ed. J. I. Catto (1984); 2: *Late medieval Oxford*, ed. J. I. Catto and R. Evans (1992); 3: *The collegiate university*, ed. J. McConica (1986); 4: *Seventeenth-century Oxford*, ed. N. Tyacke (1997); 5: *The eighteenth century*, ed. L. S. Sutherland and L. G. Mitchell (1986); 6–7: *Nineteenth-century Oxford*, ed. M. G. Brock and M. C. Curthoys (1997–2000); 8: *The twentieth century*, ed. B. Harrison (2000)]

HJ — *Historical Journal*

HMC — Historical Manuscripts Commission

Holdsworth, *Eng. law* — W. S. Holdsworth, *A history of English law*, ed. A. L. Goodhart and H. L. Hanbury, 17 vols. (1903–72)

HoP, *Commons* — *The history of parliament: the House of Commons* [1386–1421, ed. J. S. Roskell, L. Clark, and C. Rawcliffe, 4 vols. (1992); 1509–1558, ed. S. T. Bindoff, 3 vols. (1982); 1558–1603, ed. P. W. Hasler, 3 vols. (1981); 1660–1690, ed. B. D. Henning, 3 vols. (1983); 1690–1715, ed. D. W. Hayton, E. Cruickshanks, and S. Handley, 5 vols. (2002); 1715–1754, ed. R. Sedgwick, 2 vols. (1970); 1754–1790, ed. L. Namier and J. Brooke, 3 vols. (1964), repr. (1985); 1790–1820, ed. R. G. Thorne, 5 vols. (1986); in draft (used with permission): 1422–1504, 1604–1629, 1640–1660, and 1820–1832]

IGI — *International Genealogical Index*, Church of Jesus Christ of the Latterday Saints

ILN — *Illustrated London News*

IMC — Irish Manuscripts Commission

Irving, *Scots.* — J. Irving, ed., *The book of Scotsmen eminent for achievements in arms and arts, church and state, law, legislation and literature, commerce, science, travel and philanthropy* (1881)

JCS — *Journal of the Chemical Society*

JHC — *Journals of the House of Commons*

JHL — *Journals of the House of Lords*

John of Worcester, *Chron.* — *The chronicle of John of Worcester*, ed. R. R. Darlington and P. McGurk, trans. J. Bray and P. McGurk, 3 vols., OMT (1995–) [vol. 1 forthcoming]

Keeler, *Long Parliament* — M. F. Keeler, *The Long Parliament, 1640–1641: a biographical study of its members* (1954)

Kelly, *Handbk* — *The upper ten thousand: an alphabetical list of all members of noble families*, 3 vols. (1875–7); continued as *Kelly's handbook of the upper ten thousand for 1878* [1879], 2 vols. (1878–9); continued as *Kelly's handbook to the titled, landed and official classes*, 94 vols. (1880–1973)

LondG — *London Gazette*

LP Henry VIII — J. S. Brewer, J. Gairdner, and R. H. Brodie, eds., *Letters and papers, foreign and domestic, of the reign of Henry VIII*, 23 vols. in 38 (1862–1932); repr. (1965)

Mallalieu, *Watercolour artists* — H. L. Mallalieu, *The dictionary of British watercolour artists up to 1820*, 3 vols. (1976–90); vol. 1, 2nd edn (1986)

Memoirs FRS — *Biographical Memoirs of Fellows of the Royal Society*

MGH — Monumenta Germaniae Historica

MT — *Musical Times*

Munk, *Roll* — W. Munk, *The roll of the Royal College of Physicians of London*, 2 vols. (1861); 2nd edn, 3 vols. (1878)

N&Q — *Notes and Queries*

New Grove — S. Sadie, ed., *The new Grove dictionary of music and musicians*, 20 vols. (1980); 2nd edn, 29 vols. (2001) [also online edn; see also Grove, *Dict. mus.*]

Nichols, *Illustrations* — J. Nichols and J. B. Nichols, *Illustrations of the literary history of the eighteenth century*, 8 vols. (1817–58)

Nichols, *Lit. anecdotes* — J. Nichols, *Literary anecdotes of the eighteenth century*, 9 vols. (1812–16); facs. edn (1966)

Obits. FRS — *Obituary Notices of Fellows of the Royal Society*

O'Byrne, *Naval biog. dict.* — W. R. O'Byrne, *A naval biographical dictionary* (1849); repr. (1990); [2nd edn], 2 vols. (1861)

OHS — Oxford Historical Society

Old Westminsters — *The record of Old Westminsters*, 1–2, ed. G. F. R. Barker and A. H. Stenning (1928); suppl. 1, ed. J. B. Whitmore and G. R. Y. Radcliffe [1938]; 3, ed. J. B. Whitmore, G. R. Y. Radcliffe, and D. C. Simpson (1963); suppl. 2, ed. F. E. Pagan (1978); 4, ed. F. E. Pagan and H. E. Pagan (1992)

OMT — Oxford Medieval Texts

Ordericus Vitalis, *Eccl. hist.* — *The ecclesiastical history of Orderic Vitalis*, ed. and trans. M. Chibnall, 6 vols., OMT (1969–80); repr. (1990)

Paris, *Chron.* — *Matthaei Parisiensis, monachi sancti Albani, chronica majora*, ed. H. R. Luard, Rolls Series, 7 vols. (1872–83)

Parl. papers — *Parliamentary papers* (1801–)

PBA — *Proceedings of the British Academy*

Pepys, *Diary*	*The diary of Samuel Pepys*, ed. R. Latham and W. Matthews, 11 vols. (1970–83); repr. (1995) and (2000)
Pevsner	N. Pevsner and others, Buildings of England series
PICE	*Proceedings of the Institution of Civil Engineers*
Pipe rolls	*The great roll of the pipe for . . .*, PRSoc. (1884–)
PRO	Public Record Office
PRS	*Proceedings of the Royal Society of London*
PRSoc.	Pipe Roll Society
PTRS	*Philosophical Transactions of the Royal Society*
QR	*Quarterly Review*
RC	Record Commissions
Redgrave, *Artists*	S. Redgrave, *A dictionary of artists of the English school* (1874); rev. edn (1878); repr. (1970)
Reg. Oxf.	C. W. Boase and A. Clark, eds., *Register of the University of Oxford*, 5 vols., OHS, 1, 10–12, 14 (1885–9)
Reg. PCS	J. H. Burton and others, eds., *The register of the privy council of Scotland*, 1st ser., 14 vols. (1877–98); 2nd ser., 8 vols. (1899–1908); 3rd ser., [16 vols.] (1908–70)
Reg. RAN	H. W. C. Davis and others, eds., *Regesta regum Anglo-Normannorum, 1066–1154*, 4 vols. (1913–69)
RIBA Journal	*Journal of the Royal Institute of British Architects* [later *RIBA Journal*]
RotP	J. Strachey, ed., *Rotuli parliamentorum ut et petitiones, et placita in parliamento*, 6 vols. (1767–77)
RotS	D. Macpherson, J. Caley, and W. Illingworth, eds., *Rotuli Scotiae in Turri Londinensi et in domo capitulari Westmonasteriensi asservati*, 2 vols., RC, 14 (1814–19)
RS	Record(s) Society
Rymer, *Foedera*	T. Rymer and R. Sanderson, eds., *Foedera, conventiones, literae et cuiuscunque generis acta publica inter reges Angliae et alios quosvis imperatores, reges, pontifices, principes, vel communitates*, 20 vols. (1704–35); 2nd edn, 20 vols. (1726–35); 3rd edn, 10 vols. (1739–45); facs. edn (1967); new edn, ed. A. Clarke, J. Caley, and F. Holbrooke, 4 vols., RC, 50 (1816–30)
Sainty, *Judges*	J. Sainty, ed., *The judges of England, 1272–1990*, SeldS, suppl. ser., 10 (1993)
Sainty, *King's counsel*	J. Sainty, ed., *A list of English law officers and king's counsel*, SeldS, suppl. ser., 7 (1987)
SCH	Studies in Church History
Scots peerage	J. B. Paul, ed. *The Scots peerage, founded on Wood's edition of Sir Robert Douglas's Peerage of Scotland, containing an historical and genealogical account of the nobility of that kingdom*, 9 vols. (1904–14)
SeldS	Selden Society
SHR	*Scottish Historical Review*
State trials	T. B. Howell and T. J. Howell, eds., *Cobbett's Complete collection of state trials*, 34 vols. (1809–28)
STC, 1475–1640	A. W. Pollard, G. R. Redgrave, and others, eds., *A short-title catalogue of . . . English books . . . 1475–1640* (1926); 2nd edn, ed. W. A. Jackson, F. S. Ferguson, and K. F. Pantzer, 3 vols. (1976–91) [see also Wing, *STC*]
STS	Scottish Text Society
SurtS	Surtees Society
Symeon of Durham, *Opera*	*Symeonis monachi opera omnia*, ed. T. Arnold, 2 vols., Rolls Series, 75 (1882–5); repr. (1965)
Tanner, *Bibl. Brit.-Hib.*	T. Tanner, *Bibliotheca Britannico-Hibernica*, ed. D. Wilkins (1748); repr. (1963)
Thieme & Becker, *Allgemeines Lexikon*	U. Thieme, F. Becker, and H. Vollmer, eds., *Allgemeines Lexikon der bildenden Künstler von der Antike bis zur Gegenwart*, 37 vols. (Leipzig, 1907–50); repr. (1961–5), (1983), and (1992)
Thurloe, *State papers*	*A collection of the state papers of John Thurloe*, ed. T. Birch, 7 vols. (1742)
TLS	*Times Literary Supplement*
Tout, *Admin. hist.*	T. F. Tout, *Chapters in the administrative history of mediaeval England: the wardrobe, the chamber, and the small seals*, 6 vols. (1920–33); repr. (1967)
TRHS	*Transactions of the Royal Historical Society*
VCH	H. A. Doubleday and others, eds., *The Victoria history of the counties of England*, [88 vols.] (1900–)
Venn, *Alum. Cant.*	J. Venn and J. A. Venn, *Alumni Cantabrigienses: a biographical list of all known students, graduates, and holders of office at the University of Cambridge, from the earliest times to 1900*, 10 vols. (1922–54); repr. in 2 vols. (1974–8)
Vertue, *Note books*	[G. Vertue], *Note books*, ed. K. Esdaile, earl of Ilchester, and H. M. Hake, 6 vols., Walpole Society, 18, 20, 22, 24, 26, 30 (1930–55)
VF	*Vanity Fair*
Walford, *County families*	E. Walford, *The county families of the United Kingdom, or, Royal manual of the titled and untitled aristocracy of Great Britain and Ireland* (1860)
Walker rev.	A. G. Matthews, *Walker revised: being a revision of John Walker's Sufferings of the clergy during the grand rebellion, 1642–60* (1948); repr. (1988)
Walpole, *Corr.*	*The Yale edition of Horace Walpole's correspondence*, ed. W. S. Lewis, 48 vols. (1937–83)
Ward, *Men of the reign*	T. H. Ward, ed., *Men of the reign: a biographical dictionary of eminent persons of British and colonial birth who have died during the reign of Queen Victoria* (1885); repr. (Graz, 1968)
Waterhouse, *18c painters*	E. Waterhouse, *The dictionary of 18th century painters in oils and crayons* (1981); repr. as *British 18th century painters in oils and crayons* (1991), vol. 2 of *Dictionary of British art*
Watt, *Bibl. Brit.*	R. Watt, *Bibliotheca Britannica, or, A general index to British and foreign literature*, 4 vols. (1824) [many reprs.]
Wellesley index	W. E. Houghton, ed., *The Wellesley index to Victorian periodicals, 1824–1900*, 5 vols. (1966–89); new edn (1999) [CD-ROM]
Wing, *STC*	D. Wing, ed., *Short-title catalogue of . . . English books . . . 1641–1700*, 3 vols. (1945–51); 2nd edn (1972–88); rev. and enl. edn, ed. J. J. Morrison, C. W. Nelson, and M. Seccombe, 4 vols. (1994–8) [see also *STC, 1475–1640*]
Wisden	*John Wisden's Cricketer's Almanack*
Wood, *Ath. Oxon.*	A. Wood, *Athenae Oxonienses . . . to which are added the Fasti*, 2 vols. (1691–2); 2nd edn (1721); new edn, 4 vols., ed. P. Bliss (1813–20); repr. (1967) and (1969)
Wood, *Vic. painters*	C. Wood, *Dictionary of Victorian painters* (1971); 2nd edn (1978); 3rd edn as *Victorian painters*, 2 vols. (1995), vol. 4 of *Dictionary of British art*
WW	*Who's who* (1849–)
WWBMP	M. Stenton and S. Lees, eds., *Who's who of British members of parliament*, 4 vols. (1976–81)
WWW	*Who was who* (1929–)

Cranfield, Lionel, first earl of Middlesex (1575–1645), merchant, financier, and government minister, was born in London, the second son of Thomas Cranfield (*d.* 1595), a London mercer and Eastland Company merchant, and his wife, Martha (*d.* 1609), daughter of Thomas's master, Vincent Randall. Lionel was educated at St Paul's School until the age of fifteen, at which point he was apprenticed to Richard Sheppard, grocer and merchant specializing in cloth, spices, silks, and taffetas. He pursued a highly successful career first as a merchant and then, increasingly, as financier inhabiting the shady world of government contracting and projecting. Having by 1612 made a sizeable fortune he turned from poacher to gamekeeper, entering government service in 1613 and rising to become lord treasurer. His campaigns of retrenchment and reform, however, made enemies and invited accusations of, at least, hypocrisy, and he fell from office in 1624, a victim of court politics as much as anything else. Despite hints of the possibility of a return to favour he lived the rest of his life away from government, although his earlier success as merchant and financier preserved him from penury.

Merchant and financier, 1594–1613 The young merchant quickly prospered. In 1594 Cranfield was in Stade, trading English broadcloths and kerseys for Italian silks and fustians. Called home by his mother in 1597 he became a freeman of the Mercers' Company and in 1598, at the age of twenty-three, estimated his total worth at £2502, more than his father had been worth in total at his death in 1595. Back in London he continued to prosper, becoming a Merchant Adventurer in 1601. At that point, according to a will he made before travelling to Middelburg that year, he was worth £6600. At the end of his apprenticeship, in 1599, following his father's example, he had married the master's daughter, Elizabeth Sheppard (*d.* 1617). His precocious success may have made his new father-in-law reluctant to accept the match—Richard Sheppard's business was by this time in some trouble. Cranfield eschewed the offer of a house at a preferential rate from his father-in-law, establishing himself and his new wife instead under his mother's roof. As Sheppard failed, however, Cranfield profited, demonstrating a superior sense of changing market conditions. He had an eye for minute detail and an appetite for profit remarked upon by many of his contemporaries. It seems also that he was not above some dubious activities—willing to trade in wet pepper, musty wheat, or batches of cloth of uneven quality. By 1611 he had made an extremely successful career as an export merchant in the cloth trade and acquired a country seat at Pishobury, Hertfordshire, to add to his town house in Wood Street. However, at that point his factors were reporting problems in the continental markets and Cranfield was increasingly attracted by other commercial opportunities. He had, for some time, been pursuing diverse activities, employing his liquid cash in speculations in pepper, ordnance, and a prize ship, the *St Valentine*. He had also offered personal loans to private individuals and did extremely well out of the injudicious borrowing of the Yorkshire gentlemen Sir Richard Gargrave and

Lionel Cranfield, first earl of Middlesex (1575–1645), by Daniel Mytens, 1620

Peter Frobisher (nephew of the explorer). One obvious further route for prosperous merchants was into the lucrative world of government credit and contracting. In order to understand these opportunities it is necessary to understand something of the structure of royal finances.

Under Elizabeth the crown had pursued a conservative financial policy, restricting expenditure rather than maximizing revenue. As a result the proceeds of a number of the central components of royal income had declined in relative terms, and some of them absolutely. Thus crown lands and the revenues arising from prerogative rights were not pressed, leading ministers preferring the political dividend of low-cost government to the risks of maximizing revenues. Some of the civil costs of government—rewards for loyal servants and so on—could be met not with cash payments but by putting people in a position from which they could make money—selling them the right to enjoy particular crown revenues or rights, or creating monopolies in the production and sale of particular commodities. This reduced revenue to the government but met political obligations at no direct monetary cost to the exchequer. As a consequence of these policies the

Jacobean regime was cash poor but asset rich. But the Jacobean regime spent more than its Elizabethan predecessor and so the need for cash was more pressing. In order to raise it more and more concessions were sold and assets alienated. In part these assets were real but in part they lay in the legal ability to create rents—creating property in particular items or trades which could then be leased or sold for cash, providing a steady income to the recipient. A necessitous crown, in other words, increasingly sold or mortgaged its assets and the terms of trade often favoured the purchaser or leaseholder. But it also licensed individuals to find out what these assets might be—paying projectors to find concealed lands or farming out duties in order to test what they might actually be worth. Projectors took a share of what they found, or raised, and this represented a loss of income to the crown but immediate cash was raised and some extra revenue produced.

The short-term advantages of these policies to the crown were immediate cash in return for these licences and farms, and freedom from the costs of administration. The long-term cost was a loss of control of assets and the near impossibility ever of raising the cash necessary to take over the management of these assets directly. For merchants like Cranfield, with ready cash, the way was open to take up these concessions, taking for themselves profits that might have been the crown's. In his forays into this world Cranfield was guided by Sir Arthur Ingram, who introduced him to a number of syndicates bidding for customs farms and other concessions. Cranfield was also part of a group of merchants profiting from the sale of crown lands between 1607 and 1610 as the crown sought to realize cash for immediate purposes. In these financial operations Cranfield was close to the seedier edges of Jacobean merchant life but was not outstandingly corrupt or venial—these opportunities were open to, and exploited by, many traders and financiers in these years. For those outside the circle of city and crown favour, however, this looked like the problem rather than its solution, and it was a world satirized by Ben Jonson. Jonson's dining circle at the Mermaid overlapped with a circle of wits with whom Cranfield dined at the Mitre, and Jonson's satirical depictions of Jacobean projectors may well have owed something to a knowledge of Ingram, if not Cranfield.

On the basis of his successful initial career as an export merchant Cranfield grew steadily rich and developed a diverse portfolio of investments. In 1606 he was worth nearly £13,000, of which only £5000 was in cloth. In 1611 he was worth at least £21,000, around £15,000 of which was land. By 1613 he estimated his own worth at £24,200, nearly £20,000 of which was in the form of lands and houses. Clearly the apprentice merchant had acquired a huge fortune and diversified well beyond his initial specialization of cloth exports. Among the diverse sources of this fortune crown finances and contracting figured significantly and like many merchants and financiers in this period Cranfield had clearly appreciated the possibilities offered by an alliance with the court. His withdrawal from the world of international trade and speculation was

imminent, however. Ingram found himself increasingly over-extended and the German markets, always volatile, were more unpredictable as a result of political uncertainties. The attractions of land and office must have seemed considerable. Cranfield's dining circle at the Mitre had included Inigo Jones, John Donne, and men with court connections and political aspirations. His wealth, his connections, his dealings in government contracts, and his awareness of the risks of the mercantile life all must have promoted a sense of the possibility of a change of direction.

Government office, 1613–1624 The transition was facilitated by the patronage of Thomas Howard, earl of Northampton, a rival for the king's favour following the death of Salisbury. They had co-operated over Cranfield's dealings in a starch monopoly and Cranfield offered Northampton the means to propose money-saving schemes to the crown. The treasury was put into commission in 1613 and the commission began to look into ways of saving the crown's parlous financial position. Schemes for increasing revenues and reducing costs or expenditures were under very active consideration and the way to favour was open for men with eye-catching proposals. Cranfield made his mark by convincingly demonstrating that higher rents could be charged for the lease of the great customs farm. Although he unsuccessfully bid for the farm himself, his bid pulled up the value of the successful syndicate headed by Sir John Swinnerton. By revealing some of the commercial secrets of the London merchant world, however, Cranfield had made himself unpopular and his fate was increasingly tied to the court. His reward for bidding up the leases and suggesting a new import duty was government office. In 1613 he became chief surveyor of the customs, a new post worth £200 per annum which would produce accurate information about the state of trade and about the profits of farmers—useful both for policy and in negotiations over customs leases. Thus opened the second phase of his career: by 1612 he had pulled out of the cloth trade altogether and was concentrating on the more secure and certain returns of land, revenue farms, and office. In 1613 he was knighted and in 1614 extended his estates in Hertfordshire by acquiring Shering, a manor neighbouring Pishobury, from the earl of Sussex. At this point Cranfield increasingly belonged to the world of government projecting—offering reform schemes to government which promised savings or new revenue in return for a personal share of the proceeds. He made a handy profit from the farm of the Irish customs, for example, in which he and Ingram had been members of rival consortia which offered surprisingly similar bids for the farm. When the farm was let the two syndicates merged. Those outside the charmed circle of court and city financiers were suspicious that such arrangements were a cause, rather than a consequence, of crown financial difficulties and the parliament of 1614 failed amid factionalism and tensions over financial reform. Cranfield's post of surveyor-general was one of the positions singled out for criticism but he could have said in his defence that revenue had increased so that the crown, as well as he, had benefited from his office.

Northampton had died in 1614 but Cranfield's rise in court circles was not disturbed. He figured prominently as an opponent of the Cockayne project and attracted the attention of the same group of courtiers who were promoting George Villiers (soon to be, in succession, earl, marquess, and duke of Buckingham) in the king's favour. In the aftermath of the failed parliament of 1614 conciliar attention also turned towards retrenchment and reform. Cranfield's was an influential voice, proposing tariff changes intended to discourage the consumption of foreign luxuries, and a mastership in the court of requests was a further indication of royal favour (although Cranfield himself was already hoping to be chancellor of the exchequer). By 1615 he was enjoying Villiers's support, although this somewhat compromised his commitment to cut spending and reduce the profits available to officials and contractors as a means of increasing net revenues for the crown.

Over the next few years Cranfield played an important role in commissions which substantially reduced crown spending, although they failed to solve the financial problems. There were marked successes in reducing household expenditure in the light of a report by a 1617 subcommission. Cranfield in particular demonstrated a sharp eye for accounting irregularities and wasteful practices in procuring supplies. Elizabethan household expenditure had floated above the wished for £40,000 per annum to reach levels nearer £50,000, but this was greatly exceeded under James, reaching £77,000. Such expenses were not justified simply by the larger household of a married king or by the effects of inflation, and savings of around £18,000 brought the costs of the household to more defensible levels. A similar eye for economy was turned on the navy, where perquisites and extravagances in methods of procurement were addressed, again with considerable success. Cranfield also served on a subcommission examining the practices of the ordnance office, where it was claimed that annual expenditure had fallen from £34,000 to £14,000, although the extent of his achievements there may have been exaggerated. In 1618 Cranfield became master of the wardrobe and once again his close attention to the accounts yielded considerable savings—he ran the wardrobe for £20,000 per annum, compared to a peak of around £36,000 per annum in the early years of James's reign and an average in the period 1606–12 of £28,000. In part it was simply a matter of paying bills on time, in order to avoid paying well above the market rate, and ensuring that orders were delivered in full. At the same time another commission, on which he did not sit, was exploring abuses in the exchequer and again revealed a mixture of waste and corruption. As master of the court of wards, a position to which he was appointed in 1619, Cranfield's regime was stricter than that of some of his predecessors, but the gains were less spectacular. He also continued to be helpful to the government as an adviser in the negotiation of leases for the customs farms. In particular he secured an agreement to pay a duty on the tobacco imported from Virginia, a new and increasingly lucrative trade. Overall Cranfield in these years was associated with highly effective campaigns of retrenchment which seemed to promise the possibility of a balanced ordinary account. In 1619 he became a treasury commissioner.

All these reforms made enemies as well as friends, of course. In discovering outright frauds and extravagant rewards for little work or return they produced savings, but cut directly across vested interests. One of the biggest savings in the costs of the navy, for example, would have been to reduce the number of useless offices, but the scheme foundered on the problem of compensating people for the loss of what they had previously understood to be property. The increased duties on Virginia tobacco made Cranfield an enemy of the Virginia Company and of Sir Edward Sandys, and these enmities were expressed in the parliaments of 1621 and 1624. These enmities were also, potentially, factionalized, since Cranfield was closely associated with Buckingham, and his humble social origins provided ammunition for his critics. He was often referred to as a prentice boy, and to have such a man presiding over the wards—dealing with the inheritances of leading peers—was a matter of contemporary comment. As he rose in court circles so this kind of resentment increased. Finally, of course, as he saved money and attacked perquisites Cranfield himself was enjoying the fruits of government service. In fact, there were no major land purchases between 1614 and 1618, and his commercial activities had more or less ceased but his income in 1618, before he took up major offices, was £6000. As master of the wardrobe he at least doubled this income and he made significant, though less easily quantified profits from the wards as well. Like his associates and protectors Francis Bacon and Buckingham, Cranfield was certainly serving himself as well as the public good, and his dependence on their patronage made it difficult for him to carry through reform wholeheartedly.

Elizabeth, his first wife, died in 1617, and on 30 December 1620 Cranfield cemented his alliance with Buckingham by acquiescing in a marriage to Anne Brett (d. 1670), Buckingham's cousin, the daughter of his mother's sister. His first marriage had, it seems, been for love, albeit love for the master's daughter. His second was the result of financial and political calculation, a match encouraged by James himself, who offered a dowry and gave the bride away. Cranfield, like all other Stuart politicians, depended on successful conduct in court politics in order to carry out his policies. Reform was, therefore, expressed and interpreted in the light of court faction and by 1620 this threatened political trouble, the more so since the outbreak of European war gave an ideological or religious edge to factional politics. The plight of the palatinate jeopardized the protestant interest in central Europe and threw doubt on the wisdom of the Spanish alliance being pursued by James and his advisers. But the pursuit of war threatened financial ruin or, if the money was not forthcoming, military disaster.

These issues came together in the parliament of 1621.

The House of Commons was reluctant to grant supply for a war which was not yet declared, fearing, in part, that the money would simply be used to repair the holes in royal finance caused by court extravagance. Shortage of money gave rise to a number of bills designed to improve trade and this concern with the state of the economy led into criticism of patents and monopolies. Similarly, a concern with the state of royal government might easily come to focus around particular ministers as indeed it did. It was the parliament of 1621 which revived the process of impeachment, not used since the fourteenth century, in which the high court of parliament heard a case against a servant of the crown who had abused his position of trust. The victim was Bacon, who was successfully accused of accepting bribes and dismissed from office. A leading figure in this was Sir Edward Coke, a long-time rival of Bacon, and Cranfield helped in the prosecution. Parliament became, therefore, a platform for his further rise. When the Commons demanded redress of grievances before supply Cranfield seems to have supported them, and spoke in favour of law reform as well as supporting the attacks on monopolists. He could not go too far down this road, however, without losing favour at court, and Sandys won some victories over him in relation to the Virginia trade, something conflated with anti-Spanish feeling—and hence of ideological significance. From the point of view of his career Cranfield evidently trod this line successfully, though, for in July 1621 he was elevated to the peerage as Baron Cranfield and in September he succeeded Henry Montague, Lord Mandeville, as lord treasurer. In the following year he became the first earl of Middlesex. He had risen a long way, but he had also made powerful enemies and his time at the top was to be all too brief.

The interpretation of events in parliament is contentious, affecting as it does a sense of the inevitability or otherwise of civil conflict in the generation before the English civil wars. Cranfield served as a prominent spokesman in the Commons on behalf of the crown in the first session of the 1621 parliament, and his support for the attacks on monopolies is seen as a sign that James I was willing to see these grievances redressed. So too, the acquiescence in the downfall of Bacon, a government servant convicted of accepting bribes and hence indefensible. But with his elevation to the peerage Cranfield was also moved to the Lords and in the second session of the parliament business ran less smoothly in the Commons. There was no successful legislation against monopolies and the supply granted in anticipation of a war with Spain was not compensated by redress of country grievances. How far unease about the relative failure of this parliament reflected a principled commitment to a particular vision of parliament's constitutional role is controversial. The reluctance to finance war has been interpreted as a desire to use financial power to increase the political importance of the institution of parliament or simply as a quite proper expression of the interests of the houses to protect their countries from unnecessary expense. The revival of impeachment clearly served some court interests as much as it was a means for the houses to establish oversight of ministerial conduct, and in any case the interests of the crown, and of court factions in parliament, meant that disputes in parliament were a product of politics in those other arenas as much as an expression of an independent parliamentary will. Whatever is made of the events of the 1621 parliament, however, it is clear that Cranfield was a winner both politically and in career terms. As an opponent of royal extravagance and waste he was quite at home as an opponent both of some monopolies and of a Spanish war. He, more than most, knew how ill-equipped the realm was to bear the burdens of such a war.

Cranfield's achievements in government predate his tenure as lord treasurer, which lasted only two and a half years. His term of office coincided with the unsuccessful second session of the 1621 parliament which, crucially, yielded no supply. He was forced to try to trim spending, but exercised no real control over it, and to try to enforce economies across all departments. In this he was unsuccessful, and in the departments where he had previously succeeded spending began once again to increase. Meanwhile the costs of foreign embassies escalated as a diplomatic path was pursued through the increasingly dangerous world of European politics and his suggested reforms generated more grievances than cash. His radical suggestion of a suspension of pension payments and an end to renewals of pensions was not implemented but such measures as were applied began to cut against the interests of Buckingham and his hungry adherents. He had also begun a campaign to make the Irish kingdom pay for itself, an imaginative recognition of where an asset capable of improvement might be found, but like all his predecessors he failed. As a result of his close acquaintance with these difficulties he was, unsurprisingly, against war and in favour of the Spanish marriage which would at least realize a large dowry. In all, the financial position of the crown probably worsened under his treasurership, although he may deserve some credit for the fact that it only worsened to the extent that it did.

Although he did little for the financial solvency of the crown in these years Cranfield certainly did no harm to his own fortune. In 1621 he had owned real property worth £33,400. Just after his fall from office he had converted profits into large houses and estates and these were, by his own most conservative estimate, worth £102,400. He had large houses and lands at Chelsea, Copt Hall (Essex), Wiston (Sussex), and Milcote (Warwickshire). He had flirted too with establishing an estate in Ireland. On the eve of his fall his income was between £25,000 and £28,000 per annum, on the level of some of the richest peers of the realm. This had been done by buying up estates on credit secured against his public position at the court of wards and as treasurer. In both places his profits were comparable with previous incumbents. He sold offices, received gifts, and claimed his perquisites as his predecessors had done. In acquiring his estates, however, he had preferred not to pay in cash, but to borrow. The extent to which he had stayed the right side of the line between using his own profits, rather than the king's assets, to secure his borrowing was not always clear and some of his land transactions attracted attention during his impeachment. This vast private wealth insulated him from the consequences of his fall, although he had to struggle to fight the corrosive effects his own family had upon it.

Impeachment and retirement, 1624–1645 It may not be clear how much long-term significance to attach to the difficulties of the 1621 parliament but it is clear that some trouble was stored up which made for difficulties in the next parliament of the reign, which met in 1624. It was made more difficult by a serious rift within the court, between the pro-war camp and those who sought to placate Spain and protect English interests by diplomatic means. Middlesex (as Cranfield now was), who had made enemies in his rise and reform, was to fall foul of these disputes. From this perspective the key political event was the transformation of Buckingham's position. As part of the diplomatic moves to placate Spanish interests a marriage had been mooted between Charles and the Spanish infanta. As a part of these negotiations Charles and Buckingham had decided to go to Madrid in 1623, a trip which had momentous consequences. The humiliations that the pair received in Spain turned them entirely against the pro-Spanish lobby and in favour of war while at the same time Buckingham successfully established himself as a favourite of the heir apparent. James, on the other hand, continued to favour diplomacy with the Spanish so that the dispute between the two lobbies became at the same time a generational difference within the court. The reversionary interest, as it were, now favoured a war policy. When parliament met in 1624 these court disputes spilt over into parliamentary debate since Buckingham was willing to try to press for a war through parliament. In doing this Buckingham was also clear that he needed to bring down Middlesex. While Buckingham was in Madrid with Charles, Middlesex had seemed to manoeuvre against him. A marriage had been mooted between Middlesex's family and that of the earl of Southampton, one of Buckingham's court opponents, and Middlesex seemed also to be trying to introduce a rival for James's favour—his own brother-in-law Sir Arthur Brett. It was also clear that Middlesex would oppose a Spanish war for financial reasons. In so obviously contradicting the wishes of the coming man Middlesex may well have been acting in what he saw as the public interest—it is certainly difficult to see how he could have thought it to be in his own interest. In any case, Buckingham had two clear aims for the 1624 parliament—to press for war and to bring down Middlesex.

Buckingham appealed to popular sentiment and to parliament in order to persuade the king to break the treaties with Spain, and he did so successfully. The instrument of Middlesex's downfall was impeachment. Accused of corruption in misusing the stamp of the court of wards and in accepting bribes, Middlesex put up some defence. He was not the most popular man in parliament, however: as

James himself had said 'all Treasurers, if they do good service to their master, must be generally hated' (Prestwich, 448). Buckingham's intent, in any case, was fairly plain and he had ready allies in Coke and Sandys. Middlesex complained of a conspiracy against him, but could not afford publicly to name Buckingham as its mastermind. The hearings gave great latitude to his critics to speak and less opportunity for him to defend himself. The upshot was his exclusion from public office, exile from the court, and a fine of £50,000. Once again the king could not defend someone accused of straightforward corruption, although he did seek to clarify for parliament the difference between a bribe and a gratuity, and he let Middlesex fall. Once more it would be difficult to see this as an assertion of the political independence of parliament, still less of the Commons, since the fall of Middlesex was so intimately connected to court politics and because the king himself left him to his fate. In fact, the king went so far as to point out that it was Buckingham who had raised him and so it was Buckingham who should have protected him. The charges were complicated and the evidence incomplete but most authorities agree that Middlesex was harshly dealt with. The crimes of which he was committed were by the standards of the day fairly venial and his fall was part of a much larger game over European politics and the direction which foreign policy would take under the next king.

Middlesex had a vast private fortune to fall back on and exclusion from office did not entail private ruin. At his fall he moved to Copt Hall to maintain the estate of a great nobleman, but he had been fined £50,000 and lost the income from his offices, half of his total income by his own account. He lobbied successfully to have the fine reduced, first to £30,000 and then to £20,000. To pay this fine and satisfy other creditors he was forced to sell Chelsea, relinquish his farm of the duties on sugar, as well as jewellery and plate, other estates, and government concessions. Fate seemed to deal him a strong hand when Buckingham was impeached in 1626, because if anyone knew where the bodies were buried it was Middlesex. He prevaricated, hoping for rich returns for his silence, but in the end he received only a pardon, although that did promise him security in the ownership of those assets he had retained. A big-spending Villiers wife and a large marriage portion to secure the marriage of his elder daughter, Elizabeth, to the earl of Mulgrave in 1629 took further heavy tolls on his denuded income, however, and he was plagued by debts into the early 1630s. In 1632 investigations into his actions as master of the wardrobe were reopened, despite the pardon issued in 1627, and a further fine of £12,000 was imposed by Star Chamber. By 1635, although he was living in Copt Hall, his annual income was around £5000, somewhat less than it had been in 1618.

In business and public life Middlesex was a blunt man, evasive to his creditors but unswerving in the pursuit of his debtors. He revealed a streak of stubbornness in refusing to trim to Buckingham's wishes, a characteristic upon which many remarked and not usually favourably. The portrait of him as lord treasurer by Daniel Mytens reveals a man of strong, perhaps rough, features with a strong jaw and keen eyes under a receding hairline. In his retirement he revealed the same qualities in relation to his servants and in relation to the business of his own household. Having lost the protection of high office he was the frequent object of legal suits. Business papers naturally reveal these qualities rather more than they reveal his personal tastes. In religion he supported the 'beauty of holiness' and he kept a relatively ornate chapel at Copt Hall. He also took great pleasure in his gardens both at Chelsea and Copt Hall. To his family he was a loving, and much loved, father. He secured good marriages for two of the three daughters of his first marriage—Martha became countess of Monmouth and Elizabeth countess of Mulgrave. But the cost of such a dowry without high office was prohibitive and Mary, unable to attract a suitor of similar status, remained unmarried to her death in 1635. He candidly admitted that his second marriage had been entered for financial reasons, but it seems to have been an affectionate one. With Anne, his second wife, he had three sons (James, Lionel, and Edward) and two daughters (Frances and Susanna). Despite his financial straits he was able to marry Frances to the earl of Dorset's heir, somehow avoiding payment of the £10,000 dowry for ten years. His sons received some education but did not attend the universities or inns of court and neither did James, the eldest, undertake the grand tour.

Middlesex's final years were melancholy at best. In 1636 he moved out of Copt Hall for reasons of economy and took up residence in Milcote. In 1637 he considered various land sales and even the sale of Copt Hall, but he managed to avoid it, perhaps encouraged by hopes of a return to royal favour. At court interest was turning once again to household economies and Middlesex was clearly being considered as a possible agent of this reform but he was not, in the end, called back into office. In 1640 his inside knowledge of public affairs once again promised to make him politically powerful and he hoped to gain concessions for loyalty. As in 1626, however, he seems to have misplayed his hand and he got little help from the king while throwing in his lot with the opposition too late to gain real gratitude. His neutrality in the civil war simply made him an object of suspicion to both sides and his estates were attacked while exactions of all kinds were imposed on his denuded holdings. Having lost his business and office revenues he was now steadily losing his lands. In December 1644 Milcote was fired by parliamentarian troops fearful that it was about to be seized and garrisoned by the royalists. Middlesex did not live long after this cruel blow. He died on 5 August 1645 at the earl of Dorset's house in the Strand and was buried in Westminster Abbey nine days later, although he had wanted to be buried in Gloucester. Despite the tribulations of the years after his fall from office he was able to bequeath to James estates worth £76,500, producing an annual revenue of £4600. Copt Hall was remodelled but Middlesex's life was marked by the house at Wiston and the grand memorial in Westminster Abbey. He had, in the final analysis, risen much further than he had fallen. MICHAEL J. BRADDICK

Sources M. Prestwich, *Cranfield: politics and profits under the early Stuarts* (1966) · R. H. Tawney, *Business and politics under James I* (1958) · C. Russell, *Parliaments and English politics, 1621–1629* (1979) · R. Lockyer, *The early Stuarts: a political history of England, 1603–1642* (1989) · G. E. Aylmer, 'Attempts at administrative reform, 1625–40', *EngHR*, 72 (1957), 229–59 · M. B. Young, 'Illusions of grandeur and reform at the Jacobean court: Cranfield and the ordnance', *HJ*, 22 (1979), 53–73 · D. C. Beaver, 'The great deer massacre: animals, honor and communication in early modern England', *Journal of British Studies*, 38 (1999), 187–216 · *Calendar of the manuscripts of Major-General Lord Sackville*, 2 vols., HMC, 80 (1940–66)
Archives E. Sussex RO, accounts · LPL, household book | CKS, Sackville papers, personal, official, and business corresp. and papers
Likenesses D. Mytens, oils, 1620, Knole, Kent [*see illus.*] · N. Stone, tomb effigy, 1645, Westminster Abbey, Chapel of St Benedict · W. Hollar, etching, BM
Wealth at death £76,500: Prestwich, *Cranfield*, 587

Cranford, James (1602/3–1657), Church of England clergyman, was the son of James Cranford, master of the free school of Coventry. He matriculated from Balliol College, Oxford, aged fifteen, on 20 November 1618, graduated BA on 17 October 1621, and proceeded MA on 10 June 1624. In 1623 he was incorporated into Cambridge University. Cranford was ordained and was rector of Brockhall in Northamptonshire from 25 October 1627 to 4 May 1643. During this period he was also administering to the spiritual needs of the Spencer family chapel at Althorp. By 1628 he had married his wife, Abigaell; their eldest son, James, was born at Daventry late that year or early in 1629.

Like many puritan clergymen Cranford supported the Scottish war against the imposition of Archbishop Laud's religious ceremonies. The Laudian minister Robert Sibthorpe denounced Cranford and other Northamptonshire puritan ministers in June 1639 for refusing to aid the king against the Scots, Cranford stating that the invasion of the Scots was 'only for peace' (Webster, 232). His support of the Scots probably brought him into contact with the network of like-minded London puritan clergy. In September 1641 the parishioners of St Christopher-le-Stocks, London, appointed Cranford as their parish lecturer. It appears from the parish records, however, that he was employed to fill the place of the absentee and pluralist rector John Hansley, who resigned the living in 1643 in his favour. From his earliest days in London, Cranford was a supporter of parliament's cause. In 1642 he edited *The Tears of Ireland*, a pamphlet graphically reporting the alleged atrocities committed by Irish Catholic rebels against protestants. He also wrote prefaces to a number of puritan and parliamentarian tracts and on 20 June 1643 was made one of the parliamentarian licensers for the press.

From the mid-1640s Cranford was an important member of the movement that campaigned to establish presbyterianism in the Church of England. This brought him political censure in June 1645 when he acted as an agent of the Scottish commissioner Robert Baillie to discredit a number of Independent MPs and lords who opposed a presbyterian settlement. At the instigation of Baillie,

Cranford spread rumours at the Royal Exchange that a number of lords, including Viscount Saye and Sele, were going to betray the parliamentarian cause to the royalists. For his pains the House of Commons committed Cranford to the Tower for a month, fined him a total of £2000, and forced him publicly to recant. However, in furtherance of the presbyterian cause, in November that year Cranford was also a signatory of a report to London's common council, which recommended that the council petition parliament for the 'presbyteriall Government' to be 'forthwith established amongst us according to the Word of God and the example of the best Reformed Churches' (CLRO, Journals of the common council 40, fols. 151v–152v). In summer 1646 he established a presbytery within his parish and instituted godly discipline, agreeing with parishioners to catechize their children and servants. Later in that year he acted with the seventh London classis and from May 1647 he was often delegated to attend the London provincial assembly. During the session between November and May 1651 Cranford was elected as the province's moderator. He was also involved with Sion College, which gained notoriety as a club for London presbyterians during the period 1643–60; between 1653 and 1655 he was the college's president.

Cranford was one of the leaders of the presbyterian campaign against the toleration of heterodox opinion. On 1 February 1646 he preached a sermon before the lord mayor and City, published as *Haereseo-machia, or, The Mishchiefe which Heresies Doe* (1646). This sermon, on 2 Timothy 2: 17, taught that 'Erroneous and unsound doctrine is of a devouring nature: Their word … will eat as doth a gangrene' (sig. A2). This sermon provoked a broadsheet reply from a disgruntled sectary. Cranford also licensed many pamphlets attacking heresy, including Thomas Edwards's *Gangraena* (1646), to which he wrote the prefaces. Throughout the interregnum he was often the presbyterians' champion in disputations with advocates of sectarian belief. In December 1645 he and Edmund Calamy arranged to debate with the Baptists Benjamin Cox, William Kiffen, and Hansard Knowles, but the debate was stopped by the lord mayor, who feared that disorder would break out. In summer 1650 Cranford moderated two disputations between the Arminian John Goodwin and the Calvinist Independents Vavasour Powell and John Simpson. By 1652 he was debating with Dr Peter Chamberlen, a seventh-day Baptist, on the right of the laity to preach and the validity of the presbyterian ministry's ordination.

Like many other presbyterians Cranford was a fierce opponent of the republic that replaced the Stuart monarchy. He provided the imprimatur to the *Vindication* of the members secluded by Pride's Purge and so on 16 March 1649 the Rump Parliament revoked his publishing licence. On 27 June 1650 he and William Jenkyn were brought before the committee for plundered ministers and questioned for ignoring an official day of public humiliation. Like many London presbyterian ministers, he was implicated in the covenanter conspiracy of Christopher Love.

Cranford died from illness on 22 April 1657 and was buried on 27 April at St Christopher-le-Stocks, where he was succeeded by his son and namesake, who died in 1659. His will, drawn up on 14 April, shows that his estate did not amount to much, but he attempted to divide his few possessions fairly among his wife, Abigaell, five sons, James, Joseph, Nathaniell, Jonathan (destined on his return 'backe into England' to be apprenticed to a surgeon), and Josias, and five daughters, Elizabeth (wife of Henry Smith), Abigaell, Rebecca, Hepzibah (bound apprentice to 'an Exchange man'), and Mary. However, with such a small estate, Cranford could only forgive the debts of his older children and leave the proceeds of his library to his younger children. E. C. VERNON

Sources E. C. Vernon, 'The Sion College conclave and London presbyterianism during the English revolution', PhD diss., U. Cam., 1999 · P. Chamberlen, *The disputes between Mr Cranford and Dr Chamberlen* (1652) · *Truths conflict with error* (1650) · M. Mahony, 'The presbyterian party in the Long Parliament', DPhil diss., U. Oxf., 1972 · V. Pearl, 'London puritans and Scotch fifth columnists', *Studies in London history presented to Philip Edmund Jones*, ed. A. E. J. Hollender and W. Kellaway (1969), 317–31 · E. Freshfield, ed., *Minutes of the vestry meetings and other records of the parish of St Christopher* (privately printed, London, 1886) · journals, CLRO, court of common council, 40, fols. 151–152v · H. I. Longden, *Northamptonshire and Rutland clergy from 1500*, ed. P. I. King and others, 16 vols. in 6, Northamptonshire RS (1938–52), vol. 3, p. 285 · Foster, *Alum. Oxon.* · Venn, *Alum. Cant.* · *Mercurius Politicus* (27 June–4 July 1650), 50–52 · BL, Add. MS 70006, fol. 63 · will, PRO, PROB 11/264, fols. 133v–134v · T. Webster, *Godly clergy in early Stuart England: the Caroline puritan movement, c.1620–1643* (1997)

Cranford, William (d. c.1645), composer, is of unknown origins. He is known as a proficient, minor musician of the pre-Commonwealth period, though little is recorded about his life. He was active as a composer at least from the second decade of the seventeenth century and appears to have been based in London throughout his career. On the death of Prince Henry in 1612 he wrote an elegy for six voices, 'Weep, Brittaynes, weep', and he contributed the psalm tune 'Ely' to Thomas Ravenscroft's *The Whole Booke of Psalmes* of 1621. At this time he was probably associated with St Paul's Cathedral; certainly by 1624 he was a lay vicar there, and he continued to hold that post until the 1640s. Little of Cranford's church music survives, and much of this is incompletely preserved. His verse anthems include the simple 'O Lord, make thy servant Charles', which dates probably from the early years of Charles I's reign. The text of one of his anthems was included at the Restoration in James Clifford's *The Divine Services and Anthems* (1663).

Cranford's secular music consists mainly of catches and instrumental works. The former, of which John Hawkins thought highly, include 'Boy come back', which appears in some of John Playford's anthologies with a companion piece, 'Boy go down', by Simon Ives, a fellow singer at St Paul's. Another catch, 'Let's live good honest lives', was later adapted by Henry Purcell (Hawkins claimed that Purcell added the words). Although he held no position at court, Cranford wrote much music for viol consort; the twenty surviving examples include fantasias, dances, and variations, most of them composed in or before the 1630s.

Later writers have noted in these works a distinctive harmonic style and interesting textural effects, and in these respects his consort music has much in common with that of one of the major composers in the field, William Lawes. Cranford died probably about 1645, in which year his name was not recorded with those of other vicars-choral at St Paul's. PETER LYNAN

Sources A. Ashbee, 'Cranford, William', *New Grove*, 2nd edn · J. Hawkins, *A general history of the science and practice of music*, new edn, 3 vols. (1853); repr. in 2 vols. (1963), 584 · P. Le Huray, *Music and the Reformation in England, 1549–1660* (1967); repr. with corrections (1978)

Cranke, James (1746–1826), painter, was born on 21 February 1746 and baptized on 9 March at St George's Church in Bloomsbury, London, the second son of the seven children of the painter James Cranke (1707–1780) and his wife, Elizabeth (1729/30–1791), née Essex. When Cranke was nine his family settled in Urswick, Lancashire, his father's birthplace, where it is believed that he attended the local grammar school. It is supposed that he received his initial training in his father's studio before travelling to the continent to study at the galleries of Dresden and Antwerp. Gaythorpe noted that his altarpiece at Queen's College, Oxford, is a copy of Leonardo da Vinci's *Adoration of the Shepherds* at Dresden and that his copy of Rubens's *Saviour after his Resurrection* at Antwerp is at Pembroke College, Oxford (Gaythorpe, 137). By 1773 Cranke had returned to England and was practising in Warrington, Lancashire, where he was commissioned to paint a copy of Andrea del Sarto's *Holy Family*, which was placed above the altar of Trinity Church in that town. During this period Cranke also began to establish himself as a portraitist, primarily undertaking work for local gentry families in Lancashire and Cheshire. One of his best-known portraits dating from this interval is that of Thomas Peter Legh of Lyme, colonel of the 3rd Lancashire light dragoons, which was later engraved by Hardy.

In April 1775 Cranke entered the Royal Academy Schools when his age was given as twenty-seven and is recorded as having exhibited twelve works there between this date and 1798. Although a number of London addresses are cited for him during this period, it is uncertain whether he worked exclusively in the capital or continued to accept commissions in Warrington. By 1800, however, Cranke had moved to Gainford, co. Durham, in order to care for his ailing clergyman brother. While in Gainford he turned his attention to creating religious compositions in addition to painting the royal arms for the vestry of the church. Upon the death of his brother, the artist returned to Urswick, where he lived the remainder of his life with his nephew at Hawkfield in the village. In his old age Cranke began to suffer from impaired eyesight before eventually succumbing to blindness. Shortly before his death his portrait was painted by Daniel Gardner. The parish register for Urswick contains the record: 'James Cranke of Hawkfield, passed away, 1826, aged 80 years'. He was apparently unmarried. He was buried in Urswick churchyard on 24 January 1826. Both during his lifetime and after, Cranke has been confused with the miniaturist Joseph Cranke as well as with his father, James Cranke sen., who was at one time thought to be his uncle. For this reason it has proved difficult to establish conclusively works by his hand. HALLIE RUBENHOLD

Sources B. Stewart and M. Cutten, *The dictionary of portrait painters in Britain up to 1920* (1997) · H. Gaythorpe, 'Two "old masters": the Crankes of Urswick', *Transactions of the Cumberland and Westmorland Antiquarian and Archaeological Society*, new ser., 6 (1905–6), 128–42 [incl. list of paintings] · M. Hall, *The artists of Cumbria* (1979)
Archives Cumbria AS, Barrow, account book and book of designs
Likenesses D. Gardner, portrait, priv. coll.; repro. in Gaythorpe, 'Two "old masters"', facing p. 137

Cranko, John Cyril (1927–1973), ballet dancer and choreographer, was born on 15 August 1927 in Rustenburg, about 60 miles from Johannesburg, South Africa, the only child of Herbert Cranko, a lawyer who later went on to practise in Johannesburg itself, and his wife, (Hilda) Grace, daughter of Thomas Hinds, farmer at Magaliesberg, Transvaal, of English ancestry. She had a daughter from a previous marriage. The father's family were of Dutch ancestry, their name originally having been Krankoor. John Cranko spent his childhood in Johannesburg. After attending the co-educational Highlands North state high school and studying ballet privately with Marjorie Sturman, at the age of seventeen he joined the University of Cape Town Ballet School in 1944 and went to London to attend the Sadler's Wells Ballet School in 1946. Largely for ideological reasons, he never worked in South Africa again.

In 1947 Cranko danced with the Sadler's Wells Ballet and was encouraged to choreograph by Ninette de Valois. In 1951 he achieved popular success with *Pineapple Poll*, a cheerful retelling of a Sir W. S. Gilbert absurdity with more than a hint of *HMS Pinafore*, to a medley of tunes by Sir Arthur Sullivan, and this willingness to refashion material well within his audience's theatregoing experience became a characteristic of his later work. Whereas the Diaghilev company seemed almost embarrassed at the success of their potboiling *Boutique fantasque* (1919), that kind of success was far more representative of Cranko's achievements. It was a crucial difference. His *Beauty and the Beast* (1949) remade in dance Jean Cocteau's more successful film. His *Harlequin in April* (1951), and the well-known *Lady and the Fool* (1954), both used *commedia dell'arte* themes. In 1957 with *Prince of the Pagodas* (which had a specially commissioned score by Benjamin Britten) and in 1961 with *Antigone* he attempted a level of creativity he could not sustain. His intimate revue *Cranks* in 1955 had been very successful, enlarging the dance content of this popular but overworked genre, but his attempt to repeat the formula in 1960 with *New Cranks* was unsuccessful, as was his involvement in a musical, *Keep your Hair on* (1958).

A scandal in his private life (a prosecution for homosexuality) as well as these artistic set-backs led him to change direction and become director of the Opera Ballet in Stuttgart in 1961, where Nicholas Beriosoff as previous director had already begun to raise standards. Cranko made the company a popular success, the focus for a

John Cyril Cranko (1927–1973), by Sir Cecil Beaton, 1956

general renaissance of ballet in Germany, and choreographed a series of works for it, achieving an increasing reputation until his tragically early death in 1973.

His artistic set-backs from 1957 to 1960 were a watershed in his career. The Stuttgart Ballet audience had little experience of ballet, particularly of British ballet, and in the pressure for new works, itself a symptom of an unsophisticated public, Cranko inclined to opt for what was artistically the easy way out: to borrow other people's ideas and achievements, which a more knowledgeable audience might have been less willing to accept. His Neapolitan dance in his *Swan Lake* (1963), for example, came as close to being a crib of the Neapolitan of Sir Frederick Ashton as possible without being a straight copy, and these borrowings were too often apparent in Cranko's work. He tended also not to worry about an occasional clumsiness in the pressure to complete work and get it on stage, rather than revise and refine, particularly as he increasingly became aware that his Stuttgart audiences were easily pleased. He was most acclaimed for his 'story' ballets, making much use of effects from legitimate theatre, showing a shrewd sense of what worked in theatrical terms, and using broad effects with skill. In *Swan Lake* his prince was finally engulfed in a watery grave, appearing and disappearing in the waves in fine Romantic style, and his *Romeo and Juliet* (1962) showed a sensitive understanding of how to arrange dance transitions from scene to scene. His best works for Stuttgart depended on other people's achievements: *Romeo and Juliet*, *Swan Lake*, *Onegin* (1965), *Taming of the Shrew* (1969), and *Carmen* (1971).

Stuttgart, as an industrial centre, lacked the activity in all the arts which stretched Cranko's capacity and imagination in London, and his Stuttgart company tended to exist as an artistic enclave. This made for a family atmosphere and Cranko, who was extrovert and emotionally insecure, came to depend very much on his dancers as a substitute family. He increasingly relied on his principals and his ballet *Initials RBME* (1972) was created for and by

them—Richard Cragun, Birgit Keil, Marcia Haydée, and Egon Madsen. The long-term effects of this gifted quartet dancing most of the leading roles may not have been altogether healthy for the company's development as a whole. Cranko, impulsive and idealistic, had great charm, and in his curtain speeches achieved an impressive personal relationship with his German audience.

The Stuttgart ballet company's achievements were based on a long-term and sensible plan worked out by Cranko. He encouraged choreographers, including John Neumeier and Jiri Kylián, to develop within the company, and also encouraged Kenneth MacMillan to work there as well. MacMillan's major work *The Song of the Earth* (1965), originally turned down at Covent Garden, was performed by the Stuttgart company. Cranko also developed a ballet school to serve the company. His company and his narrative ballets won considerable praise and popular success, at the Edinburgh Festival in 1963, in South America in 1967, in New York at the Lincoln Center, on tour in America in 1969 and 1973, and at Covent Garden just after his death.

While returning to Stuttgart by plane from Philadelphia with his company after a successful tour, on 26 June 1973 Cranko succumbed to a vomiting fit brought on by a sleeping drug, and choked to death. He was unmarried.

NICHOLAS DROMGOOLE, *rev.*

Sources H. Kögler and others, *John Cranko und das Stuttgarter Ballett* (1969) · J. Percival, *Theatre in my blood* (1983) · personal knowledge (1986) · *CGPLA Eng. & Wales* (1973) · D. Craine and J. Mackrell, eds., *The Oxford dictionary of dance* (2000) · *The Times* (27 June 1973) **Likenesses** C. Beaton, photograph, 1956, NPG [*see illus.*] · photographs, Hult. Arch.
Wealth at death £37,554: probate, 17 Dec 1973, *CGPLA Eng. & Wales*

Crankshaw, Edward (1909–1984), writer and commentator on Soviet affairs, was born on 3 January 1909 in London, the elder son (there were no daughters) of Arthur Crankshaw, later chief clerk to Old Street magistrates' court, and of his wife, Amy Bishop. He was small in stature and suffered from a weak chest, and the family soon moved out to Letchworth in Hertfordshire for the sake of his health. He was educated at Bishop's Stortford College. His parents wished him to go to university, but in a first display of his romantic and headstrong side he went alone to Vienna, aged eighteen, and taught English in the Berlitz School. Here began the deepest intellectual attachment of Crankshaw's life. He learned excellent German, and immersed himself in German and Austrian history and culture, developing not only his talent as a writer but his particular sense of politics as an expression of inherited 'national character'. On his return, he worked in the advertising department of *The Times* and began to write reviews—mostly musical—for *The Spectator*, *The Bookman*, and other periodicals.

In 1931 Crankshaw married Clare, daughter of Ernest Carr, a civil servant; the marriage was childless. After 1933, at their home in Hampstead, London, the Crankshaws gathered around them many of the German and

Austrian intellectual refugees from Hitlerism. Crankshaw began to translate German plays and his versions were staged; when the revolutionary Ernst Toller arrived in England, he 'adopted' Crankshaw and his wife, and Crankshaw put five of Toller's plays into English in the next few years. He was by now writing his own books: *Joseph Conrad: some Aspects of the Art of the Novel* appeared in 1936, and in 1938 he published *Vienna: a Culture in Decline* and *Nina Lessing*, the first of his three novels. In spite of these successes, the Crankshaws were existing on erratic scraps of income, and in the mid-1930s they left London for a cottage in Kent. Most of the rest of Crankshaw's life was spent in the village of Sandhurst, in west Kent; he worked alone and found the research and contacts which he needed on regular forays to London.

A man who was a friend both of Toller and of the novelist Ford Madox Ford was hard to catalogue politically. Crankshaw has been called a 'romantic conservative', but his gesture of joining the territorials in 1936, which dismayed some left-wing friends, turned out to be only too practical. 'If there is going to be a war', he observed, 'I might as well learn how to do it.' When war came, his knowledge of German brought him into military intelligence. Then, to his surprise, he was posted to the British military mission in Moscow. He had to learn Russian, and was in the country for less than three years. But, while deploring the regime, he came to love the Russian people as they fought for their survival, and to understand the historic roots of their political system in the tsarist autocratic tradition.

When Crankshaw joined *The Observer* in 1947 he was at first reluctant to write about Soviet affairs. He felt his strength lay not in political analysis but in literary and especially musical criticism (Artur Schnabel was a close friend). However, he let himself be tempted, and within a few years had become Britain's most authoritative and persuasive commentator on the USSR and its 'sphere of influence'. He wrote almost weekly until his retirement in 1968, and not much less frequently after that.

Crankshaw was not a true 'Kremlinologist', remarking once that 'the difference between Brezhnev and his colleagues seemed of no more interest than the difference between a number of stale buns'. Instead, he treated Soviet affairs much in the manner of the theatre reviewer he had once been. Nor was he an ideological 'cold warrior', but—for all his loathing of the Soviet system and his pessimism about its capacity for reform—a firm advocate of peaceful coexistence. His real testament is the preface, written when he was a dying man, to *Putting up with the Russians* (1984), his aptly named collection of shorter writings. In this preface, he furiously attacked the contemporary American ambition to evict the Soviet Union from all influence outside its own borders.

Crankshaw published numerous books on the changing Soviet scene, and his book on Nazi terror, *Gestapo* (1956), was widely read. But in 1963 he began to produce the ambitious, deeply researched books which are his main literary work. *The Fall of the House of Habsburg* appeared in

that year; *Maria Theresa* in 1969; and his masterly *The Shadow of the Winter Palace*, a study of nineteenth-century Russia, in 1976.

Slight and gentlemanly in appearance, Crankshaw controlled a wild and independent nature. But even at the height of his fame, his modesty was phenomenal. He justified his own retirement by saying that he hated the Brezhnev leadership too much to be able to be fair to it. The Austrian government awarded him the Ehrenkreuz für Wissenschaft und Kunst in 1964, and the British followed with a series of prizes for his books including the Heinemann award in 1977 and the Whitbread prize in 1982 (for his *Bismarck*, 1981). He died at his home, Church House, Sandhurst, Hawkhurst, Kent, after a long illness, on 30 November 1984, continuing to write even when he was too sick to leave his bed. NEAL ASCHERSON, *rev.*

Sources *The Times* (3 Dec 1984) · *The Observer* (2 Dec 1984) · personal knowledge (1984) · *CGPLA Eng. & Wales* (1985)
Archives NRA, priv. coll., corresp. and literary papers · RS | Royal Society of Literature, London, letters to Royal Society of Literature · U. Reading L., letters to Bodley Head Ltd
Wealth at death £111,621: probate, 21 Jan 1985, *CGPLA Eng. & Wales*

Cranley, Thomas (*c*.1337–1417), archbishop of Dublin and administrator, probably came from Cranleigh in Surrey. He was a student at Oxford and proceeded to the degree of doctor in divinity, his name first appearing in 1366, as a fellow of Merton College. He was ordained by William of Wykeham, bishop of Winchester, and was admitted rector of Cranleigh, Surrey, on 16 May 1380, readmitted on 4 December 1381. Under Wykeham's patronage, he was nominated first warden in the foundation charter of St Mary's College of Winchester, 20 October 1382; but as the foundation had not yet fully taken effect he did not leave Oxford and in 1384 was renting Hart Hall. On 12 May 1389 he resigned the wardenship of Winchester College and was the next day collated to the wardenship of Wykeham's New College, Oxford, a post he held until 25 February 1396. In 1390 he was made chancellor of the university. He held various benefices, including Havant in Winchester (2 December 1390) and Bishopsbourne, near Canterbury (10 September 1396), and was collated to the prebend of Knaresborough in York (3 July 1395). He was one of the assessors at the trial of Walter Brut for heresy in 1393. He apparently impressed Richard II with his preaching and served him abroad, being absent on an embassy to Paris in June–July 1395, and in Rome from February to December 1397. In September 1397 he was promoted to the vacant archbishopric of Dublin and received restitution of the temporalities in December 1397.

Cranley was appointed chancellor of Ireland on 24 April 1398, the post being exercised by a deputy until he arrived in Ireland on 7 October. He was confirmed in the office after the accession of Henry IV and held it until 4 January 1400, although his successor Alexander Balscot, bishop of Meath, was appointed on 18 November 1399. In February 1401 he was sent by the Irish parliament with John Colton, archbishop of Armagh, to report to the king on the dangerous state of the lordship. He was again made chancellor on 4 July 1401, apparently when still in England. During serious illness in 1402 a deputy was commissioned to act for him as chancellor. In 1406 a deputy was again required, as Cranley was occupied, presumably in defence of the Dublin marches. In July 1406 he was replaced by Laurence Merbury, although the great seal was not passed to the new chancellor until September. He clearly had the confidence of many in the lordship and in 1411 was again nominated as messenger from a great council to the king, an occasion which showed him allied to critics of the justiciar of Ireland, Thomas Butler, prior of Kilmainham. On 20 April 1413 he was appointed chancellor once more and was in office when, on the death of the lieutenant, John Stanley, in January 1414, the Irish council elected him justiciar, to be assisted by two military governors. He was replaced as chancellor by Laurence Merbury on 2 March 1414, but remained justiciar until Sir John Talbot, appointed in February, arrived in November 1414. He served again in early 1416 as Talbot's deputy in his absence in England.

In 1417 Cranley was again chosen to present to the king the grievances of the Irish parliament, but the chancellor refused to seal the complaint, an indication of his own position within the current factional interests in Ireland. Cranley went to England on 30 April 1417 and died at Faringdon, Berkshire, on 25 May. He was buried before the altar of New College chapel in Oxford, with a memorial brass, bearing an inscription; the brass is now in the antechapel.

In a petition of 1421 from the Irish parliament to the king Cranley was praised for his conduct as justiciar, and his administration singled out as a good example. Exceptional qualities are indicated in his continued selection for office into old age. Henry of Marlborough also refers to his character, learning, generosity, and interest in building. The difficulties Cranley faced in administrative office were described in a complaint to the king, expressed in a poetical epistle consisting of 106 verses, which Leland saw but which is no longer extant. Nine volumes of theological works survive from his donation to the library of New College in 1393.   D. B. JOHNSTON

Sources Chancery records · E. Tresham, ed., *Rotulorum patentium et clausorum cancellariae Hiberniae calendarium*, Irish Record Commission (1828) · *The whole works of Sir James Ware concerning Ireland*, ed. and trans. W. Harris, rev. edn, 2 vols. in 3 (1764) · J. Buxton and P. Williams, eds., *New College, Oxford, 1379–1979* (1979) · T. F. Kirby, ed., *Wykeham's register*, 2 vols., Hampshire RS, 11 (1896–9) · H. F. Berry and J. F. Morrissey, eds., *Statute rolls of the parliament of Ireland*, 4 vols. (1907–39), vol. 1 · Henry of Marlborough, 'Chronicle of Ireland', *The historie of Ireland*, ed. [J. Ware] (1633); repr. as *Ancient Irish histories*, 2 (1809) · *Fasti Angl., 1300–1541*, [York] · Emden, *Oxf.* · W. W. Capes, ed., *Registrum Johannis Trefnant*, CYS, 20 (1916) · F. W. Steer, *The archives of New College, Oxford* (1974) · *Commentarii de scriptoribus Britannicis, auctore Joanne Lelando*, ed. A. Hall, 2 vols. (1709) · PRO, Exchequer enrolled accounts, E 364/41/3 · A. Wood, *The history and antiquities of the colleges and halls in the University of Oxford*, ed. J. Gutch (1786)
Likenesses monumental brass effigy, c.1417, New College, Oxford

Cranley, Thomas (*fl.* 1613–1635), poet, was the author of *Amanda, or, The reformed whore, composed and made by Thomas Cranley gent. now a prisoner in the kings-bench* (1635), which was dedicated 'To the worshipfull his worthy friend and brother-in-law, Thomas Gilbourne, Esquire'. In 1639 the work was reissued under the title of *The Converted Courtezan, or, The Reformed Whore*. It is valuable for the vivid description that it gives of the town life of the time, and the verse is not ill written. Shakespeare's *Venus and Adonis* is mentioned as one of Amanda's books in her unregenerate days. In 1613 George Wither, in *Abuses Stript, and Whipt*, addressed a copy of verses 'To his deare friend Thomas Cranley'. The complimentary verses prefixed to Wither's satire, subscribed 'Thy deare Friend Th. C.', were probably written by the same Cranley, and it seems safe to identify him as the author of *Amanda*. A reprint of *Amanda* was issued by Frederic Ouvry in 1869.

A. H. BULLEN, *rev.* MATTHEW STEGGLE

Sources G. Wither, *Abuses stript, and whipt* (1613) · *STC, 1475–1640*

Cranmer, George (1564–1600), administrator and scholar, was born in Kent, the eldest son of Thomas Cranmer (*d.* in or after 1600) and his wife, Anne Carpenter. Thomas was the son of Edmund Cranmer, archdeacon of Canterbury, and the nephew of Archbishop Thomas Cranmer; he may have been the registrar of the archdeaconry of Canterbury. Anne Carpenter's brother, John, married the sister of William Davison, who was briefly secretary of state in 1586–7. George Cranmer attended Merchant Taylors' School, London, while Richard Mulcaster was headmaster, being admitted on 6 April 1571. His entrance was registered on the same day as that of his younger brother Thomas, and Edwin Sandys, son of the bishop of London; George Cranmer and Edwin Sandys remained closely associated. On 10 January 1578 Cranmer entered Corpus Christi College, Oxford. He was a Merchant Taylors' exhibitioner from 1581 to 1583 and graduated on 29 May 1583, in the same year being elected fellow of his college. On 11 July 1589 he proceeded MA.

In 1579 Cranmer had been joined at Corpus Christi by Sandys, and both were placed under the tuition of the theologian Richard Hooker. According to Dr King, bishop of Chichester, 'betwixt Mr. Hooker and these his two Pupils there was a sacred Friendship made up of Religious Principles' and 'elemented in Youth'. In order that they might 'become the more serviceable unto their own' Cranmer and Sandys were compelled to 'leave Mr. Hooker to his College' as they departed Oxford to travel on the continent. They returned some time before March 1585, on their way visiting their old tutor at Drayton Beauchamp in Buckinghamshire where Hooker then had the living (Walton, sig. C8v). Dismayed by the circumstances of their friend's marital life there, however, they departed the next day. Cranmer continued his association with Hooker and in a letter dated February 1598 (published in 1642 under the title *Concerning the New Church Discipline*) discusses the arguments raised in Hooker's work on ecclesiastical polity, proffering support and advice. Among other things he suggests that Hooker answer the nonconformists' criticism of non-residences by comparing these to the situation in 'the Civil State' where a man can 'have a great and gainful Office in the North, himself continually remaining in the South' (Walton, sig. O7v).

Although his father wished him to enter the church, it was in this 'civil state' that Cranmer sought and found employment. He found his first position in October 1586 with the assistance of his maternal uncle John Carpenter, who persuaded his brother-in-law Davison, then joint secretary of state with Sir Francis Walsingham, to take Cranmer into his service. Unfortunately, a few months later in February 1587 Davison was dismissed from his post, accused of being over-hasty in sealing the warrant for the execution of Mary Stuart, and Cranmer was forced to look for employment elsewhere. He found this as secretary to Henry Killigrew during his embassy to the Low Countries. He continued to correspond with his previous, now disgraced, employer and in April 1588 wrote to Davison from The Hague informing him of developments there. On 6 November 1597 Cranmer and Sandys registered at the academy of Geneva. Cranmer's final employment was as secretary to Charles Blount, Lord Mountjoy, whom he accompanied on his military campaign in Ireland. He left England early in 1600. In a letter thanking Henry Cuffe, secretary to the earl of Essex, for his introduction to Cranmer, Anthony Standen described him as 'a mild, modest man and as I see chief about his Lord' (CSP Ire., 39).

Cranmer was killed in Ireland on 16 July 1600 during a skirmish with Irish rebels at Carlingford, at which Dr Latewar, Mountjoy's chaplain and another former pupil of Merchant Taylors' School, also died.

PATRICIA BREWERTON

Sources I. Walton, *The life of Richard Hooker: the author of those learned books of the laws of ecclesiastical polity* (1665) · Foster, *Alum. Oxon.* · *CSP dom., 1581–90* · *CSP for., 1588* · W. Camden, *The historie of the most renowned and victorious princesse Elizabeth*, trans. R. N. [R. Norton] (1630) · G. M. Bell, *A handlist of British diplomatic representatives, 1509–1688*, Royal Historical Society Guides and Handbooks, 16 (1990) · *CSP Ire., 1600* · H. B. Wilson, *The history of Merchant Taylors' School from its foundation to the present time*, 2 vols. (1812) · C. J. Robinson, ed., *A register of the scholars admitted into Merchant Taylors' School, from AD 1562 to 1874*, 1 (1882) · Wood, *Ath. Oxon.*, 1st edn · G. Cranmer, *Concerning the new church discipline* (1642) · Tanner, *Bibl. Brit.-Hib.* · *Le livre du recteur: catalogue des étudiants de l'académie de Genève, 1559–1878* (Geneva, 1959–)

Cranmer, Margaret (d. c.1575), wife of Archbishop Thomas Cranmer (1489–1556), was German by origin, the niece of Katharina Preu, wife of Andreas Osiander, Nuremberg's leading Lutheran preacher and reformer. Thomas *Cranmer visited Nuremberg intermittently from March to August 1532 on his mission to win the support of Emperor Charles V for Henry VIII's divorce. He became intimate with Osiander, visiting his house frequently, and a long-term friendship developed based on common interests. He also met and married Margaret, an extraordinary step for an ordained priest, and one entailing incalculable risks for husband and wife.

Margaret remained in Germany while Cranmer continued his mission, but two months later Henry recalled him to be consecrated archbishop. Some time later Margaret slipped into England. Yet though she bore a daughter, Margaret, and perhaps other children who did not survive, the marriage remained hidden throughout Henry's reign. To explain those hidden years, Elizabethan recusants gleefully circulated stories of Cranmer's 'pretty nobsey' travelling in a ventilated chest. Essentially, however, it was the loyalty of friends, a happy marriage, and a harmonious household that protected them from gossip. Margaret herself never revealed what this marriage meant to her, but her influence can plausibly be seen on Cranmer. In his innovative marriage service of 1549 the couple now vowed to love and cherish each other, and Cranmer added a third reason for marriage, as well as the traditional procreation and avoidance of sin. It was for 'the mutuall societie, helpe and coumfort, that the one oughte to have of thother, both in prosperitie and adversitie'.

Until the Act of Six Articles was passed on 5 June 1539 the Cranmers were protected from earlier attacks on clerical marriage by wording which limited prosecution to openly known marriages. But the new act was uncompromisingly conservative: married priests, unless they divorced, were declared felons without benefit of clergy. Margaret returned to Germany with the children before the final deadline expired on 12 July. The conservatives were riding high, and sought to brand Cranmer a heretic. Early in autumn 1543 in a private conversation aboard the royal barge (for which Margaret herself may have been the source) the king challenged Cranmer on the six articles, whose adoption he had opposed in the Lords. Cranmer assured him of his compliance, and Henry asked him 'merily' whether 'his inner or privie bed were free from those articles'. The king clearly knew of his marriage, and Cranmer confessed its circumstances, whereupon the king, reassured of his loyalty, named his accusers and appointed Cranmer for searching out his own cause (Parker, 392–3). Margaret subsequently returned.

Under Edward VI protestantism flourished. Retrospectively the Catholic author of *Cranmer's Recantacyons* (almost certainly Nicholas Harpsfield) charged Margaret with undue influence over her husband. Certainly she had as strong an interest in the legalization of clerical marriage as he did. After the act sanctioning it was passed in 1549 she appeared in public, and on 1 June 1550 Stumphius reported to Bullinger in Zürich that Cranmer had 'lately taken a wife' (Robinson, *Original Letters*, 2.466). The Cranmers now had a son, Thomas, and were thinking dynastically. Kirkstall Abbey and Arthington Nunnery, which Cranmer held from the crown, were put in trust for his own use for life, with remainder to the executors of his will for twenty years, and then to his son Thomas.

After the accession of Mary on 19 July 1553 things changed dramatically. Within two months Cranmer, implicated in the Jane Grey fiasco following Edward's death, was imprisoned, charged with treason. In November he was convicted and his estates forfeited. What happened to Margaret between this time and Cranmer's death at the stake on 21 March 1556 is uncertain. Some scholars have assumed she simply abandoned him. It seems, however, that she lingered in England, even though no contact between the couple is known. When the archbishop's goods and chattels were sold off after the treason trial, enough was reserved to provide Margaret with a modest lifestyle. She also had friends. Thomas Norton remembered the great kindness John Scott showed her 'in the time of her adversitie after the Archbishop's troble and deathe' (PRO, C3/217/30).

Clergy children were legally bastards even in Edward's reign, and responsibility for hers fell on Margaret. She and young Thomas fled to Europe, and there she remarried. Edward *Whitchurch (d. 1562) was such a man as protestant martyrs advised their wives to take in their widowhoods: godly men who would be good fathers to their children. He was also Cranmer's favoured publisher, and he made Margaret's interests his own. Using his connections with the book trade Whitchurch engineered a grant of Cranmer's attainted properties to protestant printers John Gawen and Reyner Wolfe, acting covertly for Margaret. Following the accession of Elizabeth the properties were renegotiated in favour of young Thomas.

Back in London the Whitchurches shared their house with Thomas Norton, whose marriage Edward arranged to the younger Margaret Cranmer. About the end of 1561 they moved to Camberwell, near Lambeth, where they leased the manor house of Edward Scott, with whom they shared it, and where Margaret turned farmer. Whitchurch died in late November or early December 1562 and Margaret was an executor of the will. Under it she received her widow's thirds and 'her' lands at Kirkstall. So empowered, she prosecuted one of its tenants. Early in 1564 both Thomas, a minor, and his sister, now adult and married, were restored in blood.

A chancery lawsuit (PRO, C3/217/30) reveals the history of Margaret's last years, although the manuscript is sometimes deficient, and the order of events uncertain. Margaret married her third husband, Bartholomew Scott, on 29 November 1564. His family moved in the Whitchurch circle: his father was John Scott, his brother Edward Scott, and Thomas Norton his friend. Before the marriage Thomas Norton drew up an extensive book of covenants to protect Margaret's interests, with a penalty of £500 for contraventions, and Norton and Wolfe were to be responsible to Margaret for suing for the penalty if need arose. Scott demurred: the terms were too stiff, too 'dark'. Norton assured him they would not be narrowly interpreted, and he capitulated. Scott had won Margaret, it was alleged, by flattery and expressions of deepest sympathy, but after marriage he dissembled no more. The marriage was without love, comfort, or mutuality. Taking money and jewels, Margaret fled secretly 'in fear of her life' to Kirkstall, where her tenant George Foxcroft sheltered her, and she summoned her son, Thomas, from Cambridge to relieve her. Scott found her, having impoverished himself in the search, as Thomas recorded. He successfully sued Foxcroft for wrongful detention, and Thomas refunded Foxcroft. Scott broke some of the covenants and Margaret urged Norton to sue him. Norton refused, claiming the

infringements were trivial. He adopted a high moral stance, demanding that she be reconciled to her husband: 'Whoever fomented such unkind and unnatural disagreement and departure were ungodly persons and workers of a wicked art'. Margaret complained of Norton to Archbishop Parker, and Wolfe shouldered the case. To avoid prosecution Scott went abroad. John Hunne, Wolfe's son-in-law, tells another story. 'In fear of her life' she complained about her husband to the archbishop and the queen's commissioners, who sequestered her for security to the house of Reyner Wolfe, where she lived for four or five years.

Norton continued to advocate reconciliation, and offered Margaret a home, but only if quarrels ceased and she had her husband's consent. Norton came to believe that ultimately she was weary of dissension and would have accepted this offer had Scott reappeared and Thomas been treated reasonably. 'Wherein', Norton remarked cryptically, 'this defendant cannot charge any man'. But Thomas was not worthy of her devotion. Fortunately she may have died before he was charged with adultery. Reyner Wolfe died about the end of 1573, and his wife the next August. Their executor John Hunne was making an inventory of household goods when he found a small chest he did not recognize. He was about to open it when Margaret broke into the room, claiming it and refusing to let him examine its 'secrets'. Next day she relented. The chest revealed a psalter, 'a little tablet made like a book for a gentlewoman to hang down to her futte with a chain', two other chains, some trifles, and five rings which Hunne thought had belonged to the archbishop:

> And this defendant Hunne having nothing to do further she took the chest and goods out of the house and conveyed it away whether this defendant knoweth not. Only the little saltre which she left behind her … in consideration of 3li she was behind me for money lent and laid out for her necessaries. (PRO, C3/217/30)

It is not known when Margaret Cranmer died, but a date in the mid-1570s seems likely. Bartholomew Scott died in 1600. A fine monument in Camberwell parish church once showed him and his third wife at prayer, with an inscription stating that Margaret Cranmer, the widow of Archbishop Cranmer, was his first wife. It was destroyed when the church was rebuilt in the 1840s.

MARY PRIOR

Sources D. MacCulloch, *Thomas Cranmer: a life* (1996) · chancery pleadings, series II, C3/217/30 (B. Scott v. T. Norton, T. Cranmer, J. Hunne); C3/170/81 (E. Scott v. B. Scott); C3/191/68 (M. Whitchurch v. J. Mylne); PRO · wills, PRO, PROB 11/45, sig. 31 [E. Whitchurch]; PRO, PROB 11/56, sig. 32 [J. Wolfe]; PRO, PROB 11/34, sig. 30 [J. Sandford] · *CPR, 1549–51; 1555–7; 1558–60* · [N. Harpsfield (?)], *Bishop Cranmer's recantacyons*, ed. Lord Houghton, Philobiblon Society Miscellany, 15 (1877–84), 8, 12 · *The acts and monuments of John Foxe*, ed. S. R. Cattley, 8 vols. (1837–41), vol. 6, pp. 692–4; vol. 7, p. 116; vol. 8, p. 173 · Bodl. Oxf., MS Jesus 74, fol. 299v · BL, Add. MS 28571, fol. 46 · R. Holinshed, 'Chronicles, &c.', c.1720–1729, Bodl. Oxf., MS Sigma 10.46 ['the excised pages'], 1475–6 · M. Parker, *De antiquitate Britannicae ecclesiae et privilegiis ecclesiae Cantuarensis* (1572), 390–93 · exchequer, king's remembrancer, inventories, PRO, E 154/2/39, fol. 77r; 154/2/41; 154/6/41 no. 7 • H. Robinson, ed. and trans., *Original letters relative to the English Reformation*, 1 vol. in 2, Parker Society, [26] (1846–7) • *Miscellaneous writings and letters of Thomas Cranmer*, ed. J. E. Cox, Parker Society, [18] (1846), 219–20, 550 • N. Harpsfield, *A treatise on the pretended divorce between Henry VIII and Catharine of Aragon*, ed. N. Pocock, CS, new ser., 21 (1878), 275 • D. Allport, *Collections illustrative of the geology, history, antiquities and associations of Camberwell and the neighbourhood* (1841), 142–7 • R. E. C. Waters, *Genealogical memoirs of the extinct family of Chester of Chicheley* (1878), 368–96, 434–50 • *London: except the cities of London and Westminster*, Pevsner (1952), 74–5 • M. A. R. Graves, *Thomas Norton: the parliament man* (1994), 35–7 • Borth. Inst., CP 1575

Wealth at death probably under £100; incl. 3 chains, one worth £23; various trifles; five rings which may have belonged to Archbishop Cranmer: PRO C3/217/30

Cranmer, Peter (1914–1994), cricketer and rugby player, was born at 18 Westfield Road, Acock's Green, Birmingham, on 10 September 1914, the son of Arthur Henry Cranmer, manager of an insurance company, and his wife, Lilian Annie, *née* Phillips. He was born into a musical family: his father later became a professional singer, and his younger brother Philip (*b.* 1918) was a gifted pianist who became professor of music at Queen's University, Belfast, and then the University of Manchester. At St Edward's School, Oxford, Peter Cranmer shone at games. In the summer of 1932 he made 911 runs with an average of 56, and was recommended to Warwickshire by one of its former players, E. P. Hewetson. On the football field he captained one of the strongest school sides. After going up to Christ Church, Oxford, in the autumn of 1933 he won a rugby blue in his first term as a fast, thrustful centre three-quarter with a devastating tackle. He had a surfeit of energy, and as an undergraduate was said to have found a game to play in—any sort of game and for anyone—every day of the week. The following season, aged nineteen, he was chosen to play rugby for England and gained the first of sixteen consecutive caps. He was always remembered as the man who gave Prince Alex Obelensky the scoring pass for both the England tries whereby in 1936 England gained her first ever victory over the All Blacks. The second was the famous one wherein 'the flying prince' on the right wing, after receiving the ball around the half-way line, wrong-footed the defence at great speed, and touched down midway between the posts and the left corner flag. Cranmer was the complete player, not only a dangerous runner and an accurate kicker but, according to the celebrated Wilfred Wooller, of Cambridge and Wales, the best defensive centre three-quarter he ever played against. England twice won the international championship during his five years in the centre.

Cranmer's cricket was modest in comparison, but in 1938 the Warwickshire committee, after deciding that R. E. S. Wyatt's leadership lacked inspiration, created a sensation by appointing Cranmer in his place. At twenty-three he was rugby football captain of England and cricket captain of Warwickshire, a double honour otherwise only achieved by the then chairman of the rugby union selectors, John Daniell. There could have been no greater contrast in outlook and disposition than between Wyatt and Cranmer. Wyatt was a serious cricketer, a notably courageous batsman behind a distinctly lugubrious expression. He was by far the best bat in the side, with forty-four hundreds for Warwickshire in the scorebook, no fewer than eight of them in the season preceding his demotion. Cranmer, strongly built and fair-haired, was an ever cheerful extrovert of much natural talent who plainly enjoyed every moment spent on both the football and cricket fields. Asked whether the presence of a previous captain in his side who had played forty times for England had caused any embarrassment, Cranmer replied that 'Bob was splendid. He could not have been more helpful', a state of affairs which reflected credit on them both.

Cranmer led Warwickshire for four seasons, two before the Second World War and the first two afterwards. Warwickshire enjoyed only modest success under his captaincy, and lacked the resources to do any better. What he provided was aggressive batting in the middle of the order, utmost keenness in the field, and an unquenchable spirit of enjoyment which communicated itself to the spectators. He thus fulfilled the expectations of the Warwickshire president, Sir Charles Hyde, who told members at a widely attended annual general meeting that Cranmer 'has a breezy personality which should ginger up Warwickshire county cricket' (Duckworth, 237). He made 5853 runs in first-class cricket, with an average of 21. There were four hundreds and his unselfishness cost him another when with only 2 more runs needed he declared. After his first season *Wisden* wrote of 'the inspiring leadership of Peter Cranmer, one of the most popular county captains' under whom 'the eleven showed plenty of keenness and a happy spirit', adding that 'by his bold declarations and willingness to attempt a task however difficult' he fulfilled the hopes expressed at his appointment.

No academic, Cranmer's residence at Christ Church lasted for only four terms, after which he joined a stockbroking firm in Birmingham. On 21 April 1939 he married Constance Pegler Appleton (*b.* 1911/12), chartered masseur, the daughter of Leonard Pegler Appleton, secretary for a trust. They had a son and a daughter. When war came Cranmer was commissioned into the Royal Warwickshire regiment. In 1941 he became aide-de-camp to General Sir Kenneth Anderson. After serving in Egypt he was seconded to the West Yorkshire regiment, with whom he saw action in the latter years of the war in Burma. He was demobilized as a temporary major.

It was said of Cranmer that whereas in the first years of his life nothing much went wrong, in the latter part nothing much went right. He resumed the county captaincy immediately after the war, and helped to reconstruct the team, which in the first two seasons, for all the enthusiasm of the captain, finished respectively fourteenth and fifteenth in the championship. In 1946 no fewer than twenty-four amateurs were called upon to support the admirable Tom Dollery and Eric Hollies and the rest of a limited professional staff.

After giving up the captaincy Cranmer chaired the club selection committee and captained the second eleven during years when he vainly sought more financial security than was provided by freelance cricket broadcasting and some sports reporting for the *Daily Telegraph* and *Sunday*

Telegraph. His health began to fail, and in 1976 a stroke severely impaired his left side. Even after both legs had been amputated he retained to the end the cheerfulness and good nature which in the palmy days had won him a host of friends. He died following a further stroke, on 29 May 1994, at the Royal Sussex County Hospital, Brighton. He was survived by his second wife (whom he had married following the death of his first) and by his two children. A memorial service was held at Edgbaston Old Church, Birmingham, on 10 July 1994.   E. W. SWANTON

Sources *Wisden* · L. Duckworth, *The story of Warwickshire cricket* (1974) · A. R. McWhirter and A. Noble, *Centenary history of Oxford University Rugby Football Club* (1969) · U. A. Titley and R. McWhirter, *Centenary history of the Rugby Football Union* (1970) · *The Times* (11 June 1994) · b. cert. · m. cert. [Constance Pegler Appleton] · d. cert.
Likenesses photograph, repro. in *The Times* · photographs, repro. in Duckworth, *Story of Warwickshire cricket*
Wealth at death under £125,000: administration, 2 Aug 1994, *CGPLA Eng. & Wales*

Cranmer, Thomas (1489–1556), archbishop of Canterbury, was born, according to his first, anonymous, biographer, on 2 July 1489, at Aslockton, Nottinghamshire. The Cranmers were an old armigerous family; Thomas's father, also Thomas (*d.* 1501), styled himself esquire in his will of 1501, although his wealth was probably dangerously modest to claim such a status, and the curiously fluid nature of Cranmer's later heraldic display reflected this slightly uncertain social position. His father's will reveals unusually strong traditional piety, with close links to the Premonstratensian monastery of Welbeck, Nottinghamshire; two of three sons, Thomas and Edmund, were prepared for a clerical career, and one sister, Alice, became a Cistercian nun at Stixwold, Lincolnshire. Among Cranmer's gentry relatives, several of whom also demonstrate a marked attachment to clerical and academic advancement, the most important family links appear to have been with Lincolnshire (from where the family had come a century before), and two of his closest lifelong friends were Lincolnshire men: Thomas Goodrich and Cranmer's later chaplain, John Whitwell.

Cambridge career, 1503–1529 Archbishop Matthew Parker's biography talks of Cranmer's father encouraging him to hunt, hawk, shoot, and enjoy the sports of a gentleman in order to preserve his enthusiasm for his studies; this may suggest education at home. Cranmer's early anonymous biographer says that he learned his grammar 'of a rude parishe clerke', no doubt in Aslockton or its mother parish of Whatton (Nichols, 218). Later, his widowed mother, Agnes, daughter of Laurence Hatfield of Willoughby, Nottinghamshire, sent him to a grammar school, possibly at Southwell, also in Nottinghamshire, or near his various Lincolnshire relatives. However, at the age of fourteen, his torments at the hands of a 'mervelous severe and cruell scolemaster' ended when in 1503 he was admitted to Jesus College, Cambridge (ibid., 239). Jesus was one of the colleges patronized and enriched by Lady Margaret Beaufort, whose entourage had many Lincolnshire connections. Perhaps the family of Cranmer's schoolfriend and later fellow evangelical Sir John Markham recommended him

Thomas Cranmer (1489–1556), by Gerlach Flicke, 1545

to Jesus; the Markhams were relatives and clients of Lady Margaret. Probably also during his early Cambridge years, Cranmer got to know James Morice, Lady Margaret's clerk of the kitchen and surveyor of much of her Cambridge building works, father of his future faithful secretary Ralph Morice, and an early evangelical.

Cranmer took eight years to 1511, a surprisingly long time, to acquire the degree of BA: perhaps his acknowledged problems in absorbing information quickly, or family financial worries, delayed his progress. There may be hints of trouble in two later negative reminiscences. In 1551 he spoke contemptuously of one of his lecturers from forty years before: 'an ignorant reader … who, when he came to any hard chapter which he well understood not, he would find some pretty toy to shift it off, and to skip over unto another chapter, which he could better skill of' (*Writings*, 1.305). His early anonymous biographer provides a famous description of Cranmer as 'nosseled [nuzzled, trained] in the grossest kynd of sophistry, logike, philosophy morall and naturall (not in the text of the old philosophers, but chefely in the darke ridels and quidites of Duns and other subtile questionestes)' (Nichols, 218–19). Certainly his embryonic library was founded on medieval scholastic textbooks; whatever Cranmer's later opinion of them, he preserved them faithfully amid his collections. Already, in his meticulous annotations, he was using the arabic numeration that he favoured throughout his life.

Cranmer graduated BA in 1511 and MA in 1515 (this time showing no special delay). Soon afterwards he married a girl named Joan. Little is known about the marriage, not even its precise date between 1515 and 1519, although it is likely to be earlier than later during that period. It was a decision in striking contrast to his characteristic caution, only paralleled in its abrupt trespass on a conventional career pattern by Cranmer's even more rash second marriage in 1532. Although not yet deacon or priest he still had to forfeit his fellowship of Jesus for marriage; he became the common reader at Buckingham College (the Benedictine university college, refounded in 1542 as Magdalene). He turned to a relative in Cambridge, the landlady of one or other of two Cambridge inns called The Dolphin, to provide lodging for his wife.

Joan died in childbirth, and the child was also lost. If they had lived, Cranmer would not have been ordained, and the course of the English Reformation would have been very different. Cranmer was later so reticent about his first wife, no doubt feeling the pain of his double loss, that not even Joan's surname is certain, although the interrogatories at his trial in 1555 seem to say that it was Black or Brown. The archbishop's later admirers John Foxe and John Strype tried to improve her image by calling her the daughter of a gentleman, but her pedigree has not emerged. The marriage's length is also uncertain; Joan's death came 'within one yere', according to Ralph Morice (Nichols, 240), but Archbishop Parker gave it longer than a year, perhaps with an eye to the innuendo that hasty marriage had followed an unwise pregnancy.

Jesus College showed its esteem for Cranmer by readmitting him to a fellowship after Joan's death—in later years, when archbishop, Cranmer showed a singular lack of gratitude to the college for its past favour, doubtless because of the theological gulf that by then had opened up between the traditionalist-minded fellowship and the evangelical convert. However, for the moment, he was not in the vanguard of religious reformism. His anonymous biographer records that about 'the tyme that Luther began to wryte' (presumably about 1518), Cranmer considered 'what great contraversie was in matters of religion' and 'applyed his whole studye iij yeares unto the … scryptures. After this he gave his mynde to good wryters both newe and old … This kynde of studie he used till he were made doctor of divinitie', that is, 1526 (Nichols, 219). In fact, this was in accord with the deliberate bias in Jesus College towards theology and with its early emphasis on biblical study. At some stage (after his grant of his doctorate of divinity in 1526 according to Morice), Thomas Cranmer held Sir John Rysley's college lectureship in the Old and New testaments. By 1520 he had proceeded to holy orders, for that year the university named him one of the preachers whom they were entitled by papal grant to license for preaching throughout the British Isles.

During the 1520s Cardinal Wolsey procured the migration of bright young Cambridge scholars to his new foundation, Cardinal College at Oxford. Cranmer, after initial hesitation, held back. His refusal was later represented by John Foxe as a principled stand bringing him danger: a misleading interpretation, since many of those who went turned out to be among the earliest enthusiasts for Lutheran ideas, and suffered severely as a result. Given the sort of people who left for Oxford, it could be argued more convincingly that Cranmer's change of heart showed conservative sympathies. Indeed, positive indications of any evangelical inclination in Cranmer during the 1520s are non-existent, while there is good contrary evidence. Most striking are his annotations in his copy of John Fisher's attack on Luther's theology, *Assertionis Lutheranae confutatio*, published in Antwerp in 1523 (now BL, C.81.f.2). These include horrified condemnation of Luther for criticizing the pope and dismissing the authority of a general council—the latter remark provoking Cranmer to explain 'oh, the arrogance of a most wicked man!' (MacCulloch, *Thomas Cranmer*, 27). Overall, he is revealed as a loyal papalist, but even more a believer in the importance of councils of the church. Long after his papal loyalty evaporated, this reverence for the general council remained a golden thread in his theological outlook.

Entry into royal service, 1527–1533 Entirely consistent with this discriminating conservatism was Cranmer's first appearance on a wider stage: as a don talent-spotted for Wolsey's overseas service. Two of his letters to the Polish humanist and diplomat Johannes Dantiscus, surviving in Polish royal correspondence, reveal that in the late spring of 1527 he joined the English diplomatic mission to the emperor Charles V in Spain. This embassy had been led from late 1525 by Dr Edward Lee, a former Cambridge don who was probably an old friend of Cranmer, having graduated MA in the same year, but who, as archbishop of York in the 1530s, did not leave his conservatism behind as Cranmer did. While in Spain, Cranmer made friends with Dantiscus and several other diplomats and imperial courtiers, relationships that assumed renewed significance in his later and more senior diplomatic missions. On his return to London in June, after an epically bad voyage from Spain, as he told Dantiscus, he was given a welcome appropriate to one of great importance. This culminated in the ultimate reward for royal service, a half-hour-long interview with the king. Among other presents Henry VIII gave him rings of gold and silver: a strange pre-echo of the royal rings that saved Cranmer's life in the 1540s. Probably already on returning to Cambridge in 1527, he began advocating the annulment of the king's marriage to Katherine of Aragon—the 'king's Great Matter'—now the all-important issue in English national politics and diplomacy.

Over the next two years Cranmer kept busy with university administration which increasingly shaded into national politics. For instance, in October 1528 he travelled from London to Ipswich bearing a business letter for William Capon, the master of his college, who doubled as dean of Wolsey's new college at Ipswich: the agent of Wolsey who had written the letter was Thomas Cromwell. Here was yet another relationship to shape a new pattern of Cranmer's life, once the two men emerged from the fallen cardinal's shadow. It was thus not entirely unexpected when, in summer 1529, his role in the king's Great Matter suddenly took on new prominence. The papal hearing of the king's case by Campeggi and the resident papal legate Wolsey had closed on 30 July. It was deliberately sabotaged by Campeggi, who, probably under instructions to ensure no decision was taken before the queen's appeal against the hearing had reached Rome, finally confirmed his previous formal declaration that by Roman custom the court must adjourn until October.

The king and his advisers embarked on a fretful summer progress north and west of London, and during these journeyings a coincidental meeting took place between Cranmer and two Cambridge colleagues working on the annulment. Cranmer avoided an outbreak of plague at Cambridge by staying at Waltham Holy Cross, Essex, with relatives called Cressy, whose two sons he was tutoring. Stephen Gardiner and Edward Foxe were also lodged with the Cressys. Probably on 2 August 1529 they told Cranmer over dinner of the royal impasse. Cranmer suggested switching energy in the campaign from the legal case at Rome towards a general canvassing of university theologians throughout Europe, which would prove more cost-effective.

In reality, the idea of consulting theologians was a humanist commonplace of the previous decade, and the annulment controversy had already been picked over by plenty of university theological experts. However, Gardiner and Foxe were desperate, and Henry showed interest when they talked to him two days later. Ralph Morice says that 'by and by' Cranmer met Henry at Greenwich; Sir Thomas More subsequently remembered Cranmer as among the theological troubleshooters sent to him with the latest statement of the king's case, very soon after More replaced Wolsey as lord chancellor, on 25 October 1529. By the time of this meeting, or soon afterwards, Cranmer was in high favour with the Boleyn family, and lodged in the entourage of Anne Boleyn's father, Thomas (soon to be earl of Wiltshire), at Durham Place.

Cranmer now began producing arguments for the annulment, a task to which the king sent him back repeatedly over the next four years whenever he was in England. It is difficult to be precise on what he wrote. Gardiner and Foxe said that they used Cranmer's writings when they went to Cambridge in February 1530, to extort an opinion favourable to the king from the university. By then Cranmer had set off with his old patron Edward Lee and the earl of Wiltshire, on an embassy designed to tackle the emperor while Charles V and the pope were conveniently both at Bologna for the imperial coronation. It was probably intended from the start that Cranmer should go to Rome for a long stay, among other things to help other royal agents in his suggested strategy of rounding up university opinions. With effect from 17 April 1530 the English government tripled his daily wage, together with that of his colleague Edward Carne; probably this reflects a rise in his status to orator to the apostolic see, anticipating the pope's return to Rome from Bologna, and probably also now he was granted the complementary title of penitentiary-general of England—traditionally appointed on a recommendation by the king of England to the

pope, and with a watching brief over papal dispensations that might affect England.

In Rome, Cranmer began accumulating his first official positions outside Cambridge, including his first promotion in the English church. Geronimo de' Ghinucci, permanent English representative in Rome, gave Cranmer the rich rectory of Bredon, Worcestershire, in his gift as bishop of Worcester; Cranmer was called rector of Bredon by 22 August 1530, when he used his status as penitentiary to obtain papal licence to hold four benefices. Ghinucci and Cranmer had previously been colleagues in the Spanish mission of 1527. It is unlikely that Cranmer ever spent much time in his sole known parochial charge. In Italy he seems to have been a patient and subtle negotiator on a hopeless cause, doing much to smooth over rows caused by the irascibility and ineptitude of his old Cambridge acquaintance Richard Croke. He left Rome to reach Bologna by 16 September, no doubt relieved to rendezvous with Croke's *bête noire* John Stokesley for the journey home. Stokesley and Cranmer officially ended their mission on 23 October 1530. Although much remains obscure about the next year, it was crucial for Cranmer's future development. Many involved in the annulment business began to see more clearly the wider religious issues behind it, and now hints of the evangelical outlook central to Cranmer's later achievements become apparent.

Straight away there was work on the annulment controversy, including continued research in primary sources. The king's team was now preparing material for publication to win hearts and minds at home and abroad, and one of Cranmer's major assignments was to edit other people's material into decent readable English. So he began developing the skills that bore lasting fruit in his greatest editorial task, the Book of Common Prayer. The research team produced two major works. One was a manuscript compilation for official use, termed the *Collectanea satis copiosa* ('Sufficiently abundant collections'), a battery of supposedly historical extracts (much of it Arthurian fantasy) designed to embody the king's disillusionment with papal authority. The idea running through the collection was that history proved that the king, not the bishop of Rome, exercised supreme jurisdiction of all descriptions within his realm: the contents fuelled the extraordinary self-confidence of the king's break with Rome. The *Collectanea* still needed supplementing when Cranmer returned from Rome, and he probably helped to complete it. The other work was first published in Latin for an international scholarly audience in April 1531, as *Gravissimae … academiarum censurae*. In English translation, with Cranmer probably undertaking the whole work and (on John Stokesley's testimony) certainly making the alterations that only appear in the English, the work appeared in November 1531 as *The determinations of the most famous and most excellent universities of Italy and France, that it is unlawful for a man to marry his brother's wife; that the pope hath no power to dispense therewith.*

These eight opinions favourable to Henry, the results of Cranmer's proposal to consult European universities and already published in English in a proclamation of late

1530, in fact prefaced a far longer treatise. This remodelled the *libellus* or summary of royal arguments that Henry's lawyers had presented to the Blackfriars tribunal in late spring 1529. Out of various other contemporary propaganda works, only the certainty that Cranmer edited and altered the *Determinations* permits a glimpse of the future master of English prose at work. His struggle to render this formidably dull text readable contains five first uses of English words earlier than those recorded in the old *Oxford English Dictionary*, at least six apparent attempts to coin English words or phrases with no subsequent linguistic careers, and about twenty-three meanings of common English, Latinate, or Norman-French words not recorded in the *Oxford English Dictionary*. Some of his modifications of the Latin also hint at developing evangelical sympathies.

Cranmer's research work for the king was encouraging him to question papal authority: now, having seen the holy father at first hand, he made his first recorded contacts with evangelical reformers. The Basel evangelical Simon Grynaeus was in England from March into the early summer of 1531, ostensibly to investigate English libraries, but also to see what capital might be made for the Reformation out of Henry VIII's marital difficulties. He became friends with Cranmer during his visits to the court; in subsequent letters to Martin Bucer at Strasbourg, Grynaeus emphasized the influence that Cranmer had with the king, and also Cranmer's evangelical sympathies. Although Grynaeus's mission bore no diplomatic fruit, Cranmer's friendship with Bucer, born of this contact, proved lifelong.

During 1532 Cranmer (now archdeacon of Taunton, in succession to his Cambridge colleague and future enemy Stephen Gardiner) went on a further diplomatic mission to Germany. He replaced Sir Thomas Elyot as ambassador, since Henry VIII considered Elyot unsound on the Aragon annulment (Elyot had his revenge the following year with his unflattering portrait of Cranmer as the cowardly and silent Harpocrates in his satirical conversation piece *Pasquil the Playne*). In the conservatively Lutheran city of Nuremberg, Cranmer befriended the leading pastor Andreas Osiander, and at some stage during a summer of diplomacy, probably in July, married Margaret [see Cranmer, Margaret (*d. c.*1575)], niece of Osiander's wife, Katharina Preu; reportedly Osiander himself officiated. Much remains mysterious about the marriage; it is uncertain whether Cranmer's wife was the daughter of a sister or brother of Katharina, so Margaret's maiden name remains uncertain. But the marriage was a decisive affirmation that Cranmer rejected the old church's tradition of compulsory celibacy, and it marked his adherence to the evangelical cause. In early autumn, leaving his new wife in Nuremberg, he followed Charles V's court into Italy and here he learned to his alarm (probably in late October) that, after the death of William Warham, Henry VIII had chosen him as the next archbishop of Canterbury, confident that Cranmer would do the royal bidding in presiding over the end of the Aragon marriage. He kept quiet about his own marriage and accepted the summons,

although he took his time returning, arriving in January 1533.

The Boleyn years, 1533–1536 Events now had to move swiftly, because Anne Boleyn was pregnant after nearly six years of keeping Henry from his heart's desire. Cranmer, now archbishop-elect, plunged into a ferment of committees thrashing out solutions to the problem of securing an annulment without Roman interference. He was not present at the secret marriage of the king and Anne in late January 1533. Perhaps, in a feeble attempt at preserving proprieties, it was felt inappropriate that the judge who would hear the annulment of one marriage should already have officiated at the celebration of the other. Despite the frantic efforts of the imperial ambassador Eustace Chapuys to be obstructive, the eleven papal bulls authorizing Cranmer's provision to Canterbury, completely traditional in form, were dispatched to England in March.

On Passion Sunday (30 March) Cranmer was consecrated archbishop of Canterbury in St Stephen's College in the palace of Westminster. Cranmer's preliminary oath of loyalty to the papacy was immediately followed with a solemn protestation declaring that his oath would not override the law of God and his loyalty to the king, or act to the hindrance of 'reformation of the Christian religion, the government of the English Church, or the prerogative of the Crown or the well-being of the same commonwealth' (*Writings*, 2.560). In a procedure reflecting no credit on him, Cranmer formally benefited from papal bulls while equally formally rejecting their authority. Immediately he took up presidency of the convocation of Canterbury, which forwarded the annulment business, and shortly afterwards he forbade unauthorized preaching, to quell opposition.

On 11 April Cranmer wrote two letters to the king, bearing the difficult and delicate burden of accusing Henry of creating a public scandal with Queen Katherine and inviting him to ease his conscience with a hearing of his plight before a church court. This trial opened on 10 May at Dunstable Priory, Bedfordshire, perhaps chosen because its aged prior Gervase Markham was a relative of Cranmer, but no doubt also because of its distance from London. The task, which had to be speedy if Anne's coronation was not to be delayed, was made easier by Katherine's refusal to appear; two days into the proceedings Cranmer definitively pronounced her contumacious, and on 23 May pronounced final sentence. A hasty hearing of a petition from Henry and Anne to have their marriage judged valid was completed on 28 May. On Whitsunday (1 June), the archbishop played the principal role in the coronation and was principal male guest at the subsequent state banquet. When, in September, Princess Elizabeth was born, Cranmer followed Bishop John Stokesley's baptism by confirming her.

Soon after the coronation Cranmer was confronted with the embarrassing prospect of forwarding an evangelical theologian, John Frith, to be burnt at the stake for denying eucharistic real presence; he presided over Frith's examinations by a commission of bishops and noblemen.

Whatever his sympathies with a fellow reformer, Cranmer certainly believed at this time (as did Martin Luther) in the corporal presence of Christ in the eucharist, and there was nothing inconsistent in his treatment of Frith. Politically more useful as well as congenial was his increasing involvement in the struggle to silence a female visionary, Elizabeth Barton (the Maid of Kent), a focus of opposition to the Aragon annulment and to religious change generally. He repeatedly interviewed Barton, and during the autumn of 1533 her morale collapsed. Her downfall led to the round-up of her leading clerical supporters, among whom were some of the most powerful clergy in Cranmer's own diocese, former clients of his predecessor Archbishop Warham. It was the perfect opportunity for him to clear out traditionalist opponents from the diocesan machine and introduce his own supporters. These included relatives from the midlands, and also represented a broad shift from Oxford to Cambridge men. Symbolic of both these new groups was Cranmer's younger brother Edmund (also a secretly married cleric), who replaced William Warham the younger as archdeacon of Canterbury and provost of Wingham College early in the spring of 1534.

Amid a growing campaign against papal obedience Cranmer was enthroned in Canterbury Cathedral on 3 December 1533, his first chance to display his full authority. Within a week he began his first diocesan visitation. At the beginning of 1534 he re-established the Canterbury mint which by ancient right the archbishops maintained. During 1534 he was prominent in parliamentary moves sealing the breach with Rome; these included the Act of Dispensations, which set up a faculty office for Cranmer to issue dispensations in place of the papal bureaucracy. The seal designed for this office (possibly by Holbein) is notably accomplished in its Renaissance and evangelical iconography, with type and antitype of serpent and cross as set out in scripture in Numbers 21: 4–9 and John 3: 14–15; it is likely that Cranmer, who frequently displayed advanced artistic taste, was active in inspiring the design.

Cranmer also initiated the national campaign to gather signatures to the Act of Succession with the aim of uniting the realm behind the king's new marriage and heir; this was an important part of his effort to assert his authority within his province by a metropolitical visitation. The visitation, begun in May 1534, met with fierce and probably co-ordinated opposition from traditionalist bishops, notably John Stokesley of London and Stephen Gardiner of Winchester. Cranmer led much of the work in person in those dioceses where he would not confront a resident bishop. On 11 November he sought to meet some of his colleagues' objections based on his continuing use of a papal title: he announced to a specially convened business meeting of convocation that from now on, in addition to his title of primate of all England, he was substituting the title of metropolitan for that of legate of the apostolic see.

This did not solve the problem that Cranmer could not act as religious leader for the whole realm, given that he had no specific jurisdiction in the province of York;

another strategy, ultimately more effective, drew on Henry VIII's newly revealed powers as supreme head of the Church of England by delegating those powers to Cranmer's colleague Thomas Cromwell. By January 1535 Cromwell was named as vicegerent or vicar-general of the king, and this soon overrode Cranmer's own jurisdiction. The metropolitical visitation staggered on into early summer, but it formally ended on 1 August. Yet there is no evidence that Cranmer resented the new situation. The previous few years had revealed both his strengths and weaknesses. He had been a popular and successful diplomat, and an exceptional researcher and deviser of texts for a complex and difficult problem, but he was no politician. He lacked the ruthlessness or deviousness to outface even clerical politicians like Stokesley and Gardiner who were now his ideological enemies. Such manoeuvres were best left to Cromwell: the two men valued each other's skills as complementary in striving for shared evangelical goals.

More important to Cranmer than personal power was what he saw as a life-and-death struggle against evil. On 6 February 1536 he preached the first in a series of weekly episcopal sermons at Paul's Cross extending through the new parliamentary session; his main theme was that the pope was Antichrist. This was a bold step, for the only previous English commentator publicly to make that identification was William Tyndale, recently judicially murdered in the Low Countries with Henry VIII's tacit approval. Cranmer had clearly come to hate the papacy while working on the Aragon annulment, probably since he believed sincerely in the rightness of the king's cause of matrimony which the pope opposed. This hatred may have stimulated his devotion to the royal supremacy, by now at the centre of his theological stance: he needed the supremacy to fill the chasm of authority which opened up when he rejected the pope. Later that Lent he preached in support of destroying the smaller monasteries, and denounced chantries and masses for the dead, apparently even rejecting purgatory. However, such boldness was at least temporarily curbed by renewed political turbulence.

Thomas Cromwell and evangelical advance, 1536–1538 Cranmer was at first unaware of the crisis that destroyed Anne Boleyn through an unlikely alliance of conservative courtiers and Thomas Cromwell. Only on Tuesday 2 May, when Anne was rowed from Greenwich to the Tower, did Cromwell summon Cranmer to Lambeth. Dependent on rumours and as yet unable to see Henry face to face, on Wednesday he wrote the king one of his most celebrated and controversial letters, in which he frankly admitted 'that next unto your Grace I was most bound unto her of all creatures living', expressed his hopes that the queen was innocent of the accusations against her, and also begged Henry not to abandon religious reform, even if Anne were guilty (*Writings*, 2.324). His later part in the proceedings was passively to co-operate with Henry's destructive fury: he saw Anne in person in the Tower to hear her confession on 16 May, the day before he formally pronounced the marriage null and void and Princess Elizabeth consequently a bastard. On Friday 19 May, the day of

Anne's execution, Cranmer's Scottish evangelical client Alexander Alesius found him walking restlessly in Lambeth Palace gardens: 'she who has been the Queen of England on earth will today become a Queen in heaven' was all that the archbishop could say before breaking down in tears (MacCulloch, *Thomas Cranmer*, 159). Clearly Anne's confession had revealed no dreadful sexual secrets. On the same day he signed a dispensation from prohibitions of affinity for a marriage between the king and Jane Seymour.

These depressingly unheroic procedures at least preserved the evangelical cause, thanks to Cromwell's political ruthlessness. A practical expression of Cranmer's debt to his friend for survival came in a parliamentary Act of Exchange in June 1536: Cranmer surrendered ancient archiepiscopal Surrey estates at Wimbledon and Mortlake. Cromwell took his baron's title from Wimbledon when created Lord Cromwell in July, a neatly symbolic transfer from primate of all England to vicegerent. In return, the archbishop received lands of the priory of St Radegund near Dover, of markedly lesser value. This was a first taste of the unequal property exchanges that became a feature of Henry VIII's relations with his bishops—comparatively modest compared with what Cranmer experienced over the next decade. Against such pressure he was little inclined to resist. After Cromwell and the crown initiated further major exchanges in 1537, he did revert to a policy of granting very long leases of many of his remaining properties, deliberately to make them less attractive targets for outside interests, but he was not an acquisitive man: his lack of involvement in the dissolution of the monasteries is noticeable, and he did not acquire even modest grants of former monastic lands until he openly had a family to support in Edward VI's reign.

During the Lincolnshire rebellion and the Pilgrimage of Grace in the autumn of 1536 and winter of 1537 Cromwell and Cranmer were prime targets of the rebels' fury. Only a day or two after trouble began, on 3 October, Cranmer headed the list of leading evangelicals to be murdered that was announced by the Lincolnshire Captain Porman at Caistor Hill, and after that, hostile references to him are legion. The famous rebel song denouncing 'Crim, Cram and Rich' was apparently first heard at the remote abbey of Sawley in the West Riding of Yorkshire. Cranmer, evidently instructed to keep a low profile, spent most of the autumn in Kent. Once the rebels had been defeated he emerged to take a full part in preparing a new doctrinal statement to replace the previous summer's ten articles. This was initiated in a synod for the Church of England inaugurated by Cromwell as vicegerent in February 1537; published in September, it was a substantial book entitled *The Institution of a Christian Man*, informally known from its first issue as the Bishops' Book. Probably at this time the archbishop set his secretaries to work compiling a source collection of quotations and comments on a classified list of theological topics; this survives in the British Library as two massive volumes (BL, Royal MS 7 B. xi, xii). Cranmer and his secretarial team continued adding to them until the end of Henry VIII's reign; they became the anchor of his omnivorous theological reading.

Although the studied compromises of the Bishops' Book might be considered an evangelical success, and the official authorization of an English Bible (thanks to Cromwell) delighted Cranmer, he was not so lucky in asserting his position in Kent. An acrid exchange of letters during 1537 with the leading conservative Kentish magnate Sir Thomas Cheyne, his own high steward, ended inconclusively, while at the same time, in another unequal 'exchange', Cranmer lost major ancient estates to the crown, including three palaces, Otford, Knole, and Maidstone. His Canterbury mint also closed for the last time. By contrast, in further exchanges of the 1540s, estates granted to Cranmer helped concentrate lands conveniently for his remaining palaces at the extremes of his jurisdiction at the far north (Lambeth and Croydon), and in the far south-east, around Canterbury. Finally under Edward VI, when many episcopal estates came under renewed pressure and many experienced grave losses, the slimmed-down estate of the archbishopric suffered no further erosion: a remarkable achievement, reflecting Cranmer's enhanced political status in the Edwardian regimes.

Nationally, Cranmer cautiously confronted King Henry in late January 1538 when the theologically minded monarch turned to a personal revision of the Bishops' Book in the aftermath of Jane Seymour's death. Cranmer's comments on Henry's revisions reveal that he was not only prepared to correct the king's frequently clumsy verbal emendations, but was also determined to spell out an evangelical message of justification by faith in the face of Henry's studied hostility to the doctrine. In his extended commentary an essential feature of his theology may also be perceived: he was a thoroughgoing exponent of predestination. Admittedly, he had no success in changing Henry's mind on justification, as is apparent from the revised King's Book (the *Necessary Doctrine and Erudition for any Christian Man*) ultimately issued in 1543. Once he had put his arguments, he did not resist the king's will; given his reverence for royal authority, he was both ideologically and temperamentally disinclined to challenge the monarch in public.

Contacts with the wider European Reformation Cranmer played a vital role in linking religious change in England to the various official reformations developing abroad. Even though his links to Lutheranism were naturally strong, his early contact with Basel through Simon Grynaeus made him open to different agendas of reformers in Switzerland and southern Germany. During English diplomatic overtures to the Lutheran Schmalkaldic League in the autumn of 1535, Martin Bucer began urging other European evangelical leaders to approach Cranmer; Bucer himself lavished praise on the archbishop, particularly when dedicating his major Romans commentary to him in 1536. Heinrich Bullinger, leader of the Zürich Reformation, entered a warm correspondence with Cranmer: they arranged for young English evangelicals to pay extended visits to Zürich, and one of these was accompanied by a Zürich protégé of Bullinger, Rudolf Gwalther, on a visit to England in 1537.

However, these contacts were disrupted for the time being by the problem of eucharistic theology. Henry VIII remained firmly wedded to the traditional theology of the mass; Cranmer and the English evangelical establishment rejected the medieval scholastic doctrine of transubstantiation, but they shared Martin Luther's adherence to the idea that the body and blood of Christ were corporally present in the eucharistic elements of bread and wine, and they were suspicious of theologians who weakened or denied the idea of presence. Cranmer expressed his hostility to such notions in a letter of spring 1537 to the St Gallen reformer Joachim von Watt (Vadianus): he said (innocent of his later change of mind on eucharistic theology) 'you will certainly never convince me, nor I think any unprejudiced reader, that … ancient authors are on your side in this controversy' (MacCulloch, *Thomas Cranmer*, 180). Similar rebuffs followed to the Strasbourg reformer Wolfgang Capito in July 1537. Cranmer's own quasi-Lutheran formulation of the question in this period seems to have centred on the idea of 'true presence', echoing the Augsburg confession's use of the phrase *vere adsint* ('are truly present').

The end result of renewed diplomatic overtures to the Lutherans in 1538 was equally indecisive. Cranmer presided over extended discussions with a Lutheran delegation from June onwards, attempting to reach theological agreement, but with Cromwell distracted by factional court politics, negotiations languished; the work was sabotaged by the conservative members of the English negotiating team, and by the king's conservative adviser Cuthbert Tunstall. The Germans had all left in despair by 1 October, carrying away no substantial achievement. In one respect, however, the negotiations were associated with a document with a great bearing on the future of the Church of England: Cranmer's first traceable experiment in changing the liturgy. In 1538–9 Cranmer produced the first of two attempts to reform the breviary. The text replaced the eightfold structure of offices by two—a morning and an evening service—as in the later Book of Common Prayer. It is enterprisingly eclectic in its sources: it draws on the breviary revision of Cardinal Francisco de Quiñones (1535–6) and the Latin hymnary of Josse Van Clichthoven, *Elucidatorium ecclesiasticum* (1516), but also on the order prepared for the Lutheran church of Denmark in 1537 by Johann Bugenhagen. The surviving manuscript is in Latin, perhaps so that it could be scrutinized by the Lutheran diplomats, but a reference in a letter of 8 March 1539 written to Zürich makes it clear that Cranmer was by then turning his liturgical work into the vernacular. Undoubtedly much of this initiative survives in the text of the prayer book services of matins and evensong.

Factional struggle and Cromwell's fall, 1539–1540 The breviary reform scheme is unfinished in the manuscript, and it is likely that it was abandoned during the political turbulence of the spring of 1539 which led to the passage of the religiously conservative Act of Six Articles. Henry VIII, worried about diplomatic isolation from the Catholic powers of Europe, irritated by clumsy diplomatic demands from the German Lutheran princes, and increasingly annoyed by extrovert popular evangelical activity, decided to demonstrate the traditionalist side of his church settlement. Cranmer opposed the proceedings, while the king was present in the House of Lords. Yet as always, he was not prepared to stand up to Henry once their respective positions had been made clear. He was in a particularly weak position, with his commissary in his peculiar jurisdiction of Calais, the outspoken evangelical John Butler, under attack for heresy from the conservative secular administration there. Moreover, as a married priest, he was directly affected by the six articles' reaffirmation of clerical celibacy, and Margaret Cranmer (with whom Cranmer by now had at least one daughter, a second Margaret) was forced to flee the country.

This was one of Cranmer's worst moments in Henry's reign. Alexander Alesius records that, early one morning in Lambeth Palace gardens at the end of June, Cranmer persuaded him to flee England. Handing Alesius a souvenir, Wolsey's ring that the king had given him, the archbishop lamented:

> I repent of what I have done, and if I had known that my only punishment would have been deposition from the Archbishopric (as I hear that my Lord [Hugh] Latimer is deposed), of a truth I would not have subscribed. (MacCulloch, *Thomas Cranmer*, 251)

Yet the king was sensitive to Cranmer's unhappiness, ordering a dinner at Lambeth Palace for him to be reconciled with his conservative opponents. On this occasion Ralph Morice overheard Cromwell say to Cranmer:

> You were borne in a happie hower I suppose … for, do or sey what you will, the Kyng will alweies well take it at your hande. And I must nedes confesse that in some thinges I have complaynyd of you unto his majestie, but all in vayne, for he will never give credite againste you, what soever is laied to your charge. (Nichols, 258)

Yet another encouraging incident reported by Morice can probably be dated to parliamentary debates around the six articles: when Sir John Gostwick, knight of the shire for Bedfordshire, made accusations in the Commons about the archbishop's sermons and lectures at Sandwich and Canterbury, Henry furiously called him a 'varlet' and roundly declared that if he did not personally apologize to Cranmer 'I will suer both make hym a poore Gostewycke, and otherwise punishe hym, to th'example of others' (ibid., 254).

Soon the atmosphere improved so much for evangelicals that Cromwell proposed a new marital alliance for the king with Anne, sister of Duke Wilhelm of Cleves, who was already brother-in-law to the elector of Saxony. Notes preserved by Lord Herbert of Cherbury's amanuensis Thomas Master (Bodl. Oxf., MS Jesus 74) reveal that Cranmer opposed going further with the Cleves enterprise, despite being one of the principal negotiators for it. Perhaps already knowing of the king's feelings for Katherine Howard, he said that he 'thought it most expedient the King to marry where that he had his fantasy and love, for that would be most comfort for his Grace', and speaking from his own experience of a German wife, he commented 'that it would be very strange to be married with her that he could not talk withal' (MacCulloch, *Thomas Cranmer*, 258). Cromwell brushed aside his objections, setting the scene for the disastrous marriage which led to his own execution in summer 1540. When Henry, aghast at the first sight of his new bride, tried to wriggle out of the marriage the day before the wedding of 6 January 1540, Cranmer combined with his fellow commissioner the conservative Cuthbert Tunstall in insisting that, on the evidence available, there was no legal reason for the marriage not to go ahead.

As the political crisis gathered momentum Cranmer made two contributions to religious change: first, writing a celebrated preface to the official Great Bible, published in its second edition of May 1540 (thus giving rise to the inaccurate nickname Cranmer's Bible), and second, presiding over the remodelling of Canterbury and Rochester cathedrals as non-monastic corporations. He only partially got his own way in remodelling the cathedrals: he disapproved of devoting such a large proportion of endowment to funding prebendaries, showed no enthusiasm for the liturgical and musical function of the institutions, and unsuccessfully urged that more should be spent on educational provision. His one success was to prevent the first admissions of scholars to the refounded Canterbury Cathedral school from being dominated by younger former monks or former novices and sons of gentry; he was determined to allow the school to be open on the basis of merit.

After Cromwell's arrest on 10 June 1540 Cranmer was one of the few to make any effort to defend him to the king; his brave letter, of which Lord Herbert preserved a fragmentary outline, is significantly similar to his pleas for Anne Boleyn in 1536. The same three elements are there: warm praise of the victim, horror conditional on the charges' being proved true, and pastoral concern for the king in the loss of a brilliant adviser. Yet otherwise his role in the affair was not heroic; duly voting for Cromwell's attainder with the rest of the House of Lords, he delivered his judgment on the nullity of the Cleves marriage (assisted by all other leading English churchmen) on 9 July. Additionally, he was probably saved from serious trouble in association with Cromwell because the new bride, Katherine Howard, knew of his initial opposition to the Cleves adventure.

Struggling to survive, 1540–1543 Cranmer's role in secular politics and administration beyond his own ecclesiastical sphere began to grow now that his close political ally had been destroyed. After being made formally first in precedence as the privy council took institutional shape on 10 August 1540, the archbishop remained in London when Henry VIII left for his first northern progress in June 1541, as a member of the caretaker council liaising with the king's advisers. During the months that followed, a number of religious changes and political moves demonstrated that the evangelicals were once more taking the initiative, while the archbishop became embroiled in

fierce rows with the conservative majority among the staff of his remodelled cathedral.

In the middle of this political turbulence came the exposure and conviction of Queen Katherine Howard on (justified) charges of adultery. When the evangelical courtier John Lascelles revealed the evidence to Cranmer, he and his fellow London councillors waited until Henry returned from the north. Inevitably they decided that Cranmer was the one man who could get away with delivering Henry such a devastating blow, but even he could not face presenting the news by word of mouth; he handed over a letter with the information at the All Souls' day mass (2 November 1541). Henry had only just given thanks for his marriage, and his reaction was stunned disbelief. After so many years of mutual trust and intimate confidences from the king, Cranmer seems to have been at his best in moments of face-to-face emotion, and he managed to avoid any immediate explosion of royal fury. In the following secret investigations it was Cranmer who eventually broke down Katherine's indignant denials, and who secured her confession in writing, leading to her execution on 13 February 1542. To look on this as a political triumph for Cranmer is misleading: Katherine was not his enemy, she did not really represent the conservative cause, and it is unlikely that the bearer of such devastating news would get much credit for his pains.

Skirmishing between religious conservatives and the evangelical party, of which Cranmer was now the obvious leader, continued through 1542—notably in the convocation of Canterbury's winter session, but also in the precincts of his own cathedral. Cranmer's leadership in London government was renewed while the king campaigned in Scotland in the autumn of 1542, but this kept him away from his own diocese, where trouble was becoming acute. In his cathedral's first six months of settled secular existence from April 1541, two of its staff had landed up in prison, two had been the subject of a formal complaint, and two others had been involved in a furious row with their archbishop. During 1543 these tensions erupted in a full-scale attempt to destroy Cranmer: the so-called prebendaries' plot. This was orchestrated by a combination of disaffected Canterbury Cathedral clergy and their allies at Oxford University, together with conservative Kentish gentry—all united by nostalgia for the late Archbishop William Warham, and with Bishop Gardiner as discreet patron. The problem for Cranmer's enemies was that they were too widely dispersed, and their schemes against him consequently lacked co-ordination. By contrast, throughout the affair, Cranmer's faithful secretary Ralph Morice saved situations at their most threatening by activating his court contacts in the archbishop's favour.

On Easter eve (24 March 1543) accusations were gathered against Cranmer himself, and probably shown to the king during April. Against this unpromising background the conservative revision of the Bishops' Book which became the King's Book was finalized in convocation (despite Cranmer's protests against many of the changes); it was followed by parliament's passing an act 'for the advancement of true religion' which restricted the reading of the Bible on a status basis. It was probably Cranmer's reluctant acceptance of these unwelcome *faits accomplis* that steadied the king's confidence in him. Henry took no action all through the spring and summer, then (probably in early September 1543) he took an evening's boat trip from Whitehall. The archbishop met Henry at Lambeth; Henry chaffed him 'Ah, my chaplen, I have newis for you: I knowe nowe who is the gretest heretique in Kent', and pulled out a paper summarizing the charges (Nichols, 252). Against Cranmer's protestations, the king told him to appoint himself as chief investigator of the affair and choose his colleagues in commission.

Those revealed as plotters included two of Cranmer's officials, Richard Thornden and Dr John Barber. Typically, he put them through an immediate humiliation, forgave them, and continued to rely on their services, even making Thornden his suffragan bishop two years later. Probably in November came a final ordeal, when the king granted the conservative privy councillors their chance to present heresy charges, while that same night he secretly summoned Cranmer to his presence and gave him his personal ring. The following morning the archbishop was summoned to the council, and was kept waiting outside the door 'emonges servyng men and lackeis' for more than three-quarters of an hour (Nichols, 256). Then he allowed his council colleagues curtly to inform him that he was under arrest before courteously delivering the king's ring to them, and accompanying them to their humiliation before the king.

Shaping future reformation, 1543–1547 'Nevermore after no man durste spurne [Cranmer] duryng the kyng Henry's life', exulted Morice (Nichols, 258). Cranmer's most highly placed enemies were allowed to survive as well, and only small fry suffered. On 18 December 1543 the archiepiscopal palace at Canterbury was virtually destroyed by fire (killing one of Cranmer's brothers-in-law); Cranmer showed particular concern to rescue one large chest from the flames. It is likely that this contained the evidence gathered of the plot, but later Cranmer's Catholic enemies (first Nicholas Harpsfield, Marian archdeacon of Canterbury) drew on his observed agitation to create the legend that Mrs Cranmer was habitually carried in such a box during the reign of Henry VIII. A more positive lasting memory arose in August 1545, when the archbishop played an impressive part in local Kentish defence: French naval galleys threatened a landing at Dover, and the archbishop was there at five o'clock in the morning with 100 horse, 'in his privy coat with his dagger at his saddle bow, his page waiting on him with his morion [helmet] and long piece [gun]' (MacCulloch, *Thomas Cranmer*, 323). This martial display by a man who always loved hunting and prided himself on his horsemanship may have done Cranmer's reputation in Kent more good than all the previous decade of evangelical sermons.

In national politics Cranmer's alignment with Edward Seymour, earl of Hertford, was of great future significance, together with his close relationship with the principal tutors of his godson Prince Edward: Richard Cox, John Cheke, and Roger Ascham. Moreover, although the relationship between the archbishop and Henry VIII's last queen, Katherine Parr, is so obscure as to suggest deliberate discretion, it is tempting to suggest that it was during the summer of 1544, with Henry absent on French campaigning, and Katherine as regent in daily contact with Cranmer, that the queen developed her strong commitment to evangelical piety. Among the fruits of Cranmer's strengthened position was the publication in 1544 of the litany, England's first officially authorized vernacular service, in connection with Henry VIII's war with France. In substance, it remains in the Book of Common Prayer. Probably about this time Cranmer produced an abortive revision proposal for the breviary, less radical than his scheme of 1538–9 but notable for ranking among the saints characters from the Old Testament, especially heroes and heroines or authors of books. He was also much involved in preparing an official primer, published first solely in English in May 1545: this also provided liturgical texts for the future prayer book.

Amid this cautious evangelical advance Cranmer commissioned a portrait from the German artist Gerlach Flicke, which since the late seventeenth century has remained the standard image of him—at first sight, a more decorously Anglican image than the later bearded portrait by which he was remembered during the Reformation itself. Dated 20 July 1545, and modelled deliberately in contrast to a portrait of Archbishop Warham, it is a remarkable piece of evangelical humanist iconography, employing a variety of theological symbolism: its domestic interior setting employs modish French grotesque motifs in the decoration, while the various books depicted emphasize an Augustinian and Pauline position on the theology of justification.

The last attempt by religious conservatives to wrest back political initiative before the old king's death resulted in the arrest of a number of Cranmer's associates on heresy charges in May 1546; some were burnt during that summer. Cranmer himself kept a low profile; it is possible that about this time he abandoned belief in the real eucharistic presence, instead affirming a spiritual presence of Christ to which the eucharistic elements witnessed—a departure from Lutheranism as well as from traditional eucharistic theology. This issue of sacramentalism was the charge on which others were executed. It is known that he arrived at his new stance in consultation with his chaplain Nicholas Ridley, but precise dating is impossible; certainly he was corresponding with Martin Bucer on the eucharist during 1547. He may have been encouraged by Henry's mood-swing away from the conservatives during negotiations for peace with France in summer 1546, when Henry told him that he intended to revise the mass in conjunction with the French king.

Cranmer continued to distance himself from political turmoil in Henry's last months, but was summoned to minister to the king as he died, on 28 January 1547:

> Then the archbishop, exhorting him to put his trust in Christ, and to call upon his mercy, desired him, though he could not speak, yet to give some token with his eyes or with

his hand, that he trusted in the Lord. Then the King, holding him with his hand, did wring his hand in his as hard as he could. (*Acts and Monuments*, 5.689)

Henry thus—significantly—died without any traditional rites of the Western Catholic church.

The protectorate of Somerset, 1547–1549 The regime of the boy king Edward VI was led by the archbishop's close ally Edward Seymour, now duke of Somerset and lord protector; from the beginning it planned a radical break with the medieval church. Cranmer himself signalled this not only by openly acknowledging his married state, but also by growing a beard. Supposedly a sign of grief for the dead King Henry, it also represented a break with the clean-shaven appearance of most late medieval celibate clergy: a deliberate gesture made by many clerical reformers. At Edward's coronation Cranmer seems to have given a short address; it was a brief but forceful statement of royal supremacy against Rome, as well as an emphatic call to the young king to imitate his 'predecessor Josiah', the Old Testament destroyer of idolatry (MacCulloch, *Thomas Cranmer*, 349).

Soon Cranmer was orchestrating commissions to carry out a new royal visitation of the whole realm, and, although action was delayed until late August, he presided meanwhile over the production of a cycle of official homilies. Reliable tradition asserts that he wrote four of the twelve: the opening 'Exhortation to the reading of holy scripture', salvation, faith, and good works. All these gave him opportunity clearly to expound the central Reformation theme of justification by faith only, and to delineate the relationship of good works to it, carefully separating them out from the means of salvation. In the autumn Cranmer began inviting to safety in England prominent reformers threatened by the military triumphs of the emperor Charles V. The first to appear, in December 1547, were Peter Martyr (Pietro Martire Vermigli) and Bernardino Ochino. The archbishop's long-term ally and correspondent Bucer was eventually forced out of Strasbourg to cross to England in April 1549.

On Easter day (1 April 1548), 'the order of the Communion', an English version of the section of the mass in which the laity took communion, was made compulsory; this was Cranmer's first published experiment with the eucharistic liturgy, perhaps drafted in the summer of 1546. A further publication under Cranmer's direction proved an embarrassment: an official catechism published probably in June 1548. It was a free translation with additions and significant modifications of a work first published in German at Nuremberg in 1533, the original principal author being Cranmer's relative Andreas Osiander. Most serious of many small signs of haste in the production are various statements on the eucharist proclaiming an uncompromisingly Lutheran position. These were hastily modified in a third edition, but provided much annoyance to Reformed observers, and ammunition for conservatives.

Throughout the autumn Cranmer presided over discussions preparing the Book of Common Prayer, ostensibly seeking consensus with more conservative colleagues, while conniving at aggressive moves against traditional eucharistic devotion. He was probably closely involved in publishing a devotional and polemical work, *A treatise of the right honouring and worshipping of our Saviour Jesus Christ in the sacrament of bread and wine*; it bore the name of an obscure Calais parish priest, Richard Bonner, was dedicated to the archbishop, and contained large sections of a eucharistic treatise by Bucer in translation. During a four-day debate on eucharistic presence held in the House of Lords from 14 December 1548 he made clear his conversion to a spiritual-presence view of the eucharist, and rejected Lutheran interpretations of it.

The first prayer book and its aftermath, 1549 Cranmer's greatest achievement, his English prayer book, was issued in March 1549; its use was compulsory from Pentecost or Whitsunday (9 June). Its contents were avowedly conciliatory to conservative opinion, but evangelical insiders were privately reassured that this was purely temporary. The sources were various, reflecting Cranmer's research in his magnificent library, probably the largest in England at the time. He drew much on the medieval use of Salisbury (the Sarum rite), but used it in creative tension with Archbishop Hermann von Wied's scheme of evangelical reform, the *Pia deliberatio* (1543, 1545), which itself synthesized many renewed liturgies of Germany and central Europe. Many other lesser sources can be traced, including English liturgical texts of the previous two decades, but all are united by a sense for sonorous rhetorical prose which is Cranmer's own. His most interesting and effective compositions are short collects (prayers) for the liturgical year, which he composed to supplement his retranslations and editing of earlier collects to produce a complete liturgical cycle.

After Bucer and his Strasbourg colleague the Hebrew scholar Paul Fagius had arrived, Cranmer embarked on an ambitious project to co-operate in creating a new Latin text of the Bible with accompanying commentary. Fragments remain at Corpus Christi College, Cambridge, but the scheme seems to have been overtaken by the multifaceted unrest affecting southern England throughout the summer of 1549. In contrast to his discreet withdrawal during the risings of 1536–7 Cranmer had a high profile in restoring order, sending his associates to preach in the home counties and East Anglian camps of demonstrators who showed themselves sympathetic to reformed theology, himself preaching a major keynote sermon against these insurgents at St Paul's on 21 July 1549, and writing a bitter answer to rebels in Devon and Cornwall who in contrast to those nearer London wished to restore the old religion. His efforts were probably put in print, though no copies apparently survive.

Even after all unrest had been ruthlessly suppressed, and Cranmer was presiding over the trial of the conservative Bishop Edmund Bonner of London, a new crisis arose: a *coup d'état* of privy councillors against Protector Somerset. Action was led by John Dudley, earl of Warwick; Somerset panicked, and from 5 October tried to rally forces to himself and the king, first at Hampton Court and then at

Windsor Castle. Cranmer, with Thomas Smith and William Paget, was among the few councillors to rally to Somerset, but from the beginning his purpose may have been to defuse the situation and safeguard the king's person. Somerset's protectorship was revoked on 13 October and he was committed to the Tower. In discreet co-operation with Warwick, Cranmer outfaced conservative politicians who had been enlisted against Somerset, and established the regime's continuing evangelical character. In December Warwick was able to exploit Cranmer's influence with his royal godson to defeat attempts by Thomas Wriothesley, earl of Southampton, and Henry Fitzalan, earl of Arundel, to engineer the execution of both Somerset and Warwick himself.

Accelerated reform, 1550–1552 From now on evangelical ascendancy was unchallenged, and during 1550 Cranmer enjoyed unprecedented room for manoeuvre in national government. He promoted protégés to sees vacated by conservatives, and used intervening vacancies in see to promote reform, for instance pioneering destruction of stone altars in the vacant diocese of Norwich in February–March 1550. He also oversaw the publication of forms of ordination for bishops, priests, and deacons (the ordinal) which had not been included in the 1549 prayer book; these were partly based on an earlier work by Martin Bucer. But his main work was to publish in summer 1550 the first full-length book to bear his name: *A defence of the true and Catholic doctrine of the sacrament of the body and blood of our saviour Christ*. The work is divided into five sections, whose polemical architecture is dependent on the relatively brief first section, setting out the nature of the eucharistic sacrament (defined in terms of natural substance of bread and wine, and spiritual presence of Christ). Cranmer then turns to the 'confutation of sundry errors' all related to beliefs of the medieval western church. These are four: transubstantiation; other general misunderstandings about eucharistic presence, metaphor, and sacrament; the belief that 'evil men eat and drink the very body and blood of Christ'; and the assertion of a repeated daily sacrificial offering of Christ (MacCulloch, *Thomas Cranmer*, 464). Each of the remaining four sections of the book, seven-eighths of the whole text, takes each of these errors in turn and refutes them at length.

During the spring of 1550 Cranmer faced confrontation about the pace of change with his more impatient colleague John Hooper. Hooper complained about features of the new ordinal soon before being nominated as bishop of Gloucester, and persuaded King Edward personally to strike out a reference to the saints in the oath of supremacy taken by (among others) clergy or bishops. However, at the end of July, despite Hooper's confirmation as bishop, Ridley and Cranmer blocked any further progress in his promotion if he continued to refuse to wear the prescribed rochet and chimere when consecrated. They were ultimately successful in persuading the privy council that Hooper was being seditious; in January 1551 he was imprisoned (supposedly even threatened with death), and he capitulated in February. This was a major victory for

Cranmer's principle that the English Reformation should proceed at the pace set by the king in parliament.

During this conflict Cranmer faced much more thoroughgoing radicals, mostly unitarian in belief, having been consistent in his attack on them since the mid-1530s. Most prominent was Joan Bocher (Joan of Kent), whom Cranmer had imprisoned in 1549; after many disputations with his colleagues she was burnt at the stake on 2 May 1550. Her fate was recalled in the wake of Cranmer's own fiery death, and was a matter of regret to Cranmer's great admirer John Foxe; it is noticeable that the account of her trial and condemnation has been extracted from Cranmer's archiepiscopal register. A further Unitarian, George van Parris, was burnt in 1551, identified as a heretic by the London Stranger Church: this grouping of émigré protestant congregations had been given its royal charter of privileges of 1550 with Cranmer's enthusiastic encouragement, partly so that it could act as a policeman on radical refugees from abroad.

While still contending with Hooper, Cranmer began the trial on 15 December 1550 of his former colleague and long-term rival Bishop Gardiner of Winchester: Gardiner was deprived of his see and returned to the Tower of London. During the trial Gardiner produced the manuscript of a book, *An explication and assertion of the Catholic faith touching the most blessed sacrament of the altar*, a major refutation of Cranmer's *Defence*, soon printed abroad. The consequence was twofold: Gardiner had disingenuously commended aspects of the 1549 prayer book that were capable of traditionalist interpretations and thus rendered urgent the liturgical revision that had been intended from the outset, but Cranmer also felt compelled to write a riposte to defend his treatise. The result was published by the end of September 1551: *An Answer to a Crafty and Sophistical Cavillation Devised by Stephen Gardiner*. To it was appended his brief but pungent answer to another attack on the *Defence* written by the former regius professor at Oxford, Richard Smith. The contentious title shows that the tone of the *Answer* was markedly different from that of the *Defence*: it could bear comparison with the most savage Edwardian polemicists.

Tensions within government, 1551–1553 The duke of Somerset's rehabilitation ended with his rearrest on 16 October 1551. Cranmer's involvement in politics had dwindled that summer, either because of his concentration on writing the *Answer*, or because sweating sickness had broken out in his Croydon household. He probably did not object to the removal of Somerset, whose increasingly irresponsible conduct threatened the evangelical cause, and indeed the government now took trouble to forward two of Cranmer's favourite projects, reforming canon law, and encouraging Somerset's community of French protestant weavers at Glastonbury. However, his attitude changed as John Dudley (now duke of Northumberland) manoeuvred to strengthen his political ascendancy, and as Somerset was condemned to death; execution followed on 22 January 1552. Cranmer and Ridley desperately tried to prevent it, much to Northumberland's displeasure.

This rift was further widened by the process in parliament intended to deprive Bishop Cuthbert Tunstall, a move linked both to Northumberland's personal aggrandizement in the north and to further depredations on church lands which leading protestant clergy, particularly Cranmer, found increasingly offensive. The archbishop voted against the bill depriving Tunstall in the Lords, and a letter of Northumberland to his fellow councillors on 26 April 1552 reveals a serious though unidentifiable quarrel between the two men. Thus a serious contradiction began to open up in government religious policy: a growing tide of personal mistrust between Northumberland and Cranmer, yet a continuing pursuit of evangelical revolution. William Cecil did much to prevent a full breach, since remarkably he retained the full confidence both of the duke and the archbishop until the collapse of Northumberland's regime in 1553.

Prominent in ongoing religious changes was the comprehensive scheme for revising canon law (later called by John Foxe the *Reformatio legum*), led by Cranmer; in this work he included both his refugee friends John à Lasco and Peter Martyr, and (revealing his uncommon ability to forget former quarrels) Bishop John Hooper. The foreigners' inclusion was a mark of Cranmer's ambitions to see England lead an international protestant reformation; in March 1552 he sent invitations to Bullinger, Calvin, and Melanchthon to gather at an international church council in England to rival the Council of Trent. Nothing came of these overtures, and, as delay became apparent, Cranmer abandoned his hope of a common statement of doctrine in favour of articles of belief designed for the church in England. After much consultation on these, which appears to have begun as far back as 1549, they became the forty-two articles issued in 1553, somewhat modified as thirty-nine in 1563; the Church of England still affirms their doctrinal importance.

A third project reached completion in the winter of 1551–2: comprehensive revision of the 1549 prayer book, authorized in a new Act of Uniformity passed in April 1552. As in the original 1549 compilation, much remains obscure about the revision, although Cranmer steered its development, and both Martyr and Bucer made comments upon which Cranmer drew for the final version. The book removed ambiguities and Catholic survivals, particularly in restructuring holy communion, which more clearly expressed Cranmer's rejection of real presence ideas; and also in shortening and amending the burial service, in order to remove the sense of continuing communion between living and dead which was such a striking feature of late medieval religion. A little modified in 1559 and rather more substantially in 1662, Cranmer's second prayer book remains at the heart of all Anglican liturgical forms. However, as an English exile remarked in the reign of Mary, it is likely that if Cranmer had lived he would have been inclined by his search for continuing Reformation to have 'drawn up a book of prayer a hundred times more perfect than this that we now have' (MacCulloch, *Thomas Cranmer*, 512).

However, both canon law reform and prayer book were delayed throughout 1552; the prayer book was not published until October, following a last-minute disagreement. This was caused by the émigré Scots preacher John Knox, whom Northumberland had brought to London. He strongly attacked the new liturgy's retention of kneeling at communion, and so on 27 September the privy council in Cranmer's absence ordered Richard Grafton to stop printing the prayer book 'untill certain faultes therein be corrected'—principally kneeling (*APC, 1552–4*, 131). Cranmer's subsequent long letter to his council colleagues is a masterpiece of controlled fury. His final *coup de grâce* highlighted the consequences of a 'scripture alone' view of the problem: the archbishop sarcastically pointed out that first-century dining practice was 'as the Tartars and Turks use yet at this day, to eat their meat lying upon the ground' (MacCulloch, *Thomas Cranmer*, 526). As a result, kneeling remained in the prayer book, with a last-minute explanatory 'black rubric' inserted (initially on a slip tipped into the text): this emphasized that kneeling was 'a signification of the humble and grateful acknowledging of the benefits of Christ given unto the worthy receiving, and to avoid the profanation and disorder which about the Holy Communion might ensue', and did not represent any theology of corporal presence or eucharistic adoration (Ketley, 283). The rubric reflected Cranmer's own eucharistic outlook; it represented a defeat for Knox and a renewed assertion of the Cranmerian principle that religious change should be decided in the forum of parliament and not after some private initiative.

Soon afterwards Cranmer left the capital's uncongenial politics to investigate religious radicalism in Kent: Anabaptists and loosely organized groups with the nickname 'freewillers', since they rejected the increasing evangelical commitment to predestination. This occupied him until February 1553, by which time the political atmosphere at court had badly deteriorated. Leading preachers were mounting a high-profile campaign against the greed of politicians, particularly against their interest in acquiring church lands, and this caused fury in Northumberland's circle. Probably in retaliation, Northumberland intervened in the House of Lords in March to halt Cranmer's cherished scheme for canon-law reform. Although a new catechism and primer were published in May alongside the finalized forty-two articles, even that provoked a fresh row between Cranmer and his privy council colleagues, because without his knowledge they misleadingly published the articles as formally authorized by the convocation of Canterbury. Cranmer's anger stemmed from the knowledge that such inaccuracy would give conservatives a perfect excuse for refusing to accept the new articles, which proved to be the case as he began attempting to secure subscriptions.

The background to this neurotic political mood was the collapse of the young King Edward's health; his death would spell disaster to the protestant cause, since his heir was his Catholic half-sister the Lady Mary. The solution devised by the king and Northumberland was to divert the succession to a protestant member of the royal family, Lady Jane Grey. It is not certain when Cranmer was brought into the scheme; it was after 17 June, when the king made his will leaving his throne to Jane. Cranmer's own later story to Queen Mary (a story that he insisted the marquess of Northampton and Lord Darcy could verify) was that he demanded to speak alone to his royal godson, to dissuade him from diverting the succession, but permission was refused; he had to speak to the king in the presence of his fellow councillors. He was told that the judges had confirmed the legitimacy of Edward's action, and the king himself sharply commented that he 'trusted that I alone would not be more repugnant to his will than the rest of the council were' (*Writings*, 2.443). After that, his continuing reluctant adherence to the plan was secured by various promises of accelerated reform: considerable government expenditure on an effort to settle Philip Melanchthon in Cambridge University, and a projected revival of his restructuring of canon law.

The rapid popular rejection of Queen Jane after Edward's death on 6 July came as a complete surprise to the political establishment; Lady Mary (inexplicably left at liberty) rallied East Anglian support, and only a fortnight later was proclaimed queen in London. Cranmer was prominent in the formal pronouncements of Jane's regime, and he contributed at least 20 men of his 100-strong private army to Northumberland's failed expeditionary force against Mary. It is therefore particularly surprising that he remained nominally at liberty at Lambeth Palace for the rest of the summer; the most plausible explanation is that he was useful in expediting business while protestantism was still officially the established religion. Thus he presided over Edward VI's funeral in Westminster Abbey on 8 August, without traditional Catholic ceremony. It may have been at this time that he ordered a clerk to inscribe all his books 'Thomas Cantuariensis', perhaps with some notion of keeping the collection intact. He made no attempt to escape to the continent, unlike other leading protestants.

Arrest, imprisonment, and trial, 1553–1555 On 5 September 1553 Cranmer appeared before royal commissioners at St Paul's deanery to answer questions about his role in the Jane Grey coup. Any intention of allowing him quiet retirement was dashed by his sharp reaction to the quickening pace of Catholic restoration. Cranmer's suffragan, Richard Thornden, resumed the mass in Canterbury Cathedral: the archbishop expressed his fury in a private letter which probably accompanied a proposed draft of a public declaration. Also on 5 September this declaration was distributed in Cheapside, apparently copied by a friend (named by Foxe as Bishop John Scory of Chichester), before Cranmer himself was ready to go public with it. Cranmer, at first annoyed, was soon himself promoting further distribution of the text through the capital.

Cranmer was ordered to appear in Star Chamber on 14 September. He was able to have a farewell meal at Lambeth Palace with Peter Martyr (now in retreat to the continent once more), but that night was lodged in the Tower. He was restored to the public world only to stand trial for treason (with the Dudley brothers Guildford, Henry, and Ambrose, and Guildford's wife, the former Queen Jane) at

Guildhall on 13 November, on charges of helping to seize the Tower for Jane and of levying troops for Northumberland's expeditionary force against Mary. Robert Wingfield (admittedly an unfriendly observer) said that Cranmer 'was put to utter dismay after hearing [William] Staunford, the Queen's counsel, outline his treachery to him, and openly confessed his crime' (MacCulloch, 274); certainly Cranmer was confused and unhappy about what he had done, and later he said of his trial that he had 'confessed more … than was true' (*Writings*, 2.212). Now his household was broken up, much of his goods sold off (with reasonable provision for his family), most of his protestant books apparently destroyed, and the bulk of his magnificent library given to the earl of Arundel, his turncoat former colleague on Jane's privy council. However, many of his most important personal manuscripts and notebooks were secured by his household and preserved privately.

After the failure of Sir Thomas Wyatt's Kentish protestant rebellion in February 1554 the crowded state of the Tower prisons resulted in Cranmer's sharing apartments with Nicholas Ridley, John Bradford, and Hugh Latimer. Now they were able to make preparations for a public show of strength with Catholicism. In early March Cranmer, Latimer, and Ridley were taken to Oxford to stand trial for heresy, and lodged in Bocardo, the town prison. Their initial confrontation in the university church was not a trial but a disputation (14–20 April) against a Catholic team led by Dr Hugh Weston. In a disorderly and partisan event, Cranmer in particular made a strong showing with his arguments on the nature of the eucharist. After this, they were separated for the next few months: Cranmer returned to Bocardo, Ridley to the mayor's house, and Latimer to the home of one of the town bailiffs. They were deprived of contact with their own servants, and also of pen and paper; Cranmer's conditions seem to have been most restrictive, although he was soon removed to the other bailiff's house.

Few details are known of Cranmer's confinement over the next months. It is certain that he was able to revise the Latin version of his *Defence* to cover more of the points raised against it by Stephen Gardiner and to tackle criticism of his citations at the disputation of April 1554; later he managed to get it smuggled out of Oxford, which resulted in an Emden edition in 1557. The last surviving writing from his hand probably dates from the opening two months of 1555: a short note to Peter Martyr (by then in Strasbourg), affirming his conviction that the desperate situation of the church was a proof of its imminent divine deliverance, and regretting that he had not produced a definitive answer to Stephen Gardiner.

On 19 June 1555 the trial mandate was issued in Rome; it was served on Cranmer on 7 September, and included a formal requirement that he appear in Rome within eighty days. In fact his trial before Brooks, Martin, and Story opened in the university church on 12 September. Cranmer was at a greater disadvantage than in the previous disputation, which had concentrated on the eucharistic question of which he had become the master: now his whole career, with all its changes of personal, political, and theological direction, was open to scrutiny. Cranmer arrived showing studied respect for the royal proctors, but studied lack of deference to the papal representative, and his first speech centred on a careful distinction between obedience that he owed to the crown and his complete rejection of the pope. However, he found himself trapped by his own respect for the role of the prince in the church into an absurd admission that the emperor Nero had been head of the church in his day. After this, his dignity returned, in the face of a string of witnesses who simply confirmed that Cranmer was the symbol of everything that had changed in the church between 1533 and 1553.

Cranmer had appealed to the queen in September, making an offer of further discussion, and this was taken up in October; the Catholic spokesman chosen was the Spanish Dominican theologian, Pedro de Soto, an able theologian and former confessor to the holy Roman emperor. There was little result, and on 16 October Ridley and Latimer were burnt in Broad Street, causing terrible distress to their friend, who was made to watch from his prison. Cranmer was now left to preserve his spiritual identity with no human help to hand.

Final imprisonments and death, 1555–1556 The last few months are illuminated by two diametrically opposed sources: Foxe's admiring biography of Cranmer in his *Acts and Monuments*, and the equally polemical anti-biography, *Cranmer's Recantacyons*, probably by Archdeacon Nicholas Harpsfield. The latter source claims that one of Cranmer's sisters who was a devout Catholic lobbied for his better treatment; this resulted in his transfer (11 December 1555) to much easier house arrest at Christ Church. Once more a Spanish Dominican, Juan de Villagarcia, was deputed to debate with him. These arguments succeeded in badly unsettling the archbishop. In an isolation spiritual rather than physical, he cast in the role of friend and confidant the attendant guarding him, Nicholas Woodson: an Oxford tradesman and university servant closely linked to some of the most activist Catholic Oxford academics. This friendship came to be his only emotional support, and, to please the devoutly Catholic Woodson, he began giving way to everything that he had hated.

Cranmer began attending services in the cathedral, including the mass, but then bitterly argued with Villagarcia about the significance of what he was doing. Furious at his obstinacy, Woodson threatened to cut off all contact with him. The prospect appalled Cranmer, and in a state of prostration on 28 January he signed his first hesitant submission to papal authority. Amid violent mood-swings, he signed a second submission and then attended the Candlemas ceremonies (2 February). Nevertheless on 14 February 1556 he was formally if farcically degraded from sacred ministry (interrupting the proceedings with a formal appeal to a general council) and taken back to Bocardo. Once there, and faced with browbeating from Bishop Bonner, John Harpsfield, and Villagarcia, he signed the third and fourth of his submissions on 15 and 16 February, but in fact they gave little ground to his opponents.

Within ten days a dramatic shift took place, prompted by the writ issued on 24 February to the mayor of Oxford for Cranmer's burning; the accompanying messengers announced that the date set for the execution was 7 March. Suddenly the reality of his position hit Cranmer: it is not necessary to speculate that he was physically tortured into a change of heart. The result on 26 February was a statement that was truly a recantation. He probably did not write it himself; the Catholic commentary on it merely says that Cranmer was ordered to sign it. He subsequently even asked for sacramental absolution—a vital capitulation to Roman authority—and commended Thomas More's *Dialogue of Comfort*, which had been given him to read.

There was growing popular excitement about Cranmer's fate, encouraged by the appearance of a comet in southern England; the government's worry about unrest led to the postponement of his execution. Mary sent Dr Henry Cole, provost of Eton, to emphasize that delay meant no prospect of clemency: this interview, on 17 March, crushed Cranmer, and precipitated a nightmare in which he saw Henry VIII and Christ, symbols of the two authorities in his life, both rejecting him. Accordingly, on 18 March, now without hope of reprieve, he embarked on the sixth, longest, and most wretched of his successive statements. It is worth noting that he signed this when there was no possibility of his being pardoned and spared. What happened next, his dramatic reversal of his recantation, was therefore not simply an act of spite by a desperate man who felt that he had nothing to lose by defying the regime and the old church. It represented a considered recovery of twenty years of integrity.

Cranmer's last full day on earth (20 March) was oddly tranquil: he spent it preparing a final discourse for the government to publish. On the following day he signed more copies of his sixth statement, and was visited by another of his sisters—this time, says *Cranmer's Recantacyons*, not the Catholic sister. Only in retrospect did this and other little clues indicate that his purpose and convictions might again be changing. Once brought to the crowded university church, after a sermon from Dr Cole, he began his discourse. After following the written text, he finally embarked on explaining 'the great thing, which so much troubleth my conscience'. This was not, as the authorities expected, his Edwardian 'untrue books and writings' about the eucharist, but 'all such bills and papers which I have written or signed with my hand since my degradation'. Amid growing commotion he denounced his old adversary Stephen Gardiner (lately deceased), before being pulled from the pulpit and hurried through the rain to the fire in front of Balliol College. In the flames Cranmer achieved a final serenity, and fulfilled the promise made in his last shouts in the church: 'forasmuch as my hand offended, writing contrary to my heart, my hand shall first be punished there-for'. He stretched it into the heart of the fire, repeating 'his unworthy right hand', 'this hand hath offended', and also, while he could, the dying words of the first martyr Stephen: 'Lord Jesus, receive my spirit … I see the heavens open and Jesus standing at the right hand of God'. 'He was very soon dead', said an anonymous observer, J. A. (MacCulloch, *Thomas Cranmer*, 601–4).

Preserving Cranmer's legacy The sensational and controversial circumstances of Cranmer's execution mocked the publicity coup hoped for by the Catholic church. Dr Cole began trying to redeem the situation the following day (Passion Sunday) by preaching a denunciation of Cranmer in the church still haunted by the archbishop's cries. In London the government published all six of Cranmer's recantations plus the text of the speech that he ought to have made in the university church, without publicly acknowledging any further developments; observers such as the Venetian ambassador in London did not feel that this was a successful manoeuvre. Neither side could make Cranmer's death the basis for simple propaganda. Various of his letters were published, and, as well as the new Latin edition of the *Defence* (1557), there was a brave if not altogether successful attempt to turn part of Cranmer's theological notebooks into a readable work of propaganda, the *Confutation of Unwritten Verities* (1556).

The task of looking after Cranmer's family was undertaken by the evangelical printers of London, led by Cranmer's favourite publishers Reyner Wolfe and Edward Whitchurch. The young Thomas was taken to the continent, and steps were taken to retrieve his landed property in Yorkshire. His restitution in blood after his father's attainder waited on a special act of parliament in 1562–3. Edward Whitchurch married the widow Margaret Cranmer, and also negotiated a marriage for Mrs Cranmer's daughter Margaret to Thomas Norton. Norton moved in with his parents-in-law in London, and was proud of his link to the old archbishop: he led an unsuccessful attempt to authorize Cranmer's revision of the canon law in the parliament of 1571. On his first wife's death Norton married her cousin Alice, daughter of Archdeacon Cranmer. Whitchurch and his wife retired to a rented property in Camberwell, leased from an old friend of his, Edward Scott; the couple shared the house with Scott (as they had shared with Norton in London). On Whitchurch's death Margaret swiftly married Bartholomew Scott, possibly a brother of Edward Scott. She died some time during the later 1570s.

The adult life of Cranmer's son Thomas was certainly not happy; living either in Yorkshire or in London, he was involved in a series of lawsuits, and never seems to have obtained full benefit out of the Yorkshire properties. His career contrasts with that of his workaholic and deeply religious brother-in-law Norton: he cannot be traced in any public office, which, however minor, should have been his for the asking. It is as well that the archbishop did not live to see his son summoned by church courts on successive charges of fornication and adultery in York diocese. The younger Thomas's widow was sister to Richard Rogers, bishop of Dover, one of the Cranmer penumbra of relatives, and her first husband, Hugh Vaughan, may also have had family links. She survived Thomas's death in London in 1598 to marry a third time, but passed her last days in poverty, requiring a charitable collection in St Olave Jewry in 1607. Neither of the archbishop's surviving adult children produced heirs.

Posthumous reputation and influence The wider aftermath of Cranmer's death is the history of the later English Reformation. Yet his theology and assumptions do not sit altogether comfortably with the still later Anglican communion. His predestinarianism has been left behind in the Anglican tradition. His theology of eucharistic presence was close to the symbolist notions of Reformed central Europe, perhaps most akin to the views of Heinrich Bullinger; this has not commended itself to the sacramentalist strain in Anglicanism. Moreover, Cranmer's conception of a 'middle way' (*via media*) in religion was quite different from later Anglicanism: certainly not between Rome and protestantism. He sought an agreement between Wittenberg and Zürich for a united vision of Christian doctrine against the counterfeit refurbished at the Council of Trent. Undoubtedly, had he lived to steer the Church of England under Queen Jane or Queen Elizabeth, he would have helped to sweep away much that has become the familiar physical and theological furniture of the English church.

When Elizabeth did come to the throne in 1558, she shows signs of having preferred Cranmer's discredited first prayer book of 1549 to his second of 1552, but to reintroduce 1549 was not practical politics. Her settlement of 1559 established a version of the Edwardian church that proved to be a freeze-frame of the church as it had been in September 1552, ignoring later Edwardian changes. Thus the 1559 prayer book was a barely modified version of the 1552 rite, devoid of the 'black rubric' on adoration of the eucharistic elements; no government sympathy was offered to attempts in 1559 and 1571 to revive Cranmer's scheme of 1553 for wholesale replacement for canon law. The 1553 catechism and primer were set aside for ever.

The surviving Edwardian clergy now leading Elizabeth's church found themselves defending this fossilized version of the Edwardian church against criticism from former companions in Marian suffering, and increasingly also from an unsympathetic new generation. In these circumstances the memory of the Oxford martyrs became as much the property of puritans who deplored the Elizabethan church's half-reformed polity as of Cranmer's conformist former colleagues: a tussle took place for the honour of being the heirs of Cranmer, Latimer, and Ridley. Both sides chose what they wanted from the myth-making of Foxe's book of martyrs. For conformists, Cranmer's legacy was his prayer book, so that he symbolized their defence of the liturgy against puritans, just as he had done in disputes among the Marian exiles about how far they could depart from the prayer book of 1552. For puritans, this was a distortion of Cranmer's work, which had been tragically cut off half-completed. Separatists on the fringe of the puritan movement were much more equivocal towards Cranmer, but only among the conscious heirs of the radical martyrs of Edward VI's reign was there a consistent hostile tradition with no admiration for the

Oxford martyrs: radicals had scorned them even amid Marian troubles.

Another less positive view of Cranmer emerged from the 1580s onwards among churchmen (eventually nick-named Arminians) who wished to lay greater stress on sacramental life. Their predisposition to emphasize continuity rather than discontinuity in the English church through the Reformation, and their wish to restore the notion of real presence in the eucharist to a key place in Christian doctrine, made them unsympathetic to Cranmer's changes, and unenthusiastic about the implications of his liturgical work as lightly revised in 1559. Rather than openly criticize (for they made much of their loyalty to the established church), their disapproval manifested itself in a discreet lack of reference to the virtues of the Edwardian church, and also in increasing interest in the 1549 prayer book—for the very reason that Cranmer had revised it: that it offered a more extrovert Catholic practice and devotion than was possible with the 1559 rite. The 1549 rite was used to modify the 1559 prayer book when a revised liturgy was imposed on the Church of Scotland, with dire consequences, in 1637.

Correspondingly, the Arminians' opponents made use of Cranmer in resisting Arminian innovation. In the dispute between William Laud and Bishop John Williams in the late 1630s over the correct positioning of the communion table, and the symbolism that the positioning might imply, Williams drew heavily on the phraseology and rubrics of the 1559 Book of Common Prayer, on the homilies, and on Cranmer's *Defence* and *Answer*. Yet from the outbreak of civil war in 1642 attitudes to the Marian prelate-martyrs became more divided. William Prynne, for instance, can be found re-evaluating the deaths of Cranmer and Ridley, whom he had previously seen as symbolic allies in his campaigns against Laudian prelacy. Most hostile of all was John Milton, in his bitter attacks on the whole notion of episcopacy during the interregnum. Conversely, moderate defenders of the pre-war established church redoubled their praise of bishops who could be seen as redeeming episcopacy from Laud's follies.

However, perhaps the most impressive interregnum verdict on the martyred archbishop was a widespread if unobtrusive continuing use of the Book of Common Prayer (flexibly adapted to local needs as Elizabethan puritans had hoped), although it was officially illegal and replaced by the *Directory for the Publique Worship of God*. Given this testimony to the prayer book's place in the fabric of English protestantism, the nature of Charles II's Restoration settlement of 1660–62, with its startling triumph of militant Anglicanism, becomes more comprehensible; Cranmer played his part in that victory. Whether he would have been happy with the consequences is debatable; he might have looked askance at the delicate subversion of his sacramental outlook by the revisers of his prayer book in 1662. Likewise, he is unlikely to have been happy that the new, more narrowly drawn identity of Anglicanism excluded many protestants who would have found a home in the pre-Laudian church. In the nineteenth century came a revival of coldness towards

Cranmerian religion among Anglican heirs of the Arminian tradition: the Tractarians, the Oxford Movement, and Anglo-Catholics. They had one escape route from the worst consequences of Cranmer's work. Like the Arminians, they could (quite mistakenly) see Cranmer's first prayer book as a refuge from the theological implications of his second. Reorderings of the eucharistic rite in the mould of 1549 became common in Anglo-Catholic parishes and convents, particularly in the church beyond England created by the worldwide spread of Anglicanism in the wake of the successive British empires.

The widest aftermath of Cranmer's life and work is in the realm of language and of cultural identity. Cranmer could not have known in 1552 that he would provide a vehicle for English worship almost unchanged for four centuries, and it was a happy coincidence that this ecclesiastical functionary, propelled into high office by the accidents of politics, had a natural feel for formal English prose. Cranmer was happily and healthily aware that he could not write successful English verse, but he was a prose connoisseur, unafraid to borrow from some of the most distinguished English liturgical craftsmen of his own time, to create a text which has remained the most frequently performed drama in the English language. At the moment when printing was fixing the forms of vernacular language, and when humanist scholarship was bombarding the language with Latin and Greek neologisms, his sense of restraint and rhythm created a vehicle for expression which now lies at the heart of global communication.   DIARMAID MACCULLOCH

Sources D. MacCulloch, *Thomas Cranmer: a life* (1996) • A. Alane [Alesius], *Of the auctorite of the word of God agaynst the bisshop of London* (1537?) • P. Ayris, 'Preaching the last crusade: Thomas Cranmer and the "devotion" money of 1543', *Journal of Ecclesiastical History*, 49 (1998), 683–701 • P. Ayris and D. Selwyn, eds., *Thomas Cranmer: churchman and scholar* (1993) • P. Ayris, ed., *The archiepiscopal register of Thomas Cranmer* (2000) • P. M. Black, 'Matthew Parker's search for Cranmer's "Great notable written books"', *The Library*, 5th ser., 29 (1974), 312–22 • P. N. Brooks, *Thomas Cranmer's doctrine of the eucharist: an essay in historical development*, 2nd edn (1992) • T. Cranmer, correspondence with Johannes Dantiscus, Muzeum Narodowe w Krakowie, Cracow, Bibl. Czartoryskich MS 1595, 9–12, 13–16 • *Writings and disputations of Thomas Cranmer*, ed. J. E. Cox, Parker Society, [17] (1844) • *The acts and monuments of John Foxe*, ed. S. R. Cattley, 8 vols. (1837–41) • F. A. Gasquet and E. Bishop, *Edward VI and the Book of Common Prayer* (1890) • B. A. Gerrish, 'Sign and reality: the Lord's supper in the Reformed confessions', *The old protestantism and the new* (1982), 118–30 • *Four political treatises: the 'Doctrinal of princes' (1533); 'Pasquil the Playne' (1533); 'The banquette of Sapience' (1534); 'The image of governance' (1541) by Sir Thomas Elyot*, ed. L. Gottesman (1967) • C. P. Hammer, 'The Oxford martyrs in Oxford: the local history of their confinements and their keepers', *Journal of Ecclesiastical History*, 50 (1999), 235–50 • *Bishop Cranmer's recantacyons*, ed. R. M. Milnes and J. Gairdner (1877–84) • W. Harrison, *The description of England: the classic contemporary account of Tudor social life*, ed. G. Edelen (1968) • J. A., account of Cranmer's death, BL, Harley MS 422, fols. 48–52 • A. Alesius, reminiscences to Elizabeth I, PRO, Secretaries of state, state papers foreign, Elizabeth I, SP 70/7/659 • D. M. Loades, *The Oxford martyrs* (1970) • J. G. Nichols, ed., *Narratives of the days of the Reformation*, CS, old ser., 77 (1859) [accounts of Ralph Morice and of the anonymous biographer of Cranmer (Dr Stephen Nevinson?)] • A. Null, *Thomas Cranmer's doctrine of repentance* (2000) • Bodl. Oxf., MS Jesus 74 [Thomas Master, collections for Edward, Lord Herbert of Chirbury, *The life and raigne of King Henry*

the Eighth, 1649] · M. Parker, *De antiquitate Britannicae ecclesiae et privilegiis ecclesiae Cantuarensis* (1572) · [J. Raine], ed., *Testamenta Eboracensia*, 4, SurtS, 53 (1869) [will of Thomas Cranmer senior] · 'The letters of Richard Scudamore to Sir Philip Holby, September 1549 – March 1555', ed. M. Dowling, *Camden miscellany, XXX*, CS, 4th ser., 39 (1990), 67–148 · D. G. Selwyn, 'A neglected edition of Cranmer's catechism', *Journal of Theological Studies*, new ser., 15 (1964), 76–90 · D. G. Selwyn, 'A new version of a mid-sixteenth century vernacular tract on the eucharist: a document of the early Edwardian Reformation', *Journal of Ecclesiastical History*, 39 (1988), 217–29 · D. G. Selwyn, 'The "Book of Doctrine", the Lords' debate and the first prayer book of Edward VI: an abortive attempt at doctrinal consensus?', *Journal of Theological Studies*, new ser., 40 (1989), 446–80 · J. Strype, *Memorials of the most reverend father in God Thomas Cranmer*, 3 vols. in 4 (1848–54) · S. Tabor, 'Additions to STC', *The Library*, 6th ser., 16 (1994), 190–207 · draft papal dispensation for plurality granted to Cranmer, August 1530, Vatican Archivo Secreto Vaticano, Brevi Clemente VII, Arm. 40, vol. 30, fol. 215 · G. W. Marshall, ed., *The visitations of the county of Nottingham in the years 1569 and 1614*, Harleian Society, 4 (1871) · D. MacCulloch, 'The *Vita Mariae Angliae Reginae* of Robert Wingfield of Brantham', *Camden miscellany, XXVIII*, CS, 4th ser., 29 (1984), 181–301 · *APC*, 1552–4 · J. Ketley, ed., *The two liturgies, AD 1549 and AD 1552*, Parker Society, 19 (1844)
Archives BL, Cotton MSS; Harley MSS, corresp. and papers | CCC Cam., MSS 102, 104
Likenesses G. Flicke, oils, 1545, NPG [*see illus.*] · portrait, *c*.1547, repro. in MacCulloch, *Thomas Cranmer*, 362 · group portrait, oils, *c*.1570 (*Edward VI and the pope*), NPG · attrib. J. Belkamp, oils, Knole, Kent · T. Beza, print, NPG; repro. in *Icones* (1589) · J. Faber senior or R. Houston, mezzotint (after oil painting by G. Flicke), BM, NPG · group portrait, woodcut, NPG; repro. in *Acts and monuments of John Foxe* · oils, Trinity Cam.

Cranogwen. *See* Rees, Sarah Jane (1839–1916).

Cranston, Andrew (*d.* **1708**), creator of a public library, was born in the late 1650s in Scotland to unknown parents. He was perhaps connected to the lords Cranstoun, for the descendants of his only known brother, James, assumed the same coat of arms. There is a volume in his library inscribed to him from Dr Alexander Cranston of Edinburgh in 1676, who may be another relative.

Cranston attended Edinburgh University, graduating BA in 1673. In 1681 he was presented to the parish of Greenock, Renfrewshire, by Sir John Schaw. He received a testimonial for ordination from the presbytery at Renfrew on 1 June and was instituted on 5 July 1681. He left the parish after only nine months; he was absent for much of this time, and had refused to subscribe to the Test Act. In May 1683, about to depart a troubled Scotland, he donated 520 books to Edinburgh University Library. The gift was revoked a year later, however, for he had chosen to make his home in England. He may have joined his brother James, a fellow graduate of Edinburgh, who had been ordained at Ely in 1683.

Cranston settled at Reigate, Surrey, where on 5 May 1687 he married Mary (*c*.1662–1707), daughter of the vicar, John Williamson (*d.* 1697). The marriage licence gave Cranston's age as about twenty-seven. Several children were baptized at Reigate, but only a daughter, Elizabeth, survived infancy.

In 1693 Cranston was instituted to the parish of Shepton Mallet, Somerset, though it appears he was never resident there. He ceded Shepton when, after his father-in-law's

death, he was instituted as vicar of Reigate on 29 October 1697. Cranston also inherited the mastership of Reigate Free School, occupying both offices until his death. In 1697 he was incorporated MA at Cambridge, and from 1699 he was vicar of Newdigate.

In 1700 Cranston became a correspondent of the Society for Promoting Christian Knowledge (SPCK) and shortly afterwards began monthly catechism classes and communion services. Early in 1701 he undertook his chief work, the foundation of a lending library, since maintained in the upper vestry of Reigate parish church for over three centuries. It was initially intended for the clergy of Ewell archdeaconry, but its terms were expanded by a deed of 4 November 1708 to establish it as a public library 'for the use and perusal of the Freeholders, Vicar and Inhabitants' of Reigate, 'and of the Gentlemen and Clergymen inhabiting in parts thereunto adjacent' (Hooper, 63). Several local figures donated books, including John Evelyn, the earl of Shaftesbury, and the speaker Arthur Onslow, while Cranston himself gave some seventy works and obtained others from the SPCK. By 1705 the library contained over 1600 volumes, most concerned with contemporary theology. It remains a significant, early example of a public lending library.

Cranston died on 11 December 1708 and was buried in the vestry of Reigate church, underneath his library. A Latin epitaph claims he 'was indefatigable in his munificence, and even in death does not desist from collecting for coming generations'.   PETER SHERLOCK

Sources W. Hooper, *Reigate* (1945) · E. McClure, ed., *A chapter in English church history: being the minutes of the Society for Promoting Christian Knowledge for … 1698–1704* (1888) · *The parochial libraries of the Church of England* (1959), 95 · G. J. Armytage, ed., *Allegations for marriage licences issued by the vicar general of the archbishop of Canterbury, July 1679 – June 1687* (1890), 285 · Reigate parish registers · *Fasti Scot.*, 2/1.238 · J. Farbrother, *Shepton Mallet* (1872) · private information (2004)

Cranston [*married name* Cochrane], **Catherine** [Kate] (**1849–1934**), tea-room proprietor, was born on 27 May 1849 at 39 George Square, Glasgow. Often known as Kate, she was the only daughter and youngest of the three children of George Cranston, hotel-keeper (1817–1899), and his wife, Grace Lace (*c*.1811–1867). She had two half-brothers, William (*b.* 1840) and Robert (*b.* 1843), the offspring of her father's first marriage, to Janet Gibson. George Cranston, previously a baker and pastrymaker, kept a succession of hotels in George Square (the Edinburgh and Glasgow, the Crow, and finally the Crown) from about 1849 to 1874 when the family moved to 91 Sauchiehall Street. From 1882, when her brother Stuart married and moved to Bearsden, Kate lived at 425 Sauchiehall Street with her widowed father and older brother George, who died in 1884, staying there until or just after her own marriage in 1892. By this time the Cranston name was well known in connection with tea-rooms.

It was Kate Cranston's brother, **Stuart Cranston** (1848–1921), tea dealer and tea-room proprietor, who claimed for Glasgow the 'invention' of tea-rooms. He entered the tea trade as a teenager, and in 1871 established his own business as Stuart Cranston & Co. A passionate champion of good tea, he opened a room in 1875 at 2 Queen Street, Glasgow, and charged for sampling at 2*d*. a cup, 'bread and cakes extra'. This caught on and Cranston opened further suites of tea- and smoking-rooms alongside his dry tea business. With five branches in Glasgow's city centre, supported by substantial property investment, he formed Cranston's Tea Rooms Ltd in 1896. Further tea-rooms opened in 1898, 1907, and 1914, and fine coffee became another specialism. A restless entrepreneur with a slightly obsessive nature, Cranston was a keen musician, long-serving yeoman, a proselytizing fruitarian, and like his sister a practical if not paid-up abstainer. He retired from the business in 1915, and died on 17 October 1921 at 28 Bank Street, Glasgow, leaving a widow, Flora Mackinlay MacLachlan, and a daughter, Sybil. The company ran on until 1955.

Despite Stuart Cranston's vigorous self-promotion it was Kate Cranston who became identified as the pioneer of the tea-room phenomenon of Glasgow's golden age between 1888 and 1911. In 1878 Kate Cranston established her Crown Tea Rooms beneath a temperance hotel at 114 Argyle Street, with moral and financial support from her father's Edinburgh cousins, the Waverley Temperance Hotel Cranstons. She was also helped by her brother when she opened another branch at 205 Ingram Street in 1886. Confusion was inevitable, but after 1889 the distinction between Cranston's Tea Rooms and Miss Cranston's Tea Rooms was clearly drawn and the businesses were quite separately developed. Miss Cranston's more substantial catering (she described herself as a restaurateur) together with a feminine note in décor became the model for the typical Glasgow tea-room. In challenging social disapproval of middle-class women in business she paved the way to money-earning for many able imitators.

On 7 July 1892 Kate married John Cochrane (1857–1917), owner of an engineering works and later provost of Barrhead, a quiet, pleasant, and artistically disposed man some eight years her junior. There were no children from the marriage. From about 1893 they rented East Park, Barrhead; then from 1904 Hous'hill, a fine house at Nitshill, south-west of Glasgow. Marriage marked not a termination of her career, but an era of expansion for 'Miss Cranston' as she remained in business, though she was Mrs Cochrane in private life.

In 1894 Kate Cranston acquired property at 91–93 Buchanan Street, perhaps as a wedding present from her husband. On this site rose a lavish new building, opened in 1897. Its unconventional interior decoration by George Walton and Charles Rennie Mackintosh earned immediate notoriety. Work in 1898–9 by the same pair on the redevelopment of the whole building at Miss Cranston's original Argyle Street location (the extended lease was acquired about 1895), and by Mackintosh at Ingram Street in 1900, established a strongly 'artistic' house style for her tea-rooms. By 1901 when she catered at the Glasgow International Exhibition, 'Kate Cranstonish' had become a

Glasgow term, as Neil Munro recalled, for 'domestic novelties in buildings and decorations not otherwise easy to define' (Munro, 198). Her reputation was confirmed by Mackintosh's glittering Willow Tea Rooms on Sauchiehall Street, opened in October 1903. The stream of smaller jobs which she gave Mackintosh right up to 1916–17 were of great importance through difficult times for this isolated architect. For her sustained patronage of Glasgow's most avant-garde designers Miss Cranston, as Pevsner says, 'deserves the art historian's unstinted gratitude' (Pevsner, 538).

Kate Cranston's eccentrically old-fashioned style of dress—mid-Victorian flounces and quirky hats—betokened a characteristic readiness to flout convention in pursuit of what she liked. Described by Edwin Lutyens as 'a dark, busy, fat, wee body with black sparky luminous eyes' (*Letters of Edwin Lutyens*, 56), she had a good sense of humour and was sociable and kindly, but could also be imperious and quite formidable. As a businesswoman she was naturally aware of the publicity value of her singular tastes.

Miss Cranston became one of the most widely cherished and respected figures in Glasgow. It was she, not her brother, who entered *Who's Who in Glasgow* (1909), one of seven women and the only businesswoman. She received another accolade in 1911 when she was the subject of the 'Men you know' profile in *The Bailie* of 26 July, which accurately detailed her 'gifts of organisation, management, taste, originality, hard work, and perseverance, and her great shrewdness in judging as to what people want', crediting her with a catering revolution 'in which temperance, comfort, elegance, and economy are allied in a fine progressive form'. As an employer she was a perfectionist and disciplinarian who was keenly concerned for her girls' welfare.

The death of her husband in October 1917 shattered her, as they were 'a most devoted couple' (private information), and Cochrane had been a considerable support in business. She disposed of the tearooms, took to dressing in black, and left Hous'hill with its Mackintosh interiors to live in the North British Station Hotel back in George Square for most of the rest of her life. In her last years she became vague and alarming, and died of 'senile decay' compounded by heart problems on 18 April 1934 at 34 Terregles Avenue, Glasgow, where she had gone to live with a companion. She was buried in Neilston cemetery. The bulk of her considerable estate was left to charity.

Mackintosh's Willow Tea Rooms on Sauchiehall Street, heavily restored, in the 1990s were functioning again in part as tea-rooms. His interiors for the Ingram Street Tea Rooms, neglected and finally dismantled in 1971, have since been partially reconstructed for display, the Ladies' Luncheon Room forming the centrepiece of the Mackintosh exhibition held in Glasgow in 1996.

PERILLA KINCHIN

Sources P. Kinchin, *Miss Cranston: patron of Charles Rennie Mackintosh* (1999) · P. Kinchin, *Tea and taste: the Glasgow tea rooms, 1875–1975* (1991); repr. with new preface (1996) · *The Bailie* (2 Oct 1889) [Stuart Cranston] · *The Bailie* (26 July 1911) [Kate Cranston] · 'The story of the Glasgow tea rooms', *Glasgow today* (1909) · G. E. Todd, *Who's who in Glasgow in 1909* (1909) · A. Downie, 'Kate Cranston, by those who knew her', *Glasgow Herald* (13 June 1981), 9 · N. Munro, *The brave days* (1931), 194–9 · N. Pevsner, 'George Walton, his life and work', *RIBA Journal*, 46 (1938–9), 537–48 · Glasgow scrapbooks, Mitchell L., Glas. · private information (2004) · *The letters of Edwin Lutyens to his wife Lady Emily*, ed. C. Percy and J. Ridley (1985), 56

Archives Mitchell L., Glas., Strathclyde regional archives, drawings of tea room plans

Likenesses J. C. Annan, two photographs, *c*.1895 · J. C. Annan, photograph, *c*.1900, T. & R. Annan & Sons, Glasgow · portrait, *c*.1900, repro. in *Who's who in Glasgow* · J. C. Annan, photograph, *c*.1915, T. & R. Annan & Sons, Glasgow · S. Cranston, photograph, repro. in 'The story of the Glasgow tea rooms'

Wealth at death £67,476: NA Scot., SC/36/51, 246, pp. 192–7

Cranston, David (*c*.1480–1512), philosopher and theologian, was born in Scotland, probably in the diocese of Glasgow. Nothing is known of his parentage or of his education before he matriculated at the University of Paris in 1495. His *bursa* at the Collège de Montaigu indicates that he enjoyed relatively easy financial circumstances, although he describes himself in his will as having been a 'poor student'. A pupil of John Mair (1467–1550), Cranston graduated MA in 1499 and embarked, while teaching in the arts faculty, on the study of theology. His first publication, *Positiones phisicales* (1500), was followed by his additions to Mair's *Termini* (2nd edn, 1503). Three years later Cranston dedicated his *Questiones* on Aristotle's *Posterior Analytics* to Archbishop Robert Blackadder of Glasgow. Described on the title-page as a 'diligent investigator of dialectic' ('sedulum dialectices rimatorem'), Cranston was now a prominent member of the circle around Mair whose joint efforts were largely responsible for the brilliant Parisian revival of scholastic philosophy, especially in its nominalist and Scotist aspects, during the early decades of the sixteenth century. That revival also affected contemporary Thomism, continued in the 'school of Salamanca'. In the dialogue with Gavin Douglas (*c*.1476–1522) prefaced to Mair's 1510 commentary on book two of the *Sentences*, Cranston—now a bachelor of theology—appears as a vigorous defender of scholastic method against humanist criticism. It should be noted, however, that he was, with Mair, among those who attended in 1512 Girolamo Aleandro's Greek lectures in the university.

Cranston was by then completing his theology course: he took his doctorate in May 1512. In his published work he had turned latterly to moral philosophy, in the form of substantial additions to the *Questiones morales* of Martin Le Maistre (1432–1482) and (less extensively) to the *Moralia* of his fellow student Jacques Almain (1480–1515). Cranston's preponderant theological interest, however, was evident in his analysis of human conduct—as it had been, indeed, even in his logical and epistemological works. Thus, in his *Tractatus noticiarum* (1506), religious faith is clearly for Cranston the crucially important form of 'inevident assent'; and in such faith both human will and divine authority are necessarily involved.

David Cranston's premature death, between 7 and 14 August 1512, meant that what seems to have been regarded as brilliant promise was not fulfilled in any major work. Much of what he wrote, whatever its originality, took the form of additions to the work of others. Almain, who also died prematurely, left much more substantial writings. This difference between contemporaries of seemingly comparable ability may well have been due, in part at least, to Cranston's poor health, of which there is certainly evidence during his theological course. Intellectually he was vigorous enough, if the dialogue with Douglas reflects his style in controversy. Mair testifies to Cranston's quickness of temper, displayed when his friends Almain and Pieter Crockaert teased him 'in the courtyard of the Sorbonne' about the Scots' diet of oaten bread—which Cranston 'strove to deny as an insult to his native country' (*History of Greater Britain*, 2.ii). Similar sensitivity (to a more serious charge) is evinced when—in a rare lapse from the impersonal austerity of his writings—Cranston tries to dismiss as due to a 'corrupt text' Jerome's report of cannibalism among the Scots (*Questiones addite … de fortitudine*, sig. C 1, col. 2).

Cranston's prickly patriotism was matched by loyalty to his college: he bequeathed 450 livres tournois for a scholarship at Montaigu. He was buried in the college chapel, beside Jan Standonck, its notable if austere principal during Cranston's student days. J. H. BURNS

Sources J. K. Farge, *Biographical register of Paris doctors of theology, 1500–1536* (1980) · *A history of greater Britain … by John Major*, ed. and trans. A. Constable, Scottish History Society, 10 (1892) · J. Durkan, 'The school of John Major: bibliography', *Innes Review*, 1 (1950), 140–57 · A. Broadie, *The circle of John Mair* (1985) · A. Broadie, *The tradition of Scottish philosophy: a new perspective in the Enlightenment* (1990) · A. Broadie, *The shadow of Scotus* (1995)

Wealth at death legacy of 450 livres tournois: Farge, *Biographical register*, 124

Cranston, Maurice William (1920–1993), political philosopher, was born on 8 May 1920 at 53 Harringay Road, Tottenham, Middlesex, the only child of William Cranston, theatrical agent, and his wife, Catherine, *née* Harris (d. *c*.1933). Although the family was of Scottish origin, Cranston himself was raised in Tunbridge Wells by two maiden aunts and a Quaker godmother, following the death of his mother when he was a boy and the emigration of his father to Canada 'to seek, unsuccessfully, his fortune' in the 1930s (Cranston, 254–5). He attended a succession of schools, including the Tunbridge Wells Technical Institute and School of Art and a Jesuit college in France. Besides preparing himself to become a journalist he acquired a facility with languages, especially French, which he used to advantage throughout his life. He had planned to attend King's College, London, in 1939, but was unable to do so as the Second World War intervened.

During the war Cranston was a conscientious objector and served throughout with the London civil defence in fire-fighting and rescuing casualties of the bombing. He also worked with refugees at Bloomsbury House and recalled that one of those he assisted presented him with a copy of Spinoza's *Tractatus theologico-politicus*, which was influential in encouraging him to turn away from a career in journalism to study political philosophy. After the blitz he began taking evening courses in philosophy in the University of London, taught by the Spinoza specialist Ruth Saw. He also contributed to *Peace News* and, while advocating non-violent resistance to the Nazis, he was well aware of the difficulties of this policy. In a pamphlet entitled *Non-Violence and Germany*, published in 1944, he wrote:

> Any encouragement the pacifist may draw from the narratives in the following pages [concerned with non-violent resistance to the Nazis and especially with the Copenhagen Strike of June 1944] must be tempered by the reflection that these incidents are but tiny glimpses of light in a swiftly darkening scene: violence, discredited by everyone twenty years ago, has come to be accepted by everyone, venerated almost by countless numbers. The memory of Mr. Chamberlain should be sufficient warning against too eager plucking of flowers out of nettles.   (p. 3)

During this period Cranston attempted to break into publishing and journalism. He shared his ambitions with the writer and painter Denton Welch, whom he met in Tunbridge Wells in 1938, and they remained close friends. On 20 July 1940 he married Helga May (*b.* 1920/21), film editor, and daughter of Siegfried May, bookkeeper, but the marriage did not survive the war. Cranston's life at this time might be seen reflected in the characters of his two amusing and stylish detective novels published in 1946: *Tomorrow We'll be Sober* and *Philosopher's Hemlock*. He also published in 1949 a travel book, *Introduction to Switzerland*. When, after the war, he attended St Catherine's College, Oxford (graduating with a second-class degree in philosophy, politics, and economics in 1948), he maintained his interest in writing and publishing, and joined Ludovic Kennedy in founding the Oxford University Writers' Club, where established authors such as Evelyn Waugh, Cyril Connolly, V. S. Pritchett, and John Betjeman were invited to dine with student members and respond to their questions.

Cranston arrived in Oxford with a head full of Spinoza and seventeenth-century rationalism which he found difficult to integrate with the linguistic philosophy which had become fashionable at the time. His BLitt thesis (published in 1953 as *Freedom: a New Analysis*) attempted to use linguistic analysis without denying the reality and importance of traditional ethical, political, and metaphysical questions concerned with freedom, freedom of the will, and liberalism. Cranston was also unusual in reading contemporary continental philosophers, such as Sartre, Merlau-Ponty, Jean Wahl, and Jean Hippolyte, who contributed to his understanding of liberty. He wrote a number of works on Sartre (including *Sartre*, 1962, and *The Quintessence of Sartrism*, 1970), and on other aspects of contemporary French thought.

During the 1950s Cranston combined a part-time lectureship in social philosophy in the University of London with an active life in journalism and publishing. By the mid-fifties he was involved in the Congress for Cultural Freedom and began to publish in *Encounter*, whose editorial board he eventually joined. In 1959 he became literary adviser to the publisher Methuen. He was also active in PEN, the association of poets, essayists, and novelists, and became a permanent delegate to PEN International. He spoke and wrote eloquently for the rights of writers who were oppressed and in prison. His book on human rights, *Human Rights Today*, first appeared in 1955 and was followed by a revised edition in 1962 and by *What are Human Rights?* in 1973. He defended human rights at a time when in Britain and elsewhere the doctrine was rejected by many who wrote in the Marxist, utilitarian, and common law traditions. He adapted the Lockean doctrine of natural rights to human rights and presented strong arguments against the extension of rights to life, a fair trial, liberty, property, and so on to include social and economic rights, as had occurred in the UN declaration of universal rights of 1948. The rights Cranston defended were those which any government could secure, and did not depend on levels of economic and social development which such rights as the right to holidays with pay required. He was thus critical of governments that denied human rights, and justified this denial on the grounds of economic backwardness. He also saw a tension between an emphasis on economic progress (especially in the communist bloc) and a willingness to subordinate liberty to collective economic achievement. In this process he found the writer and intellectual especially vulnerable to oppression by governments of all kinds. In addressing a PEN congress in Dublin in 1971, he said:

> The conclusion seems to be that *all* modern systems of economy are disadvantageous from the writer's point of view ... I feel myself that the capitalist system is perhaps the least [disadvantageous] ... But I do not think we writers can have real enthusiasm for any system of economic relationships, or any form of patronage of which we have so far had experience.   (*The Changing Face of Literature*, 32)

His approach to rights and the status of writers and others oppressed by governments reflected a strong belief in individual liberty and in a minimal state. He perhaps reasserted in a different context the earlier opposition to war and to the treatment by governments of refugees from Nazi oppression.

In 1957 Cranston published *John Locke: a Biography*, which was widely praised for its scholarship and style, and was awarded the James Tait Black memorial prize. This major work followed eight years of research on Locke's papers, which had been recently acquired by the Bodleian Library. Michael Oakeshott was among the admirers of the book, and Cranston was invited in 1959 to join the government department at the London School of Economics (LSE), where he eventually succeeded Oakeshott as professor of political science in 1969. His first marriage having ended in divorce, in 1958 he married Baroness Maximiliana (Iliana) von und zu Fraunberg (*b.* 1925). This marriage was highly successful, and two sons, Nicholas and Stephen, were born in 1960 and 1962.

As a university don Cranston was an imaginative and engaging lecturer, and he continued his lectures on French political thought even after his retirement. But his main interest was in supervising his PhD students, for many of whom he was not only a teacher but a good friend. His support and personal warmth were cherished by those fortunate enough to have been his students.

Nevertheless, Cranston was not a typical political scientist. He seldom published in the learned journals, partly because he eschewed the pedantry he found there, and partly because he found that many political scientists were little more than apologists for political parties or ideologies, dressing up their theories as philosophy or science. In his inaugural lecture of 1971, published in 1972 and entitled *Politics and Ethics*, he saw the role of the political philosopher as one that resembled a drama critic in the theatre of politics, and he especially attacked the philosopher who abandoned this perspective and became a politician:

> He may grow fretful in the stalls and yearn to mount the stage himself, but just as critics are notoriously bad actors, so philosophers make wretched politicians. Think of Gentile becoming Mussolini's minister of education, or Heidegger joining the Nazi party, or Lukacs going to Moscow to support Stalin. Or perhaps we had better not think of them.   (p. 24)

Cranston was also critical of a 'positivist' or 'behaviourist' political science displacing more traditional political philosophy. Without political philosophy, he said:

> politics might well go on as merrily as ever. But the trouble is that it would not be understood, it would be a practice without consciousness of the norms which inform its activity, ignorant even of its own identity or nature. If the day ever comes when political philosophy is dead, the triumph of information over knowledge will be complete. (p. 24)

Cranston's academic career flourished in Britain, continental Europe, and the United States. Besides his steady progress up the academic ladder, he was widely regarded as one of the few academics who could reach a general audience beyond the universities. For example, he wrote a series of eight highly imaginative political dialogues between various historical figures, from Savonarola and Machiavelli on the state to Voltaire and Hume on morality, which were originally broadcast on the BBC Third Programme, frequently repeated, and subsequently published in 1968. He often contributed to the BBC World Service and Radio Free Europe and made numerous other broadcasts in Britain, France, Canada, and Italy. In Britain he was made a fellow of the Royal Society of Literature and an honorary fellow of St Catherine's College, Oxford (1984) and of the LSE (1991). He delivered the Carlyle lectures at Oxford in 1984 on the main figures of the French Enlightenment, subsequently published as *Philosophers and Pamphleteers: Political Theorists of the French Enlightenment* (1986). He often visited North America, where he was a visiting professor at Harvard University (1965–6), Dartmouth College (1970–71), the University of British Columbia (1973–4), and the University of California at La Jolla (1986–93), and a fellow at the Woodrow Wilson Center in Washington, DC (1982). He also visited France and wrote and broadcast in French. He visited the École des Hautes Études in Paris in 1977, and served as president of the Institut International de Philosophie Politique (1976–9). He was vice-president of L'Alliance Française en Angleterre from 1964. In addition he was seconded as professor of political science to the European University Institute in Florence (1978–81).

Cranston maintained his interest in the French Enlightenment in numerous essays, and made highly praised translations of Rousseau's *Social Contract* (1968) and *A Discourse on the Origins of Inequality* (1984), published as Penguin paperbacks and widely used throughout the world. In the 1970s he began research on a three-volume biography of Rousseau, utilizing the new edition of Rousseau's correspondence and much new scholarship, attempting to create a 'Lockean' biography—one in which attention to detail, meticulously presented, would reveal the character and significance of this much misunderstood figure. The first volume, *Jean-Jacques: the Early Life and Work of Jean-Jacques Rousseau, 1712-1754*, appeared in 1983, followed by *The Noble Savage: Jean-Jacques Rousseau, 1754–1762* in 1991. To the suggestion, originally made by the philosopher Richard Peters, that Cranston's interest in Rousseau followed from a similar past, he made clear that temperamentally, philosophically, and politically, he was much closer to Locke than to Rousseau. The final volume, *The Solitary Self: Jean-Jacques Rousseau in Exile and Adversity* (1997), was incomplete at the time of his death and was published posthumously with additions from his other writings on Rousseau, carefully edited and linked together by an American colleague, Sanford Lakoff.

Cranston was a prolific writer who rose early and worked through the morning; then, following advice once given to him by Bertrand Russell, he took a siesta after lunch and returned to work in the late afternoon. Even when convenor of the government department at LSE, he maintained his regimen and would perform his administrative duties before most of his colleagues had stirred from their beds. He would then leave the school for a day's writing, often before they had arrived. Although he claimed to write slowly and with difficulty, his elegant style, displaying great wit and charm, made his writing appear effortless.

Among academics Cranston was rare in being able to increase his income substantially through writing and broadcasting, but as the years passed he found this increasingly difficult. Television took its toll on the general reader, and, despite high acclaim from many reviewers, the financial return he sought from the biography of Rousseau did not meet his expectations. Radio no longer reached the same audiences as it did in the 1950s and 1960s, and Cranston seldom appeared on television. Furthermore, he was not inclined to become a political pundit. He belonged to no political party, and while he was often associated with anti-communist and libertarian conservatism, he was alert to the limitations of all political ideologies. To associate himself with Locke's political ideas, he occasionally referred to himself as a whig, and insisted that he was more at home in the seventeenth and eighteenth than in the nineteenth and twentieth centuries. He was not only cosmopolitan but also a devoted citizen of the republic of letters who defended oppressed writers throughout the world.

In appearance, Cranston was of medium height, slim and handsome. His shy exterior, once penetrated, revealed a man of great wit and warmth, much admired and loved by his friends to whom he was devoted, and with few enemies. Despite his frequent travels, he was most at home in London: in the libraries, in his flat in Kent Terrace overlooking Regent's Park, the LSE, the BBC, the publishing houses, and the Garrick Club. He died suddenly from a heart attack on 5 November 1993 following a broadcast in London for the Canadian Broadcasting Corporation on Margaret Thatcher's memoirs. He was survived by his wife and two sons. A memorial service was held at St George's, Bloomsbury, London, on 2 February 1994.

Cranston's academic legacy rests mainly on his biographies of Locke and Rousseau, his writings on liberty and human rights, and his translations of Rousseau. His postgraduate students went on to hold academic posts throughout the world, and often worked in fields Cranston originally made his own. But his writings for a wider audience had a special charm and appeal, and reflected the link between serious philosophical thought and the intelligent lay person which characterized post-war Britain as a civilized and liberal society in spite of economic decline and a diminution of its role in the world.

F. ROSEN

Sources M. Cranston, 'Postscriptum', *Lives, liberties and the public good: new essays in political theory for Maurice Cranston*, ed. G. Feaver and F. Rosen (1987), 251–8 [incl. bibliography to 1984–5] · D. D. Raphael, 'Maurice Cranston (1920–1993)', *Utilitas*, 6 (1994), 1–7 · *The Times* (9 Nov 1993) · *The Independent* (8–10 Nov 1993) · *WWW* · personal knowledge (2004) · private information (2004) · L. Kennedy, *On my way to the club: the autobiography of Ludovic Kennedy* (1989) · M. De-la-Noy, *Denton Welch: the making of a writer* (1984); repr. (1986) · b. cert.

Archives priv. coll. · U. Texas | SOUND BL NSA, current affairs recording · BL NSA, performance recording

Likenesses B. Olson, photograph, repro. in Feaver and Rosen, eds., *Lives, liberties and the public good* · photographs, London School of Economics

Wealth at death £385,867: probate, 14 March 1994, *CGPLA Eng. & Wales*

Cranston, Robert (1815–1892), founder of temperance hotels, was born on 9 August 1815, at East Calder, near Edinburgh, the son of James Cranston, mason and innkeeper, and his wife, Janet Garvie. His grandfather Robert had moved there from Jedburgh about 1778 to act as factor for the earl of Buchan. Robert's parents kept the Bay Horse inn in East Calder before moving into Edinburgh in 1822.

Cranston was educated in Edinburgh and then apprenticed at the university printing office. After losing his left leg, however, following an act of bravado at the age of sixteen, he moved to a more sedentary apprenticeship with a tailor at 43 Princes Street (later the site of Cranston's first hotel). This proved a valuable extension to his education—he was often chosen to read aloud to his fellow workers, and it was here that he developed his fondness for the novels of Sir Walter Scott. There was also much lively discussion of current affairs. It was following arguments about the newly prominent temperance issue that Cranston and two friends embarked on a trial dry period of three months, after which they assessed themselves as better off without drink, and became total abstainers.

On 17 April 1838 Cranston married Elizabeth (1813–

1873), the eldest daughter of John Dalgliesh, carter in Leith; they set up house at South Bridge where Cranston was partner in a tailor's shop. In 1843, however, following the lead of his friend John Aitken who had opened Edinburgh's first teetotal coffee house in 1837, he abandoned tailoring to establish a temperance coffee house and lodgings at 129 High Street. Well supplied with newspapers, and commended too by Elizabeth's excellent pies, this was a success, and soon became a particular meeting place for Chartists. Cranston himself was actively involved in this movement for political reform, editing its paper the *North British Express* for some time, and was twice briefly arrested.

Five years later in 1848 the Cranstons sold the coffee house and opened the Waverley Temperance Hotel at 43 Princes Street. Many thought its prime site and high-quality fittings commercial madness, but the Cranstons had shrewdly spotted a gap in the market. While the temperance rule was strictly enforced, the hotel aimed for the first class and was immediately successful. The roll of its notable visitors was proudly kept. Temperance hotels spread rapidly from these beginnings, especially in Scotland, in the second half of the nineteenth century.

Despite heavy financial loss in the crash of the Royal Bank of London in 1849, Cranston recovered fast enough to exploit the opportunities presented by the Great Exhibition in 1851: he opened a Waverley in London at 37 King Street, Cheapside, and co-operated with Thomas Cook, another temperance man, to cater for his excursions to London. The next expansion was into Glasgow with the Waverley at 185 Buchanan Street in 1860. In 1868 the New Waverley was opened in Waterloo Place, Edinburgh, after which what became known as the Old Waverley on Princes Street was enlarged, and finally reconstructed in 1884. The scale of charges was the same in each hotel.

The success of the hotels, which made Cranston wealthy and supported his political activity, was mainly due to the skills of Elizabeth Cranston, remembered in the family biography as 'a large-hearted woman, remarkably able and phenomenally rapid and accurate with figures' (Mein, 3). Elizabeth died in 1873. On 23 April 1877 Cranston married Mary Ann, daughter of James Ryan of Gullane; she also predeceased him, dying in 1890.

Cranston was himself always ready to acknowledge the capacities of the women of his family. He was an early supporter of women's suffrage and spent freely on the education of his two daughters, Mary (1846–1932) and Elizabeth ('Liebe'; 1848–1941), as well as on that of his two sons, Robert (1843–1923), later Sir Robert, lord provost of Edinburgh, and John Dalgliesh (1845–1916). He recognized Mary's business talents by giving her the Washington Temperance Hotel on Sauchiehall Street on her marriage to the Glasgow photographic dealer George Mason in 1872, and naming her in his will chief trustee, with his oldest son, of the Waverley empire. He also financed the business start-up of his cousin's daughter, Catherine (Kate) *Cranston, whose Glasgow tearooms were renowned.

Cranston brought his progressive views to bear on local politics, serving from 1868 to 1890 on Edinburgh's town council, interesting himself particularly in the reform of the fire brigade, and in efforts to provide public baths and wash-houses and improve housing. He became a burgess of Edinburgh and a freeman of London. His passion for improving was exercised on his home, Waverley Park, Abbeyhill, and he also put up model dwelling houses. He was a vigorous, charitable, and genial man, but stern enough if his wishes were crossed. From his long service on the bench, from 1875 to 1887 and again in 1889-90, he became widely known as Bailie Cranston. He was much respected for his integrity and intellectual clarity, and it was his boast on retirement that none of his judgments had ever been appealed. Cranston was several times pressed to stand for the provostship, and for parliament, but declined partly because of his inability to kneel on ceremonial occasions.

Cranston died at his home, Waverley Park, 18 Spring Gardens, Abbeyhill, Edinburgh, on 11 May 1892 as a result of pneumonia and cardiac failure. Accorded a public funeral, he was buried at Grange cemetery, Edinburgh.

PERILLA KINCHIN

Sources E. Mein, *Through four reigns: the story of the Old Waverley Hotel and its founder* (1948) · P. Kinchin, *Tea and taste: the Glasgow tea rooms, 1875-1975* (1991) · private information (2004) · Boase, *Mod. Eng. biog.* · parish register (marriage), Edinburgh, St Cuthbert's, 17 April 1838 · m. cert. · Edinburgh directories · d. cert.

Likenesses portrait (as a young man), repro. in Mein, *Through four reigns* · portrait, repro. in Mein, *Through four reigns*; formerly in Edinburgh Council Chambers

Wealth at death £16,433 8s. 1d.: confirmation, 14 July 1892, CCI

Cranston, Samuel (1659-1727), colonial governor, was born on 7 August 1659 in Newport, Rhode Island, the eldest of the ten children of John Cranston (1625-1680), colonial governor, and his wife, Mary (1641-1711), daughter of Jeremiah Clarke of Newport and his wife, Frances. Cranston was born into one eminent political family—his father and his uncle, William Clarke, were both Rhode Island governors—and his marriage in 1680 to Mary Hart (1663-1710), granddaughter of Roger Williams, connected him to another. These family ties undoubtedly assisted his early career, but Cranston was also an extraordinarily talented politician. During his nearly thirty-year tenure as Rhode Island's governor, from 1698 to 1727, Cranston held the fractious colony together and, against long odds, successfully defended the Rhode Island charter of 1663 against two concerted efforts by English officials to revoke it.

Cranston assumed the governorship at such a young age, thirty-eight, and held it for so long, that he may have been the only colonial Rhode Island official who made public life a primary occupation. He was educated at home, and was apprenticed to a goldsmith in his teenage years, but no record exists of his ever plying the trade. He went to sea instead and had a short career as a sailor. Cranston had captained at least two ships by his mid-twenties, before coming ashore at the age of thirty. Hereafter he devoted himself primarily to government service. Like most successful New Englanders, Cranston also farmed, speculated in land, and dabbled in trade.

Rhode Island's colonial records are lost for the early 1690s, but by at least 1695 Cranston was elected a member of the governor's council, which served as the upper house of the legislature and the highest court in the colony. He also informally advised the governor on matters of state. It was the eruption of a long-simmering political crisis which catapulted Cranston into the governor's chair in 1698. For over fifteen years a group of aggrieved Rhode Island citizens—'the adverse party' (Turner, 16)—had complained to royal officials that the colony's government regularly flouted English law and custom. When the earl of Bellomont was appointed royal governor of Massachusetts and New Hampshire, the adverse party found a friendly ear and forceful advocate. Bellomont's commission gave him vaguely defined powers to command the militia throughout New England, including Rhode Island. Under this authority he prepared a lengthy report to the Board of Trade that specifically charged Rhode Island with twenty-five offences. Some—that 'the attorney general was a poor, illiterate mechanic' and the deputy governor 'a brutish man' (James, *Colonial Rhode Island*, 126)—could not be taken seriously. Others, however, proved more substantive, and, if sustained, would have justified revoking the charter. Rhode Island 'usurped admiralty authority', Bellomont wrote, 'raised taxes illegally', and 'countenanced and harbored pirates' (Bartlett, 3.387).

Rhode Islanders revered their charter because it made them virtually a self-governing commonwealth. But this status (shared only with Connecticut) was now threatened on account of Rhode Island's infamous reputation for political bickering, and the suspicion in England that many of its inhabitants, including Cranston's uncle and the then governor, William Clarke, were Quaker pacifists unwilling to involve the colony in imperial conflicts. Clarke felt compromised by his reputation, which he feared would weaken the credibility of any reply he made to Bellomont. On his resignation in March 1698 the council elected Cranston governor for the interim until the next election. Although he was relatively unknown to Bellomont and other English officials, Cranston's moderate religious and political views were judged the best means of easing the situation. He prepared a detailed report that admitted certain errors in Rhode Island's past, denied others, defended some policies, and explained many alleged problems as misunderstandings or inadvertent mistakes. Cranston's soothing tone and measured response defused the crisis. By 1700 the Board of Trade seemed disposed to take no action against Rhode Island. A grateful general assembly doubled Cranston's salary that year in a resolution that specifically thanked him for defending the charter.

Two years later, in 1702, the threat re-emerged when Governor Joseph Dudley of Massachusetts tried to take control of Rhode Island's militia. Dudley wrote to the Board of Trade that Rhode Island's government 'in the present hands is a scandal' (Turner, 36). This time Cranston appeared to be on a more solid footing. He defended his authority as commander on the grounds that the charter specifically gave the colony control of its own militia and that Rhode Island exercised that control responsibly. He was again victorious.

For the rest of his governorship Cranston used his considerable skills as a conciliator to keep Rhode Island intact and relatively harmonious. One feature of this approach was the colony's involvement in Queen Anne's War, which required high levels of military expenditure. Discussions over the financial consequences of the war led to a divisive contest between advocates of a paper currency and their critics, including Cranston. In 1715 he lost control of the general assembly to sponsors of paper currency, but he continued to be re-elected annually as governor, with comfortable margins.

Historians have little sense of Cranston's personality other than the sure knowledge that he had a knack for negotiation and compromise. Naturally conservative, he seems to have been apathetic about religion and attended no church regularly as an adult. With his first wife, Mary, he had seven children. She died on 17 September 1710, and in 1711 he married Judith Parrott (1670–1737); they had no children. Samuel Cranston died in office on 26 April 1727, having carefully guided his colony through a period of political turbulence. He was buried next to his father in the common burial-ground, Farewell Street, Newport, with a stone which described him as 'Thy country's father and thy country's friend' (Turner, 50). In the following decade Rhode Islanders resumed their vicious partisan battles, and weary citizens would often nostalgically refer to the peaceful years of Governor Cranston's long tenure.

BRUCE C. DANIELS

Sources S. V. James, *Colonial Rhode Island: a history* (1975) · J. R. Bartlett, ed., *Records of the colony of Rhode Island and Providence plantations, in New England*, 10 vols. (1856–65), vols. 3–4 · H. E. Turner, *The two governors Cranston* (1889) · Rhode Island Historical Society, Providence, Samuel Cranston MSS · B. C. Daniels, *Dissent and conformity on Narragansett Bay: the colonial Rhode Island town* (1983) · I. B. Richman, 'Cranston, Samuel', *DAB*, 4.512–13 · S. V. James, 'Cranston, Samuel', *ANB*
Archives Rhode Island Historical Society, Providence | Judicial Centre, Rawtucket, Rhode Island, general court of trials records · Mass. Hist. Soc.
Wealth at death prosperous but not wealthy; owned considerable land in Providence, East Greenwich, and Narragansett; house and property in Newport

Cranston, Stuart (1848–1921). *See under* Cranston, Catherine (1849–1934).

Cranston, William (c.1513–1562), logician, is first recorded at Paris, where he became a regent in arts and then rector of the university. He later returned to his native Scotland, to the University of St Andrews, where he was provost of St Salvator's College from 1553 to about 1560. He was also provost of Seton collegiate church from 1549. A friend of John Mair and George Buchanan, he remained a Roman Catholic after the Reformation in Scotland in 1560, until his death in 1562.

In 1540 Cranston dedicated to David Beaton, cardinal archbishop of St Andrews, a book entitled *Dialecticae compendium* ('A compendium of logic'), which was only seven folios long. In this work, which was published at Paris,

Cranston seems to have made a determined effort to discard his medieval heritage. The *Compendium* begins by stating, diagrammatically, that a term is a subject or predicate of a proposition, and that it can 'usefully' be classified under one of only five headings. Cranston adds that he omits all other divisions and definitions because they are of little use to philosophers.

In the light of the immense advances made by logicians in the preceding centuries, this is an extraordinary claim, especially coming from a man who had been brought up on the powerful logic that Mair and his Scottish colleagues at Paris had done so much to advance. For the logic Cranston had been taught listed dozens of divisions and definitions, and much of the power of that logic derived from the multitude of fine distinctions that it was, in consequence, able to make. All these fine distinctions were necessary because theologians, forever making the finest of fine distinctions, needed a correspondingly subtle logic. Among the important distinctions that Cranston jettisons is that between categorematic and syncategorematic terms. Yet this is the distinction between terms which signify things, and terms such as 'every', 'some', 'no', 'and', 'or', and 'if'; in other words, all the terms in which logicians are interested. Cranston also fails to mention the logical concept of supposition, even though many of the valuable advances made by logicians in the medieval period had been made in connection with their theory of supposition.

In large measure Cranston's *Compendium* involves a return to the *Organon*, the collection of logical works by Aristotle. But not entirely; a conspicuous exception is the brief mention he makes of the so-called 'hypothetical syllogism'. This is an inference in which at least one of the premises contains a complex proposition—that is, one composed of two propositions linked by 'and', 'or', or 'if'. Inferences of this sort are not discussed by Aristotle, though later writers such as Boethius made a detailed study of them. In the first edition of the *Compendium* there is no reference to those later logicians, but in the second edition (published in 1545) Cranston states both that Aristotle did not discuss hypothetical syllogisms, and also that he, Cranston, is basing his remarks on the subject on Boethius.

Another major difference between the two editions is their length. Evidently Cranston decided that the brevity of his first edition was a drawback for the students for whom he had written the *Compendium*. They needed more exposition of his definitions and distinctions and they needed illustrations also. The result was a much more discursive edition in 1545 than he had been prepared to offer in 1540, when he clearly regarded the sheer brevity of his exposition as a virtue. Furthermore the second edition leaves us in no doubt that he was deeply influenced by the humanist programme that Rudolph Agricola set out in his *De inventione dialectica*, first published in 1515.

In Cranston's time logic was a compulsory element of the arts curriculum, and if the compulsion was to remain then the subject had to be seen to contribute towards fitting the students for the new age of rapid economic expansion in which more and more students were aiming to become merchants, secular lawyers, and holders of civic office. Melanchthon had famously described scholastic logic as 'these waggonloads of trifles', and had looked to a grand simplification of logic. Melanchthon articulated the new mood, and William Cranston was in tune with it—and in Scotland no one moved faster to provide the new sort of logic book required in the changed climate.   ALEXANDER BROADIE

Sources W. Cranston, *Dialecticae compendium* (1540) · W. Cranston, *Dialecticae compendium*, 2nd edn (1545) · A. Broadie, *The tradition of Scottish philosophy* (1990)

Cranstoun, David. *See* Cranston, David (*c.*1480–1512).

Cranstoun, George, Lord Corehouse (*d.* 1850), judge, was the second son of the Hon. George Cranstoun of Longwarton, seventh son of the fifth Lord Cranstoun, and Maria, daughter of Thomas Brisbane of Brisbane, Ayrshire. His second sister, Jane Anne, afterwards countess of Purgstall, was a correspondent of Sir Walter Scott, and his youngest sister, Helen D'Arcy *Stewart, was an author and the second wife of Professor Dugald Stewart.

Cranstoun was originally intended for the military profession, but he preferred law and passed advocate at the Scottish bar on 2 February 1793. He was appointed a depute-advocate in 1805, and sheriff-depute of the county of Sutherland in 1806. He was chosen dean of the Faculty of Advocates on 15 November 1823, and was raised to the bench on the death of Lord Hermand in 1826, under the title Lord Corehouse; this name came from his beautiful residence near the fall of Corra Linn, Lanarkshire, on the River Clyde. In January 1839, while apparently in perfect health, he suffered a sudden stroke which forced him to retire. Lord Cockburn, while taking exception to the narrow and old-fashioned legal prejudices of Corehouse and his somewhat pompous method of legal exposition, characterizes him as 'more of a legal oracle' than any man of his time. 'His abstinence', he states,

> from all vulgar contention, all political discussion, and all public turmoils, in the midst of which he sat like a pale image, silent and still, trembling in ambitious fastidiousness, kept up the popular delusion of his mysteriousness and abstraction to the very last. (*Memorials*, 221)

Cranstoun possessed strong literary tastes, which occupied much of his free time, both before and after retirement. His accomplishments as a Greek scholar secured him the warm friendship of Lord Monboddo, who used to declare that he was the 'only scholar in all Scotland'. While attending the civil law class in 1788, Cranstoun made the acquaintance of Sir Walter Scott, and the friendship continued throughout his life. Scott read the opening stanzas of the 'Lay of the Last Minstrel' to Erskine and Cranstoun, whose apparently cold reception of it greatly discouraged him; however, discovering a few days afterwards that some of the stanzas had 'haunted their memory, he [Scott] was encouraged to resume the undertaking' (Lockhart, 100). While practising at the bar Cranstoun wrote a clever *jeu d'esprit*, entitled *The Diamond Beetle Case*,

George Cranstoun, Lord Corehouse (*d.* 1850), by Benjamin William Crombie

in which he caricatured the manner and style of several of the judges in delivering their opinions. Cranstoun died on 26 June 1850.   T. F. HENDERSON, *rev.* ERIC METCALFE

Sources Irving, *Scots.* · J. Kay, *A series of original portraits and caricature etchings … with biographical sketches and illustrative anecdotes*, ed. [H. Paton and others], new edn [3rd edn], 2 (1877), 438 · *GM*, 2nd ser., 34 (1850), 328 · *Memorials of his time, by Henry Cockburn* (1856), 221 · H. Cockburn, *Life of Lord Jeffrey, with a selection from his correspondence*, 2 vols. (1852) · J. G. Lockhart, *Memoirs of the life of Sir Walter Scott*, [new edn] (1842), 40, 100
Likenesses J. Kay, cartoon, 1810, NPG; repro. in J. Paterson and J. Kay, *Portraits*, 2: *Kay's Edinburgh* (1885) · B. W. Crombie, pencil drawing, Scot. NPG [see illus.]

Cranstoun, Helen D'Arcy. *See* Stewart, Helen D'Arcy (1765–1838).

Cranstoun, James, eighth Lord Cranstoun (*bap.* 1755, *d.* 1796), naval officer, son of James Cranstoun, sixth Lord Cranstoun (*d.* 1773), and his wife, Sophia, *née* Brown (*d.* 1779), was baptized at Crailing, Roxburghshire, on 26 June 1755. He entered the Royal Navy and received a lieutenant's commission on 19 October 1776. In command of the *Belliqueux* (64 guns) he took part in the action fought by Sir Samuel Hood with the comte de Grasse in Basseterre Road off St Kitts on 25 and 26 January 1782, and was promoted captain on 31 January.

Cranstoun commanded Sir George Rodney's flagship, the *Formidable*, at the battle of the Saints (12 April 1782), which resulted in the total destruction of the French West India squadron. He was mentioned by Rodney in the dispatches which he carried to England. He succeeded to the peerage on the death of his brother William in 1788 and on 19 August 1792 married Elizabeth (c.1770–1797), youngest daughter of Lieutenant-Colonel Lewis Charles Montolieu. Under Vice-Admiral William Cornwallis, Cranstoun commanded the *Bellerophon*, one of a squadron of five ships of the line, which on 17 June 1795, off Point Penmarch on the west coast of Brittany, repulsed an attack by a French squadron consisting of thirteen ships of the line, fourteen frigates, two brigs, and a cutter. On 10 November the vice-admiral and his subordinates received the thanks of parliament. Cranstoun's 'activity and zeal' were commended by Cornwallis in his dispatch.

In 1796 Cranstoun was appointed governor of Grenada and vice-admiral of the island, but he died before taking up his new duties on 22 September 1796 at Bishop's Waltham, Hampshire, at the age of forty-two. His death was a result of drinking cider which had been kept in a vessel lined with lead. He was buried in the garrison church at Portsmouth. He was survived by his wife who died on 27 August of the following year.

J. M. RIGG, rev. CLIVE WILKINSON

Sources *GM*, 1st ser., 52 (1782), 254 · *GM*, 1st ser., 62 (1792), 960 · *GM*, 1st ser., 66 (1796), 798 · *GM*, 1st ser., 67 (1797), 803 · *Scots peerage* · B. Burke, *A genealogical history of the dormant, abeyant, forfeited and extinct peerages of the British empire*, new edn (1883) · *Annual Register* (1796), 80–81

Cranstoun, William Henry (*bap.* 1714, *d.* 1752), alleged murderer, fifth son of William, fifth Lord Cranstoun (*d.* 1727), and his wife, Lady Jane Ker (*d.* 1768), eldest daughter of William, second marquess of Lothian, was baptized on 12 August 1714 at Crailing, near Jedburgh. While a captain in the army he married privately at Edinburgh, on 22 May 1745, Anne Murray, daughter of David Murray of Leith, with whom he had a daughter. In 1746 he disowned the marriage, but his wife insisted on its lawfulness, and on 1 March 1748 the commissaries granted a decree in her favour, with an annuity of £40 sterling for herself and £10 for her daughter so long as she was supported by her mother. Cranstoun's behaviour was explained by his having fallen in love with Mary *Blandy (1718/19–1752), the daughter of an attorney from Henley-on-Thames. Mr Blandy objected to the relationship on the grounds that Cranstoun was already married, and, resenting his interference, Mary Blandy poisoned her father on 14 August 1751. She afterwards alleged that the powder she administered had been sent to her by Cranstoun from Scotland as a love potion; but apart from her statement there was nothing to connect him with the murder. She was tried, found guilty, and executed at Oxford on 3 March 1752. Cranstoun died on 2 or 9 December 1752 at Furnes, in Flanders. He was said to have left £1500 to his daughter.

T. F. HENDERSON, rev. HEATHER SHORE

Sources *Memoirs of the life of William Henry Cranstoun, esq; in which his education and genius are consider'd* (1752) · *Capt. Cranstoun's account of the poisoning [of] the late Mr. Francis Blandy, of Henley upon Thames, Oxfordshire* (1752?) · *Miss Mary Blandy's own account of the affair between her and Mr. Cranstoun: from the commencement of their acquaintance in the year 1746 to the death of her father in August 1751* (1752) ·

[M. Blandy], *The case of Miss Blandy consider'd as a daughter, as a gentlewoman, and as a Christian* (1752) · *Scots peerage*, vol. 2

Likenesses B. Cole, line engraving, BM, NPG

Wealth at death £1500 bequeathed: *Capt. Cranstoun's account of the poisoning [of] the late Mr. Francis Blandy*

Cranwell, John (1725/6–1793), poet, was born at St Ives, Huntingdonshire, the son of Tyrell Cranwell, a vintner. He attended Eton College between 1737 and 1741 before moving to Oakham School. He was admitted to St John's College, Cambridge, in 1743, aged seventeen, but emigrated to Sidney Sussex College where he graduated BA in 1747 and MA in 1751. Having taken orders he was elected to a fellowship by his college, and became vicar of Histon, Cambridgeshire, in 1751 before receiving the living of Abbots Ripton, Huntingdonshire, which he held for twenty-six years. He died on 17 April 1793.

Cranwell translated two Latin poems into heroic couplets: Isaac Hawkins Browne's *De animi immortalitate* (*A Poem on the Immortality of the Soul*, 1765), and, after conquering his fears that the original was tainted by 'a few errors of the Romish Church', *The Christiad* (1768), originally by Marcus Hieronymus Vida.

SARAH ANNES BROWN

Sources BL *cat.* · Venn, *Alum. Cant.* · R. A. Austen-Leigh, ed., *The Eton College register, 1698–1752* (1927) · R. F. Scott, ed., *Admissions to the College of St John the Evangelist in the University of Cambridge*, 3: *July 1715 – November 1767* (1903) · ESTC · *European Magazine and London Review*, 23 (1793), 399 · *DNB*

Cranworth. For this title name *see* Rolfe, Robert Monsey, Baron Cranworth (1790–1868).

Crapper, Thomas (1837–1910), plumber, was born at Thorne, Yorkshire, one of five sons of Charles Crapper, mariner, and his wife, Sarah. Although only eleven at the time, he is reputed to have walked the 165 miles to London, where he was apprenticed in 1848 to a plumber in Robert Street, Chelsea. By 1861 he was able to set up as a sanitary engineer, with his own brass foundry and workshops, in the nearby Marlborough Road. The installation of London's first main sewers, which over the next few years were extended throughout the capital, brought in its train an enormous demand for water-closets and made the decade a golden age for plumbers. Riding on this prosperity, Crapper married in 1867 Maria Green (*d.* 1902), a cousin with whom he had grown up in Thorne. Their only son died soon after birth.

In 1872 the Metropolis Water Act was passed, obliging the various water companies to conform to a single set of regulations. One aim of this act was to reduce the waste of water through defective water-closet flushes; Crapper succeeded in making the flush both economical and tamper-proof. His design caused a volume of water in the cistern to be discharged at a velocity sufficient to cleanse the basin, with no further leakage as the cistern refilled. The device consisted of an internal circular chamber connected to a siphon; pulling the chain raised a plate within the chamber and filled the siphon. All the water in the cistern then flowed through the siphon and down to the basin. The down-flow then ceased until the next time the chain was pulled. Crapper also endeavoured to reduce the

Thomas Crapper (1837–1910), by Edith Bertha Crapper

noise of the flush, eventually being able to advertise his Marlboro Silent Water Waste Preventer, and he designed various traps to prevent bad smells from backing up the sewage pipes.

The first of four royal warrants came Crapper's way in the 1880s when he was called in to reconstruct the sanitary fittings and sewage system at Sandringham House in Norfolk, for Edward, prince of Wales. He also put in drains at Westminster Abbey. With no children of his own to succeed him, Crapper employed his nephew George Crapper as foreman and another acquaintance of his Yorkshire youth, Robert Wharam, to whom he eventually made over the company, as manager. Just before he retired, he moved the business to larger premises at 120 King's Road, Chelsea.

The Crappers lived for many years at 12 Thornsett Road, Anerley, south-east London, where Thomas enjoyed gardening. After Maria's death, two maiden nieces went to live with him. Thomas Crapper was of medium height, neatly bearded, genial, and kindly in nature. As befitted his station, he invariably wore a frock coat and a billycock hat, and carried a cane. He was a freemason. He died at home on 27 January 1910 and was buried at the nearby Elmers End cemetery.

Crapper's name and trade were blazoned across the façade of his King's Road premises, leading to a certain ribaldry as 'crap' came into popular use as a term for defecation and the word 'crapper' for the lavatory itself. While the first was in former times applied to various sorts of rubbish, 'crapper' is more common in the USA, where it

may have been introduced by American troops who first encountered Thomas Crapper's sanitary fittings in Britain.   ANITA MCCONNELL

Sources W. Reyburn, *Flushed with pride: the story of Thomas Crapper* (1969) · *CGPLA Eng. & Wales* (1910) · d. cert.
Likenesses E. B. Crapper, miniature, watercolour on ivory, V&A; on loan to NPG [*see illus.*] · photograph, repro. in Reyburn, *Flushed with pride*, 54
Wealth at death £14,909 7s.: probate, 31 March 1910, *CGPLA Eng. & Wales*

Crashaw, Richard (1612/13–1648), poet, was born in London, the son of William *Crashawe or Crashaw (*bap.* 1572, *d.* 1625/6), preacher, polemicist, and devotional writer, and his first wife, whose identity is not known.

Background and early life The Crashaw family originated from Handsworth, near Sheffield (where the name often appears as Crawshaw), and the poet's grandfather and great-grandfather, both named Richard, came from there. It was also the birthplace of his father. At the time of Richard's birth his father was preacher at the Temple. By 1614 the family had moved to Burton Agnes, near Bridlington, Yorkshire, where William Crashawe had been granted the living. Late in 1618 they returned to London when his father was given the living of St Mary Matfelon, Whitechapel, and where he remained until his death in 1626. No details of Crashaw's mother have emerged, but he appears to have been her only child. She died early in his life, for his father remarried in 1619. This second wife, Elizabeth, died in childbirth in 1620. A testimony to her celebrates 'her singular motherly affection to the child of her predecessor' (*The Honour of Vertue*, n.d., A3v).

William Crashawe was an important Anglican polemicist and devotional writer. Fiercely anti-papal, he was extremely energetic in promoting the Church of England's claim to be the true Catholic church, based on its maintenance and restitution of the norms that governed the early church as opposed to the present corruptions of Rome. His many pamphlets particularly attack the Jesuits. However, his devotional writings reveal a less confrontational stance. In his *Manuale catholicorum* (1611) he translates and imitates mostly medieval hymns and devotional poems. These employ affective language that readily combines sensual and spiritual experience, a notable feature of his son's later poetry. Father and son, too, show similar liturgical interests in their devotional writing and both were committed to the ideals of worship established in the Book of Common Prayer.

William Crashawe was a bibliophile, claiming he 'spent my patrimonye in bookes, and my time in purusinge them' (*Poems*, ed. Martin, xviii). He had amassed more than 300 printed books and 500 manuscripts by the time of his death and left many of them to St John's College, Cambridge, where he had been a student. Like his son, William Crashawe enjoyed academic life. He celebrated his time at the Temple as 'the most comfortable and delightfull company for a scholler, that (out of the Universities) this kingdome yeelds' (ibid., xvi). He was well connected with some of the important figures in the English church of his day, notably James Ussher, who baptized Richard. So Richard Crashaw spent his early years in an environment conducive to his subsequent academic, poetic, and even religious direction. The long-standing view that William Crashawe was a puritan and his son a ready convert to Roman Catholicism has suggested that the poet rejected his paternal background. This perspective is no longer sustainable. Certainly William Crashawe was more committed to a Calvinistic theology and he was far more hostile to Rome than his son's later Laudianism found appropriate. Devotionally, though, the prominence accorded to an Anglican continuity with the early church is very similar to that propounded by his son. His anti-papal rhetoric, too, reflects his era's greater preoccupation with fears about Roman Catholicism. By the time Richard came to maturity the dominant Anglican view that Rome was either a false church or no church at all had shifted so that it was increasingly perceived as a true church but in error.

Richard Crashaw was about fourteen when his father died and was an executor of his will. No special legacy was made to him but he appears to have been provided for. William Crashawe, however, was not rich, and his son's inheritance was not large. In 1631 Richard's income was enhanced when he was left some property and £20 by his godfather, also Richard Crashaw, master of the Goldsmiths' Company. It is clear, though, that Crashaw's income was always modest.

There is no indication of where Crashaw was educated before and immediately after his father's death. In 1629 he entered Charterhouse School, located just outside London's walls, as a foundation scholar. His sponsors at the school appear to have been two lawyers, Sir Henry Yelverton and Sir Randolph Crew. It was at Charterhouse that Crashaw started to forge his reputation for poetry. Among the dedications to his first published collection, the *Epigrammata sacrorum liber* of 1634, Crashaw records his debt to Robert Brook, the master of Charterhouse, for prescribing exercises in imitating Latin and Greek authors. In addition to any regular exercises foundation scholars in their final year were also expected to post four Greek and four Latin verses in the school's great hall each Sunday.

Cambridge In July 1631 Crashaw entered Pembroke College, Cambridge, as exhibitioner and holder of a Watt scholarship. The college admissions book describes him as born in London and eighteen years old. Charterhouse had close connections with Pembroke, but Crashaw's poetic abilities probably helped him to win the Watt scholarship, as one of its duties was to write Latin epigrams on scriptural subjects. Crashaw clearly took this requirement very seriously as most of the epigrams of the *Epigrammata sacrorum liber* published by Cambridge University Press in 1634 originate from this required writing. In September 1631 the deaths of three Cambridge fellows occurred. These occasioned the first of several funeral elegies or commemorative poems from Crashaw that found their way into the Latin collections published by the university press in the 1630s. Crashaw arrived in Cambridge

with a reputation for writing academic verse and rapidly emerged as one of the university's finest neo-Latin poets.

Pembroke was a centre of Laudianism in Cambridge, and Crashaw appears to have readily associated himself with the movement. His collection of Latin epigrams contains dedications both to Benjamin Laney, the college's master, and to John Tourney, his tutor, both of whom were adherents of Laudianism. William Laud, archbishop of Canterbury from 1633, was the primary exponent of a reformist movement within the English church that came to particular prominence during the 1630s. Theologically it sought to moderate strict Calvinistic perspectives on belief: notably around predestination and the issue of whether faith alone justified belief in attaining salvation. Laudians emphasized that actions, too, played an important role among believers. However, it was the movement's attention to restoring ornate liturgical ceremonies that particularly provoked its opponents. Laudians seeking to emphasize order and continuity with the early church promoted activities that included setting up elaborate images in churches, restoring communion rails, using ornate robes, and emphasizing ceremonial actions: all of which its critics saw as a relapse into popery.

In his poetry Crashaw was principally involved with issues surrounding the celebration of religion, but he also took part in defending Laudian theological positions. At least two of his Latin epigrams originate from disputations (the main academic exercise) in which he participated at Pembroke and which were probably set by his tutor, Tourney, and deal with Laudian doctrinal arguments. One of these, 'Fides quae sola justificat, non est sine spe & dilectione', addresses a topic in which Tourney himself was publicly embroiled with more puritan elements in the university. Crashaw also wrote a supporting dedicatory poem for the *Five Pious and Learned Discourses* (1635) of the Laudian Robert Shelford. This book raised enormous protest from opponents of Laudianism for favouring charity's primacy over faith in achieving salvation and for refusing to accept the pope as Antichrist.

Epigrammata sacrorum liber illustrates how highly Crashaw's neo-Latin poetry was regarded by his contemporaries, as the university press did not usually publish such volumes by individuals. As is typical of such verse from this period, recent continental models of poetic *eloquentia* are readily apparent, acknowledging the predominance of European standards within neo-Latin writing. In the prose addition to his *Lectori*, Crashaw paid tribute to his Jesuit 'instructors' for providing him with patterns, though he carefully distinguished between 'their holy things and ours'. He also condemned those who ignored native English excellence and too readily favoured only foreign works. This distinction between style and content is important. Crashaw has long been noted as an English poet who employed continental baroque poetic models, many of them originating in Counter-Reformation writers. This has been felt to reveal the poet's predisposition to Roman Catholicism. However, many Cambridge neo-Latin and English poets of the

1630s, both Laudians and those with dramatically opposing religious views, employed such continental models in their work. Jesuit handbooks for Latin eloquence were widely employed at both Cambridge and Oxford. For example Crashaw used a Latin poem of the Jesuit Famianus Strada as the basis for his long poem 'Musicks Duell'. The Strada poem appears in his *Prolusione academicae*, first published in Rome but widely used throughout Europe, an edition being published at Oxford in 1631. Strada's work was recommended to students at Cambridge as an example of 'raised and pollish'd styles' by Richard Holdsworth, fellow and later master of the puritan inclined Emmanuel College during the 1630s (Healy, 50).

Peterhouse fellow Crashaw received his BA at Pembroke in 1634, and in 1635 moved to Peterhouse, where he was elected to a fellowship. Shortly after his election he was also made college catechist and curate of St Mary-the-Less, a church that adjoins the college. Peterhouse was at the heart of the Cambridge Laudian movement. John Cosin, who became its master in 1634, embarked on an elaborate embellishment of the chapel, and Crashaw contributed money to this scheme and wrote two Latin poems appealing for financial assistance in its rebuilding. As well as decoration Cosin instituted elaborate religious observance in the chapel, including an extensive musical accompaniment to services. Cosin had published *A Collection of Private Devotions* in 1627 (based on the Elizabethan primer the *Orarium*), and Crashaw's poetic sequence of liturgical hours, *Upon our b. Saviours Passion*, may have been directly influenced by Cosin's collection. Both show a central concern with practical piety in a liturgical setting and a strong inclination to ritual grounded in ancient traditions. A good deal of Crashaw's poetry, too, celebrates religious music, presenting worshippers joining in song to celebrate the divinity. It is possible that Crashaw's sequence was set to music and used in Peterhouse chapel.

During Crashaw's early years at Cambridge he became acquainted with Nicholas Ferrar's religious community at Little Gidding, a short distance from Cambridge. This group also favoured a highly ritualized religious celebration. The relationship appears to have been a profound one for the poet, and he often visited Little Gidding. He seems to have been particularly close to Mary Collet, who became mother of the community in 1632, though there is no evidence that their relation was any other than friendship. One of Crashaw's first pupils at Peterhouse was Ferrar Collet, younger brother of Mary, and Crashaw initially sought refuge from the civil war with relatives of the Collets in Leiden.

Crashaw wrote of Cambridge as his 'little contentfull kingdom' (*Poems*, ed. Martin, xxix), and it would appear that his time at Peterhouse was indeed spent largely in intellectual and devotional pursuits. David Lloyd, his first biographer in the 1660s, claimed that his sermons at St Mary-the-Less were 'thronged on each Sunday and Holiday' (Lloyd, 618), but there is no evidence that he had a reputation for preaching. Opponents of Laudianism cited him on a number of occasions for introducing superstitious practices, and he was involved in a couple of Laudian

attempts to thwart puritans in the university. But in all these instances his role was minor, and he appears to have aroused relatively little attention among the vast majority of his contemporaries. His closest friend at Cambridge was almost certainly Joseph Beaumont, another Peterhouse fellow and poet who paid warm tribute to Crashaw's influence on him, both poetically and personally.

Poetry It is certain that Crashaw's English poetry was mostly written during his years in Cambridge. He wrote both on secular as well as sacred themes, but it is for his devotional poetry that he is rightly best remembered. His poetry was published in *Steps to the Temple: Sacred Poems, with other Delights of the Muses* by the royalist publisher Humphrey Moseley in 1646, with an expanded edition in 1648. As the title indicates Crashaw is presented as heir to George Herbert, another poet with Cambridge roots. But the styles of the two poets are different. Crashaw's devotional celebrations focus on believers as part of a large congregation, adding their voices to a chorus that stretches across liturgical history.

A number of his poems originate in well-known medieval hymns, which he adapts rather than translates precisely. Crashaw has a preoccupation with female saints (the Virgin, Mary Magdalen, St Teresa), and this has generally supported a view of his Roman Catholicism. His thorough devotion to the Virgin, including accepting a version of her Assumption, would certainly have been frowned on by many within the English church, while St Teresa is one of the most celebrated of Counter-Reformation saints. However, interest in these figures was not particularly exceptional within Cambridge and Oxford Laudian circles. Crashaw's devotional orientation and his poetic manner are distinctive when placed within the larger body of contemporary writing, but are less so when witnessed alongside the preoccupations of Laudian Cambridge.

Crashaw's poetic voice is a conspicuous one in English, however, and possesses an exuberant, often ecstatic quality that builds over many lines, celebrating an emotional excitement that greatly surpasses the tenor of the scriptural or medieval texts on which the poems are often founded. Crashaw's version of the medieval 'Sancta Maria dolorum' readily exemplifies this. Imploring Mary, witnessing her son's crucifixion, to teach the poet an appropriate fervour to share in the event, he asks that the poet, the Virgin, and by implication the reader may 'study him so, till we mix / Wounds; and become one crucifix', and concludes with a desire for an emotional merging that sees him become the child suckling on his saviour.

Much of Crashaw's English writing, both sacred and secular, builds on the epigram, the genre in which he gained his initial reputation. A number of his English poems are indeed versions of the Latin epigrams published in his *Epigrammata*. In his longer poems Crashaw frequently writes what can virtually seem a series of extended epigrams. For instance, each of the thirty-one stanzas of 'The Weeper', Crashaw's poem on Mary Magdalen, is effectively a separate epigram commemorating the penitent saint's tears. This allows the poet full exercise in varying rhetorical exaggeration and invention around a theme, a common feature in contemporary neo-Latin verse. It is less usually employed to this extent in accomplished English poetry and has sometimes resulted in Crashaw's work being critically censured as ridiculously extravagant:

And now where're he strayes
Among the Galilean mountains,
Or more unwelcome wayes,
He's follow'd by two faithful fountains;
Two walking baths; two weeping motions;
Portable, & compendious oceans.
('The Weeper', *Poems*)

Exile Parliament's troops occupied Cambridge in the spring of 1643, but it seems that Crashaw had left the town by this stage and gone into exile to Mary Collet's relations in Leiden in the Netherlands, possibly with her there too. He would have had no sympathies with parliament's endeavours, and the troops quickly purged Cambridge churches and college chapels of Laudian decoration. It was from Leiden on 20 February 1644 that Crashaw wrote to Joseph Beaumont his sole surviving letter. Crashaw presented himself as short of money in a city given over to worldly pursuits. The principal design of the letter was to explore how some of the money from his Cambridge fellowship might be made available to him. Circumstances at Cambridge had already made impossible any such arrangement, though, and it was just over a month later that Crashaw was formally expelled from his fellowship, along with all but two of the other Peterhouse fellows.

It seems possible that Crashaw returned to England in 1644 and went to Oxford, but there is no firm evidence. He may also have spent time in the English College in Liège, as there are records of his receiving payments from Father Richard Barton when in Paris, and Barton had been rector of the Liège college. Crashaw was living in Paris in 1645 and by this time had converted to Roman Catholicism. It was probably through the offices of his friend and fellow poet Abraham Cowley, in Paris as secretary to Lord Jermyn, that he was presented to the court of Henrietta Maria, which was resident in the city. He also met Susan, countess of Denbigh, who was with the queen, and he wrote his last substantial English poem to her 'perswading her to resolution in Religion' as she, too, was inclining to Rome.

On 7 September 1646 Henrietta Maria wrote to the pope on Crashaw's behalf, asking him to provide him with a post. Crashaw journeyed to Rome and became resident in the English College, alongside four other Peterhouse fellows who had converted to Rome. There is no evidence, however, that Crashaw sought to enter the Roman Catholic priesthood. Papal employment was not forthcoming, and Crashaw was apparently in financial distress. Eventually he gained a post attending on Cardinal Palotto. In 1647 John Bargrave, another former Peterhouse fellow, found him in Rome. Bargrave reported that Crashaw's life in the Palotto retinue was not comfortable, though he was now receiving a salary. Crashaw complained to the cardinal about the impious lifestyle of some of his Italian followers, objections that not surprisingly were ill received. Bargrave suggested that the cardinal then found Crashaw a 'small imploy' (*Alexander the Seventh*, ed. Robertson, 37) at Loreto, a famous pilgrimage centre to the Virgin. It was apparently as a result of illness contracted while travelling there from Rome in the summer of 1648 that Crashaw died, unmarried, at Loreto, some four weeks after arriving. He was buried there.

Reputation While in Paris in 1646 Crashaw met Thomas Car (or Carre), founder and confessor of the Monastery of the Canonesses of St Augustin. After his death Car edited the edition of Crashaw's poems called *Carmen Deo nostro* that was published in Paris in 1652, dedicated to the countess of Denbigh. Crashaw had obviously left a manuscript of his poems in Paris, but Car seems to have taken pains to have the poems presented in such a way as to emphasize Crashaw's Roman Catholicism, using titles for instance that often do not agree with the poems' arguments and thus are unlikely to be authorial. This is an early instance of the manipulation of Crashaw's life and reputation for sectarian purposes. In contrast David Lloyd presents him as a sufferer for the protestant cause. Abraham Cowley's elegy to his friend, *On the Death of Mr Crashaw*, apologizes to the English church for his conversion but plays down its significance: 'His faith perhaps in some nice tenets might / Be wrong; His life, I'm sure, was in the right'. Tantalizingly another Cambridge contemporary, John Worthington, wrote from Lincolnshire in 1667 that he had met an unnamed figure with whom Crashaw had left his poems, 'writ in his own hand' before he went abroad (*Diary and Correspondence of Dr John Worthington*, 2.230–31). In his letter Worthington showed his acquaintance with both English and French editions of Crashaw, and asked for a copy of *Steps to the Temple* (1648) to be sent to him so that he could correct it and add poems yet unpublished. This project was never realized, and this authorial manuscript appears to have been lost. The best modern edition of Crashaw's work is *The Poems, English, Latin and Greek of Richard Crashaw*, edited by L. C. Martin. THOMAS HEALY

Sources *The poems, English, Latin and Greek of Richard Crashaw*, ed. L. C. Martin, 2nd edn (1957) · T. Healy, *Richard Crashaw* (1986) · C. Warwick, 'Love is eloquence: Richard Crashaw and the development of a discourse of divine love', PhD diss., U. Cam., 1994 · D. Lloyd, *Memoires of the lives … of those … personages that suffered … for the protestant religion* (1668), 618 · *The diary and correspondence of Dr John Worthington*, ed. J. Crossley, 2/1, Chetham Society, 36 (1855), 230–37 · *Pope Alexander the Seventh and the College of Cardinals, by John Bargrave …; with a catalogue of Dr Bargrave's Museum*, ed. J. C. Robertson, CS, 92 (1867), 34–7 · P. J. Wallis, *William Crashaw: the Sheffield puritan* (1963) · A. Warren, *Richard Crashaw: a study in baroque sensibility* (Baton Rouge, 1939) · K. Larsen, 'Some light on Richard Crashaw's final years in Rome', *Modern Language Review*, 66 (1971), 492–6 · J. Roberts, ed., *New perspectives on the life and poetry of Richard Crashaw* (Columbia, MO, 1992) · J. Cosin, *A collection of private devotions*, ed. P. G. Stanwood (1967) · J. M. Hughes, *Musical manuscripts at Peterhouse Cambridge* (1953) · admissions book, Pembroke Cam., manuscripts collection

Crashawe [Crashaw], **William** (*bap.* 1572, *d.* 1625/6), Church of England clergyman and religious controversialist, was born at Handsworth, near Sheffield, Yorkshire, and baptized there on 26 October 1572. He was the second of the four children of Richard Crashawe (d. in or before 1608) and his wife, Helen (d. 1608), daughter of John Routh of Waleswood. In all likelihood he attended the grammar school at Sheffield, and then in June 1588, following in the steps of his elder brother, Thomas, he matriculated from St John's College, Cambridge, which he later described as his 'deere Nurce & spirituall Mother' (will, quoted in Wallis, *Sheffield Puritan*, 9). There he was enrolled on 1 May 1591 as sizar to Henry Alvey, future provost of Trinity College, Dublin, and graduated BA early the following year. When the bishop of Ely's fellowship at St John's fell vacant, the see being unoccupied, the right of nomination was vested in the queen. In a letter to the fellows on 15 January 1594 Elizabeth stated that she had been 'crediblie enformed of the povertie and yet otherwise good qualities and sufficiencie' of Crashawe, who was accordingly admitted on the 19th (Baker, 1.187, 291, 438). He proceeded MA in 1595 and BD in 1603.

After ordination at places and dates unknown Crashawe became a preacher in his native county, 'ffirste at Bridlington then at Beverley' (Wallis, *Sheffield Puritan*, 5), where he served the minster from at least August 1599 until 1605, receiving the generous stipend of £32. 10s. His talent in the pulpit played a large part in determining his future career. In May 1600 he was presented to the nearby vicarage of Burton Agnes, which was worth some £20 per annum, but the queen claimed an interest and he was removed by her attorney in June 1601. Following appeals to James I he was granted the living for life in May 1608, in due course obtaining the 'next avoydance' also (ibid., 12). In 1604 he became chaplain to Edmund Sheffield, Baron Sheffield, president of the council of the north, and by August was appointed to the second prebend of the newly refounded collegiate church of Ripon, retaining his stall there until death. Early in 1606 he petitioned Lord Salisbury for confirmation of its endowment.

On 10 February 1605 Crashawe obtained the post of preacher to the Inner and Middle Temples in London, where he was to lecture each Sunday and Thursday for the sum of £10 per term from either house. There he found 'the most comfortable and delightfull company for a scholler, that (out of the Universities) this kingdome yeelds' (W. Crashawe, *Romish Forgeries and Falsifications*, 1606, sig. ¶3). The connections that he now formed with influential people in various walks of life are witnessed by the sometimes multiple dedications of his printed tracts and by surviving letters to Sir Robert Cotton, James Ussher, Thomas James, and Sir Julius Caesar. He shared the enthusiasm of his fellow Templars for colonial expansion and invested in the Virginia Company, delivering on 21 February 1610 a farewell sermon at Lord De La Warr's departure that was printed without his leave as *A Sermon Preached in London* (1610) and later helping to publicize the discovery of the Bermudas. By this time he had already embarked on his life's work of practical and controversial theology with editions (1605–7) of three works by the puritan theologian William Perkins. Believing, as his will puts it, that 'the Religion now professed in England … is the

same Religion in substance which was taughte by Christe Jesus' (Wallis, *Sheffield Puritan*, 7), he set himself to demonstrate the errors of Roman Catholicism 'as nowe it is' by study of the church fathers and medieval theologians. In *Romish Forgeries and Falsifications* (1606), advertised as 'tom. I. lib. I' of his grand scheme, he discussed doctrinal changes made by the Catholic authorities in some scriptural commentaries written by the Franciscan Johann Wild, or Ferus (d. 1554). The address to Prince Henry prefacing his *The Sermon Preached at the [Paul's] Crosse Feb. xiiii 1607 [1608]* (1608) dismissed the notion that 'they and we by a reasonable mediation might well be reconciled' (sig. P2v).

Crashawe now issued what was to prove his most popular work, *Newes from Italy of a Second Moses* (1608), a translation of Niccolo Balbani's account of the Geneva conversion of an Italian marquess that was reprinted six times over the next eighty years. In the following year he published editions of John Redman's *Complaint of Grace* [n.d., 1556?] and of *Consilium delectorum cardinalium*, the deliberations of the reforming commission set up in 1537 by Pope Paul III. On 4 July 1610 he was censured in convocation for publishing an erroneous book (Cardwell, 2.591n., 592). In a letter dated 19 July the previous year he had sought advice from Cotton, complaining that 'The griefe & anger that I should be so malitiously traduced to my lords the Byshops (whom I honour) hath made me farr out of temper & put me into an ague, which in these canicular days is dangerouse' (BL, Cotton MS Julius C. III, fol. 126). According to a contemporary, the cause was 'Jealousie with some of our Bishops, by reason of some points that hath fallen from his Pen and his Tongue in the pulpit' (Fisher, 'Predicament', 270). But the rebuke may have been owed to his recent circulation, though with a view to suppression, of a copy of 'that damnable libell the Prurit-anus', in reply to which on 14 August he sent to Lord Salisbury a list of 100 instances of alleged corruptions of scripture by the Romanists (PRO, SP 14/47/169, 170). The same approach was adopted in his undated tract *A Discoverye of Popishe Corruption Requiringe a Kingely Reformation*, in which he volunteered '5000 places corrupted (de facto) in the Authors that wrote within these 200 yeares' and in the councils and fathers of the church (BL, Royal MS 17. B. IX, fol. 3v). He also took the opportunity of requesting access to the Royal Library.

From the very first year of Crashawe's preachership the Inner Templars had been in arrears with their half of his stipend, and in January 1610, meeting widespread resistance from members to a proposed increase in the levy, discontinued it altogether. Crashawe struggled to retain his post through five years of petitions and negotiations, during which, despite the fact that family residence at the Temple was frowned upon, he took a wife, of whom no details are known. Their son, the future poet and Catholic convert Richard *Crashaw, was probably born in the autumn of 1612. The event fell in an unusually poetical period for Crashawe himself. *The Jesuites Gospell* (1610) was his English version with line-by-line refutation of the Latin rapture of 1606 on the Virgin of Halle written by

Carolus Scribanius, whose style and doctrine, ironically, was to influence his son's work. The *Manuall for True Catholickes* (1611) included verse-translations of four medieval Latin religious poems 'Gathered out of certaine ancient Manuscripts, written 300 yeares *ago, or more*', and these were reprinted in 1613 with the first translation into English of St Bernard's supposititious *Querela, sive, Dialogus* of the soul and body.

The same year saw the publication of *The Embassador between Heaven and Earth*, a collection of meditations and prayers by 'W. C.' that had been entered in the Stationers' register in the previous October. On 13 May, having already moved his wife and child up to Burton Agnes, Crashawe formally surrendered his preachership and set about disposing of what he rightly termed 'one of the most complete libraryes in Europe' in private hands. This valuable resource was housed in the extension that he had built in 1607, without permission and at a cost of £240, to his official lodgings 'over parte of the Temple Church' (Fisher, 'Library'; Fisher, 'Middle Temple globes'). In 'A memorable monument of antiquitye' he had written of having 'employed much of my poore stipend to procure, & of my time to peruse the antient Manuscripts that are to be had' of 'the antient records of truthe' (Durham University Library, MS Cosin v. iii. 6). His concern for the fate of such treasures led him to urge on Isaac Casaubon the purchase of the collection of Henry Savile of Banke for the Royal Library. His own library comprised, in addition to 4000 or so printed books, at least 200 manuscripts, several of them distinguished by his motto 'Servire deo regnare est' ('To serve God is to reign'), along with 'one of the fairest paire of globes in England'. Its acquisition had cost him in all £2000. Although booksellers offered him more than half that sum he made overtures for its preservation as a 'publicke and perpetual' library to the Templars, to whom he had already donated volumes, and to his old university, which proceeded no further than the expense of an appraisal. By mid-1615 he had lodged 'almost 200 volumes of manuscripts in Greeke, Lattine, English, & about 2,000 printed books' with his fellow collegian Henry Wriothesley, third earl of Southampton, through whose widow they eventually reached the newly built library at St John's. Even so, as late as February 1620 we find him authorizing William Trumbull at Brussels to pay £10 or £12 for a copy of the Biblia Regia (BL, Add. MS 72357, fol. 52), and his will includes bequests of books that he had left at Burton Agnes. Four of Crashawe's manuscripts later found their way to Sir Simonds D'Ewes and subsequently to the British Library (Harley MSS 105, 207, 372 and 628), while his pair of Molyneux globes went to the Middle Temple.

While exercising his pastoral function in the 'rude countrye' of Yorkshire (Fisher, 'Middle Temple globes', 106) Crashawe added to his Ripon prebend in April 1617 that of Osbaldwick in the church of York, with an annual value of almost £33. He continued to visit London, and while staying with Lord Sheffield in May preached a series of five sermons published in 1618 as *The Parable of Poyson*.

His practical catechism, *Milke for Babes*, licensed in December 1617, also appeared in this year, as did *Fiscus papalis*, his translation of a catalogue of papal indulgences compiled by 'a Catholicke divine'. He may already have taken up residence in Whitechapel when on 13 November he was formally presented by Sir John North and William Baker to the vicarage of what his will calls the 'too greate Parishe' of St Mary Matfelon (St Mary, Whitechapel), worth upwards of £32 annually (BL, Add. 36776, fol. 303). As a widower of forty-six, he married at All Hallows, Barking, on 11 May 1619 a woman half his age, Elizabeth, daughter of Anthony Skinner, a local haberdasher. She died in childbirth on 8 October of the next year, and her funeral sermon was delivered by Ussher, who had baptized her stepson. She was commemorated in a privately printed tract entitled *The Honour of Vertue* (1620) and by a lapidary inscription in the church.

Crashawe resumed his theological work with editions of John Healey's translation of St Augustine's *City of God* (1620) and of a sermon by Samuel Cottesford which he dedicated to Sir Edward Sackville MP for his efforts on behalf of imprisoned debtors. In 1622 he issued *The New Man*, a translation completed in 1616 of a Catholic tract seeking support from James I for a general council to limit papal power, and his catechetical *Meate for Men*, which defended infant baptism and kneeling at communion. In 1623, when the increasing congregation at his sermons forced the building of a new gallery in the church, Henry Rogers's answer to the Jesuit Fisher incorporated Crashawe's *Dialogue Concerning this Question, Where was your Church before Luther and Calvin*. However, *The Fatall Vesper* by 'W. C.', the earliest registered tract on the Blackfriars accident of October, was not in fact his work. In the next year he published a letter, dated 1611, *Ad Severinum Binnium*, criticizing his edition (1606) of the councils of the church, and resumed his attack on indulgences in *A Mittimus to the Jubilee at Rome* (1625).

This was also a plague year, when between March and August over 1100 of Crashawe's parishioners died. *Londons Lamentations for her Sinnes*, while blaming the decline of public morals and the growth of the theatres, includes strictures on diet and hygiene. 'When the worst was over' (Balleine, 15) Crashawe himself died, probate of his will being granted to his executor, Robert Dixon, on 16 October 1626, with power reserved for his son Richard. This extraordinary document, written in November 1621, is remarkable for its long preamble affirming his creed, rejecting post-Tridentine Catholicism, and declaring the purity of his life.   W. H. KELLIHER

Sources P. J. Wallis, *William Crashaw: the Sheffield puritan* (1963), 37–49, 111–21, 169–93, 245–62 • P. J. Wallis, 'The library of William Crashawe', *Transactions of the Cambridge Bibliographical Society*, 2 (1954–8), 213–28 • R. M. Fisher, 'William Crashawe and the Middle Temple globes, 1605–1615', *GJ*, 140 (1974), 105–12 • R. M. Fisher, 'The predicament of William Crashawe, preacher at the Temple', *Journal of Ecclesiastical History*, 25 (1974), 267–76 • R. M. Fisher, 'William Crashawe's library at the Middle Temple', *The Library*, 5th ser., 30 (1975), 116–24 • T. Baker, *History of the college of St John the Evangelist, Cambridge*, ed. J. E. B. Mayor, 2 vols. (1869) • E. Coke, *A booke of entries* (1614) • E. Cardwell, *Synodalia: a collection of articles of religion, canons* and proceedings of convocation in the province of Canterbury (1842), 2.591n., 592 · G. Hennessy, *Novum repertorium ecclesiasticum parochiale Londinense, or, London diocesan clergy succession from the earliest time to the year 1898* (1898) · J. Stow, *The survey of London*, ed. A. M. [A. Munday] and others, rev. edn (1633) · G. R. Balleine, *The story of St. Mary Matfelon* (1898) · *History of Ripon*, 2nd edn (1806) · A. Freeman, 'The fatal vesper and The doleful evensong: claim-jumping in 1623', *The Library*, 5th ser., 22 (1967), 128–35 · R. Crashaw, *The poems, English, Latin and Greek*, ed. L. C. Martin (1957) · *Calendar of the manuscripts of the most hon. the marquess of Salisbury*, 24, HMC, 9 (1976) · Venn, *Alum. Cant.*

Archives Middle Temple, London, personal papers · St John Cam.

Craster, Sir (Herbert Henry) Edmund (1879–1959), librarian and historian, was born at the family seat, Beadnell Hall, Northumberland, on 5 November 1879, the third son (but only child of the second marriage) of Edmund Craster (1824–1898), formerly of the Bengal civil service. His mother, who died a fortnight after Edmund's birth, was Barbara Stewart, daughter of the Revd H. T. Lee, of Dinas Powys, Glamorgan. He was educated at Clifton College and as a scholar of Balliol College, Oxford (1898–1903), where he took first classes in Greats and in modern history, and in 1903 he was elected to a prize fellowship at All Souls College, to which he remained attached for the rest of his life. He married on 25 April 1912 a fellow Northumbrian, Alice Ida, only daughter of Gilfrid George Baker-Cresswell, of Preston Tower, Chathill. They had a son (who became an inspector of ancient monuments) and two daughters.

The Craster family had been established at Craster Tower, near Embleton, since the twelfth century, and Edmund Craster's Northumbrian affinities determined the course of his historical interests. His antiquarian ability showed itself early in mature and accomplished archaeological and numismatic articles stimulated particularly by the major Romano-British excavations of the time at Corstopitum (Corbridge). Craster's keen eye for detail and ability to discern the historical significance of archaeological or documentary evidence were put to good use as editor of volumes 8 to 10 (1907–14) of the spaciously conceived *History of Northumberland*. The first two volumes, dealing with the south-east corner of the county, were dominated respectively by the regality and monastery of Tynemouth and by the history of the Delaval family of Seaton Delaval. Craster prepared the bulk of the text himself, efficiently marshalling charter and documentary materials. Volume 10, on Corbridge, was timely after an exciting period of excavation, and equally well prepared.

In 1912 Craster was appointed sub-librarian of the Bodleian Library in Oxford, working especially on the *Summary Catalogue of Western Manuscripts*, started by Falconer Madan. Craster was responsible for the volume on the more recent accessions (1924), and for those on the collections acquired by the university in the seventeenth century, published in 1922, and (with collaborators) in 1937. Discoveries made in the course of redescribing the manuscripts were published frequently in the *Bodleian Quarterly Record*. He was promoted keeper of Western manuscripts in 1927 and in 1931 succeeded Sir Arthur Cowley as Bodley's librarian.

Gross congestion and under-funding made it a very difficult time to have taken charge of the Bodleian. Craster had to see through a programme of library extension that had after prolonged discussion been agreed by the university. This deliberate and retiring scholar, who moreover suffered from a severe speech impediment, immediately showed himself thorough and decisive, good at delegation, and equal to the administrative tasks ahead. His own strong but dutifully understated preference had been for a completely new library on an extendable site then available, but he followed his curators' wishes in overseeing the construction of the 'New Bodleian' bookstack at the end of Broad Street and its co-ordination with the existing central buildings. Designed by Sir Giles Gilbert Scott and built with substantial support from the Rockefeller Foundation, its foundation stone was laid in June 1937 and it was ready for opening by June 1940, though its official opening had to be postponed until 24 October 1946. Craster directed the systematic planning of the building with great skill. His sure touch was seen also in improvements in staffing levels and salaries, in the finances of the Bodleian, and in its catalogues. He retired under the age rule in 1945, and later wrote a *History of the Bodleian Library, 1845–1945* (1952), a full and perspicacious account notable for its candour when dealing with recent events in Bodleian history.

In retirement Craster resumed historical work that had been decreased but never suspended during his library career, and he succeeded Sir Charles Oman as librarian of the Codrington Library at All Souls. There too he carried out some much needed reforms, including the reclassification of the books and the provision of a bookstack. At the time of his death, in Oxford on 21 March 1959, he had written much of *The History of All Souls College Library*, which was completed by E. F. Jacob and eventually published (with the text of Jacob's memorial address on Craster) in 1971.

Craster, who became a fellow of the Society of Antiquaries in 1911, had taken a DLitt in 1916, and was awarded an honorary LittD by Cambridge in 1934. He was knighted in 1945. Several portraits of him by Augustus John exist, but the small carved head forming a corbel on the south exit of the Bodleian quadrangle is reckoned the best likeness of this great figure in the history of the Bodleian Library.

ALAN BELL

Sources E. F. Jacob, 'Edmund Craster', in H. H. E. Craster, *The history of All Souls College library*, ed. E. F. Jacob (1971), 112–19 · I. A. Richmond, 'Sir Edmund Craster', *Archaeologia Aeliana*, 3rd ser., 37 (1959), 355–7 · *The Times* (23 March 1959) · Burke, *Gen. GB* (1965) · I. Elliott, ed., *The Balliol College register, 1900–1950*, 3rd edn (privately printed, Oxford, 1953), 57 · *WWW, 1951–60* · *CGPLA Eng. & Wales* (1959)
Archives Bodl. Oxf., Curtis MSS, Craster letters · LUL, Ker MSS, Craster letters
Likenesses A. John, oils, 1944, Bodl. Oxf. · W. Stoneman, photograph, 1946, NPG · A. John, pencil drawing, repro. in Craster, *History of All Souls College library*, ed. Jacob, pl. 7 · corbel sculpture, Bodl. Oxf. · negative, Bodl. Oxf.
Wealth at death £11,855 6s. 2d.: probate, 11 June 1959, *CGPLA Eng. & Wales*

Cratfield, William (*d.* 1415), abbot of Bury St Edmunds, presumably came from Cratfield, Suffolk. Having professed at Bury St Edmunds, he studied at Gloucester College, Oxford, with an allowance of 4s. 4d. from the sacristy. He was recalled during the peasants' revolt in 1381, and before 1389 was appointed chamberlain. Abbot John Timworth died on 16 January 1389. Richard II issued the licence for the election of a new abbot on 20 January, and on 28 January the monks elected Cratfield by way of scrutiny. The king restored the temporalities on 8 October 1389.

Cratfield proved an able abbot who did much to restore the fortunes of Bury St Edmunds Abbey after the catastrophes of the previous decade. Abbot Timworth left enormous debts. The abbey had suffered serious loss of revenue because, during the monks' prolonged dispute with the papal provisor, Edmund Bramfield, over Timworth's election to the abbacy, the king had held the abbey's temporalities. Meanwhile Timworth had the cost of repairing the terrible damage inflicted on the abbey's property by the insurgents in 1381. Cratfield excused himself on these grounds from attending the general chapter of Benedictines of the southern province held at Northampton on 30 June 1390.

Cratfield relieved the abbey of two especially onerous financial burdens. The first was the abbey's obligation to pay the king 1200 marks at each vacancy for the monks' custody of their portion of the abbey's temporalities. On 6 August 1396 Richard II granted that henceforth the abbey should pay £40 annually instead of the lump sum, and that the prior and convent should have custody of both the abbot's temporalities and their own during a vacancy. Secondly, Cratfield obtained a similar concession from the pope, on 25 April 1398 obtaining commutation of a service tax of 1500 florins, and of more than 500 florins for petty services, for an annual payment of 20 marks. Boniface IX also conceded that an abbot-elect of Bury St Edmunds, once confirmed in office, might choose the bishop who was to bless him (and thus save himself the journey to the papal curia). Cratfield obtained these royal and papal concessions 'at his own labour and expense' (CUL, MS Ff.2.29, fol. 61): the first cost him £149 3s. 4d., besides £100 contributed by the convent, and the second £756 1s. 3½d., besides £30 which he took from St Edmund's shrine. To pay the two annual charges Cratfield obtained licences for the appropriation of two of his churches, at Harlow and Thurston in Suffolk, together worth £40 net in most years.

Defence of the property and jurisdictional rights of the abbey occupied much of Cratfield's time. Most serious were two long-standing disputes, one with Canterbury and the other with Ely. The dispute with Canterbury, over the cathedral priory's claim to return of writs in its vills of Harlow and Monks Eleigh, was brought to a satisfactory conclusion by final concord in November 1408. Unfortunately, Cratfield died before he could end the litigation over Ely's claim to return of writs in those of the latter priory's vills which lay within the liberty of Bury St Edmunds Abbey. A typical prelate of his age, Cratfield recognized the need for influential friends. An amusing contemporary account describes how he entertained Archbishop Thomas Arundel when he made an unexpected visit to Bury St Edmunds on 1 October 1400. Cratfield had to protect the abbey's privilege of exemption from the archbishop's authority, but without antagonizing so powerful a figure. In the event, he contrived to make the archbishop's visit both honourable and very convivial, while avoiding any derogation of the said privilege. Cratfield also granted confraternity to magnates, for example John of Gaunt, duke of Lancaster (the donor of six glass windows to the abbey church), Gaunt's son Thomas Beaufort, earl of Dorset, and Edmund Mortimer, earl of March. Moreover, in 1390–91, a monk of Bury St Edmunds at the command of Richard II composed a history of England from Brutus to Richard's accession. The text survives in Cambridge, Corpus Christi College, MS 251, a beautifully illuminated copy possibly intended for presentation to Richard.

Cratfield was a good Benedictine by the standards of that time. On 13 November 1394 he obtained a papal licence to have a portable altar. He took an active part in the affairs of the general chapter of the Benedictines of the southern province, and served as president in 1408 and 1411. He endowed chantries in two of the Bury hospitals, those of St John and St Nicholas, and established an anniversary for himself on which the prior was to have a noble (6s. 8d.) and each monk 40d. During his last two years he was unwell and stayed on his manor of Elmswell, performing his duties in the abbey by proxy; it was probably there that he died, on 18 November 1415. His register survives as BL, Cotton MS Tiberius B.ix; though damaged in the fire of 1731 in the Cottonian Library, it remains legible.

ANTONIA GRANSDEN

Sources BL, Cotton MS Tiberius B.ix · abbey's vestry register, CUL, MS Ff.2.29 · abbey's vestry register, CUL, MS Ff.2.35 · BL, Add. MS 14849 [one of the abbey's registers], fol. 100v · CCC Cam., MS 251 · R. M. Thomson, 'Obedientiaries of St Edmunds Abbey', *Proceedings of the Suffolk Institute of Archaeology and History*, 35 (1981–4), 98 · R. M. Thomson, *The archives of the abbey of Bury St Edmunds*, Suffolk RS, 21 (1980), 33–4, 39, 50, 56, 130–31, 134–5 · Bibliothèque de la Ville, Douai, MS 553, fol. viiiv [Kitchener's register] · *CPR* · *Polychronicon Ranulphi Higden monachi Cestrensis*, ed. C. Babington and J. R. Lumby, 9 vols., Rolls Series, 41 (1865–86), vol. 9, pp. 202, 212 · *Thomae Walsingham, quondam monachi S. Albani, historia Anglicana*, ed. H. T. Riley, 2 vols., pt 1 of *Chronica monasterii S. Albani*, Rolls Series, 28 (1863–4), vol. 2, p. 180 · 'Visitatio Thomae de Arundell archiepiscopi', *Memorials of St Edmund's Abbey*, ed. T. Arnold, 3, Rolls Series, 96 (1896), 183–8 · 'Contentio inter monasterium S. Edmundi et episcopum Eliensem', *Memorials of St Edmund's Abbey*, ed. T. Arnold, 3, Rolls Series, 96 (1896), 188–211 · W. A. Pantin, ed., *Documents illustrating the activities of … the English black monks, 1215–1540*, 3 vols., CS, 3rd ser., 45, 47, 54 (1931–7), vol. 2, p. 4; vol. 3, pp. 92–4, 205–6, 209 · M. R. James, *On the abbey of St Edmund at Bury*, Cambridge Antiquarian RS, 28 (1895), 167 · M. R. James, *A descriptive catalogue of the manuscripts in the library of Corpus Christi College, Cambridge*, 2 (1912), pt 1, pp. 1–2 · W. E. Lunt, *Financial relations of the papacy with England, 1327–1534* (1962), 235–6, 812 · *CEPR letters*, vol. 4 · C. Harper-Bill, ed., *Charters of the medieval hospitals of Bury St Edmunds*, Suffolk RS, Suffolk Charters, 14 (1994), 73–4, 91

Archives BL, register, Cotton MS Tiberius B.ix

Crathorne. For this title name *see* Dugdale, Thomas Lionel, first Baron Crathorne (1897–1977).

Crathorne [*alias* Yaxley], **William** [*alias* Augustin Shepherd] (**1670–1740**), Roman Catholic priest, born in October 1670, was the son of Ralph Crathorne and his wife, Anne Tunstall. Descended from the ancient family of Crathorne of Crathorne in Yorkshire, he was educated in the English College at Douai, where he was a professor for several years. On being ordained priest (before 2 October 1705) he assumed the name Yaxley, and after he returned to England in September 1707 on the mission he appears to have used the alias Augustin Shepherd. The scene of his missionary labours was Hammersmith, and he spent the rest of his life as chaplain to the nuns there.

Crathorne's first published work was *A Catholick's Resolution, Shewing his Reasons for not being a Protestant* (n.d. [1718?]). He resided with Bishop Giffard, who commissioned him to edit the *Spiritual Works* of John Goter (or Gother). These appeared in sixteen volumes in 1718. Drawing on a manuscript of Goter's, he published a Roman missal for the use of the laity. Other works included a historical catechism (1726), as well as lives of St Francis of Sales (1726) and of Jesus (1739). One of his devotional works, *The Daily Companion, or, A Little Pocket Manual* (1743), went through innumerable editions. Crathorne died at Hammersmith on 11 March 1740.

THOMPSON COOPER, *rev.* ROBERT BROWN

Sources G. Anstruther, *The seminary priests*, 4 vols. (1969–77) · Gillow, *Lit. biog. hist.*

Craufurd, Sir Charles Gregan (**1761–1821**), army officer, was the second son of Sir Alexander Craufurd (*d.* 1797), of Newark, Ayrshire, who was created a baronet in 1781, and his wife, Jane (*d.* 1794), daughter of James Crokatt of Luxborough, Essex; he was the brother of Sir James Craufurd, baronet, who was British resident at Hamburg from 1798 to 1803, and afterwards minister-plenipotentiary at Copenhagen, and of Robert *Craufurd, the famous commander of the light division in the Peninsula. He was born on 12 February 1761, educated partly at Harrow School (1776), and entered the army as a cornet in the 1st dragoon guards on 15 December 1778. He was promoted lieutenant in 1781, and captain into the 2nd dragoon guards, or Queen's Bays, in 1785. In 1787 he was appointed an equerry to the duke of York, whose intimate friend he became. He studied his profession in Germany, obtained a good command of German, and translated into four large volumes, illustrated by numerous plates, J. G. Tielke's great work *Beytraege zur Kriegs-Kunst*, as *An account of some of the most remarkable events of the war between the Prussians, Austrians, and Russians, from 1756 to 1763: and a treatise on several branches of the military art*, which he completed with the assistance of his brother Robert, and published in 1787; it was his only publication.

Craufurd accompanied the duke of York to the Netherlands as aide-de-camp, and was attached to the Austrian headquarters as representative of the British commander-in-chief. With the Austrian staff he was at all the earlier battles of the war, including Neerwinden, Raismes,

Famars, Caesar's Camp, Landrecies, Roubaix, and Lannoy, and in May 1793 was promoted major for his services, and in February 1794 lieutenant-colonel. In the middle of 1794 he left the Austrian headquarters, and was appointed deputy adjutant-general to the British army. In this capacity he equally distinguished himself, especially by one daring charge, when, with only two squadrons of dragoons, he took three guns and 1000 prisoners. He had been so useful at the Austrian headquarters during the campaign that, in 1795, when the British army evacuated the continent, he was sent on a special mission back to the Austrian headquarters. He was an acute observer, and his reports (now in the Public Record Office) are valuable historical documents. Craufurd took part in the battles of Wetzlar, Altenkirchen, Nordlingen, Neumarkt, and finally Amberg, where he was so severely wounded in August 1796 that he was invalided home. His wound prevented him from undertaking further active service, but he was promoted colonel on 26 January 1797, and major-general on 25 September 1803. He was lieutenant-governor of Tynemouth and Cliff Fort from 1796 until his death, deputy quartermaster-general at the Horse Guards (1795–9), and colonel of the Rutland fencibles (1799). In 1801 he applied for and obtained a pension.

Craufurd was elected MP for the venal freeman borough of East Retford, Nottinghamshire, in October 1806; he owed his election to his marriage, on 7 February 1800, to Lady Anna Maria (1760–1834), youngest daughter of William *Stanhope, second earl of Harrington [*see under* Stanhope, William, first earl of Harrington], and widow of Thomas Pelham Clinton, third duke of Newcastle, which secured for him the great Newcastle influence. He supported the Grenville, Portland, and Perceval ministries. A still unsatisfied beneficiary of 'old corruption', he unsuccessfully requested in 1811 a governorship of the Royal Military College, and the governorship of Plymouth, and in 1812 a British peerage. He resigned his seat in 1812, after the fourth duke had come of age, and retired from public life. He was made colonel of the 2nd dragoon guards in 1807, promoted lieutenant-general on 25 July 1810, and was made a GCB on 27 May 1820, in the coronation honours. He was groom of the bedchamber to the duke of York (1813–16). He died at his seat, Ranby Hall, near Retford, Nottinghamshire, on 26 March 1821, and left no children. His wife, the dowager duchess of Newcastle, survived him by thirteen years.

H. M. STEPHENS, *rev.* ROGER T. STEARN

Sources Craufurd's dispatches, PRO, War Office MSS · HoP, *Commons* · J. Philippart, ed., *The royal military calendar*, 3 vols. (1815–16) · GEC, *Peerage* · Burke, *Peerage* · A. B. Rodger, *The war of the second coalition: 1798–1801, a strategic commentary* (1964) · T. C. W. Blanning, *The French revolutionary wars, 1787–1802* (1996) · A. J. Guy, ed., *The road to Waterloo: the British army and the struggle against revolutionary and Napoleonic France, 1793–1815* (1990)

Archives BL, letters to Lord Grenville and William Windham, Add. MSS 37874–37886, 59028 · Hants. RO, Wickham MSS · Morgan L., letters to Sir James Murray-Pulteney

Craufurd, James, Lord Ardmillan (**1805–1876**), judge, was born at Havant in Hampshire, the eldest son of Major

Archibald Clifford Blackwell Craufurd of Ardmillan, Ayrshire, and his wife, Jane, daughter of John Leslie. He was educated at the academy at Ayr, at the burgh school, Edinburgh, and at the universities of Glasgow and Edinburgh. In 1829 he passed his examination in Roman and Scots law, and became an advocate. He married in 1834 Theodosia (1813?–1883), daughter of James Balfour, who before her marriage was known as Beauty Balfour. She died on 29 December 1883.

Craufurd's progress at the bar was not at all rapid, but he nevertheless acquired a considerable criminal practice both in the court of justiciary and in the church courts. He never had much civil business, though he could address juries very effectively. On 14 March 1849 he became sheriff of Perthshire, and four years later, on 16 November 1853, he was appointed solicitor-general for Scotland under the administration of Lord Aberdeen. He was made a lord of the court of session on 10 January 1855, when he took the courtesy title of Lord Ardmillan, after the name of his paternal estate. On 16 June in the same year he was also appointed a lord of justiciary, and he held these two posts until his death. His speeches and other literary utterances were not great performances. His lectures to young men on ecclesiastical dogmas were open to hostile criticism, but bore the cardinal merit of sincerity and were not without literary polish. In the court of justiciary his speeches were effective and eloquent, thanks to his rather discursive study of English and Scottish poetry. The best remembered of his judgments is that which he delivered in connection with the Yelverton case, when, on 3 July 1862, acting as lord-ordinary of the outer house of session, he pronounced against the legality of the supposed marriage between Maria Theresa Longworth and Major William Charles Yelverton. Craufurd died of stomach cancer at his residence, 18 Charlotte Square, Edinburgh, on 7 September 1876. G. C. BOASE, rev. ERIC METCALFE

Sources Irving, *Scots.* · *The Scotsman* (8 Sept 1876), 5 · *Law Times* (16 Sept 1876), 344–5 · *The Times* (9 Sept 1876), 8 · *The Graphic* (23 Sept 1876), 308 · *ILN* (23 Sept 1876), 284 · *Journal of Jurisprudence*, 20 (1876), 538–9 · *CGPLA Eng. & Wales* (1876)
Likenesses portrait, repro. in *The Graphic*, 308 · wood-engraving (after photograph by J. Hasburgh), NPG; repro. in *ILN*
Wealth at death £10,844 16s. 7d.: confirmation, 17 Oct 1876, CCI

Craufurd, John Walkinshaw, of Craufurdland (1720/21–1793), army officer, was the son of John Craufurd (d. 10 Jan 1763), laird of Craufurdland, Ayrshire, and his first wife, Robina, heir of John Walkinshaw of Walkinshaw. He entered the army in 1741 as cornet in the north British dragoons, later the 2nd dragoons, the Royal Scots Greys, and was present at Dettingen in 1743, and Fontenoy in 1745, where he distinguished himself. Having been promoted to lieutenant, he returned to England in the summer of 1745 on sick leave. In August 1746 he accompanied his Jacobite friend, William Boyd, fourth earl of Kilmarnock, to the scaffold on Tower Hill, for which act of friendship his name, it was said, was placed at the bottom of the army list. During the years 1748–50 he spent a good deal of time in London, representing the interests of his friend William, seventeenth earl of Sutherland.

He subsequently served in North America during the Seven Years' War, with the rank of captain, and, it is said, was present at the capture of Quebec in 1759. He returned to England in the following year. The *Army List* for 1763 records a commission as major-commandant, dated 19 October 1761, and describes him as 'late of the 115th foot', about whom little is known. Presumably this regiment was raised for service in North America and then disbanded. He was subsequently placed on half pay. In 1772 he was promoted to the rank of lieutenant-colonel (*Army List* for 1772). In 1761 he was appointed his majesty's falconer for Scotland, and in 1762 he received the freedom of the city of Perth. He died, unmarried, in Edinburgh, on 19 February 1793. The estates to which he succeeded on the death of his father in 1763 he settled on Thomas Coutts, the London banker, but the deed was disputed by his aunt, Elizabeth Craufurd, the next heir, who died in 1802, aged ninety-seven. After a long litigation the case was finally decided in 1806 in favour of the natural heir, her daughter Elizabeth Houison Craufurd, twenty-second laird of Craufurdland, who died on 1 April 1823.

T. F. HENDERSON, rev. JONATHAN SPAIN

Sources Burke, *Gen. GB* (1952) · Irving, *Scots.* · J. Paterson, *History of the counties of Ayr and Wigton*, 3 (1866), 426–33 · *Archaeological and historical collections of Ayr and Wigtown, 1878–99*, Craufurdland MSS, 2.156–84 · *Army List* (1763) · *Army List* (1765) · *Army List* (1772) · *Scots Magazine*, 55 (1793), 102

Craufurd, Patrick [Peter], **of Auchenames** (c.1704–1778), politician and landowner, was the first surviving son of Patrick Craufurd (d. 1733), a wealthy Edinburgh merchant, and his second wife, Jean (d. 1740), daughter of Archibald Craufurd of Auchenames and Crosbie. The younger Patrick (or familiarly, Peter) Craufurd began life as a merchant like his father, and inherited a substantial fortune on the latter's death. About 1740 he married Elizabeth Middleton (d. 1746), daughter and coheir of George *Middleton of Errol, Perthshire, a London banker. By his marriage he acquired another fortune and a life interest in the estate of Errol, where he chiefly resided after his father-in-law's death in 1747. The couple had two sons, John (1742?–1814) and James (c.1744–1811). Elizabeth died on 19 July 1746, and on 22 April 1750 Craufurd married Sarah—also known as Sally—Sempill (d. 1751), eldest daughter of Hew, twelfth Baron Sempill. This marriage produced one daughter, Sarah (1751?–1796), before the elder Sarah's death on 25 April 1751.

For much of his life Craufurd appears to have been a good-hearted and colourful, if rather naïve, individual. While James Boswell described him as 'a very honest and a very generous man' (*Boswell's London Journal*, 9 Jan 1763, 130), Lord Eglinton wrote of him in 1760, when Craufurd was in his mid-fifties:

[he] is drinking, hunting and whoring *com un possede*. I am an eye witness to the drinking, an ear witness to the whoring, and as he has just bought a terrier from a tailor in Ayr I can make no doubt he intends to commence foxhunter. Lord have mercy upon what Peter will cut flying over a five bar gate, with his flowing bob, jackboot, holster, bit and housing. (Eglinton to Bute, 26 Jan 1760, Bute MS 134/1)

Craufurd had no compunction about using his wealth to

help forge a political career. In 1740 he was adopted as opposition candidate for Ayrshire, and was elected in 1741, following a contest. In 1747 he was re-elected without a contest, but in 1754 faced serious opposition from James Mure Campbell, Lord Loudoun's cousin, and from Archibald Montgomerie, brother of the tenth earl of Eglinton. Despite using bribery on a massive scale Craufurd was eventually forced to join Eglinton in a coalition, but still suffered defeat when the duke of Argyll and the ministry threw their full support behind Campbell.

Out of parliament Craufurd divided his time between Scotland and London, where, through his close friend William Mure of Caldwell—to whose judgement he deferred throughout his political life—he became connected with the Bute circle. In 1758, with Bute's support, Mure proposed Craufurd as candidate for Ayr burghs; Argyll regarded Bute's intervention as a challenge to his own authority as 'manager' of Scotland and a bitter quarrel resulted. Argyll used his interest against Craufurd, whose campaign, despite the use of extensive bribery again, appeared to be doomed. However, the accession of George III in October 1760 tipped the scales in Bute's favour, forcing Argyll to negotiate a series of electoral compromises that included Craufurd's return as MP in 1761, albeit for Renfrewshire rather than Ayr burghs.

In parliament, while relying on Mure for advice on Scottish affairs, Craufurd faithfully supported the Bute and subsequent administrations, with the exception of that of Rockingham, who listed Craufurd as 'doubtful'. Craufurd disapproved of but did not oppose the window tax, and, while supporting the creation of a Scottish militia, felt that this should not happen until it could form part of a unified British militia.

Notwithstanding his own unruly behaviour, Craufurd was a thrifty man as regards his own fortune and estates, and deplored what he perceived as the profligate behaviour and extravagance of his sons: despite his evident affection for his elder son, John, he repeatedly quarrelled with him over financial matters. In 1766, to protect the Errol estate, Craufurd took out an inhibition against John, requiring him to entail the estate and prohibiting anyone from lending to him. A reconciliation followed, whereby the Errol revenues were made over to John, who in return assisted his father in his campaign for the 1768 general election. Craufurd's hold on Renfrewshire was insecure: his only residence there was the ruined castle of Auchenames and he was regarded as an Ayrshireman. He prepared for an expensive campaign, but when two opponents challenged him he seems to have handed over the management of the election entirely to John. After prolonged negotiations he stood down and gave his interest to William MacDowall, on condition that John should be the candidate at the next general election.

Thereafter Craufurd lived mainly in Edinburgh and in Bath. In 1771 he put John in possession of the Errol estate but later once again became increasingly and obsessively anxious about the need to provide safeguards in the form of an entail. He insisted on John's entailing his estates along with Craufurd's own, a step which John said 'I know

I shall repent all the rest of my life' and begged Mure to assist him in undoing (Mure, 2.217). He was successful, but at the cost of another rift with his father. It was reported by David Hume in 1774 that Craufurd 'wanted nothing from you [John] except your friendship which he was sorry he could not obtain and it was the circumstance that embittered his remaining days' (*Letters*, 2.283–4). Hume's intervention nevertheless seems to have healed the breach, and Craufurd, despite failing powers, assisted John at the 1774 general election. Patrick Craufurd died in Edinburgh on 10 January 1778.   ANDREW M. LANG

Sources E. Haden-Guest, 'Craufurd, Patrick', HoP, *Commons* · [W. Mure], ed., *Selections from the family papers preserved at Caldwell*, 3 vols., Maitland Club, 71 (1854) · *Boswell's London journal, 1762–63*, ed. F. A. Pottle (1950), vol. 1 of *The Yale editions of the private papers of James Boswell*, trade edn (1950–89) · A. Murdoch, *'The people above': politics and administration in mid-eighteenth-century Scotland* (1980) · *Scots Magazine*, 8 (1746), 350 · *Scots Magazine*, 12 (1750), 205 · *Scots Magazine*, 40 (1778), 53 · J. Foster, *Members of parliament, Scotland … 1357–1882*, 2nd edn (privately printed, London, 1882) · *Scots peerage* · Burke, *Peerage* (1921) · Anderson, *Scot. nat.* · *The letters of David Hume*, ed. J. Y. T. Greig, 2 vols. (1932) · Mount Stuart Trust, Isle of Bute, Bute MS 134/1

Craufurd, Quintin (1743–1819), author and friend of the French royal family, was born on 22 September 1743 at Kilwinning in Ayrshire, the second son of Quintin Craufurd of Newark (d. 1749), justiciary baillie for the west seas of Scotland, and his wife, Ann, daughter of James Robinson of Irvine. He was taught arithmetic and bookkeeping in Edinburgh to qualify him for the East India Company's service, in which he became a writer on the Madras establishment in September 1760.

Soon after arriving in India in September 1761, Craufurd went on the expedition that captured the Spanish settlement at Manila in the Philippines in the following year. He remained at Manila for a time after the withdrawal of the British forces before returning to Madras and taking up an appointment further along the coast at Masulipatam, where he stayed until 1773. In 1765 Masulipatam became the administrative centre of the territory ceded to the East India Company known as the Northern Circars. Company servants posted there were able to extract money for themselves from those paying the tribute due to the company. It is likely that Craufurd made the most of his opportunities at Masulipatam; he was later to be accused of having taken over £15,000 in a single year.

In 1773 Craufurd returned to Britain on leave, being reappointed to India as second in charge of Masulipatam in 1775. By then his financial interests seem to have shifted to the notorious loans being made at high rates of interest to the British satellite ruler of the south-east coast of India, Muhammad Ali, the nawab of the Carnatic. Craufurd gave up his post at Masulipatam to remain at Madras, where he was actively involved in devising a settlement to safeguard the interests of the creditors. In 1780, on grounds of ill health, he left India for the last time. By then he was reputed to have made a large fortune, although he continued to press for repayment of money by the nawab.

Craufurd returned to Europe with (Anna) Eleonora, *née*

Franchi (c.1750–1833), the daughter of a Tuscan tailor. She was a dancer and trapeze artist who, at a young age and after a brief marriage to the dancer Martini, had become the mistress of Duke Carl-Eugen of Württemberg, with whom she had two children, a son who died in 1793 and a daughter, Eleonore, who were ennobled under the name of de Franquemont. A French diplomat had then brought her to Paris, where she married Mr Sullivan, an Irishman. She had accompanied Sullivan to India in search of a fortune, and it was there that she was introduced to Craufurd. Eleonora's striking looks and her knowledge of Europe proved deeply attractive to Craufurd, for whom she agreed to keep house, though she retained the name of Sullivan.

After a stay in England the couple visited the United Provinces, Germany, and Italy, finally settling in Paris in 1783 at the Hôtel Rouillé d'Orfeuil, 18 rue de Clichy, where they installed an impressive collection of paintings and sculpture acquired in Italy. A salon formed around Mme Sullivan, who was described as 'une belle brune fort opulente, aux yeux d'onyx, aux traits délicats et au teint frais' (Dard, 23). Craufurd took advantage of the climate of Anglophilia that pervaded Parisian society. His aristocratic bearing, his knowledge, his taste, and his wealth opened many doors. He lent money to Talleyrand and others. He made frequent visits to London, and the plausible suggestion that he was also a British spy has been made but not substantiated. He was introduced to Queen Marie Antoinette by his friend Lord Strathavon, later the marquess of Huntly, with whom the queen practised Scottish dances.

The outbreak of the French Revolution had two consequences for Craufurd. First, the queen's intimate friend the Swedish nobleman Count Axel Fersen became the lover of Mme Sullivan, perhaps to deflect attention from his relationship with the queen. Second, they and Craufurd formed an alliance to save the queen and the royal family. Fersen's diary for the period prior to 11 June 1791 has been lost, but it is known that he borrowed 300,000 livres from Mme Sullivan in order to prepare the flight of the royal family to Varennes. He paid interest of 6 per cent on the loan, the sum of which was reimbursed by Louis XVIII at the restoration. Much of the money went on the purchase of the large and ostentatious berlin which was kept in the courtyard of Craufurd's house for use on the fateful journey to Varennes. Craufurd left for England on 17 June, bearing to safety a sum of money belonging to Louis XVI. After the failure of the flight to Varennes, Craufurd joined Fersen in Brussels, whence he returned to London to seek William Pitt's support for a military intervention in Normandy. After failing in his mission, he went to Paris in December 1791 and was immediately received in secret by Marie Antoinette at the Tuileries. Craufurd later proposed to the queen that she should leave France with the dauphin, but she refused. With the approach of war between France and the emperor in April 1792, Craufurd and Mme Sullivan resolved to depart, placing their Parisian residence in the safekeeping of one of her friends.

Craufurd took leave of Marie Antoinette on 14 April, again at a secret meeting at the Tuileries. He never saw her again, though he remained one of her channels of communication with the outside world.

In Brussels the pair, reunited with Fersen, watched the depressing unfolding of events in Paris. With the French invasion of the Austrian Netherlands, they fled to Düsseldorf, where they learned of the execution of Louis XVI a few weeks later. Lord Auckland was British ambassador to the Netherlands, and during February–May 1793 Craufurd kept him informed from Düsseldorf about the intentions and decisions of the émigrés and the planned movements of Austrian troops. With the recapture of the Netherlands by Austrian troops, Fersen and Craufurd hoped, in August 1793, to save the queen by means of a financial arrangement with Danton. Craufurd and Mme Sullivan went to London in order to raise the necessary funds. The trial and execution of the queen on 16 October dashed their hopes and broke up the trio. Mme Sullivan wished to leave Craufurd and to live with Fersen. Craufurd, by now British commissioner with the Austrian troops, resented Fersen's presence. With the second return of French troops to Brussels, the trio moved to Frankfurt in October 1794. Fersen finally returned to Sweden in 1795. That Craufurd could have been ignorant for many years of the liaison between Eleonora Sullivan and Fersen is difficult to believe, yet he claimed to have learned of it only at this time, through opening a letter destined for the count. He broke with Fersen but not with Mme Sullivan.

On 21 May 1799 Craufurd sent a request to the Directory asking to be crossed off the list of émigrés, on which his name had been placed in 1793. The Directory refused, and he was not allowed to return to France until 1802. Between those dates he was living in Vienna, where he saw a great deal of the prince de Ligne and of a French émigré, the former intendant and writer Sénac de Meilhan. It was Sénac who gave the manuscript of the memoirs of Mme de Pompadour's lady-in-waiting Mme du Hausset to Craufurd, who published them in 1809. With the signing of the treaty of Amiens in March 1802 Craufurd was allowed to return to Paris. The house in the rue de Clichy had been destroyed, and he filed a request for the return of its furniture and works of art, which had been confiscated. He finally married Mme Sullivan in three ceremonies: a civil marriage at the municipality of Paris, an Anglican wedding in the chapel of the reopened British embassy, and a Catholic marriage in the church of St Germain-en-Laye. After the 18 Brumaire Mme Craufurd's daughter and son-in-law, the comte and the comtesse d'Orsay, joined the couple in Paris in a splendid house, the Hôtel de Matignon (now the residence of French prime ministers), in the rue de Varennes. In 1801 the comtesse d'Orsay gave birth to a son, Alfred *d'Orsay, later the celebrated dandy, and in the following year to a daughter, Ida, who later married the duc de Guiche and was the mother of Napoleon III's penultimate and fatal foreign minister, the duc de Gramont.

Craufurd's return to France did not mark the end of his difficulties during the consulate and the empire. Within a year war broke out again with England, and British citizens in France were considered prisoners of war. In addition to his acquired family, Craufurd was also surrounded by his own relatives: his brother George, who had been consul in Holland, and four of his nephews, the sons of his elder brother, Sir Alexander Craufurd, bt (*d.* 1797), including Sir James Craufurd (1761–1839), who had been British minister in Copenhagen. Thanks to his old and close friendship with the now powerful Talleyrand, Quintin Craufurd was able to get his relatives out of France, while staying there himself, despite his wife's penchant for counter-revolutionary intrigue. In 1806 Talleyrand was ordered by Napoleon to negotiate with Charles James Fox, and he used the good offices of Craufurd, who entertained Fox's envoys lords Yarmouth and Lauderdale. In January 1808 Craufurd exchanged the Hôtel de Matignon for Talleyrand's residence at 21 rue d'Anjou, but a year later the minister fell from favour and had to borrow 200,000 francs from his friend. Napoleon distrusted Craufurd despite the latter's friendship with the Empress Josephine. Under the empire Craufurd never succeeded in recovering his works of art, many of which adorned ministerial offices. He slowly constituted another collection.

The restoration of the Bourbons was Craufurd's salvation. In 1815 he obtained an indemnity of 1,344,000 francs for the loss of his house and his collections and in return for the financial aid which he and his wife had given to the royal family. On 21 January 1816 two Italian paintings from the ministry of justice were returned to him. Despite their dwindling resources, the Craufurds had continued to live in great style. He may still have had investments in Jamaica. Mme Craufurd, now almost spherical in shape, was a familiar sight at great receptions, wearing a jet-black wig covered in diamonds. Craufurd's last years were troubled by the conduct of his nephew Sir James Craufurd. The diplomat sought to prevent his uncle's fortune from falling into the hands of Mme Craufurd. His initial recourse to the courts having proved unsuccessful, Sir James became belligerent, and his conduct led to an order for his expulsion from France in 1818. This was not carried out. The following year Sir James tried to break into Craufurd's residence in the rue d'Anjou, only to be arrested and sentenced to six months' imprisonment. He also threatened to expose the murky links between Louis XVIII and Robespierre.

Quintin Craufurd died in his house on 23 November 1819. His widow sold the library and the art collections and offered part of the house to let to, among others, Lord and Lady Blessington. On 18 January 1821 Sir James Craufurd was finally expelled from France. Mme Craufurd continued to hold her salon, albeit in reduced circumstances. She died at the age of eighty-three or eighty-four on 14 September 1833. Her daughter had died in 1829, and her closest relatives were Alfred d'Orsay and the duchesse de Gramont. Her papers appear to have been destroyed and with them much of the secret history of Marie Antoinette and of the attempts to save her.

No account of Quintin Craufurd would be complete without a mention of his writings. He had produced his *Sketches chiefly relating to the history, religion, learning and manners of the Hindoos, with a concise account of the present state of the native powers of Hindostan* in London in 1790, and he reverted to the subject of India towards the end of his life with his *Researches Concerning the Laws, Theology, Learning, Commerce, etc. of Ancient and Modern India*, published in two volumes in 1817. It was during his stay in Vienna and under the influence of Sénac de Meilhan that his literary talents developed. He wrote in French, and his *Essais sur la littérature française*, which he published in Paris in 1803, were a paean to that language, which he regarded as the most concise of all. He published an essay on Jonathan Swift with the aim, so he wrote to the countess of Albany, 'de faire mieux apprécier cet homme célèbre' (letter of 15 Dec 1808, Bibliothèque Municipale de Montpellier, MSS 62, A 20 (4)). On Craufurd, Sénac de Meilhan's verdict may serve as an epitaph:

> Il a l'esprit juste et en même temps actif et étendu; il joint à de profondes connaissances dans la littérature anglaise et française, le goût qui est plus rare que la science. Son cœur est généreux et sensible. Ses manières sont simples et polies. Il sait écouter avec intelligence, et ces diverses qualités l'ont rendu cher aux pays qu'il a parcourus. (Dard, 88–9)

J. M. J. ROGISTER

Sources DNB · Archives Nationale, Paris, F 7 5879 (Craufurd file); BB 17A 1; BB 18 9994, dossier 523 · Bibliothèque Municipale de Montpellier, MSS of the countess of Albany, MSS 62, A 20 (4) · BL, Auckland MSS, Add. MSS 34448–34449, 34451, 34462 · BL, Hardwicke MSS, Add. MS 35652 · [Q. Craufurd], *Mélanges, d'histoire, de littérature, etc., tirés d'un porte-feuille* (Paris, 1809) · GEC, *Baronetage* · J.-F. Barrière, 'Notice sur M. Craufurd', in J.-F. Barrière, *Bibliothèque des mémoires relatifs à l'histoire de France*, ed. A. de Lescure, 31 vols. (Paris, 1846–81), vol. 3, pp. 17–32 · E. Dard, *Un rival de Fersen: Quintin Craufurd* (Paris, 1947) · H. A. Barton, *Count Hans Axel Fersen: aristocrat in an age of revolution* (Boston, 1975) · W. Connely, *Count d'Orsay: the dandy of dandies* (1952)
Archives Archives Nationales, Paris, F 7 5879; BB 17A 1; BB 18 9994 | BL, Auckland MSS, Add. MSS 34448–34449, 34451, 34462 · BL, letters to Lord Grenville, Add. MS 59028 · BL, Hardwicke papers, Add. MS 35652 · CKS, letters to duke of Dorset

Craufurd, Robert (1764–1812), army officer, third son of Sir Alexander Craufurd, first baronet (*d.* 1797), of Newark, Ayrshire, and his wife, Jane Crokatt (*d.* 1794), and brother of General Sir Charles Gregan *Craufurd, was born on 5 May 1764 at Newark Castle, near Ayr. He was educated at Harrow School (1779), and later at Göttingen University (1787). He entered the army as an ensign in the 25th regiment in 1779, was promoted lieutenant in 1781, and captain into the 75th regiment in 1783. He served with this unit in India in Lord Cornwallis's campaigns against Tipu Sultan between 1790 and 1792, establishing a reputation as a good regimental officer.

On his return to Europe, Craufurd joined his brother Charles, Britain's representative at the Austrian headquarters, remaining there after Charles was severely wounded. He returned to England in December 1797 and was promoted lieutenant-colonel. In 1798 he was appointed deputy quartermaster-general in Ireland, and his services during the suppression of the uprising there, especially his contribution to the operations against General Humbert's French corps, were praised by General Lake. In

1799 he acted as Britain's military attaché to General Suvorov's headquarters during his campaign in Switzerland. He served on the staff in the expedition to The Helder in the Netherlands. On 6 February 1800 he married Mary Frances Holland (d. 1842), daughter of the architect Henry Holland of Hans Place, Chelsea, London. They had three sons and a daughter. In 1802 he was elected MP for East Retford in Nottinghamshire through the influence of his brother Charles, who had married the dowager duchess of Newcastle (whose family owned the borough).

Craufurd was promoted colonel on 30 October 1805 and gave up his seat in 1806 in the hope of going on active service. In 1807 he was sent to South America under General Whitelocke, and he took command of a light brigade, consisting of a battalion of the 95th rifle regiment and the light companies of several other battalions. His brigade led the advance upon Buenos Aires and, in the attack on the city, achieved its objectives. However, on orders from Whitelocke, he halted and surrendered with the rest of the army. During this expedition he acquired a reputation as a leader of light troops and, in October 1807, sailed with Sir David Baird for the Iberian peninsula at the head of a light brigade. Baird's corps joined Sir John Moore's army at Mayorga on 20 December, and Craufurd's command was repeatedly engaged, especially at Castro Gonzalo on the 28th. On 31 December the light division was ordered to leave the main army for Vigo, where it embarked for England.

In 1809 Craufurd returned to the Peninsula, with the rank of brigadier-general, to take command of a light brigade consisting of the 43rd, 52nd, and one battalion of the 95th regiment. While on his way to join the army of Sir Arthur Wellesley (later the duke of Wellington), he heard rumours that a great battle had been fought at Talavera on 27–28 July and that Wellesley had been killed. He hurried forward and reached Talavera on the day after the battle, having covered 62 miles in 26 hours in heavy fighting order. This truly remarkable forced march was but one of many brilliant feats which, under Craufurd's leadership, his soldiers performed over the next thirty months of the Peninsular War. In early 1810 Wellesley (now Viscount Wellington) reorganized his army; Craufurd's old light brigade became the core of a new 'light division', which, under his command, played a particularly prominent role in the operations along the Coa, at the battle of Busaco, and in Wellington's retreat to the lines of the Torres Vedras. Craufurd's headstrong nature occasionally got him into trouble. His imprudent decision to risk an engagement on the Coa on 24 July 1810, for instance, led to Wellington rebuking him for getting his outposts embroiled in 'foolish affairs'. Nevertheless, Craufurd was so valuable a subordinate that Wellington tended to turn a blind eye to his intermittent rashness, contenting himself with the odd caustic comment. Such was Craufurd's sense of self-assurance, however, that even these mild censures were seen by him as evidence that Wellington could be 'damned crusty'.

When the army went into winter quarters in the lines of the Torres Vedras, Craufurd went home to Britain on leave. During his absence the light division was commanded, to poor effect, by Sir William Erskine; and, on Craufurd's return to the army on the very morning of the battle of Fuentes d'Oñoro on 5 May 1811, he was greeted with ringing cheers by his soldiers. In the fighting the light division again played a distinguished part, covering the change of front which Wellington found it necessary to make when outflanked by the French.

Craufurd was promoted major-general on 4 June 1811 and, in the siege of Ciudad Rodrigo the following winter, led the light division in the attack on the smaller breach when the fortress was stormed on 19 January. At the very beginning of the assault he was mortally wounded in the abdomen, lingering in great agony until 24 January. He was buried in the breach itself. His death was marked by tributes in both houses of parliament, and, at public expense, a monument was erected to him and General Mackinnon, who was killed in the same siege, in St Paul's Cathedral, London.

Craufurd was unquestionably the finest commander of light troops who served in the Peninsula. Many of the men who fought under him had been trained at Shorncliffe camp, where Sir John Moore and his assistants had taken a paternalistic, enlightened approach to the question of discipline, believing that this motivated soldiers far better and was essential for the production of skirmishers who could function without the physical and mental constraints of orthodox tactical drills. Indeed, this ethos was to slowly percolate throughout the service and eventually become a hallmark of the British army. Craufurd, however, was very much a product of the attitudes that dominated military life throughout the eighteenth century and for much of the nineteenth. Placing order above all else, he flogged his units into obedience, ensuring that they were more afraid of their officers than of any foe. While many of his contemporaries had identical attitudes, 'Black Bob' (as he was known) stands out as a particularly fearsome martinet, both as a soldier and a man. As his friend George Napier concluded:

Brilliant as some of the traits of his character were, and notwithstanding the good and generous feelings which often burst forth like a bright gleam of sunshine from behind a dark and heavy cloud, still there was a sullenness which seemed to brood in his innermost soul and generate passions which knew no bounds. (Napier, 225)

H. M. STEPHENS, rev. DAVID GATES

Sources A. H. Craufurd, *General Craufurd and his light division* (1891) · J. W. Cole, *Memoirs of British generals distinguished during the Peninsular War*, 1 (1856) · D. Gates, *The British light infantry arm, c.1790–1815* (1987) · *Correspondence of Charles, first Marquis Cornwallis*, ed. C. Ross, 3 vols. (1859), vol. 2 · W. Cope, *The history of the rifle brigade* (1877) · G. Simmons, *A British rifle man*, ed. W. W. C. Verner (1899) · E. Costello, *The adventures of a soldier* (1841) · W. Surtees, *Twenty-five years in the rifle brigade* (1833) · *Supplementary despatches (correspondence) and memoranda of Field Marshal Arthur, duke of Wellington*, ed. A. R. Wellesley, second duke of Wellington, 15 vols. (1858–72), vol. 6 · *The Croker papers: the correspondence and diaries of … John Wilson Croker*, ed. L. J. Jennings, 1 (1884) · G. T. Napier, *Passages in the early military life of General Sir George T. Napier: written by* *himself*, ed. W. C. E. Napier (1884) • Burke, *Peerage* (1959) • P. A. Symonds and R. G. Thorne, 'Craufurd, Robert', HoP, *Commons*

Archives BL, corresp., Add. MSS 69440–69441 | BL, letters to Lord Grenville, Add. MS 59028 • BL, letters to William Windham, Add. MSS 37882–37890 • Hants. RO, corresp. with William Wickham • PRO, intelligence reports to Galbraith Lowry Cole, PRO 30/43/52

Likenesses bust

Craufurd [Crawfurd], **Thomas** (*d.* 1662), university teacher and historian, was educated at St Leonard's College in the University of St Andrews, where he matriculated in 1618 and graduated MA in 1621. In 1625 he was an unsuccessful candidate for the professorship of philosophy in the University of Edinburgh, but following a public examination on 27 March 1626 he was inducted professor of humanity on 29 March. He left this post following his appointment by the town council of Edinburgh on 26 February 1630 as rector of the high school. In 1633 he assisted John Adamson, principal of the university, and William Drummond of Hawthornden in devising the pageants and composing the speeches and verses used to celebrate Charles I's visit to Scotland for his coronation. These were published as *Musarum Edinensium in Caroli regis ingressu in Scotiam* (1633).

Craufurd returned to the university on 30 December 1640 following his election as public professor of mathematics, and on 6 January 1641 he was made one of the regents of philosophy at a combined salary of 600 merks. In a document in the university library he is styled 'a grammarian and philosopher, likewise profoundly skilled in theology, and a man of the greatest piety and integrity' (*DNB*). On 8 April 1650 he was made an Edinburgh burgess and guild member by act of the city council. He continued to teach at the university during the wars of the 1640s and 1650s until his death, which probably occurred in November 1662. He was buried on 1 December in Greyfriars churchyard, Edinburgh, where a son, Thomas, had also been interred, on 19 June 1659. His widow, Margaret Pearson, was buried there on 7 November 1688.

Several historical works by Craufurd were published posthumously. *Locorum nominum propriorum gentilitium vocumque difficiliorum, quae in Latinis Scotorum historiis occurrunt, explicatio vernacula* (1665) was edited with additions and emendations by C. Irvine. *Notes and Observations on Mr. George Buchanan's 'History of Scotland'* was published in 1708 from a manuscript in the Advocates' Library. However, his most famous work did not appear until 1808: *History of the University of Edinburgh from 1580 to 1646* was taken from a transcript in the university made by Matthew Crawford from the original then in the hands of Professor Laurence Dundas of the university. His annalistic approach was later continued by Andrew Dalzell in his *History of the University of Edinburgh from its Foundation* (1862).   T. F. HENDERSON, *rev.* STUART HANDLEY

Sources T. Craufurd, *History of the University of Edinburgh from 1580 to 1646* (1808) • A. Dalzel, *History of the University of Edinburgh from its foundation*, 2 vols. (1862) • H. Paton, ed., *Register of interments in the Greyfriars burying-ground, Edinburgh, 1658–1700*, Scottish RS, 26 (1902), 150 • C. B. B. Watson, ed., *Roll of Edinburgh burgesses and guild-*

brethren, 1406–1700, Scottish RS, 59 (1929), 130 • D. B. Horn, *A short history of the University of Edinburgh, 1556–1889* (1967)

Craven. For this title name *see* individual entries under Craven; *see also* Elizabeth, margravine of Brandenburg-Ansbach-Bayreuth [Elizabeth Craven, Lady Craven] (1750–1828); Brunton, Louisa, countess of Craven (1782x5–1860).

Craven, Abigail. *See* Watson, Abigail (1685–1752).

Craven, Charles (1682–1754), colonial governor, was born on 6 May 1682, a younger son of William Craven, Baron Craven of Combe Abbey (*d.* 1695), and his wife, Margaret Clapham (*d.* 1711). His father was one of the original eight lords proprietors of Carolina and his older brother Sir William Craven (1668–1711) inherited his father's title and share of the Carolina proprietary.

The family share in the Carolina proprietary probably aided Charles to secure the appointment of deputy governor in February 1711. He arrived at Charles Town in March 1712 and held office until April 1716. Despite considerable political trials and a devastating war with local American Indians called the Yemassee War, Governor Craven was recognized as one of the best proprietary-era governors. He worked constructively with a contentious Commons house of assembly to enact important local legislation. The Reception Act of 1712 integrated English statutes and common law into the Carolina legal system, and election laws expanded the authority of the colonial general assembly. Craven's chief contribution was his leadership during the Yemassee War. Hard pressed by traders' debts, threats of enslavement, and settlers' encroachments, south-eastern American Indian tribes, led by the Yemassee, launched simultaneous attacks on 15 April 1715 against South Carolinians. Craven led the Carolinian militia during the first critical year of the conflict. The Yemassee War threatened the survival of the European colony but after one year it diminished into isolated skirmishes that continued for the remainder of the decade.

Despite his local successes Craven clashed with the proprietors in England. A pro-proprietary faction in Carolina, led by Nicholas Trott, laboured to undermine his authority at home and in England. In April 1716 Craven left the province to address in person the proprietors' complaints. He appointed Robert Daniell acting governor, with the intention of returning to Carolina and resuming his post. However, he never returned to the province and died in Berkshire on 26 December 1754.   ALEXANDER MOORE

Sources J. W. Raimo, 'Charles Craven', *Biographical directory of American colonial and revolutionary governors, 1607–1789* (1980) • J. A. Moore, 'Royalizing South Carolina: the revolution of 1719 and the evolution of early South Carolina government', PhD diss., University of South Carolina, 1991 • A. Collins, *The peerage of England: containing a genealogical and historical account of all the peers of England*, vol. 3

Craven, Elizabeth. *See* Elizabeth, margravine of Brandenburg-Ansbach-Bayreuth (1750–1828).

Craven, Hawes (1837–1910), scene painter, was born Henry Hawes Craven Green on 3 July 1837 at Kirkgate, Leeds. His parents, James Green (*d.* 1881), a comedian, and Eliza

Hawes Craven (1837–1910), by Henry van der Weyde, c.1890

S. Craven *Green (1802/3–1866), an actress and, later, a poet, were performers on the York circuit. Young Henry acted with his father, and shortened his name to Hawes Craven. In his youth he was also a keen observer and recordist of nature. Fascinated by scene painting, Craven attended the Government School of Design in London from 1851 to 1853 where he won many prizes. Apprenticed in 1853 to John Gray, scene-painter of the Britannia Theatre, Hoxton, London, he later moved with his master to the Olympic. In 1857 Craven had his first success. Gray had rheumatic fever, so Craven was asked to provide the Eddystone lighthouse set for Wilkie Collins's *The Lighthouse* (not Collins's *The Frozen Deep*, as most obituaries state). He worked from a painting by the noted seascape artist Clarkson Stanfield, so accurately that, in reward, Stanfield gave him his original and the Olympic raised his salary. Later (1867–75) Craven exhibited seven seapieces at the Suffolk Street Galleries, London.

In the late 1850s and early 1860s, Craven assisted William Roxby Beverley, the great transformation-scene exponent, on Drury Lane pantomimes and Covent Garden opera seasons. From 1862 to 1864 he was principal scene-painter for Dublin's Theatre Royal, where, according to Percy Fitzgerald, an eyewitness, his work possessed all 'the breadth and effect of rich water-colour drawings somewhat of the Prout school'. In the summer vacation of 1863 and again in 1864 he worked for Charles Fechter at the Lyceum on some elaborate set scenes, after the new mode of mounting plays which Fechter inaugurated.

From Dublin, Craven passed successively in London to the Olympic (under Horace Wigan), where he distinguished himself by his scenery for *The Frozen Deep* (October 1864), and to the Adelphi (under Benjamin Webster). He soon increased his reputation by his work for *Play* and *School*, both produced at the Prince of Wales's Theatre (15 February 1868, and January 1869), and by *The Enchanted Isle*

in the Covent Garden pantomime *Robinson Crusoe* (December 1868). On 3 June 1866 Craven married a principal dancer, Mary Elizabeth Watson Tees (1838–1891), daughter of Alexander Tees, a civil servant; they had three sons and three daughters.

From 1871 to 1901 Craven was principal scene-painter to the Lyceum, first under 'Colonel' H. L. Bateman, then his widow (1875–8), and finally under Henry Irving (1878 to 1899, when Irving sold the Lyceum rights). In Craven's early years the theatre employed him; latterly he was freelance and rented the Lyceum's paintshop. Irving was key to this theatre's success, with Craven creating many of his plays' settings. In the first season Leopold Lewis's *The Bells* (1871), with its vision scene, was a triumph for both, and the work went to Sandringham for Queen Victoria (29 April 1889), with Craven painting 'scenery of suitable size' (Stoker, 375) for its drawing-room. In 1874 and 1878 Craven set Irving's two productions of *Hamlet*. *The Merchant of Venice* (1879), created with the scene-painters William Telbin and Walter Hann, was an 'artistic display which will never be seen again' (Darbyshire, 101–2). The 'unparalled beauty' of *Romeo and Juliet* (1882) 'not even the sternest critic disputed' (Irving, 386), though Clement Scott did find settings and lighting 'all beautiful enough, but they are a trying background for the central figures' (Booth, 55).

Irving believed in restraint, harmony, and archaeological accuracy, so would invite other artists to oversee plays' designs: Craven solved the problems of realization. The journal editor and architect Sir James Knowles supervised Tennyson's *The Cup* (1881); the book illustrator and landscape painter Keeley Halswelle, *Macbeth* (1888); the genre painter John Seymour Lucas, *Henry VIII* (1892); Ford Madox Brown, *King Lear* (1892); Sir Edward Burne-Jones, *King Arthur* (1895), by Wills and Comyns Carr; and Sir Lawrence Alma-Tadema, *Cymbeline* (1895) and *Coriolanus* (1901). For *The Cup*'s temple of Artemis, Craven created 'a speciousness of proportion' (Terry, 154), while *King Arthur*'s pastoral scenes were of such 'transcendent beauty' (Stoker, 165) that Ellen Terry recalled Craven painting 'the flicker of golden sunlight ... better than anyone' (*Daily Telegraph*, 27 July 1910). Craven varied his style in keeping with the lighting at the various theatres in which he worked. For example, the Lyceum used subtly controlled gas and there Craven's sunset, fading over Martha's three-dimensional garden in Nuremberg, provided in 1886 'one of the most beautiful' scenes in Wills's *Faust* (Booth, 110). By contrast, he adapted his technique for the electric-lit Savoy and Royal English Opera, where he worked on six Gilbert and Sullivan operettas (1884–93) and Sullivan's opera *Ivanhoe* (1891) respectively. At Her Majesty's, also lit electrically, Craven produced sets for Herbert Beerbohm Tree's sumptuous Shakespearian productions, and, for Stephen Phillips's *Ulysses* (1902), Craven 'used black velvet ... to paint on with striking effect' (*South Eastern Herald*, 27 July 1910) in his creation of Hades.

Craven worked for over fifty years, and was remarkable for his Yorkshire grit, his care, his unflappability, and his good nature. Some design sketches are preserved in the

Victoria and Albert and the Theatre museums, and an act drop at Craig-y-nos Castle, Brecknockshire. However, on 18 February 1898 the sets of over forty productions were burnt in Irving's Southwark scene-store fire. In 1905 Craven was appointed president of the Scenic Artists' Association. He died of acute bronchitis at his home, Fairlight, 246 Brockley Road, Brockley, London, on 22 July 1910 and was buried in Brockley protestant cemetery. Newspapers widely reported his death. The *Manchester Guardian* suggested Craven was 'the greatest scene-painter' (27 July 1910); certainly he was the equal of William Telbin and the younger Joseph Harker. His 'scenes were real pictures, with the atmosphere and charm of fine paintings' (*The Standard*, 27 July 1910).

[ANON.], *rev.* RAYMOND INGRAM

Sources B. Stoker, *Personal reminiscences of Henry Irving*, 2 vols. (1907) • A. E. Wilson, *The Lyceum* (1952) • M. R. Booth, *Victorian spectacular theatre, 1850–1910* (1981) • L. Irving, *Henry Irving: the actor and his world* (1951) • E. Terry, *Memoirs* (1933) • S. Rosenfeld, *A short history of scene design in Great Britain* (1973) • D. Castle, 'Sensation' Smith of Drury Lane (1984) • R. Manvell, *Ellen Terry* (1968) • A. Darbyshire, *The art of the Victorian stage* (1907) • 'Famous scenic artists: Hawes Craven', *The Era* (8 Oct 1904) • G. Rowell, *The Victorian theatre, 1792–1914* (1978) • R. Mander and J. Mitchenson, *Gilbert and Sullivan* (1962) • *Evening News* (25 July 1910) • *Daily Telegraph* (27 July 1910) • *South Eastern Herald* (27 July 1910) • *The Standard* (27 July 1910) • b. cert. • m. cert. • d. cert.
Archives Theatre Museum, London, autograph, letter, and notes on scenery
Likenesses H. van der Weyde, photograph, *c*.1890, Theatre Museum, London [*see illus.*] • AB, caricature, repro. in Irving, *Henry Irving* • photograph, repro. in *ILN* (30 Aug 1910) • photograph, repro. in *The Era* (8 Oct 1904)
Wealth at death £13,710 13s. 1d.: probate, 1910, CGPLA Eng. & Wales

Craven, Henry Thornton [*real name* Henry Thornton] (**1818–1905**), playwright and actor, was born on 26 February 1818 in Great Poland Street, London, the son of Robert Thornton, a schoolteacher in Holborn. After working as a publisher's clerk in Paternoster Row, Henry was amanuensis to Bulwer Lytton, and began writing for *Bentley's Miscellany*. In 1840 he made his first appearance on the stage, at York, and in 1841 he appeared on the Sunderland circuit, and at the Theatre Royal, Liverpool, Rochester, and Tunbridge Wells. In 1842 he made his London début at Fanny Kelly's theatre in Soho, and his first play, *Bertram the Avenger*, was produced at North Shields. His second play, *Miserrimus*, was produced at Portsmouth late in 1843.

From 1842 to 1850 Craven performed at the Adelphi, Strand, Covent Garden, Lyceum, City of London, Marylebone, and Princess's theatres. His plays were produced at the Theatre Royal, Liverpool, the Adelphi, Edinburgh, and the City of London, Strand, Grecian, and Adelphi theatres in London. In 1850 he was engaged at Drury Lane, where, at William Macready's farewell on 26 February 1851, he played Malcolm to Macready's Macbeth. On 12 June 1851 he appeared in his operetta, *The Village Nightingale*, at the Strand. **Eliza Nelson** (1827–1908), singer and actor, daughter of Sydney Nelson, the composer, and his wife, Sarah, took the leading female role. In November 1851 the two were engaged by Lloyd of Edinburgh for the Theatre Royal

company, Craven as principal stage director. They were married in Edinburgh on 12 May 1852.

In June 1854 the Cravens left for Australia. From 1854 to 1856 they were engaged at the Royal Victoria Theatre, Sydney. As well as performing in a standard repertoire of comedy and farce (including Craven's plays *My Daughter's Debut*, *The Card Case*, and *Tic doloreux*), the Cravens appeared in special seasons with Australian theatrical manager George Coppin, and tragic actor Gustavus Vaughan Brooke. In April 1857 the Cravens made their farewell at Coppin's Theatre Royal, Melbourne. On their return to London, Eliza Nelson withdrew from performing, while Henry Craven continued to write and perform his own comedies, including the successful *The Post Boy* (Strand, 1860) and *The Chimney Corner* (Olympic, 1861), both written for Frederick Robson. Craven's plans for retirement were changed with the sudden death of Robson on 6 August 1864. His play *Milky White* had opened at the Prince of Wales's, Liverpool on 20 June 1864 with Robson in the title role. Craven took over the part for the London production at the Strand (28 September 1864), and established the most memorable role of his career. In the dual role of actor and playwright Craven scored again at the new Royalty on 17 October 1866 with *Meg's Diversion*, which ran for 330 nights, with himself as Jasper Pidgeon. In 1873 he made his last provincial tour. His last play, a historical drama, *Too True*, was produced at the Duke's on 22 January 1876, and in this he made his final appearance on the stage.

Henry Craven's career was typical of the theatre of the mid-nineteenth century. He was a versatile actor, performing in high and low comedy, as well as tragedy, and was prepared to travel extensively. He was a prolific playwright, producing twenty-nine plays between 1842 and 1876, many of them published by Lacy, Duncombe, and French, and a novel, *The Old Tune* (1876). His plays, mostly domestic comedies with a strong love story, produce humour from differences in class and education between lovers. Eliza Nelson combined success in domestic comedy with abilities as a singer of popular songs and opera.

Craven died at his residence, Thorntonville, Clapham Park, London, on 13 April 1905, and Eliza Nelson died at Eastbourne on 20 March 1908. Both were buried in Norwood cemetery, London. Two of their four children survived them, a daughter and a son, Tom Sidney Craven (*b.* 1864), who became a playwright and actor.

KATHERINE NEWEY

Sources *Daily Telegraph* (14 April 1905) • B. Hunt, ed., *The green room book, or, Who's who on the stage* (1906) • J. Parker, ed., *The green room book, or, Who's who on the stage* (1909) • *The Times* (14 April 1905) • *The Times* (24 March 1908) • Adams, *Drama* • A. Nicoll, *Early nineteenth century drama, 1800–1850*, 2nd edn (1955), vol. 4 of *A history of English drama, 1660–1900* (1952–9) • A. Nicoll, *Late nineteenth century drama, 1850–1900*, 2nd edn (1959), vol. 5 of *A history of English drama, 1660–1900* (1952–9) • *Sydney Morning Herald* (Nov 1854–Nov 1856) [amusements, advertisements] • *The Age* [Melbourne] (April 1857) [amusements, advertisements] • C. E. Pascoe, ed., *The dramatic list* (1879) • J. C. Dibdin, *The annals of the Edinburgh stage* (1888) • playbills, BL • D. Mullin, ed., *Victorian plays: a record of significant productions on the London stage, 1837–1901* (1987) • J. Coleman, *Fifty years of an actor's life*, 2 (1904) • M. Williams, *Some London theatres past and present* (1883)

Likenesses Packer & Griffin, lithograph (after a photograph), Harvard TC · caricature, woodcut, Harvard TC; repro. in *Entr'acte* (7 July 1877)

Craven, John, Baron Craven (*bap.* 1610, *d.* 1648). *See under* Craven, Sir William (*c.*1545–1618).

Craven, Keppel Richard (1779–1851), traveller, the third and youngest son of the six children born to William Craven, sixth Baron Craven (1738–1791), and Elizabeth Berkeley (1750–1828), later *Elizabeth, margravine of Brandenburg-Ansbach-Bayreuth, writer and daughter of Augustus Berkeley, fourth earl of Berkeley, was born on 1 June 1779. In 1783 his parents separated, and Lady Craven shortly afterwards went to France, taking Keppel with her on condition that she return him to his father when he was eight years old. This condition was not fulfilled, and his mother placed him at Harrow School under a feigned name, where, however, he was soon recognized by his likeness to her, and henceforth was called by his family name. A month after his father's death on 27 September 1791, his mother married her lover, Christian Frederick Charles Alexander, margrave of Brandenburg-Ansbach-Bayreuth. After the margrave's death in 1805 Craven went to live with his mother at Naples. In 1814 he was briefly chamberlain to the princess of Wales, but six months later was left by her at Naples when she went on to Geneva. In 1820 he gave evidence at her trial stating that during six months' service he saw no impropriety in her conduct at Milan or Naples, or improper familiarity on the part of Bergamo.

Craven published in 1821 *A Tour through the Southern Provinces of the Kingdom of Naples*, in 1825 *Italian Scenes*, and in 1838 *Excursions in the Abruzzi and Northern Provinces of Naples* (2 vols.). The first two contain views from his own sketches. Although not particularly original, they were pleasantly written and well reviewed.

Having received a considerable addition to his fortune, Craven in 1834 purchased a large convent in the mountains near Salerno, which he fitted up as a residence, and there received a succession of literary and society visitors with much hospitality. He was for many years the close friend and companion of Sir William *Gell whom he attended with unwearying kindness during his long illness, and particularly from 1835 until Gell's death in 1836. Gell was buried in Craven's mother's tomb in Naples having left Craven many of his papers and drawings—Craven later bequeathed the latter to the British Museum. Another close friend was the diplomatist and scholar Sir William Drummond, and an acquaintance was Lady Blessington, who arrived in Naples in July 1823. Craven died unmarried at Naples on 24 June 1851, apparently leaving an illegitimate son, Augustus Craven (1806–1884).

G. C. BOASE, rev. ELIZABETH BAIGENT

Sources Burke, *Peerage* · *GM*, 2nd ser., 36 (1851), 428–9 · E. Craven, *Memoirs of the margravine of Anspach*, 2 vols. (1826) · R. R. Madden, *The literary life and correspondence of the countess of Blessington*, 3 vols. (1855) · Allibone, *Dict.* · *Men of the time* (1885) · Boase, *Mod. Eng. biog.*
Archives BL, accounts, corresp., and journals, Add. MSS 63609–63616 · Bodl. Oxf., diary | BL, letters from Queen Caroline, Add.

MS 63127 · NA Scot., letters to George Mercer · NL Scot., letters to Lady Charlotte Lindsay · NL Scot., letters to Robert Liston
Likenesses R. Page, stipple, pubd 1821, BM, NPG · Count D'Orsay, pencil and chalk drawing, 1832, NPG · portrait, repro. in Craven, *Memoirs of the margravine of Anspach*
Wealth at death quite wealthy

Craven, Louisa. *See* Brunton, Louisa (1782x5–1860).

Craven [*née* de La Ferronnays], **Pauline Marie Armande Aglaé** (1808–1891), writer, was born on 12 April 1808 at 36 Manchester Street, London, of Breton parents, Comte Auguste de La Ferronnays and his wife, Comtesse Marie Charlotte, *née* Sources de Monsoreau, Catholics who had taken refuge in England after losing their estates in the French Revolution. Pauline was one of four daughters and three sons (the others being Eugénie, Olga, Albertine, Charles, Albert, and Fernan). Born in England, and married to an Englishman, Pauline Craven lived much of her life (forty years) in Italy, thought, spoke, and wrote in French, and died in France. She considered herself 'at home in three different countries' (Bishop, vol. 2).

In 1814 the family returned to France from where Pauline's father's position in the diplomatic service took them to Russia and to Italy, with a brief interlude from 1827 to 1828 when he served as foreign minister under Charles X. In St Petersburg the de La Ferronnays met Sir Richard Acton, who was an attaché there, and lifelong friendship developed between the two families. The de La Ferronnays settled in Naples, next to Villa Acton alla Chiaja, and in the private chapel there on 24 August 1834 Pauline married Augustus Craven (1806–1884), attaché at the British legation in Naples, and the illegitimate son of Keppel Richard *Craven (1779–1851) of the court of Queen Caroline, consort of George IV. He became the heir of his grandmother *Elizabeth (1750–1828), margravine of Brandenburg-Ansbach-Bayreuth, born Elizabeth Berkeley. After his marriage Augustus Craven embraced his wife's religion, a step later accepted by his father, who also gave them a generous settlement of £17,000. As a consequence of Augustus's diplomatic postings, the Cravens lived briefly in Lisbon, Brussels, Stuttgart, and Paris, until he resigned from the service to contest (unsuccessfully) the parliamentary constituency of Dublin in the whig interest in the general election of 1852.

In 1853 Pauline and Augustus Craven settled in Naples, undertaking charitable work there in aid of such causes as a clean water supply for the city. With friends and relatives they raised money by amateur performances in a theatre they built onto their house, Casa Craven. Later they built themselves a house at Castagneto.

Influenced by her brother Albert de La Ferronnays, who was an admirer of the publication *Avenir* (1830) and an earnest follower of Lacordaire, De Lamennais, and De Montalembert, Pauline Craven became a fellow disciple. Her friendship with De Montalembert (and after his death, with his wife and daughters) lasted all their lives and she often stayed at La Roche en Breny. Her natural liberal Catholicism later led her to sympathize with Italian nationalist aspirations. Pauline was connected by ties of

Pauline Marie Armande Aglaé Craven (1808–1891), by
unknown photographer

true direction, with which she chronicles her impressions of Mr Gladstone or her views of the Italian revolution. (Ward, 454–82)

After its success, and partly as a result of her husband's worsening financial affairs, Pauline Craven wrote (in French) several novels: *Anne Severin* (1868), *Fleurange* (1870), *Eliane* (1882), *Valbriant* (*Lucia*) (1886), all published serially in *Le Correspondant*. *Récit* and *Fleurange* received awards from the Académie Française. She also produced many articles on political and religious events and crises such as the unification of Italy, the Vatican Council of 1870, and the Irish Home Rule Bill of 1886, along with reviews such as that of Margaret Oliphant's *Life of De Montalembert*, and of General Gordon's *Reflections in Palestine* (1884), and articles on, for example, Fanny Burney (1881), General Booth (1883), and Father Damien (1889). Notwithstanding the success of Pauline's writing, the Cravens' pecuniary circumstances continued to be strained, and an annuity from the Bavarian government in lieu of a claim of Craven's grandmother does not seem to have helped much. In 1880, therefore, Pauline Craven made an arrangement with her publisher Didier to pay her £240 a year for six years on works already published, and to pay as before for any new ones. Her writings generally show not only the brilliant, amusing, and spiritual side of her temperament, but also her deep interest in religious issues and related political struggles. But her literary reputation rests on her authorship of *Récit d'une sœur*.

Augustus Craven died in 1884; his literary works included a life of Palmerston in French, and translations into English of a life of De Montalembert, and into French of Queen Victoria's life of the prince consort. In 1883 Queen Victoria asked Pauline Craven for the gift of signed copies of her works, in return for which the queen sent Pauline Craven two of her own books. The queen then asked for her *Meditations*, a work that Pauline had previously omitted, thinking it of no interest to the queen. Lady Georgiana Fullerton was a close friend of Pauline Craven; she translated some of her works, and in her 1844 will left her an annuity. Pauline, in turn, wrote a memoir of Lady Georgiana, made up of autobiographical writings, extracts from Lord Granville's journals, and letters. At her own death at 28 rue Barbet de Jouy, Paris, on 1 April 1891, Pauline Craven left all her estate to her nephew Albert le Mun. She was buried at Boury in Normandy with her husband.

G. A. ELWES

relationship and friendship with many prominent families, including the Leveson-Gowers, Palmerstons, Granvilles, Actons, and Grant Duffs. Another close friend (who wrote a memoir of Pauline Craven in Italian after her death) was the Duchess Ravaschieri to whose daughter, Lina, Pauline Craven had acted as godmother.

Financial problems meant that the Cravens had to sell Castagneto in 1873. They settled in Paris, in the faubourg St Germain, at 28 rue Barbet de Jouy, and Pauline Craven became a regular contributor to *Le Correspondant*, the voice of French liberal Catholicism. The early deaths of her brother Albert, his wife, Alexandre, and Pauline's sisters Eugénie and Olga inspired her to publish the three-volume *Récit d'une sœur* (1866), a candid record of their private lives 'given to religion and study and love'. It is made up of reminiscences, diary excerpts, reflections, and letters, a story of love and devotion fascinating in its unselfconscious self-revelation. It went through nine editions in a few months, and Wilfrid Ward, in a thirty-page review in the *Quarterly Review*, wrote:

> This clever Frenchwoman, so shrewd in her judgments of men and things, so capable of political enthusiasm, so sensitive to all the pleasures of art and of intellect, an excellent amateur actress, and for years delighting, apparently, in the whirl of social amusements, was living throughout a deep inner life of the mind and the affections, which she describes with the same vividness, the same realism, the same intense eagerness, and the same strong practical and unsentimental judgment as to its import and

Sources M. C. Bishop, *A memoir of Mrs Augustus Craven-Pauline de La Ferronays … with extracts from her diaries and correspondence*, 2nd edn, 2 vols. (1894) • P. M. A. A. Craven, *Life of Lady Georgiana Fullerton*, trans. H. J. Coleridge, 2nd edn, revised (1888) • P. M. A. A. Craven, *Réminiscences: souvenirs d'Angleterre et d'Italie* (1879) • P. M. A. A. Craven, *A sister's story*, trans. E. Bowles, 3 vols. (1868) • T. Filangieri Ravaschieri Fieschi, *Paolina Craven e la sua famiglia* (1892) • P. Gunn, *The Actons* (1978) • [W. Ward], review of *Récit d'une soeur*, QR, 182 (1895), 454–82

Archives BL, corresp., Add. MS 63622

Likenesses photograph, repro. in Bishop, *A memoir of Mrs Augustus Craven*, 2, frontispiece [*see illus.*] • portrait, repro. in Bishop, *A memoir of Mrs Augustus Craven*, 1, frontispiece

Wealth at death £195 1s. 11d.: administration with will, 2 Nov 1891, CGPLA Eng. & Wales

Craven, Peter Theodore (1934–1963), speedway rider, was born at Oxford Street Maternity Hospital, Liverpool, on 21 June 1934, the second son of Benjamin Harold Craven (1902–1999), master window cleaner, later biscuit packing-machine operator, and his wife, Edna May, *née* Stevens (1905–1976), florist, of 24 Prestbury Road, West Derby, Liverpool. He was one of twins, though the other died aged three-and-a-half; he also had an elder brother and four sisters. After attending Ranworth Square infant and junior schools, Norris Green, and then Abbotsford Road senior school, he entered Walton Technical College at the age of thirteen.

Craven first rode a speedway motorcycle the day after his sixteenth birthday, in 1950, when he borrowed his brother Brian's machine at the newly reopened Stanley Park stadium in Liverpool. He crashed after a dozen laps, sustaining concussion, but returned to the saddle several months later at Ainsdale Sands practice circuit for training under one of the team sponsors of the Liverpool Chads, the former rider Charlie Oates, at whose Liverpool garage Craven worked as a motorcycle mechanic. After progressing he made eight appearances for Liverpool in division two in 1951, and the following year five appearances apiece for Liverpool and, after the Chads went defunct, for the first division Belle Vue Aces of the Zoological Gardens, Hyde Road, Manchester. After a brief spell with Fleetwood, Craven joined Belle Vue officially in 1953; he travelled from army camp at weekends in the course of the first of his two years of national service in order to fulfil twelve league appearances in that year for the Aces.

Though Craven's raw talent was obvious, at this stage 'the problem with the wee fellow was that he could not stop falling off' (Rogers, 87). But guided by the Belle Vue manager, Johnnie Hoskins, the New Zealander who had introduced speedway to Britain in 1928, and equipped with machinery which his father had worked overtime for four years to provide, he improved hugely in 1954. He twice broke the Belle Vue lap record and qualified for the individual world final, the first of his ten successive appearances, though after falling in his first ride he scored three points, finishing only above another débutant, the later multiple world champion and legendary Swedish rider Ove Fundin. Out of uniform Craven's ascent was complete. He rode in all twenty-four of Belle Vue's matches in 1955, topping the club's averages for the first of nine successive seasons, and replaced the great Jack Parker as the team's ace as they finished runners-up in the league. Craven again broke the Manchester track record, and caused a sensation at the end of that season when as a rank outsider and at the age of only twenty-one he won the world title on 15 September before a crowd of 54,000 at Wembley Stadium.

Craven finished fourth when defending the title in 1956, after unluckily blowing a motor while leading in his second ride, but won his first Golden Helmet match race title, awarded on a challenge basis to the best rider in the domestic leagues. At the end of that season, on 17 October 1956, he married at St Lawrence's Church, Kirkdale,

Peter Theodore Craven (1934–1963), by unknown photographer, 1955

Brenda Pauline Williams (*b*. 1934), a typist, the daughter of Arthur Williams, a freight clerk; they had a son and a daughter, born in 1957 and 1961 respectively. In the winter of 1956–7 Craven went on a honeymoon tour of South Africa, where he was outstandingly successful, breaking numerous track records and winning the prestigious West Rand title. He returned for the 1957 season an improved rider for his experience on different surfaces, but was disappointed to finish third in the world championship after finishing joint top scorer, with Ove Fundin and the great New Zealander Ronnie Moore, but last of the three in the consequent run-off heat. Having finished fourth in 1958, and third again in 1960, Craven won the world championship for a second time on 8 September 1962 in front of 62,000 spectators at Wembley.

Craven first rode for England in 1954, and was the country's top scorer in the series of annual tests against Australasia held between that year and 1960; he also proved almost unbeatable in tests against Poland in 1958 and 1960. Representing England (after 1962, Britain) in the world team cup inaugurated in 1960, Craven was also the side's top scorer in 1960 and 1961. In a total of forty-seven career internationals, he amassed 621 points at an incredible 13.2 average, top-scoring for his country in ten of the fourteen series. Among the myriad domestic titles and trophies which Craven also accumulated were the Golden Helmet match race title (variously between 1956 and 1963), the British championship (1962, 1963), the Champagne Derby (1954, 1955, 1956, 1959, 1960), Pride of the Midlands (1957, 1959), the Kings of Oxford trophy (1957, 1961, 1962), Pride of the East (1958, 1959, 1961), the Northern cup (1959), the CTS trophy (1959), the Tom Farndon memorial trophy (1959, 1960, 1961), the Champion of Champions cup (1959), the Internationale Derby (1959), the Metropolitan cup (1960), and Best Pairs (with Gerald Jackson, 1962). As well as the league title in 1963, his Belle Vue side won the national trophy in 1958 and the Britannia trophy in 1957, 1958, and 1960, with Craven making a total of 218 appearances and scoring 2318 points. He was one of the 'big five' world riders, and the only Englishman, to ride off the maximum 20 yard handicap introduced in the British leagues in 1962.

In 1963 Belle Vue finally broke the stranglehold of the metropolitan clubs Wimbledon and Wembley and won the national league, but their success that season was eclipsed by one of speedway's greatest tragedies. On Friday 20 September Craven was racing for the Aces in a challenge match at the Old Meadowbank stadium in Edinburgh. In heat twelve, having already won his first three heats in style, Craven lined up with his Belle Vue teammate Billy Powell against the Edinburgh riders George Hunter and Willie Templeton. Hunter had a slight lead over Craven on the first bend of the second lap when his engine seized, locking the rear wheel, and as he tried to swerve Craven clipped Hunter's machine and crashed heavily into the safety fence. He was rushed to Edinburgh's Royal Infirmary, where he lay unconscious in an iron lung, his wife at his bedside, until his death at 9.10 p.m. on the following Tuesday, 24 September 1963. The cause of death was certified as severe head and brain stem injuries. There was a large attendance and over 250 wreaths were received at Craven's funeral; he was buried on 30 September at the West Derby cemetery, Liverpool. His brother, Brian, then riding for the Newcastle Diamonds, retired from speedway. Some thirty years later, on 11 April 1992, Craven's widow, Brenda, married his former friend and pit helper, Leon Leat.

Peter Craven was arguably the country's best ever speedway rider, and, of the five Englishmen to win the individual world championship since its inauguration in 1936, the only one to do so twice. Unusually diminutive, at 5 feet 2 inches and under 8 stone, he also differed from most racers of his era in that he rarely drank, never smoked, and went regularly to the gym. But Craven's real distinction was his fearlessness, fine throttle control, and exceptional balance, permitting a daring and spectacular style which was hugely popular with fans both at home and abroad, by whom he was known variously as the Mighty Atom, the Pocket Rocket, and, most appositely, the Wizard of Balance. Off the track he was known for his gentle manners, modesty, and kindness to fans and fellow riders, and it was universally noted that he died trying to avoid another rider. His name was immortalized in the sport's Peter Craven memorial trophy, raced for annually at Belle Vue and presented by his widow, Brenda, and the Craven shield, the prestigious knock-out trophy for which British speedway's élite teams have competed since its inception in 1997. A plaque in his memory was unveiled in a ceremony at the Old Meadowbank stadium, Edinburgh, on 7 March 1998.   S. A. SKINNER

Sources E. Hancock, ed., *Peter Craven: tribute to a great little champion* [1963] · *Speedway Star and News*, 12/29 (5 Oct 1963), 4 · *Manchester Evening News* (25 Sept 1963), 14 · *Liverpool Echo* (25 Sept 1963), 9 · private information (2004) [Mrs Brenda Leat, widow] · b. cert. · m. cert. · d. cert. · P. Morrish, *British speedway leagues, 1946–1964* (1984) · J. Chaplin, *Speedway: the story of the world championship* (1979) · M. Rogers, *The illustrated history of speedway* (1978) · *Speedway Gazette*, 10/48 (24 Sept 1955), 6–11; 10/49 (1 Oct 1955), 4, 5, 11; 11/1 (29 Oct 1955), 5 · *Speedway Star and News*, 11/25 (8 Sept 1962), 24; 11/26 (15 Sept 1962), 5–6, 17; 11/27 (22 Sept 1962), 1, 11–14; 11/28 (29 Sept 1962), 9–10, 12, 19; 12/8 (28 Sept 1963), 16; 12/30 (12 Oct 1963), 5; 12/31 (19 Oct 1963), 10, 22–3; 12/32 (26 Oct 1963), 12; 12/35 (16 Nov 1963), 2; 12/36 (23 Nov 1963), 5; 12/41 (28 Dec 1963), 6 · *Manchester Evening News* (10 Sept 1962), 8; (24 Sept 1963), 16 · *Liverpool Echo* (12 Oct 1956), 9; (10 Sept 1962), 12; (21 Sept 1963), 1; (26 Sept 1963), 3 · D. Lanning, ed., *50 golden years of speedway* (1978) · R. Hoare, *Speedway panorama* (1979) · scrapbooks in family possession

Archives *Vintage Speedway Magazine*, Clipsham, Rutland

Likenesses photograph, 1955, *Vintage Speedway Magazine*, Rutland [*see illus.*] · photographs, *Vintage Speedway Magazine*, Rutland

Wealth at death £8255: probate, 1964, *CGPLA Eng. & Wales*

Craven, Sir William (*c.*1545–1618), merchant and local politician, the second son of William Craven and his wife, Beatrix, the daughter of John Hunter, was born about 1545 at Appletreewick, a village in the parish of Burnsall, near Skipton in the West Riding of Yorkshire. He was apprenticed to the London merchant taylor Robert Hulson, and became free of the company in 1569. Craven seems to have started business with Hulson, who gave him his shop and warehouse at the intersection of Bread Street with Watling Street for a period of three years after his death. He never engaged in overseas trade, and his fortune was made through the domestic wholesaling of cloth. He supplied cloth worth almost £600 for Queen Elizabeth's funeral. Later in his career his activities extended to moneylending on a major scale, and his debtors included Sir Robert Cecil, the second earl of Essex, and the ninth earl of Northumberland. For much of his career he was in partnership with his fellow merchant taylor William Parker (*d.* 1616) and Parker's brothers, John and Robert, the latter of whom had been apprenticed to Craven. Craven's associations with the Parker family were very close, as he requested to be buried near his 'well beloved friend' William Parker, and left a life-interest in the lease of his shop in Watling Street to the two surviving brothers. He was one of the tycoons of his day, his personal fortune at his death being conservatively estimated at £125,000.

In 1582 Craven was living in the parish of All Hallows, Bread Street, hard by his former master's widow. From 1588 he leased a great mansion house in Watling Street in the parish of St Antholin from the Mercers' Company, and it seems that he continued to carry out the bulk of his business from there until his death, but from 1607 he lived in Leadenhall Street in the former Zouche's Inn, recently fashionably rebuilt by alderman Sir Robert Lee. With its sixty-two rooms and external yards, its blue and white marble paving, its elaborately carved chimneypieces, its fine hall screen, its flower garden, and summer pleasure house, this property, from 1648 the site of the headquarters of the East India Company, was a fitting location for Craven's mayoralty.

Sir William Craven (*c.*1545–1618), by unknown artist

Craven was relatively uninvolved in the affairs of his livery company, serving only in the office of second warden in 1593, but he enjoyed a long and distinguished career in civic politics, which began with his election to the court of common council for Bread Street ward in 1582. On his move to St Antholin he represented Cordwainer Street ward. It was only on his tenth nomination as alderman in 1600 that he was elected to the court, and he served successively the wards of Bishopsgate (1600–02), Cordwainer Street (1602–12), and Lime Street (1612–18). He was sheriff in 1601, and a beneficiary of the bonanza of honours at the accession of the new Stuart king, from whom he received a knighthood in 1603. His mayoralty in 1610–11 does not seem to have been characterized by major policy initiatives. The court of aldermen busied themselves with advancing the king's project for the plantation of Londonderry, with the usual gamut of social problems such as the proliferation of inmates and the regulation of apprentice dress, as well as with the inevitable complaints of trade abuses, among which the most prominent in that year were directed against the silk dyers.

Craven should be counted among the more godly of the London élite, a commitment he shared with his former master Hulson and with his long-standing business associate William Parker. His will refers to confidence in his election; he was the dedicatee of a posthumous work by the radical puritan Paul Baynes; and he enjoyed good relations with the more evangelical clergy of James I, such as Nicholas Felton, later bishop of Ely, who was also rector of St Antholin. Over the course of his career he was associated with the conventional charitable projects through which Londoners proved their godly credentials. He subscribed to the new Merchant Taylors' almshouses on Tower Hill in 1595 and founded a grammar school in his native parish of Burnsall in 1605, for the support of which he conveyed properties in the London parishes of St Mary Woolnoth and St Michael, Cornhill, in 1615. Another object of his benefactions was Christ's Hospital, of which he was a governor from 1593 and a most assiduous president from 1611 to 1618, scarcely missing a meeting. In 1611 he gave the hospital £1000, a gift which he unsuccessfully attempted to keep anonymous, and the money was used in the purchase of the parsonage and advowson of Ugley in Essex. In 1613 St John's College, Oxford, with which the Merchant Taylors were closely associated, received from him the living of Creeke in Northamptonshire, on condition that it should be reserved for one of the ten senior fellows of the college. Craven laid the foundation stone of the rebuilt Aldersgate on 31 March 1617, bringing to fruition a project cherished by his friend William Parker. It was typical of their interest in the beautification of the City and its churches, for Craven had been involved in the rebuilding of Holy Trinity-the-Less in 1606, and left £100 for the repair of the church of St John the Evangelist, where he had been apprenticed. His will also included bequests to the London hospitals and prisons, the poor of a number of London parishes, his native Burnsall, and Tiverton in Devon, but the stern face of godly charity showed in his determination 'for avoyding of Tumultes which be usuallie occasioned at Buryalls' that 'nothing be given to idell persons in the streates on the day of my funerall' (PRO, PROB 11/132, sig. 75, fol. 70).

Craven married in or before 1597 Elizabeth (*d.* 1624), the third daughter of William Whitmore, and the sister of Sir George Whitmore (lord mayor, 1631–2). There were four sons and three daughters, although one of the sons and one of the daughters died in childhood, and another of the sons at the age of eighteen. Although Craven himself had not invested in land, his enormous fortune ensured that his widow and the surviving sons, William *Craven, Viscount Craven of Uffington and earl of Craven (*bap.* 1608, *d.* 1697), and John, Baron Craven of Ryton [*see below*], were able to carve out sizeable estates after his death. When Lady Craven died in 1624 it was reported that she had left an estate of £8000 per annum to her eldest son and £5000 per annum to the younger, 'the richest widow that ever died of a London lady' (*Letters of John Chamberlain*, 2.572, 576). The daughters married well—Elizabeth in 1622 to Sir Percy Herbert, bt, later second Baron Powis of Powis Castle, and Mary in 1627 to Thomas Coventry, later second Baron Coventry of Aylesborough. Sir William Craven died on 18 July 1618 and was buried in the church of St Andrew Undershaft, London, on 11 August 1618.

The younger surviving son, **John Craven**, Baron Craven

(*bap.* 1610, *d.* 1648) was baptized on 10 June 1610 in St Andrew Undershaft. He was a student at the Middle Temple, where he was bound with Bulstrode Whitlock. He married on 4 December 1634 Elizabeth, the daughter of William Spencer, second Baron Spencer of Wormleighton, and his wife, Penelope, the daughter of Henry Wriothesley, earl of Southampton; her marriage portion was £6000. He seems to have forged close associations with his wife's family, and retreated to live with them after a quarrel with Lord Maynard in 1637. A strong loyalist, he may have been the Lieutenant John Craven who was listed as a commander of a company to be raised for service in Leinster in April 1640. In October he was elected MP for Tewkesbury in the Long Parliament, possibly through the patronage of his brother-in-law Thomas, Lord Coventry, but the election was contested and subsequently voided. Craven's royalism showed its colours at an early stage in the developing conflict, when he offered to lend £1000 towards the expenses of the army in March 1641. His continuing support for the king was recognized by his elevation to the title of Baron Craven of Ryton, Shropshire, on 21 March 1643. He died childless in 1648. The major beneficiaries of his will were his wife, whose share was £3000, and an uncle, the early Arminian and leading Kent royalist Sir Richard Spencer of Orpington, whose family, taking into account specified bequests to his wife and children, received £2300. There were numerous bequests in poor relief amounting to nearly £2500, directed at parishes in London, Northamptonshire, Warwickshire, and Yorkshire, as well as at the London hospitals and prisons. Craven also allocated the profits of the manor of Cancerne, near Chichester, to supply four scholarships of £25 per annum each at Oxford and Cambridge, with preference being given to his kinsmen, the surplus revenue being applied to the redeeming of captives in Algiers. There were difficulties in implementing this bequest because of the sequestration of his lands by parliament, but the sequestration was discharged in 1654.

IAN W. ARCHER

Sources G. E. Cokayne, *Some account of the lord mayors and sheriffs of the city of London during the first quarter of the seventeenth century, 1601–1625* (1897) · M. Benbow, 'Index of London citizens involved in city government, 1558–1603', U. Lond., Institute of Historical Research, Centre for Metropolitan History · R. G. Lang, 'The greater merchants of London in the early seventeenth century', DPhil diss., U. Oxf., 1963 · wills, subsidy assessments, PRO · repertories of the court of aldermen and journals of common council, CLRO · Christ's Hospital governors' minutes, GL · C. M. Clode, *The early history of the Guild of Merchant Taylors of the fraternity of St John the Baptist, London*, 2 vols. (1888) · J. Schofield, *Medieval London houses* (1994) · GEC, *Peerage* · Keeler, *Long Parliament* · W. J. Stavert, 'Notes on the pedigree of the Cravens of Appletreewick', *Yorkshire Archaeological Journal*, 13 (1894–5), 440–80 · M. E. Finch, *The wealth of five Northamptonshire families, 1540–1640*, Northamptonshire RS, 19 (1956) · *The letters of John Chamberlain*, ed. N. E. McClure, 2 vols. (1939) · will, PRO, PROB 11/132, sig. 75 · will of John, Baron Craven, PRO, PROB 11/203, sig. 20
Likenesses circle of M. Gheeraerts the elder, oils, 1611, Corporation of London, Guildhall Art Gallery · portrait [*see illus.*]
Wealth at death £125,000—est. based on size of testator's third: PRO, PROB 11/132, sig. 75

Craven, William, earl of Craven (*bap.* 1608, *d.* 1697), army officer and royal servant, was baptized on 26 June 1608 at St Andrew Undershaft, London, the eldest son of the London alderman Sir William *Craven (*c.*1545–1618) and his wife, Elizabeth (*d.* 1624), daughter of another London alderman, William Whitmore. The elder William Craven, who had been knighted by James I on 26 July 1603 and served as lord mayor in 1610–11, was one of the small élite of great London financiers engaged in the lucrative business of advancing major loans to the crown. He died in 1618, leaving three sons and three daughters, including Mary, who married Thomas Coventry, later second Baron Coventry of Aylesborough, and Elizabeth, who married Percy Herbert, later second Baron Powis. Elizabeth Craven, then one of the richest widows in England, fended off a marriage proposal from Edmund Sheffield, first Baron Sheffield, in 1618, while continuing to invest her late husband's wealth. She advanced loans totalling £4360 to Lionel Cranfield, third earl of Middlesex, and in 1622 purchased Coombe Abbey from Lucy Russell, countess of Bedford, for £36,000.

Craven's mother died in 1624, leaving him in possession of the greatest part of his parents' immense fortune, which was ultimately converted into a landed estate with a rental value in excess of £10,000 per annum, valued at £250,000 shortly after its sequestration in 1652. This made Craven one of the nine wealthiest peers in England and his lands were spread over several counties, including Berkshire, Warwickshire, Oxfordshire, Somerset, Sussex, and Shropshire; he also retained property in London, including East India House.

Education and early career On 11 July 1623 Craven matriculated at Trinity College, Oxford; he did not graduate with a bachelor's degree, but was created MA on 31 August 1636. He had interrupted his studies to join the army of Maurice of Orange, in which he served with distinction. Upon returning to England he was knighted by Charles I on 4 March 1627 and created Baron Craven of Hampstead Marshall, Berkshire, eight days later, an honour for which he paid £7000. Craven also found himself named to the permanent council of war. In 1629 rumours circulated that he would soon marry Ann Cavendish, daughter of the earl of Devonshire, but in the same year he obtained leave to travel abroad in Italy and France; in November a correspondent of Thomas Hobbes reported that, although the prospective bride was willing enough, 'because I hear nothing of him [Craven] having been in England this month, I fear his hands are already full' (*Correspondence of Thomas Hobbes*, 1.7). He had, in fact, gone to the Netherlands, where he fell dangerously ill (SP 84/140/45). Whether for this or some other reason the match fell through, leaving Craven a lifelong bachelor.

During the Christmas season of 1630 Craven spent £3000 freeing poor debtors from London prisons. The following August he was reported to be about to join the army of Gustavus Adolphus when he received 'a command to the contrary' (*Gawdy MSS*, 136) and a commission as an officer of the forces being raised by the marquess of Hamilton to assist in the recovery of the Palatinate. Early

William Craven, earl of Craven (*bap.* 1608, *d.* 1697), by Gerrit van Honthorst

in 1632 he accompanied the elector palatine, Prince Frederick, as he led the English recruits from The Hague into Germany, where they linked up with the Swedes at Frankfurt am Main on 10 February. Craven witnessed Frederick's interview with the Swedish king at Höchst the following day and was wounded during the taking of Kruznach on 22 February, while fighting with a courage that led Gustavus to remark that he 'adventured so desperately, he bid his younger brother fair play for his estate' (*DNB*). Craven's offer to raise an independent force to complete the conquest of the Palatinate was, however, refused by the Swedish monarch. This campaign marked the beginning of a lifetime of devoted service to the family of the elector palatine and his wife, Elizabeth of Bohemia, the daughter of James I.

Craven returned to England by 31 August 1633, when he was named to the council of Wales. He was one of seven lords deputed to carry the canopy during the baptism of James, duke of York, during the following November. But although he had withdrawn from active campaigning, he remained a staunch supporter of the palatine's cause. In May 1633 he had engaged himself to provide security for a loan of £31,000 that Elizabeth's agent, Sir Francis Nethersole, sought to raise from two London merchants. The transaction collapsed when the lord treasurer, Portland, who disliked English involvement in the German war, persuaded Charles I to forbid it. The following March Craven's record of support for the cause of German protestantism led to his selection as one of four individuals who rode in the coach with Henrik Oxenstierne, son of the famous Swedish chancellor Axel Oxenstierne, to his first audience with the king on an embassy seeking greater English involvement in the Thirty Years' War.

Charles briefly became more receptive to schemes for military action against the Habsburgs in the autumn of 1636, after the collapse of negotiations by the earl of Arundel to secure a peaceful restoration of the Palatinate from Emperor Ferdinand II. Craven again stepped forward by offering to contribute as much as £30,000 to a plan to outfit a fleet of ships lent by the Royal Navy using contributions from English noblemen that would be placed under the command of the Elector Charles Lewis, who had succeeded his father in 1632, for use against Spanish commerce. Although this scheme briefly appeared ready to come to fruition early in the new year it soon collapsed because, as Sir Thomas Wentworth reported in March, 'the backwardness of everybody else in following this example [by Craven] hath quite dashed his designs' (Wentworth Woodhouse MSS, Sheffield Archives, StrP9, 421). Ralph Verney, more caustically, remarked that Craven's munificence had succeeded only in making him 'the subject of every man's discourse' for 'prodigality' and 'folly' (*DNB*).

Undeterred by these setbacks, Craven joined Charles Lewis and his brother, Prince Rupert, in June 1637 in command of a troop that landed in the Netherlands and marched up the Rhine to join a small army at Wesel. However, this combined force of about 4000 men was soon surprised and overwhelmed by the imperial general Hazfield as it attempted to reach the main Swedish army. Craven reportedly saved Rupert's life in this action, when both were taken prisoner. Although at first refusing to ransom himself so as to remain near the prince, Craven finally purchased his freedom in 1639, reportedly for £20,000, after consistently being denied access to Rupert. He returned to the court in London, where Charles Lewis was once more engaged in futile efforts to enlist military support from his British royal cousin. Toward the end of summer the prince gave up and abruptly left London, accompanied only by 'four or five confidantes, whereof one was the Lord Craven, the constant follower of his fortunes' (Finet, 263). The intention of travelling incognito to France was thwarted when a very large Spanish fleet was sighted as the electoral party neared the Downs and Charles Lewis, in his eagerness to see it, boarded the admiral of the English navy. This action elicited a salute, promptly answered by the Dutch fleet, which had moved into English waters to encounter its enemy, and the Spanish ships. Despite the unwelcome publicity the elector and his entourage continued on to Dover and the continent. Craven was at The Hague with Elizabeth in January

1640 and was presumably still abroad in April, when the king excused his absence from the Short Parliament.

The civil-war period and sequestration Although Craven evidently returned to London shortly thereafter, he left again for the continent before the outbreak of the civil war, probably in February 1642, as he later claimed. He spent most of the next eighteen years with Elizabeth at The Hague, reportedly supporting her financially once she stopped receiving her pension of £10,000 a year from the English crown. He developed a particular friendship for Elizabeth's daughter Sophie, attempting to promote her marriage to Prince Charles and taking charge of the arrangements for her removal from The Hague in 1650.

Although he took no direct part in the civil war, Craven had royalist sympathies and he remained in contact with leading politicians and officers of Charles's party. On the eve of the regicide he wrote to Prince Rupert that he feared the king's fate was sealed, 'considering what persons now rule the roost' but hoped that 'yet God perchance may direct you and do that which we do not deserve and make us happy in the re-establishment of the King and his' (*Hodgkin MSS*, 107, 110). A few years later Charles II used Sophie as an intermediary to extract financial assistance from Craven, who ended up contributing £50,000 to the exiled monarchy and its supporters during the interregnum. Not surprisingly, this involvement with leading royalists and financial assistance to the Stuarts provoked retaliation by the Commonwealth against Craven's English properties. Some of his horses had been seized and one of his servants imprisoned by local parliamentarian troops as early as 1648. In 1650 Major Richard Falconer informed the council of state that Craven had presented a petition by several officers to Charles II, asking him to accept their services against parliament. The case was referred to the committee for compounding on 6 February 1651, when two additional witnesses testified that Craven had performed various services for the exiled king at Breda, including arranging for the care of an illegitimate daughter, though they did not specifically corroborate Falconer's testimony. A week later the county committees of Warwickshire, Shropshire, Sussex, Oxfordshire, Middlesex, Herefordshire, and Gloucestershire and the authorities in London were ordered to seize his estates, although it was not until 4 March that the committee for compounding asked the council of state whether Craven's conduct actually provided legal grounds for sequestration. On 6 March parliament voted him an offender and ordered the confiscation of his properties.

The Commonwealth government, no doubt with an eye to the contribution Craven's vast wealth could make to alleviating its own financial problems, moved energetically to have the order executed. The committee for compounding proceeded within weeks to obtain accurate valuations of various clusters of manors, but nevertheless received a letter on 30 April chiding it for dilatoriness and directing it to speed up the sequestration as a matter 'of extraordinary use and concernment to the exigencies of

the State' (Green, 438). A postscript in the hand of President Bradshaw further enjoined that the committee's agents use 'speed and privacy till the work be done' (ibid.). Over the next year agents appointed by various county committees proceeded, under the watchful eye of the London authorities, to survey Craven's properties and oversee the felling of standing timber on several of them.

By early summer 1652 a decision was reached to sell Craven's estate to raise money for the Commonwealth's fleet in the impending war with the Netherlands. Craven's agents fiercely contested this plan but on 4 August parliament approved a bill authorizing the sale by the narrow margin of twenty-three to twenty. The same day a commission was appointed to dispose of his properties. Unlike most royalists who had suffered similar confiscations, Craven did not attempt to repurchase his lands but instead continued to lobby to have the sequestration reversed. He had begun his campaign in June 1651 by trying to persuade parliament to reverse the vote declaring him an offender, on the grounds that it had been taken before formal charges had been drawn up, giving him no chance to mount a defence. But this and all subsequent efforts failed, even though Falconer's testimony was eventually discredited and despite the Dutch government's intercession on his behalf, after prompting by Elizabeth and Charles Lewis. In 1654 Craven's agents produced *The Lord Craven's Case Briefly Stated* in an effort to publicize his cause. In this he claimed always to have been defeated by narrow votes after influential figures who hoped to purchase his lands intervened against him. Although Cromwell reopened the case the properties were not restored until 1660, when a series of orders passed between March and June 1660 finally reversed the sequestration. By then the estate had undoubtedly suffered considerable damage, as indicated by John Evelyn's remark in June 1654 that he had seen Craven's house at Caversham in ruins while the nearby woods were being felled.

Craven during the Restoration Craven soon recovered sufficiently, however, to engage in new building projects. He retained the services of Sir Balthazar Gerbier, the former architect and purchasing agent of the first duke of Buckingham, to design a new house at Hampstead Marshall, Berkshire. When Gerbier died during construction Craven switched his patronage to the much younger William Winde, who in 1682 also designed a new wing for Craven's mansion at Coombe Abbey, Warwickshire, which incorporated a superb plaster ceiling in the hall by Edward Gouge.

Meanwhile Craven continued his generosity to Elizabeth of Bohemia and her children. In 1661, after Charles II ungraciously failed to provide Elizabeth with a London residence, Craven invited her to move into his house in Drury Lane, where she lived until a few weeks before her death on 23 February 1662. He acted as the informal head of her household, escorted her to the theatre, and spent so much time in her company that he was rumoured to have secretly become her husband. During Elizabeth's funeral in Westminster Abbey he was one of the heralds who bore her crown. Her will left him her papers and collection of

Stuart and palatine family portraits, which he installed in Coombe Abbey, where she had once lived when a child. Craven also remained close to Rupert and was named executor of his will in 1682. He continued to correspond with Sophie, sometimes acting as an intermediary on her behalf at the English court, for example by being entrusted in January 1666 with a memorandum concerning the proposed marriage of her daughter, the Princess Elizabeth Charlotte. In addition to political affairs he advised Sophie on paintings, including a series she wished to commission commemorating the life of her brother Rupert, in which she assured Craven that his own exploits would be represented.

During the same period Craven assumed numerous duties under the restored monarchy. His military background and political loyalty won him a series of commissions, as colonel of a regiment of foot (1 September 1662), lieutenant-general in the king's army (1667), and from 1670 commander of the Coldstream Guards. In January of the same year he was also appointed to succeed George Monck, duke of Albemarle, as lord lieutenant of Middlesex, having already been named a justice of the peace for the county. Through these various appointments Craven became closely involved in the policing of the Stuart metropolis. He played an energetic role in supervising the shutting up of infected houses and burial of victims during the great plague of 1665 and drew up notes on measures to prevent future outbreaks. He helped supervise a contingent of sailors sent to fight the fire of London and was one of four commissioners of streets and highways involved in appointing a master paviour for the capital in 1667. In March the following year Pepys went to Lincoln's Inn Fields in hope of witnessing apprentice riots that had just broken out in the western suburbs but instead found 'the fields full of soldiers … and my Lord Craven commanding them, and riding up and down to give orders, like a madman' (Pepys, 9.129). During 1670 Craven worked closely with the lord mayor and the lieutenant of the Tower, Sir John Robinson, to co-ordinate the troops around London during a period of renewed anxiety about apprentice riots and possible risings by disaffected religious minorities. The following September he was given military command of the capital during a temporary absence of the king. He was also named to a commission to assist the duke of York in ordering the army after Albemarle's death.

On 16 March 1665 Craven had been elevated to the title of Viscount Craven of Uffington, Berkshire, and earl of Craven, Yorkshire. The next year he was named to the privy council and in 1667 he was rumoured to be about to succeed Sir George Carteret as treasurer of the navy. Although this appointment never materialized he did receive a number of other administrative and honorific posts, including high steward of Cambridge University (1667) and master of Trinity House (1670). He was in addition named a proprietor of Carolina (1663), a governor of the Hudson's Bay Company (1670), and a commissioner for Tangier (1673). His interest in commercial ventures and overseas expansion is indicated by his efforts, in partnership with Rupert and Albemarle, to promote the 1668 expedition to seek a north-west passage to the Pacific, after encouraging reports had been received from French explorers in the region of the Great Lakes. His role in colonial projects, especially the Carolinas, brought him into partnership with the future whig leader Anthony Ashley Cooper, earl of Shaftesbury, and his secretary, John Locke.

Despite his personal loyalty and devotion to duty, Craven does not seem to have impressed contemporaries as a man of great stature. Pepys, who regarded him as a patron, nevertheless recorded several distinctly unflattering vignettes of Craven in his *Diary*, presiding over 'very confused and very ridiculous' committee discussions, diverting his colleagues with bawdy analogies during deliberations over colonial policies and engaging in 'silly talk' with the duke of Albemarle (Pepys, 5.299; 6.264). Members of the electoral family also expressed reservations about their devoted servant. When he failed to persuade Charles II to invite Elizabeth to return to London in 1661, Rupert told a correspondent that 'Craven hath not done very well in my mother's business and my brother's; she therefore is not very willing he should have the doing of anything about it till she herself be acquainted' (*Dartmouth MSS*, 4). Sophie could be even more critical. She reportedly made fun of Craven behind his back in the 1650s, and when her husband, Karl Ludwig, employed him as an intermediary with Charles II in 1674 she expressed surprise that he would 'confide serious affairs to our milord, who does not have much common sense' ('conferer des affaires serieuse avec nostre Mylord, qui n'a pas trop le sens commun'). She changed her mind only after recalling Craven's talent for engaging the king in light conversation, even if only about 'a dog or a bitch' ('un chien ou d'une chaine'), remarking that 'these animals are better for scratching at a door than a German sovereign' ('ses animaux sont plus propres pour gratter a une porte qu'un souerain d'Allemagne'; *Briefwechsel*, 184, 186). Although coloured by Sophie's acute sense of social superiority, these comments may also reflect a feeling that Craven's character lacked depth and gravity. Further evidence of an eccentric personality is perhaps provided by his habit of rushing out to observe fires whenever they broke out in London, no matter what time of day or night, on a horse he had trained to smell out the flames and gallop directly toward them through the capital's labyrinthine streets. It is possible, however, that this seemingly bizarre hobby was actually another example of his devotion to duty, since the crown continued to call upon his services in fighting large fires in London and he may voluntarily have involved himself in combating smaller conflagrations as well.

Craven's loyalty to the Stuarts and eclipse after 1688 Craven's personal idiosyncrasies may explain why he never gained a post of the first rank. Yet he remained a trusted servant of Charles II and his brother James, duke of York, particularly after political tensions heightened at the end of the 1670s. A slanderous paper intercepted by the government in February 1679 named him as one of James's 'twelve disciples ... [who] sit at the helm and steer him [the King] as they please' (*CSP dom.*, 1678–9, 68). During the Oxford session of parliament in 1681 he was again placed at the head of the troops commanding London, with instructions that should an insurrection break out he was to suppress it with as much force as necessary, 'forbearing no act of hostility permitted by the usages of war' (*CSP dom.*, 1680–81, 679). Throughout the period of the exclusion crisis and its aftermath Craven was involved in investigating incendiary rumours and supervising measures to assure that any tumults in the capital would be quickly suppressed.

At James II's accession Craven was reappointed to the privy council and, in June 1685, named lieutenant-general of the king's forces. He was present at the birth of James Edward Stuart and provided a deposition in October 1688 testifying that the young prince was indeed the child born to the queen. In the same month, as England awaited the invasion of William of Orange, Craven took command of an English regiment and an Irish battalion guarding Westminster. Despite his great age he remained a loyal and energetic commander. On 11 December, after James's first flight from the capital, he wrote to William of Orange informing him that he would endeavour to preserve order in the capital, but, after the king's capture and enforced return to London, Craven continued to serve him with devotion. Craven's troops deserted him on the 19th when he tried to lead them to Rochester, for fear that they would be embarked for France. Eight days later he was in command at Whitehall as the Dutch army entered London. Refusing an order to withdraw, he prepared to mount a last-ditch defence, until James personally instructed him to capitulate.

William III promptly relieved Craven of his commands and offices, leaving him to devote the remainder of his life to private pursuits, including architectural projects and gardening at his three country seats of Hampstead Marshall, Benham, and Coombe Abbey, and his London house in Drury Lane. A beautiful engraving by I. Kip shows the first of these houses and its grounds as they looked in this period (BL, Add. MS 28676 A, fols. 248–9). He died on 9 April 1697 at his house on Drury Lane and was buried at Binley, near Coventry. Since he had no direct heirs his death extinguished his earldom but the baronial title descended to his nephew William under stipulations of a grant of 1665.

Although never a figure of the first rank, Craven had a long and distinguished career spanning more than sixty years, involving him in military and political events of prime importance in England and central Europe. A man of great physical courage and unshakeable devotion to duty, he never wavered in his adherence to the protestant religion, the English crown, and the Stuart family. In a quieter period these qualities would probably have resulted in a distinguished and successful, if fairly uneventful, career, perhaps as an officer and administrator responsible for military logistics. Instead Craven's life epitomizes the pitfalls of unbending consistency during a period as fraught with religious upheaval and cynical political manoeuvring as the seventeenth century. Although probably the most outspoken and generous aristocratic supporter of English aid for German protestantism in the 1630s, he found himself branded an enemy to the state when the godly came to power in the 1650s. The vast wealth that he had used to support the cause of the elector palatine was confiscated to help finance the war that a puritan regime had decided to wage against another Calvinist state. His second career of service to the crown after the Restoration ended in a futile effort to defend the popish James II against William of Orange, the one British monarch of the seventeenth century who fully shared his commitment to the military defence of European protestantism. Craven was at his best in situations calling for acts of courage and generosity in the service of uncomplicated moral principles and individuals to whom he had given his loyalty. Unfortunately these simple virtues repeatedly failed him amid the treacherous currents of seventeenth-century politics.

R. MALCOLM SMUTS

Sources DNB · Burke, *Peerage* · *The Lord Craven's case briefly stated out of the report: with observations upon the several parts of the same* (1654) · private information (2004) [Paul Gladwish] · *Briefwechsel der herzogin Sophie von Hanover*, ed. E. Bodeman (Leipzig, 1885) · BL, Add. MSS 63743, 63744 · *CSP dom.*, 1660–85 · *Memoiren der herzogin Sophie*, ed. A. Koecher (Leipzig, 1879) · L. Stone, *The crisis of the aristocracy, 1558–1641* (1965) · S. R. Gardiner, *History of England from the accession of James I to the outbreak of the civil war*, 7–8 (1884) · J. Finet, *Ceremonies of Charles I: the note books of John Finet, 1628–1641*, ed. A. J. Loomie (1987) · Pepys, *Diary* · Evelyn, *Diary* · M. A. E. Green, ed., *Calendar of the proceedings of the committee for compounding ... 1643–1660*, 1, PRO (1889), 438; 2 (1890), 1616–26, esp. 1617 · *The manuscripts of J. Eliot Hodgkin ... of Richmond, Surrey*, HMC, 39 (1897) · *The manuscripts of the earl of Dartmouth*, 3 vols., HMC, 20 (1887–96), vol. 1 · *Report on the manuscripts of Lord Montagu of Beaulieu*, HMC, 53 (1900) · *The manuscripts of S. H. Le Fleming*, HMC, 25 (1890) · *Report on the manuscripts of the family of Gawdy, formerly of Norfolk*, HMC, 11 (1885) · *Seventh report*, HMC, 6 (1879) · *The manuscripts of the Earl Cowper*, 3 vols., HMC, 23 (1888–9), vol. 2 · N. Luttrell, *A brief historical relation of state affairs from September 1678 to April 1714*, 1–2 (1857) · E. Godfrey, *A sister of Prince Rupert: Elizabeth princess palatine and abbess of Hereford* (1909) · *The correspondence of Thomas Hobbes*, ed. N. Malcolm, 1 (1994); pbk edn (1997) · M. Prestwich, *Cranfield: politics and profits under the early Stuarts* (1966)

Archives BL, papers, Add. MSS 6373, 6374; Add. MS 63743 · Bodl. Oxf., corresp.

Likenesses attrib. Princess Louise, oils, 1647, NPG · line engraving, 1791, BM, NPG · G. P. Harding, ink and wash drawing (after unknown artist, 1650), NPG · G. van Honthorst, oils, unknown collection; copyprint, NPG [*see illus.*] · engraving, repro. in BL, Add. MS 28676 A, fol. 252 · oils, NPG

Crawfie. See Crawford, Marion Kirk (1909–1988).

Crawfoot [Crowfoot, Crawford], **James** (1758?–1839), leader of the Magic Methodists, was born at Clotton, Cheshire, the second of two sons of Thomas Crowfoot and his wife, Ann, and was baptized in June or July 1759. He lived in Tarvin parish, Cheshire, except from about 1800 to about 1814, when he moved to Bryn, near Delamere Forest, Cheshire. He was described as a farmer's labourer in 1809, but after 1814 had a small business, and in 1816 described himself as a farmer. He acquired enough education to read and write. Crawfoot had six children with his first wife, Phoebe Billington of Newchurch, Cheshire

(1758/9–1807), whom he married on 28 August 1780; and one child with his second wife, Hannah Mountford (c.1785–1841), a domestic servant of Tarvin parish, whom he married on 3 January 1816, and who survived him.

Crawfoot's significance lies in his religious activities and associations. Of Anglican parentage, early religious impressions and dreams led to an evangelical conversion on 7 February 1783. Having joined the Wesleyan Methodists in Duddon Heath by 1789, he was a class leader by 1796 and a local (lay) preacher in the Northwich circuit (not Chester circuit as often claimed).

He was expelled for irregular preaching in 1807. Because of their visions Crawfoot's followers were known as the 'Forest' or 'Magic' Methodists. From 1807 he was associated with Hugh Bourne, a leader of a revivalist group which from 1812 formed part of the new Primitive Methodist Connexion. Bourne's diary (unlike his highly critical later autobiography) shows that he was deeply impressed by the visions and Crawfoot's religious insights, and on 17 November 1809 he hired Crawfoot as his first travelling preacher, apparently because of his spiritual gifts (not, as he later claimed, merely to relieve his poverty). The Methodist doctrine of entire sanctification was prominent in Crawfoot's sermons. Several Magic Methodists, mostly women, had visions of favoured preachers with trumpets and cups, in varying orders of merit. Crawfoot, though always foremost in the visions, seems not to have experienced them himself. Some followers also claimed to convey spiritual power by laying on hands. The visions ceased to be recorded after July 1811. In 1813 Crawfoot was expelled, ostensibly for failing to keep his appointments, though he probably clashed with Bourne's leadership claims and it is possible that unspecified moral failings were another cause. Continuing to preach until his death, he had 'followers bearing his name' as late as 1831.

Crawfoot's significance for Primitive Methodist origins remains debatable. His charismatic personality and visionary followers exemplified (rather than introduced) a supernaturalist strain constantly recurring in Methodism, but here helped to promote local revivals. Claims that he proposed the name Primitive Methodist in 1812, as having been used by John Wesley, are dubious, though Crawfoot used it to defend himself against criticism in 1807. Bourne was much indebted to him for theological and spiritual guidance in directions which marked later Primitive Methodism. The problems caused by Crawfoot and the visionaries probably encouraged Bourne to emphasize close supervision and less spectacular spiritual gifts. No portrait is known of Crawfoot. He was described as 6 feet tall, with a 'long visage', 'high forehead', and kindly eyes, eccentric in speech and Quaker in dress. He died on 23 January 1839 at Barrow, Cheshire, and was buried in Tarvin churchyard on 27 January.

HENRY D. RACK

Sources G. Herod, *Biographical sketches of some of those preachers whose labours contributed to the origination and early extension of the Primitive Methodist Connexion* [n.d., c.1855], 241–71 • H. Bourne, 'Autobiography', 1845–51, JRL, Methodist Archives and Research Centre, MSS DDHB 2/1–3 • H. Bourne, 'Journal', 1808–13, JRL, Methodist Archives and Research Centre, MSS DDHB 3/3–7 • M. Sheard, 'The origins and early development of Primitive Methodism in Cheshire and South Lancashire 1800–60', PhD diss., University of Manchester, 1980, 59–80 • parish registers, Tarvin, Ches. & Chester ALSS • Chester Wesleyan Methodist circuit schedules, 1788–1803, Ches. & Chester ALSS, CR 55/7, 8 • H. B. Kendall, *The origin and history of the Primitive Methodist church*, 2 vols. [n.d., c.1906] • J. Petty, *History of the Primitive Methodist Connexion … to 1860*, new edn (1880) • W. Antliff, *The life of the Venerable Hugh Bourne* (1872) • J. Walford, *Memoirs of the life and labours of the late Venerable Hugh Bourne*, ed. W. Antliff, 2 vols. (1855–6) • J. T. Wilkinson, *Hugh Bourne, 1772–1852* (1952)

Crawford. *See also* Craufurd, Crawfurd.

Crawford. For this title name *see under* Lindsay family, earls of Crawford (*per. c.*1380–1495) [Lindsay, David, first earl of Crawford (*d.* 1407); Lindsay, Alexander, second earl of Crawford (*d.* 1438/9); Lindsay, David, third earl of Crawford (*d.* 1446); Lindsay, Alexander, fourth earl of Crawford (*d.* 1453); Lindsay, David, fifth earl of Crawford and duke of Montrose (1440–1495)]. *See also* Lindsay, David, tenth earl of Crawford (1526/7–1574) [*see under* Lindsay, David, eleventh earl of Crawford (*d.* 1607)]; Lindsay, David, eleventh earl of Crawford (*d.* 1607); Campbell, Katherine, countess of Crawford (*d.* 1578); Lindsay, David, master of Crawford (*bap.* 1576, *d.* 1620) [*see under* Lindsay, David, eleventh earl of Crawford (*d.* 1607)]; Lindsay, Ludovic, sixteenth earl of Crawford (*d.* 1652); Lindsay, John, seventeenth earl of Crawford and first earl of Lindsay (1596–1678); Lindsay, William, eighteenth earl of Crawford and second earl of Lindsay (1644–1698); Lindsay, John, twentieth earl of Crawford and fourth earl of Lindsay (1702–1749); Lindsay, Alexander, sixth earl of Balcarres and *de jure* twenty-third earl of Crawford (1752–1825); Lindsay, Alexander William Crawford, twenty-fifth earl of Crawford and eighth earl of Balcarres (1812–1880); Lindsay, James Ludovic, twenty-sixth earl of Crawford and ninth earl of Balcarres (1847–1913); Lindsay, David Alexander Edward, twenty-seventh earl of Crawford and tenth earl of Balcarres (1871–1940); Lindsay, David Alexander Robert, twenty-eighth earl of Crawford and eleventh earl of Balcarres (1900–1975).

Crawford, Adair (1748–1795), physician and chemist, son of Thomas Crawford (1695/6–1782), minister, and his wife, Anne, *née* Mackay, an aunt of Elizabeth Hamilton (1758–1816), was born in Crumlin, co. Antrim. William *Crawford (1739/40–1800) was his brother. Crawford matriculated at Glasgow University in 1764 and went on to study theology, arts, and medicine. He became MA in 1770. During his studies in Glasgow, Crawford heard William Irvine, who had been appointed lecturer in chemistry in 1770, present his theory that heat was 'physically contained in substances having varying capacities for it'; this opposed Joseph Black's theory, which proceeded from the assumption that 'the absorption of heat is a chemical process' (Donovan, 94). Crawford supported Irvine's theory and in 1777 began a series of experiments designed to determine the specific heats of gases. He gave an account of his findings to the student medical society at Edinburgh University, where he had enrolled to study medicine in 1777, and later to Thomas Reid and William Irvine at Glasgow. His results were published as *Experiments and Observations on Animal Heat, and the Inflammation of Combustible Bodies* in 1779. In 1780 Crawford became MD at Glasgow, but he left the city soon after to practise medicine in London. This he did with some success and, through the influence of friends, he became a physician at St Thomas's Hospital, and professor of chemistry at the Royal Military Academy, Woolwich.

In *Experiments and Observations* Crawford proposed that 'air inhaled into the lungs contains more absolute heat than the air exhaled from the lungs … that the arterial blood leaving the lungs contains more absolute heat than the venous blood pumped into the lungs', and 'that a body's capacity for heat is reduced by the chemical fixation of phlogiston and is increased by the separation of phlogiston' (Donovan, 95). The book attracted considerable attention. William Hey, surgeon to the General Infirmary in Leeds, published in 1779 *Observations on the Blood*, in which he expressed his approval of Crawford's views. In 1781 William Morgan published *An Examination of Dr Crawford's Theory of Heat and Combustion*, in which he raised numerous objections to Crawford's conclusions. However, J. H. de Magellan in his *Essai sur la nouvelle théorie du feu élémentaire* (1780) wrote that 'we owe the birth of this branch of natural philosophy to the publication of this excellent work by Dr Adair Crawford' (Donovan, 95). In 1788 Crawford published a second edition of his book, by which time the work of Lavoisier and Laplace had cast doubt on Irvine's theory. It still, however, remained influential in Britain until 1812 when the work of François Delaroche and J. E. Bérard showed it to be untenable.

Crawford also wrote on medical topics. In 1790 he published a treatise entitled *On the Matter of Cancer and on the Aerial Fluids*; his *Experimental inquiry into the effects of tonics and other medicinal substances on the cohesion of animal fibre* appeared posthumously in 1816. Crawford attracted the attention of his medical colleagues by being the first to recommend the muriate of baryta (barium chloride) for the cure of scrofula. He was elected a fellow of the Royal Society in 1786.

At the age of forty-six, owing to poor health Crawford retired to the estate of the marquess of Lansdowne at Lymington, Hampshire, where he died on 29 July 1795. A friend who knew him well wrote of him in the *Gentleman's Magazine* as:

> a man who possessed a heart replete with goodness and benevolence and a mind ardent in the pursuit of science. All who knew him must lament that aught should perturb his philosophical placidity and shorten a life devoted to usefulness and discovery.

CLAIRE L. NUTT

Sources Munk, *Roll* · *GM*, 1st ser., 65 (1878), 789 · Watt, *Bibl. Brit.* · A. Novak, 'Ideas on respiration and Adair Crawford', *Janus*, 47 (1958), 180–97 · A. Donovan, 'Crawford, Adair', *DSB*, vol. 15 · W. I. Addison, ed., *The matriculation albums of the University of Glasgow from 1728 to 1858* (1913)
Archives RS

Crawford, Ann. *See* Barry, Ann (*bap.* 1733, *d.* 1801).

Crawford, David (1665–1726), historian, was born at Drumsoy, Ayrshire, the only son of David Crawford and his wife, a daughter of James Crawford of Baidland (afterwards of Ardmillan). He was probably educated at the University of Glasgow, where a David Crafford matriculated in the fourth class on 31 January 1679. There is no evidence in the records of the Faculty of Advocates to support the traditional claim that he was later called to the bar, nor is anything known about his activities during the 1680s and 1690s. It is nevertheless evident that Crawford harboured literary ambitions. His intentions were initially signalled by two mediocre comic dramas, *Courtship-a-la-mode* (1700) and *Love at First Sight* (1704), and by *Ovidius Britannicus* (1703), a collection of poems in the style of Ovid. However, with serious scholarly pretensions, and being of a suitably tory disposition, in 1704 he secured the important post of historiographer of Scotland from Queen Anne. His tenure was crowned by a single innovative work which enjoyed significant celebrity in the eighteenth century.

The *Memoirs of the Affairs of Scotland* (1706) was presented to Crawford's readers as an account of the Scottish revolution of 1567 based on a contemporary manuscript acquired from an unnamed episcopalian source. It portrayed the deposed Mary, queen of Scots, in a favourable light, the luckless victim of a conspiracy between an unscrupulous aristocratic faction and her zealous Calvinist enemies. Freed from the strong Presbyterian prejudices of most previous authors, Crawford's revisionism was timely, seeming to represent an inspirational early example of that self-consciously even-handed historiography that was to characterize the Scottish Enlightenment of later decades. Indeed, Crawford's account of what he described as 'the misfortunes of Mary' (*Memoirs of the Affairs of Scotland*, p. i) was crucial to her subsequent rehabilitation, paving the way for William Robertson's *History of Scotland* (1759) and David Hume's *History of England under the House of Tudor* (1759), where the compassionate and often sentimental depiction of this most famous of Catholic monarchs reached new heights. In doing so, they not only affronted eighteenth-century Scottish Presbyterian opinion but unwittingly ensured that Crawford's sympathy for Mary would continue to colour all later treatments.

Crawford's learned readers had, however, been duped. As Malcom Laing conclusively demonstrated in his 1804 edition of the manuscript *Historie and Life of King James the Sext*, Crawford had employed this text, though with the insertion of supportive additions and, even more seriously, the careful excision of all passages potentially unfavourable to James's mother, Mary. In seeking to overthrow a dominant Presbyterian historiography rooted in George Buchanan's *Rerum Scoticarum historia* (1582), still an important source of political inspiration to his early eighteenth-century Scottish whig contemporaries, Crawford's toryism had led him to accomplish 'the earliest, if not the most impudent literary forgery ever practised in Scotland' (Laing, vi). His reputation has never fully recovered from this disclosure. Crawford married a daughter of Gordon of Craiglaw and, at his death at Dromsoy in 1726, he left a single surviving daughter, Emilia (*d.* 1731). DAVID ALLAN

Sources T. Thomson, ed., *Biographical dictionary of eminent Scotsmen*, 1.395–6 · Anderson, *Scot. nat.*, 1.717 · D. E. Baker, *Biographia dramatica, or, A companion to the playhouse*, rev. I. Reed, new edn, rev. S. Jones, 1 (1812), 155 · Burke, *Gen. GB* · M. Laing, ed., *The historie and life of King James the Sext* (1804) · J. Paterson, *History of the county of Ayr: with a genealogical account of the families of Ayrshire*, 1 (1847), 327–9 · K. O'Brien, *Narratives of enlightenment: cosmopolitan history from Voltaire to Gibbon* (1997) · J. D. Mackie, *The University of Glasgow, 1451–1951: a short history* (1954), 127 · C. Innes, ed., *Munimenta alme Universitatis Glasguensis / Records of the University of Glasgow from its foundation till 1727*, 3, Maitland Club, 72 (1854), 135 · F. J. Grant, ed., *The Faculty of Advocates in Scotland, 1532–1943*, Scottish RS, 145 (1944) **Archives** NL Scot., letters of appointment in favour of subject, Adv. MS 29.2.11, F.200

Crawford, Edmund Thornton (1806–1885), landscape and marine painter, was born at Cowden, near Dalkeith, Midlothian, on 7 June 1806 and baptized there on 23 July, the son of William Crawford and his wife, Margaret Henderson. His father and grandfather were both land surveyors in Edinburgh. Crawford was apprenticed to an Edinburgh decorative painter named Dickson, but did not complete his term and enrolled instead in the Trustees' Academy, where he studied under the landscape painter Andrew Wilson. William Simson was a fellow student who remained a close friend. Crawford first exhibited two landscapes at the Association for the Promotion of the Fine Arts in Scotland (later the Royal Association) in 1824, and in 1826 one of his exhibits, *A Group of Trees* (NG Scot.), was bought by the institution. He exhibited at the Scottish Academy from 1831 and thereafter with scarcely a break until 1877, when ill health forced him to retire. He last exhibited in 1880. Crawford married in Edinburgh, on 21 March 1835, Eliza Paton, who died young (*c.*1847). The couple had one daughter, but she died aged only thirteen.

Crawford's address in Edinburgh changed regularly until in 1858 he moved to Greenbank, Lasswade, where he remained for the rest of his life. In 1826 he became one of the first elected associates of the new Scottish Academy. He was elected academician in 1829, but in 1832 he resigned. This may have reflected the turbulent early history of the institution, though it did not prevent his exhibiting there. He was re-elected ARSA in 1839 and RSA in 1848. In 1833 he travelled to the Netherlands for the first time, and that same year he exhibited two Dutch scenes at the academy, a *View at Helvoetsluys* and a *View of Dort*. He returned several times to the Netherlands and exhibited paintings of Dutch river and canal landscapes throughout his life. His vision of the country was based closely on his study of Dutch seventeenth-century landscape and marine painters. This links him to his friend William Simson and to such contemporaries as John (Old Jock) Wilson and Patrick Nasmyth, though his work is also occasionally touched by the more romantic style of the Revd John Thomson of Duddingston. Crawford worked in both oil and watercolour and is best known for his paintings of shipping, though he also painted landscapes. His first

major success was a painting of *Eyemouth Harbour*, exhibited at the Royal Scottish Academy in 1848 and engraved for the Royal Association for the Promotion of the Fine Arts. He exhibited in the south only once, showing at the Royal Academy in 1836 a *View of the Fortifications at Callao with the Capture of the Spanish Frigate Esmeralda*. His pictures are tonal, usually directly observed, simply constructed, and sometimes quite bold in handling. His style changed little, and when he last exhibited, in 1880, it would have seemed old-fashioned except that by then it found echoes in the tonal landscapes of the Hague school.

Crawford was a keen sportsman, enjoying both shooting and fishing. According to his obituary, he was of 'a gentlemanly bearing and amiable disposition … [and] was a genial and entertaining host' (*The Scotsman*, 3 Oct 1885). He died at Greenbank, Lasswade, on 27 September 1885 after some years of ill health and was buried at Dalkeith on 2 October. DUNCAN MACMILLAN

Sources DNB · *The Scotsman* (3 Oct 1885) · W. D. McKay, *The Scottish school of painting* (1906) · J. L. Caw, *Scottish painting past and present, 1620–1908* (1908) · Thieme & Becker, *Allgemeines Lexikon* · P. J. M. McEwan, *Dictionary of Scottish art and architecture* (1994) · IGI · bap. reg. Scot.

Crawford [*née* Johnstone], **Emily** (1831?–1915), journalist, was born, possibly on 31 May 1831, at Corboy, co. Longford, Ireland, one of four daughters and seven sons of Andrew Johnstone (1798–1863) and his wife, Grace-Anne Martin (*d.* 1883); the family were Church of Ireland. Educated at home, mainly by her mother who taught her to read, by the age of eight she was reading a *Dictionary of the Lives of Illustrious Women* and, while still a child, she devoured Sir Walter Scott's poetry and novels, as well as Shakespeare and biographies of European kings. On Andrew Johnstone's death in 1863 his widow and her two daughters moved to Paris.

Emily remedied her lack of formal education by attending lectures at the Sorbonne and studying painting. Her initiation into journalism was prompted by another Emily, the sister of Dr Elizabeth Blackwell, showing some of her letters to a friend who then recommended her to write a Paris letter for a San Francisco newspaper, and she also sent one to the London *Morning Star*. Since Emily Johnstone counted four American newspapermen among her relatives and one, Melville E. Stone, who founded the Chicago *Daily News*, later employed her, her choice of profession might not have seemed unusual, except for the fact that she was a woman.

Writing in 1864, her future sister-in-law, Mary Eleanor Crawford, described Emily as 'a literary lady and wonderfully clever making £400 a year with her pen!! She writes articles in the Scotch Quarterly' (family archive). A friend described Emily around this time as 'a small, exquisitely-poised figure, brilliant complexion, true blue Irish eyes, and brown hair making up a striking personality' (*Young Woman*).

In 1864 Emily married George Morland *Crawford (1812–1885), whose friendship with William Makepeace Thackeray had earned him the post as assistant to the Paris correspondent of the *Daily News* in 1850. During her

Emily Crawford
(1831?–1915), by
Denys Puech, 1896

childhood Emily had become deeply conscious of her mother's legal inferiority to her father, so in her marriage contract Emily Crawford stipulated that if any serious disagreement should arise, both parties were free to leave and lead separate lives. Yet this never occurred in their twenty-one years of happy marriage, which produced three sons and a daughter.

When Henry Labouchere arrived in Paris in 1870, as one of the new proprietors of the *Daily News*, the couple were recognized as a journalistic team—so much so that Labouchere dispatched them, with their family, to the safety of Tours on the outbreak of the Franco-Prussian War. They returned to report on the events of the commune and Emily gained a great scoop by interviewing Communard leaders as they sat in council on 23 March 1871. Regarded by fellow journalists as the equal of Henri de Blowitz as an interviewer, Emily frustrated Blowitz's attempt to usurp George Crawford's prestigious position in the press gallery of the national assembly, where, despite advancing years, George continued to devil for her until his sudden death in 1885.

Having inherited her husband's position on the *Daily News*, Emily also contributed to the New York *Tribune* as well as to *Truth*, a weekly started in 1877 by Labouchere, where he told her to 'spread her wings' and where, she thought, her best writings appeared. She was also a correspondent for the *Weekly Dispatch*, the *Calcutta Englishman*, and the Chicago *Daily News*, as well as a contributor to the *Contemporary Review*, *Macmillan's*, and the New York *Century*. Her contributions reflected her wide reading, on a daily basis, on politics and literature, of more than a score of newspapers. 'Observe, reflect, and be genuine' (*Young Woman*, 184) was her journalistic motto. She kept herself informed, developed an expertise on the works of Emile Zola, and maintained close friendships with George Sand, Victor Hugo, and George Meredith (to whom she was also related). But Emily Crawford also reported on, and explained, great political events in France such as the Panama Canal scandal, the Boulanger crisis, and the Dreyfus affair, which she played down in her *Daily News* articles, despite the efforts of her son Robert to support the Dreyfusards in the same paper.

Emily's articles were enhanced by the background knowledge the Crawfords had gathered from their friendship with many leading French politicians, such as Adolphe Thiers, Leon Gambetta, Sadi Carnot, and Georges Clemenceau. Gambetta was even godfather to Emily's only daughter, who tragically drowned in her late teens. As president of France, Sadi Carnot, the son of one of her earliest Parisian friends, Hippolyte Carnot, offered the Légion d'honneur to Emily Crawford, which she declined, asking that it be awarded to her son Robert.

Politicians' views of Emily Crawford varied. Gladstone, after meeting her in Paris during 1883, described her as a somewhat careless and inaccurate journalist (Gladstone, *Diaries*). To the American-schooled Clemenceau, however, Emily was 'a ripper. Most men [journalists] in tackling questions look merely at their frontage, [but she] gets behind, beneath, inside and through and through. I have never seen anyone like her' (R. Crawford, 61).

Emily's fellow journalists in England elected her a life fellow of the Institute of Journalists in 1890, and in 1901 she was president of the Society of Women Journalists. One of her last articles, for the *Fortnightly Review*, 'United States of Europe', reveals her longing for 'the emancipation of Europe from the military machine [which] would free her genius and enable it to soar to heights yet undreamt of' (*Fortnightly Review*, 74, 1903, 992–1001).

After retiring from the *Daily News* in 1907, Emily continued her weekly letters to *Truth* until her death. Although she was disabled, requiring a wheelchair, her son Robert effected her evacuation to England before the advancing German army in 1915. She died from apoplexy on 30 December 1915 at 5 Vyvyan Terrace, Clifton, Bristol, aged eighty-four.   FRED HUNTER

Sources M. E. Stone, *Fifty years a journalist* (1921) · R. Whiteing, *My harvest* (1915) · J. O. Baylen, 'Dreyfusards and the foreign press: the syndicate and the *Daily News* February–March 1898', *French Historical Studies*, 7 (1972), 332–48 · [M. E. Stone], *Some notes on the history of the Fox family of Kilcoursey in the King's county, Ireland* (1890) [privately printed] · interview with Emily Crawford, *Women's Penny Paper* (1 March 1890), 1–2 · *Young Woman* (1894–5), 183–5 [interview with Emily Crawford] · R. Crawford, 'The late Mrs Crawford', *Truth* (12 Jan 1916), 60–62 · Gladstone, *Diaries*, 10.404 · E. Crawford, *Victoria, queen and ruler* (1903) · *Daily News* (3 Jan 1916), 1, 6 · *Daily News* (4 Jan 1916), 4 · *Manchester Guardian* (4 Jan 1916), 5 · *New York Times* (4 Jan 1916), 8 · *The Dial* (16 March 1916), 263–6 · *The Times* (3 Jan 1916), 8 · *Truth* (5 Jan 1916), 16–18 · family archive, priv. coll. · d. cert.

Likenesses D. Puech, cast of medallion, 1896, priv. coll. [see illus.] · E. Crawford, self-portrait, priv. coll. · photograph (with George Crawford), priv. coll.

Wealth at death £6699 3s. 2d.: probate, 19 Jan 1916, CGPLA Eng. & Wales

Crawford, George Morland (1812–1885), lawyer and journalist, was born on 6 December 1812 at Chelsfield Court Lodge, Kent, the eldest of the three sons and six daughters of Robert Crawford (1789–1860) and Elizabeth (1788–1850), eldest daughter of Samuel and Sussanah Elvy. Little is known about his education, but he was known to be well-versed in the Latin classics and a competent French speaker. He began work at fifteen in the counting-house of John Benjamin Heath (1790–1879). Then, either bored with banking or as a result of some unrecorded scrape, he enlisted in the army, and several months passed before he was discovered and bought out. Influenced, perhaps, by the success at the bar of one of his friends, Barnes Peacock (1810–1890), he accepted the suggestion from his father's cousin, Edward Sidebottom (1788–1857), a barrister, that he try the law as a profession, and enrolled in his chambers at Lincoln's Inn in May 1833. Called to the bar of the Inner Temple on 5 May 1837, Crawford practised as an equity draughtsman and conveyancer.

Like other young heirs to estates, Crawford lived beyond his means. He joined the Garrick Club in 1840 and belonged to a set known as the Deanery, meeting in a tavern near St Paul's, originally under the watchful eye of one of its canons, the Revd R. H. Barham, author of the *Ingoldsby Legends*. William Makepeace Thackeray also attended, and it is most likely that his friendship with Crawford began at the Garrick. They were both members of the Eccentric Society, and, through Thackeray, Crawford met Dickens and Laman Blanchard (1769–1838). Thackeray was noted for making veiled, but unmistakable, allusions to his contemporaries in his novels. Thus, in presenting a copy of *Pendennis* to Crawford, Thackeray wrote:

> You will find much to remind you of old talks and haunts … there is something of you in Warrington, but he is not fit to hold a candle to you; for, taking you all around, you are the most genuine fellow that ever strayed from a better world into this. You don't smoke, and he is a consumed smoker of tobacco. Bordeux and port were your favourites at the 'Deanery' and the Garrick, and Warrington is always guzzling beer. But he has your honesty, and like you, could not posture if he tried. You have a strong affinity for the Irish. May you someday find an Irish girl to lead you to matrimony; there is no such good a wife as a daughter of Erin. (*Letters and Private Papers*, 2.721)

By 1850 Crawford's debts were so vast that he was excluded from the Garrick for non-payment of bills and was constrained to quit the bar and look for other employment. At this point Thackeray is alleged to have recommended Crawford for a position in the Paris office of the *Daily News*, where he went in 1850 as assistant to Savi[l]le Morton, helping him by translating French documents and newspaper reports. Together they witnessed the end of the Second French Republic by Prince Louis Napoleon's *coup d'état* in December 1851. After Morton's murder by Harold Elyott Bower, correspondent of the *Morning Post*, on 1 October 1852, Crawford took Morton's place as Paris correspondent of the *Daily News*.

Crawford never believed in the durability of the Second Empire, established by Napoleon III, and allegedly rejected the emperor's attempt to buy his support by offering him the post of inspector of railways at a salary of 30,000 francs a year, even though he knew nothing about railways. Crawford's marriage in 1864, the year after Thackeray's death, to Emily Johnstone [see Crawford, Emily (1831?–1915)], an Irishwoman of mixed Scottish and American descent, brought him not only companionship but also professional help. Emily was already earning about £400 a year from her journalism and from then on they worked as a team reporting for the *Daily News*.

Together the Crawfords raised a family of four children

and extended their friendships among prominent French writers and politicians. During the Franco-Prussian War of 1870 they left Paris, but returned to witness the ruthless suppression of the Paris commune of 1871 and the execution of many communards by General Gaston de Galliffet. Crawford's report on this bloody event in the *Daily News* was quoted by Karl Marx in his *Civil War in France*. With private telegrams suspended during the commune, Crawford's close friendship with the politician and journalist Adolphe Thiers (1797–1877) enabled his dispatches to reach London by using Thiers's special wire. The year after Thiers became president of the Third Republic in 1871, Crawford was made a member of the Légion d'honneur. The Crawfords were friends of John Bigelow (1817–1911), the American minister to France and owner of the New York *Evening Post*, after whom they named their eldest son, just as their only daughter, Leona, was named after her godfather, Leon Gambetta (1832–1882). In his diary Bigelow mentions dining at the Crawfords' with the Utopian socialist Louis Blanc (1811–1882) on 17 September 1877, and then driving with them, at 9.30 p.m., to call on Victor Hugo (whose letters to Mrs Crawford remain in the possession of the family, unpublished and untranslated). Crawford's fellow Paris correspondents elected him their representative in the chamber of deputies in preference to Henri de Blowitz (1825–1903), the renowned Paris correspondent of *The Times*. Crawford died on 23 November 1885 in his Paris home, 79 boulevard de Courcelles, of blood poisoning caused by a wasp stinging his carotid artery. He was buried on 27 November, probably at the English church, rue Agueassen, Paris. FRED HUNTER

Sources [Theodore G. Brown], *Half-lights on Chelsfield Court Lodge* (1933) · *Daily News* (25 Nov 1885) · *Daily News* (26 Nov 1885) · *Daily News* (28 Nov 1885) · M. E. Stone, *Fifty years a journalist* (1921), 7, 8, 90 · J. Bigelow, *Retrospections on an active life*, 5 (1872–9), 16, 153, 346 · private information (2004) · *The letters and private papers of William Makepeace Thackeray*, ed. G. N. Ray, 2 (1945), 721 · G. N. Ray, *Thackeray*, 2 vols. (1955–8), 211, 285 · H. S. Edwards, *Personal recollections* (1900), 30–34 · Boase, *Mod. Eng. biog.* · *Annual Register* (1852) · R. S. Lambert, *When justice faltered: a study of nine peculiar murder trials* (1935), 48–69 · d. cert. [Emily Crawford]
Archives priv. coll.

Crawford, Isabella Valancy (1850–1887), writer, was born on 25 December 1850 in Dublin, the sixth of the twelve children of Stephen Dennis Crawford (1807–1875) and Sydney Scott. Isabella studied English, Latin, and French and began writing from a young age. Her childhood was one of financial insecurity and domestic upheaval, however, largely owing to her father's alcoholism and financial irresponsibility. The Crawford family endured poverty, hardship, and tragedy: only three children survived to adulthood—Isabella Valancy, Emma Naomi, and Stephen Walter.

About 1857, in search of better prospects, Stephen Crawford moved his family to Paisley, Ontario, where, despite questionable qualifications, he became the village doctor. Following his conviction for embezzling public funds while township treasurer, in 1862 he moved his family to North Drouro (now Lakefield), Ontario, where Isabella became acquainted with the literary sisters Susannah

Moodie and Catherine Parr Traill. The Crawfords moved once more in 1868, to Peterborough, Ontario, where Isabella's father and sister Emma died within six months of each other in 1875.

Before her father's death Crawford had begun writing commercially to augment the family income, and from 1872 her short stories, fairy tales, and romances were published in a variety of American and then Canadian magazines and newspapers, including *Fireside Weekly*, the *Toronto Globe*, and the *Toronto Evening Telegram*. Her current literary reputation is based primarily on her poetry, and particularly on the one book she published during her lifetime: *Old Spookes' Pass, Malcolm's Katie, and other Poems* (1884). This collection of narrative and lyric poems received critical but not commercial success—published at Crawford's expense, it sold only fifty copies out of the 1000 that James Bain & Son had commissioned. *Malcolm's Katie*—arguably her best poem—illustrates Crawford's fascination with native mythology and her use of anthropomorphic imagery by placing a conventional love story about two young sweethearts in the context of Indian legend. Other poems that demonstrate her empathy with the Canadian landscape and native culture include 'The Camp of Souls' (published 1880), 'The Canoe' (1884), 'The Dark Stag' (1905), and 'Said the West Wind' (1905). *Old Spookes' Pass*, a narrative poem written in cowboy dialect, describes a supernatural encounter that takes place during a midnight cattle stampede. 'Gisli the Chieftain' makes use of myth—this time Russian and Icelandic—to tell a tale of love, betrayal, murder, and ultimate forgiveness, and again conveys Crawford's view of the universe as a place of destructive opposites that clash until reconciled by love. Good and evil, shadow and light, winter and summer, life and death: all these feature in her poetry as much as nature imagery and native legend.

Though Crawford is now recognized as one of Canada's most important nineteenth-century poets, she did not live to enjoy either financial or critical success, dying suddenly of a heart attack at her small flat at 57 John Street, Toronto, on 12 February 1887. An edition of Crawford's collected poems appeared in 1905 by John Garvin, who took liberties with her text; it was reprinted in 1972 with a new introduction by James Reaney. In 1923 Katherine Hale produced a selected anthology which reproduced some of the infelicities of Garvin's edition. *Hugh and Ion*, an unfinished narrative poem, was edited by Glenn Clever in 1977. Crawford's prose largely remains unpublished, with the exception of that reproduced in *Selected Stories* (1975) and *Fairy Tales* (1977), both edited by Penny Petrone, and *The Halton Boys: a Story for Boys* (1979), by Frank M. Tierney.

EMMA PLASKITT

Sources I. V. Crawford, *The collected poems of Isabella Valancy Crawford*, ed. J. W. Garvin (1905) · W. Toye, ed., *The Oxford companion to Canadian literature* (1983) · Blain, Clements & Grundy, *Feminist comp.*, 247–8 · www.lib.sfu.ca/canadaswomenwriters · E. Waterston, 'Crawford, Tennyson and the domestic idyll', *The Isabella Valancy Crawford symposium*, ed. F. Tierney (1979) · www.nlc-bnc.ca/2/12/h12-219-e.html [National Library of Canada] · eir.library.utoronto.ca/rpo/display/poet85.html [selected poetry of I. V. Crawford from *Representative poetry on-line*] · D. Familoe, *Isabella Valancy Crawford: the life and the legends* (1983) · E. McNeill Galvin, *Isabella Valancy Crawford: we scarcely knew her* (1994)
Archives Queen's University, Kingston, Ontario, Lorne Pierce collection, MS
Likenesses photograph, repro. in Crawford, *Collected poems*, frontispiece

Crawford, John (1816–1873), poet, was born in Greenock on 31 August 1816, the son of Alexander Crawford, a carpenter, and his wife, Mary, *née* McPherson. His birth took place in the same apartment in which his cousin, Mary Campbell, the 'Highland Mary' of Burns's song, had died thirty years earlier. Crawford learned the trade of a housepainter, and at eighteen moved to Alloa, where he married Jean McDougal on 26 March 1835. They had at least four children: Alexander Hope Crawford (b. 1841), William Motherwell Crawford (b. 1845), Mary McPherson Crawford (b. 1852), and Andrew Mcdougal Crawford (b. 1855).

In 1850 Crawford published *Doric Lays, being Snatches of Song and Ballad*, which met with high praise from Lord Jeffrey; a second volume appeared in 1860. Towards the end of his life Crawford was engaged on a history of the town of Alloa, which was later published, with a memoir of the author by Charles Rogers. Perhaps due to his drinking Crawford latterly contracted several serious illnesses, the frustrations of which led him to commit suicide at his home—in Broad Street, Alloa—on 13 December 1873.

T. F. HENDERSON, rev. JAMES HOW

Sources Boase, *Mod. Eng. biog.* · C. Rogers, 'Memoir of the author', in J. Crawford, *Memorials of the town and parish of Alloa* (1874) · C. Rogers, *The modern Scottish minstrel* (1857) · J. Crawford, *Doric lays*, 2nd ser. (1860) · *IGI* · d. cert.
Archives U. Glas. L., songs, with letters to David Robertson
Likenesses photograph, repro. in Crawford, *Memorials of the town and parish of Alloa*

Crawford, John Scott (1889–1978), army officer and military supplies administrator, was born on 6 February 1889 at 13 Clifton Road, West Derby, Lancashire, the son of John Paton Crawford, an assistant manager at a marine engine works, and his wife, Ellen Edith Scott. Crawford was educated at Liverpool College, then at Campbell College, Belfast. He was apprenticed in a marine engineering works and from 1911 to 1915 he travelled widely on the continent and in the Far East. On 19 December 1916 he married Amy Middleton Andrews (b. 1891/2), daughter of William Henry Middleton Andrews, a company director; they had two sons.

Crawford was gazetted a temporary lieutenant in the Army Service Corps and ordnance services on 25 November 1918 and rose rapidly to acting major (1 October 1920); he was a brevet lieutenant-colonel when rearmament began in 1934, and an acting major-general on 1 July 1940 (confirmed in that rank on 17 November 1941). Between 1928 and 1932 he had advanced himself professionally from inspector of mechanical transport second class in the Royal Army Ordnance Corps (RAOC) to deputy assistant director of mechanization at the War Office, and on 22 August 1935 he became deputy director. When war broke out in 1939 he left the RAOC to join the new Ministry of Supply, where he became director of mechanization, then deputy director-general of tanks and transport and in

1943 deputy director of armaments production. Unfortunately in that position, and as an engineer entirely concerned with the technical aspects of equipment, especially tanks and armoured fighting vehicles, he had to bear the consequences of the parsimonious system under which British tanks were developed, and in 1943, when equipment proved defective, he was moved sideways within the ministry until 1946.

After the war, Crawford joined the boards of Guy Motors Ltd and the Sunbeam Trolleybus Company Ltd. He was a member of the council of the Society of Motor Manufacturers and Traders Ltd, of which he was vice-president (1948–50) and treasurer (1953–7), a member of the Institution of Engineering Inspection and president (1953–4), as well as president of the Rubber Research Association (1952–4), vice-president for life from about 1949 of Liverpool College, and a member of the court of the Worshipful Company of Carmen, of which he was master (1957–8). In addition he was a lifetime member of the Institution of Mechanical Engineers and a member of the Institution of Marine Engineers. His honours included CBE 1940, CB 1945, and commander of the order of Leopold II of Belgium in 1963.

Crawford enjoyed golf and fishing and was a member of the United Service Club and the Royal Automobile Club. From about 1950 he was settled in Richmond upon Thames, Surrey; he died of a heart attack on 4 June 1978 at his home, 11 Glenmore House, Richmond Hill. He was cremated and his ashes were scattered in the gardens on top of Richmond Hill.   ROBIN HIGHAM

Sources *The Times* (8 June 1978) · *WW* (1950) · *WW* (1970) · B. H. Liddell Hart, *The tanks: the history of the royal tank regiment and its predecessors*, 2 vols. (1959) · M. M. Postan, D. Hay, and J. D. Scott, *The design and development of weapons* (1964) · J. D. Scott and R. Hughes, *The administration of war production* (1955) · G. MacLeod, *The business of tanks* (1977) · Regimental Association of the Royal Logistics Corps, *Our predecessors: an historical perspective* (1995) · CAC Cam., Crawford MSS · *Wartime tank production, 1945–1946* (1946), cmd 6865 · private information (2004) · b. cert. · m. cert. · d. cert.
Archives CAC Cam., diaries and papers | PRO, War Office and Ministry of Supply records, WO 32, WO 194
Likenesses photographs, CAC Cam. · photographs, priv. coll.
Wealth at death £19,913: probate, 25 Aug 1978, *CGPLA Eng. & Wales*

Crawford, Lawrence (1611–1645), parliamentarian army officer, was born in November 1611, the sixth son of Hugh Crawford of Jordanhill, near Glasgow, and Elizabeth Stirling. He early entered foreign service, passing eleven years from 1626 onwards in the armies of Denmark and then Sweden. For three years he was a lieutenant-colonel in the service of Charles Lewis, elector palatine.

In 1641 Crawford was employed in Ireland by the English parliament, and in December 1641 he appears as commander of a regiment of 1000 foot. He distinguished himself as an active officer in this war, but the cessation of 1643 brought Crawford into opposition with the king's commander, the marquess of Ormond. He objected to the cessation itself. Although following the English or

Scottish forms of worship when in their respective territories, he refused to take the oath renouncing presbyterianism which Ormond imposed on the Irish army. Above all, though willing to continue his service in Ireland, he would not turn his arms against parliament. For this he was threatened with imprisonment, and lost all his goods, but in December he contrived to escape to Scotland. The committee of the English parliament at Edinburgh recommended Crawford to the speaker of the House of Commons, and on 3 February 1644 he made a relation of his sufferings to the Commons and was thanked by them for his good service. His narrative was published under the title *Irelands ingratitude to the parliament of England, or, A remonstrance of Colonell Crawfords, shewing the Je[s]uiticall plots against the parliament, which was the onely cause he left his imployment there*. 'None but a Scott could have writt so many scandalous lyes', sneered the royalist, Lord Byron, as he forwarded a copy of the pamphlet to Ormond (Bodl. Oxf., MS Carte 14, fol. 247v).

A few days later Crawford was appointed third in command of the army of the eastern association under Edward Montagu, earl of Manchester, with the rank of sergeant-major-general and the command of his own regiment of foot. 'Proving very stout and successful,' Robert Baillie wrote, 'he got a great head with Manchester, and with all the army that were not for sects' (Baillie, 2.229). Crawford's rigid presbyterianism speedily brought him into conflict with the Independents in that army, and on 10 March 1644 Lieutenant-General Oliver Cromwell wrote him an indignant letter of remonstrance on the dismissal of Henry Warner, Crawford's own lieutenant-colonel. Cromwell also protested when Crawford arrested Lieutenant William Packer, a reputed Baptist. In time Cromwell would become more and more convinced of the threat posed by intolerance such as that evinced by Crawford, and by parliament's Scottish allies.

At the siege of York, Crawford marked himself out by assaulting without orders. 'The foolish rashness of Crawford, and his great vanity to assault alone the breach made by his mine without acquainting [David] Leslie and [Sir Thomas] Fairfax' led to a severe repulse (Baillie, 2.195). A fortnight later, at the battle of Marston Moor, Crawford commanded Manchester's foot. His kinsman, Lieutenant-Colonel Skeldon Crawford, who commanded a regiment of dragoons on the left wing, brought a charge of cowardice against Cromwell. Later Lawrence Crawford himself, in conversation with Denzil Holles, told a story of the same kind. After the capture of York, Manchester sent Crawford to take the small royalist garrisons to the south of it, and he took in succession Sheffield, Staveley, Bolsover, and Welbeck.

In September 1644 the quarrel with Cromwell broke out with renewed virulence, exacerbated not a little by the jealousies of the horse under Cromwell's command regarding the fact that the foot soldiers of the association were receiving more regular pay than they were. But the quarrel focused on Cromwell's commissioning of Independent officers at the expense of more orthodox godly men, clearly apparent when the lieutenant-general attempted to purge the army after the fall of York. As well as demanding the dismissal of numerous officers of Crawford's faction Cromwell demanded that Crawford himself should be cashiered, and threatened that in the event of a refusal his own colonels would lay down their commissions. These were among the opening shots in the war between the presbyterian and Independent wings of the parliamentarian cause, and in the short term the exchanges ruined Cromwell's close relationship with his commander-in-chief, Manchester. Although Cromwell was obliged to abandon his demand, the second battle of Newbury gave occasion for a third quarrel. Cromwell accused Manchester of misconduct. Crawford wrote for Manchester a long narrative detailing all the incidents of the year's campaign, which could be used as counter-charges against Cromwell.

The passing of the self-denying ordinance put an end to the separate command of the earl of Manchester. At the new modelling of the parliamentarian armies Crawford's command was the subject of controversy, the House of Lords vainly attempting to stem the tide of political Independency by insisting on the wholesale retention of four Scottish regiments in the new force. The attempt failing, the Scots commanders, Crawford included, resigned their commissions in the New Model Army, probably on the instruction of the Scottish commissioners to the committee of both kingdoms. While some of them may have wished to return home to deal with the resurgent marquess of Montrose, Crawford remained in the English service. He next appears as governor of Aylesbury, Buckinghamshire, in which capacity he earned a name for himself as the 'sole plunderer and oppreisor of the county' (Holmes, 148). In the winter of 1644–5 he twice defeated Colonel Thomas Blagge, the royalist governor of Wallingford, Berkshire. On 17 August 1645, while taking part in the siege of Hereford, Crawford was killed by a chance bullet; he was buried in Gloucester Cathedral on 5 September. His monument was removed at the Restoration.

C. H. FIRTH, rev. SEAN KELSEY

Sources L. Crawford, *Irelands ingratitude to the parliament of England* (1643/4) · J. Bruce and D. Masson, eds., *The quarrel between the earl of Manchester and Oliver Cromwell*, CS, new ser., 12 (1875) · J. L. Sanford, *Studies and illustrations of the great rebellion* (1858) · C. Holmes, *The eastern association in the English civil war* (1974) · C. H. Firth and G. Davies, *The regimental history of Cromwell's army*, 2 vols. (1940) · *The letters and journals of Robert Baillie*, ed. D. Laing, 3 vols. (1841–2) · J. Rushworth, *Historical collections*, new edn, 8 vols. (1721–2) · *A true relation of several overthrows given to the rebels by Colonel Crayford, Colonel Gibson, and Captain Greams* (1642) · Bodl. Oxf., MSS Carte 6, 8, 9, 14 · S. Murdoch and A. Grosjean, 'Scotland, Scandinavia and Northern Europe, 1580–1707', www.abdn.ac.uk/ssne/ · *The life and times of Anthony Wood*, ed. A. Clark, 5 vols., OHS, 19, 21, 26, 30, 40 (1891–1900) · *The writings and speeches of Oliver Cromwell*, ed. W. C. Abbott and C. D. Crane, 1 (1937) · *History of the Irish confederation and the war in Ireland … by Richard Bellings*, ed. J. T. Gilbert, 1 (1882) · D. Holles, *Memoirs of Denzil Lord Holles … from … 1641 to 1648* (1699), 16 · S. R. Gardiner, *History of the great civil war, 1642–1649*, new edn, 4 vols. (1901–5), vol. 1 · J. Vicars, *The burning-bush not consumed* (1646), 98, 116 · J. Le Neve, *Monumenta Anglicana*, 5 vols. (1717–19), vol. 1, p. 220

Crawford [*married name* Buthlay], **Marion Kirk** [*called* Crawfie] **(1909–1988)**, royal governess and author, was born on 5 June 1909 at Woodside Cottage, near Kilmarnock, Ayrshire, the daughter of John Inglis Crawford of Earlston, Ayrshire, and his wife, Margaret (later Mrs Robert Kirk). The family moved to New Zealand, where Crawford's father was killed in an accident installing electric tramlines when she was one year old. Five years later they returned to Scotland, and she was brought up in Dunfermline, Fife. Her mother married again; her second husband was a sanitary engineer. Crawford was educated at Moray House Training College, Edinburgh, studying behavioural science and psychology, and planned to undertake child psychology work with poor children.

But Crawford was diverted to teach history to the children of the tenth earl of Elgin at Broomhall, Dunfermline. She also gave lessons to Mary Leveson-Gower, whose mother, Lady Rosemary Leveson-Gower (later Countess Granville), was a sister of the duchess of York (later Queen Elizabeth). At this stage Crawford was known by the nickname Cuppie.

On Lady Rosemary's recommendation Marion Crawford was engaged as governess to Princess Elizabeth and Princess Margaret of York in 1933 and she remained in royal service until 1949. She established the schoolroom routine at 145 Piccadilly, the Yorks' London home, and was particularly effective at teaching the children history. There is no doubt about her benign influence on the young princesses, and she became a confidante to both: on Princess Elizabeth's eighteenth birthday *The Times* wrote that Marion Crawford had 'upheld through the years of tutelage the standards of simple living and honest thinking that Scotland peculiarly respects' (Pimlott, 21). From later revelations it is clear that all three had fun together. Sensitive to the remoteness of court life, she took her charges on educational visits, most famously a trip on the London underground, and she persuaded the king and queen to allow a guide troop to be set up at Buckingham Palace. The princesses called her Crawfie, the name by which she was later known in the press after her fall from grace.

On 16 September 1947 Marion Crawford married Major George Main Buthlay (1893–1977), a bank executive and businessman who had worked in Ceylon. She was appointed CVO in January 1949 for 'personal services to King George VI and Queen Elizabeth', one of only ten women so honoured by George VI.

The years after her departure from the royal household were less felicitous. The American press was hungry for royal stories: in particular, Bruce and Beatrice Blackmar Gould, co-editors of the *Ladies' Home Journal*, a large-circulation American magazine, approached Buckingham Palace for access to the British royal family and, when they were rejected, turned to the Foreign Office in London. They were directed to the *Times* leader writer Dermot Morrah, who had been authorized to produce an account of Princess Elizabeth's upbringing and similar works. The romantic novelist Dorothy Black heard that Crawford was irritated at being asked to help Morrah and felt that she had been pushed aside with a modest pension and some inferior wedding gifts. The Goulds offered Crawford $80,000 for her memoirs; she put her predicament to Queen Elizabeth. While the queen did not object to her assisting Morrah, nor to her being paid for this, she was adamant that nothing must appear over Crawford's own name. She noted her total discretion during her years of royal service.

Crawford none the less entered into a contract with the Goulds, though apparently in the belief that the articles would be published only with Queen Elizabeth's approval. When the queen read the governess's saccharine prose, as communicated to Dorothy Black, she declined to give this. But Crawford was under contract regardless, and the articles were duly published in the *Ladies Home Journal* in December 1949, then in *Woman's Own* in London, and finally in book form by Cassell as the bestselling *Little Princesses* (1950). These memoirs, though effusively loyal and inoffensive by the standards of fifty years later, provide an invaluable insight into the upbringing of the future Queen Elizabeth II. The book was reprinted in 1993 with an introduction by A. N. Wilson, who noted that, albeit in a mawkish tone, they were written with 'obvious love' (Pimlott, 164).

Despite the undoubtedly beneficial effect of these revelations on the royal family's public relations in the United States and Britain, Crawfie became *persona non grata* with the royal family and the court, and was never restored to favour. Among the royals the expression 'doing a Crawfie' became a byword for the selling of secrets by trusted servants. In the aftermath of her revelations the palace press secretary, Richard Colville, followed a highly restrictive policy on access to the royal family. This line was followed for many years, ensuring that the media would continue to place a high premium on court gossip. One example was a BBC programme entitled *The Young Queen*, which was heavily censored by the palace; an interview with Crawfie was excised completely (Pimlott, 197).

In the autumn of 1950 Crawfie retreated from her grace and favour home, Nottingham Cottage, at Kensington Palace, to Aberdeen. Thereafter, under the influence of her husband, she leased her name to further articles in *Woman's Own* (not written by her) and to further ghosted books: *The Queen Mother*, a life of Queen Mary (1951); *Queen Elizabeth II* (1952)—originally a series in *Woman's Own* called 'Princess Elizabeth: the woman'—which was in its sixth impression by February 1953; *Happy and Glorious!* (1953); and *Princess Margaret* (1953), another series of articles converted into book form.

Woman's Own had a six-week deadline, and Crawfie's column was always ghosted in the office, phrased in suitably vague terms, in advance of the events it covered. The edition of 16 June 1955 carried descriptions of trooping the colour and royal Ascot, which, due to a rail strike, had been cancelled at the last moment. Media rivals exposed Crawfie as a fraud and she retreated into further obscurity at her home, a whitewashed cottage in Hillhead Road, Bieldside, Aberdeen.

Thereafter Marion Buthlay's general policy was to reject all enquiries and requests for information. If she responded, it was in the negative, by way of a typed letter with an illegible signature stating: 'She has always said no to such requests and this policy she is to continue'. Nor did she ever seek to explain her actions. George Buthlay died in 1977, and in the years that followed she made at least one suicide attempt. She spent her last years at Hawkhill House Nursing Home in Milltimber, Aberdeen, where she died on 11 February 1988. HUGO VICKERS

Sources D. Morrah, *Princess Elizabeth* (1950) · B. Gould and B. Gould, *American story* (1968) · *Crawfie, the royal nanny who wouldn't stay mum* [Channel 4, 26/6/2000] · Bruce and Beatrice Blackmar Gould corresp., Princeton University, CO673 · Harold Albert papers, priv. coll. · private information (2004) [R. Lacey] · B. Pimlott, *The queen: a biography of Elizabeth II* (1996) · *The Guardian* (18 Feb 1988) · V. Thorpe, 'Queen mother was "ruthless" to royal nanny', *The Observer* (25 June 2000) · Kelly, *Handbk*

Archives Princeton University, Bruce Blackmar Gould and Beatrice Blackmar Gould corresp., CO673

Wealth at death £126,872 10s.: confirmation, 25 April 1988, court books of the commissariat of Grampian, Highland, and Islands

Crawford, Osbert Guy Stanhope (1886–1957), archaeologist, was born on 28 October 1886 at Breech Candy, Bombay, where his father, Charles Edward Gordon Crawford, was an Indian civil servant; he was later a judge at Ratnagiri. His mother, Alice Luscombe Mackenzie, died a few days after his birth, and his father in 1894. He was brought up by two of his father's unmarried sisters, first in London, then in Hampshire, near Newbury. He went to school at Park House, Reading, then Marlborough College, which he considered an internment, on one occasion running away. Despite this, it was his membership of the Marlborough natural history society and its archaeological section which first encouraged his interest in the countryside and its antiquities.

Crawford went up to Keble College, Oxford, where he obtained a third class in honour moderations (1907), began reading for *literae humaniores*, but changed to the diploma in geography. By this time his interest in archaeology was developing strongly, and his change of course owed something to the influence of H. J. E. Peake, whom Crawford first met in the autumn of 1908. 'Going from Greats to Geography', he wrote, 'was like leaving the parlour for the basement; one lost caste but one did see life' (Crawford, 44). He rowed for his college and was captain of boats in his last year. He graduated in 1910 and was offered by A. J. Herbertson the post of junior demonstrator in the school of geography which he held until the end of 1911. At Oxford, J. L. Myres, R. R. Marett, Arthur Evans, and Herbertson were the main formative influences; outside, Peake and J. P. Williams-Freeman, whose 'solid common-sense and scientific outlook' Crawford greatly valued (ibid., 64).

In 1913 Crawford set out on a three-year expedition to Easter Island led by Mr and Mrs Scoresby Routledge, but quarrelled with them and left the ship at St Vincent. In the same year he joined the excavation staff of Henry Wellcome in Sudan, working at Jebel Moya and Abu Geili.

Crawford always retained an interest in Sudan, and particularly the Fungs, publishing in 1951 *The Fung Kingdom of Sennar*. In 1914 he excavated (with E. A. Hooton) an unchambered long barrow on Wexcombe Down, and was digging when the First World War broke out. He enlisted in the London Scottish, went to France in November 1914, and transferred in 1915 to the survey division of the Third Army, serving as a photographer. In 1917 he joined the Royal Flying Corps as an observer and was shot down and captured in February 1918. He was a prisoner of war at Holzminden, from which, as at Marlborough, he tried to escape, though he later claimed to have been happier at the former than the latter.

After the war a period of uncertainty and odd jobs followed, which ended in October 1920 when Sir Charles (Arden-) Close appointed Crawford the first holder of the post of archaeology officer in the Ordnance Survey. It was a role for which he was pre-eminently suited, and which he held until his retirement in 1946. His job was to revise and compile the Ordnance Survey maps from the point of view of archaeological information; but in addition to this work on the standard topographical maps he started a special survey of megalithic monuments, and initiated a series of period maps beginning with the *Map of Roman Britain* (1924). His megalithic surveys led him to write *The Long Barrows of the Cotswolds* (1925). One of his many ideas was to publish geographical memoirs for the Ordnance Survey sheets, but this did not get beyond the first memoir: *The Andover District* (1922), which he wrote himself.

In and out of his professional occupation and throughout his life Crawford was a field archaeologist *par excellence* in the sense defined by Williams-Freeman in his *Field Archaeology as Illustrated by Hampshire* (1915): his prime interest was the face of the countryside in its archaeological aspects. He summarized his ideas on this subject in *Field Archaeology* (1932) and *Archaeology in the Field* (1953). A keen and very gifted photographer, he had taken panorama photographs during the war, and soon realized the value of air photography to archaeologists and historians. He gave an important lecture on this 'powerful new technique of discovery' (Crawford, 168) at the Royal Geographical Society in March 1922, illustrating his talk with a batch of aerial photographs taken mostly of Celtic field systems in Hampshire. The lecture helped to establish his reputation as an archaeologist and as a pioneer in the development of the civilian use of aerial photography, and he went on to write *Air Survey and Archaeology* (1924), *Air Photography for Archaeologists* (1929), and, with Alexander Keiller, *Wessex from the Air* (1928).

Crawford was particularly anxious to interest others in the remote past and archaeological remains of humankind, and to relate these studies to the whole general study of human existence. *Man and his Past* (1921), which he began writing during the war, sets out his credo in these matters. In 1927 he founded *Antiquity: A Quarterly Review of Archaeology* which he edited for thirty years until his death. It was, and remained, the only independent archaeological journal in the world. In *Antiquity* he was able to publish many aerial photographs, articles on archaeology from all parts of the world, and examples of modern folk culture and the culture of modern primitive peoples to illumine the mute documents of the past. A man of strong character, likes and dislikes, prejudices and enthusiasms, he found in the editorial columns of his journal a place to vent his views, to the delight and fury of a wide circle of readers.

Crawford was elected FBA in 1947 and appointed CBE in 1950; he received the Victoria medal of the Royal Geographical Society in 1940 and honorary degrees from Cambridge (1952) and Southampton (1955). He was president of the Prehistoric Society in 1938, and a member of the Royal Commission on Historical Monuments (England) from 1939 to 1946. His last two books—*Castles and Churches in the Middle Nile Region* (1953) and *The Eye Goddess* (1957)—reflect the width of his interests as an enthusiastic and untiring traveller. In 1951 he was presented with a Festschrift edited by W. F. Grimes, *Aspects of Archaeology in Britain and Beyond*, which included an account of his career by his former teacher, Sir John Myres, entitled 'The man and his past'. The foreword to this volume begins: 'No single scholar has done more than O. G. S. Crawford to place the study of the remoter past, and of the past of Britain in particular, on the secure and sound basis upon which it now rests' (Grimes, iii). Crawford was one of the handful of British archaeologists—Sir Cyril Fox, Sir Mortimer Wheeler, Sir Thomas Kendrick—who revolutionized and revivified British archaeology in the decade after 1918. Wheeler wrote of him: 'He was our greatest archaeological publicist, he taught the world about scholarship, and scholars about one another' (*Antiquity*, March 1958, 4).

In 1955 Crawford published *Said and Done*, a vivacious and amusing autobiography in which his character comes clearly through. A bachelor, he lived with a housekeeper and his cats at Nursling, Hampshire; one of his last acts was to give a broadcast entitled 'The language of cats'. He died at his home, Hope Villa, Nursling, in his sleep on the night of 28–9 November 1957 and was buried at Nursling. Crawford did not suffer fools gladly but had a great capacity for friendship, a genuine delight in encouraging and helping young archaeologists, and an infectious enthusiasm for anyone who shared his interest in aerial photographs and field archaeology, or his belief that archaeology, properly studied as a branch of world history and anthropology, was one of the most important subjects. To old and young alike, friends and foes, he was known as Ogs or Uncle Ogs.   G. E. DANIEL, *rev.* MARK POTTLE

Sources O. G. S. Crawford, *Said and done: the autobiography of an archaeologist* (1955) • *The Times* (30 Nov 1957) • W. F. Grimes, ed., *Aspects of archaeology in Britain and beyond: essays presented to O. G. S. Crawford* (1951) • *Antiquity*, 32 (March 1958) • G. Clark, 'O. G. S. Crawford, 1886–1957', *PBA*, 44 (1958), 281–96 • personal knowledge (1971) • private information (1971) • *CGPLA Eng. & Wales* (1958)
Archives Bodl. Oxf., corresp. and papers • Bodl. Oxf., lists of places on ordnance survey maps of dark age Britain • Hants. RO, lists and corresp. • U. Oxf., Griffith Institute, drawings, maps, and plans • U. Oxf., Sackler Library, drawings, maps, and plans • U. Oxf., Sackler Library, typescript article on early Bronze Age | Alexander Keiller Museum, Avebury, corresp., annotated maps,

and papers · Bodl. Oxf., corresp. with Sir John Myres · Cheltenham Art Gallery and Museum, letters to Sydney Harrison · Hants. RO, letters from him concerning excavations · photographic negatives, Southampton Central Library · S. Antiquaries, Lond., corresp. and papers relating to Beaker pottery · S. Antiquaries, Lond., letters to C. F. Tebbutt · S. Antiquaries, Lond., letters to Commander Alexander Woolner and Diana Woolner · U. Oxf., Research Laboratory for Archaeology and the History of Art, papers · U. Oxf., Sackler Library, archaeological photographs **Likenesses** I. Scollar, photograph, 1954, repro. in *Antiquity*, frontispiece **Wealth at death** £4785 8s. 2d.: probate, 25 Feb 1958, *CGPLA Eng. & Wales*

Crawford, Robert (1695?–1732/3?), poet, was the second son of Patrick Crawford, merchant in Edinburgh (third son of David Crawford, sixth laird of Drumsoy), and his first wife, a daughter of Gordon of Turnberry. Patrick Crawford purchased the estate of Auchinames in 1715, as well as Drumsoy in Renfrewshire about 1731, which explains the probably inaccurate topographic of Robert Crawford 'of Achnames' in a statement by Robert Burns (Chambers, 4.38). Robert Crawford's brother, Thomas, was a diplomat. Crawford wrote a number of songs that were popular in eighteenth-century Scotland, the best of which include 'Cowdieknowes', a version of an older song, of which Jacobite variants were popular; and 'Tweedside', a vivid portrait of spring written in honour of the prodigious beauty Mary Lilias Scott, who was known as the second Flower of the Yarrow. Crawford's pieces in Scots, the most famous being 'Bush Abune Traquair' and 'Doun the burn, Davie', are rather mediocre, though Burns produced an improved version of the second of these.

Crawford was a contributor to Allan Ramsay's *Tea-Table Miscellany* (1724–37) under the signature C. During the eighteenth century C had often been thought to be Robert's elder brother, Colonel George Crawford, but the true attribution was firmly established by Robert Burns with his interest in the Scottish archaeology of his own art as a songwriter. Writing in his 'Notes to Johnson's musical museum', Burns relates that he is assured by Alexander Fraser Tytler of Woodhouselee that C

> was a Robert Crawford ... of the house of Achnames, who was unfortunately drowned coming from France. As Tytler was most intimately acquainted with Allan Ramsay, I think the anecdote may be depended upon. (Chambers, 4.38)

In a letter of early September 1793 Burns instructs George Thomson to make sure that the index to his *Select Collection of Original Scottish Airs* acknowledges the name of Robert Crawford (*Letters*, 2.240). According to an obituary manuscript that was in the possession of Charles Mackay, professor of civil history in the University of Edinburgh, the date of Crawford's death was May 1733; however, though his sources seem now to be untraceable, the usually reliable literary historian Lauchlan Maclean Watt gave Crawford's dates as 1695–1732.   GERARD CARRUTHERS

Sources L. M. Watt, *Scottish life and poetry* (1912) · J. Veitch, *The history and poetry of the Scottish border*, new edn, 2 (1893) · *The letters of Robert Burns*, ed. J. de Lancey Ferguson, 2nd edn, ed. G. Ross Roy, 2 vols. (1985), vol. 2 · *The life and works of Robert Burns*, ed. R. Chambers, rev. W. Wallace, [new edn], 4 vols. (1896), vol. 4 · A. Ramsay,

The tea-table miscellany, sel. edns (1724–37) · *The poems and songs of Robert Burns*, ed. J. Kinsley, 3 vols. (1968)

Crawford [Craufurd], **Thomas** (*d.* 1603), soldier, was the sixth son of Lawrence Crawford of Kilbirnie, north Ayrshire, who died in 1541, and his wife, Helen, daughter of Sir Hugh Campbell of Loudoun. He is remembered as a professional soldier in Scotland at a time when military affairs were handled largely on an amateur basis and there were few paid opportunities for specialists. He was employed by the government as a captain of mercenaries in the civil wars of 1571–3 when the supporters of Mary, queen of Scots, were finally rooted out, with English help, from their last stronghold in Edinburgh Castle, and later in 1579 when the earl of Morton turned against the powerful Hamilton family. Crawford is generally referred to in documents of the time as captain, and his company in 1572 consisted of 150 men, of whom twenty were hagbutters (armed with long guns) mounted on horses, with two hagbuts of found (light pieces of artillery) also carried by horse. In June of that year the English ambassador, Sir William Drury, reported that Crawford had acquired the nickname Gauntletts, both 'for manhood and skill as able as any of his coat in Scotland' (*CSP Scot.*, 1571–4, no. 348).

Crawford is first recorded as involved in war in 1547, when he turned out to serve in the host and was one of the prisoners taken by the English at the battle of Pinkie on 10 September. He is said by George Crawfurd, writing early in the eighteenth century, to have gone to France in 1550 and to have served in the French king's Scots guard. After his return to Scotland in 1561 he appears in the personal service of the earl of Lennox, father of Henry, Lord Darnley, who married Mary, queen of Scots, in 1565. Crawford was sent by Lennox to represent him at the meeting between the estranged queen and Darnley when the latter lay sick at Glasgow in January 1567. His account of this meeting, as reported to him by Darnley, was later used at the first trial of the queen in December 1568 as evidence against her, but his deposition is so close to the account allegedly given by Mary in the second of the casket letters that the two cannot be considered independent. One or other, perhaps both, must be forgeries. After Darnley's murder the following month Crawford's allegiances meant he was always to be found serving with the factions opposing the queen. On 3 September 1569, presumably at Lennox's prompting, Crawford made a dramatic entry to a privy council meeting at Stirling and accused Maitland of Lethington and Sir James Balfour of playing a part in Darnley's murder.

After his appointment as regent in July 1570, Lennox resolved on capturing Dumbarton Castle, apart from Edinburgh Castle the main stronghold of the supporters of the deposed Queen Mary. This royal stronghold, set on a rock guarding the mouth of the River Clyde, was considered to be one of great strength, well supplied with food and munitions. The task was entrusted to Crawford, who made his plans for the early morning of 2 April 1571. He was provided with information on the arrangements for guarding the castle and where best to scale the rock by a former member of the garrison. He organized a supply of ladders, ropes, and grappling irons, and his men were told of the task ahead only as they set out. With his party of foot soldiers he left Glasgow on the evening of 1 April, horsemen having been sent ahead to secure the 16 miles to Dumbarton and to prevent news of their coming preceding them. This strategy worked successfully and Crawford was able to commence his attack on the castle without being detected.

The highest part of the castle rock had been selected for the assault, but even with all the ladders lashed together they were some distance short of the base of the castle wall. In a letter to John Knox, Crawford describes how he and his guide managed to climb a further 'twenty steps' and secure some ropes to a tree so that his men could haul themselves up. All this took some time and it was already light when they set ladders on the castle wall itself and the first man climbed onto the battlements. He was immediately spotted by the castle guard, who raised the alarm. In the ensuing confusion Crawford got his men over the wall and some of the garrison were slain before the castle's guns were turned against them. The rest of the garrison failed to make a stand, and those that could were soon fleeing whichever way they could. The enterprise was a complete success although the keeper, Lord Fleming, managed to escape by boat. Those captured included the French ambassador, De Virac, and John Hamilton, archbishop of St Andrews, who was shortly afterwards hanged.

This enterprise singled out Crawford as a soldier of ability and his activities in the next two years are often the subject of report. In June 1571 he was with a force of mercenaries and volunteers, a few hundred strong, marched out of Leith by the earl of Morton to oppose a party of the queen's supporters from Edinburgh, escorting the English ambassador, Sir William Drury. Despite an attempt at reconciliation by Drury the two forces took arms, the Marians being seen off with 50 killed and 150 taken prisoner. In the following August Crawford's soldiers were involved in an attempt to take the town of Edinburgh from Mary's supporters by trying to gain entry disguised as mealmen, and when the Hamiltons raided Stirling the following month to avenge the archbishop, Crawford was there, gathering men from the castle and chasing the Hamiltons out of town. His master Lennox, however, was shot and killed.

In June 1572 Crawford took Calder House, near Glasgow, recently captured by the Hamiltons, before taking his foot soldiers to Hamilton itself, where he suffered a reverse at the hands of that family. Thereafter he was stationed at Leith or at Edinburgh in the struggle to gain Edinburgh Castle from the Marians. He formed part of the combined English and Scottish assault force which scaled the outwork known as the spur on 26 May 1573 and, according to an English report, he was hard at the breach, ready to assail the castle when the garrison capitulated.

The fall of Edinburgh Castle meant that Crawford's company could be disbanded, but he was required to take up arms again in 1579 as part of the expedition sent to take the Hamiltons' strongholds of Hamilton (Cadzow) and Draffen (Craignethan) in Lanarkshire. He was hurt in the foot at Hamilton but was left with his company to supervise its destruction. His employment as a military hardman was still being mooted in the 1580s.

There was evidently more to Crawford than the soldier. He served a year (1577–8) as provost of Glasgow, but was then put off the council altogether, apparently with some acrimony. Perhaps his establishment in the previous year of a bursary at Glasgow University for students of philosophy does more credit to his memory. He received several rewards for his services including lands and an annual pension of £200. The mill of Partick near Glasgow was specifically granted to him for his services at the taking of Dumbarton Castle and Edinburgh Castle. Crawford married twice. With his first wife, Marion, daughter of Sir John Colquhoun of Luss and widow of Robert, fourth Lord Boyd, whom he married about 1558, he had a daughter, Marion, who married Sir Robert Fairlie of that ilk. The elder Marion had died by October 1571, when Crawford is recorded as married to Janet, eldest daughter and heir of Robert Ker of Kersland in north Ayrshire. She died about 1600. They had two sons, Daniel, who succeeded to Kersland after adopting his mother's surname and arms, and Hew, who succeeded to Jordanhill, an estate near Glasgow which his grandfather had bestowed upon the chaplainry of Drumry, but which Crawford recovered through a grant under the great seal of 8 March 1566. Crawford also had a daughter, Susanna, who married Colin Campbell of Elengreg. Crawford died on 3 January 1603 and was buried in Kilbirnie churchyard, in or beside a mausoleum erected for himself and his second wife in 1594.

DAVID H. CALDWELL

Sources R. Bannatyne, *Memoriales of transactions in Scotland, 1569–1573*, ed. [R. Pitcairn], Bannatyne Club, 51 (1836) · *CSP Scot.*, 1569–81 · G. Crawford, *A general description of the shire of Renfrew*, ed. G. Robertson (1818) · D. Calderwood, *The history of the Kirk of Scotland*, ed. T. Thomson and D. Laing, 8 vols., Wodrow Society, 7 (1842–9), vol. 3 · W. Fraser, *The Lennox*, 2 vols. (1874) · J. D. Marwick, ed., *Extracts from the records of the burgh of Glasgow, AD 1573–1642*, 1, Scottish Burgh RS, 11 (1876) · C. T. McInnes, *Compota thesaurariorum regum Scotorum / Accounts of the lord high treasurer of Scotland*, ed. J. B. Paul, 11–13 (1916–78) · *Reg. PCS*, 1st ser., vols. 2–3, 5 · J. M. Thomson and others, eds., *Registrum magni sigilli regum Scotorum / The register of the great seal of Scotland*, 11 vols. (1882–1914), vols. 3–5 · M. Livingstone, D. Hay Fleming, and others, eds., *Registrum secreti sigilli regum Scotorum / The register of the privy seal of Scotland*, 6–7 (1963–6) · M. H. A. Davison, *The casket letters* (1965)

Crawford, Thomas Jackson (1812–1875), Church of Scotland minister and theologian, was born on 13 February 1812 at St Andrews, Fife, the youngest son of William Crawford, professor of moral philosophy at the University of St Andrews. He was educated at Edinburgh high school and at the University of St Andrews, receiving his MA in 1831. He went on to study divinity at the same university, and was licensed as a minister of the Church of Scotland and ordained to the parish of Cults, Fife, on 13 June 1834. He was translated to Glamis in 1838, and subsequently to St Andrew's church, Edinburgh, in 1844. He remained in the Church of Scotland after the Disruption of 1843 and wrote *Reasons of Adherence to the Church of Scotland* (1843). Crawford not only ministered to a large city parish but also served as convenor of several church committees, as well as writing some significant works of orthodox theology. His sermons were renowned for being 'doctrinal in the extreme', being described by a contemporary wit as being 'all shirt and no frill' (Porter, 87). He received a DD from St Andrews in 1844, and in September 1859 became professor of divinity at Edinburgh University. In 1861 he became the chaplain-in-ordinary to Queen Victoria, and subsequently became a dean of the Chapel Royal. His many contributions to the Church of Scotland and to Scottish theology were recognized by his election as moderator of the general assembly in May 1867; his celebrated closing address to that assembly was a call for Christian unity.

Although Crawford's early writing was to argue the case of presbyterianism against prelacy, his most famous work was the product of a dispute with a fellow presbyterian. In 1866 he became involved in a controversy with Robert Smith Candlish, one of the leading figures in the Free Church of Scotland and the principal of New College, Edinburgh. The subject of their disagreement was Candlish's Cunningham lectures on the doctrine of the fatherhood of God; Crawford published *The Fatherhood of God Considered in its General and Special Aspects* (1866), and while the precise differences between the two theologians are subtle, Crawford's text has been called 'one of the most important contributions to the literature on a side of Christian truth that was very widely discussed in the third quarter of the nineteenth century by different schools of theology' (MacLeod, 268). He also wrote *The Doctrine of Holy Scripture Respecting the Atonement* (1871), which is considered to be a standard statement of the orthodox position of the nineteenth-century Church of Scotland on this doctrine.

Crawford was married twice; his first marriage, on 23 August 1848, was to Mary Rankine (*d.* 17 Sept 1853), and their one child died as a baby. His second marriage was on 25 September 1855 to Elizabeth Robertson (*d.* 3 Nov 1908), and they had two sons, William Thomas and George. Crawford died on 11 October 1875 in Genoa, Italy.

JAMES LACHLAN MACLEOD

Sources *Fasti Scot.* · W. H. Porter, *Cults and its ministers* (1906) · H. Watt, *New College, Edinburgh: a centenary history* (1946) · J. R. Fleming, *A history of the Church in Scotland, 1875–1929* (1933) · J. Macleod, *Scottish theology in relation to church history since the Reformation*, [3rd edn] (1974) · T. Trumper, '"The good news of adoption": a comparative study of John Calvin and 19th century Scottish and American Calvinism', PhD diss., U. Edin., [forthcoming]
Likenesses engraving, repro. in Watt, *New College, Edinburgh*, following p. 224
Wealth at death £13,963 15s. 10d.: inventory, 24 Nov 1875, NA Scot., SC 70/1/175/815

Crawford [*née* Smith], **Virginia Mary** (1862–1948), party in the Dilke divorce case and social worker, was born on 20 November 1862 at Gosforth House, Northumberland, the sixth of the ten children of Thomas Eustace Smith (1831–1903), Newcastle shipping magnate and Liberal MP for Tynemouth (1868–85), and his wife, Martha Mary (1835–1919), daughter of Captain W. H. C. Dalrymple EICS, of North Berwick, East Lothian. Smith left the management of his shipping interests to his second son, and he and his wife, a leading London hostess, travelled widely and were patrons of Pre-Raphaelite and other painters. Virginia and her five sisters were educated by a Calvinist governess at home and abroad at Lausanne, where Virginia acquired a European outlook, an interest in literature, and a talent for languages.

Marriage was then almost the only career open even to well-educated young women and on 27 July 1881, when still just eighteen, Virginia, having refused two suitors found by her strong-willed mother, married Donald Crawford (1837–1919), fellow of Lincoln College, Oxford, a Scottish advocate and later (1885–95) MP for North-East Lanarkshire. He was twenty-five years her senior; the marriage gave her a degree of financial and personal independence. When in London she led a social life with her two eldest married sisters, Maye and Helen, lapses in propriety contrasting sharply with practical social work in the East End. She met a Captain Henry Forster, with whom her husband suspected her of infidelity. Confronted by her husband on 17 July 1885, Virginia named the politician Sir Charles *Dilke as her lover. Dilke had been an intimate friend of the family and was also related through the marriage in 1876 of his younger brother, Ashton Wentworth Dilke (1850–1883), MP for Newcastle (1880–83), proprietor of the *Weekly Dispatch*, to Virginia's sister Maye.

Donald Crawford sued for divorce, the case *Crawford v. Crawford and Dilke* being heard on 12 February 1886 when Crawford, on Virginia's unsworn confession, obtained a decree nisi. The case against Dilke was, however, dismissed, the judgments thus implying, paradoxically, that Virginia had committed adultery with Dilke but he had not done so with her. Dilke's failure to deny the charges in court damaged his reputation and in July, against the advice of friends and counsel, he sought to clear his name by contesting Crawford's decree absolute. The second case, *Crawford v. Crawford* (the queen's proctor intervening), on 16–23 July 1886, revealed actionable evidence against both Virginia, who admitted adultery with Forster, and Dilke likewise with Mrs Smith, Virginia's mother. Although Virginia almost certainly fabricated details of her allegations, she was self-assured in court, and the jury upheld Crawford's decree.

The motives which induced Virginia to accuse Dilke are still debated; in his intimacy with the Smith family Dilke may well have behaved improperly towards her. Dilke suspected a female conspiracy. Virginia, who was anxious to shield Forster, never wavered in her allegations, and the courts and the country both believed her. But in the process she ruined Dilke's career, discredited her family, and made herself a social outcast.

After her separation from Crawford in 1885 Virginia retained her marriage settlement, travelled in Europe, lived for a time in Italy, and when in London stayed with her sister Maye, whose testimony in the divorce case was loyal to Virginia. Maye introduced her to W. T. Stead, then editor of the *Pall Mall Gazette*, who employed her as a journalist, though she refused to assist his campaign against Dilke. Stead introduced her to Henry Parr Liddon, canon of St Paul's, with whom she corresponded during 1888–9 on religious beliefs, and who gave her the *Confessions of St Augustine* to read. On 10 March 1888, on Stead's behalf, she interviewed Cardinal Manning, who became her firm friend and mentor. Virginia's spiritual journey ended with her reception into the Roman Catholic church on 4 February 1889. Evidently no retraction of her charges against Dilke was required and Manning, also a friend and confidant of Dilke, counselled silence on all concerned.

Manning introduced Virginia to Wilfrid Meynell, whose friendship enabled her to regain a limited social life, and also to Father David Fleming OFM, for her spiritual guidance. Through Manning's contacts abroad Virginia Crawford met many of the pioneers of Catholic social action in Europe, whose work she later described in *Catholic Social Doctrine, 1891–1931* (1933). In 1896 she visited Rome, Assisi, and Perugia, and studied Franciscan influences in art, on which she published articles and her books *Fra Angelico* (1900) and *Raphael* (1904). In 1899 she published *Studies in Foreign Literature*, reviewing the works of Daudet, Maeterlinck, Huysmans, D'Annunzio, Sienkiewicz, and others. In 1897 Stead recommended her to George Moore as a researcher for *Evelyn Innes* (1898) and so began their lifelong friendship. She became a prolific author, contributing more than 130 articles to periodicals between 1895 and 1947.

Mrs Crawford, as she was now publicly known, also followed Manning's advice in resuming practical social work in London, describing her experiences and advising on training for such work in *Ideals of Charity* (1908). She was elected a poor-law guardian for Marylebone in 1898 and re-elected until the end of the poor law in 1930. Her experience as a visitor to the workhouse and infirmary and on the outdoor relief committee led her to conclude that the poor-law system tended to create a permanent class of paupers, able-bodied as well as helpless, unmarried mothers, deserted wives, orphans, and abandoned children. As early as 1908 she recommended the transfer of infirmaries to metropolitan boards, the pauper schools to education authorities, and the workhouses themselves to municipal councils. She was especially concerned for the spiritual welfare of Catholic inmates and for children settled by the Catholic Emigration Society in Canada, which she visited in 1902.

Mrs Crawford's activities in Catholic charitable and social organizations included the chairmanship of St Joseph's Home for Girl Mothers in London, where mother and child could stay together, and where the mother could train to earn a living to keep the child. She was a founder member of the Catholic Social Guild in 1909 to promote the church's teaching on social questions and to educate Catholic working men through study clubs, summer schools and, from 1921, at the Catholic Workers' College in Oxford. She was the guild's secretary from 1912 to 1919, and her *Ideals of Charity* (1908) and *The Church and the Worker* (1916) were among the guild's basic texts.

In 1919 Mrs Crawford was elected a Labour Party councillor on Marylebone borough council, and re-elected until 1930. In 1920 she was asked to visit Dublin to report on the unrest there. From 1919 to 1929 she was prominent in St Joan's Social and Political Alliance, formerly the Catholic Women's Suffrage Society, and when chairman in 1925–6 she organized a national meeting in London demanding equal franchise rights for women. She was its delegate to the 1929 Berlin conference of the International Women's Suffrage Alliance.

Between the wars Mrs Crawford took part in the Christian Democratic Union, which brought together leaders of Christian political parties in Europe. She was among the first to see the dangers of fascism and edited *Italy Today* (1929–32), pamphlets issued by the Friends of Italian Freedom, her campaigning against Mussolini earning her *persona non grata* status in Italy. The Spanish Civil War presented a dilemma for left-wing Catholics, and Mrs Crawford devoted her energies to promoting the peace plans drafted in 1937 by the British and French committees for civil and religious peace in Spain. In 1936 she founded the People and Freedom Group to apply Christian principles in national and international life, the group continuing into the 1940s.

Although she never disguised her identity, few people in later years associated her with the notorious Mrs Crawford of the 1886 Dilke case. From about 1905 she suffered increasing deafness but retained much of the boyish vitality which endeared her to her many lifelong friends. She never forgot her debt to Stead, Liddon, and above all Cardinal Manning for her spiritual regeneration, and after her conversion led an exemplary single life. She followed the Franciscan ideal and supported the Franciscan nuns at Mill Hill, whose convent she entered briefly in 1903. Mrs Crawford outlived all her brothers and sisters and all those involved in the Dilke case, and died at 48 Holland Park, London, on 19 October 1948. ROBIN M. GARD

Sources Churchill College, Cambridge, Dilke-Crawford-Roskill Collection · F. Bywater, 'The Dilke story', priv. coll. · F. Bywater, 'Virginia Crawford', priv. coll. · R. Jenkins, *Dilke: a Victorian tragedy* (1965) · B. Askwith, *Lady Dilke: a biography* (1969) · D. Nicholls, *The lost prime minister: a life of Sir Charles Dilke* (1995) · F. Bywater, 'Cardinal Manning and the Dilke divorce case', *Chesterton Review*, 18/4 (Nov 1992), 539–53 [Cardinal Manning special issue] · V. Green, *Love in a cool climate: the letters of Mark Pattison and Meta Bradley, 1879–1884* (1985) · *The Times* (13 Feb 1886) · *The Times* (20 Feb 1886) · *The Times* (17 July 1886) · *The Times* (19–24 July 1886) · *Weekly Dispatch* (14 Feb 1886); (4 July 1886); (25 July 1886) · b. cert. · d. cert. · *Christian Democrat*, 28/12 (Dec 1948) · *Catholic Citizen* (15 Nov 1948) · LMA, St Marylebone board of guardians archives · Marylebone borough council records, City Westm. AC · *Crawford v. Crawford*, queen's proctor intervening, evidence with notes, 1891?, BL, ref. 1609/1569 · *CGPLA Eng. & Wales* (1948)

Archives CAC Cam., corresp. and publications | BL, Dilke papers · Bodl. Oxf., J. E. C. Bodley papers

Likenesses photograph, *c*.1886, BL · photograph, 1910, CAC Cam. · watercolour sketch (as a child), CAC Cam.

Wealth at death £11,071 13*s*. 4*d*.: probate, 27 Nov 1948, *CGPLA Eng. & Wales*

Crawford, William (1739/40–1800), minister of the Presbyterian General Synod of Ulster, was born at Crumlin, co.

Antrim, the eldest of the four sons of Thomas Crawford (1695/6–1782), Presbyterian minister at Crumlin for fifty-eight years, and Anne Mackay. He was fourth in a direct line of distinguished Presbyterian ministers. His mother was the sister of the Revd Thomas Mackay and aunt of the writer Elizabeth Hamilton. His brothers all entered the medical profession: John (*d.* 1813), who was a surgeon in the service of the East India Company and then physician at Demerara; Adair *Crawford (1748–1795); and Alexander (1755/6–1823), who was a physician in Lisbon. William Crawford studied for the ministry at Glasgow University, where he graduated MA in 1763 and received the degree of DD in 1784. On 6 February 1766 he was ordained minister of Strabane, co. Tyrone, a charge which had been vacant since the death of Victor Ferguson in 1763.

Like his father Crawford was a latitudinarian in theology but he took no part whatsoever in ecclesiastical polemics; his tastes were literary and political. He published, first, a critique of Lord Chesterfield's *Letters to his Son*; his plea, in the form of a dialogue, for a more robust morality attracted notice at Oxford University. He next translated a treatise on natural theology by the Genevan theologian John Alphonso Turretine. He zealously promoted the volunteer movement, which he believed would lead to national independence, was chaplain to the 1st Tyrone regiment, and published in Strabane two stirring sermons to volunteers. A more significant publication was *A History of Ireland from the Earliest Period to the Present Time* (1783), which he dedicated to the earl of Charlemont. Though largely derivative the work provides an interesting example of the protestant tradition of patriotism that combined reverence for the revolution principles of 1688 with a defence of Old English and Gaelic institutions.

At the same time as calling for a free parliament, liberal Presbyterians were campaigning for an Irish university in the north that would be open to protestants of all denominations. While William Campbell was negotiating for government support for his plan James Crombie, at Belfast, and Crawford, at Strabane, were making strenuous efforts to start the project on the basis of private enterprise. Crawford's academy, though short-lived, fulfilled the common aim more perfectly than Crombie's. The Strabane Academy was opened in 1785 with three professors. The curriculum was enlarged as the plan progressed, and the General Synod of Ulster placed the institution for a time on the footing of a university and appointed periodic examinations. In 1795, during the brief administration of Earl Fitzwilliam, Crawford was advised that there was a prospect of a parliamentary grant 'to establish a university for the education of protestant dissenters'. Under the direction of a committee of synod Crawford and two others went to Dublin to press the matter, but with the recall of Fitzwilliam the opportunity passed away.

The new turn given to the volunteer movement by the rise of the United Irishmen in 1791 perhaps contributed to the ruin of the Strabane Academy, for it divided the Ulster Presbyterians into hostile sections. Alexander Crawford became a well-known United Irishman and was imprisoned in 1797 with other northern radicals. William

opposed the movement and regretted that some Presbyterians had deserted 'the good old Whig principles' of their forefathers; he believed, however, that responsibility for the rising of 1798 lay with an inflexible government (William Crawford to William Campbell, 7 Sept 1799, Presbyterian Historical Society, Belfast). In the first half of 1797 Arthur McMahon, minister of the non-subscribing congregation at Holywood, near Belfast, fled the country for political reasons, and on 9 May 1798 the Antrim presbytery declared the congregation vacant. Crawford received a call to Holywood in September, resigned the charge of Strabane and his connection with the general synod in October, and on 21 November was admitted into the Antrim presbytery.

Crawford died on 4 January 1800, aged sixty; he was survived by his wife, who died on 20 February 1806. His funeral sermon was preached by William Bryson.

ALEXANDER GORDON, *rev.* I. R. McBRIDE

Sources *The manuscripts and correspondence of James, first earl of Charlemont*, 2 vols., HMC, 28 (1891–4) · *Records of the General Synod of Ulster, from 1691 to 1820*, 3 vols. (1890–98) · W. I. Addison, *A roll of graduates of the University of Glasgow from 31st December 1727 to 31st December 1897* (1898) · W. I. Addison, ed., *The matriculation albums of the University of Glasgow from 1728 to 1858* (1913) · T. Witherow, *Historical and literary memorials of presbyterianism in Ireland*, [2 vols.] (1879–80) · J. McConnell and others, eds., *Fasti of the Irish Presbyterian church, 1613–1840*, rev. S. G. McConnell, 2 vols. in 12 pts (1935–51) · I. R. McBride, *Scripture politics: Ulster Presbyterians and Irish radicalism in the late eighteenth century* (1998) · DNB
Archives Presbyterian Historical Society of Ireland, Belfast, Campbell MSS · PRO NIre., Stewart of Killymoon MSS

Crawford, William (1788–1847), prison inspector, the youngest son of Captain Robert Crawford and his wife, Mary Haw of Great Yarmouth, was born on 30 May 1788 in London, where his father ran a wine retail business. He was educated for a business career, but from 1805 to 1815 he worked at the Naval Transport Office, London. At this time Crawford was deeply influenced by the evangelical revival of the period: in 1810 he joined the British and Foreign School Society, and also campaigned against the slave trade and the penal code of maximum severity.

In 1812 Crawford fell under the influence of Peter Bedford (1780–1864), a well-known Quaker philanthropist who founded the London Refuge for the Destitute, which received abandoned or orphaned children in London. Witnessing the gross neglect of children which, in his view, led to their later criminality, Crawford was deeply affected by the execution of an apparently innocent boy and thus began a lifelong commitment to the reform of young offenders. In May 1815 he and Bedford set up the Society for Investigating the Causes of the Alarming Increase of Juvenile Delinquency in the Metropolis. In 1816 this society reported that large numbers of London children and young people were maltreated and neglected by their parents, and left wholly ignorant of spiritual, moral, and educational knowledge. Addicted to gambling and sexual promiscuity, living by begging or crime, they were *habitués* of liquor halls and houses of prostitution, and were in and out of prison, where they learned to admire and emulate older criminals. Crawford believed that the roots of crime lay in parental and educational neglect, which created a moral vacuum; in this urban culture, wholly sealed off from religious and moral truths, children formed naturally depraved habits and associations which led to criminal conduct. He advocated the placement of young offenders in severe disciplinary and educative reformatory institutions, followed by transportation to the colonies to begin a new life based on experience in a fresh and natural environment.

In 1815 Crawford was a founder member and secretary of the Society for the Improvement of Prison Discipline and Reformation of Juvenile Offenders. At that time he was closely associated with Henry Grey Bennet, the whigs' leading penal spokesman, and was a regular visitor to the London prisons. This new society was joined by representatives of the Quaker banking families of Fry, Gurney, and Hoare, and leading Anglican evangelicals. Crawford edited the eight reports of that society which appeared between 1818 and 1832 and he won over the support of aristocrats, bishops, and MPs. The society advanced a radical critique, based on the rational, reformatory, and uniform system of measured deterrence embraced by the penologists of the Enlightenment: British prisons were accused of undermining morals by uncontrolled association, idleness, lack of reformatory programmes, and the poor quality of staff.

In 1833 the whig home secretary, Viscount Melbourne, sent Crawford to the United States to consider possible import of American penal ideas. Crawford found two systems in transatlantic prisons: on one hand there was the Auburn 'silent system' which allowed associated labour and dining, but prevented contamination by silence enforced by flogging; on the other hand was the Philadelphia 'separate system' which combined cellular confinement throughout sentence with visits from a battery of reformatory personnel, such as chaplains, teachers, and trade instructors, whose message of forgiveness would hopefully be well-received by prisoners softened by enforced solitude. Crawford was entranced by what he saw as the perfect prison system, and criticized the silent system which, in his view, led to vengefulness and hatred among prisoners. Separation alone, in his view, could deter by its awesome severity and reform by its irresistible impact on the individual conscience.

Crawford was appointed prison inspector to the home district along with Whitworth Russell, former chaplain of Millbank penitentiary, under the 1835 Prison Act which created the inspectorate: these two men dominated prison policy for over a decade. Unlike the other three inspectors they had a national remit, and they used their influence to campaign for separation in all prisons and to drive localities to set up severe, moralistic, and disciplinary regimes which (in their view) were absent from most prisons. With Russell, who was an intransigent separatist, Crawford produced annual reports to parliament extolling the separate system and damning the silent. They castigated local magistrates for inertia, devised new law, certified new regulations, and crusaded unrelentingly

against prison hulks. Together they planned special projects, such as the model separate system at Pentonville opened in 1842, which was for a time the wonder of the age, and the state-of-the-art Parkhurst prison for young convicts opened in 1838, in which Crawford's vision of discipline, religion, training, education, and eventual transportation to Australasia was attempted.

Whig home secretary Lord John Russell was won over to separation, and localities increasingly came under pressure from hostile published annual reports, circular instruction backed up by new laws, and refusal to certify prison regulations where compliance was not forthcoming. In the 1840s the single-cell prison, with its tiers of corridors radiating from a central headquarters block, mushroomed throughout the country. In 1837 the Home Office seconded Joshua Jebb (1793–1863), a royal engineer, to survey this huge building programme. Whitworth Russell was in almost continuous conflict with Jebb, whom he saw as invading the inspectors' prerogative, while Crawford unsuccessfully sought to reconcile them. By the mid-1840s Crawford was also working extremely long hours on his special projects at Pentonville and Parkhurst, and experiencing great disappointment that the Parkhurst experiment was proving very problematic. Despite failing health he continued to drive himself until, on 22 April 1847, he had a fatal heart attack in the board-room of Pentonville prison.

Crawford was unmarried, and a friend described him as a remarkably gentle and amiable man. He was immensely diligent and, although he published no books, the annual reports of the prison inspectors for the home district constituted a major literary output. He had a major and enduring impact on the reconstruction of the English and Welsh prison systems in the period from 1835 to 1847: the single-cellular prison dominated the prison system of the nineteenth and early twentieth centuries long after the enticing reformatory claims which Crawford and his associates had so enthusiastically embraced had been shown to be groundless.

BILL FORSYTHE

Sources L. Radzinowicz and R. Hood, *A history of English criminal law and its administration from 1750*, rev. edn, 5: *The emergence of penal policy in Victorian and Edwardian England* (1990) · S. McConville, *A history of English prison administration*, 1: *1750–1877* (1981) · W. Forsythe, *The reform of prisons, 1830–1900* (1987) · E. Stockdale, 'The rise of Joshua Jebb, 1837–1850', *British Journal of Criminology*, 16 (1976), 164–70 · 'Inspectors of prisons for the home district', *Parl. papers* (1835–47) [reports 1–13] · PRO, HO/20, HO/21 · *Reports of the Committee of the Society for the Improvement of Prison Discipline, and Reformation of Juvenile Offenders*, 8 vols. (1818–32) · M. Ignatieff, *A just measure of pain: the penitentiary in the industrial revolution, 1750–1850* (1978) · 'Select committee … on gaols and houses of correction: first report', *Parl. papers*, 11 (1835), 11.3–14, no. 438 [evidence on prison discipline] · 'Report of William Crawford on penitentiaries of the United States', *Parl. papers* (1834), 46.349, no. 593 · 'Papers on Parkhurst Prison', *Parl. Papers Annual* (1838–47) · DNB
Archives PRO, HO MSS

Crawford, William (1822–1869), portrait and genre painter, was born at Ayr on 9 August 1822, the second son of Archibald *Crawfurd, or Crawford (1784–1843), poet and auctioneer, the author of such popular lyrics as 'Bonnie Mary Hay', and his wife, Catherine or Catharine Craig.

In boyhood he showed a talent for art and was at an early age sent to Edinburgh to study under Sir William Allan at the Trustees' Academy. His success in copying one of William Etty's paintings secured for him a travelling bursary, thus enabling him to visit Rome. He studied there for two or three years, and from Rome he contributed occasional papers and reviews to some Edinburgh newspapers. On his return he settled in Edinburgh and enrolled as a student of the life school of the Royal Scottish Academy between 1840 and 1843. He found an influential patron in Lord Meadowbank, and from 1844 to 1858 he was employed as a teacher of drawing in the school of design which was part of the Trustees' Academy until its absorption into the Department of Science and Art based in South Kensington, London.

Crawford was an indefatigable worker, and both a regular and prolific exhibitor at the annual exhibitions of the Royal Scottish Academy. Among his contributions were various religious subjects, and many genre pictures, the most successful of which were centred on female figures. These were executed with a technical finesse acquired during his years in Rome. Many of these works were bought by the Royal Association for the Promotion of the Fine Arts in Scotland. However, he achieved his greatest success with his portraits in crayon, especially those of children and young women. These were executed with a sense of grace and a delight in femininity which made them much sought after in his own lifetime.

Crawford was an original member of an artists' club called the Smashers Club, which was formed in Edinburgh in 1848. He also exhibited portraits and figure subjects such as *A Highland Keeper's Daughter* (exh. 1865) at the Royal Academy in London between 1852 and 1868. In 1860 he was elected an associate of the Royal Scottish Academy. He married Theodosia Yonge Muller (c.1838–1922) on 24 October 1862, and died suddenly at his home, 2 Lynedoch Place, Edinburgh, on 1 August 1869. His wife survived him and remarried. R. E. GRAVES, rev. JOANNA SODEN

Sources *The Scotsman* (3 Aug 1869) · *Art Journal*, 31 (1869), 272 · *Annual Report of the Council of the Royal Scottish Academy of Painting, Sculpture, and Architecture*, 42 (1869), 10 · C. B. de Laperriere, ed., *The Royal Scottish Academy exhibitors, 1826–1990*, 4 vols. (1991), vol. 1, pp. 362–5 · Graves, *RA exhibitors*, 2 (1905), 196 · R. Brydall, *Art in Scotland, its origin and progress* (1889), 388–9 · P. J. M. McEwan, *Dictionary of Scottish art and architecture* (1994), 150 · Wood, *Vic. painters*, 2nd edn · bap. reg. Scot. · m. cert. · d. cert. · life school records, Royal Scot. Acad.

Archives Royal Scot. Acad., corresp. · Royal Scot. Acad., life school records

Likenesses two photographs, Royal Scot. Acad.

Wealth at death £1921 5s. 8d.: inventory, 19 Oct 1869, NA Scot., SC 70/1/145, 187–93 · £78: due deceased

Crawford, William (1833–1890), trade unionist and politician, was born at Whitley in Northumberland, the son of William Crawford, a miner. Little is known of his early years, except that he suffered a serious injury when sent to work in the pits at about the age of ten. Doctors wanted to amputate his leg but his father refused. He was able to attend Seaton Sluice School during convalescence and as a result was somewhat better educated than most miners'

sons. At the age of twenty-four, when he married Sarah Ann, daughter of John Townson of Tamworth, he was already a Primitive Methodist preacher and an advocate of temperance and social reform.

By the early 1860s Crawford was an active trade unionist, and in 1863 he played a key role in the formation of the Northumberland and Durham Mutual Confident Association. Towards the end of that year colliery owners threatened to reintroduce the yearly bond (or contractual arrangement) into Northumberland but met with stern resistance from the pitmen. Spurred by the thought of collective strength the pitmen agreed to form a union at the end of December; Crawford was elected general secretary. The union was much stronger in Northumberland than in Durham and Crawford worked with considerable success to encourage interest in unionization in the Auckland district of Durham. In the same year, 1863, he was nominated as delegate to the famous conference of the National Association of Coal, Lime, and Ironstone Miners. There he argued the case for improved inspection of mines, but urged rejection of the proposal for an eight-hour bill in mining. Crawford was vehemently opposed to the disruption of working practices in the region which would be entailed by limiting the hours worked by boys.

In 1864 the Northumberland miners seceded from the joint association, and this led to a campaign by Durham miners to establish their own trade union. Crawford remained secretary and agent of the Northumberland Association until June 1865 when he became secretary of the Cowpen co-operative store at Blyth, Northumberland. He was succeeded in the union by Thomas Burt. Earlier in the same year, shortly before leaving the Northumberland union, Crawford gave evidence before the select committee on the regulation and inspection of mines and miners' complaints. He worked for about a year for his co-operative society and then began business on his own account at Bedlington.

The creation of the Durham Miners' Association (DMA) in 1869 was to prove pivotal to Crawford's future career. In Durham as in Northumberland, miners were becoming increasingly aware of their common problems and the possibility of finding solutions in united action. They shared a common detestation of the yearly bond and the realization of the need to protect their rates of pay and conditions of work. The issue came to a head at Monkwearmouth colliery in 1869 when four men were charged before the courts for breach of contract. They had signed the 'bond' but had then withdrawn their labour on the grounds that the low wages which the colliers were being paid did not provide anything like a living wage. Their dispute provided a focal point for the widespread discontent which had been growing in the Durham coalfield for many years. On 20 November 1869 a decision was made in the Market Hotel in Durham to form a Durham miners' union. Crawford became involved somewhat later, but was appointed a full-time agent in May 1870. Thereafter his position and influence grew considerably. He was invited to become president at the end of 1870 and from 1872 acted in addition as secretary of the DMA, itself on the way to becoming the largest separate miners' union in the United Kingdom. In 1872 the DMA secured replacement of the yearly bond by a fortnightly agreement.

The union was formed at an opportune time. Trade was beginning to boom and continued to do so until 1873 when conditions quickly changed. During 1873 coal prices fell. Demand was far lower than the industry's capacity to produce coal and this was reflected in the continued reduction of wage rates. The union's early responses to these troubled times bore the mark of Crawford's influence. Although he had a lasting concern to improve legislative regulation over coalmining accidents and workmen's compensation, he was driven in his regular dealings with miners and colliery owners by more personal and powerful instincts. Committed to the cause of improving the position of working men through trade union action, he consistently opposed unconstitutional strike action. As a religious nonconformist he was opposed to industrial militancy; only by moderation and tolerance did he foresee negotiations being maintained with the coal owners on the basis of mutual respect. He worked hard to establish and maintain conciliation boards and representative committees to establish wage levels in general and colliery price lists and tonnage rates in particular.

Under Crawford the Durham Miners' Association had a highly developed system of collective bargaining based on a sliding scale of wages and defence of traditional working hours and shift systems. Crawford acquiesced in the coal owners' view that wages should vary with the selling price of coal in both an upward and downward direction. This issue, together with the question of the length of the working day, affected Durham's relationship with other mining associations and ultimately with the Miners' Federation of Great Britain (MFGB), formed in 1888. Sliding-scale wage agreements fell out of favour in other coalfields during the 1880s: the MFGB resisted their continuation and remained determined to secure legislative limitation of miners' daily working hours to a maximum of eight. The dispute over the statutory working day led Durham to refuse to join the MFGB, a divide which left the Durham miners in a vulnerable position in their major strike of 1892. Crawford remained convinced, however, that his duty was to protect the interests of the Durham miners as he saw them.

Better suited to the detailed complexity of committee work rather than to platform oratory, Crawford was nevertheless skilful in negotiation and a man of considerable executive power; he was a solver of problems, as well as a manager of men. Short-tempered and intolerant at times, he remained utterly convinced of the power of trade unionism. In politics he was a firm Liberal, and sat on the parliamentary committee of the TUC from 1878 to 1890 and was its chairman in 1881 and again in 1888. He was elected to parliament in 1885 for Mid Durham, and re-elected in 1886, serving as its MP until his death. For some years he was an alderman of the Durham county council.

Although he contributed to committee work in the House of Commons, Crawford participated very little in parliamentary affairs, never once speaking on the floor of the house. Nevertheless he held strong views, consistently rejecting socialism as invalid in favour of a radical brand of Liberalism by which people like himself could stand for parliament as a candidate in the Labour interest, but with Liberal sponsorship. Up to the time of his death he remained committed to mining affairs. He was secretary of the Miners' National Association from 1877 to 1890, and in the year of his death he attended the international miners' conference in Belgium. He joined the freemasons in 1878 and was worshipful master of his local lodge in 1886. He died at his home, 15 North Road, Durham, on 1 July 1890. He was survived by his wife.   W. R. GARSIDE

Sources R. Fynes, *The miners of Northumberland* (1873) · E. Welbourne, *The miners' unions of Northumberland and Durham* (1923) · *DLB* · J. Wilson, *A history of the Durham Miners' Association, 1870–1904* (1907) · *Durham Chronicle* (4 July 1890) · R. F. Wearmouth, *The social and political influence of Methodism in the twentieth century* (1957) · R. Moore, *Pitman, preachers and politics* (1974) · R. P. Arnot, *The miners: a history of the Miners' Federation of Great Britain*, 1: … *1889–1910* (1949) · *CGPLA Eng. & Wales* (1890) · d. cert.

Wealth at death £204 6s. 2d.: probate, 31 July 1890, *CGPLA Eng. & Wales*

Crawford, Sir William (1840–1922), industrialist and philanthropist, was born on 19 May 1840 at Maine Mount, Randalstown, co. Antrim in Ulster, the youngest of the ten children of the Revd Alexander Crawford (1790–1856), missionary and Presbyterian clergyman, and his wife, Anna, *née* Gardner (1803–1882). His parents were both Scottish, but settled in Ireland in 1836, after spending seven years in India, where Alexander was a missionary, and a further four years in England. Alexander took up the position of minister of the First Randalstown Presbyterian Church in January 1837.

Crawford was educated privately and at the Royal Belfast Academical Institution. In 1856, the year his father died, he began work as an apprentice at the York Street Flax Spinning Company Ltd in Belfast, the world's leading linen producer at that time. He remained with this firm for the rest of his working life. During his apprenticeship Crawford showed exceptional aptitude, initiative, and diligence, so much so that in 1862, when he was just twenty-two, he was given the task of reorganizing the Paris branch of the firm. Having successfully completed this task, he remained in Paris as the firm's representative there until 1887, when he was appointed as a managing director of the company. During his period in Paris, Crawford was elected president of the Paris British chamber of commerce in two consecutive years. In 1866 he married Annie Coulson, *née* Glasgow, daughter of a Presbyterian missionary to India. They had four sons and a daughter.

On his return to Belfast to take up his new position of managing director of the York Street firm, William Crawford made his home at Mount Randal, off the Malone Road. He remained managing director of the York Street Flax Spinning Company Ltd for thirty years. In carrying out his duties he not only exhibited 'great business ability' and a 'unique knowledge of the linen trade' but also worked with 'untiring energy and perseverance'. He was renowned for working long hours, being at the York Street Mill early and late. Furthermore, in all his business dealings he acted with transparent honesty and uprightness of character. As one commentator pointed out, 'Everyone who knew him realised that his word was as good as his bond' (*Belfast News-Letter*, and *Northern Whig*, 13 May 1922). On the death of R. H. Reade, the chairman of the company, in 1913, Crawford was appointed chairman. He retained this position until 1918, when poor health forced him to retire.

Throughout his working life Crawford had been an active member of many of the commercial associations connected with the linen industry and had held office in the Linen Merchants' Association, the Flax Supply Association, and the linen section of the Textile Institute. In 1910 he was the president of the Belfast chamber of commerce. In that year he published a pamphlet, *Irish Linen and some Features of its Production*, in which he warned of the increasing threat of cotton to the linen industry and emphasized the need to develop new uses for linen. He himself suggested that it could be used in mesh underwear.

As well as being a very busy and effective businessman, William Crawford was a particularly active supporter of the Presbyterian church and held office on numerous church committees. He was particularly interested in the home and foreign missions and supported them liberally. He was also one of the founders and first chairman of the Central Presbyterian Association and was a member of the general assembly.

However, perhaps Crawford's greatest contribution to society, and the reason for his knighthood in 1906, was his involvement in the development of the new Belfast Royal Victoria Hospital. He had a long and prominent association with the old hospital in Frederick Street, and was very active in promoting the building of the new hospital on the Grosvenor Road. It was 'one of the largest and best equipped hospitals of its kind' at the time (*Belfast News-Letter*, 13 May 1922).

Crawford's health deteriorated after 1918 and he died at his home, Mount Randal, Malone Road, Belfast, on 12 May 1922, a week before his eighty-second birthday. He was buried in the city cemetery in Belfast. EMILY BOYLE

Sources *Belfast News-Letter* (13 May 1922), 5 · *Northern Whig and Belfast Post* (13 May 1922), 5 · E. Boyle, 'The economic development of the Irish linen industry, 1825–1913', PhD diss., Queen's University Belfast, 1979 · R. Allen, *The history of the first Randalstown Presbyterian church* (1955) · R. M. Young, *Belfast and the province of Ulster* (1910)
Wealth at death £42,000

Crawford, William Sharman (1781–1861), politician and landlord in Ireland, was the eldest son of William Sharman (*d.* 1803), of Moira Castle, co. Down, a protestant landowner, MP for Lisburn (1783–90), and colonel of a union regiment of volunteers. His mother was Arminella, daughter of Hill Wilson of Purdysburn, co. Down. His father advanced progressive causes and also upheld the interests of the linen trade in the Irish House of Commons. Very little is known of his early life. He was born at

William Sharman Crawford (1781–1861), by John Prescott Knight, exh. RA 1843

Moira Castle on 3 September 1781 and inherited substantial landed property from his father in 1803. On 5 December 1805 he married Mabel Fridiswid (*d.* 1844), daughter of John Crawford of Crawfordsburn and Rademon, co. Down; they had seven sons and four daughters. In 1811 he was high sheriff of co. Down. During the following years he advocated Catholic emancipation and also sought to improve the condition of tenants on his estates, giving recognition to the Ulster custom which allowed them to sell their interest in a holding. When his brother-in-law died without children, he came into possession of an even larger landed estate and under the terms of the will assumed by royal licence in 1826 the additional surname of Crawford.

Sharman Crawford was now one of the wealthiest commoners in Ulster, and in 1850 he enjoyed an income of some £8000 per annum. About 1830 he began to agitate for the legal enactment of the Ulster custom and its extension to the rest of Ireland. His views on emancipation and tenant-right led Daniel O'Connell to solicit his support in 1831 for repeal of the union. Though acknowledging that 'a national principle for local legislation' was consistent with his outlook, he could not uphold 'two parliaments with equal powers in all matters' (Kennedy, 237).

Sharman Crawford's political interests led him to seek a seat in the House of Commons. He unsuccessfully contested County Down at the general election of 1831, then experienced a similar fate when seeking the representation of Belfast at the general election of 1832, before finally capturing Dundalk borough in the 1835 general election. During his first two parliamentary sessions he introduced abortive bills to compensate evicted tenants for improvements. Increasingly, he adopted advanced or radical positions on a range of issues and on 31 May 1837 attended a Chartist meeting in London, identifying himself with the movement's aims; in the following year he joined the committee which drafted the People's Charter of 1838. Despite having already been approached by O'Connell, his relationship with the Liberator was never harmonious. O'Connell's influence was employed against him in Dundalk; he did not seek re-election in the general election of 1837 and never again represented an Irish constituency. After the passage in 1838 of the Irish Tithe Bill, which had O'Connell's full backing, he took issue with it because of provisions that in his opinion jeopardized tenants' financial interests. At a public meeting in Dublin where he 'bearded the lion in his own den' (*Northern Whig*, 25 Oct 1861), he further accused O'Connell of sacrificing Ireland to an alliance between himself and the whig government of Lord Melbourne, an accusation he repeated in his public letters of November 1844. O'Connell's abusive retort further soured their relations.

While out of parliament Sharman Crawford continued to promote radical reforms. In 1841 at Birmingham he joined Joseph Sturge (1793–1859) in launching the complete suffrage agitation, and found warm support among English sympathizers. Admirers in Rochdale persuaded him to stand for the borough at the general election of 1841, and agreed to pay his election expenses; he represented the constituency until 1852. During this second stint in the House of Commons, he proved an active member, promoting a range of general issues, including free trade, reduced taxation, mitigation of the effects of the poor law, and separation of church and state. In 1842 he pressed for parliamentary reform; in 1843 he moved rejection of the Arms Act while also supporting the Irish nationalist William Smith O'Brien's demand for the redress of Irish grievances. Following the report of the Devon commission in 1844, he tried to secure legislation to codify the Ulster custom and extend it to all of Ireland; he took charge of this issue for some years in the House of Commons. Meanwhile O'Connell's repeal agitation had been gaining ground in Ireland. He had addressed a series of highly successful 'monster' meetings. Fearful of the campaign, the ministry of Sir Robert Peel in 1844 proclaimed the meeting at Clontarf to be illegal. Sharman Crawford criticized the government's action in the House of Commons. His attitude led to a reopening of communication between O'Connell and himself. In the *Northern Whig* in November 1844 he published a series of four public letters outlining the case for a federal union between Ireland and Great Britain, influenced by the Canadian model. On lines replicated by the federalist movement of the 1870s, he insisted that

> whilst I advocate the principle of local legislation for local purpose, I am equally convinced of the necessity of Imperial representation, and that the combined operation of these two principles is the greatest bulwark of strength and prosperity of a great empire, and the surest means of preserving its integrity. (*Northern Whig*, 19 Nov 1844)

O'Connell momentarily appeared persuaded to substitute federalism for repeal but, faced with hostility from his own ranks, he had by late November 1844 distanced himself from the scheme. Although Sharman Crawford's concept attracted some support from whig newspapers, his attitude towards federalism ultimately was vacillating.

In 1846 Sharman Crawford returned forcefully to the Irish land question, forming under his aegis the Tenant Right Association in Ulster. He was quickly alive to the consequences of the famine that gripped Ireland in 1846. As early as March 1847 the Newtownards Union, under his chairmanship, petitioned parliament without effect to amend legislation so that boards of poor-law guardians could give temporary outdoor food relief to the able-bodied poor. In 1847 and 1848 he once more introduced Irish land bills in the House of Commons and was equally adamant in denouncing Lord John Russell's Coercion Bill for Ireland in this latter session. Although popular with his Catholic countrymen, his vote for the Ecclesiastical Titles Bill in 1850 disappointed many. Interest in the land problem continued to mount in Ireland; in August 1850 he occupied the chair at the founding of the Tenant League of Ireland which adopted as its platform the three Fs (fair rent, fixity of tenure, and free sale of an occupier's interest), but found fixity of tenure difficult to swallow. In 1852 he made a last attempt to mount a land bill. At the general election that year he stood unsuccessfully for County Down.

Although he did not re-enter parliament, Sharman Crawford remained active in public affairs. He was a magistrate, a grand juror noted for attending to his duties, a deputy lieutenant for County Down, chairman of quarter sessions, and vice-president of the Royal Belfast Academical Institution. In his role as chairman of the Newtownards Union he presided at its regular meeting held only two days before his death. He routinely opened his house and estate to visitors. He died on 17 October 1861 at his home, Crawfordsburn, co. Down. After his funeral, on 21 October, which was conducted by the Unitarian minister of Holywood, he was interred in the family vault at Kilmore, co. Down. In his later years, and especially after his death, both the man and his ideas were a potent factor in Ireland's politics. He was revered especially as 'the father of tenant right'. His proposals found expression in the Land Acts of 1870 and 1881, while nationalists from the 1870s effectively co-opted his legacy for the 'patriotic' cause. He was succeeded by his eldest son, James Sharman Crawford, who sat as Liberal MP for County Down from 1874 until his death in 1878.

SIDNEY LEE, *rev.* ALAN O'DAY

Sources *Northern Whig* (12 Nov 1844) • *Northern Whig* (14 Nov 1844) • *Northern Whig* (16 Nov 1844) • *Northern Whig* (19 Nov 1844) • *Northern Whig* (18 Oct 1861) • *Northern Whig* (21–2 Oct 1861) • *Northern Whig* (25 Oct 1861) • *The Times* (19 Oct 1861) • *The Nation* (30 Oct 1861) • *Dod's Parliamentary Companion* • WWBMP • Burke, *Gen. Ire.* • *Thom's directory* (1859) • J. Bardon, *A history of Ulster* (1992) • M. Kinoulty, *A*

biographical dictionary of Ireland from 1500 (1992) · K. Newmann, *Dictionary of Ulster biography* (1993) · B. A. Kennedy, 'Sharman Crawford's federal scheme for Ireland', *Essays in British and Irish history*, ed. H. L. A. Cronne, T. W. Moodey, and D. B. Quinn (1949), 235–54 · G. Boyce, 'Federalism and the Irish question', *The federal idea*, ed. A. Bosco, 1 (1991), 119–38 · E. D. Steele, *Irish land and British politics: tenant-right and nationality, 1865–1870* (1974) · B. M. Walker, ed., *Parliamentary election results in Ireland, 1801–1922* (1978)
Archives PRO NIre., corresp. and papers, autobiographical memorandum | Durham RO, Vane-Tempest-Stewart MSS · W. Sussex RO, Goden MSS
Likenesses J. P. Knight, oils, exh. RA 1843, Ulster Museum, Belfast [*see illus.*] · T. Lupton, mezzotint, pubd 1844 (after oil painting by J. P. Knight, exh. RA 1843), NG Ire., NPG
Wealth at death £14,000: resworn probate, Nov 1864, *CGPLA Ire.*

Crawford-Lindsay. For this title name *see* Lindsay, John, seventeenth earl of Crawford and first earl of Lindsay [*known as* earl of Crawford-Lindsay] (1596–1678).

Crawford, Archibald (1784–1843), poet, was born in Ayr, Scotland, on 15 January 1784, the son of William Crawfurd, hairdresser, and his wife, Robina, *née* Thomson. In his thirteenth year, after limited schooling in Ayr, he went to London to train as a baker with his sister's husband. After eight years he returned to Ayr, and at the age of twenty-two attended writing classes at Ayr Academy for a few months. He went to Edinburgh, where he was for some time employed in the house of Charles Hay, after which he obtained an engagement in the family of General Hay of Rannes. In honour of General Hay's daughter, who had nursed him through typhus fever, he composed the popular song 'Bonnie Mary Hay', which originally appeared in the *Ayr and Wigtonshire Courier*. After returning to Ayr with his earnings in 1810 or 1811 he set up as a grocer, but after this proved unsuccessful he became an auctioneer and furniture seller. On 23 March 1816 he married Catharine or Catherine Craig (*d.* 1857), the daughter of an Ayr vintner, and they started a family; their second son was William *Crawford, portrait and genre painter. The use of his former employers' libraries had encouraged Crawfurd's literary interests, and in 1819 he published anonymously *St James's in an Uproar*, of which 3000 copies were sold in Ayr alone, and for which the printer was apprehended and compelled to give bail for his appearance. In the same year Crawford began to contribute prose and verse pieces to the *Ayr and Wigtonshire Courier*, including a series of sketches published as *Tales of a Grandmother* (1824), and enlarged in 1825. Shortly afterwards, with one or two friends, he began a weekly serial in Ayr called *The Correspondent*, which was soon discontinued following a disagreement between them. In 1826 he brought out *The Gaberlunzie*, which ran to sixteen issues, and to which he contributed a number of tales and poems including the popular song 'Scotland, I have no home but thee'. He also wrote at least four plays during his career. His financial situation suffered from the bankruptcy of John Constable, his publisher, after the economic crisis of 1826. In his later years he contributed articles in prose and verse to the *Ayr Advertiser*. He died at Ayr on 6 January 1843. His widow died in December 1857.

T. F. HENDERSON, *rev.* SARAH COUPER

Sources A. Crawford, 'The Huntly casket' and other tales and lyrics, ed. J. Paterson (1861), 3–31 · Anderson, *Scot. nat.* · C. Rogers, *The modern Scottish minstrel, or, The songs of Scotland of the past half-century*, 6 (1857), 31–2 · R. Inglis, *The dramatic writers of Scotland* (1868), 32 · Irving, *Scots.*
Likenesses pencil sketch, repro. in Crawford, *Huntly casket*, prefaces

Crawfurd, George (*b.* in or before 1695, *d.* 1748), genealogist and historian, was the third son of Thomas Crawfurd (*b.* in or before 1669, *d.* 1695), landowner of Cartsburn, Renfrewshire. In June 1716 he married Margaret (*d.* in or after 1748), daughter of the patriotic Scottish historian James *Anderson (1662–1728) and his wife, Jean Ellies. The couple had four daughters, and a son who died young.

Crawfurd was the author of a *Genealogical history of the royal and illustrious family of the Stewarts from … 1034 to … 1710* (1710), and, largely at his father-in-law's prompting, *The Peerage of Scotland* (1716). His *Genealogical History* contained a description of Renfrewshire, which was published separately with a continuation by David Semple at Paisley in 1788, and again in 1818, with a continuation by George Robertson. He also wrote a biographical account of the crown officers who had served Scotland from the reign of David I to the Union of 1707.

In the late 1720s Crawfurd was employed by Simon Fraser to investigate the case for Fraser's claim to the barony of Lovat, and to supply materials to support his claim. It is said that the successful outcome of Fraser's claim was due to Crawfurd's researches, but Fraser refused to pay him anything for his trouble, even though Crawfurd was desperately short of money. Justly indignant at Fraser's meanness, Crawfurd used to call him one of the greatest scoundrels in the world, and threaten if he met him to break every bone in his body. Crawfurd died at Glasgow on 24 December 1748.

T. F. HENDERSON, *rev.* ALEXANDER DU TOIT

Sources *The Spottiswoode miscellany*, 2 vols. (1844), 1.397–406 · W. Anderson, *The Scottish nation*, 3 vols. (1868) · *Scots Magazine*, 10 (1748), 614
Archives NL Scot., genealogical papers · NL Scot., notes for his *Peerage of Scotland*, incl. another of his annotated copies · corresp. and historical notes and papers, incl. his annotated copy of *Peerage of Scotland* | NA Scot., MS history of the Argyll family

Crawfurd [*née* Jack; *other married name* Anderson], **Helen** (1877–1954), suffragette and communist, was born at 175 Cumberland Street, Glasgow, on 9 November 1877, the fourth of seven children of William Jack, a prosperous master baker, and his wife, Helen Kyle. Her parents had been married in Glasgow in 1872, but Helen spent most of her childhood in Ipswich, and returned with her family to Glasgow only at the age of seventeen when her schooling finished.

Helen's political education was fostered by the involvement of her parents with the Conservative Party; both occupied platform seats at the large Conservative Party meetings in Ipswich and her father represented tory interests in his union, the Operative Bakers' Association. The family's political discussions were combined with religious fervour. William Jack was a strict Presbyterian, in the Church of Scotland, and his wife was a devout Methodist. Their Glasgow upbringing encouraged a strong antipathy towards Irish Catholics. Helen read the Bible avidly and also attended evangelical Sunday school meetings in Glasgow. On 19 September 1898 Helen married a widower, the Revd Alexander Montgomery Crawfurd (1829/30–1914), a staunch campaigner for temperance reform in Scotland and an opponent of militarism.

Against this background Helen developed an early interest in the women's movement. Inspired by Josephine Butler's works on the Contagious Disease Act of 1867, she joined the suffrage movement about 1900 and lent her burgeoning debating skills to group discussions on sexual inequality and political and educational discrimination. In 1910 she joined the Women's Social and Political Union (WSPU), formed seven years earlier to secure the franchise for women, and she soon became a proponent of the militant tactics adopted by the Pankhursts. In 1912 she was sentenced to one month's imprisonment in Holloway gaol in London for smashing the windows of the residence of the Liberal minister of education in Piccadilly. She was given the same penalty in Glasgow in the following year, for a similar attack on the army recruiting office and for fighting with police at a meeting attended by Mrs Emmeline Pankhurst at St Andrew's Hall. This gave rise to her first hunger strike, which lasted for eight days before she was released under the so-called Cat and Mouse Act (the Prisoners' Temporary Discharge Act of 1913). Hardened by these experiences, before the First World War Helen Crawfurd became one of the most popular speakers in the Scottish suffragette movement. She continued to campaign and to suffer imprisonment, most notoriously for her alleged responsibility for a bomb explosion at Glasgow Botanic Gardens in the summer of 1914. On each occasion she used the hunger-strike technique for propaganda purposes, buoyed up other female prisoners such as Sylvia Pankhurst. She left the WSPU soon after the outbreak of the war, however, owing to its pro-war position.

As with many other women in this period Crawfurd's feminist efforts merged with socialist principles. Her political awareness was influenced partly by the radical plays of Henrik Ibsen, George Bernard Shaw, Maksim Gorky, and others performed by the Glasgow repertory theatre. She was also deeply affected by the disparity in living standards of people in the slums of Glasgow compared with those of Ipswich's inhabitants. 'These skilled creators of the city's wealth were living in squalor, in houses unfit for human beings', she wrote in her memoirs. 'I began to think there must be something wrong with a system that could allow this' (Memoirs, 29). Although she had in the course of her married life gradually rebelled against much of her religious upbringing, because of the perceived low status accorded women in the Bible, Crawfurd held on to the scripture's egalitarian pronouncements to produce a form of Christian socialism. In 1914 she joined the Independent Labour Party (ILP).

During the First World War, Crawfurd established herself as a national political figure. This was based on her leading role in the anti-war movement and her activities to improve Glasgow's housing for the working classes. In November 1915 she and Agnes Dollan, a close friend and fellow suffragette, established the Glasgow branch of the Women's International League—a predominantly middle-class pressure group opposed to the war, without party affiliations. In June 1917 they helped to form the Women's Peace Crusade, with Crawfurd as honorary secretary, in order to forge a more working-class and militant opposition to militarism. The two women also worked together in the Glasgow rent strikes of 1915. As secretary of the Glasgow Women's Housing Association, Crawfurd became a high-profile figure in urging housewives at mass rallies in Govan and Partick to resist rent increases. This resulted in the Rent Restriction Act in December 1915 and, along the way, Crawfurd's forging of strong links with the shop stewards' movement.

A measure of Crawfurd's increased standing was her appointment as vice-chairman of the Scottish divisional council of the ILP in 1918. In the immediate aftermath of the war, however, she grew increasingly disillusioned with what she saw as the ILP's lack of radicalism, and she was attracted instead by the movement to set up a British Communist Party, headed by Tom Bell and Arthur MacManus. Initially she worked to establish a communist faction within the ILP and travelled in her official capacity as a visitor to Moscow in July 1920 to attend the Second Congress of the Third Communist International. There she met a number of friends, including Sylvia Pankhurst and Willie Gallacher. During her stay she even managed to interview Lenin, who spoke of recruiting women into the Communist Party.

When the vote for the affiliation of the ILP to the Communist International was rejected at the national conference of the ILP in 1920, Crawfurd left to join the recently established Communist Party of Great Britain (CPGB). She was appointed to the executive committee within a year and concentrated from the outset on increasing female membership in the party. Her propaganda expertise led to her editing a separate women's page in the CPGB's official newspaper, the *Communist*, and a part in the creation of the *Sunday Worker*, which disseminated left-wing views in the labour movement.

Throughout the 1920s Crawfurd's political activities ranged further afield. In 1922 she became secretary of the Workers' International Relief Organisation, formed to assist economically distressed areas such as the Volga province in Russia. Her international reputation as a political organizer grew as she visited countries such as Ireland, where she supported the quest for home rule, and Germany, where in 1924 she addressed an audience of 10,000 people on behalf of the German Communist Party. She also helped to set up a number of international trade union and socialist conferences, such as the League Against Imperialism in Brussels in 1927. Following several further visits to Russia, Crawfurd consistently expressed loyal admiration for Stalinism, dismissing the Trotskyists as 'disgruntled elements' (Memoirs, 341). At home she gave active support to the 1926 general strike in terms of food distribution and speeches. She also stood (unsuccessfully) as a Communist candidate in general elections: first in 1929, for the Bothwell division of Lanarkshire, where she polled 1677 votes; and second in 1931 for North Aberdeen, obtaining 3980 votes.

During the 1930s Crawfurd was closely associated with the Communist Party's front organization, Friends of the Soviet Union. However, she switched the bulk of her attention to fighting the spread of fascism in Europe. In 1933 she became honorary secretary of two committees to combat fascism and antisemitism in Scotland, and in 1938 she organized the Peace and Empire Congress which sought to launch a co-ordinated peace movement throughout the British Commonwealth. When war broke out, like many members of the CPGB her stance was somewhat ambiguous. Answering critics who argued that the Communist Party only supported Britain's war effort when Germany attacked Russia in 1941, she retorted that her fellow communists had to be convinced that Britain was prepared to fight fascism and not to co-operate with it (Memoirs, 374). Her ambivalence was perhaps illustrated by her retirement during the war to a cottage in Dunoon.

Helen Crawfurd was tall and robust and renowned for wearing stark, black dresses at public meetings. A personal assessment of her career as a feminist and leading radical was made by a fellow party member, who praised her high intelligence and sterling character as a militant and fighter. 'A fluent speaker and sympathetic personality', wrote Tom Bell, 'she is just as at home addressing a meeting of thousands as she is in conversation with the working class housewife … Had she been self seeking and opportunist I feel certain she could have been among the first women members of Parliament' (Bell, 258).

Crawfurd's last years included a two-year stint as Dunoon's first woman councillor, immediately after the end of the war, and she continued her commitment to the communist cause through the establishment of a local discussion group on Marxist literature. Having lost her first husband in 1914, she married a steel-master and CPGB member from Coatbridge, George Anderson (d. 1951). She died childless at her home, Mahson Cottage, Kilbride Avenue, Dunoon, on 18 April 1954. HELEN CORR

Sources H. Corr, 'Crawfurd, Helen', Scottish labour leaders, 1918–39: a biographical dictionary, ed. W. Knox (1984) · T. Bell, Pioneering days (1941) · memoirs of Helen Crawfurd, Marx Memorial Library, London · W. Gallacher, Revolt on the Clyde: an autobiography (1936) · b. cert. · m. cert. · d. cert.

Archives Marx Memorial Library, London

Crawfurd, John (1783–1868), orientalist and colonial administrator, was born on 13 August 1783 on the island of Islay, Inner Hebrides, the son of Samuel Crawfurd, a medical doctor from Ayrshire, and his wife, Margaret, née Campbell, whose family owned a small estate on the island. At the village school in Bowmore, Crawfurd acquired a lifelong curiosity and a passion for learning, but in 1799 he moved to Edinburgh to study medicine, a profession for which he had little enthusiasm. In April 1803 Crawfurd left for Calcutta as assistant surgeon in the East India Company's Bengal medical service and was immediately plunged into active military service as an army doctor in war-torn northern India. His first wife (née Robertson) was invalided home from India; she perished in a shipwreck along with their child on the journey back to Britain.

In 1808 Crawfurd was posted to the more peaceful island of Penang, where he acquired an extensive knowledge of the Malay language and people, and then accompanied Governor-General Lord Minto's 1811 expedition to seize Java from the Dutch. Throughout the company's occupation of Java (1811–16) Crawfurd held senior administrative posts, notably as resident at the central court of the sultan of Jogjakarta, and he accompanied political missions to Bali and Celebes (Sulawesi) in 1814. Befriending Javanese aristocratic literati, he studied both ancient Kawi and contemporary Javanese and collected scores of manuscripts. He became a fellow of the Royal Society on returning to Britain in 1817 and published his first major work, a much acclaimed three-volume History of the Indian Archipelago (1820). On 25 November 1820 he married for a second time; his wife was the beautiful Anne Horatia Perry (d. 1855).

On resuming service in India in 1821 Crawfurd was appointed to head a mission to Siam and Vietnam, with the primary objective of opening up commerce. He made little headway with the suspicious local authorities and achieved no political and little commercial advantage, despite instructions to seek trade on liberal terms without demanding the exclusive privileges customary in the past. But the official report, which he submitted on his return to Calcutta in December 1822, provided invaluable information.

When Sir Stamford Raffles retired from the residency of Singapore in June 1823, he appointed Crawfurd as his successor. Crawfurd was impatient and quick-tempered, but Singapore prospered under his stewardship. An ardent free trader, he pruned administrative expenses, abolished port fees, and confined taxes to pleasures, vices, and extravagance, such as opium, alcohol, and gambling. His major achievement was to propose and negotiate a treaty of friendship and alliance, signed with the local chiefs on 2 August 1824, ceding the whole island to the East India Company.

In March 1826 Crawfurd was posted to be civil commissioner in Rangoon at the end of the First Anglo-Burmese War and was appointed by the governor-general to head a mission to the Burmese court at Ava, 500 miles up the Irrawaddy River. He was warned to adopt a conciliatory attitude and negotiate a commercial treaty on the basis of equality. He left Rangoon in September 1826, and on his journey along the Irrawaddy he made notes on geology and collected seven large chests of wood, bone, and rock specimens. He was received fairly courteously by the Burmese king but encountered many frustrations in Ava. The commercial treaty concluded on 23 November 1826 offered little, but Crawfurd presented a comprehensive report on Burma on his return to Calcutta in February 1827.

The following year Crawfurd retired permanently to England, where he published the accounts of his various missions: *Journal of an Embassy from the Governor General of India to the Courts of Siam and Cochin China* (1828) and *Journal of an Embassy from the Governor General of India to the Court of Ava* (1829). These were well received, and both volumes were reprinted in more popular format a few years later. Crawfurd presented his collections of specimens to various scientific societies, and William Buckland, professor of mineralogy and geology at Oxford University, hailed him as the pioneer of geology of southern Asia.

Crawfurd supported the successful campaign to break the East India Company's China trade monopoly in 1833, and acted as the paid agent of the Calcutta merchants in their disputes with the company. But his efforts to enter parliament failed. After unsuccessfully contesting Glasgow in 1832, Paisley in 1834, Stirling in 1835, and Preston in 1837, he remained on the fringe of British politics, continuing to lobby on behalf of the Calcutta merchants for many years and later for the Singapore commercial community. By the 1850s Crawfurd was the doyen of an influential London group of retired Straits Settlements officials and merchants, and he lobbied hard against the unpopular measures foisted on the Straits Settlements by the company. In 1857 the Singapore merchants commissioned his portrait in oils, costing nearly £300, for the new Singapore town hall, and one of three stained-glass windows in the new St Andrew's Church was dedicated to Crawfurd, 'whose sound principles of administration during the infancy of the Settlements formed a basis for that uninterrupted prosperity which the Colony thus gratefully records' (*Straits Times*, 3 March 1857). Following the Indian mutiny in 1857 the Singapore merchants petitioned the British government to take the Straits Settlements under the direct rule of the crown. For the next ten years Crawfurd steered the flagging transfer movement to a successful conclusion, repeatedly putting pressure on the reluctant British authorities, and he was elected first president of the Straits Settlements Association, which was founded in London in January 1868 to safeguard the interests of the new crown colony.

Increasingly Crawfurd devoted his time to the languages, geography, and ethnology of south-east Asia. *A Grammar and Dictionary of the Malay Language* (2 vols., 1852), which was a culmination of forty years' research, not only compared the various Indies languages but also incorporated a comprehensive study of peoples, migrations, trading patterns, and the diffusion of language. *A Descriptive Dictionary of the Indian Islands and Adjacent Countries* (1856), which was a sequel in encyclopaedia form to his *History of the Indian Archipelago*, focused heavily on Java but included much about the Malay peninsula, Siam, and the Philippines archipelago.

Crawfurd became the president and driving force of the Ethnological Society in 1861, was a popular public lecturer, and a regular and lively participant at meetings of the Royal Geographical Society. A prolific writer, he contributed many papers to the journals of learned societies, wrote frequently to reviews and weekly newspapers, and left sixteen unpublished manuscripts at the time of his death.

A tall, sprightly figure, vigorous in body and mind, and blessed with robust health, Crawfurd mellowed in old age from the brusque resident of Singapore into a 'fine old gentleman, somewhat of the old school', respected for his 'singularly simple and unostentatious bearing' (*The Times*). In the quarrelsome world of science he was considered a model of forbearance, forthright in his opinions but courteous in debate. A sparkling conversationalist, genial and gregarious, he had a wide circle of friends, old and young, and held court at the Athenaeum most afternoons.

Crawfurd was widely respected by contemporary experts: the crucial help of 'der talentvolle Verfasser' ('the highly talented author') received fulsome acknowledgement in Wilhelm von Humboldt's monumental *Über die Kawi-Sprache auf den Inseln Java* (3 vols., 1836–9). At the Royal Geographical Society's annual meeting held a fortnight after Crawfurd's death the chairman, Sir Roderick Murchison, spoke warmly of Crawfurd, his friend of more than forty years, who had 'perhaps written more than it has been given to any one author of this century to accomplish' (*Proceedings*). And *The Times*, in a substantial obituary, hailed Crawfurd as a 'distinguished orientalist, scholar and ethnologist'.

Throughout his life Crawfurd read widely and was keenly interested in new ideas. He was not always right. Presiding at the February 1868 meeting of the Ethnological Society, three months before his death, he spoke rationally at considerable length, claiming that Darwin's theory of natural selection 'except in so far as it provokes inquiry is of no value to ethnology or the natural history of man' (*GM*, 4th ser., 5, 375–6). Yet much of Crawfurd's work remained valid. His *Mission to Siam* was reprinted in 1967 and *A Descriptive Dictionary* in 1971, while his findings at Singapore were praised by a late twentieth-century geologist for the 'surprising modernity of the interpretations' (Khoo).

Crawfurd suddenly succumbed to pneumonia and died at his home at Elvaston Place, South Kensington, London, on 11 May 1868; he was buried in London. From his second marriage he left a son, (John) Oswald Frederick *Crawfurd, a consul in Porto, and two married daughters.

C. M. TURNBULL

Sources *The Times* (13 May 1868) · *Proceedings* [Royal Geographical Society], 12 (1867–8), 234–8 · *DNB* · J. Bastin, 'Malayan portraits: John Crawfurd', *Malaya*, 3 (1954), 697–8 · J. Crawfurd, *Journal of an embassy from the governor general of India to the courts of Siam and Cochin China* (1828); repr. with an introduction by D. K. Wyatt (1967) · J. Crawfurd, *Journal of an embassy from the governor general of India to the court of Ava* (1829); 2nd edn (1834) · A. Munshi, *Hikayat Abdullah* (Singapore, 1849); ed. and trans. A. H. Hill, *Journal of the Malayan Branch of the Royal Asiatic Society*, 28 (1955); pubd separately (1970) · C. B. Buckley, *An anecdotal history of old times in Singapore*, 2 vols. (1902); repr. in 1 vol. (1965); new edn (1984) · W. von Humboldt, *Über die Kawi-Sprache auf der Inseln Java*, 3 vols. (1836–9) · C. M. Turnbull, *The Straits Settlements, 1826–67* (1972) · C. M. Turnbull, *A history of Singapore, 1819–1975* (1977) · C. M. Turnbull, *A history of Singapore, 1819–1988* (1989) · W. Makepeace, G. E. Brooke, and R. St J. Braddell, *One hundred years of Singapore*, 2 vols. (1921); repr. (1991) · T. T. Khoo, 'Comments on John Crawfurd's observations', *Journal of the Malaysian Branch of the Royal Asiatic Society*, 69/2 (1996), 61–70 · A. Lamb, 'British Missions to Cochin China, 1788–1822', *Journal of the Malayan Branch of the Royal Asiatic Society*, 34/3–4 (1961) [whole

double issue] · C. E. Buckland, *Dictionary of Indian biography* (1906) · *GM*, 4th ser., 5 (1868) · *GM*, 5th ser., 1 (1868), 127 · *CGPLA Eng. & Wales* (1868) · *IGI*
Archives BL, dictionary of English and Javanese, Add. MSS 18577–18578 · BL, Oriental MSS 12273–12401 [bought from Crawfurd 1842] · BL, papers, Add. MS 33411 · BL OIOC, corresp. relating to India · BL OIOC, documents relating to service with East India Company in Java, Singapore, etc. · BL OIOC, draft descriptions of India, MS Eur. D 457 · National Library of Thailand, Bangkok, papers relating to mission to Siam, 1915 | BL OIOC, letters to H. H. Wilson, MS Eur. E 301 · RGS, letters to Royal Geographical Society
Likenesses oils, c.1857–1858, National Museum, Singapore
Wealth at death £5000: resworn probate, Dec 1869, *CGPLA Eng. & Wales* (1868)

Crawfurd, (John) Oswald Frederick [*pseud.* John Dangerfield] **(1834–1909)**, writer and diplomatist, born in Wilton Crescent, London, on 18 March 1834, was the son of John *Crawfurd (1783–1868), diplomatist, and his wife, Anne Horatia (*d.* 1855), daughter of James *Perry, editor of the *Morning Chronicle*, and god-daughter of Horatio Nelson. Educated first at Eton College, Crawfurd then matriculated at Merton College, Oxford, in 1854 but left the university without taking a degree. Appointed on 23 January 1857 to a junior clerkship in the Foreign Office, he was sent in April 1866, having served in Madeira, as acting consul to Porto in Portugal. He became consul there on 13 January 1867 and filled the post competently, though not energetically, for the next twenty-four years. On 1 January 1890 he was made CMG.

While in Porto, Crawfurd spent his leisure time mainly in sport and literary work. In addition to several novels he published three sympathetic but sketchy studies of Portuguese life which are of interest for their accounts of the Portuguese peasantry and rural customs: *Travels in Portugal*, under the pseudonym John Latouche (1875; 3rd edn, 1878), *Portugal Old and New* (1880), and *Round the Calendar in Portugal* (1890).

Crawfurd's last two years in Portugal (1890–91) were a period of great controversy. The 'ultimatum' of Lord Salisbury to Portugal of 11 January 1890, the result of a dispute between Britain and Portugal over the territories known later as Zambia and Malawi, led to a wave of anti-British feeling, more violent in Porto than in other areas of Portugal. Crawfurd's house on the east side of the city was stoned, and there were demands for the withdrawal of his exequatur, co-ordinated by the Portuguese pressure group the Patriotic League of the North. He carried on with his duties until the demonstrations subsided, and then resigned on 17 June 1891. He then returned to England and spent his retirement in writing.

Crawfurd married Margaret (*d.* 1899), younger daughter of Richard *Ford, author of the *Handbook to Spain*; they had one son, who died in infancy. In 1902 he married again, this time to Amelia (Lita) Browne, daughter of Hermann von Flesch Brunningen.

Although writing was for Crawfurd merely a recreation, his literary activity was diverse. A novelist, essayist, poet, and anthologist, the author of around forty volumes, he was also a frequent contributor under his own name and under pseudonyms to *The Times* and leading reviews. He edited the *New Quarterly Magazine* for some years, as well as *Chapman's Magazine of Fiction*. He was also a publisher, being an original director of *Black and White*, founded in 1891, and, through his friendship with Frederic Chapman, was a director and then managing director of Chapman and Hall—a post for which he lacked obvious qualifications. Of his novels, *Sylvia Arden* (1877) was once the best-known. In others, such as *The World we Live in* (1884), *In Green Fields* (1906), and *The Mystery of Myrtle Cottage* (1908), he dealt with political and social questions, and a penchant for settings in remote parts of Britain is often shown. In the 1870s he published some fiction under the pseudonym John Dangerfield, and he also used the pseudonym George Windle Sandys. His verse plays, *Two Masques* (1902) and *The Sin of Prince Eladane* (1903), show competence in diction and prosody but lack dramatic values. He also compiled *Laws of Opposition Bridge* (1906).

Crawfurd was a typical minor writer of the later Victorian era, who also played a small but significant role in diplomatic history. He died at Montreux, Switzerland, on 31 January 1909; his second wife survived him.

S. E. FRYER, *rev.* C. A. R. HILLS

Sources *The Times* (2 Feb 1909) · *The Athenaeum* (4 Feb 1909), 164 · Allibone, *Dict.* · *FO List* (1900) · *Black and White* (5 Feb 1909) · *WW* (1908) · private information (1912) · H. Livermore, 'Consul Crawfurd and the Anglo-Portuguese crisis of 1890', *Portuguese Studies*, 8 (1992), 170–88 · *CGPLA Eng. & Wales* (1909)
Archives Balliol Oxf., corresp. with Sir Robert Morier · Merton Oxf., letters to Max Beerbohm · Richmond Local Studies Library, London, corresp. with Douglas Sladen
Wealth at death £2371 18s. 2d.: administration with will, 17 March 1909, *CGPLA Eng. & Wales*

Crawfurd, Sir Raymond Henry Payne (1865–1938), physician and medical historian, was born at East Grinstead, Sussex, on 9 November 1865, the sixth son of the Revd Charles Walter Payne Crawfurd, and his wife, Mary, daughter of James Adey *Ogle, regius professor of medicine at Oxford. He was educated at Winchester College, New College, Oxford, and King's College Hospital, London, at all of which he gained scholarships or prizes. He qualified BCh (Oxon.) in 1894 and DM in 1896. After holding resident appointments at his hospital and at the Victoria Hospital for Children, Chelsea, he became in 1898 assistant physician to King's College Hospital and later (1905) full physician, as well as lecturer there and at the London School of Medicine for Women. He continued with active work at King's College Hospital until 1930.

Crawfurd took a keen interest in the history of medicine and played a leading part in the foundation of the section of the history of medicine of the Royal Society of Medicine, of which section he became president. He contributed to the *Proceedings* of the society many interesting papers such as 'Martial and medicine' (1913), 'Oliver Goldsmith and medicine' (1914), and 'Superstitions concerning menstruation' (1915). He also published *The Last Days of Charles II* (1909). Besides his historical work he was the author of a thesis on exophthalmic goitre, and was joint editor with Farquhar Buzzard of Burney Yeo's *Manual of Medical Treatment* (1913).

Crawfurd took an active part in the affairs of the Royal

College of Physicians, of which he was elected a member in 1894, a fellow in 1901, and registrar in 1925, holding this post until his death in 1938. He also gave the Fitzpatrick lectures in 1911–12, which were expanded and published as *The King's Evil* (1911) and as *Plague and Pestilence in Literature and Art* (1914), and he delivered the Harveian oration in 1919. His skill as an organizer, for which he was knighted in 1933, was shown by the active part which he took in the transfer of King's College Hospital from its position near the Strand to its new site on Denmark Hill. He was an effective chairman of the council of Epsom College (1923–36), though permitting 'undue prolixity in debate' (*BMJ*, 652).

Crawfurd married in 1898 Ethelberta Ormrod, youngest daughter of Colonel Arthur Bailey JP, of Bolton; they had three sons. He died at 11 Beaumont Street, London, after a few days' illness, on 9 March 1938, his wife surviving him.

J. D. ROLLESTON, *rev.* H. C. G. MATTHEW

Sources *The Times* (10 March 1938) · *BMJ* (19 March 1938), 651 · *The Lancet* (19 March 1938), 697–8 · *CGPLA Eng. & Wales* (1938)
Likenesses photograph, repro. in *BMJ*
Wealth at death £29,226 18s. 3d.: probate, 17 May 1938, *CGPLA Eng. & Wales*

Crawfurd, Thomas. *See* Craufurd, Thomas (*d.* 1662).

Crawhall, Joseph [*known as* Joseph Crawhall the second] (1821–1896), wood-engraver and promoter of the arts, was born at West House, Newcastle upon Tyne, the son of Joseph Crawhall the first (1793–1853), rope maker, well-known lover of the arts, local politician, and mayor of Newcastle in 1849–50. Crawhall came from a large family, with his brother Thomas also gaining a reputation in the art world and his sister Jane Ann becoming the mother of Abel Chapman (who was to play a role in the development of southern Africa). Crawhall was involved with his brother Thomas and another brother, George, in the family rope works for a number of years. By the middle of the 1870s their partnership had dissolved and his only business interests lay in investment in and disposing of real estate. For the last twenty-five years of his life he had a free hand to devote time to artistic pursuits. He was fascinated by the past. This led to a specific interest in reproducing the kind of woodcuts and engravings associated with ancient chapbooks and ballad sheets. Although medieval glass and manuscripts were part of his inspiration, other decisive influences included the work of Thomas Bewick, which he much admired, and the rich tradition of producing chapbooks and ballad sheets which was attached to his native Newcastle.

By 1859 Crawhall had begun to produce books illustrated with his own engravings. These were after the style of the old 'comic cuts' hacked out with a knife, and proofs were often hand coloured. Some of his works were reprinted in the second half of the twentieth century, provoking interest because of the intriguing nature of their contents. At the age of sixty, when many consider retirement, Joseph entered the most creative and productive phase of his life. His capacity for work seemed limitless

and he added Valentine cards, Christmas cards, and children's books to an ever growing list of woodcuts and chapbooks. Many of his works reflected his wide interests. He was a keen angler, and a number of his early books were on fishing, including the *Newcastle Fisher's Garland* of 1864, a collection of songs and poems about the pastime. He was also a musician with a love of the Northumbrian pipes and north-eastern songs. His *Beuk o' Newcassel Sangs* (1888) was produced by subscription and reprinted in 1965 at the time of the 'folk revival'. His love of art alone may have gained him a lasting reputation. His close connections with the Bewick family enabled him to place many of Bewick's works in his personal collection as well as to bring them to the attention of fellow Novocastrians. As a leading member of the Newcastle Arts Association he helped to organize a number of successful exhibitions and is held responsible for much of the groundwork for the city's current art collections. Along with his brothers he was a keen rower and supporter of aquatics at a time when Tyneside was a world centre for the sport. He also found time to collect books and follow developments in archaeology. Another interesting aspect of Crawhall's life was the work emanating from his friendship with the *Punch* cartoonist Charles Keene. Crawhall's sharp wit and lively sense of humour led to a heavy involvement with Keene. For more than twenty-five years he provided his friend with rough drawings and 'punch' lines which the cartoonist then completed and published.

Crawhall married Margaret Boyd (*c.*1833–1928), a Berwickshire woman, in Edinburgh on 30 November 1854. They had at least five children brought up in Morpeth and, later, central Newcastle. The ever-increasing reputation of one of his sons, Joseph *Crawhall the third (1861–1913) [*see under* Glasgow boys], led twentieth-century academics to label the 'three Josephs'. The youngest Joseph was one of the Glasgow school of artists and his work enjoyed a large exhibition in Glasgow in 1990. In his career he was well supported by both father and mother.

Crawhall endured poor health for the last ten years of his life. In 1890 he moved close to his eldest daughter, Elspeth, in Ealing, London. In 1891 he completed his last paste-up. Three years later, on discovering he had cancer, he sold off most of his collections. After a brief stay in the English Lake District he returned south to the West End of London, where he died, at his home, 27 Kildare Terrace, Bayswater, on 7 July 1896. His body was returned to Morpeth, where he was buried on 9 July. His reputation has remained intact for over a century. At his death he was described as 'one of the North of England's most conspicuous and interesting figures' (*Newcastle Daily Leader*). In 1990 his son's biographer confirmed him as 'one of the most fascinating characters of the Victorian era' (Hamilton, 4).

KEITH GREGSON

Sources V. Hamilton, *Joseph Crawhall (1861–1913)—one of the Glasgow Boys* (1990) · C. S. Felver, *Joseph Crawhall: the Newcastle wood engraver, 1821–96* (1972) · A. Bury, *Joseph Crawhall: the man and the artist* (1958) · *Newcastle Daily Chronicle* (8 July 1896) · *Newcastle Daily Leader* (9 July 1896) · W. Wallace, 'Joseph Crawhall: a short biography', in J. Crawhall, *A beuk o' Newcassel sangs* (1965) · D. P. Bliss, *History of wood engraving* (1928)

Archives Newcastle upon Tyne Central Library · U. Cal., Berkeley | priv. coll.
Likenesses J. Crawhall, self-portrait, pencil drawing, Scot. NPG · J. Guthrie, portrait, repro. in Felver, *Joseph Crawhall*, 45
Wealth at death £847 15s. 3d.: probate, 10 Nov 1897, *CGPLA Eng & Wales*

Crawhall, Joseph [Joseph Crawhall the third] (1861–1913). *See under* Glasgow Boys (*act.* 1875–1895).

Crawley, Aidan Merivale (1908–1993), politician and television executive, was born on 10 April 1908 at the vicarage, Benenden, near Cranbrook, Kent, the third of the five children of Arthur Stafford Crawley, vicar of Benenden (later canon of Windsor), and his wife, Anstice Katharine, *née* Gibbs. His paternal grandfather was an entrepreneur, specializing in overseas railways; his mother's roots lay in west-country farming. Both families had a tradition of service in the Church of England. As a result his childhood was dominated by clergymen, especially Archbishop Cosmo Lang, of York, whom his father later served as chaplain and after whom his elder brother was named.

Crawley began his education in London in the summer of 1917 in preparation for enrolment at Farnborough School, a boarding preparatory school, in September 1917. He entered Harrow School in 1920, completing his education there in the summer of 1926. At Harrow he shone academically—winning the top history scholarship to Trinity College, Oxford, on his departure—but above all on the cricket field. Tall, rugged, with a jutting chin and sharply-defined face, he was the stereotypical gifted schoolboy, an inter-war hero. In the Harrow XIs of 1924, 1925, and 1926 he missed out on the captaincy only because of his youth. The headmaster's son became captain in his stead. As an undergraduate studying history at Trinity College, Oxford (1926–30), he again shone, especially as a batsman, scoring 1137 runs in 1928 (including five centuries) against first-class opposition. He was also a leading member of Oxford's Bullingdon Club, becoming friends with Frank Pakenham (later Lord Longford). In later life he recalled that Evelyn Waugh's *Brideshead Revisited* reflected much that he remembered about his time at university. In 1929 his college extended his scholarship and he graduated in 1930 with a second class degree. That summer his name was listed in an England XII against South Africa, but he was not chosen to play. He had some success as an amateur for Kent but left full-time cricket at the end of the year, though it remained his chief recreation. He was a co-founder of the national village cricket championship in 1971, and president of the MCC in 1973.

In October 1930 Crawley began work as a cub reporter at the *Daily Mail*, entering the Commons lobby in 1931 or 1932. In the latter year he began a series of jobs at regional papers in the Harmsworth group, visiting the United States in 1933 to report on the 'new deal'. This was a sign of his growing tilt towards socialism, encouraged by his work in recession-hit south Wales. In 1936 he left the Harmsworth group, unable to stomach its fascist sympathies. He then began an involvement in factual film-making that lasted for the rest of his life. Early in 1937 he left for Palestine, to make films about life there; these

Aidan Merivale Crawley (1908–1993), by Elliott & Fry, 1950

were shown with limited success in 1938. On his return he joined the Auxiliary Air Force, though he cautioned against active British involvement in the Spanish Civil War, then a cause for many on the left, including his future wife, (Harriet) Virginia Spencer *Cowles, a foreign correspondent and gifted writer whom he met in 1937. He joined the Labour Party late the same year. He wrote to Hugh Dalton and found himself in agreement with the latter's campaign for rearmament. Dalton helped him achieve selection as Labour candidate for the then Conservative seat of North Buckinghamshire.

When the Second World War broke out Crawley was serving as an auxiliary with 601 squadron. In February 1940 he joined the Balkan intelligence service, based in Istanbul, with the aim of keeping Turkey neutral. Late in that year he moved to Sofia, fleeing in March 1941 as Germany attacked Bulgaria. As a result he returned to air force service, flying Hurricanes with 73 fighter squadron in the western desert, before being shot down and captured by a German truck convoy, flown to Greece, and held at a prisoner of war camp in Salonika. Anxious to hide his work in the Balkans, he registered with a false forename—Stafford—when formally taken prisoner and sent to Germany. He was held at a succession of camps, ending at Schubin in Poland. There he took part in an attempt to escape by tunnelling under the perimeter: on 5 March 1943 he broke out and, using false documents, headed for Switzerland. After a remarkable journey across the Reich he was recaptured by the Gestapo on the Swiss border. After interrogation he was returned to Schubin.

He played a peripheral part in another escape, later described by Eric Williams in his book *The Wooden Horse* (1949) and by Crawley in his *Escape from Germany* (1956). In May 1945 the camp was liberated and he returned to England.

On his return Crawley was almost immediately thrown into campaigning as Labour candidate for North Buckinghamshire. Unexpectedly he won with a majority of 3845—part of the Labour landslide of July 1945. He also resumed his relationship with Virginia Cowles. They were married by his father on 30 July 1945 at St George's, Hanover Square. She was the daughter of Edward Spencer Cowles, a physician. They had three children, Andrew, Reginald, and Harriet. Like his fellow new MPs Woodrow Wyatt and Christopher Mayhew, Crawley represented the technocratic face of the Labour Party, ensuring that it could claim to represent progressives of all classes. Looking back in his memoirs he recalled the spirit of the time: 'we were not only going to build a new world, but we could see no reason why we should not be in power for the next thirty years' (Crawley, 209). A gilded high flyer, he served as parliamentary private secretary to two colonial secretaries, George Hall and Arthur Creech-Jones. In February 1950 he was re-elected at the general election, with a reduced majority of 1500, and appointed under-secretary at the Air Ministry. He toured RAF bases in Asia before returning to fight the October 1951 general election, losing his seat by fifty-four votes.

Crawley's response was to return to film-making. With three other former Labour ministers (Mayhew, Wyatt, and John Freeman) he became a star documentary maker with the BBC, travelling to India to make a series shown in 1953. His face became synonymous with the new medium, especially as a presenter on *Viewfinder* in 1954. In this he was ahead of his political generation. In February 1955 he was named editor-in-chief of Independent Television News (ITN), due to come on air in September. In this role he insisted—to the point of threatened resignation—on freedom in selecting presenters, choosing Robin Day, Christopher Chataway, and Reginald Bosanquet, all to become famous. Day described his appointment in his memoir, *Grand Inquisitor* (1989), making much of the makeshift facilities available to ITN and Crawley's inspiring role. The channel was launched successfully but ITN's budget and air time immediately came under fire. Crawley threatened to resign unless ITN retained at least 20 minutes of broadcasts a day. Air time was safeguarded but after failing to overturn budget cuts Crawley resigned as editor in January 1956. In leaving, he ensured that the honour for ITN's success went to others—though Day paid ample tribute to him in his memoirs. The departure also marked the end of Crawley's heyday, his promise not quite fulfilled.

By this stage Crawley was becoming disillusioned with socialism in the face of what he saw as trade-union obstructionism. He resigned from the Labour Party in 1957 and joined the Conservative Party late the same year. He later traced the roots of his disillusionment to his suggestion to Hugh Gaitskell in 1951 that the party drop clause 4 of its constitution. After resigning from ITN he returned to documentary-making and spent increasing amounts of time on his farm in Buckinghamshire, which he had bought in 1947. This was sold in 1962 after losses mounted. He also ranged across Africa, and was a member of the Monckton commission on the future of the Federation of the Rhodesias and Nyasaland, in 1960.

Crawley's friendship with Conservative politician Iain Macleod led to his selection in 1962 as Conservative candidate for the vacant seat of West Derbyshire. He was chosen from a shortlist which included Norman St John-Stevas. He narrowly won the by-election with a majority of 1220 over the Liberals. The result was a relief not just to Crawley but to Macleod, who, controversially, had promoted his candidature. At the general election of 1964 he was re-elected with a larger majority. Nevertheless, in parliament for a second time Crawley made little impact, apparently content that his election was proof enough that his talents had not departed after the ITN debacle. He served on the public accounts committee and an ad hoc committee of the Conservative Party which aimed to reform trade unions, by this time his major political interest.

By 1963 Crawley was considering applying for an independent television franchise and in 1966 he formed a consortium to apply for the London weekend franchise. This was awarded on 6 May 1967, and in October that year Crawley left parliament. London Weekend Television (LWT) went badly from the start; disagreement within the broad-based consortium, which included Rupert Murdoch, led to prolonged dispute. Crawley was forced out of the chairmanship in 1971, remaining as nominal president until 1973. In 1969 he published a well-reviewed biography, *De Gaulle*, following this with *The Rise of Western Germany, 1945–72* in 1973.

From 1974 Crawley lived mainly abroad, in France, Spain, and Italy. In 1983 his wife, Virginia, died in a car crash; in 1988 his two sons were killed in a mountain air crash, flying their own plane near Turin in Italy. He moved to live with his remaining daughter, Harriet, in Northamptonshire; she survived him when he died, at Horton General Hospital, Banbury, Oxfordshire, on 3 November 1993, following a stroke. A memorial service was held at St Michael's, Chester Square, London, on 10 February 1994.

MATTHEW PARRIS

Sources A. Crawley, *Leap before you look* (1988) · R. Day, *Grand inquisitor* (1989) · *The Times* (4 Nov 1993) · *The Independent* (5 Nov 1993) · *WWW, 1991–5* · b. cert. · m. cert. · d. cert. · *CGPLA Eng. & Wales* (1994)
Archives SOUND BL NSA, Bow dialogues, 1 Feb 1966, C 812/6 C4 · BL NSA, performance recording
Likenesses photograph, 1949, repro. in *The Independent* · Elliott & Fry, photograph, 1950, NPG [*see illus.*] · photograph, repro. in *The Times*
Wealth at death £157,467: probate, 14 June 1994, *CGPLA Eng. & Wales*

Crawley, Sir Francis (1574/5–1650), judge, was probably born at Luton, Bedfordshire, the eldest son of Thomas Crawley, a husbandman of Luton, and Dorothey, daughter and coheir to John Edgerley of Milton, Oxfordshire. The register of Gonville and Caius College, Cambridge, where

Crawley matriculated on 2 May 1592, suggests, however, that he was born in Norton, Leicestershire, then attended school there and in Luton. According to Lloyd, Crawley's 'dexterity in logic at the university promised him an able pleader at the Inns of Court' (Lloyd, 290). Leaving Gonville and Caius in 1595, he entered Staple Inn, then Gray's Inn, where he was admitted on 26 May 1598.

In 1607 Crawley married Elizabeth (b. c.1576), daughter of Sir John Rotheram of Luton. They had five children who survived to adulthood, a daughter, Ann (b. 1623), and four sons, all educated at Cambridge: John (1609–1638); Francis (1611–1683); Thomas (c.1618–1678); and Robert (1619–1695). John and Francis were admitted to Gray's Inn, where the former was called to the bar on 29 May 1633 and the latter on 11 February 1638; Francis was appointed cursitor baron of the exchequer in 1679. Thomas (BA 1635/6; MA 1639; DD 1661) served as rector of Amersham, Buckinghamshire, in 1660–78, and of Barton in the Clay, Bedfordshire, 1662–78. Robert (MD 1660) became an extra-licentiate of the Royal College of Physicians on 11 July 1656, and practised medicine at Luton.

Crawley's own career progressed slowly. His early offices appear to have been few and minor, the only one known being that of escheator of Bedfordshire and Buckinghamshire, a position he held in 1607. He achieved the bar on 12 November 1617, but never gained the bench at Gray's Inn. Nevertheless, in the early 1620s he began to advance more rapidly, possibly with the earl of Salisbury and Lord Wentworth as his patrons. He became a serjeant-at-law on 26 June 1623, shortly after having been elected summer reader at Gray's (he had served as assistant to the reader in 1622). In 1626 he was among the counsel that the earl of Bristol sought to represent him at his trial in the Lords. Two years later he successfully represented the earl of Cork in a case before the Commons.

Raised to the bench as justice of the common pleas on 11 October 1632, and knighted by Charles I at Whitehall on 4 November, Crawley supported the crown as it sought to enhance its revenue through extra-parliamentary means. In November 1635 he advised that the king had authority to fix the price of corn, thereby creating a situation in which the crown could obtain revenue by selling licences to exceed the set maximum. Of greater consequence, for both the kingdom and himself, was the position that Crawley took on ship money. In February 1636 he joined the other judges in resolving in favour of the levy, and in January 1638 he not only supported the crown position in Hampden's case, but stated that parliament lacked the power to limit the king in regard to the levy. Basing his argument on the need of the king to maintain the nation in a powerful military posture, he accepted the government's case that:

> the whole kingdom is in peril … and that the danger is present, imminent and instant … whether must the king resort to parliaments? No … But let us resort to our pious and just king, whose prerogative and right to sovereignty is to defend the realm. (State trials, 3.1087)

Crawley's statement on that occasion represented perhaps the most radical assertion of royal prerogative.

In December 1640 the Lords proceeded against Crawley and the other judges who had favoured the crown against Hampden. After Lord Keeper Finch fled, the others were bound for £10,000 apiece to assure their continued presence. In July 1641 the judges were impeached. Waller opened the case against Crawley by declaring that his 'progress through the law has been like that of a diligent spy through a country into which he meant to conduct an enemy' (State trials, 3.1305). On 5 August 1641 Crawley was barred from riding circuit. Although at first he, like the other impeached judges, was prohibited from leaving London, the Lords allowed him to depart for Luton at Christmas 1642, and at the new year he received a summons from the king. By 21 January 1643 he was at Oxford, for on that date he was awarded the degree of DCL. While at Oxford he continued to serve as a justice of common pleas, but on 24 November 1645 parliament deprived him and four other royalist judges of their places. He appears to have returned to Luton in 1646. On 12 November 1646 he petitioned to compound, and on 11 December he was fined £958, a relatively high figure. Crawley died at Luton on 13 February 1650 and was buried at Luton church on 20 February.

PAUL E. KOPPERMAN

Sources DNB · State trials · R. J. Fletcher, ed., The pension book of Gray's Inn, 1 (1901) · Venn, Alum. Cant. · F. A. Blaydes, ed., The visitations of Bedfordshire, annis Domini 1566, 1582, and 1634, Harleian Society, 19 (1884) · Baker, Serjeants · M. A. E. Green, ed., Calendar of the proceedings of the committee for compounding … 1643–1660, 5 vols., PRO (1889–92) · R. C. Johnson and others, eds., Proceedings in parliament, 1628, 6 vols. (1977–83) · Foss, Judges · private information (2004) [N. Lutt, Beds & Luton ARS] · D. Lloyd, Memoires of the lives … of those … personages that suffered … for the protestant religion (1668) · parish register, Luton, Beds. & Luton ARS [burial] · VCH Bedfordshire, vol. 3

Archives Beds. & Luton ARS, answer to articles of impeachment; deeds, etc.

Crawley, Leonard George (1903–1981), sportsman and golf journalist, was born at Nacton, Suffolk, on 26 July 1903, the eldest in the family of three sons and a daughter of John Kenneth Crawley, land agent, and his second wife, Cecily Frances Booker. He was educated at Harrow School and Pembroke College, Cambridge, where he showed himself a celebrated player of games. After making a hundred for Harrow against Eton at Lord's in 1921, he missed by two runs equalling his Uncle Eustace's record as the only player to have scored a hundred in the Eton and Harrow cricket match and in the university match. At Cambridge he studied for the ordinary BA degree (not the tripos) but he did not complete this.

After Cambridge Crawley became a schoolmaster at Farnborough and in 1929 he married Elspeth, daughter of Rear-Admiral John Ewen Cameron; they had two sons. In 1932 he started his own preparatory school, Warriston, at Moffat, Dumfriesshire, in the Scottish borders. He played county cricket for Worcestershire (1922–3) and Essex (1924–37) and went on the MCC tour of the West Indies in 1925–6, but his working life as a schoolmaster meant that his appearances were limited to the summer holidays. Nevertheless, he made eight first-class hundreds, and hit Maurice Tate onto the pavilion roof twice in one innings at

Leyton (1927). Less enviable was the task of opening the innings for Essex in 1932 after Yorkshire had declared, having made a world record of 555 for the first wicket. He played cricket with Jack Hobbs, Walter Hammond, and Frank Woolley. He was a great admirer of Hobbs, whom he invited to coach the boys at his preparatory school, for Crawley was a strong advocate of the importance of good teaching at games. He was also a fierce critic of how poor the standard of teaching was for both cricket and golf.

Crawley was a natural stylist, someone to whom the art of hitting any ball was automatic. He had an elegance and power that people appreciated. One Glamorgan fast bowler of his day said that the only way to bowl at him was to deliver from 27 yards and hide behind the umpire. This was probably the result of Crawley's 222 against Glamorgan in 1928. Crawley abhorred the bodyline tour of Australia, for which he was nearly picked in 1932, a year in which he averaged 51.87. He had a letter printed in *The Times* on the subject.

Crawley was the last of the great all-rounders and perhaps the best. He played golf with Ouimet, Sarazen, Snead, and Cotton. In addition, he was an outstanding rackets player, won the northern lawn tennis doubles championship with an uncle, and captured a gold medal for skating. He was also a good and keen shot. Yet, like many a fine player of games, he was totally unaware of how good he was or how much pleasure he gave to others. Unless asked, he never talked about his achievements, but he presented an imperious figure at the crease or on the golf course, immediately recognizable in his younger days by his ginger moustache. In later years an occasional irascible streak contrasted with a tendency to mislay things, but he was also enormously kind.

In 1932 Crawley went with the British Walker cup golf team to the United States, where his singles victory over George Voigt gained the team's only point. By that time he was established more as a golfer than a cricketer, having won the English championship at Hunstanton in 1931, although it was, he always maintained, 'before I was anything like any good'. He played in the first victorious British team in 1938, when he won his foursome with Frank Pennink—a feat he repeated in 1947 with Percy Belgrave (Laddie) Lucas as a partner. It was Lucas who, in his book *Five up* (1978), suggested that Crawley was the best all-round sportsman of all, adding 'I would put C. B. Fry a loser in the final against him'. Although Crawley was runner-up in the English championships of 1934 and 1937 and, when he retired, had made more appearances for England than anyone, he may not quite have done his huge talent justice. Some ascribed this to the fact that his lovely, rhythmic swing rubbed off on others, inspiring them to play above themselves.

For a short spell before the Second World War Crawley abandoned schoolmastering for stockbroking. During the war he served in the RAF. In 1946 he was appointed golf correspondent of the *Daily Telegraph*, thus maintaining his wide-ranging interest in sport. He wrote felicitously for the paper until 1971 and also contributed regular articles to *The Field*. He loved helping the young with their golf and had a lot to do with improving coaching standards and urging the adoption of the American-sized ball in Europe. Crawley died at his home in Worlington, Suffolk, on 9 July 1981.

DONALD STEEL, *rev.*

Sources *The Times* (10 July 1981)
Likenesses S. R. Gaiger, double portrait, photograph, 1932 (with Roger Weathered), Hult. Arch.

Crawley, Richard (1840–1893), translator and writer, was born at Bryngwyn rectory on 26 December 1840, the eldest son of William Crawley (*d.* in or after 1890), archdeacon of Monmouth, and his wife, Mary Gertrude (*d.* 1854), third daughter of Sir Love Parry Jones *Parry (1781–1853) of Madryn, Caernarvonshire. From 1851 to 1861 Crawley was educated at Marlborough College, before matriculating at University College, Oxford, as an exhibitioner on 22 May 1861. He graduated BA in 1866, having taken a first class both in moderations and in *literae humaniores*. The following year he was elected a fellow of Worcester College, Oxford, a position he held for fourteen years, and in 1868 he published *Horse and Foot, or, Pilgrims to Parnassus*, a witty satire on contemporary literature in the manner of Pope, which many suspected to be the work of Swinburne or Browning, and Crawley merely a *nom de plume*. But ill health plagued Crawley, and though he was called to the bar at Lincoln's Inn on 7 June 1869, he never practised, residing instead in Switzerland and Italy, where he wrote a more serious endeavour, *Venus and Psyche*, in 1871. In Italy too, Crawley wrote his most important work, a translation of Thucydides' *History of the Peloponnesian War* which, though it had appeared in 1866, he reworked entirely while convalescing in Florence, reissuing the whole in 1874. It was an able and vigorous piece of work, which, though it secured little recognition at the time, became the most widely read translation of the next century, remaining in print more than one hundred years after his death.

While in Italy, Crawley published several more works, including *The Younger Brother: a Comedy* (1878), with a touching dedication to his father, and *Election Rhymes* (1880). Neither attained the stature of his Thucydides, however, partly because after April 1875 Crawley was forced by circumstance to become the director of a life insurance company. After his wedding about 1881, he ceased to write entirely, living with his wife, Marian, in Switzerland for ten years. He died of heart disease at his London home, 45 Great Marlborough Street, on 30 March 1893. He was survived by his wife. A short biography, with a collection of his verse, was issued by his family in 1905.

SIDNEY LEE, *rev.* KATHARINE CHUBBUCK

Sources *In memoriam: letters and poems of Richard Crawley* (privately printed, Woking, [1905]) • R. F. McCausland, 'A satire of the later sixties', *The Speaker* (19 May 1900) • *The Athenaeum* (8 April 1893), 445 • R. Crawley, *Horse and foot, or, Pilgrims to Parnassus* (1868) • R. Crawley, *The younger brother: a comedy* (1878), v–vi [preface to his father] • Foster, *Alum. Oxon.* • R. B. Strassler, ed., *The landmark Thucydides: a comprehensive guide to the Peloponnesian War, using the Richard*

Crawley translation (1996), xxx–xxxi · Thucydides, *History of the Peloponnesian War*, trans. R. Crawley (1990) · d. cert.
Likenesses photograph, repro. in *In memoriam*
Wealth at death £50,466 1s. 3d.: resworn probate, May 1895, *CGPLA Eng. & Wales* (1893)

Crawshay, George (1821–1896), ironmaster and politician, was born on 5 February 1821 in Russell Square, London, the eldest son of George Crawshay (1794–1873), iron merchant, of Stoke Newington, and his wife, Josephe Louise Dufaud (1802–1883) from Paris. He was the grandson of William *Crawshay (1764–1834), the 'Iron King' of south Wales, from whom he inherited both wealth and entrepreneurial skill. His mother's family owned the largest ironworks in France at Fourchambault. He studied classics at Trinity College, Cambridge, 1839–42, and although he never graduated (possibly because he may have been a dissenter), he subsequently read for the bar at the Inner Temple. However, in 1843 the sudden death of his brother-in-law Francis William Stanley disrupted his promising legal career.

Crawshay and his younger brother Edmund were obliged to take over the management of Hawks, Stanley & Co., an established ironworks at Gateshead on the Tyne previously run by members of the *Hawks family (*per. c.*1750–1863). The senior partner, George Hawks, retired soon afterwards and the rapid expansion that followed can be largely attributed to the Crawshays' expertise in securing government contracts. By the mid-1840s the ironworks of Hawks, Crawshay & Sons had become the largest on Tyneside, employing more than one thousand workers. It produced a vast range of iron goods, including anchors, chains, and boiler plates, but its growing reputation primarily accrued from lucrative contracts to supply quality ironwork for bridges and lighthouses. Among the most notable of these was the commission for Newcastle upon Tyne's High Level Bridge in 1849, an ambitious structure requiring some 5050 tons of ironwork. The firm also worked on the Iron Bridge at Sunderland and the Lendel Bridge, which spans the Ouse at York. Foreign contracts quickly followed, and impressive bridges were constructed in Constantinople and Burma, and for the India State Railway. By mid-century, Crawshay's enterprises had earned him the popular nickname King of Gateshead.

Crawshay's stature as a local businessman inevitably drew him into the realms of municipal government, not least because George Hawks had been Gateshead's first mayor in 1836. Moreover, marriage on 25 February 1847 to Elizabeth (1826–1889), the youngest daughter of Sir John Fife, greatly enhanced Crawshay's already powerful political and social connections. The couple had two sons and one daughter. Crawshay was elected town councillor for West Gateshead in 1854 and appointed mayor three times, in 1856, 1859, and 1863.

Crawshay's political interests, however, stretched far beyond the boundaries of the municipality. Shortly after settling in the north Crawshay involved himself in the Anti-Corn Law League and, by 1845, had become the leading spokesman of the local branch. As an avowed radical

he supported the Chartists in 1848 and took an active interest in the nationalist struggles of the Poles, the Italians, and the Danes. As a result, he became a close associate of the Russophobic politician David Urquhart (1805–1877) and, as the Crimean War escalated, Crawshay helped to promote the establishment of foreign affairs committees in numerous towns and cities. In 1854 the Newcastle foreign affairs committee, with Crawshay as a major subscriber and leading spokesman, was one of the first to be set up. Although his outspoken defence of the oppressed Turkish people placed him increasingly at odds with W. E. Gladstone and official Liberal policy, especially during the Eastern crisis of the mid-1870s, nevertheless he continued to support their cause. Midhat Pasha became a personal friend and was a frequent visitor at the family home, Haughton Castle, North Tyne. Crawshay was so highly regarded that he later acted as Turkish consul in Newcastle and, interestingly enough, is thought to have been the first person to introduce Turkish baths into England, installing a bath at his Northumberland home, Tynemouth House.

Crawshay firmly believed in the principle of religious toleration, and his beliefs led to membership of the Anti-State Church Association, his vociferous defence of the Muslim Turks, and denunciation of the mischievous 'greased cartridge' affair, which precipitated the Indian mutiny (1857–9). His business and political interests nevertheless collided over India in the late 1850s. Although a principal stock holder, Crawshay vehemently opposed ministerial plans to usurp the power of the East India Company. A number of his speeches were published separately.

A man of eclectic interests, Crawshay was an able mathematician and scientist with an acknowledged flair for foreign languages. He also exhibited considerable literary talents, and wrote poetry and romantic drama as well as critical prose, some of which was published in the *Newcastle Chronicle*. The manuscript of a semi-autobiographical romance, *A Silver Shape*, was finally published in 1980.

His extensive involvement in political affairs, general ill health, and old age all eventually exacted their toll on Crawshay. By the 1870s and 1880s the overcrowded Gateshead site, home to a great diversity of processes and product lines, compared unfavourably with the more streamlined and specialized engineering yards established along the Tyne by entrepreneurs such as Sir William Armstrong. A crisis was reached in 1889, when the 'New Greenwich' ironworks of Hawks, Crawshay & Sons at Gateshead was suddenly closed. Crawshay was accused of incompetence and neglect in investing too heavily in new plant and failing to specialize, but the circumstances of the collapse remain somewhat mysterious. Having paid off all his creditors he retired to his daughter's home at Hazelwood, Horsted Keynes, Sussex, where he died on 13 March 1896. Crawshay's estate at the time of his death was valued at just £25. JOAN ALLEN

Sources F. W. Manders, *History of Gateshead* (1973) · I. C. Carlton, *Short history of Gateshead* (1974) · *History, topography, and directory of*

the county palatine of Durham, F. Whellan & Co. (1856); 2nd edn (1894) · *Ward's directory* (1867) · *Ward's directory* (1879–80) · *Ward's directory* (1889–90) · M. Taylor, 'The old radicalism and the new: David Urquhart and the politics of opposition, 1832–1867', *Currents of radicalism: popular radicalism, organised labour, and party politics in Britain, 1850–1914*, ed. E. F. Biagini and A. J. Reid (1991), 23–43 · M. Taylor, *The decline of British radicalism, 1847–1860* (1995) · *The Times* (23 March 1896) · *Newcastle Weekly Chronicle* (21 March 1896) · *Newcastle Daily Chronicle* (16 March 1896) [editorial] · G. Crawshay, *A silver shape*, reprint (1980) · E. Mackenzie and M. Ross, *An historical, topographical, and descriptive view of the county palatine of Durham*, 1 (1834) · J. Hugman, 'Joseph Cowen of Newcastle and radical liberalism', PhD diss., University of Northumbria, 1993 · D. J. Rowe, ed., *Bibliography of northern business history* (1979) · D. J. Rowe, 'Crawshay, George', *DBB* · Burke, *Gen. GB* · J. P. Addis, *The Crawshay dynasty: a study in industrial organisation and development, 1765–1867* (1957) · M. S. Taylor, *The Crawshays of Cyfarthfa Castle: a family history* (1967) **Archives** NL Wales, corresp. and papers | Sandon Hall, Staffordshire, Harrowby MSS · Tyne and Wear Archives Service, Newcastle upon Tyne, Cowen MSS **Likenesses** pen-and-ink sketch, repro. in *Newcastle Weekly Chronicle* **Wealth at death** £25 11s. 8d.: probate, 26 June 1896, *CGPLA Eng. & Wales*

Crawshay, Richard (1739–1810), ironmaster and merchant, was born in Normanton, Yorkshire, the first child of William Crawshay (1713–1766), a farmer, and his wife, Elizabeth (1714–1774), *née* Nicholson. He had three sisters. According to family tradition a bitter quarrel with his father led to the sixteen-year-old Crawshay setting out for London. Once in the capital he apprenticed himself to a Thames Street ironware merchant named Bicklewith, selling, so legend has it, the pony which had carried him from Yorkshire to furnish a premium. Whatever the truth of this, Crawshay's career was certainly an exercise in self-improvement in the classic Smilesian mould. Indeed, he was the subject of an encomium in Samuel Smiles's *Lives of the Engineers* (1861–2). The young man's resourcefulness and application were soon evident, for by 1763 Crawshay was in sole possession of Bicklewith's business, and as if to mark his independence, he married Mary Bourne (1745–1811), the daughter of a London stonegrate maker, on 13 June 1763. They had a son, William *Crawshay (1764–1834), and three daughters, Anne, Elizabeth, and Charlotte.

During the 1760s and 1770s Crawshay traded as an iron merchant and a dealer in cast-iron wares from a variety of wharfs and warehouses, before settling at George Yard, Upper Thames Street, which was to be the London base of the Crawshay family firm until 1864. By the 1780s Crawshay was probably London's leading iron merchant. However, his pre-eminence in the capital was not enough. Although he had made much of his fortune by importing iron from the Baltic, he was irresistibly attracted by the idea of becoming an ironmaster in his own right, in Britain. His opportunity came in 1786 with the death of Anthony Bacon, master of the Cyfarthfa ironworks at Merthyr Tudful, with whom Crawshay had been in partnership as a supplier of guns to the Board of Ordnance during the American War of Independence. The guns had been

Richard Crawshay (1739–1810), by unknown artist, *c.*1800

cast at Cyfarthfa and Crawshay must have been well aware of the potential of the iron industry in mineral-rich south Wales. Accordingly, he leased Cyfarthfa from Bacon's estate and devoted an increasing amount of his time to the development of the works. He had, he told a visitor there, 'bent his whole mind upon being a perfect ironmaster' (Manners, 69).

By 1793 Crawshay claimed to have laid out £50,000 on new plant at Cyfarthfa. He did so with effect. A survey of pig iron production in 1796 identified Cyfarthfa as by far the largest ironworks in Britain, casting 7204 tons when average output per works was a mere 1562 tons. The expansion of smelting was more than matched by a massive growth in forge capacity at Cyfarthfa. Indeed, it was in the field of iron refining that Crawshay made his most signal contribution to the British iron trade. He was the sponsor of the 'iron puddling' technique of Henry *Cort, which was pioneered as a commercially viable process at his works in the late 1780s and which revolutionized the production of malleable bar iron in Britain. It was small wonder that Cyfarthfa attracted industrialists and technologists from across Europe, anxious to view what was referred to locally as the domain of 'Moloch the Iron King'. For his part, Crawshay relished the attention. His ambition was overweening: 'I must do more than any other Man or my Emulation is not gratify'd' (Gwent RO, D2.162, fol. 233, R. Crawshay to T. Erskine, 3 Nov 1797).

Crawshay's imperiousness did little to endear him to his

fellow ironmasters at Merthyr. Their relations were famously sour. He was, an admirer conceded, 'overbearing in his manners & more unfortunately at variance … with several others who are embarked in the same class of trade' (PRO, HO 42/61, fol. 529, G. Hardinge to the duke of Portland, 11 April 1801). The 'Tyrant', as Crawshay was dubbed by one of his neighbours, could brook no local opposition (NL Wales, Maybery 2466, R. Hill to J. Powell, 5 Aug 1793). Yet Crawshay was also alert to the sense of corporate fraternity that was so prominent a feature of the eighteenth-century iron trade. His commissioning of a set of portraits of the chief iron founders in the kingdom in 1796 was one expression of this amity. He was indefatigable in protecting the interests of the iron trade, putting to good use the many political contacts he had acquired during his years among the mercantile élite of the City of London, and he played a notable part in the campaign to avert the threatened taxation of iron in 1797.

Crawshay's interests were not exclusively in iron. He was a tireless advocate of agricultural improvement and canvassed schemes of general enclosure during the 1790s. He took a leading role in the development of canal and road communications in south Wales. He was also a devout churchman. His circle included high-churchmen such as William Stevens, an erstwhile partner at Cyfarthfa, as well as evangelicals from the Clapham Sect. His was a highly conservative Anglicanism, which had him at odds with the 'fanatick Sectarys' of Merthyr with their radical sympathies.

Crawshay died on 27 June 1810. He was buried at Llandaff Cathedral, attended by vast crowds from Merthyr. His estate was valued at £1.5 million. His ironworks were divided between his son, William, his son-in-law Benjamin Hall (1778–1817), and his nephew Joseph Bailey (1783–1858). To the end, Crawshay was without social pretension. Unlike some of his ironmaster neighbours, he did not aspire to social grandeur. He adopted a simple family motto: 'Perseverance'.   CHRIS EVANS

Sources J. P. Addis, *The Crawshay dynasty: a study in industrial organisation and development, 1765–1867* (1957) · C. Evans, *The labyrinth of flames: work and social conflict in early industrial Merthyr Tydfil* (1993) · M. S. Taylor, *The Crawshays of Cyfarthfa Castle: a family history* (1967) · J. H. Manners, *Journal of a tour through north and south Wales* (1805), 69 · R. Crawshay to T. Erskine, 3 Nov 1797, Gwent RO, D2.162, fol. 233 · G. Hardinge to duke of Portland, 11 April 1801, PRO, HO 42/61, fol. 529 · R. Hill to J. Powell, 5 Aug 1793, NL Wales, Maybery 2466
Archives Gwent RO, Cwmbrân, letter-book | NL Wales, Maybery 2466 · Oxf. U. Mus. NH, corresp. with William Smith · PRO, HO 42/61, fol. 529
Likenesses Wilson of Birmingham, oils, 1796, Cyfarthfa Castle Museum, Merthyr Tudful, Wales · oils, *c*.1800, NMG Wales, Cardiff [*see illus.*]
Wealth at death £1,500,000: will, PRO, PROB 11/1513/362

Crawshay, Robert Thompson (1817–1879), ironmaster, was born at Cyfarthfa, Merthyr Tudful, Glamorgan, on 8 March 1817, the second of the nine children of William *Crawshay (1788–1867), ironmaster, and his second wife, Isabel Thompson (*d.* 1827). He was educated at Dr Prichard's school at Llandaff until 1835, and from an early age

manifested a great interest in his father's ironworks. During his early adult years he spent much of his time learning practically the various aspects of the business, assisting in all the major departments, including the puddling furnaces and the rolling mills. On the death of his half-brother William by drowning at the old passage of the Severn in 1839 he became acting manager at Cyfarthfa. On 15 May 1846 Robert married Rose Mary Yeates (1828–1907) [*see* Crawshay, Rose Mary], a gifted organizer, and a lover of music and literature, who exuded sensibility and foresight, something in which her husband was particularly lacking. They had three sons, William Thompson (1847–1918), Robert Thompson (1853–1944), and Richard Frederick (1859–1903), and two daughters, Rose Harriette Thompson (1848–1943) and Henrietta Louise (1851–1883). In 1847, on the semi-retirement of his father to Caversham Park, he assumed full managerial control at Cyfarthfa.

It was at Robert Crawshay's insistence that his father, who had been in favour of giving up the business and allowing the family to enjoy the fruits of their success, renegotiated the Cyfarthfa lease, which was due to expire in 1864. A new lease was duly agreed in 1862, potentially securing Crawshay control of Cyfarthfa for a further sixty years from 25 March 1864. Part of William's reluctance to enter negotiations stemmed from Robert's poor state of health, which began to fail in the late 1850s. He suffered a stroke, which left him semi-paralysed, and by January 1860 he was stone deaf. Although Robert had controlled Cyfarthfa since 1847, his father had retained overall control of the business, particularly of sales conducted through George Yard, London, and from time to time influenced policy at Cyfarthfa. Following the successful renegotiation of the lease, William became concerned over some of his son's policies, particularly in regard to excessive expenditure (most notably that of holding large amounts of unnecessary stock), poor furnace management, and an inability to deal firmly with the workforce.

After his father's death, Robert Crawshay assumed full control of the business but, owing to his own failings, both of health and of business sense, and to the unfavourable economic climate, Cyfarthfa declined as a powerful force in the iron industry. The iron era in south Wales was drawing to a close, and Cyfarthfa was increasingly unable to compete, with either the new methods of producing steel or producers from other regions. During the early 1870s Crawshay began to seek buyers for the business, but his asking price was too high. In 1874 he was forced to close the works due to the south Wales coal strike. Although the strike ended in May 1875 and the Cyfarthfa collieries reopened, the ironworks remained closed, in part due to Crawshay's stubbornness over accepting unions, and partly due to his failing health. For the last two years of his life he took little interest in the business; he had become completely deaf and broken down by other physical infirmities.

While on a visit to Cheltenham for the benefit of his health Crawshay died suddenly at the Queen's Hotel on 10

May 1879 after contracting bronchitis. He was buried at Vaynor church, Brecknockshire, the building of which he had financed in 1870, under a tablet of Radur stone bearing the inscription 'God Forgive Me'. He left estate valued at under £1,200,000, his eldest son, William Thompson, succeeding to his father's estate at Caversham and to joint control of the business with his two brothers. Operating under the title Crawshay Brothers & Co., they reopened the works in October 1879 and proceeded to effect a changeover to steel production at Cyfarthfa. This move, however, did not prove to be an unqualified success and was insufficient to secure long-term survival of the works, which eventually closed during the early twentieth century following its acquisition by Guest, Keen, and Nettlefolds Ltd in 1902.   G. C. BOASE, rev. TREVOR BOYNS

Sources J. P. Addis, *The Crawshay dynasty: a study in industrial organisation and development, 1765–1867* (1957) · *Merthyr Tydfil: a valley community*, Merthyr Teachers Centre Group (1981) · NL Wales, Cyfarthfa papers · m. cert. · d. cert.
Archives Glamorgan RO, Cardiff, letters · Gwent RO, Cwmbrân · NL Wales
Likenesses portrait, repro. in Addis, *Crawshay dynasty*, 115; at Llanfair Court, 1957
Wealth at death under £1,200,000: probate, 20 June 1879, *CGPLA Eng. & Wales*

Crawshay [*née* Yeates], **Rose Mary** (1828–1907), educationist and feminist, was born at Caversham Grove, Oxfordshire. Her mother died when she was young and her father, Wilson Yeates, remarried two years later. She was educated at home by a governess. At the age of eighteen she met her husband, the 29-year-old Robert Thompson *Crawshay (1817–1879), at the Reading county ball. He was one of the 'iron dynasty' which owned and ran the Cyfarthfa ironworks at Merthyr Tudful in south Wales. His father, William Crawshay II, lived at Caversham Park, close to the Yeates's home. They married on 15 May 1846 at St Peter's Church, Caversham.

From 1846, therefore, Rose Crawshay's home was industrial Merthyr, where the Crawshays had built, in a medieval style, Cyfarthfa Castle. In a strategic position above the town, looking down on the homes of the ironworkers, it boasted seventy-two rooms and fifteen towers. The Crawshays had five children: William Thompson (1847–1918), Rose Harriette Thompson (1848–1943), Henrietta Louise (1851–1883), Robert Thompson (1853–1944), and Richard Frederick (1859–1903).

It was an unhappy marriage, exacerbated by Robert Crawshay's paralytic stroke in 1860 which left him completely deaf. Rose Mary Crawshay advocated marriage reform. She was also an early member of the London National Society for Women's Suffrage and in the early 1870s a vice-president of the Bristol and West of England National Society for Women's Suffrage (which encompassed south Wales). She spoke at Merthyr meetings in favour of women having the vote, and her friends included Millicent Fawcett, the suffragist leader, and her sister Dr Elizabeth Garrett Anderson. According to the *Woman's Herald* (19 March 1892), Mrs Crawshay was 'one of the most enlightened pioneers of women's emancipation'. Like many later feminists, she argued that the vote would mark the beginning not the end of widening equality for women, and she understood the need for women to permeate the structures of local government.

Rose Crawshay seized her opportunity when women became eligible for election to the new school boards established in the wake of the 1870 Education Act, and was one of the first people in Britain to sit on such a board. In 1871 she became the sole woman representative on the Merthyr Tudful school board and she was also elected to and chaired the Vaynor school board in Brecknockshire, making her the only woman in the nineteenth century to sit simultaneously on two school boards. At Vaynor she presided over twelve men, having polled the highest number of votes. She was a regular attender, twice re-elected, and served until 1879. Unafraid of dissenting from majority views, she was instrumental in simplifying the religious diet meted out to children at schools in her districts, expressed concern over compulsory attendance, instigated a rewards system in place of corporal punishment, and even advocated the use of decimal coinage and simplified spelling. She helped establish Swansea Training College (1872), enabling women to train as teachers for the first time within Wales.

In the same year Rose Crawshay addressed 800 local people on the iniquities of widows not being guardians of their children. She also established seven free cottage libraries, all open on Sundays long before the better-known Sunday opening of the Birmingham Free Library. Books could be taken home, and her schemes were carefully developed for the enjoyment and instruction of both sexes. She also involved herself in some of the charitable work expected of ironmasters' wives, for example, establishing a long-running soup kitchen.

Rose Crawshay's 1874 paper to the Social Science Association, *Domestic Service for Gentlewomen*, was published. She opened a register office in London's West End where prospective employers could register their need for 'lady helps', and took on five such distressed gentlewomen at Cyfarthfa Castle. Always a keen publicist—with a number of letters in *The Times*—some of her advanced views earned her criticism. She was a founder member of the council of the Cremation Society of England from 1874 and also publicly defended euthanasia.

Increasingly estranged from her husband, Rose Crawshay spent much of her later life in London, the south of France, and at Cathedin, a home near Llan-gors Lake, Brecknockshire. Despite her Welsh connections, unlike Lady Charlotte Guest, Merthyr's other eminent English wife of an ironmaster, Rose Crawshay evinced little interest in Welsh culture. She was, however, a devotee of the English Romantic poets, endowing a poetic memorial prize for the study of poets and awarding an annual prize for the best essays on Byron, Shelley, and Keats. Photographs show her to have been tall and dark, slender when young, with strong features and a slightly square face. After her husband's death in 1879, Rose Crawshay moved to Cathedin and died at her home there, Rose Cottage, on 2

June 1907. Cremation had finally been fully legalized in 1902, and her wish to be cremated at Golders Green crematorium in Middlesex was fulfilled on 6 June.

ANGELA V. JOHN

Sources M. S. Taylor, *The Crawshays of Cyfarthfa Castle: a family history* (1967) · A. V. John, 'Beyond paternalism: the ironmaster's wife in the industrial community', *Our mother's land: chapters in Welsh women's history, 1830–1939*, ed. A. V. John (1991), 43–68 · NL Wales, Cyfarthfa MSS · Cyfarthfa Castle Museum, Merthyr Tudful, Wales, transcript of part of diaries of Rose Harriette Thompson Crawshay · J. P. Addis, *The Crawshay dynasty: a study in industrial organisation and development, 1765–1867* (1957) · *The Times* (1871–4) · *The Times* (1907) · *Western Mail* [Cardiff] (June 1907) · d. cert.
Archives NL Wales, Cyfarthfa MSS | BL, letters from John Gray, Add. MSS 40140–40141 · Cyfarthfa Castle Museum, Merthyr Tudful, diaries of Rose Harriette Thompson Crawshay [transcript]
Likenesses C. Leslie, portrait, 1829 (aged two), Cyfarthfa Castle Museum, Merthyr Tudful, Wales · double portrait, *c.*1871 (with Richard Frederick), Cyfarthfa Castle Museum, Merthyr Tudful, Wales · R. T. Crawshay, seven photographs, Cyfarthfa Castle Museum, Merthyr Tudful, Wales
Wealth at death £19,852 0*s.* 3*d.*: probate, 29 June 1907, *CGPLA Eng. & Wales*

Crawshay, William (1764–1834), ironmaster and merchant, was the only son, in a family of one son and three daughters, of the ironmaster Richard *Crawshay (1739–1810) and his wife, Mary Bourne (1745–1811). Little is known of Crawshay's early life and education, only that he joined his father's business as a young man. It was the beginning of a tempestuous career. Like his father, William Crawshay was a masterful character and he found it difficult to work under the direction of a man of Richard Crawshay's autocratic temper. This led to repeated estrangements. A visitor to the Crawshay ironworks at Cyfarthfa, near Merthyr Tudful, in 1797 reported that the two

> would not sit in the same room together—the young one however kept possession of the parlour, & the old gent took possession of the counting house & the business they were about was transacted by letters sent from the old Crawshay in the counting house to the young one in the parlour & vice versa. (Gilbert Gilpin to William Wilkinson, 19 July 1797, Shropshire Records and Research Centre, 1781/6/25)

About 1784 Crawshay married Elizabeth (Eliza), *née* Couzens (1760–1825); they had three sons, Richard (1786–1859), William *Crawshay (1788–1867), and George (1794–1873), and two daughters, Elizabeth (1790–1877) and Mary (1793–1881). Increasingly, William Crawshay was entrusted with running the firm's merchant house at George Yard in London, while his father remained at Cyfarthfa. Their physical separation could not, however, ameliorate relations completely. A fresh quarrel in 1809 led to the old man's revising his will. William Crawshay was replaced as his father's executor and residuary legatee by Benjamin Hall (1778–1817), his brother-in-law, and left without a share in the ironworks. A belated reconciliation ensured William Crawshay's partial reinstatement, but he still acquired only a three-eighths share in the Cyfarthfa works upon his father's death in 1810, an outcome he described as 'disinheritance'.

For much of the next decade Crawshay strove to reverse this humiliation and make himself the undisputed master of Cyfarthfa. His cousin Joseph Bailey (1783–1858), who had inherited a two-eighths share in the works, was bought out for £32,000 in 1813. Hall was more difficult to dislodge and Crawshay does not seem to have acquired his share in the works before Hall's death in 1817. Crawshay had more success in his dealings with Anthony Bacon, the illegitimate son of Anthony Bacon (*c.*1717–1786), the founder of Cyfarthfa, to whom a royalty on the works' output was due. Through a mixture of intimidation and bluff—including a deliberate running down of production at Cyfarthfa—Crawshay persuaded Bacon to sell his interest in the site for £95,000 in 1814.

The Cyfarthfa ironworks was the largest in Britain, producing 24,200 tons of pig iron from eight blast furnaces in 1823, yet the functioning of the Crawshay firm was far from smooth. William Crawshay adhered to the policy of his father, that George Yard should be the exclusive outlet for iron produced in Merthyr. Unfortunately, his partners in the London house saw no reason why they should carry large stocks of Cyfarthfa iron when trade was slack. And his manager at Cyfarthfa, his son William Crawshay, had no wish to be tied to George Yard if he could command a higher price as an independent seller. Yet Crawshay was committed to using the financial resources of the merchant house to stockpile iron for which there was no immediate market, allowing the Crawshay firm to stand aloof from the price wars which afflicted the early nineteenth-century iron trade. It was a policy which fomented dissension within the Crawshay firm until William Crawshay's death—an event which his partners and sons awaited with ill-disguised eagerness.

William Crawshay, the Iron King, died on 11 August 1834 at his suburban mansion at Stoke Newington, Middlesex. He was afterwards a rather forgotten figure. Normally resident in the vicinity of London, he did not live on in the folk memory of south Wales as his father and his son were to. Nevertheless, Crawshay's guile and ruthlessness were characteristic of the Crawshay clan and he used these qualities to the full to maintain the family's position at the head of the British iron trade.

CHRIS EVANS

Sources J. P. Addis, *The Crawshay dynasty: a study in industrial organisation and development, 1765–1867* (1957) · J. D. Evans, 'The uncrowned iron king: "the first William Crawshay"', *National Library of Wales Journal*, 7 (1951–2), 12–32 · M. S. Taylor, *The Crawshays of Cyfarthfa Castle: a family history* (1967) · G. Gilpin, letter to William Wilkinson, 19 July 1797, Shrops. RRC, 1781/6/25
Archives NL Wales, Cyfarthfa MSS
Likenesses J. Hoppner, portrait, priv. coll.

Crawshay, William (1788–1867), ironmaster, born on 27 March 1788, was the second son of William *Crawshay (1764–1834) and his wife, Eliza. He had two brothers and two sisters. He was from the age of twenty-two the manager of his father's ironworks at Cyfarthfa near Merthyr Tudful, at that time the world's largest. By upbringing and disposition Crawshay was equipped for the task. In common with so many of his family he was a commanding personality. Lady Charlotte Guest, the wife of his arch-rival, Sir Josiah John Guest, considered him as 'beyond all rule and description … one of those meteoric beings whom it is quite impossible to account for' (Guest and John, 27).

When Crawshay assumed business responsibilities Welsh iron was in its heyday and Cyfarthfa prospered under his charge: the four blast furnaces producing approximately 11,000 tons of pig iron annually, which he took over in 1810, grew to nine furnaces producing 29,000 tons in 1830. These early years were marked by a perennial battle with his father over the extent of his authority at the works. The elder Crawshay was determined to keep Cyfarthfa subordinate to the family's merchant house at George Yard, London. This his son could not endure; he was intent on selling Cyfarthfa iron as he saw fit, without reference to his father and brothers in London. Yet despite the repeated tendering (and hasty withdrawals) of his resignation young William was unable to overcome his father. 'My Dear Will, don't play the fool,' his father told him after one threatened resignation in 1820, 'You are now Vice-Roy of Cyfarthfa and will be Sovereign early enough if you will be content to allow his present Majesty some shadow of Royalty' (Evans, 19). Upon his father's death in 1834 Crawshay did indeed become the king of Cyfarthfa, inheriting the works in Wales, as well as a share in the London house. Yet having spent twenty years chafing against the connection between the works and the merchant house, he now performed a volte-face: by 1843 he had bought out his brothers and his father's old partners in the London house, running Cyfarthfa and George Yard as one business, as his father had always intended.

By the time Crawshay entered into his inheritance the pre-eminence of Cyfarthfa was slipping. He could not prevent his works being overhauled by neighbouring Dowlais, where the Guests were more sensitively attuned to the crucial market for rails in the 1830s and 1840s. Indeed, the aloofness of the Crawshay dynasty was fast becoming an impediment to continued success: little notice was taken, for example, of the new steel-making technology of the 1850s. In William Crawshay's last years it was clear that the great days had passed. 'I do not see any way very clear for the Welsh Iron trade for the future,' he conceded in 1862, '[t]hose cheap ores in the Cleveland district, the Cumberland and Northampton are making awfully cheap iron' (Addis, 132). Many south Wales ironworks turned to selling coal in the 1840s and 1850s to counteract their loss of competitive edge, but uncertainty over the renewal of the Cyfarthfa lease prevented Crawshay from following suit until the mid-1860s.

As a young man Crawshay inclined to radicalism in politics. Hostile to the Anglican church, he associated with the Unitarian caucus that came to dominate parochial affairs in Merthyr in the 1820s and he declared for manhood suffrage and the ballot. He was also a firm supporter of anti-truck legislation, sensing an opportunity to embarrass the Guests, who operated a truck system at Dowlais. During the Reform crisis he actively promoted the cause of parliamentary reform—while simultaneously introducing a programme of sudden wage cuts at depression-hit Cyfarthfa. This was a volatile course of action, and one to

which contemporaries attributed the insurrectionary riots which swept Merthyr in June 1831, obliging Crawshay to write a hasty defence of his role in local affairs, *The Late Riots at Merthyr Tydfil* (1831). During the later 1830s he swung abruptly into the tory camp, although this was a plainly opportunistic manoeuvre to unseat Sir Josiah John Guest, who had been returned for the newly enfranchised borough of Merthyr in 1832 on a radical ticket. He retained enough of his liberal sympathies to subscribe £500 for the support of Hungarian refugees in Turkey after the collapse of the revolutionary outbreaks of 1848.

At Merthyr Crawshay lived at Cyfarthfa Castle, a Gothic mansion built in 1825 to the design of Robert Lugar at a cost of £30,000. In later life he spent an increasing amount of time at his seat at Caversham in Oxfordshire, which he leased for many years and bought outright in 1848. He was married three times, each time to a bride with connections in the iron trade. He married first, in 1808, Elizabeth, the daughter of Francis *Homfray (1725–1798) of Stourbridge, a member of the midland iron-making dynasty [see under Homfray family]. They had three sons, and Elizabeth died in 1813 giving birth to a daughter. Crawshay married second, in 1815, Isabel, the daughter of James Thompson of Grayrigg, Westmorland. Her uncle William Thompson (1793–1854), MP, lord mayor of London in 1828, was a partner in the Penydarren ironworks at Merthyr, and her uncle Robert Thompson was the proprietor of the Tintern Abbey ironworks in Monmouthshire. Isabel died in 1827, having given birth to two sons and seven daughters. Crawshay married third, in 1828, Isabella (*d*. 1885), the sister of Thomas Johnson, a partner in the Bute ironworks in the Rhymni valley, and they had a daughter.

Crawshay died at Caversham on 4 August 1867, leaving a personalty sworn at under £2 million. It had once been his intention that the Cyfarthfa works should pass to his eldest son, William (*b*. 1810), but this son was drowned crossing the Severn in 1839. Crawshay's other sons from his first marriage, Francis (1811–1878) and Henry (1812–1879), had been provided with iron and coal estates of their own, at Trefforest in Glamorgan and Cinderford in the Forest of Dean respectively. The Cyfarthfa estate therefore passed to the elder son of his second marriage, Robert Thompson *Crawshay (1817–1879).   CHRIS EVANS

Sources J. P. Addis, *The Crawshay dynasty: a study in industrial organisation and development, 1765–1867* (1957) · M. S. Taylor, *The Crawshays of Cyfarthfa Castle: a family history* (1967) · G. A. Williams, *The Merthyr rising* (1978) · G. A. Williams, 'The Merthyr election of 1835', *The Welsh in their history* (1982), 95–133 · R. Guest and A. V. John, *Lady Charlotte: a biography of the nineteenth century* (1989), 27 · J. D. Evans, 'The uncrowned iron king: "the first William Crawshay"', *National Library of Wales Journal*, 7 (1951–2), 12–32 · Burke, *Gen. GB*
Archives Glamorgan RO, Cardiff · Gwent RO, Cwmbrân · NL Wales, corresp. and papers; accounts, corresp., and papers
Likenesses portrait, Cyfarthfa Castle Museum and Art Gallery, Merthyr Tudful, Wales · portrait, priv. coll.
Wealth at death under £2,000,000: probate, 23 Aug 1867, CGPLA Eng. & Wales

Craxton, (Thomas) Harold Hunt (1885–1971), pianist and teacher, was born on 30 April 1885 at 6 Dorchester Place,

Marylebone, London, the first son of Thomas Robert Craxton (1858–1908), a surveyor's assistant, and his wife, Sarah Jane Hunt (1852–1905). The Craxtons originated in Northamptonshire. Before marriage Sarah Jane Hunt had been headmistress of a girls' school, and she sang in a forerunner of the Royal Choral Society. By Harold's first birthday the family had moved to Devizes, Wiltshire, where his father set up as a publican. At the age of seven Harold passed the first grade of the Trinity College of Music examinations, entering the room nervously because he thought that two dummy knights guarding the entrance were the examiners.

Thomas Robert Craxton's business proved unsuccessful. The family moved to the poorer part of the town while the father sought work in London; there were now five boys to support. By 1898 they were reunited in London, and a Miss Collins of Trinity received '£1. 8s 0d for 12 pianoforte and theory lessons for Master Harold Craxton (plus 2s 6d for Beringer's Technical Studies)' (private information). 'Master Craxton's First Grand Evening Concert' took place at Hammersmith town hall on 23 January 1901. The *West London Observer* reported that he was 'the possessor of exceptional qualities'. From 1902 he worked in light-music ensembles. His early training thus took place far from the great musical centres, and not until 1907 did he enter the Tobias Matthay School, studying with Cuthbert Whitemore and Matthay himself.

From 1909 to 1911 Craxton was accompanist to Emma Albani. The year 1911 also saw the publication of his first compositions. Extensive tours on both sides of the Atlantic with Dame Clara Butt and her husband, Kennerley Rumford, made him the most celebrated accompanist in the United Kingdom. Dame Clara performed several of his compositions and also smoothed the way for his marriage on 12 December 1914, initially opposed by her parents, to

the violinist Essie May Faulkner (1890–1977), daughter of Charles W. Faulkner, an art publisher. In 1919 Craxton became professor of piano at the Royal Academy of Music; thereafter his career was London-based.

Craxton also undertook performances as a soloist; but although as an accompanist he covered an enormous range of music, this and his work as a teacher left him little time to enlarge his solo repertory. He had a great love of early English music—invariably beginning recitals with a group of such pieces—and was reported to have found a rare magic in them. Chopin, Schumann, Brahms, and Debussy were also especially dear to him, and he was proud of his collaboration with Sir Donald Tovey in the Associated Board edition of the Beethoven piano sonatas (1931). He no longer performed publicly after 1954. However, Craxton's work as accompanist was preserved on several recordings; his largest project was a recording of the Delius cello sonata with Beatrice Harrison (1926). In addition, his recordings of lieder with Elena Gerhardt (1924–7), and also of Purcell songs with Astra Desmond in the 1940s, were innovative in their day. He recorded many lighter pieces with the violinist Jacques Thibaud.

Yet however significant Craxton was as a pianist, it is as a teacher that he will be remembered. He jocularly remarked, 'the right Bach at the right time for the pupil or trouble always happens' (autobiography); and the secret of his whole approach can be divined from this phrase. He was acutely aware that each pupil had a completely different set of needs, which he diagnosed with exceptional capacity. Craxton had absorbed from Matthay fundamental ideas such as economy of movement, a relaxed wrist, and a strong first joint, and the pupil who did not possess these by nature did exercises until he or she obtained them. Craxton knew that standards in England were fairly amateurish, and if attitudes towards the technical side of

(Thomas) Harold Hunt Craxton (1885–1971), by unknown photographer, late 1960s

musical studies had improved by the time he retired, no small credit was due to him. Very often his method consisted simply in selecting the right piece of music at the right time. A pupil might realize only long afterwards why a particular piece had been chosen. The final analysis is of almost underhand teaching, outwardly benign and democratic, which none the less stemmed from a clear idea of where each pupil had to go, and got him there. On his retirement from the Royal Academy of Music in 1960 Craxton was awarded the OBE.

A collateral aspect was the legendary Craxton hospitality. Blessed with a large house post-war in Kidderpore Avenue, Hampstead, and with a still larger pre-war one in Grove End Road, St John's Wood, Craxton virtually adopted some students, the dinner table was always crowded, and the upstairs rooms were permanently full of pails of soaking students' socks. Presiding over the household was Essie, the 'universal mother' to family and students alike, and even to her husband, whom she escorted to the Royal Academy of Music in the battered Rolls-Royce he was unable to drive himself. After retirement he still received students privately and always showed interest in their careers. The novelist Elizabeth Jane Howard, who was taught by him, has given a memorable description of Craxton in 1936:

> His appearance was unusual and fascinating. He wore his hair much longer than other people. He had a broad and noble brow, large, pale blue eyes whose blandness often concealed an acute sense of humour and a degree of perception that I was unused to; a long nose, a long, indented upper lip below which curled a delicately sardonic mouth, a purposeful chin and large elegant ears.　(Howard)

Craxton was modest about his compositions, yet showed a genuine melodic gift, and the four unpublished Shakespeare settings (1944) achieve the lucidity upon which he insisted in his playing and teaching. The mixture of old and new in such very free transcriptions of early English pieces as 'The Plaint of Love' and 'Siciliano and Rigadon' (1935) has its own fascination. His editions of old English keyboard compositions brought the music to a wider public.

Harold Craxton died on 30 March 1971 in New End Hospital, Hampstead. He was cremated at Golders Green crematorium. A memorial concert was held at Fairfield Hall, Croydon, on 17 September 1971, and several years later his ashes were scattered on Hindhead golf course. His wife survived him. Of their six children only Janet *Craxton (1929–1981), an oboist, became a professional musician; Antony (1918–1999), for long a distinguished BBC producer, brought classical music to the television; and John (b. 1922) became a noted painter.

CHRISTOPHER HOWELL

Sources incomplete autobiography, printed in programme for Craxton memorial concert, Fairfield Hall, 17 Sept 1971 · documents, press cuttings, priv. coll. · private information (2004) [family; pupils] · E. J. Howard, 'A voyage round my teacher', *Daily Express* (8 Sept 1982) · A. Richardson, 'Pen portrait: Harold Craxton', *MT*, 101 (1960), 356–7 · P. Jenkins, 'A few good lessons', *Royal Academy of Music Magazine*, 239 (1985), 9–19 · D. Matthews, 'Harold Craxton, 1885–1971', *Music Teacher* (June 1971) · b. cert. · m. cert. · d. cert. · website.lineone.net/~matthew.brailsford/cmt/family.htm [Craxton Memorial Trust website], 2001

Archives Craxton Studios, London, MSS, published works, letters, press cuttings, notebooks, concert programmes, photographs | FILM BFI NFTVA, documentary footage | SOUND BL NSA, documentary recordings · BL NSA, *Mining the archive*, BBC Radio 3, 2 May 1997, H8912/3 · BL NSA, oral history interviews · BL NSA, 'Tribute to Janet Craxton', NP5281 BW BD1

Likenesses photograph, 1966–9, priv. coll. [*see illus.*] · G. Argent, photograph, 1970, NPG · bust, Craxton Studios, London · photographs (from later years), Craxton Studios, London

Craxton, Janet Helen Rosemary (1929–1981), oboist and teacher, was born on 17 May 1929 at 8 Grove End Road, London, the only daughter and the youngest of the six children of (Thomas) Harold Hunt *Craxton (1885–1971) and his wife, Essie May Faulkner (1890–1977). Her father was the eldest son of Thomas Robert Craxton of Devizes, Wiltshire, and senior piano professor at the Royal Academy of Music. Previously at the Matthay School, he was an outstanding pianist, accompanist, and music editor. Her mother was an intelligently modest, 'saintly' woman. They married in 1914.

Few musicians have had a more fortunate background than Janet Craxton, except perhaps Mozart himself, or Craxton's Hampstead neighbour and near contemporary at the academy, the remarkable horn player Dennis Brain (1921–1957). Indeed, there are many similarities in their lives and careers: each was brought up in an exceptionally musical family, with the father a notable teacher, and became an outstanding wind instrumentalist at the academy; each became a leading soloist, orchestral principal, and chamber music player, and had major works composed for him or her; and each died suddenly and was greatly missed.

Janet Craxton had five elder brothers, which may explain why she was something of a tomboy: she spoke in low, sonorous, oboe-like tones, and was tall and willowy. Anthony, her eldest brother (1918–1999), became a senior television producer. John, the artist (b. 1922), settled in Hania, Crete, in 1948. She grew up at 8 Grove End Road, in north-west London; the family's post-war home was 14 Kidderpore Avenue, Hampstead. By 1930 the Craxtons had become the most talked-about and most loved family in musical London.

After attending Francis Holland School, Baker Street, and King Alfred's School, Hampstead, Craxton entered the Royal Academy of Music, where between 1945 and 1948 she studied the oboe with Helen Gaskell, the piano with her father, and musicianship with Priaulx Rainier; she then went to the Paris Conservatoire as a pupil of Pierre Bajeux (1948–9), each Wednesday afternoon attending Nadia Boulanger's seminar in the rue Ballu. In 1958 she was appointed both oboe professor at the academy and tutor to the National Youth Orchestra. The oboe faculty at the academy was a remarkable and cohesive group with such luminaries as Leonard Brain (Dennis's brother), Neil Black, and Michael Dobson, who said: 'The lovely sound that she produced was a reflection of the naturalness and warmth of her own personality' (private information). Another was Evelyn Barbirolli, who remembered her as 'a

Janet Helen Rosemary Craxton (1929–1981), by unknown photographer, 1960s

very dear loyal friend, a great musician, inspired teacher and performer' (ibid.).

Craxton was principal oboist in the Hallé Orchestra (1949–52), the London Mozart Players (1952–4), the BBC Symphony Orchestra (1954–63), the London Sinfonietta (1969–81), and the orchestra of the Royal Opera House (1979–81). She toured the USA with the Royal Philharmonic Orchestra and the USSR with the English Opera Group. In 1957, while on a tour of Canada, Léon Goossens chanced to overhear a radio broadcast, not knowing which orchestra was playing. He suddenly remarked: 'It must be the BBC from home: only Janet can play like that' (private information). And so it was.

A perfectionist, Janet Craxton preferred to make her own reeds. Once, being dissatisfied with her own performance in an orchestral concert, she returned her performer's fee. She was determined: having decided to do something, she had that rare ability to make things happen. In 1967 Craxton formed the London Oboe Quartet; she was fortunate in having a personal following which ensured her a good audience, and the quartet gave many concerts and broadcasts. She also played in the London Concertante among other ensembles.

Janet Craxton was sought after as a soloist, and gave a number of world premières. These works included Ralph Vaughan Williams's *Ten Blake Songs* (1958) with the tenor Wilfred Brown, and three compositions by Lennox Berkeley: the sonatina for oboe and piano, op. 61 (1962), dedicated to Janet and her brother John; the oboe quartet, op. 70 (1967); and the *Sinfonia concertante*, op. 84, with large

chamber orchestra (commissioned by the BBC for the 1973 Promenade Concerts). Other commissions were from Alan Rawsthorne, Elisabeth Lutyens, Elizabeth Maconchy, Richard Stoker, and Priaulx Rainier.

On 17 July 1961 Janet Craxton married Alan Richardson (1904–1978), composer, piano professor at the academy, and a former pupil of her father. At their summer cottage, High Latch, in the Lammermuir Hills south of Edinburgh, she pursued wide interests, including cycling, gardening, golf, and organic cooking. Craxton was an environmentalist, loved animals, and was an excellent draughtsman, but photography took first place among these activities: her camera went with her everywhere. After many happy years, she made time to nurse both parents and husband during their final illnesses.

Janet Craxton died suddenly and unexpectedly on 18 July 1981 at Lodge Farm Cottage, Rossway, Berkhamsted, Hertfordshire. It was impossible to ascertain the cause of death. She left her body to science. There was a service shortly after her death. She left funds to the Craxton memorial trust and to the Royal Academy of Music. A thanksgiving concert was given at the Wigmore Hall on Saturday 24 April 1982; the performers included Sir Peter Pears, who spoke about her, Denis Matthews, Nina Milkina, Celia Nicklin, Bernard Roberts, the London Sinfonietta, the Trio Cannello, the Philip Jones Brass Ensemble, and remaining members of the London Oboe Quartet. Works by Alan Richardson and Neil Saunders were performed.

Craxton's pupil Valerie Taylor Lockwood has said:

> Janet hated pretentiousness and anyone in music for their own ends. She was caring and understanding of shortcomings, but had the highest musical standards so she could be quite exacting. Her sense of humour was wicked. She loved cats and children, talking to both in their own language. As an oboist Janet had a completely different tone; although Paris-trained it was a darker Germanic sound with total control. (private information, V. Taylor Lockwood)

Asked if she had any shortcomings, Valerie Taylor Lockwood replied: 'No, in my opinion she was perfect. I find myself thinking of her almost every day in my teaching' (ibid.). Janet Craxton was an outstanding person in every way, dedicated, caring, intensely musical, deeply conscientious.   RICHARD STOKER

Sources M. Kennedy, *The Oxford dictionary of music*, 2nd edn (1994); rev. edn (1997) • *New Grove* • Grove, *Dict. mus.* • J. O. Ward, ed., *The concise Oxford dictionary of music*, 2nd edn (1964) • *WWW, 1971–80* • *WW* (1970) • *WW* (1995) • *International who's who* (1998) • *Chambers biographical dictionary* (1998) • *Cambridge biographical dictionary* (1998) • *Who's who in music*, 5th edn (1969) • A. Jacobs, ed., *The music yearbook, 1972–3* (1972) • *Handbook and register of members, 1974/75*, Incorporated Society of Musicians (1974) • programme, thanksgiving concert, Wigmore Hall, 24 April 1982 (privately printed, 1982) • programme, thanksgiving concert for Essie Craxton, St John's, Smith Square, London, 1978 (privately printed, 1978) • *The Times* (21 July 1981), 16 • B. Campbell, *RAM Magazine*, 227 (autumn 1981) • M. Dobson, *RAM Magazine*, 227 (autumn 1981) • R. Stoker, *Open window—open door* (1985) • *The 80th year of Sir Lennox Berkeley*, Chester Music (1983) [tribute booklet] • programme booklet, seventy-fifth birthday concert for Sir Lennox Berkeley, Park Lane Group, Park Lane Group Publication (1971) • m. cert. • d. cert. • *CGPLA Eng. &*

Wales (1982) · personal knowledge (2004) · private information (2004) [Michael Craxton, brother]

Archives FILM BBC Television (*c*.1980–81), Covent Garden orchestral rehearsal, with conductor Sir Colin Davis | SOUND BBC Gram Library, White City, London W8 · BBC Music Archives, Broadcasting House, London W1, broadcasts and documentary programmes · BBC World Service Gram Library, Bush House, London WC2 · British Institute of Recorded Sound, London · British Music Information Centre, London W1

Likenesses photograph, 1960–69, priv. coll. [*see illus.*] · double portrait, photograph (with Alan Richardson), repro. in *Composer*, 40 (1971) · five photographs, repro. in *Double Reed News*, 17 (1991) · photograph, repro. in *RAM Magazine*

Wealth at death £144,000: probate, 14 Oct 1982, *CGPLA Eng. & Wales*

Crazy Gang (*act.* 1931–1962), comedians, came to prominence in the early 1930s. They comprised the double acts of Bud *Flanagan and Chesney Allen [*see* Allen, (William Ernest) Chesney (1894?–1982)], Jimmy *Nervo and Teddy Knox [*see* Knox, Edward Albert Cromwell], Charlie Naughton [*see below*] and Jimmy Gold [*see below*], and the comedy juggler and droll 'Monsewer' Eddie Gray [*see* Gray, Edward Earl]. They first appeared together (minus Flanagan and Allen who joined in the following year) in a *Crazy Week* in 1931 at the London Palladium. For the next thirty years they appeared in a series of highly successful revues and films and became a regular feature of royal variety shows, enjoying a nationwide reputation for their original brand of comedy. Although they formed a distinct group, the members of the Crazy Gang maintained parallel careers as separate acts. Flanagan and Allen in particular enjoyed enormous popularity as sentimental elegists for the depressed 1930s and as wartime exemplars of the indomitable, irreverent British spirit.

Although Flanagan came to be seen as the animating spirit of the gang, its format and style were based on a type of comedy that had been pioneered by Nervo and Knox in the 1920s. In a series of shows, beginning with *Young Bloods of Variety* in 1925, Nervo and Knox, often working with Gray, had developed a style which gave an impression of spontaneous mayhem throughout the theatre, with performances spilling into the auditorium and constant 'interruption gags' in which the performers would intrude into other acts on the bill. This style informed the first *Crazy Week*, which began on 30 November 1931 at the instigation of George Black, manager of the London Palladium, and involved, along with Gray and Nervo and Knox, the double acts of Glaswegians **Charles John** [Charlie] **Naughton** (1886–1976) and **Jimmy Gold** [*real name* James McGonigal] (1886–1967) and the husband-and-wife act of Billy Caryll and Hilda Mundy. Caryll and Mundy adapted sportingly to the format but left the gang after the inclusion of Flanagan and Allen in 1932. Naughton and Gold proved immediately adept, having been working toward a similar style in their own extensive variety and pantomime career. The pair had first met on a Glasgow building site and had made their work experience the basis of a slapstick act, begun in 1908 and billed as 'The Comedy of the British Working Man'. Their routine was hardly

Crazy Gang (*act.* 1931–1962), by Sir Cecil Beaton [Bud Flanagan, Jimmy Nervo, Teddy Knox, Charlie Naughton, and Jimmy Gold]

innovative, but it was expertly timed. Perhaps their greatest asset, one that was exploited in turn by the Crazy Gang, was the comic resemblance of the bald, lisping Charlie Naughton to an overgrown, if rather accident-prone baby (René Cutforth memorably described Naughton as having the appearance of 'a hamster who's swallowed a tennis ball').

After the success of a number of *Crazy Weeks* and *Crazy Months* the group began, with *Round about Regent Street* in 1935, a series of revues, each running for about eight months, that filled the Palladium throughout the 1930s. *All Alight at Oxford Circus* (1936), *O-Kay for Sound* (1936), *London Rhapsody* (1937), *These Foolish Things* (1938), and *The Little Dog Laughed* (1939) were renowned for their high production values and the quality of the support acts and were significant in establishing in the public mind the Crazy Gang's unique blend of anarchic physical comedy, playful vulgarity, and musical whimsicality. The gang became famed for their beautifully timed slapstick (with Charlie Naughton frequently featured as the fall guy), their outrageous drag performances such as the popular 'Shadow of Eros' in which they appeared as rather matronly Piccadilly Circus flower-sellers singing 'Six Broken Blossoms', and the glowingly melancholic songs of Flanagan and Allen. The gang also gained a formidable reputation as on-stage and off-stage practical jokers. Jimmy Nervo was recklessly prone to setting various parts of Charlie Naughton's costume on fire and the gang would routinely sabotage other acts on the bill. On one occasion they dyed the face of their understudy George Lane an indelible red and blue after tampering with his make-up; on another they sent the trainer of a canine act due to support them on a quest round London after persuading her that her dogs needed to be fireproofed in order to appear on stage. The gang attempted to replicate their stage successes in several films, *Okay for Sound* (1937), *Alf's Button Afloat* (1938), *Gas Bags* (1940), and *Life is a Circus* (1962). While not flopping, these films were recognized as having been only partially successful in capturing the spirit of the gang's stage act.

After a wartime hiatus the Crazy Gang performed with continued acclaim under the aegis of Jack Hylton at the Victoria Palace. They now appeared without Allen, who had retired at the end of the war, although he continued to appear with the gang in royal variety performances and acted as their agent and manager, and Gray, who rejoined in 1956. Their revue *Together Again* opened on 17 April 1947 and ran for a record-breaking 1566 performances. This was followed by a series of shows, all of which enjoyed phenomenal runs of over 800 performances: *Knights of Madness* (1950), *Ring out the Bells* (1952), *Jokers Wild* (1954), *These Foolish Kings* (1956), and *Clown Jewels* (1959). Their final show, *Young in Heart*, ran for 826 twice-nightly performances from December 1960 until an emotional farewell on 19 May 1962. This final performance was commemorated by the poet laureate, John Betjeman, in his 'To the Crazy Gang' and was the subject of a moving tribute on BBC radio by René Cutforth. According to Cutforth, the audience were all agreed 'some of us in tears, that something English, human, and admirable had departed from this mortal scene' (Green, 305).

With an unprecedented longevity at the top of their profession the Crazy Gang had managed the rare trick of articulating in comedy and song the solidarity and spirit of mid-century Britain. The particular affection in which they were held by their audiences was based on a shared sense of having weathered difficult times with a ready smile. Their popularity reputedly stretched to the royal family, for whom they performed fifteen official and several other unofficial royal variety performances. The influence of their anarchic, borderline surreal style, analogous to the contemporaneous American *Hellzapoppin*, can be traced in British humour in shows such as *The Goons* and *Monty Python's Flying Circus*, but they are probably most fondly remembered for their populist strain of heartening vulgarity and heartwarming sentimentalism.

DAVID GOLDIE

Sources M. Owen, *The Crazy Gang: a personal reminiscence* (1986) · J. Fisher, *Funny way to be a hero* (1973) · R. Wilmot, *Kindly leave the stage!* (1986) · B. Flanagan, *My crazy life* (1961) · B. Green, ed., *The last empires: a music hall companion* (1986) · R. Busby, *British music hall: an illustrated who's who from 1850 to the present day* (1976) · R. Hudd, *Roy Hudd's cavalcade of variety acts* (1997) · I. Bevan, *Top of the bill* (1952) · R. Mander and J. Mitchenson, eds., *Revue* (1971) · *The Times* (9 Oct 1967) [Jimmy Gold] · *CGPLA Eng. & Wales* (1976) [Charlie Naughton] · *The Times* (12 Feb 1976) [Charlie Naughton] · b. cert. [Charlie Naughton]

Archives FILM BFI NFTVA, news footage · BFI NFTVA, performance footage |SOUND BBC WAC · BL NSA, 'The Crazy Gang: a celebration', T6225WR TR2 · BL NSA, oral history interview · BL NSA, performance recording

Likenesses photographs, c.1937–1962, Hult. Arch. · C. Beaton, group portrait, photograph, NPG [*see illus.*]

Wealth at death £4076—Charlie Naughton: probate, 9 April 1976, *CGPLA Eng. & Wales*

Creagh, Sir Garrett O'Moore (1848–1923), army officer, the seventh son of Captain James Creagh RN and his wife, Grace Emily, daughter of Garrett O'Moore of Cloghan Castle, co. Kerry, was born at Cahirbane, co. Clare, in Ireland, on 2 April 1848. He was educated privately, at the Royal Naval School, New Cross, and finally at the Royal Military College, Sandhurst. He married twice: first, in 1874, Mary Letitia Longfield, daughter of John Brereton of Oldcourt, co. Tipperary, who died two years later; second, in 1891, Elizabeth (*d.* 1945), daughter of Edward Reade of Kelverton, Buckinghamshire, with whom he had a son and a daughter.

Creagh was commissioned ensign in the 95th foot in October 1866 and went to join the regiment in India in 1869. In February 1870 he transferred to the Indian army, taking up an appointment on the Bombay staff corps as a lieutenant. He served briefly with the marine battalion, 25th Bombay light infantry, Deoli irregular force, and the Merwara battalion. He was promoted captain in 1878 and served during the Second Afghan War of 1879–80. He was sent with 150 men to protect the village of Kam Dakka on 21 April 1879, where he was attacked by 1500 Mohmands. He retired to a position in a nearby cemetery where his men repulsed every enemy assault until they were relieved late in the afternoon. He was awarded the Victoria Cross for his actions. The commander-in-chief in India, General Sir Frederick Haines, reported that but for Creagh's coolness and gallantry his detachment would probably have been destroyed. He was mentioned in dispatches, and promoted brevet major.

Between 1882 and 1886 Creagh commanded the Merwara battalion and in the latter year was promoted major. In 1890 he participated in the Zhob valley expedition on the north-west frontier of India. He assumed command of the 29th Bombay infantry later the same year and was promoted lieutenant-colonel in 1892. In 1896 he was promoted colonel and became assistant quartermaster-general at Bombay. Creagh was promoted brigadier-general in 1899 and appointed political resident and general officer in command at Aden. In 1900 he led the 2nd brigade during the China expedition, and in the following year became general officer commanding the British expeditionary force in China.

Creagh then commanded a first-class district in India. He was promoted major-general in 1902 and in the same year became a KCB. In 1904 he took over the command of the 5th division and was promoted lieutenant-general. In 1906 Creagh assumed command of the 2nd division, but the following year returned to England on special duty, and in July 1907 was appointed military secretary at the India Office. Creagh, promoted general in November 1907, remained at the India Office until 1909, when he was appointed to succeed Lord Kitchener as commander-in-chief in India. During his tenure of command Creagh did not introduce many new reforms, being primarily occupied defending changes made by his predecessor in the organization and deployment of the army in India as pressure for retrenchment in the military budget mounted following the 1907 Anglo-Russian convention. In 1911 he was

Sir Garrett O'Moore Creagh (1848–1923), by London Stereoscopic Co.

appointed GCSI and was made aide-de-camp to George V. He retired in May 1914 and lived in London. He died at his residence, 65 Albert Hall Mansions, Kensington Gore, on 9 August 1923, and was buried in East Sheen cemetery two days later. C. V. OWEN, *rev.* T. R. MOREMAN

Sources *The autobiography of General Sir O'Moore Creagh, with an introduction and notes*, ed. C. E. Callwell (1923) · *Quarterly Indian Army List* (July 1913) · W. M. Lummis, 'Sir O'Moore Creagh, Victoria Cross biography', NAM, c. 108
Archives CUL, corresp. with Lord Hardinge · PRO, private corresp. with Sir E. Satow, PRO 30/33/9/19
Likenesses London Stereoscopic Co., photograph, repro. in S. H. Shadbolt, *The Afghan campaigns of 1878–80* (1882), vol. 1, pl. 20 [*see illus.*] · portrait, repro. in *Autobiography of General Sir O'Moore Creagh*, frontispiece
Wealth at death £1317 14s. 6d.: probate, 5 Sept 1923, *CGPLA Eng. & Wales*

Creagh, Peter [Piers] (1642–1705), Roman Catholic archbishop of Dublin, was born in Limerick. His father's name was also Peter Creagh; that of his mother has not been preserved. The family was of Gaelic Ulster origin, but by this date had been a leading merchant family in Limerick for approximately three centuries. They had been prominent recusants and contributed many recruits to the Counter-Reformation priesthood. The most distinguished of these was Peter's granduncle, Richard Creagh, archbishop of Armagh, who died in the Tower of London after a long imprisonment at the end of 1586 or the beginning of 1587.

About 1656 Creagh was sent to study in the Jesuit college at Poitiers under the care of a Jesuit uncle, also, if confusingly, named Peter Creagh. In 1660 he went to Rome, where another uncle, John Creagh, was a domestic chaplain to Pope Alexander VII. Here he entered the Irish College to study for the priesthood. He was ordained priest in February 1666 and said his first mass on 14 February, presumably the following day, in the basilica of St Mary Major. After a further year's study he was awarded a doctorate in divinity in the Jesuit Collegio Romano.

Creagh then set out for Ireland. Though conditions fluctuated from time to time, after the Restoration in 1660 it was normally possible for the Roman Catholic clergy to minister discreetly. Creagh seems to have distinguished himself particularly in reconciling those who had lapsed in the 1650s, either under pressure or for lack of pastoral care. A hierarchy was also being discreetly restored, headed by Archbishop Oliver Plunket of Armagh. In 1671 the Irish bishops appointed Peter Creagh to be their agent in Rome. He arrived there early in 1672. In 1676 a petition arrived from the chapter of the diocese of Cork, asking that he be named their bishop. He was provided on 22 April to the united sees of Cork and Cloyne, and consecrated on 26 May in the Irish Franciscan church of St Isidore's.

Back in Ireland Creagh at first faced a tacit toleration, but this was shattered by the Popish Plot, sprung by Titus Oates in September 1678. Though Creagh was not named as implicated in the plot, local vendettas forced him to give up his ministry and go into hiding in the house of his brother John at Killaloe, near Limerick. Early in March 1680 he was betrayed and captured. The order from Dublin was that he be sent there, but for most of a year he was too ill to travel. After more than another year in gaol in Dublin he was sent to Cork to stand trial at the end of August 1682. The charge was not treason, but the less dangerous (but legally defenceless) one of *praemunire*. However, by now the Popish Plot was beginning to run out of credibility. One witness withdrew his sworn statement. Then, dramatically, the floor of the courtroom collapsed. The story spread across Europe, losing nothing in the telling. More practically, other witnesses began to withdraw statements, and the bishop was acquitted.

The accession of James II in 1685 allowed Creagh to minister openly, take over many churches, and attend a provincial synod at Cashel. He also enjoyed a crown pension of £150 a year. But William of Orange landed in England in November 1688, and James fled to Ireland. The Williamite forces arrived in August 1689, and after the battle of the Boyne on 1 July 1690 James fled to France, followed by his deputy, the earl of Tyrconnell.

There were divided counsels in Ireland. Tyrconnell had wished to seek terms, but a group in the army, heartened by heroic defence actions at Athlone and Limerick, wanted to seek further French help and fight on. In October 1690 a delegation was sent to France to urge this plan. Bishop Peter Creagh was one of its four members. It is not possible to say how deeply he was involved in general politics, but it would appear that he was included in the delegation by the duke of Berwick, now James's representative in Ireland, in the hope that he would be a moderating influence.

It is not certain if Creagh returned to Ireland, where resistance ended with the treaty of Limerick on 3 October 1691. A surviving letter shows him at James's court in St Germain in February 1692. On 2 November James nominated him to the see of Dublin, vacant since the death of Archbishop Russell in July. James had been nominating to Irish Roman Catholic bishoprics since 1688, and though the practice was not liked in Rome it was not resisted, and Creagh was provided to Dublin on 9 March 1693. Return to

Ireland was impossible, but he was offered asylum by the cardinal-bishop of Strasbourg. He arrived there on 4 July 1694, and for the rest of his life acted as assistant bishop. In 1703 he suffered a stroke, which left him with impaired speech. He died in Strasbourg on 20 July 1705, and was buried before the high altar in the choir of the church of St Stephen, Strasbourg. Even the location of his grave was lost in the depredations of the French Revolution, but the tomb inscription survived in an eighteenth-century copy.

PATRICK J. CORISH

Sources L. F. Renehan, *Collections on Irish church history*, ed. D. McCarthy, 1 (1861) [incl. account of Creagh in MS history of Limerick priest James White, *d.* 1768] · C. Mooney, 'The library of Archbishop Piers Creagh', *Reportorium Novum*, 1/1 (1955), 117–39 [list, with analysis and biographical memoir] · W. P. Burke, *The Irish priests in the penal times, 1660–1760* (1914) [civil records of Creagh's imprisonment and trial, since destroyed] · E. Bolster, *A history of the diocese of Cork*, 1: *From the earliest times to the Reformation* (1972) · M. Lenihan, *Limerick: its history and antiquities* (1866) · *The letters of Saint Oliver Plunkett, 1625–1681*, ed. J. Hanly (1979) · J. Hanly, 'Records of the Irish College Rome under Jesuit administration', *Archivium Hibernicum*, 27 (1964) · C. Giblin, 'The Processus datariae and the appointment of Irish bishops in the 17th century', *Father Luke Wadding: commemorative volume*, ed. Franciscan Fathers dún Mhuire, Killiney (1957), 508–616 · C. Eubel and others, eds., *Hierarchia Catholica medii et recentioris aevi*, 5, ed. P. Ritzler and P. Sefrin (Passau, 1952) · B. Jennings, ed., 'Miscellaneous documents, 1588–1715 [pt 3]', *Archivium Hibernicum*, 15 (1950), 1–73, esp. 59, 67–9 · B. Jennings, ed., 'Ireland and Propaganda Fide, 1672–6', *Archivium Hibernicum*, 19 (1956), 1–60 · *Collectanea Hibernica*, 2 (1959) · *Collectanea Hibernica*, 3 (1960) · *Collectanea Hibernica*, 16 (1973) · *Collectanea Hibernica*, 18–19 (1976–7)

Archives Archivio Vaticano, Vatican City · Irish College, Rome, archives · Sacra Congregazione di Propaganda Fide, Rome

Creagh [Crevagh], **Richard** (*c.*1523–1586?), Roman Catholic archbishop of Armagh, was born in Limerick, one of at least three children of Nicholas Creagh, a merchant, and his wife, Joan White. Having been apprenticed to a merchant in Limerick he began to trade in his own right until, at about the age of twenty-five, he abandoned commerce to follow a scholarly and religious vocation. Already fluent in English, Irish, and French, he studied Latin in Limerick and migrated to Louvain, where, on 28 February 1549, he matriculated as a *pauper* in Le Porc College of the university. Supported by a bursary from the almoner of Charles V, he studied in the arts faculty at Standonk House and graduated MA in 1551; afterwards he studied theology in the Pontifical College, and proceeded BTh in 1555.

In that year Creagh came to the attention of Ignatius of Loyola, general of the Society of Jesus, as a fit candidate for the Roman Catholic bishopric of Limerick, which was then occupied by William Casey, a 'public Lutheran' (Loyola, 9.378). Creagh refused the proffered promotion and returned as a priest to Limerick about 1557. There he opened a grammar school and was joined as teacher after May 1560 by Thomas Leverous, the deposed bishop of Kildare. In 1562 Creagh was adjured by David Wolfe SJ, the papal emissary, to go to Rome and accept appointment to either of the vacant archiepiscopal sees of Cashel or Armagh.

While resident in Rome in 1563–4 Creagh befriended Thomas Goldwell, the exiled bishop of St Asaph, and took an interest in the closing session of the Council of Trent. Creagh had hoped to join the order of the Theatines in Italy but was eventually appointed archbishop of Armagh on 22 March 1564. On appointment he was granted special faculties by Pope Pius IV to carry out his mission and to found schools and a university in a country where protestantism was now the official state religion.

In Flanders Creagh was joined by William Good SJ and Edmund Daniel, a Jesuit scholastic, for the final part of the journey to Ireland. He was separated from the others at Dover, travelled by way of London to the west coast of Britain and took a ship to Ireland. Almost as soon as he entered his ecclesiastical province he was arrested by an English captain and examined before the Irish council in Dublin. He was sent in chains to London and committed to the Tower on 18 January 1565. On 22 February he was interrogated at length by Sir William Cecil about his sojourn on the continent and the purpose of his mission. He was again examined before the recorder of London on 17 March, and for a third time on 23 March. He continually stressed his loyalty to Elizabeth I and the transparency of his motives.

On the octave of Easter 1565 Creagh escaped from the Tower and boarded a ship for Antwerp. He was received with great kindness by the Jesuits there and by Michel Baius, president of the Pontifical College at Louvain. He stayed in Brabant until late 1565, receiving duplicates of his documents of appointment and accreditation from Rome in preparation for the resumption of his mission. He travelled to Madrid, where he briefed Philip II on his plans, and with financial assistance from the king he set out for Ireland in the summer of 1566. He was robbed and maltreated by pirates in the Bay of Biscay and left for dead by them at Blavet near Nantes. Recovered, he proceeded on his journey and arrived in the north of Ireland in the autumn of 1566.

The paramount chieftain of central Ulster, Shane O'Neill, who had vainly expected the archbishop to support his rebellion against the crown, refused to allow Creagh to take up his episcopal temporalities. Creagh attempted to convoke the Catholic bishops and clergy of the region to promulgate the decrees of the Council of Trent. At Christmas 1566 he offered in a letter to the lord deputy, Sir Henry Sidney, to act as mediator between O'Neill and the crown but was rebuffed. Having been joined by David Wolfe, Creagh journeyed from Ulster into Connaught. While passing near Roger O'Shaughnessy's castle, he was captured on 27 April 1567 and sent to Dublin. He was said to be not more than forty-four years old about this time.

Creagh broke gaol in Dublin Castle for a brief period but was recaptured by Meiler Hussey, the steward of the earl of Kildare. He was transferred to London in late 1567 and questioned closely about his alleged traitorous relations with Shane O'Neill, who had been killed the previous June. For two and a half years he was held in irons in the Tower of London, during which period the Spanish ambassador reported to Philip II on his captivity. On 5 March 1570 he was returned to the custody of Sir Henry Sidney in Dublin and put on trial for treason. He defended himself against charges of conspiracy and was found not guilty by the jury. His imprisonment in Dublin was continued, however, until February 1575 when Lord Deputy William Fitzwilliam requested that he be transferred to London because, as he stated, the work of the Reformation was being hindered by the presence of a revered Roman Catholic in Dublin.

A plea from Creagh to the privy council for his release was turned down, but the conditions of his captivity for his last twelve years were not as severe as formerly. Creagh was vindicated of a charge of sexual misconduct with the young daughter of a gaoler, and for the final phase of his life he was a confessorial figure in the Tower prison, debating issues of theology and strengthening the faith of correspondents. He was questioned in 1580 about his connections with a Portuguese agent, Antonio Fogaza, but established his innocence of conspiracy. His release was denied because the authorities concluded that he was a 'dangerous man to be among the Irish' (PRO, SP 12/178, no. 74). Eventually he died in prison, probably by poisoning, about December 1586. It was suspected that Robert Poley, the *agent provocateur* of Sir Francis Walsingham in the Babington plot, administered poisoned cheese to Creagh. He is said to have been buried in the Tower.

Because of his reputation for holiness, Creagh's importance as an icon for contemporary Irish Roman Catholics was widely acknowledged. His early biographers had no doubts about his sanctity and they also stressed his role as a pioneer of Roman Catholic education both as teacher and visionary of third-level training for Irish youth. Despite his short ministry as archbishop, Creagh vigorously promoted Tridentine norms among the Irish clergy and laity. While rejecting any compromise with protestantism, he remained professedly loyal to the English crown. As a scholar perhaps his major contribution lay in his treatment for the first time of the Irish language scientifically, and his use of it as a tool of instruction in his catechism of about 1560. He also wrote on cases of conscience and on ecclesiastical history, including the lives of the Irish saints. He was above all a champion of the rights of the Roman Catholic church in Ireland against all obtruders, whether in the form of crown officials, ill-disciplined clergy, or intrusive Irish magnates such as Shane O'Neill.   COLM LENNON

Sources D. Rothe, *De processu martyriali quorundam fidei pugilum in Hibernia, pro complemento sacrorum analectorum* (1619), 1–47 · P. F. Moran, ed., 'Some documents connected with Dr Creagh, archbishop of Armagh, with notice of his life', *Spicilegium Ossoriense*, 1 (1874), 40–58 · letters of Richard Creagh to and from Jesuit correspondents, 1564–8, Irish Jesuit Archives, Dublin, MacErlean transcripts, MSS A, B · 1567–8, 1575, state papers, Ireland, PRO, SP 63/12/32–3, 59, 50; 20/13(ii); 22/50; 23/8; 48/86 · J. H. Pollen, ed., 'Tower bills', *Miscellanea, III*, Catholic RS, 3 (1906), 4–29 · C. Lennon, *Archbishop Richard Creagh of Armagh, 1523–1586: an Irish prisoner of conscience of the Tudor era* (2000) · R. Creagh, 'On the origins of the O'Neills and Creaghs', c.1583, TCD, MS 568, fol. 61 · J. Linchaeo [J. Lynch], *De praesulibus Hiberniae*, ed. J. F. O'Doherty, IMC, 1 (1944), 130–35 · P. O'Sullivan-Beare, *Historiae Catholicae Iberniae compendium* (1621), fols. 89r–90r · R. Creagh, 'De lingua Ibernica', c.1560, TCD, MS 664, fols. 121r–127v · *APC*, 1577–8, 31, 43–4 · I. Loyola, *Epistolae et instructiones*, ed. M. Lecina, V. Agustí, and D. Restrepo (1903–11), 9.378 · M. Gonçalves da Costa, ed., *Fontes inéditas Portuguesas para a história de Irlanda* (Braga, 1981), 140 · Archivio Segreto Vaticano, acta vice-cancellarii, 9, fol. 156r

Creagh, William (1828–1901), army officer in the East India Company, was born on 1 June 1828 at Newry, co. Down, the second son of the seven children of General Sir Michael Creagh (1787–1860), and his wife, Elizabeth, only daughter of Charles Osborne, judge of the king's bench, Ireland, and niece of Sir Thomas Osborne, eighth baronet, of Newtown Anner, co. Tipperary. He came of an old Roman Catholic family, and his father, who entered the army at the age of fourteen, saw much service with the 86th regiment, and was at his death in 1860 colonel of the 73rd regiment; he was the first in the family to become a protestant. His eldest brother, General Charles Creagh-Osborne (d. 1892), after service in India, was commandant of the Staff College, Camberley, from 1878 to 1886; his youngest brother, Major James Henry Creagh (d. 1900), served in the 27th regiment during the Indian mutiny, and retired as a result of illness contracted at that time.

William Creagh was educated for six years at Mr Flynn's private school in Dublin. After attending the Royal Military College, Sandhurst, from January 1842 to December 1844, he became a cadet in the East India Company's service, and joined his regiment, the 19th (later the 119th) Bombay infantry, in June 1845. In 1847, being then stationed at Karachi, he was placed by General Walter Scott RE in charge of a district in Upper Sind. He was recalled from administrative duties by the outbreak of the Second Anglo-Sikh War in the Punjab (April 1848), and served with his regiment through the campaign of 1848–9. His regiment, the 119th Bombay infantry, was called the Mooltan regiment (later the 2nd battalion 9th Jat regiment). Creagh came home early in 1856, and on 29 April 1857 married Haidée Sarah Rose, daughter of John Dopping, of Derrycassan, co. Longford; they had five sons and two daughters. She predeceased him. On his wedding trip in 1857 at Killarney, Creagh learned of the uprising and returned to duty, but sailed round the Cape and so did not reach India until Delhi had fallen. However, with his regiment, under Sir Hugh Rose in central India, he took part in the pursuit of Tantia Topi and was present at Tantia's defeat near Jhansi on 1 April 1858, and, a year later, at his capture.

Gazetted captain on 3 February 1860, Creagh successfully administered, by commission from Sir Richmond Shakespear, resident at Indore, the princely state of Dhar, during the minority of its raja (1861–2). On 10 November 1877 Creagh married Dora, younger daughter of Edwin Sturge of Gloucester; they had one son and two daughters. Having been promoted major in 1865, lieutenant-colonel in 1871, and colonel in 1876, he was in command of his regiment when the Second Anglo-Afghan War broke out in 1878. He had earlier shown an aptitude for engineering and had made the first road up to the hill station of Matheran, near Bombay. From 16 December 1878 to 26 February 1879 he was employed with his men in making a military road from Jacobabad to Dadhar, a distance of 109 miles; he then built a further roadway, to the Bolan Pass and on to Dadhar.

For private reasons, Creagh retired in December 1879, with the rank of major-general. He returned to England early in 1880, where he lived at St Leonards, Sussex. Anglican and Conservative, he took an active though unostentatious part in religious, philanthropic, and political affairs. He died at his home, 6 Charles Road, St Leonards, on 23 May 1901, and was buried in the Hastings borough cemetery. He was survived by his second wife. His four sons who reached manhood all entered the army. The eldest, Ralph Charles Osborne, Royal Marines and 5th Punjab infantry, served with distinction in Burma, in Manipur, at the relief of Chitral, in the Kurram valley, and in South Africa, and died at Netley on 27 January 1904.

H. C. MINCHIN, rev. JAMES LUNT

Sources S. H. Shadbolt, ed., *The Afghan campaigns of 1878–1880*, 2 vols. (1882) · historical record of the 86th regiment (2nd bn royal Ulster rifles · B. Robson, *The road to Kabul: the Second Afghan War, 1878–1881* (1986) · *Hart's Army List* (1845–79) · C. Hibbert, *The great mutiny, India, 1857* (1978) · B. Bond, ed., *Victorian military campaigns* (1967) · *CGPLA Eng. & Wales* (1901) · private information (1912)
Likenesses oils (aged twenty-eight); priv. coll., 1912 · oils (aged forty); priv. coll., 1912
Wealth at death £4137 8s. 2d.: probate, 19 June 1901, *CGPLA Eng. & Wales*

Creak, Edith Elizabeth Maria (1855–1919), headmistress, was born on 26 July 1855 at 118 Lansdowne Place, Hove, Sussex, daughter of Albert Creak, an early graduate of London University, nonconformist minister and successful proprietor of a boys' school in Hove. Her mother was Bertha Creak (formerly Shelly). After a thorough education in her father's school, Edith Creak took the Cambridge higher local examination, set up in 1869 for women intending to teach. Having won a scholarship established by John Stuart Mill and Helen Taylor she was enabled, at only sixteen, to register in 1871 as one of the first five students at what became Newnham College, Cambridge. Although taking a second-class honours in classics and a third in mathematics in 1875, as a woman she was not eligible for a Cambridge degree. In 1878, 1879, and 1880 respectively, she took honours in the London University general examination for women, gained a first class in the intermediate examination, and was in the first batch of women admitted to the London degree.

In teaching, Edith Creak was equally a pioneer. Having been an assistant mistress at Plymouth high school from 1875 to 1876, she was appointed, at the age of only twenty, headmistress of the new Brighton High School for Girls, the tenth school founded by the Girls' Public Day School Company. She appointed the staff and organized the school, which opened in June 1876. Gifted, plump, and jolly, she apparently inspired 'lively enthusiasm and sound scholarship', as she did at King Edward VI's High School for Girls in Birmingham, of which she became the first headmistress in 1883. She grew very proud of this ancient educational foundation which had broken new ground in 1880 by establishing an endowed high school

for girls. Her highly praised role in the design and organization of new premises for the girls' high school illustrated her authority over her governors, her perception of the educational needs of her pupils, and her attention to their health. She secured cookery facilities despite the governors' misgivings over teaching domestic subjects in a high school, excellent science facilities, and all-in-one desks which could be adjusted so that the girls need neither stoop nor be uncomfortable.

Miss Creak admired Edward Thring, headmaster of Uppingham, whose conference of headmistresses she had attended in 1887, and emulated him in achieving discipline through pupils' self-respect and the internalization of the school ethos rather than by proliferating formal rules. Her school was known for its serene, quiet order: she was strict, but highly respected. She gave the senior girls in particular much responsibility for their own learning. Like Thring she stressed attention to all pupils whatever their abilities and, accordingly, catered for the development of practical skills, as her 'beautiful pendant', made and designed in 1910 by girls working in the jewellery section (the only girls' school to have one), illustrated. Keenly interested in all subjects, she stimulated a broad, liberal education.

A Congregationalist and deeply religious, Miss Creak was a pioneer in religious education, but it was in science that King Edward's was outstanding. She appointed excellent science teachers, ensured the requisite facilities, and used the local expertise of Dr Crosskey and Mason College. In sport she was less adventurous, allowing gymnastics and tennis but not hockey. Rejecting the athleticism of boys' schools, she paid more attention to the principles of sound bodily health, including proper ventilation, heating, lighting, and sanitary arrangements. She also wanted annual medical inspections. Her dread of pupils overworking led her to issue timetables for homework and wish for an eight-hour bill for both them and staff. She was one of the first headteachers to stop examinations lower than matriculation, yet the school's academic standing steadily rose, and from the early days came a stream of academic distinctions at school and later university, particularly at Newnham and London, and especially in science. She was an associate of Newnham from 1893 to 1900 and she founded the Newnham College Club in Birmingham.

Miss Creak's generous gifts to the library and system of free hours there for the older girls, like her encouragement of art, music, drama, and debates, were a model of high school education for girls. She was, indeed, among a new breed of headmistresses who developed girls' secondary schools with classical ideals of academic excellence and self-realization through public service. In many ways she exemplified the new professionalism of women graduate teachers in her relationships with staff, governors, and parents and in her membership of the Headmistresses Association. She was one of the headmistresses interviewed for the Bryce commission in 1894. In her written submission to this she voiced her particular concerns for the registration and proper training of secondary teachers, for keeping elementary education and secondary education strictly apart, and for closing higher-grade elementary schools.

In some respects, indeed, Miss Creak was quite conservative. Pleased personally with the new areas opening for women's energy and enterprise, she remained, none the less, sure that women's best sphere was in the home. In 1885 she had supported the Women's Suffrage Bill, but by the 1900s she was adamant in her opposition to both women's suffrage and the educational ladder which could take the poor to secondary education and university. Her patriotism in the Second South African War was strident, and her character, once humorous, sympathetic, and full of *joie de vivre*, became irritable, dictatorial, and abrupt as her health deteriorated. This and her lack of adaptability eventually led to her resignation in 1910. Nevertheless, at her best she was clear-sighted, courageous, patient, and innovative, and wielded natural authority. She had wide and keen interests including classics, botany, mountaineering, art, needlework, lace-making, and collecting alpine flowers, which she grew in her beloved garden at Barnt. Edith Creak died at her home, 55 Hagley Road, Edgbaston, Birmingham, on 20 May 1919. RUTH WATTS

Sources W. I. Candler, *King Edward VI High School for Girls, part I* (1971) · R. Waterhouse, *King Edward VI High School for Girls, 1883–1983* (1983) · [A. B. White], ed., *Newnham College register*, 1: *1871–1923* (1964), 48 · E. Archibald, 'In memoriam Edith E. M. Creak', *Newnham College Roll Letter* (1920), 74–5 · *Birmingham Faces and Places*, 5 (1893) · Birmingham biography newpaper cuttings, 1909–1911; 1917–1922; 1941–1942, Birm. CL · 'Royal commission on secondary education: report', *Parl. papers* (1895), 48.439, C. 7862-VI · *The historical record, 1836–1912: being a supplement to the calendar completed to September 1912*, University of London (1912) · M. G. Mills, *Brighton and Hove high school, 1876–1952* (1953) · J. Sondheimer and P. R. Bodington, eds., *GPDST, 1872–1972: a centenary review* (1972) · J. S. Pederson, *The reform of girls' secondary and higher education in Victorian England* (1897) · b. cert. · d. cert.
Archives King Edward Resources Centre, Edgbaston Park Road, Birmingham, King Edward VI Foundation archives · Newnham College, Cambridge, archives
Likenesses portrait, King Edward High School for Girls
Wealth at death £4019 5s. 3d.: probate, 26 June 1919, *CGPLA Eng. & Wales*

Creak, (Eleanor) Mildred (1898–1993), child psychiatrist, was born on 11 August 1898 in Swann Lane, Cheadle Hulme, Stockport, Cheshire, the elder daughter of Robert Brown Creak, mill engineer, and his wife, Ellen, *née* McCrossan. She knew from an early age that she wanted to be a doctor and work with children. She entered the London School of Medicine for Women at the age of eighteen years but after a year transferred to University College Hospital (UCH), London, and qualified MB, BS (London) in 1923. While a medical student she developed an admiration for two psychiatrists on the staff at UCH, Bernard Hart and A. F. Tredgold. This led her to want to specialize in psychiatry.

At the time that Creak qualified it was difficult for women doctors to obtain employment, and she made ninety applications before securing a post. While a medical student she had become a Quaker, and in 1924 she was appointed assistant physician to the Quaker mental hospital, The Retreat, in York. She remained there for four years and then in 1929 was appointed to the Maudsley Hospital, London. There she helped to lay the foundations for what became an internationally recognized centre for research into child and adolescent psychiatric disorders. In 1932 she was awarded a Rockefeller Fellowship for postgraduate training in the United States, where she spent most of her time at the Philadelphia Child Guidance Clinic. On her return she engaged in clinical and academic work with children, specializing in those whose problems had a biological basis. At this stage in her career she published articles on organic psychoses, chorea, tics, compulsive utterances, and hysteria in childhood. In the mid-1930s, she was involved in planning the first psychiatric in-patient unit for children in the country at the Maudsley Hospital, but war was declared when it had been open for just a month, and the patients were evacuated to Mill Hill Hospital. Creak herself joined the Women's Army Corps and rose to the rank of major. Much of her service was in India.

At the end of the war Creak was offered a post at the Maudsley but declined, disliking what she felt was an over-emphasis there on statistical research, for which she felt she was not fitted. Instead in 1946 she took up the offer of a post at the Hospital for Sick Children, Great Ormond Street, London, where she established a thriving, clinically active department with a strong training role. From the time of her appointment to her retirement in 1963 she worked tirelessly to establish the credibility of the speciality of child psychiatry in the world of paediatrics, a world in which many of her paediatric colleagues questioned the importance of emotional factors in the lives and illnesses of their patients. Her success can be gauged by the fact that the department that she founded became one of the largest in the hospital.

Perhaps Creak's best-known contribution was in autism. Many autistic children were referred to her, and she developed what was then the unfashionable concept that it stemmed not from parental inadequacy, as was commonly believed by her child psychiatric colleagues, but from constitutional or what were later called genetic factors. This view was based on studying 100 children with autism, many of whom turned out to have evidence of brain dysfunction. She chaired a working party to establish criteria for the diagnosis of autism, and her 'nine points' were for some time the agreed basis for this diagnosis. She was highly respected both by paediatricians and psychiatrists. She gave the Charles West lecture at the Royal College of Physicians in 1958 and had a number of child psychiatric units named after her during her lifetime. These included a unit in Perth, Western Australia, and the child psychiatric in-patient unit at Great Ormond Street.

Creak's outstanding characteristic was her gentleness. Paradoxically she was both highly puritanical and exceptionally tolerant. When a psychotherapist in her department bought a comfortable couch for his child patients (and doubtless to rest on himself in exhausted moments), she caught sight of it and exclaimed 'you're turning this place into a brothel'. With her complete lack of make-up, her horn-rimmed spectacles, and her skirt length that made no concession at all to prevalent fashion it is difficult to imagine a person less likely to have any idea what a brothel was really like. Yet she was totally non-judgemental when it came to parents who behaved deplorably, and merely tried to do her best for their children.

Creak had a wide circle of friends but few interests outside her work. She never married. She was a committed Christian and an active Quaker. After her retirement she went to live in Welwyn Garden City and attended Friends' meetings there regularly. She suffered from Alzheimer's disease for most of the last two decades of her life, and latterly from cancer, but she continued to attend meetings until her last months. She died, of breast cancer, at her home, Martins House, Jessop Road, Stevenage, Hertfordshire, on 27 August 1993.   PHILIP GRAHAM

Sources *The Independent* (6 Nov 1993) · S. I. Elmhirst, *Psychiatric Bulletin*, 18 (1994), 318–19 · personal knowledge (2004) · private information (2004) · b. cert. · d. cert.
Likenesses photograph, repro. in *The Independent*
Wealth at death £569,308: probate, 5 May 1994, *CGPLA Eng. & Wales*

Crealock, Henry Hope (1831–1891), army officer, artist, and author, born on 31 March 1831, was the son of William Betton Crealock of Langeston, Littleham, near Bideford. Crealock entered Rugby School in February 1844. He was commissioned in the 90th light infantry on 13 October 1848, and promoted lieutenant on 24 December 1852 and captain on 29 December 1854. On 5 December 1854 he landed at Balaklava and served at the siege of Sevastopol. He was mentioned in dispatches for his bravery during the attacks on the Redan on 18 June and 8 September 1855, and was appointed deputy adjutant quartermaster-general at headquarters on 17 September and at Constantinople in December. He received the brevet rank of major and the Mejidiye (fifth class). On 26 December 1856 he was promoted major, and in March 1857 he was appointed deputy adjutant quartermaster-general to the China expeditionary force. He was present at the operations at Canton (Guangzhou) in December 1857 and January 1858, and received the brevet rank of lieutenant-colonel. On 20 July 1858 he was promoted lieutenant-colonel. He served in the Indian campaigns of Rohilkhand, Biswara, and Trans-Gogra during 1858 and 1859 on the staff of Sir William Rose Mansfield, was present at the actions of Bareilly and Shahjahanpur, and was mentioned in dispatches. In March 1860 he was appointed military secretary to Lord Elgin during his Chinese embassy. He was attached to the headquarters of the army during the ensuing war, and was present at actions from Sinho to the capture of Peking (Beijing). On 6 July 1864 he received his colonelcy and in 1869 a CB, and on 2 January 1870 he was promoted major-general. During the Austro-Prussian War he was military attaché at Vienna, and from 1874 to 1877 quartermaster-general in Ireland. In the Anglo-Zulu War of 1879 he commanded the 1st division in the second invasion, and for his

services was created CMG. He retired from the army on 4 September 1884 with the rank of honorary lieutenant-general.

Crealock was an accomplished draughtsman, and his sketches of scenes in the Indian mutiny, China campaign, and Anglo-Zulu War are valuable records. Sketches of the Zulu campaign in the *Illustrated London News* have been misattributed to him; they were by his brother, John North *Crealock. In 1885 he republished his 1870–79 anti-Russian articles as *The Eastern Question*. At the time of his death he was working on his *Deer-Stalking in the Highlands of Scotland*, illustrated by his drawings, which was edited by his brother and published in 1892. Crealock died at his residence, 20 Victoria Square, Pimlico, London, on 31 May 1891, and was buried at Littleham, near Bideford, Devon.

E. I. CARLYLE, *rev.* M. G. M. JONES

Sources *The Times* (4 June 1891) · *Army List* · Elgin's letters and papers, priv. coll. [Broomhall, Dunfermline] · I. Knight, *Brave men's blood: the epic of the Zulu War, 1879* (1990) · D. R. Morris, *The washing of the spears* (1966) · *ILN* (13 June 1891) · [F. Temple], ed., *Rugby School register from 1675 to 1867 inclusive* (1867), 142 · W. Ashe and E. V. W. Edgell, *The story of the Zulu campaign* (1880) · T. Day, *But burdens shouldered: Anglo-Zulu war graves and memorials in the United Kingdom* (Zulu Study Group, Victorian Military Society, 1995) · R. A. Brown, ed., *The road to Ulundi: the water colour drawings of John North Crealock (the Zulu war of 1879)* (1969) · J. P. C. Laband, ed., *Lord Chelmsford's Zululand campaign, 1878–1879* (1994)
Archives NRA, priv. coll., corresp. with Drummond family
Likenesses H. H. Crealock, self-portrait, pen-and-ink drawing, 1858, NAM · R. Russ, oils, 1869, NPG · Spy [L. Ward], watercolour study, NPG; repro. in *VF* (15 March 1879) · engraving or photograph, repro. in *ILN* (13 June 1891) · marble effigy on a monument, Littleham Church, near Bideford, Devon
Wealth at death £65,797 8s. 2d.: probate, 24 June 1891, *CGPLA Eng. & Wales*

Crealock, John North (1836–1895), army officer and artist, was born on 21 May 1836, the second son of William Betton Crealock of Langeston, Littleham, near Bideford. Educated at Rugby School, he was commissioned as ensign in the 95th (Derbyshire) regiment on 13 October 1854 and promoted lieutenant on 9 February 1855. From May 1855 to June 1856 he was inspector of musketry at Aldershot. He served with his regiment in the Indian mutiny (1858–9), and was present at the siege and capture of Kotah, Chundaree, and Gwalior, and at the battle of Kotah-ki-sarai, where he was wounded. He was mentioned three times in dispatches. On 6 May 1859 he was promoted captain and was aide-de-camp to the lieutenant-general, Bombay, from 16 December 1862 to 11 March 1864. He passed staff college in 1868 and was promoted brevet major on 5 July 1872, becoming a major in the 95th regiment on 30 March 1875. Between 1870 and 1878 he held a series of staff appointments, first as aide-de-camp to the general officer commanding the forces, headquarters, Ireland, between 1 August 1870 and 15 November 1871, then as deputy assistant adjutant-general at Aldershot from 16 November 1871 to 19 May 1875, and finally as deputy assistant quartermaster-general, intelligence branch of the army at Adair House, London, from 30 September 1877 to February 1878.

On 25 February 1878 Crealock was appointed assistant

John North Crealock (1836–1895), by unknown engraver

military secretary, Cape of Good Hope, to Lieutenant-General the Hon. F. Thesiger (later Lord Chelmsford), the officer commanding in South Africa, and accompanied him to the Cape. In recognition of his services in the Cape Frontier War of 1878 he was made a brevet lieutenant-colonel on 11 November 1878. During the 1879 Anglo-Zulu War he continued on Chelmsford's personal staff and was promoted military secretary in May 1879. He served as senior staff officer to the Eshowe relief column and was slightly wounded at the battle of Gingindlovu on 2 April 1879. He was present at the battle of Ulundi on 4 July 1879 which ended the campaign. He returned with Chelmsford to England when the general resigned his command in July 1879, and was made CB on 27 November 1879.

During his service in South Africa, Crealock had been Chelmsford's constant companion and was suspected of wielding undue influence over the general and of shielding him by withholding information. Yet he was not noted for his efficiency as military secretary nor for the legibility of his dispatches. Crealock was privately critical of the general's military capabilities, but he always staunchly defended him in public, gaining a reputation for haughtiness, facetiousness, and sharp retorts. His overbearing manner did nothing to ease Chelmsford's always difficult relations with the local colonial officials upon whom he relied for transport and supplies, and alienated many of his fellow officers.

Promoted lieutenant-colonel in the 95th regiment on 21 July 1880 and colonel in the army on 11 November 1882, Crealock commanded his regiment (which became the 2nd battalion, Sherwood Foresters, in 1881) from 1880 to 1885 while it was deployed in Gibraltar, Egypt, and India. During the Egyptian expedition of 1882 he was commandant at Alexandria and at El Mex. Subsequently he held senior staff appointments, first as assistant adjutant-general at Aldershot from 1 April 1887 to 22 May 1890, and then from 23 May 1890 to 29 February 1892 as assistant quartermaster-general, headquarters of the army. On 24 December 1891 he was promoted major-general, and on 1 April 1892 given command of the 3rd infantry brigade at Aldershot. Crealock returned to India as major-general,

Madras, first-class district commander, a post he held from 13 November 1893 until his retirement on 5 March 1895. He never married, and died at Rawalpindi on 24 April 1895.

Crealock excelled at watercolour paintings and sketches, many executed while on campaign and, presumably, to the detriment of his military duties. On his death, 189 of his watercolours of the eastern Cape, Natal, and Zululand, executed during 1878–9, were given to the Sherwood Foresters Museum, Nottingham. They depict landscapes, camp scenes, forts, battles, and military and civilian personalities (both black and white) during the Cape Frontier War and the Anglo-Zulu War. They are a valuable historical record of the campaigns and of the South African countryside, besides being of pleasing artistic quality. Their detail, wit, and accurate sense of topography have been commended by historians, botanists, and geographers alike.   J. P. C. LABAND

Sources R. A. Brown, ed., *The road to Ulundi: the water colour drawings of John North Crealock (the Zulu war of 1879)* (1969) · S. Clarke, ed., *Zululand at war: the conduct of the Anglo-Zulu war* (1984) · J. P. C. Laband, ed., *Lord Chelmsford's Zululand campaign, 1878–1879* (1994) · *Army List* (1895) · *The frontier war journal of Major John Crealock, 1878*, ed. C. Hummel (1988) · *CGPLA Eng. & Wales* (1895)
Archives Rhodes University, Grahamstown, South Africa, Cory Library for Historical Research, journal written during frontier war in South Africa · Sherwood Foresters Museum, Nottingham Castle, watercolour drawings | Brenthurst Library, Johannesburg, Alison MSS · NAM, Chelmsford MSS
Likenesses J. N. Crealock, self-portrait, pen and wash, 1879, Sherwood Foresters Museum, Nottingham Castle · photograph, 1879, NAM · engraving, repro. in *ILN* (27 Dec 1879), 605 · engraving, repro. in Crealock, *Frontier war*, frontispiece [see illus.]
Wealth at death £22,165 14s. 5d.: probate, 27 June 1895, *CGPLA Eng. & Wales*

Cream, Thomas Neill (1850–1892), doctor and murderer, was born in Glasgow on 27 May 1850, the eldest son of William Henry Cream (*c*.1823–*c*.1891) and Mary Elder. The family emigrated to Canada, where William became manager of Gilmour & Co., a major Quebec shipbuilding and lumber merchant in Wolfe's Cove. Thomas attended the company's school, taught at Chalmer's Sunday school, and was later apprenticed to the shipbuilding firm of Baldwin & Co.

From there Cream went to study medicine at McGill University, Montreal, from 1872 to 1876, graduating on 31 March 1876. His thesis was on the effects of chloroform. The prophetic title of the address to the graduating class was 'The evils of malpractice in the medical profession'. Dr Craik, the professor of chemistry, recalled him as 'rather wild and fond of ostentatious displays of clothing and jewelry'. He had a reputation as a 'fast and extravagant liver' and was suspected of setting fire to his rooms at 106 Mansfield Street in April 1876 hoping to collect on the insurance (report by Inspector Jarvis, 14 July 1892, PRO, MEPO 3 144).

Cream became engaged to Flora Eliza Brooks, the daughter of Lyman H. Brooks, owner of the main hotel in Waterloo, Quebec. Flora fell ill on 9 September 1876 and Dr Phelan, her physician, told her father that she had been surgically aborted. A face-saving shotgun wedding on 11

September, presided over by Archdeacon Lindsay, ensued, but Cream left for England the next day, leaving his wife behind.

In the autumn of 1876 Cream continued medical studies at St Thomas's Hospital in London, finishing in 1878. He served as an obstetrical clerk, but failed the examinations of anatomy and physiology in 1877, and was also denied entry to the Royal College of Surgeons. He was, however, admitted to the Royal College of Physicians and Surgeons in Edinburgh, with a licence to practise midwifery. On 12 August 1877 his wife died in suspicious circumstances, having taken medicine which he had sent her; he collected $200 from the marriage settlement. From 1879 to 1881 he practised in London, Ontario, and in Chicago with a licence granted by the Illinois state board of health and was thought to have caused the deaths of two prostitutes, although nothing was proved against him. He was accused of passing scurrilous postcards through the mail, but jumped his bail, which had been put up by Mrs Mary McClellan, the mother of his newly betrothed, and went to Canada. He was arrested at Belle Rivière, Ontario, and tried in Illinois for the murder of a patient, Daniel Stott, whose wife he had seduced. He was found guilty on 23 September 1881, thanks largely to the testimony of Mary McClellan against him, and sent to the state penitentiary at Joliet on 1 November for life.

Cream's brother, Daniel, was successful in having his sentence reduced to seventeen years for good behaviour, although he had become a foul-mouthed, frightening, drug addict, and he was released on 31 July 1891. He inherited $16,000 on the death of his father and left for London in September. He booked in at Anderton's Hotel, Fleet Street, and then took a room at 103 Lambeth Palace Road. He was described at this time as lonely and restless, talking endlessly of women, money, and poison, carrying pornographic photographs, and taking drugs. He had a bushy moustache, a marked squint, and dressed in a caped coat and a silk top hat.

When two prostitutes, Ellen Donworth and Matilda Clover, died in October 1891, the crimes were not immediately solved. Shortly afterwards, Cream left for America to see to his father's estate, leaving a will in favour of one Laura Sabbatini, to whom he had become engaged. He now included whisky among his addictions and was not welcomed by his brother in Quebec City. He returned to London on 2 April 1892 to lead a rackety life among the lowlife of the town, giving out that he was the local representative of the Harvey Drug Company, and using the name of Neill.

In April 1892 Cream murdered by strychnine Emma Shrivell and Alice Marsh, two prostitutes living close by, telling his landlady's daughter, Miss Sleaper, that a fellow lodger and medical student named Harper was responsible for their deaths. He rashly proceeded to blackmail Harper's father, a doctor in Barnstaple, who complained to the police. At this time the police viewed Cream as a blackmailer who used the gossip of prostitutes as his weapon, but increasingly suspected him of the murders. An Inspector Jarvis was sent to make inquiries in North America, and his findings led to Cream being charged with blackmail and the murder of Matilda Clover. Further charges were subsequently added to cover the deaths of Donworth, Marsh, and Shrivell, and the attempted murder of one Louisa Harris.

Cream was tried at the central criminal court on 17–20 October 1892, when evidence was produced about his purchase of strychnine, a visit which he had paid to Clover, and an eye-witness account of his handing pills to Harris. It was not alleged that he profited from any of the crimes. Cream was found guilty and sentenced to death on 20 October. A plea of insanity was dismissed under the McNaughten rules, although Cream's behaviour was bizarre and drug induced. He was hanged before a crowd of 4000–5000 people by Billington at Newgate prison at 9 a.m. on 15 November 1892. By 23 October there was already a display at Tussaud's depicting the murders, the effigy wearing Cream's own clothes, for which the museum had paid £200. He is the subject of a late twentieth-century biography, in which he is referred to as 'the most geographically energetic of villains' (McLaren, vii).   J. GILLILAND

Sources A. McLaren, *A prescription for murder* (1993) · W. T. Shore, ed., *Trial of Thomas Neill Cream* (1923) · R. D. Altick, *Victorian studies in scarlet* (1970) · D. J. D. Perrin, *St Thomas's Gazette*, 47 (1949), 229–32 · Boase, *Mod. Eng. biog.* · J. Cashman, *The gentleman from Chicago* (1973) [a novel] · G. Kohn, *Dictionary of culprits and criminals* (1995) · C. Wilson and P. Pitman, *Encyclopaedia of murder* (1961) · *Penny Illustrated Paper* (16 July 1892) · *The Spectator* (29 Oct 1892), 590 · PRO, Central criminal court sessions MSS, minutes of evidence, 1892, 116.1417–60 · *The Times* (13 April 1892) · *The Times* (16 Nov 1892) · *Daily Graphic* (18 Oct 1892) · *Lloyd's Weekly Newspaper* (17 April 1892) · *Reynold's* (17 April 1892) · *Daily Advertiser* [London, Ont.] (8 May 1879) · *Daily Advertiser* [London, Ont.] (14 May 1879) · *Chicago Daily Tribune* (23 Aug 1880) · *The Lancet* (29 Oct 1892), 1003 · McGill University Archives, Montreal, Canada · *Illustrated Police News* (29 Oct 1892) · *Illustrated Police News* (5 Nov 1892) · *Illustrated Police News* (19 Nov 1892)
Archives McGill University, Montreal · PRO, CRIM 1/38/1 · PRO, MEPO 3 144
Likenesses W. Armestead, photograph, BL; repro. in Shore, ed., *Trial of Thomas Neill Cream* · photograph, repro. in *Daily Graphic* · print, repro. in *Penny Illustrated Paper* · waxwork, Madame Tussaud's, London

Crean, Thomas [Tom] **(1877–1938)**, polar explorer, was born at Gurtuchrane, Anascaul, co. Kerry, on 20 July 1877, one of the ten children of Patrick Crean, farmer, and his wife, Catherine Courtney. He grew up speaking both Gaelic and English. Educated at Brackluin School, Anascaul, he enlisted in the Royal Navy on 10 July 1893, aged fifteen, and underwent training on board HMS *Impregnable* at Devonport, Plymouth. He was promoted to petty officer second class in September 1899 and on 15 February 1900 was assigned to HMS *Ringarooma* in the Australia–New Zealand squadron. On 18 December 1900 he was demoted for an unknown offence, and it was as an able seaman that he volunteered to join Captain Robert Falcon Scott's Antarctic expedition ship *Discovery* at Lyttelton, New Zealand, on 10 December 1901. Nearly 6 feet tall, with broad shoulders and a robust constitution, he emerged as one of the strongest sledgers on the expedition. Scott thought highly of Crean, and when the *Discovery* returned to England he recommended him for promotion to petty officer first class, which took effect from 9 September 1904.

Crean's polar experience and love of adventure made him an automatic choice for Scott's second Antarctic expedition. He joined the expedition ship *Terra Nova* in the spring of 1910, along with two companions from the mess deck of the *Discovery*, Chief Stoker William Lashly and Petty Officer Edgar Evans. *Terra Nova* arrived at its Antarctic anchorage in January 1911, and Crean again impressed Scott with his enthusiasm and industry. On 1 March he showed great courage in trying to rescue ponies and sledges caught on breaking sea ice off Cape Armitage. With Lieutenant Henry Robertson (Birdie) Bowers and Apsley Cherry-Garrard, Crean coaxed the animals and gear across the gaps between the moving floes and towards safety. Bowers afterwards wrote: 'Very little was said. Crean, like most bluejackets, behaved as if he had done this sort of thing often before' (Seaver, 185).

A forthright character, Crean had a welcoming grin and friendly greeting, delivered in a rich brogue, which made him a popular member of the expedition. He marched south with the main polar party on 1 November 1911, reaching the foot of the Beardmore Glacier on 9 December. There the last of the ponies was shot. Progress now depended upon man-hauling in three teams of four men, and Crean joined Bowers and Lashly in that led by Lieutenant Edward Evans. On 21 December the first returning party, led by Dr Edward Atkinson, departed, and on 3 January 1912 Scott announced that the summit party would comprise his own team, with the addition of Bowers. The inclusion of a fifth man was unexpected: it 'over-staffed the polar party, and under-staffed the returning party', with serious consequences for both (Seaver, 246).

Edward Evans, Crean, and Lashly turned back on 4 January 1912, with Crean deeply affected by the farewells. They faced a return journey of between 750 and 800 miles. Scott was comforted by the thought that they would make quick progress, but the odds were now heavily against this. They were fatigued, malnourished, and dehydrated, while the loss of Bowers meant that each had a heavier load. In bad visibility they lost the outward track and the journey down the Beardmore Glacier became a series of 'hairbreadth escapes' as they were forced to shun detours in favour of direct routes (Lashly, diary, quoted in Cherry-Garrard, 390). After traversing one vast crevasse on an ice-bridge barely wide enough to take the sledge, Crean remarked that they had travelled 'along the crossbar to the H of Hell' (Evans, 220). When they eventually reached the foot of the glacier on 22 January, he 'let go one huge yell, enough to frighten the ponies out of their graves of snow' (Lashly, diary, quoted in Cherry-Garrard, 393).

That night Lieutenant Evans reported a stiffness in his knees, and within a week it was certain that he had scurvy. In spite of intense pain he continued to march, but on 13 February he could proceed no further and told Crean and Lashly to leave him: 'this we could not think of', Lashly wrote. 'We shall stand by him to the end one way or other, so we are the master today' (Lashly, diary, quoted in Cherry-Garrard, 400). Strapping Evans onto the sledge,

they hauled him along until, on 18 February, the surface conditions and overwhelming fatigue finally defeated them. They then made a final camp, and while Lashly tended Evans, by now seriously ill, Crean set out to walk the 34 miles that remained to Hut Point. He arrived exhausted eighteen hours later to raise the alarm: within half an hour a blizzard closed in that delayed the rescue of Evans and Lashly by a day. Crean, who had covered about 1500 miles on foot since 1 November, had shown extraordinary powers of mental and physical endurance, as indeed had Lashly; both were awarded the Albert medal for saving Evans, who dedicated his memoir *South with Scott* (1921) to the two men.

At Cape Evans that winter Crean and Lashly were included in the councils of the upper deck and both were members of the relief expedition that found Scott's final camp at 79°50′ south on 12 November 1912. When the *Terra Nova* returned to England, Crean was posted to the naval barracks at Chatham. He had risen in stature with each of Scott's two expeditions, and on 23 May 1914 was assigned by the Admiralty to the Imperial Trans-Antarctic Expedition led by Sir Ernest Shackleton. He joined the expedition ship *Endurance* as second officer and thus became one of the few polar explorers to serve under both Scott and Shackleton. While he had a high regard and affection for Scott, he enjoyed a special rapport with Shackleton, 'the Boss'.

After the wreck of the *Endurance* in ice in the Weddell Sea in November 1915, Crean's polar experience became a vital asset to the survival of the 28-man party. On the voyage to Elephant Island (9–15 April 1916) he was second in command of one of the three small boats salvaged from the wreck of the *Endurance*, and when Shackleton undertook a second, infinitely more perilous journey to South Georgia, over 800 miles away, Crean was in his crew of five. The *James Caird* endured sixteen days 'of supreme strife amid heaving waters' before making land on the uninhabited west coast of South Georgia on 10 May (Shackleton, 167). The memory of Crean singing at the tiller stayed with Shackleton always: 'nobody ever discovered what the song was. It was devoid of tune and as monotonous as the chanting of a Buddhist monk at his prayers; yet somehow it was cheerful' (ibid., 176). In moments of inspiration he would attempt 'The Wearing of the Green'. With Frank Worsley, Crean accompanied Shackleton on the epic trek over the previously unexplored interior of the island to the Norwegian whaling station at Stromness, 19–20 May, and when 'the Boss' finally returned to Elephant Island to rescue his men on 30 August 1916, Crean was at his side.

Crean returned to Britain early in November 1916 and resumed his naval career. He served in the war and was promoted to acting boatswain on 11 August 1917. On 5 September 1917 he married, at Anascaul, Eileen (Nell) Herlihy (*d.* 1968), daughter of a local publican; they had three daughters, one of whom died in childhood. On 24 March 1920 he was invalided out of the navy with defective vision following a fall at Rosyth while serving in HMS *Fox*. His commanding officer called it 'a great loss' to the service (Smith, 304).

Crean contemplated a fourth polar expedition, with Shackleton, but eventually decided against and settled in Anascaul, where in 1927 he opened the South Pole Inn. A modest man, he rarely talked about his polar exploits. He died on 27 July 1938 at Bon Secours Hospital, Cork, of a perforated appendix, and was buried in the family tomb that he had built in the cemetery at Ballynacourty, close to his birthplace. He was survived by his wife and two daughters. Tom Crean is commemorated by Mount Crean (77°53′ S, 159°30′ E) in the Antarctic and by the Crean Glacier (54°08′ S, 37°01′ W) on South Georgia.

MARK POTTLE

Sources M. Smith, *An unsung hero: Tom Crean, Antarctic survivor* (2000) · J. Lee Hallock, 'Tom Crean: Antarctic explorer', *Polar Record*, 22/141 (Sept 1985), 665–78 · F. Debenham, *Polar Record*, 3/17 (Jan 1939), 78–9 · E. Shackleton, *South: the story of Shackleton's 1914–1917 expedition* (1999) · F. A. Worsley, *Shackleton's boat journey* (1940) · E. R. G. R. Evans, *South with Scott* (1921); repr. (1962) · R. F. Scott, *The diaries of Captain Robert Scott: a record of the second Antarctic expedition, 1910–1912*, 6 vols. (1968), vol. 2 · A. Cherry-Garrard, *The worst journey in the world: Antarctic, 1910–1913* (1951) · C. Alexander, *The Endurance* (1998) · G. Seaver, *'Birdie' Bowers of the Antarctic* (1938) · G. C. Gregor, *Swansea's Antarctic explorer: Edgar Evans, 1876–1912* (1995) · H. G. Ponting, *The great white south* (1921) · S. Solomon, *The coldest March: Scott's fatal Antarctic expedition* (2001) · *The Norwegian with Scott: Tryggve Gran's Antarctic diary, 1910–1913*, ed. G. Hattersley-Smith (1984) · *Under Scott's command: Lashly's Antarctic diaries*, ed. A. R. Ellis (1969) · *Edward Wilson: diary of the 'Terra Nova' expedition to the Antarctic, 1910–1912*, ed. H. G. R. King (1972) · S. Wheeler, *Cherry: a life of Apsley Cherry-Garrard* (2001)

Likenesses portrait, 1912, repro. in Smith, *Unsung hero*, 141 · F. Hurley, portrait, *c*.1914–1915, repro. in Smith, *Unsung hero*, 241 · photographs, repro. in Smith, *Unsung hero*

Creasy, Sir Edward Shepherd (1812–1878), historian, was born at Bexley in Kent, where his father, Edward Hill Creasy, was a land agent. In the boy's early youth the father removed to Brighton, where he set up in business as an auctioneer and started the *Brighton Gazette*, chiefly with a view to publishing his own advertisements. Young Creasy, having displayed intellectual leanings, was placed on the Eton foundation, and won the Newcastle scholarship in 1831. He was a loyal if critical Old Etonian, publishing *Some account of the foundation of Eton College and of the past and present condition of the school* (1848) and *Biographies of Eminent Etonians* (1850). He won a scholarship to King's College, Cambridge, in 1832, becoming a fellow in 1834; he was called to the bar at Lincoln's Inn in 1837. For several years he went on the home circuit, and he was for some time assistant judge at the Westminster sessions court. He wrote articles for *Bentley's Miscellany* and verse squibs for the *Tipperary Hall Ballads*. In 1840 he was appointed professor of modern and ancient history in London University and in 1846 married Mary, second daughter of G. Cottam, a civil engineer. They had five children. She may have predeceased him. In 1860 he was appointed chief justice of Ceylon, and was knighted. He was chief justice until 1875, visiting Britain as a result of ill health in 1869.

Creasy became a lucid and extreme whig historian, emphasizing the peculiarity of English institutions—the

Sir Edward Shepherd Creasy (1812–1878), by Lock & Whitfield, pubd 1876

mixed monarchy, parliament, and trial by jury—in *The Text-Book of the Constitution* (1848) and then in *The Rise and Progress of the English Constitution* (1853), the latter becoming a best-selling textbook, widely used in schools and colleges until the end of the century. He set out to amplify his views in his *History of England*, but work was interrupted by his departure for Ceylon. He published two of the planned five volumes from Ceylon in 1869. Creasy was also interested in battles, publishing an account of invasions of England (1852) and his memorably entitled *Fifteen Decisive Battles of the World* (1852), which went into many editions. His well-timed *History of the Ottoman Turks, Chiefly Founded on von Hammer* (2 vols., 1854–6) was highly regarded by contemporaries. While in Ceylon, Creasy also wrote *The Old Love and the New* (3 vols., 1870), a novel based on Greek texts, and a competent survey, *The Imperial and Colonial Institutions of the Britannic Empire* (1872). Continued ill health forced his return to England and he died at his home, 15 Cecil Street, London, on 27 January 1878.

Creasy was not an important historian, but he was influential, reflecting parliamentarianism at its most typical.

H. C. G. MATTHEW

Sources *Men of the time* (1856) · Boase, *Mod. Eng. biog.* · *CGPLA Eng. & Wales* (1878) · *DNB*

Likenesses Lock & Whitfield, woodburytype photograph, pubd 1876, NPG [*see illus.*]

Wealth at death under £600: probate, 28 Nov 1878, *CGPLA Eng. & Wales*

Creasy, Sir George Elvey (1895–1972), naval officer, was born on 13 October 1895 at Badulla, Ceylon, the second of the three sons (there were no daughters) of Leonard

Creasy, a civil engineer, the son of the judge, historian, and author Sir Edward Shepherd *Creasy (1812–1878), and his wife, (Ellen) Maud, the eldest daughter of Sir George Job *Elvey, organist of St George's Chapel, Windsor. George's elder brother, Robert, was killed in France in 1918; his younger brother, Sir Gerald Creasy, became governor and commander-in-chief respectively of the Gold Coast from 1947 to 1949 and of Malta from 1949 to 1954.

George Creasy joined the Royal Naval College, Osborne, in September 1908. On completion of his naval training in May 1913, he was promoted midshipman and joined the battleship *Conqueror* in the second battle squadron. On promotion to sub-lieutenant in September 1915, he was appointed to the destroyer *Lively* in the 9th flotilla of the Harwich force under Commodore Reginald Tyrwhitt. Later he transferred successively to the *Milne, Recruit,* and *Nonsuch.* On 15 December 1916 he was promoted to lieutenant and when the war ended in November 1918 he joined the *Vernon,* the torpedo school ship, to undergo the long (T) course. He spent the next ten years in various appointments requiring his specialized knowledge. In 1924 while serving on the staff of the *Vernon,* he met and married Monica Frances (*d.* 1975), daughter of Wilfred Ullathorne, businessman, of Melbourne, Australia. They had a daughter who died in 1934 at the age of nine and a son.

On 30 June 1930 Creasy was promoted to commander. There followed two years on the staff of the tactical school and a further two years as staff officer (operations) on the staff of the commander-in-chief, Mediterranean Fleet. In July 1934 he joined the cruiser *Sussex* as her executive officer and second in command. In December 1935 he was promoted to captain and joined the Admiralty plans division as an assistant director. Two years later, in June 1938, he returned to sea in the *Grenville,* in command of the first destroyer flotilla in the Mediterranean Fleet. Soon after the outbreak of the Second World War in September 1939 the Admiralty concentrated all available destroyers in home waters where they were needed for a great variety of duties. While so employed the *Grenville* was mined and lost. She was replaced by the *Codrington* and it was in this ship that on the invasion of the Netherlands in May 1940 Creasy rescued Princess Juliana and her family. For the skill and initiative he displayed during this and subsequent operations for the evacuation of the British army from Dunkirk on 11 July 1940, he was appointed to the DSO.

For a short time thereafter he served as personal assistant to the first sea lord, Admiral Sir Dudley Pound, before taking up the important post of director of anti-submarine warfare at the Admiralty in September 1940. Creasy, ably assisted by C. R. N. Winn, played an important part in countering the moves made by Admiral Dönitz, head of the U-boat section of the German navy. After just over two years in this post he returned to sea in command of the *Duke of York,* flagship of the commander-in-chief, Home Fleet. His tenure of this important command was, however, cut short by his early promotion to rear-admiral on 8 July 1943. Admiral Sir Bertram Ramsay, who had been entrusted with the conduct of the naval side of the

re-entry into Europe, immediately applied for Creasy as his chief of staff and it was on the latter's shoulders that the task of drafting the detailed orders for the movement of some 5000 ships was to fall. The success of the landings was mainly due to the careful planning which preceded them.

His next appointment was that of flag officer (submarines). War experience had persuaded the Admiralty of the need for more British and allied submarines in the Far East. Rear-Admiral C. B. Barry, his predecessor, had fallen sick and Creasy's first task was to implement this policy. He arrived back on 26 March 1945. With the surrender of Germany on 7 May 1945 followed by that of Japan three months later, he then had to concern himself with the disposal of the enemy submarines as they arrived in British ports.

His next appointment was that of flag officer (air) in the Far East which he assumed on 8 March 1947. Ten months later, on 4 January 1948, he was promoted to vice-admiral. Soon afterwards he rejoined the Admiralty as fifth sea lord and deputy chief of the naval staff. On 30 November 1949 he became vice-chief of the naval staff, a post he was to occupy for almost two years. Meanwhile, on 15 January 1951 he was advanced to admiral and a year later, on 3 January 1952, he hoisted his flag in the *Vanguard* as commander-in-chief, Home Fleet. On 22 September 1954 he took up his last appointment, that of commander-in-chief, Portsmouth, and on 22 April 1955 he was promoted to admiral of the fleet.

Creasy was appointed MVO (1934), CBE (1943), CB (1944), KCB (1949), and GCB (1953). He was commander of the American Legion of Merit, of the Dutch order of Orange Nassau, and of the Polish order of Polonia Restituta.

In 1957 Creasy and his wife settled in the Old House, Great Horkesley in Essex, where he spent the last sixteen years of his life. He took a great interest in local affairs and especially in the Essex branch of the Royal British Legion of which from 1958 to 1969 he was the president. He was an avid reader, kept himself up to date with world affairs, and made many friends locally. A keen fisherman and a good shot, he pursued these activities until his health began to fail in the mid-1960s. He died at his home in Great Horkesley on 31 October 1972 and was buried in the churchyard at Little Horkesley.   B. B. SCHOFIELD, *rev.*

Sources *The Times* (2 Nov 1972) · *WWW* · personal knowledge (1986) · S. W. Roskill, *The war at sea, 1939–1945,* 3 vols. in 4 (1954–61) **Archives** FILM IWM FVA, actuality footage **Likenesses** W. Stoneman, photograph, 1945, NPG

Creech, Thomas (1659–1700), translator and classical scholar, was born in Blandford, Dorset, the only son of Thomas Creech (*d.* 1720) and his wife, Jane (*d.* 1693). Creech, who had one sister, Bridget, was educated at the free grammar school in nearby Sherborne (later Sherborne School), under Thomas Curgenven (Curganven), a noted classicist whose 'unweary'd Diligence, and regular Carriage' Creech was to acknowledge gratefully in later life (*The Odes, Satyrs, and Epistles of Horace,* sig. A6r). Since his parents' financial circumstances would not allow him an

Thomas Creech (1659–1700), by William Sonmans

academic education, an apparently well-connected Dorset personality, Colonel Strangways (possibly Giles Strangways, MP for Dorset in 1661), took care of Creech, who had shown an early 'Disposition and Capacity for Learning' (Jacob, 39), and arranged for him to go to Oxford. Aged sixteen, Creech matriculated on 23 February 1677 as a commoner from Wadham College, to whose founder, Nicholas Wadham, the Strangways family were related. Robert Pitt and Peter Balch, both fellows of Wadham, were his tutors. Creech was admitted as a scholar on 28 September 1677, and on 27 October 1680 graduated BA, an occasion on which he first seems to have demonstrated his considerable eloquence in public. He took his MA on 13 June 1683.

During these early years at Oxford, Creech acquired the reputation of being 'a most severe Student' (*Remarks*, 9.81), whose industry and hard work was to produce a spate of publications in the first half of the 1680s. A commendatory poem, 'To Mr. DRYDEN, on *Religio Laici*', published in November 1682, was preceded, probably in July or August 1682, by the translation which established Creech as a philosopher and a poet, *T. Lucretius Carus the Epicurean philosopher, his six books De natura rerum done into English verse, with notes*, the first almost complete translation, in heroic couplets, to be published in English. (Lucy Hutchinson's and most of John Evelyn's ambitious but ill-fated attempts, in the 1650s, at rendering the difficult *De rerum natura*—the fullest exposition we possess of the Epicurean system—into English remained unpublished until the twentieth century.) The success of Creech's translation was as immediate as it was sensational. It was reprinted in quick succession in 1682-3, both in London and Oxford, and, after the current demand had been satisfied, again in

1699 and 1700, as well as several times throughout the eighteenth century. The third edition of 1683 was acclaimed by no less than thirteen commendatory poems, by Aphra Behn, Tom Brown, John Evelyn, Thomas Flatman, Thomas Otway, and Nahum Tate, among others, not to mention old college friends such as Humphrey Hody, later regius professor of Greek at Oxford, who was Creech's chamber fellow of 'five happy years' (*Miscellany Poems*, 1685, 38). At Oxford generally, as Matthew Tindal underlined as late as 1712, 'he was look'd on as a raw Lad that had not read the *Lucretius* of *Creech*' (*The Nation Vindicated from the Aspersions Cast on it in a Late Pamphlet*, pt 2, 1712, 39). Indeed, according to one eighteenth-century account, the translation of *De rerum natura* 'succeeded so well, that Mr. Creech had a party formed for him, who ventured to prefer him to Mr. Dryden, in point of genius' (Cibber, 3.187).

The translation won Creech a fellowship at All Souls in 1683, some fierce competition from John Glanvill notwithstanding. Creech was one of the first to benefit from Archbishop Sancroft's electoral reform, and although he 'had nothing to recommend him but his talents' (Burrows, 318), the fellows accepted the poor student after he had given 'singular proof of his classical learning and philosophy before those that were his examinants' (Wood, *Ath. Oxon.*, 4.739). However, Creech's election as fellow may have been the last genuine moment of happiness in what was about to turn into an ever more troubled existence.

Creech's first major set-back occurred in 1684 when he published, presumably by late spring or early summer, not only a new translation of the pastoral poems of Theocritus and poetic renderings of selected eclogues and elegies by Virgil and Ovid (*Miscellany Poems ... by the most Eminent Hands*, 1684, 15–29, 107–10, 125–33, 138–40) but also the *Odes, Satyrs, and Epistles of Horace*, a new translation which he had offered to Jacob Tonson and upon which he embarked immediately after finishing the *De rerum natura*. While the first of these do not seem to have left much of an impact on the reading public, the translation of Horace, 'for which [Mr. *Creech*] was the most unfit man in the World', as the critic Charles Gildon put it bluntly (*Laws of Poetry*, 1721, 318–20), was a spectacular failure. In fact, it is fair to say that Creech lost as much reputation by his Horace as he had gained by his Lucretius, even though it ran into at least five more editions, all brought out by the Tonsons (1688, 1711, 1715, 1720, 1737). His lack of success was all the more piquant as the translation was dedicated to John Dryden, and as Dryden's enemies were only too eager to circulate the rumour that the poet laureate, being jealous of Creech's rising fame, 'trepann'd the honest Translator of *Lucretius*' by engaging him 'in a Province, where he ha[d] not stock enough to carry on the Plantation' ([Tom Brown], *The Late Converts Exposed*, pt 2, 1690, 53). The gossip may have had its foundations in Dryden's own miscellany volume of 1685, *Sylvae*, for which Dryden translated selected passages from Lucretius, among others, and in which he demonstrated how easily he could outshine Creech if he so chose. Whatever the truth of the matter,

Creech remained unsuspecting, and relations between the two men, as far as we know, continued to be friendly. After having already contributed 'The life of Solon' (1683), Creech resumed his contributions to a project orchestrated by Dryden for Tonson: 'The life of Pelopidas' and 'The life of Cleomenes' to *Plutarch's Lives* (1683–5), 'The life of Cleomenes' being reprinted, with a fulsome compliment from Dryden, before the prologue to Dryden's tragedy *Cleomenes, the Spartan Heroe*, in 1692. In addition Creech supplied translations of 'Laconick apophthegms', of 'A discourse concerning Socrates his daemon' (both 1684), and of the especially extensive 'Plutarch's symposiacks', in two instalments, for *Plutarch's Morals* (1684–90).

This impressive amount of translation easily disposes of a contemporary report that Creech 'grew lazy' soon after his election to All Souls (*Remarks*, 9.81). Moreover, he was active as a member of the Oxford Society, which, like the Royal Society, was concerned with the development of natural philosophy. Finally, having dedicated considerable attention to a Greek biographer and moral philosopher in the 1680s, Creech returned to Latin literature in 1692–3. He not only translated, and annotated, the thirteenth satire for Dryden's *The Satires of Decimus Junius Juvenalis: Translated into English Verse*, published in 1692 (dated 1693); by June 1692 he had also taken up work on both an edition of the demanding Latin text of Lucretius and a new translation of what is arguably the most difficult of all Latin texts, the *Astronomica* of Marcus Manilius. Although the edition of *De rerum natura*, complete with an *interpretatio* after the manner of the Delphin editions, a copious commentary, and a glossary, carries the imprint Oxford, 1695, it was published late in 1694, and went on to become the standard Latin edition of Lucretius in the eighteenth century. According to one contemporary reviewer, 'No one more accurately studied and better understood the System and Diction of Lucretius than Creech' (E. Harwood, *A View of the Various Editions of the Greek and Roman Classics*, 1775, 153). It was only later that classical scholars tended to belittle its use. *The Five Books of M. Manilius, Containing a System of the Ancient Astronomy and Astrology* followed two years later, in 1697, and was immediately hailed as an imposing poetic feat:

> But Smile, my Muse, once more upon my Song;
> Let *Creech* be numbred with the Sacred Throng.
> Whose daring Soul could with *Manilius* fly,
> And, like an Atlas, Shoulder up the Sky.
> (S. Cobb, *Poetae Britannici: a Poem*, 1700, 23)

Yet even if Creech seemed to be back on the road to renown with his last two achievements, there had been signs since the early 1690s that he was dissatisfied with his life, and that he was trying to reorientate himself. Thus when in early September 1694 Creech's old classics tutor, Thomas Curgenven, tendered his resignation as headmaster of Sherborne School, he seems to have put himself forward as successor. Thereupon the warden and governors chose Creech 'to be Master in the said Schoole to succeed the said Mr Curgenven and to come at our Ladyday next', but, as the minutes of the Sherborne School governors

continue, 'hee afterwards refused the said place and came not' (Real, *Untersuchungen*, 26).

Instead, Creech now opted for a career in the church. He took his BD on 18 March 1696, and on 25 April was presented by All Souls to the living of Welwyn, Hertfordshire, presumably a sinecure which did not involve residence there. At any rate Creech's correspondence of 1698 and 1699 shows him to be in Oxford (Bodl. Oxf., MS Ballard 20; MS Tanner 22), where he embarked on a new scholarly project, an edition of Justin Martyr, one of the early fathers of the church. However, in July 1700 the news spread that Creech had committed suicide. As a contemporary chronicler noted in lurid detail: 'He was found dead in a Garret … on July 19, 1700 … but he had hung some days, as was guess'd, for the body then stunk' (*Remarks*, 9.80).

Speculation about Creech's motives was rife among contemporaries. One explanation imputed the deed to Creech's desire to imitate in a grand, sympathetic gesture his idol, Lucretius, who was said to have killed himself. Another view pointed to the failure of Creech's Horace, of some sixteen years earlier, as the occasion for his suicide—a view that Swift was to echo in 1734:

> *Creech* murder'd *Horace* in his senseless Rhymes,
> But hung himself to expiate his Crimes.
> (*The Poems of Jonathan Swift*, ed. H. Williams, 2nd edn, 3 vols., 1958, 666)

A third account, first propagated by Grub Street pamphleteers and subsequently endorsed by French sources, argued that the real reason was an unrequited love affair (R. P. Nicéron, *Mémoires*, 31, 1735, 44; see also *A step to Oxford, or, A mad essay, &c.; an essay upon amorous madness: or, in other words, to lament Mr. Creech's ridiculous passion to hang himself, for the sake of a woman*, 1700; [J. Froud], *Daphnis, or, A Pastoral Elegy upon the Unfortunate and Much-Lamented Death of Mr. Thomas Creech*, 1700).

However, the version that approximates to the truth is that Creech, who was described by people close to him as a proud, morose, and quarrelsome man, killed himself during a bout of depression. In an apologetic letter of 8 May 1698 to Arthur Charlett, master of University College, Oxford, Creech confessed to suffering from a mental 'disturbance' (Bodl. Oxf., MS Ballard 20, fol. 27), a disclosure that Charlett intended 'to make good use of' whenever he found Creech relapsing, hoping to 'teach Him better manners and better sense' (Bodl. Oxf., MS Tanner, 22, fol. 34; 4, fol. 26). At the coroner's inquest Creech was found to have been *non compos mentis*. This verdict notwithstanding, Creech's final decision to kill himself may have been caused by despair about his debts, allegedly 'occasiond by a too rash engagement for a Spendthrift cheating Relation' (Bodl. Oxf., MS Ballard 20, fol. 27), and the simultaneous departure of his wealthy friend and supporter, Christopher Codrington, for the West Indies, where Codrington had become governor-general. Deeply hurt by the rumours that Creech's suicide was due to his refusal of financial aid, Codrington, to whom the 1695 edition of *De rerum natura* had been dedicated, thereupon affected 'to despise what [he could] not prevent' (Harlow, 60–64). In his will Creech, not being 'in a condition to give legacies', stipulated that all his goods were to be sold and that a portion of what little was left after the sale was to go to 'his dear sister Bridget Bastard of Blandford', yet not before 'his debts [had been] paid' (Kippis, 4.433 n [E]).

Creech's reputation continues to rest on his translation of Lucretius. At its best it is surprisingly readable, although uneven, wooden, and laboured at times. However, Creech did miss the chance of rescuing Lucretius from the centuries-old denunciations that he was the prince of atheists and the prophet of wantonness. Creech even reaffirmed these charges, not only by inserting passages of his own invention into the translation but also by adding a commentary that is less an explication than an antidote against the supposed poison of Epicurean doctrine. Only where the ancient system had anticipated the discoveries of the New Science, such as the existence of atoms and the demonstration of a vacuum as well as the disclosure of an infinite universe populated by a multiplicity of worlds—where, in other words, Lucretius had been enthroned as the new scientific authority of the Moderns—did Creech render his source faithfully.

HERMANN J. REAL

Sources M. Burrows, *Worthies of All Souls: four centuries of English history illustrated from the college archives* (1874) · R. Shiels, *The lives of the poets of Great Britain and Ireland*, ed. T. Cibber, 5 vols. (1753) · R. Clutterbuck, ed., *The history and antiquities of the county of Hertford*, 2 (1821) · B. Fabian, 'Lukrez in England im siebzehnten und achtzehnten Jahrhundert', *Aufklärung und Humanismus*, ed. R. Toellner (Heidelberg, 1980), 107–29 · P. France, ed., *The Oxford guide to literature in English translation* (2000) · R. B. Gardiner, ed., *The registers of Wadham College, Oxford*, 2 vols. (1889–95) · C. A. Gordon, *A bibliography of Lucretius* (1962) · G. D. Hadzsits, *Lucretius and his influence* (1935) · P. Hammond, 'The integrity of Dryden's Lucretius', *Modern Language Review*, 78 (1983), 1–23 · V. I. Harlow, *Christopher Codrington, 1668–1710* (1990) · *Remarks and collections of Thomas Hearne*, ed. C. E. Doble and others, 11 vols., OHS, 2, 7, 13, 34, 42–3, 48, 50, 65, 67, 72 (1885–1921) · J. Hutchins, *The history and antiquities of the county of Dorset*, 3rd edn, ed. W. Shipp and J. W. Hodson, 4 vols. (1861–74) · G. Jacob, *An historical account of the lives and writings of our most considerable English poets* (1720) · H. Jones, *The Epicurean tradition* (1989) · A. Kippis and others, eds., *Biographia Britannica, or, The lives of the most eminent persons who have flourished in Great Britain and Ireland*, 2nd edn, 5 vols. (1778–93), vol. 4 · H. MacDonald, *John Dryden: a bibliography of early editions and of Drydeniana* (1939) · B. Nugel, *A new English Horace: die Übersetzungen der horazischen 'Ars Poetica' in der Restaurationszeit* (Frankfurt, 1971) · H. J. Real, 'The authorship of some anonymous recommendatory poems of Creech's translation of Lucretius', *N&Q*, 213 (1968), 377–8 · H. J. Real, *Untersuchungen zur Lukrez-Übersetzung von Thomas Creech* (Bad Homburg v.d.H., Berlin, Zürich, 1970) · H. J. Real, 'A taste of composition rare: the *Tale's* matter and void', *Papers from the third Münster symposium on Jonathan Swift*, ed. H. J. Real and H. Stöver-Leidig (Munich, 1998), 73–90 · S. E. Sprott, *The English debate on suicide: from Donne to Hume* (LaSalle, Illinois, 1961) · *Jacob Tonson in ten letters by and about him*, ed. S. L. C. Clapp (Austin, Texas, 1948) · J. A. Winn, '"Dryden's epistle before Creech's Lucretius": a study in restoration ghostwriting', *Philological Quarterly*, 71 (1992), 47–68 · Wood, *Ath. Oxon.*, new edn, 4 · *The life and times of Anthony Wood*, ed. A. Clark, 5 vols., OHS, 19, 21, 26, 30, 40 (1891–1900)

Archives BL, Add. MSS · Bodl. Oxf., MSS Ballard · Bodl. Oxf., MSS Tanner

Likenesses W. Sonmans, oils, Bodl. Oxf. [*see illus.*] · engraving (after W. Sonmans), Wadham College, Oxford · engraving (after W. Sonmans), repro. in Jacob, *Historical account*

Wealth at death in debt; goods sold to pay debts; bequests to sister and Miss Philadelphia Playdell of Oxford: Kippis, *Biographia Britannica*

Creech, William [*pseud.* Theophrastus] (1745–1815), bookseller and magistrate, was born in Newbattle, Edinburghshire, on 12 May 1745, the son of the Revd William Creech (1705–1745), minister of Newbattle, and his wife, the Calvinist Mary Buley (d. 1764) of the English family of Quarme, Devon, sometime ushers of the black rod in the House of Lords. His father died when Creech was only months old, and he was raised by his mother; he also survived two sisters, Margaret and Mary, who died in September 1749. Creech was educated as a gentleman in Perthshire and at Dalkeith Academy by Mr Barclay, tutor to Viscount Melville, and the Revd John Robertson of Kilmarnoch, tutor to Lord Glencairn's sons, boarders at Mrs Creech's. Intended as a physician, Creech went to medical lectures at the University of Edinburgh from 1761, but, on becoming co-founder in 1764 of the Speculative Society, reconceived himself as a member of the literati, establishing friendships with Hugh Blair, Alexander Duncan, and William Cullen. That year he became apprenticed to the royal printer for Scotland, Alexander Kincaid and John Bell. He formed professional alliances with William Strahan, Thomas Cadell, and others by travelling to London, Paris, and Holland for two years, and returned to Edinburgh in 1768. After a grand tour of France, Holland, Switzerland, and Germany with Lord Kilmaurs in 1770, in May 1771 he joined Kincaid in the firm of Kincaid and Creech, becoming in May 1773 the sole partner. Unmarried, Creech was an elegant, self-conscious man, with a passion for socializing. This he nourished in the homosocial milieu of the Edinburgh élite by hosting book auctions and weekly breakfasts in the room over his shop, known as 'Creech's levees', where he charmed such lifelong friends as Lord Kames, Henry Home, and Dr James Beattie with his irony and anecdotes.

As a bookseller, Creech was patriotic, ambitious, and ostentatiously high-minded, contributing greatly to the contemporary popularity of Scottish literature. He published works by Blair, Beattie, Cullen, Gregory, Ferguson, and Robert Burns, as well as Henry Mackenzie's periodicals *The Mirror* (1779–80) and *The Lounger* (1785–7), and belonged to the Mirror Club with Mackenzie, the lords Craig, Abercrombie, Bannatyne, and Cullen, George Home, and George Ogilvie. Publishing nationalistic, if unprofitable, texts, including Sir John Sinclair's *Statistical Account of Scotland* (1791–9) containing his own *Account of the Manners and Customs of Scotland between 1763 and 1783*, updated to 1791, he enraged Burns by his delay in settling his account with Burns for the publication of his *Poems*, turning the poet from flattering him as 'witty' to deriding him as

A little, upright, pert, tart, tripping wight,
And still his precious self his chief delight.

Under the pseudonym Theophrastus, Creech disparaged modern manners in the newspapers, and in 1791 published his own collection of satires garnered from the

Edinburgh Courant, *Edinburgh Gazette*, and *Caledonian Mercury*, entitled *Edinburgh Fugitive Pieces*, and reissued with a biographical sketch of Creech in 1815.

In later life Creech entered politics. Founder with John Bell of the Society of Booksellers of Edinburgh and Leith, and a fellow of the Antiquaries Society of Edinburgh, he was a member of the Edinburgh town council, helping to form the Chamber of Commerce and Manufactures of Edinburgh in 1786, and serving as magistrate in 1788, 1789, 1791, and 1792, when he also founded the Corporation of Booksellers. A moderate and supporter of Pitt and Lord Melville, while he was provost from 1811 to 1813 the Edinburgh town council legislated for increases in trade pensions, noise curfews, a Charity workhouse, and the publication of studies on recent water and grain shortages. Famous throughout Edinburgh for his well-placed bookshop near St Giles's Church and his well-born friends, Creech was a businessman whose obituary, appearing in the *Edinburgh Courant* five days after his death in Edinburgh on 14 January 1815, praises his scholarship and social eminence.   BARBARA M. BENEDICT

Sources B. M. Benedict, 'William Creech and sentiment for sale', *Eighteenth-Century Life*, 15 (1991), 119–46 • A. Constable, 'An account of his life', in W. Creech, *Edinburgh fugitive pieces* (1815), xi–xlii • *Edinburgh Evening Courant* (19 Jan 1815) • NA Scot., Dalguise muniments, microfilm copy, W. Creech, correspondence, 1751–1793 • J. C. Carrick, *William Creech: Robert Burns' best friend* (1903) • *Fasti Scot.*, new edn • Chambers, *Scots.* (1868–70), 1.398 • [W. Creech], *Edinburgh fugitive pieces* (1791); [another edn] (1815) • W. Creech, *Letters, addressed to Sir John Sinclair, Bart. respecting the mode of living, arts, commerce, literature, manners, &c. of Edinburgh, in 1763, and since that period* (1793) • *Regulations for the tronmen, chimney-sweepers and firemen of Edinburgh*, 27 Feb 1811, BL, Edinburgh session papers, Edinburgh 1811.80, Ry. 1.1.30, fol. 2 • J. Brown, *Contract of agreement … for building and endowing the Charity Work-House*, BL, Edinburgh 1812.80, 1959.16, fol. 8 • *By order of the … Lord provost and magistrates of Edinburgh*, BL, Edinburgh 1814.40, 6.1699, fol. 96 • *Act of the right honourable the lord provost, magistrates, and council of the city of Edinburgh*, Edinburgh, 1813, Macc. 1537, fol. 3 • T. Telford and T. C. Hope, *Reports on the means of improving the supply of water for the city of Edinburgh*, Edinburgh, 1813, BL, 5.142, fol. 13 • *The petition of William Creech, bookseller in Edinburgh, against Lord Abercromby's interlocutor* (14 Feb 1794) • *A capital collection of books, to be sold by auction … above Mr. Creech's shop* (1780) • *William Creech's sale catalogue* (1791) [sale catalogue, Edinburgh, 1791] • R. H. Cromek, *Reliques of Robert Burns* (1808), no. 19, 23–7 • S. W. Brown, 'Life of Creech', *The British Library book trade, 1700–1800*, ed. J. K. Bracken and J. Eiliver (1995)
Archives BL • Edinburgh Central Reference Library, journal, letter-books, inventory of stock, etc. [journal: copy] • NA Scot., corresp. • NA Scot., Dalguise muniments • NL Scot., corresp. • NRA Scotland, priv. coll., corresp. and papers • Signet Library, Edinburgh, business diary
Likenesses H. Raeburn, oils, 1806, Scot. NPG

Creed, Cary (*bap.* 1708, *d.* 1775), etcher, was baptized on 25 November 1708, the son of Cary Creed (1687–1775) and his wife, Elizabeth (1689–1737), and grandson of the Revd John Creed, vicar of Castle Cary, Somersetshire. He etched and published a number of plates from the marble statues and bas-reliefs in the collection of the earl of Pembroke at Wilton House, near Salisbury, working with a light but skilful touch in imitation of Perrier. Four editions of the work are known: with sixteen etchings, with forty etchings (1730), with seventy etchings (1731), and with seventy-four etchings (1731). With his wife, Mary, whom he probably married about 1750, Creed had a son, Cary (*bap.* 1755) and a daughter, Jane (*bap.* 1757). He died on 16 January 1775, and was buried at Castle Cary.

L. H. CUST, *rev.* ANITA MCCONNELL

Sources J. Collinson, *The history and antiquities of the county of Somerset*, 2 (1791); repr. (1983), 57 • Redgrave, *Artists*, 2nd edn, 105 • parish register, Castle Cary, Somerset, 25 Nov 1708 [baptism] • *GM*, 1st ser., 45 (1775), 46 • T. Dodds, 'History of English engravers', BL, Add. MS 33398, fol. 227

Creed, Charles Southey (1909–1966), couturier, was born on 25 May 1909 at 29 rue Singer, Paris, the third son and sixth child of Henry Creed (*b.* 1863), tailor, and his wife, Aimée Nathalie Josephe, *née* Landrin (*d.* 1917). The tailoring house of Creed can be traced to the beginning of the eighteenth century, when John Creed, a tailor from Leicester, moved to London. In 1870 Creed's grandfather Henry Creed opened a branch of Henry Creed & Co. in Paris. Charles Creed was proud of his ancestry and described himself as 'born and bred' a tailor.

After his mother's death Creed was sent to England to be educated. He attended Aldro preparatory school at Eastbourne from 1918 to 1923 and Stowe School from 1923 to 1925. To prepare him for entering the family business of H. Creed & Co. in Paris he was apprenticed briefly to a tailor in Vienna. This was followed by eight months at Linton Tweeds in Carlisle, where he learned to weave and understand the structure of cloth, and developed an appreciation of colour. In 1929 he travelled to New York to work for Bergdorf Goodman, where he had his first experience of designing womenswear. He then worked as a designer for the wholesale houses A. Beller & Co. and Philip Mangone. Working in America gave him an understanding of the organization and economics of mass production, and of the commercial value of public relations.

On his return to Paris he was put in charge of womenswear and won a reputation for his sophisticated tailored suits and blouses. He also designed models for wholesale reproduction for the American market, which he presented to buyers in New York rather than in Paris, as was customary at the time. During the Second World War, after the occupation of Paris by the Germans in 1940, he moved to London, where he designed exclusively for Fortnum and Mason of Piccadilly. In December 1940 he took an export collection to New York and presented a group of sketches to the Museum of Costume Art (now the Costume Institute at the Metropolitan Museum of Art); further sketches of Creed designs were presented to the museum by Bergdorf Goodman in 1966. In 1942 he became an early member of the Incorporated Society of London Fashion Designers. He was later vice-president of the society. In 1943 he joined the Royal Artillery but his fluent French and competent German enabled him to transfer to field intelligence. After the war he secured a contract to design models for wholesale production for Philip Mangone in New York. In 1946 he set up his own house, Charles Creed Ltd, at 31 Basil Street, Knightsbridge, London.

On 1 September 1948 Creed married Patricia Aileen Cunningham (b. 1921) in the chapel of the Assumption Convent in Kensington. She was a fashion editor for British *Vogue* and later a freelance fashion consultant. They had no children. In 1949 he opened a boutique department at 27 Basil Street but this closed in 1954. In 1950 he set up a company called Creedation Ltd, which traded as ladies' tailors from 27 Basil Street until 1954, and from 31 Basil Street until 1956. In 1952 he presented a joint collection with the furrier S. London Ltd, of 185 Sloane Street, and during the 1950s the firms displayed each other's work in their collections. In 1953 he was commissioned to design a dress by the Cotton Board, which is now in the collection of the Gallery of Costume, Manchester. From 1957 to 1964 he shared his Basil Street premises with the dressmaker Giuseppe Gustavo *Mattli (1907–1982). In 1959 he set up another company, Charles Creed (London) Ltd, to sell ready-to-wear jersey and knitwear alongside his couture collections. In 1964 he moved his business to 30 Ebury Street. In 1966 he retired from couture to concentrate on his ready-to-wear company. On his retirement he donated a small group of garments to the Victoria and Albert Museum.

Creed's strength lay in the creation of immaculately tailored daywear made in high quality British woollen fabrics. His designs were influenced by his interest in military uniforms and his passion for lead soldiers, which he had collected since childhood. This interest revealed itself in suit jackets designed with turnback skirts, coats and suits trimmed with frogging and braid, and waistcoat-fronted tailored blouses. His clients included the duchess of Abercorn, the duchess of Westminster, Lady Rendlesham, and Margot Fonteyn.

In his youth Creed was criticized for his conceit and relentless pursuit of women and pleasure, which distracted him from work. In later life he declared himself 'only interested in his profession and the opposite sex' (Creed, *Maid to Measure*, 217) but his friends praised his wit and affability. In 1961 he published his autobiography, *Maid to Measure*, which was written by Elspeth Grant. His lecture in 1958 for the Royal Society of the Arts, 'The trend in wool fashions', was published by the department of education of the International Wool Secretariat (1960). Creed died on 17 July 1966 at his home, 19 Cambridge Street, Westminster. The administration of his will was granted to his widow and his estate valued at nil. Charles Creed Ltd was dissolved on 14 November 1967. Creedation Ltd was dissolved on 31 October 1968. Charles Creed (London) Ltd was dissolved on 9 July 1981.

EDWINA EHRMAN

Sources C. Creed, *Maid to measure* (1961) · *Daily Telegraph* (19 July 1966) · *New York Times* (19 July 1966) · *Vogue* (Oct 1940), 37 · *Vogue* (Feb 1946), 43 · *The Times* (19 July 1966) · *Kelly's Post Office London directory* (1946–66) · C. Creed, *The trend in wool fashions* (1960) · private information (2004) [Old Stoic Society; Musée de la Mode de la ville de Paris] · papers, Companies House, Cardiff · b. cert. · m. cert. · d. cert. · will · *CGPLA Eng. & Wales* (1966) · *Almanach du commerce* Paris (1870–73) · G. Waddell, 'The Incorporated Society of London Fashion Designers: its impact on post-war fashion', *Costume*, 35 (2001), 95ff.

Archives Chicago Historical Institute, clothing · Metropolitan Museum of Art, New York, Costume Institute, designs · V&A, clothing | V&A, department of prints and drawings, S. London Ltd deposit
Wealth at death estate valued at nil

Creed [*née* Pickering], **Elizabeth** (c.1642–1728), artist and philanthropist, was probably the eldest daughter of Sir Gilbert *Pickering, first baronet (1611–1668), of Titchmarsh, Northamptonshire, and his first wife, Elizabeth (d. 1679), only daughter of Sir Sidney Montagu of Hinchingbrook, Huntingdonshire, and hence the sister of the first earl of Sandwich. According to her cousin Samuel Pepys she was 'a very well-bred and comely lady, but very fat' (Pepys, 4.308). With no great prospects her mother hoped to use her Montagu relations to provide a fitting marriage. In April 1665 Pepys learned that one of Sandwich's officials, John *Creed (d. 1701), had made known his interest in Elizabeth Pickering, telling Lady Sandwich that he depended on her to get a reasonable settlement from her parents. Despite initial opposition from Lady Sandwich, the couple were married on 6 October 1668. They settled at Oundle, Northamptonshire, and had eleven children, only two sons and three daughters surviving to adulthood, and only one son and one daughter surviving their mother.

Following the death of her husband on 18 September 1701, Elizabeth Creed moved to Barnwell All Saints, Northamptonshire, where she continued to entertain, and to paint, draw, and produce fine needlework, as well as offering instruction in these fine arts. The chancel of Titchmarsh church was decorated with her 'flying angels, small decorative designs of flowers and the emblems of mortality' (Esdaile, 24); she also provided an altarpiece in 1714. Creed wrote the inscriptions for several monuments in the church (often providing contradictory clues to her own age), including one to another cousin, John Dryden. Other work decorated Barnwell church and Canons Ashby House, Northamptonshire, and a portrait by her of Sandwich survives at Drayton. Creed was buried on 16 May 1728 at Titchmarsh, Northamptonshire. In her will she left money to supplement her daughter Jemima's (d. 1704?) charity school at Ashton, near Oundle.

STUART HANDLEY

Sources Pepys, *Diary* · PRO, PROB 11/622, fols. 322v–323r · PRO, PROB 11/459, fol. 341r · Redgrave, *Artists*, 102 · K. A. Esdaile, 'Cousin to Pepys and Dryden: a note on the works of Mrs. Elizabeth Creed of Titchmarsh', *Burlington Magazine*, 77 (1940), 24–7 · W. Smalley Law, *Oundle's story: a history of town and school* (1922), 91–111 · GEC, *Baronetage* [Pickering] · H. I. Longden, *The visitation of the county of Northampton, 1681*, Harleian Society, 87 (1953), 171–2 · J. Bridges, *The history and antiquities of Northamptonshire*, 2 vols. (1953), vol. 2, p. 386 · M. Hunter, *The Royal Society and its fellows, 1660–1700: the morphology of an early scientific institution* (1982), 188–9 · *The manuscripts of the duke of Leeds*, HMC, 22 (1888), 15 · F. R. Harris, *The life of Edward Montagu, … first earl of Sandwich*, 1 (1912), 123, 164 · *CSP dom.*, 1655–60

Creed, Frederick George (1871–1957), inventor and manufacturer of telegraph equipment, was born on 6 October 1871 in Mill Village, Nova Scotia, one of six sons of John R. Creed, a poor Scottish émigré, and attended school in the village. At fourteen he became a telegraph operator, working in Canada, the USA, Peru, and Chile. In 1896 Creed married Jane (Jeannie) Russell (1868/9–1945), a missionary in Chile; they had three sons and three daughters. In 1897 he moved to Glasgow, and worked for the *Glasgow Herald* until 1904. The constant laborious operation of the Morse three-key tape perforator permanently deformed his right hand, and he became convinced that he could design a more efficient system. By late 1897 he had produced a perforator utilizing a typewriter keyboard instead of three plungers to punch dots and dashes into the outgoing signal tape. He then developed a reperforator which recorded incoming signals as tape perforations, and a printer which translated the tape into letters. These machines formed his 'high speed automatic printing telegraph system'. In 1902 the Post Office bought twelve perforators, and Creed became obsessed with winning further large orders for them. In 1906 the *Glasgow Herald* adopted the system, pronouncing it three times faster than the Morse apparatus.

In 1909, partly to be closer to the Post Office, Creed and his partner, Harald Bille, a talented Danish engineer who died in a train crash in 1916, moved their business from Glasgow to Croydon, near London. Orders from the *Daily Mail* in 1912 and the Press Association in 1920 were the company's major successes, prompting numerous sales. In 1923, responding to the American Morkrum Teletyper, Creed developed his teleprinter, which directly printed incoming signals as letters, initially working on a five-unit signalling code. In 1925 he acquired the patents for the more efficient Murray code, which became the standard signalling code. Creed's system significantly increased news transmission speeds for the newspapers and press bureaux who bought it, and telegraph rooms became known as 'Creed rooms'. In 1928, seeking an order for the Post Office's new public telegraph system, he produced the Model 3 Tape Teleprinter, combining a transmitter with the earlier teleprinter. However, large Post Office orders came only after Creed & Co. had been bought by the International Telephone and Telegraph Corporation (ITT) for £250,000 in 1928. Creed resigned from the board in 1931 over the use of company sports fields on Sundays, his strict religious values at odds with those of ITT's American directors.

Deeply devout, Creed hated smoking, abuses of the Sabbath, and particularly drink. He insisted that employees sign a pledge of abstinence, and he would sometimes visit Croydon pubs and remove any staff he found there. Over 6 feet tall, often dressed in black, he could be intimidating, but he had a genuine concern for his workforce, and personally visited sick employees. He was not a natural businessman—in 1916 he expressed a wish to be relieved of financial responsibilities, and his relationships within the industry were often difficult. Following his resignation he poured resources into designs for giant catamarans and floating platforms, called 'seadromes', and other unsuccessful projects, which brought him close to bankruptcy in his final years. In 1947 Creed married Valerie Leopoldine Gisella Layton, *née* Franzky (1906–1994). He died at his home, 20 Outram Road, Addiscombe, Croydon, on 11 December 1957. He was cremated at Croydon on 18 December.

TIM PROCTER

Sources J. Rackham, 'Creed, Frederick George', *DBB* • papers, Croydon Archives Service, collection no. AR53 • P. W. Bower, 'The breath of invention', *Print Out* [ITT Creed Ltd magazine] (Dec 1971), 2–9, 13–21 • *Croydon Guardian and Croydon Express* (13 Dec 1957) • 'Frederick George Creed, 1871–1957: the man, the inventor, the company', *Private Wire* [ITT Creed Ltd magazine] (Sept 1971), 2–3 • *Croydon Times* (20 Dec 1957) • 'Notable Croydonians no. 19', *Croydon Advertiser* (5 Oct 1956) • M. Thornton, 'Success, frustration, and now, perhaps, recognition', *Hovering Craft and Hydrofoil*, 18/11 (1979), 4–8 • A. E. Stone, 'Start-stop printing telegraph systems (cont.)', *Post Office Electrical Engineers' Journal*, 22 (1929–30), 1–10 • 'He put out 80 candles in one puff', *Croydon Times* (13 Oct 1957) • 'City freeman', *Croydon Advertiser* (1 Feb 1957) • *Croydon Advertiser* (20 Dec 1957) • private information (2004) • d. cert. [Jane Creed]
Archives Croydon Archives Service, corresp., drawings, MSS, and patents, collection no. AR53 | BT, London, Post Office Telegraphs files, archives
Likenesses photograph, repro. in Rackham, 'Creed, Frederick George' • photographs, Croydon Archives Service, collection no. AR53 • photographs, ITT Creed Ltd archives; now presumed lost

Creed, John (*d.* 1701), naval administrator, was probably born at Oundle, Northamptonshire. He took service with Edward Mountagu, and is first mentioned in public business in April 1656. In April 1659 he sailed to the Baltic with Mountagu as secretary to the fleet. Later that year he urged his master to enter politics to save 'this poor broken nation' (Harris, 1.123). In March 1660, as Mountagu prepared to go to sea again, he retained Creed as deputy treasurer, but the normally concurrent secretaryship went to Mountagu's cousin Samuel Pepys. The two men became social companions and correspondents, but the relationship was increasingly soured by rivalry. Despite superior intellectual skills and possibly some private means, Creed was to be eclipsed by Pepys in Mountagu's favour and in the pursuit of public office. Creed held appointments as muster master between 1660 and 1663. In 1661–2 he went as deputy treasurer with Mountagu (now earl of Sandwich) in the voyage to take possession of Tangier and to bring Catherine of Braganza to England. His letters back to Pepys are full of naval information and political gossip. The experience qualified him for appointment as secretary of the Tangier committee from 1662. In 1663 he was elected FRS. Further professional advance was perhaps checked by the taint of religious radicalism, which he had espoused when it had been the fashion, but he quickly adjusted his lifestyle. In May 1661, after a convivial outing in Creed's company, Pepys mused that a year before he 'might have been got to hang himself almost, as soon to go to a drinking-house on a Sunday' (Pepys, *Diary*, 2.99). Yet in 1664 Creed was examined by the council on suspicion of being a 'serviceable friend' to fanatics (ibid., 5.107–8). Pepys did his best to blacken Creed's character, having persuaded himself that he was 'a crafty and false rogue' (ibid., 5.119). He schemed to prevent Creed's further employment should Sandwich return to sea, and told his countess that Creed was 'as shrewd and cunning a man as any in England' (ibid., 6.15). The two nevertheless continued to associate, sharing interests in music, scientific experiment, and women. Pepys gleefully noted that Creed's viol was poorer than his own, and was shocked by rumour of an attempted rape. Creed's romantic requirements were eventually and triumphantly satisfied by marriage in October 1668. Elizabeth *Creed (c.1642–1728) was the daughter of Sir Gilbert Pickering, bt, of Titchmarsh, Northamptonshire, and the niece of Sandwich. Pepys, who had previously described the bride as 'comely … but very fat' (ibid., 4.308), was stupefied, and was obliged thereafter to call Creed cousin. Creed retained his Tangier post until the colony was abandoned in 1684, when he received £93 compensation for personal property left there. On 25 September 1677 he was named an assistant in the charter of the Royal Fishery Company. But chiefly he became a local worthy: JP for Northamptonshire, high sheriff of the county in 1690–91, and feoffee of the Oundle charities in 1700. He died, probably at Oundle, on 18 September 1701, and was buried at Titchmarsh on the 28th. Five of his eleven children survived him. His sons Richard and John served together as army officers; Richard was killed at Blenheim, and was commemorated in Westminster Abbey. Elizabeth lived on at Barnwell until May 1728, achieving local celebrity as a painter and philanthropist. She erected a memorial in Titchmarsh church recording her husband's service to Charles II at home and abroad. She was herself remembered as a 'beautiful conjunction of Chearfulness and gravity' (Wilford, 764).

John's brother **Richard Creed** (*fl.* 1652–1660) was a servant of the Cromwellian Major-General Harrison. He was a clerk in the admiralty by 1652, and on 21 August 1654 was appointed to succeed his friend John Poortmans as secretary to the generals-at-sea and deputy treasurer. He was still at the admiralty in March 1660, and there is uncertainty over which of the brothers some papers refer to. Richard, like John, was a religious radical, and was recommended to Cromwell as registrar of wills. He is to be distinguished from Major Richard Creed, republican opponent of Charles II. C. S. KNIGHTON

Sources F. R. Harris, *The life of Edward Montagu, … first earl of Sandwich*, 1 (1912), 123, 164 • Pepys, *Diary*, esp. 10.79–80 • *CSP dom.*, 1655–6, 249; 1659–60, 551; 1660–61, 146; 1664–5, 250; 1690–91, 194; 1654, 319; 1697, 2; 1700–02, 527 • W. A. Shaw, ed., *Calendar of treasury books*, 1–8, PRO (1904–23), esp. vol. 6, p. 2 and vol. 8, p. 304 • *The manuscripts of J. Eliot Hodgkin … of Richmond, Surrey*, HMC, 39 (1897), 153–85 • H. I. Longden, *The visitation of the county of Northampton in the year 1681*, Harleian Society, 87 (1935), 172 • J. Bridges, *The history and antiquities of Northamptonshire*, ed. P. Whalley, 2 vols. (1791), esp. vol. 2, pp. 386–7 • J. Wilford, *Memorials and characters … of divers eminent and worthy persons* (1741), 762–4 • W. S. Law, *Oundle's story: a history of town and school* (1922), 91, 100, 110–11 • G. E. Aylmer, *The state's servants: the civil service of the English republic, 1649–1660* (1973), 70 • B. Capp, *Cromwell's navy: the fleet and the English revolution, 1648–1660* (1989), 125 • *The journal of Edward Mountagu, first earl of Sandwich, admiral and general at sea, 1659–1665*, ed. R. C. Anderson, Navy RS, 64 (1929), 4n., 46, 148 • *The letters of Robert Blake*, ed. J. R. Powell, Navy RS, 76 (1937), 380, 463 • S. R. Gardiner and C. T. Atkinson, eds., *Letters and papers relating to the First Dutch War, 1652–1654*, 6 vols., Navy RS, 13, 17, 30, 37, 41, 66 (1898–1930), vol. 3, p. 430; vol. 4, pp.175–6; vol. 5, p. 107; vol. 6, p. 220 • *DNB* • PRO, PROB 11/459, fols. 341–341v [John Creed]
Archives PRO | Bodl. Oxf., Carte MSS
Wealth at death owned land at Oundle, Northamptonshire, and property in Yorkshire and Norfolk: Law, *Oundle's story*, 110–11

Creed, John Martin (1889–1940), university professor, was born in All Saints' parish, Leicester, on 14 October 1889, the eldest son of Colin John Creed, vicar of All Saints' Church, and his wife, Etheldreda Wright, daughter of Frederick Robert Spackman, a doctor of Harpenden, Hertfordshire. Sir Thomas Percival *Creed was his brother. John Creed was educated at the Wyggeston grammar school, Leicester, and, from 1908, at Gonville and Caius College, Cambridge, where he was admitted as a scholar and obtained first classes in part one of the classical tripos (1911) and in part two of the theological tripos (1912). In 1913 he was ordained as assistant curate at St Paul's Church, Manningham, Bradford, and in 1914 was elected a fellow of Caius, where he returned as chaplain in 1915. From 1917 to 1919 he was a chaplain to the British forces in France.

After the First World War, in 1919, Creed was elected a fellow of St John's College, Cambridge, and appointed dean and lecturer in theology. Although not good with students, in 1926 he succeeded A. E. Brooke as Ely professor of divinity and honorary canon of Ely Cathedral. In 1927 Creed married May Geraldine, the younger daughter of Alfred Leslie Lilley, canon of Hereford. They had one son and three daughters, the youngest of whom died in childhood. Creed held his post as Ely professor and canon of the cathedral until his death, at the Evelyn Nursing Home in Cambridge, on 17 February 1940. He had been elected a fellow of the British Academy in 1939.

Creed's historical and theological outlook was very much that handed down by the so-called Cambridge 'triumvirate' of J. B. Lightfoot, B. F. Westcott, and F. J. A. Hort. His main scholarly contributions were in the field of New Testament studies and the early Christian age; they included his *The Gospel According to St. Luke: the Greek Text with Introduction, Notes, and Indices* (1930), a critical commentary concerned especially with the composition of St Luke's narrative and its stage in the development of the gospel tradition, and journal articles, especially in the *Journal of Theological Studies*, which he edited from the end of 1935. One of his more noteworthy articles was a discussion of the early Christian document known as the Didache (*Journal of Theological Studies*, 39, 1938, 370–87). He was also increasingly interested in the history of religious thought of the eighteenth and nineteenth centuries which, although widely separated from the early Christian era, shed light upon it in his view, as was shown in his *Religious Thought in the Eighteenth Century Illustrated from Writers of the Period* (1934, written in collaboration with J. S. Boys Smith), and his Hulsean lectures delivered at Cambridge in 1936 and published in 1938 as *The Divinity of Jesus Christ: a Study in the History of Christian Doctrine since Kant*.

Creed was deeply interested in the history of the Church of England and in the meaning of Anglicanism and was considered a sound representative of Anglican values. He believed that a national church was a natural counterpart to the political and social order of a world in which the nation was the fundamental political and cultural unit. Being strongly pro-monarchist, he also thought that the association of church and state in England had fostered a wholesome contact between the sacred and the secular. This position, stated in a number of published articles and sermons, gave added weight to his views as a member of the archbishops' commission on Christian doctrine, the report of which was published in 1938 as *Doctrine in the Church of England*.   J. S. B. SMITH, *rev.* GERALD LAW

Sources J. S. Boys Smith, 'John Martin Creed', *Journal of Theological Studies*, 41 (1940), 113–18 · C. E. Raven, *Cambridge Review* (1 March 1940), 310 · J. F. Bethune-Baker, 'John Martin Creed, 1889–1940', *PBA*, 26 (1940), 517–30 · *The Times* (21 Feb 1940) · *The Times* (22 Feb 1940) · J. S. B. S. [J. S. Boys Smith], *The Eagle*, 52 (1941–7), 51–3 · *CGPLA Eng. & Wales* (1940) · private information (1949) · personal knowledge (1949)
Likenesses W. Stoneman, photograph, 1940, NPG · portrait, repro. in Bethune-Baker, 'John Martin Creed', 517
Wealth at death £9921 15s. 7d.: probate, 24 May 1940, *CGPLA Eng. & Wales*

Creed, Richard (*fl.* 1652–1660). *See under* Creed, John (*d.* 1701).

Creed, Thomas. *See* Creede, Thomas (*b.* in or before 1554, *d.* 1616).

Creed, Sir Thomas Percival (1897–1969), lawyer and educationist, was born in Leicester on 29 January 1897, the third son in the family of five children of the Revd Colin John Creed, curate of St Peter's, Leicester, and later rector of Farthinghoe, Northamptonshire, and his wife, Etheldreda Wright, daughter of Frederick Robert Spackman MD of Harpenden, Hertfordshire. He was educated at Wyggeston School, Leicester, joined the Artists' Rifles in 1915, and served in France with the Leicestershire regiment, being twice wounded and winning the MC (1917).

After demobilization in 1919 Creed was awarded a classical scholarship at Pembroke College, Oxford, taking third-class honours in *literae humaniores* in 1922. He then entered the Sudan political service, and read for the bar while serving as assistant district commissioner in Berber Province (1923) and Darfur (1925). After being called to the bar (Lincoln's Inn) in 1925, in 1926 he was seconded to the legal department of the Sudan government as district judge of the first grade and permanently transferred to this post in 1929. In 1928 Creed married (Agnes) Margaret, elder daughter of Arthur Brewis, solicitor, of St Helens in Lancashire; they had one son (who also went into practice as a solicitor) and two daughters.

Creed was seconded to the Iraqi government under the Anglo-Iraqi judicial agreement in 1931. There, after a short period as additional judge in Baghdad, he served as president of the courts in Kirkuk (1932) and Mosul (1934) before returning to Sudan as a judge of the high court, Khartoum, in 1935. He was appointed chief justice of Sudan in 1936, and legal secretary, with a seat on the governor-general's council, in 1941. He was awarded the order of the Nile, second class, in 1939, appointed CBE in 1943, and KBE in 1946. In 1947 he was chief representative of the Sudan government at the hearing of the Anglo-Egyptian dispute by the Security Council at Lake Success.

Shortly before his retirement from Sudan in 1948 Creed took silk, but preferred to seek an educational career, like other members of his family. One of his brothers, John

Sir Thomas Percival Creed (1897–1969), by Godfrey Argent, 1968

Martin *Creed, had been Ely professor of divinity at Cambridge, and another, (Richard) Stephen, a fellow of New College, Oxford. Their sister, Mary, was a lecturer at Aberystwyth College (University of Wales), and the fourth brother, Edward, a senior pathologist at King's College Hospital. Thomas Creed became secretary to King's College, London, in 1948, and principal of Queen Mary College in 1952, a post he was to hold for fifteen years. From 1964 to 1967 he was vice-chancellor of London University.

During this period Creed also served as chairman of the Medical Appeal Tribunal under the National Insurance (Industrial Injuries) Act, chairman of the committee of inquiry into the administration of the Forest of Dean (1955), chairman of the Burnham committee for the assessment of pay scales for teachers (1958–64), and chairman of Oxford House social settlement in Bethnal Green. He was made an honorary fellow of Pembroke in 1950, a freeman of the Drapers' Company (with which Queen Mary College had close ties) in 1963, an honorary LLD of Leicester in 1965, and an honorary bencher of Lincoln's Inn, a distinction which he prized especially highly, in 1967. He was also a member of the education committee of the Goldsmiths' Company.

The key to Creed's character lay in his unswerving integrity. As chief justice he could forgive an error of judgement but admit no excuse for careless or slipshod behaviour in a magistrate, however hard-worked he might be. As legal secretary he regarded himself as a watchdog for the Sudanese people, ensuring that their constitutional rights were not infringed and firmly refusing to agree to any project, however well-intentioned, for which no clear legal authority existed. As adviser to the governor-general, and as his representative from time to time in his absence, he would not tolerate evasion, or failure to clarify the true nature and purpose of any proposed act or policy. He would have disliked being a professional diplomat or a politician, and to the end of his life he was accustomed to use the correspondence columns of *The Times* to convey trenchant and uninhibited criticism of the policy of the British government in Middle Eastern affairs.

Creed's headship of Queen Mary College happily coincided with a period of expansion; he took full advantage of this, trebling the size of the student body and providing the college with a whole range of new buildings. He resisted for some time pressure to let his name go forward for the vice-chancellorship, although he served as deputy vice-chancellor from 1958 to 1961, but his supporters finally convinced him, in 1963, that his leadership and wisdom were needed at a time when the future of London University had become a live issue. Creed firmly believed that the particular excellence of the university lay in retaining its broadly based federal structure. He was among those who feared that the threat of an independent commission of inquiry into the future of the university might lead to its premature dismemberment or to a regrouping which would result in a loss of the identity of some of its smaller institutions. The threat was not averted, but Creed's work, in close accord with the officers of the Senate House, did not go unrewarded, for the outcome of the independent inquiry left the federation intact.

As *The Times* said on his death, Creed:

> seemed to embody everything that is excellent in the law … He was the embodiment of impartiality; he had a deep and abiding concern for the rights of individuals; yet he was determined that decisions, once taken, should be strictly and honourably carried out. (13 May 1969)

He seldom minced his words. His strictures were devastating, without respect of persons, but where he considered praise deserved, he bestowed it unstintingly. Creed died at his home, 18 Wynnstay Gardens, Allen Street, London, on 11 May 1969. K. D. D. HENDERSON, rev.

Sources *The Times* (13 May 1969) • personal knowledge (1981) • *WWW* • *CGPLA Eng. & Wales* (1969)
Likenesses P. Greenham, portrait, 1967, Queen Mary and Westfield College, London • G. Argent, photograph, 1968, NPG [see illus.]
Wealth at death £36,449: probate, 25 Aug 1969, *CGPLA Eng. & Wales*

Creed, William (1614/15–1663), Church of England clergyman, the son of John Creed, was a native of Reading, Berkshire. He was elected a scholar of St John's College, Oxford, in 1631, matriculating on 24 May 1633 at the age of eighteen, and became a fellow there in 1634. He graduated BA on 23 April 1635 and MA on 29 April 1639, was appointed proctor in 1644, and proceeded BD in 1646. Creed sided with the royalists during the civil war, preaching many sermons to the king and parliament at Oxford. Anthony Wood states that Creed was one of those delegates appointed by the university to draw up the 'Reasons' against the covenant, negative oath, and *Directory for the Publique Worship of God*. The parliamentarian visitors expelled him from his fellowship on 2 October 1648. He held the Wiltshire rectories of Codford St Mary from 1645 and Stockton from 1658.

Early in 1660 Creed published *The refuter refuted, or, Doctor Hammond's Ektenesteron defended against the impertinent cavils of Mr. Henry Jeanes* (which in turn called forth a further riposte from Jeanes the following year). Later in 1660,

Creed published two loyalist sermons, *Judah's Return to their Allegiance: and David's Returne to his Crown and Kingdom* (preached in St Mary Woolchurch, London, on the day of thanksgiving for the king's return) and *Judah's Purging in the Melting Pot* (preached at the Wiltshire assizes in September).

The Restoration brought Creed preferment. In July 1660 he became archdeacon of Wiltshire and prebendary of Lyme and Halstock in Salisbury Cathedral. At Oxford, he was created DD on 7 August 1660 and appointed regius professor of divinity and canon of Christ Church in July 1661. As an appointee of Gilbert Sheldon, Creed with his Arminian views was to act as a countervailing influence to the generally Calvinist Lady Margaret professors. He and his immediate successors as regius professor, Richard Allestree and William Jane, shifted clerical attention in Oxford away from divisive theological disputation, instead placing the emphasis on practical religion and uniting the church against the twin threats of international Catholicism and parochial dissent. Creed died at Oxford on 19 July 1663 and was buried in the cathedral there. There is a dedication to him on a pillar in Christ Church. Nothing is known of his wife, but he was survived by three sons, Robert, William, and John.

EDWARD VALLANCE

Sources Foster, *Alum. Oxon.* • *DNB* • *Walker rev.*, 372 • *Fasti Angl.* (Hardy), 2.657; 3.493, 510 • W. Creed, *The refuter refuted, or, Doctor Hammond's Ektenesteron defended against the impertinent cavils of Mr Henry Jeanes* (1660) • R. A. Beddard, 'Restoration Oxford and the making of the protestant establishment', *Hist. U. Oxf.* 4: *17th-cent. Oxf.*, 803–62 • M. Burrows, ed., *The register of the visitors of the University of Oxford, from AD 1647 to AD 1658*, CS, new ser., 29 (1881) • F. J. Varley, ed., 'The Restoration visitation of the University of Oxford and its colleges', *Camden miscellany, XVIII*, CS, 3rd ser., 79 (1948) • A. Wood, *The history and antiquities of the University of Oxford*, ed. J. Gutch, 2 (1796), 508, 588, 846

Creede, Thomas (*b.* in or before **1554**, *d.* **1616**), printer, was made free of the Stationers' Company on 7 October 1578 by his master, Thomas East. His first wife, Dorothy, with whom he had at least three children, died on 18 January 1588, and on 7 July 1588 he married Margery King (*d.* 1615), with whom he had another eleven children. Creede ran one of the smaller printing houses in London, mainly producing books of a literary or religious nature. He is best known for issuing works of dramatic authors such as Shakespeare, Dekker, Chapman, and Marston, as well as other literary figures such as Greene, Lodge, and Breton.

For the first fifteen years after attaining his freedom Creede was apparently a journeyman printer with a residence in the parish of St Giles Cripplegate. In 1593 he opened his own printing house at the sign of the Catherine Wheel, near the Old Swan in Thames Street. At this establishment he produced a number of important literary works, including the first quarto editions of Shakespeare's *2 Henry VI* (1594) and *Henry V* (1600). Creede financed from his own resources a significant amount of the production during this time, with roughly two-thirds of his total output from 1593–1600 self-published. In 1597 he was one of four 'yonge men' of the Stationers' Company to receive a £5 loan from the bequest of Thomas Stuckey (Greg and Boswell, 57). He was for the most part a law-abiding businessman, although in 1599 he was listed among fourteen printers who were warned not to reprint a number of banned satires.

By the summer of 1600 Creede had moved closer to St Paul's and the centre of the bookselling trade, relocating his house to the Old Change at the sign of the Eagle and Child near Old Fish Street. He also apparently maintained a separate bookshop in Watling Street for a time, but only one imprint survives bearing this address. The move marked the beginning of a shift in Creede's business practices, and he began to function as a trade printer, sharing more jobs with other printers and printing more books financed by other stationers. As Creede's business practices changed, so too did the type of materials he printed. Fewer literary works issued from his office, while he began to produce books about politics and current events, and his output of religious titles increased markedly. In 1612 he was fined by the Stationers' Company court for binding an apprentice contrary to ordinances, as he had been for a similar offence in 1595. A year later he printed a counterfeit copy of a popular satire by George Wither for a group of three stationers, but other than these events he seems to have done little to attract the attention of trade, state, or ecclesiastical authorities.

At the end of his career Creede took as a partner Bernard Alsop, a young stationer who had been made free of the company in 1610 by William White. On 22 August 1615 Creede's second wife was buried in the church of St Mary Magdalen, Old Fish Street. A little over a year later, on 22 November 1616, Creede was buried in the same churchyard. Two of his children received regular payments from the company until 1619.   DAVID L. GANTS

Sources A. Yamada, *Thomas Creede, printer to Shakespeare and his contemporaries* (1994) · W. C. Ferguson, 'Thomas Creede's pica roman', *Studies in Bibliography*, 23 (1970), 148–53 · *STC, 1475–1640* · W. A. Miller, 'Printers and stationers in St Giles Cripplegate, 1561–1640', *Studies in Bibliography*, 19 (1966), 15–38 · W. W. Greg and E. Boswell, eds., *Records of the court of the Stationers' Company, 1576 to 1602, from register B* (1930) · W. A. Jackson, ed., *Records of the court of the Stationers' Company, 1602 to 1640* (1957) · private information (2004) [P. Blayney] · W. C. Ferguson, 'The Stationers' Company poor books, 1608–1700', *The Library*, 5th ser., 31 (1976), 37–51

Creedy, Sir Herbert James (1878–1973), civil servant, was born on 3 May 1878 in London, the elder son (there were no daughters) of Robert Henry Creedy, head of the trustee department of the National and Provincial Bank, and his wife, Eliza Horn. He was educated at Merchant Taylors' School, London, and won a scholarship to St John's College, Oxford, where he took a double first in classical honour moderations (1898) and *literae humaniores* (1900). He was a senior scholar of the college from 1901 to 1905 but decided that an academic career would be too sheltered.

Creedy joined the War Office as clerk of the higher division in 1901 and was seconded for special duty in South Africa in 1903. In the same year he became private secretary to Sir Edward Ware, then permanent under-secretary of state for war, and five years later he was promoted to take charge of the War Office central management branch. In 1913 he became private secretary to the secretary of state and thus began his long service to seven war ministers including Asquith, Kitchener, and Winston Churchill.

In 1920 Creedy succeeded the ailing Sir Reginald Brade as secretary of the War Office, becoming also a member and secretary of the army council, and four years later he became the sole permanent under-secretary of state for war, a post which he held until his retirement in 1939. Thus for thirty-six years (1903–39) Creedy was never far removed from the central controls of the War Office; indeed, his was a longer continuous association with one department than even the justly celebrated service of Sir Maurice Hankey with the secretariat of the committee of imperial defence and the cabinet.

Creedy's period as permanent under-secretary covered the drastic run-down of the army in the 1920s and its hectic rearmament in the 1930s so there were numerous occasions for quarrels with the generals and Treasury officials. Creedy's method was to avoid confrontations by patient diplomacy behind the scenes. In private he might hint that some of the generals, markedly less intelligent and well-educated than himself, needed delicate handling and tutoring in the mysteries of War Office procedures, but he achieved this without a trace of condescension. He seems to have been universally liked and respected by the soldiers who worked with him, more than one recalling that his successor, Sir P. James Grigg, was more acerbic and also more forceful and dynamic.

Though fascinated by his work, Creedy felt strongly that it should not dominate his whole life. He cultivated a wide circle of friends from many professions, travelled a good deal, and kept up his classical studies. Inevitably he had strong personal opinions about some public issues; he is known, for example, to have opposed the creation of a Ministry of Defence, and he disliked the RAF's strategic bombing policy; but he hated intrigues and was a man of monumental discretion. Characteristically he did not preserve letters or documents and wrote no memoirs.

Creedy continued to enjoy robust health and to pursue an active life for many years after his retirement. During the Second World War he was a member, and in 1943–5 chairman, of the security executive. Among many other activities he was a governor of Wellington College (1939–53), a commissioner of the Royal Hospital, Chelsea (1945–57), and a trustee of the Imperial War Museum (1942–59). He was admired and much consulted as doyen by later generations of public servants and men of affairs. He eventually retired to Oxford where he had many friends, particularly at his old college which had made him an honorary fellow in 1931. Creedy was appointed MVO (1911), CVO (1917), KCVO (1923), CB (1915), KCB (1919), and GCB (1933).

In appearance Creedy was short and plump with an almost globular head and small, well-cut features. A model of urbanity, he could nevertheless inspire awe with his quickness of mind and uncanny ability to detect the tiniest error in what he read or heard. His skill in mastering files, seizing on the main points, settling acrimonious disputes in a conciliatory manner, and hitting upon the right phrase in minutes and reports became legendary.

Creedy married in 1904 Mabel Constance (*d.* 1958), daughter of Samuel James Lowry, of Grove Park, Kent, who worked in the City; they had one daughter. Creedy died in the civil service home, Oakhill House, Eady Close, Horsham, Sussex, on 3 April 1973.　　　BRIAN BOND

Sources *WW* · *WWW*, 1971–80 · *The Times* (5 April 1973) · B. Bond, *British military policy between the two world wars* (1980) · G. C. Peden, *British rearmament and the treasury, 1932–1939* (1979) · P. J. Grigg, *Prejudice and judgement* (1948) · private information (2004) [Hilary Creedy, daughter; Sir James Marshall Cornwall; Ronald Adam, Viscount Bridgeman] · *Chief of staff: the diaries of Lieutenant-General Sir Henry Pownall*, ed. B. Bond, 2 vols. (1972–4) · *CGPLA Eng. & Wales* (1973)
Archives HLRO, corresp. with J. C. C. Davidson and Andrew Bonar Law · King's Lond., Liddell Hart C., corresp. with Sir B. H. Liddell Hart · Lpool RO, corresp. with seventeenth earl of Derby · PRO, War Office MSS · U. Newcastle, Robinson L., Runciman MSS, corresp. with Walter Runciman
Likenesses W. Stoneman, two photographs, 1919–33, NPG · photograph (in old age), repro. in *The Times*
Wealth at death £38,219: probate, 1 Aug 1973, *CGPLA Eng. & Wales*

Thomas Creevey (1768–1838), by Abraham Wivell, *c.*1821–4

Creevey, Thomas (1768–1838), politician, was born in School Lane, Liverpool, on 5 March 1768, the second child and only son of William Creevey, captain of a slave ship, and his wife, Phoebe Prescott. His father died soon after Thomas was born. Mrs Creevey married again; she died as Mrs Lowe in 1812. The evidence that Creevey was the natural son of Lord Molyneux, later first earl of Sefton, is suggested but not conclusively proven. His rise in the exclusive society of the whig party was rapid, and he called the Molyneux his 'real' family. Creevey was educated at Newcome's school, Hackney, which favoured 'the sons of noblemen and gentlemen', from about 1780 to 1787, when he was admitted to Queens' College, Cambridge. He graduated in 1789 as seventh wrangler. In November 1789 he was admitted as a student of the Inner Temple, transferring to Gray's Inn in 1791.

While practising at the chancery bar, he kept up an interest in Liverpool through Dr James Currie, whose circle included many local Liberals like William Roscoe, as well as rising whig politicians such as Samuel Romilly and James Scarlett (later first Baron Abinger). His political career was helped by an old school friend, Charles Western, who introduced him to Eleanor Ord, widow of William Ord, and a distant cousin of Charles Grey, the future prime minister. She had five children and an independent income, and Creevey married her in 1802. In the same year he used his interest with the tenth Baron Petre to secure the parliamentary seat of Thetford (thirty-one electors) with the approval of Petre's guardian, Charles Howard, eleventh duke of Norfolk.

Creevey described his political creed as 'devotion to Fox'. During Pitt's second administration he was an outspoken critic, especially of its Indian policy. He was one of the managers who drew up the articles of impeachment of Henry Dundas, first Viscount Melville. In the 'ministry of all the talents' his reward was to be made secretary to the Board of Control, 1806–7. On the death of Fox in 1806, Creevey became dissatisfied with the party's leaders, and his attacks on the Grenvilles helped weaken whig unity. In 1812 he accepted an invitation to stand for Liverpool with his friend Henry Brougham. The candidature of two whigs in tandem lost both the election. In 1813 Creevey was found guilty of a libel on a Liverpool inspector of taxes and fined £100. Heavily in debt, following the failure of his appeal to the king's bench, he had to be rescued by his friends Western and Samuel Whitbread, the latter paying him an annuity of £1000.

From 1814 to 1819 the Creeveys lived in Brussels. Creevey left a vivid account of his experiences before and during the battle of Waterloo, which ended Napoleon's 'hundred days'. He also came to know and admire Arthur Wellesley, first duke of Wellington. Mrs Creevey died in May 1818. In the same year the duke of Norfolk gave Creevey notice to quit Thetford, receiving a long but futile rebuke in return. Creevey returned with his stepdaughters to England in the autumn of 1819.

Creevey was returned to parliament in 1820 as MP for Appleby, through his friend Brougham's good offices with Sackville Tufton, ninth earl of Thanet; he held the seat until 1826. He was thus a witness of the political crisis engendered by the 'trial' of Queen Caroline in that year. But his speeches in parliament were now less frequent and more restrained. In 1825 Thanet died, and with him went Creevey's political ambitions. Thereafter he lived for society and gossip, projecting the writing of a history of his times, the materials for which were to be his long, delightfully observant letters to his favourite stepdaughter, Elizabeth Ord. The book was never written and his only publications were two pamphlets, *A Guide to the Electors of Great Britain, upon the Accession of a New King* (1820), and

Letters of Lord John Russell, upon the Original Formation of the House of Commons (1826), in which he declared for a thorough reform of the closed boroughs he had always represented. His term as MP for Appleby ended in 1826.

When Grey became prime minister in 1830, Creevey got the post of treasurer of the ordnance at £1200 a year. He was MP for Downton from 1831 to 1832, but the borough was destined for abolition in the Reform Act of 1832. When his post at the ordnance was abolished in 1834, Creevey's luck held, with the auditorship of Greenwich Hospital, which he retained until his death. He died on 5 February 1838; he had no children of his own.

Creevey's charm and good humour made him both popular and a delightful guest; his fame derives from the amusing letters preserved by the Ord family. His importance as a historical source is considerable. No one described more graphically the appearance, or recorded more faithfully the looks and the talk, of the royal personages and major politicians of the time. His nicknames for leading characters have often stuck. But he was, after 1819, an observer more than a participant. While he was politically active, his judgement was vehement and unsteady, oscillating between adulation and disillusionment, but not equipped for the small gains and reverses of political routine. As his political prospects faded, his assets as a gossip grew. His rootless life did, however, colour the descriptions he left. He had an acute eye for absurdity, and some power of describing the surface of events and places, but he is incurious about the underlying processes shaping them. It is a cartoonist's talent, sharp, but not deep or lasting. He had not, as a source, the shrewdness of his friend Charles Greville, nor the sharp asperity of his contemporary J. W. Croker; but he had a greater sense of humour than either.

WILLIAM THOMAS, *rev.*

Sources *The Creevey papers*, ed. H. Maxwell, 2 vols. (1903) · *Creevey's life and times: a further selection from the correspondence of Thomas Creevey*, ed. J. Gore (1934) · [T. Creevey], *Creevey*, ed. J. Gore (1948) · *The Greville memoirs, 1814–1860*, ed. L. Strachey and R. Fulford, 8 vols. (1938)
Archives Northumbd RO, Newcastle upon Tyne, corresp. and papers | Beds. & Luton ARS, letters, mainly to Samuel Whitbread · BL, letters to James Currie, Egerton MS 3020 · Lambton Park, Chester-le-Street, co. Durham, corresp. with first earl of Durham · Lpool RO, Currie MSS · Lpool RO, corresp. with William Roscoe · U. Durham L., letters to second Earl Grey
Likenesses A. Wivell, drawing, c.1821–1824, priv. coll. [*see illus.*]

Cregeen, Archibald (*bap.* 1774, *d.* 1841), lexicographer, was born in the village of Colby, Isle of Man, and baptized in the parish church of Arbory on 20 November 1774, the third of four sons of William Cregeen, a cooper and small farmer, and his wife, Mary Fairclough (Faircliff in the marriage register of the adjoining parish of Malew, 13 November 1764), who is reported to have come from Ireland. Of his education nothing is known. He was apprenticed as a monumental mason and so must have added literacy in English to his native Manx. After his marriage to Jane Crellin (1775/6–1844) in the parish church of German on 8 March 1798, he built in Colby a house for himself and his

family (six daughters and two sons), later called Ravenstone. In alternate years from 1813 he held the office of coroner for the sheading of Rushen in addition to his ordinary occupation.

Cregeen began work about 1814 on what was to be the first published Manx dictionary, collecting words from the Manx Bible (1770–75), for which he often gave references, from the Book of Common Prayer, and from other printed sources, but also gathering material, words, phrases, scraps of traditional verse, and proverbs, from current usage. He marked stress, the gender and plural of nouns, the stems of verbs, and included old case-forms and all the pronominal prepositions. To this catalogue of inflectional variations he added a generous number of illustrations of the initial mutations. The dictionary is preceded by a sketch of grammar, again concentrating on morphology. In this work of at least twenty years' duration Cregeen was encouraged and assisted by the Revd John Edward Harrison (1784–1858), vicar of Jurby, whose hand has been detected in the preface and the opening paragraphs of the grammar. The dictionary, published in 1835, though not the most copious, is the most serviceable, the most reliable and soundly based, ever produced. It has been reprinted several times, beginning in 1910.

Cregeen died on Good Friday, 9 April 1841, and was buried on 13 April in Arbory churchyard, where his elegant box-tomb is still to be seen south-east of the church.

R. L. THOMSON, *rev.*

Sources J. M. Jeffcott, 'Archibald Cregeen, the Manx lexicographer', *N&Q*, 7th ser., 10 (1890), 181–3 · R. L. Thomson, 'The study of Manx Gaelic', *PBA*, 55 (1969), 177–210 · parish registers · *International encyclopaedia of lexicography*, 2349

Creighton, Charles (1847–1927), medical scholar, was born on 22 November 1847 at Peterhead, Aberdeenshire, a son of Alexander Creighton, a prosperous saw-miller and wood merchant, and his wife, Agnes Brand. He was educated at the local elementary school, and then at the Gymnasium in Old Aberdeen. At the age of seventeen he won eighth place in the open bursary competition for King's College, Aberdeen, from which he graduated MA in 1867.

Creighton moved to Marischal College, Aberdeen, to study medicine, and obtained his MB in 1871. The chronological details of his early career are somewhat uncertain. He seems to have spent the last months of 1871, and 1872, in Vienna, where he studied pathology under Karl von Rokitansky and Rudolph Virchow. Early in 1873 he took up the post of surgical registrar at St Thomas's Hospital, London; in 1874 he was medical registrar at Charing Cross Hospital. Between 1874 and 1878 he was apparently associated with the Brown Animal Institution, then under the directorship of John Burdon Sanderson, while he also undertook several research projects for the medical department of the privy council. In 1876 he moved to Cambridge as demonstrator in anatomy under Sir George Humphry, and there took an active part in the university's scientific life, becoming an editor of the *Journal of Anatomy and Physiology* in 1879 and an early member, and secretary, of the Cambridge Medical Society in 1880. In October 1881, however, his Cambridge career came to an abrupt and mysterious end, and he moved to London. Although a friend, the bacteriologist William Bulloch, later recorded that Creighton left Cambridge with some sort of grievance, no confirmatory evidence of this has been found.

In London Creighton pursued a somewhat isolated career as an independent scholar. It is possible that the move to London was associated with the decision to undertake the first great scholarly project of his career, the *Handbook of Geographical and Historical Pathology*, which he translated from the German work by August Hirsch, of which the first volume appeared in 1881. The three substantial volumes of Creighton's translation were published by the New Sydenham Society between 1883 and 1886. During this period Creighton was regarded with respect by the medical community, and delivered an address to the British Medical Association in 1883. He contributed several entries to the ninth edition of the *Encyclopaedia Britannica* (1879–88). Publication of his encyclopaedia entry on vaccination in 1888 precipitated the major crisis of Creighton's career, and his fall from scientific grace. While researching for the article, he became convinced not only that Edward Jenner, the originator of vaccination against smallpox, was a rogue and a charlatan, but also that vaccination itself was valueless. This view, expressed in a popularly regarded authoritative text, outraged the medical profession, which was at that time well engaged in a struggle to maintain the practice of compulsory infant vaccination in the effort to control one of the most dangerous and repulsive diseases then known. Creighton compounded the offence in the following year by publishing *Jenner and Vaccination*; there he accused the profession of self serving, of self-interest, and of being 'perseveringly wrong' in promoting 'a grotesque superstition' (pp. 352–3). Thereafter he became known as 'Creighton the Anti-vaccinator', and was ostracized by the profession.

Anti-vaccinationism did not, however, become a personal crusade. Throughout his professional life Creighton regarded himself as a pathologist and continued his pathological researches. These focused on breast tumours, tuberculosis, and cancer, and resulted in several publications. His conclusions were, however, uniformly individual, being deeply rooted in the science he had been taught as a young man. He seemed unable intellectually to accommodate the astounding developments in disease theory after c.1880, and was especially out of sympathy with the new discipline of bacteriology, notwithstanding the friendship with Bulloch, begun in 1898. This was notably evident in the crowning achievement of his scholarly career, the two-volume *History of Epidemics* published in 1894. Even on publication, despite Creighton's reactionary views, the *History* was recognized as an outstanding work of scholarship, the distillation of a vast mass of sources into an exact and readable account. It also marked the emergence of a new approach to medical history, diverging from the tradition of annual chronologies to integrate the story of disease into the wider events of British national history. The first volume dealt with pestilences from antiquity to the great plague of London; the second with infectious diseases, including smallpox, measles, whooping cough, influenza, and the various intestinal disorders. Cherished and esteemed for many years by certain scientists, the *History* acquired classic status and wider recognition when reprinted in 1965. It remained an authoritative scholarly resource beyond the end of the twentieth century.

The *History* was Creighton's last historical work. He paid a visit to India to study the plague pandemic, continued his pathological studies on cancer, and began to publish idiosyncratic studies on Shakespearian themes. In 1918 he disposed of his books and pathological collections, and retired to The Yews at Upper Boddington, Northamptonshire.

Tall, with a commanding presence, and meticulously dressed, Creighton was described as being 'a gentleman in all things', and of great personal integrity (Underwood, 134). Yet he was inflexible in his views and undeterred by hostile opinion, and cared little for worldly success. He did not tolerate fools; the anti-vaccinationists, who regarded him as a hero, found him difficult: 'he had even a certain acerbity for members of our own party when they outran what he deemed scientific discretion' ('A dead hero'). A regular churchgoer, he led a most frugal life, of wide and unostentatious charity. He never married. He died from a cerebral haemorrhage at his Northamptonshire home on 18 July 1927.   ANNE HARDY

Sources E. A. Underwood, 'Charles Creighton, the man and his work', in C. Creighton, *A history of epidemics*, 2nd edn (1965), vol. 1, pp. 43–135 · W. Bulloch, 'Charles Creighton', *The Lancet* (30 July 1927), 250–51 · W. Bulloch, 'Charles Creighton', *Aberdeen University Review*, 15 (1928), 112–18 · M. Greenwood, 'Charles Creighton', *BMJ* (6 Aug 1927), 240–41 · 'A dead hero', *Vaccination Inquirer and Health Review*, 49 (1927), 115 · C. Creighton, *Some conclusions on cancer* (1920) · C. Creighton, *Jenner and vaccination* (1889) · E. A. Underwood, *Proceedings of the Royal Society of Medicine*, 41 (1948), 869–76 · bap. reg. Scot. · d. cert.

Likenesses photograph, repro. in Bulloch, 'Charles Creighton' · photograph, repro. in Underwood, 'Charles Creighton, the man and his work', facing p. 133

Wealth at death £770 12s. 3d.: probate, 1927, CGPLA Eng. & Wales

Creighton, James (1739–1819), Wesleyan Methodist minister, was born on 5 February 1739 at Moyne Hall, co. Cavan, Ireland, of Scottish-Irish descent. His parents, though dissenters, attended the Church of Ireland, and his mother gave him a pious upbringing. Educated at Cavan grammar school, Creighton was admitted sizar at Trinity College, Dublin, on 2 July 1760, graduating BA in 1764. Though doubting his call to the ministry, he was ordained deacon on 28 October 1764 and priest on 28 October 1765 by the bishop of Kilmore. After a curacy with the bishop and teaching at his old school in 1764–6, in 1769 he became curate of Swanlinbar, co. Cavan.

Worried about his sins, Creighton knew little about Methodism despite correspondence with John Wesley in 1773 and reading Methodist pamphlets. However, old Anglican writings in 1775 convinced him that justification and sanctification were not new doctrines. He felt the need to be saved by faith alone and in 1776, influenced by dreams and a feeling like 'the shock of electric fire' (*Arminian Magazine*, 301), he was converted. For seven years he preached his new faith in his own parish and far beyond, aided the Methodists, and alienated clerical friends. In 1781–2 he preached in seven counties and walked 4000 miles. Though Wesley failed to persuade him to become John Fletcher's curate in Madeley in 1779, in October 1783 Creighton became Wesley's assistant at City Road Chapel, London.

In the deed of declaration of 28 February 1784, which legally defined the Methodist conference, Creighton was named immediately after the Wesleys and Thomas Coke among the 100 legal members of conference and assisted Wesley in the first ordinations for America on 1–2 September 1784. Creighton claimed that Wesley later regretted ordaining, at least for Scotland, though the ordinations continued, and in 1792 he asserted that Methodist sacraments contradicted Wesley's original plan and his claim not to separate from the Church of England. In 1787 Creighton asked Charles Wesley to approach Lord Mansfield with a plan (probably by Coke) to ask the Anglican hierarchy to keep Methodism within the Church of England by giving Wesley and his successors power to ordain preachers to supervise Methodism under its own rules.

From 1788 to 1792 Creighton edited the *Arminian Magazine* and continued to minister at Wesley's chapel until shortly before his death. Here he upheld dignified worship, the use of music, and choral processions for funerals, deploring noisy Methodist behaviour in worship. He was a diligent pastor, especially among the poor. Creighton's publications included poems, sermons, writings on liturgical worship and domestic duties, and *An Enquiry into the Origins of True Religion* (2nd edn, 1817), ascribing the origins of religion and culture to the Jews. He declared himself free of bigotry, though he opposed Catholic emancipation. Disgusted with the behaviour of warring factions in Methodism in the 1790s, he took a moderating line on the power struggles between preachers and people. Though upholding conference control against anarchy, he thought local societies should have some control over preachers. Creighton was married, though details of his wife, who died in 1816, are unknown; the couple had at least two sons. He died on 26 December 1819 at his home at Hoxton Square, London, and was buried in his family grave in Henley.　　　Henry D. Rack

Sources 'A short account of the experience of Rev. James Creighton', *Arminian Magazine*, 8 (1785), 241–4, 297–302, 354–9, 398–403 · F. Baker, *John Wesley and the Church of England* (1970), 228, 265–6, 268, 279, 281–2, 386–7, 394–5, 397–9 · letters by Creighton, JRL, Methodist Archives and Research Centre, PLP 30/11/2–12; Brown Folio, Wesley Family II, 88–9 · G. J. Stevenson, *History of City Road Chapel* (1872), 147–9, 282–3, 587 · *The letters of the Rev. John Wesley*, ed. J. Telford, 8 vols. (1931), vol. 6, pp. 28, 356; vol. 8, pp.121, 129, 160, 235 · J. Wesley, letter to J. Creighton, 26 Feb 1779, JRL, Methodist Archives and Research Centre, MAM JW 2.67 · *Methodist Magazine*, 43 (1820), 694–5 · Burtchaell & Sadleir, *Alum. Dubl.*, 2nd edn
Archives JRL, Methodist Archives and Research Centre, letters, PLP 30/11/2–12 · World Methodist Building, Lake Junaluska, North Carolina, 'Extracts from Rev. James Creighton's letters to his sister'

Likenesses T. Hodgetts, mezzotint, exh. RA 1816 (after John Renton), BM · engraving (aged forty-five), NPG, JRL, Methodist Archives and Research Centre, PLP 30/11/1

Creighton [*née* von Glehn], **Louise Hume** (1850–1936), social activist and writer of popular history and biography, was born on 7 July 1850 at Peak Hill Lodge, Sydenham, on the outskirts of London, tenth child of Robert William von Glehn (1801–1885) and Agnes Duncan (*c*.1813–1881). Louise's godmother was Elisa Hume, daughter of radical MP Joseph Hume (1777–1855). Robert von Glehn, of German and Scottish ancestry, was born in Reval, Estonia. He emigrated to England as a young man and established an import–export business in London, soon afterwards marrying Agnes Duncan, the Scottish stepdaughter of a successful London merchant. Louise grew up in a reasonably prosperous but careful middle-class family, liberal in religion and in politics. Her early life was shaped by strict but caring parents, strong-willed brothers and sisters, and a German governess. Educated at home, although she took classes at the Crystal Palace, she entered and passed with honours the first London University higher examination for women. However, she was always to regret having missed formal schooling, and was to become a keen promoter of women's education.

Louise von Glehn grew up in a lively, cultivated, and cosmopolitan atmosphere. There were always visitors at Peak Hill Lodge, the house was full of music, and the family went to concerts and to study the sculpture casts at Crystal Palace. She herself had no musical talent, although she was to develop a certain facility in sketching and watercolour. John Ruskin (1819–1900) was her prophet. Louise claimed that the strongest intellectual influence in her girlhood was her friendship with the historian J. R. Green (1837–1883), who often visited her home and who advised her on her reading. Family life was loving but intense: all its members seem to have been critical of one another, over-sensitive, and prone to take themselves rather too seriously. Louise felt that this had reinforced her own self-consciousness, yet as an adult she was equally exacting in her expectations of people.

On a visit to Oxford in February 1871 she met Mandell *Creighton (1843–1901), a fellow of Merton College, who had admired her boldness in wearing a yellow scarf to one of Ruskin's lectures. They were engaged the following month, and were married on 8 January 1872 at St Bartholomew's, Sydenham. They were an extremely happy and close couple, always sharing interests and commitments. Their first home was in St Giles', Oxford, a new rented villa which they named Middlemarch after George Eliot's novel. This they took much pride in decorating and furnishing, with a yellow drawing-room and blue china setting off the white Persian cat. A painting of her done shortly after her marriage by her friend Bertha Johnson shows a serious, handsome woman, with deep-set dark eyes and strong eyebrows, standing in a Pre-Raphaelite garden. She was enchanted by Oxford, and she and her husband had a busy and stimulating social life. Nearly every afternoon they went for a walk together. Meanwhile she began to read—principally history—in the Bodleian

Louise Hume Creighton (1850–1936), by Glyn Philpot, 1918

Library, sharing a desk with William Stubbs (1825–1901), who leaned over to joke with her or to ask her the meaning of a German word. She took over the translation of a volume of Ranke's history of England which Mandell had undertaken with four other tutors. (It none the less still appeared under his name.) He also encouraged her to write a series of historical primers. She became involved in religious work, volunteering as an Anglican district visitor in one of the poorest areas of the city, and was among the founders of a women's committee which encouraged tutors to offer history and literature courses for women. During this period she and Mandell began the custom of taking their holidays in Italy, which they both loved. At Oxford the first two of their seven children were born, Beatrice in 1872 and Lucia in 1874.

In 1875 they moved to Embleton in Northumberland, a Merton College living to which Mandell Creighton had been appointed. Although at first this seemed a social exile, Louise came to see the ten years which they spent there as a major turning point in their lives. They both came to parochial work for the first time, and threw themselves into visiting. Louise started a mothers' meeting and a branch of the Girls' Friendly Society, of which she was elected first diocesan president. She gained much experience of dealing with people and of speaking in public, although she never felt enthusiastic about the Girls' Friendly Society either there or elsewhere. She became interested in Ellice Hopkins's writings, and gave some talks on purity. Four more children were born during this period (Cuthbert in 1876, Walter in 1878, Mary in 1880, and Oswin in 1883), and Louise taught them herself, reading up on modern educational theory. At the same time she

established herself as an accomplished writer, producing historical biographies, a very successful *Child's First History of England* and other historical stories for children, and a novel, *The Bloom off the Peach*, which she published under the pseudonym Lois Hume.

In 1884 the Creighton family moved to Cambridge, where Mandell took up the Dixie chair of ecclesiastical history. He was appointed a canon of Worcester in the following year. During the Cambridge years (1884–91) Louise emerged as a national figure. Besides her literary and social work, she became caught up in the movement against female suffrage. She helped Mrs Humphry Ward (1851–1920) to organize signatures for a petition against female suffrage which was published in the *Nineteenth Century* in 1889. Her opposition, she claimed, rested on the belief that there were benefits from having a large body of intelligent and influential opinion outside party politics; she said that she changed her mind when she realized how involved in party politics women were even without the vote, so that it would be better for them to have full responsibility. She publicly announced her change of position in 1906. At Cambridge Louise Creighton also began her long association with the National Union of Women Workers (NUWW), a non-political organization of middle-class women dedicated to improving the lives of working women. She served as its first president in the 1880s and held a number of executive posts thereafter. Her last child, Gemma, was born in 1887.

In 1891 Mandell Creighton was appointed bishop of Peterborough, and in 1897 was promoted to the see of London. It fell to Louise to run the episcopal households and to provide an ever-increasing range of hospitality. She missed the close daily companionship with Mandell, which was no longer possible, but developed her own independent interests and kept up her writing. As well as continuing her work for the NUWW and the Mothers' Union, she addressed women's sessions at church congresses. In London she revitalized the Women's Diocesan Association and initiated the Girls' Diocesan Association, of which her daughter Beatrice was the first president. She maintained her interest in rescue work, and was on the London Council for the Promotion of Morality from its inception.

Louise Creighton was only fifty when her husband died (on 14 January 1901). She was granted a grace-and-favour apartment at Hampton Court, and lived there until 1927. Within months of Mandell's death she embarked on her greatest literary achievement, the two-volume *Life and Letters of Mandell Creighton* (1904), which received justified acclaim. She also collected and edited nine volumes of his speeches, sermons, lectures, and essays. Of the twenty-four books which she wrote or edited during her life, thirteen were written during her years as a widow. They included biographies, a monograph on missions, lectures on household economy delivered at the London School of Economics, and lectures on the theory of the state given in 1916. She served on two royal commissions—the London University commission (1909) and the venereal disease commission (1913)—and also on the joint committee of insurance commissioners (1912). In 1908 she chaired the women's meetings at the Pan-Anglican Congress. She became increasingly involved in the Society for the Propagation of the Gospel, and worked hard to get the work of women and men amalgamated. She participated in the Edinburgh World Missionary Conference in 1910. During the First World War she supported the National Mission of Repentance and Hope, and the Life and Liberty Movement, which urged increased self-government and reform of the Church of England. With the passage of the Church of England Assembly (Powers) Act (1919), which created the first national assembly, Louise became a charter member from 1920 to 1930. By then she was recognized as a moderate voice in the women's movement.

Louise Creighton moved to Oxford in the late 1920s, where she served on the governing board of Lady Margaret Hall. After a period of declining health, she died on 15 April 1936 at 5 South Parks Road, Oxford. Her ashes were buried in her husband's grave in St Paul's Cathedral. As a wife, Louise had been highly protective and supportive of her husband and his career. She exhibited an extraordinary devotion to him, for in her eyes he could say nothing dull, do nothing wrong. As a mother, she loved her children, but found it difficult to express tenderness towards them. She was to wonder whether she had praised them too little; certainly none of them matched up intellectually to her expectations. As an author, she wrote effectively for a wide public, biography proving her most successful genre. As a social activist, she showed consummate skills in organization. In this context her reputation for being alarming, which she herself related to her social awkwardness, could be turned to good effect. She continued to promote women's primary role within the family, seeing church work as an extension of this; she saw women as having a distinctive and influential contribution to make. She increasingly came to feel that more responsibility and freedom should be given to women in church affairs; only then would the most intelligent women be drawn to this sort of work. In her later life she pondered the question of the priesthood of women. She recognized that her opposition to it was rooted in instinct and prejudice, and she could find no logical reason against it.   JAMES THAYNE COVERT

Sources J. Covert, *A Victorian marriage: Mandell and Louise Creighton* (2000) · *A Victorian family as seen through the letters of Louise Creighton to her mother, 1872–1880*, ed. J. T. Covert (1998) · *Memoir of a Victorian woman: reflections of Louise Creighton, 1850–1936*, ed. J. T. Covert (1994) · L. von Glehn Creighton, *Life and letters of Mandell Creighton*, 2 vols. (1904) · *The Times* (16 April 1936) · priv. coll., Louise Creighton MSS [Creighton family] · LPL, Louise Creighton corresp.

Archives LPL, family corresp. · priv. coll.

Likenesses B. Johnson, oils, 1872?, repro. in Covert, ed., *Memoir of a Victorian woman* · G. Philpot, oils, 1918, unknown collection; copyprint, NPG [*see illus.*]

Creighton, Mandell (1843–1901), bishop of London and historian, was born in Carlisle on 5 July 1843, the elder son of Robert Creighton (*d.* 1878), who built up a family business in Carlisle, and Sarah Mandell (*d.* 1850/51), of a farming family in Cumberland. He had a brother and two sisters. Of the sister who survived infancy little is known, but

Mandell Creighton (1843–1901), by W. & D. Downey, pubd 1893

Creighton kept in touch with his brother, James, who continued the family's prominence in Carlisle, and on the latter's death in 1896 Creighton and his wife opened their home to his children. Creighton's own mother had died when he was seven. His father was a stern parent and, despite companionship at school, Creighton seems to have had a solitary adolescence, taking long walks, a relaxation that he enjoyed throughout his life (in his youth he walked from Oxford to Durham in three days), and forming decided, independent opinions. He went first to the cathedral school in Carlisle in 1852 and in 1858, with a scholarship, to the grammar school of Durham.

Merton College, 1862–1874 In October 1862 Creighton went into residence at Merton College, Oxford, with a classical postmastership. In a small college he was one of a handful who did not come from a leading public school and who took their studies seriously. His intellectual prominence and his moral convictions provoked criticism from some of his contemporaries and won admiration from others, among them 'athletes' with some of whom he made lasting friendships. His powers of concentration and flair for literary composition were already evident. He took a first class in *literae humaniores* in 1866 and was elected as probationer for a Merton fellowship in December that year. After a mere few months of preparation he was tutoring undergraduates in modern history in 1867.

Throughout the seven years of Creighton's fellowship, Merton was experiencing the stresses of the recent reforms which affected the whole university. At the same time Oxford was absorbing the controversies over ritual and doctrine brought about by the Tractarians and Darwin. His appointment was part of a steady improvement in the intellectual quality of Merton's governing body in line with reforming interests; as tutor and, shortly afterwards, principal of the postmasters responsible for undergraduate discipline and performance, he promoted the raising of standards in accordance with the college's policy. By helping to initiate the sharing of lectures among like-minded colleges, and as an examiner, he promoted these improvements more generally. The minutes of college meetings show the continuing preoccupation with the character of chapel services and the requirement on undergraduates to attend. Changes in the status of clerical fellows in these years were even more directly related to Creighton's own position. The changing environment in the university was matched by significant changes in his own life. In 1870 he was ordained deacon, as required by his fellowship but also fulfilling a long-settled purpose: as a schoolboy at Durham he had told the wife of the headmaster that he intended to become a bishop. He was priested at Christmas 1873. In 1871 he had met his future wife, Louise (1850–1936) [see Creighton, Louise Hume], daughter of Robert von Glehn (d. 1885), a naturalized merchant from Estonia, and Agnes Duncan (d. 1881). They were married on 8 January 1872, and Creighton applied to retain his fellowship. The change required in the statutes to retain a fellowship after marriage was duly conceded, not without opposition although it accommodated other members of the college. In these same years Creighton showed his ability as a popularizer of the study of history, partly in extramural lectures to non-academic audiences. The scholarly standards which he brought to this new discipline from his earlier studies in classics led to his wish to give more time to writing history than his college duties allowed. In 1874, not without misgivings and in the face of a petition from all the senior undergraduates, he and his wife decided to accept the college living of Embleton in Northumberland. There he expected to have leisure to write a history of the papacy on the eve of the Reformation, a theme which had become the main preoccupation of his university lectures because other tutors chose to offer more attractive topics.

Embleton, 1874–1884 Embleton was a remote rural parish on the Northumbrian coast close to Dunstanburgh Castle. Yet it provided a more than comfortable stipend and all the time that he was there Creighton had a curate. Despite being urged to stay in Oxford, Creighton anticipated that the burden of university business, combined with the business of his college and teaching, would prevent him completing the extended piece of work which he had in mind. In his view Embleton offered 'the opportunity for uninterrupted work … and concentration of intellectual energy on one subject'. In March 1875 the Creightons settled into the large vicarage with its garden full of trees. Parochial responsibilities were a challenge because they were unfamiliar. Apart from one or two landed families like the Greys at Fallodon and Howick, Creighton moved among poorly educated parishioners: quarrymen in Embleton village, farmers and labourers in the surrounding countryside, and the families of the fishermen on the coast. A northerner himself, he knew better than to take his people for granted and in the course of his incumbency he won their friendship and trust. He set a pattern for his later ministry by forging confident relations with successive Presbyterian colleagues and encouraging the largely Methodist fishermen to be active in their church. As early as May 1875 he had established the routine of working in his study in the mornings and spending the afternoon until seven visiting parishioners, taking them as he found them at home or at work. There were not so many of them (Mrs Creighton estimated seventeen hundred), but Creighton preferred to cover the 7 miles of his parish on foot. From Embleton he published the first two volumes of the *History of the Papacy* (1882) and upwards of half a dozen of the papers reprinted in *Historical Essays and Reviews* (1902), mainly on figures of the Italian Renaissance. To complete this work he depended largely on books which he bought himself, emphasizing original sources, such as his valued copy of Muratori's *Rerum Italicarum scriptores* (1723–51), and others to be found in the citations and appendices of his volumes on the papacy.

Cambridge, 1884–1891 Surrounded by his growing family (four daughters and three sons), producing work of historical and literary merit to satisfy both scholarly and general readers, Creighton's years at Embleton were happy; but he knew that they would not and should not last, and he was thinking of moving as he became increasingly involved in the administration of the new diocese of Newcastle. Nevertheless, the summons from Cambridge to be the first Dixie professor of ecclesiastical history in May 1884 came out of the blue. He doubted his qualifications for the position, although he had been enquiring about the succession to William Stubbs in Oxford when the invitation reached him. In accordance with the new foundation, his purpose was to establish the history of the church as a subject with appeal to students of politics, to lawyers and theologians, and to the merely curious, as much as to budding historians. His aim was to treat this field in the same fashion as any other historical topic, without prejudice or ulterior purpose. 'I turn to the past to learn its story', he wrote, 'without any preconceived opinion what that story may be' (*Life and Letters*, 1.280). As a historian he was concerned with what the past had to tell about the character of the actors and their times rather than with the accumulation of information.

Being a newcomer to Cambridge, Creighton did not push himself forward. However, he was sought out for his advice and political sense, contributing from his arrival to changes in the historical tripos and its examination, with more choice and more open-ended questions. His standing among his colleagues was shown when, in 1885, prolonged discussions about the publication of an English journal of history came to fruition and he was invited to be the first editor of the *English Historical Review*. Creighton had no illusions about the work this would entail, and he accepted out of duty, before any editorial policy had been framed, quite apart from his goal of promoting interest in the discipline and improving research. The *Review* took a lot of time and energy, finding and corresponding with contributors on subjects from Homer to recent British politics and keeping in close touch with Longmans, who undertook its publication and were concerned about the early failure to recover their costs. Among others, articles were obtained from celebrities such as Gladstone, Viscount Bryce, and Lord Acton without evident results in increased circulation. As far as possible Creighton avoided university duties, but he was an active member of his college, Emmanuel, which had provided the endowment for the Dixie chair. In 1886 he was chosen as its representative to contribute to the 250th anniversary of Harvard College, since John Harvard had been at Emmanuel before emigrating. In a sense, though, Creighton was but a part-time Cambridge man. In June 1885 he was appointed a canon of Worcester Cathedral and he and his household lived in the close there during university vacations, until his appointment as bishop of Peterborough. He contributed actively to the intellectual and liturgical life of the cathedral, lecturing himself, bringing visiting scholars to lecture to the clergy, preaching, leading the three-hour devotion on Good Friday (a practice which he brought to Peterborough and St Paul's, London), and as examining chaplain.

Creighton and the episcopate Worcester rather than Cambridge prepared Creighton for the remainder of his career, as a bishop. He was nominated to Peterborough in March 1891: at the age of forty-eight he entered once more into an unfamiliar dimension. Bishops at all times are of uneven quality; none gains universal approval. Of those whom he had encountered earlier in his career only Lightfoot at Durham and Wilberforce at Newcastle had impressed Creighton. He saw himself as more than the bishop of a diocese: he was a bishop of the Church of England with a historic sense of the identity of church and nation. Beyond that nation, he came to office at a time when the Anglican church was becoming aware of itself as a worldwide communion. While not wholly enthusiastic about them, Creighton was in demand at the sequence of church congresses in the 1880s and 1890s where, as well as being secretary for a time, he delivered many of the addresses which reflect his view of the church's role in national affairs in the past and in the present. As a bishop he was a regular participant at the informal council of bishops which met regularly under the chairmanship of archbishops Benson and then Temple. Little of Creighton's experience in Oxford, Embleton, Cambridge, or even Worcester had prepared him for episcopal office. On the other hand, the formation of his character had equipped him very completely.

Character and appearance As a schoolboy Creighton's brother gave him the nickname Homer; friends of his undergraduate days knew him as the Professor (or the P) and deferred to his intellectual and moral judgement for the most part; after marriage he was known in the family circle as Max. These bynames reflect different aspects of Creighton's character: the scholar concerned with achievements of the past and the man of the world comfortable in dealing with the present. After leaving school he wrote a guide for his successor as head monitor of remarkable authority and moral certainty. He was a sophisticated and opinionated undergraduate of aesthetic tastes, in sympathy with the high-church interest. His assurance about standards of behaviour, which won both respect and opposition as an undergraduate, continued as a young fellow charged with college discipline; and this moral earnestness and certainty were not lessened by ordination. There were grounds for his self-accusation that as a young man he was a prig. His conviction of the church's position as the soul of the nation, and the place of the church by law established as that soul's keeper, governed his political views, which veered from moderate Liberal to moderate Conservative, as Gladstone's policies seemed to threaten the established church. It gave rise, too, to misguided views about the independence of the medieval English church from Rome, which were widespread among the clergy of his time. The necessary identity of church and nation, a topic for many of his addresses, was complemented by his belief in his country's mission at home and overseas in guarding and promoting the humane values of civilization which had been revived in the Renaissance, the historical period to which he was most attached. He was a man of his time: the Victorian head of his family who lectured his young bride with a kindly patronage on intellectual and aesthetic taste; or who wrote offhandedly to his mother-in-law that the interruptions from the birth of a second child were now over and, as an afterthought, that he had another daughter. He could be very direct, as when he had written earlier to the same lady that she should only expect to hear from him when there was a precise purpose in writing. In another aspect this was perhaps a reflection of his concentrated efficiency and disciplined use of his time. As bishop he kept up with personal correspondence during meetings while contributing effectively to the business at hand. He had great powers of absorption which served him both in scholarship and in practical affairs. From the time of his Merton fellowship contemporaries were impressed by his ability to isolate the central issues in a discussion, and without delay propose a moderate settlement which sized up both the situation and the parties involved in it.

This sketch conveys an effective but hardly an attractive personality. Yet Creighton inspired as much affection as admiration. The other side of him was found in the romping parent who enchanted his own children and others with his boisterous play and fanciful imagination. On a visit to Sandringham the bishop alarmed bystanders by the freedom with which he repeatedly tossed the future Edward VIII into the air, to the child's delight. All his life he puzzled or shocked those of more conventional outlook by the paradoxes of his conversation, throwing off epigrams as they occurred to him in the exchanges of dialogue. He had a great sense of fun, he was approachable, and even in his reproofs he usually retained the victim's friendship. Despite these abilities he was modest in his own estimate of them: 'my reputation is always a surprise to myself', he wrote shortly before going to London, 'I never tried to make a hit, and never consider anything but the need for simplicity and straightforwardness. But I am writing a panegyric of myself' (*Life and Letters*, 2.200). About the same time he wrote to a friend who had sought his advice:

> Life is a sum of relationships. There is no independent or self-centred existence … The Christian claim is that my life, my capacities, my relationships are part of an eternal order running through the universe, beginning and ending in God. Nothing short of this conception gives happiness or strength or reality. (ibid., 2.211)

At the centre of this far from simple man was his faith in his risen Saviour.

The two sides of Creighton's personality may be discerned in his appearance. There were the striking head with its prominent brow and nose below the receding hair, the level gaze, the full but carefully nurtured beard. At the same time there was a playful quality in the expression of his refined mouth, in his lively eyes, and the positioning of the gold-rimmed lenses which are a feature of so many photographs. His eldest son recorded his father's capacity to overawe and enchant his children at the same time. He was tall enough to be imposing in clerical robes, erect and trim, and he was fully aware of the impression which he could make. He could project his voice without effort.

Bishop of Peterborough, 1891–1897 The diocese of Peterborough, to which Creighton was consecrated on 25 April 1891, was a comfortable place to find his feet as a bishop. Not too large, it was homogeneous in its rural population with two considerable industrial towns, Leicester and Northampton, for variety. When he left for London in 1897 the bishop could justly recall the sense of solidarity which he and his clergy had shared. He gave a lot of thought and effort to guiding their ministries. He recognized the importance of their not being left behind in the currents of popular knowledge or theological change and he built up a library in the palace for their use. He brought them to Peterborough on retreat. He urged them to get to know their parishioners and identify with their hopes and problems. He emphasized the importance of the daily offices, the value of their regular and public observance having been evident to him during his time at Embleton. He gave close attention to ordinands and delighted in confirmations: not every bishop was careful about these standard duties. Recognizing the church's opportunity and its obligation to evangelize the industrial classes, he took up residence in Leicester for a period each year. He encouraged church extension and missions, although he had been doubtful about the value of the latter when he had a parish of his own. As at Embleton he had excellent relations with nonconformists, for he understood that the need for Christian ministry overwhelmed the resources available

for it. Particularly, his concern and advice were instrumental in helping to settle the bitter strike of 1895 in the boot and shoe trades in Leicester and Northampton.

This fortunate period was punctuated by the completion of his *History of the Papacy* (volume five being published in 1894), the preparation and delivery of the Hulsean lectures at Cambridge, in 1893–4, the Rede lecture in 1895, and a short visit to Moscow in 1896 to attend the coronation of Nicholas II as representative of the Church of England, a visit from which he drew a favourable impression of the close association of church and state in Orthodox Russia. In an official visit, for which the tsar's minister responsible for the Orthodox was his guide, he did not get beyond surface impressions.

Bishop of London, 1897–1901 Creighton was enthroned as bishop of London on 30 January 1897. If Peterborough was a tranquil charge, the bishopric of London was the opposite. Its problems, social and ecclesiastical, resulted from the unceasing growth of the capital: the churches of the City of London were too many and too rich, while those of the sprawling suburbs and crowded slums were too few and often too poor. Every form of ecclesiastical taste was represented amid its population, with church attendance ranging from crowded to deserted according to the charisma and capacity of the incumbent and the nature of the parish. Issues which troubled the national church at large were generally more acute in the metropolitan diocese. To the discussions at the council of bishops between 1897 and 1901, before whom Archbishop Temple laid the problem of keeping Anglican clergy loyal to the order prescribed in the prayer book, Bishop Creighton contributed his concerns about ritual, theological training, and the more manageable question of the conservation of episcopal and parochial records. By virtue of his office he had responsibility for Anglicans in parts of Europe and in the colonies overseas. He was too ill in the autumn of 1900 to conduct the routine visitation of his diocese himself; but the questions to which he sought answers indicate the wide range of his concerns. In addition to the inevitable questions about church order and discipline, he wanted to know about the state of parish schools and other parochial organizations, how his clergy and people got on with other denominations, their relations with labour organizations, and their contribution to the work of local authorities. His official act books record the continual preoccupations of his formal functions: ordinations, collations, resignations and institutions, grants of licences for various purposes, commissions to act on his behalf, and the appointment of diocesan officers. The unrelenting pressure of private correspondence is evident in the dozen or so large volumes in which inward letters are preserved and which his widow digested so effectively in the second volume of her memoir. London had more than its share of 'difficult' clergymen. Thirty folios of the collection of letters for 1898, for example, convey the successive grievances of one cantankerous priest, the Revd William Adamson of Old Ford. Quarrels, many provoked by the combative Protestant Truth Society and its leader John Kensit, and questions about ritual took much more of the bishop's time than he wished. His replies on these and other matters of pastoral guidance had to be fitted into the crowded calendar of functions which he could not refuse; and letters alone were frequently insufficient.

Death In face of the burden of these daily trivialities Creighton strove to retain his settled vision of the church's purpose, his keen intelligence, his confidence in the capacities of human nature guided by Christian faith, his trust in common sense (his own and other people's), his sense of humour, and his service to a Lord who bade his followers to love one another. After earlier discomfort at the end of 1899, ulcers put him to bed in September 1900 for prolonged rest. Confined to Fulham Palace, he still conducted some diocesan business. Notably he brought together under his own roof those who held opposing views about the celebration of holy communion so that they might understand each other's positions. By Christmas he had undergone a second operation, and he died on 14 January 1901 at his palace, eight days before the death of Queen Victoria, when his wife had been writing to her sister of her hopes for his recovery. He was buried in St Paul's Cathedral on 17 January.

The memorial to Creighton in St Paul's carries two inscriptions: 'He tried to write true history', his own choice; and 'I determined to know nothing among you save Jesus Christ', which his widow also used on the title-page of her memoir. Creighton's reputation as a bishop was soon obscured by his more enduring reputation as a historian. Yet the mind of the churchman had fruitfully informed his historical work throughout his life.

Creighton as historian Creighton was a great figure of the late-Victorian Church of England—when he went to London not a few thought that he was due to succeed Benson at Canterbury; but he is remembered as a historian. Fashion no longer gives pride of place to the subjects which interested Creighton; yet because his concern was with the discipline as much as with the content of his work, and because he avoided the advocacy of causes, his work as a historian has continued to be respected. Opinion about the quality of his contribution to historical studies therefore has not altered much since his death. His great Catholic contemporary, Lord Acton, attributed Creighton's detachment as a commentator to his 'serene curiosity'; and he criticized him for evoking the ephemeral personalities of fifteenth-century popes at the cost of appreciating the tradition of the institution. He looked for much more explicit censure on the Renaissance popes. Creighton's moral conviction was no less certain, but as historian he refused to stray far from contemporary sources and aimed for clear-sighted analysis of complicated issues, reducing them to connections which a general reader could follow. Lytton Strachey found the result a dry biscuit, but Canon Jenkins noted the 'zest and vigour' with which Creighton painted pictures of men and events in their contemporary setting. His repeated holidays abroad familiarized him with many of those places. His historical output was the result of a clear intellect and an artistic imagination, but his standards and methods were honed

by his ability to read the work of the leading German historians of his time. He translated into English a volume of Ranke, and at Cambridge he introduced what Mrs Creighton demurely calls 'conversation classes'—seminars on the German model—as a regular part of his teaching.

In 1893–4 Creighton delivered the Hulsean lectures on 'Persecution and tolerance' and in 1895, also in Cambridge, the Rede lecture on 'The early Renaissance in England'. A year later in Oxford he gave the Romanes lecture on 'The English national character'. In November 1896 he accepted the invitation to write an introductory chapter for the projected Cambridge Modern History; but two years later he had to admit that the church's business left him no time for it. The five volumes of the *History of the Papacy* are certainly his chief contribution, a work which stands up to critical scrutiny for its judgements, selection, and compression; but he was equally concerned with the impact of the Reformation in England. While far from confined to ecclesiastical questions, his successive studies of Wolsey (1888) and the reign of Elizabeth I (1896)—a period which he noted as barely suitable for undergraduate study because everything in England was then undergoing such rapid change—are limpid interpretations of those times, and influenced the understanding and curiosity of the generation which followed him. As well as editing the *English Historical Review* for its first five years, he edited two series of historical outlines. By intention none of this historical production was beyond the range of the educated general reader. Outstanding as his abilities were, Creighton never lost sight of ordinary men and women.

C. M. D. CROWDER

Sources L. von Glehn Creighton, *Life and letters of Mandell Creighton*, 2 vols. (1904) · DNB · QR, 193 (1901), 584–622 · W. G. Fallows, *Mandell Creighton and the English church* (1964) · C. Jenkins, 'Bishop Creighton's view of history', *Church Quarterly Review*, 109 (1930), 193–238 · G. Carnell, 'Mandell Creighton, bishop, 1891–1897', *The bishops of Peterborough, 1541–1991* (1993) · O. Chadwick, *Creighton on Luther: an inaugural lecture* (1959) · D. L. Edwards, 'Creighton and Davidson', *Leaders of the Church of England, 1828–1944* (1971) · J. T. Covert, 'Mandell Creighton and English education', diss., University of Oregon, 1967 · E. A. Knox, *Reminiscences of an octogenarian* (1934) · M. C. Burson, 'Historical judgement and the Victorian churchman: a study in the historical thought and outlook of Mandell Creighton', MA diss., Graduate Theological Union, Berkeley, California, 1971 · E. W. Gosse, 'Mandell Creighton', *Portraits and sketches* (1912) · L. Strachey, 'Six English historians: Hume, Gibbon, Macaulay, Carlyle, Froude, Creighton', in L. Strachey, *Portraits in miniature, and other essays* (1931), 139–218 · *Memoir of a Victorian woman: reflections of Louise Creighton, 1850–1936*, ed. J. T. Covert (1994) · [J. R. L. Highfield], 'Merton in the nineteenth century', in G. H. Martin and J. R. L. Highfield, *A history of Merton College, Oxford* (1997), 279–324

Archives GL, bishop's act book, MS 9532A/10, 11 · LPL, corresp. and papers as bishop of London | Borth. Inst., corresp. with second Viscount Halifax · CUL, letters from first Lord Acton; letters to Lord Acton · GL, episcopal visitations, 1900, MS 9539/24 · JRL, letters to E. A. Freeman · LPL, records of bishops' meetings, MS BM4 · LPL, Louise Creighton, collection of her letters, MS 3677 · LPL, corresp. with Edward Benson · Merton Oxf., register 1.5 · Merton Oxf., Wagner's album · NL Ire., corresp. with Alice Stopford Green

Likenesses H. H. Brown, oils, exh. RA 1896, Emmanuel College, Cambridge · H. H. Brown, portrait, 1896, Peterborough Cathedral Palace, Peterborough · H. von Herkomer, enamel on metal, 1896,

Merton Oxf. • H. von Herkomer, oils, 1902, Fulham Palace; version, NPG • W. H. Thornycroft, bronze statue on monument, exh. RA 1906, St Paul's Cathedral, London • W. & D. Downey, woodbury-type photograph, NPG; repro. in W. Downey and D. Downey, *Cabinet portrait gallery*, 4 (1893) [*see illus.*] • F. T. D. [F. T. Dalton], watercolour study, NPG; repro. in *VF* (22 April 1897) • W. H. Thornycroft, bronze bust, LPL • photograph, NPG • photographs, repro. in Creighton, *Life and letters*

Wealth at death £30,741: resworn probate, July 1901, *CGPLA Eng. & Wales*

Creighton [Creyghton], **Robert** (1593–1672), bishop of Bath and Wells, was born at Dunkeld, Perthshire, son of Thomas Creighton and Margaret Stuart, who claimed kinship with the earls of Atholl, and therefore with the royal house. In 1614 he was elected from Westminster School to Trinity College, Cambridge, graduating BA in 1618 and becoming a fellow in 1619. He proceeded MA in 1621, and on 27 February 1622 was one of the opponents in a philosophical disputation held before the Spanish ambassador, Don Carlos Coloma, and other noble visitors. His earliest publication was a contribution to the Cambridge collection of verses at the death of James I. In 1625 he was made regius professor of Greek, and on 27 February 1627 he succeeded his friend George Herbert as public orator of the university, holding both these offices until his resignation of them in 1639. On 15 July 1628 he was incorporated MA at Oxford.

On 18 March 1632 Creighton was installed prebendary in the cathedral of Lincoln, and on 17 December of the following year he was made canon residentiary and treasurer of Wells, to which he was appointed by Archbishop Abbot during the vacancy of the see. He added the archdeaconry of Stowe and the rectory of Huggate, Yorkshire, in 1641, and the following year the deanery (or rectory) of St Buryan in Cornwall, and the vicarage of Greenwich. About 1638 he married Frances (1615–1683), daughter of William Walrond of Ile Brewers; they had three sons, Robert *Creighton (1636/7–1734), Thomas (d. 1674), and George (d. 1685), and a daughter, Katherine, who married Francis, son of John, first Baron Poulett of Hinton St George.

At the outbreak of the civil war Creighton appears to have remained in Wells, but an entry by him in the steward's book referring to the completion of a transaction in August 1642 'whilst I was prisoner in Bristoll' (Bailey, ix, n. 3) suggests that at an early stage he was in trouble on account of his royalist sympathies. He was present on 28 January 1645 at the last recorded meeting of the Wells chapter before the residentiaries were compelled to leave. He then retired to Oxford, where he had been made DD in 1643, and acted as the king's chaplain, holding the same office under Charles II. On the fall of Oxford he escaped into Cornwall disguised as a labourer and embarked for the continent.

Creighton was a member of the court of Charles II in his exile, and Evelyn heard him preach at St Germain on 12 September 1649. From 1653 to 1655 he was at Utrecht, acting as tutor to Sir Ralph Verney's son Edmund (*Verney MSS*). It was there, together with Michael Honywood, that Creighton ministered to an Anglican congregation and

Robert Creighton (1593–1672), by unknown artist, *c.*1670–72

defended both the Laudian tradition and the royalist cause. The exiled clergy who sought refuge in France and the Low Countries frequently moved around but maintained contact with each other and church leaders in England. But they faced attacks from two sides: the presbyterian claim that after the Westminster assembly it was now the legitimate church in England and the persistent attempts by Roman Catholics to win converts. Creighton, while acting as chaplain to the king at The Hague, 'preached very liberally before him against the presbyterians, and the murderers of King Ch. I' (Wood, 1.444). He shared the conviction of many against what they termed 'the cursed Genevan tyranny'. His anti-presbyterianism is evident in *Akolouthos, or, A Second Faire Warning to Take Heed of the Scotish Discipline* (1651), which brought together tracts produced in exile by John Bramhall, bishop of Derry, and Richard Watson, and to which is prefixed his introductory letter. Together with George Morley, later bishop of Worcester, Creighton also engaged the Jesuit Father Darcy in a debate at Brussels before a group of nobility on the differences between the two churches, maintaining that the Church of England was catholic in continuing the apostolic faith, ministry, and sacraments. For his loyalty the king is said to have appointed him dean of Wells during the exile.

On 18 July 1660 Creighton was instituted as dean of Wells but he discovered that the deanery was still claimed by the puritan divine Cornelius Burgess, who had purchased it with part of the episcopal estates and who, since

1650, had been preacher at the cathedral. Creighton was compelled to bring an action of ejectment; when the case came to trial, Burgess lost his claim. In 1664 Creighton received the benefice of Uplowman, in Devon, and the following year the chapter presented him to the living of Cheddar. As dean he was instrumental, in 1667, in securing the pre-election of his son Robert (who already held a prebend) to the next vacant canon residentiary, thereby later securing for him a better position and greater authority. Creighton took an active part in repairing the damage done to the cathedral during the Commonwealth, presenting the church with an impressive brass lectern and Bible and having installed a painted window at the west end (in which he is depicted as bishop) at a cost of £400.

Creighton preached often before the king and before the House of Commons, and Evelyn, who gives several notices of his sermons, pronounced him 'most eloquent' (*Diary of John Evelyn*, 1.364). Pepys, who also admired his preaching, nevertheless called him 'the most Comical man that ever I heard in my life—just such a man as Hugh Peters', and gave a description of a very plain-spoken sermon he heard from 'the great Scoch man' on 7 March 1662 on the subject of the neglect of 'the poor cavalier' (Pepys, 1.42). He also recorded, on 3 April 1663, 'a most admirable, good, learned, and most severe sermon, yet comicall', in which Creighton 'railed bitterly ever and anon against John Calvin and his brood, the Presbyterians' (ibid., 4.92–3). Creighton was a forthright man, full of originality and vigour, and in July 1667 preached 'a strange bold sermon' before the king

> against the sins of the Court, and perticularly against adultery … and of our negligence in having our castles without ammunition and powder when the Dutch come upon us; and how we have no courage nowadays, but let our ships be taken out of our Harbour. (ibid., 8.362–3)

His sermons against the vices of the times were, according to Wood, 'well taken by some tho' sneared at by others', but his boldness and 'comical' manner in the pulpit seem, unfortunately, to have turned at times to an aggressive testiness in his relations with the Wells chapter and certain of its members.

There is general testimony to Creighton's scholarship as an 'admirable Grecian', and the quality of his Latin was remarked upon by contemporaries. He published *Vera historia unionis non verae inter Graecos et Latinos, sive, Concilii Florentini exactissima narratio*, a translation into Latin from the Greek of Sylvester Sgouropoulos with a long preface (The Hague, 1660); this was answered by the Jesuit Leo Allacci in *In R. Creyghtoni apparatum, versionem et notas* (1665), and to this Creighton is supposed to have made a reply. Wood also mentions some published sermons.

In 1663 Creighton took the oaths for his naturalization. On the supposed death of Bishop William Peirs in 1668 the warrant to begin his election as bishop of Bath and Wells was issued, but the actual death did not occur until 1670. Creighton was elected on 25 May 1670 and consecrated the next month (19 June) at Lambeth. He died at Wells on 21 November 1672 and was buried in the chapel of St John the Evangelist in his cathedral. His marble tomb and effigy had been prepared by himself at great expense.

JOHN S. MACAULEY

Sources D. S. Bailey, ed., *Wells Cathedral Chapter Act Book, 1666–83* (1973) · Venn, *Alum. Cant.* · Wood, *Ath. Oxon.: Fasti*, new edn · Foster, *Alum. Oxon.* · *Walker rev.* · *Fasti Angl., 1541–1857*, [Bath and Wells] · Pepys, *Diary*, vols. 1, 4, 8 · *The diary of John Evelyn*, ed. W. Bray, new edn, 2 vols. (1907); rev. edn (1952) · Seventh report, HMC, 6 (1879) · *Calendar of the manuscripts of the dean and chapter of Wells*, 1, HMC, 12 (1907) · R. S. Bosher, *The making of the Restoration settlement: the influence of the Laudians, 1649–1662* (1951) · CSP dom., 1661–71

Archives CUL, letters and speeches as public orator, Add. MSS 3126, 4021 | Claydon House, Buckinghamshire, Verney MSS

Likenesses oils, *c.*1670–1672, Wells town hall [*see illus.*] · copy of oil painting at Wells town hall, bishop's palace, Wells · enamel on painted glass, great west window, Wells Cathedral · marble monument and effigy (designed by Creighton), Wells Cathedral, chapel of St John the Evangelist

Creighton [Creyghton], **Robert** (1636/7–1734), Church of England clergyman and composer, was the son of Robert *Creighton (or Creyghton) (1593–1672) and his wife, Frances Walrond (1615–1683). The elder Creighton was professor of Greek at Cambridge from 1625 to 1639; after exile with the court of Charles II he became dean of Wells at the Restoration in 1660 and finally bishop of Bath and Wells in 1670; like his son he was an amateur musician and was probably responsible for compiling the vocal and keyboard music now in Paris (Bibliothèque Nationale, Conservatoire MS Rés. 1186), some of whose contents are signed 'R. Cr.'.

Like his father the younger Creighton was elected from Westminster School to Trinity College, Cambridge, where he was admitted pensioner on 23 May 1655 and matriculated at Easter 1656, graduating BA in 1659, the same year that he became a fellow of the college; he proceeded MA in 1662. He was professor of Greek at Cambridge from 1666 to 1672. From 1662 he was a prebendary of Wells Cathedral, holding successively the prebends of Timberscombe (from 1662) and Yatton (from 1667 until his death), becoming canon residentiary in 1667 and precentor on 2 May 1674. He became rector of Uplowman, Devon, in 1670 and held the living of Ashbrittle, Somerset, from 1670 until his death. He was one of the king's chaplains-in-ordinary and was created DD at Cambridge in 1678. In 1682 he published a sermon on *The Vanity of the Dissenters' Plea for their Separation from the Church of England*, preached before the king at Windsor. In 1719 he presented an organ to the parish of Southover, near Wells, and on two occasions gave money to almshouses in the same parish.

Creighton's wife is named as Frideswide in 1685 when she was recompensed (on 7 October) for money paid out under threat from men of Monmouth's rebellion that summer. There were at least a son and daughter of the marriage. Creighton died at Wells on 17 February 1734, aged ninety-seven, and was buried at the cathedral there five days later. A son Robert (1673/4–1732) and, in turn, his son Robert (1704/5–1755), also held prebends in the diocese.

Creighton was well placed to indulge his talents as a

church composer at Wells. In all it seems as if he may have written nine, or even eleven, services, though only six now survive. Similarly eleven anthems are known, though only five survive. As a composer of church music he was not markedly inferior to many of his professional contemporaries, or, indeed, his fellow churchman Henry Aldrich, dean of Christ Church, Oxford, whose musical accomplishments are more renowned. Creighton's service in E♭ was widely performed in cathedrals during the eighteenth and nineteenth centuries, and was printed in E. F. Rimbault's *Cathedral Music* (1847); one in B♭ was printed in F. A. Ouseley's *Cathedral Services* (1853). The anthem 'I will arise', a canon 'three in one', has also been highly praised. Sources of his music are in the British Library (Harley MSS 7338–7339), the Royal College of Music, London (MS 673), and the Bodleian Library, Oxford (MSS Tenbury 793 and 795–796). Also in the British Library is an autograph manuscript (Add. MS 37074) dating from 1727, containing instrumental and vocal music signed 'R. C.'. These seem mostly to be in the nature of composition exercises and do not create such a favourable impression as his church music. IAN SPINK

Sources *Fasti Angl., 1541–1857,* [Bath and Wells] · *Calendar of the manuscripts of the dean and chapter of Wells,* 2, HMC, 12 (1914) · Venn, *Alum. Cant.* · *Old Westminsters,* 1.230–31

Cremer, John [nicknamed Rambling Jack] (**1700–1774**), merchant navy officer and author, was born in East Lane, Rotherhithe, Bermondsey, the third of five children of Edmund Cremer (d. 1707/8) and his wife, Elizabeth, née Cantor (d. 1715). Almost all that is known about Cremer's life comes from memoirs which his great-great-grandson, Richard Reynall Bellamy, edited and published in 1936. Even his memorial, which used to stand outside the church of Charles the Martyr in Plymouth, was destroyed by enemy action in 1941. The memoirs, however, in spite of or possibly because of the idiosyncratic language in which they are written, give a unique picture of life at sea in the early eighteenth century. They are the living yarns of a gifted story-teller.

John Cremer's father, Edmund, was a captain in the merchant service of whom John saw little and who died when John was only seven. His widowed mother could not cope with a wild and difficult child who even killed a parrot because it told him to go to school. So John was sent to sea under the care of his uncle, Lieutenant Peter Franklin, in the *Dover* (48 guns). While his uncle was away, pressing seamen for the ship, John was left under the charge of a servant, and he suffered a weekly flogging at the gun for the past week's 'crimes'. Things did improve and he was put in a 'class' with four other boys including the captain's son who led them into all kinds of mischief.

It was the time of the War of Spanish Succession, and the *Dover* was involved in convoy duty. This included a running battle with a Spanish privateer, involving heavy losses on both sides. The *Dover* later ran ashore and nearly became a total loss. By the age of nine John Cremer had already encountered much death and destruction. When peace came in 1713 there were few openings in the Royal Navy and the rest of his seafaring career was spent in merchant vessels. However, on more than one occasion he narrowly avoided being pressed into the king's service.

Although in many respects wild and irresponsible, Cremer was also wedded to the sea life and often proved himself an excellent seaman. When it came to the well-being of a ship or its crew he was utterly dedicated and reliable. Authority, however, was respected only in so far as he considered it to be deserved.

Cremer's nickname 'Rambling Jack' was most appropriate. His two brief shore jobs as a youth were first an apprenticeship to a carpenter, from which he was dismissed when he insulted a maid, and then to a wine merchant in whose service he got helplessly drunk (his uncle consequently sent him back to sea). He served a somewhat turbulent apprenticeship in various merchant ships in the Mediterranean and across the Atlantic. In one the captain deliberately smashed his sextant believing that Cremer had ambitions beyond his station.

Cremer achieved his first position as an officer as the gunner of the *Samuel* and he then became second mate of the *Goodfellow*. He served as the second in a duel at Leghorn and spent a time in prison. Also at Leghorn he quarrelled with two British army officers over a girl in a Spanish bawdy house and was nearly killed. On another occasion he was allowed to pay his respects to James Francis Edward Stuart (the Old Pretender) and his wife, Princess Clementina. At the same time he worked hard to improve his professional knowledge, even of aspects such as book-keeping, essential if he was to achieve his ambition of commanding his own ship.

Cremer's memoirs end in 1727, just before he became master of the *Galley Amsterdam*. In that year he wrote a will leaving everything to Rose Hayes of Plymouth and a year later he married her. Little is known of the rest of his life. He had a son, Peter Franklyn Cremer (b. 1732), named after the uncle who had supported him over so many years. His wife died in 1752, and two years later he married Grace Bath of Helstone in Cornwall. They had two boys and two girls. John Cremer died on 19 March 1774, aged seventy-three, and was buried at the church of Charles the Martyr in Plymouth. HENRY BAYNHAM

Sources *Ramblin' Jack: the journal of Captain John Cremer, 1700–1774,* ed. R. R. Bellamy (1936)

Cremer, Robert Wyndham Ketton- (**1906–1969**), biographer and county historian, was the elder son of a Norfolk squire, Wyndham Ketton-Cremer (1870–1933) of Beeston, and his wife, Emily (1882–1952), daughter of Robert Bayly, timber merchant. Born on 2 May 1906, at his mother's family home in Plymouth, he lived always near Cromer where his father's land adjoined that of an eccentric bachelor great-uncle, Robert Ketton of Felbrigg Hall. At Harrow School and at Balliol College, Oxford, where he was an exhibitioner from 1924, bouts of rheumatic fever permanently impaired his health. For that reason, after obtaining a second-class degree in English in 1928, he decided to live at home, write books, and help his father to nurse the Felbrigg estate back to life. Robert Ketton had made that property over to the boy's father early in 1924 before flitting suddenly to Kent, on condition that the family should change its name to Ketton-Cremer.

The family moved with deep misgiving into Felbrigg. The lovely seventeenth-century house had been left, like everything else, in a state of such appalling neglect that restoration could only be an arduous work of many years. It was promptly transformed, nevertheless, into a scene of happiness and hospitality, and when young Ketton-Cremer inherited it on his father's death in 1933 his first book had been well received. It was entitled *The Early Life and Diaries of William Windham* (1930), a remote collateral predecessor, who had been Pitt's secretary at war and a friend of Burke and Johnson. His literary output branched thereafter into the two channels of full-scale biography and local history.

Ketton-Cremer published two major biographies, *Horace Walpole* (1940) and *Thomas Gray* (1955). The latter book won the James Tait Black memorial prize and the Heinemann Foundation award. He felt an affinity with both subjects because, like himself, they never married and came to terms with the fact that they were natural celibates. He did not live to write a projected biography of Matthew Prior, but his contribution to the history of Norfolk is unlikely ever to be surpassed. It consists partly of five volumes of collected essays (1944–61), descriptive of personalities and events, and composed in an urbane style of polished but pungent lucidity. It consists also of a long work entitled *Norfolk in the Civil War* (1969) and *Felbrigg: the Story of a House* (1962), which he alone could have written, and which is much the most personal and revealing of his books. He was his own land agent and, with Donovan Purcell, restored the house. In 1941 he approached the National Trust about it and on his death the house and its policies were bequeathed to the trust.

Ketton-Cremer's sense of duty matched his sense of history. His public role as a prominent landowner and man of letters was conducted against a background of many unrecorded kindly offices. His more conspicuous activity included service as a major in the Home Guard (1941–5), as chairman of his magistrates' bench (1948–66), and as high sheriff (1951–2), in which capacity he was required to witness two hangings. He was a trustee of the National Portrait Gallery, and he combined chairmanship of the Norwich Diocesan Council for the Care of Churches with membership of the regional committee of the National Trust. A fellow of the British Academy (1968), and a governor of Gresham's School, Holt, Norfolk, he helped to promote the University of East Anglia which conferred on him an honorary degree (1969). He derived much pleasure from his election as a fellow-commoner of Christ's College, Cambridge (1966), and gave the Rede lecture at Cambridge (1957) on Matthew Prior, the Warton lecture for the British Academy (1959) on lapidary verse, and the Lamont memorial lecture at Yale (1960) on Gray as a letter writer.

Ketton-Cremer's gentleness and modesty earned a rare measure of affection and respect. He was a practising Christian and devout churchman, sustained by an unshakeable Anglican religious faith which he did not ask his friends to share. He kept a wide range of friendships in repair on both sides of the Atlantic, and took a warm personal interest in the individual welfare of everyone who worked or lived on his estate. Loving the fine arts, and fascinated by antiquarian studies, he possessed knowledge and instant command of illuminating detail that were extraordinary. But his most absorbing passion was forestry, and he planted on a substantial scale. His appearance, personality, and library all strongly suggested the eighteenth century, in which he would have been thoroughly at home.

The most bitter sorrow of Ketton-Cremer's life was the death on active service in Crete in 1941 of his younger brother, Dick, while serving in the Royal Air Force. Despite differences in tastes and temperaments they exhibited the same serenity and charm and were completely in accord. When their mother died in 1952 Ketton-Cremer became the last survivor of a family circle which had always been exiguous. Although faithfully served, he experienced increasing frustration as his health, which worried his friends more than it did him, visibly deteriorated. On 12 December 1969 he died peacefully in hospital in Norwich.   PHILIP MAGNUS, *rev.* H. C. G. MATTHEW

Sources M. Lascelles, 'Robert Wyndham Ketton-Cremer, 1906–1969', *PBA*, 56 (1970), 403–6 · J. Madison, *Felbrigg Hall* (1995) · B. Ford, 'Staying at Felbrigg Hall as a guest of Wyndham Ketton-Cremer', *National Trust Year Book* (1977–8), 52–62 · R. W. Ketton-Cremer, *Felbrigg: the story of a house* (1962) · personal knowledge (1981)

Archives Herts. ALS · Norfolk RO, antiquarian corresp. and papers | CUL, corresp. with Sir Samuel Hoare · Norfolk RO, letters to Bryan Burstall · Norfolk RO, letters to Gilbert Thurlow

Likenesses A. Gwynne-Jones, portrait (unfinished), Felbrigg Hall, Norfolk

Wealth at death £891,236: probate, 23 Nov 1970, *CGPLA Eng. & Wales*

Cremer, Sir William Randal (1828–1908), peace campaigner, born on 18 March 1828 at Fareham, Hampshire, was the son of George Cremer, a coach-painter, and his wife, Harriet Tutte, daughter of a local builder. Deserted by her husband, Cremer's mother, a devout Methodist, brought up William in great poverty.

At the age of twelve Cremer began work as a pitchboy in a shipyard. Three years later he was apprenticed to a carpenter. In 1846 he moved to Brighton, where he came under the influence of Frederick Robertson at his Workmen's Institute. In 1852 Cremer moved to London as a carpenter and became involved in politics and trade unionism. A good speaker, he campaigned for the nine-hour day as representative of the building trades committee in 1858, and he led the lock-out of 70,000 men in 1859–60. Out of this dispute Cremer helped found both the Amalgamated Society of Carpenters and Joiners, on 4 June 1860, and the London Trades Council. In that year he married Charlotte (*d.* August 1876), daughter of J. Wilson of Spalding.

Cremer was secretary to the workmen's committee formed to support the north in the American Civil War, and organized the 1863 meeting in St James's Hall, addressed by John Bright, which attacked the British government's role in the *Alabama* affair. He was appointed the first secretary of the British section of the International Working Men's Association (IWMA) in September 1864 and was a delegate to its 1865 Geneva conference. Although he supported the general council on the questions of unionism, strikes, and the eight-hour day and in its opposition to the Proudhonists, Cremer also opposed any revolutionary activity and Marx effected his removal from the secretaryship. Cremer left the organization, though in 1869 he urged the delegates at the second Trades Union Congress to affiliate with it and the same year joined the IWMA-dominated Land and Labour League.

Cremer was a supporter of Mazzini and helped to organize the 1863 demonstrations in support of Garibaldi; he also addressed a meeting in London in July 1863 in support of Polish nationalism and in 1870 formed a committee of working men to press for British neutrality during the Franco-Prussian War. This committee became the Workmen's Peace Association in 1871 (later the International Arbitration League). Cremer was its secretary until his death, and he travelled on its behalf repeatedly to America and the continent, bearing petitions and appeals for international arbitration, and becoming a well-known international figure as a consequence. He was also on the executive of John Stuart Mill's Land Tenure Reform Association in 1873 and in 1889 became British secretary to the Inter-Parliamentary Union. For his tireless service in the cause of international arbitration (especially the 1897 Anglo-American arbitration treaty) he was awarded the Nobel peace prize in 1903 and gave £7000 of the prize money in trust to the International Arbitration League. For his work in the cause of peace he also received the French cross of the Légion d'honneur, was made commander of the Norwegian order of St Olaf in 1904, and was knighted in 1907.

A political radical, Cremer was a member of the Reform League from its inception in 1864, though also supportive of the National Reform Union and the reform bills of 1866–7, and as an executive committee member of the league he was a moving force behind the 1866 Hyde Park demonstrations. In 1868 he accepted an invitation to stand as radical parliamentary candidate for Warwick. He was defeated by the Liberal candidate, but received only 260 votes and lost there again as representative of the Labour Representation League in 1874, when he won only 183 votes. Twice he failed in his candidature for the London school board, in 1870 and 1873; but in 1884 he was elected to the St Pancras vestry. Under the widened parliamentary franchise Cremer was elected MP for the working-class Haggerston division of Shoreditch in 1885. He retained his seat in 1886 and 1892, but was defeated in 1895 by thirty-two votes. He recovered the seat in 1900 despite his unpopular hostility to the Second South African War, and kept it until his death. He vigorously opposed the rise of the independent labour movement and remained within the Liberal Party. Cremer was never endorsed by the Trades Union Congress or the Labour Representation

Committee and let his membership of the carpenters' union lapse after it affiliated to the Labour Party. However, he continued to campaign on labour issues in parliament.

Following the death in August 1884 of his second wife, Lucy Coombes of Oxford, Cremer lived in his office at 11 Lincoln's Inn Fields. He died at 59 Weymouth Street, London, on 22 July 1908, and was buried in Hampstead cemetery after cremation. He had no children. Cremer's autobiography remained in manuscript note form and his literary work was confined to the pages of *The Arbitrator*, a monthly peace journal which he edited from its appearance in 1889.   MATTHEW LEE

Sources H. Evans, *Sir Randal Cremer: his life and work* (1911) · *The Times* (23 July 1908) · *DLB* · B. A. Cook, 'Cremer, William Randal', *BDMBR*, vol. 3, pt 1 · C. Hirschfield, 'Cremer, William Randal', *Biographical dictionary of modern peace leaders* (1985), 181–3 · H. Collins and C. Abramsky, *Karl Marx and the British labour movement* (1965) · H. L. Malchow, *Agitators and promoters in the age of Gladstone and Disraeli: a biographical dictionary* (1983), 54 · E. W. Sagar, 'The working-class peace movement in Victorian Britain', *Histoire Sociale/Social History*, 12 (1979), 122–44 · *DNB*

Archives HLRO, letters to Herbert Samuel · Mondcivitan Republic, 27 Delancey Street, London, International Arbitration League MSS · United Nations Library, Geneva, International Peace Bureau archives

Likenesses B. Stone, photograph, 1904, NPG · P. R. Montford, bronze bust, exh. RA 1911, Palace of Westminster, London · P. R. Montford, bust, possibly Palace of Peace, The Hague

Wealth at death £2241 4s. 1d.: probate, 16 Oct 1908, *CGPLA Eng. & Wales*

Crespin, Paul Daniel (1693/4–1770), goldsmith, was born in London, the son of the Huguenot Daniel Crespin of St Giles-in-the-Fields, Westminster. In June 1713, at the late age of nineteen, Paul Crespin was apprenticed to Jean Pons, goldsmith. Between July 1720 and December 1721 he entered his first two marks at Goldsmiths' Hall as a freeman of the Longbowstringmakers' Company. He was working in Compton Street, Soho, London, at the sign of the Golden Ball. In the 1720s Crespin married Margaret (Mary) Branboeuf; by 1743 they had five children.

Crespin's mature apprenticeship explains the high quality of his earliest work. A 1721 cruet set (Colonial Williamsburg, Virginia) reveals his mastery of the different goldsmiths' skills. The octagonal cruets have pierced covers; their sides are chased with flowers, fruit, and birds; their handles are formed of cast figures of harpies. The stand has a finely chased border.

In 1724 Crespin received an order for a silver bath for King João V of Portugal. This important commission may have come through his younger brother, who was royal goldsmith in Lisbon. A contemporary described the full-size bath as supported on three dolphins, their tails curling up around the outside surface, while inside three mermaids' bodies followed the curve of the tub. The two sides were decorated with scenes of Diana bathing and Perseus and Andromeda. Weighing 6030 ounces, the bath was shown at Kensington Palace to George I, 'who was well pleased with so curious a Piece of Workmanship, which can scarcely be match'd in all Europe' (*Weekly Journal*, July 1724). It was destined for the royal palace, Lisbon, but was destroyed in the 1755 earthquake. An unusually large circular basin of 1722 (BM) may have been associated with this commission and used as a footbath.

In 1726 Crespin contributed to a large service for Empress Catherine I of Russia a silver-gilt cup and cover (Hermitage Museum, St Petersburg). Such important royal commissions attracted noble clients. These included Richard Temple, Viscount Cobham, for whom Crespin made a large sideboard dish with applied profile medallions of classical philosophers (1727). Charles, third duke of Marlborough, commissioned a pair of silver-gilt wine coolers in 1733. Their shape, the faun supporters, and the wave ornament on the base are influenced by contemporary French silver. Crespin's landlord in Soho, the second duke of Portland, ordered large quantities of table silver. A manuscript list of plate supplied by Crespin to Viscount Townsend between 1740 and 1759 illustrates the range of his stock.

Silver centrepieces and tureens provided the most appropriate vehicles for Crespin's mastery of the craft. A tureen and stand made for Charles Seymour, sixth duke of Somerset, in 1740 (Toledo Museum of Art, Ohio) is supported by recumbent figures of hinds and the cover is decorated with grapes, plums, apples, and pears. The design is close to the centrepiece (V&A) made for John, second earl of Ashburnham, by Nicholas *Sprimont (bap. 1715, d. 1771). The elaborate marine silver-gilt centrepiece (1741), bearing Crespin's mark, made for Frederick, prince of Wales, may have been produced in collaboration with Sprimont. The wave ornament, supporting mermen, and presiding figure of Neptune recall the Portuguese royal bath and the Marlborough wine coolers.

The *General Advertiser* declared Crespin's bankruptcy in 1747, the year in which Nicholas Sprimont left the goldsmiths' trade to concentrate on the Chelsea Porcelain Manufactory. Crespin's stock intended for the export market was sold by the auctioneer John Heath. It consisted of gold and silver toys, snuff boxes, étuis, watches, jewels, and rings. Crespin's second son, Elias David, educated at Merchant Taylors' School, London, and Caius College, Cambridge, was ordained and became dean of Guernsey in 1765. His eldest daughter Magdalen (1729–1795) married the Huguenot watchmaker Francis Barraud (1727–1795) of St Andrew's Street, Seven Dials, London.

In the 1760s Paul Crespin retired to Southampton, where he died in 1770. He was survived by his wife, who was dead by April 1775. A portrait of Crespin (c.1730; V&A) descended in the Barraud family. TESSA MURDOCH

Sources T. Murdoch, 'Harpies and hunting scenes: Paul Crespin, 1694–1770, Huguenot goldsmith', *Country Life* (29 Aug 1985), 556–8 · A. Delaforce, 'Paul Crispin's silver-gilt bath for the king of Portugal', *Burlington Magazine* (1997), 38–40 · A. Grimwade, 'Crespin or Sprimont? An unsolved problem of rococo silver', *Apollo*, 90 (1969), 126–8 · A. Grimwade, *London goldsmiths, 1699–1837: their marks and lives* (1976) [3rd rev. edn 1990] · E. M. Barraud, *The story of a family* (1967) · E. A. Jones, 'Paul Crespin, Huguenot goldsmith', *Proceedings of the Huguenot Society*, 16 (1938–41), 1–6 · P. A. S. Phillips, 'Huguenot goldsmiths in England, 1687–1737', 1933, Library of the Worshipful Company of Goldsmiths [typescript] · will, PRO, PROB 11/955, sig. 95 · will of Mary Crespin, PRO, PROB 11/1011, sig. 337

Archives Blenheim Palace · BM, Wilding bequest · Colonial Williamsburg Foundation, Virginia · Hermitage Museum, St Petersburg · Royal Collection · Toledo Museum of Art, Ohio · V&A
Likenesses oils, c.1730, V&A

Cressener, Drue (*bap.* 1642, *d.* 1718), Church of England clergyman, and religious controversialist, was baptized in St James's parish, Bury St Edmunds, on 13 January 1642, the son of Thomas Cressener, a druggist. He entered Christ's College, Cambridge, in March 1658 and migrated to Pembroke College in 1661. He graduated BA in 1662 and MA in 1665 and became a fellow of Pembroke College in 1669. He was ordained in January 1677 and was rector of Waresley in Huntingdonshire from 1677 to 1679. He became proctor of the University of Cambridge in 1678. In 1679 he transferred to the vicarage of Soham in Cambridgeshire, a position he retained until his death. He was made DD in 1680. In 1700 he also became a prebendary of Ely. He and his first wife, Faustina, had one son, Henry (*b.* July 1682). After the death of his first wife, Cressener married Frances Cockain on 11 November 1689; they had four children. A son, Drue, was born in December 1691; two other sons, Thomas (*b.* March 1693) and John (*b.* October 1694), both died in early infancy, and another child was stillborn (buried on 4 June 1690). Cressener died in Soham on 20 February 1718 and Frances died there in September 1747.

Cressener's only two published works were printed in the immediate aftermath of the events of 1688 and 1689. These are among a body of works by English authors such as the congregationalist Thomas Beverley, the Baptist Benjamin Keach, and the Anglican ministers Benjamin Woodroffe, John Butler, and Walter Garett, among others, that presented the fall of James II and the accession of William and Mary as a fulfilment of prophecies in the book of Revelation. The *Judgments of God upon the Roman-Catholick Church* was published in 1689, and Cressener's efforts to confirm that this work had been written before the climactic events began in 1688 demonstrated his belief that his interpretation of apocalyptic scripture found special application in the circumstances of the revolution of 1688. Dedicating this book to William III, Cressener ascribed the role of deliverer of protestantism to the new king, and expected a revived reformation to go out from England to conquer Europe. He anticipated the near approach of the end times, with William's actions fulfilling apocalyptic expectations. Assigning great import to the year 1689, Cressener paid particular attention to the details of Louis XIV's actions against French protestants. His interpretation also connected the growth of suppression of religious dissent and the power of civil magistracy over religious worship with the beginning of apostasy in the Christian church. He stressed the significance of religious liberty and declared that apocalyptic resolution would not be achieved until freedom of conscience was extended to all protestants, advanced by the efforts of William III.

Cressener's second published work was entitled *A Demonstration of the First Principles of the Protestant Application of the Apocalypse* (1690). This time dedicated to Queen Mary, the book continued Cressener's expositions of Revelation and Daniel. He emphasized again the prophetic relevance of the circumstances of protestants in France, although he had to adapt his interpretation somewhat to accommodate the fact that there had not yet been a great resurgence of French protestantism. Also continuing his arguments asserting the necessity of freedom of conscience and his denunciation of the restraint of religious liberty, Cressener criticized the enforcement of erroneous canons and claims of universal jurisdiction by the Church of Rome.

WARREN JOHNSTON

Sources Venn, *Alum. Cant.*, 1/1.417 · will, PRO, PROB 11/563, fol. 32r–v · J. van den Berg, 'Glorious revolution and millennium: the "apocalyptical thoughts" of Drue Cressener', *Church, change and revolution*, ed. J. van den Berg and P. G. Hoftijzer (1991), 130–44 · register, Soham, Cambridgeshire, Cambs. AS [baptisms, marriages, and deaths]
Wealth at death £40 owed to him; later memorandum mentions debts of £50 and £60, and £120 and 30 guineas on behalf of younger son: will, PRO, PROB 11/563, fol. 32r–v

Cressey [Cressy], **John** [Robert] (*d. c.*1450), prior of Boston and theologian, joined the Carmelite order at Boston, Lincolnshire, and was ordained priest on 23 December 1424 in the Carmelite church, York. He completed his studies at Oxford, where he incepted as DTh, and lectured for some years in the Carmelite studium there. In later life he returned to be prior of the Boston convent, and eventually died there, about the middle of the fifteenth century. Bale records two of his writings, a collection of sermons and, based on information derived from John Leland, a work in praise of the Virgin Mary. Nothing further is known of Cressey, and even his first name is uncertain, Leland giving it as Robert, whereas Bale, in an early notebook recording a list of burials at the Carmelite house at Boston, has John.

The Cressey family lived in the Lincolnshire parish of Surfleet, and it has been suggested that John Cressey was related to, or even identical with, another Carmelite theologian, **William Surfleet** (*d.* 1466). But the two men are clearly different individuals, and their names are recorded separately in Bale's list of burials at Boston. Like Cressey, Surfleet joined the Carmelites at Boston. He studied in York, and was ordained priest there on 24 September 1418. He continued his theological studies at Cambridge, and had incepted as DTh there by 1444, when he was elected a diffinitor for the English province at the general chapter at Chalon-sur-Saône. In 1446 he was one of four doctors chosen to represent the York distinction in the meeting called to discuss the reform of the province. In 1453 and 1454 he preached at Tatershall College, Lincolnshire. He died in Boston on 13 November 1466, and was buried in the Carmelite chapel there. Bale attributes two works to him, a book on the vices and virtues and a collection of sermons, but neither is known to survive.

RICHARD COPSEY

Sources J. Bale, Bodl. Oxf., MS Bodley 73 (SC 27635), fol. i v · J. Bale, BL, MS Harley 3838, fol. 208 · J. Bale, BL, MS Harley 1819, fol. 200v · Bale, *Cat.*, 2.97, 99 · *Commentarii de scriptoribus Britannicis, auctore Joanne Lelando*, ed. A. Hall, 2 (1709), 482 · G. Wessels, ed., *Acta*

capitulorum generalium ordinis fratrum B. V. Mariae de Monte Carmelo, 1 (Rome, 1912), 198 · C. de S. E. de Villiers, ed., *Bibliotheca Carmelitana*, 2 vols. (Orléans, 1752), vol. 1, p. 615 · Emden, *Oxf.*, 1.513 · Emden, *Cam.*, 566 · 'Cressy, Robert', *DNB* · Borth. Inst., Reg. 5A, Sede vacante, fol. 393v · Borth. Inst., Reg. 17, Bowet, fol. 401

Cressingham, Hugh of (*d.* 1297), administrator and justice, took his name from Great Cressingham in Norfolk. He was of illegitimate birth, the son of William of Cressingham and a woman named Emma. Many times referred to as a cleric, he must have taken at least minor orders. But his earliest employment appears to have been as a clerk in the courts at Westminster, where he is also recorded as an attorney, acting for the bishop of Norwich in 1273. In 1282 he became the bishop of Ely's steward, and held this office until 1286, when he entered the service of Queen Eleanor, as the steward of her lands, and also as a member of her council. He appears to have retained grateful memories of Queen Eleanor afterwards, for in 1293 he endowed prayers for her soul at Spinney Priory, Cambridgeshire.

Eleanor died on 28 November 1290. Cressingham had already been employed as a commissioner and justice of assize, and now he became increasingly important in the king's government. Early in 1292 he was one of the commissioners appointed to audit the debts still owed to Henry III. Shortly afterwards he became a justice itinerant. Edward I's purge of the judiciary in 1290 had left a shortage of qualified personnel for the eyres which began two years later. In spite of his never having previously acted in this capacity, on 16 April 1292 Cressingham was appointed senior justice for the circuit in the north of England, a post he retained until the Yorkshire eyre was prorogued, never to be resumed, on 12 June 1294. There is no evidence that he and his colleagues were less than competent in their management of proceedings. None the less, Cressingham was never employed as a justice in the Westminster courts, though he might act as the king's spokesman or prosecutor there. Instead he became engaged in raising troops for the suppression of the Welsh revolt of 1294–5, being active in Chester and East Anglia, as well as in Wales, where he was also engaged in military operations.

That Cressingham had already won the king's trust is shown by the presentments to livings, and occasional gifts of venison, with which his services were rewarded from 1291 onwards. Others began to regard him as a man worth cultivating. The abbot of Peterborough gave him an annual pension of 66s. 8d., while in 1294 the archbishop of York granted him 100s. per annum, until a prebend could be found for him. On 1 August 1295 Cressingham was among the justices and councillors summoned to parliament, and on 22 August 1296 he was appointed treasurer of Scotland in the administration established to govern that country after the deposition of King John. For this he was to have an English-style exchequer set up at Berwick, which may account for his having had a collection of English statutes prepared for his own use. The Scots hated him, describing him as the king's treacherer, not treasurer (*non thesaurarium sed traiturarium*) (*Chronicle of Walter of Guisborough*, 303). There can be no doubt that he was heavy-handed, since the English government several times intervened to moderate the pressure he exerted upon Scottish debtors. But he also attracted a particular animus by virtue of his emergence as the effective head of the English administration in occupied Scotland, closely involved in efforts to keep the peace and control rebels and dissidents. By July 1297 he was writing to the king regretting his inability to report good news of the struggle to contain William Wallace, and to his deputy commenting on the failure of their subordinates to raise money. An anonymous letter of 24 July praised Cressingham's efforts, advising King Edward to give him the church of Douglas, since 'he does not grow slack in your service, but takes the greatest pains to make things succeed' (Stevenson, 2.205). But success remained elusive, and during that summer Cressingham found it necessary to raise extra troops in Northumberland.

In the catastrophe that eventually befell the English in 1297, Cressingham played a prominent part. This is heavily emphasized by the chronicler Walter of Guisborough, whose north Yorkshire monastery stood very near to Rudby, of which Cressingham was rector, raising the possibility of personal animosity as well as of firsthand knowledge. The English army, confronting the Scots at Stirling on 11 September, and hampered by the earl of Surrey's weak leadership, was urged to take the initiative by Cressingham, who rejected expert advice to send men round to the enemy rear. He had already dismissed approaching reinforcements in order to save money. In the event it was the Scots who attacked, splitting the English forces as they crossed a narrow bridge over the Forth, and killing nearly all the men who had gone over it. Cressingham himself was one of them, slain, according to Peter Langtoft, when he fell off his horse. After the battle the Scots flayed the treasurer's body and divided the skin into strips. Wallace is said to have made a sword-belt of his portion.

The disaster of his death and the ignominious treatment of his remains have cast a retrospective shadow over the whole of Cressingham's career, deepened by the hostility of Guisborough's account of him, as proud, pompous, smooth, and avaricious, a pluralist who preferred armour to church vestments. There is some truth in these charges, but the chronicler overstates them. Cressingham was certainly a pluralist, holding the prebend of Neasden in St Paul's, London, and at least nine other livings. Probably he was careless about the spiritual welfare of his benefices, since he took the vicar of one of them with him to Scotland. Although a clerk, he seems to have had a daughter, Alice, and perhaps also a son, Hugh. He was guilty of sharp practice at the expense of Queen Eleanor's tenants when he was her steward, and at his death owned a house in London and lands in several counties, as well as a small property in Wales. But pluralism, incontinence, and venality were the typical shortcomings of Edward I's administrators, and there is no evidence that Cressingham's offences were exceptional. His estates were mostly small, and he was hardly a pluralist on a grand scale. A handsome man, though overweight, he maintained a harper, who accompanied him to Scotland. The likelihood is that Cressingham was an energetic and able man, killed on the threshold of what might have been a notable career. HENRY SUMMERSON

Sources PRO, court of common pleas, plea rolls, CP 40/1 A m.10 · PRO, assize rolls, JUST/1/1290 · *Chancery records* · F. Palgrave, ed., *The parliamentary writs and writs of military summons*, 1 (1827), pt 2 · *The chronicle of Walter of Guisborough*, ed. H. Rothwell, CS, 3rd ser., 89 (1957) · CDS, vol. 2 · J. Stevenson, ed., *Documents illustrative of the history of Scotland*, 2 (1870) · RotS, vol. 1 · *The chronicle of Pierre de Langtoft*, ed. T. Wright, 2, Rolls Series, 47 (1868), 298–9 · CIPM, 3, no.405 · E. B. Fryde, ed., *Book of prests of the king's wardrobe for 1294–5* (1962) · RotP, 1.30–31, 85 · W. C. Bolland, ed., *Year books of Edward II, 16: 7 Edward II*, SeldS, 39 (1922), 36–43 · G. O. Sayles, ed., *Select cases in the court of king's bench*, 5, SeldS, 76 (1958), xxxn · *The register of John le Romeyn … 1286–1296*, ed. W. Brown, 2 vols., SurtS, 123, 128 (1913–17) · E. King, *Peterborough Abbey, 1086–1310: a study in the land market* (1973) · E. Miller, *The abbey and bishopric of Ely*, Cambridge Studies in Medieval Life and Thought, new ser., 1 (1951) · J. C. Parsons, *Eleanor of Castile: queen and society in thirteenth-century England* (1995) · J. C. Parsons, ed., *The court and household of Eleanor of Castile in 1290*, Pontifical Institute of Medieval Studies: Texts and Studies, 37 (1977) · 'Communication by Mr Doubleday', *Archaeologia*, 25 (1834), 589–622, esp. 607–9 · F. Watson, *Under the hammer: Edward I and Scotland, 1286–1306* (1998)
Wealth at death see CIPM

Cresswell, Madam (d. c.1698), bawd and brothel keeper, of unknown origins, was made infamous by the slanders and libels of court wits and pamphleteers on account both of her prominence in the vice trade of Restoration London and her whig politics during the exclusion crisis. As a result her image was fixed by tory pamphleteers as a wizened old crone who would stoop to any ruse in order to corrupt the virtue of young countrywomen.

Madam Cresswell probably began her career as a prostitute in London during the 1650s. By the early 1660s she was already well established as the owner of brothels in Camberwell, Clerkenwell, and Moorfields, and was effectively shielded from prosecution through the complicity of those of her clients who sat on the boards of City companies and who filled the offices of local government in the capital. However, her increasing wealth, near monopoly of the vice trade, and immunity from the law rendered her a particular hate figure to the apprentices of London. These youths, unable to marry by the terms of their employments, or to afford the high prices paid for the services of Cresswell and her girls, took out their rage and frustration upon her establishment in Moorfields. During the May day celebrations of 1668, the apprentices broke into the cathouse—scattering the 'Poxed and Painted' whores, ripping up the linen and absconding with a quantity of plate, before tearing down the very fabric of the building (F. O., 8). This incident promoted the publication of a flurry of scurrilous pamphlets, and a bogus petition which had Madam Cresswell and her fellow bawd Damaris Page begging the king's mistress the countess of Castlemaine—on behalf of their 'sisters'—to recoup their losses, out of taxpayers' money, and to form a guard of 'French, Irish and English Hectors' in order to protect the brothels from further violence (*Whores Petition*).

Madam Cresswell
Vne Maquerelle
Vecchia rufiana

52

Madam Cresswell (*d. c.*1698), by Pierce Tempest, pubd 1711 (after Marcellus Laroon the elder)

Unfortunately Cresswell's troubles with the apprentices were not at an end and, on the night of 2 April 1670, a citizen was accosted by an angry mob who vowed that 'on Monday next they would assemble … with swords and lances, and raze the brothel house [where a friend of theirs had been murdered, and] … also one house opposite, occupied by Mrs. Cressell' (*CSP dom., 1670,* 147). Although the deployment of beadles prevented this from happening the remainder of the decade saw Cresswell involving herself far more closely in the politics of the capital. She believed—and actively promoted—Titus Oates's allegations of a popish plot, and enjoyed the friendship and protection of Sir Thomas Player, the whig chamberlain of the City of London. However, although Player was a man of enormous sexual appetites, and certainly frequented her brothels, there is no evidence that the two were ever lovers. Allegedly through her 'spies and emissaries', who kept a lookout for 'rising beauties in different parts of the kingdom', she controlled a valuable network of intelligence and correspondence, which was put to good use for the whig cause during the exclusion crisis.

The price of Cresswell's political activism and strong protestantism was the continual traducing of her name in tory satires and the increasing attempts of the duke of York's supporters to secure her prosecution for vice. Thus she figured in the prologue of Thomas Otway's *Venice Preserv'd*—satiating Player's needs for young flesh—and was mercilessly satirized in the anonymous pamphlets: *A Letter from the Lady Cresswell to Madam C.* [Cellier] *the midwife* (London, 1680) and *The Whore's Rhetorick* (London, 1683). In the former she begs her friend to forsake playing 'at State Politicks and Sham Plots' and to return to the 'honourable calling of prostitution', while in the latter she cynically instructs a young noblewoman to feign 'ejaculations, aspirations, sighs [and] intermissions of words' in order to please her would-be clients (*A Letter,* 2; *Whore's Rhetorick,* 96). She was convicted in 1681 for 'above thirty years' practice of bawdry' and was conceivably fined £300 for prostitution three years later—although this allegation probably refers to Player's failure to honour his bedroom debts (Fraser, 469).

There is nothing, however, to suggest that Cresswell suffered a long-term decline in her fortunes. She continued to run two houses within the City limits and a home in the country, where she spent the summer months and 'provided convenient lodgings for her customers, some of whom were persons of distinction' (Granger, 4.219). As she grew older she sought to protect herself by assuming the outward trappings of respectable society, dressing soberly and attending regular prayer meetings. She died about 1698, or shortly before the turn of the century, and was probably buried in St Bride's churchyard, London. It is alleged that in her will she offered to pay £10 to the Anglican clergyman who delivered her funeral service on the proviso that he would 'say nothing but what was well of her'. After some difficulty a willing preacher was found, who—after delivering an inordinately long sermon on the subject of public morality—concluded with a few brief words about the deceased: 'She was born well, she lived well, and she died well; for she was born with the name of Creswell, she lived in Clerkenwell, and she died in Bridewell' (Granger, 4.219). Recorded in numerous versions there is much that is apocryphal about this tale. In a patriarchal society Madam Cresswell was a rarity. Though she raised herself out of the shackles of poverty through criminality and the exploitation of other women she gained a fortune and played her part in the struggles to bar the duke of York from the throne, achievements which were largely independent of the whims of any man.

JOHN CALLOW

Sources J. Granger, *A biographical history of England, from Egbert the Great to the revolution,* 2nd edn, 4 (1775) · F. O. [F. Ouvry], *Petitions and answers* (privately printed, London, 1870) · *A letter from the Lady Cresswell to Madam C. the midwife* (1680) · *The whores petition to London 'prentices* (1668) · *CSP dom., 1667–8; 1670* · *The complete works of Thomas Otway,* ed. M. Summers, 3 vols. (1926) · K. H. D. Haley, *The first earl of Shaftesbury* (1968) · *The poems of John Dryden,* ed. J. Kinsley, 4 vols. (1958), vol. 4 · N. Thompson, *A collection of one hundred and eighty loyal songs,* 4th edn (1694) · *The whore's rhetorick* (1683) · [J. Garfield?], *The wandring whore,* 5 pts (1660–61) · T. Harris, *London crowds in the reign of Charles II: propaganda and politics from the Restoration until the exclusion crisis* (1987)

Likenesses P. Tempest, line engraving (after M. Laroon the elder), BM; repro. in P. Tempest, *The cryes of the city of London* (1711) [*see illus.*]

Wealth at death owned at least two houses

Cresswell, Sir Cresswell [*formerly* Cresswell Easterby] (1793–1863), judge, was born Cresswell Easterby on 20 August 1793 at Bigg Market, Newcastle, the fourth of five sons born to Francis Easterby (*d.* 1834) of Blackheath, a merchant and sailor, and Frances Dorothea Cresswell (1768–1832), daughter of John Cresswell (1748–1781) of Morpeth, Northumberland. The Cresswell family claimed great antiquity, and traced direct descent from twelfth-century forebears seated in the north of England and mentioned in the annals of the crusades. Frances together with her sister inherited the considerable family fortune, and her husband adopted her family name in 1807. Cresswell, their son, was educated from 1806 to 1810 at Charterhouse School, where he counted Thirlwall, Grote, and Havelock among his schoolfellows. He went on to study at Emmanuel College, Cambridge, having migrated there from Trinity, and was tutored by the future Mr Justice Maule who in later life owned that he could barely remember having taught him. Cresswell's unremarkable academic talents were confirmed by the award of the lowest place in the honours list for the university. During his later career it was often remarked by contemporaries that the award of a 'wooden spoon' at university was no guarantee of lack of ability later in life. He graduated BA in 1814 and MA in 1818. He joined the Inner Temple and was called to the bar in 1819, and became a member of the northern circuit, of which Brougham and Scarlett were the leaders. Brougham especially treated the young barrister with great affection and supplied him with briefs. Cresswell's first successes in the Liverpool courts were in shipping and mercantile law, where the nautical knowledge learned from his father served him in good stead and soon attracted a satisfactory business. From 1822 to 1830 he edited a series of king's bench *Law Reports* with Richard Vaughan Barnewall which bears their name, and is to this day regarded as a model of accuracy and intelligent commentary. After Brougham and Scarlett had left the northern circuit Cresswell and Alexander became the leaders. In 1830 Cresswell was appointed recorder of Hull, in 1834 was made a king's counsel, and from 1834 to 1842 was also solicitor-general for the county palatine of Durham. He was counted at this time a 'violent Tory' in politics, and the Conservative electorate of Liverpool chose him as their member in the general election of 1837. He was returned as member of parliament again in 1841, defeating the whig William Ewart and also Lord Palmerston. He was knighted on 4 May 1842.

In his political behaviour Cresswell was moderate and cautious, always supporting Sir Robert Peel and Peelite policies. He spoke little in the House of Commons, but always plainly and well; his best speech concerned the Danish claims over Schleswig-Holstein. On the retirement of Mr Justice Bosanquet, Sir Robert Peel made Cresswell a puisne judge of the court of common pleas, in a time when political appointments to the bench were common enough. Cresswell quickly established himself as a fair, respected, austere, and efficient justice of common pleas,

a post he held for the next sixteen years. In court he could have an acid tongue, could be cold and supercilious to counsel and witnesses, and disliked rhetoric unsupported with good reasons and precedents. Brusque common sense and technical proficiency mark most of his common bench judgments. He was particularly skilled at mercantile cases at *nisi prius* on circuit, and less impressive in reserved judgments. Cresswell generally avoided taking a lead in the common pleas, deferring to Chief Justice Tindal, one of the strongest lawyers of the age, who effortlessly dominated the court. Cresswell's correct sense of judgment was usually accompanied by a marked caution; Cresswell typically stated limited reasons for decision and thereby gave few hostages for appeal. The result was that he contributed to the fairness and efficiency of the court but made little intellectual contribution to the development of the common law. For example, Cresswell participated in the important nuisance case of *Piggot* v. *Eastern Counties Railway Company* (1846), determining the respective liabilities of farmers and rail companies for social costs caused by locomotives. Cresswell declined the opportunity to analyse the weighty issues of policy discussed by his judicial brethren, and merely concurred with the rest of the court. By contrast in *Smith* v. *Kenrick* (1849), Cresswell wrote an important judgment on the law of nuisance and natural property rights, holding that mine owners working their land could impose damage on each other within reasonable bounds. This decision proved influential throughout the next century and formed a basis for the celebrated doctrine of *Bradford* v. *Pickles* (1895). In *Ackroyd* v. *Smith* (1850), he held that new species of rights and duties unconnected to the enjoyment of land could not be created and annexed to land— another influential theoretical contribution to the modern law of property. Cresswell's judgment in *Sampson* v. *Hoddinott* (1857) was a notable restatement of the natural right theory of riparian use. In *White* v. *Great Western Railway Company* (1857), Cresswell reduced the liability of railway companies, holding that contracts of carriage eliminated their status as common carriers so that consequential economic loss for failure to deliver was irrecoverable at law. There were few other important judgments.

Had Cresswell's career been completed in the common pleas, it would scarcely have commanded attention. But in January 1858, when the probate and divorce court was created, he was appointed the first judge-in-ordinary, presiding over the divorce jurisdiction. It was rumoured that a peerage had been offered to him at that time and declined, but he did become a privy councillor. The new court had been created to replace the ecclesiastical jurisdiction over probate and family law, and was a modernizing measure. Lord Palmerston, the architect of the scheme, had to force the legislation erecting the court through a hostile parliament, with Gladstone leading a strong opposition to the bill on grounds of conscience and religion. The recognition of civil divorce by this new common legal process made dignified divorce available to the poor for the first time. The rich already could divorce by resort to complex annulment and private bill methods, but the new system benefited them too. The private bill process had regularly resulted in both houses of parliament debating the full evidence of individual marriage breakdowns and discussing the parties' merits and demerits before the whole nation; the new procedure guaranteed some privacy and expertise in the adjudication of matrimonial causes. The sensitive nature of the new jurisdiction meant that the quality of initial leadership was crucial. Cresswell was appointed to lead the divorce court by Lord Palmerston with bipartisan support, and despite the occasional doubter who wondered if a confirmed bachelor with an irascible judicial temper could succeed, he performed brilliantly in the job for six years until his death. Lord Campbell, who as chancellor had helped design the divorce jurisdiction and who sat in early hearings of the court, at one stage expressed fears that the court would be a 'Frankenstein' and undermine marriage in England. In the first hearings 300 cases came forward, compared to an average of three applications per year for divorce *a vinculo matrimonii* beforehand. But all fears of deluge and disorder were conquered by Cresswell's creative leadership of the new court. He used juries to decide particularly sensitive issues of cruelty and infidelity. He could be both stern and delicate as the case required. His summing-up was always excellent. He upheld the sanctity of marriage while vindicating the rights of outraged spouses. It was said that he became the most important judicial and political figure of his age, for Cresswell in his court represented five million married women and had a say in the running of two out of every three households in England. The four volumes of reports of divorce court decisions edited by Swabey and Tristam record his work. A review of the precedents cited in any divorce cases of the late nineteenth and twentieth centuries will show how the case reports of Cresswell's pioneering court, especially the first volume (1858–9), laid the procedural and intellectual foundations of the new jurisdiction. In *Hope v. Hope* (1858), and also *Keats v. Keats* (1858), Cresswell followed the great case of *Reg. v. Millis* (1844) to hold that canon-law rules whether concerning marriage or other matters were not part of the common law of England. It followed that mutual adulteries did not cancel out and restitution of conjugal rights to the wife in such a case was not permitted; mutual forgiveness was not condonation; there must be a legal intention to release the wrongdoer, as in release of a debt. This decision helped steer marriage away from notions of sacrament towards a more legalistic contractual model. In *Iredale v. Ford* (1859), it was held that admissions or confessions of a respondent are not evidence against the co-respondent. In *Mette v. Mette* (1859), Cresswell held that naturalized, as well as native, Englishmen cannot marry sisters of deceased wives, inverting the Mosaic law of levirite marriage. In *Tollemache v. Tollemache* (1859), Cresswell ruled that Scots courts cannot dissolve marriages of Englishmen; and in *Brook v. Brook* (1858), it was held by Vice-Chancellor Stuart and Justice Cresswell that in the case of a marriage prohibited by the country of domicile, the law of the country where the ceremony took place cannot confer validity. The judgments in this last decision were especially

sophisticated, scholarly, and clear, making a notable contribution in the difficult area of matrimonial causes in the conflict of laws. The decision was newsworthy enough to be reprinted in a widely circulated pamphlet by Wildy's of Lincoln's Inn. In *Ward v. Ward* (1858), Cresswell held that desertion in law must be without the consent or condonation of the victim. In *Tomkins v. Tomkins* (1858), it was held that legal cruelty as a ground for divorce is generally encompassed by bodily injury, apprehension of such, or injury to health. This clutch of cases demonstrates the profundity of Cresswell's work as the first and greatest family lawyer of his day. He worked enormously hard and disposed of cases at great speed, sitting from November to August and hearing more than one thousand cases over six years, only one of which was reversed on appeal.

Cresswell was tall, slim, pale, and arrogant in bearing, and was known as a martinet in court who could treat counsel with contempt; yet he retained the respect of his peers, largely because of his humane wisdom and occasional flashes of wit. Once in court a witness to a marriage ceremony stated: 'My Lord, I can testify to having seen the marriage duly consummated'; Cresswell replied: 'Sir, it is not usual to require a witness for that purpose.' He would stop the court applauding him when he gave illuminating instructions or speeches from the bench, insisting that the judge was only an agent of justice and was not to receive praises or acclaim. He achieved in family law what Lord Mansfield had done in commercial law in the prior century. On 11 July 1863 Cresswell was riding down Constitution Hill in London when he was knocked down by horses frightened at the breakdown of the carriage they were hauling. His kneecap was broken, and he was taken to St George's Hospital and thence to his home at 21 Prince's Gate, Hyde Park, to recover. He was recovering from his fracture, but the shock of the accident may have contributed to his death from heart failure on 29 July, aged sixty-nine. Being unmarried, he left a large fortune, and was found to be as charitable in his will as he had been in life. He was buried on 5 August at Kensal Green. He may now be counted as one of the most creative legal figures of the high Victorian age. JOSHUA S. GETZLER

Sources E. Walford, *Law Times* (22 Aug 1863), 535–7 · ER, vols. 8, 65, 134–40, 164 · E. Manson, *Builders of our law during the reign of Queen Victoria*, 2nd edn (1904), 124–31 · Foss, *Judges*, 9.184–7 · A. H. M. [A. H. Manchester], 'Cresswell, Sir Cresswell', *Biographical dictionary of the common law*, ed. A. W. B. Simpson (1984) · H. E. Fenn, *Thirty five years in the divorce courts* (1910), 15 · Venn, *Alum. Cant.* · Burke, *Gen. GB* (1914) · *CGPLA Eng. & Wales* (1863) · IGI
Archives Glamorgan RO, Cardiff, opinion on the Criminal Law Consolidation Bill · PRO, notebooks, PROB
Wealth at death under £35,000: will, 1 Sept 1863, *CGPLA Eng. & Wales*

Cresswell, Daniel (1776–1844), Church of England clergyman and mathematician, was the son of Daniel Cresswell, a native of Crowden-le-Booth, in Edale, Derbyshire, who lived for many years at Newton, near Wakefield, Yorkshire. He was born at Wakefield and educated in the grammar school there and at Hull. In 1793 he matriculated at Trinity College, Cambridge, graduating BA in 1797 (seventh wrangler) and MA in 1800. He became a fellow of

Trinity in 1799, and was proctor in 1813 and taxor in 1814. In addition to collegiate and university duties he took private pupils. He was curate of Great St Mary's, Cambridge, from 1817. In December 1822 he was presented to the vicarage of Enfield, one of the most valuable livings in the gift of his college, and in the following year he was appointed a justice of the peace for Middlesex and elected a fellow of the Royal Society. In 1827 he married Anne, daughter of Peter Thompson of Enfield. He died at Enfield on 21 March 1844, his wife surviving him.

Cresswell published *The Elements of Linear Perspective* (1811), a translation of Giuseppe Venturoli's work on the elements of mechanics (1822), and several mathematical works, chiefly geometrical. He also published *Sermons on Domestic Duties* (1829) and other sermons, and a discourse on duty to dumb animals.

THOMPSON COOPER, rev. H. C. G. MATTHEW

Sources J. H. Lupton, *Wakefield worthies* (1864) · GM, 2nd ser., 21 (1844), 655 · Venn, *Alum. Cant.*

Cresswell, (Addison) Joe Baker- (1901–1997), naval officer, was born on 2 February 1901 at 3 Hereford Gardens, Mayfair, London, the younger son in the family of two sons and two daughters of Major Addison Francis Baker-Cresswell (1874–1921), army officer, and his wife Idonea, second daughter of Major Shalcross Fitzherbert Widdrington, of Newton Hall, Northumberland. Baker-Cresswell came from an old Northumbrian landowning family. His father was an officer in the Grenadier Guards and then the 60th rifles. His elder brother, John (b. 1899), a lieutenant in the Royal Navy, was drowned at Portsmouth in 1920 in the execution of his duty. Joe Baker-Cresswell went to Gresham's School before joining the navy in 1919, his first ship, as a midshipman, being the battle cruiser *Tiger*. He then served in the light cruiser *Castor* at Queenstown, at a time of IRA troubles in Ireland, and in the sloop *Veronica*, based in New Zealand. There he met, and on 24 August 1926 married, Rona Eileen Vaile, daughter of H. E. Vaile, of Glade Hall, Epsom, Auckland. They had two daughters, Jocelyn (b. 1928) and Pamela (b. 1931), and a son, Charles (b. 1935).

Baker-Cresswell specialized in navigation in 1927 and was appointed to the minelayer *Adventure* and the battleship *Nelson*, followed by three happy years as navigating officer of the battleship *Rodney*, during which he was twice commended for his skill in piloting that famously unwieldy ship in and out of harbour. He was promoted commander in 1937. At the outbreak of the Second World War he was in Cairo, as the naval member of General Wavell's planning staff, and was involved in missions to Turkey and Greece. He then returned to Britain. His first command, in 1940, was the destroyer *Arrow*. Late in 1940 he was appointed captain of the destroyer *Bulldog*, leading the 3rd escort group, based in Iceland.

On 9 May 1941, the 3rd escort group was in the Atlantic, escorting convoy OB 318, outward bound from Liverpool, when it was attacked by *U-110*—commanded by a notable U-boat 'ace', *Kapitänleutnant* Julius Lemp, whose U-boat sank the liner *Athenia* on the first evening of the war. Lemp sank two merchant ships in the starboard columns of OB 318, but his periscope was sighted by the nearest escort, the corvette *Aubretia*, which gained a firm asdic contact and dropped a pattern of ten depth charges. *Bulldog* and the destroyer *Broadway* were about to join the attack when the U-boat surfaced, with men already pouring out of the conning tower. Having just lost two ships in his convoy, Baker-Cresswell literally 'saw red' for a moment and steered to ram, but then (remembering a staff course lecture on the *Magdeburg*, the capture of whose signal-book by the Russians in 1914 enabled British naval intelligence to decode German signals) collected himself and steered away again. For a moment it seemed that the U-boat sailors were manning their gun, so *Bulldog* opened fire with all weapons down to small arms. The U-boat survivors (Lemp was not among them) were then picked up by *Aubretia* and quickly hustled below decks. They saw, and were told, nothing. Meanwhile, OB 318 steamed onwards and out of sight, thus removing possibly awkward eyewitnesses from the scene.

U-110 was then boarded by a party from *Bulldog*, who methodically stripped the boat of all the equipment they could remove—binoculars, sextants, books, logs, charts, diaries, pictures, tools, and instruments. A telegraphist noted down the tuning positions of all the radio sets in the wireless office. *Bulldog's* whaler had to make several trips, back and forth, loaded with treasures. Baker-Cresswell realized there was a good chance of saving the U-boat and of keeping any information gained from it secret from the Germans. He decided to take *U-110* in tow, but the weather worsened overnight and *U-110* sank the next morning.

Baker-Cresswell was bitterly disappointed to lose his prize, but the cryptanalytical gains from *U-110* were beyond price—far more valuable than the U-boat itself. The experts from Bletchley Park went up to Scapa Flow to meet *Bulldog*, taking with them small briefcases, expecting only a few papers. When they saw two large packing cases, they could hardly believe their eyes. They handled the contents like men in a daze. Here were items they had only dreamed of, including *U-110's* Enigma cipher machine, with the settings for 9 May still on its rotors, the special code settings for high-security *Offizierte* (officer only) traffic, and the current code book for U-boats' short-signal sighting reports.

Baker-Cresswell was awarded the DSO and promoted to captain. At the investiture for his DSO, King George VI told him that the capture of the cipher material was 'the most important single event in the whole war at sea' (*The Guardian*).

After *Bulldog*, Baker-Cresswell joined the joint intelligence staff at Storey's Gate in London, and was then appointed training captain, western approaches, in command of Tom Sopwith's steam yacht *Philante*, working up Atlantic escorts in Lough Larne. Late in 1943 he was appointed chief of staff to the commander-in-chief, western approaches, Admiral Sir Max Horton, but after a volcanic clash of personalities he asked to be relieved, and went out to command the East Indies escort force until the end of the war. In 1946, he commanded the cruiser *Gambia* for a two-year commission in the Far East. For his last three years in the navy, he was deputy director of naval intelligence. He retired in 1951, and was appointed aide-de-camp to King George VI the same year.

In retirement Baker-Cresswell went back to his native Northumberland. He farmed near Bamburgh, became a JP and chairman of the bench, and was high sheriff of Northumberland in 1962. He was devoted to fishing, and was an honorary naval member of the Royal Yacht Squadron. He died at Budle Hall, Bamburgh, Northumberland, on 4 March 1997. He was survived by his wife, Rona, his son, and one daughter, the other daughter having predeceased him.

The story of *U-110*'s capture was kept secret for many years. The formal letter the Admiralty sent Baker-Cresswell on his retirement, summarizing his naval career, did not mention it. The official naval historian Captain Stephen Roskill, who published his first volume on the Second World War in 1954, knew nothing of it then, but published an account, *The Secret Capture*, dedicated to Baker-Cresswell and the officers and men of the 3rd escort group, in 1959. Even then Roskill was not permitted to reveal precisely what Baker-Cresswell had succeeded in capturing. Only after the 'Ultra' secret became public knowledge in the 1970s did the full significance of the capture of *U-110* become clear.   JOHN WINTON

Sources S. W. Roskill, *The secret capture* (1959) · J. Winton, *Ultra at sea* (1988) · R. Lewin, *ULTRA goes to war: the secret story* (1978) · *Daily Telegraph* (7 March 1997) · *The Times* (6 March 1997) · *The Guardian* (19 March 1997) · *Navy List* · Burke, *Gen. GB* · private information (2004) · b. cert. · d. cert.

Likenesses photograph, 1940–44, repro. in *The Times*

Wealth at death under £180,000: probate, 25 July 1997, *CGPLA Eng. & Wales*

Cresswell, Joseph. *See* Cresswell, Joseph (1556–1623).

Cresswell, Nicholas (1750–1804), diarist, was born on 5 January 1750 at Crowden-le-Booth in Edale parish, Derbyshire, the eldest son of Thomas Cresswell, a local landowner and sheep farmer, and his wife, Elizabeth (Betty; 1727/8–1801), the daughter of Richard Oliver of Smalldale, Derbyshire. It is probable that he received his earliest education at a school established by his father, and that he thereafter attended Wakefield grammar school.

In 1774 at the age of twenty-four, armed with a letter of introduction to a Mr James Kirk of Alexandria, Virginia, formerly of Edale parish, Cresswell sailed from Liverpool on the *Molly* for America, where he spent the next three years. During this period he kept 'a daily and impartial Journal' (*Journal*, ed. Thornely, 2) filled with observations on the nature of the terrain and the character of the towns and people he encountered, interspersed with comments on political events. Virtually everything known about Cresswell derives from this journal. Cresswell's motives for leaving England are not clear. His parents, family, and friends did not support his decision but were resigned to his going. His expectations of America were high but his timing was poor. For a young man of slender means, indifferent education, and weak connections, he lacked the economic resources to establish himself as a gentleman

farmer, an ambition initially reinforced by his observations on the poor state of American agriculture.

As a diarist, however, Cresswell excelled. As colonial hostility to Britain intensified following the aggressive British measures adopted in response to the Boston Tea Party, Cresswell witnessed British power collapsing around him as popular resistance grew and military preparations were organized. After only two months in Virginia, and ill, Cresswell ventured to Barbados in the hope of generating funds to underwrite his American land schemes, only to be disappointed. His prospects brightened in January 1775 when, back in Virginia, he was engaged to view a large tract of land in the Illinois country in return for 5000 acres. Travelling at his own expense, his hopes of an appointment as surveyor dashed owing to the uncertainty of the times and the Illinois Company's title to the land, he carried with him some silver trinkets should the plan come to nothing. He set out from Alexandria on 26 March 1775 and at Winchester joined others travelling west. His journey carried him through the region where General Braddock had been defeated at the hands of a French and American Indian force in 1755, arriving at Fort Pitt on 16 April. Using canoes, Cresswell's party descended the Ohio River, reaching the mouth of the Great Kanawha on 9 May and the Kentucky River on 21 May. On 6 June Cresswell split off from the group which had little interest in the Illinois country. From Fort Pitt he set out to trade on his own account in 'the Indian Country' (*Journal*, ed. Thornely, 102) where he took and a month later abandoned 'a temporary [American Indian] wife', whom he called Nancy (ibid., 102, 112).

Believing that the American War of Independence would be short-lived and fearful of the reception he would receive at home, Cresswell reconciled himself to remaining in Virginia despite deteriorating conditions there. He spurned some offers of employment, deeming them inconsistent with his loyalty to the crown, but undertook small tasks for his neighbours. He tried his hand at making saltpetre and building a mill; the latter feat led to the offer of a commission in the American army which he refused. Cresswell had little understanding of the American patriot cause and attributed the rebellion to the activities of a conniving few, aided and abetted by the Presbyterian clergy—'Bellows of Sedition and Rebellion' he called them (*Journal*, ed. Thornely, 261). Increasingly desperate and under constant suspicion for his outspoken views against the patriot cause, he resolved to escape. His acute sense of personal failure is the dominant theme of this part of his narrative. He repeatedly referred to his idleness and ill health in northern Virginia, his loneliness, heavy drinking, and mounting debts. His various schemes for quitting the province—via Bermuda, through 'Indian Country' to Canada where he contemplated joining the British forces, and overland to New York—all proved abortive. 'I am now in an enemy's country', he lamented in October 1776, 'forbidden to depart' (ibid., 166). In early May 1777 Cresswell finally secured a passage to British-occupied New York and only then did he give full rein to his antipathy towards the American patriots. He also derided the failure of British military leaders who, confronted by the supposedly ragtag army under George Washington, 'a Negro-driver' (ibid., 251), had been forced to retreat.

On his return to England, Cresswell failed to gain a commission from John Murray, fourth earl of Dunmore, Virginia's ousted royal governor, and so went back to Edale, where he resumed farming. He married Mary (d. 1824), youngest daughter of Samuel Mellor, at Wirksworth parish church, Derbyshire, on 21 April 1781; he died at nearby Idridgehay on 26 July 1804 at the age of fifty-four leaving six children. He was buried at Wirksworth parish church, in the Mellor family vault.

GWENDA MORGAN

Sources *The journal of Nicholas Cresswell, 1774–1777* (1924) [incl. preface by S. Thornely] · *The journal of Nicholas Cresswell, 1774–1777*, 2nd edn (New York, 1928) [incl. introduction by A. G. Bradley] · 'Journey to Kentucky in 1775: diary of James Nurse', *Journal of American History*, 19 (1925), 121–38, 251–60, 351–64 · H. B. Gill, 'Nicholas Cresswell acted like a British spy. But was he?', *Colonial Williamsburg*, 16 (1993), 26–30 · G. M. Curtis and H. B. Gill, 'A man apart: Nicholas Cresswell's American odyssey, 1774–1777', *Indiana Magazine of History*, 96 (2000), 169–90 · T. D. Clark, ed., *Travels in the old south: a bibliography*, 3 vols. (Norman, Oklahoma, 1956), 1 · W. Holton, *Forced founders: Indians, debtors, slaves, and the making of the American Revolution in Virginia* (Chapel Hill, North Carolina, 1999) · R. Isaac, *The transformation of Virginia, 1740–1790* (Chapel Hill, North Carolina, 1982)
Archives Colonial Williamsburg Foundation, Rockefeller Library, MS
Likenesses oils, c.1780, Colonial Williamsburg Foundation, De Witt Wallace Building

Cressy, Hugh de (d. 1189), administrator, derived his name from the village of Cressy, a dependency of the Warenne honour of Bellencombre, in upper Normandy. Cressy settlement on Warenne lands in East Anglia and Surrey dates almost certainly from the late eleventh century. Nothing is known of Cressy's father and mother, Roger and Eustacia, except their names. His brother, Berengar, was married to Isabel of Gressenhall, the daughter of another Warenne tenant, Wimar the Sewer. The family's rise to prominence began when Hugh de Cressy joined the household of William FitzEmpress, Henry II's brother, some time in the early 1150s. Cressy accompanied William on his travels between Normandy and England and attested his lord's charters. For his service, Cressy received from William the manor of Harrietsham in Kent, part of the old honour of Peverel of Dover. The honour's heir, Countess Isabel de Warenne, was betrothed to William in late 1163 and on his unexpected death in January 1164 married another royal sibling, Hamelin of Anjou. As a representative of one of the leading families of the Warenne honours in England and in Normandy and a former member of William FitzEmpress's household, Cressy easily gained Hamelin's confidence, taking over the chief administrative office (seneschal) in the Warenne Surrey earldom. He appears in the pipe rolls for the first time in 1167, offering a fine of 100 marks for custody of the land of his nephew in the honour of Tickhill.

Cressy's income, direct and indirect, must have been substantial, and was derived, in part, from an advantageous marriage arranged for him by the king in 1174 to Margaret de Chesney, heir to Blythburgh, Suffolk, and hereditary claimant to the shrievalty of Norfolk and the custodianship of Norwich Castle. All in all, the Cressy and Chesney lands brought together into one estate nine knights' fees in the honour of Warenne, eleven in the honour of Eye, two in the Giffard earldom, three in Tickhill, two in Little Dunmow, and additional fees in the honours of Peverel of Dover, Gant, Clare, Musard, Kentswell, and Bury St Edmunds, for a total of thirty knights' fees held in mesne. These fees collectively may have been worth about £600 per year. If Hugh's own income was about a third of this figure, his wealth would have been matched by few contemporary English barons. Some evidence of the territorial influence built up by Cressy in East Anglian counties is found in the pipe roll of 1187–8 where he is excused from fines in no less than six hundreds. The unity of the Cressy holdings, however, was ephemeral, as the estate descended in the next generation to Hugh and Margaret's sons Roger and Stephen and Margaret's second husband, Robert fitz Roger, who in 1192 became sheriff of Norfolk in right of his wife.

Cressy's star rose steadily when he left Hamelin's entourage in 1170 for the royal court. He attended the coronation of Henry the Young King at Westminster in June, where he was included among the witnesses of Henry II's charter to Waltham. He again witnessed royal charters in 1171 in Normandy, 1172 in Ireland, and 1173 in England, marking the advent of his almost continuous presence with the king or involvement with the king's business. A study of witness lists from the reign ranks Cressy ninth overall as an attestor, one place below the more renowned justiciar Ranulf de Glanville. He was active on Henry II's behalf during the 1173–4 rebellion of the king's sons. He provisioned Norwich Castle against the attacks of Hugh (I) Bigod, earl of Norfolk, fought with distinction at the battle of Fornham, and made at least two channel crossings at this time paid for by the exchequer. After the war Cressy became deeply involved in the evolving English judicial system, being appointed a justice in the great eyre of 1176 which followed the Council of Northampton. Soon afterwards he was appointed constable of the Tower of Rouen under a general policy of filling key positions within the duchy of Normandy with new men of proven loyalty and strong ties to England. As constable he is found on several occasions sitting in judgment with the ducal court, and alternatively commanding elements of the king's armies on expeditions as far away as Poitou. His last stay in England is recorded by the pipe roll for 1186–7. Cressy died some time in early 1189 only a few months before the lord king he had come to serve and love. One of his last acts as he lay sick at Rouen was a grant of lands in Walberswick to Blythburgh Priory for his own soul, the souls of his mother, father, ancestors, and those of Henry II and his brother, William FitzEmpress. The witnesses to this charter, including two archbishops and an earl, offer a glimpse of the high regard and position Hugh de Cressy had come to enjoy within the Angevin inner court circle. Cressy's career was typical of the men who, with Henry II, made the 'Angevin empire'. THOMAS K. KEEFE

Sources L. Delisle and others, eds., *Recueil des actes de Henri II, roi d'Angleterre et duc de Normandie, concernant les provinces françaises et les affaires de France*, 4 vols. (Paris, 1909–27) · *Chronica magistri Rogeri de Hovedene*, ed. W. Stubbs, 4 vols., Rolls Series, 51 (1868–71) · W. Farrer, *Honors and knights' fees … from the eleventh to the fourteenth century*, 3 (1925) · L. F. Salzman, ed., *The chartulary of the Priory of St Pancras of Lewes*, 2 vols., Sussex RS, 38, 40 (1932–4) · M. Bouquet and others, eds., *Recueil des historiens des Gaules et de la France / Rerum Gallicarum et Francicarum scriptores*, new edn, 23 (Paris, 1894), 640c, 708j · *Pipe rolls*, 13 Henry II – 2 Richard I · C. Harper-Bill, ed., *Blythburgh Priory cartulary*, 2 vols., Suffolk RS, Suffolk Charters, 2–3 (1980–81) · L. C. Loyd, *The origins of some Anglo-Norman families*, ed. C. T. Clay and D. C. Douglas, Harleian Society, 103 (1951); repr. (1975) · H. C. M. Lyte and others, eds., *Liber feodorum: the book of fees*, 3 vols. (1920–31) [PRO] · *VCH Norfolk*, vol. 2 · I. J. Sanders, *English baronies: a study of their origin and descent, 1086–1327* (1960) · J. H. Round, ed., *Calendar of documents preserved in France, illustrative of the history of Great Britain and Ireland* (1899) · *Reg. RAN*, vol. 3 · H. Hall, ed., *The Red Book of the Exchequer*, 3 vols., Rolls Series, 99 (1896) · T. Stapleton, ed., *Magni rotuli scaccarii Normanniae sub regibus Angliae*, 2 vols., Society of Antiquaries of London Occasional Papers (1840–44) · P. Brown, ed., *Sibton Abbey cartularies and charters*, vols. 1–2, Suffolk RS, Suffolk Charters, 7–10 (1985–6) · J. Verneir, ed., *Chartes de l'abbaye de Jumièges*, 2 vols., Société de l'Histoire de Normandie (1916) · R. Ransford, ed., *The early charters of the Augustinian canons of Waltham Abbey, Essex, 1062–1230* (1989) · F. M. Stenton, ed., *Facsimiles of early charters from Northamptonshire collections*, Northamptonshire RS, 4 (1930) · *Jordan Fantosme's chronicle*, ed. and trans. R. C. Johnston (1981) · B. R. Kemp, ed., *Reading Abbey cartularies*, 2 vols., CS, 4th ser., 31, 33 (1986–7) · C. J. Holdsworth, ed., *Rufford charters*, 4 vols., Thoroton Society Record Series, 29, 30, 32, 34 (1972–81) · J. H. Round, ed., *Rotuli de dominabus et pueris et puellis de XII comitatibus* (1185), PRSoc., 35 (1913) · *CClR* · 'Register of Castle Acre Priory', BL, Harley MS 2110

Cressy, Hugh Paulinus [*name in religion* Serenus] (1605–1674), Benedictine monk, was born at Thorp Salvin in Yorkshire, the son of Hugh Cressy, barrister of Lincoln's Inn and judge of the king's bench, and his wife, Margerie, the daughter of Thomas *D'Oylie, an eminent London physician. Although he is sometimes called de Cressy, as on the title-page of the first edition of his apologetic *Exomologesis*, he firmly disavows this style in the second edition. He was sent in Lent term 1619 to Oxford where he graduated BA in 1623; he was first a member of Magdalen Hall, then of Merton College, where he was elected to a fellowship in 1626. After proceeding MA on 10 July 1629 and then taking holy orders Cressy was chaplain to Thomas, Lord Wentworth, while Wentworth was president of the council of the north and, through Laud's intercession, when Wentworth became lord deputy of Ireland and earl of Strafford. Resident in Merton until 1638, however, Cressy also held a variety of offices including bursar and chaplain, and in January 1631 he delivered a funeral oration for Henry Briggs, Savilian professor of mathematics. This work, the only one he seems to have written before he became a monk, does not survive.

Cressy was a member of the Great Tew circle, that 'university bound in a lesser volume' (Clarendon, *Hist. rebellion*, 3.187–9) which met at the house in Great Tew of Lucius Cary, second Viscount Falkland, and included Edward Hyde (later earl of Clarendon), John Earle, John Hales, Gilbert Sheldon, George Morley, Henry Hammond, William Chillingworth, and Thomas Barlow. Writing in 1673 Clarendon says that he has known Cressy 'very near fifty years' (Clarendon, *Animadversions*, 8). During this period, through Elizabeth Cary, Lady Falkland, Cressy met the Benedictine Cuthbert Fursdon, disciple of Augustine Baker, a scholarly lawyer-convert to Rome and, a mystic himself, a considerable student of that tradition; Fursdon was spiritual director to Lady Falkland, four of whose daughters were later professed as Benedictines. From 1634 Cressy was in Dublin, where on 26 January 1636 he was installed as prebendary of St John's, Christ Church; in February 1636 he received the prebend of St Patrick's, Dublin, and on 11 August 1637 he was installed as dean of Leighlin. When he returned to England he obtained through the help of Falkland a canonry of Windsor in 1642, but was never installed. He may also have met Queen Henrietta Maria during her residence in Oxford at Merton in 1643–4, a meeting which would in part account for her later attention to him. After the death of Falkland at the battle of Newbury, Cressy travelled in 1644 as tutor to Charles Berkeley, afterwards earl of Falmouth, who later gave financial help to his old tutor. His lifelong interest in peace and church unity was reinforced by his association with the Tew circle, whose heroes were Erasmus and Grotius. Although Cressy later engaged in controversy, sometimes with the men of Tew, he remained for the most part on amiable terms with them.

As the opening of his *Exomologesis* (1647) suggests, Cressy was disillusioned by the war and by what he considered the failure of the Church of England. In Rome on 21 July 1646, 'being the vigile of the Feast of St. Mary Magdalen', he was reconciled in the offices of the Inquisition (Baker, sig. a2v). After proceeding to Paris he studied theology under Henry Holden, whose positions were essentially Gallican. At Douai in 1647 Cressy wrote his *Exomologesis*, an apologia for his conversion that argued against William Chillingworth's *Religion of Protestants* and the scandal of disunity, and for the importance of tradition and ecumenical councils as sources of authority. This work was widely read and there were many responses, not least among the men of Tew: Thomas Barlow annotated the copies now in the Bodleian Library and replied in papers which remain unpublished in Queen's College, Oxford. 'Well known to the Queen of England, Lord Aubigny, Lord Abbot Montague, and other English Noble Catholicks … [Cressy] procur'd … their protection and favour … obtaining … many Benefactours by his acquaintance and Interest … particularly with the Messieures de Port Royal' ('Sketch', 290). Henrietta Maria, for instance, gave him 100 crowns for a journey to a monastery. Cressy's own religious preference was for the Carthusians (the perception of whose holiness was a strong factor in his conversion) but, realizing that he did not have a vocation for a contemplative life, he was professed at St Gregory's, Douai, as a Benedictine on 22 August 1649 where he took the name Serenus, an allusion to his lifelong commitment to peace. During his noviciate he wrote the very dark 'Treatise on the passion' (1648), still in manuscript at Ampleforth Abbey, Yorkshire. It is dedicated to the Oratorian Stephen Gough, an important figure among Catholics in Paris, whom Cressy had probably met at Merton.

In 1651 the Benedictine congregation directed Cressy to accompany nuns from Cambrai to a new foundation in Paris, where he acted for a year as chaplain. The community included Clementia and Mary Cary (to whom Cressy had dedicated his *Arbor virtutem* in 1649), sisters to Falkland and influential among Catholics. As a result St Benedict's Priory at Colwich, the later home of the Parisian Benedictine convent, still held many of Cressy's works at the start of the twenty-first century. Cressy revised the *Exomologesis* in 1653, evidently under pressure, removing some praise of the Church of England and considerably extending his discussion and praise of mystical theology, and of Baker. He displays great familiarity with other mystics like Suso, Tauler, Ruysbroek, and Blosius. The 1653 edition of *Exomologesis* also includes an answer to John Pearson's preface to Falkland's *Discourse of Infallibility* (1651). The very rare third edition of 1659 differs from the 1653 edition only in some changes on the title-page, which alert the reader to the important appendices and to the influence of Holden. This alteration reflects Cressy's habit. Reading, as he observes in his preface to *Arbor virtutem* (1649), always with pen in hand, he aims to instruct his readers, translating, editing, and condensing texts. In 1657 he edited a digest of Baker's voluminous works, *Sancta Sophia*, which includes a prefatory life, and in 1659 Walter Hilton's *Scale of Perfection*.

In 1660 Cressy went on the mission in the southern province of England and became one of Catherine of Braganza's chaplains after her arrival in England. Living chiefly at Somerset House he was appointed definitor of the southern province (1666) and cathedral prior of Rochester (1669). Both titles testify to the regard in which he was held, as does the chapter's grant to him in 1653 of five years' seniority in the Benedictine habit. He formed an important association with Thomas, first Lord Clifford of Chudleigh, who was obliged, upon his own conversion to Catholicism, to resign as lord high treasurer. Cressy, intellectually influential in Clifford's conversion, spent time at Ugbrooke Park, Clifford's estate in south Devon, one of the two houses alleged to be the site of Dryden's composition of *The Hind and the Panther*. Clifford's manuscript commonplace book cites *Exomologesis* four times, once in a long section labelled 'Unio', demonstrating the importance of church unity for both men. It was in a letter to Clifford that Cressy used, uniquely, the pseudonym of H. Clark. Cressy gave Clifford a short reading list, including Alford's history of the church in England, and the works of Bede and St Bernard, and together they devised schemes for unity which included substantial concessions about matters like clerical marriage, communion in both kinds, and Latin in the liturgy. (These papers were placed, with other family documents, including the secret treaty of Dover, among the Clifford manuscripts in the British Library.) Cressy reflects seriously on the knotty matter of the oath of allegiance, both in the Clifford papers and in *Reflexions on the Oathes of Supremacy and Allegiance* (1661).

In 1670 Cressy became the first editor of Julian of Norwich's *XVI Revelations of Divine Love* (1670), dedicated to Lady Mary Blount. Augustine Baker and Cressy were together largely responsible for the preservation of the early English mystics in English and it was this tradition that Cressy defended against the attacks of Edward Stillingfleet in *Fanaticism Fanatically Imputed* (1672). In addition to his controversial work, and the edition of Julian, Cressy abridged the Jesuit Michael Alford's Latin ecclesiastical history of England as *The Church History of Brittany* (that is, Britain), in 1668, a volume half the size of the original, occasionally adding material to emphasize the monastic contribution to English ecclesiastical history. Cressy's intention, as his title-page indicates, was to demonstrate that 'the present Roman Catholick religion hath from the beginning, without interruption or change, been professed in this our island'. Wood observed approvingly that Cressy tried to look at miracles carefully. The importance of Cressy within his own order and as part of the history of controversy is highlighted by the chapter's levy to support this work. A second part, in manuscript, was placed at the municipal library, Douai, and includes elaborate praise of Merton College. Oxford remained central to Cressy, not only because of personal attachment, but also because, as his visits with Wood and the Catholic Ralph Sheldon indicate, he was, like Baker, preoccupied with antiquarian matters as part of his argument about his order and his church. According to Wood it was Cressy who introduced Sheldon to him. This concern with the past also emerges in Cressy's lesser controversial works, like *Roman-Catholick Doctrines No Novelties* (1663).

Cressy's last letter (now among the Wood manuscripts in the Bodleian Library), written at the Sheldon house in Worcestershire three weeks before his death, was directed to John Mallet, a fellow Benedictine, and concerned Fell's inappropriate editing of Wood. Cressy died on 10 August 1674 at the house of Richard Caryll, of another ancient Catholic family, in West Grinstead, Sussex.

Dryden mentions Cressy in the preface to *Religio laici*, mistakenly assuming that he sympathized with those allegedly plotting against the monarchy. In addition to remaining in touch with his distinguished Oxford friends Cressy was associated with important Catholic writers of his day, among them the Franciscans Vincent Canes and Christopher Davenport, who shared his pacific and accommodating views. It is not surprising to find him as a character in the Anglican Joseph Henry Shorthouse's novel *John Inglesant* (1881) or his works, with Davenport's, in the Pusey House Library, Oxford. His inclination to disregard what he considered small matters of difference between the churches of England and Rome, and his arguments about peace and reconciliation, appealed both to more liberal Roman Catholics and to the members of other churches.   PATRICIA C. BRÜCKMANN

Sources 'A sketch of the history of the Benedictine community now residing at St Benedict's Priory, Colwich, Stafford [pt 3]', *Ampleforth Journal*, 12 (1906–7), 287–303 • C. H. Hartmann, *Clifford of*

the cabal (1937) • C. H. Hartmann, *The king's friend* (1951) • H. T. Roper, *Catholics, Anglicans and puritans* (1987) • H. Cotton, *Fasti ecclesiae Hibernicae*, 6 vols. (1845–78) • R. Clark, *Strangers and sojourners at Port Royal* (1932) • battels and register, Merton Oxf. • Wood, *Ath. Oxon.*, new edn • *The life and times of Anthony Wood*, ed. A. Clark, 5 vols., OHS, 19, 21, 26, 30, 40 (1891–1900) • B. H. G. Wormald, *Clarendon: politics, historiography and religion, 1640–1660* (1961) • A. Allison, 'An English Gallican: Henry Holden', *Recusant History*, 22 (1995), 319–49 • S. Cressy, *The life of … Augustine Baker*, ed. J. McCann (1933) • A. Baker, *Sancta Sophia*, ed. S. Cressy (1657) • G. Tavard, *Seventeenth-century tradition: a study in recusant thought* (1978) • B. Green and P. Spearritt, *English Benedictines, 1558–1850* (1978) [microfilm] • Athanasius [P. A. Allanson], *Biography of the English Benedictines*, ed. A. Cramer and S. Goodwill (1999) • miscellaneous papers, Downside Abbey [includes Profession Book; 'Biography … English Benedictines'; 'History of the English Benedictine congregation'; 'Records and letters in the history and biography'] • W. Knowler, *Letters and dispatches*, 2 vols. (1740) • P. Spearritt, 'The survival of medieval spirituality among the exiled black monks', *American Benedictine Review*, 25 (1974), 287–316 • G. Scott, 'Oxford and the Benedictines: from the Restoration until Catholic emancipation', in H. Wansbrough, H. Marett-Crosby, and A. Marett-Crosby, *Benedictines in Oxford* (1997) • [E. Hyde, earl of Clarendon], *Animadversions upon a book* (1673) • Clarendon, *Hist. rebellion* • *DNB* • S. Cressy, *Exomologesis* (1647)

Archives Australian National University, Canberra • Downside Abbey, near Bath | BL, letters, etc. to Lord Clifford, Add. MS 65139

Cressy, Robert. *See* Cressey, John (*d. c.*1450).

Crestadoro, Andrea (1808–1879), bibliographer, was born at Genoa and educated at the public school there. An industrious student, he proceeded (*c.*1825) to the University of Turin, where he graduated PhD, and soon after was appointed professor of natural philosophy. Here he published a *Saggio d'istituzioni sulla facoltà della parola* and a small treatise on savings banks, advocating their establishment in Italy. He also translated part of George Bancroft's *History of the United States of America*. Throughout his life he was fond of mechanical experiments, and in 1849 he moved to Britain in order to promote his inventions. Between 1852 and 1873 he patented various mechanical devices, none of which came into practical use. One related to aerial locomotion, and a model of his metallic balloon was shown at the Crystal Palace in June 1868; a description of it was printed.

The failure of his early patents led Crestadoro to seek work with the publishing firm of Sampson Low & Co., compiling the *British Catalogue of Books* and the *Index to Current Literature* (1859–61). This led him often to the British Museum, where the question of a printed catalogue to its holdings was under discussion, and in his treatise on *The Art of Making Catalogues* (1856) he recommended transcribing the title pages of books and compiling an index of the 'key words' used therein. The British Museum did not, however, take up his suggestion.

In 1862 Crestadoro was engaged by the corporation of Manchester to compile a catalogue of the Free Reference Library, on which work had come to a halt after staff difficulties. In 1864 he was appointed chief librarian of the Manchester Free Libraries. The 'index-catalogues' which he completed in 1863 and had printed in 1864 were widely adopted as models, first by other Manchester libraries and then by other municipal libraries throughout Britain. They followed the system he had expounded in 1856, but modified by a supervisory committee. He participated in the International Congress of Librarians in 1877 and was a founder member of the Library Association of the United Kingdom in 1877, serving on its first council. He also attended the Social Science Congress in 1878, at which he presented a paper on taxation levying. The king of Italy in 1878 sent him the order of the Corona d'Italia. He had earlier (1861) published a work on the relations between lay and spiritual authority, which was said to have influenced developments in Italy. He died at his home, 155 Upper Brook Street, Charlton upon Medlock, Manchester, on 7 April 1879, after a brief illness, and was buried at Ardwick cemetery. He left a widow, but no children. His manuscript on joint-stock companies was never published. Crestadoro, who was naturalized British in the 1860s, exerted a marked and beneficial influence upon the progress of the free library movement, and as a bibliographer was skilled in organization. With his early suggestions on the use of 'key word indexes' he has been hailed by some as the forerunner of computer catalogues based on this system (Firby, 24). In private life he was a pleasant and genial companion.

W. E. A. AXON, rev. ELIZABETH BAIGENT

Sources N. K. Firby, 'Andrea Crestadoro, 1809–1879', *Manchester Review*, 12–13 (1971–4), 19–25 • *Manchester Guardian* (8 April 1879) • *CGPLA Eng. & Wales* (1879) • *Momus* (20 March 1879) • *Manchester Guardian* (19 March 1878) • *Manchester City News* (13 April 1929) • J. Minto, *A history of the public library movement* (1932), 168

Likenesses W. G. Baxter, cartoon, repro. in *Momus*

Wealth at death under £100: probate, 30 May 1879, *CGPLA Eng. & Wales*

Creswell, Frederic Hugh Page (1866–1948), politician in South Africa and mining engineer, was born on 13 November 1866 in Gibraltar, the youngest of the thirteen children of Edmund Creswell (*d.* 1877), then deputy postmaster-general of Gibraltar, and his wife, Mary Fraser of Belrain, Inverness. At the age of nine he was sent to Bruce Castle, England, then to Derby School for his education, before training as a mining engineer at the Royal School of Mines. After working briefly in Venezuela as an engineer in 1888–9 he became assistant manager of a mine in Turkish Syria, but was enticed to south Africa by news of the spectacular development of the goldmines on the Witwatersrand. When he arrived in Cape Town in 1893 he joined an expedition to Rhodesia, where he surveyed a new railway line before in 1894 settling on the Witwatersrand; there he became manager of the Durban Deep mine. Before the Second South African War he was active in the Uitlander Reform Committee, and when war broke out he joined the Imperial light horse and served as a lieutenant, fighting in the battle of Elandslaagte, at Ladysmith, and in Transvaal. In November 1900, with Transvaal under British rule, he became general manager of the Village Main Reef mine.

Creswell's first significant involvement in politics

occurred on the Chinese labour issue. Given white unemployment, he rejected the plan to import Chinese labourers, and instead advocated employing only whites, skilled and unskilled, in the goldmines. When he attempted to implement this at the Main Reef mine, he was at first allowed to experiment, but when the experiment was rejected by both miners and the company headquarters he resigned in 1903. His white labour policy, which he set out in a pamphlet, *The Chinese Labour Question from within*, published in London in 1905, was not practical, given that most white miners wanted to be members of a labour aristocracy and that the mine owners wanted to employ as many low-paid African labourers as possible. When in England early in 1906 he campaigned strongly for the Liberals against Chinese labour, and urged the prime minister, Sir Henry Campbell-Bannerman, to grant self-rule to Transvaal.

Back on the Rand, Creswell spoke for the white mine workers against the capitalists and what he claimed was their kept press. Though twice defeated in elections for the new Transvaal parliament, standing for a pro-Botha British party, he was returned for Jeppe in September 1910 in the first Union parliament. He had joined the South African Labour Party that June, and had probably been promised that he would become leader of the parliamentary party if elected. As leader he worked closely with his friend Thomas Boydell, whose political career paralleled his own in many respects.

When the mine workers struck in 1913–14 Creswell was arrested and imprisoned for distributing pamphlets, and was released only so that he might attend the opening of parliament. His attack on Smuts for deporting nine leading strikers to Britain was published in Cape Town as *The Attempt to Crush Labour: a Reply to General Smuts* (1914). When war broke out he served with the Rand rifles in the German South-West Africa campaign, and then in 1916 in German East Africa, where he was promoted lieutenant-colonel of the 8th South African infantry regiment and made a DSO. Despite his support for Britain he became increasingly friendly with General J. B. M. Hertzog, leader of the National Party. Both men claimed in speeches to favour total territorial separation between black and white.

Defeated in Jeppe in 1915 because of his support for the war, Creswell was elected for Troyeville in 1916. Five years later he lost that seat, but was returned for Stamford Hill, Durban, in 1922 and 1924. In July 1922 he held talks, as leader of the Labour Party, with Hertzog, which led to an agreement to form a united opposition against Smuts. This produced the formal pact between the National and Labour parties in April the following year. In 1924 the pact won the general election on a platform built around 'Civilised Labour'. Creswell was given the key portfolio of labour, as well as defence, in Hertzog's cabinet. He began to build up the new department of labour, and introduced segregationist measures, most notably the Colour Bar Act of 1926. Creswell was given strong support in his later political career by his wife, Margaret Philippa Bingham Groenewald, *née* Boys, whom he married on 1 December 1920.

The widow of Albert Groenewald, a medical man, she was twenty years younger than Creswell but they were admirably suited to each other.

By 1928 the Labour Party had split, with a majority section believing that the party's national council should be able to dictate to Labour members of parliament. Creswell rejected this and lost the leadership of the party, but kept Hertzog's support, and was retained in the cabinet after the 1929 general election. His career as a minister ended early in 1933 when Hertzog joined Smuts, who would not have Creswell in his cabinet. Creswell was returned as member of parliament for Bellville in 1933 and remained in parliament until 1938. In 1933 he was elected vice-president of the International Labour Organization conference in Geneva, and in 1935 became its chairman.

Though not a 'man of the people', Creswell tried to hold the Labour Party together, but with the rise of Afrikaner nationalism there was no long-term future for a party of white labour. His key ideas—all-white labour in the mines and total territorial segregation—were impractical, and his main political significance lies in the way he helped bring the National Party to power in 1924, enabling it to implement more segregationist legislation. He was a competent minister and a man of integrity and culture, who had a wide circle of friends among English-speaking and Afrikaner whites, though he did not suffer fools gladly. Inclined to be autocratic, he was derided by critics, one of whom called him 'the pregnant sardine' (Nicholls). Creswell retired to Kuilsriver, outside Cape Town, and died there of a stroke on 25 August 1948. He was cremated at Epping, Cape Town. His widow wrote a memoir of her husband which was published in 1956.

CHRISTOPHER SAUNDERS

Sources M. Creswell, *An epoch of the political history of South Africa in the life of Frederic Hugh Page Creswell* (Cape Town, 1956) • F. Creswell, *The Chinese labour question from within: facts, criticism and suggestions; impeachment of a disastrous policy* (1905) • L. E. Neame, *Some politicians* (Cape Town, 1929) • W. K. Hancock, *Smuts*, 2: *The fields of force, 1919–1950* (1968) • C. F. Nieuwoudt, 'Creswell, Frederic Hugh Page', *DSAB* • D. Ticktin, 'The origins of the South African labour party', PhD diss., University of Cape Town, 1973 • D. Ticktin, 'The war issue and the collapse of the South African labour party, 1914–15', *South African Historical Journal*, 1 (Nov 1969) • B. J. Liebenberg and S. B. Spies, eds., *South Africa in the twentieth century* (Pretoria, 1993) • *WWW* • G. H. Nicholls, *South Africa in my time* (1961)

Archives National Archives of South Africa, Pretoria, Transvaal archives depot, MSS | CUL, Smuts MSS • National Archives of South Africa, Pretoria, Hertzog MSS • National Archives of South Africa, Pretoria, Union archives | FILM National Film Archive, South Africa

Likenesses two photographs, 1931–6, repro. in Creswell, *An epoch* • Quip, caricature, repro. in Neame, *Some politicians*, 25

Creswell, Joseph [*formerly* Arthur] (1556–1623), Jesuit, was born in 1556 at Nunkeeling Priory, Holderness, East Riding, Yorkshire, son of Percival Creswell (*d.* 1558) and his second wife, Cassandra (*d. c.*1579). His father managed the estates of such absentee landlords as the Greshams of London and William Rastell, nephew of Thomas More. By Percival's will Cassandra received the leasehold of houses in London so that after her second marriage, to William Lacy of Beverley, she brought the family there. Privately educated, Creswell, a recusant, did not attend a university but he later wrote that before leaving London he had been engaged in business.

In July 1580, after escorting Campion and Persons to visit Catholic families in the London region, Creswell left to study at the English College in Rome. Here he received news in August 1582 that his stepfather, who had studied for the priesthood in France, had been executed in Yorkshire. On 10 October 1583 Creswell entered the Society of Jesus in Rome, at which time he chose to change his forename from Arthur to Joseph. In early 1588 Cardinal Allen asked him and William Holt to serve as chaplains for the troops gathered under Parma in Flanders and, at the duke's request, Creswell wrote an English proclamation that was printed for distribution in the event of an invasion; however, no copies have survived. He then returned to Rome to be rector of the English College, where he wrote his first book, a response in Latin to a proclamation of 1591 denouncing English colleges overseas as schools of sedition. Addressing William Cecil, while concealing his name as Joannes Penius, he insisted that the students were trained only for a peaceful mission of assisting the faithful at home.

In the spring of 1592 Persons called Creswell to Spain to seek funds for two new colleges. For years Creswell was the advocate at the court of Spain for the support of colleges at Valladolid and Seville, in addition to those at Douai and St Omer in Flanders. Fortunate in gaining the trust of certain courtiers he submitted numerous reports on the treatment of Catholics in England and Flanders which were read by officials. To increase public interest he wrote in Spanish in 1596 a tribute to Henry Walpole, who had been executed two years before in England; this was also translated into French. He then provided many narratives of the mistreatment of recusants for the large tome published by Bishop Diego de Yepez in 1599 as the *Historia particular de la persecucion de Inglaterra*.

Unfortunately, Creswell's zeal outran his discretion in two serious incidents. His independence of Spanish Jesuits, particularly in Seville, led to damaging complaints to the father-general; and he had poor judgement in 1602-3 in trusting Guy Fawkes and other messengers from England who vainly sought aid for an uncertain military 'enterprise' on behalf of Catholics. They told him of their petitions to the Spanish council of state before the death of Elizabeth, but he learned in 1606 that in their statements after the Gunpowder Plot he became part of their 'Spanish Treason' (Loomie, 'Fawkes', 22-7). Previously, in June 1605, at the ratification of the peace between England and Spain, Creswell had amicable talks with the earl of Nottingham, whom he invited to visit the English College in Valladolid. Charles Cornwallis, the ambassador, was gratified at first by Creswell's news of court politics, until the printing in 1606 in Madrid of a misleading summary of the recent penal laws prompted his repeated protests at the misconduct of English exiles in Spain. This led to Creswell's *Carta escrita al embajador*, an apologia to the court which stressed that penal laws created excessive burdens on the consciences of Catholics. In 1608 Creswell gave a copy of his English letter to Cornwallis, who offered it to Robert Cotton's manuscript library (BL, Cotton MS Vespasian C XIII, fols. 342ff.).

Creswell's Jesuit critics later found new allies in Lerma, the king's favourite, and the English ambassador, John Digby. Lerma mistrusted his friendship with members of the queen's court faction, while Digby wanted to undermine his plan to found a new college in Madrid for which a legacy was given. Misleading allegations about his conduct were sent to the father-general, who asked Creswell to leave Spain. Although later exonerated in Rome, it was decided that his financial and administrative skills were needed in Flanders, where in 1615 he was appointed vice-prefect. While still corresponding with the secretary of state in Rome, or Gondomar in England, both close friends, Creswell completed the plans for the new noviciate in Liège and then arranged for the improvement of the printing press at the St Omer college so that production rose from seven books in 1611 to fifteen in 1622. Here was printed his only English book, a translation of Salvian's *Quis dives salvus* in 1618, and two years later his Spanish translation of it appeared. Finally, after a grave illness, he died at the Jesuit college in Ghent on 19 February 1623. He was buried at Ghent. In his summary of his career Allison considered him a person 'with a sense of divinely ordained mission that made him impatient of all secondary considerations' (Allison, 131). A. J. LOOMIE

Sources A. F. Allison, 'The later life and writings of Joseph Creswell, SJ (1556–1623)', *Recusant History*, 15 (1979-81), 79–144 · A. J. Loomie, *The Spanish Elizabethans* (1963) · *English polemics at the Spanish court: Joseph Creswell's 'Letter to the ambassador from England'*, ed. A. J. Loomie (1993) · A. J. Loomie, 'Guy Fawkes in Spain: the "Spanish treason" in Spanish documents', *BIHR*, special suppl., 9 (1971) [whole issue] · A. F. Allison and D. M. Rogers, eds., *The contemporary printed literature of the English Counter-Reformation between 1558 and 1640*, 2 vols. (1989-94) · J. C. H. Aveling, 'Yorkshire notes', *Recusant History*, 6 (1961-2), 238-40 · T. M. McCoog, ed., *Monumenta Angliae*, 1: *English and Welsh Jesuits, catalogues, 1555-1629* (1992) · M. Murphy, *St Gregory's College, Seville, 1592-1767*, Catholic RS, 73 (1992) · E. Henson, ed., *The English college at Madrid, 1611-1767*, Catholic RS, 29 (1929) · W. Kelly, ed., *Liber ruber venerabilis collegii Anglorum de urbe*, 1, Catholic RS, 37 (1940)
Archives PRO | BL, Cotton MS Vespasian C XIII, fols. 342 ff.

Creswick, Thomas (1811–1869), landscape painter, was born at Sheffield, Yorkshire, on 5 February 1811, one of the large family of Thomas Creswick and his wife, Ann Fox; he was baptized on 15 March at the church of St Peter and St Paul, Sheffield. He received his education at Hazelwood, near Birmingham, and rapidly developed a talent for drawing, studying for some years in Birmingham under John Vincent Barber. In 1828 he moved to London, settling in Edmund Street, St Pancras. In that year, two of his works were exhibited at the Royal Academy, where he was to show 139 works during a long career; he also exhibited eighty paintings at the British Institution and forty-six at the Society of British Artists. His unchallenging but competently executed landscapes found ready patrons at these exhibitions. Early in his career he also produced drawings for engraving: his illustrations to Thomas Roscoe's *North Wales* (1836) are conventional in composition, while those for Leitch Ritchie's *Ireland Picturesque and Romantic* (1837–8) are more originally conceived. His etchings, such as those for *Songs and Ballads of Shakespeare, Illustrated by Members of the Etching Club* (1843), demonstrate a secure grip of the technique and conventions of etching but little imaginative flair. He contributed to Edward Moxon's illustrated edition of Tennyson's poetry (1857) alongside works by the Pre-Raphaelites.

After various moves in St Pancras and Pentonville, Creswick settled permanently at 7 Linden Grove, Bayswater, in 1836. With the Royal Academy exhibits of 1841, the *Art Journal* noted that 'he seemed to have struck into a new path, one uniting vigour and boldness of handling with delicacy, and greater variety of harmony of tints with the freshness and verdure of Nature' (*Art Journal*, 1856, 142). One of the most vigorous in this new manner is *Land's End, Cornwall* (1842; exh. British Institution, 1843; Victoria and Albert Museum, London). In 1842 the director of the British Institution awarded him a premium of 50 guineas for the general merit of his works. Many of Creswick's finest works were painted in the north of England during the 1840s. A series of paintings of Haddon Hall, Derbyshire (such as *On the Terrace*, 1840, Yale U. CBA), deploy figures in period costume in a carefully observed setting. He was elected an ARA in 1842 and Royal Academician in 1851. His later works lacked the precision and vibrancy of their predecessors, leading the *Art Journal* in 1856 to criticize the 'low and dingy scale of colouring' which he had recently adopted.

Creswick often collaborated with other artists such as William Powell Frith and Richard Ansdell, who added figures and animals to his landscape compositions; *Trentside* (exh. RA, 1861; Royal Holloway and Bedford New College, University of London, Egham), includes cattle by John William Bottomley. Little is known of Creswick's methods: Richard and Samuel Redgrave suggest that 'he was accustomed to paint only what may be called the eye of his pictures out of doors and on the spot', though 'to secure exactly what he wanted he would brave cold and wet and all other trials' (Redgrave and Redgrave, 335).

Creswick was a committed member of the academy and seems to have revelled in its cliquish institutional politics. Allies such as Frith recalled him as an 'intimate friend— and good nature personified' (Frith, 1.125), whereas Thomas Sidney Cooper, though admitting 'he *could* paint' (Cooper, 2.93), described him as 'self-willed and insincere. He did all he could to keep me from getting full honours of the Royal Academy [and was] ignorant, vindictive and unsociable' (ibid., 95). Scruffy and unkempt, with a ragged beard, Creswick was known as 'big unwashed' among his detractors. There seems to be some truth in the idea that he schemed to keep other landscape painters out of the Royal Academy.

Creswick died at Linden Grove, Bayswater, London, on 28 December 1869, leaving a widow, Anne. He was buried in Kensal Green cemetery in London. While *Blackwood's Edinburgh Magazine* in 1861 admired his works as 'essentially English in subject and in sentiment' (J. Chapel, *Victorian Taste*, 1982, 78), even his champions, Richard and

Samuel Redgrave, admitted that 'his touch is inclined to mannerism and there is a good deal of sameness in his work', a fact which became apparent at the memorial exhibition of his work held at South Kensington in 1873. In describing his work as 'anodyne in treatment' and characterizing *A Summer's Afternoon* (1844; Victoria and Albert Museum, London) as 'a banal pastoral', Michael Rosenthal articulates the consensus of modern opinion on Creswick (*British Landscape Painting*, 1982).   TIM BARRINGER

Sources 'British artists, their style and character: no. XIV, Thomas Creswick', *Art Journal*, 18 (1856), 141–4 • Redgrave, *Artists* • R. Redgrave and S. Redgrave, *A century of painters of the English school*, 2nd edn (1890) • H. N. O'Neill, *The Phillip and Creswick Collection at the International Exhibition and other subjects relating to art: a lecture* (1873) • C. Collins Baker, 'Thomas Creswick and mid-Victorian landscape painters', *Art Journal*, new ser., 28 (1908), 104–7 • T. S. Cooper, *My life*, 2 (1890) • W. P. Frith, *My autobiography and reminiscences*, 1 (1887) • IGI • CGPLA Eng. & Wales (1870)

Likenesses H. N. O'Neill, group portrait, oils, 1869 (*The Billiard Room of the Garrick Club*), Garr. Club • M. Jackson, woodcut (after T. Scott), BM • J. & C. Watkins, carte-de-visite, NPG • photograph, repro. in J. Maas, *The Victorian art world in photographs* (1984), p. 23 • wood-engraving (after photograph by J. Watkins), NPG; repro. in *ILN* (8 Jan 1870) • woodcut (after photograph by J. Watkins), NPG; repro. in *The Graphic* (8 Jan 1870)

Wealth at death under £10,000: probate, 18 Jan 1870, CGPLA Eng. & Wales

Creswick, William (1813–1888), actor, was born on 27 December 1813 in Long Acre, Covent Garden, London. As Master Collins he appeared in 1831 at a theatre in the Commercial Road, playing Martin Heywood, an Italian boy, in the drama *Rent Day*. After practice with travelling companies in Kent and Suffolk, he played leading business on the York circuit, where he met Elizabeth Page (d. 1876), performing as Miss Paget, whom he married on 14 May 1838. His first appearance in London was at the Queen's Theatre, Tottenham Street, under Louisa Nisbett, on 16 February 1835, as Horace Meredith in Douglas Jerrold's *Schoolfellows*. He took part in a failing experiment under William Penley at the Lyceum, joined Downe's company on the York, Leeds, and Hull circuit, then spent the years between 1839 and 1842 on a visit to the USA and Canada.

On 25 July 1846 Creswick joined Samuel Phelps's company at Sadler's Wells, playing Hotspur, and afterwards one or two other parts. On the reappearance of Fanny Kemble, he performed in April 1847, at the Princess's, Master Walter in Sheridan Knowles's *The Hunchback* to her Julia, and subsequently supported her in other characters. At the same house he played with Macready. At the Haymarket he appeared in July 1847 as Claude Melnotte to the Pauline of Helen Faucit in Bulwer-Lytton's *The Lady of Lyons*. On 4 October he was the first Vivian Temple in Marston's *The Heart and the World*. He was also seen as Trueworth in Knowles's *The Love Chase*, Mordaunt in Marston's *The Patrician's Daughter*, Proteus in *The Two Gentlemen of Verona* (December 1848), the Ghost in *Hamlet*, and Cassio.

With Richard Shepherd, Creswick began, on 17 September 1849, the management of the Surrey Theatre (1849–62), where he opened as Alasco in Knowles's *The Rose of Aragon*. At the Surrey he appeared as the first Laroque in H. F. Chorley's *Old Love and New Fortune* on 18 February 1849, and was seen as Damon in Richard Edwards's *Damon and Pythias*, and Adam Bede, among other parts. After retiring from management in 1862, he starred in London and the provinces. However, he joined Shepherd in management again in 1866, and on 8 September played Martin Truegold in Slous's prize nautical drama, *True to the Core*.

In 1871 Creswick went for the second time to America, made his first appearance as Joe in *Nobody's Child*, a part in which he had been seen at the Surrey on 14 September 1867, and played with Charlotte Cushman and Edwin Booth. His wife, Elizabeth, died on 16 February 1876, and in May 1877, after accepting a benefit at the Gaiety, in which he played Macbeth, he went to Australia, visiting Sydney, Adelaide, and Hobart Town. He opened at Melbourne as Virginius, and was very popular. Creswick was occasionally seen in London thereafter, chiefly in Shakespeare. His younger son, Charles Edward Creswick, also an actor, died in August 1885 at the age of thirty-five. Shortly afterwards, on 29 October 1885, William Creswick appeared at Drury Lane in a scene from *King Lear*, for his farewell benefit. He died at 12 The Terrace, Kennington Park, on 17 June 1888, leaving his second wife, Janet. He was buried at Kensal Green. His autobiography, copies of which are very rare, was published posthumously.

William Creswick belonged to the old-fashioned and oratorical school, of which he was one of the last survivors. He was popular in tragedy and won acceptance in melodrama, but had little subtlety or insight.

JOSEPH KNIGHT, rev. KATHARINE COCKIN

Sources *An autobiography: a record of fifty years of the professional life of the late William Creswick* [1889] · C. E. Pascoe, ed., *The dramatic list*, 2nd edn (1880) · Adams, *Drama* · T. A. Brown, *History of the American stage* (1870) · Hall, *Dramatic ports.* · Boase, *Mod. Eng. biog.* · CGPLA Eng. & Wales (1888) · m. cert. · personal knowledge (1901)
Archives Wellcome L., letters to Henry Lee
Likenesses A. Bryan, watercolour drawing, NPG · prints, BM, NPG · ten prints and caricatures, Harvard TC · woodbury-type, NPG
Wealth at death £2115: probate, 20 July 1888, CGPLA Eng. & Wales

Cresy, Edward (1792–1858), architect and civil engineer, was born on 7 May 1792 at Dartford, Kent, the only child of Edward Cresy (bap. 1764, d. 1838), a prosperous builder, and his wife, Lydia (bap. 1765, d. 1848), daughter of William and Lydia Muggeridge, farmers, of nearby Horton Kirby. He was educated at Rawes's academy, Bromley, Kent, before being articled in 1808 to James T. Parkinson, a London architect then engaged in laying out the Portman estate. He subsequently served two years with George Smith, surveyor to the Mercers' Company. The summer of 1816 was passed with his colleague and lifelong friend George Ledwell Taylor in a walking tour through England, measuring and drawing cathedrals and other notable buildings. For the next three years the two men pursued similar studies on the continent, travelling, mainly on foot, through France, Switzerland, Italy, Greece, Albania, Malta, and Sicily. Their chief aim was to present the dimensions of buildings in English measurements, with the ornamentation one quarter actual size. The results were published as *The Architectural Antiquities of Rome* (2

vols., 1821–2; new edn, 1874) and *The Architecture of the Middle Ages in Italy* (1829). The latter publication included the first modern survey of the leaning tower of Pisa. A third work, on the architecture of the Renaissance, was abandoned after the publication of two parts from lack of encouragement.

On 17 March 1824 Cresy married Eliza Taylor (bap. 1798, d. 1877), to whose translation from the Italian of F. Milizia's work of architectural biography *The Lives of Celebrated Architects, Ancient and Modern* (2 vols., 1826) he contributed additional material. Their five children—Edward, Eliza, Adelene, Bertha, and Theodore Grant—were born over the next six years, the youngest in Paris, where their father was engaged in building the Square d'Orléans, artists' apartments at 80 rue Taibout. His experiences here during the July revolution of 1830 were recorded by Charles Knight. Although successful, this venture interfered with his professional prospects at home. His practice was mostly private, since he was out of sympathy with contemporary trends, disapproving of the system of open competitions on artistic grounds and deprecating the growing separation between architecture and engineering. From c.1836 to 1847, as estate surveyor, he supervised the development of Rutland Gate, Knightsbridge. He undertook commissions for friends, among them Charles Darwin, at Down House, Kent, and the collector William Cotton, for whom he gothicized The Priory, Leatherhead, Surrey, and built his own houses at 6 Suffolk Street, Westminster (part of John Nash's rebuilding scheme of the 1820s), and Holmesdale at South Darenth, Kent. Here, as well as farming 170 acres, he busied himself with local improvements. These included the construction of a gasworks, a bridge, and a village school, and some church restoration. However, he was mainly occupied in his extensive library, writing a series of books and articles on bridge-building (1839), on cottages for agricultural labourers (with C. W. Johnson, 1847), on Gothic architecture, and, most important, *An Encyclopaedia of Civil Engineering* (1847; new edns, 1856 and 1861), which long remained a standard work.

In the 1840s Cresy became an enthusiastic participant in the new movement for sanitary reform, giving evidence before the health of towns and metropolitan sewers commissions. Because of his expertise in hydraulics—a branch of engineering then in its infancy—Cresy was among the first five superintending inspectors appointed by Edwin Chadwick to the General Board of Health, for which he prepared sixteen reports on urban water supply and drainage (1849–51). His remaining years were devoted to his architectural and antiquarian studies—he had been elected fellow of the Society of Antiquaries in 1820, and was a member of the British Archaeological Association and of John Britton's Architects' and Antiquaries' Club. An original member of the Institute of British Architects, he resigned early on policy grounds. An edited version of his final work, a 'Memorandum' on Horton Kirby, was issued in 2000 by its local history society. He died from a stroke at South Darenth, Kent, on 12 November 1858 and was buried at St Mary's Church, Horton Kirby, Kent. His elder son, Edward Cresy jun. (1824–1870), architect and administrator, having trained as an architect with his father and in Paris, became principal assistant clerk at the Metropolitan Board of Works, and architect to the London Fire Brigade, for which he designed twenty-six fire stations.

GORDON GOODWIN, rev. DIANA CRESSY BURFIELD

Sources G. L. Taylor, *The auto-biography of an octogenarian architect*, 2 vols. (1870–72) • E. Cresy, 'Memorandum relating to my tour round the parish', 1857, CKS, MS deposit from Dartford PL, uncataloged • *The Builder*, 16 (1858), 793–4 • G. L. Taylor, *The Builder*, 17 (1859), 166 • *The Engineer* (16 Dec 1870) • *The correspondence of Charles Darwin*, ed. F. Burkhardt and S. Smith, 2–13 (1987–2002) • *GM*, 1st ser., 94/1 (1824), 367 • *GM*, 1st ser., 94/2 (1824), 639 • gravestone inscriptions, Holy Trinity, Dartford, Kent • gravestone inscriptions, St Michael's, Wilmington, Kent • gravestone inscriptions, St Mary's, Horton Kirby, Kent • *Bailey's British Directory* (1784), vol. 4 • *Universal British Directory* (1793–8) • *Pigot's Directory* (1823–39) • *Kelly's directory* (1859) • IGI • census returns, 1841, 1851 • C. Knight, *Passages of a working life during half a century*, 3 vols. (1864–5), vol. 2, pp. 144–5 • C. Greenwood, *Kent* (1838), vol. 1 of *Epitome of county history*, 70, 82 • G. H. Gater and F. R. Hiorns, *The parish of St Martin-in-the-Fields*, 3: *Trafalgar Square and neighbourhood*, Survey of London, 20 (1940) • Dartford Gas Lights, minutes, vol. 1, 1826–7, CKS • Society of Architects and Antiquaries, Proceedings, 1820 • *CGPLA Eng. & Wales* (1858) • E. Cresy, letters to A. J. Dunkin, Dartford PL, ALSs • d. cert. • Colvin, *Archs.* • fellows' nomination papers, RIBA BAL, Fv1, p.1 • D. Burfield, *Edward Cresy, 1792–1858: architect and civil engineer* [forthcoming] • D. Burfield, 'Edward Cresy: polymath president of the Geologists' Association, 1864–5', *6A Magazine of the Geologists' Association*, 3/1 (2002), 22–3 [on Edward Cresy junior]

Archives BM, MS notes, cat. 1401.g.34.(4), 1401.g.34.(3*), 1401.g.34.(1) • RIBA BAL, cat. EW 72-03:92 | CKS, deposit from Dartford Public Library • CUL, Darwin MSS • Dartford Public Library, Kent, Horton Kirby collection

Wealth at death under £7000: probate, 10 Dec 1858, *CGPLA Eng. & Wales*

Creton, Jean (*fl.* 1386–1420), historian and poet, was probably a native of the Île-de-France. Nothing is known of his family, his early life, or the place and date of his birth and death. By 1386 he had entered the service of Philip, duke of Burgundy, supplying him with a book, possibly his own composition. In April 1399 he was sent by Charles VI of France (*r.* 1380–1422) to accompany Richard II on his fateful expedition to Ireland. When news of Henry Bolingbroke's invasion reached Richard in Ireland, Creton sailed for north Wales with the earl of Salisbury, 'for the sake of song and merriment' (Creton, 'Metrical history', 314). After Richard II had rejoined the earl, Creton remained in his entourage until his capture at Conwy. Creton returned to France in September 1399, where he composed an account in verse and prose of *La prinse et mort du roy Richart*, presented to the duke of Burgundy before July 1402. The *Prinse* reported the official story of the death of Richard II by starvation, but expressed Creton's belief that the body buried with royal pomp and circumstance was that of Richard Maudeleyn, who strongly resembled the king. He believed that Richard himself was alive and in prison. Shortly after completing his work, however, news arrived at the French court that Richard was at liberty in Scotland. In the spring of 1402 Creton was dispatched there by the duke of Burgundy to ascertain the truth of this report. The letter he wrote upon his return reveals that he was now convinced that Richard II was dead. In 1403 Creton was rewarded for his efforts by the honourable position of *valet de chambre* of the duke of Burgundy. By 1410 he was also *valet* to the king of France, and in the following year was given the important post of *clerc payeur des œuvres du roy* in the provostry of Paris, a post he held in 1413 and again in 1420, when he was given assistance in paying his ransom. His terms of office coincided with periods of Burgundian ascendancy in Paris, so he may, as a servant of the duke of Burgundy, have been seized during the Armagnac proscription of 1413. Nothing is known of his subsequent career.

Creton's historical importance rests on his history of 'the capture and death of King Richard' and his letters recounting his Scottish journey. The former contains a vivid account of Irish customs and manners, but its principal interest is the light it throws upon the Lancastrian usurpation. For many of the key episodes Creton is the sole witness, and for others his testimony conflicts with the official story propagated by English sources. Creton alone, for instance, reports the circumstances in which news of Bolingbroke's invasion was received in Ireland, and he is the sole source for the division of Richard's army, and for the activities of the earl of Salisbury in north Wales. Creton, too, is the only authority for the situation of the king and his tiny entourage in north Wales. Above all, however, Creton is responsible for the circumstantial eyewitness account of the capture of the king and of 'how he was falsely enticed out of his fair and strong castles in Wales' (Creton, 'Metrical history', 423) by the promise, given by the earl of Northumberland under oath, that nothing was intended against him, and that Bolingbroke asked only for the return of his inheritance and the punishment of traitors in parliament. This is entirely at odds with the official report of Richard's promise to renounce the crown, given while at liberty at Conwy. Creton was aware of the significance of what he had witnessed or had been told by the earl of Salisbury. While still in England he trembled for his life. But he solemnly declared that he wrote only the truth, which he feared would otherwise be suppressed. He was probably right to think so.

J. J. N. PALMER

Sources J. Creton, *Histoire du roy d'Angleterre Richard*, ed. J. A. C. Buchon, Collection des Chroniques Nationales Françaises, 23 (1826), 321–466 • [J. Creton], 'Translation of a French metrical history of the deposition of King Richard the Second … with a copy of the original', ed. and trans. J. Webb, *Archaeologia*, 20 (1824), 1–423 • P. W. Dillon, 'Remarks on the manner of the death of King Richard II', *Archaeologia*, 28 (1840), 75–95 • P. Cockshaw, 'Mentions d'auteurs, de copistes, d'enlumineurs et de libraires dans les comptes généraux de l'état bourguignon (1384–1419)', *Scriptorium*, 23 (1969), 122–44 • M. Rey, *Le domaine du roy et les finances extraordinaires sous Charles VI, 1388–1413* (1965) • F. Lehoux, *Jean de France, duc de Berri: sa vie, son action politique (1340–1416)*, 4 vols. (1966–8), vol. 2 • J. J. N. Palmer, 'The authorship, date and historical value of the French chronicles on the Lancastrian revolution', *Bulletin of the John Rylands University Library*, 61 (1978–9), 145–81; 398–421 • B. A. Pocquet du Haut-Jussé, *La France gouvernée par Jean sans Peur* (1949)

Crèvecoeur, J. Hector St John de (1735–1813), writer on America and farmer, was born on 31 January 1735 in Caen, Normandy, and baptized Michel-Guillaume Jean de Crèvecoeur. The son of Guillaume-Augustin Jean de Crèvecoeur, a substantial landowner and member of the provincial nobility, and Marie-Anne-Thérèse Blouet, the daughter of a prosperous banker, Crèvecoeur spent much of his early life in comfort at the family estate in Pierrepont, a farming village north-west of Caen. Probably tutored at home until he was eleven or twelve years old, Crèvecoeur then attended the Jesuit Collège Royal de Bourbon. Although he would later characterize his years at the boarding-school as confinement in a 'dark and cold hovel' (Allen and Asselineau, 5), Crèvecoeur was an excellent student who not only distinguished himself in language and literature but mastered the practical skills of cartography and surveying. He graduated in 1750, and perhaps as early as 1751 travelled to Salisbury, England, to continue his education, apparently driven into exile by his father's autocratic rule at home.

About 1755 Crèvecoeur migrated to Canada and enlisted in the French colonial militia. His service as a surveyor and cartographer in the region of the Great Lakes during the French and Indian War enabled Crèvecoeur more speedily to acquaint himself with the land and native inhabitants of the area. The map he drew for the marquis de Montcalm in preparation for the battle at Fort William Henry won Crèvecoeur high praise and helped gain him a commission in 1758 as a lieutenant in the regular French army. The following year, however, during the siege of Quebec by the forces of General James Wolfe, Crèvecoeur was wounded, and after the French surrender, at the insistence of his fellow officers, resigned from the regiment and sold his commission. His military career abruptly cut short, Crèvecoeur decided against returning to France, and in December 1759 moved to New York.

In *Letters from an American Farmer* (1782) Crèvecoeur poses his famous question: 'What then is the American, this new man?' His answer appears in the question itself. The American is a 'new man', a European immigrant who, having shed 'all his ancient prejudices and manners, receives new ones from the new mode of life he has embraced, the new government he obeys, and the new rank he holds' (Crèvecoeur, 39). Starting a new life in New York, Crèvecoeur was the archetypical American. After 1759 he fashioned a new identity for himself by adopting a new name, J. Hector St John; a new national allegiance, naturalized citizen of New York; a new occupation, farming; and a new language, English. He married Mehetable Tippet (*d.* 1781), the daughter of a substantial landowner in Westchester county, on 20 September 1769, and later that year purchased 120 acres of land in Orange county. Over the next half-dozen years he turned his property into a productive farm, which he dubbed Pine Hill, built an attractive two-storey frame house on it, fathered a daughter, America-Francès (Fanny), and two sons, Guillaume-Alexandre (Ally) and Philippe-Louis, continued to make

J. Hector St John de Crèvecoeur (1735–1813), by L. Massard, after 1786

excursions into the surrounding countryside to improve his knowledge of the geography and people of the region, and lived the idyllic life of the freeholders he celebrated in *Letters*. He became, like his fictional Scot 'Andrew, the Hebridean', an independent 'tiller of American soil' (ibid., 79).

The onset of the American War of Independence ended this placid phase of Crèvecoeur's life and commenced a period of personal turmoil. James, his fictional American farmer in *Letters*, beset by partisans on both sides, found it impossible to 'say this side is right, that side is wrong'. He was certain of one thing only: 'I was happy before this unfortunate Revolution. I feel I am no longer so; therefore I regret the change' (Crèvecoeur, 196–7). The once-contented farmer was transformed into a distressed 'frontier man'. The fictional husbandman ponders abandoning his farm and seeking safe haven among hospitable Native Americans. In fact Crèvecoeur decided to return to France, ostensibly to secure his inheritance in Normandy. Ironically, the 'American farmer' chose to shed his American identity at the very moment that his adopted country's national identity was taking shape.

In early 1779, toting a bundle of manuscript essays he

had written over the past decade and accompanied only by his six-year-old son, Ally, Crèvecoeur left Orange county for British-occupied New York city hoping to catch a ship bound for Europe. Soon after his arrival in the city, however, he was suspected of being an American spy and gaoled for three months. After his release Crèvecoeur struggled to keep himself and Ally alive through winter by occasionally working for firewood and subsisting on stale vegetables. In September 1780 father and son finally set sail for Britain, but they were shipwrecked off Ireland. Leaving Ally in Dublin, Crèvecoeur travelled alone to London in search of a publisher for his essays and succeeded in selling a collection that later appeared as *Letters*. In August 1781, nearly two and a half years after leaving Pine Hill, the weary voyagers arrived in Normandy.

The publication of *Letters*, which became an international best-seller, changed Crèvecoeur's fortunes in France. His reputation as an authority on America quickly established, Crèvecoeur was appointed by Louis XVI in 1783 to serve as French consul in New York. On his return, Crèvecoeur was devastated to discover that Mehetable had died in 1781, that Pine Hill had been burnt, and that Fanny and Louis had disappeared. A frantic search revealed that both children were being cared for by a Boston family whose efforts, Crèvecoeur later recorded, had been inspired by the aid he had once given to five American seamen on the Normandy coast.

By mid-1784, his family secure for the first time in many years, Crèvecoeur immersed himself in consular activities. He improved commercial relations between France and the United States, facilitated scientific exchanges, helped found several botanical gardens, wrote articles on agricultural subjects for American newspapers, encouraged the formation of medical societies in Cambridge and New Haven, and got Louis XVI to make donations to American colleges and scientific societies. All of his successes notwithstanding, Crèvecoeur longed to return to France. The erstwhile American farmer was homesick.

Crèvecoeur took a leave of absence from his official duties in July 1785, and spent the next two years in France, where he prepared a second French edition of *Letters*. After returning to his consular duties in New York in the summer of 1787, Crèvecoeur was interested in the work of the constitutional convention and hopeful that the federal government would be strengthened. Meanwhile factions within the French government, including some that did not share his enthusiasm for the revolutionary republic, and the appointment of a French ambassador who was critical of what he perceived to be Crèvecoeur's 'prejudices in favor of English customs and laws' (Allen and Asselineau, 150) discouraged further attempts to boost trade between France and the United States. Still Crèvecoeur's reputation in America continued to improve, and in January 1789 he was elected to membership of the American Philosophical Society.

By the spring of 1790 Crèvecoeur was anxious to return to France. Increasingly troubled by the revolutionary unrest there and worried about the safety of his sons, both of whom were residing in Normandy, he applied for and

was granted another leave from his consular duties. For the next four years, especially after the onset of the terror, Crèvecoeur remained as inconspicuous as possible while he arranged to have Ally and Louis relocated outside France. Ordered to return to his post in 1792, he chose instead to resign his consulship. Finally, in October 1793 Ally secured passage to Hamburg, and in April 1794 Louis, with the assistance of Governeur Morris, the American ambassador to France, embarked for the United States. As for Crèvecoeur himself, unsuccessful in his bid to secure a governmental pension and unable to gain another diplomatic assignment to the United States, he moved in with Ally for a year (1795–6), spent three years (1806–9) with Fanny in Munich, and lived out the rest of his life in relative obscurity in France. Although he continued to write, he never approached the success of *Letters*. Crèvecoeur died in Sarcelles of a heart ailment on 12 November 1813.

MELVIN YAZAWA

Sources G. W. Allen and R. Asselineau, *St John de Crèvecoeur: the life of an American farmer* (1987) · T. Philbrick, *St John de Crèvecoeur* (1970) · J. P. Mitchell, *St Jean de Crèvecoeur* (1916) · J. H. St J. de Crèvecoeur, *Letters from an American farmer*, ed. W. B. Blake (1957) · K. Emerson and E. Emerson, 'Crèvecoeur', *ANB* · S. T. Williams, 'Crèvecoeur', *DAB* · M. Jehlen, 'Crèvecoeur', *American writers before 1800: a biographical and critical dictionary*, ed. J. A. Levernier and D. R. Wilmes (1983)
Archives Archives Nationales, Paris, consular papers · L. Cong. | L. Cong., William Short MSS, corresp. · Maryland Historical Society, Baltimore, Maryland literary MSS, corresp.
Likenesses L. Massard, engraving, after 1786, repro. in R. de Crèvecoeur, *St John de Crèvecoeur* (1883) [*see illus.*] · Valière, portrait, 1786, repro. in Allen and Asselineau, *St John de Crèvecoeur*, frontispiece

Crew, Francis Albert Eley [Frank] (1886–1973), animal geneticist, was born on 2 March 1886 at 227 Dudley Port, Tipton, Staffordshire, on the outskirts of Birmingham. His father, Thomas Crew, was a small grocer who later prospered in business. Both his father and his mother, Annie (*née* Eley), were devout nonconformists. Crew was the third of their five children but the only one to survive beyond infancy. He was educated at the King Edward VI School in Birmingham from 1896 to 1906. From an early age Crew was passionately interested in pets, and he bred bantams very successfully, winning prizes at local shows. Believing a medical qualification to be the gateway to biological research, from 1907 he studied medicine at the University of Edinburgh, graduating MB ChB in 1912. In the following year Crew married Helen Campbell Dykes (*c*.1886–1971), a fellow medical student in Edinburgh. They had one son and one daughter.

During the First World War Crew served in the Royal Army Medical Corps, reaching the rank of major in 1917. After the war he returned to Edinburgh and obtained the post of assistant in the department of natural history, where he taught genetics. His flair for teaching was described by his colleague and close friend Lancelot Hogben:

> In the lecture theatre he was a spell binder. Handsome, well built, equipped with a mellifluous voice and a ready but rarely uncharitable wit, he had histrionic talent worthy of a

Shakespearean actor and—how rare a combination—an irreproachably lucid gift of exposition. (Hogben, 136)

In 1920 Crew was appointed as the first director of the Institute of Animal Breeding, then being set up in Edinburgh. Although it was linked to the department of animal breeding, the department existed only in name (and had neither staff, nor accommodation). By persuasive begging he obtained funds for a new building and for the endowment of a new chair, staff, and funds for research. In 1928 he was appointed to the new Buchanan chair of animal genetics.

Under Crew's leadership the institute did pioneering work on sex determination, reproductive physiology, and many aspects of the husbandry and breeding of sheep, cattle, pigs, horses, and poultry, and on the genetics of mice and budgerigars' colours. Crew's own most notable work centred on sex determination and sexual abnormalities such as sex reversal and intersexes in birds and mammals. This work, which was described in his book *Sex Determination* (1933), led to an understanding of how secondary sexual characters (such as the feathering of fowls) are determined during development.

The Seventh International Congress of Genetics was held in Edinburgh from 23 to 30 August 1939, when the Second World War was imminent. In the absence of the president-elect, the Russian N. Vavilov, Crew was chosen to be president in his place. This congress was the culmination of Crew's career in genetics.

Crew's influence on genetics was not so much through his own research, but through his infectious enthusiasm which attracted many able biologists to the subject, and through his success in obtaining funds. Crew's successor in the Buchanan chair, C. H. Waddington, described his influence on genetics as 'an achievement on a heroic scale' (*The Times*). During the Second World War, Crew served in the War Office as director of biological research, with the rank of brigadier. He was charged with producing the official *Army Medical History of the War*, much of which he wrote himself. It was published between 1953 and 1966 in five volumes. Crew resigned from the Buchanan chair in 1944 and was appointed in 1945 to the chair of public health and social medicine in Edinburgh. During his tenure of this chair he laid the foundations of medical genetics. His book *The Measurement of Public Health* (1948) outlines his teaching in the department. After retiring in 1955 he went on missions to Egypt, Burma, and twice to India, teaching and advising on medical genetics. After the last of these journeys, in 1967, he settled at Upton Mill, Framfield, Sussex.

Crew was elected fellow of the Royal Society in 1939, and he received many other marks of distinction and honours. In 1972, following the death of his first wife, he married Margaret Whithof-Keus, a medical graduate and friend who had given him much help and support in his later work. Crew died on 26 May 1973.

D. S. FALCONER

Sources L. Hogben, *Memoirs FRS*, 20 (1974), 135–53 · C. H. W. [C. H. Waddington], *The Times* (2 June 1973) · F. A. E. Crew, 'The genealogy

of the Poultry Research Centre, Edinburgh', *British Poultry Science*, 121 (1971), 289–95 · b. cert. · *WWW*, *1971–80*
Archives CUL, corresp. with Charles C. Hurst · Rice University, Houston, Texas, Woodson Research Center, corresp. with Sir Julian Huxley
Likenesses photograph, repro. in Hogben, *Memoirs FRS*, 135
Wealth at death £11,716: probate, 7 Dec 1973, *CGPLA Eng. & Wales*

Crew, John, first Baron Crew (1597/8–1679), politician, was the eldest son of Sir Thomas *Crewe (1566–1634), lawyer and politician, and Temperance (1580/81–1619), daughter of Reginald (or Reynold) Bray of Steane, Northamptonshire. Admitted to Gray's Inn in 1615, he matriculated from Magdalen College, Oxford, aged eighteen, on 26 April 1616. He was called to the bar in 1624 and about 1623 married Jemimah (1601/2–1675), daughter of Edward Waldegrave of Lawford Hall, Essex, with whom he had six sons, including Nathaniel *Crew, and two daughters.

Crew was MP for Amersham, Buckinghamshire, in 1624 and 1625, for Brackley, Northamptonshire, in 1626, for Banbury in 1628–9, and for Northamptonshire in the first parliament of 1640. In the Long Parliament he sat for Brackley. In May 1640 he was committed to the Tower for refusing to surrender papers in his possession as chairman of the committee on religion but, making submission in the following month, was released. A decidedly moderate Long Parliamentarian, he is said to have preferred primitive episcopalianism, he voted against the attainder of Strafford in 1641, and he spoke against the motion to commit Geoffrey Palmer for protesting against the publication of the grand remonstrance. Nevertheless, on the outbreak of the civil war he subscribed £200 in plate, engaged to maintain four horses for parliament, and in due course became a 'middle group' advocate of the war's vigorous prosecution. He was one of the commissioners appointed by parliament for the treaty of Uxbridge in 1644–5. He subsequently supported the self-denying ordinance by which it was proposed to disable members of parliament from holding places under government. A member of the committee of both kingdoms, he was also one of the commissioners who conducted the negotiations with the king at Newcastle upon Tyne and Holdenby in 1646, and in the Isle of Wight in 1648. From there in November he wrote to his colleague and ally in the Commons, John Swynfen, promising that he and his fellow treaty commissioners 'shall use our utmost endeavours here to bring the King nearer the Houses, and you will do good service at London in persuading the House to come nearer the king' (*CSP dom.*, 1648–9, 319). As one of the prime movers behind the treaty of Newport he was arrested among the secluded members on 6 December 1648. He was, however, released on the 20th.

Crew was returned to parliament for Northamptonshire in 1654, was a member of the committee for raising funds in aid of the Piedmontese protestants, and helped to draw up the new statutes for Durham College in 1656. In 1657 he received a peer's writ of summons to parliament, but does not appear to have taken his seat. On the secluded members' usurping power he was nominated one of the council of state (23 February 1660), and subsequently moved a resolution condemnatory of the execution of the king. At the general election which followed he was again returned for Northamptonshire. A prominent political presbyterian, he was one of the deputation that met Charles II at The Hague. In the king's coronation honours of 1661 he was created Baron Crew of Steane, retiring from public prominence thereafter. However, he continued to feature in the political gambits of the Cavalier Parliament, is known to have frowned upon its Anglican policies, and was marked as 'an opposition peer' from 1675 (HoP, *Commons, 1660–90*, 2.168). The presbyterian earl of Bedford held his proxy in the upper house until Crew's death. Crew is frequently referred to by Pepys, who seems to have entertained a very high respect for him. Clarendon describes him as a man of the 'greatest moderation'. He died on 12 December 1679 and was probably buried at Steane. He was succeeded in his title and estates by his eldest son, Thomas. His eldest daughter, Jemimah, married Sir Edward Mountagu, afterwards Lord Sandwich and lord high admiral.   J. M. RIGG, *rev.* SEAN KELSEY

Sources GEC, *Peerage*, 3.532–3 · J. Bridges, *The history and antiquities of Northamptonshire*, ed. P. Whalley, 1 (1791), 200 · Keeler, *Long Parliament*, 147 · D. Underdown, *Pride's Purge: politics in the puritan revolution* (1971), 15–16, 63–4, 71, 102, 104, 111, 114, 138, 147, 168n., 233, 352 · M. W. Helms and J. P. Ferris, 'Crew, John', HoP, *Commons, 1660–90*, 2.168 · P. Seaward, *The Cavalier Parliament and the reconstruction of the old regime, 1661–1667* (1989), 281 · A. Swatland, *The House of Lords in the reign of Charles II* (1996), 44, 124, 150, 152 · R. J. Fletcher, ed., *The pension book of Gray's Inn*, 1 (1901), 264 · W. A. Shaw, *The knights of England*, 2 (1906), 231 · Foster, *Alum. Oxon.* · J. Foster, *The register of admissions to Gray's Inn, 1521–1889, together with the register of marriages in Gray's Inn chapel, 1695–1754* (privately printed, London, 1889), 136 · W. E. Riley, *The parish of St Giles-in-the-Fields*, ed. L. Gomme, 1, Survey of London, 3 (1912), 75 · will, PRO, PROB 11/561, fols. 253v–254r
Archives Beds. & Luton ARS, letters to John Swynfen · PRO, letters to J. Swynfen, SP 16/516
Likenesses wash drawing, AM Oxf., Sutherland collection
Wealth at death see will, PRO, PROB 11/561, fols. 253v–254r

Crew [Crewe], **Nathaniel**, third Baron Crew (1633–1721), bishop of Durham, was born on 31 January 1633 at Steane, Northamptonshire, one of eight children and fifth of the six sons of John *Crew, afterwards first Baron Crew (1597/8–1679), and his wife, Jemimah (1601/2–1675), daughter of Edward Waldegrave of Lawford, Essex. Following an education at home and, in 1648, at Mr Azall's school, Chenies, Amersham, Buckinghamshire, Crew was admitted to Gray's Inn on 2 February 1652, and matriculated at Lincoln College, Oxford, on 8 June 1653. He graduated BA on 1 February 1656 and was elected fellow of the college on 9 May, proceeding MA on 29 June 1658. He was incorporated at Cambridge in 1659. That year he was elected fellow in canon law at Lincoln College, where he was sub-rector from 1659 to 1661 and 1663 to 1668.

Under the Commonwealth and protectorate Crew passed as a presbyterian, but when he sensed that the restoration of Charles II was imminent he shaved off his beard, dressed fashionably, and wore a surplice in chapel before the college made it compulsory. He became senior university proctor in 1663 and on the occasion of Charles

Nathaniel Crew, third Baron Crew (1633–1721), by Sir Godfrey Kneller, 1698

II's visit to Oxford on 23 September that year Crew's welcoming speech greatly impressed him. Crew was offered a knighthood by the king, but declined as the honour was incompatible with the holy orders he was expected to take as a fellow of Lincoln. He continued to acquire distinctions, being appointed an associate to the bench on 15 May 1663 and DCL on 2 July 1664. Following a long period of hesitation, perhaps connected with his family's presbyterian history and the prospect of a career at court, he was ordained deacon and priest the same day in Lent 1665. On 5 November 1666 he became a king's chaplain and in 1667 was preferred by the king to the rectory of Gedney, Lincolnshire, a sinecure with no cure of souls, which he held until 1671. On 12 August 1668 he was elected rector of Lincoln College, in recognition of his abilities as an administrator as well as of his links with the court.

At court Crew made the acquaintance of the king's brother, James, duke of York, and became his close friend. Through James's influence he was made dean and precentor of Chichester in 1669. In April 1671 he was elected bishop of Oxford, and in May was appointed rector of Witney, with an income of £600 p.a., to help support him in episcopal style. Following criticism that holding a bishopric and the headship of an Oxford college was inappropriate he resigned as rector of Lincoln in October 1672.

Crew's early biographer, John Smith, wrote that Crew had disapproved of James's conversion to Catholicism, but Crew was happy to act as the face of James's professed benevolence towards the Church of England, and on 21

November 1673 he solemnized James's unpopular marriage with Mary Beatrice of Modena according to the Anglican rite. In return he was promised James's influence on his behalf, and requested the wealthy see of Durham, vacant since the death of John Cosin in 1672. Despite the opposition of many at court, who wanted to keep the see vacant until the bishop's palatine authority in co. Durham had been dismantled, Crew was elected bishop on 18 August 1674. A pamphlet in 1675 alleged that Crew had paid Louise de Kéroualle, duchess of Portsmouth, Charles II's mistress, several thousand pounds to secure the see, and in 1715 Richard Lumley, first earl of Scarbrough, told a similar story where the beneficiary was Nell Gwyn. In 1674 Crew was also made a member of the Inner Temple, and on 4 November 1674 was appointed lord lieutenant of Durham. The following year he baptized James's daughter Catharine Laura, and on 26 April 1676 he was sworn a privy councillor.

Crew first entered his diocese in 1675, and made his first formal visitation the next year. He watched his palatine privileges strictly. He appointed the civil officers of the county, which included the judiciary, attorney-general, and solicitor-general as well as the high sheriff and under-sheriff. He held regular confirmations, and kept lavish hospitality. In 1679 he entertained James Scott, duke of Monmouth, the eldest illegitimate son of Charles II, at Auckland Castle on his way to command the army in Scotland, and greeted him yet more lavishly at Durham Castle on his return journey south. In November that year he entertained the duke and duchess of York at Durham Castle on their way to Scotland. His close relationship to James was already costly to his career; he had been James's candidate to succeed Sheldon as archbishop of Canterbury in 1677, but James's support itself doomed his chance. In 1679, during the agitation surrounding the Popish Plot, Crew was excluded from Sir William Temple's privy council of thirty, drawing attention to his supposed Catholic sympathies. In 1683, following the discovery of the Rye House plot, Crew organized raids on the houses of potential rebels, including both Catholics and opponents of James. That year he declined the archbishopric of York.

The county and city of Durham had both been enfranchised in 1673, and Crew was the first bishop of Durham to be concerned with parliamentary elections. Both county and city usually returned candidates favoured by Crew. In August 1684, Durham surrendered its 1602 charter to the king, and Crew, then in London, advised on the city's new charter, including the clause directing that the mayor, aldermen, and councillors must conform to the Church of England. He was on good terms with the corporation, presenting plate including a silver tankard, six silver candlesticks, a silver loving cup and cover, and a silver whistling pot with cover attached. Paintings show his coach with six black horses and his gondola on the river with gardens sloping to the water. In the castle he extended the upper chapel of about 1502 eastwards, placed rooms within the Norman gallery, extensively altered the great hall, added fine spout heads bearing his arms, and built a house, subsequently the master's lodging of University College, Durham. His personal wealth had increased when, in 1681, he inherited an estate at Newbold Verdon, Leicestershire, worth about £500 per annum, on the death of his brother John.

When James II became king Crew continued as a privy councillor and was one of his chief advisers on church affairs, often causing injury or offence, which he usually sought to redress by small favours. On 29 December 1685 he became dean of the Chapel Royal. In June 1686 James revived the ecclesiastical commission. William Sancroft, archbishop of Canterbury, refused to serve but Crew, who became the senior churchman on the commission, was delighted. It suspended Henry Compton, bishop of London, and Crew was called also to administer his diocese with Thomas Sprat, bishop of Rochester, and Thomas White, bishop of Peterborough, also servile to James II. Crew said that now his name would be recorded in history. When friends warned him of his danger, he replied he 'could not live if he should lose the King's gracious smiles' (Whiting, 147). When in 1686 Samuel Johnson, a protestant theologian, was condemned to flogging for writing against the king, Crew, Sprat, and White degraded him from holy orders despite their not constituting an ecclesiastical court. In 1687 Crew was one of the ecclesiastical commissioners who suspended Dr John Peachell, vice-chancellor of Cambridge University, for refusing to confer, at the king's request, the degree of MA on Alban Francis, a Benedictine monk who declined to take the required oaths of allegiance.

Crew's willingness to enforce the king's policies led to rumours that he was a secret Catholic, but he showed his reservations about James's Catholicism in his own way. When the papal nuncio was received in state at Windsor, scandalizing protestants, it was rumoured that Crew was present but although his carriage was seen he was absent. After November 1687, when Father Edward Petre was sworn of the privy council, Crew ceased to attend. In Durham, in 1688, after severely reprimanding two distinguished clergymen for refusing to read in church the declaration of indulgence he accompanied them to the castle gate, rebuking the porter for opening only the little wicket gate. One of them said immediately: 'No, my lord, we'll leave the broad way to your lordship; the strait way will serve us' (Whiting, 176).

In October 1688, when the ecclesiastical commission was dissolved, Crew was pardoned for any acts of illegality he had undertaken. He was one of the bishops who attended James on 1 November 1688 to assure him, in Crew's case truthfully, that they had not invited William of Orange to invade. He realized that James's overthrow was probable, and on 10 November 1688 was reconciled with those of his colleagues who had opposed James, telling Sancroft 'that he was sorry for having so long concurred with the court, and desired now to be reconciled with his grace and the other bishops' (W. Kennett, *A Complete History of England*, 3 vols., 1719, 3.527). On 14 November 1688 he presented James with a paper advising that James withdraw his protection from Catholic chapels and call a free parliament, refusing again the archbishopric of York, but this advice came too late. In December William of Orange dismissed Crew as clerk to the closet and dean of the Chapel Royal. In the House of Lords on 29 January 1689 he voted for a regency during James's absence, but on 6 February was one of only two bishops, with his old adversary Compton, to vote that the throne was vacant by James's flight. He then spent five months in the Netherlands. He returned in July to take the oath of allegiance to the crown, but was omitted from the Act of Grace the next year, implicitly threatening him with prosecution. Archbishop John Tillotson interceded and secured a separate pardon for Crew, who retained his bishopric, but without the patronage of the cathedral stalls, and without the lord lieutenancy, which was awarded to the earl of Scarbrough. Crew attempted to buy off the animosity of those he had injured, such as Johnson, by large gifts of money.

Crew retired to Durham and tried to make amends for the past. He was a capable administrator of his see, and made himself popular in the diocese by his generosity. On 21 December 1691 he married Penelope (1655/6–1699), widow of Sir Hugh Tynte and daughter of Sir Philip Frowde of Kent and his wife, Margaret, née O'Neile. His brother Thomas died without issue in 1697 and Crew inherited the peerage and the estate of Steane, now much diminished in value from the £3000 annual income it had once provided. Following Penelope's death in 1699, on 23 July 1700, at Durham, he married Dorothy (1672/3–1715), daughter of Sir William Forster, of Bamburgh in Northumberland, whom he had courted in 1691, when her parents had refused consent because of her youth. She was now twenty-seven and he was sixty-seven. The Forsters were a leading family in his bishopric. After marriage to Dorothy, Crew entertained Durham guilds at the castle. She persuaded him to cover the beautiful Norman hall doorway with lath and plaster, since removed.

After her brothers died Dorothy was coheir with her nephew Thomas Forster (afterwards a leader of the 1715 Jacobite rising which Crew did not support) to the manors of Bamburgh, Blanchland, Shotley, and Thornton. In 1704 they were heavily encumbered, and after the court of chancery agreed that year to sell them to discharge the debts only £1028 remained to be divided between Thomas and Dorothy. Crew bought the estates gradually for £20,679.

Crew enjoyed a revival of his political standing in the later years of Queen Anne's reign. In 1712 he was restored as lord lieutenant of co. Durham, and was one of the clerical supporters of the Oxford ministry. He proclaimed George I in 1714, and waited on him and the prince and princess of Wales (afterwards George II and Queen Caroline) but was again displaced by Scarbrough as lord lieutenant of Durham. His wife died, according to Lady Cowper, of 'convulsions' (GEC, *Peerage*, 2.534) brought on by fear of her nephew's arrest, on 16 October 1715, and was buried in the chapel at Steane, where Crew spent hours meditating at her tomb. He remained physically active for some years, and on 24 and 25 June 1717 he attended both days of the trial of Lord Oxford in the House of Lords, although the two had become estranged. He died at Steane on 18 September 1721, and was buried there. As he was childless the barony of Crew became extinct.

By his long and detailed will Crew devised his Northumberland estates for charitable purposes to five trustees: Dr John Montagu, Dr John Morley, rector of Lincoln College, Dr William Lupton, Dr Thomas Eden, and Dr John Dolben. On the death of any trustee another in holy orders was to replace him, one always to be the rector of Lincoln College. He left them considerable discretion. His provisions included annual gifts to midland schools and charities; others to augment small benefices in Durham diocese; funds to found charities local to his estates, including an apprentice charity in Durham city; and annual allowances to the almspeople of Durham and Auckland, and to schools. This was the basis for Lord Crewe's Charity. Lincoln College devoted part of Crew's annual benefaction to Oxford University, and the Crewian oration is delivered in alternate years by the public orator or the professor of poetry at the commemoration of university benefactors. The trustees kept for themselves Crew's new coach and six black horses, used in visiting tenants. They added to Crew's original provisions, establishing schools, repairing Bamburgh Castle as a landmark for sailors, and undertook other charitable schemes. These provisions established Crew's lasting reputation as a philanthropist, balancing his notoriety as the churchman who was James II's principal collaborator.　　　MARGOT JOHNSON

Sources Foster, *Alum. Oxon., 1500–1714*, 1.349 · Venn, *Alum. Cant.*, 1/1.418 · W. Hutchinson, introduction, *The history and antiquities of the county palatine of Durham*, 1 (1785) · C. E. Whiting, *Nathaniel, Lord Crewe, bishop of Durham, 1674–1721, and his diocese* (1940) · [J. Smith], 'Memoirs of Nathaniel, Lord Crewe', ed. A. Clark, *Camden miscellany, IX*, CS, new ser., 53 (1895) · *An examination of the life and character of Nathaniel Lord Crewe* (1790) · C. J. Stranks, *The charities of Nathaniel, Lord Crewe and Dr John Sharp, 1721–1976* (1976) [Durham Cathedral lecture, 1976] · *The history of King James's ecclesiastical commission: containing all the proceedings against the lord bishop of London* (1711) · VCH Berkshire, 3.41–2 · D. Baldwin, *The Chapel Royal ancient and modern* (1990), 235–7, 410 · G. Hampson and G. Jagger, 'Durham county', 'Durham city', HoP, *Commons, 1660–90*, 1.225–8 · GEC, *Peerage*, new edn, 3.532–34
Archives Yale U., Beinecke L., queries put by the bishop of Durham to the clergy of his diocese
Likenesses oils, c.1675–1685, Bishop's Palace, Chichester; version, NPG · G. Kneller, oils, 1698, Bodl. Oxf. [*see illus.*] · J. Faber junior, mezzotint, 1727 (after G. Kneller), BM, NPG · R. Dunkarton, mezzotint, pubd 1874 (after unknown artist), NPG · G. Kneller, oils, NPG · G. Kneller, oils, Lincoln College, Oxford · Lely?, portrait · D. Loggan, line engraving (after G. Kneller), BM, NPG · F. Place, mezzotint (after oils, c.1675–1685), BM, NPG · J. Riley, portraits, Bamburgh Castle · portraits, Durham Cathedral · portraits, U. Durham
Wealth at death see will, repr. in Whiting, *Nathaniel, Lord Crewe*, 332–358; Stranks, *Charities*

Crew [Crewe], **Randolph** [Randall, Ralph] (**1631–1657**), cartographer, was born on 6 April 1631, at Westminster, the second son of Sir Clipsby (Clippesby) Crew (or Crewe; 1599–1648), serjeant-at-law and MP, and Jane, daughter of Sir John Poultney. Sir Clipsby was a friend of the poet Robert Herrick, who addressed several odes to him and his wife. He was the grandson of Sir Randolph (Ranulphe or Randall) *Crewe (Crew) (*bap*. 1559, *d*. 1646). He attended Westminster School, as did his only brother, John (1626–1684), and was admitted a fellow-commoner at St John's College, Cambridge, on 15 June 1646. He was admitted at Lincoln's Inn on 30 October 1647.

Crew's only known work is a map which was published in Daniel King's *The Vale Royall of England, or, The County Palatine of Chester Illustrated* (1656). In this volume were published two historical tracts by William Smith and William Webb respectively, each being at the time of their first publication more than forty years old. King's was the first published history of Cheshire and is of very considerable interest despite the fact that its approach was already rather dated by the time of its publication. William Smith's manuscript history of Cheshire had been deposited with Sir Randolph Crew, the lawyer, and it was from the grandson of the elder Sir Randolph, that is, the subject of this memoir, that King obtained the manuscript. Randolph Crew the younger added one of two maps to the history (the other was a 'Ground plott' of Chester engraved by Wenceslas Hollar and was a freely adapted copy of John Speed's earlier town plan). Crew's map, which was extravagantly praised by Fuller in his *Worthies of England*, vol. 1, p. 193, appears to have been copied from William Smith's own map of 1603. This was until recently known as 'the anonymous map' of 1603, but has since been securely attributed to Smith. Smith's map was itself based on the earlier county map of Christopher Saxton but it was updated and filled out to incorporate details known well to Smith, a native of the county. In an inscription in the corner of Crew's version of this map the 'Eruditissimi et generosissimi Randolphi Crew' ('the most learned and generous') is said to have drawn the map with his own pen and had it engraved at his own expense, but it seems not to be the original work that earlier authors assumed.

Crew came to a sad end. He travelled abroad to complete his education but on 19 September 1657, while walking in the streets of Paris, he was set upon by footpads and sustained wounds of which he died two days later. He was buried in the Huguenots' burial-ground in the Faubourg St Germain at Paris. ELIZABETH BAIGENT

Sources J. B. Harley, 'From Saxton to Speed', *Cheshire Round*, 1/6 (1966), 174–84 • Venn, *Alum. Cant.* • J. B. Harley, 'Cheshire maps, 1787–1831', *Cheshire Round*, 1/9 (1968), 290–305 • J. B. Harley, 'Ogilby and Collins', *Cheshire Round*, 1/7 (1967), 210–25 • G. Ormerod, *The history of the county palatine and city of Chester*, 2nd edn, ed. T. Helsby, 3 vols. (1882) • E. Berry, 'The vale royal of England', pt 1, *Cheshire Round*, 1/9 (1968), 305–10; pt 2, 1/10 (1968), 338–43 • H. Whitaker, *A descriptive list of the printed maps of Cheshire, 1577–1900* (1942) • Fuller, *Worthies* • *DNB* • admin., PRO, PROB 6/33, fol. 240r

Crew, Sir Ranulphe. *See* Crewe, Sir Randolph (*bap*. 1559, *d*. 1646).

Crew, Thomas. *See* Crewe, Sir Thomas (1566–1634); Crewe, Thomas (*fl*. 1580).

Crewdson, Gertrude Gwendolen Bevan (1872–1913), college administrator and benefactor, was born on 28 March 1872, in Manchester, the second daughter among the four children of William Crewdson, a manufacturer and a member of the Society of Friends, and his wife, Ellen Waterhouse, sister of Alfred Waterhouse, the architect. She was left an orphan in 1881 and was thereafter brought up by a housekeeper, Miss Loader, who was also a governess with considerable experience of preparing students for Cambridge. At first they lived in Reading, and then at Bournemouth, in the hope of improving Gertrude's health: she had a tendency to consumption all her life. Her formal education began late. Because of its bracing air, and on the advice of Elizabeth Welsh, mistress of Girton College, Cambridge, she chose to go to St Leonard's School, St Andrews, at the age of twenty-one. She went as a by-pupil in a house which then trained teachers, to prepare herself for university entrance. She made rapid progress there and in 1894 entered Girton, whose buildings had been designed by her uncle. Mistrusting woolly abstractions, she had a penchant for expressing ideas in diagrammatic form, and she chose to read for the natural sciences tripos part I. She then took a fourth year at the college to study geology. Her beauty and charming personality, together with great talent as a pianist, ensured the respect and affection of her fellow students, who elected her senior student during her final year (1897–8), to represent them in college affairs.

When she left Cambridge, Gertrude Crewdson was elected by the former students who had received certificates that they had fulfilled the conditions necessary for a Cambridge degree, as their representative on the governing body of Girton College. In 1906 she graduated MA, taking advantage of the offer of Trinity College, Dublin, between 1904 and 1907, to confer degrees on women with appropriate qualifications. She had returned to Girton in 1900 as librarian and registrar, becoming junior bursar in 1902. A woman of means, she was a quiet and generous donor, providing the college with small requisites of plants and books. She resigned in 1905 to live in her own home.

From 1892 to 1899, Miss Crewdson had her permanent home with her older brother, Wilson Crewdson (1856–1918) and his wife, Mary Bevan, in Reigate, Surrey. In 1899, she bought her own house, Homewood, Aspley Heath, near Woburn Sands in Bedfordshire. She furnished it with great taste and care, buying antique furniture, Japanese pictures and ornaments, some of these being curios from her travels abroad. She opened the house and its extensive garden during the summer months as an inexpensive holiday home for professional women, putting aside the small sums raised. On her death these amounted to £250, which she left to Girton College, resulting in the Frances Buss Loan Fund. Among her other benefactions to the college was a large piece of land to the north of the buildings, which she had purchased in 1902 to save it from housing development.

Her Quaker upbringing had instilled in Gertrude Crewdson a high sense of purpose and service. A teetotaller, she had firm principles, but never obtruded them on her associates. She supported the non-militant women's suffrage movement. She took a particular interest in the Quaker School for Artisans at Sibford, near Banbury. She travelled widely in Greece, Crete, Sweden, and Norway, but her first love was for Egypt and its ancient past. Characteristically, she took a course in Egyptology before spending a winter and spring in Khartoum. On her death, Girton was the recipient of her collection of Egyptian antiquities.

Gertrude Crewdson was active, to the point of being restless, all her life, an attribute consonant with her life-long battle with tuberculosis, of which she died, at home, on 14 October 1913, at the early age of forty-one. A memorial brass was unveiled in her memory in the chapel at Girton College. Her successor as bursar, Eleanor Allen, when she died in 1929, bequeathed money to the college to found the Crewdson memorial prize for natural sciences. BARBARA E. MEGSON

Sources K. T. Butler and H. I. McMorran, eds., *Girton College register, 1869–1946* (1948) · *Girton Review* (1913), 10–15 · W. Crewdson, ed., *Gwendolen Crewdson* (privately printed, 1914) · *CGPLA Eng. & Wales* (1913)
Likenesses photographs, 1894, Girton Cam. · portrait, Girton Cam.
Wealth at death £61,460 3s. 4d.: probate, 1 Dec 1913, *CGPLA Eng. & Wales*

Crewdson, Isaac (1780–1844), Quaker seceder, was the elder son of Thomas Crewdson and Cicely (*née* Dillworth) of Kendal, Westmorland. He was born there on 6 June 1780, and at fourteen settled at Ardwick, Manchester, where he became a successful textile manufacturer. On 27 July 1803 he married Elizabeth (1779–1855), daughter of John Jowitt and Susannah (*née* Dickinson) of Leeds. A strict Quaker in his earlier years, he opposed slavery and ministered in the society from 1816 to 1836. However, after a serious illness, having heard a strong Calvinist preacher in Manchester, he became more evangelical. In his *Beacon to the Society of Friends* (1835) he protested that Friends placed the authority of the Spirit (or the inward light) above that of scripture, and the publication provoked a major crisis among Quakers. In other pamphlets Crewdson criticized the Quaker rejection of biblical ordinances such as the Lord's Supper and water baptism. Although moderates like Joseph Gurney supported him at the yearly meeting, his confrontational approach aroused local opposition. In November 1836 he resigned from the society with about fifty sympathizers and established, in Grosvenor Street, an assembly of Free Evangelical Friends, loosely associated with the so-called 'Plymouth' Brethren. In 1837 Crewdson was baptized and also administered baptism to other Quakers. He died at Bowness, Westmorland, on 8 May 1844 and was buried at Rusholme Road cemetery, Manchester. His surviving daughter, Mary, married Henry Waterhouse in 1832. His quiet and unsophisticated sincerity attracted followers, but with his death the new assembly was dissolved and many members became Brethren or Anglicans. TIMOTHY C. F. STUNT

Sources 'Dictionary of Quaker biography', RS Friends, Lond. [card index] · I. Crewdson, *Glad tidings for sinners* [1860] [with memoir of the author] · E. Isichei, *Victorian Quakers* (1970), 45–51 · R. M. Jones, *The later periods of Quakerism*, 2 vols. (1921) · M. Grubb, 'The Beacon separation', *Journal of the Friends' Historical Society*, 55 (1983–

9), 190–98 · T. C. F. Stunt, *Early Brethren and the Society of Friends* (1970), 6–7, 14 · *DNB*
Archives RS Friends, Lond., archives
Likenesses B. R. Haydon, group portrait, oils, 1841 (*The Anti-Slavery Convention, 1840*), NPG · F. C. Lewis, mezzotint, pubd 1843 (after B. R. Faulkner, 1840), NPG

Crewdson [*née* Fox], **Jane** (1808–1863), poet and hymn writer, was born at Perran-ar-worthal, Cornwall, on 22 October 1808, the second daughter of George Fox of Cornwall. Little is known about her early life before her marriage at Exeter on 12 October 1836 to Thomas Dillworth Crewdson (1803–1869), a Manchester cotton manufacturer. She was best-known for her hymns, which appeared in various American and British anthologies such as Lovell's *Selection of Scriptural Poetry* (1848) and B. H. Kennedy's *Hymnologia Christiana* (1863). In 1851 she published *Aunt Jane's Verses for Children*, which was reprinted with additions in 1855 and 1871. This volume contained poems about heroes of the Bible and the Reformation, as well as more secular pieces intended to 'cultivate a kindly sympathy towards all living things' (Crewdson, 'Preface', 1851). In 1860 she issued a second work, *Lays of the Reformation and other Lyrics, Scriptural and Miscellaneous*. Crewdson died after a long illness on 15 September 1863 at her residence, Summerlands, Whalley Range, Manchester, and was buried at Sale, near Manchester. A posthumous collection of her hymns, entitled '*A Little While', and other Poems*, was published in 1864, and went through several editions. One source identifies Crewdson's religious denomination as Church of England (Long, 538); however, there are indications that she had Quaker connections: her marriage was recorded in the *Digest Register of Marriages* of the Devon quarterly meeting of the Society of Friends, and her children's verses and collected hymns were published in the US by the Association of Friends. C. W. SUTTON, *rev.* CLARE COTUGNO

Sources Boase & Courtney, *Bibl. Corn.*, 1. 97; 3. 1141 · J. Julian, ed., *A dictionary of hymnology*, rev. edn (1907); repr. in 2 vols. (1915), 268–9, 622, 830, 1162 · J. Crewdson, introduction, in J. Crewdson, 'The little while' and other poems', 3rd edn (1870), 3–4 · E. M. Long, *Illustrated history of hymns and their authors*, 538 · J. Crewdson, preface to the first edn, *Aunt Jane's verses for children*, 2nd edn (1855), 8

Crewe. For this title name *see* individual entries under Crewe; *see also* Milnes, Robert Offley Ashburton Crewe-, marquess of Crewe (1858–1945).

Crewe [*née* Greville], **Frances Anne**, Lady Crewe (*bap.* 1748, *d.* 1818), political hostess, was baptized at Newton Toney, Wiltshire, on 28 November 1748, the only daughter of Fulke Greville (1717–1805), diplomat and man of fashion, and his wife, the poet Frances *Greville, *née* Macartney (1727?–1789). She was educated privately. On 4 April 1766, at St George's, Hanover Square, she married John *Crewe, afterwards first Baron Crewe of Crewe (1742–1829), MP for Stafford and later for Cheshire.

By the time she was twenty Mrs Crewe was one of the best-known of the whig hostesses and was accustomed to entertaining lavishly both at Crewe Hall, her husband's country seat, and at their villa in Hampstead. In 1773 she visited Paris, where she made a positive impression on

Frances Anne Crewe, Lady Crewe (*bap.* 1748, *d.* 1818), by Sir Thomas Lawrence, *c.*1810

Marie de Vichy Chamrond, marquise du Deffand, correspondent of Horace Walpole. Her husband established an enduring friendship with Charles James Fox during the 1770s, and this relationship shaped Mrs Crewe's career as a political hostess. Fox dedicated a booklet of verses to her in 1775, and following the Westminster election in 1780 she hosted 'a great public company met … expressly to celebrate the success of his election' (*Memoirs of … Wraxall*, 2.17). Mrs Crewe's place at the centre of Fox's circle was emphasized by her enthusiastic part in his election campaign in Westminster in 1784. She coined the term 'mince-pie administration' for the Pitt ministry formed in December 1783, and during the campaign led one of the controversial ladies' canvassing parties. On the evening of Fox's victory at the hustings, on 18 May 1784, she hosted a celebration at her house in Lower Grosvenor Street, London, with all attending, including the prince of Wales (afterwards George IV), in Fox's colours of blue and buff. The prince proposed the toast 'True blue and Mrs Crewe', to which Mrs Crewe responded equally laconically 'True blue and all of you' (ibid., 3.350). The toast was often cited as capturing the fellowship of the Foxite whigs.

Mrs Crewe's notoriety in public life was impossible to separate from her effect on the private lives of some of her circle. For some, her good looks established the criterion of feminine beauty. She was painted three times by Joshua Reynolds. Frances Burney wrote in 1779 that 'the elegance of Mrs Sheridan's beauty is unequalled by any I ever saw, except Mrs Crewe' (*Diary and Letters of Madame D'Arblay*, 118–19). The comparison between Elizabeth Sheridan and

Frances Anne Crewe was often made in the late 1770s and early 1780s, spice being added to the reference by the awareness that Mrs Crewe and Sheridan were conducting an affair at that time. In May 1777 Sheridan dedicated his play *The School for Scandal* to Mrs Crewe, with 124 lines of rhyming verse concluding 'To Thee my Inspirer—and my Model—CREWE'. Presumably he meant that the character of Lady Teazle in the play was modelled on her. He also addressed her as

Amoret … for 'neath that name
In worthier verse is sung thy beauty's fame …

the 'worthier verse' and the name 'Amoret' having been included by Elizabeth Sheridan in a half-bantering, half-anguished letter to her husband in 1775 at the point where she realized that Mrs Crewe had become a serious rival for his affections. None the less both Sheridans remained regular visitors at Crewe Hall, and even as late as 1785 Elizabeth wrote from there to her friend Mary Anne Canning:

S is in Town—and so is Mrs Crewe. I am in the Country and so is Mr Crewe—a very convenient Arrangement, is it not? Oh the Tiddlings and Fiddlings that have been going on at Chatsworth. 'Twas quite a Comedy to see it. (Sichel, 2.64)

Three years later, however, the affair was apparently over. In the spring of 1788 Sheridan complained to the duchess of Devonshire of Mrs Crewe's self-pitying and depressive nature and of her irresponsibility and lack of discretion: 'she is of an unhappy disposition and there are moments when, in spite of her behaviour, I feel inclined to pity her' (ibid., 2.102).

Mrs Crewe continued to maintain and extend her political connections in the 1780s and beyond. About 1790 the future diplomat Charles Arbuthnot met her, thinking her 'a comfortable kind of creature that has read a great deal and is amazingly well-informed' (GEC, *Peerage*). Following the breach between Fox and Edmund Burke over the whig response to the French Revolution, she acted as an intermediary between the two. Burke regarded her as a friend and a valuable source for the latest state of opinion in Foxite circles. In 1793 she organized a committee of ladies to raise money for refugee French clergy, and in 1796 she acted as Burke's emissary in his successful bid for ministerial support in his scheme to start a school for French children at Penn, although her desire for continued influence at the school infuriated both Burke and the superintending French clergyman, Jean-François de la Marche, bishop of St Pol. She was also highly regarded by William Windham, maintained friendships with the Burneys, and made the acquaintance of younger politicians such as George Canning.

Lady Crewe, as she became when Fox made her husband a peer in 1806, died in Liverpool on 23 December 1818, and was buried near Crewe Hall, in the Crewe family vault in the parish church at Barthomley, Cheshire. She was remembered as 'one of the most brilliant constellations in the hemisphere of fashion' (GM, 1st ser., 88/2, 1818, 648). She was survived by her husband, her son John, later second Baron Crewe (1772–1835), and her daughter Elizabeth

Emma (1780–1850), who married Foster Cunliffe-Offley (d. 1832); two other children, Richard and Frances, died in infancy.   ERIC SALMON

Sources A. Chedzoy, *Sheridan's nightingale* (1997) · F. O'Toole, *A traitor's kiss* (1997) · *Diary and letters of Madame D'Arblay*, ed. C. Barrett, 1 (1893) · R. B. Johnson, *Fanny Burney and the Burneys* (1926) · *Fanny Burney: selected letters*, ed. J. Hemlow (1986) · W. Sichel, *Sheridan*, 2 vols. (1909) · *Memoirs of the life of the Right Honourable Richard Brinsley Sheridan*, ed. T. Moore (1825) · A. Foreman, *Georgiana, duchess of Devonshire* (1998) · *The correspondence of Edmund Burke*, ed. T. W. Copeland and others, 10 vols. (1958–78), vols. 4–8 · *The historical and the posthumous memoirs of Sir Nathaniel William Wraxall, 1772–1784*, ed. H. B. Wheatley, 5 vols. (1884), vols. 2–3 · Walpole, *Corr.* · W. Windham, *The Windham papers*, 2 vols. (1903) · GEC, *Peerage* · IGI · G. Ormerod, *The history of the county palatine and city of Chester*, 2nd edn, ed. T. Helsby, 3 vols. (1882)
Archives BL, corresp. and travel journals | BL, letters to Caroline Fox, Add. MSS 51960–51961 · Yale U., Burney family collection, corresp.
Likenesses J. Macardell, mezzotint, pubd 1762 (after J. Reynolds), BM, NPG · J. Marchi, mezzotint, pubd 1770 (after J. Reynolds), BM, NPG · T. Watson, mezzotint, pubd 1773 (after J. Reynolds), BM, NPG · T. Watson, stipple, pubd 1780 (after D. Gardner), BM, NPG · T. Lawrence, drawing, c.1810, priv. coll. [*see illus.*] · J. Reynolds, three portraits, oils, priv. coll.

Crewe, John, first Baron Crewe (1742–1829), politician, was born in London on 27 September 1742, the first son of the six children of John Crewe (1709–1752), MP for Cheshire from 1734 until his death, and Anne, daughter of Richard Shuttleworth of Gawthorpe, Lancashire. He was educated at Westminster School and matriculated at Christ Church, Oxford, on 19 February 1760, leaving without a degree. After a grand tour in 1761–3 to France and Italy, he returned to his Cheshire estates, where he would establish a reputation as one of the leading agriculturists of his day. On 4 April 1766 he married Frances Greville [*see* Crewe, Frances Anne (*bap.* 1748, *d.* 1818)], daughter of Fulke Greville, of Wilbury, Wiltshire, and Frances Macartney, poet. They had four children, two sons and two daughters.

In 1765 Crewe was elected MP for the borough of Stafford, and from 1768 to 1802 was returned unopposed as one of the county members for Cheshire. Although only one vote is recorded between 1765 and 1774, he seems from the beginning to have been a follower of the duke of Grafton. He followed Grafton into opposition, over American affairs, in 1775 and thereafter consistently voted against North's administration. Crewe spoke infrequently in the house, mostly in support of his bills to exclude revenue officers from parliamentary elections. Passed in 1782, Crewe's Act was one of the Rockingham administration's main evidences of reform. Crewe went on to support Shelburne's government, and then the Fox–North coalition.

Long a loyal friend to Charles James Fox, Crewe went into opposition with Fox when the latter was dismissed from office in 1783. Among the raffish young blue bloods who frequented Almack's, and afterwards Brooks's, each new generation produced recruits to a Fox fan club for whom he could do no wrong. Crewe was a charter member (as well as a founder member of Brooks's), and his

adoration never waned. By 1773 he was already saddled with a £1200 annuity on Fox's behalf. Before the end of the Fox–North coalition, Crewe's annual expenditure for Fox's benefit was said to have grown to £12,000; and thereafter whenever there was an appeal to rescue his idol, Crewe always dug deep into his pockets. Nor was Crewe's tolerance of Fox limited to his spendthrift ways. The beautiful Frances Crewe appears to have been the sweetheart of the whole Foxite party, not least its leader. The relationship seems to have been one of perfect propriety, but might have been resented for all that. Crewe gave no sign of any pique.

Not only was Crewe indulgent with Fox, he was prepared to fight for him, quite literally. Early in 1784 William Pitt, the new prime minister, was granted the freedom of the City of London. An exuberant crowd insisted on drawing his carriage home, and as they went up St James's Street, they suddenly tried to turn the whole procession into St James's Place, to break the windows of Fox's house. The effort was, however, deflected by a flanking attack from Brooks's, with Crewe prominently in the lead.

In 1806, when Fox returned to power, Crewe's unswerving loyalty and friendship was rewarded in the form of a peerage. In his twenty-three years as a peer, Crewe stayed true to his early habits. There is no record of his ever speaking in the Lords, though this was hardly unusual in the upper house. He was, however, a loyal whig and ready with his vote or proxy, especially on questions of religious liberty, which constituted the majority. Fanny Burney said of him in 1813, that he 'seems always pleasing, unaffected, and sensible, and to possess a share of innate modesty that no intercourse with the world, nor addition of years can rob him of' (HoP, *Commons*).

Crewe died on 28 April 1829, aged eighty-six, in his house in Grosvenor Street, and was succeeded by his only surviving son, John, as second Baron Crewe.

                                                R. W. DAVIS

Sources GEC, *Peerage* · Hansard 1 · Hansard 2 · M. M. Drummond, 'Crewe, John', HoP, *Commons, 1754–90* · D. R. Fisher, 'Crewe, John', HoP, *Commons, 1790–1820* · S. Ayling, *Fox: the life of Charles James Fox* (1991) · J. Ingamells, ed., *A dictionary of British and Irish travellers in Italy, 1701–1800* (1997) · DNB
Likenesses W. Lane, group portrait, chalk, c.1810 (*Whig statesmen and their friends*), NPG · W. Say, mezzotint (after T. Lawrence), BM, NPG · J. G. Wood, etching, BM

Crewe, Nathaniel. *See* Crew, Nathaniel, third Baron Crew (1633–1721).

Crewe [*formerly* Dodds], **Quentin Hugh** (1926–1998), writer on food and travel, was born at 27 Welbeck Street, London, on 14 November 1926, the second son of Major (James) Hugh Hamilton Dodds, British consul in Tripoli, and his wife, formerly Lady Annabel Hungerford O'Neill (d. 1948), daughter and heir of Robert Offley Ashburton Crewe-*Milnes, marquess of Crewe. The whole family took the name Crewe in 1945. Lady Annabel had five other children from her first marriage, to the Hon. Arthur O'Neill, who was killed in the First World War. Quentin Crewe was fond of saying that his grandfather was the first secretary of state for India who found it worth the trouble to visit the country. He realized that his mother, all too aware of her own grand connections, looked down on his father's Scottish covenanter forebears.

While his parents lived abroad on a series of diplomatic postings Quentin was in the care of various relatives in England, one of whom noticed, when he was six, that he had difficulty walking and fell down frequently. His mother took him to a neurologist in Harley Street, who diagnosed muscular dystrophy and said that the child would die before he was sixteen. Lady Annabel took him to tea with a cousin and never mentioned the subject again. Crewe remembered being disappointed when he reached sixteen and nothing happened; he did not see a doctor between the ages of six and eighteen.

Having been expelled from Eton College after one year, for escaping to London with the aid of a copied key to a fire door, he was tutored by an impoverished vicar near Henley-on-Thames before going up to Trinity College, Cambridge. There he read law and was spare cox for the university crew before being sent down for sheer indolence. He went to work at Southeran's, the London antiquarian bookshop, then as a statistics clerk in a Technicolor film factory and in the publicity department of the shipping company French Lines. It was at this time that he nearly married Sarah Macmillan, the daughter of Lady Dorothy Macmillan and Lord Boothby. It ended badly, and by 1952 Crewe's illness made normal work almost impossible—he could move one hand only by grasping it with the other. So he went to Lerici, in Italy, where he read aloud to the almost blind literary scholar Percy Lubbock and wrote some *Times Literary Supplement* reviews actually commissioned from Lubbock—which gave him the ambition to be a writer himself.

In the following year Crewe returned to England, where Bob Boothby, who was interested in the good-looking young man with flaxen curls and the face of a cherub, introduced him to John Junor, deputy editor of the *Evening Standard*. Junor assigned Crewe to fly to Nice to investigate rumours that Aristotle Onassis intended to make a virtual takeover bid for Monaco and that Prince Rainier intended to sell him his tiny principality. There was of course no evidence of any such plan but the resulting article was so funny that Crewe was hired at £15 a week. He was soon writing leaders, 'Londoner's diary', and features, and was not hampered in 1955 by having to squeeze his 6 feet 1 inch frame into a wheelchair. In 1956 he married Martha Sharp, an American heiress, and started a new column for the paper called 'In London last night', which took him to two or three parties every evening. A commission for a book in 1958 (*A Curse of Blossom*, 1960) took the couple to Japan, where Crewe learned Japanese and travelled with Arthur Koestler. Having had a son and a daughter, the Crewes divorced.

Back in England in 1959 Crewe joined Jocelyn Stevens's magazine *Queen*, where he found his métier as a new kind of restaurant critic when he filled an empty half-page by describing his lunch at Wiltons, in St James's, where members of the aristocracy were served nursery food by waitresses dressed as nannies, and the bill, as befitted the clientele, was so large that it had to be paid out of capital. The resulting column was called, somewhat tastelessly, 'Meals on wheels'.

In 1961 Crewe published *Frontiers of Privilege*, a slight book about changing attitudes in society as reflected in *Queen*, and married journalist Angela Maureen Huth (*b.* 1938), with whom he had a daughter, and a son who died in infancy. At their flat in Wilton Crescent they entertained a social circle dominated by Princess Margaret and Lord Snowdon that encompassed George Melly, a couple of the Rolling Stones (Bill Wyman and Keith Richards), Peter Sellers, Arthur Koestler, Kenneth Tynan, and Bernard Levin. Despite this giddy whirl Crewe was a man of principle, and when *Queen* ran an advertising supplement promoting apartheid-ruled South Africa he resigned and went to the *Daily Mail*. On that paper he doubled as film critic and, as 'Charles Greville', gossip columnist. From 1964 to 1971 he wrote a free-ranging column in the more left-wing *Sunday Mirror*.

Crewe's second marriage also having ended in divorce, on 5 March 1970 he married Susan Anne (Sue) Cavendish (*b.* 1949/50), a cousin of the duke of Devonshire and later editor of *House and Garden*. They had a son and a daughter, and divorced in 1983. Crewe had travelled a good deal for his various jobs in journalism; now he wanted to travel for its own sake, and in 1966 he set off with Jeremy Fry, inspired by the writing of Wilfred Thesiger, to cross the 'empty quarter' of Saudi Arabia. There was a bad moment once, when they were lost—'The desert claims you with a smile', he wrote, 'I had never been so afraid' (*The Times*)— and an even worse one, when one of the guides went mad and slit his own throat in four places.

In 1978 Crewe's *Great Chefs of France* appeared. This was far from being a trivial work, for Crewe had spotted that a revolution had taken place in the restaurant kitchens of France, and he was one of the first British journalists (the American journalist Raymond Sokolov had noticed the trend as early as 1972) to write about the *nouvelle cuisine* and introduce its practitioners to the non-Francophone world. To his further credit Crewe got it exactly right, from his choice of chefs to his descriptions of their techniques, and the book is a historical document of real importance. There followed in 1980 the tiny *Pocket Book of Food*, which is still valuable to the traveller who wants to know what local dishes to order in Indonesia, India, or even Italy.

For two years Crewe and a series of friends and young helpers travelled the Sahara from Tunisia to Mauritania, and on to Khartoum, Cairo, and Siwa. In Mauritania one of the trucks hit a landmine and Crewe was catapulted out, going up 'with the happy ease of a shuttlecock' but coming down and 'spraining a dreary ankle' (*The Times*). The journey is detailed in *In Search of the Sahara* (1983). He had become a fine travel writer, and there followed a book about India, *The Last Maharaja* (1985); *Touch the Happy Isles* (1987), about the West Indies; *In the Realms of Gold* (1989); *Well, I Forget the Rest* (1991), his funny, touching autobiography; *The Food of France* (1993); and his final book, *Letters from India* (1993). In that year his losses at Lloyd's, a broken back, and generally worsening health forced him to abandon his house in a hilltop village in France and return to England, where with the help of the former wives, with whom he remained on the best of terms, he moved to the Cotswolds to live in a flat at Bliss Mill, a former industrial mill in Chipping Norton. It was there that he died on his seventy-second birthday, 14 November 1998.

PAUL LEVY

Sources *The Times* (16 Nov 1998) • *Daily Telegraph* (16 Nov 1998) • *The Guardian* (16 Nov 1998) • *The Independent* (16 Nov 1998) • b. cert. • m. cert. [A. Huth] • m. cert. [S. A. Cavendish] • d. cert. • personal knowledge (2004) • Burke, *Peerage* (1939) • *WW*
Likenesses photograph, 1966, Mirror Syndication International, London • photograph, repro. in *The Times* • portrait, repro. in *Daily Telegraph* • portrait, repro. in *The Guardian* • portrait, repro. in *The Independent*
Wealth at death under £200,000: probate, 19 March 1999, *CGPLA Eng. & Wales*

Crewe [Crew], **Sir Randolph** (*bap.* 1559, *d.* 1646), judge, was baptized in Nantwich, Cheshire, on 10 January 1559, the second son of John Crewe (*d.* 1598), a tanner of Nantwich, and his wife, Alice, daughter of Hugh Mainwaring, also of Nantwich. Sir Thomas *Crewe (1566–1634) was his brother. After attending Shrewsbury School, Crewe matriculated at Christ's College, Cambridge, in May 1576, but left without a degree. He subsequently credited Thomas Egerton with his admission to Lincoln's Inn from its satellite Furnival's Inn on 14 November 1577, and Crewe's gratitude for the continued 'favour, countenance, and protection' of his fellow countryman can hardly be doubted (Baker, *Serjeants*, 323).

After his call to the bar (minuted on 8 November 1584), Crewe's professional career seems to have blossomed only in the later 1590s, when Gilbert Talbot, tenth earl of Shrewsbury, employed him as legal adviser and counsel, and Egerton secured his return for the seat of Brackley in the parliament of 1597, where he generally kept a low profile. On 20 July 1598 Crewe married Julia Clipsby (1574–1603), the heir of a Norfolk landowner and maid to the countess of Shrewsbury. With this 'deare and vertuous wife' Crewe had a male heir and two other children before her death, probably in childbed, on 19 June 1603 (Ches. & Chester ALSS, DAR/I/18).

Crewe had joined the governing body of Lincoln's Inn as a bencher in 1600, delivering his reading on the Henrician Statute of Enrolments (27 Hen. VIII c. 16) in August 1602. In 1604 he acted as spokesman for the House of Commons in conference with the Lords, though not an elected MP, and in 1608 he became recorder of Great Yarmouth, where he had previously served as steward. On 12 April 1607 he had married for a second time; his new wife was Julia Hesketh, *née* Fasey, the widow of a prosperous Gray's Inn lawyer. Crewe's flourishing practice in chancery and other Westminster courts also enabled him to pay over £6000 for a large Cheshire estate formerly belonging to Sir Christopher Hatton, which centred on the manor of Crewe: as he later proclaimed, 'it hath pleased God of his abundant goodness to reduce the house and Mannor of the name to the name againe' (Ches. & Chester ALSS, DCR 1/4/2, 4–5, 9; PRO, PROB 11/196).

Sir Randolph Crewe (*bap.* 1559, *d.* 1646), by Sir Peter Lely, *c.*1645

Crewe was elected in 1614 to represent the crown-controlled borough of Saltash; his 'wisdome, moderation and discretion' (Baker, *Serjeants*, 324) as speaker of that turbulent parliament earned him a knighthood the day after its dissolution. Within three weeks he was also called to the rank of serjeant and granted a patent as king's serjeant; the customary gold rings he presented bore the inscription *Rex lex loquens* ('The king is the speaking law'; Baker, *Serjeants*, 324–5). By now Crewe was among the busiest counsel appearing in chancery before his patron Ellesmere. His practice extended to other superior courts and various special commissions, including those appointed to examine Edmond Peacham, and to prosecute the murderers of Sir Thomas Overbury. However, his involvement as assize judge in the execution of nine supposed witches in Lancashire in 1616 hardly enhanced his reputation, when the king himself exploded the slender evidence that had led to their conviction. Having been reluctantly obliged to ride the assize circuit of his kinsman Sir Edward Coke, following the chief justice's suspension, Crewe was among the learned counsel before whom Coke appeared to defend his law reports in October 1616; much later he served as one of Coke's executors. He also attended at Whitehall in January 1617 when the king tried to settle an inheritance dispute between the earl of Dorset, his wife, Anne Clifford, and her uncle. Crewe did not sit in the parliament of 1621, but led the prosecution in the politically charged trials of Attorney-General Yelverton, the monopolist Sir Francis Michell, and the civilian judge Sir John Bennet. In 1624 he opened the impeachment of Sir Lionel Cranfield before the House of Lords.

On 26 January 1625, shortly before James I died, Crewe was appointed to succeed Sir James Ley as chief justice of king's bench. While this promotion was evidently unsought and not particularly welcome, he did not enjoy it long after delivering a celebrated passage of judicial rhetoric to the House of Lords in the Oxford peerage case:

> Where is Bohun, where's Mowbray, where's Mortimer? &c. Nay, which is more and most of all, where is Plantagenet? They are entombed in the urns and sepulchres of mortality. And yet let the name and dignity of De Vere stand so long as it pleaseth God. (82 ER 53)

In November 1626, after twice heading a delegation which conveyed the judges' collective refusal to endorse the forced loan, Crewe was summoned before the king, suspended from office, and then dismissed. This 'heavy, sudden and unexpected' action (*Diary of Sir Richard Hutton*, 66) caused some political damage, although Crewe declined nomination to the parliament of 1628 and successfully prevailed upon friends such as John Hampden to prevent the promotion of his case as a grievance. Despite this restraint, and appeals to the duke of Buckingham, royal favour proved elusive. Crewe continued to hope for reinstatement, or recompense, well into the 1630s. As he pointed out in a draft petition (Ches. & Chester ALSS, DAR/D/98), no other judge had been punished for their collective stand, although his accompanying request for compensation in the form of a baronetcy was hardly realistic.

Crewe divided his forced retirement between a Westminster house and his mansion of Crewe Hall which, says Fuller, 'first brought the model of excellent building into these remoter parts' (Fuller, *Worthies*, 273). There he rode over his extensive estates and pursued antiquarian interests, as well as the numerous lawsuits that must have made him a formidable neighbour. Given the well-attested protestant piety of this 'Religious good man' (Malbon, 193–4), Crewe's strong support for the parliamentarian cause can hardly be attributed merely to resentments arising from his mistreatment sixteen years earlier. He died at Westminster on 13 January 1646, was buried on 5 June at Bartholmley, Cheshire, and was mourned as 'the glorie of his profession' and 'the grace of his Countrey' (Hall, 455).   WILFRID PREST

Sources J. Hall, *A history of the town and parish of Nantwich, or Wich-Malbank, in the county palatine of Cheshire* (1883); repr. (1972) · W. R. Prest, *The rise of the barristers: a social history of the English bar, 1590–1640*, 2nd edn (1991) · W. J. Jones, 'Crewe, Sir Randolph', HoP, *Commons, 1558–1603*, 1.669–70 · G. Ormerod, *The history of the county palatine and city of Chester*, 2nd edn, ed. T. Helsby, 3 vols. (1882) · W. P. Baildon, ed., *The records of the Honorable Society of Lincoln's Inn: the black books*, 2–3 (1898–9) · Baker, *Serjeants* · *The diary of Sir Richard Hutton, 1614–1639*, ed. W. R. Prest, SeldS, suppl. ser., 9 (1991) · will, PRO, PROB 11/196, fols. 100r–103r · 'Inventory in my fyrst wyffes tyme', Ches. & Chester ALSS, DAR/I/18 · Fuller, *Worthies* (1840), vol. 1 · T. Malbon and E. Burghall, *Memorials of the civil war in Cheshire and the adjacent counties*, ed. J. Hall, Lancashire and Cheshire RS, 19 (1889)

Archives Ches. & Chester ALSS, DCR 1–25 | BL, Harley MSS · BL, MSS relating to legal suit between Crewe and the City of Chester, Stowe MS 812

Likenesses portrait, *c.*1626 · P. Lely, portrait, *c.*1645, Christ's College, Cambridge; photograph, NPG; two versions [*see illus.*] · W. Hollar, etching (after unknown portrait), repro. in W. Dugdale, *Origines juridiciales* (1666) · oils, Palace of Westminster, London · portrait, Harvard U., law school; version, Gov. Art Coll. · portrait, priv. coll.

Wealth at death substantial landholdings in Cheshire and elsewhere; income as chief justice approx. £2000 p.a.: Ormerod, *History of the county palatine*; will, PRO, PROB 11/196, sig. 65

Crewe, Thomas (*fl.* 1580), translator, is known only for and from *The nosegay of morall philosophie, lately dispersed among many Italian authors and now newely and succinctly drawne together into questions and ansueres and translated into Englishe by T.C.* (1580). This is a translation of *Le bouquet de philosophie moral* (1568) by Gabriel Meurier (*c.*1530–1602). Only four copies of Crewe's version are known to have survived. It is a threadbare and repetitive compilation of aphorisms, notable for dullness even in its tedious genre. At the end the translator adds some conventional verses of his own— 'Of a Blessed Life', 'Of Worldly Wealth', 'For Wisdome'. Crewe dedicated his work to 'The right worshipfull and his singular good Lady and mistris the Lady Martin of London'. This was presumably Dorcas Ecclestone (1536/7– 1599), wife of Sir Richard Martin (1533/4–1617), goldsmith, master of the mint, alderman, and twice lord mayor of London, whom she married some time before 1562. It seems possible that Crewe was or had been tutor to one or more of the Martins' family of five sons and a daughter. He had at some time visited Paris, where (he says in his dedicatory epistle) he had—in Meurier's book—'met with 'branches' from '[t]he slips hereof', which 'were set in sundry Italian gardens'. No further particulars of his life have been ascertained.   J. H. BURNS

Sources T. Crewe, *The nosegay of morall philosophie* (1580) · G. Meurier, *Le bouquet de philosophie moral* (1568) · *DNB* · 'Martin, Sir Richard', *DNB*

Crewe, Sir Thomas (1566–1634), lawyer and speaker of the House of Commons, was born in Nantwich, Cheshire, the third son of John Crewe (*d.* 1598), a tanner, and his wife, Alice Mainwaring, and brother of Sir Randolph *Crewe, politician and judge. He married, in 1596, Temperance (1580/81–1619), the daughter and heir of Reginald (or Reynold) Bray of Steane; they had nine children, of whom the eldest son, John *Crew (1597/8–1679), also followed a parliamentary career. A reader at Barnard's Inn in 1599, Thomas Crewe was called to the 'grand company' of Gray's Inn in 1603, and was elected Lent reader in 1612. He was made serjeant in 1623. His parliamentary career bridged both houses and five constituencies: he sat for Lichfield in 1604, Bere Alston, Devon, in 1614, Northampton in 1621, Aylesbury in 1624, and Gatton, Surrey, in 1625.

In King James's first parliament, although a member for the first time, Crewe sat on more than a hundred committees and spoke often. His opposition politics began here, probably with the committee to draft legislation against the collection of impositions. He also played a part in drafting a bill against recusants, arguing that 'nothing may be declared heresy until it be confirmed by parliament' (Foster, 1.127). Throughout his political career ecclesiastical matters were important to Crewe, who commended his father in his will for raising him in 'true religion' (PROB 11/165, fol. 45). Employing his legal skills he also spoke on the *post nati* question of Scottish naturalization after the union of the crowns under James VI and I. In 1614, when his older brother Ranulph was speaker, Crewe again sat on numerous committees and spoke regularly, arguing from case and precedent in the debates on impositions. After the session the privy council ordered him and others who had prepared the debate against impositions to bring in their notes and papers to be burned.

Crewe's parliamentary maturity is evident in 1621 in his role in the proceedings against Francis Bacon, Viscount St Albans, and in the debate on monopolies and the subsequent impeachment of Sir Giles Mompesson. In the same session he preferred a bill to support hospitals and working places for the poor, which he successfully secured as a statute in 1624. Later, in his will, he left bequests to the poor of Brackley, Banbury, and Nantwich. In 1622 he was appointed to a commission to inquire into the state ecclesiastical and temporal in Ireland. He served in Ireland until November 1622, working in particular on compiling reports on the courts and the church. Inclusion on the commission had been labelled a banishment by some but in 1625 Crewe rejected that term, noting that he was subsequently (21 February 1625) made a king's serjeant. He had also been knighted, on 17 November 1623. The council board again relied on his opinions about Ireland when in August 1628 he was called on to consult about preparations for an Irish parliament.

In 1624 Crewe, although he had previously opposed crown policy, particularly with regard to impositions and taxation, was nominated speaker of the lower house by a crown servant, Sir Thomas Edmondes, treasurer of the king's household. Crewe was known to be 'a great lover of the laws of the land and the liberties of the people' (Ruigh, 157, n. 15). He could also depend on the support of the puritan members of the house. He was re-elected speaker in 1625. Sir John Eliot reported that Crewe's:

> former carriage in that place and the success thereof after so many nullities and breaches, making again as it were a new marriage and conjunction between King and people, gave such satisfaction in all hope as all men were affected with the choice. (Bidwell and Jansson, 1625, 494)

Having been made king's serjeant, Crewe was appointed to the ecclesiastical high commission in 1625, an appointment renewed in 1626, 1629, and 1633. His advancement to the position of king's serjeant marked a change in his parliamentary responsibilities. He was called on to examine legislation in the upper house, and to serve as a messenger between the houses. Besides those tasks in 1626 he served, with the attorney-general, Sir Robert Heath, as counsel for Robert Bertie, Lord Willoughby, in the dispute over the earldom of Oxford. In 1628, along with the routine work of serjeant, Crewe delivered the impeachment charge against Roger Mainwaring.

Crewe's career outside parliament was centred in Northamptonshire. He sat on county commissions, for charitable uses in 1603, gaol delivery (1612–16), subsidy (1621), and martial law (1628), and served as a justice of peace from 1616 until his death. From 1626 he sat on the midlands commission of oyer and terminer. He built up an impressive legal practice and served in 1631 as counsel in the trial of Mervin Touchet, earl of Castlehaven. He acted as a feoffee for impropriations from 1632 and was a friend to the notable puritan divine, Robert Bolton, whose works he undertook to publish after Bolton's death. Richard Sibbes, who preached his funeral sermon, described Crewe as 'a marvellous great encourager of honest, laborious, religious ministers' (Prest, 229). Crewe died at Steane in February 1634, leaving his estates and the religious oversight of his younger children to his eldest son, John, later first Baron Crew. He was buried in a chapel in Steane, a marble monument of himself in serjeant's robes in a recumbent position beside his wife, Temperance, marking the tomb.

MAIJA JANSSON

Sources The visitation of Cheshire in the year 1580, made by Robert Glover, Somerset herald, ed. J. P. Rylands, Harleian Society, 18 (1882), xli, 69 • R. J. Fletcher, ed., The pension book of Gray's Inn, 1 (1901), 146, 156, 196 n.1 • W. A. Shaw, The knights of England, 2 (1906), 183 • W. Notestein, The House of Commons, 1604–1610 (1971), 156, 227, 386 • E. R. Foster, Proceedings in parliament, 1610, 1 (1966), 127; 2 (1966), 95, 201, 226, 273 • JHC, 1 (1547–1628), 1028 • The parliamentary diary of Robert Bowyer, 1606–1607, ed. D. H. Willson (1931), 357, 384 • The letters of John Chamberlain, ed. N. E. McClure, 1 (1939), 539 • W. Notestein, F. H. Relf, and H. Simpson, eds., Commons debates, 1621, 5 (1935), 42, 385 • APC, 1621–3, 113; 1628–9, 111 • M. Jansson and W. B. Bidwell, eds., Proceedings in parliament, 1625 (1987), 476, 494 • R. E. Ruigh, The parliament of 1624: politics and foreign policy (1971), 157 • E. W. Kirby, 'The lay feoffees: a study in militant puritanism', Journal of Modern History, 14 (1942), 1–25 • R. G. Usher, The rise and fall of the high commission (1913), 349 • W. B. Bidwell and M. Jansson, eds., Proceedings in parliament, 1626, 4 vols. (1991–6) • R. C. Johnson and others, eds., Proceedings in parliament, 1628, 6 vols. (1977–83) • DNB • T. W. Mellows, ed., Peterborough local administration … 1541–1689, Northamptonshire RS, 10 (1937), 207 • J. C. Cox and C. A. Markham, eds., The records of the borough of Northampton, 2, ed. J. C. Cox (1898), 495 • J. Wake, ed., A copy of papers relating to musters, beacons, subsidies, … Northampton, Northamptonshire RS, 3 (1926), 174 • PRO, PROB 11/170, fols. 103–104v • V. Treadwell, Buckingham and Ireland, 1616–28: a study in Anglo-Irish politics (1998) • W. R. Prest, The rise of the barristers: a social history of the English bar, 1590–1640 (1986)
Archives BL, commonplace book, RP154 [photocopy]
Likenesses marble monument, Steane Chapel, Northamptonshire • print, Palace of Westminster, London

Cribb, Tom (1781–1848), pugilist, was born at Hanham in the parish of Bitton, Gloucestershire, on 8 July 1781, the son of Thomas and Hannah Cribb (he had three brothers and three sisters). He moved to London at the age of thirteen and worked as a bellhanger, then became a porter at the public wharves, and was afterwards a sailor. From the fact of his having worked as a coal porter he became known as the Black Diamond. He won his first public contest against George Maddox at Wood Green on 7 January 1805 in seventy-six rounds (two hours ten minutes), and won three more the same year. On 20 July, however, against George Nicholls, he experienced his first and last

Tom Cribb (1781–1848), by Douglas Guest, 1810–11

defeat. The system of milling on the retreat which Cribb generally practised with so much success in this instance failed, and at the conclusion of the fifty-second round he was unable to carry on. In 1807 he was introduced to Captain Robert Barclay Allardice, better known as Captain Barclay, who quickly perceived his natural good qualities and took him in hand. Captain Barclay trained him under his own eye, and backed him for 200 guineas against the famous Jem Belcher. The contest took place on 8 April, and the fighting was so severe that both men were completely exhausted; but in the forty-first round Cribb was proclaimed the victor. Belcher had lost an eye four years earlier; only this handicap allowed Cribb to overcome a far more skilful fighter through strength and endurance, saying, 'He'll break his hand on my head' (Lynch, 31) (which Belcher did).

The marquess of Tweeddale now backed Bob Gregson to fight Cribb, who was backed by Paul Methuen; this battle came off on 25 October, but in the twenty-third round Gregson, who was severely hurt, was unable to come up to time—fortunately for Cribb, since he himself passed out immediately afterwards. Jem Belcher, still smarting under his defeat, next challenged Cribb to a rematch, the stakes being a belt and 200 guineas. The contest took place at Epsom on 1 February 1809, when, much to the astonishment of his friends, the ex-champion was beaten and had to resign the belt to his adversary. Cribb now seemed to have reached the highest pinnacle of fame as a pugilist, when a rival arose from an unexpected quarter. Tom Molineaux, an athletic black American, challenged him, probably prompted by the retired black fighter Bill Richmond, an old opponent with whom Cribb had almost come to

blows again when Richmond was acting as Gregson's second. Cribb could not afford to lose to a man he called an 'ebony imposter' (Prestidge, 21), but he probably would have done so, had not someone cut the ropes when Molineaux had him pinned against them, and had not his seconds distracted the referee with bogus complaints on an occasion when Cribb was unable to recover his feet. The fight, on 18 December 1810, concluded, however, with Molineaux's collapse after thirty-three rounds and fifty-five minutes. Molineaux, not at all satisfied, sent another challenge, and a second meeting was arranged for 28 September 1811 at Thistleton Gap, Leicestershire. This match was witnessed by more than 20,000 spectators, a quarter of whom belonged to the upper classes. The fight much disappointed the spectators, as in the ninth round Molineaux's jaw was fractured, and in the eleventh he was unable to stand; the contest lasted only twenty minutes but did testify to the power of Cribb's blows, enhanced by severe training under Barclay since the first fight. On the champion's arrival in London on 30 September he was received with a public ovation, and Holborn was completely blocked by the assembled crowds. At a dinner on 2 December 1811 Cribb was the recipient of a silver cup worth 80 guineas, subscribed for by his friends.

After an unsuccessful venture as a coal merchant at Hungerford Wharf, London, Cribb 'underwent the usual metamorphosis from a pugilist to a publican' (Miles, 3.262), and took the Golden Lion inn in Southwark, then the King's Arms at the corner of Duke Street and King Street, St James's, and subsequently the Union Arms, 26 Panton Street, Haymarket. Byron met Cribb through John Jackson—not that Cribb could compare with that luminary; he found Cribb 'now a publican and, I fear, a sinner'; he 'has a wife and a mistress, and conversations well, barring some sad omissions and misapplications of the aspirate' (*Byron's Letters and Journals*, 3.221). The wife was apparently Elizabeth Warr: they married on 12 December 1809 at St Pancras Old Church. Apart from the occasional ejections entailed by a publican's duties, Cribb's life was peaceful, although on 15 June 1814 he sparred at Lord Lowther's house in Pall Mall before the emperor of Russia, and again two days afterwards before the king of Prussia. On 24 January 1821 it was decided that Cribb, having held the championship for nearly ten years without receiving a challenge, ought not to be expected to fight any more, and was to be permitted to hold the title and belt of champion for the remainder of his life. Further challenges were diverted to his protégé, Thomas Winter, alias Spring, though in 1824 Cribb had to pay £100 damages for an unofficial assault on Tom Belcher, Jem's brother. On the day of the coronation of George IV, Cribb, dressed as a page, was among the prize-fighters engaged to guard the entrance to Westminster Hall. Lured into gambling, he was obliged in 1839 to give up the Union Arms to his creditors. He died of a disease of the stomach in the house of his son (a baker), 111 High Street, Woolwich, on 11 May 1848. Supposedly Cribb sat up when Spring visited him and punched the air, with the last words, 'The action's still there but the steam's all gone'. He was buried in St Mary's churchyard, Woolwich, where, in 1851, a monument representing a lion grieving over the ashes of a hero was erected to his memory. G. C. BOASE, *rev.* JULIAN LOCK

Sources *GM*, 2nd ser., 29 (1848), 674 • 'Tom Cribb', www. readysnacks.mcmail.com/cribb.htm, Jan 2003 [referring to family information from Alan Bartlett] • D. Prestidge, *Tom Cribb at Thistleton Gap* (1971) • H. D. Miles, *Pugilistica: being one hundred and forty-four years of the history of British boxing*, 3 vols. (1880–81), vol. 1, pp. 242–77 • P. Egan, *Boxiana, or, Sketches of ancient and modern pugilism*, 1 (1812), 386–423 • [F. Dowling], *Fistiana* (1868) • J. Ford, *Prizefighting: the age of Regency boximania* (1971) • J. C. Reid, *Bucks and bruisers: Pierce Egan and Regency England* (1971) • *Byron's letters and journals*, ed. L. A. Marchand, 12 vols. (1973–82) • D. Johnson, *Bare fist fighters of the 18th and 19th century: 1704–1861* (1987) • B. Lynch, *Knuckles and gloves* (1922) • H. Cleveland, *Fisticuffs and personalities of the prize ring* (*c.*1923)
Likenesses D. Guest, portrait, 1810–11; Sothebys, 27 June 1973, lot 108 [*see illus.*] • J. Emery, etching, pubd 1811, NPG • C. Warren, line print, pubd 1812 (after painting by S. De Wilde), BM, NPG; repro. in Prestidge, *Tom Cribb at Thistleton Gap*, 15 • watercolour and brown ink, 1812, NPG • P. Roberts, stipple (after J. Sharples), BM; repro. in P. Egan, *Boxiana* (1818–29), vol. 4 • T. Rowlandson, cartoon, Brodick Castle, Garden and Country Park, Isle of Arran • E. Woodnaker, Staffordshire figurine, repro. in Prestidge, *Tom Cribb at Thistleton Gap*, 27 • cartoon, repro. in Prestidge, *Tom Cribb at Thistleton Gap*, 41 • engraving (after statue), repro. in Egan, *Boxiana*, 1, facing p. 281 • print, repro. in Prestidge, *Tom Cribb at Thistleton Gap*, 37 • print, repro. in N. Fleischer, *The heavyweight championship* (1949), facing p. 50
Wealth at death negligible; lost all money on horses and had to be supported by subscription of admirers

Crichton. *See also* Creighton.

Crichton, Sir Alexander (1763–1856), physician and author, was born in Newington, Edinburgh, on 2 December 1763, the second surviving son of Alexander Crichton (1721–1808), a Newington coachmaker, and his wife, Barbara Boyes (1739–1787). He was educated at the Canongate and Edinburgh high schools, apprenticed to the surgeon Alexander Wood on 23 September 1779, and studied medicine at Edinburgh University from 1779 to 1784, when he became a member of the Royal Physical Society. In 1784 he spent a year in London with the surgeon William Fordyce, attended hospitals, and joined the Lyceum Medicum Londinense, a society founded in 1785 by John Hunter and George Fordyce. After graduating MD at Leiden University in July 1785 with the thesis *De vermibis*, he passed a year's broadly based medical studies in Paris, followed by two years' attendance at leading clinical hospitals in Stuttgart, Vienna, Halle, Berlin, Prague, and Göttingen.

On his return to London Crichton practised as a member of the Company of Surgeons from May 1789 until May 1791, but became a licentiate of the Royal College of Physicians in June 1791 and a member of the Society of Collegiate Physicians in September 1792. In 1791 he and Thomas Bradley were elected physicians to a large public dispensary at Featherstone Buildings, Holborn, and, in 1794, physicians to Westminster Hospital. At both these institutions they gave public clinical lectures, modelled on those of Göttingen University, in medicine, materia medica, and chemistry, and Crichton later lectured with Charles Badham, physician to the Westminster Infirmary. In 1804 he published *A Synoptical Table of Diseases*, designed for his medical students and as a text for his public lectures. His chemical analysis helped confirm the efficacy of a substitute devised by Richard Chenevix for Dr James's famous fever powder (*Philosophical Transactions*, 1801), and on 2 March 1801 Count Rumford invited him to lecture at the Royal Institution in place of Thomas Garnett, the indisposed professor of chemistry and natural philosophy. Samuel Parkes, reproducing Crichton's formula in his *Chemical Catechism* (1808), maintained that Crichton was the first chemist to elucidate and demonstrate certain advanced views of combustion in his public lectures.

In 1792 Crichton translated, as *An Essay on Generation*, a work by Johann Blumenbach, the outstanding Göttingen physiologist. The essay, its title better rendered as *Biological Drive*, was central to contemporary physiology and inspired Crichton's book, *An Inquiry into the Nature and Origin of Mental Derangement* (1798) which was translated into Dutch, German, and (partly) French, and reprinted in 1971. A seminal text of early modern psychiatry, it profoundly influenced French pioneers such as Pinel and Esquirol by highlighting German research in the field, by the scientific objectivity and clinical precision of its observations, and by linking physiology with psychological manifestations. It also introduced the principles of associationism to neurology and psychiatric medicine before the advent of cortical localization. Crichton was called on to testify about the sanity of James Hadfield, who attempted to assassinate George III in May 1800. On 8 May 1800 Crichton was elected a fellow of the Royal Society. In September of that year he married Frances (1772–1857), daughter of Edward Dodwell, of West Molesey in Surrey, and heir to an Irish estate. Resigning his post at Westminster Hospital in April 1801 to be its consultant, he was appointed physician to the duke of Cambridge, later retaining both titles. Notes of his treatment of George III for his mental illness (in 1801?) survive in private family papers.

On 17 May 1803 Crichton was elected a foreign corresponding member of the Russian Academy of Sciences. He received a jewelled ring from Tsar Alexander for his book on mental illness, and was invited to become physician-in-ordinary to him and to Maria Federovna, the dowager empress. Crichton took up duties in September 1804 that also involved him in Maria's foundling hospitals and charities for the sick poor. On 9 September 1807 he was appointed physician-general to the Russian civil medical department. For his services, and his efforts to combat a severe cholera epidemic in 1809 in the country's south-eastern provinces, he received the knight's grand cross of St Vladimir's order, third and second classes, in 1809 and 1814. These and other awards, together with the titles of actual councillor of state (pre-1814) and aulic councillor (1816), also reflected his considerable skill as a physician to the imperial family, who sponsored three baptisms of the four of his children named after them.

Mrs Crichton was a talented musician and artist. Several pictures from the family collection, some of which were sold during 1817, are in the Hermitage Gallery. Crichton became a member of the Moscow Physico-Medical Society in 1805 and of the Natural History Society in 1806. On 11 June and 9 July of that year, six human foetuses, other preserved anatomical specimens, and twenty-one freak zoological items were purchased for him at the Leverian Museum sale in London, possibly by his colleague William Babington. He was elected an honorary member of the Academy of Sciences in 1814, having given it a spiny anteater and duck-billed platypus in 1807. That year he and the chemist Konstantin Kirchof, using sulphuric acid, won the Free Economic Society's first prize in a competition for refining vegetable oil, and they established a factory at St Petersburg which had a maximum daily output of 4400 lb of the oil. In 1807 Crichton compiled a now rare *Pharmacopoeia* for use by the Hospital for the Poor at St Petersburg; its chemical preparations and compositions incorporated Lavoisier's nomenclature. Ten years later he wrote a pamphlet on treating patients at the hospital with tar vapour for pulmonary consumption; with a new title and a dedication to Maria Federovna it was republished in an extended version in 1823, having been translated into French in 1817 and German in 1819. In addition he co-edited a short-lived but valuable compendium, in German, for the natural sciences and medicine (1816–17), which aimed to extend knowledge of Russian natural and medical history. Crichton retired from Russia in 1819, returning briefly in 1820 in order to treat the Prussian born Grand Duchess Aleksandra Fyodorovna, the wife of Nicholas, who became tsar in 1825, at St Petersburg and Berlin. He retained his title of physician to the Russian emperor, was created a knight of the grand cross of the Red Eagle by Frederick William of Prussia in December 1820, and was made a knight bachelor by George IV in March 1821. At some stage he is known to have written a confidential memoir of his treatment of Queen Caroline, George's wife, who died in August 1821. Granted land in the Vitebsk region of Belorussia in 1812, he was given a pension in 1826 by Tsar Nicholas, who also conferred on him the knighthood of the grand cross of St Anne (first class) in 1830.

Resuming medical practice in Harley Street, Crichton later bought a home near Sevenoaks in Kent. His correspondence (1819–32) with Count, later Prince, Christopher Lieven, Russian ambassador in London, reveals that he declined a permanent post as physician to the embassy in 1827, and maintained excellent relations with the Russian imperial family. During the summer of 1831 he treated Helena Pavlovna (1807–1873), the wife of Grand Duke Michael of Russia, at Sidmouth and Cheltenham, her health having been undermined by frequent pregnancies. His course of treatment was approved by Sir Henry Halford and Drs Maton, Babbington, and Chambers, leading consultant physicians.

As an honorary member of the Caledonian Horticultural Society from 1812, he supplied it and the Royal Botanical Gardens at Edinburgh and Kew with several packets of rare seeds from Siberia and southern Russia between 1815 and 1818, being chosen as a member of the medico-botanical and royal medical and chirurgical societies

about 1821. Robert Jameson, later professor of natural history at Edinburgh University, commented on Crichton's collection of 'fossils' which he saw several times during 1793. Elected a fellow of the Linnean Society in 1793 as 'well skilled in mineralogy', he sent it a large Siberian crystal emerald in September 1812, with plants, a hedgehog, and botanical works from naturalists in Russia. In August 1807 he wrote to William Babington about an unusual complete Siberian mammoth and a large meteorite that had reached the Russian capital. In the same year he obtained subscriptions from Count Stroganov and other noblemen which, combined with Babington's efforts in London, resulted in the publication of Count De Bournon's monograph on carbonate of lime in 1808. In 1811 Crichton was elected a member of the Geological Society of London; he became a fellow in 1819, served on its council for six years between 1824 and 1837, and was a vice-president from 1825 to 1827.

Between 1820 and 1830 Crichton donated many minerals and fossils from Russia and elsewhere, several of which were transferred in 1911 to the British Museum (Natural History). Between 1822 and 1838 he contributed four papers to the society's journals. His paper 'On the climate of the antediluvian world and … the formation of granite' appeared in the *Annals of Philosophy* (1825) as well as in French and German journals. In 1813 De Bournon named the rare mineral crichtonite after him. Crichton's own collection was described in 1818 by the expert Joseph Wagner as the finest private collection of Siberian minerals in Russia. It also contained specimens from other European countries, South America, Greenland, and Madagascar. In December 1826 G. B. Sowerby the elder publicized the main contents of Crichton's cabinet of minerals, which in 1827 was sold by auction in 2600 lots, having been catalogued by Sowerby, possibly assisted by Henry Heuland, from whom Crichton had purchased specimens. Henry Sowerby, son of G. B. Sowerby, dedicated his *Popular Mineralogy* (1850) to Crichton, his patron. In addition to minerals acquired from the sale of Crichton's collection, a significant new suite of his specimens was discovered at Chatsworth House in 2002. A portion of Crichton's library was sold in 1894.

Crichton was elected foreign corresponding member of the Royal Academy of Medicine, Paris, in 1835 and a member of the Royal Institution of Great Britain in 1842, serving on its visitors' committee from 1853 to 1856. He published four papers in medical journals between 1789 and 1814, a pamphlet advocating financial provisions for the Roman Catholic clergy in Ireland (1834), and a well-received book entitled *Commentaries on some doctrines of a dangerous tendency in medicine and on the general principles of safe practice* (1842). Characterized as frank and manly, Crichton, versatile and cosmopolitan in his intellectual interests, died at his home, The Grove, Seal, Sevenoaks, Kent, on 4 June 1856 and was buried at Norwood cemetery. His wife died on 20 January 1857.　JOHN H. APPLEBY

Sources E. M. Tansey, 'The life and works of Sir Alexander Crichton', *Notes and Records of the Royal Society*, 38 (1983–4), 249–50 · J. H. Appleby, 'Sir Alexander Crichton, FRS (1763–1856), imperial physician at large', *Notes and Records*, 53 (May 1999), 219–30 · D. B. Weiner, 'Mind and body in the clinic', *The languages of Psyche: mind and body in Enlightenment thought* (1990), 331–402 · S. Finger and H. W. Buckingham, 'Disorders of fluent speech and associationist theory', *Archives of Neurology*, 51 (1994), 498–503 · M. P. Cooper, 'The Devonshire mineral collection, Chatsworth House', *Mineralogical Record*, no. 5 (2002–3) · J. F. Wagner, *Notizen über die Mineralien-Sammlung des Herren Drs. Alexander von Crichton* (1818) · G. B. Sowerby, *Notice of the principal contents of Sir Alexander Crichton's cabinet of minerals* (1826) · A. Crichton and others, *Pharmacopoeia in usum nosocomii pauperum petropolitani* (1807) · A. Crichton, J. Rehmann, and K. Burdach, eds., *Russische Sammlung für Wissenschaften und Heilkunst*, 2 vols. (1816–17) · G. B. Sowerby, *Catalogue of a magnificent collection of minerals, and precious stones* (1827) · *Catalogue of the Leverian Museum* (1806) · J. M. Sweet, 'Robert Jameson in London, 1793', *Annals of Science*, 19 (1963), 81–116 · De Bournon, *Catalogue de la collection minéralogique du Comte de Bournon* (London, 1813) · De Bournon, *Traité complet de la chaux carbonatée et de l'arragonite*, 1 (1808) · I. Macalpine and R. Hunter, *George III and the mad-business* (1969) · bap. reg. Scot. · d. cert. · Burke, *Gen. Ire.* (1976), 290 · GL, MS 11, 192 · J. E. Portlock, *Quarterly Journal of the Geological Society*, 13 (1857), lxiv–lxvi · *DNB* · *GM*, 1st ser., 70 (1800)

Archives GL, MS 11, 192 · Russian State Historical Archives, St Petersburg | BL, corresp. with Prince Lieven, Add. MSS 47290–47296 · Linn. Soc., general minute book 1 and certificates · NHM, department of palaeontology, catalogues and lists of untraced specimens transferred from Geological Society, nos. 6 and 30 · RBG Kew, inward books · Royal Botanic Garden, Edinburgh, minutes, Caledonian Horticultural Society, vol. 1 · Royal Institution of Great Britain, London, minutes and committee of visitors **Likenesses** G. Harlow?, oils, Wellcome L. · H. Room, oils, priv. coll. **Wealth at death** property in Britain; wife inherited property in Ireland: will, June 1866, PRO

Crichton, Andrew (1790–1855), biographer and historian, youngest son of a small landed proprietor, was born in the parish of Kirkmahoe, Dumfriesshire, in December 1790. He was educated at Dumfries Academy and at the University of Edinburgh. After becoming a licensed preacher he taught for a time in Edinburgh and North Berwick. In 1823 he published his first work, the *Life of the Rev John Blackader*, which was followed by the *Life of Colonel J. Blackader* (1824) and *Memoirs of the Rev Thomas Scott* (1825). To Constable's Miscellany he contributed five volumes—*Converts from Infidelity* (2 vols., 1827) and a translation of a work by C. G. de Koch, *History of the Revolutions in Europe* (3 vols., 1828). For the Edinburgh Cabinet Library he wrote the *History of Arabia* (2 vols., 1833) and, with H. Wheaton, *Scandinavia, Ancient and Modern* (2 vols., 1838).

Crichton began his connection with newspaper publishing in 1828 by editing (at first in conjunction with De Quincey) the *Edinburgh Evening Post*. From 1830 to 1832 he edited the *North Briton*, and from 1832 until June 1851 the *Edinburgh Advertiser*. He contributed extensively to periodicals, including the *Westminster Review*, *Tait's Edinburgh Magazine*, the *Dublin University Magazine*, *Fraser's Magazine*, the *Church Review*, and the *Church of Scotland Magazine and Review*. In 1837 the University of St Andrews conferred on Crichton the degree of doctor of laws. He was a member of the presbytery of Edinburgh, being ruling elder of the congregation of Trinity College Church, and sat in the general assembly of the Church of Scotland as elder for

the burgh of Cullen (1852–5). He disputed Thomas MacCrie's view of John Knox, and in 1840 published a critical edition of MacCrie's *Life of John Knox*, with a memoir of MacCrie.

Crichton married first, in July 1835, Isabella Calvert, daughter of James Calvert of Montrose; she died in November 1837. He married for a second time, in December 1844; his new wife was Jane, daughter of the Revd John Duguid, minister of Erie and Kendall. Crichton died of paralysis at 33 Bernard Crescent, Edinburgh, on 9 January 1855 and was buried in the new Calton cemetery, Edinburgh.   G. C. BOASE, *rev.* H. C. G. MATTHEW

Sources *GM*, 2nd ser., 43 (1855), 654 · Boase, *Mod. Eng. biog.* · d. cert.

Crichton, Sir Archibald William (1791–1865), physician in Russia, the eldest son of **Patrick Crichton** (1762–1823) and his wife, Margaret Lambie, was born in Gayfield Square, Edinburgh, on 10 April 1791. His father, a well-known figure, distinguished himself with the army in America during the American War of Independence before returning to partner his father, Alexander Crichton (1721–1808), in the family's coachbuilding firm. Elected an Edinburgh city councillor and treasurer, he also commanded the Royal Edinburgh volunteers' first regiment from 1794 to 1796, as featured in John Kay's *Original Portraits*, and an Edinburgh militia regiment, besides publicizing his inventions for conveying troops and sick or wounded personnel.

Archibald William Crichton was educated at Edinburgh high school and Edinburgh University where, in 1810, he contributed a paper on alkaline salts to the Royal Medical Society. He graduated MD with 'De melancholia', a thesis dedicated to his father and his uncle Alexander *Crichton (1763–1856), Tsar Alexander's physician and director-general of the Russian civil medical branch, whom he joined at St Petersburg soon afterwards. Through his uncle Crichton obtained in May 1811 the post of medical supervisor, responsible for developing a mineral spa resort in the Caucasus mountain area, and his success in controlling a plague outbreak earned him the knight cross of the order of St Vladimir (fourth class). Following Napoleon's abortive invasion of Russia, he volunteered for army service and in 1813 became physician to a hospital for French prisoners at Riga. Transferred at his own request to his uncle's headquarters by his compatriot James Wylie, the tsar's physician and inspector-general of the military medical department, Crichton took part, as a member of the tsar's suite, in two battles for the French capital. On Napoleon's withdrawal from Paris, the British hosted a dinner in April 1814 for their Russian allies. It was attended by Wylie, Crichton (now promoted to physician-in-chief of the Russian hospitals in the city), Count Platov, generals Chernikov and Barclay de Tolly, and many other senior officers. In 1814 Crichton was awarded the campaign medal and the knight cross of the order of St Anne (second class), as well as the Légion d'honneur by Louis XVIII. After a short period as regimental surgeon to the

Sir Archibald William Crichton (1791–1865), by unknown artist

renowned Preobrazhensky guards, in 1816 he was appointed physician-in-ordinary to Grand Duke Nicholas, who became tsar in 1825.

In addition to his medical duties, Crichton often performed the role of a courtier. He escorted Grand Duke Nicholas on his four months' tour of Britain between 1816 and 1817. They stayed, *inter alia*, at Chatsworth House (6–9 December 1816) as guests of the sixth duke of Devonshire, and reached Glasgow at Christmas. It was Crichton and not, as recorded, his uncle who accompanied the grand duke and interpreted when Robert Owen, the social reformer, invited them to spend a night at his New Lanark community home late that December. Owen declined Nicholas's offer to help resettle two million surplus British workers in Russia with a view to expanding the country's manufacturing industry (Owen, 115–20). In 1817 Crichton received honorary doctorates in medicine and law from Glasgow and Oxford universities respectively, and he was knighted by the prince regent in the same year. He corresponded from Russia in 1818 with the London ambassador Prince Lieven and the duke of Devonshire about the birth of the tsarevich Alexander, whom he safely vaccinated, and about the grand duchess's health. On 20 May 1820 he married, at St Petersburg, Sophia Louisa Kimmel (1798–1869), a widow, daughter of Nicholas Suthoff (d. 1836), court physician and obstetrician. In 1825 Crichton treated Maria Federovna, the dowager empress.

Crichton, known as Vasily Petrovich Kreyton in Russia, played a significant part in monitoring the serious cholera epidemic in Russia during 1830–31. His knowledge and medical advice on the subject were sought by colleagues such as Joseph von Hamel, the distinguished Russian academician and scientific writer, and Nicholas Arendt, one of the most important surgeons before Pirogov.

Co-ordinating information sent from all over Russia, Crichton made a report on the epidemic to the Russian medical council towards the end of 1831, and this in turn formed the basis of two reports compiled by the Royal College of Physicians of London for the privy council. These and accounts by other British doctors of the Russian 'cholera morbus' were relayed to the central board of health in London. Crichton's letter to Sir Alexander Crichton in England, describing the treatment of cholera by German doctors at six St Petersburg hospitals, was published in 1832. He was decorated with the order of St Stanislas (first class) on the birth of Grand Duke Michael in 1832, and was accorded a special badge for '20 years' impeccable service' two years later.

Compelled by ill health to relinquish his post of physician to Tsar Nicholas and his wife Charlotte, Crichton retired in 1837 with the rank of councillor of state, equivalent to a major-general, and, presumably, with a pension. He was presented with a snuffbox on the tsar's twenty-fifth wedding anniversary in 1847, and was an elected honorary member of the Physico-Medical Society of Moscow University from 1838 to 1848. A portrait represents Crichton as a pleasant man of shrewd intelligence, wearing several insignia on a smart green coat and around his neck. In addition to the honours mentioned he was awarded the higher Russian orders of St Vladimir (second class) in 1834 and St Anne (first class) in 1837, and, successively, in 1829, in 1834, and about 1837, two classes and a star of the grand cross of the order of the Red Eagle of Prussia. According to the *Scottish Antiquary*, which published excerpts from his father's family history, he intended to 'make out his title to the Frendraught peerage' (pp. 12–16), but evidently he decided against pursuing this claim to an Aberdeenshire viscountcy conferred upon James Crichton in 1642. Four of his six children died young, but his son Nicholas (1825–1885) became a councillor of state and married Helena Johanna Augusta Nieroth, a wealthy countess of German origin. Their son Nicholas (1869–1916) served as gentleman of the bedchamber to the imperial court in 1911. Crichton died at St Petersburg on 27 February 1865, and was buried at the Smolensk evangelical cemetery on 2 March.   JOHN H. APPLEBY

Sources P. Crichton, 'The Crichton papers: with supplementary notes by A. W. Crichton', *Scottish Antiquary*, 13 (1899), 12–16 • E. M. Tansey, 'The life and works of Sir Alexander Crichton', *Notes and Records of the Royal Society*, 38 (1983–4), 249–50 • Burke, *Gen. Ire.* (1976) • *Rossysky meditsinsky spisok* (1812–63) [Russ. medical list] • A. W. Crichton, letters to Dr Hamel, Tsarskoye Selo, St Petersburg, and Peterhoff, St Petersburg, 1830–36, NL Scot., MS Acc. 7365 • A. W. Crichton, to the duke of Devonshire, 30 April and 7 June 1818, Chatsworth House, Derbyshire, sixth duke series, nos. 309 and 314 • J. Kay, *A series of original portraits and caricature etchings … with biographical sketches and illustrative anecdotes*, ed. [H. Paton and others], new edn [3rd edn], 2 (1877), 390–92 • N. K. Shildera, *Imperator Nikolay Pervy* [Emperor Nicholas the first], 2 vols. (St Petersburg, 1903) • R. D. Owen, *Threading my way: twenty-seven years of autobiography*, 2 vols. (1874), 115–20 • P. I. Bartenev, ed., *Arkhiv kniazia Vorontsova* [Archives of Prince Vorontsov], 40 vols. (1870–95), vols. 15, 17, 19, 22–3, 37, 40 • J. Lees-Milne, *The bachelor duke: a life of W. S. Cavendish, 6th duke of Devonshire, 1790–1858* (1991) • *Some account of my life and writings: an autobiography by the late Sir Archibald Alison*, ed. Lady

Alison, 1 (1883), 93 · W. Steven, *The history of the high school of Edinburgh* (1849), 215 · parish register, St Petersburg English Church, GL · *Peterburgsky nekropol*, 1912, vol. 2 [St Petersburg necropolis]
Archives GL, registers · NL Scot. · St Petersburg English Church | U. Edin., Royal Medical Society dissertations [microfilm]
Likenesses oils, priv. coll. [*see illus.*]
Wealth at death probably substantial: Crichton, 'The Crichton papers'

Crichton, Charles Ainslie (1910–1999), film director, was born on 6 August 1910 at 25 Montpellier Crescent, Liscard, Wallasey, Cheshire, one of six children of John Douglas Crichton, iron and steel merchant, and his wife, Hester Wingate Ainslie. He was educated at Oundle School, Northamptonshire, and New College, Oxford, where he read history, graduating with a second in 1932. Seeking to enter the film industry, he accepted an unpaid job in the cutting rooms of the Korda brothers' company, London Films, at Denham. He was soon assistant editor on several films, such as the acclaimed *The Private Life of Henry VIII* (1933), before editing a number of notable Korda productions. These included *Sanders of the River* (1935); the science fiction epic *Things to Come* (1936), based on H. G. Wells's novel; *Elephant Boy* (1937), based on Kipling's novel; *Prison without Bars* (1938); and *The Thief of Baghdad* (1940). On 24 December 1936 he married Vera Pearl Harman-Mills (*b.* 1916/17), daughter of Percy Harman-Mills, journalist. They had two sons, David and Nicholas.

In 1940 Crichton joined the documentarist Cavalcanti to edit the propaganda 'shorts' *The Young Veterans* and *Yellow Caesar*. Being involved in such work, he was not called up; he and Cavalcanti moved to Ealing, 'the studio with the team spirit', whose films were often to concentrate on the pluck and resilience of ordinary people, capturing exactly the mood of the times. There he co-edited Charles Frend's *The Big Blockade* (1941), about the use of economic warfare, and edited and produced Harry Watt's *Nine Men* (1943), a gripping tale of British soldiers stranded in the north African desert. Michael Balcon offered Crichton his first directing job, on the film *For those in Peril* (1944). It was semi-documentary in style, as was his next, *Painted Boats* (1945). This style touched a number of his feature films. The former was co-written by T. E. B. (Tibby) Clarke, who contributed much to Crichton's Ealing output.

After directing the 'golfing' episode, the weakest of five ghost stories, in *Dead of Night* (1945), Crichton scored a great success with *Hue and Cry* (1947). Scripted by Clarke, it was the first 'Ealing comedy', and Crichton's personal favourite. Innovatively shooting much on location, he showed a huge gang of children scrambling across the bomb-sites of London to corner the crooks who had been using their favourite comic to communicate plans for robberies. *Against the Wind* (1948), about the resistance in Belgium, was good, but not successful. Crichton then completely re-edited *Whisky Galore!* (1948), unpaid, an act which its director, Alexander Mackendrick, believed saved his nascent career, and which was typical of the mutual co-operation between Ealing's creative staff. After *Dance Hall* (1950) came his greatest success, Ealing's finest

comedy, *The Lavender Hill Mob* (1951). Alec Guinness played a mild bank clerk who steals £1 million in gold bars and, with a souvenir manufacturer played by Stanley Holloway, melts them down to smuggle out of the country as Eiffel Tower statuettes. The film won the British Academy award as best film of the year, and an Oscar for Clarke's screenplay; Crichton received a Directors' Guild award nomination.

On loan to Rank, Crichton made the tense and touching *Hunted* (1952) with Dirk Bogarde before, back at Ealing, collaborating again with Clarke on *The Titfield Thunderbolt* (1953). In the latter, villagers unite against bureaucracy to prevent the closure of their local railway line: the film 'brought out the Ealing ideology of smallness and insularity with breezy aplomb' (*The Guardian*), but perhaps revealed that Ealing was no longer quite so well in step with a changing Britain. *The Love Lottery* (1953) was fairly inconsequential, but *The Divided Heart* (1954), sensitive and poignant, was a critical if not a popular success. More solid films followed: *The Man in the Sky* (1957) was his last Ealing film, as that studio dissolved, although *Law and Disorder* (1958), his final collaboration with Clarke, was very similar to the Ealing style. He also directed and co-wrote *Floods of Fear* (1959); *The Battle of the Sexes* (1959), from a James Thurber story, was also Ealing-like, as a Scottish tweed company accountant played by Peter Sellers attempted to thwart an American efficiency expert played by Constance Cummings.

Following *The Boy who Stole a Million* (1961), Crichton was invited to Hollywood to direct *The Birdman of Alcatraz* but clashed with its star, Burt Lancaster, and withdrew. His first marriage having ended in divorce, on 30 June 1962 he married the French-born Nadine Charlotte Flossie Hazé (*b.* 1917/18). He made only two more feature films in the 1960s: *The Third Secret* (1964) and *He who Rides a Tiger* (1965). He found much more work in television, directing episodes of such series as *The Avengers*, *Man of the World*, *Danger Man*, *Man in a Suitcase*, *Strange Report*, and, in the 1970s, *The Adventures of Black Beauty*, *The Protectors*, *Space: 1999*, *The Professionals*, *The Return of the Saint*, and *Dick Turpin*.

In the early 1980s Crichton's directorial services were sought by John Cleese, whose company, Video Arts, was producing a series of successful (and funny) management training films. He and Cleese developed a story which became the hugely successful film *A Fish called Wanda* (1988), the first feature Crichton had directed for twenty-three years. It won an Oscar for one of its stars, Kevin Kline. Crichton, too, was Oscar-nominated, and won the British Academy and *Evening Standard* best director awards and another Directors' Guild award nomination.

Away from film-making, Crichton was a keen photographer, and enjoyed fishing, particularly on Scottish and Welsh rivers. He died of lung cancer at his home, 1 Southwell Gardens, Kensington, London, on 14 September 1999. His second wife and his two sons survived him.

ROBERT SHARP

Sources *The Times* (15 Sept 1999) · *The Times* (1 Oct 1999) · *The Independent* (16 Sept 1999) · *The Guardian* (15 Sept 1999) · *Daily Telegraph* (15 Sept 1999) · *The Scotsman* (22 Sept 1999) · WWW · E. Katz, *The* *international film encyclopaedia* (1980) · D. Quinlan, *Illustrated guide to film directors* (1983) · C. Barr, *Ealing Studios* (1977) · b. cert. · m. certs. · d. cert.

Archives BFI, annotated scripts

Likenesses photograph, *c*.1945, repro. in *The Independent* · photograph, *c*.1980–1989, repro. in *The Scotsman* · photograph, 1987, repro. in *The Times* (15 Sept 1999) · photograph, 1989, repro. in *Daily Telegraph*

Wealth at death £247,515—gross; £245,546—net: administration with will, 1999, *CGPLA Eng. & Wales*

Crichton [*née* Grierson], **Elizabeth** (1779–1862), founder of the Crichton Royal Hospital, Dumfries, was born in 1779 at Rockhall, Dumfriesshire, the fourth daughter of Sir Robert Grierson, fifth baronet (1733–1839), of Lag and Rockhall, and Margaret Dalzell. She married, on 14 November 1810, James Crichton (1765–1823) of Friars Carse, Dumfriesshire. Crichton had obtained his medical degree at the University of Edinburgh and entered the service of the East India Company; he rose to be physician to the viceroy, Lord Mornington. He amassed a large fortune from the proceeds of his medical practice and his successful trading ventures in India and China, and returned to Scotland in 1808. There were no children of the marriage and, after various bequests had been made to family and friends, Crichton's will provided £100,000 to be 'applied in such charitable purposes … as might be pointed out by my wife, with the approbation of the majority of the trustees' (Easterbrook, 11). Mrs Crichton knew that her husband had a particular wish to encourage poor scholars, and in 1829 she submitted her proposal for 'Founding and Endowing a College at Dumfries … for the education of poor Scholars and others resorting thereto' (ibid., 10), with the condition that the government should take charge of the college and give it the status of a university. Crichton's trustees approved this proposal for a fifth Scottish university but, following four years of negotiation and with opposition from the existing universities and a change of government, the scheme had to be abandoned. Notwithstanding the size of the bequest a project of this size could not have survived without government support.

In 1833 Mrs Crichton submitted a proposal for 'Founding and Endowing a Lunatic Asylum in the neighbourhood of Dumfries upon the most approved plan' (Easterbrook, 10), which was unanimously approved by the trustees, although initially there was some local opposition. The trustees purchased 40 acres of land, 1 mile south of Dumfries, in 1834, commissioned architects, and built Crichton Hall, the original building of the Crichton Institution (later the Crichton Royal Hospital). Mrs Crichton appointed Dr William A. F. Browne as the first medical superintendent; he is remembered as the father of occupational therapy and enlightened treatment. The hospital opened in June 1839. Mrs Crichton wished it to be 'the most perfect in Europe' (ibid., 11), with quality built into its site, setting, architecture, and medical treatment. It was certainly well ahead of its time in offering a range of treatments for patients of all social classes, acknowledging the importance of beautiful surroundings, both within the buildings and in the magnificent parklands,

and encouraging the patients to become involved in art, drama, and music therapy. The first theatrical performance ever given in a lunatic asylum took place in 1843, with all the parts and music played by patients. In 1844 the Crichton Royal Hospital's own journal, *New Moon*, began; it was published regularly by patients for the next ninety-two years.

From first to last Mrs Crichton took an active and personal interest in the affairs of the Institution. Sir James Crichton-Browne, in his foreword to the story of the hospital, wrote:

> I well recollect Mrs Crichton in the forties and early fifties of last century, a prim little lady in a black gown with a frilled collar and frilled widow's cap, of a somewhat sombre manner, as was the fashion of the time, but genial and kindly withal, highly intelligent and well-informed, and with a sweet voice in which traces of Scottish dialect and cadence still lingered. I recall her visits to the Crichton Royal Institution in her yellow and black C-spring coach for monthly meetings or conferences with my father or to make calls on lady patients in whom she was specially interested. I recall picnics arranged at Friar's Carse, when parties of patients were hospitably entertained and personally conducted to Burns Hermitage and through its beautiful wood and gardens. (Easterbrook, foreword)

The quality of the hospital and its international reputation for humane and forward-thinking treatment was well established before Mrs Crichton's death, on 11 October 1862 at Friars Carse. She was buried in St Michael's churchyard, Dumfries.

The Crichton Royal Hospital subsequently expanded to cover 85 acres of parkland and gardens, with 27 buildings housing over 1400 patients, its own farm, artesian well, a hydrotherapy pool, a concert hall, and a magnificent cathedral-style church. In the 1980s, with the development of psychiatric medicine and community care, Dumfries and Galloway Health Board declared all the buildings, apart from the original Crichton Hall and the hospice building, to be redundant. The remainder of the estate was sold, part for development as a business park, the rest as Britain's first multi-university campus, housing the universities of Glasgow and Paisley; Bell College, Hamilton; Dumfries and Galloway College; Barony Horticultural College; and the Scottish Agricultural College (in the former hospital farm). In May 2000 the prince of Wales unveiled a statue of Elizabeth Crichton on the campus beside the Crichton Memorial Church, symbolizing the fulfilment of Dr Crichton's legacy and his widow's dream of a university in the south of Scotland.

CAROL GODRIDGE

Sources C. Cromhall Easterbrook, *The chronicle of Crichton Royal, 1833–1936* (1940) · New Monkland register of deaths, NA Scot., 651/2 (122)

Archives Crichton Royal Hospital, Dumfries, Crichton Royal Museum

Likenesses B. Scott, bronze statue, 2000, Crichton Park, Dumfries · oils, Crichton Museum, Dumfries

Crichton, George, of Cairns, earl of Caithness (*d*. 1454). *See under* Crichton, William, of that ilk, first Lord Crichton (*d*. 1453).

Crichton, George (*c*.1555–1611), classical scholar and civil lawyer, was born in Scotland, but left his country at an early age in order to attend university in France, first in Paris (*c*.1577) and then in Toulouse (from 1578). There he studied jurisprudence and also taught both canon and civil law for four years. He mentioned his presence in Toulouse in 1579 in his *Oratio habita in Collegio Harcuriano* (1584). In 1582 he left Toulouse for Paris with the idea of enjoying the city before going back to Scotland. He was at Ste Barbe during the same year and for several months he practised at the bar. Soon his compatriots, the Scottish student John Hamilton among them, recommended he leave a profession in which he could not succeed as a foreigner. Hamilton also advised him not to return to Scotland, where he would not be allowed to lead a quiet life in the Catholic religion he professed. Therefore Crichton accepted the post of regent in the Collège d'Harcourt on 12 November 1583, and on the occasion he delivered a speech (printed as the *Oratio*) in which he indicated that he was born on 1 January. He was then about twenty-eight years old.

In 1586 Crichton started teaching in the Collège de Boncourt and he stayed there several years. After the death in 1590 of Jacques Hélias, professor of Greek, he was appointed by the duc de Mayenne to succeed him; but he never took the position, for Henri IV gave it to François Parent instead. However, another professor of Greek, Daniel d'Auge, died soon afterwards and Crichton was given his post and wages in the Collège Royal in 1595. The mathematician *père* Mersenne was then one of his students. Crichton's appointment to the Collège Royal was the origin of an argument between himself and Parent pursued in *Causa Crittonianae conjectio, in senatu habita idibus Septembris 1597* (1597). He went to Rome for the jubilee of 1600. The same year he was also in the Collège de Lisieux. The thesis he defended on 17 and 18 January 1607 in both civil and canon law was denounced as being contrary to the old doctrine of France and of the Sorbonne, but he was finally made doctor of canon law at the University of Paris on 10 January 1609. At an unknown date Crichton married a daughter of Adam Blackwood, his compatriot and presidial counsel in Poitiers. He died in Paris on 8 April 1611 and was buried in the Église des Jacobins in the rue St Jacques. Later his widow married François de la Mothe le Vayer.

Nicéron enumerated twenty-nine works by Crichton, including a poem on the election of Henri de Valois, duc d'Anjou: *In felicem Ser. Poloniae regis inaugurationem Georgii Crittonii, Scoti, congratulatio* (1573). His *Orationes duae habitae in auditorio regio, anno 1608* was published in Paris in 1609; one of the speeches is on the laws of Draco and Solon, the other on the title *De judiciis* in Hermenopulus. His speech about the death of Henri IV was published the following year as *Parentalia Henrico IV. Franciae Navarraeque regi inscripta & recitata a Georgio Crittonio die 24. Maii 1610.*

MARIE-CLAUDE TUCKER

Sources L. Moreri, *Dictionnaire historique*, new edn (1759); (Geneva, 1995), 226–7 · P. Nicéron, *Mémoires des hommes illustres*, 37 (1727), 346–57 · P. Bayle, *Dictionnaire historique et critique* (1740) · C. Jourdain, *Histoire de l'Université de Paris au XVIIe et au XVIIIe siècle*, 2 pts (Paris, 1862–6), 47 · J. Durkan, 'The French connection in the sixteenth and early seventeenth centuries', *Scotland and Europe, 1200–1850*, ed. T. C. Smout (1986), 41–3

Crichton, James, of that ilk, earl of Moray and second Lord Crichton (*d.* 1454). *See under* Crichton, William, of that ilk, first Lord Crichton (*d.* 1453).

Crichton, James [*called* the Admirable Crichton] (1560–1582), rhetorician and soldier, was born on 19 August 1560, probably at Eliock near Sanquhar, Dumfriesshire, the son of **Robert Crichton** (*d.* 1582), lawyer.

Scotland: law and learning In February 1552 Robert Crichton had a lease of the lands of Eliock, an estate which since the 1460s had been held by the Crichtons of Sanquhar, the family to which he clearly belonged (though his parentage is uncertain). In 1558 he married the first of his three wives, Elizabeth Stewart of Beath in Fife (through whom their children could claim descent from the Scottish royal house); they had three sons—James, Henry (who died young), and **Sir Robert Crichton** (*c*.1569–*c*.1620)—and two daughters. In 1562, by a transaction already envisaged in 1558, Robert Crichton, now queen's advocate (jointly with John Spens), acquired the estate of Clunie in Perthshire. This belonged to the see of Dunkeld: Bishop Robert Crichton (of another branch of the family) had the chapter's consent for an arrangement with his namesake seemingly intended to avert annexation following the religious revolution of 1560. By a further manoeuvre in 1566 the bishop conveyed the estate to the six-year-old James Crichton, who probably spent much of his childhood in the little castle on the Loch of Clunie. There, or in nearby Dunkeld, he received the first stages of his education, from the schoolmaster Alexander Hepburn, author of *Grammaticae artis rudimenta* (1568). It is also likely that some of his early education was in Edinburgh, with the resolutely Roman Catholic schoolmaster William Robertson as his teacher.

Robert Crichton's prosperity during the personal reign of Mary Stewart is evinced by a number of advantageous property transactions in the mid-1560s. In public life he acted for the crown in the proceedings against the murderers of Riccio in the spring of 1566, and a year later for the prosecution in the somewhat anomalous trial of Bothwell for the murder of Darnley. He supported the queen in the conflict following her enforced abdication in July 1567 and was among those proscribed in summer 1568 for taking the field with her at Langside. In July 1569, nevertheless, he attended the estates as king's advocate; but his position was far from secure in the unstable situation after the assassination of the regent Moray in January 1570. In September he was summoned to appear before the council; and during the winter of 1570–71 the new regent, Lennox, took steps to keep him in Edinburgh when Mary wished him to take part in the abortive negotiations in England for her conditional return to the throne. Crichton continued in office as lord advocate, but his situation was still uneasy: as late as February 1574, with Morton firmly in control as regent, he was again summoned

James Crichton [the Admirable Crichton] (**1560–1582**), by unknown artist

before the council to answer charges. Meanwhile, some time before February 1572, his first wife had died: he married, secondly, Agnes Mowbray of Barnbougall, with whom he had a daughter.

During this troubled time for his father, James Crichton's academic career had begun: he matriculated at St Andrews, aged ten, in 1570. His college, St Salvator's, was then presided over by a humanist of some note, John Rutherford (1520–1577), author of *Commentariorum de arte disserendi libri quatuor* (1557). Crichton graduated BA in 1573, and MA in 1575. The fifteen-year-old graduate probably spent much of the next two years in Edinburgh. His signature appears on a deed dated 20 June 1575 forming part of a transaction to secure possession of the Clunie estate from the protestant bishop of Dunkeld (Bishop Crichton having been forfeited in 1571). This was confirmed on 22 March 1576 in 'Mr Robert's foir chalmer at Bell Wynde heid' in the High Street near Parliament House (Stuart, 108): James Crichton was the principal beneficiary, with reversion to his brother and father. It must have been during this Edinburgh sojourn that James encountered George Buchanan, whom he named later as one of his teachers. Buchanan was then tutor—and a terror—to the boy king, and Crichton is said to have been one of several older youths to have shared that experience. The supposition is plausible, though unconfirmed: certainly Crichton's education, or self-education, must have continued apace. His career, however, was now to take a new direction.

The Scot abroad It was probably in autumn 1577 that James Crichton left Scotland. He later attributed his departure to disputes with his father that were acrimonious enough to be called *intestinas seditiones et praelia domestica* ('inner discord and domestic strife'; Tytler, 290), and his exile was in some measure involuntary. The issues dividing father and son may have had a public or semi-public dimension. This was an uneasy period in both politics and religion, and the younger Crichton had spent five years in a university then by no means reliably loyal to the prevailing order. He seems to have remained a Roman Catholic, whereas his father, whether from conviction or convenience, had accommodated himself to the establishment in the Scotland of Andrew Melville. However, the division in the family must not be exaggerated; in 1579 Robert Crichton (now married to his third wife, Isobell Borthwick) took further steps to consolidate his elder son's tenure of Clunie, and three years later James was named as an executor of his father's will and his return to Scotland was still expected.

The usual destination for the Scot abroad—at least for Scots with intellectual ambitions—was Paris; and thither, accordingly, it has been supposed that James Crichton went, though there is no reliable independent evidence. Crichton himself said, two or three years later in Italy, that he had spent two years as a soldier in France 'with the honour of a command' (*con carico honorato*; Tytler, 290). This may be mere rodomontade: it was certainly part of a campaign of self-promotion. On the other hand, there is later evidence to suggest that Crichton had acquired some military experience and skill beyond the swordsmanship befitting his social status. He certainly arrived in Genoa in the spring of 1579, his fortunes evidently at a low ebb, but within a few months had established himself sufficiently in the city to be invited to deliver on 1 July the ceremonial oration on the biennial election of magistrates. The printed text of this encomium on republican virtue and its exemplification in Genoa was the first—and was to be the most substantial—of Crichton's few publications. It is said to have earned him a substantial financial reward and an invitation to remain in Genoa. The latter he declined, choosing instead to try his fortune in the other (and greater) Italian mercantile republic. By summer 1580 he was in Venice.

It was here that the legend of the Admirable Crichton was born: the midwife was the scholarly publisher Aldo Manuzio, who seems to have seen at once that here was a phenomenon to be promoted—exploited may be too harsh a term for a process from which its subject gained considerably. The promotion of *Lo scozzese, detto Giacomo Critonio* was extravagant enough: fluent in ten languages (including Hebrew and Chaldean); learned in philosophy, theology, mathematics, astrology, and statecraft; dazzling in disputation, equipped with an almost miraculous memory; eloquent, handsome, courtly, witty in conversation; and soldierly and athletic, as much a master of horsemanship and jousting as of the dance. And withal he was, through his mother, of royal blood! How much of this was then, or can now be, believed is hard to gauge. The handbill in which it is all proclaimed was probably Crichton's own work, the text later revised and expanded by Manuzio—evidently a publicist of considerable calibre. Yet, if the lily was being opulently gilded, there was clearly a remarkable reality behind the showy appearance. Others were independently impressed by what they saw and heard of the Scottish *Wunderkind*. Learned and sophisticated critics were not hard to find in Venice or in the wider world of Italian culture to which Manuzio could make his new protégé known, and his correspondence reflects the success of his efforts. Within a few months of Crichton's arrival in Venice, his reputation had reached the learned cardinal Guglielmo Sirleto. By midsummer 1581 Crichton had been invited to Rome by the erudite Spanish historian of the papacy, Alfonso Chacón. He may have accepted that invitation, but it was primarily in Venice and Padua that he sought to enhance his reputation.

Triumphs and tragedy in Italy Soon after reaching Venice, doubtless through Manuzio's influence, Crichton, on his twentieth birthday (19 August 1580), addressed the council of ten: his oration earned him 100 gold crowns and launched a brief but brilliant career in the city. Among other episodes, this included a debate in the house of the patriarch of Aquileia on the procession of the Holy Ghost. Crichton's success was somewhat offset by a prolonged illness during the winter of 1580–81. The chronology is not clear, but it seems that Crichton's withdrawal to a villa on the Brenta was partly to convalesce and partly to prepare for a major exhibition of his dialectical skills in the church of Santi Giovanni e Paolo (perhaps originally planned for the autumn of 1580). In any case, in mid-March 1581 he displayed his talents to a formidable academic audience in Padua under the patronage of Giacomo Luigi Corner. It may have been at this time that Crichton met and impressed the octogenarian Sperone Speroni, from whom a letter in flattering terms survives. Applause was not universal: the cancellation of a projected public disputation in Padua prompted some unfriendly comment. To this Crichton's response was the postponed performance in Venice at Pentecost (14 May)—reported by Manuzio as a triumph. It was probably later in 1581 that Crichton met, and was worsted by, his most distinguished opponent, the philosopher Jacopo Mazzoni (1548–1598). A later account of this indicates that, in defeat, Crichton took refuge in the somewhat disingenuous plea that his profession was arms rather than learning. It may well be that such setbacks led him to seek new outlets for his talents and ambitions.

One of Crichton's dialectical exploits had been a theological debate in the presence of Cardinal Luigi d'Este; and it was the cardinal's secretary, Annibale Capello, who recommended Crichton to the duke of Mantua's secretary, Aurelio Zibramonti, and thus brought about his migration to the ducal court. By early February 1582 Crichton had established himself there with what seems to have been characteristic facility. He was commissioned by Duke Guglielmo Gonzaga to draw up a plan for the fortification of the city—which may tend to confirm the hypothesis that Crichton had indeed had some military experience in France; and this would lend colour to his

claim that his professional skill lay in that field. Other tasks in the court came his way, however. Towards the end of March he was sent back to Venice on business connected with the marriage of the duke's daughter to Archduke Ferdinand of Austria. Crichton seemingly spent much of April in Padua, where he renewed his contact with Giacomo Luigi Corner—whose comments after Crichton's death suggest that the patron found the client at least as trying as he was 'admirable'.

Back in Mantua by 7 May 1582, Crichton soon found that his situation at court, advantageous though it was, had its problems. The evidence is by no means clear, but letters in late June and early July from Crichton in the city to Zibramonti at the duke's summer residence indicate that the new favourite had incurred jealous resentment. Though the name is not mentioned, it seems clear that Crichton's chief enemy was the duke's son and heir, Vincenzo Gonzaga. Only a day after his last letter, that enmity—whether by chance or by design—had bloody consequences. In the small hours of 3 July 1582—on a moonlit night following a stiflingly hot day—Crichton was roaming the streets of Mantua. His object and that of the two other young men he encountered may have been merely some respite from the heat, but their hot-tempered brawling ended fatally. Crichton inflicted a mortal wound on Vincenzo's disreputable companion, Hippolito Lanzone. Vincenzo in turn gave Crichton the wound from which he later died. Crichton, it seems, had not recognized his princely adversary until after he was wounded. He was buried by his servants the same day in an unmarked grave in the nearby church of San Simone. Vincenzo's account of the affray was widely disbelieved in the city, where Crichton seems to have been popular; but in default of other evidence 'a general mist of error' seems as likely an explanation of the tragedy as anything more sinister.

Scottish aftermath In Scotland meanwhile a period of political flux had begun in the spring of 1578. Formal regency came to an end. Morton was arrested in December 1580, and Robert Crichton appeared for the prosecution in the trial which led to his condemnation and execution. Crichton had become sole lord advocate and a lord of session on 1 February 1580. He seems to have been in good standing with the faction who shared the royal favour enjoyed by Esmé Stewart, soon to be duke of Lennox. This is suggested by some of the names mentioned in the will Crichton made on 18 June 1582, a fortnight before his son's death in Mantua. This, with James Crichton as one of the executors, made careful provision for the advocate's wife, his younger son, and his five unmarried daughters. Robert Crichton was by then a sick man: by 27 June he was dead.

Uncertainty as to James Crichton's fate may explain the puzzling fact that his father's will was not confirmed until 24 January 1586. (It may also help to explain his being sometimes confused with another James Crichton (*fl.* 1585–1587), schoolmaster and author in the archdiocese of Milan. In 1586 James's brother Robert, heir to the Eliock and Clunie estates, was then not yet of full age—years of discretion he perhaps never attained. His career was one of aristocratic thuggery, including the violent kidnapping of his half-sister Marion in July 1592. The murder of the laird of Moncoffer in 1598 was part of a campaign of revenge for the slaying of Crichton's kinsman, 'the bonny earl of Moray'. Four years later, failure to answer a charge of assault committed in the king's presence cost him the forfeiture of his remaining estates: necessity had compelled him to sell Eliock to his brother-in-law Robert Dalzell (later earl of Carnwath) in 1595. Although seemingly knighted in the late 1590s, Sir Robert Crichton's life after 1602 seems to have been a combination of property dealing and violence. In 1616—not for the first time, though perhaps for the last—he was imprisoned following a 'tumult' in Edinburgh. His stormy career ended some time between then and 1620.

James Crichton alone, then, gives this branch of the family a claim to substantial biographical interest, if hardly historical significance. (His father played more of a part, however small, in the public domain.) It may be harsh to say that nothing in James's life did as much for his reputation as his premature and melodramatic death. Was he 'likely, had he been put on, to have proved' if not 'most royal' then at least more than a transient prodigy? Neo-classical Latin verse and rhetorical prose would have to be of more dazzling excellence than Crichton's to sustain an affirmative answer. His fame rested on reported brilliance in forms that have, necessarily, left no adequately objective record. Yet in James Crichton there was perhaps a conjuncture of precocious talents in a youth who died before finding the vocation they might have served. Incongruously, *The Admirable Crichton* is widely remembered as the title of J. M. Barrie's Edwardian social comedy. Less inaptly, Crichton's story was seized upon and inflated by Sir Thomas Urquhart (in *The Jewel*, 1652); but the larger-than-life figure in those ornate pages would here be out of place, as well as out of proportion.

J. H. BURNS

Sources 'Lo Scozzese, detto Giacomo Critonio' (1580) [anonymous handbill] · A. Manuzio, *Relatione della qualità di Jacomo di Crettone*, 8 vols. (Venice, 1581) · A. Manuzio, 'Dedication', in *In M. Tullii Ciceronis de officiis libros tres Aldi Mannucij, Paulli F. Aldi N. commentarius: item in dialogos de senectute, de amicitia, paradoxa, somnium scipionis*, ed. A. Manuzio and others (Venice, 1581) · Thomae Dempsteri Historia ecclesiastica gentis Scotorum, sive, De scriptoribus Scotis, ed. D. Irving, rev. edn, 1, Bannatyne Club, 21 (1829), 187–9 · J. Imperialis, *Museum physicum* (1640), 62, 122 · J. Imperialis, *Museum historicum et physicum* (1640), 140–43, 242 · P. F. Tytler, *Life of the admirable Crichton* (1823) · J. Stuart, 'Notices of Sir Robert Crichton of Cluny and of his son James, "The admirable Crichton"', *Proceedings of the Society of Antiquaries of Scotland*, 2 (1854–7), 103–18 · D. Crichton, *The admirable Crichton: the real character* (1909) · D. Crichton, 'James Crichton of Eliock', *Votiva tabella: a memorial volume of St Andrews University* (1911), 339–61 · *Reg. PCS*, 1st ser. · *CSP Scot.*, 1547–69; 1586–1603 · J. M. Thomson and others, eds., *Registrum magni sigilli regum Scotorum / The register of the great seal of Scotland*, 11 vols. (1882–1914), vols. 3–8 · M. Livingstone, D. Hay Fleming, and others, eds., *Registrum secreti sigilli regum Scotorum / The register of the privy seal of Scotland*, 4–8 (1952–82) · C. T. McInnes, ed., *Accounts of the treasurer of Scotland*, 12 (1970) · J. Stuart, ed., 'Papers from the charter chest of the earl of Airlie', *The miscellany of the Spalding Club*, 4–5, Spalding Club, 20, 24 (1849–52)

Likenesses oils, 1600–40, priv. coll. · oils, 1600–40, priv. coll. · eleventh earl of Buchan, pencil and chalk drawing (after unknown artist), Scot. NPG · attrib. J. Medina, junior, version of oil painting in Royal Collection, Lennoxlove, East Lothian · engraving (after portrait), repro. in Stuart, 'Notices of Sir Robert Crichton' · oils, Royal Collection [*see illus.*]

Crichton, James, first Viscount Frendraught (*c.*1620–1664/5), royalist nobleman, was the eldest son of James Crichton (*d.* in or after 1667) of Frendraught and his wife, Lady Elizabeth, daughter of John Gordon, twelfth earl of Sutherland. He was descended from William Crichton, Lord Crichton, the celebrated lord chancellor. His father was of very turbulent disposition, and in October 1630 several friends whom he had urged to stay in his house to protect him from the threatened assault of his enemies were burnt to death there under circumstances which threw suspicion on himself. His chief enemies were the Gordons of Rothemay, who repeatedly plundered Frendraught.

Crichton was educated at King's College, Aberdeen, where he matriculated in 1635. In 1639 he married Lady Janet (*d.* 1640), third daughter of Alexander and Agnes Leslie, third earl and countess of Leven. Reputedly granted a new charter of the territorial barony of Frendraught in 1641, he was certainly made Viscount Frendraught and Lord Crichton by patent dated at Nottingham on 29 August 1642. His first wife having died on 24 November 1640, he married Marion, daughter of Sir Alexander and Lady Margaret Irvine of Drum, on 8 November 1642. Crichton sold the Frendraught estate on 20 July 1647. He took part in the last expedition of the royalist marquess of Montrose and was present at the battle of Invercharran, or Carbisdale, on 27 April 1650. In the rout Montrose's horse was wounded, and it is reputed that Frendraught gave him his own, which enabled Montrose to make good his escape. However, there is no truth in the story that Frendraught died by his own hand on the field of battle in order to evade capture. In fact, having been severely wounded, he languished for a time at Dunrobin. 'Having expressed penitence for his manifold defections from the covenant, he was, on 3 October 1651, admitted an elder of the kirk sessions at Forgue' (GEC, *Peerage*). He took his seat in the Scottish parliament on 25 January 1661. He died some time between 14 July 1664 and 17 August 1665, and was succeeded by his son by his second marriage, James.

J. M. RIGG, *rev.* SEAN KELSEY

Sources GEC, *Peerage*, new edn · R. Douglas, *The peerage of Scotland*, 2nd edn, ed. J. P. Wood, 2 vols. (1813)

Crichton, Patrick (1762–1823). *See under* Crichton, Sir Archibald William (1791–1865).

Crichton, Robert (*d.* 1582). *See under* Crichton, James (1560–1582).

Crichton, Robert (*d.* 1585). *See under* Castilians in Edinburgh (*act.* 1570–1573).

Crichton, Robert, eighth Lord Crichton of Sanquhar (*c.*1568–1612), nobleman and murderer, was the son of Edward Crichton, seventh Lord Crichton of Sanquhar (*c.*1542–1569), and Margaret Douglas (*c.*1545–*c.*1605), of Drumlanrig. On 10 April 1608 he married Anne (*c.*1593–

1675), daughter of Sir George Fermor of Easton, North-amptonshire. His Catholic religion, and status as a baron of the Scottish west march with properties in and around Dumfries and Nithsdale, shaped his career. The success he doubtless believed to be his due eluded him; his impetuosity and poor judgement always let him down, as in 1599 when after a conciliatory audience with the king he kidnapped two of his enemies, for which he was briefly gaoled. From 1590 he followed a pattern whereby failure at home was followed by a withdrawal abroad, where his religion might be an advantage. Reports of his associations with Scottish Jesuits and military service under the archdukes in Flanders led Robert Cecil, among others, to warn King James against him. Nevertheless James used him for minor diplomatic missions to France, Venice, and other Italian states, hinting at future leniency towards Catholics.

From 1601 Sanquhar attached himself to Queen Anne's circle. He prospered somewhat, being named in 1603 with Lord Lindore as having some rights of attendance in the king's English bedchamber. Then in 1604 he lost an eye, and nearly died, in a fencing match with an English fencing master, John Turner, at Lord Norris's house in Oxfordshire. Eight years later he hired two Scots to murder Turner, whom they shot and killed on 11 May 1612. One of the assassins was caught red-handed. Within days Sanquhar surrendered. As a Scottish nobleman he was refused trial before the House of Lords, and appeared in the king's bench on 27 June. He pleaded guilty, offering a lengthy speech in mitigation. Despite the efforts of his friends at court, James refused to pardon him. The murder of Turner was the final straw in a succession of violent scandals involving Englishmen and Scots close to the king. James made an example of Sanquhar, who was hanged in a silken halter at the gates of Great Palace Yard, Westminster, on 29 June 1612. On the scaffold Sanquhar affirmed his Catholic faith, which led some Catholic propagandists to try unsuccessfully to portray him as a martyr. His marriage was childless; in 1609 he had obtained legitimation of his natural son William, then at school in Paris. Nevertheless, his cousin William Crichton of Ryhill was recognized as ninth Lord Crichton of Sanquhar in 1619. His widow married Barnaby O'Brien, the sixth earl of Thomond, in 1615; she died on 13 April 1675.

M. J. BOWMAN

Sources Scots peerage, vol. 3 · GEC, Peerage, new edn, vol. 3 · Reg. PCS, 1st ser., 6.44, 46, 47, 49–51, 103, 114–16, 444–5, 844–8; 8.153, 215, 347–8, 363, 377, 380, 382, 386, 390, 399, 400, 402, 405–6, 408, 434, 449, 517–18, 525, 598, 719, 720–21 · CSP Scot., 1597–1603, 54–5, 155, 261, 363, 532, 564, 569, 575, 579, 591, 628, 661, 700–01, 829–30, 843, 888, 908, 960, 977–8, 982, 1003, 1012, 1015, 1031, 1033–4, 1118 · Calendar of the manuscripts of the most hon. the marquis of Salisbury, 14, HMC, 9 (1923), 95, 139–41, 233 · CSP Venice, 1603–7, 52, 63, 85–7, 114, 118, 123 · The letters of John Chamberlain, ed. N. E. McClure, 1 (1939) · State trials, 2.92 · The ninth part of the reports of Sir Edward Coke (1738) [9 Co Rep] · Report on the manuscripts of the marquis of Downshire, 6 vols. in 7, HMC, 75 (1924–95), vol. 3 · 'John Jackson alias Nelson to T. More', Westm. DA, XI, 565 · Reg. PCS, 1st ser., 9.740
Wealth at death dues in kind from various tenants, 900 merks and £100 Scots in money [£58 6s. 6d.]: 1612, Masson, ed., Register of the privy council, vol. 9, p. 740

Crichton, Sir Robert (c.1569–c.1620). See under Crichton, James (1560–1582).

Crichton, William, of that ilk, first Lord Crichton (d. 1453), administrator and courtier, was the eldest son of Sir John Crichton of that ilk and his spouse, thought to have been Christian Grimslaw (who survived her husband). The family's principal seat was at Crichton in Edinburghshire, and there were important estates in Dumfriesshire, as well as in Peeblesshire and Roxburghshire. William Crichton was knighted at the coronation of James I, in May 1424. In May 1426, described as a gentleman of the king's bedchamber, he was sent with two others to treat with Erik, king of Norway and Denmark, concerning the annual payment owed to Norway since 1266 for the Scottish Western Isles. Thereafter Crichton clearly profited from the favour of James I, who in the 1430s relied mainly on barons from Lothian to act as his daily council. In 1429 Crichton began to witness crown charters and by March 1432 he had been created master of the king's household, an office he retained until at least June 1437. He was also appointed sheriff of Edinburgh and captain of Edinburgh Castle (for which he received a sizeable annual pension) about 1433, holding both posts until his death. The influence of Archibald, fifth earl of Douglas, cannot be discounted as a factor behind Crichton's promotion, but the earl was seldom at court, which allowed Crichton to strengthen his position there.

After the murder of James I in 1437 Crichton was increasingly prominent in the administration which ruled Scotland in the name of the young James II, especially after the earl of Douglas, who was lieutenant-general, died in June 1439. In May of that year Crichton had become chancellor, and the seal tags of many engrossed charters bear his signature, suggesting that he carefully controlled the use of the great seal. In his capacity as chancellor he was the means whereby the king's council blocked the claim of Sir Robert Erskine to the earldom of Mar, a substantial prize which in 1457 was to be denied to Erskine's son Thomas by a verdict in the crown's favour. Crichton's main rival was an unlikely one, Sir Alexander Livingston of Callendar, who had not been a court regular, but who now benefited from having control of the young king, after imprisoning the queen mother in Stirling Castle in August 1439. However hostile to each other they may have been, Crichton and Livingston came to terms, and may have co-operated in the judicial murder of the sixth earl of Douglas on 24 November 1440. The seventh and eighth earls of Douglas were antipathetic to Crichton, but sympathetic to Livingston. About 1444 Crichton was forced from office, and indeed in June 1445 he was besieged in Edinburgh Castle by forces nominally led by the king himself, though in actuality controlled by Douglas, after a year in which both sides had ravaged the other's lands.

An accommodation was reached: Crichton returned to court and assumed (at the same time as the heads of various other major Scottish landed families) a peerage title, making the small but significant change from the style lord of Crichton, which he had used before, to that of Lord Crichton. But he held no office, as the Livingstons and their supporters were now dominant. However, following the death in 1447 of Bishop James Bruce, who had succeeded him as chancellor, Crichton resumed his former post, before November in the same year. In 1448 he travelled to Burgundy, one of the king's ambassadors sent to arrange James II's marriage to Mary, daughter of Arnold, duke of Gueldres. On his return to Scotland, after negotiations were concluded in the spring of 1449, Crichton founded a collegiate church at Crichton. It is also thought that he transformed the tower-house of Crichton Castle into an impressive courtyard castle.

In September 1449 the Livingstons were dramatically ousted. Their power had been based on office holding, and Crichton now sought similar rewards for his own family. He had never been slow to attend to their interests. In the late 1430s he seems to have encouraged Sir Alexander Seton of Tullibody, later first earl of Huntly, to marry his daughter Elizabeth Crichton, after Seton divorced his first wife; Crichton cannot have been displeased when Seton then entailed his lands on his and Elizabeth's first son, excluding from the succession the son of his first marriage, greatly to the latter's chagrin. An important beneficiary of Crichton's patronage in the 1450s was his cousin **George Crichton of Cairns**, earl of Caithness (*d.* 1454). The elder son of Stephen Crichton of Cairns, Edinburghshire, and an unknown mother, George had before his father's death in 1434 built up an estate mostly (but not entirely) in south-west Scotland and Lothian; his territorial designation was sometimes 'of Blackness', Linlithgowshire, later his main estate, rather than Cairns. Knighted by 1438, George witnessed a few crown charters during William Crichton's first tenure of office as chancellor, and was ambassador to Brittany in 1441, to negotiate the marriage of James II's sister Elizabeth. By then he was admiral of Scotland (an office he held until his death) and had succeeded his father as sheriff of Linlithgow.

George Crichton was involved in the troubles affecting his cousin William in 1444–5, and his activities are rarely recorded thereafter until 1450. But from February in that year he was a frequent witness of crown charters and was also present on the king's council in judicial matters and in parliament as an auditor of causes. Shortly after the fall of the Livingstons he became sheriff of Stirling and keeper of Stirling Castle, and by late 1452 he was justiciar south of Forth. In June that year he was created earl of Caithness. Particularly after his elevation to the peerage (and probably at the king's instigation) he began to entail his estates, to the effect that his son and heir, James Crichton, would not succeed to either title or lands after George's death. James resented this, and incarcerated his father in Blackness Castle, which the king had to besiege in person in order to relieve the earl. A settlement was reached whereby James received the Cairns estate and (from the king) some crown lands in Perthshire, but the rest of the earl's property, along with his title, fell to the crown on George's death, which took place at Edinburgh in August 1454. George married twice. James, who was

often present in parliament under James III, was the son of George's first marriage, about 1425, to a daughter (name unknown) of Sir William Douglas of Strathbrock. About 1450 George married Janet, daughter of Sir William Borthwick of that ilk, widow of Sir James Douglas of Dalkeith and former wife of Sir Colin Campbell of Glenorchy; they had a daughter, Janet, who married Robert, Lord Maxwell.

The records of the exchequer show sundry other minor Crichtons obtaining fees or pensions while William Crichton was dominant in government. But the fountain dried up in 1453–4, when William, his son and heir, James, and his cousin George all died. William witnessed his last crown charter on 16 September 1453 and probably died shortly afterwards. His wife, Agnes (surname unknown), is presumed to have been the mother of all his known children, a son, James, and two daughters: Elizabeth married Sir Alexander Seton, while Agnes married Alexander, second Lord Glamis. **James Crichton of that ilk**, earl of Moray and second Lord Crichton (*d.* 1454), was knighted in October 1430, on the occasion of the baptism of James II. Another beneficiary of his father's patronage, he was appointed chamberlain by March 1451, though he does not appear to have been active in that post. He was also captain of Kildrummy Castle from late 1450 until 1452 and in 1453–4 keeper of Dunbar Castle. By 1445 he had married Janet, elder daughter and coheir of James Dunbar, fourth earl of Moray. Her sister Elizabeth married Archibald Douglas, third son of James Douglas, seventh earl of Douglas, who assumed the title earl of Moray until his forfeiture about 1452, while Crichton was styled Lord Frendraught by right of his spouse until he was created earl of Moray in the parliament of June 1452. While there has been doubt about the status of this grant, he is clearly styled earl on a number of occasions, though he certainly did not transmit his title to his son. Crichton died at Dunbar in August 1454. His spouse survived him and by 1459 married John Sutherland. Active in the land market until her death about 1500, she is unusual in being a medieval Scotswoman who demonstrated the ability to sign her name.

The eldest of James and Janet Crichton's three sons, **William Crichton of that ilk**, third Lord Crichton (*d.* 1493), succeeded to the lordship in 1454. He witnessed a few charters of James III in 1469–70 and 1476, and was normally present in parliament between 1467 and 1479; he was sheriff of Edinburgh in 1469–71, and perhaps for a longer period. However, he became a follower of Alexander Stewart, duke of Albany, in the latter's intrigues against his brother, James III, and supported the coup of July 1482 against the king. Accordingly he suffered the consequences once King James regained control of government in the following spring. Under an indenture of 19 March 1483 between the king and Albany, Crichton was banished from Scotland for three years; then, as Albany continued to plot with England, Crichton and others were forfeited in the parliament of February 1484 (the sentence was given in his absence, as he may have been in sanctuary in Tain). James III may have had personal grounds for disliking Crichton. The sixteenth-century historian George Buchanan tells of the king seducing Crichton's wife, Janet Dunbar (actually his mother), though there is no contemporary evidence for this. But there seems to be no doubt that Crichton formed a relationship with James's younger sister, Margaret, which resulted in the birth of a daughter.

Crichton may have fled Scotland after his forfeiture. Nevertheless he was among the rebel forces which held Dumbarton and Duchal castles against James IV in the summer of 1489. In September 1489 he obtained a safe conduct from Henry VII to pass to England and elsewhere, but he was certainly in Scotland in September 1492. He had died by October 1493, possibly in Inverness, where he may have been buried. Before 1478 he married Marion, daughter of James, Lord Livingston, a union presumably intended to settle the previous rivalry between the families. They appear to have had one son, James. Crichton's forfeiture meant that the peerage title became extinct; and following a resignation of property in his favour in November 1493 by his grandmother, Janet Dunbar, James Crichton assumed the designation 'of Frendraught', which became the family style.   ALAN R. BORTHWICK

Sources J. M. Thomson and others, eds., *Registrum magni sigilli regum Scotorum / The register of the great seal of Scotland*, 11 vols. (1882–1914), vol. 2 · APS, 1424–1567 · G. Burnett and others, eds., *The exchequer rolls of Scotland*, 23 vols. (1878–1908) · various collections of manuscript estate and other papers in archive offices and in private hands in Scotland and England · *The Asloan manuscript*, ed. W. A. Craigie, 2 vols., STS, new ser., 14, 16 (1923–5) · W. Bower, *Scotichronicon*, ed. D. E. R. Watt and others, new edn, 9 vols. (1987–98), vol. 8 · *Buchanan's History of Scotland*, 2 vols. (1733) [trans.] · [T. Thomson] and others, eds., *The acts of the lords of council in civil causes, 1478–1503*, 3 vols. (1839–1993) · M. Brown, *James I* (1994) · C. McGladdery, *James II* (1990) · N. Macdougall, *James III: a political study* (1982) · *Scots peerage*, vol. 3 · South Leith Kirk Sessions MSS, Class I, no. 3, Edinburgh · Floors Castle, Roxburghe Muniments, bundle 692 · NA Scot., Eglinton Muniments, GD 3/1/492 · M. Brown, *The Black Douglases: war and lordship in late medieval Scotland, 1300–1455* (1998)

Crichton, William, of that ilk, third Lord Crichton (d. **1493**). *See under* Crichton, William, of that ilk, first Lord Crichton (d. 1453).

Crichton, William (c.**1535–1617**), Jesuit, was the son of Patrick Crichton of Camnay in the barony of Meigle in east Perthshire and a kinsman of Robert Crichton, eighth Lord Crichton of Sanquhar (d. 1612). He matriculated at St Andrews University in 1552, graduated in arts as bachelor in 1554 and as master in 1555. In 1561 he matriculated at Louvain. In 1562 he and his cousin Edmund Hay had decided to enter the Society of Jesus, each being described as son of a 'confessor', that is, one who had continued to profess Catholicism.

Crichton returned to Scotland to wind up his affairs and to await the arrival of Hay and the papal envoy, the Jesuit Nicholas of Gouda. From 18 June to 3 September 1562 the two cousins acted as the envoy's guides and Crichton was present at his interview with William Crichton, bishop of Dunkeld. When the envoy left Scotland, with great secrecy as all the ports were being watched, Crichton

accompanied him. Towards the end of the year the two cousins went together to Rome.

Crichton's progress in the Jesuits was swift. He had studied in several continental centres of learning and was versed in several languages. Having entered the noviciate at Rome on 5 December 1562 he made his religious vows on 6 January 1563 and was ordained priest in Rome around Whitsun that year. Sent to Aquitaine, in 1565–77 he was rector of the Jesuit colleges at Lyons and Avignon, then again at Lyons, and in 1574–80 was vice-provincial. On 29 August 1568 he was professed of the four vows. In February 1581 he attended the fourth Jesuit general congregation in Rome and was instructed to inform the pope about Scottish affairs. His career now underwent a complete change. The Scots Jesuit Robert Abercromby had compiled a report on Scotland and Robert Persons had sent priests to Scotland to see the situation there. It seemed a very opportune time, as the strongly protestant regent Morton had been deposed and executed, while the duke of Lennox, reputed to be a Catholic, had great influence over the teenaged James VI.

Crichton travelled to Rouen in January 1582 to receive instructions from Persons, then went on to Scotland. In April he returned to France with letters from Lennox, who was willing to lead the enterprise of restoring Catholicism in the two kingdoms if given a very generous support of Spanish troops and money. After a series of meetings with Catholic leaders in France, Crichton was sent to treat with the pope. Plans and projects were drawn up, including a scheme to assassinate Queen Elizabeth, but were shelved when the raid of Ruthven put James in the hands of protestants, while Lennox was forced to leave Scotland. The reality was that Philip II of Spain had more important and pressing projects in hand.

Following a request by Archbishop James Beaton, Queen Mary's ambassador in Paris, Crichton and another Jesuit, James Gordon, set off for Scotland in September 1584 but were captured at sea by Dutch protestants. Gordon was released but Crichton was taken to Flanders, where according to his own narrative he narrowly escaped being hanged for complicity in the recent murder of William of Orange. Instead he was handed over to the English authorities and imprisoned in the Tower of London, where he remained for over two years. With him he had papers outlining the schemes of 1582, which he succeeded in only partially destroying. They were, however, no longer very relevant as the plans had been abandoned after the exile and death of Lennox, though Crichton when interrogated admitted they could be revived.

Eventually he was released, for he was not an English subject and there was one important factor in his favour, namely that he had insisted to the double agent, William Parry, that killing Elizabeth was completely unlawful. In May 1587 he travelled from London to Paris and went on to Rome. Later that year he was in Scotland, where he remained until the summer of 1589. After the failure of the armada to invade England, he was sent after the Spanish ships to invite them to invade Scotland but failed to make contact. At this time, too, he made a notable convert in the earl of Crawford and was distributing money from the duke of Parma, Philip II's deputy in the Netherlands, to Catholic nobles.

In the winter of 1589–90 he was in Flanders and considered the time ripe for a pro-Catholic coup in Scotland, as James was in Denmark for his wedding with the king's daughter. After this Crichton was in Spain. In the last days of 1592 the mysterious episode of the Spanish blanks took place. A Scots Catholic, George Kerr, was captured as he was about to embark on a ship leaving Scotland, and in his possession were various letters including blank sheets signed by the Catholic earls. Under torture Kerr confessed that they were to be filled in by Crichton in Spain, pledging help for a Spanish invasion of Scotland. There are various suspicious features casting grave doubts on the plot as it was publicly portrayed, but the main factor pointing to Crichton's non-involvement is that several months before, in August 1592, he had grown tired of Philip II's temporizing and had left Spain for Rome.

In 1593 Crichton assumed charge of the little Scots seminary at Douai, which moved to Louvain in 1595. It is not clear whether he was among the Jesuits present in October 1594 at the battle of Glenlivet, where the Catholic earls were victorious. He was in Rome in early 1595 and thereafter worked with energy on behalf of the seminary until he left Flanders in July 1598. Before leaving he compiled a register of past and present students.

The beheading of Queen Mary in 1587 had profoundly affected the politics of English Catholic exiles on the continent, and their choice of a successor on the English throne was a Spanish Catholic and not the protestant James VI, by now an adult. During his stay in Spain in 1590–92 Crichton too favoured Philip, but his otherwise constant policy was to organize the support of the Scottish Catholic nobles and to promote James's claim to the throne of England as well as of Scotland, always in the hope of his becoming a Catholic. This brought him into conflict with William Holt, a strongly pro-Spanish English Jesuit, and he also vigorously condemned Robert Persons's publication of 1594 advocating Philip's daughter as successor to the English throne. Following on other harsh criticisms of James VI, Crichton in 1598 oversaw, if he did not actually write, an apology in the king's defence. It was this stance that ended his work in Louvain, which lay in the Spanish Netherlands.

James's one overriding aim was to secure the English throne for himself. To obviate papal opposition to this, he sent Crichton with a conciliatory letter to the pope dated 4 September 1599 requesting that the Scottish bishop of Vaison in France, William Chisholm III, be made a cardinal. Crichton then, despite advancing old age, occupied various advisory and spiritual posts in the province of Lyons, though in June 1603 he was at Calais, planning to cross to England, where James was now king, and in 1615–16 he was at Paris and Rouen. The Jesuit general and others still sought the benefit of his long experience and in 1611 and 1613 he compiled reports on Scottish affairs. He died at Lyons on 9 July 1617. Although a recent scholar has described Crichton as 'the most distinguished of all

Scottish Jesuits' (Anderson, 'Macpherson', 164), Jesuit and other Catholic writers have made adverse judgements on his career and character which may appear somewhat subjective rather than based on the recorded facts and the words that he wrote. MARK DILWORTH

Sources CSP Scot. • T. M. McCoog and L. Lukács, eds., *Monumenta Angliae*, 3: *England, Ireland, Scotland, and Wales, documents, 1541–1562* (2000) • T. G. Law, 'Father William Crichton, SJ', *Collected essays and reviews of Thomas Graves Law*, ed. P. H. Brown (1904), 305–12 • F. Shearman, 'The Spanish blanks', *Innes Review*, 3 (1952), 81–103 • F. Shearman, 'Father Crichton and the Spanish blanks', *Innes Review*, 4 (1953), 60 • J. H. Pollen, ed., *Papal negotiations with Mary queen of Scots during her reign in Scotland, 1561–1567*, Scottish History Society, 37 (1901) • *The letters and memorials of William, Cardinal Allen (1532–1594)*, ed. T. F. Knox (1882), vol. 2 of *Records of the English Catholics under the penal laws* (1878–82) • T. G. Law, ed., 'Documents illustrating Catholic policy in the reign of James VI', *Miscellany … I*, Scottish History Society, 15 (1893), 3–70 • W. Forbes-Leith, ed., *Narratives of Scottish Catholics under Mary Stuart and James VI* (1885) • P. J. Anderson, ed., *Records of the Scots colleges at Douai, Rome, Madrid, Valladolid and Ratisbon*, New Spalding Club, 30 (1906) • W. J. Anderson, ed., 'Abbé Paul MacPherson's history of the Scots College, Rome', *Innes Review*, 12 (1961), 3–172, esp. 12–13, 146 • T. M. McCoog, *English and Welsh Jesuits, 1555–1650*, 2 vols., Catholic RS, 74–5 (1994–5) • D. McRoberts, ed., *Essays on the Scottish Reformation, 1513–1625* (1962) • J. M. Anderson, ed., *Early records of the University of St Andrews*, Scottish History Society, 3rd ser., 8 (1926) • A. I. Dunlop, ed., *Acta facultatis artium universitatis Sanctiandree, 1413–1588*, 2 vols., Scottish History Society, 3rd ser., 54–5 (1964) • A. L. Martin, *The Jesuit mind* (1988)

Archives Archivum Romanum Societatis Iesu, Rome, De missione Scotica (1611); memoir on missions of De Gouda (1562) and Fr Hay (1566) (1613); letters [transcripts in Archives of the British Province of the Society of Jesus, London]

Crichton, William (1733–1782), merchant and politician, was the son of Patrick Crichton, a saddler and merchant of Edinburgh. Details of Crichton's early life and career cannot be established with any great certainty but it is likely that he was the William Crichton who entered an apprenticeship as a goldsmith with Dougal Ged of Edinburgh in 1752. In the 1750s and 1760s several Crichtons, most notably David Crichton, a merchant and insurer of Heydon Square, Minories, were active in trade in London and this no doubt assisted in the establishment of William Crichton in business in the capital by 1765. At first he was located at Nag's Head Court, but by 1774 he had moved to Brabant Court, Philpot Lane.

Crichton's main line of business was the West Indies trade but he diversified his activities to include the purchase of property in Edinburgh and London, marine insurance broking, lending on mortgage, and investment in stocks and securities. The last activity provided him with an entry into City politics, for the purchase of £500 of East India Company stock in September 1767 allowed him to take a leading part in company affairs during a critical phase in the development of British India. In the four years before the passage of Lord North's Regulating Act of 1773, Crichton made more recorded speeches than any other stockholder at the company's general court of proprietors. This earned him the nickname Orator Crichton from one observer, but others complained that his repeated and lengthy interventions served only to test the patience of those who were trying to steer the company through difficult times. As a self-appointed watchdog over the company's affairs, Crichton played a leading part in exposing financial malpractice among the directors of the company in 1773.

Of much wider significance, however, was the fact that Crichton suggested in January 1773 that the company might look to Europe and North America for a market where it could dispose of the ever-increasing stockpiles of tea that were being stored in its London warehouses. Crichton's specific proposal for the removal of the duty on tea imported into North America prompted lengthy debate within the company and the House of Commons but it was not endorsed by the North ministry for political reasons. In the event, the alternative arrangements that were put in place by the government alongside the highly unpopular Townshend duty served only to increase tension in the colonies. The colonists believed that taxed tea was to be forced upon them by the British and consequently a consignment of company tea was dumped into Boston harbour during the course of the events known as the Boston Tea Party. This set in motion the chain of events that eventually led to the outbreak of hostilities between Britain and her American colonies in 1775.

Although he never became a director of the East India Company, Crichton continued to play a leading role in company affairs until the time of his death in 1782. At the same time, he broadened the range of his public activities. He served on several charitable committees, helped to promote the interests of West Indies merchants as they attempted to overcome the difficulties caused by the American War of Independence, and he was appointed to office in a number of different institutions. This kept him in the public eye and he was able to develop a broad base of political support in the City where, as a member of the Company of Fishmongers, he was made a freeman in January 1775. In September 1780, following the death of John Kirkman, Crichton was elected alderman of Cheap ward and shortly afterwards he became one of the two sheriffs of the City of London. His one-year term of office was eventful because it coincided with the Gordon riots, and Crichton found himself with responsibility for the control of public order. He was widely praised for his handling of a difficult situation, and this served to raise his political stock even higher in the City. Indeed, had it not been for the fact that as sheriff he was electoral returning officer and thus debarred from declaring himself as a candidate, Crichton would have stood for election as member of parliament for the City following the death of George Hayley in August 1781.

Crichton's personal life appears to have been as colourful as his public life. By the time he wrote his will in July 1774, his relationship with Ann Jeffries had produced a son (Robert Crichton), while Esther Stokes had given birth to two daughters (Anna and Henrietta Crichton) and was expecting a third child. In spite of this, Crichton's will stated that he was about to marry Priscilla, whose surname was probably Warriner, a widow of Great Baddow in Essex. A codicil added to the will indicates that he did indeed marry Mrs Warriner because her son, John, was

granted income from a trust fund as part of a legacy of £1000 destined to be left to him by Crichton. Crichton died as a widower on 30 July 1782 at Chillingham Barns, Northumberland, having become ill during a journey on horseback to London from Edinburgh where his brother, Alexander, lived and worked as a coachmaker.

H. V. BOWEN

Sources *GM*, 1st ser., 52 (1782), 406 · will, PRO, PROB 11/1094, fols. 101–3 · *London Evening-Post* (1767–82) · *St James's Chronicle* (1780–82), *passim* · 'Eighth report from the committee of secrecy appointed to inquire into the state of the East India Company', *Reports from Committees of the House of Commons*, 4 (1772–3), 383, 388–9, 394, 396 · Index for Edinburgh Sasines, NA Scot. · Inventory of debts and property of William Crichton, 22 Nov 1782, NA Scot., CC8/8/125/2 · J. Gilhooley, ed., *A directory of Edinburgh in 1752* (1988) · Journal of Court of Crown Council, CLRO, CFI/1025, vol. 68 (1780–83) · H. V. Bowen, *The Indian problem in British politics, 1757–1773* (1991), 33, 44, 152–4

Wealth at death considerable: will, PRO, PROB 11/1094, fols. 101–3; inventory, 22 Nov 1782, NA Scot., CC8/8/125/2

Cricklade, Robert of (*d.* in or after 1174), prior of St Frideswide, theologian, and hagiographer, was a man of Saxon stock (his grandfather bore the name Sesogel son of Colmann) from Cricklade in Wiltshire, where he may have taught before entering the religious life. He was successively an Augustinian canon regular at Cirencester Abbey (his *De connubio patriarche Jacob* was composed there between 1131 and 1140) and prior of St Frideswide, Oxford (1141–74), where he was engaged in biblical scholarship, preaching and perhaps teaching in the priory, and where he acquired a reputation for sound learning. He went to Rome on official business in 1158, travelling by way of Sicily and Paris, and may have visited the papal curia in Rome in 1141 and in Paris in 1147. He was in Scotland in the early 1160s, and he also scoured England for Hebrew texts of the works of Josephus. At Oxford he was not 'chancellor of the university' (which did not yet exist), as earlier writers thought, but superior of an Augustinian house in close physical proximity to the Oxford schools, whose students probably listened to his sermons.

Robert's surviving works, which remain unedited, reveal a man of conservative theological tastes, well acquainted with the writings of Bernard of Clairvaux and William of Malmesbury, and critical of the teaching of some of the Parisian masters. He dissented from Richard of St Victor's exegesis of Ezekiel's vision, and he opposed the Christological teaching of Peter Lombard's *Sentences*, the most widely used textbook for the teaching of theology, recording his satisfaction that Roger, later bishop of Worcester (*d.* 1179), was attending the school of Master Robert de Melun instead of 'that heretic's' (Hunt, 31–3, 37–8; Smalley, 197). The manuscript survival of the biblical works attributed with certainty to him suggests a modest influence in monastic circles, but the lost life and miracles of St Thomas the Martyr (Thomas Becket), which he wrote *c.*1173–4, after experiencing a cure at Becket's tomb, achieved a remarkable success through being translated into Old Norse *c.*1200, and then incorporated into *Thómas saga*, which was compiled in Iceland from Norwegian and

Latin sources in the late thirteenth century. The saga identifies him as 'príórs Roberths af Cretel'—the name being a faulty transmission of the abbreviated form Crecel (Cricklade). From him the Icelandic life received excerpts from letters and details about Becket's life not otherwise known; and the *Vie de Thomas Becket* by Beneit of St Albans (c.1184) was also largely dependent on his life. To this same period (1171–3) belong the series of forty-two homilies on Ezekiel, composed for Reginald, prior of Church Gresley, Derbyshire, which contain commendations of 'Thomas, glorious bishop and martyr', probably written before Becket's canonization in February 1173 (Smalley, 198). Nothing is known of Robert after c.1174. He probably died at Oxford and was buried at St Frideswide. Manuscripts of his works survive in Cambridge (Corpus Christi College, Pembroke College), Eton College, Hereford (cathedral library), London (British Library), and Oxford (Balliol College, Bodleian Library).   A. J. DUGGAN

Sources Emden, *Oxf.* · M. Orme, 'A reconstruction of Robert of Cricklade's *Vita et Miracula S. Thomae Cantuariensis*', *Analecta Bollandiana*, 84 (1966), 379–98 · *Gir. Camb. opera* · E. Magnússon, ed. and trans., *Thómas saga Erkibyskups*, 2 vols., Rolls Series, 65 (1875–83) · R. W. Hunt, 'English learning in the late twelfth century', *TRHS*, 4th ser., 19 (1936), 19–42 · B. Smalley, *The Becket conflict and the schools* (1973) · S. R. Wigram, ed., *The cartulary of the monastery of St Frideswide at Oxford*, 1, OHS, 28 (1895), nos. 15, 22–3, 30, 367; 2, OHS, 31 (1896), nos. 792, 943, 1121–5, 1187 · W. Holtzmann, ed., *Papsturkunden in England*, 3 (Berlin), Abhandlung der Gesellschaft der Wissenschaften zu Göttingen, 3rd ser., 33 (1952), 164–5 · C. D. Ross and M. Devine, eds., *The cartulary of Cirencester Abbey, Gloucestershire*, 3 vols. (1964–77) · D. Knowles, C. N. L. Brooke, and V. C. M. London, eds., *The heads of religious houses, England and Wales*, 1: 940–1216 (1972)

Cridiodunus, Fridericus. *See* Fredericus (*d.* 838).

Crighton, David George (1942–2000), applied mathematician and fluid dynamicist, was born on 15 November 1942 in the Maternity Home, Oxford Road, Llandudno, Caernarvonshire, the elder child of George Wolfe Johnston Crighton (1899–1976), a civil servant in the stamp duty office, and his wife, Violet Grace, *née* Garrison (*b.* 1912). His sister, Frances, was born in 1946. David was educated at the primary school in Abbots Langley to the age of eleven, then at Watford Boys' Grammar School from 1953 to 1961. He studied a broad range of subjects including modern languages and classics, eventually concentrating on mathematics, spurred on, as he used to enjoy relating in later life, by a schoolmaster who said that it was the one subject in which he would not succeed. He was an all-rounder at school, captain of rugby, an enthusiastic runner and cyclist, and head boy in his final year.

Crighton read mathematics as an undergraduate of St John's College, Cambridge, from 1961 to 1964. He achieved first-class honours in part two (1964) of the mathematical tripos. The course offered a broad range of options in pure and applied mathematics, and Crighton specialized on the applied side, and particularly on the courses involving the dynamics of fluids. He could have continued with part three mathematics, the normal route to research and an academic career, but chose instead to leave Cambridge to take a job as a lecturer at Woolwich Polytechnic (later the University of Greenwich). The teaching load was heavy, and at a fairly basic level; after two years, however, he was taken on as a research assistant at Imperial College, London, by John Ffowcs Williams (later professor of engineering at the University of Cambridge and master of Emmanuel College, Cambridge). He worked with Ffowcs Williams on the effect of bubbles on the propagation of sound through water in turbulent motion, a problem of great importance for the US Navy which supported the research. The work was published in 1969, and Crighton received his PhD degree in the same year.

Within a further five years, continuing at Imperial College, Crighton had written or co-authored a series of sixteen influential papers on jet noise, the scattering of sound waves, acoustic beaming and reflection from wave-bearing surfaces, and related topics. The need to control engine noise during take-off and landing of the supersonic aircraft Concorde made this research urgent. Crighton's involvement in the Concorde research team of that period is described in detail by Ffowcs Williams (Williams, 'Commentary').

Crighton's subsequent research remained within the broad field of aero- and hydro-acoustics and wave theory; he was a pioneer in studies of the generation of sound and vibration by underwater structures (important in naval architecture and for submarine detection); of intense sound waves, as generated by supersonic aircraft, and the manner in which shock waves develop when these sound waves propagate over large distances; and of the phenomenon of Anderson localization, whereby wave disturbances in the neighbourhood of periodic structures can remain trapped near the region of excitation.

On 2 March 1968 Crighton married Mary Christine West, a professional musician, with whom he shared a passion for music and opera, and whom he had first met at the Bayreuth Festival in 1964. Their son, Ben, was born in 1970, their daughter, Beth, in 1971. In 1974, at the early age of thirty-three, Crighton was appointed to the chair of applied mathematics at Leeds (previously held by T. G. Cowling); there his organizational and administrative talents were soon evident. The department, which in 1974 was modest in its achievements and expectations, was transformed under his influence over the next twelve years into one of the top three or four departments of its kind in the country. Crighton's successive spells as head of department, chairman of school, and chairman of the science board, left in every case indelible marks of his imagination and effectiveness, tough decisions being invariably coupled with a caring interest in those individuals affected.

In 1985 Crighton's marriage was dissolved, and on 6 September 1986 he married Johanna Veronica Kooij, *née* Hol, an independent education consultant from the Netherlands, whom he had met some years earlier. In that same year he was elected professor of applied mathematics at the University of Cambridge. Here his boundless energy and talents found full scope. In 1991 he became head of the department of applied mathematics and theoretical physics and immediately took steps to establish new professorships, first in the rapidly emerging field of nonlinear dynamics, and then in the field of solid mechanics. The department continued to flourish under his inspired leadership. He played a key role in planning the move of the two departments of the Cambridge faculty of mathematics from their antiquated buildings on the Old Press site in the centre of town to the new Centre for Mathematical Sciences in west Cambridge (a move finally completed in 2002, two years after his death), and in the massive fund-raising campaign that this entailed.

From 1979 Crighton had been an associate editor of the *Journal of Fluid Mechanics*, the premier international journal of the subject. This was a position of great exposure, involving an immense correspondence with contributors from all over the world; from 1996, he gradually took over the editorship from the founding editor, G. K. Batchelor, whose health was failing. Crighton was elected to fellowship of the Royal Society in 1993, and for two years (1994–6) took on the additional burden of editing the *Proceedings (A)* of the Royal Society. Within Cambridge, Crighton was a fellow of St John's College from 1986 until his appointment as master of Jesus College in 1997. In this latter role, as in his role as head of the department of applied mathematics and theoretical physics, he governed with consummate diplomatic skill, great good humour, and a selfless concern for the members and staff of the college at all levels.

Crighton was widely respected outside Britain: he was president of the European Mechanics Society until 1997, and then continued to serve as vice-president. He was elected a member of Academia Europeae in 1999, in recognition as much for his services to European science as for his own considerable achievements in research. Institutions in the US and Europe awarded him medals and honorary doctorates.

Outside science, David Crighton's enduring passion was for the operas of Wagner, on which he became an authority. He never missed an opportunity to attend the Bayreuth Festival, and would always seek to incorporate at least one opera in each of his many lecturing engagements around the world. A final achievement that gave him great personal satisfaction just a few weeks before his death was to conduct his college orchestra in a moving performance of the overture to *Tannhäuser*. His infectious enthusiasm, and the twinkle in his eye, were endearing for all who worked with him.

Crighton died of cancer at Addenbrooke's Hospital, Cambridge, on 12 April 2000, aged fifty-seven, following fifteen months of illness which he endured with great courage, relinquishing none of his heavy responsibilities. He was cremated at Cambridge crematorium following a service in Jesus College chapel. A memorial service was held at Great St Mary's, Cambridge. His early death was a shock for the worldwide community of fluid dynamics, of which he had been an influential and greatly respected member.　　　　　　　　　　H. K. MOFFATT

Sources H. E. Huppert and N. Peake, *Memoirs FRS*, 47 (2001) · J. F. Williams, 'David Crighton, 1942–2000: a commentary on his career and his influence on aeroacoustic theory', *Journal of Fluid Mechanics*, 437 (2001), 1–11 · *The Times* (19 April 2000) · G. I. Barenblatt, 'George Keith Batchelor (1920–2000) and David George Crighton (1942–2000), applied mathematicians', *Notices of the American Mathematical Society*, 48/8 (2001), 800–06 · WW (2000), 471 · CGPLA Eng. & Wales (2000) · b. cert. · m. certs.

Likenesses L. Riley-Smith, oils, 1999, Jesus College, Cambridge; copy, department of applied mathematics and theoretical physics, U. Cam.

Wealth at death £192,013—net £189,935: probate, 2000

Crippen, Hawley Harvey (1862–1910), murderer, was born in Coldwater, Michigan, the only child of storekeeper Myron Augustus Crippen (1827–1910) and his wife, Andresse Skinner (d. 1909). After studying in Michigan, London, and the Homoeopathic Hospital College, Cleveland, Ohio, he qualified as a homoeopathic doctor in 1884. In 1887 he married a nurse, Charlotte Jane Bell (d. 1892). Their son Otto was born in 1889, but Charlotte died three years later. Crippen placed Otto with Myron and Andresse and entered general practice in New York. There he married on 1 September 1892 Kunigunde (1873–1910), daughter of Joe Mackamotzki, a Pole who had kept a fruit stand in Brooklyn. She was at this time someone else's mistress and was known as Cora Turner.

In 1894 Crippen's practice failed and he took employment with Munyon's Homoeopathic Remedies. They sent him to establish a branch in London in 1897, but fired him in 1899 for managing his wife's indifferent career as a music-hall singer. He was London manager of the disreputable Drouet's Institute for the Deaf from 1901 until its bankruptcy in 1908. From 1908 Crippen was partner in a dental practice called the Yale Tooth Specialists at Albion House, 61 New Oxford Street.

At Drouet's, Crippen employed as a typist Ethel Clara Le Neve (1883–1967) and about 1903 they fell in love. In 1905 the Crippens moved from a flat near Oxford Street to 39 Hilldrop Crescent, Holloway, and took in lodgers. In December 1906 Crippen found Cora (who now called herself Belle Elmore) in bed with a lodger. She had cuckolded Hawley for several years, but this incident provoked him to consummate his hitherto blameless love for Ethel. Belle maintained her shaky connection with the stage by serving the charitable Music Hall Ladies' Guild, whose office was also in Albion House. This led to occasional confrontations between Belle and Ethel.

Overtly the Crippens' marriage was happy. In reality Belle Elmore was a tipsy, plump, and unfaithful shrew with inordinate vanity and a miserly streak; her docile and submissive husband chafed at her dominion. On Monday 31 January 1910 two friends of Belle's dined with the Crippens before leaving Hilldrop Crescent at 1.30 a.m. Belle Elmore was never seen again. Crippen said she had gone to America for a few months. In February Ethel was seen wearing a piece of Belle's jewellery. In March Crippen moved her into Hilldrop Crescent and gave out that Belle had died in California. He proved evasive about details, and the Music Hall Ladies' Guild suspected foul

Hawley Harvey Crippen (1862–1910), by unknown photographer, c.1890

play. They established that no Belle Elmore or Cora Crippen had crossed the Atlantic or died in California.

Crippen took two short holidays in Dieppe with Le Neve, and brought back a French maid for her. But his lies led vaudevillians John and Lil Nash to Scotland Yard, and Detective-Inspector Walter Dew was sent to interview Crippen on 8 July. Crippen told a plausible tale of being deserted by Belle, and lying because he felt humiliated. But panicked by Dew's visit, he fled the following day. The police searched the house, but found nothing until Dew took up the flooring of the kitchen coal cellar. Underneath was a woman's headless, limbless, desexed, and boneless flesh, wrapped in a man's pyjama jacket. It contained hyoscine, a poison Crippen had bought shortly before Belle's disappearance. A two-week international hunt for Crippen and Le Neve followed.

They had bought boy's clothes for Le Neve and gone to Brussels. On 20 July they sailed from Antwerp to Montreal on the *Montrose*, with Crippen posing as John Philo Robinson, taking his sixteen-year-old son. The ship's captain, Henry Kendall, mistrusted the Robinsons' loving hand-holding and decided that they were Crippen and his paramour. When he informed his owners by Marconigram they contacted Scotland Yard, and passed all Kendall's subsequent descriptions of the runaways to the press, which followed Dew's pursuit of them in the faster liner *Laurentic* to reach Montreal three days ahead of the *Montrose*. Dew arrested the pair before they could disembark.

Crippen's lackadaisical defence at his trial (18–22 October 1910) was that the remains must have been in the cellar when he bought the house. The prosecution, however, proved that the pyjamas were made after he came to Hilldrop Crescent. Pathologist Bernard Spilsbury, in his first widely publicized case, demonstrated that the flesh bore an abdominal scar matching Belle's ovariectomy. Crippen, who was imperturbable but unconvincing under cross-examination, and showed a brand of heroism in his determination to protect Le Neve, was sentenced to death. But he had achieved his purpose of minimizing the damage to Le Neve, who was acquitted in a separate trial on 25 October of a charge of being an accessory after the fact.

From prison Crippen exchanged love letters with Ethel until his execution at Pentonville prison on 23 November 1910. He was buried within the prison precincts. His posthumous reputation as one of the most frightful murderers of his generation was unjustified. Everyone who knew him was astonished by this polite little man's crime. He was deeply in love with Ethel and not the calculating seducer portrayed at her trial. He refused to mount any serious defence, as that might have compromised her, and he was the first murderer caught by ship's radio-telegraph. Crippen was a commonplace, bespectacled little man, with a sandy moustache and domed forehead, who abstained from tobacco, wine, and spirits. He was courteous and considerate socially, though his professional life as a quack dealing in patent medicines must sometimes have been calculating and predatory. He proved a bungling murderer, who covered his victim's remains in slaked lime, which preserves human flesh, rather than quick lime, which destroys them. His essentially sordid *crime passionnel*, committed in a humdrum backwater of London suburbia, excited an intense and enduring notoriety.

MARTIN FIDO

Sources T. Cullen, *Crippen: the mild murderer* (1977) · F. Young, *The trial of Hawley Harvey Crippen* (1920) · W. Dew, *I caught Crippen* (1938) · CGPLA Eng. & Wales (1911)
Archives PRO, MEPO and HO MSS | Madame Tussaud's Ltd, London, letters | FILM BFI NFTVA, documentary footage | SOUND BL NSA, 'Dr Crippen', 1993, 1GA 0024466D253BD1
Likenesses photograph, c.1890, Hult. Arch. [*see illus.*]
Wealth at death £268 6s. 9d.: probate, 8 Feb 1911, CGPLA Eng. & Wales

Cripps, Arthur Shearley (1869–1952), missionary and poet, was born on 10 June 1869 at Mount Calverley Lodge, Tunbridge Wells, Kent, the younger son and third child in the family of two sons and two daughters of William Charles Cripps (1821–1882), solicitor, and his wife, Catherine Charlotte Mary (*d.* 1913), daughter of William Shearley, surgeon. Four other children died in childhood. It was a high-church family, and his mother converted to Roman Catholicism after her husband's death. Cripps was educated at Charterhouse School, and in 1887 went to Trinity College, Oxford, where he was awarded a second in modern history in 1891. As well as rowing, running, and winning a half-blue for boxing, he wrote poetry, publishing *Primavera* (1890) with his friend Laurence Binyon and others, and, most importantly, coming under the influence of Charles Gore, principal of Pusey House and a leading Christian socialist. Cripps joined the Oxford branch of the Christian Social Union, and decided to train for the Anglican ministry, entering Cuddesdon theological college in 1891. He was ordained in 1893, and in 1894 took up a living at Ford End, a country parish in Essex. Cripps loved Ford End and the Essex countryside, but after reading Olive Schreiner's novel *Trooper Peter Halket of Mashonaland* (1897), an attack on Cecil Rhodes and the seizure of African land by the British South Africa Company, he resigned his living to become a missionary, and offered his services to the Society for the Propagation of the Gospel. He arrived in Southern Rhodesia in 1901, and was put in charge of a new mission at Wreningham, in Mashonaland, near Enkeldoorn, 95 miles south-west of Salisbury.

Cripps devoted the rest of his life to the Africans. At the heart of his Christianity was the Franciscan ideal, and wanting to join the poor in their poverty he adopted the African way of life, living in a thatched hut and eating African food. He gave away his possessions, including most of his clothes, to those poorer than himself, and travelled around his huge district on foot, either walking or running, wearing boots tied up with string and repaired with metal from bully beef tins, and carrying his remaining possessions in a biscuit tin. From the start he took up the cause of the Africans, walking to Salisbury in 1903 to protest to the Anglican diocesan synod about the raising of the hut tax by the British South Africa Company, and writing an *Ode in Celebration of the Proposed Quadrupling of the Hut Tax* (1903). Using money given him by his mother, in 1911 Cripps bought a farm at Maronda Mashanu, halfway between Wreningham and Enkeldoorn, to which he added three more farms during the next decade, and he gave the land rent-free to tenant Africans who had converted to Christianity. He built schools, and a new church, completed in 1913, which was constructed out of stones, mud, and grass, with a clay floor strewn with pebbles. Inspired by the ruins of the temple at Great Zimbabwe, the Church of the Five Wounds had round walls and five pillars of stones. In 1915 Cripps volunteered to serve as an army chaplain during the east African campaign, but he returned to Mashonaland when the fighting ended: his book of poems *Lake and War* (1917) expresses his disillusionment with the war, and especially the sacrifices made by the Africans.

Realizing the importance of giving land back to the Shona people so that they could be self-sufficient and not be forced to work as cheap labour for the white settlers, Cripps began campaigning in 1917, when the imperial commission on the native reserves of Southern Rhodesia submitted its report recommending that the area of the native reserves be reduced by 1 million acres. He published a pamphlet, *One Million Acres* (1918), which he distributed in Britain. Concentrating his efforts on a 12-mile strip of land in the Sabi reserve, in his own district, which lay along the route of a proposed new railway line, he devoted his leave in England in 1919–20 to putting the case for the Africans before officials in the Colonial Office, writing letters to the press, and distributing *The Sabi Reserve* (1920). His campaign culminated in an interview with the under-secretary of state for the colonies, Leo Amery, and an audience with the archbishop of Canterbury. In the end, the railway was never built, and the land was restored to the Sabi reserve in 1930, although this was the result more of economic factors than of Cripps's intervention. At the same time he was pressing the government to set aside native purchase areas where the Africans could buy land, pleading his case unsuccessfully in *Africa for Africans* (1927).

While in England in 1926 Cripps resigned his post at the Wreningham mission, and took up his former living at Ford End, which had just become vacant: he turned the vicarage into a boys' club and a home for tramps, and moved into a small cottage. While the main reason for his return was to raise money to clear his African farms of debt and build up some reserves, he was also despondent over his constant battles with the colonial and church authorities, especially over his refusal to accept government grants for his mission schools for fear that mission education might be taken over by the state. He had also clashed with the Anglican church over the annual tax imposed on African Anglicans, and over the practice of denying the sacrament to those who did not pay. He blamed himself for failing to have any impact on the injustice done to Africans by the white settlers, especially after Southern Rhodesia became a self-governing colony in 1923, and the rights of the Africans were progressively reduced. In 'The black Christ's crusade' (*Africa: Verses*, 52) he wrote that to him,

> Christ hath reveal'd Himself—not as to Paul
> Enthroned and crown'd, but marr'd, despised, rejected,
> The Divine Outcast of a terrible land,
> A Black Christ with parch'd lips and empty Hand.

Cripps returned to Maronda Mashanu in 1930 as an independent 'Christian missionary in Mashonaland'. He was no longer officially part of the diocese, as he had refused the bishop's licence, and he had no salary, but he continued to take services, and to prepare candidates for confirmation by the bishop. In 1932 he established a refuge at Maronda Mashanu for Africans suffering from venereal disease. He continued his campaigning, keeping in close touch with the colonial bureau of the Fabian Society in London, and writing letters to the *Manchester Guardian*. He testified to the royal commission appointed in 1938 to consider the amalgamation of Nyasaland, Northern Rhodesia, and Southern Rhodesia, which he opposed because of the colour bar in Southern Rhodesia: his pamphlet *Is our Colour Bar to Cross the Zambezi?* (1942) was widely read. Although the royal commission opposed amalgamation, the federation of Rhodesia and Nyasaland was created in 1953.

Throughout his life Cripps wrote poetry almost daily, and some of his poems were included in the *Oxford Book of Mystical Verse* (1916). His first collection of African poems, *Lyra evangelistica: Missionary Verses in Mashonaland* (1909), ran to three editions, and in 1939 Oxford University Press published *Africa: Verses*, a collection of some of his best poems, with an introduction by his friend John Buchan. In 1902 he won the Oxford University prize for a poem on a sacred subject with 'Jonathan', a success he repeated in 1926 with 'Judas Maccabeus'. His poems were included in anthologies, and were widely read in Rhodesian schools. He was also a prolific writer of short stories, beginning with *Magic Casements* (1905), and he published two sets of stories about the white settlers in Africa, *Faerylands Forlorn* (1910) and *Cinderella in the South* (1918). He wrote a play, *The Black Christ* (1901), and eight novels, one of the best of which is *Lion Man* (1928).

In 1938 Cripps suffered a stroke, and in 1941 he had his left eye removed; he became totally blind in 1942. He died, unmarried, on 1 August 1952 in Enkeldoorn Hospital,

Southern Rhodesia, and after a funeral attended by thousands his coffin was carried to Maronda Mashanu, where on 3 August he was buried in the nave of the Church of the Five Wounds. He became a legend in Mashonaland, and his grave became an object of pilgrimage.

ANNE PIMLOTT BAKER

Sources D. V. Steere, *God's irregular: Arthur Shearly Cripps* (1973) · M. Steele, '"With hope unconquered and unconquerable …": Arthur Shearly Cripps, 1869–1952', *Themes in the Christian history of central Africa*, ed. T. O. Ranger and J. Weller (1975), 152–75 · D. E. Finn, '"Kambandakoto": a study of A. S. Cripps, 1869–1952', *Rhodesiana*, 7 (1962) · D. E. Finn, 'An early Rhodesian poet: Arthur Shearley Cripps, 1869–1952', *Chirimo*, 2/1 (Sept 1969), 29–31 · D. Jenkins and D. Stebbing, *They led the way: Christian pioneers of central Africa* (1966), 38–43 · C. F. Andrews, *John White of Mashonaland* (1935), 117–27 · *Arthur Shearley Cripps: a selection of his prose and verse*, ed. G. R. Brown, A. J. Chennells, and L. B. Rix (1976) · T. O. Ranger, *Rhodes, Oxford and the study of race relations: an inaugural lecture* (1989) · T. O. Ranger and J. Weller, eds., *Themes in the Christian history of central Africa* (1975) · A. Hastings, *The church in Africa, 1450–1950* (1994) · b. cert.
Archives Bodl. RH, Aborigines Protection Society files, letters · Bodl. RH, corresp. and papers relating to Southern Rhodesia · National Library of Zimbabwe, Harare, corresp. and literary papers · United Society for the Propagation of the Gospel, London, archives, papers | Bodl. Oxf., corresp. with L. G. Curtis · Bodl. RH, corresp. with Margery Perham · JRL, letters to *Manchester Guardian*
Likenesses photograph, 1941, repro. in Ranger and Weller, eds., *Themes*, no. 9 · photograph, repro. in Steere, *God's irregular*, frontispiece

Cripps, Charles Alfred, first Baron Parmoor (1852–1941), lawyer and politician, was born on 3 October 1852 at West Ilsley, Berkshire, the sixth of the eleven children of Henry William Cripps (1815–1899), a prominent ecclesiastical lawyer, and his wife and cousin, Julia (*d.* 1912), daughter of Charles *Lawrence, the agriculturalist. Cripps had an impressive academic career as a scholar both at Winchester College (1865–71) and at New College, Oxford (1871–5), where he obtained four first classes in mathematical moderations, history, jurisprudence, and civil law. He also played for the university at Association Football. He held a fellowship at St John's College, Oxford, from 1875 until 1881, when he relinquished it on his marriage on 27 October to Theresa Potter (1852–1893), sister of (Martha) Beatrice *Webb and Catherine *Courtney; they had four sons and one daughter, the youngest son being (Richard) Stafford *Cripps.

Cripps followed his father into a professional legal career, winning a senior studentship to the inns of court in 1876. Called to the bar by the Middle Temple in 1877, he published *A Treatise on the Principles of the Law of Compensation* (1881), which long remained a standard work. He established a large and lucrative practice at the parliamentary bar (until he entered parliament) and in rating, patent, railway, and ecclesiastical cases. With Haldane and Asquith among his juniors, in 1890 he became a queen's counsel. He was made a bencher of his inn in 1893, was appointed attorney-general to three successive princes of Wales from 1895 to 1914, and created KCVO in 1908. He succeeded his father both as vice-chairman and, from 1910 to 1925, as chairman of Buckingham quarter sessions.

Charles Alfred Cripps, first Baron Parmoor (1852–1941), by Elliott & Fry

Cripps was proud of a long ancestry, his memoirs printing a pedigree dating from 1207, and as heir to his father's estate of about 2000 acres he counted farming as his chief recreation. He began with conventional beliefs in the priorities of private property, individualism, and personal effort, and equally conventional disapproval of the socialism of his sister- and brother-in-law Beatrice and Sidney Webb. From a strongly religious background, he had a benevolent, tolerant, and optimistic outlook, judged by the Webbs to be the characteristic complacency of a wealthy lawyer. He also had a high-church attachment to existing institutions in church and state. In contrast to his father's political Conservatism his early political opinions were Liberal, but the 1886 home-rule crisis and fear for the church turned him into a Liberal Unionist and then a Conservative. He was elected Conservative MP for the Stroud division of Gloucestershire in 1895, but lost his seat to a Liberal in the 1900 general election. He was returned for the Stretford division of Lancashire at a by-election in 1901, but was again defeated by a Liberal in the 1906 general election. After being out of parliament for four years, he was elected for the Wycombe division of Buckinghamshire in January 1910 and held the seat until January 1914, when he entered the House of Lords. As an MP he served on the select committee on the Jameson raid and the royal commission on local taxation, and hoped for appointment to one of the government law offices. During the tariff reform controversy he remained a free-trader, and during the constitutional crisis of 1910–11 provided a moderating influence, helping to organize support for Balfour and Lansdowne against the Unionist radicals.

Cripps was most prominent in ecclesiastical issues, becoming a leading lay churchman. A representative from 1890 in the house of laymen of the Canterbury convocation, he served as its chairman from 1911 to 1919. He was chancellor and vicar-general of York province from 1900 to 1914, and from 1902 to 1924 vicar-general of Canterbury province, in which capacity he resisted objections on doctrinal grounds to two controversial episcopal appointments, Charles Gore as bishop of Winchester in 1902 and H. H. Henson as bishop of Hereford in 1918. He was a leading campaigner in defence of church schools, in 1908 opposing Archbishop Davidson's proposed compromise on the Liberal government's Education Bill and carrying a resolution in the Representative Church Council which effectively forced the bill's withdrawal. He also criticized what he considered to be Archbishop Davidson's temporizing attitude towards the government's proposals for Welsh church disestablishment. Dissatisfied, like other high-churchmen, with parliament's interference in church matters, he took a leading part in altering the relationship. In July 1913 he successfully moved a resolution in the Representative Church Council calling for measures to secure the church's 'spiritual independence'. From this emerged the archbishop's committee on church and state from 1913 to 1916, of which he was a member, and which recommended the establishment of the church assembly. After this had been established by the 1919 Enabling Act, he served from 1920 to 1924 as first chairman of the assembly's house of laity.

Although Cripps entered parliament as a Conservative, he received his peerage from a Liberal government and obtained office in a Labour government. Faced with a shortage of senior judges, Haldane and Asquith negotiated a special arrangement by which, in January 1914, Cripps was sworn of the privy council in order to serve as an unpaid member of its judicial committee, and was made Baron Parmoor of Frieth to enable him to undertake judicial work in the House of Lords, while retaining the freedom to continue as an active politician. During the First World War his judicial work included chairmanship of the committee to assess damage by enemy naval raids on the north-east coast, and membership of the appeal committee to hear Admiralty prize cases. But the war also began a shift in his political allegiances. He criticized Britain's entry into the war as unnecessary, disliked the war jingoism and its anti-German expressions, and came to regard the war as incompatible with Christian morality. He applied his legal expertise to assist the cause of conscientious objectors, and during 1917 publicly approved the Lansdowne letter and became chairman of a committee supporting the efforts of Archbishop Söderblum of Uppsala to restore peace by means of an International Christian Conference. A co-founder in 1915 of the League of Nations Society, in March 1918 he opened the House of Lords debate supporting the formation of a League of Nations. After the armistice he led deputations urging President Wilson and British ministers to establish the league. As chairman of a Fight the Famine council formed in January 1919, he campaigned around Britain for easier treatment of former enemy countries, visited Germany and Austria to view conditions for himself, and participated in three annual international conferences on economic recovery and world peace, as a result of which he advocated revision of the treaty of Versailles to alleviate the burden upon Germany. In 1920 he was appointed president of the Peace Society. His political reorientation was confirmed by his second marriage on 14 July 1919 to a member of a prominent Quaker family and a co-worker on his various peace committees, Marian Emily *Ellis (1878–1952), daughter of John Edward Ellis, colliery owner and Liberal MP. Lady Parmoor was a vice-president of the World Young Women's Christian Association from 1921, and president during 1924–8.

The 'horrors of the war, and the vengeful spirit' had turned Parmoor 'into something very like an international socialist' (*Diary of Beatrice Webb*, 3.346). In the early 1920s he also criticized the coalition government's repressive policies in Ireland and, where discretion allowed, his judicial decisions revealed increased sensitivity towards social injustice and religious intolerance. In these respects he was 'an intriguing appellate judge' (Stevens, 259). Without becoming an economic socialist, his involvement in peace movements had brought him into contact with leading Labour politicians, notably MacDonald. When the opportunity of forming a Labour government unexpectedly arose after the 1923 election, MacDonald was hard-pressed to secure ministers in the House of Lords—where the Labour Party had no recognized members—and offered a choice of offices to Parmoor. After obtaining assurances on MacDonald's commitment to international reconciliation, he resigned his church positions and joined the cabinet as lord president of the council with specific responsibility for League of Nations affairs. He participated in the preparations for the London conference on German reparations, and was British representative on the League of Nations council. At the September 1924 meeting of the league assembly he strongly supported the Geneva protocol, the ultimately abortive Anglo-French proposal to establish mechanisms of international arbitration and collective security. After the government's defeat he did not return to judicial work but continued as a Labour spokesman in the House of Lords and remained active in Christian and peace movements, addressing Archbishop Söderblum's international Life and Work Conference at Stockholm in 1925.

On Haldane's death in 1928 Parmoor was elected Labour leader in the Lords, so when reappointed as lord president in the second Labour government in June 1929 his additional responsibility was leadership of the House of Lords rather than his previous role in League of Nations affairs. Now in his late seventies, he was too old to keep pace with an increasingly aggressive Conservative opposition, and in debates tended to become prolix and confused. In early

1931 ill health disabled him for three months, and Mac-Donald would have replaced him had there not been an intractable problem of inadequate numbers of possible ministerial recruits in the Lords. During the August 1931 cabinet crisis, he was one of six ministers who resisted a revenue tariff as a means of bridging the budget deficit, but was absent when the fatal vote was taken over the alternative, a cut in unemployment benefits. After the cabinet's resignation, he retired from the leadership of the Labour peers and withdrew from public life. He died at Parmoor, Henley-on-Thames, on 30 June 1941, and was buried at nearby Frieth church.   PHILIP WILLIAMSON

Sources *The Times* (2 July 1941) · *The Times* (5 July 1941) · *The Times* (10 Jan 1942) · Lord Parmoor [C. A. Cripps], *A retrospect* (1936) · GEC, *Peerage* · *The diary of Beatrice Webb*, ed. N. MacKenzie and J. MacKenzie, 4 vols. (1982–5) · G. K. A. Bell, *Randall Davidson, archbishop of Canterbury*, 2 vols. (1935) · P. Williamson, 'The labour party and the House of Lords, 1918–1931', *Parliamentary History*, 10 (1991), 317–41 · R. Stevens, *Law and politics: the House of Lords as a judicial body, 1800–1976* (1979)

Archives BLPES, letters to the Courtneys · Bodl. Oxf., letters to Lord Ponsonby · Bodl. Oxf., corresp. with Gilbert Murray · LPL, Archbishop R. Davidson MSS · PRO, corresp. with Ramsay MacDonald, PRO 30/69

Likenesses W. Stoneman, photograph, 1917, NPG · Elliott & Fry, photograph, NPG [*see illus.*] · J. Lavery, oils, Church House, Westminster · Spy [L. Ward], chromolithograph caricature, NPG; repro. in *VF* (10 April 1902)

Wealth at death £48,093 1s. 10d.: probate, 5 Jan 1942, CGPLA Eng. & Wales

Cripps [*née* Swithinbank], **Dame Isobel**, **Lady Cripps** (1891–1979), overseas aid organizer, was born at Denham, Buckinghamshire, on 25 January 1891, the second daughter and youngest of three children of Commander Harold William Swithinbank (1858–1928), landowner, of Denham Court, and his wife, Amy, daughter of James Crossley Eno, of Dulwich, founder of the firm of that name which manufactured a well-known brand of fruit salts. She was educated privately and at Heathfield School, near Ascot.

Isobel Swithinbank met Stafford Cripps [see Cripps, Sir (Richard) Stafford (1889–1952)] in January 1910. His father, Charles Alfred *Cripps, was standing in the Conservative interest at Wycombe, and Stafford was supporting his father's candidature with his customary zeal. Among the campaign helpers was Isobel Swithinbank. C. A. Cripps was elected but his success did not see the end of his son's acquaintanceship with Miss Swithinbank. They corresponded; Isobel visited the Cripps home at Parmoor and stayed in the family's London house. The following year both were members of a family party which went to the winter sports in Switzerland and they soon became engaged. Cripps had earlier shown great promise as a scientist and had attracted the attention of Sir William Ramsay, the experimentalist chemist, but, as he wished to marry, he turned from science to the bar for which he had already begun to read.

The young couple—he was twenty-two and she twenty—were married at Denham parish church on 12 July 1911. It was in every sense a marriage of true minds, a close and sympathetic partnership. Both held firm Christian beliefs. Throughout his sometimes stormy political

Dame Isobel Cripps, Lady Cripps (1891–1979), by unknown photographer, 1949 [with her husband, Sir Stafford Cripps]

career—he was for a time expelled from the Labour Party—Isobel remained his unswerving supporter. Above all she was the protector of his always indifferent health. After his death she came in for much praise for the care she had bestowed on him but it would be a mistake to regard her as solely an admirable wife and mother. She was a woman of commanding presence. She was tolerant and she listened but she went her own way. She was not a political animal and she did not entertain much when Cripps was in office, though they gave occasional small dinner parties. When Cripps was ambassador in Moscow during the Second World War she spent a year with him in conditions that were restrictive and socially far from rewarding.

Isobel's true bent was for helping others. More than one political contemporary of her husband later recalled her shrewd kindness. She was, for example, a source of much comfort to the first wife of Herbert Morrison whose life was not always easy. But she was not narrow in her friendships, bore no malice to her husband's political enemies, and had friends in all political parties.

During the Second World War, Isobel was president of the British United Aid to China Fund. She was an able and active leader and in June 1946 was appointed GBE for her public services. Later that year she undertook an extensive and arduous tour of China where she was the guest of General Chiang Kai-shek and Madame Chiang. At Nanking (Nanjing) she pointed out that the fund did not confer its benefits on nationalist China alone. During her tour she was invited by Mao Zedong to visit Yenan (Yan'nan). This she did and was welcomed on her arrival by Madame Mao. The word arduous in connection with her trip is rightly used for the journey, one of 30,000 miles which included travel by air, sea, road, rail, and truck. Most of the great cities of China were visited and to see co-operative work in rural areas the Gansu Desert was crossed by lorry. Her interest in China did not wane and she was to hold the chairmanship of the Sino-British Fellowship Trust for some years.

Throughout life Isobel's aim, simple and never proclaimed, was to do good in the world. After her husband's death she kept up with many of those friends at home and abroad in whose lives Stafford Cripps had shown interest. She also developed an interest in affairs in Ghana after the marriage of her daughter Peggy to Joe Appiah, lawyer and politician. In 1962 she visited him in Accra at a time when he was being held under a preventive detention order.

Though not witty, Isobel laughed easily and was never dull. It has sometimes been said that she and her husband were vegetarians and food cranks. This was untrue. For reasons of health Cripps was compelled to be a vegetarian and abstainer. Isobel followed his lead but at her table guests were given the usual kinds of hospitality and, except in times of national shortages, drinks of all sorts were available. To the last she thought in Christian terms, and acted in accordance with Christian standards.

In addition to her appointment as GBE Isobel was given the special grand cordon of the order of the Brilliant Star of China, first class. In 1946 she was given the award of the National Committee of India in celebration of International Women's Year. Of her marriage to Stafford Cripps there was a son, Sir John *Cripps, who was for many years editor of The Countryman, and three daughters. She died on 11 April 1979 in Minchinhampton, Gloucestershire. COLIN WATSON, rev.

Sources private information (1986) • Burke, Gen. GB (1937) ['Swithinbank'] • WWW
Archives SOAS, corresp. with H. V. Hodson | FILM BFI NFTVA, news footage
Likenesses photograph, 1949 (with her husband, Sir Stafford Cripps), Popperfoto, Northampton [see illus.]
Wealth at death £354,973: probate, 3 Sept 1979, CGPLA Eng. & Wales

Cripps, John Marten (1780–1853), traveller and antiquary, was born in Sussex, the son of John Cripps. He was entered as a fellow-commoner at Jesus College, Cambridge, on 27 April 1798, and came under the care of Edward Daniel Clarke. Cripps was wealthy: by a will of 1 October 1797 he inherited the property of his maternal uncle, John Marten, which included land in Sussex. On 20 May 1799 he set out on a tour with his tutor, to whom he paid a salary. The tour, originally intended for only a few months, lasted for three and a half years. In the first part of their journey to Norway and Sweden they were accompanied by the Revd William Otter, afterwards bishop of Chichester, and Malthus, the political economist, both Jesus men. An account of their journey was published by Clarke in his Travels (6 vols., 1810–23), in which he describes Cripps as 'the cause

and companion of my travels'. Cripps and Clarke travelled all through Denmark, Sweden, Norway, and Finland, including the far north. They went on to Russia and central Asia, Turkey and Greece, and the Near East. Cripps brought back large collections of statues, antiques, and oriental flora, some valuable portions of which he presented to the University of Cambridge and to other public institutions. Cripps's father rescued much of Clarke's collection which was shipwrecked off his land in England.

In 1803 Cripps was created MA per literas regias; he was elected fellow of the Linnean Society in 1803 and of the Society of Antiquaries in 1805. On 1 January 1806 he married Charlotte, third daughter of Sir William Beaumaris Rush of Wimbledon, and elder sister of Angelica, who married Clarke. Cripps and his wife had at least two sons. Having built Novington Lodge on the Stantons estate, near Lewes, in Sussex, which he had inherited from his uncle, Cripps settled there, and devoted much of his time to horticulture. His investigations brought to notice several varieties of apples and other fruits. From Russia he introduced the kohlrabi, a useful vegetable. He died at Novington on 3 January 1853. Clarke named Rubus crippsii in his honour.

GORDON GOODWIN, rev. ELIZABETH BAIGENT

Sources Venn, Alum. Cant. • GM, 1st ser., 76 (1806), 87 • GM, 2nd ser., 39 (1853), 202–3 • Burke, Gen. GB • Proceedings of the Linnean Society of London, 2 (1848–55), 231–2 • W. Otter, The life and remains of … Edward Daniel Clarke (1824) • M. A. Lower, The worthies of Sussex (1865) • T. W. Horsfield, The history and antiquities of Lewes and its vicinity, 2 vols. (1824–7) • E. D. Clarke, Travels in various countries of Europe, Asia and Africa, 6 vols. (1810–23) • Desmond, Botanists, rev. edn

Cripps, Sir John Stafford (1912–1993), journalist, was born at Fernacres Cottage, Fulmer, Burnham, Buckinghamshire, on 10 May 1912, the only son and eldest of the four children of Sir (Richard) Stafford *Cripps (1889–1952), politician, and Dame Isobel *Cripps, née Swithinbank (1891–1979), overseas aid organizer. The family was long established in west Oxfordshire and Gloucestershire, and Cripps lived for all but the first few years of his life at Filkins, just inside Oxfordshire. Educated at Winchester College and at Balliol College, Oxford, he took a brilliant first in modern Greats, chaired the university Labour Club, and was secretary of the Oxford Union. In the general election of 1935 he was unsuccessful for Labour at Exeter. With friends such as the future Labour leader Michael Foot (whom he claimed to have helped convert from Liberalism), he seemed set for a political career on the left. But in 1938, determined on a course distinct from his father's, he was led by his concern for countryside communities to take a post on the advertising staff of The Countryman, then edited by J. W. Robertson Scott at Idbury, near Filkins. During the war this was perforce a part-time job; as a conscientious objector Cripps was required to work some days a week as a market gardener on the family's 500 acre farm at Filkins. Cripps's pacifism reflected his Quakerism and during the war he helped to revive the Burford Friends' meeting, of which he remained a member (noted more for silence than speech) for the rest of his life. He was editor of The Countryman from 1947 to 1971. In 1946 he began his forty-one years on Filkins parish council and was elected to the Witney rural district council; he was still a member at its demise in 1974. On 29 December 1936 he married Ursula Davy; they had four sons and two daughters. They were divorced in 1971 and Cripps married Ann Elizabeth Farwell, a journalist, on 14 August 1971.

Cripps made *The Countryman* an authoritative and influential voice for the countryside, as much concerned for employment, schools, shops, and transport as for conservation; the quarterly's circulation peaked at 88,895 in 1954. Backed by a talented and devoted staff, he found time to pursue the magazine's objectives through his work in local government. He chaired his district council from 1959 to 1962 and the Rural District Councils' Association from 1967 to 1970; he was appointed CBE for his services to local government in 1968, and was deeply involved in the campaign to 'keep local government local' before the changes of 1974.

From 1970 to 1977 Cripps chaired the Countryside Commission, then at the height of its influence. With sympathies in both camps, he sought to reconcile farmers and conservationists. He persuaded ministers and civil servants, whom the demands of farming had dominated since 1945, to take countryside conservation more seriously. Under his chairmanship the commission offered a first tentative challenge to the prevailing orthodoxy that efficient farming is necessarily beautiful farming. In close alliance with the commission's forceful director, Reg Hookway, he achieved the settlement of national park administration in 1974. This compromise angered conservationists because it left the parks ultimately under local-authority control; but it proved a long-term success because it gave them their own staff and considerable autonomy. He was knighted in 1978.

Cripps left his mark on many aspects of rural life and amenities. He served on the government-appointed committee in 1968 which ruled against rationalization of the public-path network; he was a notably awkward member of the defence lands committee in the early 1970s, refusing to join the majority in favour of military training on beautiful landscapes, and he produced the radical report on accommodation for gypsies for the government in 1976. Despite his early abandonment of party politics he remained a socialist and a believer in public ownership of land. In the 1980s this took practical form when he used the sale of a farmhouse on his Filkins property to finance the development of a redundant farmyard and buildings for light industrial and retail units. He served on many Oxfordshire bodies concerned with rural life, education, and voluntary work; and on such national organizations as the Council for the Preservation of Rural England and the Nature Conservancy.

Despite his years in journalism and public life Cripps was neither an orator nor a flashing wordsmith. He spoke in an austere but compelling Quaker style and wrote similarly, often with difficulty but striving always for clarity and honesty of expression. He was a socialist active in rural affairs, in which leaders and opinion formers during his lifetime were overwhelmingly Conservative. He died of leukaemia on 9 August 1993 at his home, Fox House, Filkins, and is buried in Filkins cemetery.   CHRIS HALL

Sources personal knowledge (2004) · files and papers, *The Countryman*, Burford, Oxfordshire · private information [Lucy Cripps, widow, colleagues] · *The Countryman* [Christmas], 98/6 (1993) · *The Times* (19 Aug 1993) · *The Independent* (28 Aug 1993) · b. cert. · m. cert. [Ursula Davy] · m. cert. [Ann Elizabeth Farwell] · d. cert. · *WW*

Likenesses photograph, repro. in *The Countryman*, 98/6 · photograph, repro. in *The Times* · photograph, repro. in *The Independent*

Wealth at death £1,777,393: probate, 1994, *CGPLA Eng. & Wales*

Cripps, Marian Emily. *See* Ellis, Marian Emily (1878–1952).

Cripps, Sir (Richard) Stafford (1889–1952), politician and lawyer, was born at Elm Park Gardens, London, on 24 April 1889. He was the fifth and youngest child of Charles Alfred *Cripps (1852–1941) and his wife, Theresa (*née* Potter) (1852–1893). His father, a successful and prosperous barrister, became a Conservative MP and later (as first Baron Parmoor) a Labour cabinet minister. His mother was the sister of Beatrice Potter, who became Beatrice Webb. But for Stafford Cripps these political connections were, in his early years, much less significant than his parents' strong Christian values. His mother died suddenly when he was four; in line with her express wishes, he and his siblings were brought up to be 'undogmatic and unsectarian' (Estorick, 21) in their faith, and to take their religious inspiration directly from the spirit of the New Testament.

Early life and the law Cripps's high intelligence and capacity for hard work showed itself early. After attending preparatory schools at Reigate and Rottingdean, he moved on to Winchester College. He won a scholarship to New College, Oxford, in 1907, the first ever offered in chemistry. But instead of taking it up, he was persuaded by Professor Sir William Ramsay to study at University College, London. Cripps once more excelled, taking the MSc degree and subsequently co-authoring a research paper published under the auspices of the Royal Society. He was also personally popular, as shown by his election as president of the Student Union. But he was not quite the youthful paragon that biographers have made out. He enjoyed gambling, and, as he later admitted, exaggerated his own illnesses in order to gain sympathy.

During the first general election of 1910, when helping out with his father's campaign in South Buckinghamshire, he met Isobel Swithinbank (1891–1979) [*see* Cripps, Dame Isobel], whom he married on 12 July the following year, and with whom he had four children, including Sir John Stafford *Cripps. He later accounted for his presence at the Conservative headquarters by saying that at this time he was 'almost entirely politically unconscious' (Estorick, 43–4). In fact, he was politically ambivalent. A patriotic, anti-Liberal imperialist, he was none the less sympathetic to the plight of 'the poor slum-beings' (diary, 26 July 1910, Cripps MSS) and had occasional emotional spasms in the direction of socialism. But he did not have any clear idea of how the problem of poverty could be

Sir (Richard) Stafford Cripps (1889–1952), by Yousuf Karsh, 1943

solved, and he retained many strong conservative instincts, for example, against the suffragettes.

His career was to be made in the law. He was called to the bar by the Middle Temple in 1913, but his progress was interrupted by the outbreak of war in August 1914. Still under medical treatment from a breakdown he had suffered in June, Stafford did not join up, accepting the view that married men were not yet needed. But he did become an active recruiter and in October crossed to France on a freelance mission to deliver winter comforts to the troops. Once there he determined on joining the Red Cross, and soon became driver of a lorry which Isobel persuaded her father to donate. After twelve months' arduous but unskilled ambulance service, evacuating wounded men through Boulogne, Cripps offered his expertise as a chemist to the newly created Ministry of Munitions, and was posted to Queensferry, near Chester. Here, during the illness of the superintendent in the early months of 1916, he took on full responsibility for one of the biggest munitions factories in Great Britain and worked very long hours. He consequently suffered a more significant physical breakdown, eventually diagnosed as colitis (inflammation of the colon), and spent much of the rest of the war as an invalid.

This may have served to inhibit his inclination towards the Labour Party, given his sensitivity about his enforced dependence on unearned income. He noted: 'I could never go into Political life as a representative of Labour, being myself one who toils not neither does he spin!' (diary, 5 Oct 1918, Cripps MSS). After he returned to the bar in 1919, he thus concentrated his surplus effort not on politics but on religious work, most especially for the World Alliance

for Promoting International Friendship through the Churches, of which he became treasurer. Work at the bar was initially slack, and the purchase and refurbishment of his country house, Goodfellows, in Gloucestershire, put him under financial strain. But his career soon took off, aided by an appearance for the London county council before the railway rates tribunal in 1924–6, and he became Britain's youngest king's counsel in 1927.

Entry into politics Cripps's work before the tribunal had brought him to the attention of Herbert Morrison, the Labour leader in London. In 1929, with Morrison's encouragement, Cripps joined the Labour Party, now in office, and was soon adopted as prospective parliamentary candidate for West Woolwich. In 1930, however, he accepted an invitation to join Ramsay MacDonald's Labour government immediately as solicitor-general; he received the customary knighthood and in January 1931 won a by-election at Bristol East. Parachuted into a safe seat as a front-bencher, Cripps quickly showed strong parliamentary ability. When MacDonald formed the National Government in August 1931, he invited Cripps to continue as solicitor-general. Cripps declined politely, and, after the government's landslide election victory in October, was one of only three ministers from the previous administration left on the Labour benches in the Commons. Thrown into political prominence, he quickly became intimate with the other two, George Lansbury and Clement Attlee, who became party leader and deputy leader respectively. But the Commons atmosphere made him uncomfortable and he became a teetotaller 'as a protest against the alcoholism' of the Parliamentary Labour Party (Beatrice Webb, diary, 2 Sept 1934, Passfield MSS, BLPES). Although his initial impetus towards Labour had been born of the desire to act as a moderating influence, he now swung sharply to the left. The risk of isolation was mitigated, however, when he deployed his legal skills, without asking a fee, on behalf of the miners in the inquiry into the Gresford colliery disaster of 1934.

As a prominent member of the newly formed Socialist League (and, after 1933, as its chairman), Cripps attempted to rally Labour's rank and file against the 'reactionary' policy of the trade unions and the party's national executive. He made numerous extreme statements, suggesting, for example, that a future socialist government would be unlikely 'to maintain its position of control without adopting some exceptional means such as the prolongation of the life of Parliament for a further term without an election' (Cripps, 'Can socialism come by constitutional methods?', in Addison and others, 39). He described the League of Nations as an 'International Burglars Union' (*Labour Party Annual Conference Report*, 1935, 158)—a position which even the Soviet ambassador wanted him to moderate—and, although he bitterly opposed appeasement of Germany, he refused until 1938 to countenance rearmament. This was because he supposed the National Government 'far more likely to be the allies of Fascism than the allies of Russia or any working-class country' (*Hansard 5C*, 18 Feb 1937). The German take-over of Austria and, in particular, the Munich crisis helped bring Cripps to the realization that, if war came, he would feel compelled to do whatever he thought he could for his country, whatever the political complexion of its government. In retrospect this appears as the beginning of his transition from the heedless (albeit well-heeled) class warrior of the 1930s to the detached national figure with cross-party authority that he would become later.

In the immediate term, however, Cripps seemed bound on a trajectory of political self-destruction. His advocacy of a 'united front' with the Communist Party and the Independent Labour Party brought him onto a collision course with Labour's executive and led, in 1937, to the forcible winding up of the Socialist League. In January 1939, desperate to rid the country of the National Government, he put forward the idea of a 'popular front', now to include Liberals as well. He launched a highly personalized campaign to this end, in open defiance of the executive, which expelled him from the party. The annual party conference in May endorsed this decision by 2,100,000 votes to 402,000.

The start of the Second World War, 1939–1940 The outbreak of war in 1939 caught Cripps off guard. He immediately threw up his practice at the bar and offered the government his services, presumptively in a technical or administrative role. With this offer spurned, and driven by a conviction that India, China, Russia, and the USA were the countries of the future, Cripps decided to embark on a world tour, undertaken with a young colleague, Geoffrey Wilson. In India Cripps was warmly received as the friend of Jawaharlal Nehru, an exact contemporary with a provokingly similar background to Cripps's own. Though unofficial in status, Cripps's visit was undertaken with the cognizance of the India Office and was intended to explore the prospects of an agreed plan for progress towards Indian self-government. Encouraged by his reception, and undoubtedly benefiting to some extent from Nehru's good offices in securing this, Cripps evidently hoped to enlist Gandhi's influence, writing after their first meeting: 'I feel there is a much better chance of solution of the problem while he is still alive and in control than there will be if and when he goes' (diary, 20 Dec 1939, Cripps MSS). The viceroy and the India Office, however, remained unmoved.

From India, Cripps moved on to China, currently resisting Japanese invasion. He based himself for two months at the beginning of 1940 in Chungking (Chongqing), the nationalists' wartime headquarters, where he established some degree of rapport with their leader, Generalissimo Chiang Kai-shek, whose influential wife apparently shared Cripps's reforming instincts. Indeed, Cripps was invited to stay on as a personal adviser to the generalissimo, an offer that briefly tempted him, although the nationalists' increasing friction with the communists was a problem that he could not ignore. From Chungking, Cripps launched his own exploratory visit to Moscow, where he was *persona grata* as a rare Western apologist for the Soviet Union's actions in recent months, in first concluding its pact with Germany and then occupying Finland. His meeting with the foreign minister, Molotov, was

the first British contact since the withdrawal of the ambassador at the end of 1939. Cripps made a report to the foreign secretary, Lord Halifax, with whom he maintained good relations, though without achieving much impression.

Returning to London via the USA at the end of April 1940, Cripps resumed his efforts for what he called a government of national unity. Despite the fall of Chamberlain in May 1940, after a parliamentary debate on Norway to which Cripps had contributed critical comments, he found himself excluded from the Churchill coalition government, which was constructed on strict party lines. An official posting to the Soviet Union, however, was now offered by the Foreign Office, largely through the good offices of Halifax, supported by his junior minister, R. A. Butler.

Ambassador in Russia, 1940–1942 Cripps served as British ambassador to the Soviet Union from June 1940 to January 1942. He left Goodfellows, now too large a commitment once his legal income was gone, and subsequently lived in a more modest but comfortable country home at Frith Hill, near Stroud; Isobel joined him in Moscow, with their daughters Peggy and Theresa, from October 1940 to June 1941. Cripps had initially been charged with a special mission limited to possible economic or strategic co-operation, but the Russians forced the hand of the British government by agreeing to accept him only provided he were a full ambassador. Exceptionally, he remained a member of parliament, thus permitting his easy re-entry to British politics at a moment of his choosing. After one introductory meeting with Molotov, Cripps found himself officially snubbed. With Britain fighting for its very survival, the Russians chose to keep their distance, especially from an ambassador in whom the Foreign Office establishment betrayed some lack of confidence.

Cripps saw himself as a major political figure with his own mission to accomplish—to ease relations between Britain and Russia pending the eventual 'divorce' between Hitler and Stalin—and proposed an initiative over the status of the Baltic states (Latvia, Lithuania, and Estonia). Their occupation by Russia struck Cripps as evidence of Russia's security worries rather than of its own imperialist expansion. In the middle of October 1940 Halifax persuaded the war cabinet to support the proposals that Cripps now put forward. His optimism was soon deflated with the announcement on 9 November that the elusive Molotov was off to Berlin for the first top-level talks since the signing of the Nazi–Soviet pact, fifteen months previously. Having spent four months persuading the Foreign Office to offer concessions over the Baltic states, Cripps found that it could not abruptly be unpersuaded, even though by December his own line had changed. His critics erred, however, in putting down everything to 'disillusionment'. He had written at the outset: 'One thing has been proved here—so far—and that is that you cannot leap into Utopia in one bound' (letter to his daughter Diana, 8 Sept 1940, Cripps MSS). But perhaps his realism about the Soviet Union became infused with a degree of cynicism. Correspondingly, his conviction that his own government was doing the right thing, if often in the wrong way, was strengthened.

One incident that has bulked disproportionately large is Churchill's charge that Cripps failed to ensure that Stalin received a personal warning of Hitler's plan ('Barbarossa') to attack Russia. The fact is that Cripps long sought unavailingly to alert the Foreign Office to such a possibility, without appreciable success, and that Stalin had a range of much more circumstantial intelligence reports available, which he ignored.

Early in June 1941 Cripps was recalled to London, as a disciplinary step, since the Foreign Office had built up a formidable dossier against the behaviour of their eccentric ambassador. Vindication came with the launch of Barbarossa on 22 June. Churchill and Eden now found it easy to close ranks with Cripps, who was summoned at once to Chequers. The prime minister's broadcast that night, balancing emotion with realism in its support of Russia, tallied with Cripps's own analysis. On his return to Moscow, Cripps was joined by a British military mission, and an agreement on mutual assistance was finalized with unwonted speed. Its signature on 12 July was the high point of Cripps's diplomatic career. Though Cripps vigorously represented the demands of the Soviet government, he was by no means its creature. In economic negotiations, Cripps chided the Foreign Office as 'still imbued with the appeasement attitude and dont see that people respect you if you stand up to them in a dignified way' (diary, 11 Aug 1941). Cripps's tough tactics in handling the Russians went along with his strategy for forging a robust alliance of equals.

Successful in pressing for an Anglo-American conference with the Russians, as finally convened in Moscow at the end of September, Cripps found that the entire discussion of supplies for Russia was to be kept in the hands of the visiting dignitaries: the British minister of supply, Lord Beaverbrook, and the American roving ambassador, Averell Harriman. His personal treatment by Beaverbrook left Cripps wary of him as a colleague and, more important, deplorably under-informed about the course of discussions from which he had been excluded. Moreover, within days, the whole war situation deteriorated in ways that further marginalized Cripps, with the enforced evacuation of the embassy on 15 October to Kuibyshev, 500 miles to the east on the River Volga. Worst of all, though the diplomatic corps was now in Kuibyshev, the Soviet government was not.

For the first time since going to Russia, Cripps looked hard at his own political prospects. His increasingly sharp clashes with Churchill had a political undertone of which both men were aware. Cripps now saw himself as a political exile, and submitted what was virtually his resignation. With Eden now about to visit Moscow, Cripps was browbeaten or charmed, yet again, into staying at his post. The Moscow talks, starting on 16 December, saw him as a participant throughout, flanking Eden and facing Stalin and Molotov. But, following the dramatic entry into the war of the USA, Churchill came to think Cripps a bigger menace in Russia than at home and sent permission for him to return to London, which he did in January 1942.

Churchill's colleague, 1942–1945 Cripps was now widely hailed as the man who had brought Russia into the war. Churchill, his own position weakened by a string of British set-backs, notably the fall of Singapore, sought to conciliate Cripps, and in late February 1942 brought him into the government as lord privy seal and leader of the House of Commons. A novice in the war cabinet, Cripps had neither a strong department nor a secure party base—only the evanescent support of public opinion. He chose to invest his windfall political capital in an initiative to break the political impasse in India, now a crucial theatre of war in the path of Japanese advance.

Cripps exploited US pressure to secure Churchill's reluctant agreement to the 'Cripps offer'. This was a promise of self-government for India via a post-war constituent assembly, subject only to the right of any province not to accede. Only a month after joining the war cabinet, Cripps flew out to Delhi. There he threw himself into a whirlwind of negotiation, in order to win consent from all sections of Indian opinion, reporting nightly to a sceptical viceroy (the second marquess of Linlithgow). Within days Gandhi's aphorism—that the Cripps offer was 'a post-dated cheque'—was in circulation. What Cripps offered was not only a post-war promise, however, but a substantial payment on account in the form of an immediate approximation to cabinet government. There were two provisos: that strategic defence issues would remain in British hands for the duration of the war and that the viceroy's co-operation in operating the new conventions would be forthcoming.

The Muslim League under Mohamed Ali Jinnah was ready to accept the package, provided that Congress would too. Here agreement seemed tantalizingly close, the more so after intervention from President Roosevelt's representative in Delhi, Colonel Louis Johnson, who helped Cripps devise a formula on defence acceptable to Nehru and the Congress president, Abul Kalam Azad. Only Linlithgow failed to co-operate; but this proved enough to undermine Congress's faith in Cripps's assurances about how the conventions of cabinet responsibility would be operated by the viceroy. It was this, rather than sharp practice on Cripps's part or sabotage from London, that doomed the Cripps mission.

The aftermath of the Cripps mission was piquant. The political vacuum was filled by Gandhi's Quit India campaign, soon accepted by Congress. Conversely, Cripps saw the opportunity to redeem his disappointment in Delhi by a propaganda triumph, aimed particularly at the USA, with the aim of unmasking Gandhi as the cause of failure. One result of the Cripps mission, then, was to embitter attitudes in India, not least towards Cripps himself, while influential sections of American opinion swung to a less critical view of British policy. In this respect, Churchill owed a substantial, if largely unacknowledged, debt to Cripps.

Their working relationship in the war cabinet was not happy. Cripps chafed under a regime which he considered inefficient, while his own talents were largely wasted as leader of the house, a role in which he was weakened by his lack of either party allegiance or political finesse. That he seriously thought that he could displace Churchill remains unlikely, but he showed himself prepared to risk his career in an attempt to remodel the structure of government. Failing to carry his proposals by the autumn of 1942, Cripps patriotically deferred his resignation while the military outcome in the north African desert remained in doubt. Once the victory at El Alamein had strengthened Churchill's hand, a reinvigorated prime minister was ready for a showdown with Cripps, who left the war cabinet in November, accepting the less glamorous post of minister of aircraft production.

Cripps's dedication and powers of rapid comprehension suited him well for the technical tasks that faced him at his new ministry, in spite of early clashes with its highly able chief executive, Sir Wilfrid Freeman. Cripps's time at the Ministry of Aircraft Production alerted him to the complexities of industrial planning. In contrast to his pre-war dogmatism, he now became convinced of the need for varying degrees of nationalization and control in different industries. One significant innovation was the idea of joint production committees of workers and employers, an experiment in industrial democracy which contributed to his new-found belief in 'democratic planning', dependent for its success on all social classes working together voluntarily in the national interest. It was this kind of emphasis on common efforts to tackle economic problems that became his great theme upon his return to the Labour Party in 1945. Appointed president of the Board of Trade by Attlee after Labour's victory of that year, his emphasis on collective self-denial—by restraining consumption to promote economic recovery—made his name a byword for austerity.

The transfer of power in India, 1946–1947 For eighteen months the Board of Trade had to compete for Cripps's attention with India, now being extricated from the thralls of empire. It is striking here how far the historiography has diminished Cripps's role. For it was Cripps who arguably offered India its last chance to avert partition and bloodshed, as Indian politicians as diverse as Vallabhbhai Patel and Chakravarti Rajagopalachari came to appreciate. From March to June 1946 Cripps made his third and longest visit to India charged with seeking agreement on the transfer of power from Britain to an independent government. Though part of a cabinet delegation with two colleagues (Lord Pethick-Lawrence as secretary of state and Albert Alexander as first lord of the Admiralty), Cripps was seen as the man in charge.

It was Gandhi's proven ability to thwart a settlement that made his position pivotal. Cripps decided that no trouble was to be spared in courting him, despite the qualms of the viceroy, Lord Wavell, who sat with the ministers through protracted formal meetings with all parties. Cripps saw the alternatives starkly: either a negotiated settlement or bloodshed. When the talks adjourned to Simla, in the cool of the hills, hopes of a rapprochement between Nehru and Jinnah seemed to blossom, only

to be blighted by a sudden frost. Back in Delhi, everyone waited instead upon an initiative from Cripps.

The cabinet delegation's statement of 16 May was essentially Cripps's attempt to build on the measure of agreement revealed at Simla and to erect this into a system of government. His strategy was to accommodate the Muslim demand for some kind of self-government by means of a three-tier structure, in which provinces could opt for grouping at an intermediate level below that of a union of all India, which would be responsible for certain common functions, including defence. The underlying problem was that Congress found the notion of grouping repugnant, and therefore refused to grant it the sort of legitimacy necessary to entice the Muslim League into such constitutional arrangements. Within days of this statement, Cripps faced a crisis that was both political and personal. Having set great store by gaining Gandhi's approval, Cripps suddenly found that he could not rely upon it; and his own physical collapse at this point was hardly coincidental. On his sickbed Cripps sent a personal appeal to Gandhi, only to find it rebuffed with a clear imputation on his probity.

Securing the Muslim League's acceptance of a scheme for an all-India union was actually the cabinet delegation's greatest achievement. Despite the league's commitment to Pakistan, it was induced into a constitutional scheme providing for a united India—on certain conditions, the most important of which was a recognition of grouping. Cripps trusted Congress to make a reality of that inducement; the league soon concluded that the behaviour of the Congress leaders left it with no basis for such trust, and thus with no reason to compromise its own aim of Pakistan. At the time neither Nehru nor Patel, much to Cripps's exasperation, was prepared to counter Gandhi's influence, which was crucial in determining this outcome. Wavell, for his part, blamed Cripps for dishonesty and duplicity in accepting Congress's qualified assurances as consent. The issue was really how far political finesse could be justified in brokering a messy compromise from which each side naturally hoped to gain different advantages. Like early steps in any peace process, the cabinet delegation's scheme did not tie up all the historically generated loose ends at once, but opened the way to incremental co-operation in creating, building, and sustaining trust.

The fact that the crux of the whole issue now lay within the ambit of Indian politics was recognized by Cripps. By the end of 1946 Indian policy had reached an impasse which was broken only when Attlee made a striking move: the appointment of the glamorous figure of Admiral Lord Mountbatten as the last viceroy (in place of Wavell), combined with setting a date for British withdrawal. It was not, contrary to his later claims, Mountbatten himself who imposed a deadline for British withdrawal; at most he tinkered with the date itself. Attlee had already fixed on this plan by the time he decided to appoint Mountbatten, as is now generally accepted. But the records suggest that this proposal actually came from

Cripps, who was also largely responsible for bringing forward the name of Mountbatten, to whose subsequent efforts he gave unwavering support throughout the transfer of power in 1947.

Economic supremo, 1947–1950 Getting back into his stride at the Board of Trade, Cripps emerged as an increasingly strong figure in an increasingly beleaguered government. He introduced legislation which allowed the creation of development councils, intended to facilitate 'tripartite' co-operation between government, employers, and workers at an industry-wide level, although the innovation proved largely unsuccessful. He also played a key role in drafting the landmark *Economic Survey for 1947*, a government white paper in which he reiterated his belief that planning should be reconciled to the maximum possible extent with free individual choice.

The fuel and convertibility crises of 1947, however, contributed to a sense that the government was drifting, perhaps sinking. Eager to see control restored, Cripps attempted that September to replace Attlee with Ernest Bevin as prime minister. Attlee coolly faced Cripps down, offering him instead a new post as minister for economic affairs, independent of the Treasury, and responsible for economic planning. Cripps accepted, but the arrangement lasted only six weeks. Hugh Dalton resigned as chancellor after a budget leak, and Cripps replaced him, while retaining the economic affairs portfolio—a unique concentration of authority in determining economic policy.

Cripps's priorities were: exports first, capital investment second, and the needs, comforts, and amenities of ordinary consumers last. However, his belief in 'democratic planning' made him reluctant to achieve his ends via compulsion, so he increasingly relied on exhortation, both of workers and employers. This had some notable results, in particular the Trades Union Congress's acceptance of a two-year wage freeze after 1948. But, as the war-weary public's forbearance dimmed, it was hardly surprising that this proved to be a strategy of progressively diminishing returns. Moreover, owing to the inadequacies of its propaganda, the government had difficulty getting its message across.

Cripps and his colleagues had, then, failed to create the detailed and effective system of physical planning that Labour thinkers had envisaged before 1945. It was logical, therefore, to try another policy—a less *dirigiste* form of economic control based on the restraint of aggregate demand. Cripps thus deliberately and explicitly achieved large budgetary surpluses as a means to this end; his 1948 budget is generally considered a landmark of applied Keynesianism. Arguably the real architects of this policy were two of Cripps's key officials, Edwin Plowden and Robert Hall. Hall believed that Cripps's skill as a barrister enabled him to make more of the arguments of his subordinates than they ever would themselves, leading to the paradoxical judgement: 'He did not really understand the basis of economic planning as we developed it under his regime, but he was entirely responsible for its development' (*Hall Diaries*, 222). Never a bookish man, Cripps had

neither read Keynes nor assimilated his theoretical analysis.

The chancellor's authority was undermined by the devaluation crisis of 1949. The decision to devalue sterling—which Cripps announced on 17 September—was in fact taken by a triumvirate of less senior ministers, approved by the cabinet, and conveyed to him in Zürich, where he was convalescing. He acquiesced, although he was by no means convinced of the rightness of the action. The episode also led to a breach with Churchill, who accused Cripps of dishonesty, given that he had previously stated that devaluation would not take place. Cripps, of course, had had little other option.

Now gravely ill, and with his reputation damaged, Cripps found his macroeconomic strategy being increasingly questioned by his colleagues, including even the prime minister. The most serious challenge came from Hugh Gaitskell, who had played a key role in the decision to devalue. Early in 1950 Gaitskell wrote a memorandum that criticized the tendency to move from direct physical controls to indirect budgetary methods of economic management. This view won wide support from other ministers, and Cripps was obliged to endorse Gaitskell's general line. This is not to say that there was any immediate threat to Cripps's position; but, with Gaitskell emerging as an obvious successor, Cripps was no longer clearly indispensable.

Final illness Sickness finally forced Cripps's resignation, both as chancellor and as an MP; this was announced on 20 October 1950. He travelled to his habitual retreat, the Bircher Benner clinic in Zürich, and also received treatment in Lausanne. Not only was he suffering from tubercular spondylitis, a spinal infection, but he also developed stomach tumours and was later diagnosed as having a form of bone marrow cancer, which ultimately proved fatal. He put up a remarkable physical fight, and in the autumn of 1951 was briefly able to return to Britain. A relapse early in 1952 compelled him to go back to Switzerland; he died at the Bircher Benner clinic, Keltenstrasse 48, Zürich, on 21 April of that year, and was cremated in Zürich three days later.

There were many contradictions or at least paradoxes. Latterly Cripps's public image was constructed, especially through the press, in ways that positively emphasized his leadership potential during the war but rebounded negatively against him afterwards. In the 1940s his lean appearance, his rimless spectacles, his well-known vegetarianism, and his teetotalism contributed to an impression of asceticism; and he ultimately gave up his only 'vice', heavy smoking, on doctor's orders. Yet Cripps had another side—personally warm and privately tolerant—which suggests that he was no narrow-minded killjoy. It was a major propaganda coup for the Conservatives to suggest that post-war privations were imposed on the hard-pressed British people not through necessity but through choice: that Cripps as economic supremo relished the hair-shirt measures that he preached with such high-minded fervour. In death as in life, his reputation hinged on one inescapable word: austerity.

Cripps was a man from a background of established wealth, who gave up an income of £30,000 a year in 1939; whose early political career was as a prominent left-wing rebel and fellow-traveller of the communists. Conversely, in the 1940s he emerged as a central figure in the establishment of a new post-war consensus, especially in economic policy. His wartime role as ambassador in Moscow propelled him into the top rank of British politics, alone able to rival Churchill as a wartime leader, albeit briefly and perhaps not wholly deservedly. Yet Cripps's insight into the great unresolved problem of India was far less blinkered and flawed than that of Churchill, and here Cripps surely deserved better for his tireless commitment in pursuit of a peaceful resolution of the impasse. In many ways he is remembered for the wrong reasons.

PETER CLARKE and RICHARD TOYE

Sources P. Clarke, *The Cripps version: the life of Sir Stafford Cripps* (2002) • S. Burgess, *Stafford Cripps: a political life* (1999) • E. Estorick, *Stafford Cripps: a biography* (1949) • *The Robert Hall diaries, 1947–53*, ed. A. Cairncross (1989) • *DNB* • C. Bryant, *Stafford Cripps: the first modern chancellor* (1997) • P. Strauss, *Cripps: advocate and rebel* (1943) • *Economic survey for 1947* (1947) [cmd 7046] • C. Addison and others, *Problems of a socialist government* (1933) • *Labour Party Annual Conference Report* (1935) • *Hansard 5C* • *CGPLA Eng. & Wales* (1952) • Bodl. Oxf., MSS Cripps
Archives Bodl. Oxf., papers • Nuffield Oxf., papers • PRO, corresp. and papers, CAB 127/57–154 | BLPES, Passfield MSS, Beatrice Webb diary • Bodl. Oxf., corresp. with Clement Attlee • Bodl. Oxf., corresp. with Lord Monckton • Bodl. RH, corresp. with Arthur Creech Jones • Bristol RO, corresp. with Bristol South East Labour Party and its secretary H. E. Rogers • CAC Cam., corresp. with A. V. Alexander • Inst. EE, corresp. with Dame Caroline Haslett • King's Lond., Liddell Hart C., corresp. with Sir B. H. Liddell Hart • NL Wales, corresp. with Huw T. Edwards; corresp. with Thomas Jones • Nuffield Oxf., corresp. with Lord Cherwell | FILM BFI NFTVA, current affairs footage • BFI NFTVA, documentary footage • BFI NFTVA, news footage • BFI NFTVA, propaganda film footage (ministry of information) • IWM FVA, actuality footage • IWM FVA, documentary footage • IWM FVA, news footage | SOUND BL NSA, current affairs recording • IWM SA, 'What has become of us?', Channel 4, November 1994, 15271 • IWM SA, oral history interview • priv. coll., recording of Cripps
Likenesses I. M. Cohen, oils, *c.*1931, NPG • M. Cohen, portrait, *c.*1931, NPG • W. Stoneman, three photographs, 1931–49, NPG • F. Man, photograph, 1939, NPG • H. Coster, photographs, 1940–49, NPG • Y. Karsh, photograph, 1943, NPG [*see illus.*] • F. Man, photograph, 1943, Hult. Arch. • photograph, 1949 (with his wife, Dame Isobel Cripps), Popperfoto, Northampton; *see illus. in* Cripps, Dame Isobel, *Lady Cripps (1891–1979)* • S. White, oils, *c.*1950, Gov. Art Coll. • S. Charoux, bust, priv. coll. • J. Epstein, bronze bust, St Paul's Cathedral, London • W. Lewis, pen and ink, and watercolour drawing, Cecil Higgins Art Gallery, Bedford • photographs, Nuffield Oxf.
Wealth at death £15,190 17s. 11d.: probate, 12 Aug 1952, CGPLA Eng. & Wales

Cripps, Wilfred Joseph (1841–1903), writer on silver, was born on 8 June 1841 in London, the eldest surviving child of William Cripps (1804/5–1848), barrister and MP for Cirencester, and his wife (and cousin), Mary Anne Harrison, daughter of Benjamin *Harrison (1771–1856), treasurer of Guy's Hospital. The Cripps family, whose wealth came from the wool trade, had been prominent citizens of Cirencester since the sixteenth century. Cripps's grandfather Joseph Cripps (1765–1847) sat as an independently

minded MP for the town in 1806–12 and 1818–41. He was succeeded in the representation by his son William Cripps (Wilfred's father). A Conservative, he was made a lord of the Treasury in 1845, supported Peel over the repeal of the corn laws, and died on 11 May 1848.

Wilfred Joseph Cripps was educated at Kensington grammar school and at King's College, London, and Trinity College, Oxford, where he was admitted in 1859 and graduated BA in 1863 before proceeding MA in 1866. He took an active part in the volunteer movement, frequently attending the rifle competitions at Wimbledon. In May 1865 he was called to the bar at the Middle Temple and, like his father, practised for a few years on the Oxford circuit. On 31 May 1870 he married Maria Harriet Arabella Daniel-Tyssen (d. 1881), second daughter of John Robert Daniel-Tyssen.

It is for his research and publications in the field of decorative arts, specifically silver studies, that Cripps deserves to be remembered. His interest in old silver began in the early 1870s, when he was introduced by William, fifth Earl Bathurst, to Charles Octavius Swinnerton *Morgan, the antiquary, who entrusted Cripps with his notes on the subject. In 1878 Cripps published *Old English Plate*, his major scholarly work. This drew on the researches of Sir Augustus Wollaston Franks, Morgan himself, William Chaffers, and others, but brought them to a wider audience, and thereby greatly stimulated the demand for antique silver. Nine editions of the manual appeared between 1878 and 1906, with each new edition containing fresh material; there were subsequent reprints in 1927, 1967, and 1977. Cripps's interest in the subject was broad: in 1880 he published *Old French Plate* (2nd edn, 1893), and in 1881 he produced *College and Corporation Plate: a handbook to the reproductions of silver plate in the South Kensington Museum, from celebrated English collections*. His paper on the old church plate of Northumberland and Durham, read before the Society of Antiquaries of Newcastle upon Tyne, was later published (*Archaeologia Aeliana*, 1st ser., 16, 249–67).

Cripps was recognized as a leading authority on silver, and became an adviser to the South Kensington Museum (now the Victoria and Albert Museum). In October 1880, with the museum's director, Sir Francis Philip Cunliffe-Owen, he persuaded the Russian government to allow the reproduction of plate from the magnificent imperial collection using the electrotyping process. The success of their enterprise did much to advance the study of silver, through the copies that were lent to art schools and used to illustrate textbooks. He also helped to acquire important silver for the museum, notably Elizabethan plate from the Mostyn family in 1885. In 1880 Cripps was a member of the English subcommission connected with the exhibition of gold and silver work at Amsterdam (*The Athenaeum*, 28 Feb 1880, 289).

Cripps was also interested in archaeology. He excavated Roman sites in Cirencester and reported on them to the Society of Antiquaries, of which he became a fellow in 1880. He served in the Royal North Gloucester militia, from which he retired with the rank of major, and completed the regimental history begun by Sir J. Maxwell Steele-Groves (published in 1875). He was made a CB in 1889, and in 1894 received the honorary freedom of the Goldsmiths' Company. He took in a keen interest in local affairs, especially education, and in politics he was active in the Conservative cause.

Following the death of his first wife in 1881, Cripps married, on 2 December 1884, Helena Augusta Wilhelmine, Countess Bismarck, daughter of Count Bismarck of Scherstein, Prussia, a relative of the Iron Chancellor. There were no children of either marriage. Cripps died at his residence, Cripps Mead, Cirencester, on 26 October 1903, and was buried in Cirencester cemetery. He was survived by his second wife.

CHARLES WELCH, rev. ANN EATWELL

Sources J. Culme, 'Attitudes to old plate, 1750–1900', *The directory of gold and silversmiths, jewellery and allied trades, 1838–1914*, 1 (1987), xvi–xxxvii • C. Oman, *The Victorian period* (April 1965), vol. 1 of *A hundred years of English silver*, 18–28 • P. Glanville, *Silver in England* (1987) • P. Glanville, ed., *Silver* (1996) • D. R. Fisher, 'Cripps, Joseph', HoP, *Commons, 1790–1820* • Foster, *Alum. Oxon.* • CGPLA Eng. & Wales (1903)

Archives Birm. CA, corresp., MSS, and notes, mainly relating to plate

Wealth at death £84,552 18s. 9d.: probate, 22 Dec 1903, CGPLA Eng. & Wales

Crisp, (Charles) Birch (1867–1958), financier, was born on 5 September 1867 at Dove Street, Bristol, the son of Charles Birch Crisp, common-law clerk, and his second wife, Clara Isabella, daughter of James Peterkin, solicitor. His paternal grandfather, Charles Crisp, was a corn merchant. He was raised in Bristol and initially worked as a journalist. He was a newspaper manager in London by 1893, the year in which he married Beatrice Marion, daughter of Edwin Chapple. They had at least two sons, Charles Birch and Christopher Norman Birch, and at least one daughter, Phyllis Crowhurst, later Mrs Archer. He was a self-styled 'Tory Democrat' who stood unsuccessfully as Unionist candidate at Oldham in the general elections of 1900 and 1906.

Known usually as Birch Crisp, he became a member of the London stock exchange in 1897, and was active as a company promoter for several years. His most important domestic transaction was the acquisition in 1917 of the Siemens electrical factory at Stafford, which had been confiscated from German ownership under the trading with the enemy acts. Crisp and his long-term associate Almeric Paget MP (created Lord Queenborough in 1918) superintended an elaborate capital reconstruction of Siemens, which was merged with the English Electric Company in 1919.

Crisp had ambitions as an international financier. After visiting St Petersburg in 1909, he was instrumental in placing on the London market £3.5 million of railway bonds, and he made contacts at this time with other financiers interested in Russia. He became chairman in 1910 of the Anglo-Russian Trust which had a 30 per cent holding in the Russian Commercial and Industrial Bank (Russki Torgovi Promishlenni Bank), of which he also became London director. In 1911 he launched the Anglo-Russian Bank, the name of which was changed to the British Bank for Foreign Trade (BBFT) in 1912; he was its chairman until 1927. He intended his BBFT to imitate the French and German practice of making 'tied loans' whereby in return for British investment the Russians would place industrial orders in Britain. Between 1908 and 1914 Crisp's banking interests placed £20 million of Russian bonds and other securities in London, and at the outbreak of the world war BBFT held over £1 million of Russian government and municipal bonds.

In 1910 an international consortium of bankers, supported by their respective governments, had agreed a system to regulate the haphazardly expanding indebtedness of the Chinese government. The Hongkong and Shanghai Bank was initially the sole British bank in this concern until Barings joined in 1912, and the consortium enjoyed the British government's exclusive support. Crisp however assailed this monopoly with a syndicate which in 1912 agreed to loan £10 million to China in defiance of consortium policy. After public acrimony and Foreign Office hindrance of the flotation of the first instalment of £5 million, the Chinese paid £150,000 to Crisp for surrendering his right to issue a second instalment and for waiving his option to handle a £25 million reorganization loan. He thus received £150,000 of the loan's proceeds for the privilege of breaking his own contractual obligations. Crisp made other attempts to break the consortium policy, notably in 1918 when he organized the so-called Marconi loan of £600,000 to be spent on erecting wireless stations. The Chinese predictably defaulted on interest payments.

Crisp in his prosperity bought Moor Close, an imposing red-bricked house built in 1881 at Binfield, a village on the edge of Windsor Park, with easy rail links to the City and convenient for racing. A 'Spy' cartoon of him published in *Mayfair* in 1911 shows a sharp, self-assured, resilient-looking man with glossy tailoring but no physical distinction. He sat several times for this portrait, 'in spite of the fact that he is an extremely busy man and rarely to be found out of his office', wrote Sir Leslie Ward, of whose work Crisp 'made a representative collection … which hangs in his beautiful house near Ascot' (Ward, 338).

After the revolution in 1917, the BBFT bought Russian securities on the open market in an attempt to protect the value of its own holdings. By the early 1920s Crisp's stock-broking firm was the largest individual holder of Russian securities in Britain. He was a member of the Russian committee of the Foreign Bondholders Council until 1924, when he was forced to resign on the discovery that he had been negotiating privately with Soviet officials. Crisp saw the Conservative Party's anti-bolshevism as an obstacle to debt settlement, and therefore contested Windsor unsuccessfully as a Liberal in the general elections of 1922 and 1923. After a minority Labour government took office under Ramsay MacDonald in 1924, he visited Russia, and discussed Anglo-Soviet settlement and the abandonment of the Chinese consortium policy with MacDonald and other Labour leaders. When a general election was called before the Anglo-Russian commercial treaty was signed,

Crisp's bank lent £5000 to the Labour Party, and he personally paid £750 for Labour to fight the three parliamentary seats in Berkshire. These were the first Labour candidacies in the county: his son Christopher stood at Windsor, also unsuccessfully. Crisp wrote to Hugh Dalton on 21 July 1930, 'When I resigned from the Carlton Club my firm lost many clients, and when I fought the Windsor Division as a Liberal Free Trader more clients fell away, and when my son stood … as a Labour candidate my business suffered an eclipse which led me later to leave the Stock Exchange' (PRO 30/69/676).

Crisp retired in 1927 and went to Australia for a few years. His supporters turned away in his misfortune, and such was his obscurity that his entry was deleted from *Who's Who* in 1948. He died of coronary disease on 7 November 1958 at Tooting Bec Hospital, London, and was cremated at Streatham Vale.

RICHARD DAVENPORT-HINES

Sources R. P. T. Davenport-Hines, 'Crisp, Charles Birch', *DBB* · L. Ward, *Forty years of 'Spy'* (1915), 338 · F. W. S. Craig, *British parliamentary election results, 1918–1949*, rev. edn (1977) · PRO, 30/69/676 · d. cert. · b. cert.
Archives HLRO, Bonar Law MSS, 33/2/30 · Mitchell L., NSW, George Ernest Morrison MSS · PRO, Ramsay MacDonald papers · University of Sheffield, W.A.S. Hewins MSS, 59/102–112
Likenesses Spy [L. Ward], cartoon, 1911, repro. in *Mayfair*

Crisp, Donald (1880–1974), actor and film director, was born on 27 July 1880 in Aberfeldy, Perthshire, the son of a country doctor. When he was ten he twice sang before Queen Victoria with the choir of St Paul's Cathedral, and he continued his choral career at Eton College and Oxford, where he also excelled at cross-country running. He enlisted in the 10th hussars on the outbreak of the Second South African War, seeing action at Kimberley, Ladysmith, and the Tugela Heights, after which he received the Distinguished Conduct Medal for his courage while wounded.

Crisp embarked in 1906 for New York, where his performance in a benefit concert persuaded John C. Reilly to cast him in the Broadway hit *Floradora*. During his year with the Fisher-Reilly opera company he toured Cuba and Mexico, as well as singing in the chorus of two musical plays, *The Silver Slipper* by Owen Hall and *San Toy* by Edward Morton. In 1907 he made his first appearance before the cameras in *The French Maid*, a saucy short which was produced by the Mutoscope company exclusively for its peep-show viewers. In the following year he served as George M. Cohan's stage manager on *The Yankee Prince* and *The Little Millionaire*, while also finding time to make movies for Pathé Frères.

Crisp joined American Biograph late in 1909 and began appearing regularly in the films of the pioneer director D. W. Griffith, most notably teaming with Mary Pickford in *The Adventures of Billy* (1911). Soon he was doubling as Griffith's assistant and made his own directorial début with *Her Father's Silent Partner* (1914). He also claimed to have directed Charlie Chaplin in *The Little Country House*, but Chaplin does not mention this in his meticulous autobiography. Crisp parted company with Griffith in 1915 after being denied an on-screen credit for directing the

impressive battle sequences in the controversial and immeasurably influential civil-war epic *The Birth of a Nation* (in which he also played General Grant). However, they would reunite for *Broken Blossoms* (1919), in which he gave a memorable display of malevolence as Lillian Gish's drunken tormentor, Battling Burrows.

Contracted to producer William H. Clune, Crisp developed into a steady if unremarkable director with such melodramas as *Ramona* (1916), in which he also acted under the pseudonym James Needham. But his career was briefly side-tracked towards the end of the First World War, when he was dropped into Russia by British intelligence to report on conditions in the wake of the 1917 revolution. He later held a commission with US army intelligence, while serving as a captain in the California state guard.

After the war Crisp joined Famous Players-Lasky, returning to Britain to direct *Beside the Bonnie Briar Bush* (1920). Adolph Zukor, the president of the company, was so impressed by his resolve and efficiency that he entrusted him with the foundation of studio facilities in London, Berlin, Paris, and Bombay. It was also in this period that Crisp was hired by the Bank of Italy (later the Bank of America) to advise on loans to film companies, a lucrative post he continued to hold well into old age.

On returning to Hollywood, Crisp abandoned Zukor to co-direct Buster Keaton's *The Navigator* (1924). He then collaborated twice with Douglas Fairbanks, as his director on *Don Q, Son of Zorro* (1925) and his co-star in *The Black Pirate* (1926). In 1927 he became the first director granted access to West Point for *Dress Parade* (1927). However, following *The Runaway Bride* (1930) he gave up directing in protest at the growing nepotism of investors. As he later complained: 'So many children wanted to be picture stars. And it was just like trying to make a picture without tools' (*Films and Filming*).

Having broken into talking pictures with *The River Pirate* (1928), Crisp re-established himself as an actor with *Svengali* (1931) and *Red Dust* (1932). He freelanced around Hollywood, often appearing in authoritarian or patriarchal roles, although he was also capable of unswerving professionalism and no-nonsense loyalty. He told one interviewer:

> I read scripts very carefully before I accept a role. The part suggested for one must be real, not a stuffed shirt. I demand that the character be true to life. That doesn't mean that he necessarily has to be sympathetic and lovable. Just believable and honest. (*Picturegoer*)

Although Crisp made *Mutiny on the Bounty* (1935) for MGM and co-starred with Katharine Hepburn in *The Little Minister* (1933) and *Mary of Scotland* (1935) at RKO, he was most effectively employed by Warner Bros., where he supported Errol Flynn on six occasions and Bette Davis on five, most notably as Francis Bacon in *The Private Lives of Elizabeth and Essex* (1939). Yet his greatest success came at Twentieth Century Fox, where he won the Oscar for best supporting actor for his work as Gwilym Morgan in John Ford's *How Green was my Valley* (1941).

Crisp was twice married. His first marriage to Marie

Stark ended in divorce in 1912. A second, in 1932 to the screenwriter Jane Murfin, also ended in divorce, in 1944. He divided his later years between travelling (he owned a holiday island in British Columbia), his extensive charitable activities, and acting. He came to specialize in wholesome family entertainment, often working with animals. In addition to a trio with Hollywood's favourite collie, including *Lassie Come Home* (1943), Crisp also demonstrated a softer side in *National Velvet* (1944), *A Dog of Flanders* (1959) and *Greyfriars Bobby* (1961), his second outing for Walt Disney, following *Pollyanna* (1960). He retired having completed *Spencer's Mountain* (1963), which brought his career total to about 450 films. He died in Van Nuys, California, on 25 May 1974, and was buried in the Wee Kirk churchyard of Forest Lawn, Glendale.   DAVID PARKINSON

Sources J. Vinson, *The international dictionary of film and filmmakers: actors & actresses* (1986) · *Variety* (29 May 1974) · *Daily Telegraph* (28 May 1974) · *The Times* (28 May 1974) · Warner Bros. publicity for *Oil for the lamps of China*, 1935, BFI [microfiche] · *Cinema* (July–Aug 1971) · *Films and Filming* (Dec 1960) · *Film Dope* (Oct 1975) · *Film Weekly* (4 March 1939) · *Picturegoer* (9 Dec 1944)
Likenesses photographs, Kobol collection, London · photographs, Ronald Grant archive, London · photographs, Huntley archive, London

Crisp, Sir Frank, first baronet (1843–1919), lawyer and microscopist, was born in London on 25 October 1843, the only child of John Shalders Crisp (1811–1896), a printer, and his first wife, Harriet (d. 1846), daughter of John Filby *Childs, the Congregationalist campaigner against church rates and owner of the printing business for whom her husband worked. His mother died when he was not yet three and he was brought up by his grandfather. He was educated at private schools, then at University College School. Shortly before leaving school he decided to take up law and, having been introduced to John Morris by his uncle, he was articled to the firm of Ashurst and Morris at the age of sixteen. Besides his duties with the firm, Crisp studied privately for the London University examinations; he matriculated in 1862, graduated BA in 1864 and LLB in 1865, and found time to take holidays in Switzerland. On 27 August 1867 he married Catherine (1845/6–1931), daughter of George Durrant Howes of St Mary Bungay, Suffolk; they had four sons and two daughters.

Crisp was admitted as a solicitor in 1869, with honours. As his legal reputation grew, he was brought into partnership in 1871, and in 1877 the name of the firm became Ashurst, Morris, Crisp & Co. His interest lay in company law, and he acted for such important clients as foreign railway companies and the Imperial Japanese Navy (in the purchase of its first British-built battleship). He wrote the contract for the expert who was to cleave the Cullinan diamond. He sat on two commissions for the revision of company law, and for his part in connection with the Companies (Consolidation) Act of 1906 he was knighted on 7 November 1907. Crisp was legal adviser to the Liberal Party and for this service he received a baronetcy on 5 February 1913.

Besides his town house in Lansdowne Road, Holland Park, Crisp acquired in 1895 the house and gardens of Friar Park, Henley-on-Thames. He was lavish in his hospitality, entertaining King Edward VII and Queen Alexandra, King George V, and other royalty during Henley week. Crisp's passion for landscape gardening preceded his purchase of Friar Park; he was a member of the Linnean Society from 1870 and in 1904 his wife was among the first women to be elected fellow. He served as vice-president and was treasurer from 1881 to 1905 and in 1919 received the society's Victoria medal of honour, its highest award. Over the years he was a generous benefactor, meeting various costs including that of the installation of electric light at the society's rooms in Burlington House and endowing awards for research. His garden was divided into the usual specialist areas, but the alpine garden was further embellished with a 20 foot high model of the Matterhorn, to scale, capped by a piece of rock from the original, and there were three highly decorated underground caverns. The public were admitted during the summer, with proceeds from ticket and guide sales going to charity. His weekend hobby was to gather material for a book on medieval gardening, which was seen through the press by his daughter after his death.

In parallel with his horticultural activities, Crisp joined the Royal Microscopical Society in 1870, was elected to its council in 1874, and was appointed one of its secretaries in 1878, holding that office until he took up the treasurership in 1890 before serving as vice-president between 1893 and 1897. From 1879 he laboured to expand and improve the society's journal, organized a supply of specimens for the meetings, and over the years donated more than one hundred books and various items of furniture. Aware that English scientists were failing to advance their understanding of the theoretical principles involved in microscopy and also the systematic investigation of microscopic phenomena, he set about translating the revised edition (1877) of the three-volume standard German text, *Das Mikroskop*, by C. Nägeli and S. Schwendener. A fire at the printers destroyed all but the first 374 pages and a few of the numerous woodcuts, but as Crisp was by this time occupied elsewhere, this partial account was issued in 1887 as *The Microscope in Theory and Practice*, with a second edition in 1892.

By 1890 Crisp had acquired a notable collection of microscopes and related material. But although he wrote description sheets for many of these, and had numerous engravings made, no complete list exists of instruments which passed through his hands. At his death Stevens auction house disposed of his holdings in five sales, but no proper catalogue was made for that event. It seems that between his death and the sales many instruments and their parts had become separated or were wrongly combined, and that the instruments were not accompanied by their descriptions. Crisp attended to his law work until a few days before his death, at Friar Park on 29 April 1919. He was buried at Henley parish church. His eldest son, Frank Morris Crisp (1872–1938), succeeded as second baronet.   ANITA McCONNELL

Sources J. Insley, 'Sir Frank Crisp, baronet (1843–1919)', *Microscopy*, 35 (Jan–June 1984), 10–24 · *The Times* (1 May 1919) · *The Times* (5

May 1919) · *Solicitors' Journal*, 63 (1918–19), 484 · B. D. Jackson, *Proceedings of the Linnean Society of London*, 131st session (1918–19), 49–51 · *WWW* · Burke, *Peerage* (1939) · m. cert. · d. cert.
Archives MHS Oxf., papers relating to his collection of microscopes
Likenesses Spy [L. Ward], caricature, repro. in *VF* (31 May 1890)
Wealth at death £179,213 12s. 9d.: administration with will, 24 July 1919, CGPLA Eng. & Wales

Crisp, Sir Nicholas, first baronet (*c.*1599–1666), merchant and royalist, was the son of Ellis Crisp (*d.* 1625) of Hammersmith (but descended from a Gloucestershire landed family), a prominent merchant, alderman, and sheriff of London in 1625, and his wife, Hester. Crisp married Anne Prescott, the daughter and heir of a London merchant, Edward Prescott, and she survived him. Although a member of the Merchant Adventurers' Company, and also trading to the Mediterranean, Crisp's main commercial interests were in the trades to India and Africa. Like his father he was a substantial stockholder in the East India Company. He served several year-long terms on its governing body from 1623 onwards and was an unsuccessful candidate for election as deputy governor in September 1635 and as governor in November 1641. From time to time he purchased large quantities of East India Company commodities, principally cloves and indigo, but also silks, pepper, elephant tusks, calicoes, cassia lignum, and shells. The shells were specially purchased on his behalf by the company's agents and intended for resale in west Africa, perhaps to finance the purchase of black slaves. Crisp's purchase of a hundred barrels of gunpowder from the company in September 1634 may have been connected with his activities as a shipowner, and on more than one occasion in the 1630s he operated under letters of marque. Over his long career he had interests in at least nine ships, either as sole or as part owner.

Crisp had been a prime mover in the breaking up of a Jacobean monopolistic company for trade to Guinea, and in the flotation of a new company in 1631 with a monopoly of trade between the Cape of Good Hope and Cape Blanco. Following an indifferent start, a spectacularly successful voyage in 1636 more than cleared the company's substantial debt. In May 1638 Maurice Thomson and Oliver Cloberry, merchants with extensive transatlantic and interloping interests, attempted to break into this trade. Crisp's company complained against this violation of its monopoly of transporting 'nigers' and the government intervened on its behalf. In the same month another group of merchants led by Crisp received a monopoly of trade with Morocco, dealing in, among other things, sugar and saltpetre.

In November 1638 Crisp and Roger Charnock were appointed as collectors of impositions in western ports. About the same time Crisp's concessionary interests were significantly diversified by his venture into the business of customs farming. During the summer and autumn of 1637 Lord Treasurer Juxon had been striving to arrange a merger between the existing syndicate of farmers of the great customs, dominated by the great financier Sir Paul Pindar, and another group, led by the courtly concessionaire Lord Goring and including Crisp. For a variety of reasons, not

Sir Nicholas Crisp, first baronet (*c.*1599–1666), by Cornelius Johnson

the least of which was Pindar's distrust of Goring and his proposals for management of the farm, the proposed merger fell through. Pindar and all but one of his partners withdrew, and a new lease was made to Goring and the remainder, to run from Christmas 1638 at an annual rent £12,500 above the existing rent of £160,000. The rent of the petty farm of duties on wines and currants was raised by the same amount above the existing £60,000, and the farm was let to a new syndicate which included Crisp's brother Samuel. However, in 1640, with Charles I in desperate need of loans, the two farms were amalgamated. Goring withdrew but Pindar reluctantly yielded to royal persuasion to join the consolidated syndicate, which now made a supreme effort to meet the royal demand for loans. Their post-Restoration claim that £253,000 was due to them on this account may be an overstatement and probably includes tallies directed on, but not honoured by, the syndicate.

Unlike Pindar, Crisp had not hitherto been a prominent individual lender to the crown, though he was associated with Abraham Chamberlain in a loan of around £8000 in 1625, and was repaid £12,000 of a sum of £15,000 due to him when he joined the king at Oxford in 1643. On new year's day 1640 Charles both recognized past services and anticipated Crisp's further services with the award of a knighthood. In November, Crisp's concessionary interests as customs farmer and East India Company magnate came together when he and another farmer, Sir John Nulls, were entrusted with the task of purchasing for the king more than £63,000 worth of pepper from the company, which was to be paid in arrears by tallies on the customs farm. These proved largely worthless since the farm was abrogated by parliament in May 1641.

Crisp had been elected to both the Short and Long parliaments as MP for Winchelsea, but his concessionary interests earned him the disapprobation of the latter, from which he was expelled on 2 February 1641 as a monopolist of redwood and African copperas ore. In addition, along with the other customs farmers, he had to find his share in the fine of £150,000 imposed by parliament in May as the price of compounding for their delinquency in collecting duties not voted by parliament. Following such experiences it is somewhat surprising to find him investing in 1642 in the parliamentary Sea Adventure to Ireland. Thus by the outbreak of the civil war Crisp's customs farming and monopolistic interests had been smashed, his Guinea Company was under attack, while his Irish adventure was to prove profitless, he being assigned, as he later complained, coarse and boggy land in return for his investment of £1000. Nevertheless, Clarendon describes him as 'a citizen of good wealth, great trade and an active spirited man' (Clarendon, *Hist. rebellion*, bk VII, para. 59) and extols his services in providing money, intelligence, and support for the king. For these purposes he had remained in London after the outbreak of civil war, but in January 1643 he was questioned by the House of Commons about £3700, which an intercepted letter revealed as owed to him 'for secrett service done for his Majestie' (BL, Harleian MS 164, fol. 277b), and he slipped away to Oxford, where he was warmly welcomed by the king. In the meantime his houses at Hammersmith and in Lime Street were ransacked, the latter ultimately being sold by the candle in 1645, and although in 1643 only £300 was found there, a further £5300 in gold and coin was discovered in the Tower and elsewhere in the city and confiscated, and his estates in the Guinea and East India companies sequestered. Despite his enforced absence from London, Crisp was the centrepiece of a royal plan in March 1643 to issue a commission of array authorizing him and named London royalists to organize a force to take over the capital. The failure of the enterprise was skilfully exploited by Pym to discredit the peace party at Westminster.

Thereafter Crisp's militant royalism found expression in a variety of activities, some unsuccessful, such as his apparent failure to effect a commission in November to raise an infantry regiment of 1500. At sea, however, he was more successful. On 6 May 1644 he was commissioned to equip fifteen warships at his own and his partner's expense and granted a tenth of any prizes taken by them. Operating from west country ports, he was in 1645 under orders to have ships ready for royal service such as the ferrying of troops from Ireland. He also played a very important part in shipping tin and wool to the continent, often on the queen's behalf, and sometimes bringing back arms and ammunition as a return cargo. He also held the important position of deputy controller-general of posts.

At the end of the first civil war in 1646 Crisp fled to France, but in May 1648 his son Ellis petitioned on his behalf that he should be allowed to compound on the terms of the Exeter articles, a request which was, rather

surprisingly, granted. During the Commonwealth he performed secret services such as raising money for the maintenance of the prince, with whom his real allegiance lay, not to mention clandestine support for royalist conspiracies such as the abortive plot of 1650 to land forces from the Scillies on the Cornish coast. On the eve of the Restoration he displayed his hand more openly. In May 1660 he signed the London royalists' declaration in favour of Monck and was selected as a member of the committee sent to meet Charles II at Breda. However, by July he was temporarily in prison for debt, much of which had been incurred in the service of Charles and his father, quite apart from royal debts due to the customs farmers of 1640, which, in Crisp's case (so he claimed), amounted to £30,000. Towards the end of 1653 and early in 1654 there had been a proposal that the government would offer security for the repayment of the money which the former farmers had lent to Charles I in 1640; but they had been unable to meet the stipulated condition that they should advance a further sum equivalent to the current amount of the royal debt to them, making the total debt around £552,000. These debts were ultimately satisfied after the Restoration by assignments on the newly farmed customs revenue, which the survivors of the farming syndicate, along with Sir John Shaw, undertook for five years from Michaelmas 1662, having previously, in June 1661, been appointed commissioners for customs.

In the meantime Crisp had stood unsuccessfully for election to the Cavalier Parliament as one of the MPs for the City of London. However, in other respects the Restoration brought the expected renewal of his fortunes with a golden shower of concessions, of which the revived customs farm was only one. These included the grants of the farm of the duties on sea coal (with Sir John Shaw) in June 1661; of the farm of the duties on spices imported from the Netherlands, in December 1662; of salaried collectorships of customs revenue in April 1661; of a lease of the Yorkshire alum works in 1665; and a contract to supply the king with bricks, in the manufacture of which Crisp acquired an unrivalled reputation for high quality. On 6 April 1665 Charles II honoured him with a baronetcy. He died in London on the following 26 February and was buried in the church of St Mildred, Bread Street. His heart was deposited in a monument to the memory of Charles I which he had erected in the chapel of his great house at Hammersmith, and on 18 June 1898 his other remains were exhumed and reinterred in the churchyard of St Paul, Hammersmith.   ROBERT ASHTON

Sources CSP dom., 1625–68 • State Papers, PRO, 1625–68 • CSP col., 1622–34 • E. B. Sainsbury, ed., *A calendar of the court minutes ... of the East India Company*, 11 vols. (1907–38) [vols. 1–2] • BL, Stowe MSS, 326 • W. A. Shaw, ed., *Calendar of treasury books*, 1–2, PRO (1904–5) • M. A. E. Green, ed., *Calendar of the proceedings of the committee for advance of money, 1642–1656*, 3 vols., PRO (1888) • M. A. E. Green, ed., *Calendar of the proceedings of the committee for compounding ... 1643–1660*, 5 vols., PRO (1889–92), 1643–60 • Declared Accounts, PRO, E351/642, 677; AO.3/297 • B. M. Gardiner, ed., 'A secret negociation with Charles the First, 1643–4', *Camden miscellany, VIII*, CS, new ser., 31 (1883) • Clarendon, *Hist. rebellion*, 3.41–2 • JHC • S. R. Gardiner,

History of the great civil war, 1642–1649, new edn, 1 (1893) • R. Ashton, *The crown and the money market, 1603–1640* (1960) • R. Ashton, *The city and the court, 1603–1643* (1979) • D. Brunton and D. H. Pennington, *Members of the Long Parliament* (1954) • J. Burke and J. B. Burke, *A genealogical and heraldic history of the extinct and dormant baronetcies of England, Ireland and Scotland*, 2nd edn (1841); repr. (1844) • J. P. Prendergast, *The Cromwellian settlement of Ireland*, 3rd edn (1922) • A. Kippis and others, eds., *Biographia Britannica, or, The lives of the most eminent persons who have flourished in Great Britain and Ireland*, 2nd edn, 3 (1784) • A. B. Beaven, ed., *The aldermen of the City of London, temp. Henry III–[1912]*, 2 vols. (1908–13) • K. N. Chaudhuri, *The English East India Company: the study of an early English joint-stock company* (1965) • R. Brenner, *Merchants and revolution: commercial change, political conflict, and London's overseas traders, 1550–1653* (1993) • *DNB* • will, PRO, PROB 11/319, sig. 42

Archives BL, Stowe MSS, corresp. with Sir John Harrison
Likenesses R. H. Cromek, line engraving, pubd 1785 (after unknown portrait), BM, NPG • C. Johnson, miniature, Institut Néerlandais, Paris, France, Fondation Custodia • C. Johnson, oils, Parham Park, West Sussex [*see illus.*]

Crisp, Quentin [*real name* Dennis Charles Pratt] (1908–1999), writer and actor, was born on 25 December 1908 at Wolverton, Egmont Road, Sutton, Surrey, the youngest of the four children of Spencer Charles Pratt, a feckless and frequently insolvent solicitor, and Frances Marion, *née* Phillips, a former nursery governess. In his autobiography, *The Naked Civil Servant*, he recounts that his childhood ambition was to be a chronic invalid. He enjoyed the drama of illness because it made him the centre of everyone's attention, especially that of the servants who came and went. He was indeed frail and sickly, to such an extent that he incurred his father's undisguised loathing. His more tolerant mother realized that Dennis was an unusual child, never more so than when she dressed him in green tulle to play a fairy in a school production of *A Midsummer Night's Dream*.

Pratt was educated at a local school in Sutton, and then won a scholarship to Denstone College, a boarding-school in Staffordshire. This grim establishment, where canings were regular and bullying an everyday business, provided him with the fortitude to cope with the privations he endured with such stoicism for much of his adult life. His attempts to charm the staff failed, though an Indian boy invited him to bed. This was the first of many unsatisfactory sexual encounters, establishing a pattern that continued until the 1940s, when he found romance and something like love in the arms of handsome American servicemen.

After taking a course in journalism at King's College, London, Pratt drifted onto the streets near Piccadilly Circus, where he earned a living as a prostitute for a year or so. As a 'dilly boy', he discovered that the men who availed themselves of his body (in doorways and dingy alleys) were coarse, brutal, and invariably drunk. There followed art courses at Battersea Polytechnic and in High Wycombe, but he soon decided he was happiest painting his face, his fingernails and—in summer when he wore sandals without socks—his toenails.

Pratt lived in a variety of furnished rooms before settling into 129 Beaufort Street, where Chelsea meets Fulham. The room he occupied on the first floor became famous for its squalor, since he had at an early age abandoned the housewifely duties of cleaning and dusting. It inspired Harold Pinter to write his first play, *The Room*. The only thing that needed to be washed and kept in good condition was himself. He was always beautifully turned out, in elegant cast-offs passed on by friends of both sexes. In 1931 he changed his name to Quentin Crisp.

Working variously as a map tracer, selling commercial art—he published a book on window dressing, *Colour in Display*, in 1938—and in the art department of a publishers, Crisp wrote a musical, a novel, and a play about Helen of Troy; all were unpublished and unperformed. Although he volunteered for military service in 1940 he was too obviously effeminate to be called up. In 1943 he wrote the anti-war *All this and Bevin too*, which was illustrated by Mervyn Peake. He found employment as an artist's model thanks to the shortage of young men during the Second World War. He made the best of his physical defects—he was skinny, but with a pronounced pot belly—and had the ability to remain still for long periods. He enjoyed posing for crucifixion scenes, and liked to tell new acquaintances that he made crucifixions his speciality. Because his employer was London county council he was effectively a civil servant, hence the title of the book that brought him fame.

Crisp was in his sixtieth year when *The Naked Civil Servant* (1968) came out. The publisher Tom Maschler, of Jonathan Cape, had commissioned it after hearing Crisp being interviewed on radio by Philip O'Connor. The book was praised for its elegance and wit, and for its absence of bitterness and self-pity. It told of a man determined to proclaim his effeminacy in the streets of London, not on the stage, where he would have been applauded and accepted. For three decades he was abused verbally and physically, and was frequently spat on for asserting his individuality. He had no desire to look like a woman, or even become one—*pace* the transsexual April Ashley—although he sometimes wondered whether a sex-change operation might have helped: 'I could have opened a knitting shop in Carlisle and my life would have been quiet and happy' (*The Independent*).

The rest of his life was not quiet, as a result of the television film of *The Naked Civil Servant*, written by Philip Mackie, directed by Jack Gold, and starring John Hurt. It took Mackie and Gold six years to find the money to make it, and when it appeared in 1975 it was an instant and justified success. Its subject was now fêted and celebrated, instead of being regarded as a freak and an outcast. People now wanted to shake his hand, to boast that they had met him in King's Road, Chelsea, the scene of some of his worst humiliations. His book *How to have a Life Style* was published in the same year as the release of the film.

In 1978 Crisp became the star of his own one-man show, *An Evening with Quentin Crisp*. The formula was simple: he reminisced about his life and times for the first half, and answered questions from the audience in the second. Its success meant that at the age of sixty-nine he achieved his ambition of visiting America, which for him meant New York. He was radiantly happy in Manhattan, where he was treated with the respect and tolerance so long denied him. Three years later he returned to New York, staying in the Chelsea Hotel, and after achieving resident alien status he moved into a tenement room on the lower East Side, which quickly became as surreally filthy as the one in Beaufort Street.

Crisp continued to perform on stage and off, and to write. When not being taken to dinner by his host of admirers, he lived on a diet of Guinness and Complan. He played Queen Elizabeth I in Sally Potter's film of Virginia Woolf's *Orlando* (1992), and in the following year he was a party guest in *Philadelphia*, and invited by Channel 4 to deliver an alternative queen's speech. He also starred in the less well known *To Wong Foo, Thanks for Everything! Julie Newmar* (1995) and *Homo Heights* (1998). He provided film criticism for the magazine *Christopher Street*, and contributed to *New York Native*. He wrote a Gothic novel, *Chog* (1979), about sexual repression and bestiality; *How to Become a Virgin* (1981), a second volume of autobiography; and, best of all, *Resident Alien* (1996), a selection from his New York diaries. The literary finesse that informs these books was not inspired by the work of other writers, since Crisp on his own admission did not enjoy reading. He spent his formative years in the cinema, delighting in the often preposterous dialogue of Hollywood films. His rather manicured style is rooted in the lines Miss Garbo, Miss Dietrich, and Miss Crawford (as he always politely referred to them) had to say to their various screen lovers and victims.

Days before embarking on a British tour of his one-man show Quentin Crisp died, on 21 November 1999. The venue was a suburb of Manchester, not his beloved lower East Side. The hated English had claimed him again. His ashes, however, were scattered over Broadway, Manhattan. Crisp was unfailingly courteous and sweet-tempered, though pretentiousness of any kind inspired him to exquisitely phrased sarcasm. He was his own creation, and by being such did much more for tolerance than many militants. The unique human being who disposed of Dennis Pratt ('as my name was before I dyed it') and wore mascara, lipstick, and powder in order to be Quentin Crisp, will be remembered for that grand assumption.

PAUL BAILEY

Sources Q. Crisp, *The naked civil servant* (1968) · *The Independent* (22 Nov 1999) · personal knowledge (2004) · b. cert. · d. cert.
Likenesses M. Evans, oils, *c*.1943, NPG · A. M. Parkin, etching and drypoint, 1978, NPG · D. Gamble, colour print, 1988, NPG · E. Barber, photograph, repro. in Crisp, *Naked civil servant* (Flamingo, 1985), cover · C. Beaton, photograph · A. Macpherson, photograph, repro. in *Guardian Weekend* (12 Dec 1998) · photographs, Hult. Arch.

Crisp, Samuel (1707–1783), playwright, was baptized on 14 November 1707, at Hurst, Berkshire. His mother was Florence, *née* Williams (1672?–1720); his father was Samuel Crisp (1671?–1718), a London merchant who owned property in three counties and was a grandson of Tobias Crisp

Samuel Crisp (1707–1783), by Edward Francis Burney, 1782

(1600–1643), the antinomian theologian. Samuel and Florence married in 1696 and had five daughters; young Samuel was a late and only son; he lost both parents by the age of thirteen.

Crisp entered Eton College in 1718; it is not known when he left. As the residuary legatee of quite wealthy parents, he enjoyed the leisured life of a virtuoso and dilettante; there is no evidence of his ever following a profession or trade. He studied the fine arts and music for some years in Italy and returned to England in the summer of 1740, where he associated with the aristocratic connoisseur and gambler Fulke Greville (*c*.1717–*c*.1804), at whose house in the autumn of 1747 he met Greville's young protégé Charles Burney (1726–1814), the musicologist. Burney later testified that Crisp was 'a man of infinite taste in all the fine Arts, an excellent Scholar … possessed of a fine tenor voice' (*Memoirs of Dr Charles Burney*, 70), and that Crisp and Greville were the 'travelled and heterodox gentlemen' who taught Burney to appreciate modern Italian music (*Letters of Dr Charles Burney*, 328).

Crisp began a translation of the *Vita* of Benvenuto Cellini, planned a biography of Philippe de Comines, and wrote poems, but his only literary work to come before the public in his lifetime was *Virginia*, a tragedy in blank verse based on the story of Appius and Virginia. David Garrick accepted the play reluctantly, under pressure from the countess of Coventry, but improved it with cuts, and wrote and delivered an amusing prologue which lightly mocks Crisp, 'stiff in classic knowledge' (l. 5); Garrick also wrote the comic epilogue spoken by Susanna Maria Cibber. Thanks to their acting and popularity *Virginia*, which opened at Drury Lane Theatre on 25 February 1754, had a moderately successful run of eleven nights, with average nightly takings of £160 and three author's benefit performances. Though Crisp made alterations for a revival, advertised for April 1755, the play was never acted again. Crisp blamed Garrick for this. The printed edition of *Virginia* (1754) was dedicated to the sixth earl of Coventry and his countess, and was damned in the *Monthly Review* (10, 1754, 225–31).

At this time Crisp was living in Hampton, Middlesex, but shortly afterwards, with his inherited fortune dwindling alarmingly, he gave up the Hampton house, sold his collection of books, musical instruments, artworks, and antiquities, and joined his ruined friend Christopher Hamilton at Chessington Hall, Surrey, a decayed rambling mansion said to date from 1520, set among muddy fields and difficult of access. The two men shared household expenses and when, after Hamilton's death in 1759, his unmarried sister Sarah (1705–1797) set up a boarding-house in the hall, Crisp became her first boarder. He called himself Lem and affected to share Gulliver's opinion that men are yahoos, though in reality he remained kindly and sociable.

After an intermittent correspondence Charles Burney and Crisp met again in London in 1763 and renewed a close friendship for the remainder of Crisp's life, during which time Chessington Hall became a regular country retreat for Burney and members of his family. Fanny Burney (1752–1840) said Chessington 'is a place of peace, ease, freedom & cheerfulness, & all its inhabitants are good humoured & obliging—& my dear Mr Crisp alone would make it, to us, a Paradise' (*Early Journals and Letters*, 1.164). She and her father wrote some of their best work in retirement there: by contrast, Crisp published only a review of Charles Burney's *Italian Tour* in the *Critical Review* (1771) and perhaps reviews of Burney's *German Tour* (1773) and *History* (1776) in the same periodical. Crisp's portrait was painted at Chessington in 1782 by Charles Burney's nephew Edward Francisco Burney.

Crisp enjoyed a particularly close relationship with Fanny, forty-five years his junior: he became her dear second 'Daddy' while she was his dear 'Fannikin'. She idolized him and regularly sent him long instalments of her brilliant journals, receiving in reply 'most delightful long, & incomparably clever Letters' (*Early Journals and Letters*, 1.319), giving frank advice on her conduct, deportment, marriage prospects, and finances, as well as her writings. With her father's help Crisp persuaded her in 1779 to abandon her comedy 'The Witlings', because its satire of bluestockings might cause resentment and retaliation, but he enthusiastically encouraged her 'journalizing' and novel-writing. Some of her *Cecilia* (1782) was written at Chessington. Crisp was in some respects the original of Mr Villars in her *Evelina* (1778) and of Sir Jaspar Herrington in her *The Wanderer* (1814).

During the last twenty years of his life Crisp suffered from gout and rheumatism. His death, on 24 April 1783, was caused, it was said, by gout extending to the head and breast (d'Arblay, 2.315); he was buried on 2 May, leaving Charles Burney and Fanny full of grief. Charles wrote his obituary in the *Gentleman's Magazine* and the long verse eulogy on his monument in Chessington church. Crisp never married. He is not to be confused with Samuel Crisp (1705–1784), 'the Greenwich traveller', described in the *Gentleman's Magazine* (54, 1784, 73).   JAMES SAMBROOK

Sources *The early journals and letters of Fanny Burney*, ed. L. E. Troide, 3 vols. (1988–94) • *Memoirs of Dr Charles Burney, 1726–1769*, ed. S. Klima, G. Bowers, and K. S. Grant (1988) • F. A. Crisp, *Family of Crispe: genealogical memoranda* (1882–97), 1.53–5, 68–9, 100; 4.43, 65 • *Memoirs of Dr Burney* (1832), 1.47–55, 172–84, 207–10; 2.315–24 • *Diary and letters of Madame D'Arblay (1778–1840)*, ed. C. Barrett and A. Dobson, 6 vols. (1904–5) • *Burford papers, being the letters of Samuel Crisp to his sister at Burford*, ed. W. H. Hutton (1905) • *The early diary of Frances Burney, 1768–1778*, ed. A. R. Ellis, rev. edn, 2 vols. (1907) • *The journals and letters of Fanny Burney (Madame D'Arblay)*, ed. J. Hemlow and others, 12 vols. (1972–84) • G. W. Stone, ed., *The London stage, 1660–1800*, pt 4: 1747–1776 (1962), 411–18, 481 • *The letters of Dr Charles Burney*, ed. A. Ribeiro, 1 (1991) • A. I. Macnaghten, 'An Englishman in Italy, 1738–1740', *N&Q*, 193 (1948), 559–62 • *VCH Surrey*, 3.265 • *The letters of David Garrick*, ed. D. M. Little and G. M. Kahrl, 3 (1963), 939–40 • Walpole, *Corr.*, 35.167 • R. A. Austen-Leigh, ed., *The Eton College register, 1698–1752* (1927), 90 • C. Burney, *GM*, 1st ser., 53 (1783), 452 • J. Hemlow, J. M. Burgess, and A. Douglas, *A catalogue of the Burney family correspondence, 1749–1878* (1971) • IGI

Archives BL, corresp. and MSS, Add. MS 47463 • NYPL, letters | BL, corresp. with C. A. Burney, Egerton MS 3700A, fols. 135–49 • BL, corresp. with F. Burney, Egerton MS 3694, fols. 2–136 • BL, letters to Mrs Sheppard, Add. MS 47458, fols. 72–81b • Essex RO, letters to T. Payne and his daughter Sarah • Yale U., letters to C. Burney

Likenesses E. F. Burney, oils, 1782 [*see illus.*] • print (after E. F. Burney), NPG; repro. in J. Hemlow, *The history of Fanny Burney* (1958), facing p. 16

Crisp, Stephen (1628–1692), Quaker activist and writer, was born in Colchester, the son of Stephen Crisp (d. 1671), a clothier, and his wife, Elizabeth (d. 1666). Crisp was religiously inclined from an early age. In an account of his life published posthumously he reveals how at the age of nine or ten he sought 'the Power of *God* with great diligence' in order to obtain power over his 'Corruptions'. By the age of eleven he was, he says, an assiduous hearer of the 'best Ministers' (Crisp, *Memorable Account*, 4–5). The parental household in particular probably exercised a great influence over the young Crisp: his father and mother were presented at the church courts for repeated failure to attend communion, an offence for which they were subsequently excommunicated. After visiting several separatist congregations Crisp had joined the Baptists by the age of eighteen, and in 1648 he married Dorothy (1625–1683). Together they had two children, both of whom died of the plague in Colchester in 1665–6.

Crisp was converted to the Quakers in 1655 by James Parnel, followed by his parents and wife. In 1659 he resolved to take up service in the Quaker ministry—a move which was initially opposed by his wife and family—and became an eloquent, well informed, and effective proponent of Quakerism. His ministry was a practical one: he helped widows and the needy members of the society, and often acted as the scribe when Friends made their wills (extending this role to include non-Quakers as well). He undertook a number of private family visits among Colchester Friends in order to raise their understanding as to what were the implications of following the Quaker faith. His missionary zeal was striking, even when in later years his body was infirm through ill health and constant travelling. His first calling in 1659 took him to Scotland and back by way of Lincolnshire, Yorkshire, Westmorland, Lancashire, and London. In subsequent years he was to be in particular a frequent visitor to the north, evangelizing there in 1663, 1667, 1671, 1678, and 1681. He travelled widely in England, including several visits to the west country, and extensively around his native East Anglia. His missionary efforts sometimes met with abuse, as at York in 1659 and Cambridge in 1660, and he suffered several periods of imprisonment, most notably in his own county of Essex in 1662 where he was gaoled for organizing an illegal meeting at Harwich, and in Colchester the following year.

What marks Crisp out as an important figure to historians of Quakerism is that his life—and prodigious output of published works—spanned the first and second generations of the movement. Like the earliest Friends, Crisp denounced the clergy as 'greedy dumb dogs', especially for what he considered was their unjustified reliance on tithes and scriptures, and their hostility to the Friends' doctrine of the 'inner light' (S. Crisp, *A Word of Reproof to the Teachers of the World*, 1658, 69). However, with the consolidation of the movement other issues assumed a great importance and Crisp was concerned more to urge members to follow without question the central tenets of Quaker faith. The most significant of his works in this regard was *An Epistle to Friends Concerning the Present and succeeding Times* (1666), which encouraged purity in language, unity among Friends, and preparedness for loss and suffering on behalf of the faith. When in 1666 the 'First yearly meeting epistle' was issued by senior Quakers, Crisp was one of the signatories. His *Plain Path-Way Opened to the Simple-Hearted* (1668) was another heartfelt plea to Quakers to remain loyal to the movement's truth. The most printed of his writings, however, was the Bunyanesque *Short History of a Long Travel, from Babylon to Bethel*, first published posthumously in 1711 and which appeared in at least seventeen subsequent editions. His sermons, taken down in shorthand by his listeners, were also published after his death.

Although Crisp played a significant role in the development of the Quaker movement in England his most notable contribution was probably his role in the planting and growth of the Quaker faith in the Low Countries, building on the initial missionary work of the Quaker William Caton. He first visited the Low Countries in 1663, and by 1670 had made three separate trips. Over time his preaching, writings, and organizational skills were to make a significant impact. In the late 1660s he developed the Quaker meeting system for good order and government, and in the early 1670s he was responsible for the expulsion of a number of 'apostate' Friends from Quaker communities in Friesland, Haarlem, and Leiden. Crisp became a central figure in the society in the Low Countries, travelling there from England during most years of the 1670s, and again in 1680 and 1683. Not only did he master Dutch sufficiently to preach in it but he also had a dozen of his works published in Dutch during the 1670s,

mostly exhortations to Friends, attacks on persecuting officials, or ripostes to rival religious groups such as the Baptists. He held a particular affection for Friesland. He also made a number of trips further up the Rhine, visiting Heidelberg in 1669 and Hamburg in 1670.

In 1685 Crisp married a Dutch friend, Gertruid, or Gertrude, Derricks (d. 1687), who was the sister of Caton's widow, in Colchester. In 1691 he was present among those Quakers who attended Fox in the days before the Quaker leader's death. Crisp himself died in London in 1692, and was interred in the Quaker burial-ground at Bunhill Fields. His last words expressed a confidence that he had fulfilled God's mission: 'I have a full Assurance of my Peace with god in Jesus Christ, my integrity and uprightness of heart is known to the Lord' (Tomkins, 1.112). He left money for the help of the parish poor in St Buttolph's, Colchester.   ADRIAN DAVIES

Sources S. Crisp, *A memorable account of the Christian experiences, gospel labours, travel and sufferings of that ancient servant of Christ, Stephen Crisp* (1694) · W. I. Hull, *Benjamin Furly and the rise of Quakerism in Amsterdam* (1941) · C. Fell Smith, *Stephen Crisp and his correspondents, 1657–1692* (1892) · A. Davies, *The Quakers in English society, 1655–1725* (2000) · S. Crisp, *Several sermons or declarations of Mr. Stephen Crisp*, 2 vols. (1693) · S. H. G. Fitch, *Colchester Quakers* [1962] · J. Tomkins, *Piety promoted in a collection of the dying sayings of many of the people called Quakers*, ed. W. Evans and T. Evans, 1 (Philadelphia, 1854) · will, 1692, Essex RO, Chelmsford, D/ACR 16/15 · Quaker register of births, marriages, and burials, RS Friends, Lond. · H. Barbour, 'Crisp, Stephen', Greaves & Zaller, *BDBR*, 1.190–91
Archives RS Friends, Lond., letters and treatises · University of Essex, Colchester, corresp.

Crisp, Tobias (1600–1643), Church of England clergyman and stimulator of religious controversy, was born in Bread Street, London, the third son of Alderman Ellis Crisp (d. 1625) and his wife, Hester, and younger brother of Sir Nicholas *Crisp (c.1599–1666). After attending Eton College as a scholar he matriculated from Christ's College, Cambridge, in 1621 and graduated BA in 1624. He married at Merton, Surrey, on 11 April 1626, Mary, daughter of Rowland Wilson, a London merchant, and sister of Rowland *Wilson (bap. 1613, d. 1650). Crisp was incorporated in February 1627 at Balliol College, Oxford, and proceeded MA the same month. That year he became rector of Newington, Surrey. Two years later he was presented to the rectory of Brinkworth, Wiltshire. There he became famous for his hospitality, entertaining up to 100 guests at a time, and raised a large family. Although apparently uninterested in further preferment, in 1638 he proceeded BD from Oxford and DD from Cambridge.

At the outbreak of civil war Crisp inclined to the parliamentarianism of his brother-in-law Wilson rather than to the royalism of his brother Nicholas. In August 1642 he returned to London 'to avoid the insolence of the cavalier soldiers', according to John Gill, his first biographer. He preached diligently twice on Sunday, and then repeated the material to others at home in the evening. According to his son and editor, Samuel, his diligence cost him his life. He died of smallpox on 27 February 1643, and was buried in the family vault in St Mildred, Bread Street. He was survived by Mary, who died in 1673, and by eleven of his thirteen children.

Crisp's sermons were published posthumously from shorthand notes in a series of volumes, all with the title *Christ Alone Exalted*. Three of the volumes were published between 1643 and 1648 with introductions by Robert Lancaster. A complete version, prepared by Crisp's son Samuel, contains extra sermons published from manuscript authenticated by a number of prominent nonconformist divines. Together with a life by Dr Gill and an engraved portrait dated 1643, it appeared in 1690. It was with these publications that Crisp's reputation became established. For the next fifty years, and well into the eighteenth century, his name became synonymous with the doctrines preached in the sermons—free grace, or antinomianism—though Lancaster denied that 'we' were antinomian. These are the doctrines of the radical Reformation, potentially revolutionary, and particularly associated with the preaching of the army chaplains William Dell and John Saltmarsh from 1643 onwards. While the Westminster assembly regarded both Crisp and Lancaster as heterodox, Crisp himself seems to have been a quiet, conscientious, and unrevolutionary figure, moving gradually towards an emphasis on the absolute, unconditional consequences of Christ's atonement. According to his son Samuel, his targets were 'Grotian Divinity'; he was unhappy with the Arminianism of John Goodwin (only just emerging as Crisp died) as well as Socinians and papists because 'all three jostle out Christ's righteousness'. If Christ alone has satisfied the demands of the law, argued Crisp, the way man behaves is the consequence of salvation, not the way to it. That move, it was argued at the time, paved the way for the Anabaptists and Ranters. Crisp himself preached one sermon entitled 'Christian liberty no licentious doctrine', anticipating such objections.

In the 1690s 'Crispianism' again became an object of controversy in nonconformist congregations and was blamed by some for the failure of the London congregations to unite. Crisp's works were republished a number of times in the eighteenth century, where the distance between Crisp and the more revolutionary antinomians had become more obvious. However, in 1773, an eight-page pamphlet of extracts, with the title *Doctor Crisp's ghost … being a bridle for antinomians and a whip for Pelagians and Arminian-Methodists*, showed that Crisp was still a recognizable figure, useful for a controversy that still reverberated over 100 years after his death.

ROGER POOLEY

Sources J. Gill, preface, in T. Crisp, *Christ alone exalted*, 4th edn (1791) · J. F. Maclear, 'Tobias Crisp', Greaves & Zaller, *BDBR*, 191–2 · G. Huehns, *Antinomianism in English history* (1951) · Wood, *Ath. Oxon.*, 2nd edn · Venn, *Alum. Cant.*, 1/1 · Foster, *Alum. Oxon.* · *IGI* [parish register of Merton, Surrey]
Likenesses engraving, 1643, repro. in T. Crisp, *Christ alone exalted* (1690) · A. Soly, line engraving, BM, NPG; repro. in T. Crisp, *Sermons* (1696)

Crispin, Edmund. *See* Montgomery, (Robert) Bruce (1921–1978).

Crispin, Gilbert (*c*.1045–1117/18), theologian and abbot of Westminster, was the son of William Crispin and Eva, sister of Amaury (III), lord of Montfort l'Amaury. On his father's side he came of an outstanding Norman family, descended from another Gilbert Crispin, who may have been the grandson of Duke Richard (I) (*d.* 996) and who was the first patron of the abbey of Bec. William Crispin, who was made vicomte of the Vexin by Duke William (II) (*d.* 1087), held lands in the region of Bec, was an active friend and patron of Herluin (*d.* 1078), its first abbot, and himself retired to end his days as a monk there. William's wife, with two of her friends, thereupon took up residence near the abbey. Gilbert Crispin the younger was given to Bec at an early age—he is fifty-ninth on the roll of its monks. In a letter of the 1070s Anselm celebrates the close ties between the Crispins and Bec, describing Gilbert's mother as thinking of Anselm as her son, and her children as treating him as their own elder brother. Other Crispins would later be associated with Bec. Another Gilbert appears on the Bec roll about 1112, while Miles Crispin (*d. c.*1150) was precentor of the abbey and author of a life of Lanfranc.

Gilbert Crispin seems to have been one of the most notable of the scholars trained at Bec by Anselm, who wrote to congratulate him when he was made abbot of Westminster about 1085 at the wish of Archbishop Lanfranc (*d.* 1089). Eadmer describes how, early in Lent 1108, Crispin was sent to discuss with Anselm the consecration of Hugh of Fleury as abbot of St Augustine's, Canterbury. Although Anselm had asked Lanfranc if he might have his former pupil back, Crispin remained at Westminster for over thirty years until his death, which took place in either 1117 or 1118. There is in fact a problem about this date, because Crispin's *Disputation with a Jew* is dedicated to Alexander, bishop of Lincoln (*d.* 1148), who received that office only in 1123, but it may be postulated that this is the result of interference by a later editorial hand.

Gilbert Crispin was the fourth abbot of Westminster. It had not been a distinguished house until Edward the Confessor chose to be buried there, rebuilt the church, and provided handsome endowments. (As abbot, Crispin seems to have been instrumental in having Edward's body exhumed; it was said to be found to be free of decay.) There was evidently expansion in the late eleventh century, with the foundation of new cells in such places as Great Malvern, Worcestershire, Hurley, Berkshire, and Sudbury, Suffolk. Crispin's abbacy also saw the extension of the buildings of the abbey—cloisters, a dormitory, and perhaps a refectory were built. The abbot himself began to need a hall and a kitchen to enable him to discharge his duties of hospitality, and this too may be a mark of the success of Crispin's abbacy.

This new 'high profile' of the abbey had results which were almost certainly instrumental in shaping the direction of Crispin's writings. The building operations needed finance, and the raising of the necessary money may well have brought Gilbert into active contact with the Jewish community. It was a real Jew with whom he held the discussions that form the basis of his *Disputation with a Jew*.

There are contemporary parallels. William of Malmesbury describes a disputation held in London between Jews and bishops under the patronage of William II.

The *Disputation with a Jew* is of particular interest, not only because it was Crispin's most finished and most widely disseminated work, but also because it can be linked with the writing of Anselm's *Cur Deus homo*. Anselm stayed quietly with Crispin at Westminster in the winter of 1092–3, during the period when the replacement for Lanfranc as archbishop of Canterbury was under discussion. Issues raised by the theology of the incarnation in debates with the Jews are central to Anselm's solution of the question why God became man, for it was the Jews above all in Anselm's day who were shaping a challenge to Christian orthodoxy on the matter.

Crispin thus became one of surprisingly few pupils of Anselm to make his mark as a theologian in his own right. He was also a good Latin stylist—not up to Anselm's high standard, but perhaps influenced by him in this as in much else. He had begun to write, while he was still at Canterbury, a treatise on the monastic life which he sent to a fellow monk, who is likely to be the Ralph d'Escures who was first a monk and then abbot of Séez, became bishop of Rochester in succession to Gundulf (another former monk of Bec) in 1108, and succeeded Anselm as archbishop of Canterbury in 1114. A second treatise followed, also sent to Ralph d'Escures. It discusses the problem of the identities of the three Marys of the gospels. Ralph d'Escures was already abbot of Séez at the time when Crispin sent him this. Of *Disputation with a Jew*, involving a Jewish scholar from Mainz (which can be dated about the time of Crispin's winter conversations with Anselm, but which Crispin certainly revised and polished subsequently), over thirty manuscripts survive. This was no doubt partly because it belongs to a genre which had some contemporary popularity. But it was drawn upon in its own right by theologians throughout the twelfth century.

Crispin wrote a companion piece, a *Disputatio* with a gentile (*gentilis*), who represents the position of the pagan philosophers. It was not as easy to meet with such a person in contemporary London as with an educated Jew. Crispin describes a philosophical debating society where a discussion takes place in which some are prepared to take the position of a man who will accept only what appeals to his reason. Crispin seems also to have written a dialogue, *De angelo perdito*, on the fall of Satan. This must have been inspired by Anselm's *De casu diaboli*. It preserves additional ideas, which he may have taken from Anselm's teaching at Bec, but also reflects topics of current debate at the school of Laon. A *De spiritu sancti* was sent to Anselm with a request for a solution to the final question raised by the 'pupil' in the dialogue. The *De altaris sacramento* (probably the work listed as Crispin's in the oldest catalogue of the Bec Library under the title *De veritate corporis et sanguinis domini*), includes a discussion of the validity of simoniacal consecration. This subject is taken up and developed in Crispin's *De simoniacis*. A *De anima* is also likely to be his. It is of particular interest as it deals with a subject Anselm

had wished to write on. Also extant are a sermon for Septuagesima and some verses, including a verse letter written to Anselm in exile in 1105, begging the shepherd to return to his sheep. Late in his life, certainly after the death of Anselm in 1109, Crispin completed a life of Herluin, the first abbot of Bec, which is also an important source for the life of Lanfranc; it is less detailed on Anselm, but perhaps Crispin deliberately left to Eadmer the task of describing Anselm's period at Bec.

For several of these works the only direct evidence of Crispin's authorship is their inclusion in a unique twelfth-century manuscript of his writings, now BL, Add. MS 8166. But, taken as a whole, the corpus is remarkably coherent and consistent. It is the work of an author with a lively interest in contemporary theological controversies, who wants to make his own contribution to them. The treatises are profoundly influenced by the method Anselm developed at Bec. Crispin had nothing like Anselm's stature, but he was certainly an able theologian in his own right and a man who liked to keep up with and contribute to the lively scene of contemporary debate in England and northern France.   G. R. EVANS

Sources R. W. Southern, *Saint Anselm: a portrait in a landscape* (1990) · D. Knowles, C. N. L. Brooke, and V. C. M. London, eds., *The heads of religious houses, England and Wales*, 1: 940–1216 (1972) · J. A. Robinson, *Gilbert Crispin, abbot of Westminster: a study of the abbey under Norman rule* (1911) · *The works of Gilbert Crispin, abbot of Westminster*, ed. A. S. Abulafia and G. R. Evans (1986) · B. Harvey, *Westminster Abbey and its estates in the middle ages* (1977) · W. R. Lethaby, *Westminster Abbey and the king's craftsmen* (1906) · *De nobili Crispinorum genere* [PL158] · R. W. Southern, 'St Anselm and his English pupils', *Medieval and Renaissance Studies*, 1 (1941), 3–34 · G. R. Evans, 'Gilbert Crispin on the eucharist, a monastic postscript to Lanfranc and Berengar', *Journal of Theological Studies*, new ser., 31 (1980), 28–43
Archives BL, Add. MS 8166

Cristall, Anne Batten (*bap.* 1769), poet, was born in Penzance and baptized there on 7 December 1769, the elder daughter and second of the four children of Alexander Cristall (*d.* 1802) of Arbroath in Scotland, a mariner and later maker of sails, masts, and blocks with yards at Fowey and Penzance in Cornwall and later at Rotherhithe, and his second wife, Elizabeth, the daughter of John Batten, a Penzance merchant. Alexander Cristall already had two sons by the time of his second marriage. When Anne was young, the family moved to London and later to Blackheath. Alexander Cristall apparently had a jealous disposition and family life was unpleasant when he was ashore. He also had a 'dread of the arts', but his wife was a 'woman of education and taste' (Roget, 179); she paid school fees from a small independent income of her own and appears to have had a significant influence on the artistic development of her children. Much of what is known about Anne Cristall's life is due to the modest fame enjoyed by her brother Joshua *Cristall (*bap.* 1768, *d.* 1847), who became a founder member of the Society of Painters in Water Colours in 1804, although he seems to have suffered financial difficulties all his life. Anne and Joshua were very close. They 'studied together as children, and hand in hand did they daily walk to London and back for their schooling when the family lived at Rotherhithe' (ibid., 179).

Anne Cristall evidently became a schoolteacher but seems, to some extent, to have been financially dependent on Joshua. By the late 1780s she had become a friend of Mary Wollstonecraft and her sister Everina, and there are several references to her in Wollstonecraft's correspondence. In March 1790, Wollstonecraft wrote to Joshua: 'I know that you earnestly wish to be the friend and protector of your amiable sister and hope no inconsiderate act or thoughtless mode of conduct will add to her cares—for her comfort very much depends on you' (*Collected Letters*, 188). Elsewhere, Wollstonecraft refers to Anne's 'tender affectionate heart' (ibid., 196), and in a letter to Joshua dated 9 December 1790 wrote: 'I fear her situation is very uncomfortable. I wish she could obtain a little more strength of mind. I am afraid she gives way to her feelings more than she ought to' (Roget, 184).

In 1795 Anne Cristall's *Poetical Sketches*, published by Joseph Johnson, appeared. Subscribers included both Wollstonecrafts, Anna Letitia Barbauld, John Aikin, Amelia Alderson (later Opie), Samuel Rogers, Mary Hays, and George Dyer, suggesting a fairly distinguished circle of intellectual acquaintances. The poems were often melancholic pieces and mostly concerned with nature. Contemporary reviewers criticized her technical imperfections but praised her 'genius, and Warmth of imagination' (P. Feldman, ed., *British Women Poets of the Romantic Era: an Anthology*, 1997, 214). The poet George Dyer became a close friend, and in a letter to Mary Hays suggested a collaborative effort—a *'poetical novel'*—between the two female writers. He praised Anne Cristall's 'very fine talent for poetry: one or two of her songs are, I think, as beautiful as any I know' (Wedd, 238–9). In 1797 she was introduced to Robert Southey, who declared in a letter to Joseph Cottle, dated 13 March 1797: 'the literary circles say she has no genius; but she has genius, Joseph, or there is no truth in physiognomy' (*Life and Correspondence*, 1.306). In May 1799 Southey wrote that Dyer had promised him a piece by Anne Cristall for his *Annual Anthology* (1799–1800), but she appears not to have contributed.

Very little is known about Anne Cristall's later life, and she appears to have dropped out of intellectual circles after the 1790s. She seems not to have married and is listed under her own name in *A Biographical Dictionary of the Living Authors of Great Britain and Ireland* (1816). In 1841 Joshua Cristall returned to London, where his household consisted of 'two lady wards, between whom and himself there existed a strong attachment' (Finch, 67). These were presumably Anne and another sister, Elizabeth, who died in 1851, aged about eighty. There is no record of Anne Cristall's date of death.   LEYA LANDAU

Sources *The life and correspondence of Robert Southey*, ed. C. C. Southey, 6 vols. (1849–50), vol. 1, pp. 305–6; vol. 2, p. 16 • J. L. Roget, *A history of the 'Old Water-Colour' Society*, 1 (1891), 178–91 • *Collected letters of Mary Wollstonecraft*, ed. R. M. Wardle (1979) • E. Finch, *Memorials of F. O. Finch* (1865), 67–75 • A. F. Wedd, ed., *The love-letters of Mary Hays* (1925), 238–9 • R. Lonsdale, ed., *Eighteenth-century women poets: an Oxford anthology* (1989) • W. G. S. Dyer, *Joshua Cristall* (1959) • W. G. S. Dyer, *Joshua Cristall*, rev. edn (1962) • B. Taylor, *Joshua Cristall* *(1768–1847)* (1975), 11–30 [exhibition catalogue, V&A, February–April 1975] • [J. Watkins and F. Shoberl], *A biographical dictionary of the living authors of Great Britain and Ireland* (1816) • DNB

Cristall, Joshua (*bap.* **1768**, *d.* **1847**), watercolour painter, was baptized at St Botolph, Aldgate, London, on 22 April 1768, the eldest of the four children of Captain Alexander Cristall (*c.*1722–1802), mariner, and his second wife, Elizabeth Batten (1745–1801), daughter of John Batten (1709–1792), merchant, of Madron, near Penzance, in Cornwall. His father, a Scot from Monifieth near Dundee, was master of a coastal vessel trading from London. He already had two sons: John, with his first wife; and Alexander, who was born in the year before his marriage on 24 April 1767 at Madron parish church. Accounts differ over Joshua's birthplace, either in Camborne, Cornwall, or in London; one, by W. G. S. Dyer, asserts, without disclosing a source, that he was born on 18 December 1767.

At the time of Cristall's baptism his parents were living in Swan Street, off The Minories at Aldgate; his two sisters and younger brother were baptized alternately at Madron and St Botolph. The family settled at Rotherhithe on the Thames, where his father established a yard at Hanover Stairs for making masts, blocks, and sails. Cristall attended a school at Greenwich and his mother used her private income, secured by her marriage settlement, to foster his interest in music and classical literature and to encourage his talent for drawing. After his death, his sister Elizabeth described their father to J. J. Jenkins as a jealous man, whose times ashore from his voyages were 'periods of trouble and discomfort' for the family (Roget, 1.179). He believed the boy's wish to become an artist would lead to penury—an accurate prophecy—and had him apprenticed to an Aldgate dealer in china and glassware named Hewson. Joshua Cristall became so highly regarded by his master as to be offered the business. In an angry scene with his father he declared that he would rather paint china than sell it, and left home.

Cristall soon found work at Thomas Turner's porcelain factory at Caughley, near Ironbridge, Shropshire. Engaged as a salesman, he travelled widely, using his sketch pad more often than his order-book. He took advice on his career from Mary Wollstonecraft, a friend of his sister Anne Batten *Cristall; she urged him to determine whether drawing was to be the business or the amusement of his life, and in 1792 he enrolled as a part-time student engraver at the Royal Academy Schools in London. In 1795 he illustrated Anne's volume of verse, *Poetical Sketches*, published by Joseph Johnson. He was then lodging with his sister Elizabeth at 28 Surrey Street (now Blackfriars Road); befriended by a family named Clayton, he became godfather to their granddaughter. He was also taken up by Dr Thomas Monro, whose 'academy' was more encouraging of an emerging generation of watercolourists than was the Royal Academy. Cristall scraped a living with his work, but he was very poor. His career did not really begin until the deaths of his parents; they left him a small legacy which allowed him to journey to north Wales in 1802. He was already thirty-four, his early years, according to his sister Elizabeth, being 'cruelly wasted' (Roget, 1.188).

At Dolgellau, in Merioneth, Cristall sketched alongside John and Cornelius Varley, and the following year—when he exhibited a portrait (*Mr G. Adams*) at the Royal Academy—he returned there with Cornelius Varley. Through these associations he was invited to become a member of the Sketching Society, and a founder member of the first watercolour society (referred to as the Old Watercolour Society and later called the Royal Society of Painters in Water Colours). His eight pictures at the first Old Watercolour Society exhibition in 1805 were of contemporary landscapes and subjects drawn from history and literature, two interests which would be reflected in his exhibits over the next forty-one years, and they demonstrated his talent—some said genius—for drawing the human figure. He had a major success with a series of pictures of the Kent coast where he had convalesced from a breakdown in his health. For its size and complexity, his *Fishmarket on the Beach at Hastings* (exh. 1808; Victoria and Albert Museum, London) set a precedent in watercolour painting which others were to follow. His classical pictures, such as *Nymphs and Shepherds Dancing* (City Museum and Art Gallery, Hereford), became less popular than his studies of contemporary figures, country girls, and children in pastoral settings derived from his trips to Wales, the Lake District (1805), Scotland (1818), and beauty spots nearer home.

In 1812, while living in the rural outskirts of Marylebone, Middlesex, as a neighbour of his good friends George Barret, Cornelius Varley, and William Sawrey Gilpin, Cristall was married on 10 June at St James's, Paddington, to Elizabeth Cossins (*c.*1771–1839). His bride ran a boarding- and day school for young ladies in Barret's childhood home, the Manor House on Paddington Green. She had lived in France as a girl and her sophistication and small private income were a useful counterfoil to Cristall's naïvety and money troubles. He renewed the lease on the Manor House and for a while the couple's home became a salon, the resort of musicians, authors, and artists. Well liked for his modesty and unselfish interest in the work of others, Cristall was made president of the Old Watercolour Society in 1816, again in 1819, and from 1821 to 1831. But in 1822 he announced that he and his wife were to leave London in search of purer air and to gratify their desire for a rural life.

The childless Cristalls' choice of Herefordshire was influenced by their close attachment, *in loco parentis*, to two sisters, Mary Anne and Matilda Lovett, who had boarded at Mrs Cristall's school. When the girls went to live with their reputed father, Edward Wallwyn, on his Hellens estate at Much Marcle, the Cristalls followed. With Elizabeth's money they bought Granton Cottage at Goodrich, a simple house with a studio in the garden and a stable, in the idyllic landscape of the Wye valley. Here for eighteen years Cristall did much of his best work and was probably at his happiest. In 1827 he staged the first arts exhibition in the county, at Ross-on-Wye; he also formed a circle of like-minded friends. Visiting London only at the time of the annual exhibitions, he fell out of touch with changing technique and fashion. Following the death of

his wife in 1839, however, he finally returned to London (1841), accompanied by two servants he described in a letter as his 'maidens', Mary Cox and Sarah Woore. They had been educated by his wife and looked after him in his declining years.

Cristall was warmly welcomed back by old friends in the Sketching Society and he tried to renew his career with oil paintings and portraits. At the Old Watercolour Society a new generation saw him as a silver-haired patriarch—courteous, dignified, and with an endearing simplicity of manner, but whose work was irrelevant. He died on 18 October 1847 at 11 Douro Cottages, Circus Road, St John's Wood, London; he was buried twelve days later beside his wife in St Giles's churchyard, Goodrich. A three-day sale of his remaining works and equipment at Christie and Manson, London, in April 1848 raised less than £200.

Cristall's work remained largely disregarded for another hundred years until art historians identified him as an innovative figure of central importance in watercolour history and traced his influence on his contemporaries, notably John Sell Cotman. Graham Reynolds, who promoted a Cristall exhibition at the Victoria and Albert Museum in 1975, also detected in his work an anticipation of Cézanne and cubism. There are collections at the Victoria and Albert Museum and the British Museum, London; the City Museum and Art Gallery, Hereford; the Victoria Art Gallery, Bath; the National Galleries of Scotland; and the Yale Center for British Art, New Haven, Connecticut. However, much of his exhibited work still remains untraced.   JOHN TISDALL

Sources Bankside Gallery, London, Royal Watercolour Society archive, J. J. Jenkins MSS, 1851 · B. Taylor, *Joshua Cristall (1768–1847)* (1975) [exhibition catalogue, V&A, February–April 1975] · J. Tisdall, *Joshua Cristall: in search of Arcadia* (1995) · J. L. Roget, *A history of the 'Old Water-Colour' Society*, 2 vols. (1891) · R. Redgrave and S. Redgrave, *A century of painters of the English school*, 2 vols. (1866) · W. G. S. Dyer, 'Joshua Cristall', *OWCS Club Journal*, 50th annual (1975) · *DNB* · private information (2004) · G. Reynolds, *An introduction to English watercolour painting* (1950) · M. Hardie, *Water-colour painting in Britain*, ed. D. Snelgrove, J. Mayne, and B. Taylor, 2nd edn, 3 vols. [1967–8] · E. Finch, *Memorials of the late Frances Oliver Finch* (1865), 71–5 · parish register, London, Aldgate, St Botolph, 22 April 1768 [baptism] · parish register, Goodrich, Herefordshire, St Giles's, 30 Oct 1847 [burial]

Archives Bankside Gallery, London, Royal Watercolour Society archive, Jenkins MSS · FM Cam., letters to W. Turton · Herefs. RO, Hellens MS, Much Marcle, E69 · priv. coll., letters to Mary Ann Lovett and Matilda Lovett

Likenesses J. Cristall, self-portrait, *c.*1800, Bankside Gallery, London, Royal Watercolour Society collection · C. H. Lear, pencil drawing, 1846, NPG · J. Cristall, self-portrait, oils, Royal Society of Painters in Water Colours, London · J. Linnell, group portrait, drawing (*A group of artists*, 1820), BM; Bankside Gallery, London, Royal Watercolour Society collection · D. Maclise, chalk drawing, V&A · J. Varley, chalk drawing, V&A · J. Varley, pencil drawing, Victoria Art Gallery, Bath · group portrait (*Artists 1825*), NPG

Wealth at death insignificant: will, PRO, PROB 11/2064-262

Critchett, George (1817–1882), ophthalmic surgeon, the elder son of Richard Critchett (1777–1865), and his wife, Elizabeth, was born at Highgate, near London, on 25 March 1817. After attending a private school in Highgate, he studied at the London Hospital under John Scott, and became MRCS in 1839 and FRCS (by examination) in 1844. He was successively demonstrator of anatomy, assistant surgeon (1846), surgeon (1861–3), and professor of surgery to the London Hospital. He was a skilful surgeon and operator, introducing some valuable types of treatment of ulcers, and orthopaedic procedures. From 1841 he was attached to the Royal London Ophthalmic Hospital, Moorfields, becoming a distinguished eye surgeon, and working with his colleague William Bowman to raise the standard of British ophthalmology, and to make Moorfields one of the leading ophthalmic hospitals in Europe. Numerous important eye operations were much improved by him. He published *Lectures on Ulcers of the Lower Extremities* (1849) and a course of lectures, 'Diseases of the eye', in *The Lancet* (1854).

Critchett was elected a member of the council of the College of Surgeons in 1870, was president of the Hunterian Society for two years, and president of the International Congress of Ophthalmology held in London in 1872. In 1876 he was appointed ophthalmic surgeon and lecturer at the Middlesex Hospital, and when the Ophthalmological Society of the United Kingdom was formed in 1880, he was elected a vice-president.

Critchett was extremely kind, courteous, and generous; he was fluent in French, and had a refined artistic taste, and great love for athletic sports. He died on 1 November 1882 at his home at 21 Harley Street, London, after a short illness, leaving from his marriage to Martha, daughter of Captain Booker RN, a daughter and two sons, the elder of whom, Sir George Anderson Critchett (1845–1925), became ophthalmic surgeon to St Mary's Hospital. The younger son was (Richard) Claude *Carton (1856–1928), actor and playwright.

G. T. BETTANY, rev. HUGH SERIES

Sources A. M. Ramsay, 'George Critchett, FRCS, 1817–1882', *British Journal of Ophthalmology*, 7 (1923), 353–8; pubd separately (1923) • Boase, *Mod. Eng. biog.* • *BMJ* (4 Nov 1882), 907, 921 • *List of candidates* (1848–1940) • CGPLA Eng. & Wales (1883) • Burke, *Peerage*
Likenesses G. Jerrard, photograph, 1881, Wellcome L. • portrait, repro. in Ramsay, 'George Critchett, FRCS, 1817–1882'
Wealth at death £9567 17s. 2d.: administration, 15 March 1883, CGPLA Eng. & Wales

Critchley, Alfred Cecil (1890–1963), greyhound racing promoter and aviation administrator, was born at Stapleton ranch, near Calgary, Alberta, Canada, the first of the two sons of Oswald Assheton Critchley (d. 1935), ranch owner, and his first wife, Maria Cecil, née Newbolt (d. 1891). Following his early boyhood in Canada, Critchley was privately educated at St Bees Boys' School in Cumberland. In 1908 Critchley was commissioned into Lord Strathcona's Horse, after training at the Royal Military College at Kingston, Ontario. He served on the western front from 1914 with the 7th Canadian infantry brigade. Wounded at Ypres in 1916 while acting brigade major, Critchley was subsequently awarded the DSO. On his return to active service he was put in charge of basic training for new Canadian troops. He undertook this role so successfully that in February 1918 he was seconded to the Royal Flying Corps to undertake a similar training role.

By the end of the war Critchley had the rank of brigadier-general, but then left the army. He spent the years from 1919 to 1923 in South America, involved in a number of commercial activities: in his memoirs he described how he unsuccessfully prospected for oil in Mexico, and was almost kidnapped by the bandit Pancho Villa in 1920. Returning to England in 1922, he and his friend Henry Horne were convinced of the investment potential of the cement industry, and borrowed £300,000 from the Guaranty Trust to begin Associated and British Portland Cement Manufactures, which soon amalgamated almost sixty companies. Critchley and Horne held 600,000 shares between them, and through the directors they nominated to the board played an important role in the affairs of the cement giant. Critchley later claimed to be responsible for first suggesting that a blue circle should be put around all the company's products for advertising purposes, and as a seal of quality. 'Blue Circle' was subsequently adopted as the company's name.

In 1926 Critchley actively helped defeat the general strike by co-ordinating the distribution of Winston Churchill's *British Gazette*. Critchley later claimed credit for the effective circulation of the *Gazette*, which grew from 232,000 on 5 May to over 2,200,000 by 12 May. The same year also saw the introduction of the electric hare into Britain, thanks to the efforts of Critchley and his business associates who grouped together to form the Greyhound Racing Association Limited (GRA). They built the first electric greyhound stadium in Britain at Belle Vue, Manchester, and the GRA's operations soon expanded to White City in London, and to other tracks in Birmingham, Leeds, Liverpool, and London. Although the new sport was greeted with popular enthusiasm, Critchley had to contend with disapproval, if not hostility, from the middle and upper classes, and in order to obviate the latter he shrewdly 'gathered round him figures of standing in other spheres of sport' (*The Times*, 11 Feb 1963). Much of the later integrity of the sport's controlling body, the National Greyhound Racing Society of Great Britain, 'owes much to his early influence' (ibid.).

Critchley attempted a political career, and stood unsuccessfully as a Conservative candidate at Gorton, Manchester, in 1929. In 1930, he unsuccessfully contested the Islington by-election for Max Aitken's United Empire Party. In a 1934 by-election, however, he was elected as the Conservative MP for Twickenham. However, 'his explosive manner in debate did not make him a good parliamentarian' (*The Times*, 11 Feb 1963). He did not stand as a candidate in the 1935 general election, instead choosing to concentrate on the business of cement and dogs.

Between 1939 and 1943 Critchley resumed his role as trainer of air crew for the RAF with the rank of air commodore. He was again very effective in this role: many of his staff were sporting personalities, and he created training centres at empty seaside resorts. In 1943, having built up an adequate reserve of trained men, he was appointed director-general of the British Overseas Aircraft Corporation (BOAC) at the suggestion of Lord Beaverbrook. His dynamic energy soon made itself felt: while commuting to London from his home at Sunningdale, Berkshire, he had the idea of converting thousands of acres of flat land near Staines into a major airport for London which he intended to name 'Churchill Field'. Labour members of the national government objected to this, but he was given clearance for his project, and by mid-1944 the national press was excited about the now public plans for a London airport.

By early 1946 the new London airport was established at what subsequently became better known as Heathrow, and the corporation had also become profitable. However, it was clear that the Labour government was determined to split BOAC into a number of nationalized corporations. This prompted Critchley's resignation in January 1946. He then moved back into the commercial sector and established a private airline, Skyways, with Captain Ronald Ashley. They bought a number of York aircraft from A. V. Roe, and operated scheduled services to Asia and Africa, but the business did not prove to be long-lasting. Critchley later blamed the restrictive effect of the civil aviation legislation of the 1940s, arguing that it was intended to crush private enterprise by removing licences, and thus profitable routes, from private operators. 'The death of Skyways', he wrote, was due to 'nothing else but socialist dogma practised by the Labour Government. All that is left is the glory of the pioneering work we did' (Critch!, 234).

Critchley married three times. His first wife, whom he married on 19 January 1916, was Maryon, daughter of John Galt, president of the Union Bank of Canada; they had a daughter and a son (killed on active service in Libya in 1941). On 22 December 1927 he married Joan Kathleen Welsh Lee, daughter of Mrs Reginald Foster, and this marriage produced a further son and daughter. Critchley married his third wife, Diana Fishwick, in 1938; with her he had another son and daughter. A celebrated golfer, Critchley won a number of amateur championships, including the French (1933) and the Belgian (1938). His third wife, Diana, was also his golfing partner, and they jointly won a number of contests. One of Critchley's other passions was hunting chamois in the Austrian Alps.

In April 1953 Critchley went blind, a tragedy against which he fought bravely. He maintained his roles as a director of the Greyhound Racing Association, and of Associated Portland Cement. He became president of the British Golf Foundation in 1953, and was captain of Wentworth Golf Club from 1953 to 1956.

Critchley died aged seventy-three on 9 February 1963, at Cherry Garth, Firwood Road, Wentworth, Surrey, of a cerebral thrombosis and of arteriosclerosis; his third wife survived him. A well-attended memorial service was held for him at St Martin-in-the-Fields, London, on 21 February 1963.   MARK CLAPSON

Sources *Critch! the memoirs of Brigadier General A. C. Critchley* (1961) · *The Times* (11 Feb 1963) · *The Times* (22 Feb 1963) · *Greyhound Owner and Breeder* (14 Feb 1963) · *Sporting Life* (11 Feb 1963) · d. cert. · will · CGPLA Eng. & Wales (1963) · WWW · m. certs.
Archives CAC Cam., corresp. with Sir E. I. Spears
Likenesses photographs, repro. in *Critch!*

Wealth at death £23,331 10s. od.: probate, 6 Dec 1963, *CGPLA Eng. & Wales*

Critchley, Sir Julian Michael Gordon (1930–2000), politician, was born on 8 December 1930 at the Royal Northern Hospital, Islington, London, the elder of the two sons of Macdonald *Critchley (1900–1997), neurologist, and his first wife, Edna Auldeth, *née* Morris (1899/1900–1974), who had been a midwife before her marriage. Although he was a sensitive, stammering child, from an early age it was clear that Critchley would kick against conformity. After Brockhurst preparatory school he was educated at Shrewsbury School, the University of Paris at the Sorbonne, and Pembroke College, Oxford, where he read philosophy, politics, and economics, and where his best friend was Michael Heseltine. Two years younger than Critchley, Heseltine had also attended Shrewsbury. They shared lodgings, and became so close that they were dubbed Critcheltine. They won their first headlines in the national press when they returned to Shrewsbury to support a motion criticizing public schools. But although many contemporaries thought Critchley the more talented of the pair, Heseltine achieved higher academic grades and became president of the Oxford Union. Critchley (who graduated with a fourth-class degree in 1955) rose no higher than secretary of the Oxford University Conservative Association, in which Heseltine also secured a junior office; but even there Critchley and Heseltine were suspected of heterodox opinions, and had initially been refused membership.

Even before Critchley's year at the Sorbonne he had been struck by a misfortune which added to the sense of inferiority induced by his social origins. He later described Heseltine and himself as 'first generation public school, first generation Oxbridge—middle-class boys on the make' (*The Times*). He contracted polio, which lamed him and caused more deep-seated physical damage which reduced him to near paralysis forty years later. It also ended his promising career as an amateur boxer, though he retained a keen interest in the sport (and would later serve as a steward for the British Boxing Board of Control). He consoled himself that, coupled with his attractive appearance, the limp qualified him as 'sub-Byronic'. He was also charming, and ambitious. For a while he pursued a career in advertising, and by 1956 was a senior executive with Lintas. Meanwhile, on 15 October 1955 he married Paula Joan Baron (b. 1932/3), an advertising visualizer and daughter of Paul Hillman Baron, company director. They had two daughters.

In 1957 Critchley was selected as Conservative candidate for Rochester and Chatham, and at the general election of 1959 he narrowly toppled the sitting Labour MP, Arthur Bottomley. At twenty-nine he was the youngest MP, part of the same intake as Margaret Thatcher. For once he had a head start on Heseltine, who was beaten in 1959 and did not join the Commons until 1966. But the situation was quickly reversed. Rochester and Chatham was highly vulnerable to a Labour revival, which duly arrived in 1964. Critchley was defeated. In the house he had supported 'permissive' measures of social reform, sponsoring a bill

Sir Julian Michael Gordon Critchley (1930–2000), by Jillian Edelstein, 1991

outlawing racial discrimination, and campaigning for homosexual law reform and the abolition of capital punishment. Such activities, combined with the dissolution of his first marriage in 1965, did not endear him to his activists. Not for the last time he escaped de-selection, but he was defeated again in the general election of 1966 and decided to look elsewhere. Even his calculated attempts to build a 'reliable' profile within his party backfired; elected chairman of the Bow Group in 1966, he caused offence by inviting the Liberal leader, Jo Grimond, to the Carlton Club. His party's central office pointedly refused to help him find a new berth.

In the meantime Critchley scraped a living from journalism. A third of his income went to his first wife, Paula, following their divorce, and on 11 June 1965 he married her best friend, Heather Anne Goodrick (b. 1933/4), daughter of Charlie Moores, hotelier; they had a daughter and a son. To add to these commitments, Critchley, while not absurdly extravagant, did have expensive habits; he collected Victorian china, and relished good food and wine. After the election of 1966 he briefly edited Heseltine's glossy and innovative magazine *Town*, but the circulation fell and his old friend sacked him after two years. Critchley's financial saviour was William Rees-Mogg, editor of *The Times*, who contracted him to write television criticisms. But financial security always eluded Critchley.

Shortly before the general election of 1970, Critchley was chosen as the Conservative candidate for the safe seat of Aldershot and North Hampshire. Back in the Commons, he had good reason to expect promotion under the new prime minister, Edward Heath. They were on the same wing of the party, and Critchley was a strong supporter of the EEC. His main qualification for office was his interest in defence; his views on this subject were sufficiently hardline to please the substantial army faction in Aldershot—and the duke of Wellington, whose influence in this constituency was a distant echo of the days when his ancestor had resisted the Great Reform Act. Critchley believed that Europe should contribute more to its own defence, an idea congenial to Heath. Even so, the call never came.

Critchley was disillusioned well before the Heath government came to grief in February 1974. Unfortunately for him, he still depended on journalism to support his lifestyle; and the ability to coin memorable phrases, which made him popular with the newspaper editors, also guaranteed the disapproval of Conservative power brokers. In 1973, for example, he predicted that if his party lost office at the next election and ideologues took over, 'we could become the party of the aggrieved motorist' (*Political Quarterly*, Oct–Dec 1973, 410). When the Conservatives did indeed lose power—and were beaten again in October 1974—Critchley decided that it was time for a change at the top. He supported Margaret Thatcher in the ensuing leadership election, thus helping to bring about precisely the development he had feared. There was an almost poetic symbolism when, towards the end of the 1970s, Thatcher delivered a speech which Critchley had written for her. All the jokes fell flat, and Critchley was informed of his leader's displeasure.

Thatcher was forced to find room in her shadow cabinet for 'grandees' who had no liking either for her or her policies. There also had to be a place for Heseltine, who had attained junior office and a high public profile under Heath. But Critchley was clever, witty, and liberal. With powerful, faithful patrons he could have overcome these impolitic virtues; but Critchley's friends were mainly independent-minded, irreverent characters like David Walder, who described Thatcher as resembling the wife of his own constituency chairman 'writ hideously large'. Critchley might still have forced his way into office if his ambition had been matched by a burning commitment to some cause. But although he was ranked among the tory 'wets', and joined Francis Pym's short-lived ginger group Centre Forward in 1985, he was not of the generation which had witnessed deprivation in the 1930s. In his own life he often faced insecurity, but he never experienced poverty; and the pose he adopted in his writings—whimsical, if not sardonic—made him an unlikely champion of social justice.

Critchley made his best-known contribution to the literature of detraction in February 1980, when an unsigned article in *The Observer* ridiculed Thatcher's economic pretensions. Although the subsequent revelation of Critchley's authorship did him no good at Westminster—or in Aldershot—it was rather like a man hanging himself after he has swallowed arsenic. Critchley still hoped for a ministerial post, but realistically his only chance was for Heseltine to succeed Thatcher—and even then he would have had to rely on friendship proving stronger than political calculation. His chances became even more remote when he cashed in on their chequered relationship by publishing an unauthorized biography of Heseltine in 1987. Heseltine's loyalty was never put to the test; by the time of his appointment as deputy prime minister, Critchley was too ill to be considered for office. Given what had already passed between them, he would have been better served by hitching his wagon to a different star.

In the last two decades of his life Critchley produced several light-hearted books on politics, two novels, and an autobiography. The last of these, *A Bag of Boiled Sweets* (1994), contained numerous brilliant character sketches, as well as an account of his own life which struck the perfect balance between dignity and self-effacement. When it appeared, the author had been diagnosed with prostate cancer, and was finding attendance at the Commons increasingly difficult because his right leg was now almost immobile. Yet he was far happier with John Major as prime minister. In his autobiography he wrote that knighthoods in politics were almost invariably the reward for prolonged and taciturn service on the back benches. On the second of those grounds he was an unlikely candidate, but Major granted the honour in 1995. Critchley had also moved to Ludlow, a town which he had always loved. Having separated from his second wife, he shared his elegant home on Broad Street with Mary Prudence (Prue) Bellak, *née* Marshall, with whom he had enjoyed an idyllic affair while he was at the Sorbonne. They had met by chance in the Commons, when both of their marriages were breaking up. The romance gave Critchley an Indian summer which effaced the memory of so many false steps. The couple remained generous hosts to the end.

Critchley's last book, *Collapse of Stout Party* (1997; co-written with his friend Morrison Halcrow), chronicled the disastrous Conservative defeat of May 1997. He escaped that conflagration, having decided to leave the house before the election. At least Major had tried to resist the Euro-sceptics, but Critchley thought that the same was not true of William Hague, and he felt unable to support the party in the European elections of 1999. As a result he was formally expelled. This petty gesture from the new leadership gave a new lease of life to his journalism. But his health deteriorated further, and he died in Hereford on 9 September 2000 and was buried in Wistanstow, Shropshire. He was survived by Prue Bellak, and by the four children of his two marriages.

Critchley's long-term political significance lies in the fact that in the 1980s he pioneered and maintained a continuous undercurrent of scepticism in the face of the missionary zeal that Thatcher had temporarily imported into the Conservative Party. 'It is curious how moralistic the party has become', he wrote in October 1980; 'it has acquired a tinge of Buchmanism': since 1975 it had taken on 'a flavour that was part-revivalist, part-ideological and almost wholly foreign' (*The Listener*, 9 Oct 1980, 454). With comments such as this, he made his small but distinctive contribution towards the pressures within the party

which in 1990 came together to overthrow her. Yet, looking back on his political career, Critchley made no secret of his disappointment. By the time of his death he was better remembered for his quips than for any constructive achievements at Westminster. Even these remarks were not always original—'The Great She-Elephant' was borrowed from Bernard Shaw, 'Is he One of Us?' came (at third hand) from Thatcher herself, and the origin of 'Essex Man' is contested. Undoubtedly, though, Critchley was capable of excellent one-liners; he was the first to call Thatcher's leadership victory 'The Peasants' Revolt' (although he had been one of the peasants); he (belatedly) claimed that Heseltine 'could not see a parapet without ducking below it', and in the mid-1980s (referring to Norman Tebbit and Norman Fowler on the one hand, and Kenneth Baker and Kenneth Clarke on the other) he complained that 'There are too many Normans in the Tory Party but not enough Kens' (*The Observer*, 8 Sept 1985). He must have been conscious of a tendency to repetition which was forced on him by his pose as the gadfly of the Conservative Party; if his political career had left him with nothing more than a limited stock of good stories, he would keep on using these until the commissioning editors declined to answer his calls. His books, even the delightful *Bag of Boiled Sweets*, were written in a style which suggests that the author expected their impact to prove as transient as his journalism. But it is to be hoped that at least part of him believed that he would prove an exception to his own rule, when he wrote that 'Few if any MPs of whatever party leave anything tangible behind them' (Critchley, *A Bag of Boiled Sweets*, 151).   MARK GARNETT

Sources J. Critchley, *A bag of boiled sweets* (1994) · *The Times* (11 Sept 2000) · *Daily Telegraph* (11 Sept 2000) · *The Guardian* (11 Sept 2000) · *The Independent* (11 Sept 2000) · WWW · personal knowledge (2004) · private information (2004) · b. cert. · m. certs.
Archives King's Lond., Liddell Hart C., corresp. with Sir B. H. Liddell Hart
Likenesses J. Edelstein, bromide print, 1991, NPG [*see illus.*] · photograph, repro. in *The Times* · photograph, repro. in *Daily Telegraph* · photograph, repro. in *The Guardian* · photograph, repro. in *The Independent*
Wealth at death under £210,000: probate, 13 Nov 2000, *CGPLA Eng. & Wales*

Critchley, Macdonald (1900–1997), neurologist, was born on 2 February 1900 at 4 Lime Tree Villas, Ashley Down, Bristol, the son of Arthur Frank Critchley, gas collector, and his wife, Rosina Matilda, *née* White. Educated at the Christian Brothers' College, Bristol, he matriculated at fifteen at Bristol University. Too young to be admitted, he spent the following year studying German and Greek. In 1917 he enlisted as a private soldier and in 1918 became a cadet in the Royal Flying Corps. He returned to university after the war and graduated in 1922 with first-class honours, having found the time also to perform on stage in and around Bristol.

After a brief period as a house physician in Bristol, Critchley moved to London, first to the Hospital for Sick Children at Great Ormond Street, then to the Maida Vale Hospital, and finally in 1923 to the National Hospital, Queen Square. He was trained there as a neurologist by

Macdonald Critchley (1900–1997), by Godfrey Argent, 1969

physicians such as Sir Gordon Holmes, James Collier, Samuel Alexander Kinnier Wilson, and Risien Russell. In 1924, the year he proceeded MD, Critchley published seven papers, including three on disorders of movement and three on disorders of calcium metabolism. His interests then shifted to those which came to dominate his later work: in 1927 he published on defects in reading and writing in children, a prelude to one of his major books, *The Dyslexic Child* (1970), for which he received the Sam T. Orton prize in 1974. It was Critchley who, in diagnosing dyslexia in Michael Heseltine's son Rupert, diagnosed it also in the father. 'You do realize that you are a classic dyslexic?' was his question, which confirmed what had been, with Michael Heseltine, a slowly growing suspicion (Heseltine, 14). He married on 16 April 1927 Edna Auldeth Morris (1899/1900–1974). They had two sons, the elder of whom was Sir Julian Michael Gordon *Critchley (1930–2000), MP. Critchley's first book, *On Mirror Writing* (1928), was published in the same year that he was appointed to the consultant staff at both the National Hospital, Queen Square and King's College Hospital. Elected fellow of the Royal College of Physicians at the early age of thirty, he gave the Goulstonian lecture to the college in 1931 on the neurology of old age, a topic which sixty years later became a major concern of neurology.

Increasingly in the 1930s Critchley's writings reflected a growing concern with higher cerebral function: the dementias, hallucinatory states, and aphasia. The Second World War radically, if temporarily, changed his direction. As surgeon captain he organized the neurological

and psychiatric services for the Royal Navy. His observations in the Arctic and in the tropics provided the substance of his Croonian lecture to the Royal College of Physicians in 1945: 'Problems of naval warfare under climatic extremes'. After the war he returned to his clinical studies of higher cerebral function and in 1953 published *The Parietal Lobes*, a landmark in the field of cognitive neurology.

Critchley was a brilliant teacher and was internationally renowned as a lecturer. His eminence in the profession was recognized by, among other things, his election as president of the World Federation of Neurology (1965–73). He was the first elected vice-president of the Royal College of Physicians (1964). He was appointed CBE in 1962 and retired from the National Health Service in 1965, but continued to see patients for another two decades.

Critchley wrote extensively throughout his life. His essays were collected in three volumes: *The Divine Banquet of the Brain* (1979), *The Citadel of the Senses* (1986), and *The Ventricle of Memory* (1990); they covered topics as diverse as self-portraiture, gesture, Indian mythology and dance, criminal trials, and human attitudes to the nose. Critchley wrote biographies of the two neurologists who had influenced him most: Sir William Gowers (1949) and John Hughlings Jackson (1998). The latter was written with his second wife, Eileen Audrey Hargreaves, née Bristow (b. 1926/7), whom he married on 23 April 1974, and was completed just before he died.

Critchley's manner was that of the distinguished physician of the mid-twentieth century—quiet, elegant, unhurried, and always civil. An apparent aloofness of manner reflected a natural reticence which concealed from most a concern for others prompted by shrewd insight into their personalities. He avoided any unnecessary movement and counselled against exercise. In later years in his office in Queen Court, he would sit surrounded by cushions in an armchair at his desk, in the side-shelves of which were memorabilia of Oscar Wilde, pieces from his collection of paste jars, and curious objects collected in the Far East.

Critchley died suddenly on 15 October 1997 at his home, Hughlings House, Mill Lane, Nether Stowey, Bridgwater, Somerset, and was cremated. His second wife survived him.   W. I. McDONALD

Sources archives, RCP Lond. · WWW · S. J. Gillam and W. I. McDonald, eds., *Lives of the fellows of the Royal College of Physicians of London continued to 1997* (2000) · *Medical Register* (1997) · *Migraine News* (spring 1998) · *BMJ* (7 Feb 1998), 478 · *The Independent* (24 Oct 1997) · *The Times* (16 Oct 1997) · *The Guardian* (16 Oct 1997) · *Daily Telegraph* (27 Oct 1997) · M. Heseltine, *Life in the jungle: my autobiography* (2000) · b. cert. · m. certs. · d. cert.
Archives RCP Lond. | FILM Institute of Neurology, Queen Square, London
Likenesses oils, 1965, Institute of Neurology, Queen Square, London · G. Argent, photograph, 1969, NPG [*see illus.*] · photograph, RCP Lond.

Crittall, Francis Henry (1860–1935), metal window manufacturer, was born on 27 July 1860 at 27 Bank Street, Braintree, Essex, the eighth of the eleven children of Francis Berrington Crittall (d. 1879), an ironmonger, and Fanny

Morris, *née* Godfrey (d. 1879). His parents, from Kent and Rutland respectively, had settled in Braintree in 1849.

Crittall was brought up in a strict nonconformist household and attended private schools in Braintree and Witham. His scholastic achievements were undistinguished, and in 1876 he joined his father and elder brother, Richard, in the family business in metal working and retailing. In 1881, two years after both his parents died, Francis Henry left for Birmingham where he found employment at a manufacturer of metal bedsteads. He attended evening classes in drawing at Birmingham School of Art while there. After a year he started an ironmonger's shop in Chester but in 1883, when his brother decided to give up the family business, Crittall returned to Braintree. In the same year he married Ellen Laura Carter (d. 1934), daughter of a middle-class Baptist family from Birmingham; they had five children. With financial help from a local grocer, Crittall then began to rebuild the Bank Street firm.

Crittall was mainly interested in the practical side of the business, and he concentrated his efforts on the manufacturing of metal products for engineering and architectural purposes from a workshop on the premises. The company's professionalism and the quality of its work established its reputation, and by the late 1880s substantial commissions were being obtained from as far away as Lancashire. Realizing that the future lay in specialized production he persuaded his partners to form a second company, the Crittall Manufacturing Company Ltd, in 1889, specifically for the manufacture of windows and doors. In 1894 this activity moved to a purpose-built factory, the Manor Works, in Braintree.

Under Crittall's energetic leadership, and with an enhanced production capacity, the company prospered, winning several prestigious contracts for specialist metalwork. By the turn of the century a nationwide sales network had been established and in 1904 Crittalls opened an office and showroom in Finsbury Square, London. Three years later the company ventured abroad and started the Detroit Steel Products Company, which first introduced steel windows to the United States. Crittall's two eldest sons, Valentine George (1884–1961) and Walter Francis (1887–1956), were elected to the board at this time.

The firm steadily expanded, and the formation of a casting company in 1911, which by the following year employed 500 people, consolidated Crittall's manufacturing base. With annual sales of £100,000 the company had secured a leading position in the British metal window industry but, despite considerable technical progress, its products were still confined to the luxury market. Crittall was keen to produce domestic windows for mass consumption, but the development was interrupted by the First World War. In 1915 Crittall helped form the East Anglia Munitions Company, comprising forty-two private manufacturing companies, which successfully challenged the monopoly of the official 'armaments ring', with considerable efficiency gains in armaments production. He remained its joint manager for the duration of the war and had the Crittall factories converted for the

mass production of munitions components, employing up to 2000 personnel.

The experience thus gained of large-scale production techniques proved useful to the company during the post-war redevelopment phase, as did the Crittall family's many links with progressive architectural and planning circles. The firm played a key role in the campaign to have standardized metal windows accepted in the general domestic market and government housing schemes: Crittall was co-founder and chairman of the Steel Window Association, a combination of twenty-one manufacturers, which from 1919 to 1921 promoted this cause. Some of the company's individual efforts to find practical application for the new technology were also significant, notably the prefabricated houses erected through its subsidiary, the Unit Construction Company (1919–20), and Silver End, the self-sufficient garden village built 1926–32 for its employees.

The 1920s brought rapid growth. Two new Essex factories were added to the expanding Braintree works and in 1924, when Crittalls was floated as a public company, its workforce totalled nearly 2000. It was double that before the end of the decade. In 1922 Crittall stepped down as managing director, a position he had held since 1898, in order to direct the company's overseas development programme. Accompanied by his wife he undertook several world tours between 1921 and 1933 to promote Crittalls' interests, which are described in their joint publication, *Fifty Years of Work and Play* (1934). By the time of his death the firm had a global export trade, subsidiaries in eight countries and an authorized share capital of £1.5 million.

Crittall maintained an active involvement in the management of the firm until 1933 but the last years of his life were devoted increasingly to the development of Silver End (where he moved in 1927) and welfare schemes for the Crittall workers. In the latter, as in other matters, he was a progressive, yet he showed little inclination for active political service during his life. He died of heart failure on board ship returning from the Caribbean on 9 March 1935 and was cremated at Golders Green crematorium. The family connection with the company he founded lasted until 1980.   HENTIE LOUW

Sources F. H. Crittall and E. L. Crittall, *Fifty years of work and play* (1934) · D. J. Blake, *Window vision: Critall, 1849–1989* (1989) · E. Crittall, 'Crittall, Francis Henry', *DBB* · *The Times* (12 March 1935) · *The Builder*, 148 (1935), 493
Archives Crittall Windows Ltd, Braintree, Essex
Likenesses A. John, oils, 1919, NPG · A. J. Munnings, pencil sketch, 1919, priv. coll. · R. Dick, bronze bust, 1930, priv. coll.
Wealth at death £18,225—gross: Crittall, 'Crittall, Francis Henry'

Critz, Emanuel de (1608–1665). *See under* Critz, John de, the elder (d. 1642).

Critz, John de, the elder (d. 1642), serjeant-painter, was a son of Troilus de Critz (d. 1582), a broker of Antwerp, and his wife, Sara (d. 1590), the daughter of Jacob van Meteren of Breda, a printer, and Ottilia Ortels, a relative of the cartographer Abraham Ortelius, whose family had moved to Antwerp from Augsburg. His parents were granted the right of denization in England in 1552, perhaps indicating that they had arrived somewhat earlier to establish their credentials. The only evidence about their family is in a few ambiguously worded aliens' returns of dubious accuracy—probably because of language difficulties and misunderstandings between English assessors and foreign-born immigrants. The first return, dated 1568, lists Troilus and Sara and five children, Susan (Susanna), Oliver, John, Sara, and Magdalen, who must have been born in England. Returns of 1571 show that the sons were apprenticed, to an immigrant merchant and painter respectively, and lodged with them in the customary manner. John appears to have completed four years of his service with the immigrant painter Lucas de Heere in the parish of St Benet Fink. His parents, living in the parish of St Mary Staining, near Cripplegate, were now 'of the Englishe churche', not the Dutch—thoroughly assimilated. Troilus was buried at St Andrew Undershaft in 1582 and Sara in 1590.

In the 1580s and 1590s ministers sometimes recruited foreign-born residents in London to revisit the continent as couriers of official letters. One was John de Critz, who in the 1580s enjoyed the patronage of Sir Francis Walsingham. In 1582 he was in Paris, and three letters from him to the secretary of state survive (quoted in *DNB* and Edmond, 47). In the third, dated 14 October, he says he is thinking of spending the winter in France and then, if Walsingham agrees, going on to Italy. It is not known whether he did so. That he was in Paris again several times between 1583 and 1588 is evident from fees noted in the accounts of the treasurer of the chamber. There is only one known portrait type of Walsingham (*d*. 1590), and de Critz may well have been responsible for the unsigned likenesses of his former patron. No signed portraits commonly attributed to de Critz survive: a few manuscripts show that he wrote his 'de' with a small letter, not a capital as supposed hitherto.

Portraits of Robert Cecil also seem to be confined to one face pattern, with de Critz probably the 'purveyor' or provider (Strong, *Tudor and Jacobean Portraits*, 273–5). Cecil was a small and slightly deformed man (Queen Elizabeth sometimes called him her 'elf'). He was understandably sensitive about his appearance and ensured that only a carefully edited image was circulated. A bill of 1607 from de Critz to Cecil (since 1605 earl of Salisbury) includes a charge of £4 each for 'making' five 'pictures' (Cecil papers, Box U/81, Hatfield House, Hertfordshire). One was given to the constable of Castile, one was for Lady Elizabeth Guildford, one for Sir Henry Wotton, ambassador at Venice, and two were given to the French ambassador in London—one of Cecil, the other of his father, Lord Burghley. It has been assumed that de Critz was producing 'his standard three-quarter length portrait of Robert Cecil', of which a version at Hatfield House measures 35 by 27 inches. Salisbury, approving payment in his fluent hand at the bottom, writes 'pay this byll so farr', implying that there were more to come: de Critz's signed receipt is dated 16 October. (Some orders from less exalted men may have been copies.)

For some time there had been much intermarrying within the protestant artistic community in London, immigrants 'for religion' from France and the Spanish Netherlands. The complexities, as set out in Edmond, in particular in the pedigree, show the importance of the marriages of de Critz's sisters Susanna and Magdalen (which he probably promoted). In 1571 Susanna became the second wife of Marcus *Gheeraerts the elder, a widower who had arrived from Bruges with his young son Marcus *Gheeraerts the younger. The boy later became the most fashionable portrait painter of his day and in 1590 married de Critz's sister Magdalen, becoming his stepmother's brother-in-law. Marcus Gheeraerts the elder and Susanna had two surviving daughters—here correctly identified as de Critz's nieces—Sara, who became the second wife of the miniaturist Isaac Oliver in 1602 but died in 1605, and Susanna (called after her mother), who in 1604 was married to Maximilian *Colt, a sculptor, of a French family from Arras. He and de Critz became close colleagues at court.

De Critz's main importance was as serjeant-painter, a court appointment to James I from his accession in 1603, and then to his son Charles I until his death in 1642. After the death of his predecessor, Leonard Fryer, in 1605, and the appointment of Robert Peake as portrait painter to the short-lived Prince Henry, heir to the throne, de Critz formally achieved his goal, becoming the sovereign's sole serjeant-painter for life. The word serjeant, as used in de Critz's case, then prefixed the titles of heads of some specific departments within the royal household. In the sixteenth and seventeenth centuries portrait painters were usually called picturemakers, or variants of this; the word painter was generally used for men who used paint to embellish surfaces of all objects, sizes, and descriptions, and often made of wood or stone. De Critz and his men worked, not only in London, embellishing objects from garden seats, royal barges, ships, and road vehicles to 'dials' and interiors of palaces, the last involving much gilding and use of 'rich colours'. Horace Walpole was surely right in concluding that de Critz's life could be better traced 'from office-books [the office of works accounts] than from his works or his reputation' (Walpole, 2.15; see also Edmond, 162–74). There he appears repeatedly but never as a painter in the sense of portrait painter.

In 1606 Colt and de Critz were given a commission of prime importance, to complete the great tomb of Elizabeth I in the Henry VII chapel at Westminster Abbey. Colt is presumed to have been recommended by Lord Salisbury, by whom he was employed at Hatfield House, and received an initial contract of £600 for carving the stone (very much higher than supposed earlier) and further payments later, the work to be completed by 1607. De Critz received £100 for painting the stonework. Nicholas Hilliard sought the stone-painting commission, but ruefully reported to Salisbury that de Critz had told him the task was his responsibility 'within the Patent'—as Hilliard put it (letter, 1606, Hatfield House, CP 119/8). This supports the present assessment of the serjeant-painter's full-time court responsibilities. A fine full-length portrait of James

I, shown at the Tate Gallery exhibition 'Dynasties' (1995, catalogue no. 125), was there tentatively dated c.1606 and attributed to John de Critz. This would not have been within his patent, and attribution to the admired portrait painter Marcus Gheeraerts the younger would surely have been more appropriate (see Edmond, 137–8).

John de Critz married three times and had sixteen children in all. His first wife, Helen Bower, was English and of a wealthy City family called Woodcock; dates and places of marriage and baptisms of the first four children are unknown—the family was probably living in the parish of St Sepulchre without Newgate, of which early registers were lost in the great fire of London. From 1607 they appear in the neighbouring parish of St Andrew, Holborn, where they remained for thirty years, living at the north end of Shoe Lane, which links Holborn to Fleet Street. The last three baptisms were of Thomas (1607), Emanuel [see below] (1608), and a short-lived Elizabeth. Their English mother was buried on 4 April 1609, and on 14 May de Critz married a widow and mother of painters, Sara de Neve. She and John had four children. Sara died in 1618, and about 1621 de Critz married Grace Palmes of Hampshire (who was probably English) and fathered his last five children. In 1637 the family moved to the parish of St Martin-in-the-Fields, where de Critz, a wealthy man now 'sick and full of yeares', died in 1642 and his widow in 1648: both had expensive funerals and were buried in St Martin-in-the-Fields, John de Critz on 14 March 1642. His will opens with the resounding words 'I John Decretts Esquire Serjeant Paynter to our Soveraigne lord king Charles'—underlining his pride in his long-standing court appointment.

John de Critz the younger (d. 1642×5) was the eldest son of John de Critz, who in 1610 had paid to ensure him the office of serjeant-painter after his own death. In fact the son never succeeded to the office: his father was buried on 14 March 1642 and he was sworn in four days later, but civil war broke out in August and he soon joined Charles I at Oxford and lost his life. He may have helped his father during his long career, but there is no substantial evidence of this.

Emanuel de Critz (1608–1665) was the youngest son of John de Critz and his English first wife, Helen. At the restoration of Charles II in 1660 he was among the first to seek recompense for loss of royal earnings during the Commonwealth, but from the state papers it is clear that he never became serjeant-painter, although it is often assumed that he did. When Charles I's art treasures were dispersed in 1649–51 he made strenuous but largely unsuccessful attempts to buy many of them. At some point he moved to the parish of St Margaret, Westminster, where he succumbed to the great plague of 1665. 'Mr Emannewell Decreets' was buried there that year on 2 November. There is no consensus about works to be attributed to him.

MARY EDMOND

Sources M. Edmond, 'Limners and picturemakers', *Walpole Society*, 47 (1978–80), 60–242 • R. L. Poole, 'An outline of the history of the De Critz family of painters', *Walpole Society*, 2 (1913), 45–68 • R. L. Poole, 'Marcus Gheeraerts, father and son', *Walpole Society*, 3 (1914), 1–8 • J. L. Nevinson, 'Emanuel van Meteren, 1535–1612', *Huguenot Society Proceedings*, 19 (1953–9) [incl. trans. of the Welbeck MS: E. van Meteren's 'Ghedachtenis Boeke ofte register Van my Emanuel Demetrius', 136–45] • accounts, treasurer of the chamber, PRO, E 351/542, fols. 54, 67, 79, 82v, 95v, 114 [see Edmond, 144 and 206 n. 368] • accounts, office of works, PRO, E 351/3239 • parish register, Holborn, St Andrew's, GL, MS 6667/1 [baptism] • parish register, Holborn, St Andrew's, GL, MS 6668/1 [marriage] • parish register, Holborn, St Andrew's, GL, MS 6673/1 [burial] • parish registers, Dutch Church, Austin Friars, GL, MSS 7381, 7382 • registers, poorrate books, churchwardens' accounts, City Westm. AC [see Edmond, 155, 207–8, n. 412, nn. 414–16] • will, PRO, PROB 11/188, fol. 34 • will, PRO, PROB 11/113, fol. 51 [Helen de Critz] • will, PRO, PROB 11/318, fol. 139 [Emanuel de Critz] • R. Strong, *Tudor and Jacobean portraits*, 2 vols. (1969), 273–5 • R. Strong, *The English icon: Elizabethan and Jacobean portraiture* (1969), 259 • H. Walpole, *Anecdotes of painting in England*, new edn, ed. R. N. Wornum, 3 vols. (1888), vol. 2, p. 15 • K. Hearn, ed., *Dynasties: painting in Tudor and Jacobean England, 1530–1630* (1995) [exhibition catalogue, Tate Gallery, London, 12 Oct 1995 – 7 Jan 1996] • H. M. Colvin and others, eds., *The history of the king's works*, 3–4 (1975–82) • M. Whinney, *Sculpture in Britain, 1530 to 1830*, rev. J. Physick, 2nd edn (1988), 59–63, 433 n. 47

Wealth at death salaried as serjeant-painter • well off: will, PRO, PROB 11/188, fol. 34

Critz, John de, the younger (d. 1642×5). *See under* Critz, John de, the elder (d. 1642).

Crocker, Charles (1797–1861), poet, was born at Chichester, Sussex, on 22 June 1797. His parents could not afford to send him to school after the age of seven, but some generous friends enabled him to attend the Grey Coat School in Chichester for four years. At the age of twelve he was apprenticed to a shoemaker, and he worked at this trade for thirty years (1809–39), while also composing verses which he wrote down during his leisure time. Some lines which he sent to the *Brighton Herald* having attracted considerable attention, a list of subscribers was obtained for the publication of a volume of his poems called *The Vale of Obscurity, The Lavant, and other Poems* (1830; 2nd edn, 1834; 3rd edn, 1841), from which a large profit was obtained. Among his warmest friends was Robert Southey, who asserted that the sonnet 'To the British Oak' was one of the finest in the English language. In 1837 he published another volume entitled *Kingley Vale and other Poems*.

In 1839 Crocker obtained employment from Hayley Mason, the publisher of his works, in the bookselling department of the business, but in 1845 he resigned this situation for that of sexton in Chichester Cathedral, to which was soon afterwards added that of bishop's verger. He thoroughly mastered all the architectural details of the building, and his descriptive account of it to visitors was generally followed with more than usual interest. In 1848 he also published a small handbook on the building entitled *A Visit to Chichester Cathedral* (2nd edn, 1849; enlarged and continued by W. Hayden in 1874 under the title *The Visitor's Chichester Guide*). A complete edition of his *Poetical Works* appeared in 1860. He died in South Street, Chichester, on 6 October 1861; he was survived by his second wife, Mary, and three children. He was buried in the subdeanery, without the Northgate of Chichester Cathedral.

T. F. HENDERSON, *rev.* REBECCA MILLS

Sources C. Crocker, preface, in C. Crocker, *The vale of obscurity, The Lavant, and other poems* (1830), ixff. • W. E. Winks, *Lives of illustrious shoemakers* (1893) • *CGPLA Eng. & Wales* (1862) • *GM*, 3rd ser., 12 (1862), 782–3 • Allibone, *Dict.* • Boase, *Mod. Eng. biog.* • D. Bank and others, eds., *British biographical archive* (1984–98), 28.337–41 [microfiche; with index, 2nd edn, 1998]

Wealth at death £300: probate, 15 March 1862, *CGPLA Eng. & Wales*

Crocker, Henry Radcliffe- (1846–1909), dermatologist, was born Henry Radcliffe Crocker on 6 March 1846 at Western Road, Hove, Sussex, the son of Henry Radcliffe Crocker, a chemist and druggist, and his wife, Maria, formerly Walters. He was generally called by his middle name, Radcliffe, rather than his first name, Henry; in time this usage suggested the compound surname Radcliffe Crocker or Radcliffe-Crocker. He was educated at a private school in Brighton until, aged sixteen, he became an apprentice with a general practitioner, possibly Dr Ralph Goodall, in Silverdale, Staffordshire. Crocker's initial intention was presumably to follow his father as a pharmacist but, despite straitened circumstances, he studied hard and in 1870 gained entry to University College Hospital medical school in London. Part-time employment as a dispenser to a doctor in Sloane Street helped to support his brilliant undergraduate career. He was awarded the gold medals in materia medica and clinical medicine in 1872, which were followed two years later by the university scholarship and the gold medal in forensic medicine together with honours in medicine and obstetrics. He obtained his MRCS in 1873, LRCP and BS (London) in 1874, and his MD the following year.

Crocker's first appointment was as resident obstetric physician and physician's assistant at University College Hospital. The delayed start to his medical career gave that institution a more mature and confident junior doctor than was normally found. These qualities were also recognized by his fellow practitioners and he was able to supplement his income by tutoring as he progressed through the posts of clinical assistant at the Brompton Hospital for Consumption and Diseases of the Chest and a further six months as resident medical officer at Charing Cross Hospital. His training continued in 1875 with his return to University College Hospital as resident medical officer and one year later he became the assistant medical officer in its dermatology department. There he came under the influence of William Tilbury Fox who inspired in Crocker the abiding interest in skin disease that developed into his career.

Crocker continued to broaden his experience by taking appointments as assistant physician and pathologist to the East London Hospital for Sick Children at Shadwell in 1878 and six years later he became honorary physician there, an association he maintained until 1893. He became a member of the Royal College of Physicians in 1877 and a fellow ten years later.

The tragic death in 1879 of William Tilbury Fox at the early age of forty-two gave Crocker the opportunity to succeed him as physician and dermatologist to University College Hospital. There were very few dermatologists in England and prejudice against the continental practice of specialization persisted among physicians. However, Crocker had acquired a wide base of medical knowledge and he steadily evolved a method of considering a skin disorder as part of the patient's overall condition which led him to direct therapy through both topical and systemic modalities. In so doing he retained his colleagues' respect and, as the necessity for specialization in the light of increasing medical knowledge was slowly accepted they credited Crocker and Tilbury Fox with 'bringing some semblance of order to the subject' (Gold, 23). Crocker was one of the first to appreciate the value of microscopic examination of a skin biopsy and undertook some of the earliest thorough epidemiological investigations of skin disease. His many scientific publications included the first descriptions of a number of important skin disorders including granuloma annulare and erythema elevatum diutinum, and he is credited with the identification of micrococci as the causative agents of impetigo. In England he pioneered the application of X-rays in the management of inflammatory skin disease and the use of Koch's treatment of lupus vulgaris with tuberculin. Concern for his patient, though, always tempered his thirst for innovation with a sober assessment of its value.

On 3 April 1880, established in his substantive post, Crocker married Constance Mary, the daughter of Edward Francis Fussell, medical officer of health for east Sussex and physician at Sussex County Hospital. Crocker's developing reputation attracted increasing numbers of private patients and, from 1889, he consulted from rooms at 121 Harley Street. The couple had no children but, in 1898, their increased prosperity allowed the purchase of a country residence at Bourne End, Buckinghamshire.

Crocker was a member of the court of examiners of the Society of Apothecaries from 1880 to 1896. An active interest in medical politics encouraged him to take office within the British Medical Association. He began as honorary secretary of the metropolitan counties branch (1889–91), he was appointed to council from 1890 to 1904, and high esteem for his business and organizing abilities resulted in his election as treasurer (1905–7). He was deeply involved in the redevelopment of the association's headquarters in the Strand and participated in the management of the *British Medical Journal*. His regular contributions on dermatological and ethical matters to this journal and its rival, *The Lancet*, were well received by their readers and for many years he taught the fundamentals of medical ethics to each new intake of students at University College Hospital.

For the last twenty years of his life Crocker was the doyen of British dermatologists; his professional stature has been compared with that of his contemporary Ernest Besnier in Paris. He was founder member of the Dermatological Society of London which functioned as the training ground for these new specialists. He was also an early participant in the Dermatological Society of Great Britain and Northern Ireland, later serving on its council and as its president in 1899. When, in 1905, these two societies were merged to form the Royal Society of Medicine, Radcliffe-Crocker was elected as the first president of its dermatological section. Nevertheless, he was able to maintain his position in mainstream medicine, as evidenced by the invitation in 1903 to deliver the prestigious Lettsomian lectures to the Medical Society of London and by his position on the council of the Royal College of Physicians from 1906 to 1908.

Crocker's avid reading and retentive memory facilitated the production of his textbook *Diseases of the Skin: their Description, Pathology, Diagnosis and Treatment*, which was first published in 1888 and exemplified his lucid and comprehensive writing style. For many years it was the most highly regarded on the subject in English and it ran to several editions. It was followed between 1893 and 1896 by the monthly instalments of *The Atlas of Diseases of the Skin*. Dermatological societies in America, France, Germany, and Italy recognized his pre-eminence in the speciality, elected him to their membership, and valued his attendance and contributions to their meetings.

As a young man Crocker went about his work with an air of grave determination, but he was not aloof and remained generally good humoured and capable of sharing a joke. Above middle height he had a fine physique and participated in a number of sporting activities including cycling, sculling, and lawn tennis. He particularly enjoyed travel but in later life his health was undermined by recurrent attacks of erysipelas, of which the final and most severe precipitated his resignation from his posts at the British Medical Association and induced a desire to step down from his duties at University College Hospital. His colleagues persuaded him to reconsider and, in the summer of 1909, he embarked on a holiday to the Swiss alpine village of Engelberg, where he hoped to complete his recuperation. On 22 August he died suddenly from heart failure while sitting in his hotel. His burial took place at Engelberg. In 1912 Mrs Radcliffe-Crocker donated his extensive library of dermatological works in various languages to University College Hospital medical school together with £1500 for the foundation of a dermatological travelling scholarship.

WILLIAM A. BRANFORD

Sources DNB · BMJ (11 Sept 1909), 729–32 · *The Lancet* (4 Sept 1909), 758–60 · *British Journal of Dermatology*, 21 (1909), 331–3 · E. Graham-Little, 'Celebrated British dermatologists of the past fifty years', *British Journal of Dermatology and Syphilis*, 50 (1938), 503–18 · A. M. H. Gray, 'Dermatologists at University College Hospital', *British Journal of Dermatology*, 75 (1963), 457–64 · C. B. Bunker and P. M. Dowd, 'Henry Radcliffe Crocker, M.D., F.R.C.P., (1845–1909), physician to the skin department of University College Hospital', *International Journal of Dermatology*, 31 (1992), 446–50 · S. Gold, *A biographical history of British dermatology* (1995) · W. B. Shelley and J. T. Crissey, *Classics in clinical dermatology* (1953) · b. cert. · m. cert.
Archives Royal Free Hospital, London, medical school, Crocker Chest, original drawings of cases studied by subject · UCL, July 1879 appointment as University College Hospital skin department medical officer · University College London Hospitals, department of dermatology, part of subject's collection of histology sections
Likenesses photograph, c.1896, repro. in Graham-Little, 'Celebrated British dermatologists' · H. Ernst, photograph (in academic robes), repro. in BMJ, 2 (1909), 729–32 · H. Ernst, photograph (in academic robes), repro. in Graham-Little, 'Celebrated British dermatologists' · photograph, University College Hospital, London; repro. in Gray, 'Dermatologists at University College Hospital'
Wealth at death £17,778 8s. 2d.: probate, 31 Aug 1909, *CGPLA Eng. & Wales*

Crocker, Sir William Charles (1886–1973), lawyer, was born at 8 Tytherton Road, Upper Holloway, London, on 19 May 1886, the son of Thomas Edward Crocker, a law clerk, and his wife, Emma, *née* Whyte. Crocker served his articles of clerkship with his father and was admitted as a solicitor in 1912. Shortly before his admission, on 25 January 1911, he married Mary Madeline (1884/5–1953), daughter of Alfred Harris Tailby, a draughtsman, with whom he had one son and five daughters. He served in the First World War, first in the Artists' Rifles and later as a second lieutenant with the 4th Dorset regiment, winning the Military Cross.

Crocker practised with various firms in the City of London during his professional life. Throughout his career he was concerned to raise and maintain the status of solicitors, and to that end he was actively involved in the affairs of the Law Society. He first served on the society's council in 1932, and he remained a member of that body for the next twenty-three years. He was a member of the disciplinary committee under the Solicitors Act from 1949 to 1960, the committee being responsible for policing the standards of the profession. He was one of the first within the Law Society to see the value of publicity, and with this end in mind he reorganized the *Law Society Gazette*, the journal of the Law Society, as a monthly publication, and was responsible for establishing the public relations department of the society. His long service was rewarded with the vice-presidency of the society in 1952 and the presidency in 1953. He received a knighthood in 1955.

Professionally Crocker was renowned for acting for insurers and gained notoriety from a number of high-profile cases. His greatest success was in the so-called 'fire raising' case of 1933. A series of conspirators planned frauds on insurers by taking premises, stocking them with over-insured goods and then setting fires so as to allow a claim against the insurers. The conspirators, led by Leopold Harris, made claims amounting to £270,000. Crocker, whose suspicions were aroused by previous cases that had come to him in the course of his business, communicated with representatives of the insurance companies and Lloyds, and he was retained as solicitor to investigate further. As a result of his work sixteen members of the gang that had 'plundered the insurance offices' were put on trial before Mr Justice Humphreys. One of the longest criminal trials that the Old Bailey had seen, it lasted thirty-three separate days, and the summing-up to the jury took twelve and a half hours. Harris was sentenced to fourteen years' imprisonment, while the other gang members received sentences between six years and fourteen months. At the end of the trial Crocker was complimented by the judge for his efforts in tracking down the gang. Although this was his best-known case, he was engaged in other successful detective enterprises, one involving the disappearance of £54,000 worth of diamonds in Egypt during the Second World War, for which he was dubbed the Sherlock Holmes of insurance. His exploits were documented in two semi-autobiographical works, *Far from Humdrum* (1967) and *Tales from the Coffee House* (1973).

After the death in 1953 of his first wife, in 1956 Crocker married Ruth Boswell, daughter of Harry Chandler of Los Angeles and widow of Colonel James G. Boswell. He retired from active practice in 1966 and spent much of his time in California, where his presence had already been acknowledged by the bestowal of honorary membership of the American Bar Association in 1958. He died in California on 29 September 1973. Although he was responsible for important reforms within the Law Society, he is best remembered for being 'outstandingly successful in directing private enquiries into the origins of incidents giving rise to [insurance] claims' (*Solicitors' Journal*, 718).

MARK LUNNEY

Sources *Law Society Gazette*, 70 (14 Nov 1973), 2526 [address by Sir Desmond Heap] · *The Times* (1 Oct 1973) · *Solicitors' Journal*, 117 (1973), 718 · *Law Society Gazette* (1933) · *Law List* (1933) · *Law List* (1963) · W. C. Crocker, *Far from humdrum: a lawyer's life* (1967) · W. C. Crocker, *Tales from the coffee house: stories about Lloyds* (1973) · b. cert. · m. cert. [Mary Madeline Tailby] · d. cert.

Wealth at death £122,490: probate, 7 Feb 1974, *CGPLA Eng. & Wales*

Samuel Rutherford Crockett (1859–1914), by Elliott & Fry

Crockett, Samuel Rutherford [*formerly* Samuel Crocket] (1859–1914), Free Church of Scotland minister and novelist, was born Samuel Crocket on 24 September 1859 at the farm of Little Duchrae, Balmaghie, Stewartry of Kirkcudbright, natural son of Annie Crocket (1828–1879), dairymaid, daughter of William Crocket (1784–1875), tenant farmer, and his wife, Mary Dickson (1802–1884). Crockett gave his father's name as 'David Blaine Crockett, farmer' on his marriage certificate. His grandparents, although Cameronians, made his country childhood very happy. Stories of covenanting forebears were adventures to him: he acted them out like cowboys and indians. From the Free Church school at Castle Douglas he won in 1876 an annual £20 bursary to Edinburgh University, supplementing it by miscellaneous journalism.

Thereafter Crockett explored Europe as a travelling tutor, and in 1881 entered New College, Edinburgh, as a Free Church divinity student, evangelized in slums, added Rutherford to his name, and continued his ever-increasing journalism. In 1886 he was called to the Free Church in Penicuik, Midlothian, and published *Dulce cor*, his poems. On 10 March 1887 he married Ruth Mary Milner (1861–1932), daughter of a Manchester philanthropist and mill owner, whom he had met through his writing. They had four children, on whom Crockett based his six humorous books for children.

Crockett continued his journalism, rising early to write before starting his pastoral duties, which included literary and scientific talks to his congregation, following Free Church policy. Missions to miners and paper mill workers increased his warm sympathy for the poor; he was a leader in relief work after the 1889 Mauricewood pit disaster, and

a hard-working, well-liked minister. Sketches of ministers and congregations, slyly mocking humbug in both, which he contributed to a Glasgow religious weekly, were so popular that twenty-four, published in 1893 as *The Stickit Minister*, brought Crockett immediate fame. The success in 1894 of *The Raiders* and *The Lilac Sunbonnet*, an adventure story and a romance, both evoking Galloway's wild beauty, encouraged him, impatient with Free Church narrowness, to risk full-time writing.

Often dismissed as merely a kailyard writer of sentimental, old-fashioned tales of Scottish rural life, Crockett inclined rather to the sensational, borrowing plots from experience, tradition, and his enormous library, taking liberties with history and exaggerating. He called himself a romancer but his hatred of cruelty, his sardonic humour, and his vigorous description and characterization in Scots and English came through with gusto, whether about covenanters (*The Men of the Moss Hags*), sixteenth-century Ayrshire feuds and Sawny Bean the macabre Scottish cannibal (*The Grey Man*), Edinburgh slums (*Cleg Kelly*), the tragic fifteenth-century Douglases (*The Black Douglas*, *Maid Margaret*), his own childhood melodramatically heightened (*Kit Kennedy*), or nineteenth-century Italian banditti (*The Silver Skull*). His range was wide and varied—sixty-three books in twenty years, mostly novels and collections of short stories—but every Crockett was different; many readers were disappointed.

Of immense stature, an alpine climber, golfer, and far-travelled photographer, Crockett was, however, never strong; weakened by recurrent malaria and enteritis, he nevertheless had to write, wintering abroad and returning home to Penicuik, Peebles, or Auchencairn in summer. His letters show cheerful courage, but his novels display strain and flagging power. He died suddenly at Villa Philip, Tarascon, near Avignon, southern France, on 16 April 1914, and was brought home to Balmaghie churchyard for burial on 23 April.

ISLAY M. DONALDSON

Sources I. M. Donaldson, *The life and work of Samuel Rutherford Crockett* (1989) • E. Black, ed., *The Black Collection*, Penicuik Public Library, vol. 57 'The Free Church'; vol. 18 'S. R. Crockett' • M. McL. Harper, *Crockett and Grey Galloway: the novelist and his work* [preface dated 1907] • *Kirkcudbrightshire Advertiser* (24 April 1914) • F. R. Hart, *The Scottish novel: a critical survey* (1978), 114–53 • 'Christian Leader', Mitchell L., Glas. • Broughton House, Kirkcudbright, collection of Crockettiana and catalogues of Sotheby's sales of his books, 1912–14
Archives Hornel Library, Broughton House, Kirkcudbright, letters mainly to Mr and Mrs Macmillan of Newton Stewart • Mitchell L., Glas. • NL Scot., corresp. and literary papers • U. Edin. L.
Likenesses Elliott & Fry, photograph, NPG [*see illus.*] • F. R., cartoon ('The stickit minister'), repro. in *VF* (5 Aug 1897) • Moffat, photograph, repro. in J. J. Wilson, *A fifty years retrospect: a short history of the Free Church Congregation in Penicuik* (1893) • photographs, priv. coll.
Wealth at death £9734 13s. 2d.; also house in Auchencairn: will, General Register Office for Scotland, Edinburgh

Crockford, John (1824/5–1865), publisher of *Crockford's Clerical Directory*, was perhaps born in Taunton, though his origins and parentage are obscure. No baptism has been traced, but his marriage certificate records him as the son of John Crockford, schoolmaster. By his early twenties he was in business as a printer and publisher at 29 Essex Street, Strand, and it was from that address that *Crockford's Directory* was first published in 1858.

Crockford's long association with Edward William *Cox had begun by 1843, when the *Law Times* first appeared. The two men shared the same business address in Essex Street, and were joint founders of a number of periodicals, including *The Critic* and *The Field*. Cox, as the elder, more established, and richer man, was the financial backer and often the named publisher. When the *Clerical Directory* came to be planned, Cox's professional ethics (he was then recorder of Helston and Falmouth) forbade the use of his name in the title. However, the legend that he therefore picked, almost at random, the name of one of his office clerks, is far from the truth. Crockford was manager of the joint enterprises, 'a splendid man of business'. It was he who bought the embryonic *Field* 'for a trifling sum', and within a short time achieved profits amounting to £20,000 a year.

The *Clerical Directory* was first published in weekly parts from 1855 to 1857, initially as a supplement to the *Clerical Journal*. The first full edition seems to have been assembled in a very haphazard fashion, with names added as fast as they could be obtained, out of alphabetical order, and with an unreliable index. The 1858 volume stated that the 1859 edition would be in a more orderly sequence; in fact the 1860 volume was the first to be entitled *Crockford's Clerical Directory*, and in its new format was a very much more useful work of reference, with excellent bibliographical as well as career information. By 1917, with the absorption of its only serious rival, the *Clergy List*, *Crockford's Clerical Directory* reigned supreme. The famous 'prefaces', with sometimes sharp comments on the condition of the Church of England, began in 1869, after Crockford's death. From 1921 *Crockford*, as it had become known, was published by Oxford University Press.

No more than glimpses survive of Crockford's personality. John C. Francis (of *The Athenaeum*) recorded that, 'I had occasion to call on him a short time before his death, when we joined in a hearty laugh over his former furious attacks upon *The Athenaeum*. "Dilke's Drag" he used to call it' (*The Athenaeum*, 29 Nov 1879, 695).

Crockford married Annie Ellam on 24 December 1847 at St Pancras Old Church. No children are recorded. His sudden death occurred at his home, 10 Park Road, Haverstock Hill, London, on 13 January 1865, when he was aged forty. His will, proved on 6 February 1865, left everything to his widow. His personal effects were valued at less than £1000, but the family must have lived in some style, since one of the witnesses to the will was the resident coachman. BRENDA HOUGH, *rev.* H. C. G. MATTHEW

Sources *The Times* (16 Jan 1865) • J. L. Altholz, 'Mister Serjeant Cox, John Crockford, and the origins of *Crockford's clerical directory*', *Victorian Periodicals Review*, 17 (1984), 153–93, esp. 153–8 • *N&Q*, 9th ser., 11 (1903), 82–3 • Oxford University Press • m. cert. • d. cert.
Archives Oxford University Press
Wealth at death under £1000: probate, 1865

Crockford, William (*bap.* 1776, *d.* 1844), gambling club proprietor, was baptized in February 1776, the son of William Crockford, fishmonger, and his wife, Mary Ann, whose fish stall was at the eastern end of the Strand, Westminster. It is supposed that young William acquired a taste for gambling at Billingsgate fish market and in the less salubrious taverns in nearby Fleet Street, where whist, piquet, and cribbage were the favourite games. Crockford's success at dice and cards soon made him a rich man. He also backed horses, and by 1809 he was a familiar figure at Tattersalls and Newmarket, where his cronies told him about other rich and fashionable gamesters who soon became his town clients. Blessed with a good memory, he had an up-to-date awareness of their various financial situations which was part of the tools of his trade. Despite his move into high society, Crockford, who was barely literate when young, never lost his cockney accent.

Crockford kept his private life well away from his public activities. It was said that his wife, Sarah Frances, had been governess to the family of a wealthy lady, and that Crockford had enjoyed the favours of the mistress, with whom he had four children, and her servant. The date of their marriage is not known, but Crockford and his family of fourteen children resided in a house at 26 Sussex Place, which was decorated by architects Benjamin and Philip Wyatt. Rumours abounded of his sexual exploits elsewhere. Nevertheless he gave his children good educations, sending his sons to public schools such as Harrow, and to the universities of Oxford and Cambridge, and his daughters made good marriages.

As his status among London's gaming fraternity rose, Crockford migrated westward to Mayfair and St James, where he frequented such fashionable dining and gambling clubs as Almack's in King Street and Watier's in Bolton Row; he was at one time briefly a partner of Joshua Taylor, then Watier's proprietor. After many complaints from the residents about the nightly affray at the King

Crockford the Shark
Keeper of Hell
gaming House
Piccadilly

William Crockford (*bap.* 1776, *d.* 1844), by Thomas Rowlandson

Street houses, Crockford confined himself to a house in St James's Street, later extended to four houses in a row, where his brother was in partnership, and on this site he in 1826 commissioned the Wyatts to build his 'palace of gambling', which survives as the finest example of their work.

When 'Crockford's' doors opened in 1828, revealing the superbly decorated interior, all fashionable London clamoured for admission. Its lofty saloons and magnificent dining-room were ancillary to the all-important 'playroom' with its table for hazard, by then the favourite game. Membership was limited to 1000 or 1200, exclusive of ambassadors and distinguished foreign visitors, who enjoyed temporary membership. Benjamin Disraeli, when a friend proposed putting his name forward, thought it likely he would be blackballed; he was elected only in 1840. Crockford bore with wise tolerance the label of 'Fishmonger's Hall' bestowed on his mansion and the various stinging satires on himself that soon circulated. He could afford to do so: other gaming clubs failed to compete with this new venture, and opposition would have been futile as virtually all the men of power were members. Vast sums of money followed the fall of the dice or the facing of a card. It was recounted that 'one notorious gambling nobleman, known as "Le Wellington des Joueurs", lost £23,000 at a sitting, beginning at twelve at night and ending at seven the following evening' (Timbs, 240). In the first year, over £300,000 was plucked from count and commoner, peer and professional, most of it ending up in Crockford's coffers. One of Crockford's sons

was the house manager. The famous chef Louis Eustache Ude presided for ten years over the club's exquisite table and the best wines, all provided gratis to the clients. When he was dismissed in 1838, after a row at Crockford's, it was revealed that Ude had been paid the vast sum of £4000 annually for his services.

At Newmarket, Crockford acquired Panton House, in the High Street, with 50 acres of ground, where he stayed during the racing season. He also bought a large farm where at considerable expense he constructed a pig-rearing unit. This caused some guffaws among the farming community, for Crockford's ignorance of anything other than fish or horseflesh was common knowledge. He owned several racehorses, but the pig farm was never a success. Nor was his essay into commercial property: seeing how successful the new bazaars had become, he decided that the residents of Mayfair would enjoy similar facilities. He leased some crown land on the corner of King Street and St James's Street, and after some difficulty in evicting its occupants, the building was completed in 1832, at a cost of over £20,000. It flourished for a season or two, as customers were drawn to this novel way of shopping, but when they tired of it, the stallholders abandoned it as unprofitable. It stayed open for a further year, housing exhibitions and entertainers, then closed. The only benefit to Crockford was that he used its cellars as his wine store, also selling wines by the bottle to his members. After his death three of his sons continued this line of business.

In his earlier days, Crockford was regularly charged with keeping a common gambling-house, but by slipping sufficient money into the right hands, he always avoided having to make a court appearance, which would probably have led to imprisonment or even transportation. Crockford's, however, remained immune from prosecution, for the sworn evidence which was required from two householders resident in the parish was never forthcoming. Challenged by a parliamentary select committee on gaming in 1844, the police commissioner declared that Crockford's was a 'general club' and that many members did not play. The same could have been said about many clubs that were raided and Crockford was undoubtedly protected by his more powerful members.

In 1842 Crockford bought 11 Carlton House Terrace, London, from Baron Monson and moved his family into the limelight and literally within sight of the royal palace of Buckingham House. But his last days were unhappy. He was persuaded to invest heavily in a mining venture in Flintshire, which produced only dross. He was mortified by the knowledge that he had made bad investments and lost a great deal of money, and his health deteriorated. He survived the Derby Day of 1844, in which his horse Ratan ran. In a famously dirty race Ratan, doped or deliberately misridden, came in seventh. Crockford died at 11 Carlton House Terrace, appropriately on the day of the Oaks, 24 May 1844.

Crockford, in a brief will, left everything to his wife, 'trusting her to do what is right' (PRO, PROB 11/1999, sig. 446). Despite his recent losses, his personal property approached £200,000, his real estate a further £150,000. Sarah Crockford sold the residence at Carlton House Terrace, let the remainder of the Crockford's lease, reconstructed the bazaar, and converted it into chambers. The fortunes of the club went downhill immediately after his death; the building went through several hands before emerging with a cleansed reputation as the Devonshire Club. Sarah retired to end her days in comfort and obscurity.

ANITA MCCONNELL

Sources H. Blyth, *Hell and hazard* (1969) · A. L. Humphreys, *Crockford's, or, The goddess of chance in St James's Street, 1828–1844* (1953) · H. T. Waddy, *The Devonshire Club and 'Crockford's'* (1919) · 'Crockford and Crockfords', *Bentley's Miscellany*, 17 (1845), 142–55, 251–64 · J. Timbs, *Clubs and club life in London: with anecdotes of its famous coffee houses, hostelries, and taverns, from the seventeenth century to the present time* (1872) · W. F. Monypenny, *The life of Benjamin Disraeli*, 1 (1910), 292 · W. F. Monypenny, *The life of Benjamin Disraeli*, 2 (1912), 39 · will, PRO, PROB 11/1999, sig. 446 · d. cert. · *DNB*

Likenesses T. Jones, etching, pubd 1828 (after his portrait), BM, NPG · R. S., lithograph, BM, NPG · T. Rowlandson, pen-and-ink drawing, BM [*see illus.*]

Wealth at death personal property valued at £200,000, and real estate valued at £150,000: *DNB*

Croft, (Noel) Andrew Cotton (1906–1998), army officer and Arctic explorer, was born on 30 November 1906 at Abbey Cottage, Essex Road, Stevenage, Hertfordshire, the only son and fourth child of the Revd Robert William Croft, curate of Stevenage, and his wife, Lottie Alice Bland Clayton. His father, a gentle, saintly man and a classical scholar, took a living in a remote hamlet on the Essex coast before becoming vicar of Kelvedon, and a canon of Chelmsford Cathedral. Croft attended two preparatory schools before going to Lancing College, where he was in the house of J. F. Roxburgh, who recognized his potential and took him with him as one of his senior pupils when he became first headmaster of Stowe School in 1923. He went to Christ Church, Oxford, in 1925, and took a pass degree in 1928. New interests, developed at Oxford, led to his working in Geneva with the American committee at the League of Nations in 1927. There he met the polar explorer Fridtjof Nansen, and also Gustav Stresemann who had brought Germany into the league. Stresemann's right-hand man, Werner Kissling, became a lifelong friend.

Croft intended to go into the cotton trade, and studied at the Manchester School of Technology. But he spent a brief unhappy time in the textile industry in Carlisle until he was invited by the headmaster of Eton College to join his staff, provided that he first became fluent in German. He spent a year in Europe, learning German and French. Happening to be in Berlin on 28 February 1933, he was a witness to the Reichstag fire, and to the fact that the watching Brownshirts made no attempt to put it out. He taught briefly in a preparatory school, but in autumn 1933 he was invited to join Martin Lindsay's three-man expedition across Greenland. Croft put in much of the preparatory work in west Greenland, essential to the expedition's success, and he was principal dog-driver on what remains the longest self-supporting dog-sledge journey on record, at 1080 miles. The expedition crossed the ice cap in 1934, and mapped Greenland's highest mountains.

Croft spent 1934–5 as aide-de-camp to the young maharaja of Cooch Bihar, before joining the Oxford University Arctic expedition to Nordaustland, the most northerly of the Spitsbergen group, as deputy leader under Alexander (Sandy) Glen. The team were all awarded the polar medal for the expedition, for their contributions to radar development by research on the ionosphere, and glaciological discoveries and survey. From 1937 to 1939 Croft was secretary to Louis Clarke, the director of the Fitzwilliam Museum, Cambridge, and he accompanied an ethnographical expedition to Swedish Lapland in 1938. He published *Polar Exploration* in 1939.

His time in Germany had left Croft in no doubt that war was likely and from summer 1939 he was involved in the secret and intelligence organizations then being improvised. He was initially engaged in the War Office mission to the Finno-Soviet war, and then in attempts to frustrate the German invasion of Norway. He was in Bergen as the Germans invaded, and, in ordinary clothes, evaded them and walked over the mountains to Voss, eventually joining the evacuating British forces. With the rank of major, he was sent to Stockholm in 1941, ostensibly as an assistant military attaché, actually with the Special Operations Executive (SOE). From the Shetland Islands he undertook long-range reconnaissance flights to map the sea ice edge with Sandy Glen, in support of the north Russian convoys. In 1943 Croft was posted to the Mediterranean, to launch commando raids on Italy and the south of France, first from north Africa and then, after the fall of Italy, from Corsica, and to infiltrate SOE agents into occupied France. He personally led twenty-four sorties into enemy territory, and in 1944 parachuted into France to work with the resistance. He ended the war in Denmark, and was awarded the DSO.

After the war Croft was internationally recognized as an expert on cold-weather warfare, and on special operations more generally. He stayed with the army, and was attached to the Canadian Operation Musk Ox in 1945–6, testing equipment in Canada's frozen northern territories, and to the north-west frontier trials in India in 1946–7, where he witnessed the communal massacres after partition later that year. By now a lieutenant-colonel in the regular army, he served as liaison officer headquarters continental army in the United States (1952–4). On 24 July 1952 he married Rosalind Madden, *née* de Kantzow (1917/18–1996); they had three daughters. A skilled soldier, and a perfectionist, Croft found other talents, during these years, in training and human development, especially with the young. In 1954 he took over and reorganized the boys' infantry battalion at Plymouth, transforming a hitherto dispirited unit with such success that in 1957 he was promoted colonel and commandant of the army apprentices school at Harrogate. He retired from the army in 1960, and was asked to create and run a training college for the Metropolitan Police at Hendon. He organized the college along public-school lines, and encouraged the cadets to take GCE examinations. It was, he said, the most exciting job he had taken on: 'parachuting had nothing on it' (*Independent*, 1 July 1998). He was appointed OBE in 1970, and retired in 1971 to his home, River House, 52 Strand-on-the-Green, Chiswick, where he and his wife entertained generously. He published his autobiography, *A Talent for Adventure*, in 1991. Andrew Croft died in Charing Cross Hospital, Fulham, on 26 June 1998.

ALEXANDER R. GLEN

Sources A. Croft, *A talent for adventure* (1991) · *The Independent* (1 July 1998) · *The Times* (3 July 1998) · *The Guardian* (14 July 1998) · *WWW* · personal knowledge (2004) · private information (2004) · M. R. D. Foot, *SOE: an outline history of the Special Operations Executive, 1940–46* (1984) · b. cert. · m. cert. · d. cert.

Likenesses photograph, *c*.1933, repro. in *The Times* · photograph, 1933–4, repro. in *The Independent*

Wealth at death £431,999—gross; £359,549—net: probate, 26 Nov 1998, *CGPLA Eng. & Wales*

Croft, Edward (*d.* 1601). *See under* Croft, Sir James (*c*.1518–1590).

Croft, George (1747–1809), Church of England clergyman and religious writer, second son of Samuel Croft (*b.* 1711), was born on 29 March 1747 at Beamsley, a hamlet in the chapelry of Bolton Abbey, in the parish of Skipton, West Riding of Yorkshire, and baptized on the same day at Bolton Abbey. His elder brother, John, died in youth of consumption. In spite of his father's poor financial circumstances Croft received a good education at Bolton Abbey grammar school under the direction of the Revd Thomas Carr. Of uncouth appearance and a sufferer from a 'slight paralytic affection of the head' (Kennedy, 1.xxvi), Croft was intelligent and of quick mental apprehension, the retentiveness of his memory being demonstrated by an ability to quote from the gospels at an early age. Carr not only taught his gifted pupil without fee, but solicited subscriptions from affluent friends and neighbours in order to send him to university.

Croft was admitted a servitor of University College, Oxford, at the age of fifteen, on 23 October 1762. He matriculated on 23 November 1762, was chosen Bible clerk of University College on 6 December, and a scholar of the college on 9 May 1768. In 1768, the first year of its institution, he gained Oxford University's chancellor's prize for an English essay entitled 'Artes prosunt reipublicae'. He graduated BA on 16 February 1768, and MA on 2 June 1769. On 6 December 1768 he was appointed master of Beverley grammar school. After being ordained he was elected fellow of University College on 16 July 1779. On 11 December 1779 he was instituted by his college to the vicarage of Arncliffe in the West Riding of Yorkshire. On 19 and 21 January 1780 he took the degrees of BD and DD respectively. On 12 October 1780 he married Ann Grimston, daughter of William Grimston of Ripon. They had one son and six daughters.

Croft became chaplain to the earl of Elgin about 1780. He left Beverley at Michaelmas 1780, on being appointed headmaster of Brewood School, Staffordshire, a post which he resigned in 1791 in order to take up the lectureship of St Martin's Church, Birmingham, to which was later added the chaplaincy of St Bartholomew. At college Croft had become a friend of John Scott, the future Lord Eldon who in 1802, as lord chancellor, awarded him the

rectory of Thwing in the East Riding, which he was allowed to hold, by a dispensation, with the vicarage of Arncliffe.

Croft's credentials as an educationist were demonstrated by his *A plan of education, delineated and vindicated, to which are added a letter to a young gentleman designed for the university and for holy orders; and a short dissertation upon the stated provision and reasonable expectation of public teachers* (1784), in which he aimed to 'remove the prejudices of those, who think the education of a grammar school too circumscribed' (p. 12). In an unpublished treatise, 'General observations concerning education', Croft defended the study of ancient authors and the value of learning more than one language. In 1797, as an addition to another work, he published *Observations on the Duties of Trustees and Conductors of Grammar Schools*, and in *An Address to the Proprietors of the Birmingham Library* (1803) he further propagated his educational views. A recurrent theme in his writings was the necessity for high standards of clerical learning and scholarship.

Croft was invited regularly to preach from the university pulpit of St Mary's, Oxford; one sermon on Proverbs 24: 21, delivered on 25 October 1783, was published in Stafford in 1784. By 1786 his reputation as a preacher earned him the invitation to deliver the prestigious Bampton lectures. In these lectures, published in 1786, his high-church principles, in vindication of the Church of England against dissenting sects, and in support of 'the authority of the Fathers' and against the abuses of human reason found lucid expression (G. Croft, *Eight Sermons Preached before the University of Oxford*, 1786, 3). Croft was distinctively eirenical in his references to the Church of Rome, complaining at the puritans' 'excessive prejudice against everything that wore the aspect of Popery' (ibid.), and regretting that the reformed Church of England had not retained 'somewhat more of the Romish ritual, or of outward decoration' (ibid., pp. 96, 139). He praised Archbishop Laud, implying that he had been a martyr to puritan 'malignity and invective' (ibid., p. 139). While not a consistent feature of all his writings, his relative tenderness towards the Church of Rome found an outlet in a sermon supposedly commemorating the anniversary of the deliverance from the Gunpowder Plot, preached at St Mary's on 5 November 1783, in which he claimed that there were elements of truth in almost every Roman Catholic doctrine and practice.

In Birmingham, Croft, along with Spencer Madan, the rector of St Philip's, became an active leader of the Church and King party. Although not directly involved in the town's Church and King mob riots against the Unitarian Dr Joseph Priestley and nonconformist meeting-houses in 1791, Croft later castigated Priestley for 'deep-rooted malignity' (G. Croft, *A Short Commentary, with Strictures, on Certain Parts of the Moral Writings of Dr Paley and Mr. Gisborne*, 1797, xix). He also urged the inhabitants of every district to give a 'true account' of the behaviour of protestant dissenters to the civil authorities, and called for civil restraints on those 'speaking indecently of the doctrine of the Trinity' (G. Croft, *The Test Laws Defended*, 1790, 5.xi). His antipathy towards dissenters, Methodists, rationalists, political radicals, and parliamentary reformers also found expression in *Plans of Parliamentary Reform, Proved to be Visionary, in a Letter to the Reverend C. Wyvill* (1793), and *Thoughts Concerning the Methodists and Established Clergy* (1795). His hostility to nonconformity and evangelicalism, sharpened by his experience of 'enthusiastic preachers' in Hull, led him to contemplate writing 'an account of the Puritans, Presbyterians, and Independents from the beginning of Elizabeth's reign', in order to show that the 'Dissenters have neither in the present nor in former times, deserved the indulgence they claim with so much confidence' (J. Hobson, *A Series of Remarks, upon a Sermon Preached ... by George Croft*, [1790], 14–15); a plan which he never fulfilled. He was also an implacable opponent of parliamentary reform, defending inequality in representation on the ground that the great proprietor was better educated, more independent, and liable to 'have more enlarged ideas' than a forty-shilling copyholder (G. Croft, *Plans of Parliamentary Reform*, 1793, 25). He recommended that the clergy avoid politics, but insisted that the dangers to the constitution were a legitimate subject of clerical concern which justified his own foray into political debates. Croft accused dissenters of what he called 'laxation bigotry' which 'by annexing no guilt to religious opinions, however absurd, has given a sanction to such an innundation of licentious comment on the Word of God' (*The Test Laws Defended*, 29). Although he conceded that Methodists were 'real friends to the King and Constitution', he deplored what he regarded as their introduction of a levelling principle in religion by apparently decrying the claims of learning 'in order to understand the Word of God more perfectly' (G. Croft, *Thoughts Concerning the Methodists and Established Clergy*, 1795, 50). Croft died at Birmingham on 11 May 1809, aged sixty-two, and was buried in the north aisle of St Martin's Church, where a memorial monument was erected. He was survived by his wife.

PETER B. NOCKLES

Sources Foster, *Alum. Oxon.* · *GM*, 1st ser., 79 (1809), 494 · R. Kennedy, 'Life of George Croft', in G. Croft, *Sermons: including a series of discourses on the minor prophets*, 2 vols. (1811) · *DNB* · *IGI* · J. Overton, *The true churchman ascertained* (1801)
Likenesses F. Egington, stipple (after G. Heape), BM, NPG · monument, St Martin's Church, Birmingham

Croft, Henry Page, first Baron Croft (1881–1947), politician, was born at Fanhams Hall, Ware, Hertfordshire, on 22 June 1881. He was the second son and youngest of the eight children of Richard Benyon Croft (1843–1912), an officer in the Royal Navy from 1858 to 1873, who later joined the business of Henry Page (1843–1912), a prosperous Hertford grain trader and maltster, after marrying Page's only child and heir, Anne Elizabeth (1843–1921), Henry Page Croft's mother. On his father's side, he was descended from the Croft family of Croft Castle, baronets. Raised in relative luxury, he attended St David's School, Reigate, Eton College, and Shrewsbury School, where he showed plenty of prowess in rowing but more modest academic ability. With his father's encouragement he went to Trinity Hall, Cambridge, to study chemistry. He captained

the boat club, but left to join the family business in 1902 without taking a degree, his elder brother, Richard Page Croft (1872–1961) having been severely wounded in the Second South African War. Quickly mastering the demands of both the corn trade and the brewing industry, he also gained valuable political insights into many of the problems then facing British commerce. On 10 July 1907 he married Nancy Beatrice (d. 1949), daughter of Sir Robert Hudson Borwick (later first Baron Borwick), a businessman, and had three daughters and a son.

The empire and tariff reform Like so many other young Conservatives of his generation, Croft was drawn into the world of politics by Joseph Chamberlain's tariff reform campaign. His memoirs liken his frequent trips to Highbury to a 'pilgrim going to Mecca' (Croft, *Life of Strife*, 46–7); and the combination of Joe's organizational crusading zeal and intense imperial patriotism was to leave an indelible imprint on him. Thereafter, enthusiasm for empire (in particular for its self-governing regions), a fear of at first the dominions and then later India spinning out of the imperial orbit, and a deeply rooted belief in the capacity of the colonies to contribute to Britain's economic and spiritual well-being, were consistently at the centre of his political outlook.

But Croft's imperialism was of the constructive variety: for idle imperialists he had no time at all. Like a thriving business, the empire needed close attention, careful management, and an eye constantly on the future. The passivity of the state, or of its political leaders, was thus to be condemned. What was required was creative and dynamic government, with administrative and legislative programmes aimed at furthering 'imperial unity'. Bringing the self-governing dominions into closer contact with Britain was the major theme of his *The Path of Empire* (1912), which had an introduction by Joseph Chamberlain. This, in turn, demanded attention to the form as well as the substance of political life, and it was here that Croft was to excel. His organizational and campaigning skills were harnessed to a variety of pre-war right-wing political movements—the Tariff Reform League (TRL), the Confederacy, Reveille, and the Imperial Union—all of which saw the Chamberlainite policy of preferential tariffs as crucial to the ability of Britain and the empire to survive in an increasingly competitive and hostile international environment. Possibly for the first time in British politics, here was a cause which could so inspire a group of men (and women) that they would make party serve the interests of empire, not the other way round. Whether within or beyond the pale of the Unionist Party, Croft showed throughout his life a facility for experimenting with new types of political organization which made for a turbulent and tortuous but not entirely unrewarding parliamentary career.

Before the First World War, Croft's contribution to the tariff reform campaign was immense. He began by traversing east Hertfordshire—in a dog cart with a stout cob belonging to his father—to set up local branches of the TRL. Within months fifteen branches were established with a combined membership of 2036. These branches remained among the most active within the league a decade later. In 1906 he contested the parliamentary constituency of Lincoln, whose sitting member, Charles Seely, was a strong Unionist free trader. Croft came bottom of the poll, but Seely was also defeated, the split Conservative vote letting a Liberal in. Defending his stand Croft stated, 'I much prefer an open enemy as a member for Lincoln than a professing friend who will stab me in the back' (Witherell, 43). This intransigent attitude thrust Croft to the centre of the Confederacy, a secret society of fifty or so youthful and ardent tariff reformers who from 1907 to 1909 pressed the party leader, Arthur Balfour, to commit himself to their cause, while trying to purge or purify the parliamentary party of free trade MPs and candidates. In 1910 Croft was elected by a narrow majority to the Christchurch division of Hampshire (having campaigned there vigorously for the previous three years). He remained in the House of Commons for thirty years, retaining the Bournemouth half of his constituency when it was divided in 1918.

The successors to the Confederacy were the Reveille movement and the Imperial Union. The former was founded by Croft in the summer of 1910 out of frustration with 'the sleeping sickness' to which he felt the Unionist Party had succumbed. Its aim was to shift party policy from a negative defence of the *status quo* to a positive programme of national defence, tariff reform and imperial union, small ownership, and poor law reform. In effect, this amounted to a frontal attack on Balfour as party leader. Indeed, Balfour's tactical pledge in December 1910 not to impose food duties until submitting them to the verdict of a referendum had so incensed Croft and his co-organizer, Lord Willoughby de Broke, that, like Leo Maxse, they were convinced that he 'must go'. The Imperial Mission, an empire-wide movement active from 1911 to 1913, which Croft chaired, was particularly concerned with the danger of a trade reciprocity agreement between Canada and the USA (Croft visited Canada to support Robert Borden's campaign against such an agreement), but also organized rallies in England, especially in the north. In 1912 Croft became vice-chairman of the Tariff Reform League's organizing committee (he became its chairman in 1916), and in 1913 he succeeded George Wyndham as head of the league's Lancashire, Cheshire, and north-west counties federation, and was one of the few Unionist MPs to refuse to put his name to the memorial stating full confidence in Bonar Law's tariff policy. Croft believed that the tariff reform campaign would best be advanced by grass roots political activism, and that constituency work was vital in proving that preference was potentially a popular cause.

The National Party In November 1914 Croft went to France with the 1st volunteer battalion of the Hertfordshire regiment, which he had joined as an undergraduate, and which he was to command within a year. He had previously written on national defence, arguing for the necessity of a 'national citizen army' as an integral part of military policy (H. P. Croft, 'A citizen army', in Lord Malmesbury, ed., *The New Order: Studies in Unionist Policy*, 1908, pp.

255–68). He fought on the Somme in 1916 as commander of the 68th infantry brigade and was twice mentioned in dispatches. After spending twenty-two months at the front—longer than any other MP—he returned to Britain to take up his seat in the House of Commons. His wartime experience hardened the political opinions which he had formed over the previous decade. Having witnessed the selflessness and bravery of men at the front he became more intolerant of the pragmatism and opportunism of politicians at home. Having felt at first hand the spirit of patriotism in the trenches, he was outraged at the pettiness and sordidness of the party system, not least at Lloyd George's sale of honours for party funds. Having watched the damage inflicted by German U-boats on Britain's food supplies, he was more than ever convinced of the need for an economic policy which would secure the greatest possible production of all the necessities of life under the British flag. And having seen the soldiers of Britain's dominions spill their blood on the battlefields of France he insisted that this be recognized by increasing the involvement of their political leaders in the management of the empire's affairs.

Determined that Britain should learn the lessons of the war, Croft resigned from the Tariff Reform League (along with its chairman, Viscount Duncannon) in August 1917 to form a new National Party, in order to oppose the 'corrupt compromises' of the coalition, and to strive for the principles of 'National Production and Imperial Unity'. In addition to tariffs, the National Party advocated neo-corporatist ideas (for example trade associations and a 'standard comfort wage') to deal with unemployment and poverty; a strict peace treaty with Germany; stiff restrictions on alien immigration; and publication of the details of party funds. It briefly claimed seven MPs and eighteen peers, as well as press support from the *Morning Post*, *The Globe*, and its own monthly journal, *National Opinion* (published from October 1917 to November 1922). Twenty-five candidates were fielded at the 1918 election, but only two (Croft and Sir Richard Ashmole Cooper) were returned. None the less, the National Party received just over 94,000 votes—one of the highest polls (in percentage terms) achieved by any minor party in the twentieth century. In January 1921 it was decided not to contest any more seats, and shortly afterwards the National Party was absorbed into the ranks of the Conservative 'die-hards' who, while divided over domestic policy, were united against the coalition's policy of buying off Irish, Indian, and Egyptian nationalists with constitutional concessions. Following the fall of Lloyd George, the die-hards lost momentum and Croft returned to the Conservative fold (his Bournemouth constituency association had remained loyal to him throughout this period). He was created a baronet in February 1924.

Tariffs and India between the wars As chairman of the influential Empire Industries Association (EIA), Croft took a leading part in the revived agitation for tariffs from 1927 to 1931. Like the TRL, the EIA's propaganda emphasized the importance of developing the resources of Britain's colonies and expanding trade within the empire—

'Empire Trade saves Great Britain', as he was apt to declare (H. P. Croft, *The Crisis: How to Restore Prosperity*, 1931, 1). But it also made even greater play of the need to safeguard home industries and to prevent the domestic market from being 'exploited' by foreign producers. Its campaigning on this issue was unremitting, and often took the form of protests on behalf of specific industries: iron and steel, lace and embroidery, motor vehicles, for example. Under his guidance the EIA quickly became a force to be reckoned with. Little attempt was made to enlist the support of the trade unions, his attitude to organized labour having hardened since the war. The EIA was also more accommodating towards the Conservative Party leadership: its message was disseminated by the press and platform, but it decided to work locally through existing party organizations rather than to form rival EIA branches. The EIA likewise avoided a confrontation with the Conservative leadership on the issue of food duties and preference, despite its frustrations with the limitations imposed by Baldwin's election pledge. Croft's own contribution to this campaign was huge, and it was partly owing to him that pro-tariff resolutions were secured at Conservative Party conferences in Scarborough (1926), Cardiff (1927), and Yarmouth (1928). By late 1928 an EIA memorial on the steel industry attracted the signatures of 200 MPs. Of course, the Ottawa tariff agreements (1932)—a series of bilateral agreements between Britain and the dominions establishing a system of imperial preference—were ultimately a response to world depression. But the vigorous lobbying and propaganda activity of the EIA had helped to promote the idea that a solution to Britain's economic problems lay in the empire. Croft, who was a key figure in this process, later reflected that the decisions of the Ottawa conference had placed a seal on the great policy which Joseph Chamberlain had given to the empire, and completed the main objective of his own political life.

In the early to mid-1930s Croft joined Churchill in the fight against Indian constitutional reform—what was the use of campaigning for thirty years to promote imperial unity, he asked, only to stand by and watch the end of British rule in India? To Croft, the policy of granting India greater self-government was a total anathema, a betrayal of the providential mission bestowed by God on the British nation in the form of its empire. His faith in Britain's right and duty to govern India was unshakeable:

> our ideal of government is the nearest approach to Christianity, and to exchange it for government which may lean towards the precepts of the Hindu religion and the ideals of the worship of Shiva or Kali is quite definitely, in my view, a 'spiritual abdication'. (Studdert-Kennedy, 349)

He also firmly believed that India's problems were economic, not political, and that the reforms would 'sharpen not soften communal strife' (Croft, *Life of Strife*, 237). These convictions brought him into conflict yet again with the Conservative leadership. Before its annual conference in Birmingham in 1933 he circulated a pamphlet entitled *The Salvation of India* to every delegate of every constituency body, an infringement of an unwritten rule that MPs must not attempt to interfere with constituency affairs. He was

typically unapologetic, stating that he would 'never hesitate personally to address any communications to Conservatives at any time when I consider that there is a danger to British or Imperial interests' (*Memoirs of a Conservative: J. C. C. Davidson's Memoirs and Papers, 1910–37*, ed. R. R. James, 1969, 396).

Even with Churchill's emergence as their leader, however, the die-hards of the 1930s fared little better than their predecessors a decade before. The more liberal direction of Baldwin's and Hoare's India policy was not to be changed, and the Government of India Act was passed in 1935, Croft having spoken against it in parliament nearly 300 times. He never wavered in his belief that the British empire was 'the greatest instrument for the advancement of Christian ideals in the world' (Studdert-Kennedy, 350). From 1936 to 1939 he continued to agitate on imperial affairs, along with Amery, George Lloyd, Alan Lennox Boyd, and Austen Chamberlain. A mass meeting was staged at the Albert Hall in July 1936 to mark the centenary of Joseph Chamberlain's birth, and to launch a new national campaign for empire unity.

War Office and peerage Though Croft found himself temporarily estranged from Churchill and his friends when he supported the Munich agreement in 1938, his contribution to the India Defence League, and his earlier co-operation with the anti-appeasement rebels, were not forgotten, and after Churchill became prime minister, Croft was elevated to the peerage as Baron Croft of Bournemouth in May 1940, and was made joint parliamentary under-secretary for war (with Edward Grigg), answering for the War Office in the House of Lords. His earlier advocacy of a citizen army made him 'a true believer' in the Home Guard, formed in May 1940 in response to the German invasion threat. He attracted ridicule, though, for his defence in the House of Lords (4 February 1942) of distributing pikes to the Home Guard in the absence of sufficient firearms; these became known as 'Croft's pikes' (Mackenzie, 179, 100). He retained his post in Churchill's short-lived caretaker government of 1945. He died at the Middlesex Hospital, London, on 7 December 1947.

Croft was described as a 'tower of strength', 'indefatigable worker' and 'stalwart fighter' by Leo Amery, who lamented that Croft had never received the recognition that he deserved (Amery, vol. 3). His boundless energy, organizational flair, and passionate commitment to the empire helped to sustain a succession of right-wing movements; these encountered mixed fortunes but are integral to the history of twentieth-century Conservatism. This left little time for recreation or even, perhaps, for his family; his son-in-law, Manfred Uhlman, described Croft's attitude toward his children as 'correct, cool and reserved' (Uhlman, 208). Not surprisingly, Uhlman, a socialist and Jewish refugee from Germany, who married Croft's second daughter, Diana (1912–1999) [*see* Uhlman, (Nancy) Diana Joyce, *under* Uhlman, Manfred], was not welcomed into the family. Croft apparently considered the union tantamount to 'social suicide', though, to his credit, he subsequently visited the couple and their children. Croft was succeeded as second baron by his son, Michael Henry Glendower Page Croft (1916–1997).

ANDREW S. THOMPSON

Sources L. Witherell, *Rebel on the right: Henry Page Croft and the crisis of British conservatism, 1903–1914* (1997) • W. D. Rubinstein, 'Henry Page Croft and the national party, 1917–22', *Journal of Contemporary History*, 9 (1974), 129–47 • H. P. Croft, *My life of strife* (1948) • H. P. Croft, *Twenty-two months under fire* (1916) • Burke, *Peerage* (1999) • L. S. Amery, *My political life*, 3 vols. (1953–5) • A. Morrison, *British business and protection, 1903–32* (1996) • A. Thompson, *Imperial Britain: the empire in British politics, 1880–1932* (2000) • G. Studdert-Kennedy, 'The Christian imperialism of the die-hard defenders of the raj, 1926–35', *Journal of Imperial and Commonwealth History*, 18 (1990), 342–62 • M. Gilbert, ed., *Winston S. Churchill*, companion vol. 5/2 (1981) • F. Uhlman, *The making of an Englishman* (1960) • S. P. Mackenzie, *The home guard: a military and political history* (1995) • G. R. Searle, *Corruption in British politics, 1895–1930* (1987) • CGPLA Eng. & Wales (1948)

Archives CAC Cam., MSS | CAC Cam., notes and corresp. with E. Spears • HLRO, corresp. with Lord Beaverbrook; letters to R. Blumenfeld

Likenesses portrait, 1910, repro. in Witherell, *Rebel* • H. Coster, photographs, NPG • W. Stoneman, photograph, NPG

Wealth at death £101,738 0s. 3d.: probate, 12 March 1948, CGPLA Eng. & Wales

Croft [Crofts, Craftes], **Sir Herbert** (*c.*1565–1629), administrator and landowner, was the eldest surviving son of Edward *Croft (*d.* 1601) [*see under* Croft, Sir James] of Croft Castle, Herefordshire, and his first wife, Anne (*d.* 1575), daughter and heir of Thomas Browne of Attleborough, Norfolk. Both his father and his grandfather, Sir James *Croft, lord deputy of Ireland and one of Elizabeth's privy council, had very chequered careers, suffered imprisonment and exile, and had been reduced to selling family lands. Herbert, according to his son, Colonel Sir William Croft, was an undergraduate at Christ Church, Oxford, but there is no trace of him in the college records. Croft was granted a post at court at some point during the 1580s, and served with Robert Dudley, earl of Leicester, in the Netherlands during 1585–6. An attempted match with a Welsh heiress, Barbara Gamage, was thwarted by a rival suitor, Robert Sidney, in 1584; however, in 1590 or 1591 Croft married Mary (1573×6–1659), youngest daughter and coheir of Anthony Bourne of Holt Castle, Worcestershire, with whom he had a family of four sons and five daughters. He succeeded his grandfather to the diminished family estates in 1594, in which year he was admitted to the Middle Temple. During the 1590s he seems to have had three patrons: Henry Herbert, earl of Pembroke; Robert Devereux, earl of Essex; and Sir Robert Cecil. When James VI of Scotland made his royal entry into England, Croft was among those who waited upon the new king at Theobalds in Hertfordshire, and there, on 7 May 1603, he was knighted. He clearly had high hopes of promotion in this new era.

Croft had first entered parliament in 1589 for Carmarthenshire, where not only had he inherited lands from his great-aunt, Joyce Gamage, but where he also had a strong alliance with Gelly Meyrick, steward and political manager for the earl of Essex. But Croft's support for Essex was always rather ambivalent, and when Essex's rebellion of 1601 failed Croft eventually joined the rush for the forfeited estates. From 1592 to 1614 he followed the family tradition of representing Herefordshire in parliament except for one occasion in 1597 when he was ousted by the rival Herefordshire family of the Coningsbys, with whom the Croft family had long been in conflict, and was forced to find another seat, in the Cornish borough of Launceston. Croft was a determined participant in parliament, where he was a highly active member of many of its committees; from 1604 he was 'one of the leading members' of the House of Commons and was described by his contemporary John Chamberlain as one of the 'prime parlement men' (Ham, 138).

Locally too Croft was fast becoming a figure of some consequence. By 1600 he had not only recovered, but had augmented his family estates. In May 1605 he was entrusted by the privy council with suppressing the 'Whitsun riot', a petty skirmish in south-west Herefordshire after some local Catholics had commandeered the churchyard at Allensmore for a burial according to their rites. The government's exaggerated fears of the danger posed by this little affray reveal its nervousness in the year of the Gunpowder Plot. But Croft, though powerful, was not altogether popular: in 1600, despite Cecil's backing, he failed in his bid for the stewardship of Leominster, a post that had often been in his family, in the face of local opposition marshalled by the Coningsbys. In the following year Croft was one of twelve local grandees appointed to the council of Wales. However, he soon became very critical of that body and spent himself and his fortunes in a pertinacious campaign to remove from its jurisdiction the four English counties of Herefordshire, Worcestershire, Gloucestershire, and Shropshire, whose links to it were due to their being the successors to the turbulent marcher lordships. His obsession with this issue led, as he himself acknowledged, to his losing the favour of both the king and Cecil, who were only too sensitive to attacks on a court of royal prerogative. Croft too was not without a strong personal interest in this matter, given that in 1608 Lord Eure, the president of the council of Wales, was investigating excessive exactions that Croft was imposing on the queen's tenants in the stewardship of Leominster, a post he had finally obtained. In 1607 Croft was put down from the council of Wales (*CSP dom.*, *1603–10*, 370).

Croft felt acutely the loss of the royal favour when the king refused to knight his son, while his costly campaign against the council of Wales and his wife's extravagances made the family finances still worse. With 'almost everything he had fought for … [having] been lost', by the end of 1615 Croft had decided to leave England (Ham, 277). However, he seems not to have departed until 1617, when his movements (under at least two aliases) in France and the Spanish Netherlands were reported to Cecil by Sir Dudley Carleton, ambassador at The Hague. Croft, a typical specimen of the thrusting and grabbing gentry of his time, surprised everyone in 1617 when he 'turned popish', although John Chamberlain noted 'yt is no great marvayle, for desperation hath made more monckes than him' (Ham, 279).

Croft was in Rome shortly after his conversion, but returned to the Spanish Netherlands by August 1618. By the following year he had settled in St Omer. It was to there that he summoned his third son, Herbert *Croft, who was himself a recent convert to Catholicism, to be educated at the local Jesuit college; the son later returned to Anglicanism and eventually became bishop of Hereford. Croft retired to the English Benedictine monastery of St Gregory's at Douai in Flanders, where on 2 February 1626 he received 'letters of confraternity', which entitled him, though not formally a monk, to share in the spiritual life and benefits of the community.

There he spent the rest of his life in recollection and strict religious observance. He wrote several works printed at Douai in highly limited editions of eight copies each (one for the monastery, and seven for his family) justifying his own conversion and encouraging his family to follow suit. He died at St Gregory's on 1 April 1629 (not 1622 as claimed by Wood) and was buried in the church of the monastery before the altar of St Benedict where an epitaph praises Croft for following the example of his eleventh-century ancestor, Bernard de Croft, who had become in the last years of his life a monk of the Cluniac priory of Thetford.   DAVID DANIEL REES

Sources R. E. Ham, *The county and the kingdom: Sir Herbert Croft and the Elizabethan state* (1977) · Wood, *Ath. Oxon.*, new edn, vol. 1 · O. G. S. Croft, *The house of Croft of Croft Castle* (1949) · H. Foley, ed., *Records of the English province of the Society of Jesus*, 6 (1880) · R. Mathias, *Whitsun riot* (1963) · R. Weldon, *Chronological notes containing the rise, growth and present state of the English congregation of the order of St Benedict* (1881) · J. E. Neale, *The Elizabethan House of Commons* (1949) · Gillow, *Lit. biog. hist.* · M. Questier, *Conversion, politics and religion in England, 1580–1625* (1996) · W. J. Tighe, 'Herbert Croft's repulse', *BIHR*, 58 (1985), 106–9 · A. H. Dodd, 'Croft, Herbert', *HoP, Commons, 1558–1603* · *CSP dom.*, 1603–18 · BL, Add. MS 32102, fol. 145v · *Calendar of the manuscripts of the most hon. the marquis of Salisbury*, 24 vols., HMC, 9 (1883–1976), vol. 11, pp. 61, 114, 413, 567; vol. 13, p. 360 · G. D. Owen, *Wales in the reign of James I* (1988)
Archives BL, Cotton MSS
Likenesses two portraits, Croft Castle, Herefordshire

Croft, Herbert (1603–1691), bishop of Hereford, was born on 18 October 1603 at Great Milton, Oxfordshire, the third son of Sir Herbert *Croft (*c*.1565–1629) of Croft Castle, Herefordshire, and his wife, Mary (1573x6–1659), daughter of Anthony Bourne of Holt Castle, Worcestershire. He was educated first in Herefordshire, and then in 1616 at Oxford, though he did not then matriculate.

Jesuit period and return to Anglicanism In May 1617 his father, a prominent, though ultimately unsuccessful, national and local politician, had left England to become a Roman Catholic, and by 1619 had settled at St Omer. Eventually, in 1626, he was admitted as a lay brother at St Gregory's Benedictine Monastery, Douai, and wrote polemical material in the hope of converting his family, but he had already had what was to be his sole success, with young Herbert. By 1619 the latter, partly inspired by his father, partly by Newton, a Catholic layman in a London prison to

Herbert Croft (1603–1691), by unknown artist, *c*.1670

whom he took 'alms for a certain lady', had been converted by a priest named Chadwick (Kenny, *Responsa scholarum*, 390). Soon afterwards he went to St Omer to visit his father, who sent him to the Jesuit college there. Here he studied from about 1622 to 1626, and reputedly showed proficiency in poetry and rhetoric. By 1626 the Jesuits, using Ignatius of Loyola's *Spiritual Exercises*, persuaded him, against his father's wishes, to join the order. He now intensified his already thorough and protracted theological education. Under the assumed name of John Harley he became a student at the English College at Rome where he stayed until 1628, the year before his father's death in Douai.

While visiting England on family business Croft was persuaded to return to the Church of England by Thomas Morton, from 1632 bishop of Durham and renowned for the number of his conversions. William Laud further encouraged Croft to go to Christ Church, Oxford, where he now matriculated. He had already had ten years' intensive theological training abroad, and in November 1635 he successfully requested the university to take this into account. He consequently graduated BD in 1636.

John Davenant, bishop of Salisbury, ordained Croft deacon and priest on 12 January 1638. His family's once close connections with royalty—Yorkist, Tudor, and Stuart—had been temporarily weakened by his father's vigorous political campaign to have Herefordshire and three other shires exempted from the jurisdiction of the council of the marches, but his eldest brother, William, had accompanied the future Charles I and the duke of Buckingham on their ill-fated marriage expedition to Spain in 1623. These re-established connections now bore fruit. Almost immediately after ordination in 1638 Croft was instituted into the crown living of Uley, Gloucestershire, but the incumbency was brief; records show he had already resigned by the following January. Other preferments followed rapidly in 1639—he was appointed chaplain to the earl of Northumberland for his Scottish campaign, in May he became rector of Harpsden, Oxfordshire, and in August he became prebendary of Major Pars Altaris in Salisbury Cathedral. The following year, 1640, he proceeded DD at Oxford, and became a prebendary of Worcester Cathedral; in 1641 he gained a canonry of Windsor. Towards the end of 1644 he was made dean of Hereford, and that year became a chaplain to Charles I, after preaching before him 'with great approbation' (PRO, LC5/135, 13). The king approved of him enough to use him for conveying secret commands to leading royalist generals, often at great personal risk.

The civil war Naturally the civil war, in which three of his brothers fought for the king, and the ensuing interregnum severely disrupted Croft's fortunes. Soon after parliamentarian troops captured Hereford he showed exemplary physical courage when from the pulpit of his cathedral he 'inveighed boldly and sharply against [the] sacrilege' (Croft, iii) of the musketeers who had forced their entry into the building. Some levelled their firearms at him, and it was only by the intervention of the presbyterian governor of Hereford, Colonel John Birch, that he was saved. In the interregnum that followed, like many others, he was deprived of all his preferments, including the deanery, and thus lost his total ecclesiastical income. He spent these years with Sir Rowland Berkeley at Cotheridge, Worcestershire. The death of his eldest brother in 1645 enabled him to live off part of the Croft family revenues, his second brother, James, died in 1659, and he inherited the whole estate, then valued at £2000 a year. By 1651 he had married Anne, daughter of Jonathan Browne, dean of Hereford. Their son Herbert was born in late 1651 or early 1652.

Bishop of Hereford In 1660 Croft was reinstated to his deanery and other preferments, but not for long. Despite his undoubted loyalty to the royalist cause, surprisingly he had not appeared in the exiled government's promotion lists in 1658, nor was he one of the seventeen recommended for the see by Richard Baxter in 1660. However, his chance came in 1661 when Nicholas Monck, the newly consecrated bishop of Hereford, died. Croft was nominated to replace him on 27 December and was consecrated at Lambeth on 9 February 1662. The see was not a rich one, being worth only £800 a year, but Hereford was his home county and, with his newly inherited family estates he was happy to refuse offers of further preferment. He had a spell at court, eventually as dean of the chapels royal from 8 February 1668 to March 1670. During this time Samuel Pepys records that the king himself approved of Croft's preaching, but Gilbert Burnet was more critical: 'Crofts [sic] was a warm, devout man, but of no discretion in his conduct; so he lost ground quickly. He used much freedom with the king: but it was in the wrong place, not in

private, but in the pulpit' (Croft, v). Later, 'finding but little good effect of his pious endeavours there' (Wotton, 362), the bishop became so disillusioned with life at court that he withdrew to his see.

At Hereford he vigorously devoted himself to his duties as bishop, and earned a great reputation in his sprawling diocese that covered not only Herefordshire, but half Shropshire. He spent much time at Croft Castle, his family seat on the Hereford–Shropshire border, rather than in Hereford, but this, far from providing cause for criticism, made strategic sense: it was more central to his diocese than was the cathedral city. He ordained regularly throughout his episcopate, at first at the small church adjoining Croft Castle, but after 1677 invariably at Hereford, either in the cathedral or in the palace chapel nearby; he constantly demanded high standards of his ordinands. Diocesan administration was efficient. Despite the interruption caused by his predecessor's premature death, Croft was one of the first bishops after the Restoration to conduct an urgently needed episcopal visitation. He visited the Wenlock deanery on 2 May 1662, a mere four months after his consecration. From then onwards he always conducted his triennial visitations in person at least until the 1680s, when he was over eighty. The complicated procedures required under the Act of Uniformity (1662), whereby all clergy had to subscribe afresh, were managed with remarkable efficiency, and yet he showed sincere sympathy towards clergy ejected by the act. For instance, he regarded Richard Hawes, the puritan vicar of Leintwardine, so highly that he allowed him to continue preaching a month beyond the legal limit. He declared it was 'contrary to his inclination to have such as he removed, saying it was the law who turned him out and not he' (Marshall, 21).

Croft made little public show of his charitable works, but those who knew him realized his personal generosity in augmenting small livings and relieving many in distress. If he was not resident in Hereford himself, he had a weekly dole distributed among sixty poor people at his palace gate there. Until the late twentieth century there was a charity for the poor named after him at Yarpole. His correspondence shows he was still active in the diocese in the 1680s, even if the matter was a small one concerning an usher at Monmouth School in 1682. He took personal interest in charity briefs; in 1684 he was infuriated by one deanery official who lost all the briefs for French protestants in that year. He was lucky to have had efficient senior officials, Timothy Baldwin, his chancellor, and Griffith Reynolds, his registrar, but time and again he was prepared to admonish them for over-zealous execution of their duties. He was also much concerned with the welfare of his clergy. Normally he reserved prebends solely for clergy from inside the diocese, and in one case, to maintain efficiency, he refused to allow an archdeacon to hold a Windsor canonry simultaneously.

Anti-Catholicism, publication, and last years On the other hand, trained as a Jesuit himself, Croft seemed frenetic to prevent the growth of popery, always a potent force in the diocese, especially in Hereford itself, in Monmouth, and among the county families. His ardour was so extreme that in July 1678 the covert father provincial of the Jesuits ordered 'the assassination of Dr. Herbert Croft, the Bishop of Hereford, an apostate of the faith' (Foley, 5.101). In the following year Croft sent his men to take and plunder the Jesuit seminary of St Francis Xavier at Combe, near Monmouth. The seminarians escaped, but many books were seized and taken to the cathedral library.

After his departure from the court in 1670 Croft ceased to be politically active, and from then on hardly attended the Lords, although he preached a fast sermon there on 4 February 1674, and before the king at Whitehall on 12 April the same year. Instead, he turned for the first time to publication. His two sermons appeared in 1674 and 1676, and *A Second Call to Farther Humiliation* in 1678. Much of his work reflects his hostility to, even hatred of, popery. *A Letter to a Friend Concerning Popish Idolatrie* (1674) was followed in 1675 by *The Naked Truth*, originally anonymous, which 'made a great noise at the time of its publication' (Wotton, 363). *The Legacy of the Right Reverend Father in God the Bishop of Hereford* (1679) summarized the controversies between the Church of England and Rome, while in the same year he published *A Short Narrative of the Discovery of a College of Jesuits at Combe*. The second declaration of indulgence of 1688, occurring when Croft was eighty-five, caused him much anguish. A staunch monarchist, he had known James II personally; he wrote to Adam Ottley that he felt a 'very great kindness as well as a duty and obedience to my king' (NL Wales, Ottley MSS) and yet he protested he was prepared to die for the Church of England. In his last publication, *A Short Discourse Concerning the Declaration of Indulgence* (1688), he reveals both the torture of conscience and the inflexibility of age. After a night of torment, in 'a perfect agony' (p. 4), he agreed to allow the reading of the indulgence in his diocese. Reading, he equivocated, did not indicate assent. In this he disagreed with Archbishop Sancroft. Later he was tormented by papist rumours in London that he 'would come over to them' (NL Wales, Ottley MSS). This he firmly denied both to the king and the archbishop. He assured Sancroft he would retain the tests and do nothing 'prejudicial to the Church of England' (ibid.). In Henson's words, his writings of that year reveal a 'confused and troubled intellect' (Croft, vi). Croft's will, drawn up on 4 January 1689, lamented 'these evil dayes wherein wee have lived to see such sad Revolutions and dismall Catastrophes' (PRO, PROB 11/405, fols. 187–90). Eventually, later that year, he agreed to take the oaths to the new monarchs. He died in his palace in Hereford on 18 May 1691, and was buried in the cathedral on 28 May. His wife was living at the time he made his will, but his executor was their son Herbert (d. 1720), who had been created baronet in 1671 and who was MP for Herefordshire in 1679, 1690, and 1695.

Character and reputation Anthony Wood was not complimentary about Croft's writings, observing that 'the books that he wrote do show that he was not altogether conversant in divinity' (Wotton, 363). However, he wrote that Croft was 'much venerated by the gentry and commonalty of that diocese for his learning, doctrine, conversation and good hospitality; which rendered him a person, in their esteem, fitted and set apart by God for honourable and sacred function' (ibid., 362). Certainly he was not only a conscientious, painstaking, and caring bishop, but a genuine pastor, visiting the sick and relieving the poor in the parishes near his home, while his frequent use of Croft Castle as his base made strategic sense. Yet it is clear that the traumatic memory of his own early Jesuit training bulked large in his mind. In his will he thanked God for recalling him from 'the darknesse of popish errors and grosse superstitions, into which I was seduced in my younger dayes' (PRO, PROB 11/405, fols. 187–90). His hostility, fear, even hatred, of popery seemed to grow rather than diminish as the years passed. A more recent writer was ambivalent about his character:

> Loyal, affectionate, and zealous, he was also dictatorial and prejudiced. His candour was matched by his obstinacy. He was neither a great man nor a learned divine, but he had seen much of the world, and his conscience was more considerable than his understanding. (Croft, vi)

His father had always been single-minded in pursuit of a chosen cause, however disastrous the outcome, but Bishop Croft in old age, unlike his father, was prepared to trim during the cataclysmic events of 1688 and 1689, despite his violent antipathy to popery. This he frequently justified by referring to prophet Elisha's advice to Naaman to bow the knee in the house of Rimmon.

WILLIAM MARSHALL

Sources W. M. Marshall, 'The administration of the dioceses of Hereford and Oxford, 1660–1760', PhD diss., University of Bristol, 1979 · R. E. Ham, *The county and the kingdom: Sir Herbert Croft and the Elizabethan state* (1977) · Foster, *Alum. Oxon.* · *Fasti Angl.* (Hardy), vols. 1–3 · H. Croft, *The naked truth*, ed. H. H. Henson (1919) · diocesan records, Herefs. RO · Walker rev. · Wood, *Ath. Oxon.*, new edn, 4.309, 880 · T. Wotton, *The baronetage of England*, ed. E. Kimber and R. Johnson, 3 vols. (1771) · G. Holt, *St Omers and Bruges colleges, 1593–1773: a biographical dictionary*, Catholic RS, 69 (1979), 77 · A. Kenny, ed., *The responsa scholarum of the English College, Rome*, 2, Catholic RS, 55 (1963) · J. Wadsworth, *The English Spanish pilgrime* (1629); facs. edn (1970) · T. M. McCoog, *English and Welsh Jesuits, 1555–1650*, 1, Catholic RS, 74 (1994) · P. R. Harris, ed., *Douai College documents, 1639–1794*, Catholic RS, 63 (1972) · H. Foley, ed., *Records of the English province of the Society of Jesus*, 7 vols. in 8 (1875–83) · B. Willis, *A survey of the cathedrals*, 3 vols. (1742) · Oxon. RO, Oxfordshire diocesan papers, c. 78, fol. 161 · BL, Egerton MS 2542 · PRO, LC 5/135,13 · *Reliquiae Baxterianae, or, Mr Richard Baxter's narrative of the most memorable passages of his life and times*, ed. M. Sylvester, 1 vol. in 3 pts (1696) · will, PROB 11/405, fols. 187–90

Archives NL Wales, letters to Adam Ottley

Likenesses oils, c.1665–1670, Croft Castle, Herefordshire · oils, c.1670, Croft Castle, Herefordshire [*see illus.*]

Croft, Sir Herbert, fifth baronet (1751–1816), writer and lexicographer, was born at Dunster Park, Berkshire, on 1 November 1751 and was baptized the following day at St Andrew's Church, Holborn, London, the eldest son of Herbert Croft (1717/18–1785) of Stifford in Essex, the receiver to the Charterhouse, and his first wife, Elizabeth, daughter of Richard Young of Midhurst, Sussex. He was the grandson of Francis Croft, second son of the first baronet, and on the death, without a legitimate heir, in 1797, of Sir John Croft, the fourth baronet, he succeeded to the title. Unfortunately, however, the third baronet, Sir Archer

Croft, had cut off the entail, the family estates had passed into other hands, and Croft Castle itself had been sold to the father of Thomas Johnes, the translator of Froissart. Pecuniary pressure hampered Herbert Croft from the commencement of his life, but his difficulties were increased by his volatile character, which prevented him from settling into a profession, or dealing responsibly with his finances.

In March 1771 Croft matriculated at University College, Oxford. Intending to pursue a legal career, he entered himself at Lincoln's Inn, where he became the constant companion of Thomas Maurice, the oriental scholar, and Frederick Young, the son of Edward Young, the author of *Night Thoughts*. He was called to the bar in 1775, and is said to have practised in Westminster Hall with some success. On 17 April 1779 he married Sophia (1754–1792), the daughter and coheir of Richard Cleave, with whom he was to have three daughters. He gave up his legal practice (perhaps unwisely, as his later financial difficulties would demonstrate), and about 1782 he returned to University College, Oxford, where under the advice of Lowth, the bishop of London, he decided to study with a view toward taking orders. In April 1785 he took the degree of BCL, and in 1786 his episcopal patron conferred on him the vicarage of Prittlewell, in Essex, a living which he retained until his death in 1816.

For some years after his appointment, however, Croft lived at Oxford, busying himself in the collection of the materials for a proposed English dictionary. Croft had had a long-standing interest in lexicography, and in Johnson's *Dictionary* in particular. An unfinished 'Letter to the Right Hon. William Pitt concerning the New Dictionary of English' pointed out some of the defects of Johnson's dictionary, and Croft also published several papers in the *Gentleman's Magazine* on the topic. In 1787 his manuscripts commenting on the dictionary amounted to 200 quarto volumes, and in 1790 he claimed to have amassed 11,000 words used by the highest authorities, but missing from Johnson. He proposed to publish a new edition of Johnson's *Dictionary* in 1792, in four large volumes priced at 12 guineas. As Jonathon Green points out, however, 'his timing was bad and his labours pointless' (Green, 229). The subscribers' names were so few that Croft announced in the *Gentleman's Magazine* for 1793 that he would not be able to continue with the project without further pecuniary assistance, and, this not being forthcoming, he was forced to abandon the project. This was unfortunate, particularly as Joseph Priestley, who had himself considered compiling 'a large treatise on the structure and present state of our language', had dropped the scheme and given the unused materials to Croft.

These years of work were unremunerative for Croft, to say the least, and as he was naturally extravagant, he was soon embroiled in financial difficulties. His whole income consisted of his small vicarage in Essex, which produced about £100 p.a., and the balance of the salary assigned to his position of chaplain to the garrison of Quebec (where his personal attendance was not enforced) and his expenditure quite exceeded his means. His first wife died

on 8 February 1792, and on 25 September 1795 he was married by special licence to Elizabeth (d. 1815), daughter of David Lewis of Malvern Hall in Warwickshire; they were to have no children. On the day after his second marriage, however, Croft was arrested for debt and thrust into the common gaol at Exeter. He was obliged to withdraw to Hamburg, and his library was sold at King's in King Street, Covent Garden, in August 1797. While in Hamburg, he published *A Letter from Germany to the Princess Royal of England on the English and German Languages* (1797), which was a rambling commentary ranging on topics from Johnson's *Dictionary*, to the process of translating from German and the connection of the two languages, to an outline of the charms of Hamburg.

At the close of 1800 Croft seems to have returned to England, and during the next year he resided at the Royal Terrace, Southend, discharging in person the duties attached to his living and superintending the publication of two sermons which he preached at Prittlewell. When promotion came neither from lay nor clerical hands, Croft again withdrew to the continent in 1802, and there he spent the remainder of his days. His first settlement on his second trip abroad was at Lille, and on the renewal of the war between England and France he was one of those detained by Bonaparte, but, as a literary man, he was released and permitted to live where he pleased. He then lived for some years in a pleasant country retreat near the château in the vicinity of Amiens which belonged to a Lady Mary Hamilton, daughter of the earl of Leven and Melville. At a later period he removed to Paris, where he haunted libraries and sought the society of book lovers. While in France he wrote several works on the country and its language, including *Horace éclairci par la ponctuation* (1810), a whimsical production which printed a few of Horace's odes on the new system of punctuation on which he had also attempted to base an abortive edition of *Télémaque: réflexions soumises à la sagesse des membres du congrès de Vienne* (1814); and *Commentaires sur les meilleurs ouvrages de la langue française* (1815), which comprised a commentary on the *Petit-carême* of Massillon.

Croft's acknowledged works are numerous, but he is chiefly remembered for the life of Edward Young which he contributed to Johnson's *Lives of the Poets*. His other writings include *A Brother's Advice to his Sisters* (signed 'H.', 1775; 2nd edn 1776) and a paper called by the whimsical name of the *Literary Fly*. 10,000 copies of the first number were distributed gratuitously on 18 January 1779, but the journal soon died of inanition. Another of Croft's more popular works was the anonymously published *The Abbey of Kilkhampton, or, Monumental Records for the Year 1780* (1780). A satirical collection of epitaphs on a number of Croft's famous or notorious contemporaries, it ran to fourteen editions, and in 1822 a sequel entitled *The Abbey of Kilkhampton Revived* was issued. *Love and madness, a story too true, in a series of letters between parties whose names could perhaps be mentioned were they less known or less lamented* was published anonymously in 1780. This rather sensational volume went through seven editions, with many variations in the text, and deals with the clandestine love of James Hackman, a one-time army officer and Norfolk clergyman, for Martha Ray, the mistress of Lord Sandwich, who was shot by Hackman as she was leaving Covent Garden Theatre on 7 April 1779. Into this work Croft inserted a huge interpolation on Chatterton, and the fifth edition contained a postscript on Chatterton. Many years later this circumstance inflicted an indelible stain on Croft's reputation. In a letter inserted in the *Monthly Magazine* for November 1799 he was accused by Robert Southey of having obtained in 1778 Chatterton's letters from the boy's mother and sister under false pretences, of having published the letters without consent, and without awarding to the owners an adequate remuneration from the large profits he had himself made by their publication, and of having kept the originals for twenty-one years. To these charges Croft made a very unsatisfactory answer in the pages of the *Gentleman's Magazine* (1st ser., 70, 1800, 99–104, 222–6, 322–5), which was subsequently published separately as *Chatterton and love and madness: a letter from Denmark to Mr Nichols, editor of the Gentleman's Magazine, 1800*.

Croft was also a prolific contributor to the periodical publications of his day. Several sets of his verses in English and Latin appeared in the *Gentleman's Magazine*, and a paper on chess, communicated by him to Horace Twiss, and published in Twiss's *Book on Chess*, was reprinted in volume 57 of that journal. His epitaph on Bishop Hurd is printed in Nichols's *Literary Anecdotes*, and a printed letter from him to a pupil is criticized in Boswell's *Life of Johnson*. The faults of Croft's character are perceptible at a glance, but his linguistic attainments—he knew Latin, Greek, Hebrew, and Anglo-Saxon, and spoke French, Italian, and German—exceeded the power of most of his contemporaries. A warm tribute to his charitable disposition was paid by the author of a *Poetical Description of Southend*, who had been his curate for some years.

Croft died at Paris on 25 April 1816, and a white marble monument to his memory was placed on the north wall of Prittlewell church.

W. P. COURTNEY, rev. REBECCA MILLS

Sources Foster, *Alum. Oxon.* · J. Foster, *The peerage, baronetage, and knightage of the British empire for 1883*, 2 [1883] · *European Magazine and London Review*, 25 (1794), 251 · [J. Watkins and F. Shoberl], *A biographical dictionary of the living authors of Great Britain and Ireland* (1816) · P. Benton, *The history of Rochford hundred* (1867–8), 593–5 · T. Maurice, *Memoirs of the author of Indian antiquities* (1819), pt 2, 156 · J. Boswell, *The life of Samuel Johnson*, ed. A. Napier, new edn, 6 vols. (1884), vol. 3, pp. 188–9 · *Life and correspondence of Joseph Priestley*, ed. J. T. Rutt, 1 (1831), 46; 2 (1832), 42, 49 · Allibone, *Dict.* · C. J. Robinson, *A history of the mansions and manors of Herefordshire* (1873), 80–83 · W. P. Baildon, ed., *The records of the Honorable Society of Lincoln's Inn: admissions*, 1 (1896), 457 · *Annual Biography and Obituary*, 2 (1818), 1–15 · *The life and correspondence of Robert Southey*, ed. C. C. Southey, 6 vols. (1849–50), vol. 2, pp.185–6 · Watt, *Bibl. Brit.* · *GM*, 1st ser., 86/1 (1816), 470–72 · *GM*, 1st ser., 86/2 (1816), 487 · *N&Q*, 4th ser., 1 (1868), 353, 467 · *N&Q*, 4th ser., 7 (1871), 319–20 · *N&Q*, 4th ser., 12 (1873), 237 · M. Novak, 'The sensibility of Sir Herbert Croft', *Age of Johnson*, 8 (1997), 189–207 · B. Goldberg, 'Romantic professionalism in 1800: Robert Southey, Herbert Croft, and the letters and legacy of Thomas Chatterton', *ELH: a Journal of English Literary History*, 63 (1996), 681–706 · J. Green, *Chasing the sun: dictionary-makers and the dictionaries they made* (1996) · IGI · CGPLA Eng. & Wales

Archives BL, Egerton MS 2186 · BL, corresp. with earl of Liverpool, Add. MSS 38215–38221, 38308–38309, 38470–38471
Likenesses L. F. Abbott, oils, Croft Castle, Herefordshire · Drummond, etching (after sculpture by Farn), repro. in *European Magazine*

Croft, Sir James (*c*.1518–1590), lord deputy of Ireland and conspirator, was the eldest surviving son of Richard Croft (*d.* 1562) of Croft Castle, Herefordshire, and his second wife, Katherine, daughter of Sir Richard Herbert of Montgomery. His great-grandfather Sir Richard *Croft (*d.* 1509) had been treasurer of Henry VII's household and steward of Prince Arthur's household; his grandfather Sir Edward (*d.* 1547) was seven times sheriff of Herefordshire and also, from 1525, one of Princess Mary's learned counsel. His father was esquire of the body to Henry VIII. Croft was thus well-connected both at court and in the Welsh marches, a fact which explains his easy rise to prominence as a soldier-administrator during the decade before Edward VI's death. Yet the subsequent rebuilding of his career perhaps owed more to Elizabeth's special trust in him following his refusal to incriminate her during Mary's reign.

Early career James Croft first served as knight of the shire for Herefordshire in 1542. In 1544 he served as captain to John Dudley at the siege of Boulogne, where two of his brothers were killed; and he was later water bailiff (1544–5) and under-marshal (1546–7) there, losing an arm while attacking Hardelot Castle. He was knighted at Westminster on 24 November 1547. His growing military reputation was acknowledged by his appointment in summer 1549 as captain of Haddington, then the chief English garrison in the Scottish lowlands and besieged by the French, where he acquitted himself well before its final abandonment. In 1550 his appointment to the council in the Welsh marches, then as vice-president (1550–51), marked a first association with the wider government of Wales and the marches, a position resumed under Elizabeth when, from 1570, he was reappointed to the council, and served as constable or steward of numerous castles and manors there and also, from 1573, as justice of the quorum for most Welsh and marcher counties.

In February 1551 Croft was dispatched with an expeditionary force to Ireland, where the government was worried by rumours of French and Scottish intrigues with Gaelic chiefs. Landing at Cork, he was ordered to fortify the Munster and Ulster ports, but growing fears of invasion and Croft's close association with Dudley prompted his appointment as lord deputy in May. His salary was £1000 a year, with an increased garrison of 2134 English troops and 484 Irish, the largest throughout the mid-Tudor period. As governor, Croft faced serious difficulties. The coinage debasement was ruining trade, fuelling dissent in the towns. The Irishry had been thoroughly unsettled by the government's increasing resort to coercion since 1547, notably the planting of garrisons in marcher districts and the expropriation of the O'Mores and O'Connors from King's and Queen's counties for colonization. Operating within the context of traditional Tudor reform strategy, Croft initiated surrender and regrant

SIR IAMES CRAFTS   CONTROLER

Sir James Croft (c.1518–1590), by unknown artist

agreements with several Munster chiefs, and appointed the earl of Desmond to head a peace commission there. Yet his strategy also included a more coercive strand. He developed settlements around Newry and Lecale and in Kavanagh's country, completed the leasing of King's and Queen's counties, and unsuccessfully recommended another English colony at Baltimore, co. Cork. He also issued new regulations for the garrisons at Carlow and Leighlin to reduce the burden on local inhabitants.

More importantly, in Ulster the expansion of clan Donald into Clandeboye—precipitated by the collapse of their own Gaelic lordship in the Western Isles—was misinterpreted as an attempt by the French-dominated Edinburgh government to open a second front in Ireland. Croft toured Ulster, persuaded the Tyrone O'Neills to permit an English garrison at Armagh, and placed the ageing earl of Tyrone in protective custody in the pale. He proclaimed a hosting from Carrickfergus to expel clan Donald. Most Irish chiefs submitted and proffered aid, but the 'Scots' melted away and Croft's attempt to seize Rathlin, the island stronghold of James MacDonald of Dunyvaig, failed for lack of shipping. In November, Edward appointed him a gentleman of the privy chamber. Yet after a second expedition against the MacDonalds ended in heavy defeat at Belfast the following summer, Croft sued for recall.

The other major task entrusted to Croft was to enforce the Edwardian Reformation, particularly to ensure the bishops 'give good example' rather than winking at the retention of Catholic ceremonies. Despite orders to enforce the Book of Common Prayer, and proposals for Latin and Gaelic versions outside Anglophone districts, the mass was still widely celebrated throughout 1550.

Croft, however, was much more vigorous in enforcing the English prayer book, and he also established a printing press in Dublin to address the shortage of copies. Vigorous action against Archbishop Dowdall of Armagh, who had hitherto refused to implement any of the Edwardian reforms in his diocese, precipitated Dowdall's flight, whereupon the deputy requested a religious adviser to 'direct the blind and obstinate bishops' (Ellis, 221). His pleas eventually prompted the privy council's nomination of Hugh Goodacre for Armagh and John Bale for Ossory, but they only arrived after Croft's final departure on 4 December 1552. By then the annual deficit had soared to Ir£52,000, but the deputy remained overstretched, particularly in the most Gaelic province of Ulster. His failure as deputy is unsurprising. Croft himself recognized that he was sitting on a powder keg: his army kept the country quiet, but diplomacy was needed for a political solution. He never returned to Ireland, but under Elizabeth was influential on Irish affairs. He later advised his relative and Munster planter, Sir William Herbert, who dedicated a tract to him, and in 1583 wrote a discourse on Irish reform. Comparing the situation to Spanish rule in the Indies, he observed that 'Ireland, consisting of a warlike and well-armed people, is not so easy to be subdued' (Quinn, 30). He disapproved of the 'inhuman cruelty' shown during the Desmond wars, pointedly remarking that 'good government causeth good obedience, not contrariwise' (ibid., 28).

A career blighted Although close to Dudley, and appointed deputy constable of the Tower in May 1553, Croft did not sign the device to alter the succession, and was mysteriously removed from office immediately after Edward's death. Yet he defected from Dudley's army to Mary only at the last moment, and his well-known protestantism rendered him suspect to the new regime. By late November he was a leading conspirator in what became Wyatt's rebellion, entrusted with raising the Welsh marches. While frustration at his exclusion from office perhaps played a part, Croft's actions were presumably motivated mainly by religion. The leaking of the conspirators' plans, however, forced them to act prematurely. Croft sought French aid, then left London (c.24 January 1554) to raise troops, then did nothing. Arrested in Herefordshire, he was committed to the Tower (21 February), indicted of treason (7 April), and tried at the Guildhall (28 April). Not 'passing viii[te]' of the jurors were willing to convict him, 'so they were fayne to sende for Hartropp and serten curryars and others' to secure his conviction on 29 April (Nichols, 76). Sentenced to death and remanded to the Tower, he was 'marvellously tossed and examined' (HoP, *Commons, 1558–1603*, 1.672), but refused to incriminate Princess Elizabeth, to whom he had had access, as leading councillors had hoped. Eventually, in January 1555, he was bound over to a 'good abearinge', fined £500, and released. He was pardoned on 16 February, but was regranted only some of his goods, plus a pension of £100 from King Philip.

Renewed hostilities with Scotland prompted Mary, in August 1557, to send Croft north to advise the earl of

Shrewsbury and Lord Wharton on the conduct of the war. Following her accession, Queen Elizabeth employed him to supervise the defence of Berwick, then threatened by French forces. On 3 March 1559 he was restored in blood and then appointed governor of Berwick, being commissioned in August, with the earl of Northumberland and Sir Ralph Sadler, to settle border disputes with the Scots. In practice, Croft's brief was much wider. He was already in touch with John Knox, before Sadler's arrival, about financial aid for the lords of the congregation, and secretly disbursed money following Elizabeth's instructions. Sadler accounted him 'a wise man, secret and diligent' (Clifford, 1.409), although he was later reprimanded about indiscipline in the Berwick garrison. Neither trusted the two wardens, Northumberland and Lord Dacre, 'being indeed rank papists' (ibid., 449), and in September, Sadler recommended Croft as Northumberland's replacement. Croft weakly excused himself on grounds of poverty and the harsh climate, but in February 1560 Elizabeth unexpectedly ordered him to accompany Lord Grey, as second in command, with the English army sent to besiege Leith. He advised against the assault and his company failed to attack as instructed. Subsequently Grey and Norfolk, the lieutenant-general, charged him with secret negotiations with the besieged. Norfolk had him recalled and sent up to court: he had 'used hymself so suspiciouslye in this Your Majesties last Servyes', besides his 'unsatiable pilling and pollinge' at Berwick (*Collection of State Papers*, 1.321). He was blamed especially for the army's disorderly conduct. The council's subsequent inquiry diplomatically focused on Croft's shortcomings at Berwick, for which he was dismissed from office and briefly imprisoned.

Now deep in debt, Croft spent the next decade rebuilding his local influence. From 1563 he represented Herefordshire in every parliament until his death. He also nominated one burgess (and sometimes both) for nearby Leominster where he was steward. About 1540 he had married Alice, daughter of Richard Warnecombe of Ivington, Herefordshire, and widow of William Wigmore of Shobdon. They had three sons and four daughters. The eldest son, Edward [*see below*], represented Leominster in parliament in 1571 and, with his half-brother Thomas Wigmore, in 1584 and 1586. Croft's daughter Eleanor's marriage to John Scudamore cemented good relations with another of the county's three leading families, allowing Croft to dominate the shire against the rival Coningsby faction. His wife died in 1573, being buried at Croft on 4 August, and he later married Katherine, daughter of Edward Blount, esquire. He manoeuvred relatives and supporters onto the peace commission, having himself been justice of the quorum since 1559. Croft was also a powerful critic of successive presidents of the Welsh council, Sir Henry Sidney and the earl of Pembroke.

Restored to favour Croft's unexpected appointment as comptroller of the household in January 1570 announced his return to favour, followed four months later by appointment to the privy council. He proved a regular attender, and was also active in succeeding parliaments both in public and private matters. Substantial grants of land in Herefordshire and Kent followed. The middle years of Elizabeth's reign offered few opportunities for his particular talents, however. He openly supported a pro-Spanish policy, receiving a pension from Philip II whom he professed himself ready to serve in everything 'he honestly could' (HoP, *Commons, 1558–1603*, 1.674). In 1583 he petitioned, on grounds of poverty, for a grant of concealed lands. Three years later he was granted lands worth £100 a year, with the reversion of a leasehold worth £60, and in December 1586 he presented remembrances for a reform of the royal household. He was one of the commissioners to try Mary, queen of Scots, in October 1586, and in November made an unpopular speech in parliament, interpreted as opposing her execution. On 28 March 1587, he alone of these commissioners sat in Star Chamber at the trial of Secretary Davison, made scapegoat for Mary's execution, where he courageously protested his good opinion of the secretary.

By now Croft was virtually isolated in council. Burghley had lost confidence in him, and Croft's political stance set him against his earlier patron, the earl of Leicester, and the faction favouring active support for Dutch protestants. Yet his stance frequently matched Elizabeth's changing moods. Probably for this reason, in January 1588 Elizabeth included him with the earl of Derby and Lord Cobham on the commission to treat with the duke of Parma at Bourbourg, notwithstanding that, as she later admitted, he had 'been more trained in martial affairs than acquainted with matters of treaties' (BL, Add. MS 4160, fol. 85). Consequently, the commissioners were riven by jealousies even before Croft, sensing that the Spanish negotiators were simply dragging out time, saw the duke privately, without authority, to discuss a document drawn up by himself and purporting to be Elizabeth's negotiating position. Parma was unimpressed, describing Croft as 'a weak old man of 70 with very little sagacity' (HoP, *Commons, 1558–1603*, 1.674). The queen, wrongly advised by Croft that Parma had agreed an armistice, condemned 'such an extraordinary attempt by a counsellor of your years' (BL, Add. MS 4160, fol. 82v). Examined by the privy council on his return, Croft was briefly confined in the Fleet prison. Meanwhile Edward Croft, blaming Leicester for his father's disgrace, allegedly procured the earl's death by means of a London conjuror: he was so charged, following examination by the council, but apparently did not stand trial. Sir James Croft was not involved, and Elizabeth readily forgave the excess 'zeal he had to further the peace' (ibid., fol. 85). He was back in council by January 1589. He died on 4 September 1590 and was buried in the chapel of St John the Evangelist, Westminster Abbey.

Croft was that rare bird, an expert and successful military commander with an acute sense of the limitations and risks of warfare. These skills particularly commended him to Elizabeth who brought him back from the political wilderness in one of her typical balancing acts. She trusted him implicitly while recognizing his weaknesses, so that Croft could take risks in accordance with her preferences for peace and compromise which would have ruined other ministers. He was afterwards remembered in Ireland for his 'honourable dealing towards the Irish' (Campion, 124). Yet his general honesty hindered his political advancement. 'The man has not the readiest way to do good to himself as other courtiers have', so Northumberland informed Burghley in 1578 (HoP, *Commons, 1558–1603*, 1.672). Croft himself acknowledged his 'unskilfull manor of delyng for my selfe': by 1583 he was again reduced to 'selling of lande to releive my necessyte' (BL, Lansdowne MS 37, fol. 94). And despite the considerable perquisites of office, he still died 'pauperrimus miles' (HoP, *Commons, 1558–1603*, 1.672). For the historian, Croft's long and varied career presents considerable problems of interpretation. His particular aims and ambitions have to be conjectured from patchy sources since, apart from a short autobiography, few of Croft's own writings have survived.

Croft's eldest son, **Edward Croft** (d. 1601), was educated at the Middle Temple. He married Anne (d. 1575), daughter of Thomas Browne of Attleborough, Norfolk, but perhaps because of his unstable character was excluded from his father's estates in Herefordshire, which were regranted to their eldest son, Sir Herbert *Croft (c.1565–1629), by Sir William Herbert and Thomas Wigmore, the feoffees, in 1594. Edward was imprisoned for debt after his father's death, and on release in 1592 he fled to the Netherlands. He settled at Stranehage, in the south, from where he wrote to Lord Burghley in 1596 seeking employment. By his will (22 June 1600), he left his seal to his son Herbert, a sword to another son, and rings to two daughters. His second wife, Mareen, received the rest of his property and an annuity of £40. He died on 29 July 1601, and Mareen was granted administration of his estate in 1607.

Sir James's third son, **Sir James Croft** (d. 1624), was educated at Gray's Inn. In 1580 he married Margaret (d. 1587), daughter of Thomas, first Baron Wentworth, and widow successively of John, first Baron Williams of Thame, Oxfordshire, and Sir William Drury, governor of Ireland, whom he had served in Ireland as captain (1578–9). The couple lived on an estate at Weston on the Green in Oxfordshire which Margaret acquired through her first marriage. James was JP there by 1582, and sat in parliament in 1584 and 1586 for Brackley, probably returned through his father's influence. He accompanied Sir James on his peace commission to the Netherlands in 1588. By then he was a gentleman pensioner and spent the rest of his life at court. He was knighted on 23 July 1603, and eventually died of a fever on 4 September 1624.

STEVEN G. ELLIS

Sources *The state papers and letters of Sir Ralph Sadler*, ed. A. Clifford, 2 vols. (1809) • *Collection of state papers … left by William Cecil, Lord Burghley*, 2 vols.; 1, ed. S. Haynes (1740); 2, ed. W. Murdin (1759) • J. G. Nichols, ed., *The chronicle of Queen Jane, and of two years of Queen Mary*, CS, old ser., 48 (1850) • APC, esp. 1554–6 • J. Strype, *Annals of the Reformation and establishment of religion … during Queen Elizabeth's happy reign*, 2 vols. (1709–25); 2nd edn, 4 vols. (1725–31) • D. MacCulloch, 'The Vita Mariae Angliae Reginae of Robert Wingfield of Brantham', *Camden miscellany, XXVIII*, CS, 4th ser., 29 (1984), 181–301 • R. Keith, J. P. Lawson, and C. J. Lyon, *History of the affairs of church and state in Scotland from the beginning of the Reformation to the year 1568*, 3 vols., Spottiswoode Society (1844–50) • N. H. Nicolas, 'Sir James Croft, privy counsellor and comptroller of the household of Queen Elizabeth', *Retrospective Review*, 2nd ser., 1 (1827), 469–98 • R. E. Ham, 'The autobiography of Sir James Croft', *BIHR*, 50 (1977), 48–57 • O. G. S. Croft, *The house of Croft of Croft Castle* (1949) • C. Brady, *The chief governors: the rise and fall of reform government in Tudor Ireland, 1536–1588* (1994) • S. G. Ellis, *Ireland in the age of the Tudors* (1998) • W. Herbert, *Croftus, sive, De Hibernia liber*, ed. A. Keaveney and J. A. Madden (1992) • HoP, *Commons, 1509–58*, 1.724–5 • HoP, *Commons, 1558–1603*, 1.670–74 • C. Brady, *Shane O'Neill* (1996) • BL, Add. MS 4160 • BL, Lansdowne MS 37, fol. 94 • D. B. Quinn, 'Ireland and sixteenth-century European expansion', *Historical Studies: Papers Read Before the Irish Conference of Historians*, 1 (1958), 20–32 • M. L. Bush, *The government policy of Protector Somerset* (1975) • W. T. MacCaffrey, *The shaping of the Elizabethan regime: Elizabethan politics, 1558–1572* (1968) • E. Campion, 'Histories of Ireland', *The historie of Ireland, collected by three learned authors*, ed. J. Ware (1633), 124 • P. Williams, *The council in the marches of Wales in the reign of Elizabeth I* (1958) • J. E. Neale, *The Elizabethan House of Commons* (1963) • D. G. White, 'The reign of Edward VI in Ireland: some political, social and economic aspects', *Irish Historical Studies*, 14 (1964–5), 197–211 • C. G. Cruickshank, *Elizabeth's army*, 2nd edn (1966) • D. M. Loades, *Two Tudor conspiracies* (1965) • DNB

Archives U. Nott. L., autobiographical writings, Portland MS PwV83

Likenesses oils, Croft Castle, Herefordshire [*see illus.*]

Wealth at death seven manors and other lands, mainly in Herefordshire: Croft, *House of Croft*, 52–3, 76

Croft, Sir James (d. 1624). *See under* Croft, Sir James (c.1518–1590).

Croft, John (1732–1820), wine merchant and antiquary, was born on 29 February 1732 at Stillington, Yorkshire, the fifth son of Stephen Croft (1683–1733) and Elizabeth (d. 1771), daughter of Sir Edmund Anderson, fourth baronet (bap. 1629, d. 1703). The Crofts were part of a long-established, aristocratic, wealthy landowning Yorkshire dynasty. His great-great-grandfather was Sir Christopher Croft, alderman and lord mayor of York, whom Charles I had knighted in 1641. His father, who was descended from a younger, relatively impoverished branch of the Croft family, died the year after John was born. Not being the eldest son, it was necessary for John to seek his own fortune and, since several members of the family had worked in the wine trade, he was sent to Oporto, where he worked for several years. Following his return to Britain he became a partner in the firm of Messrs George Suttrell & Co., an old established firm of wine merchants in York, which dealt principally with the wines of Portugal. He was admitted to the freedom of that city in 1770 and in 1773 acted as one of its sheriffs. On 16 June 1774 he married Judith (1746–1824), daughter of Francis Bacon, an alderman of the city and lord mayor in 1764 and 1777, and his second wife, Catherine Hildrop. They had two sons. It is reputed that he read aloud to his wife all of *Don Quixote* in Spanish, of which she did not understand a word, but she liked to listen to it because it was so sonorous.

Croft's reputation is based primarily on his literary contributions, which encompassed a wide variety of topics although they were of little long-term significance. His first publication consisted of a two-part work, *A treatise on the wines of Portugal, and dissertation on the nature and use of wines in general imported into Great Britain*, printed in York in

1787 and dedicated to William Constable of Burton Constable of Holderness. An enlarged, extensively revised edition was produced in the following year. In 1792 he published *A Small Collection of the Works of Shakespeare*, which he dedicated to the Society of Antiquaries. In the same year his notebook of witticisms and jests *Scrapeana, Fugitive, Miscellany, Sans souci*, dedicated to the Polish dwarf Count Joseph de Boruwlaski, was issued. This earned him the nickname of Scrapeana, which remained with him for the rest of his life. It is probable that Croft also contributed to an edition of *Macbeth*, 'with notes by Harry Rowe, Trumpet major to the High Sheriffs of Yorkshire', published in 1797, a text which is more frequently ascribed to Dr Alexander Hunter.

In 1797 Croft's research into the foundations at York were published in a small volume, *Excerpta antiqua, or, A Collection of Original Manuscripts*, which was dedicated to the Society of Antiquaries. Among these reprints is a copy of the York Corpus Christi pageant plays, which had been transcribed for him from the original manuscript retained at that time in the city archives in the Guildhall. In 1808 he published anonymously a twelve-page pamphlet *Rules at the Game of Chess*. Two years later York press published his *Annotations of the Plays of Shakespeare*, a text which was considered by one Shakespeare critic to be of more value than those compiled by Jackson, Becket, or even John Lord Chedworth and Henry James Pye. His last publication was a small volume, *Memoirs of Harry Rowe, constructed from materials found in an old box after his decease. By Mr John Croft, wine merchant. Together with the 'Sham Doctor', musical farce by Harry Rowe, with notes by John Croft*. The subject of his study had also been master of a puppet show who died in York workhouse in 1799. The publication was undertaken in order to assist York Dispensary, the finances of which were in a precarious state.

In the latter part of his life Croft devoted most of his time to antiquarian researches and became a well-known figure in the local book and curiosity sales, where his bidding was strictly regulated by financial considerations. According to one of his contemporaries who knew him between 1806 and 1809:

> His personal appearance was singularly grotesque. A figure made by one of Nature's journeymen was usually invested in a dress half English, half Portuguese; under this exterior there was a certain kind of elegance, and an extraordinary avidity for information, especially historical and Shakespearian. He was a great questionist, and every third question which he asked was *Unde derivatur*. (Davies, 310)

His eccentric manner and dress made him a well-known figure in York society, his popularity no doubt enhanced with his continuing association with the wine trade.

Following a brief illness, Croft died on 18 November 1820 at his house in Aldwark, York, which was located close to the city wall adjoining the hall of the Merchant Taylors' Company. His remains were interred in York Minster on 24 November. Judith died four years later and was buried close to her husband; their two sons had both predeceased their parents.

W. P. COURTNEY, *rev.* JOHN MARTIN

Sources R. Davies, *A memoir of the York press: with notices of authors, printers, and stationers in the sixteenth, seventeenth, and eighteenth centuries* (1868) • *Yorkshire Gazette* (25 Nov 1820) • J. Foster, ed., *Pedigrees of the county families of Yorkshire*, 3 (1874) • GEC, *Baronetage* • J. Delaforce, *The factory house at Oporto*, new edn (1990)
Likenesses engraving, repro. in Delaforce, *Factory house*, 14

Croft, John (1833–1905), surgeon, son of Hugh and Maria Croft (*d.* 1842), was born on 4 August 1833 at Pettinghoe, near Newhaven, Sussex. His grandfather Gilmore Croft, a successful medical practitioner in the City of London, had left Hugh Croft a competence, much of which was spent in farming. After the death of his first wife, Croft's father married again and moved to Lower Clapton, London. John Croft was educated at the Hackney Church of England school, and throughout his life held earnest religious views. He served a short apprenticeship with Thomas Evans of Burwash in Sussex, and entered St Thomas's Hospital in 1850. He was appointed dresser to Le Gros Clark in 1852.

Admitted MRCS and in 1854 made a licentiate of the Society of Apothecaries, Croft served as house surgeon at St Thomas's Hospital. After spending five years (1855–60) as surgeon to the *Dreadnought* hospital ship, he returned to St Thomas's to become demonstrator of anatomy and surgical registrar. He became resident assistant surgeon in December 1863 and in the following year he married Annie Douglas, daughter of Alexander Douglas Douglas; they had no children. On 1 January 1871 Croft became both assistant surgeon and surgeon, when the new buildings of the hospital were opened on the Albert Embankment. In the medical school he was in succession demonstrator of anatomy, lecturer on practical surgery, and lecturer on clinical surgery. Croft resigned his appointments in July 1891, when he was elected consulting surgeon. He was also surgeon to the Surrey Dispensary, the National Truss Society, the Magdalen Hospital at Streatham, and the National Provident Assurance Society. Croft was elected FRCS in 1859, and was a member of the council from 1882 to 1890, vice-president in 1889, and a member of the court of examiners from 1881 to 1886.

Croft was one of the earliest hospital surgeons in London to adopt Listerian methods. His name is chiefly associated with the introduction of 'Croft's splints', which were plaster of Paris cases made with scrubbing flannel and shaped to the limb. They were employed in place of the ordinary splints and the 'gum and chalk' bandages which had previously been used in the treatment of fractures of the leg. Croft strongly advocated the early excision of the joint in cases of hip disease. Throughout his career, Croft contributed numerous articles to *St Thomas's Hospital Reports* and the *Transactions* of the Royal Medical and Chirurgical Society, the Clinical Society, and other societies.

Croft died on 21 November 1905 at his home, 1 Fitz James Avenue, West Kensington, London, and was buried in Kensal Green cemetery. He was survived by his wife.

D'A. POWER, *rev.* JEFFREY S. REZNICK

Sources *BMJ* (5 Dec 1905), 1494–5 • *The Lancet* (2 Dec 1905), 1655–6 • *St Thomas's Hospital Report*, new ser., 34 (1906) • private information (1912) • personal knowledge (1912) • *CGPLA Eng. & Wales* (1905) • V. G.

Plarr, *Plarr's Lives of the fellows of the Royal College of Surgeons of England*, rev. D'A. Power, 2 vols. (1930)
Archives BL, corresp. with Florence Nightingale and H. Bonham-Carter, Add. MSS 47718–47719, 47724
Likenesses H. J. Brooks, group portrait, oils (*The Council of the Royal College of Surgeons of England, 1884–5*), RCS Eng. · portrait, RCS Eng. · portrait (as a young man), repro. in Fellows Album, RCS Eng. · portrait, repro. in *St Thomas's Hospital Report*, frontispiece · portrait, repro. in *The Lancet*
Wealth at death £8009 15s. 4d.: probate, 20 Dec 1905, *CGPLA Eng. & Wales*

Croft, (John) Michael (1922–1986), founder and director of the National Youth Theatre, was born in Oswestry on 8 March 1922, the child of Constance Croft, who was unmarried. As a young child he moved with his elder sister to live with his mother's sister in Manchester, where he was educated at Burnage grammar school from 1933 to 1940. His adolescence was dominated by two passions, for literature (in particular, poetry, for which he had an almost photographic memory), and for team games. He played games with extreme gusto, but achieved a limited effectiveness only in cricket, the rich lore of which always fascinated him.

Croft had little satisfaction or security from his home. He soon developed an uncompromising individualism and volunteered for aircrew duties in the Royal Air Force in 1940. He became a sergeant-pilot and took part in daylight bombing raids over occupied France, but his manual dexterity proved unequal to the demands of flying, and he was offered the option of a discharge. He had a variety of casual occupations, as an actor, professional 'fire-watcher' in air-raid precautions, credit salesman, and lumberjack, before he volunteered for the navy in 1943. After service in Mediterranean convoys, he finished the war as a radar operator on merchant ships.

In 1946 Croft went to Keble College, Oxford, to read English. He was a member of an exceptionally talented generation of former service students, and revelled in being able to indulge his love of literature, theatre, writing, and sport, while, at the same time, breaking university regulations by living in licensed premises. He took a special short-course degree and achieved a third class in English in 1948.

An unsettled period followed graduation. Croft did occasional journalism, poetry writing, broadcasting, and acting, and worked as a private tutor and a supply teacher. From teaching he gathered the material for his novel *Spare the Rod* (1954), a minor *cause célèbre* among liberal educationists, which, after skirmishes with the British Board of Film Censors, was filmed in 1961 with Max Bygraves as the sexually ambivalent schoolteacher. He also wrote *Red Carpet to China* (1958). Croft's final teaching post was at Alleyn's School, Dulwich (1950–55), where he staged a series of epic Shakespearian productions, involving the majority of the school's pupils, that aroused the interest of the London press and the professional theatre. His work was characterized by spectacle, vigour, commitment, and an unusual concern for verse speaking: he wanted to envelop everybody in his huge enthusiasm and to make them share his fascination with the works of Shakespeare. *Spare the Rod* gave him sufficient financial independence to resign from teaching, ostensibly to devote himself to writing, but it seems that he was persuaded by a group of former pupils, disconsolate at the loss of their Shakespeare play, to direct them in an out-of-term production of *Henry V* at Toynbee Hall in 1956. In effect, this was the first youth theatre production and it determined the course of the rest of his life. The venture was self-supporting: ticket sales and donations were the only funding until, in 1958, King George's Jubilee Fund gave a grant which was continuous. Subsequently, the British Council and the Department of Education and Science provided support. There was a long and fairly acrimonious battle with the Arts Council before any funding was secured, only for it to be withdrawn after a few years. By 1970 Croft was able to claim, 'We have three companies touring in Europe, four in London, and one in the northeast of England—the whole being run by a full-time staff of four, with a handful of voluntary helpers.' Ahead lay the televising and broadcasting of youth theatre productions, the commissioning of new works (significantly from Peter Terson and Barrie Keeffe in the 1970s), the visit to America, the acquiring of the Shaw Theatre (1971), and, in 1977, official recognition of the National Youth Theatre of Great Britain (NYTGB). Croft gained an increasing reputation as an internationally respected director, and his companies added to the lustrous reputation of the English theatre, but the NYTGB struggled against inadequate funding. He saw his creation as the victim of national parsimony to the arts and he became more obviously an abrasive, militant publicist, enjoying a bare-knuckle approach to negotiation. He had a flair for discovering stars, such as Derek Jacobi, Helen Mirren, Ben Kingsley, and Diana Quick.

Croft was appointed OBE in 1971. After the straitened circumstances of his early days, his later success introduced him to an expansive lifestyle, which he delighted in sharing generously with his vast number of friends and acquaintances. He was homosexual, but he had many friends of the opposite sex and, particularly in his early years, led a bisexual existence. He had few intimates, apparently finding it difficult to break down his core of loneliness. He was a man of gargantuan appetites in every way, especially for food and drink, and his eventual failure to control these proclivities, allied to a dread of surgery, contributed to his comparatively early death. He died of a heart attack at his home, 74 Bartholomew Road, Kentish Town, London, on 15 November 1986. A characteristic instruction in his will provided a party for a vetted list of some hundreds of his friends, 'at which the food shall be wholesome—and the drink shall not be allowed to run out'.

GEOFFREY SYKES, *rev.*

Sources priv. coll., Croft MSS · M. Croft, *Spare the rod* (1954) · *The Times* (17 Nov 1986)
Archives priv. coll.
Wealth at death £260,961: probate, 3 Dec 1986, *CGPLA Eng. & Wales*

Croft, Sir Richard (1429/30–1509), royal official, was the second son of William Croft of Croft Castle, Herefordshire, and of his wife, Margaret Walwyn. Croft's father and his elder brother, John, died in 1439, and John's posthumous daughter, Joan, in 1445, bringing him the inheritance of a modest but ancient estate. His guardian was Walter Skull. He had two younger brothers (possibly half-brothers), another Richard, and Thomas *Croft (c.1435–1488). A sister, Agnes, married Philip Domulton of Brockhampton, near Bromyard, Herefordshire. A complaint by Edward and Edmund, sons of Richard, duke of York, of 'the odieux rule and demenying of Richard Crofte and his brother' in 1454 has been cited as evidence that he was tutor to the future Edward IV, but the reference (possibly jocular) is more likely to the younger Richard (Davies, 243). Croft is likely to have held a post on York's estates and to have fought for him at Ludford Bridge (12 October 1459). He was pardoned in December 1459 and appointed to administer York's forfeited estates. He rejoined York's cause after the battle of Northampton (10 July 1460), and fought for Edward IV at Mortimer's Cross (2 or 3 February 1461). About this time he married Eleanor, née Cornewall (d. 1519), widow of Sir Hugh Mortimer of Kyre, Worcestershire (d. between April and June 1460). Croft was JP in Worcestershire from 1464, and became sheriff of Hereford in November 1469. That appointment was confirmed by the restored Lancastrian government in October 1470, but not renewed in November. Edward IV on his return from exile reappointed him sheriff on 11 April 1471, and he fought at Tewkesbury. Tudor sources credit him with the capture of the Lancastrian prince of Wales, though they exonerate him from responsibility for the prince's death. He was knighted after the battle and was granted lucrative and important receiverships, most notably that of the earldom of March. He was a member of the council of Edward, prince of Wales, at Ludlow, and, probably from 1473, treasurer of his household. A later tradition names his wife as 'governess' to the prince. He was MP for Herefordshire in 1478. Despite these connections with Edward V, Richard III appointed him treasurer of his household in May 1484. There is no record of his role in the Bosworth campaign, but his appointment as sheriff of Hereford, the grant of a seven-year farm of the royal manor of Woodstock, and reappointment as treasurer of the household, all in September–October 1485, suggest an understanding with Henry Tudor. His bastard, Thomas, and his stepson, John Mortimer, fought for Henry, and his brother Thomas may have helped finance Henry's campaign.

Croft's rivalry with Sir William Stanley erupted into violence in Hereford and in the marches in 1487. He ceased to be treasurer of the household in 1494, but was steward of the household to Arthur, prince of Wales, by February 1495, until Arthur's death in 1502. He held the March receivership and other offices in Wales and the border counties until his death on 29 July 1509. He had accumulated sufficient land, from the profits of office and advantageous marriages, to establish his three surviving legitimate sons, Edward, John, and Robert, as landed gentlemen, to arrange good marriages for his five surviving daughters, and several granddaughters, and to make modest provision for his bastard's family. Croft's success was founded on a family solidarity which encompassed his

brothers, bastard, and stepson, and indeed his former guardian, Sir Walter Skull, who, after the death of his own son, arranged a series of marriages to convey his property and a large part of that of his stepdaughters to the Crofts. Croft's wife, Eleanor, survived him until 1519. She was alleged to have headed an armed force of followers and outlaws during the feud with Stanley in 1487. She and her husband are buried in an alabaster tomb of fashionable Westminster workmanship, with effigies, in Croft church, which he rebuilt.

Sir Richard should be distinguished from his brother, also Richard, who appears in the records as 'the younger' before Sir Richard's knighthood, thereafter as 'esquire'. He was closely associated with his younger, probably full, brother, Thomas. The younger Richard was probably the Richard Crofte of the letter of 1454 cited above, and may have been a clerk in the Ludlow household. After Edward IV's accession he gained lands and offices in Oxfordshire, was MP for the county (1472–5), and esquire of the body from 1482. He lost his offices with the accession of Henry VII and died on 26 May 1502.   C. S. L. Davies

Sources C. S. L. Davies, 'The Crofts: creation and defence of a family enterprise under the Yorkists and Henry VII', Historical Research, 68 (1995), 241–65 · O. G. S. Croft, The house of Croft of Croft Castle (1949) · W. R. B. Robinson, 'A letter from Sir Richard Croft to Sir Gilbert Talbot in 1486 concerning Sir James Tyrell's offices in Wales', Historical Research, 67 (1994), 179–89 · J. C. Wedgwood and A. D. Holt, History of parliament, 1: Biographies of the members of the Commons house, 1439–1509 (1936), 237–40 · CEPR letters, 15 · Chancery records · will, PRO, PROB 11/16, fol. 168 · C. G. Bayne and W. H. Dunham, eds., Select cases in the council of Henry VII, SeldS, 75 (1958), cxxiii–cxxiv, 78–87 · C. Ross, Edward IV (1974), 48; appx 2, p. 436 · D. E. Lowe, 'The council of the prince of Wales and the decline of the Herbert family', BBCS, 27 (1976–8), 278–97 · D. E. Lowe, 'Patronage and politics: Edward IV, the Wydevills, and the council of the prince of Wales, 1471–83', BBCS, 29 (1980–82), 545–73 · PRO, E 101/412/16, 18, 19 · R. Horrox and P. W. Hammond, eds., British Library Harleian manuscript 433, 4 vols. (1979–83) · VCH Oxfordshire · J. R. H. Weaver and A. Beardwood, eds., Some Oxfordshire wills, Oxfordshire RS, 39 (1958), 72–3
Likenesses double portrait, effigy on tomb (with Lady Croft), Croft Castle, Herefordshire; Croft Church; repro. in Royal Commission on Historical Monuments—Hereford, 3 (1934), pl. 95–6
Wealth at death impossible to calculate; substantial landed holdings in Herefordshire (at least £100 p.a.), similar holdings in Worcestershire, plus considerable cash resources: will, PRO, PROB 11/16, fol. 168, summarized in Davies, 'The Crofts', 258–9

Croft, Sir Richard, sixth baronet (1762–1818), physician and man-midwife, was born on 9 January 1762, the youngest of eleven children of Herbert Croft (1717/18–1785), clerk to the court of chancery and later receiver and treasurer in the Charterhouse, and his wife, Elizabeth, daughter of Richard Young of Midhurst, Sussex. The Croft family was a wealthy and ancient one in Herefordshire, where Croft Castle had been in the possession of the family from the time of Edward IV.

After schooling in London, Croft went to Mr Manlover's academy in Derby to complete his education. He received his medical education at St Bartholomew's Hospital, London, was awarded his diploma from the Barber-Surgeons' Company on 17 May 1781, and graduated MD from Aberdeen on 27 July 1789.

After qualifying Croft became a partner of Rupert Chawner at Tutbury, Staffordshire. Chawner was the brother of Croft's father's second wife, Mary Chawner. When his partner moved to Burton upon Trent, Croft continued single-handed at Tutbury for another five years. While he was there he became a friend of Dr Joseph Denman. After moving to Oxford, a gambit that proved to be a failure, he obtained a letter of introduction from Denman to Thomas *Denman in London, who was an accoucheur of very considerable distinction. Denman wrote extensively including aphorisms on the use of forceps and midwifery practice in general. His teaching was conservative, avoiding unnecessary interference in the normal course of labour. Croft inherited these principles and applied them in his own practice which grew successfully. In 1810 Harriet, countess of Granville, wrote of her prospective accoucheurs, Sir Walter Farquhar and Croft, 'I fear Farquhar and Croft as I do viper and vixen and I shall expire of fright at being left at their mercy' (Askwith, 73). In 1792 Croft was appointed physician and man-midwife to the 'Charity for attending and delivering poor married women in their lying in at their respective habitations', and later to the Royal Maternity Charity. At Hereford on 3 November 1789 he married Margaret (1779–1833), Denman's elder twin daughter. The younger twin married Matthew Baillie, the morbid anatomist. In 1816 Croft succeeded to the baronetcy on the death of his elder brother Sir Herbert *Croft (1751–1816). On 3 November 1817 he was appointed surgeon-in-ordinary to the prince of Wales and Prince Leopold.

Croft made no significant contributions to medical literature or to medical knowledge and practice. His name and notoriety stem mainly from his involvement in the events leading to the tragic death of Princess Charlotte in 1817. The disastrous marriage of the prince of Wales and Princess Caroline of Brunswick, which ended three months after the birth of their daughter, kept the young princess apart from her mother so that she became somewhat isolated and lonely. As she grew up, a beautiful and attractive girl, she attracted a great deal of sympathy from the public which grew to treat her with a degree of affection, and her popularity increased while that of her parents diminished. However, at the age of eighteen she made a happy marriage to Prince Leopold. Croft was nominated to attend her confinement assisted by Matthew Bailie and Sir Everard Home. The pregnancy took a normal course and labour started on 4 November 1817. The labour was long and tedious and after some time Croft became suspicious that interference might become necessary. He sent for John Sims, who had been nominated to attend in case of any complications. However, Sims advised against the use of forceps and so the labour was allowed to continue until after fifty-two hours a stillborn baby was delivered without artificial assistance. It became necessary to remove the afterbirth manually because of haemorrhage. This however was not thought to be sufficient to cause the death of the mother, which took place five hours later. The exact cause of death was never fully explained, but

was probably due to the effects on the heart of the haemorrhage as it became very irregular some hours before death.

News of the tragedy soon reached the public and there was an immediate state of consternation and grief that was quite incredible and almost hysterical. Now the hopes for the succession to the throne were destroyed, and the extent to which the public loved Princess Charlotte was summed up later by Byron in these lines:

> … in the dust
> The fair-haired daughter of the Isles is laid,
> The love of millions, how we did entrust Futurity to her …

Very soon after the announcement of the tragedy all the doctors involved in the care of Princess Charlotte, but especially Croft himself, were accused in some quarters of the press of ignorance, neglect, and mismanagement and there was even a demand by Jesse Foot, a well-known surgeon, for a public inquiry into the causes of the death of the princess and her child. Croft was criticized especially for allowing the labour to last so long without interference. But medical opinion at that time was very divided about the indications for the use of forceps and other instruments, which was so often followed by equally disastrous results. It is interesting, however, that he received every sympathy and consideration from the royal family, most of the members of his own profession, and his patients.

Croft continued in practice but never managed to throw off the depression and despair which overtook him immediately after the tragedy. He felt deeply that the criticisms to which he was subjected were unjust. After three months, while he was in attendance in Wimpole Street on another patient whose labour was pursuing a course similar to that of the princess, he retired to an adjoining room and shot himself on 13 February 1818. At the coroner's inquest it was disclosed that in the room to which he retired a copy of Shakespeare's *Love's Labour's Lost* lay open with the words 'Good God, where is the Princess?'. A memorial to Croft and his wife was erected in St James's Church, Piccadilly, London.   JOHN PEEL

Sources F. Crainz, *Birth of an heir to the 5th duke of Devonshire* (1989) · E. Holland, *The Princess Charlotte of Wales: a triple obstetric tragedy* (1951) · H. Graham, *Eternal Eve* (1950) · J. Dewhurst, *Royal confinements* (1980) · B. Askwith, *Piety and wit: a biography of Harriet Countess Granville, 1785–1862* (1982) · P. J. Wallis and R. V. Wallis, *Eighteenth century medics*, 2nd edn (1988) · C. F. Mullett, 'Sir Richard Croft and the regimen of expectant mothers', *Bulletin of the History of Medicine*, 17 (1945), 195–202 · private information (2004) [J. London] · *IGI*

Archives NRA, priv. coll., papers

Likenesses W. Wall, stipple, 1801 (after G. Hayter), Wellcome L. · J. J. Halls, oils, *c*.1810, Croft Castle, Herefordshire · W. Holl, stipple (after G. Hayter), BM

Croft, Thomas (*c*.1435–1488), customs official, shipowner, and patron of Atlantic exploration, was the son of William Croft (*d*. 1439) of Croft Castle, Herefordshire, and Isabella, presumably a second wife. He was born during the 1430s, the youngest of four brothers, including Sir Richard *Croft (1429/30–1509), John, and another Richard. He was probably serving in the household of the sons of Richard, duke of York, at Ludlow in 1454. York's defeat in October 1459 probably accounts for his admission to Lincoln's Inn, in autumn 1459. The Yorkist victory of 1461 brought him, jointly with the younger Richard Croft, lands and offices in Oxfordshire and the designation 'king's servant'. He was sheriff of Merioneth in 1464, though he claimed never to have exercised the office. An unidentified Croft was clerk in the royal signet office from November 1461 to July 1470. Thomas Croft was readmitted to Lincoln's Inn in Trinity term 1469. In April 1470 he was commissioned to seize the lands of the rebels Warwick and Clarence. The Croft brothers lay low during Henry VI's readeption, but resumed their Oxfordshire offices on Edward IV's return in 1471. In 1472 Thomas married Elizabeth (d. 1500), the daughter (probably of her mother's second marriage, to John Wysham) and one of three coheiresses of Margaret Beauchamp (d. 1452x6), who had inherited the estate of her father, Sir John Beauchamp, of Holt, Worcestershire (d. 1420). The marriage was probably arranged by Sir Walter Skull, Margaret's last husband, and former guardian of the Crofts. Thomas Croft was seneschal of Llantwit, Glamorgan, in 1474, and MP for Leominster in 1478.

Croft became a customer of Bristol in 1472, adding responsibility for the wine customs at Exeter and Topsham in 1475. In 1482 he was accused of not rendering account for his Merioneth shrievalty of 1464 or for the commission of 1470, and of improperly engaging in trade while a customs officer. He produced a licence to trade issued in 1480 and claimed that his share in two ships in 1481 was not for commerce but was 'to serch and fynd a certaine Ile callid the Isle of Brasile' (Carus-Wilson, 164). This substantiates William Worcester's evidence of early Bristol involvement in exploration. Worcester records a search for the island of 'Brasylle' to the west of Ireland in 1480 (Itineraries, 308–9). Croft's venture of 1481 was also unsuccessful. But these voyages were part of a continuing and possibly successful Bristol enterprise. Reporting on the Cabot voyage of 1497 to a Spanish admiral, possibly Columbus, John Day mentioned the admiral's prior knowledge of the earlier discovery by Bristol men of the isle of 'Brasil'.

Croft retained his offices under Richard III, but disappeared from the Bristol scene about the end of 1484. He may have joined Henry Tudor in France, perhaps handing over the customs revenues. In 1486 Henry exempted him from accounting at the exchequer for the Bristol customs, and remitted all arrears. His nephew and namesake fought for Henry at Bosworth. Croft was not reappointed customer by Henry VII, but retained estate offices and property in Oxfordshire. He was trading with Seville in 1486. By his will, made in October 1485, the bulk of his property, lands at Woodstock and South Weston in Oxfordshire, and tenements in Bristol, was left to found a chantry at Woodstock, with lodging for a priest and two poor men, worth £8 9s. gross when it was suppressed in 1548. Croft died, leaving no children, in 1488 (his will was proved on 15 November), and was presumably buried in his foundation. His widow, Elizabeth, subsequently married Nicholas Crowmer and died, still childless, in 1500.

The younger Thomas Croft was a bastard of Sir Richard Croft. For his part at Bosworth, he was granted property in Hereford after the battle of Stoke (1487), and is later designated 'armiger' and 'gentleman of London'. His offices and property were confiscated by act of parliament in October 1491 after he allegedly committed a murder. He was dead by 1509.   C. S. L. DAVIES

Sources C. S. L. Davies, 'The Crofts: creation and defence of a family enterprise under the Yorkists and Henry VII', *Historical Research*, 68 (1995), 241–65 · O. G. S. Croft, *The house of Croft of Croft Castle* (1949) · J. C. Wedgwood and A. D. Holt, *History of parliament*, 1: *Biographies of the members of the Commons house, 1439–1509* (1936), 239–40 · *Chancery records* · J. R. H. Weaver and A. Beardwood, eds., *Some Oxfordshire wills*, Oxfordshire RS, 39 (1958), 37–8 · E. M. Carus-Wilson, ed., *The overseas trade of Bristol in the later middle ages*, Bristol RS, 7 (1937) · P. McGrath, 'Bristol and America', *The Westward enterprise: English activities in Ireland, the Atlantic, and America, 1486–1650*, ed. K. R. Andrews, N. P. Canny, and P. E. H. Hair (1978), 81–102 · D. B. Quinn, 'Columbus and the North', *William and Mary Quarterly*, 49 (1992), 278–97 · W. P. Baildon, ed., *The records of the Honorable Society of Lincoln's Inn: admissions*, 1 (1896), 14 · W. P. Baildon, ed., *The records of the Honorable Society of Lincoln's Inn: the black books*, 1–4 (1897–1902) · J. Otway-Ruthven, *The king's secretary and the signet office in the XV century* (1939), 158, 188 · PRO, PROB 11/16, fol. 168 [will of Sir Richard Croft] · *Itineraries [of] William Worcestre*, ed. J. H. Harvey, OMT (1969)
Wealth at death property in Woodstock and South Weston, Oxfordshire; also four tenements in Bristol: will, Davies, 'The Crofts', 254

Croft, William (*bap.* 1678, *d.* 1727), organist and composer, was born presumably at the Shirley Manor House in Nether Eatington, Warwickshire, the fourth of seven children of William Croft (1614–1690) and his wife, Jane Brent, daughter of the late vicar of Nether Eatington, John Brent. He was baptized there on 30 December 1678.

Croft's paternal lineage dates back to Domesday Book and by the seventeenth century was distinguished by the strength of its widespread ecclesiastical connections, among them Bishop Herbert Croft (1603–1691) of Croft Castle, patriarch of the Croft family and dean of the Chapel Royal under Charles II from 1668 to 1670. Croft was a chorister in the Chapel Royal under John Blow, and his dedicatory verses to Blow in *Amphion Anglicus* (1700) suggest that he was also Blow's student. Although Croft is not listed in Sanford's account of the coronation of James II in 1685, it is more than likely that he entered the Chapel Royal in 1686. He remained there until no later than 1698, by which time his voice is reported to have changed. In 1700 Croft was installed as organist at St Anne's Church, Soho, following King William's donation in the previous year of the organ from the queen dowager's chapel of St James, and in the same year he was made gentleman-extraordinary at the Chapel Royal along with Jeremiah Clarke. Croft and Clarke jointly succeeded Francis Piggott as organist on 25 May 1704. Upon Clarke's death in 1707 these posts were consolidated under Croft's leadership. In October 1708, upon the death of his mentor John Blow, Croft succeeded to Blow's post as organist of Westminster

William Croft (*bap.* 1678, *d.* 1727), by Thomas Murray, *c.*1720

Abbey, master of the children of the Chapel Royal, and composer to Queen Anne. Croft married on 7 February 1705 Mary George, the daughter of Robert George (or Georges) of Westminster, and in their marriage document she is indicated as 'Mrs Mary George', suggesting that she may have been an actress or singer, or perhaps an older bride. The couple appear to have had no children. About 1715 the Crofts retained a house in Charles Street, Westminster, very near St James's Palace, and at his death they were resident in Kensington. Records from 1726 of the Academy of Vocal Music confirm the attendance of Croft and the children of the Chapel Royal at the society's second meeting, thus placing him as one of its earliest members. Croft died on 14 August 1727 in Bath and was buried on the 23rd of that month near the head of Henry Purcell's tomb in Westminster Abbey. Mary Croft appears to have died some years later, but in any event no later than 28 July 1734, when her father was given full administrative responsibilities for the estate of the Crofts.

Despite Croft's achievements as an organist, it is mainly through his church compositions that his significance is measured, even though his secular output is not inconsiderable. Croft's early compositional interests are evident in two surviving composition notebooks, one of 1697 and another of 1700, both now in the British Library. His presumed earliest publications are in fact secular and appeared as songs in 1699, in the *Twelve New Songs* and *Mercurius Musicus* of William Pearson and John Playford. Secular instrumental compositions from this period include music for *Courtship alamode* (1700), *The Funeral* (1702), *The Twinn Rivals* (1702), and *The Lying Lover* (1704). Other secular compositions include numerous songs, a small number of

odes, music for harpsichord and organ, a set of three sonatas for violin and basso continuo and three for flute and basso continuo (1700), six sonatas for two flutes and basso continuo (1704), and miscellaneous dances for strings. In July 1713 Croft submitted successfully to Oxford University for the degree of DMus two secular odes for solo voices, chorus, and orchestra which celebrate the treaty of Utrecht, *Laurus cruentas* and *With Noise of Cannon*. These works are extant in the university and appear in published form in *Musicus apparatus academicus* (1715). The greater part of Croft's œuvre of sacred compositions comprises anthems, upon which his reputation is mostly based. His collection of anthems, *Musica sacra* (1724), is distinguished by being possibly the earliest publication to be engraved and in the form of a score rather than in individual parts. Croft also composed various hymns, three morning and communion services, one morning and evening service, and a burial service which he appended to *Musica sacra*. He is generally considered to have codified the verse anthem, in which verses for solo voices with instrumental accompaniment generally alternate with sections for full choir. A small group of anthems, known as 'full' anthems, reflect a great indebtedness to sixteenth-century polyphonic style, owing to their use of imitative counterpoint and less overtly sectional construction; 'Hear my prayer, o Lord' (1724) is one such example. These attributes reflect Croft's admiration for the 'solemnity and gravity' of earlier music, denoted in his preface to *Musica sacra*. Such words might well summarize Croft himself, whom Hawkins described as a 'grave and decent man' (J. Hawkins, *A General History of the Science and Practice of Music*, 5 vols., 1776, 2.797). BENNETT MITCHELL ZON

Sources J. F. Harrison, 'The secular works of William Croft', PhD diss., Bryn Mawr College, 1977 · B. J. Durost, 'The academic and court odes of William Croft (1678–1727)', DMA diss., Claremont Graduate College, 1997 · M. E. Atkinson, 'The orchestral anthem in England, 1700–1775', DMA diss., University of Illinois, 1991 · R. L. Scandrett, 'The anthems of William Croft (1778–1727)', PhD diss., University of Washington, 1961 [pt 2: 'The anthems of William Croft for voices with organ accompaniment'] · W. Shaw, 'Croft, William', *New Grove* · L. M. Roe, *William Croft, 1678–1727: tercentenary celebrations* (1978) · DNB · L. Roe, 'A note on Croft's secular music', *MT*, 119 (1978), 501–4 · N. Temperley, 'Croft and the charity hymn', *MT*, 119 (1978), 539–41 · BL, records of Academy of Vocal Music, Add. MS 11732 · marriage document, PRO, R.68 110 ERD/1941 · parish register (baptism), 30 Dec 1678, Nether Eatington parish church

Archives Bibliothèque Nationale, Paris · BL · Christ Church Oxf. · Dulwich College, London · Durham Cathedral · FM Cam. · Folger · L. Cong. · NYPL · Royal College of Music, London · St Michael's College, Tenbury · U. Cal., Los Angeles, William Andrews Clark Memorial Library · Westminster Abbey | Bodl. Oxf., Mus. MS C 399

Likenesses oils, *c.*1690 (William Croft as a boy?), NPG · T. Murray, oils, *c.*1720, U. Oxf., faculty of music [*see illus.*] · J. Caldwell, engraving (after T. Murray), repro. in J. Hawkins, *A general history of the science and practice of music*, 5 vols. (1776) · G. Vertue, line engraving (after T. Murray), BM, NPG; repro. in W. Croft, *Musica sacra* (1724) · marble bust on monument, Westminster Abbey

Crofton, Morgan William (1826–1915), mathematician, was born on 26 June 1826 in Dublin, the eldest of twelve children of the Revd William Crofton (1795–1851), rector of Skreen, co. Sligo, and his first wife, Melesina (1799?–1881), daughter of the Revd Henry Woodward. He was educated at Edgeworthstown School, Mostrim, co. Longford, and entered Trinity College, Dublin, in October 1843, graduating with honours in spring 1848 as senior moderator and gold medallist in mathematics and physics.

From 1849 to 1852 Crofton was professor of natural philosophy (physics) at the newly founded Queen's College, Galway. On 15 July 1851 he was received into the Roman Catholic church by John Henry Newman, for whom he retained a lasting reverence, whereas his brother, the Revd Henry Woodward Crofton (1827–1894), made his career in the established church. Crofton moved in 1852 to the Catholic University College, Dublin, where Newman was then rector, as professor of mathematics. In August 1857 he married Julia Agnes Cecilia (1826–1892), third daughter of J. B. Kernan of Cabra, co. Monaghan. Newman resigned the rectorship in 1858 and Crofton also departed, taking employment at Jesuit colleges in France before being appointed mathematics master at the Royal Military Academy, Woolwich, in February 1864.

James Joseph Sylvester FRS (1814–1897), a mathematician of international renown and professor of mathematics at the academy from 1855 to 1870 'stimulated into activity the exceptional mathematical prowess of his colleague, and communicated some of his original work to the Royal Society … with the result that at his first nomination, in 1868, [Crofton] was elected a Fellow' (Larmor, xxix). Crofton sent only one paper to the society, its lengthy title explaining what is now known as geometric probability: 'On the theory of local probability, applied to straight lines drawn at random on a plane, the methods used being also extended to the proof of certain new theorems in the integral calculus' (*PTRS*, 158, 1868, 181–99).

The subject of geometric probability had originated in France about 1777 as the Buffon needle problem and was attracting growing interest in Britain due to numerous notes in the *Educational Times* and important questions posed by Sylvester and published in the British Association *Report* for 1865. Characteristically, one seeks the probability of a convex disc intersecting a line when tossed at random onto a plane ruled by parallel lines. French scholars took up Crofton's ideas; eventually two theorems bore his name and the subject became of applied importance. In their day his contributions were viewed as a new methodology of integral calculus. Crofton recapitulated his own contributions in 'On local probability', the last section of his major article, 'Probability', published in the ninth edition of the *Encyclopaedia Britannica* (1885), 19.768–88.

On Sylvester's departure from the academy Crofton, although a junior member of the mathematical staff, was appointed professor in February 1870. His subsequent research focused more on statics and mechanics, in line with his teaching responsibilities. He was on the council of the London Mathematical Society in 1871–3, serving as its vice-president in 1872 and published in its *Proceedings* from the inception of the journal in 1866. He published at least twenty articles after 1862, in addition to his contributions to the *Educational Times*. When the Royal University of Ireland was created in 1882 he served as one of the Catholic fellows for about a decade.

Crofton retired from the academy in March 1884. He appears to have been estranged from his wife, for shortly after her death in Dublin on 27 March 1892 he married Catherine (Kate) Charlotte (1853?–1945), daughter of Holland Taylor. Crofton was an exceedingly private individual. According to Larmor he 'had a large acquaintance with the classical and general literature. This, in addition to a most amiable and kind-hearted disposition, endeared him greatly to those who had the privilege of his acquaintance' (Larmor, xxx). Of Crofton's five children William John Camille Crofton (1858–1940), born at Orléans, France, became a teacher and astronomer within the Jesuit order; his daughters, Marie Robertine Crofton (*b.* 1860) and Josephine Adrienne Crofton (1862–1890), were at the time of the 1881 census nun and scholar respectively at the Convent of the Sacred Heart, Putney, London. Little is known of John Louis Crofton (*b.* 1863, *d.* after 1910), who was specifically excluded from his father's will; Henry Joseph Crofton (1865–1887) joined the Royal Engineers and died of a fever in Bangalore, India. The Croftons were living in Worthing, Sussex, in 1899, in Ryde, Isle of Wight, in 1906, and were at 23 Montpelier Place, Brighton, Sussex, when Morgan Crofton died at his home on 13 May 1915. According to his obituarist in *The Tablet*, Crofton 'remained to the end a staunch and uncompromising Catholic, singularly pious and devout in his bearing and in his habits'.   EUGENE SENETA and IRENE N. JOHNSON

Sources H. T. Crofton, W. B. Wright, and H. A. Crofton, *Crofton memoirs* (1911) • J. Larmor, 'Morgan William Crofton', *Proceedings of the London Mathematical Society*, 2nd ser., 14 (1915), xxix–xxx • R. Deltheil, *Probabilités géométriques* (Paris, 1926) • H. Salomon, *Geometrical probability* (Philadelphia, 1978) • R. E. Miles and J. Serra, eds., *Geometrical probability and biological structures* [Paris 1977] (1978) • *The war office list and directory for the civil departments of the British Army, 1863–1937* (1986) [list for 1905] • J. S. Crone, *A concise dictionary of Irish biography* (1928) • F. C. Burnand, ed., *Catholic who's who and yearbook* (1915) • 'Father William Crofton', *Our dead: memoirs of the English Jesuits who died between June 1939 and December 1945*, 1 (1947–8), 108–12 • *The Tablet* (22 May 1915), 662 • CGPLA Eng. & Wales (1915) • Burtchaell & Sadleir, *Alum. Dubl.* • *The letters and diaries of John Henry Newman*, ed. C. S. Dessain and others, [31 vols.] (1961–), vol. 4, pp. 308–10 • census returns, 1881 • British Civil Registration Index, June quarter 1892 • CGPLA Eng. & Wales (1945) [Catherine Charlotte Crofton] • V. G. Plarr, rev., *Men and women of the time* (1899) • d. cert.

Wealth at death £6553 13s. 1d.: probate, 7 July 1915, CGPLA Eng. & Wales

Crofton, Sir Walter Frederick (1815–1897), prison administrator and penal reformer, was born at Courtrai, Flanders, on 27 February 1815. His father, Walter Crofton, a captain in the 54th foot regiment, was killed shortly afterwards at the battle of Waterloo. No details of his mother have been discovered. Like his father, and like many of the leading officials in the Victorian penal system, Crofton had a military background. He was educated at the Royal Military Academy, Woolwich, and entered the Royal Artillery as second-lieutenant in 1833. Having married Anna

Maria, only daughter of the Revd Charles Shipley of Twyford House, Hampshire, on 24 November 1840, he retired with the rank of captain in 1845. As a magistrate in Wiltshire he became interested in prisons and reformatories, and in 1853 was a commissioner of inquiry into Irish prisons. In the following year he was appointed chairman of the directors of Irish convict prisons and it was in this position, which he held until 1862, that he came to public attention.

Crofton introduced a variant of the 'progressive stages' system of penal discipline into the Irish convict prisons, as first developed by Captain Alexander Maconochie, superintendent of the Norfolk Island penal colony in the 1840s. Though unable to introduce his ideas in their entirety, Maconochie sought to reform convicts by rewarding their labour and good behaviour with 'marks' and putting them through a series of stages—different penal regimes with attendant privileges—according to their moral progress. Crofton applied these ideas in Ireland, adding the innovation of the 'intermediate stage', a final preparation for release during which convicts were given considerable liberty and responsibility to test their fitness for freedom. On release they were found work and kept under routine supervision. Crofton and his supporters made many claims for the success of the so-called Irish system, some of which were certainly bogus.

Crofton's administration of the Irish convict prisons came to the attention of English penologists at a singular moment in the mid-1850s when public confidence in the penal system was low and diminishing. The ending of transportation to the colonies in 1853 necessitated a new system of domestic penal servitude, and it was widely believed that under this system convicts were being set free too soon, without evidence of personal reformation and without supervision after release. A wave of public concern about the dangers posed by the release of convicts at home—the so-called ticket-of-leave panic of 1856–7—led to calls for the return of transportation. This was opposed by members of the reformatory movement, among them Lord Brougham, Matthew Davenport Hill, Thomas Barwick Lloyd-Baker, and Mary Carpenter, who opposed transportation as inhumane and inefficient, and whose work establishing reformatory schools for young offenders since 1849 had led them to believe that it was possible to reform not only juvenile but also adult offenders, thus negating public concern over the release of prisoners into the community. Organized in several bodies, among them the National Reformatory Union and, from 1857, the Social Science Association, the reformatory movement fell upon Crofton's scheme as a proven model of their principles in operation and propagandized for its adoption in English convict prisons, which had nothing comparable to Crofton's intermediate stage and arrangements for supervision after release. Their public campaign came to a climax at the London congress of the Social Science Association in June 1862 in direct debates between Crofton, who had recently resigned his position, and the chairman of the board of convict prison directors in England, Sir Joshua Jebb.

Over the next decade the English prison regime came closer to the Irish system, though it never adopted all its features. Crofton, meanwhile, became one of the leading penal experts of the age. He published his ideas, spoke frequently at the Social Science Association (whose penal policies he largely determined), and was engaged by several administrations in different capacities: as a commissioner of the county and borough gaols in England during 1865–8 to assist in the implementation of the 1865 Prisons Act; as a special commissioner of prisons and reformatory schools in Ireland (1868–9), during which period he introduced industrial schools there; and as chairman of the new Prisons Board in Ireland in 1877–8. He also worked closely with Henry Herbert, fourth earl of Carnarvon, the leading Conservative minister of the 1860s and 1870s, on a range of penal questions, especially the reorganization of Winchester gaol in 1864–5, which Carnarvon, in his capacity as chairman of the judicial committee of quarter sessions in Hampshire, wished to establish as a national model. Crofton, like many such experts in this period, sought aristocratic patronage, not least because the modest pension for his services in Ireland and his army half pay did not amount to a large sum. But the earl, in common with many leading politicians at this time, was slow to recognize and recommend the talents of his adviser. Nevertheless, Crofton was made CB in 1856, knighted in 1862, and appointed a privy councillor in Ireland in 1868. He also attained an international reputation. The Irish system attracted interest in Europe and America, the support of foreign statesmen including Cavour, and of foreign penologists such as the Germans Mittermaier and Holtzendorff. Many distinguished foreign experts came to see it in operation, visiting especially the intermediate prisons at Smithfield, in Dublin, and at Lusk. The prince consort and the elder princes, Edward and Albert, also visited Smithfield in August 1861 during a royal visit to Ireland. Crofton gave evidence to a committee of the French national assembly at Versailles in 1873.

Crofton's most important legislative contribution was little appreciated at the time and has been little recognized since. He was at the centre of a group of penal reformers in the Social Science Association who drafted the bill that became the 1869 Habitual Criminals Act and who worked for the legislation's improvement in the 1871 Prevention of Crimes Act. This group, including Lloyd-Baker and the former prisons inspector Frederic Hill, benefited from the association's close relations with the then Liberal home secretary, Henry Austin Bruce, who largely acted at their behest. As an opponent of the 1869 measure explained to the House of Lords, 'The real author of this bill is Sir Walter Crofton' (*Hansard 3*, 194.710, 5 March 1869). The two acts extended the system for the supervision of released convicts and established a register of convicted criminals, though they were criticized at the time and subsequently for their unworkable provisions, their infringement of civil liberties, and for essentially creating precisely the class of 'habitual criminals' which they were designed to control. Their passage brought to a close the period of readjustment in penal policy after the end of transportation, which Crofton, both directly and through his well-placed supporters, had influenced very considerably. The reformed system remained in place until the next major legislation of the 1890s.

Crofton was one of those civil servants and experts of the mid-Victorian period, before the development of full bureaucracy and of stricter conventions governing officials' behaviour, whose experience of social problems, use of the press and platform, and cultivation of ministers and men of influence enabled them to project their ideas and shape social policies. He died of heart disease at his home, 25 Winchester Road, Oxford, on 23 June 1897, survived by his wife.　　　　　　　　LAWRENCE GOLDMAN

Sources *Biograph and Review*, new ser., 1 (1882), 183–6 · *Transactions of the National Association for the Promotion of Social Science* (1857–86) · UCL, MSS of Henry Peter, Lord Brougham and Vaux · UCL, MSS of Henry Herbert, fourth earl of Carnarvon, esp. Add. MS 60844 · papers of T. B. L. Baker, Glos. RO, Hardwicke papers · BLPES, Jebb MSS · S. McConville, *English local prisons, 1860–1900: next only to death* (1995) · L. Radzinowicz and R. Hood, *A history of English criminal law and its administration from 1750*, 5: *The emergence of penal policy in Victorian and Edwardian England* (1986) · M. J. Wiener, *Reconstructing the criminal: culture, law and policy in England, 1830–1914* (1990) · L. Goldman, *Science, reform, and politics in Victorian Britain: the Social Science Association, 1857–1886* (2002) · M. W. Melling, 'Cleaning house in a suddenly closed society: the genesis, brief life and untimely death of the Habitual Criminals Act, 1869', *Osgoode Hall Law Journal* [York University, Toronto], 21/2 (June 1983), 315–62 · *Hansard 3* (1869), 194.710 · *The Times* (25 June 1897), 10 · m. cert. · d. cert. · Boase, *Mod. Eng. biog.*, 4.806 · *Men of the time* (1875)
Archives BL, corresp. with Lord Carnarvon, Add. MS 60844 · U. Lpool L., corresp. with William Rathbone · UCL, Brougham MSS
Wealth at death £3826 18s. 9d.: probate, 20 July 1897, *CGPLA Eng. & Wales*

Crofton, Zachary (1626–1672), nonconformist minister, was born in Dublin, the son of Daniel Crofton and a relative of Sir Edward Crofton. He was admitted as a student of Trinity College, Dublin, on 16 July 1641 but later fled to England to escape the Irish rising. Crofton arrived in England almost penniless and in 1644 served in the parliamentary army in Lancashire and Cheshire. He was appointed as curate to the congregation at Newcastle under Lyme in Staffordshire in 1646 and signed the ministers' *Testimony* in 1648 in support of a reformation of church and state according to the solemn league and covenant. At an unknown date he married Hannah Eaton.

Edmund Calamy described Crofton as a man of 'warm and hasty temper' (*Nonconformist's Memorial*, 1.103) and this is perhaps best illustrated by his regular changes of clerical position. In 1649 he was appointed the vicar of Dilhorne, Staffordshire, and moved to become the curate of Wrenbury in Cheshire in 1650. He was not popular at Wrenbury and was ejected on 9 October 1651 by order of the committee for compounding for refusing and preaching against the engagement. In December 1651 Crofton moved to London where he took up a brief and troubled appointment as the rector of St James Garlickhythe. He left, arguing over money, in June 1654 to become rector of the parish of Gravely in Hertfordshire. This appointment was also brief and Crofton returned to London to become

the curate of St Botolph, Aldgate, by order of Lord Protector Cromwell on 30 April 1655; he was administering to the congregation by June that year.

Crofton was an uncompromising presbyterian and a member of the eighth London classis and a delegate to the London Provincial Assembly. His vehemence for presbyterian doctrine was such that he entered into disputations with prominent Independents including John Rogers and John Simpson. Crofton was particularly violent against Simpson (who was one of the preachers at St Botolph's) and prevented him from preaching in the parish. The conflict became so intense that the protector and council ordered him to stop obstructing Simpson. His presbyterianism also manifested in staunch support for parochial discipline and he wrote a long pamphlet supporting the Provincial Assembly's call to use rigorous catechizing as the first step to admission to holy communion. Nevertheless, his rigour was overtaken by public scandal and sexual innuendo in 1661 when he was accused of physically mistreating a young female servant.

Extreme even by presbyterian standards, Crofton was a passionate supporter of the solemn league and covenant, and this manifested as opposition to both the Cromwellian and Restoration regimes. In July 1659 he preached in Chester and was arrested on the rumour that he had helped stir up Sir George Booth's royalist rising. Yet the restoration of Charles Stuart and the re-establishment of episcopacy meant that he was equally alienated from the new government. Of the London presbyterians, only Crofton and Arthur Jackson refused to sign the address of gratitude for Charles II's declaration of Breda because it might appear to countenance assent to episcopacy. Crofton was removed from St Botolph's in 1660 and became an itinerant preacher, raging against the bishops and arguing that the solemn league and covenant was still binding upon the nation. His position led to a protracted controversy with Bishop John Gauden who was among those asserting the abrogation of the oath. In Crofton's *A Serious Review of Presbyters Re-Ordination by Bishops* (1661) he invoked the memory of one of the puritans' most hated figures, Archbishop Laud, in describing his opponents as the '*Laudenses* of our age' (p. 15). Moreover, he praised a recently republished work of William Prynne and its Erastian arguments against *jure divino* claims for episcopacy. After '2000 in the streets … could not get in to the Tantling meeting-house to hear him bang the bishops', Crofton was arrested in March 1661 and imprisoned in the Tower of London on a charge of high treason (*Calamy rev.*, 144). He remained in the Tower, supported by nonconformist donations, until 14 July 1662. After his release he left London for Cheshire; by November 1662 he was briefly imprisoned in Chester Castle for sedition.

In 1664 Crofton became a member of the Grocers' Company and freeman of the City of London. Although he traded between London and Chester, he lived at Little Barford in Bedfordshire. His foray into commerce does not appear to have been successful and a chancery action was commenced against him in 1666 for the value of a cargo of tobacco that had been damaged on its way to Chester fair.

At the same time, Crofton's eldest son and daughter (who had a business in London) fled to his Bedfordshire home to escape the plague. They were not allowed into the village and, being infected, soon died. With the collapse of his business and the loss of his children, Crofton returned to London, setting up a school in East Smithfield. The school seems to have been popular and Calamy claimed that it sometimes attracted over a hundred students. Crofton took advantage of the royal indulgence of 1672 and was licensed as a presbyterian at his house in Tower Hill on 25 July. He died in December 1672 and was buried at St Botolph, Aldgate, on 26 December. He was survived by his wife, Hannah, to whom he left his land in Weaverham, Cheshire, and six children—five sons and one daughter.

E. C. VERNON

Sources Calamy rev., 144–5 · The nonconformist's memorial … originally written by … Edmund Calamy, ed. S. Palmer, [3rd edn], 3 vols. (1802–3) · D. Neal, The history of the puritans or protestant nonconformists, repr. (1990), vol. 4, p. 302 · minutes of the London provincial assembly, DWL, MS 201.12 · Z. Crofton, Catechizing Gods ordinance (1656) · Z. Crofton, Bethshemesh clouded (1653) · Z. Crofton, Berith-anti-Baal (1661) · The presbyterian lash, or, Noctrof's maid whipt (1661) · J. A. Dodd, 'Troubles in a city parish under the protectorate', EngHR, 10 (1895), 41–54 · J. Houston, Catalogues of ecclesiastical records of the Commonwealth, 1643–1660, in the Lambeth Palace library (1968) · W. M. Lamont, Godly rule: politics and religion, 1603–60 (1969)

Wealth at death property at Weaverham in Cheshire: Calamy rev.

Crofts, Elizabeth (b. c.1535), impostor, is of unknown origins. Nothing is known of her before 1554, when she was involved in a cause célèbre that led to her being accused of attempting to undermine the church and the crown. The episode is reported in both Catholic and protestant sources, with no significant variation in detail. On 14 March that year, aged about eighteen, Crofts, a serving maid whose own religious views are not recorded, was persuaded, or perhaps paid, by protestant zealots to conceal herself behind the false exterior wall of a house on Aldersgate Street, in a part of London with a considerable reformist population. There she uttered anti-Catholic propaganda which many of her hearers took to be the words of an invisible spirit; believing her to be some kind of angel, they dubbed this mysterious voice 'the bird in the wall'. Using a special whistle given her by one Drake, described as a servant of Sir Anthony Nevill or (more plausibly) Knyvet, she spoke heresies and treason against Queen Mary, King Philip, and the Catholic church. But when the onlookers said 'God save the Lady Elizabeth', referring to the queen's younger (protestant) sister, the voice answered 'So be it'. She attracted huge crowds, her audience apparently reaching 17,000 by the second morning. It was several days before the imposture was discovered, the wall pulled down and the young vocalist arrested. She was imprisoned first in Newgate and then at Bread Street.

On 6 July (or perhaps the 15th) Crofts appeared at Paul's Cross to answer her accusers and atone for her sins. In the presence of the preacher, John Wymunsley, archdeacon of Middlesex, she confessed to having offended 'God and the Queenes majestie … and to be a gasyng stocke to the

hoale worlde to my gret shame' (Hogarde, 120). She also denounced her accomplices, or corrupters, who included 'Miles, clarke of Saint Butolphs in Aldersgate street, a plaier, a weaver, Hill, clarke of S. Leonards in Foster lane'; during her imposture these men had apparently gone among the entranced crowds and 'tooke upon them to interpret what the spirit said' (Stow, 1059). Following her penance Crofts was briefly returned to prison but soon released. It is possible that Drake had links with the conspirator Sir Peter Carew, and even with Sir Thomas Wyatt. Whether the affair of 'the bird in the wall' had such grandiose connections it is impossible to say, but it was clearly well prepared and very successful in attracting attention, giving it a significant place in a growing wave of questioning and dissent. Although at least one of Crofts's collaborators was set in the pillory, she herself was never held fully responsible for her actions. Londoners apparently found it easier to countenance the idea that she had been led astray or that, as many suggested, she was simply mad. After this episode nothing further is known of her.

DANIEL HAHN

Sources C. Wriothesley, A chronicle of England during the reigns of the Tudors from AD 1485 to 1559, ed. W. D. Hamilton, 2 vols., CS, new ser., 11, 20 (1875–7) · J. G. Nichols, ed., The chronicle of Queen Jane, and of two years of Queen Mary, CS, old ser., 48 (1850) · J. G. Nichols, ed., The chronicle of the grey friars of London, CS, 53 (1852) · CSP Spain, 1554 · M. Hogarde, The displaying of the protestantes (1556) · J. Stow, Chronicles of England (1592) · G. Burnet, The history of the Reformation of the Church of England, rev. N. Pocock, new edn, 2 (1865) · S. Brigden, London and the Reformation (1989)

Crofts, Ernest (1847–1911), history painter, was born in Leeds, Yorkshire, on 15 September 1847. He was the second son of John Crofts JP, a manufacturer, and his wife, Ellen Wordsworth, who was a descendant of the poet William Wordsworth. Crofts attended Rugby School and was also schooled in Berlin. Having decided to become a professional artist he remained in Germany, studying in Düsseldorf under Professor Hünten, who was himself a pupil of the history and military painter Horace Vernet. It was also in Düsseldorf that Crofts met his future wife, Elizabeth Wüsthofen, whom he married in 1872. They had one daughter. After returning to London, Crofts studied under another painter of military scenes, Alfred Borron Clay. Given such tutelage, it is hardly surprising that by the time Ernest Crofts ended his studies he, too, had come to specialize in military and historical subjects. In this field he found financial success, if not universal artistic acclaim.

The paintings of Ernest Crofts can be grouped into three main subject areas, the first of which is English civil war scenes. These include Cromwell at the Sign of the Blue Boar (1883; Dudley Museum and Art Gallery), The Funeral of Charles I (Bristol Art Gallery), and Cromwell after the Battle of Marston Moor (Townley Hall Art Gallery, Burnley). His second area of interest was the Napoleonic era; his paintings in this category include On the Evening of the Battle of Waterloo (Walker Art Gallery, Liverpool). His third theme comprised military, political, and civic scenes, both historical and contemporary, such as King Edward VII Distributing

South African War Medals and *The Funeral of Queen Victoria* (1903), and Crofts's largest work, *Queen Elizabeth Opening the First Royal Exchange* (Royal Exchange, London).

Crofts was a fine draughtsman, and his paintings reveal his keen interest in the most minute accuracy of costume detail. Yet his work was neither dry nor academic. Indeed his particular talent lay in the way that he imbued his imagined historical scenes with dramatic intensity: they are feasts of action-packed theatre, and proved tremendously popular. The numerous internet sites that sell reproductions of his paintings testify to his continued popularity among military enthusiasts.

Crofts exhibited regularly at the Royal Academy from 1874, his first painting accepted there being *A Retreat: Episode in the Franco-German War*. He followed this with numerous submissions on his favoured themes, such as *Napoleon and the Old Guard at Waterloo*, exhibited in 1895. Crofts was elected an associate member of the Royal Academy in 1878 and a full academician in 1896. His diploma work was entitled *To the Rescue*. Succeeding Phillip Hermogenes Calderon, who died in 1898, Crofts was appointed keeper and trustee of the Royal Academy; he is included in Sir Hubert von Herkomer's large portrait group of the Royal Academy council of 1908 (Tate collection). Crofts was also elected a fellow of the Society of British Artists on 1 March 1900. In later life such administrative duties took up much of his time and his paintings perhaps suffered as a result. They lacked the colour and vitality of his earlier work.

Crofts died in London, on 19 March 1911, and was buried at Kensal Green cemetery; his wife survived him. Exactly nine months later Christies salesrooms in London held a sale of the contents of his studio.

Jennifer Melville

Sources DNB · Graves, *RA exhibitors* · Bénézit, *Dict.*, 3rd edn · G. M. Waters, *Dictionary of British artists, working 1900–1950* (1975) · CGPLA Eng. & Wales (1911)
Likenesses H. von Herkomer, group portrait, oils, 1908 (*The council of the Royal Academy*), Tate collection · R. W. Robinson, photograph, NPG; repro. in *Members and associates of the Royal Academy, 1891* (1892) · A. G. Wyon, memorial plaque, Holy Trinity Church, Suffolk · wood-engraving, NPG; repro. in *ILN* (20 July 1878) · woodcut, BM
Wealth at death £3736 3s. 8d.: probate, 24 May 1911, CGPLA Eng. & Wales

Crofts, Freeman Wills (1879–1957), railway engineer and writer of detective stories, was born at 26 Waterloo Road, Dublin, on 1 June 1879, the son of Freeman Wills Crofts, a surgeon-lieutenant in the Army Medical Service, who died before his son's birth, and his wife, Celia Frances Wise. Both parents were of Irish protestant descent from the Cork area. When young Freeman was aged three his mother married Jonathan Harding, Church of Ireland vicar of Gilford, co. Down (1865–1900), and archdeacon of Dromore. Brought up in his stepfather's Ulster vicarage, Crofts attended the Methodist College in Belfast (1891–4), then completed his education at Campbell College in that city. In 1896 he was apprenticed to his uncle, Berkeley Deane Wise, who was then chief engineer of the Belfast and Northern Counties Railway. In 1899 Crofts was appointed assistant engineer constructing the Londonderry and Strabane Railway, and in 1900 he became district engineer of the Coleraine, Belfast and Northern Counties Railway. He became chief assistant engineer of his company, now the LMS Northern Counties Committee, in 1923.

A keen amateur musician, Crofts was a church organist and choirmaster at Coleraine parish church and later at St Patrick's, Jordanstown. On 12 September 1912 he married Mary Bellas (1876–1964), daughter of John J. C. Canning of Coleraine, a bank manager. There were no children of the marriage.

In 1919 Crofts suffered a severe illness and, encouraged by his doctor, Adam Mathers, he occupied his time writing a book subsequently published as *The Cask* (1920). Set in Edwardian London and Paris, this detective story soon became a classic of the genre and 'a milestone in the history of the detective novel' (Binyon, 82). Encouraged by his agent he continued writing detective stories, producing a book nearly every year for the next three decades. His fifth book, *Inspector French's Greatest Case* (1925), introduced that portly, dour, but methodical and meticulous Scotland Yard detective who was to feature in most of his later books, plays, and short stories. In 1931 a critic wrote that 'The alibi was Crofts's first love and the pivot of his plots … [he] exploited to the full his knowledge of the railways and found in Bradshaw a *vade mecum*' (Thomson). Julian Symons saw him as of 'the humdrum school' but Raymond Chandler admired him as 'the soundest builder of them all' (Barnes, 270–71). Crofts's carefully constructed alibis for the murderers (often involving railway timetables) could be demolished only by French's careful attention to detail, and such was his reputation for breaking apparently unbreakable alibis that French was included with Sherlock Holmes and Hercule Poirot in Agatha Christie's parody of 'the great detectives', *Partners in Crime* (1929). The strain of producing an annual novel while following his engineering profession affected Crofts's health, so he resigned his railway career in 1929 and moved to the quiet village of Blackheath, near Guildford, in Surrey, to write full time.

Crofts was recalled to Ulster in 1930 when the government of Northern Ireland appointed him to inquire into the 'objections lodged against the draft scheme for the drainage of the River Bann and Lough Neagh'. He reported within a month, finding 'nothing which could not be met by compensation or slight modification of detail'. 1930 also saw the publication of *Sir John Magill's Last Journey*, set in Ulster as was the dénouement of his ingenious *Fatal Venture* (1939). Following his move to Surrey, Crofts generally used locations in the home counties, visiting local scenes with notebook and camera to aid authenticity—the victim of *The Hog's Back Mystery* (1933) was buried in the cutting of the new main road through that feature just outside Guildford. Several other novels were set near his Blackheath cottage.

By 1930 Crofts was, with Agatha Christie and Dorothy L. Sayers, an active member of the Detection Club. They funded their Gerrard Street premises, and their formal dinners, by publishing stories with the chapters serially written by the members. Crofts contributed to the club's *The Floating Admiral* (1931) and *Double Death* (1939); his account of the 1933 Lakey murder case as 'A New Zealand tragedy' formed a part of the club's non-fiction collection *The Anatomy of Murder* (1936). He was made a fellow of the Royal Society of Arts in 1939 and in that year he wrote in support of Moral Re-Armament (*Guildford City Outlook*, February 1939).

Crofts continued his annual Inspector French books through the Second World War, his villains often now working for the enemy cause or the settings being wartime England. Most of his books were also published in the United States, occasionally with their titles slightly modified for the American market. Translations appeared in ten languages, including two, *The Cask* and *Sir John Magill's Last Journey*, into Gaelic and *Death of a Train* into Esperanto. His short stories in *Murderers Make Mistakes* (1947) were the twenty-three plays that had originally been broadcast in 1943–5 by the BBC Home Service in 30 minute episodes as *Chief Inspector French's Cases* while *Many a Slip* (1955) contained fuller versions of the twenty-one Inspector French stories that had appeared in the *Evening Standard*. Crofts also wrote one story, *Young Robin Brand, Detective* (1947), for children and a single religious volume, *The four gospels in one story, written as a modern biography with difficult passages clarified and explanatory notes* (1949). His more successful books went into numerous reprints, fifteen titles being issued in the 'green' Penguin Crime series (1945–59). His books show a cohesion and continuity as Inspector French frequently refers to his previous cases and some of the police officers reappear.

In 1953 Crofts and his wife moved to the Sussex coast at Worthing. His final book, *Anything to Declare?*, featuring the now Chief Superintendent French, appeared in 1957. Crofts died of bowel cancer at a nursing home, 2 Farncombe Road, Worthing, Sussex, on 11 April 1957. His popularity with readers of the golden age of English detective fiction is occasionally revived and, in 2000, all thirty-six of his classic works were reprinted in paperback.

ROBIN WOOLVEN

Sources M. Barnes, *Twentieth-century crime and mystery writers*, ed. L. Henderson, 3rd edn (1991), 270–71 · T. J. Binyon, 'Murder will out': *the detective in fiction* (1989), 82 · H. Haycraft, *Murder for pleasure: the life and times of the detective story* (1941) · H. R. F. Keating, *Whodunit? A guide to crime, suspense, and spy fiction* (1982) · H. R. F. Keating, *The bedside companion to crime* (1989) · b. cert. · d. cert. · *WW* (1940–57) · *Irish Book Lover*, 18 (1930), 132 · H. D. Thomson, *Masters of mystery: a study of the detective story* (1931) · J. Symons, *Bloody murder: from the detective story to the crime novel, a history* (1984) · J. Cooper and B. Pike, *Detective fiction: the collector's guide* (1994) · *The Times* (13 April 1957) · *ILN* (27 April 1957) · *Belfast Telegraph* (17 Feb 1941) · *Belfast News-Letter* (11 Aug 1953) [in press cuttings bks in Belfast City Library] · B. Benstock and T. F. Staley, eds., *British mystery writers, 1920–1939*, DLitB, 77 (1989) · m. cert.
Archives BL, corresp. of Crofts and his executors with Society of Authors, Add. MS 56685
Wealth at death £21,737 19s. 6d.: probate, 16 Aug 1957, CGPLA Eng. & Wales

Crofts [Croft], **George** (d. 1539?), Roman Catholic ecclesiastic, was the son of Sir Edward Croft of Hereford. He was elected probationary fellow of Oriel College, Oxford, on 10 October 1513 (holding the fellowship until 4 February 1519) and determined for the degree of BA the same year. His MA came before 1518 and in 1522 he matriculated at Louvain. In 1520 he was junior proctor at Oxford. Ordained deacon on 3 April 1518, he was admitted rector of Mappowder, Devon (15 December 1519); rector of Upper Sapey, Herefordshire (28 August 1523, vacated 1524); rector of Winsford, Somerset (admitted on 19 September 1524); rector of Deane, Hampshire (13 March 1525, vacated in October 1527); master of St Bartholomew's Hospital, Bristol (admitted on 31 July 1525); canon of Chichester and prebendary of Hova Ecclesia (4 May 1526, vacated by 1529); rector of Broughton, Oxfordshire (19 September 1527 until death); bursal prebendary in Chichester (13 August 1529, vacated in August 1531); rector of Shepton Mallet, Somerset (20 September 1529 until death); and rector of Newton Ferrers, Devon (8 March 1537 until death). He became chaplain to and preached before Henry VIII in 1531. By 1538 he was chancellor of Chichester Cathedral. Later that year he was arrested in the wake of Sir Geoffrey Pole's interrogation, which implicated Crofts in the Courtenay conspiracy, and revealed that he was an opponent of the Henrician reformation. He was from the first linked to Lord de la Warr. At his first interrogation Crofts admitted to having frequently talked to Sir Geoffrey and expressed his discontent with the direction of royal policy on religion, especially the abolition of papal authority. Although Crofts had taken the oath of supremacy, he was later reported to have said that 'none act or thing that ever he did more grieved his conscience' (*LP Henry VIII*, 13, pt 2, 829). According to Pole's examination, Crofts was also privy to Sir Geoffrey's communications with his brother Cardinal Pole, had endorsed Sir Geoffrey's actions and approved of the cardinal's, and at one point had recommended that Sir Geoffrey go to his brother, although Crofts denied most of this. But Crofts confessed that he disapproved of many religious changes, and wrote to his father from the Tower that he was a traitor. Indicted for saying Henry was not supreme head, he pleaded guilty on 4 December 1538 and was presumably executed shortly thereafter, probably in early 1539.

T. F. MAYER

Sources Emden, *Oxf.* · *LP Henry VIII*, 13/1, no. 1009; 13/2, nos. 695(2–3), 771(2), 803–4, 821–2, 826, 828–9, 830(5), 831(2), 957, 960, 986(6, 10, 13)
Archives PRO, records of the 'Courtenay conspiracy', SP 1/138

Crofts, James. *See* Scott, James, duke of Monmouth and first duke of Buccleuch (1649–1685).

Crofts, William, Baron Crofts (d. 1677), courtier, was the eldest son of Sir Henry Crofts (c.1590–1667) of Little Saxham, Suffolk, and his wife, Elizabeth (c.1595–1642), daughter of Sir Richard Wortley, of Wortley, Yorkshire. His sister Cicely was, by 1630, a maid of honour to the queen and about that time Crofts may have gone to court, where, according to Sir Edward Hyde, he was 'too much favoured' (Ollard, 53).

In 1635 Crofts was sent on a mission to Elizabeth, queen

of Bohemia, at The Hague, and on his return she recommended him to Charles I and Henrietta Maria for a position with one of the princes. However, in 1634 he had quarrelled with George, Lord Digby, and in 1636 was expelled from court for a time. Nevertheless, prior to the civil war he was appointed master of the horse to James, duke of York, and captain of the guards to the queen. Crofts was one of the king's servants declared by parliament, in February 1642, to be an enemy of the state who should be removed from court. He was with the court during the civil war and in March 1645 was granted several manors in Essex and Suffolk. In 1646 his aunt Eleanor Wortley married Robert Rich, second earl of Warwick, commander of the parliamentarian fleet, and in 1648 Crofts was sent to persuade him to negotiate with the royalists, but Warwick would not receive him.

In September 1649 Charles II dispatched Crofts and Sir John Denham to the Baltic to seek assistance in regaining his throne. The mission, in Poland, Danzig, Lithuania, and Königsberg, lasted until February 1652. Crofts returned to the court at Paris and in 1652 Charles II appointed him a gentleman of the bedchamber, to the annoyance of Hyde, who resented his influence with the king. Crofts held the post until his death and used his position to advance the career of his cousin, Henry Bennet (later earl of Arlington), who became secretary to the duke of York in 1654. In 1652 Crofts took a house near Paris, where he entertained Charles in April and May 1654, and he was also host to the duke of Gloucester, dissuading him from converting to Roman Catholicism. He fought a duel in 1652 and his behaviour at the exiled court prompted James Hamilton to refer to him as 'that mad fellow Crofts' and to describe him and Lord Carlingford as 'those insipid buffoons' (*Memoirs … Grammont*, 308).

By a patent dated at Brussels 18 May 1658 Crofts was created Baron Crofts of Saxham. Towards the end of that year he was entrusted with the care of James Scott, Charles's illegitimate son by Lucy Walter, who had died that autumn. The boy was passed off as Crofts's nephew and was known as James Crofts. After the Restoration he was taken to England by Crofts and presented at court. When he was created duke of Monmouth in 1665 Crofts was appointed one of the commissioners to manage his affairs. Monmouth's four children by his mistress Eleanor Myddleton bore the name of Crofts.

In 1660 Charles directed Crofts to acquaint the French court of his restoration and, although it was thought that Louis XIV would not grant him an audience because of Charles's treatment of Antoine de Bordeaux, the French ambassador in London, Crofts was able to smooth over any resentment. He also presented Charles's congratulations on Louis's marriage to Maria Teresa and in 1661 returned to Paris to convey the king's congratulations on the birth of the dauphin, when he was cordially welcomed and entertained. Having previously carried news of the Restoration to Poland, in January 1662 he was sent with Edward Montagu, earl of Sandwich, to bring Catherine of Braganza from Portugal.

Crofts married, on 1 April 1661, Dorothy (*bap.* 1620, *d.* 1663), widow of Sir John Hele, and also previously of Hugh Rogers of Conington, Somerset, and possibly of Sir Thomas Hele. She was the daughter of Sir John Hobart and his wife, Philippa, daughter of Robert Sydney, first earl of Leicester. Dorothy was buried on 7 February 1663 at the church of St Andrew, Holborn. Crofts then married, in or before December 1664, Elizabeth (1618–1672), widow of the Hon. Henry Howard and before that of John, Baron Craven of Ryton. She was the daughter of William, Baron Spencer of Wormleighton, and Penelope, daughter of Henry Wriothesley, earl of Southampton. She died on 11 August 1672 and was buried at Little Saxham on 18 August.

In 1662 Crofts was granted a pension of £1000 per annum as a gentleman of the bedchamber. Payment fell into arrears and in 1665 it was replaced by £1500 per annum to him and his wife, and the longer lived of them, payable out of receipts from the dues on Newcastle coal and the revenues of the duchy of Lancaster. In 1663 he was awarded the remaining sixty-five years of a lease of the manor, mansion, and park of Holdenby in Northamptonshire, granted to Henrietta Maria in 1629. He also entered into partnerships to improve crown land in Kent that had been damaged by the sea and in Whittlewood Forest in Northamptonshire. In 1667 he succeeded to his father's estates, and he had a house at Spring Garden in St Martin-in-the-Fields, Westminster, which, in his will, he directed should be sold to pay his legacies and debts.

Crofts died, childless, on 11 September 1677, and the peerage became extinct. He allocated £1000 for his funeral charges if he should die in London, and £500 if elsewhere, but the location of his death is unknown. However, he was buried at Little Saxham on 13 September, having allowed £500 for the erection of a monument to him and his wife in the aisle where he was buried. The monument, of black and white marble, was made by Abraham Storey and has been judged his best work. It has a life-size, semi-recumbent figure of Crofts, in his peer's robes, with that of his wife on a lower table forward of his, and his coat of arms on a panel on the front of the monument.

STEPHEN PORTER

Sources CSP dom., 1634–5, 81; 1635, 267; 1641–3, 274; 1661–2, 128, 546, 588; 1663–4, 67, 105, 125, 648; 1664–5, 32, 121, 125, 151, 182–4, 223; 1665–6, 143; 1666–7, 202; 1670, 406 · CSP Venice, 1659–61, 158, 174, 178, 183, 191; 1661–4, 66–7, 72, 168 · Clarendon, *Hist. rebellion*, 1.527; 4.365; 5.343 · Calendar of the Clarendon state papers preserved in the Bodleian Library, 2: 1649–1654, ed. W. D. Macray (1869), 124, 130 · Calendar of the Clarendon state papers preserved in the Bodleian Library, 5: 1660–1726, ed. F. J. Routledge (1970), 44–50 · R. Ollard, *Clarendon's four portraits* (1989), 44, 53 · DNB · GEC, *Peerage*, 3.544 · will, PRO, PROB 11/354, sig. 95 · G. M. Bell, *A handlist of British diplomatic representatives, 1509–1688*, Royal Historical Society Guides and Handbooks, 16 (1990), 114–5 · Memoirs of the court of Charles the Second, by Count Grammont, ed. W. Scott (1846), 308 · J. Gage, *The history and antiquities of Suffolk: Thingoe hundred* (1838), 134, 136–7, 159 · R. Gunnis, *Dictionary of British sculptors, 1660–1851* (1953); new edn (1968) · J. Nichols, *The progresses, processions, and magnificent festivities of King James I, his royal consort, family and court*, 2 (1828), 407

Likenesses A. Storey, marble monument, Little Saxham church, Suffolk · engraving, repro. in Gage, *History and antiquities* · oils, priv. coll.

Wealth at death see will, PRO, PROB 11/354, sig. 95

Croghan, George (*d.* 1782), colonial official and land speculator in America, was born in Dublin, though further details of his parents and upbringing are uncertain. Before moving to America in 1741 he is known to have married. His daughter Susannah was born in 1750. In later life he lived with the daughter of a Mohawk chief, with whom he had a second daughter, Catherine. Once in America, Croghan entered the fur trade, working both independently and for merchants in Philadelphia. His success as a trader owed much to his willingness to engage with the Indians of the Ohio and Great Lakes in their villages, rather than waiting for them to come to Philadelphia. He soon learned the language of the Delaware, and probably also Mohawk, and discovered a talent for diplomacy. In 1744 he obtained his own licence and established his post at the head of the Ohio River, the future site of Pittsburgh. Five years on he employed a hundred traders and claimed 200,000 acres as a gift from his Indian friends. However, expansion also brought problems: attacks from rivals and thieves were extensive in the lawless region, and by the early 1750s Croghan faced bankruptcy. His trading position was further threatened by the outbreak of the French and Indian War during which he served as General George Washington's interpreter in the Fort Necessity campaign; in July 1755 Croghan led a detachment of Indians who served as scouts during General Edward Braddock's ill-fated march on Fort Duquesne, one of the French strongholds built to counter Croghan's expanding trading empire. He was also present with Washington at Braddock's death following an ambush by French forces composed principally of American Indians.

In 1756 Croghan was appointed deputy to Sir William Johnson, the newly created superintendent of Indian affairs in the northern department, a position he held until 1772. In 1758 he led an Indian scouting party in the failed British assault on the French Fort Ticonderoga on Lake Champlain. Later he participated in General John Forbes's successful march on Fort Duquesne, subsequently renamed Fort Pitt, and is credited with negotiating the important treaty of Easton (1758), which promised to halt westward colonial expansion and secured the allegiance of several tribes including the powerful Iroquois nation. In 1763, with the war over, Croghan travelled to England, partly to secure approval for his 200,000 acre land grant and partly to propose Johnson's ideas on Britain's future policies towards the extensive interior lands and native peoples of which Britain had gained control.

On his return, Croghan was charged with securing a final peace with the American Indians who had risen in opposition to the imposition of British rule (1763–5). Although ultimately unsuccessful, the rising demonstrated that, although Britain claimed the Ohio region, the American Indians controlled it. During his first attempt to meet the leader of the rising, Pontiac, Croghan and his party were captured, but his adept diplomacy managed to save his party and secure a settlement.

During this time of relative peace Croghan, like many officials involved with the American Indians, sought financial benefit from his post, becoming heavily involved in a variety of land grant schemes for the creation of colonies in the Ohio. Such ventures operated with high risks, because the British had stripped the colonists and their governments of the ability to purchase or seize lands from the American Indians—a policy thought crucial to the stability of British-Amerindian relations. Freedom of movement in the interior for purposes of trade and survey was also restricted by royal proclamation. Croghan became an instrumental figure for the competing land companies because he had both the authority to move freely in the interior and the known talent for successful negotiation with American Indians. As a result, Croghan became a much sought man. He was a key source of information for Benjamin Franklin, who was then in London pressing for colonization of the interior; when writing his *History of America* (1777), William Robertson quizzed him on American Indians; and during his trips down the Ohio River he managed to collect and send to London a substantial number of fossilized bones of the then-undiscovered mastodon, causing a transatlantic stir and making an important step in early palaeontology. British opposition to the colonization of the Ohio region remained steadfast until 1772, when Lord Hillsborough, the secretary of state for America, resigned in protest to a grant of 20 million acres to the Grand Ohio Company, of which Croghan was a stockholder. However, rising Anglo-American tensions caused further postponements and prevented this and other grants from materializing into the huge profits investors had hoped for.

Facing renewed demands from creditors, Croghan retired to his residence near Fort Pitt and devoted his efforts to keeping the peace, despite the constant encroachment of settlers on Indian lands. In 1774 he could not prevent the governor of Virginia, Lord Dunmore, from waging a punitive war against the Shawnees in an attempt to secure that colony's claim to the Ohio territory. At the outset of the American War of Independence he sided with the patriots, and later he was imprisoned during the British occupation of Philadelphia. None the less, after the British evacuation he was required to clear his name with the Pennsylvania authorities, who suspected him of sympathizing with the loyalists and charged him with treason in June 1779. Declining health kept Croghan in Philadelphia, where he continued to hope for the resurrection of his plans for western expansion in an attempt to fend off his creditors. However, rising debts forced him to sell off much of his remaining land and so, in poverty, to abandon proposals the validity of which the American government refused to acknowledge. Croghan's death in Philadelphia on 31 August 1782 went unrecorded in the newspapers, and the inscription on his gravestone in St Peter's churchyard, Philadelphia, was soon obliterated.

EDWARD J. CASHIN

Sources N. B. Wainwright, *George Croghan: wilderness diplomat* (1959) · A. T. Volwiter, *George Croghan and the westward movement, 1741–1782* (1926) · J. M. Sosin, *The revolutionary frontier, 1763–1783* (1967) · R. A. Billington, *Westward expansion: a history of the American frontier*, 3rd edn (1967)

Archives Hist. Soc. Penn., Cadwalader collection, papers · Hunt. L., Loudon and Abercomby papers · New York Historical Society, Banyar papers · U. Mich., Clements L., corresp. with Thomas Gage **Wealth at death** £50 13s. 6d.: Wainwright, *George Croghan*, 307

Croke, Sir Alexander (1758–1842), lawyer and author, was born on 22 July 1758 at Aylesbury, Buckinghamshire, the son of Alexander Croke of Studley Priory, Oxfordshire, and Anne, daughter of Robert Armistead, rector of Ellesborough, Buckinghamshire. After spending some years at a private school at Bierton, Buckinghamshire, he matriculated at Oriel College, Oxford, on 11 October 1775, and was called to the bar at the Inner Temple in 1786. Ten years later he married Alice Blake of Brackley, Northamptonshire; the couple had three daughters and five sons. Croke had returned to Oxford about 1794 and he proceeded BCL on 4 April 1797 and DCL three days later. He was admitted a member of the College of Advocates on 3 November 1797. Sir William Scott (later Lord Stowell), whose acquaintance Croke had made at Oxford, employed him in 1800 to report one of his judgments. The case (*Horner v. Liddiard*) related to the marriage of illegitimate minors, and Croke published his report with an essay on the laws affecting illegitimacy. The publication brought Croke to notice, and in 1801 he was employed by the government to reply to a book by a Danish lawyer that attacked the action of the British admiralty court in its relations with neutral nations.

In the same year the system of vice-admiralty courts in the British colonies was reconstructed, creating a number of new judgeships. Croke was offered a choice of Nova Scotia, Jamaica, or Martinique. He chose the first, preferring the climate. During his service as president of the vice-admiralty court he was engaged in numerous controversies and earned the enduring dislike of the Canadians. His rigid enforcement of the Navigation Acts did not endear him to the merchant community, and in 1813 his vocal opposition to Walter Bromley's interdenominational charity school, which many of the Halifax élites supported, provoked a heated public controversy.

Croke was knighted on his return to England in 1816. For the rest of his life he lived at Studley, where he entertained his Oxford friends and amused himself with drawing and painting. A man of strong tory opinions, he also published widely on various subjects: his works include numerous legal reports and commentaries, poetry, letters on politics and religion, an Anglican catechism, and the ambitious *Genealogical History of the Croke Family* (1823). Croke died at Studley Priory on 27 December 1842.

SIDNEY LEE, *rev.* TROY O. BICKHAM

Sources C. A. Janzen, 'Croke, Sir Alexander', *DCB*, vol. 7 · A. Croke, *The genealogical history of the Croke family*, 2 vols. (1823) · G. Gilmore and C. L. Black, *The law of the admiralty* (1957) · J. Fingard, 'English humanitarianism and the colonial mind: Walter Bromley in Nova Scotia, 1813–25', *Canadian Historical Review*, 54 (1973), 123–51 · L. Laing, 'Nova Scotia's admiralty court as a problem of colonial administration', *Canadian Historical Review*, 16 (1935), 151–61 · C. A. Janzen, 'Tentacles of power: Alexander Croke in Nova Scotia, 1801–1815', MA diss., University of New Brunswick, 1978 · *GM*, 2nd ser., 19 (1843), 315–17
Archives BL, corresp., Add. MSS 16569, 34568–34572, 59377, 59383 · Bodl. Oxf., corresp. and papers

Croke, Charles (1590/91–1657), Church of England clergyman, was the third son of Sir John *Croke (1553×6–1620), lawyer, of Studley, Oxfordshire, and Chilton, Buckinghamshire, and his wife, Katherine Blount (*b*. 1563). Sir Henry *Croke (1588–1659) and Unton *Croke (1594/5–1670/71) were his brothers. After attending Thame School, on 8 June 1604, aged thirteen, he matriculated from Christ Church, Oxford. He graduated BA on 16 April 1608 and the following year, as was the practice in his family, was admitted to the Inner Temple, but he remained at Oxford, where he became a respected tutor and lecturer at his college and proceeded MA on 18 April 1611. Through the influence of his father (who had been city recorder) and of Bishop John King of London, in January 1613 Croke was appointed professor of rhetoric at Gresham College, London. For the next few years he seems to have divided his time between the two cities. In 1616 he was instituted rector of St Olave, Silver Street, London, but that year he also served as junior proctor in the University of Oxford and was, on the presentation of his uncle Sir George Croke, for a few months rector of Waterstock, until he resigned it in favour of his cousin Henry Croke (1597/8–1642). From 1617 he was a fellow of Eton College; he was licensed to preach on 16 April 1618. At some point he married Anne, daughter of Sir William Grene of Great Milton, Oxfordshire; she died on 24 July 1619 and was buried at Beckley, near Studley.

Croke's marriage had already marked the end of academic ambitions at Oxford. By May 1619 he had also resigned his Gresham professorship, the beneficiary again being his cousin Henry. Some financial support came through his fellowship at Eton (resigned 1622), but family wealth may have enabled him to live comfortably and he probably did not lack patrons. By licence dated 10 July 1620 he married Amy or Anne Rivett of All Hallows Staining, Middlesex, daughter of John Rivett or Revett of Brandston, Suffolk; they had a son, John, who died young. The following year Croke was presented by the earl of Bedford to the rich living of Amersham, Buckinghamshire, still within the orbit of his prosperous and extensive south midlands cousinage. He became BD and DD on 20 June 1625 and was subsequently a chaplain to Charles I.

Through his reputation and connections Croke set up what was effectively a school at his rectory. Students included local boys like William Drake and John Gregory (1607–1646) (later chaplain to Bishop Brian Duppa), kin like his nephew Robert Croke (1609–1681), and others who travelled a considerable distance, such as Henry, son of Sir Patricius Curwen of Warkington, Cumberland. When Henry died aged fourteen in 1638, Croke preached the funeral sermon at Amersham; *A Sad Memorial of Henry Curwen* (1638), his only publication, is a conventional celebration of a sickly but pious and dutiful youth. An appended note of the funeral and accompanying verses by friends of the deceased suggest that the earl of Manchester's sons George and Sidney Montagu were contemporaries of Curwen among Croke's students.

With the coming of civil war the Croke family, hitherto

renowned for its collective piety, was divided in its political allegiance. John Ward claims that Charles Croke was 'very zealous for the king' (Ward, 308), although the nature of his loyalty is not clear. In a petition to the protector of 2 March 1655 Croke revealed that he had an estate in Ireland. Requesting permission to settle there, he announced an intention to 'employ my talent in preaching the Gospel' (*CSP dom.*, *1655*, 63). His suggestion of a substitute at Amersham, Edward Terry of University College, Oxford, was endorsed by Thomas Goodwin and by Thankful and John Owen; it was accepted, and his request approved, on 20 March. Croke is said to have taken up residence at Feathard, co. Tipperary, but he died at Carloe, near Dublin, on 10 April 1657.   VIVIENNE LARMINIE

Sources A. Croke, *The genealogical history of the Croke family*, 2 vols. (1823), 506–10 · Foster, *Alum. Oxon.* · J. Ward, *The lives of the professors of Gresham College* (1740), 306–8 · *CSP dom.*, *1655*, 63 · W. H. Cooke, ed., *Students admitted to the Inner Temple, 1547–1660* [1878]

Croke, Charles (*fl.* 1652–1686). *See under* Croke, Unton (1594/5–1670/71).

Croke, Sir George (*c.*1560–1642), judge and law reporter, was the third son of John Croke (*d.* 1608) of Chilton, Buckinghamshire, and Elizabeth (*d.* 1611), daughter of Sir Alexander Unton of Chequers. Educated at the parish school in Thame, he matriculated at Christ Church, Oxford, in 1575, but was admitted in the same year to the Inner Temple, evidently intending to follow in the footsteps of his elder brother, the future judge Sir John *Croke (1553x6–1620). By the time he was called to the bar in 1584 he had already established habits of study that he perfected during the next fifty years. He actively collected manuscript copies of older law reports while at the same time assembling new material either from his own observations in court or by borrowing from other younger lawyers, including Sir Edward Coke.

Croke established a lucrative practice that enabled him by 1620 to purchase estates in Buckinghamshire and at Waterstock in Oxfordshire. He maintained a connection with the Hampden family, and in 1597 became member of parliament for Brere Alston (Devon) thanks to the patronage of his relative, Charles Blount, eighth Lord Mountjoy. He was made a bencher at the Temple in 1597, served as reader in 1599 and 1618, and was elected treasurer of the inn in 1609. At about the same date he surprised his friends and acquaintances by marrying Mary, a daughter of the former lord mayor of London, Sir Thomas Benet, who was some thirty years younger, and with whom he had one son and three daughters.

Although he failed to become a serjeant-at-law in 1614 because he was unwilling to give the king money in return for the distinction, Croke was knighted and made a serjeant (gratis) in 1623, naming Lord Keeper Williams and Lionel Cranfield, the earl of Middlesex, as his patrons. Now in his sixties, he was promoted quickly. When he was appointed a justice of the common pleas in 1625, Lord Keeper Coventry declared in a speech that the king had

Sir George Croke (*c.*1560–1642), by unknown artist, 1626

advanced Croke because of his universally acknowledged integrity and great learning. On the death of Sir John Dodderidge in 1628 he was transferred to the court of king's bench. During the 1630s Croke emerged as one of the few judges willing to question royal financial measures. When the king asked the judges in 1635 and 1637 for opinions about the legality of ship money, his approval was qualified. Although his decision reflected some encouragement from his relatives, and especially his wife, he was one of only two judges who ruled clearly against the exaction when John Hampden's test case came to trial in 1637. Declaring that the question would have been better decided before a 'public assembly of the state', Croke repeatedly stressed that according to both the statute and common laws of England, a man had a freedom and property in his goods and estate that could be taken from him only with his personal consent, or by his consent as expressed in parliament. In reply to the argument that ship money was necessary for the immediate defence of the kingdom, he held that no 'necessity nor danger can allow a charge, which is a breach of the laws' (*State trials*, 3.1134).

Croke's argument circulated widely in manuscript and was printed, along with that of Sir Richard Hutton, in 1641. It became a commonplace that ship money 'may be gotten by Hook, but not by Crook' (Fuller, *Worthies*, 1.202), and though he was also vigorously defended by his son-in-law, Harbottle Grimston, the reputation served him well when the Long Parliament began drawing up articles of impeachment against the surviving Caroline judges in late 1640. One committee report notes that, quite apart from his record on ship money, Croke had always displayed zeal for 'Parliamentarie waies of goverment' (Gorhambury MS XII, B. 25). He had been willing to bail the members of parliament arrested for holding down the speaker in 1629, had been disciplined by the council for accepting grand jury presentments that muster-master charges were being made contrary to the petition of right, and had been willing to issue prohibitions to restrict the jurisdictional pretensions of the ecclesiastical courts.

Sir John Bramston the younger alleged that Croke was treated leniently because he was allied to Hampden, and of the 'Puritan perswasion and partie, which was now the prevailing side' (*Autobiography*, 80). However, already suffering from the gout in the late 1630s, he had by this time largely withdrawn from public life. In June 1641 King Charles acceded to his request that he be allowed to retire on the grounds of age and ill health, stipulating that he should continue to receive the salary and fees of a judge. He died at Waterstock on 16 February 1642, and was buried in the parish church there. Though Croke requested that his funeral should involve no 'heraldry', 'hearse', or 'unnecessary ceremonies' (PRO, PROB 11/189, fol. 117r), his widow erected an elaborate monument to his memory. Among a number of bequests, which included the establishment of a chapel and 'hospital' for the poor in the hamlet of Studley in Buckinghamshire, Croke left his manuscript and printed law books to Harbottle Grimston. His manuscript collections of reports contained notes on increasingly complete runs of cases stretching from the reign of Elizabeth up to 1640, and Grimston translated them from Norman French into English and prepared them for publication as *The Reports of Sir George Croke, Knight*. Since they covered a period that was relatively poorly served by printed reports, and because the collection contained cases that had been tried when Croke himself was sitting on the bench, Grimston began by publishing in 1657 those covering the reign of Charles I. Two further volumes—one for James I, and another for the reign of Elizabeth—were published in 1659 and 1661, and the whole went through two further editions before 1685. Croke had approached his work within the tradition of Plowden and Coke, law reporters who were interested in arguments, and the names of those who made them, as well as the substance of the decision, but as Grimston noted in his preface, Croke's mature style was notable for its concision:

> here the Case is shortly stated according to the points in Law, therein to be discussed and adjudged, the reasons plainly and succinctly laid down, and yet the matter intended truly uttered, and, as near as may be, in the name and words of the party who delivered it, and the former Authorities to warrant the same summarily vouched.   (Croke, A3)

CHRISTOPHER W. BROOKS

Sources DNB · *State trials*, vol. 3 · *The autobiography of Sir John Bramston*, ed. [Lord Braybrooke], CS, 32 (1845) · B. Whitelocke, *Memorials of the English affairs*, new edn (1732) · *The diary of Bulstrode Whitelocke, 1605–1675*, ed. R. Spalding, British Academy, Records of Social and Economic History, new ser., 13 (1990) · *Liber famelicus of Sir James Whitelocke, a judge of the court of king's bench in the reigns of James I and Charles I*, ed. J. Bruce, CS, old ser., 70 (1858) · Baker, *Serjeants* · Fuller, *Worthies* (1840) · *The diary of Sir Richard Hutton, 1614–1639*, ed. W. R. Prest, SeldS, suppl. ser., 9 (1991) · E. Wells, 'Common law reporting in England, 1550–1650', DPhil diss., U. Oxf., 1994 · Herts. ALS, Gorhambury MS XII, B. 25 · *The reports of Sir George Croke, knight, late, one of the justices of the court of kings bench and formerly one of the justices of the court of common bench of such select cases as were adjudged in the said courts, the time that he was judge in either of them*, ed. and trans. H. Grimston, 3 vols. (1657) [incl. biographical material] · will, PRO, PROB 11/189, sig. 58

Archives Herts. ALS, Gorhambury collection, autograph law reports and other papers

Likenesses oils, 1626, Inner Temple, London; version, Royal Collection · portrait, 1626, priv. coll. [*see illus.*] · Gaywood, engraving · W. Hollar, oils, NPG · R. Vaughan, oils, repro. in H. Grimston, ed. and trans., *The first part (though last publish't) of the reports of Sir George Croke* (1661) · R. White, engraving · funerary monument, Waterstock, Oxfordshire · oils; in possession of Sir Alexander Croke in 1823

Wealth at death very wealthy but unspecified; landed property in Oxfordshire and Buckinghamshire: will, PRO, PROB 11/189, sig. 58

Croke, Sir Henry (1588–1659), exchequer official, was the second son of Sir John *Croke (1553x6–1620), lawyer, of Chilton, Buckinghamshire, and of his wife, Katherine Blount (*b*. 1563). He matriculated from St John's College, Oxford, in January 1605, and in 1607 followed family tradition by being admitted to the Inner Temple, where ten years later he was called to the bar at the request of his father, then a judge.

Meanwhile he had married Bridget (*d*. 1638), one of the daughters and coheirs of Sir William Hawtrey of Chequers, Buckinghamshire; their elder son Robert was born in 1609. Like Sir John Croke, Henry became an MP, sitting for Shaftesbury, Dorset, in the 1614 parliament, and was knighted, in October 1615. Partly through the influence of his father and his uncle Sir George *Croke, also a judge, and partly through the payment of £3600, he was granted on 20 July 1616, with Anthony Rous, the office of clerk of the pipe in the exchequer. Although he was to hold this office almost continuously until his death forty-two years later, his tenure of it was controversial as he was reputed to be exceptionally venal.

By September 1617 Croke and Rous were in the course of reforming the many abuses they listed in the clerks' office, but were caught between vociferous external critics, principally Edmund Sawyer, and the internal hostility of established officers newly deprived of accustomed fees. Resentment increased over the next eight years, as the 'reformers' were accused of profiting on their own account, raising the value of their office by fivefold over this period. Sir Henry's personal wealth was further augmented in 1625 when his wife inherited the manor of Chequers and half the manor of Hampton Poyle, Oxfordshire. Additional property from the Hawtreys accrued to him subsequently.

In the 1628 parliamentary elections Croke compensated for an unsuccessful initial candidature in Oxford City by gaining the seat of Christchurch, Hampshire, apparently with the assistance of his elder brother, Sir John Croke (1586–1640), deputy lieutenant of Dorset, who this time took the Shaftesbury seat. Sir Henry spoke in the house only to defend his conduct in the exchequer, still under scrutiny. From the mid-1630s accusations of corruption began to come to a head, thanks probably to his subordinate, Christopher Vernon, first secondary of the pipe, and his activities were officially investigated. In 1638, however, although he lost his wife Bridget, he obtained a royal pardon and kept his office, albeit at the cost of paying £4300 compensation.

Through the 1640s and 1650s Croke was beset by money problems, which he pleaded to escape taxation and his son Robert's delinquency fines. Marriage in 1648 to Judith Wroth, a widow, coincided with the sale of Hampton Poyle, though debts charged on the estate caused lawsuits for some years afterwards. Return to office in 1654 after an enforced absence of five years failed to repair his fortunes: in December 1657 he, like other exchequer officials, petitioned that his payment was greatly in arrears.

Dame Judith having died some eighteen months earlier, when Sir Henry himself died, 'of the stone' (Croke, 500), on 1 January 1659, he was buried at Ellesborough, Buckinghamshire, beside his first wife. Their son Robert, heavily indebted despite an advantageous marriage into the Vanlore family, continued as a clerk of the pipe until his death in 1681. VIVIENNE LARMINIE

Sources A. Croke, The genealogical history of the Croke family, 2 vols. (1823) • will, PRO, PROB 11/297, fol. 5 • PRO, PROB 11/268, fol. 398 [Judith Croke] • Bodl. Oxf., MS Top. Oxon. b.87 • G. E. Aylmer, 'Studies in the institutions and personnel of the English central administration, 1625–42', DPhil diss., U. Oxf., 1954, esp. 564–71, 605–18 • G. E. Aylmer, The king's servants: the civil service of Charles I, 1625–1642, rev. edn (1974) • G. Lipscomb, The history and antiquities of the county of Buckingham, 4 vols. (1831–47), vol. 2, p. 185 • CSP dom., 1611–18, 385, 486; 1631–3, 141; 1635–6, 433; 1636–7, 272; 1637–8, 587; 1645–7, 564–5; 1648–9, 2; 1657–8, 207, 263 • M. A. E. Green, ed., Calendar of the proceedings of the committee for advance of money, 1642–1656, 1, PRO (1888), 340 • M. A. E. Green, ed., Calendar of the proceedings of the committee for compounding … 1643–1660, 1, PRO (1889), 609, 611 • Foster, Alum. Oxon. • VCH Buckinghamshire, 2.336; 4.71, 75 • VCH Oxfordshire, 6.162, 164 • W. A. Shaw, The knights of England, 2 (1906), 157 • R. C. Johnson and others, eds., Proceedings in parliament, 1628, 6 vols. (1977–83) • W. R. Prest, The inns of court under Elizabeth I and the early Stuarts, 1590–1640 (1972), 57

Archives Bodl. Oxf., MS Top. Oxon. b.87 | Bucks. RLSS, Chequers MSS

Wealth at death see will, PRO, PROB 11/297, fol. 5

Croke, John (1489–1554), legal official, was born at Banbury, the son of Richard Croke, otherwise called Le Blount or Le Blountez, of Easington, Buckinghamshire, and his wife, Alice. He has sometimes been confused with his contemporary Dr John Croke (d. 1549×51), advocate of the arches and member of parliament, who had more conventional qualifications for some of the chancery offices that he held. The chancery official, however, was a layman who was educated at Eton College from 1503 to 1507, and King's College, Cambridge, from 1507 to 1509. The interval between his leaving Cambridge in 1509 and his special admittance to the Inner Temple in 1515 is probably explained by his having become in the meantime a clerk of the chancery. He was certainly a chancery clerk by 1518, and is named as a six clerk in a statute of 1523.

Croke practised as a six clerk for over twenty-five years, acquiring in addition the offices of clerk of the hanaper

(1528–49) and clerk of the enrolments (1534–41), until in 1549 he was appointed a master in chancery. Towards the end of his life he wrote some notes on the chancery officials entitled Orders … upon the Estate of the Chauncery Courte, edited by Sir Alexander Croke in 1823 from BL, Lansdowne MS 163; there is another manuscript text at Harvard. He is also credited with a verse translation, Thirteen Psalms, printed by the Percy Society in 1844.

Croke had always lived in Buckinghamshire, like his father, and was a justice of the peace for that county from 1539 until his death. But it was he who in 1529 purchased the estate at Chilton and built the family mansion house there. To the family estates he also added Studley Priory, bought for over £1180 in 1539, and he bought a house in Fleet Street in 1541. His wife, Prudence, third daughter of Richard Cave and sister of Sir Ambrose Cave, predeceased him. Their son Sir John (d. 1608) was father of the two judges Sir John Croke and Sir George Croke.

Croke died in office on 2 September 1554, and was buried at Chilton, where there is a monumental brass. Among other legacies, he left £10 to 'my olde companyons the feloweshipp of the six clerkes', to be spent partly on necessaries for their house and partly on a dinner for all the chancery officials. J. H. BAKER

Sources A. Croke, The genealogical history of the Croke family, 1 (1823), 393–407; 2 (1823), 819–21 • W. Sterry, ed., The Eton College register, 1441–1698 (1943), 91 • Cooper, Ath. Cantab., 1.118 • HoP, Commons, 1509–58, 1.726 • will, PRO, PROB 11/37, sig. 33 • LP Henry VIII, 4, no. 4801(19); 7, no. 922(6); 16, no. 779(24) • PRO, C1/390/4 • CPR, 1553–4, 454 • A. Luders and others, eds., Statutes of the realm, 11 vols. in 12, RC (1810–28), vol. 3 • J. H. Baker, English legal manuscripts in the United States of America: a descriptive list, 2 (1990), p. 117, no. 559 (u) • G. Lipscomb, The history and antiquities of the county of Buckingham, 4 vols. (1831–47), vol. 1, pp. 131, 145 • W. Lack, H. M. Stuchfield, and P. Whittemore, The monumental brasses of Buckinghamshire (1994), 42–3 • W. J. Jones, The Elizabethan court of chancery (1967)

Likenesses brass effigy on monument, c.1554, Chilton church, Buckinghamshire

Croke, Sir John (1553×6–1620), judge and speaker of the House of Commons, was the eldest son of Sir John Croke (d. 1608) of Chilton, Buckinghamshire, and Elizabeth (d. 1611), daughter of Sir Alexander Unton of Chequers in the same county, and grandson of John *Croke (d. 1554). His younger brother George *Croke (c.1560–1642) also became a bencher of the Inner Temple and a king's bench judge; there are kneeling effigies of both brothers in their judicial robes on their father's tomb at Chilton. After some time at Oxford, where he graduated BA in 1571 (he later served as under-steward of the university), the younger John was admitted to the Inner Temple in 1570 and subsequently called to the bar. He was added to the commission of the peace for Buckinghamshire in 1591, became a judge of the Brecon circuit and member of the council in the marches in 1594, and in 1595 was elected to the important position of recorder of the City of London, which until 1603 he held concurrently with his Welsh judgeship. A law student noted a quip in 1602, when someone remarked that the recorder was the mouth of the city, 'then the city hath a black mouth … for he is a verry blacke man' (Diary

Sir John Croke (1553x6–1620), by unknown artist, 1618

of *John Manningham*, 114), apparently alluding to Croke's complexion.

Croke became a bencher of the Inner Temple in 1592 and in March 1596 gave his reading on the statute 14 Eliz. I c. 8, concerning feigned recoveries; the autograph text, with speeches, is preserved at Cambridge (CUL, MS Mm.6.64, fols. 126–47). From 1599 to 1607 he presided as chief justice of the Brecon circuit. He married Katherine (*b*. 1563), daughter of Michael Blount of Mapledurham, Oxfordshire, lieutenant of the Tower, and they had five sons, including Sir Henry *Croke, exchequer official, Charles *Croke, Church of England clergyman, and Unton *Croke, lawyer and politician. They lived for a time at Studley Priory in Oxfordshire, part of which he rebuilt; his arms were carved over the chimney in the old drawing room and over the porch, with the date 1587. However, he lived beyond his means, and was obliged to alienate Studley to his brothers in 1598 and to mortgage his manor of Easington to George; he even sold his father a silver-gilt bowl given him by Sir Christopher Hatton for counsel. He did not redeem Studley until after his father's death.

Croke represented New Windsor in the parliament of 1584 without attracting notice, but was more active in the parliaments of 1597 and 1601, as member for the City of London, when he served on numerous committees. He was elected speaker in October 1601, and in his presentation speech inveighed against the king of Spain, the pope, and the rebels in Ireland, all of whom he said 'were like a snake cut in pieces, which did crawl and creep to join themselves together again' (Croke, 463). Although inclined to be subservient to the crown and to the secretary of state, Sir Robert Cecil, and a weak chairman, he was obliged by the will of the House of Commons to preside over the warm debates on monopolies, which culminated in the statue 43 Eliz. I c. 1. The session also produced significant legislation dealing with poor relief and charitable trusts, but was marked by disorderly behaviour for which Croke was criticized. Croke nevertheless had the pleasure of thanking the queen for her 'golden speech' at Whitehall on 30 November 1601, and of earning her praise at the end of the short session for his wisdom and discretion. At this time he presented twenty-seven books to the Bodleian Library. In 1602 Croke edited for publication a series of law reports (1496–1519) from a manuscript belonging to his step-grandfather Robert Keilwey. The author was well known to be John Caryll, but the printed edition was anonymous and came to be cited as Keilwey's reports; the volume also included some Inner Temple moots from the 1480s, and some older matter from the reigns of Edward II and Edward III. Several of Croke's own speeches survive in manuscript.

Croke was knighted on 22 May 1603 and created a serjeant-at-law on 24 May. Although his knighthood was probably intended to give him precedence over his fellow new serjeants, the judges insisted that he take his place in accordance with seniority. He gained his precedence nevertheless on 29 May by virtue of a patent to be one of the king's serjeants. Four years later, on 25 June 1607, he was appointed a justice of the king's bench to fill the vacancy created by Sir Lawrence Tanfield's promotion to the exchequer. Among his judicial speeches was a charge to the grand jury in the king's bench in 1613, when he said it was a damnable offence to portray God as a man with a grey beard. He was the senior puisne judge, or secondary justice, when he died at his house in Holborn on 23 January 1620. An anonymous obituarist described him as 'un mylde home et de eloquent speech' (Harvard law school, MS 106, fol. 54*v*). He was buried at Chilton, where there is a brass monumental inscription. By a will of 1617, written in Latin, he left Chilton to his wife. She was succeeded by the eldest son, Sir John (*d*. 1640), whose heir (another Sir John) sold the Chilton estates and died in disgrace and poverty after becoming involved in a conspiracy to charge the local vicar with robbery.   J. H. BAKER

Sources HoP, *Commons, 1558–1603*, 1.677–8 · A. Croke, *The genealogical history of the Croke family*, 1 (1823), 459–84 · Foster, *Alum. Oxon.* · minutes of will, 28 Oct 1617, BL, Add. MS 6209, fol. 279 · speech, 1601, BL, Egerton MS 2222, fol. 248*v* · Sainty, *Judges*, 31 · Sainty, *King's counsel*, 17 · Baker, *Serjeants* · obit., Harvard U., law school, MS 106, fol. 54*v* · reading, CUL, MS Mm.6.64, fols. 126–47 · *The diary of John Manningham of the Middle Temple, 1602–1603*, ed. R. P. Sorlien (Hanover, NH, 1976) · father's will, PRO, PROB 11/113, fols. 389–92 · *DNB* · monument, Chilton church, Buckinghamshire
Archives BL, notebook of speeches
Likenesses oils, 1618, Holkham Hall, Norfolk [*see illus.*] · oil on panel, 1619, Harvard U., law school · effigy, Chilton church, Buckinghamshire · oils (in robes), Palace of Westminster, London

Croke, Richard (1489–1558), Greek scholar, was born in London. Nothing is known about his family, except that he had a brother, Robert, who was living in Coltishall in

Norfolk in 1538 and in Water Orton, Warwickshire, in 1558, when he was named as one of the executors of Richard's will. Croke studied at Eton College and on 4 April 1506 was admitted as a scholar at King's College, Cambridge. Probably before his first spell in Cambridge, or possibly after his admission to a BA about 1510, he was the servant-pupil of the humanist William Grocyn in London. It may have been through his connection with Grocyn that he made the acquaintance of Thomas More, whom he certainly knew by 1516 and who wrote to him familiarly in 1519. He may also have met Erasmus in this period; by the autumn of 1511 Croke was studying humanistic subjects under Erasmus and Girolamo Aleandro in Paris. On 13 September of that year Erasmus wrote positively of him to John Colet, asking Colet if he had access to funds to support Croke; the polite answer was negative. Croke was also on friendly terms in Paris with Guillaume Budé, with whom he later corresponded, and with the printer Gilles de Gourmont, with whom he worked on the publication of the first edition of Erasmus's *Moriae encomium*; the author would later complain that the edition was shoddy.

It is not clear when Croke left Paris but, after a spell in Louvain, he matriculated at the University of Cologne on 20 March 1515. In both places he taught Greek before arriving in the same year in Leipzig, where he was to enjoy major success as a humanist lecturer, introducing Greek studies to the university almost for the first time and publishing works of Greek grammar and philology. Several accounts dating to this period attest to his high popularity and reputation, not only in Leipzig itself but in a wider Germany. In 1516 Erasmus, a number of whose German supporters Croke came to know or teach, wrote warmly of his achievements at Leipzig to Thomas Linacre. His students and friends included Joachim Camerarius, Petrus Mosellanus, Conrad Mutianus Rufus, Ulrich von Hutten, and Heinrich Stromer. Such was his reputation that the University of Wittemburg attempted to poach him for itself, and he was retained in Leipzig only through the generosity of the Leipzig faculty of arts and of Georg, duke of Saxony. While there he published a Latin edition of Ausonius (*Ausonii opera*, 1515); an oration in praise of Leipzig University (*Achademiae Lipsensis encomium congratulatorium*, which is sometimes found bound with the Ausonius); a book of tables of Greek grammar (*Tabulae Graecas literas compendio discere cupientibus*, 1516; a second edition was published in 1521 prefaced by a letter from Philipp Novenianus to Georg, duke of Saxony); and a Latin edition of the last book of Theodore Gaza's Greek grammar (*Quartus liber & ultimus de constructione*, 1516, which includes a dedicatory letter by Croke to Albert, archbishop of Magdeburg and Mainz). In a letter of 3 September 1516 to Johannes Reuchlin, Croke promised to send him one of these works, which was shortly to appear, hoping that in return Reuchlin would dedicate his own *De arte cabalistica* to John Fisher, bishop of Rochester. In the event Reuchlin's ambitions were higher, and this work, published in the following year, was in fact dedicated to Pope Leo X. Nevertheless,

Croke's association with Reuchlin forms part of the background to Croke's brief appearance in the notorious satirical manifesto of German humanism, the *Epistolae obscurorum virorum*.

Through the influence of Fisher, Croke journeyed back to England in the spring of 1517, passing through Frankfurt and visiting Erasmus in Antwerp, where he seems to have left his books with Peter Gillis; after Erasmus insisted on looking at them, they went missing. He was certainly in England by November 1517, and acquired an MA at Cambridge in that year. On 23 April 1518 Erasmus wrote to Croke congratulating him on his new post in Cambridge, which suggests that he already believed him to be a lecturer in Greek there, a position which he definitely held from 1520 with an annual stipend of £10 from the crown. In association with this position he delivered two important orations in praise of Greek studies. These note the centrality of Greek learning for theology and a range of other subjects; the practical and political achievements of the ancient Greeks; the superiority of their sciences to those of the Romans; and their moral excellence. Croke exhorts his Cambridge students to embrace the subject, warning that unless they do so Oxford will outshine them. The *Orationes duae* were printed in 1520 by Simon de Colines in Paris, with Croke's dedicatory letter to Nicholas West, bishop of Ely, a letter from Gilbert Ducher to Antoine Des Prez, and a second letter from Ducher to Croke. In the same year there appeared at Cologne Croke's *Introductiones in rudimenta Graeca*, dedicated to William Warham, archbishop of Canterbury.

In the meantime Croke had been ordained subdeacon on 9 April 1519, deacon on 23 April 1519, and priest on 18 June 1519. Through the influence of John Fisher he had gained a sinecure post at Strood Hospital at about the same time, and a fellowship of Fisher's Cambridge foundation, St John's College. Besides the lectureship in Greek, Croke also held other university positions: in the period 1521–3 he was public orator, in 1523/4 he was lecturer in theology, and in 1524/5 he was a university auditor. He graduated DTh from Cambridge in 1523.

After a conflict with Fisher in early 1526, Croke gravitated away from Cambridge and into royal service. In June 1526 he was granted a pension at the king's request from the abbot of Llanthony, which was probably connected with his position from late 1526 as the tutor of Henry Fitzroy, duke of Richmond, Henry VIII's illegitimate son, with whom he lived at Sheriff Hutton Castle near York. Between late 1529 and late 1530 he was in Italy as part of the royal mission to find support for Henry VIII's divorce, working closely with other crown servants, in particular Giovan Battista and Gregorio Casale, Girolamo Ghinnucci, John Stokesley, and Thomas Cranmer. His task, which took place mainly in Bologna, Venice, and Padua, included acquiring a range of supporters for Henry VIII's contention that the pope should not have made a dispensation permitting the king to marry Katherine of Aragon. Through persuasion, the exploitation of contacts, and monetary incentive, Croke and his co-workers enlisted the support of a number of Italian universities, prominent philosophers, canonists, theologians, humanists, and rabbis. In addition, with considerable energy and determination Croke investigated Venetian and Paduan libraries for patristic and other early Christian writings which could bolster the king's cause. Copious details of his successes and tribulations in Italy are documented in his many letters to colleagues and to the king, and some of his finds, together with the subscriptions of the universities in favour of the king, appeared in the government's propagandistic tracts of 1531, the *Gravissimae censurae academiarum* and its English translation, *The Determinations of the Moste Famous and Mooste Excellent Universities of Italy and Fraunce*, both printed by Thomas Berthelet.

Back in England, Croke was made a canon, subdean, and professor of divinity at King Henry VIII College in Oxford in 1532, supplicating at that time for incorporation at Oxford of his Cambridge doctorate in theology. He had acquired the rectorship of Hurworth, co. Durham, in 1528. Now, in 1532, he added to this benefice the rectorship of Long Buckby, Northamptonshire, by royal grant. This and his Oxford appointment were partly rewards for his services in Italy. In the same year he wrote to Thomas Cromwell, reporting on his distribution of copies of the government's latest propagandistic treatise, the *Glasse of Truth*, and giving an account of the responses to the work which he had encountered. And he continued to advocate the royal cause in the 1530s, telling Cromwell in 1537 about the many sermons he had delivered against papal authority. (In other doctrinal matters he seems to have remained an orthodox Catholic.) He listed for Cromwell thirty-seven churches at which he had preached, probably in the wake of the Pilgrimage of Grace. By way of reward he was made a royal chaplain by March 1538.

Thereafter his career stagnated. In the same year Croke failed to secure the deanship of King Henry VIII College, and when the college was dissolved in 1545 he was not made a canon of its successor foundation, Christ Church, being granted instead in 1546 an annual pension of £26 13s. 4d. from the crown. For a decade he then rented rooms in Exeter College, Oxford, and was present at the public disputation on the sacrament in Oxford, attended by Thomas Cranmer, Nicholas Ridley, and Hugh Latimer, in the spring of 1554. But he seems to have returned to his birthplace in the last years of his life and his nuncupative will of 21 August 1558 was proved on 29 August in London.

Historical opinion has been decidedly negative about Richard Croke. For Thomas Baker he was 'an ambitious, envious and discontented wretch' (Baker, 1.97); for J. T. Sheppard his character was 'suspicious, touchy, conceited, zealous' (Sheppard, 23); for J. J. Scarisbrick he was 'a whining, tiresome man, who seems to have been able to quarrel with anybody' (Scarisbrick, 256–7); for Diarmaid MacCulloch he was 'a fussy and self-righteous Cambridge don who was more skilled at Greek than he was at human relationships' (MacCulloch, 51). Croke did indeed argue with and alienate any number of contemporaries, including John Leland, who wrote a poem against him; Giovan

Battista Casale, and other Italians involved with him during his mission in Italy; and the duke of Richmond's servants, about whose laxity and disrespect he complained to Cardinal Wolsey in 1527–8. According to Croke, the other pupils whom he taught with the duke mocked and insulted him. Frustration, paranoia, indignation, and self-justification are the dominant tones of Croke's letters, especially those from Venice. Particularly unfortunate for his reputation has been his conflict with, and betrayal of, martyrs on both sides of the religious divide. In September 1555 he testified to the heresy of his former colleague Thomas Cranmer as the first witness at the trial which led to Cranmer's execution. In 1526 he accused his patron John Fisher, who was to be executed for his opposition to Henry VIII's divorce and royal supremacy, of using Lady Margaret Beaufort's bequest for St John's College to further his own kin or men from his own locality. Fisher replied with a defence of his actions and a series of counter-accusations about Croke's bad behaviour at St John's. According to Fisher, Croke and Robert Wakefield (another innovating humanist and supporter of Henry VIII, whose career contains striking parallels to Croke's own) were ingrates undeserving of their stipends.

Despite the reputation which has accrued to him, Croke was an important innovator in the early stages of the institutionalized study of Greek in England. Through teaching, research, and publications he advanced the humanistic project of Grocyn, More, Colet, and Erasmus in significant ways in England and Germany, activities for which he gained the respect of contemporaries in the early part of his career, before less attractive character traits set in.

JONATHAN WOOLFSON

Sources J. Woolfson, 'A "remote and ineffectual don?": Richard Croke in the Biblioteca Marciana', *Bulletin of the Society for Renaissance Studies*, 17/2 (2000), 1–11 · J. T. Sheppard, *Richard Croke, a sixteenth-century don* (1919) · H. de Vocht, *History of the foundation and rise of the Collegium Trilingue Lovaniense, 1517–1550*, 1 (1951), 274–7 · G. Przychocki, 'Richard Croke's search for patristic MSS in connexion with the divorce of Catherine', *Journal of Theological Studies*, 13 (1911–12), 285–95 · R. Rex, *The theology of John Fisher* (1991) · *Opus epistolarum Des. Erasmi Roterodami*, ed. P. S. Allen and others, 12 vols. (1906–58) · *LP Henry VIII*, vol. 4 · *DNB* · Emden, *Oxf.*, 4.151–2 · C. F. G. and P. G. B., 'Richard Croke of London', *Contemporaries of Erasmus: a biographical register*, ed. P. Bietenholz and T. B. Deutscher, 1 (1985), 359–60 · T. Baker, *History of the college of St John the Evangelist, Cambridge*, ed. J. E. B. Mayor, 2 vols. (1869) · J. J. Scarisbrick, *Henry VIII* (1968) · D. MacCulloch, *Thomas Cranmer: a life* (1996) · will, PRO, PROB 11/40

Archives BL, Cotton MSS, diplomatic corresp.

Croke, Sir Richard (1624/5–1683). *See under* Croke, Unton (1594/5–1670/71).

Croke, Thomas William (1823–1902), Roman Catholic archbishop of Cashel, was born on 19 May 1823 at Dromin, Castlecor, co. Cork, the third child of William Croke (1792–1834), estate agent, and his wife, Isabelle Plummer (1796–1854). His father was a Roman Catholic, but his mother, who was descended from Thomas Fitzgerald, sixteenth knight of Glin, Glin Castle, co. Limerick, was a protestant until a few years before her death, when she became a Roman Catholic. There were eight children, two daughters and six sons: the girls and three of the boys entered the service of the church. After the death of Thomas's father in 1834 the family moved to Charleville, co. Cork, where Thomas spent five years in the endowed school (1834–9). He was a fine sportsman and excelled in handball, a game he continued to play in adult life. In 1839 he successfully gained a scholarship to the Irish College, Paris, and spent the next six years there studying philosophy and theology. In 1845, being too young for ordination, he was sent for a few months to teach English and mathematics in the diocesan seminary at Menin, Belgium. He then went on to Rome, where he spent the next two years studying theology at the Gregorian University (1845–7). He was ordained priest on 29 May 1847, for the diocese of Cloyne, and awarded a doctorate in theology on 15 July of that year.

Croke returned to Ireland in November 1847, and spent one year on the staff of Carlow College before being recalled to teach theology in his former alma mater, the Irish College, Paris. In August 1849 he returned once more to Ireland, this time as curate of Charleville, succeeding his older brother William, who had died from famine fever. For the next nine years Croke served as curate in various parishes in the diocese of Cloyne: Charleville (September 1849 to June 1853), Midleton (June 1853 to July 1857), and Mallow (August 1857 to September 1858). During these years he became well-known throughout Ireland as a preacher of charitable sermons and a champion of the poor. He also became involved in Irish politics, writing articles for *The Nation* newspaper. In 1857 he inherited a large fortune from an uncle, James Croke, who had been crown solicitor in Port Melbourne, Australia. In 1858 the bishop of Cloyne, William Keane, appointed Croke first president of the newly established diocesan seminary of St Colman's, Fermoy, co. Cork, a position he held until February 1866, when he became parish priest of Doneraile and vicar-general of the diocese of Cloyne. Croke was in Rome from December 1869 until June 1870, acting as theological adviser to Bishop Keane during the First Vatican Council.

While Croke was in Rome the diocese of Auckland, New Zealand, became vacant. Croke's name had been proposed to the Roman authorities by Cardinal Paul Cullen, the archbishop of Dublin. His official appointment to Auckland is dated 15 June 1870. He apparently made an agreement with the Roman authorities that he would stay in Auckland only for as long as was needed to put the diocese on a sound financial footing. He was consecrated bishop of Auckland in Rome on 10 July 1870, and arrived in Auckland on 17 December 1870. Almost immediately he set about putting the affairs of the diocese in order, as can be seen from the detailed diary which he kept of his administration. Within two and a half years he had bought back the property which had been mortgaged, and is said to have restored discipline and religious fervour among his priests and flock. He departed from Auckland on 28 January 1874 and arrived back in Ireland at the end of May. The Roman authorities were somewhat surprised at Croke's sudden departure from Auckland, but were forced to accept the *fait accompli*.

When Patrick Leahy, the archbishop of Cashel, died on 26 January 1875, Croke's name was among those mentioned as a possible successor. He was appointed archbishop of Cashel on 25 June 1875, and administered the diocese until his death in 1902. He was a very able administrator, and soon became the leading spokesperson for the Irish Catholic church. He became deeply involved in the Irish Land War (1879–92), the struggle for home rule, and the founding of the Gaelic Athletic Association in 1884. He counted among his friends many eminent public figures, including William Gladstone, Cardinal Manning, Charles S. Parnell, and Michael Davitt. In 1895 Croke celebrated his silver jubilee as a bishop amid great festivities throughout Ireland. He died in Thurles, co. Tipperary, on 22 July 1902. His funeral took place on 26 July 1902, and he was buried in a vault in his cathedral at Thurles.

Croke was a well-built man, well over 6 feet tall, with a cheerful and impressive appearance, as can be seen from his portrait, in Archbishop's House, Thurles. He maintained a special interest in sport throughout his life, and the national stadium for Gaelic games in Dublin, Croke Park, was named after him. But it was in the political and social life of his day, and in the creating of an Irish national identity, that he made his real mark. He had a very independent mind, and on many issues was reputed to be 'unchanged and unchangeable'. His only publications were a few pastorals, and the letters and poems written for *The Nation* newspaper. He was greatly admired and loved throughout his life and familiarly referred to as Croke of Cashel. D. MARK TIERNEY

Sources M. Tierney, *Croke of Cashel: the life of Archbishop Thomas William Croke, 1823–1902* (1976) · 'A short-title calendar of the papers of Archbishop Thomas William Croke [pt 1]', ed. M. Tierney, *Collectanea Hibernica*, 13 (1970), 100–38 · 'A short-title calendar of the papers of Archbishop Thomas William Croke [pt 2]', ed. M. Tierney, *Collectanea Hibernica*, 16 (1973), 97–124 · 'A short-title calendar of the papers of Archbishop Thomas William Croke [pt 3]', ed. M. Tierney, *Collectanea Hibernica*, 17 (1974–5), 110–44 · J. F. Hogan, 'The archbishop of Cashel', *Irish Ecclesiastical Record*, 4th ser., 12 (1902), 301–11 · alumni register of Irish College, Rome · parish register (baptism), Ballyclough, 6 June 1823 · Thomas Fennelly, diary

Archives Archbishop's House, Thurles · Bishop's House, Auckland, New Zealand · Cashel Roman Catholic Diocesan Archives, corresp., notebook, papers, and sermons | Archbishop's House, Dublin, Walsh MSS · Irish College, Rome, Kirby MSS · Sacra Congregazione di Propaganda Fide, Rome, Irlanda and Oceania, archives

Likenesses J. B. Brennan, portrait, 1885, Archbishop's House, Thurles · E. D. Jones, statue, 1922, town square, Thurles, co. Tipperary

Wealth at death £663: administration, 23 Sept 1902, *CGPLA Ire.*

Croke, Unton (1594/5–1670/71), lawyer and politician, was the fourth son of Sir John *Croke (1553×6–1620), lawyer, of Chilton, Buckinghamshire, and Studley, Oxfordshire, and his wife, Katherine Blount (b. 1563, d. in or after 1620); Sir Henry *Croke (1588–1659) and Charles *Croke (1590/91–1657) were his elder brothers. He was admitted with Charles to the Inner Temple during the year 1609–10, when his uncle Sir George Croke was treasurer. Although he matriculated from Charles's college, Christ Church, Oxford, on 2 March 1610, aged fifteen, it seems likely that his legal studies continued uninterrupted, for in 1616 he was called to the bar. On 8 November 1617 he married Anne (1601/2–1670), daughter and heir of Richard Hore of Marston, just outside Oxford; they had ten children.

In the year 1619–20 Croke was made deputy steward of Oxford University and by 1624–5 he had acquired a house at Grandpont, not far from Christ Church. He also rebuilt the Hore family house at Marston and in time made it his residence when not in London. He soon acquired further land and became the leading gentleman in the village, but his prosperity led to conflict with the Whorwood family of nearby Holton and to decades of rivalry in estate management and local politics. By the mid-1620s Croke and Sir Thomas Horwood or Whorwood were at suit in chancery. When, probably through the influence of his south Oxfordshire and Berkshire kin, Croke was returned to the 1626 parliament as MP for Wallingford, Sir Thomas not only pursued the suit but also alleged that his adversary had obtained his seat by bribery and corruption. The House of Commons found on 28 April that Horwood's action against Croke breached parliamentary privilege. Croke did not sit in the 1628 parliament, but he became a JP for Oxfordshire and in 1635 a bencher of his inn. In 1640 he was Lent reader at the Inner Temple and took the Wallingford seat again in the Short Parliament.

With the coming of civil war Croke and his sons conspicuously supported parliament. His house was used as Sir Thomas Fairfax's headquarters when the general arrived to besiege Oxford in 1645; in May and June the following year it was the scene of negotiations for, and the signing of, the royalist surrender. In June 1655 Croke was created serjeant-at-law by Oliver Cromwell. According to Anthony Wood, like Thomas Hearne later a bitter critic of the Marston Crokes because of their identification with the interests of Oxford city as against those of the university, this was a reward for the treacherous services of his son and namesake Unton Croke [see below] in the aftermath of the Penruddock rebellion. Others at Oxford were better disposed towards Croke: on 2 October that year John Owen, dean of Christ Church, wrote to Cromwell reminding him of a favour granted to him on Croke's behalf and asking further that Croke be made a judge. The second request was not granted, but in the following year Croke appeared high on a list of commissioners for the security of the protector, named by act of parliament, and served as a justice of assize in Surrey.

Croke had been engaged on repairing his lands from the depredations arising from the siege of Oxford. In 1655 he was the first-named participant in a process to enclose by agreement two open fields in Marston. Following the Restoration, when Croke was not re-created serjeant and may thus have seemed vulnerable, the former royalist and serving Oxford senior MP Brome Whorwood (son of Croke's old adversary Sir Thomas) challenged the enclosure, but a judgment in chancery in favour of the innovation seems to have been upheld. Croke's wife died on 10

June 1670, and was buried the next day at St Nicholas's Church, Marston. Croke himself survived her only a few months. His funeral monument at St Nicholas's records his death as having taken place on 28 January 1671, though the parish register has a burial entry for 3 January.

Sir Richard Croke (1624/5–1683), lawyer and politician, was the second but eldest surviving son of Unton and Anne Croke. In 1636, aged eleven, he was a pupil at Winchester College, but on 24 January that year he gained admittance to the Inner Temple, his father having just become a bencher. He was called to the bar on 5 November 1646. In autumn 1649, with his younger brother Unton and others, he was appointed to survey the former royal palace and lands at Woodstock and to arrange their sale. A royalist plot to frighten away the unwelcome commissioners by means of 'poltergeists', and their consequent humiliation, is recounted in *The Just Devil of Woodstock* (1660) and a ballad, 'The Woodstock Scuffle'.

At some date in the early 1650s Richard Croke married Elizabeth (c.1624–1683), daughter of Martin Wright, alderman and goldsmith of the parishes of All Saints and St Martin, Oxford. On 12 December 1653 Croke, as one of the city justices, was given his freedom and formally chosen deputy recorder. By now a powerful figure in Oxford, he was in a position to lend effective support to the candidatures of his cousins Bulstrode and James Whitelocke for the city seats in the parliamentary elections of July 1654; the successful (and grateful) Whitelockes subsequently ceded one of them to Croke when Bulstrode went on embassy to Sweden. Subsequently less accommodating to the Whitelockes' aspirations to an Oxford seat, Croke was returned again as MP in 1656 and 1659, on the latter occasion with his younger brother Unton.

On the eve of the Restoration, Croke failed to gain election to parliament in April 1660, but was sufficiently untainted by his civil war activities to be chosen recorder on 12 June and to be returned again as city MP with the former royalist Brome Whorwood in April 1661. While Whorwood, a moderately active MP, gravitated towards 'country' opposition and ultimately exclusionism, the less active Croke in contrast 'ran with the times' (*Life and Times of Anthony Wood*, 1.196) and found favour with the court. What Wood characterized as a 'smooth, false and flattering tongue' (ibid.) served him well when he delivered speeches on royal visits to Oxford in August 1661, September 1663, and March 1681, and gained him in June 1670 a gratuity from a council grateful for his 'readiness to maintain the liberties of the city on all occasions' (Hobson, 39). Having become a bencher of his inn in 1662, he was created serjeant-at-law in April 1675. In the parliamentary elections of 1679 Croke lost his seat to his brother-in-law William Wright (1619–1693), a prominent whig, and he did not sit again, but his conduct and publicly expressed sentiments at the time of the Oxford parliament earned him a knighthood from the king on 16 March 1681.

During this time Richard Croke had divided his time between All Saints' ward in Oxford, of which in 1665 he was by far the wealthiest inhabitant, and Marston, where he inherited his father's property in 1671. Wood claims that in October 1666 Croke and Canon Sebastian Smith 'got an incredible mass of money' (*Life and Times of Anthony Wood*, 2.90–91) as executors of John Wall of Christ Church, but this is not evident from the will. When Croke drew up his own will on 3 April 1682 he seems to have considered that his most prosperous days, when he had been able to 'do well' for his relations, were past; his property was left to his wife to divide among their two surviving sons, Wright and Charles. In the event, she died first, on 27 March 1683, and was buried with her parents at St Martin's Church. Croke died in the same house behind All Saints' Church 'a little before midnight' (ibid., 3.40) on 14 September the same year, and was buried the next day at Marston. The claim of his funeral monument, erected by Wright Croke, that he was 'beloved by King Charles I and II and by all good men' and 'always devoted to the true Catholic religion' provoked Wood's fury: 'Charles I knew him not' and 'his religion was as venal as his tongue' (ibid., 1.196).

Unton Croke (*d.* 1694), parliamentarian army officer and lawyer, was the second surviving son of Unton and Anne Croke. While Charles I still had his headquarters at Oxford, Croke, as a young lieutenant in the parliamentarian garrison at Abingdon, was one of a party who daringly seized royalist horses grazing in meadows near Magdalen College. In the year 1646–7 he was admitted to the Inner Temple, but he combined legal studies with continuing military service as captain of a troop, initially in and around Oxford, where in 1649 he was created a BCL. During this period he married Bridgett, probably daughter of Sir Charles Wise, with whom he had at least one daughter before she died early in 1649; she was buried on 8 February at St Mary Magdalen, Oxford. Having accompanied his brother Richard on the survey of Woodstock that autumn, Croke was by April 1650 on the militia commission for Oxfordshire.

In spring 1651 Unton Croke was with his troop in Scotland, where he was instrumental in the capture at Dumbarton of Alexander Seton or Montgomerie, earl of Eglinton—a notable pre-emptive strike since the earl was apparently on the point of raising a substantial military force for Charles II. Although the regiment remained in the north until September 1653 Croke may have returned earlier. In that year he was called to the bar, and in November he received special permission from Oliver Cromwell to accompany his cousin Bulstrode Whitelocke on embassy to Sweden as one of his nominated committee of assistants.

Following his return to England in June 1654 Croke went with his troop to the west country, and by February 1655 was in Exeter. From here, though he failed in an attempt to capture the conspirator Colonel Edward Sexby and disaffection with the regime was detected in one of his own officers, he played a prominent role in pursuing the participants in John Penruddock's unsuccessful rising. On 14 March he surprised the main royalist force at South Molton, Devon, and imprisoned its leaders. When the latter were condemned to death they accused Croke of breaking his undertakings given at their surrender that

their lives and estates would be spared and even that they would be immune from prosecution. No such undertakings could be proved, and were probably beyond Croke's competence to grant, still less secure. His letters to secretary John Thurloe of 20 March and 12 April pleaded strongly the case of five men for whose lives he had promised to intercede, but they were 'the most inconsiderable of the company, not one of them being of estate or quality' (Thurloe, 3.281). Wherever the truth lay, Croke's reputation among royalists was irreparably damaged but his prompt and decisive action earned him the government's gratitude.

By June 1655 Croke was back in Oxford, from where he reported seizing more 'dangerous and disaffected persons' (Thurloe, 3.521), including Lord Lovelace, Sir John Burlace, Lord Falkland, and Thomas Whorwood. He was subsequently promoted to the rank of major. In 1657 he was made a freeman of Oxford. His career reached its height in 1658 when following his success in preventing an expected anabaptist rising in the city in May, and already serving as a JP, he was also made sheriff of Oxfordshire. However, his dignity was soon compromised: he and his brother were pelted with carrots and turnips by young scholars when on 6 September they proclaimed Richard Cromwell as lord protector. In January 1659, despite being sheriff, he was elected with Richard as one of the Oxford MPs. Some time before this he was married again, possibly to Grace, the wife mentioned in his will; she was probably the daughter of one Mallet, an Exeter merchant. A son, Unton, was baptized and buried at St Aldates in March 1659; there were several daughters of the marriage.

Despite his shrievalty Unton Croke spent much of 1659 in the west country, and in August he acquired from parliament lands in Wiltshire formerly belonging to Thomas Mompesson. In December he was in Sarum, where his troop declared for the restoration of the last parliament and for liberty of conscience. On 10 January 1660 he was made colonel of his regiment, following the cashiering of James Berry, and at his own request was discharged of his shrieval duties. He went to restore order in Exeter, but on 29 February the regiment declared for General George Monck on his arrival in London and was then disbanded. Petitions from Arundell Penruddock and others that Croke be excluded from the terms of the Act of Indemnity and Oblivion on the grounds of his perceived perfidy did not succeed in their object, but in December 1660 Unton Croke senior was bound with his son in a bond of £4000 to guarantee the latter's good behaviour.

Croke continued on Oxford council until deprived of his place there on 24 March 1663. Thereafter he seems to have divided his time between the Croke house at Grandpont, which he had inherited, and the Inner Temple. Wood reported him as suffering from gout in his later years. His will, dated from the Inner Temple on 7 February 1694 and witnessed by the whig and republican Slingsby Bethel, gave only token sums to his daughters 'Drury' and Bridgett, and divided most of the remainder of his estate between his other daughters, Gratious, Charity, and Eleanor Snow. He died soon afterwards and was buried in the Temple Church on 2 March.

Charles Croke (*fl.* 1652–1686), scapegrace and author, was the youngest surviving son of Unton and Anne Croke. He was admitted to the Inner Temple in 1652, but this must have been a special admission for in the same year he went to the school kept by his uncle Charles Croke at Amersham, Buckinghamshire. From November 1653 to June 1654 he was a page on Bulstrode Whitelocke's embassy to Sweden. Then aged, as he later recalled, about fifteen or sixteen he was briefly at Christ Church, Oxford, although his account is not entirely consistent with that given by Unton Croke the younger, who in March 1655 asked Cromwell to grant colours to a brother (usually taken to be Charles) 'well disposed and of a gratious spirit' (Thurloe, 3.194) who had been in his troop for some years. Given the description Charles gave of himself in his thinly disguised autobiography, *Fortune's Uncertainty, or Youth's Inconstancy* (1667), as a young man prone to dangerous childish pranks, Unton's view seems optimistic.

Charles soon grew impatient of regimental life and temporarily absconded to Plymouth, but after persuasion to return he was given a cornetcy in August 1659. Unreformed, he ran up debts, and after a few months at the Inner Temple was first shipped off to Virginia and then, having survived shipwreck on the way home, served as a soldier in Portugal before returning to his sister's house at Hammersmith. Here he married, and his autobiography, which reveals the generosity of a seventeenth-century family towards a troublesome younger son and yields insights into life in 1650s Oxford, America, and Iberia, ends. Wood reported in July 1684 that Charles Croke (or just possibly his nephew Wright) was 'posted up for a shark and a coward in Day's coffey house' (*Life and Times of Anthony Wood*, 3.108). In 1686 he was 'living by gaming' (ibid., 1.196) to maintain his wife and children. The date of his death is unknown.   VIVIENNE LARMINIE

Sources A. Croke, *Genealogical history of the Croke family* (1823) • W. H. Cooke, ed., *Students admitted to the Inner Temple, 1547–1660* [1878] • Foster, *Alum. Oxon.* • *The life and times of Anthony Wood*, ed. A. Clark, 1–3, OHS, 19, 21, 26 (1891–4) • M. G. Hobson and H. E. Salter, eds., *Oxford council acts, 1626–1665*, OHS, 95 (1933) • M. G. Hobson, ed., *Oxford council acts, 1665–1701*, OHS, new ser., 2 (1939) • Thurloe, *State papers*, 3.165, 193–4, 281, 368–9, 521, 4.274 • *CSP dom.*, *1650–61* • C. H. Firth and G. Davies, *The regimental history of Cromwell's army*, 2 (1940), 242–53 • Baker, *Serjeants*, 190, 196, 402, 507 • Oxford parish registers, Bodl. Oxf., MS Top. Oxon. c. 172 • parish register, Marston, 1653–c.1720, Oxon. RO • will of Sir Richard Croke, PRO, PROB 11/374, fol. 137 • will of Unton Croke, 1694, PRO, PROB 11/420, fol. 96 • [C. Croke], *Fortune's uncertainty, or youth's inconstancy, wherein is contained a true and impartial account of what happened in the space of few years to the author, whom you will know in this ensuing discourse by the name of Rodolphus* (1667) • L. Naylor and G. Jagger, 'Croke, Sir Richard', 'Wright, William', HoP, *Commons, 1660–90* • L. Naylor and G. Jaggar, 'Whorwood, Brome', HoP, *Commons, 1660–90* • *The diary of Bulstrode Whitelocke, 1605–1675*, ed. R. Spalding, British Academy, Records of Social and Economic History, new ser., 13 (1990) • *VCH Oxfordshire*, 5.214–20 • M. Toynbee and P. Young, *Strangers in Oxford* (1973), 138–140 • Wood, *Ath. Oxon.* • *Remarks and collections of Thomas Hearne*, ed. C. E. Doble and others, 11 vols., OHS, 2, 7, 13, 34, 42–3, 48, 50, 65, 67, 72 (1885–1921), vols. 1–2 • *Parochial collections made by Anthony à Wood and Richard Rawlinson*, ed. F. N. Davis, 2, Oxfordshire RS, 4 (1922), 203–5 • sheriff's accounts, 1658, Bodl. Oxf., MS rolls Oxon. 61 • J. E. Thorold Rogers, ed., *Oxford city documents, financial and judicial, 1268–1665*, OHS, 18 (1891), 88 • M. A. E. Green, ed., *Calendar of the proceedings of the committee for compounding … 1643–1660*, 5 vols., PRO (1889–92), vol. 1 • *Seventh report*, HMC, 6 (1879), 97a, 110b, 112b • *The manuscripts of the duke of Somerset, the marquis of Ailesbury, and the Rev. Sir T. H. G. Puleston, bart.*, HMC, 43 (1898), 91

Croke, Unton (d. 1694). *See under* Croke, Unton (1594/5–1670/71).

Croker [*née* Sheppard], **Bithia Mary** (c.1848–1920), novelist, was born in Ireland, the second child and only daughter of the Revd William Sheppard (1811–1860) and his wife, Bithia, *née* Watson. Her father, who had begun his career as a barrister, then entered the Church of Ireland, and was rector of Kilgefin, co. Roscommon. She was educated at Rock Ferry in Cheshire, and at Tours in France. On her return to Ireland she continued to indulge her passion for riding and acquired a considerable reputation as a horsewoman. On 16 November 1871 at Rathangan, co. Kildare, she married Lieutenant John Croker (1844–1911) of the Royal Scots Fusiliers, who came from another Anglo-Irish family. Their only child, a daughter Eileen, was born in 1872.

In 1877 Lieutenant Croker was posted with his regiment to India where he and his wife spent in all some fourteen years in different areas, including south and north India and Burma. The latter part of his service, after returning from home leave in 1882–4, was with the Royal Munster Fusiliers. With only one child to occupy her in cantonments with limited resources, Bithia Croker turned to writing, for which she had from her schooldays been noted for her ease and fluency. In 1880 in the hot season in Secunderabad in south India she wrote her first novel, *Proper Pride*, set largely in India; the original manuscript was lost, but with a determination which was typical of her, she rewrote the work, which was published in England in 1882. Its success was sealed when Gladstone was noted reading it during wearying hours in the House of Commons.

A second Indian novel, *Pretty Miss Neville*, followed quickly in 1883, setting Bithia Croker firmly on the path to a long and prolific career as a romantic novelist, during which she wrote some forty-four novels and six collections of short stories, all of which closely reflected the worlds she knew. She was best remembered for her seventeen novels set in India, and one in Burma. Seven other novels were set in Ireland, notably *Beyond the Pale* (1897) and *Lismoyle* (1914). The remaining novels reflected the lives of the professional, well-to-do, and travelled British upper classes, and feature such varied locations as France, Spain, Italy, Switzerland, Norway, Egypt, and Australia.

Bithia Croker's novels were renowned for their wit, vivacity, and fluency. She was a born story-teller, with a strong grasp of character and plot. She also had a sensitive ear for speech, for idiom and the diction of different classes, which she reproduces in lively and entertaining dialogue. A sense of place, whether in Ireland, particularly co. Kerry, or the many areas she knew in India is another notable feature of her novels. Her view of colonial society is for the most part conservative, and her interest in peasant life is reflected most clearly in her short stories, notably *Village Tales and Jungle Tragedies* (1895). Dramatic tension is often created by threats to the established order in societies bound by convention. The issues of class and gender in British India provide the plot of several novels. In *The Company's Servant* (1907) the hero, a 'gentleman', has to surmount the social disgrace of working on the railways in order to win the heroine. *The Cat's Paw* (1902) narrates the story of a girl who refuses to marry the man for whom she has come to India, and, without family, connections, or money, places herself in an impossible social predicament—which is finally resolved after lively accounts of her employment as a companion, a nurse in a plague camp, a housekeeper in a Eurasian boarding-house, and a royal governess.

The Crokers left India in 1892 and settled in London, and at 5 Radnor Cliff, Folkestone. Lieutenant-Colonel Croker died in 1911. His widow carried on with her stream of writing, producing one or more novels a year until her death. She reached a wider audience through translation, some of her novels appearing in French, German, and Norwegian. An Irish novel, *Terence* (1899), ran for two years as a play in the United States, while her novel about Burma, *The Road to Mandalay* (1917), was made into a film in 1926. Meanwhile she pursued her interests of reading, the theatre, and travelling. She was a friend of many writers— *Angel* (1901) was dedicated to another creator of Indian fiction, Alice Perrin—and assisted many aspiring authors.

Bithia Croker died on 20 October 1920 at 30 Dorset Square, London, and was buried in Folkestone three days later. A tribute on her death noted, 'jealousy was not in her nature, and her generous admiration for all of the best in other people's efforts was one of her many fine characteristics' (*The Times*, 22 Oct 1920, 13). She left the bulk of her estate in England and Ireland to her daughter, who was said to have been the model for many of her heroines. Among the personal items she specially asked her to keep were her writing-table, and her diamond and ruby ring, with the request that she should wear it occasionally.

ROSEMARY CARGILL RAZA

Sources A. T. C. Pratt, ed., *People of the period: being a collection of the biographies of upwards of six thousand living celebrities*, 2 vols. (1897) · H. Cox, *Who's who in Kent, Surrey, Sussex* (1911–12) · *WWW, 1916–28* · *WWW, 1941–50* · *The lady's who's who: who's who for British women … 1938–9* (1939) · L. Sage, *The Cambridge guide to women's writing in English* (1999) · R. Hogan, ed., *Dictionary of Irish literature*, rev. edn, 2 vols. (1996) · R. Welch, ed., *The Oxford companion to Irish literature* (1996) · *The Times* (22 Oct 1920), 13 · Burke, *Gen. Ire.* (1899), 409 · army records, PRO, WO 25/3244, fol. 525 · *India Office List* · *Indian Army List* · *Retford, Gainsborough and Worksop Times* (16 May 1947), 8 [death of daughter] · will · d. cert.

Wealth at death £8421 10s. 9d.: probate, 28 Dec 1920

Croker, John [*formerly* Johann Crocker] (1670–1741), engraver of coins and medals, was born at Dresden, Saxony, on 21 October 1670, the son of a woodcarver and cabinet-maker to the electoral court of Saxony who died

when he was young. Croker and his younger siblings were brought up by their mother, Rosina Frauenlaub, who saw to their education. Croker was apprenticed to his godfather, a goldsmith and jeweller of Dresden, and during his leisure hours sought to improve his knowledge of drawing and modelling. His journeyman years as a jeweller were spent travelling in Germany and then in the Netherlands, from where he arrived in England in 1691.

In England, Croker took employment with a jeweller, then learnt die-sinking and began to work exclusively as a medallist. In 1697 he was appointed assistant to Henry Harris (1633/4–1704), chief engraver at the Royal Mint (then located at the Tower), the arrangement being that Harris would pay him £175 out of his own salary and he would live in the graver's house in the mint but pay for his diet and assist in instructing other workmen. In fact Harris seems to have generally handed over to Croker, who was required to make the original dies for obverses of the fourteen standard coins of William III. In the same year Croker produced his first-known English medal, relating to the peace of Ryswick. In 1702 he made Queen Anne's coronation medal, and in 1704 the Queen Anne's Bounty medal, the first to be signed 'I. C.', which became his usual signature.

Following Harris's death, on 7 April 1705, Croker was appointed to succeed him. At this time he married a lady surnamed Franklin (d. 1735); they had one daughter, who died young. Croker engraved all the dies for the gold and silver coins current during the reigns of Anne and George I, as well as the dies for the gold coins of George II until 1739; for the silver coins with the 'young head' from 1727 to 1741; and in copper the pattern halfpennies and farthings for George I and the first coinage of George II. He made some of the Queen Anne halfpennies and farthings, including the 1714 specimen with the Britannia reverse. Three of the reverse types of pattern farthings refer to the peace of Utrecht, and it appears that Croker was following Dean Swift's recommendation, supported by the lord treasurer, that the English copper coins should allude to notable events in the queen's reign.

From 1702 to 1732 Croker was constantly engaged in medal-engraving. His designs commemorated events rather than persons and were always struck, not cast. The obverses were in low relief and very pictorial, with much detail. Zacharius von Uffenbach, who visited him in 1710, was unimpressed by this aspect of Croker's work and noted that he had no conversation. With the accession of George I in 1714 his work was increased by demands for medals and change in the entire coinage; the peace of Utrecht brought much gold and silver into the kingdom that needed coining. Besides his official duties Croker was permitted to make and sell gold and silver medals unrelated to state affairs, and those medals awarded by the monarch for personal services.

During his working life Croker took several apprentices who stayed on as his assistants. Vertue noted that 'towards his latter end of life he grew grosse and heavy,— lethargick—did little, was much assisted in his business of the Mint by Mr Tanner' (Vertue, *Note books*, 3.101); this was

John Sigismund Tanner, apprenticed in 1729, who was to succeed him. When infirmity prevented his working at the mint Croker passed his time reading instructive and devotional works. His bequest to the minister of the Lutheran chapel indicates the nature of his beliefs. He died on 21 March 1741 and was buried, as his wife had been, in the church of St Peter ad Vincula, in the Tower.

ANITA MCCONNELL

Sources C. E. Challis, ed., *A new history of the royal mint* (1992) · 'Croker, John', *Biographical dictionary of medallists*, ed. L. Forrer, 1 (1902); rev. edn (1904); repr. (1979), 472–9 · J. G. Pfister, 'Memoir of Johann Croker', *Numismatic Chronicle*, 15 (1852–3), 67–73 · P. A. Rayner, *The designers and engravers of the English milled coinage, 1662–1953* (1954) · Vertue, *Note books*, 3.101 · J. Redington, ed., *Calendar of Treasury papers*, 6 vols., PRO (1868–89), 1696–7, 358; 1697i, 75, 186; 1697ii, 21, 40; vol. 3, pp. 297, 445 · *London in 1710: from the travels of Zacharias Conrad von Uffenbach*, ed. and trans. W. H. Quarrell and M. Mare (1934), 43–4 · will, PRO, PROB 11/708, sig. 61 · *DNB*

Croker, John Wilson (1780–1857), politician and writer, was born in Galway on 20 December 1780, the son of John Croker, an exciseman who rose to be surveyor-general of the port of Dublin, and his second wife, Hester Rathbone, the daughter of a protestant clergyman. He went to James Knowles's school in Cork where his parents hoped he would be cured of a stammer; then to a school, also in Cork, kept by French émigrés, where he acquired his fluent French and his interest in the French Revolution which later helped to shape his politics and his historical work; and finally to two schools in Portarlington (Willis's and then the Revd Richmond Hood's), where he was well grounded in the Greek and Latin classics. In 1796, still no more than fifteen, he entered Trinity College, Dublin, where he came to know Thomas Moore the poet, John Leslie Foster who became Irish advocate-general, and Percy Smythe, later Lord Strangford, the diplomat. He retained close friendships with other Trinity men who achieved distinction if not fame, notably his tutor Bartholomew Lloyd (1772–1837), later provost of Trinity, the lawyer William Henry Ellis (1774–1847), and Thomas Casey the doctor (*b.* 1779). It was while he was at Trinity that the uprising of 1798 broke out, and it left Croker with a strong sense of the fragility of polite society, and the power of French arms to disrupt it. He also became convinced that Ireland's stability required the granting of full political rights to the Roman Catholics and the payment of the Catholic priesthood. Although he was a typical product of the protestant ascendancy, sharing its proprietary view of political and legal patronage, and looking to England for leadership and example, his liberal views on 'Catholic emancipation' as it came to be called, put him in advance of many English tories.

Croker was looked on by his contemporaries as outstandingly gifted, but his slender means made a legal career the obvious road to fame. To qualify for legal practice in Ireland he kept terms at Lincoln's Inn from 1800 to 1802, when he was called to the Irish bar. His first practice was on the Munster circuit, where he met Daniel O'Connell. But the Act of Union, which brought to an end the parliament in Dublin, meant that any Irishman with ambition now looked further afield. Croker always spoke

John Wilson Croker (1780–1857), by Sir Thomas Lawrence, 1825

of himself as Irish, but the lure of London was strong, and like Swift, Goldsmith, Sheridan, and Burke before him, he was drawn to its larger stage and more sophisticated cultural life. Burke indeed was a kinsman by marriage, and his writings were a vital influence on Croker's outlook. In Dublin his first literary efforts had been pamphlets, squibs, and humorous verse about Irish society and the Irish stage. But he was a prudent man, and he had no illusions about the struggles of Grub Street.

Political début In May 1806 Croker married Rosamund Carrington Pennell, daughter of William Pennell of Waterford. William Pennell's eldest son later (in 1820) married Catherine Croker, a daughter of John Croker by his first wife, while another daughter, Margaret, married Lovell Pennell, a nephew of William. Pennells and Crokers were therefore linked by three marriages in a single generation. In addition, Rosamund Croker's first cousin, Harriet Pennell, married Ambrose Hardinge Giffard, son of John Giffard, a staunchly protestant loyalist and friend of J. W. Croker's father. Any young man of promise, connected with such a clan, must have been aware of giving hostages to fortune, and Croker's family loyalties were, as with most ascendancy families, unusually strong. He knew he must have a competence before he could hope for literary fame, and he took the first tide of fortune at the flood. A few months after his marriage he was acting as legal adviser to the Rowley family in an election for Downpatrick, when Captain Rowley the candidate was posted to Mauritius, and Croker stood in his place. He was defeated, but at the general election which followed in 1807, he stood again and won, after appealing successfully for the support of the new chief secretary for Ireland, Sir

Arthur Wellesley. The following year Wellesley was appointed to command the new army in Portugal and arranged for Croker to deputize as chief secretary in his absence. He did this very well. One of his first services to the administration was in the Commons debate over the Mrs Clarke scandal. Mary Anne Clarke had been the mistress of the duke of York, then commander-in-chief, and she had used her position to promise officers commissions and promotions in return for bribes. In an unruly debate Croker did something to expose Mrs Clarke's motives, and although the government failed to exonerate the duke, who was obliged to resign, there was a general feeling that no one on the government side had shown a greater mastery of detail than Croker.

Soon after this, in October 1809, Croker was offered the post of secretary to the Admiralty. The appointment of a novice to such an important office in time of war was a symptom of the government's desperation. The war was going badly. Two cabinet ministers, Castlereagh and Canning, had just fought a duel. The duke of Portland had resigned the premiership. His successor, Spencer Perceval, was hard pressed to form a united administration. Croker himself thought his tenure would be short, and it was some years before he gave up his legal practice in Ireland or sold his house in Dublin. Yet he was to hold the office with conspicuous success through four premierships, until 1830.

Croker was an excellent secretary, whose probity and competence were both soon tested. His first act was to expose a high-placed official, the Hon. George Villiers, who as paymaster of the marines since 1792 had appropriated £250,000 of public funds to his own use. When Villiers represented Croker to the king as an ignorant novice and a busybody, George III referred the matter to Perceval, and Croker resigned his office rather than give up his conviction that he had exposed a serious defalcation. He was reinstated when his opinion was upheld, and complimented by the king for his integrity. The Napoleonic blockade begun by the Berlin decrees was met by the orders in council, which in turn provoked a war with the United States, and gave the opposition an opportunity to attack the Admiralty for incompetence. Croker had frequently to explain and defend Britain's naval policy in parliament and the press. His complete mastery of his brief in debate was shown in 1816, when the opposition, having just gained a victory over the income tax, sought to gain another on the navy estimates. In a speech meant to spearhead a concerted assault on the Admiralty, the whig leader Tierney asked why the estimates for 1815, the first year of peace, were higher than for 1814, the last year of war. He should have been answered by the treasurer of the navy, Sir George Warrender, but he was at a loss, and at short notice Croker had to reply for him. He showed that at every declaration of peace the expenses for active service were much reduced, and what remained of them was always charged to the establishment, which therefore showed an increase, that this had been so for every first year of peace since 1714, and that it was last done in 1803 when Tierney himself had been treasurer of the navy. The

reply destroyed the opposition's case and was long remembered by witnesses as a *tour de force*.

With the coming of peace, Croker could have had a distinguished political career. He was too valuable to the administration to be left out of the Commons for long. When he was defeated at Downpatrick in 1812, the Liverpool administration found him a seat at Athlone, which he held until 1818. In that year he was a candidate for his own university, but his rival Plunket was a member of the Grenville group which the government wished to enlist in its support, and so Croker fought the election without the official backing he thought his due, and lost by four votes. He was shortly after this offered a seat for Yarmouth, Isle of Wight, in the gift of his friend and patron, the marquess of Hertford. Hertford controlled six seats and frequently put them at the disposal of the ministry. Croker moved within a year to another of these, Bodmin, which he held for six years, and later to a third, Aldeburgh, Suffolk. He achieved his ambition to sit for Trinity College, Dublin, in May 1827, and kept the seat for three years, letting it be known that he would like the post of chief secretary for Ireland, but his support for Catholic emancipation was unpopular with a majority of the seventy fellows and scholars who comprised the electors, and he was defeated in 1830. Again Aldeburgh was his safety net, and he sat for that borough through his last two years in parliament.

Aldeburgh was due to lose its representation under the Reform Act, but that need not have ended Croker's political career. He had acquired great administrative experience, and though not a frequent speaker, he was adept at mastering any complex body of information and he could easily have held a ministerial portfolio. He was moreover well known to leading politicians. He was a favourite of George IV, who made a special request that Croker accompany him on his state visit to Dublin in 1821. He was a close friend of the duke of Wellington and Peel, and a much sought-after guest at the houses of leading tory politicians. In 1828 he was made a privy councillor. He had a shrewd appreciation of political issues, great administrative skill, and a trenchant way of expressing himself which led grandees like Lord Hertford and Viscount Lowther to rely on him for help and advice. But he lacked the key ingredient of ambition. A daughter had died an infant, and in 1820 his only other child, Spencer Perceval Croker, died aged only three years. The blow was severe. Mrs Croker had a prolonged depressive illness and Croker himself said that he only stayed in office to preserve his sanity. So the critical acerbity for which he acquired a reputation was really a carapace for a sensibility happiest in a domestic circle and easily bruised by the strife of party politics.

Literary career Croker's political career may have been too prolonged to allow him to fulfil his other ambition, to make his mark in literature. There are hints in other writers' references to Croker that he was a little too well connected with parliament and the beau monde, a little too ready with opinions backed by inside knowledge and the authority of office, to be easy company among humble men of letters. His position moreover enabled him to dispense a certain amount of patronage, which of all kinds of help is the hardest to acknowledge. But he had a wide appreciation of all varieties of literature and art, which made him a valuable intermediary between the politicians and the public, and he was an able writer, lucid, fluent, and always well informed.

Croker's own writings cover a huge range. As a politician, he had written pamphlets on the exchange of prisoners, on the orders in council, and on the state of Ireland. He briefed and sometimes contributed to government newspapers such as *The Courier*, and later *The Standard*. He wrote a poem in the style of Scott's *Marmion* on the battle of Talavera, of which Wellington said that he did not think 'that a battle could be turned into anything so entertaining' (*Croker Papers*, 1.25). He was a compulsive writer of light verse like his friend Canning, though his anti-whig verses in *The New Whig Guide* (1819) have not lasted as well as Canning's contributions to *The Anti-Jacobin*.

Official duties and the political situation, however, drew Croker more and more into serious criticism and historical research. In 1809 the *Quarterly Review* was founded, specifically to provide an official riposte to the successful whig venture, the *Edinburgh Review*. Croker contributed regularly until 1854. Altogether he wrote or shared authorship of 270 articles, often providing three and occasionally four in a single number. Before 1827 he contributed articles on literature and politics, especially events in France. During Gifford's editorship he had not much influence on the *Quarterly*'s line in domestic politics, which was largely prompted by Canning, but when J. G. Lockhart became editor in 1829, Croker, mainly through his connections with the tory front bench, and especially Peel, became the *Quarterly*'s main political writer. Under Gifford he had gained a reputation as the severest critic of the romantic poets, especially of Keats, Croker's review of *Endymion* being wrongly supposed to have hastened the poet's death. Under Lockhart, his heaviest strictures were against the whig ministries of Grey and Melbourne, and it was this which led the whig wit Sydney Smith to call him 'the calumniator general of the human race' (*Letters of Sydney Smith*, ed. N. C. Smith, 1953, 680). Actually, Croker was capable of generous and humane reviews even of whig politicians, as his pieces on Sir James Mackintosh and Sir Samuel Romilly show very well. Though he was a severe critic, who struck as hard as any writer during a period of bitter partisanship in periodical literature, he did not make great claims for his articles, and with the exception of eight on the French Revolution, he did not seek to reprint them in book form. 'I have no amour propre d'auteur', he once told Peel (25 Jan 1835, BL, Add. MS 40321, fols. 64–5), and he often admitted to Lockhart that a review left him feeling that he had failed to do justice to his subject. He knew that his forte was mastery of detail. 'I do nothing at all approaching to well but what I understand *in its details*' (Brightfield, *Croker*, 331), he told John Murray.

The keynote of all Croker's periodical writing is a sense of tradition under attack. He thought that in poetry the standard had been set by Dryden and Pope. Among his contemporaries he most admired the poetry of Scott and Crabbe (who was one of his electors at Aldeburgh). He thought the romantics culpably ignorant of their predecessors, and only Byron struck him as an exception. He was not a good judge of fiction, and once said he preferred 'an ounce of fact to a ton of imagination'. Even Scott's novels, he thought, took too many liberties with the historic past. More popular novelists left him cold. He confessed he could not get far with *Nicholas Nickleby*, and even that he had read none of the novels of his friend Theodore Hook though some of them had been written under his own roof. His later reviews deal more and more with history and biography, and these bulk largest in his work after 1830.

In 1815, soon after Waterloo, Croker paid a visit to Paris with Peel and Vesey Fitzgerald, and on this and subsequent visits he began to gather materials on the history of the French Revolution. In 1823 he published an edition of three *Royal Memoirs on the French Revolution*. He corresponded with Madame de Genlis, with Chateaubriand, and with Guizot. He accumulated a huge collection of revolutionary pamphlets, including the entire library of Jean Paul Marat, to whose surviving sister he paid a small pension. The pamphlet collection was subsequently given to the British Museum. Croker became the best-informed British historian of the French Revolution of his day. But he saw the period through the eyes of Burke. He thought the revolution had inspired all the democratic movements of his day, and his historical work, though accurate and scrupulously documented, was subordinated to the long-term aim of discrediting these.

Not that Croker disapproved of reform. In fact, he called himself a 'rational reformer' (Croker to Brougham, 22 Aug 1842, Brougham MSS, UCL). But he liked reform to come from above, from those best informed about the fault and best placed to find a remedy. Peel's reforms, as home secretary, of the criminal code and Metropolitan Police were the sort of centrally directed improvements he approved of. He had himself suggested to Lord Liverpool the transfer of parliamentary seats from certain corrupt boroughs to four new industrial towns, and he later thought that if this advice had been taken, it would have avoided the upheaval of 1831–2. Like many officials, familiar with the difficulties of stirring up people to address urgent issues, he refused to believe there was a popular demand for political reform, seeing only interested parties inciting popular feeling for their own ends.

The French Revolution provided the pattern. Starting with well-meaning aristocratic attempts to reform the finances, it soon fell under the influence of philosophers and light-headed enthusiasts who could not resist the demands of the mob or arrest the inevitable slide into anarchy. The excesses of democracy in turn generated a yearning for strong military rule, so that the French became more enslaved under Napoleon I than they had ever been under the Bourbons. Britain by contrast with its mixed constitution had achieved order with freedom, and the issue facing those who wanted to preserve this heritage from critics of a Francophile radical and whig persuasion was

> whether, in a free press, the force of reason and truth, and the principles of order, good morals and true religion, are a match for the adroitness and the audacity of the philosophers of the Revolution and their disciples—the loose in morals, the factious in politics—the preachers of liberty, the practisers of despotism. (Brightfield, *Croker*, 323)

This provided the underlying theme of his reviewing in the *Quarterly*. A new public was emerging all too responsive to sensationalism and trash. The critic had the high moral and social responsibility of holding up the higher standards of literature. Croker did not confine his conception of a writer's responsibility to his criticism: he saw that literature and art would be more responsible if their practitioners enjoyed a closer collaboration and higher status, and to this end he gave the initial impulse which led to the foundation of a club for writers, artists, and men of science, the Athenaeum.

Croker as historian The features of Croker's work on the French Revolution which strike a modern reader are its elaborate factual detail and its inexhaustible moral revulsion against the revolutionaries. He saw that the horrors of the period exercised a fascination with uninformed readers which was fed by writers willing to distort and invent, and that to confute these, only a detailed knowledge of the original evidence would suffice. So he took great care to establish the exact time and place of particular episodes so as to be able to expose carelessness and fabrication. His knowledge of the topography of revolutionary Paris was meticulous. He collected contemporary gazetteers and maps and had measurements made of particular buildings so as to be able to check the accuracy of contemporary narratives of, for example, the execution of Louis XVI and his queen, or the death of Robespierre. He saw that as events recede into the past men's memories lose their immediacy, and the agents' motives are blurred and condoned, especially by writers like Thiers and Mignet, who published smooth and colourful narratives long after the events described. To maintain both factual accuracy and moral alertness, his own method was to take a single topic or episode, such as the royal family's flight to Varennes, or the invention of the guillotine, dwelling analytically on all the evidence available. The result is fascinating, sometimes tedious, but never easy or popular.

In his criticism of English writers of memoirs, Croker applied the same concerns, especially if they were liberals. His review of Wraxall's *Historical Memoirs of his Own Time* in the *Quarterly* for 1815 is a merciless exposure of a self-important gossip whose anecdotes improved with telling. In 1851 and 1852/4 he gave the same treatment to Lord Holland's posthumous *Foreign Reminiscences* and *Memoirs of the Whig Party*. In both cases he treats slipshod and careless assertions as libels on historic figures, which it is the duty of the historian to correct. He was not content to be a mere critic, however. His sense that in the historical process 'trifles float and are preserved' while 'what is solid and valuable sinks to the bottom, and is lost forever', led him to take on the role of historical editor. In 1821 he published an edition of the letters of Mary Lepel, Lady Hervey (1700–1768), which was followed in 1824 by an edition of those of Henrietta Howard, Lady Suffolk (1681–1767), and in 1825 by one of Horace Walpole's letters to the earl of Hertford. None of these named him as editor. Two more weighty editorial undertakings did. In 1831 Croker published a new edition of Boswell's *Life of Johnson* including the *Journal of a Tour to the Hebrides*, which was vindictively attacked by Macaulay in the *Edinburgh Review*, but which remained the best edition until superseded by the work of George Birkbeck Hill. In 1848 Croker published from the original manuscript a two-volume edition of *Lord Hervey's Memoirs*, similarly superseded in the twentieth century by a complete scholarly edition. But Croker as an editor had two handicaps not experienced by modern scholars. He had to beware of giving offence to the relatives and descendants of the historical figures he studied, especially if they owned the materials he used or helped him with information; and he had to present the work for a lay readership in such a way as to ensure a profit to his publisher, in the process being his own transcriber, compiler, and annotator. In these circumstances, his productivity was extraordinary. At the very end of his life, in failing health, he was still busy preparing an edition of Pope.

Political retirement Already by the 1820s Croker's literary projects were exerting a strong pull away from politics, and there are signs that he wanted to have more time from his official duties. In April 1827 the coalition which had ruled Britain since 1812 began to break up when Lord Liverpool had a stroke, and forty-one ministers and senior officials resigned rather than work with his successor, Canning. Croker was torn between approval of Canning's policies (especially Catholic relief) and loyalty to Wellington. His efforts to unite the antagonists failed and led to a temporary estrangement from Peel. One of the seceders was Croker's chief at the Admiralty, Lord Melville, and instead of a first lord, Canning appointed the duke of Clarence, the future William IV, as lord high admiral. The duke quarrelled with Sir George Cockburn, who would normally have been Melville's successor, and with Croker himself. Croker therefore had no reason to look forward to the new reign, especially as Wellington's premiership failed to heal the breach of 1827. But his wish to retire from politics to his writing was frustrated by the fall of Wellington in November 1830 and the crisis over parliamentary reform which followed. When the Reform Act was law, his declared reason for refusing a seat in the reformed house was that it would have been inconsistent with his opposition to reform. But the vehemence of that opposition may well have been due to the fact that he had already determined to retire. Early in 1830 he was disinclined to accept Wellington's offer of the treasurership of the navy because it would affect his retirement pension.

At the general election in August 1830 Croker was defeated at Trinity College, Dublin. Like Peel, he did not regret the fall in November of a ministry which had become too weak to control the Commons. But the Grey ministry which followed took him by surprise with the radicalism of its parliamentary reform proposals. As the whigs had always disagreed on the issue, Croker thought their proposing it once in office was a piece of cynical opportunism. He feared that the ending of proprietary boroughs would deal a severe blow to executive government, making the Commons too responsive to the electorate and too hostile to the House of Lords. Besides, the framers of the bill turned out to be flagrantly partisan in the boroughs they chose to deprive of representatives. Croker decided, despite recurrent illness, to fight the Reform Bill with all the vigour he could muster, and he became the most formidable of its critics on the opposition benches, destroying Jeffrey, harassing Russell, and humiliating Macaulay. In this way he proved his ministerial mettle, just when he was hoping to leave politics altogether.

Croker resisted the remonstrances of his friends and refused several offers of safe seats in the reformed House of Commons. But he could not long ignore the political scene, and he reconciled his retirement and his former loyalties by writing the political articles in the *Quarterly*, of which he became virtually co-editor with J. G. Lockhart. Croker's reputation as a tory partisan dates from 1830 and his attacks on the whig ministry and its supporters, but the ingredients of his criticism were all present in his earlier articles. He saw the whig aristocracy as the infatuated leaders of an English *révolte nobiliaire*, leading to a plebeian revolution. But he was never a party politician in the modern sense of one who has no opinions but those of his party. He thought party feeling a peculiarly English failing and the device of using a parliamentary party to force the monarch's hand a peculiarly whig one. By conservatism he meant the preservation of the monarchy, the landed interest, and the church, not the narrow parliamentary party. In this he agreed with Peel, whose supposedly Fabian policy, from 1835 to 1841, of keeping the whigs in office, was really an echo of the arguments of Croker's *Quarterly* articles, which he often approved and revised. If Peel used a parliamentary majority to gain office he would, Croker thought, be playing the whig game and weakening the crown. Peel's famous demand over the ladies of the bedchamber in May 1839 reflects Croker's view, as does the practice with which he and Peel had been familiar before 1832, that a minister, being chosen by the crown, had a right to expect some outward sign of the crown's approval. Neither thought it right for the minister to be a nominee of a parliamentary party; and Peel's notorious disdain for party supporters is Croker's doctrine put into practice.

During Peel's ministry from 1841, Croker supported him in all the measures which the tory back-benchers most disliked, the alteration of the sliding scale for corn, the 1842 budget, the factory legislation, the Charitable Bequests Act, and the Maynooth grant. On the last issue, which prepared and perhaps ensured the great split of the following year, Croker even carried his own opinion against those of Lockhart and their publisher, Murray. It was only on Peel's conversion to the repeal of the corn laws that Croker rebelled, and then what he deplored was not the split in the parliamentary party but the separation of that party's leaders from the landed interest, the most stable form of property in the country, and the class (as he thought) which had made it great. His thirty-five year friendship with Peel came to an end in January 1847 with an exchange of letters, conciliatory on Croker's part, frigid and dismissive on Peel's.

Croker's reputation suffered heavily from his habit of putting private friendship before political expediency. In March 1842 the third marquess of Hertford, after a decade of increasing eccentricity and dissipation, died leaving a tangled will. Croker was an executor and was himself left £26,000; but when it was suspected that Hertford's valet, Suisse, had stolen £80,000 from his master, the executors decided to prosecute, and most of the direction was left to Croker. Suisse's counsel, Thesiger, argued that as his client knew he would be handsomely rewarded in Hertford's will, he had no motive to defraud, and that the missing money was amply explained by Hertford's dubious tastes which it was the valet's job to satisfy. Suisse was acquitted, and though the executors later recovered the money from Suisse in the French courts, the fact was largely ignored in England. Two novelists paid close attention to the trial of Suisse and used it in their writings, Disraeli in *Coningsby* (1844) and Thackeray in *Vanity Fair* (1847–8). In the former Hertford figures as Lord Monmouth and Croker as Rigby. Disraeli's portrayal of the latter seems to have been part of his campaign against Peel, since he thought, on the basis of gossip and the *Quarterly*, that Croker was Peel's *éminence grise*, and that while attacking the prime minister might be politically hazardous, attacking his retiring friend was fair game. Croker almost certainly never read *Coningsby* even when he and Disraeli found themselves together in the Protectionist Party, but it became a habit among writers who wanted to discredit Croker to cite *Coningsby* as proof, as G. O. Trevelyan did when attempting to justify Macaulay's hatred of his old rival.

In fact Croker, as his two biographers showed, was not the obsequious toady portrayed by Disraeli. Prominent men sought his company because he was witty, clever, and amusing, and his advice because he was clear-headed and practical. He was generous to improvident writers and artists, like Theodore Hook, and even when they differed from him in politics, as did Thomas Moore, he recognized their talent. He was not vindictive. Certainly he pursued Lord John Russell with great venom, but that was a prejudice derived from Burke, and later amply reinforced by his experience of Lord John's part in the Reform Act. But with other political antagonists like Sir Francis Burdett and Lord Brougham, Croker enjoyed close and cordial friendships. He was certainly a staunch supporter of the aristocratic order, but he was not self-seeking. His ambition from 1809 had been to earn a competence and devote himself to literature. What kept him involved in politics was loyalty, to Perceval, Wellington, Hertford, and finally to Peel. The severity of his reviewing made him many enemies, but posterity would condone this (as it has Macaulay's) if he had left some one enduring work. Instead, most of his work was anonymous and was only identified with certainty as his in the twentieth century, long after the image of the savage reviewer had become established.

Croker had no surviving children, but he adopted as his own child his wife's youngest sister, Rosamund Hester Elizabeth Pennell, who married George, the son of his Admiralty colleague Sir John Barrow, and he regarded her six children as his own grandchildren. In 1828 he bought a cottage with 15 acres at West Molesey which he called Molesey Grove, and made a family home. Here he had his large library and wrote his reviews. In 1841 he employed the architect Decimus Burton to build Alverbank, on Stokes Bay near Gosport, which he used as a summer retreat, and which still stands. It bears the characteristic motto *Parva sed apta*. With Lord Hertford's legacy he bought a 336 acre farm near Cheltenham with an income of £648 p.a. These, along with the official apartment in Kensington Palace, gave him the way of life of a prosperous Victorian gentleman, which is undoubtedly what he wanted to appear. But he retained his early fear of revolution and social chaos, and became more and more out of touch with the Conservatism of Disraeli's party. In 1854 he formally gave up his connection with the *Quarterly Review*. He died at Molesey Grove soon after going to bed, on 10 August 1857.   WILLIAM THOMAS

Sources *The Croker papers: the correspondence and diaries of … John Wilson Croker*, ed. L. J. Jennings, 3 vols. (1884) · M. F. Brightfield, *John Wilson Croker* (1940) · G. Breiseth, 'British conservatism and French revolutions: John Wilson Croker's attitude to reform and revolution in Britain and France', PhD diss., Cornell University, 1984 · *Wellesley index* · H. Shine and H. Shine, *The Quarterly Review under Gifford: identification of contributors, 1809–1824* (1949) · J. Shattock, *Politics and reviewers: The Edinburgh and The Quarterly in the early Victorian age* (1989), chap. 3 · B. Disraeli, *Coningsby* (1844) · H. Ben-Israel, *English historians on the French Revolution* (1968), chap. 11 · R. Stewart, *The foundation of the conservative party, 1830–1867* (1978) · J. L. Clive, *Thomas Babington Macaulay: the shaping of the historian* (1973) · M. F. Brightfield, *Theodore Hook and his novels* (1926) · B. Falk, '*Old Q's*' daughter: the history of a strange family' (1951) · J. Ingamells, *The 3rd marquess of Hertford as a collector* (1983) · T. H. Ward, *The Athenaeum* (1925) · W. Thomas, *The quarrel of Macaulay and Croker* (2000)

Archives BL, corresp. and papers, Add. MSS 22630, 38078–38079, 41124–41129, 44895–44899, 52465–52472, 56367, 60286–60289 · Bodl. Oxf., letters · Duke U., Perkins L., corresp. and papers · Hunt. L., letters and papers · NL Scot., corresp. · U. Mich., Clements L., corresp. and papers · University of Florida Libraries, Gainesville, Florida, corresp. · Yale U., Beinecke L., corresp. and papers relating to Louis Philippe | All Souls Oxf., corresp. with Charles Richard Vaughan · Alnwick Castle, letters to Henry Drummond · Balliol Oxf., letters to Lady Alice Peel · BL, corresp. with Lord Aberdeen, Add. MS 43196 · BL, corresp. with Sir Hardinge Gifford, Add. MS 56367 · BL, corresp. with John Charles Herries, Add. MS 57403 · BL, corresp. with Lord Liverpool, Add. MSS 38248–38327, 38572–38576, *passim* · BL, corresp. with Sir Thomas Byam Martin, Add. MSS 41367, 41369, 41389, *passim* · BL, corresp. with B. E. O'Meara, Add. MSS 20124, 20145–20146, 20218 · BL, letters to Sir Robert Peel, Add. MSS 40183–40184, 40319–40321 · BL, letters to Lord Wellesley, Add. MSS 37298–37313, *passim* · BL, letters to Charles Philip Yorke, Add. MSS 45038, 45046 · Bodl. Oxf., letters to Sir Francis Burdett · Bodl. Oxf., letters to Sir James Burges · Bodl. Oxf., corresp. with Isaac D'Israeli · Bodl. Oxf., letters to Theodore Hook · Bodl. Oxf.,

letters to Horace Twiss and Mrs Twiss · Bodl. Oxf., corresp. with Wilberforce family · Cork City Library, letters to Thomas Crofton Croker · Cumbria AS, Carlisle, letters to Lord Lonsdale · Derbys. RO, letters to Sir R. J. Wilmot-Horton · Durham RO, letters to Lord Londonderry · Exeter Cathedral, archives, letters to Henry Phillpotts, bishop of Exeter · Hunt. L., letters to Sir Francis Beaufort · Lpool RO, letters to fourteenth earl of Derby · NA Scot., corresp. with Lord Melville · NL Ire., letters to Thomas Casey · NL Scot., letters to Blackwoods · NL Scot., corresp. with Edward Ellice · NL Scot., corresp. with J. G. Lockhart · NL Scot., corresp. with John Rennie · NL Scot., letters to Sir Walter Scott · NL Scot., letters to Sir Charles Stuart, later Lord Rothesay · NMM, corresp. with Sir George Cockburn · NMM, letters to Charles Yorke · NRA, priv. coll., corresp. with Sir George Sinclair · Pembroke College, Oxford, letters to G. W. Hall · RA, corresp. with Thomas Lawrence · Suffolk RO, Bury St Edmunds, letters to Lord Arthur Hervey · Suffolk RO, Ipswich, corresp. with Sir James Saumarez · TCD, letters to Sir William Betham · TCD, corresp. with Lord Donoughmore · TCD, letters to Herbert Francis Hore · TCD, corresp. with William Shaw Mason · U. Glas. L., special collections department, corresp. with James Watt jnr and Charles Hampden Turner · U. Southampton L., corresp. with Henry John Temple, third Viscount Palmerston, relating to military and political matters · U. Southampton L., letters to first duke of Wellington · University of Chicago Library, department of special collections, corresp. with Lord Ripon · W. Yorks. AS, Leeds, Canning MSS · Yale U., Beinecke L., corresp. with Edward Locker

Likenesses drawing, *c*.1810, NPG · W. Owen, oils, exh. 1812, NPG; repro. in Jennings, ed., *The Croker papers* · T. Lawrence, oils, 1825, NG Ire. [*see illus.*] · T. Blood, stipple (after S. Drummond), BM, NPG; repro. in *European Magazine* (1812) · F. Chantry, marble bust, Athenaeum Club, Pall Mall, London; repro. in F. R. Cowell, *The Athenaeum* (1975) · Kirkwood, etching, NPG · D. Maclise, lithograph, BM, NPG; repro. in *Fraser's Magazine*, 1st ser., 4 (Sept 1831), 240

Croker, Margaret Sarah (*bap.* **1773**), poet and novelist, was baptized on 4 March 1773 at Holbeton in Devon, the daughter of Captain Richard Croker (*d.* 1816) and his wife, Mary. The high cost of a brother's education prompted Croker to contact the Royal Literary Fund just before her father's death in 1816, in the hope of earning a living by her pen.

Croker's published poems include *A Monody on the Lamented Death of Princess Charlotte Augusta* (1817), *A Tribute to the Memory of Sir Samuel Romilly* (1818), and *Monody on his Late Royal Highness the Duke of Kent* (1820), expressing her hopes for the future reign of his daughter Victoria. These verse tributes are 'well-written, feeling, but not remarkable' (Blain, Clements & Grundy, *Feminist comp.*, 249). Croker also published a volume of verse, *Nugae canorae* (1818), by subscription.

Croker's only surviving novel, *The Question, who is Anna?* (3 vols., 1818), treats the question of illegitimacy with unusual frankness for its time. Its heroine, born to unmarried young parents, is portrayed sympathetically, rather than condemned. Croker may also have published two other novels, *Henry de Courtenay* and *The Widow of Wingfield*, and written a further unpublished novel in 1825 (see Blain, Clements & Grundy, *Feminist comp.*, 249), but these cannot be traced. It is not known when she died.

MEGAN A. STEPHAN

Sources Blain, Clements & Grundy, *Feminist comp.*, 249 · *IGI* · 'Margaret Sarah Croker', *The Cambridge bibliography of English literature*, ed. J. Shattock, 3rd edn, 4: *1800–1918* (1999), 326 · N. Cross, *The*

Royal Literary Fund, 1790–1918 (1984), 42 · D. J. O'Donoghue, *The poets of Ireland: a biographical and bibliographical dictionary* (1912)

Croker, Marianne (1791/2–1854). *See under* Croker, Thomas Crofton (1798–1854).

Croker, Temple Henry (1729–1790?), writer, was born at Sarsfield Court, co. Cork, Ireland, the son of Henry Croker. He was admitted to Westminster School in October 1741, and became a king's scholar in 1743. In 1746 he was elected to a scholarship at Trinity College, Cambridge; but he chose to study at Christ Church, Oxford, from where he matriculated on 25 November 1746 and graduated BA (1750) and MA (1760). He was appointed chaplain to the earl of Hillsborough, and seems to have helped William Huggins (1696–1761) in a translation of Ariosto's *Orlando Furioso*, which was first published anonymously in 1755, with a dedication to the prince of Wales signed by Croker. An edition of 1757 claimed the work for Huggins. A translation of Zappa's Italian sonnets (1755), also attributed to Huggins, has a manuscript dedication by Croker on the copy in the Dyce Library. He translated the second and seventh satires in *The Satires of Lodovico Ariosto* (1759), and he published a work criticizing Archibald Bower's *History of the Popes* in 1758, and a paper that supported Charles Mason's assertions on magnetism in 1761. He also designed an instrument, built by Jeremiah Sisson, that he claimed was a perpetual motion machine. He was the principal editor of *The Complete Dictionary of Arts and Sciences* (1766), a work of three folio volumes, which boasts a subscription list of more than 1000.

In August 1769 Croker became rector of St Peter's Church in Ightam, Kent, which he vacated in 1773, probably because of his bankruptcy. He became rector of St John's, Capisterre, St Kitts, in the West Indies, where he published a collection of four sermons (*c*.1790). He probably died in 1790 in St Kitts.

THOMPSON COOPER, rev. ADAM JACOB LEVIN

Sources *Old Westminsters*, 1.233–4 · Venn, *Alum. Cant.* · Foster, *Alum. Oxon.* · *GM*, 1st ser., 43 (1773), 416 · E. Hasted, *The history and topographical survey of the county of Kent*, 2 (1782), 249 · D. J. O'Donoghue, *The poets of Ireland: a biographical and bibliographical dictionary* (1912), 88 · P. Fara, *Sympathetic attractions: magnetic practices, beliefs, and symbolism in eighteenth-century England* (1996), 58–60 · Boswell, *Life*, 4.473–5

Croker, Thomas Crofton (1798–1854), antiquary, was born in Buckingham Square, Cork, on 15 January 1798 to a respectable family of limited means. His father, Thomas Croker (1761–1818), had seen extensive active service in the army and retired in ill health as a brevet major in 1802; in 1786 he had married Maria Fitton, the daughter of Croker Dillon of Baltidaniel, co. Cork. Croker's only sibling, Caroline (or Catherine), married Charles Eyre Coote (1801–1858) and died in 1878. Croker's mother died just three years before he did.

After an irregular local education, Croker entered the Cork mercantile firm of Lecky and Mark in 1813, but soon displayed greater interest in artistic and antiquarian pursuits. His excursions in the Munster countryside between 1812 and 1815, and again (with members of the Nicholson family) in 1821, provided the materials for his early and best publications. After Major Croker's death his widow applied on behalf of her only son to John Wilson Croker, then secretary to the Admiralty, who obtained a clerkship for him in February 1819. (There seems to have been no family connection between the secretary and the new clerk.) Introduction of lithography into the Admiralty's office practice was an early achievement of Croker, who contributed several articles to the *Gentleman's Magazine* about the time of his marriage in 1830 to Marianne [**Marianne Croker** (1791/2–1854)], daughter of the watercolourist Francis Nicholson (1753–1844); they had one son, Thomas Francis Dillon Croker (1831–1912). Like her father, Marianne Croker was a painter, and apparently exhibited two Scottish landscapes in 1815. As well as providing illustrations, she was a substantial collaborator in her husband's literary work, but received little public acknowledgement. She died on 6 October 1854, less than two months after he did.

Apart from some effusions as a teenager, Croker's significant work began after his removal from Ireland to London. *Researches in the South of Ireland* (1824) included a valuable memoir (by Mrs Jane Adams) of events in co. Wexford during the 1798 rising. *Fairy Legends and Traditions of the South of Ireland* (3 vols., 1825–8) first appeared anonymously. Said to be the first collection of oral legends published in the British Isles, it was praised by Walter Scott and translated into German by the brothers Grimm (1826); a French edition was published in 1828. Other historical and ethnographical publications followed sporadically, together with contributions to Irish archaeology and the study of English drama. In 1827 Croker was elected fellow of the Society of Antiquaries of London and member of the Royal Irish Academy. In scholarship he is remembered as the first editor of Philip Massinger's *Believe as you List* (written *c*.1631, published 1849), though John Payne Collier (1789–1883) criticized the edition severely at the time. His *The Memoirs of Joseph Holt* (2 vols., 1838), long used by historians of the 1798 rising and of the early penal settlements in Australia, has recently been exposed as editorially unsound and a misrepresentation of its subject. Croker's original literary compositions do not reward scrutiny.

An assessment of Croker's diverse interests might initially focus on his relationship with Thomas Moore (1779–1852). When Moore's *Irish Melodies* were in train, young Croker had sent the poet some material gathered in his Munster travels, and received an invitation to England in return. For over thirty years he combined several careers—as minor writer and literary host, as indefatigable researcher, as Admiralty clerk—without ever transcending the emotional and intellectual limitations of drawing-room song. At the end of his life Croker (by his own account) was working on a biography of Moore, whom he termed 'an actor—a hypocrite—a swindler—a sensualist and a habitual liar' (*Irish Book Lover*, 50). Moore was two years dead, but Croker's *Life* never saw the light of day.

Between 1837 and 1846 the Crokers lived at Rosamond's Bower, Fulham, near London, entertaining extensively and collecting antiquities. (A brief account of the house, privately circulated in 1842, was later incorporated into *A Walk from London to Fulham*, 1860.) Croker helped to found the Camden Society in 1839, and was even more energetic in setting up the Percy Society, of which he was an active member for many years. He joined the committee of the British Archaeological Association on its establishment in 1843. To these (sometimes fractious) activities was added extensive contribution to journals, notably *Fraser's Magazine*. His salary at the Admiralty rose to £800 p.a., before he was required to retire in February 1850 as senior clerk, first class, on a pension of £580.

Croker was of slight build and was described by Walter Scott as 'little as a dwarf, keen-eyed as a hawk, and of easy, prepossessing manners' (Hogan, 297). His last years were troubled by gout, which had attacked him as early as 1828. His mother's death in 1851 led to a strange correspondence (see BL, Egerton MS 2845, fols. 278–81) with the head of the British Museum's manuscript department, Sir Frederic Madden, to whom Croker announced the likely discovery of a *Tempest* by Shakespeare written before 1588, preserved in his parents' library. In September 1853 he was planning a trip to Ireland, but neither this nor the *Tempest* text appears to have materialized. After a short illness Croker died on 8 August 1854 at 3 Gloucester Road, Old Brompton, Middlesex, his home for several years. His son, Thomas Francis Dillon Croker, was employed by a shipping agency, and did not share his interests. The prompt auctioning of Croker's books and antiquities, conducted just before Christmas 1854, suggests a need for funds. Two lots constituted collections of material for works in progress—a history of ballads and popular song in Ireland (lot 275) and 'a history of the origin and progress of the art of lithography' (lot 869 in two boxes). The former was purchased, together with miscellaneous papers, by the British Museum. The National Library of Ireland possesses a bound collection of *c*.200 letters and sundry documents (Joly MSS 1): other materials have been dispersed.

As an ethnographer, Croker had insufficient interest in comparisons: his library contained virtually no foreign books. Though he knew some Gaelic, he was greatly inferior to scholars such as John O'Donovan (1809–1861), who were revolutionizing the study of Irish antiquity. In 1888 W. B. Yeats, who had drawn on Croker's *Fairy Legends*, wrote of him harshly and inaccurately as having 'the dash as well as the shallowness of an ascendant and idle class'. He also charged Croker with being 'continually guilty of that great sin against art—the sin of rationalism' (Thuente, 93). Douglas Hyde (1860–1949) was more sympathetic in *Beside the Fire* (1890).   **W. J. McCormack**

Sources *DNB* · R. Welch, ed., *The Oxford companion to Irish literature* (1996) · M. H. Thuente, *W. B. Yeats and Irish folklore* (1980) · B. G. MacCarthy, 'Thomas Crofton Croker, 1798–1854', *Studies*, 32 (1943), 539–56 · R. Hogan, ed., *Dictionary of Irish literature*, rev. edn, 1 (1996), 297–8 · R. O'Donnell and B. Reece, 'A clean beast: Crofton Croker's fairy tale of General Holt', *Eighteenth-Century Ireland*, 7 (1992), 7–42 · D. Hyde, *Beside the fire* (1890) · T. C. Croker, *Fairy legends … with a short memoir of the author by his son* (1859) [T. F. D. Croker] · T. C. Croker, *A walk from London to Fulham*, ed. T. F. D. Croker (1860) · Irish *Book Lover*, 15 (1925), 49–52 · 'Nicholson, Francis (1753–1844)', *DNB* · d. cert. [Marianne Croker]

Archives BL, collections relating to Irish ballads, Add. MSS 20091–20099 · Cork City Library, corresp. · Harvard U., Houghton L., collection of materials etc · NL Ire., letters · Princeton University Library, New Jersey, papers · S. Antiquaries, Lond., diary | BL, letters, as a sponsor, to the Royal Literary Fund, loan no. 96 · Bodl. Oxf., letters to Disraeli · Bodl. Oxf., letters to Isaac Disraeli · Dublin corporation, letters to Richard Caulfield · GL, corresp. with Frederick William Fairholt · Hammersmith and Fulham Archives and Local History Centre, corresp. with T. E. Hook and T. E. Bayliss · NL Scot., corresp. with William Blackwood & Sons · RBG Kew, letters, mostly to Sir William Hooker · TCD, letters to Sir W. Betham and Herbert Hore · U. Edin. L., corresp. with James Halliwell-Phillipps

Likenesses D. Maclise, drawing, 1827, V&A · Irish school, etching (after C. Grey?), NG Ire.; repro. in *Dublin University Magazine*, 34 (1849) · D. Maclise, lithograph, BM, NPG; repro. in *Fraser's Magazine*, 2 (1831) · D. Maclise, pencil study, V&A · D. Maclise, watercolour study, Norwich Castle Museum · oils, NPG

Crokesley, Richard de. *See* Croxley, Richard of (*d*. 1258).

Croll, Francis (*bap*. **1826**, *d*. **1854**), engraver, was baptized on 5 February 1826 in Musselburgh, Midlothian, the son of Francis Croll and his wife, Elspeth, *née* Baird. At a very early age his talent for drawing attracted the notice of the Scottish sculptors Alexander and John Ritchie, who urged his friends to cultivate it. He was accordingly articled about 1841 to the draughtsman and naturalist Thomas Dobbie of Edinburgh, who was not well known as an engraver. The death of his master about 1846 before the completion of his apprenticeship led to Croll's being placed for two years to study line engraving under Robert Charles Bell, and during the same time he also attended the Trustees' Academy, then under the direction of Sir William Allan. Croll engraved both figures and portraits for Edinburgh publishers. His earliest works included some plates of animals for Henry Stephens's *Book of the Farm* (3 vols., 1844), numerous portraits for *Hogg's Weekly Instructor* (1845–59), and a small plate from James Drummond's picture of *The Escape of Hamilton of Bothwellhaugh*. Between 1850 and 1852 he exhibited at the Royal Scottish Academy mostly sketches from nature in Argyll and Perthshire. In 1852 he executed for the *Art Journal* an engraving of *The Tired Soldier*, after the picture by Frederick Goodall formerly in the Vernon Gallery, which was published in *The Vernon Gallery of British Art*, ed. S. C. Hall (3 vols., 1854). He also engraved for the Royal Association for the Promotion of Fine Arts in Scotland one of a series of designs by John Faed to illustrate *The Cottar's Saturday Night* of Robert Burns. During the progress of this plate Croll developed heart disease, and soon after its completion a promising career was ended by his premature death, in Edinburgh, on 12 February 1854, at the early age of twenty-seven. Two of his engravings are in the City of Edinburgh collection. Others may be found in the print rooms of the Victoria and Albert Museum and the British Museum.

R. E. Graves, *rev*. Greg Smith

Sources *The Scotsman* (18 Feb 1854) · *Art Journal*, 16 (1854), 119 · B. Hunnisett, *A dictionary of British steel engravers* (1980) · B. Hunnisett, *An illustrated dictionary of British steel engravers*, new edn (1989) · P. J. M. McEwan, *Dictionary of Scottish art and architecture* (1994)

Archives BM, department of prints and drawings · Museum of Edinburgh, City of Edinburgh collection · V&A, department of prints and drawings

Croll, James (1821–1890), geologist and climatologist, was born on 2 January 1821 at St Martin's, Perthshire, the second of four sons of David Croll, a stonemason of Little Whitefield, Perthshire, and his wife, Janet Ellis of Elgin. Both his parents were devout Scottish Congregationalists. Croll attended the village school, then stumbled from occupation to occupation—journeyman millwright, joiner, shopkeeper, hotelier, life assurance agent—in part due to injuries and illnesses; he returned to Scotland in 1858 from his last post in Leicester, because the health of his wife, Isabella, daughter of John Macdonald of Forres, whom he had married on 11 September 1848, had begun to fail.

In 1859 Croll obtained a position as keeper at the Andersonian Museum in Glasgow through the intervention of Walter Crum of Thornliebank, father-in-law of William Thomson (Lord Kelvin). Turning over most of the position's duties to his disabled younger brother David, whom he supported, Croll was left with the leisure to pursue varied scientific interests and develop his, at times, metaphysical, principally theistic, views. In the 1860s he began publishing several series of papers, primarily in the *Philosophical Magazine*, that had a profound impact on physical geology. This impact, measured, in part, by his showing the efficacy of applying simple mathematical arguments to geological questions and spurring further the development of quantitative methods, is especially surprising as Croll was largely an autodidact with no formal training in mathematics, physics, or geology. The value of his researches was quickly recognized by such leading Scottish scientists as Archibald Geikie (1835–1924), Andrew Ramsay (1814–1891), and Thomson, who were instrumental in securing Croll a job as secretary to the geological survey of Scotland in 1867. His various series culminated in the duly influential *Climate and Time in their Geological Relations* (1875). The following year he became FRS as well as an LLD of St Andrews. Over the years he also won three funds' awards from the Geological Society of London. Persisting ill health and a mild stroke forced his early retirement from the geological survey after 1880.

Croll's final ten years were as difficult financially as his earlier ones had been, with a niggardly pension and an annuity purchased with the help of his scientific colleagues. However, the heart disease from which he suffered did not affect his mind, and he continued publishing geological, cosmological, and metaphysical speculations. In addition to *Climate and Time*, Croll published two other, largely cumulative, scientific books, two treatises on metaphysics, and some eighty-seven scientific papers. He died from heart disease in Perth on 15 December 1890.

Croll's odd genius lay in striking a reverberant chord in several key problem areas of the 1860s and thereby successfully carving out a peculiar niche in the scientific environment, aided by the fluidity of disciplinary boundaries of his time. Among his contributions are papers on the influence of the tidal wave on the earth's rotation, his estimation of the rate of subaerial denudation, and his general advocacy of a limited geological time-scale (Croll was an early convert to Thomson's 100 million year geochronology). However, Croll's most important work focused on physical climatology: the physical causes of climatic change during geological epochs, the question of the Glacial submergence, and physical theories of ocean currents in which he engaged W. B. Carpenter's thermohaline, or density, theory with his own advocacy of wind stress.

The 1860s and 1870s saw renewed interest in astronomical and physical causes of glaciations. Geologists had long laboured to explain the existence of extremely cold glacial conditions in now-temperate latitudes, and the remains of subtropical flora in polar regions. Following an abandoned 1830 suggestion of Sir John Herschel, Croll advanced in a seminal *Philosophical Magazine* paper of 1864 (on the physical cause of the change of climate during geological epochs) the theory that global weather patterns would be indirectly affected by the periodic changes in the eccentricity of the earth's orbit about the sun, for a winter occurring when the earth was in the aphelion of its most eccentric orbit would be bitterly cold, and this would set in motion a chain of large-scale climatic changes resulting in large tracts of glacial land ice—an ice age. Croll postulated a global climatic feedback system, resting on the combined proven physical phenomena of the variation of eccentricity, the precession of the equinoxes, and the motion of the apsides of the orbit itself. Such a system accounted for cyclic global climate patterns, explaining both the occurrence of glaciations and intervening equable periods such as the Carboniferous. Indeed, Croll believed that if enough land ice formed, the earth's centre of gravity could shift, making the ensuing climatic changes even more severe. Croll's various theories proved influential at the time, attracting the attention, and often the approbation, of Charles Darwin, Archibald and James Geikie, Sir Charles Lyell, A. R. Wallace, and Thomson, among others. Although Croll left unanswered many questions in this new branch of physical geology and proffered numerous insupportable speculations, his kernels of insight into the accumulation of subtle variations affecting climate over time have regrettably been forgotten.

DAVID KUSHNER

Sources D. Kushner, 'The emergence of geophysics in nineteenth century Britain', PhD diss., Princeton University, 1990 · J. Horne, *Transactions of the Geological Society of Edinburgh*, 6 (1892), 170–87 · J. D. Burchfield, *Lord Kelvin and the age of the earth* (1975) · H. C. Burstyn, 'Croll, James', *DSB* · J. C. Irons, *Autobiographical sketch of James Croll with memoir of his life and work* (1896) · D. Kushner, 'Sir George Darwin and a British school of geophysics', *Osiris*, 2nd ser., 8 (1993), 196–223 · C. Smith and M. N. Wise, *Energy and empire: a biographical study of Lord Kelvin* (1989) · C. Hamlin, 'James Geikie, James Croll, and the eventful Ice Age', *Annals of Science*, 39 (1982), 565–83 · *CCI* (1891) · *DNB*

Archives BL, corresp., Add. MS 41077 | BGS, letters to B. N. Peach · CUL, G. H. Darwin MSS · RS, Herschel MSS · U. Edin. L., special collections division, corresp. with Sir Charles Lyell

Likenesses photograph, repro. in Horne, *Transactions of the Geological Society of Edinburgh* · portrait, repro. in Irons, *Autobiographical sketch*

Wealth at death £388 0s. 6d.: confirmation, 19 Jan 1891, CCI

Crolly, William (1780–1849), Roman Catholic archbishop of Armagh, was born at Ballykilbeg near Downpatrick, co. Down, on 8 June 1780, the son of John Crolly, a tenant farmer, and his wife, Mary, née Maxwell. He was educated at the classical school in Downpatrick, which was conducted by Dr James Neilson, the Presbyterian minister of the town. In 1801 he entered St Patrick's College, the recently established Roman Catholic seminary at Maynooth, and five years later was ordained priest. From 1806 to 1812 he taught logic, ethics, and metaphysics in Maynooth. In 1812 he took charge of the parish of Belfast, where Catholics numbered about one-sixth of the population of 28,000.

Crolly's urbane and conciliatory manner greatly eased his way into the predominantly Presbyterian society of Belfast. He participated actively in the social and welfare societies of the town and served on the board of governors of schools, public charities, and the General Hospital. Inter-denominational relations were good and protestants contributed generously to the collection for the erection of a second Catholic church in Belfast in 1815.

On 1 February 1825 Crolly was appointed bishop of his native diocese of Down and Connor—an appointment that was warmly received by both Catholics and protestants—and remained in charge of Belfast. The movement for Catholic emancipation was gathering strength, and to promote it he worked closely with the leading liberal Presbyterians, one of whom, Henry Montgomery, advocated it at public meetings in St Patrick's Catholic Church in 1828 and 1829. Opposition to emancipation, the expansion of biblical and educational societies hostile to Catholicism, and the growth of the Catholic proportion of the population to one-third increased sectarian tensions. By the time of Crolly's appointment as archbishop of Armagh, on 12 April 1835, relations between protestant and Catholic in Belfast had deteriorated. In Armagh, Crolly founded St Patrick's College, a Catholic secondary school for boys, in 1838, and on 17 March 1840 he laid the foundation stone of St Patrick's Cathedral. But work on this project was interrupted by the great famine of 1845–9.

Unlike the majority of his episcopal colleagues Crolly did not support O'Connell's campaign for the repeal of the Union in the 1840s. He became involved in public controversy with his colleagues on three issues that split the hierarchy in that decade: national education, the Charitable Bequests Act, and the Queen's Colleges. In the first he defended the national system of education, which was founded in 1831 to educate children of all denominations together for moral and literary subjects but separately for religion, against Archbishop MacHale of Tuam, who charged that the system was dangerous to the faith of Catholic children. Crolly headed the majority of the prelates who won from Rome in 1841 permission to continue supporting the system, provided they adopted certain safeguards.

But as suspicion of British legislation among the bishops grew, Crolly found himself in a minority on the other two issues. The dispute over the Bequests Act (1844) centred on its refusal to recognize bequests to religious orders and on its non-recognition of legacies in land or property made within three months of the testator's death. To the annoyance of many of his colleagues Crolly accepted the act and became a commissioner of charitable bequests. The majority of the bishops opposed the Queen's Colleges (dubbed 'godless' by a tory MP in 1845) on the grounds that they had no real voice in the appointment of staff and in the material taught, especially in sensitive areas such as history, moral philosophy, and metaphysics, and that the arrangements for residence did not afford sufficient moral protection for Catholic students. The question was examined at length in Rome, and in a rescript sanctioned by Pope Pius IX and dated 9 October 1847 the bishops were admonished not to take any part in establishing the colleges, as institutions of that sort proved detrimental to religion. Instead, they were exhorted to found a Catholic university on the model of Louvain. Further representations to Rome by Crolly's party did not alter this decision.

Crolly contracted cholera, a pandemic which struck Ireland in December 1848, and died in Drogheda, co. Louth, on 6 April 1849. He was buried under the sanctuary of his unfinished cathedral in Armagh on 8 April 1849.

AMBROSE MACAULAY

Sources A. Macaulay, *William Crolly, archbishop of Armagh, 1835–49* (1994) · D. A. Kerr, *Peel, priests, and politics: Sir Robert Peel's administration and the Roman Catholic church in Ireland, 1841–1846* (1982) · P. J. Corish, *Maynooth College, 1795–1995* (1995) · D. A. Kerr, *A nation of beggars* (1994)

Archives Archives of the Sacred Congregation for the Evangelization of Peoples, Rome · Armagh Diocesan Archives, Armagh, episcopal corresp. and papers · Down and Connor Diocesan Archives, Belfast · NRA, corresp. and papers · Pontifical Irish College, Rome

Likenesses portrait, Archbishop's House, Ara Coeli, Armagh · portrait, Bishop's House, Somerton Road, Belfast · statue, St Patrick's Cathedral, Armagh

Croly, George (1780–1860), writer and Church of England clergyman, was born in Dublin on 17 August 1780 to a physician there. Of his ancestry, sources mention only a family long settled in northern Ireland, characterizing Croly himself as 'a living type of the Protestant and Orange party' (*Some Account*, 2.272). At fifteen he entered Trinity College, Dublin, where he distinguished himself in classical scholarship, composition, and speaking. His talents had been destined for the bar, but Croly inclined to the church and, on earning his MA in 1804, was ordained in the Church of Ireland by Bishop T. L. O'Beirne of Meath. His first curacy, in northern Ireland, affording little scope for ambition, Croly moved to London about 1810, accompanied by two unmarried sisters and his mother (d. 1832), now a widow.

By 1813 Croly had emerged as a theatre critic for *The Times* and later for the *New Times* (published 1817–28). His own verse tragedy of 1822, *Catiline*, failed when staged in 1827, but his comedy of 1824, *Pride Shall have a Fall*, enjoyed a successful run. In April 1813 *The Times* assigned him as foreign correspondent to Hamburg or Paris. He had

George Croly (1780–1860), by William Brockedon, 1832

returned to London by 1817, when William Jerdan became editor of the *Literary Gazette* and invited Croly to contribute poetry and criticism. That year witnessed Croly's first successful poem, *Paris in 1815* (1817, 1821). This, like his later verse tales, appropriates the Byronic manner for a tory argument, thus unifying (according to John Wilson Croker's review) the 'splendid in imagination' with 'what is right in politics' (Croker, 229). The poem earned Croly a lampoon in *Don Juan* but also an influential position in the Royal Society of Literature.

In 1819 Croly married the daughter of a Scottish official with the Board of Trade, Margaret Helen Begbie (d. 1851), a minor fellow contributor to the *Literary Gazette*. Accounts disagree, but their family probably grew to five sons and two daughters.

In 1819–20 Croly edited a tory weekly, *The Constitution*, and then in 1820 joined the writers for *Blackwood's Magazine*. For thirty-six years he contributed poetry, fiction, historical essays, and reviews, prolifically and staunchly promoting ultra-toryism and ultra-protestantism. These views were delivered with notorious fierceness, heightened when delivered in person by his formidable, bulky features. Equally reputed for eloquence, Croly's style, as George Gilfillan put it, 'loves the magnificent too exclusively' and 'wants repose' (p. 232). None the less, his exaggerated rhetoric and bitter satire can prove strengths in his fiction. He wrote many short tales for *Blackwood's*, as well as the *Tales of the Great St. Bernard* (1828); *Marston* (1843–5), a romance of the French Revolution; and the novel *Salathiel* (1828), his most enduring work, which traces the Wandering Jew through history.

Croly's theatricality and ferocity were contradicted by his personal reserve. A 'shy' and 'ungainly' man as recalled by Croker (J. W. Croker, *Correspondence and Diaries*, 2 vols., ed. L. J. Jennings, 1884, 2.60), Croly incessantly admonished *Blackwood's* to safeguard his anonymity, and he repulsed offers by Samuel Carter Hall to write a biographical sketch of his career. Croly must have shunned publicity lest it jeopardize his preferment in the Church of England, which had long eluded him. According to the *Gentleman's Magazine*, an attempt by Jerdan to intercede with the lord chancellor, John Scott, Lord Eldon, ironically foundered on confusion of Croly's name with that of a convert from Roman Catholicism. Later, in 1834, while serving as temporary vicar of Romford, Essex (1832–5), Croly was offered the living of Bondleigh by Lord Chancellor Henry Brougham (a whig, but a relative of Croly's wife). Croly refused, however, to be banished to a remote edge of Dartmoor. At last, in 1835, Brougham's successor, John Singleton Copley, Lord Lyndhurst, appointed Croly to the combined London parish of St Benet and St Stephen, with its fine Wren church in Walbrook.

Now appointed rector of St Stephen and awarded an honorary DD by Trinity in 1831, 'Dr Croly' secured dignity and more liberty to pursue theological writing. His sermons and commentaries, given to interpreting political events as apocalyptic signs—as in the *Apocalypse of St John* (1827) and *Divine Providence, or, The Three Cycles of Revelation* (1834)—seemed to James Grant to sacrifice evangelical to political causes. Croly persisted in writing leading articles for the tory weekly *Britannia* between 1839 and 1846 and may have been its editor. He also at various times edited literary annuals, the *Universal Review*, and, possibly, the *New Monthly Magazine*; and he contributed to the *London Magazine*, *Morning Herald*, *The Standard*, *Church Quarterly Review*, and *Bentley's Miscellany*.

Croly's influence proved ultimately negative, even on sympathizers. A frequent house guest of the Ruskins, and a contributor to literary annuals that were introducing the young John Ruskin, Croly must have impressed the elder Ruskin as an ideal model for his son. Here was an ambitious tory clergyman who, as John James Ruskin hoped for his son, could write 'poetry as good as Byron's, only pious' (Ruskin, *Works*, ed. E. T. Cook and A. Wedderburn, 1903–11, 35.185). As Ruskin matured, however, he came to regard Croly as prone to sensationalism and lacking in 'earnestness' (*Ruskin in Italy*, ed. H. I. Shapiro, 1972, 241).

In the 1840s Croly was tried by controversy and bereavement. For some years after 1843 his income suffered in litigation against a dishonest and powerful churchwarden, Alderman Michael Gibbs. In 1847 Croly was appointed afternoon preacher at the Foundling Hospital, only to resign within a few months, indignant that his sermons were criticized as too abstruse. In 1845 his eldest son, George, was killed at the age of twenty-three in India when in action against the Sikhs; and in 1851 he lost both his wife and his youngest daughter. Croly's final years, however, were quiet and contented. He died suddenly of heart disease on 24 November 1860 while walking alone in Holborn and was buried in his own church, St Stephen Walbrook. DAVID C. HANSON

Sources F. W. Croly, 'Biographical sketch', in G. Croly, *The book of Job* (1863), v–xxviii · *GM*, 3rd ser., 10 (1861), 104–7 · R. Herring, *A few personal recollections of the late Rev George Croly, with extracts from his speeches and writings* (1861) · *DNB* · W. R. Thompson, 'The letters of George Croly to William Blackwood and his sons', 2 vols., PhD diss., Texas Technological College, June 1957 · D. C. Hanson, 'George Croly', *British short-fiction writers, 1800–1880*, ed. J. R. Greenfield, DLitB, 159 (1996), 69–83 [incl. the most complete bibliography] · *Some account of my life and writings: an autobiography by the late Sir Archibald Alison*, ed. Lady Alison, 2 (1883), 272–3 · [J. W. Croker], review of *Paris: a poem*, *QR*, 17 (1817), 218–29 · G. Gilfillan, *Sketches of modern literature, and eminent literary men*, 2 vols. (New York, 1846), 231–7 · *CGPLA Eng. & Wales* (1861) · *Literary Gazette*
Archives BL, letters, as a sponsor, to the Royal Literary Fund, loan no. 96 · Bodl. Oxf., William Jerdan corresp. · NL Scot., letters to William Blackwood & Sons
Likenesses W. Brockedon, chalk drawing, 1832, NPG [*see illus.*] · W. Stevenson, line engraving, pubd 1840 (after J. Kirkwood), NPG · W. Behnes, marble bust, c.1855, St Stephen's Church, Walbrook · C. Baugniet, lithograph, BM · R. Beard, photograph, repro. in *ILN* (29 April 1854) · engraving? (after photograph), repro. in Herring, *A few personal recollections*, frontispiece · engraving?, repro. in *ILN* (20 April 1844) · print (after daguerreotype by R. Beard), NPG; repro. in *ILN* (1854)
Wealth at death under £8000: probate, 4 Feb 1861, *CGPLA Eng. & Wales*

Crom, Mattheus (c.1505x10–1546?). *See under* Mierdman, Steven (c.1510x12–1559).

Cromarty. For this title name *see* Mackenzie, George, first earl of Cromarty (1630–1714); Mackenzie, George, styled third earl of Cromarty (c.1703–1766); Mackenzie, John, Lord Macleod, and Count Cromarty in the Swedish nobility (1727–1789).

Crombie, Alexander (1760–1840), philologist and schoolmaster, was born in Aberdeen, the son of Thomas Crombie. He was educated at Marischal College, Aberdeen, where he graduated MA in 1778, and he received the degree of LLD from the same source in 1794. Although licensed by the Church of Scotland, Crombie did not proceed to ordination but pursued a successful career as a schoolmaster. With a Mr Hogg, he briefly ran an academy in Aberdeen before moving to Highgate, Middlesex, where he also officiated as pastor of a Presbyterian meeting-house in Southwood Lane. He later kept a school at Greenwich, where he purchased a mansion on the site of the old powder magazine. When Crombie gave up the school, after seventeen years, the mansion and its grounds were sold piecemeal and for considerable profit. His cousin Alexander Crombie (d. 1832), an advocate and land agent in Aberdeen, was also laird of Phesdo and Thornton in Kincardineshire. His estates, which had undergone considerable improvements over a period of years, passed to Crombie on his death. Crombie married Jane Hendry and was survived by her, a daughter, and three sons, the eldest of whom, Alexander (d. 1877), succeeded him in his estates.

Early in life Crombie became acquainted with eminent men such as Alexander Geddes, Richard Price, and Joseph Priestley. His first major published work, *An Essay on Philosophical Necessity*, appeared in 1793 but Crombie was perhaps best known for his *Gymnasium, sive, Symbola critica* (1812) which laid down rules for Latin composition and went through numerous editions, as did his *Etymology and Syntax of the English Language Explained* (1802). His two-volume *Natural Theology* (1829) was hailed as 'the most comprehensive view of the whole science of natural theology that has hitherto appeared' (*QR*, 213) and a significant development of the arguments of William Paley. In addition to these more substantial works, Crombie also contributed articles to the *Analytical Review* and issued a number of publications addressing themselves to matters of current controversy, such as *A letter to D Ricardo, esq., containing an analysis of his pamphlet on the depreciation of bank notes* (1817). His last such work, in 1837, was on the demoralizing effects of the ballot.

His friend John Grant wrote of Crombie as 'a man of the most inflexible honour and integrity. He possessed in the highest degree a keen and penetrating intellect'. Yet while Grant considered him a friend of civil and religious liberty, that view was tempered by the fact that:

> as a sound Christian divine, and a sincere admirer of the British constitution, he honestly despised, and indignantly repudiated, the cant of spurious liberality, both in religion and politics, which has in later years so extensively tainted the human mind. (*The Times*)

Crombie died at his home in York Terrace, Regent's Park, London, on 11 June 1840, and was buried at Marylebone church. LIONEL ALEXANDER RITCHIE

Sources *The Times* (16 June 1840) · *GM*, 2nd ser., 18 (1842), 433–4 · *GM*, 2nd ser., 14 (1840), 216 · Burke, *Gen. GB* (1886) · C. A. Mollyson, *The parish of Fordoun* (1893), 250 · W. R. Fraser, *History of the parish and burgh of Laurencekirk* (1880), 93 · F. H. Groome, ed., *Ordnance gazetteer of Scotland*, 6 vols. (1882–5), vol. 6, p. 437 · *The new statistical account of Scotland*, 11 (1845) · *QR*, 51 (1834), 213–28 · *EdinR*, 54 (1831), 147–59 · personal knowledge (1888) [*DNB*] · Allibone, *Dict.* · U. Aberdeen, Fasti of Marischal College
Likenesses portrait, pubd 1832 (after miniature by W. Booth) · R. J. Lane, drawing on stone

Crombie, Alistair Cameron (1915–1996), historian of science, the second son of William David Crombie (d. 1949) and Janet Wilmina, *née* Macdonald (d. 1975), was born on 4 November 1915 in Brisbane, Australia. His parents, who were of Scottish extraction, had established a farmstead at the remote Maranthona, near Longreach (precisely on the tropic of Capricorn, in Queensland). After school at Geelong grammar school Crombie began his university career at Trinity College, University of Melbourne, as a medical student, graduating in zoology in 1938. Continuing his studies in England at Jesus College, Cambridge, he proceeded to a doctorate in 1942 with a dissertation on population dynamics—a fact that helps to explain his lifelong interest in the history of Darwinism. By this time he was occupying a temporary research position with the Ministry of Agriculture and Fisheries in the Cambridge Zoological Laboratory. He married on 3 December 1943 Nancy Hey (1914–1993), a graduate of Girton College who undertook war work in Cambridge collecting statistics for the Ministry of Agriculture; she was the daughter of Donald Hey, a wool manufacturer, of Helperby, Yorkshire. In 1944 they both became converts to Roman Catholicism, she first and he later 'with difficulty'.

At Cambridge, Crombie studied philosophy informally with C. D. Broad, who helped to turn him in the direction of the history and philosophy of science. In 1946 he was appointed to teach and direct research in those subjects at University College, London, then one of the main centres in Britain for the teaching of the history and philosophy of science. While there he helped to found the British Society for the History of Science (1946), of which he was made president in 1964. He was also a founder of its Philosophy of Science Group, which later became an independent body as the British Society for the Philosophy of Science. He was the first editor of its journal, the *British Journal for the Philosophy of Science* (1949), and was later a joint founder and editor of another influential journal, *History of Science* (1962).

In 1953 Crombie was appointed lecturer in the history of science at Oxford, where there were already plans afoot to teach the subject to undergraduates in science, history, and philosophy. He moved to Oxford in 1954, after a year as visiting professor at the University of Washington, Seattle. He soon established an influential seminar in the history of science; although originally intended for philosophy undergraduates, it quickly became the centre of gravity of the subject for people from other faculties. It was always well attended by a number of notable senior scholars, several of them visitors to Oxford from elsewhere. First held in the Old Ashmolean building, and later in All Souls, the seminar was moved in 1969 to Trinity College, when Crombie was made a fellow there.

The ambitions that had prompted the rapid growth of the history and philosophy of science in the 1950s changed in many respects during the following decade. Crombie found himself faced with the disparate wishes of three very different social groups, for whose needs it was impossible to cater simultaneously. Some of the most regular attenders at his weekly seminar (for many years run jointly with J. D. North and later Wilma Crowther) were from the natural sciences. They valued the subject for its bridging function between 'the two cultures', one of the reasons why the intellectual net was cast very wide. Crombie's broad outlook did not, however, always fit comfortably with the needs of the various honour schools that called on his services. He established successful undergraduate courses for the faculties of history and the natural sciences, but he left the teaching to others. The scientists, the historians, and the philosophers all had very different interests and expectations, and—despite the efforts of such enlightened colleagues as Friedrich Waismann, William Kneale, George Temple, and his nearest colleague in the philosophy of science, Rom Harré—it proved impossible to hammer out the notion of a single discipline that could hold the allegiance of those in the university whose support he most needed.

Some opposed the subject on the grounds that it was an administrative inconvenience. Crombie's earlier concern with medieval science, combined with his low-key Catholicism, was presented by some as a sign of a Catholic plot to infiltrate the curriculum. Others had their own plans for academic dominion, and Crombie was not always a good judge of the territorial ambitions of his colleagues. He was happiest creating a focus for research at an advanced level and was not greatly attracted to undergraduate teaching, nor was he successful at that level. His idea of a diploma in the history and philosophy of science, meant as a prior qualification for doctoral work, had limited success. It introduced many now senior historians of science to the field; but again there arose the problem of enforced breadth, and not a few students from the direction of history and the then fashionable social sciences made known their displeasure at the idea that they should be obliged to study philosophy of science. When the Oxford chair in history of science was eventually created and filled (1971–2), the part Crombie had played in building up the subject counted for little on a committee that had a narrower view of the field than his. To the great surprise of most outsiders, he was passed over. He nevertheless continued to act as a magnet to scholars from elsewhere who knew him either personally or through his writings, and, as far as reputation was concerned, the subject in Oxford continued to be associated with him more than any other person.

As a historian of science Crombie's central interest was in the methods and modes of scientific thinking and reasoning as these developed within the intellectual context of medieval and early modern Europe. This was his outlook when writing his first book, *Augustine to Galileo: the History of Science, AD 400–1650* (1952, expanded in 1959). Translated into seven languages, it became one of the world's most widely used textbooks in its subject. He took a similar approach in his *Robert Grosseteste and the Origins of Experimental Science, 1100–1700* (1953), where he made an analysis of the question of continuity and change in the European scientific tradition from the middle ages to the seventeenth century. Crombie's view of his subject is nowhere more evident than in his monumental *Styles of scientific thinking in the European tradition: the history of argument and explanation especially in the mathematical and biomedical sciences and arts* (3 vols., 1994). In this he made a detailed comparative analysis of the forms of scientific reasoning developed within European intellectual culture, beginning with the Greek search for the principles of nature and argument, and adopting a similar approach to an ever wider variety of historical material.

This three-volume summary of a lifetime's work and ideals, which was well received within his profession, reveals also Crombie's abiding interest in the history of theories of the senses—echoing his earlier work in biology—and in particular the physiology and epistemology of vision and hearing, and their relation to the visual and musical arts. These are subjects touched upon in his numerous other publications—for example, in the two published volumes of his collected essays—but they run through another of Crombie's studies, one that occupied much of the last thirty years of his life. Awarded the Galileo prize by the Domus Galileana in Pisa in 1964 for an essay on Galileo, Crombie became a leading authority on that crucially important figure. His Galileo interest also made Oxford a natural place to set up the Harriot Seminar in 1967, which was done with the collaboration of several distinguished Harriot scholars and the financial support of the London mathematician Cicely Tanner.

Crombie long planned to publish two other books, 'Galileo's arguments and disputes in natural philosophy' and 'Marin Mersenne: science, music and language'. His final illness took him unawares, and they were never completed. He became involved in much invigorating controversy in the course of writing on Galileo, with the result that his main theses are well known to a wide scholarly public. The essence of most of his unpublished material may be found in one form or another in his published writings. Throughout he treats of science as a rational and not merely a social activity.

Alistair Crombie was a writer of vision who influenced an entire generation, and he left his signature on the practice of the history of science in the world at large, as well as in Oxford. His circle of friends was great, nationally and internationally. He was president of the Académie Internationale d'Histoire des Sciences from 1968 to 1971. After retirement he took up a half-time appointment as professor of history of science and medicine at Smith College, Northampton, Massachusetts. He held several other visiting professorships and lectured in many countries. He was a fellow of the British Academy and held honorary doctorates of the universities of Durham, Paris X, and Sassari. Shortly before his death he was awarded the prestigious premio europeo Dondi (jointly with his old friend Marshall Clagett) for his life's work.

Crombie was a warm-hearted and unstinting friend to a large number of younger scholars, and a generous supporter of causes that he thought worthy. Among his recreations was landscape gardening, which he and his wife put into practice over forty years in the garden of their home, Orchard Lea, Boars Hill, Oxford. He died at home on 9 February 1996, and was buried beside his wife on 19 February at Ramsgill church in Yorkshire. He was survived by a daughter, three sons, and six grandchildren.   J. D. NORTH

Sources J. D. North and J. J. Roche, eds., *The light of nature: essays in the history and philosophy of science presented to A. C. Crombie* (Dordrecht, 1985) [incl. partial bibliography] · J. D. North, *PBA*, 97 (1998), 257–70 · personal knowledge (2004) · private information (2004) [Sophie Plender, daughter] · J. J. Roche, *The Independent* (8 April 1996)

Archives priv. coll., papers

Likenesses photograph, repro. in North, *PBA*

Wealth at death £748,170: probate, 30 April 1996, *CGPLA Eng. & Wales*

Crombie, James (1730–1790), non-subscribing Presbyterian minister and founder of the Belfast Academy, was born on 4 December 1730 at Perth, the eldest son of James Crambie, mason, and his wife, May Johnstoun. In 1748 he matriculated at St Andrews, and he graduated MA in 1752. He studied for a short time at Edinburgh on leaving St Andrews. He was licensed by Strathbogie presbytery on 8 June 1757 at Rothiemay, where he acted as parish schoolmaster. On 1 July 1760 he was presented to Lhanbryd, near Elgin, by the earl of Moray, in whose family he had acted as tutor, and having been duly called was ordained at Lhanbryd on 11 September by Elgin presbytery. Almost immediately he obtained permission from the Strathbogie presbytery to return to his studies, this time at Glasgow, where he matriculated in the same year and attended four sessions. A licentiate, James Thompson, was ordained by Strathbogie presbytery to supply his pulpit in Lhanbryd, but the protests of the Elgin presbytery, culminating in a formal censure on 1 March 1763, compelled Crombie to return to his parish.

In February 1768 a colleagueship in the First Presbyterian Congregation of Belfast became vacant. This was a New Light or non-subscribing congregation, and it seems very likely that Crombie was recommended for the position by Professor William Leechman of Glasgow, the leader of the moderate party in Scotland, who had himself earlier declined a call to the similarly non-subscribing Second Congregation in Belfast. Crombie did not, however, desert his charge at Lhanbryd until 22 October 1770, when he was already settled in Belfast as colleague to James Mackay. Four years after arriving in Belfast he married Elizabeth Simson (d. 1824), on 23 July 1774. Together they had four sons and one daughter. On Mackay's death (22 January 1781) Crombie became sole pastor. The congregation, which worshipped in a dilapidated meeting-house, was declining; Crombie met a suggestion for amalgamation with the Second Congregation by proposing the erection of a new meeting-house. The new church was designed by the local architect Roger Mulholland and cost £1923 7s. 9d., towards which Crombie gave a donation of 10 guineas and lent a sum of £276 18s. 5½d. John Wesley preached in the new building in 1789, when it was the only meeting-house in Belfast open to him, and described it as 'the completest place of worship I have ever seen' (8 June 1789, *Works of … John Wesley*, 4.461).

Crombie generally avoided theological disputes, though he went into print in 1777 with an *Essay on Church Consecration* to answer a charge of schism made by the vicar of Belfast. He was also a keen supporter of the volunteer movement and preached largely political and patriotic sermons before the Belfast companies on several occasions. Some of these sermons were printed, including a *Sermon on the Love of Country* (1778) and *The Expedience and Utility of Volunteer Associations for National Defence and Security* (1779). Most controversial, however, was *The propriety of setting apart a portion of the sabbath for the purpose of acquiring the knowledge and use of arms in times of public danger* (1781), which incurred the displeasure of many Presbyterians and was answered by Sinclair Kelburn, minister of the Third Congregation and himself also a volunteer, in *The Morality of the Sabbath Defended* (1781). In September 1783 he was made DD of St Andrews.

Crombie's most lasting contribution to his adopted home town was his founding of the Belfast Academy, one of the first attempts to establish an unsectarian higher educational college in Ulster. In 1784 the General Synod of Ulster, meeting at Magherafelt, Crombie being present, proposed that its members should consider establishing an academy, principally for the training of ministers. Crombie had been receiving students from Scotland and may have been already contemplating founding an academy. However, William Crawford of Strabane, another New Light minister and enthusiastic volunteer, was the first to open an academy and received the approval of the general synod in 1785. In September 1785 Crombie issued the prospectus for his academy (*Belfast News-Letter*, 9 Sept 1785), and soon secured the warm support of representatives of all denominations in Belfast. Funds were subscribed, the Killyleagh presbytery (then the most latitudinarian of those under the general synod) sending a donation of 100 guineas. The prospectus contemplated academic courses extending over three sessions. The scheme was ambitious, and included a provision of preparatory schools. The academy was opened in Donegall Street on 1 May 1786 with Crombie, as principal, undertaking classics, philosophy, and history. The Belfast Academy soon lost its collegiate classes, but as a high school it maintained itself, acquired great vogue under Crombie's successor, William Bruce (1757–1841), and flourished, acquiring the designation 'royal' in 1887.

Crombie's labours broke his strength, and his health declined; yet he continued to discharge all his engagements with unflagging spirit. On 10 February 1790 he attended a meeting of the Antrim presbytery, at which two congregations were added to its roll, and he was appointed to preside at an ordination on 4 March. On 1 March 1790 he died, and was buried in Belfast two days later.   ALEXANDER GORDON, *rev.* A. D. G. STEERS

Sources bap. reg. Scot. • A. Gordon, 'James Crombie, D.D.', *The Disciple*, 3 (1883), 93–101 • *Belfast News-Letter* (5 March 1790) • J. Bryson, 'Funeral sermon', Antrim Presbytery Library, MS QUB B3 XI 13 • J. M. Anderson, ed., *The matriculation roll of the University of St Andrews, 1747–1897* (1905), 2 • W. I. Addison, ed., *The matriculation albums of the University of Glasgow from 1728 to 1858* (1913), 63 • *Fasti Scot.*, new edn, 6.401 • minute books of the presbytery of Antrim, First Presbyterian Church archives, Rosemary Street, Belfast • minute books of the First Presbyterian Church, PRO NIre. • Belfast Academy prospectus, *Belfast News-Letter* (9 Sept 1785) • *The works of … John Wesley*, 4 (1872), 461 • *Records of the General Synod of Ulster, from 1691 to 1820*, 3 (1898), 69, 76, 80–81 • *The Drennan–McTier letters*, ed. J. Agnew, 3 vols. (1998–9)
Likenesses pencil drawing, First Presbyterian Church, Rosemary Street, Belfast

Crome, Edward (*d.* 1562), Church of England clergyman and religious controversialist, was probably born in Norfolk, and was educated at Cambridge, taking the degrees of BA in 1505, MA in 1508, BD in 1518, and BTh in 1526. In 1516 he was university preacher. He was a fellow of Gonville Hall (its refounder, John Caius, witnessed his will), and president of its dependency, Physwick Hostel. Years later Thomas Cranmer remembered that Crome's house was 'better ordered' than all others at the university. (*Miscellaneous Writings*, 161–2).

Like Cranmer, Crome spent much of his career quietly at Cambridge, until the urgency of the king's great matter plucked him away to greater and more dangerous opportunities. Crome was a prompt supporter of Henry VIII's divorce, and thus enjoyed Anne Boleyn's protection, but the erratic nature of Henry's shifts in religious policy meant that most protestant leaders had publicly to retract their opinions at least once. As the supreme practitioner of the equivocal recantation, Crome abjured four times, hedging and prevaricating, seeming to obey and deny simultaneously, a sophisticated strategy which many reformers, including Latimer and Cranmer, also employed.

By the beginning of 1531 Crome's evangelical sermons made him a favourite among London reformers, who felt that he spoke 'true' while all of the other preachers at Paul's Cross uttered 'nothing but lies and flatterings' (*Acts and Monuments*, 5.32). None of his sermons survives and the tenets he promoted must be glimpsed in the texts of his various recantations, biased though they are. He habitually preached against purgatory, the intercession of saints, pilgrimages, fasting, images, masses, and prayers for the dead, and the papal supremacy. Conservative critics, led by Archbishop William Warham and Bishop John Stokesley of London, levelled charges against him in March 1531. Astutely, Crome appealed to Henry to hear his case as supreme head of the church. Valuing Crome's abilities to preach in favour of the expansion of royal authority, and lending an ear to Anne's entreaties, the king released him with the proviso that he retract those opinions Henry felt were incorrect. Crome signed a prepared retraction, yet at Paul's Cross he denied the import of its articles. He issued his own written account of his positions to challenge the version printed by Stokesley, to obfuscate his opinions for his enemies. At this and his later recantations Crome relied upon his ability to say one thing, while all the while allowing his supporters to appreciate that he meant the exact opposite.

Although James Bainham (executed 1532) felt Crome 'spake against his conscience', and that his printed recantation was 'a very foolish thing' (*Acts and Monuments*, 4.699), a politic submission was no bar to further advancement. Crome was already the incumbent of St Antholin's in London. In May 1534 Anne obtained for him the living of one of the wealthiest churches in the city, St Mary Aldermary, so that he might encourage 'the furtherance of virtue, truth, and godly doctrine', an appointment he greeted with so much reluctance that she had to write to urge him to take up the living. (BL, Harley MS 6148, fols. 79v–80r). Prominent Londoners, including Humphrey Monmouth, asked Crome to preach at their funerals as a substitute for the traditional masses. On 9 February 1537 Bishop Nicholas Shaxton of Salisbury collated Crome to the prebend of South Grantham, seizing the opportunity to introduce him into an ecclesiastical peculiar in Lincolnshire, which formed part of the endowment of his own cathedral chapter. Under Crome's influence, Grantham became a pocket of reform inside a largely conservative diocese. Cranmer tried, without success, to make Crome dean of the new foundation of Canterbury in 1541.

Crome was among the few who dared to oppose the passage of the Act of Six Articles in 1539. When bishops Latimer and Shaxton resigned under duress, he preached in defence of their integrity. The next year Crome's colleagues Barnes, Garrard, and Jerome were burnt following Thomas Cromwell's execution. A wave of arrests took place in London, and Crome's parishes were cited for irregularities. Preaching 'with more zeal than ordinary' during moments of crisis, Crome interceded with the king on behalf of those arrested. During Advent, he was accused of preaching against the six articles by arguing 'it is a superstition to say masses for the dead' (Robinson, *Original Letters*, 1.208–15). Again Henry offered him mercy in exchange for submission. In early 1541 Crome appeared at Paul's Cross and attempted to satisfy the king while cultivating the impression that he was advancing reform as usual. He was not permitted to preach again for several years.

In 1546, as Henry's health waned, the struggle between conservatives and evangelical reformers for control over policies reached a new stage of intensity. In Lenten sermons delivered at St Mary Aldermary, and at the Mercers' chapel, St Thomas Acon, Crome attacked the doctrine of transubstantiation, arguing that the mass was a remembrance of Christ's death. Again he was accused of heresy and seemed to capitulate, but before he could appear at Paul's Cross, a throng of reformers, led by Latimer and Shaxton, urged him not to submit. Consequently, on 9 May he announced that he would not recant, and repeated his belief that the mass was only a commemoration. Now he was threatened by the privy council, and keenly questioned by royal chaplains Nicholas Ridley and Richard Coxe, who warned him to do the king's will. His subsequent appearance at Paul's Cross on 27 June was meant to be an unambiguous apology, but one of the witnesses referred to 'Dr Crome's canting, recanting, decanting, or rather double canting' (Ellis, 2nd ser., 2.176–8). At least twenty people were investigated, another sixty fled, some were tortured, and Anne Askew (who had attended his sermons) was burnt with three others on 16 July. Shaxton broke ranks, and returned to the conservative fold for good. These events intensified the debate among reformers as to whether it were better to die for the testimony of their faith, or endure the rigours of exile, rather than dissimulate. Under Edward VI, Crome remained a controversial figure. The tract *I Playne Piers* accused him of surrendering a martyr's crown for 'a pair of asses ears'.

Following Mary's accession, Crome was arrested for unlicensed preaching at Christmas 1553, and committed to the Fleet. With other leaders, he signed a defiant declaration of protestant doctrine in May 1554, and he was mentioned warmly for his constancy in the letters of other prisoners, including Ridley. But Cardinal Pole's register contains pardons for him and for Shaxton. The time of his release is uncertain. Early in Elizabeth's reign encroaching age kept Crome from the pulpit. He died in June 1562, making 'a godly end and constant confession of the truth' (Coverdale, fol. 46), and was buried in the chancel of St Mary Aldermary, under a marble stone engraved with verses from Job.

Within a few years the Nicodemites who dissembled seemed less heroic than those who had died in the Henrician and Marian purges. When John Foxe reconsidered Crome's legacy, he omitted much of the favourable information about his life and faith that he had planned for the 1570 edition of the book of martyrs. Thus a useful strategy that had served a generation of reformers was dismissed, obscuring Crome's sizeable contribution to the survival of protestantism in England at several dangerous junctures. SUSAN WABUDA

Sources *The acts and monuments of John Foxe*, new edn, ed. G. Townsend, 4 (1846), 699; 5 (1846), 32, 446–8, appx 16 · R. H. Brodie, 'The case of Dr Crome', *TRHS*, new ser., 19 (1905), 295–304 · will, PRO, PROB 11/45, fols. 138r–139v · GL, MS 9531/10, fols. 123v, 127v · GL, MS 9531/12, pt 1, fol. 26r–v · BL, Harley MS 6148, fols. 79v–80r · BL, Harley MS 425, fols. 65r–66r · *I playne Piers which can not flatter* (1550?) · *Miscellaneous writings and letters of Thomas Cranmer*, ed. J. E. Cox, Parker Society, [18] (1846), 161–2, 396–9 · H. Robinson, ed. and trans., *Original letters relative to the English Reformation*, 1, Parker Society, [26] (1846), 208–15 · H. Ellis, ed., *Original letters illustrative of English history*, 2nd ser., 2 (1827), 176–8 · Pole's register, Bibliothèque Municipale, Douai, MS 922, vol. 2, fols. 49r–50v (Shaxton); vol. 4, fols. 97v–98r · M. Coverdale, ed., *Certain most godly, fruitful, and comfortable letters* (1564), 44–9 · A. Pettegree, *Marian protestantism: six studies* (1996), 86–117 · S. Wabuda, 'Equivocation and recantation during the English Reformation: the "subtle shadows" of Dr Edward Crome', *Journal of Ecclesiastical History*, 44 (1993), 224–42

Wealth at death see will, PRO, PROB 11/45, fols. 138r–139v

Crome, John (1768–1821), painter and etcher, was born on 22 December 1768 in Norwich, the son of John Crome, a publican and journeyman weaver, and his wife, Elizabeth. He was baptized on Christmas day in the church of St George, Tombland.

Education and marriage The history of Crome's early years has often been embellished with anecdote, but a few facts do emerge. In 1783 Crome was apprenticed to the house, coach, and sign painter Francis Whisler, his indentures taking effect from 1 August (though dated 15 October). In common with his Norwich contemporaries Charles Catton, John Ninham, and James Sillett, whose beginnings lay in the field of heraldic painting, Crome's early artistic training was as a journeyman painter.

Crome continued his trade for some time after finishing his apprenticeship in 1790, and is known to have painted numerous public-house signboards. As late as May 1803, the year of the foundation of the Norwich Society of Artists, he submitted a bill of £2 4s. to one J. Thompson for 'Painting Lame Dog writing and gilding Board for ye Lamb and gilding name of ye Maids Head' (Reeve collection, BM). Crome harnessed his considerable artistic talents to a keen business acumen. He was the first among his peers to undertake picture restoration, and was paid £40 for cleaning the civic portraits in St Andrew's Hall, Norwich. In 1820, when he was both prosperous and successful, he earned another 12 guineas for repeating the work (ibid.).

On 2 October 1792 Crome married Phoebe Berney (d. 1845) in the church of St Mary, Coslany. The witnesses included Robert Ladbrooke, with whom Crome sketched,

John Crome (1768–1821), by Denis Brownell Murphy, exh. Norwich Society of Artists 1821

and the bride's sister, Mary Berney, who were married exactly a year later. Crome's first year of marriage was one of ill health, and he was twice admitted to Norwich hospital with hydrocele. His and Phoebe Crome's first child, a daughter, also Phoebe, was born within a month of the wedding, but died in infancy; of their eleven children four died young. Of those who survived, John Berney *Crome (1794–1842), Frederick James (1796–1832), William Henry (1806–1867), and Emily (1801–1840) all became painters. John Crome was sometimes called Old Crome to distinguish him from his eldest son.

Crome's early influences   Although Crome did not enrol as a pupil to any specific master, it would be wrong to infer that he was purely self-taught, or received at most only rudimentary tips from the other painters he met. He made his first oil sketch in 1790 and furthered his artistic training as the decade proceeded. The Revd William Gunn, of Smallburgh near Norwich, in a letter to the sculptor John Flaxman of 4 May 1821, provides an insight into the early influences on Crome's career. Prominent among them was William Beechey, who had lived and worked in Norwich for several years in the early 1780s. Crome's oils suggest a definite study of Beechey's work and the artists of Beechey's milieu. Another Royal Academician to have a discernible influence was John Opie, who painted a portrait of Crome, probably about the time of his visit to Norwich in 1797 (Norwich Castle Museum and Art Gallery).

But perhaps the foremost influence on Crome at this critical stage was Thomas Harvey of Catton, Norwich, a wealthy master weaver and member of one of the principal mercantile families in Norwich. As well as being an art patron and a collector, Harvey was an amateur artist in his

own right, and Crome later owned several of his paintings. His style owed much to Gainsborough, whose work was represented in his substantial collection. Harvey also owned numerous paintings from the continent, including Dutch seventeenth-century masters, purchases facilitated by his marriage to the daughter of a Rotterdam merchant. Crome, who was given access to Harvey's studio and collection, was drawn to these Dutch works and especially Meindert Hobbema's *Landscape* (Foundation E. G. Bührle collection, Zürich). According to the Yarmouth banker and art collector Dawson Turner, he later copied the painting, and also Harvey's Gainsborough, *The Cottage Door* (Hunt. L.).

Another significant influence on Crome were the paintings of Richard Wilson—which were to be found in the collections of both Harvey and Turner, as well as that of the Norwich landscapist Daniel Coppin, a house painter and glazier by trade. This influence may be seen, for example, in Crome's *Norwich from Mousehold Gravel Pits* (priv. coll.). Wilson continued to be an important influence on Crome to the end of his career, as a number of his later works reveal.

Crome the collector   Crome's contact with Thomas Harvey encouraged him to take up collecting himself, and he built up a valuable portfolio. In September 1812, in straitened circumstances, he held a three-day sale of his collection at Yarmouth. The pictures were noticed in the local press as 'the genuine and entire property of Mr CROME, of Norwich, a great part of whose life has been spent in collecting them' (*Norwich Mercury*, 12 Sept 1812). The catalogue doubtless included a proportion of hopeful attributions, but the auctioneer could nevertheless claim with some justice that it was: 'a collection as is well worth the attention of connoisseurs, amateurs, artists, and the public of every description, and such as, it is presumed, was never before exposed to sale in the County of Norfolk'. It included a few old masters, and drawings and prints, including impressions by Rembrandt and Anthonie Waterloo. The sale is said to have raised some £200 or £300 and evidently helped Crome to recover his finances. In 1812 he had debts with the Gurney family (bankers) of Earlham Hall of over £220, but by the end of 1815 his bank account showed a very healthy credit.

As well as collecting, Crome dealt in pictures. Dawson Turner records purchasing *Rocky Landscape*, by Isaac Moucheron, from him for £12, as well as *Vase of Flowers*, attributed to John Baptist Monnoyer. It is not clear when in his career Crome began, or indeed ceased, dealing. He bought £195 worth of pictures at the sale of John Patteson of Surrey Street, Norwich, on 28 and 29 May 1819. Not all these were in the sale of his own collection after his death, suggesting that he continued dealing until the very end of his life. This business also appears to have been a secondary motive for Crome's visit to Paris in 1814, his only trip abroad. He wrote to his wife from the French capital: 'I shall make this journey pay ... I shall be very cautious [how I lay] out my money' (art department archive, Norwich Castle Museum and Art Gallery). The principal purpose for the visit, in which he was accompanied by Daniel

Coppin and the Norwich artist and framer William Freeman, was to see the magnificent artwork collected in Paris by Napoleon's conquering armies.

Crome the drawing-master After a short-lived attempt to establish himself in London, Crome set up as a drawing-master in Norwich. The seven daughters of the banker John Gurney were among his earliest pupils. Richenda Gurney wrote in her journal of a lesson on 17 January 1798: 'I had a good drawing morning, but in the course of it gave way to passion with both Crome and Betsy—Crome because he would attend to Betsy and not to me, and Betsy because she was so provoking' (A. J. C. Hare, *The Gurneys of Earlham*, 1895, 1.74).

Crome favoured instruction from nature rather than through copybooks, and when opportunity allowed would take his pupils in to the countryside with the cry 'This is our Academy' (Mallalieu, *Watercolour artists*, 11). Crome accompanied the Gurney family on summer tours through England and Wales, and in 1802 went with them to the Lake District. In 1804 he visited Wales with Robert Ladbrooke. Views painted on these trips were shown by Crome at the inaugural exhibition of the Norwich Society of Artists in 1805. His profession was given in the exhibition catalogue as drawing-master, and thus it continued to be recorded until 1819. His address in 1805 was given simply as St George's, but this was later amplified to St George's, Colegate. Crome returned to the Lake District with the Gurneys in 1806. He also spent time at Great Yarmouth, where he was employed by Dawson Turner to teach his daughters drawing. He was succeeded in this post by John Sell Cotman, but continued his work as drawing-master at Norwich grammar school.

That Crome was an enthusiastic and serious teacher may be judged from one of his few extant letters to his pupil James Stark, dated January 1816. In it he exhorted Stark to attend to the qualities for which he believed an artist should strive:

> Brea[d]th must be attended to; if you paint a muscle give it brea[d]th. Your doing the same by the sky, making parts broad and of a good shape, that they may come in with your composition, forming one grand plan of light and shade, this must always please a good eye and keep the attention of the spectator and give delight to everyone. Trifles in Nature must be overlooked that we may have our feelings raised by seeing the whole picture at a glance, not knowing how or why we are so charmed. (BM, Add. MS 43830, fol. 73)

Crome's technique The qualities of breadth and dignity that Crome recommended to Stark, and which were displayed with such virtuosity in his own work, did not, however, find universal acceptance. Like John Sell Cotman and J. M. W. Turner, Crome had his detractors. He first exhibited at the Royal Academy in 1806, when Joseph Farington recorded in his diary for 5 May the response of two art critics, Taylor of *The Sun* and James Boaden of *The Oracle*, to the opening of the exhibition:

> The *latter* after looking round the room sd. He had never seen so many bad pictures. On looking at Turner's *Waterfall at Schaffhausen* He sd. 'That is Madness'—'He is a Madman' in which Taylor joined.—In the anti-room, looking at an

Upright landscape by Croom, Boaden said, 'There is another in the new manner', 'it is the scribbling of painting.—So much of the *trowel*—so mortary—surely a little more finishing might be born?' (Moore, 21)

This was a common enough criticism among those seeking a greater degree of 'Dutch finish' in their pictures. The public was not yet receptive to the monochromatic range deployed to such magnificent effect in paintings such as Crome's *View of Carrow Abbey, Near Norwich* (Norwich Castle Museum and Art Gallery), which was exhibited in Norwich in 1805. Although he later lightened his palette, the 'unfinished' appearance of Crome's works continued to attract adverse comment to the end of his career. It was said of *The Fishmarket at Boulogne*, exhibited with the Norwich Society of Artists in 1820, that: 'the artist loses "half the praise he would have got" had he but discreetly bestowed a little more pains upon the finishing of it' (*Norfolk Chronicle*, 29 June 1820). Crome's thin-glazed shadows and broadly applied lights drew on a painterly tradition before which even his best students faltered. In his watercolours and soft-ground etchings one can see a sureness of touch, of design and draughtsmanship, that bears witness to the influence of artists such as Gainsborough, Rembrandt, and Waterloo.

When precisely Crome began etching is uncertain. It was his practice to take test impressions which were quite lightly bitten, and few of the originals have survived. The earliest dated example is a soft-ground etching from 1809, entitled *Colney*. The total extant œuvre is nine soft-grounds and twenty-five pure etchings, a few of which bear the dates 1812 or 1813. The soft-ground etchings are almost all landscapes and are more successful than the ordinary, hard-ground etchings, which are mostly intricate studies of trees and their foliage. Crome was reputedly dissatisfied with his etchings and did not publish them, although in 1812 he issued a publishing prospectus that attracted a number of subscribers. It was not until 1834 that a volume of thirty-one plates, entitled *Norfolk Picturesque Scenery*, was published on behalf of Mrs Crome. Four years later seventeen of these were included in a volume with a memoir by Dawson Turner. These and subsequent impressions were all later states, bearing additional work by Henry Ninham and also W. C. Edwards. All Crome's original plates are now in Norwich Castle Museum and Art Gallery and show signs of re-biting and engraving.

Crome's best etchings display a delicate command of line. Small though their number is, they place him at the forefront of the English revival in etching. His influence went far beyond Norwich and can be seen in the nineteenth-century tradition of painter–etchers. Attempts to isolate the single influences at work upon him ultimately pale before the fresh vision, clear colour, and strong design that lie at the heart of his technique in all his chosen media. It is also difficult to discern a straightforward development within Crome's œuvre. His reference to other artists and his choice of subject matter throughout his career defy an easy categorization or sense of specific development.

Crome and the Norwich school Crome was undoubtedly the leading spirit behind the formation of the Norwich Society of Artists on 19 February 1803. He was credited in the contemporary press with being the founder of both the society and the 'Norwich school'. The *Norwich Mercury* announced the arrival of the new society, in which Robert Ladbrooke was also closely involved, on 26 March 1803: 'An Academy has lately been established in this city by a society of gentlemen for the purpose of investigating the rise, progress, decline and revival of the fine arts'. The Norwich society was among the first in the provinces to follow the example of the Royal Academy in London. But although other societies were founded along similar lines in Edinburgh, Liverpool, Bath, and Leeds, none gave rise to an autonomous school of painting as in Norwich.

Crome showed pictures annually at the society exhibitions until his death. He exhibited 288 works in all, seldom sending fewer than ten pictures, and once sending more than thirty. By contrast thirteen works at the Royal Academy, and five at the British Institution, were the sum total of his London exhibits. Crome was vice-president of the Norwich Society of Artists in 1807 and again in 1820, and president in 1808. The Norwich school is mainly represented by landscape paintings that portray tranquil rural scenes, usually of the landscape of Norfolk, and John Crome, along with John Sell Cotman, must be credited as its leading practitioners. The society survived the secession of several important members in 1816, and the death of Crome himself in 1821, but it could not outlive the move of Cotman to London in 1833.

Death and reputation Crome's last years were spent in relative comfort and prosperity. A jovial and sociable man, he enjoyed an evening drink at a favourite inn on the Market Place in Norwich, and in his later years was said to be 'sometimes more convivial than was prudent' (*DNB*). He worked to the last, and at the time of his death was preparing a large canvas, *Yarmouth Water Frolic*, an ambitious picture of Wroxham regatta which he had sketched a week earlier. He died on 22 April 1821 at his home at 17 Gildengate Street, Norwich, and was buried in St George's Church, Colegate, on 27 April. Despite occasional criticism of his work his brilliance was recognized in his day: he achieved a considerable reputation locally, and increasingly in London as well. Shortly after his death, on 4 May 1821, the Revd William Gunn wrote to John Flaxman:

> The fine arts are not forgotten at Norwich; we too have an annual exhibition. We are now deploring the loss of one of its first ornaments Crome who died a fortnight ago. He was a poor lad who laid the foundation of his celebrity in cleaning brushes for Beechey … People are now crazy for his pictures which are bought with avidity and sell high. (Moore, 19)

According to Henry Ladbrooke, at the close of the Norwich Society exhibitions 'there was not a picture of his that had not the world "sold" upon it' (ibid.).

Yet Crome's subsequent reputation has suffered from that very success. He did not sign his paintings, and the identification of his works remains bedevilled by problems of misattribution. The existence of numerous contemporary copies both by his pupils and, more problematically, by copyists whose own stylistic personalities remain obscure, increases the uncertainty. Yet those oils that may be securely identified on either stylistic or documentary grounds reveal a body of work entirely original and confident in execution. Crome's œuvre represents a landmark contribution to the history of British landscape painting. Norwich Castle Museum and Art Gallery holds the largest extant collection of securely attributed works, thanks largely to the researches of James Reeve, curator of the Norwich Castle Museum from 1851 to 1910. Reeve advised the Colman family on its purchases, and the Russell James Colman bequest now forms the substantial core of the Norwich Castle collections.

ANDREW W. MOORE

Sources A. W. Moore, *The Norwich school of artists* (1995) • D. Clifford and T. Clifford, *John Crome* (1968) • D. Turner, *Outlines in lithography, from a small collection of pictures* (privately printed, Yarmouth, 1840) • W. F. Dickes, *The Norwich school of painting* (1905) • M. Rajnai and M. Stevens, *The Norwich Society of Artists, 1805–1833: a dictionary of contributors and their work* (1976) • H. S. Theobald, *Crome's etchings: a catalogue and an appreciation with some account of his paintings* (1906) • D. B. Brown, A. Hemingway, and A. Lyles, *Romantic landscape: the Norwich school of landscape painters* (2000) [exhibition catalogue, London, Tate Britain, 24 March – 17 Sept 2000] • F. Hawcroft, 'Crome and his patron: Thomas Harvey of Catton', *The Connoisseur*, 144 (Dec 1959) • T. Fawcett, 'John Crome and the idea of Mousehold', *Norfolk Archaeology*, 38/2 (1982), 168–81 • L. Binyon, *John Crome and John Sell Cotman* (1897) • *DNB* • H. Mallalieu, *The Norwich school: Crome, Cotman and their followers* (1974)

Archives BM, James Reeve MSS, 167–c.8

Likenesses J. Opie, oils, c.1800, Norwich Castle Museum • J. S. Cotman, sketch, 1809, BM • P. Mazotti, plaster bust, c.1820, NPG • D. B. Murphy, watercolour and pencil, exh. Norwich Society of Artists 1821, NPG [*see illus.*] • M. W. Sharp, oils, 1821, Norwich Castle Museum • H. Gurney, pencil and wash with bodycolour, Norwich Castle Museum • D. B. Murphy, related drawing, Norwich Castle Museum • J. T. Woodhouse, oils, Norwich Castle Museum

Crome, John Berney (1794–1842), landscape painter, was born on 8 December 1794 in Norwich, and baptized there on 14 December at St George Colegate, the eldest of the seven surviving children of John *Crome (1768–1821), painter, and his wife, Phoebe (d. 1845), daughter of James Berney, a Norwich weaver. He attended Norwich grammar school, where he became head boy and 'attained considerable classical acquirement' (*Norwich Mercury*, 17 Sept 1842). His father was drawing-master at the school, which James Stark and George Vincent also attended. All three became pupils of John Crome, the founder of the Norwich school of artists. At the age of twelve in 1806 he was already exhibiting with the Norwich Society of Artists, and was a regular and prolific contributor until it broke up in 1833. During this time he played an important role in the society, serving four times as vice-president and three as president. While very young he exhibited at the Royal Academy in 1811 and again in 1814. He soon began assisting his father as a drawing-master and took over the teaching practice after John Crome's death in 1821. In 1814 he accompanied his father on a sketching trip to Ipswich and from there the two artists went by boat along the River

John Berney Crome (1794–1842), by unknown engraver

Orwell to Harwich. This journey provided him with subjects for several paintings. He went further afield in 1816 to France, in the company of George Vincent and Benjamin Steel, his future brother-in-law. While he was in Paris his father urged him 'Pray see as much of Modern Art as you can' (John Crome to J. B. Crome, 28 Dec 1816, MS letter, Norwich Castle Museum and Art Gallery, 1951.220). One result of this visit was a series of paintings of Rouen, the finest of which is *Rouen, Looking from the Base of Mont Ste Catherine towards the Bridge of Boats*, which was purchased by Countess de Grey in 1821 (Sothebys, 14 July 1999, lot 27). John Berney Crome exhibited regularly in London from 1820 to 1842 with the British Institution and later with the Society (later Royal Society) of British Artists (1825–42) and the Royal Academy (1839–42). He also exhibited extensively in the provinces and in Ireland. In 1821, a few months after his father's death, he exhibited in Norwich the large and impressive painting, *Yarmouth Water Frolic—Evening; Boats Assembling Previous to the Rowing Match* (Kenwood House, London), possibly left unfinished by the father and completed by the son. It was believed Crome would take on his father's mantle, but his work varies in quality and he never fulfilled his early promise. He was capable of fine interpretations but too often he produced coarsely painted works with colours laid on thickly. However, his paintings were favourably received wherever they were exhibited and appear to have sold reasonably well. He painted landscapes and coastal views in Norfolk, particularly of the River Yare and Great Yarmouth (for

example *Great Gale at Yarmouth on Ash Wednesday*, 1836; Norwich Castle Museum and Art Gallery), and the subjects of his other paintings indicate continued travel abroad in France, Belgium, and the Netherlands, most notably Rotterdam and Amsterdam. In the early 1820s he began specializing in moonlight scenes in the manner of the seventeenth-century Dutch master Aert Van der Neer, 'which earned for him both fame and profit' (*Norwich Mercury*, 30 July 1831). He rarely painted in watercolour but several drawings in pencil and black and white chalk are known. His work is well represented in Norwich Castle Museum and Art Gallery. On the rare occasions that he signed his paintings he used the signature J. B. Crome.

In 1822, like his father before him, Crome was initiated into the freemasons. Two years later, in 1824, he was appointed landscape painter to the duke of Sussex, a patron of the Norwich Society of Artists, whom Crome had escorted round the exhibition during his year of presidency in 1819. Later that year, on 28 December 1824, he married Dorcas Sarah Burcham (1806–1827) of Norwich, but tragically she died three years later at the age of twenty-one 'after an affliction of more than two years' (*Norfolk Chronicle*, 1 Sept 1827). He was described as a man of culture and literary attainments and an eloquent speaker, and throughout the 1830s he was actively involved in the artists' conversaziones in Norwich. He served as a steward with John Sell Cotman and also addressed some of the meetings. The relationship between painting and poetry was of particular interest to him, and the manuscript survives of a paper he read at the Norwich Philosophical Society, 'Essay on painting and poetry' (*c*.1828, Norwich Castle Museum and Art Gallery, 1958.1). It was also the theme of his poem *Prologomena* (MS, n.d., Norwich Castle Museum and Art Gallery), presumably the prologue to the talk. In 1830 Crome married his second wife, Sarah Ann Clipperton (1799/1800–1879), of Braydeston, Norfolk. There were no children from either of his marriages. By 1834 he was in financial difficulties caused by an extravagant lifestyle, probably combined with declining sales of paintings and pupils to teach. On 5 August 1834 he was declared bankrupt. The bankruptcy notice described him as 'drawing master, stationer, dealer and chapman' (*Norfolk Chronicle*, 9 Aug 1834). From 3 to 5 September 1834 a three-day bankruptcy sale was held of the contents of his home in Middle Street, St George Colegate, where he had continued to live after the death of his father. Soon after he moved to Great Yarmouth. It is significant that these events occurred about the time of the breakup of the Norwich Society of Artists in 1833 and suggests that they may have been a contributory factor.

Dawson Turner described Crome as a man with a 'joyous, buoyant, warm-hearted, generous' disposition ('Biographical memoir' in J. Wodderspoon, *John Crome and his Works*, 1876, 6). His portrait in watercolour by Horace Beevor Love (*c*.1830; Norwich Castle Museum and Art Gallery) shows him as a portly man, and in 1837 he wrote self-mockingly to his wife from Paris how at his hotel his 'slender form' had prompted the offer of 'un plus grand' bath

(MS letter, 8 July 1837, Norwich Castle Museum and Art Gallery, 1951.220). Ill health, apparently caused by a 'stone, said to have been brought on by too great fondness for port wine' (Dickes, 160), dogged his final years. He received financial help from his friend and patron James Norton Sherrington, an amateur artist from Great Yarmouth, who accompanied him to France in 1837. Sherrington was an avid collector of paintings by John Crome, and bought more of his paintings from the son. Sherrington also paid Crome to restore pictures and on occasion lent him money. Crome died of 'fistula' at his home on Row 81, King Street, Great Yarmouth, on 13 September 1842, having maintained 'much of his original vivacity amid his suffering. He had an elegant and classical turn of mind and deserved a better fortune' (*Norwich Mercury*, 17 Sept 1842).   NORMA WATT

Sources priv coll., Rajnai Norwich Artists archive · W. F. Dickes, *The Norwich school of painting: being a full account of the Norwich exhibitions, the lives of the painters, the lists of their respective exhibits, and descriptions of the pictures* [1906] · A. W. Moore, *The Norwich school of artists* (1985) · A. Hemingway, *The Norwich school of painters, 1803–1833* (1979) · H. A. E. Day, *East Anglian painters*, 3 vols. (1967–9) · parish register, Norwich, St George Colegate, 14 Dec 1794 [baptism] · BM, Reeve Collection · *Norfolk Chronicle* (1 Sept 1827) · d. cert. · *Norwich Mercury* (2 March 1845) · *Norfolk Chronicle* (1 Jan 1825)
Archives Norwich Castle Museum, MSS | BM, Reeve collection
Likenesses H. B. Love, pastel and watercolour drawing, 1830, Norwich Castle Museum and Art Gallery · Dawe, engraving (after H. B. Love) · mixed-method engraving (after H. B. Love), BM, NPG [*see illus.*]

Cromek, Robert Hartley (1770–1812), engraver and literary entrepreneur, was born at Kingston upon Hull, the son of Thomas Cromek (*d.* 1802), stonemason, and Martha Hartley (*d.* 1811). When he was a young man his family moved to Manchester, where he briefly studied law but soon turned to literary and artistic pursuits. In 1788 he moved to London and studied engraving under Francesco Bartolozzi; he then undertook engraving book illustrations, among them many by Thomas Stothard and Henry Fuseli. On 24 October 1806 Cromek married Elizabeth Hartley Charge (1779–1848), with whom he had two children, Maria and Thomas Hartley *Cromek.

In 1805 Cromek engaged William Blake to produce designs for an illustrated edition of Robert Blair's *Grave*. Initially Blake was to engrave his designs, but Cromek subsequently decided upon Luigi Schiavonetti as the engraver, a decision that Blake considered double-dealing especially as Cromek acquired most of the 589 subscribers by exhibiting Blake's designs in provincial cities. The volume was published in 1808, with a disappointed Blake receiving 20 guineas for his designs and nothing more. In 1807 Cromek had begun collecting previously unpublished Burns manuscripts, which he published as *Reliques of Robert Burns, consisting chiefly of original letters, poems, and critical observations on Scottish songs*, in 1808. The Society of Scottish Antiquaries elected Cromek a correspondent member in 1808. He subsequently edited and published *Select Scottish songs, ancient and modern; with critical observations and biographical notices, by Robert Burns* (1810). In 1809,

while searching Scotland with Stothard for more Burns materials, Cromek met the poet and songwriter Allan Cunningham in Dumfries. Over several months Cunningham provided Cromek with the contents for *Remains of Nithsdale and Galloway song, with historical and traditional notices relative to the manners and customs of the peasantry* (1810). Cunningham had in fact invented almost all of the purportedly ancient songs.

Cromek had engaged Stothard in 1806 to paint *The Pilgrimage to Canterbury*, and announced a plan to publish a print of it by subscription. After exhibiting the painting for several months in London, he travelled with it to provincial cities over the next two years in search of subscribers. Blake included his competing *Chaucer's Canterbury Pilgrims* in his public exhibition of 1809. It is not possible to determine definitely whether Cromek or Blake first conceived the idea of painting and engraving this subject. Blake's engraving was completed in 1810; Schiavonetti died in 1810 before finishing his engraving of the Stothard painting, and the work was continued by William Bromley and Francis Engleheart, and then Niccolo Schiavonetti, James Heath, and W. H. Worthington, before it reached a final state in 1817.

In 1810 Cromek, as secretary of the Chalcographic Society, also promoted a scheme to sell twenty engravings of British art to 170 subscribers for 100 guineas, under the aegis of the impromptu Society for the Encouragement of the Art of Engraving. In response Blake wrote a vituperative draft 'Public address to the Chalcographic Society' in his notebook. The plan, however, was abandoned and the societies were dissolved in 1811. By this time Cromek was suffering from an advanced stage of consumption and he died at his home, 64 Newman Street, London, on 14 March 1812. In 1813 his widow sold the copyright of Blake's designs for £120 to Rudolph Ackermann, who that same year published a new edition, with summary biographies of Cromek and Schiavonetti. In 1829 Elizabeth Cromek sold the copyright of the *Pilgrimage to Canterbury* engraving, along with remaining proofs and prints, to the printsellers Boys and Graces for £400.

Cromek's reputation has suffered largely through his highly charged disputes with Blake. His quick temper and his brashness did not serve him well. In a letter to John Murray, Scott called him 'a perfect Brain-sucker' (H. J. C. Grierson, *Letters of Sir Walter Scott*, 1932, 2.409). However, many prominent artists and patrons of the arts were his friends and defenders, among them Benjamin West, William Roscoe, John Hoppner, and Thomas Hope. In his short career Cromek accomplished a great deal, with ambitions to do a great deal more.   DENNIS M. READ

Sources G. E. Bentley, *Blake records* (1969) · G. E. Bentley, *Blake records supplement* (1988) · D. M. Read, 'The context of Blake's public address: Cromek and the Chalcographic Society', *Philological Quarterly*, 60 (1981), 69–86 · D. M. Read, 'The rival Canterbury pilgrims of Blake and Cromek: Herculean figures in the carpet', *Modern Philology*, 86 (1988–9), 171–90 · A. Ward, 'Canterbury revisited: the Blake–Cromek controversy', *Blake: an Illustrated Quarterly*, 22 (1988–9), 80–92 · G. E. Bentley, jun., '"They take great liberty's": Blake reconfigured by Cromek and modern critics—the argument from

silence', *Studies in Romanticism*, 30 (1991), 657–84 • D. M. Read, 'Practicing "the necessity of purification": Cromek, Roscoe, and *Reliques of Burns*', *Studies in Bibliography*, 35 (1982), 306–19 • D. M. Read, 'Cromek, Cunningham, and *Remains of Nithsdale and Galloway song*: a case of literary duplicity', *Studies in Bibliography*, 40 (1987), 171–90 • *The Examiner* (22 March 1812) • private information (2004) [P. Warrington; M. Warrington] • 'Biographical sketch', *The Grave* (1813)
Archives BM, department of prints and drawings • priv. coll., 'Memorials of the life of R. H. Cromek', ed. T. H. Cromek, 1865 | Free Library of Philadelphia, George Frederick Lewis collection • Liverpool City Library, William Roscoe letters • NL Scot., grangerized copy of *Reliques of Robert Burns* • Sheff. Arch., letters to James Montgomery
Likenesses J. Flaxman, pencil sketch, 1804, FM Cam. • T. Stothard, pencil sketch, BM, department of prints and drawings, Cromek collection

Cromek, Thomas Hartley (1809–1873), painter, was born at 64 Newman Street, London, in late July 1809, the only son of the engraver and book illustrator Robert Hartley *Cromek (1770–1812) and his wife, Elizabeth, *née* Hartley (1779–1848). Following his father's death in London, his mother took him to live with his grandfather at Bridge House, Wakefield; he attended the Moravian school at Fulneck, near Leeds, from 1820 and Wakefield grammar school from 1821. His early interest in drawing was greatly encouraged by James Hunter, a local portrait painter, and Joseph Rhodes of Leeds who accompanied him on sketching tours. In 1827 Thomas Teale, a Leeds surgeon, commissioned Cromek to make some detailed anatomical drawings, for each of which he was paid 5*s*.: Cromek observed later that 'to the very minute attention which these drawings required I attribute careful and accurate drawings' which became his 'principal merit as an artist' (Cromek, 'Reminiscences', fol. 5).

For the sake of his mother's health Cromek set out in June 1830 for Florence and Rome, armed with letters of introduction from the duchess of Leeds. Before leaving he met John Constable who lectured him about 'young men going to Italy to study', supposing that 'England was not large enough for an artist now a days' (Cromek, 'Reminiscences', fol. 13). After a short stay in Florence he quickly moved on to Rome and there met Edward Cheyney and later Robert Henry Cheyney: these two brothers figured among Cromek's most important patrons, giving him many introductions and becoming his lifelong friends. In the spring of 1831 he sketched fragments in the Vatican Museum and in the forum and the ruins of the colosseum, Caesar's palace, and the Farnese Gardens, subjects which proved to be significant and regular sources for his commissions. He visited the Roman campagna and many towns and villages such as Frascati, Assisi, Tivoli, and Ariccia, and was shown the excavations at Pompeii by the archaeologist Sir William Gell. By the winter of 1832 he was admitted to a private Russian sketching society which concentrated on sketching figures in costume; the influence of this group can be seen in many of his watercolours. While in Rome he also met many British artists, including the sculptors John Gibson, M. C. Wyatt, and Joseph Gott, and the painters Joseph Severn, Penry Williams, and Thomas Uwins. In 1834 Cromek journeyed to

Greece; he had intended to go to Palestine but upon reaching Syria he was forced back by the plague then raging in the Levant and returned to Greece. He spent time in Mycenae and Argos, and then stayed for two months in Corfu before returning to Venice to join Edward Cheyney for a sketching tour. Arguably this journey to Greece prompted some of his finest drawings, many of which were sketched *en plein air*; they reveal a freshness of colour and an originality of method somewhat lacking in his later, more finished, drawings.

Cromek returned to England in 1835 and in January 1836 was received into the Roman Catholic church. Soon afterwards, in July 1836, he married Anastasia Priestman; they had three daughters. In September 1836 he made another visit to Florence, where, in the following year, he continued to sketch all the prominent views and buildings of the city. Cromek's memorialist, James Fowler, recorded that by now his reputation was fully established, and that he gave lessons to Edward Lear at about this time. On 5 July 1837 he was invited to the Palazzo Pitti to present his work to the grand duke and duchess of Tuscany; they selected seven views of Greece. He wrote: 'In consequence of this patronage I am much talked about and I expect it will lead to an increase in my connections and commissions' (Cromek, 'Reminiscences', fol. 41). These expectations were indeed fulfilled, as his career flourished between 1840 and 1849: in both Florence and Rome he received a constant flow of commissions and gave lessons to many of the distinguished visitors then flocking to Italy. By 1845 he was able to undertake a second visit to Greece. As Fowler proclaimed, 'these were prosperous days', and Cromek 'moved in the most intellectual society in Rome'. Back in London in the summer of 1843 he was summoned to Buckingham Palace to show his drawings to the queen and Prince Albert. Victoria bought two drawings: when the artist Peter DeWint heard of this he jealously remarked that 'the Queen has no taste'. Appalled, Cromek wrote that he 'was so disgusted with de Wint's illiberality and apparent friendship that I never saw him more' (Cromek, 'Reminiscences', fol. 96).

The outbreak of the civil war in Italy in 1849 compelled all English residents to leave Rome, and thus Cromek returned to England. In 1850 he exhibited four major drawings at the Royal Academy and he was elected an associate of the New Society of Painters in Water Colours. Despite sympathy and help from many of his friends, especially Clarkson Stanfield, he never maintained in England the level of success he had achieved in Rome. By 1861 his health had so deteriorated that he had lost the use of his hands and no paintings are recorded after this date. He died in Hatfield Street, Wakefield, Yorkshire, somewhat impoverished, on 10 April 1873.

MICHAEL WARRINGTON

Sources T. H. Cromek, 'Reminiscences at home & abroad, 1812–1855', unpublished MS, priv. coll. • J. Fowler, 'A biographical notice of Thomas Hartley Cromek, esq', *Wakefield Express* (19 April 1873) • T. H. Cromek, 'Memorials of the life of R. H. Cromek esq. FSA Edin.', unpublished MS, priv. coll. • will, 30 Jan 1862, W. Yorks. AS, Wakefield • letters between T. H. Cromek and Thomas Fenteman,

1856–73, Central Library, Leeds · 'Cromek, Robert Hartley', *DNB* · 'Cheyney, Edward', *DNB* · *CGPLA Eng. & Wales* (1873)
Archives U. Edin. L., corresp. | Central Library, Leeds, corresp. with Thomas Fenteman
Likenesses M. Hohl, watercolour, 1845, priv. coll.
Wealth at death under £450: probate, 1 May 1873, *CGPLA Eng. & Wales*

Cromer. For this title name *see* Baring, Evelyn, first earl of Cromer (1841–1917); Baring, Rowland Thomas, second earl of Cromer (1877–1953); Baring, (George) Rowland Stanley, third earl of Cromer (1918–1991).

Cromer, George (d. 1543), archbishop of Armagh and lord chancellor of Ireland, is of uncertain background, but it has been plausibly suggested that he was a member of 'a solidly established Kentish family' (Gwynn, 53–4). He was a scholar of Oxford University in 1497 and graduated MA. He was referred to as Dr Cromer in Henry VIII's book of payments in 1518.

Cromer secured a number of benefices in Canterbury, London, and Chichester dioceses about the turn of the sixteenth century. In 1512 Henry VIII presented him to the mastership of Cobham College in Rochester diocese. Cromer was one of the king's chaplains. He may well have been consulted by Henry VIII while the king was writing his *Assertio septem sacramentorum adversus Martinum Lutherum* (1521). It was on the monarch's recommendation that Cromer was provided to the archdiocese of Armagh on 2 October 1521. It has been proposed that Henry VIII favoured him because 'he was a priest of some ability and ambition, who had shown his devotion to the king in person, and who could be relied upon to be a conscientious, resident pastor in Ireland, and politically useful too' (Jefferies, *Priests*, 83–4).

Cromer had arrived in Ireland before November 1523. He found himself the ordinary of a diocese which was sharply divided: the southern parishes encompassed part of the English pale in Ireland, while the northern parishes and his cathedral were in part of the exclusively Irish lordship of Tyrone. As an Englishman, Cromer was inevitably viewed with some suspicion by the Irish élites, yet he managed to use the *modi operandi* established by his predecessors to overcome the divide between the two 'nations' and to administer the archdiocese successfully.

It has been shown that the church in Armagh was well ordered and pastorally effective during Cromer's episcopate on the eve of the Henrician Reformation. Within that portion of the archdiocese in the pale, in particular, there was a dense network of churches and chapels served by resident priests to meet the pastoral needs of the laity. The clergy and their congregations there were intensively supervised by the archbishop and his archdeacon, and grievous sins were dealt with in an efficient manner in Armagh's consistory court. The evidence available to study the church in the Ulster portion of the archdiocese is less voluminous than that for the southern parishes, yet there too it seems that the church was far better ordered than conventional accounts of the church in the Gaelic

lordships had supposed. Indeed, recent work has revealed that the church in the diocese of Armagh was going through a period of remarkable renewal on the very eve of the Henrician Reformation.

Cromer's synodal legislation shows him to have been a conservative reformer. He constantly challenged his priests to strive for the highest standards in their priestly lives and ministries. None the less, he was very much opposed to the Reformation. He was very distressed to witness Henry VIII's escalating campaign against the papacy during a visit to England in 1530–32. He employed his next synod in Ireland to prepare the clergy in his diocese against the religious maelstrom which was sure to cross the Irish Sea.

When Thomas Fitzgerald, son and heir of the ninth earl of Kildare, rebelled in 1534, ostensibly in a Catholic crusade against the heretical Henry VIII, Primate Cromer and Magister Cormac Roth, his archdeacon cum official principal, were both implicated in the rebellion. Cromer was removed from the office of lord chancellor of Ireland, a post which he had held since 1532, and was very fortunate to escape with his life. It is likely that the primate's high ecclesiastical office made his execution politically inexpedient. It has been suggested too that Cromer came to an arrangement with Deputy Grey, a viceroy who was conservatively inclined in religion, whereby the primate conformed outwardly to the Henrician religious settlement without being obliged to implement the more radical religious decrees in his diocese.

The English crown effectively displaced the papacy in juridical terms in the 'English' parishes of Armagh, but beneath the veneer of conformity Archbishop Cromer worked hard to preserve the Catholic faith and practices against Henry VIII's decrees. The agendas set before the priests in the annual diocesan synods were resolutely conservative. The royal injunctions against images were largely ignored in the southern parishes of Armagh, and the efficacy of pilgrimages continued to be endorsed by the primate. The Ulster parishes of the archdiocese were largely immune to the Henrician Reformation.

In Primate Cromer's last years he was beset by debilitating illness. He employed George Dowdall, former prior of the dissolved community of crutched friars at Ardee, as his chief commissary. Dowdall was a prominent conservative Catholic who, like his ordinary, conformed reluctantly to Henry VIII's schismatic church. Primate George Cromer died on 16 March 1543, and was probably buried at Termonfeckin, in co. Louth. He was succeeded as archbishop and primate by Prior Dowdall.

HENRY A. JEFFERIES

Sources H. A. Jefferies, *Priests and prelates of Armagh in the age of reformations, 1518–1558* (1997) · H. A. Jefferies, 'Dr George Cromer, archbishop of Armagh, and Henry VIII's Reformation', *Armagh: history and society*, ed. A. Hughes (2000) · G. Cromer, register, PRO NIre., MS DID 4/2/11 · exchequer inquisitions, NA Ire., MS R.C.19 · V. M. Buckley and D. Sweetman, eds., *Archaeological survey of county Louth* (1991) · *The whole works of Sir James Ware concerning Ireland*, ed. and trans. W. Harris, rev. edn, 1 (1764) · state papers, Ireland, Henry

VIII, PRO, SP 60 · A. Gwynn, *The medieval province of Armagh, 1470–1545* (1946) · Emden, *Oxf.*, vol. 4

Cromleholme, Samuel (1618–1672), headmaster, born in Wiltshire, was the son of Richard Cromleholme, who was rector of Quedgeley, Gloucestershire, from 1624. Samuel was seemingly educated at the King's School, Gloucester, during the mastership of John Langley (afterwards high master of St Paul's and the agent of Cromleholme's advancement). He was admitted to Corpus Christi College, Oxford, on 13 November 1635 at the age of seventeen, graduating BA on 27 June 1639 and proceeding MA on 15 June 1642.

In 1644 Cromleholme became master of the Mercers' Chapel school, London, and in 1647 was appointed surmaster of St Paul's School, London. Pepys, who was a pupil there at this time, respected his learning, but came to find him in his later years 'a conceited pædagogue … so dogmaticall in all he doth and says'. He was dismayed by Cromleholme's pleasure in the bottle and the neglect of his pretty, but childless, wife (who 'looks as if her mouth watered now and then upon some of her boys') (Pepys, 4.133; 6.53). His wife's name was Mary, but nothing else is known about her. By Langley's means Cromleholme obtained the headmastership of the grammar school at Dorchester, Dorset, on 19 October 1651. He returned to St Paul's as high master on 14 September 1657, having had Langley's deathbed recommendation to the Mercers' Company.

Renowned as a linguist, and 'very curious in books' (Knight, 326), at the burning of the school in the great fire of 1666 Cromleholme lost a valuable library, reputed the best private collection of its time in London. Until the school was reopened in 1671 the masters were paid retainers and allowed to take temporary employment elsewhere; Cromleholme opened a school at Wandsworth in 1668 or 1669. He died in London on 21 July 1672, having seen the school restored but still distraught at the loss of his own books. His funeral was held in the Guildhall chapel, the sermon given by Dr John Wells of St Botolph, Aldersgate. Cromleholme was buried in the Mercers' Chapel, London, on 26 July. His wife survived him.

C. W. SUTTON, *rev.* C. S. KNIGHTON

Sources J. Hutchins, *The history and antiquities of the county of Dorset*, 3rd edn, ed. W. Shipp and J. W. Hodson, 2 (1863), 368–9; facs. edn (1973) · S. Knight, *The life of Dr John Colet*, new edn (1823), 325–6 · M. McDonnell, ed., *The registers of St Paul's School, 1509–1748* (privately printed, London, 1977), 226–7 · Pepys, *Diary*, 3.199; 4.133; 6.53; 7.297 · *The obituary of Richard Smyth … being a catalogue of all such persons as he knew in their life*, ed. H. Ellis, CS, 44 (1849), 96 · N&Q, 2nd ser., 11 (1861), 403

Crommelin, Andrew Claude de la Cherois (1865–1939), astronomer, was born on 6 February 1865 at Cushendun, co. Antrim, Ireland, the third son of Nicholas de la Cherois Crommelin. His family was of Huguenot descent; one of his ancestors had helped found the linen trade in Ulster. He was educated in England—first at Marlborough College, then at Trinity College, Cambridge, where he took the mathematics tripos and in 1886 graduated as twenty-

seventh wrangler. Crommelin had always been interested in astronomy: when an additional post of assistant was created at the Royal Observatory at Greenwich, in 1891, he applied and was appointed.

Crommelin's work at Greenwich involved a combination of observation and computation. His computational responsibilities lay in the reduction of lunar observations and the calculation of cometary orbits. The British Astronomical Association was set up just before he went to Greenwich, and he served for many years as director of its comet section. In 1925, under his guidance, the association published a comet catalogue that rapidly became the standard reference source for cometary orbits. The best-known of his cometary calculations related to Halley's comet. This had last been seen in 1835 and was expected to return in 1910, but the exact date was uncertain. Crommelin collaborated with a colleague at the observatory, Philip *Cowell, in developing a simplified but more accurate way of calculating the orbit of a comet when subject to the gravitational perturbations of the planets. The comet passed the sun in 1910 just three days before the time predicted by Cowell and Crommelin. They commented that the difference might be due to non-gravitational forces—a suggestion that was confirmed when the comet returned in 1986. By extrapolating backwards in time, they were able to identify returns of the comet back to 240 BC. For their studies of Halley's comet, the two were jointly awarded the Lindemann prize of the Astronomische Gesellschaft, and both received honorary degrees from Oxford. The methods used with Halley's comet were also applied by Cowell and Crommelin to studying the orbit of the eighth satellite of Jupiter, discovered by their colleague P. J. Melotte at Greenwich in 1908.

In 1929 Crommelin's knowledge of past cometary orbits enabled him to identify a comet observed in the previous year as being identical with others seen in 1818 and 1873. In 1948, long after Crommelin's death, it was decided to call this comet after him—a rare honour, since a comet is almost always called after the person who observes it rather than the one who computes its orbit.

Another topic that attracted Crommelin's interest was the study of eclipses. His most important observations were certainly those made at the eclipse in 1919. Einstein published his general theory of relativity during the First World War. The then astronomer royal, Sir Frank Dyson, pointed out that the theory could be subjected to an observational test at the solar eclipse due in 1919. Consequently, two observing parties were sent out from Greenwich—one to Brazil and the other to west Africa. Crommelin was a leading member of the former party, which obtained the better results. The photographs brought back were measured rapidly, and found clearly to favour Einstein's predictions.

Crommelin was originally a member of the Church of England, and stayed on at Cambridge after the tripos examinations, intending to take holy orders. However, he gave up this intention, and, in 1891, became a Roman

Catholic. He had joined the Royal Astronomical Society before leaving Cambridge, and served it in various capacities throughout his life, being president from 1920 to 1930. In 1897 he married Letitia (*d.* 1921), the daughter of the Revd Robert Noble, and they had two sons and two daughters. His wife predeceased him, as did his elder son and younger daughter, who were killed in a mountaineering accident. Crommelin continued to live in London after his retirement from the observatory. He died at Twyford Abbey, West Twyford, Ealing, on 20 September 1939.

A. J. MEADOWS

Sources C. R. Davidson, *Monthly Notices of the Royal Astronomical Society*, 100 (1939–40), 234–6 · A. J. Meadows, *Greenwich observatory: the story of Britain's oldest scientific institution, 2: Recent history (1836–1975)* (1975) · *DSB* · d. cert. · *CGPLA Eng. & Wales* (1939)
Archives NMM, Royal Observatory, Greenwich, archives · RAS, letters to Royal Astronomical Society
Likenesses photograph (as president of Royal Astronomical Society), RAS
Wealth at death £2904 17s. 9d.: probate, 20 Dec 1939, *CGPLA Eng. & Wales*

Crommelin, (Samuel-)Louis [Samuel-Lewis] (1652–1727), linen manufacturer, was born in May 1652 at Armandcourt, near St Quentin, Picardy, the son of Louis Crommelin and his wife, Mary (Marie), *née* Mettayer. The Crommelin family had long been landowners and flax growers in the region. Louis Crommelin was sufficiently wealthy to leave £10,000 to each of his four sons, Samuel-Louis, Samuel, William, and Alexander. The younger Louis Crommelin, who, on his father's death, appears to have dropped the prefix Samuel, provided employment for many hands in flax spinning and linen weaving. The family was protestant, and the revocation of the edict of Nantes in 1685 proved the ruin of their business. Crommelin for some years endeavoured to hold his ground; he had reconciled himself to the Roman Catholic church in 1683, but, on his becoming again a protestant, his estates were forfeited to the crown and his buildings wrecked. With his son and two daughters (his wife, Anne, was dead) he made his way to Amsterdam. Here he became partner in a banking firm, and was joined by his brothers Samuel and William.

Many exiled Huguenot linen workers had been attracted to settle near to or in Lisburn (formerly Lisnagarvey), a cathedral town on the borders of counties Antrim and Down, where already there was considerable manufacture of linen, established by weavers from the north of England in the decades following the English civil war. In 1696 the English parliament passed an act (7 and 8 Will. III, c. 39) inviting foreign protestants to settle in Ireland, and admitting all products of hemp and flax duty free from Ireland to England. The Irish parliament in November 1697 passed an act for fostering the manufacture of linen. William III, in reply to an address from the English Commons on 9 June 1698, expressed his determination, while discouraging the Irish woollen trade, to do all in his power to encourage the linen manufactures of Ireland. With this view the king wrote to Crommelin, asking him to inquire into the condition of the French colony at Lisburn, and to

(Samuel-)Louis Crommelin (1652–1727), by unknown artist, *c.*1690–95

outline the terms on which he would agree to act as director of the linen manufacture. Crommelin arrived at Lisburn in the autumn of 1698. He set out his ideas respecting the best mode of improving the linen industry in a memorial dated 16 April 1699, and addressed to the commissioners of the Treasury. The Treasury, together with the commissioners of trade and plantations, recommended the adoption of Crommelin's proposals, and effect was at once given to them by a royal patent. Crommelin, who was made 'overseer of the royal linen manufacture of Ireland', advanced £10,000 to carry out the necessary works, the Treasury paying him 8 per cent on this sum for ten years. He was to have £200 a year as director, and £120 a year for each of three assistants. A grant of £60 was added towards the stipend of a French minister, and early in 1701 Charles Lavalade (whose sister had married Alexander Crommelin) became the pastor of the colony. The death of William III in 1702 imperilled the rising enterprise, but the royal patent and grants were renewed under Anne.

Crommelin began by ordering 300 looms (afterwards increased to 1000) from Flanders and Holland. Until his death a premium of £5 was granted for every loom kept going. He considered the old Irish spinning wheel superior to any in use abroad; but he employed skilled workmen to improve it still further. His reed maker was Henry Mark du Pré (*d.* 1750), one of the best reed makers of Cambrai. Baron Conway donated a site for weaving workshops, and, in addition to the Huguenot weavers, Irish apprentices were taken on. Dutch workers were engaged to teach improved methods of flax growing to farmers, and to superintend bleaching operations. Crommelin deserves limited credit for raising the levels of technical skills in Ulster, although his claims far exceeded his achievements. These, and those of the Huguenots in general, must be set against a wider background, including favourable factory endowments and the efforts of local landlords to encourage linen manufacture.

Crommelin published an *Essay towards the Improving of the Hempen and Flaxen Manufactories in the Kingdom of Ireland* (1705) containing many details of historical and scientific interest. It is perhaps best read today as a testimony to Crommelin's ability as a self-publicist.

Crommelin was effectively assisted by his three brothers. In 1705 a factory was opened at Kilkenny, under the management of William Crommelin. In 1707 the thanks of the Irish parliament were voted to Crommelin. The minutes of the linen board, a body of trustees appointed on 13 October 1711 by the Irish government for the extension of the linen manufacture, bear frequent testimony to Crommelin's 'invaluable service'. He pursued his work bravely, although his private life was blighted by the death of his only son, Louis, born at St Quentin, who died at Lisburn on 1 July 1711, aged twenty-eight. This event also cost him a pension of £200 per annum, which had been offered to Crommelin, but at his desire was given to his son. On 24 February 1716 the linen board recommended that a pension of £400 per annum be granted him by the government. In December 1717 Crommelin extended his operations by promoting settlements for the manufacture of hempen sailcloth at Rathkeale, Cork, Waterford, and later at Rathbride (1725). His energy ceased only with his life; he died at Lisburn on 14 July 1727, aged seventy-five, and was buried, with other Huguenots, in the eastern corner of the graveyard of the cathedral church. He left a daughter, married to Captain de Bernière.

ALEXANDER GORDON, rev. L. A. CLARKSON

Sources W. H. Crawford, 'The origins of the linen industry in north Armagh and the Lagan valley', *Ulster Folk Life*, 17 (1971), 42–51 · C. N. Purdon, 'The Huguenot colony at Lisburn', *Ulster Journal of Archaeology*, 1 (1853), 209–20 · E. R. R. Green, *The Lagan valley, 1800–50: a local history of the industrial revolution* (1949), 57–8 · C. Gill, *The rise of the Irish linen industry* (1925), 16–20

Likenesses portrait, c.1690–1695, Ulster Museum, Belfast [*see illus.*]

Crompton, Sir Charles John (1797–1865), judge, was born on 12 June 1797 at Derby, the third son of Peter Crompton (b. 1767), medical practitioner and son of a Derby banker, and Mary Crompton (b. 1759), daughter of John Crompton of Chorley Hall, Lancashire. His parents, who were second cousins, were descended from an old Lancashire puritan family that included the regicide John Bradshaw. His father, who moved the family to Eton House at Eaton, near Liverpool, after Charles was born, was a well-liked local gentleman, who donated medical services to the poor and dispensed hospitality to society. His mother was noted for her beauty, intellect, and advanced liberal opinions. A partisan in the Horne Tooke trial, she won the friendship of the poet Coleridge. Both parents saw continuity between contemporary political reform and the Good Old Cause of the seventeenth-century parliamentarians, and were hostile to 'old corruption'. Charles's deep-seated liberalism and satirical, caustic wit may be traced to his family descent and upbringing. He was respectably radical in opinion and style, and resented all pretence and claims to privilege. He would joke that 'the last judge in his family had tried a very illustrious prisoner' (Peel, 3).

Crompton made his career in the law by talent alone, without patronage. He had a distinguished undergraduate career at Trinity College, Dublin, from 1813 to 1816 (BA 1818, MA 1821), and after a year at a Liverpool solicitor's office he entered the Inner Temple in London to read for the bar. He mastered the art of special pleading, or the formal presentation of cases for litigation, learning from the leading barristers Joseph Littledale and John Patteson. After being called to the bar in 1821, he went to the northern and western circuits. He built an excellent reputation, particularly in mercantile and local government law; but his Liverpool practice took some time to flourish, and he knew the sting of failure. He twice stood unsuccessfully as a Liberal candidate for parliament, being defeated at Preston in 1832 and at Newport, Isle of Wight, in 1847. In 1832 he married Caroline, fourth daughter of Thomas Fletcher, a Liverpool merchant.

In time Crompton attracted offices, reporting exchequer decisions from 1830 to 1836 (with John Jervis and then with Roger Meeson and Henry Roscoe), becoming tubman and postman in the exchequer, counsel for the board of stamps and taxes, and assessor of the court of passage in Liverpool from 1836. He was appointed a member of the commission of inquiry into the court of chancery in 1851.

In February 1852, before he had taken silk, he was made a judge of queen's bench by Lord Truro, and knighted. He was a very successful appellate judge *in banco* for fourteen years, an equal of his eminent brethren of the court, though not their intellectual leader. His profound knowledge of the law and his honed skills of language revealed a cultivated and well-read mind. His store of learning was prodigious, though his judgments remained terse and clear. He soon won the admiration and esteem of his profession. He did not have the tall, dignified mien of a trial judge, but was quick-witted, sarcastic, kind, and humane.

Crompton delivered many leading judgments, most notably *Lumley* v. *Gye* (1853), where he held that a third party maliciously inducing a breach of contract was liable to tort damages independent of the contract—a doctrine used to devastating effect against trade unions at the turn of the century. His judgments generally reveal a classical liberal mind, devoted to individual freedom under the law. He applied private law concepts to public bodies and corporations, and did not develop a jurisprudence for the nascent collectivist age. He interpreted statutes strictly according to the worded intention of parliament, as if they were private contracts. In criminal and taxation cases he staunchly protected the legal rights of the defendant. His commercial law judgments were sound, elegant, learned, and utterly orthodox; for example he refused to expand agency, estoppel, and family entitlement as substitutes for the strict requirements of contractual agreement with bargained consideration (*Howard v. Hudson*, 1853; *Fitzmaurice v. Bailey*, 1856; *Tweddle v. Atkinson*, 1861). He preferred tort concepts of individual responsibility over concepts of strict liability derived from property law, and thereby limited the expansion of nuisance remedies for pollution (*Laing v. Whaley*, 1858).

Crompton died at his home, 22 Hyde Park Square, on 30 October 1865, aged sixty-eight, within weeks of the onset of stomach cancer. He was buried in Willesden churchyard, London. He was the archetype of the liberal-minded, supremely competent mid-Victorian judge. His five sons and three daughters included Henry *Crompton and Caroline Anna Croom *Robertson.

JOSHUA S. GETZLER

Sources L. Peel, 'The late Mr Justice Crompton', *Law Magazine*, new ser., 23 (1867), 1–30 · ER, 157.118–22 · E. Manson, *Builders of our law during the reign of Queen Victoria*, 2nd edn (1904), 294–301 · Foss, *Judges*, 9.187–8 · DNB
Likenesses portrait, repro. in *ILN* (1852), 356
Wealth at death under £60,000: probate, 30 Nov 1865, CGPLA Eng. & Wales

Crompton, Henry (1836–1904), barrister and positivist, was born at Liverpool on 27 August 1836, the second of five sons and three daughters of Sir Charles John *Crompton (1797–1865), judge of the queen's bench, and his wife, Caroline Fletcher. The eldest son, Charles Crompton (1833–1890), QC, was briefly a Gladstonian Liberal MP for Staffordshire (Leek division), and the fourth son, Albert Crompton (1843–1908), manager of the Ocean Steamship Company, was the founder of the positivist church at Liverpool. Of his sisters, the eldest, Mary, married the Christian socialist clergyman John Llewelyn Davies; the second, Caroline Anna [see Robertson, Caroline Anna Croom], married the philosopher George Croom Robertson; and the third, Emily, married the positivist Edward Spenser Beesly. The Crompton parents were Unitarians but brought up their children as Anglicans.

Crompton attended University College School, London, and then a private school at Bonn, before entering Trinity College, Cambridge, in 1854. He graduated BA as junior optime in the mathematical tripos in 1858. Through his father's influence he was appointed in 1858 clerk of assize on the Chester and north Wales circuit, a post he held until retirement in 1901; he was called to the bar at the Inner Temple on 6 June 1863. His familial legal connections were strengthened by marriage, on 8 November 1870, to the Hon. Lucy Henrietta (d. 1923), daughter of John *Romilly, first Lord Romilly, master of the rolls. They had two sons.

During a long period of illness in 1861, Crompton read Harriet Martineau's edition of Comte's *Philosophie Positive* and became a convert to the secular religion of positivism. After meeting E. S. Beesly in 1864, and through him Richard Congreve, he joined the positivist community in London. Like other followers of Comte, he studied medicine and biology, attending classes at St Mary's Hospital, Paddington. He was active in denouncing the oppression of subject races, and became a member of the Jamaica committee in 1867 to prosecute Governor Eyre; he also signed the petition on behalf of the Fenian prisoners in the same year. He later urged British intervention to protect the French republic in 1871, and attacked the immorality of wars of colonial conquest in a pamphlet edited by Congreve and published in 1879. His *Letters on Social and Political Subjects* were published in 1870. He was active in the movement in 1868 to establish lectures open to women at University College, London, his mother, Lady Crompton, being a founder member of the London Ladies' Educational Association. He belonged to the circle of John Russell and Katherine Russell (Lord and Lady Amberley); one of their more conservative relatives, deploring Crompton's defence of the Paris commune, pronounced him 'one of the biggest fools I ever met' (Russell and Russell, 2.462).

Crompton's particular contribution to the positivist project of social reconstruction lay in his assistance to the Trades Union Congress in its campaign between 1871 and 1875 to place employers and workers in a position of equality before the law and to remove the criminal law from the conduct of industrial relations. His numerous publications during the controversy included articles in the trade union paper *The Beehive* and pamphlets on the Criminal Law Amendment Act (1871) and the law of conspiracy in the TUC's series of Tracts for Trade Unionists. At the Congress held in Leeds in 1873 he contributed to the drafting of the TUC legislative programme, and later described its successful outcome in an article on 'The workmen's victory', published in the *Fortnightly Review* (1875). His professional insight into the criminal law and its administration made his counsel particularly valuable, but his influence lay as much in his even-tempered and sympathetic character. Unlike the more abrasive and outspoken positivists Beesly and Frederic Harrison, he established good relations with the secretary to the TUC parliamentary committee, George Howell, who regarded him as a personal friend. After 1875 he encouraged the TUC to support the extension of trial by jury and the codification of the criminal law. His articles on the subject, published during 1875–6 and reprinted after his death as *Our Criminal Justice* (ed. K. Digby, 1905), though critical in detail, were ultimately preservative in their intent, namely, to stimulate popular interest in and loyalty to the law. His failure in 1881 to persuade the TUC to oppose the government's policy of coercion against the leaders of the Irish Land League led to a more distant relationship with the labour movement.

Crompton was a well-informed and influential analyst of contemporary trends in industrial relations. His pamphlet *The Labour Laws Commission* (1875) sharply exposed the divergence between legal assumptions and the facts of industrial life, and this approach was developed in his *Industrial Conciliation* (1876), an optimistic account of the development of collective bargaining in British industry. It was described by Sidney and Beatrice

Webb as 'the classic work' on the subject (*The History of Trade Unionism*, 1920 edn, 338 n.), and its evolutionary approach was drawn upon by Arnold Toynbee in his account of the industrial revolution. His methods also helped to inspire his cousin Charles Booth to embark upon a programme of social investigation.

Crompton was among those who followed Congreve after the schism in the English positivist movement in 1878, and assumed responsibility as his successor as director of the Church of Humanity at Chapel Street, London, where he was known for his piety and religiosity. His leadership was challenged by Malcolm Quin, the positivist leader in Newcastle and, in poor health, he resigned in 1901, despairing at the divisions within the movement. Crompton died on 15 March 1904 at his home, Churt House, near Farnham, Surrey. His widow, also a positivist, published a volume of *Selections of Prose and Poetry by Henry Crompton* in 1910.

M. C. CURTHOYS

Sources E. S. Beesly, 'Henry Crompton', *Positivist Review*, 12 (1904) · DNB · J. E. McGee, *A crusade for humanity: the history of organized positivism in England* (1931) · R. Harrison, *Before the socialists: studies in labour and politics, 1861–1881* (1965) · A. Kadish, *Apostle Arnold: the life and death of Arnold Toynbee, 1852–1883* (1986) · R. O'Day and D. Englander, *Mr Charles Booth's inquiry: 'Life and labour of the people in London' reconsidered* (1993) · Venn, *Alum. Cant.* · *Wellesley index* · T. R. Wright, *The religion of humanity: the impact of Comtean positivism on Victorian Britain* (1986) · B. Russell and P. Russell, eds., *The Amberley papers: the letters and diaries of Lord and Lady Amberley*, 2 vols. (1937)
Archives Bishopsgate Institute, London, letters to George Howell · BL, corresp. with R. Congreve · Castle Howard, Yorkshire, letters to countess of Carlisle · LUL, corresp. with E. S. Beesly
Likenesses photograph, repro. in Harrison, *Before the socialists*, facing p. 275
Wealth at death £16,203 0s. 3d.: probate, 30 July 1904, CGPLA Eng. & Wales

Crompton, Hugh (*fl.* 1652–1658), poet, was probably a member of a Lancashire family, born a gentleman and well educated, who initially wrote poetry for his own amusement. When his father's business failed, he tried some genteel employment. When this failed him, he wrote to become self-sufficient. His first work may have been *The Glory of Women, Translated into Heroicall Verse*, from Agrippa, published in 1652. But the work that brought recognition for its liveliness was *Poems … Being a fardle of fancies or a medley of musick, stewed in four ounces of the oyl of epigrams* of 120 pages, published in 1657. It was dedicated to his kinsman Colonel Thomas Crompton. The first part includes sixty-seven poems, normally on a theme of love, and the second part of ten pages includes twenty-one epigrams. A year later he published *Pierides, or, The Muses Mount*, dedicated to Mary, duchess of Richmond and Lennox, containing 110 light poems covering the emotions of love, despair, and hope. An engraved oval portrait of Crompton with flowing hair faces the title-page. Before 1687 he emigrated to Ireland, and he may have been responsible for *The Distressed Welshman* in verse published in 1688.

F. D. A. BURNS

Sources DNB · W. Winstanley, *The lives of the most famous English poets* (1687), 191 · T. Corser, *Collectanea Anglo-poetica, or, A … catalogue of a … collection of early English poetry*, 4, Chetham Society, 77 (1869), 521–6

Likenesses A. Hertochs, line engraving (aged eighteen), BM · line engraving, BM; repro. in H. Crompton, *Pierides, or, The Muses mount* (1658), facing title-page · pen-and-ink drawing (after A. Hertochs), BM

Crompton, John (*bap.* 1611, *d.* 1669), clergyman and ejected minister, was born in Bolton, Lancashire, and baptized there on 29 September 1611, a younger son of Abraham Crompton of Breightmet, Bolton, and his wife, Alice, *née* Roscoe. Admitted as a sizar at Emmanuel College, Cambridge, in July 1629, Crompton graduated BA in 1633 and MA in 1636. After being ordained a deacon at Chester on 25 September 1636, he was appointed curate (or possibly lecturer) of All Hallows, Derby, on 30 November of the same year. While there he gained substantial respect for ministering to the people throughout a major outbreak of the plague, attributing his own good health during that time to a plaster applied to his stomach. At Lichfield on 1 March 1640 Crompton was ordained a priest and licensed to preach in the diocese.

Following William Greaves's ejection, Crompton was appointed rector of Brailsford, Derbyshire, where he had arrived by 13 September 1645. However, Greaves refused to relinquish the living, forcing the county committee, which accused him of scandalous living and neglect of his responsibilities, to remove him on 5 May 1646. Unlike many other intruded ministers, Crompton was assiduous in paying his predecessor's family the fifth of his income allowed by parliament. He also assigned the revenue from the chapel at Osmaston, worth £40 per annum, to another minister in order to devote his own full attention to the Brailsford congregation, where he preached twice on Sundays and then repeated both sermons in the evening to his family and neighbours.

The interregnum discomfited Crompton. Ignoring the Rump Parliament's abolition of monthly fasts in 1649 he observed one on the first Wednesday of every month throughout most of the interregnum, for which activity he was kept under surveillance by magistrates. With his neighbours he hoped to aid Sir George Booth's rebellion in August 1659 by supporting the attempt by Colonel Charles White and Lord Byron to take control of Derby, but the uprising there was very brief. Although some of Crompton's associates were imprisoned, he avoided this punishment, but had five or six soldiers quartered in his house. On the eve of the Restoration seven ministers signed a certificate, dated 22 February 1660, attesting his good behaviour, but he was ejected from his living notwithstanding the support of aldermen, local clergy, and people of substance. Edward Love succeeded him at Brailsford.

Crompton moved to Arnold, Nottinghamshire, where he served as vicar until his ejection in 1662. According to Edmund Calamy his farewell sermon was published as the ninth in a collection of similar sermons by country ministers, but this seems not to be extant. For three years Crompton continued to live at Arnold, renting the vicarage-house and preaching when no one else was available. Generally, however, he worshipped at nearby Gedling and Basford. Because of the Five Mile Act (1665) he relocated to Mapperley, Derbyshire, where he attended Church of England services. He died on 9 January 1669, probably at Mapperley, and was buried three days later at West Hallam, Derbyshire, following a sermon by Robert Horne. Nothing is known of any wife, but Crompton presumably married, as his nuncupative will, proved on 8 June 1669, left possessions valued at £83 17s. 6d., divided equally among his children, Abraham, Joshua, Samuel, and Rebecca. Samuel (1650–1735) was a dissenting minister at Doncaster, Yorkshire, and Crompton's nephew, John (1640–1703), son of Henry and Rebecca Crompton of Breightmet, was a Presbyterian minister at Bolton. An unidentified conformist remarked that John Crompton was 'always chearful, tho' mostly of the losing side' (*Nonconformist's Memorial*, 2.278). RICHARD L. GREAVES

Sources *Calamy rev.* · *The nonconformist's memorial ... originally written by ... Edmund Calamy*, ed. S. Palmer, 2 vols. (1775) · Venn, *Alum. Cant.* · Burke, *Gen. GB* (1833–8) · J. Hunter, *Familiae minorum gentium*, ed. J. W. Clay, 4 vols., Harleian Society, 37–40 (1894–6) · *Walker rev.*
Archives BL, Add. MS 15669, fol. 170 · BL, Add. MS 15670, fol. 81
Wealth at death £83 17s. 6d.: *Calamy rev.*, 146

Crompton, Richard (*b. c.*1529, *d.* in or after 1599), legal writer, was the son of Richard Crompton (*d.* 1530), citizen and mercer of Honey Lane, London, and his wife, Elizabeth Gyrling, of Norfolk. He was admitted to the Middle Temple on 19 April 1553 at the instance of Robert Brown, baron of the exchequer, who acted as his pledge. Called to the bar before 26 June 1563, he was appointed to provide the reader's feast in 1571. Autumn reader in 1573, he became a bencher of the inn in the same year, and read again in Lent 1579 on the Statutes of the Staple.

Crompton's father had been born at Fradswell, Staffordshire, and by 1583 at the latest Crompton was living at Checkley in the same county. He was regularly a justice of the peace for Staffordshire from 1586 at the latest, making his last appearance in the calendar of justices in 1599. At an unknown date he married Katherine, daughter of Oliver Richardson, grocer of London, and his wife, Katherine Rawson, who had previously been married to Crompton's uncle William Crompton (*d.* 1564), also a citizen and mercer of London. Their children included John Crompton of Stone Park, Staffordshire (*d.* 1663).

It is said that for his legal abilities Crompton might have been created serjeant-at-law, 'had he not preferred his private studies and repose before public enjoyment and riches' (Wood, *Ath. Oxon.*, 1.634), but his 'private studies' gave rise to a number of books. His considerable enlargement of Sir Anthony Fitzherbert's *Loffice et authoritie de iustices de peace*, dedicated to Sir Thomas Bromley, lord chancellor, and the author's companions in the Middle Temple, which contained a number of references to matters concerning the commission of the peace in Staffordshire, was printed by Richard Tottell in 1583, and again in 1584, 1587, and 1593. Charles Yetsweirt printed it in 1594, and further printings were undertaken by Adam Islip for the Stationers' Company in 1606 and 1617. In 1587 appeared *A Short Declaration of the Ende of Traytors, and False Conspirators Against the State*, concerning the fate of traitors and the duty of subjects to their sovereign, which put into

circulation material which the author, as he said, had 'lately published' to acclaim at the general sessions of the peace in Staffordshire. It was printed by John Charlewood for Thomas Gubbin and Thomas Newman, and dedicated to John Whitgift, archbishop of Canterbury.

These works were followed by Crompton's principal contribution to legal writing, his *L'authoritie et iurisdiction des courts de la maiestie de la royne*, printed by Yetsweirt in 1594, and again in 1637 by the assigns of John More. Dedicated to Sir John Puckering, lord keeper, and to 'all my companions of the Middle Temple' it had been, as Crompton said, written for the solace of his old age, for the ease of others, and to demonstrate that he had not been an entirely unprofitable member of the inn. In contrast with William Lambard's *Archeion*, completed in 1591 and published in 1635, Crompton's volume on the central courts was legal rather than political, owing much to Fitzherbert's and Brooke's abridgments, and being largely a digest of cases. Roger North recommended it to law students, regarding it as one of the 'institutionary' works which 'must be read at one time or another' (North, 17). In 1630, and again in 1641, appeared *Star-Chamber Cases*, collected 'for the most part' out of Crompton's volume on the courts, and printed for John Grove. Crompton's last work was *The Mansion of Magnanimitie*, concerning the defence of the realm; dedicated to Robert Devereux, earl of Essex, earl marshal of England, it was printed for William Ponsonby in 1599, and issued again twice in 1608.

Virtually nothing is known of Crompton's death. He was apparently still listed as a magistrate for Staffordshire in January 1599, and was mentioned in the 1601 marriage settlement of his cousin, William Crompton of Stone Park, although it is not clear whether he was still living at that time. N. G. JONES

Sources H. A. C. Sturgess, ed., *Register of admissions to the Honourable Society of the Middle Temple, from the fifteenth century to the year 1944*, 1 (1949) · C. T. Martin, ed., *Minutes of parliament of the Middle Temple*, 4 vols. (1904–5) · S. Grazebrook, ed., 'The visitation of Staffordshire [sic] ... 1583', *Collections for a history of Staffordshire*, William Salt Archaeological Society, 3/2 (1882) · H. S. Grazebrook, ed., 'The heraldic visitations of Staffordshire ... in 1614 and ... 1663 and 1664', *Collections for a history of Staffordshire*, William Salt Archaeological Society, 5/2 (1884) · S. A. H. Burne, ed., *The Staffordshire quarter sessions rolls*, 1–4, William Salt Archaeological Society, 3rd ser. (1929–35) · *STC, 1475–1640* · Holdsworth, *Eng. law*, vol. 5 · J. B. Williamson, ed., *The Middle Temple bench book*, 2nd edn, 1 (1937) · Wood, *Ath. Oxon.*, new edn, vol. 1 · *Report on the manuscripts of the late Reginald Rawdon Hastings*, 4 vols., HMC, 78 (1928–47), vol. 1 · G. Ormerod, *Additions and index to parentalia and genealogical memoirs* (1856) · R. North, *A discourse on the study of the laws* (1824)

Crompton, Richmal. See Lamburn, Richmal Crompton (1890–1969).

Crompton, Robert (1879–1941), footballer, was born at his parents' home, 1 Harwood Street, Blackburn, Lancashire, on 26 September 1879, the son of Robert Crompton, an innkeeper, and his wife, Alice Utley. He learned his football on the streets of Blackburn and at his schools, Moss Street board school and the higher grade school, to which he went in the 1880s. He became an apprentice plumber and was initially spotted playing in the local Sunday

OGDEN'S CIGARETTES.

R. CROMPTON.

Robert Crompton (1879–1941), by unknown engraver, 1908

school league. He also played for the Rose and Thistle (which does not have the ring of the bible class) and Blackburn Trinity, before joining the mighty Blackburn Rovers, for whom he played as an amateur for two years because he did not want to jeopardize his amateur status in swimming and water polo.

Crompton was associated with his home town club from the time he first signed for them in 1896 until his death, save for a few years in the 1930s. After the institution of the maximum wage in 1901 a move to another club would not bring more money, but money was not everything. Some clubs appeared more likely to win cup and league than others, and there were rumours that Crompton was wanted by Everton. But he remained with Blackburn Rovers and was captain of the side which in the four years immediately preceding the abandonment of professional football in the First World War, had won the championship of the first division twice, in 1911–12 and 1913–14, and had finished fifth and third in 1912–13 and 1914–15. He was still playing when football resumed after the war, but injury forced his retirement at the age of forty in 1920.

Bob Crompton must have been a remarkable footballer, if for no other reason than that he played forty-one times for England between 1902 and 1914, when the number of international matches was much lower than in later years. This record number of appearances was not exceeded until Billy Wright won his forty-second cap, in 1952. Moreover in Crompton's time the selection committee was fickle and inconsistent, never choosing the same eleven twice. He played in every England v. Scotland game in this period except 1905, when he was unfit, and became the first professional to captain an England side which also included an amateur player.

Crompton was a right full-back. He played under the old offside law, which gave the two full-backs more responsibility for central defence than after 1925, when the law was relaxed, reducing from three to two the number of players who had to be between the receiver of the pass at the moment it was made and the opposition goal line. After this change the centre half was withdrawn from midfield to become the third back, playing between those on the right and left, whose main job was now to mark the wing forwards. Crompton himself had begun as a centre half but converted to full-back in the late 1890s. He had a reputation for robust tackling combined with a use of the shoulder charge, which would be penalized as rough play in more recent times. At his peak he was quick enough to recover if beaten or drawn out of position.

Crompton maintained his trade as a plumber and was successful enough not only to be the first footballer to drive a car, in 1908, but also to become a director of a local firm of building contractors. In many respects he was a model professional, successful and upwardly mobile. He was sceptical about the players' need for a trade union and accepted the view of management that commercialized football was not like other businesses and was run in the best interests of all by the wise men at the Football League and the Football Association.

In June 1921 the Football Association granted the special permission necessary for this ex-professional to become a director of Blackburn Rovers. By the end of 1926 Crompton was team manager and led the team to a surprise victory in the 1928 cup final. He was then an early victim of player discontent and in the spring of 1931 lost both his job as manager and his seat on the board. He briefly managed Bournemouth and Boscombe Athletic during 1935–6, but when Blackburn were threatened with relegation to the third division in 1937–8 he was recalled as 'honorary' team manager. The club escaped and in May 1938 he was back on the payroll. Under his charge Rovers won the championship of the second division but war then intervened.

Crompton died suddenly at 24 Eldon Road, Blackburn, on 15 March 1941, after having watched a wartime fixture between Rovers and Burnley. By then he and his wife, Ada, had been living in Blackpool for several years. She, along with two sons and a daughter, survived him. He was buried in Blackburn cemetery on 20 March 1941.

TONY MASON

Sources T. Mason, *Association football and English society, 1863–1915* (1980) · A. Gibson and W. Pickford, *Association football and the men who made it*, 4 vols. [1905–6], vol. 1 · F. Wall, *Fifty years of football* (1934) · *Northern Daily Telegraph* (17 March 1941) · *Northern Daily Telegraph* (20 March 1941) · J. Harding, *For the love of the game* (1991) · b. cert. · d. cert. · J. A. H. Catto, 'Celebrities at association football', *Ideas* (23 Jan 1914)

Likenesses print on Ogden cigarette card, 1908, BM [*see illus.*] · photographs, repro. in Gibson and Pickford, *Association football* · photographs, Blackburn Rovers football club

Wealth at death £8871 6s. 7d.: probate, 24 July 1941, *CGPLA Eng. & Wales*

Crompton, Rookes Evelyn Bell (1845–1940), engineer, was born at Sion Hill, near Thirsk, on 31 May 1845, the fourth son and youngest child of Joshua Samuel Crompton and his first wife, Mary, daughter of Sir Claud Alexander, and a friend and pupil of Mendelssohn. The names Rookes Evelyn record his kinship through the Rookes, his grandmother's family, with the diarist John Evelyn.

During the Crimean War, Crompton, aged only eleven, was enrolled as a naval cadet and allowed to accompany Captain William Houston Stewart, his mother's cousin, commander of the *Dragon*. He visited his elder brother in the trenches and actually came under fire, thus earning himself the Crimean medal and Sevastopol clasp.

School at Elstree (1856–8) prepared Crompton for Harrow (1858–60). During his holidays he built, in a workshop at home, a full-size steam-driven road engine; but before his true engineering career began he served for four years in India (1864–8) as an ensign in the rifle brigade. Even there, however, he equipped a travelling workshop, and had his machine tools sent out from England. His strong views on the inefficiency and slowness of the bullock trains impressed R. S. Bourke, earl of Mayo, then viceroy, and within a short time Crompton introduced steam road haulage, receiving a government grant of £500 for his services.

Crompton married, on 16 June 1871, Elizabeth Gertrude (d. 1939), daughter of George Richard John Clarke, of Tanfield, near Ripon; they had two sons, one of whom predeceased his father, and three daughters. His wife was his constant companion, keenly interested in all his enterprises.

In 1875 Crompton retired from the army and bought a partnership in a Chelmsford engineering firm. While adviser at the Stanton ironworks belonging to the Derbyshire branch of his family, he purchased some of the new Gramme dynamos in order to improve the lighting of the foundry. Their success provided a turning point; from that date (1878) electricity and engineering became for him almost inseparable. Co-operating with Emil Bürgin, of Basel, who was then working on dynamo design, Crompton obtained the rights of manufacture and sale of Bürgin's machine, improved it, and developed it to commercial success. From 1878 to 1882 he restricted his business to the manufacture of electrical-arc plant. One of his early contracts was to light St Enoch's Station, Glasgow. This was followed in due course by contracts at the Mansion House and Law Courts in London and the Ringtheater in Vienna. At the Paris Electrical Exhibition of 1881 the firm of Cromptons was awarded the first gold medal ever given for electric lighting plant.

Towards the end of 1886 Crompton formed the Kensington Court Company, financed by a few friends, for electricity supply to neighbouring premises. This pioneer enterprise, one of the first of its kind, became the Kensington and Knightsbridge Electric Supply Company. Crompton advocated the direct current system; S. Z. de Ferranti, engineer of the London Electric Supply Corporation, believed in alternating current and led the opposing school. The resulting 'battle of the systems', with these

two as friendly antagonists, has its place in electrical history.

Between 1890 and 1899 Crompton revisited India, advising the government on electrical projects. On his return he took charge of a volunteer corps of electrical engineers, and by May 1900 was in South Africa with his men, whose efficiency in maintaining communications and skill in emergencies won high praise. Crompton had gone out as captain; on his return, later that year, he was promoted lieutenant-colonel, appointed CB, and retained as consultant to the War Office on the development of mechanical transport.

Although electrical matters still claimed much of his time, Crompton became increasingly occupied with road transport. He had been a founder member of the Royal Automobile Club in 1896, and was one of the judges in 1903 at the first motor show; as engineer member of the road board appointed by the government in 1910, he improved road construction practice and materials. In the early part of the First World War, Churchill consulted Crompton upon the design of an armoured vehicle capable of crossing trenches, and he was responsible for producing a type of 'landship' which later evolved, under various hands, into the tank.

In his laboratory at Thriplands, his Kensington home, Crompton spent many hours at research. He served on the committee of the National Physical Laboratory, and his advocacy of a closer understanding between all countries on electrical affairs resulted in the founding of the International Electrotechnical Commission in 1906, of which he was the first secretary.

In 1927 Cromptons merged with another firm under the title Crompton, Parkinson, & Co. Ltd. 'The Colonel' was then over eighty, but still active, and he retained a directorship in the new concern. A dinner in his honour, held in London in 1931, was attended by probably the largest gathering of distinguished scientists and engineers ever recorded at a personal function. Each of the three principal engineering bodies, the Civil, Mechanical, and Electrical, made him an honorary member; he was twice president of the Institution of Electrical Engineers, in 1895 and again in 1908. He was awarded the Faraday medal in 1926 and was elected FRS in 1933. His ninetieth year was celebrated by another banquet, at which Sir James Swinburne presented him with his portrait by George Harcourt, later in the possession of the Institution of Electrical Engineers.

Professionally, Crompton was the expert, commanding respect and admiration; socially, a host of friends regarded him with affection. Young men benefited by his cheerful attitude to life, his resource and originality, and often by his generous help. He died at Azerley Chase, Kirkby Malzeard, near Ripon, on 15 February 1940.

W. L. RANDELL, *rev.* ANITA McCONNELL

Sources R. E. B. Crompton, *Reminiscences* (1928) · J. H. Johnson and W. L. Randell, *Colonel Crompton* (1945) · A. Russell, *Obits. FRS*, 3 (1939–41), 395–403 · *Journal of the Institution of Civil Engineers*, 14 (1939–40), 245–7 · personal knowledge (1949)

Archives Sci. Mus., corresp., diaries, and papers | CUL, corresp. with Lord Kelvin
Likenesses W. Stoneman, photograph, 1933, NPG · G. Harcourt, oils, *c*.1935, Inst. EE · G. Hall, drawing, Institution of Mechanical Engineers, London · Who, caricature, Hentschel-colourtype, NPG; repro. in *VF* (30 Aug 1911) · oils, Inst. EE · portrait, repro. in *Obits. FRS*, facing p. 395
Wealth at death £15,329 14s. 0d.: probate, 4 June 1940, *CGPLA Eng. & Wales* · £13,000: further grant, 3 Oct 1940, *CGPLA Eng. & Wales*

Crompton, Samuel (1753–1827), inventor of the spinning mule, was born at Firwood Fold, Tonge, near Bolton, Lancashire, on 3 December 1753, the eldest son of George Crompton (1726–1758) and Elizabeth Holt (1725–1799) of nearby Turton. Firwood Farm had been held by Cromptons since Tudor times; Samuel's father began his working life as a farmer–weaver but he was forced to sell the property and to become a mere tenant. At his death his widow was left to rear three small children, but she was able, industrious, and proud. She stayed in the area, moving the family to the old black and white timbered mansion of Hall-in-the-Wood, where they remained from 1758 until 1781. Samuel was schooled locally in arithmetic, algebra, and geometry. From an early age he was set to work, spinning yarns by hand for Marseilles quiltings, a new local product. At the age of eleven he rose to the more elevated status of weaver, but continued to spin his own yarn. Bettey Crompton with her two daughters, Rebekah and Mary, seems to have prospered through industry and frugality, leasing Hall-in-the-Wood in 1764 for an annual rental of £9 18s. She remained a widow for forty years and was buried in 1799, leaving less than £100, of which one-third passed to Samuel.

The mule The details of Samuel Crompton's life are of limited importance in comparison to the magnitude of his achievement in inventing the spinning mule (so called because it combined the rollers of Richard Arkwright's water frame with the moving carriage of James Hargreaves's jenny). Crompton's invention was, none the less, wholly his own since he had no predecessors in the field and was never assailed by rival claimants. No alternative device could fulfil the functions performed by the mule, or spin yarn equal in quality to its product. Contemporaries paid ample homage to his achievement by seeking to discover its secrets, laying siege to his home, invading his privacy, spying upon his activity, and seducing his workers.

Crompton fulfils all the criteria appropriate to the heroic theory of invention, whereby new devices are produced by individual minds and not by impersonal social forces. The story of the invention is related at length in a letter written on 30 October 1807 to Sir Joseph Banks. From 1768 Crompton had used the new jenny in place of the spinning-wheel. He seems to have tried to spin warps on a machine designed to spin weft. The brittle quality of his jenny-spun yarn drove him first to despair and then to creative invention. From 1772 he devoted all his considerable ingenuity to improving the process of spinning and ensuring, as he confided to Sir Joseph Banks, 'that every thread of cotton yarn should be (as near as possible)

Samuel Crompton (1753–1827), by Samuel William Reynolds senior, pubd 1828 (after Charles Allingham)

Eaqually good'. Before he could finally decide which plan to adopt, six years had passed—three in contemplation and three in experiment. Crompton was not a practical mechanic and his funds were very limited. Fearing that the employment of a mechanic risked the disclosure of his device, he himself constructed the entire pioneer machine during a period of eighteen months in 1778–9. That creation 'was to be the standard on which to rest all my future hopes both as to good yarn and profit to myself' (Crompton to Banks, 30 Oct 1807, Bolton Central Library, Crompton MS ZCR 11/4). Machine-breaking riots spread eastwards from Wigan to reach Bolton on 5 October 1779, greatly disturbing Crompton and compelling him to conceal the new invention. From 1779 to the beginning of 1780 he spun both warp and weft for his own use on the 48 spindle machine and discovered that it functioned best when it was kept in constant operation. He therefore abandoned weaving to concentrate on spinning.

The mule remains the most important of 'the most sensational series of epoch-making mechanical inventions, which has ever been compressed into so short a period in the history of civilization' (S. J. Chapman, 'Cotton', *Chambers's Encyclopedia*, 1918, 3.510). Its value may best be measured by comparison to earlier machines, though it is unnecessary to depreciate the achievements of his predecessors, from John Wyatt and Lewis Paul to Hargreaves and Arkwright. Both types of spinning-wheel were limited in the type of yarn they could produce. Their early successors, the jenny and the water frame, remained similarly restricted. The roller-spinning frame could spin a coarse warp, but could not spin weft of any kind or fine twist. The jenny could spin only weft, but could spin higher counts (that is, finer, with more threads to the inch) of weft than the water frame could of warp. The finest yarn in the world was spun in Bengal by hand spinners. Crompton combined the spindles of the jenny with the rollers of the frame, transferring the spindles to a mobile carriage and placing the gearing to the side of the machine. The hybrid machine undertook a five-stage cycle of operations, like the jenny. In essence it combined drafting by rollers and drawbar with the insertion of twist by the revolution of the spindle. Its inventor called it 'a machine or Spinning Wheele'; others termed it the double jenny, the Hall-in-the-Wood wheel, the muslin wheel, and, finally, the mule. The machine proved to be much more versatile than its predecessors because the relationship between the speed of the three working parts—spindles, rollers, and carriage—could be varied and because its intermittent action replicated that of the human hand in spinning. Its motion imposed minimum strain upon the yarn until it had been strengthened by twisting, a procedure which also served to eliminate fibre-mass faults. A cop of yarn was built up on the bare spindle and the tension was carefully controlled during the operation of winding, as on the jenny. Thus it avoided the labour of rewinding since a weft cop could be skewered directly into a weaver's shuttle. The mule could spin both hard and soft yarns, suitable for either warp or weft, and could spin warps superior in hardness to those of the water frame. Above all it could spin finer counts of yarn than either of its rivals. It was also highly productive since it employed forty-eight spindles, or sixfold the number on Hargreaves's original jenny. Whichever type of yarn it spun, the product remained perfectly uniform throughout. The machine was an immediate success, a remarkable achievement for an invention without any precedent.

The impact of the mule The mule proved to be a machine of immense merit which gave the greatest impulse to the trade, as Thomas Bazley, the chairman of the Manchester chamber of commerce, noted in 1852. In effect it created a wholly new cotton industry. Imports of raw cotton quintupled in volume between 1779 and 1790 in order to supply the needs of what became from 1784 the largest cotton industry in Europe. The value of its product increased even faster than its consumption of raw material. It is, however, misleading to suggest that the spread of the mule completed the process of decline in domestic spinning. Indeed it stimulated an immediate competitive improvement in the jenny as well as in the water frame. The jenny enlarged its spindleage and was improved by Crompton himself in 1783, but it faced increasing competition from the mule from the 1790s and thereafter was relegated to the spinning of the lowest and coarsest counts of yarn, made from the waste of inferior cottons and usually known as jenny-weft. The water frame also upgraded its capacity and by 1788 was spinning yarn of a degree of fineness which would have been incredible a decade earlier.

In versatility and productivity the mule embodied all the dynamic features favouring rapid propagation which the water frame lacked. It was unrestricted in the range of its products and remained unshackled by any patent or monopoly. Being compact in form, light in weight, and, above all, cheap, it was accessible to persons with the least amount of capital. It was both hand-powered and hand-controlled and could easily be worked at home. The demand for mule-spun yarn was well-nigh insatiable. That demand was met first in the 1780s by small masters, and only in the 1790s by factory masters. During the decade 1779–89, mules were set to work in garrets, cow houses, stables, and barns. A large number of householders acquired a single mule and began operations. Thus the trend initiated by Arkwright of restricting the industry to capitalists was reversed (A. Mallalieu, 'The cotton manufacture', *Blackwood's Edinburgh Magazine*, March 1836, 408). A new democratic era dawned wherein small-scale producers catered for the swelling demand. In that respect, the diffusion of the mule would have satisfied Crompton, who disliked the factory system. The increasingly fine mule-spun yarns created a range of new trades, especially the manufacture of muslin, enabling Lancashire and Scotland to compete with Bengal and reducing the price of East-India muslins from 1784, though the mule never produced yarns as fine as those made by the hand spinners of Bengal. Nor did the new muslins use mule-spun yarn for both warp and weft; the preference during the 1780s was to combine roller-spun warps with mule-spun wefts. The new machine nevertheless gave a great impetus to the increase in the numbers of hand-loom weavers, virtually creating an army of such domestic workers at the same time as vast numbers of spinners lost their employment. 'It was the introduction of mule yarns … that gave such a preponderating wealth through the loom' (W. Radcliffe, *Origin of the New System of Manufacture*, 1828, 65).

From 1780 the price of cotton yarn and cloth began to decline. British cotton cloth became competitive with imports from the East Indies, the prices of which sank sharply from 1783–4 onwards. Yarn prices were affected more than cloth prices and the price of fine yarn most of all. The reduction in price was initiated by technical innovation, but was carried further by the extension of cotton cultivation in America. The price of fine yarns was reduced progressively and the markets for such yarns enlarged in proportion to the fall in price, cheapness promoting consumption without any definite limit. Thus arose a wholly new trade in the large-scale export of yarn from 1793. Those exports brought to an end the golden age of the hand-loom weaver which had lasted for a decade (1785–94) and initiated a debate over the morality of supplying foreign weavers rather than British weavers with their materials. The mule established British supremacy in the markets of Europe through the supply first of fine muslin and then of fine warp yarns.

Within Lancashire the advent of the mule marked the beginning of the true industrial revolution, since it established the superiority of the region over the midlands and enabled it to capitalize upon the humidity of its atmosphere for the purpose of spinning fine yarns. The use of the mule was extended as it was improved and integrated into a whole new factory-based process of production. In 1783 Crompton's wooden rollers were replaced by more effective metal cylinders. The first mule mill was built in Manchester by the merchant Peter Drinkwater in 1789, with 144 spindle hand-mules and carding engines driven by a Boulton and Watt steam engine. The width of the mill was increased by a half in order to accommodate the new machines. Mules were driven first by a water-wheel at New Lanark in 1790–92 and then by a steam engine at the mill of M'Connel and Kennedy in Ancoats, Manchester, in 1796–7. In 1791 Henry Whitehead of Bury introduced the technique of piecing or rejoining broken strands of yarn while the mule remained in motion, so greatly enhancing the productivity of both workers and machine. From 1792 the gearing was shifted from the side to the centre of the mule, in order to drive spindles sited upon both sides of the headstock, by 1796 more than doubling the numbers of spindles carried per mule. A new aristocracy of labour emerged in the form of the male mule spinners, who devoted their strength and their skill to the intricate operations of the hand mule. They founded their first union in 1792 and so set the example which made the cotton industry a cradle of combinations. The mule became the spinning machine *par excellence*, stimulating the growth of spinning firms, spinning towns, and the spinning trade in general.

The Crompton censuses The successful completion of the mule encouraged Samuel Crompton to marry Mary Pimlott (*d.* 1796) on 16 February 1780. Of their eight children, five sons and one daughter reached maturity. Crompton never patented his invention of the mule, perhaps because it incorporated the rollers used by Arkwright or perhaps because he could not afford the fee of £100. He made no effort to seek out a wealthy partner, but followed the advice offered by John Pilkington, a local merchant-manufacturer. On 20 November 1780 Crompton allowed the use of the mule by the trade in return for what he hoped would be 'a generous and liberal subscription'. In the event he was bitterly disappointed. Eighty-four spinners raised 100 guineas, but paid over to Crompton only £50–£60 in recognition of the 'utility and importance' of the machine. No satisfactory explanation of this niggardly response has ever been offered. In 1802 a second subscription following the intense boom of 1800–02 in mule spinning in Manchester promised £872 (including no contributions from Bolton) but raised only £444, which was paid out between 1803 and 1807. A parliamentary grant of £10,000 in 1809 to Edmund Cartwright for the invention of a power loom which had never proved a commercial success stimulated a third bid by Crompton to secure some measure of recompense. In 1810 he appealed to Sir Robert Peel for a parliamentary grant. In pursuit of that grant he undertook the first census of the cotton spinning industry. He was aided by nineteen correspondents and concluded his labours in November 1811. The census listed the numbers of mule, jenny, and throstle spindles operated, by firm and by township. It embraced more

than 650 factories in England alone, but it excluded significant sectors such as a large area of Lancashire (Blackburn, Rossendale, and the Calder valley) and the whole of Ireland, as well as the woollen industry and all the water frames operating in the midlands, north Wales, and Scotland. Inevitably it underestimated the number of both throstle spindles and jenny spindles. Despite its imperfections, however, the census provided a mass of new information, revealing that England alone had 3,875,966 cotton-spinning spindles, of which 3.4 million, or 88 per cent, were mule spindles, and that 70,000 persons were employed in spinning.

Unfortunately the time proved unpropitious for Crompton. Not only did he have to prepare a whole dossier of evidence in order to justify his claim, he also had to spend six months in London in the distasteful task of lobbying for the support of the influential. In addition he had to overcome the prejudice of parliament against Bolton which seemed to have become, in the opinion of the secret committee of the House of Lords appointed to inquire into the disturbances in Nottingham, which reported in 1812, the 'very fountain and focus of disaffection and riot'. Local Luddites had destroyed a power-loom factory near Bolton at Westhoughton, on 24 April 1812. The House of Commons established a committee to enquire into the merits of Crompton's claim and, on 24 June 1812, awarded him £5000. Thereupon he left the capital in disgust.

Business activities Crompton undertook a variety of business ventures without success. He neither manufactured the mules, nor prospered from their use. Indeed he suffered from the continual seduction of his workers and was condemned to the perpetual labour of 'teaching green hands' (Crompton to Banks, 30 Oct 1807, Bolton Central Library, Crompton MS ZCR 11/4). He could not expand his operations because he could not retain his workforce. He therefore abandoned spinning and found it much more profitable to make rovings or 'slipings' (the strands produced during the preparatory stage between carding and spinning) for sale. He remained a merchant–manufacturer, operating a hand-loom manufactory in Bolton from 1791 to 1815 and making a range of luxury fabrics for the London market. He was undertaking finishing operations by 1799, and he handled bills of exchange averaging £455 per annum between 1802 and 1807. He took into partnership his son William (1786–1834), and Richard Wylde, a fellow-Swedenborgian. He opened a warehouse in Manchester and employed sixty-three domestic weavers in 1810–11. He always preferred independence to employment by others, declining the offer of a post as a mill manager in Scotland in 1805. His native ingenuity became manifest once more in the invention of an improved loom in 1808 and of a domestic wringer in 1812, though he suffered from the piracy of his cloth patterns. In 1813 he used his parliamentary grant to set up in business as a bleacher at Darwen, Lancashire, together with his sons George (1781–1858) and James (1793–1836). After the Darwen venture failed in 1822, he ceased to keep any further annual accounts. A third and final subscription during the Bolton boom of 1820–25 raised a capital sum of £431, which included contributions from France and Switzerland and which supplied the ageing Crompton with an annuity of £63 15s. In 1825–6 he fell into the toils of John Brown, a historian of Bolton, a bitter critic of the factory system and of Peel, its leading representative, and author of the propagandist tract, *A Memoir of Robert Blincoe* (1832). Brown drew up a petition to the House of Commons, seeking a supplementary remuneration and portraying Crompton as borne down by 'the weight of age and sorrow'. The petition was dated 6 February 1826 but apparently not presented. Brown tried, however, to persuade Crompton that Peel was 'your primitive enemy' and 'your secret foe' (Brown to Crompton, 22 April 1826, Crompton MS ZCR 44/13), so creating a tradition bequeathed to the grandson of the inventor.

Character and beliefs Crompton's profound interests and affections lay largely outside and above the mundane world of affairs. By 1791 he had joined the New Jerusalem Church Society, a Swedenborgian church founded in 1787, and in its service he found true fulfilment. He served as treasurer to the church and also, until 1823, as choirmaster. In 1803 he contributed £100 (or one-quarter of the cost) to enable a chapel to be built in Little Bolton. For the new chapel he built an organ which remained in use until 1846. He also served as organist and composed twenty-five hymn tunes, including two entitled 'Meditation' and 'Contemplation'. Religious influence was manifest in his lifelong abhorrence of the use of oaths and curses. The distinctive nature of his character is further demonstrated in the range of peculiar opinions enumerated by his biographer. Thus he did not hunt, shoot, or fish, regarding fly-fishing as a treacherous and deceitful practice. He condemned the consumption of lamb, veal, and new potatoes as an Epicurean indulgence. He strongly objected to boys being taught Latin or Greek unless they were destined for the learned professions. He took little interest in politics, but favoured the principles of 'church and king', incongruously coupled with a degree of support for reform and the abolition of sinecures. He always opposed the military bias of his two eldest sons, George, and Samuel (1782–1840).

Crompton shared the lot of many inventors and benefactors in so far as he was 'more or less misunderstood, thwarted, wronged and persecuted' (*Spectator*, 3 Sept 1859, 909). He did not, however, fall victim to malignant powers but always remained the master of his own fate. The reasons for his misfortunes seem to have lain in his own character. In essence he lacked the qualities necessary for success in business and especially the indomitable energy and perseverance characteristic of Arkwright. The originality of his great invention remains indisputable and serves as lasting testimony to his immense and wide-ranging ingenuity. But Crompton was wholly innocent of the ways of the world and, as a person of great originality, he may well have required more knowledge of the world than ordinary mortals. He was modest, shy, and sensitive, presenting to the world a mask of 'icy diffidence' (French, 157). He valued his independence to the highest degree and detested the prosaic process of marketing: he could

not bear to haggle or to bargain over price. He found solace in his love for music, in his circle of friends meeting in the Black Horse Club, in 'those thick brooding fancies which mark alike the poet and the inventor', and in meditation upon the doctrines of Swedenborg, especially as manifest in the mystical scientist's *Treatise upon the Last Judgment* (1766). Thus in the end he secured what he liked best, 'etherial satisfaction instead of solid cash' (H. Dunckley, *Manchester Examiner and Times*, 3 Sept 1859, 7i). He never left the country of his birth.

Samuel Crompton died in Bolton on 26 June 1827 at his home, 17 King Street, and was buried locally, in St Peter's churchyard, on 29 June. He had attained neither riches nor status, but still retained 'a paramount claim upon the country' (*Bolton Chronicle*, 30 June 1827, 4iii). An inventory valued his household goods at £8 10s. 4d. His estate was less than £450 and was shared among six children. In 1842 Sir Robert Peel made a grant of £200, to be divided between the three surviving children. That grant encouraged applications for a similar bounty from the descendants of John Kay in 1843 and of James Hargreaves in 1845. During the 1850s Bolton surpassed even Manchester to become the largest spinning town in Lancashire, but was suddenly reminded of a debt unpaid. The rise of the cotton trade had produced 'the most remarkable leap in population, trade, wealth, social comfort and, we may add, in political opinion and power that the world has ever beheld' (*Manchester Examiner and Times*, 3 Sept 1859, 7i). But the memory of Samuel Crompton had been 'almost forgotten'. Gilbert French (1804–1866) determined to amend the verdict of history and published in 1859 a biography of Crompton. Therein he reminded his fellow citizens that 'Crompton's invention is the fulcrum which sustains that mighty lever the Cotton Trade, the most valuable and the most powerful of our national resources' (French, 225). A public subscription raised £200 and, on 24 January 1861, a granite tomb replaced the modest flagstone over Crompton's grave at St Peter's. On 24 September 1862 a statue of Crompton was unveiled in Nelson Square in the presence of more than 10,000 working people and twenty-three brass bands, endowing Bolton with its first public statue. The sculptor was William Calder-Marshall. The cost of £2000 was raised wholly from local subscriptions. Palmerston paid a gratuity of £50 to John Crompton (1791–1864), a warper at Arrowsmith's mill and the sole surviving son as well as the ancestor of the Cromptons of the twentieth century. Hall-in-the-Wood was presented to the borough by Lord Leverhulme in 1900 and transformed into a museum of technology, opened in 1902. Three further celebrations were held in Bolton: in 1927, to mark the centenary of Crompton's death; in 1953, to commemorate the bicentenary of his birth; and in 1979, to commemorate the bicentenary of the invention of the mule. D. A. FARNIE

Sources G. W. Daniels, *The early English cotton industry, with some unpublished letters of Samuel Crompton* (1920) · G. W. Daniels, 'Industrial Lancashire prior and subsequent to the invention of the mule', *Journal of the Textile Institute*, 18 (1927), 71–86 [Mather lecture] · G. J. French, *The life and times of Samuel Crompton*, 2nd edn

(1860); facs. repr. (1970) • S. Crompton, letter to Sir Joseph Banks, 30 Oct 1807, Bolton Central Library, Crompton MS ZCR 11/4 • [S. Smiles], review, *QR*, 107 (1860), 45–85, esp. 65–80 • A. P. Wadsworth, 'The inventor of the spinning mule', *Manchester Guardian* (26 May 1927) • A. P. Wadsworth, 'Autobiography of Crompton: a new discovery', *Manchester Guardian* (3 June 1927) • A. P. Wadsworth, 'The Crompton centenary', *Manchester Guardian* (7 June 1927) [leader] • S. Crompton, 'Crompton, Samuel', *The imperial dictionary of universal biography*, ed. J. F. Waller (1857–63) • G. W. Daniels, 'Samuel Crompton's census of the cotton industry in 1811', *Economic History*, 2 (1930–33), 107–10 • J. Kennedy, 'A brief memoir of Samuel Crompton', *Memoirs of the Literary and Philosophical Society of Manchester*, 2nd ser., 5 (1831), 318–53 • J. Kennedy, *Miscellaneous papers* (1849) • 'Brown, John (*d.* 1829)', *DNB* • H. Catling, *The spinning mule* (1970) • M. E. Rose, 'Samuel Crompton (1753–1827)', *Transactions of the Lancashire and Cheshire Antiquarian Society*, 75–6 (1965–6), 11–32 • M. M. Edwards, *The growth of the British cotton trade, 1780–1815* (1967) • R. L. Hills, *Power in the industrial revolution* (1970) • T. Thompson, *Crompton's way* (1947) • John Brown, letter to S. Crompton, 22 April 1826, Bolton Central Library, Crompton MS ZCR 44/13

Archives BL, corresp. and papers, Egerton MS 2409 • Bolton Central Library, family and business corresp. and papers • JRL, letters | FILM Manchester Metropolitan University, North-West Film Archive, Crompton centenary celebrations, Bolton, 1927, 6 minutes

Likenesses C. Allingham, portrait, 1803, NPG • Eccles of Bolton, bust, 1827, repro. in French, *Life and times*, 213 • S. W. Reynolds senior, mezzotint, pubd 1828 (after C. Allingham), BM, NPG [*see illus.*] • W. Calder-Marshall, statue, 1862, Nelson Square, Bolton, Lancashire • J. F. Skill, J. Gilbert, W. Walker and E. Walker, group portrait, pencil and wash (*Men of science living in 1807–08*), NPG • engraving (after C. Allingham, 1803), repro. in E. Baines, *History of Lancashire* (1824)

Wealth at death under £450: will, Bolton Central Library, Crompton MSS, ZCR 45/18

Crompton, Sir Thomas (1558–1609), civil lawyer, was born in London, the second son of William Crompton (*d.* in or before 1577), a London mercer who had purchased lands in London, Staffordshire, and Kent, and his wife, Elizabeth, daughter and heir of Thomas Boughton, of Mardyke, in Essex. He may have attended school in Shrewsbury. The family's landed property was left to his elder brother, William, but Thomas received an annuity of £20 which he used to pay his way through Oxford, where he entered St Alban Hall in 1577. Having graduated BA (1579) and MA (1582), his grace for the degree of DCL (1584) was refused on the grounds of 'suspected backwardness in religion'. Five years later, admitting that he had earlier not been 'so well settled' as he should have been, he was now willing to take the oath of supremacy and to conform to the established church, and was allowed to proceed both BCL and DCL. In the same year, 1589, he married Barbara Hudson of Yorkshire.

Crompton entered Doctors' Commons and over the next twenty years his name figures in a wide range of administrative and judicial records. James I on one occasion said that he was as good a man as Sir Edward Coke. Expert in maritime law, and proficient in languages, he served both Elizabeth and James as advocate for foreign causes in the admiralty court. He accompanied Cecil to France in 1598 and acted for him in cases involving piracy and shipping disputes. Crompton also specialized in ecclesiastical law, and was personally close to Richard Bancroft,

bishop of London and later archbishop of Canterbury, to whom he left a small token in his will. He was advocate-general for ecclesiastical causes (1603); attended the Hampton Court conference as 'a doctor of the Arches' (Cardwell, 85); and served as chancellor of the diocese of London and vicar-general, with Sir Edward Stanhope, of the archbishop of Canterbury (1605–9).

In the House of Commons, Crompton sat for Shaftesbury, Dorset (1589), by patronage of the earl of Pembroke; Boroughbridge, Yorkshire, through Cecil (1597); Whitchurch, Hampshire (1601), through episcopacy; and Oxford University (1604–9). In the parliament of 1601 he opposed the bill against pluralities, and he met with a hostile reception when in 1604 he spoke in favour of commissaries' courts, narrowly avoiding censure after revealing that he had consulted with some of the bishops about the proposed legislation against them. In these matters as in others Crompton, like other civil lawyers, was a natural ally of the crown and the church against common lawyers and (in his view) anti-clerical reformers in the House of Commons. He criticized the common lawyers for their use of prohibitions which, he argued, conflicted with their oaths to maintain the liberties of the church: as he saw it, the ecclesiastical courts were being hindered from imposing effective church discipline. Similarly, Crompton prepared a wide-ranging defence of the crown's right to impositions (BL, Cotton MS, Titus FIV, fols. 242–3). In the controversy over the oath of allegiance he refuted papist claims that the pope had power to depose princes and their subjects the right to take up arms against them as infidels or heretics.

Crompton accumulated enough capital to invest in commerce and purchase lands and manors at Millwich and Cresswell in Staffordshire. He was granted arms in 1595 and was knighted in 1603. He left lands to his sons John, Richard, and Thomas after the death of his wife, 1000 marks for the marriage of his first daughter, 500 marks for the marriage of the second, and £200 to his daughter Barbara. Crompton died in January or February 1609.

P. O. G. WHITE

Sources B. P. Levack, *The civil lawyers in England, 1603–1641* (1973) • HoP, *Commons, 1558–1603* • M. B. Rex, *University representation in England, 1604–1690* (1954) • *JHC*, 1 (1547–1628) • J. E. Neale, *Elizabeth I and her parliaments*, 2: *1584–1601* (1957) • *Calendar of the manuscripts of the most hon. the marquis of Salisbury*, 7–8, HMC, 9 (1899); 12 (1910); 18 (1933); 18 (1940) • A. Wood, *The history and antiquities of the University of Oxford*, ed. J. Gutch, 1 (1792), 235–6 • *Reg. Oxf.*, vol. 2/1. 38, 116, 157 • E. Cardwell, *A history of conferences and other proceedings connected with the revision of the Book of Common Prayer* (1840) • R. G. Usher, 'James I and Sir Edward Coke', *EngHR*, 18 (1903), 664–75 • BL, Cotton MS, Titus FIV, fols. 242–3 • BL, Cotton MS, Cleo FII, fol. 427 • Inner Temple Library, London, Petyt MS 538/38, fols. 47–8 • *Grants of arms*, Harleian Society, 1 (?), xvi, 66 • will, PRO, PROB 11/99, sig. 18

Archives BL, Cotton MS, Cleo FII, fol. 427 • BL, Cotton MS, Titus FIV, fols. 242–3 • BL, Lansdowne MS 145, fols. 59–60 • Bodl. Oxf., Tanner MS 427 • Inner Temple, London, Petyt MS 538/38, fols. 47–8

Crompton, William (1599/1600–1642), Church of England clergyman, was born in the parish of Leigh near Wigan, Lancashire, the son of Richard Crompton. He was educated at the local grammar school before matriculating from Brasenose College, Oxford, on 28 March 1617, aged seventeen. He graduated BA on 9 November 1620 and proceeded MA on 10 July 1623. By 1624 he had become preacher at Little Kimble, Buckinghamshire, where the vicar was the ecclesiastical controversialist Richard *Pilkington (d. 1631). Following in the footsteps of Pilkington, whose daughter Mary he married, he published that year *St Austin's religion, wherein is manifestly proved out of the works of that learned father … that he dissented from popery, and agreed with the religion of protestants, contrary to the slanderous position of the papists, who affirm that we had no religion before the times of Luther and Calvin*. This was a reply to a work of James Anderton, who wrote under the name of John Brereley, priest. A second edition was published in 1625. Contradictory accounts survive of the final stages of this work. Dr Daniel Featley claimed that he corrected faults in it before licensing it but that he and Crompton were then summoned before James I to justify the book's orthodoxy and that James, when satisfied, rewarded Crompton. A different account comes from the diary of the future Archbishop William Laud, who recorded that the king had found fault with some passages in the book and so the duke of Buckingham, to whom it was dedicated, sent Crompton to Laud with the book. Laud gave his opinions on it and was later required by the king to correct it to accord with the doctrines of the Church of England.

Subsequently Crompton was persuaded by another controversial writer, Dr George Hakewill, rector of Heanton Punchardon, Devon, to become lecturer at Barnstaple. Hakewill could have learned of Crompton from his brother William Hakewill, the lawyer and antiquary, who lived at Wendover, near Little Kimble. Crompton's appointment at Barnstaple was made by the corporation, who paid his stipend. He was approved before the death of the aged vicar in November 1627 and so managed the parish until the new vicar, Martin Blake, arrived in December 1628. However, he retained links with Little Kimble, where his son William was born on 13 August 1633.

At first relations between Crompton and Blake were amicable but soon a dispute arose over psalm singing, which Blake, a moderate puritan, favoured while Crompton opposed it. The situation deteriorated in 1630 when Blake was required as rural dean to present at the archdeacon's visitation any lecturer in his deanery who did not read divine service according to the prayer book in hood and surplice before his lecture, and any lecturer who did not also hold a cure of souls. Under these terms Blake had to present Crompton and in doing so he offended the more radical puritans. Feelings rose when Crompton accused Blake of pluralism, on the ground that he was also vicar of King's Nympton, but it was theological differences which were the main cause of dispute and of the creation of divisions in the town with Crompton contradicting on Sunday afternoons what Blake had said on Wednesday evenings. In 1636 Blake attempted to end Crompton's engagement but in this he was interfering with the powers of the corporation, who ultimately agreed to refer the matter to Bishop Joseph Hall of Exeter.

He persuaded Crompton to accept the living of St Mary Magdalene, Launceston, in place of the lectureship. He held this from 1638 until his death in January 1642. His funeral sermon, delivered on 5 January and later published as *The Art of Embalming Dead Saints* (1642), was preached by George Hughes, who referred to Crompton's 'Bosome-day-book', wherein he noted every sin of which he accused himself. Crompton was survived by his wife, two sons, and three daughters; his elder son William *Crompton (1630/1633?–1696) was later vicar of Cullompton until his ejection in 1662.

C. W. SUTTON, *rev.* MARY WOLFFE

Sources DNB • 'Featley or Fairclough, Daniel', DNB • 'Hakewill, George', DNB • 'Hakewill, William', DNB • 'Anderton, James', DNB • J. F. Chanter, *Life and times of Martin Blake BD* (1910) • Wood, *Ath. Oxon.*, new edn • G. Hughes, *The art of embalming dead saints discovered in a sermon preached at the funerall of Master William Crompton* (1642) • will, PRO, PROB 11/188, sig. 23 • J. A. Vage, 'The diocese of Exeter, 1519–1641: a study of church government in the age of the Reformation', PhD diss., U. Cam., 1991 • Foster, *Alum. Oxon.* • VCH *Buckinghamshire*, vols. 2–3
Wealth at death bequests totalling £300 to children, residue to wife: will, PRO, PROB 11/188, sig. 23

Crompton, William (1630/1633?–1696), clergyman and ejected minister, was born or baptized either on 3 January 1630 or 13 August 1633, the eldest son of William *Crompton (1599/1600–1642) and his wife, Mary Pilkington, at Little Kimble, Buckinghamshire. William Crompton the elder had been preacher at Little Kimble where Mary's father, Richard Pilkington, was vicar, and she had evidently gone to her parental home for the birth of their first child; William the elder by that time was lecturer at Barnstaple, later moving on to become vicar of Launceston. The younger William was admitted to Merchant Taylors' School in 1647 and to Christ Church, Oxford, by the authority of the parliamentary visitors, in 1648, graduating BA in 1650 and MA in 1652.

Approved by the Westminster assembly in June 1651, Crompton became a member of the Devon association and in June of the same year was presented to the living of Cullompton, Devon, from which he was ejected for nonconformity on 30 October 1662. He continued to live at Cullompton, preaching there in 1669 to a meeting of 'nigh 500' (Gordon, 246). After ejection there is reference to his living at Exeter, where he was licensed as a presbyterian minister on 11 April 1672. Towards the end of his life he was evidently very poor for he received a grant from the Common Fund during the years 1690–96, when he was described as 'an aged and very poor' man ministering at Exeter (Gordon, 31). In the early 1690s there was no fixed meeting at Cullompton, where Crompton has been credited as founder of the Pound Square congregation.

Crompton wrote a number of tracts, including *An useful tractate to further Christians … in the practice of the most needful duty of prayer* (1659) which discussed the nature, necessity, and fruits of prayer; *A Remedy Against Superstition* (1667) which warned against idolatry; *A Brief Survey of the Old Religion* (1672), a guide to salvation; and *The Foundation of God*, in 1682. He died in 1696, having for some years been troubled by a fistula in the breast, and was buried in Cullompton on 22 July. His wife had died before him, but he left a daughter, Elizabeth. CAROLINE L. LEACHMAN

Sources Calamy rev., 146–7 · A. Gordon, ed., Freedom after ejection: a review (1690–1692) of presbyterian and congregational nonconformity in England and Wales (1917), 246 · Wood, Ath. Oxon., new edn, 3.23; 4.626 · E. Calamy, ed., An abridgement of Mr. Baxter's history of his life and times, with an account of the ministers, &c., who were ejected after the Restauration of King Charles II, 2nd edn, 2 vols. (1713), vol. 2, p. 247 · The nonconformist's memorial ... originally written by ... Edmund Calamy, ed. S. Palmer, 1 (1775), 346–7 · Wood, Ath. Oxon.: Fasti (1820), 120 · Mrs E. P. Hart, ed., Merchant Taylors' School register, 1561–1934, 1 (1936)

Cromwell, Bridget. See Fleetwood, Bridget, Lady Fleetwood under the protectorate (bap. 1624, d. 1662).

Cromwell, Edward, third Baron Cromwell (c.1559–1607), soldier, was the son and heir of Henry Cromwell, second Baron Cromwell (c.1538–1592), landowner, and Mary (d. 1592), daughter of John Paulet, second marquess of Winchester. His early life is obscure but he appears to have spent some time at Jesus College, Cambridge, as the pupil of Richard Bancroft. He did not matriculate; his award of the degree of MA in 1594 was one of a number given to followers of Robert Devereux, second earl of Essex. He commanded a company in Dutch pay in the Netherlands, having possibly served under his kinsman, Ralph *Cromwell, in 1584; he served under the sponsorship of Elizabeth I in 1585. He was a follower of Essex by the early 1590s at the latest, commanding a company during the expedition to Normandy in 1591. Cromwell served in the embassy of 1596; he also served on the Cadiz expedition of 1597, and two years later followed Essex to Ireland. In Ireland his military reputation was bolstered by his victory in August 1599 over 6000 of the rebels of Hugh O'Neill, second earl of Tyrone, one of the few successes of that campaign.

In 1592 Cromwell succeeded to the title on the death of his father but was plagued by a legacy of expensive and protracted legal disputes. The most costly of these, against All Souls College, Oxford, concerned lands in Leicestershire that had been granted to his great-grandfather, Thomas *Cromwell, earl of Essex, by Henry VIII. Cromwell married first Elizabeth (d. 1593), daughter of William Upton of Pusliach, Devon, serjeant-at-arms, and Mary, daughter of Thomas Kirkham of Blakedon, Devon, with whom he had a daughter, Elizabeth. His wife died on 5 January 1593 and was buried in Launde Abbey, Leicestershire, on 15 January. Soon afterwards he married Frances (d. 30 Nov 1631), eldest daughter of William Rugge of Felmingham, Norfolk, and Thomasine, daughter of Sir Thomas Townshend. They had a son, Thomas, and two daughters, Frances and Anne. In 1598 Cromwell tried to obtain the office of governor of Brill through his patron but Essex was unable to secure it for him. In 1599 Cromwell petitioned the queen for a determination of his many causes at law as 'the weakness of his estate cannot bear such extraordinary charges' (CSP dom., 1598–1601, 326). These financial difficulties and the failure of his petition to the queen may have combined with his military links with Essex in persuading him to join the earl's abortive

rebellion in 1601. Faced with charges of high treason, Cromwell was imprisoned in the Tower of London. He submitted to the queen's mercy in May, however, and was pardoned and fined £6000.

Cromwell was restored to favour by James I, being sworn of the privy council and serving as a magistrate for Rutland and Lincolnshire, counties in which he was a landowner. He raised soldiers in Lincolnshire in 1591. His continued financial difficulties, however, forced him to quit England for the prospect of advancement through military service in Ireland. His Leicestershire manors (as well as his horses and carriage) were seized to pay his creditors, and in September 1605 he exchanged lands in England for the barony of Lecale in co. Down. At the same time he also received lands from the Irish chieftain Phelim McCartan on the proviso that he educated and provided for McCartan's son in his household. On 26 September his new position was recognized by the crown and he was made governor of Lecale and other lands in co. Down with the power to exercise martial law. His time in Ireland was short-lived as he died at Lecale in September 1607; he was buried in Down Cathedral.

Thomas Cromwell, first earl of Ardglass (1594–1653), soldier and politician, was the only son and heir of Edward Cromwell, third Baron Cromwell, by his marriage to Frances. Before going to Ireland in 1599, Lord Cromwell asked William Cecil, Lord Burghley, the lord treasurer, to grant his son's wardship to his wife, Frances. Thomas Cromwell's wardship was granted to his mother in consideration of their poor estate. He served in a military capacity in Ireland, being created Viscount Lecale in November 1624. In 1617 it had been rumoured that 'Young Lord Cromwell' would marry 'Lady Lower' (CSP dom., 1611–18, 504), probably the widow of Sir William Lower of Cornwall. However about 1625 he married Elizabeth (d. 1653), daughter and heir of Robert Meverell, of Ilam, Staffordshire, and Elizabeth, daughter of Sir Thomas Fleming, chief justice of the king's bench. In 1625 Cromwell was given command of a regiment in Ernest von Mansfeld's abortive expedition to the Palatinate, raising men in his wife's lands in Staffordshire. He was a staunch supporter of the Stuart monarchy and in the civil war commanded a regiment of horse, being rewarded with the Irish earldom of Ardglass in April 1645. He was fined £460 after the war by parliament for his commitment to the royalist cause and retired to the old family estates in Rutland, dying some time before 26 March 1653 at Tickencote. He was succeeded by his son and heir, Wingfield Cromwell (1624–1668). DAVID GRUMMITT

Sources GEC, Peerage · CSP dom., 1598–1601; 1611–18 · CSP Ire., 1601–8 · CSP for. · P. E. J. Hammer, The polarisation of Elizabethan politics: the political career of Robert Devereux, 2nd earl of Essex, 1585–1597 (1999) **Archives** PRO, R. Cecil, SP 14/19/28 · PRO, Robert Cecil, SP 78/38, fols. 55, 91, 105 · R. Cecil, earl of Salisbury, SP 14/18/63 **Wealth at death** see CSP Ire., 1606–8, 291–2

Cromwell [née Bourchier], **Elizabeth** (1598–1665), lady protectress of England, Scotland, and Ireland, consort of Oliver Cromwell, was one of twelve children of Sir James

Bourchier (c.1574–1635), merchant and furrier, and his wife, Frances, daughter of Thomas Crane of Newton Tony, Wiltshire. James, an only son, was knighted at Whitehall on 23 July 1603. He inherited from his father substantial property in Essex, especially the recently acquired manor of Little Stambridge, but also had property at Felsted in Essex and Tower Hill, London, as well as connections with Newton Tony in Wiltshire, for it was there on 19 June 1596 that he married Frances Crane. Elizabeth Bourchier, born in 1598, was probably the eldest of Sir James's twelve children (nine sons and three daughters), though neither the exact date nor the place of her birth is recorded. In his will, dated 5 March 1635, Sir James divided his properties in and around Stambridge between several younger sons; the will contains no mention of his eldest son, Thomas, by that time married to the widow of Richard Cromwell (son of Oliver Cromwell's uncle Henry), who was presumably provided for elsewhere, of Sir James's wife, who had presumably predeceased him, or of his daughter Elizabeth.

On 22 August 1620 Elizabeth Bourchier married Oliver *Cromwell (1599–1658), the future lord protector, at St Giles Cripplegate, London. The match may have sprung from mutual connections with the Cranes of Newton Tony, for in 1614 Elizabeth's maternal aunt, Eluzai or Eluiza Crane, had married as her second husband Henry Cromwell of Upwood, uncle of Oliver Cromwell. Alternatively the Bourchiers and the Cromwells may have come into contact through Essex society, for Sir James Bourchier held land in the county and the Cromwells had connections with several Essex families. For example Oliver's aunt Joan had married Sir Francis Barrington of Barrington Hall in Essex, though the suggestion that there was thus a direct family link via the Barringtons between Cromwell and his wife-to-be is erroneous; although Sir Francis's sister married Sir William Bourchier, this family was not related to that of Cromwell's bride. Nor, it seems, was Elizabeth descended from the Bourchier family who were earls of Essex during the fifteenth and sixteenth centuries, for her own ancestry has been traced back to the fifteenth century, when the family lived in Worcestershire, and no link has been found with the Bourchier earls of Essex. Upon his marriage Cromwell received a dowry of £1500; for his part, in August he contracted to convey to his wife as her jointure the parsonage house, with its glebe lands and tithes, in Hartford, Huntingdon.

Surviving sources reveal little beyond a sparse factual outline of Elizabeth Cromwell's married life. Between 1621 and 1638 she had nine children, five boys and four girls: Robert (1621–1639), Oliver (1623–1644), Richard *Cromwell (1626–1712), Henry *Cromwell (1628–1674), James (born and died 1632), Bridget *Fleetwood (bap. 1624, d. 1662), Elizabeth *Claypole (bap. 1629, d. 1658), Mary *Belasyse (bap. 1637, d. 1713), and Frances *Russell (bap. 1638, d. 1720). With her growing family she lived in Huntingdon until 1631, St Ives from 1631 until 1636, and Ely from 1636 until the mid-1640s. During the civil war Cromwell ensured that part of his pay was directed to Ely to support Elizabeth and his family, which included his children and his widowed mother. In late 1646 he moved his now somewhat smaller family (by this time three of the sons had died and two of the daughters had married) to London.

In 1649 Elizabeth Cromwell planned to cross to Ireland, to be with or near her husband while he was on campaign there. Although she travelled west, visiting her elder surviving son, Richard, and his new bride at Hursley in Hampshire, and saw her husband embark from Milford Haven in August, she probably did not, in fact, cross. She was certainly back in London before he returned, for on 31 May 1650 she was one of a throng who travelled out from London to Windsor to meet and greet the victorious general on his journey back from Ireland. There seem to have been no plans for Elizabeth to join her husband for any part of his Scottish campaign of 1650–51, and it is from this period that we have the only correspondence between husband and wife to have survived—three letters from Oliver to his wife, and one from her to him. In his letters Oliver expresses a love and tenderness which sound a little gruff to a modern ear—'Thou art dearer to me than any creature; let that suffice' (Writings and Speeches, 2.329)—but which appear deep:

> My Dearest, I could not satisfy myself to omit this post, although I have not much to write; yet indeed I love to write to my dear, who is very much in my heart. It joys me to hear thy soul prospereth; the Lord increase His favours to thee more and more … The Lord bless all thy good counsel and example to all those about thee, and hear all thy prayers, and accept thee always. (Writings and Speeches, 2.412)

In her one surviving letter, written in December 1650, she gently chides him for not writing more often both to herself and to others in London, claiming that she had written three to him for every one she received, as well as expressing a longing to see him again, if it be the Lord's will:

> I should rejoys to hear your desire in seing me, but I desire to submit to the provedns of God, howping the Lord, houe hath separated us, and heth oftune brought us together agane, wil in heis good time breng us agane, to the prase of heis name. Truly my lif is but half a lif in your abseinse, deid not the Lord make it up in heimself, which I must ackoleg to the prase of heis grace. (J. Nickolls, Original Letters and Papers of State Addressed to Oliver Cromwell, 1743, 40)

By late 1650 Elizabeth Cromwell and her remaining family were living in lodgings assigned to them by parliament in The Cockpit, adjoining Whitehall Palace. Soon after her husband's elevation as lord protector she and her family took up residence in Whitehall Palace itself, on 14 April 1654 moving into apartments redecorated for them. She and her remaining children also gained apartments at Hampton Court. From time to time before the protectorate Elizabeth had been present at some public or state events. For example, she and Sir Thomas Fairfax's wife rode together in a coach when the army marched into London in August 1647. But from December 1653, as the wife of the head of state and often herself styled her highness the lady protectress, she played a slightly larger public role. Thus she frequently had her own table at official receptions or dinners, entertaining the wives of councillors, ambassadors, and other dignitaries. But even as protectress, her public role was limited and she did not, for example, play a significant part at the two installations of her husband as protector or at the opening and closing of the protectorate parliaments; indeed, she may not have been present at many of the state ceremonies of the protectorate.

After her husband's death on 3 September 1658, the new protectoral government made generous provision for 'her Highness dowager'. Elizabeth was to receive payment of £20,000 and perhaps also an annuity of £20,000, and St James's House was to be prepared for her. Even after Richard Cromwell's fall in spring 1659 the army officers treated her respectfully and agreed to propose to the recalled Rump that she be allocated £8000 per annum. Such a generous settlement, if ever paid, ended at the Restoration. She left London in April 1660, vehemently denying rumours that she either had with her or had hidden various jewels and other goods belonging to the royal family. Within a few months of the Restoration she petitioned Charles II, denying possession of any royal goods, claiming that the baseless accusations were rendering her liable to 'disrepute' and to 'many violences and losses under pretence of searching for such goods', so making 'her abode in any place unsafe', and stressing her obedience to the new monarchical government. She also refers to 'the many sorrows wherewith it hath pleased the all wise God to exercise' her and to her hope that 'now in her old age' she might have 'a safe retirement' (*CSP dom.*, 1660, 392; the petition is reproduced in Waylen, 2–3). In fact, the restored monarchy did not molest her and she lived out her final years in quiet retirement with her son-in-law John Claypole at Northborough in Northamptonshire. Following a long illness—after one visit, her daughter Mary wrote that 'my poor mother is so affecting a spectacle as I scarce know how to write … The Lord knows best what is best for us to suffer, and therefore I desire we may willingly submit to His will, but the condition she is in is very sad; the Lord help her and us to bear it' (ibid., 102)—she died there in November 1665 and was buried in Northborough church on 19 November. No will is extant, though a report of 1666 suggests that Jeremiah White, formerly one of the protector's chaplains, was acting as executor for such property as she retained at her death.

As a public figure, from the late 1640s until the Restoration and beyond, Elizabeth Cromwell was from time to time attacked in print. *Newes from the New Exchange* of January 1650 alleges sexual immorality, claiming that she 'hath run through most of the Regiment, both Officers and Souldiers', while *A Tragi-Comedy called New Market Fayre* has her trading base insults with Fairfax's wife. More often, she was mocked for her simple ways. *Mercurius Elencticus* of July 1649 makes her a preposterous figure when attending a dinner given by the City of London for Cromwell: 'Pusse Rampant of Ely, cloathed all over in Innocent white (her Beloved's owne colours) with the Clerke of the Kitchen both in a Coach' (*Mercurius Elencticus*, 9–16 July 1649, 93). A woodcut in *The Case is Altered* of

August 1660 shows her with a round face in a simple black hood and necklace, while in the accompanying text Oliver's ghost refers to her as 'Queen Joan' or 'Jugg'. But most famously and quotably, *The Court and Kitchen of Elizabeth, Commonly called Joan Cromwell, the Wife of the Late Usurper* of 1664 alleges that her 'indigent' background so coloured her character that, when opportunity arose during the 1640s, she used her husband's position to amass ill-gotten plunder, actively encouraging and then reselling gifts, accepting bribes, and through Oliver distributing and selling offices. As protectress she found it hard 'to lay aside those impertinent meannesses of her private fortune' and for a time 'like some kitchen maid preferred by the lust of some rich and noble dotard, was ashamed of her sudden and gaudy bravery', keeping cows in St James's Park to make her own butter, and generally running the protectoral court in a mean and parsimonious way (*The Court and Kitchen of Elizabeth*, reprinted as *Mrs Cromwell's Cookery Book*, 1983, 34).

The accusations of corruption and influence in *The Court and Kitchen of Elizabeth* stand out because they were exceptional. Most contemporary commentators said remarkably little about Elizabeth Cromwell and did not claim that she played a significant role in the protectoral regime or in shaping Cromwell's military and political career. Thus, despite his strong anti-protectoral bias, Ludlow says very little about her beyond the assertion that during the protectorate she was at first 'unwilling to remove' to Whitehall Palace, 'tho afterwards she became better satisfied with her grandeur' (*The Memoirs of Edmund Ludlow*, ed. C. H. Firth, 2 vols., 1894, 1.379); Lucy Hutchinson goes no further than a single sneer that she was ill suited to the socially elevated position she held (*Memoirs of the Life of Colonel Hutchinson*, ed. C. H. Firth, 1906, 298); while, from a royalist perspective, the earl of Clarendon largely ignores her. In short, the accusations of humility and of feeling out of place in her elevated position as protectress ring truer than those of personal ambition and corruption. No member of her own family, the Bourchiers, appears to have won senior office, fortune, or clear advancement through her, either before or during the protectorate, and the principal historian of the protectoral court and household not only highlights a relatively low level of corruption there but also specifically dismisses *The Court and Kitchen of Elizabeth* as hopelessly biased (Sherwood, *Court of Cromwell*, 147). It is harder to reach firm conclusions about Elizabeth's wider influence and the degree to which, within a long, close, and loving marriage, she helped to shape the ideas and aspirations of her husband. It would be surprising if she had had no influence, directly or indirectly, in these matters. However, our knowledge of Cromwell points to other individuals, experiences, and sources which played a much larger role in shaping his career; the surviving correspondence between Oliver and Elizabeth does not suggest that he was seeking or she was offering advice on public affairs—though he certainly did seek her advice on the marriage settlement of their eldest surviving son—and protectoral central government, and its written constitutions did not, of course, ascribe her any political role. In her petition to Charles II, Elizabeth claimed that she 'never intermeddled in any of those public transactions which have been prejudicial to your Majesty's royal father or yourself', and Charles seems, probably correctly, to have accepted her plea, acceding to her request that he 'be pleased to distinguish betwixt the concernment of your petitioner and those of her relations who have been obnoxious' (CSP dom., 1660, 392).

PETER GAUNT

Sources The writings and speeches of Oliver Cromwell, ed. W. C. Abbott and C. D. Crane, 4 vols. (1937–47) · J. Waylen, The house of Cromwell and the story of Dunkirk (1897) · M. Noble, Memoirs of the protectoral-house of Cromwell, 2 vols. (1787) · R. Boucher, 'Notes on the family of Elizabeth (Bourchier), wife of the protector, Oliver Cromwell', The Genealogist, new ser., 28 (1911–12), 65–75 · R. Sherwood, The court of Oliver Cromwell (1977) · R. Sherwood, Oliver Cromwell: king in all but name, 1653–58 (1997) · L. Knoppers, Constructing Cromwell: ceremony, portrait and print, 1645–61 (2000) · CSP dom., 1658–60; 1665–6 · will of Sir James Bourchier, PRO, PROB 11/167/32

Likenesses S. Cooper, watercolour on vellum miniature, repro. in D. Foskett, Samuel Cooper and his contemporaries (1974) [exhibition catalogue, NPG, 1974]; priv. coll. · attrib. P. Lely, oils, Cromwell Museum, Huntingdon · woodcut, BL; repro. in The case is altered, or, Dreadful news from hell (1660) [Thomason Tract]

Cromwell, Elizabeth. See Claypole, Elizabeth (bap. 1629, d. 1658).

Cromwell, Frances. See Russell, Frances, Lady Russell (bap. 1638, d. 1720).

Cromwell, Henry (1628–1674), soldier, politician, and lord lieutenant of Ireland, was born on 20 January 1628 at Huntingdon and baptized there at All Saints' Church on 29 January, the fifth of nine children and fourth among the five sons of Oliver *Cromwell (1599–1658), lord protector of England, Scotland, and Ireland, and his wife, Elizabeth (1598–1665), daughter of Sir James Bourchier [see Cromwell, Elizabeth].

Early life and career, 1628–1654 Historians are able to recover a portrait of Henry far fuller and richer than that of any of Oliver Cromwell's other children, in large part because there survives vastly more correspondence to and from Henry than for all his siblings put together. Nevertheless, little is known of his childhood and adolescence. He presumably spent his early years in the family home at Huntingdon until 1631, St Ives in 1€31–6, and Ely from 1636, and then—like his elder brothers—he probably attended Felsted School in Essex. He does not appear to have entered university and instead by his late teens was serving as an officer in the parliamentary army. In October 1647 a newspaper reported that Oliver Cromwell's two surviving sons, Richard *Cromwell and Henry, were both then serving as captains in the army, one in Lord General Fairfax's life guard, the other in the regiment of Thomas Harrison. Although James Heath and other near-contemporaries, followed a century later by Mark Noble, suggested that the Cromwell in Fairfax's life guard was Henry, modern historians more reliably place him in Harrison's New Model horse regiment. That regiment saw service in northern England during the second civil war, and Henry and his troop played a significant role in a skirmish

Henry Cromwell (1628–1674), by Christiaan Janszoon Dusart

at Appleby in mid-July 1648. He presumably fought in the battle of Preston on 17 August, in which Harrison's regiment was prominent. He was in London by the end of the year, on 15 December 1648 attending a council of war at Whitehall, but he is not listed at any other army meetings between November 1648 and February 1649, and apparently played no part in the political developments of that time.

In late 1649 Henry was commissioned a colonel and given command of a newly created regiment of horse, dispatched to Ireland to reinforce the English military campaign led by his father. After a short delay he crossed from Pembrokeshire to Youghall late in February 1650. He quickly linked up with Roger Boyle, Baron Broghill, and campaigned with him in Munster, falling upon and mauling Inchiquin's troops outside Limerick in late March. He remained in Ireland after his father's departure in May 1650 and continued to campaign there, first under Lord Deputy Henry Ireton, and then under Charles Fleetwood; both men were also Henry's brothers-in-law, having successively married his sister Bridget [see Fleetwood, Bridget]. There are only occasional glimpses of Henry in Ireland over this period—in April 1651 he was jointly leading a military expedition into King's county, and at about the same time he was observed by Thomas Patient, a preacher attached to Ireton's headquarters, who reported to Oliver Cromwell on his son's spiritual condition:

> your sonne, to my great rejoiceing, it hath pleased God, I am perswaded, to begin a work of grace in his soule; I have had great incouradgment that the word of God takes greate effect upon him; he hath had inward temtations in his soule, and many words of grace made very precious and

comfortable to his soule, and I watch him, and he is much crieing to God in secrett, and very forward to propound doubts and cases of conscience, betwixt him and I.
(J. Nickolls, ed., *Original Letters and Papers of State Addressed to Oliver Cromwell*, 1743, 6–7)

The following autumn Henry was present at the siege of Limerick and was with Ireton when the latter died at Limerick on 26 November 1651. Some time in the following year Oliver Cromwell asked Fleetwood to 'commend me to Harry Cromwell. I pray for him, that he may thrive, and improve in the knowledge and love of Christ' (*Writings and Speeches*, 2.602).

Early in 1652, with Henry apparently still in Ireland, his sister Mary [*see* Belasyse, Mary] worked for a match between him and the eldest daughter of Lord Wharton. His father, while not opposed, was unconvinced that the affair was serious, ascribing it to 'little Mall's fooling', and rightly predicting that it would come to nothing (*Writings and Speeches*, 2.561). Instead Henry, who left Ireland and returned to England some time later in 1652 or early in 1653, had expressed affection for Dorothy Osborne; in April 1653, just after Oliver Cromwell's ejection of the Rump Parliament, she wrote that 'if I had bin soe wise as to have taken hold of the offer was made mee of H. C., I might have bin in a faire way of prefferment, for sure they [the Cromwells] will bee greater now than ever' (Osborne, 38). However, by spring 1653 she had clearly rejected his advances and on 10 May that year at Kensington church Henry married Elizabeth (1637–1687), eldest daughter of Sir Francis Russell, second baronet (*c*.1616–1664), of Chippenham in Cambridgeshire, and Catherine, daughter of John Wheatley. Russell was a close friend and comrade in arms of Oliver Cromwell and had campaigned with him in East Anglia and elsewhere during the civil wars, succeeding him as governor of Ely. Henry and Elizabeth had seven children—Elizabeth (1654–1659), Oliver (1656–1685), Henry (1658–1711), another Elizabeth (1660–1711), Francis (1663–1719), Richard (1665–1687), and William (1667–1692).

In the spring of 1653 Henry was named as a representative of Ireland in the nominated assembly. He was one of the more prominent members of that body, frequently appointed to committees and on nine occasions serving as teller in formal divisions. In June he was assigned lodgings nearby in Whitehall. He was elected to the assembly's second and short-lived council of state at the beginning of November 1653 and was one of its most diligent members, attending thirty-two of the thirty-six meetings. Although he did not play a recorded role in the resignation of the assembly on 12 December, a contemporary list of members marks him down as a non-radical, as 'for the Godly Learned Ministry and Universities' (*A Catalogue of the Names of the Members of the Last Parliament*, 1654, 3), and the assembly's foremost historian identifies Henry both as a moderate and as one of the most active members of the house (A. H. Woolrych, *Commonwealth to Protectorate*, 1982, 414–15).

Henry's position did not formally change when his father became lord protector in December 1653. He did

not, for example, become a member of the protectoral council of state, nor was he given any office in the protectoral administration. However, as the younger son of the new head of state, his status clearly had changed and contemporary commentators began taking notice of Oliver Cromwell's two surviving sons, on occasion referring to them respectfully (or sneeringly) as lord or prince. Although Henry had no role in the inauguration ceremony of 16 December 1653, he accompanied his father when he was entertained by the City of London on 8 February 1654. On 22 February Henry was enrolled at Gray's Inn, but this was merely an honorary registration.

By then more serious work was at hand, for Henry Cromwell was *en route* for Ireland, sent there by his father to investigate and report on the political and religious allegiances among the parliamentary army; with hindsight, Edmund Ludlow wrote that Cromwell had really been sent 'to feel the pulse of the officers there touching his coming over to command in that nation' (*Memoirs of Edmund Ludlow*, 1.380). Travelling via Chester and Holyhead, Cromwell landed near Dublin on 4 March 1654; he stayed in Ireland less than three weeks, for he landed back on the north Wales coast on 21 March and was in London by 29 March. In Ireland he met and had discussions with Fleetwood, the civic dignitaries of Dublin, assorted judges and lawyers, and above all with the disaffected republican Ludlow—what is extant is, via a highly interventionist editor, a detailed if at times rather suspect account of a tense discussion with Henry about the legitimacy of the new regime—and with many other army officers. Within a few days of his arrival he had formed a clear impression of the state of affairs in Ireland, which he conveyed to secretary of state John Thurloe in a characteristically brisk manner. Apart from 'some few inconsiderable persons of the anabaptiste judgment', he found the army to be loyal to, and satisfied with, the protectoral regime. However, he was bitterly critical of Ludlow, who had attempted to stir up opposition to the regime and who 'hath not spared any company or opportunitie to vent his venomous discontents'. Henry also believed that Ludlow's fellow commissioner John Jones opposed the protectorate, though he was 'more cuninge and close in it'. Henry suggested that Ludlow be dismissed and that the Irish administration should be overhauled, for the present government 'does verry little unless it be to make orders to give away the publique lands, of which they have given large proportions to each of themselves'. Cromwell cut even closer to the knuckle in an enclosed note written in cipher, in which he criticized Fleetwood for being 'too deeply ingaged in a partial affection to the persons of the Anabaptists to answer your end; though I doe believe it rather to proceed from tenderness then love to their principles'. Having 'taken the freedom to be very plain' with his brother-in-law, Henry believed him to be loyal to the protectorate but reported 'his desire rather to returne than to continue here' (Thurloe, *State papers*, 2.149).

Henry was at Chippenham in June and July 1654, but was back in London later in the summer. Over the summer he was returned as MP for the University of Cambridge in the first protectorate parliament. He accompanied his father during the opening ceremonies on 3 and 4 September. Appearing in the *Commons Journal* as 'Lord Henry Cromwell', he was named to about a dozen committees spread fairly evenly over the twenty weeks of the session. He served as teller in formal divisions three times, all in the closing days of the parliament; in two of these he was partnered by Broghill. All this suggests that Henry was one of the more active members of the house but was not in the first rank, and was not one of those who took a very prominent or leading role during the session. The single parliamentary diary of this session is brief, incomplete, and rarely identifies individual speakers, so it is impossible to know how far or to what ends he contributed to particular debates. There is a single report of a speech by him, a claim that in late December 1654 he and a protectoral councillor spoke in the house in support of a proposal by another MP that Oliver Cromwell be made king, but the matter was quickly dropped and 'nothing was done in it more' (C. H. Firth, ed., *The Clarke Papers*, 4 vols., 1891–1901, 3.16). In any case, this report is highly suspect, for it conflicts with Henry's own letters of spring 1657 which show him urging his father to refuse parliament's offer of the crown.

Chief administrator of Ireland, 1655–1659 In August 1654, prior to the opening of parliament, the protectoral council had recommended to Oliver Cromwell that Henry be appointed commander of the English army in Ireland and be added to the Irish council. In late October Broghill and other 'Irish gentlemen' attended the council to support this appointment (*CSP dom.*, *1654*, 382). After some delay, perhaps caused by a reluctance to be seen advancing his son, the protector commissioned Henry major-general of the forces in Ireland and formally added him to the Irish council in December 1654. Henry and his family did not cross to Ireland until the following summer; leaving London in mid-June 1655 and travelling via Chester, they embarked from Holyhead and landed near Dublin on 9 July. In a letter to Fleetwood of 22 June the protector had vigorously denied rumours that he would be recalled, with Henry made lord deputy in his place, but the largely unspoken assumption on both sides seems to have been that Henry would, in fact, replace his brother-in-law as effective administrator of and in Ireland. Thus while Henry received assurances prior to leaving England that he would be empowered to appoint to 'places and offices' in Ireland and consulted on judicial appointments, the protector's letter to Fleetwood made clear that if Fleetwood had 'a mind to come over' he would be most welcome in London (Thurloe, *State papers*, 3.440; *Writings and Speeches*, 3.756). Over the early summer Fleetwood undertook an extensive final tour of inspection around Ireland 'to the better settlement of affaires', and by early July he was suggesting mid-September as the likely date of his departure (Thurloe, *State papers*, 3.363). Early in August, having received 'his highnes positive commands to returne into England', Fleetwood reported that he was seeking to leave things in good order for Henry, 'who

though he may have sometimes some melancholy thoughts, yet I hope he will find it much better then he may at present expect' (ibid., 3.697). Fleetwood and his family left Ireland, never to return, early in September 1655.

From summer 1655 until spring 1659 Henry was in Ireland, never once leaving its shores. He and his growing family—two of his sons were born while he was in Ireland—resided principally at Cork House in Dublin and, especially during the summer, at Phoenix House or 'the Phoenix' outside the city. The state rooms at Dublin Castle were used for some public and ceremonial events. Henry also acquired by allocation or purchase land and property in Ireland, notably the Portumna estate in Galway, formerly held by the earl of Clanricarde. Although Henry spent most of the year in Dublin, at the centre of government and administration, each year from 1655 to 1658 inclusive he undertook a tour of inspection around Ireland in the late summer.

From the departure of Fleetwood in September 1655 until his own departure in June 1659 Henry Cromwell was in effect, though not always in name, chief administrator of Ireland. There is a wealth of information from this phase of his life, the one time he exercised extensive, though limited and essentially devolved, political power. However, his status and position changed during this period. Initially he was merely commander of the armed forces in Ireland and one of a six-man Irish council, and Fleetwood, though now absent from Ireland, remained lord deputy until his three-year commission expired in September 1657. The result, described by one historian as one of protector Cromwell's 'least satisfactory compromises' (Barnard, *Cromwellian Ireland*, 20), was to deny Henry full power and control to bring about political, religious, and military change in the English administration of Ireland, and repeatedly to compel him to consult, defer to, or win the grudging acquiescence if not active support of the absent Fleetwood. This quickly soured an already tense relationship with Fleetwood, who as lord deputy, as a protectoral councillor, and as a senior military and political figure whose approach and preferred policies were often very different from Henry's could and at times did serve (wittingly or unwittingly) both as a hindrance to Henry's reforms and as a rallying point for Henry's critics and opponents on both sides of the Irish Sea. In some ways those difficulties were alleviated in autumn 1657, for in November, several weeks after Fleetwood's appointment had expired, Henry was commissioned lord deputy of Ireland in his stead and empowered to govern Ireland for a term of three years. In November 1658 the new protector, Richard Cromwell, made his brother lord lieutenant of Ireland; Henry wrote that 'I had great strivings within my breast, before I could prevail with myself to accept and open the commission' (Thurloe, *State papers*, 7.492). In practice, Henry's difficulties continued even after Fleetwood's direct influence in Irish affairs greatly diminished in autumn 1657, for as lord deputy Henry was required to work with the Irish council, and several members of that small but apparently powerful body opposed some of his central plans, especially in religion. The surviving records of the Irish council in the 1650s are much thinner than those of the (English) protectoral council and it is not possible to reconstruct a detailed picture of the day-to-day operation of the Irish executive and central administration, or of the power structure and struggles within it. On the one hand, the sources which do survive, including Henry's own correspondence, his position as commander of the army in Ireland, and his close relationship with the protectoral administration in England all suggest that from September 1655 onwards he headed the Irish central administration, sitting perhaps as *primus inter pares* in the Irish council but not as someone who could completely dominate or disregard that body. For, on the other hand, Henry's letters of complaint about the opposition he was encountering within the Irish council, several times naming his opponents there, and his repeated requests that new and supportive councillors be appointed to ensure a secure majority for him and his proposals—requests which largely fell on deaf ears in London—together suggest that as lord deputy Henry was abiding by the terms of his formal, written instructions from the protector. These required him to govern Ireland by the 'advice and counsel' of the Irish council 'in all our affairs' and empowered lord deputy and council jointly to run Ireland (Dunlop, 2.437–43, 578–86, 672–3).

Henry's overriding goal in Ireland was to ensure that the country and its people, especially those given military, political, and administrative power under the English regime, were unswervingly loyal to the protectorate. He set out to crush disloyalty and opposition, but he also sought to win over the established protestant community by pursuing policies which would gain its support. Thus his rule was marked by moderation, civilianization, a return to some of the traditional forms, and a greater sensitivity to the needs of the 'old protestants', whatever their former allegiance. Henry adopted a practical approach to governing, not tied to any overriding secular ideologies or spiritual beliefs. He seems to have had no sense of a divine mission driving him forward, and although his correspondence points to a sincere personal faith, it is not loaded with the sort of religious language which often dominates the letters of his father and Fleetwood.

Key traits of Henry's approach became apparent during his opening year in Ireland as he pursued his first main goal, to break the hold which the Baptists had gained over the English army and administration during the pusillanimous governorship of Fleetwood. Henry stressed that he had no quarrel with Baptism as a faith, offering Baptists 'equal liberty in their spiritual and civil concernments with any others' (Thurloe, *State papers*, 4.433). But he was determined to reverse the favoured and elevated position which they had achieved under Fleetwood, because he rightly suspected that Baptism, which had gained a strong hold among town governors, garrison commanders, and senior officers in the English army, was a cover for, and

itself encouraged, republicanism and disaffection towards the protectorate regime, and was thus a grave political threat:

> liberty and countenance they might expect from me, but to rule me, or to rule with me, I should not approve of ... I doe not thinke that God has given them a spiritt of government; neither is it safe they should have much power in their handes. (ibid.)

There ensued a dour power struggle, as many of the civilian and military Baptists agitated against Henry in Ireland and also turned to London, petitioning for Fleetwood's return to Dublin and seeking to lay their case directly before the protector. Henry was sometimes unsure of his position, feeling that his father and the London government were not supporting him as fully as he expected; he was embarrassed when friends and allies in Ireland petitioned for his appointment as lord deputy in place of Fleetwood, correctly predicting that it would win him many enemies and would not be supported by his father; and he was forced for a time into an uncomfortably close alliance with a group of Independent ministers in and around Dublin led by Samuel Winter. However, by late 1656 the battle was won; four leading Baptists in the English army had resigned their commissions, and others either left Ireland, fell silent, or actively courted Henry on his terms. When in 1656 Quakerism showed its face in Ireland, Henry's response was initially very harsh, for fear that it could become the new Baptism and spread in the army as a cover for political disaffection. However, when it became apparent that he had successfully stifled its appeal to the English army in Ireland and that the civilian Quakers were politically loyal, he relaxed his stance.

The power of the radical sects broken, the latter half of Henry's period in Ireland was marked by his cautious and conservative plans for protestantism in the country. Although initially suspicious of the loyalty of the Ulster Scots—'our Scots in the north are a packe of knaves' (Thurloe, *State papers*, 4.198)—Henry went out of his way to conciliate the Presbyterians in the north, enabling them to consolidate their dominance of Ulster's religious life, allowing Presbyterian ministers to preach elsewhere in Ireland, appointing a Presbyterian as one of his chaplains, and inviting another to become minister at St Katherine's Church in Dublin. Increasingly distancing himself from Winter's Dublin-based group of Independents, Henry came to support the work of an association of ministers based in and around Cork, many of them former Anglicans and episcopalians, led by Edward Worth, and to see in their regional organization a possible blueprint for a new national protestant church in Ireland, arranged on broadly presbyterian lines. Henry convened a small convention of ministers which met in Dublin in spring 1658 and which, as intended, proved supportive of these plans. Although Worth was dispatched to England to seek support there, in reality the proposals aroused fierce, Independent-backed opposition in both Ireland and England and little had been achieved by the time that Henry fell from power.

Henry's treatment of the majority Irish Catholic population was mixed. The policies of land seizure and transplantation had been established and largely executed before September 1655, and Henry was left merely to resolve remaining issues, such as the allocation of available land to adventurers and soldiers. Suspicious of the Irish Catholics, and especially of possible collusion with Spain after the outbreak of the Spanish war, he continued a policy of keeping watch over them, of arresting leading Catholics at times of tension, of mounting occasional military and police operations in the provinces, and of lobbying for an effective naval guard around the Irish coast. He regretted the legislation passed by the second protectorate parliament which required Irish Catholics to take an oath of abjuration, denying the pope's power, transubstantiation, and the validity of the Roman church, writing that 'I wish this extreme course had not been so suddenly taken, comeing like a thunder-clapp uppon them. I wish the oath for the present had provided … for their renounceing all forreign jurisdiction' (Thurloe, *State papers*, 6.527). In practice the new oath, like the rest of the existing anti-Catholic legislation, was enforced by Henry only very fitfully, and he continued the well-established policy of English governors in Ireland of largely ignoring the faith of the majority of the Irish, with no serious attempt to undermine or extirpate Catholicism through either sustained and extensive persecution or peaceful mass conversion. On the other hand, his lack of feeling for the Irish Catholics was revealed by the rather callous way in which he planned during the autumn of 1655 to dispatch to Jamaica 'a supply of young Irish girles'—:

> although we must use force in takeing them up, yet it beinge so much for their owne goode, and likely to be of soe great advantage to the publique, it is not in the least doubted that you may have such number of them as you shall thinke fitt. (ibid., 4.23-4)

—together with up to 2000 young boys from the Irish Catholic population: 'it may be a meanes to make them English-men, I meane rather Christians' (ibid., 4.40).

Henry's preference for a return to more traditional and civilian government in Ireland was reflected in other policies. In summer 1655 he inherited from Fleetwood and brought to fruition moves to restore the established central judicial system, based upon the Four Courts, and in 1655-6 he oversaw not only the restoration of commissions of the peace and much of the local and provincial judicial system but also the re-establishment of civilian urban administration under new town charters, creating or cementing protestant control over local government. He sought to strengthen the material and financial position of the protestant church in Ireland by amalgamating parishes to increase the salaries of incumbents, and in 1658-9 he restored in some parishes the payment of tithes directly to the incumbent, in part superseding the existing system under which the government collected tithes into a separate treasury and then paid stipends centrally. Seeking to win over the old protestants, he chose not to enforce and collect the fines which the English government had imposed on former royalists. Peaceful elections

were held in Ireland in summer 1656 and winter 1658-9 to the second and third protectorate parliaments—Henry himself did not stand for election to either—and more generally there were signs of a modest economic and commercial recovery in the country in the latter half of the 1650s.

But Henry's record in Ireland was decidedly mixed. As well as the continuing divisions between several protestant groups, the failure to establish a broadly supported new protestant church settlement, and the failure to engage with the majority Catholic population, little was achieved in repopulating and reviving many towns, well-intentioned ambitions to improve state education and to establish a new college in Dublin came to naught—though Henry did save Archbishop Ussher's library for Ireland, the collection later passing to Trinity College, Dublin, of which Henry had been installed as chancellor in August 1655—and requests to protector and council in London to curb English restrictions upon Irish trade and commerce, to protect Irish shipping and coasts from pirates, and to reform the debased Irish coinage met little response. Above all, Henry, like many of his predecessors and successors, was stymied by the fiscal weakness of the English administration in Ireland. He argued long but in vain for a thorough review and more favourable settlement of the country's finances. Instead, the protectoral government progressively reduced the subsidy which Ireland received from England, while attempts to increase the direct and indirect taxes raised in Ireland were thwarted by the continuing poverty of much of the country, though farming out customs did usefully boost government income. Although Henry cut to the bone the already modest civil costs of the Irish administration, he was able to do no more than tinker with the principal item of expenditure, the military budget of about £330,000 per year, for in the wake of a major reduction of the army in Ireland undertaken in summer 1655, the implementation of which Henry oversaw on succeeding Fleetwood, no further large-scale disbandment of the 16,000-strong army was possible. As a result, expenditure consistently exceeded income during Henry's time in Ireland, leading to an accumulating deficit and increasing military arrears.

Of the English protectoral government of Ireland few official records survive, but the extensive correspondence to and from Henry reveals much about government policy and its imposition, success, or failure, as well as about Henry himself. One historian has described Henry's letters as 'a long series of complaints' and felt they showed him to be 'absurdly sensitive to criticism' (*DNB*; Firth, 2.128). They certainly reveal that he often felt isolated and unsure of himself and of the support which his father and the protectoral government in London would give him. As early as October 1655, with the battle against the Baptists just beginning, he wrote to the protector acknowledging 'that by reason of my youthe and inabilitie, that my tryalls and temptations are too great for me, as well as my employment', and in mid-December, in the face of Baptist complaints to the protector, he wrote, 'Let his Highness doe with me as he please, send me into a Welch cottage, if it be for his service' (Thurloe, *State papers*, 4.72–3, 327). In the summer of 1656, despondent at the alleged support which his Baptist enemies had received in England and Ireland as well as at the alleged lack of support which the London government was giving him, he sent his father via secretary Thurloe two letters of resignation:

> according to the apprehension I have of the present state of thinges I cannot judge it good either for the publique or myselfe to be longer here. I knowe not howe thinges are managed, but sure I am, my enemyes (whoe have bin hitherto designinge to supplante me and to caste their reproaches uppon me) insult, my friends droop, myself thereby rendered contemptible, and altogether uncapable of doeing further service. (ibid., 5.177)

The protector and Thurloe reassured Henry and persuaded him to stay. Yet doubts remained. His correspondence with Fleetwood turned into a catalogue of accusations and complaints from Henry, met by a mixture of denials, counter-complaints, and oozing protestations of affection mixed with religious exhortation from Fleetwood. Moreover, at times Henry was justified in feeling that the protectoral regime might have done more to support him. His complaints about the financing of Ireland, the Irish coinage, and the need for more councillors were well founded but largely ignored; Henry was understandably hurt when in December 1655 the protector wrote an amicable letter to Colonel John Hewson, one of Henry's leading Baptist opponents, who promptly circulated the letter and claimed that it showed the protector supporting his position; protector and council do not appear to have supported a scheme drawn up by Henry in 1656 for a new horse and foot militia in Ireland; and in 1658, when further modest reductions were made to the army in Ireland, the English protectoral council imposed its own scheme for disbandment and overruled Henry's alternative—and, he felt, far better—plans for saving money.

Henry was all too aware of his own shortcomings in Ireland, pointing to his youth and inexperience, and knew that at times he could be impatient and quick-tempered. Towards the end of 1655 he admitted that upon his arrival in Ireland he had on occasion showed 'too much of my own spirit (which through grace I am sencible of as my burden)', and a few weeks later he noted his own strength in the face of Baptist assaults, 'beyond what I ever expected, both in respect of my youthe and naturall temper' (Thurloe, *State papers*, 4.349, 376). Apart from fairly impersonal letters of recommendation, the few surviving letters from Oliver Cromwell to his son over this period seek to reassure and support but also to guide and warn Henry. In April 1656 the protector advised his son to:

> study still to be innocent, and to answer every occasion, roll yourself upon God … Cry to the Lord to give you a plain single heart. Take heed of being over-jealous, lest your apprehensions of others cause you to offend. Know that uprightness will preserve you.

At the same time Henry was not to be 'too hard' in dealing with his opponents, men who were 'weak, because they are so peremptory in judging others', for 'being over-concerned may train you into a snare'. Another snare to be avoided, the protector advised, was 'studying to lay for yourself the foundation of a great estate … they will watch you; bad men will be confirmed in covetousness. The thing is an evil which God abhors. I pray you think of me in this' (*Writings and Speeches*, 4.146). The protector returned to the theme of Henry's over-harsh approach in a letter of October 1657, criticizing his son for implying that Fleetwood was an enemy of the regime, and condemning him for court-martialling and cashiering an officer, a former ally of Hewson, on insufficient evidence—'I am afraid you have erred in this. If you can, I pray you give a remedy for my sake, and let the poor man be handsomely restored'. The protector also advised his son to be 'humble, and patient, place value where it truly lies, viz., in the favour of God, in knowing Him, or rather in being known of Him' (ibid., 4.647, 646).

Throughout his time in Ireland Henry maintained a close interest in political developments in England, kept well informed by a range of London-based correspondents. He, in turn, was not slow to share his advice and opinions with his father, Thurloe, and others. Thus in the spring of 1657 he warmly supported the proposed new constitution, though he advised against the restoration of kingship. Under the new constitution he was named by the protector a member of the new second parliamentary chamber, but his absence in Ireland meant that he never took his seat, either in the second session of the second protectorate parliament or in his brother's one parliament. In September 1658 Henry warmly supported Richard's succession to the protectorship, though he soon began expressing a strong wish to go over to London, in part on health grounds, in part to be on hand to advise and support the new protector. These plans were successfully opposed not only by the military group which eventually overthrew Richard but also by the friends of Henry and the regime, who believed that Henry would be safer in Ireland and better able to support the regime from his Irish power base. In fact, when his brother and the protectorate fell in spring 1659, Henry's own position in Ireland quickly collapsed.

By early May 1659 Henry had heard news of the enforced dissolution of parliament and the military coup against his brother. There followed several weeks of uncertainty in Dublin, as Henry attempted to discover what was happening in London and elsewhere, and cautiously explored what support there might be among military and civilian circles in Ireland for direct action in support of the protectorate. Late in May he dispatched several commissioners to London, sent a neutral letter to Fleetwood, promising his 'endeavours for the peace of this nation', and also wrote to his brother, addressing him still as lord protector, reporting that he and the officers were 'in a waiting frame to see what God or our superiors would command us' and seeking clear guidance from Richard 'upon these matters' (Thurloe, *State papers*, 7.674). When it became evident that neither the army in Scotland nor the fleet would oppose the new military regime, and that Richard was unable or unwilling to make a decisive stand, Henry, too, decided to bow to events. Unwilling or unable to call upon the army or the old protestants in Ireland to mount physical resistance, and turning a deaf ear to royalist approaches and intrigues, he decided to go quietly. On 15 June he wrote a long letter of resignation to the speaker of the recalled Rump Parliament, professing that 'I am soe unwilling to interrupt the peace of these nations', reporting that he had heard 'nothing expressly' from his brother but had received 'credible notice of his acquiescing in what providence had brought forth', and signalling that he, too, would 'acquiesse in the present way of Government, although I cannot promise soe much affection to the late changes as others very honestly may'. Refusing to continue in office in circumstances which 'hath beene looked upon as an indignity to those my nearest relations … [and] which inferres the diminution of my late father's honour & meritt', Henry concluded that 'I have a tenderness to peace which … renders me content to wait upon providence in the expectation of that mercy, being ready to yeeld up my charge to any whom you shall send to receive itt' (ibid., 7.683). A week later he wrote again, confirming that he had received and would obey parliament's orders to return to London and was handing over control of Ireland to parliamentary commissioners. On 27 June 1659 he took ship from Ireland, never to return. He arrived in London on the evening of Saturday 2 July and in the following week he reported on Irish affairs to the Rump's council of state and then retired with his family to Chippenham. At thirty-one his political and military career was over.

Later life, 1659–1674 Henry was not seriously harassed either by the returning republican regime or by the restored Stuarts, and passed the remainder of his life quietly in Cambridgeshire. In 1660–61 he actively sought to protect himself and his family, and to retain as much of his land as possible, writing to Monck, petitioning the king, and welcoming the support he received from influential royalists such as Broghill, Falconberg, Clarendon, and Ormond. In his petition to the king Henry stressed that 'all his actions have been without malice either to the person or to the interest of your majesty, but only out of natural duty to his late father', and he stressed that during his time in Ireland he had consistently sought to:

> study to preserve the peace plenty and splendour of that Kingdom, did encourage a learned ministry, giving not only protection but maintenance to several Bishops there, placed worthy persons in the seats of Judicature and magistracy, and to his own great prejudice upon all occasions was favourable to your majesty's professed friends.

He requested that the king 'would not suffer him his wife and children to perish from the face of the Earth, but rather live and expiate what hath been done amiss with their future prayers and services for your Majesty' and asked that 'no distinction between himself and your Majesty's other good subjects may be branded on him to posterity that so he may without fear and as well out of interest as duty serve your Majesty all his days' (Waylen, 25–6). Henry was not excluded from the general pardon and, although he lost land in Ireland and England, he managed

to retain considerable property in both countries, including much of the Portumna estate. In surviving letters to Clarendon and Ormond, written in the early 1660s, Henry was at pains to stress his gratitude for their help, his absolute loyalty to the king, and his distance from any plots and conspiracies.

In 1662–3 Henry bought from his wife's family, the Russells, Spinney Abbey at Wicken in Cambridgeshire, and there he spent his final decade. Noble and others relate colourful but unlikely stories of Charles II visiting him there at least once while travelling to or from Newmarket. In July 1664 Henry invited the minister Isaac Archer to Wicken, to preach there and to serve as his personal chaplain, and over the following months, until his departure in 1665, Archer's diary makes occasional reference to Henry and throws considerable light upon the faiths of both men. Archer found Henry to be 'a patron of piety … neither was he and his lady religious only by countenancing religion … but by their private examples and duties did shame those of their quality round about'. Archer had uneasily and unhappily conformed to the Church of England, but at Wicken, with Henry's support, he was able to focus on a preaching ministry and employed the prayer book 'as little as was possible'. This rekindled thoughts of 'quitting conformity' which he shared with Henry, who 'did not urge mee still to conforme; for he was not much for those things'. In the spring of 1665 Henry dispensed with Archer's services, for in the wake of enquiries whether he had a 'conformable' chaplain, he had concluded that 'it would have bin a prejudice to us both' to retain Archer (Storey, 97–103). While he was not apparently willing to prejudice his own and his family's safety by standing out against the established church and instead wishing to maintain a level of bare conformity within the Church of England, the episode shows that Henry's faith was deep and sincere, that he favoured a simple, preaching ministry, and that he was in sympathy neither with Restoration religious policy nor with significant elements of the restored Church of England.

Henry visited his dying mother at Northborough in 1665, and his unmarried paternal aunt, Elizabeth Cromwell, spent her last years with him and died at Spinney Abbey in September 1672. In the following year Henry himself drew up his will. A short, brisk, and typically business-like document, with no reference to his faith, his soul, or the disposal of his body, it left everything to 'my deare and wel beloved wife', who was empowered to share the estate among their surviving children as she saw fit. Henry died at Spinney Abbey of the stone on 23 March 1674 and was buried two days later in Wicken church beneath an inscribed marble slab which still survives. His widow, who outlived him by thirteen years and died in April 1687, lies beside him.

Reputation Like his father and his elder brother Richard, Henry Cromwell appears to have left no diary, memoir, or other autobiographical account. However, his extensive surviving correspondence provides a rich and rounded picture of him when he was at the height of his powers in the 1650s. He comes across as a decent, honest, and hard-working young man who applied himself, learned quickly, and was able swiftly and usually accurately to weigh up people and circumstances. But Henry's real importance rests upon his period as chief administrator of Ireland from 1655 to 1659, and it is upon his record in Ireland that historical judgements must be grounded. In Ireland he oversaw and helped to shape a civilianized and moderate English regime, which restored many of the traditional forms of colonial rule and the well-established policies of the English government of Ireland. Sensitive to the needs of the established protestant population, Henry's period in Ireland was also marked by growing stability, a modest economic recovery, and greater recognition of the needs of the old protestants; his re-establishment of civilian urban and local government also served to cement the protestants' hold on power. On the other hand he came up with few new or radical policies and, just as most of the problems he encountered in governing Ireland and the Irish were not new, so his responses tended to be traditional and, in many cases, limited or unsuccessful. He reversed the imbalances created during the governorship of Charles Fleetwood and won wider support for the protectorate in Ireland. But when put to the test in spring 1659, he was unable or unwilling to bring Ireland out in support of his brother's tottering regime and, opposed to royalism, he had no alternative but to make way for a very different non-monarchical regime in England and Ireland. He may, consciously or unconsciously, have helped to prepare for the protestant ascendancy in Ireland but he failed to establish a durable Cromwellian ascendancy there.

PETER GAUNT

Sources Thurloe, *State papers* · BL, Lansdowne MSS 821–823 · T. Barnard, *Cromwellian Ireland* (1975) · T. Barnard, 'Planters and policies in Cromwellian Ireland', *Past and Present*, 61 (1973), 31–69 · *The writings and speeches of Oliver Cromwell*, ed. W. C. Abbott and C. D. Crane, 4 vols. (1937–47) · C. H. Firth, *The last years of the protectorate, 1656–1658*, 2 vols. (1909) · R. W. Ramsey, *Henry Cromwell* (1933) · J. Waylen, *The house of Cromwell and the story of Dunkirk* (1897) · M. Noble, *Memoirs of the protectoral house of Cromwell*, 2 vols. (1787) · O. Cromwell, *Memoirs of the protector, Oliver Cromwell, and of his sons Richard and Henry* (1820) · J. Caulfield, ed., *Cromwelliana: a chronological detail of events in which Oliver Cromwell was engaged, from the year 1642 to his death, 1658* (1810) · A. Clarke, *Prelude to restoration in Ireland* (1999) · J. Ohlmeyer, ed., *Ireland from independence to occupation, 1641–60* (1996) · R. Dunlop, ed., *Ireland under the Commonwealth*, 2 vols. (1913) · *The memoirs of Edmund Ludlow*, ed. C. H. Firth, 2 vols. (1894) · *CSP dom.*, 1649–61 · *CSP Ire.* · [D. Osborne], *The letters of Dorothy Osborne to William Temple*, ed. G. C. M. Smith (1959) · M. Storey, ed., *Two East Anglian diaries, 1641–1729* (1994) · will, PRO, PROB 11/346, fol. 123 · GEC, *Baronetage* · D. Foskett, *Samuel Cooper and his contemporaries* (1974)

Archives BL, corresp., Lansdowne MSS 821–823 · Bodl. Oxf., MSS · Cambs. AS, Huntingdon, corresp., papers, and letter-book | Bodl. Oxf., Thurloe state papers, Rawl. MSS

Likenesses R. Dunkarton, two mezzotints, pubd 1814 (after unknown artist), NPG · R. Earlom, mezzotint, pubd 1814 (after unknown artist), NPG · T. Athow, wash drawing (after miniature by unknown artist), AM Oxf. · S. Cooper, watercolour on vellum miniature, priv. coll. · C. J. Dusart; oils; Sothebys, 24 Nov 1971 [*see illus.*] · C. P. Harding, wash drawing, AM Oxf. · attrib. R. Walker, portrait, priv. coll.; repro. in Ramsey, *Henry Cromwell*, frontispiece · two portraits, NPG

Wealth at death see will, PRO, PROB 11/346, fol. 123

Cromwell, Henry (1659–1728), translator and poet, was born on 15 January 1659 at Clifton, Bedfordshire, the second son and third child of Thomas Cromwell (1609–1660), a first cousin of Oliver Cromwell, the lord protector, and Elizabeth Dixie (b. 1627?). It is probable that he was educated at home.

Cromwell owned lands in Beesby, 9 miles south-east of Louth, Lincolnshire, where he sometimes passed the summer months. The rest of the year he spent principally in London, visiting coffee houses, attending the theatre, and playing ombre and piquet in fashionable salons. He also translated Latin poets and wrote his own verse. He contributed a number of amorous songs, and a rendering of Martial (i.67), to Charles Gildon's *Miscellany Poems upon Several Occasions* (1692), and versions of half a dozen of Ovid's *Amores* (i.7, 8, 10, 15) to *Examen poeticum* (1693), the last of which, 'Of the Immortality of the Muses', was 'Inscrib'd to Mr. *Dryden*' (p. 282). The volume also contains translations of *Amores*, iii.2 and 3; a manuscript copy of the latter is to be found in the West papers (BL, Add. MS 34744), where it accompanies an interpretation of *Amores*, i.5, in the same hand. And 'To his Mistress' and 'The Dream', renderings of *Amores*, ii.16 and iii.5, were published in Bernard Lintot's collection *Miscellaneous Poems and Translations* (1712), the volume which further contains *The Rape of the Locke*, the first edition of that poem. Cromwell is also known to have translated Voiture. His published works, both the translations and original lyrics, reveal a competent, if slightly mechanical, facility for versification.

Womanizing was the other great love of Cromwell's life. Courteously old-fashioned in manner, he was none the less a fashion plate, wearing nosegays, favouring a high, full-bottomed wig, and walking with a mincing step or dancing gait. To an unprepossessing appearance (a long, thin countenance and a sallow complexion: 'a Satyr in his Face', in Wycherley's view) were added 'creeping advances, clinging embraces', as the playwright put it to Pope (14 June 1709, *Correspondence of Alexander Pope*, 1.65), and by Cromwell's own account a thoroughly raffish demeanour: one of his favourite anecdotes recalled his competing with Dryden for the favours of a Drury Lane prostitute. This and suchlike lubricious tales he rehearsed for a younger circle of friends, including Alexander Pope, whom he had met probably through Wycherley, possibly as early as 1705, and a group which comprised Nicholas Rowe, Eustace Budgell, William Fortescue, and John Gay, to whom he was introduced for the first time in the autumn of 1710, on his return from Lincolnshire. (Shortly afterwards, Cromwell was responsible for introducing Gay to Pope.)

For a brief period Cromwell and Pope corresponded on matters literary and carnal. In addition to replies in prose which allowed the young poet to demonstrate, and to apply, his self-education in the ancients, Pope composed verse letters animated by a deal of characterful detail: from 'An Epistle to Henry Cromwell, Esq.' (1707), for example, we learn that the recipient was somewhat deaf, was particular in his snuff-taking and penmanship, and kept company with the unheralded poetasters Brocas and Fouler, and the gamester Pentlow. In 'Mr Popes Welcome from Greece' (1720), moreover, John Gay imagines 'honest, hatless *Cromwell*, with red breeches' (l. 136), the source of Johnson's exiguous character of the roué in his life of Pope. Cromwell further commented on Pope's translation of Statius, and his is probably the hand which supplies a marginal commentary of approving and monitory Latin exclamations, and the occasional note drawing attention to departures from Ovid's model, to the autograph of Pope's rendering of *Sapho to Phaon* (c.1707; published 1712). The annotations show Cromwell to be a scrupulous critic attentive to the nicest points of grammar. That a scurrilous epigram alluding to him appears on the verso of the Ovid manuscript exemplifies the cooling of his friendship with Pope, probably but not certainly to be attributed to Cromwell's increasing association with John Dennis, of whom he was to become a long-term friend and admirer, but who was one of Pope's most persistent literary enemies. Cromwell and Pope remained casual friends after 1711, but ceased to correspond.

From about 1717 Cromwell appears to have curtailed his metropolitan socializing; throughout his life Epsom was a favourite resort. In 1726, however, he returned to public attention when Edmund Curll, another of Pope's longstanding literary adversaries, published the poet's youthful, unguarded correspondence with Cromwell, embarrassing letters he had obtained from Elizabeth Thomas. Thomas was (and has continued to be) referred to in print as Cromwell's mistress—when she is not remembered as 'Curll's Corinna', Pope's scatological revenge on her in *The Dunciad Variorum* (1729), II.66—but eighteenth-century senses of the term have been apt to mislead: a literary-minded gentlewoman living with her widowed mother and grandmother in impoverished but respectable circumstances, Thomas had been a friend of Cromwell, but nothing more intimate, perhaps since 1700. He paid court to her, shared Pope's writings with her after 1708, and introduced her to the poet, who esteemed her as a free-spirited literary friend. Thomas pestered Cromwell to be allowed to keep the letters he had shown her, and which she continued to hold, regarding them as relics, or prizes, of her acquaintance with the poet, in which request he eventually acquiesced. He forgot the affair as they drifted apart after 1717; he was reminded of the autographs, and his part in their dissemination, only when he learned that Thomas, indigent after the deaths of her mother and fiancé, had sold the letters to Curll, who published them in a two-volume collection, *Miscellanea* (1726), together with a handful of his uncollected verses. If Pope replied to the two mortified letters Cromwell appears to have addressed to him (but which are known only from the poet's published correspondence), the dispatches have not survived.

It is probable that Pope and Cromwell had no further contact. For a short time, at the beginning of Pope's literary career, the friendship and exacting criticism of Cromwell, a man nearly thirty years his senior, whose other pursuits earned him a reputation as a '*louche boulevardier*' (Nokes, 53), fulfilled an important need; later, already alienated by Cromwell's association with Dennis, Pope dropped him as his confidence in his abilities, and his fame, grew. Cromwell died on 29 June 1728 and was buried in London at St Clement Danes, on the Strand, as he had requested in his will.   JONATHAN PRITCHARD

Sources M. Mack, *Alexander Pope: a life* (1985) · G. Sherburn, *The early career of Alexander Pope* (1934) · *The correspondence of Alexander Pope*, ed. G. Sherburn, 5 vols. (1956) · T. R. Steiner, 'Young Pope in the correspondence of Henry Cromwell and Elizabeth Thomas ("Curll's Corinna")', *N&Q*, 228 (1983), 495–7 · T. R. Steiner, 'The misrepresentation of Elizabeth Thomas, "Curll's Corinna"', *N&Q*, 228 (1983), 506–8 · V. Rumbold, *Women's place in Pope's world* (1989), 163–5 · *Parish register of Clifton, 1539–1812*, Bedford Parish Register, 62 (1985), 19, 53 · *Pylades and Corinna, or, Memoirs of the lives, amours and writings of Richard Gwinnett esq, of Great Shurdington in Gloucestershire, and Mrs Elizabeth Thomas junr of Great Russel Street, Bloomsbury ... to which is prefixed, the life of Corinna, written by her self*, 2 vols. (1731–2) · D. Nokes, *John Gay: a profession of friendship* (1995) · *The last and greatest art: some unpublished poetical manuscripts of Alexander Pope*, ed. M. Mack (1984), 72–90 · D. Clay Jenkins, 'Scribbling on the backside of 'Sapho to Phaon': an unpublished Pope epigram?', *Scriblerian*, 8/2 (1975–6), 77–8 · S. Johnson, *Lives of the English poets*, ed. G. B. Hill, [new edn], 3 vols. (1905) · J. Spence, *Observations, anecdotes, and characters, of books and men*, ed. J. M. Osborn, new edn, 2 vols. (1966), item no. 103, 1–43

Wealth at death owned lands in Beesby, Lincolnshire, which he left to 'cousin', Henry Greene, clerk, son of Cromwell's 'cousin German', John Greene; estate mortgaged to Elizabeth Godolphin for £1200; left various bequests of life annuities (£40) chargeable to the estate; books and portraits: will, PRO, PROB 11/623, fols. 40v–41

Cromwell, Mary. *See* Belasyse, Mary, Countess Fauconberg (*bap.* 1637, *d.* 1713).

Cromwell, Oliver (1599–1658), lord protector of England, Scotland, and Ireland, was the second son of Robert Cromwell (*d.* 1617) and his wife, Elizabeth Steward (*d.* 1654); he was born in Huntingdon on 25 April 1599 and was baptized in St John's Church there four days later. He was named after his father's elder brother, Sir Oliver Cromwell of Hinchingbrook and of Ramsay, who almost certainly stood as his godfather.

Family background and life to 1628 The Cromwell fortune and name derived from Cromwell's great-grandfather, Morgan Williams, a Welshman from Glamorgan who had settled in Putney as an innkeeper and brewer and who had had the good fortune to marry the elder sister of Henry VIII's great minister Thomas Cromwell before the latter's rise to greatness. Williams and his son Richard were beneficiaries of this relationship and received enough confiscated church lands to become one of the most prominent families in Huntingdonshire. In slightly defiant gratitude (Thomas Cromwell having been beheaded in 1540) Richard changed his family name to Cromwell. Conscious of the circumstances, Oliver, throughout his life and even as lord protector, occasionally described himself as Williams alias Cromwell. Richard's son Sir Henry Cromwell ('the golden knight', 1536–1604) built substantial houses on the sites of a dissolved Benedictine convent (Hinchingbrook, half a mile from Huntingdon) and a dissolved Benedictine

Oliver Cromwell (1599–1658), by Samuel Cooper, c.1650

abbey (Ramsey, 15 miles away in the fenland). Sir Oliver (1563–1655), uncle and godfather of the future lord protector, thus inherited a large but debt-laden estate (debt made worse by over-frequent receptions of members of the royal family as they travelled up the Great North Road, less than a mile away). Cromwell's father in contrast inherited a modest cluster of urban properties and impropriations in and around Huntingdon, but no manors or freehold land. With an income of perhaps £300 per annum and a seven-room town house, Robert Cromwell was a substantial inhabitant of a secondary town. He represented it in the parliament of 1593. None the less, as the eldest (surviving) son of the younger son of a knight Cromwell's social status was ambiguous.

Oliver Cromwell's mother was the daughter of William Steward. William's father in the early days of the Reformation had secured from his own brother, as prior of Ely, long leases of abbey (later dean and chapter) lands. Those leases passed to Elizabeth's childless brother Thomas, and eventually to Oliver.

Very little is known about Cromwell's first forty years. Only four of his personal letters survive, together with the précis of a speech he made when the House of Commons was in grand committee in 1628. He made only fleeting and impersonal appearances in public records. During his first decade there is the record of his baptism and of his having been a boy at the town grammar school, sitting at the feet of Thomas Beard, a pluralist and rather complacent conformist, whose reputation rested principally on his having written a best-seller on the way God visited divine justice in this world on scandalous sinners. There is a story that when the future Charles I, aged three, stayed at

Hinchingbrook on his way south to join his father, Sir Henry brought his four-year-old grandson Oliver to play with him; and that they squabbled and Oliver punched the prince on the nose and made it bleed. The story was recorded only after Oliver had orchestrated Charles's death, and it seems just too good to be true.

During Cromwell's second decade there is the record of his matriculation at Sidney Sussex College, Cambridge, on 23 April 1616 and of his departure from the college on 24 June 1617, immediately after the death of his father. Some early biographers claimed that he then attended Lincoln's Inn, but there is no trace of him in its records and no evidence of a common-law training in his later discourse. With a widowed mother and seven unmarried sisters the eighteen-year-old Oliver is more likely to have returned home. The next ten years would have necessarily been spent in coping with being the only man in a household of women. In effect, it meant trying to find husbands for his sisters who would be worthy of family honour and not ask for too much by way of dowry. Since his mother did not marry again and lived on as a widow until 1654, this was a major drain on the attenuated family fortune.

During Cromwell's third decade (April 1619 to April 1629) there is slightly more evidence. His marriage on 22 August 1620 is recorded in the registers of St Giles Cripplegate, London, as is his return in at least some of the annual elections to the common council of Huntingdon (the records are too incomplete for greater precision about how often). The subsidy rolls for the mid-1620s place him among the top twenty householders in the town. A brief and secular letter in 1626 to Henry Downhall—an old university friend, now a minister with Arminian leanings—inviting him to stand as godfather to Richard, his third son, suggests that Oliver's puritan conversion lay before him. In 1627 his uncle Oliver, who had massive debts, sold Hinchingbrook to Sidney Montagu, brother of the first earl of Manchester and, like him, a thrusting lawyer with court aspirations, and retreated to the family's larger house at Ramsey. Initially this led to a new honour for Cromwell, as he was selected in 1628 to represent the borough of Huntingdon as junior member behind a scion of the Montagus. He made virtually no impact on the very full records of that parliament except for one gauche speech, which fell like a stone, against the Arminian Bishop Richard Neile.

The crucial event of this decade was his marriage to Elizabeth Bourchier (1598–1665) [see Cromwell, Elizabeth]. She was the eldest of twelve children of Sir James Bourchier, a retired London fur trader with extensive land in Essex (and elsewhere) and with strong connections with the godly gentry families there. The marriage was probably arranged by Oliver's father's sister Joan, wife of Sir Francis Barrington, who certainly brokered many other family matches. It brought Oliver into contact with the Barringtons, the Mashams, and the St Johns and also with leading members of the London merchant community, and behind them all the great interest of the Rich family, headed by the earls of Warwick and Holland. Cromwell's marriage was to be long and stable. There were nine children: five boys and four girls. One son (James) died as an infant (1632), and two others on the eve of manhood—the eldest, Robert (1622–1639), while away at school and the second, Oliver (1623–1644), of camp fever while serving as a parliamentarian officer. But two sons—Richard *Cromwell (1626–1712) and Henry *Cromwell (1628–1674)—and four daughters—Bridget (*bap.* 1624, *d.* 1662) [*see* Fleetwood, Bridget], Elizabeth (*bap.* 1629, *d.* 1658) [*see* Claypole, Elizabeth], Mary (*bap.* 1637, *d.* 1713) [*see* Belasyse, Mary, Countess Fauconberg], and Frances (*bap.* 1638, *d.* 1721) [*see* Russell, Frances, Lady Russell]—played their part in the great affairs of the 1650s. Little is known of the relationship between Oliver and Elizabeth beyond the unmannered deep affection of their letters to one another in the early 1650s and her apparent utter loyalty and discreet public presence on state occasions under the protectorate.

A personal crisis, 1628–1631 There is evidence that Cromwell was suffering from physical and mental stress by 1628. He took the waters at Wellingborough for severe stomach cramps, and the papers of Sir Theodore de Mayerne, a London doctor, record his seeking treatment on 19 September 1628 for *valde melancolicus* (depression). According to a much later report, in 1628 or 1629 he experienced the religious conversion which henceforth dominated his life and was recorded graphically in a letter of 1638 to his cousin. Following on from this he became involved in a number of confrontations, all of which he lost. He became embroiled in a local feud that is chronicled in the records of the Mercers' Company over several years from 1628. The Mercers were trustees of a bequest left for the benefit of Huntingdon by a member of the company, Richard Fishbourne, who had been born in the town. Cromwell can be found lobbying for the money to be used not to underwrite an existing lectureship held by his old conformist schoolmaster Beard but a new one to be held by a firebrand puritan, Robert Procter. Then in 1630 the Montagus procured a new charter for Huntingdon, and replaced the council elected annually by the freemen with a closed oligarchy, from which Cromwell was excluded. His public accusations of malpractice against the Montagus and their lawyer led to his being called before the privy council in December 1630 and forced to admit his error. On 7 May 1631 Cromwell (and his mother and his wife) entered into a deed of sale of almost all their properties in and around Huntingdon for the sum of £1800, which suggests an annual value of about £100. Oliver, Elizabeth, and the children moved to a farmstead in St Ives, 4 miles away. For the next five years he may have remained a gentleman by birth but he was a plain russet-coated yeoman by lifestyle.

St Ives and Ely, 1631–1640 The next few years are no less murky than the previous ones. Yet the silence of the records about Cromwell is itself striking. There is no suggestion that he was ever presented before the church courts for any form of recusancy or nonconformity, and cryptic (but unexplained) memoranda in the papers of

Matthew Wren, the Laudian bishop of Ely, for November and December 1638 and March 1640 suggest that he was using Cromwell in helping to resolve a number of disputes. Cromwell was not included in any sheriffs' list for non-payment or obstruction of ship money, nor was he reported to the council for any more ill-advised words. In 1637 he is reported to have offered legal advice to commoners in the Isle of Ely whose livelihoods were threatened by the drainage of the fens, but there is no shred of evidence that he opposed the principle of the land improvement, let alone that he condoned riot or extralegal protest against it.

From 1631 to 1636 Cromwell lived and worked as a farmer in St Ives, suffering from an intractable chest infection that led him to wear a red flannel around his throat, even to church. Perhaps his move stemmed from an accumulation of debt from having too many sisters to marry off, compounded by having lost status, honour, and such authority as he had possessed in Huntingdon. But there is another intriguing possibility: when he moved to St Ives in 1631 he became a tenant of the godly Henry Lawrence, just after Lawrence had become one of the ten patentees of Connecticut in New England, and had committed himself to moving to this colony as soon as he could; Cromwell's selling up and moving when he did could well indicate his intention to move there with him. In 1634 Lawrence and his co-patentees wrote to John Winthrop, the governor of Massachusetts, and announced their imminent departure from England. But they never arrived, either because Winthrop would not meet their preconditions, or because the privy council prevented this particular group from travelling. This is the allegation that several later royalists and the New England minister Cotton Mather later made with respect to Cromwell himself and others. In the event, Lawrence went instead to Arnhem in the Netherlands, where he became a noted lay preacher and wrote against paedobaptism. Perhaps he was becoming too radical for New England. There may have been many reasons why Cromwell did not go with him, but one is almost certainly the happenstance that in January 1636, just as Lawrence was emigrating, Oliver's childless and widowed maternal uncle Sir Thomas Steward died. Cromwell—who may have been spending time securing a court order to protect his inheritance by having the old man declared a lunatic (probably because senility was advancing)—inherited from him leases on tithes held by the dean and chapter of Ely, and he and his family moved to a substantial glebe house in the shadow of the cathedral. His income increased dramatically to some £300 a year. The tide had turned.

In addition, there are tantalizing hints in two letters written in 1636 and 1638 that Cromwell had established himself within an East Anglian puritan network emanating from his extended family. On 11 January 1636 Cromwell wrote to a London mercer, George Storie. He reminded Storie (who, he did not realize, had just migrated to New England) that he was late with his subscription for a lectureship in Godmanchester, which abuts Huntingdon but lies across the River Ouse in a different diocese; the lectureship had been set up after the failure of the godly to secure the Fishbourne bequest in 1629. The peremptory tone of a working farmer to a rich London merchant is startling. In an age where recognizing relative social status mattered, this was an inappropriate letter, unless Cromwell was writing on behalf of a group which included Storie's betters. Furthermore, in prompting Storie to pay up, Cromwell spoke of the need for such lectureship posts 'in these times wherein they are suppressed with too much haste and violence by the enemies of God his truth', clearly a snarling reference to the bishops (*Letters and Speeches*, 1904, letter 1).

A second letter, written on 13 October 1638, is much stronger evidence of a fierce puritan faith. It is addressed to his 22-year-old cousin Elizabeth, the young bride of Oliver St John (1598–1673), Cromwell's exact contemporary at Cambridge and principal attorney to Cromwell's cousin John Hampden in the ship-money trial just concluded. It is a passionate account of how after having been 'a chief, the chief of sinners', driven to the depths of despair, he had been called to be among 'the congregation of the firstborn [the firstborn son of God, Christ]' so that 'my body rests in hope, and if here I may serve my God either by my doing or by my suffering, I shall be most glad' (*Letters and Speeches*, 1904, letter 2). His religious journey had begun before 1630 but it is possible that he had been further radicalized by Job Tookey, the curate of St Ives, hounded out by Bishop John Williams of Lincoln in 1635. His link to Lawrence also makes plausible a claim made in a report in other respects very accurate that by the later 1630s Cromwell regularly preached in other men's houses as well as in his own.

By the end of 1639, then, Cromwell was a radicalized puritan with powerful links through the families of his father and of his wife to leading puritan families in Essex and London and to some of the leading figures who had emigrated to New England, including Robert Hooke, whose marriage had been arranged by Joan, Lady Barrington. His own personal fortunes—and his health—had waned in the 1620s, reached a low plateau in the early 1630s, and had waxed in the later 1630s. Providence had smiled on him. If in the years in and immediately after his conversion he had served God by his suffering, he was about to find out how he could serve him by his doing.

From the private to the public man If Cromwell had died in his fortieth year he would have made no mark on history, and would be unknown except to the antiquaries of Huntingdonshire. Yet from this lowly position he was to emerge as the most powerful figure in revolutionary times, and this made him loved and reviled in equal measure. He was in his own day, and has remained ever since, one of the most contended of Englishmen. He was a man born on the cusp of the gentry and the middling sort who became a head of state. He was a general whose brutal conquests of Scotland and (particularly) Ireland have cast a long dark shadow. He was a king-killer who agonized about whether to be king; a parliamentarian who used military force to break and to purge parliaments. He was a passionate advocate of religious liberty who stood by and

let books be burnt and blasphemers be publicly tortured. He was an advocate of equitable justice who imprisoned not only those who challenged his powers to raise extra-parliamentary taxation but also the lawyers who had the temerity to represent them. To his admirers he overthrew tyranny and strove to promote liberty. To his detractors he was an ambitious hypocrite who betrayed the cause of liberty he claimed to represent. And it all began with his very surprising return to the parliaments of 1640 as MP for the city of Cambridge.

Parliamentarian, 1640–1642 Cromwell must have been the least wealthy man returned to both the Short and the Long parliaments, and he was returned for a borough that had always returned a prominent client of the lord keeper and a prominent resident of the borough. Only one existing account makes any sense of his selection. An anonymous report, integrated into the wholly scurrilous and unreliable *Flagellum* after the death of the first compiler, James Heath, is full of verifiable detail. It tells how a group of godly freemen, headed by the mayor's brother-in-law (who, like Cromwell, held a tenancy in St Ives) and inspired by Cromwell's 'preaching' at a conventicle, persuaded the mayor on 7 January 1640 to make Cromwell a freeman on the mayor's own nomination. This made him eligible to stand for election as MP for Cambridge, and the same group subsequently pressed his cause, securing his return in March 1640 in second place behind the lord keeper's nominee and in October in first place ahead of a prominent puritan common-councilman to the exclusion of the court candidate. Less reliable, but also quite possible, is a later memoir that claimed that when in September 1640 a group of twelve opposition peers refused to obey Charles I's summons to York, Oliver St John brought Cromwell into the small group that helped to draft the peers' petition and to carry it to the north.

This trajectory—a well-connected man with passionate views about the way that the godly were being driven out of the church or persecuted if they sought to witness within it—helps to explain the prominent part Cromwell played in the early months of the Long Parliament. It would explain how he came to be trusted with responsibility in the very first week for presenting the petition of one of the great puritan martyrs of Star Chamber, John Lilburne, for securing his release from prison and the promise of compensation for his savage flogging. It would explain how he came to be the man who in May 1641 moved the second reading of the Annual Parliaments Bill, and how soon afterwards he came to take so leading a part in drafting the bill for the suspension of episcopacy. In those opening months he served on eighteen high-profile committees, especially those concerned with investigating religious innovation and abuse of ecclesiastical power. His faith and trust in God made him fearless. And more than once he spoke his mind too forcefully and was reproved by the house (as in his unvarnished attack on episcopacy in February 1641). Sir Philip Warwick memorably recalled him as wearing a plain cloth suit, and plain linen shirt, its collar spotted with blood. It is an image of a man short of a change of clothes and without a servant to shave him: a man on the margins socially and not entirely at ease with himself. As a result he was dropped from the opposition front bench speaker's panel after May 1641. He remained a useful man on committees, pushing for religious reform and a strong line against the Irish rebels. But as time went on he spoke less in the full house.

Soldier, 1642–1644 In the high summer of 1642 king and parliament were increasingly provoking one another into trial by battle. The Rubicon was finally crossed when Charles I raised his standard at Nottingham on 22 August. He had written on 25 July to the vice-chancellor of Cambridge University inviting the colleges to assist him by the 'loan' of their plate. Cromwell was sent down by the Commons to prevent them from doing so. On 10 August, accompanied by perhaps 200 lightly armed countrymen who had volunteered to help him, he blocked the exit road from Cambridge that led to the Great North Road. He went on to intimidate his way into Cambridge Castle and to seize the arms stored there, and halt the movement of silver. At a time when most Englishmen were dithering and waiting upon events, it was a bold and unhesitating act. Within a fortnight he had raised a company of sixty cavalry, recruiting his cousin Edward *Whalley and his brother-in-law John *Disbrowe to be his lieutenants, and he used his troopers to search the houses of suspected royalists. In mid-October he was instructed to take his troop to join the army assembled by the earl of Essex, the captain-general of the parliamentarian forces; he arrived at some point during the battle of Edgehill and may have taken some part in its end-game. He remained with the earl until 13 November at Turnham Green (5 miles west of London): the stand-off there caused the king to abandon his attempt to enter his capital and to withdraw first to Reading and then to Oxford. Cromwell's movements for the rest of the year are unknown, but a return to Ely and to organizing the defence of the area seems likelier than a return to the House of Commons. Certainly from 6 January to 13 March 1643 he was in Cambridgeshire and west Suffolk.

In the course of February 1643, without being in more than the odd skirmish, Cromwell was inexplicably promoted from captain to colonel. Parliament had appointed William Grey, Lord Grey of Warke, as major-general of the forces for the defence of the six eastern counties, and Cromwell's appointment was to one of the regiments Grey now sought to raise. But the appointment quickly took on a greater significance because on 7 April Grey took the great bulk of his force, some 5000 men, and set off to join the earl of Essex at the siege of Reading. He never returned. For the rest of 1643 Cromwell was effectively the senior officer in the six parliamentarian heartland counties of East Anglia: Essex, Hertfordshire, Huntingdonshire, Cambridgeshire, Suffolk, and Norfolk. He had no experience as a militia captain, let alone as a deputy lieutenant—he had learned nothing of war from his father, his grandfather, his uncles. He was a gentleman by birth but he was not the equal of any of the men who ran the county committees or the lieutenancies of the six associated counties. Yet from the outset he, and he alone, seems

to have formed a strategic plan for the defence of the region with the fierce insistence of a sergeant-major dealing with a bunch of officer cadets who had yet to realize that war was a life-and-death matter: 'you must act lively; do it without distraction. Neglect no means' (*Letters and Speeches*, 1904, letter 14, 6 Aug 1643); 'Service must be done. Command you and be obeyed!'—this in a letter endorsed, 'to the deputy-lieutenants of Essex: these, haste, haste, posthaste' (ibid., 3.316, 6 Aug 1643).

In a sense, Cromwell's task was simple: there was no threat from the east (the sea), from the south, or from the west. But there were all kinds of pockets of anti-parliamentarian sentiment within the region, and there was a threat that grew steadily throughout the spring and summer from the north as the royalist army of the earl of Newcastle inexorably took control of Lincolnshire and of the Great North Road as far south as Stamford. With no more than 2000 men to hand at any one time, Cromwell had reason to be fearful.

Cromwell had three priorities. His first was to act decisively and firmly to deal with any royalist stirs (hence his rapid march and seizure of Lowestoft on 13–14 March 1643 and King's Lynn the following week). His second was to secure and defend all the bridges and routes across first the Great Ouse and then the Nene (which involved the bombardment and occupation of small royalist outposts like Crowland and Burghley House). It is astounding that he could write with such confidence in June that 'two or three hundred men in these parts are enough' (*Calendar of the Wynn (of Gwydir) Papers, 1515–1690*, 1926, no. 1722A [p. 280]), a judgement borne out by the fact that a royalist regiment under Colonel Sir John Palgrave was repulsed by the small garrison he had left in Peterborough. No one else was attempting to do anything. By his own strenuous efforts and intuitive strategic sense Cromwell secured East Anglia for the parliament. The coping stone to this effort was the establishment of military headquarters for the region at Ely and his own appointment as governor of the Isle of Ely. This was achieved in July 1643.

Cromwell's third priority was to establish an effective supply system to ensure a steady flow of new soldiers and of regular pay and provisions. That meant galvanizing the various county committees, each of which was more concerned with its own defence than with the defence of the wider region. In addition, each county found itself more focused on sending money off to Lord Grey's brigade serving with the earl of Essex than on supplying Master Cromwell's troopers. As the latter's sense of military achievement grew, so did his self-confidence. His pleading turned to peremptory command. And the staccato notes began to have an effect.

The most striking aspect of Cromwell's letters from the summer of 1643 was his insistence that no religious test be applied to those volunteering for service. He needed more men, and the more committed to the cause the better. He later recalled advising John Hampden that a reliance of 'old decaying serving men and tapsters' would not secure victory; rather he called on him to 'get men of a spirit … that is like to go as far as a gentleman will go, or else I am sure you will be beaten still' (*Speeches*, 134, 13 April 1657). His most famous statement in this respect is that 'I had rather have a plain russet-coated captain that knows what he fights for, and loves what he knows, than that which you call a gentleman and is nothing else. I honour a gentleman that is so indeed' (*Letters and Speeches*, 1904, letter 16, 11 Sept 1643). Better a godly commoner than an inactive gentleman, for sure; but better a committed commoner than a committed gentleman? That is not so clear. If, as seems possible, in the lost original Cromwell wrote 'I honour a gentleman who is so in deed' rather than 'indeed', the social animus is stronger—he will honour only a gentleman who is fully active in the cause. And then there are the implications of his statement that 'if you choose honest men to be captains of horse, honest men will follow them, and they will be careful to mount such' (ibid.). If gentlemen are followed by their retainers, then honest men are followed by honest men. But the 'honest man' he had in mind was Ralph Margery, a farmer from Walsham-le-Willows, Suffolk. Margery and his wife had been outspoken and principled puritan nonconformists in the 1630s, and Margery was an unreconciled excommunicate from 1638 onwards. He was quick to volunteer once the war started and had gained notoriety for exceeding orders in the arbitrary seizure of horses from suspected royalists. Both his religious enthusiasm and this freedom in implementing orders against delinquents made the county committee distrust him. Twice Cromwell commanded the Suffolk committee to confirm his appointment and look for more like him. As Newcastle's army came ever closer, Cromwell's insistence became ever more shrill.

Having thus created a strong defensive line across the southern fenland, radiating out from Ely, Cromwell offered his services to the beleaguered forces to the north, and he made a number of sallies from his redoubt to help to push back royalist probes. Twice he joined up with an improvised body of troops from other counties—once at Sleaford, Lincolnshire, early in May 1643, and once at Nottingham early in June, with a view to a concerted advance into royalist areas, but each time the mission was aborted. A sweep through Lincolnshire in July did culminate in a stiff skirmish at Gainsborough on the 27th, Cromwell's first real experience of what it was to lead a cavalry charge and maintain discipline through and after the charge. The ability to regroup victorious cavalry and to redirect them against other opponents, so crucial to his part in the victories of Marston Moor and Naseby, was learned at Gainsborough. Much of the summer was spent either at regional headquarters in Cambridgeshire or in strengthening Lincolnshire against the royalists, culminating in another important (though rash) cavalry charge at Winceby as, in conjunction with Yorkshire forces under Sir Thomas Fairfax, he routed a significant royalist force sent out from Newark. After this battle Cromwell came to be known in the royalist press as 'the Lord of the Fens' (*Mercurius Aulicus*, 4–11 Nov 1643).

Grey's secondment to Essex's army, the lack of co-ordination within the six East Anglian counties, and the threat posed by Newcastle's advances caused parliament to rethink its policies for the region. Early in August Edward Montagu, second earl of Manchester, was given military command over the eastern association, a much stronger and more centralized committee system was established, and conscription was introduced (this is a context for some of Cromwell's tough letters about the need for more russet-coated captains and honest men). Cromwell was initially just one of the many colonels appointed by Manchester as he struggled to raise an army of 14,000 men, but from the beginning he was in *de facto* command of the cavalry, and this was formalized in February 1644 when he was appointed lieutenant-general of Manchester's army. Throughout the winter of 1643–4 he was busy in and around Cambridge and in the counties to the west (as far as Northampton), although this involved little military action. The entry of the Scots into the war caused the marquess of Newcastle to look north and this relieved pressure on Lincolnshire and therefore on the association. Cromwell—working closely with Manchester—was released to assist the parliamentarian war effort first in Yorkshire and then in the midlands. Cromwell thus felt able to return briefly to parliament (mid-January to mid-February 1644), long enough to bring a series of charges against Lord Willoughby of Parham for the inefficiency and mismanagement of the defence of Lincolnshire, resulting in Willoughby's resignation and the extension of Manchester's commission to cover that county. Cromwell then, belatedly, took the solemn league and covenant and was immediately appointed a member of the committee of both kingdoms which had been charged with managing the whole strategy of war and peace. He was clearly recognized as a rising man.

Cromwell continued to seek out those most committed to the cause, and that certainly did include dedicated presbyterians as well as sectaries. In January 1644 he supported the energetic presbyterian Edward King for promotion in Lincolnshire, and twice he dissuaded Lieutenant-Colonel William Dodson from resigning in protest at having to serve with sectaries. But this goodwill was not reciprocated. In March 1644 Lawrence Crawford, the Scottish major-general responsible for the foot in Manchester's army, sought for good reason to dismiss William Packer, a Baptist junior officer, and engaged in heated exchanges with Cromwell over it. Initially Manchester stood aloof from these disputes, being a man temperamentally both drawn to a reformed Erastian episcopal settlement and willing to commission and support William Dowsing as his agent for systematic orderly iconoclasm across Suffolk and Cambridgeshire. But eventually he came to side with Crawford.

Late in February 1644 Cromwell returned to his command and set out to expand the frontiers of the parliamentarian eastern redoubt: he took Hillesdon House (Buckinghamshire) on 9 March, and was involved both in the storm of Lincoln (6 May) and in the repulse of George Goring's attempt to relieve the town. Manchester and Cromwell then joined up with the northern army under the Fairfaxes and the Scots to take York. In response the king's principal marching army marched north to combine with the marquess of Newcastle to relieve the town.

That in due course led to the greatest of all civil-war battles, at Marston Moor on 2 July 1644. Cromwell's role in that battle remains contentious. He commanded the left wing of the allied army, consisting of his own eastern cavalry and three regiments of Scots cavalry. Cromwell himself received a nasty flesh wound in the neck early on and needed treatment, but he returned in time to take responsibility for the final, decisive charge. The official English reports gave all the praise to Cromwell and none to the Scots—Cromwell himself, in a private letter, spoke only of 'a few Scots in the rear' (*Letters and Speeches*, 1904, letter 21, 5 July 1644)—and David Leslie, who commanded the wing in his absence and whose regiments were crucial to disrupting the royalist centre, and his fellow Scots took great umbrage. That the London press should henceforth call Cromwell 'Ironside' and in due course his troops the Ironsides, in recognition of his victory, rubbed salt into the wound. Cromwell himself neither claimed nor disclaimed responsibility for the victory; he ascribed it entirely to God. In a moving letter to his brother-in-law Valentine *Walton, breaking to him the news of the agonizing death from a shattered and amputated leg of Valentine's oldest son, Cromwell spoke of it as 'an absolute victory obtained by the Lord's blessing upon the godly party principally … Give glory, all the glory, to God'. And, in one of his most memorable metaphors, he wrote that 'God made them as stubble to our swords' (ibid., letter 21, 5 July 1644). The process by which he came to see himself and his cause as peculiarly blessed by God was well in train. Cromwell had no doubt that he was no longer serving God by his suffering but by his doing, and he was most glad.

Those who served over and alongside Cromwell failed to exploit the victory. For two months Manchester dallied over the siege of Doncaster, and he then unhurriedly moved back into the eastern association. By now the tensions and resentments both over the composition of the army and the need to help out wherever the cause was under pressure had become seriously debilitating, and Crawford and Cromwell went up to London and presented their alternative accounts of their relationship one with another. Each sought the dismissal of the other, and each had too much political support to be sacked. The Commons established a committee to 'consider the means of uniting presbyterians and Independents', which was a startling admission of the scale of the problem. But their stated willingness to 'endeavour of finding out some way how far tender consciences … may be borne with' was a considerable concession to Cromwell's position (*JHC*, 3, 1642–4, 626). Manchester broke the deadlock by calling on both parties to unite in common service but they returned to their military duties deeply antagonized.

In the spirit of the uneasy concord Manchester and Cromwell began the process of squeezing the royalist headquarters at Oxford by taking out its satellite garrisons in Oxfordshire, Berkshire, and Northamptonshire. Then, as the king returned from his triumph over the earl of

Essex in Cornwall, Manchester joined Sir William Waller's army of the southern association to block his passage at Newbury. The result was an unsatisfactorily drawn battle in which Cromwell unaccountably delayed engaging his cavalry until it was too late to make an overall victory possible. He then sulked for two days and failed to carry out a direct order from Manchester to prevent the king from relieving and securing Donnington Castle. He also took part in a council of war in which he was scathing about Manchester's failings. Relations between the two men were beyond repair and, within a month, on and after 23 November both were back at Westminster hellbent on destroying each other.

The creation of the New Model Army   The feud between Manchester and Cromwell was symptomatic of parliamentarianism in almost every region—and if not every major-general had recalcitrant subordinates, most of them were unwilling to take orders from or show respect to the captain-general himself. Essex, stranded and cut off in Cornwall, was forced into an abject surrender at Lostwithiel that brought disgrace upon his head. It was therefore in the interests of his friends to spread the responsibility for the failures of the cause since Marston Moor as widely as possible. His friends laid the blame for the failure of the Newbury campaign on those who put godly enthusiasm ahead of 'wisdom and valour'. Godliness versus aristocratic prudence was now the crunch issue. Stung by public and private criticism which seemed more directed at them than at Manchester, Waller and Cromwell decided to take the initiative. On 25 November they reported to the Commons that all the failings of the past three months resulted from Manchester's inability or unwillingness to take decisive action at the right time. Perhaps Cromwell expected Manchester to roll over as Willoughby had done in January. But there was nothing indecisive or lacklustre in Manchester's response. On 28 November he rebutted the charges of incompetence, implicating Waller and Cromwell in all the mistaken decisions, and accusing them of failing to carry out direct orders to the detriment of the cause. He then accused Cromwell in particular of vilifying the Westminster assembly, displaying a violent animosity towards the Scots, and being opposed in principle to the hereditary peerage. Each house now set up a committee to investigate the claims of its own member. Meanwhile Essex convened a meeting of his own friends, of Manchester's allies, and of the Scots, to see if under the terms of the solemn league and covenant the Scots could impeach Cromwell as an incendiary.

As the temperature rose and mutual recrimination mounted, some men remembered there was a common enemy who hoped to see their heads on poles or their bodies dangling from ropes. God would not bless a cause so divided, nor give victory to men who had failed to honour him consistently. 'The chief causes of division are pride and covetousness', the presbyterian Zouch Tate told the house (*Writings and Speeches*, 1.314). Let all those who had held commissions surrender them; let all MPs return to Westminster and let there be a fresh start. Cromwell was quick to accept the proposition. Over the next four months the principles of self-denial and of the rationalization of the armies operating in the areas firmly under parliamentarian control (viz., the armies of Essex, Manchester, and Waller) were rarely questioned. Who was to decide on a new command structure, and whether, and if so in whose favour, exceptions to the principle of self-denial were to be made, became and remained bitterly divisive questions. It is possible that Cromwell was privy to, and ready to promote, the self-denying ordinance; it is unlikely (but not impossible) that he hoped and planned to be excepted from its operation. When he said that he hoped 'no Members of either House will scruple to deny themselves, and their own private interests, for the public good' (ibid., 1.314–15) he was probably speaking from the heart. There can be no doubt that he was one of those who prevented Essex from being excepted, and one of those who strenuously supported Sir Thomas Fairfax's elevation to command the New Model Army; but his own exemption was never fully approved by both houses, and seemed against the odds until after Prince Rupert's sack of Leicester on 30 May 1645 threatened a major escalation of the war. When the struggle over the list of officers was being fought out within and between the houses Cromwell was away, serving under Waller. Waller later recalled that Cromwell was blunt in his manner, but that he did not bear himself with any pride or disdain, and that he had never disputed Waller's orders. In the event the failure of the two houses to agree on a lieutenant-general led on 3 April and 12 May to Cromwell's being granted two forty-day appointments. As the second came to an end Fairfax moved, at a council of war on 13 June 1645, that Cromwell be appointed for the duration of the war. The Lords would not agree to it and in the event his commission was renewed for periods of three, four, and finally six months, so that he remained in the army until mid-July 1646. No other MP was exempted from the self-denying ordinance to serve in the New Model Army, although two provincial commanders were given similar temporary extensions. By early 1646 many New Model officers were securing positions in the Commons as a result of the 'recruiter elections' by which the places of secluded royalists were filled via by-elections. Cromwell was not the sole MP in the army for long.

Soldier, 1645–1646 Cromwell's part in the victories of the New Model Army in the last eighteen months of the war was striking. His role at the battle of Naseby (14 June 1645) in driving half the royalist cavalry from the field and regrouping to break the discipline and will of the royalist infantry was pivotal. His role at Langport (10 July), where his own troopers stormed a narrow ford in the face of concentrated enemy fire with complete self-belief and passion, demonstrates that their faith in Cromwell was as great as his faith in God. He then took part in the sieges of Bridgwater, Sherborne, Bristol, Devizes, and Winchester; and, with Fairfax, he succeeded in brushing aside 20,000 Clubmen on the Dorset/Wiltshire border. This relentless phase culminated in the brutal assault, destruction, and pillaging of the Catholic marquess of Winchester's

380-room castle and mansion at Basing on 14 October. Cromwell entered Devon on 24 October 1645 and remained there and in Cornwall until 12 April 1646. He met serious resistance only at Bovey Tracey (9 January), where he dispersed Thomas, Lord Wentworth's horse troop; Dartmouth (18 January), where he joined Fairfax in a carefully planned amphibious assault; and Torrington (16 February), where Ralph, Lord Hopton's force of 5000 men was dispersed. Otherwise it was an inexorable progress, occupying towns (the most important of which was Exeter) and castles from which the defenders had fled or were winkled out by delicate negotiation. After reporting briefly to parliament he returned to his command for the final seven-week siege of Oxford. Both Exeter and Oxford surrendered on extremely generous terms, with the royalists made liable only to minimal fines, lower than those set by parliamentary ordinance. It is worth noting Cromwell's strong support for these generous terms. He wanted to win the war as quickly as possible, not humiliate the losers.

As this campaign progressed Cromwell's conviction that he was fighting God's cause became ever clearer to him. After the taking of Bletchingdon House in Oxfordshire in April 1645 he told his colleagues on the committee of both kingdoms that 'this was the mercy of God … God brought them to our hands when we looked not for them' (*Letters and Speeches*, 1904, letter 25, 9 April 1645). After Langport he was even more emphatic: 'thus you can see what the Lord hath wrought for us. Can any creature ascribe anything to itself? Now can we give all the glory to God!' But he added that when the 'mercy' of Langport be added to the 'mercy' of Naseby, then, 'is it not to see the face of God?' (ibid., 3.246–7, July 1645). It was in this 'chain of providences' that Cromwell saw himself as the instrument of God's deeper purpose in bringing England through civil war: and Cromwell linked God's providential guidance more and more to the cause of religious liberty. Thus after Naseby Cromwell wrote to the speaker and after a staccato account of the battle pleaded for religious liberty for all who served in a cause so obviously upheld by God: 'he that ventures his life for the liberty of his country, I wish he trust God for the liberty of his conscience, and you for the liberty he fights for' (ibid., letter 29, 14 June 1645). After the taking of Bristol in September he was plainer still: 'Presbyterians, Independents, all had the same spirit of faith and prayer … they agree here, know no names of difference: pity it should be otherwise anywhere. All that believe have the same unity' (ibid., letter 31, 14 Sept 1645). The response of the Commons to these heartfelt pleas (as it was to be after the most passionate plea of all from the battlefield of Preston in 1648) was to censor the letters and to publish them with their pleas for liberty omitted, though in each case Lord Saye and other friends in the Lords procured the unlicensed printing of the whole letter some time later.

Cromwell returned to Westminster in July 1646 to face new challenges. As a soldier—and as an MP—he had spent four years committed to one overwhelming objective: to win the war. He had seen in councils of war and in parliamentary committees all too many of his colleagues reluctant to make the sacrifices necessary to secure victory. They were reluctant to tolerate the necessary requisitioning of supplies or the rough justice of war, reluctant to continue the fighting if there was a glimpse of a settlement by negotiation, reluctant to make use of men from less reputable social backgrounds or with fierce religious commitment. The rigidities of formal religion, the proscription on lay preaching, the inflexible Scottish demand for a strict, bureaucratic, and mandatory uniformity of belief and practice across the three kingdoms—all these things appalled him. While (as the artillery pounded out the prelude to a push of pike and a charge of horse) he meditated on how free prayer, free testimony, and the improvisation of worship had made God's immanence so clear, he must have been struck by the irrelevance and impropriety of the commitment to replacing one confessional state by another. But nothing in the molten politics of war prepared him for the low-temperature physics that were to constitute 'the politics of peace and the limits of the possible' (Davis, 141).

Shuttle diplomacy, 1646–1647 The twenty-two months between Cromwell's return to Westminster in July 1646 and the renewal of war in May 1648 saw him constantly on the move between London and wherever army headquarters were to be found. His commission as lieutenant-general formally lapsed in July 1646, but Fairfax paid no heed. He spasmodically signed pay warrants for Cromwell in the months that followed, and in May 1647 Cromwell submitted a statement of all his arrears to that point which was counter-signed and honoured. He attended some sessions of the army council as a parliamentary commissioner, but others (including Putney in October–November 1647) as 'lieutenant-general'. He was rewarded by parliament with estates in England and Ireland worth £2000 a year, and there were persistent rumours that as part of any settlement with the king made by the alliance of 'Independents' in parliament and their allies in the army, he would be created earl of Essex (the title held both by his own ancestor Thomas Cromwell and by the Bourchiers, and therefore assumed (erroneously) by many at the time to have been held by Elizabeth's ancestors). In the summer of 1646 his immediate family moved up from Ely to London to a town house in Drury Lane, where they remained until he was allocated rooms in the Cockpit, adjacent to the palace of Whitehall, after his return to London from the battle of Worcester in September 1651.

In the second half of 1646 Cromwell was one of the most active and dynamic members of parliament, serving on many central executive committees and acting as one of the most active tellers in the increasingly frequent divisions. But little is recoverable of his contribution to debates, although he can be seen to have remained close to those who had constituted the war party throughout the civil wars: Henry Vane, Oliver St John, Nathaniel Fiennes in the Commons, William Fiennes, Viscount Saye and Sele, and Philip, Lord Wharton, in the Lords. He seems to have been constantly in the Palace of Westminster until

overwhelmed with a life-threatening (but unidentified) illness that kept him housebound throughout February 1647 and on half-throttle for some weeks thereafter. Few of his letters from the second half of 1646 and the first half of 1647 have survived, though those that have reveal continued support for godly, honest folk persecuted because they would not attend their parish churches.

By the time Cromwell was back in the political saddle in March 1647 a crisis had erupted in the relations between parliament and the army. A majority in both houses was determined to bring about a settlement of the three kingdoms. The Scots would be paid off and sent home; most of the New Model would be disbanded and the rest restructured and dispatched to put an end to the Irish rebellion; and intense negotiations with the king would settle the remaining issues. Those negotiations would seek to honour the solemn commitment to replace the Elizabethan church settlement with a presbyterian settlement enshrined in the proposals that had been hammered out in the Anglo-Scottish Westminster assembly. The king would lose the freedom to choose his own ministers and the right to control the armed forces; and the proponents of this settlement would promote themselves to high political and court offices. There was much here for Cromwell and his parliamentary allies, and even more for the army, to resent. But when the army petitioned against the proposals, the Commons declared their very act of petitioning unlawful. This inaugurated a six-month-long crisis, during which Cromwell's role was consistent: to prevent a formal rupture; to persuade the houses that the anger in the army was considerable and reasonable; and to persuade the army that men like himself could bring parliament to listen to their grievances. The rumours picked up and reported by the French ambassador that Cromwell was considering abandoning England in the spring for a senior command under the elector palatine amid the dying embers of the Thirty Years' War were almost certainly false. Cromwell was working to prevent the parliamentarian movement from disintegrating.

Thus from 2 to 20 May 1647 Cromwell was one of the four officers/MPs sent down from parliament to army headquarters in Saffron Walden to discuss how the army's grievances about arrears, indemnity, and war pensions could be addressed. On 21 May he and Charles Fleetwood reported back to the Commons on the state of the army. The document he carried bore the legend 'the heads of a report … in the name of themselves and the rest of the officers in the army and the members of that House lately sent down' (*Works*, 1.94–9). Like a classic negotiator he understated to each party the disaffection of the other towards it. And the result, late in May, was disaster. Having assured the houses that the army would disband quietly if its legitimate concerns about arrears and indemnity were addressed, Cromwell watched in horror as the Commons voted the immediate disbandment of most of the army on the basis of meagre concessions. Perhaps the Commons thought that since the Scots had sulkily returned home and disbanded on the basis of a small down-payment and vague promises for the future, so would the New Model. It was not to be.

From the time he returned to London, Cromwell's house in Drury Lane was constantly visited by a stream of sectaries and officers. There they were 'frugally entertained by Mrs Cromwell with small beer, bread and butter [as] they laid bare to the lieutenant general their fear of the presbyterians and their ideas for the army's salvation' (Gentles, 169). There was nothing unique, therefore, in a visit by a cornet in Fairfax's regiment of horse, George Joyce, on 31 May. What he and Cromwell discussed is not known for sure. Most likely it was a request that the 'presbyterian' officers guarding the king at Holdenby House in Northampton be replaced by more reliable officers, who were less likely to be at the beck and call of the 'presbyterian' politicians at Westminster. It is likely that Joyce informed Cromwell that he had gathered 1000 horse (almost two full regiments) and that he sought Cromwell's informal authorization for him to surprise Colonel Graves and his 100 men at Holdenby and remove the distrusted officers. But to commission—however informally—a cornet to humiliate a colonel seems incredible. Perhaps Cromwell was not told the whole story; or perhaps he was asked to put himself or someone of appropriate rank in charge of the expedition and declined to do so, only for Joyce to undertake it anyway. What is almost certain is that Joyce originally intended to keep the king at Holdenby under his own authority, but that after the escape of Graves he panicked and started moving Charles across the country to army headquarters at Newmarket. As the news broke, Fairfax sent Colonel Edward Whalley to intercept Joyce and the king and to return the latter to Holdenby. But Whalley acceded to the king's stated preference to be taken to Newmarket. Cromwell and the other generals both at the time and later solemnly protested to both king and parliament that Joyce had acted 'without their privity, knowledge or consent' (Warwick, 229). Joyce later maintained otherwise and there were plenty at the time and later who were unconvinced by Cromwell's denials. It was the first of a whole series of occasions (the king's escape from Hampton Court to the Isle of Wight, Pride's Purge, the dissolution of the Rump, the self-immolation of the nominated assembly, the offer of the crown in February 1657) when Cromwell solemnly denied something which other principals and other contemporary witnesses asserted—that he was guilty of underhand dealing to secure his goals. And as with all the others, conclusive proof either way is lacking.

The seizure of the king escalated the crisis at Westminster. Cromwell now stayed with the army and took a leading part in the debates among the general officers and in the general council of the army: generals, regimental commanders, and representatives (or adjutators) of the junior officers and of the rank and file who met at least fortnightly over the following months. With ever greater determination the general council clarified the terms of the future settlement of the kingdom and their right to articulate those terms. On 7 June 1647, at Childerley House near Cambridge, Cromwell had his first interview with King Charles. He was to have several more during August and September. From mid-July, with the explicit consent of the general council, Commissary-General Henry *Ireton (Oliver's close colleague in the defence of the Isle of Ely, and since 15 June 1646 his son-in-law), together with Cromwell and other senior commanders, and in close liaison with their friends in the two houses, drafted *The Heads of Proposals*. These were to be simultaneously proffered to the king and converted into a series of parliamentary bills to be passed by the houses and then formally assented to and made binding by the royal assent.

This orderly stratagem was shaken by the violent mass demonstrations in favour of peace and disbandment in London on 26 July 1647 that caused sixty-five MPs to withdraw from London to the protection of the army. This led to the army's occupation of London, its reinstatement of the sixty-five, and its removal of the eleven leading presbyterians whom the army called 'incendiaries'. Cromwell probably resumed his seat in the wake of this *putsch* but he spent more time at army headquarters at Putney than in the house until late September. Thus in August he was central to the failed head-to-head negotiations with a king who would never say yes and never say no. In September and October a different tack was tried. The houses—the presbyterians now cowed and in a minority—worked steadily on the bills that would enact the proposals. Cromwell was then pivotal to pushing several of those bills, especially a toleration bill, which repealed the Elizabethan statutes requiring church attendance and permitted anyone who wished 'to hear the word of God preached elsewhere'. He still expected to be able to bounce both king and parliament into a settlement.

The Heads of Proposals would have exempted very few 'malignant' royalists from pardon, they would have placed time-limited restrictions on Charles's freedom to choose his own ministers or control the armed forces, and they would have restored the episcopalian church as the Church of England but without the right to require either attendance or obedience to its forms or beliefs. Under these proposals parliaments would have been elected regularly on a rationalized franchise but would not have been omnicompetent or omnipresent. They would have met for a limited period every two years. Much of *The Heads of Proposals* foreshadowed the 'Instrument of government' under which Cromwell became lord protector in December 1653. Until mid-October, Cromwell and his allies seemed to be holding the ring. But then, in quick succession, he was to find himself defied by parliament, by large sections of the army, and by the king.

The Putney debates The post-war settlement to which Cromwell was now firmly committed assumed a divided sovereignty between king and parliament. There were many who felt that this was no longer sufficient. Foremost among these were the London pamphleteers shortly to become known as the Levellers. These men argued with ever greater force for a literal 'agreement of the people', whereby all householders would sign up to put themselves under a new form of government in which all those who exercised authority—above all the chief and lesser magistrates, and members of parliament—were accountable to those who elected them. The king would not be party to the making of the agreement but would be offered a limited role within it on a take-it-or-leave-it basis. Most of the adjutators had worked closely with the generals and had consented to their face-to-face negotiations with the king. But some of them now began to doubt the probity of Cromwell and Ireton—perhaps influenced by the growing disaffection towards the 'grandees' in the army and the parliament expressed in the writings of the Leveller leader John Lilburne, beginning with the characterization of Cromwell and Vane as 'the sons of Machiavel' (J. Lilburne, *Jonah's Cry out of the Whale's Belly*, July 1647, 3). From about 29 September some regiments began to choose additional 'agents' who would make that case more forcefully. The result was a tense series of debates in and around Putney church from 28 October to 11 November 1647. The debates were covered by a news blackout so complete that there is no contemporary discussion of them. The secretary to the council of the army, William Clarke, used a team of stenographers to cover the opening days of the debate, but from 2 November tensions rose so high that even this recording was discontinued. His minutes were never published and were unknown until rediscovered in 1890 by Sir Charles Firth.

Cromwell's role at Putney was first and foremost to be chairman and ringmaster. His mission statement for all four recorded days was 'let us be doing, but let us be united in our doing' (*Works*, 1.259). He extracted a retraction of the charge that he and his son-in-law had negotiated in bad faith. The *Agreement of the People*, tabled on 28 October, proposed that the discredited king and the discredited parliament be ignored and a new constitution introduced in a new social compact signed by all those who wished to enjoy rights of citizenship. Cromwell subsequently persuaded a committee of eighteen, made up of grandees, officer adjutators, and soldier adjutators to whom the most contentious issues were referred, unanimously to reject that proposition in favour of a proposal that the army lobby the Long Parliament to dissolve itself after making provision for a redistribution of seats 'according to some rule of equality of proportion' (ibid., 1.365), and for biennial elections on a franchise consisting of all those previously qualified plus all those who had secured a stake by offering their lives in the parliamentarian armies up to and including the date of the battle of Naseby. This compromise, acceptable to all sections of the army, was made possible by Cromwell's careful diplomacy.

Up to the evening of 31 October tempers were frayed but things were going reasonably well. Unity had been maintained. But Cromwell had more difficulty in controlling things on and after 1 November. Now the subject turned to the right of the king and the Lords to veto legislation approved by the Commons. This drifted into the wider and even more contentious issue of whether the king should be a party to the settlement and even whether Charles should be deposed (by implication even executed). Adjutator Edward Sexby proclaimed that 'we have gone about to heal Babylon when she would not' (*Works*,

1.377); Cromwell responded by saying that there were many problems with Charles—'we all apprehend danger from the person of the king'—and that there could be no safety in such a person 'having the least interest in the public affairs of the kingdom', but they should not jump to the conclusion that 'God will destroy these persons' (kings in general) or 'that power' (monarchy) (ibid., 1.378–82). He did not rule out deposition, but he did not see any immediate divine encouragement to proceed with it.

Clearly by November 1647 Cromwell's patience with Charles was running out. But he also argued that the army should not be 'wedded and glued to forms of government' and that 'forms of government are (as St Paul says) dross and dung in comparison of Christ' (*Works*, 1.277, 370). Using the Old Testament as his sole source he argued that the Jewish people had done well and badly under all forms of government. A bad king did not discredit monarchy itself. Cromwell's speeches on 1 November 1647 testify to the development of an unsophisticated political thought which owed nothing to Aristotle or Edward Coke and everything to the Old Testament. They are also testimony to his growing impatience with Charles and his willingness to wait upon God's pronouncement of a judgment against the king. The debates on 1 November spiralled out of control and somebody told William Clarke to stop recording them. Debate continued for another ten days, during which Ireton stormed out but Cromwell stayed. The debates seem to have centred on the role of the king in the making of the settlement and increasingly on whether he should be deposed. In a fascinating fragment left in his papers for 11 November, Clarke records that Colonel Harrison called Charles 'a man of blood', and that 'they were to prosecute him'. Cromwell replied by 'putting several cases in which murder was not to be punished', citing the case of King David's refusal to put his nephew Joab on trial for killing Abner, because his other nephews, as military governors with more force at their disposal than David himself had, would rise up to prevent or to avenge Joab's death: 'the sons of Zeruiah were too hard for him' (ibid., 1.417). Charles I, Cromwell implies, no longer deserved to reign; but it was not feasible or prudent at present to get rid of him.

The Putney debates broke up acrimoniously. But in the ensuing recriminations the fault-line lay not between those who wanted a cautious extension of the franchise and a radical one but—a very different alignment—between those who wanted to break off all personal negotiations with the king and those who did not. Fairfax and Cromwell struggled to maintain army unity, and they strove to do so by holding a series of separate army rendezvous. They succeeded, but only at the expense of a tense confrontation with mutineers who appeared against orders at the first rendezvous at Ware. Cromwell, riding among sullen ranks of troopers, pulled copies of the *Agreement of the People* from their hatbands and ordered them back to their quarters. The mutiny did not spread from the initial two (of twenty-four) regiments. By 18 November order was restored.

Putney seems to have been a turning point for Cromwell. He came to realize that his brokering a settlement with Charles was not acceptable to large sections of the army, and he may well have recognized that the king had not been negotiating in good faith. On 12 November his growing distrust was massively reinforced. Charles, breaking his word, escaped from Hampton Court and fled to the Isle of Wight. There was plenty of contemporary speculation that Cromwell encouraged him in this escapade, but there are compelling reasons for doubting it. When a few days later Sir John Berkeley, a royalist intermediary who had formed good relations with Cromwell and Ireton over recent months, arrived with a letter from Charles, he found an army council meeting in progress. He later recalled that 'I look'd upon Cromwell and Ireton and the rest of my acquaintance, who saluted me very coldly, and had their countenance quite changed towards me'. Berkeley was then told by an unnamed officer that at the afternoon meeting of the council Ireton and Cromwell had called for the king to be transferred as a close prisoner to London where the army would then 'bring him to a tryal'; and that 'none be allowed to speak to' (negotiate with) the king, 'upon pain of death' (The Memoirs of Sir John Berkeley, 1699, 70, 72).

The second civil war Between 11 November 1647 and 3 May 1648 Cromwell can be glimpsed sometimes in London, sometimes at army headquarters. There are extant only fragmentary parliamentary diaries from this time, but one of them offers a single glimpse of Cromwell's unfolding views. Speaking in the Commons on 3 January 1648 (according to a much-repeated royalist canard rattling his sword in its scabbard as he spoke) he passionately demanded a suspension of all 'addresses' to the king for the foreseeable future. He asserted that they 'shalt not suffer a hypocrite to reign' and that they 'should not any longer expect safety and government from an obstinate man whose heart God had hardened'. Even more dramatically, he said that 'we declared our intentions for monarchy … unless necessity enforce an alteration' (D. Underdown, 'Parliamentary diary of John Boys, 1647–8', BIHR, 39, 1966, 156). (Necessity for Cromwell meant seeking out and obeying God's will in his providences: the authority to settle the kingdom, he told his nominated assembly in 1653, came to them 'by way of Necessity, by the way of the wise Providence of God' (Speeches, 20, 4 July 1653).) Later the same day Cromwell wrote to his cousin by marriage Colonel Robert Hammond, custodian of Charles in Carisbrooke Castle, that the king's flight and subsequent developments represented 'a mighty providence to this poor kingdom and to us all'. This gives a rather chilling menace to his concluding words: 'we shall (I hope) instantly go upon the business in relation to [the king], tending to prevent danger' and his request that Hammond 'search out' any 'juggling' by the king (Letters and Speeches, 1904, letter 52, 3 Jan 1648).

Cromwell's realization at Putney that the king did not deserve restoration but that the army must await a sign from God about when and how to proceed against him was powerfully reinforced by the king's escape. During 1648 there are indications that Cromwell was considering how the king might be induced to abdicate in favour of one of his sons. The generally well-informed Roman agent in London, writing on 17 January, names Cromwell and Oliver St John as favouring direct negotiation with the prince of Wales which could have led to Charles's abdication or deposition. The French ambassador and material in the papers of the duke of Hamilton support the suggestion that there was such a plan, although they do not name the men behind it. Later in the year ambassadorial sources indicate that Cromwell was looking to replace Charles by the king's youngest son, Henry, duke of Gloucester.

For much of the spring, as a series of regional revolts rocked the parliamentarian regime, and as the Scots prepared for an invasion to restore the king on the rather vague terms he had agreed in a secret treaty signed on 26 December 1647, Cromwell's whereabouts are not generally known. He was, however, present for some but not all of the three-day prayer meeting at Windsor held from 29 April to 1 May 1648. It ended with the council of officers binding themselves to call 'Charles Stuart, that man of bloud, to an account, for that bloud he had shed, and mischief he had done, to his utmost, against the Lords cause and people in these poor Nations' (W. Allen, A Faithful Memorial, 1659, 5).

On 3 May Fairfax divided the New Model Army, keeping the larger part in the south-east to deal with the bush fires of rebellion in Kent and East Anglia and sending Cromwell with five regiments to deal with revolts in south Wales. Cromwell quickly took Chepstow and Tenby, but without heavy artillery he found no way to storm the great castle of Pembroke. It took him six weeks to starve it into surrender. By then the Scots were marching on England and he had hastily to march north. He joined up with northern regiments under the command of John Lambert at Knaresborough, and together they crossed the Pennines and fell upon the Scots as they marched down through Lancashire. Preston was his first battle in full command. It was a messy three-day affair (17–19 August 1648) in which he secured a complete victory, aided by very poor communication among the Scottish commanders and by torrential rain that soaked the powder of the Scottish infantry and rendered it useless. But the outcome owed most of all to Cromwell's decisive and bold leadership. By the end of 19 August the army of the Scottish engagers had been annihilated: Cromwell reckoned 2000 killed and 9000 taken prisoner. He promptly set off and made straight for Edinburgh. There he found that the marquess of Argyll—who had always opposed the English adventure—had seized power. Leaving Lambert and three regiments (at Argyll's request) to shore up this regime, Cromwell moved south and quickly reduced Carlisle and Berwick, but became bogged down in stamping out the embers of revolt in Yorkshire.

Cromwell and the Bible As Cromwell campaigned in 1648 there was a dramatic development in his religious thinking. His letter to his cousin Elizabeth St John in 1638 describing his religious conversion had been saturated in biblical images, but his letters throughout the 1640s used the Bible only as glancing asides. Suddenly in 1648 his letters become meditations on how particular scriptures were helping him to find his way through the constitutional mire. Private letters to Fairfax, to Philip Wharton, Lord Wharton, to Robert Hammond, and to Oliver St John were epistolary sermons exploring the will of God. After parliament had voted to reopen negotiations with the king Cromwell, from the siege of Pembroke, wrote to Fairfax and told him that 'surely it is not [the mind of God] that the poor people of this kingdom should still be made the object of wrath and anger, nor that our God would have our necks under a yoke of bondage'. And he continued:

> for these things that have lately come to pass have been the wonderful works of God, breaking the rod of the oppressor as in the day of Midian, not with garments much rolled in blood but by the terror of the Lord; who will yet save His people and confound His enemies as in that day. (*Letters and Speeches*, 1904, letter 61, 28 June 1648)

This is a paraphrase of Isaiah chapter 9 and contains a cross-reference to the victory of Gideon and the Midianites described in the book of Judges. Gideon was the farmer called from the plough to winnow and lead the armies of Israel. He defeated the Midianites, executed their kings, and then returned to his farm. It is one of several references to the Gideon story in Cromwell's letters in 1648—suggesting that he saw himself as the new Gideon. After the battle of Preston meditations on Psalms 17 and 105 led him to tell parliament that 'they that are implacable and will not leave troubling the land may be speedily destroyed out of the land' (ibid., letter 64, 20 Aug 1648). Who else could he mean but the king? Once again the Commons published his letter with the lecture at the end omitted. In a private letter a week later to Wharton he called down God's mercy on 'the whole society of saints, despised, jeered saints' (ibid., letter 68, 2 Sept 1648) and on the same day told Oliver St John that 'this scripture hath been great stay with me: read it; Isaiah eighth [chapter], [verses] 10, 11, 14, read all the chapter' (ibid., letter 67, 2 Sept 1648). Isaiah predicted Ahaz's turning from God would condemn his kingdom to inevitable collapse, but that a godly remnant would survive the holocaust. Cromwell was using the scriptures to discern God's will, and he was ever more convinced that one way or another Charles I had to be removed from the land.

Regicide As he mopped up royalist resistance in the north Cromwell was at least spasmodically aware of the fast-moving events in the south, above all of the content of the *Remonstrance* of the army (20 November 1648). This was both an unwavering repudiation of the parliament's decision to reopen negotiations with a king who would dishonour any treaty he made, and a demand that 'the capital and grand author of our troubles, the person of the king … may be speedily brought to justice for the treason, blood and mischief he is guilty of' (pp. 62–5). It also demanded that the king's elder sons, the prince of Wales and the duke of York, surrender themselves for trial on pain of being declared incapable of governing and sentenced to die if found in England. The phrase 'person of the king' and the careful wording of the section on the princes Charles and James suggest that Ireton and his colleagues may have envisaged not the end of monarchy but the replacement of Charles by Prince Henry, duke of Gloucester, who was in their custody. Cromwell's letters showed that he supported the *Remonstrance*. Two letters written to Hammond in November pleaded with him to take his orders from his military and not his parliamentary masters and study the 'so constant, so clear and unclouded' providences of God. He called the Newport treaty on which the houses were embarked 'this ruining, hypocritical agreement' and begged Hammond to consider what good could come from a treaty with the king, 'this man against whom the Lord hath witnessed' (*Letters and Speeches*, 1904, letter 85, 25 Nov 1648; ibid., 3.389–92, 6 Nov 1648).

There is no further reliable evidence of Cromwell's intentions until after he had returned to Westminster, upon a peremptory order from Fairfax, late on 6 December, hours after Pride's Purge during which some MPs were arrested and many more turned away following the Commons' defiant vote to continue negotiating with the king. He took his seat in the Commons the next morning and immediately tried to calm things down and to prevent any hasty action. Foreign ambassadors clearly thought he hoped to induce the king to abdicate, and his role in sending the earl of Denbigh (who had been involved in earlier attempts to get Charles to abdicate in favour of the prince of Wales) to negotiate with the king on an unknown brief points that way. Bulstrode Whitelocke, whose evidence was committed to paper shortly afterwards, appears to confirm that the mission was intended to offer the king his life in return for an abdication. It was not that Cromwell had any constitutional scruple about a trial and deposition, even about execution; rather, he had the overwhelming sense that such action would be counterproductive, that there would be an internal and international reaction so violent as to sweep away those who had engineered it. The sons of Zeruiah would be too strong for them. Presbyterians thundered from their pulpits. The king of France, the Dutch estates (who had just made a naval treaty with the king's lord lieutenant in Ireland), and the Scottish estates all threatened and cajoled the army leaders and the Rumpers to spare the king. Cromwell sought desperately to broaden the support for the 6 December coup and to delay a trial. As the king refused to contemplate abdication, a trial became inevitable, a trial during which negotiation under duress could continue. For six weeks Cromwell worked for a settlement without a regicide, but once he concluded that Charles would not abdicate, not only the king's trial but his death became inevitable. To try to put someone else on the throne so long as the king lived was even worse than to attempt, in the face of the inevitable backlash across the British Isles and western Europe, to establish a kingless Commonwealth. And so, in the final ten days of January, he worked for the latter. He attended every day of the trial and was the third to append his name to the death warrant. Legends attached themselves to Cromwell's actions, but none are reliable. Algernon Sidney later claimed that Cromwell told him the army would cut off the king's head with the crown upon it. Colonel Isaac Ewer claimed that Cromwell and Henry Marten flicked ink at one another in a childish game after signing the warrant. Clarendon claimed that Cromwell and others compelled Richard Ingoldsby and others to sign, holding their hands to the parchment. The only credible story of this kind is the testimony of Philip Warwick that as Cromwell looked down on the dismembered royal corpse, he murmured: 'Cruel necessity'. God's providences were not always comfortable.

Cromwell in January 1649 Cromwell was now the single most powerful man in England. Fairfax was still the lord general and Cromwell his lieutenant-general. But the events of the previous three months had knocked the stuffing out of Fairfax. He had hoped against hope that the king would see sense but when the crunch came and he had to decide whether to assert his authority as head of the army to attempt to halt the trial, or more particularly the regicide, he had alternately wrung his hands and sat on them. Before him stretched a decade of irresolution. He did not resign his command for another sixteen months, but Cromwell was *de facto* general from the moment the king's head was cut off on 30 January 1649. In parliament, Cromwell was prominent but not dominant.

In the public eye this position was also consolidated. Cromwell's image was one of the best known by 1649, appearing in many pamphlets and broadsheets. For example, as early as 1644 he was pictured among the successful generals in *The Parliament's Kalendar of Black Saints*, and he makes a prominent appearance in John Vicars's *England's Worthies* (1647). His name was much more familiar than his image. Between his first appearance in the early summer of 1643 and the end of 1648, Cromwell's name had appeared on the title-pages of 119 pamphlets, 79 of them in the year 1648. This was low visibility in comparison with the attention given to Fairfax (named on 654 title-pages before the end of 1648) but it was high compared with others who were still alive. In total about 90 per cent of commentators gave a broadly sympathetic account of his military career (just as every engraved image of him portrays him in the armour of a cavalry commander). Press coverage of his disagreements with army colleagues was short-lived in 1643–5, but from June 1647 he became the target of sustained personal abuse. It began with Lilburne, who singled out Cromwell, together with Henry Ireton, for criticism in a string of polemical pamphlets beginning with *Jonah's Cry out of the Whale's Belly* (July), and *The Juglers Discovered* (late September). But simultaneously there came criticism from royalist and (renewed) criticism from presbyterian sources, and a personal crusade mounted by William Prynne (*The Hypocrite Unmasked* and *Articles of the Impeachment for High Treason*). And there was a flurry of short, witty satires (*A Coppie of a Letter* by John Worth-rush, *Cromwell's Panegyrick*, *Craftie Cromwell*, *The Machiavellian Cromwellist*, and *A Case for Nol Cromwell's*

Nose). The charges brought from all sides were the same: vaunting ambition, machiavellianism, hypocrisy, insincerity. He was accused specifically of using a personal treaty with the king to line his own pocket and secure the earldom of Essex, the title's having lapsed with the death of the third earl. He was also accused of manipulating Fairfax—'Sir Thomas Fairfax was but a cypher with you, Cromwell, only your conductor' (*The Hypocrite Unmasked*, 2).

Rather surprisingly, in the years immediately after the regicide Cromwell's name receded from public view, appearing on title-pages forty-one times in 1649 (entirely related to his campaigns in Ireland), twenty-nine times in 1650, nineteen times in 1651, and fourteen times in 1652. Once again it was his military role and achievements that dominated and apart from Leveller and royalist protests about his role in the early months of 1649 most of the coverage was positive or at least neutral and descriptive.

Cromwell did not commit to paper his ideas for the settlement of the kingdom in the wake of the regicide. He had come to see the need to eliminate Charles I but there is no evidence that he believed in the permanent eradication of monarchy. It might not be feasible immediately, but nothing about the Rump Parliament was a blueprint for the future. When he helped to draw up *The Heads of Proposals* in July 1647 he was clearly committed to the constitutional and religious settlement there provided for, and all that changed between July 1647 and January 1649 was an unwillingness to have Charles I as the man to serve as constitutional monarch within that framework. He was thus a soldier whose pragmatism had driven him to king-killing. He had become a hesitant politician, all too aware of the huge risks associated with regicide: the extreme difficulty of creating any stability on the basis of an act bound to cause widespread revulsion and a tidal wave of international protest. His instincts were to do everything possible to broaden the basis of support for the embattled regime, opening the doors to anyone willing to walk through them.

Cromwell's social thought was no more impetuous. In 1643 he had shown a willingness to promote men for the vigour and strength of their commitment to the cause of liberty without regard to their social status. But he had not shown that hostility towards the peerage and gentry of which he was accused by Manchester and Crawford. On the contrary, throughout the period from 1644 to 1648 he worked closely with individual peers, especially Saye and Wharton, and many of his close allies in the Commons, including Nathaniel Fiennes and Oliver St John, were related to peers. On 1 November 1647, as Ireton struggled to hold the line at Putney against the calls for manhood suffrage by arguing for a franchise based on the possession of a 'fixed permanent interest', Cromwell sat mute. More than forty speeches were delivered that day before he joined in, and the argument had by then progressed beyond the argument for social prudence.

Cromwell's religious views are better chronicled but not straightforward. He was always in favour of a national church to which the great majority should be attached. He believed in a publicly approved and appointed ministry supported by some form of mandatory levy on all householders—tithes until a better system could be worked out. He believed that all sincere protestants who wished to dissociate themselves from that national church and worship God in the light of their own consciences should be permitted to do so. He came over time to define more precisely but not necessarily more strictly how to prevent the liberty he strove to promote from being (in his own eyes) abused. He was suspicious of all clerical claims to special or reserved powers, and believed that gifted laymen should be allowed to preach and lay people to prophesy. He believed that membership of the national church should not privilege anyone in the distribution of offices and responsibilities in civil and military affairs. He expected all those who claimed liberty for themselves to be willing to grant it to others. Beyond that, little is clear. There is nothing to indicate how he himself worshipped. He was married in a London parish church in 1620, almost certainly in accordance with the Book of Common Prayer. The registration of all his children in parish registers in the 1620s and 1630s suggests a continued willingness to participate at some level in the life of the church. But he seems also to have played a leading part in a house-conventicle and to have preached at it. It is not known whether he continued to exercise the gift of preaching as an army officer. It cannot be shown that he ever in his life received holy communion. It is likely but not certain that he sometimes attended divine worship in a parish church after 1640, and he probably worshipped in the old Chapel Royal at Whitehall in the 1650s and heard sermons there. Most of the ministers who were his chaplains were Independents, but of the kind who were willing to hold livings in the state church as reconstituted in and after 1650. One of his sisters, who married John Wilkins, the warden of Wadham College, Oxford (and after the Restoration bishop of Chester), almost certainly married in his presence in the Chapel Royal in 1656 using the marriage service from the Book of Common Prayer. Within a period of four weeks in 1647 he appears openly to have supported the restoration of an episcopate shorn of all coercive power, the introduction of what Robert Baillie called 'a lame erastian presbytery' for an experimental period, and the right of laymen to preach and to administer the sacraments.

Cromwell, then, was no more wedded to forms of government in the church than in the state. They too were dross and dung in comparison with the authentic search for Christian living, and God would not be confined in his choice of instruments. In the 1640s Cromwell struggled within the puritan movement to liberate those who could not in good conscience abide the rules being made by the godly men in power. In the 1650s he had to decide what to do with those who abused the liberty he strove to nurture: what to do about the licentious, the blasphemous, and the idolatrous. It made him appear more restrictive but it is not self-evident that he was.

The Rump Parliament, 1649–1651 Over the next four years Cromwell combined the demanding business of war with the demanding business of sustaining a fragile political system and of seeking to develop viable long-term political and institutional forms. He was away from London, campaigning in Ireland and in Scotland, from July 1649 to mid-September 1651. But he kept in close touch with events there during his absences, and after 12 September 1651 he never left the environs of the capital (except for two brief excursions into Kent in May 1652) for the rest of his life, moving first to the Cockpit and then, early in 1654, into the royal palaces at Whitehall and Hampton Court.

Cromwell's role in the Rump Parliament was an uncomfortable one. For some he was God's chosen instrument, the man manifestly enjoying the Lord's favour and therefore one who could deliver the fruits of revolution. To others he was the man who had the ultimate say in what happened because he had the army behind him, and the army had shown in July 1647 and in December 1648 that its patience could snap and that it would have its way. And so everyone looked to him for a lead and he found himself pulled in different directions. The central tension in him which cruelly tugged at him in the internal forum was the tension 'between on the one hand his taste for constitutional respectability and on the other his hunger for godly reformation' (Worden, *Rump Parliament*, 274). This was vividly expressed in the external circumstances that he brought about: after

> the trial and execution of the king, he helped to ensure that the settlement which followed was as respectable as possible, and that power would remain in the hands of unrevolutionary men. Enthusiasm for godly reformation was not the criterion he adopted when he sought to determine the character and composition of the Rump government. When he later demanded such reformation of the Rump, it not surprisingly declined to grant it. (ibid., 19)

From the moment he returned to London on 6 December 1648 Cromwell was desperate to broaden the basis of support for the new regime. Before the regicide little could be accomplished, although he worked to secure the early release of those imprisoned. But from 1 February 1649 onwards he actively encouraged those who had been excluded in December, or who had excluded themselves in protest, to return. He targeted especially the 'Royal Independents', those like Lord Saye and his son Nathaniel Fiennes with whom he had worked closely in 1647 and who had wanted a settlement with the king along the lines of *The Heads of Proposals*. Even though only one of them, Oliver St John, was persuaded to take his seat, Cromwell continued to work on the others and keep their seats warm for them. His aim was to tell them that what was done was done, and that sulking would not bring the king back. Therefore they should face the reality that the king was dead and work for the programme of social, legal, and religious reform to which they had so long been committed. Even more dramatic was his doomed attempt to save the House of Lords from abolition, and his successful subversion of Ireton's attempt to make all those who served on the Rump's executive, the council of state, take an oath that recognized the legitimacy of the purge and the regicide. As a result twenty-two of its forty-one members failed to give any assent to the actions that had brought into being the regime they headed. Cromwell was, of course, himself on the council—indeed its president in its first weeks until 8 March 1649—though his closest military colleagues at this time, Henry Ireton and Thomas Harrison, were pointedly excluded.

Cromwell's aim was simple: to prevent the regime from collapsing and all the forces of vengeance and reaction from overwhelming the new Commonwealth. The spectre of foreign intervention, the prospect of royalist invasion from Ireland and Scotland, and the need to get men of goodwill up and down the land to collect the taxes and mobilize the supplies that would allow the regime to protect itself, all demanded an embrace of the offended. This in turn led him to abandon the commitment of the previous eighteen months to an orderly transfer of power to a new parliament elected by a reformed franchise. This had to await the stabilization of the regime. Thus the second *Agreement of the People*, hammered out by Ireton and other army officers, by radicals in parliament and the City of London, and by the Levellers in the weeks either side of the Purge, and with much, perhaps all, of which Cromwell was in sympathy, had also to be shelved for the time being. When the Levellers inevitably took this as the ultimate proof of Cromwell's (and Ireton's) duplicity they subjected the generals to a blistering series of attacks, most notably in *England's New Chains Discovered* and *The Hunting of the Foxes by the Five Small Beagles*. They launched their own third *Agreement of the People* and looked to their friends in the army to mutiny against their traitorous generals, linking the failure to promote the second agreement to the understandable reluctance of many soldiers to go on the impending expedition to Ireland. Fairfax and Cromwell were compelled to march with 4000 men to the Cotswolds in a short, fierce campaign in late April and early May to put down these mutinies at Burford.

Thus Cromwell in 1649 stood full-square behind the cruel necessity of executing Charles I and the current necessity of governing through the remnant of the Long Parliament who had accepted the purge or who had been willing to contaminate themselves by re-entry after the regicide. He neither approved nor disapproved of the Rump at this stage: it was an interim expedient that was keeping open the prospect of a new freedom from royal and clerical tyranny.

Over the next two years Cromwell was away on campaign. He did not try to exercise much influence over what happened in the Rump or the council of state (declining to become involved, for example, in the debate about whether to go to war with the Dutch), but he was much lobbied by all groups. Far more of his incoming correspondence than of his outgoing letters has survived, and it is clear that he was courted by all those groups who were conforming to the new regime. He in turn continued to write to old friends who had washed their hands of the revolution. Thus he wrote a striking letter to Lord Wharton from winter quarters in Ireland, likening his chastening work there to the action of Phinehas who thrust his spear through an Israelite and a Midianite concubine as they were copulating and thus brought to an end the

plague that was a sign of God's wrath. He also defended what the Rump was achieving despite itself: 'good kept out; most bad remaining. It hath been so these nine years, yet God has wrought. The greatest work lasts; and is still at work' (*Letters and Speeches*, 1904, letter 117, 1 Jan 1650).

Cromwell in Ireland, 1649–1650 Cromwell had no known connection with Irish affairs before the outbreak of the Irish rising in November 1641. He can then be seen making a generous gift (£300 on 1 February 1642) and a significant loan against confiscated Irish land (£500—more than his annual income is supposed to have been—in April 1642). In the months before the outbreak of civil war in England he was one of the most active members of the committee for the affairs of Ireland and two other committees charged with funding the Anglo-Scottish military expedition. For example, he attended thirty-three of the thirty-nine meetings of the main committee in the months from April to July 1642. When he was in London during the years 1643–6 he played little part in Irish affairs and he was not appointed to committees for Irish affairs. There is evidence that he wished to be appointed to command the new military expedition to Ireland in 1647, but that post went to Philip Skippon. In 1648 he handed over two-thirds of the £1680 per annum income awarded him out of the earl of Worcester's estates for the Irish war. When Fairfax declined to command the expedition to overthrow the loyalist alliance of the marquess of Ormond and the Catholic confederates in 1649, the position fell to Cromwell as much because of his seniority as because of his developed interest in Ireland.

Cromwell was appointed in May 1649 to be lord lieutenant of Ireland and to be general of the army there, although technically as part of the New Model Army still under Fairfax's nominal command. He had three principal objectives in crossing to Ireland. The first was to eliminate the threat of military support for Charles II from those loyal to him—principally the Old English (protestant and Catholic) supporters of the long-time loyalist lord lieutenant James Butler, marquess of Ormond, and the Old English and Irish Catholic supporters of the confederation of Kilkenny. The second was to carry through the confiscation of land from all those involved in rebellion against the English parliament since 1641 and the redistribution of confiscated land to those who had invested (as 'adventurers') in various military expeditions since 1642. The third was to reform the institutions of Ireland not only (or specifically) to introduce the instruments of English civility, but to improve on them. This commitment can most clearly be seen in his proposals for law reform. On 31 December 1649 Cromwell wrote to invite John Sadler, a Cambridge don and civil lawyer, to become chief justice of Munster to establish 'a way of doing justice amongst these poor people which, for the uprightness and cheapness of it, may exceedingly gain upon them' (*Letters and Speeches*, 1904, 3.267, 31 Dec 1649). Sadler turned him down but his offer was accepted by John Cook, prosecutor of the king at his trial. Cook set to work to provide swift and cheap justice, dispensing with most court officials, radically reducing fees, dispensing with all lawyers except himself, and deciding all cases and moving from county to county providing summary justice biased in favour of the poor. Edmund Ludlow confessed that to Cromwell 'Ireland was a blank paper' and that his 'supersedeas to the old courts there' would be an example from a 'younger sister' to an older, so that 'England might have been the learner and gainer by her' (*Memoirs of Edmund Ludlow*, 1.246–7).

Cromwell's campaign in Ireland in 1649–50 is the stuff of legend—legend rooted in part-truths. In forty weeks (from 15 August 1649 to 26 May 1650) he occupied twenty-five fortified towns and castles (and visited five more already in English hands) on a progress that began in Louth and moved through counties Dublin, Wicklow, Wexford, Waterford, Cork, Kilkenny, and Tipperary, and the east tip of co. Limerick. In other words he spent thirty-four of his forty weeks clearing Munster of royalist garrisons. He never moved north of Drogheda, nor south of Kinsale, nor west of Mallow. For the most part he followed up the ferocity at Drogheda and Wexford by startlingly generous surrender articles (as at Mallow, Fethard, and Kilkenny). Blood was shed on only five occasions even though several towns defied him for days or weeks (he was even forced by the atrocious weather and disease to abandon a siege of Waterford). Two episodes from this phase of his career have given rise to the black legend: his sack of Drogheda and of Wexford. At Drogheda on 11–12 September Cromwell stormed a town that had refused a summons and his troops killed perhaps 3000 royalist troops in hot and cold blood, all the Catholic clergy and religious he could identify (mainly in cold blood), and an unknown number of civilians (probably all in hot blood). He followed the laws of war as they had operated in Ireland for the previous century and not as he had operated them in England. The royalist commander, Sir Arthur Aston, was clubbed to death, and 300 of his men, who had surrendered to mercy (that is, put their lives at the discretion of their vanquishers), were executed. Cromwell justified the massacre on three grounds. The first was by reference to the laws of war. The second was that it was as 'a righteous judgment of God upon these barbarous wretches who have imbrued their hands in so much innocent blood' (*Letters and Speeches*, 1904, letter 105, 17 Sept 1649). This was an inappropriate reference to the massacres of 1641–2: Drogheda had never been a confederate town and many of those killed—including most of the officers—were English, while the rest were men of Munster who had fought with Ormond against the rebels. And third, he justified the massacre on the grounds that it would terrorize others into immediate surrender and thus save lives in the long run.

In Wexford on 11 October his troops stormed a town still negotiating surrender articles (although with deliberate tardiness); again more than 2000 people were slain, including a larger number of civilians. The fact that as the assault began the defenders sank a hulk in the harbour, drowning 150 protestant prisoners-of-war, and that the Cromwellians found the bodies of more prisoners starved to death in a locked chapel, heightened their fury. Cromwell neither ordered nor sought to halt the indiscriminate killing that followed. Those soldiers who were not killed were sent to be slaves in Barbados. Drogheda was Cromwell's Hiroshima, and Wexford was his Nagasaki. These massacres did not bring an end to the war, only to atrocity. Resistance elsewhere led to more selective enforcement of the laws of war. At Gowran, for example, Ormond's own regiment surrendered on 21 March 1650. Cromwell ordered the officers to be shot but the common soldiers spared; and although he lost 2000 men at Clonmel in May, he offered and honoured generous terms to both town and garrison.

On 26 May 1650 Cromwell embarked at Youghal for England. His personal responsibility for the subsequent Irish settlement, and the 'Cromwellian confiscations', is very uncertain. Much hangs on the sincerity of his 'Declaration of the lord lieutenant of Ireland for the undeceiving of deluded and seduced people' (January 1650), in which he repudiated the claim made by twenty Catholic bishops gathered at Clonmacnoise that he had come to Ireland to 'extirpate the Catholic Religion'. Cromwell was withering in his denunciation of the episcopate in particular and of Catholic superstition and clerical tyranny in general (*Letters and Speeches*, 1904, 2.15). But while he stated that 'I shall not, where I have the power … suffer the exercise of the Mass', he also promised that:

> as for the people, what thoughts they have in the matter of religion in their own breasts I cannot reach; but I shall think it my duty, if they walk honestly and peaceably, not to cause them in the least to suffer for the same.   (ibid., 2.16–17)

Summary executions would be visited only on those taken in arms; no other killing would take place except after trial by due process for cause known to the law; and he promised that only those in arms would be banished or transported. There was to be no general confiscation of property, other than that of men who were still in arms. Those who had long since laid down their arms could expect merciful treatment, those who laid down their arms immediately could expect some mercy, while such private soldiers as laid down their arms 'and shall live peaceably and honestly at their several homes, they shall be permitted so to do' (ibid., 2.22). There is nothing in Cromwell's declaration to suggest that he favoured different principles of retribution from those that had applied to the royalist party in England. It is far from clear how far he subsequently changed his view and supported the Act of Settlement of 1652 that envisaged up to 100,000 executions, mass emigration, and ethnic cleansing on a scale unknown in western European history.

The final campaigns against the Scots, 1650–1651 Cromwell was recalled from Ireland specifically to command the New Model Army—as commander-in-chief of all the land forces of the Commonwealth following Fairfax's resignation—in a war with the Scots. He had supported the policy of early 1649 to permit the Scots to resume an existence independent of England that they had enjoyed before

1603. Cromwell had no objection to their retaining monarchy for themselves. But he could not accept their determination to recognize Charles II as king of all Britain and Ireland and to fight to place him on all his thrones, and their determination to see confessional presbyterianism throughout the archipelago. When it became clear in the spring of 1650 that Argyll was willing to commit Scottish arms to that enterprise and that Fairfax had no stomach to command against them, Cromwell was recalled. He was in London for only three weeks before setting off for the north on 28 June to launch a pre-emptive strike.

The harshness of the terrain and the climate, compounded by plague, had made the Irish campaign tougher than anything Cromwell had known. In Scotland he met fiercer resistance, was hindered by his own intermittent poor health, and, at least initially, made serious strategic errors. Entering Scotland late in July, he sought to bring to battle the swelling number of covenanters under Alexander Leslie, earl of Leven. But having stripped the Lothians of young men and all provisions, Leven was content to refuse him battle. Cromwell could neither afford to storm the strongholds, being unable to risk casualties, nor to lock his army away in garrisons. Essentially he had not thought through what to do if Leven would not come into the field. He took out some of his frustration in an attack on the Scottish presbyterian clergy at least as vicious as his attack on the Catholic clergy in Ireland. Accusing them of arrogance and 'spiritual drunkenness', he urged them to read 'the twenty-eighth of Isaiah, from the fifth to the fifteenth verse'. It was a passage which describes dissolute priests vomiting over the altar of the Lord. Theirs was, he said, not a covenant with God, but with 'carnal and wicked men'. Consider, he said, whether yours be a 'covenant with death and hell' (*Letters and Speeches*, 1904, letter 136, 3 Aug 1650). This was a phrase he had also hurled at the Irish bishops. After a month, Cromwell's forces were depleted by desertion and disease to 11,000 and Leven's had grown to 22,000. Cromwell was stranded on the coast at Dunbar dependent on inadequate supplies from the sea. Leven occupied a strong defensive position cutting off his lines of retreat. It looked all too likely to be Cromwell's Lostwithiel. Leven (and the younger David Leslie, who was increasingly taking over from his ailing namesake) assumed he would try to break out with his cavalry and leave his infantry to make what terms they could. He was not prepared for what happened. For having got his strategy completely wrong, Cromwell showed a tactical brilliance beyond anything shown by other commanders in these wars. Very early on 3 September, well before first light, he launched the greater part of his force against the right wing of the Scots, and having broken the stiff resistance of that wing, he wheeled to his right against the centre and eventually against the left of the Scots and destroyed them. It was the greatest of his victories. He claimed that 3000 Scots were killed and 10,000 were captured. Before the battle it was said that Cromwell was so tense that he bit his lips until blood covered his chin. He began the battle by emitting a great shout: 'let God arise and his enemies shall be scattered' (Psalm 51). After the

battle, he laughed uncontrollably. Normally God had given the victory to the side that had providentially brought the greater number to the field. Never had God made himself so visible, so immanent. Cromwell's ecstatic letter to Speaker William Lenthall beseeched parliament to see how great was God's blessing upon them: 'God puts it more into your hands to give glory to him … own His people more and more, for they are the chariots and horsemen of Israel. Disown yourselves, but own your authority'. They were, he added, to relieve the oppressed, reform the abuses of the professions (the lawyers and clergy), and 'if there be any one that makes many poor to make a few rich, that suits not a Commonwealth' (could this be a dig at the MPs themselves?) (*Letters and Speeches*, 1904, letter 140, 4 Sept 1650).

There followed twelve difficult months. Leslie's troops were holed up in very strong fortresses that Cromwell lacked the strength in depth to storm, and he himself was intermittently incapacitated by illness. Meanwhile the Scots were bitterly divided over how far to tie themselves to an unregenerate Charles II. When Cromwell was fit he oscillated restlessly between the Lothians and Strathclyde. He did occupy Leith and Edinburgh but he failed to lure Leslie back into a major engagement. With the embers of resistance in Ireland now extinguished, more men could be put into the Scottish theatre, and by July 1651 Cromwell felt able to send a force to occupy Fife and cut off David Leslie's connections to the highlands. He then moved the great bulk of his army north of Leslie's army with the deliberate intention of tempting him into a desperate invasion of England. On 4 August he wrote to Lenthall that although a Scottish dash on London 'will trouble some men's thoughts and may occasion some inconveniences' (*Letters and Speeches*, 1904, letter 180), it was preferable to another winter in Scotland with the Scots playing peekaboo with his army. Leslie swallowed the bait. He crossed into England on 9 August and headed south. Cromwell pursued, incorporating fresh English troops as he went, as Leslie shed his own. By the time they both reached Worcester, Cromwell had the same numerical advantage over Leslie as Leslie had had over him at Dunbar. On the anniversary of that battle, Cromwell won the inevitable and even more crushing victory, the 'crowning mercy' as he put it. Once again, his paean of praise for God's providential assistance led on to a demand that 'the fatness of these continued mercies may not occasion pride and wantonness as formerly, [but that] justice righteousness, mercy and truth may flow from you as a thankful return to our gracious God' (ibid., letter 183, 4 Sept 1651). Leaving others to mop up in Scotland, Cromwell returned to London on 12 September to be formally received in a triumph that echoed those of Roman generals, even Roman emperors.

The Rump Parliament, 1651–1653 From the moment of Cromwell's return in triumph from Worcester he and his close colleagues in the army sought to galvanize the Rump. He had four objectives. First, he sought to persuade the Rump to set a time for it to dissolve itself and to hold new elections. Second, he sought to achieve a greater acquiescence from the large number of former royalists by a broad and generous amnesty. Third (and this was a change of heart), he supported the settlement that united the three former kingdoms into a single polity. And fourth (in the words of his declaration of 22 April 1653 justifying his dissolution of the Rump), he sought 'to encourage and countenance God's people, reform the law, and administer law impartially … the fruits of a just and righteous reformation' ('A declaration of the lord general and his council', 1–2, *Writings and Speeches*, 3.5–8).

Immediately upon Cromwell's return the Rump abandoned its desultory plans to hold elections to recruit itself up to strength and began work on a bill for fresh elections. But the magnitude of Cromwell's problem can be seen in the fact that the house agreed on 14 November 1651 (though only by a majority of two and notwithstanding a passionate speech by Oliver) to fix a date for its own dissolution, but then to his dismay four days later settled on ending their sitting 'by' 3 November 1654, three years hence. After that the bill got caught up in a hundred procedural delays and prevarications.

Cromwell also gave his support to the proposal for an act of indemnity and oblivion that would safeguard all former royalists from any new proceedings for past actions. But again, while the principle was very quickly conceded, the devil entered into the detail and it finally emerged a much more pusillanimous act than Cromwell had hoped for and intended. And, over Cromwell's protests, the number of royalists named as 'malignants' whose estates were to be sold to offset the debts of the state grew steadily, from 73 to 780.

Cromwell was also influential in the plans to incorporate Scotland into an enlarged English state. When he first set out on campaign there the plan had been only to occupy strong points in the lowlands and to create a cordon sanitaire for the future security of England. But as Cromwell encountered the factionalism and fanaticism of the hardline covenanters he became a convert to a union of the former kingdoms, although he hoped that the Scots would agree to a consensual union, and supported the proposal that delegates from the major shires and burghs, having first agreed to the principle of union, be sent south to take part in the agreeing of the detail. This turned out to be little more than a *fait accompli*. They were simply shown a draft bill and asked to comment on it before a final decision was made by the English council. The Rump wished to avoid a rhetoric of conquest and imposed union, but they made sure they got what they wanted.

It is far from clear what Cromwell's role was in the much harsher settlement imposed on Ireland. Under the Act of Settlement (September 1652) more than 100,000 Irish Catholics were made liable to the death sentence; all Catholics were made subject to penalties 'according to their respective demerits'; and no Catholic was to be allowed to reside, let alone to own property, in the provinces of Leinster, Munster, or Ulster, but would be herded into Connaught and co. Clare. Even then they would be liable to summary execution if discovered within 1 mile of the coast or of the River Shannon. This settlement was so much at odds with that envisaged by Cromwell in 1650 and with the policy he later pursued as lord protector that he probably disapproved strongly of it. S. R. Gardiner, the only scholar to study the passage of the legislation in detail, concluded that 'as far as the act of 1652 is concerned, there is no evidence whatsoever to connect it with Cromwell' (Gardiner, 'Transplantation', 707).

Dearest of all to Cromwell in these years, however, were those 'fruits of a just and righteous reformation' for which his letters from the fields of Dunbar, Inverkeithing, and Worcester had pleaded. Religious toleration was in place, and no one he approved of as 'honest' and 'godly' was suffering for his or her faith. But there was also concern to sustain a broad national church with no requirements as to forms of worship or pietistic practice, but with a loose definition of core beliefs (such as the fifteen 'fundamentals' of faith that a committee under Cromwell's chaplain John Owen proposed in the wake of the publication—in a translation in which John Milton had a hand—of the anti-Trinitarian Racovian catechism). He could also approve the Rump's intention to distinguish those beliefs that men and women could be allowed the freedom to evangelize from those that they should be required to keep to themselves; and he sought recognition of the principle that God's truth could be promulgated by persuasion but not by persecution. But parliament's failure to follow up Cromwell's plea to extend and adapt the commissions for the propagation of the gospel from 'the dark corners of the land' to the whole of England, the failure to explore an alternative to tithes for the maintenance of the ministry, and the defeat of his proposal for a non-presbyterian rite of ordination all sapped Cromwell's patience. In essence, the Rump had done something towards embedding negative liberty, but little towards inculcating positive Christian liberty, the freedom of God's children to resist vice and embrace godliness through a programme of moral evangelism and of sanctions against the sins of the flesh. He felt much the same about the slow progress made with answering the call of his letter from the battlefield of Dunbar for an examination of inequities in legal process. He presided over the panel that appointed the extra-parliamentary Hale commission, but as its recommendations for reform of judicial process and of the substantive law of property began to come back to the Rump in the summer of 1652, they too ran into endless procedural delay.

Cromwell wanted an early end to the Rump, the hand of forgiveness if not of friendship to old enemies, fresh elections on a broad franchise, measures to promote godliness and equity. And beyond that? Did he want to see the restitution of some form of monarchy? Here above all the evidence is fragmentary, treacherous—and retrospective. And yet it cannot just be discounted. It takes two forms: one consists of the conversations Cromwell is said to have had with individuals and groups floating the idea of restoring the house of Stuart in the person of Henry, duke of Gloucester, still of impressionable years and in the hands of the regime. The other is the idea of Cromwell himself becoming king or at least occupying the kingly office.

The evidence for the former is to be found both in the known views of men to whom Cromwell was drawing closer at this time—especially Oliver St John—and in the testimony (probably near-contemporary) of Bulstrode Whitelocke in his *Memorials* that on 10 December 1651 Cromwell convened a meeting at which some present argued that the idea of a parliamentary grant of the title to Henry was feasible and desirable. Whitelocke records much said on both sides, but concludes that Cromwell summed up by saying that:

> this will be a business of more than ordinary difficulty! But really I think, if it may be done with safety, and preservation of our rights, both as Englishmen and Christians, that a settlement with somewhat of monarchical power in it would be very effectual. (Whitelocke, *Memorials*, 491–2)

As one historian puts it: 'before Worcester, the royalist threat had made it unthinkable that the Rump should voluntarily restore monarchy. Now the government could undertake such an initiative on any terms to which it could persuade the army to agree' (Worden, *Rump Parliament*, 276). If Cromwell's words were carefully recorded, then they were carefully chosen: 'somewhat of monarchical power' implies not necessarily a new king, but someone who would act as protector of a written constitution in the intervals between elected parliaments, someone who would prevent powerful legislatures from overreaching themselves, someone who was elected to ensure that the actions of executive bodies worked effectively. He had wanted no more in 1647 or 1648; he created that role for himself from 1653 to 1658. And it is worth linking this to the fact that at the time he made these remarks he hoped for an early dissolution and fresh elections. Perhaps he looked to a new, broader, elected parliament to negotiate this difficult but desirable outcome.

The belief that Cromwell was considering becoming king himself rests on the testimony of the disillusioned Edmund Ludlow, and on a further recollection by Bulstrode Whitelocke of a private conversation with Cromwell in Hyde Park in November 1652. Cromwell, Whitelocke recorded, expressed great weariness with the pride, sloth, and self-seeking of the Rump and then blurted out the question: 'what if a man should take upon him to be king?' Whitelocke's response was that there were far more difficulties in the way of such a move than in restoring the house of Stuart (*Diary of Bulstrode Whitelocke*, 281–2). But that the thought was in other sympathetic minds can be seen from the journal of a German diplomat, who wrote down at the time a conversation with John Dury, a key figure in the civil administration. Discussion turned to the adulation that Cromwell had received during his triumphal entry into London after the battle of Worcester. Herman Mylius had observed that perhaps Cromwell would be made England's doge: so great is he, replied Dury, that 'he is unus instar omnium, et in effectu rex' ('he is a man set above all others, and, in effect, our king'; L. Miller, ed., *John Milton & the Oldenburg Safeguard*, c.1985,

49). It is unlikely that this was the only such conversation.

The dissolution of the Rump Parliament By August 1652 Cromwell felt it was time to move on constitutionally, and that the fruits of the revolution were not being garnered in. His own patience was wearing thin, but that of the army was wearing thinner and Cromwell could feel the weight of their expectation. After a nine-hour meeting of the army council on 2 August 1652 the officers published their demands in the aggressively titled 'Declaration of the armie to the lord general Cromwell for the dissolving of this present parliament'. It called for an early dissolution and fresh elections, for a purge of unworthy men from the parochial ministry, the replacement of tithes, the implementation of the recommendations of the Hale commission, a non-parliamentary commission to look into corruption in public office, and a fundamental reform of taxation and of provision for the poor, and especially for ex-soldiers and war widows. Cromwell can only have agreed with every word, but his reaction was to nudge the Rump into responding responsibly. Over the next few months he convened something like twelve informal meetings of leading officers and MPs. He tried his best, but he failed. Finally his self-restraint snapped and he undertook that which, he had told quartermaster John Vernon late in 1652, 'the consideration of the issue whereof made his hair to stand on end' (*Memoirs of Edmund Ludlow*, 1.346).

If Cromwell's letters from the fields of Dunbar and Worcester reveal his yearnings for constitutional settlement and godly reformation, then the Rump had utterly failed him. They had not disowned themselves but they had disowned their call to bring liberty and equity to the people; and the fatness of God's continued mercies had occasioned more pride and wantonness than righteousness, mercy, and truth. Cromwell's fundamental disappointment with them was further fuelled by new prevarications over a range of other issues. For example, he failed to persuade the house to address the £31,000 a month deficit on the army wage bill; and he was deeply irritated by their constant privileging of the adventurers and of friends of Rumpers over the army in the detailed arrangements for the redistribution of Irish land. He was losing patience, and was failing to contain the army's impatience. On 11 March 1653 he had to speak powerfully to defeat a vote in the council of officers to expel the Rump immediately. He did so by saying it would be easier to leave a dissolution until after a peace treaty was made with the Dutch. So it was added wormwood to him that he failed on 15 March 1653 to persuade the Rump to open negotiations. He ceased attending both the house and the council of state.

Despite all the warnings it had received, the Rump had no sense of urgency. Day after day was spent tinkering with the Irish Land Bill, and giving the bill for a new representative desultory attention. By 19 April Cromwell had had enough; and he was well aware that many in the army were more exasperated than he was. Exactly as in 1649 he wanted due form to be followed if at all possible: the Rump's abdication was better than its deposition. He demanded that the Rump establish a caretaker government of forty drawn from itself and from the army, entrust all power to it as a constituent assembly, and then abdicate. He put this as something midway between a demand and an order to a cross-section of the members who sulkily agreed to suspend work on the new representative until his own plan had been debated. But the next morning, to his incredulity, Cromwell heard that they had gone back on their word and were debating a bill of their own. Four years of prevarication appeared to be being replaced by a day of defiant decisiveness. Arranging for troops to follow and wait outside the chamber, he went to the house and took his seat. There were twice as many members present as usual, a clear sign that those who opposed his demand had called in all their friends. He was in a white anger and his words scourged his opponents one by one. With the help of about forty musketeers with lighted match, he cleared the chamber and carried off the mace and the papers that lay on the table. What precisely had been in the bill the Rump was rushing through is now irretrievable. In a declaration published two days later Cromwell claimed that they had done something even worse than continue with the bill for a new representative, and had reverted to the plan to recruit to themselves. This was probably a lie intended to increase the popularity of his act (although it just might have been a ghastly misunderstanding on his part). He dropped the claim once it had served his immediate purpose. If he was lying, it is the only occasion on which he can be shown to have done so.

Why should Cromwell dissolve the Rump when it was finally doing what he had so long demanded of it: making urgent arrangements for a new representative? It is likely that he thought the political tests to be applied to the electorate or to those eligible to sit were inadequate. It is likely that the bill provided for 'perpetual parliaments'— one damn parliament after another, each exercising full control over the legislative and executive activities of government, an arrangement that the Rump itself had taught Cromwell to be disastrous. It may have intended to make Rumpers alone responsible for vetting returns and deciding who was qualified and who was not qualified to sit in the next parliament. And it may be that the Rump's intention to delay its own dissolution until 3 November 1653 was intolerable to Cromwell in the light of the previous day's discussion. At any rate, he used strong language and brute force to dissolve the Rump. Cromwell had longed to see the back of it, but to the end he had hoped for an orderly transfer of power. When he acted as he did on 20 April he had no plan ready to implement. If he had wanted personal power then and there he could have taken it. His determination, in the days and weeks that followed, to avoid a leading role for himself is testimony to his lack of ambition.

The nominated assembly—Barebone's Parliament Instead, power passed immediately to the council of officers, and it was they who decided how to proceed from where they were. They set up a council of state of seven senior officers, headed by Cromwell, and six civilians to run civil government and foreign policy on a day-to-day basis.

Meanwhile the council of officers themselves took responsibility for constitutional reform. They debated the merits of the scheme put forward by Major-General John Lambert for a council of state of forty with limited legislative powers and the plea of Major-General Thomas Harrison for a sanhedrin of saints. Harrison was a believer in the imminent second coming of Christ and the thousand-year rule of the saints predicted by the biblical books of Daniel and Revelation—the latter making the reconstitution of the Jewish ruling council of seventy men (the sanhedrin) a precondition of Christ's arrival. Few members of the council of officers subscribed either to this Fifth Monarchist package or to the fall-back position of Fifth Monarchist preachers like John Rogers that Cromwell was in a very real sense the new Moses chosen to lead the people of Israel from slavery in Egypt, through the Red Sea (regicide), across the desert to the Promised Land. But the council did like the idea of a constituent assembly made up of a cross-section of men drawn from 'the various forms of godliness in this nation', and Cromwell would seem to have been influential in giving precise shape to this assembly. He was, it is clear, behind the proposal that no serving army officer and no lawyer was to sit in the assembly. Gathered churches around the land, no doubt encouraged by what they heard, spontaneously sent in lists of names, but the council of officers seems to have acted principally on its own knowledge in the final nomination of 140 men to serve in the assembly. They were men of social substance—80 per cent were born into gentry families—and all had been active in the parliamentarian cause and were known for their commitment to religious liberty.

Neither in the writ of summons, nor in the place of its first meeting (the council chamber in Whitehall, not the parliament house in Westminster), nor in Cromwell's opening address is there any implication that the officers saw it as a parliament. It was an assembly, and its task was over a maximum period of eighteen months to prepare the people for the responsibilities of self-government.

From the years between 1653 and 1658 there survive what purport to be full versions of more than twenty speeches by Cromwell to the nominated assembly, to the protectorate parliaments, and to a committee of parliament seeking to persuade him to accept the title of king. Seven of these speeches (those of 4 July 1653, 4 and 12 September 1654, 22 January 1655, 17 September 1656, and 25 January and 4 February 1658) were major set-piece reviews of the political world as he saw it, and most took between two and three hours to deliver. They were printed verbatim, having the cadences of spoken rather than written speech. None of them was as upbeat, optimistic, and passionate as that of 4 July 1653. Cromwell clearly had the highest hopes for the nominated assembly. Far more than the others this speech is a sermon, containing significant meditations on passages from the Psalms, Hosea, Isaiah, and Romans. It began with a rehearsal of 'that series of providences wherein the Lord hitherto hath dispensed wonderful things to these nations, from the beginning of our troubles to this very day' (*Speeches*, 9). This section culminated in an analysis of why the dissolution of the Rump was just and necessary and how the army had lit upon the idea of the assembly. 'Truly God hath called you to this work by, I think, as wonderful providences as ever passed upon the sons of men in so short a time' (ibid., 20). He called upon them to:

> love all the sheep, love the lambs, love all and tender all, and cherish all, and countenance all in all things that are good. And if the poorest Christian, the most mistaken Christian, should desire to live peaceably and quietly under you, soberly and humbly desire to lead a life in godliness and honesty, let him be protected. (ibid., 22)

Then he charged them to come up with a reform programme that would turn the people from the things of the flesh to the things of the spirit, make themselves capable of taking responsibility for their own freedom. Towards the end the apocalyptic language intensifies and he called this 'a day of the power of Jesus Christ' (ibid., 23). But it was a this-worldly fulfilment of the promise of God to be with his people as he had been with Israel in their days of obedience; it was not evidence that Cromwell thought that the end of the world was nigh.

Cromwell then left the members to their own devices. They moved to the Commons chamber, announced they were a parliament, and began to act like one (hostile, royalist pamphlets soon lampooned it as Barebone's Parliament, after the name of one of its 'fanatic' members, the Baptist Praisegod Barbon). They invited Cromwell and three other officers to join them, but he firmly declined (although he did attend the council of state it set up to administer the Commonwealth day by day). As they wrangled and disputed, he just watched with dismay. Some radical bills were approved, but there was no progress on the essential matter that they had been constituted to address: a long-term constitutional arrangement that combined freely elected parliaments with advancing godliness and Christian liberty. By early December a clear majority of the members knew that they would not fulfil their commission. In collusion with Major-General Lambert—but not with Cromwell, whose protestation that he had no foreknowledge of it carries conviction—they voted themselves out of existence on 12 December and marched to Cromwell to tell him so. His experiment had failed.

Becoming lord protector, 1653–1654 This time there was no great delay. Lambert had been preparing for this moment and stepped forward with a fully formed paper constitution, the 'Instrument of government', very clearly based on *The Heads of Proposals* of 1647. Senior members of the council of officers, including Cromwell, had already considered a draft of the 'Instrument', and Cromwell himself had insisted that the elected head of government should not be called king. But they were taken by surprise by the events of 12 December and over the next three days continued to refine the document in a series of long, tense, and inconclusive meetings. When Cromwell was formally sworn in as head of state on 15 December some passages of

the 'Instrument' were not agreed, and had to be mumbled so as to be inaudible to the ambassadors and others present. It took several more days for the new constitution to be finally agreed and published.

For the remaining four years and nine months of his life Oliver Cromwell was to exercise as lord protector 'the chief magistracy and the administration of the government over [the Commonwealth of England, Scotland and Ireland and of the dominions thereunto belonging] and the people thereof' (Gardiner, *Constitutional Documents*, 406). As lord protector for life he had some freedom to act on his own, as in proroguing and dissolving parliaments once they had met for the prescribed minimum five-month period. He used this power in January 1655 and February 1658, on neither occasion consulting his councillors. But in most matters of governance he was constrained to act with and through the majority will of a council of state consisting of between thirteen and twenty-one members, over whose membership he had limited control. He and the council were given the authority to make law for the period before the next ensuing parliament, after which he would be required to make law in and through parliament, with a limited power of veto over bills approved by them. It was the council that selected and removed judges and all other civil magistrates.

The shape of the protectorate Cromwell became lord protector on 16 December 1653. Between then and the meeting of the first protectorate parliament on 4 September 1654 he and the council of state ruled by decree, issuing 180 ordinances (only eighty-two of them published at the time), sixty of them in the fortnight up to 2 September. When parliament met the council had plucked out about a dozen very obvious royalists as not being men 'of known integrity, fearing God, and of good conversation' (Gardiner, *Constitutional Documents*, 411). After some initial gestures of co-operation—such as approving without discussion all the appointments Cromwell had made that required their confirmation—parliament began a systematic review of the constitution. Cromwell, on the advice of the council, called them to a meeting and harangued them on how a 'cloud of witnesses' (a phrase from the epistle to the Hebrews) had underwritten the 'fundamentals' (*Speeches*, 42, 51; 12 Sept 1654). His cloud of witnesses included the army, the City of London, and all those who had written congratulatory petitions—even the MPs themselves, by seeking election on the writs of the protectorate. And the fundamentals were the separation of powers between protector and parliament, their joint control of the armed forces, that parliaments should meet for limited periods and were not 'perpetual', and religious liberty. He then ordered all members to subscribe to a 'Recognition' of the protectorate, causing about a quarter of the members to withdraw (ibid., 41–56). Parliament then worked on a solid body of 'Commonwealth' legislation (bills which regulated social, economic, and cultural life, dealing with such matters as parish boundaries and the local provision of welfare) and on a revised constitution, with a view to offering them as a package to Cromwell at the end of five calendar months. Cromwell, claiming that the reference to five months as the minimum duration of a parliament in the 'Instrument' meant five lunar and not calendar months, dissolved the house without warning on 22 January 1655 to prevent a showdown in which he would have had to reject their constitutional bill.

In the eighteen months before the summoning of the next parliament Cromwell was preoccupied with two matters above all. One—in the wake of the series of abortive royalist risings in late February and early March—was national security, and the introduction of the major-generals; the other was foreign policy. This was the period during which Cromwell was most active in the council. He took a close personal interest both in the efforts of the major-generals to encourage 'a reformation of manners' and in persuading a sceptical council to back the amphibious expedition against the Spanish West Indies.

The second parliament met on 17 September 1656, well before the triennial stipulation of article 11 of the 'Instrument', in order to provide taxation for the war against Spain. On this occasion the council ruled that more than 100 of those elected were ineligible, but the remainder chose not to make a fuss and for three months there was little friction within the house or between the house and the council. There was an unspoken agreement that Cromwell would leave them alone and that they would leave the constitution alone. He even kept out of furious debates during two weeks in December about how to deal with the Quaker James Nayler, whom many believed to have blasphemously claimed to be Christ (by riding into Bristol on a donkey in imitation of Jesus's entry into Jerusalem on Palm Sunday). But behind the scenes a group of councillors and members of parliament were planning to bounce Cromwell into taking the crown, and they brought in a draft bill to this effect on 23 February 1657. For the next four months the house perfected a revised constitution built around a King Oliver. After much hesitation he rejected the crown but accepted the rest of the revised constitution, and after a period of equal hesitation parliament agreed to this compromise. Under the 'Humble petition and advice', a new upper house of Cromwell's own nominees would restore a bicameral parliament, Cromwell was given the responsibility of nominating his own successor, and the council was made more firmly answerable to parliament.

From July 1657 to January 1658 Cromwell, acting alone, struggled to give effect to the provisions of the 'Humble petition', and acting with the council he focused on the complex affairs of the Baltic and on the Spanish war. When parliament reconvened in January 1658, with the secluded members restored to the Commons and about fifty of Cromwell's friends translated to the upper house, it was clear there would be no co-operation, and after a short-tempered harangue had failed to recall them from determined constitutional obstruction (they challenged the title and powers of the 'other house'), he unceremoniously dissolved this, his last parliament. His final months were months of drift, except for a last great victory for British arms at the battle of the Dunes near Dunkirk on 4 June 1658. Cromwell's health deteriorated exponentially throughout the year and he died peacefully enough on 3 September.

The limits of protectoral authority, 1653–1658 Too many studies of the period have assumed that almost everything that the three arms of government attempted and achieved while Cromwell was lord protector were the result of his initiative or had his consent. In fact he was often embattled and overborne by his councillors, by his parliaments, and perhaps by his army colleagues. This problem is compounded by a significant shift in the nature of the evidence about what Cromwell himself thought. The flow of private letters dries up once he had moved into the palaces of Whitehall and Hampton Court. It is replaced by the survival of full versions of about twenty-five public speeches. These certainly represent very personal, largely unwritten and unrehearsed expressions of passionate opinion, but their rhetorical structures and awareness of a wide audience are very different.

Cromwell's precise part in the shaping and articulation of government action is difficult to establish. There is no record of discussion at the council board; only its minutes of matters discussed and decisions reached are extant. He attended less than half of the more than 800 meetings up until his death—surprisingly, only a third of those in the period preceding the meetings of the first protectorate parliament (4 September 1654), and less than a third in the last nine months of his life. He was most attentive in the middle period of the protectorate, between the two parliaments (January 1655 to September 1656). At times it is hard not to conclude that he was deliberately absenting himself at a time of decisions with which he wished not to be associated (such as the selection of those to be excluded from the parliament as unqualified under the 'Instrument'). As head of state he did not attend parliamentary sessions. He formally opened and closed each session, and otherwise occasionally summoned the members to meet him on neutral ground such as the painted chamber within the palace of Westminster.

Cromwell was often dragged along reluctantly by what his councillors and principal officers of state advised him to do. The first fifteen councillors were named in the 'Instrument' and three more were soon chosen by Cromwell and the council in collaboration. The striking thing about the council is that it was not dominated by the army that established it. Only three senior officers (John Lambert, Cromwell's son-in-law Charles *Fleetwood, and his brother-in-law John Disbrowe), together with Philip Skippon, elderly, retired, and largely apolitical, were among the eighteen. Three more were colonels who conjoined garrison commands with seniority in regional government. A clear majority were civilians, only one of whom— Henry Lawrence, his old landlord at St Ives in the 1630s— had a long and close relationship with Cromwell, although others had been allies in the Rump or had recently shown good sense during their time in the nominated assembly. They were a cross-section of the godly, essentially a band of strong Calvinists, although their ecclesiological preferences represented a spectrum from primitive episcopacy to Baptist. They were all men, in Cromwell's characteristic phrase, 'with the root of the matter' in them. Perhaps the most influential figure to emerge, however, is John Thurloe, who acted as sole secretary of state and head of the security services, a man whose instincts inclined towards normalizing government by the restoration of the kingship with Cromwell in it and towards gradually reducing the power and influence of the generals at court and of the army itself in the country.

Cromwell was constantly spending time discussing public affairs with a remarkable cross-section of preachers whose views he respected: a spectrum that ran from the former archbishop of Armagh, James Ussher, to the Quaker George Fox, all of whom found him a good listener and sincere discussant. But little is said, because little is known, about what happened at the weekly dinners to which Cromwell invited all army officers currently in London—up to 120 at any time. There was very little turnover in the officer corps (as against the rank and file) in the course of the 1650s. Almost a third of those who served as colonels in 1649 were cashiered for disaffection at some point in the 1650s, but they were replaced by men who were already majors or captains. So were these unminuted dinners an opportunity for reminiscence about battles won? Were they an opportunity for political lobbying and the pricking of Cromwell's conscience? Or were they an opportunity for him to get his colleagues to understand the complexity of the problems facing him and the integrity of his own and the council's response? Probably a bit of each. Certainly there are a few glimpses of how frustrated he could get when the army did interfere with politics. In an astonishing outburst to a deputation of 100 officers in London on 28 February 1657 he blamed them collectively for a series of miscalculations (he said they had made him their 'drudge upon all occasions'). And most notably he blamed them for the clumsy attempt to have the authority of the major-generals, the regional governors responsible for local security and 'a reformation of manners', placed on a statutory footing: 'who bid you go to the House with a bill and there receive a foil?' (*Speeches*, 111–12, 28 Feb 1657).

Aspirations as lord protector The protectorate consisted of two distinct phases divided by the great debate on the kingship (February to May 1657) and the replacement of the 'Instrument' by the 'Humble petition' (June 1657), under which Cromwell became king in all but name. In the first phase Cromwell represented himself more like the governor of Massachusetts than the king of England. He wore sober dark suits with collars unspotted with blood. His installation in December 1653 was very much a swearing-in, not a surrogate coronation, and in his short acceptance speech he put first among his tasks to make the gospel 'flourish in all its splendor and purity' (*Writings*

and Speeches, 3.138). He took up permanent residence in the palace of Whitehall (Mondays to Thursdays) and Hampton Court (Fridays to Sundays). He endured being called 'his highness' (and allowed his daughters to take the title princess) and by 1656 he was dubbing knights, but the drift towards a monarchical style was slow and gradual. Evocations of royalty accelerated in 1657: his second investiture as lord protector (and there was no need for one beyond the taking of a new oath) self-consciously appropriated some aspects of a coronation and eschewed others. He sat in the coronation chair used since 1308, moving it to Westminster Hall from the abbey; he wore a robe of purple velvet lined with ermine; and he received a sword of justice and a sceptre (but not an orb or a crown). Henceforth his council was called a privy council, he created peers as well as an increasing number of knights, and his ritual behaviour on state occasions represented a dilution of royal practice.

Cromwell's public performance became more king-like. But whenever he described his own role he downplayed it. He described himself as a good constable, set to keep the peace of the parish. He likened himself to a watchman set on a watchtower to espy threats to security and peace. He reiterated that he had not called himself to the place that he occupied, saying that he saw it as a duty laid upon him by God and not as something he sought and enjoyed (*Speeches*, 40, 4 Sept 1654; 133, 13 April 1657; 174, 25 Jan 1658). With every speech there was less expectation that England was moving closer to the attainment of those things made possible by the overthrow of Stuart and episcopal tyranny, and more frustration at the lack of progress towards those goals. By the final speeches he was old, tired, and disillusioned.

In his speeches as lord protector Cromwell never drew on pre-civil-war history and never compared himself or his situation to that of English kings—or for that matter to continental kings or Roman emperors. There are a number of implied parallels between himself and Moses—especially extended metaphors about the people of England being like the people of Israel after the Exodus, 'repining in the desert'—and more obliquely between himself and David. Official publications, engravings, and the multiple copying of paintings by Lely and Walker emphasize his martial qualities and pedigree. Those currying favour and seeking to justify his actions again fail to draw on English history but are more evenly divided between biblical images of Cromwell (as Gideon, as Moses, or as David—only with his death did the image of Josiah, iconoclast, temple-restorer, and doomed warrior come into prominence) and images of Cromwell drawn from imperial Rome (Julius Caesar and Augustus predominantly, but also, in a double-edged way, Brutus). His critics focused on less deserving Romans such as Sejanus but by far the most favoured hostile typology was with the Machiavel.

Cromwell's attempts to realize his vision of a godly reformed nation abandoning the things of the flesh for the things of the spirit were constantly frustrated by those he was constrained to work with and through. He was frustrated with the council, who used their power under the 'Instrument' to remove far more of those returned to parliament than he wished, both in 1654 and in 1656. He was very reluctant to follow their insistence in the summer of 1656 that a parliament be called earlier than necessary. He was much more disillusioned by the failure of both parliaments to keep their eye on the task of providing the legislative framework for a reformation of manners, and by their interference with the rights of those who wished to exercise freedom of conscience outside the church. He was frustrated by the failure of the royalists to draw a line under the past and to accept that there would be no new penalties for old offences, and he was much more frustrated with the sects for refusing to live peaceably and quietly with one another and with the great number of sober, godly folk living out their lives in and around their parish communities.

All Cromwell could do was to mitigate the failure of all parties. When John Biddle was imprisoned on the Scilly Isles by the council for persisting in publishing anti-Trinitarian views, Cromwell made clear that he could not condone the public advocacy of such blasphemy, and would not overrule the council's decision; but in his horror of persecution he arranged for 10s. a week of his own money to be sent to Biddle to alleviate the conditions of his imprisonment. More dramatic was his intervention in the case of John Southworth, who was hanged, drawn, and quartered in June 1654, the only priest executed in Britain during the protectorate. Southworth had been condemned to death in 1627 under the Elizabethan laws making it treason to be a Catholic priest in England. His sentence had been commuted to perpetual banishment on pain of death if he returned. Arrested and identified by a pursuivant in June 1654 during a routine security sweep, he spurned the judge's advice that he refuse to confirm or deny that he was the same John Southworth (which would have allowed him to be released for lack of proof that he was) and he went to his death. Again Cromwell felt unable to overrule the court, but he did arrange for Southworth's quartered body to be reassembled and given to his seminary at Douai for Catholic obsequies. Indeed Cromwell's attitude to English Catholics was much milder than is usually recognized. He wrote to Cardinal Mazarin on 26 December 1656 and told him it was not politically possible to decree liberty for Catholics but that he personally had helped many to escape persecution and that he wanted to see an end to 'the raging fire of persecution, which did tyrannise over their consciences' and that he would, when he could, 'remove impediments' (*Writings and Speeches*, 3.368–9). Catholics, like protestant sectaries, benefited from the repeal of all the statutes that required attendance at divine worship in their parish churches, and there was little disturbance of the private exercise of Catholic rites, even in central London. Cromwell operated a double tier of religious freedom. There was an active encouragement of those who came under the umbrella of evangelical protestantism and who affirmed the scriptures and the creeds; and a grudging acknowledgement of a right of unfettered private assembly granted to those who denied

the authority of scripture or credal statements about the Trinity. Such groups were not in general compelled to witness against conscience, but nor were they allowed to proselytize their beliefs. This is one of the contexts in which to place Cromwell's strong personal advocacy of readmitting the Jews. He encouraged the Amsterdam rabbi Manasseh ben Israel, in his embassy to London, to plead for the formal readmission of the Jews, and when it became clear that a majority of the council would not support it Cromwell ruled that since their exclusion had been based solely on a royal edict, he could readmit them without consulting council or parliament.

Nothing caused Cromwell more pain or gradual disillusionment than his uphill struggle against the narrow-mindedness of a majority of MPs (and of his councillors) over the extension of religious liberty, especially given the continuing shrill demands for special privilege from so many of the sects. A comparison between his vision of 1653 and his nightmare of 1658 is especially poignant. He exhorted the nominated assembly to:

> be faithful with the Saints; to be touched with them … In my pilgrimage and some exercises I have had abroad, I did read that Scripture often in Isaiah 41:19 … what would [God] do. To what end? That he might plant in the wilderness the cedar and the [acacia] tree, and the myrtle and palm tree together. To what end? That they might know and consider and understand together that the hand of the Lord hath done this. (*Speeches*, 22, 4 July 1653)

It was a vision of 'the various forms of godliness in this nation' respecting one another, learning from one another, growing together in trust and love.

Eighteen months later, reproving the first protectorate parliament as he dissolved it, Cromwell said he had hoped that they would have 'upheld and given countenance to a Godly ministry, and yet would have given a just liberty to Godly men of different judgments'. Yet:

> is there not yet upon the spirit of men a strange itch? Nothing will satisfy them, unless they can put their finger upon their brethren's consciences, to pinch them there … Is it ingenuous to ask liberty, and not to give it? What greater hypocrisy than for those who were oppressed by the bishops to become the greatest oppressors themselves so soon as their yoke was removed? (*Speeches*, 66–7, 22 Jan 1658)

And by January 1658 the irritation at the pinching of conscience had become something much more disturbing:

> What is that which possesses every sect? What is it? That every sect may be uppermost … we have an appetite to variety, to be not only making wounds, but as if we should see one making wounds in a man's side and would desire nothing more than to be groping and grovelling with his fingers in those wounds. This is what all men will be at … They will be making wounds, and rending and tearing and making them wider than they are. (ibid., 180–81, 25 Jan 1658)

Cromwell continued to aspire to see the law reformed, and in particular to see a greater equity and social justice introduced into legal proceedings. As he put it to his second parliament on 17 September 1656:

> The great grievance lies in the execution and administration … The truth of it is there are wicked abominable laws that will be in your power to alter. To hang a man for sixpence, thirteen pence, I know not what; to hang for a trifle and

pardon a murder, is in the ministration of the Law, through the ill framing of it. I have known in my experience abominable murders quitted; and to come and see men lose their lives for petty matters. (*Speeches*, 99)

How far Cromwell personally influenced the parliament, or the council, or the judges, to address this beyond such exhortations is not clear. Perhaps significantly, this outburst immediately follows within the speech of 17 September 1656 his passionate defence of what the major-generals had achieved in respect to the 'reformation of manners'—by the stricter enforcement of the legislation against fornication, drunkenness, gambling, sabbath-breaking. He linked this campaign by a statement of his fundamental social conservatism, his desire to maintain the social order but to make every person more aware of the duties and responsibilities of their station:

> We would keep up the nobility and gentry; and the way to keep them up is, not to suffer them to be patronizers nor countenancers of debauchery or disorders; and you will be hereby but as labourers in the work ... The liberty and profaneness of this nation depends upon reformation, to make it a shame to see men to be bold in sin and profaneness. And God will bless you. (*Speeches*, 98)

In foreign policy, too, disillusionment gradually set in. Cromwell had a grand design in foreign affairs that he outlined to his second parliament: to use his influence and naval power to bring peace to protestant princes warring against one another (above all, peace among the Baltic protestant princes), and to renew the onslaught on Spanish power—'your great enemy is the Spaniard. He is. He is a natural enemy, he is naturally so' (*Speeches*, 81, 17 Sept 1656). He wanted peace with the Dutch, an alliance with France, and a war with Spain. Most of the details were left to the council. His own personal obsession, the expedition to seize Hispaniola (Dominica), was a disastrous failure, the occupation of Jamaica being taken as no substitute. Cromwell saw in that failure a rebuff from God, and it troubled him that God was displeased with him. But the hammering out of foreign policy cost him dearly. It led to serious divisions in the council, difficult and protracted negotiations, and unwelcome compromises. Thus the alliance with France, bearable because French protestants enjoyed a liberty of religion denied to subjects of the Spanish king, was utterly compromised when the duke of Savoy, a creature of the French government, undertook a massacre of his protestant subjects in the Valltelline in Piedmont. The worldly compromise over this matter that allowed Cromwell to remain in alliance with France troubled his conscience. As he lay dying, according to an anonymous letter to William Clarke, secretary to the army, he cried out 'what will they do with the poor protestants of the Piedmont, in Poland and other places' (F. Henderson, 'New material from the Clarke papers', DPhil diss., University of Oxford, 1998, 430–31). Cromwell took similar responsibility for the shaping of policy in Scotland and Ireland while leaving those on the ground and in his secretariat to work out the details. His concern at the very harsh settlement that the Rump had introduced into Ireland, reinforced by the tough militarism of Major-General Charles Fleetwood as lord deputy,

led Cromwell to send his younger son, the assured and pragmatic Henry Cromwell, to bring an end to the plan to herd all the Catholics into the west of Ireland and to soften the policies against the Catholic religion and the participation of Catholics in trade and agriculture. More dramatically, it was very much at his own insistence that two men who had supported the king in Ireland in the period leading up to 1647—Major-General George Monck and Roger Boyle, Lord Broghill, younger brother of the earl of Cork—were won over to the Commonwealth regime in Ireland and then brought over to head the military and civil establishments in Scotland. Cromwell interfered counter-productively in the feuding among Scottish presbyterians, and gave too much authority over religion in Scotland to one faction of 'protesters' who lacked the strength in depth and social clout to be able to bring any stability.

The rule of law The protectorate was successful in achieving the widespread acquiescence of the English people, and towards its end there were only 6000 men in arms in England to maintain order. But Cromwell still needed 40,000 men to police Scotland and Ireland. The high taxation needed to fund them (and the expeditionary force serving with the French in Flanders, and by the time of his death garrisoning Dunkirk on a semi-permanent basis) nourished a low-level unpopularity of the regime. However much Cromwell might present himself in smart, sober, civilian clothes, he was still thought of as General Cromwell. The garrisons around the country were a law unto themselves: they were kept under strict and severe military discipline, but when their officers used them to menace civil magistrates into releasing Quakers from prison, or to assist in the distraint of taxes, or to press local freemen to vote a certain way in a local election, there was little civilian redress.

The abject failure of the royalist risings in the spring of 1655 showed how acquiescent the English had become, but it also showed how little active support Cromwell could count upon among the county élites. If few rose in arms to challenge the regime, few rose in arms to support it. Everyone outside the army waited upon events. Cromwell was persuaded by Lambert to embark on a bold experiment. If people disliked the regime because there were too many soldiers and too much tax, then let both be halved and replaced by efficient, well-trained and equipped 'select militias', made up mainly of demobilized veterans and paid for by a 10 per cent 'decimation' tax on the income of all convicted royalists. And let the scheme be under the management of eleven senior officers (the major-generals) each responsible for a bloc of counties, and assisted by bodies of activist shire commissioners. To Lambert's brief Cromwell added his own: they were to wage war on vice and promote the reformation of manners. It was in that aspect of their work that he took a close personal interest.

When the scheme came under remorseless attack in December 1656 and January 1657 it was principally because the major-generals, and the decimation tax they collected, were unconstitutional and against law and custom. To levy discriminatory taxation on ex-royalists was a clear breach of the Indemnity Act that Cromwell had campaigned for so vigorously in 1652. To levy taxation without parliamentary consent was against both the ancient and the modern constitution. There was a deep principle at stake here. If he and the council could arbitrarily tax ex-royalists, could he not arbitrarily tax everyone? In his speech of 17 September 1656 Cromwell tried to brazen it out:

> There was a little thing invented, which was the erecting of your major generals … we invented this, so justifiable [as] to necessity, so honest in every respect. Truly, if ever I think anything were honest, this was, as anything that ever I knew; and I could as soon venture my life with it as anything I ever undertook. (*Speeches*, 92)

The ends justified the means. There was in Cromwell no respect for the past, no sense of the integrity of the law, no legitimation to be found in antiquity or custom, just as there was no legitimacy to be found in majoritarian consent. God looked to the future not the past. His providences did not seal moulds but broke them. And God spoke through the remnant and not through the reprobate majority. Despite a longing for all to be freed from slavery to the flesh for freedom in the spirit, until that time came, legitimation would be found not in a hallowed past or a consensual present but a yearned-for future.

In this speech Cromwell defended not only the creation of major-generals and the levying of arbitrary taxes, but also the imprisonment of men without trial in gaols in the Scilly Isles and the Isle of Wight—beyond the reach of writs of habeas corpus. He defended the making of law outside parliament: 'if nothing should ever be done but what is according to law, the throat of the nation may be cut while we send for some to make a law' (*Speeches*, 100, 17 Sept 1656). George Cony refused to pay customs duty on the silk he was importing on the strong ground that the protector's right to customs lapsed with the dissolution of the first parliament. To ensure that Cony lost the case, the council, with Cromwell's consent, imprisoned both Cony and his lawyers until they agreed to withdraw their suit. It was for attitudes such as these that the lawyers and pragmatic gentry of his second parliament sought to make him king. For (although given their wars with Charles I this was not without irony), a king was shackled by the past, to act in accordance with ancient law and custom, and bound to seek the consent of the people through parliament in the making of law, the establishment of penalties, and the granting of taxation. Parliament's vote in December 1656 to have James Nayler publicly mutilated for his blasphemy only added to the cry for a return to known ways. Cromwell was shaken by their action, but powerless to prevent it. The timing of the offer of the crown, just after the Nayler affair and the debates on the major-generals, is indicative. Cromwell was in large part offered the crown not to further enhance his authority but to circumscribe the power of the protectorate itself, as well as the power of its ill-defined executive, legislative, and judicial bodies.

King Oliver Rumours that Cromwell was to be made king can be found throughout the protectorate. Cromwell had aired it with Whitelocke late in 1652, but he ruled it out when it was in the first draft of the 'Instrument'. Yet rumour continued to flourish. For example, the Swedish ambassador sent a long dispatch home on 1 June 1655 carefully laying out twelve arguments for and three against Cromwell's becoming king: his prediction was that Cromwell would assume the title shortly thereafter. So it was not a bolt out of the blue when Alderman Sir Christopher Packe, acting for a group within and far beyond the council, proposed on 23 February 1657 that Cromwell be king under a contract that modified the terms of the 'Instrument', strengthening his personal authority as against that of the council but prescribing his power in relation to the ancient constitution and unshackled parliaments. Indeed, he was to have one new power greater than that of the old monarchy: the freedom to nominate his own successor. Cromwell from early on indicated a willingness to accept everything except the title. Parliament tried to bluff him into it by maintaining it was all or nothing. In the battle of wills that followed the house cracked first. Cromwell was to become king in all but name.

Cromwell spoke to the Commons, or to its negotiating committee, on nine occasions between 31 March and 25 May 1657. There is no reason to doubt his agony of mind and conscience. It is true that his colleagues in the army, those he had fought alongside in battle after battle, lobbied relentlessly against the title. It is not right, however, to conclude that he was intimidated out of becoming king. Intellectually, he was fully persuaded: 'I am hugely taken with this word "settlement"' (*Speeches*, 144, 21 April 1657); 'I cannot take upon me to refel [refute] those grounds, for they are strong and rational' (ibid., 129, 13 April 1657). Yet his conscience would not give him leave: 'it would savour more to be of the flesh, to proceed from lust, to arise from arguments of self-love … it may prove even a curse to these three nations' (ibid., 136, 13 April 1657). He waited upon a clear sign from God (a great victory over the Spaniard?) and it never came:

> God has seemed providentially not only to strike at the family but at the name … He hath blasted the title … I would not seek to set up that which Providence hath destroyed and laid in the dust, and I would not build Jericho again. (ibid., 137, 13 April 1657)

And so he turned it down. He just could not see how it could be God's will that he accept the title. But five times in his speech of 13 April 1657 (*Speeches*, 128–37) he repeats: God has blasted the title and the name. But what of the office that the name signified? Would God have the kingly office renamed, as he had had the jurisdiction of bishops in the primitive church retained but in offices which no longer bore the name of bishop? Could he, Cromwell, discharge the duties and responsibilities of king as the earthly surrogate of Jesus, the only true king? This tortured logic may have persuaded him to be king-like in power and display but without the blasted title. God would have his vicar ruling, an upper house consisting of a spiritual aristocracy nominated by this vicar-protector, and a restoration of that which could bring healing and settling to a still-broken people.

Cromwell's death and its aftermath Then the dusk of life closed in, and with the dusk a sea-mist. The last few months were months of idling. Cromwell's health declined steeply, and he became much preoccupied by the terrible suffering and death from cancer of his beloved daughter Elizabeth. Despite rumour at the time that what the assassin's bullets had failed to achieve, insidious poisons did achieve, it is overwhelmingly likely that the malarial fevers that had troubled him at time of stress ever since the early 1630s came back to haunt him and triggered a chest infection and pneumonia from which he died. Alternating between fevered dreams and moments of lucidity, he died at Whitehall at three in the afternoon on 3 September 1658, on the anniversary of the 'eminent mercy' at Dunbar and the 'crowning mercy' of Worcester.

Under the 'Humble petition and advice', Cromwell had the duty to nominate his successor. There was no other mechanism for the transfer of power. Amazingly there was no written designation. Thurloe reported that he had been told that there was one sealed up but that he could not find it. Can Cromwell have been so careless? He had seen too much of sudden death to be unmindful of his own mortality. Indeed he carried a loaded musket with him whenever he went out for fear of assassins and once, in 1654, he almost killed himself when his musket exploded as he was dragged behind some bolting horses. Conspiracy theories—that John Thurloe broke the seal of the written nomination, did not like what he read in it, (the likely names were John Lambert or Charles Fleetwood) and destroyed it—should not be lightly dismissed. However, recent discoveries in the shorthand letters of William Clarke strengthen the case for Cromwell's having made a lucid and clear nomination of his eldest surviving son, Richard, in the presence of witnesses, during his final hours.

After his death a wooden effigy of Cromwell with a wax mask lay in state at Somerset House vested with his robe of estate, a sceptre placed in one hand, an orb in the other, with a crown laid on a velvet cushion a little above his head. The ceremony was modelled on the lying-in-state of James I. Thus was Cromwell crowned in death, his scruples no longer carrying weight. The fact that it was not Cromwell himself was because embalmers had bungled. When the body began to putrefy it was decided to proceed rapidly with burial; it was secretly interred, probably on 4 or 5 September in Westminster Abbey. It was thus the effigy, not the corpse, which made a sombre and ill-planned progress on 23 November through the streets of London—largely deserted, say the contemporary diarists, all predisposed to wish it so—so that it arrived at Westminster Abbey at nightfall; and no-one had organized candles. So there was no ceremony in the abbey. The coffin was placed on a sumptuous catafalque—again based on Inigo Jones's design for that of James VI and I—in Henry VII's chapel in the abbey.

There Cromwell remained—his body and his effigy, presumably—until after the Restoration. Then the vengeful Convention Parliament decreed that he, like others who signed the king's death warrant, should suffer the fate of traitors. It was decided that Cromwell, Ireton, John Bradshaw, and Thomas Pride should be exhumed and their bodies desecrated on the twelfth anniversary of the regicide, 30 January 1661. For reasons never adequately explained except by conspiracy theorists, Cromwell's body was removed from the abbey on 26 January and moved to the paddock behind an inn in Holborn. From there it was taken to Tyburn on 30 January. Unsurprisingly it has long been claimed that this was to allow another body to be substituted for his actual body (Bradshaw's body was brought directly from the abbey, his grave being opened only on 29 January). A body purporting to be Cromwell's was hanged in its cerecloth for several hours, then decapitated. The body was put into a lime-pit below the gallows and the head, impaled on a spike, was exposed at the south end of Westminster Hall for nearly two decades before being rescued during the exclusion crisis. Descendants of his daughter Mary have the best of several similar claims that the bodies were exchanged and that Cromwell's undivided body lies in their family vault in Newburgh Park, near Coxwold in the North Riding of Yorkshire. Another tradition has the skull rescued from Westminster Hall in or about 1688 and surviving with a fairly complete itinerary—as a fairground exhibit, or one brought out at dinner parties in great houses—until it was acquired by Cromwell's descendants and by them donated to Sidney Sussex, Cromwell's college in Cambridge, where it was interred in an unmarked grave in 1960.

Posthumous reputation Cromwell's reputation has ebbed and flowed. Since the death of the generation that knew him as their head of state more than 160 full-length biographies have appeared, and more than 1000 separate publications bear his name. In 1929 Wilbur Cortez Abbott, limbering up to produce his four-volume, 3400-page, 2-million-word edition and commentary, *The Writings and Speeches of Oliver Cromwell*, produced a bibliography of 3520 pamphlets, books, and essays in which Cromwell makes a prominent appearance. An updated list would probably be in excess of 6000 items. There was a crescendo of interest in the later nineteenth century, triggered by the appearance of Thomas Carlyle's edition of Cromwell's letters and speeches in December 1845.

It had not been ever thus. In the immediate aftermath of Cromwell's death several journalistic biographies appeared, together with Henry Daubeny's edgy attempt to find thirty lengthy parallels between Cromwell's life and that of Moses. There was then a moment of republican scorn in the winter of 1659–60 which was overtaken by sensationalist synthetic royalist rage. This reached its apogee in James Heath's *Flagellum* (6 edns, 1662–81), but from the 1660s Cromwell's name rather dropped into the background. Fewer titles invoking it appeared between 1663 and 1700 than in the years 1660–63. The whigs did not seek to rehabilitate him and the tories used him as a bogeyman more than as someone whose career needed rehearsal. When there was a brief revival of interest in the 1690s it took the form of hostile parallels between Cromwell and William III: such parallels were promoted both by Jacobite authors and by those deist-republicans around John Toland who re-edited the work of Edmund Ludlow to highlight the parallels between the two military 'tyrants'.

As personal memory faded and death carried away those who could testify from experience, and with the tracts of the 1640s and 1650s locked away in private libraries and little known to a new generation of pamphleteers, Cromwell became less known than at any later period. When Britain became once more sucked into major wars in the 1690s with the mobilization of huge armies and a financial and administrative revolution to sustain them, memories of the previous military dictatorship were revived by the publication of the memoirs of many of the men at the heart of the period: to those of Bulstrode Whitelocke (1682) were added between 1696 and 1704 those of Richard Baxter, Edmund Ludlow, and Denzil Holles, and Clarendon's *History of the Rebellion*. This represents a wonderful cross-section of opinion. All (with the exception of Ludlow) were men who both admired and deplored Cromwell. Their memoirs set the tone for eighteenth-century discussions. Gentlemen of letters were unanimous in seeing him as dangerous and fanatical, although the degree of his self-interested dissimulation differs as between the unrelieved contempt of the tories and the regretful whigs. John Hampden and John Pym, fortunate in the time of their deaths, were the respectable witnesses against royal and episcopal tyranny. As David Hume put it, Cromwell was the 'most frantic enthusiast … most dangerous of hypocrites … who was enabled after multiplied deceits to cover, under a tempest of passion, all his crooked schemes and profound artifices' (Richardson, 64–5). There was a blunter, unvarnished literature generated within and for the dissenting communities that recognized his strivings for a religious liberty grounded in religious and civil egalitarianism. There were, above all, three biographies, by Isaac Kimber (1724), John Banks (1739), and William Harris (1762), which were never noticed outside dissenting circles but may well have been influential within them. Thus while it is not easy to find Cromwell being evoked in any systematic way in any political campaign during the radical awakening of 1770–1830 (although the bogey of regicide was used by government agents against both the Wilkites in the 1770s and the Foxites in the 1790s), Elizabeth Gaskell could write that in the nonconformist villages of the West Riding in the 1820s the phrase 'in Oliver's days' denoted a time of prosperity, and in 1812 an anonymous threat was sent to the government noting that 'it was time a second Oliver made his appearance' (Richardson, 99).

The transformation of Cromwell into a dominant figure in British public memory can be closely linked to the publication of Thomas Carlyle's *Letters and Speeches of Oliver Cromwell* in December 1845. It was to remain continuously in print in inexpensive editions for exactly 100 years. At a conservative estimate more than 100,000 copies were sold, and many were handed down from generation to generation. Thomas Macaulay had begun the process of rehabilitation twenty years before, but Carlyle's edition took the world by storm. It is a passionate defence of Cromwell's sincerity, of his faith in God, in his living out his vocation and his mission. Carlyle's Cromwell had a contempt for democracy, an unreflective belief in spiritual aristocracy, a rough-tongued, cloudily articulated integrity. Deficiencies of scholarship and Carlyle's own obtrusive interpolations disfigure his text, but did not dull its impact. It emboldened the views of Congregational historians like John Forster who had earlier taken a more cautious line on Cromwell. Now—in the best available summation of Carlyle's Cromwell—he hailed the new Cromwell as:

> no hypocrite or actor of plays … no victim of ambition, no seeker after sovereignty or temporal power. That he was a man whose every thought was with the Eternal—a man of a great, robust, massive, mind and an honest, stout, English heart. (Lang, 133–4)

One unintended consequence of Carlyle's edition was certainly to make Cromwell the champion of a particular denomination—Congregationalism—and of its history. His preference for a broad national church with a public ministry within which the great majority would hear the word of God, sing his praises, and submit themselves to gentle correction for their sins passed the Victorians by. He became first and foremost the spokesman for Victorian middle England and of responsible self-reliant nonconformity. It is striking that when in 1899, for the very first time, commemorative events to mark a major Cromwellian anniversary were held, they were all organized through and controlled by the Congregational and Baptist churches. At the London ceremony David Lloyd George proclaimed that he believed in Cromwell because 'he was a great fighting dissenter' (*The Times*, 26 April 1899, 12). Rather more preposterously, another nonconformist MP, R. W. Perks, claimed on the same occasion that:

> the modern equivalent of the seventeenth-century Puritan, was the possessor of the Non-conformist conscience, who now raised his voice against the desecration of the Lord's Day, against the gambling saloon, the drink bar, the haunt of vice, and the overwhelming power of brute force. (*The Times*, 28 April 1899, 8)

In addition the tercentenary of 1899 also stabilized Cromwell's academic reputation. Both Samuel Rawson Gardiner and Sir Charles Firth wrote biographies. Supervised by Firth, Mrs S. C. Lomas re-edited Carlyle, checking and correcting his transcriptions and adding more than 200 pages of material that had come to light since 1845. It was unfortunate that this edition—welcome though it was and is—appeared more or less simultaneously with a truly scholarly edition of the speeches by C. L. Stainer (based on an Oxford DPhil dissertation). That edition remains the benchmark and finally gained acceptance when used as the basis of Ivan Roots's popular edition in 1989 (though without Stainer's scholarly apparatus). This, together with the new editions—mainly by Firth—of many little-known papers in which Cromwell played a prominent part (the Putney debates, rediscovered by Firth in 1890, and the memoirs of Lucy Hutchinson and Edmund Ludlow), brought a new solidity to Cromwell studies. In the course of the twentieth century the American scholar W. C. Abbott undertook a fundamental new edition of all Cromwell's words on the page and in reported speech. Unfortunately, his scholarship was sloppy, his way of organizing the material requires the patience of a saint from all its users, and Abbott became one of several leading scholars shallowly convinced that Cromwell was a forebear of the Fascist dictators. So a great opportunity was missed. Since 1945 Cromwell biographies have become gradually more sympathetic in tone. Even Christopher Hill, who in *God's Englishman* (1970) portrayed a Cromwell who came increasingly to betray the revolution he had done so much to create, rooted himself firmly within Cromwell's own terms of reference and self-representation. For that was the key. The twenty most widely read biographies—from John Buchan's and Antonia Fraser's accounts aimed at a general readership, through Robert Paul's account, which echoes at a high level of sympathy and engagement the denominational tradition of the nineteenth-century Congregationalists, to those aiming principally at a student audience (the most recent of which are those of Barry Coward, Peter Gaunt, and J. C. Davis)—work within a very clear set of conventions. The authors have read all the letters (some 500 of which can be confidently said to have been Cromwell's own work), twenty major and many minor speeches, and the much less reliable summaries by others of what he is reported to have said. They weigh the evidence of his self-representation against the testimony of contemporary tracts and of personal memoirs. All the serious biographies have drawn on very similar bodies of evidence. And although the judgement of the vast majority of his peers is harsh in its assessment of his honesty, integrity, and credibility, historians have opted to take him much more at his own valuation, finding in his words an openness and striving that usually appeals and just sometimes appals.

Yet throughout the period during which Cromwell's reputation in England was gaining ground, his name was becoming reviled in Ireland. For the first 200 years after the conquest he had been subsumed in Catholic—at least in English-language Catholic—writing in a long list of English men of violence, and in ascendancy writing his religious fanaticism relegated him as hero to a status far below that of King Billy. But with the recovery of Irish-language folklore in the nineteenth century, and with the emergence of a new kind of Irish nationalism, Cromwell was demonized. This new harsh view was adumbrated in J. P. Prendergast's *The Cromwellian Settlement of Ireland* (1865), and reinforced by Father Denis Murphy's *Cromwell in Ireland* (1883), a book which became the basis of a century of Irish school textbooks, popular novels (of which Walter Macken's best-selling *Seek the Fair Land*, 1959, was the culmination), and popular songs (such as 'Once upon a Time', sung by Sinéad O'Connor at a demonstration outside the British embassy in Dublin in August 1989).

Cromwell was memorialized not only in print but on canvas, in woodcut and engraving, and in marble and bronze. He is one of the most familiar of Englishmen, more familiar to more people certainly than all but a handful of English monarchs or British public figures. The first statue of him by Matthew Noble was erected in Manchester in 1875 followed by three more statues in his tercentenary year: the Hamo Thornycroft statue erected outside the palace of Westminster after testy parliamentary debate in 1899; in Warrington a statue presented by a local businessman, which shows Cromwell addressing his troops and Scottish prisoners after the battle of Preston, a statue which inappropriately has 'Holy Bible' engraved on the back not the front of the book he is holding; and perhaps the finest of them all, the statue by Frederick William Pomeroy in St Ives, raised opportunistically after the town council of Huntingdon had declined it. The statue by Thornycroft of Cromwell, Bible in one hand, sword in the other, which has stood on Cromwell Green since the tercentenary of his birth in 1899, is one of the most visible and noticeable statues in the country. The contemporary portraits by Robert Walker (two of them), Samuel Cooper (four miniatures), and Peter Lely have been endlessly reproduced not only in lives of Cromwell but in lives of the men and women of his time. They in turn inspired many of the 750 engravings listed by W. C. Abbott in his catalogue which includes work noticed by him in 1930. The vast majority show him as a soldier, as a martial man of God, evoking (sympathetically or unsympathetically) his puritanism, either through the characteristic plain style of his collars protruding from his armour or his holding of a Bible. There was at least one Victorian Staffordshire pottery figurine manufactured as a chimney ornament; but it does not seem to have caught on. More surprisingly he is memorialized in stained glass, in prominent windows in the Victorian Congregational church in St Andrews Street, Cambridge, and in the chapel of Mansfield College, Oxford.

Cromwell is memorialized musically. A folk song bearing his name was edited by Benjamin Britten in 1938. A nursery rhyme which can be first traced back to the late seventeenth century begins 'Oliver Cromwell lay buried and dead, hee-haw, buried and dead', and tells how his wraith rose and 'gave a drop' to an old woman gathering apples that had fallen on his grave. The most extraordinary musical evocation is undoubtedly the rendering of a John Cleese prose poem by the Monty Python team (on the recording *Monty Python Sings*, 1989) that tells the life of Cromwell set to the music of a polonaise by Chopin.

Cromwell is memorialized institutionally. Isaac Foot, prominent liberal politician of the 1920s and 1930s, established in 1935 the Cromwell Association. It has always had a membership of hundreds rather than of thousands, but it has worked effectively to extend knowledge and understanding of Cromwell and of his age. It has erected memorial plaques on battlefields and other Cromwellian sites; it has promoted publications about Cromwell and has held competitions to encourage the study of Cromwell by adults and children; and it holds an annual service of thanksgiving by the Thornycroft statue. The association in its early days collected many artefacts associated with Cromwell and these, together with a larger group owned by his descendants, form the basis of the collection held by the Cromwell Museum, which is in the Huntingdon schoolroom he once attended. The house he owned in Ely is also a museum, and an information and education centre. The Cromwell Association and the Cromwell Museum jointly set up a website in 1999 which promotes his memory and jointly co-ordinated the activities of more than thirty museums, galleries, and sites during the Cromwell quatercentenary year. It is doubtful if any other non-royal Englishman is so diversely commemorated.

Cromwell is also memorialized by name. George V prevented Churchill, as first lord of the admiralty, from naming a battleship the *Cromwell* in the First World War, but royal influence was less persuasive elsewhere. The first colleges established by the Congregational Church for training ministers in Australia, Canada, and South Africa bear his name. More than 250 roads in Britain bear his name, in all the metropolitan boroughs except for Birmingham and in most county towns; a great majority of these roads and streets comprise Victorian or Edwardian terraces, the backbone of late nineteenth-century nonconformity (though Cromwell Road in South Kensington was given its name at the suggestion of Prince Albert). No lay person other than Wellington approaches him in this respect. On the other hand, on the 400th anniversary of his birth on 25 April 1999 only three inns and public houses bore his name, although there were more than 400 websites on the internet bearing it. These included one devoted to Cromwell as an exemplar of good family values, one devoted to exploring his institutionalized violence against the people of Ireland, several devoted to making available key passages from his letters and speeches, and one devoted to commemorating a black slave who had been given the name Oliver Cromwell and had been decorated for his courage in the American Civil War.

Cromwell's role in fiction is also extensive. The earliest play bearing his name was George Smith Green's *Oliver Cromwell: an Historical Play* (1752), followed by the anonymous *Cromwell, or, The Days of the Commonwealth* (1832). He is the hero of Victor Hugo's melodrama *Oliver Cromwell* (1828), although it seems that a 1923 London production was the play's first staging in England. Six other plays that either bear his name or in which he is the central figure were staged in the West End (most of them in the 1920s). He was the anti-hero of Henry William Herbert's *Oliver Cromwell: a Historical Novel* (1838), and he had more than a walk-on part in Alexandre Dumas's *Vingt ans après* (1845)—a sequel to *The Three Musketeers*, Captain Marryat's children's classic, *Children of the New Forest* (1846), James Kirke Paulding's *The Puritan and his Daughter* (1849), by an effectively anti-British American writer, and G. J. Whyte-Melville's *Holmby House* (1860). In all of them he is a grim, unsmiling, self-righteous puritan, a literary equivalent of 'when did you last see your father?' In contrast most Victorian realizations of civil-war scenes in which he

appears, such as Daniel Maclise's *Interview between Charles I and Cromwell*, Ford Madox Brown's *Cromwell on his Farm*, or Edward Croft's *Cromwell after Marston Moor* show him as grim, determined, but virtuously purposeful. Although actors playing Cromwell have appeared in a number of feature films (such as Alan Howard's portrayal of him in *The Return of the Musketeers*), only one feature film has been made specifically about him—*Cromwell*, which improbably cast the Irish tearaway actor Richard Harris as the hero (although Alec Guinness's charismatically prim Charles I stole the show). But Cromwell has been the subject of much television drama, from John Hopkins's *Cruel Necessity* in 1962, in which Patrick Wymark bore an uncanny likeness to him, onwards. Between 1985 and 2000 at least six programmes devoted to him were produced for British terrestrial television. He remains one of the most recognizable of Englishmen.

Conclusion Recognizable for what? Cromwell was not a great thinker. In 1638 he told his young cousin 'that if here I may serve my God either by my doing or by my suffering, I shall be most glad' (*Letters and Speeches*, 1904, letter 2, 13 Oct 1638). It was his motto and his epitaph. He did not enjoy power. It was thrust upon him. He was not especially intelligent, and was quite unintellectual, lacking a deep understanding of law, of the classics, of theology. He had a deep sense of being propelled by God into leading his people towards a promised land. He had an imperfect sense of what the promised land would look like, and only a magpie instinct for picking up the latest bright and shiny idea of how to make the next move towards it. Those whose ideas he took up all too briefly felt the warm glow of his approval. He then moved on to the next idea, and abandoned the people as well as the ideas that had not worked. This is why he was so resented and so distrusted by those he affirmed and then abandoned—John Lilburne and Charles's intimates in 1647, the Independent politicians in 1648, Sir Henry Vane in 1653, Thomas Harrison in 1653, John Lambert in 1657. He could never make the adjustment from war where the objective was always clear and the victory unambiguous. The pragmatism and compromise of the political arena constantly dismayed him and ground him down. All this cost him in personal terms. He yearned to 'keep a flock of sheep under a woodside', to emulate Gideon who led the armies of Israel and then returned to his farm. But God would not let him go. God would have him serve. And still there was before him the mirage of a perfected humanity. He had seen that corrupted institutions could not deliver a humanity more obedient to the will of God. He was called to overthrow tyranny and pride and replace it with humility and a common concern to share the fragments of truth that so many men of goodwill had been granted. But instead pride and self-interest kept on taking over. As he climbed another barren hill and peered over the next sun-baked valley, the mirage reappeared. What makes Oliver Cromwell endlessly appealing and endlessly alarming is that he was true to his own vision. He never doubted his call to service or to salvation. He knew enough of the Bible to know that all those whom God called, he chastened. The fierceness of his determination to free all those whose sense of God shared elements of his own experience drove him into uncomfortable action. He was not wedded and glued to forms of government. He was not bound by human law. If God called upon him to be the human instrument of his wrath, he would not flinch. His sense of himself as the unworthy and suffering servant of a stern Lord protected him from the tragic megalomanias of others who rose to absolute power on the backs of revolutions. Cromwell's achievements as a soldier are great but unfashionable; as a religious libertarian great but easily mis-stated; as a statesman inevitably stunted. No man who rises from a working farmer to head of state in twenty years is other than great. To achieve that and still to be able to say that 'if here I may serve my God either by my doing or by my suffering, I shall be most glad' is a man of towering integrity. He was to himself and to his God most true, if at great cost to himself and others. JOHN MORRILL

Sources *The letters and speeches of Oliver Cromwell with elucidations by Thomas Carlyle* (1845–) [cited by item no., which remains constant] • *The letters and speeches of Oliver Cromwell*, ed. T. Carlyle and S. C. Lomas, 3 vols. (1904) • *Speeches of Oliver Cromwell*, ed. I. Roots (1989) [based on the texts prepared for an Oxford DPhil by C. L. Stainer, pubd 1901] • *The writings and speeches of Oliver Cromwell*, ed. W. C. Abbott and C. D. Crane, 4 vols. (1937–47) • W. C. Abbott, *Bibliography of Oliver Cromwell* (1929) • J. Heath, *Flagellum, or, The life and death, birth and burial of O. Cromwell, the late usurper*, 4th edn (1669) • J. Bruce and D. Masson, eds., *The quarrel between the earl of Manchester and Oliver Cromwell*, CS, new ser., 12 (1875) • *The Clarke papers*, ed. C. H. Firth, 4 vols., CS, new ser., 49, 54, 61–2 (1891–1901) • *The diary of Bulstrode Whitelocke, 1605–1675*, ed. R. Spalding, British Academy, Records of Social and Economic History, new ser., 13 (1990) • [B. Whitelocke], *Memorials of the English affairs* (1682) • *The memoirs of Edmund Ludlow*, ed. C. H. Firth, 2 vols. (1894) • S. R. Gardiner, *Constitutional documents of the puritan revolution, 1625–1660*, 3rd edn (1906) • P. Gaunt, *A Cromwellian gazetteer* (1987) • P. Gaunt, *Oliver Cromwell* (1996) • J. C. Davis, *Oliver Cromwell* (2001) • J. S. Morrill, ed., *Oliver Cromwell and the English revolution* (1990) • B. Coward, *Oliver Cromwell* (1991) • R. S. Paul, *The lord protector: religion and politics in the life of Oliver Cromwell* (1958) • R. Howell, *Cromwell* (1977) • C. Hill, *God's Englishman: Oliver Cromwell and the English revolution* (1970) • C. H. Firth, *Oliver Cromwell and the rule of the puritans* (1900) • S. R. Gardiner, *Cromwell's place in history* (1898) • P. Warwick, *Memoires of the reign of King Charles I* (1701) • J. Buchan, *Oliver Cromwell* (1934) • A. Fraser, *Cromwell, our chief of men* (1973) • J. Gillingham, *Portrait of a soldier: Cromwell* (1976) • A. Woolrych, *Oliver Cromwell* (1964) • C. H. Firth, *Cromwell's army*, 3rd edn (1921) • J. P. Prendergast, *The Cromwellian settlement of Ireland* (1865) • D. Murphy, *Cromwell in Ireland: a history of Cromwell's Irish campaign* (1883) • T. Reilly, *Cromwell the honourable enemy: the untold story of the Cromwellian invasion of Ireland* (1999) • J. S. Wheeler, *Cromwell in Ireland* (2000) • T. Barnard, *Cromwellian Ireland*, rev. edn (2000) • J. D. Grainger, *Cromwell against the Scots: the last Anglo-Scottish war, 1650–1652* (1997) • C. H. Firth, ed., *Scotland and the Commonwealth: letters and papers relating to the military government of Scotland, from August 1651 to December 1653*, Scottish History Society, 18 (1895) • D. Stevenson, *Revolution and counter-revolution in Scotland, 1644–1651*, Royal Historical Society Studies in History, 4 (1977) • F. D. Dow, *Cromwellian Scotland, 1651–1660* (1979) • I. Roots, ed., *Cromwell: a profile* (1973) • J. Morrill, ed., *Reactions to the English civil war, 1642–1649* (1982) • S. R. Gardiner, *History of the great civil war, 1642–1649*, new edn, 4 vols. (1893) • A. Woolrych, *Britain in revolution, 1625–1660* (2002) • C. Holmes, *The eastern association in the English civil war* (1974) • A. Woolrych, *Soldiers and statesmen: the general council of the army and its debates, 1647–1648* (1987) • M. Mendle, ed., *The Putney debates of 1647: the army, the Levellers and the English state* (2001) •

J. Peacey, ed., *The regicides and the execution of Charles I* (2001) • R. Ashton, *Counter-revolution: the second civil war and its origins, 1646–8* (1994) • I. Gentles, *The New Model Army in England, Ireland, and Scotland, 1645–1653* (1992) • S. R. Gardiner, *History of the Commonwealth and protectorate, 1649–1656*, new edn, 4 vols. (1903) • C. H. Firth, *The last years of the protectorate*, 2 vols. (1911) • G. E. Aylmer, ed., *The interregnum* (1973) • C. Jones, M. Newitt, and S. Roberts, eds., *Politics and people in revolutionary England* (1986) • D. Underdown, *Pride's Purge: politics in the puritan revolution* (1971) • B. Worden, *The Rump Parliament, 1648–1653* (1974) • D. Norbrook, *Writing the English republic* (1998) • S. Kelsey, *Inventing the republic* (1997) • A. Woolrych, *Commonwealth to protectorate* (1982) • R. Sherwood, *The court of Oliver Cromwell* (1977) • R. Sherwood, *Oliver Cromwell: a king in all but name, 1653–1658* (1997) • C. Durston, *Cromwell's major generals: godly government during the English revolution* (2001) • S. Pincus, *Protestantism and patriotism: ideologies and the making of English foreign policy, 1650–1668* (1996) • T. Venning, *Cromwellian foreign policy* (1995) • L. Knoppers, *Constructing Cromwell: ceremony, portrait and print, 1645–1661* (2000) • T. Lang, *The Victorians and the Stuart inheritance* (1995) • R. C. Richardson, ed., *Images of Oliver Cromwell* (1993) • P. Karsten, *Patriot heroes in England and America* (1978) • D. Armitage, 'The Cromwellian protectorate and the languages of empire', *HJ*, 35 (1992), 531–55 • G. E. Aylmer, 'Was Cromwell a member of the army in 1646 and 1647 or not?', *History*, 56 (1971), 183–8 • A. N. B. Cotton, 'Cromwell and the self-denying ordinance', *History*, 62 (1977), 211–31 • C. H. Firth, 'The court of Oliver Cromwell', *Cornhill Magazine*, new ser., 3 (1897), 349–64 • C. H. Firth, 'Cromwell and the crown [2 pts]', *EngHR*, 17 (1902), 429–42; 18 (1903), 52–80 • J. McElligott, 'Cromwell, Drogheda and the abuse of Irish history', *Bullan* (2002) • J. Morrill, 'Textualising and contextualising Cromwell', *HJ*, 33 (1990), 629–39 • G. Nuttall, 'Was Cromwell an iconoclast?', *Transactions of the Congregationalist Historical Society*, 12 (1933–6), 51–66 • D. Piper, 'The contemporary portraits of Oliver Cromwell', *Walpole Soc.*, 34 (1958), 27–41 • A. Woolrych, 'The Cromwellian protectorate: a military dictatorship?', *History*, 75 (1990) • B. Worden, 'Toleration and the Cromwellian protectorate', *Persecution and toleration*, ed. W. J. Sheils, SCH, 21 (1984), 199–233 • A. B. Worden, 'Oliver Cromwell and the sin of Achan', *History, society and the churches*, ed. D. Beales and G. Best (1985), 125–45 • S. R. Gardiner, 'The transplantation to Connaught', *EngHR*, 14 (1899), 700–34 • P. Gaunt, 'To Tyburn and beyond: the mortal remains of Oliver Cromwell', *Cromwelliana* (1986) • P. Gaunt, ed., *Cromwell 400* (2000) • M. Noble, *Memoirs of the protectoral house of Cromwell*, 2 vols. (1787) • J. Waylen, *The house of Cromwell* (1897)

Archives BL, letters, Egerton MS 2620 • Bodl. Oxf., letters and papers • Boston PL, letters • Cambs. AS, Huntingdon, letters and papers [copies] • Cromwell Museum, Huntingdon, corresp. and papers • NRA, priv. coll., letters written during the protectorate • S. Antiquaries, Lond., corresp. and papers • Warks. CRO, letters • Yale U., Beinecke L., papers | BL, letters to Fairfax, etc., Sloane MSS • BL, autograph letters collected by Countess Spencer • Bodl. Oxf., Bishop Wren's abstract of letters, MS Rawl. C 368, fols. 12, 13, 18 • CAC Cam., letters to Sir Arthur Hesilrige • HLRO, MS of the 'Substance of what passed at the council table the 1st of August 1656 betweene the lord protector and the Lord Bradshawe' • Leics. RO, letters to Sir Arthur Hesilrige • NL Scot., letter to the committee of the army on commemoration of the battle of Dunbar • Pembrokeshire RO, Haverfordwest, letters to Haverfordwest corporation • V&A NAL, letters incl. to Lord Wharton with papers

Likenesses English school, mezzotint, 1600–69, NG Ire. • R. Walker, oils, 1649, Leeds Art Gallery; version, NPG • line engraving, c.1649 (after unknown artist), NPG • S. Cooper, miniature, c.1650, Buccleuch estates, Selkirk [*see illus.*] • T. Simon, silver medal, 1650, NPG • T. Simon, silver medal, 1650, Scot. NPG • T. Simon, silver medal, c.1651, BM; electrotype, NPG • P. Lely, oils, 1653–4, City Museum and Art Gallery, Birmingham • attrib. P. Lely, oils, c.1654, Uffizi, Florence, Italy • T. Simon, medal sculpture, 1654, BM • E. Pierce, marble bust, c.1654–1658, AM Oxf.; bronze cast, NPG • by or after S. Cooper, miniature, 1655, Chatsworth,

Derbyshire · S. Cooper, miniature, second version, 1656, NPG · E. Mascall, portrait, 1657, Cromwell Museum, Huntingdon; repro. in Knoppers, *Constructing Cromwell*, 131 · plaster death mask, 1658, AM Oxf.; version, NPG · J. Richardson?, oils, 1700–50 (after drawing by S. Cooper), Boscobel House and the Royal Oak, Shropshire · line engraving, pubd 1739, NPG · M. Ford and A. Miller, mezzotint, pubd 1745 (after portrait by R. Walker, c.1655), NG Ire. · J. Caldwell, line engraving, pubd 1810, NPG · R. Cooper, stipple, pubd 1810 (after miniature by S. Cooper, c.1650), NG Ire. · mezzotint, pubd 1899 (after P. Lely), NPG · R. Brookshaw, mezzotint (after drawing by S. Cooper, c.1655), NG Ire. · R. Dunkarton, mezzotint (after unknown artist), NPG · English school, mezzotint (after R. Walker), NG Ire. · T. Simon, medal sculpture, NPG · attrib. T. or A. Simon, funeral effigy, Bargello, Florence, Italy · L. Stocks, line engraving (after P. Lely), NPG · J. Van de Velde senior, stipple and line engraving (after R. Walker), NG Ire. · brass medallion, Scot. NPG · electrotype sculpture (after dunbar medal by unknown artist, 1650), NPG · line engravings, BM · mezzotint (after P. Lely), NPG · mezzotint, BM · mezzotint (after R. Walker), NPG · oils, Hazelrigg House, Northampton · oils (after S. Cooper), NG Ire. · oils (after R. Walker), Scot. NPG · stipple and etching (after unknown artist), BM, NPG

Wealth at death see S. Roberts, 'The wealth of Oliver Cromwell', *Cromwell 400*, ed. Gaunt

Cromwell, Oliver (c.1742–1821), biographer and lawyer, was one of six children of Thomas Cromwell (1699–1747/8), of Bridgewater Square, London, and his second wife, Mary (1708–1813), daughter of the London merchant Nicholas Skinner. He was the great-great-grandson and last of the direct male descendants of Oliver Cromwell, lord protector of England. Cromwell was trained for the legal profession and became a well-respected solicitor in Essex Street, Strand, and was also clerk to St Thomas's Hospital. He married Mary (b. 1743), daughter of Morgan Morse, solicitor, at All Hallows Barking on 8 August 1771. They had two children: Oliver, who was born on 24 September 1782 and died on 18 April 1785, and Elizabeth-Oliveria (b. 1777), who married, at Cheshunt, Thomas Artemidorus Russell on 18 June 1801.

As a result of the will of his unmarried cousins Elizabeth, Anne, and Lettia, daughters of his father's elder brother, Richard, Cromwell succeeded to the manor of Theobalds and the estate of Cheshunt Park, Hertfordshire. There in 1795 he built a house in which he lived for the remainder of his life. In the year before his death he published *Memoirs of Oliver Cromwell, and his Sons Richard and Henry* (1820). A second edition in two volumes appeared the same year and a third edition was published in 1823. Despite this apparent popularity the book had little value as a work of history and has been described as 'unbounded panegyric' (Allibone, *Dict.*, 1.454) and by Thomas Carlyle as 'incorrect, dull [and] insignificant' (*Oliver Cromwell's Letters and Speeches*, ed. T. Carlyle, 2nd edn, 1846, 2.161n.) Cromwell died at his home at Cheshunt Park on 31 May 1821. GORDON GOODWIN, rev. M. J. MERCER

Sources GM, 1st ser., 83/1 (1813), 286 · GM, 1st ser., 91/1 (1821), 569–70 · R. Clutterbuck, ed., *The history and antiquities of the county of Hertford*, 2 (1821), 95–8 · C. J. Palmer, *The perlustration of Great Yarmouth*, 3 (1875), 286–7 · Allibone, *Dict.* · IGI

Cromwell, Ralph, third Baron Cromwell (1393?–1456), administrator, came of a long-established midland family.

Soldier and diplomat One of Cromwell's ancestors, a king's thegn named Alden, had held land at Cromwell in Nottinghamshire as part of his knight's fee at the time of the Domesday inquest (1086), while his grandfather, another Ralph (d. 1398), had been summoned to parliament as Lord Cromwell in 1375. The son of Ralph, second Baron Cromwell (d. 1416), and his wife, Joan, the third Lord Cromwell did not come into the barony of Tattershall, with which he is normally associated, until the death of his paternal grandmother, Maud Barnack, in 1419. As a youth he gained a place in the household of Henry IV's second son, Thomas, duke of Clarence (d. 1421), and the connection with Clarence soon led to the expanding of Cromwell's horizons. The civil war that broke out in France in 1410 between the dukes of Burgundy and Orléans led to English intervention. Cromwell was part of the army which under Clarence's command crossed to Normandy in August 1412 and campaigned into the duchy of Orléans. When, in November, arrangements were made by which the English were given a substantial payment to be on their way home, Clarence, with Cromwell, went into Gascony to wait out the winter, and returned to England early in April 1413.

The French wars of Henry V's reign offered Cromwell an opportunity for further advancement, and he participated in the capture of Harfleur and fought at Agincourt in 1415. In the Normandy campaign of 1417 Cromwell was present at the capture of Caen. Notice must have been taken of Cromwell's talent for administration, for Clarence appointed Cromwell to be his lieutenant in command of the garrisons of Bec, Poissy, and Pontoise; then in 1421 Cromwell became captain of Harfleur. He must also have shown a talent for diplomacy, since he was one of the men appointed to negotiate the treaty of Troyes of 1420. Cromwell had become one of Henry V's most trusted diplomats and captains and, following the sudden death of the king in 1422, it is no surprise that Cromwell was given one of the four places for knights on the council established by parliament in 1422 for the governance of England during the minority of Henry VI. This parliament was the first to which Cromwell was summoned, and thereafter he concentrated on administration and finance. In this period he married Margaret (d. 1454), coheir with her sister of the valuable midland estates of John, Lord Deincourt (d. 1422). Furthermore, he established what would be a long political association with Henry Beaufort, bishop of Winchester (d. 1447), and Cromwell's political fortunes tended to wax and wane with those of Beaufort.

Treasurer of England, 1433–1443 Cromwell was summoned to Rouen in 1431 during the trial of Jeanne d'Arc, and probably witnessed her death at the stake. He was also in France for Henry VI's coronation in Paris on 16 December 1431. Some time in the late 1420s or early 1430s Cromwell had become the king's chamberlain. But on 1 March 1432 he lost that office, as part of a move against Beaufort and his associates by the king's uncle Humphrey, duke of Gloucester. However, when the king's senior uncle, John, duke of Bedford, interrupted his labours as regent of Lancastrian France to attend to business in England, he secured Cromwell's promotion to be treasurer of England on 11 August 1433, replacing Gloucester's friend, John, Lord Scrope of Masham. As head of the exchequer Cromwell faced extreme fiscal problems. According to the estimate he prepared on taking office, the indebtedness of the crown amounted to £164,000, with an estimated level of annual expenditure of £56,000, and an anticipated annual income of only £38,000. The greatest single drain on crown resources was the French war, which dominated Cromwell's treasurership. In his decade as treasurer, Cromwell did not succeed in bringing stability to government finances, and the crown debt expanded to an alarming size.

Cromwell's personal wealth, however, grew steadily during his treasurership, in part because he seized upon opportunities made available to him as one of the great officers of state to acquire lands, wardships, reversions, and other fruits of patronage and power. During his treasurership Cromwell was able to lend the crown over £4000, as well as to embark on impressive building projects. At his death, Cromwell left over £21,000 in goods and money alone, while his executors subsequently returned to their owners lands worth £5500 of which Cromwell had unjustly deprived them. That is not to say that Cromwell was not an energetic and conscientious treasurer, for by all indications he was, but his desire to hold down governmental spending was not shared by enough of the king's councillors. That Cromwell was treasurer of England longer than any man since William Edington (treasurer from 1344 to 1356) is suggestive of his mastery of the demands of his office as well as a tribute to his political abilities.

It was changes in the political climate that led to Cromwell's resignation as treasurer on 6 July 1443, and his replacement the next day by Ralph Boteler, Lord Sudeley (d. 1473). In particular, this was the period which saw William de la Pole, earl of Suffolk (d. 1450), emerge as the most prominent of the king's councillors. Cromwell, unlike Sudeley, was not one of Suffolk's supporters, hence his replacement as treasurer. The reasons given for his resignation, ill health and the burdens of office, are belied by his continuing activity and vigour. In any case, Cromwell retained his place on the king's council, and continued to attend meetings on a regular basis. He remained as well one of the two chamberlains of the exchequer, an office he had obtained while treasurer, and arrangements Cromwell had set up for the repayment of loans he had made to the crown were allowed to stand.

Political difficulties, 1443–1456 Cromwell thus ceased in 1443 to be one of the great officers of state, but was not utterly stripped of influence and position. Although there seems as yet to have been no rancour between Cromwell and Suffolk, Cromwell was nevertheless outside the most influential circle in government. The gradual withdrawal of Beaufort from government in the 1440s, and his death in 1447, did nothing to aid Cromwell's position. Cromwell had established ties with Richard, duke of York (d. 1460), becoming one of York's annuitants before 1441, but York was far from influential during Suffolk's ascendancy.

Indeed, York was appointed lieutenant of Ireland in 1447, probably as a way of removing him more completely from the scene (though he did not take up the post until March 1448).

A change in Cromwell's political life began abruptly with a physical assault upon his person, on 28 November 1449. While parliament was in session, and as Cromwell came from a council meeting in the Star Chamber at Westminster, he was set upon by a band of men with murderous intent led by William Tailboys (d. 1464). With the aid of his retainers Cromwell escaped the assault. Tailboys, a wealthy, well-connected Lincolnshire squire, who already had a record of violent behaviour, was a neighbour of Cromwell, and may have attacked Cromwell to protect himself from punishment for earlier crimes. Cromwell initiated legal action against Tailboys following the assault, but it was blocked by Suffolk, who was a patron of Tailboys. Outraged by Suffolk's actions, it seems that Cromwell set in motion the process of impeachment against Suffolk that was completed by the Commons in January 1450. The inclusion in the articles of impeachment of detailed financial information concerning Suffolk's administration suggests Cromwell's influence, and the mention of Tailboys among the charges against Suffolk reinforces the veracity of contemporary reports of Cromwell's efforts against Suffolk. Suffolk was subsequently murdered crossing the channel, and Tailboys was placed in the Tower of London while the legal proceedings against him ran their courses. He was convicted in February 1450 of the charges brought against him by Cromwell, and was ordered to pay damages of £2000. Tailboys did not, however, abandon his efforts to destroy Cromwell, and in 1451 and 1452 he used rumours and bills to accuse Cromwell of being a party to the loss of English lands in France, in what amounted to a campaign of character assassination against him. Cromwell's reappointment as king's chamberlain in the summer of 1450 made him seem more a part of an unpopular government than he actually was, or recently had been—there is little evidence for friendship between Cromwell and Edmund Beaufort, duke of Somerset (d. 1455), who was emerging as the king's principal councillor.

The links between Cromwell and the duke of York served to diminish Cromwell's influence at the centre of power. He was suspected by the council of being involved in York's rising of February 1452, and he was suspended from the council for several months in late 1452 and early 1453 until he could clear himself. Nor was this his only difficulty. A quarrel of several years' standing between himself and Henry Holland, duke of Exeter (d. 1475), over lands in Bedfordshire became extremely bitter in 1452, with outbreaks of violence in June 1452 and again the following spring. In an effort to retrieve his position, Cromwell established ties with the Neville family and strengthened his connection with the duke of York. Cromwell was childless, and his heirs were his two nieces, the daughters of his sister Maud. One of those nieces, Maud Stanhope, widow of Robert (III), sixth Lord Willoughby of Eresby (d. 1452), was married in the summer of 1453 to Sir

Thomas Neville, second son of Richard Neville, earl of Salisbury (d. 1460). In the same summer Cromwell became a feoffee of lands to York's use. The connection with York made Cromwell less tolerable to Somerset, and this in turn tied Cromwell's fate more closely to York's. Thus Cromwell could hope to benefit when, following Henry VI's collapse into insanity in August 1453, York was appointed protector and defender of the realm on 27 March 1454. And with his patron he came under threat when the king recovered his senses and Somerset returned to power at the end of 1454. York took up arms, and on 22 May 1455 defeated and killed Somerset at the first battle of St Albans. Cromwell arrived on the scene the day after the battle, and his tardiness may indicate that he had misgivings about York's violent courses. York was subsequently appointed protector again on 19 November, and it was during this second protectorate that Cromwell died at his Derbyshire manor of South Wingfield on 4 January 1456.

Cromwell as builder Cromwell's activity in public life was complemented by equal activity as a builder. Without children to provide for, and comfortably wealthy, he was able to finance some impressive architectural projects. The southernmost of these was Collyweston in Northamptonshire, of which today nothing remains although the site is well established. Here he considerably augmented a house which he purchased in 1441, and which had been begun earlier in the century by Sir William Porter. South Wingfield, an impressive stone manor house overlooking the Amber valley, was built by Cromwell over a decade, or perhaps longer, beginning in 1439 or 1440. A building account for the period from 1 November 1442 to Christmas 1443 notes expenditures of £222 16s. 11¾d., but this in no way represents the total cost of construction, of which impressive remains can still be seen. Cromwell also had a manor house at Lambley, Nottinghamshire, which had been in the family since the eleventh century, but nothing remains of it today. The parish church of Lambley was the final resting place of his parents and grandparents, and perhaps of other ancestors as well. Cromwell left instructions in his testament that the church be rebuilt from his estate, and that a marble slab with brass images of his parents be placed over their grave. The rebuilding was carried out under the direction of his executors after his death.

At Tattershall, where he had inherited an early thirteenth-century castle, Cromwell undertook to build or refurbish an entire complex of buildings, and to make this his principal residence. The centrepiece of the domestic buildings was, and remains, an imposing brick tower begun in 1434 and completed in 1446. The tower-house was built on six levels, and was designed for the comfort of its owner, and also to provide a dramatic expression of his distinction and power. Within the castle the surviving chimney-pieces suggest a taste for sumptuous display as well as family pride, for they are carved with heraldic shields of Cromwell and kindred families, and also with pouch-like purses, a favourite decorative device probably representing Cromwell's eminence as treasurer of England. Beyond the castle moat Cromwell founded a college of seven chantry chaplains, for which he obtained a charter in 1440. The old parish church was not adequate for Cromwell's grander purposes, and it was taken down to make way for a new stone-built church dedicated to the Holy Trinity. Cromwell and his wife were buried in the church, and their canopied memorial brass, though damaged, remains one of the most impressive in Lincolnshire. In addition to the chantry chaplains using the choir of Holy Trinity (the nave was for parochial use), the ecclesiastical personnel included six secular clerks and six choristers, and two brick lodgings were constructed for all these men. There were also built two bede-houses or almshouses, with hall and chapel, for thirteen elderly poor men and the same number of women. If Lord Cromwell wished to leave a physical legacy of his life and eminence, it must be admitted that he succeeded.   A. C. REEVES

Sources A. Emery, 'Ralph Lord Cromwell's manor at Wingfield, 1439–1450: its construction, design and influence', *Archaeological Journal*, 142 (1985), 276–339 · R. L. Friedrichs, 'The career and influence of Ralph Lord Cromwell, 1393–1456', PhD diss., Columbia University, 1974 · R. L. Friedrichs, 'Ralph Lord Cromwell and the politics of fifteenth century England', *Nottingham Medieval Studies*, 32 (1988), 207–27 · R. L. Friedrichs, 'The two last wills of Ralph, Lord Cromwell', *Nottingham Medieval Studies*, 34 (1990), 1–20 · J. L. Kirby, 'The issues of the Lancastrian exchequer and Lord Cromwell's estimates of 1433', *BIHR*, 24 (1951), 121–51 · R. Marks, 'The glazing of the collegiate church of the Holy Trinity, Tattershall (Lincs.): a study of late fifteenth-century glass-painting workshops', *Archaeologia*, 106 (1979), 133–56 · R. Marks, 'The rebuilding of Lambley church, Nottinghamshire', *Transactions of the Thoroton Society*, 87 (1983), 87–9 · E. M. Myatt-Price, 'Ralph Lord Cromwell, 1394–1456', *Lincolnshire Historian*, 11/4 (1957), 4–13 · S. Payling, *Political society in Lancastrian England* (1991) · [J. Raine], ed., *Testamenta Eboracensia*, 2, SurtS, 30 (1855), 196–200 · W. D. Simpson, ed., *The building accounts of Tattershall Castle, 1434–1472*, Lincoln RS, 55 (1960) · M. W. Thompson, 'The architectural significance of the building works of Ralph, Lord Cromwell, 1394–1456', *Collectanea historica: essays in memory of Stuart Rigold*, ed. A. P. Detsicas, Kent Archaeological Society (1981) · M. W. Thompson, 'The construction of the manor at South Wingfield, Derbyshire', *Problems in economic and social archaeology*, ed. G. de G. Sieveking, I. H. Longworth, and K. E. Wilson (1976), 417–37 · M. W. Thompson, *Tattershall Castle, Lincolnshire* (1974) · R. Virgoe, 'William Tailboys and Lord Cromwell: crime and politics in Lancastrian England', *Bulletin of the John Rylands University Library*, 55 (1972–3), 459–82 · C. Weir, 'The site of the Cromwells' mediaeval manor house at Lambley, Nottinghamshire', *Transactions of the Thoroton Society*, 85 (1981), 75–7 · K. B. McFarlane, *The nobility of later medieval England* (1973), 49 · K. B. McFarlane, 'The Wars of the Roses', *England in the fifteenth century: collected essays* (1981), 231–61, esp. 240, n.21 · PRO, chancery, early chancery proceedings, C1 · PRO, special collections, rentals and surveys, SC 11 · PRO, exchequer, king's remembrancer, accounts various, E 101
Archives Magd. Oxf. · Sheffield Central Library, estate records and records of public service | CKS, De L'Isle and Dudley MSS · Sheff. Arch., Copley deeds
Wealth at death over £21,000: McFarlane, *England*, 240, n.21

Cromwell, Ralph (*fl.* 1568–1585), soldier, was from a cadet branch of the family of the barons Cromwell; his parentage is unknown. He was a minor but notable player in some of the great events of Elizabeth's reign. In 1568 Cromwell was one of the first English soldiers to join William of Orange. By 1574, he was lieutenant of a company of volunteers in a regiment raised by Edward Chester, his captain being the poet George Gascoigne. At the very outset of the famous siege of Leiden most English troops 'failed … in vertue' (Camden, 2.347), surrendering or taking to their heels when the Spanish attacked. Dutch historians typically describe (and celebrate) Leiden's garrison as entirely local militiamen, but, in fact, Cromwell made a fighting retreat with part of the company into Leiden where, as documents in the municipal archives reveal, they fought throughout the celebrated siege. Cromwell and his men were the only foreign troops present during these momentous events.

In 1575 they received a special bonus from the states of Holland, which commissioned Cromwell as captain. He helped quell a dangerous mutiny in south Holland in 1576 and on 1 August 1578 fought in the great victory at Rijmenam. The balance of war shifted south and in 1580 the states of Holland arranged to transfer his employment to the states of Flanders. Cromwell joined his company to the new regiment of John North in summer 1582, but later that year he obtained a commission for his own battalion, one company of which was commanded by his kinsman, Edward (later third Baron) Cromwell. Thanks partly to the backing of the principal secretary of state, Sir Francis Walsingham, Cromwell's force was kept in Dutch pay in 1583 when some English regiments were being paid off. Cromwell remained in Dutch employ until the time of the royal intervention in 1585, when he seems to have retired, after receiving a last reward from the Dutch.

In some ways typical of many other, almost anonymous, English captains, Ralph Cromwell was more resolute and a more skilful soldier than most.   D. J. B. TRIM

Richard Cromwell (1626–1712), by unknown artist, c.1650–55

Sources BL, Harley MS 253 · BL, Lansdowne MS 1218 · Baron Kervyn de Lettenhove [J. M. B. C. Kervyn de Lettenhove] and L. Gilliodts-van Severen, eds., *Relations politiques des Pays-Bas et de l'Angleterre sous le règne de Philippe II*, 11 vols. (Brussels, 1882–1900), vol. 7 · warrant of February 1574, Geemente Archief Leiden, archief der secretarie, lias 1334 · Den Haag, Nationaal Archief, The Hague, Archief van de staten van Holland, 11–13 · F. J. G. ten Raa and F. de Bas, eds., *Het staatsche leger, 1568–1795*, 1 (Breda, 1911) · *CSP for.*, 1575–8; 1581–4 · W. Camden, *Annales: the true and royall history of the famous Empresse Elizabeth*, trans. A. Darcie (1625), bk 2 · T. Churchyard and R. R[obinson], *A true discourse historicall of the succeeding governors in the Netherlands and the civil wars there begun in the yeere 1565* (1602)

Archives PRO, Cromwell to Walsingham, 12 Dec 1583, SP 83/20/99 | BL, Harley MS 253, fol. 116

Cromwell, Richard (1626–1712), lord protector of England, Scotland, and Ireland, was born in Huntingdon on 4 October 1626 and baptized at St John's Church on 19 October, the fourth of nine children and the third of five sons of Oliver *Cromwell (1599–1658), lord protector, and his wife, Elizabeth *Cromwell (1598–1665), daughter of Sir James Bourchier.

Early life and career, 1626–1653 For all but a few months during a life of nearly eighty-six years Richard Cromwell was a minor figure of little national importance. He was born and brought up a younger son of a struggling provincial gentleman. Little is known of his childhood and adolescence, though he presumably spent much of his early

years in the family home—at Huntingdon until 1631, St Ives in 1631–6, and Ely from 1636. Mark Noble and other early biographers suggest that, like his elder brothers before him, he attended Felsted School in Essex. He does not appear to have entered or attended university. By the mid-1640s his two elder brothers had died and he had become the eldest surviving son and heir of a man who was rapidly gaining substantial military and political influence, but Richard remained firmly in the background, with no political or serious military role. On 27 May 1647, a few months before his twenty-first birthday, he was enrolled at Lincoln's Inn. In October 1647 a newspaper reported that Oliver Cromwell's two surviving sons, Richard and Henry *Cromwell, were both serving as captains in the army, one in Lord General Fairfax's lifeguard, the other in the regiment of Thomas Harrison. As other sources confirm that Henry was in Harrison's regiment around this time, it seems possible that Richard saw military service in the lord general's lifeguard in 1647. However, the absence of Richard's name from other military records and accounts of the latter half of the 1640s, the indications that by the time of his marriage negotiations in 1648–9 he was a civilian and bore no military rank or title, and slightly later reports that he had played no part in the civil wars all suggest that any military service was very brief and limited.

In spring 1648 Oliver Cromwell opened negotiations for his son's marriage to the daughter of Richard Maijor, a member of the Hampshire gentry who had played no part in national politics and who, though an active parliamentarian administrator in his home county, did not take up arms in the civil war. The two families were probably introduced to each other via a mutual friend, Richard Norton, a wealthy Hampshire gentleman, colonel of a parliamentarian cavalry regiment, and (from 1645) recruiter MP for Hampshire. It was through Norton, and employing him as an intermediary, that Cromwell began negotiating with Richard Maijor in February 1648. Cromwell noted that he had already received an alternative marriage proposal for his son which was financially more lucrative, but he foresaw 'difficulties' there and 'not that assurance of godliness' which a Major match offered. In any case, Richard Major's estate was 'more than I look for, as things now stand'. Cromwell as usual professed that he looked to 'Providence' to decide the issue, for 'If God please to bring it about, the consideration of piety in the parents, and such hopes of the gentlewoman in that respect, make the business to me of a great mercy; concerning which I desire to wait upon God' (Abbott, 1.585). In reality he took a very keen interest in the material terms of the marriage settlement, and when he and Major met at Farnham in late March, Cromwell was not satisfied by the latter's offer, though he found him to be 'very wise and honest' and 'exceedingly liked the gentleman's plainness and free dealing with me' (ibid., 1.590); Norton was given detailed instructions to continue negotiations and urged to secure a more generous provision of land and money. For his part, Major clearly held some reservations not about Richard—who had reportedly 'left himself very much to the guidance and direction of his father' (BL, Add. MS 24860, fol. 17)—but about Oliver Cromwell, for 'some things of common fame did a little stick' with him. Cromwell felt sure that God would 'in His own time vindicate' him of 'all ill reports' (ibid., 1.590). However, for the time being the marriage negotiations stalled.

They revived a year later, in the opening months of 1649, both through direct correspondence between Cromwell and Major and via another intermediary, the Revd Robert Stapleton. Richard Cromwell, described by Norton the previous year as a 'young man of wil enough … very civil, free, and open-hearted' (BL, Add. MS 24860, fol. 17), was also dispatched to visit Major and his daughter, to see 'if God dispose the young ones' hearts thereunto' (Abbott, 2.21). As in 1648, his father stressed the 'gentlewoman's worth', her 'virtue and godliness', and 'the piety of the family' (Abbott, 2.9), but he still looked to 'the dispensation of Providence' (ibid., 2.21) and sought a sound financial and property settlement—'I may not be so much wanting to myself nor family as not to have some equality of consideration towards it' (ibid., 2.29). By early April terms were almost concluded and Richard was anxious to be with his intended bride—'my son had a great desire to come down and wait upon your daughter. I perceive he minds that more than to attend business here. I should be glad to see him settled' (ibid., 2.52). Richard Cromwell and Dorothy Major (1627–1676), elder daughter of Richard Major (1604–1660) and Anne, daughter of John Kingswell, were at last married on 1 May 1649 at Hursley in Hampshire; Oliver Cromwell attended the ceremony.

With his new wife, Richard Cromwell lived with Richard Major and his wife at their principal estate at Hursley and settled down to life as a member of the Hampshire landed élite. During the 1650s he and Dorothy had nine children, only four of whom survived into adulthood: Elizabeth (1650–1731), Anne (1651–1652), an unnamed son (b. and d. 1652), Mary (b. and d. 1654), an unnamed daughter (b. and d. 1655), Oliver (1656–1705), Dorothy (1657–1658), another Anne or Anna (1659–1727), and another Dorothy (1660–1681). Following his marriage, Richard was named a Hampshire JP and, like his father-in-law, from

time to time he attended meetings in Winchester and elsewhere, and was present at about a dozen quarter sessions in 1651–7. He was placed on various county committees and, with other magistrates, was occasionally required by the council of state to undertake administrative and judicial tasks in Hampshire. However, almost all we know of Richard's life in Hampshire in the years following his marriage is drawn from a series of letters that Oliver Cromwell wrote to his son and daughter-in-law and to Richard Major in 1649–51. Cromwell was clearly concerned about his son and looked to Richard Major to watch over him and to correct perceived faults. Cromwell saw his son not only as lacking true devotion to God and to business but also as being too fond of good and expensive living. These faults he collectively labelled 'idleness', and urged his son to be 'serious, the times requiring it' (Abbott, 2.95), and to knuckle down:

> I would have him mind and understand business, read a little history, study the mathematics and cosmography: these are good, with subordination to the things of God. Better than idleness, or mere outward worldly contents. These fit for public services, for which a man is born.   (ibid., 2.103)

In 1649 he exhorted Dorothy to 'provoke your husband' to search for God's guidance (Abbott, 2.103), and warned Richard, who was to 'seek the Lord and His face continually', to 'take heed of an unactive vain Spirit', urging him to study history and 'to understand the estate I have settled; it's your concernment to know it all, and how it stands' (Abbott, 2.236). In 1650 he was still worried that 'my son is idle' and in need of 'good counsel' for 'he is in the dangerous time of his age, and it's a very vain world' (ibid., 2.289). Cromwell's forebodings proved well founded, for by summer 1651 he had heard that 'my Son hath exceeded his allowance, and is in debt'. Cromwell condemned this, not because he begrudged him 'laudable recreations, nor an honourable carriage of himself', but because

> if pleasure and self-satisfaction be made the business of a man's life, so much cost laid out upon it, so much time spent in it, as rather answers appetite than the will of God, or is comely before His Saints, I scruple to feed this humour; and God forbid that his being my son should be his allowance to live not pleasingly to our Heavenly Father.

Major was to reprove Richard and urge him 'to seek grace from Christ'. Cromwell repeatedly stressed that he would provide for the couple's 'comfort' and 'encouragement' but would not 'feed a voluptuous humour' in Richard 'if he should make pleasures the business of his life, in a time when some precious Saints are bleeding, and breathing out their last, for the safety of the rest' (ibid., 2.425).

The lord protector's son, 1653–1658 Unlike his father-in-law and his younger brother Henry, Richard Cromwell was not named a member of the nominated assembly in 1653. His position did not formally change when his father became lord protector at the end of the year, for he was not given office within the protectoral executive or central administration, he did not play any role in the public and state occasions of the opening year of the protectorate—thus it was Henry and not Richard who accompanied the new protector when he was entertained by the City in

February 1654 and when he formally opened the first protectorate parliament in September—and he was not generally looked upon as a likely future candidate for the elective protectorship established by the new constitution. None the less, as the eldest surviving son and heir of the new head of state, Richard's status had changed. Contemporary commentators began taking a little more notice of him, occasionally referring to him respectfully or sneeringly as 'lord' or even 'prince', and he was returned to both the first and second protectorate parliaments. In summer 1654 he was elected for both Hampshire and Monmouthshire and chose to sit for the former. Appearing in the *Commons Journal* as Lord Richard Cromwell, he was named to about a dozen committees spread fairly evenly over the twenty weeks of the session. He served as teller in formal divisions twice. All this suggests that Richard, though one of the more prominent members of the house, was neither in the first rank of parliamentary activity nor one of those who took a leading role during the session. As the single parliamentary diary of this session is brief, incomplete, and rarely identifies individual speakers, it is impossible to know whether, how far, or to what ends Richard may have contributed to particular debates.

During the twenty months between the dissolution of the first and the meeting of the second protectorate parliaments Richard Cromwell divided his time between the apartment he had been assigned in Whitehall Palace and his family at Hursley. He attended several meetings of the Hampshire quarter sessions over this period. In November 1655 he wrote from Hursley to his brother Henry, apologizing for failing to write more often—'writing to my unskilfull hand is very irksome'—as well as conveying his 'love and honour ... [and] ardent affections' and letting Henry know that he was sending him some hounds (BL, Lansdowne MS 821, fol. 38). This, the earliest extant letter by Richard, was the first of a series written to Henry in Ireland during the latter half of the 1650s. Further letters followed from Hursley or Whitehall during 1656-7, many of them recommending individuals for office or land in Ireland, though intermingled with more personal expressions of love and affection for his brother. Over this period, too, there survives one further letter from Oliver Cromwell to Richard, of May 1656, a short note regarding the sale of part of the estate that he had assigned him on his marriage.

In summer 1656 Richard Cromwell was elected to the second protectorate parliament for both Hampshire and Cambridge University and chose to sit for the latter. The *Commons Journal* suggests that he was quite active in the house during the opening months of the long first session, for he was teller in one division, on 9 October, and was nominated to about eighteen committees down to mid-December, but that thereafter he played a much more limited role—he was named only to a handful of committees from January to June 1657 and never served as a teller during that period. Thomas Burton's parliamentary diary suggests that Richard spoke only rarely and that

his brief interjections were generally on minor procedural matters—for example, on 9 December he proposed that a petition be referred to an existing committee on Cambridge University and on the following day that further MPs be added to that committee. But Burton also records having dinner with Richard on 12 December, in the course of which 'Lord Richard was very clear in passing his judgment that Nayler deserves to be hanged ... He, for his part, was clear in that Nayler ought to die', suggesting that Richard took a very firm line against the alleged blasphemy of James Naylor, though one that he is not recorded as having expressed in the chamber during the long debates on Naylor's guilt and punishment (*Diary of Thomas Burton*, 1.126). Burton's diary also reveals that Richard was absent 'sick' when the house was called on 31 December (ibid., 1.284). The impression that Richard may have been attending parliament only intermittently during the latter half of the session is strengthened both by his letter to his brother Henry from Whitehall on 7 March, in which he implied that he was learning of developments in parliament only as an outside observer—'I know noe newes ... Only I heare that the Howse hath made themselves the Commons by voting another Howse' (BL, Lansdowne MS 821, fols. 324-5)—and by his presence at the Hampshire quarter sessions in spring 1657. One reason for Richard's apparent reduced activity in parliament during the opening months of 1657 may be that he found distasteful and uncomfortable the heated and prolonged debates over the new constitution in general and the restoration of kingship in particular; he hinted at this in his letter to Henry of 7 March, writing of 'the peevish world' and commenting that his brother was fortunate to be away from 'the spatterring dirte which is throwen aboute here' (ibid.). However, neither there nor in the clutch of letters that he wrote to Henry over the summer, once the new constitution had been finalized and the parliamentary session ended, did Richard make explicit his own views on the revised constitutional position of the head of state and on the arrangements for the appointment of future heads of state. On the other hand, he did criticize unnamed

> persons, whose designe hath been for a long time layed to take roote for the hindring nationall advantadges in settlement, where it might occation difficulty to them getting into the saddle, respecting there owne ambitious mindes and advantadges before religion, peace, or what else thay may stand in there way.   (BL, Lansdowne MS 822, fols. 100-1)

The new constitution empowered and required Oliver Cromwell to nominate his successor as protector and, although there was no requirement that he name his eldest son, his deliberate promotion of Richard from summer 1657 onwards suggests that this was on his mind. In contrast to the initial installation of the protector in December 1653, in which Richard had played no part, he was prominent at his father's second installation of late June 1657; he rode with his father in the state coach and stood by him during the ceremony. In July he was elected chancellor of Oxford University in succession to his father, and an elaborate installation ceremony was held at Whitehall on 29 July. During the autumn Oliver Cromwell appointed Richard, who was convalescing in Hampshire after breaking his leg in a riding accident, a member of the new, nominated second chamber of parliament, and in December he was appointed to the council of state. He proved himself conscientious in both capacities, attending every meeting of the 'other house' during the brief and unproductive second session of the second protectorate parliament of 20 January to 4 February 1658, and attending forty-eight of the seventy-three council meetings held between his admittance to that body on 31 December 1657 and the beginning of September 1658. In his capacity as a member of the 'other house', *A Second Narrative of the Late Parliament* provided a satirical description of Richard about this time, portraying him as a person 'skilled in Hawking, Hunting, Horse-racing, with other sports and pastimes', who had done little 'for the cause' beyond 'the drinking of King Charles's … health', who was 'no very good Scholar', and who was

> not judged meet (not having a Spirit of Government for it) to have a Command in the Army when there was fighting, or honest and wise enough to be one of the little Parliament. Yet is he become a Colonel of Horse now fighting is over; as also taken in to be one of the Protector's Council, and one of the Other House, and to have the First Negative Voyce over the good People of the Commonwealth. (*A Second Narrative of the Late Parliament*, 1659, 13; BL, Thomason tract, E977 (3))

Indeed, in January 1658 Oliver Cromwell had appointed Richard commander of a cavalry regiment. In May 1658 he attended the launching at Woolwich of a new ship, named the *Richard* in his honour, and in June and early July he, his wife, and assorted courtiers were warmly entertained on a semi-official and almost regal visit to the west of England, especially to Bath and Bristol.

On 29 July, soon after his return to London, Richard Cromwell wrote to Henry to relate that their sister Elizabeth *Claypole, though very ill, was showing signs of rallying, so 'now things beginn to have a blessing put onto them, that our darke and disconsolate famuly may once againe revive and live'; however, 'His Highness having soe much afflicted himselfe is not very well' (BL, Lansdowne MS 823, fols. 81–2). When he wrote again on 24 August, his mood was much gloomier, for Elizabeth was dead and his father was very ill:

> Since oure late, great stroacke … it hath pleased God to vissett our sorrowes with greater feares; for it is one thinge to have the greatest bowe lopt offe, but when the axe is layed to the roote, then there is noe hopes remaining … We have been a famuly of much sorrow all this summer, and therefore we deserve not the envy of the world. (ibid., fols. 89–90)

Although by this stage many commentators were reporting that Richard was likely to succeed his ailing father, at no point in his surviving letters did Richard himself talk of his succession or speculate on his future role.

The vagaries and inconsistencies of surviving sources have led to considerable historical debate about whether Oliver Cromwell nominated Richard to succeed him as head of state—alternative theories would have it either

that he died without naming a successor or that at some point in 1657–8 he nominated someone else, perhaps his son-in-law Charles Fleetwood—and, if he did nominate his eldest son, precisely when and to whom he did so. According to a contemporary newsletter, on or about 26 August Cromwell sent for Richard and the former speaker of the second protectorate parliament to consult about the form in which Richard should be nominated and proclaimed his successor, but the meeting was inconclusive. On 30 August Thomas *Belasyse, Lord Fauconberg, reported that he believed no nomination had yet been made, though John Thurloe, the secretary of state, was summoning up the courage to press the protector to do so. During the evening of the same day, 30 August, Thurloe himself wrote a letter claiming that over a year before, in summer 1657, Cromwell had sealed up a paper or will containing the name of his chosen successor but that the document could not now be found, creating fears that he would die before making a clear nomination; no such nomination had yet been made. However, in a letter written after Cromwell's death Thurloe claimed that he had verbally nominated Richard as his successor (presumably very late) on 30 August. Other contemporary and near contemporary accounts suggest that one or more verbal nominations of Richard were not made until 1 or 2 September, to Thurloe and Thomas Goodwin, possibly repeated in the presence of a slightly larger group of councillors and senior officers. In short, although no written document of nomination was ever publicly produced, several contemporary or near contemporary sources agree that Oliver Cromwell did name Richard as his successor verbally, if not in writing, and perhaps more than once, in the days before he died. This would be consistent with his deliberate promotion of his eldest son during 1657–8, when he apparently groomed him to succeed him, as well as with the record of what occurred in the council of state on the afternoon of 3 September, after Cromwell's death.

Succession Lord Protector Oliver Cromwell died about 3 p.m. on 3 September. The council of state immediately convened and met for several hours before, in the evening, first the lord chamberlain (Sir Gilbert Pickering) and then the lord president (Henry Lawrence) and other councillors met Richard to inform him formally that he had been nominated by his father, had therefore succeeded as head of state, and was to be proclaimed as such. A contemporary newsletter and a slightly later account both claimed that there had been some discussion in council before all the members had pledged to accept Richard and had agreed that he should be the new lord protector. The formal minutes show the council expressing itself satisfied both that Oliver Cromwell was dead and,

> by what was now exhibited to the Councell, as well by writing as by word of mouth, by certain members of the Councell, and others who were called in, that his late Highness did, in his life time, appoint and Declare the Lord Richard Cromwell to succeed him in the Government of these nations.

The council then resolved 'nemine contradicente That it appears to the Councell that his late Highness hath appointed and declared' Richard to succeed him in government according to the written constitution. But significantly, the minutes immediately reiterated this point—'That the former Vote be entered, and notice taken therein, that the same passed nemine contradicente' (PRO, PRO 31/17/33, unpaginated). The council moved on to more procedural matters surrounding the succession, including instructing Fleetwood to call the army officers together to inform them of the day's developments, to require them to be vigilant in maintaining peace and order, and to gain their signatures of support to the document proclaiming Richard protector.

When, on the evening of 3 September, Richard Cromwell met a delegation of councillors who informed him of his succession to the protectorship, he responded with his first speech as head of state, a brief oration not only thanking the members of the council for the support they had given his father but also acknowledging his own inexperience and the onerous task ahead and stating that he looked to the council and to God for support, strength, and guidance. On 4 September Richard was proclaimed in London, and during the afternoon he met the lord mayor and aldermen to receive their condolences and congratulations and to be offered the sword of the City, which he immediately returned, again with a short speech. In the presence of the lord mayor and aldermen, the councillors, many army officers, and others, Richard then took the oath of office as protector. Over the next week he was proclaimed protector in towns and other public places in England and Wales, Scotland, and Ireland. Contemporary reports suggest that his succession received wide public support, and by the end of September he had received addresses of support from many towns and counties, as well as from the armed forces; to those presented in person, he often responded with brief but effective and well-received speeches of thanks. Messages of condolence, congratulation, and support also began to be received from many of the states of Europe. His father's death had upset Richard and distracted him during the opening weeks of his protectorship—early in September Thurloe wrote that Oliver's death was 'soe soare a stroake unto him, and he is soe sensible of it, that he is in noe condition to write or doe yet' (Thurloe, *State papers*, 7.373), and the council order book indicates that he did not begin attending formal council meetings until the last week of September, though he and his councillors met on other occasions earlier in the month, including a day of fasting and humiliation on 10 September. However, all the evidence suggests that Richard's succession had been smooth and unopposed and that in many quarters his protectorship was welcomed with genuine warmth. As Thurloe put it to Henry Cromwell in a letter of 7 September, 'There is not a dogge that waggs his tongue, soe great a calme are wee in' (ibid., 7.374).

The army and the council of state As protector, Richard Cromwell had to begin handling a mass of business, much of it minor or routine, some of it—the continuing war with Spain and other diplomatic affairs, together with preparations for Oliver's state funeral, for example—

more weighty. However, two issues came to dominate the opening months of his protectorate. The first was the position and command of the army. In stark contrast to his predecessor as protector, Richard had no real military experience, background, or pedigree upon which he could draw to win the trust and obedience of the army. Indeed, many in the army clearly questioned his commitment to the parliamentary and godly cause and feared that the army and the beliefs which it held dear might be sidelined by this young country gentleman of uncertain political and religious outlook and his civilian allies. Accordingly, before the end of September many junior and some senior army officers were holding meetings at which Richard's right to command the armed forces was questioned. As early as 7 September Thurloe had foreseen difficulties, reporting 'some secret murmurings in the army as if his highnes were not generall of the army as his father was' (Thurloe, *State papers*, 7.374); a week later Fauconberg had claimed that a 'caball there is of persons and great ones, held very closely, resolved, it's feared, to rule themselves, or set all on fire' (ibid., 7.386). By early October some in the army were pressing for Charles Fleetwood to be appointed commander-in-chief, with power to issue military commissions; twinned with this was the demand that no one should be dismissed from the army except by court martial. Several meetings of the officers were held during October, some chaired by Fleetwood, who was ostensibly steering a middle course, keen to maintain his dominant military position while also professing loyalty and obedience to the protector, some attended and addressed by Richard himself. Thus on 18 October Richard met the officers and delivered a speech that Thurloe may have helped him prepare, in which he professed his pursuit of liberty and godliness and his desire to keep the army in the hands of godly men, sought the loyalty, support, and prayers of the army, and pledged that he would do all he could to clear the military arrears and ensure prompter payment henceforth. However, he forcefully reiterated a line which he had taken from the moment his military position had first been questioned, that under the written constitution he was commander-in-chief of the armed forces and that, while he would consult with and support Fleetwood as lieutenant-general of the army under him, he was determined to retain the position and full power of commander-in-chief. The tactful but firm stance taken by Richard, together with moves by protector and council during the latter half of October to meet some of the arrears of military pay, quietened the army for a time, though murmurings and meetings of officers continued. In mid-November Thurloe referred to these undertones of military discontent when he wrote that 'sometymes the fire seemes to be out; then it kindles againe' (ibid., 7.510). Accordingly, on 19 November Richard summoned the officers to Whitehall and addressed them once again. He pointed out that God's providence had placed the civil and military government of the nations in his hands, that he was bound by oath to uphold the written constitution, and that several senior officers had explicitly supported his succession and proclamation as protector. He acknowledged his own youth and inexperience and called upon the army and others to support him in his task of governing. He stressed that he sought a 'good correspondency' between himself and the army, suggesting to the officers that they could use rooms in Whitehall Palace for any future meetings, and urged them to lay aside 'all jealousies and misconstructions' (Firth, 3.168–9). As before, Richard's intervention by no means resolved the issue, but for a time at least it mollified the army, and the announcement soon after that a parliament was to be summoned also served to focus military attention elsewhere.

The military issue may also have affected the broader operation of central government during the opening months of Richard Cromwell's protectorate. Like his father, Richard clearly worked closely with the executive council of state, the surviving order book of which, covering the period down to mid-January 1659, indicates that he attended part or all of thirty-eight of the seventy-four meetings recorded between 3 September and 18 January, that is slightly over half the meetings held during that four-and-a-half-month period. When Richard attended only part of a meeting, his presence often coincided with consideration of the most important items dispatched at that meeting. The formal record of many of the meetings of October and November is surprisingly brief and sparse, suggesting that the council was handling a limited quantity and range of business or, perhaps more likely, that much of the business at those meetings was not being minuted. The record becomes fuller during December 1658 and January 1659, more closely resembling the very wide range of business, national and local, important and mundane, recorded as being handled by the protectoral council of Oliver Cromwell. Although neither the order book nor other official sources reveal it, a number of other commentators reported that the military question spilled over into a power struggle within, and for control of, Richard's council during autumn 1658. Some commentators suggested growing divisions between a pro-army military group within the council, headed by Fleetwood and John Disbrowe, whose loyalty to Richard was sometimes questioned, and a civilian group, including Thurloe, Lawrence, and Nathaniel Fiennes, whose supposed influence upon Richard was viewed with dismay by many senior officers; indeed, such was the intensity of the ill feeling that during November Thurloe offered to resign, though the offer was declined by Richard. As well as divisions among the existing thirteen councillors, all of whom Richard had inherited from his father, there were reportedly clashes over the possible appointment of new councillors, with the military faction wishing to see further senior officers added to the council of state and opposing the appointment of civilian-minded figures such as lords Fauconberg and Broghill, who were thought to be close to Richard and whose appointment was supported by the existing civilian councillors. In fact, Richard appointed no new councillors during his protectorate.

Parliament The second major issue that had to be addressed during the opening months of Richard Cromwell's protectorate was the financial position of the regime. Financial weakness had undermined the protectoral regime from the outset, and in September 1658 Richard inherited not only an annual deficit but also an accumulated debt estimated at up to £2 million, much of it comprising arrears of military pay. Within weeks of Oliver Cromwell's dissolution of the second protectorate parliament there had been rumours that another parliament would have to be called shortly to address these financial problems, and, although Oliver's illness and death had intervened before anything had been decided, there was an expectation that the new protector would promptly be forced to summon parliament. In fact, the decision to call a parliament was not firmly taken until late November. In the interim Cromwell, who perhaps wished to delay meeting parliament until the army was more firmly under his control, initiated through the council a thorough review of existing revenues—this issue first appears in the council minutes of 7 September, and many of the thinly minuted meetings of October and November may have been dominated by discussions of financial problems as well as possible solutions, including the role and composition of a parliament—while he sought loans from abroad, especially from France. The completion of Oliver Cromwell's state funeral and signs that army unrest had subsided may have encouraged Richard to proceed, and on or about 29 November the decision was taken to summon a parliament to meet late in January; strangely, not until its meeting of 3 December did the council minute that it was advising the protector to call a parliament. In a letter to his brother Henry on 30 November Richard wrote that his 'affaires … are very heavy, and difficult' and, drawing attention particularly to financial problems and to arrears of military pay in England, Scotland, and Ireland and in the navy, he reported that 'these with other waighty considerations hath caussed us to call a Parliament' (BL, Lansdowne MS 1236, fol. 119). It was decided to revert to the pre-protectorate franchise and distribution of seats for the House of Commons, though retaining not only MPs sitting for Scotland and Ireland but also the nominated 'other house' of the 1657 constitution. The elections were often hotly contested but passed off reasonably peacefully and, as the 1657 constitution made no provision for the pre-session vetting and exclusion of MPs, all those duly elected were entitled to take their seats when parliament opened on 27 January 1659.

The meeting of his only protectorate parliament and its immediate consequences dominated the second half of Richard Cromwell's protectorate. He arrived at Westminster by water on 27 January to attend a special service in Westminster Abbey, and then took his place in the Lords chamber to deliver his opening speech. Once more contemporaries noted that he spoke clearly and effectively; his opening speech, which lasted about fifteen minutes, was certainly much briefer and more tightly structured than the great orations with which his father had opened his protectorate parliaments. He began by thanking God that the nation was at peace internally and in good order, despite 'the great and unexpected change' that had recently occurred with the passing of his father; he paid tribute to his father's achievements and legacy. Turning to the coming parliament, he said that he had summoned it in accordance with the written constitution and looked forward to working with it to further 'the Peace, Laws, Liberties, both Civil and Christian, of these Nations'. He drew parliament's attention to the threat posed by enemies at home and abroad, to the need to address the great arrears of pay owed to the army—'the best Army in the world'—and to the necessity both of continuing war against Spain and of defending the country against land and sea attacks from other states. He closed by recommending to parliament's care 'the People of God in these Nations, with their Concernments', 'the good and necessary work of Reformation, both in Manners and in the Administration of Justice', and 'the Protestant cause abroad, which seems at this time to be in some danger'. He hoped that parliament would show 'the Spirit of Wisdom and Peace … and to this let us all add our utmost endeavours for the making this an happy Parliament' (*The Speech of His Highness the Lord Protector*, 1659, 1, 5, 6, 8–9; BL, Thomason tract, E968 (1)). The address was widely praised, and many contemporaries were surprised by Richard's ability confidently to deliver such a crisp speech.

Like his father before him, Cromwell then withdrew and appears to have left the parliament free to run its own affairs without further intervention. Although in due course a grouping emerged in parliament which was sometimes referred to by contemporaries as 'courtiers' or 'the court party', there is little sign that either directly or through his councillors the protector generally sought to guide or shape the session. Like his father, he appears to have stood back and waited upon parliamentary developments. Indeed, during Richard's protectorate parliament of January to April 1659, as during the sessions of the first and second protectorate parliaments of his father, official and unofficial sources tend to focus on events in parliament, particularly the House of Commons, and throw little light upon the protector himself. Richard continued to oversee the executive arm of government, and the council continued to meet and to transact business, though, as no council order book appears to survive for the period after 18 January 1659, we know far less about the work of Richard and his council over these months; a sketchy picture may be reconstructed from a surviving index to the missing order book and from other supporting papers.

Until the end of March much parliamentary time was absorbed by long debates in the Commons on a number of key issues. Should they recognize Cromwell as lord protector (a bill to this end was introduced by Thurloe on 1 February, suggesting that a limited degree of planning and parliamentary management was being attempted) and in the process accept the provisions of the written constitution of 1657? Should there be a second parliamentary chamber, and, if so, what should its composition and role be? Should the Commons recognize and transact business with the existing 'other house', and should the sixty MPs representing Scottish and Irish seats continue to be permitted to sit and vote in the House of Commons? All these proposals were strongly opposed by an anti-protectoral, republican minority in the Commons, though even these critics of the regime in general and of the existence of a single person as head of state in particular were at pains to stress that they held no personal animosity towards Richard and had found him a pleasant and honest young man. However, despite the vociferous opposition of the republicans, pro-protectoral majorities were eventually secured in the Commons on all these main points. Moreover, parliament also began the process of inquiring into state finances and their shortcomings, and, by recognizing Richard's control of the armed forces, cleared the way during February for protector and council to dispatch a fleet to the Baltic to counter Dutch activity in the area; it sailed at the end of March.

On the other hand, there were growing signs not only of continuing discontent in the army but also of links between the army and the radical minority in parliament, with soldiers seeking the right to petition parliament to air their grievances and the republican faction in the Commons only too keen to encourage military unrest and to make common cause with the army against the alleged deficiencies of the protectoral regime. In mid-February Cromwell addressed another meeting of officers, this time at Fleetwood's house, to emphasize once more that he would not give up his position as commander-in-chief, and to make clear that he would not allow the army to go behind his back and petition parliament against the government, either alone or in conjunction with other civilian or religious groups. As before, his personal intervention temporarily quelled but did not resolve the problem or end military discontent.

The fall of the protectorate, April–May 1659 A combination of republican and radical propaganda, continuing and unaddressed military arrears, and growing distrust of Cromwell were exacerbated by anti-military sentiments emanating from the conservative majority in parliament during the closing weeks of the session. The army feared that parliament might not only reorganize the military, perhaps greatly reducing the existing army and relying more heavily upon an expanded militia, ostensibly a cost-cutting exercise—a financial report of early April confirmed a huge debt of nearly £2½ million and an annual deficit of £⅓ million—which would serve to break the power of the army, but also push ahead with a more conservative religious settlement, whittling away the religious liberties held dear by many within the army; in both areas there was an expectation that Richard would support parliament rather than the army. Early in April Richard permitted a meeting of the general council of officers which, with his concurrence, called for parliament to act against royalists and to settle arrears of military pay; indemnity for parliamentarian soldiers was also urged. But parliament conspicuously failed to support the higher taxes which would be needed to meet army arrears and to support the existing military budget; instead the Commons launched proceedings against a senior army officer who had allegedly maltreated a royalist conspirator, and it rebuffed a petition seeking relief for ailing imprisoned Quakers.

There were rumours that during the third week of April senior officers considered seizing Cromwell and holding him in their custody, and that various officers and civilian politicians loyal to the protector had sought his consent to their plans to seize or assassinate the senior officers, but that he had declined to endorse the plans. On 17 April he again met the officers to try to heal a growing breach between the army and the conservative majority in parliament but, apparently pessimistic at the outcome, he seems to have supported a dual strategy which the Commons voted through on 18 April—on the one hand, parliament would move against royalists and would seek to pay military arrears, but, on the other, the general council officers should henceforth assemble only if authorized by protector and parliament and all officers must take an oath against forcible coercion of parliament. However, the 'other house', which comprised many senior officers such as Fleetwood and Disbrowe, did not vote to support these Commons resolutions. Nothing daunted, Richard ordered the general council dissolved. At first the officers obeyed, and on 20 April Fleetwood and Disbrowe pledged their loyalty to Richard. When, however, on 21 April the Commons pressed on with moves to reorganize the army and form a militia, perhaps under parliamentary control, the obedience of the army was at an end. When Cromwell refused an initial request from the senior officers to dissolve parliament, they began gathering troops around St James's; when he in turn called an alternative rendezvous at Whitehall, many of the regiments on whose loyalty he thought he could depend deserted him, the rank-and-file and junior officers deciding instead to attend the St James's rendezvous. After several hours of further resistance and agonizing over what he could and should do, Richard bowed to army pressure and felt compelled to do as the officers commanded. His parliament was dissolved by his enforced command on 22 April and effective power passed to the army.

Cromwell remained for a further month in powerless limbo at Whitehall Palace, still protector in name though no longer in command of events and under a form of house arrest. At first some of the senior officers, including Fleetwood, may have envisaged retaining Richard as protector with reduced powers, but the harder line taken by other officers, together with the removal from their commands in late April of the officers who had supported Richard and the promotion or reinstatement of more radical officers in their stead, strengthened arguments in favour of a republican settlement. During the first week of May the officers agreed to recall the Rump, thus completely ending the position and role of Richard as lord protector, though laying down certain conditions, including the honourable treatment of him, the payment of the debts which he had incurred in the service of the state, and the allocation to him of a pension and a London residence. About this time Thurloe was writing that Cromwell was to be excluded from any share in government and would be compelled to retire as a private gentleman. Meanwhile everyone, including Richard, awaited news from outside England, to see how Henry Cromwell, George Monck, William Lockhart, and Edward Montague, who respectively commanded the army in Ireland, Scotland, and Dunkirk and the fleet, would respond to news of Richard's fall. However, Richard failed to give a clear lead, and in due course all four commanders and their forces acquiesced in the changes and recognized the authority of the new republican regime. Similarly, he did not respond decisively to offers of French military and financial support made via the French ambassador.

Cromwell may have held back from encouraging and supporting active resistance for fear of unleashing widespread bloodshed or perhaps because he judged that such resistance would be futile and unsuccessful. It is possible that he was being kept under tight, armed seclusion in Whitehall Palace, and so was unable to communicate freely with the outside world, though in mid-May he did manage to dispatch two heavily coded letters to his brother Henry which give some insight into his state of mind at this time. In the first, written about 12 May, Richard acknowledged his own sins and weaknesses, while noting that 'I could not have beleved that religion, relation and selfe interests would have deceved me'. He urged his brother to 'be wary what you doe for youre owne sake and the sake of those that shall have an affection with you', but he also made clear that only armed intervention from outside England could reverse recent developments; he had heard nothing yet from Scotland, Dunkirk, or the fleet. Parts of the letter suggest that he was quietly resigned to his fate—'I am now in daly expectation what course they wil take with me. My confidence is in God and to Him wil I put my cause … I knowe not whether a liberty or a prisson [awaits me]'; though elsewhere he appeared angry: 'I believe Fleetwood and Desborough are not longe lived' (BL, Lansdowne MS 823, fols. 371–2). In the second letter to Henry, written about 17 May, Richard appeared more bitter, reporting that he had been forsaken by his council, friends, and relations and was 'in the duste with my mouth as to God'. Urging Henry to 'have a care whoe you trust, the world is false', Richard noted that 'those my father's friends, pretended ones only, were myne' had 'tripped up my heels before I knew them, for though they were relations yet they forsooke me'; he called Fleetwood and Disbrowe 'pittiful creatures. God will avenge inocency'. As Monck had sent a 'poore' reply, indicating that he would not intervene, and no word had been received from the fleet, Richard seemed resigned to his fate: 'Greate severities are put upon me and I expect the greatest … These men intend nothing lese then ruen to us boeth'. He concluded by exhorting Henry to join him in relying 'upon the God of oure father; and it will be as much our honor to know how to' (ibid., fol. 370).

On 14 May the Rump had Richard Cromwell's protectoral seal smashed and the protectoral arms removed from buildings. The Rump agreed to pay Richard's debts, by this time amounting to about £29,000, and undertook both to cover his removal expenses from Whitehall Palace and to provide him with an annual pension. At length, bowing to what was now inevitable, he signed a formal letter of resignation, written by or for him, which was delivered to the Rump on 25 May. In it he pledged to accept the new regime, noting that 'I trust my past Carriage hitherto hath manifested my acquiescence to the Will and disposition of God, and that I love and value the Peace of this Common-Wealth much above my own concernments'; he undertook to continue to submit quietly 'to the hand of God'. He closed by making explicit that, although he had played no part in the establishment of the new government,

> through the goodness of God I can freely acquiesce in it being made, and do hold myself obliged, as (with other men) I expect Protection from the present Government, so to demean myself, with all peaceableness under it, and to procure to the uttermost of my Power, that all in whom I have any Interest do the same. (*His Late Highnes's Letter to the Parlament of England*, 1659; BL, Thomason tract 669, fol. 21 (32))

With the signing and submission of this letter, Richard Cromwell's protectorate formally came to an end on 25 May; in practice, it had effectively ended several weeks before.

Later life, 1659–1712 Cromwell lingered at Whitehall Palace for several weeks, and even visited Hampton Court and hunted deer there, until in July he was eventually forced by the Rump to vacate his former protectoral properties and retire to Hursley. During the political turmoil of the autumn and winter of 1659–60 there were rumours that he was to be recalled and the protectorate re-established—at one point he may even have been temporarily reinstalled at Hampton Court to be on hand close to London if needed—but nothing came of them. His return to family life at Hursley with his wife and children proved short-lived, however, for the Rump failed to cover his debts and to provide him with a pension and he was increasingly troubled by creditors. On 18 April 1660 he wrote to George Monck, reporting that his 'present exigencies' were forcing him 'to retire into hiding-places to avoid arrests for debts contracted upon the public account', and seeking the help of Monck and of the new parliament in this matter (Ramsey, 116). On 8 May he gave up his last public office, that of chancellor of Oxford University, writing ruefully that 'since the all-wise providence of God, which I desire always to adore and bow down unto, has been pleased to change my condition, that I am not in a capacity to answer the ends of the office', he was resigning his chancellorship (ibid., 117). Perhaps as much to elude his creditors as to avoid harassment by the restored Stuart regime—he had, after all, played no part in the civil wars or the regicide—Richard went into semi-voluntary exile soon after the Restoration. Leaving behind his heavily pregnant wife (his last child was born in August) and his children, in July 1660 Richard took boat from Sussex to a new life on the continent.

We catch only occasional glimpses of Cromwell while he was living abroad from 1660 until 1680 or 1681. He spent most of those years in France, especially Paris, though he probably passed through Geneva and may have lived for a time in Italy or Spain. From time to time during the 1660s Samuel Pepys recorded in his diary reports of Cromwell's life abroad, supported by friends and living under a pseudonym but making no real attempt to disguise himself or to deny his true identity if challenged. In 1666 Richard successfully persuaded the government not to recall him to England. On his behalf it was claimed in March that he was living very quietly, peacefully, and modestly in Paris, changing his name and his abode from time to time 'that he may keep himself unknown beyond the seas', having no contact with 'Fanatics nor with the King of France or States of Holland', avoiding the company of English, Scots, and Irish, and keeping clear of plots against Charles II. Instead, Richard, who was reportedly spending his time reading, drawing landscapes, and being 'instructed in the sciences', often prayed for the king and expressed his loyalty. His financial position remained precarious—he was 'not sixpence the better or richer for being the son of his father'—and 'his debts would ruin him in case he should be necessitated to return into England' (*CSP dom.*, 1665–6, 299). He did not even return in the mid-1670s when he heard that his wife was seriously ill, though in the first of a series of surviving letters to his eldest daughter, Elizabeth, he did express concern for Dorothy's health, recommending various remedies and the love of God and expressing great frustration that he could not do more to help. He asked Elizabeth to 'Pray imbrace thy mother for me, I doe love her, she is deare to me. Desire her to keepe up her spirits, beg her to be cheerfull' (Ramsey, 133). Dorothy died in January 1676, nearly sixteen years after she had last seen her husband, and control of the Hursley estate passed to Richard's eldest surviving son, Oliver.

In 1680 or 1681 Cromwell quietly returned to England. After some delay and apparent reluctance, from the late 1680s onwards he began visiting the family estate and some of his children at Hursley from time to time. However, he never took up residence there and instead spent the last thirty years of his life as a lodger in other households. By 1683 he had become a paying boarder with the merchant Thomas Pengelly and his wife, Rachel, at Finchley, Middlesex, an arrangement that continued for the rest of his life. He lodged with Rachel Pengelly after her husband's death in January 1696 and moved with her to the house of one of her relatives in Cheshunt, Hertfordshire, in 1700. During the 1680s and 1690s Richard's modest income of £120 per annum, drawn from the Hursley estate, covered his rent and other items, including clothes and a wig, wine, sherry, and brandy, tea and coffee, pipes and tobacco, spectacles, and a horse and dogs. In later years, though still a boarder, he maintained his own man-servant. He also took a fatherly interest in the Pengellys' son Thomas, and supported his education and budding legal career.

During his time in England, as in his earlier years on the continent, Cromwell generally employed a variety of pseudonyms, signing his letters to his daughter Elizabeth variously Clarke, Canterbury, Crandberry, Cranmore, Cranbourne, or Cary. Soon after his return in 1683 he fell under some suspicion of involvement in the Rye House Plot, and an order was issued that he be secured and questioned, but he could not be found. In 1690 he became alarmed when his son Oliver sought to pursue his disputed election as MP for Lymington, fearing that, however justified his case might be, it would be unwise to draw attention to the family. Indeed, Richard became increasingly concerned about his son's running of the Hursley estate, his financial affairs, his personal life, his marriage prospects, and the company he was keeping, as well as (in the early 1700s) his growing estrangement from his surviving sisters. Oliver died unmarried and childless in May 1705, leaving large debts—Richard's own allowance from the Hursley estate had fallen into arrears—as well as a complex dispute over whether his elderly father or his eldest sister should succeed him in control of the estate. There followed a bitter legal dispute between Richard and his daughter Elizabeth, egged on by members of the family by marriage and by other associates, for the administration of Hursley, which both angered and hurt Richard. It is noticeable that by 1706 he felt able and compelled to proceed at law under his own name. In December 1706 the court found in his favour and he gained control of Hursley, though he continued to live not there but with Mrs Pengelly in Cheshunt. Richard and his daughter had sought to stay on good terms personally throughout the dispute and during his last years he resumed his warm correspondence with Elizabeth and Anne, now his only surviving children.

Financially now more secure, Cromwell enjoyed a few more years at Cheshunt before his health broke down in 1712. In May 1712 Mrs Pengelly noted that he was 'not very well—he decaes, the hot weather makes him out of order' (Ramsey, 221). By early June he 'hath no mind to stire neither indeed is he fit to stire without these walls at present' (ibid.). On 1 July he made his will, a brief and simple document in which he recommended his 'soul to my gracious God trusting I shall be saved by the alone merits of my blessed Saviour Jesus Christ' and then, having made small bequests to various friends, servants, and suppliers—including a London tobacconist—and a larger bequest to his late brother Henry's only surviving son, left the bulk of his estate to 'my beloved sister Mary, Countess of Falconberg', who was also appointed sole executrix (PRO, PROB 11/528, sig. 150). On 2 July he worsened: 'his distempers seem to have got fast hold of him & don't goe of as they use to doe & he declines. I think sometimes he maye Rub on a whill longer & some times I think he will be gone quickly' (Ramsey, 223). In fact, he lingered a further ten days and died on 12 July 1712. According to some reports he was visited by his daughters during his last days and exhorted them to 'Live in Love. I am going to the God of love' (ibid., 224). He was buried on 18 July in the chancel of Hursley church, beside his wife. If a contemporary tablet marked the grave, it perished in the Victorian restoration of the building. However, there survive within the church both a large, later eighteenth-century monument to the Maijor and Cromwell families, including Richard and Dorothy and six of their children, and a modern inscribed tablet recording the presence near by of the mortal remains of Richard Cromwell.

Assessment Richard Cromwell appears to have left no journal, memoir, commonplace book, or other biographical writings, and apart from the formal and official correspondence which he signed or which was addressed to him as protector, there survives only a small number of more personal and revealing letters written by or to him. Accordingly, biographers often struggle to paint a full, rounded, and even portrait of Richard, to give an account of his eighty-six years in which he remains centre-stage throughout. Overall, he comes across as decent and honest, a pleasant and reasonably intelligent man, well suited to the life of a good husband, father, and country gentleman into which he was settling in the early and mid-1650s. Developments beyond his control, and which there is no evidence that he actively sought, brought that to an end and cast him in a new role to which he was ill suited, and which overshadowed and permanently changed the remainder of his long and in some ways rather sad life. It is noticeable that friends and opponents alike found little to fault in his personality and character; most found him to be worthy, dignified, and personally engaging. Although both during and after his protectorate he was often attacked in printed works, most mocked or lampooned him rather than levelled accusations of dishonesty or corruption, personal ambition, cruelty, or vindictiveness. Most portrayed him as too gentle and a little too naive for his own good, a 'meek knight', 'Queen Dick'. *Margery Good Cow* of May 1659 argued that he should receive a generous financial settlement from the returning Rump 'as a reward of his own Virtues, his modesty, true serenity, gentle and manly deportment' (p. 1; BL, Thomason tract E984 (9)), while *Fourty Four Queries to the Life of Queen Dick* of June or July 1659 asked 'Whether Richard Cromwell was Oliver's sonne or no?', so great were the differences between them (p. 1; BL, Thomason tract E986 (18)). Richard bore his sufferings with equanimity and, excepting a brief show of bitterness and impotent rage in April and May 1659, calmly accepted and made the best of his lot. Despite early rumours of a weak religious faith, he was clearly supported and strengthened by a genuine and deep belief in an active and providential God who had some divine purpose in all the twists and turns of his life. In his intensely personal letters to his eldest daughter during his later life, as well as in some of his more public pronouncements during his protectorate, he repeatedly looked to God's will and sought divine guidance, while encouraging others to do the same. Reverses he often interpreted as the Lord's just retribution for his own sins and shortcomings. There is no clear evidence about where and how he worshipped during the closing decades of his life, no evidence that he did not conform to the Church of England before or after the Toleration Act.

Most historical judgements of Cromwell focus not upon his character or religious faith in general, but upon his abilities and performance as lord protector in 1658–9. Despite limited preparation and previous experience upon which he could draw, in many respects he was a successful head of state. He was conscientious and dedicated, carried himself with calm dignity, and made good and effective speeches, both formal and informal. Many contemporaries noted his engaging manner, his strong interpersonal skills, his ability to charm. He was modest and unassuming: time and again he sought to disarm critics by adopting a self-deprecating line, stressing his youth and inexperience and calling on his audience to come to his aid and to work with him. For a time he just about held his own in his struggle with the army. But, however pleasant the speeches, however charming the personality, his protectorate was in severe difficulties from the outset, overshadowed by problems which were largely not of his making and which he could do little to resolve. That he had no real military background and no standing in the army, that he was obviously more civilian than soldier, and that he could do little to meet the military arrears or to sort out the state finances soon became apparent to everyone, inside and outside the army. Faced with growing military insubordination, in spring 1659 he went too far in supporting the civilian parliament against the army and in trying to confront the military, and he lacked the power and resources to survive the military backlash. But it is hard to see how successfully he could have contained in the longer term the centrifugal forces of the protectorate and maintained the regime and constitution that he had inherited from his father. Although Lucy Hutchinson's assessment of Richard and his rule is in places rather sharp and unfair, it is hard to disagree with her conclusions: Richard 'was so flexible to good counsels, that there was nothing desirable in a prince which might not have been hoped in him, but a great spirit and a just title' and he 'was pleasant in his nature, yet gentle and virtuous, but became not greatness' (Hutchinson, 304, 298).

PETER GAUNT

Sources R. W. Ramsey, *Richard Cromwell, protector of England* (1935) · J. Waylen, *The house of Cromwell and the story of Dunkirk* (1897) · M. Noble, *Memoirs of the protectoral house of Cromwell*, 2 vols. (1787) · O. Cromwell, *Memoirs of the protector, Oliver Cromwell, and of his sons Richard and Henry* (1820) · *The writings and speeches of Oliver Cromwell*, ed. W. C. Abbott and C. D. Crane, 4 vols. (1937–47) · Thurloe, *State papers* · Henry Cromwell, correspondence, BL, Lansdowne MSS 821–823 · J. A. Butler, *A biography of Richard Cromwell, 1626–1712, the second protector* (1994) · E. M. Hause, *Tumble down Dick: the fall of the house of Cromwell* (1972) · *CSP dom.*, 1657–66 · A. S. Burn, 'Correspondence of Richard Cromwell', *EngHR*, 13 (1898), 93–124 · D. Hirst, 'Concord and discord in Richard Cromwell's House of Commons', *EngHR*, 103 (1988), 339–58 · I. Roots, 'The tactics of the Commonwealthsmen in Richard Cromwell's parliament', *Puritans and revolutionaries*, ed. D. Pennington and K. Thomas (1978), 283–309 · order book of Richard Cromwell's council, Sept 1658–Jan 1659, Longleat House, Wiltshire, Longleat MS 67a [photocopy at PRO, PRO 31/17/33] · will of Richard Cromwell, 1712, PRO, PROB 11/528, q. 150 · G. Davies, *The restoration of Charles II, 1658–1660* (1955); repr. (1969) · G. Davies, 'The army and the downfall of Richard Cromwell', *Huntington Library Bulletin*, 7 (1935), 131–67 · *The Clarke papers*, ed. C. H. Firth, 4 vols., CS, new ser., 49, 54, 61–2 (1891–1901) · L. Hutchinson, *Memoirs of the life of Colonel Hutchinson*, ed. J. Hutchinson, rev. C. H. Firth, new edn (1906) · F. Guizot, *History of Richard Cromwell and the restoration of Charles II*, trans. A. R. Scoble, 2 vols. (1856) · A. B. Nourse, 'The nomination of Richard Cromwell', *Cromwelliana* (1979), 25–31 · R. Hutton, *The Restoration: a political and religious history of England and Wales, 1658–1667* (1985) · F. M. S. Henderson, 'New material from the Clarke manuscripts: political and official correspondence and news sent and received by the army headquarters in Scotland, 1651–60', DPhil diss., U. Oxf., 1998 · A. Woolrych, 'The last quests for settlement, 1657–60', *The interregnum*, ed. G. E. Aylmer (1972), 183–204 · R. Tangye, *The two protectors: Oliver and Richard Cromwell* (1899) · *Diary of Thomas Burton*, ed. J. T. Rutt, 4 vols. (1828) · I. Roots, 'The short and troublesome reign of Richard IV', *History Today*, 30 (1980) · quarter session records, 1649–60, Hants. RO, QO/2–4 · D. Hall and N. Barber, *Colonel Richard Norton's regiment of horse* (1989) · N. Barber, 'Richard Maijor, esquire', diss., Portsmouth Polytechnic, 1979 · Richard Maijor's papers, BL, Add. MS 24860

Archives BL, Henry Cromwell corresp., Lansdowne MSS 821–823 · Bodl. Oxf., Thurloe state papers, MSS Rawl. · Cambs. AS, letters mostly to his daughter Elizabeth on family matters · Harvard U., Houghton L., letters to Elizabeth Cromwell

Likenesses miniature, watercolour on vellum, *c.*1650–1655, NPG [see illus.] · engraving, 1659, repro. in *Some farther intelligence of affairs of England* (1659) · S. Cooper, miniature, watercolour on vellum, repro. in D. Foskett, ed., *Samuel Cooper and his contemporaries* (1974), no. 44 [exhibition catalogue, NPG, London]; priv. coll. · S. Cooper, miniature, watercolour on vellum, repro. in D. Foskett, ed., *Samuel Cooper and his contemporaries* (1974), no. 45 [exhibition catalogue, NPG, London]; priv. coll. · P. Stent, engraving, repro. in Clarendon, *Hist. rebellion* · R. Walker, oils, Cromwell Museum, Huntingdon · attrib. R. Walker, oils, Chequers Court, Buckinghamshire · miniature (after Walker), Cromwell Museum, Huntingdon

Cromwell, Thomas, earl of Essex (*b.* in or before 1485, *d.* 1540), royal minister, was the son of Walter Cromwell of Putney, Surrey, who made his name there as a blacksmith, fuller, and cloth merchant, as well as the owner of both a hostelry and a brewery. All that is known of his mother is that she was the aunt of Nicholas Glossop of Wirksworth in Derbyshire, and that she reportedly lived in Putney in the house of a local attorney, John Welbeck, at the time of her marriage to Walter Cromwell in 1474.

After Archbishop John Kemp granted the lease or ownership of a fulling mill to William Cromwell (probably Walter's grandfather) in 1452 the cloth trade had become something of a family business. Walter Cromwell's modest success as a tradesman is reflected by his frequent service as a juryman and his appointment as constable of Putney in 1495. He secured good marriages to local men for his daughters: the elder, Katherine, married Morgan Williams, an aspiring Welsh lawyer; her younger sister, Elizabeth, married a farmer, William Wellyfed. Katherine and Morgan's son Richard changed his name to Cromwell and worked in his uncle's service, being particularly active in the suppression of the monasteries. Richard's great-grandson was Oliver Cromwell, the lord protector.

Early life, c.1485–1520 The precise date of Thomas Cromwell's birth is uncertain, but could not have been after 1485. Very little is known about his early life in Putney apart from his own declaration to Archbishop Thomas Cranmer much later as to what a 'ruffian he was in his young days' (*Acts and Monuments*, 5.365). He is even said to have been imprisoned for a short while. Certainly life at

Thomas Cromwell, earl of Essex (*b*. in or before 1485, *d*. 1540), after Hans Holbein the younger, *c*.1533–4

home was not easy. Despite his property and local influence Cromwell's father drank heavily and was regularly in trouble. Between 1475 and 1501 Walter Cromwell was fined 6*d*. by the manor court on forty-eight occasions for breaches of the assize of ale, and he was also often reprimanded for allowing his cattle to graze too freely on public land. More seriously, in 1477 he was convicted of assault and fined 20*d*., and he was finally evicted from his manorial tenancy in 1514 after fraudulently altering documents concerning his tenure.

Whether it was his own bad behaviour, an argument with his father, or some other reason which prompted his decision, Cromwell left his family in Putney to travel the continent. Accounts of precisely what he did and where he went are both sketchy and contradictory, but it is most likely that after crossing the channel he first joined the French army and marched with them to Italy, fighting in the battle of Garigliano on 28 December 1503. At some point after this he parted from the French army and entered the household of the merchant banker Francesco Frescobaldi. The Italian novelist Bandello tells how the destitute Cromwell confronted Frescobaldi in Florence, begging for his assistance. Frescobaldi is said instantly to have taken pity on him and invited him to stay in his household, where he provided clothes and money. Bandello also records that when Cromwell decided to return to England, Frescobaldi gave him sixteen gold ducats and a strong horse. However, it is likely that instead of travelling straight home Cromwell went instead to the Netherlands, where he worked as a cloth merchant. George Elyot, a mercer writing from Calais in 1536, claimed that he had enjoyed Cromwell's 'love and

true heart since the Syngsson Mart at Middelburgh in 1512', implying that it was there that they had first met (*LP Henry VIII*, 10, no. 1218). Cromwell certainly spent time touring the Low Countries, visiting such leading mercantile centres as Antwerp and Bruges. There he learned his trade living among the English merchants and was able to develop an important network of contacts, as well as learning several languages. He must also have returned to Italy for a while, as the records of the English Hospital in Rome show that he stayed there in June 1514.

Some time during these years Cromwell returned to England. He married Elizabeth Williams, *née* Wykys (*d*. 1527), with whom he had his only surviving son, Gregory. It was a good match for him. Elizabeth was the widow of Thomas Williams, a yeoman of the guard, and her father, Henry Wykys, was another Putney shearman who had also served as a gentleman usher to Henry VII. The marriage enabled Cromwell to seek his father-in-law's assistance in obtaining a foothold in the English cloth trade. Cromwell was also becoming established as a business agent, a role which often strayed into fringe work in the law. Usually described at the time as 'soliciting', this did not imply any professional training, but was similar to the work of a French *homme d'affaires*. It is not surprising, therefore, to find him enhancing his earnings from this source by a little moneylending as well. However, his travelling days were not yet over. John Robinson, alderman of Boston and a close acquaintance of Cromwell's, in 1517–18 asked him to travel to Rome with one Geoffrey Chambers on behalf of the town's guild of Our Lady, in order to obtain indulgences from Pope Julius II. The concessions sought were of a kind which could be granted only by papal authority. Cromwell gained access to the pope without having to spend the usual tedious amount of time waiting around by surprising him as he returned from a hunting expedition with a performance of an English 'three man's song'. Knowing the pope's predilection for fine foods he then presented him with a selection of fine English sweetmeats and jellies 'such as kings and princes … only in the realm of England use to feed upon' (*Acts and Monuments*, 5.364). The pope was suitably impressed and instantly granted all the guild's requests.

A London lawyer, 1520–1529 By 1520 Cromwell was firmly established in London mercantile and legal circles. Most significantly he began to act for clients in several important suits, including an appeal from the prerogative court of Canterbury to the papal curia in October that year. Then in 1521 he acted for Charles Knyvett, formerly surveyor to Edward Stafford, third duke of Buckingham, who had resigned from Buckingham's service shortly before the duke's execution for treason on 17 May, and gave evidence against him. Knyvett now sought to recover offices he had lost following his resignation, as well as release from bonds to the value of £3100 which he had been forced to undertake on Buckingham's behalf. Cromwell prepared and corrected numerous petitions on behalf of his client, some of which were delivered to the king and some to Cardinal Thomas Wolsey. He failed on this occasion, but for the first time he had succeeded in making his name known in the highest circles of government. During the next few years he came increasingly into contact with the cardinal over legal matters. For instance, in 1521 he was employed by the London bakers' guild to draft petitions to both Wolsey and the lord mayor for licence to reform their craft. The following year he was instructed as an attorney in a case before the king's council and in another in which Wolsey was personally involved.

In 1523 Cromwell entered the House of Commons for the first time, though his constituency has not been identified. A speech survives in the hand of one of his clerks, in which he attacks the war against France for which the parliament had been called, although it is not recorded whether it was ever delivered. In it Cromwell declares that he is as committed as anyone to reclaiming France for the king, but that an invasion will inevitably fail as a result of both logistical and financial considerations. Instead he suggests conquering Scotland, whose union with England will in turn make France more submissive. Such a policy was unlikely to be adopted, but it was one which would draw attention to him without offending either the taxpayer or the king. It was a tempestuous parliament, with strongly divided opinions. In a letter to his friend John Creke, composed shortly after the close of the session, Cromwell wrote wittily of having:

> indured a parlyament which contenwid by the space of xvii hole wekes wher we communyd of warre pease Stryffe contencyon debatte murmure grudge Riches poverte penurye trowth falshode Justyce equyte dicayte [deceit] opprescyon Magnanymyte actyvyte foce [force] attempraunce [moderation] Treason murder Felonye consyli ... [conciliation] and also how a commune welth myght be ediffyed and a[lso] contenewid within our Realme. Howbeyt in conclusyon we have d[one] as our predecessors have been wont to doo that ys to say, as well we myght and lefte wher we begann ... (Merriman, 1.313)

Cromwell's rise in social status at this time is shown by his moving from his residence in Fenchurch Street some time after September 1522 to another 'against the gate' of the Austin Friars in Broad Street (*LP Henry VIII*, 7, no. 1618). Soon after arriving in the new ward of Broadstreet he was elected as a senior officer, probably secretary, in the wardmote inquest set up at the end of 1523 to send an annual report on the ward to its alderman. This represented an unusually swift advancement, as it was normally necessary to hold several less distinguished positions in a ward before promotion to senior office. Then in 1524 Cromwell was appointed a subsidy commissioner in Middlesex, determining the value of people's lands and goods for taxation, while success as a lawyer was recognized by his election as a member of Gray's Inn. He was also involved in a number of high profile land cases which influenced the course of the rest of his career. In February Sir Robert Ughtred, a Yorkshire knight, sold the manor of Kexby to John Aleyn, a London alderman and a senior member of the Mercers' Company. The manor was then sold on immediately to Cardinal Wolsey, with Cromwell acting for Aleyn. His considerable skill in conveyancing was noticed by Thomas Heneage, one of Wolsey's main agents in the sale, who asked Cromwell to represent him

in several of his own transactions. The two men became close, and by the summer Cromwell had joined Heneage in Wolsey's service.

At this time Wolsey was heavily preoccupied with the building projects which were intended to be his principal legacy: the construction of Cardinal College at Oxford and of a grammar school in Ipswich. As might have been expected of the cardinal the plans were extravagant and the costs exorbitant. Although there were several precedents for the suppression of religious houses and the diversion of their revenues to similar establishments, Wolsey's project was on an unprecedented scale. Nearly thirty monasteries were to be dissolved and their lands and goods sold. This in turn created a considerable amount of legal work, and Cromwell's skill in land conveyancing marked him out as the best man for the job. On 28 July 1524 he supervised the resignation by Sir John Longevile to Wolsey of his patronal rights in Bradwell Priory, Buckinghamshire. Another twenty-eight monasteries followed, with Cromwell and his team responsible in each case for selling their lands and goods. By August 1526 the documents relating to the houses which had been suppressed to fund the Oxford college alone filled thirty-four bags.

Cromwell's enthusiasm for his work is very apparent. On 2 April 1528 he wrote to Wolsey concerning Cardinal College:

> The buyldinges of your noble colledge most prosperouslye and magnyfycentlye dothe arryse in suche wise that to every mannes judgemente the lyke thereof was never sene ne ymagened having consideracyon to the largeness beautee sumptuous Curyous and most substauncyall buylding of the same.

He added that the daily services in the chapel were 'so devuoute solempne and full of Armonye that in myne opynyon it hathe fewe peres' (Merriman, 1.319). The ruthlessness with which Cromwell and his men went about their business was also much remarked upon. Foxe records Cromwell's efficiency, but that he 'procured to himself much grudge with divers of the superstitious sort, and with some also of noble calling about the king' (*Acts and Monuments*, 5.366). Dr William Knight, the king's secretary, made the same point in a letter to Wolsey, informing him: 'I have herd the Kyng, and noble men, speke thinges incredible of thactes of M[r] Alayn [John Allen, later archbishop of Dublin] and Cromwell' (*State papers*, 1.261), and the king himself demanded that Wolsey supervise more closely the work of those involved in the dissolution. Cromwell was widely accused of corruption for the number of gifts and fees he received as receiver-general for the colleges. Any administrator at this time might reasonably expect to receive gifts as a form of payment for his services. The criticism was primarily an attempt by Wolsey's enemies to discredit the dissolutions. But Cromwell does seem to have overstepped the mark in this area, if less flagrantly than his accusers suggested.

Wolsey, however, was very satisfied with Cromwell's work and some time after 1526 appointed him to his council. While Cromwell never held a senior formal position in the cardinal's household and was rarely involved in matters of state, he increasingly supervised Wolsey's legal affairs and exercised considerable ecclesiastical patronage. By 1529 he was recognized as one of the cardinal's most senior and trusted advisers, as well as managing to maintain a prosperous private legal practice. The will he drafted in July 1529 testifies to his success. His wife had died two years previously, but he made generous bequests to her sister Joan; his son, Gregory (now studying at Pembroke College, Cambridge); his daughters, Anne and Grace (neither of whom survived childhood); and to his sisters' families. However, this stability did not last. By the end of October Wolsey had fallen from power. Cavendish records meeting a distraught Cromwell on All Hallow's day in the morning, standing against a window in the Great Chamber at Esher. In a rare display of emotion and piety tears poured down his cheeks as he clutched his primer and recited 'our lady mattens'. Cromwell feared that he would go down with Wolsey, and lamented that he had never been provided with an income or office. But this expression of self-pity was short-lived. After regaining his composure he announced to Cavendish:

I do entend (god wyllyng) this after none, whan my lord hathe dyned to ride to london and so to the Court, where I wyll other make or marre or I come agayn, I wyll put my self in the prese [press] to se what any man is Able to lay to my charge of ontrouthe or mysdemeanor.   (Cavendish, 105)

It was this dogged determination to make something of himself that had characterized Cromwell's entry to the cardinal's service and which now took him much further.

'Make or marre', 1529–1530 On New Year's day 1527 Henry VIII finally won the heart of Anne Boleyn after more than a year of persistent courting, and from this date he sought to have his marriage to Queen Katherine annulled. As well as being driven by a desire to consummate his love Henry was also plagued by concern that God was punishing him for having broken the biblical commandments laid down in Leviticus 18 and 20 by having married his dead brother's wife. Securing an annulment from Rome would not be an easy process. While scholars worked to defend the king's position Wolsey was charged with attending to the practical matters. After two years of careful diplomatic negotiation a trial opened at Blackfriars on 18 June 1529 to prove the illegality of the marriage, presided over by cardinals Wolsey and Campeggi. The trial was adjourned by Campeggi on 30 July to allow the queen's petition to reach Rome. This instantly and considerably weakened Wolsey's position, giving the hostile coterie of courtiers who flocked around Anne the leverage they needed to topple him. Nevertheless he fought hard to retain office, and the king's evident reluctance to lose his services enabled him to cling to power until the autumn. It was not until 18 October that Wolsey resigned the great seal, and even then Henry protected him against complete ruin.

Cromwell's anxiety that he would go down with his master was not paranoia. Wolsey had protected him against the onslaught he had faced over monastic dissolutions, but now he faced his enemies on his own. There were even rumours circulating in London that he had been imprisoned in the Tower. Yet within a few days of his telling Cavendish that he was resolved to go to court to 'make or marre' (Cavendish, 105), Cromwell was able to return to inform him that he had just been returned as a burgess in the new parliament which opened on 4 November. He had moved quickly. A hasty request to the third duke of Norfolk (then the leading councillor) for the king's consent was granted on condition that he could find a seat at this late stage and that he would comply with royal instructions. Cromwell asked his secretary, Ralph Sadler, to approach Thomas Russhe, a friend with connections with the Willoughby family, to see if he could help him obtain the Suffolk seat of Orford. Nothing came of this, but Cromwell also had the option of falling back on his influence with Sir William Paulet, Wolsey's steward for the bishopric of Winchester, who was able to nominate members to seats in that diocese. Although he would have preferred not to have had to use his connection with Wolsey, as the new member for Taunton Cromwell now had a base from which he could rebuild his career.

Cromwell participated in the business of the house from 4 November until the close of the first session of the new parliament on 17 December. There is little evidence on exactly what he did apart from sitting on a committee investigating the misuse of the king's protection by merchants, and no bill came of this. It is also possible that he took a leading role in the Commons' campaign against the clergy which culminated in the supplication against the ordinaries in 1532. Cavendish records that Cromwell successfully defended Wolsey against a bill of attainder, but as the proceedings against the cardinal were heard in the court of king's bench in October, well before the opening of parliament, this cannot be true (it is more likely that a confession by Wolsey was submitted as a substitute for the attainder that his enemies failed to achieve). Since Henry did not want Wolsey to be attainted he would certainly have approved of Cromwell's speaking in his defence, and may even have instructed him to do so.

Cromwell also acted as a go-between for the disgraced cardinal and the king, travelling to court on several occasions. He was in a difficult position, attempting to advance his own career and reputation while remaining loyal to his disgraced master. Wolsey's enemies were in the ascendant at court and Cromwell had to do business with them. But there was no conflict of interest. Cavendish records that 'by ther wytty hedes' Wolsey and Cromwell worked together 'to bryng by ther pollecyes mr Cromwell in place & estate where he myght do hymeself good and my lord myche profet' (Cavendish, 126). It was almost entirely due to Cromwell's intercession for Wolsey that the king eventually granted the cardinal a pardon in February 1530. The colleges were not yet under threat, and Cromwell's position as their receiver-general was probably little affected. He was also able to continue his private legal and business interests.

On 30 October 1529 Cromwell's friend Stephen Vaughan had written to him from Antwerp to console him in the wake of Wolsey's fall from power, assuring him: 'You are more hated for your master's sake than for anything which I think you have wrongfully done against any man' (*LP Henry VIII*, 4/3, no. 6036). By the end of November, however, another correspondent had heard 'comfortable tydynges that you be in favour hilie with the Kynges grace, lordes and comunalytie aswell spirituall as temporall' (Elton, *Tudor Revolution*, 88). And in a letter of 3 February 1530 Vaughan himself was able to celebrate: 'You now sail in a sure haven' (*LP Henry VIII*, 4/3, no. 6196). In the following June Sir John Russell sent word of the king's approval after Cromwell had helped the lord chamberlain, William, Lord Sandys, to become keeper of Farnham Castle, one of Wolsey's forfeited properties, informing him: 'After your departure from the Kyng his grace hadd very good Comunycacion of you, whiche I shall advertise you at our next metyng' (Elton, *TudoR revolution*, 85).

Cromwell's entry into the king's service is shrouded in myth. He has been credited with whispering into the king's ear a blueprint for all the revolutionary developments of the 1530s, whereupon he was immediately offered the task of putting his grand scheme into action. In reality his progress into the royal service was somewhat more prosaic. In order to advance at court three things were necessary: the backing of a group of influential courtiers, favour from the king, and talents of obvious use in a particular task. Cromwell managed all these with remarkable speed. After Wolsey's fall he quickly set about cultivating contacts with extraordinary skill. He formed particularly good relationships with the king's lawyers, and it was apparently the attorney-general, Sir Christopher Hales, who first introduced him to the very sceptical king. Cromwell could also rely on the support of former servants of Wolsey like Thomas Heneage and Dr Stephen Gardiner. By June 1530 Cromwell had also won over the king, and soon afterwards a task was found for him which suited his abilities. Yet again it involved conveying land.

Although Wolsey had forfeited all his properties and goods to the crown the legal position of the colleges was not clear. Almost a year after the cardinal's fall they continued to function, albeit facing bankruptcy after their possessions and revenues had been gradually reduced. It was easy enough for Henry to seize their valuables, and his lawyers also succeeded in diverting to the crown some of the proceeds from their leases. This left the ownership of their lands unaffected, and for the crown to obtain this proved very complicated. The difficulty seems to have been that the papal permission required to dissolve the monasteries that financed the colleges had been granted only because the proceeds were going to be used to fund educational establishments, while Henry had himself ratified every step in the process, even agreeing to protect the colleges from legal challenge. After so much controversy surrounding the initial dissolutions the king was reluctant to convert the lands to secular use too hastily. However, his lawyers had discovered a legal loophole which would allow him to obtain possession of the lands, and eventually Henry decided to act on it, arguing that the original land grants were invalid because Wolsey had been in breach of the *praemunire* laws and thus unable to receive them. From June 1530 commissioners were

appointed and inquests held to facilitate the crown's receipt of these monastic estates. As Cromwell had managed all the original transactions he was the obvious choice to supervise the dispatching of the commissions and to draft the inquests' verdicts. A letter which Wolsey wrote to him in August, referring to his 'opportunities of access' to the king, is the first indicator that Cromwell had now officially entered Henry's service (*LP Henry VIII*, 4/3, no. 6554).

In the period after his fall from power Wolsey repeatedly expressed his gratitude to Cromwell, describing him in one letter as 'Myn onely ayder in thys myn intollerable anxiete and hevynes' (*LP Henry VIII*, no. 6098). Cromwell remained loyal to his master until the end, but moments of tension may be discerned in their relationship once the king began to take possession of the college lands. Wolsey appreciated that it would only be a matter of time before this happened, and when Cromwell informed him of his involvement in it Wolsey was understanding and recommended his 'poore estat and Collegys to your and other goode friendes helpe and releff' (*State papers*, 1.362). However, as he watched his life's work being dismantled the cardinal became increasingly distraught, at one point provoking Cromwell to write an explosive letter demanding to know whether he still enjoyed the cardinal's confidence. Wolsey assured him that he did, and that he had rejected rumours to the contrary after friends had relayed Cromwell's loyalty in his dealings concerning the colleges and archbishopric. Nevertheless the situation was becoming increasingly difficult for Cromwell, and when Wolsey died at Leicester Abbey on 29 November 1530, on his way to the Tower on a charge of treason, this probably came as a merciful release to them both.

Progress at court, 1531–1532 At some point during the closing weeks of 1530 Cromwell became a member of the council. Wolsey's death had freed him to undertake more legal and administrative business for the king. It is likely that he acted as receiver-general and supervisor of the newly acquired college lands from early 1531, though he was not officially appointed until 9 January 1532. (By then the grammar school in Ipswich had closed. The Oxford college struggled on until it was re-founded in July as King Henry VIII College, before becoming the present Christ Church in 1546.) Other work included the sale and receipt of land for the king; the supervising of building works at Westminster and the Tower of London; and involvement in various matters of law enforcement, such as hearing appeals and deciding the fate of prisoners and felons brought before him. His perceived influence with the king is reflected in the large number of requests for assistance that he received, even from magnates like the second earl of Essex and the duke of Suffolk, who was the king's brother-in-law.

Cromwell's advance was also apparent in the new session of parliament between January and March 1531. When it ended he took home with him the twenty-nine bills that had reached the statute book, and by the summer the rumour that 'one Mr. Cromwell penned certain matters in the Parliament house, which no man gainsaid' was circulating as far afield as Derbyshire (*LP Henry VIII*, 5, no. 628). Soon everyone wanted to take advantage of his legal skills. Corporate bodies, religious houses, and individuals paid him freely—both off as well as on the books—for his advice and help in securing the passage of measures in their favour. Of most value to the king was Cromwell's assistance in drafting legislation concerned with the continuing attempts to obtain a royal divorce. Yet there is nothing to suggest that he acted in any way other than as Henry's agent and draftsman, working to execute policy formulated elsewhere.

At the centre of the campaign to secure the divorce was the emerging doctrine of the royal supremacy. From 1530 Dr Edward Fox led a team of scholars in collecting a number of sources known as the *Collectanea satis copiosa*. These biblical, early Christian, and ancient English texts were brought together in order to argue that since Anglo-Saxon times kings of England had always enjoyed both secular *imperium* and complete spiritual authority. As diplomatic attempts continued to fail Henry became increasingly convinced of his right to complete jurisdiction, spiritual as well as temporal, over the church. Towards the end of January 1531 he issued a writ of *praemunire* against the entire English clergy and demanded a subsidy of £100,000 from convocation in return for a general pardon. In the ensuing exchanges between the king and his clerics the latter demanded several clarifications and assurances, while Henry further insisted that they acknowledge him as the 'supreme head' of the church in England. It was the task of Cromwell and Thomas Audley, the speaker of the Commons, to persuade William Warham, the archbishop of Canterbury, to accept the king's title. This proved difficult, not least because nobody was sure what it actually meant. Warham was also rightly suspicious of Cromwell's assurances that the king was not taking on any new powers. Eventually convocation consented to a much weaker version of the title and accepted the king's supreme headship only as far as the law of Christ allowed, a qualification probably thought up by Cromwell or Audley. This calmed clerical fears for the time being, but the supremacy was now recognized in law, and Henry had new, if vague, rights over the English church. Moreover they had the potential for extension.

By the autumn Cromwell had taken control of the supervision of the king's legal and parliamentary affairs, working closely with Audley, and about this time he also joined the inner ring of the council. Shortly before the beginning of the Michaelmas term instructions were issued by the king 'unto his trustie Counsailor Thomas Cromwell, to be declared, on his behalf, to his Lerned Counsaill, and indelayedlie to be put in execucyon, the Terme of Saynt Michael, in the 23ti yere of his moct victoryous reigne' (*State papers*, 1.380). A diverse array of briefs was included, from the supervision of criminal prosecution to customs duties, payments due to the king, and the drafting of parliamentary legislation on matters ranging from treason to sewers. By the following spring he had also begun to exert some influence over elections to the Commons.

The third session of what has become known as the Reformation Parliament had been scheduled for October 1531, but was postponed until 15 January 1532, due to government indecision as to the best way to proceed. This uncertainty is reflected in the conflicting legislation drafted by Cromwell and his team: one bill proposed to grant convocation the power to annul the royal marriage, while another sought to remove convocation's independent jurisdiction. Attempts were also made by the duke of Norfolk to get influential peers to support the proposition that the annulment could be granted by parliament, and that Warham might pronounce one in defiance of the pope. Both efforts failed. In the end the best that the king and his leading councillors could come up with was a plan to put pressure on the pope by ending annates (payments made to Rome by senior clerics of the first year's revenue from their benefices). Although Cromwell probably drafted the bill he did not hide his scepticism, confessing to Gardiner that 'for what ende or effecte it will succede suerlie I know not' (Merriman, 1.343). So vehement was the opposition in both houses that a clause had to be added to the bill which would delay its effect until Henry ratified it. Finally passed as the *Act for the Conditional Restraint of Annates*, it was little more than a threat of possible future action.

Meanwhile Cromwell had come around to the solution favoured by Anne Boleyn and her circle: the assertion of the royal supremacy over the church. He successfully manipulated the mood of the Commons by resurrecting their anti-clerical grievances as expressed in the session of 1529. On 18 March the Commons delivered a 'supplication against the ordinaries' to the king, denouncing clerical abuses and the power of the ecclesiastical courts. By describing Henry as 'the only head, sovereign lord, protector, and defender' the supplication would inevitably force convocation to define what it understood by 'headship as far as the law of Christ allows' (Bray, 59). The clergy fell straight into the trap. Refuting the attack in a courageous reply drafted by Gardiner convocation declared: 'we, your most humble servants, may not submit the execution of our charges and duty, certainly prescribed by God, to your highness' assent' (ibid.). Henry was livid. Faced with the threat of parliamentary reprisal in the form of another *praemunire* charge the church had little option but to surrender.

Break from Rome, 1532–1534 On 14 May 1532 parliament was prorogued. Two days later Sir Thomas More resigned as lord chancellor, recognizing that the battle to save the marriage was lost. There is little doubt that in his support for the royal supremacy Cromwell was influenced by genuine evangelical convictions. He was probably also acting with the enthusiasm of a recent convert. Before he joined the court Cromwell appears to have been comfortable expressing orthodox religious beliefs. His will of July 1529 made traditional provision for his spiritual well-being, requesting intercession by the saints and leaving money for various charitable causes as well as for masses for his soul. After Wolsey's fall Cavendish had found him resorting to traditional devotional practice by reciting 'our lady mattens' (Cavendish, 105) with a primer clasped in his hand. On 17 May 1530 Cromwell also declared in a letter to Wolsey that 'The fame is that Luther is departed this life. I would he had never been born', though this need not denote strict orthodoxy (*LP Henry VIII*, 4/3, no. 6076). Yet the seeds of burgeoning evangelicalism are also evident. On the same evening as the emotional outburst at Esher, Cavendish also records an explosion of anti-clerical resentment. When Wolsey admitted he had no money to offer his lay servants Cromwell demanded that the cardinal's chaplains should make a contribution. He complained bitterly about the 'profettes and avuntages' enjoyed by the priests, and declared that Wolsey's lay servants had 'taken myche more payn for you in oon day than all your Idell chapleyns hathe don in a yere' (Cavendish, 106).

During the late 1520s Cromwell had also begun to discuss new ideas about religion with notable reformers like Stephen Vaughan and Miles Coverdale, both his close friends. In a letter which cannot be later than 1527 a young and eager Coverdale wrote to Cromwell requesting books to help advance his studies, and in a eulogy laden with evangelical catch phrases he praised Cromwell for 'for the fervent zeall, that yow have to vertu and godly study' (*State papers*, 1.384). Coverdale was now at the Austin Friars in Cambridge and mixed with passionate reformists like his mentor, Robert Barnes, who were dedicated to what they saw as the reconstruction of true religion through the study of scripture. Coverdale's praise of Cromwell was not mere flattery. John Oliver also later thanked Cromwell for evenings he had spent at his house in 1531 or 1532, 'where in verie dede I did here such communicacion which were the verie cause of the begynnynge of my conversion'; here they would pore over translations of the New Testament and evangelical texts, and Oliver 'found allwaies the conclusions you mayntenyd at yor borde to be consonent with the hollie worde of god' (Brigden, 'Thomas Cromwell', 41).

Throughout the 1530s Cromwell persistently encouraged Henry to consider evangelical reforms. In early 1531, for instance, he persuaded the king to allow William Tyndale safe passage back to England only months after Henry had denounced him as a heretic. Stephen Vaughan was given the task of negotiating this with Tyndale in Antwerp. It looked possible until Vaughan enclosed a copy of Tyndale's *Answer* to Thomas More, defending his enthusiasm for an English Bible. Henry was furious and Cromwell sent a strongly worded letter ordering Vaughan to have nothing further to do with Tyndale. Nevertheless Vaughan's reply indicates that he had somehow got the impression that Cromwell had actually encouraged him to remain in contact with Tyndale, suggesting that Cromwell had added a secret postscript to his original letter instructing him to keep the channels of communication open, but to be more tactful. Vaughan then reported two further meetings with Tyndale in May and June, before Cromwell eventually conceded defeat and dropped the matter.

Sir Thomas More's resignation from the council on 16

May 1532 represented a triumph for Cromwell and the reform faction at court. On the following day the king rewarded Cromwell with a grant for himself and his son, Gregory, in survivorship of the lordship of Romney in Newport, south Wales. As Cromwell's influence increased so did his wealth. About the same time he also took out a ninety-nine-year lease of two recently constructed messuages within the precinct of the Austin Friars in London, where he had lived for the past decade. It was undoubtedly now that Cromwell perpetrated the remarkably arbitrary act later recorded by John Stow. Not only did he move the palings of his neighbours' gardens 22 feet back without permission, warning, or compensation, but he also set Stow's father's house upon rollers and moved that as well, before starting to build upon the land thus cleared.

Cromwell was also appointed to his first significant offices during this period. On 14 April 1532 he had become master of the jewels, to which he added the clerkship of the hanaper on 16 July, before being appointed chancellor of the exchequer on 12 April 1533. Each of these offices was comparatively minor, and none offered much of an income, but the mastership of the jewels allowed Cromwell the most influence in that it permitted access to the king's coffers and enabled him to administer government finance from the funds brought under his control. The king's granting him these offices for life constituted a further indication of royal favour, and one which gave Cromwell a position in three major institutions of government: household, chancery, and exchequer.

From spring 1532 Cromwell was thus in a much stronger position to influence the king. Archbishop Warham's death on 22 August 1532 removed another conservative opponent. Since Thomas Cranmer, who was nominated as the new archbishop of Canterbury, had long worked to secure the divorce, Cromwell knew that securing an archiepiscopal verdict on the case would no longer be a problem, and the king was now willing to lend his support to this possibility. With Audley's assistance Cromwell began to draft proposals which would allow parliament to ratify Cranmer's expected ruling. By January 1533, however, Anne was pregnant and the marriage could be postponed no longer. The dating of the wedding is unclear. Some sort of unofficial ceremony may have taken place when Anne was with the king in Calais in November 1532, but it seems likely that a priest was present for the first time in a secret service conducted on 25 January 1533. In any case Henry was now ecstatic at the prospect of a son, and it became essential to legitimize the union without further delay. Henry had no option but to rely on Cromwell to achieve this.

Parliament was recalled immediately to pass the necessary legislation. On 26 January Sir Thomas Audley was appointed lord chancellor and would now officiate over the House of Lords. Cromwell also increased his control over the membership of the Commons through his continued management of by-elections. It was far from being a 'packed' parliament, but several of the new members were known to be close to him, men such as Thomas Alvard, Sir Francis Bigod, David Broke, Sir Roger

Cholmley, Thomas Derby, John Goodall, and Robert Southwell. The session began on 4 February and Cromwell introduced a new bill restricting the right to make appeals to Rome. He acted quickly and took little notice of opposition; even the king's alterations of his draft were ignored. Lists of names survive which are thought to represent an attempt to identify and control people who dared to speak out. One of the leading dissenters was Sir George Throckmorton, who had also irritated the king by spreading rumours that Henry had not only slept with Anne Boleyn's sister Mary (which was common knowledge) but also with her mother. His letter to Cromwell of 29 October shows that Throckmorton had been instructed 'to live at home, serve God, and meddle little', and it is unlikely that he was the only one (*LP Henry VIII*, 6, no. 1365).

In the first week of April 1533 the bill became law as the Act in Restraint of Appeals, ensuring that Cranmer's verdict was now final and unchallengeable. The famous preamble to the act declared the realm of England to be an empire, in which the king as supreme head had complete mastery over the bodies and souls of his subjects. In the various drafts of the bill Cromwell had persistently removed many of Henry's references to jurisdiction over the church as emanating from his 'imperial' crown, but this should not be taken as evidence that king and minister subscribed to fundamentally different constitutional theories. In order to reduce clerical opposition Cromwell had merely adopted the pragmatic strategy of emphasizing the threat which appeals to Rome constituted to the king's temporal position, while still asserting the royal supremacy.

A few days beforehand, on 30 March, Cranmer had been consecrated archbishop of Canterbury. Immediately afterwards convocation agreed that the marriage of Henry and Katherine had been unlawful, and on 11 April the archbishop sent the king a pro forma challenge to its validity. A formal trial of its legitimacy opened on 10 May in Dunstable, and on the 23rd Cranmer was able finally to pronounce sentence declaring Henry's marriage to Katherine illegal, while five days later he pronounced his marriage to Anne to be lawful. On 1 June Anne was crowned queen. Having assisted Cranmer throughout this process Cromwell now moved to the fore again to enforce acceptance of the new queen. During the late summer they both interrogated Elizabeth Barton, a self-styled visionary who had repeatedly spoken out against the divorce. In September and October a clear signal was sent that dissent would no longer be tolerated when Cromwell had Barton and a group of her supporters rounded up and imprisoned in the Tower. The move contributed to the complete breakdown in diplomatic relations with Rome that autumn, and Clement VII refused to issue any more papal bulls for the appointment of English bishops.

In December Henry finally permitted Cromwell to unleash all the resources of the state in discrediting the papacy. In one of the fiercest and ugliest smear campaigns in English history the minister showed his mastery of propaganda techniques as the pope was attacked throughout the nation in sermons and pamphlets. In the new year

another session of parliament was summoned to enact the necessary legislation to break formally the remaining ties which bound England to Rome, again under Cromwell's meticulous supervision. Cranmer's judgment took statutory form as the Act of Succession; the Dispensations Act reiterated the royal supremacy; the Act for the Submission of the Clergy incorporated into law the surrender of 1532; and a new Act in Restraint of Annates brought the former one into effect. The session closed on 30 March when Audley gave the royal assent to the legislation in the presence of the king.

King's secretary, 1534–1536 In April 1534 Henry confirmed Cromwell as his principal secretary and chief minister, a position he had held in all but name for some time. Cromwell's style of administration represented a marked departure from what had been before, and Hans Holbein was careful to demonstrate this in a portrait for which Cromwell had sat some time after his appointment as master of the jewels. Although the original has since been lost several copies were made, of which the best now hangs in the Frick collection in New York. Turned slightly to the right, Cromwell is depicted apparently deep in thought. He was a man driven by ideas, and his thirst for knowledge is reflected by the finely bound book placed on the desk in front of him. Yet he was no unworldly academic lost in the cavities of his own mind, but a shrewd pragmatist driven to reform. Everything about the scene suggests utility. Cromwell is portrayed at work in his office, not basking in the splendour of his London home. The cap and gown he is wearing are finely made, but they are hardly the attire of an elegant courtier. Most significantly, the desk in front of him is covered with his letters, while he clutches another in his hand. Cromwell's style of administration was very personal, and he was not always good at delegating.

Yet this very attention to detail was also one of his greatest strengths as an administrator, as is shown, for instance, by his skilful control of crown finance from 1532 onwards. Here his operations were essentially flexible and pragmatic. Cromwell was certainly capable of radical innovation in this area, as with the subsidy act of 1534, where for the first time a tax was justified not on the grounds of war but as the reward for the achievement of peace. But more often he was content to use his various offices to receive and spend money as the need arose. He exercised his creative talents in much the same spirit, most notably with the establishment of the court of augmentations in 1536 to handle the massive windfall brought into the royal coffers by the dissolution of the monasteries. Two more financial institutions, the court of wards and the court of first fruits and tenths, were also set up immediately after the minister's death as an attempt to formalize the legacy of his personal regime.

Cromwell also spent a considerable amount of time drafting reforms to improve the 'common weal', and here his motivation was largely evangelical and humanistic. The reformers of the 1530s saw their time as one of regeneration rather than destruction, and Cromwell remained dedicated to introducing wide-ranging social reform until his death. It was his habit to keep 'remembrances' (or memoranda) of initiatives to be introduced or discussed with the king, and these papers contain a plethora of schemes and proposals for reforms in education, agriculture, trade, industry, poor relief, and the common law. It is true that there was a general humanist drive for social reform throughout Europe supported by Catholics as well as protestants, but Cromwell's willingness to embrace and encourage these new ideas is important. It was to this end that he employed a number of intellectuals in his large household—men such as Thomas Starkey, William Marshall, and Richard Morison—who helped develop reformist ideas for him to implement. Not all his attempts succeeded—none of his repeated efforts to fix food prices by statute had any effect—but Cromwell was still able to introduce several important social and economic reforms in the 1530s. Thus he took action against enclosures, and promoted English cloth exports. But his greatest achievement in this area was the poor relief legislation of 1536, which made parishes responsible for measures to combat local poverty. Although this statute was far from resolving the problem and soon lapsed, it nevertheless marks the first occasion on which an English government had recognized a responsibility to those on the fringes of society.

Enforcing the royal supremacy, 1534–1535 In April 1534, however, Cromwell's overwhelming priority was to enforce the legislation of the recently prorogued parliamentary session. Before the members of both houses returned home on 30 March they had all sworn an oath accepting the Act of Succession. In an unprecedented move all the king's subjects were now required to swear to the legitimacy of Henry's marriage to Anne, which also implied acceptance of the king's new powers following the break from Rome. On 13 April the London clergy were presented with and accepted the oath. The same day commissioners also offered it to Sir Thomas More and John Fisher, bishop of Rochester, at Lambeth, but both refused it. More was taken into custody on the same day, and was moved to the Tower on 17 April. Fisher joined him there four days later. On 18 April an order was issued that all the citizens of London were to swear, the city's officers doing so that day as well as making arrangements to receive the oaths of the rest of the city after the weekend. On Monday 20 April the seventeen commissioners each saw that all the members of their guilds swore. In order to make it clear that dissent would not be tolerated Cromwell organized a spectacle for them. Elizabeth Barton and five of her supporters were dragged through the streets of London from the Tower to Tyburn where they were executed for treason. In deference to her sex Barton was left to hang until dead before her head was hacked off, though as a woman she should have been burnt. Her followers were less fortunate, experiencing the full horrors of a traitor's death. The only concession they received as clerics was that their corpses were merely decapitated rather than quartered.

Elizabeth Barton was well known to the crowds through whom she passed on the way to death. One of the most powerful propaganda tools of the conservatives opposed to the royal divorce, she had predicted all sorts of terrible calamities that would occur should Henry marry Anne Boleyn. She enjoyed considerable influence while Archbishop Warham was alive and able to protect her, but her support began to dwindle as the tide turned against the conservatives. The first victim of the English Reformation, her demise showed not only that dissent would not be tolerated, but also the lengths to which the king was prepared to go to root out opposition. In November 1533 Eustache Chapuys, the imperial ambassador, had reported with glee the extreme reluctance of the judiciary to convict her, informing Charles V that 'some of the principal judges would sooner die' than declare against her (*LP Henry VIII*, 6, no. 1460). It was for this reason that the treason verdicts were secured through an act of attainder in parliament rather than in court. Sir Christopher Hales's shock at Cromwell's investigation of the four men he had been asked to arrest in Canterbury in September 1533 on suspicion of colluding with Barton is also apparent. After he had arrested the first two men, Dom Edward Bocking and Dom William Hadley, he asked Cromwell, 'If no cause appear to the contrary, I pray you send home the religious men as soon as you can' (ibid., no. 1149). When Cromwell informed him a few days later of Bocking's guilt Hales accepted it tactfully, describing Bocking as 'more worthy of punishment than others who are destitute of learning' (ibid., no. 1169). Yet it is also apparent that he did not expect so many to be executed. He was palpably uneasy with the whole investigation, and three days before the executions at Tyburn pleaded with Cromwell, 'for God's sake be ye mean to the King's highness to be merciful to them all' (*LP Henry VIII*, 7, no. 496).

The executions of Elizabeth Barton and her supporters marked a turning point in the administration of justice in the Henrician period. Cromwell controlled everything from the centre, and their fate shows that he was prepared not only to crush anyone who was perceived to be a significant threat, but also to make public examples of men and women who had become unwittingly caught up in events. That Bocking manipulated Barton is almost certain, but there were men executed that day who had done no more than accept the endorsement of a woman recognized as a remarkable mystic by their recently deceased and much respected archbishop. As 1534 unfolded similar investigations ceased to elicit such surprise.

After swearing the capital to the Act of Succession Cromwell now organized similar commissions throughout the rest of the country. Even more was demanded of the clergy. When Rowland Lee was elevated to the see of Coventry and Lichfield and Thomas Goodrich to that of Ely, in March and April 1534 respectively, each had to swear acceptance of the royal supremacy as well as of the Act of Succession, and thereafter all new bishops were required to do the same. From the summer, ecclesiastical corporations and colleges (including those of the universities) swore corporate oaths to a similar effect, while the secular and parish clergy merely signed declarations that 'the bishop of Rome has no greater power conferred on him by God in this realm than any other foreign bishop'

(*LP Henry VIII*, 7, no. 1025). Most people, lay and clerical, accepted the words thrust before them, though many continued to express their disapproval afterwards. When parliament reconvened in November, Cromwell overcame fierce opposition to guide through a new treason act, which not only facilitated the enforcement of the previous session's legislation, but also constituted the most significant revision of the treason laws since 1352. It was now treasonous to speak rebellious words against the royal family, to deny their titles, or to call the king a heretic, tyrant, infidel, or usurper. The Act of Supremacy also clarified the king's position as head of the church, and the Act for Payment of First Fruits and Tenths substantially increased clerical taxes.

Many of the words spoken against the king came from the pulpit, where members of religious orders were particularly outspoken in attacking the supremacy. Several ended up in the Tower; others fled the country. Nobody escaped the arm of the law, and in a further demonstration of his personal style as an administrator Cromwell investigated accusations against people from every level of society. No washerwoman was safe who called the king a rude name or suggested in passing that the pope's enormities might not be quite as detestable as Henry would have his subjects believe. Writing from the safety of Brussels at the end of 1534 Stephen Vaughan begged his friend to reform the judicial system so that he did not have to spend so much time dulling his wit 'with the continual travail of common causes' (Elton, *Reform and Renewal*, 45). However, Cromwell understood well that it was one thing to instigate reform, but quite another to enforce it.

The direct manner in which Cromwell pursued opponents was born less of choice than of necessity. While the allegations he investigated may now appear trivial, at times almost farcical, dissent in a period of such instability could not be allowed to ferment. By scrutinizing every accusation Cromwell was able to determine the strength of local discontent so that further action could be taken if necessary, and his robust approach also served as a useful deterrent. The insults levelled by ordinary people which came to his attention tended to be directed particularly at Anne Boleyn. A particularly notorious incident was reported in February 1535 in Suffolk. Cromwell was informed that one Margaret Chanseler had attacked the divorce and said that the new queen was 'a noughtty hoore', according to her own admission, or 'a goggyll yed [eyed] hoore', according to her accusers. It appears that no punishment was imposed (as often happened), but her remarks were still considered serious enough to warrant an inquiry where witnesses were examined by the abbot of Bury St Edmunds and no fewer than nine other JPs (*LP Henry VIII*, 8, no. 196).

One of those JPs was Christopher Jenney, a king's serjeant-at-law who also sat as an assize judge with Sir John Spelman on the northern circuit during the following summer. His report of the cases heard at the York assizes held in August 1535 illustrates Cromwell's involvement in judicial process. Spelman and Jenney condemned George Lazenby, a monk of Jervaulx, to be executed for high treason, but they felt less competent to rule on a number of other indictments for treason. Jenney informed Cromwell that they were unable to decide whether the evidence in these cases amounted to high treason, and so 'we have foreborne to arraign them till we communicate with you and other of the Council' (*LP Henry VIII*, 9, no. 37). It has been calculated that in the years 1532–40 a total of 883 people in England, Wales, and Calais came within the compass of the treason laws, of whom 308 were executed. However, the vast majority of these were involved in open rebellion against the crown, or were victims of high dynastic or court politics. Only some sixty-three people suffered for the new offence of speaking against the supremacy. While Cromwell was capable of manipulating the system in order to remove people like Elizabeth Barton, who were regarded as a significant threat, very few fell into this category. Most of those investigated were not punished, and the rule of law remained intact. These were extraordinary times, and the statistics reflect more the instability of the period than Cromwell's desire for butchery.

As well as securing the acceptance of the king's new powers Cromwell also worked in 1535 to strengthen his own control over the church. On 21 January 1535 the king appointed him royal vicegerent, or vicar-general, and commissioned him to organize two visitations, one of all the country's churches, monasteries, and clergy, the other limited to monasteries. Cromwell did not attempt to exercise his full powers while Cranmer was attempting to hold an archiepiscopal visitation, but within two years his power had eclipsed that of both archbishops. Meanwhile, in April 1535 he circulated royal letters to bishops, nobility, and JPs instructing them to imprison clergy who persisted in defending the power of the pope, and thereafter this was Cromwell's chosen method of exerting his authority. Such letters adopted a standard format, with instructions issued under the king's stamp being immediately followed by Cromwell's own to reinforce the impact. While he demanded a swift and effective response from his recipients he also flattered them by emphasizing that they had been 'elected and chosen' for their tasks.

A few weeks after the first letters were sent a further series of executions was organized to emphasize that the price for loyalty to the pope was death. On 4 May three Carthusian priors, a learned monk, and the vicar of Isleworth were executed at Tyburn. Three more Carthusians followed them on 19 June, while on the 22nd a stunned and silent crowd at Tower Green witnessed the axe falling on John Fisher. On 6 July Sir Thomas More also placed his head on the block. Cromwell did not desire the death of his fellow lawyer and had done everything in his power to try to persuade him to accept the supremacy, but in the end his loyalty to the king took precedence. More put up a skilful defence, but Cromwell took no chances. It is possible that his prosecution rested on perjured evidence, and the verdict was certainly delivered by a rigged jury. Standing on the scaffold More exhorted the crowd to remember that he was to suffer 'in and for the faith of the holy chatholick churche' (Roper, 103). Both he and Cromwell knew that this was just the beginning.

The vicegerency and the monasteries, 1535–1536 Although Henry VIII's religious instincts were essentially conservative he took his responsibilities as supreme head of the English church very seriously, and was determined to play an active role in determining its reform following the break from Rome. He had always taken a keen interest in theology, and like Sir Thomas More he had long admired Erasmus. But with the conservatives at court implacably opposed to the severance of links to the papacy, the initiative lay with leading evangelicals to advise on the nature of the new religious settlement. During 1534 Cromwell's first priority was to attack the authority of the pope and not until the following year did he become actively engaged in further reform. The monastic visitation commissioned under his vicegerency in January did not get under way until summer 1535, as he first had to implement the more general commission issued at the same time, which produced the census of church lands and revenues now known as the *valor ecclesiasticus*—an administrative *tour de force*, completed with remarkable accuracy within a year. Meanwhile Cranmer was still attempting to complete his own visitation of the province of Canterbury, albeit with limited success since a number of bishops refused to co-operate.

Cromwell moved into action on 3 June 1535 by issuing a circular letter to all the bishops ordering them to preach in support of the supremacy, and to ensure that the clergy in their dioceses did so as well. A week later he sent further letters to JPs ordering them to report any instances of his instructions being disobeyed. In the following month he turned his attention to the monasteries. Since early June the king and queen had been engaged on a magnificent progress to the west country which occupied them until the end of September. Cromwell caught up with the court at Winchcombe on 23 July and travelled with it for two months. Encouraged by Anne, Henry took the unusual decision to put business before pleasure and used the trip as an opportunity to visit towns where there was strong support for reform, and bestowed rewards on the local gentry who were largely responsible for this. Cromwell took this opportunity to launch his own visitation of religious houses by organizing the inspection of the monasteries in the west country, even investigating a few himself. In September he increased the pace by suspending the authority of every bishop in the country so that the six canon lawyers he had appointed as his agents could complete their surveys. When a newly established vicegerential court gradually restored power to individual bishops they were declared to be officers of state. When the king died their powers too would expire. Cromwell also withheld indefinitely certain rights which brought with them lucrative fees, such as those of visitation and probate, in the hope that their temporary loss would furnish incentives to obedience.

Early in 1536, towards the end of a long list of scribbled notes, Cromwell wrote a memo to himself concerning the 'abomination of religious persons throughout this realm, and a reformation to be devised therein' (*LP Henry VIII*, 10, no. 254). The final session of the Reformation Parliament began on 4 February, and about 6 March a bill was introduced to dissolve the religious houses with a gross income of less than £200 per annum, supported by the commissioners' (grossly exaggerated) reports—the so-called *comperta*—of sordid corruption and vice in these smaller monasteries. By 18 March the bill had passed through both houses as the Act for the Suppression of the Lesser Monasteries. Cromwell did not plan the entire dissolution process as soon as he became vicegerent. The census of 1535 was intended to enable the government to tax church property more effectively. And while the subsequent visitation was designed to smooth the way for the act of 1536 the commissioners' report went to great lengths to emphasize the high moral standards of the wealthier houses. Furthermore, several of the poorer houses were eventually spared (albeit usually in return for the payment of significant fines), while many of the monks and nuns who wished to continue in the religious life were permitted to do so: the king even re-founded two houses (Bisham Abbey and the nunnery of Stixwould) in his own name. None of this is likely to have happened had there been a plan for the wholesale destruction of religious life at this stage.

The destruction of Queen Anne, 1536 However, while Cromwell's success in obtaining parliamentary acceptance for the suppression of the smaller religious houses represented a significant political achievement, it also caused a clash with Anne Boleyn which threatened to undermine his position completely. Anne was angry that the proceeds of the dissolution were to be paid into the king's coffers and not redeployed for charitable purposes, and instructed her chaplains to preach against the vicegerent. On Passion Sunday (2 April) 1536 John Skip, her almoner, denounced Cromwell before the entire court as an enemy of the queen, comparing him to Haman, the evil and greedy adversary of Queen Esther in the Old Testament. Furthermore, in the following month Anne subverted Cromwell's previously accepted policy of breaking England's reliance on France in order to allow the forging of closer ties with the empire, by insisting that Charles V accept the royal supremacy. Cromwell was now in grave danger, and it was apparent that he would have to move against the queen to save himself.

Removing Anne was unlikely to be easy, but Cromwell hatched a plan which would dispose of both the queen and the leading members of her powerful faction at court. Like Katherine before her Anne's weakness was her failure to produce a male heir. In a cruelly ironic twist, on 29 January 1536 she had miscarried of a son on the same day as Katherine of Aragon's funeral, and Henry was growing impatient. While the king showed no interest in divorcing Anne, he also made little attempt to hide his fondness for the young and amenable Jane Seymour. Without any success a faction of conservative courtiers led by Sir Nicholas Carew had been attempting to regain the initiative at court by plotting to replace the reformers' patron with the more pliant Jane. When Cromwell decided to make peace (temporarily) with them, their prospects improved dramatically.

Anne was well known for conducting herself with her courtiers in an informal and flirtatious manner, and Cromwell calculated that he could twist the language of courtly love to support an accusation of adultery. When Anne had a very public argument with Henry Norris, Cromwell's leading rival at court, he saw his opportunity. On 30 April Cromwell arrested Mark Smeaton, one of Anne's musicians. After rigorous interrogation Smeaton confessed to an illicit affair with her, and over the next few days the queen and several of her closest courtiers (including Norris and Anne's own brother, Viscount Rochford) were rounded up and sent to the Tower. The charge of adultery was almost certainly without substance, but it was extremely effective. Carew would have left Anne alive to pour scorn on her successor as Katherine of Aragon had done. By charging Anne with a treasonous offence not only was Cromwell able to remove her permanently, he could also get rid of her closest supporters. The queen and her brother stood trial on Monday 15 May, while the four commoners accused with them were condemned the Friday beforehand. The evidence for the prosecution was embarrassingly weak, but Cromwell managed to contrive a case based on Mark Smeaton's questionable confession, a great deal of circumstantial evidence, and some very salacious details about what Anne had allegedly got up to with her brother. The men were all executed on 17 May. On the same day Cranmer declared the marriage invalid, a completely illogical ruling but one which secured the bastardization of Princess Elizabeth. Two days later Anne suffered herself, a mere three weeks from the date of Smeaton's arrest. Henry married Jane on 30 May and was now free to continue the arduous process of trying to father a son.

Cromwell had acted with such ruthless determination because he was under threat. Conservative opposition at court was becoming more effective. With both Katherine and Anne dead the political necessity for reform had receded. But Cromwell had not taken such drastic action simply to bring Carew and his friends to power. When they then attempted to restore Princess Mary to legitimacy he persuaded the king that they were responsible for her stubborn refusal to submit to the supremacy and threatened them with treason charges. Mary responded by finally announcing her submission on 15 June 1536 to save the lives of her supporters, though Cromwell was still able to have the marquess of Exeter and Sir William Fitzwilliam expelled from the council, as well as others from the court. While Carew was safe for the time being in the privy chamber Cromwell also began to exert more control over this vital department in the royal household by appointing loyal supporters like Ralph Sadler and Peter Mewtas to the vacancies created by the recent executions.

Doctrinal debate and the Pilgrimage of Grace, 1536–1537 After a couple of very testing months Cromwell's position was now stronger than ever. On 18 June 1536 Anne Boleyn's father surrendered the office of lord privy seal, to which

Cromwell succeeded on 2 July, resigning the mastership of the rolls which he had held since 8 October 1534. A few days later, on 8 July, the brewer's boy from Putney was raised to the peerage as Baron Cromwell, of Wimbledon. However, although he had succeeded in gaining ascendancy over his opponents for the time being, there were still plenty who were determined to thwart Cromwell's reformist agenda at every turn. In attempting to strike some sort of balance Henry was merely vacillating between the two camps. Not only did this result in incoherent policy, but, more destructively, it also afforded hope to both sides.

The first attempt to clarify religious doctrine came in July 1536. On 8 June a new parliament opened, with convocation following a day later. Parliament had little business and the main reason for summoning it was to pass the second Act of Succession, which secured the rights of Queen Jane's heirs to the throne. Convocation on the other hand was a hive of activity. A few days into the session Cromwell's lay representative Dr William Petre began to sit alongside Cranmer to symbolize the royal supremacy, and the vicegerent also attended in person on several occasions. Early in July Bishop Edward Fox returned from an unsuccessful embassy to the Lutheran princes in Saxony, which it had been hoped would achieve a political and religious alliance. Although the talks had collapsed Fox tabled proposals in convocation based partly on the draft theological agreement known as the Wittenberg articles, with strong backing from Cromwell and Cranmer. These met fierce opposition, but the king demanded that a compromise should be reached before the summer recess. Eventually Henry was able to endorse ten articles of religion, which were printed in August and were followed by injunctions circulated by Cromwell for their enforcement.

The ten articles were mildly evangelical. While they expressed reservations about the doctrine of purgatory, included the words 'justification' and 'faith' in close proximity, and promoted only three (out of the medieval seven) sacraments as essential for salvation (baptism, the eucharist, and penance), they were hardly radical. A traditional definition of the real presence in the eucharist was still asserted, and the articles even encouraged the use of images and ceremonies, although with certain restrictions. A few days after agreeing these convocation also enacted a canon which abolished certain saints' days. Cromwell's injunctions instructed the clergy to enforce all the summer's decisions, and urged parents and masters to catechize every member of their family in the creed, the Lord's prayer, and the ten commandments. But he went beyond what had been agreed in convocation by ordering that every parish church should provide copies of the Bible in both English and Latin—an evangelical priority. The language he used to attack the cult of the saints and the use of images is also far harsher than anything in the ten articles. Far from reassuring public opinion as Henry had intended, Cromwell succeeded in aggravating fears.

Throughout northern Lincolnshire in September 1536 a

combination of opposition both to commissioners attempting to implement Cromwell's injunctions and to another set of commissioners collecting tax, and widespread concern that traditional religious life in the parishes would soon be completely destroyed, caused enough resentment to prompt a rebellion. On 1 October Thomas Kendall, the vicar of Louth, used his Sunday sermon to incite his parishioners to defend their church against Cromwell's agents, who were expected in the town the following day. Rumours ran rife that they were planning to pillage all the local churches as they were the monasteries. Within days most of northern Lincolnshire was up in arms. However, when the king sent the duke of Suffolk north with an expeditionary force he found it relatively easy to persuade the rebels to stand down. But the troops started to disperse too soon. Beyond Lincolnshire revolt was breaking out throughout the six northern counties. Widespread popular and clerical risings were apparently attracting the support of the gentry and even of some of the nobility, most notably Thomas, Lord Darcy.

The insurrections are known collectively to history as the Pilgrimage of Grace, though this name was used only of the risings in Yorkshire and the north led by Robert Aske. By the end of the month the duke of Norfolk had tactfully ignored the king's instructions to defeat the rebels (who greatly outnumbered his forces) and negotiated a truce, promising that the king would listen to their grievances. Throughout the winter the north remained effectively under the control of the rebels, but when the unstable Sir Francis Bigod decided to raise a fresh rebellion early in the new year Henry acted swiftly to quash the rebels once and for all. Believing that this betrayal released him from his former promises, he ordered exemplary executions in the north and that the leaders of the original pilgrimage should be brought to London.

The grievances of the rebels were wide-ranging. Several were political in nature, for instance the unpopular Statute of Uses, which was carried through parliament by Cromwell early in 1536, and which safeguarded the crown's feudal rights by redefining the terms on which settlements of land were made by the process known as enfeoffment to uses. But by far the greatest was the suppression of the monasteries, and for this they blamed the king's 'evil counsellors', principally Cromwell and Cranmer. The extent of the hatred felt for Cromwell was made particularly clear at the investigations of the leading rebels afterwards. During an interrogation on 19 April 1537 Lord Darcy dared to tell Cromwell:

> it is thou that art the very original and chief causer of all this rebellion and mischief, and art likewise causer of the apprehension of us that be noble men and dost daily earnestly travail to bring us to our end and to strike off our heads, and I trust that or thou die, though thou wouldest procure all the noblemen's heads within the realm to be stricken off, yet shall there one head remain that shall strike off thy head. (*LP Henry VIII*, 12/1, no. 976)

Reform and reaction, 1538 The suppression of the risings only spurred reform. In February 1537 Cromwell ordered a vicegerential synod of bishops and doctors from both provinces, which was held in the currently vacant parliament house in Westminster. About 18 February he made the opening speech in the king's name asking for a calm debate about the current theological controversies, though this did not prevent him from gently steering the debate along evangelical lines. After the first few meetings to thrash out the broad outline of an agreement the relatively small synod acted more like a committee, and met more informally elsewhere in London. Cromwell increasingly left Cranmer and Fox to co-ordinate sessions, ensuring that the initiative remained with the reformers.

By July a comprehensive draft of *The Institution of a Christian Man*, more commonly known as the Bishops' Book, was ready. By October it was in circulation, despite the fact the king had been unable to grant it his full assent, perhaps because he was too preoccupied with the preparations for Jane's childbearing—his long-awaited son, Prince Edward, was born on 12 October. Although the conservatives had achieved concessions, principally a (qualified) acceptance of seven sacraments, Cromwell, Cranmer, and Fox had taken the evangelical cause subtly forward in key areas. For instance, the article on justification emphasized the role of faith and played down the efficacy of good works, though without either explicitly affirming Lutheran or compromising Catholic beliefs. And while the doctrine of the real presence was unconditionally asserted, the doctrines of transubstantiation and the sacrifice of the mass were not mentioned, a position not incompatible with Lutheran eucharistic teaching. But the reformers' most significant achievement was to re-edit and renumber the traditional ten commandments along lines favoured by many protestants, in that they now gave greater emphasis to the divine prohibition on the making and worshipping of 'graven images'. Without royal backing the Bishops' Book was destined to have little impact on attempts to define the doctrine of the English church. It did, however, prepare the way for a more substantial attack on the cult of the saints.

Cromwell's success in advancing evangelical reform in the months following the northern risings was not always matched in the political sphere, and his position was now weakened by the emergence of a 'privy council', making him even more dependent on the favour and support of the king. This was another development arising from the impact made by the Pilgrimage of Grace. The rebels had been very critical of the low birth of the minister and of several of Henry's other leading councillors, particularly Cranmer and Audley. It became essential that Cromwell should keep out of the limelight during the suppression of the risings, and this was in any case too big a task for the king and his minister to manage on their own. As a result, leading magnates had formed a special war council to issue instructions. Having proved its effectiveness during the risings, this was then developed into a corporate board of nobles and office-holders during the spring of 1537. Henry had no intention of removing Cromwell as his chief minister, and confirmed his support for him by electing him to the Order of the Garter on 5 August. But while the privy council did not achieve its own bureaucratic machinery until after the death of Cromwell, who did not have to share power with anyone, he was nevertheless forced to accept the existence of an executive body dominated by his conservative opponents.

In January 1538 Cromwell again attempted to put pressure on Henry to countenance further reform by pursuing an extensive campaign against idolatry, in which statues, roods, and images were attacked. Commissioners were sent round the country to seize relics and shrines which had been abused by popular devotion. Notorious examples were brought to London where they were publicly shown to be fakes, such as the famous Rood of Grace of Boxley Abbey. Upon closer inspection this miraculous talking crucifix was revealed to be little more than a puppet, worked by 'certain engines and old wire, with old rotten sticks in the back of the same' (*LP Henry VIII*, 13/1, no. 231). Spontaneous outbreaks of iconoclasm accompanied Cromwell's official campaign, and during the summer an attack was also launched against the great shrines, culminating in September with the dismantling of perhaps the most revered of all, that of St Thomas Becket at Canterbury.

In May 1538 evangelicals were also heartened by the arrival of a new delegation from the Lutheran Schmalkaldic League of north German princes. The king was very receptive to the possibility of an agreement with them, but though it was Cranmer and a team of theologians who were left to conduct the actual talks the original initiative had been Cromwell's, and he did not inform Henry of his every move. Early in September the minister completed a new set of vicegerential injunctions which greatly intensified the reformist line of his 1536 injunctions. Open war was now declared on 'pilgrimages, feigned relics, or images, or any such superstitions', and so by implication on the fraternities which had largely maintained them, while correspondingly heavy emphasis was laid on scripture as 'the very lively word of God'. The order of 1536 that churches should acquire English bibles had been virtually ignored, but Coverdale's Great Bible was now almost ready for circulation, and Cromwell was determined that this time his instructions would be obeyed, commanding that 'one book of the whole Bible of the largest volume in English' should be set up in every church. And in a measure with far-reaching consequences for the study of the English past he ordered that every clergyman should 'keep one book or register, wherein ye shall write the day and year of every wedding, christening, and burying, made within your parish for your time' (C. H. Williams, 811–14). Nor was this all, for following the 'voluntary' surrender of the remaining smaller monasteries during the previous year, the larger monasteries were now also 'invited' to surrender throughout 1538, a process legitimized in the 1539 session of parliament and completed in the following year. The king's anger at the involvement of monks and friars in the Pilgrimage of Grace had caused him to lose all interest in the 'religious life'.

Yet there were also signs that Henry was becoming increasingly unhappy about the extent of recent reforms. In January 1538 he had provided Cranmer with a list of 250 emendations to the Bishops' Book. But it was the king's choice of Cuthbert Tunstall, the conservative bishop of Durham, to be his theological companion throughout the court's summer progress which was the first significant indicator that he was becoming cooler towards reform. Furthermore, this was a particularly peripatetic and isolated progress, making communication with Cromwell harder. It also coincided with a written request from the Lutheran delegation in August that in order to speed up the talks Henry should outline his views on the key issues of theological dispute, as outlined in Philipp Melanchthon's *Apologia*. By the time Henry presented his thoughtful objections at the end of September, the talks had already fizzled out, and the Lutherans went home early in October. Their decision to write to the king in August had proved a bad move, and the mistake was compounded when another letter was sent from Hesse on 25 September drawing the king's attention to the problem of Anabaptism in his country. Cromwell acted immediately by issuing a heresy commission on 1 October in order to allow the reformers to show their willingness to root out Anabaptists and sacramentaries. Nevertheless the letter deepened Henry's concern that evangelical reform was also creating space for radicals and heretics.

During the autumn it also became evident that the conservative faction was becoming a stronger and more cohesive force. Perceiving the threat Cromwell again lashed out at his opponents at court. In November, using evidence acquired from Sir Geoffrey Pole under interrogation in the Tower, he imprisoned the marquess of Exeter, Sir Edward Neville, and Sir Nicholas Carew on charges of treason; all were executed in the following months. On 16 November the king presided in person over the public trial of the evangelical John Lambert. Dressed in white for purity he used the opportunity to deliver a powerful speech defending transubstantiation before consigning the unrepentant Lambert to the flames. To reinforce the point Henry issued a proclamation on the same day which defended the real presence and clerical celibacy, as well as banning heretical books. He had left the reformers with little doubt that persuading him to further their cause would now be a much tougher task.

The governance of Ireland The kingdom which Henry VIII inherited was not united. If enforcing the royal supremacy and subsequent religious reform in the heartlands of England had been perilous and bloody, it was much more so in the peripheral regions. Successive monarchs had attempted to assert their authority there with varying degrees of success. When the task fell to Cromwell as chief minister, the comparative instability of the regime raised the stakes considerably. His main concern was to extend the authority of the legal and judicial institutions associated with the English crown, and to increase the control exercised from the centre by empowering councils under royal figure-heads at the expense of local lords.

In Ireland, after a decade in which the office of deputy changed hands several times, the ninth earl of Kildare was appointed on 5 July 1532, largely through the influence of the duke of Norfolk. But by the end of the year Kildare's power showed signs of waning after he suffered an incapacitating gunshot wound. As Cromwell began to take an increasing interest in Ireland he communicated with Kildare's rivals, the Butlers and Archbishop Alen of Dublin, and in September 1533 the earl was summoned back to England, eventually arriving there in February 1534. Cromwell then worked to place new men in the Dublin council and to secure the allegiance of the immigrant New English and loyalist Anglo-Irish, and by late May 1534 there was widespread acceptance both of the royal supremacy and of the restoration as deputy of the septuagenarian Sir William Skeffington, Kildare's most recent predecessor. Cromwell had prepared for him copies of a pamphlet, intended for circulation, entitled *Ordinances for the Government of Ireland*. Furnishing interesting evidence for Cromwell's use of the printing press as an agent of policy, it advocated modest solutions to traditional problems, but these were never implemented.

On 11 June Kildare's son Thomas, Lord Offaly ('Silken Thomas'), who had been asked to deputize in his father's absence, denounced the king's policies before the council and began a rebellion. Offaly probably intended only to put pressure on the king to restore Kildare, but at a time when domestic politics were so volatile Cromwell did not construe it that way. On 29 June Kildare was imprisoned in the Tower, where he died on 2 September. Offaly responded by mounting a full-scale revolt, murdering Archbishop Alen together with all his chaplains and servants as they attempted to set sail for England on 27 July, and then storming Dublin Castle. Having become tenth earl of Kildare after his father's death, he surrendered on 24 August 1535 and was escorted back to London by the marshal of the army, Lord Leonard Grey.

Cromwell had been preparing for a new Dublin parliament since June 1535, but because of Skeffington's death on 31 December it did not meet until 1 May 1536, with Lord Leonard Grey presiding as the new deputy. The Irish Reformation Parliament sat until 20 December 1537, enacting all the major English reform legislation and also attainting Kildare and his supporters. On 8 September 1537 four high-ranking officials arrived to assess and correct abuses in all aspects of government, departing in the following April. But although over half Cromwell's surviving correspondence for these months consists of letters to them there were no major reforms. The main policy decisions were to extend the control of the Dublin council to the whole area of English lordship (but not beyond), and to establish a permanent garrison to support this. However, as crown resources were still insufficient Grey continued to adopt the traditional policy of dealing with the Gaelic chiefs by a mixture of short campaigns and negotiations. This resulted only in a large-scale attack upon the pale by the so-called Geraldine league of Irish lords in August 1539. Order was not restored until Grey was summoned home to face a long list of treason charges and replaced as deputy by Sir Anthony St Leger in July 1540. Cromwell had succeeded in extending royal power in Ireland and in introducing religious reform, but the costs of keeping a garrison were enormous and his policy of centralized control did not last.

The Scottish borders and Wales More successful was Cromwell's approach to the north of England, where he continued earlier policies of attempting to assert royal authority. In 1533 the lieutenant of the north was the weak Henry Percy, sixth earl of Northumberland. What power he had was restricted to the middle and eastern marches, and this was declining, largely as a result of his indebtedness. In the north-west, feuding between the Dacres and the Cliffords also made governance much less effective. While there was no deliberate policy of undermining the powerful northern nobility Henry did take action against powerful nobles of whom he was suspicious. In 1534 Cromwell himself arranged that William, third Baron Dacre, should be charged with treason for developing cross-border ties with Scottish lords, even though these arguably benefited both nations. Although Dacre's peers acquitted him at his trial in July, Cromwell had succeeded in breaking his control of the west march, where Henry Clifford, first earl of Cumberland, was appointed warden in September.

Then in 1536 Cromwell began to act against the liberties of the region—privileged areas from which the agencies of royal government had hitherto been largely or wholly excluded. While he could not abolish all of them as he had hoped, local jurisdictional anomalies were curtailed significantly, both by act of parliament and through the suppression of the monasteries, which had held many liberties. Most significantly the palatinate of Durham now retained only a nominal independent jurisdiction under Bishop Cuthbert Tunstall. A partial solution was also found to the problem of weak governance in the north-east when the earl of Northumberland died in June 1537. As the earl had no natural heirs and was in dispute with his brothers he had left most of his estates to the crown. On all the marches Henry and Cromwell would have preferred strong noblemen to impose royal authority, but at least Northumberland's legacy gave them increased control on and near the border, which they tried to build on by promoting able men from the local gentry to act as deputy wardens—Sir Thomas Wharton, Sir John Widdrington, and Sir William Eure on the west, middle, and east marches respectively. They also used grants of pensions to create a royal affinity in the border region.

When the Pilgrimage of Grace broke out in autumn 1536 the duke of Norfolk became lieutenant in the north. The subsequent failure of the rebellions and the crown's inheritance of the Percy lands in 1537 gave Cromwell the opportunity to reform the council of the north. Originally the council served Norfolk as lieutenant, but Cromwell thwarted his desire to obtain the same authority as the Percys had enjoyed. He persuaded the king to grant power to leading members of the local gentry, over whom he was then able to exert pressure through regular correspondence. In June 1538 Cromwell appointed Bishop Tunstall as lord president of the council and reconstituted it as a permanent institution. He was also careful to include the local nobility and gentry to exclude the possibility of rival influence. The pilgrimage had almost cost Henry his crown, but its defeat allowed Cromwell to increase substantially the control of the north by the centre, not least by maintaining regular contacts with the council's officials, who successfully enforced both royal justice and religious reform. As the council dealt with issues such as land enclosure, the maintenance of private armies, and food supplies, it was also able to address effectively the grievances of the king's humbler subjects.

Cromwell also had much success in implementing a similar policy of reform in Wales. In 1534 he appointed Rowland Lee, bishop of Coventry and Lichfield, to succeed John Veysey, bishop of Exeter, as president of the council in Wales. He also had a number of statutes enacted which gave Lee more power to apprehend felons who were still able to escape justice by exploiting the complex independent jurisdictions of the marcher lordships. Lee set about fulfilling his mandate with enthusiasm and soon obtained a reputation as a hanging judge. Yet despite his own protestations to the contrary there was little possibility of any real success without more substantial reform. In 1536, at the same time as securing the act restricting liberties, Cromwell supervised the passage through parliament of an 'act for laws and justice to be ministered in Wales in like forms as it is in this realm'. This reaffirmed the traditional union of England and Wales as it dated back to Edward I's reign, and enacted that the Welsh were now to enjoy the same rights under the law as their English neighbours. Five new counties were to be created where the old marcher lordships (now abolished) had been, each with parliamentary representation. Boundary commissions were established to consider the new boundaries of shire and hundred, as well as to decide what local customs should be incorporated into law, and an exchequer and chancery were to be established at Brecon and Denbigh.

However, the implementation of the act proved to be considerably more difficult, not least because in 1537 Henry decided to invoke powers of veto written into the act, perhaps in order to give more authority in the principality to the newborn prince of Wales. The resulting problems remained unresolved at the time of Cromwell's death, and his policy was not fully implemented until a lengthy act in 1543 defined the union in much greater detail. Nevertheless, during his lifetime Cromwell succeeded in promoting stability and gaining acceptance for the royal supremacy in Wales. His policy of centralization was also extended in 1536 to Calais, where Cromwell introduced a series of measures to make the pale more like a normal English borough, including the introduction of parliamentary representation. Finally, a council in the west was created in 1539, but this had little effect and was dissolved in 1540 after Cromwell's fall.

March to the scaffold, 1538–1540 During the relatively quiet winter months of 1538–9 the recently increased tensions slackened temporarily. Cromwell's main concern was with the preparation of Coverdale's Great Bible, in the final stages of production in Paris. On 17 December the inquisitor-general of France ordered work to cease, and

Cromwell had to beg the French king to release the unfinished books so that printing might continue in England. Revealing his personal interest in the project he admitted to the French ambassador that he had contributed £400 of his own money. After much negotiation the presses, type, and workers were all transported to London in February 1539. The following month Cromwell also planned 'a device in the Parliament for the unity in religion', and seemed comfortable in discussing preparations with the king (LP Henry VIII, 14/1, no. 655). In April the first edition of the Great Bible was finally available, printed by Richard Grafton and Edward Whitchurch, two enthusiastic evangelicals. Cromwell had long been passionately interested in the Bible—he was said to have learned Erasmus's translation of the New Testament by heart after buying a copy in 1517. The publication of the Great Bible was the culmination of his persistent pressure for an authoritative version in English, and represents one of his most significant achievements.

The king, however, remained committed to holding back reform. During Holy Week and Easter (early April) he made a point of being seen to perform traditional ceremonies, and celebrated Ascension day (15 May) in extravagant style. With terrible timing Cromwell was ill for the opening of parliament, and was not well enough to sit in the Lords until 10 May. On 5 May the lord chancellor, Audley, delivered a speech there repeating the king's desire to control 'diversity of opinions'. Cromwell had lost the initiative, and a committee was established to examine doctrine. On 16 May the duke of Norfolk suddenly announced that the committee could not reach a decision and presented six questions for the house to consider. Despite Cranmer's strong opposition the duke received the answers he was expecting. These were duly passed as the Act of Six Articles. The articles required an orthodox understanding of the mass, opposed the practice of communion in both kinds for the laity, ruled against clerical marriage, upheld vows of chastity, and asserted the efficacy of private masses and auricular confession. They therefore promoted the traditional view of the priesthood and allowed Henry to present his conservative credentials to Catholic Europe. On 7 June he declared two days of official mourning for Isabella, the wife of the emperor Charles V and niece of Katherine of Aragon. Franz Burchard, the leader of yet another Lutheran delegation, took this as his cue to go home the same day.

At the same time a crisis was developing in Calais. Cromwell had clashed with Lord Lisle, the king's deputy, on several occasions during the past few years over the activities of reformers in the pale. The problem was largely that while Lisle, his wife, and the leading members of the council there were all ardent conservatives implacably opposed to religious reform Cranmer had found it expedient to move some evangelical ministers there away from England. When the earl of Hertford had made a visit to inspect the defences earlier in the year Lisle took the opportunity to complain about Cranmer's evangelical commissary John Butler and others whom he regarded as sacramentaries—deniers of the real presence in the eucharist. By the beginning of May the news had spread round the court, and on the 6th Cromwell, still convalescing, wrote to Lisle asking him to look into the matter. Encouraged by the developments at Westminster the deputy rounded up his opponents and sent them to London for investigation. Incensed by what he saw as a witchhunt Cromwell appealed unsuccessfully to Lisle to halt it. On 12 June one of the MPs for Calais, Thomas Broke, made an over-impassioned speech in the Commons against the six articles and joined the others under investigation.

At this time of evangelical despondency it took very little to raise spirits. Cromwell was able to carry a contentious Statute of Proclamations, giving proclamations issued by king and council the same legal force as parliamentary statutes, and in the last week of June both houses of parliament agreed on minor concessions on clerical marriage and chastity. These, and Cromwell's positive view of the Calais evangelicals' chances, were enough to give him hope, but overall the situation remained very bleak. The six articles were passed shortly before the session ended on 28 June. Their positions now untenable, bishops Latimer and Shaxton resigned immediately. Foxe recounts a story that when the king organized a reconciliatory dinner in Cranmer's honour at Lambeth Palace shortly afterwards, Cromwell became embroiled in a bitter argument with a leading noble, probably Norfolk, who had impugned Cardinal Wolsey's honour. The first weeks of July marked a new low point for Cromwell. Most of the evangelicals before Cranmer for investigation following the new act had been reported by Lisle, who continued to provide a stream of new charges; the archbishop had no option but to imprison many of the accused. On 12 July the French ambassador Marillac informed François I that Henry had 'taken up again all the old opinions and constitutions, excepting only papal obedience and destruction of abbeys and churches of which he has taken the revenue' (*LP Henry VIII*, 14/1, no. 1260).

But then Cromwell's influence with the king suddenly began to revive. During July the conservative bishops gradually returned to their dioceses. In August an outburst from Bishop Gardiner, in which he called the evangelical Robert Barnes a heretic, was enough for Cromwell to have him expelled from the privy council, and Bishop Sampson also went at the same time. By the autumn Henry's mood had changed noticeably and the Lutheran Burchard was back. Cromwell was very much in favour again. After two years of indecision Henry finally accepted his proposal that he should marry Anne, the sister of Duke Wilhelm of Cleves, agreeing to the treaty in early October. While the duke was no protestant, neither was he close to either pope or emperor, and the treaty considerably increased the prospects for an alliance with the Schmalkaldic League of Lutheran princes. Henry also showed more support for Cromwell in his enthusiasm for promulgating the Great Bible. He commissioned Cranmer to compose an official preface to the second edition, and in a proclamation released on 14 November granted the vicegerent responsibility for licensing all Bible translations for the next five years. The situation also improved

radically for the Calais evangelicals. Taking advantage of the death of Bishop Stokesley of London on 15 September, Cromwell and Cranmer released the vast majority of them in mid-November, while delaying proceedings against the others.

On 27 December Anne of Cleves arrived at Dover, greeted with lavish celebrations. On New Year's day 1540 the king caught his first glimpse of her at Rochester. However, it was immediately obvious that she was not the beauty Holbein had portrayed, and Henry found her physically repulsive. The wedding ceremony on 6 January at Greenwich was unavoidable and Cromwell took the blame. The conservatives instantly saw this as a chance to topple him, and there were pulpit confrontations across the country. In March Robert Barnes was imprisoned in the Tower together with two other notorious evangelicals, William Jerome and Thomas Garrett. After his stand-off with Gardiner over Barnes in the previous August, Cromwell recognized the danger the bishop now posed and arranged a conciliatory dinner in an attempt to resolve their differences. In Calais, Lisle was in close contact with the conservatives in London, and the duke of Norfolk arranged for a new commission of carefully chosen conservatives to investigate heresy there. Appointed on 9 March, on 5 April they reported 'great division' in the pale. Thirteen heretics were sent back to London, five of whom were recipients of the vicegerent's direct patronage. Cromwell was in deep trouble.

On 10 April Ambassador Marillac reported that Cromwell was 'tottering', and even speculated about who would succeed to his offices. Two days later parliament opened with another speech by Audley repeating the king's demand to find a middle way in religion, and the appointment of two new committees to resolve this was announced. On 17 April Lord Lisle arrived from Calais at Norfolk's invitation. Yet still Cromwell enjoyed the king's protection. Although he resigned the duties of the secretaryship to his protégés Ralph Sadler and Thomas Wriothesley about this time he did not lose any power: indeed, on 18 April Henry confirmed his standing by granting him the earldom of Essex and the senior court office of lord great chamberlain. Cromwell set in motion the process of setting up the court of wards (the bill was read in the Lords for the first time on 3 June), and with renewed vigour he lashed out again at his conservative opponents. Lisle had come to London in the expectation of promotion in the peerage. Instead, on 19 May, he was taken to the Tower on suspicion of treason, never to leave it. By the end of the month two leading conservative members of the current parliamentary committees, Sampson and Dr Nicholas Wilson, had joined him. But Cromwell's attempts to rid himself of his opponents were looking increasingly desperate. At the same time Norfolk and Gardiner plotted his own downfall. On 1 June Marillac reported that 'Things are brought to such a pass that either Cromwell's party or that of the bishop of Winchester must succumb' (*LP Henry VIII*, 15, no. 737). With further arrests expected drastic action was required.

On 10 June Cromwell arrived slightly late for a meeting

of the privy council. As he entered the chamber the captain of the guard came forward and arrested him, presenting charges of treason and heresy. Surprised and furious Cromwell threw down his bonnet, appealing to the consciences of those present. But realizing this was useless he begged for a speedy dispatch. Norfolk went over and ripped the George from around his neck, relishing the opportunity to restore this low-born man to his former status, while the earl of Southampton untied the Garter from his knee. Finally the prisoner was led out through a side door which opened down onto the river and taken by boat the short journey from Westminster to the Tower.

The news of the arrest was announced by Audley to a silent House of Lords in the afternoon, while men appointed by the king seized Cromwell's house at Austin Friars. A week later a bill of attainder was introduced into the Lords. Containing a long list of indictments ranging from treason, heresy, and corruption to plotting to marry Princess Mary, it was passed on 29 June. Cromwell's last service to Henry was to confirm details of their private conversations which could be used as evidence that the marriage with Anne of Cleves had not been consummated. Terrified for his life he closed the letter with the plea, 'Most gracyous prynce I crye for mercye mercye mercye', though he of all people should have known the futility of this (Merriman, 2.273). But by 28 July, when Cromwell walked out onto Tower Green for his execution, he had recovered his composure. In his speech from the scaffold he denied that he had aided heretics, but acknowledged the judgment of the law. He then prayed for a short while before placing his head on the block. He suffered a particularly gruesome execution before what was left of his head was set upon a pike on London Bridge as the usual warning to traitors.

Cromwell's fall cannot be attributed to any one mistake or decision, although the Cleves marriage was the single most important factor in undermining the king's confidence in him. It was also a problem particularly difficult for Cromwell to resolve, as Henry's divorce from Anne would only lead to the king's marrying Norfolk's niece, Katherine Howard, thereby further threatening the minister's position. When he made his final desperate bid to strike out his conservative opponents Cromwell was forcing the king to decide between the two competing factions. As Henry dispatched his minister he was probably thinking more about the future than the past. With so committed an evangelical as his chief minister there would be little chance of achieving the religious unity he sought. Two days after Cromwell suffered, in a blunt statement intended to show his determination to end the years of religious strife since the break from Rome, Henry ordered the executions of the three evangelicals arrested in March, as well as three conservatives loyal to Rome. As Barnes prepared to perish in the flames he asked the sheriff if he had 'any articles against me for the which I am condemned' (Acts and Monuments, 5.43). There was none.

Historiography Until the twentieth century perceptions of Cromwell were largely coloured by religious belief. The process started in his own lifetime when Cardinal Reginald Pole portrayed the minister in his *De unitate* (1536) as 'an agent of Satan sent by the devil to lure King Henry to damnation' (p. 123). Denying that Cromwell held genuine evangelical convictions, Pole claimed that he was moved instead by greed and a Machiavellian desire to serve the king. No more objective, though far more reliable because of his access to Cromwell's contemporaries, was the martyrologist John Foxe. The first to attempt a full life of Cromwell, Foxe, in his *Acts and Monuments*, stresses Cromwell's importance in shaping the beginning of the English Reformation: his whole life, he concludes, 'was nothing else but a continual care and travail how to advance and further the right knowledge of the gospel and reform of the house of God' (*Acts and Monuments*, 5.384).

Roman Catholic writers in the second half of the sixteenth century, such as Nicholas Sander and Robert Persons, though more willing than Pole to accept Cromwell's evangelicalism, still attacked him for hypocrisy and political ruthlessness. But Foxe's favourable portrait remained largely intact. It seems to have influenced the play *The True Chronicle Historie of the Whole Life and Death of Thomas Cromwell* (1602, 1613) by W. S., implausibly identified with William Shakespeare by the editors of the third and fourth folios, in which the ambitious young Cromwell rises to a fame and fortune which never cause him to forget the benefactors who helped him on his way, before his destruction is engineered by Bishop Gardiner in revenge for the dissolution of the monasteries. And it certainly underlay the scholarly accounts of Henry VIII's reign which began to appear from the middle of the seventeenth century, by writers like Edward, Baron Herbert of Cherbury, and Gilbert Burnet. Burnet, for instance, assessed Cromwell as 'a man of mean birth but noble qualities', who was brought down by enemies of reform 'under the weight of popular odium rather than guilt' (*Bishop Burnet's History of his Own Time*, ed. G. Burnet and T. Burnet, 2 vols., 1724–34, 1.281–2, 454). In the eighteenth century, too, Cromwell continued to be seen in an essentially positive light, alike by the Anglican priest John Strype and by the agnostic David Hume.

The early nineteenth century saw a striking change of emphasis, as the campaign for Catholic emancipation and the developing Romantic movement together began to inspire more favourable attitudes towards England's pre-Reformation religion. As monasticism, in particular, came to be seen in a kindlier light, so Cromwell was attacked for his role in destroying it. William Cobbett was particularly influential in this respect. In his *History of the Protestant Reformation in England and Ireland* (1824–7) Cobbett denounces the 'tyrant' king and his agent 'the brutal blacksmith', and concludes of Cromwell that 'Perhaps of all the mean and dastardly wretches that ever died, this was the most mean and dastardly' (1.157, 189). The most powerful response to the indictment formulated by Cobbett, and repeated by historians like S. R. Maitland, was that of J. A. Froude. For Froude, a committed protestant, the English Reformation was the victorious culmination of a moral crusade to free the country from the corruption of the Catholic church. In his *History of England from the Fall of Wolsey to the Defeat of the Spanish Armada* (1856–70), he asserted that Cromwell 'pursued an object, the excellence of which, as his mind saw it, transcended all other considerations—the freedom of England and the destruction of idolatry'. For Froude the fact that Cromwell 'did the thing that England's true interests required to be done' justified the 'despotic' methods he employed (3.340).

By the beginning of the twentieth century Froude's religious determinism was coming to look increasingly unconvincing in the light of the increasingly scientific scholarship of historians such as R. B. Merriman and A. F. Pollard, based as it was on the close analysis of contemporary sources. This did not, however, lead to agreement about Cromwell's aims and methods. For Merriman the minister was a wholly secular figure, and as such the subservient hireling of a despotic king, with no higher motive than that of continuing Henry VIII's policy of raising the crown 'to absolute power on the ruins of every other institution which had ever been its rival' (Merriman, 1.164). Pollard saw the political initiative as lying solely with the king, though he blamed Cromwell for influencing 'Henry's progress to despotism', and for attempting to pack parliament (A. F. Pollard, *Henry VIII*, 1902 and later editions). It was in keeping with this attitude that Cromwell's fall should be presented in the context of a struggle between the minister and his religious opponents at court, which continued until Henry moved against Cromwell in June 1540 for attempting to force his views on the nation.

In 1905 Paul van Dyke attempted to rehabilitate Cromwell, describing him not as a tyrant but a 'statesman working hard to give England an efficient government, and to guide her safely during the difficult transition from the medieval to the modern world' (P. van Dyke, *Renascence Portraits*, 1905, 257). For him, though Cromwell was a supporter of religious reform his motives were essentially secular and patriotic. But such theories made little impact until Geoffrey Elton began his reassessment of Cromwell. In his highly influential PhD dissertation, published in 1953 as *The Tudor Revolution in Government*, Elton argued that Cromwell planned and introduced a new model of government, no longer controlled by the king through the royal household, but directed by bureaucratic departments of state. For more than forty years Elton developed his thesis, claiming that Cromwell set about reforming every aspect of government in an attempt to realize his vision of a limited constitutional government, in which king and parliament worked in close partnership. For Elton, Cromwell was not driven by religious reform, nor was he a tyrant. Despite modifying his position from time to time Elton consistently maintained that Cromwell's main ambition was to reform secular government, 'working in effect to a master-plan' (Elton, *Thomas Cromwell*, 32).

Despite his enormous influence Elton's view of Cromwell has never been universally accepted and historians have questioned his work from every angle. Most significantly further research into the workings of the court has contradicted Elton's bipolar division of government into household and bureaucratic (or national) departments. It is now generally accepted that the court, and in particular the privy chamber, played a far more important role in Henrician government than that for which Elton gave them credit. Furthermore there is also a greater willingness to accept the significance of such informal power structures as patronage, faction, and affinity in determining policy and events. Consequently Elton's pivotal argument that Cromwell reformed government institutions according to a preconceived model has had to be reconsidered. Yet there remains little consensus about the intricate details of government bureaucracy in the 1530s, and the subject remains controversial. Elton wrote of Cromwell 'Wherever one touches him, one finds originality and the unconventional, and his most persistent trait was a manifest dissatisfaction with things as they were … he remained all his life a questioner and a radical reformer' (Elton, *Reform and Reformation*, 169). At the beginning of the twenty-first century few would dispute the minister's radicalism, but historians are once more inclined to stress his commitment to the cause of evangelical reform, together with his desire to serve the king, as his principal motivating forces.

Assessment A public figure with a very private life, Thomas Cromwell remains strangely elusive. In part this can be attributed to an imbalance in the surviving sources—in his huge correspondence, mostly preserved in the Public Record Office, London, letters to Cromwell greatly outnumber those which he sent. But he nevertheless remains a man of opposites, a pragmatic idealist who could be extremely kind or extraordinarily ruthless, depending on the occasion. Holbein's portrait reinforces the impression of Cromwell as the stern, hard-working bureaucrat as which he is often characterized, but he was also well known for his wit and generosity. The few glimpses that there are of the minister away from his desk indicate that he combined a love of art, literature, music, and fine objects with a keen interest in gardening and falconry. Late in 1535 Chapuys reported of him: 'He speaks well in his own language, and tolerably in Latin, French, and Italian; is hospitable, liberal with his property and with gracious words, magnificent in his household and in building' (*LP Henry VIII*, 9, no. 862). As well as telling how Cromwell appropriated his neighbours' land Stow also emphasized how 'in that declining time of charity', he often saw him providing 'bread, meate and drinke sufficient' for two hundred poor people twice every day outside his gate (Stow, 1.89). That this was not some cynical attempt to obtain popularity is shown by Cromwell's commitment to social reform.

It was his desire for reform, complemented by a driving ambition and a keen sense of duty, which drove Cromwell in the 1530s. His skill as a lawyer, merchant, and businessman initially enabled him to escape from his relatively humble origins, but it was through a life of service that he was able to become one of the richest and most powerful men in England, his loyalty to the king never compromised by his dedication to the cause of religious reform. Attempts at a precise definition of Cromwell's religious convictions have proved inconclusive. There is evidence for an interest in Lutheranism in the 1530s, but no indication that he ever denied the real presence or promoted the doctrine of justification by faith alone. Consequently his position is best described as evangelical.

As the king's minister Cromwell occupied a position very different from that of Cardinal Wolsey before him. After taking personal control of the divorce proceedings in 1527 Henry continued to intervene in government far more than he had done before. There was no formal office of chief minister, and Cromwell's advancement as the king's business and parliamentary manager was far removed from Wolsey's upward passage through the church and chancery. Cromwell's initial promotion relied on his ability to execute and enforce the royal supremacy, rather than to create policy. Although as time passed he played an increasing role in policy making he never approached Wolsey's influence over the king. Even after he had reached the peak of his power, with the destruction of Anne Boleyn and her leading supporters at court, his position still rested on his ability to manipulate factional politics and on his controversial authority over the church as vicegerent in spirituals. With a powerful faction of conservative courtiers strongly opposed to evangelical reform it is little wonder that after several attempts to overthrow him Cromwell's enemies finally succeeded in June 1540.

Cromwell's relationship with the king has always been a matter of debate and probably always will be. While historians are fortunate that so many of the minister's papers survived as the result of their confiscation at the time of his arrest, the comparative lack of other sources means that there is often only half the story recorded. Nevertheless, it is clear that both Henry and Cromwell were active in creating policy. While the king was responsible for the general thrust of decision making during the 1530s his minister enjoyed considerable influence. Not only was Cromwell able to shape decisions by first advising the king and then developing policy through its execution, but Henry also showed a willingness to tolerate the initiatives of others either as long as he agreed with the broad principles involved, or where the issues involved held little interest for him.

Although Henry took control of the divorce process after 1527, he allowed Cromwell a significant amount of freedom in the implementation and enforcement of the royal supremacy. Despite his personal commitment to the development of religious policy following the break from Rome, the king was very willing to allow his minister and the other leading reformers to take much of the initiative during the earliest years of the English Reformation. Towards the end of 1538, however, Henry was clearly becoming concerned about the pace of reform, and Cromwell's influence consequently began to decline. In those areas where the king was less interested, such as social reform, Cromwell enjoyed greater freedom, but that does not mean that Henry did not monitor his actions carefully and intervene where he had objections. A good example is

Henry's decision in 1537 to halt the strengthening of the union between England and Wales.

Thus the relationship between king and minister can be understood as an unequal partnership in which they both used similar means to achieve different objectives. While Henry was primarily concerned with asserting his new powers and purging the church of any elements which might suggest papal authority, Cromwell was more interested in exploiting the development of the royal supremacy to advance evangelical reform. It also appears that Cromwell's fiscal objectives were fundamentally different from those of the king: he planned to use the proceeds of the dissolution of the monasteries to create a permanent landed endowment which would strengthen the new 'imperial' monarchy along the lines argued during the reigns of Henry VI and Edward IV by Sir John Fortescue. By contrast Henry's decision during the 1540s to sell much of the land thus acquired in order to fund his French and Scottish campaigns suggests that he had other priorities.

Cromwell succeeded not only in enforcing the royal supremacy and strengthening the 'imperial' crown both politically and financially, but also in using his position to pursue his own reforming agenda. Against significant opposition he secured acceptance of the king's new powers, created a more united and more easily governable kingdom, and provided the crown, at least temporarily, with a very significant landed endowment. Parliament also became a more permanent and significant institution as the result of the legislation which Cromwell drafted, and he certainly understood that the king was at his most powerful when working in collaboration with the three estates through statute. But here too Cromwell's instincts were primarily pragmatic, and he did not go so far as to endorse the developing notion of the sovereign state, as defined in the 1530s by the lawyer Christopher St German, in which the king worked as an equal partner with Lords and Commons.

Despite the significance of some of his measures for social reform, not least as models for the future, Cromwell's most notable achievement was in the end religious, his furtherance of the evangelical cause. Through the dissolution of the monasteries, and by his attacks on pilgrimages, shrines, ceremonies, and images, Cromwell succeeded in removing much of the culture of Catholicism, as well as attacking the doctrine of purgatory. More positively he was also able to offer patronage and protection to reformers throughout the country, and he made effective use of the printing press to circulate evangelical literature and propaganda. By far the most notable publication for which he was responsible was the Great Bible of 1539. At the heart of the evangelical message was the total predominance of scripture as religious authority. Its wide availability in parish churches throughout the country meant that for the first time ordinary people would have direct access to the word of God without having to rely on the authority and interpretation of the church. Although Henry slowed the pace of reform after 1538 he was reluctant to reverse it entirely; indeed, subsequent measures included the levying of a fine in 1541 on parishes which failed to buy a copy of the Great Bible.

Both the life and the legacy of Thomas Cromwell have aroused enormous controversy. While opinions of him vary his effectiveness and creativity as a royal minister cannot be denied. And although he often worked to further his own ideas and ambitions his loyalty to Henry VIII cannot be doubted. Perhaps the minister's most appropriate epitaph came from the king himself: in a letter to the constable of France dated 3 March 1541, Ambassador Marillac reported that Henry was now said to be lamenting that 'under pretext of some slight offences which he had committed, they had brought several accusations against him, on the strength of which he had put to death the most faithful servant he ever had' (Kaulek, 274).

HOWARD LEITHEAD

Sources G. Bray, ed., *Documents of the English Reformation* (1994) • G. Cavendish, *The life and death of Cardinal Wolsey*, ed. R. S. Sylvester, EETS, original ser., 243 (1959) • *The acts and monuments of John Foxe*, ed. S. R. Cattley, 8 vols. (1837–41) • J. Kaulek, ed., *Correspondance politique de MM. de Castillon et de Marillac, ambassadeurs de France en Angleterre (1537–1542)* (Paris, 1885) • W. Roper, *The lyfe of Sir Thomas Moore, knighte*, ed. E. V. Hitchcock, EETS, 197 (1935) • *English historical documents*, 5, ed. C. H. Williams (1967) • *LP Henry VIII* • *State papers published under ... Henry VIII*, 11 vols. (1830–52) • J. Stow, *A survay of London*, rev. edn (1603); repr. with introduction by C. L. Kingsford as *A survey of London*, 2 vols. (1908) • J. M. W. Bean, *The decline of English feudalism, 1215–1540* (1968) • B. W. Beckingsale, *Thomas Cromwell: Tudor minister* (1978) • G. W. Bernard, 'Elton's Cromwell', *History*, 83 (1998), 587–607 • G. W. Bernard, 'The making of religious policy, 1533–1546: Henry VIII and the search for the middle way', *HJ*, 41 (1998), 321–49 • *HoP, Commons, 1509–58* • S. Brigden, 'Thomas Cromwell and the "brethren"', *Law and government under the Tudors: essays presented to Sir Geoffrey Elton*, ed. C. Cross, D. Loades, and J. J. Scarisbrick (1988), 31–49 • S. Brigden, *London and the Reformation* (1989) • S. Brigden, *New worlds, lost worlds* (2001) • C. Coleman and D. Starkey, eds., *Revolution reassessed: revisions in the history of Tudor government and administration* (1986) • C. Cross, D. Loades, and J. J. Scarisbrick, eds., *Law and government under the Tudors: essays presented to Sir Geoffrey Elton* (1988) • A. G. Dickens, *Thomas Cromwell and the English Reformation* (1959) • *DNB* • E. Duffy, *The stripping of the altars: traditional religion in England, c.1400–c.1580* (1992) • S. Ellis, *Tudor frontiers and noble power* (1995) • S. G. Ellis, *Ireland in the age of the Tudors* (1998) • G. R. Elton, 'A new age of reform?', *HJ*, 30 (1987), 709–16 • G. R. Elton, *Policy and police* (1972) • G. R. Elton, *Reform and Reformation: England, 1509–1558* (1977) • G. R. Elton, *Reform and renewal* (1973) • G. R. Elton, *Studies in Tudor and Stuart government*, 4 vols. (1974–92) • G. R. Elton, *The Tudor constitution*, 2nd edn (1962) • G. R. Elton, *The Tudor revolution in government* (1953) • G. R. Elton, *Thomas Cromwell* (1991) • GEC, *Peerage*, 3.555–7 • S. J. Gunn, ed., *Early Tudor government* (1995) • J. A. Guy, *The Tudor monarchy* (1997) • J. A. Guy, *Thomas More* (2000) • J. A. Guy, *Tudor England* (1988) • C. Haigh, *English reformations* (1993) • R. W. Hoyle, *The Pilgrimage of Grace and the politics of the 1530s* (2001) • E. W. Ives, *Anne Boleyn* (1986) • J. G. Jones, *Early modern Wales, c.1512–1640* (1994) • S. E. Lehmberg, *The Reformation Parliament, 1529–1536* (1970) • D. Loades, *Tudor government: structures of authority in the sixteenth century* (1997) • D. MacCulloch, ed., *The reign of Henry VIII* (1995) • D. MacCulloch, *Thomas Cranmer: a life* (1996) • R. McEntegart, *Henry VIII, the league of Schmalkalden, and the English Reformation* (2002) • *Life and letters of Thomas Cromwell*, ed. R. B. Merriman, 2 vols. (1902) • A. Neame, *The holy maid of Kent* (1971) • R. O'Day, *The debate on the English Reformation* (1986) • R. O'Day, *The Longman companion to the Tudor age* (1995) • R. A. W. Rex, *Henry VIII and the English Reformation* (1993) • R. A. W. Rex, *The Tudors* (2002) • J. J. Scarisbrick, *Henry VIII* (1968) • P. Slack, *The English poor law, 1531–1782* (1990) • D. Starkey and others, eds., *The English court: from the Wars of the Roses to the civil war* (1987) • D. Starkey, ed., *A European court in London* (1991) • D. Starkey, *The reign of Henry VIII* (1991) • D. Starkey, 'A reply: Tudor government: the facts?', *HJ*, 31 (1988), 921–31 • D. Starkey, *Six wives: the queens of Henry VIII* (2003) • R. Strong, *Tudor and Jacobean portraits*, 2 vols. (1969) • G. Williams, *Renewal and Reformation: Wales, c.1415–1642* (1993) • A. S. Bevan, 'The role of the judiciary in Tudor government, 1509–1547', PhD diss., U. Cam., 1985 • D. Grummitt, 'Calais 1485–1547: a study in early Tudor government and politics', PhD diss., U. Lond., 1997 • M. L. Robertson, 'Thomas Cromwell's servants: the ministerial household in early Tudor government and society', PhD diss., U. Cal., Los Angeles, 1975 • P. J. Ward, 'The origins of Thomas Cromwell's public career: service under Cardinal Wolsey and Henry VIII, 1524–30', PhD diss., U. Lond., 1999

Archives BL, corresp. and papers • PRO, corresp. • Worcs. RO, letters

Likenesses after H. Holbein the younger, portrait, c.1533–1534, Frick collection, New York [*see illus.*] • after H. Holbein the younger, portrait, versions, incl. NPG • W. Hollar, portrait, NPG

Cromwell, Thomas (c.1540–1610/11), parliamentary diarist, was the third son of Gregory Cromwell, first Baron Cromwell (d. 1551), and Elizabeth, sister of Edward *Seymour, duke of Somerset, and widow of Sir Anthony Oughtred. Thomas *Cromwell, Henry VIII's minister, was his grandfather. He attended St John's College, Cambridge, and in August 1580 married Katherine, daughter of Thomas Gardner of Coxford. Cromwell sat in five of Elizabeth's parliaments, for Fowey (1571), Bodmin (1572), Preston (1584), and Grampound (1586 and 1589), seats often available to the well connected. He is best remembered for the diaries he kept for the sessions of 1572, 1576, 1581, and 1584, now in Trinity College, Dublin. These reveal a love for parliamentary process and the details of legislative business at a key time in the development of the English parliament. Where they can be checked against other sources, Cromwell's diaries are shown to be an accurate, if at times incomplete, record of bill proceedings, peppered with details of measures and often quite extensive reports of debates. In 1572 he took pains to report the Commons' actions against Thomas Howard, fourth duke of Norfolk, and Mary, queen of Scots; the remaining diaries consist largely of bill proceedings.

Cromwell was intimately acquainted with the workings of parliament. He was an active committee man, being named to almost a hundred committees considering a wide range of matters. In the last two weeks of March 1585, for example, he was appointed to the Commons' committees dealing with cloth making, malt, apprentices, church ministers, leases of land, copyhold lands in Ely, and a bill concerning a debtor. On occasion he notes that his afternoon committee work necessitated his absence from the floor of the house. He seems to have had a special interest in electoral returns, being entrusted with reporting the work of the relevant committees, and in legal matters. In 1585 Cromwell was one of three members chosen to argue before the lord chancellor, unsuccessfully, that members' privilege of freedom from arrest should extend to being unavailable to receive subpoenas.

According to his own diaries, and the journal of Elizabeth's parliaments compiled from a number of original sources by Sir Simonds D'Ewes in the seventeenth century, Cromwell made several speeches to the house. In 1572 he spoke in favour of bringing minstrels under the terms of the vagabonds bill and, in 1581, on the subject of children born to foreigners. In 1587 Cromwell made a well-received motion thanking the queen for her response to the Commons' petition urging the execution of Mary Stuart. He was no sycophant, however. When a leading government minister urged caution after an MP moved that the whole house should attend the queen to request Norfolk's execution in 1572, Cromwell 'misliked to have any delay from so necessarie a motion' (Hartley, 1.314). He supported Paul Wentworth's 1581 motion for a public fast, a move considered by the queen to be a breach of her royal prerogative. Cromwell also objected to the queen's imprisonment of MPs in 1587 for promoting a radical alternative to the Book of Common Prayer.

Cromwell's will requested 'that noe pompe or sumptuousnes be used in about or by reason of my buriall, beinge not willinge to have vanities continued for me after my deathe whereto I have beene too much subiect in my lifetime'. He was one of those moderate puritan MPs with a compromising marriage, for his brother-in-law was a Jesuit priest. Nevertheless, his marriage to Katherine Gardner was evidently a happy one. His will repeatedly acknowledged his 'beloved' wife, and required his children's obedience to her if they hoped to receive their inheritances. Cromwell assisted the privy council on local matters in Norfolk, where he retired to property near King's Lynn. His land dealings and agricultural activities were complicated, troubled, and rather unsuccessful. This, he claimed in his will, was due to his preoccupation with the affairs of his brother and nephew, the second and third barons Cromwell. He died between February 1610 and April 1611.   DAVID DEAN

Sources HoP, Commons, 1558–1603 · T. E. Hartley, ed., Proceedings in the parliaments of Elizabeth I, 3 vols. (1981–95) · S. D'Ewes, ed., The journals of all the parliaments during the reign of Queen Elizabeth, both of the House of Lords and House of Commons (1682) · APC · JHC · J. E. Neale, Elizabeth I and her parliaments, 2 vols. (1953–7) · PRO, PROB 11/117/135, fols. 280v–282r · G. R. Elton, The parliament of England, 1559–1581 (1986) · GEC, Peerage
Archives TCD, parliamentary diaries, MS 1045

Cromwell, Thomas, first earl of Ardglass (1594–1653). See under Cromwell, Edward, third Baron Cromwell (c.1559–1607).

Cromwell, Thomas Kitson (1792–1870), Unitarian minister and writer, was born on 14 December 1792, and at an early age joined the literary department of Longmans, the publishing house. A small volume of verse, The School-Boy, with other Poems (1816), was followed four years later by a few privately printed copies of Honour, or, Arrivals from College: a Comedy. The play had been produced at Drury Lane on 17 April 1819 and was twice repeated. A second drama, The Druid: a Tragedy (1832), was never acted. A more ambitious undertaking was Oliver Cromwell and his Times (1821; 2nd edn, 1822), which is described by Thomas Carlyle as 'of a vaporous, gesticulating, dull-aërial, still more insignificant character, and contains nothing that is not common

elsewhere' (Letters and Speeches of Oliver Cromwell, 2nd edn, 2, 1846, 161–2n.).

Although originally a member of the Church of England, of which his elder brother was a clergyman, Cromwell joined the Unitarians about 1830. At the end of 1838 he preached as a probationer at the old chapel on Stoke Newington Green, and in March 1839 was 'inducted' by neighbouring ministers. He officiated there for twenty-five years and introduced a modified form of the Church of England liturgy. He also held during the greater part of his ministry the somewhat incompatible office of clerk to the local board of Clerkenwell, from which he retired with a pension. He had married the daughter of Richard Carpenter, JP and deputy lieutenant for Middlesex; there were no children. In 1864 he resigned the pulpit at Stoke Newington, and soon afterwards took charge of the old Presbyterian congregation at Canterbury, over which he presided until his death. During the last two years of his life he acted as honorary secretary of the Birmingham Education League.

In December 1838 Cromwell became a fellow of the Society of Antiquaries, and a few years previous to his death accepted an honorary PhD from the University of Erlangen. He was also a master of arts, but of what university is unknown. Besides contributions to the Gentleman's Magazine, Chambers's Journal, and other periodicals, he supplied the text for the four volumes of James Storer's History and Antiquities of the Cathedral Churches of Great Britain (1814–19) and for Excursions through England and Wales, Scotland, and Ireland, a series of attractive views published in numbers (1818–22). He published topographical works on Chichester (1825), Clerkenwell (1828), and Islington (1835). The Soul and the Future Life (1859) is an assertion of the older Unitarian view that descended from Joseph Priestley, which was under serious attack from a new generation of Unitarian teachers and theologians. At the climax of this confrontation in 1866 Cromwell published a letter in The Inquirer that in its pamphlet version, Whither are we tending? To transcendental deism, or conservation of the Christianity of the New Testament?, contains direct attacks on John James Tayler and James Martineau, the leaders of the 'new school', for their rejection of the Unitarian name and for a philosophy based on intuition rather than fact. Cromwell died on 22 December 1870 at home at 11 St Dunstan's Terrace, St Dunstan's, Canterbury, and was buried in the nonconformist burial-ground in Canterbury on 28 December.

GORDON GOODWIN, rev. R. K. WEBB

Sources The Inquirer (31 Dec 1870) · The Inquirer (7 Jan 1871) · The Inquirer (14 Jan 1871) · S. Lewis jun., The history and topography of the parish of St Mary, Islington (1842), 319 · N&Q, 4th ser., 7 (1871)
Wealth at death under £200: probate, 14 Feb 1871, CGPLA Eng. & Wales

Crónán moccu Éile (d. 665). See under Munster, saints of (act. c.450–c.700).

Crone, Robert (c.1718–1779), landscape painter and collector, was born in Dublin; he is of unknown parentage. He was educated at the Dublin Society Schools under Robert Hunter, Robert West, and Philip Hussey and won prizes in 1748 and 1750. Hussey, a relative, sent him to Italy in 1755, where he studied landscape painting for about a year under Richard Wilson RA. He also trained at the Accademia del Nudo in Rome with John Plimer; after Plimer's death in 1760, he finished two of his landscapes, *The Landing of Aeneas in Africa* and *Dido Flying with Aeneas from the Storm*, commissioned by James Grant of Grant. As well as his studies, he was engaged in procuring artworks for Dublin connoisseurs and collectors. He was regarded as a highly promising painter by the traveller James Martin, who called him 'very clever in his profession … a most excellent drawer of landskip' (Ingamells, 256), and by Richard Dalton, who mentioned Crone's physical deformity in a letter to Lord Bute when he described him as 'a little crooked Irishman' (ibid.).

Crone returned to London in 1767, and in 1768 exhibited two landscapes at the Society of Artists. In 1770 he exhibited four paintings at the Royal Academy, and up to 1778 contributed several more, most of which were Italian landscapes in the Claudean manner and many of which were drawings. These, often executed in black and white chalks on blue-grey or buff paper, recall similar works by Wilson, although they are stiffer in execution. The superiority of his drawing to his paintings is credited by Crookshank and the knight of Glin to the lack of training in oils at the Dublin Society Schools (Crookshank and the Knight of Glin, *Watercolours*, 59). He only contributed once to a Dublin exhibition, sending a landscape with figures to the Irish Society of Artists in 1770.

Crone's career was considerably hampered by epilepsy. After an initial fit when he was fifteen, he experienced a recurrence fifteen years later while copying a picture at the Palazzo Barberini, causing him to fall from some scaffolding. He survived this, but his attacks continued until a severe fit caused his death early in 1779.

L. H. Cust, *rev.* Kate Retford

Sources J. Ingamells, ed., *A dictionary of British and Irish travellers in Italy, 1701–1800* (1997), 255–6 · A. Crookshank and the Knight of Glin [D. Fitzgerald], *The watercolours of Ireland: works on paper in pencil, pastel and paint, c.1600–1914* (1994), 58–9, 300 · A. Crookshank and the Knight of Glin [D. Fitzgerald], *The painters of Ireland, c.1660–1920*, 2nd edn (1979), 120, 123 · W. G. Strickland, *A dictionary of Irish artists*, 1 (1913); facs. edn with introduction by T. J. Snoddy (1969), 233–4 · E. Edwards, *Anecdotes of painters* (1808); facs. edn (1970), 59 · W. G. Constable, *Richard Wilson* (1953), 37, 137 · Graves, *Soc. Artists*, 67 · Graves, *RA exhibitors* · G. Breeze, *Society of Artists in Ireland: index of exhibits, 1765–80* (1985), 8 · W. Fraser, ed., *The chiefs of Grant*, 2 (1883), 538 · Redgrave, *Artists* · Waterhouse, *18c painters*

Cronin, Archibald Joseph (1896–1981), novelist, was born on 19 July 1896 at Cardross, Dunbartonshire, the only child of Patrick Cronin, a clerk and commercial traveller, and his wife, Jessie Montgomerie. When he was seven his father died and Cronin and his mother went to live with her family. His mother became a travelling saleswoman and the first woman public health inspector with Glasgow corporation.

Cronin was educated at Dumbarton Academy and at Glasgow University, where he studied medicine. He graduated MB ChB with honours in 1919. His years at Glasgow were interrupted by service in 1916 as surgeon sub-

Archibald Joseph Cronin (1896–1981), by Bassano, 1931

lieutenant in the Royal Naval Volunteer Reserve, and by three months at the Rotunda Hospital in Dublin, where he took his midwifery course. His first practice was in a mining district in Wales. He married Agnes Mary Gibson (*b.* 1897/8) on 31 August 1921. She was the daughter of Robert Gibson, a master baker, of Hamilton, Lanarkshire, and Agnes Thomson, *née* Gilchrist. They had three sons, the eldest of whom, Vincent, became a writer. Cronin also obtained a diploma in public health (London, 1923), was admitted MRCP (London, 1924), and graduated MD (Glasgow, 1925)—a considerable achievement which involved unremitting work. In 1924 he was appointed medical inspector of mines for Great Britain. His work at this time led to two reports on dust inhalation and first aid in mines.

Between 1926 and 1930 Cronin practised in London, but ill health took him to the west highlands, and there he wrote *Hatter's Castle* (1931). It made him famous overnight; he was able to give up his medical practice and become a full-time writer, as he had always wished to do. The choice of publisher was determined by his wife, who picked out the name of Victor Gollancz with a pin from a list of publishers. His second novel, *Three Loves* (1932), was 'torture to write', as he expressed it, and did not do well. However, *The Stars Look Down* (1935), which drew attention to the miserable working conditions of coal miners and the risks they ran from injury and occupational diseases, was an instant favourite with his public. His next book, *The Citadel* (1937), which fiercely attacked the greed and charlatanism in Harley Street, caused a sensation. Launched with a brilliant publicity campaign by Gollancz, it probably played some part in creating the climate of opinion which led to the recommendations of the Beveridge report (1942) and subsequently to the establishment of the National Health Service.

In July 1939 Cronin went with his family to the United States—a move which led to considerable criticism in Britain. Two of his novels were filmed in Hollywood at about this time (several of his books were made into successful films). Between 1941 and 1945 he worked in Washington for the British Ministry of Information and wrote *The Keys of the Kingdom* (1942) and *The Green Years* (1945). After the war he lived permanently in Switzerland, writing novels at roughly two-yearly intervals, notably *The Spanish Gardener* (1950). He was an honorary DLitt of Bowdoin and of Lafayette University.

Cronin's strength as a novelist lay in his narrative skill, his acute observation, and his graphic powers of description. His plots were often over-dramatic and his characters were in general unremarkable—he needed, as he himself remarked, to have real people to base them on (the tyrannical James Brodie, in *Hatter's Castle*, is said to be a portrait of his maternal grandfather, which caused consternation in the family). But as a craftsman he was highly professional, and there is some refreshing humour in his books. He was not an intellectual, and enjoyed simple pleasures such as watching cricket matches and talking to the people round him, the kind of people who might have been his patients, and who often became characters in his novels. He loved travelling, and this gave him material for his books which he used to good effect.

Cronin was a Roman Catholic, and several of his novels are concerned with religion and matters of conscience. The example of his mother, a devout Roman Catholic who continued to live with him after his marriage, and of a favourite uncle, Canon Montgomerie, combined with happy early years in a Roman Catholic school to make his religious beliefs important to him. Having suffered from a then prevalent bigotry, particularly at the time of his marriage—since his wife's family were Plymouth Brethren—his Roman Catholicism was tolerant and ecumenical before such attitudes became commonplace. Though extremely tough in business dealings, in private life he was a good-humoured person to whom each day was an adventure. His last years, however, after his wife became ill, were lonely, for he had always been a solitary individual and his wealth cut him off from other people.

Cronin's experiences in Glasgow and Wales made him keenly aware of the evils of extreme poverty, and his skill in combining romantic, compelling narrative and vivid, realistic portrayal of life among the poorer members of society is one of the most striking facets of his novels. Nearly all his books have a strong autobiographical element, returning again and again to his childhood in Dumbarton, which is thinly veiled under the fictitious name of Levenford. Episodes in his semi-autobiographical *Adventures in Two Worlds* (1952) are repeated in his novels, making it difficult to disentangle fact from fiction. A collection of short stories, *Adventures of a Black Bag* (1969), was made into the immensely popular television and radio series *Dr Finlay's Casebook*. Extremely hard-working, he liked to average 5000 words a day, planning all the details of his plots meticulously in advance.

Although Cronin's powers flagged in his later years, the best of his novels are extremely readable and accomplished, and during his lifetime they had deservedly large sales, especially in Europe. Like many writers of fiction he suffered a loss of popularity after his death, except in the Far East and the former communist bloc where his style of writing, by then old-fashioned in the West, was still enjoyed. He was a middlebrow writer *par excellence*, and above all a masterly story-teller. Cronin died of bronchitis on 6 January 1981 at Glion, near Montreux, Switzerland, and was buried at La Tour de Peilz.   SHEILA HODGES

Sources *The Times* (19 Jan 1981) · private information (1990) · personal knowledge (2004) · *WW*

Archives NL Scot., papers · NRA, corresp. and literary papers · Purdue University Library, West Lafayette, Indiana | Georgetown University, Washington, DC, corresp. with Bruce Marshall

Likenesses Bassano, photograph, 1931, NPG [*see illus.*]

Cronshaw, Cecil John Turrell (1889–1961), industrial chemist and businessman, was born on 13 June 1889 at Heywood in Lancashire, the son of William Robert Cronshaw, a commercial traveller, and his wife, Anne Elizabeth, *née* Turrell. He was educated at Bury grammar school and apprenticed for a time to J. H. Leicester at the Manchester chamber of commerce testing house. He subsequently attended the Victoria University of Manchester and in 1913 graduated with first-class honours in chemistry. After a short spell with the synthetic rubber manufacturers, Strange and Graham, in 1915 he joined the dyestuff firm of Levinstein Ltd, based at Blackley, Manchester. There he acted as assistant to James Baddiley, who was developing a research team at the firm. On 1 December 1917 he married Annie, the daughter of John Downham, a consulting engineer; they had two sons.

Cronshaw worked first on oleum manufacture, but his most important achievements were connected with organic chemicals, notably dyestuffs and pharmaceuticals. He was one of the generation of industrial chemists educated in Britain who rebuilt the country's synthetic dyestuff industry during and after the First World War, following its earlier eclipse by Germany. Only a handful of small British dyestuff firms had survived and Levinsteins was perhaps the leader of these. Cronshaw undertook some chemical work himself, at Levinsteins and later, but his major contribution was in management, and the promotion and organization of research. In 1916 he was placed in charge of the synthetic indigo plant at Ellesmere Port which had been appropriated from the German firm of Meister, Lucius and Brüning, and with his colleagues brought it into operation in three months. The main focus of his work was the production of intermediaries required for the process, notably phenylglycine, which had previously been imported from Germany. The range of his activities soon widened. He was involved in technical negotiations with the American firm of Du Pont for the purchase of manufacturing processes from Levinstein. After the armistice he was, for a year, controller of chemical factories in the Rhineland area. When he returned to Britain in 1919 he became assistant to Herbert Levinstein, managing director of the newly formed British Dyestuffs Corporation, which incorporated the two major companies, Levinstein and British Dyes Ltd, of Huddersfield. Cronshaw was quickly appointed head of production control and then works manager at Blackley, and by 1924 he was technical manager of the company.

British Dyestuffs Corporation was one of the four main firms which merged to form ICI in 1926. Cronshaw's acknowledged range of experience led to his appointment as technical director of ICI's Dyestuffs Group, which represented the major organic element in the company's business. From this position and, later, as managing director on its delegate board, he widened the group's technical interests into synthetic rubber and pharmaceuticals. The latter area was eventually constituted as a separate division (groups were renamed divisions in ICI in 1943). The growth of the Dyestuffs Group was influenced by Cronshaw's emphasis on research and his recruitment of high-calibre graduates, an approach which was met with scepticism in some quarters, but supported elsewhere in ICI, notably by F. A. Freeth of the Alkali Group. During the mid-1930s Cronshaw promoted the exploitation of a major new chromogen (that is, a chemical structure common to numerous dyestuffs) based on phthalocyanine. For this work, twenty-five years later, he received the Perkin medal of the Society of Dyers and Colourists. Outside the technical domain Cronshaw negotiated the entry into Dyestuffs Group of such firms as the British Alizarine Company, and the group's administrative structure was largely his creation. From 1939 until 1943 he was chairman of the delegate board. He joined the main board of ICI in 1939 and remained a member until his retirement in 1952. During this time he promoted new technical initiatives of many kinds, extending from new drugs to the development of plant for the cracking of oil fractions on Teesside.

Despite increasing administrative and commercial responsibilities, Cronshaw retained a strong professional and technical involvement in the industry. He acted as president of the Society of Dyers and Colourists from 1939 to 1946 and received a variety of honours, including an honorary DSc. from the University of Leeds (1938), and the silver medal of the Royal Society of Arts (1940). He was a small man, of mercurial disposition and quick wit, with interests in music, cricket, and yachting. Indeed, his wit was said to be too barbed for the taste of some of his junior colleagues, though he was not intentionally unkind. He had an interest in and respect for young people and was a governor of his old school and university. For most of his life he lived at Prestwich, Manchester, and latterly at Alnwick, Prestwich Park. After a prolonged illness, he died in Cheadle Royal Infirmary on 5 January 1961.

JAMES DONNELLY

Sources *Journal of the Society of Dyers and Colourists*, 77 (1961), 163–4 · *The Times* (7 Jan 1961) · *The Times* (11 Jan 1961) · *Manchester Guardian* (7 Jan 1961) · WWW · *ICI Magazine*, 31 (1953), 53–4 · *Hexagon Courier* [ICI Dyestuffs Division] (Feb 1961), 3 · M. R. Fox, *Dye-makers of Great Britain, 1856–1976: a history of chemists, companies, products, and changes* (1987) · W. J. Reader, *Imperial Chemical Industries, a history*, 2 vols. (1970–75) · *ICI Magazine*, 39 (1961), 87–8 · P. Allen, 'Cronshaw, Cecil John Turrell', *DBB* · d. cert.
Archives Ches. & Chester ALSS, ICI materials · ICI Central Archives, Millbank, London · Zeneca Limited, Blackley, Manchester, archive
Likenesses photograph, ICI Central Archives, Millbank, London · photograph, Zeneca Limited, Blackley, Manchester, archive
Wealth at death £70,717 13s. 6d.: probate, 21 March 1961, *CGPLA Eng. & Wales*

Crook, John (1616/17–1699), Quaker leader and writer, was born in the north of England of wealthy parents. Educated in London from the age of ten until he was seventeen, he was subsequently apprenticed, possibly to a lace merchant. During the civil war he served as a captain in the parliamentarian army, and in 1647 he married Margaret Mounsell (d. 1685) of Weymouth, whose brother, a parliamentary officer, had been killed in the fighting. The Crooks had six children, one of whom died young. With three other officers, in 1650 Crook purchased Beckerings Park, near Ridgmont, Bedfordshire, an estate sequestered from John Ashburnham. Crook became a justice of the peace, and on 13 May 1653 was recommended for a seat in the nominated assembly by William Dell and other Bedfordshire men, but the council of state selected Edward Cater. Crook, his supporters had argued, was opposed to tithes and taxes. During these years Crook experienced religious turmoil, likening himself to one lost in the wilderness and buffeted by storms:

> I was as one that once went astray and wandered upon the barren Mountains, and when I had wearied my self with wandring, I went into the Wilderness, and there I was torn as with briars, and pricked as with thorns, sometimes thinking this was the way, and sometimes concluding that was the way, and by and by concluding all was out of the way, and then bitter morning came upon me, and weeping for want of the interpreter; for when I sought to know what was the matter, and where I was it was too hard for me; then I thought I would venture on some way where it was most likely to find a lost God, and I would pray with them that prayed, and fast with them that fasted, and mourn with them that mourned, if by any means I might come to rest, but found it not, until I came to see the candle lighted in my own house. (Penington, 12)

'Convinced' to become a Quaker by William Dewsbury in 1654, Crook welcomed George Fox to Beckerings Park in 1655, arranging for local gentry to meet him. Hostile reaction to the Quakers soon swept Bedfordshire, resulting in Crook's dismissal from the commission of the peace. With Fox he visited Cambridge and Warwick in 1655, briefly suffering imprisonment at the latter. James Nayler held a general meeting at Beckerings Park in 1656, and in May 1658 as many as 3000, including Fox, reportedly attended a meeting there. Crook and other prominent Friends petitioned Richard Cromwell and the council of state in October 1658 for release of 115 Quakers and for reform of laws, courts, and officials. The following April he led a Quaker delegation that unsuccessfully petitioned parliament for relief of incarcerated Friends. The same year he published the first four of his more than two dozen works, including *A Declaration of the People of God*, directed primarily to magistrates and written with Thomas Aldam and fourteen others. In *Tythes No Property* he manifested modest legal knowledge, citing statutes and Coke as well as John Foxe; Michael Benyon of Gray's Inn replied in *Antitythe-Monger Confuted* (1662). In *A Defence of the True Church* Crook deftly distinguished Friends from other nonconformists. Equally polemical was *Unrighteousness No Plea for Truth*, which refuted James Pope's *Plea for Truth*.

At the Restoration Crook's primary concern was the nation's spiritual condition. In *An Epistle of Love* (1660) he urged rulers to remember that God had restored them to wreak vengeance on a hypocritical generation. He argued the Quakers' opposition to oaths in *The Case of Swearing* (1660), reinforcing his argument by example when he was imprisoned at Huntington in January 1661 for refusing to take the oaths. *Sixteen Reasons* (1661) against swearing restated the case. With Francis Howgill, Samuel Fisher, and Richard Hubberthorne he wrote *Liberty of Conscience* (1661), presenting copies to members of parliament on 31 May. By September Crook had been confined at Aylesbury for holding a conventicle near Stony Stratford, Buckinghamshire. From prison he sent *An Epistle for Unity* (1661) to Friends, suggesting ways to avoid internal dissension. One threat to Quaker unity was posed by John Perrot, with whom Crook was sympathetic; Crook was present at the meeting on 19 November that found Perrot innocent of fomenting division. After being arrested at a London meeting on 13 May 1662, Crook was tried at the Old Bailey on 25 June before Chief Justice Robert Foster, Sir Matthew Hale, and others. Refusing to take the oath of allegiance, Crook insisted he had been illegally arrested and demanded due process. The trial is powerfully recounted in *The Cry of the Innocent* (1662), which denounces the judges' severity. Adjudged guilty of *praemunire*, Crook was remanded to Newgate and his estate at Beckerings Park was confiscated. A warrant for his release was issued on 16 October. Crook published several other works in 1662, including an epistle, *To All Dear Friends and Brethren*, written with Edward Burrough and Isaac Penington, and *An Apology for the Quakers*, articulating the Friends' case for religious liberty. One of his most influential works, *Truth's Principles* (1662), a primer of Quaker principles, was often reprinted and was published in French at Rotterdam in 1675.

Crook was in London in February 1663 when he completed *Glad-Tydings Proclaimed*, warning Friends to remain faithful to the peace principle and not 'stir out of their Tents' (*Glad-Tydings*, 6). For refusing to take the oath of allegiance, he was imprisoned at Ipswich in March. He was still there in May 1664, when he wrote *An Epistle of Peace and Good-Will* to Friends, proclaiming the 'Birth of the Morning of the everlasting Day of the Most High'. The same year he published *A True and Faithful Testimony* about John Samm, who had died in Northampton gaol. For violating the Conventicle Act by attending a London meeting

in July, Crook was incarcerated in Newgate; he provided an account of the act's enforcement in London and Southwark in *A True Information to the Nation* (1664). On 1 October Crook completed *Truths Tryumph*, defending Friends against an attack by the congregationalist Francis Holcroft. By July 1665 Crook was in Reading gaol, where he wrote *Some Reasons* in defence of the Quakers' refusal to attend the Church of England or swear. As he explained in *Compassion to All the Sorrowful* (1665), he found comfort in believing that God was about to raise up his children. As Crook attempted to sustain the Quakers' resolve amid persecution, he remained sensitive to the threat of internal divisions, a subject he addressed in *Truth's Progress* (1667). The same year he propounded *Twenty Cases of Conscience* to the bishops, querying their grounds for insisting that Quakers violate their consciences by conforming. When the congregationalist William Haworth boasted about a Quaker's defection in *The Quaker Converted to Christianity* (1674), Crook and William Bayly responded in *Rebellion Rebuked* (1673 [1674]). Crook also joined Bayly in composing *The Counterfeit Discovered* (1674?). After Bayly died, Crook wrote a testimony for *A Collection* (1676), an edition of his works.

As the Quaker movement matured, its senior members had to explain anew the reasons for its distinctive way of life. Crook and Thomas Green contributed to this effort in *An Epistle to All that's Young* (1673). Crook revisited this theme in *An Epistle to Young People* (1686). In a related work, *An Epistle to All that Profess the Light* (1678), he warned children and servants not to embrace Quakerism simply because their parents and masters were Friends. Green was Crook's companion on a visit to Quakers in the Netherlands during the early 1670s; the two men jointly addressed two works to the Dutch.

By 1678 Crook had settled in Luton, where Fox visited him in April. He and Fox spoke at meetings in Middlesex during the summer of 1686 and at Waltham Abbey, Essex, in July 1687. Crook was still at Luton in 1686, but some time thereafter he apparently went to live with his daughter, Mary Fairman, in Hertford. His last works were composed at Hertford: *The Way to a Lasting Peace* (1697), calling on people to follow the peace of Ryswick with an internal war against the corruption that causes external conflicts, and *An Epistle to Friends, for Union* (1698). After his death at Hertford on 26 April 1699, aged eighty-two, he was buried at Sewel, Bedfordshire. His autobiography, *A Short History of the Life of John Crook*, was published in 1706, five years after an edition of his works, *The Design of Christianity*. A prolific author, Crook was also a loquacious speaker; for talking three hours beyond his 'leading', the Hertford meeting reprimanded him, prompting his silence in meetings for several years. His contemporary, Gerard Croese, remarked that Crook was 'famous for all manner of Learning, an eloquent, neat and accurate Man' (Croese, 1.61).

RICHARD L. GREAVES

Sources *The journal of George Fox*, ed. N. Penney, 2 vols. (1911) • *CSP dom.*, 1654, p. 334; 1661–2, p. 519 • 'Dictionary of Quaker biography', RS Friends, Lond. [card index] • J. Smith, ed., *A descriptive catalogue of Friends' books*, 2 vols. (1867); suppl. (1893) • I. Penington, *To all such* as complain that they want power (1661), 12–13 · The short journal and itinerary journals of George Fox, ed. N. Penney (1925) · W. C. Braithwaite, The beginnings of Quakerism, ed. H. J. Cadbury, 2nd edn (1955) · W. C. Braithwaite, The second period of Quakerism, ed. H. J. Cadbury, 2nd edn (1961) · G. Croese, The general history of the Quakers (1696) · H. G. Tibbutt, 'John Crook, 1617–1699, a Bedfordshire Quaker', Bedfordshire Historical Record Society, 25 (1947), 110–28 · H. L. Ingle, First among Friends: George Fox and the creation of Quakerism (1994) · W. Penn, Judas and the Jews combined against Christ and his followers (1673), 71–2 · Original letters and papers of state addressed to Oliver Cromwell ... found among the political collections of Mr John Milton, ed. J. Nickolls (1743) · H. Barbour, 'Crook, John', Greaves & Zaller, BDBR · J. Crook, A short history of the life of John Crook (1706)

Archives RS Friends, Lond., Swarthmore MSS

Crooke, Andrew (c.1605–1674), bookseller, was the son of William Crooke (d. in or before 1634), a husbandman of Kingston Blount in the Oxfordshire parish of Aston Rowant. He was apprenticed on 4 February 1622 to the London bookseller Roger Potts, himself the son of the clerk of Aston Rowant parish. Crooke was made free of the Stationers' Company on 26 March 1629 and was trading at 'the sign of Green Dragon' by the following February; he would continue to operate under this sign for the rest of his life, first in St Paul's Churchyard and later, after the fire of London, 'without Temple Bar', by Devereux Court, in the Strand near Fleet Street. On 17 May 1630, in St Benet Paul's Wharf, London, Crooke married Susan Rancle, who was buried in St Faith's Church on 17 April 1646. At some point between 1649 and 1656 he married Elizabeth Needham (d. 1681), the widow of the London stationer Lawrence Needham.

Crooke rose in the hierarchy of the Stationers' Company. He took the livery on 5 March 1638, and on 26 March 1653 he was elected to the company's governing body. He served as under-warden for 1660–61, as upper warden in 1663–4, and for two successive terms as master (1665–7). He also served on the city's common council as a representative of the ward of Farringdon Within for 1656–7, 1659–63, and 1667. As a bookseller, he chiefly sold plays, including ones by Jonson, and Beaumont and Fletcher. He published the first authorized edition of Sir Thomas Browne's Religio medici. In 1662 he is recorded as making a payment to the philosopher John Locke via an Oxford bookseller. Over his career, Crooke took a number of apprentices, the most notable being **William Crooke** (bap. 1639, d. 1694), who was not Andrew's son as is sometimes said, but was almost certainly his nephew. William had been baptized in Aston Rowant on 22 December 1639, the son of William Crooke, a yeoman. He was apprenticed to Andrew on 24 January 1656 and was freed on 2 November 1663. On 29 or 30 June of the latter year, William married Andrew's nineteen-year-old stepdaughter, Rebecca Needham (b. 1644), at St Benet Paul's Wharf. William set up independently in 1664 at the Three Bibles, Fleet Bridge; after the fire he rejoined his former master, now at Temple Bar, and traded there until his own death. A printed catalogue of Crooke's stock in 1675 included books of plays and poems, travel, gardening, physic, and law.

From 1637 until 1679 virtually all Thomas Hobbes's authorized publications in England were issued by either Andrew or William. Chief of these was Leviathan, whose bibliographical history is complex. Andrew entered it into the Stationers' register on 20 January 1651. Three imprints bear his name and the year 1651; today, these three are distinguished as the 'head', the 'bear', and the 'ornaments' editions. The last two are reprints of the first edition, although they contain textual variants; it is probable that they were printed later but falsely dated. One clue in this is that the spelling in these two is more modern. Republication of Leviathan had been forbidden since the mid-1660s, and on 3 September 1668 Samuel Pepys reported that the book was selling at three or four times its original price of 8s. The 'bear' edition may have been printed in the Netherlands, and it and the 'ornaments' edition may date from the 1670s. Certainly, Andrew attempted a clandestine reprinting of the work in 1670 through his regular printer, John Redmayne, at whose printing house sheets were seized by the authorities on 6 October. The Stationers' Company records show a further 'damasking' (defacing) of the printed sheets of Leviathan on 24 October 1674. When, on 22 February 1675, William assigned the rights of a number of books that had previously been entered by Andrew to John Wright, the company's court of assistants ordered that Leviathan was not to be entered in the company's register.

Hobbes's correspondence reveals much about Andrew Crooke, who evidently acted as the philosopher's man of business. Letters were addressed to Hobbes care of Andrew Crooke's shop from 1654 to 1671 (although sometimes by mistake to the bookshop of Andrew's brother John). In 1656 François du Verdus wrote to Crooke in Latin from Bordeaux to disconfirm a rumour that Hobbes was dead. In 1657 Hobbes got Crooke to send books to Samuel Fermat, the mathematician's son, at Paris. In the same year, François Peleau wrote that Crooke had sent him a letter in Latin: 'your bookseller is a learned man, but I think you make him partake of your own learning', probably meaning that Hobbes had dictated a letter that had gone over Crooke's name (Correspondence of Thomas Hobbes, 1.439). In 1659 Crooke sent copies of Leviathan and De homine to Charles du Bosc at the French court. In 1661 John Aubrey relied on Crooke to tell him when Hobbes would be in Derbyshire, and in 1667–9 Pieter Blaeu, printer at Amsterdam, quarrelled with Crooke over earnings from Hobbes's books.

Andrew Crooke died intestate on 20 September 1674 and was buried in St Peter and St Paul Church in Aston Rowant on 29 September; a memorial tablet, erroneously giving his year of death as 1675, survives in the church floor. He left three daughters, and the administration of his estate was granted to his widow, Elizabeth, on 5 October 1674. An inventory of December 1674 gave the total value of his estate as £2071 5s. 8d., with debts of nearly £5000 owing to him. The Stationers' Company appointed a committee to examine his accounts and decided in May that Elizabeth owed the company £110. When she died in 1681, her estate was divided between three daughters from her previous marriage and one daughter surviving from her marriage to Andrew. Besides William, two of her sons-in-law also belonged to the book trade: Cassandra Needham had married the typefounder Thomas Grover, and Mary Crooke had married the typefounder Robert Andrews.

From 1673 William took over Andrew's role in helping Hobbes. In the following year he wrote to Anthony Wood about errors in the printing of an item by Hobbes; but the letter sounds very like Hobbes himself, and it is suspected that Hobbes dictated it to Crooke in the bookshop. In 1679 Hobbes wrote to Aubrey via Crooke, 'at whose shop I suppose you sometimes look in as you pass the street' (*Correspondence of Thomas Hobbes*, 2.770). Four letters by Hobbes to Crooke from Chatsworth survive from 1679, one of them forbidding publication of *Behemoth*, of which a pirated edition had just appeared. Before that, however, Crooke had allowed people to read Hobbes's manuscripts in his shop and sold manuscript copies of them. In February 1673 Aubrey wrote to Locke about Hobbes's *Dialogue of the Common Laws*, saying,

> I never expect to see it printed, and intended to have a copy, which the bookseller will let me have for 50s ... When you go by the Palsgrave-head Tavern be pleased to call on Mr W. Crooke at the Green Dragon and remember me to him ... and he will show it to you. (*Correspondence of John Locke*, 1.375)

Similarly, in 1678 the deist Charles Blount saw a manuscript copy of Hobbes's *Historical Narration Concerning Heresy* by 'Mr Crooke's favour' (*Correspondence of Thomas Hobbes*, 2.759). As soon as Hobbes died in 1679 Crooke sought out his literary remains, and was sent Hobbes's prose autobiography. He consulted Charles Hatton about the worth of publishing it, and was reassured that it would have a market. In 1681–2 he issued two volumes of Hobbes's tracts, including *Behemoth*; these contain prefaces by Crooke. When Aubrey was constructing his life of Hobbes, he had trouble sorting out Hobbes's bibliography: 'Dr Blackburn, W. Crooke, and I will lay our heads together to set these things right' (*Brief Lives*, 1.360). William Crooke died intestate in 1694. His second wife, **Elizabeth Crooke** (*d.* in or after 1696), who may have been the Elizabeth Miskin who married a William Crooke in St James's, Duke's Place, on 31 May 1680, carried on his bookselling business for two years before selling up in 1696.

Two of Andrew's brothers were also apprenticed to members of the Stationers' Company. The younger of the two, Edmond, was baptized on 4 August 1616 at Aston Rowant and was bound on 3 March 1634 but never freed. However, he was active as a bookseller in Dublin, where he died in 1638. The elder, **John Crooke** (*bap.* 1613, *d.* 1669), was baptized in the same parish as Edmond on 5 September 1613. He was apprenticed on 26 March 1628 and freed on 6 April 1635. About 1637 he set up a bookselling partnership with his brother Edmond, Thomas Allot, and Richard Sergier in Dublin; he was also operating a bookshop in St Paul's Churchyard from 1638 onwards. He appears to have been in Dublin between 1642 and 1647 but, once back in London, he continued to issue Irish books throughout the 1650s. In 1652 he married Mary

Tooke (*fl.* 1652–1685), the sister of the bookseller Benjamin Tooke. In July 1660 he petitioned for and was granted the office of printer-general in Ireland; however, he does not seem to have returned permanently to Dublin. He died intestate in Duck Lane, London, on 20 March 1669; the administration of his English estate was granted to Mary a month later, while in Dublin administration was granted to his primary creditor. Although John was formally succeeded as king's printer by his brother-in-law Benjamin Tooke, Mary took over the business until 1684, in partnership with her sons John (*c.*1657–1683), who shared the patent with Tooke from 1679 to 1683, and Andrew (*c.*1659–1732). Andrew took over the business, and formally held the patent for king's printer in Ireland from 1689 to 1731.   MARK GOLDIE

Sources *The correspondence of Thomas Hobbes*, ed. N. Malcolm, 2 vols. (1994) · M. Pollard, *A dictionary of members of the Dublin book trade 1550–1800* (2000) · M. Pollard, 'Control of the press in Ireland through the king's printer patent, 1600–1800', *Irish Booklore*, 4 (1980), 79–95 · R. Tuck, introduction, in T. Hobbes, *Leviathan* (1991) · *Brief lives, chiefly of contemporaries, set down by John Aubrey, between the years 1669 and 1696*, ed. A. Clark, 2 vols. (1898) · H. Macdonald and M. Hargreaves, *Thomas Hobbes: a bibliography* (1952) · J. S. T. Hetet, 'A literary underground in Restoration England: printers and dissenters in the context of constraints, 1660–1689', PhD diss., U. Cam., 1987 · *The correspondence of John Locke*, ed. E. S. De Beer, 2 (1976) · *A catalogue of books newly printed for William Crook* (1675) · J. W. Phillips, *Printing and books in Dublin, 1670–1800* (1998) · A. H. Stevenson, 'Shirley's publishers: the partnership of Crooke and Cooke', *The Library*, 4th ser., 25 (1944–5), 140–61 · H. R. Plomer and others, *A dictionary of the booksellers and printers who were at work in England, Scotland, and Ireland from 1641 to 1667* (1907) · H. R. Plomer and others, *A dictionary of the printers and booksellers who were at work in England, Scotland, and Ireland from 1668 to 1725* (1922) · private information (2004) [M. Treadwell, Trent University, Canada; R. Baxendale] · parish register, Aston Rowant, Oxon. RO [burial] · parish register, Aston Rowant, Oxon. RO [baptisms: William Crooke, John Crooke] · IGI · D. F. McKenzie, ed., *Stationers' Company apprentices*, 3 vols. (1961–78), vols. 1–2 · R. C. F. Besch, *The church of St Peter and St Paul Aston Rowant, Oxon* (1978)

Wealth at death £2071 5s. 8d.: inventory, 1674, court of orphans, common serjeants book 2, fols. 367b, 403b, box 14

Crooke, Elizabeth (*d.* in or after **1696**). *See under* Crooke, Andrew (*c.*1605–1674).

Crooke, Helkiah (1576–1648), physician and anatomist, born in Suffolk, was the third son of Thomas *Crooke (*c.*1545–1598), puritan rector of Great Waldingfield, Suffolk, and preacher to Gray's Inn, London, after 1582. Crooke matriculated as a sizar at St John's College, Cambridge, on 7 October 1591. In the following November he was admitted scholar on a foundation established by Sir Henry Billingley. Despite his father's fame as a preacher there was little money to pass on to a large family. While his older brother, Samuel *Crooke (1575–1649), received all his father's divinity books in Thomas Crooke's will of 1595, Helkiah was left 'all my humanitie books'. Crooke was passionate about classical literature. His tutor at St John's was the notable Greek scholar John Bois. Crooke graduated BA in 1596 and registered as a medical student at the University of Leiden on 6 November 1596. A pupil of the anatomy professor, Pieter Paaw, Crooke defended thirteen theses 'De corpore humano' on 16 April 1597 (a manuscript copy of the theses was deposited in the library of the Royal Society of Medicine). The theses were dedicated to Crooke's father and to other relations of Crooke, the puritan preacher Stephen Egerton and Robert Dexter. Egerton and Dexter were engaged in editing the complete works of the puritan saint Richard Greenham, and to this end recruited the young Helkiah Crooke who, in 1598, brought out *Paramthion: Two Treatises of the Comforting of an Afflicted Conscience*, 'written by M. Richard Greenham'. Crooke's identity was not revealed until the work was reprinted by Egerton and Dexter, but it clearly foreshadowed Crooke's interest in the problems of mental illness. As editor, in both an introduction and some verses, Crooke showed a genuine compassion for the afflicted.

Crooke did not graduate MD at Leiden, but by 1599 had returned to Cambridge, where he graduated MB. The Cambridge grace book indicates that he studied medicine for seven years. This study began under Bois, who had himself once considered a medical career. Crooke took his MD at Cambridge in 1604. A period of country practice may have followed, probably in Suffolk, but by 1610 Crooke was in London applying for candidacy in the College of Physicians, which ultimately rejected him in 1611. Contentiousness and personal disputes shadowed Crooke's entire medical career. With a scant majority of votes he was finally elected a candidate on 7 May 1613. Anatomy remained a powerful interest and he may have given occasional lectures at the Barber–Surgeons' Hall on his favourite subject. He burst into public awareness in 1615 with the publication of *Microcosmographia: a Description of the Body of Man*. It was the first English language anatomy written by a physician, rather than a surgeon, and outraged many of his colleagues at the College of Physicians with its plates depicting the parts of the body involved in generation. The efforts of the bishop of London, the president of the college, Sir William Paddy, and other fellows, to have the book suppressed were unsuccessful. Crooke had a stronger ally in James I, and in his printed epistle to the king Crooke attacked physicians for their lack of reverence for the body in their own lectures to the barber–surgeons. Crooke never claimed originality, only the desire to make the best anatomical knowledge of the day available for the use of the surgeons. The book was enormously successful and was reprinted (along with an epitome by the Scottish surgeon Alexander Reid) in 1616 and 1618. Whatever its shortcomings, the *Microcosmographia*'s place in history remains secure as 'the largest and fullest anatomical work produced in England up to its day and for a considerable time to follow' (O'Malley, 11).

Buoyed by his fame and the continuing support of James I, Crooke was able, in 1619, to secure, through his own election by the Bridewell governors, the ouster of Thomas Jenner, the sitting keeper of the Bethlem Hospital. Attacking Jenner's lack of medical skill and compassion for his patients, Crooke secured the keepership for himself and brought in reforms: the separation of the hospital from Bridewell Hospital, and the introduction of the hospital's surgeons. But Crooke and the governors of the hospital were at odds from the first: Crooke insisted that the governors had given him insufficient funds to run the hospital; the governors suggested that Crooke had lined his own pockets with fees and contributions that should have gone to patient care. A royal commission, appointed by Charles I, ultimately secured Crooke's removal in 1634, but he was fighting for his reinstatement as late as 1642. The greedy mad-doctor, Alibius, in Thomas Middleton's play *The Changeling*, first performed in 1622, may have been modelled on the public and stormy tenure of Crooke at Bethlem.

Still unpopular with the College of Physicians, Crooke was not elected a fellow until 21 April 1620, and even then with a number of dissenting votes. Once in the college, Crooke was an active fellow and was chosen as censor for five consecutive years from 1627 to 1631. He was prevailed on to give the extraordinary lectures in morbid anatomy, which he did on 11, 12, and 14 December 1629. Although he never incorporated William Harvey's discovery of the circulation of the blood into his published work, he also never criticized Harvey, with whom he worked closely on a number of college occasions. Quite the contrary, his comments on Harvey the man in the 1631 edition of *Microcosmographia* constitute one of the earliest appreciations of Harvey in print and occur in his dedication to Charles I: 'The anatomical part [of medicine] has indeed been elucidated by me in this very work, but more deeply cultivated and enriched by your Harvey, a man alike most gifted and observant' (Keynes, 74). Crooke was also the author of the short tract on surgical instruments, largely based on the works of Ambroise Paré, appended to this edition.

Crooke's movements in London can be followed from the prefaces to his anatomy which place him in St Anne's Lane in 1615—no doubt attending the sermons of his brother-in-law, Stephen Egerton, the puritan lecturer at St Ann Blackfriars—and in Coleman Street in 1631, where he lived in the most radical puritan parish in the City, St Stephen, Coleman Street, from 1630 to 1634. A rare reference to Crooke as a father occurred in the will of his sister, Sara Egerton, a Blackfriars resident, with the brief mention of 'my niece Alice Crooke daughter to my brother Dr Crooke'. Crooke's own likeness is thought to be that of the anatomy lecturer in Martin Droeshout's elaborate title page to the *Microcosmographia* of 1631.

At the height of his fame in this year, Crooke's fall was no less sudden. The expensive new edition of his anatomy, to which he may have contributed his own funds, was a relative failure next to the popularity of the 1615 edition, which had been reprinted in 1616 and 1618. The legal proceedings at Bethlem Hospital, begun in 1632, were long and costly. Crooke maintained that his keepership had cost him £1000, and by his removal in 1634 he seems to have become a weary and broken man, driven to selling his fellowship back to the College of Physicians for £5. Crooke resigned his place on 25 May 1635 and disappeared into obscurity beyond the City of London's walls, with only one further notice of him, that for his burial in the parish of St James's, Clerkenwell, on 18 March 1648. A brilliant and compassionate physician, Crooke's virtues, progressiveness, and accomplishments were obscured by an almost pathological inability to get along with other people or to manage his money; which in turn raises the possibility that Crooke himself may have suffered from the depression or melancholia he tried so hard to relieve in others, and to which he seemed so genuinely sympathetic.   WILLIAM BIRKEN

Sources C. D. O'Malley, 'Helkiah Crooke, MD, FRCP, 1576–1648', *Bulletin of the History of Medicine*, 42 (1968), 1–18 • E. G. O'Donoghue, *The story of Bethlehem Hospital* (1914) • P. Allderidge, 'Management and mismanagement at Bedlam, 1547–1633', *Health, medicine and mortality in the sixteenth century*, ed. C. Webster (1979), 141–64 • R. Hunter and I. Macalpine, *Three hundred years of psychiatry, 1535–1860* (1963) • G. Keynes, *The life of William Harvey* (1966) • Vicar-General's book of the consistory court of the bishop of London, LMA, DL/C/337, fol. 77 • G. Clark and A. M. Cooke, *A history of the Royal College of Physicians of London*, 3 vols. (1964–72) • Munk, *Roll* • Venn, *Alum. Cant.* • R. W. Innes Smith, *English-speaking students of medicine at the University of Leyden* (1932) • F. B. Williams, *Index of dedications and commendatory verses in English books before 1641* (1962) • W. Haller, *The rise of puritanism: … the New Jerusalem as set forth in pulpit and press from Thomas Cartwright to John Lilburne and John Milton, 1570–1643* (1938) • J. Andrews and others, *The history of Bethlem* (1997) • London consistory court wills, LMA, 185 Sperin [Thomas Crooke] • *DNB*

Crooke, John (*bap.* 1613, *d.* 1669). *See under* Crooke, Andrew (*c.*1605–1674).

Crooke, Samuel (1575–1649), Church of England clergyman and author, was born at Great Waldingfield, Suffolk, on 17 January 1575, the son of Thomas *Crooke (*c.*1545–1598), clergyman, and older brother of Helkiah *Crooke (1576–1648). Educated first at Merchant Taylors' School, London, he was then admitted as a scholar to Pembroke College, Cambridge, from where he graduated BA in 1593. After his election as a fellow of Pembroke was blocked by the master, Lancelot Andrewes, about 1596 he was elected a foundation fellow of Emmanuel College, from where he proceeded MA in 1596; he also appears in college papers as BD. Already greatly respected for both his scholarly and his personal qualities he was appointed reader, first in rhetoric and then in philosophy. A disciple of William Perkins he was 'acute in the Greek, and well skilled in the Hebrew and Arabick' (Clarke, 203), read and spoke Italian, French, and Spanish, and studied history, politics, and medicine. A good singer, he 'composed severall hymns of his own' (W. G., 3–4).

In accordance with college statutes, on 24 September 1601 Crooke was ordained; immediately he began preaching in the villages around Cambridge, especially in Coxton, giving twenty-eight sermons in eleven months. After his departure from Cambridge in 1602 he donated works by the church fathers to Pembroke, Emmanuel, and the university library. On 27 September of that year he was presented by Sir Arthur Capel to the rectory of Wrington, Somerset, and soon afterwards married Judith, eldest daughter of M. Walsh, a Suffolk minister who was well regarded among the godly. She proved a supportive wife; they had no children.

Crooke remained at Wrington for the rest of his life, undertaking, like his friend Edward Chetwynd, an innovative and energetic preaching ministry in this area of the west country. He soon found himself before the church courts following a complaint that he had refused to use the sign of the cross in baptism. The case continued for many months, during which Crooke showed himself a robust defendant. Taken to task for speaking before the bishop, John Still, 'more than did become you', he retorted that 'my lord spake more than did become him, for he reviled me, & told me that I lied'. His response to the chancellor of the diocese, Francis James, who had apparently threatened to replace Crooke at Wrington with 'an honester man', was that he was 'honester than any that ever you placed anywhere' (Stieg, 208). In 1606 he was pronounced contumacious, but thereafter the case against him seems to have fizzled out: Still avoided substantial deprivations of clergy during this period; both men seem to have had more important preoccupations.

Crooke's strong pastoral concern is evident both in *The Ministeriall Husbandry and Building* (1615), a sermon preached to 'my reverend Fathers, and Brethren, and fellow-labourers in the worke of the Gospell' at the triennial visitation at Bath on 30 July 1612, and in his first publication, *The Guide unto True Blessednesse* (1613). Dedicated to his patron Capel and emphasizing personal faith and knowledge of the scriptures the latter work sets out the fundamentals of the Christian faith and supplies both prayers for different occasions and an abridgement 'for the private use of Christian families, and help of the weaker sort'. Located squarely within the Jacobean mainstream it gives due place to the covenant of grace with God's elect, while urging that there be no separation from 'churches which are sick of heresy' while signs of life survive; there should be separation from the current church of Rome but not from its well-meaning members (pp. 61–70). Another aid to personal faith was embodied in a sermon delivered to 'an honourable assembly at Bath' on 19 September 1613, published as *The Discovery of the Heart* (1615) with a dedication to Sir John Tonstal, gentleman usher to the queen. It was reissued early the following year, together with *The Ministeriall Husbandry* and *The Waking Sleeper* ('intended to stir my self and others for the coming of the Lord Jesus Christ'), as *Three Sermons*, dedicated to 'my singular good friend' Sir James Lancaster.

At an unknown date, in company with Chetwynd, Crooke became a chaplain to Queen Anne—a fact significantly omitted from W. G.'s and Samuel Clarke's later accounts of Crooke's life. His *Death Subdued* (1619) is 'the only surviving text of a sermon for Anne's court by one of her ordinary chaplains' (McCullough, 173). Dedicated to Robert Sidney, earl of Leicester, 'and to my much honoured friends, the rest that were of the family of our late Gracious Mistresse' it is a conventional work, positive in tone, which emphasizes equality in death because all are mortal.

Over the next twenty years Crooke preached about

three times a week, catechized his congregation, and dispensed hospitality. Evidence that he had horizons beyond north Somerset exists tantalisingly in Venn's assertion that he went to Batavia, and in his biographers' comment that he mourned deeply the death in 1632 of Gustavus Adolphus of Sweden. In the wake of Bishop William Piers's 1633 visitation of the Bath and Wells diocese Crooke's weekday lecture was suppressed because of his refusal to wear a surplice or to read the authorized service before preaching but, according to W. G., at some date 'God set it on going again' (W. G., 36). With the death of his friend Chetwynd in 1639 Crooke and John Harrington of Kelston, as executors, were given the task of superintending the education of their godson, Chetwynd's fourteen-year-old son John *Chetwind.

In the spring of 1642 Crooke was chosen as one of the two Somerset representatives in the Westminster assembly, although when it finally convened he did not sit. Like Harrington he was apparently active in forwarding the parliamentary cause in the early stages of the civil war but, on the shift of power in the county to royalist forces in the summer of 1643 and in the aftermath of the quartering of soldiers in his house, he signed in September 'a submission in which he declared that all resistance to the king was unlawful, that he had always abhorred the defacing of churches and images, and the contemning of the Common Prayer' (Hunt, 208). Crooke was a signatory to *The County of Somerset Divided into Severall Classes* (1648), a scheme for the introduction into Somerset of a presbyterian system, and on 9 August 1648 to *The Attestation of the Ministers*, which petitioned for the speedy implementation of the 'much longed for settlement of church government' and for an end to 'unwarrantable toleration' (Wroughton, 119).

Already 'weake in bodie' when he drew up his will on 26 October 1649, Crooke died on 25 December, leaving his widow, Judith, as his executor and his 'brother' William Gregory, minister of Barkwell, and his friend Thomas Baynard of Blagdon as overseers. 'His funerals were extraordinarily celebrated' (W. G., 41) on 3 January 1650, with a crowded church and many hundreds outside. A testimony given there compared him to the biblical Samuel, and fellow ministers then and later paid tribute not only to his exemplary life but also to its demonstration, at a period when their position was perceived as being under attack, of the indispensability of the godly, publicly maintained preaching pastor. W. G.'s *Anthologia: the Life and Death of Mr Samuel Crook*, dated 20 May 1650 and published in 1651 with licence from John Downham, who described Crooke as 'my intimate acquaintance and dearest friend', was dedicated to the author's godfather William Purefoy, MP and member of the council of state, who had known Crooke at Emmanuel. This portrait of 'a wise Master builder' (W. G., 28) was also accompanied by Latin endorsements and by epitaphs from the ministers C. B., A. P., and W. T. In *The Dead Speaking* (1653) Crooke's neighbour William Thomas, pastor at Ubley, and his godson John Chetwind, by this time pastor at Wells, in reproducing respectively their exhortation at Crooke's funeral

and memorial sermon of 12 August 1652, brought to the reader's attention the need 'to make men sensible of the benefit of a Ministry'. While Thomas referred not just to Crooke's plain, popular, and profitable preaching but also to the lawfulness of tithes Chetwind noted both his role in the conversion of souls to God and 'the Excellency of the Ministeriall employment' (Thomas and Chetwind, 34). In *Ta diapheronta, or, Divine characters* (1658) C. B. and W. G. finally brought to publication a substantial treatise on hypocrisy, the *magnum opus* on which 'that burning and shining Lamp' and 'our Christian Gamaliel' had been working before 'the iniquity of the times ... disabled him from finishing' (W. G., 18–19). VIVIENNE LARMINIE

Sources W. G. [W. Garret], *Anthologia: the life and death of Mr Samuel Crook, late pastor of Wrington in Sommerset-shire* (1651) • S. Clarke, *The lives of thirty two English divines*, in *A general martyrologie*, 3rd edn (1677), 202–14 • W. Thomas and J. Chetwind, *The dead speaking, or, The living names of two deceased ministers of Christ* (1653) • Venn, *Alum. Cant.* • W. Hunt, *The Somerset diocese of Bath and Wells* (1885), 202–16 • M. Stieg, *Laud's laboratory: the diocese of Bath and Wells in the early seventeenth century* (1982) • P. E. McCullough, *Sermons at court: politics and religion in Elizabethan and Jacobean preaching* (1998), 172–3, 178 [incl. CD-ROM] • J. Wroughton, *The civil war in Bath and north Somerset* (1973) • Edward Chetwynd, will, PRO, PROB 11/180, fol. 379 • will, PRO, PROB 11/211, fols. 280v–281v • [W. Prynne], *The county of Somerset divided into severall classes* (1648) • F. W. Weaver, ed., *Somerset incumbents* (privately printed, Bristol, 1889), 304

Crooke, Thomas (c.1545–1598), Church of England clergyman, was born at Cransley, Northamptonshire. After schooling at Stamford School he matriculated sizar at Trinity College, Cambridge, in May 1560. Elected scholar in 1562, he graduated BA early in 1563 and was chosen fellow that year. He commenced MA in 1566 and BD in 1573.

Ordained priest at Norwich on 11 June 1568, Crooke was instituted rector of Great Waldingfield, Suffolk, on 3 April 1571 at the presentation of Edward Colman. To judge from his will he preached strenuously in the surrounding countryside, leaving money to the poor of nearby Assington, Suffolk, and also to those of Elmstead, Fingringhoe, and Wivenhoe, all Essex parishes near Colchester.

Crooke and his wife, Samuel (*sic*), can have married no later than 1568 since their daughter Sara herself married in 1585. Their eldest son, Thomas [see below], was born about 1574. Their second and third sons, Samuel *Crooke and Helkiah *Crooke, were born at Great Waldingfield in 1575 and 1576 respectively.

By now Crooke's nonconformity was known to the authorities. He appears on an undated list of clerics who had not been observing order but now promised 'a conformity requiring respite of time', which was submitted to John Parkhurst, bishop of Norwich (*Letter Book*, 221).

Crooke commenced DTh from Pembroke College, Cambridge, in 1578. He resigned Great Waldingfield to become preacher at Gray's Inn, London, being 'specially admitted' there on 4 January 1582 (Foster, 60). He was also appointed lecturer at St Mary Woolchurch, deriving a comfortable annual salary of £60 or more from both appointments until he gave up the latter in 1591. He was soon associated with London's radical religious leaders, John Field and Thomas Wilcox, and, evidently at about the same time as his future son-in-law, Stephen Egerton, joined their London clerical conference. First convened in 1570, this was by now discussing methods of introducing the presbyterian Book of Discipline into a programme of ecclesiastical reform.

Suspicious as the government always remained about the activities of such prominent radicals, it did not hesitate to harness their energy and learning whenever the protestant cause came under threat. Crooke was one of those nominated at this time by the privy council to take part in debates with apprehended Jesuits and was also one of the twenty-five learned divines who submitted their 'opinion concerning the Jesuits' thereafter (Inner Temple, Petyt MS 538/47, fol. 19r). The latter included not only seven future bishops but also William Fulke, Walter Travers, John Reynolds, and William Charke, all leading evangelicals.

In 1583 Crooke was one of many who urged Thomas Cartwright to publish his confutation of the Rheims New Testament, published in the previous year, yet he does not seem to have been active within the network of clerical conferences and provincial and national 'synods' which it was Field's self-imposed task to co-ordinate. His precise relationship with the militant nonconformity of the 1580s thus remains equivocal. His privileged position at Gray's Inn perhaps saved him from the attentions of John Aylmer, bishop of London, but there is no evidence either that he ever fell foul of John Whitgift, archbishop of Canterbury.

There is, however, no doubt that from the beginning of his career Crooke was a privileged member of the godly élite. A Latin letter to John Foxe, dated at Great Waldingfield on 15 September 1575, survives among Foxe's papers (BL, Harley MS 417, fols. 126v–127r). His daughter Sara married Stephen Egerton at St Ann Blackfriars on 4 May 1585 and he was one of eight London preachers, including Field and Wilcox, who in 1586 received a monetary bequest in the will of Richard Culverwell.

Crooke's own will, drawn up on 8 January 1595, reveals a network of godly friendships. There were bequests of a book to Emmanuel College, Cambridge, to his 'good brother', Laurence Chaderton, the master, and to others who shared Crooke's religious allegiance. His overseers included Sir John Hart, Anthony Culverwell, and his son-in-law, Egerton. The will is an extraordinarily detailed document, occupying four folio pages in a registrar's transcript (London Metropolitan Archives, DL/C/359, fols. 185v–187v). Crooke made it as 'professor of divinity and preacher of the word of God in the house and fellowship of Gray's Inn in London'. A full Calvinist confession of faith was followed by the directive that he should be buried 'without superstition and vanity' in the chancel of St Mary Woolchurch, since it was there that 'some good part of my poor labours for many years hath been bestowed'. He requested a sermon on Hebrews 13: 7, 'Bear in mind those that have had the guiding of you and have declared unto you the word of God'.

The large number of Crooke's family bequests included seven to brothers or sisters and their families and to his 'good mother Mrs Joyner', perhaps his father's second wife. Of his sons, Thomas received £40; Samuel all his divinity books in Greek, Hebrew, Latin, and French; and Helkiah all his 'humanity' books. His fourth and fifth, John and Richard, and his younger daughters, Rachel, Anne, and Elizabeth, received £20 each. All were still minors. His wife was left the residue and was appointed sole executrix. In an attached schedule Crooke carefully noted that the cash legacies added up to £146 1s. 8d.

Crooke survived his will-making by nearly three years and even took up a third London lectureship, at St Peter Westcheap, in 1597. He revised his will in November that year, died in London, and was duly buried in the chancel of St Mary Woolchurch on 5 October 1598.

Despite his learning Crooke appears to have published nothing. He wrote against opinions expressed by Hugh Broughton in the latter's controversial *Concent of Scripture* (1588), but the work is lost.

Sir Thomas Crooke, first baronet (*c*.1574–1630), was admitted to Gray's Inn at his father's petition on 1 March 1597. He migrated to Ireland, establishing a protestant colony at Baltimore, co. Cork, where he was granted substantial estates. He was created a baronet in 1624. The title became extinct at the death of his son, Samuel, in 1666.

BRETT USHER

Sources Venn, *Alum. Cant.*, 1/1.424 • institution to Great Waldingfield, Norfolk RO, REG 13, fol. 168v • J. Foster, *The register of admissions to Gray's Inn, 1521–1889, together with the register of marriages in Gray's Inn chapel, 1695–1754* (privately printed, London, 1889) • P. S. Seaver, *The puritan lectureships: the politics of religious dissent, 1560–1662* (1970) • parish register, St Ann Blackfriars, GL, MS 4509/1 [unfoliated] • GEC, *Baronetage* • *The letter book of John Parkhurst, bishop of Norwich*, ed. R. A. Houlbrooke, Norfolk RS, 43 (1974–5) • G. Keynes, *Dr Timothie Bright, 1550–1615* (1962) • J. Strype, *The life and acts of John Whitgift*, new edn, 3 vols. (1822) • will, LMA, DL/C/359, fols. 185v–187v [registered, CCL] • BL, Harley MS 417, fols. 126v–127r

Archives BL, Harley MSS, corresp. with John Foxe

Wealth at death £146 1s. 8d. in monetary bequests; residue to widow; total estate of £400?: will, LMA, DL/C/359, fols. 185v–187v

Crooke, Sir Thomas, first baronet (*c*.1574–1630). *See under* Crooke, Thomas (*c*.1545–1598).

Crooke, William (bap. 1639, d. 1694). *See under* Crooke, Andrew (*c*.1605–1674).

Crookenden, Isaac (b. 1777), writer, was born on 19 October 1777, the youngest of nine children of Caleb (b. 1730) and Mary Crookenden; his father was perhaps the shipbuilder of Itchenor, Sussex, whose bankruptcy was recorded in 1789 (*GM*, 186). Isaac Crookenden married Elizabeth Pelham Fillary on 25 December 1798 at Arundel; they had one son, Adolphus Pelham (1800–1870). In 1802 Crookenden published *Berthinia, or, The Fair Spaniard*, a chapbook of forty-eight pages which also included a second tale. Nine further titles of a similar type are known; one of them, *The Skeleton* (1805), describes Crookenden as 'Late assistant at Mr Adams' Academy in Chichester'. Frederick Frank identifies Crookenden as 'probably the most notorious counterfeiter of legitimate Gothic novels' (Frank, 59). Thus Crookenden's *The Skeleton* was a 'refabrication' of the anonymous *Animated Skeleton* (1798) and his *Horrible Revenge, or, The Monster of Italy!!* (1808) was 'another shilling shocker based loosely upon [Edward] Montague's *The Demon of Sicily* of 1807' (ibid., 59). Crookenden also derived materials from Ann Radcliffe, Matthew ('Monk') Lewis, and Charlotte Dacre to produce his series of 'gothic novels in miniature' (Neuburg, 165). His only deviation from the Gothic mode is *Venus on Earth* (1808), an 'examination' of the 'passion of love'. He worked for four publishers successively: S. Fisher, A. Neil, J. Lee, and R. Harrild. It is difficult to date the end of his career as the later chapbooks are undated: *The Spectre of the Turret* is conjecturally dated between 1810 and 1820. None of his work was reviewed, but *The Mysterious Murder* (1806) was reprinted in New York in 1827.

PAUL BAINES

Sources F. S. Frank, 'The Gothic romance: 1762–1820', *Horror literature: a core collection and reference guide*, ed. M. B. Tymn (1981), 59 · M. Summers, *A Gothic bibliography* (1940), 32, 319, 371, 437, 504, 507, 512, 576, 606 · V. E. Neuburg, *Popular literature: a history and guide* (1977), 164–5 · G. Kelly, *English fiction of the Romantic period* (1989), 59 · *GM*, 1st ser., 59 (1789), 186 · *IGI* · private information (2004) [family]

Crookes, Sir William (1832–1919), chemist and science journalist, was born on 17 June 1832 at 143 Regent Street, London, the eldest son of the sixteen children of Joseph Crookes (1792–1884), a tailor from Yorkshire, and his second wife, Mary Scott of Aynhoe, Northamptonshire. (There were another five children from Joseph's first marriage.) He regarded himself as a family 'sport', since no other sibling showed the slightest interest in science. He was educated at Prospect House School, Weybridge, and began his scientific career at the age of sixteen when he entered the Royal College of Chemistry in Oxford Street, London, under the directorship of August Wilhelm Hofmann. By then his father, having established a successful gentlemen's outfitters in Regent Street, had moved to Hammersmith, and Crookes commuted to Oxford Street every day from there.

Scientific career, 1849–1873 From 1849 to 1854 Crookes was one of Hofmann's personal assistants, in which capacity he was able to begin an original investigation of new compounds of selenium, the selenocyanides. These formed the subject of his first publications in 1851. Hofmann's connections with the Royal Institution, however, brought Crookes to the notice of Faraday, who, with his friends Charles Wheatstone and George Stokes, turned him away from Hofmann-type organic chemistry towards chemical physics, then exemplified by the optical problems of photography and, later, spectroscopy.

Crookes left the Royal College and became in 1854 superintendent of the meteorological department of the Radcliffe (Astronomical) Observatory in Oxford, where his photographic skills were fully deployed; the following year he was appointed lecturer in chemistry at the Chester Anglican teachers' training college, and on 10 April 1856 he married Ellen, daughter of William Humphrey, of Darlington, with whom he had ten children, though only three sons and a daughter survived into adulthood. Soon afterwards the couple moved back to London, and from then on, apart from extensive European travels, his life

Sir William Crookes (1832–1919), by Albert Ludovici, *c*.1884–5

was spent in the capital and was devoted mainly to independent research, journalism and consultancy. In 1854, with John Spiller, he had devised the first dry collodion process and for some ten years he worked enthusiastically at photography, editing journals on the subject, investigating the spectral sensitivity of the wet collodion process, and attempting to apply photography to the scientific recording of polarization, astronomical objects, and spectra.

Shortage of money as a young man does much to explain the catholicity of Crookes's interests, many of which were clearly motivated by the possibility of commercial rewards. Science and business were integrated activities throughout his life. In the world of commerce he drove many a hard bargain, but although he eventually made a comfortable living from such ventures as the sodium amalgamation method of gold extraction (which he worked in north Wales) and the chemical exploitation of sewage as a fertilizer (which he exploited at Crossness), as well as electric lighting, achieving this financial success was hard. By the early 1880s he was comfortably off, and could afford to entertain on an impressive scale. Apart from running a successful analytical consultancy from a laboratory at his home at 20 Mornington Road (where the Crookes family lived until 1880, when they moved to 7 Kensington Park Gardens, the first house in England to be lit by electricity), the foundation of his financial success came through the launch of the weekly *Chemical News* in 1859, and journalistic ventures with James Samuelson's *Popular Science Review* in 1861 and, three years later, with the *Quarterly Journal of Science*. *Chemical News*, which he edited regularly himself until 1906, was conducted on much less formal lines than other commercial journals; it eventually closed in 1932.

That Crookes took some years to abandon the idea of an academic position is clear from his abortive attempt in 1862 to obtain a chair of chemistry at the Royal Veterinary College in London. Ironically, he would have been in a better position three years later when his efforts to promote carbolic acid (phenol) as a germicide during the great cattle plague (rinderpest) of 1865–6 brought him considerable prominence in government and veterinary circles. His growing family and his increasingly complex instrumental researches in the 1870s were sustained by relentless hard work in journalistic ventures, and his success in obtaining analytical contracts as sanitary and food adulteration legislation provided increasing business. In particular, the water companies, besieged by criticisms of water quality, provided handsome retainers and regular consultancy work.

Crookes's life was one of unbroken scientific and business activity. He worked regularly in his laboratory in the mornings, and after dinner through the evening into the early hours. He was eclectic in his interests, ranging over pure and applied science, economic and practical problems, and psychic research. All of these interests collectively made him a well-known personality within the late Victorian scientific community. He received many public and academic honours. He was knighted in 1897 and in 1910 appointed to the Order of Merit. At various times he was president of the Chemical Society (1887–9), the Institution of Electrical Engineers (1890–94), the Society for Psychical Research (1897), the British Association for the Advancement of Science (1898), and the Society of Chemical Industry (1913). Each of his presidential addresses proved a *tour de force*, gaining him worldwide publicity. He was a Davy and Copley medallist of the Royal Society (1888, 1904), its foreign secretary (1908–13), and its president (1913 to 1915), having been elected FRS in 1863. He was also closely involved in the affairs of the Royal Institution until 1912, when a quarrel with its director, Sir James Dewar, over his son, Henry Crookes, led to his resignation.

The work of Crookes extended over the regions of both chemistry and physics. Its salient characteristic was the originality of conception of his experiments, and the skill of their execution. Frequently aided at the theoretical level by colleagues such as George Stokes, his speculations were equally imaginative and stimulating. He was an able syncretist of other scientists' hints and suggestions, and by weaving these together imaginatively he acquired a well-deserved reputation as a Victorian sage. Nevertheless, he was always more effective at experiment than in interpretation. Spectroscopy, introduced by Bunsen and Kirchhoff in 1859, was received by Crookes with great enthusiasm, and, on applying it to the examination of the seleniferous chimney deposits from a sulphuric acid factory, he discovered an unknown green line in the spectrum. The isolation of the new metallic element, thallium, followed in 1861. Through this work and the controversy with French scientists over C. A. Lamy's claim to

have discovered the element at the same time, his reputation became firmly established. A decade's work produced the atomic weight of thallium which confirmed his reputation for meticulous analytical precision in 1873.

Cathode rays and lanthanides Two lines of research then occupied Crookes's attention for many years. These were the properties of highly rarefied gases, with which he began to occupy himself immediately, and the investigation of the elements of the 'rare earths', upon which he embarked shortly after 1880. His attention had been attracted to the first problem in using a vacuum balance during the course of the thallium researches. Believing, erroneously, that he had uncovered a relationship between gravity and heat, he was led to the phenomenon upon which depended the action of the 'lightmill' or radiometer. In this popular instrument a system of vanes, each blackened on one side and polished on the other, is set in rotation on a pivot in an evacuated space when exposed to radiant energy. This apparent attraction and repulsion resulting from radiation, which Crookes initially attributed to a psychic force, was explained in terms of the kinetic theory of gases by Stokes, Maxwell, and others. His work on this phenomenon led Crookes to investigations of fundamental importance in understanding the nature of matter, for in seeking a mechanism for the rotation, he passed electrical discharges through the rarefied gases. He then quickly discovered, with the aid of his young assistant, Charles Gimingham (d. 1890), that as the attenuation of the gas was made greater the dark space around the cathode (negative electrode) extended, while rays (soon termed cathode rays) proceeded from the anode (positive electrode).

In a series of spectacular and ingenious experiments Crookes showed that these rays travelled in straight lines, cast shadows, caused phosphorescence in objects upon which they impinged, and produced heat by their impact. Following an earlier hint of Michael Faraday's, he believed that he had discovered a fourth attenuated state of matter, which he called radiant matter. It remained for J. J. Thomson in 1897 to demonstrate that the rays were not streams of particles of ordinary molecular magnitude, but subatomic particles of negative charge whose mass was only $\frac{1}{1800}$ that of an atom of hydrogen. However, it was Crookes's success in producing a vacuum of the order of one millionth of an atmosphere that made possible the discovery of X-rays as well as of the electron; his experimental work in this field was the foundation of nuclear physics and of the electronic theory that altered the whole conception of chemistry and physics at the beginning of the twentieth century. 'Crookes's dark space' and the 'Crookes tube' have become part of the vocabulary of modern physics. It was characteristic of Crookes that, though already in his sixties, he readily and enthusiastically accepted the new interpretation of his work.

For many years Crookes conducted laborious experiments on the rare earth elements (lanthanides), elements so similar to one another in chemical properties that special methods for their separation had to be devised. Throughout this exacting work with his assistant, James

H. Gardiner, he employed spectroscopic methods for following the course, and testing the completeness, of the separation of one element from another. What had been one of the most obscure regions in inorganic chemistry gradually became clear. In the course of these years Crookes was increasingly led to speculate on the existence of 'meta-elements', clusters of elements resembling one another so closely that in most ways the cluster behaved like a single individual or element. Further stimulated by Darwin's theory of evolution and N. J. Lockyer's speculations concerning the dissociation of the elements in the sun and stars, Crookes daringly speculated that he had found evidence of the evolution of the elements, which was the theoretical underpinning of Mendeleyev's periodic law and table.

Further experimental work and psychic research Crookes's 'meta-elements' bear a superficial similarity to isotopes, a concept which arose in 1912–13 from the phenomenon of radioactivity—another field into which Crookes threw himself wholeheartedly. In 1900 he achieved the separation from uranium of its active transformation product, uranium-X. He observed the gradual decay of the separated transformation product, and the simultaneous reproduction of a fresh supply in the original uranium. His own explanation, in terms of energy gained from the atmosphere, was soon superseded by that of Rutherford's and Soddy's disintegration theory. Crookes also observed that when alpha particles, ejected from radioactive substances, impinge upon zinc sulphide, each impact is accompanied by a minute scintillation. This observation became the basis of a detection instrument (spinthariscope) that played an invaluable role in early work on radioactivity until the invention of the Geiger counter in 1908.

Crookes published numerous papers on spectroscopy, a subject which always held a great fascination for him, and he made researches on a host of minor subjects. In addition to various technical books and translations, he wrote a standard treatise, *Select Methods in Chemical Analysis* (1871), and a small book, *Diamonds* (1909), a subject to which he had devoted some study during two visits to South Africa in 1896 and 1905. He frequently served the government in an advisory capacity, and his work on the production of an anti-polarising glass for safety spectacles in 1909–14 (the basis of sun-glasses) was one of many contributions to public welfare.

The most controversial aspect of Crookes's career was his investigation of mediums in the 1870s and 1880s. Following the death of a much-loved brother at sea (which also led him into a libel action) Crookes attended seances, becoming interested in the kinetic, audible, and luminous phenomena that could be witnessed in fashionable seances of the period. To the disgust of members of the scientific community such as W. B. Carpenter, J. Tyndall, and T. H. Huxley (but supported by A. R. Wallace), Crookes was persuaded that the mediumship of some practitioners was genuine. In 1870 he subjected D. D. Home to a number of tests, and convinced himself that Home possessed a psychic force that could be used to modify gravity,

produce musical effects, and perform feats unknown to science or conjuring. When the Royal Society rejected his papers on the subject on the grounds that the experimental conditions were insufficiently exacting, Crookes reported them in his own *Quarterly Journal of Science*. Even more sensational was Crookes's support for the pretty young medium Florence Cook, who materialized a phantom called Katie King. Contemporary debate, that has continued to the present day, questions whether Crookes lied under the spell of infatuation. Was he duped; and, if he ever understood this, was he too embarrassed to confess? There can be no doubt of Crookes's sincerity or that he staked his very considerable scientific reputation on the validity of the extraordinary phenomena he described. He genuinely believed that a scientific investigation of psychic phenomena held out the promise of data and theories that were unseen and unknown in contemporary natural philosophy.

Crookes was a great experimentalist. His material discoveries were of lasting and fundamental value. His ventures into psychical research were strongly criticized by contemporaries and certainly led him into some curious company, but they demonstrate that he thought all natural phenomena worthy of investigation, and that he refused to be bound by tradition and convention. Although Lord Kelvin believed Crookes started more hares than any other scientific contemporary, he was a man of science in the broadest sense, an influential personality, and a doyen of his profession.

Crookes died at 7 Kensington Park Gardens, London, on 4 April 1919, less than three years after his wife, to whom he had been devoted, and was buried in Brompton cemetery six days later.

W. H. BROCK

Sources E. E. Fournier d'Albe, *Sir William Crookes* (1923) · W. H. Brock, 'Crookes, William', *DSB* · R. G. Medhurst and K. M. Goldney, 'William Crookes and the physical phenomena of mediumship', *Proceedings of the Society for Psychical Research*, 54 (1963–6), 25–157
Archives Royal Institution of Great Britain, London, laboratory notebooks, papers · RS, letters to Royal Society · Sci. Mus., laboratory books · Sci. Mus., notebooks, letters, and papers | Air Force Research Laboratories, Cambridge, Massachusetts, Strutt MSS · BL, letters to Alfred Russel Wallace, Add. MSS 46437–46442 · CUL, corresp. with Sir George Stokes · ICL, letters to Henry Armstrong; letters to S. P. Thompson · Sci. Mus., letters to C. H. Gimingham, assistant · Sci. Mus., corresp. with Oswald John Silberrad · Society for Psychical Research, London, corresp. with Sir Oliver Lodge · Wellcome L., letters to John Spiller
Likenesses A. Ludovici, oils, c.1884–1885, NPG [*see illus.*] · G. C. Beresford, photograph, 1906, NPG · C. Dessler, bronze bust, 1908, RS · W. Strang, chalk drawing, 1910, Royal Collection · E. A. Walton, oils, 1911, RS · Elliott & Fry, photogravure photograph, NPG · Spy [L. Ward], caricature, chromolithograph, NPG; repro. in *VF* (21 May 1903) · W. Stoneman, photograph, NPG · five photographs, RS · photographs, priv. coll.; repro. in Fournier d'Albe, *Sir William Crookes*
Wealth at death £29,013 18s. 4d.: probate, 11 July 1919, CGPLA Eng. & Wales

Crooks, William [Will] (1852–1921), politician, was born on 6 April 1852 at 2 Shirbutt Street, a one-roomed house near the docks at Poplar in the East End of London. He was the third of seven children of Caroline, *née* Coates (b.

William Crooks (1852–1921), by Sir Benjamin Stone, 1905

*c.*1821), and George Crooks (*b. c.*1821). The family experienced extreme poverty after George, a ship's stoker, lost his right arm in an accident and was reduced to occasional casual work. At one time they were forced into Poplar workhouse. Will Crooks recalled that his mother took in additional sewing to maintain the family, but could not afford the fare to deliver it. The bitter experience of poor-law schooling and separation from his parents never left him. Crooks was baptized a Congregationalist and briefly attended George Green elementary school, Crisp Street. From the age of seven he worked at labouring jobs until his mother insisted on his apprenticeship to a cooper. In 1871 Crooks married Matilda South (1854–1892), a shipwright's daughter. They endured difficult times; of their ten children only six survived. He tramped twice to Liverpool to find work as employers in Poplar victimized him as a political agitator.

By the 1890s, with his broad-shouldered figure, long sinewy arms, and full-bearded face, Crooks was a familiar and beloved personality in his locality. He spoke every Sunday morning outside the East India Dock gates. These well-attended democratic gatherings, known as 'Crooks College', inaugurated various campaigns for a free library, tunnels under the Thames, and poor-law reform. He was an unsung hero during the London Dock strike, while continuing to work his own trade, but the strain of his dual endeavours led to illness, and he afterwards spent three months in the London Hospital close to death.

In 1892 Matilda died, aged thirty-eight. The following year Crooks married a widow, Elisabeth Coulter, *née* Lake (1854–1932), and their home (28 Northumberland Street and later 81 Gough Street) became a haven of local politics. His remarkable appeal as a people's politician was exemplified by his matchless skill in public speaking: his power to sway audiences combined the inspiration of the evangelist and the everyday humour of the cockney comedian. Although he was against drink and gambling, he once jested memorably to a priest that all ordinary folk wanted to hear about in sermons was 'beer, work and football' (Jones, 105). He was no intellectual, but was an omnivorous reader of Dickens, Scott, and Bunyan. Instead of visiting the pub, he purchased Homer's *Iliad* for 2*d.* at a bookstall. He wrote several tracts on politics and religion, as well as one on cask making (1896).

Before the First World War, Will Crooks and George Lansbury were leading pioneers of the labour and socialist movement in Poplar. Crooks joined the Fabian Society in 1891, but his main backing for his election to the London county council (1892) and the Poplar board of guardians (1893) came from the Poplar labour electoral committee, formed by representatives from the new unions and progressive clergy. Later named the Poplar Labour League, this body established a voluntary Crooks wages fund, which gave him financial independence as a working-class politician. A Poplar councillor from 1900, he became mayor in 1901, the first Labour mayor in London. On the London county council up to 1910, he formed a Labour bench, which included Will Steadman and John Burns, and co-operated with middle-class Progressives. His causes included fair wages, open spaces, technical education, and the construction of the Blackwall Tunnel.

As Poplar guardians, despite being in a minority and sometimes at odds over policy, Lansbury and Crooks (who was chairman from 1897 to 1906) dominated the proceedings. Their radical measures, which used the poor law to reform the workhouse system and defend working-class living standards, marked the beginnings of 'Poplarism' in the deprived East End. The resultant conflict with the municipal alliance of local ratepayers led to an official inquiry by the Local Government Board in 1906. In 1903, as the Labour Representation Committee candidate, Crooks won a sensational by-election at Woolwich, a tory constituency. Though he had enjoyed official Liberal support, his victory demonstrated the electoral potential of the newly founded Labour Party. Crooks was a hard-working constituency MP, interested in poor-law schooling, old-age pensions, and Woolwich arsenal issues. In 1905 Will and Elisabeth Crooks organized a march of 6000 working women to Westminster to lobby for unemployment assistance. He retained his seat in 1906 but lost it in January 1910, having arrived home on the eve of poll from New Zealand after a five-month recuperative world tour. Though victorious in December 1910, Crooks was now a controversial Labour politician, criticized by socialists for his continued links with Liberalism. In 1911 the Trades

Union Congress roundly censured Crooks for not consulting the movement about his support for the Labour Disputes Bill to curtail strikes.

Although he had been a vigorous opponent of the Second South African War, the patriotic Crooks greeted British entry into the First World War by leading the singing of the national anthem in the House of Commons. A vice-president of the British Workers' National League, he toured extensively for recruitment and visited front-line troops. In 1916 George V made Crooks a privy councillor and visited him in hospital. He was re-elected unopposed in 1918, but extreme ill health ended Crooks's parliamentary career in February 1921, when he resigned his seat. He had never recovered from the horror of the bombing of a Poplar school in June 1917, when eighteen pupils perished. He died in Poplar Hospital on 5 June 1921 and was buried four days later in Tower Hamlets cemetery, after an impressive funeral service at All Saints' Church.

Popular with different social classes, Will Crooks was more typical of the early Lib–Lab MPs in Labour history than his independent socialist contemporaries. No revolutionary theorist, he upheld the monarchy and empire. With a deep religious faith, he extolled the Victorian values of self-improvement and gradual reform. Above all, as an indefatigable and respected pioneer of working-class representation, he remained quintessentially an East End politician moulded by his practical experience of working life. In 1995 his neglected grave, with the original epitaph to the Labour servant of Poplar and Woolwich, was restored with a council grant of £540.

JOHN SHEPHERD

Sources newspaper cuttings, correspondence, obituaries, cartoons, etc., Bancroft Road Library, Tower Hamlets, London, Local History Collection · P. R. Thompson, *Socialists, liberals and labour: the struggle for London, 1885–1914* (1967) · D. E. Martin, 'Crooks, William', *DLB*, vol. 2 · G. Haw, *From workhouse to Westminster: the life story of Will Crooks, MP* (1908) · P. A. Ryan, '"Poplarism" 1894–1930', *The origins of British social policy*, ed. P. Thane (1978), 56–83 · P. A. Ryan, 'Politics and relief: east London unions in the late nineteenth and early twentieth centuries', *The poor and the city: the English poor law in its urban context*, ed. M. E. Rose (1985), 134–72 · W. Crooks, *Working men and gambling*, 1 (1906) · W. Crooks and others, *Social ideals* (c.1909) · J. O. Stubbs, 'Lord Milner and patriotic labour, 1914–18', *EngHR*, 87 (1972), 717–54 · J. R. Clynes, *Memoirs*, 1 [1937] · J. Jones, *My lively life* (1928) · *DNB* · P. Tyler, 'Will Crooks, local activist and Labour pioneer: Poplar to Woolwich, 1852–1921', PhD diss., London Metropolitan University, 2002 **Archives** Bancroft Road Library, Tower Hamlets, London, miscellany · BLPES, Fabian Society archives, letters to Fabian Society · BLPES, corresp. with the Independent Labour Party · Greenwich Local History Library, London, Woolwich Labour Party records · JRL, Labour History Archive and Study Centre, papers · People's History Museum, Manchester, Labour Party corresp. files · priv. coll. | BL, Burns MSS · BLPES, Beveridge MSS · LUL, Senate House Library, Broth collection **Likenesses** B. Stone, photograph, 1905, NPG [*see illus.*] · W. Stoneman, photograph, 1918, NPG · H. Furniss, pen-and-ink sketch, NPG · Spy [L. Ward], chromolithograph caricature, NPG; repro. in *VF* (6 April 1905) · photographs, Bancroft Road Library, Tower Hamlets, London, Local History Collection **Wealth at death** £1863 8s. 10d.: probate, 11 Aug 1921, *CGPLA Eng. & Wales*

Crookshank, Harry Frederick Comfort, first Viscount Crookshank (1893–1961), politician, was born in Midan Bab-al-Louk, Cairo, Egypt, on 27 May 1893, the only son and first child of Harry Maule Crookshank (1850–1914), a physician and surgeon, and director-general of the Egyptian prisons administration, who was created pasha in 1890, and his wife, Emma Walraven (d. 1954), daughter of the American businessman Samuel Comfort. In 1897 Crookshank Pasha was made controller of the Daira Sanieh administration; he retired in 1907. After his father's death in March 1914 Harry, his mother, and his sister, Betty, continued as one household, from 1937 at 51 Pont Street, London.

After two years at Summer Fields School, Oxford, Crookshank went to Eton College in 1906. At Eton, where he was a king's scholar, Crookshank excelled in most areas with the exception of games. In 1912 he went up to Magdalen College, Oxford. Owing to a weakness in Greek he narrowly missed a first in honour moderations in 1914. Following in the footsteps of his father he became a passionate freemason, joining the Apollo Lodge as soon as he arrived in Oxford.

In summer 1914 Crookshank was studying in Germany, and narrowly escaped internment. On repatriation he volunteered for the Hampshire regiment but soon transferred to the Grenadier Guards. In August 1915, while serving with the 2nd battalion, he was buried alive by the explosion of a mine in an orchard near Givenchy. In October 1915, as he prepared to go out on a wiring party, he was shot in the left leg by a German sniper. He rejoined his unit in August 1916. He commanded the battalion's Lewis guns at the attack on Lesbœufs on 15 September 1916, when he was seriously wounded by a shell explosion. He returned to active duty between September 1917 and June 1918 at Salonika as aide-de-camp to General Charles Corkran, head of the British military liaison mission to the Serbian army.

In February 1919 Crookshank sat the Foreign Office examination, passing with ease. In October 1920 he was offered a permanent commission in the grenadiers. Despite his own desire to return to the army the Foreign Office refused to release him. In 1921 he was posted to the high commission in Constantinople. In September 1922 he was co-author of a pro-Turkish memorandum that was considered by the cabinet. In the following month he refused to entertain the visiting Ramsay MacDonald. The Chanak crisis convinced Crookshank that important decisions were made by politicians rather than by diplomats. In September 1924 he was adopted as candidate for Gainsborough, Lincolnshire; he won the seat in the general election held in the following month, and retained it until 1956.

Crookshank soon established himself as a Commons 'character'. He was thought closely to resemble William Shakespeare, was a natty dresser, and was drawn to quixotic affairs. His first parliamentary set piece was an attempt to wreck a government bill relieving MPs from seeking re-election when they became ministers. He was also associated with the parliamentary revolt in 1927 against the revised Book of Common Prayer. In the early 1930s he served as Sir Austen Chamberlain's representative to the League of Nations Union. He was parliamentary under-secretary at the Home Office from July 1934 until June 1935, when he was appointed minister of mines. 'Promotion of course,' he recorded, 'but just about the least pleasant department and one in which I start with no interest at all' (Bodl. Oxf., Crookshank papers). Nevertheless, in December 1935 he persuaded the miners and mineowners to agree on a pay deal. His 'whole-hogging' Coal Bill, which aimed to give the state extensive control over the industry, was, however, howled down in the House of Commons in May 1936. At the end of 1937 the bill was re-introduced; although it became law its provisions were overtaken by the outbreak of war.

Crookshank considered resigning from the government when Anthony Eden was forced out of the Foreign Office in February 1938. He had a private meeting with Neville Chamberlain to express his qualms at the direction of British foreign policy but agreed to remain in office. He did submit his resignation over Munich. Following another private meeting, however, Chamberlain persuaded him to withdraw that resignation. In December 1938 his private criticisms of Leslie Hore-Belisha were leaked to the press, and he apologized to Chamberlain for becoming involved in the so-called 'under-secretaries plot'. In April 1939 Crookshank was transferred to the Treasury as its financial secretary, in peacetime a plum job but in wartime a backwater.

Crookshank's combination of carping and caution meant that he was trusted by neither Chamberlain nor Churchill: he voted with the government in the Norway division in May 1940. In February 1942 Churchill asked him to go to the Lords as minister of works. Believing this to be a deliberate insult (the wounds he had sustained at the Somme precluded his fathering an heir to the peerage), he refused. In May 1942 Churchill offered him the post of minister resident in West Africa; this offer too he turned down. In December 1942 he accepted the office of postmaster-general, in war little more than a sinecure. Churchill declined to offer him a senior position in the administration he formed in May 1945: they viewed each other with mutual dislike. It was to 51 Pont Street that James Stuart was summoned in 1947 to hear demands for Churchill's resignation from a group of senior Conservatives.

For Harry Crookshank the Conservative election débâcle of July 1945 was most fortuitous. He was first and foremost a House of Commons performer and the Conservatives badly needed such talents in opposition. He made a number of high profile attacks on left-wing ministers such as Bevan, Strachey, and Shinwell. He enjoyed his greatest success in exposing the government's incompetence in securing food supplies, particularly the gullibility of ministers in dealing with the Peronist tyranny in Argentina.

Crookshank entered the cabinet in October 1951 as minister of health and deputy leader of the House of Commons. He had little interest in the health portfolio and his tenure was not considered a success. In May 1952 he became lord privy seal and leader of the House of Commons. His transition into full-time parliamentary management was not altogether smooth, and he was criticized for allowing the Steel Bill to be counted out. He continued to search for opportunities to unseat Churchill. In July 1954 he led a walkout of ministers from the cabinet in response to Churchill's decision to build a British H-bomb after consultation with selected ministers only. He supported Lord Salisbury when the latter accused the prime minister of deliberately flouting constitutional norms in his pursuit of a summit with the Soviet Union. Churchill subsequently failed in his attempt to persuade Harold Macmillan to replace Crookshank as leader of the house. In the end it was Anthony Eden, in whom Crookshank had invested much hope for advancement, who sacked him in order to install R. A. Butler as leader of the house at the end of 1955. In compensation Crookshank was offered a seat in the cabinet as deputy leader of the House of Lords: he accepted the peerage (he was created a viscount in January 1956) but refused further political office. He was appointed CH in 1955.

Although his career was not lacking in worldly success Harry Crookshank remained disappointed in his own progress. Even in the freemasons, who had installed him as a provincial grand master in September 1954, he felt he might have risen higher. His career testifies to the declining importance of the House of Commons as a power base, though his own propensity to be troublesome to the party leadership without ever sticking to a principle and resigning, retarded his own political advancement.

Following the death of his sister in 1948 and of his mother in 1954, Crookshank was a lonely man. He established the Crookshank lectures at the Royal College of Radiologists in his sister's memory. He too was to be killed by cancer. The whiff of scandal was brought to his door in 1958 when his lover was adopted, then ejected, as prospective Conservative parliamentary candidate for Grimsby at a time when Conservative anxieties about homosexuality in the party were particularly acute. Crookshank died at his London home on 17 October 1961. As he had since 1960 been high steward of Westminster, his funeral took place in Westminster Abbey; he was buried in Lincoln Cathedral, where a simple plaque is his memorial.   S. J. BALL

Sources Bodl. Oxf., MSS Crookshank · grenadier guards records, Wellington Barracks, London · *DNB* · *The Times* (18 Oct 1961) · *The Times* (20 Oct 1961) · *The Times* (25 Oct 1961) · b. cert. · Burke, *Peerage* (1959) · J. Ramsden, *The age of Churchill and Eden, 1940–1957* (1995) · *CGPLA Eng. & Wales* (1961)

Archives Bodl. Oxf.

Likenesses photograph, 1932, Hult. Arch. · Weldman?, photograph, NPG

Wealth at death £235,134 4s.: probate, 16 Nov 1961, *CGPLA Eng. & Wales*

Crookshanks, John (1708–1795), naval officer, entered as a volunteer on the *Torbay* with Captain Nicholas Haddock in the autumn of 1725. While serving in her he seems to have found favour with the Hon. John Byng, whom he followed to the *Gibraltar*, the *Princess Louisa*, and the *Falmouth*.

In August 1732 he passed his examination for the rank of lieutenant, but it was not until March 1734 that he received a commission as third lieutenant of the *Montagu*. On 13 December 1734 he was appointed lieutenant of the *Rose* when she was commissioned station guardship at South Carolina. Crookshanks remained with the *Rose* until she returned home before the outbreak of war with Spain in 1739. In June 1739 he was made second lieutenant of the *Orford* and in September he was promoted first lieutenant of the *Greenwich*. On 2 February 1740 he took up the post of sixth lieutenant on the first rate *Royal George*. He worked his way up to second lieutenant by February 1741 and at last, on 3 July 1742, he achieved post rank when appointed captain of the new ship *Lowestoft* (24 guns), which was launched at Deptford five days later. From Plymouth he was ordered to cruise southwards, and on 17 September 1742, in company with the *Medway* (60 guns), she fell in with a French ship in the straits. In the chase, as night came on, the *Lowestoft* far outsailed the *Medway*, and came up with the enemy; but Crookshanks, preferring to wait until the weather moderated, wrapped himself in his cloak and went to sleep. When he woke the chase was not to be seen. Crookshanks's explanation focused on the crew's misunderstanding of his orders, their fatigue, and the failings of the *Medway*, and this was accepted by the Admiralty.

During 1743 Crookshanks cruised around Gibraltar, from where the Admiralty again started to hear complaints about his failure to engage potential enemy vessels. By March 1744 Crookshanks felt compelled to defend himself against these 'base and barbarous' accusations, (PRO, ADM 1/1601 Crookshanks to secretary of the Admiralty board, 15 March 1744). His explanations were again accepted and he appears to have had the support of the commander-in-chief in the Mediterranean, Admiral William Rowley, who appointed him captain of the *Dartmouth* on 12 December 1744. In May 1746 he was appointed to the temporary command of the *Sunderland* (60 guns), then on the Irish station. On 2 July, off Kinsale, she fell in with three ships judged to be French men-of-war. Crookshanks estimated that they were 40-gun vessels, and, considering the *Sunderland* to be no match for the three together, made sail away from them. His men were angry and violent; they had not estimated the French force so high, and proposed to take the ship from Crookshanks and appoint the first lieutenant as captain, to take them back to fight the French. They were quieted, though not without some difficulty; and Crookshanks, if indeed he knew of the uproar, conceived it best to pass it over. Two days afterwards the crew broke out into open mutiny, claiming that the captain was a coward. One man who had been in the *Lowestoft* brought up the story of what had happened four years before. Crookshanks took his pistols in his hands and went on deck. 'Damn you', roared the ringleader of the mutineers, 'you dare not show the pistols to the French.' The man was put in irons, tried by court martial, and hanged; others were ordered two hundred and fifty lashes; and the first lieutenant was dismissed the service.

Crookshanks was relieved of the command of the *Sunderland*, but in the following January appointed to command the *Lark* (40 guns). Lord Anson, then one of the lords of the Admiralty, as well as commander-in-chief of the Channel Fleet, had misgivings, defending the first lieutenant while questioning Crookshanks's sense and intelligence.

In June 1747 the *Lark*, in company with the *Warwick* (60 guns), sailed from Spithead for the West Indies. On their way, near the Azores, on 14 July, they met the Spanish ship *Glorioso* (70 guns and 700 men), homeward bound with treasure said to amount to nearly £3 million in value. The *Warwick* attacked the *Glorioso* at close quarters, but the *Lark* kept a more prudent distance. The *Warwick*, unsupported, was reduced to a wreck, and the *Glorioso* got away to land her treasure safely at Ferrol. The damage the *Warwick* had sustained rendered it necessary to bear up for Newfoundland, where her captain, Robert Erskine, charged Crookshanks with neglect of duty. It was not until the following year that a court martial could be held, by which time the squadron was at Jamaica. Crookshanks was dismissed from the command of the *Lark*, and cashiered during the king's pleasure. In October 1759 the Board of Admiralty submitted that he might, after twelve years, be restored to the half pay of his rank, which was accordingly done. About the same time he published a pamphlet in which he charged Admiral Charles Knowles, who was commander-in-chief at Newfoundland and later at Jamaica, during the period of Crookshanks's court martial, with influencing the decision of the court, out of personal ill-feeling. Knowles refuted the charge, which indeed appears to have been groundless, and other pamphlets followed. Again, in 1772, Crookshanks brought a similar but more scurrilous charge against Knowles's secretary, the judge advocate at his trial, who retaliated by publishing a complete set of the minutes of the court martial. These give no reason for supposing that the verdict was not perfectly just. In addition Crookshanks's manner and temper towards both men and officers seem to have been harsh and overbearing. Crookshanks did not serve after 1748. He appears to have lived his life in London. His will refers to two daughters, though no details of their mother exist. He died in London on 20 February 1795.

J. K. LAUGHTON, *rev.* RICHARD HARDING

Sources PRO, ADM 1/1601 [captain's letters, 1741–3] · PRO, ADM 1/1602 [captain's letters, 1744–5] · PRO, ADM 1/1603 [captain's letters, 1746–7] · *A refutation of Captain Crookshanks charge against Admiral Knowles* (1759) · PRO, ADM 8/19, 20, 21 [Fleet disposition lists] · 'Account of all the ships in Ordinary', PRO, SP 42/23 [state papers–naval], fol. 411 · PRO, ADM 6/13, 110 · PRO, ADM 6/14, 171, 198 · PRO, ADM 6/15, 222, 375, 415 · PRO, ADM 6/16, 13, 21, 72 · PRO, ADM 6/17, 164, 193

Archives PRO, ADM 1/1601–1603 · PRO, ADM 6/13–17 · PRO, ADM 8/19–21 · PRO, SP 42/23

Croone, William (1633–1684), physician, was born in London on 15 September 1633 and admitted into Merchant Taylors' School, London, on 11 December 1642. On 13 May 1647 he was admitted as a pensioner of Emmanuel College, Cambridge, where he graduated BA in 1650, gained a fellowship in 1651, and graduated MA in 1654. He was incorporated at Oxford University in the same year. In

William Croone (1633–1684), by Mary Beale, c.1680

1659 Croone was elected professor of rhetoric at Gresham College, London, where he was an active participant in the group of chemical and physiological experimenters that formed the nucleus of the nascent Royal Society. At their first meeting, on 28 November 1660, after they had formed themselves into a regular body, he was appointed their registrar, a post he held until the granting of their charter, at which time John Wilkins and Henry Oldenburg were nominated joint secretaries. On 7 October 1662 Croone was created MD at Cambridge by Charles II, and on 20 May 1663 he was elected one of the first fellows of the Royal Society. Croone was admitted as a candidate of the College of Physicians, London, on 7 October 1663, becoming a fellow on 29 July 1675 and censor in 1679. On 28 August 1670 the Barber–Surgeons' Company appointed Croone their anatomy lecturer on muscles, in succession to Sir Charles Scarborough. Croone retained the position for life and resigned his Gresham professorship. In addition to maintaining an active experimental life in the 1660s and 1670s, Croone developed a lucrative medical practice in London during his later years.

Croone, whom a contemporary described as 'little in person, but very lively and active, and remarkably diligent in his inquiries after knowledge' (Ward, 320), pursued research in several important physiological subjects of his day, including respiration, muscular motion, and generation. During the summer of 1664 several members of the Royal Society performed experiments that attempted to elucidate the mechanical importance of air in respiration. Before members of the society in June 1664 Croone

choked a chicken until it appeared dead and then revived it by blowing air into its lungs through a slender glass pipe inserted down its throat. In the same year he produced a brief tract, *De ratione motus musculorum* (published in London in 1664, and in Amsterdam in 1667), in which he argued for a modified chemical explanation of muscle contraction. Briefly, Croone wrote that when the volatile components derived from the nerves and arteries mixed in the spaces between muscle fibres, the resulting effervescence caused the belly of the muscle to swell, thereby shortening its length. In 1665 he visited France and met other men interested in natural philosophy. On 15 November 1666 Pepys recorded that he saw Croone, who told him that earlier in the evening he had witnessed a

> pretty experiment of the blood of one dog let out, till he died, into the body of another on one side, while all his own run out on the other side. The first died upon the place, and the other very well, and likely to do well. This did give occasion to many pretty wishes, as of the blood of a Quaker to be let into an Archbishop, and such like. (*Diary and Correspondence*, 3.336)

Croone also read several papers before the Royal Society, including 'A discourse on the conformation of a chick in the egg before incubation' on 28 March 1672.

Croone married Mary, daughter of John Lorymer, a London alderman. Croone died of fever on 12 October 1684 and was buried at St Mildred Poultry in a Lorymer family vault. In his sermon preached at Croone's funeral John Scott spoke of him as being:

> an accurate linguist, an acute mathematician, a well read historian, and a profound philosopher. [He] was a very generous and careful Practitioner, for though his Practice was large among those of the better Rank and Quality, yet his Ears were always open to the Cries and complaints of the Poor … Thus while he lived Dr Croun was a Publick good, and a great and eminent benefactour to the world; so that his loss is like the breaking up of a common treasury, in which we all of us share. (Scott, 26–9)

Mary Croone later married Sir Edwin Sadlier, of Temple Dinsley, Hertfordshire, and died on 30 September 1706. Croone left plans, but no money, for two lectureships. One was to be delivered annually at the Royal College of Physicians, with a sermon to be preached at St Mary-le-bow; the other, on the nature and laws of muscular motion, was to be delivered before the Royal Society. His widow carried out his intention by devising in her will the King's Head tavern in Lambeth Hill, Knightrider Street, in trust to her executors to settle four parts out of five on the Royal College of Physicians to found the annual lecture now called the Croonian lecture, and the fifth part on the Royal Society. Lady Sadlier also commemorated her first husband by endowing algebra lectures at Emmanuel, King's, St John's, Sidney, Trinity, Jesus, Pembroke, Queens', and St Peter's colleges at Cambridge. On 13 June 1738 Croone's grandson, William Woodford, regius professor of physic at Oxford, presented his portrait, painted by Mary Beale, to the Royal College of Physicians.

ROBERT L. MARTENSEN

Sources DNB · Munk, *Roll* · R. G. Frank, *Harvey and the Oxford physiologists* (1994) · Venn, *Alum. Cant.* · J. Scott, *A sermon preached at the funeral of Dr William Croun on the 23rd October 1684* (1685) · *The record*

of the Royal Society of London, 4th edn (1940) · *Diary and correspondence of Samuel Pepys*, ed. R. N. G. Braybrooke, 3rd edn, 5 vols. (1848–9), 336 · J. Ward, *The lives of the professors of Gresham College* (1740)
Archives BL, corresp. with H. Power, etc., Sloane MSS
Likenesses M. Beale, oils, *c*.1680, RCP Lond. [*see illus.*]

Crophill, John (*d.* in or after **1485**), medical practitioner, is one of the few rural doctors of the middle ages whose intellectual interests and practical concerns can be traced in any detail. He compiled and owned what is now BL, Harley MS 1735, a volume written on parchment and paper, which contains several pieces in his handwriting, as well as others written by a professional scribe and afterwards annotated by Crophill. His main occupation was that of bailiff of Wix Priory, a small but well-endowed house of Benedictine nuns in Essex; he took up the post in 1455. Two years later his salary was apparently 40*s*. per year. He continued as bailiff until at least 1477 and his activities, principally the collection of rents and administration of the demesne lands, are recorded in the court rolls. His additional medical activities would not be known, were it not for his manuscript. The first part, on parchment, is written by a scribe and deals with such concerns as perilous days, the zodiacal signs governing parts of the body, the planets and their influences, the four prime qualities and elements, the four complexions and their effect throughout the year, the cycle of the moon, uroscopy, prognostics, and divination. By the mid-fifteenth century texts of this character were widely available in Middle English, many of them having been translated out of Latin. They prove that a man of business like Crophill, who is not known to have received any university training, might still have access to the practical sciences of medicine, astrology, and divination.

The second part of the manuscript, written mostly by Crophill himself, contains lists of patients treated by him, rents owing, and a variety of other practical texts, with a focus on medical treatment and prognostication. Crophill, like the university-trained doctors of the period, was happy to include in his therapeutic armoury charms for childbirth and a wound-charm, alongside herbal recipes and a regimen of health. He notes the occupations of several of his patients: these include carpenters, a cordwainer, a sheepman, a shearman, a herdsman, a merchant, a tailor, and a sexton. Crophill clearly treated many of them when riding his rounds as bailiff and some of his patients would have been able to afford only very small fees. His income as medical practitioner would have been only marginal in comparison with his income as bailiff. He must have been a convivial man, as he composed some doggerel verses, addressed to five named ladies of Wix, telling how a certain Friar Thomas Stanfeld has made a gift of drinking cups to him; and he in turn presents each lady with a cup. It is clear that Crophill not only brewed ale himself at home in 1457, but liked a good drinking party. He is last recorded in 1485.

PETER MURRAY JONES

Sources BL, Harley MS 1735 · court rolls, Wix Priory court records, PRO, Special Collections, SC2/174/26, 27 · L. G. Ayoub, 'John Crophill's books: an edition of British Library MS Harley

1735', DPhil diss., Centre for Medieval Studies, University of Toronto, 1994 · E. W. Talbert, *The notebook of a fifteenth-century practising physician*, Texas Studies in English, 22 (1942), 5–30 · J. K. Mustain, 'A rural medical practitioner in fifteenth-century England', *Bulletin of the History of Medicine*, 46 (1972), 469–76 · R. H. Robbins, 'John Crophill's ale-pots', *Review of English Studies*, new ser., 20 (1969), 181–9
Archives BL, Harley MS 1735

Cropper, James (1773–1840), merchant and philanthropist, was born at Winstanley, Lancashire, the son of Thomas Cropper and his wife, Rebecca, *née* Winstanley. The Croppers were birthright members of the Society of Friends and small-scale farmers. James, however, was sufficiently ambitious to leave home at the age of seventeen to become apprenticed to Rathbone Brothers, a Quaker enterprise and the first Liverpool merchants trading regularly with America. Here he developed considerable business acumen, to the point when he was able to establish his own mercantile house—Cropper, Benson & Co. In 1796 he married Mary Brinsmead (*d.* 1838). They had two sons, John and Edward, who survived them, and one daughter, who married the Quaker philanthropist Joseph Sturge of Birmingham, and died in giving birth to her first child.

Cropper's trading links were initially with Ireland and North America, but by the end of the Napoleonic wars he was importing a wide range of products, including textiles and spices from India and China. Cropper, Benson & Co. also established the first line of packets to carry mail to North America. The company engaged in common trading ventures with Rathbone Brothers, extending to the joint ownership of vessels. The story is told that when one such ship, the *Bengal*, was due to sail from Liverpool to Calcutta in 1814, Cropper's Quaker conscience refused to countenance the arming of the vessel, but he reconciled his fears of attack by the French with the placing of wooden cannon at the port-holes.

Cropper, Benson & Co. proved to be a highly prosperous concern, and the wealth generated enabled Cropper to engage in a number of religious and philanthropic activities. The focus of his attention was the campaign for the abolition of slavery in the West Indies, and he addressed William Wilberforce at an early stage in the anti-slavery agitation by sending him pamphlets with a high polemical content. Cropper was incensed not only by the inhumanity and injustice of slavery but also by its economic irrationality. In the latter context, the heavy protective duties imposed on sugar imported from the Far East in order to sustain the interests of slave owners in the West Indies were the subject of his incessant attacks in the belief that once protection was removed the institution of slave labour would collapse. As an abolitionist, Cropper associated himself with the advanced wing of the anti-slavery movement, demanding immediate and unconditional extinction of what he regarded as a national crime. His activities were by no means popular in Liverpool with his fellow merchants, some of whom possessed substantial commercial interests in the West Indies. In 1823–4 he was subject to a series of attacks in the columns of the *Liverpool Courier* and *Liverpool Mercury* by Sir

John Gladstone, bt, a senior partner in Corrie & Co. and himself the owner of 1609 slaves. In 1831 Cropper joined forces with his son-in-law, Joseph Sturge, to form the Young England Abolitionists, distinguished from other anti-slavery groups by its unconditional arguments and vigorous campaigning tactics.

The anti-slavery campaign did not absorb all of Cropper's energies. The poverty of the Irish peasantry also engaged his attention, even to the extent of establishing cotton mills in Ireland with a view to providing remunerative employment. In that connection he studied political economy assiduously, and as an advocate of freedom of trade campaigned publicly and successfully for the repeal of the orders in council (issued in 1807 and 1809 in reply to Napoleon's Berlin decrees) which, in damaging Liverpool's trade with the United States, adversely affected the city's prosperity. In the late 1820s Cropper became interested in the business of railway projection in the hope of improving Liverpool's internal communications. He was a founder director of the pioneering Liverpool and Manchester Railway and maintained a close interest in the company's affairs until his death.

In pursuing his philanthropic interests Cropper embarked on an educational project in the form of an agricultural school for boys, and in 1833, after a lengthy tour in Germany and Switzerland to obtain information on the subject, he built a school and orphan house on his estate at Fearnhead, near Warrington, together with a house for himself so that he could personally supervise the undertaking. He resided there until his death, occupying himself chiefly with the affairs of the school. His pen, however, was not idle, and during the last years of his life he published pamphlets on the condition of the West Indies, and especially on the inequalities of the 'negro apprenticeship' system, the sugar bounties, and other protective duties. He died in 1840 of apoplexy, and was buried in the Quaker burial-ground at Liverpool by the side of his wife, who had died two years before him. No monument marked his grave, but the house in which he lived and died at Fearnhead bore the following inscription:

> In this house lived James Cropper, one, and he not the least, of that small but noble band of christian men who, after years of labour and through much opposition, accomplished the abolition of West Indian slavery; and thus having lived the life of the righteous, he died in the full assurance of faith on the 26th of Feby. 1840.

M. W. KIRBY

Sources K. Charlton, 'James Cropper and Liverpool's contribution to the anti-slavery movement', *Transactions of the Historic Society of Lancashire and Cheshire*, 123 (1971), 57–80 · R. Furneaux, *William Wilberforce* (1974) · J. Walvin, ed., *Slavery and British society, 1776–1846* (1982) · R. M. Jones, *The later periods of Quakerism*, 1 (1921) · C. Bolt and S. Dretcher, eds., *Anti-slavery, religion and reform* (1980) · D. Eltis and J. Walvin, eds., *The abolition of the Atlantic slave trade* (1981) · C. Taylor, *British and American abolitionists: an episode in transatlantic understanding* (1974) · P. H. Emden, *Quakers in commerce: a record of business achievement* (1939) · d. cert. · *DNB* · will, PRO, PROB 11/1927, sig. 318

Cropper, James (1823–1900), paper manufacturer and politician, was born on 22 February 1823 in Duke Street, Liverpool, the eldest of the three surviving sons and six daughters of John Cropper (1797–1874), merchant of Liverpool, and his wife, Anne (1797–1876), daughter of John and Mary Wakefield of Sedgwick, Kendal. His grandfather was James *Cropper (1773–1840), philanthropist and slavery abolitionist. The family were of Lancashire Quaker yeoman stock from Bickerstaffe from at least the early seventeenth century.

Cropper passed his boyhood at the family home of Dingle Bank on the Mersey where he was introduced early to the world of letters through family connections with Lord Macaulay, whose sister Margaret (d. 1834) was the second wife of Cropper's uncle Edward Cropper (1799–1877). After school in Liverpool he went on to Edinburgh University, where he decided against going into the family business in Liverpool in favour of paper manufacture, which he learned first with Alex Cowan & Sons at Penicuik, near Edinburgh.

At the same time Cropper made the other important decision of his career: to leave the Society of Friends and enter the Church of England. Both actions, in business and in religion, were not entirely uninfluenced by his devotion to his cousin Fanny Alison Wakefield (1825–1868), whom he had known since childhood and to whom he was formally engaged in 1843. At her wish he was baptized and they were married at Heversham parish church, near Kendal, on 25 November 1845. Fanny was the second of four daughters and two sons of John Wakefield (1794–1866) of Sedgwick House, Kendal, and was born at Broughton Lodge, Cartmel, on 10 April 1825. The marriage consolidated the close links with the leading banking and manufacturing family in Westmorland.

The Croppers lived near Kendal, first at the mill house adjoining the Cowen Head paper mill until after the birth of their elder daughter, Frances Anne (1846–1934), when they moved to a new house, Ellergreen, they had built in 1847 at Burneside; there a second daughter, Mary Wakefield (1849–1943), and a son, Charles James (1852–1924), were born. The marriage was close and happy but cut short by the early death of Fanny on 3 February 1868. Cropper filled the gap left by this loss largely by devoting himself to a prodigious range of public service in education, religion, and politics. He built and endowed a new hospital in Kendal in her memory in 1870, later the Westmorland County Hospital.

The basis of Cropper's power and influence lay in his paper-making business, which he entered in July 1845 by leasing the Cowen Head and Burneside mills from Cornelius Nicholson. He did not gain full control until 1854, but had formed a private company in 1852 and set about expanding and modernizing the mills, aided by an increase in demand for paper and by improved transport links (the Kendal to Windermere line opened in 1847 alongside the Burneside mill and he was an influential director of the Lancaster and Carlisle Railway Company). Despite heavy losses when a fire destroyed the Burneside mill in 1886, production reached 3000 tons by the time the limited company was established in 1889 and had doubled to 6000 tons by 1900 when the firm was established as a leading paper manufacturer in the north of England.

Cropper came to exert great influence in the community, but as an *arriviste* in local gentry terms, though well connected, he felt it necessary to build up a landed estate to give greater substance to his social position and political interests. Over 2000 acres had been acquired by 1900, centred on Ellergreen. Under his energetic leadership he dominated every aspect of social life in the locality, providing housing for his workforce, building the new school, and influencing moral standards through the temperance movement, the Mutual Improvement Society, and the church. His strong sense of social duty was based on Christian principles, but he did not care for his leadership to be questioned. He was strongly opposed to disestablishment.

Cropper had long wished to enter parliament. His public service began early with the chairmanship of the Kendal board of guardians (1853) and as JP (1863), but as an active Liberal of great organizational ability he was an obvious potential candidate. Following the death of John Whitwell shortly after the 1880 general election, he served as the last MP for the borough of Kendal (1880–85), but although he contested the new county division of South Westmorland in December 1885 he lost to the Conservative, Lord Bective, by 277 votes. His political position shifted in 1886 when hostility to home rule pushed him into the Liberal Unionist camp, although his respect for established authority did not sit easily with Liberal demands for change. However, his appetite for public service was undimmed when in 1889 the first Westmorland county council was elected and he became its chairman (1889–1900) and threw himself indefatigably into the work of its committees. He also served as high sheriff of Westmorland in 1875–6 and was a deputy lieutenant.

Cropper was ever hopeful of improving the human condition and was a tireless pamphleteer and lecturer for education and the church. Among many benefactions he founded an open scholarship at Lady Margaret Hall, Oxford. He was taken ill while visiting the Paris Exhibition and died at 157 rue de la Pompe, Paris, of acute pneumonia after four days on 16 October 1900. He was buried in Burneside churchyard beside his wife on 20 October.

RICHARD HALL

Sources J. Cropper, *Notes and memories* (1900) · T. Jones and H. A. Willink, *James Cropper & Co. Ltd and memories of Burneside, 1845–1945* (1945) · C. A. M. Press, *Westmorland lives: social and political* (1895) · *Westmorland Gazette* (1845–1901) · *Westmorland Gazette* (27 Oct 1900) · K. Laybourn, 'A comparative study of Holme and Burneside: two industrial communities in south Westmorland, c.1790–1916', MA diss., University of Lancaster, 1969 · Burneside paper mills, title deeds, 1746–1901, Cumbria AS, Kendal, WDX 577 · Westmorland parish registers, Cumbria AS, Kendal, Burneside 1868, 1900, WPR 54; and Heversham, 1845, WPR 8 · Kendal elections, 1843–92, Cumbria AS, Kendal, WD/PW/A 2181 · family papers, diary, correspondence, etc., priv. coll.
Archives Cumbria AS, Kendal, James Cropper & Co. deeds · priv. coll.

Likenesses photograph, 1895, repro. in Press, *Westmorland lives* (1895) · C. Lucchesi and E. Rawnsley, bronze medallion, 1901, Abbot Hall recreation ground, Kendal · C. Lucchesi and E. Rawnsley, copper medallion, 1901, Cumbria County Council, Kendal, County Offices · oils, priv. coll.
Wealth at death £82,130 12s. 7d.: probate, 21 Nov 1900, CGPLA Eng. & Wales

Crosbie, Andrew (1736–1785), lawyer and antiquary, was probably born at Holm, near Dumfries. He was the surviving son (the elder died young) of Andrew Crosbie (d. 1762), provost of Dumfries (like his father, John), and Jean, daughter of James Grierson of Capenoch and Catherine Sharpe. Educated at Dumfries grammar school and at the University of Edinburgh, Crosbie was admitted to the Faculty of Advocates on 6 August 1757. He quickly developed an excellent practice both in civil and criminal law and as a pleader in the courts of the Church of Scotland where he supported the popular side. In *Thoughts of a Layman Concerning Patronage and Presentations*, published anonymously in 1769, he maintained the superior authority of the church courts in conferring appointments.

Crosbie's success enabled him to build a handsome house at St Andrew Square, in the New Town, Edinburgh. It was scarcely roofed in when he was ruined by the failure in 1772 of the Douglas, Heron & Co. Bank at Ayr, in which he was a partner. Unyielding, he occupied the new house until his death, though he was beset by creditors.

Crosbie was a discriminating book collector and a founder and first fellow of the Society of Antiquaries at Edinburgh. He was also a habitué of taverns; and clumsy of figure, awkward among women in polite society, he married a woman of ill repute, Elizabeth Barker (d. in or after 1814). His unbridled wine drinking led to an early physical and even intellectual decline, yet Crosbie's ability was still so much respected that he was elected vice-dean of the Faculty of Advocates on 24 December 1784, just two months before his death. Animated by this expression of confidence, he proposed 'A treatise on the office, duty, and powers of judges and magistrates in Scotland', which William Creech announced at 1 guinea, by subscription, in the *Edinburgh Advertiser* for 12–15 February 1785. Ten days later, on 25 February 1785, Crosbie died, impoverished, at Edinburgh, and was interred the following day at the Greyfriars churchyard. His library was sold at auction on 4 July 1785. The Faculty of Advocates granted his widow an annuity of £40; in 1814 she presented the portrait by David Martin of Crosbie gesturing broadly as he addressed the court, a portrait which still hangs in the Parliament House.

Learned (Samuel Johnson was pleased by his knowledge of alchemy), fearless, eloquent, and witty, Andrew Crosbie was considered in his time the best criminal lawyer at the bar. John Ramsay of Ochtertyre, his schoolmate, wrote of him in *Scotland and Scotsmen in the Eighteenth Century* that Crosbie would have been raised to the bench had he lived. The assumption is unrealistic because Crosbie was a nonconformist and defender of the underdog. Sir Walter Scott probably drew useful hints from him for Paulus Pleydell in *Guy Mannering*; the irreverent opinions and personality

Andrew Crosbie (1736–1785), by David Martin

of the man himself survive in the journal, correspondence, and legal papers of James Boswell, Crosbie's intimate friend, distant relation, and admirer. Crosbie defended the Kilmarnock Common against the trustees' plan to build upon it, and served tenaciously as counsel to sheep- and horse-stealers, often as Boswell's associate and guide. Together they sent munitions to the Corsican rebels under General Pasquale Paoli and shared the extra costs of unmet subscriptions to the fund they had raised. During the anti-Catholic riots of February 1779 Crosbie was prepared to resist by gunfire the mob that besieged his house because it thought him the author of a bill relaxing many penal laws against Catholics, an attribution affirmed by Boswell. We also learn from Boswell that Crosbie thought Jesus only a 'very able and very good man' who pretended to have supernatural powers in order to influence a 'most superstitious people' (*Boswell in Extremes*, 219). Perhaps equally as damaging as Crosbie's Enlightenment views was his composition, with Boswell, of 'The justiciary opera', an unpublished rhymed parody of the criminal court, sung, with topical alterations, by many generations of Scottish advocates.   IRMA S. LUSTIG

Sources F. Miller, *Andrew Crosbie, advocate: a reputed original of Paulus Pleydell in 'Guy Mannering'* [1919], 1–22 · *Scotland and Scotsmen in the eighteenth century: from the MSS of John Ramsay, esq., of Ochtertyre*, ed. A. Allardyce, 1 (1888); repr. with introduction by D. J. Brown (1996) · *Catalogue of the papers of James Boswell at Yale University*, ed. M. S. Pottle, C. C. Abbott, and F. A. Pottle, 3 vols. (1993) · *Boswell in search of a wife, 1766–1769*, ed. F. Brady and F. A. Pottle (1956), vol. 6 of *The Yale editions of the private papers of James Boswell*, trade edn (1950–89) · *Boswell for the defence, 1769–1774*, ed. W. K. Wimsatt and F. A. Pottle (1960), vol. 7 of *The Yale editions of the private papers of James Boswell*, trade edn (1950–89) · *Boswell's journal of a tour to the Hebrides*

with Samuel Johnson, ed. F. A. Pottle and C. H. Bennett (1963), vol. 9 of *The Yale editions of the private papers of James Boswell*, trade edn (1950–89) · *Boswell: the ominous years, 1774–1776*, ed. C. Ryskamp and F. A. Pottle (1963), vol. 8 of *The Yale editions of the private papers of James Boswell*, trade edn (1950–89) · *Boswell in extremes, 1776–1778*, ed. C. M. Weis and F. A. Pottle (1970), vol. 10 of *The Yale editions of the private papers of James Boswell*, trade edn (1950–89) · *Boswell, laird of Auchinleck, 1778–1782*, ed. J. W. Reed and F. A. Pottle (1977), repr. (1993), vol. 11 of *The Yale editions of the private papers of James Boswell*, trade edn (1950–89) · *Boswell: the applause of the jury, 1782–1785*, ed. I. S. Lustig and F. A. Pottle (1981), vol. 12 of *The Yale editions of the private papers of James Boswell*, trade edn (1950–89) · Boswell, *Life*, vols. 2, 5 · F. A. Pottle, *James Boswell: the earlier years, 1740–1769* (1966) · F. Brady, *James Boswell: the later years, 1769–1795* (1984) · F. Brady, 'So fast to ruin: the personal element in the collapse of Douglas, Heron & Company', *Ayrshire Collections*, 11/2 (1973) [whole issue]

Likenesses D. Martin, oils, Faculty of Advocates, Parliament House, Edinburgh [*see illus.*]

Wealth at death died impoverished: *DNB* · library sold at auction shortly after Crosbie's death, on 4 July 1785: Miller, *Andrew Crosbie*, 15; Lustig and Pottle, *Boswell: the applause*, 66 and n.1

Crosby, Allan James (1835–1881), record scholar, was the only son of James Crosby, gentleman, of the parish of St Lawrence in the City of London. He was educated at Worcester College, Oxford, and graduated BA in law and history in 1858. He obtained a nomination for the competitive examination for clerkships in the Public Record Office and was one of the group of talented graduates who refreshed the staff of the office in 1861–3. He was called to the bar at the Inner Temple on 1 May 1865. He assisted Joseph Stevenson in the preparation of the *Calendar of State Papers, Foreign Series*, for the period beginning in 1558, and on Stevenson's resignation to join the Roman Catholic priesthood succeeded him as editor in 1871. Crosby was promoted senior clerk in 1874 and might well, as the senior admitted barrister on the staff, have been further promoted to inspecting officer for legal records. However, he was stricken by paralysis and had to resign; his death followed shortly afterwards, on 5 December 1881 at Holmbush, in Ide, near Exeter. With his colleague John Bruce he edited *Accounts and Papers Relating to Mary Queen of Scots* (Camden Society, 1867).   ALAN BELL

Sources *The Athenaeum* (17 Dec 1881), 815 · *The Times* (2 May 1881), 14 · Foster, *Alum. Oxon.* · J. D. Cantwell, *The Public Record Office, 1838–1958* (1991) · *DNB*

Wealth at death £9175 13s. 8d.: probate, 6 Jan 1882, *CGPLA Eng. & Wales*

Crosby, Brass (1725–1793), lawyer and politician, was born on 8 May 1725 in Stockton-on-Tees, the elder son in the family of five children of Hercules Crosby (d. 1761), burgess, and his wife, Mary (1704/1705–1769), the daughter and coheir of John Brass, of Blackhalls, Hesleden, co. Durham, and his first wife, Mary Watson. After serving his apprenticeship to an attorney in Sunderland, Mr Hoskins, Crosby practised as an attorney in London, first in the Little Minories, then from about 1752 in Seething Lane. His parents followed him to London and settled in Stoke Newington, his father having squandered the income from his wife's property on a coalmining project. Crosby married three times, each of his wives being a rich widow. He married first Sarah Walraven, on 7 May 1748 at St Ethelburga,

Bishopsgate, with whom he had one daughter; second, he married a Mrs Cook, the widow of a collar-maker to the ordnance. His third wife, whom he married on 9 February 1772, was Mary, the widow of John Tattersall, rector of Gatton, and the daughter of James Maud, a wine merchant of London; she brought him a large fortune of some £25,000 as well as the manor of Chelsfield, near Orpington, Kent.

Crosby's career in City politics started in earnest when he was elected a member of the common council for Tower ward in 1758, and he held a succession of City offices, including that of remembrancer, which he purchased for £3600 in 1760 and sold the following year. He served as sheriff in 1764–5 and in February 1765 was elected alderman of Bread Street ward, replacing Alderman Janssen. Three years later he bought his entry into national politics when he was returned as MP for Honiton, a notoriously venal borough, at the general election of 1768. He sided with the opposition and gave wholehearted support to his fellow alderman John Wilkes, whom the government was trying to expel from the Commons on grounds of seditious and obscene libel. The Wilkites gained a considerable victory when Crosby was elected lord mayor on 29 September 1770, whereupon he declared that at the risk of his life he would protect the just privileges and liberties of the City of London. One of his first acts after taking office in November was to refuse to back the Admiralty warrants for press-ganging men into naval service, declaring that 'the city bounty was intended to prevent such violences' (*Annual Register*, 1770, 169).

Crosby gained greater celebrity in the following year for his role in the 'Printers' case'. In March a proclamation was issued for the arrest of John Wheble and Roger Thompson for printing reports of parliamentary debates in the *Middlesex Journal* and *The Gazetteer*, a breach of privilege. Wheble and Thompson were subsequently discharged when they appeared before the City magistrates, Wilkes and Richard Oliver. When a messenger from the Commons was sent to command another printer, John Miller, of the *London Evening-Post*, to appear before the house, the messenger was arrested by a City constable, and Crosby, supported by Wilkes and Oliver, refused to release him. Crosby was now ordered to attend the Commons, which he accordingly did on 19 March and again on the 25th; he defended himself by arguing that he was bound by his aldermanic oath to protect the rights of the City. A severe attack of gout delayed his final hearing until the 27th, when, accompanied by huge crowds of disorderly supporters, Crosby was committed to the Tower of London for his continued defiance of the Commons, by a majority of 202 votes to thirty-nine. During his imprisonment with Oliver, Crosby was visited by City politicians and the leaders of the opposition and received a stream of public addresses and thanks from all parts of the country. To confirm his radical credentials, he was admitted to the Society of Supporters of the Bill of Rights on 30 April. When the parliamentary session closed on 8 May, Crosby and Oliver returned to the Mansion House in a triumphal procession, having stubbornly thwarted the Commons and indirectly secured the right to report parliamentary debates.

Crosby stood for election on a radical Wilkite platform in the City of London at the general election of 1774, but was defeated; he failed to regain his seat at a by-election in January 1784. He accumulated further offices—the presidency of Bethlem and Bridewell Hospital (1782) and the governorship of the Irish Society (1785)—and was chair of four City committees at the time of his death. He died after a short illness on 14 February 1793 at his house in Chatham Place, Blackfriars Bridge, and was buried on the 21st in Chelsfield church. An obelisk which was erected to him during his mayoralty in the centre of St George's Circus, Blackfriars Road, was later moved to a position outside Bethlem Hospital, Lambeth, now the Imperial War Museum.   G. F. R. BARKER, *rev.* S. J. SKEDD

Sources *Memoir of Brass Crosby, esq., alderman of the City of London and lord mayor, 1770–1771* (1829) • I. R. Christie, 'Crosby, Brass', HoP, *Commons, 1754–90* • *GM*, 1st ser., 63 (1793), 188–9 • A. B. Beaven, ed., *The aldermen of the City of London, temp. Henry III–[1912]*, 2 (1913), 53, 133, 199, 216 • P. D. G. Thomas, *John Wilkes: a friend to liberty* (1996) • *City biography*, 2nd edn (1800) • A. T. Brown, *Brass Crosby, lord mayor of London, 1770–71* (1933) • IGI
Likenesses W. Dickinson, mezzotint, pubd 1771 (after R. E. Pine), BM, NPG • J. S. Copley, oils, Art Institute of Chicago

Crosby, Sir John (*d.* 1476), merchant and diplomat, inherited from his father the manor of Hanworth, which had also been held by his grandfather. He was apprenticed to the prominent London grocer John Young, and became a freeman in 1454. By that date Young, who was a wealthy exporter of wool, was a leading member of the Yorkist faction in the Grocers' Company. Crosby, too, became a wool merchant, and apparently also adopted Young's political allegiance, because in April 1459 he found it expedient as a 'grocer and woolman' to purchase a pardon from Henry VI, most probably to protect himself against the charges which were soon to be levelled against prominent Yorkists for giving illegal credit. Crosby was purchasing large amounts of wool by 1460 and he was also giving substantial credit in partnership with the Yorkist alderman and grocer Richard Lee. Later he clashed with his old master, John Young, over debts owed for wool. By 1465 Young was accusing Crosby of counterfeiting his seal and making a false indenture; 'scandalous and opprobrious words' were spoken, and the disputes were only resolved when they agreed to accept arbitration by the mayor and aldermen.

In 1464 Crosby was one of the merchants of the staple who had purchased a pardon from Edward IV. He was also importing through Southampton damasks and satin, which may possibly have been return cargoes for exports of wool to the Mediterranean, of the kind he was licensed to export from Southampton on an Italian carrack in 1469. The success of his Italian connections appears from the legacy of £50 he bequeathed to a Florentine merchant 'for the good faith and truth that he hath borne towards me afore this time … as my confidence thereof is right especial in him' (Gough, 2, appx iv).

Crosby was chosen as a member of parliament for London in 1466, became an alderman in 1468, and the following year was master of the Grocers' Company when the earl of Warwick first challenged Edward IV. The choice of John Young as master in 1470 suggests that the leadership of the Grocers' Company remained committed to Edward IV throughout his exile, and Crosby may have been chosen as sheriff that year to assist in his return. He must certainly have influenced the decision of the aldermen to commit the city to Edward while Warwick's forces were still in the field. When Warwick's ally Thomas Fauconberg tried to retake the city in May 1471, Crosby distinguished himself with other grocer aldermen in its defence, and he was one of those knighted by Edward IV later that month. His extensive commercial experience and loyalty made him the king's choice as ambassador in 1472, and again the following year, to re-establish commercial relations with Burgundy.

Crosby's wealth enabled him in 1466 to lease the land from St Helen's Priory in Bishopsgate on which he shortly afterwards began to build his house, which was described by Stow as 'verie large and beautiful and the highest at that time in London' (Stow, 1.172). It was afterwards occupied by Richard III, and early in the twentieth century its hall was moved to a site in Chelsea. It remains the only extant example of domestic architecture built for a London merchant in the middle ages. When he died in either January or February 1476 Crosby was buried beside his first wife, Agnes, in St Helen's Church. Crosby made monetary bequests of over £3200, besides all his property and merchandise. He left £2000 in money to his second wife, Anne, the daughter of William Chedworth; his manor of Hanworth he left to his daughter Joan, as John, his son by his second wife, had predeceased him, and he gave £400 to fund a chantry in St Helen's for forty years.

PAMELA NIGHTINGALE

Sources S. L. Thrupp, *The merchant class of medieval London, 1300–1500* (1948) · P. Nightingale, *A medieval mercantile community: the Grocers' Company and the politics and trade of London, 1000–1485* (1995) · J. Schofield, *The building of London from the conquest to the great fire* (1984) · J. Stow, *A survay of London*, rev. edn (1603); repr. with introduction by C. L. Kingsford as *A survey of London*, 2 vols. (1908); repr. with addns (1971) · J. A. Kingdon, ed., *Facsimile of first volume of MS archives of the Worshipful Company of Grocers of the city of London*, AD 1345–1463, 2 (1886) · R. R. Sharpe, ed., *Calendar of letter-books preserved in the archives of the corporation of the City of London*, [12 vols.] (1899–1912), vol. L · *CPR, 1452–77* · *CClR, 1461–8* · PRO, C 241 · chancery, extents for debts, PRO, C 131 · chancery, certificates of statute merchant and statute staple, PRO, C 1/27/261 · chancery, early chancery proceedings, PRO, C 1/29/369 · will, PRO, PROB 11/6, sig. 179 · GL, MSS 11, 592 · Journals, 7, CLRO · R. Gough, *Sepulchral monuments in Great Britain*, 2 (1796), pt 3, appx

Likenesses line engraving, 1794 (after tomb effigy), NPG · tomb effigy, St Helen's, Bishopsgate, London

Wealth at death over £3200 in cash legacies; also bequeathed merchandise, household possessions, the manor of Hanworth: will, PRO, PROB 11/6, sig. 179

Crosby, Thomas (*d.* in or after **1749**), historian, lived at Horselydown, Southwark, London, where he kept a mathematical and commercial school, and also was deacon of the local Baptist church. Between 1738 and 1740 he published his four-volume *History of the Baptists from the Restoration to the Beginning of the Reign of George I*, which provided valuable biographies of early Baptist ministers. Crosby showed less scholarly vigour in his failure to describe the denominational differences within the church, an omission that caused considerable offence to Baptist readers. Much of the material used had been collected by Benjamin Stinton (*d.* 1718), a Baptist minister whose original intention it had been to write the *History* himself. Crosby for his part supplied Daniel Neal with information on the Baptist church for his *History of the Puritans* (1732–6). Crosby's other works are *A Brief Reply to Mr John Lewis's History of the Rise and Progress of Anabaptism in England* (1738) and his last study, *The Bookkeeper's Guide*, published in 1749.

A. C. BICKLEY, *rev.* PHILIP CARTER

Sources W. Wilson, *The history and antiquities of the dissenting churches and meeting houses in London, Westminster and Southwark*, 4 vols. (1808–14)

Crosdill, John (1751/1755–1825), cellist, was born in London, in 1751 or 1755 (sources differ), the son of Richard Crosdill (1698–1790), also a cellist; it is believed that some of the activities formerly associated with John may well have been confused with his father's career. Although he was reputed to have been educated at Westminster School, he does not appear in its admission books. He was a Westminster Abbey choir member under John Robinson and Benjamin Cooke. He studied with the influential French cellist Jean-Pierre Duport (1741–1818), but it is unclear whether the lessons took place in the early 1760s in Paris or in 1769 when Duport was in London. Crosdill's standing rose with his ability: in 1776 Charles Burney wrote to Lord Mornington that he was 'very much improved: The great Performers whom he has constantly heard & with whom he has been associated at Bach and Abel's Winter Concerts have polished his taste' (*Early Journals and Letters*, 1.213); Burney went so far as to compare him favourably with his former master Duport.

Crosdill was principal cellist at the Three Choirs festival each year (except 1778) from 1769 until his retirement, at the Concerts of Antient Music from 1776, and at the Professional Concerts; at the last he played many concertos, concertinos, continuo sonatas, and chamber music. He also performed in private concerts for the nobility and organized Friday afternoon ladies' concerts. From about 1778 he was a member of the king's band of music and from 10 March 1778 until his death he was violist in the Chapel Royal. In 1782 he is listed as principal player at the King's Theatre in place of James Cervetto and from that year, in his capacity as chamber musician to the royal household, he taught cello to the prince of Wales. In May and June 1784 he performed at the Handel commemoration concerts, a project closely associated with the court. He became composer and master of the king's band in Ireland in 1784; the post was desired by Burney and the appointment caused some scorn, expressed in the *Public Advertiser* (9 March 1785). Crosdill also performed in Paris, as a member of Viotti's orchestra for the Concert de la Loge Olympique (1780) and at the Concert Spirituel (15

John Crosdill (1751/1755–1825), by William Daniell (after George Dance)

August 1784). He married Elizabeth Colebrooke, a wealthy septuagenarian widow with interests in Yorkshire, at St Marylebone on 31 May 1785. Thereafter he played only where he chose and accepted hardly any engagements from 1787, though he remained active in London musical life; he was an honorary member of the Royal Academy of Music and met Joseph Haydn in 1791. In 1821 he performed at the coronation of his pupil George IV.

Crosdill lived at various London addresses, including 14 Upper Harley Street, Titchfield Street, where William, second Earl Fitzwilliam often stayed as his guest, and Grosvenor Square, where his fellow lodger was Beilby Thompson of Escrick, MP for Hedon. His will was signed at Berners Street in Marylebone on 30 August 1825 and he may have died there that October, if not in a house in Escrick, Yorkshire, belonging to Thompson's nephew. It seems likely that he remarried following the death of Elizabeth Colebrooke, since his only son, Lieutenant-Colonel Crosdill, of the East India Company, gave the Royal Society of Musicians £1000 when his father died. Crosdill enjoyed a successful career that allowed him, with the help of a good marriage, to attain the status of a gentleman. He was clearly highly regarded by contemporaries and remained a professional musician long enough to teach leading cellists of the next generation, such as Robert Lindley and John Gunn. FIONA M. PALMER

Sources Highfill, Burnim & Langhans, *BDA*, 4.55–7 · V. Walden, *One hundred years of the violoncello: a history of technique and performance practice, 1740–1840* (1998) · *The letters of Dr Charles Burney*, ed. A. Ribeiro, 1 (1991) · T. B. Milligan, *The concerto and London's musical culture in the late 18th century* (1983) · M. Campbell, 'Masters of the

baroque and classical eras', *The Cambridge companion to the cello* (1999) · S. McVeigh, *Concert life in London from Mozart to Haydn* (1993) · K. Geiringer, *Haydn: a creative life in music*, 3rd edn (Berkeley, 1982) · C. Pierre, *Histoire du Concert Spirituel, 1725–1790* (Paris, 1975) · C. F. Pohl, *Mozart und Haydn in London*, 2 vols. (Vienna, 1867) · W. H. Husk, 'Crosdill, John', Grove, *Dict. mus.* (1927), 760 · C. Price, J. Milhous, and R. D. Hume, *Italian opera in late eighteenth-century London*, 1: *The King's Theatre, Haymarket, 1778–1791* (1995) · [J. S. Sainsbury], ed., *A dictionary of musicians*, 1 (1825); repr. (New York, 1966), 1.190 · G. Sadler, 'Crosdill, John', *New Grove* · W. J. von Wasielewski, *The violoncello and its history*, trans. I. S. E. Stigand (1894) · W. T. Parke, *Musical memoirs*, 2 vols. (1830); repr. (New York, 1970) · R. Elkin, *The old concert rooms of London* (1955) · L. Forino, *Il violoncello, il violoncellista e i violoncellisti* (Milan, 1905) · A. M. Clarke, *Fiddlers ancient and modern* (1895) · E. van der Straeten, *History of the violoncello*, 2 vols. (1915) · will, dated 30 Aug 1825, proved, 25 Oct 1825 · J. Doane, ed., *A musical directory for the year 1794* [1794]

Likenesses W. Daniell, engraving (after G. Dance), NPG [*see illus.*] · T. Gainsborough, portrait

Wealth at death £1000 bequest to the Royal Society of Musicians: will, 1825, proved 25 Oct 1825

Crosfield, George (1785–1847), botanist and Quaker publicist, was born on 26 May 1785 at Warrington, the son of George Crosfield (1754–1820) and his wife, Ann. His parents left Warrington in 1799, leaving the fourteen-year-old Crosfield to work in a grocery business there, a chain of events which gave him remarkable self-reliance. He acted as secretary to the Warrington Botanical Society, and in 1810 published *A Calendar of Flora, Composed during the Year 1809 at Warrington*. He used the nomenclature of Sir J. E. Smith. At the age of thirty he became an elder in the Society of Friends, for whom he was an active publisher. His publications included the *Letters of W. Thompson of Penketh* (1818) as well as John Wilbur's *Letters to a Friend on the Primitive Doctrines of Christianity* (1832) and the *Memoirs of S. Fothergill* (1837). He moved to Liverpool in 1819. In 1844 he took a political stance on behalf of the Friends by publishing *An address on behalf of the Society of Friends complaining about acts of vandalism against those who refused to pay tithes*. He died at Liverpool on 15 December 1847.

G. S. BOULGER, *rev.* ALEXANDER GOLDBLOOM

Sources Desmond, *Botanists*, rev. edn, 179 · G. Bridson, *The history of natural history* (1994) · *Annual Monitor* (1849), 33–8

Archives NL Wales, papers · RS Friends, Lond., letters

Likenesses silhouette, repro. in J. Kendrick, *Profile of Warrington worthies* (1853)

Crosfield, John (1832–1901), chemical manufacturer, was born in Warrington, Lancashire, on 11 February 1832, the youngest in the family of five sons and three daughters of Joseph Crosfield and his wife, Elizabeth Goad. He received a Quaker education in Penkelt, Cheshire, and at Bootham School, York, before going on to Glasgow high school. In 1847 he followed his elder brothers, George and Morland, into the family soap business, Joseph Crosfield & Son, founded by their late father at Bank Quay, Warrington. In 1853 he became a partner, and after the death of Morland and George's move to London in 1875, he became solely responsible for the firm. The abolition of excise duty in 1853 heralded a period of growth and prosperity for the soap industry. Many improvements were made to the

Bank Quay works, and Crosfields' products were marketed throughout the world. In 1883 Crosfields was one of the first factories to install electric light.

In 1874 John Brunner and Ludwig Mond began the production of soda at Winnington, Cheshire, by a new and cheaper process (ammonia-soda) than the traditional Leblanc method. Crosfield became their largest buyer of soda. In 1881, when Brunner, Mond & Co. became a public company, he invested in it, became its first chairman, and remained a director until his death. In 1896 Joseph Crosfield & Son became a public company, with Crosfield as chairman, and his two sons, Arthur and Joseph, and Dr Karl Markel (transferred from Brunner, Mond & Co.) as directors. Markel was a German-educated chemist, who was responsible for significant technical improvements.

Crosfield was an enlightened employer in the paternalistic tradition, deeply influenced by his Quaker upbringing. Works outings to Llangollen and Blackpool, bowls competitions, and social evenings indicated an industrial harmony far from common at the time. Crosfield campaigned against intemperance, improvidence, and vice. He contributed time and money generously to Warrington: he was mayor in 1882, alderman in 1885, and freeman in 1891; he built a working men's mission, and supported schools, the library, the infirmary, and other institutions. He was a dedicated Liberal, helping to start the local club and association, and the Liberal newspaper, the *Warrington Examiner*. In the general election of July 1886 he was narrowly beaten by the tory Sir Gilbert Greenhall, head of the local brewing family—a bitter disappointment to a temperance advocate.

Crosfield married Eliza Dickson, from an Ulster protestant family in the cotton trade, in Belfast in 1864; they had five sons and four daughters. She died in 1882, and in 1890 he married her sister Gertrude, in Jersey; they had no children. He relinquished control of the company to his three surviving sons, but remained chairman until his death, on 26 December 1901, at his home near Warrington, Walton Lea, Cheshire.   N. J. TRAVIS, *rev.*

Sources A. E. Musson, *Enterprise in soap and chemicals: Joseph Crosfield & Sons Limited, 1815–1965* (1965) • P. N. Read, 'Crosfield, John', *DBB*, vol. 1, pp. 841–4 • *Warrington Examiner* (28 Dec 1901)
Wealth at death £155,490 13s. 3d.: probate, 18 Feb 1902, *CGPLA Eng. & Wales*

Crosfield, Margaret Chorley (1859–1952), geologist, was born on 7 September 1859 at Wray Park, Reigate, Surrey, the daughter of Joseph Crosfield, tea merchant, and his wife, Sarah Swatridge, *née* Lowe; both were members of the Society of Friends. Crosfield attended the Mount School, York, and entered Newnham College, Cambridge, in 1879. Her studies there were interrupted by ill health and after her return, from 1880 to 1883, she read only geology.

All Crosfield's research was undertaken in a private capacity, often with friends. With Dr Ethel G. Skeat (later Woods) she surveyed a 4 mile radius round Carmarthen, and in examining the syncline discovered new aspects of stratigraphy and collected a new species of trilobite. In 1906 Professor John Marr suggested that Crosfield and Skeat should examine the little-known series of Denbighshire Grits and Flags in the Clwydians, in order to establish a sequence by means of the graptolite fauna. In 1906–9 and again in 1911 they covered an area of 72 square miles; there was then a delay until 1922, when they recorded the palaeontology. These investigations were published in the *Quarterly Journal of the Geological Society*, volumes 52 (1896) and 81 (1925) respectively. With M. S. Johnston, Crosfield surveyed the Wenlock Limestone, written up for the *Proceedings of the Geological Association* (1914), and she provided a short account of geology in Surrey for C. E. Salmon's flora of Surrey.

Crosfield was elected to the British Association for the Advancement of Science in 1894 and attended its meetings at home and abroad. She was a member of the Palaeontological Society from 1907 to 1932 and served on its council; she was also a member of the Geological Association, serving on its council in 1919 and as librarian in 1919–23. In 1919 she was one of the first six women to be elected as fellows of the Geological Society. In Reigate she lectured to the local history society on scientific and social topics, being an ardent advocate of women's suffrage. She served on the Reigate borough educational committee from 1919 until failing memory obliged her to resign, and she was a governor of Reigate County Girls' School from 1926. Crosfield amassed a large collection of specimens, all meticulously place-marked, while her accuracy, artistry, and industry were displayed in her voluminous notebooks. She died, unmarried, at her home, 78 Doods Road, Reigate, on 13 October 1952. Her funeral took place at the Friends' meeting-house, Reigate, on 18 October.

ANITA MCCONNELL

Sources *Proceedings of the Geological Association*, 64 (1953), 62–3 • *Surrey Mirror* (17 Oct 1952), 1 • [A. B. White and others], eds., *Newnham College register, 1871–1971*, 2nd edn, 1 (1979) • b. cert. • d. cert. • *CGPLA Eng. & Wales* (1953)
Wealth at death £9754 19s. 0d.: probate, 3 Jan 1953, *CGPLA Eng. & Wales*

Crosfield, Thomas (1602–1663), diarist and Church of England clergyman, was born on 14 May 1602 at Stricklandroger, in the parish of Kendal, Westmorland, the only son of Robert Crosfield (*b.* 1573), scrivener, and of Barbara Philipson who died in his infancy. His father, who married secondly in 1606 Dorothy Gilpin of Katterton near York, rose in his son's maturity to be twice mayor of Kendal and was reputed a gentleman. Crosfield, who had probably attended Kendal grammar school, matriculated at Oxford on 15 May 1618 from the Queen's College, with which the Gilpins had connections, graduating BA on 9 December 1622 and proceeding MA on 30 June 1625. He was elected fellow on 20 October 1627. From 1626 onwards he preached occasionally in nearby parishes. On 29 January 1630 he was pre-elected by the college to the proctorship for 1635–6, his father having promised money for the library if he obtained the office, but in 1635 someone else was chosen. Crosfield incorporated his MA at Cambridge in 1634, and proceeded BD on 17 December 1635.

The main run of Crosfield's manuscript diary, Queen's College MS 390, stretches, with gaps, from January 1626 to

January 1640. There are also accounts of conversations between provost and fellows, or among the fellows, from 1632 to 1638, and analyses of books. Much of the diary proper and some other portions, but by no means all that is of significance, was edited in 1935 by F. S. Boas. The text, in English and Latin, with some passages in idiosyncratic French, throws light on collegiate and university life in a period which included William Laud's chancellorship. Christopher Potter, provost from 1626 to 1646, who favoured the diarist, comes to life in table-talk, theological views, disciplinary measures, careful husbanding of resources, and efforts to beautify the chapel. Crosfield witnessed the spread of 'Pelagianismi cancer' (Queen's College, MS 390, fol. 19r) after King James's death. He was interested in town politics and assizes, and particularly in theatrical performances. A keen observer of national and international events, he frequently summarized 'currantos' and letters. His diary offers incidental evidence for the study of French, Hebrew, Arabic, mathematics, and astronomy; the royal visit to Oxford in August 1636 is also described.

On 18 December 1631 Crosfield claimed he had 'printed & translated' Grotius, 'Of the True religion' (Diary of Thomas Crosfield, 59), commended to him by Potter. True Religion Explained (1632) appeared without a translator's name, but the Stationers' register on 28 January 1632 gave that of Francis Coventry, Lord Keeper Coventry's son, a fellow-commoner at Queen's. Crosfield, whose diary at this point suggests preoccupation in other business, was probably largely responsible.

In 1633 Crosfield published anonymously A Letter, relating the Martyrdome of Ketaban, mother of Teimurases prince of the Georgians, & withall a notable imposture of the Iesuites upon that occasion, translated from the Greek text of the monk Gregory, dated 1626. He also contributed poems to university collections on royal occasions.

Possibly responsible for the 1635 broadsheet Synopsis of Laud's provisional university statutes of 1634, Crosfield was certainly entrusted with the handbook abridgement of the definitive 1636 statutes, published at Laud's request to 'direct the younger sort in matter of manners and exercise' (Works, 5.171), and printed anonymously in January 1638 as Statuta selecta e corpore statutorum universitatis Oxoniensis. Frequent editions, later known as Parecbolae, appeared over the next two centuries. On 30 December 1639 Potter wrote thanking Laud for 'good intentions toward our Mr. Crosfield' (PRO, SP 16/436, fol. 117v).

In 1638 Crosfield became vicar of the Queen's College living of Godshill, Isle of Wight, which was sequestered by parliament in 1644. He may have been vicar of Windermere, Westmorland, between September 1644 and February 1645. On 7 April 1645 he married Helen, daughter of Francis Wyvill, rector of Spennithorne, Yorkshire, and granddaughter of Sir Marmaduke Wyvill, of Burton Constable, to whom he may have been related. The couple had two sons and three daughters. In August 1648 Crosfield obtained the rectory of Chale, Isle of Wight, and in 1649 became rector of Spennithorne, in the Wyvills' gift, after his father-in-law's death. In September 1652 Crosfield paid

a fine of £72 to discharge the estate of his late father, Robert Crosfeild, a committed royalist who had fallen foul of parliament for delinquency.

Diary entries recommence in February 1653 and run until February 1654, replete with concern about money and litigation, debts and tithes, but also touching on Quakers. They suggest that Crosfield had come to accept Cromwell. He was buried at Spennithorne church on 15 February 1663, leaving by will his Westmorland estate to his elder son, Robert, and purchased lands at Bellerby near Spennithorne to his other son, Francis.

A. J. HEGARTY

Sources diary of Thomas Crosfield, Queen's College, Oxford, MS 390 · The diary of Thomas Crosfield, ed. F. S. Boas (1935), esp. introduction and notes · T. G. Fahy, 'Thomas Crosfield's diary', Transactions of the Cumberland and Westmorland Antiquarian and Archaeological Society, new ser., 64 (1964), 382–5 · J. Crosfield, The Crosfield family: a history of the descendants of Thomas Crosfeld [sic] of Kirkby Lonsdale who died in 1614 (privately published, 1980) · Reg. Oxf., 2/2.368; 2/3.413 · The works of the most reverend father in God, William Laud, 5, ed. J. Bliss (1853), 168–9, 171, 189–90 · PRO, SP 16/436, fols. 117r–118v · Walker rev., 182 · M. A. E. Green, ed., Calendar of the proceedings of the committee for compounding … 1643–1660, 3, PRO (1891), 1658 · F. Madan, Oxford books: a bibliography of printed works, 1–2 (1895–1912) · W. Farrer, Records relating to the barony of Kendale, ed. J. F. Curwen, 3 vols., Cumberland and Westmorland Antiquarian and Archaeological Society, record ser., 4–6 (1923–6)
Archives Queen's College, Oxford, diary, MS 390
Wealth at death estate in Westmorland with moveable goods and several houses there left to elder son; lands purchased near Spennithorne, Yorkshire, from father-in-law and others, to younger son; mother was to raise money from these in her sons' minorities in order to provide each of three daughters with £200 apiece at the age of twenty-five: Diary of Thomas Crosfield, ed. Boas, xvii–xviii

Croskery, Thomas (1830–1886), minister of the Presbyterian Church in Ireland and journalist, son of Thomas Croskery and Agnes Cosby (d. 1883), was born in the village of Carrowdore, co. Down, on 26 May 1830. Most of his childhood was spent in Downpatrick, where his family had moved after opening a shop. He was educated in the classics by two local clergymen and then in November 1845 he entered the old college in Belfast, with a view to becoming a minister of the non-subscribing body to which his father belonged.

Croskery's religious views soon changed under the influence of some of his student friends, and he determined to enter the ministry of the Presbyterian Church in Ireland. His father's financial difficulties, which forced him to support himself, resulted in his learning shorthand and becoming a newspaper reporter in Belfast. He thus got through the six years of his college course, and on 6 May 1851 was licensed to preach by the presbytery of Down. Shortly after he went to America, where he remained for two years preaching. Returning to Belfast, he resumed his connection with the press, becoming first a reporter and subsequently editor of the Banner of Ulster. He also officiated on Sundays, but used laughingly to tell that he preached in twenty-six vacant churches before he received a 'call'. Eventually he was invited to undertake the charge of the congregation of Creggan, co. Armagh, and on 17 July 1860 was ordained. Croskery was married to Mary Emily Dickson, youngest daughter of Dr Dickson of Belfast, in the same year. They had three sons and two daughters. He was translated to Clonakilty, co. Cork, and installed on 24 March 1863. In 1866 he received a call to the newly formed congregation of Waterside in the city of Londonderry, and was installed there on 20 March in that year. In all three charges he was an active and hard-working minister. In 1875 he was appointed by the general assembly to the professorship of logic and belles-lettres in Magee College, Londonderry, and in 1879, on the death of Richard Smyth (1826–1878), Croskery was transferred at his own request to the chair of theology, an office which he held until his death. In 1883 he received the honorary degree of DD from the Presbyterian Theological Faculty, Ireland. He died in Londonderry on 3 October 1886 and was buried on 5 October in Londonderry cemetery.

Croskery's literary life began early with contributions to newspapers. His first work of importance was *A Catechism on the Doctrines of the Plymouth Brethren*, which ran through several editions. In 1879 he published a larger work of considerable ability, entitled *Plymouth Brethrenism: a Refutation of its Principles and Doctrines*. In 1884 appeared his *Irish Presbyterianism: its History, Character, Influence, and Present Position*. He had charge of the homiletical portion of the Pulpit Commentary on Galatians (1885). But his main strength as an author was given to periodical literature. He was a contributor of articles on varied topics to the *Edinburgh Review*, the *British Quarterly*, *Fraser's Magazine*, the *London Quarterly*, the *British and Foreign Evangelical Review*, and the *Princeton Review*, and of leaders to such Irish newspapers as *The Witness* and the *Northern Whig*. Croskery was a prolific writer and a popular preacher. He was one of the best-known figures of the Presbyterian Church in Ireland.

THOMAS HAMILTON, *rev.* DAVID HUDDLESTON

Sources *Presbyterian Churchman* (1886), 313–20 · C. H. Irwin, *A history of presbyterianism in Dublin and the south and west of Ireland* (1890) · W. T. Latimer, *A history of the Irish Presbyterians*, 2nd edn (1902) · *A history of congregations in the Presbyterian Church in Ireland, 1610–1982*, Presbyterian Church in Ireland (1982)
Archives Presbyterian Historical Society of Ireland, Belfast
Likenesses woodcut, repro. in *Presbyterian Churchman*, 313
Wealth at death £2761 7s. 8d.: probate, 27 Oct 1886, *CGPLA Ire.*

Crosland, (Charles) Anthony Raven (1918–1977), politician and writer, was born on 29 August 1918 at St Leonards, Sussex, the only son and the second of three children of Joseph Beardsell Crosland (1874–1935), under-secretary, War Office, and his wife, Jessie Raven, lecturer in Old French at Westfield College, University of London. He was educated at Highgate School and, as a classical scholar, at Trinity College, Oxford, where he obtained a second class in classical honour moderations in 1939. His university years were interrupted by the Second World War, in which he served from 1940 to 1945. He was commissioned in the Royal Welch Fusiliers in 1941, transferred to the Parachute regiment in 1942, and subsequently served in north Africa, Italy, France, and Austria. His most notable

(**Charles**) **Anthony Raven Crosland (1918–1977)**, by Ron Case, 1965

military exploit was to land by parachute on the casino at Cannes, during operation Anvil in the summer of 1944.

At Oxford Crosland had a notable career, both academically and as an undergraduate politician. He lost interest in classics and turned to philosophy, politics, and economics (primarily economics). After his return to the university he secured a first class in philosophy, politics, and economics in 1946, and was elected a lecturer and later a fellow in economics at Trinity. He held this position from 1947 to 1950, and in 1966 became an honorary fellow. Before the war he was an active and orthodoxly Marxist member of the Labour Club. In the early months of the war, however, he found himself increasingly out of sympathy with its fellow-travelling and neutralist line, and in May 1940 he joined with others to lead the successful breakaway of the Democratic Socialist Club, which was much closer to the national Labour Party position. He was elected treasurer of the Union Society, but was defeated for the presidency. Six years later, however, on his return from the army, he redressed this set-back and secured the higher office.

Crosland was an imposing undergraduate, apparently self-confident, irreverent, and even glamorous, with striking good looks, intellectual assurance, a long camel-hair overcoat, and a rakish red sports car. Later, as a young don, he, with one or two contemporaries, formed something of a cult group, of which the distinguishing characteristic was the unusual combination of hard intellectual endeavour and undisciplined, even riotous, relaxation. Crosland was, and remained, a puritan (his family were Plymouth Brethren), shot through with strains of self-indulgence.

In 1950, at the age of thirty-one, Crosland was first

elected an MP, for the constituency of South Gloucestershire, which he was able to win for the Labour Party and hold for the next five years because it contained a good deal of Bristol suburb as well as south Cotswold countryside. He gave up his Oxford fellowship a few months later, and never returned to professional academic life, although he remained very much an intellectual in politics. In the House of Commons he had a considerable, although not perhaps a remarkable, success. He was an economic specialist, and a close friend and assistant of Hugh Gaitskell, who for most of that period was shadow chancellor of the exchequer. In 1952 Crosland married Hilary Anne Sarson of Newbury, the daughter of Henry Sarson, a member of the vinegar family, but the marriage was short-lived and was finally dissolved in 1957.

Before the 1955 general election the boundaries of South Gloucestershire were redrawn in a way unfavourable to Labour, and Crosland decided to seek another seat. This was a mistaken move, for the one which he found, Southampton, Test, produced a larger Conservative majority than the one he had left. He was not, however, greatly disconcerted by his exclusion from parliament, for, although devoted to politics in a broader sense, he regarded the trappings and life of the House of Commons with some indifference.

Crosland had other things to do. In 1953 he had already published his first book, *Britain's Economic Problem*. This was a lucid but fairly conventional analysis of the country's post-war trading difficulties. By 1955 he was already well into a much more original and substantial work, which he completed in the next year and published in the autumn of 1956. *The Future of Socialism* was well received at the time, but only gradually, over the next decade or so, achieved its position as the most important theoretical treatise to be written from the moderate left of British politics in the first twenty-five post-war years. It assumed the triumph of Keynesianism, and with it a future of broadening abundance and the withering of the Marxist class struggle. It disputed the importance of nationalization and challenged the bureaucratic socialism of the Fabian tradition of Sidney and Beatrice Webb: 'Total abstinence and a good filing system are not now the right sign-posts to the socialist Utopia; or at least, if they are, some of us will fall by the wayside'. It was at once libertarian and strongly egalitarian. It saw no conflict which could not be resolved by the flowing tide of continuing economic growth. It was in the mainstream of the optimism, many would now say the complacency, of the English liberal tradition. It influenced a generation.

Political theory having been disposed of with imagination, even if not total prescience, Crosland showed his practical sense by devoting the next two years to acting as secretary (under Gaitskell's chairmanship) to the independent committee of inquiry into the co-operative movement and writing a good report. Then he re-entered the House of Commons in 1959 as member for Grimsby, the constituency which he represented for the remaining seventeen and a half years of his life. He was quickly involved in all the Labour Party disputes which followed

that lost election, urging Gaitskell on in his desire to modernize the party and dump some out-of-date ideological baggage, supporting him against unilateral disarmament, and sharply disagreeing with him over his reticence towards Macmillan's initiative for British entry to the European Community. Even apart from the European issue, however, he was in no way a client of his leader. He had too strong a personality and too critical a judgement for that. In some ways Gaitskell sought him more than he sought Gaitskell, and he appeared less thrown by Gaitskell's early death in 1963 than were some others in the circle. In the election to the leadership which followed he supported James Callaghan, who ran a bad third, rather than George Brown, who was the candidate of the majority of the 'Gaitskellites'.

In 1964 Crosland married again and also entered government for the first time. His second marriage was to Mrs Susan Barnes Catling, daughter of Mark Watson, of Baltimore, Maryland, who subsequently (sometimes under the name of Susan Barnes) became a prolific writer of skill and perception; unlike the first marriage, it was a great and continuing success and brought Crosland two stepdaughters. His initial government post was minister of state in the newly created Department of Economic Affairs, but after only three months he filled an unexpectedly early cabinet vacancy and became secretary of state for education and science. He was sworn of the privy council in 1965.

The combination of his second marriage and entry into government, some close observers felt, produced a considerable change in Crosland's personality. He had a happier and more rounded life, and became somewhat more benign. He also became more of a party politician, more stirred by ambition, less the uninhibited and fearless commentator. He was a successful departmental minister, a master of various subjects, but occasionally lacking in decisiveness, always believing that a decision had so carefully and logically to be thought through that he sometimes missed the moment at which to make it. His popular impact was also limited, and, surprising though this may seem in retrospect, he was frequently confused in the public mind with Richard Crossman.

Crosland stayed at education for two and a half years. The great departmental issue of the time was the furtherance of comprehensive secondary schools. Michael Stewart, Crosland's Labour predecessor, who had just been promoted to the foreign secretaryship, had given priority to such reorganization. He had accepted a cabinet decision not to legislate on the subject, partly because of the government's minuscule majority and partly because it looked unnecessary, most local authorities being willing to respond to a firm steer. To this end he had prepared a draft circular, which under the famous number of 10/65 Crosland was soon to issue. The main point which the new secretary of state had to decide was whether it should 'require' or 'request' local authorities to go comprehensive. He decided in favour of the latter, softer word, but he was none the less most vehemently in favour of the policy. The policy was not at the time particularly controversial.

Edward Boyle, the previous Conservative education secretary of state, had been broadly in favour of it, and Margaret Thatcher, who became Edward Heath's education secretary in 1970, continued to implement it. No alternative to Crosland in 1965 or successor between 1967 and 1970 could in a Labour government have resisted it. He, however, approached the task with a characteristic extremity of expression. He was, to turn a tag round, to be *fortiter in modo* but not *suaviter in re*. His expletive-rich desire to destroy every grammar school, although authenticated in his wife's sympathetic posthumous biography, should be seen in the context both of his natural liking for not too serious phrases designed to shock and of the conventional wisdom of the time.

Crosland, although with some misgivings, accepted his transfer to the presidency of the Board of Trade in September 1967, hoping that this would lead on to the exchequer. When the vacancy in the chancellorship occurred a few months later and this did not follow, he was deeply disappointed. His relations with Harold Wilson were not close, and in the autumn of 1969 there was some doubt about his survival in the government. But he was too able a man to lose, and for the last few months of that government occupied a co-ordinating role over unmerged departments as secretary of state for local government and regional planning.

There followed nearly four years in opposition. Crosland worked hard as a party spokesman, and published another book, *Socialism Now*, in 1974 (which, like its 1962 predecessor, *The Conservative Enemy*, was a collection of political essays, but more circumscribed in scope by his housing and local government responsibilities), but he surprised and disappointed many of his friends by failing to vote with sixty-eight Labour MPs in favour of Britain's entry to the European Community in the decisive division of October 1971; he did not vote against, but abstained. This probably accounted for his poor result in the deputy leadership election of 1972.

In the 1974 Wilson government Crosland became secretary of state for the environment, essentially the same job but with a different name, tighter control over his subordinate ministers, and a more senior position at the cabinet table than he had occupied in 1969. His experience as an upper-middle-rank departmental minister was unrivalled. The great offices of state continued to elude him. He responded by being increasingly effective in his department and by exercising more authority in the cabinet than in the previous government, while moving consciously away from the right and towards the centre of the party. In March 1976, when Harold Wilson resigned as prime minister, Crosland was determined to contest the succession. He ran fifth of five candidates, securing only seventeen votes. Yet the contest did not damage him. He succeeded to the Foreign Office in the new Callaghan administration with an unimpaired authority, and had he lived might well have been a stronger rival to Michael Foot in 1980 than Denis Healey proved to be.

Crosland was foreign secretary for only ten months. Although he had always tried to think and write in an internationalist context, his experience was insular. He was unacquainted with the intricacies of foreign or defence policy. He was impatient of many of the nuances of the game. He knew foreign sociologists rather than foreign statesmen. Yet, after a hesitant start, he impressed most of his officials and his foreign colleagues by his authority, his wit, and his intellect. His personality, if not his fame, was a match for that of his principal confrère, Henry Kissinger. He was no longer the glamorous *enfant terrible* of his Oxford days, or even the adventurous thinker of *The Future of Socialism*. He was not old, but he had become a little tired in body, heavy and hooded-eyed, yet mordant of phrase, contemptuous of pomposity, and capable of a still dazzling charm.

Crosland was pleased to be foreign secretary, but he still wanted, as ten years before, to be chancellor of the exchequer, and devoted some of his over-taxed and waning energy to preparing for that job, which he was never to hold. This was a last but typical manifestation of the paradox of Anthony Crosland. His intellect was one of the strongest in post-war British politics, and he fortified it by exceptional powers of application. But it was weakened by some uncontrolled demon of discontent, which marred his satisfaction in his own particular roles of excellence. He died at Oxford on 19 February 1977, in office and at the age of fifty-eight, six days after a massive cerebral haemorrhage.   ROY JENKINS

Sources S. Crosland, *Tony Crosland* (1982) • personal knowledge (2004) • *The Times* (21 Feb 1977)
Archives BLPES, corresp. with the editors of the *Economic Journal*; papers | Nuffield Oxf., corresp. with Philip Williams | FILM BFI NFTVA, current affairs footage • BFI NFTVA, party political footage | SOUND BL NSA, current affairs recordings • IWM SA, recorded talk
Likenesses V. Weisz, ink and wash, 1960, NPG • R. Case, photograph, 1965, Hult. Arch. [*see illus.*] • I. Showell, photograph, 1974, Hult. Arch. • photographs, 1974–7, Hult. Arch. • T. McGrath, photograph, 1976, Hult. Arch.
Wealth at death £116,933: probate, 2 May 1977, *CGPLA Eng. & Wales*

Crosland [*née* Toulmin], **Camilla Dufour** (1812–1895), writer, was born on 9 June 1812 at 45 Aldermanbury, London, daughter of William Toulmin (d. 1820), a solicitor, and his wife, *née* Wright (d. 1862), who was related to the author Mary Berry (1763–1852). She had a younger brother, Edward (d. 1845) and a much older half-brother, Henry (d. 1838). She was a precocious child who apparently could read at the age of three. After her father's death in 1820 the family was left in straitened financial circumstances: they moved lodgings several times, and Mrs Toulmin attempted unsuccessfully to start a boarding-house. Camilla Toulmin's education was interrupted by illness and limited by poverty, although she attended a ladies' academy for a time. She began to earn her living by making jewellery, before becoming a daily governess in 1834.

In 1837 some of Camilla Toulmin's verses were accepted by Lady Blessington for inclusion in the *Book of Beauty*; she also published poetry and short stories in *The Keepsake*, *Bentley's Miscellany*, the *Court Magazine*, and *Friendship's Offering*, for which she was sub-editor from 1842 to 1844. She became a friend of the Chambers brothers, whom she visited in Edinburgh in 1845, and contributed to *Chambers's Journal* until her death. Many of the poems which she published in these early years were reprinted in her *Poems* (1846), among them 'On the Completion of the Thames Tunnel'; they show her mediocre talent and taste for topical subjects. Her editors and publishers introduced her to a range of literary and artistic circles: her acquaintances came to include Samuel Carter Hall and his wife, the Brownings (whom she visited in Florence in 1857–8), Douglas Jerrold, Grace Aguilar, Richard Hengist Horne, Mary Mitford, Geraldine Jewsbury, and Margaret Fuller.

By the late 1840s Camilla Toulmin was writing for a variety of annuals and journals, as well as publishing novelettes such as *Partners for Life: a Christmas Story* (1847) and *The Little Berlin Wool Worker* (1844). Despite her modest literary success, she never forgot the 'gnawing anxiety' of these difficult years (N. Crosland, 348): living with her mother in lodgings in New Ormond Street, she rarely made more than £60 a year by her teaching and £50 a year by her pen. Her concern with the economic plight of women was reflected in her topical fiction such as 'The Orphan Milliners' (1844) and 'A Story of the Factory' (1846).

When Camilla Toulmin became engaged in 1848 to Newton Crosland (d. 1899), a London wine merchant, she was unwell and in debt. The marriage took place on 22 July 1848: Crosland had vacillated between Toulmin and Dinah Mulock, later Craik, who was their bridesmaid. The couple lived in London: for fourteen years at 3 Hyde Vale Cottages in Greenwich, before moving in 1863 to Lynton Lodge in Blackheath. In 1885, after Crosland had sold his business, the couple moved to a smaller house, 29 Ondine Road, in East Dulwich, London.

In 1854 Camilla Crosland published *Memorable Women*, a collection of short biographies of famous women including Fanny Burney, Rachel, Lady Russell, and Margaret Fuller: she stressed that her subjects were as eminent for their domestic as their intellectual qualities, which ensured *The Athenaeum*'s praise for the work as one which 'may be placed with safety in the hands of young women' (*The Athenaeum*, 4 March 1854, 278). In 1857 Camilla Crosland published the poorly received *Light in the Valley*, a fervent defence of spiritualism, which she and her husband had been investigating since 1854. Part 1 argued that spiritualism could be reconciled with Christianity, while part 2 dwelt on the experiences of the Croslands themselves and their circle of spiritualist friends, among whom were Sophia De Morgan and the Howitts.

Camilla Crosland continued to publish fiction: *Lydia: a Woman's Book* (1852) presented a critique of contemporary education. *Mrs Blake: a Story of Twenty Years* (1862) contained a thinly veiled account of her early years as an impoverished writer. This novel and *Hubert Freeth's Prosperity* (1873)—the tale of an upwardly mobile family—represent her best fiction: 'well-written, high-toned works' (N. Crosland, 367) as her husband described them, they are intelligent and painstaking examples of the mid-century realist novel. However, Crosland's more considered works did not meet with great acclaim. Steeped in contemporary

sensation novels, *The Athenaeum* critic damned *Hubert Freeth's Prosperity* with faint praise, commenting that it was 'life-like; though the life is for the most part of a humdrum and unromantic colour' (*The Athenaeum*, 25 Oct 1873, 524).

In the last fifteen years of her life Camilla Crosland was in bad health, suffering from asthma, a weak heart, and impaired vision. She translated the dramatic works of Victor Hugo (1887), and in 1893 she published *Landmarks of a Literary Life*, a fascinating memoir of her literary acquaintances. She gave little detail here of her writing career, which was more fully treated in her autobiographical fragments published by Newton Crosland in his *Rambles Round my Life* (1898): together, they provide an unusually full picture of the career and literary milieu of a mid-nineteenth-century female hack writer. She died at 29 Ondine Road on 16 February 1895: as her husband quaintly put it, 'at half past seven she had a cup of tea; and at a quarter to eight she was in Paradise' (N. Crosland, 370). She was buried in Camberwell cemetery, London, and a window was erected in her memory in St Albans Cathedral.

ROSEMARY MITCHELL

Sources Mrs N. Crosland [C. Toulmin], *Landmarks of a literary life, 1820–1892* (1893) · N. Crosland, *Rambles round my life: an autobiography*, 2nd edn (1898) · Blain, Clements & Grundy, *Feminist comp.* · *The Athenaeum* (4 March 1854), 278 · *The Athenaeum* (25 Oct 1873), 524–5 · J. Kestner, *Protest and reform: the British social narrative by women, 1827–1867* (1985) · *DNB*
Archives BL, letters as sponsor to the Royal Literary Fund, loan no. 96 · NL Scot., letters | NL Scot., letters to William Blackwood & Sons · U. Reading L., letters to George Bell & Sons
Likenesses engraving (after miniature by Mrs Petit), repro. in Crosland, *Landmarks* (1893), frontispiece
Wealth at death £177: administration, 14 March 1895, *CGPLA Eng. & Wales*

Crosley, David (1669/70–1744), Particular Baptist minister, was born in Heptonstall, near Hebden Bridge, of unknown parentage. Initially worshipping with the presbyterians, he was brought up by a devout aunt, called Mitchell, in Barnoldswick. He did not readily sever ties with the presbyterians because as late as 1692, even after his baptism as a believer, he was still contemplating ordination among them.

In his youth Crosley worked as a stonemason at Walsden, preaching in the neighbourhood in the evenings. About 1687 he began an itinerant ministry; in 1691 he preached to John Bunyan's congregation in Bedford, and was impressed by the teachings of the great man himself. A sermon on Samson of the same year, preached in a presbyterian meeting-house in Spitalfields, was to his surprise published and brought the preacher some fame. In the following August Crosley was both baptized as a believer and set aside for ministry by the Bromsgrove Baptist Church. The form of ordination was interesting in that the language deployed related not to a settled pastorate but was rather a commissioning 'to preach the gospel and baptize, wheresoever the providence of God shall open a door to his ministry' (Ivimey, 3.362).

Under this commission Crosley returned to the northwest of England where, with his cousin, William Mitchell, he had already begun his evangelistic work as early as 1687 or 1688. By 1696 he had constituted 'the Church of Christ in Rossendale', starting with a chapel erected in Bacup in 1692, which was followed by others in Barnoldswick and Tottlebank, all registered under his or his cousin's name. These congregations, however, only slowly moved to an exclusively Baptist position. During the period 1692 to 1705 Crosley and Mitchell established congregations or house churches not only in Rossendale but in the Calder, Aire, and Wharfe valleys and further into Yorkshire. Crosley was the flamboyant pioneer, known as 'the Evangelist of the Pennines', Mitchell the more careful nurturer and consolidator; while Crosley was itinerating throughout the country Mitchell steadily built up the church in Rossendale.

In 1695 questions were raised about Crosley's ordination as an itinerant evangelist, and the Yorkshire and Lancashire Baptist Association concluded that such roving commissions were not legitimate. After 1705 these associated northern congregations increasingly formed themselves into separate churches, partly because of the large distances separating them, partly as a consequence of Crosley's move to London following Mitchell's death that year, and later because of the impact of news of Crosley's moral failures, which unfortunately proved to be more than an isolated aberration.

Crosley took up the pastorate of the congregation meeting in the Currier's Hall in Cripplegate, once ministered to by Hansard Knollys, in 1705, and is reported to have returned to Tottlebank about 1710. His sexual indiscretions seemed to validate accusations of antinomianism, and churches which he had founded refused him fellowship; he therefore established new churches and for a short while a separate association in Yorkshire.

At the end of Crosley's life true repentance seems to have come about and he established a school near Goodshaw, one of whose graduates was John Butterworth, the noteworthy minister in Coventry, who bears testimony to Crosley's impact as a popular Calvinist preacher. A large man weighing over 20 stone, he preached without difficulty to some 4000 people in the open air when seventy-two years of age. Some of his later devotional works, published in the year of his death in August or September 1744 at Tatop Farm, near Goodshaw, Lancashire, attracted a preface from the pen of George Whitefield.

J. H. Y. Briggs

Sources D. Crosley, introduction, in W. Mitchell, *Jachin and Boaz* (1707) · J. Ivimey, *A history of the English Baptists*, 4 vols. (1811–30), vols. 2–4 · C. E. Shipley, ed., *The Baptists of Yorkshire* (1912) · W. T. Whitley, *The Baptists of north west England* (1913) · I. Sellars, ed., *Our heritage: the Baptists of Yorkshire, Lancashire and Cheshire* (1987) · *DNB* · Blomfield, 'The Baptist churches of C17 and C18', *The Baptists of Yorkshire*, ed. C. E. Shipley (1912)

Archives Man. CL, Mitchell–Crosley corresp.

Cross, Sir Barry Albert (1925–1994), physiologist, was born on 17 March 1925 at West Combe, Windermere Road, Coulsdon, Surrey, the second of the three sons of Hubert Charles Cross, a life assurance cashier, and his wife, Elsie May, *née* Richards. He was educated at Reigate grammar school, and after gaining a London University BSc in veterinary science in 1947 while studying at the Royal Veterinary College in London he moved to St John's College, Cambridge, where he read physiology and in 1949 was awarded a BA (class two, division one) in part two of the natural sciences tripos. On 6 August 1949 he married Audrey Lilian (*b*. 1926/7), a schoolteacher, daughter of Victor Crow, a cost accountant: they had one son and two daughters.

As an ICI research fellow at the physiological laboratory in Cambridge from 1949 to 1951, Cross worked for a PhD under G. W. Harris (1913–1971), who was responsible for establishing the new discipline of neuroendocrinology, the study of the interaction of the nervous system and the hormone-secreting glands. With Harris he studied the neural control of lactation and the suckling reflex of mammals. In 1951 he was appointed a university demonstrator in applied anatomy, and in 1955 became a university lecturer in veterinary anatomy. He spent 1957–8 as a Rockefeller fellow at the University of California at Los Angeles, learning how to record the electrical impulses of single neurones, and went on to establish the relationship between the electrical activity of the brain and the secretions of the pituitary gland.

In 1967 Cross was appointed professor of anatomy at the University of Bristol, where he was responsible for both veterinary and human anatomy, and he built up a strong neuroendocrinological research team before going back to Cambridge in 1974 as director of the Agricultural Research Council's (from 1983 the Agricultural and Food Research Council) Institute of Animal Physiology at Babraham (usually known as the Babraham Institute). At Babraham, which had been set up for fundamental research on animals as a basis for the medical, veterinary, and agricultural sciences, Cross developed neuroendocrinological research, and expanded the institute, which won an international reputation for its work on animal physiology. While there he became the focus of personal attacks from animal rights campaigners who were protesting about experiments on animals; this was despite the report of the Commons select committee on agricultural research, which commended the high quality of animal care at Babraham, and despite his own commitment to animal welfare. He helped to influence the drawing up of the Animals (Scientific Procedures) Act of 1986, which replaced the Cruelty to Animals Act (1876). After the reorganization of the Agricultural and Food Research Council institutes in 1986 Cross was appointed head of the new Institute of Animal Physiology and Genetics Research, with establishments at Babraham and Edinburgh, and he helped to incorporate the council's unit of reproductive physiology and biochemistry into the institute in 1989. He retired in 1989.

Throughout his career Cross enjoyed teaching undergraduates: he was supervisor in physiology at St John's College, Cambridge, from 1955 to 1967, and fellow of Corpus Christi College from 1962 to 1967 and from 1974 to 1987. He was also tutor for advanced students at Corpus from 1964 to 1967, and on his return from Bristol he was appointed warden of Leckhampton, the college's graduate student community, from 1975 to 1980. He was president of Corpus from 1987 to 1992. In addition to his research, and his university and college commitments, Cross served on many advisory committees, including the research and policy advisory committee and the management board of the Agricultural and Food Research Council, and the university grants committee working party on veterinary education. He was chairman of the Physiological Society from 1974 to 1975, and president of the International Society for Neuroendocrinology from 1976 to 1980.

A member of the council of the Zoological Society of London from 1985, Cross was elected secretary in September 1988. Although it was an honorary position, the secretary was responsible for the day-to-day management of the society at a time when falling attendance at the London Zoo in Regent's Park was causing an annual deficit of £2 million. As the financial crisis deepened the council of the Zoological Society considered various options, and in June 1992 the decision was taken to close London Zoo, in order to save Whipsnade Park and the programme of captive breeding of endangered species, and the society's research at the Institute of Zoology. After considerable public outcry, and a campaign led by the Reform Group formed by several fellows of the Zoological Society, the decision was reversed in September 1992, but following a vote of no confidence in the council and management of the society, Cross, who had supported the closure of the zoo, announced his intention to resign, and stepped down in December 1992. He had been elected a fellow of the Royal Society in 1975, and an honorary fellow of the Royal Agricultural Society in 1987. He was knighted in 1989. He died on 27 April 1994 in Addenbrooke's Hospital, Cambridge.   ANNE PIMLOTT BAKER

Sources R. B. Heap and R. G. Dyer, *Memoirs FRS*, 44 (1998), 93–108 · *The Times* (5 May 1994) · *The Independent* (12–27 May 1994) · *WW* · *Cambridge Historical Register* · b. cert. · m. cert. · d. cert.
Likenesses Godfrey Argent Studio, photograph, 1976, repro. in Heap and Dyer, *Memoirs FRS*, 94
Wealth at death £19,747: probate, 15 July 1994, *CGPLA Eng. & Wales*

Cross, Charles Frederick (1855–1935), industrial chemist, was born on 11 December 1855 at Brentford, Middlesex, the second son of Charles James Cross JP, of Brentford, who was at first a schoolmaster and later a director of T. B. Rowe & Sons, soap makers, of Brentford, and his wife, Ella Mendham. He was educated at King's College, London where he graduated BSc in 1878, and spent some time at Zürich university and polytechnic and Owens College, Manchester. He thus had two outstanding teachers—Georg Lunge in Zürich and H. E. Roscoe in Manchester. Thereafter he devoted his life to the field of cellulose technology. After early work on jute fibre in Barrow in Furness and Kew, in 1885 he set up in business in Lincoln's Inn in partnership with Edward J. *Bevan, his fellow student at Manchester, as analytical and consulting chemists. In 1890 he married Edith Vernon, daughter of Major-General

Charles Roper Stainforth, Madras cavalry. They had two sons and one daughter.

Cross's popular reputation was based upon his discovery in 1892 of viscose, which made possible the manufacture of artificial silk, afterwards called rayon, and was also used in the manufacture of photographic film. His achievement was no less esteemed by chemists. The discovery consisted in treating cellulose with aqueous caustic soda and then with carbon bisulphide, producing a golden yellow viscous liquid. This liquid when projected or spun through fine nozzles into a precipitating bath of sulphuric acid yielded fibres. These, after further treatment to remove the sulphur, left a pure regenerated cellulose. Initially, his interest in the fibre was not as a new textile but as a basis for the fine filaments needed for the newly developed electric lamp. Cross's patent remained a chemical master patent for its full term of years and was extended for a further term in view of its outstanding merit. It was soon worked throughout the world, and over the years 1893–1900 his process was developed through proprietary companies in London, Breslau, and Paris. With C. H. Stearn he founded the Viscose Spinning Syndicate, which developed the spinning of artificial silk. This was later acquired by Courtaulds.

Cross was also a pioneer in the production of transparent viscose films (cellophane), used in huge quantities by the packaging industry. In addition he initiated the production of cellulose acetate, later associated in the public mind with the name Celanese: he took out the first industrial patent for its manufacture in 1894. Although less spectacular than his discovery of viscose, this work was likewise of remarkable influence, in the development of the paper trade.

Cross, who was far ahead of his time in working with a substance so unusual in its chemical behaviour, never ceased to be actively interested in the theoretical as well as the practical chemistry of cellulose. When he began his research its chemical identity was obscure: by the 1920s his work had contributed largely to elucidating the basic features of its structure. He published his researches in book form as well as in contributions to scientific journals. His book *Cellulose* (written in collaboration with Bevan, 1895) is unique, full of imagination and stimulating ideas. He also published four volumes of *Researches on Cellulose* (1901–22), the first three in collaboration with Bevan, the last with Charles Dorée. Although he achieved so much on the technical side, at heart he was a scientist, chiefly interested in the pursuit of pure knowledge.

Cross was elected FRS in 1917, with the unusual citation, 'as the founder of a great industry … based on scientific work' (Royal Society Election Certificate). He was awarded the medal of the Society of Chemical Industry in 1916, the research medal of the Dyers' Company in 1918, and in 1924 the Perkin medal of the Society of Dyers and Colourists, of which he was president (1918–20). Owing to ill health he retired to Hove about eight years before his death. He was fortunate in his artistic temperament and happy in his musical gifts—he was an organist of ability. A man of striking appearance, cultured, and with broad interests, he was widely popular. He died at his home, 4C King's Gardens, Hove, Sussex, on 15 April 1935.

E. F. ARMSTRONG, *rev.* TREVOR I. WILLIAMS

Sources E. F. Armstrong, *Obits. FRS*, 1 (1932–5), 459–64 · *JCS* (1935), 1937 · *Journal of the Society of Chemical Industry* (July 1931), 97 [jubilee number] · *The Times* (16 April 1935) · *The Times* (22 April 1935) · *CGPLA Eng. & Wales* (1935) · *WWW*
Archives Sci. Mus., papers relating to his work with Edward Bevan
Likenesses photograph, repro. in *Obits. FRS*
Wealth at death £22,691 10s. 6d.: probate, 21 June 1935, *CGPLA Eng. & Wales*

Cross, Edward (*bap.* 1774, *d.* 1854), zoo proprietor, was born in London and baptized on 3 February 1774 at St Andrew's, Holborn, the son of Walter Cross and Jane (*née* Callow). Nothing is known of his life until he became proprietor of the Exeter 'Change Menagerie in the Strand, following the death of Stephen Polito in 1814. This menagerie had been in existence since about 1780 on the first floor of a complex of small shops. The animals were mostly big cats and birds, but there were also ungulates and reptiles. Cross established relations with painters such as Edwin Landseer and Jacques-Laurent Agasse, as well as scientific figures such as Joshua Brookes and J. E. Gray (who named *Rhinoceros crossii* after him). George IV patronized him both as a dealer and adviser on his own animals. He also befriended and encouraged the future superintendent of London Zoo, Abraham Dee Bartlett (1812–1897), who was allowed to walk about the beast room and developed his skill in taxidermy by mounting birds which Cross gave him when they died. Even in the late Georgian period, the 'disgusting receptacles' for animals at the Exeter 'Change had been the subject of criticism. This became particularly vocal after the bloody destruction of the bull Asiatic elephant Chunee in March 1826, which took more than an hour and some 180 musket shots by soldiers from Somerset House. Shortly after this Cross attempted to sell his collection and offer his services to the newly formed Zoological Society of London, an offer which was repeated in 1828, but which failed because the society required only certain specimens.

The Exeter 'Change was demolished to widen the Strand and Cross found temporary quarters in the King's Mews (on the site of the National Gallery). Then, in 1831, he held a public meeting at the Horns tavern in Kennington at which the Surrey Literary, Scientific and Zoological Institution was founded. Cross sold his animals to this body for £3500 and became superintendent of the enterprise. The grounds of Walworth Manor House, Kennington, were laid out as a zoological garden and the patronage of Queen Adelaide and the archbishop of Canterbury was granted. In addition to a 3 acre lake, there was a circular glass house, 300 feet in diameter and with 6000 square feet of glass, housing the big cats. In 1832 these gardens were said to be both more suitable and more imposing than those at Regent's Park. The collection increased: an Indian rhinoceros in 1834, an orang-utan in 1835, and three giraffes in July 1836. Other attractions included firework displays,

Edward Cross (*bap.* 1774, *d.* 1854), by Jacques-Laurent Agasse, 1838

flower shows, Promenade Concerts, and balloon ascents. Cross retired in 1844 and died a widower at his home, 45 Newington Place, Kennington, on 26 September 1854, just over a year before the animal collection was auctioned. His wife's name was Mary but nothing more is known of her.

J. C. EDWARDS

Sources Southwark Local Studies Library, London, Surrey Zoological Gardens archives · Theatre Museum archives, 1e Tavistock Street, London · Zoological Society of London archives · *IGI* · 'London and its vicinity', *GM*, 1st ser., 96/1 (1826), 266 · *GM*, 2nd ser., 42 (1854), 534 · R. D. Altick, *The shows of London* (1978) · A. D. Bartlett, *Wild animals in captivity: being an account of the habits, food, management, and treatment of the beasts and birds at the 'Zoo' with reminiscences and anecdotes*, ed. E. Bartlett (1898) · parish register, London, St Andrew's Holborn, 3 Feb 1774 [baptism] · census returns, 1851 · d. cert.
Archives Southwark Local Studies Library, London, Surrey Zoological Gardens material · Theatre Museum, London · Zoological Society of London, archives
Likenesses J.-L. Agasse, group portrait, oils, 1827 (including Cross?), Royal Collection · J.-L. Agasse, oils, 1838; Christies, 9 July 1993, lot 49 [*see illus.*]

Cross, Frank Leslie (1900–1968), Church of England clergyman and patristic scholar, was born on 22 January 1900 at home in the High Street, Honiton, Devon, the eldest of three children of Herbert Francis Cross (1868–1957), a pharmacist, and his wife, Louisa Georgina (1869–1946), daughter of William Joseph Randall. His father sold his pharmacy and retired to Bournemouth in 1911. Cross attended Allhallow's School, Honiton (1908–11), and then Bournemouth School (1911–17), from where he won the domus scholarship for natural science at Balliol College,

Oxford. After war service, he read the honour school of chemistry, in 1920 obtaining honours in part one with crystallography. He then switched to theology, in which he took a first in 1922. Winning the senior Denyer and Johnson prize enabled him to spend two years in Marburg and Freiburg working on a thesis on Husserl. In 1925 he was ordained deacon to the title of tutor and chaplain of Ripon Hall (priest in 1926). In 1927 he was invited to become a priest–librarian at Pusey House. For a time he combined this office with that of chaplain of Ripon Hall, apparently unworried by differences in churchmanship. He was appointed university lecturer in the philosophy of religion in 1934 and from 1935 to 1938 he was also Wilde lecturer in natural and comparative religion. In 1944 he was elected Lady Margaret professor of divinity. To this chair was attached a canonry in Christ Church and a large house. He tried to persuade the principal of Mirfield College to set up a theological college in the house. After the death of his mother, his father and younger sister came to live there, but he continued to provide cheap lodging for pious students.

Cross's first book was *Religion and the Reign of Science* (1930), but his main interest gradually moved from the philosophy of religion to the church fathers. In 1933 he published a study of J. H. Newman; in 1935 (with P. E. More) a collection of extracts from the works of seventeenth-century Anglican divines; and in 1939 a students' edition of Athanasius's *De incarnatione*. On the death of Darwell Stone in 1941 he took over for five years the editorship of the future *Patristic Greek Lexicon* and wrote a life of Stone (1943). He produced an edition, with English translation, of Cyril of Jerusalem's *Lectures on the Christian Sacraments* (1951). He had meanwhile embarked on the book eventually to be published in 1957 as *The Oxford Dictionary of the Christian Church*. This quickly became a standard work of reference. It was formally commissioned by Geoffrey Cumberlege in 1939, but the diaries of Tom Parker (at one time co-editor) suggest that work had begun earlier and that from the start Cross's enthusiasm was the driving force. The final shape was certainly due to his persistence. He wrote many of the entries himself and those he commissioned from others were nearly all reworked by him to give the book uniformity of style. His wide interests and enthusiasms led him to turn from one project to another. The book on Athanasius foreshadowed in his inaugural lecture was never written, and his main contribution to scholarship in the narrower sense lay in articles which drew attention to things which were obvious once they had been pointed out. He had a keen sense of how people behave. Thus he saw how the second recension of Dionysius Exiguus's *Codex canonum* had conflated material from different councils of Carthage and by sorting out the documents in a pioneer article (*Journal of Theological Studies*, new ser., 12, 1961, 227–47) he made sense of the history of the African councils from 393 to 419. Similarly, he recognized the difference in character between literary and liturgical manuscripts, comparing the latter to timetables compiled for practical use, not to preserve an archetype (*Journal of Theological Studies*,

new ser., 16, 1965, 61–7). He had taken the degrees of DPhil in 1930 and DD in 1950 and in 1967 he was elected a fellow of the British Academy.

At the end of the Second World War, Cross was involved in re-establishing contact with German Christians. He went to Germany and invited German academics to Oxford, arranging seminars and lectures. When Patrick McLaughlin suggested to him that a gathering of scholars interested in the period before the division of Christendom into East and West would foster reunion, he readily agreed to convene such a meeting. The first international conference on patristic studies took place in 1951, to be followed by five others in Cross's lifetime. He arranged publication of their proceedings in *Texte und Untersuchungen*, helping many to get their first works in print. A parallel concern to bridge the gap between academic theologians and the parish clergy led to conferences called 'Theology and ministry' which developed into international congresses on New Testament studies held in the years between patristic conferences. Towards the end of his life he arranged conferences for members of religious orders, both active and enclosed.

Intensely shy, Cross was known for his silence. His lectures and sermons were painful. He found social contact difficult, but once the initial barrier was penetrated, his sincerity and goodwill were so apparent that he inspired devotion, and he had a great capacity for persuading people to do things. He was diligent both in work and worship; as a canon he attended every office in the cathedral when he was in Christ Church, and laid on extra services in term time. He was a frequent visitor of religious houses at home and abroad. He was found dead on the morning of 30 December 1968 at the Priory House, Christ Church, Oxford, and his ashes were interred in the cathedral garth.

ELIZABETH A. LIVINGSTONE

Sources T. M. Parker, 'Frank Leslie Cross, 1900–1968', *PBA*, 55 (1969), 369–75 · T. Parker, ed. K. Mcnabb, diary, Pusey Oxf. · 'Life', *The Oxford dictionary of the Christian church*, ed. F. L. Cross, 2nd edn, ed. E. A. Livingstone (1974) [preface] · *CGPLA Eng. & Wales* (1969) · b. cert. · d. cert. · personal knowledge (2004) · private information (2004)

Archives priv. coll., papers concerning the early patristic conferences

Likenesses R. S. Ashworth, photograph, repro. in *Oxford children's encyclopedia* [under 'Academic dress'] · Oxford Mail and Times, photograph, repro. in *PBA*, 368

Wealth at death £94,665: probate, 25 April 1969, *CGPLA Eng. & Wales*

Cross, (Arthur) Geoffrey Neale, Baron Cross of Chelsea (1904–1989), judge, was born in London on 1 December 1904, the elder son and elder child of Arthur George Cross, quantity surveyor, of Hastings, and his wife, Mary Elizabeth Dalton. He was eight years older than his brother, Rupert *Cross, a distinguished academic lawyer. He was a scholar of Westminster School, where his classical learning was firmly grounded. He then won a scholarship to Trinity College, Cambridge. First-class honours in both parts of the classical tripos (1923 and 1925) and the Craven scholarship (1925) followed. He was elected to a fellowship of Trinity, which he held from 1927 to 1931. His book *Epirus*, published in 1932, became a classic. But while he might have aspired to be a successor to Richard Porson or Sir Richard Jebb, he decided in favour of a career at the Chancery bar. He was called to the bar by the Middle Temple in 1930 and started to practise in Lincoln's Inn. His abilities were soon recognized. He built up a large junior practice, especially in the somewhat esoteric field of estate duty, which amply justified him in taking silk in 1949. At that time the Chancery bar was exceptionally strong. His contemporaries and rivals included Charles Russell, Milner Holland, and Andrew Clark, all formidable advocates. Cross's talents were less spectacular or rhetorical, but sometimes the more effective for that reason. Promotion to the Chancery bench was stagnant in the 1950s. There was no compulsory retirement age. Incumbents showed a marked reluctance to accept the limitations of increasing age, and the inevitability of promotion was thus delayed. Ultimately, however, there were retirements and Milner Holland's refusal of the proffered appointment facilitated the promotion of Russell, Cross, and others. Thus the strong Chancery bar of the 1950s became the strong Chancery bench of the 1960s.

Cross's practice had been wide-ranging. He had been leading counsel for the Bank of England before the bank rate leak inquiry in 1956. He was for many years closely involved on behalf of C. S. Gulbenkian and his family in the intricacies of the various agreements concerning the production and distribution of Middle East oil. Those who were involved with him at that time never ceased to admire his gifts for converting the complex into the simple. His advice was widely sought because of his gifts of clarity of thought and expression. From 1960 (the year in which he was knighted) to 1969 he served as a judge of the Chancery Division, always charming and courteous to those appearing before him, quick to see the point and to reach his decisions. By chance, cases involving champagne, sherry, and toffee-apples came before him, and not only brought him unaccustomed publicity, but revealed an enjoyment of life which had hitherto been known only to his family and friends.

Cross bought a house at Aldeburgh in Suffolk. This led him to sit as a deputy chairman of Suffolk quarter sessions and to acquire for him the novel experience of the workings of the criminal law. He was fond of saying that the criticism of Chancery lawyers with their supposed love of technicality was misdirected. The criticism should be directed at criminal lawyers. Promotion to the Court of Appeal came in 1969. After only two years, in 1971 he was promoted to the House of Lords as a lord of appeal in ordinary. But he decided to retire in 1975 upon the completion of his fifteen years' service. His relatively short time in the two appellate tribunals did not enable him to leave his mark as an appellate judge. He and his wife retired to Herefordshire, where they lived happily for the remainder of his life. He served for five years after his retirement as chairman of the appeal committee of the Takeover Panel (1976–81), and occasionally chaired a select committee in the House of Lords. He had become a bencher of the

Middle Temple in 1958, and an honorary fellow of Trinity College, Cambridge, in 1972. In his last years at the bar he was an admirable and sensitive chairman of the bar's charity, the Barristers' Benevolent Association. He was sworn of the privy council in 1969.

Cross had not only his intellectual gifts, but also warmth and charm. He was nearly 6 feet in height and somewhat short-sighted, but his thick lenses did not conceal his smile. He possessed a real humility, and often wondered why so much had come his way when others had been less fortunate. He married in 1952 Joan, widow of Thomas Walton Davies and daughter of Lieutenant-Colonel Theodore Eardley Wilmot, who was killed in France in March 1918. They had one daughter. Cross died in hospital in Hereford on 4 August 1989.   ROSKILL, rev.

Sources *The Independent* (17 Aug 1989) · *The Times* (7 Aug 1989) · *WWW* · personal knowledge (1996) · private information (1996) · *CGPLA Eng. & Wales* (1990)
Wealth at death £110,963: probate, 9 Feb 1990, *CGPLA Eng. & Wales*

Cross, Herbert Shepherd (1847–1916), bleacher and landowner, was born on 1 January 1847, at Mortfield, Halliwell, Bolton, Lancashire, the third surviving son of Thomas Cross (1805–1879), a bleacher, cotton spinner, and banker, of Bolton, and his first wife, Ellen, the daughter of Joseph Mann of Liverpool. He was educated at Worksop and Harrow schools and Exeter College, Oxford, and entered the Inner Temple in 1867; however, illness ended his law studies, and he later joined the family business. On 22 June 1870 he married Lucy Mary, the only child of the Revd Shepherd Birley, of the Birleys of Kirkham, Lancashire; the adoption of the name Shepherd in 1884 was a requirement of his father-in-law's will, and concerned his wife's inheritance. Following Lucy's death, in 1891, he married, on 23 January 1895, Patty Penelope, the daughter of James Hortor, gentleman, of Edinburgh.

The three Cross brothers inherited their father's personal estate of nearly £350,000 and formed a partnership to run the Mortfield bleaching interests. Illness removed Alfred (1849–1886), leaving control to Herbert and, principally, James Percival Cross (1843–1906). The Crosses were known for their paternalism, the development of an extensive area of alcohol-free working-class housing, and the provision of public buildings. The bleaching process, with its heavy demand for water, inevitably meant the family had extensive landed interests. In 1884 Herbert added to the land he owned in Bolton the large Hertfordshire estate of Hamel's Park, Buntingford. Later he owned land at Sheen in Surrey.

Behind Cross's move to Hertfordshire—he also acquired a house in Kensington—lay politics. He served on the Bolton school board (1873–81), became a JP (1874) and a major in the Duke of Lancaster's Own yeomanry, and actively supported the Anglican church's education and temperance movements. The Crosses ranked among Bolton's leading tory families, and in 1884 Cross was nominated for one of the town's seats. He was elected in 1885 and remained in parliament until illness—some said differences with his supporters over Chamberlain's programme—led to his retirement in 1906. He spoke in the house seven times, supported his party in the division lobbies, and whiled away parliamentary tedium by playing chess. He was also a member of the Carlton and Junior Carlton clubs. He was reputedly a good constituency member and he did not neglect his base; the Crosses' strength as employers and landlords, particularly in the Victory and Chorley Old Road districts of Bolton, where street names reflected his influence, was combined with generous gifts to the town. Cross's wife, Lucy, was a founder of the Adult Deaf and Dumb Society, and in 1885 she was influential in establishing the Bolton Habitation of the Primrose League. His second wife was also active in the league.

Cross, described at the time of his first marriage as a 'gentleman', and at his death as a 'landowner and JP', illustrates the attraction of rural society to industrialists of the period. At Hamel's Park—purchased from Charles Frederic Villiers MP—he brought up two families, enjoyed farming, fishing, and shooting, and entered into country life. He took an interest in agriculture and the management of his home farm, was a member of Hertfordshire county council, chairman of the Buntingford magistrates' bench, the Braughing council school, and the parish council, and president of the Braughing, Standen, and Puckeridge Nursing Association. On one occasion he arranged for more than a thousand of his Bolton constituents to attend an immense picnic at his Hertfordshire home.

Politics did not end Cross's business career. His participation as chairman in two small mining ventures, on the Gold Coast (1896–1902) and in British Columbia (1898–1901), suggests other interests. However, he was best known as a bleacher. In 1900 Thomas Cross & Co. was the third largest of the fifty-three concerns which merged to form Bleachers Association Ltd, one of Britain's largest industrial companies. A family account credits Cross with the association's inception. To the trade's members the new combine offered reduced competition, less risk, and the opportunity to convert some of their assets. Cross became the first chairman. He was resented for interfering in matters which were the concern of the general managers and, following reorganization in 1904 and 1906, became a nominal chairman, a post he retained until his death.

Cross died from cancer at Hamel's Park on 9 January 1916, and was buried at Braughing parish church on 13 January. In a complex will he settled his estate on his wife, the two sons and a daughter of his first marriage, and the son and two daughters of the second.　　　　J. J. MASON

Sources J. J. Mason, 'Cross, Herbert Shepherd', *DBB* · E. F. Audland, 'Shepherd-Cross pedigree', 1975, Bolton Reference Library · A. J. Sykes, *Concerning the bleaching industry* (1925) · 'Pillars-of-Bolton: Mr H. Shepherd-Cross, MP', *Bolton Review* (1897) · *Bolton Chronicle* (1 Nov 1879) · *Bolton Chronicle* (24 April 1886) · *Bolton Chronicle* (30 May 1891) · *Bolton Chronicle* (10 Feb 1906) · *Bolton Chronicle* (15 Jan 1916) · Foster, *Alum. Oxon.* · H. W. Macrosty, *The trust movement in British industry* (1907) · P. Joyce, *Work, society and politics* (1980) · d. cert.

Archives Quarry Bank Mill, Styal, Whitecroft collection
Likenesses photograph, repro. in *Bolton Chronicle* (15 Jan 1916) · portrait, repro. in 'Pillars-of-Bolton'
Wealth at death £336,000: probate, 12 April 1916, *CGPLA Eng. & Wales*

Cross, Joan Annie (1900–1993), opera singer and teacher, was born in London on 7 September 1900, and was adopted by an aunt and uncle. She was educated from 1913 at St Paul's Girls' School (where Gustav Holst was among her music teachers, and where she played in the first performance of Holst's *St Paul's Suite*) and Trinity College of Music, where, after studying the violin, she was taught singing by Dawson Freer, whose ability to establish firm vocal foundations she continued to praise to the end of her life. In 1923 she joined the chorus of Lilian Baylis's Old Vic, and by 1924 had graduated to principal status with, where Miss Baylis was concerned, a not untypically haphazard selection of leading roles, including Cherubino, Second Lady in *The Magic Flute*, Elisabeth in *Tannhäuser* (later alternating with Venus), Lola in *Cavalleria Rusticana*, both Mercedes and Frasquita in *Carmen*, and Alisa in *Lucia di Lammermoor*. The title role in *Aida* (alternating with the Priestess) preceded her biggest success to date in the role of Elsa in *Lohengrin* (1928), learned as an emergency replacement in the space of ten days. Evidence of her ability to soar above the chorus in the finale of *Lohengrin*'s act I and, in the act II scene with Ortrud, to project tone as well as conveying the ecstatic side of Elsa's character, was captured in recordings made at a performance in October 1933 and published in a retrospective album entitled *The Old Vic and Sadler's Wells*. 'Does the Wells public know its luck in having so rare a soprano?' wrote Richard Capell in the *Daily Telegraph* that year.

By the end of the 1920s Cross had added what became the basis of her repertory as a leading lyric soprano: Pamina, Donna Elvira, Mimi, Desdemona, Tatyana, Marguerite, Micaela, and Violetta, the last named after a full year of study. Capell wrote:

> Verdi's *Traviata* was given last night at the Old Vic … with such a singer in the title role as must have amazed any casual visitor … who might happen not to be aware that the Old Vic has the luck to claim the services of one of the best lyric sopranos of the day.

In 1930 came Leonora in *La forza del destino*, of which role Francis Toye wrote in the *Morning Post*: 'Joan Cross, at her best, reached heights of vocal beauty and expressiveness that entitle her to rank among some of the best exponents of the art.' According to her erstwhile colleague Clive Carey (writing twenty-three years later in the magazine *Opera*), in this role she 'matured from a promising singer to an operatic artist of first-rate potentialities'.

The opportunity to realize those potentials came after the opening in 1931 of the Sadler's Wells Theatre, where the Old Vic's chief conductor, Charles Corri, was soon succeeded by Lawrance Collingwood, whose standards were high and who would influence much of the remainder of Joan Cross's life. Butterfly, Dido, and Antonia and Giulietta in a new production of *The Tales of Hoffmann* soon followed, and in September 1931, after singing Pamina at a matinée at Sadler's Wells, she made an impromptu début at Covent Garden as Mimi. *The Times* wrote:

> She showed herself a credible Mimi, sympathetic but not too pathetic, who maintained in the bigger theatre the purity of line and subtle inflexions of tone which she employs on the smaller stage of the Old Vic and Sadler's Wells.

Her pre-war activities at Covent Garden were to be sporadic: Mimi, Elsa, Micaela (with Conchita Supervia as Carmen), and a single Desdemona opposite Lauritz Melchior in 1934 ('Better forgotten', she later said; 'We met for the first time on stage when I addressed him as "Mio superbo guerrier"!'). At Sadler's Wells she created Arthur Benjamin's *The Devil Take her!* (under Beecham) and sang Collingwood's *Macbeth*, missing the première because of illness; figured in revivals of Stanford's *Travelling Companion* and Vaughan Williams's *Hugh the Drover*; sang in the first British performances of Rimsky-Korsakov's *Snow Maiden* and *Tsar Saltan*; and added to her repertory Marěnka in *The Bartered Bride*, Amelia in *A Masked Ball*, Donna Anna, Fiordiligi, and Rosalinda, and, less probably, Gilda and Nanetta. In the seasons immediately preceding the war she registered what were to date possibly her two greatest successes, whose nature suggested a future which was never realized. In December 1937, only days after the sudden death of Lilian Baylis, came the first performance of *The Valkyrie*, in which Joan Cross sang Sieglinde to great critical acclaim, and in March 1939 there followed *Der Rosenkavalier* with her as the Marschallin. 'This and Sieglinde were her finest and most mature achievements', Clive Carey later wrote; and these roles pointed the direction for an international career which surely beckoned but which the advent of war in 1939 effectively prevented.

Sadler's Wells was bombed during the blitz on London, and autumn 1940 saw a skeleton company embarking on a programme of touring, at first with productions so small that they could be fitted into a lorry, and in towns often hit by bombing, but later, as civilian life stabilized, of a more ambitious nature. Joan Cross was seen as the obvious successor to Lilian Baylis, and soon after the start of wartime touring, Tyrone Guthrie, director of the Old Vic and Sadler's Wells, appointed her manager of the opera company. Seasons alternated between the New Theatre in London's St Martin's Lane and provincial theatres all over the country (in sixty-nine different towns in five years), and by 1943 the company had grown sufficiently to undertake a highly successful revival of *The Bartered Bride*, followed by *Così fan tutte* with Joan Cross as Fiordiligi. Her management was skilled enough to ensure that the company emerged from the war years in a solvent condition, something of a triumph for a manager singing roles in *Dido and Aeneas* and *The Beggar's Opera*, as well as giving regular performances of Butterfly, Violetta, the Countess, and Mimi.

The post-war years brought disappointments as well as triumphs for Joan Cross, and Sadler's Wells Theatre reopened with a mixture of the two. The première of Benjamin Britten's *Peter Grimes* in June 1945 had Peter Pears in the title role and Joan Cross in the female lead of Ellen Orford, a role conceived by the composer specially for her.

He drew on the compassion of a mature Violetta, harnessed the fire of Sieglinde, and reinvented the grand statement of the Marschallin in one great role to form the apogee of her career and the herald of the start of its last phase. Her choice, as manager, of *Peter Grimes* can with hindsight be perceived not only as the beginning of a new era for British opera but also as a triumph for the Sadler's Wells ensemble itself, but in fact it disrupted the company, who felt the choice as baffling as the music. Within a year Peter Pears, Reginald Goodall (who conducted the new opera), Eric Crozier (who directed it), Anna Pollak, and Joan Cross herself had left the company. She was henceforth to sing on stage very little opera apart from new works by Benjamin Britten, all tailored to her particular talents.

Glyndebourne, where Cross had rather surprisingly never sung before the war, was the scene of Britten's next two operas, *The Rape of Lucretia* (1946) and *Albert Herring* (1947), and the formation by Britten of the English Opera Group, which Cross joined. She sang respectively the Female Chorus and Lady Billows, the former a compassionate commentator on the brutal events of the story, the latter a comic representation of one side of her own character, a *grande dame* of considerable splendour and panache. In 1947 she produced for the newly formed Covent Garden Opera *Der Rosenkavalier* (but was sadly not asked to sing even a handful of performances of the Marschallin, her favourite role, which she had sung only seven times), and the same year sang Ellen Orford in a new production of *Peter Grimes*, a role which she had sung in Zürich in 1946 and was to repeat at Covent Garden in two more seasons. A late climax to her career came with Britten's coronation opera, *Gloriana* (1953), whose première in front of the young Queen Elizabeth was not without controversy, but whose title role, like that of Ellen Orford in *Peter Grimes*, was composed with Joan Cross's qualities very much in mind. It was written in an easy soprano tessitura, but its demands on a singer's expressive resources ran the gamut from the domineering monarch in public to the sensitivity of a woman of experience in the scenes with Essex, taking in the humility of a ruler praying for guidance, the serenity of a queen confident in her subjects' affections, and the agony of a woman confronting a decision which will eliminate danger but with it her last emotional prop. These demands she met, fortified perhaps for the extensive dialogue of the last scene by her Mary Stuart a few years earlier in Tyrone Guthrie's radio production of Schiller's play.

In 1954 Cross sang the last of her five Britten premières when she was Mrs Grose in *The Turn of the Screw*, an important role but secondary none the less. She took the hint and the following year bade farewell to the stage, initially with the Countess in *The Marriage of Figaro* at Covent Garden, a late backward glance at past Mozartian glories. 'Joan Cross's Countess … is a wonderful example of a character created *through* the music', wrote Andrew Porter in *Opera* magazine in July 1955;

> One cannot pretend that she sang her first aria well but thereafter schooling told; in many an ensemble passage, and

particularly in 'Dove sono', the voice was beautifully placed, the tone often lovely. By handling Mozart's phrases as if they were precious objects, beautifully arranged, which the audience was to share in enjoying, she went to the heart of the music and the drama.

After her last Mrs Grose at London's Scala Theatre in September 1955, Desmond Shawe-Taylor wrote regretfully in *Opera* (November 1955): 'the long narrative in the first act, in some ways the core of the whole work, was handled with such skill and subtlety, she was moreover in such fine voice.'

Cross continued to work in the service of opera, but now as director, more often abroad (in the Netherlands, Scandinavia, and Canada) than in England, and as principal of the new Opera Studio, which she and Anne Wood had founded in 1948. About her work as a teacher, to which a large number of successful singers paid tribute, she said:

> I like to suggest ... I've no patience or time unless there's talent ... I do love talent! You can't teach people how to act; it must be in them. You can teach only the mechanics—how to move, how to stand still.

Her time with the Opera Studio and its successor ended when she and Anne Wood resigned in 1964 after a dispute with the board, which may have accounted for her appointment as CBE in 1951 never being followed up by the damehood which much of the operatic world, though never that nebulous entity known as the establishment, believed she deserved.

Joan Cross was a singer noted for subtle inflection of music and text rather than bold vocal assault, and for purity of singing line more than overwhelming vocal plenitude, and as an actress, for constant care for the development of character, in the manner of a stage play, rather than reliance on sheer physique, in the manner of film. She placed great emphasis as both performer and teacher on operatic craft, the matching of music and words, voice and movement, and, as well as a singer of real importance, she became an actress of consummate skill, in comedy as well as tragedy. Her place in English operatic history is substantiated not only by records—although she was not a natural denizen of the studio—but by more than a dozen premières and British first performances in a career lasting over forty years. She remained a formidable though much loved presence into her nineties, an involved observer of the operatic scene, and a keen, though usually constructive, critic. She died at her home, Garrett House, Park Road, Aldeburgh, Suffolk, on 12 December 1993, following a stroke, and was buried in Aldeburgh on 17 December. As a young woman she had married James Armstrong, but the marriage did not last long and she seldom referred to it. She had no children.

HAREWOOD

Sources unpublished autobiography, Britten–Pears Library, The Red House, Aldeburgh, Suffolk · S. Sadie, ed., *The new Grove dictionary of opera*, 4 vols. (1992) · R. Capell, *Daily Telegraph*, various articles · F. Toye, *Morning Post, passim* · *The Times, passim* · C. Hardy, *Opera*, 1 (1950) · C. Carey, 'Sadler's Wells', *Opera*, 4 (1953) · A. Porter, 'The marriage of Figaro', *Opera*, 6 (1955) · D. Shawe-Taylor, 'The turn of the screw', *Opera*, 6 (1955) · *The Independent* (14 Dec 1993) · *The Times* (15 Dec 1993) · WWW, 1991–5 · personal knowledge (2004) · private information (2004) · d. cert.

Archives BL NSA, current affairs recording · BL NSA, documentary recording · BL NSA, performance recording · Britten–Pears Library, The Red House, Aldeburgh, Suffolk | SOUND BL NSA, interview, B7469/01

Likenesses photographs, 1935–47, Hult. Arch. · photograph, repro. in *The Independent* · photograph, repro. in *The Times*

Wealth at death under £125,000: probate, 2 Feb 1994, CGPLA Eng. & Wales

Cross, Sir John (1766?–1842), judge, was the second son of William Cross of Scarborough (or perhaps Manchester). He matriculated from Trinity College, Cambridge, in 1789 and in August 1790 joined Lincoln's Inn, where he was called to the bar on 16 November 1795. He was appointed a serjeant-at-law in 1819, and had a considerable practice in the court of common pleas. In 1827 he petitioned that his name be taken off the books of Lincoln's Inn. The same year he was appointed a king's serjeant and attorney-general of the duchy of Lancaster. On 2 December 1831 he was appointed a judge of the court of bankruptcy, and was knighted. Subsequently he became chief judge. He returned home from his court at Westminster on 5 November 1842, and suddenly died. On his death the separate court of bankruptcy was abolished, and its jurisdiction transferred to the court of chancery, vice-chancellor Sir James Knight-Bruce becoming chief judge.

J. A. HAMILTON, *rev.* HUGH MOONEY

Sources *Annual Register* (1842) · *Jurist*, 6/2 (1842), 466 · Venn, *Alum. Cant.* · W. P. Baildon, ed., *The records of the Honorable Society of Lincoln's Inn: the black books*, 4 (1902)

Cross, John (1819–1861), historical genre painter, was born at Tiverton, Devon, in May 1819. His father, foreman in Heathcoat's lace manufactory, moved the family to France when he became superintendent of a branch manufactory at St Quentin in Picardy. He hoped that his son would develop mechanical skills; but his wife, who had a maternal sympathy for their son's artistic bent, arranged for him to attend the drawing-school founded by the pastellist Maurice Quentin de La Tour. Having done well, Cross proceeded to Paris and entered the atelier of François-Edouard Picot, a history painter and former pupil of Jacques-Louis David. Among his compatriots in Paris was Ford Madox Brown, who became one of his friends.

Cross returned to England in 1843 and sent to the Fine Arts Commission's second competition (1844) a cartoon, *The Death of Thomas à Becket*, which attracted little notice. In the final competition (1847) he fared much better: his *Richard Coeur de Lion Forgiving Bertrand de Gourdon*, one of 120 oil paintings exhibited in Westminster Hall, London, won one of the three second-class premiums of £300; it was purchased for £500 by the commission and engraved at its expense. From this high point in his career, Cross declined into ill health, aggravated by anxiety over the low estate of history painting and his own future. During the 1850s, however, he had five historical works on exhibition at the Royal Academy. These included *The Burial of the Young Princes in the Tower* (exh. 1850), which was engraved for the Art Union and reproduced in the *Illustrated London News*, and *The Assassination of Thomas à Becket* (exh. 1853), noticed in the *Art Journal* as Cross's best picture since *Richard Coeur de*

Lion. Yet all five works remained unsold, and in 1860 his two offerings to the Royal Academy were rejected. Disappointed and far from well, he tried teaching.

Not yet forty-two years of age, Cross died on 27 February 1861 at his home, 38 Gloucester Road, Regent's Park, London, after a long illness. A small civil-list pension was granted to his widow, Mary (originally from Botham, near Tiverton, Devon), in consideration of his merits as a painter. Several fellow artists raised a fund to help the needy family; they arranged an exhibition at the Society of Arts and purchased some of the remaining pictures. *The Assassination of Thomas à Becket* was placed in Canterbury Cathedral; *The Burial of the Young Princes* was presented to the Albert Memorial Museum in Exeter, to honour Cross as a Devonian.   DAVID ROBERTSON

John Kynaston Cross (1832–1887), by unknown engraver, pubd 1874

Sources Redgrave, *Artists* · *DNB* · D. Robertson, *Sir Charles Eastlake and the Victorian art world* (1978) · F. M. Hueffer [F. M. Ford], *Ford Madox Brown: a record of his life and work* (1896), 28, 38, 72, 125 · *Art Journal*, 15 (1853), 150 · T. S. R. Boase, *English art, 1800–1870* (1959), 279 · Bénézit, *Dict.*, 3rd edn · *CGPLA Eng. & Wales* (1861) · *ILN* (10 March 1861) · *The Builder*, 19 (1861), 181
Wealth at death £300: probate, 31 July 1861, *CGPLA Eng. & Wales*

Cross, John Kynaston (1832–1887), industrialist and politician, was born on 13 October 1832 in Bolton, the eldest son of John Cross, cotton manufacturer, and his wife, Hannah, daughter of Richard Kynaston, another Bolton mill owner. He was educated privately, and on 3 June 1858 married Emily Jane (*b.* 1837/8), daughter of James Carlton, a merchant, of Manchester. They had three sons and three daughters.

The family business was one of the main employers in Bolton, and Cross was secretary of the masters' association during the bitter trade dispute of 1861. He later became a town councillor and a JP for both the borough and the county. He was an Anglican and a moderate Liberal and at the 1874 general election stood, reluctantly but successfully, for Bolton and survived a subsequent petition against his return. Cross was not politically ambitious and spoke only eight times during his first five years in parliament, but he gradually established a reputation as an expert in commercial and Indian affairs. During an Indian finance debate on 12 June 1879 Cross's speech, bracketed by *The Times* with those of Gladstone and Goschen, showed an impressive mastery of the complex subject (India was a 'silver standard' economy at a time when there was a widespread movement towards gold). Cross believed that lower import duties would help the Indian poor as well as the Lancashire cotton industry, and he was scathing about the rising burden of military and administrative costs. He reaffirmed his belief in free trade on 12 April 1881, in a speech on the renegotiation of the French trade treaty, which was later reprinted as a Cobden Club pamphlet.

In January 1883 Gladstone persuaded Cross with some difficulty to become under-secretary for India, serving under Lord Kimberley. Unlike the previous secretary of state, Lord Hartington, Kimberley was in the House of Lords, and Cross had to cope in the Commons with a flow of detailed and sometimes hostile questions (over 400 during the three parliamentary sessions 1883–5) which involved him in regular exchanges, by telegraph and letter, with the viceroy, Lord Ripon. In December 1884 Cross declined an offer of promotion to the Treasury on health grounds, and by the time the government left office in June 1885 he was exhausted. When he lost his seat at the general election in November he was ready to abandon politics. Heavily bearded and distinctively bald and suffering from diabetes and nervous depression, Cross seemed older than his fifty-three years. After an extended continental holiday his health seemed better, but on the morning of 20 March 1887 he was found hanged in his bedroom at Fernclough, Heaton, near Bolton. The inquest jury returned a verdict of suicide while temporarily insane. At the funeral on 24 March the cortège was over a mile long and ten thousand people crowded into Deane churchyard.   PATRICK JACKSON

Sources *The Times* (31 June 1879) · *The Times* (21 March 1887) · *The Times* (23 March 1887) · *The Times* (25 March 1887) · *Bolton Weekly Journal and District News* (26 March 1887) · *Bolton Guardian* (19 Jan 1878) · Hansard 3 (1874–85) · Boase, *Mod. Eng. biog.* · m. cert.
Archives BL, corresp. with W. E. Gladstone and others · BL, Ripon MSS
Likenesses engraving, pubd 1874, NPG [*see illus.*] · E. Papworth, bust, 1895, Bolton town hall · portrait, repro. in *Bolton Guardian* · portrait, repro. in *Bolton Journal and District News* (7 Nov 1885)
Wealth at death £156,462 3*s.* 3*d.*: resworn probate, March 1888, *CGPLA Eng. & Wales* (1887)

Cross, Kenneth Mervyn Baskerville (1890–1968), architect, was born at 71 Parliament Hill Road, Hampstead, London, on 8 December 1890, the eldest son of Alfred William Stephen Cross (1858–1932), architect, and his wife, Emily Thursfield. A. W. S. Cross was himself the son of an architect, Alfred Cross, of Greenwich, and practised in Hastings, Weston-super-Mare, and London. He specialized in the design of swimming baths, public libraries, and schools, including baths in Dulwich, Hoxton, and Hampstead. In 1906 he restored Shoreditch town hall following a fire.

Kenneth Cross was educated at Felsted School (1902–9), where he captained the cricket eleven. He then went up to Gonville and Caius College, Cambridge. He obtained a third class in both parts of the historical tripos (1911 and

1912) and proceeded MA in 1921. He studied at the university school of architecture, in the founding of which his father had played an important part. He completed his professional training in articles to his father, setting up in private practice in 1919, and becoming his father's partner in 1922. In a wide-ranging general practice he acted as architect for a number of local authorities including Westminster city council, Newcastle upon Tyne council, and Bournemouth council. He also carried out commissions for the Barbers' Company and for the Grocers' Company, the London Hospital, St John's College, Cambridge, and Barclays Bank.

By the late 1930s Cross had, like his father before him, earned a reputation as a specialist in the design and construction of swimming baths, and, with his father, had written a book on the subject: *Modern Public Baths and Wash-Houses* (1930), of which a new edition appeared in 1938. He had previously revised his father's *Practical Notes for Architectural Draughtsmen* (2nd and 3rd series, 1922, 1923), a useful guide for students, in whom he was always interested. In architecture he was a solid traditionalist with a good appreciation of modern structural techniques. Cross was best-known for his devoted work for the Royal Institute of British Architects (RIBA), of which he became a fellow in 1931 and was president from 1956 to 1958, having previously served as honorary secretary (1952–5) and as vice-president (1955–6). He was chairman of the board of architectural education from 1950 to 1952, chairman of the competitions' committee from 1937 to 1949, and served on a number of the royal institute's other committees. He was chairman of the committee on the constitution of the council, and also of the committee on the architects registration acts.

Kenneth Cross was a quiet, soft-spoken, and unassuming man of friendly aspect. In private life he was interested in English literature, gardening, and walking. He seemed to come from a generation older than himself, and, although somewhat diffident in conversation, below the surface his standards were high and his opinions firmly based. He became president of the RIBA at a time when the senior members, who had seen the royal institute through the Second World War, attempted to re-establish it as it had been, predominantly a learned society, inward-looking and comfortably unaware of the changes taking place in architecture and the building industry. They were, above all, unaware of, or perhaps just not interested in, the aspirations of the generation of architects trained after the war, which felt that the older generation was essentially out of date and that the profession needed total reorganization within an efficient and aggressive institute. It fell to Cross as honorary secretary to attend, and afterwards as president to preside over, meetings at which these views were forcefully made known. The annual general meeting of the RIBA changed during Cross's time from a peaceful, badly attended, and unquestioning affair to a crowded battlefield where officers of the institute were attacked and received little support from the floor. Few regretted the passing of the old

order and the introduction of important electoral, educational, and administrative reforms which followed. The importance of Kenneth Cross's part in these reforms should not be underestimated. His manner in the chair was impeccable. He was urbane but firm, tolerant, even-tempered, and procedurally correct. He could be witty but sometimes there was a glint of steel in his remarks. He retained control at all times, and his wisdom ensured the introduction of constructive change. Whatever his personal feelings were, he met the storms graciously and with understanding. During his presidency and largely on his own initiative, he made a world tour of the royal institute's allied societies which much improved relations between the RIBA and its overseas members.

Cross was an honorary DCL of Durham University, an honorary fellow of the Royal Architectural Institute of Canada, the American Institute of Architects, and the New Zealand Institute of Architects, and a life fellow of the Royal Australian Institute of Architects. He died at Chelmsford Hospital on 16 January 1968. He was unmarried.   GONTRAN GOULDEN, rev. KAYE BAGSHAW

Sources *The Times* (18 Jan 1968) · J. Venn, ed., *Biographical history of Gonville and Caius College*, 4 vols. (1897–1912) · *Building*, 214 (26 Jan 1968), 98 · *RIBA Journal*, 75 (1968), 102 · personal knowledge (1981) · private information (1981) · *The Builder* (6 Jan 1933) · *CGPLA Eng. & Wales* (1968)
Archives RIBA BAL · RIBA nomination papers
Likenesses A. R. M. Todd, oils?, 1958, RIBA · photograph, RIBA
Wealth at death £89,218: probate, 4 March 1968, *CGPLA Eng. & Wales*

Cross, Letitia (*bap.* 1682?, *d.* 1737), singer and actress, was, according to a statement in 1712, the daughter of Ann Cross; she may have been the daughter of Leonard and Ann Cross baptized on 6 March 1682 at St Martin's, Dorking, Surrey. A prologue which she spoke in spring 1696 included the words 'Look to't, ye Beaus, my Fifteen is a coming' (Danchin, *Restoration*, 3.289), which would place her birth in 1681 or 1682. She described herself as 'having from her Childhood been educated in the theatre' (Milhous and Hume, 'Theatrical politics', 428), and by 1694 she was a member of London's only theatre company. In spring 1695, when Thomas Betterton and other star players seceded, she remained with the Drury Lane / Dorset Garden company and was a leading performer of the music which Henry Purcell wrote in the last few months of his life. She sang new songs by him in *The Indian Queen*, by Robert Howard and John Dryden, *The Mock Marriage*, by Thomas Scott, *The Rival Sisters* by Robert Gould, and John Dryden's version of *The Tempest*, where she played Dorinda and sang 'Dear pretty youth'. As the doomed young Bonvica in an anonymous adaptation of Fletcher's *Bonduca* she sang 'O lead me to some peaceful gloom', as Altisidora in Thomas D'Urfey's *Don Quixote Part 3* she performed Purcell's great mad song 'From rosy bowers', and in Thomas Southerne's *Oroonoko* she sang a *faux-naïf* dialogue with the boy Jemmy Bowen. The theatre exploited her youth and charm in teasing prologues and epilogues, and she became an accomplished comic actress. In *The Female Wits*, an anonymous theatrical satire performed in

1696, Mrs Cross appeared as herself. She was called 'pretty Miss' and 'a little inconsiderable Creature', sang, danced, and threatened (aside) to kick an admiring fop 'i'th' Chops'. In November 1696 she created Miss Hoyden in John Vanbrugh's *The Relapse*. When Peter the Great visited England early in 1698 he went to the theatre and she became his mistress; on his departure he sent her 500 guineas, which she thought insufficient. She gave a concert at York Buildings on 1 June 1698, but by the end of the year had left the stage for 'an Excursion into *France*, with a certain Baronet' (Egerton, 2).

On 2 January 1705 Mrs Cross, 'Famous for Singing and Acting in the last Reign' (*Diverting Post*), returned to Drury Lane to perform 'several Entertainments of Singing and Danceing' (*Daily Courant*, 2 Jan 1705). On 16 January she sang in the first all-sung English opera in the Italian style, Thomas Clayton's *Arsinoe*. On 8 February she appeared as Florimel, the role written for Nell Gwyn in Dryden's *Secret Love*, and in April she created Mrs Clerimont, a lady returned from the continent with French affectations, in Richard Steele's *The Tender Husband*. In *The Tempest* she sang 'her Original Song of Dear Pretty Youth' (*Daily Courant*, 1 Jan 1707), and later new roles included Miranda in the première of Susanna Centlivre's *The Busybody*, on 12 May 1709. On 31 March 1706, at St Benet Paul's Wharf, she married Martin Weir, who died fighting in Flanders soon after. She signed a five-year contract with Owen Swiny in 1709, but a year later Swiny was joined in management by Colley Cibber, Robert Wilks, and Thomas Doggett, and the new managers refused to employ her. The following March they received a letter from seventy-three gentlemen, threatening to wreck Doggett's benefit if she was not reinstated. In a letter to the lord chamberlain she denied instigating this and claimed that she had dissuaded them. *The Spectator* of 6 April 1711 reported that Mrs Cross had visited Holland, where she was not computed as handsome as a Dutch soprano 'by near half a Tun'. In 1712 she took out a lawsuit against Swiny, making a strong case, but he was in debt and fled abroad. Her return to the London stage came only in the 1714–15 season, when a new theatre managed by John Rich opened at Lincoln's Inn Fields. She acted, spoke saucy prologues and epilogues, danced, and sang. Mrs Cross was away from the stage for three seasons (1717–20) and after October 1725 made only a single appearance, as Monimia in Thomas Otway's *The Orphan*, for her benefit on 8 May 1732. She died at her lodgings in Leicester Fields on 4 April 1737, and was buried on 8 April at St James's, Piccadilly. She left mourning rings to a number of friends and the share in the Lincoln's Inn Fields theatre which she had inherited from her mother to her friend and residuary legatee Elizabeth Barker.   OLIVE BALDWIN and THELMA WILSON

Sources W. Van Lennep and others, eds., *The London stage, 1660–1800*, pts 1–2 (1960–65) · *Post Man* (28–31 May 1698) · *Diverting Post* (9–16 Dec 1704) · *Daily Courant* (2 Jan 1705) · *Daily Courant* (1 Jan 1707) · *The Spectator* (6 April 1711) · *Daily Post* [London] (8 May 1732) · J. Milhous and R. D. Hume, eds., *A register of English theatrical documents, 1660–1737*, 2 vols. (1991) · J. Milhous and R. D. Hume, eds., *Vice Chamberlain Coke's theatrical papers, 1706–1715* (1982) · J. Milhous and R. D. Hume, 'Theatrical politics at Drury Lane: new light on Letitia Cross, Jane Rogers and Anne Oldfield', *Bulletin of Research in the Humanities*, 85 (1982), 412–29 · O. Baldwin and T. Wilson, 'Purcell's stage singers: a documentary list', *Performing the music of Henry Purcell* [Oxford 1993], ed. M. Burden (1996), 277 · P. Danchin, ed., *The prologues and epilogues of the Restoration, 1660–1700*, 7 vols. (1981–8), vol. 3 · P. Danchin, ed., *The prologues and epilogues of the eighteenth century: a complete edition* (1990–), vols. 1–2 · *The female wits* (1704) · J. Mottley, *The history of Peter I, emperor of Russia*, 1 (1739) · W. Egerton [E. Curll], *Faithful memoirs of the life, amours and performance of … Anne Oldfield* (1731) · parish register, St Benet Paul's Wharf [marriage] · parish register, St James's, Piccadilly [burial] · will, PRO, PROB 11/683, fol. 43r–v · admin., PRO, PROB 6/113, fol. 58r

Likenesses J. Smith, mezzotint (after T. Hill), BM, Harvard TC · J. Smith, mezzotint (after G. Kneller), BM

Wealth at death share in the Lincoln's Inn Fields Theatre and residue of estate to Elizabeth Barker; also twelve mourning rings to various friends: will, proved 13 May 1737, PRO

Cross [Crosse, Crass], **Michael** [Miguel de la Cruz, Michaell de la Croy, Michaell La Croix] (*fl.* **1633–1660**), painter, is of unknown parentage, place of birth, and training. In 1633 Carducho called him someone 'que anticipa obras a su edad', and said he was employed to copy paintings by Titian in the palace (the Alcázar) at Madrid and at El Escorial for Charles I. In 1633–5 Sir Arthur Hopton's correspondence from Madrid, referred several times to the 'king's painter', payments to whom were Hopton's responsibility, and implied that the artist was not native to that city (Du Gué Trapier). Cross returned to London with Hopton in 1636, being given £110 as a gift by Charles I in August, while Hopton was repaid the sums he had paid to Cross at the end of May. The only reference in van der Doort's inventory of the collections of Charles I is to a Madonna at Whitehall 'coppied at the Schuriall in Spaine after Raphell Urbin by Michaell de la Croy' ('Abraham van der Doort's catalogue', 53). The inventories taken (1649–51) for the sale of Charles I's collection mention six copies by Cross after Titian, but not the Raphael. The soldier and diarist Richard Symonds saw one of these, a *Mary Magdalene*, with an unnamed painter near Aldgate and another, *The Burial of Christ*, with the painter Emanuel de Critz and said Cross was English. Sanderson, however, called him La Croix and said he 'out-went' all as a copyist (Sanderson, 16 and 20). An inventory made for Charles II *c.*1666 includes three other Cross copies of paintings by Titian, a *Venus and the Organist*, an *Adoration of the Magi*, and *The Marquis del Guasto's Family* (known today as the *Allegory of Alfonso d'Avalos*). The *Adoration* also appears in the inventory of James II, as does a *Venus and Adonis* (not previously mentioned), while there are two versions of the *Allegory of Alfonso d'Avalos*. Including a *Last Supper*, *Agony in the Garden*, *St John*, and *Paradise*, all after Titian, which appear only in the sale inventories as by Cross, a copy of the now lost *Annunciation*, formerly at Aranjuez (referred to only by Hopton), and a *Rape of Europa* (mentioned in De Piles but the other information given there appears unreliable), Charles I commissioned from Cross at least eleven copies after works by Titian either in Spain or in his own collection. (A *Paradise* mentioned by van der Doort as doubtfully attributed to Titian is referred to in the sale inventories without attribution.) Various other references to unattributed copies after Titian in the sale inventories could relate to Cross. Wethey (vol. 1) also proposed Cross as the painter of a *Madonna and Child with SS. Dorothy and George* (Royal Collection), an attribution rejected by Shearman in 1983. Of the paintings mentioned above, Shearman proposed Cross as the copyist of *The Allegory of Alfonso d'Avalos* and a *Venus with an Organist* (both Royal Collection), but these attributions remain speculative. In the *Dictionary of National Biography* Lionel Cust noted that: 'it is on record that he made copies of Vandyck's "Charles I on a Dun Horse"', though no further reference to these has been traced, and it should be noted that all other copies by Cross are after Old Master paintings not contemporary works. In 1660 Cross petitioned Charles II for a promise the king made at Caen to renew a pension of £200 per annum granted by Charles I for twenty-eight years' service copying in Spain 'and in Italie in making newe collections' (Sainsbury, 323); he is not otherwise recorded among those active purchasing on the king's behalf. Cross may have trained the copyist Simon Stone.

SUSAN BRACKEN

Sources PRO, E 403/2755, 2756 · inventory of paintings made for Charles I, *c*.1666, Royal Collection, Surveyor's office MSS · inventory of paintings made for James II, 1688, BL, Harley MS 1890 · V. Carducho, *Dialogos de la pintura* (1633) · M. Beal, *A study of Richard Symonds* (1984) · 'Abraham van der Doort's catalogue of the collections of Charles I', ed. O. Millar, *Walpole Society*, 37 (1958–60), esp. 53–4, 206 · O. Millar, ed., 'The inventories and valuations of the king's goods, 1649–1651', *Walpole Society*, 43 (1970–72), 1–432, esp. 186–7, 206, 301 · E. Du Gué Trapier, 'Sir Arthur Hopton and the interchange of paintings between Spain and England in the seventeenth century', *The Connoisseur*, 164 (1967), 239–43; 165 (1967), 60–63 · W. N. Sainsbury, 'Artists patronized by King Charles II', *Fine Arts Quarterly Review*, new ser., 2 (Jan–June 1867), 319–34 · W. Sanderson, *Graphice: the use of the pen and pensil, or, The most excellent art of painting* (1658) · H. E. Wethey, *The paintings of Titian*, 1: *The religious paintings* (1969) · H. E. Wethey, *The paintings of Titian*, 2: *The portraits* (1971) · H. E. Wethey, *The paintings of Titian*, 3: *The mythological and historical paintings* (1975) · J. Shearman, *The early Italian pictures in the collection of her majesty the queen* (1983) · M. K. Talley, *Portrait painting in England: studies in the technical literature before 1700* (1981) · [B. Buckeridge], 'An essay towards an English school of painters', in R. de Piles, *The art of painting, and the lives of the painters* (1706), 398–480 · Vertue, *Note books*, 2.146–7 and 4.96

Cross, Nathaniel (1688/9–1751), musical instrument maker, was one of the earliest violin makers in London whose work survives in sufficient quantity for some assessment to be made. Little is known of his early life, but it appears that he probably learned the essentials of his craft from Richard Meares, who was best-known as a maker of viols. Cross was one of the first to copy the much favoured, highly-arched model of the Tyrolean violin maker Jacob Stainer, and on some of his earlier labels added the word 'Stainero', to make clear to his buyers that the instruments were in the latest fashion. He tended to use plain wood, but the overall quality of his workmanship is good.

About 1715 Cross went into partnership with the outstanding Barak Norman, a maker renowned for his bass viols, violas, and cellos. Cross's work is widely thought to have improved during the ten years or so that this arrangement lasted. Their joint label reads 'Barak Norman and Nathaniel Cross, at the Bass Viol in St Paul's

Churchyard, London, fecit 172-'. Cross's cellos have a good reputation, though they are smaller than is the norm for full-size cellos and tend to be somewhat squat in appearance. Sandys and Forster, in their pioneering critique of old English instruments (1864), describe his varnish as 'of a light yellow colour, the vehicle or body varnish is considered to be made of one of the soft gums, mastic or sandarac dissolved in alcohol, which renders them of easy blemish and disfigurement by any slight scratch', and add that 'the tone is clear and penetrating in quality' (Sandys and Forster, 261).

Cross's labels give evidence of a somewhat itinerant London existence, and thus of economic instability. Some of his instruments were produced with inked, simulated purfling and integral bass bars, short cuts to minimize time and cost. He kept a workshop at 'the Cross near St James' in Piccadilly in 1725, where the fashionable maker Peter Wamsley had his workshop, and then moved to The George inn, Aldersgate Street, about 1731, and to Aldermanbury in 1733. Cross was baptized as an adult at St Peter Cornhill on 12 July 1722, and married Martha Waite on 25 January 1723 at St Mary Magdalen, Old Fish Street. He died in Clerkenwell in 1751 at the age of sixty-two and was buried there.

BRIAN W. HARVEY

Sources J. Dilworth, 'Cross examination', *The Strad*, 98 (1987), 592–5 · W. Sandys and S. A. Forster, *The history of the violin* (1864) · B. W. Harvey, *The violin family and its makers in the British Isles: an illustrated history and directory* (1995) · J. Liivoja-Lorius, 'Cross, Nathaniel', *The new Grove dictionary of musical instruments*, ed. S. Sadie, 1 (1984)

Cross, Nicholas [*name in religion* Nicolaus à Santa Cruce] (1614/15–1698), Franciscan friar, missionary, and writer, was born in Derbyshire. It is not certain that Cross was his family name: as a Recollect he was called Nicolaus à Santa Cruce (Nicholas of the Holy Cross). A contemporary minister provincial, confused with Nicholas, was referred to as John of the Holy Cross; he was also called More, which could have been his mother's maiden name. In 1670 Nicholas signed the dedication of his *Cynosura* with a simple 'Nicolas Cross' (sig. ***2r); and in 1695 he described himself as 'B[r]. Nicolas of the holy Cross' (*Pious Reflections*, sig. A5r.). Little else is known of his early life before he joined the English Franciscans probably in Douai. He was ordained a priest about 1640, only one year after his religious profession, which could mean either that he had already studied theology or that he would do so after ordination. In the 1650s and early 1660s he was appointed a confessor, became guardian of the London friary twice, was a procurator for the province, and twice a provincial definitor or counsellor. The records concerning Cross are scarce until he became minister provincial in 1662, when he found himself embroiled in the problem of the validity of the previous chapter.

In 1670 Cross published in London *The Cynosura, or, A Saving Star that Leads to Eternity*, a lengthy folio, also issued in octavo, dedicated to the duchess of Shrewsbury; it is a paraphrase on the Miserere or Psalm 50, and its table of contents provides a handy armoury for preachers. About that time, too, he became chaplain to Anne Hyde, duchess of York and wife to the future James II, and was instrumental in getting financial help from her for the English Franciscan nuns in the Princenhoff at Bruges. When he was provincial in 1672 the decision was taken to send some Franciscans to Maryland in America; and in 1674 the English friars officially embraced the strict observance of the Recollects. He was elected provincial for the third time in 1680 at Bruges.

After the revolution in 1688 Cross accompanied James's second wife, Mary of Modena, into exile at St Germain-en-Laye; she had previously favoured him with a position at court as preacher and chaplain, and he had published in 1687 *A Sermon Preach'd before Her Sacred Majesty, the Queen*. He may have returned to England for a few years as he was elected provincial for a fourth time in 1689—a testimony to his worth and good reputation—but resigned for health reasons in May 1691. He lived at Douai from about 1692, and in 1695, encouraged by the queen, he published *Pious Reflections and Devout Prayers on Several Points of Faith and Morality*, 'the products of a winter season and soyl' (his old age), including a hymn of thanksgiving for the newborn prince of Wales (*Pious Reflections*, sig. A3v). He died among the English Franciscans at Douai on either 21 March or 8 August 1698, and was buried before the high altar in the church there. He was eighty-three years old, and had spent forty-eight years as a priest in England where (it is said) he had been imprisoned three times, and exiled to Scotland once, but no details nor dates are given.

IGNATIUS FENNESSY

Sources N. Cross, *The Cynosura, or, A saving star that leads to eternity … paraphrase upon the Miserere* (1670) • N. Cross, *Pious reflections, and devout prayers* (1695) • R. Trappes-Lomax, ed., *The English Franciscan nuns, 1619–1821, and the Friars Minor of the same province, 1618–1761*, Catholic RS, 24 (1922) • Father Thaddeus [F. Hermans], *The Franciscans in England, 1600–1850* (1898) • J. Gillow and R. Trappes-Lomax, eds., *The diary of the 'blue nuns' or order of the Immaculate Conception of Our Lady, at Paris, 1658–1810*, Catholic RS, 8 (1910) • Gillow, *Lit. biog. hist.*, vol. 1 • T. H. Clancy, *English Catholic books, 1641–1700: a bibliography*, rev. edn (1996) • J. Berchmans Dockery, *Christopher Davenport: friar and diplomat* [1960] • *DNB*

Archives BL, letters, 8621, fols. 19–22

Cross, Peter [Lawrence Crosse] (*c.*1645–1724), miniature painter, was the fourth son and youngest of seven children of Anthony Cross (*c.*1585–1651/2), freeman of the Drapers' Company (1614), and of his wife, Margaret, *née* Thrall (whom he married in 1616), who lived 'at the sign of the Golden Cross' in the parish of St Edmund the King, Lombard Street, London. The date of Peter's birth is unknown but his father directed in his will that Peter be made apprentice when old enough to some 'fittinge' trade. This and the evidence of dates on his earliest surviving miniatures suggest that he was born about 1645. He married, first, Arabella (daughter of the sculptor Thomas *Burman, 1617/18–1674), on 23 September 1669, with whom he had three surviving children. She died in August 1700. He then married, on 3 February 1713, Elizabeth, the widow of Arabella's brother Balthasar; she died in December 1714. The family lived 'at the sign of the Blue Anchor' in Henrietta Street, the same street as Samuel Cooper. Cross, describing himself as 'weake in body' and now living with

his daughter Elisabeth Chase in Lower John Street, Golden Square, made his will on 9 June 1721. He was buried at St James's, Piccadilly, on 3 December 1724.

Peter Cross is the artist who used to be called Lawrence Crosse on the strength of the apparent form of his monogram, which was modelled on that of Sir Peter Lely, and of scattered and contradictory notes by George Vertue (Murdoch, 'Hoskinses and Crosses'; *English Miniature*; *Seventeenth-Century English Miniatures*). The latter culminate correctly, however, in a transcription of the monogram and the note 'Peter le Croix, limner [X] his Mark. originally french-name. tho he was English born & bred. here. tho' he always went by [name] of [blank] Cross' (Vertue, *Note books*, 6.19). On 23 July 1678 he succeeded Nicholas Dixon as 'Lymner in Ordinary to his Ma[jesty] with Fee' (private information).

It has been suggested that there were close connections between the Cross and Cooper households in Henrietta Street, founded on a common connection with the Drapers' Company; Cooper's Yorkshire in-laws were also drapers. This has led to the suggestion that Cross learned the art of miniature from Cooper. But Cross's technique, by which he builds up forms by a minutely variegated polychrome stipple, is significantly different from that of Cooper. It is likely that Cross learned his technique elsewhere—possibly, depending on his age, as a theoretical exercise—from John Hoskins, after the latter had ceased practice; or from Alexander Cooper, who was back in England by 1658; or in France, where miniature painting in bright polychrome stipple remained standard after it was supplanted by red-brown hatching in England, largely under Samuel Cooper's influence. Nevertheless the overall appearance of the early Cross works shows a strong consciousness of Samuel Cooper's manner of composition and presentation during the 1660s. A portrait traditionally identified as the earl of Sandwich, in the Victoria and Albert Museum, London, and an *Earl of Romney* at Welbeck Abbey, both of 1669 and painted in Cross's polychrome stipple but bearing apparently genuine Cooper signatures, show the possibilities of confusion. Cross is even known to have owned the *Romney*. Other works from 1660–80, which presently sit awkwardly in the *œuvres* of better-known artists, may be attributable to the early Cross on the basis that multi-coloured stipple combined with high compositional sophistication are his characteristics. The touchstone is the *Robert Kerr, Marquis of Lothian* of 1667, signed with the PC monogram in gold on the front and fully inscribed 'Peeter Cross fecitt' on the back (V&A). For the later Cross the touchstone is the *Lady Katherine Tufton* (V&A), signed on the front in gold with the monogram that looks like LC and helpfully inscribed on the back 'P Cross fec 1707'.

Cross's later works, familiar in the older histories under the name of Lawrence Crosse and bearing the monogram described by Vertue, date from about 1680 to 1716. Compared with the early works the stipple is larger, softer, and more sombre, the head emerging from the dark background with a blurred silhouette and the face simplified in its structure and strongly lit from the front. The warts-

and-all naturalism of Lely when painting public men has evolved into an almost judicial impersonality, expressing that which is ideally common, in terms of appearance, between members of a governing caste. In terms of the history of portraiture the late Cross relates to Willem Wissing and Sir Godfrey Kneller; in terms of technique he looks back to Hilliard, Peter Oliver, and the elder Hoskins. There is evidence that Cross, a collector and connoisseur, was interested in early miniatures. The revival of miniature painting by Bernard Lens and his sons after Cross's death drew on the increasingly widespread consciousness among connoisseurs of the early miniaturists and reproduced their jewel-like colours and clear outlines against solid blue backgrounds. But in his own work Cross avoided such 'primitive' brightness and hard focus.

Good miniatures from all phases of Cross's career may be seen at the Victoria and Albert Museum but the later works are faded. Late works in an excellent state of preservation, with the fugitive reds in the sitters' cheeks still present, are preserved at Welbeck Abbey and catalogued, with good illustrations, in Goulding.

JOHN MURDOCH

Sources Vertue, *Note books*, 1–6 · R. W. Goulding, 'The Welbeck Abbey miniatures', *Walpole Society*, 4 (1914–15) [whole issue] · J. Murdoch, 'Hoskinses and Crosses: work in progress', *Burlington Magazine*, 120 (1978), 284–90 · J. Murdoch and others, *The English miniature* (1981), 157–162 · J. Murdoch, *Seventeenth-century English miniatures in the collection of the Victoria and Albert Museum* (1997), esp. 235–50 · M. Edmond, 'Peter Cross, limner: died 1724', *Burlington Magazine*, 121 (1979), 585–6 · private information (2004) [Katherine Gibson] · PRO, Lord Chamberlain's papers, LC5/143, fol. 129; LC3/28, fol. 123

Cross, Richard Assheton, first Viscount Cross (1823–1914), politician, was born at Red Scar, near Preston, Lancashire, on 30 May 1823, the fifth of six children of William Cross (1771–1827), of Red Scar, and his wife, Ellen, eldest daughter of Edward Chaffers, of Liverpool and Everton, a collateral relative of Richard Chaffers, the well-known potter and rival of Josiah Wedgwood, and of William Chaffers, the authority on hallmarks and potters' marks. Cross was educated at Rugby School under Thomas Arnold, and at Trinity College, Cambridge, where he rowed in the first Trinity eight at the head of the river, and in 1845 was president of the Cambridge Union. Called to the bar by the Inner Temple in 1849, he went on the northern circuit. As his father and grandfather had held legal office in the county palatine court of common pleas at Preston, he started with the advantage of a well-known name, and quickly built up a substantial practice. In 1852 he married Georgiana (d. 1907), third daughter of Thomas Lyon of Appleton Hall, near Warrington. They had four sons and three daughters.

Cross became leader of the Preston and Salford quarter-sessions bar; wrote a book on pauper settlement (1853); and collaborated in a work on the jurisdiction of quarter sessions in non-criminal matters (1858), which remained the standard manual for practitioners until that jurisdiction was almost completely abolished on the creation of county councils. In 1857 his position was sufficiently

Richard Assheton Cross, first Viscount Cross (1823–1914), by Sir Hubert von Herkomer, 1882

assured to allow him to stand for parliament. He won Preston as a Conservative and held the seat until 1862. The only pledge on which his supporters insisted was that he would not join the Carlton Club; and he signalized his independence by being the only Conservative member to vote in favour of Gladstone's repeal of the paper duties, as well as by voting against the same proposal when Gladstone unconstitutionally, as he held, tacked it to a money bill in order to circumvent opposition in the House of Lords.

In 1860 the death of his father-in-law led to Cross's becoming a partner in Parr's Bank at Warrington, a step which involved giving up both his practice at the bar and his seat in parliament. But the years 1862–8 were of great importance in his career; for to the legal ability which he had already shown he was now to add financial experience as partner in a great bank in times of exceptional difficulty (the 'cotton famine'), and an intimate knowledge of the problems of local government. In 1865, when Parr's Bank was one of the pioneers of limited liability as applied to banking, Cross became deputy chairman, and he succeeded to the chairmanship in 1870. During these years he also became chairman or deputy chairman of every local-government body then existing in his neighbourhood, including two courts of quarter sessions, a highway board, a board of guardians, and the governing bodies of many charitable institutions. The eminent services which he afterwards rendered to the state were based on the intimate knowledge thus gained of local conditions in an industrial area.

In the general election of 1868 Cross again stood for parliament, this time for the new constituency of South-West Lancashire, where he achieved a sensational success by defeating Gladstone, then at the height of popularity and power, and heading the poll. Family connections and the influence of his old school and college friend, the fifteenth earl of Derby, had their share in this, but Cross's personal popularity was the decisive factor. Returning to parliament a marked man, he was active with W. H. Smith and Viscount Sandon in harrying Gladstone's government, and, with fellow Lancashire members, in pressing in 1871–2 for a more positive Conservative policy based on social, administrative, and economic reform and on colonial questions. Yet he lacked sparkle in debate, and Disraeli performed, as he said, an 'act of almost unexampled confidence' in 1874 in making Cross home secretary without his having undergone a probation in some minor post.

From the very start, however, Cross was an unqualified success as home secretary. Disraeli had shown in his early novels, and in his Manchester speech of 1872, an appreciation of the need for social reform; but he had little idea what direction it should take, and the only promise on the subject made in his election address of 1874 was that he would give the country a rest from 'incessant and harassing legislation'; moreover, he not only allowed but expected his colleagues to have policies of their own. It is certain, therefore, that Cross was not merely responsible for the details, but had a large part in shaping the principles of the social reforms which are perhaps the greatest achievement of the ministry of 1874–80.

Cross's first measure, the Licensing Bill of 1874, seemed too obviously framed to conciliate the drink interest and had to be substantially modified: 'not much to be proud of' was his own admission in after years. A measure more congenial to him was the Artisans' Dwellings Act of 1875, which empowered municipal authorities, by compulsory purchase if necessary, to clear slums and to let or sell the land for the provision of new working-class housing. It forbade the enhancement of compensation on the ground of compulsion; and it substituted the award of a departmental arbitrator for the proprietary and local sympathies of juries. At the same time a Home Office order was issued requiring all local authorities to appoint medical officers of health and sanitary inspectors. Cross was anxious, however, to forestall the charge of collectivism, insisting that 'it is not the duty of the Government to provide any class of citizens with any of the necessaries of life'. The costs of implementing the act restricted its impact, though Joseph Chamberlain afterwards said that the reforms which made a model city of Birmingham would have been impossible without it. Cross was subsequently regarded as an authority on housing problems, and published articles on the subject in the *Nineteenth Century* in 1882 and 1884.

The Factory Act of 1874 dealt with the employment of women and children in textile factories; and the Factories

and Workshops Act, 1878, consolidated and codified the mass of legislation on this subject. The latter embodied the recommendations of a royal commission appointed in 1876. The Employers and Workmen Act, 1875, and its associated Conspiracy and Protection of Property Act, on the other hand, owed little to the royal commission which preceded them. It was Disraeli who said that the policy of these acts was initiated by Cross and would have been vetoed by the rest of the cabinet but for his own support. Largely relieving workers of the threat of imprisonment for breach of contract, and trade unions of the possibility of prosecution for conspiracy and restrictions on peaceful picketing, the measures were warmly welcomed by the labour movement. Cross also legislated to preserve open spaces near large towns, and transferred the management of prisons and the cost of their upkeep from local to central government. His last proposal, to acquire and transfer to a single authority all the undertakings which supplied London with water, was sharply criticized on the ground of excessive compensation and had to be dropped; but the idea was sound.

In opposition (1880–85) the school of businessmen in politics to which Cross belonged was speedily thrown into the shade by Lord Randolph Churchill, whose dislike for them was open and violent. Accordingly, although Cross returned to the Home Office in the short-lived ministry of 1885, it was no surprise when in 1886 that department was given to Lord Randolph's nominee, and Cross received the lighter India Office, being at the same time raised to the peerage as Viscount Cross of Broughton in Furness. His tenure of the India Office, which lasted until 1892, was uneventful, its only important piece of legislation being the Indian Councils Act, 1892, which enlarged the membership of the Indian legislative councils—though without formally introducing the elective principle, which Cross opposed—and proved highly successful. In 1895 he accepted the office of privy seal, which he retained until 1900, and he finally retired in 1902. After this his appearances in parliament were few, and he does not appear to have spoken in the Lords after 1909. He died on 8 January 1914, following a bronchial attack, at Eccle Riggs, Broughton in Furness, his family home since 1860.

Cross was a fellow of the Royal Society, a bencher of the Inner Temple, and an ecclesiastical commissioner, and was keenly interested in the affairs of the church. His honours included, besides the viscountcy, the GCB (1880) and GCSI (1892). He was among the small band of her ministers to whom Queen Victoria gave her close personal friendship, and he was a trustee of more than one royal marriage settlement. But the story that he was the queen's confidential business agent is unfounded. Very far from being a brilliant man, Cross was yet gifted with unfailing good sense; and he had the knack of securing the affection and trust of his subordinates. His speeches were of a type which the House of Commons listened to with respect rather than enjoyment, well-documented and clear statements such as might be made at a meeting of a business company. Only twice did he rise to a note of passion in oratory—when introducing the Artisans' Dwellings Act

(1875) and when repudiating on behalf of the cabinet the charge of indifference to the sufferings of Bulgaria. The latter speech (7 May 1877) contained a cogent defence of the whole policy of the government in the Eastern crisis, and created a widespread impression.

To Cross's reputation as an outstanding home secretary and a model of the hard-working, efficient departmental head has been added the suggestion that he and his Lancashire associates built on their local experience to pursue a version of tory democracy based on combination between the middle classes and the aristocracy to supply such social and administrative reform as would preserve paternalistic government against popular pressure. Cross however, was too pedestrian and, in Disraeli's and Salisbury's cabinets, too middle-class a figure to achieve more than moderate influence in the inner councils of his party.

S. V. FITZ-GERALD, *rev.* PAUL SMITH

Sir (Alfred) Rupert Neale Cross (1912–1980), by Ramsey & Muspratt

Sources *The Times* (9 Jan 1914) · *Annual Register* (1914) · R. A. Cross, *A family history* (privately printed, 1903) · R. A. Cross, *A political history* (privately printed, 1903) · D. J. Mitchell, *Cross and tory democracy: a political biography of Richard Assheton Cross* (1991) · F. J. Dwyer, 'R. A. Cross and the Eastern crisis of 1875–8', *Slavonic and East European Review*, 39 (1960–61), 440–58 · P. Smith, *Disraelian Conservatism and social reform* (1967) · R. Shannon, *The age of Disraeli, 1868–1881: the rise of tory democracy* (1992) · E. J. Feuchtwanger, *Disraeli, democracy and the tory party: conservative leadership and organization after the second Reform Bill* (1968) · W. F. Monypenny and G. E. Buckle, *The life of Benjamin Disraeli*, 5–6 (1920) · S. Gopal, *British policy in India, 1858–1905* (1965)

Archives BL, corresp. and papers, Add. MSS 51263–51289 · BL OIOC, corresp. and papers relating to India, MS Eur. E 243 · Lancs. RO, corresp. and papers | BL, corresp. with W. E. Gladstone, Add. MSS 44469–44482 · BL OIOC, letters to Sir Owen Tudor Burne, MS Eur. D 951 · BL OIOC, letters to Arthur Godley, MS Eur. F 102 · BL OIOC, corresp. with Lord Harris, MS Eur. E 256 · BL OIOC, letters to Lord Wenlock, MS Eur. D 952 · Bodl. Oxf., letters to Benjamin Disraeli · CKS, letters to Aretas Akers-Douglas · CKS, letters to Edward Stanhope · Hants. RO, letters to Arthur Bower Forwood · LPL, corresp. with Archbishop Benson · LPL, corresp. with Edward Benson · LPL, corresp. with A. C. Tait · Lpool RO, corresp. with Lord Derby · LUL, corresp. with Sir Edwin Chadwick · PRO NIre., corresp. with Lord Dufferin · Suffolk RO, Ipswich, letters to Lord Cranbrook · W. Sussex RO, letters to duke of Richmond

Likenesses H. von Herkomer, oils, 1882, NPG [*see illus.*] · S. Hodges, oils, exh. RA 1891, Lancaster Castle · Ape [C. Pellegrini], caricature, chromolithograph, NPG; repro. in *VF* (16 May 1874) · G. Cook, stipple and line print (after photograph by London Stereoscopic Co.), NPG · Fradelle & Young, photograph, NPG; repro. in *Our Conservative and Unionist Statesmen*, 2 · Lock & Whitfield, woodburytype photograph, NPG; repro. in T. Cooper, *Men of Mark: a gallery of contemporary portraits* (1880) · Russell & Sons, woodburytype photograph, NPG · H. T. Wells, print, NPG · lithograph, BM; repro. in *Civil Service Review* (1877) · prints, NPG · woodburytype photograph, NPG

Wealth at death £91,617 6s. 4d.: probate, 16 April 1914, *CGPLA Eng. & Wales*

Cross, Sir (Alfred) Rupert Neale (1912–1980), jurist, was born at Chelsea, London, on 15 June 1912, the second son and younger child of Arthur George Cross, quantity surveyor, of Hastings, and his wife, Mary Elizabeth Dalton. His elder brother, (Arthur) Geoffrey Neale *Cross, became Baron Cross of Chelsea, lord of appeal in ordinary.

Cross was one year old when he was operated on for cancer of the eyes and he became totally blind. His mother, however, inculcated in him a sturdy independence. His school, the Worcester College for the Blind, reinforced this. He rowed for the school at Henley in 1927 and took up chess. He became proficient enough to captain Oxford University chess club and to come fourth in the British chess championship in 1935. He was disappointed to obtain only a second class in history (1933) at Worcester College, Oxford, but redeemed this by a first in jurisprudence in 1935. He soon acquired a deep love and knowledge of the law. With the help of G. S. A. Wheatcroft he became articled to a firm of solicitors and, before admission, married in 1937 (Aline) Heather Chadwick, herself a solicitor and the daughter of a solicitor, Robert Agar Chadwick, who practised in Leeds. Without her staunch and loving support his later success would have been unthinkable. They had no children.

In 1939 Cross was admitted a solicitor and during the Second World War he practised in London, mainly in family law. After the war he turned his mind to law teaching. In 1945 he became a full-time lecturer at the Law Society school of law. He had a talent for lecturing, in which he combined great lucidity with a keen sense of the limitations of his audience. In 1946 he began to help with the law teaching at Magdalen College, Oxford. He became an excellent tutor, and was a fellow of the college from 1948 to 1964. Though forthright and outspoken, he had a sensitive feeling for the needs of his pupils, several of whom attained high office, and possessed an impressive mastery of many branches of law which was aided by an almost infallible memory. With the help of his wife, his secretaries, and books in braille he read widely and soon began to publish. An elementary but popular *Introduction to Criminal Law*, written with P. Asterley Jones in 1948, made him known to a wide circle of lawyers; but it was *Evidence*, published in 1958, that established his reputation in Britain and the Commonwealth as one of the leading academic lawyers of the day. It was the first time that the subject had been treated scientifically in England. Based on a wide range of sources, legislative, judicial and literary, domestic and foreign, it expounded the law of evidence with virtually perfect precision. Though it attracted hardly any reviews it was immediately recognized by judges, practitioners, and law teachers as an indispensable guide to the pitfalls of the subject. What had been a confused jumble of doctrines, statutes, and decisions became an academic discipline.

Though evidence was thenceforth Cross's main speciality he had wide interests. Jurisprudence attracted him, and he wrote books entitled *Precedent in English Law* (1961) and *Statutory Interpretation* (1976). These married an exact knowledge of the authorities to wide reading in legal philosophy. In later life his thoughts turned more and more to penology. His inaugural lecture, published as *Paradoxes in Prison Sentences* (1965), is a plea to those who profess criminal law to widen their horizons. He wrote a successful book entitled *The English Sentencing System* (1971). For his Hamlyn lectures (1971) he chose as a topic what their published title summarized as *Punishment, Prison and the Public*. He called himself merely an 'armchair penologist' but he devoted himself to bodies such as the Criminal Law Revision Committee, in whose deliberations his provocative advice, conceived in a Benthamite spirit, and backed by an unrivalled mastery of detail, often carried great weight.

Cross's status was recognized by his election to the Vinerian chair of English law at Oxford University in 1964. In this he owed something to the self-effacement of his colleague J. H. C. Morris, who had himself a strong claim to the chair. Cross held this, the most ancient and prestigious of English law chairs, for fifteen years with great distinction. He shirked none of the chores of college and university life, such as examining. Indeed he could establish a rapport with a student at a *viva voce* examination more quickly than most sighted people. He enjoyed life immensely, though he would remark ironically that it was bearable only as long as he knew where the next bottle of champagne was coming from. With his zest for wine, food, gossip, chess, and long walks one could easily overlook his regular routine and steady output. He had a wide circle of friends many of whom claimed him as in a special sense their own. He was invited abroad to Australia, Africa, and America and was honoured by the Middle Temple, who made him an honorary bencher in 1972, and by the award of a knighthood in 1973. He was a doctor of his own university (DCL, 1958) and an honorary LLD of Edinburgh (1973) and Leeds (1975). He was elected FBA in 1967. In 1973, however, his cancer returned in a painful form and, though he faced and in the end dominated the pain, he was conscious that his career was drawing to a close. Yet he remained buoyant and, the day before he died, was still planning a book on Sir James Fitzjames Stephen and taking pleasure in the news of a volume of essays (*Crime, Proof and Punishment*, 1981) which his friends were preparing in his honour. He died at Oxford on 12 September 1980.

Cross was unusual among English academic lawyers in the degree to which he spoke the language of judges and practitioners without sacrificing scholarly rigour or theoretical insight. But it was as a blind man that his achievement was most striking. To his undaunted spirit blindness was not a barrier, nor even a handicap, but just a nuisance to be overcome. He refused to submit to it, and by his courage rose to the summit of his chosen profession.

TONY HONORÉ, *rev.*

Sources T. Honoré, ed., *Crime, proof and punishment* (1981) · personal knowledge (1986) · *CGPLA Eng. & Wales* (1980)
Archives SOUND BL NSA, performance recording
Likenesses Ramsey & Muspratt, photograph, British Academy [*see illus.*]
Wealth at death £142,358: probate, 15 Oct 1980, *CGPLA Eng. & Wales*

Cross, Thomas (*fl.* 1644–1682), engraver, produced a great number of portraits of authors for frontispieces as well as title pages for books published in London in the middle of the seventeenth century. He seems hardly ever to have worked for the publishers of single-sheet prints. His style shows no attempt at artistic refinement, and his plates are executed in a dry and stiff manner. He was a specialist in engraving shorthand manuals, and was the inventor of a system himself. In the preface to Ratcliff's *New Art of Short and Swift Writing without Characters* he claimed that he had engraved 'more of short-hand books than all the engravers in England'. He also made the plates for Josiah Rycraft's *Peculiar Characters of the Oriental Languages*.

Among the few documents on Cross's life that are known are two payments from Sir William Dugdale in 1664 for plates of arms made for the *Origines juridiciales* of 1666. His work has been catalogued by M. Corbett and M. Norton, who list 144 plates by him, eighty-four of which are portraits, forty-five frontispieces, and only two of independent subjects (a *memento mori* and a pious broadsheet from 1672).

Cross had a relation (probably a son or nephew) of the same name who shared his profession and was working at least by 1682, when the elder began to sign his work as 'senior'. The younger man became a specialist music engraver and publisher, and had a virtual monopoly of the music engraving trade at the end of the seventeenth century. He is best known as the engraver of Purcell's music. He must have been born between 1660 and 1665 and died between 1732 and 1735.

ANTONY GRIFFITHS

Sources A. M. Hind, *Engraving in England in the sixteenth and seventeenth centuries*, 3, ed. M. Corbett and M. Norton (1964), 277–326 · F. Kidson, W. C. Smith, and P. W. Jones, 'Cross, Thomas', *New Grove*

Cross, Victoria. *See* Cory, Annie Sophie (1868–1952).

Crosse, Andrew (1784–1855), electrician, was born on 17 June 1784 at Fyne Court in the parish of Broomfield, Somerset. He was the son of Richard Crosse (*d.* 1800), high sheriff of Somerset, and his second wife, Susanna (*d.* 1805), daughter of Jasper Porter of Blaxhold, Somerset. The Crosse family had occupied the manor house from its construction in 1629. At the age of four Andrew was taken to France by his parents. On returning four years later to England he was sent to the Revd White's school at Dorchester, and in 1793 he was placed under the care of the Revd Samuel Seyer of the Royal Fort School, Bristol. In 1802 he entered as a gentleman commoner Brasenose College, Oxford, which he found 'a perfect hell on earth' (*Memorials*, 32). After taking his degree in 1805 he retired to his estates.

At Fyne Court, Crosse passed the quiet life of a country gentleman. He began to study electricity, chemistry, and mineralogy, and became acquainted with George John Singer, the maker of electrical apparatus and author of *Elements of Electricity*, who spent some time at Fyne Court. The first recorded experiment made by Crosse was in 1807, the subject being the formation of crystals under the influence of electricity.

Crosse married, in 1809, Mary Anne (*d.* 1846), eldest daughter of Captain John Hamilton. In the succeeding ten years the couple had seven children, three of whom died in childhood. The household was happy, but unsettled and in confusion, Crosse 'not ever being used to domestic affairs' (*Memorials*, 46). He erected a mile and a quarter of insulated copper wire in his grounds, and observed the spectacular electrical phenomena exhibited by this apparatus. Crosse became well known in local literary and philosophical circles, and associated with Humphry Davy, Theodore Hook, John Kenyon, and Robert Southey. In politics he was a republican, campaigning on behalf of candidates who advocated radical reform.

In 1836 Crosse's experimental work became nationally celebrated through the meeting of the British Association for the Advancement of Science at Bristol. Conversations with eminent men of science led to his being invited to address the geological section. He described his experiments on the formation of crystalline bodies under the influence of a voltaic current generated in a water battery. In the chemical section he also spoke of his improvements on the voltaic battery, and of his observations on atmospheric electricity. Crosse returned home from the meeting a scientific philosopher of eminence.

At the end of 1836 while pursuing experiments on electro-crystallization, Crosse observed the appearance of life in immediate connection with his voltaic arrangements. The creatures proved to be mites belonging to the genus *Acarus*, and were observed in metallic solutions supposed to be destructive to organic life. Publication of this sensational result (without Crosse's permission) led to an international controversy in which he was accused of being a Frankenstein and a 'disturber of the peace of families' (Secord, 337). To use his own words, Crosse 'met with so much virulence and abuse … that it seems as if it were a crime to have made them'. He eventually communicated to the London Electrical Society a full account of the conditions under which the mites were developed, and said '*I have never ventured an opinion on the cause of their birth*, and for a very good reason: I was unable to form one' ('Description', 10).

Crosse's experiments played a major role in contemporary controversies about miracles, materialism, and natural law. In a widely circulated report, Michael Faraday was said to have repeated the result, but this was not the case, for he thought the subject beyond the limits of science. Several others did attempt to replicate Crosse's finding, and the Kentish surgeon William Henry Weekes claimed success.

In 1850 Crosse married his second wife, Cornelia Augusta Hewitt of Exeter, who aided in his electrical researches. The couple had a son in 1852. She published *Memorials* (1857) of her husband and lively recollections of intellectual life in *Red-Letter Days of my Life* (1892).

Crosse experimented on a method of extracting metals from their ores and on the purification of sea water and other fluids by electricity. He also communicated to the Electrical Society a paper 'On the perforation of nonconducting substances by the mechanical action of the electric fluid', and endeavoured to trace the connection between the growth of vegetation and electric influence.

After a tour in England with his wife Crosse returned to Broomfield in 1855 and arranged an experiment with John Frederic Daniell's sustaining battery. This was the last scientific act of his life. On the morning of 28 May he had a paralytic seizure, and died on 6 July 1855, in the room in which he had been born. He was buried in Broomfield churchyard. ROBERT HUNT, *rev.* J. A. SECORD

Sources *Memorials, scientific and literary, of Andrew Crosse, the electrician*, ed. [C. Crosse] (1857) · J. A. Secord, 'Extraordinary experiments: electricity and the creation of life in Victorian England', *The uses of experiment: studies in the natural sciences*, ed. D. Gooding, T. Pinch, and S. Schaffer (1989), 337–83 · O. Stallybrass, 'How Faraday "produced living animalculae": Andrew Crosse and the story of a myth', *Proceedings of the Royal Institution of Great Britain*, 41 (1966–7), 597–619 · A. Crosse, 'Description of some experiments', *Transactions and Proceedings of the London Electrical Society*, 1 (1838), 10–16 · Burke, *Gen. GB* (1952) [Hamilton of Fyne Court] · d. cert.
Likenesses lithograph, 1838, repro. in Stallybrass, 'How Faraday "produced living animalculae"', 598

Crosse, John (1739–1816), Church of England clergyman, was born in the parish of St Martin-in-the-Fields, London, the son of Hammond Crosse of Kensington, London. He was educated in a school at Hadley, near Barnet, Hertfordshire. While resident in London he appears to have undergone an evangelical conversion through the ministry of a Methodist preacher and to have joined a Methodist class. In October 1762 he matriculated as a member of St Edmund Hall, Oxford, subsequently graduating BA on 18 February 1768. He served two brief curacies: one in Wiltshire and one at the Lock Hospital in London. In 1765 he travelled for three years through a great part of Europe in the company of John Thornton, the cousin of John Thornton of Clapham. They visited Voltaire and also the University of Halle, by which Crosse was later awarded the degree of MA for a dissertation on the ruins of Herculaneum.

Soon after Crosse's return from the continent he was presented to the small adjacent livings of Todmorden in the parish of Rochdale and to Cross-Stone in the parish of Halifax. He ministered there for six years and during this period, on 1 March 1774, married his first wife, Grace Sutcliffe (*d.* 1811), described by Morgan as a 'good, plain, pious woman' (p. 143). In 1774 Crosse became incumbent of White Chapel, Cleckheaton, Yorkshire. In 1776 he was incorporated BA at the University of Cambridge, and he took the degree of MA as a member of King's College there. Crosse's father had bought for him the next presentation of the vicarage of Bradford, Yorkshire, and Crosse became incumbent there in 1784 and he remained there until his death in 1816.

In theology Crosse was an evangelical Arminian and a close friend of John Wesley, to whom he offered the use of his pulpit. He maintained a wide circle of friends, however, including Calvinistic evangelicals such as Thomas Robinson and high-churchmen such as Dr Gaskin, the secretary of the Society for Promoting Christian Knowledge. Crosse was an extremely active parish priest who preached and catechized regularly, both on Sundays and during the week. He established a Sunday school and also a religious society for adults that met on Friday evenings, under his direction in the vicarage kitchen. His afternoons were devoted to visitation of his extensive parish; this provided the occasion for charitable giving and also for the impromptu cottage services, or 'parsonings', for which he became famous. This combination of evangelistic energy and assiduous pastoral care was the keynote of Crosse's ministry and it seems to have borne considerable fruit. The parish church was frequently crowded and twice had to be enlarged by the construction of galleries. Crosse also promoted the construction of two further churches: one in the outlying settlement of Great Horton in 1808 and the other in Bradford in 1813.

Crosse rarely ventured into print, but he did produce two publications: one, in 1790, a response to a personal attack on himself and the other, in 1798, a defence of the Church of England against charges brought by the influential dissenting propagandist Michaijah Towgood. In 1811 his first wife died and on 6 December in the following year Crosse married again; his second wife, Martha Hopkinson from his own parish, also predeceased him. Towards the end of his life Crosse became blind, but this does not seem to have hampered his ministry; he remained a fully active clergyman until two weeks before his death at home on 17 June 1816 after a short illness. He was buried in Bradford, probably on 23 June. Beyond the confines of his parish Crosse supported both local charities, including the Leeds Infirmary, and a range of national organizations, such as the Bible Society and the Society for Promoting Christian Knowledge. In his will he left £10,000 in trust 'for promoting the cause of true religion', which was subsequently divided among a number of causes, including the foundation of three Crosse theological scholarships in the University of Cambridge.

MARK SMITH

Sources W. Morgan, *The parish priest portrayed in the life, character, and ministry of the Rev John Crosse* (1841) · Venn, *Alum. Cant.* · W. W. Stamp, *Memoir of Revd John Crosse* (1844) · IGI
Likenesses Topham, engraving (after portrait by J. Hunter) · J. Wilson, engraving, repro. in Morgan, *Parish priest portrayed*
Wealth at death over £10,000: Morgan, *Parish priest portrayed*

Crosse, John (1786–1833), writer on music, was born on 7 July 1786 in Hull. In 1825 he published his only work, *An account of the grand musical festival held in September 1823, in*

the cathedral church at York, with a brief history of music festivals in Great Britain. Crosse died in York on 20 October 1833, and was buried at St James's Church, Sutton, Yorkshire.   W. B. SQUIRE, *rev.* ANNE PIMLOTT BAKER

Sources Grove, *Dict. mus.* · private information (1888)

Crosse [*formerly* Cross], **John Green** (1790–1850), surgeon, was born on 6 September 1790 at Boyton Hall, Great Finborough, Suffolk, the son of William Cross (1762–1836), a landowner and farmer, and his wife, Sarah Green (1760–1838). At an early age he was apprenticed to Thomas Bayly, a surgeon apothecary in Stowmarket, whose daughter Dorothy he married on 18 May 1816; among their children was Lavinia *Crosse. When his apprenticeship was finished he went to London, and studied at St George's Hospital and at the Great Windmill Street school of anatomy, where he was noted for his skill in dissection. This led to his first appointment. James Macartney, professor of anatomy in Trinity College, Dublin, asked Benjamin Brodie to recommend a demonstrator to him, and Brodie nominated Crosse, who proved as successful a teacher as he had been a pupil.

However, Crosse failed the examination at the Royal College of Surgeons in Ireland and left Dublin for Paris, where he spent the winter of 1814–15. He wrote letters describing the work of the Parisian hospitals to friends in London and Dublin, and on his return he published them as a book, *Sketches of the Medical Schools of Paris* (1815), which gives an interesting account of surgical and anatomical education in Paris in comparison with that offered in London and Dublin. He heard Guillaume Dupuytren lecturing on inguinal hernia to twelve hundred students, and thought such a class more flattering to the lecturer than useful to the students; he found François Chaussier's lecture of an hour on methods of opening the skull for purposes of dissection prolix. Crosse was disappointed to find the French anatomists using no cases of surgery as illustration, but he found the lectures on medical jurisprudence a significant step forward.

In March 1815 Crosse settled in Norwich, and in 1817 he published *An Attempt to Establish Physiognomy upon Scientific Principles*. This was followed in 1820 by *A History of the Variolous Epidemic which Occurred in Norwich in the Year 1819*, which gave an account of the progress of vaccination in the eastern counties and of its beneficial results. In 1823 he became assistant surgeon to the Norfolk and Norwich Hospital, and in 1826 surgeon. Norwich was the centre of a district in which bladder stones were common, and nearly every great Norwich surgeon has also been skilled as a lithotomist. Crosse was no exception and soon gained a large practice as a surgeon. In 1833 he won the Jacksonian prize at the Royal College of Surgeons for his work on urinary calculus, and *The Formation, Constituents, and Extraction of the Urinary Calculus* was subsequently published in 1835, containing original observations and a full list of previous works on stone. In the following year he was elected FRS.

Crosse published several papers in the *Transactions of the Provincial Medical and Surgical Association*, of which he was president in 1846, and some cases of midwifery described by him were published posthumously in 1851 by E. Copeman, one of his pupils. Crosse had a series of forty apprentices, among them G. M. Humphry, later professor of surgery at Cambridge University; several recounted his enthusiasm for acquiring medical and surgical knowledge, and his untiring energy. In his later years he undertook a series of financial speculations which turned out disastrously and in 1848 he began to be afflicted by a cerebral condition. Crosse died on 9 June 1850, and was buried in Norwich Cathedral five days later.

NORMAN MOORE, rev. CHRISTIAN KERSLAKE

Sources V. M. Crosse, *A surgeon in the early nineteenth century: the life and times of John Green Crosse, 1790–1850* (1968) · G. M. Humphry, *Medical Times*, 1st ser., 20 (1850), 311 · private information (1888)
Archives Norfolk RO, diaries, letters, and papers · Norwich Central Library · Royal Society of Medicine, London · Wellcome L., case books
Likenesses line engraving, 1846 · F. Sandys, lithograph, Wellcome L. · lithograph, repro. in Crosse, *Surgeon* · lithograph (after F. Sandys), NPG · portraits, Norwich Central Library

Crosse, Lavinia (1821–1890), Anglican nun, was born on 16 December 1821 at 45 St Giles', Norwich, the third daughter of John Green *Crosse (1790–1850), surgeon and physician, and his wife, Dorothy Anne, *née* Bayly or Bayley (1792–1870). She had three sisters and four brothers. She inherited many of her father's personal traits: decisiveness, determination, and a concern for the poor. Educated at home, her friendship with E. H. Hansell of Magdalen College, Oxford, led her to read works by Anglican divines and contemporary Tractarians. Together with Catherine Hansell she worked as a district visitor among the poor in the parish of St Peter Mancroft. In 1854 she heard John Armstrong speak at the Norwich assembly rooms in support of a penitentiary at Shipmeadow to rescue girls and women in moral danger; shortly after, on 9 January 1855, Lavinia Crosse was asked by the council of the penitentiary to supervise this home, as the founder wished to withdraw.

Visits to similar penitentiaries at Clewer, Bussage, and Wantage, as well as to convents on the continent, convinced Lavinia Crosse that the best way forward was as a religious sisterhood: new year's eve 1855 saw the inauguration of the Community of All Hallows by T. T. Carter of Clewer—Mother Lavinia and two novices being received. Despite accusations of 'Romanism' by the local press and the reservations of the ruling council, the sisterhood began to grow. In September 1859 a new penitentiary was opened at Ditchingham, Norfolk, having been moved there from Shipmeadow. A new convent was also completed in 1877, and the community added an orphanage, a school, and a hospital. They expanded their activities to include also mission work in Norwich and the surrounding area, and work among Native Americans in British Columbia.

Lavinia Crosse remained mother superior throughout her life, despite a long and painful illness. Nearly 600 women passed through the penitentiary during that time. In the words of her obituarist her 'attractiveness of disposition; her character—spiritual-minded—yet most practical; her tender heartedness and great love of justice; her indomitable energy … all had their full results' (*The Guardian*). Although 'she could not endure slovenly or careless work and so was sometimes esteemed severe', this was balanced by 'a strong love of fun and humour which never failed even in later life'.

Mother Lavinia's friend and mentor the Revd William Scudamore, rector of Ditchingham and first warden of the sisterhood, died early in 1881 (he had exercised a strong influence on the community's development). Her own death on 26 June 1890 occurred at Aldeburgh, whence she had gone for rest and recuperation. She was buried in the Ditchingham parish cemetery on 1 July. The strength of character and single-mindedness of Mother Lavinia ensured that the community overcame all the difficulties which beset its early years. Although the work of the community has changed with the needs of society, its survival into the twenty-first century is a lasting tribute to its first mother superior.

VALERIE BONHAM

Sources Sister Violet, *All Hallows, Ditchingham: the story of an East Anglian community* (1983) · *The Guardian* (2 July 1890) · P. F. Anson, *The call of the cloister: religious communities and kindred bodies in the Anglican communion*, 2nd edn (1964) · J. Crosse, commonplace book, letters, and memoirs, Norfolk RO · private information (2004)
Archives Community of All Hallows, Ditchingham, Norfolk, community diary and minutes of Shipmeadow penitentiary · Norfolk RO
Likenesses photographs, *c*.1855–1889, Community of All Hallows, Ditchingham, Norfolk

Crosse, Lawrence. *See* Cross, Peter (*c*.1645–1724).

Crosse, Richard (1742–1810), miniature painter, was born at Knowle, near Cullompton, Devon, on 24 April 1742, the son of John and Mary Crosse, of an old Devon family. Like one of his sisters he was born deaf and mute. About 1778 he formed an attachment to Miss Sarah Cobley (*d*. 1808), who refused him and subsequently married Benjamin Haydon, and was mother of B. R. Haydon, the famous historical painter. This was a great blow to Crosse and a cause of his living in retirement from general society. Having developed ability as a miniature painter he moved to London, and in 1758 obtained a premium at the Society of Arts. He studied at Shipley's Drawing School and in the duke of Richmond's sculpture gallery. He exhibited from 1760 to 1791 at the Society of Artists (of which he was a member from 1763); at the Free Society of Artists from 1761 to 1766; and at the Royal Academy from 1770 to 1796. During this time he lived in Henrietta Street, Covent Garden. In 1789 he was probably appointed painter in enamel to George III.

In 1798 it appears that Crosse gave up active practice and retired to Wells, in Somerset, where he lived with Mr Cobley, prebend of Wells, a brother of Sarah Haydon. There in 1808 he encountered his old love. Haydon in his diary gives a touching account of the interview between his mother and Crosse, which was quite unexpected and took place after an interval of thirty years; it was their last meeting, as Mrs Haydon died on her subsequent journey to London, having stopped at Wells to see her brother *en route* from Exeter.

Richard Crosse (1742–1810), self-portrait, c.1780

Crosse died at Knowle on 30 May 1810, aged sixty-eight. He ranks very highly as a miniature painter, especially for his delicate and natural colouring, and was held in great esteem by his contemporaries. He also tried painting in watercolours, and in 1788 exhibited a portrait of the opera singer Mrs Billington. He also occasionally painted portraits in oil, for instance a group of six members of his family (ex Christies, London, 3 March 1922). A miniature self-portrait was engraved by R. Thew and published on 1 September 1792; a portrait of the marchioness of Salisbury was engraved by Benjamin Smith in 1791; and another, of Gregory Sharpe, master of the Temple, was engraved in mezzotint by Valentine Green in 1770. Crosse's manuscript ledger, containing a list of the portrait miniatures that he painted between 1775 and 1798, survives in the National Art Library at the Victoria and Albert Museum, London. The artist is there revealed as having produced about 100 miniatures a year between 1777 and 1780; during the following two decades he painted a decreasing number of miniatures each year. The prices he set were modest, remaining about 8 guineas for small miniatures and 10 guineas for larger works. In a good year he could expect a turnover of nearly £1000. His painting-box survives (V&A).

While Crosse cannot be classed in the front rank of late eighteenth-century miniaturists with Richard Cosway, John Smart, and George Engleheart, the quality of his production places him alongside Jeremiah Meyer, Ozias Humphry, and Andrew Plimer. Some of the most striking miniatures of the period were painted by Crosse. Foremost among these is the large miniature of Mrs Siddons, painted in 1783 (V&A); equally accomplished—and almost as large—is his *Self-Portrait* (V&A; c.1780). Among his other most important miniatures are *William Henry, Duke of Gloucester* (Royal Collection; reproduced in Walker, 106), which was probably exhibited at the Royal Academy in 1771; the exquisite *Mrs. Johnstone* (FM Cam.; reproduced in Bayne-Powell, 54), almost certainly painted in 1779; and the official portrait of George III (Gilbert Collection; reproduced in Coffin and Hofstetter, 129), which is documented as having been painted in 1793. Highly unusual in Crosse's *œuvre* is his portrait miniature of the Revd Thomas Gibbons (FM Cam., reproduced in Bayne-Powell, 55). Not only is this one of his finest character studies but it is also exceptionally rare in being signed ('R. Crosse Fect.' on the reverse). Crosse also painted a small number of enamels; among the finest of these is the portrait of his brother, James or Edward (c.1780; priv. coll.; reproduced in Foskett, *Dictionary of British miniature painters*, 2, pl. 71, fig. 201).

L. H. CUST, *rev.* STEPHEN LLOYD

Sources R. Bayne-Powell, ed., *Catalogue of portrait miniatures in the Fitzwilliam Museum, Cambridge* (1985) · S. Coffin and B. Hofstetter, *Portrait miniatures in enamel: the Gilbert collection* (2000) · P. Caffrey, *Treasures to hold: Irish and English miniatures, 1650–1850, from the National Gallery of Ireland collection* (Dublin, 2000) · R. Walker, *The eighteenth and early nineteenth century miniatures in the collection of her majesty the queen* (1992) · G. Reynolds, *English portrait miniatures* (1952); rev. edn (1988) · B. S. Long, *British miniaturists* (1929) · B. S. Long, 'Richard Crosse: miniaturist and portrait painter', *Walpole Society*, 17 (1928–9), 61–94 · D. Foskett, *A dictionary of British miniature painters*, 2 vols. (1972) · D. Foskett, *Miniatures: dictionary and guide* (1987) · administration, PRO, PROB 6/186, fol. 271*v* · *Mortimer's Directory* (1763)

Archives V&A NAL, corresp. and papers, ledger-book

Likenesses R. Crosse, self-portrait, oils, c.1760–1769, Royal Albert Memorial Museum, Exeter · R. Crosse, self-portrait, watercolour on ivory miniature, c.1780, V&A [*see illus.*] · R. Thew, stipple, pubd 1792 (after R. Crosse, c.1780), BM, NPG

Wealth at death under £25,000: administration, PRO, PROB 6/186, fol. 271*v*

Crosse, Sir Robert (c.1547–1611), naval commander, was born at Charlinch, near Bridgwater, Somerset, the second of seven sons of William Crosse, gentleman, and Elizabeth, his wife, who also bore five surviving daughters. His earliest known employment was as a soldier with the regency army during the siege of Edinburgh Castle in 1573; he was wounded, 'and shall carry the mark to my dying day' as he claimed much later (*Naval Tracts of Sir William Monson*, 1.213; *Salisbury MSS*, 18.297). His first recorded command at sea was of the bark *Bond* in Sir Francis Drake's West Indies raid of 1585. In the fleet list he was identified as Sir Christopher Hatton's man: one 'who long sense hathe medled at Sea but not of late, very lyke to do well' (Keeler, 49). On 2 October Crosse volunteered as a hostage during negotiations with the governor of Bayona to allow the English fleet to revictual there; and on 10 February 1586, at Cartagena on the Spanish main, he commanded part of a force, led by the expedition's vice-admiral Martin Frobisher, in a diversionary assault upon a harbour chain, while English troops took the city from the landward side.

In 1587 Crosse sailed in Drake's Cadiz expedition as a land captain. On 27 April he was sent back to England with dispatches announcing the success of the assault, and subsequently gave testimony during the investigation of William Borough's 'mutiny' against Drake. In a list dated 22 December 1587 Crosse was one of fourteen men appointed to have charge of the queen's ships. He commanded the ship *Hope* as rear-admiral of Drake's squadron during the Armada campaign, and was mentioned in the unofficial 'Relation of proceedings' as having done good service in the fight off Gravelines. During the early part of the campaign the *Hope* and Thomas Fenner's *Nonpareil* patrolled the coast of northern France, seeking intelligence of the approaching Armada. In May 1589 Crosse was appointed admiral of a fleet of seventeen sail to resupply the expedition of Drake and Sir John Norris off the coast of Spain. Separated from the expedition by storms he took several of his ships to the island of Porto Santo, which he captured, sacked, and ransomed back to its governor before returning directly to England.

In 1591 Crosse commanded the *Elizabeth Bonaventure* in Lord Thomas Howard's Azores squadron, a voyage notable only for the last fight of the *Revenge* and death of Richard Grenville. In the following year, now enjoying the patronage of Sir Walter Ralegh, he commanded the queen's ship *Foresight* in the memorable capture of the carrack *Madre de Dios*. The *Foresight* played a leading role in the fight, lashing herself to the Portuguese vessel's bow to prevent her crew from grounding her, until the remainder of the English squadron could come up to assist. Following the carrack's capture Crosse and his crew joined, or led, a general plundering of her cargoes, though his subsequent report of the episode to Lord Burghley (BL, Lansdowne MS 70, fol. 86) tactfully omitted this detail. Several days later he met with the ship of his admiral, Sir Martin Frobisher, who accused him of having boasted of taking some £10,000 worth of plunder (of which Crosse later admitted to only £2000). Departing the fleet against orders Crosse returned to England to dispose of his booty. At Dartmouth, the Isle of Wight, and Gosport he sold some of his spoils (scenes during the latter occasion were compared to those at Bartholomew fair), but much was subsequently confiscated at Chatham by customs officials. In some grief Crosse wrote to his brother John a few days later: 'All my things are stayed and seized, and so tell Sir Walter Raleigh if he be not good to me, I shall be the worse by this voyage' (*Salisbury MSS*, 4.226). However, he appears to have retained sufficient prize-money to have acquired a ship, the *Exchange* of Southampton, later that year. She was outfitted as a privateer under the command of John Crosse, whose subsequent seizure of a Bayonne ship was deemed unlawful in the admiralty court.

In 1595 Crosse commanded the ship *Swiftsure*, which was sent with the *Crane* to rendezvous with Drake and Hawkins off the Portuguese coast—again, with the intention of intercepting a plate fleet. However, the main English fleet had already moved out into the Atlantic before Crosse arrived in October, and he returned to England soon after without significant prizes. In a long letter to 'my master', Robert Cecil (the first reference to his new patron), he begged not to be judged by his ill success. In the following year, in the *Swiftsure* once more, Crosse served in the Cadiz expedition of Essex and Howard, and, with most of his fellow officers, was knighted by the lord admiral following the town's capture. In 1597 he was patrolling the narrow seas in the *Vanguard*, gathering intelligences from Dieppe and elsewhere and acting as courier for letters between Essex and Cecil. From January to March 1598 Crosse served as admiral of a channel squadron of sixteen ships without notable incident. As captain of the *Nonpareil* he was in 1599 part of the fleet under the lord admiral that was hurriedly assembled at the rumour of an impending Spanish invasion attempt.

Crosse appears to have retired from the sea soon afterwards on the grounds of ill health. In 1600 he was awarded some £2700 from exchequer forfeits in recognition of his services, but this was largely consumed by his purchase of property at Marten Abbey in Wiltshire. He spent much time at court thereafter, particularly outside Cecil's chambers, attempting to obtain preferment. In 1601, following the arrest of the earl of Essex, a Captain Lee attempted to involve Crosse in a plot to imprison the queen in her privy chamber until she agreed to release her former favourite from the Tower. Crosse promptly betrayed the plot, and testified at Lee's trial. In July 1603 Sir Walter Ralegh asked Crosse to ride with him to Windsor to visit the new king, James I. This fateful occasion marked the start of Ralegh's long imprisonment; prudently, perhaps, Crosse confined himself to bed for a month thereafter with an unspecified illness.

In 1604 Crosse married Dorothy, the twice widowed daughter of Mitchell Green, a yeoman of the stirrup. By his own admission, he took this drastic step solely to 'have meat to eat the remainder of my years' (*Salisbury MSS*, 19.45–6); however, on 11 February 1606 he was petitioning Salisbury to halt the confiscation of Dorothy's estate by reason of her recusancy. His subsequent attempts to turn her from her fiscally irresponsible convictions by filling his house with protestant divines was wholly unsuccessful, as he admitted. It is not known how Crosse's petition was answered, but his later years appear to have been relatively penurious, despite further pleas to Salisbury to obtain for him a safe parliamentary seat. Crosse's last known entreaty to his old mentor, in 1610, was for the arrest of a man said to have owed him £335 for more than five years. The plea was probably unanswered; in July of that year he petitioned the king, somewhat disingenuously, to allow him relief from his debts or otherwise to permit him to live abroad to avoid the shame of his poverty.

Crosse died on 18 October 1611 at Moulsham, Essex, where he was also buried, without known heirs. His wife probably predeceased him, as the sole benefactor named in his will was Gregory Fenner, of the Sussex seafaring family with whom he appears to have had long-standing associations. Crosse's career exemplified the vacillating fortunes that Elizabethan and Jacobean patronage conferred. Physically courageous and a talented sea commander, but indifferently honest and morbidly fearful of poverty, he appears to have been regarded as good company, both personable and likeable—qualities that kept him at the door of powerful men when less endearing supplicants would have been dismissed as nuisances.

JAMES MCDERMOTT

Sources *Calendar of the manuscripts of the most hon. the marquis of Salisbury*, 24 vols., HMC, 9 (1883–1976), esp. vols. 4–24 · *The naval tracts of Sir William Monson*, ed. M. Oppenheim, 5 vols., Navy RS, 22–3, 43, 45, 47 (1902–14) · J. K. Laughton, ed., *State papers relating to the defeat of the Spanish Armada, anno 1588*, 2 vols., Navy RS, 1–2 (1894) · E. W. Bovill, 'The *Madre de Dios*', *Mariner's Mirror*, 54 (1968), 129–52 · PRO, E351/2234–7 [declared accounts for the navy] · BL, Lansdowne MS 70, fols. 68, 86 · M. F. Keeler, ed., *Sir Francis Drake's West Indian voyage, 1585–6* (1981) · M. Oppenheim, *A history of the administration of the Royal Navy* (1896) · C. L. Kingsford, 'The taking of the *Madre de Dios*, anno 1592', *The naval miscellany*, 2, Navy RS, 40 (1912) · *CSP for., 1591–2* · R. B. Wernham, ed., *The expedition of Sir John Norris and Sir Francis Drake to Spain and Portugal, 1589* (1988) · *Letters from Sir Robert Cecil to Sir George Carew*, ed. J. Maclean, CS, 88 (1864) · J. S. Corbett, ed., *Papers relating to the navy during the Spanish war, 1585–1587* (1898) · PRO, PROB 11/118, fol. 199v · PRO, SP 14/63, 32
Archives BL, corresp. with Lord Burghley, Lansdowne MS 70, fol. 86 · Hatfield House, Hertfordshire, corresp. with R. Cecil

Crosse, Robert (1604/5–1683), writer on philosophy and Church of England clergyman, was the son of William Crosse of Dunster, Somerset. He matriculated from Lincoln College, Oxford, as a commoner on 13 December 1622 aged seventeen. He graduated BA on 6 July 1625, was elected a fellow of his college in 1627, proceeded MA on 10 May 1628 and was ordained that year, and in 1637 became BD. Wood comments that at Oxford Crosse 'became a great tutor and Aristotelian, and [was] much noted in the University for a learned man' (Wood, *Ath. Oxon.*, 4.122). Crosse supported the parliamentarians during the civil war, being taken prisoner in 1643 and interrogated. The same year he was nominated one of the assembly of divines at Westminster. He took the covenant, and in 1648 submitted to the parliamentary commissioners, when he was nominated a canon of Christ Church, Oxford. The committee for the reformation of the university subsequently appointed him to succeed Robert Sanderson as regius professor of divinity but he declined the post and shortly afterwards resigned his university fellowship. In 1652 he was instituted as vicar of Chew Magna, Somerset, and two years later was appointed an assistant to the commissioners for ejecting scandalous ministers in the county. He conformed at the Restoration and remained incumbent at Chew Magna.

Crosse is chiefly known for his promotion of Aristotelian philosophy, which he elucidated in his 1655 publication *Exercitatio theologica de insipientia rationis humanae, gratia Christi destitutae in rebus fidei*. This work led to a prolonged disputation with Joseph Glanvill, who criticized Crosse's adherence to a deductive method of reasoning rather than the experimental philosophizing which had been promoted by Francis Bacon and was then in vogue among members of the Royal Society, to which Glanvill had been elected in 1664. In 1667 Glanvill visited Crosse in

Chew Magna, and in the following year attacked him in print: in *Plus ultra, or, The Progress and Advancement of Knowledge since the Days of Aristotle* he ridiculed Crosse's philosophical interpretations and his criticisms of the Royal Society. Crosse's reply, 'Logou alogia', which Glanvill considered full of 'incomparable railing and impertinence', was rejected by the licensers. Glanvill secured a copy of the tract, and a further 100 copies of it were privately printed by the theologian Nathaniel Ingelo, under the title of the *Chew Gazette*. According to Glanvill, Crosse subsequently wrote ballads against the Royal Society and composed a guide to writing biographies, intended as a critical commentary on John Fell's biography of Henry Hammond, but none of these works appears to have survived. Crosse died at Chew Magna on 12 December 1683. His will mentions neither wife nor children.

HENRY LANCASTER

Sources Wood, *Ath. Oxon.*, new edn, 4.122–3 · *Walker rev.*, 315 · will of Robert Crosse, PRO, PROB 11/375, fol. 212 · Northants. RO, Finch-Hatton papers, MS 577
Archives Northants. RO, interrogation as a prisoner in 1643, MS 577

Crosse, William (*b.* 1589/90), poet and translator, was born in Somerset, 'the son of sufficient parents', and educated at St Mary Hall, Oxford. He matriculated on 28 November 1606, aged sixteen, graduated BA on 14 May 1610 and MA on 9 July 1613, and took holy orders. Soon after this he left Oxford and went to London, 'where he exercised his talents in history and translation, as he had before done in logic and poetry' (Wood, *Ath. Oxon.*). In 1612 he had contributed verses on the death of Henry, prince of Wales, to *Justa Oxoniensium*, and in the following year to *Epithalamia*, a similar collection, in honour of the marriage of the Princess Elizabeth to Frederick, count palatine.

In 1625 Crosse published a poem of little merit but some interest, divided into two books and entitled *Belgiaes troubles and triumphs, wherein are … related all the most famous occurrences, which have happened betweene the Spaniards and Hollanders in these last foure yeares warres of the Netherlands*; it was dedicated to the earl of Essex and Lord Mountjoy. Crosse had accompanied the army as chaplain to the regiment of Colonel Sir John Ogle, and in his poem he celebrates events of which he was himself an eyewitness. In the dedication of the second book he acknowledges, with some modesty, that he has written 'rather a discourse then a poeme' and professes to have treated events 'truely and historically', without unduly indulging in poetic licence. (Wood knew nothing of this work.) Crosse published a second history of the wars in the Netherlands in 1625, *The Dutch Survey*. Under the title *A Continuation of the Historie of the Netherlands, from … 1608 till … 1627* the work appears at page 1276 of Edward Grimestone's *General Historie of the Netherlands* (1627). Grimestone was at first inclined to grumble at this division of labour, 'the printer's hast preventing myne owne desire, having had always an intent to continue what I had begun', but in a subsequent passage he speaks very handsomely of his partner's share in the undertaking.

Crosse's last known publication was *The Workes of C. Crispus Salustius*, in three parts (1629). In the dedication prefixed to the second part he makes quaint allusion to the fact that 'the royall pen of Queene Elizabeth hath beene formerly verst in this translation, but this being like to herselfe, and too good for the world, was never published'. His life was passed in poverty, no better preferment having apparently fallen to his lot than wretchedly paid army chaplaincies. In 1626 he appears as 'preacher to Sir Edward Horwood's regiment in the expedition to Cadiz', in 1630 as 'preacher to the company of the Nonsuch in the last expedition to Rochelle'. Lord Herbert of Cherbury refers to Crosse in his autobiography as 'master of arts, soldier, who hath written and printed the history of the Low Countries' (E. Herbert, *Autobiography*, ed S. L. Lee, 1886, 119). GORDON GOODWIN, *rev.* JOANNA MOODY

Sources Wood, *Ath. Oxon.*, new edn, 2.481–2 • T. Corser, *Collectanea Anglo-poetica, or, A … catalogue of a … collection of early English poetry*, 4, Chetham Society, 77 (1869), 533–9 • Foster, *Alum. Oxon.* • *CSP dom.*, 1625–6, 527; 1629–31, 227

Crossgrove, Henry (1683–1744), printer and newspaper proprietor, was born on 14 August 1683, the son of Patrick Crossgrove, an Irish merchant who died in the revolution of 1688, and his wife, Elizabeth (*fl. c.*1660–*c.*1720), daughter of Henry Gutteridge of Low Leyton, Essex, and Elizabeth, widow of John Fellows. He was bound apprentice to the London printer Thomas Milbourne on 5 August 1700, but never completed his time. Following the death in November 1706 of Francis Burges, proprietor of the *Norwich Post*, Samuel Hasbart, a Norwich distiller, established a printing office in Magdalen Street and employed Crossgrove (who was also known as, and who signed himself as, Cross-grove) as a journeyman to print a rival newspaper, the *Norwich Gazette*. He became a freeman of Norwich by purchase on 18 June 1710.

Crossgrove was in sole charge of the editing and production of the newspaper until March 1718, when he split with Hasbart following a dispute. Crossgrove then set up his own press and published the *Gazette* from premises in St Giles's parish. He also undertook small-scale publishing and bookselling, but remained primarily a newspaper proprietor. For his first twelve years Crossgrove had to compete with two or three rival Norwich newspapers. These included titles produced by Burges's various successors, including Edward Cave, William Chase, and briefly Robert Raikes, who succeeded to Hasbart's press and printed yet another newspaper. However, by the summer of 1718 the *Norwich Gazette* and Chase's *Norwich Mercury* had emerged as the victors, and the rivals had disappeared.

As an outspoken tory with unconcealed Jacobite sympathies (a relatively unusual position for an early Hanoverian printer to adopt), Crossgrove used his newspaper as a vehicle for criticizing both local and national politics in a predominantly whig city. As a result he had frequent brushes with the authorities, and was twice threatened with prosecution for high treason and sedition (1715 and 1730). In each case he was able to avoid prosecution, although he frequently sailed close to the wind. He was also the lifelong enemy of William Chase, and constantly used his newspaper to ridicule or expose his rival's dubious business practices. From 1728 until his death he served as a common councillor, but never obtained influence or profit due to his political allegiances and outspoken views.

Crossgrove's publications were unusually well produced compared with most contemporary provincial printing. He was also a man of some education, and limited literary talent, printing his own verses in his newspaper. In the early days of the *Norwich Gazette* he devoted two columns to answering readers' questions, which were republished in 1708 as *The Accurate Intelligencer* and *Apollinaria* respectively. He was also a friend and correspondent of the ecclesiastical historian John Strype.

Crossgrove was twice married. His first wife, Judith, died in February 1742, and he decorated an issue of his newspaper in her memory. In September 1742 he married Mary, aged nineteen. He had one daughter, Pleasance, who married the printer Robert Davy. Henry Crossgrove was also the master of the Norwich printer Stephen White. He died on 12 November 1744 aged sixty-two, and was buried in St Giles's parish; his newspaper was continued by his widow and son-in-law. DAVID STOKER

Sources J. Williams, 'Henry Cross-grove, Jacobite, journalist and printer', *The Library*, 3rd ser., 5 (1914), 206–19 • D. Stoker, 'The establishment of printing in Norwich: causes and effects, 1660–1760', *Transactions of the Cambridge Bibliographical Society*, 7 (1977–80), 94–111 • D. Stoker, 'The Norwich book trades before 1800', *Transactions of the Cambridge Bibliographical Society*, 8 (1981–5), 79–125 • G. A. Cranfield, *The development of the provincial newspaper press, 1700–1760* (1962) • H. R. Plomer and others, *A dictionary of the printers and booksellers who were at work in England, Scotland, and Ireland from 1668 to 1725* (1922), 88 • D. Stoker, 'Prosperity and success in the eighteenth-century English provincial book trade: the firm of William Chase & Co.', *Publishing History*, 30 (1991), 31–88 • D. F. McKenzie, ed., *Stationers' Company apprentices*, [2]: 1641–1700 (1974) • P. Millican, *The register of freemen of Norwich, 1548–1713* (1934) • [J. Chambers], *A general history of the county of Norfolk*, 2 (1829), 1288–91 • R. M. Wiles, *Freshest advice: early provincial newspapers in England* (1965)

Crossing, William (1847–1928), antiquary, was born on 14 November 1847 in Plymouth, Devon, the second son of Joseph Crossing, a canvas mill owner. He was educated at a clergyman's school in Plymouth, the Independent college at Taunton, and Mannamead School at Plymouth. He then joined the family business in Plymouth and later worked at the South Brent mill. Here, his lifelong fascination with Dartmoor lured him away from his job to explore the moorlands.

The mill failed, and Crossing decided to earn his living by writing about Dartmoor. On 14 March 1872 he married Emma Witheridge of Ivybridge (there were no children of the marriage), and about this time he began to keep detailed notes of his expeditions and of the prehistoric and historic remains which he had found. His early researches were directed mainly towards medieval stone crosses, many of them almost forgotten and neglected; he wrote several books on the subject, the earliest being *The Ancient Crosses of Dartmoor* (1887). A popular figure, Crossing made friends with farmers and moormen wherever he went: he would entertain the local people around a peat fire with his tin whistle or with improvised rhymes describing his day on the moor. He usually walked clad in leather gaiters and tweeds.

By the 1890s Crossing was in some financial difficulties. A frequent contributor of articles to local journals, he now turned to journalism to pay his way. Two of his series of newspaper articles about Dartmoor were subsequently published as books, *A Hundred Years on Dartmoor* (1901) and *Gems in a Granite Setting* (1905). These titles were reprinted in 1967 and 1986 respectively, and others have appeared since.

Crossing's numerous soakings on the moor were now beginning to affect his health and writing abilities (he was stricken with rheumatism), but in 1906 a benefactor, W. P. Collins, engaged him as tutor to his three sons. While he was thus employed, he was able to write his *magnum opus*, the *Guide to Dartmoor* (1909, 1912, and 1914). This book ran to 528 closely printed pages and continues to be the standard topographical account of upland Dartmoor. It was reprinted in facsimile in 1965 with a lengthy introduction and is still in print at the beginning of the twenty-first century.

Crossing's last years were saddened by the death of his wife, on 6 June 1921, while she was a patient in the Tavistock Institution, the local workhouse. Later his landlady destroyed his notes and papers gathered over a lifetime, and he in turn had a spell in the workhouse. Once again, he was rescued by Collins, who installed him in Cross Park House, a nursing home in Plymouth, and paid all the bills until Crossing's death there on 3 September 1928. On 6 September he was buried with his wife in Mary Tavy churchyard on the western edge of Dartmoor.

BRIAN LE MESSURIER

Sources W. Crossing, *Crossing's guide to Dartmoor* (1965) [1912 edn repr. with new introduction by Brian Le Messurier] · W. H. K. Wright, ed., *West-country poets* (1896) · P. Hamilton-Leggett, *The Dartmoor bibliography, 1534–1991* (1992) · *Western Morning News* (4 Sept 1928) · W. Crossing, *Crossing's Dartmoor worker*, ed. B. Le Messurier (1966) · W. Crossing, *Crossing's hundred years on Dartmoor*, ed. B. Le Messurier (1967) · W. Crossing, *Crossing's amid Devonia's alps*, ed. B. Le Messurier (1974) · W. Crossing, *The land of stream and tor* (1994) [with an introduction by Brian Le Messurier] · W. Crossing, *Echoes of an ancient forest* (1994) [with an introduction by Brian Le Messurier] · E. Hemery, *High Dartmoor* (1983) · B. Nicholls, 'William Crossing and the Ivybridge connection', *The Devon Historian* (April 1989), 20–21
Archives Exeter Central Library, Westcountry Studies Library, Hamlyn Parsons MSS
Likenesses photograph, repro. in Wright, ed., *West-country poets* · photograph, repro. in Crossing, *Crossing's Dartmoor worker* · photograph, repro. in Hemery, *High Dartmoor* · photograph, repro. in Crossing, *Crossing's hundred years on Dartmoor*

Crosskey, Henry William (1826–1893), Unitarian minister, social reformer, and geologist, was born in Lewes, Sussex, on 7 December 1826, the eldest of four sons and one daughter of William Crosskey, a prominent Unitarian draper in Lewes, and his second wife, Elizabeth (*née* Rowland). After attending schools run by Unitarian ministers he entered Manchester New College in 1843, where his teachers included James Martineau, Francis Newman, and William Gaskell. In his first pastorate, at Derby, from 1848 to 1852, he served a poor congregation at the Friar-Gate Chapel, founded the Derby Working Men's Institute, and helped establish the National Public School Association, which advocated free, compulsory, secular education supported by local rates and managed by local committees. On 7 September 1852 he married Hannah (*b.* 1825/6), a governess, daughter of Richard Aspden, an accountant and assistant secretary of Manchester New College. In the following month he became pastor of the Unitarian church in Glasgow, where he remained until 1869, overcoming prejudice against Unitarians. He gained a reputation for advocating humanitarian and radical causes such as complete manhood suffrage and suffrage for women.

In 1869 Crosskey responded to a call from the church of the Messiah in Birmingham, the successor to Joseph Priestley's eighteenth-century New Meeting, and during the following twenty-four years he became one of the period's great preachers. As a social reformer he worked alongside such national nonconformist figures as John Bright, R. W. Dale, and Joseph Chamberlain, vigorously championing Chamberlain's programme of municipal reform, serving on the Birmingham school board (1876–92) and on the executive of the National Education League (1869–71), and becoming joint secretary to the Central Nonconformist Committee (1870). A committed Liberal and skilled polemicist, he was sometimes ahead of his party, as in his presidency of the Birmingham Women's Suffrage Society for ten years, and his advocacy of state-supported old-age pensions. He broke with Gladstone over the religious education provisions of the 1870 Education Bill; a second break, over Irish home rule in 1886, brought a virtual end to his national political activities.

A thoroughgoing nonconformist—a proud political dissenter—Crosskey was on the executive committee of the Liberation Society, promoting its unsuccessful campaign to disestablish the Church of England. Expert on the vexed issues of disendowment, he argued with relentless logic that, since the Church of England 'is in reality the State exercising ecclesiastical functions', it followed that, if disestablishment terminated those functions, the funds with which they were carried out should be restored to the nation and applied to public purposes such as education. Crosskey's religious teaching was equally libertarian and controversial. He stood for a humanistic theism free of dogma, authoritarianism, and bibliolatry, and insisted that social reform and scientific research were not only consistent with, but were required by, genuine religious faith. From the moment that he daringly dedicated *A Defence of Religion* (1854) to the secularist George Jacob Holyoake, praising his 'reverence for truth and justice', it was said that Crosskey bore 'the mark of the heretic'.

In the midst of his political and religious commitments, Crosskey pursued his avocation as a self-taught geologist, an interest shared by his wife. During his Glasgow years he headed the city's Geological Society, classifying fossils in order to reconstruct the geological history of western Scotland, and lecturing to the Glasgow Mechanics' Institute. In his Birmingham years he virtually trained a school of midland geologists and presided over the Birmingham Philosophical Society and Natural History Society. He became an expert fly-fisherman and field botanist. In addition to demonstrating his mastery of glaciology and a sustained scientific productivity (some seventy publications), Crosskey advanced a series of prophetic educational proposals, calling for science classes in elementary schools, technical education in mechanics' institutes and teacher training colleges, merit pay increases for teachers, and a midland university that anticipated the University of Birmingham. Recognizing his contributions to science and education, Glasgow University conferred the degree of LLD on him in 1882.

Crosskey died of heart failure on 1 October 1893 at Thirlmese, 24 Wheeleys Road, Edgbaston, Birmingham, survived by his wife. Of his five children, two sons predeceased him. ALBERT R. VOGELER

Sources R. A. Armstrong, *Henry William Crosskey, LLD, FGS, his life and work* (1895) · R. V. Holt, *The Unitarian contribution to social progress in England* (1938) · H. McLachlan, *The Unitarian movement in the religious life of England: its contribution to thought and learning, 1700–1900* (1934) · A. R. Vogeler, 'Crosskey, Henry William', *BDMBR*, vol. 3, pt 1 · *The Times* (3 Oct 1893) · *Birmingham Daily Post* (3 Oct 1893) · *Birmingham Weekly Mercury* (7 Oct 1893) · d. cert.
Archives Birm. CL, Church of the Master MSS · U. Birm., Joseph Chamberlain MSS, corresp.
Likenesses H. J. Whitlock, photograph, repro. in Armstrong, *Henry William Crosskey*, frontispiece
Wealth at death £5,500 8s. 11d.: probate, 11 Nov 1893, CGPLA Eng. & Wales

Crossland, William Henry (1835–1908), architect, was born in Huddersfield and baptized at nearby Elland on 10 May 1835, the son of Henry Crossland, a stonemason, and his wife, Eleanor, *née* Wilkinson. He was a pupil of Sir George Gilbert Scott, and worked under him at Akroydon, near Halifax. On 1 October 1859 he married Lavinia Cardwell Pigot (1837–1879) at St Pancras Old Church in London; they had one daughter. His wife died at Boulogne on 7 January 1879 and was buried at Highgate cemetery, though by this time Crossland was involved with an actress many years his junior, Ruth Elizabeth Hatt, *née* Tilley (1853–1892), with whom he then lived until her death in 1892, and with whom he had several children.

Crossland's architectural development started at Akroydon (now Boothtown), when Edward Akroyd undertook an experiment in social housing. Scott was engaged to prepare initial designs for a model village, while Crossland was employed to work up the detail. An architectural practice centred on the Yorkshire towns of Halifax, Huddersfield, and Leeds followed. For the Church of England Crossland designed at least sixteen new churches and restored ten others. For Sir John William Ramsden he designed the Kirkgate Buildings (1878–85), Byram Arcade (1878–81), and the Ramsden estate office (1868–74) in the centre of Huddersfield. He was also responsible for designing Rochdale town hall (1864–71), on the other side of the Pennines in Lancashire, a building which celebrated Rochdale's rise to fame as a textile borough.

Crossland then shifted his allegiance to the south of England and to Thomas Holloway, a man who had made a fortune from the sale of patent medicines, but who then set about spending his fortune on others. In 1872 Crossland, with John Philpott-Jones (*d.* 1875) and Edward Salomons (1827–1906), entered, and won, an architectural competition for a middle-class asylum which Holloway wished to erect. However, before building work started, Philpott-Jones had died and Salomons had lost interest, leaving Crossland to inherit the commission. What emerged from the Surrey heathland at Virginia Water between June 1873 and 1885 was, at least in part, a recreation of Rochdale town hall and its large central hall (it is now a private housing development and known as Virginia Park).

Crossland's next commission was Royal Holloway College at Egham (now part of the University of London), a women's college, and one which was intended to give women the same educational opportunities as men. The inspiration came from Vassar College in the United States, and the architectural precedents from the châteaux of the Loire, and particularly from Chambord. The first brick was laid in 1879, the skyline was up by 1881, and the college was opened by Queen Victoria on 30 June 1886.

Shortly after completing Royal Holloway College, Crossland slipped into obscurity. He stopped designing, and his name disappeared from RIBA records in the 1890s. He died of a stroke in a north London lodging-house, 57 Albert Street, Regent's Park, on 14 November 1908 and left just £29. JOHN ELLIOTT

Sources L. J. Whitaker, 'W. H. Crossland: his architectural development', MA diss., University of Manchester, 1984 · *Building News* (7 Feb 1890), 221 · biographical file, RIBA BAL · J. Elliott, *Palaces, patronage and pills: Thomas Holloway, his sanatorium, college and picture gallery* (1996) · RIBA BAL, Edward Law MSS · parish register (baptism), 10 May 1835, Elland · census returns, 1861, 1871, 1881, 1891 · parish register (marriage), 1 Oct 1859, St Pancras Old Church · Highgate cemetery records · trade directories · will, 1908
Archives RIBA, nomination papers · RIBA BAL, biography file · RIBA BAL, photographs collection · Royal Holloway College, Egham, Surrey, RIBA archive, biographical file
Likenesses lithograph, repro. in *Building News*, 202 · portrait, Holloway sanatorium, Virginia Park · portrait, Royal Holloway College, Egham, Surrey
Wealth at death £29 2s. 9d.: probate, 6 Jan 1909, CGPLA Eng. & Wales

Crossley, Sir Francis, first baronet (1817–1872), carpet manufacturer and philanthropist, was born at Halifax, Yorkshire, on 26 October 1817, one of the eight children of John *Crossley (*c.*1772–1837) [*see under* Crossley, Martha], a carpet manufacturer at the Dean Clough Mills, Halifax, and his wife, Martha *Crossley (1775–1854), daughter of Abraham Turner of Upper Scout Farm, Northowram, near Halifax, Yorkshire. The fifth and youngest son, Francis was from the earliest age trained to habits of industry. He was sent to school at Halifax, but while still a schoolboy his pocket money was made dependent on his own work. A loom was set up for him in his father's mill, which he tended when not at school, and thus he learned the value of money. In John Crossley's time the carpet factory was a modest affair, but it became, under the management of his sons, John *Crossley (1812–1879), Joseph, and Francis Crossley, who constituted the firm of J. Crossley & Sons, the largest concern of its kind in the world. Crossley married, on 11 December 1845, Martha Eliza, daughter of Henry Brinton of Kidderminster. Their only son, Savile Brinton, became second baronet, and MP successively for Lowestoft and for Halifax.

The buildings at Dean Clough Mills covered an area of 20 acres, and the firm gave employment to between five and six thousand persons. Its rapid growth followed the installation of steam power and machinery. Steam power had already been used extensively in the manufacture of other textile fabrics, and the Crossley firm saw at once its value to their own business. They acquired patents, and then devised and patented improvements which placed them at once far in advance of the whole trade, and gave them the monopoly of a brand of carpet which was subsequently for many years manufactured in greater quantity than any other. One type of loom, for which they owned the patent, had six times the output of the old hand loom. The possession of this loom and the acquisition of other patents compelled the manufacturers of tapestry and Brussels carpets to abandon their hand looms, and to apply to Crossley for licences to work the firm's patents. Very large sums thus accrued to them from royalties alone. In 1864 the concern was changed into a limited liability company and, with a view to increasing the interest taken by the employees in the working of the business, a portion of the shares in the new company were offered to them on favourable terms, and were widely accepted. Crossley was elected in the Liberal interest as MP for Halifax on 8 July 1852; he sat for that borough until 1859, when he became the member for the West Riding of Yorkshire. On the division of the riding in 1868 he was returned for the northern division, which he continued to represent until his death. His generosity was on a princely scale. His first great gift to Halifax consisted in the erection of twenty-one almshouses in 1855, with an endowment yielding a small allowance to each person. On his return from America in 1855 he announced his intention of presenting the people of Halifax with a park, and on 15 August 1857 this park was opened. It consisted of more than 12 acres of ground, laid out from designs by Sir Joseph Paxton, and, with a sum of money invested for its maintenance in 1867, cost the donor £41,300. About 1860, in conjunction with his brothers John and Joseph, he began the erection of an orphan home and school on Skircoat Moor. This was completed at their sole united cost, and endowed by them with a sum of £3000 a year; it was designed to accommodate four hundred children who had lost one or both parents. In 1870 he founded a loan fund of £10,000 for the benefit of deserving tradesmen of Halifax, and in the same year presented to the London Missionary Society the sum of £20,000, the noblest donation the society had ever received. At about the same period he gave £10,000 to the Congregational pastors' retiring fund, and a similar amount towards the formation of a fund for the relief of widows of Congregational ministers. He was mayor of Halifax in 1849 and 1850, and was created a baronet on 23 January 1863. After a long illness he died of heart disease at his home, Belle Vue, Halifax, on 5 January

1872, and was buried in the general cemetery on 12 January, when an immense concourse of friends followed his remains to the grave.

G. C. BOASE, rev. ANITA McCONNELL

Sources *Statesmen of England* (1862) · 'Sir F. Crossley bart.', Religious Tract Society: Biog. Series, 1028 (1873) · S. Smiles, *Thrift* (1875), 205–17 · *Illustrated News of the World and Drawing-Room Portrait Gallery*, 3 (1859) · *The Times* (6 Jan 1872), 12a · *ILN* (20 Jan 1872), 55, 57 · *ILN* (15 June 1872), 587 · *Family Friend*, new ser., 1 (1870), 39–43 · d. cert. · *CGPLA Eng. & Wales* (1872)
Archives V&A NAL, inventory of Somerleyton Hall and its estates | Balliol Oxf., corresp. with Connoley Working Men's Committee *re* the Turkish commercial treaty
Likenesses C. Baugniet, lithograph, 1856, NPG · J. Durham, statue, exh. RA 1861, People's Park, Halifax · Moira & Haigh, carte-de-visite, NPG · stipple and line engraving (after photograph by Mayall), NPG; repro. in *Illustrated News of the World and Drawing-Room Portrait Gallery* · portrait, repro. in *Statesmen of England* · portrait, repro. in *Family Friend* · stipple and line engraving, NPG · wood-engraving, NPG; repro. in *ILN* · woodcut, NPG
Wealth at death under £800,000: probate, 27 May 1872, *CGPLA Eng. & Wales*

Crossley, Francis William (1839–1897), engine manufacturer and philanthropist, and his brother, **Sir William John Crossley**, first baronet (1844–1911), were born in Antrim, the sons of Major Francis Crossley (1787–1846) of Glenburn, Dunmurry, Antrim, and his second wife, Elizabeth Helen Irwin, whom he married in 1837. William, and probably Francis, more affectionately known as Frank, attended the Royal School, Dungannon, from where William went to Bonn for his further education—later to prove of great value in the brothers' association with their German partners. Both trained as engineers, Frank at the works of Robert Stephenson in Newcastle and later working as a draughtsman in Liverpool, and William at the works of W. G. Armstrong & Co., Elswick.

In 1866 the two brothers formed a partnership and with financial help from an uncle, Hastings Irwin, purchased a small engineering business in Great Marlborough Street, Manchester, which manufactured products for the rubber industry. Frank proved to have excellent design as well as technical skills and one of his inventions revolutionized the manufacture of indiarubber thread. Later, his patent thread lathe was adopted by every rubber manufacturer in Britain. William played a part in the technical development of the small firm but was more involved with management matters. The manufacture of internal combustion engines, meanwhile, had gathered pace in Germany. This was largely due to the work of Nikolaus August Otto and his partner, Eugen Langen. In 1867 their engine, referred to as an atmospheric gas engine, was awarded a gold medal at the Paris Exhibition. Following agreements with N. A. Otto & Co., the Crossley brothers began manufacturing gas engines in 1869.

Industry was badly in need of a small power source as an alternative to steam engines that could be used to drive machinery, but the engine was a noisy, cumbersome contraption and Frank immediately instigated improvements in design and operation. An estimated 1300 of these engines, ranging from 0.5 to 3 horsepower, were manufactured and sold to a wide range of industries. The Crossley

Gas Engine quickly became a household name. Otto's invention in 1876 of the four-stroke cycle engine—the principle of all modern internal combustion engines—was a major turning-point in the history of the Crossley firm. More efficient and quieter in operation than its predecessor, the atmospheric engine, it was more economical in use and capable of producing much higher power. As a consequence, demand for the new engine increased rapidly. Larger premises were obtained in Pottery Lane, Openshaw, in 1881, where the firm remained throughout the twentieth century. Engine sales rose from a few hundred in 1869 to over 25,000 in 1897. A wide variety of industries benefited from their use including printing, food, textiles, and engineering.

The private lives of the Crossley brothers were somewhat different. Both, however, had a seemingly overwhelming desire to be of service to others, helping in whatever capacity they could. Frank was a man of deep religious convictions. Work at the factory often started with a service in the specially built chapel which his workers were invited to attend. Away from the works he did much to help the poor and needy of Manchester. William, on the other hand, was very public-spirited and active on numerous committees throughout Manchester and Cheshire.

Frank Crossley's sincere religious belief led him to prevent the sales of engines to breweries and to theatres and public houses, where they could be used to generate electricity. He later softened his views, allowing engines to be sold, but his profits were donated to various charities. His marriage on 1 June 1871 to Emily Kerr (1849–1928) served to strengthen his charitable nature. Her views, so similar to his own, enabled both of them to become even more active in social work. Frank was particularly involved in the work of the Salvation Army movement and General Booth was a frequent visitor to the Crossleys' home in Bowdon, Cheshire. Frank became affectionately known in Salvation Army circles as 'the Paymaster', his gifts to the movement being estimated at over £100,000.

With the help of his wife, Frank Crossley's work continued in earnest throughout the poorer areas of Manchester. An old and disreputable music hall in Ancoats, known as the Star, was pulled down and a new hall erected for meetings. It included bathrooms, dining rooms, and residences attached for the workers. The cost, paid for by the Crossleys, was £20,000. After a few months their home in Bowdon was sold. The Crossleys moved into the new building in Ancoats soon after its opening in 1889 to be nearer 'his people'. Various similar halls were built with Frank bearing the cost in all cases. His unstinting devotion and desire to help others earned him the title St Francis of Ancoats.

Frank Crossley died at a comparatively young age on 25 March 1897, many would say of exhaustion. On the day of his funeral, a crowd of 15,000 people turned out to pay tribute to someone they had come to love dearly. Some people came from Ireland, some from Scotland and other distant parts of Britain. True to his nature, he asked to be buried among the poor people of Ancoats, in Phillips Park

cemetery. He was survived by his wife and four of his five children, Helen (1872–1966), Alan Hastings (1878–1917), Erskine Alick (1880–1918), and Francis Marshall (1884–1938); Richard Frank, born in 1873, died in 1884.

William Crossley was no less sparing in his efforts to be of service to the community. He became a highly respected and successful businessman and was of immense help to his brother in steering the firm through difficult times—in particular, the numerous High Court actions against infringers of the Otto patent for the four-stroke engine. Such actions went totally beyond the principles and beliefs of the Crossleys and were initiated only as a last resort to ensure the continued growth of the firm and the employment of many hundreds of workers. His marriage on 20 April 1876 to Mabel Gordon (d. 1943), daughter of Francis Anderson, produced five children: Kenneth Irwin (1877–1951), Eric (1883–1889), Brian (1886–1915), Lettice (1879–1889), and Ciceley (b. 1880).

In 1901, William Crossley was elected a member of the Cheshire county council and served on numerous committees. He was chairman of the Manchester Hospital for Consumption and Diseases of the Throat and the Crossley Sanatorium, which he founded at Delamere in Cheshire. He also became chairman of the Boys' and Girls' Refuges, at Strangeways, Manchester, president of the Young Men's Christian Association, and founder of the Crossley Lads' Club and Openshaw Lads' Club. In 1902 he became a director of the Manchester Ship Canal Company.

In recognition of his public service, the corporation of Manchester conferred upon William Crossley the freedom of the city in 1903. He became a member of parliament for the Altrincham division of Cheshire in 1908 and was made a justice of the peace in 1907. In 1909 he received a baronetcy but had little time to enjoy the honour. He died at his home, Elmfield, Anson Road, Rusholme, south Manchester, on 12 October 1911.

K. A. BARLOW

Sources Crossley Brothers company records, priv. coll. [firm in Pottery Lane, Openshaw [1996]] · Crossley Brothers, Daybook, 1881–6, priv. coll. [firm in Pottery Lane, Openshaw [1996]] · d. cert. · m. cert. · d. cert. [Sir William John Crossley] · m. cert. [Sir William John Crossley]
Archives BLPES, corresp. with E. D. Morel · priv. coll., Crossley Brothers company records
Wealth at death £624,456 16s. 2d.: probate, 19 May 1897, CGPLA Eng. & Wales · £591,636 17s. 7d.—Sir William John Crossley: probate, 1 Dec 1911, CGPLA Eng. & Wales

Crossley, James (1800–1883), writer and book collector, was born on 31 March 1800 at The Mount, Halifax, the second son of James Crossley (1767–1831), a merchant in the wool manufacturing trade, and his wife, Anne (1772–1813), daughter of William Greenup, a merchant. He received a grounding in classical literature at the grammar schools of Heath and Hipperholme, supplemented by the contents of his father's library. His interest in book collecting was encouraged by Thomas Edwards, a local bookseller, and his precocious knowledge became a curiosity exhibited to his father's friends and dinner guests. The shape of his future life was determined on a visit to Manchester at the age of sixteen when he first visited Chetham's Library, and became absorbed with the unique collection of old volumes, reading through the Latin poets in the course of a six-month vacation after leaving school.

In 1817 Crossley became articled to Thomas Ainsworth, a Manchester solicitor, and began what was to be a life-long friendship with his employer's son William Harrison Ainsworth, who later found fame as a writer of historical romances. Between 1819 and 1821 Crossley wrote articles for several journals, most notably *Blackwood's Magazine* and the *Retrospective Review*. John Gibson Lockhart invited him to contribute to the *Quarterly Review*, but there is no clear evidence that he did so. The *Blackwood's* articles include 'Cheetham's [sic] Library', an affectionate memoir in a style whose maturity belies the youth of the writer, and 'Manchester poetry', ostensibly a review of a poem by W. D. Paynter, which contains satirical comments on the Peterloo massacre of 1819, written from an extreme tory viewpoint.

In 1822 Crossley went to London to complete his legal training under Jacob Phillips, a specialist in conveyancing, at King's Bench Walk. While there he managed to find time to broaden his literary experience with visits to the British Museum and to Charles Lamb and his circle. Crossley's first venture as an editor emerged in 1822, published by Blackwood in the form of a small volume of three tracts by Sir Thomas Browne. It is clear from the preface that a biography of Browne, together with a definitive edition of his works, was planned. In this Crossley was pre-empted by Simon Wilkin, who published a new edition of Browne in 1834–5. Crossley collaborated with Wilkin to some extent, but mischievously included a 'Fragment on Mummies' which he claimed was copied from a manuscript in the British Museum, but was in fact a skilful pastiche from Crossley's own pen, which Wilkin unfortunately published in good faith. The piece was at first accepted as original, but was omitted from subsequent editions of the work.

Crossley was recalled to Manchester in 1823 to become a partner in the firm of Ainsworth, Crossley, and Sudlow. He continued in the legal profession until his retirement in 1860, being elected as the first president of the Manchester Law Association in December 1838, and serving again in that office in 1857. Working in the Conservative interest, he was actively involved in the parliamentary elections of 1832, 1835, and 1837. The following year, Crossley became the legal representative of the movement against the incorporation of Manchester as a municipal borough. Passions ran high at this time, as exemplified in one memorable clash with John Edward Taylor, the editor of the *Manchester Guardian*, which resulted in Crossley challenging the bemused editor to a duel. Fortunately the challenge was declined, but politics might have played a larger part in Crossley's life had not the causes he espoused been doomed to failure.

The second half of Crossley's life was centred on his involvement with the Chetham Society, which also constitutes his foremost claim on posterity. Conceived after a dinner at Crossley's house given for like-minded friends,

the society was dedicated to publishing the 'Remains historical and literary connected with the palatine counties of Lancaster and Chester'. As president of the Chetham Society, a position he held from 1847 to his death in 1883, Crossley was the driving force behind all the publishing, always striving to maintain the society's commitment to its subscribers of three volumes per year. This may have restricted the amount of editorial work he was able to complete, but he nevertheless produced twelve titles for the society, including scholarly editions of Thomas Potts's *The Wonderfull Discoverie of Witches in the Countie of Lancaster* (1845) and the first two volumes of *The Diary and Correspondence of Dr John Worthington* (1847–86).

For more than thirty years there was hardly a literary event in Manchester in which Crossley did not play a major part, one of his most prestigious offices being the chairmanship of the committee for selecting and buying books for the Manchester Free Library, which opened in 1852. He was president of the Athenaeum from 1847 to 1850, donated rare volumes to the Portico Library, and served as honorary librarian at Chetham's Library from 1877. Outside Manchester, he was a member of the Abbotsford Club as well as the Camden, Surtees, Spenser, and Philobiblon societies, and was elected a fellow of the Society of Antiquaries in 1852. His antiquarian interests provided source material for several of Harrison Ainsworth's novels: a hitherto unknown piece by Defoe, discovered by Crossley, *Due Preparations for the Plague*, for example, formed the foundation for Ainsworth's very successful *Old St Paul's* (1841). Similarly, Crossley's edition of Potts furnished the raw material for one of Ainsworth's best-known novels, *The Lancashire Witches* (1849). Ainsworth returned the compliment by depicting Crossley as the benign physician Dr Foam, in *Mervyn Clitheroe* (1858).

A portrait of Crossley, said to be an excellent likeness, was commissioned in 1875 from John Hanson Walker, and can be found in the reading-room of Chetham's Library. A large man in every sense of the word, in the latter part of life he cut a striking figure in the streets of Manchester as he made his daily excursion to Chetham's Library, enveloped in a dark cloak, with a broad-brimmed hat covering his large head, silvery locks falling to his shoulders. Crossley earned a reputation as an accomplished public speaker as well as an erudite and entertaining dining companion, and was more than once described as Manchester's Doctor Johnson. In 1878, when he moved out of the city to a larger property, Stocks House in Cheetham Hill, Crossley estimated the size of his library at about 50,000 volumes, including many rare tracts and manuscripts. He was often consulted by fellow bibliophiles on a wide variety of subjects, and his contributions to *Notes and Queries* between 1850 and 1878 testify to the vast extent of his knowledge. He made a lasting contribution to Defoe scholarship by identifying some sixty works that had not previously been attributed to that author. A few of these have subsequently been challenged, but most are accepted as legitimate parts of the Defoe canon.

Crossley died at Stocks House on 1 August 1883 following a fall at Euston Station some months earlier, and was buried at St Paul's parish church, Kersal, Manchester. He was never married. His vast collection was broken up and sold at auction, first in Manchester in May 1884, and then by Sothebys in July 1884 and June 1885—the total sale taking up 22 days, with a total of 8625 lots.

STEPHEN COLLINS

Sources Manchester Guardian (2 Aug 1883) · Manchester Courier (2 Aug 1883) · S. Crompton, 'The late Mr James Crossley', Palatine Note-Book, 3 (1883), 221–9 · W. H. Ainsworth, December tales (1823), 183–92 · J. Evans, Lancashire authors and orators (1850), 67–72 · S. M. Ellis, 'A great bibliophile: James Crossley', Wilkie Collins, Le Fanu, and others (1931) · R. J. Kane, 'James Crossley, Sir Thomas Browne, and the Fragment on mummies', Review of English Studies, 9 (1933), 266–74 · P. N. Furbank and W. R. Owens, The canonisation of Daniel Defoe (1988) · A. Crosby, 'A society without equal': the Chetham Society, 1843–1993 (1993) · W. R. Credland, The Manchester free public libraries (1899) · S. F. Collins, 'James Crossley: publisher, critic, collector, and bibliographer', PhD diss., Manchester Metropolitan University, 2000

Archives Chetham's Library, Manchester, MS coll. and notes · Man. CL, papers | BL, life of Girolamo Cardano · BL, annotations on Hartlib–Worthington corresp. · BL, letters to W. C. Hazlitt and others

Likenesses C. Mercier, oils, 1857; formerly in Free public library, Manchester · photograph, c.1870 · J. H. Walker, oils, 1875, Chetham's Library, Manchester

Wealth at death £4736 14s. 2d.: administration with will, 19 Oct 1883, CGPLA Eng. & Wales

Crossley, John (c.1772–1837). See under Crossley, Martha (1775–1854).

Crossley, John (1812–1879), industrialist and philanthropist, was born on 16 May 1812 in Halifax, the sixth of the eight children of John *Crossley (c.1772–1837) [see under Crossley, Martha], carpet manufacturer, and his wife, Martha *Crossley (1775–1854), daughter of Abraham Turner (1747–1805) of Upper Scout Farm, Northowram, near Halifax. His father, a former carpet weaver, had founded the family carpet manufacturing business at Dean Clough, Halifax, in 1822, following two decades in partnership with other carpet manufacturers. After his death in 1837 the firm continued as John Crossley & Sons under the direction of his three youngest sons, John, Joseph, and Francis *Crossley, and by the time of John's death in 1879 it had become the largest carpet manufacturing firm in the world.

It is not easy to distinguish the individual contributions to the success of the firm of the three brothers, who maintained an effective and harmonious business partnership. Joseph, who unlike his brothers played no prominent role in public life, is often characterized as the partner most closely involved in the day-to-day management of the firm, while Francis has been portrayed as the most enterprising and innovative, taking the initiative in the development of steam-powered tapestry carpet production, which provided the springboard for the firm's mid-century expansion. However, John's association with the firm, extending over a half a century, was the longest, including forty years as senior partner and chairman of the board of directors. During this period the firm became a pioneering joint-stock company, with the primary aim of enabling employees to become shareholders, achieving by the early 1870s annual carpet sales of £1,100,000, including exports to the United States valued at nearly £500,000. On his retirement John Crossley expressed particular satisfaction that for nearly forty years 'no dispute or misunderstanding has occurred but such as was there and then, by mutual compromise, adjusted' (Halifax Courier, 19 April 1879). Later, Uriah Bairstow, a former employee, contrasted the management styles of Francis, 'the shrewd businessman', and Joseph, 'a terror to evil doers', with the more sympathetic approach to personnel of John, whose 'great kindness and his great regard for the people and their great regard for him' was universally acknowledged (Calderdale District Archives, DC 1737).

Samuel Smiles, the apostle of Victorian self-help, commending the approach of the Crossley brothers' father to parenting, observed: 'when at home, he always had one of his sons near him; or when he went from home, he always took one of them with him', thereby equipping them with 'a great deal of practical knowledge of life' (Smiles, 238). As John Crossley later revealed, 'when he was about twelve years of age his father, finding that he was not making much progress at school, thought it would be a good thing to put him in his factory for twelve months', working a fifteen hour day (Hansard 3, 218, 1874, 1773–6). He received no further formal education, apart from a year at the local grammar school in 1825–6. No less significant was the influence of the boys' remarkable mother, whose earnest evangelical nonconformity and celebrated vow that 'if the Lord does bless us at this place, the poor shall taste of it' (Smiles, 240) inspired both an unremitting commitment to work and a liberal philanthropy, which characterized the lives of all three brothers.

Of the brothers, John made the most significant contribution to the life of the local community. A petitioner for Halifax's municipal charter, he served on the Halifax town council from its inception in 1848 until 1868, earning the unique distinction of serving four terms as mayor and hosting the first visit of a member of the British royal family to Halifax in 1863, when the prince of Wales opened Sir Charles Barry's magnificent new town hall. This sumptuous monument to Victorian municipal endeavour formed the centrepiece of a privately financed urban improvement scheme, commenced by John Crossley in 1851, which transformed an area of dilapidated back yards, workshops, stables, and piggeries into an elegant urban environment with wide streets and impressive stone buildings, which a visiting reporter later maintained 'would do credit to most European capitals' (Bretton, 18). Elsewhere in the town he constructed an Italianate model lodging house, with accommodation for fifty vagrants; promoted a non-profit-making model housing scheme, designed 'to encourage thrifty artisans, clerks and others to obtain freehold dwellings for themselves' (Hole, 75); and, with his brothers, founded and endowed a large orphanage, close to his ornate Gothic mansion at Manor Heath. Moreover, besides serving as a magistrate, chairman of the Halifax Commercial Banking Company, and a member of the Halifax school board, he was associated with the establishment of a building society, chamber of commerce, local newspaper, post office, and woollen market, and the construction of new reservoirs for the town.

In February 1874 John Crossley accepted nomination as parliamentary candidate for Halifax and headed the poll, even though serious injuries sustained in a carriage accident in August 1873 had precluded his taking an active part in the contest. A Gladstonian Liberal and sabbatarian, he also supported militant dissenting campaigns for the disestablishment of the Church of England and the repeal of clause 25 of the 1870 Education Act, which permitted payments from the rates to Anglican schools for the education of poor children. He was assiduous in his attendance at the House of Commons and served on the public departments (purchases) select committee in 1874, but rarely spoke in debates, experiencing some difficulty with 'spontaneous public utterance' (*Halifax Courier*, 26 April 1879). His maiden speech in May 1874, while recognizing the value of the 'ten hour system', revealed his opposition to further extension of factory regulation, and in a subsequent speech he supported an amendment designed to enable the employment of children of nine years of age in factories. He resigned his seat in February 1877 as a result of continuing ill health and financial embarrassment arising from imprudent speculative investment, motivated in the view of his mentor, Dr Enoch Mellor, by 'an undercurrent of hope that immense public benefit would accrue' (ibid.) from the development of natural mineral resources rather than any desire for personal financial gain.

John Crossley appears in photographs and portraits as a tall, soberly dressed figure, with a greying beard and whiskers, a gentle bearing, and kindly disposition. He had known personal tragedy when his first wife, Anne Child (1811–1846), the daughter of Kitchenman Child of Ovenden, whom he had married on 7 May 1839 and with whom he had a son and two daughters, died shortly after the birth of their third child. He remarried on 11 November 1847; his new wife was Sarah (1803–1879), daughter of Joseph Wheatley of Hopton and widow of John Hodgson of Halifax; they had no children. He was a devout Christian and chairman of the English Congregational Chapel Building Society, supporting numerous chapel and school building schemes, including the rebuilding in 1857 of Square Congregational Chapel, Halifax, where he was a devoted member, deacon, and Sunday school teacher. Enoch Mellor, the minister, described him in his funeral eulogy as essentially 'a plain man, simple as a child, artless, unambitious of name or honours, content to do good and to be hidden behind the good he did, and to die where his work was done' (*Halifax Courier*, 26 April 1879).

Unlike Francis Crossley, who acquired a country estate in Somerleyton, Suffolk, in 1861, and a baronetcy in 1863, John remained in Halifax until ill health and straitened financial circumstances obliged him to move to his daughter and son-in-law's home at Putney in 1878, before returning with them to Halifax, where he died at Broomfield,

Skircoat, from heart disease on 16 April 1879. He was buried at Lister Lane cemetery; his civic funeral brought the busy town of Halifax to a halt, revealing the undiminished respect of the Halifax public for the last of the Crossley brothers, who had died an invalid, leaving less than £8000, in marked contrast to his brothers, Joseph and Francis, who had left personal estates valued at £900,000 and £800,000 respectively. He was survived by his wife, who died later in the year, by his only son, Louis John (1842–1891), a pioneer electrical scientist, and by his younger daughter, Anne (1846–1925), who had married Giulio Marchetti, formerly one of Garibaldi's redshirts and subsequently a director and chairman of John Crossley & Sons Limited.

JOHN A. HARGREAVES

Sources *Halifax Courier* (19 April 1879) · *Halifax Courier* (26 April 1879) · *Halifax Guardian* (19 April 1879) · *Halifax Guardian* (25 April 1879) · *Hansard 3* (1874), 218.1773–6; 220.332 · R. Bretton, 'Crossleys of Dean Clough', *Transactions of the Halifax Antiquarian Society* (1953) · S. Smiles, *Thrift* (1875) · John Crossley and sons (Dean Clough mills), Halifax, carpet manufacturers, records 1621–1982, W. Yorks. AS, Calderdale · MSS notebook attributed to John Crossley, Calderdale Industrial Museum, Halifax · J. N. Bartlett, *Carpeting the millions: the growth of Britain's carpet industry* (1978) · R. Fletcher, *Pedigree of the Crossleys of Dean Clough* (1974) · J. N. Bartlett, 'Crossley, Sir Francis', *DBB* · J. A. Jowitt, ed., *Model industrial communities in mid-nineteenth century Yorkshire* (1986) · R. A. Innes, *Crossley mosaics* (1974) · E. Webster, *Dean Clough and the Crossley inheritance* (1988) · J. Hole, *The homes of the working classes* (1866) · M. Girouard, *The Victorian country house*, rev. edn (1979) · m. cert. · d. cert.
Archives Avena Carpets, Bankfield Mill, Halifax, carpet samples · Bankfield Museum, Halifax, mosaics · Calderdale Industrial Museum, Halifax, machinery and memorabilia · Dean Clough Galleries, Halifax, lost workers archive · W. Yorks. AS, Dean Clough archives
Likenesses J. Durham, marble bust, *c.*1860, Joseph Crossley Almshouses, Halifax, West Yorkshire, chapel · photograph, *c.*1860, W. Yorks. AS, Calderdale District Archives · J. P. Knight, portrait, 1868, Halifax Town Hall, Halifax, West Yorkshire · photograph, *c.*1868, W. Yorks. AS, Calderdale District Archives · R. Drummond, ink and wash drawing, 1872–5, Bankfield Museum, Halifax, West Yorkshire · photograph, 1877, Henry Moore Studio, Dean Clough; on loan from Mary Crossley · J. Eastham, photograph, priv. coll. · E. Greaves, composite photographs, W. Yorks. AS, Calderdale District Archives · print, Crossley Heath School, Halifax, West Yorkshire
Wealth at death under £8000: probate, 15 May 1879, *CGPLA Eng. & Wales*

Crossley, Sir Julian Stanley (1899–1971), banker, was born on 3 January 1899 in Halifax, Yorkshire, the son of Charles Wheatley Crossley, and his wife, Caroline Smedley Marsden Smedley. His father was a descendant of John Crossley, founder of the Crossley Carpet Company. He attended Wellington College and in the holidays sailed on Lake Windermere. This gave him a love of sailing, and he later owned a sloop in which he and his family sailed around Britain and beyond. From 1917 to 1919 he was a midshipman in the Royal Navy; after the war he took a short course in modern history, from 1919 to 1921, at New College, Oxford.

At Wellington and at Oxford Crossley was a good friend of William Macnamara Goodenough, son of Frederick Crauford Goodenough, chairman of Barclays Bank; this friendship shaped Crossley's life. He joined Barclays in

October 1921, at first in its Cannon Street branch, then in 1922 was sent to Barclays' New York office as assistant to Barclays' local representative. In 1925, led by Frederick Goodenough but with some input from Crossley and Will Goodenough, Barclays created Barclays Bank (Dominion, Colonial, and Overseas); its constituents were the Colonial Bank (with branches in Africa and the Caribbean), the Anglo-Egyptian Bank, and the National Bank of South Africa. Crossley in 1926 transferred to the new subsidiary, which rapidly became known simply as DCO.

Crossley's first overseas assignment was a visit to southern and central Africa to assess possibilities for DCO; on hearing (through a chance meeting with a prospector) of enormous untapped copper deposits in undeveloped country, he urged and obtained rapid DCO expansion in what became Zambia, though acknowledging that new branches would take time to become profitable. Expansion, with an eye to the long rather than the short run, was the keynote of DCO, and it was endorsed by Crossley as he moved to become assistant general manager, general manager (1935–44), executive deputy chairman (1944), and then chairman (1947) on the promotion of the incumbent, Will Goodenough, to the chairmanship of Barclays. In 1928 Crossley's ties with the Goodenough family were reinforced by his marriage to Will Goodenough's sister, Barbara Mary Goodenough. The couple had three sons and one daughter.

Crossley was a handsome, square-jawed, ex-rugby player, sometimes taciturn, sometimes forthright, but imbued with the belief that Britain, the colonies, and the emerging dominions must all benefit from closer financial and industrial ties, and that these would encourage political cohesion in an uncertain world. He had no hesitation in promoting the expansion of European-owned enterprises in Africa and elsewhere, equating this with general improvement; he was a tireless traveller to DCO's branches abroad, cramming events and visits into his schedules, and encouraging staff to seek new opportunities. Crossley relied on such visits to promote unity within DCO, since at the same time he decentralized more power to its local boards. His creation of the post of general manager (staff), while introducing more method into appointments and career moves within DCO, still allowed for some differences of practice and approach in a bank that had branches in forty countries.

Wartime exigencies often caused Crossley to accompany Will Goodenough on visits to government departments, and the contacts thus acquired were of some use when they lobbied for thirteen months for permission to create Barclays Overseas Development Corporation, which was designed to provide finance for agricultural and industrial projects in countries where DCO operated. Approval was granted in 1945: Crossley was a founding director, and subsequently its deputy chairman. Proud that Barclays DCO gave equal service to all, including Jew and Arab in the then Palestine, he was at first cautious about employment of non-Europeans in the West Indies and elsewhere. Within a few years, however, DCO trained and employed people from all ethnic groups in most countries except South Africa (a favourite country of Crossley's), where apartheid laws effectively confined non-Europeans working for DCO to cleaning and chauffeuring. Crossley resisted full corporate status for DCO's local boards, since this implied tying up capital in individual countries—a change later forced upon DCO.

Crossley also strengthened commonwealth ties in another way. From 1935 he endorsed the Goodenough family's support for London House, a residence for white male students from the empire and commonwealth; its umbrella organization was the Dominion Students' Hall Trust, which later created William Goodenough House. Crossley acknowledged before the war ended that the trust needed to alter its deeds, and it subsequently did so, opening the residences' doors to men and women of every ethnic origin. Crossley became its chairman in 1965, and he was a governor of the Pilgrim Trust and of Queen Elizabeth House, Oxford. He was also an active and valued vice-president of Wellington College from 1960 to 1966, and of the Commonwealth Institute. Crossley retired as chairman of Barclays DCO in January 1967, remaining a director of it and of Barclays Bank until his death. He died before completing his history of DCO, but the first nine chapters of *The DCO Story* (1972) are virtually as he wrote them. Barclays DCO became one of the largest and most successful of Britain's overseas multi-nationals, and Crossley played an important role in its expansion in the 1950s and early 1960s. His knighthood in 1964 was a tribute to his banking career and his energetic public life.

Sir Julian Crossley died on 26 January 1971 at Severals, his Hampshire farm at Swarraton, near Alresford. He was survived by his wife.   MARGARET ACKRILL

Sources J. S. Crossley, diaries, 1942–9, Barclays archives, Wythenshawe, Cheshire · J. S. Crossley, diaries, 1951, Barclays archives, Wythenshawe, Cheshire · J. S. Crossley, file of weekly notes, Oct 1963–June 1965, Barclays archives, Wythenshawe, Cheshire · Board minutes of Barclays DCO, Barclays archives, Wythenshawe, Cheshire · Assorted addresses about Crossley and his obituaries, Barclays archives, Wythenshawe, Cheshire · J. Crossley and J. Blandford, *The DCO story: a history of banking in many countries, 1925–71* (1975) · A. W. Tuke and R. J. H. Gillman, *Barclays Bank Limited, 1926–1969: some recollections* (1972) · [Barclay's Bank], *A bank in battledress* (1948) · CGPLA Eng. & Wales (1971) · d. cert. · G. Jones, *British multinational banking, 1830–1990: a history* (1993)

Archives Barclays, Wythenshawe, Cheshire, archives

Likenesses O. Birley, oils, Barclays Bank; repro. in Crossley and Blandford, *DCO story* · photographs, Barclays archives, Wythenshawe, Cheshire

Wealth at death £163,073: probate, 6 May 1971, CGPLA Eng. & Wales

Crossley [*née* Turner], **Martha** (1775–1854), carpet manufacturer, was born on 23 February 1775 at Folly Hall, Ambler Thorn, Northowram, near Halifax, the second of the six children of Abraham Turner (1747–1805), a yeoman farmer and former worsted manufacturer, and his wife, Sarah (1741–1814), the daughter of Charles Appleyard of Shaw Booth, Warley, Halifax, and his wife, Martha. Her father's property, although it was not extensive, had been in the family for many generations, and the land contained rich coal deposits, valued at £1000 in 1805. Martha, who was baptized at Mixenden Independent Chapel, Ovenden, Halifax, on 5 April 1775, 'could knit a stocking as long as myself' from the age of five and later knit stockings 'for my father and all the family' (Calderdale Industrial Museum, notebook, attrib. J. Crossley). Her family took up residence at Upper Scout Farm, Northowram, in 1782. Martha was educated locally at the Catherine Slack and Boothtown schools, Northowram, before entering domestic service at the age of thirteen for a spinster, Miss Elizabeth Oldfield, of Stock Lane, Warley, Halifax. She earned initially around 3 guineas a year, rising to 6 guineas after nine years' service, for doing the work of kitchenmaid, housemaid, and cook, milking six cows morning and evening, and spinning woollen yarn. During this period she managed to save £30 'by sheer thrift', according to Samuel Smiles, the Victorian prophet of honest toil, for whom she became a paradigm of prudent financial management (Smiles, 203). Her savings, a valuable source of capital for industrial enterprise, were augmented by legacies from her father in 1805 and from her former employer in 1808.

Martha Turner married the carpet manufacturer **John Crossley** (c.1772–1837) on 28 January 1801 at Halifax parish church, against the wishes of her father, who had declared 'that he would never allow his daughter to marry a weaver, or even a foreman of weavers' (Smiles, 234–5). After her marriage she became 'the backbone of the family', taking 'a full share in the labours and responsibility of her husband', in the view of Smiles, who maintained that the prosperity of the Crossley family was 'quite as much due to the Crossley women as the Crossley men' (ibid.). She later recalled that 'in addition to carpet making we carried on the manufacture of shalloons and plainbacks, the whole of which I managed myself, so far as putting out the warps and weft and taking in from the weavers'—who numbered as many as 160 when the outworking system was operating at its peak. She also 'made and stitched, with assistance, all the carpets that we sold retail', rising regularly before dawn, and sold 'brace webs and body belts … principally to the Irish, who … hawked them about the country' (Calderdale Industrial Museum, notebook, attrib. J. Crossley).

Eight children—two daughters and six sons, including John *Crossley (1812–1879)—were born to the Crossleys between 1803 and 1817, all of whom survived infancy apart from the eldest boy, who died in January 1805, a month after his birth. Their youngest son, Sir Francis *Crossley, paying tribute to his mother's memory in a public speech in Halifax in 1867, described her as 'sensitive and quick in disposition'. The oil portrait of her in later life, which he commissioned, shows her plainly attired in silk bonnet, white shawl, and dark dress. Her sympathetic dark brown eyes, neatly parted hair, and calm, resolute countenance reveal a woman of quiet determination, seated upright, her left hand clutching her spectacles and resting upon an open Bible on her lap. Her earnest evangelical nonconformity and celebrated vow that, 'if the Lord does bless us at this place, the poor shall taste of it' inspired a liberal philanthropy in her

sons, based on the biblical principle of tithing, and a compassionate commitment to sustaining employment for their employees throughout the year. 'If you can', she advised, 'go on giving employment to some during the winter … for it is a bad thing for a working man to go home and hear his children cry for bread and not be able to give them any' (Bretton, 5–6).

After her husband's acquisition of the Dean Clough lease in 1802, Martha Crossley lived in a house adjoining the carpet factory in Old Lane, Northowram, until the time of her death, from natural causes, on 26 November 1854, in her eightieth year. In her declining years she had a mirror fixed in her room so that 'while lying in bed she could see the happy countenances of those who were going to work, or coming back again'. An obituary in the *Halifax Courier* (2 December 1854) described her as 'a woman of great sagacity and of keen insight into character, of inflexible integrity … generous and benevolent and a thorough Christian in mind, heart and action', who was 'universally respected' (*Halifax Courier*, 2 Dec 1854) by the poor. Her burial at Square Congregational Chapel on 30 November 1854, conducted by the minister, the Revd Dr Enoch Mellor, was a strictly private ceremony, but many hundreds gathered around the chapel in silent tribute. John Crossley & Sons, which by 1854 had become the largest carpet firm in the country, was closed for the day of the funeral, in compliance with her request, and 'a full day's wages paid to every person employed there whether working by day or piece' (*Halifax Courier*, 2 Dec 1854).

The life of her husband, John Crossley, the founder of the family firm, who predeceased her by sixteen years, is less well documented. Indeed, the precise date of his birth remains uncertain and no likeness of him has survived. He was the fifth of the eight children of John Crossley (1741–1820), a carpet weaver, of Halifax, and his wife, Bethia (1739–1788), the eldest daughter of Richard Webster of Clay Pits, Halifax. When his mother died in childbirth in 1788, he was apprenticed as a carpet weaver at the age of sixteen to his uncle, John Webster of Clay Pits, who 'did me a great deal of good'. He subsequently worked for William Currer, the largest carpet manufacturer in Yorkshire in the late eighteenth century, at Luddenden Foot, near Halifax; following an industrial injury he transferred to loom tuning, which led to his appointment as manager of Job Lees's carpet factory, in the Lower George Yard, Halifax. He soon became a partner with Lees, and when Lees died in October 1801 Crossley formed new partnerships in rapid succession, first with Robert Abbot and Francis Ellerton, and then with his brother Thomas Crossley and James Travis, and in 1802 took out a twenty-year lease of premises at Dean Clough, Halifax. When the lease expired in 1822, the partnership was dissolved; John Crossley renewed the lease and set up his own business. He purchased the carpet manufacturing business of Messrs Abbot and Ellerton, his former partners, in 1830, and, by the time of his death, at Old Lane, Northowram, following a short illness, on 17 January 1837, the firm, with 150 looms and some 300 employees, ranked as fourth largest in the country. He left a personal estate of around £18,000 and was 'deeply lamented by his family and numerous circle of friends' (*Halifax Guardian*, 21 Jan 1837). He was later remembered by his son Francis (who, with two of his elder brothers, continued their father's business after his death) as a 'quaint, humorous, shrewd man and thoroughly upright and honest in all his dealings' (*Halifax Courier*, 19 April 1879). His dictum 'Let each carpet produced by John Crossley and Sons be its own traveller' helped to establish the Crossley reputation for quality (ibid.).

JOHN A. HARGREAVES

Sources *Halifax Courier* (2 Dec 1854) · *Halifax Guardian* (21 Jan 1837) · *Leeds Mercury* (21 Jan 1837) · R. Bretton, 'Crossleys of Dean Clough [pt 1]', *Transactions of the Halifax Antiquarian Society* (1950), 1–9 · S. Smiles, *Thrift* (1875) · John Crossley & Sons (Dean Clough Mills), Halifax, carpet manufacturers, records, 1621–1982, W. Yorks. AS, Calderdale, DC · MS notebook attributed to John Crossley, Calderdale Industrial Museum, Halifax · J. N. Bartlett, *Carpeting the millions: the growth of Britain's carpet industry* (1978) · R. Fletcher, *Pedigree of the Crossleys of Dean Clough* (1974) · J. N. Bartlett, 'Crossley, Sir Francis', *DBB* · T. Baines, *Yorkshire, past and present: a history and description of the three great ridings of the county of York*, 2 (1875), 405–6 · E. Webster, *Dean Clough and the Crossley inheritance* (1988) · J. A. Hargreaves, 'Religion and society in the parish of Halifax, c.1740–1914', PhD diss., CNAA (Huddersfield), 1991 · M. Girouard, *The Victorian country house*, rev. edn (1979) · d. cert.

Archives Bankfield Museum, Halifax, mosaics · Calderdale Industrial Museum, Halifax, memorabilia | Dean Clough Galleries, Halifax, Lost Workers archive · W. Yorks. AS, Halifax, Calderdale District Archives, Dean Clough archives

Likenesses E. Greaves, group portrait, composite photograph, 1877 (with family; after painting), W. Yorks. AS, Calderdale, DC 1715 · oils, Somerleyton Hall, near Lowestoft, Suffolk · oils, priv. coll.

Wealth at death under £18,000—John Crossley: Fletcher, *Pedigree*

Crossley, Sir William John, first baronet (1844–1911). *See under* Crossley, Francis William (1839–1897).

Crossman, Richard Howard Stafford (1907–1974), politician and diarist, was born on 15 December 1907 in Porchester Terrace, Bayswater, London, the third of six children (three boys and three girls) of Sir (Charles) Stafford Crossman (1870–1941) of Buckhurst Hill House, Essex, and his wife, Helen Elizabeth (1876/7–1961), daughter of David Howard DL. His father, appointed to the bench in 1934, was an industrious chancery barrister of strictly conservative disposition; there was little rapport between the cautious parent and his ultimately rebellious middle son. There was never any doubt, however, that more than any of the other five children Crossman inherited his father's intellectual ability and academic bent: at the age of twelve, like his father, he won a scholarship to Winchester College. His school career (1920–26), which ended with his becoming prefect of hall and winning a scholarship to New College, Oxford, was conventionally successful, but his father's hope that his son would follow him into the law did not survive Crossman's own declaration that, if so, he would want to be 'a famous criminal advocate'—an aspiration that caused his father, as a bencher of Lincoln's Inn, such pain that he readily accepted his son's alternative ambition to become a don.

Having again followed in his father's footsteps by taking

Richard Howard Stafford Crossman (1907–1974), by Bassano, 1947

first classes in both classical honour moderations (1928) and *literae humaniores* (1930), Crossman was duly offered a fellowship by his own college in 1930. To ease the transition from junior to senior common room, a condition was that he should first spend a year abroad. Crossman elected to go to Germany and, given the rise of Hitler at the time, it turned out to be a fateful choice. Though he had hitherto taken little interest in politics, his year in Germany awakened a political appetite in Crossman that was to remain unabated for the rest of his life. He also met in Berlin a twice-married German Jewess, Erika Susanna Glück (*née* Landsberg), who on 15 July 1932 became his first wife.

Back in Oxford Crossman soon made his mark, lecturing to crowded houses in the Examination Schools and acquiring renown as a brilliant tutor with a special gift for the toughest sort of dialectic. His technique of teaching is probably best preserved in the books he wrote at the time—*Plato To-Day* (1937), *Socrates* (1938), and *Government and the Governed* (1939). By the time the latter two were published he had already left the university—though he retained his links with the city through his leadership from 1936 to 1940 of the Labour group on the Oxford city council, to which he had first been elected in 1934.

The occasion of Crossman's departure from New College lay in a development in his private life. Having in 1934 ended his first marriage, on 18 December 1937 he married the divorced wife (Inezita (Zita) Hilda Baker, *née* Davis, who died in 1952) of one of his own colleagues in the New College senior common room. But the cause of his wanting to get away from Oxford had deeper roots than this personal difficulty. By the mid-1930s he had become an active participant in Labour politics, nationally as well as locally; along with Hugh Dalton and a few others he was a lonely champion of British rearmament in the Labour Party. In 1937 he unsuccessfully fought a by-election in Labour's interest at West Birmingham and a year later was adopted as the party's prospective candidate for the then single seat of Coventry.

In the ordinary course of events, Crossman could have expected to enter the House of Commons in 1940 at the latest. But the outbreak of war, and the extension of the 1935 parliament, meant he had to wait another five years. He initially used the waiting time in Workers' Educational Association lecturing and in political journalism (becoming an assistant editor of the *New Statesman* in 1938)—but in 1940 he was drafted into the Ministry of Economic Warfare by Hugh Dalton to organize the British propaganda effort against Hitler's Germany. Of the official view of his performance in this role one piece of contemporary evidence survives in the Public Record Office. It is the final character assessment written on him in 1945 by Sir Robert Bruce Lockhart, his immediate superior, who said that he lacked team spirit and defied regulations, but his energy and agility of mind had made a notable contribution to political warfare. 'I have no hesitation in saying that his virtues greatly outweigh his faults. In other words, if he doesn't win a prize for good conduct, he certainly deserves a commendation for distinguished service' (PRO, FO371/C3220). During 1944–5 Crossman was assistant chief of the psychological warfare division of the Supreme Headquarters, Allied Expeditionary Force.

The antithesis noted by Lockhart was to run right through Crossman's career and, no doubt, does something to explain why he languished for nineteen years on the back benches before being appointed to any ministerial office. Elected Labour MP for Coventry East in 1945, a seat which he held until 1974, he was offered no front-bench post throughout the six years of the Attlee government. The nearest he ever came to official favour was when he was nominated by Ernest Bevin, then foreign secretary, to serve in 1946 as a member of the joint Anglo-American Palestine commission. The report, providing for further Jewish immigration into Palestine to an upper limit of 100,000 European refugees, was, however, far from welcome to Bevin, who blamed Crossman for it, even aiming his famous 'stab in the back' reference at the following year's Labour Party conference directly at him.

Denied any regular chance to display his gifts within the House of Commons, Crossman turned to the party conference, being elected to the party's national executive committee in 1952 and staying on it for the next fifteen years. A founder member of the original Bevanite rebellion of 1951, he remained a formidable and influential lieutenant to Aneurin Bevan until the latter's resignation from the shadow cabinet in 1954, when he, virtually alone among the Bevanites, defended the right of Harold Wilson to take Bevan's place at the shadow cabinet table. Although his attitude made him very unpopular with his left-wing colleagues, it proved a shrewd investment for the future—

providing, indeed, the foundation for his subsequent close association with Harold Wilson, whose campaign for the leadership, following the death of Hugh Gaitskell in January 1963, he effectively managed.

With Gaitskell, Crossman's relationship, though personally cordial enough (they had been at Winchester and New College together), had tended to be politically bumpy. Only with Wilson's election to the leadership in February 1963 did Crossman at last become an integral part of the Labour leadership team. In 1964 he made an important contribution to constitutional debate by his controversial introduction to a new edition of Bagehot's *The English Constitution*. Appointed to the front bench as opposition spokesman on higher education and science, he had confidently expected to be made secretary of state for education and science when Harold Wilson formed his first government in October 1964. Instead, as a result of a last-minute switch, he was sent to the Ministry of Housing and Local Government, where he proved a strong, if turbulent, head. His effectiveness at the dispatch box persuaded the prime minister in August 1966 to promote him to lord president of the council and leader of the House of Commons—a post in which he started promisingly, originating the Commons departmental select committees, but finished somewhat frustratedly, even having to watch from the sidelines as his own pet scheme for the reform of the House of Lords foundered in face of a parliamentary filibuster by Labour and Conservative back-benchers alike. Crossman's last two years as a cabinet minister (from November 1968 to June 1970) were spent at the newly created mammoth Department of Health and Social Security, where he worked hard and conscientiously to weld together two former disparate ministries, though perhaps without conspicuous success. (They were to be separated again later under Margaret Thatcher.) He also had to endure the ultimate disappointment of seeing his national superannuation plan (a subject to which he had given his sporadic attention from 1957 onwards) fail to come into law as a result of Harold Wilson's defeat in the election of 18 June 1970.

But Crossman's real memorial does not lie in his brief—and often stormy—ministerial career. Instead, his fame rests on the *Diaries* he wrote from the 1950s onwards and which were posthumously published in the 1970s and 1980s. The first of them in terms of date, but last in terms of publication—his back-bench diary, begun in 1951 but not published until 1981—would not by itself have caused the relevant Whitehall authorities much anxiety. Any back-bench MP is perfectly entitled to record his daily observations and life in parliament and then, if he is lucky enough to find a publisher, to communicate them to a wider public. The problem with Crossman, so far as the Cabinet Office was concerned, arose from his determination to give what Sir John Hunt, the cabinet secretary of the time, described as 'blow-by-blow' accounts (J. Hunt to Lord Goodman, 7 Aug 1974, Young, 19) of what actually went on within the Wilson cabinet.

The authorities of the period were probably right in regarding this as setting a most disagreeable precedent—

a precedent, incidentally, that was soon to be followed by two of his cabinet colleagues, Barbara Castle and Tony Benn (and much later, from within the ranks of the Conservative Party, by the junior minister Alan Clark). Where the guardians of tradition erred was in lacking the nerve to reach for the ultimate Domesday weapon, the then still fully extant Official Secrets Act. Instead, they sought to extend the law of confidentiality (with a rather arcane pedigree reaching back to some Victorian etchings) to cover the content of cabinet discussions. The Labour attorney-general of the day, Sam Silkin, sought an injunction to prevent publication by invoking this particular aspect of the law. In a rather unsatisfactory judgment in 1975 the lord chief justice, Lord Widgery, upheld the attorney-general's contention that confidentiality could properly apply to cabinet discussions, but maintained that it was not applicable in this case as 'much of the action is up to ten years old and three general elections have been held meanwhile' (*The Times*, 2 Oct 1975).

Crossman was not alive to witness this legal victory, which permitted a three-volume series, *The Diaries of a Cabinet Minister* (1975, 1976, 1977), to be published almost without delay. Its publication did not cause the heavens to fall—though within the citadel of Whitehall a number of senior civil servants began to regard their political masters with a new wariness, and Wilson himself took his defeat rather hard by vainly trying to extract from his cabinet colleagues an agreement that no memoirs using official papers would be published within a fifteen-year term.

There can be no doubt, however, that this final victory over the establishment would have gratified Crossman. He had been working on the preparation of the *Diaries* for publication almost until the moment of his death—the necessary editorial labour providing valuable therapy for him after his abrupt dismissal from the editorship of the *New Statesman* in March 1972 (a post he had taken up only on the 1970 defeat at the polls of the Wilson government). The editorship had not been a happy experience for him, and it may be that the directors of the *New Statesman* did him a good turn by providing him with both the time and the leisure to prepare what he came to think of as his *magnum opus*. It is certainly a work which no political historian of the twentieth century will be able to ignore, even if Crossman may have exaggerated in seeing himself as a reincarnation of Samuel Pepys and Walter Bagehot rolled into one.

Crossman made a third and very happy marriage on 3 June 1954 to Anne Patricia, daughter of Alexander Patrick McDougall, farmer. The relaxed setting at Prescote Manor, near Banbury, the Oxfordshire farm inherited via his father-in-law, enabled him to prepare the diaries for publication. He underwent a major operation for cancer in 1972 and died at Prescote Manor on 5 April 1974, being survived by his third wife and a son (*d.* 1975) and daughter. There were no children of his previous marriages. Crossman was appointed OBE in 1945 and sworn of the privy council in 1964.   ANTHONY HOWARD

Sources A. Howard, *Crossman: the pursuit of power* (1990) · T. Dalyell, *Dick Crossman: a portrait* (1989) · H. Young, *The Crossman affair* (1976) · *The backbench diaries of Richard Crossman*, ed. J. Morgan (1981) · R. H. S. Crossman, 'My father', *Sunday Telegraph* (16 Dec 1962) · S. Barnes, 'The man who thinks out loud', *Sunday Times* (29 Nov 1970) · personal knowledge (2004) · private information (1986)

Archives St Ant. Oxf., Middle East Centre, corresp. and papers relating to Anglo-American committee on Palestine · U. Warwick Mod. RC, annotated speeches and papers; corresp. and papers; political corresp. | King's Lond., Liddell Hart C., corresp. with Sir B. H. Liddell Hart · U. Warwick Mod. RC, letters to Winifred Lakin | FILM BFI NFTVA, current affairs footage · BFI NFTVA, party political footage · IWM FVA, documentary footage · IWM FVA, news footage

Likenesses K. Hutton, photographs, 1938, Hult. Arch. · photograph, *c.*1940, Hult. Arch. · B. Brandt, bromide print photograph, *c.*1945, NPG · H. Magee, group portrait, photograph, 1945, Hult. Arch. · Bassano, photograph, 1947, NPG [*see illus.*] · S. O'Meara, photograph, 1964, Hult. Arch. · D. N. Smith, photograph, 1967, Hult. Arch. · D. Levine, pen-and-ink drawing, NPG · photographs, repro. in Howard, *Crossman*

Wealth at death £791: probate, 25 Oct 1974, *CGPLA Eng. & Wales* · £20,731: further grant, 20 Dec 1974, *CGPLA Eng. & Wales*

Crossman, Samuel (*bap.* 1625, *d.* 1684), Church of England clergyman, was baptized at Bradfield St George, Suffolk, on 28 September 1625, the son of Samuel Crossman (*b.* before 1600, *d.* after 1661), vicar of Bradfield St George, and his wife, Mary, daughter of Charles Willoughby of Bradfield St George. On 27 January 1642, aged sixteen, Crossman was admitted to Pembroke College, Cambridge. He graduated BA in 1645, proceeding MA in 1651. As both Samuel and his father were clergymen it is difficult to determine who served which cure. It seems likely that Samuel senior served at Bradfield St George until 1644 and then at Bradfield St Clare until his ejection in 1661, and that following ordination on 28 June 1647 by the seventh London classis Crossman himself became vicar of All Saints, Sudbury, Suffolk, pastor of a congregational church at Sudbury, and then rector of Dalham, Suffolk, and Little Henny, Essex. By September 1647, when a son, also Samuel, was baptized at Sudbury All Saints, Crossman had married his wife, Grace (*d.* in or after 1657). Crossman had five children in all, two sons and a daughter surviving him. He served as assistant to the Suffolk commission in December 1657 and was summoned to the Savoy conference in 1658. He was made BD in 1660.

Crossman was ejected in 1662 and subsequently, on 2 November 1662, he was imprisoned for preaching. Crossman's first publication, *The Young Man's Monitor*, was published in 1664. It is not known when Crossman decided to conform to the Church of England, but he was episcopally ordained deacon and priest at Norwich on 28 October 1665 as curate of St Gregory's and St Peter's, Sudbury. He became a chaplain to the king and on 19 December 1667 he became a prebendary of Bristol. On 30 December 1667 he was appointed vicar of St Nicholas's, Bristol. Crossman may well have been a controversial figure in Bristol, with its high concentration of dissenters. On 8 August 1677 he was cited in the consistory court and admonished for failure to read prayers according to canons. He then protested vigorously at his treatment in a statement of 12 September 1677, in which he complained of Bishop Carleton's treatment of him, particularly his praying for the corporation before the clergy, and his fears of being suspended. Among other good works he mentioned his tenure as treasurer, in which he claimed to have turned round the accounts, and he noted specifically his conformity in performing the liturgy. Many of Crossman's letters to Archbishop Sancroft dwelt on his difficulties with Bristol corporation's dissenting members. Perhaps it was these difficult circumstances which prompted him to solicit Sancroft for an Irish prebend in February 1678.

Carleton's death and the revelations of the Popish Plot transformed the situation in Bristol. Crossman was a believer of the plot and was instrumental in ensuring that Justice North was taken to hear William Bedloe's death-bed affirmation of his evidence. Crossman's sermons of this time seem to preach unity, such as that of 5 February 1682, *A Humble Plea for the Quiet Rest of God's Ark*. Crossman continued to write more devotional volumes: *The Young Man's Calling* (1678) was 'a mixture of a treatise on godly living, uplifting tales and religious verse' (Green, 440). Crossman was appointed dean of Bristol on 24 May 1683 and died there on 4 February 1684. He was buried in Bristol Cathedral. A few days before his death he penned *The Last Testimony, and Declaration of the Reverend Samuel Crossman DD*, which was dated 26 January 1683 (that is, 1684 NS) and was published with a preface from the tory civic leader and future MP, Sir John Knight, who wrote 'it was this gentleman's lot … to fall under the lash and scandal of several reproaches: wherein he was so solicitous to clear himself'. In his testimony Crossman praised Charles II for his 'most admired conduct of the government for our common good', and referred to 'whatever bold insolencies have been lately animated by some to the affronting the true line of succession' (Crossman). Some of his contemporaries were not inclined to be charitable, the chancellor of the diocese, Henry Jones, telling Archbishop Sancroft, 'Mr Crossman, our new Deane dyed this morning: a man lamented by few either of the citie or neighbourhood. He hath left a debt upon our Church of 300*l*' (Bodl. Oxf., MS Tanner 129, fol. 70, cited in *Calamy rev.*, 150).

In his will Crossman referred to his 'present wife Catherine', his sons Samuel and James, and his daughter Sarah, whom he appointed executor. At least two of Crossman's poems later became Anglican hymns. His widow may have survived until 1717 when the will of Catherine Crossman of Bristol, widow, was proved.

STUART HANDLEY

Sources Venn, *Alum. Cant.* · *Calamy rev.* · *Fasti Angl., 1541–1857*, [Bristol] · *IGI* [parish registers of Bradfield St George, Suffolk] · J. Barry, 'The politics of religion in Restoration Bristol', *The politics of religion in Restoration England*, ed. T. Harris, R. Seaward, and M. Goldie (1990), 163–89 · *CSP dom.*, 1677–8 · S. Crossman, *The last testimony, and declaration of the Reverend Samuel Crossman DD* [1684] · I. Green, *Print and protestantism in early modern England* (2000) · *Catalogi codicum manuscriptorum … Thomae Tanner*, ed. A. Hackman (1860), 889 · B. Willis, *A survey of the cathedrals*, 2 vols. (1742) · will, PRO, PROB 11/558, fols. 32–3 [Catherine Crossman, second wife?]

Archives Bodl. Oxf., Tanner MSS, letters

Crossman, Sir William (1830–1901), army officer, born at Isleworth, Middlesex, on 30 June 1830, was the eldest son of Robert Crossman of Cheswick House, Beal, and Holy Island, Northumberland, and his wife, Sarah, daughter of E. Douglas of Kingston upon Thames. After education at Berwick upon Tweed grammar school and Mr Jeffery's at Woolwich, he entered the Royal Military Academy at the head of his batch in January 1847. He was commissioned second lieutenant in the Royal Engineers on 19 December 1848. After serving at Woolwich, he was employed on the organization of the Great Exhibition of 1851, and the next year was sent to Western Australia to superintend the construction of public works by convicts. He was a police magistrate there and visiting magistrate for the ticket-of-leave stations, being stationed principally at Albany in King George's Sound and at Perth. He was promoted lieutenant on 17 February 1854. He married at Albany, on 3 March 1855, Catherine Josephine (*d.* 1878), daughter of John Lawrence Morley of Albany; they had two sons and three daughters. His services were commended by the governor, but the Crimean War necessitated his recall in February 1856.

After employment at Aldershot and Chatham, Crossman served at the War Office under the inspector-general of fortifications, working on surveys and designs for new defences of dockyards and naval bases (nicknamed Palmerston's Follies). He designed several of the coastal defences of Portsmouth and the Isle of Wight, of Hilsea lines and the detached forts of the Gosport advanced line, of the Verne Citadel at Portland, and Scraesdon and Tregantle forts at Plymouth. Meanwhile he was promoted captain on 12 May 1858, and was a member of the committee on the equipment of coast batteries (January 1860). In December 1861 he went to Canada to help with military preparations at the time of the *Trent* crisis, and afterwards was secretary to the royal commission, led by Sir J. W. Gordon, on the defences of Canada, visiting every post on the frontier.

Between 1866 and 1870 Crossman was engaged by the Treasury to report on the legation and consular buildings in Japan and China, and to arrange for new buildings where necessary. In the course of his mission he secured for the Admiralty the site for a new dockyard at Shanghai; he accompanied both the naval expedition to Nanking (Nanjing) and Lingling in 1869 and the force of sailors and marines which was landed in Formosa (Taiwan) and at Swatow (Shantou) in 1868 and 1869. Varied service occupied him after his return to England. Promoted major on 5 July 1872 and lieutenant-colonel on 11 December 1873, he became assistant director of works for fortifications at the War Office on 1 April 1875, but on 6 September he joined a special commission appointed by the Colonial Office to inquire into the resources and finances of the western Griqua country, South Africa. He was made CMG in May 1877. From 1876 to 1881 he served as the first inspector of submarine mining defences and as member of the Royal Engineers committee for submarine experiments and stores, visiting all the defended harbours at home and some overseas. Under his auspices mines became an important part of harbour defence. During 1879 and 1880 he was also president of an important committee on siege operations, which conducted many experiments with a view to remodelling siege operations in line with improved artillery. In 1881–2 he visited Esquimalt and various colonies and reported on their defences. On his return (July 1882) he was commanding royal engineer of the southern military district, but was absent in 1883 on a commission of inquiry with Sir George Smyth Baden-Powell into the financial condition of Jamaica and other West Indian islands. The report was published in March 1884, and in May he was made KCMG.

Crossman, who had been promoted brevet colonel on 11 December 1878 and colonel on 6 May 1885, resigned his command to stand for parliament. In June 1885 he was elected Liberal MP for Portsmouth. Rejecting home rule he joined the Liberal Unionists, and retained the seat until 1892. He retired from the army with the honorary rank of major-general (6 January 1886). In January 1883 he had succeeded to his father's estate in Northumberland, and was a JP and alderman for the county, and served as sheriff in 1894–5 and as chairman of the River Tweed commission. He married in London, on 29 June 1899, Annie, eldest daughter of Lieutenant-General R. Richards, Bombay staff corps, who survived him. Crossman died at the Hotel Belgravia, in London, on 19 April 1901.

R. H. VETCH, rev. M. G. M. JONES

Sources The Times (22 April 1901) · Royal Engineers Journal (Oct 1901) · PRO, War Office Records · Royal Engineers Institution, Chatham, Royal Engineers Records · W. Porter, History of the corps of royal engineers, 2 vols. (1889) · Burke, Gen. GB

Archives Northumbd RO, family, historical and archaeological papers

Wealth at death £54,972 14s. 5d.: probate, 5 June 1901, CGPLA Eng. & Wales

Crossrig. For this title name see Home, Sir David, of Crossrig, Lord Crossrig (1643–1707).

Crosthwaite, Sir Charles Haukes Todd (1835–1915), administrator in India and Burma, was born at Donnybrook, co. Dublin, on 5 December 1835, the second son of John Clarke Crosthwaite, vicar-choral of Christ Church, Dublin, and later rector of St Mary-at-Hill, London, and his wife, Elizabeth Haukes, daughter of Charles H. Todd MD of Sligo and Dublin. After education at Merchant Taylors' School and St John's College, Oxford, he entered the Indian Civil Service in August 1857, and served in various revenue and judicial posts in the North-Western Provinces and the Central Provinces. In these early years Crosthwaite acquired a large family and thereafter his career was dominated by the concern to provide adequately for his children. He married, first, in 1863, Sarah, daughter of William Graham, of Lisburn, with whom he had three sons and three daughters. Sarah died in 1872 and Crosthwaite married, secondly, on 29 December 1874, Caroline Alison (d. 1893), daughter of Sir Henry Lushington, fourth baronet, of Aspenden Hall, Hertfordshire, with whom he had two sons and one daughter.

In March 1883 Crosthwaite became acting chief commissioner of Burma. He returned to the Central Provinces in the following March, again as acting chief commissioner, and was subsequently confirmed in the post. In March 1887, after four months with the public service commission, he readily returned to Burma as chief commissioner in succession to Sir Charles Bernard.

Crosthwaite found that Upper Burma, annexed only two years previously, remained in a state of rebellion. Alert to the unpopularity of the British and their imported Indian police force, he concentrated on strengthening village-level administration and traditional village headships in an attempt to restore a sense of familiar government to the Burmese. At the same time he cracked down hard on guerrilla warfare and arson, thereby easing the embarrassment Britain had suffered over her latest imperial acquisition. He had already been made a CSI in February 1887; in June 1888 he was promoted to KCSI.

Crosthwaite was home member of the executive council from December 1890 until February 1891 and again from April to November 1892, at which latter date he succeeded Sir Auckland Colvin as lieutenant-governor of the North-Western Provinces and chief commissioner of Oudh. His politics were those of gruff conservatism; he saw sedition lurking in many vernacular publications and scorned the political ambitions of Western-educated Indians. When anti-cow-killing disturbances flared up in his province in 1893, he advocated repressive legislation; fortunately for his reputation, however, the less alarmist counsels of Lord Lansdowne prevailed.

Crosthwaite went home on leave in early 1895, and in the following March was appointed to the Council of India, where he served the customary ten years. In retirement he published a memoir of his Burmese years, The Pacification of Burma (1912), and Thakur Pertab Singh and other Tales (1913). In a series of articles in The Times he condemned the Morley–Minto reforms for abandoning the Indian masses to the machinations of a few irresponsible and over-educated Indian politicians. He died at his home at Long Acre, Shamley Green, Surrey, on 28 May 1915 and was buried on 2 June.

KATHERINE PRIOR

Sources The Times (31 May 1915) · D. M. Sein, The administration of Burma (1938); repr. with introduction by J. Silverstein (1973) · S. Gopal, British policy in India, 1858–1905 (1965) · C. H. T. Crosthwaite, The pacification of Burma (1912) · DNB · Mrs E. P. Hart, ed., Merchant Taylors' School register, 1561–1934, 1 (1936) · Burke, Peerage (1907)

Archives BL, letters to Lord Ripon, Add. MS 43595 · BL OIOC, Elgin MSS · BL OIOC, letters to Arthur Godley, Eur. MS F 102 · BL OIOC, Ilbert MSS · BL OIOC, Lansdowne MSS · BL OIOC, letters to Sir H. T. White, Eur. MS E 254 · McMaster University, Hamilton, Ontario, corresp. with Lord Dufferin

Likenesses P. Klier, photograph, c.1887–1890, BL OIOC · C. W. Walton, lithograph (after unknown portrait), BL OIOC

Wealth at death £8385 15s. 11d. in England: Irish probate sealed in England, 22 Oct 1915, CGPLA Eng. & Wales · £11, 779 5s. 11d.: probate, 1 Oct 1915, CGPLA Ire.

Crotch, William (1775–1847), composer and organist, was born on 5 July 1775 at Green's Lane, St George Colgate, Norwich, the only child of Michael Crotch (1735–1813), a carpenter, and his second wife, Isabella (1737–1830); he

William Crotch (1775–1847), by John Linnell, 1839

had two older half-brothers, the children of his father's first marriage to Margaret Lockton.

A prodigy Crotch was a most remarkable musical child prodigy. His father, who included music among his many interests, had built a small pipe organ, and Crotch showed an interest in it well before his second birthday. The visit of a musician friend to the house when he was two years and three weeks old prompted his first attempt to play himself, and his father was astonished the next day to discover him picking out the melody of the national anthem. The day after that he was able to add a second part to it, and on the next a bass. Despite his parents' initial reluctance to spread the news of their son's musical abilities, for fear of being disbelieved, word soon leaked out, and the family home was besieged by crowds of curious visitors anxious to hear the prodigy for themselves.

It was soon decided that Crotch's talents should be commercially exploited and that he should be exhibited further afield. In the summer of 1778, when barely three years old, he set off with his mother on a tour of Ipswich, Oxford, Framlingham, and Bury St Edmunds. Two more tours followed, and in October 1778 he made his first appearances in London. On 10 December Daines Barrington heard him play tunes 'almost throughout with chords'. He was also introduced to J. C. Bach, music master to the queen, who arranged for Crotch and his mother to visit Buckingham House. Here, on 1 January 1779, he played before George III, the prince of Wales, and the duke of Clarence. He was also heard by Samuel and Charles Wesley, themselves former child prodigies, and by Charles Burney, who on 18 February made a report of Crotch's extraordinary talents to the Royal Society, later published in the society's *Philosophical Transactions*, in the

Gentleman's Magazine, and as a separate volume. In his report Burney described in detail Crotch's extraordinary musical accomplishments, while stressing the completely untutored nature of the boy's performances, remarking that 'at present he plays nothing correctly, and his voluntaries are little less wild than the native notes of a lark or a black-bird' (Burney, 'Account of an infant musician', *PTRS*, 69, 1779, 201). Another similar report was published by Barrington in his *Miscellanies* (1781).

Crotch's life as travelling child prodigy continued for the next four years in a series of tours organized by his mother which took him to almost every large town in England and Scotland. Apart from some lessons from his half-brother John, from whom he learned the names of the notes and how to read and write, he remained almost completely uneducated. In his manuscript memoirs, written in his late fifties, Crotch was to comment:

> I look back on this part of my life with pain and humiliation … the manner in which my uncultivated abilities had been displayed to audiences who were frequently as ignorant of what was good and correct as myself and bestowed on me the most extravagant praises and dangerous flatteries, the attentions I received from the great, the noble and the fair, and the consciousness of possessing a musical ear such as everyone had not, made me think myself a most consequential being. … I was indulged in all my wishes as far as it was practicable; I was becoming a spoilt child and in danger of becoming what too many of my musical brethren have become under similar circumstances and unfortunately remained thro' life. (Crotch, memoirs)

A similar picture of Crotch's behaviour and character at this time is conveyed in a letter of 25 May 1783 from Charles Burney to Sir James Lake, in which Burney recorded his fear that the adulation Crotch had received had caused him to be 'as much satisfied with his own imperfections in performance, as contemptuous of all such instructions as his weak & vulgar mother or her connections could supply' (*Letters of Dr Charles Burney, Letters*, 362–5).

Education and early career Burney's remarks were made in the context of concern about the manner in which Crotch's talents were being exploited and a desire, evidently shared by others, that he should receive a more appropriate education and upbringing. Although Burney opined that 'this is not an age for the *solid* patronage of uncultivated genius', it was from private patronage that assistance was shortly to come. On a visit to Oxford later in the year Crotch first met Alexander Crowcher Schomberg, tutor of Magdalen College, who was to become his greatest benefactor and patron. Although initially reluctant to go to hear an eight-year-old 'jingle the keys of a harpsichord and scrape imperfect tones from the strings of a diminutive fiddle' (quoted in Rennert, 22), Schomberg was eventually persuaded to visit the Crotches at their lodgings. At first merely fascinated by the young Crotch, he was in time completely won over, and took over responsibility for his education.

Finding an appropriate way of continuing Crotch's education was a problem. Various suggestions were made, including apprenticeship to Samuel Wesley, a place at

Rugby School, and a choristership at the Chapel Royal or at Magdalen College, Oxford. Eventually, in April 1786, Crotch and his mother moved to Cambridge, where Crotch became assistant to the aged professor of music, John Randall, and furthered his general education with various members of the university.

Crotch's time in Cambridge was crucial to his wider musical education. In addition to learning the skills of an organist—his duties required him to play services at King's College, Trinity, St John's, and Great St Mary's—he was active in the city's concert life. He directed the Cambridge Concerts at Petty Cury and performed in fortnightly concerts at the Black Bear inn with Charles Hague. He also attended musical evenings held by Joseph Jowett and Richard Hey, where he became familiar with a wide range of music, old and new.

This period was also the time of Crotch's first compositions. In September 1786 Schomberg sent him the text of an oratorio, *The Captivity of Judah*. Crotch's setting, written with the aid of Hague and Pieter Hellendaal (1721–1799), was his first large-scale work. In June 1789 parts of it were performed at Trinity Hall to an audience which included Prince William of Gloucester. The Revd Thomas Twining thought it an extraordinary work for an eleven-year-old, but, while commending Crotch's command of 'grand choral effect and expression', none the less found it 'all the work of *ear*, recollection and *âtonnement*, without regular musical training' (quoted in Rennert, 30): these were views with which Crotch was later to concur. While in Cambridge, Crotch was able to pursue a number of non-musical interests, which included painting and drawing—in which he had already shown his precocious aptitude—fortifications, balloons, fireworks, geography, and astronomy.

In June 1788 Crotch moved to Oxford, following the advice of Schomberg and Jowett that he should study for the church; his mother, by now estranged from his father, remained in Cambridge. These plans were soon overturned by the breakdown of Schomberg's health in early 1790, which obliged him to reduce his previously generous financial support to Crotch; Schomberg subsequently retired to Bath, and died in 1792.

Crotch rapidly became prominent in Oxford's musical life. In September 1790, following the death of Thomas Norris, he became organist of Christ Church Cathedral, and when Haydn visited Oxford in July 1791 for the conferment of an honorary degree, Crotch played an organ recital at the cathedral to mark the occasion. He was actively involved in orchestral concerts at the Holywell Music Room, and succeeded Philip Hayes, the professor of music, as their director about 1792. In 1793 he published three piano sonatas by subscription. On 5 June 1794 he took his degree of Bachelor in Music.

During his early years in Oxford Crotch became friendly with John Malchair (1730–1812), the leader of the Holywell Music Room's orchestra and a keen collector of old and national music. Malchair was also an artist and drawing-master and the central figure in the Oxford school of artists. Through Malchair, Crotch further developed his interest in painting and drawing; later he was to be the means by which Malchair's teaching and influence was transmitted to John Constable, whom Crotch first met in London about 1806.

Professor of music In April 1797, following the death of Hayes, Crotch was elected professor of music. He was twenty-one, and was to retain the position until his death. At the same time he also took on the organistships at St John's College, the university church, and the theatre, all of which were also left vacant by Hayes's death. On 21 November 1799 he took the degree of DMus, his exercise being a setting of Warton's *Ode to Fancy*, which as professor of music he himself was obliged to examine.

On 10 July 1797 Crotch married Martha Bliss (*b.* 1776), whom he had known for five years and in whose parents' house he had been lodging; Robert Bliss, her father, was a bookseller and printer in the High Street and the son of Nathaniel Bliss FRS, who had been astronomer royal and Savilian professor of astronomy at Oxford. They had five children, only one of whom, William Robert (*b.* 1798/9), was to outlive him.

Between 1800 and 1804 Crotch gave several courses of lectures on music at Oxford. These formed no part of his official duties and were public lectures to a paying audience. The lectures originated in a suggestion from his friend the miniature painter James Roberts, who had earlier tried without success to persuade Crotch's predecessor, Hayes, to lecture, and from Crotch's own reading of the *Discourses* of Sir Joshua Reynolds. Crotch derived his system of aesthetics from Reynolds: he divided music into three categories (the sublime, the beautiful, and the ornamental) into which he attempted to fit all the music he discussed. Although Crotch's avowed aim was the improvement of public taste, his lectures were in fact conceived on historical lines. Each course followed a broadly chronological sequence, and each lecture included musical examples played by Crotch at the keyboard.

On the recommendation of William Crowe, public orator of Oxford, Crotch was subsequently invited to lecture in London at the Royal Institution, where Crowe himself lectured on poetry. The moribund Gresham lectures apart, these were the first lectures on music in London, and they were highly successful. As at Oxford, the brilliance of Crotch's score-reading was one of the chief attractions. Samuel Wesley went to a lecture in early 1807, after which he commented, in a letter to his brother Charles: 'I cannot understand how he manages to play *all* the parts of a symphony of Mozart so that you do not miss the absence of any one instrument, whether stringed or wind' (15 Jan 1807, JRL, Methodist Archives and Research Centre, DDWF 15/12). Crotch's first course at the Royal Institution was in early 1805, and he gave further courses there in 1806 and 1807. He did not lecture at the Royal Institution again until 1820, but later gave frequent courses at the Surrey and London institutions, and elsewhere in London. Between 1808 and about 1810 he published by subscription *Specimens of Various Styles of Music*, a three-volume collection of the music examples used in his lectures, and in 1831 *Substance of Several Courses of Music*, an abbreviated version of the lectures themselves.

Crotch was well paid for his lectures: for an early course at the Royal Institution he received £80 for twelve lectures, with £5 for each additional one. The prospect of the healthy income to be gained from further courses and from other professional engagements in the capital was probably the main factor in his decision in 1805 to leave Oxford and to move to London. He remained there until the end of his life, and his further visits to Oxford were restricted to occasions on which his presence as professor of music was required.

In London, Crotch's career was made up of composing, lecturing, writing about music, private teaching, and infrequent concert appearances. One of these was on 7 June 1809, when he played an organ recital of his own arrangements of Handel's music to commemorate the fiftieth anniversary of Handel's death. With Samuel Wesley, Benjamin Jacob, Vincent Novello, and others, he did much to promote the music of J. S. Bach, at this time little known in England, and participated in the celebrated series of recitals of Bach's music at the Surrey Chapel. He also performed occasionally in the provinces. He was the musical director of the 1808 Birmingham festival, where he conducted performances of Handel's *Messiah* and Haydn's *The Creation* and other miscellaneous concerts. A letter from him to the festival organizer, Joseph Moore (22 Aug 1808, Birmingham Archives 1292/1), concerning arrangements for the conduct of the concerts suggests that Crotch may have been somewhat high-handed and inflexible in his demands, and that he may have clashed with Moore as a result. At all events, he was not invited back to Birmingham to direct later festivals.

Crotch's lectures and the publication of *Specimens of Various Styles of Music* brought him a considerable reputation as a scholar. He was also the author of such elementary works of theory as *Elements of Musical Composition* (1812) and *Practical Thoroughbass* (c.1825).

As a composer, Crotch was active in most areas except the theatre. His works include music for the Anglican church; odes for a variety of official occasions; keyboard music; a large number of glees and canons, many dating from his time in Oxford; two symphonies, published in arrangements for piano duet; and three organ concertos. They show an essentially conservative style, 'learned but not pedantic' according to *New Grove*, which shows Crotch's knowledge of a wide variety of musical styles from the past and from his own time. He also published a large quantity of arrangements of works by other composers.

In 1812 Crotch completed his oratorio *Palestine*, to a text selected from the poem by Reginald Heber. It was his most ambitious work, and the only oratorio by an English composer to enjoy even a modest success since the time of Handel. Although clearly based on Handelian models, it is by no means a work of slavish imitation and contains many strikingly original passages. It was immediately

regarded as his masterpiece, and the chorus 'Lo! star-led chiefs' remains in the repertory of cathedral and parish church choirs.

It is an indication of Crotch's business acumen that he did not have *Palestine* published and retained control of the performing materials, only permitting it to be performed under his personal direction, and for the exceptionally large fee of £200. Further evidence of his hard-headed approach to music, and also of his celebrity, is the fee of £542 that he was able to negotiate at Oxford in 1810 for directing a four-day festival to mark the installation of Lord Grenville as chancellor of the university. Many years later he would invariably charge a fee for giving his opinion on their works to aspiring young composers. It was perhaps this aspect of his character that caused Samuel Wesley to remark in a letter of 1825 to Vincent Novello that Crotch 'loves Money better than real Reputation' (27 Jan 1825, BL Add. 11729, fol. 233).

The paucity of comment of any sort on Crotch in letters and memoirs of the period suggests that he was somewhat remote in his eminence, or at least a very private man. He seems to have played little part in the hurly-burly of London concert life and musical politics. It is perhaps significant that he was not among the thirty original members of the Philharmonic Society at its foundation in 1813, and was a full member of the society only between 1814 and 1819 and between 1828 and 1832. None the less he frequently conducted concerts for the society, and his symphony in F was performed at the concert of 16 May 1814.

Royal Academy and final years In 1822 Crotch was appointed by Lord Burghersh (John Fane, later eleventh earl of Westmorland) the first principal of the Royal Academy of Music. In addition to his overall responsibility for administration, he taught harmony and counterpoint and organized a number of notable concerts at the academy by leading performers; he also instigated a tradition of concerts given by the students themselves.

Crotch's relationship with the committee of management, and particularly with Burghersh, himself an amateur composer, was not easy. He later commented, 'I now *reigned* at the Academy, and had as much good music performed as I could—nevertheless mine was a *limited* monarchy' (quoted in Rennert, 67)—a reference no doubt to Burghersh's continual interference in the day-to-day running of the academy, which Crotch's pupil and successor Cipriani Potter later found equally trying. Crotch's eventual departure came about in December 1831 following an incident in which he was observed giving a female student a kiss, apparently as a reward for a particularly well-executed harmony exercise. The affair was brought to the attention of the committee of management and was used as a pretext to force Crotch's resignation.

The years leading up to and immediately following his resignation from the academy had been a time of repeated personal tragedies for Crotch and his wife. In succession they saw the deaths in early adulthood of three of their four surviving children (an infant daughter having died in 1806): Isabella in 1821, Sarah in 1826, and her twin, Jane, in 1832. In addition, Crotch's health had also started to deteriorate, and he had put on a good deal of weight. Following his departure from the academy he appears to have considered his public career largely over, although he still continued to compose, to make arrangements of the music of other composers, and to take private pupils. It was around this time that he put his personal papers in order and wrote his memoirs, which present a selective, sanitized, and disappointingly impersonal account of the events of his life. His musical activities continued in private at regular meetings at Crotch's house of a group of friends calling themselves 'The Club'.

Although Crotch remained a well-respected figure following his departure from the academy, he came in for criticism on occasion for the conservatism of his views. In 1832 he was one of the three judges (the others being William Horsley and R. J. S. Stevens) for the newly instituted Gresham prize, awarded for 'the best original composition in sacred vocal music', and he and his fellow judges were attacked for favouring composers with approaches similar to their own and their unwillingness to acknowledge the validity of some modern developments in church music. These criticisms were articulated in two articles by H. J. Gauntlett in the *Musical World* for July 1836 .

Crotch continued occasionally to appear in public. In June 1834 he was in Oxford in his official capacity as professor of music for the installation of the duke of Wellington as chancellor, an event which included three days of concerts in addition to the official ceremonies. On 11 June he directed a performance of the ode *When these are Days of Old*, which he had written for the occasion. The previous day he had directed the first performance of a new version of *The Captivity of Judah*, a fresh setting of the text which Schomberg had given him almost fifty years earlier in 1786. This new version, written between 1812 and 1828, was composed in memory of Schomberg, his friend and patron, and in recognition of the debt of gratitude he owed him. Later in the month, on 28 June, he made what was to be his final public appearance at one of the concerts in the Handel festival in Westminster Abbey. He visited Oxford for the last time in 1839.

Crotch's closing years were spent in generally poor health among his books and papers and his family. Eventually he and his wife accepted the offer of a home from their son William, by now ordained and a master at Taunton grammar school, and it was here that he died of a heart attack on 29 December 1847. He was buried in the churchyard at Bishop's Hull, near Taunton, and a memorial tablet was erected in the church. He left his music and copyrights to his son, and the rest of his property, with an estimated value of £18,000, to his wife.

PHILIP OLLESON

Sources J. Rennert, *William Crotch* (1975) · W. Crotch, memoirs, BL, Add. MSS 27639, 27646, 27691 · C. Burney, 'Account of an infant musician', *PTRS*, 69 (1779), 183–206 · C. Burney, 'Account of an infant musician', *Annual Register* (1779) · C. Burney, 'Account of an infant musician', *GM*, 1st ser., 49 (1779), 588–91 · D. Barrington, *Miscellanies* (1781), 311–16 · *The letters of Dr Charles Burney*, ed. A. Ribeiro, 1 (1991), 362–5 · A. H. Mann, 'Notes on the life and works of Dr William Crotch', *c.*1920, Norfolk RO, MS 11206 [compiled in preparation for his biography] · 'Memoir of William Crotch', *The Harmonicon*, 9 (1831), 3–5 · M. Raeburn, 'Dr Burney, Mozart and Crotch', *MT*, 97 (1956), 519–20 · S. Wollenberg, 'Music and musicians', *Hist. U. Oxf.* 5: *18th-cent. Oxf.*, 865–87 · F. Corder, *A history of the Royal Academy of Music from 1822 to 1922* (1922) · I. Fleming-Williams, 'Dr William Crotch (1775–1847), member of the Oxford school and friend of Constable', *The Connoisseur*, 159 (1965), 28–31 · P. J. Olleson, 'Crotch, Moore, and the 1808 Birmingham festival', *Royal Musical Association Research Chronicle*, 29 (1996), 143–60 · H. J. Gauntlett, 'The Gresham prize [pt 1]', *Musical World* (22 July 1836), 81–6 · H. J. Gauntlett, 'The Gresham prize [pt 2]', *Musical World* (29 July 1836), 97–101 · *The Times* (11–13 June 1834) · Birmingham Archives, letter from Crotch to J. Moore, 22 Aug 1808, MS 1292/1 · N. Temperley, 'Crotch, William', *New Grove* · *Norfolk Genealogy*, 17, 41

Archives BL, musical MSS and papers, Add. MSS 27639, 27646, 27691, 30388–30396 · Norfolk RO, lecture notes and musical arrangements

Likenesses J. Sanders, etching, pubd 1778, BM · engraving, pubd 20 Nov 1778 (after J. Sanders) · J. Sanders, painting, exh. RA 1785 · attrib. W. Beechey, oils, exh. RA 1786, Royal Academy of Music, London · W. Crotch, self-portrait, pencil and brown ink, 1801, Norfolk Museums Service · J. Constable, sketch, *c.*1806, Norfolk RO · T. Uwins, watercolour-and-pencil drawing, *c.*1814, BM · W. T. Fry, engraving, 1822, Norfolk RO · J. Thompson, engraving, 1822 (after W. Derby), repro. in *European Magazine* (1822) · Hullmandel, lithograph, 1830 (after M. A. Pears), Norfolk Museums Service · W. Crotch, self-portrait, pencil and watercolour, 1833, Norfolk Museums Service · J. Linnell, two watercolour drawings, *c.*1839, NPG [*see illus.*] · J. Fazi, plaster bust, 1853, Christ Church Oxf. · W. De La Motte, sketch, Norfolk RO · J. Fittler?, engraving (aged three), Norfolk Museums Service · Mrs Harrington, silhouette, BM · F. W. Wilkins, drawing, priv. coll. · engraving, repro. in *London Magazine* (April 1779); version, engraving, Norfolk RO · engraving (after silhouette by Mrs Harrington, 1778), BM · portrait, repro. in Rennert, *William Crotch*, frontispiece · two engravings, BM

Wealth at death approx. £18,000: *New Grove*; will, *Norfolk Genealogy*

Crotty, William (*d.* 1742), highwayman and rapparee, was active in the south of Ireland for at least four years before his death. Nothing is known for certain of his early life, though he may have been in domestic service as a young man. By 1739 he had already acquired some notoriety as a robber and had formed a small gang of accomplices. After several exploits he was finally captured near Waterford. At least one former colleague was involved in his apprehension and several others gave evidence against him at his subsequent trial. Prominent among this group was David Norris, who had acted as a receiver of Crotty's booty. Despite being wounded by his captors, Crotty survived to be hanged at Waterford on 18 March 1742. His head remained affixed to the gateway of the town's gaol for some time after his execution. Crotty had assumed his place in local mythology even before his death. His name is given to a cave and a lough in the Comeragh Mountains of co. Waterford, in which area he operated. An isolated crag, from which Crotty's distraught widow is alleged later to have jumped to her death rather than be transported, is known as Crotty's Rock. Crotty has variously been reported by chroniclers of Ireland's outlaws as having performed superhuman athletic feats, including the outrunning of horses, and as having been a noted sportsman, a great dancer, and a skilled marksman. Less amiably, he has been accused of eating human flesh and of inflicting wanton cruelty on his victims. There is, however, no contemporary evidence to support any of these conjectures. NEAL GARNHAM

Sources M. Butler, 'Crotty the robber', *Journal of the Waterford and South-East of Ireland Archaeological Society*, 18 (1915), 12–20, 56–62, 105–07

Crouch [*née* Phillips], **Anna Maria** (1763–1805), singer and actress, was born in Gray's Inn Lane, London, on 20 April 1763, the third of six children of Peregrine Phillips, a lawyer and official of the Wine Licence Office (of Welsh paternal descent, and French maternal descent and alleged relationship to Charlotte Corday), and his wife, a Miss Gascoyne, the daughter of a Worcestershire farmer. Her mother died when she was young, and she was brought up in her father's house by an aunt. She studied singing and keyboard with the organist of Berwick Street Chapel, named Wafer, and soon after she was seventeen she was articled to Thomas Linley for three years. She was then engaged at Drury Lane for six seasons at a salary rising from £6 to £12 a night (of which Linley appears to have taken half). Her début was as Mandane in Arne's *Artaxerxes* on 11 November 1780, with Sophia Baddeley in the title role. At the end of a season in which she successfully took other parts, she was engaged at Liverpool, where she appeared at the Theatre Royal on 11 June as Polly in *The Beggar's Opera*. For her first benefit, in April 1781, she sang Clarissa in Charles Dibdin's *Lionel and Clarissa*. Her beauty seems to have been already at least as striking as her singing, and on the revival of Purcell's *King Arthur* she appeared as Venus. She was also to develop a lively gift for comedy. She remained all her life connected with Drury Lane, where she appeared occasionally in speaking parts: these included Fanny Stirling in Colman's and Garrick's *Clandestine Marriage* (1784), Olivia in *Twelfth Night*, and Ophelia to John Philip Kemble's *Hamlet*. In 1781 she also played at the Smock Alley Theatre, Dublin, and elsewhere in Ireland. After returning to Ireland in 1783 she eloped with the son of an Irish peer, but they were caught, and in 1785 she married Lieutenant Rawlings Edward Crouch RN. She acted and sang for a while under her maiden name, but after the birth of a child (who lived only two days) she took her husband's name.

In March 1787 Michael *Kelly (1762–1826) returned to England from Vienna, and was schooled in English by Crouch in return for singing lessons. At his Drury Lane début she sang Clarissa to his Lionel. Kelly then went to live with the Crouches, accompanying them on tour in the country and in Ireland, and in 1790 joined them on a visit to Paris. In 1791 she separated from her husband by mutual consent, allegedly on the grounds of an association with the prince of Wales. She continued to live with Kelly, in what seems to have been a platonic relationship, and in 1792 their house at 4 Pall Mall, then another in Suffolk Street, became the scene, after the theatre, of brilliant receptions to which Crouch came in her stage costume, and where guests included the prince of Wales,

Elizabeth Billington, Sheridan, and Stephen and Nancy Storace. For the next ten years she continued to sing and act at Drury Lane in opera and oratorio, and also appeared with Kelly at provincial festivals. She was the first singer of Lady Elinor in Storace's *The Haunted Tower* (1789), of Catherine in his *The Siege of Belgrade* (1791), and of the title role in his *Lodoiska* (1794). One of her last performances was as Celia in *As You Like It*, which she played for the first time at Kelly's benefit on 14 May 1801.

Crouch's singing seems never to have created as much impression as her beauty, though contemporaries referred to her 'remarkably sweet voice and naive affecting style of singing' and a voice that 'ravishes the ear with its delicacy and melting softness'. Kelly declared that 'she seemed to aggregate in herself all that is exquisite and charming'. During her later years, when she suffered accidents and illness, she devoted herself to training singers for the stage. She had by then put on weight and lost her looks, though she always retained her charm, modesty, and good nature. She installed her father in a cottage off the King's Road, in Chelsea, where she continued to entertain. She died in Brighton on 2 October 1805 of 'an internal mortification' (presumably cancer); she was buried on 6 October in Brighton churchyard, where Kelly put up a stone to her memory. JOHN WARRACK

Sources M. J. Young, *Memoirs of Mrs Crouch*, 2 vols. (1806) · M. Kelly, *Reminiscences*, 2nd edn, 2 vols. (1826); repr., R. Fiske, ed. (1975) · 'Memoirs of Mrs Crouch', *European Magazine and London Review*, 48 (1805), 323–6 · *Oxberry's Dramatic Biography*, 5/78 (1826) · 'Mrs Crouch', *Thespian Magazine*, 1 (1792), 14–15 · T. Dibdin, *The reminiscences of Thomas Dibdin*, 2 vols. (1827) · *GM*, 1st ser., 75 (1805), 977 · Highfill, Burnim & Langhans, *BDA* · d. cert.

Likenesses G. Romney, oils, 1787, Kenwood House, London · Ridley, portrait, pubd 2 Jan 1792 (after Lawrence) · Bartolozzi, portrait (after Romney) · S. De Wilde, oils (as Polly in *The beggar's opera*), Garr. Club · E. Harding, mezzotint · R. Thomas, pencil drawing, Garr. Club · mezzotint (as Rosetta or Mandane) · portrait, repro. in Young, *Memoirs of Mrs Crouch*, frontispiece · prints, BM, NPG

Crouch, Frederick Nicholls (1808–1896), cellist and composer, was born on 31 July 1808 at Warren Street, Fitzroy Square, London, the son of Frederick William Crouch (*c*.1783–1844), cellist and author of *A Complete Treatise on the Violoncello* (1826), and his wife, Anna Maria, daughter of John Nicholls, barrister. His paternal grandfather, the composer William Crouch, was organist of St Luke's, Old Street. He played at the Royal Coburg Theatre from the age of nine, and later at the King's Theatre, Drury Lane, and elsewhere, as a member of Queen Adelaide's private band among others. He travelled in Yorkshire and Scotland, and for two years was obliged to work on coastal smacks plying between London and Leith. After tuition from William Hawes he sang in the choirs of Westminster Abbey and St Paul's Cathedral. From about 1822 he studied at the Royal Academy of Music with Crotch, Attwood, Crivelli, and Linley, among others, and played in London orchestras including the Philharmonic and those of the Antient Concerts and Royal Italian Opera. Some time after 1832 he moved to Plymouth, where he worked as a singer and as a travelling salesman for a firm of metal brokers, and invented the engraving process known as zincography. He

Frederick Nicholls Crouch (1808–1896), by unknown engraver, pubd 1896 (after Lamson)

was also musical supervisor to the London publishers D'Almaine & Co. From about 1838 he gave lecture recitals on the songs and legends of Ireland, at the same time publishing *The Songs and Legends of Ireland*, which included his most successful song, 'Kathleen Mavourneen'.

By 1849 Crouch was in America, where he played in the Astor Place Opera House, and where his (mostly unsuccessful) musical enterprises included conducting, singing, and teaching in Boston, Portland, Philadelphia (conducting Mrs Rush's Saturday Concerts), Washington, and Richmond. He joined the Confederate army in the Civil War as a trumpeter, then taught singing in Baltimore, and, from 1883, worked as a varnisher in a factory. He also wrote two operas, *Sir Roger de Coverley* and *The Fifth of November, 1670*, an *Othello Travestie*, a monody, song collections including *Songs of Erin*, *Echoes of the Past*, *Bardic Reminiscences*, *Songs of the Olden Time*, *Songs of a Rambler*, and *Wayside Melodies*, and many other songs popular in their day. A testimonial concert was given for him in Baltimore in 1883. An autobiographical memoir was published in the Boston *Folio* in January 1887. Crouch married Lydia Pearson, whom he deserted in 1845; he fathered sixteen children, including Emma Elizabeth (1835?–1886), the Parisian Second Empire courtesan known as Cora *Pearl. He died in Portland, Maine, on 18 August 1896.

JOHN WARRACK

Sources Brown & Stratton, *Brit. mus.* · *New Grove* · N. Slonimsky, *Baker's biographical dictionary of musicians*, suppl. (1971) · *MT*, 37 (1896), 411
Archives NYPL
Likenesses portrait, repro. in *Harper's Weekly*, 40 (1896), 858 · wood-engraving (after Lamson), NPG; repro. in *ILN*, 108 (1896), 486 [*see illus.*]

Crouch, Humphrey (*fl.* 1601–1657), writer, may have been the Humphrey Crouch who was apprenticed to a merchant tailor named William Sherley in May 1618 and freed in 1625. This Crouch was the son of a London cutler named Henry Crouch, and was living in Aldersgate Street near Smithfield in 1629. In 1638 a Humphrey Crouch was living in the vicinity of Scotts Alley, very near this address. On 22 June 1628 a Humphrey Crouch married Winifride Worshipp in the parish of St Mary Woolnoth, London. If Humphrey was indeed the son of Henry Crouch from London,

he could not have been closely related (if at all) to Edward, John, or Nathaniel Crouch. Edward and John Crouch were born in Standon in Hertfordshire, and Nathaniel Crouch hailed from Lewes in Sussex. Humphrey may, however, have known Edward and John Crouch. Edward Crouch was apprenticed to a Smithfield stationer named Richard Harper who published seven ballads by Humphrey Crouch between 1636 and 1646. In addition, a ballad written by Humphrey Crouch appears in John Crouch's newsbook *Mercurius Fumigosus* (no. 46, 11–18 April 1655, 364–5).

Twenty-two surviving titles bear Crouch's name or initials, although he probably wrote many more which do not survive. *Londons Vacation* and *Londons Lord have Mercy upon Us* (both printed in 1637) explain the 1636 plague in the City as a punishment for the sins of its citizens. The three other surviving titles from the 1630s display a misogynistic streak and a coarse, earthy humour which is evident in his subsequent writings.

The ballads which Crouch composed during the 1640s demonstrate his attachment to the Church of England and the Book of Common Prayer. They also highlight his distaste for Laudian innovation, protestant sectaries, and Catholics. *A Whip for the Back of a Backsliding Brownist* (*c*.1640) ascribes the turmoil of the times to the machinations of the sectaries and the Catholics. *The Greeks and Trojans Wars* (*c*.1641) suggests that Catholic powers had fomented the Irish uprising, and argues that Englishmen should 'Let all home-bred strife alone' in order to secure Ireland. In November 1642 *A Godly Exhortation* lamented the outbreak of civil war, and argued that both sides should 'all imbrace, and throw downe armes'. *A Godly Exhortation* also contains some striking images of the militarization of London at this time. *The Parliament of Graces* expresses a longing for an agreement between king and parliament. It suggests that this is unlikely, however, because 'there are adverse parties of both sides, which hinders the cause, and keepes the work unfinished' (H. Crouch, *The Parliament of Graces*, 1643, sig. A5r). Humphrey's next surviving ballad is *Come Buy a Mouse-Trap* (*c*.1647). This recounts the punishment meted out to a lecherous citizen of Rotterdam named Peters. It is hard to believe that this is not a reference to Hugh Peters, the puritan preacher who had been minister to the English church at Rotterdam during the 1630s.

Humphrey penned a number of humorous, non-political works during the 1650s. *The Lady Pecunia's Journey unto Hell* (1654), a satire on the evil effect of money on men's souls, contains a number of lines which could be interpreted as an attack on the execution of Charles I. *The Heroick History of Guy Earl of Warwick* (1655) is a verse and prose version of the popular chivalric tale, and *The Welch Traveller* recounts the misfortunes of a dull-witted individual named Taffie. *The Welch Traveller* is the last item which can definitely be attributed to Crouch, and he may well have died soon after this date. A number of items which purported to have been written by Crouch appeared in the 1670s and 1680s. The long gap between the publication of

The Welch Traveller and these later titles suggests, however, that they were fakes.

Crouch's titles evidently enjoyed a good measure of popularity during his lifetime. In 1648 the newsbook *Mercurius Pragmaticus* referred to him as one of the 'high-flying wits of balladry' and in 1656 he was ranked (along with Samuel Smithson and Lawrence Price) as one of the 'glorious three' of contemporary balladry (Rollins, 40).

JASON McELLIGOTT

Sources Wing, *STC* · D. F. McKenzie, ed., *Stationers' Company apprentices*, 3 vols. (1961–78), vols. 1–2 · T. C. Dale, ed., *The inhabitants of London in 1638*, 2 vols. (1931) · Merchant Taylors' Company court minute book, GL, 315, vol. 8a, fol. 89, microfilm · *CSP dom.* · *IGI* · J. Crouch, *Mercurius Fumigosus*, no. 46 (11–18 April 1655) · *Death in a new dress* (1650) · H. E. Rollins, *Cavalier and puritan* (1923)

Crouch, Isaac (1756–1835), Church of England clergyman, was born on 25 April 1756 at Bradford-on-Avon, Wiltshire, only son of Isaac Crouch, market gardener (*d.* 1792), and his first wife, Elizabeth Wobren (*d.* 1781). Bradford experienced a spiritual revival while the Revd Edward Spencer was curate in charge, during the period 1762–74. Crouch is said to have been converted to evangelical views during this time. It is not conceivable, however, despite contemporary statements, that Crouch was educated at Spencer's school at Wingfield (Winkfield) rectory, near Bradford. Spencer was not instituted to Wingfield until 1775. Crouch was more probably educated at the free grammar school in Bradford, founded in 1712.

Crouch matriculated at Oxford on 8 February 1774 as a member of St Edmund Hall, where the principal, Dr George Dixon, continued to encourage evangelicals, despite the vice-chancellor's expulsion of the hall's six 'methodist' students in 1768, and presently awarded Crouch a scholarship. As an undergraduate he associated with a small band of evangelical students, including their leader, Nathaniel Bridges, who became a fellow of Magdalen College in 1775, and Crouch's contemporary, Thomas Charles of Bala, then at Jesus College, who in 1804 helped to found the British and Foreign Bible Society: members of an undergraduate group visited in 1775 by Henry Venn, a well known evangelical clergyman. In 1777 Crouch took his bachelor's degree, and in 1778, on a title from Prebendary James Stillingfleet (an earlier Oxford evangelical leader while a fellow of Merton College, 1752–67) to St Martin's, Worcester, was made deacon at Oxford. In the following year Stillingfleet resigned St Martin's, and Crouch moved to a curacy with Edward Spencer at Wingfield, Wiltshire, being ordained priest in 1780, again at Oxford, as on the previous occasion, by letters dimissory (Charles Daubeney, later a notable high-churchman, being one of his sponsors), and took his MA degree. In 1781 he moved on to another, perhaps more responsible, curacy at Billericay, Essex, with the Revd Peter D'Aranda, vicar of the neighbouring parish of Great Burstead, where he remained until 1783.

In that year Crouch was recalled to Oxford, where Principal Dixon made him vice-principal and bursar of St Edmund Hall. While also acting as curate (1783–97) to Dr J. W. Peers at Chiselhampton and Stadhampton, villages near Oxford, Crouch's responsibilities lay mainly at the hall, where he lectured and instructed about thirty undergraduates at first, and rather more when his spiritual influence had become known in evangelical circles elsewhere. An early pupil, Josiah Pratt, soon became a leader as secretary of the Church Missionary Society (1802–24). William Marsh, afterwards an outstanding parish clergyman, had chosen St Edmund Hall because of Crouch's reputation. Crouch was widely read, not least in church history. During term he seldom worked less than twelve hours a day, starting at 5 a.m. Crouch and his wife, Jane (1756–1828), whom he married in 1784 (thereafter living in Holywell, not far from the hall), especially as they had no children of their own, were devoted to the welfare of his pupils, as well as members of other halls and colleges commended to him. Among the latter, introduced by letter from the Revd Dr Thomas Haweis, an evangelical leader at Oxford (1757–62), was Hugh Pearson of St John's, senior proctor in 1813, and a notable dean of Salisbury from 1823 to 1846.

Crouch established an evangelical tradition at the hall which continued until 1854. A century later Principal A. B. Emden wrote: 'Under the influence of Isaac Crouch, the Hall came to be recognised as the headquarters of the Evangelical revival in Oxford' (*VCH Oxfordshire*, 3.332). Dr Emden's successor, Dr J. N. D. Kelly, in his *St Edmund Hall: Almost Seven Hundred Years* (1989), suggested that Crouch was more influential at Oxford than his two pupils Dr Daniel Wilson, afterwards bishop of Calcutta, vice-principal of St Edmund Hall from 1807 to 1812, and John Hill, vice-principal from 1812 to 1851. In the university as a whole Crouch's influence gradually encouraged more tolerance of evangelical beliefs. Several times a pro-proctor, his not infrequent sermons at St Mary's (the university church) 'were always listened to with great respect' (*Hist. U. Oxf.* 5: *18th-cent. Oxf.*, 418, n. 2). Such a sermon of 1786 is apparently the only printed work of Crouch which has survived. Bishop Wilson's obituary of him in the *Christian Observer*, while making allowances for considerable differences in character and circumstances, does not hesitate to compare Crouch's influence at Oxford with that of Charles Simeon at Cambridge.

For no recorded reason, but later associated with dropsy and 'depression of spirits', in middle life Crouch's health began to deteriorate. He resigned as tutor in 1804, and as vice-principal in 1807. He had been an active 'country' member of the committee of the Church Missionary Society since its founding in 1799. He remained a chaplain of Merton College (1796–1817), as well as being elected a city lecturer at St Martin's, Carfax, in 1805. With considerable hesitation on account of health, Crouch accepted in 1814 the country living of Narborough, Leicestershire, remaining, however, resident partly in Oxford until 1820, assisted by a curate at Narborough. His wife died in February 1828, and he married again, on 13 October 1830; his second wife was an old friend, Mary Ann Hancock (1780–1866), widow of George Hancock (1780–1810), of St Peter-in-the-East, Oxford, coal merchant. In his lifetime he gave a school house to his parish, with an endowment to maintain a school. In 1832 Crouch suffered a second stroke, but again recovered measurably. He died at Narborough rectory on 30 October 1835, and was buried at Narborough on 6 November. News of his death reached St Edmund Hall the next day. Vice-Principal Hill recorded that Crouch had been 'able to comfort his family by his dying assurance that his faith was unshaken, and that he was rejoicing in his God and Saviour' (diary, vol. 10, 31 Oct 1835, Bodl. Oxf., MS St Edmund Hall 67). A Latin inscription in Narborough church succinctly recalls his memory.

J. S. REYNOLDS

Sources D. Wilson, *Christian Observer* (1837), 410–18 · J. S. Reynolds, 'Crouch, Isaac', in D. M. Lewis, *The Blackwell dictionary of evangelical biography, 1730–1860* (1995) · J. S. Reynolds, *The evangelicals at Oxford, 1735–1871: a record of an unchronicled movement* (1953) · J. N. D. Kelly, *St Edmund Hall: almost seven hundred years* (1989) · parish register, Bradford-on-Avon, Wilts., Wilts. & Swindon RO · rate books, Bradford-on-Avon, 1762–74 (Spencer); 1781–92 (Isaac Crouch senior), Wilts. & Swindon RO · will, Salisbury consistory court, 1792, Wilts. & Swindon RO [Isaac Crouch senior] · ordination papers, 1778, Worcs. RO [also in Oxon. RO] · ordination papers, 1780, Wilts. & Swindon RO [also in Oxon. RO] · battel books, St Edmund Hall, 1783, 1807, St Edmund Hall · J. Hill, MS diary, vol. 10, 1835, Bodl. Oxf., MS St Edmund Hall 67 · C. J. H. Fletcher, *St Martin's Carfax* (1896), 119 · G. V. Cox, *Recollections of Oxford*, 2nd edn (1870), 30–31 · C. Hole, *The early history of the Church Missionary Society for Africa and the East to the end of AD 1814* (1896) · W. Tuckwell, *Pre-Tractarian Oxford* (1909) · D. E. Jenkins, *Life of Thomas Charles*, 1 (1908) · J. Bateman, *Life of Daniel Wilson*, 1 (1860) · J. Pratt and J. H. Pratt, *Memorials of Josiah Pratt* (1849) · [C. Marsh], *The life of the Rev. William Marsh* (1867) · Mrs R. Lane Poole, ed., *Catalogue of portraits in the possession of the university, colleges, city and county of Oxford*, 3 vols. (1912–25), vol. 3 · parish register, Narborough, Leics. RO [burial]
Likenesses J. Russell?, portrait, oils, *c*.1800, St Edmund Hall, Oxford
Wealth at death £25,000: will, PRO, proved 12 Feb 1836

Crouch, John (*b. c.*1615, *d.* in or after **1680**), writer and bookseller, was born the son of a yeoman named Thomas Crouch in Standon, Hertfordshire. He had at least one brother, Gilbert Crouch, who acted as a land agent for the earl of Shrewsbury. John Crouch began an apprenticeship with the bookseller Nicholas Salisbury on 6 November 1632 and served his time until 2 December 1639. He evidently worked as a bookseller during the 1640s (McKenzie, *1641–1700*, 42) and there is no evidence that he wrote any books or pamphlets during the early 1640s. Between 1652 and 1657 he and a printer named Thomas Wilson owned and ran a print shop at the sign of the Three Foxes in Long Lane in Smithfield. During the 1650s he lived in or near Cock Lane in Smithfield. Although he and his wife, who may have been called Ann, may have had several children, the only one of whom any record survives is their son John, who became a freeman of the Stationers' Company in February 1673.

In February 1648 Crouch wrote the first part of a two-part satirical, anti-puritan pamphlet entitled *Craftie Cromwell*. Between April and November 1648 he wrote five further anti-puritan pamphlets, *The Kentish Fayre*, and four plays based on the character of Mrs Parliament. He also wrote three numbers of a royalist newsbook entitled *Mercurius Critticus* and a counterfeit edition of John Hackluyt's royalist newsbook *Mercurius Melancholicus*. In April 1649 he

wrote the first of fifty-seven issues of the *Man in the Moon*. This eight-page weekly was printed by John's kinsman Edward Crouch. It recounted little news and relied instead on obscene stories and rhymes to fill its pages. Its principal targets were parliament, the army, the council of state, and the official newsbooks. In general it had three main lines of attack: the humble social origins of England's new rulers, their alleged sexual immorality, and their contempt for, and oppression of, the poor.

John and Edward Crouch were arrested some time before 15 December 1649. On 17 December Edward was committed to Newgate to await trial for publishing 'several treasonable and scandalous books' (*CSP dom., 1649–50*, 438), but John was later released without charge. After his release John returned to writing the *Man in the Moon* and was re-arrested and sent to the Gatehouse on or shortly after 5 June 1650. He probably remained in custody until November 1651 when the council of state ordered that a Mr Crouch be released after lodging a bond of £100, with two sureties of £50 each. In January and March 1652 he penned four numbers of a pro-army newsbook *Mercurius Bellonius*, probably in return for his release. In April 1652 he wrote the first of eighty-six numbers of *Mercurius Democritus*, which was joined in June 1652 by three numbers of *Mercurius Heraclitus*. The titles of these two newsbooks referred to the ancient Greek philosophers Democritus and Heraclitus, who had respectively laughed and wept at the foolishness of the world. *Democritus* ceased publication in February 1654 and in June 1654 John Crouch wrote the first of seventy numbers of *Mercurius Fumigosus*.

The principal aim of *Democritus*, *Heraclitus*, and *Fumigosus* was to parody the lies and exaggerations of the rest of the press by deliberately peddling half-truths and hyperbole. Crouch initially used *Democritus* to attack a number of minor figures associated with the regime, but from late 1652 he began to eschew any comment on political matters. Gradually, despite himself, he came to the conclusion that the regime was preferable to the anarchy that would accompany a forcible restoration of the crown. His advice was simple:

> Lets eat, drink, play and cast off fear,
> security is best;
> Then hang up sorrow, banish care,
> 'tis sleep affords us rest.
> (J. Crouch, *Mercurius Democritus*, 45, February 1653, 1)

In the aftermath of the execution of John Gerard and Peter Vowell in July 1654 for plotting to assassinate Oliver Cromwell, he wrote: 'If this be the reward of plotting,/I'll hate all treason, hatch'd by Potting' (J. Crouch, *Mercurius Fumigosus*, 6, July 1654, 6). He was also unsympathetic to those involved in the attempted royalist rising of early 1655: 'Sure Hell's broake loose, and all the Feinds and Locusts do appear, for to no ends, base Plotting tends, and yet they will swarm here.' He argued that royalist intrigue was 'Ominous to all that attempt it' and that the result of such 'ill actions' was akin to 'an arrow shot upwards into the sky which wound[s] that eye that gave aime unto it' (ibid., 32, January 1655, 1–2).

The business that Crouch had established with Thomas

Wilson folded in 1657, probably as a result of the ordinance of September 1655 which suppressed all existing newsbooks except the officially sponsored *Mercurius Politicus*. In 1657 he wrote *An Elegie ... upon the Death of ... Anne, Countess of Shrewsbury*. Between May and August 1659 he wrote ten issues of a revived *Mercurius Democritus*. This newsbook was largely non-political and much of the material for it was lifted *verbatim* from old issues of *Mercurius Fumigosus* and the previous incarnation of *Mercurius Democritus*. Crouch returned to political pamphleteering only in June 1659. His *Democritus Turned Statesman* argued that the 'purest and safest' state was one in which 'a free Parliament [is] elected annually or twice a year ... without restraint on the wills of the free people of this nation.' He maintained that such a parliament 'ought not to be restrained, or curbed by any sort of court convention, or Council enjoying co-ordinate power'. He also believed 'factious sectaries' should be excluded from this parliament and that the militia should replace the standing army which was, he wrote, a 'ready instrument for any ... Tyrannical dictator' (*Harleian Miscellany*, 82–6).

Following the Restoration Crouch addressed *A Mixt Poem* (1660) to Charles II and *The Muses Joy* (1661) to the queen mother in an attempt to secure royal patronage. He evidently believed that his brother's association with the earl of Shrewsbury, whose second wife was 'as near the Queen [Mother] as her shadow to her Body', would ensure his success (J. Crouch, *The Muses Joy*, 1661, sig. A3v). He became increasingly resentful at the wealth and good fortune of the court circle, however, when it became clear that his efforts had fallen on deaf ears. He likened himself to a 'poor man expecting an alms at the Presbyterians gate, [who] instead of a gift shall be fed with crumbs of comfort' and was contemptuous of the fact that 'a penny in thy pocket will purchase thee many friends at Court' (J. Crouch, *Man in the Moon*, 1, 1660, 5).

Crouch wrote only a dozen or so items in the twenty years after 1660. He penned two numbers of *Mercurius Democritus* in 1661 and four numbers of the *Man in the Moon* and one of *Mercurius Fumigosus* in 1663. He wrote poems on the occasion of the Second Anglo-Dutch War, the plague of 1665, and the great fire. The majority of his output during this period, however, consisted of eulogies on the deaths of royalty and various members of the nobility. The last work which can be positively attributed to him is the 1680 *Elegie upon [Philip Herbert] the [First] Marquess of Dorchester*, in which he claimed to have been 'once his Domestick Servant'. It is not clear when or in what capacity Crouch might have been a servant to the marquess, but Dorchester had lived in Aldersgate Street from November 1649, a few hundred metres from where John Crouch lived and worked during the 1650s. Crouch does not seem to have written anything after 1680 and extensive searches have not uncovered any will made by him.

JASON McELLIGOTT

Sources J. McElligott, 'Edward Crouch: a poor printer in seventeenth-century London', *Journal of the Printing Historical Society*, new ser., 1 (2000), 49–73 · J. McElligott, 'The career and politics of John Crouch' in 'Propaganda and censorship: the underground loyalist newsbooks, 1647–2000', PhD diss., U. Cam., 188–225 · Wing, *STC* · C. Nelson and M. Seccombe, eds., *British newspapers and periodicals, 1641–1700: a short-title catalogue of serials printed in England, Scotland, Ireland, and British America* (1987) · D. Underdown, 'The *Man in the Moon*: loyalty and libel in popular politics, 1640–1660', in D. Underdown, *A freeborn people: politics and the nation in seventeenth century England* (1996) · *CSP dom.*, 1649–60 · J. Crouch, *A mixt poem* (1660) · J. Crouch, *The muses tears* (1661) · W. Oldys and T. Park, eds., *The Harleian miscellany*, 10 vols. (1808–13), vol. 7 · D. F. McKenzie, ed., *Stationers' Company apprentices*, 3 vols. (1961–78)

Crouch, Nathaniel [*pseud.* Robert Burton] (*c.*1640–1725?), bookseller and writer, the son of a tailor named Thomas Crouch, was born in Lewes in Sussex. He was apprenticed to the London bookseller Livewell Chapman in May 1656 and became free of the Stationers' Company in November 1664. In 1666 his bookshop was located at the Rose and Crown in Exchange Alley near Lombard Street, London. From 1668 to 1671 Crouch traded at 'the Cross-Keys in Bishops-gate-street, near Leaden Hall' and from 1671 until 1684 his business was located in 'Exchange-Alley, over against the Royal Exchange in Cornhill'. From 1684 onwards his imprint was 'Nath. Crouch at the Bell in the Poultry, near Cheapside'. The catalogues which he printed at the end of all his books indicate that his bookshop carried a large amount of stock. In 1669 Nathaniel bound a Samuel Crouch from Southwark in Surrey as an apprentice. When Samuel became free in 1674 Nathaniel bound a woman named Elizabeth Guard from Norton in Sussex, although there is no evidence that she successfully completed her apprenticeship. On 12 November 1711 Nathaniel's sons Thomas and Nathaniel junior were made members of the Stationers' Company by patrimony.

John Dunton praised the elder Nathaniel Crouch as 'a very ingenious person ... [who] can talk fine things upon any subject' (*Life and Errors*, 2.436). Not much is known about his personal life, but on 7 March 1684 he attended a meeting of the Royal Society with Anthony Wood and Robert Plot. In 1695 he was living in the parish of St Mildred Poultry in central London with his wife, Elizabeth, his sons Thomas and Nathaniel, a servant, and two lodgers. He does not seem to have been related in any way to Edward, Humphrey, or John Crouch.

In 1679 Crouch published one number of a newspaper entitled the *Weekly Intelligencer*. He also edited and published thirty-four numbers of a tri-weekly newspaper called the *English Post* between 14 October and 30 December 1700. Crouch's name appears as the author or publisher of at least seventy-eight books between 1666 and 1725. These titles were written in clear, simple English and almost always sold for 1s. They went through numerous editions during his lifetime and beyond. Crouch himself divided the books which he sold into three broad categories: miscellanies, divinity, and history (*Antichrist Stormed*, 1689, 232–43). The stories and riddles which comprise *Winter Evenings Entertainments* (1687) typify the ephemeral nature of the miscellanies. Crouch published more than thirty religious and spiritual titles by nearly twenty different authors. Only one of these authors, John Hall (1574–1656), had been a conforming member of the Church of England. All of the other authors of religious books who can be identified were nonconformists. Moreover, the majority of these nonconformists were either Baptists or Quakers. It is not clear whether Nathaniel shared these men's religious convictions or whether he merely published their books because there was a market for them.

Crouch was best-known to his contemporaries as the author and publisher of a number of historical works written under the pseudonym Robert Burton or R. B. This pseudonym was a reference to the author of *The Anatomy of Melancholy* (1620). *The Anatomy* became a best-seller partly because it translated hundreds of quotations from Greek and Latin into English, thereby giving many humbly educated men a passing knowledge of the classics. In a similar fashion Crouch's history books presented shortened and simplified versions of serious works to audiences that might otherwise never have read them. Indeed, John Dunton wrote of Nathaniel Crouch:

> I think I have given you the very Soul of his Character, when I have told you that his Talent lies at Collection. He has melted down the best of our English Histories into Twelve-Penny-Books, which are fill'd with Wonders, rarities and Curiosities. (*Life and Errors*, 1.206)

Crouch began to write historical works under his pseudonym from 1681 onwards. His *Wars in England, Scotland and Ireland* (1681), *Historical Remarques* (1681), *Admirable Curiosities* (1682), and *England's Monarchs* (1685) were intended to give 'a very satisfactory account' of English history 'for near sixteen hundred years past'. Crouch claimed that these works 'have received very great acceptation with the English Nation, So that many Thousands more of them have been vended, than of others which have concerned Forreign Matters' (*England's Monarchs*, A2r–3v). In the eleven years from 1685 Crouch wrote and published a number of other historical works: *The English Empire in America* (1685); *The History of the Kingdoms of Scotland and Ireland* (1686); *A View of the English Acquisitions in Guinea and the East Indies* (1687); *The English Hero, or, Sir Francis Drake Reviv'd* (1687); *The History of the Nine Worthies of the World* (1687); *The History of Oliver Cromwell* (1693); *The History of the House of Orange* (1693); *The History of the Kingdom of Ireland* (1693); *The History of the Two Late Kings, Charles ... and James* (1693); *The History of the Principality of Wales* (1695); and *The History of Scotland* (1696) were extremely successful.

Crouch probably died in 1725, the year the name Thomas Crouch, possibly his son, appears on the title-page of one of Burton's books. He must have been a wealthy man, but he seems to have left no will. In editions of his works printed after his death his pseudonym is sometimes given as Richard, instead of Robert, Burton. His historical works were reprinted many times during the eighteenth century and editions were printed in Bolton, Bristol, Dublin, Edinburgh, and London. Benjamin Franklin's *Autobiography* records that he sold the works of Bunyan to obtain a copy of 'Burton's books', and in 1784 Samuel Johnson asked the bookseller Mr Dilly to obtain copies of Crouch's histories for him. A collected edition of Crouch's historical works issued between 1810 and 1814 was reported to be fetching high prices in the 1860s (Mayer, 392–3). JASON M^c ELLIGOTT

Sources R. Mayer, 'Nathaniel Crouch, bookseller and historian: popular historiography and cultural power in late seventeenth-century England', *Eighteenth-Century Studies*, 27 (1993–4), 391–420 · Wing, STC · C. Nelson and M. Seccombe, eds., *British newspapers and periodicals, 1641–1700: a short-title catalogue of serials printed in England, Scotland, Ireland, and British America* (1987) · D. F. McKenzie, ed., *Stationers' Company apprentices*, 3 vols. (1961–78), vols. 2–3 · *The life and errors of John Dunton*, [rev. edn], ed. J. B. Nichols, 2 vols. (1818) · marriage assessment, 1695, CLRO, 81.17 · [W. Huddesford], ed., *The lives of those eminent antiquaries, John Leland, Thomas Hearne, and Anthony à Wood*, 2 vols. (1772) · DNB

Crouch, William (1628–1711), Quaker leader and writer, was born on 5 April 1628 at Penton, near Weyhill and Andover, Hampshire, the son of a prosperous yeoman and a puritan mother (their names are as yet unknown). His father died while Crouch was a young boy. After the repeated dislocations during the civil war claimed most of his inheritance, Crouch, lacking a grammar school education, went to London in 1646 and became an apprentice upholsterer in Cornhill. When his training was finished he set up shop in Spread-Eagle Court, Finch Lane. By 1656 his mother and sisters had become Quakers while in Gloucestershire, and Crouch himself, influenced by Edward Burrough and Francis Howgill, joined the Friends that year. He later described his relationship to Burrough as that of a son to his father. Following the death of his first wife, with whom he had a son and a daughter (Katherine), Crouch married Ruth (*c*.1638–1710), daughter of John Brown and his wife, Ruth, of Wood Street, London, on 6 February 1660. He and Ruth, an early convert to the Quakers, had two sons, Jasiel (*b*. 1662) and John (*b*. 1668), and three daughters, Mehetabell (*b*. 1670), Ruth (*b*. 1673), and Sarah (*b*. 1677).

For refusing to pay church rates in the parish of St Benet Fink, Threadneedle Street, Crouch had carpet from his stock distrained on 19 June 1660, and when he failed to appear at Christ Church after being cited for recusancy he was excommunicated. He was appointed scavenger for Broad Street ward in 1661, but was imprisoned in the Poultry compter after declining to take the required oath at the Guildhall. Unwilling to pay prison fees, he was confined in the hole with indigent prisoners, though he was released eight days later after appealing to the lord mayor. Crouch adamantly refused to pay tithes, and was again arrested in July 1661. Although he remained in prison for twenty-one months, by remitting a fee of 3*d*. per night for his chamber he received modest liberty to tend to his business after the first two months. As a prisoner he wrote a lengthy letter on 26 July 1662 to Samuel Clark, curate of St Benet Fink, explaining his opposition to tithes, eliciting Clark's response to this missive but not to two subsequent epistles composed in August. After the prison chaplain, William Wickins, preached on the lawfulness of oaths, Crouch submitted a written refutation of his views. Elected a constable by his parish in 1663, he paid a fine in order to be excused from serving. Crouch, Solomon Eccles, and other Friends were arrested in August 1665 for attending a conventicle at Peel Meeting-House in St John's Street, and when each of them refused to pay the £2 fine to relieve the indigent of the parish, they were incarcerated for three months in the Gatehouse, Westminster. Some of his co-religionists succumbed to the plague during this imprisonment.

After the great fire claimed Crouch's house and shop he lived in Devonshire House until new quarters were available in Crown Court, Gracechurch Street. Again apprehended for attending a conventicle in 1670, he had more goods distrained when he refused to pay a fine of £10. The following year he was a founder member of the six weeks' meeting, which handled much of the important business involving London Friends, and he continued as a member of the two weeks' meeting (established about 1656), which dealt with disciplinary cases. In 1672 the yearly meeting appointed Crouch and nine others to supervise the printing and distribution of Quaker books. In November 1675 Crouch had possessions worth £3 10s. distrained for refusing to pay tithes to John Cliffe, rector of St Benet Gracechurch. Cliffe's successor, Henry Halstead, made similar demands every year from 1676 to 1705, according to Crouch, though the amount fluctuated. In October 1681 Crouch was also fined 25s. for refusing to bear arms. Possibly an original member of the meeting for sufferings established in 1676, he was responsible for receiving accounts of persecuted Quakers in Oxfordshire, Warwickshire, Jamaica, and the Netherlands.

During the 1680s Crouch's efforts on behalf of suffering Friends increased. Between 1682 and 1684 he and eight co-religionists administered funds collected to ransom Quaker captives in north Africa and relieve persecuted Friends. In March 1683 he and George Whitehead sought to free Quakers incarcerated at Norwich, and on 23 June the two men met with Archbishop William Sancroft at Lambeth Palace to protest against the false testimony of informers, but Sancroft replied that some crooked timber was necessary to build a ship. Ten days before that meeting an informer had reported Crouch for attending a conventicle in White Hart Court, leading to the imposition of a £10 fine by Thomas Jenner, recorder of London. Jenner fined him the same amount on 21 April 1684 for attending a conventicle. During these years Crouch enjoyed close relations with George Fox, who met at Crouch's house on 1 June 1683 with Friends from Scotland, Ireland, the Netherlands, Danzig, and America. Other gatherings involving Fox in Crouch's house included several with Dutch Quakers (May 1684, April 1686) and Stephen Crisp (March and May 1686), and one involving West Jersey (February 1685). With five other Friends, Crouch petitioned James II against informers, probably in 1686.

Crouch's stature as a leading London Quaker was further evident by his selection in 1689 as one of a dozen 'interval Friends' assigned to handle important disciplinary cases between monthly meetings. In 1692 he was a signatory of *The Doting Athenians Imposing Questions No Proofs*, a response to hostile remarks about Quakers in *The Athenian Mercury*. His *Sermon Against Evil Speaking* (1694) warned against gossip and harsh criticism. About 1706 Crouch moved to Edmonton, Middlesex, and joined the Tottenham monthly meeting. His 350-page book, *The Enormous*

Sin of Covetousness Detected (1708), with an epistle by Richard Claridge, condemned fraud, oppression, and lying. Crouch's major work, *Posthuma Christiana*, including his autobiography and a valuable account of early Quakers in London, was edited by Claridge and published in 1712.

Following the death of his wife on 20 April 1710, Crouch, who had been troubled with stones for two years, died on 13 January 1711. He and Ruth were interred in the Quaker burial-ground at Winchmore Hill, Middlesex. He was survived by his son John and his daughters Mehetabell, wife of Michael Lovell, and Ruth, wife of Samuel Arnold, five grandchildren, and a great-granddaughter. A wealthy man, Crouch bequeathed two freehold farms in Cranbrook, Kent, to his son; two freehold farms at Woodham Ferrers, Essex, and two tracts of land in Pennsylvania to his daughters; profits from the sale of land in West New Jersey to all three children; a building, at the sign of the Coach and Horses, Bishopsgate Street, London, which he leased from the master and fellows of Emmanuel College, Cambridge, to Mehetabell; £730 to assorted family members, £20 to two friends, and £20 to apprentice four indigent boys. Money from the rent or sale of his houses in Crown Court, thirty shares of printing stock, and his personal goods were designated to pay his debts. A 1725 mezzotint of 'Honest *Will. Crouch*' is probably not a posthumous portrait of the Quaker, though it refers to 'pious bounties' and the subject's relief of 'the slave', possibly a reference to Friends ransomed from north Africa (*N&Q*).

RICHARD L. GREAVES

Sources W. Crouch, 'Posthuma Christiana', *The Friends' Library*, ed. W. Evans and T. Evans (1837–50), vol. 11, pp. 287–321 · *The short journal and itinerary journals of George Fox*, ed. N. Penney (1925) · J. Besse, *A collection of the sufferings of the people called Quakers*, 2 vols. (1753) · will, 1711, PRO, PROB 11/519, sig. 3 · *The Christian progress of that ancient servant and minister of Jesus Christ, George Whitehead*, ed. [J. Besse?] (1725) · Greaves & Zaller, *BDBR*, 202–4 · 'Dictionary of Quaker biography', RS Friends, Lond. [card index] · H. Barbour and A. O. Roberts, eds., *Early Quaker writings, 1650–1700* (1973) · W. R. G., 'Honest Will. Crouch', *N&Q*, 5th ser., 1 (1874), 228
Likenesses N. Tucker, mezzotint, 1725
Wealth at death £770; plus landed estates: PRO, PROB 11/519, sig. 3

Croudace, Camilla Mary Julia (1844–1926), supporter of education for women, was born on 29 January 1844 at Marsh House, Homerton, Middlesex, the daughter of Thomas Croudace and his wife, Anne Hester Vignoles. She spent part of her early life in Kiev with her mother, her older brother, and her grandfather, the civil engineer Charles *Vignoles, who was responsible for building a suspension bridge over the Dnieper River. Here she laid the foundations for her love of languages by learning French, German, and Russian. After returning to England, she attended a small school in Notting Hill Gate, in London, before entering the preparatory class of Queen's College, Harley Street, in 1856, where Dorothea Beale was one of her teachers. A year later she entered the college itself, which was to prove the centre of her life's work, and attended lectures given by F. D. Maurice, R. C. Trench, and E. H. Plumptre and others; Maurice particularly impressed her deeply, and she retained a vivid memory of his teaching to the end of her life.

On leaving the college in 1861 Camilla Croudace spent seven years as a governess to several families. After a further four years of extensive travels on the continent, she and her mother settled in Hampstead, and she secured a teaching post at Kensington high school, the first of the schools of the new Girls' Public Day School Company (later Trust). But it was not long before she was invited to return to Queen's as 'lady resident' in succession to Eleanor Grove. From 1881 until her retirement in 1906 she served under five principals. Most of the teaching was done by the male professors; her responsibilities were for discipline and for the communal life of the students, though in addition she always took a deep interest in the students' intellectual progress and encouraged them to continue with further study. She led prayers in the morning, presided over lunch, and arranged social events after the hours of teaching.

Camilla Croudace was much loved and respected by all who came under her care; they remembered her regal bearing (she always wore a lace cap), her generosity, her patience, and her sense of humour. She provided stability, a gracious atmosphere, and intellectual encouragement for generations of students, one of the most brilliant of whom was Gertrude Bell. Her very wide circle of friends from many walks of life were frequently entertained at the college, and students would often be invited to act as hostesses. At weekends she would sometimes invite girls to visit her country home in Surrey, and in the holidays she organized walking parties. It was due to her initiative that four Greek plays were presented at the college during her period of office. She was devoted to Queen's, to its tradition of liberal education, and to its founder, and it was due to her initiative that a fund was started to purchase the portrait of Maurice which was hung in the college library. At her retirement, representatives of every college generation since 1881 gathered to present her with the means to purchase an annuity. Her wide cultural and intellectual interests included a particular attraction to the ideas of Emanuel Swedenborg.

Camilla Croudace divided her retirement between homes in West Liss, Hampshire, and Haslemere, Surrey. She took a few private pupils for a time, and kept closely in touch with the Old Queen's Society. She died at Keith Cottage, Park Avenue, Worthing, of senile decay on 3 April 1926, aged eighty-two. ELAINE KAYE

Sources Queen's College Magazine, 35 (1890) · Queen's College Magazine, 36 (1891) · Queen's College Magazine, 82 (1906) · C. Croudace, 'A short history of Queen's College London', The first college for women, ed. A. Tweedie (1898) · E. Kaye, A history of Queen's College, London, 1848–1972 (1972) · R. G. Grylls, Queen's College, 1848–1948 (1948) · d. cert. · CGPLA Eng. & Wales (1926) · parish register (baptism), Hackney, St John's, 6 March 1844
Archives Queen's College, London
Likenesses portrait, repro. in Kaye, History of Queen's College, London, 49
Wealth at death £1989 6s. 5d.: probate, 8 June 1926, CGPLA Eng. & Wales

Croueste [formerly Crowhurst], **Edwin** (1841–1914), clown and circus proprietor, was the son of Alexander Crowhurst, a shoemaker, and his wife, Mary, née Finch, and was born at Bromley, Kent, on 23 May 1841. His first visit to the circus was in 1851, when he saw Batty's circus performing during the Great Exhibition. On leaving school he worked for two years at a shop in the Minories, London, but, always keen on tumbling and clowning, in 1857 he joined a circus at Stratford as a clown. His brother, Harry (d. 1891), had been a clown for some time, and Edwin had seen many travelling companies; he had also visited Astley's where 'The Battle of Waterloo', with Edward Gomersal as Napoleon and the ringmaster John Widdicombe as Wellington, made a particular impression on him. He appeared with John Clark's circus at Lambeth Baths for the winter season of 1857–8, and in 1858 joined Harry Croueste's circus in Vauxhall Gardens for what proved to be its last year.

One of the best-known circus clowns of his day, Edwin Croueste visited many continental cities, America, and the colonies. In 1863 he took part in a race along the Thames between three clowns drawn in tubs by geese, a variant of Dickie Usher's stunt. In 1879 he was advertised as 'England's Greatest Shakespearian Jester, Acknowledged the Biggest Draw in the Profession', and gave a permanent address in Leicester. He then went into business for himself, and by the late 1880s Edwin Croueste's Grand circus seems to have become well established: in the 1890s it was based in Scarborough and made regular visits to Dewsbury, Halifax, Leicester, and Bradford. In 1891 Croueste opened an iron circus in Dewsbury, which in 1894 he converted to the Empire Variety Theatre.

Croueste had a son, George John Coney Croueste, an equestrian performer, but he died in 1881 at the age of eighteen. Croueste's nephew George, known as the 'English Hernandez', was famous in the late 1870s as a clever pirouette and somersault rider, and later became equestrian director in his uncle's circus. Prosperous for many years, Edwin Croueste lost his money later in life, and died in the workhouse hospital at Horton, Bradford, on 25 April 1914. JOHN M. TURNER

Sources World's Fair (20 March 1909) · World's Fair (8 May 1909) · World's Fair (2 May 1914) · World's Fair (9 May 1914) · Era Almanack and Annual (1879) · Era Almanack and Annual (1882) · C. Keith, Circus life and amusements (1879) · Penny Illustrated Paper (26 Sept 1863) · G. Speaight, A history of the circus (1980) · Dewsbury Reporter (3 Oct 1891) · World's Fair (25 Sept 1926) · b. cert. · d. cert.
Wealth at death fund raised 'to save him from … pauper's grave': World's Fair (2 May 1914)

Crouse, John (1737/8–1796), printer and newspaper proprietor, was the son of William Henry Crouse (d. 1804) of Norwich, theatre proprietor and comedian, and his wife, Esther. William Crouse held one of the twenty-eight shares in the Theatre Royal, Norwich, where he and Esther were managers of the theatre wardrobe. On 20 April 1752 John was apprenticed to the Norwich printer and bookseller William Chase, son of the printer and local politician, also William (1692–1744). In July 1760 Crouse bought the stock of the local bookseller Robert Goodman and set up his own business at the Bible and Star in Cockey Lane, Norwich. In the following year, on 18 July, he began his first newspaper, the *Norwich Gazette*, which enjoyed only moderate success. On 6 March 1763 he was admitted to the freedom of Norwich and, three years later, he opened a printing office over Lewis's warehouse, Upper Market Place. On 14 December 1768 it was agreed that Crouse and William Chase were, on alternate months, to supply all printing materials to the town's Theatre Royal. Several months later, on 8 April 1769, Crouse began a new newspaper, the *Norfolk Chronicle*, which was distributed throughout the county. In addition to this title he printed an extensive number of books, some incorporating maps, including Robert Potter's translation *The Tragedies of Aeschylus* (1777). This volume had an impressive list of over 550 subscribers, an indication of Crouse's standing in the printing trade.

In the next decade Crouse became a major contractor for the Norwich to London mail coach (the second mail coach, introduced on 28 March 1785) to run from the King's Head in the town's market place. To Crouse goes the credit of publishing the first point-to-point timetable in Britain (*Norfolk Chronicle*, 16 April 1785). This detailed the mail coach routes—one via Colchester, the other via Newmarket—from London to Norwich, with all the horse posts connected to the new service. In the same year Crouse took as a partner William *Stevenson [*see under* Stevenson, Seth William], who helped him to run his 'medicinal warehouse' in the market place. Stevenson admired Crouse for his integrity, generosity, and goodness of heart. The partnership was enlarged at the end of September 1794 to include Chase's relative Jonathan Matchett (*c*.1771–1844) and was renamed Crouse, Stevenson, and Matchett. Between 1794 and 1796 the firm printed posters detailing 'Mail coaches; Hambro [Hamburg], Yarmouth, Norwich etc', announcing through-running to 'Hambro' by packet.

It is debatable which is Crouse's most important work. The *Norfolk Chronicle* became a major journalistic force in the county and survived until 1955. His tabulated timetable became the standard format for road and, later, rail transport, replacing the old stagecoach maxim 'if God permits' with minute-by-minute timing. Crouse was unmarried, though his 'reputed daughter', Esther Bowyer Crouse, was living with him in 1796. He became seriously ill in September of that year and died on 18 November 1796, aged fifty-eight. Crouse was buried at St Peter Mancroft Church, Norwich, on 24 November.

DERRICK HASTED

Sources *Norfolk Chronicle* (16 April 1785) [see also 1769] · Hasker Letter Books, 1794–6, post office records · committee books, 1768–1805, Theatre Royal, Norwich · Norwich Central Library, Colman collection · E. Vale, *The mail-coach men of the late eighteenth century*, new edn (1967) · R. Stedman, *Vox populi: the Norfolk newspaper press, 1760–1900* (1971) · J. Feather, 'Country book trade apprentices, 1710–1760', *Publishing History*, 6 (1982), 85–99 · parish register, St Peter Mancroft, Norwich [burial]
Archives Norfolk Central Library, Colman collection
Wealth at death property and land in Norwich and Tasburgh, Norfolk, and Wickham Market, Suffolk: will, 12 Nov 1796

Crow, Francis (1627–1692/3), clergyman and ejected minister, was the son of Patrick Crow of Heugh Head in Berwickshire, Scotland, and Elizabeth, daughter of John Clapperton, minister of Coldstream, Berwickshire. He studied theology at Sedan under Pierre du Moulin, but returned to Scotland and for a few months acted as usher under William Webb, appointed in September 1646 as first master of the grammar school at Berwick. Crow graduated MA as minister of the word from Edinburgh University on 22 July 1647. By 1653 he was minister of a parish in the presbytery of Chirnside, Berwickshire; he supported the protesting party in the church, and was convicted of irregular procedure on 8 December 1653. In 1658 it emerged that Crow had engaged in 'fornication with a woman in his own parish', and she 'being found with childe, was cited to the session to declare the father of the child; but being demanded the question, she told she could not give one'. The unfortunate woman was hauled before the presbytery but continued to protect her lover. Accordingly the presbytery:

> commanded her to be excommunicate; and the person they appointed for to do it, was the said Mr — Craw [*sic*], her minister, and the day appointed being come, he calls her by her name, but in the mean time, he being one way or another touched, left off, and told publickly that he himselfe was the man that was the father of the child; and so leaving the place, he told they should see his face no more: whereupon he left his charge and fled. (*Diary of Mr John Lamont*, 104)

Shortly afterwards Crow was in Suffolk, where he probably had relations, and was admitted as vicar of Hundon. In or before 1662 he married a wife, Frances, who predeceased him; they had at least four children, Patrick, Elizabeth, Francis, and Paul, baptized at Hundon on 27 April 1662. Crow was soon afterwards ejected from the living, where a successor was instituted on 26 September 1662, but it seems that the family were allowed to stay temporarily in the parsonage before moving to a house nearby. Later he lived at Ovington, Essex, preaching 'twice every Lord's Day, between the Times of Worship in the publick Church, the greatest Part of the Auditory in which came to hear him' (*Calamy rev.*, 151). In 1669 he was reported to be preaching to 200 or 300 people at Bury St Edmunds, and at Rede—to a congregation 'of the vulgar sort, but some of considerable quality' (Gordon, 246). On 1 May 1672 he was licensed as a presbyterian teacher at his house in Ovington. Later he preached at Clare, travelling once a month to Bury St Edmunds:

> to a numerous auditory. He has preach'd there twice on the Lord's Day, and administer'd the Sacrament to four several Tables, because of the great Number of Communicants ... Towards the latter End of the Reign of King Charles, he was taken at Bury, put into Prison in the Time of the Assizes, and had Tribulation ten Days

but was then released because his accusers got his first name wrong (*Calamy rev.*, 151).

Nevertheless, Crow experienced further harassment, and emigrated to the West Indies, arriving on 30 March 1686 at Port Royal. On 7 March 1687 he sent to Giles Firmin of Ridgwell, Essex, his impressions of Jamaica, including remarks on slavery:

> The greatest Trade of this Place, lies in bringing of these poor Creatures like Sheep from Guinea hither, to sell them to the home Plantations, and to the Spanish Factors that buy them at 20 l. per Head, or thereabouts. They come as naked as they were born, and the Buyers look in their Mouths, and survey their Joints as if they were Horses in a Market. We have few other Servants here but these Slaves, who are bought with our Money, except some from Newgate. (*Calamy rev.*, 152)

Crow was deeply unhappy:

> I am left alone, having the heavy Work of the Place on my weak Shoulders, being to preach two Sermons every Lord's Day; and yet studying and preaching one Sermon here, is more spending than three in England. The constant Heat is so consuming Night and Day, that here is a continual Summer, without the least Footsteps of a Winter, either for Frost or Snow, Cold or Rain, or any sensible Shortness of Days ... there seems small Encouragement for staying, if either England or New England were open. I am here depriv'd of Converse both with Scholars and Christians ... As the Wicked here are more prophane than in England, so the Professors (the few that there are) are more lukewarm and worldly. Most of them are Anabaptists and Independents ... [who] excuse themselves from living under any Pastoral Charge or Inspection here. (ibid., 152–3)

But he found their 'wretched Laodicean tepidity' (ibid.) more irksome than their doctrinal unsoundness.

While still in Jamaica, Crow wrote *The Vanity and Impiety of Judicial Astrology*. In its preface 'To the gentlemen, merchants and other inhabitants of Port Royal in Jamaica, that attended on my ministry in the meeting there', he explained that he had:

> found the island of Jamaica too much addicted to Judicial Astrology, and several so fond of that foolish art, as seldom to set out to sea without consulting their oracle of a star gazing astrologer for lucky days, and happy stars.

In an effort at 'undeceiving the deluded' he had 'searched the best authors I could meet with in your illiterate world'. The result of his labours was issued soon after Crow's return to England in 1690. He was offered but refused a pastorate in London, and returned instead to Clare. Here, too, he appears to have found little content, for it was reported in 1690 that 'Att Clare, they offered to allow him £25 per annum in money & £5 otherwise but he would not stay, soe they are destitute' (Gordon, 103–4). Crow died there between signing his will on 17 September 1692 and the grant of probate on 6 February 1693. He was survived by three of his children, Patrick, Elizabeth, and Francis.

STEPHEN WRIGHT

Sources *Calamy rev.* · *Fasti Scot.*, new edn, vol. 1 · *The diary of Mr John Lamont of Newton, 1649–1671*, ed. G. R. Kinloch, Maitland Club, 7 (1830) · E. Calamy, ed., *An abridgement of Mr. Baxter's history of his life and times, with an account of the ministers, &c., who were ejected after the Restauration of King Charles II*, 2nd edn, 2 vols. (1713) · E. Calamy, *A continuation of the account of the ministers ... who were ejected and silenced after the Restoration in 1660*, 2 vols. (1727) · J. Scott, *Berwick-upon-Tweed* (1888) · A. Gordon, ed., *Freedom after ejection: a review (1690–1692) of presbyterian and congregational nonconformity in England and Wales* (1917) · D. Laing, ed., *A catalogue of the graduates ... of the University of Edinburgh*, Bannatyne Club, 106 (1858) · will, PRO, PROB 11/413, fols. 180–81

Archives Bodl. Oxf., letters to R. Hill, MS Eng. Hist. D 164

Likenesses I. Smith, engraving, repro. in *Caribbeana*, 281

Wealth at death see will, PRO, PROB 11/413, fols. 180–81

Crow, Hugh (1765–1829), privateer and slave trader, was born in Ramsey, Isle of Man. He lost his right eye in infancy, but despite this was apprenticed to a boat builder in Ramsey at the age of fifteen and then, aged seventeen, went to Whitehaven, where he was apprenticed into the merchant navy. He sailed on several voyages across the Atlantic and to northern waters. In 1790, having served his apprenticeship, he made his first trip to west Africa for slaves, having overcome his scruples against the trade. He continued slaving trips and on one was captured by the French and spent a year as a prisoner in France, eventually escaping disguised as a Breton by speaking Manx. He was appointed captain in 1798 and continued in the slave trade out of Liverpool, during the course of which he had engagements with several French ships. He was a successful slaver until he retired in 1807, after the trade was outlawed. He returned to Ramsey to a small estate near the town but, disconsolate after the death of his son (whom he had got into the Royal Navy) in Lisbon in 1812, he moved to Liverpool in 1817, where he stayed until his death on 13 May 1829. He was buried in Kirk Maughold churchyard, Isle of Man. He is chiefly remembered for his *Memoirs* (1830) which are of interest because of their early descriptions of the kingdom of Bonny, on the Niger delta, and of slave trading and privateering. More recent editions (a book of 1970 and a microfiche of 1990) gave them a wider audience.

ELIZABETH BAIGENT

Sources C. W. Sutton, *A list of Lancashire authors* (1876) · A. W. Moore, *Manx worthies, or, Biographies of notable Manx men and women* (1901) · G. Williams, *History of the Liverpool privateers and letters of marque* (1897) · DNB

Likenesses portrait, repro. in H. Crow, *Memoirs* (1830)

Crow, Mitford. *See* Crowe, Mitford (*bap.* 1669, *d.* 1719).

Crowder [alias Broughton], **Arthur** [name in religion Anselm] (1588/9–1666), Benedictine monk, was born in Shropshire or Montgomeryshire, probably the son of Arthur and Mary Crowder (perhaps the couple of that name from Sparchford, Diddlebury, Shropshire) and the younger brother of the Benedictine monk John Mark Crowder, who also sometimes used the alias Broughton. He was sixteen when he entered the English College at Douai on 12 June 1605; he moved to the English College at Valladolid on 15 October 1606. At the end of 1608 Leander Jones took him to the new English monastery at Dieulouard in Lorraine (later Ampleforth) where he received the Benedictine habit on 15 April 1609 with the name Anselm. This was the last recorded move from Valladolid to a monastery. The fluid state of the English Benedictines, most of whom belonged to nominally Italian or Spanish congregations until 1619, is shown by his taking his vows at St Gregory's, Douai (later Downside), as a member of the new community there. For some years he taught at the nearby Marchienne college, where several of the monks worked, but by 1624 he was in England, where he was sometimes called Broughton. In England he acted as agent for the new convent of Benedictine nuns at Cambrai. In 1629 he was elected the first cathedral prior of Rochester, a title revived from the pre-Reformation monasteries so that someone would be ready at once to take over the property and dignity of each ancient monastery. It was supposed that James I would perhaps allow a Catholic restoration, and that a more recent and energetic order might make a stronger claim if no incumbent were ready. From 1653 he was provincial, that is superior, of all the Benedictine missioners working in the area of the province of Canterbury and in 1657 was translated, a promotion, to the priorship of Canterbury.

Crowder had great devotion to the Virgin Mary and set up a society to promote this devotion among Catholics, probably during the Commonwealth. He:

> erected the Chapel of the Rosary in London, having obtained letters patent to that end from Baptista Marina, general of the Dominicans and a privilege for his altar of Our Blessed Lady of Power from Pope Innocent X. In this chapel the relic of the holy thorn which had formerly been kept in the abbey of Glastonbury was deposited, as also a curious piece of the holy Cross which the renowned Feckenham, Abbot of Westminster, who being Clerk of the Chapel to Queen Mary, had taken from the Royal Chapel on the accession of Queen Elizabeth. Many of the nobility and gentry joined this sodality of the Rosary of which Robert Earl of Cardigan, was Prefect. (Allanson)

Robert Brudenell, earl of Cardigan, lived at Cardigan House in Lincoln's Inn Fields, which was probably the confraternity's (and perhaps Crowder's) base.

Crowder, in conjunction with Thomas Faustus or Vincent Sadler, was probably the author of three works of spiritual devotion first published between 1651 and 1657. *Jesus, Maria, Joseph, or, The Devout Pilgrim of the Ever Blessed Virgin Mary* (1657) was 'published for the benefit of the Pious Rosarists' (title-page), while the latest of the three works, entitled *The Dayly Exercise of the Devout Rosarists* (1657), went through fifteen editions by 1793 under variant titles, usually *A Dayly Exercise of the Devout Christian*. It is likely that Crowder was influenced by the teaching of Augustine Baker. Like the confraternity, the works seem to have been popular in the Restoration period, when English monks were serving the Queen's chapel at Somerset House, but did not attract much subsequent attention. Crowder died on 5 May 1666, during a meeting of the general chapter of the Benedictines, which was being held at the street called Old Bailey, which gave rise to a myth that he died in prison. The confraternity survived his death and lasted until the death of Sadler, who succeeded him as dean of the society, in 1681. The associated relics were in existence at the end of the twentieth century, the Glastonbury thorn at Stanbrook and the relic of the true cross at Downside.   ANSELM CRAMER

Sources A. Allanson, *Biography of the English Benedictines* (1999) · Gillow, *Lit. biog. hist.* · J. McCann and H. Connolly, eds., *Memorials of Father Augustine Baker and other documents relating to the English Benedictines*, Catholic RS, 33 (1933), 219 · R. H. Connolly, 'The Benedictine Chapel of the Rosary in London (c.1650–1681)', *Downside Review*, 52 (1934), 320–29 · D. Lunn, *The English Benedictines, 1540–1688* (1980) · E. Henson, ed., *The registers of the English College at Valladolid, 1589–1862*, Catholic RS, 30 (1930)

Crowder, John (1756–1830), printer and mayor of London, was born in Wyradsbury, Buckinghamshire, the son of

John Crowder (*b. c.*1720), a playing-card maker, and his wife, Frances (later Frances Scriven). Like his paternal grandfather of the same name, John Crowder was brought up in the book trades and, after moving to London, found early employment in his majesty's printing office under William Strahan. About 1780 he obtained a position with Francis Blyth, printer and part proprietor of the *Public Ledger*, a daily morning newspaper, and the *London Packet*, an evening paper published three times a week. In the year leading up to Blyth's death in 1788, Crowder took control of the *Public Ledger* and was trading from Blyth's premises at 2 Queen's Head Alley, Paternoster Row. Following Blyth's death on 27 May 1788 Crowder also became proprietor of the *London Packet*. He managed the publication of both newspapers 'with the greatest impartiality, diligence and integrity' (*GM*, 100/2, 1830, 568) until 1822, when they were taken over by T. Richards. In the same year that Crowder gained ownership of the *London Packet* he married Blyth's niece, Mary Annabella James (*d.* 1823), on 2 February at St Mary Aldermanbury, and was admitted to the freedom of the City of London by patrimony through the Playing-Card Makers' Company in July. Within two years he had moved his printing business to 12 Warwick Court, where, on 2 February 1790, Robert Crakelt was bound to him as an apprentice printer. While still maintaining publication of the *Public Ledger* and the *London Packet*, Crowder also published the *Mirror of the Times* between 1799 and 1803, was 'frequently employed in printing valuable works for the booksellers, by whom he was equally esteemed for punctuality, intelligence, and accuracy' (ibid., 568), and in 1802 was trading in partnership with another printer, E. Hemsted.

After amassing a considerable fortune through 'some successful speculations' (*GM*, 100/2, 1830, 568) Crowder relinquished his printing business in 1820 in the pursuit of a full-time civic career. As a longstanding and well-respected resident in the ward of Farringdon Within, he was first elected in 1800 as a representative of that ward in common council, and between 1814 and 1823 he served as one of two deputies. Although his wife died on 6 November 1823, Crowder maintained 'an assiduity and energy which more and more endeared him to his constituents' (ibid., 569) and was accordingly elected alderman of his ward on 24 April 1823 and sworn a week later. In that same year he joined the Stationers' Company by translation, sponsored by John Nichols, and was selected for the Stationers' Company court within a few months of being admitted to the livery; he served as under warden in 1827, as upper warden in 1828, and as master of the company in 1829. Between 1825 and 1826 Crowder was sheriff of London, and on 9 November 1829 he began his term as lord mayor, during which time he reputedly gave approximately £1000 for charitable purposes. He was known for his 'industry and integrity' in both public and private life, and he possessed a 'spirit, vivacity, and intelligence which rendered him an agreeable companion' (ibid., 570). Within months of entering his mayoralty, however, ill health forced him temporarily to abandon his civic responsibilities, and in September 1830 an asthmatic affection was aggravated by a severe cold and failure of digestion. This eventually forced him to withdraw completely from public life on 9 November 1830—exactly one year after commencing as lord mayor. Crowder died at his residence at Sudbury House, King Street, Hammersmith, in the early hours of the morning on 2 December 1830 and was buried eleven days later in the same vault as his wife at Christ Church Greyfriars. MICHAEL T. DAVIS

Sources I. Maxted, *The London book trades, 1775–1800: a preliminary checklist of members* (1977) · A. B. Beaven, ed., *The aldermen of the City of London, temp. Henry III–*[1912], 2 vols. (1908–13) · D. F. McKenzie, ed., *Stationers' Company apprentices*, [3]: 1701–1800 (1978) · *GM*, 1st ser., 100/2 (1830), 568–70 · 'Beadle's book', Worshipful Company of Stationers and Newspaper Makers, 179 · freedom admission paper, CLRO, City of London, CF1/1101
Wealth at death retired in 1820 with 'considerable fortune'; subsequent successful public career could only mean he died with this still applicable

Crowder, Sir Richard Budden (*bap.* 1796, *d.* 1859), judge, was the third son of William Henry Crowder of Montagu Place, Bloomsbury, and his wife, Ann Maidman. His exact date and place of birth are unknown, but he was baptized at St Luke's, Old Street, Finsbury, on 24 June 1796. He was educated at Eton College and Trinity College, Cambridge, but did not take a degree. He was called to the bar at Lincoln's Inn on 25 May 1821. He practised from chambers in 1 Brick Court, Temple, and joined the western circuit and the Exeter sessions. He was the leader of the sessions bar from 1829 to 1835 and leader of the western circuit from 1844 to 1854.

Both on circuit and in London Crowder enjoyed a good practice, particularly through his aptitude for influencing juries. Lord Chief Justice Coleridge considered him 'the greatest master of Nisi Prius I ever knew' (*Contemporary Review*, 57, 1890, 797). He was a very long-winded advocate, and he and Serjeant Bompas were mainly responsible for the western circuit's reputation for long-windedness at that time.

In 1837 Crowder was appointed a queen's counsel; in August 1846 he succeeded Sir Charles Wetherell as recorder of Bristol; and from 1849 to 1854 he held the appointments of counsel to the Admiralty and judge-advocate of the fleet. In January 1849 he was returned unopposed as Liberal MP for Liskeard in Cornwall, in succession to Charles Buller. In the House of Commons he spoke little and only on legal topics. In the great foreign policy debate in June 1850 he was asked to reply on behalf of the government but declined, thereby losing the opportunity for promotion, which passed instead to Cockburn. In March 1854 he was appointed a puisne justice in the court of common pleas in succession to Mr Justice Talfourd, and was knighted.

Crowder died suddenly at Southall, Middlesex, on 5 December 1859. He never married.

J. A. HAMILTON, *rev.* DAVID PUGSLEY

Sources D. Pugsley, 'Sir Richard Crowder', *Bracton Law Journal*, 28 (1996) · Boase, *Mod. Eng. biog.* · Venn, *Alum. Cant.* · *The Times* (6 Dec 1859) · *Law Magazine*, new ser., 5 (1859), 345 · *Jurist* (10 Dec 1859) · *IGI*

Wealth at death under £80,000: resworn probate, March 1860, *CGPLA Eng. & Wales*

Crowdy, Edith Frances (1880–1947), travel agent and member of the Women's Royal Naval Service, was born on 25 August 1880 at 79 Victoria Road, Wandsworth, London, one of the four daughters of James Crowdy, solicitor, and his wife, Mary Isabel Anne Fuidge. Educated at home, in 1912 she joined her younger sister Rachel Eleanor *Crowdy in the voluntary aid detachment (VAD), a nursing organization affiliated to the Red Cross, becoming deputy to Katharine Furse, commandant-in-chief. When Furse was appointed director of the newly formed Women's Royal Naval Service (WRNS) in 1917 Crowdy also left the VAD and joined Furse as deputy director. In this role she was deeply involved in drafting and implementing new regulations for the WRNS. In her tribute written after Crowdy's death in *The Wren*, the magazine of the Association of Wrens which Crowdy had helped to found in 1920, Dame Katharine Furse acknowledged Crowdy's contribution to the success of the WRNS in its brief existence, commenting that Crowdy had instilled confidence in everyone by her bold but calm behaviour. Crowdy had been made an honorary serving sister of the order of St John of Jerusalem in recognition of her work with the VAD; in 1919 she was appointed CBE for her services to the WRNS, which was disbanded at the close of hostilities.

Between the wars Crowdy worked for the travel service created by Sir Henry Lunn, and from 1926 she acted as secretary of the Hellenic Travellers Club, enjoying many voyages to the Mediterranean. Although she liked this work, Crowdy left Lunn in 1928 to become the general secretary of the World Association of Girl Guides and Girl Scouts, founded that year, and in 1930 she helped to organize the association's first world conference. But these duties did not fully occupy her, and she soon rejoined Lunn's travel business and took up again the secretaryship of the Hellenic Travellers Club. She also renewed her association with Katharine Furse, who had also joined Lunn's company.

With the outbreak of the Second World War in 1939, Crowdy joined her sister Isabel who was working as a secretary of the Children's Country Holiday Fund. She helped to organize holidays for children, especially from London, who would not otherwise have the opportunity to visit the countryside. At the same time she advised the government on evacuation plans for children under the age of five. She was still a special case worker for the fund in 1947, with a London address at 100 Beaufort Street, Chelsea, but had been living near Blandford, Dorset, when she suffered a heart attack and died at Herrison House, Charminster, Dorset, on 23 July 1947. She was buried at Blandford on 26 July 1947. LESLEY THOMAS

Sources K. Furse, *Hearts and pomegranates* (1940) · U. S. Mason, *Britannia's daughters: the story of the WRNS* (1992) · K. Furse, 'Miss Edith Crowdy, C.B.E.', *The Wren* (Oct 1947), 3 · K. Furse, *The Times* (29 July 1947), 6e · b. cert. · d. cert. · *CGPLA Eng. & Wales* (1947)
Archives NMM, corresp. with Dame Katharine Furse
Wealth at death £8246 19s. 9d.: probate, 11 Oct 1947, *CGPLA Eng. & Wales*

Crowdy, Dame Rachel Eleanor (1884–1964), social reformer, was born on 3 March 1884 at 28 Craven Hill Gardens, Paddington, London, the daughter of James Crowdy (*d.* in or before 1939), solicitor, and his wife, Mary Isabel Anne, *née* Fuidge. One of four sisters including Edith Frances *Crowdy, who were all to develop an active interest in social service in their adult lives, she was educated at Hyde Park New College in London, and at Guy's Hospital where she completed her training as a nurse in 1908. In 1911 she joined the newly formed voluntary aid detachments (VADs), volunteer nursing units attached to the Territorial Army. With characteristic thoroughness, she immediately began to study at Apothecaries' Hall for a certificate to serve as dispenser to her unit, VAD 22, London. Between 1912 and 1914 she was also a lecturer and demonstrator at the National Health Society.

It was through her work for the VADs during the First World War that Rachel Crowdy made her name. With her friend Katharine Furse she broke down the prejudices of both male administrators and professional nurses, setting up first aid and home nursing classes all over the country. The VADs had been trained for the eventuality of invasion, but they managed to send a small group to Boulogne, where they set up a rest station for wounded soldiers in a railway siding. There, during the first battle of Ypres, about twenty nurses ministered to 30,000 men. At the end of 1914 Katharine Furse returned to London and for the rest of the war Rachel Crowdy was in charge of the VADs on the continent. She set up rest stations along the lines of communication in France and Belgium, and established ambulance depots, hostels for nurses and for relatives of the sick and wounded, and hospitals and sickbays wherever they were needed. Before long the VADs had proved themselves so well that the two Crowdy sisters Rachel and Mary could set up an office in the joint war committee centre in the Hôtel Crystal in Boulogne.

Rachel Crowdy was mentioned in dispatches several times, and received the Royal Red Cross, second class, in 1916 and first class in 1917; in 1919 she was created DBE. Her experiences had tested her courage to the full. They had also helped to make her into an exceptionally firm and determined administrator. In 1919 she became chief of the social questions and opium traffic section at the League of Nations, the only woman to head a section at the league. During her twelve years there she considered a wide range of social problems, becoming best known for her inquiries into the traffic in women and children and into the opium trade. Her work won international acclaim. In 1920–21 she went with the International Typhus Commission to Poland when the epidemic was at its height, and in 1922 she was made a commander of the order of Polonia Restituta. In 1926 Smith College in the United States made her an honorary doctor of laws, and in 1931, at the end of her work for the League of Nations, the Spanish government made her a commander of the order of Alfonso XII 'for services of outstanding value in the international field of social reform'.

During the 1930s Dame Rachel's career as a 'social worker' (her own description) continued unabated. She was a member of the British delegation to the Conference on Pacific Relations at Shanghai in 1931, having attended the Conference on Pacific Affairs in Honolulu the previous year. She travelled alone to Shanghai, as she did again in 1936, when she returned to Manchuria. She revelled in the freedom to go where she wished and see what she pleased. In 1935–6 she was a member of the royal commission on the private manufacture of and trading in arms. The commission's report concluded that nationalization was impracticable, but recommended some far-reaching British and international regulations, which were not implemented. In 1937 Dame Rachel went with a parliamentary commission to observe the war in Spain. In 1938–9 she served on the West Indies royal commission, whose recommendations included the establishment of a West Indian Welfare Fund. From 1939 to 1946 she served as regions' adviser to the Ministry of Information, her last major appointment in a long and remarkably varied career.

Dame Rachel Crowdy belonged to a generation in which women had to possess very obvious strength of character if they were to attain recognition. She certainly could have been described as 'formidable', but those who knew her found much more besides. Strikingly good-looking and always well turned out, she impressed her colleagues with her incisive mind and quick wit. Her orderliness and other administrative talents tempered an abiding zest for life, a curiosity about people and places which seemed to be insatiable, and a feeling for poetry and visual beauty which was reflected in the vivid and graceful language of her many lectures to audiences all over the world. On 13 December 1939 she married Colonel Cudbert John Massy Thornhill CMG DSO (1883–1952), the son of Lieutenant-Colonel Sir Henry Beaufoy Thornhill. Dame Rachel died of coronary thrombosis at her home, Sheppards, Outwood, Surrey, on 10 October 1964, at the age of eighty.

ALICE PROCHASKA, *rev.*

Sources T. Bowser, *The story of British VAD work in the Great War* (1918) · Foreign Office, general corresp., PRO · *The Times* (12 Oct 1964), 12c · K. Furse, *Hearts and pomegranates* (1940) · P. Gibbs, *Ordeal in England* (1937) · private information (1981) · *WWW* · b. cert. · m. cert. · d. cert.

Archives University of Bristol Library, papers, incl. typescript autobiography, DM 1584 · Wichita State University Library, corresp.

Likenesses O. Edis, photograph, 1914, NPG · A. O. Spare, pastel and watercolour drawing, 1914–18, IWM · G. C. Beresford, photograph, 1923, NPG

Wealth at death £49,983: probate, 30 June 1965, *CGPLA Eng. & Wales*

Crowe [*née* Stevens], **Catherine Ann** (1790–1872), novelist and writer on the supernatural, was born in Borough Green, Kent, on 20 September 1790, the daughter of John Stevens (1758–1833), a farmer and later the proprietor of the popular Regency haunt Stevens's Hotel, and his first wife, Mary, *née* Nash (*b.* 1754). Educated at home, Catherine Stevens spent her childhood mainly in Kent. On 6 June 1822 she married Major John Crowe (1783–1860). They had one son, John William Crowe, born in 1823, but Catherine was unhappy, and sought help from Sydney Smith and his family, whom she met in Clifton, near Bristol, in 1828. By 1838 (the intervening years are obscure), she had separated from her husband and moved to Edinburgh, and moved in literary circles: her literary friends there and elsewhere came to include Francis Jeffrey, Thomas De Quincey, the Monckton Milneses, Harriet Martineau, and W. M. Thackeray. Smith also encouraged her plans to write.

Catherine Crowe's first publication was a verse-tragedy, *Aristodemus* (1838): it shows how the Messenian general Aristodemus's extreme public ambition and his wife Laodamia's extreme maternal emotions both lead to disaster. Although this play was never performed, her other, more crude drama, *The Cruel Kindness*—about a tyrannical Italian Renaissance duke's efforts to control his family—ran for a short season at the Haymarket in 1853.

Catherine Crowe first achieved prominence as a novelist, with *The Adventures of Susan Hopley, or, Circumstantial Evidence* (1841). This was followed by *Men and Women, or, Manorial Rights* (1844), *The Story of Lilly Dawson* (1847; the work best received by critics), *The Adventures of a Beauty* (1852), and *Linny Lockwood* (1854). The novels' interest in middle- and lower-class domestic life aligns them with mid-nineteenth-century realism, but they are also notable for crime, upper-class seducers, exotic locales, and complicated and coincidence ridden plots. The plotting encountered some criticism, but the novels' sheer readability was widely acknowledged. Crowe herself claimed to have written her fiction mainly for money. Indeed *Susan Hopley* was successful enough for her to resent others' exploitation of it: it was published in three volumes by Saunders and Otley in 1841, then brought out by Tait in 1842 in weekly numbers, monthly parts, and a 3s. volume. There were also a play by Dibdin Pitt (1841) and a penny serial by Prest (1842) loosely based on Crowe's text. None the less, the preface to *Linny Lockwood*, published in two volumes, offers an early challenge to the dominance of the expensive three-volume novel. Crowe contributed short stories to periodicals, including *Chambers' Journal* and Dickens's *Household Words* (some republished in her collection *Light and Darkness*, 1850). She also adapted Harriet Beecher Stowe's best-seller *Uncle Tom's Cabin* for children of two age groups (1853).

The predicament of nineteenth-century women is prominent in Catherine Crowe's novels: how they were seen as appendages to men rather than as independent beings, and so were ill-prepared for adulthood; how ignorance and social pressures fostered bad marital choices; how poverty and limited employment opportunities made women vulnerable to seduction. Crowe's female characters often become enterprising and resourceful, however, and her 'fallen' women are spared the deaths traditionally meted out to such characters in most mid-nineteenth-century novels.

Crowe's fiction sometimes features supernatural incidents, reflecting her increasing interest in the spiritual world. In 1845 she translated from German as *The Seeress of Prevorst* Kerner's account of a somnambulist clairvoyant. Then she brought out *The Night Side of Nature, or, Ghosts and Ghost Seers* (1848), also influenced by German writers. This largely comprised stories of hauntings, apparitions, premonitions, and revelations from somnambulism and hypnotism. It became Crowe's most popular work, running to many editions up to 1904. Underpinning the stories, however, was Crowe's strong conviction that her contemporaries needed to be receptive to evidence of a spiritual dimension in nature, in apparitions, and in psychological experiences giving the imagination free rein. Finding contemporary churches dogmatic, sectarian, and worldly, Crowe foreshadowed the search for more satisfying sources of religious enlightenment which would escalate in later decades. (She went on to become friendly with the mediums Sophia de Morgan and Arethusa Milner Gibson, and to attempt to communicate with a lost love of her youth.) *The Night Side of Nature* also influenced Baudelaire's theories about the imagination and the 'correspondences' between the natural and spiritual worlds.

Crowe was criticized for her credulous attitude to the incidents she recorded. Unfortunately, in February 1854, while preparing another collection of supernatural stories, she had a brief but publicized attack of insanity: she was found naked one night in Edinburgh, convinced that spirits had told her she was thus invisible. After a short stint in Hanwell Asylum she was advised to rest from writing. She resumed periodical contributions in 1857, going on to publish in *Once a Week* and the popular weekly *Bow Bells*, and brought out two children's books: *The Story of Arthur Hunter and his First Shilling* (1861) and *The Adventures of a Monkey* (1862). But her spiritualist publications for adults, *Ghosts and Family Legends*, and *Spiritualism, and the Age we Live in* (both 1859), enjoyed little success. In 1861 she sold most of her copyrights to Routledge.

From 1852 Catherine Crowe lived mostly in London and on the continent, but moved in 1871 to Folkestone, Kent. She died at her home there, 22 Upper Sandgate Road, of 'natural decay' on 14 June 1872, and her son had her buried in Cheriton Road cemetery, simply as the widow of her husband (who had died in 1860). She was, however, one of the fourteen writers included in *Women Novelists of Queen Victoria's Reign* (1897), a book of 'appreciations' by late-nineteenth-century women writers of their mid-Victorian predecessors; particularly noted were her advanced ideas about women. JOANNE WILKES

Sources University of Kent, Canterbury, Geoffrey Larken collection · A. Sergeant, 'Mrs Crowe, Mrs Archer Clive, Mrs Henry Wood', *Women novelists of Queen Victoria's reign: a book of appreciations* (1897), 147–92 · *The letters of Charles Dickens*, ed. M. House, G. Storey, and others, 2–7 (1969–93) · S. Mitchell, *The fallen angel: chastity, class and women's reading, 1835–1880* (1981) · reviews, *The Athenaeum* (1841–59) · G. T. Clapton, 'Baudelaire et Catherine Crowe', *Modern Language Review*, 25 (1930), 286–305 · R. Hughes, 'Une étape de l'esthétique de Baudelaire: Catherine Crowe', *Revue de la littérature comparée*, 17 (1937), 680–99 · A. Lohrli, ed., *Household Words: a weekly journal conducted by Charles Dickens* (1973) · A. H. Japp [H. A. Page], *Thomas de Quincey: his life and writings*, new edn (1890) · BL cat. · *Poole's index to periodical literature* (1802–82) · *The letters of Sydney Smith*, ed. N. C. Smith, 2 vols. (1953)

Archives Trinity Cam., letters · U. Cal., Los Angeles, letters · University of Kent, Canterbury, letters | New College, Oxford, letters to Sydney Smith's daughter, Lady Holland · Trinity Cam., letters to

Arethusa Milner Gibson, Cullum L81.1–6 · Trinity Cam., letters to Lord and Lady Houghton, Houghton 6.225, 237–39 · University of Kent, Canterbury, Geoffrey Larken collection, materials for biography
Likenesses sketch (after R. Sharples?, 1829), repro. in H. D. Thomson, ed., *The great book of thrillers* (1935)
Wealth at death under £800: probate, 9 July 1872, *CGPLA Eng. & Wales*

Crowe, Sir Colin Tradescant (1913–1989), diplomatist, was born on 7 September 1913 in Japan, the younger son and third of the three children of Sir Edward Thomas Frederick *Crowe (1877–1960), diplomatist, and his wife, Eleanor (*d.* 1947), daughter of William Hyde Lay, British consul at Chefoo, China. His father was commercial attaché at the British legation in Tokyo. Educated in England, latterly at Stowe School, Crowe went to Oriel College, Oxford, in 1932. He took a first in modern history in 1935 and joined the foreign service, which appointed him vice-consul in Peking. In 1938 he married Bettina Lum (1911–1983), nicknamed Peter, who as the daughter of American missionary Burt Francis Lum had lived in China since 1922. They had no children.

From 1938 until early in 1940 Crowe was vice-consul at the Shanghai international settlement. The remainder of the Second World War saw him rise from third to second secretary at the much-expanded Washington embassy. After three years at the Foreign Office (1945–8) his career continued in Paris, where he was first secretary and head of Chancery with the UK permanent delegation to the Organization for European Economic Co-operation (OEEC), created in April 1948 to administer Marshall aid. Next he served in the same capacity at the British legation in Tel Aviv (1949–50). In November 1950 Crowe returned to Peking; his rank remained first secretary and head of Chancery. Chinese 'volunteers' were fighting the Korean War and, although Britain had recognized the People's Republic of China, the communists harassed British diplomats. Crowe's brother-in-law, Antonio Riva, was executed in August 1951 on a charge of conspiring to murder Chairman Mao. After leaving Peking in April 1953, Crowe headed the Far Eastern department of the Foreign Office (as counsellor) until 1956—years during which the USA and the People's Republic of China engaged in brinkmanship over Taiwan.

Appointed CMG in January 1956 Crowe spent most of 1957 at the Imperial Defence College before being named in October as prospective chargé d'affaires in Cairo. Egypt had broken off diplomatic relations during the Suez crisis of 1956; Britain now sought their restoration in the hope of countering Soviet influence over President Nasser. Egyptian demands for war reparations deadlocked preliminary talks throughout 1958. Crowe arrived in Cairo on a tourist visa on 10 January 1959, by which time Egypt had joined Syria in forming the United Arab Republic. After Britain agreed to release Egypt's sterling balances, he became head of the British property commission in April 1959, leading a small team of diplomats working to secure the desequestration of British assets. They were barred from embassy premises until relations resumed at chargé d'affaires level on 9 December 1959. Crowe felt no nostalgia for lost British regional dominance. His style was self-effacing. Mohammed Hassanein Heikal, a prominent Egyptian journalist, crucially acted as go-between (for Nasser and Crowe never met). At length, the United Arab Republic and Britain agreed on 26 January 1961 to exchange ambassadors. Nasser freed the last British 'spy' imprisoned in Egypt as a 'farewell gift' to Crowe.

Crowe's next appointment was as deputy permanent representative to the United Nations (UN) in New York (1961–3), serving under Sir Patrick Dean. The war in the Congo loomed large during this time, and, as British spokesman on the decolonization committee of the UN general assembly, Crowe was frequently concerned with rebutting criticism of British policy in Africa. In April 1963 he became British ambassador to Saudi Arabia—the first since relations were severed in 1956. He was promoted KCMG in June 1963 and reported the power struggle between King Saʿud and Prince Faisal for eighteen months. After a sabbatical year at St Antony's College, Oxford (1964–5), Crowe worked as the chief of administration of the diplomatic service (1965–8). His careful personnel management knit together the foreign, trade commissioner, and Commonwealth services (combined in January 1965), and incorporated the colonial service too in 1966. He then spent two years in Canada as high commissioner (1968–70).

Edward Heath chose Crowe to replace Lord Caradon as permanent representative to the United Nations in New York from October 1970. Crowe was not a specialist; he was a problem solver, who saw international disputes in their widest context. Never pompous or flamboyant, this quiet bespectacled man needed his wife's moral support whenever he had to give a formal speech. His talent lay in building trust through patient negotiation. Conciliation was required as Britain's relationship with the UN reached its nadir in respect of Rhodesia: Crowe had to withdraw from the decolonization committee and veto a resolution calling for tighter economic sanctions in May 1973. His friendship with the US envoy, future President George Bush, helped limit Anglo-American tensions arising from different attitudes to the Arab–Israeli conflict. He also cultivated better understanding with the UN secretary-general, Kurt Waldheim, who knew that Britain had opposed his candidacy in December 1971. Terrorism, Cyprus, and Namibia were major issues, along with the UN membership of communist China and East and West Germany. Crowe took his turn as president of the UN Security Council in January 1971, April 1972, and July 1973. He was raised to GCMG in June 1973, prior to his retirement in September 1973.

Back in Britain, Crowe lived at Pigeon House, Bibury, Gloucestershire, his home in England since the mid-1960s. He was a director of Grindlay's Bank (1976–84) and chaired the council of Cheltenham Ladies College (1974–86). Widowed in 1983, he died of a stroke at Cirencester Hospital on 19 July 1989.   JASON TOMES

Sources *The Times* (27 March 1962) · *The Times* (24 July 1989) · *The Independent* (29 July 1989) · *Daily Telegraph* (24 July 1989) · *The Guardian* (21 July 1989) · C. Crowe, 'An account of the restoration of relations between the United Kingdom and the United Arab Republic (Egypt) after the Suez episode, 1957–61', St Ant. Oxf., Middle East Centre · *Diplomatic service list, 1972* · WWW · Burke, *Peerage* · P. Lum [B. Crowe], *Peking, 1950–1953* (1958) · A. Parsons, *They say the lion* (1986) · G. Moorhouse, *The diplomats* (1977) · d. cert.
Archives St Ant. Oxf., Middle East Centre, account of restoration of relations between Britain and Egypt after Suez crisis | PRO, Foreign Office papers, Foreign and Commonwealth Office papers
Likenesses photograph, repro. in *The Times* (24 July 1989)
Wealth at death £812,946: probate, 11 Sept 1989, CGPLA Eng. & Wales

Crowe, Sir Edward Thomas Frederick (1877–1960), public servant, was born at Zante in the Ionian Islands on 20 August 1877, the son of Alfred Louis Crowe, who later became vice-consul for the island, and his wife, Matilda Fortunata Barff. He was educated at Bedford grammar school and in 1897 joined the consular service as a student interpreter in Japan. In 1901 he married Eleanor (d. 1947), daughter of William Hyde Lay, British consul at Chefoo (Yantai), China. They had two sons and one daughter.

During the Russo-Japanese War Crowe was in charge of the consulate at Tamsui (Danshui), Taipei (Tabei), then a Japanese possession, where his ability attracted attention at Tokyo, and in 1906 he was assigned to the legation as commercial attaché. He was appointed CMG in 1911. In 1918, after the creation of the department of overseas trade and the commercial diplomatic service, he was confirmed as the first commercial counsellor at the new embassy in Tokyo. He was knighted in 1922, and was recalled to London in 1924. He never returned to the Far East, but his admiration and affection for the Japanese people remained a feature of his life. For seven years he was vice-president of the Japan Society in London, the Japanese ambassador being traditionally its president, and he took an active part in its work, on the council and at its lectures. After the Second World War he led a movement for the submission of a petition for clemency to the war crimes tribunal at Tokyo for Mamoru Shigemitsu, the former ambassador in London and later Japanese foreign minister. In 1950 Crowe became the first president of the Japan Association, formed to promote British trade interests in Japan. In 1955 he was decorated with the Japanese order (first class) of the sacred treasure.

From 1924 to 1928 Crowe served as director of the foreign division of the department of overseas trade, and in April 1928 he was chosen to succeed Sir William Clark as comptroller-general of the department. During his term of office, which lasted until the autumn of 1937, he did much to foster British trade with the Far East, and to reconcile the interests of British and Japanese cotton-goods exporters. His nine years as comptroller-general marked the period of widest influence for the department. He brought to the post a practical and sympathetic experience of the problems facing exporters and he was endowed with boundless energy, an inquisitive mind, and a remarkable capacity for winning people's confidence. Not content with the current administrative duties of his office, he got to know intimately each member of his staff, at home or overseas; he was in personal contact with the leaders in banking, industry, and commerce in London; and, unusually for a government official, he frequently took the initiative to visit the centres of industry in the provinces and to address their chambers of commerce. Single-handed he did much to reverse the previous apathy or indifference of government departments to the difficulties of exporters. Above all, he strove for the expansion of the annual British Industries Fair which provided an important showcase for British exports. For nine years he was vice-president of the International Exhibitions Bureau at Paris, and vice-president of the board of governors of the Imperial Institute. In recognition of his services he was advanced to KCMG in 1930.

Crowe retired from government service in 1937, and took up the chairmanship of Croda Ltd and directorships of W. T. Henley's Telegraph Works Company, Marconi's Wireless Telegraph Company, and the English Electric Company Ltd. He became an ardent supporter of the Royal Society of Arts, serving as vice-president (1937–60), president (1942–3), and chairman of the council (1941–3). He identified himself particularly with the society's work for the vocational education of young people and for sixteen years was chairman of its examination committee. He also served on many government committees, including Lord Goschen's on the law relating to trade marks, Lord Gorell's on art and industry, and Lord Fleming's on public schools.

Crowe was one whose character found its happier development only after his release from the ties of official life. He was not a scholar and he disliked being alone; his delight was in meeting people and drawing them to him. After his death, Sir Harry Lindsay recalled 'his sense of human neighbourliness', which 'endeared him to all with whom he came into contact' (*Journal of the Royal Society of Arts*, 298). He had a graceful facility for public speaking, enjoyed abundant health, and appeared to be incapable of fatigue. In his old age, with his mass of white hair, his monocle, and his blue beret, he was a respected and popular figure. He died on 8 March 1960 at 10 Sharia Willcocks Zamalek, Cairo, during a visit to his son Colin Tradescant *Crowe, then British chargé d'affaires in Cairo. A memorial service was held in his honour at Holy Trinity Church, Brompton, on 20 May.

R. L. NOSWORTHY, *rev.* ALEX MAY

Sources *The Times* (9 March 1960) · *The Times* (14 March 1960) · *The Times* (22 March 1960) · *Journal of the Royal Society of Arts*, 108 (1959–60), 296–8 · WWW · private information (1971) · H. Cortazzi, 'The Japan Society: a hundred-year history', *Britain and Japan, 1859–1991: themes and personalities*, ed. H. Cortazzi and G. Daniels (1991), 1–53 · I. Nish, '"In one day have I lived many lives": Frank Ashton-Gwatkin, novelist and diplomat, 1889–1976', *Britain and Japan: biographical portraits*, ed. I. Nish, 3 (1994), 159–73 · P. Lowe, *Great Britain and Japan, 1911–15* (1969) · P. Lowe, *Britain in the Far East: a survey from 1819 to the present* (1981) · personal knowledge (1971) · CGPLA Eng. & Wales (1960) · PRO, Foreign Office MSS
Likenesses W. Stoneman, photograph, 1930, NPG · W. Stoneman, photograph, 1945, NPG
Wealth at death £24,113 19s.: probate, 28 June 1960, CGPLA Eng. & Wales

Crowe, Eyre (1824–1910), painter, was born on 3 October 1824 at 141 Sloane Street, London, the eldest of the six children of Eyre Evans *Crowe (1799–1868), author and journalist, and his first wife, Margaret (d. 1853), daughter of Joseph Archer of Newtown Mount Kennedy, co. Wicklow, and his wife, Hester. His younger brother was the journalist and art historian Sir Joseph Archer *Crowe (1825–1896). His childhood was spent largely in Paris, where his father was correspondent for the *Morning Chronicle*. He was educated at home by his father and was taught drawing by William Darley and one M. Brasseur. In 1839 he enrolled at the celebrated atelier of Paul Delaroche, where he associated with many rising artists, including Jean-Léon Gérôme, with whom he formed a lasting friendship. Both were among the pupils who accompanied Delaroche to Rome after the atelier closed in 1843.

In the following year Crowe rejoined his family, now settled in London. His early work was rejected by the Royal Academy and he registered at the Academy Schools for further study. In 1846 he made his début at the academy with *Master Prynne Searching Archbishop Laud's Pockets in the Tower*. This impressed W. M. Thackeray, a close family friend, who employed Crowe to transfer his sketches for *Notes of a Journey from Cornhill to Grand Cairo* (1846) to woodblocks and to conduct research for his commentary on Louis Marvy's *Sketches after English Landscape Painters* (1850).

When his father ceased to be editor of the *Daily News* and returned to Paris in 1852, the indigent Crowe was engaged by Thackeray as his secretary and as drawing-master for his daughters. After preparing *The History of Henry Esmond Esquire* for publication Crowe was persuaded to accompany the author on a six-month (November 1852 to April 1853) lecture tour of the United States as his 'factotum and amanuensis' (Crowe, *With Thackeray in America*, 1). He did not always prove competent in this capacity but Thackeray appreciated his company as 'the kindest and most affectionate henchman ever man had' (*Letters and Private Papers*, 3.184). Crowe's American sketches, some of which appeared in the *Illustrated London News*, show a strong interest in the appearance and condition of the black community, later expressed in the painting *Slaves Waiting for Sale, Richmond, Virginia* (exh. RA, 1861; Heinz Collection).

After his return to England Crowe gradually achieved success as a painter of genre and historical subjects, often reflecting an extensive knowledge of eighteenth-century literature, for example *The Penance of Dr Johnson* (exh. RA, 1869; Dr Johnson's House). His *Defoe in the Pillory* (exh. RA, 1862) won the silver medal of the Society for the Encouragement of the Fine Arts. Modern criticism has paid greater attention to his unsentimental excursions into social realism, such as the depictions of foundrymen in *Shinglers* (exh. RA, 1869; Christies sale catalogue, 19 February 2003, there entitled *The Foundry*) and women millworkers in *The Dinner Hour, Wigan* (exh. RA, 1874; Manchester City Galleries). From 1859 he acted as occasional examiner and inspector of the government schools of art. He was commissioned by the South Kensington Museum to design mosaics of William Hogarth (1867) and Sir Christopher Wren (1869) for the south courts and to paint the lunette *Modelling from Life* (1869) for the National Competition Gallery. He exhibited annually at the Royal Academy from 1857 to 1908, was elected an associate in 1876, and lived to become its oldest member, but never attained the rank of academician.

Crowe was a sociable bachelor, from 1861 frequenting the Reform Club, which owns his painting *John Bright at the Reform Club, 1883*. He was also welcomed by the St John's Wood clique of artists as an 'honorary member' whose 'hearty laugh was … more exhilarating than champagne' (Leslie, 194–6). However, his nature grew more retiring as he outlived contemporaries and his artistic reputation. Having published two illustrated memoirs of his mentor, *With Thackeray in America* (1893) and *Thackeray's Haunts and Homes* (1897), he was himself remembered by Henry James as:

> a Thackerayan figure, but much as if the master's hand had stamped him with the outline and the value, with life and sweetness and patience—shown, as after the long futility, seated in a quiet wait, very long too, for the end. (H. James, *Autobiography*, 1956, 53)

Crowe died, unmarried, of heart failure on 12 December 1910 at his home, 88 Hallam Street, Portland Place, London, following a hernia operation; he was buried on 15 December at Kensal Green cemetery.   J. P. HOPSON

Sources E. Crowe, *With Thackeray in America* (1996) · J. Crowe, *Reminiscences* (1895) · G. D. Leslie, *The inner life of the Royal Academy* (1914) · *The letters and private papers of William Makepeace Thackeray*, ed. G. N. Ray, 4 vols. (1945–6) · J. Dafforne, 'Eyre Crowe', *Art Journal* (1864), 205–7 · J. Treuherz, *Hard times: social realism in Victorian art* (1987) [exhibition catalogue, Man. City Gall., 14 Nov 1987 – 10 Jan 1988] · J. G. Wilson, *Thackeray in the United States* (1904) · A. T. C. Pratt, ed., *People of the period: being a collection of the biographies of upwards of six thousand living celebrities*, 2 vols. (1897) · H. Ottley, *A biographical and critical dictionary of recent and living painters and engravers* (1876) · *The Times* (13 Dec 1910) · G. N. Ray, *Thackeray*, 2 vols. (1955–8), vol. 2 · E. Crowe, *Thackeray's haunts and homes* (1897) · IGI · DNB

Archives V&A NAL, corresp. and sketches; family MSS

Likenesses R. W. Robinson, photograph, 1891, NPG; repro. in J. Maas, *The Victorian art world in photographs* (1984) · Elliott & Fry, photograph, c.1900, repro. in C. Welch, *London at the opening of the twentieth century* (1905) · E. Crowe, self-portrait, oils (as young man); in possession of his sister in 1912 · W. M. Thackeray, watercolour; Sothebys, 27 July 1911 · wood-engraving (after photograph by G. Crowe), NPG; repro. in *ILN* (6 May 1876)

Wealth at death £287 9s. 1d.: probate, 2 Feb 1911, CGPLA Eng. & Wales

Crowe, Sir Eyre Alexander Barby Wichart (1864–1925), diplomatist, was born on 30 July 1864 at Leipzig, the third of the seven children of Sir Joseph Archer *Crowe (1825–1896), diplomatist and art historian, and his wife, Asta von Barby (1840–1908), daughter of Gustav von Barby and Eveline von Ribbentrop, and stepdaughter of Otto von Holtzendorff, attorney-general to Duke Ernst II of Saxe-Coburg and Gotha. He received his education at *Gymnasien* in Düsseldorf (1872–80) and Berlin (1880–82), and subsequently attended courses at both King's College and University College, London (1882–5). He never took a degree, as his ambition from an early age was to obtain a place in the Foreign Office. He concentrated on preparing for the entrance examination and became fluent in French as well as English and German. He was appointed a junior clerk in May 1885.

Crowe's initial tasks in the Foreign Office were purely clerical and gave him little opportunity to take independent action or even to offer advice. Nevertheless he quickly made a reputation for himself by his efficiency and devotion to duty, so that by the mid-1890s he had been marked out for eventual promotion to the highest ranks. From 1885 to 1897 he lived in the Foreign Office as a resident clerk and devoted much of his spare time to a study of British diplomacy during the nineteenth century. During these years he developed firm views on the aims that he believed British foreign policy should pursue and which he thought recent governments had neglected. He became convinced that Britain should be more assertive in order to maintain her command of the sea, and should use her sea-power to preserve a balance of power in Europe. In his view, Britain should always be the guardian of the independence of other nations as well as her own, opposed to the domination of any one state. With no opportunity to influence the formulation of policy, Crowe found ways of bringing these opinions to a wider public. He collaborated with his brother-in-law, the journalist and military historian Henry Spencer Wilkinson, on the writing of *The Great Alternative*, published under Spencer Wilkinson's name in 1894, and he contributed a chapter to a *Memoir of Hubert Hervey* (ed. Earl Grey, 1899), a close friend recently killed in Africa. Crowe's chapter contained his own political views, which he had shared with Hervey. On 2 February 1903 he married his cousin Clema (b. 1869), daughter of Professor Carl Gerhardt, of Gamburg, Baden, and widow of Eberhardt von Bonin. They had four children, Asta (b. 1904), Eric (b. 1905), Una (b. 1906), and Sibyl (b. 1908).

Crowe was a strong critic of the organization of the Foreign Office, feeling that the talents of even its most senior members were wasted on purely clerical tasks, and that the foreign secretary was consequently deprived of the well-informed advice that he needed. The turning point in Crowe's career came in December 1904, when he was asked to supervise a major reorganization of the Foreign Office along the lines that he had been advocating. He quickly revealed exceptional powers of organization and negotiation. He elaborated a completely new scheme and persuaded the Treasury to accept the additional costs involved. By the end of 1905 he had arranged all the details and produced lengthy instructions on how his system should be operated. The reorganization involved the devolution of the clerical work of the Foreign Office to second division clerks, leaving the first division clerks and the under-secretaries free to devote themselves to advising the secretary of state. To make this possible there was a new system of registering and keeping papers in 'jackets', on which minutes could be written. The new system came into operation in January 1906, shortly after Sir Edward Grey became secretary of state.

Crowe was able to take full advantage of the new system, because its introduction coincided with his promotion by seniority to the rank of senior clerk. He was placed in charge of the western department of the Foreign Office, which dealt with Germany and the other states of western Europe. He quickly became very influential in the formulation and execution of Grey's foreign policy. His years as head of the western department coincided with a deterioration in Anglo-German relations, which he personally very much regretted. He advised Grey during the important negotiations for a possible Anglo-German naval and political agreement (1908–12) and during the Agadir crisis of 1911. He was guided by his belief, expressed at first tentatively in his famous 'Memorandum on the present state of British relations with France and Germany' of January 1907, but then much more positively in later minutes, that the German government was consciously aiming at a general political hegemony in Europe. He argued forcefully that Britain should act firmly to maintain the balance of power and to prevent any erosion of her maritime supremacy.

In January 1912 Crowe was promoted to be an assistant under-secretary, but continued to be responsible for the western department. Then, in September 1913, he was made responsible for both the western and the eastern departments, to co-ordinate British foreign policy throughout Europe and the Middle East. He was convinced that Germany was preparing for a war against the entente powers and that it was therefore essential to maintain the fragile triple entente. He urged on Grey that the preservation of the increasingly unpopular entente with Russia would only be possible if the British government was very firm with the Russians over imperial disputes, particularly in Persia.

When the final crisis came in July 1914, Crowe had absolutely no doubt that it was in the interests of Britain herself, and of the independence of Europe as a whole, that the government should enter the war on the side of France and Russia. For Crowe himself, half-German, educated in Germany, strongly Germanophile, and with a German wife, the outbreak of the First World War was a personal tragedy. The war also had a profound impact on Crowe's career. Grey had decided that the permanent under-secretary should be transferred to the Paris embassy in the autumn of 1914, so that Crowe could be promoted in his place. At the age of only fifty, this would have placed him at the head of the Foreign Office for the final fifteen years of his career. In the event his promotion was delayed by six years, and very nearly prevented, when all diplomatic transfers were postponed for the duration of hostilities.

From 1914 to 1918 Crowe's main task was the organization of the blockade of Germany, a task for which he was particularly well qualified. As head of the western department he had made a special study of these questions and had played a very important role in the negotiations concerning the implementation of the declaration of London (1909), intended as a codification of international law in regard to maritime warfare. He created a new contraband department in the Foreign Office, which soon became larger than the rest of the office combined. In 1916 it became the nucleus of a new ministry of blockade, with Lord Robert Cecil, the parliamentary under-secretary at the Foreign Office, as the cabinet minister in charge. In recognition of his outstanding contribution to the war effort Crowe was given the rank of permanent under-secretary in the ministry of blockade in April 1917. However, his role as director of the blockade brought his name to the attention of the general public, and he suffered from the wave of Germanophobia which swept the country. Critics of the government's blockade policy, notably Emmeline and Christabel Pankhurst and other suffragettes, called attention to Crowe's German connections, alleged that he was secretly allowing the blockade to be undermined, blamed him for every failure in the war, and demanded his dismissal. Crowe was subjected to a sustained public attack, which lasted from the summer of 1915 until the end of the war. He was defended in parliament by both Grey and Cecil, but his promotion to be head of the Foreign Office was called into question. When the permanent under-secretary, Sir Arthur Nicolson, retired in June 1916 he was replaced not by Crowe, but by Lord Hardinge of Penshurst.

In January 1919 Crowe went to Paris as part of the British delegation to the peace conference. He quickly emerged as the most influential member of the Foreign Office team, and played a central role in the territorial negotiations leading to the five peace treaties. In September 1919, when only the German and Austrian treaties had been signed, he was given the vitally important position of British representative on the supreme council of the peace conference, which was chaired by Clemenceau, the French prime minister. Crowe and Clemenceau developed a personal friendship, and partly for this reason Crowe dominated the proceedings of the council until the German treaty was ratified and the peace conference came to an end in January 1920. Lord Curzon, the new foreign secretary, was amazed by Crowe's powers of negotiation and his profound knowledge of the issues involved. When Hardinge left the Foreign Office in November 1920, Curzon insisted that Crowe should be promoted permanent under-secretary.

Crowe remained head of the Foreign Office, serving under three foreign secretaries (Lord Curzon, Ramsay MacDonald, and Sir Austen Chamberlain), for the next four and a half years. He was keen that a balance of power should be restored in Europe, and that Germany should not be permanently weakened or crippled by excessive reparations. Vital to this balance was close co-operation between Britain and France, the only two powers capable of guaranteeing peace and stability in Europe after the war. Crowe advised Curzon that the only way to persuade France to co-operate with Britain and soften her attitude towards Germany was to offer a guarantee of her security on the Rhine against any future German attack. As Anglo-French relations deteriorated during 1921–2 he continued to advocate this policy, but failed to convince either Curzon or Lloyd George. When the French and Belgians

occupied the Ruhr in 1923 he argued that the occupation was illegal under the terms of the treaty of Versailles and that the repressive policy towards Germany was having disastrous consequences which threatened international peace. He drafted the note in which the government publicly condemned the Franco-Belgian action, and then played a major part in the negotiations which culminated in the Dawes plan of 1924. Before he died he had finally persuaded the new Conservative government to accept his proposal for a security pact with France. He formulated and drafted the guarantee of Germany's western frontiers which was later included in the Locarno pact. He exercised a dominant influence over Austen Chamberlain, with whom he developed a very close friendship. He was also an important influence on the foreign policy of Ramsay MacDonald. In October 1924, when he authorized the publication of the Zinoviev letter, he was distressed to discover that the prime minister had not intended the letter to be published. Nevertheless responsibility for the mistake lay with MacDonald, who had failed to make his intentions clear.

Crowe was over 6 feet tall, with blue eyes, a fair complexion, and thick, wavy, red hair. He suffered throughout his life from poor health, mainly the result of weak kidneys, made worse by constant overwork. He nearly died of kidney failure at the beginning of 1920 and continued working against medical advice. He was an exceptionally cultivated man, read very widely throughout his life, and had a great love of music. As a young man he played the piano to a high standard and composed both songs and piano pieces. His setting of Shelley's 'Arethusa' was published in 1889. His interest in military defence led him to serve as an officer in the first volunteer battalion, City of London fusiliers, from 1890 to 1902, reaching the rank of captain in 1894. His powers of argument were revealed in February 1911 when he won a spectacular forensic victory in the Savarkar arbitration case at The Hague, for which he was appointed KCMG. He was made KCB in June 1917 and advanced to GCMG in January 1920. He died of kidney failure while still in office, on 28 April 1925, in Swanage, Dorset. He was buried on 1 May in nearby Studland.

Crowe was a great administrator and a master of Foreign Office procedure, whom Baldwin referred to, on hearing of his death, as 'the ablest public servant of the Crown' (*DNB*). Public perception of his views has changed during the twentieth century. Attacked during the war as a pro-German traitor, he was later denounced by many as a rabid Germanophobe after the publication of *British Documents on the Origins of the War, 1898–1914* (1926–38). His memorandum of January 1907, published in 1928, had a wide popular appeal and aroused great interest in the academic world as a set text for generations of students of international relations. EDWARD CORP

Sources S. Crowe and E. Corp, *Our ablest public servant: Sir Eyre Crowe, 1864–1925* (1993) · E. Corp, 'The problem of promotion in the career of Sir Eyre Crowe, 1905–1920', *Australian Journal of Politics and History*, 28 (1982), 236–49 · E. Corp, 'Sir Eyre Crowe and Georges Clemenceau at the Paris peace conference, 1919–1920', *Diplomacy and Statecraft*, 8 (1997), 10–19 · G. P. Gooch and H. Temperley, eds.,

British documents on the origins of the war, 1898–1914, 11 vols. in 13 (1926–38) · L. Woodward and others, eds., *Documents on British foreign policy, 1919–1939*, 1st ser., 1–21 (1947–78) · *DNB* · *CGPLA Eng. & Wales* (1925)

Archives Bodl. Oxf., corresp. and papers · priv. coll., family papers · PRO, Foreign Office corresp., FO 800 | Bodl. Oxf., corresp. with Sir Horace Rumbold · CAC Cam., corresp. with Sir Eric Phipps · Lpool RO, corresp. with Lord Derby

Likenesses photographs, 1888–1920, repro. in Crowe and Corp, *Our ablest public servant*; priv. coll.

Wealth at death £1333 16s. 9d.: probate, 12 June 1925, *CGPLA Eng. & Wales*

Crowe, Eyre Evans (1799–1868), historian and journalist, was born at Redbridge, Southampton, on 20 March 1799, the son of David Crowe, captain in an East India regiment, and his wife, formerly Miss Hayman of Walmer. David Crowe's father was another Eyre Evans Crowe, also in the army; and an ancestor was William Crowe, dean of Clonfert from 1745 to 1766. Crowe's mother died from the effects of her confinement. He was educated at a school in Carlow, and at Trinity College, Dublin, where he won a prize for an English poem. He left college early to take to journalism in London. In 1822 he went to Italy, from where he wrote descriptive letters published in *Blackwood's Magazine* during 1822 and 1823. Also in 1823 Crowe married Margaret Archer (d. 1853), the daughter of Captain Archer of co. Wicklow, at St Patrick's Cathedral, Dublin. He then produced a series of novels, including *Vittoria Colonna*, *To-Day in Ireland* (1825), *The English in Italy* (1825), *The English in France* (1828), *Yesterday in Ireland* (1829), and *The English at Home* (1830). He wrote no other novel until 1853, when he published *Charles Delmer*, a story containing much shrewd political speculation.

Crowe contributed a *History of France* to Dionysius Lardner's *Cabinet Encyclopaedia* in 1830; and part of a series of lives of eminent foreign statesmen to the same in 1831, the remainder being contributed by the historical novelist G. P. R. James. The *History of France*, amplified and rewritten, was published in five volumes in 1858–68. In 1853 Crowe published *The Greek and the Turk*, the result of a journey made to the Levant to investigate the Eastern question. In 1854 appeared his *History of Louis XVIII and Charles X*: by then a resident of Paris, he had witnessed the revolution of 1830. In 1832 he became the Paris correspondent of the *Morning Chronicle*. The needs of a growing family compelled him to devote himself exclusively to journalism, and he returned to England in 1844. He joined the staff of the *Daily News*, a Liberal rival to the *Morning Chronicle*, on its foundation in 1846, and was its editor from 1849 to 1851, during which time the paper made slow but steady progress. He also wrote the foreign articles for *The Examiner* during the editorship of Albany Fonblanque and, later, of John Forster. Crowe died, after a painful operation, on 25 February 1868 at 56 Beaumont Street, Marylebone, London, and was buried at Kensal Green cemetery.

Crowe had six children from his first marriage: Eyre *Crowe (1824–1910), Sir Joseph Archer *Crowe (1825–1896), Eugenie Marie Crowe (afterwards Mrs Wynne), Edward Crowe (b. 1829), Amy Marianne Crowe (Mrs

Eyre Evans Crowe (1799–1868), by Daniel Maclise

Edward Thackeray; b. 1831), and Dr George Crowe, (b. 1841). He had also a family by a second wife, of whom nothing is known. [ANON.], rev. NILANJANA BANERJI

Sources private information (1888) · Boase, *Mod. Eng. biog.* · H. R. Fox Bourne, *English newspapers: chapters in the history of journalism*, 2 (1887) · D. Griffiths, ed., *The encyclopedia of the British press, 1422–1992* (1992)

Archives BL, letters, as applicant and sponsor, to the Royal Literary Fund, loan no. 96 · Cork City Library, letters to Thomas Crofton Croker · LUL, letters to the Society for the Diffusion of Useful Knowledge · NL Ire., letters to Thomas Crofton Croker · NL Scot., letters to William Blackwood & Sons

Likenesses D. Maclise, pencil and watercolour drawing, V&A [see *illus.*]

Crowe, Sir Joseph Archer (1825–1896), art historian and diplomatist, was born on 20 October 1825 at 141 Sloane Street, London, the second of the six children of Eyre Evans *Crowe (1799–1868), historian and journalist, and his wife, Margaret Archer (d. 1853). In addition to his work for the press, Crowe's father was a prolific writer of novels, and of articles for Lardner's *Cabinet Encyclopaedia*, and the author of a five-volume history of France (1858–68), and this passion for history was a great stimulus to his young son.

The Crowe family moved to France, where Crowe senior became a correspondent for the *Morning Chronicle*. His journalism provided his family with an exciting upbringing in Paris, where the young Crowe children mixed with artists and writers, and were educated at home by tutors in French, English, Latin, and Greek. Although Joseph was just four years old when the revolution of 27 July 1830 erupted, he vividly recalled hiding with his mother at their home in the rue des Carrières, while his father hurried away to record the event for the British press.

In 1840 Joseph Crowe entered the Paris atelier of the painter Paul Delaroche to train as an artist; his elder brother Eyre *Crowe (1824–1910) was already enrolled there. At fifteen, Crowe was extremely junior and found Delaroche stern, while his fellow pupils wasted little time in exerting their seniority by marking him with oil paint: 'I was partially stripped and rubbed about with Prussian blue, which I found it difficult to get rid of, especially where the colour had gone on to my scalp' (Crowe, 24). Although Crowe's limitations as a draughtsman led him to abandon his studies after just one year, while Eyre later became a noted painter and an associate of the Royal Academy in 1875, his love of the fine arts was already in place and he began making notes and sketches in continental museums for a history of the early Flemish painters.

In 1843 the family returned to London where Crowe became a correspondent alongside his father for the *Morning Chronicle* (1843–6) and the *Daily News* (1846–53), work which provided sustenance and trips to European cities where he continued to collect art-historical evidence. During a visit to Berlin in 1847 Crowe met Giovanni Battista Cavalcaselle, a young Italian with a similar interest in early Renaissance art, and the pair began a lifelong collaboration. Between 1852 and 1857 Crowe and Cavalcaselle shared lodgings near Regent Street, following Cavalcaselle's escape to London as a political refugee, and together they wrote *The Early Flemish Painters* (1857), which ran to three editions and was translated into French and German. The 1850s were an unsettled time for Crowe, however, as he was unable fully to pursue art criticism without an external income. This found Crowe accepting interesting and intrepid employment such as a posting to the Balkans to report on the Crimean War for the *Illustrated London News* (1853–6). In 1857 he left London altogether to become principal of the Sir Jamsetjee Jeejeebhoy School of Art at Bombay, a post which proved unavailable on arrival, and Crowe instead took work with *The Times* covering the Indian mutiny of 1858 and the Austro-Italian War of 1859, experiences which he recounted in *Reminiscences of Thirty-Five Years of my Life* (1865).

The insecurity of Crowe's professional life was resolved in 1860 by a chance contact with the foreign secretary, Lord John Russell, who posted Crowe to Leipzig where he became consul-general for Lower Saxony (1860–80), sending intelligence reports to Prince Albert. By 1880 he was an attaché at Berlin and Vienna, negotiating treaties of trade for Britain, and in 1882 he was promoted to represent British commercial concerns for the whole of Europe, residing in Paris until his retirement in April 1896. Crowe's contentment in this continental environment was made complete by his marriage in 1861 at Gotha, Germany, to Asta von Barby (1840–1908), with whom he had seven children. Their son Eyre Alexander *Crowe (1864–1925) was later made KCMG for his work as under-secretary of state for the Foreign Office.

Crowe's travels as an attaché enabled him to visit art collections across Europe, and he eagerly spent long periods of leisure in collaboration with Cavalcaselle, producing *A New History of Painting in Italy* (1864–6), *A History of Painting in North Italy* (1871), and monographs on Titian (1877) and Raphael (1882). He also revised two standard works, Kugler's *Handbuch* on the German, Flemish, and Dutch schools (1874) and Jacob Burckhardt's *Cicerone* (1879), and contributed regularly to *The Athenaeum* and *The Times*. Although Crowe's prose style now appears antiquated, and much in the detail of his work has been superseded by later research, his innovation lies in the stimulation of the serious study of early Renaissance art in Britain and beyond. Together with Cavalcaselle, he provided the first extensive analyses in English of works by Jan van Eyck, Giotto, Giovanni Bellini, and many other painters, combining a sensitive appreciation of the art objects with a keen antiquarian sense of their historical context and the need to reconnect them to original documents. The particular importance of the volumes on Italian painting is underlined by their revision almost forty years after their initial publication as *Early Christian Art* and *Giotto and the Giottesques* (1903), edited by Langton Douglas and S. Arthur Strong, *The Sienese, Umbrian and North Italian Schools* (1908), edited by Langton Douglas, *Florentine Masters of the Fifteenth Century* (1911), edited by Langton Douglas, and *The Umbrian and Sienese Masters of the Fifteenth Century* and *The Sienese and Florentine Masters of the Sixteenth Century* (1914), edited by Tancred Borenius. In 1904 Roger Fry made an unsuccessful bid to John Murray's publishing house to edit Crowe's published and unpublished papers on northern Italian art, but was rejected by Lady Crowe, who feared Fry's revisions would neither preserve nor respect her late husband's views. This episode perfectly illustrates the generational shift which had occurred in the connoisseurship of the Italian Renaissance by the end of Crowe's life, but which owed its stimulus to the scholarly foundations laid by Crowe and Cavalcaselle.

Though Crowe was sometimes pedantic, given to correcting unfavourable reviews by formal letter, he was also a genial man blessed with tremendous energy and a gift for recounting amusing anecdotes. His prodigious contribution to art history is all the more remarkable for its achievement within the leisure hours of a successful official career. While he was made CB in 1885 and KCMG in 1890 for his diplomatic work, his art historical legacy has never been fully acknowledged. Even within his own lifetime, Crowe contested a public misapprehension that Cavalcaselle was the expert, as an Italian, while he merely wrote the texts. Though he did provide the overall narratives as Cavalcaselle spoke no English, Crowe also supplied documentary evidence and stylistic commentary, and was perhaps the more daring of the two when identifying works. Several controversial attributions to Raphael, Giorgione, and others are still endorsed by modern critics. The specialism of Crowe's writing is signalled by an appeal from his publisher John Murray to make the Italian painters appear 'more amusing', finding their treatment 'terribly dry' (Sutton, 'Crowe and Cavalcaselle',

114). Murray's request was met with a characteristically polite yet firm refusal.

Crowe died on 6 September 1896 at Schloss Gamburg, Baden, at the home of his brother-in-law Professor Carl Gerhardt, where he was resting following his retirement from the Foreign Office in April 1896.

JENNY GRAHAM

Sources J. A. Crowe, *Reminiscences of thirty-five years of my life*, 2nd edn (1895) · J. Graham, 'A note on the early reputation of Roger Fry', *Burlington Magazine*, 143 (2001), 493–9 · D. Sutton, 'Crowe and Cavalcaselle', *Apollo*, 122 (1985), 11–17 · 'Correspondence of Eyre Crowe and others', unsorted MSS, V&A NAL · D. Levi, *Cavalcaselle: il pioniere della conservazione dell'arte italiana* (1988) · L. Moretti, *G. B. Cavalcaselle: disegni da antiqui maestri* (1973) · Boase, *Mod. Eng. biog.*, 4.816 · 'Sir Joseph Archer Crowe', *Encyclopaedia Britannica*, 11th edn, 7 (1910), 54 · *The Times* (8 Sept 1896), 4 · *The Athenaeum* (12 Sept 1896), 361 · *ILN* (12 Sept 1896), 326 · *The Academy* (12 Sept 1896), 187 · C. Whitaker, ed., *Whitaker's Almanack* (1897) · *DNB* · U. Kultermann, *The history of art history* (1993) · *Letters of Roger Fry*, ed. D. Sutton, 2 vols. (1972), 223

Archives BL, MS of autobiographical reminiscences, Add. MSS 41309, 44059–44060 · John Murray, London, archives · V&A, MSS · V&A NAL, corresp. and sketches; notes on history of art | BL, Henry Layard MSS, Add. MSS 38989, 38992, 38994–38995 · NAM, letters to Spencer Wilkinson · PRO, letters to Odo Russell, FO918 · V&A, Eyre Crowe MSS

Likenesses L. Kolitz, oils, 1877, NPG

Wealth at death £713 4s. 8d.: probate, 15 Dec 1896, CGPLA Eng. & Wales

Crowe, Mitford (*bap.* 1669, *d.* 1719), diplomat, was baptized on 18 April 1669 at Hexham, Northumberland, the son of Patrick Crowe (*d.* before 1705), justice of the peace, of Ashington, Northumberland, and his wife, Anne Mitford (*fl.* 1669–1689). He was apprenticed to a Mr Tillard, a Barbados merchant, but by January 1697 he was living in Barcelona, making himself known to the government for the first time by writing an important letter of information to William III. At much the same time he married Urania, Lady Chamberlain (*née* Sandiford?), widow of Sir Willoughby Chamberlain, a prominent Barbados planter; three sons—George Sandiford, Mitford, and William—were baptized in London between 1699 and 1703.

In December 1700 Crowe was one of the agents of Barbados who presented the need for better defences on the island to the council of trade and the plantations. By now 'an opulent London merchant', according to one source (*Caribbeana*, 3.281), Crowe was returned as MP for Southampton in the parliaments of February to November 1701, and December 1701 to July 1702. On 29 January 1702 William III appointed him governor of Barbados 'for several good services rendered the crown', but this appointment was overturned on the king's death shortly afterwards; Crowe protested, claiming that he had '[laid] aside the whole course of his affairs in Europe' and spent more than £2000 preparing for the voyage (BL, Add. MS 61301, fol. 44).

On 18 March 1705 Crowe was commissioned as envoy to Catalonia to increase support there for the Habsburg claimant to the Spanish throne; it was said that this was because 'of his being well versed in the Spanish trade, of the interest he has with his Majesty ["Charles III"], [and] the knowledge he has of the people and country' (*Bath MSS*, 1.108). His highly placed contacts also included the prince of Hesse, whom he described as 'my dear friend' (Bodl. Oxf., MS Eng. hist. D164, fol. 45). Crowe arrived at Genoa on 20 May and at Barcelona on 2 November. Although the English military commander, the earl of Peterborough, was initially wary of Crowe's seemingly over-confident style, he was soon won over. The military rank of colonel that Crowe held may have been a Habsburg commission from this period, or else a rank in the Barbados militia; he was never commissioned in a regular British unit. Crowe returned to Genoa in May 1706 to raise money for 'Charles III'. He was subsequently appointed envoy-extraordinary to make a commercial treaty with Habsburg Spain, but did not return there.

In October 1706 Crowe was finally commissioned as governor of Barbados. He arrived there on 8 May 1707, and claimed to find the island's government 'in the last distraction, nothing but corruption and parties' (*CSP col.*, 1706–8, 435). Although he attempted to improve the defences of the island, his high-handed treatment (and eventual suspension) of several of his councillors, relying on the assembly rather than the council, his dismissal of several justices and militia officers, and his attempts to end the monopoly of a small group of barristers made him many enemies, who accused him of siding with factions, possessing an arbitrary attitude, and acting as the supreme legal authority of the island. Further charges against him ranged from accepting bribes and imprisoning without trial to indecently assaulting the wife and sister of one of the planters and (perhaps most damning of all) employing a Catholic as a personal servant.

There was clearly a large amount of factional sour grapes underlying the assault on Crowe. Given his and his wife's previous associations with the island, however, he was hardly likely to be an impartial adjudicator in the vicious struggle between the two main factions on the island; indeed, one of the factional leaders called Crowe 'his bird' (*CSP col.*, 1706–8, 564). The council of trade reprimanded him twice in 1708, and in July 1709 the queen herself sent him a letter stating her resentment of his disrespect in disobeying her order to restore the councillors. When Crowe found out that all of this had been reported to England, he allegedly turned on his accusers and 'abus'd us in such scurrilous Billingsgate language as would be offensive to your Lordships' ears to hear; such as no gentleman would have given even to a footman' (ibid., 1708–9, 299); and in October 1709 he was ordered to return to England to defend himself before the privy council. He finally left Barbados on 15 May 1710.

After returning to England, Crowe seems to have moved in circles that included Jonathan Swift, whose letters of the period 1710–12 make a number of references to Crowe. He died on 15 December 1719, and his will was proved by his widow in Barbados on 7 June 1720. His brother Christopher Crowe (1682–1749), consul at Leghorn while Mitford was in Barcelona and Genoa, married Charlotte, daughter of Edward Henry Lee, first earl of Lichfield, and Lady Charlotte Fitzroy (an illegitimate daughter of Charles II), and widow of the fourth Lord Baltimore.　　　　　J. D. DAVIES

Sources CSP col., vols. 13–26 • D. B. Horn, ed., British diplomatic representatives, 1689–1789, CS, 3rd ser., 46 (1932) • Journal of the Commissioners for Trade and the Plantations (1704–15) • petition of Crowe, BL, Add. MS 61301, fol. 44 • J. M. Sanders, ed., Barbados records: wills and administrations, 3: 1701–25 (Houston, Texas, 1981) • The manuscripts of the House of Lords, new ser., 12 vols. (1900–77), vols. 6–7, 9 • BL, additional charters 76100 • Caribbeana, 3 (1914) • N&Q, 11th ser. (1910–15), 233 • Members of parliament, 1213–1702, 1 (1878) • J. Redington, ed., Calendar of Treasury papers, 3, PRO (1874) • letters to Richard Hill, 1704–6, Bodl. Oxf., MS Eng. hist. D164 • W. Brigg, The register book of the parish of Saint Nicholas Acons, London, 1539–1812 (1890), 41 • W. Musgrave, Obituary prior to 1800, ed. G. J. Armytage, 6 vols., Harleian Society, 44–9 (1899–1901) • IGI [Hexham parish register] • Calendar of the manuscripts of the marquis of Bath preserved at Longleat, Wiltshire, 5 vols., HMC, 58 (1904–80), vol. 1
Archives Bodl. Oxf., letters to Richard Hill, MS Eng. hist. D164
Likenesses J. Smith, mezzotint (after T. Murray), BM, NPG; repro. in Caribbeana, 281
Wealth at death estates in Ashington, Northumberland: will, cited in Sanders, ed., Barbados records, 88

Crowe, Sir Sackville, first baronet (c.1600–1683), entrepreneur and diplomat, was the son of William Crowe of Socketts in Kent and his wife, Anne, daughter of John Sackville of Sussex. He owed the rise of his fortunes in the 1620s to the patronage of George Villiers, first duke of Buckingham, of whose accounts he was treasurer from 1624 to 1628. Buckingham's influence was responsible for Crowe's being entrusted with the delicate mission of pawning some of the duke's and king's jewels at Amsterdam in 1626, his being created baronet in 1627, and his appointment as treasurer of the navy in March 1627. He proved incapable of meeting the financial demands of this last office, and his predecessor Sir William Russell had to step into the breach and ultimately replaced him in 1630. Crowe's long-standing ambition to secure the lease of the royal ironworks in the Forest of Dean was finally rewarded in 1635 when he and his partners obtained the lease after the existing lessees had fallen foul of the royal forest jurisdiction.

In November 1633 Crowe was appointed ambassador at Constantinople, though he was unable to take up the appointment for five years. In the meantime he engaged in a fierce dispute, both with the Levant Company, which financed the embassy but no longer nominated its occupant, and with the retiring ambassador, Sir Peter Wyche. The issue was the right to 'strangers' consulage', the duties payable by foreigners shipping goods under the protection of the English flag. The Levant Company claimed the right to these dues, but both Wyche and Crowe claimed them for the crown. Charles I provided further occasion for dispute among all three parties by formally alienating the right to Crowe in 1636, though the latter, in return for compensating payments by the company, waived it until his arrival in Constantinople in October 1638. Thereafter the dispute grew fiercer and was to be further exacerbated by Crowe's royalist and the company's parliamentarian sympathies. Believing that the merchants were responsible for his sequestration in 1644,

following the interception of a letter of his to Charles I, Crowe retaliated in 1646 by bribing the grand vizier to arrest all the company's factory at Constantinople and some of its merchants at Smyrna. However, the company's far greater resources of baksheesh soon restored them to liberty.

In January 1647 a new ambassador, Sir Thomas Bendysh, was appointed and, following his arrival in Constantinople, Crowe and his wife were forcibly deported in November. On reaching London in April 1648, Crowe was sent to the Tower, where he remained until 1656. While there he submitted to an unsympathetic government in 1652 and 1653 projects for the improvement of the manufacture of iron ordnance and for general economic improvement, similar to his later and, in the former case, more successful, schemes after the Restoration.

In other respects the Restoration did not bring the looked-for revival of Crowe's fortunes. In 1662 the royal grant of control of the tapestry manufactory at Mortlake founded by Charles I brought disaster, even though it was coupled with an annual subsidy of £1000. Writing to the countess of Rutland in 1670 from his 'uncouth cell' in the Fleet prison, where he had been committed for debt, Crowe was scathing about the quality of the tapestries produced by William, earl of Craven, and his associates, who had taken over from him at Mortlake in 1667. After his release the fairly lucrative office of secretary and clerk of the signet in Wales and the marches was bestowed upon him in October 1671. He had acquired an estate in Carmarthenshire and became a deputy lieutenant of that county in July 1674. But insolvency again intervened and he died in the Fleet prison in 1683.

One product of Crowe's connection with Buckingham in the 1620s was his spectacular marriage in 1634 into the duchess's family—to Mary, daughter of Sir George Manners and sister of John Manners, later eighth earl of Rutland. The bride's mother bitterly deplored 'my daughter's offence to God and disobedience to me' in marrying so far beneath her, but Lady Crowe seems loyally to have shared her husband's sharp vicissitudes of fortune. Crowe was succeeded by his only child, Sir Sackville Crowe, on whose death the baronetcy became extinct.

ROBERT ASHTON, rev.

Sources A. C. Wood, A history of the Levant Company (1935) • R. Lockyer, Buckingham: the life and political career of George Villiers, first duke of Buckingham, 1592–1628 (1981) • R. Ashton, The crown and the money market, 1603–1640 (1960) • R. Ashton, 'The disbursing official under the early Stuarts', BIHR, 30 (1957), 162–74 • CSP dom. • CSP Venice • Levant Company records • Twelfth report, HMC (1888) • administration, PRO, PROB 6/58, fol. 67
Archives BL, Egerton MSS, corresp. mainly relating to Turkey, 2533, 2541
Wealth at death died insolvent in the Fleet prison

Crowe, Dame Sylvia (1901–1997), landscape architect, was born on 15 September 1901 at 30 Oxford Road, Neithrop, Banbury, Oxfordshire, the daughter of Eyre Crowe, a box and cabinet manufacturer who, because of ill health, retired early to become a fruit farmer near the village of Felbridge, Sussex, and his wife, Beatrice, née Stockton. Crowe's own childhood was also marred by ill health, for after attending Berkhamsted Girls' School in Hertfordshire from 1908 to 1912 she had to stay at home receiving only spasmodic lessons as a result of her suffering from tuberculosis. None the less her memories of childhood were happy. Her parents were devoted to the countryside, their farm was in a delightful part of England beside the shores of a lake, and they often travelled in France and Corsica, where she remembered her 'fourth birthday in a Corsican forest sitting revelling in the carpet of wild cyclamen' (Harvey, *Reflections*, 31). While kept away from school in her teens she helped on her father's farm and wandered in the landscape. In her early twenties she spent several years in the beautiful countryside of Italy with her parents. She attended Swanley Horticultural College (1920–22), became a pupil of the landscape gardener Edward White (1926–7) and then worked as a garden designer for William Cutbush & Son's nurseries in Barnet. The sensitivity of her garden designs was recognized when she won a gold medal at the Chelsea flower show in 1937 for a contoured bluebell wood from which a stream flowed into a naturalistic pond. During the Second World War she served first with the Polish army in France as a volunteer ambulance driver, and then in motor transport, becoming a sergeant in the ATS. In later life she always liked to be driven by others.

After 1945 Crowe entered private practice as a landscape architect, sharing an office, but never as partner, with Brenda Colvin, whose ideas she was soon to put into practice with startling effectiveness and perception. In 1956 she wrote: 'I gratefully acknowledge my debt to all who have contributed to the present school of thought on landscape, and in particular to Brenda Colvin … and to G. A. Jellicoe' (Crowe, foreword). Crowe was the great achiever of the landscape profession in the second half of the twentieth century. Her humanity, her common touch, and her charm, combined with vigour and clarity of purpose, enabled her to persuade her numerous clients to put her ideas about landscape into practice. She wrote:

> The object of my work and writing is to reconcile the needs and aspirations of men with the welfare of the natural order and to create beauty out of the fusion of the human spirit and the workings of nature. I try to enter into the spirit of each landscape and to express its individual character. (Emanuel, 180)

She worked in Great Britain (except for once in India and a plan for the Commonwealth Gardens in Canberra, Australia), from a small office at 182 Gloucester Place, London, assisted by Wendy Powell and a few others. The 1950s to 1970s, when she was at her most productive, were a period when minimalism was important in artistic thought. Many of her works were reticent in displaying her own artistic endeavour, so that her designs for huge modifications of the landscape for human purposes have been perceived as part of the natural order of things. Many of her works were indeed great in scale. One of her first tasks after the Second World War was to work on the reclamation of sand dunes in Lincolnshire damaged by wartime gun emplacements and so by eroding.

In 1948 Crowe became consultant on landscape design at Harlow New Town, where she made real the green spaces on Sir Frederick Gibberd's master plan. This work led to work in other new towns, including Basildon in Essex, Washington in co. Durham, and Warrington in Lancashire. She was the landscape consultant for nuclear power stations at Trawsfynydd, in Snowdonia, where she had refused to support the principle of a power station in a national park, and at Wylfa head, Anglesey. In both these projects her interest in creating artificial hills helped to mask smaller elements and create a large-scale setting for the huge generators. She designed and saw completed numerous landscapes adjacent to buildings, university

Dame Sylvia Crowe (1901–1997), by Kelvin Brodie, 1975

courtyards in Oxford, hospital grounds, churchyards, and training colleges. Her gardens at the Cement and Concrete Association Research Station at Wexham Springs in Buckinghamshire, the Scottish Widows' Fund offices in Edinburgh, and the Commonwealth Institute in London, were particularly well known. She also greatly enjoyed designing landscapes for reservoirs, including Bewl Bridge and Bough Beech in Kent and Wimbleball in Somerset: 'it is very largely the recreational side I have to worry about, because the water is there anyway' (Harvey, *Reflections*, 51). A masterpiece was her design for Rutland water, a project to which she was personally attached. The landscape was planned around this beautiful lake to benefit engineering, wildlife, visitors, and nearby residents in equal measure in a new place of serenity and harmony, 'created with the three great landscape elements of landform, trees and water' (Crowe, 63).

Crowe's greatest achievement was her work as the first landscape consultant to the Forestry Commission from 1964 to 1976. 'One had to use discretion and diplomacy in the early days until gradually good landscape became accepted within the Commission … I believe that planting should be made to talk the same language as the terrain' (Harvey, *Reflections*, 44–5). She completely changed the ethos of the commission from a narrow specialism to a body able to balance the needs of timber production with wildlife, recreation, and beauty of landscape. Her ideas, communicated with an infectious smile and lucid exposition, came to be embraced by all from foresters in the field to senior civil servants. Her slim and influential book *Forestry in the Landscape* (1966) expounded her ideas on this subject. It was one of many books, including *Tomorrow's Landscape* (1956), *Garden Design* (1958), *The Landscape of Power* (1958), *The Landscape of Roads* (1960), *Space for Living*, which she edited (1961), *Shaping Tomorrow's Landscape*, which she co-wrote with Zvi Miller (1964), *The Landscapes of Forests and Woods* (1978), and *The Pattern of Landscape* (1988).

Crowe was founding honorary secretary (1948), vice-president and secretary-general (1953–9), and president (1969) of the International Federation of Landscape Architects, president of her professional body, the Institute of Landscape Architects, later the Landscape Institute (1957–9), chairman of the Tree Council (1974–6), and a founder member of the environmental planning committee of the International Union for the Conservation of Nature. She received honorary doctorates from the University of Newcastle (1976), Herriot-Watt University (1976), and the University of Sussex (1978), honorary fellowships of the Royal Institute of British Architects, the Royal Town Planning Institute, the Institute of Chartered Foresters, and the Australian Institute of Landscape Architects, and the special honours of the president's medal of the American Society of Landscape Architects (1988), the Victoria medal of honour of the Royal Horticultural Society (1990), and the gold medal of the Australian Institute of Landscape Architects (1990). She was created CBE in 1967 and DBE in 1973, the first landscape architect to be so highly honoured since Sir Joseph Paxton 122 years earlier. She lived for more than fifty years in a small basement flat in Ladbroke Grove, London, fading slowly but gracefully until her death from bronchopneumonia at St Mary's Hospital, Westminster, on 30 June 1997. She never married. Her beautiful features and earthy laugh expressed contentment with life: 'I have enjoyed being a landscape architect; I would not have wanted to be anything else' (Harvey, *Reflections*, 51).

HAL MOGGRIDGE

Sources S. Harvey, ed., *Reflections on landscape* (1987), 31–51 · G. Collens and W. Powell, eds., *Sylvia Crowe* (1999) · M. Emanuel, ed., *Contemporary architects* (1980), 179–80 · S. Harvey and S. Rettig, eds., *Fifty years of landscape design* (1985) · S. Crowe, *Tomorrow's landscape* (1956) · *Daily Telegraph* (2 July 1997) · *The Guardian* (4 July 1997) · *The Times* (10 July 1997) · *WWW* · b. cert. · d. cert. · Landscape Institute, London · personal knowledge (2004)
Archives Landscape Institute, London
Likenesses K. Brodie, photograph, 1975, News International Syndication, London [*see illus.*] · photograph, 1984, repro. in *Daily Telegraph* · A. Reevel, photograph, repro. in *The Guardian* · photograph, repro. in Harvey, ed., *Reflections on landscape*, 30
Wealth at death £500,624: probate, 16 Dec 1997, *CGPLA Eng. & Wales*

Crowe, William (1616–1675), bibliographer and schoolmaster, was born at Mutford, Suffolk, and baptized there on 3 October 1616, the eldest son of William Crow (1576–1633), son of Christopher Crow, gentleman, and his wife, Margarett, daughter of James Taylor, prebendary of Ely. His father had been a senior fellow of Gonville and Caius College, Cambridge, before taking orders in 1613 and becoming rector of Barnby and vicar of Mutford, where he also ran a small school and took pupils. Crowe was taught by his father for seven years before being admitted to the scholars' table of Gonville and Caius College, Cambridge, on 15 June 1632. Crowe graduated BA (1636), MA (1639), and was ordained on 22 December 1639.

From 1648 to 1656 Crowe worked in the same position that his father had held, that of rector of Barnby and vicar of Mutford. Presumably during this time he maintained his Cambridge contacts, and in 1663 compiled a catalogue (Bodl. Oxf., MS Tanner 274) of the manuscripts of the Lambeth Palace library, which had been relocated to Cambridge during the interregnum. He also helped catalogue the Holdsworth collection, one of the largest private collections in England at the time, which had been bequeathed to Cambridge in 1649. Crowe was paid £13 6s. 8d. to transcribe the complete catalogue (CUL, MS Ff. 4.27, 260ff.) in 1663–4.

It was while working on these catalogues that Crowe conceived the idea of compiling textual scripture indices of English, Greek, and Latin theological literature. Published anonymously in 1663, *An Exact Collection or Catalogue of our English Writers on the Old and New Testament* indexed several thousand English commentaries and sermons, consisting mostly of seventeenth-century texts but also including some earlier works that had 'lain neglected and as it were forgotten' (Crowe, *Exact Collection*). Crowe viewed bibliography as a tool by which people 'satisfie our curiosities', and described his verse-by-verse index as 'a key whereby you may unlock to yourself all the treasuries of holy Scripture'. A second edition was published in 1668 as *The Catalogue of our English Writers on the Old and New Testament*, and included a few thousand additional entries. His *Elenchus scriptorum in sacram scripturam tam Graecorum quam Latinorum* was published in 1672.

Crowe was one of two people nominated for the post of librarian for Cambridge University when it became vacant on 16 March 1668, and it must have been a great disappointment to him when the job was awarded to Robert Peachy, a much younger colleague who had also worked extensively on the Holdsworth collection. Later that year Archbishop Gilbert Sheldon, perhaps in gratitude for Crowe's work on the Lambeth manuscripts, nominated Crowe as chaplain and schoolmaster of the hospital of Holy Trinity at Croydon. Crowe had the credentials: his publications had proved him a scholar, and he had presumably taught at Mutford, when working there as vicar, as his father had before him. Crowe accepted the appointment on 4 December 1668 on a modest annual salary of £20. Although ambiguity in the school's statutes meant that Crowe could potentially augment his earnings by attracting fee-paying students to the school, it is unlikely that he had much success. Opportunities to attract wealthier pupils were greatly restricted by the actions of the nefarious vicar of Croydon, Dr William Clewer. So serious and numerous were Clewer's offences that he was officially deprived in 1684, following a petition by the citizens of Croydon submitted to the privy council in 1673. The petition charged Clewer with, among other things, fraudulency, drunkenness, and thievery, and noted that he had 'spoiled the school, so that no gentlemen's sons come at it' (*Case of the Inhabitants*, x).

Crowe killed himself in 1675, the parish record reporting that 'William Crow that was skool master of the Free skool ... hanged himselfe in the winde of one of his Chambers in his dwelin house' (*Collectanea topographica*, 3.308). Besides the difficulties caused by Clewer, Crowe's time at the school had been complicated by apparent irregularities with the leasing of school property, leading to a rebuke from the archbishop being issued both to him and to the school's warden in 1671, as well as a lawsuit being filed by one of his tenants. But what exactly brought him to suicide remains uncertain. In 1672 Crowe reflected that his happiest times had been among the books and manuscripts of the university library (Crowe, *Elenchus*); perhaps exchanging the academe of Cambridge for his adversities at Croydon had been a vicissitude too hard to bear. Despite his suicide Crowe was buried in the parish church at Croydon on 11 April 1675.   SIMON LANCASTER

Sources J. C. T. Oates, *Cambridge University Library: a history from the beginnings to the Copyright Act of Queen Anne* (1986), 281–2, 313, 326–7, 335–6, 391–4 · F. H. G. Percy, *Whitgift School: a history*, rev. edn (1991), 63–5 · [W. Crowe], preface, *An exact collection or catalogue of our English writers on the Old and New Testament* (1663) · W. Crow, preface, *Elenchus scriptorum in sacram scripturam tam Graecorum quam Latinorum* (1672) · *The case of the inhabitants of ... Croydon ... concerning the great oppressions they ly under* [1673], repr. in D. W. Garrow, *The history and antiquities of Croydon* (1818), 304–13 · J. Venn and others, eds., *Biographical history of Gonville and Caius College*, 1: *1349–1713* (1897), 305–6 · 'Further extracts from the registers of Croydon',

Collectanea topographica et genealogica (1834–43), 3.308 · Venn, *Alum. Cant.*

Crowe, William (*c.*1691–1743), Church of England clergyman, was baptized at Hope Mansell, Herefordshire, and educated at Eton College (1702–8). He then went up to Trinity Hall, Cambridge, where he matriculated in 1709 and graduated BA in 1713. He was elected to a Craven scholarship and a fellowship, and awarded an MA in 1717, having been ordained by the bishop of London on 26 February 1715.

On 6 February 1721 Crowe became rector of the united parish of St Mary Magdalen and St Gregory by Paul, London; he was also lecturer at the attached church of St Martin Ludgate. He was prebendary of Chiswick in St Paul's Cathedral in 1726–7, and of St Pancras from 1727 until his death. A staunch whig, he was accordingly created DD at Cambridge when George II visited the university in 1728. In 1730 he obtained the rectory of the newly rebuilt church of St Botolph without Bishopsgate, where he became noted for providing daily services at 11 a.m. and 6 p.m. This had been his practice also at St Mary with St Gregory. In September 1731 he was collated to the rectory of Finchley, Middlesex. He owed this preferment largely to Bishop Edmund Gibson to whom he was chaplain. He was also a chaplain-in-ordinary to George II.

Crowe died at Finchley on 11 April 1743, and was buried in the churchyard of that parish. In his will he left £3000 to his patron, Bishop Gibson, who generously gave the money to the testator's poor relatives. Crowe also bequeathed £1000 to Queen Anne's Bounty fund, and the same amount to Sir Clement Cotterell Dormer, master of the ceremonies, in remembrance of the many favours received from him when they were at college together.

William Cole, the antiquary and diarist, observed that Crowe was a good Greek scholar, and that he had lent his notes and observations to Dr Bentley, from whom he was never able to recover them (BL, Add. MS 5865, fol. 117). Crowe published some single sermons as well as *Sermons on Several Occasions* (1744). A volume entitled *Dr Crowe's Favourite and most Excellent Sermons* (1759) was probably a reissue of the 1744 work. Crowe had also contributed some Greek verses to the Cambridge University collection on the treaty of Utrecht.

THOMPSON COOPER, *rev.* WILLIAM GIBSON

Sources Venn, *Alum. Cant.* · *Fasti Angl., 1541–1857*, [St Paul's, London] · *New remarks of London* (1732) · G. B. Besant, *City churches and their memories* [1926] · BL, Add. MS 5865, fol. 117 · GL, MS 9531/19, fol. 296 · Nichols, *Lit. anecdotes*, 2.52 · *GM*, 1st ser., 13 (1743), 218 · R. A. Austen-Leigh, ed., *The Eton College register, 1698–1752* (1927)
Likenesses J. Smith, engraving
Wealth at death over £5000; incl. £3000 bequest to Bishop Edmund Gibson; plus two bequests of more than £1000: will

Crowe, William (*bap.* 1745, *d.* 1829), poet and Church of England clergyman, was born at Midgham, Berkshire, where he was baptized on 13 October 1745. During his childhood his father, a carpenter by trade, lived at Winchester, and as a boy Crowe, who was musically talented, was occasionally employed as a chorister in Winchester College chapel. At the election in 1758 he was placed on the roll for admission as a scholar at the college, and was duly elected a 'poor scholar'. He was fifth on the roll for New College, Oxford, at the election in 1764, and succeeded to a vacancy on 11 August 1765. After two years of probation he was admitted as fellow in 1767, and became a tutor of his college. On 10 October 1773 he took the degree of BCL. He continued to hold his fellowship until November 1783, although, according to Tom Moore, he had several years previously married 'a fruitwoman's daughter at Oxford' named Elizabeth; they had two boys and two girls.

In 1782, on the presentation of his college, Crowe was admitted to the rectory of Stoke Abbas in Dorset, which he exchanged for Alton Barnes in Wiltshire in 1787, and on 2 April 1784 he was elected the public orator of his university. This position, and the rectory of Alton Barnes, Crowe retained until his death, and he continued to discharge his duties as public orator until far advanced in years. According to the *Clerical Guide* from 1805 until his death he was also rector of Llanymynech on the border of Montgomeryshire and Shopshire, worth about £400 per annum, and incumbent of Saxton in Yorkshire, valued at about £80 a year, from the same date.

A grace for the degree of DCL was passed by Crowe's college on 30 March 1780, but he does not seem to have proceeded to take it. Many anecdotes are told of his eccentric speech and his rustic address, but Crowe's simplicity, says Moore, was 'very delightful'. In politics he was 'ultra-whig, almost a republican', and he sympathized with the early stages of the French revolution. His expenditure was carefully limited, and he was accustomed to walk from his living in Wiltshire to his college at Oxford where he delivered many well-received sermons at the university church of St Mary the Virgin; his command of Latin was acknowledged by his contemporaries.

Crowe was also interested in architecture, and occasionally read a course of lectures on that subject in New College hall. The merits of his lectures at the Royal Institution on poetry were extolled by Thomas Dibdin. When he visited John Horne Tooke at Wimbledon, a considerable portion of his time was spent in the garden, and horticulture was the theme on which he dilated. Owing to his skill in valuing timber, acquired from the farmers with whom he had long been associated, he was always selected by the fellows at New College as their woodman. His peculiarities marked him out as a fit subject for caricature, and his portrait as 'a celebrated public orator' was drawn by Dighton in January 1808 in full-length academicals and with a college cap in his hand.

Crowe and Samuel Rogers were intimate friends, and when the latter poet was travelling in Italy he made two authors, Milton and Crowe, his constant study for versification. 'How little', said Rogers on another occasion, 'is Crowe known, even to persons who are fond of poetry! Yet his *Lewesdon Hill* is full of noble passages.' The first edition, issued anonymously and dedicated to Shipley, the whig bishop of St Asaph, was published at the Clarendon Press, Oxford, in 1788. A second impression, with its authorship

avowed, was demanded in the same year, and later editions, in a much enlarged form, and with several other poems, were published in 1804 and 1827. Wordsworth and Coleridge, like Rogers, recognized its value as an admirable description in harmonious blank verse of local scenery, and Tom Moore confessed that some of its passages were 'of the highest order'. Crowe's other works which attracted less attention were: *A Sermon on Exodus before the University of Oxford at St. Mary's, 5 Nov 1781*; *On the late attempt on her majesty's person, a sermon before the University of Oxford at St. Mary's, 1786*; and *Oratio ex instituto ... dom. Crew* (1788). From the preface it appears that the oration was printed in refutation of certain slanders as to its character which had been circulated. It contained his views on the revolution of 1688. Crowe also published *Oratio Crewiana* (1800), on poetry and the poetry professorship at Oxford; *Hamlet and As you Like it, a Specimen of a New Edition of Shakespeare*, published anonymously with Thomas Caldecott (1819, with later editions in 1820 and 1832); *A Treatise on English Versification* (1827), dedicated to Thomas Caldecott, his schoolfellow at Winchester and friend of seventy years' standing; and *Poems of William Collins, with Notes, and Dr Johnson's Life, Corrected and Enlarged* (1828). Crowe's son died in battle in 1815, and in *Notes and Queries* (1st ser., 7, 1853, 6, 144) is a Latin monody by his father on his loss.

Crowe died after a short illness at Queen's Square, Bath, on 9 February 1829. He had spent the previous two winters there for his health.

W. P. COURTNEY, rev. REBECCA MILLS

Sources IGI · private information (2004) [C. Dalton, archivist, New College, Oxford] · will, PRO, PROB 11/1756, sig. 343 · Foster, *Alum. Oxon.* · [J. Watkins and F. Shoberl], *A biographical dictionary of the living authors of Great Britain and Ireland* (1816) · G. V. Cox, *Recollections of Oxford*, 2nd edn (1870), 229–32 · *GM*, 1st ser., 99/1 (1829), 642–3 · C. H. Mayo, ed., *Bibliotheca Dorsetiensis: being a carefully compiled account of books and pamphlets relating to ... Dorset* (1885), 120 · J. Hutchins, *The history and antiquities of the county of Dorset*, 3rd edn, ed. W. Shipp and J. W. Hodson, 2 (1863), 150–55 · *The clerical guide, or, Ecclesiastical directory* (1817), 115, 224 · *N&Q*, 2nd ser., 6 (1858), 42–3 · *N&Q*, 2nd ser., 5 (1858), 308 · T. F. Dibdin, *Reminiscences of a literary life*, 1 (1836), 245–6 · A. Stephens, *Memoirs of John Horne Tooke*, 2 vols. (1813), 2.332 · *Memoirs, journal and correspondence of Thomas Moore*, ed. J. Russell, 2 (1853), 177–8, 190, 192, 197, 200–02, 300; 5 (1854), 60, 112, 277–8; 8 (1856), 234, 245 · *Recollections of the table-talk of Samuel Rogers*, ed. A. Dyce (1856), 223–7 · Watt, *Bibl. Brit.*, 1.273

Archives Bodl. Oxf., letters and poems · NL Wales, address, letter, poems

Likenesses R. Dighton, coloured etching, caricature, pubd 1808, BM, NPG · oils, New College, Oxford

Wealth at death approx. £6000 in household goods and a library: will, PRO, PROB 11/1756, sig. 343

Crowfoot, John Rustat (1817–1875), Hebrew and Syriac scholar, was born at Beccles, Suffolk, on 21 February 1817. His father was William Henchman Crowfoot, a surgeon. He was educated at Eton College, where he obtained a foundation scholarship. He matriculated at Gonville and Caius College, Cambridge, in 1835, where he was a scholar from 1836 until 1838, and graduated BA in 1839. The following year, in which he was ordained deacon, he was elected fellow of Caius College, and was also appointed divinity lecturer at King's College. He was ordained a priest and became dean of Caius in 1842. In 1848 he competed, unsuccessfully, for the regius professorship of Hebrew although he printed his probation exercise on Jeremiah 33: 15–16. He was made BD the next year. On 27 August 1850 he married Elizabeth Tufnell, the daughter of J. C. F. Tufnell, a clergyman from Edburton in Sussex. They had one son, who died young. He worked as a curate at the university church of Great St Mary's, Cambridge, from 1851 to 1853, and in 1854 accepted the living of Southwold, Suffolk, which he held until 1860, when he became vicar of Wangford-cum-Reydon, also in Suffolk.

While at Cambridge, Crowfoot became involved in university affairs and issued pamphlets on these matters, including *On Private Tuition* (1844), *On a University Hostel* (1849), and *Plea for a Colonial and Missionary College at Cambridge* (1854). In 1870 he published *Fragmenta evangelica*, a retranslation into Greek of Cureton's early Syriac text of certain portions of the first two gospels. In order, as he put it, to get 'as near as possible to the very words of Christ', Crowfoot went to Egypt in 1873 in search of Syriac manuscripts of the gospels. Crowfoot died in Wangford-cum-Reydon on 18 March 1875 and was buried at Reydon. He was considered by those who knew him to be a diligent and devoted parish priest. As an academic, however, Crowfoot's work was soon superseded.

EDMUND VENABLES, rev. GERALD LAW

Sources Venn, *Alum. Cant.* · Crockford (1871) · *Clergy List* (1874) · private information (1888) · d. cert.
Wealth at death under £6000: probate, 27 April 1875, *CGPLA Eng. & Wales*

Crowland [Croyland], **Roger of** (*fl. c.*1200), Benedictine monk and hagiographer, was a member of his order's community of Crowland Abbey in Lincolnshire. He is known only from his reworking, at the behest of Abbot Henry de Longchamp (1190–1236), of the composite life of St Thomas of Canterbury, known as the 'second' *Quadrilogus*, which had first been compiled in the Benedictine monastery of Evesham by the monk E in 1198–9. Roger's most important contribution was the insertion into the text of the remodelled *Quadrilogus* of 241 letters, mostly taken from the great collection of Becket materials assembled at Canterbury (*c.*1174–80) by Alan, later abbot of Tewkesbury. Completed at Crowland in 1213, the work was presented by Abbot Henry of Crowland to Archbishop Stephen Langton on the occasion of Becket's translation in July 1220. Despite such illustrious associations, Roger's work survives in two manuscripts only (Bodl. Oxf., MS e Museo 133; Paris, Bibliothèque Nationale, MS Lat. 5372), both of them fragmentary, and remains unpublished.

A. J. DUGGAN

Sources A. Duggan, *Thomas Becket: a textual history of his letters* (1980), 205–23, 278–84 · J. C. Robertson and J. B. Sheppard, eds., *Materials for the history of Thomas Becket, archbishop of Canterbury*, 7 vols., Rolls Series, 67 (1875–85) · J. A. Giles, ed., *Vita Sancti Thomae Cantuariensis archiepiscopi et martyris*, 2 vols., Patres Ecclesiae Anglicanae (1845) · J.-P. Migne, ed., *Patrologia Latina*, 217 vols. (1844–55) · D. Knowles, C. N. L. Brooke, and V. C. M. London, eds., *The heads of religious houses, England and Wales*, 1: 940–1216 (1972)
Archives Bibliothèque Nationale, Paris, MS Lat. 5372 · Bodl. Oxf., MS e Museo 133

Crowland, William of (*d.* 1179). *See under* Ramsey, William of (*fl.* 1219).

Crowley, Aleister [*formerly* Edward Alexander] (1875–1947), author and occultist, was born on 12 October 1875 at 30 Clarendon Square, Leamington Spa, Warwickshire, the elder child of Emily Bertha (*née* Bishop) and Edward Crowley (*d.* 1887). A daughter died in infancy. Edward Crowley's family had owned Crowley's Ales, and he retired on his inheritance; his wife was from a family in Somerset and Devon. The elder Crowley was an evangelist for a fundamentalist Christian sect, the Plymouth Brethren, which his wife also joined. Their son was spoiled by material comfort and a belief in his spiritual superiority. His mother called him the Great Beast, the unholy monster of the Apocalypse (Therion, 666). At his father's death, the boy became truly hostile to Christianity, for he was then transferred to the care of his uncle, Tom Bond Bishop, who was publicly philanthropic but surreptitiously cruel. Crowley briefly attended Malvern College, in 1891–2, and Tonbridge School, in 1892, both of which he found uncongenial.

At the age of twenty Crowley went up to Trinity College, Cambridge, to study for the natural sciences tripos, and in his leisure time excelled at chess and at mountaineering. In October 1897 a fevered vision convinced him that all human endeavours are ephemeral, with one exception—the magical tradition. He dedicated himself to esoteric studies and sought initiation by genuine magi. Poetry greatly attracted him, and it was probably Shelley's 'Alastor, or, The Spirit of Solitude' that inspired Crowley to call himself Aleister, a deliberate repudiation of his given name. The spelling reflects a Gaelic form in keeping with the Celtic revival then popular. Crowley came into his inheritance, which he spent extravagantly. He issued deluxe volumes of his own poetry, beginning with *Aceldama* (1898), which sparked the admiration of Gerald Festus Kelly, also at Trinity but destined for knighthood and the presidency of the Royal Academy. In *White Stains*, Crowley exhibited homosexual sentiments. He was intimate with Herbert Charles Jerome Pollitt, a young stage performer who came to mistrust Crowley's 'spiritual' ambition; they separated in 1898. Crowley left Cambridge without having earned a degree.

Crowley met members of the London temple of the Hermetic Order of the Golden Dawn, a quasi-secret society which had been founded in 1888 and claimed to transmit a species of ancient cabalism. Crowley joined in November 1898 and assumed the magical name of Perdurabo (I will endure). He soon impressed Samuel Liddell Mathers, one of the order's founders, which disappointed another young initiate, William Butler Yeats, who judged Crowley to be insane. Mathers had revived obscure techniques for evoking one's guardian angel. Crowley, eager to test these operations, secluded himself at Boleskine House, on the shore of Loch Ness, but was distracted by dissension in the Golden Dawn. Superior officials heard rumours of his sexual immorality and, defying Mathers, opposed Crowley's advancement. As Mathers's power declined, Crowley lost interest in the order.

For several years Crowley wandered restlessly. In Mexico in 1900 he was joined by Oscar Eckenstein, an older and more experienced mountain climber, and they explored the local terrain. Eckenstein instructed Crowley in concentration and visualization. Crowley also undertook magical evocations in the style of John Dee, the Elizabethan magus, and his scryer, Edward Kelley, and Crowley now felt that he was the incarnation of Kelley. He resolved to advance independently through the grades of magical attainment prescribed by the Golden Dawn and travelled in Asia and practised hatha yoga. In 1902 he and Eckenstein undertook the first attempt to scale Chogo Ri (K-2), the world's second-highest peak. Crowley's sporting inclinations also included big-game hunting.

In 1903 Crowley married Rose Edith Skerrett, the widowed sister of Gerald Kelly. In Cairo in April 1904 Rose entered involuntary trances and urged her husband to prepare for supernatural communications. Subsequent sessions produced *Liber legis* ('Book of the law'), which was supposedly dictated to Crowley through the voice of a certain Aiwaz or Aiwass, perhaps the guardian angel whom Crowley had sought. The transmission was inexplicably signed by a pharaonic priest named Ankh-f-n-khonsu. (Crowley later decided that he himself was the reincarnation of this priest.) The document, while laden with enigmas, is clear in announcing the New Aeon: Christianity will yield to another spiritual movement. Crowley was charged with promoting its basic principle, the law of Thelema: 'Do what thou wilt shall be the whole of the Law'. This pronouncement was purportedly relayed from an Egyptian goddess, Nuit. In fact, the injunction had already been given in the famous story by Rabelais (*d.* 1553), whose monstrous Gargantua founded the abbey of Thélème.

At Boleskine Rose gave birth to a daughter, but in May 1905 Crowley resumed his wanderings. He conducted a Himalayan expedition that proved disastrous for his colleagues, whom he preferred to vilify rather than to help or to mourn. He summoned his wife and daughter to India, then fled the country with them as authorities were inquiring into his fatal shooting of two assailants. He dragged his family across south China but dispatched them homeward, on account of his desire to locate a former mistress. When he returned to Britain, he learned that his daughter had been taken ill and died in Burma, a death he attributed to his wife's negligence. Rose bore two more daughters but finally filed for divorce. Her charge of adultery was uncontested.

Crowley renewed his occult activities in 1909. He published *Liber 777*, which revealed the attributes of the tarot as interpreted in the Golden Dawn, and began recruiting for his own esoteric order, the Argenteum Astrum (Silver Star). This incorporated Golden Dawn rituals, some of which appeared in summary in Crowley's new journal, *The Equinox*. Mathers charged Crowley with plagiarism and petitioned the courts to prevent further publication of his secret teachings, but Crowley prevailed. He and the Golden Dawn were widely parodied, even in the *Occult Review*, while his Argenteum Astrum continued in secret. One member, before he rose to fame as a military strategist, was Captain John Frederick Charles Fuller, who encouraged occult studies by Charles Stansfeld Jones and by Victor Neuburg, a young poet (later poetry editor of the *Sunday Referee*). Neuburg and Crowley combined their magical and homosexual pursuits, producing a form of sex magic. Neuburg was a dancer in Crowley's theatrical production of *The Rites of Eleusis*, which received acclaim from critics. Crowley attracted the attention of Theodor Reuss, frater superior of the Ordo Templi Orientis (OTO), a German society that sometimes engaged in sex magic. Reuss visited Crowley and was sufficiently impressed to install him as chief of the English branch of the OTO.

During the First World War Crowley lived in America. His inheritance had long been exhausted—his travel funds probably came from the OTO. He practised sexual rituals involving a varied list of partners and in New York found employment in writing propaganda for pro-German periodicals. This deeply alienated his countrymen, who did not forgive him, even after the war.

In 1920 Crowley moved to Cefalù, in Sicily. There he rented a farmhouse, which he called the abbey of Thelema, and accepted disciples hopeful of advancing the New Aeon. The Sicilian project halted in 1923 when a young Englishman mysteriously died at the abbey. His widow accused Crowley of various crimes and sins, and the British periodical *John Bull* called him the 'wickedest man in the world'. The Italian government expelled Crowley and his Thelemites, but Crowley continued to attract students. Theodor Reuss had resigned as head of the OTO and Crowley subsequently occupied the office. His associates in this period included Karl Germer, Gerald Yorke, and Israel Regardie, all of whom became influential in occult circles. In Berlin in 1929, Crowley married Maria Teresa Ferrari de Miramar, a Nicaraguan. They soon separated.

In England during the depression, Crowley gleaned money through litigation. He sued both a bookseller who erroneously advertised the suppression of Crowley's novel, *The Diary of a Drug Fiend*, when in fact it had only gone out of print, and the publisher of Nina Hamnett's *Laughing Torso*, in which she presumed that Crowley had fostered black magic at the abbey of Thelema. Former friends refused to testify in Crowley's behalf. In the latter case, the judge was repelled by reports of Crowley's erotic literature and rituals, and Crowley lost and incurred the court costs. He was penniless. A sympathetic woman offered to have his child, and he accepted. He is said to have fathered other illegitimate children, but far from nurturing his offspring, he imposed on his paramours for his own support.

One of the circle around Crowley in the 1930s was **Greta Mary Valentine** (1907–1998), the adopted daughter of James Henry Sequeira, dermatologist, and his wife, Nellie Adams. Educated in England and on the continent, Greta was studying anthroposophy when she met Crowley in 1936. Although she did not share his interest in drugs or magic, he was fascinated by her flirtations, and soon became her close friend and confidant, while both had other lovers. Crowley declared his love for her, and in 1938 followed her to Cornwall where she was on holiday with Lamorna Birch, the landscape painter. Birch introduced Greta to Ranald Valentine (d. 1956), who ran a company in Dundee making greetings cards and calendars. When he and Greta decided to marry, Crowley declared himself desolated, but the marriage endured until Ranald's death.

A friend of Greta Valentine's was Frieda Harris, the wife of Sir Percy Harris (Liberal MP for Bethnal Green). She was devoted to Crowley, who named her as an executor of his will. In 1942 she completed watercolours for use in publishing a pack of tarot cards conforming to Crowley's concept. In his tarot, as elsewhere, he merged Western magic with exotic mysticism (such as gnosticism and tantric Buddhism) and with modern science (such as chemistry and Freudian psychology). He thereby extended the work of Éliphas Lévi, a notable French magus, who had died in 1875, the year of Crowley's birth; Crowley claimed to be Lévi's reincarnation. *The Book of Thoth* (1944) is Crowley's commentary on his tarot. He did not acknowledge the fact that his tarot's basic structure depended on Golden Dawn teachings.

In his waning years Crowley befriended John Symonds and acceded to the young writer's request that Crowley supply notes for a biography. He designated Symonds and Kenneth Grant, the youngest of his last students, as literary executors, empowered to publish his papers. On 1 December 1947, at Netherwood, a residential hotel in The Ridge, Hastings, Crowley, by this time a chronic heroin addict, died of bronchitis and heart congestion. His remains were cremated at Brighton and reportedly have been lost.

Interest in Crowley has reflected waves of curiosity in the occult. The Crowley–Harris tarot is popular, and several occult groups adhere to his law of Thelema. His most readable books on occultism are *Book Four* (1912), *The Book of Lies* (1913), and *Magick in Theory and Practice* (1929). Among sympathizers he is revered for his peculiar gifts, but others remember his reputation as a social outcast on account of his flagrant nonconformity.

RONALD DECKER

Sources *The confessions of Aleister Crowley*, ed. J. Symonds and K. Grant (1979) • I. Regardie, *The eye in the triangle* (1970) • C. Wilson, *Aleister Crowley, the nature of the beast* (1987) • F. King, *The magical world of Aleister Crowley* (1978) • G. Suster, *The legacy of the beast: the life, work and influence of Aleister Crowley* (1988) • K. Grant, *Remembering Aleister Crowley* (1991) • DNB • b. cert. • d. cert. • CGPLA Eng. & Wales (1949) • R. B. Porch and others, eds., *The Malvern College register, 1865–1914* (1915) • H. E. Steed, ed., *School register, 1826–1910* [Tonbridge School] • *Daily Telegraph* (24 Nov 1998)
Archives Ransom HRC | Warburg Institute, London, Yorke collection | FILM BFI NFTVA, *Without walls*, Channel 4, 17 May 1994 | SOUND BL NSA, 'The mischief makers', [4] B843/3; other sound recordings (occult ceremonies); performance recordings; 'The wickedest man in the world', T1141RCI
Likenesses A. John, drawing, c.1914, priv. coll.; repro. in M. Bakewell, *Fitzrovia* (1999) • E. A. Crowley, self-portrait, 1918 (*The Master Therion 666*), priv. coll.; repro. in M. Bakewell, *Fitzrovia* (1999)

Wealth at death £18 0s. 6d.: probate, 24 Jan 1949, CGPLA Eng. & Wales • £100: further grant, 1 March 1971, CGPLA Eng. & Wales

Crowley, Sir Ambrose (1658–1713), ironmaster, was born in Stourbridge, Worcestershire, on 1 February 1658, the only son of Ambrose Crowley (*bap.* 1635, *d.* 1720) and his first wife, Mary Hall (*d.* in or after 1658), the daughter of Thomas Hall of Bromsgrove, Worcestershire. His father, a Quaker, started out at Stourbridge as a semi-literate nailer, but through thrift, application, and considerable business acumen, became a manufacturer of nails on the putting-out system, an ironmonger, and an owner of iron forges. His interests extended to south Wales, where he was a part owner of an ironworks with Major John Hanbury of Pontypool, the inventor of the iron-rolling process used in the manufacture of tin plate.

The younger Ambrose, after serving an apprenticeship with a London ironmonger, became free of the Drapers' Company on 9 July 1684. He immediately became active in London as an independent wholesale ironmonger serving both home and export markets from his warehouses and residence in Thames Street, near the river. When his business outgrew these premises he acquired property in 1704 on the Thames at Greenwich, where he built a wharf, warehouses, and a spacious residence.

At the very start of his business activity Crowley recognized that there was an enormous demand for nails on the south and east coasts, particularly from shipyards, both royal and private. With land transport slow and costly, this market was inconveniently and expensively served by west midland nail makers such as his own father in Worcestershire. However, he saw his opportunity and integrated backwards, acquiring manufacturing premises in co. Durham which had readier access to the shipbuilding market: first at Sunderland (by 1685) and subsequently at Winlaton, near Newcastle upon Tyne. These proving profitable, he strengthened his market position by buying out competing works at nearby Swalwell. During the period 1707–9 his undertakings in co. Durham contained two slitting-mills, two forges, four steel furnaces, many warehouses, and innumerable smithies producing a very wide variety of ironmongery. His naval contracts alone mentioned 108 varieties of nails, plus anchors, screws, bolts, hinges, latches, files, pots, and the like, as well as hemp and pitch presumably obtained in trade.

Crowley supervised operations from his Greenwich warehouse whence he supplied the metropolitan and export markets in particular. For inland distribution he had other warehouses in London and at Blaydon-on-Tyne, Ware in Hertfordshire, Wolverhampton, Walsall, and Stourbridge. The last was also used to buy bar iron for the Durham works, while Blaydon supplied other manufacturers in the north-east with semi-manufactured iron products including steel and iron rods. The firm prospered markedly during the wars of 1689–1713, when it became a major vendor of ironmongery to the Royal Navy.

The sheer size of Crowley's ironworks and his decision to control operations from London caused serious managerial problems. The solution, laid out in the *Law Book of* the *Crowley Ironworks*, was a written constitution for the works, enumerating the duties of the principal officials and clerks. The regulatory framework, built up in the fifteen or so years after 1690, was unique for its time and embodied not only penalties for infringement but also insurance and welfare provisions for the employees.

As a large supplier to the royal dockyards, Crowley was inevitably drawn towards politics. He was a tory, and his associations helped his contracting in the 1680s when he was favoured by the duke of York, lord high admiral, with permission to bring skilled workers from Liège. Crowley was in due course elected member of the London common council (1697–1711), sheriff (1706–7), the office that brought him his knighthood on 1 January 1707, and alderman for Dowgate ward (1711–13). His status was also acknowledged by his selection as master of the important Drapers' Company (1708–9), while his political weight was enhanced by his election in 1713 as MP for Andover. As a major government contractor, he had accumulated over £50,000 in navy bills during the last stages of the War of the Spanish Succession and was one of the key figures in the City consulted by Robert Harley, earl of Oxford, on ways to relieve the government of the burden of such floating debt. Out of these consultations came the plan for the South Sea Company. With its launching in 1711, Crowley's holdings of naval bills and the like could be converted into shares in the new undertaking, of which he became one of the largest shareholders, a director (1711–13), and ultimately deputy governor (1712–13).

To support his activity as wholesale ironmonger and manufacturer, Crowley was necessarily also a merchant in foreign trade. To supply his customers and his own smithies in the north-east, he became a very large importer of Swedish bar iron at Newcastle upon Tyne— possibly the largest in the kingdom. A substantial portion of his ironmongery sales went to exporters, while he himself appears in the London customs records in the late 1690s as an exporter of nails and hardware to New England. During the tory ministerial ascendancy after 1710, the Board of Trade consulted him about both the Baltic iron trade and ways of encouraging exports of English ironwares to the American colonies.

Two of Crowley's half-sisters remained within the Society of Friends on marrying fellow Quakers of the Lloyd family: Sarah to Charles Lloyd of Dolobran; and Mary to Sampson Lloyd, a Birmingham iron-dealer. Mary's son, also Sampson Lloyd, was one of the founders of Lloyds Bank. By contrast, Crowley broke with his father's strong Quaker commitments and had become an Anglican by the time of his marriage, in March 1682, to Mary, daughter of Charles Owen, a Londoner from a Shropshire gentry family. In 1712 Sir Ambrose was named one of the commissioners for building fifty new churches and persuaded that board to give priority to rebuilding the parish church near his property at Greenwich. He died at Greenwich on 7 October 1713 and was buried at the parish church of Mitcham, Surrey. He left portions of £10,000 each to the four of his five daughters still unmarried; John Crowley (1689–1728), his only son and residuary legatee, inherited the business.

Sir Ambrose's children continued their father's tory associations. John, a suspected Jacobite, sat in the House of Commons from 1722 to 1728. Lettice (1692–1718), the second of Sir Ambrose's five daughters to reach marriageable age, married Sir John Hynde Cotton, third baronet, a prominent tory politician; the third, Sarah (1697–1759), married Humphry Parsons, a wealthy brewer and extreme tory lord mayor of London; the fourth, Anne (b. 1699), married Richard Fleming (c.1682–1740), a Hampshire country gentleman and tory MP; and the fifth, Elizabeth (1702–1769), married another tory, the eleventh Baron St John of Bletso.

The firm which Crowley founded was continued by his son John and by his grandsons and lasted well into the reign of Queen Victoria, prospering from all the wars in the century following his death. As a major supplier to the Atlantic export trades, it also gained from the great growth of population, housebuilding, and shipbuilding in the American colonies during the period from 1700 to 1775, engendering orders to the firm for nails and other building hardware. At its height in the second quarter of the eighteenth century, the firm, then worth over £100,000 and employing over one thousand workers, was reputed to be the largest iron-manufacturing concern in Europe. Its exceptional integration and scale made it, in the words of its historian, 'a giant in an age of pigmies' (Flinn, *Men of Iron*, 252). JACOB M. PRICE

Sources M. W. Flinn, *Men of iron: the Crowleys in the early iron industry* [1962] · J. G. Sperling, *The South Sea Company* (1962) · E. Cruickshanks, 'Crowley, John', HoP, *Commons* · 'Boyd's Inhabitants of London', 1939, Society of Genealogists, London, no. 15841 · London bills of entry, 1696–7, Yale U., Beinecke L. [printed] · *Journal of the commissioners for trade and plantations*, [14 vols.] (1920–38) [April 1704 – May 1782] · M. W. Flinn, ed., *The law book of the Crowley ironworks*, SurtS, 167 (1957) · S. Pollard, *The genesis of modern management* (1965)

Archives BL, law book of the Crowley ironworks, Add. MS 34555 · E. Sussex RO, Ashburnham MSS · Society of Antiquaries, Newcastle upon Tyne, arbitrators' records · Suffolk RO, Ipswich, Ashburnham MSS

Likenesses portrait on tombstone, repro. in Flinn, *Men of iron*, frontispiece

Crowley, Ann (1765–1826), Quaker minister, was born on 8 May 1765 at Shillingford, Oxfordshire, the sixth of the eight daughters of William Crowley (1717?–1783), mealman and maltster, and his wife, Catherine Stiles (d. 1795). Ann felt her Quaker family helped her to struggle with what she perceived to be spiritual weakness. 'A fondness for dress and music were some of my greatest foibles, and I am bound to acknowledge that had it not been for parental care, advice and prudent restraint, I might have gone great lengths in these gratifications' (Crowley, 4). She dated her religious awakening from the age of sixteen and found it confirmed by the shock of her father's sudden death the following year from an apoplectic fit. Ann subsequently lived with her mother and unmarried sisters 'in great harmony and tender affection' (ibid., 7) but the family was further broken up when three of her sisters married. The death of her elder sister Mary Ashby in 1791, aged twenty-eight, after less than two years of marriage also gave Ann's mind a serious turn and she began to feel that she might be called to the ministry. A few months later two visiting travelling ministers, Deborah Darby and Rebecca Young from Coalbrookdale, asked Ann to accompany them on their journey, and under their influence she first spoke in meeting.

Ann gradually extended her ministry, accompanying more experienced ministers and visiting local meetings. Her first longer journey was to Wales in 1794 with Mary Stevens and George and Sarah Dillwyn. Ann kept a careful note of the number of miles they travelled and the meetings they attended. In 1795 her mother died after a stroke and this made it necessary for the remaining sisters to move house. Ann, as the eldest at home, felt that she should organize this but she had ministerial commitments. The worry made her ill but she recovered when a house in Uxbridge and her next journey in the ministry had both been decided on. Three weeks after she had returned to her new home her family was again shaken, by the death of her sister Catherine Ashby, aged thirty-six, who left a husband and six children in need of care. The aunts took turns to stay with their bereaved brother-in-law and his family in Staines but Ann did not take much part in this arrangement. Instead, in 1797 she left home to accompany Phoebe Speakman of Pennsylvania on her travels in the ministry throughout England, Scotland, and Wales. The journey covered 4000 miles and took nearly two years, leaving Ann ill and exhausted.

In the next few years Ann continued to travel extensively but eventually her health, which 'had suffered considerably by long exposure to northern blasts' (Crowley, 29), broke down and she was forced to remain at home for three years. In 1810 she went with her fellow minister Priscilla Hannah Gurney to Essex, Suffolk, and Norfolk but her health was still in a very feeble state and she was confined to home again on her return, although this gave her the opportunity to nurse her younger sister Rebecca in her last illness. After travelling in the ministry again, in 1815 and 1816, Ann was taken ill once more, as was her youngest sister, Martha. Doctors recommended warm baths and sea air for both of them so they went together to Hastings for some months.

On her return from Hastings Ann was never strong enough to travel in the ministry away from home again, although she attended local meetings when she could and was faithful to what she called her 'little testimony' (Crowley, 40). Her health was very bad and she suffered much pain. During the last few weeks of her life her breathing was affected and she found speech difficult, so it was a relief to herself, her family, and her friends when, after extreme suffering, she died on 10 April 1826, at the age of sixty, at her home in Uxbridge. She was buried in Uxbridge on 16 April 1826.   GIL SKIDMORE

Sources A. Crowley, *Some account of the religious experience of Ann Crowley* (1842) · W. Evans and T. Evans, eds., *Piety promoted*, 4 vols. (1854), 4 · *Digest registers of births, marriages and burials for England and Wales, c.1650–1837* [1992] [Berkshire and Oxfordshire quarterly meeting; microfilm]

Crowley, Nicholas Joseph (1819–1857), genre and portrait painter, was born on 6 December 1819 in Dublin, the son of Peter Crowley. He began his training at the art school of the Royal Dublin Society at the age of eight, and then moved to the Royal Hibernian Academy in 1832. Most successful as a portraitist, he was elected a member of the academy in 1837 when aged only eighteen. He received much of his patronage from the Roman Catholic hierarchy, which had been liberated as a result of the Catholic Emancipation Act of 1829. His portraits of distinguished leaders of Irish Catholic society include *Daniel Murray, Archbishop of Dublin* (exh. RA, 1844; National Gallery of Ireland, Dublin) and *Mrs Aikenhead* (exh. RA, 1844), founder of the Irish Sisters of Charity. A year later both of these sitters appeared in a larger painting, *Taking the Veil* (exh. RA, 1845; St Vincent's Hospital, Dublin); this work shows Jane Bellew being received as a nun while the artist himself appears in the background.

By this time Crowley had moved to London: here he produced a number of portraits of the Irish statesman Daniel O'Connell, in particular one in the Richmond penitentiary (exh. RHA 1845) which was commissioned as a gift for O'Connell's friend Dr John Gray. In Richmond, Crowley also painted a portrait of the Irish nationalist Charles Gavan Duffy (1844), who was later to describe the portrait of O'Connell as 'an ideal … a tribune in the height of his vigour and inspiration, bearing only a distant and fanciful resemblance to the original'. Of his own portrait, Duffy complained that Crowley gave him 'a dreamy, poetic head which might have passed for Shelley's' (Duffy, 2.60).

Crowley also did paintings based on sentimental literature, a good example of which is a scene from Anna Maria Hall's play *The Groves of Blarney* (1836?), entitled *Tyrone Power as Conor O'Gorman* (exh. British Institution 1840; ex-Tyrone Guthrie priv. coll.). One of his most popular paintings, *Fortune Telling by Cup Tossing* (exh. Northern Irish Art Union 1842; priv. coll.), was offered as the premier prize of 1844 by the Royal Irish Art Union in Dublin, while other prize-winners won an engraving of the image by Charles W. Sharpe (1844, impression in National Gallery of Ireland, Dublin). Crowley's relationship with the union continued, as two years later they purchased *Invitation, Hesitation and Persuasion: a Group of Ladies* (exh. British Institution 1846; National Gallery of Ireland, Dublin), which was also offered as a prize: the large painting shows a successful merging of group portraiture and theatrical sentiment. Crowley was a most productive painter who exhibited widely and regularly throughout the United Kingdom: at the Royal Hibernian Academy in Dublin from 1832 (when only thirteen), the Royal Academy from 1835, the British Institution from 1839, the Belfast Association of Artists from 1836, and the Northern Irish Art Union in Belfast. Most of his adult life was spent in London, though he made occasional visits to Ireland. In the autumn of 1857 he was taken ill with diarrhoea and died at his home, 13 Upper Fitzroy Street, London, on 4 November.

FINTAN CULLEN

Sources W. G. Strickland, *A dictionary of Irish artists*, 1 (1913), 235–6 · A. Stewart, *Royal Hibernian Academy of Arts*, 3 vols. (1978) · A. M. Stewart, ed., *Irish art loan exhibitions, 1765–1927*, 3 vols. (1990–95) · E. Black, 'Practical patriots and true Irishmen: the Royal Irish Art Union, 1839–59', *Irish Arts Review Yearbook*, 14 (1998), 140–46 · A. Crookshank and the Knight of Glin [D. Fitzgerald], *The painters of Ireland, c.1660–1920* (1978) · C. G. Duffy, *Young Ireland: a fragment of Irish history, 1840–1845*, rev. edn, 2 vols. (1896) · DNB

Likenesses N. Crowley, self-portrait, oils, 1835–6, priv. coll.; repro. in Crookshank and the Knight of Glin, *Painters of Ireland*, 231

Crowley, Peter O'Neill (1832–1867), Fenian leader, was born at Ballymacoda, co. Cork, on 23 May 1832, the son of a small tenant farmer. His uncle Peter O'Neill, a priest, had been engaged in the rising of 1798 and transported to Norfolk Island in the Pacific Ocean. Released in 1802, he returned to Ireland.

Crowley, a farmer who was very popular in the Ballymacoda district, was a practising Catholic and teetotaller. He never married. Following his family's republican tradition, he was involved in the Fenian movement almost from its beginning. With Captain John McClure he led the successful raid for arms on the coastguard station at Knockadoon on 5 March 1867. The raiders remained in hiding until they dispersed when discovered by soldiers. Crowley and McClure retreated to the Kilclooney Wood, where, on 31 March, Crowley was shot in a skirmish with the constabulary; he died at Mitchelstown the same day. His funeral in Ballymacoda attracted an immense following.   J. M. RIGG, rev. BRIGITTE ANTON

Sources D. J. Hickey and J. E. Doherty, *A dictionary of Irish history* (1980) · H. Boylan, *A dictionary of Irish biography*, 3rd edn (1998) · J. Devoy, *Recollections of an Irish rebel* (1929); repr. (1969) · T. W. Moody and others, eds., *A new history of Ireland*, 5: *Ireland under the Union, 1801–1870* (1989) · R. J. Hayes, ed., *Manuscript sources for the history of Irish civilisation*, 1 (1965) · R. J. Hayes, ed., *Manuscript sources for the history of Irish civilisation: first supplement, 1965–1975*, 1 (1979) · R. J. Hayes, ed., *Sources for the history of Irish civilisation: articles in Irish periodicals*, 1 (1970) · '"Sliabh Ruadh": some Fenian anecdotes', *Catholic Bulletin*, 10/5 (May 1920), 273–4 · R. V. Comerford, *The Fenians in context: Irish politics and society, 1848–82* (1985) · L. O'Broin, *Revolutionary underground* (1976) · R. Kee, *The green flag*, 2: *The bold Fenian men* (1976); repr. (1989) [orig. pubd in 1 vol. as *The green flag: a history of Irish nationalism* [1972]] · T. Pakenham, *The year of liberty: the story of the great Irish rebellion of 1798*, rev. edn (1997) · T. J. Kiernan, *The Irish exiles in Australia* (1954)

Wealth at death prosperous farmer in Ballymacoda district: Devoy, *Recollections*, 213

Crowley, Robert (1517×19–1588), author, Church of England clergyman, and printer, was born in Gloucestershire, possibly in Tetbury; John Bale, however, describes him as a native of Northamptonshire. One source (Emden, *Oxf.*, 153) gives his age as twenty on 25 July 1539; others indicate that he was born in 1517 (Martin, *Religious Radicals*, 149). He seems to have begun his studies at Oxford about 1534, and was admitted demy of Magdalen College (25 July 1539), BA (19 June 1540), and probationer fellow (26 July 1541). Appointed a fellow of Magdalen in 1542, he left his fellowship the same year. Alongside his friend John Foxe he became one of the somewhat persecuted protestant minority at Oxford, possibly in a lightning conversion after active Catholic devotion.

Following a period as tutor to the children of Sir Nicholas Poyntz of Iron Acton, Gloucestershire, by the end of 1546 Crowley was in London, writing, and was possibly also a proof-reader to John Day, who, with William Seres, printed his three earliest works (1548). Two were attacks on Roman Catholic doctrine: refutations of Nicholas Shaxton's recanting sermon at the burning of Anne Askew (1546) and of Miles Hoggarde's advocacy of transubstantiation. The third, *An Informacion and Peticion Agaynst the Oppressours of the Poore Commons*, was a programme of legislative reform to aid the distressed, landless, and poor, addressed to the parliament currently sitting. Here Crowley followed in a tradition already established by Simon Fish (1529) and Henry Brinkelow (1542–5). He furiously attacked all those 'possessioners'—especially engrossers of farms, rack-renters, enclosers, leasemongers, usurers and owners of tithes—who failed to practise good stewardship in their ill treatment of the poor, and he anticipated as remedy the sanctions of royal edict and parliamentary statute and fear of divine punishment.

The lack of significant responses led Crowley to take advantage of the relatively permissive years of Somerset's protectorship and set up a publishing enterprise (1549–51) in Ely Rents, Holborn, to produce propaganda for his passionately held beliefs. It was underwritten (but without acknowledgement by Crowley) by Richard Grafton, the king's printer. Acting, with Latimer and Thomas Lever, as 'the social conscience of Edwardine England' (Collinson, 49), Crowley became arguably the most eloquent and vigorous of the 'commonwealth' writers, inveighing against the irresponsible accumulation of wealth. He published nineteen texts, including ten of his own authorship. Some of these were works of formal theological controversy, combining firm protestantism with compassion for the oppressed commons; but he specialized in the sale of inexpensive octavo chapbooks written in doggerel verse, and some of the earliest Welsh books, including William Salesbury's translations of the gospels (1551), carried his imprint. In addition to editions of Wyclif, Tyndale, and the renegade Augustinian friar Peter Pateshull, Crowley risked publishing (in three separate editions, 1550) the first complete version of Langland's *The Vision of Pierce Plowman*, which had enough anti-clericalism to be regarded as a proto-protestant work. It especially satirized clerical pretensions and attacked church corruption. Crowley showed fidelity to the text (apart from omitting some specifically Catholic elements of Langland's thought, on purgatory, transubstantiation, and praise for the monastic ideal), but he modernized it for the sixteenth century reader and gave it the apparatus of contemporary editions of the Greek and Roman classics, to enhance its appeal as a trustworthy authority. Its main importance lay in 'bringing into sharp focus—through the violent exaggerations and biting invective of a radical gospeller—the persuasive value of literature in the bitter controversies of the English Reformation' (King, 322). In particular, Crowley saw Edward's reign as a return to the imperial greatness of Edward III, and appeared to hope that the young king would complete the doctrinal work left unfinished by the Henrician political reformation by emulating Edward III's toleration of the Bible in English.

Of Crowley's own (almost entirely verse) contributions, a metrical version of the Psalms (1549) was obviously intended as a protestant service book. *A New Yeres Gyfte* (1549) was a harsh summary of the gospel teaching on avarice, lust, and sloth, aimed at men's social consciences. *The Voyce of the Laste Trumpet* (1549) presented a comprehensive picture of Crowley's views on the ills of English society. Focusing on selected groups such as yeomen, lawyers, and merchants, he echoed the deep conservatism about social structure shown by Langland in the fourteenth century: each estate should accept its lot, and, especially after the 1549 rebellions, the poor should look to God alone to avenge their misery. *One and Thyrtye Epigrammes* (1550) (actually thirty-three in number) satirized arbitrarily chosen subjects such as alehouses, beggars, and usurers, while *The Way to Wealth* (1550), a prose work, voiced the infuriated rejection by the poor of a French-type slavery, but also aimed to catch the atmosphere of public concern after the rebellions, and suggested how the poor, property owners, and clergy could help to restore social harmony: 'If the possessioners woulde consyder them selves to be but stuards, and not Lordes over theyr possessions … oppression woulde soon be redressed' (*Select Works*, 157). *Philargyrie* (1551), arguably Crowley's masterpiece, was a well-developed and elaborate satirical and allegorical attack on human greed, especially visible in the selfish scramble for wealth and power which followed the break with Rome. Once more it looked to Edward VI for remedy, using the Bible as a model for good government. *Pleasure and Payne* (1551) again showed Crowley's disillusionment at the lack of good stewardship from landowners, and saw him using his vision of the last judgment to frighten his readers.

In 1551, probably attracted by the potential of the church to inspire social reform, Crowley was ordained deacon by Bishop Ridley (28 September), and he abandoned his venturesome publishing career. But, perhaps because of his tenuous link to the disgraced protector, Somerset, through his patroness Lady Fane (whose metrical paraphrases of Psalms and Proverbs he published), Crowley seems to have received no ecclesiastical preferment under Edward VI. Indeed, there is no record of him after his ordination. By 1555 he was one of the Marian exiles at Frankfurt am Main; little is known of his time spent there, but by June 1557 he was clearly married, with a child.

Early in 1559 Crowley was back in England, and he was collated archdeacon of Hereford on 24 March. Although he never returned to his publishing role, in April he updated Lanquet's *Epitome of Cronicles*, in which he idealized Somerset and listed the Marian martyrs, anticipating Foxe in his desire to produce protestant substitutes for the old Catholic saints. He was clearly in great demand as a popular preacher (though only one of his sermons survives in print); he delivered three sermons at Paul's Cross (1559–63), inveighing against popish ceremonies. A canon

of Hereford (1560) and member of convocation (1562), Crowley's earlier strictures against clerical pluralism did not inhibit him from simultaneously becoming (1563) rector of St Peter-le-Poer and reader at St Antholin's, London, a canon of St Paul's (1 September), and vicar of St Giles Cripplegate (26 September 1565). After appealing (with others) in May 1565 for exemption from Archbishop Parker's new regulations on clerical vestments, in 1566 he led about a third of London's beneficed clergy in confronting him over the issue. He was suspended from St Giles and imprisoned for creating a disturbance over the wearing of surplices by lay clerks at a funeral service (2 April), only a few days after the issue of Parker's 'Advertisements' that ordered the surplice's use. Parker put Crowley in the custody of the bishop of Ely (June–October), and by 1568 Crowley had either resigned from or been deprived of all his preferments. Clearly it was the vestiarian controversy that activated him into writing *A Briefe Discourse Against the Outwarde Apparell of the Popishe Church* (1566), a statement of the position held by the dissident clergy, and termed by Collinson 'the earliest puritan manifesto' (Collinson, 77). The ensuing literary exchange saw Crowley making a number of contemptuous references to the bishops. He also published (1567) his earliest work (of 1546), *The Opening of the Wordes of the Prophet Joell*, an apocalyptic poem of nearly 3000 lines, suggesting the backsliding on reform was as true of Elizabeth as of Henry VIII.

In 1569 Crowley was living in retirement in Southwark; but by the mid-1570s he was clearly well regarded by the church hierarchy and back in the mainstream of London ecclesiastical and civic life. On 29 September 1574 he delivered a Guildhall sermon at the election of the new lord mayor; on 5 May 1576 he became vicar of St Lawrence Jewry (resigning in 1578); in 1578 he was reappointed (9 May) vicar of St Giles Cripplegate, and was admitted (27 September) to the Stationers' Company; and a privy council letter of 13 March 1579 enlisted his help to reason with some west-country separatists. During the 1570s and 1580s he also retained his reputation for contributing skilled prefaces and refurbishing old texts, and he received a number of dedications in other men's books. He wrote two anti-Catholic polemics (1581 and 1586) and in 1580 was appointed to visit (and dispute with) Catholic prisoners in the Marshalsea and the White Lion at Southwark. An offer by him to bestow 'certayne Tythes' due to him as vicar of St Giles 'on the poare in Chrystes hospytall towardes theyre releef and compfortes' prompted the city's court of aldermen to appoint a committee on 25 September 1582 to consider the matter further (Arber, *Regs. Stationers*, 2.770). In 1580 and 1584 he bound apprentices with the Stationers' Company (what may have been a third apprentice was freed by Crowley's widow four years after his death), and he preached a sermon to the company on its annual election day in summer 1586. His inclusion a few months later alongside the names of members of its governing body suggests that he may even have reached a position of some seniority within it. He acted as a licenser for books for printing from probably 1579 onwards, and he was among several formally appointed as licensers by

Archbishop Whitgift on 3 June 1588. He died on 18 June 1588, and was buried beneath the same stone in the chancel of St Giles Cripplegate as Foxe. His widow was left so poor that she was allowed a pension by the Stationers' Company in October or November 1592.

The stewardship theory of property ownership was the kernel of Crowley's social gospel under Edward VI, and he felt that only a reorganized church could bridle the avarice and exploitation of the commons by a new élite of protestant clergy and landlords in the aftermath of the monastic dissolutions. Under Elizabeth the focus of his radicalism changed, though his work (1575) to ameliorate the plight of imprisoned debtors showed social concern. Mid-century, sensitive to Catholic gibes about the lack of protestant antecedents to Luther, he had been preoccupied with the fourteenth-century foundations of English protestantism; under Elizabeth, Foxe's *Acts and Monuments* (1563) usurped this stance. Crowley was no rabble-rousing demagogue: he accepted a hierarchical society, and showed respect for the law and for orderly procedures—in his abhorrence at the 1549 rebellions, in his eventual conformity over ecclesiastical vestments, which earned him the scorn of the new generation of radicals, led by John Field, and in his refusal to be tempted into separatism. His sense of English nationalism grew stronger, especially after the papal bull of 1570 and rising concern over the activities of Jesuit missionary priests, and his stand over clerical vestments and controversion of Catholic doctrine were elements in his conviction that the poor needed not only relief from rapacious landlords, but also a new preaching clergy to divert them from adherence to superstitious ceremonies. Elton sees Crowley as a somewhat cranky figure, fuelled by the vivid, passionate indignation of the archetypal pamphleteer, not especially original or visionary, nor even clearly understanding the economic crisis which afflicted mid-Tudor England. But, as 'the first English university man to set up as a printer' (Martin, 'Publishing career', 85), Crowley had the imagination to see the possibilities afforded by the press to mould popular opinion, and the energy and burning compassion to produce a sizeable and varied body of work which was an antidote to the plethora of wordy theological tomes currently being printed. To one modern authority, although Crowley exerted no stylistic influence on major poets such as Philip Sidney or Spenser, 'he emerges as the most significant poet between Surrey and Gascoyne' (King, 320).　　　　　　　　　　　　　　　BASIL MORGAN

Sources J. W. Martin, *Religious radicals in Tudor England* (1989) · J. N. King, *English Reformation literature* (1982) · G. R. Elton, 'Reform and the "commonwealth men" of Edward VI's reign', *The English commonwealth, 1547–1640*, ed. P. Clark, A. G. R. Smith, and N. Tyacke (1979) · Emden, *Oxf.* · J. W. Martin, 'The publishing career of Robert Crowley: a sidelight on the Tudor book trade', *Publishing History*, 14 (1983), 85–98 · P. Collinson, *The Elizabethan puritan movement* (1967); repr. (1982) · *DNB* · J. W. Allen, *A history of political thought in the sixteenth century* (1928) · *The select works of Robert Crowley*, ed. J. M. Cowper (1872) · B. L. Beer, *Rebellion and riot* (1982) · W. R. D. Jones, *The Tudor commonwealth, 1529–1559* (1970) · M. M. Knappen, *Tudor puritanism* (1965) · Bale, *Cat.* · Arber, *Regs. Stationers* · W. W. Greg and E. Boswell, eds., *Records of the court of the Stationers' Company, 1576 to 1602, from register B* (1930) · W. W. Greg, ed., *A companion to Arber* (1967) · W. W. Greg, *Licensers for the press, &c. to 1640* (1962) · will, PRO, PROB 11/72, sig. 50

Wealth at death two charitable bequests, provided there was more than £120 surviving for wife after all debts paid; provision made for library to be appraised, and successor at St Giles (Launcelot Andrewes) given forty days to purchase it from executors: will, PRO, PROB 11/72, sig. 50 · widow left so poor she was allowed pension of 4 nobles p.a. by Stationers' Company: Martin, *Religious radicals*, 165; *DNB*

Crowley, Thomas [*pseud.* Amor Patriae] (*c.*1713–1787), religious controversialist and political writer, of whose date and place of birth details are unknown, appears to have been connected to those Crowleys who pioneered the iron industry of the west midlands. In any event he turned up in London by 1727, apprenticed to a linen draper. He subsequently went into business for himself and expanded his enterprises to become a general merchant, living on London's Gracechurch Street, with a country home just across the Thames in Walworth. He and his wife, Mary (*d.* 1778), had seven children between 1748 and 1759. Their second youngest child, Ann, one of three daughters, died of a lingering illness in 1774. Griefstricken but proud of her abiding faith and strength in facing death, they had her *Expressions* published to serve as an inspiration to others. The disputatious Crowley, though born and raised a Quaker, was disowned by the Devonshire House monthly meeting in February 1774. Beginning in the late 1760s with letters to friends that expanded to broadsides, newspaper pieces, and pamphlets—eventually collected as *Dissertations on Liberty of Conscience* (1774)—Crowley had criticized various Quaker practices, especially the stand against tithes and the disowning of those who paid them. Civic-minded, Crowley paid tithes and taxes gladly, including funds to support the militia. He contended that Quakers owed the state money as well as allegiance and tried, through scriptures, to prove that Christ and his apostles would have agreed with him. His appeal to 'liberty of conscience' and request for reinstatement rejected, Crowley condemned his opponents as modern-day pharisees and thereafter described himself as 'a rational Christian'. He never stopped believing that he was right and that the Quaker brethren who stood against him were wrong.

Crowley's *nom de plume*, Amor Patriae (a Lover of his Country), employed in one piece on tithes and taxes, appeared more frequently in his *Public Ledger* essays on imperial reform. Virtually all of these were later reissued under one cover as *Letters and Dissertations on Various Subjects* (1776). Crowley's interest in colonial problems dated from the Stamp Act crisis. Although he felt that the colonists were ingrates and shortsightedly petulant in their protests against imperial policy, he accepted as constitutionally valid their claims that they should not be taxed where they were not represented. Virtual representation, he warned, would never satisfy them. Initially he recommended that they tax themselves through existing representative assemblies and he computed what he considered to be equitable rates that he argued would actually raise more money than Grenville's stamp tax. He soon after shifted to the position that Americans be given seats in parliament. Because crown and parliament were supreme, he contended, no other solution was possible where the American right to representation could be combined with the American duty to pay taxes in support of the empire. He was convinced that only a legislative restructuring would prevent an American drift towards independence and stave off a crisis that could be exploited by Britain's enemies. Before taking any particulars to the public he tried—but failed—to secure the backing of prominent politicians. The papers of Benjamin Franklin and the earl of Chatham both contain copies of his plan. In it he urged that the Americans, West Indians and Canadians included, receive fifty seats in the House of Commons and ten seats for new peers in the House of Lords. Following his notion of proportional representation, the larger, more populous colonies would be granted as many as four seats each in the Commons; the smaller, less populous would be awarded fewer; with the smallest having only one apiece. The Irish too would be seated at Westminster, with thirty MPs in the Commons and ten peers in the Lords. This expanded parliament would deal with imperial affairs and leave internal matters to local assemblies. 'A wise-established Representation of all considerable Parts of the British Dominions in Europe and America, in one central Parliament', Crowley emphasized, 'would give Stability, Unity and Concord, and consequently greater Strength to the Whole' (Crowley, *Letters and Dissertations*, 79). Although he was hardly the first to call for this sort of solution, he worked it out in more detail than virtually anyone else and pushed it more persistently, so persistently that Franklin dismissed him as hopelessly obsessive. He did not give up until after the outbreak of the American War of Independence.

With his predictions realized, Crowley ceased his efforts to influence imperial policy. Never acting on his threat to build a new meeting-house for like-minded Christian rationalists at his own expense, Crowley continued to set his own religious course. Regretting that his unorthodox tendencies made life difficult for his family, who maintained their Quaker association, he was apparently a generous and loving father. He died in Walworth on 17 December 1787 'aged about' seventy-four, and left his children a substantial estate in land, buildings, stocks, and cash. He was buried on 26 December in Bunhill Fields, London, next to his wife, Mary, who had died on 9 July 1778.

NEIL L. YORK

Sources T. Crowley, *Letters and dissertations on various subjects* (1776) · T. Crowley, *Copies of Thomas Crowley's letters to the Quakers, not printed before* [1776] · RS Friends, Lond., Adverse Box C2 · Amor Patriae [T. Crowley] to William Pitt, 2 Feb 1766 and 17 Nov 1770, PRO, Chatham MSS, 30/8/97 and 30/8/82 · Amor Patriae [T. Crowley] to Benjamin Franklin, 17 Nov 1770 and 10 Dec 1770, American Philosophical Society library, Benjamin Franklin MSS, vol. 69, fol. 92 and vol. 69, fol. 93 · will, Dec 1787, PRO, PROB 11/1160, sig. 540 · P. Boyd, ed., *Roll of the Drapers' Company of London* (1934) · minutes of the (London) six weeks meeting, 1772–8, RS Friends, Lond., vol. 14 · digest registers (burials to 1837), RS Friends, Lond., [London and Middlesex quarterly meeting, no. 860], PRO, RG6/975 · nonconformist register, 1783–7, RS Friends, Lond., [London and Middlesex quarterly meeting, no. 862, 1783–7, no. 260], PRO, RG6/670 · PRO, RG6/670 · N. L. York, 'Thomas Crowley's proposal to seat Americans in parliament, 1765–1775', *Quaker History*, 91 (2002), 1–19
Wealth at death at least several thousands of pounds: will, Dec 1787, PRO, PROB 1160/12

Crowne, John (*bap.* **1641**, *d.* **1712**), playwright, was baptized on 6 April 1641 at St Martin-in-the-Fields, London, the second of the four children of Colonel **William Crowne** (*c.*1617–1683) and Agnes Watts, *née* Mackworth (*b.* 1616/17).

William Crowne As a young man William Crowne travelled with a mission from Charles I, probably serving as tutor for the earl of Arundel's grandson. In 1637, immediately on his return, Crowne published *A true relation of all the remarkable places and passages observed in the travels of Thomas, Lord Howard, earle of Arundell and Surrey*, with a flattering dedication to the earl. On 24 September 1638 the earl's patronage procured Crowne his appointment as Rouge Dragon pursuivant of arms to the king.

Crowne remained prosperous and was one of only a few knights pursuivant who remained active during Cromwell's time. Crowne was a man of extraordinary political prudence and astuteness, who managed to succeed in a career of public service whatever the politics. In 1637 or 1638 he married Agnes Watts, *née* Mackworth. The Mackworths were Shropshire's pre-eminent puritan family. Agnes's brother Humphrey was governor of Shrewsbury and three times member of parliament. Through this influence Crowne secured major offices in the parliamentary cause, and garnered enough wealth and influence to buy into a proprietorial partnership for the territory of Nova Scotia, which Cromwell signed on 10 August 1656.

In 1657 Crowne sailed to Nova Scotia with his sons. He built a successful trading post on the Penobscot River but, after troubles with his partner, settled in Boston, of which he was made freeman. In 1661 he returned to England with John to take his place as Rouge Dragon at the coronation of Charles II—and to argue for his rights to his American property, which, having been procured by Cromwell's decree, were invalidated by the Restoration. He did not prevail, and with the treaty of Breda (1667) Charles ceded the territory to France.

While at court Crowne also promoted the interests of the Massachusetts Bay Colony—so successfully that in 1662, after he returned, it 'graunt[ed] him five hundred acres of land' of his choice (*Records, Colony of Massachusetts Bay*, 4/2, 61). In 1667 he joined with others to found Mendon, where until 1673 he was registrar, magistrate, and annually elected selectman. However, in April 1674, after a dispute, the general court of Mendon ordered Crowne to 'return [to England] to his wife by the next opportunity of Shipping'. He fled to Rhode Island until their differences were resolved in September. Crowne returned to Boston for his final years and died there early in 1683.

Early years, religion, and politics John Crowne remained in England in 1661 when his father returned to America. While in America he had attended Harvard College (1657–60), but did not take a degree. As John Dennis remembered in 1719, 'The vivacity of [Crowne's] Genius made him soon grow impatient of that sullen and gloomy Education and soon oblig'd him to get loose from it and seek his Fortune in *England*' (Dennis, 2.404). At first Crowne had difficulty earning his living: in 1664 his poverty exempted him from paying the hearth tax. Dennis describes those days: '[Crowne's] necessity, upon his first Arrival here, oblig'd him to become a Gentleman-Usher to an old Independent lady. But he soon grew weary of that precise Office, as he had been before of the Discipline of [Harvard]' (ibid.). In 1665 he published *Pandion and Amphigenia, or, The History of the Coy Lady of Thessalia* (1665), a prose romance with both the defects of youth—Crowne was 'scarcely 20 years of age when [he] fancied it'—and those of the 'fungous words and lame conceits' of that prolix genre (dedication). It proved popular, however, and was read and later satirized by the court wits.

Crowne's biographers disagree about his religion and his politics. John Genest's assessment of 1832, however, that Crowne's was a 'career of loyalty' rather than conviction (Genest, 124) seems sound; Crowne followed closely in his father's politically prudent footsteps. Upon his return to England in 1661 he allied himself with his monarch, making a deposition identifying his Harvard teachers and the family who had sheltered him in his student days as among those who 'received [the visiting regicides] with great demonstrations of tenderness' (*Political Annals of the Present United Colonies*, ed. G. Chalmers, 1780, 263).

Crowne's fervour was equally strong for whatever religion or policy was ascendant. The plays he wrote during Charles's reign are those of a tory royalist; those produced under James praise Catholicism; and those under William toe the whig line. All dedicatees were shrewdly selected. Nevertheless, Crowne presented himself as a reluctant sycophant. He wrote about his 'adversions to things I saw acted [at Court] by great men', and lamented he was 'fixt … in a dependence on that Court, for I could have my compensation no where else' (dedication, *English Frier*). Dennis confirms: 'The Promise of a Sum of Money made him sometimes appear [at court] to solicit the Payment of it; But as soon as he had got it, he vanish'd, and continued a long time absent from it' (Dennis, 405). Nevertheless Crowne managed to remain in royal favour throughout his thirty-year career.

Dramatic career Six years after his early success with *Pandion and Amphigenia* Crowne produced *Juliana, or, The Princess of Poland* (performed June 1671; published 1671), a combination of heroic tragedy and comedy-romance. The play mixes heroic couplets, tragic blank verse, and comic colloquial prose, with spirited damsels in masculine garb, mistaken identity, love, jealousy, madness, court intrigue and betrayal, swordplay and blood, all in a struggle for succession to the Polish throne. Crowne chose for his hero the duke of Curland, the putative ancestor of the present duke, whose claim to Tobago Island Charles was presently championing. He dedicated his play to Roger Boyle, earl of Orrery, who, like Crowne himself, had given his support to both protector and king, and who now commanded both financial and political influence.

Crowne's next work, *The History of Charles the Eighth of France, or, The Invasion of Naples by the French* (performed November 1671; published 1672), was a heroic drama about Charles VIII's conquest of Naples and his honourable return of it to its former ruling family. It supported Charles's recent alliance with France—'Charles and France, / Names that now shake the world'—and, sounding that most royally flattering of all strains, the divine right of kings, declared that it hoped to make:

> heroic virtue shine
> In royal breasts, where it shews most divine.
> (epilogue)

Crowne's dedication to John Wilmot, earl of Rochester, indicates that his political prudence was already bringing him to the attention of the powerful and influential.

By 1674 and *Andromache* (first performed in August; published 1675), Crowne had established himself among the modish literati. Rochester satirized him in *Timon* (1674), which reveals his fastidious appearance:

> Little Starch'd Johnny C—…
> His Crevat-string new Iron'd,
> His lilly white Hand out.

Shortly afterwards John Dryden added a preface and postscript to the satire by Crowne and Thomas Shadwell on Elkanah Settle's *The Empress of Morocco* (which had attacked Dryden in the preface). Crowne later admitted writing three-quarters of *Notes and Observations on 'The Empress of Morocco', or, Some Few Errata's to be Printed Instead of the Sculptures with the Second Edition of that Play* (1674), and expressed some regret: 'I gave vent to more ill nature [then] … than I will do again' ('Epistle to reader', *Caligula*, [1698]). Rochester, perhaps flattered by the *Charles the Eighth* dedication, or perhaps motivated by 'malice', as Dennis put it, 'to mortify Mr. Dryden' (Dennis, 2.404), gained Crowne the royal commission to compose a masque for the little princesses to perform. There is, however, no evidence that Dryden wanted to write a court masque, and the good relations between the two continued. The printed text of the masque included a compliment to Dryden in the preface, and Dryden may have written, or again collaborated with Crowne in writing, the epilogue.

With its dancing, singing, and opulent costumes, that masque, *Calisto, or, The Chaste Nimph* (1675), was described by John Evelyn and others as a magnificent spectacle. Rehearsals began in September 1674, and there were open rehearsals in December and January, and several official performances in February. The masque firmly established Crowne as a court favourite. His next play, *The Country Wit* (1676), a prototypical Restoration comedy, satirizing both the country booby and the town rake in their rivalry for the hand of the spirited heroine, was also 'honour'd with the King's favour' (dedication).

Crowne turned again to Charles's favoured heroic tragedy with his *Destruction of Jerusalem* (2 parts, January 1677; published 1677). In a two-afternoon extravaganza, Crowne combined Josephus's account of events preceding the sacking of Jerusalem with Racine's rendering of the love of the Roman emperor, Titus, and the Judaic queen, Berenice. With its extraordinary spectacle and pageantry and, climactically, the temple in flames, it 'met with as wild and unaccountable Success as Mr. Dryden's *Conquest of Granada*' according to Charles St Edmonde (*Dramatic Works*, 2.218). Its triumph, however, lost Crowne the patronage of the envious Rochester. Discounting any possibility of Rochester's continuing sponsorship, Crowne dedicated the published play to the duchess of Portsmouth, Rochester's enemy and Charles's most influential mistress.

In 1679 Crowne began the first of his two lengthy campaigns for his father's lost land, petitioning Mounthope to compensate for the land Charles had signed away with the Breda treaty. Despite Charles's active support, his plea was rejected. Similarly, his petition for Boston Neck and adjoining acreage was favourably discussed by the council for trade and plantations, but was rejected in March 1680.

Concurrently, Crowne wrote *The Ambitious Statesman, or, The Loyal Favourite* (performed March 1679; published 1679), a tragedy in blank verse. In it he responded to the exclusion crisis by portraying the downfall of an insidiously ambitious protagonist and by having the dying hero say significantly:

Princes are sacred!
Whate'er religious rebels may pretend.
(act v)

The play was not a success, and Crowne turned instead to adaptations of Shakespeare: *The Misery of Civil-War* (performed December 1679 or January 1680; published 1680)— later titled *Henry the Sixth: the Second Part*—and *Henry the Sixth: the First Part, with the Murder of Humphrey Duke of Gloucester* (performed January–March 1681?; published 1681). Both adaptations, and the intervening *Thyestes* (March 1680; published 1680), a Senecan tragedy, continued to draw contemporary parallels. The first was his most polemic tory play yet, in which Edward IV (a satirized version of the Shakespeare original) represents Charles II, and the Yorkist claim to the throne is presented as unassailable. The second adaptation, however, showed a shift in its politics. It was dedicated to the whig Sedley, and Crowne overplayed the anti-Catholicism—described in the prologue to *1 Henry VI* as 'a little vinegar against the pope'—and thus, though these plays were 'acted with good applause', according to Gerard Langbaine, 'the Romish faction … got [*1 Henry VI*] supprest' (Langbaine, 29).

Crowne made another misjudgement in *City Politiques* (licensed 15 June 1683), a comic satire set in 1540s Naples, where he presents the whigs as the cuckolds, cuckolders, dupes, and witlings of conventional scatological farce. He had this time underestimated the strength of the parliamentary whigs, and on 26 June the play was suppressed. Charles intervened, and six months after the ban *City Politiques* began a run that lasted well into the next century. A few days after its opening (19 January 1684), Crowne was set upon in St Martin's Lane by a man claiming to be acting on Rochester's behalf. Rochester had, however, been dead for over two years, and the attacker was more probably working for the City whigs. Later that year, according to Dennis, Crowne 'desir'd his Majesty to establish him in some Office that might be a Security to him for Life'.

Charles agreed, but 'he would first see another Comedy' (Dennis, 2.405). Charles collapsed on the final rehearsal day and died soon afterwards, and with him Crowne's chance of an office, but *Sir Courtly Nice, or, It Cannot Be* (performed May 1685; published 1685) proved Crowne's masterpiece. It became a staple of the English stage in the seventeenth and eighteenth centuries, and was revived periodically in the nineteenth and twentieth. According to Dennis, 'the greatest Comick Poet that ever liv'd in any Age might have been proud to be the author' (ibid.). Besides the charm, wit, and topical satire of the best Restoration comedies, this commentary on the war between the sexes achieves a universal appeal in its gibes at the sanctimonious who worry about 'the great—great sinfulness of sin', at the snobbish fawner 'so respectful to every thing belongs to a Gentleman, he stand's bare to his own Perriwig', and especially at those who see love only as an appetite and women as chattels.

James with his Catholic wife was now monarch; thus, in the prologue to *Sir Courtly Nice* Crowne blames his earlier anti-Catholicism on 'a turn-coat doctor's lying Creed' and welcomes 'that Illustrious paire … Who both Reform and Grace Us by their sway'. James gave Crowne £20 for that play and another £20 for *Darius, King of Persia* (April 1688; published 1688), a ponderous tragedy of blood and spectacle, profitable only because of James's patronage on the author's benefit night. In portraying a good king surrounded by treachery, Crowne supported James just months before William's revolution with such lines as 'Leave the dispose of Crowns to Kings and Gods' (act III).

With the revolution of 1688, however, the court party changed, and Crowne, perforce, changed too. Each of the plays he wrote during William's reign contains flattering references to the new regime, is dedicated to an influential instigator of the revolution, and also attacks the administrations to which Crowne once was so loyal. *The English Frier, or, The Town Sparks* (March 1690; published 1690), for instance, is a satiric comedy against the preceding 'vicious, degenerate age … where Treachery to our country was called fidelity to the King' (dedication). This play was fresh and witty and its politics matched the court's, but Jacobite drumming and catcalling from the pit shortened its run.

In 1692 Crowne wrote two mock-heroic poems satirizing Catholics and Jacobites, *Daeneids* and *The History of the Famous and Passionate Love*, as well as a heroic tragedy, *Regulus* (performed June 1692), glorifying a military hero, like William, whom he describes as '[without] fault … approach[ing] near gods in excellence'. Despite songs by Henry Purcell, comedy, and spectacle, it too 'met with no good success', as Langbaine reports, 'though the Design is Noble' (Langbaine, 30). More successful was *The Married Beau, or, The Curious Impertinent* (performed April 1694; published 1694), a comedy developed from Cervantes, which caught the transitional mood, adding genuine emotion to Restoration brittle wit. According to Langbaine, this was 'often Acted with general Approbation' (ibid.).

In 1697 Crowne began his second petitioning campaign.

The treaty of Breda had been superseded by that of Ryswick, and the validity of land claims such as his again became pragmatically disputable. His petitions and appeals to one governmental tribunal after another dragged on until the council for trade and plantations finally validated his claim on 21 January 1701. Nevertheless, Crowne was never awarded the land.

An embittered Crowne portrayed horrors and gross injustices in his last heroic tragedy, *Caligula* (1698), demonstrating 'the dreadful consequences of lawless and boundless power', and made a plea to 'our wise and valliant king, who was born to free and do justice to opprest mankind: and I hope to myself' (dedication).

Crowne's final comedy, 'Justice Busy' (1700?), was never published, though some of its songs are extant. John Downes commented: ''Twas well acted, but proved not a living play' (Downes, 45).

Retirement and death From 1687 Crowne suffered from 'tedious sickness' which 'frequently took from [him] not only all sense, but almost all signs of life' (*Caligula*, preface), and his disappointment at the loss of his patrimony was profound. William granted him only £50 compensation at the decision, but he received at least another £50 every year afterwards from Mary, then Anne. With this pension he lived comfortably on Great Russell Street in the parish of St Giles-in-the-Fields, home of the theatrical and literary community, where later a contemporary fondly remembered, 'Many a cup of metheglin have I drank with little starch'd *Johnny Crowne*' (*GM*, 1st ser., 15, 1745). Crowne died aged seventy-one years, and was buried in the churchyard of St Giles-in-the-Fields on 27 April 1712.   BETH S. NEMAN

Sources J. Dennis, 'Letter to Mr. *** in which are some passages of the life of Mr. John Crown, author of Sir Courtly Nice', 23 June 1719, *The critical works of John Dennis*, ed. E. N. Hookier, 2 (1943) • *The dramatic works of John Crowne*, ed. J. Maidment and W. H. Logan, 4 vols. (1872–4) • G. Langbaine, 'John Crowne', in [C. Gildon], *The lives and characters of the English dramatick poets* [1699] • B. Neman, 'John Crowne', *Restoration and eighteenth-century dramatists: first series*, ed. P. R. Backscheider, DLitB, 80 (1989), 36–51 • B. Neman, 'Setting the record straight on John Crowne', *Restoration and 18th Century Theatre Research*, 2nd ser., 8 (spring 1993), 1–26 • A. F. White, *John Crowne: his life and dramatic works* (1922) • A. McMechan, 'John Crowne: a biographical note', *Modern Languages Notes*, 6 (May 1891), 278–86 • Genest, *Eng. stage*, vol. 1 • R. L. Capwell, 'A biographical and critical study of John Crowne', PhD diss., Duke U., 1964 • S. Sengupta, 'Biographical notes on John Crowne', *Restoration: Studies in English Literary Culture*, 6 (spring 1982), 26–30 • J. Downes, *Roscius Anglicanus, or, An historical review of the stage* (1708) • J. A. Winn, *John Dryden and his world* (1987) • D. Hughes, *English drama, 1660–1700* (1996) • parish register, London, St Martin-in-the-Fields, 6 April 1641 [baptism] • parish register, London, St Giles-in-the-Fields, 27 April 1712 [burial] • steward's book of Thomas Chesholme, Harvard U., 97

Crowne, William (*c*.1617–1683). *See under* Crowne, John (*bap.* 1641, *d.* 1712).

Crowquill, Alfred. *See* Forrester, Alfred Henry (1804–1872).

Crowther, Geoffrey, Baron Crowther (1907–1972), journalist and businessman, was born on 13 May 1907 at Headingley, Leeds, the eldest son of Charles Crowther (1876–

Geoffrey Crowther, Baron Crowther (1907–1972), by Howard Coster, 1937

1964), lecturer then professor of agricultural chemistry at the University of Leeds, and his wife, Hilda Louise Reed (*d.* 1950). He was educated first at Leeds grammar school and later at Oundle School, where he won a scholarship to read modern languages at Clare College, Cambridge (of which he was to become an honorary fellow in April 1958). He switched to economics, however, in his third year, became president of the union in 1928, and gained a double first. He was awarded a Commonwealth Fund fellowship and pursued further studies at Yale and Columbia universities (1929–31). These years marked the beginning of his lifelong attachment to American affairs and people. During his stay in the United States he met Margaret, daughter of E. H. Worth of Claymont, Delaware: they were married in 1932, and had two sons and four daughters, one of whom died. On the recommendation of J. M. Keynes, Crowther became economic adviser on banking to the Irish government; his report on Irish banking, written at the age of twenty-five, was the first of many distinguished public documents to come from his pen.

In 1932, on a further recommendation by Keynes to Walter Layton, then editor, Crowther joined the staff of *The Economist*; he became its editor in 1938, and put his first issue of the paper to press on the night of Munich. He held the editorship until March 1956—for a period longer than that of any of his important predecessors, including Walter Bagehot himself—saying (though few believed him) that he was then 'written out'. Crowther shared many of

Bagehot's qualities. His writing was succinct, uncomplicated, sparing of polysyllables, and always brightened by wit. He composed in a neat small hand, and with seemingly effortless facility, pellucid leading articles on questions of great inherent complication, and his envious colleagues on the paper tried as best they could to model their own style on his uncluttered prose. He thus inspired, though he never sought to impose, a quality of writing in *The Economist* which rapidly attracted readers, so that the circulation multiplied during his editorship from 10,000 to 55,000. As the paper grew in influence and resources, he attracted spirited people to join it, and he was one of the first newspaper editors to appoint distinguished women to his staff. Late in the war Crowther's concern for Anglo-American relations led him to introduce into the paper an American survey, which was intended to inform non-American readers about American affairs but which quickly became required reading for thousands of Americans, from presidents downwards. *The Economist* was indeed Crowther's monument, and under his editorship it became one of the most influential and most widely quoted papers in the world. In 1957 he was knighted for his services to journalism.

Crowther's editorship continued during the Second World War, although he was also heavily engaged in the Ministry of Supply (1940–41) and in the Ministry of Information (1941–2), and he became deputy head of the joint war production staff, Ministry of Production (1942–3). But business was beginning to attract him soon after the war. He succeeded Lord Layton as chairman of The Economist Newspaper Ltd, and remained in the chair until his death. For some time Crowther was deputy chairman of Commercial Union Assurance, and he was an important member of the team (including Commercial Union interests) that created the ambitious Trafalgar House property group, of which he later became chairman. Unfortunately it cannot be said that Crowther's achievements in business matched his outstanding successes at *The Economist*. He had the capacity for the highest responsibilities in national and international business, but his moral judgement was sorely tried in a number of companies of rather less importance. Crowther was impelled to leave Trafalgar House when it entered into the hotel business, with which he himself had been associated since 1944 as a director of Trust Houses. He created the British Printing Corporation by a merger of Hazell Sun, which he had joined in 1957, and Purnell, only to discover many things amiss on the Purnell side. Eighteen months later, in the summer of 1965, he had a bitter fight to remove the Purnell chairman from the board. Crowther had become chairman of Trust Houses in 1960 and worked hard to improve and expand its interests before the agreed merger with Forte Holdings in 1970. He then became head of the biggest hotel group in the country, but his hold on the chair of Trust Houses Forte in the ensuing year became increasingly precarious because of differences about policy and between personalities. His last despairing act was to support an offer by Allied Breweries to take over the company, but this was comfortably defeated and he and most of his former Trust

Houses colleagues resigned. Undoubtedly these bitter boardroom quarrels were a primary factor in his sudden death, on 5 February 1972, at Heathrow airport, just as he had returned from Australia.

Crowther never sought high public office, but his public service, particularly in education, was of the highest importance. Between 1956 and 1960 he was chairman of the Central Advisory Council for Education, which in 1959 recommended the raising of the school-leaving age to sixteen in what became known as the Crowther report. Between 1968 and 1971 he was chairman of the committee on consumer credit, which sought to modernize the law and practice of this phenomenally expanding business. Of the many governing bodies on which he sat he was perhaps proudest of becoming chancellor of the Open University in 1969. In that year he became chairman of the royal commission on the constitution (as well befitted Bagehot's successor), on which he was working when he died. He was created a life peer in June 1968. Seven honorary degrees were conferred upon him by English and American universities. He wrote in his early career several books on economic subjects, of which the most widely read was *An Outline of Money*, published in 1941. Crowther was of stocky build, with small hands and a dominating head well fitted to house his varied talents as economist, journalist, businessman, educationist, and reformer, working from what he would always call 'the extreme centre'.   ROLAND BIRD, *rev.*

Sources personal knowledge (1986) · private information (1986) · *The Times* (7 Feb 1972) · *The Times* (10 Feb 1972) · *The Times* (12 Feb 1972) · R. D. Edwards, *The pursuit of reason: The Economist, 1843–1993* (1993) · *CGPLA Eng. & Wales* (1972)

Archives NRA, priv. coll. | FILM BFI NFTVA, documentary footage | SOUND BL NSA, performance recording

Likenesses H. Coster, photograph, 1937, NPG [*see illus.*]

Wealth at death £423,940: probate, 22 June 1972, *CGPLA Eng. & Wales*

Crowther, James (1768–1847), botanist and porter, was born on 24 June 1768 in a cellar near the Wheat Sheaf inn, Deansgate, Manchester, the youngest of the seven children of Richard Crowther, a labourer, and his wife, Hannah. He attended three schools between the ages of six and nine before starting work as a draw-boy in petticoat weaving. For most of his working life he was employed as a porter, first in Salford, then in Manchester. His childhood interest in plants was encouraged by other working-men botanists and he began to attend their meetings, held in pubs, in order to acquire botanical knowledge. He had a strong love of nature and would often walk 20 miles at night in order to collect a particular plant, returning to work in the morning. On more extensive walks he discovered the lady's slipper orchid *Cypripedium calceolus* in Craven, Yorkshire, and the small mud-growing plant *Limosella aquatica* at Mere, Cheshire. His knowledge of the local flora was sought by John Hull and other gentlemen botanists.

Crowther formed close friendships with the artisan botanists John Dewhurst, George Caley and Edward Hobson.

His generosity in sharing information was widely acknowledged. As Leo Hartley Grindon recalled in *Manchester Walks and Wild-Flowers* ([1859]), he was a mainstay of pub botanical meetings, claiming that 'my specimens always look best through a glass!' (p. 126). For several years from 1829 he was a member of Hobson's Banksian Society, resuming his membership when this society became the natural history class of the Manchester Mechanics' Institution in 1836. Here, under the editorship of John Bland Wood, Crowther helped compile the *Flora Mancuniensis* (1840) together with Grindon, Richard Buxton, and George Crozier. Recalling this class in *Joseph Sidebotham: a Memoir* (1886), Grindon remembered 'weather-beaten old Crowther … whose deep-hued complexion always gave one the idea of a hard winter breaking up' (p. 11).

Crowther married about 1794 and raised six children. Following his wife's death in 1823 he lived first with a daughter in Salford, then with another daughter near Deansgate, Manchester. From the 1830s he suffered increasing destitution and was forced to sell his plant and insect specimens. On 1 October 1832, the Banksian Society resolved to allow him to attend meetings 'free of Expense'. He was saved from the workhouse by charitable donations from the Manchester botanist John Moore and others before becoming a recipient of a fund established by Edward William Binney in 1844 for 'the relief and encouragement of scientific men in humble life'. In attempts to encourage public support for such men a biographical account was obtained from Crowther, which Binney read at a meeting in Manchester town hall in 1843. This account was reprinted as part of Crowther's obituary in the *Manchester Guardian* (13 January 1847) and thereafter in various popular journals, thus establishing Crowther's life as an exemplar, in the genre of the 'pursuit of knowledge under difficulties'. Elizabeth Gaskell also borrowed from this account in the opening paragraphs of chapter five of her 1848 novel *Mary Barton*. However, the shoemaker and botanist Richard Buxton fondly recalled in his *Botanical Guide* (1849) that Crowther's 'heart was far superior to his head' (p. viii).

Crowther died at 17 Bridgewater Street, off Deansgate, on 6 January 1847. His funeral and gravestone (bearing a poetic tribute probably composed by his son Richard) were paid for by means of a £7 subscription, which critics argued would have better been spent in providing him with food and bedding in the last year of his life. Although a regular worshipper at St Matthew's, Deansgate, he had obtained permission several years before his death to be buried at St George's Church, Hulme, next to his closest friend, Edward Hobson, with whom he had spent his 'happiest hours'. He was buried there on 10 January 1847.

ANNE SECORD

Sources 'The late James Crowther, the naturalist', *Manchester Guardian* (13 Jan 1847) · 'Death of James Crowther, the Manchester botanist', *Manchester Guardian* (9 Jan 1847) · 'Old Crowther, the botanist', *Manchester Guardian* (16 Jan 1847) · R. Buxton, *A botanical guide to the flowering plants, ferns, mosses, and algae, found indigenous within sixteen miles of Manchester* (1849), viii–x · L. H. Grindon, *Manchester walks and wild-flowers: an introduction to the botany and rural beauty of the district* [1859], 126 · Banksian Society minutes, Man. CL, Manchester Archives and Local Studies, MS 590. 6. B3 · J. B. Wood and others, *Flora Mancuniensis* (1840) · [E. Gaskell], *Mary Barton: a tale of Manchester life*, 2 vols. (1848), chap. 5 · J. Cash, *Where there's a will there's a way! or, Science in the cottage* (1873), 11, 13, 77–89 · 'James Crowther, the naturalist', *Chambers' Edinburgh Journal*, new ser., 7 (1847), 215–17 · A. Secord, 'Science in the pub: artisan botanists in early nineteenth-century Lancashire', *History of Science*, 32 (1994), 269–315 · L. H. Grindon, *Joseph Sidebotham: a memoir* (1886), 11
Wealth at death destitute: *Manchester Guardian* (9 Jan 1847; 13 Jan 1847)

Crowther, Jonathan (1760–1824), Wesleyan Methodist minister, was appointed to the itinerant ministry by John Wesley in 1784. In 1787 Wesley sent him to Scotland at 50s. per annum; he reported that 'no man is fit for Inverness circuit, unless his flesh be brass, his bones iron, and his heart harder than a stoic's'. In 1789 Wesley empowered him to reduce to Wesleyan discipline the Glasgow Methodists, who had set up a session of ordained elders on the presbyterian model. From 1789 Crowther served on English circuits, except in 1792–3, when he was in Ireland. He was, in the period after Wesley's death in 1791, a fierce defender of the rights and privileges of itinerant ministers. He wrote two influential books in defence of the Wesleyan system, including his *Portraiture of Methodism* (1811), and a biography of Thomas Coke. Crowther was president of conference in 1819 and president of the Irish conference in 1820. For two years before his death he was paralysed. Crowther died at Warrington on 8 June 1824, leaving a wife and children, and was buried in the chapel yard at Halifax.

ALEXANDER GORDON, rev. TIM MACQUIBAN

Sources *Minutes of conference of Wesleyan Methodists* (1824) · W. Hill, *An alphabetical arrangement of all the Wesleyan Methodist preachers and missionaries*, 2nd edn (1824) · *Wesleyan Methodist Magazine*, 47 (1824), 500, 648
Likenesses W. Holl, stipple (after J. Jackson), BM; repro. in *Methodist Magazine* (1813)

Crowther, Jonathan (1794–1856), Wesleyan Methodist minister, was born at St Austell, Cornwall, on 31 July 1794. His father, Timothy Crowther, and his uncles, Richard and Jonathan *Crowther, were all Methodist preachers of Wesley's own appointment. He was educated at Kingswood School, Bath (1803–9), and began to preach when about the age of twenty. He was a master at Woodhouse Grove School, near Bradford, Yorkshire, and was briefly headmaster in 1816; he was appointed in 1823 headmaster of Kingswood School. There he was a byword for brutality and flogging. One of his pupils recalled that he inaugurated a system of 'harsh and cruel treatment which turned boys into devils, and made school a prison-house' (*Kingswood School*, 124). His regime resulted in strikes by his pupils, and in 1826 he was effectively dismissed. After this he was stationed from time to time in various Wesleyan circuits, and distinguished himself as a zealous defender of the principles and discipline of his denomination. In 1837 he was appointed general superintendent of the Wesleyan missions in India, and gave important services to this cause in Madras presidency. Returning to England in

1843 on account of impaired health, he was again employed in the home ministry. In 1849 he received the appointment of classical tutor in the Wesleyan Theological Institution at Didsbury, Lancashire. He was a respectable scholar and successful teacher. To the acquirements necessary for his chair he added a good knowledge of Hebrew and several modern languages. He acted as examiner at Wesley College, Sheffield, as well as at New Kingswood and Woodhouse Grove schools. To the periodical literature of his denomination he was a frequent contributor. His health failed some time before his death, and on 31 December 1855 he was seized with congestion of the brain while on a visit to the Revd William Willan at Leeds. In this friend's house he died on 16 January 1856, leaving a widow and family.   H. C. G. MATTHEW

Sources *Wesleyan Methodist Magazine*, 79 (1856), 191, 564, 846 · *The history of Kingswood School … by three old boys* (1898) · *DNB*
Likenesses T. A. Dean, stipple and line engraving (after J. Hill), NPG · portrait, repro. in *History of Kingswood School*

Crowther, Samuel Ajayi (*c.*1807–1891), bishop of western Africa and linguistic scholar, was born of Yoruba parents at Oshogun, in the south-west of Nigeria. Captured in war in 1821 he was sold on 7 April 1822 to a Portuguese slave ship in Lagos, but freed that evening by two Royal Navy ships. Also freed was a girl, later baptized Susanna, whom Crowther married about 1830, by which time she was a schoolmistress.

Taken to Freetown, Sierra Leone, he was cared for by missionaries of the Anglican Church Missionary Society (CMS) and quickly became literate in English. In 1825 he was baptized as Samuel Crowther, and the next year taken to England, where he attended Islington parish school. In 1827 he returned to Africa and became the first student to enrol in the new Fourah Bay College, where he was appointed tutor in 1834. His scholarly love was languages, and Freetown's liberated Africans were a living laboratory where many African tongues could be studied.

In 1841 Crowther was employed as interpreter for the ill-fated Niger expedition, which attempted to establish a model farm at Lokojo, at the confluence of the Niger and Benue, to demonstrate the benefits of 'Christianity, commerce and civilization'. There he formed a friendship with the German scholar J. F. Schön, with whom he wrote the account of the expedition published in 1843. The deaths of so many Europeans in the expedition appear to have convinced Crowther that Christianity could only be established in tropical Africa by Africans. The CMS in London, under the visionary Henry Venn, conceived the same idea. Crowther was called to London to train at the CMS Missionary College in Islington and was ordained by the bishop of London in 1843. He then joined the mission in Abeokuta, to preach and teach in Yoruba. There, by chance, he was reunited with his mother, whom he baptized in 1848.

With the publication of his dictionary and grammar of Yoruba in 1843 Crowther began to standardize Yoruba by fixing its orthography and spellings, inventing the system

Samuel Ajayi Crowther (*c.*1807–1891), by Ernest Edwards, *c.*1864

for expressing its tonality, and laying the foundation for its printed literature in his beautiful translations of the Book of Common Prayer and his Yoruba Bible. As he continued work in Yoruba Crowther pioneered studies of other Nigerian languages, using his experiences during the British Niger expeditions of 1854 and 1857, publishing a primer of Igbo in 1857, another for the Nupe language in 1860, and a full grammar and vocabulary of Nupe in 1864.

In 1851 he visited London and held meetings with Palmerston, Queen Victoria, and Prince Albert, urging assistance for Abeokuta and action against the anti-missionary ruler of Lagos (whom the British removed by force in 1852).

During the 1857 Niger expedition Crowther had established new stations in Onitsha and Igbebe, and planned further expansion northward. Venn, the CMS lay secretary, who wanted a self-sustaining 'native church' in west Africa, gave him sole authority over the Niger mission. After much delay, in 1864 Crowther was consecrated bishop of 'Western Africa beyond the limits of our dominions', in a curious arrangement which left the European clergy in Abeokuta and Lagos, who had refused to serve under an African, under the white bishop of Sierra Leone. Crowther thus presided over an all-African clergy in the Niger mission. This experiment with 'African agency' was a success. New stations were pushed into Muslim Nupe, but it was the Niger delta that saw the greatest expansion, with stations in all the main city states by the 1880s, and mass conversions in some, like Nembe. Crowther used his mission stations to demonstrate the 'new life' of Christians, with schools to influence the young towards Christianity, avoiding theological complexities. An astute diplomat, he built good relations with African rulers, both Muslim and animist.

Crowther's personal life was blameless; he was totally without ambition, a kindly, generous man. His chief weakness lay in judging others to be like himself, which made for poor discipline. The last years of his life were plagued by scandals among African clergy, which European lay missionaries exploited to argue that any African, by virtue of race, could not exercise authority responsibly. Inquiries showed that many charges were trivial or false, but a few were not, including one of murder by an African clergyman, whom Crowther had initially protected out of pity. The CMS in London continued to support Crowther, but the mission was increasingly placed under European oversight with white men as secretaries to the mission, exercising financial control. In 1889 a group of young, headstrong white zealots led by Graham Wilmot Brooke provoked a major crisis which darkened Crowther's last years. They were devotees of the Keswick movement, which stressed intense spirituality for missionaries and converts, and opposed Crowther's technique of conversion through education. They attacked the alleged luxury of mission buildings, demanding sale of the mission steamship, lower African salaries, and the resignation of Crowther, to be replaced with a white bishop. The CMS compromised by making Brooke leader of the Sudan party in the northern half of the Niger mission, outside the bishop's control. Once into the area the Brooke party made charge after charge, many frivolous, against African clergy. In August 1890 a crisis erupted when the white secretary of the finance committee overrode Crowther and suspended African clergy, including Archdeacon Dandeson Crowther, son of the bishop. The result was a rebellion of the Niger delta churches, which repudiated CMS control and declared themselves a self-governing pastorate within the Anglican communion. In the aftermath of this crisis Crowther, now in his eighties, suffered a stroke in July 1891, was moved to Lagos, and died there on 31 December 1891.   JOHN FLINT

Sources J. F. A. Ajayi, Christian missions in Nigeria, 1841–1891 (1965) • P. E. H. Hair, The early study of Nigerian languages (1967) • E. A. Ayandele, The missionary impact on modern Nigeria, 1842–1914 (1966) • E. A. Ayandele, Nigerian historical studies (1979) • C. P. Williams, The ideal of the self-governing church: a study in Victorian missionary strategy (1990) • T. E. Yates, Venn and Victorian bishops abroad: the missionary policies of Henry Venn and their repercussions upon the Anglican episcopate of the colonial period, 1841–1872 (1978) • A. N. Porter, 'Cambridge, Keswick, and late-nineteenth-century attitudes to Africa', Journal of Imperial and Commonwealth History, 5 (1976–7), 5–34 • A. N. Porter, 'Evangelical enthusiasm, missionary motivation, and west Africa in the late nineteenth century: the career of G. W. Brooke', Journal of Imperial and Commonwealth History, 6 (1977–8), 23–46 • A. N. Porter, 'The Hausa Association, the bishop of Dover, and the Niger in the 1890s', Journal of Imperial and Commonwealth History, 7 (1978–9), 149–79 • J. Page, The black bishop, Samuel Adjai Crowther (1900) • S. A. Crowther and J. F. Schön, Journal of an expedition up the Niger in 1841 (1843) • S. A. Crowther, Journal of an expedition up the Niger and the Tshada in 1854 (1855) • S. A. Crowther and J. C. Taylor, Journal of the Niger expedition of 1857 and missionary notices (1859)

Archives National Archives of Nigeria, Ibadan • U. Birm. L., Church Missionary Society archives, corresp. and journals
Likenesses E. Edwards, carte-de-visite, c.1864, NPG [see illus.] • photograph, repro. in Ayandele, Missionary impact, facing p. 237

Crowther-Hunt. For this title name see Hunt, Norman Crowther, Baron Crowther-Hunt (1920–1987).

Croxall, Rodney (1702–1754). See under Croxall, Samuel (1688/9–1752).

Croxall, Samuel (1688/9–1752), poet and Church of England clergyman, was baptized on 4 February 1689 at Walton-on-Thames, Surrey; his parents were Samuel Croxall (1655/6–1730), rector of Hanworth, Middlesex, and vicar of Walton-on-Thames, and Elizabeth, née Humfrey. The younger Samuel was the fourth of eleven children, four of whom died in infancy. He was educated at Eton College (1701–7), where he was elected a King's scholar on 4 August 1702, and at St John's College, Cambridge, where he was admitted as a sizar on 5 May 1708, aged nineteen; he graduated BA in 1712, MA in 1717, and DD in 1728. He was ordained in London diocese in 1712, instituted as rector of Bradenham, Norfolk, in 1713, appointed chaplain-in-ordinary at Hampton Court in 1715, and succeeded his father as vicar of Hampton-on-Thames, a crown living, on 9 October 1716. He retained both Hampton preferments until he died.

Croxall's first publications, in 1713 and 1714, were two anti-tory satires, purporting to be 'original cantos' of Spenser, and a welcoming ode on the arrival of George I: all three in pseudo-Spenserian language and versification. The first of these was attributed to an ancestor of Nestor Ironside (Steele's pen-name), so it was laid at Steele's door and fiercely attacked in Swift's Examiner. Croxall replied anonymously in a prose letter, The Examiner Examin'd (1713). More whig celebratory poems followed in 1715: one is addressed to the duke of Argyll on his victory at Sheriffmuir; the other, The Vision, addressed to the earl of Halifax, foresees a golden age under George I. Croxall's first published sermon, Incendiaries No Christians (1715), preached at St Paul's Cathedral, is a whiggish plea for moderation in religious disputes.

Croxall translated book 6 and parts of four other books in the version of Ovid's Metamorphoses (1717) edited by Samuel Garth: his contribution was second only to Dryden's in bulk. Croxall's version of part of the Song of Solomon, first printed in Steele's Miscellanies (1714), was expanded and published in 1720 as The Fair Circassian, a Dramatic Performance. This erotic poem is dedicated in fulsomely amorous terms to Anna Maria Mordaunt (d. 1803), niece of the earl of Peterborough, and, as a subterfuge, was attributed to an anonymous, now dead 'Gentleman-Commoner of Oxford'. The Fair Circassian was often republished and brought Croxall some notoriety, but did not check his clerical advancement. Among the shorter poems added to many later editions was the no less warm 'On Florinda, Seen while she was Bathing'. In 1718, at St James Piccadilly, Croxall married Philippa (d. 1745), daughter of Edward *Progers of Hampton, formerly

Samuel Croxall (1688/9–1752), by Clark & Pine, 1719 (after Bonawitz)

groom of the bedchamber to Charles II. It seems that the marriage was childless.

Between 1720 and 1722 Croxall edited for John Watts, the bookseller, *A Select Collection of Novels* in six volumes, comprising short stories mostly translated from French, Italian, and Spanish; the dedications, written by Croxall, were all to prominent ladies. *Fables of Aesop and Others* 'with applications and useful observations' (1722), dedicated to Lord Sunbury, son of the earl of Halifax, was a work of morality and whiggish politics which enjoyed reprints until well into the twentieth century and must be reckoned Croxall's most successful publication. It was one of the first books to influence the poet Robert Browning.

When Croxall's former Eton schoolfriend Henry Egerton, son of the earl of Bridgewater, was consecrated bishop of Hereford in Lambeth Palace chapel on 2 February 1724 Croxall preached the sermon. On 30 January 1730 he covertly attacked Walpole when he took Proverbs 25: 5 as the text for a sermon before the House of Commons in which he declared that kings should not screen wicked servants. The house snubbed Croxall by not thanking him or having his sermon printed; he was attacked in an absurd pamphlet, *Light in a Candlestick*, by John (Orator) Henley and in a polished anonymous verse satire, *Dr Croxall to Sir Robert Walpole*, which alleges that Croxall joined the opposition because Walpole would not give him a deanery or bishopric. It was expected that Croxall would lose his chaplaincy, 'but the court overruled it, as he had

always manifested himself to be a zealous friend to the Hanover Succession' (Kippis, 4.544).

Meanwhile Croxall's friendship with the bishop of Hereford was bearing fruit. He was collated to the Hereford prebend of Hinton on 7 August 1727; he exchanged it for Moreton Magna on 1 May 1730, which prebend he held to the end of his life. He was treasurer of the cathedral from 27 July 1731 to 1732 and chancellor from 22 April 1738 to his death. He was archdeacon of Shropshire from 1 July 1732 to 1738. He was a portionist (holder of a one-third share in the patronage) of the vicarage of Bromyard, Herefordshire, from 11 September 1739 to his death and a canon residentiary at Hereford from 24 March 1740, also to his death. Additionally the bishop presented him on 26 February 1731 to the rectory of the united parishes of St Mary Somerset and St Mary Mounthaw in the City of London. Croxall employed curates in his London and Middlesex livings and a deputy (from 1740) in the Hampton Court chaplaincy, all of which benefices he retained to his death. It seems that in his later years he lived mostly in Hereford, though he owned a house and other property in Crickhowell, Brecknockshire.

Though Kippis's report that Croxall 'chiefly governed' the diocese during the old age of Bishop Egerton (Kippis, 4.544) is an exaggeration, it seems that plural ecclesiastical duties left him little time for writing. His last substantial work was *Scripture Politics* (1735), a prose treatise on the political and social organization of the Israelites, as evidenced by the Old Testament. His last published sermon was *The Antiquity, Dignity, and Advantages of Music* (1741); it was preached in Hereford Cathedral on 2 September 1741, during the meeting of the three choirs of Worcester, Gloucester, and Hereford. Croxall died on 13 February 1752; he was buried in the north transept of the cathedral, but his gravestone is not now to be found. By his will, signed on 15 November 1751, a sizeable estate was left to his unmarried housekeeper, Hester Hooper, after small bequests to her relations. His wife had predeceased him; she was buried at St Mary's, Hampton, on 28 October 1745. *The Royal Manual*, a tame 'Happy the man' poem, wrongly attributed to Andrew Marvell on first publication in 1751, was included in a posthumous edition of *The Fair Circassian* (1765). The pseudo-Spenserian poem 'Colin's Mistake' attributed to Croxall by Nichols is in fact by Prior. Croxall's library was sold in 1756.

Rodney Croxall (1702–1754), Samuel's youngest sibling, was baptized on 16 November 1702 at Walton-on-Thames. He was a colleger at Eton (1713–21), where he was elected a King's scholar on 11 March 1714. He was, however, as his schoolmate Thomas Morell (1703–1784) recalled, a mere cipher, 'the very reverse of his brother *Sam*' (Nichols, *Lit. anecdotes*, 4.600). Rodney matriculated from Lincoln College, Oxford, on 18 December 1721, aged nineteen; he graduated BA at Oxford in 1725, and MA from King's College, Cambridge, in 1733. The date of his ordination is not known. On 19 February 1733 he married Elizabeth Baldwin at St Mary Somerset, London: his brother Samuel conducted the ceremony. It was a short marriage—ended, one assumes, by the wife's death, because what appears to be Rodney's first child, Anne, baptized on 11 August 1735 and buried three months later, was by his second wife, Ann, who bore him a second daughter, who also died in infancy, and shortly afterwards herself died; she was buried in Hereford Cathedral. In October 1738 Rodney married his third wife, Elizabeth Lane (b. 1718/19); they had a son, Samuel (1745–1768), and she died on 16 July 1787, aged sixty-eight. Like his brother, Rodney enjoyed patronage in the gift of the bishop and the dean and chapter of Hereford: he was vicar of Sellack from 1 March 1732, vicar of Madley and Tibberton from 15 May 1735, prebendary of Moreton Parva from 10 November 1732, and treasurer of the cathedral from 30 January 1745. He held all these preferments until his death on 9 May 1754; he was buried at Madley on 13 May.   JAMES SAMBROOK

Sources A. Kippis and others, eds., *Biographia Britannica, or, The lives of the most eminent persons who have flourished in Great Britain and Ireland*, 2nd edn, 4 (1789), 544–5 · Venn, *Alum. Cant.*, 1/1–4 · *Fasti Angl.* (Hardy), 1.484, 491, 494, 508, 516–17 · R. Shiels, *The lives of the poets of Great Britain and Ireland*, ed. T. Cibber, 5 (1753), 288–97 · J. Nichols, ed., *A select collection of poems*, 7 (1782), 345–6 · *GM*, 1st ser., 22 (1752), 92 · R. Steele, *The Englishman: a political journal*, ed. R. Blanchard (1955) · parish register, Walton-on-Thames, Surrey, 4 Feb 1689 and 16 Nov 1702 [baptism] · parish register, Madley, Herefordshire, 11 Aug 1735 [baptism] · private information (2004) [R. Caird, archivist, Hereford Cathedral] · G. Hennessy, *Novum repertorium ecclesiasticum parochiale Londinense, or, London diocesan clergy succession from the earliest time to the year 1898* (1898), 192, 197, 349 · Nichols, *Lit. anecdotes*, 3.655, 4.600, 7.295 · H. Ripley, *History and topography of Hampton-on-Thames* (1891) · D. Lysons, *An historical account of those parishes in the county of Middlesex which are not described in 'The environs of London'* (1800), 84, 87–8 · tablet in Madley church
Archives BL, letters to Jacob Tonson, Add. MS 28275, fols. 343, 491
Likenesses Clark & Pine, engraving, 1719 (after Bonawitz), NPG [see illus.] · engraving, repro. in G. Jacob, *Poetical register* (1725), 2
Wealth at death bequests of houses in Hereford and Crickhowell; also annuities of £44 p.a.; lump sum of £300; will · four houses in the parish of St Martin-in-the-Fields with combined rental value of £132 p.a.; Rodney Croxall: will

Croxley [Crokesley], **Richard of** (d. 1258), abbot of Westminster and royal counsellor, was probably a native of Croxley in Hertfordshire. He first appears as a monk of Westminster in the late 1230s, as the abbey's proctor to the papal curia. In 1242 he escorted a relic of the Virgin's girdle to the king and queen in Gascony, and thereafter, as the first recorded monastic archdeacon of Westminster, was given joint charge of the abbey's building operations. In 1242 he was himself building a chapel at Westminster. In 1244 he was sent as royal envoy to Scotland, and in February 1246 as envoy to France. Following the death of Abbot Richard of Barking on 1 December Croxley was elected abbot on 16 December 1246, apparently because of his perceived familiarity with the king. He is said to have been a great admirer of Archbishop Edmund of Canterbury (d. 1240), in whose honour he later constructed a chapel at Westminster Abbey. He is occasionally credited with the title 'master', generally reserved for graduates of the schools, and according to the chronicler Matthew Paris, was expert in both canon and civil law. As abbot he combined his responsibilities to the monastic community with service at the king's court, appearing as a baron of

the exchequer in 1249–51 and again in 1257–8, and serving as regular diplomatic envoy overseas. In 1247, for instance, he was sent to investigate the possibility of a marriage between the king's son Edward and a daughter of the duke of Brabant, and in 1257–8 he was in France for a parley with Louis IX (r. 1226–70). From 1252 onwards he had joint charge of the collection of subsidies for Henry III's proposed crusade, being appointed chief preacher of the crusade in the west country and Wales. He also acquired a supervisory role over the London house founded by the king for the reception of converts from Judaism.

Croxley's relations with the Westminster monks were punctuated by disputes over the appointment of monastic obedientiaries, the monks' food allowance, and the abbot's right to visit the monastic estates. But a journey to the papal court in 1251 led to the agreement of a final settlement with the monks in the following year, though according to Matthew Paris, Croxley was severely censured by the king, both for his attacks upon the monks of Westminster and for his acceptance of the title of papal chaplain from Innocent IV (r. 1243–54). Paris claims that Richard was deposed from the king's council, and that Henry forbade the citizens of London to lend him money to pursue his case before the pope. However, the chancery rolls continue to record a stream of royal gifts to the abbot, and in 1253 he was appointed to act as a counsellor to Queen Eleanor during the king's absence in Gascony. At Westminster he presided over the great campaign of rebuilding initiated under his predecessor, which was accompanied by the delivery to the abbey of a host of relics, vestments, and precious artefacts, for the most part gifts from the king. In 1247 Richard introduced the feast of the Annunciation of the Virgin Mary to Westminster, and he appears to have been the first to exercise a papal privilege by which the abbots of Westminster were allowed to bestow pontifical blessing during the celebration of mass, the king granting him a great pontifical ring for this purpose shortly after his election.

In 1258 Croxley is said to have abetted the king in an attempt to force the leading Benedictine monasteries to lend money for Henry's doomed bid for the throne of Sicily, the king pledging his crown and regalia to Westminster as surety for the repayment of a loan of more than 2000 marks. In July 1258 Croxley attended the reforming parliament at Winchester, having earlier been appointed one of the twelve royal counsellors who were to negotiate with the barons. But he fell ill there, according to some accounts as a result of poisoning, and died at or near Winchester on 17 or 18 July. He was buried in the chapel of St Edmund of Canterbury which he had founded at Westminster. His body was exhumed at least twice thereafter, being removed to the chapel of St Nicholas after the demolition of the chapel of St Edmund in the first half of the fifteenth century. His will included a lavish assignment of rents and manors for the celebration of his obit, reduced to a more modest scale in 1267.

NICHOLAS VINCENT

Sources Chancery records · E. H. Pearce, *The monks of Westminster* (1916) · E. Mason, J. Bray, and D. J. Murphy, eds., *Westminster Abbey charters, 1066–c.1214*, London RS, 25 (1988) · T. Madox, *The history and antiquities of the exchequer of the kings of England*, 2nd edn, 2 vols. (1769) · J. Flete, *The history of Westminster Abbey*, ed. J. A. Robinson (1909) · Paris, *Chron.* · B. Harvey, *Westminster Abbey and its estates in the middle ages* (1977) · G. Rosser, *Medieval Westminster, 1200–1540* (1989) · N. Vincent, *The holy blood: King Henry III and the Westminster blood relic* (2001)

Croxton, Thomas (c.1603–1666), parliamentarian army officer, was the son of George Croxton (d. in or before 1621) of Ravenscroft, Cheshire, and his wife, Judith, daughter of William Hassal of Burland (or Nantwich), Cheshire. Nothing is known of Thomas Croxton's education. He served in the Cheshire trained band in the years before the civil war.

Croxton was an active captain early in the war; his rise was sponsored by the Cheshire commander Sir William Brereton and he was a member of the Cheshire county committee as early as 21 March 1643. Croxton's appointment as deputy lieutenant in May 1644 was followed by his governorship of the parliamentarian headquarters at Nantwich, where he was prominent in the deliberations of the county committee. In July 1646 he was caught up in the disturbances of the Nantwich garrison, when the soldiers' discontent over arrears of pay erupted into a mutiny which targeted the excise and sequestrators. Croxton, who tried to prevent the trouble, was arrested by the mutineers.

Consistently styled colonel after December 1645, Croxton probably became field commander of Brereton's own foot regiment at this time. His radicalism propelled him to a colonelcy in 1648 when he commanded a foot regiment of 600 men under Colonel Robert Duckenfield, while in 1651 his regiment was present at the battle of Worcester. Continually finding favour in national radical circles, Croxton was appointed a militia commissioner for Cheshire in 1650 (re-affirmed in 1654–5) and was made a member of courts martial to try participants in Charles II's invasion of 1651, including that which tried and sentenced the earl of Derby on 1 October 1651.

There is no evidence that Croxton, very much a Brereton man in the 1640s, ever deviated from a pro-government stance in the 1650s. A JP between 1647 and 1659, he proved himself an assiduous supporter of the protectorate. In the 1656 election he was a candidate for the county seat on Cromwell's 'slate'. He was named to the committee for ejecting scandalous ministers in 1658 and revealed his radical credentials by tolerating the existence of sectaries in Cheshire (being one of only two magistrates who showed sympathy—albeit wavering in his case—towards a Ranter before the courts in 1652), though there is no evidence that he was himself a religious extremist. In the summer of 1659 Croxton was commander of Chester Castle when the city was seized during the Booth rising by the supporters of Charles II. He is said to have answered a summons to surrender the castle with the words,

> that as perfidiousness in him was detestable, so the castle which he kept for the parliament of England was disputable,

and if they would have it they must fight for it, for the best blood that ran in his veins in defence thereof should be as sluices to fill up the castle trenches. *(DNB)*

He defended his position against the insurgents for three weeks until relieved by General John Lambert. This action, which contributed to the rising's defeat, earned Croxton an award of £300 from parliament on 18 September 1659.

Croxton was unable to reconcile himself to the restoration of Charles II and in 1663 was arrested, along with Sir George Booth and Colonel Robert Duckenfield, on suspicion of involvement in a plot against the government. Croxton was released but was again the subject of an investigation on 9 November 1665 when he denied being privy to any plot against the government. Croxton, who married Elizabeth, daughter of Edward Holland of Denton, Lancashire, died in 1666. The inventory of the personal estate that he left, made on 16 November 1666, listed goods to the value of £384 17s.

MALCOLM GRATTON

Sources Greaves & Zaller, *BDBR* · *The letter books of Sir William Brereton*, ed. R. N. Dore, 2 vols., Lancashire and Cheshire RS, 123, 128 (1984–90) · J. S. Morrill, *Cheshire, 1630–1660: county government and society during the English revolution* (1974) · *DNB* · J. A. Atkinson, ed., *Tracts relating to the civil war in Cheshire, 1641–1659: including Sir George Booth's rising in that county*, Chetham Society, new ser., 65 (1909) · J. Morrill, 'Mutiny and discontent in English provincial armies, 1645–1647', *Past and Present*, 56 (1972), 49–74 · Thomas Croxton's inventory, 16 Nov 1666, Ches. & Chester ALSS, WS 1666 · *CSP dom.*, 1644–54 · G. J. Armytage and J. P. Rylands, eds., *Pedigrees made at the visitation of Cheshire, 1623*, Lancashire and Cheshire RS, 58 (1909), 69–70 · [H. Newcome], *The autobiography of Henry Newcome*, ed. R. Parkinson, 1, Chetham Society, 26 (1852)

Wealth at death £384 17s.: inventory, Ches. & Chester ALSS, WS 1666

Crozier, Eric John (1914–1994), opera producer and librettist, was born on 14 November 1914 in London, the son of John Crozier and his wife, Ethel Mary Wilson. Unhappy at University College School, Hampstead, Eric acquired his passion for drama at the local Everyman Theatre. The plays of Chekhov particularly attracted him. He trained at the Royal Academy of Dramatic Art (1932–4) and then gained a scholarship from the British Institute in Paris. While resident in France, he admired the amateur theatre of Henri Ghéon's *Les compagnons de jeux* and the stylized stagings of Jacques Copeau's *La compagnie des quinze*. However, an interest in experimental and poetic drama did not commend him to West End managements on his return to London in 1936. Thanks to the actor Stephen Haggard, who was a friend, Crozier secured employment producing plays for the new BBC television service based at the Alexandra Palace, Wood Green. His credits included *Once in a Lifetime* (6 December 1937), considered ambitious in its use of four sets and two studios. He married Ada Margaret Johns (b. 1914/15), an artist, on 3 July 1936; they had two daughters.

Crozier was a conscientious objector during the Second World War. After television closed down in 1939 he worked as assistant to Tyrone Guthrie, director of the Old Vic Company, then performing in Burnley, Lancashire,

Eric John Crozier (1914–1994), by Maria Austria, 1948 [left, with Benjamin Britten and Tyrone Guthrie, discussing *The Beggar's Opera*]

company with Crozier, Britten, and John Piper as artistic directors.

Librettist and composer seemed so inseparable at this time that some people mistakenly supposed Crozier to be homosexual (like Britten). He was indeed estranged from his wife, but he had fallen in love with Nancy *Evans (1915–2000), a mezzo-soprano with the EOG, married to the impresario Walter Legge. As soon as they were both divorced they married on 26 December 1949. Meanwhile, the Britten–Crozier partnership created the cantata *Saint Nicolas* (June 1948), and *Let's Make an Opera* (June 1949), incorporating *The Little Sweep*, an opera for children. Crozier also joined Britten in founding the Aldeburgh Festival of Music and the Arts, held annually in Suffolk from 1948.

Billy Budd—set aboard a warship in 1797 and first staged at the Royal Opera House, Covent Garden, on 1 December 1951—had a libretto written for Britten by Crozier and E. M. Forster; the former contributed mainly dialogue, while the latter handled longer narratives. Crozier then left the EOG, however, as his friendship with Britten was waning. The composer made a habit of dropping people, and Crozier was never thick-skinned. Short and narrow-shouldered, with a pointed nose and small chin, he aimed at perfection in personal relationships just as in his work and hated being taken for granted. He later suspected Britten of excluding his name from an authorized biography.

Alternating between a flat in Kensington and a cottage in Great Glemham, Suffolk, Crozier continued writing without attracting much further notice: his plays *The Gamblers* (1952) and *Rab the Rhymer* (1953) were followed by the libretto of *Ruth* (1956) for Lennox Berkeley, six opera translations for Sadler's Wells, three books on music for children, and a commonplace book for friends. His wife later taught (1973–90) at the Britten–Pears School of Advanced Musical Studies, which encouraged him to renew his connection with the Aldeburgh Festival. They both received OBEs in January 1991. Crozier died while on holiday at Granville, France, on 7 September 1994.

JASON TOMES

and wrote a few English adaptations of French drama. *Christmas in the Market Place*, based on a nativity play by Ghéon, was given at St Paul's Cathedral in December 1943. From early in 1942 Crozier was a stage director for Sadler's Wells Opera, presenting revivals at the New Theatre and Princes Theatre in London. His own production of *The Bartered Bride* by Smetana in November 1943, using a translation by himself and soprano Joan Cross, became a company staple. Its tenor lead, Peter Pears, introduced Crozier to composer Benjamin Britten, who consulted him about the theatrical aspects of *Peter Grimes*, his forthcoming opera. Crozier was invited to produce it at Sadler's Wells Theatre, although some in the company objected to the piece—partly because of the modernity of the music, but also because the composer, producer, lead singer (Pears), and conductor (Reginald Goodall) had all refused military service. The world première of *Peter Grimes* (7 June 1945) won instant recognition as a milestone in the history of British opera. Ill feeling nevertheless drove Crozier and Pears to leave Sadler's Wells in March 1946.

Crozier's life increasingly revolved around Britten and new operatic ventures. He suggested the subject of *The Rape of Lucretia* and less than a year later produced the work at Glyndebourne on 12 July 1946. After supervising the first American production of *Peter Grimes* at Tanglewood in August 1946 and supplying the text for *A Young Person's Guide to the Orchestra*, Crozier was delighted to be asked to write Britten's next libretto. He took as his starting point *Le rosier de Madame Husson* by Maupassant; a shift of setting from Normandy to Suffolk transformed it into *Albert Herring*, a comedy of small-town English life in 1900, in which a timid grocer rebels against his domineering mother. It opened at Glyndebourne on 20 June 1947, sung by the English Opera Group (EOG), a non-profit-making

Sources *The Times* (9 Sept 1994) · *Daily Telegraph* (9 Sept 1994) · *The Guardian* (8 Sept 1994) · *The Independent* (8 Sept 1994) · H. Carpenter, *Benjamin Britten* (1992) · *New Grove* · *The Guardian* (24 Aug 2000) [obituary of Nancy Evans] · *The Independent* (22 Aug 2000) [obituary of Nancy Evans] · M. Kennedy, *Britten* (1981) · J. P. Wearing, ed., *London stage, 1940–1949: a calendar of plays and players* (1991) · *Selected letters of E. M. Forster*, ed. M. Lago and P. Furbank, 2 (1985) · www.apts.org.uk [Alexandra Palace Television Society], 17 June 2002 · J. Law, 'Linking the past with the present: a conversation with Nancy Evans and Eric Crozier', *Opera Quarterly*, 3/1 (1985), 72–9 · M. Kennedy, *The Oxford dictionary of music*, 2nd edn (1994) · E. Crozier, *Christmas in the market place* (1945) · E. Crozier, *Albert Herring* (1947)
Archives Britten–Pears Library, The Red House, Aldeburgh, Suffolk, drafts of libretti · NRA, corresp.
Likenesses group portraits, photographs, 1947–9, repro. in Carpenter, *Benjamin Britten* · M. Austria, group portrait, photograph, 1948, NPG [*see illus.*] · group portraits, photographs, Hult. Arch.
Wealth at death £126,560: probate, 6 Jan 1995, *CGPLA Eng. & Wales*

Crozier, Francis Rawdon Moira (1796–1848), naval officer and polar explorer, was born on 17 September 1796 at Banbridge, co. Down, Ireland, the son of George Crozier (*d*. 1831), lawyer. He was the fifth son in the family and had at least two sisters. It seems probable that he was related to Francis Rawdon Hastings, earl of Moira. He entered the navy in 1810; served in the *Hamadryad* (34 guns) and *Briton* (44 guns, Captain Sir Thomas Staines); in the *Meander* (38 guns, captains John Bustard and Arthur Fanshaw), guardship in the Thames, and *Queen Charlotte* (104 guns, Sir Edward Thornborough), guardship at Portsmouth; passed his mate's examination in 1817, and in 1818 went to the Cape of Good Hope as mate of the sloop *Doterel* (18 guns, Captain James Gore). On his return to England in 1821 he was appointed to the *Fury*, discovery ship, Captain William Edward Parry. In the *Fury* and afterwards in the *Hecla* he accompanied Parry in his three Arctic voyages, 1821–7. His services were rewarded by a lieutenant's commission, dated 2 March 1826, and were marked when Parry named after him the Crozier River in 1823 and Point Crozier, overlooking Hecla Cove, in 1827.

From 1831 to 1835 Crozier served in the *Stag* on the coast of Portugal, and in December 1835 joined the *Cove*, commanded by Captain James Clark Ross, his shipmate in the *Fury* and the *Hecla*, and his close friend. Their correspondence sheds much light on Crozier's character and Crozier made his home with Ross in Blackheath, Kent, when in England, having none other of his own. The *Cove* made a summer voyage to Davis Strait and Baffin Bay in 1836, and on 10 January 1837 Crozier was promoted commander. On 11 May 1839 he was appointed to the *Terror*, in which he accompanied Captain Ross in his voyage to the Antarctic Ocean, from which they both happily returned in September 1843. Ross named Cape Crozier at the foot of Mount Terror after his friend on this expedition. Crozier had been advanced to post rank during his absence on 16 August 1841.

After a short tour of continental Europe, Crozier was on 8 March 1845 appointed to the *Terror* for Arctic exploration at the express request of Sir John Franklin who was to lead the expedition to discover the north-west passage. Franklin, like Parry and Ross, had a very high opinion of Crozier as an officer, a scientist (he was FRS and FRAS and made important scientific contributions to all the expeditions he went on), a polar explorer, and a companion. The two had met while Crozier was in the Antarctic and Franklin was lieutenant-governor of Van Diemen's Land. Crozier was a favourite in the Franklin household, but his love for Sophy Cracroft, Lady Franklin's niece by marriage and beloved companion, went unrequited. Crozier had himself been invited to lead the Arctic expedition but had declined with characteristic modesty, preferring to serve under Franklin.

The *Terror* and the *Erebus* sailed from England on 19 May 1845, but having been spotted by whalers at the head of Baffin Bay on 26 July no more was heard of them. Attempts first to relieve and then more realistically to discover the fate of the Franklin expedition dominated Arctic exploration for the rest of the nineteenth century and into the

Francis Rawdon Moira Crozier (1796–1848), by unknown photographer, 1845

late twentieth century. Although the ships were lavishly provisioned, it seems that both the quality and the quantity of the foodstuffs lay at the heart of the disaster. Autopsies carried out on bodies disinterred by Beattie in the 1980s revealed strikingly high levels of lead in the men's hair which, because the hair grows quickly, were attributable only to the effects of the voyage. It seems that canned food, hailed as a breakthrough for Arctic travel, caused the poisoning because of the lead solder used to seal the tins. The very abundance of the food might then have contributed to the men's deaths since the more they ate, the worse they became. Lead poisoning would have caused physical and mental degeneration and perhaps accounts for some apparently erratic behaviour on the part of the men. There were also signs of scurvy, which could be attributed to the facts that vitamin C deteriorates in cold weather, so their abundant supplies of lemon juice (4200 kg) were not efficacious, and that no fresh meat was eaten. Beattie's conclusions (1987) would explain the very high levels of death (nine officers and fifteen men) early on, even before the ships were abandoned, and the particularly high death rate among officers, who might have eaten more of the tinned food.

After Franklin's death on 11 June 1847 Crozier took command. The summer weather was particularly severe and the ice which had beset the ships since 12 September 1846 did not thaw. Crozier ordered the men to construct sledges and small boats so that the following season they could go in search of fresh meat. On 22 April 1848 the 105 surviving officers and men abandoned the ships. This was very early in the season and suggests that they were by this time desperate. It seems certain that provisions were low (faulty soldering might have resulted in much of the tinned food's rotting) and scurvy was becoming very severe. The men set off in a weakened condition wearing only cloth garments, no skins or furs having been supplied. Their boots wore out quickly on the rough ice. Their inappropriate dress and their emaciated condition and damaged gums were the cause of particular remark by Inuit who met them. They reached King William Island on 25 April 1848 (a spot later named Crozier's Landing by McClintock) and a note in Crozier's hand stated their intention of heading the following day for Back's Fish River which was reputedly abundant in game. They moved down the coast of King William Island, dividing at Terror Bay where hospital tents were set up to house those too weak to go on. The last known stopping place was, appropriately enough, Starvation Cove on the Adelaide peninsula. A point on the western edge of the island where skeletons were discovered by McClintock was named Cape Crozier. It is not certain where along the route Crozier himself died. There are some Inuit traditions that Agluukkaq, as he was known, survived until late on but it is very difficult to know how much weight should be placed on such accounts. Efforts such as that by Fluhmann (1976) to exonerate him from the charges of cannibalism levied against members of the expedition are impossible to substantiate. Some western commentators attribute to him the discovery of the north-west passage in the last stages of the expedition, though others credit Franklin with this.

A memorial to Crozier and the other officers was erected by McClintock at the site of Franklin's first winter quarters on Beechey Island. At Banbridge, Crozier's birthplace, the Crozier memorial, a full length statue towering over stone polar bears, and a memorial tablet in the church record his tragic death.   Elizabeth Baigent

Sources M. Fluhmann, *Second in command: a biography of Captain Francis Crozier, RN, FRS, FRAS* (1976) · *A memoir of the late Captain Francis Rawdon Moira Crozier RN, FRS, FRAS of HMS Terror* (1859) · O. Beattie, *Frozen in time: the fate of the Franklin expedition* (1987) · F. L. McClintock, *A narrative of the discovery of the fate of Sir John Franklin* (1859)

Archives Admiralty Library, London, log and proceedings of HMS *Terror* · NMM, Naval Historical library · RGS, papers | Scott Polar RI, letters in the Lefroy bequest · Scott Polar RI, letters to J. C. Ross

Likenesses T. Bock, 1840, Hobart Museum, Tasmania · photograph, 1845, NMM [*see illus.*] · Kirk, medallion, 1862, Seapatrick Museum, Banbridge, co. Down; repro. in Fluhmann, *Second in command*, facing p. 80 · Kirk, statue, 1862, Seapatrick church, Banbridge, co. Down; repro. in Fluhmann, *Second in command*, introduction · miniature, RGS · monument, Waterloo Place, London

Crozier, William Percival (1879–1944), journalist, was born at Stanhope, co. Durham, on 1 August 1879, the youngest son of the Revd Richard Crozier, a Wesleyan Methodist minister, and his wife, Elizabeth Hallimond. He was educated at Manchester grammar school and at Trinity College, Oxford, where he held a scholarship and obtained firsts in classical moderations (1900) and *literae humaniores* (1902). A year teaching at Knaresborough persuaded him that he was not cut out to be a schoolmaster.

Diverted to journalism, he joined *The Times* for a few months, and then the *Manchester Guardian* (1903). He made an impression immediately with his sharply critical analysis of the case for tariff reform. Sooner than most he won his editor's confidence and became C. P. Scott's right-hand man in charge of news gathering and the newspaper's make-up. In 1906 Crozier married Gladys Florence, daughter of George Frederick Baker, draper and furnisher, of Maidstone. They had one son and two daughters.

Years before he became editor, Crozier reorganized the foreign news service; dramatically increased the use of photographic illustrations and maps; even succeeded in introducing classification. He encouraged new features, though some, like the women's page (1922), with more reluctance than others. He encouraged contributions on a wide range of sporting activity, while the arts columns gave critical coverage to the cinema (or kinema, as Scott preferred) and broadcasting. In 1929 he introduced the daily crossword. It was due to Crozier more than any other that 'the *Manchester Guardian* was transformed from a provincial organ of opinion into a national newspaper pre-eminent also for its news' (Taylor, xix–xx).

With his friend and older colleague Herbert Sidebotham Crozier shared a devotion and commitment to Zionism. He became the leading advocate in the daily press of a Jewish national home. His Zionism was 'a secular but profound fulfilment of his strongly scriptural imagination' (Ayerst, 383). He succeeded Sidebotham as news editor in 1912, and in 1918 as military critic. This last he undertook, as all his tasks, with thoroughness and energy, but he lacked his predecessor's flair. In 1919 he was offered, but declined, the editorship of the *Daily News*. Determined not to repeat the earlier mistake that had cost him Sidebotham's services, Scott made Crozier a member of the *Manchester Guardian*'s board. Ted Scott's tragic accidental death in April 1932 sundered the dynastic succession, and Crozier was appointed editor. His choice seemed to offer some guarantee of continuity for he had served a long and faithful apprenticeship to C. P. Scott. As chairman of the board, John Scott ensured that the tradition of editorial precedence and independence was respected and maintained.

As editor, Crozier remained to an extraordinary extent what he had always been, 'a working journalist of something approaching genius' (Wadsworth, 232). He was distinguished by the close control he exercised over the paper. He frequently contributed leaders. His own style of writing was clear and precise. He persistently, if gently, censured the use of jargon and verbiage, extolling the virtues of writing that was 'simple, direct, lucid, concise and brief … the best and most effective English for newspaper purposes' (Ayerst, 197). He was as dedicated a Liberal as C. P. Scott, but Westminster was neither a favoured nor a familiar milieu. He was saved from engagement in debilitating domestic political disputes by an overwhelmingly more important issue of foreign politics. His editorship spanned the dozen years from Hitler's assumption of power to the last months before the allied invasion of Europe. No other English editor was better informed about the true nature of German national socialism. His reserved, sceptical manner masked his passionate loathing for the cruelties perpetrated by the Nazi regime. As foreign editor he had always been unduly possessive about foreign news, to the considerable irritation and exasperation of his correspondents. Now he considered it no less than his duty personally and persistently to expose the Nazis. Although he frequently asserted the contrary, he was reluctant to surrender any part of his crusade even though it undermined his frail health. He was not stopped by a perforated ulcer in 1936, any more than by the diagnosis, in 1943, of his ultimately fatal heart condition. He worked to the end.

A father's over-zealous Methodism had induced in Crozier a reluctant agnosticism. Nevertheless, the scholar-journalist maintained his biblical and classical studies. They informed the two works of historical fiction he wrote in the scanty leisure time he allowed himself: *Letters of Pontius Pilate* (1928), and the posthumously published *The Fates are Laughing* (1945). He contributed a fascinating character sketch of C. P. Scott to J. L. Hammond's biography of the editor whose name is synonymous with the *Manchester Guardian* (1934). Crozier died at his home, 23 Anson Road, Victoria Park, Manchester, on 16 April 1944. He was survived by his wife.   A. J. A. MORRIS

Sources *Manchester Guardian* (17 April 1944) · *Manchester Guardian* (18 April 1944) · *The Times* (17 April 1944) · W. P. Crozier, *Off the record: political interviews, 1933–1943*, ed. A. J. P. Taylor (1973) · D. Ayerst, *Guardian: biography of a newspaper* (1971) · [A. P. Wadsworth], ed., *C. P. Scott, 1846–1932: the making of the Manchester Guardian* (1946) · S. E. Koss, *The rise and fall of the political press in Britain*, 2 (1984) · DNB · CGPLA Eng. & Wales (1944)
Archives JRL, *Manchester Guardian* archives, corresp. and papers, mainly as editor of the *Manchester Guardian* · JRL, accounts of interviews with statesmen and politicians | Bodl. Oxf., J. L. Hammond MSS · Bodl. Oxf., letters to J. L. Howard · Bodl. Oxf., corresp. with Gilbert Murray · NL Wales, corresp. with Thomas Jones
Likenesses photograph, repro. in Wadsworth, ed., *C. P. Scott*, facing p. 160 · photograph, repro. in Ayerst, *Guardian*, facing p. 433
Wealth at death £6381 19s. 6d.: probate, 9 Sept 1944, CGPLA Eng. & Wales

Cruchley, George Frederick (1796–1880), map publisher, was born in 1796. Nothing more is known of his parentage or early life save that he described himself in his early days as 'from Arrowsmith's', having presumably been apprenticed to the celebrated Aaron Arrowsmith, the elder. In 1823 Cruchley established his own firm at 349 Oxford Street, London. In 1825 it moved to 38 Ludgate Street and in 1833 to 81 Fleet Street where it remained until its dissolution in 1877.

Initially Cruchley concentrated on publishing clear, attractive plans of London which he promoted energetically. Many were republished many times, with revisions and extensions, in varying formats, sometimes with additional information, notably about railways and postal districts. From 1826 he created a fine series of London plans which was represented at the Great Exhibition of 1851. Their popularity is shown by their frequent re-edition and

longevity. His maps of London's environs, such as *Cruchley's Environs of London Extending Thirty Miles from the Metropolis* (issued from 1824), were superior in some respects to the Ordnance Survey's one-inch sheets: for example in differentiating grades of roads and footpaths; noting distances from London; listing fairs, markets, and watermen's fares; and by their more frequent revision. He was one of the last major map publishers to undertake private estate mapping, but no examples of his estate maps are known to survive. The quality of his work resulted in his being commissioned from the late 1820s to engrave plans for official reports on railway proposals.

From the mid-1830s, however, Cruchley progressively abandoned the high standards for which his apprenticeship had prepared him and of which his early work showed him amply capable. The turning point can perhaps be traced to his 1836 revision and reissue of Christopher Greenwood's 1818 map of Lancashire. Such ready profits were to be had from making minor alterations to existing maps and publishing them as allegedly new works that Cruchley began assiduously to buy up or acquire for issue the stock of others, notably the plates of George and John Cary, acquired some time between 1846 and c.1850. His only significant updating of the Cary maps was the frequently inaccurate addition of railways and telegraphs. This was typical of his growing practice of issuing maps of doubtful reliability created from old plates using cheap lithographic transfer techniques. The Cary maps and others were also adapted to appeal to the growing market for touring and excursion maps. They were sold widely at bookstalls and railway stations and Cruchley promoted them vigorously by advertising, by offering them in different portable formats, coloured or uncoloured and by mail order, by producing special exhibition issues, and even printing them on silk or as handkerchiefs.

Cruchley extended his output through the republication of earlier atlases, such as *Outlines of the World* (1843), first published by Arrowsmiths in 1825. Some of these general atlases were aimed at the growing educational market and he boasted that his educational maps were used by the royal children. He also recognized a growing commercial market and supplied maps to merchants and traders and to institutions such as public libraries. On 16 January 1877 Cruchley's stock was sold at auction by Hodgson's whose sale catalogue revealed the high proportion of his plates which had been acquired from others. Much of the stock was bought by Gall and Inglis who continued to issue some, notably the Cary maps, until well into the twentieth century. Cruchley had lived at 12 Penn Road Villas, London, while still in business, but retired to 65 Grand Parade, Brighton, where he died on 16 June 1880. It is likely that he remained unmarried since a nephew, Alfred Frederick King, was left to execute his will, proved at the surprisingly small sum of under £2000.

Cruchley began his career by producing high-quality maps, mainly of the London area, but soon saw the opportunities for supplying an expanding market which demanded neither quality nor reliability but only cheapness. In exploiting this demand Cruchley pioneered vigorous and innovative marketing techniques later imitated by competitors. DAVID SMITH

Sources D. Smith, 'George Frederick Cruchley, 1796–1880', *Map Collector*, 49 (1989), 16–22 • J. Howgego, *Printed maps of London, circa 1553–1850*, 2nd edn (1978) • R. Hyde, *Printed maps of Victorian London, 1851–1900* (1975) • D. Smith, *Antique maps of the British Isles* (1982) • D. Smith, *Victorian maps of the British Isles* (1985) • D. Smith, 'The Cary family', *Map Collector*, 43 (1988), 40–47 • D. Smith, 'Gall & Inglis, c.1810–c.1910', *Map Collector* • CGPLA Eng. & Wales (1880) • Boase, *Mod. Eng. biog.*

Wealth at death under £2000: probate, 17 July 1880, CGPLA Eng. & Wales

Crudelius [*née* McLean], **Mary** (1839–1877), promoter of women's education, was born on 23 February 1839 at Henry Street, Bury, Lancashire, the eldest daughter of William McLean, a draper, and his wife, Mary, *née* Alexander. Both her parents were Scottish, with roots in Dumfriesshire. Brought up in relatively easy circumstances, she was well educated, latterly attending Miss Turnbull's Boarding-School for Young Ladies in Edinburgh in the late 1850s. She made the acquaintance of her future husband, Rudolph Wilhelm Crudelius, a German wool merchant of the firm of Crudelius, Hirst & Co., Leith, at the home of family friends in Leith during school holidays. She later married him on 24 September 1861. Residing at a house called Chapelside in the Trinity area of Edinburgh and later in Inverleith Terrace, Edinburgh, she had two daughters, Maud and Mary.

Although Mary Crudelius never kept in good health, her early married life was not limited to domestic affairs. The origins of her interest in the two key women's issues of the Victorian era, namely suffrage and education, are not clear but her commitment to these causes was uncompromising and lasted her lifetime. Perhaps her personality gave her this degree of commitment. She was described as someone of wisdom and intellect, a 'woman with a mission' (Burton, 13). Although tactful, she was also noted for her 'frankness of speech', perhaps unusual for her generation. She had a practical outlook, although she noted in correspondence that she had never organized anything, apart from in her role as Sunday school teacher. Correspondence was her strength and for her an all-consuming activity. Her husband was frequently away from home on business matters and the volume of correspondence between them was frequent and lengthy; in this she expressed many views and thoughts on a diverse range of subjects, including religion, suffrage, politics, and music. She was later to use this skill as her main strength. The evidence of this correspondence suggests eloquence, liveliness, and a keen sense of contemporary issues. Indeed she was proud to be one of the first 1500 women to petition parliament in 1866 on the question of women's suffrage, but she realized the difficulties of following the two campaign paths of education and politics.

Interest in women's suffrage was the catalyst for Mary Crudelius's support of the issue of higher education of women. In 1860 Edinburgh University had set up a local

examination scheme, opening it to girls in 1865. At Glasgow, Aberdeen, and St Andrews as well as Edinburgh moves were afoot to set up classes or educational associations for women. One of the first occasions Mary Crudelius spoke out publicly in favour of women's education was during her attendance at a meeting of a small but élite ladies' discussion group in Edinburgh's New Town, called the Edinburgh Essay Society, in 1867. Shortly after this meeting, along with several other ladies, including Mrs Mair, her daughter Miss Sarah Mair, Mrs Daniell, and Mrs Ranken, she called a meeting at Mrs Daniell's house, Inverleith Terrace, Edinburgh, to discuss the formation of a ladies' educational association. The ladies set up the Edinburgh Ladies' Educational Association (ELEA) in October 1867, after much discussion and planning, supported by a group of professors sympathetic to the idea of higher education. Mary Crudelius's aim was to see the 'throwing open of the University to us, not the organising of a special college for women' (Burton, 81). She wanted equal opportunities not separate learning, and remained adamant in this aim. The association was run by women for women with the specific aim of holding classes based on the curricula of the arts faculty and to university standard.

The constitution of the association allowed honorary members to include men. Mary Crudelius looked on Professor David Masson of Edinburgh University as the ELEA's mentor and chief supporter. The association ran its first lecture series in January 1868, Masson being the first to lecture in a course on the history of English literature. Over 400 women attended the opening lecture and 250 enrolled for Masson's course, which attracted the serious student as well as the 'fashionable' element. The association went on, over the next ten years, to run a regular series of classes taught by professors from the university, adding subjects as they became more established. The running of the association and its success were due mainly to Mary Crudelius, who guided the association through these early years. There were internal disputes and signs of dissension but Mary Crudelius effectively mediated, and her opinion was deferred to in committee meetings, despite suggestions of personal prejudice against her on account of her commercial background and foreign name. She realized the importance of running the association in such a way as to provide no cause for criticism from those who were suspicious of women's higher education. For this reason she opposed proposals for co-educational classes.

The association distanced itself from the campaign of the medical women, under the leadership of Sophia Jex-Blake, to secure admission to Edinburgh University, fearing that this would alienate support among the university professors. Controversy, however, did arise publicly in December 1871 when Mary Crudelius was involved in terse correspondence with Sir Alexander Grant, principal of Edinburgh University, over the issue of awarding certificates to women and the interpretation of statements made in the university court. Letters to the press followed from Grant and Masson. Misunderstandings seem to have arisen in the senatus, university court, and in the ELEA over the question of when and how the university would examine the ELEA women. The matter blew over and Edinburgh University gave the final official university recognition to the association in 1872, awarding a certificate in arts for women. Mary Crudelius regarded this compromise as a significant move towards her aim of co-equality of provision and examination, though full admission to university degrees remained her ultimate goal.

Until 1877 Mary Crudelius was at the helm as secretary of the ELEA. She described her own leadership as 'a sort of despotism but it has been the force of enthusiasm, and not of wilfulness' (Burton, 171). During much of this ten-year period she suffered frequent bouts of ill health, which meant her temporary absence from Edinburgh to visit health spas and healthier climates. She resigned as secretary temporarily in February 1872 and returned in October 1875. Her health failed to recover and she died of brain disease at her home, 14 Inverleith Terrace, Edinburgh, on 24 July 1877.

Mary Crudelius did not live to see the fulfilment of her efforts. In 1877 the association changed its name to the Edinburgh Association for the University Education of Women, which reflected the changing attitude to women's higher education; she would have been proud to see the names of her two daughters, Maud and Mary, in the class lists of the association in 1881–2. The Universities (Scotland) Act (1889) and subsequent ordinances opened the Scottish universities to women from 1892. The Crudelius name lived on for a while in the naming of the Crudelius bursary and in the opening of a hall of residence called Crudelius Hall, which later closed when the main hall of residence for women, Masson Hall, at Edinburgh University was opened in 1897. SHEILA HAMILTON

Sources M. M. Crudelius, *A memoir of Mrs Crudelius*, ed. K. Burton (privately printed, Edinburgh, 1879) · L. M. Rae, *Ladies in debate, being a history of the Ladies' Edinburgh Debating Society, 1865–1935* (1936) · U. Edin. L., special collections division, Edinburgh Association for the University Education of Women MSS, GEN 1877 · S. Hamilton, 'Women and the Scottish universities, *circa* 1869–1939: a social history', PhD diss., U. Edin., 1987 · S. Hamilton, 'The first generations of university women, 1869–1930', *Four centuries: Edinburgh University life, 1583–1983*, ed. G. Donaldson (1983), 99–115 · E. J. B. Watson, *Edinburgh Association for the University Education of Women, 1867–1967* (1967) · B. W. Welsh, *After the dawn: a record of the pioneer work in Edinburgh for the higher education of women* (1939) · b. cert. · d. cert.

Archives U. Edin. L., special collections division, Edinburgh Association for the University Education of Women, letters, GEN 1877

Likenesses photograph, repro. in Watson, *Edinburgh Association*, frontispiece

Cruden, Alexander (1699–1770), biblical scholar and eccentric, was born in Aberdeen on 31 May 1699, the second of eleven children of William Cruden (*d.* 1739), a prominent merchant and bailie in the city, and his wife, Isabel Pyper (*d.* 1740). He was educated in Aberdeen at the grammar school and at Marischal College, where he took the degree of master of arts. He also attended divinity lectures with the apparent intention of entering the ministry of the Church of Scotland. However, a disappointment

Alexander Cruden (1699–1770), by Thomas Trotter, pubd 1785 (after Thomas Frye)

in love, where an Aberdeen minister's daughter not only failed to respond to his attentions but was subsequently disgraced through becoming pregnant by her brother, appears to have unhinged him. He was confined to the tolbooth for about a fortnight, there being no more suitable asylum at that time, in November 1720. He subsequently left Aberdeen for London and returned only once, at the end of his life. In London he lived as a private tutor and then in 1726 he began work as a proof-corrector.

In 1729 the prospect of employment as a reader in French to the earl of Derby, through Mr Maddox, chaplain to the bishop of Chichester, led Cruden to visit the earl's Sussex residence at Halnaker. Cruden failed to find favour, apparently on the grounds of his inadequate grasp of pronunciation, but his eccentricity was probably already apparent. It certainly became so thereafter for he felt that he had been deceived and mistreated, and he channelled his indignation into a long series of letters to the earl, assuring him of his improved grasp of French. A personal audience was sought and Cruden travelled to Knowsley with this in view. He was repeatedly turned away but once contrived to gain access to Lord Derby, only to be removed before he had the interview that he sought. At some point (though the date is unclear) Cruden appears to have worked as a tutor in the Isle of Man, which suggests that Derby may have found some employment for him.

By 1732 Cruden was back in London as a proof-corrector and bookseller at the Royal Exchange, and in 1733 he began work on his celebrated *Complete Concordance to the Holy Scriptures*. In 1735 he received a royal warrant and now styled himself 'The Queen's Bookseller'. The *Concordance* was finished and a copy presented to Queen Caroline in November 1737, only days before her death. The demise of his royal patron and financial difficulties attending the production of the *Concordance* contributed to Cruden's mental deterioration. He paid unwelcome attentions to a widow, Mrs Pain, and was subsequently confined in Mr Wright's private madhouse in Bethnal Green in March 1738. He remained there for over nine weeks, chained to his bed, until he escaped. He was determined to take action against those whom he held responsible for his incarceration and publicized his case in a pamphlet, *The London Citizen Exceedingly Injured*. But his attempts to pursue a lawsuit came to nothing, possibly on account of the fact that he conducted the ensuing court case himself.

Returning to the business of proof correction Cruden lived quietly until in September 1753 he became involved in a street brawl at Southampton Buildings. It was his habit to intervene in such public altercations to calm the situation but on this occasion he became more actively involved in a battle of about an hour's duration. A young man with a shovel swore in front of Cruden, 'which so greatly offended him that, contrary to his usual custom, he took his shovel and corrected him with some severity' (A. Cruden, *The Adventures of Alexander the Corrector*, 3 pts, 1754–5, 1.5). At his sister's instigation he now endured a seventeen-day confinement at Inskip's Asylum in Chelsea. His indignation led him to suggest to his sister that she should endure forty-eight hours of imprisonment in Newgate as atonement for her action. Her reluctance prompted him to bring a suit for damages against her and three others but his resort to law was no more successful than on the previous occasion. His account of ill usage in Chelsea appeared as *The Adventures of Alexander the Corrector* (1754), of which two further parts were published. The title is explained by the connection Cruden made in his mind between his work as a corrector of proofs and the greater work that he felt was then required, that of a corrector of public morals. It was a role for which he felt himself not merely suited but divinely intended. However, it seemed only proper that such a corrector should be backed by the authority of king and parliament and he published an address to them on the topic. He referred to his experiences in Bethnal Green and Chelsea but argued that it was the way of providence to cast down before exalting and that, just as it had been with Joseph, son of Jacob, so it would be with Alexander, son of William. Cruden also considered that his status would be enhanced by the award of a knighthood and that he might be better placed to reform the nation's morals were he to stand as a parliamentary candidate for the City of London, but nothing came of these initiatives. An idea of what a pest Cruden could be was given in his own words when he commended the civility of Lord Poulett at St James's Palace, 'for being goutish in his feet he could not run away from the Corrector, as others were apt to do' (ibid., 3.12).

On his release from Chelsea, Cruden formed a new emotional attachment, though without first making the lady's acquaintance. Elizabeth Abney, the daughter of Sir Thomas Abney of Newington (1640–1722), lord mayor of London, lived in comfortable circumstances. Cruden conceived the idea that she was the Corrector's predestined partner but her reluctance to entertain him or to respond to his flood of letters resulted in Alexander the Corrector becoming Alexander the Conqueror, delivering a formal declaration of war to his Princess Elizabetha in July 1754. Cruden was fond at this time of using military imagery and he gave her home the emblematic name of Silesia, which he now besieged. Even flight from London was not a wholly adequate response, for Cruden waged his campaign with the single-mindedness of the true fanatic, though with a predictable lack of success. With the exception of Miss Abney most people by this time were prepared to accept Cruden's eccentricities and to see them as amusing rather than alarming. He was well received in Oxford and Cambridge during a tour in his self-appointed role of corrector in 1755, his particular concern being that of sabbath observance. He picked up on the signs of the times in *The Corrector's Earnest Address to the Inhabitants of Great-Britain* (1756), citing the Lisbon earthquake and other events as indicative of the need for a reformation of morals.

A second, revised edition of the *Concordance* appeared in 1761 and Cruden produced a third in 1769; these revised editions ensured that his work remained the most authoritative of its kind until well into the next century. In 1763 he became aware of the case of a young seaman, Richard Potter, who was facing death for the offence of claiming the prize-money belonging to another man, which in the event he did not even receive. Shocked at the severity of the sentence and convinced that Potter was guilty of no more than naivety, Cruden befriended Potter and secured, through characteristic persistence, the commutation of his sentence to one of transportation. He published the story of the case as *The History of Richard Potter* (1763). Another preoccupation in his later years was antipathy towards John Wilkes. Cruden would efface the chalked letters of 'no 45' with a piece of sponge that he carried with him for the purpose, as well as removing any other offensive scribblings encountered on his journeys.

In 1769 Cruden finally returned to Aberdeen, where he gave a public lecture and remained for about a year. On his return to London he lodged in Camden Street, Islington, where he was found dead on the morning of 1 November 1770. His preference was apparently for burial in the churchyard of St Nicholas's, Aberdeen, but he was interred instead in the dissenters' burial-ground at Deadman's Place, Southwark.

In religion Cruden remained true to his Calvinist upbringing and was for many years an attender at Dr John Guyse's Independent meeting. While seldom less than eccentric and sometimes undeniably mad Cruden was nevertheless respected for the benefits that others derived from the *Concordance*. Perhaps it required someone of Cruden's mental narrowness and indefatigable working habits to produce such a work. While often revised and updated by others over the years it is still recognized as essentially the work of one man.

LIONEL ALEXANDER RITCHIE

Sources E. Olivier, *The eccentric life of Alexander Cruden* (1934) · A. Kippis and others, eds., *Biographia Britannica, or, The lives of the most eminent persons who have flourished in Great Britain and Ireland*, 2nd edn, 4 (1789), 619–24 · A. Chalmers, 'Life of the author', in A. Cruden, *A complete concordance to the holy scriptures*, 5th edn (1805) · J. Nelson, *The history, topography and antiquities of the parish of St Mary Islington* (1811), 392–400
Archives BL, letters | Bodl. Oxf., letters to the earl of Derby, MS Rawl. C 793 [copy made by Cruden]
Likenesses T. Cook, engraving (after drawing by R. Fry), AM Oxf.; repro. in Olivier, *Eccentric life* · T. Frye, portrait, repro. in Cruden, *Complete concordance* · T. Trotter, line engraving (after T. Frye), BM, NPG; repro. in A. Cruden, *Concordance* (1785) [*see illus.*]

Cruden, Harry (1895–1967), builder and contractor, was born on 16 August 1895 at 19 Frithwick Street, Fraserburgh, Aberdeenshire, Scotland, the son of Lewis Cruden, fish curer, and his wife, Margaret Smith. He was educated in Fraserburgh and served a three year apprenticeship as an engineering draughtsman with a local firm. In 1914 he volunteered for the Gordon Highlanders, and served with them before being commissioned and transferred to the King's African rifles in Kenya. After the war he stayed in Kenya, working as a coffee planter, and later lived and worked in China until his return to Scotland in the late 1930s. There he worked in the timber trade, in a business in Musselburgh, near Edinburgh, owned by his wife, Clara Madelaine Buck (*d.* 1965). During the Second World War the firm made ammunition boxes.

In 1943 the Crudens converted their business into a limited company, Crudens Ltd. Cruden saw that Scotland's post-war housing needs could only be met by using non-traditional building techniques and materials, and he worked with a team of draughtsmen and engineers on the design of a prefabricated house which could be produced quickly and cheaply after the war. The Cruden house, steel-framed, with walls made of concrete slabs and roofs of concrete tiles, and all its internal components prefabricated, was approved by the Department of Health for Scotland in 1946. The department had guaranteed that a fixed number of houses would be contracted for by the local authorities: some were built directly by contractors while others were constructed by the Scottish Special Housing Association. Cruden formed an association with several leading Scottish building firms, Cruden Houses Ltd, and each firm was responsible for building Cruden houses in its own area. By 1954 13,000 Cruden houses had been built, and more than 25,000 by 1960.

Cruden retired as managing director of Crudens in 1957, and became chairman. Under the new managing director, M. R. A. Mathews, Crudens moved into the construction of prefabricated steel units for factories, garages, hospitals, schools, and churches, and also made pre-cut timber components. The firm began to contract for large public projects in Scotland, and was involved in the construction of housing developments in Edinburgh and Glasgow, shopping centres such as Sauchiehall Street in Glasgow, hospitals, including Ninewalls Hospital in Dundee, and other public buildings such as the David Hume tower at Edinburgh University. Crudens became one of the largest building and civil engineering firms in Scotland.

Cruden and his wife donated most of their shareholdings in the firm to charity, setting up the Cruden Trust, which became the Cruden Foundation in 1964. This supported public and educational projects in Scotland. By 1967 the foundation held 249,985 of the company's 250,000 shares. Harry Cruden died of cancer at his home, Kingswood, King's Road, Longniddry, East Lothian, on 1 March 1967 and was cremated at Mortonhall crematorium, Edinburgh, three days later.

ANNE PIMLOTT BAKER

Sources DSBB · *The Scotsman* (3 March 1967) · b. cert.
Likenesses photograph, repro. in *DSBB*, vol 1, p. 139
Wealth at death £180,208 6s.: probate, 24 April 1967, NA Scot., SC 40/40/70/415–18

Cruden, William (1726–1785), Church of Scotland minister, was the son of Alexander Cruden, beadle at Pitsligo. He graduated MA from Marischal College, Aberdeen, in 1743 and married Clementina Hadden, the first of their four children being born in 1749. He became minister of Logie-Pert, near Montrose, in 1753 and while there published *Hymns on a Variety of Divine Subjects* (1761) and *Nature Spiritualised, in a Variety of Poems* (1766). In 1773 he was elected minister of the Scottish Presbyterian church in Crown Court, Covent Garden, London, in succession to Thomas Oswald. He died on 5 November 1785 and was buried in London at Bunhill Fields cemetery. In 1787 there appeared his *Sermons on Evangelical and Practical Subjects*, published by his widow, and in 1800 Robert Carr Blackenbury brought out a revised and enlarged collection of his hymns as *Divine Hymns Composed Originally by Mr William Cruden*.

THOMPSON COOPER, *rev.* MARY CATHERINE MORAN

Sources W. Wilson, *The history and antiquities of the dissenting churches and meeting houses in London, Westminster and Southwark*, 4 vols. (1808–14) · *Fasti Scot.* · *N&Q*, 2nd ser., 3 (1857), 447, 516 · J. A. Jones, ed., *Bunhill memorials* (1849)
Archives BL, Add. MS 28518a, nos. 1710, 1711
Likenesses T. Trotter, line engraving (after D. Allen), repro. in W. Cruden, *Sermons on evangelical and practical subjects* (1787), frontispiece

Cruft, Charles Alfred (1852–1938), founder of Crufts Dog Show, was born on 28 June 1852, the son of Charles Cruft, jeweller and goldsmith of Hunter Street, Brunswick Square, Bloomsbury, London. He was educated at Ardingly College, Sussex, one of the Church of England schools founded by Nathaniel Woodard. At the age of fourteen he left school and worked for his father for a short period, at the same time studying an evening course at Birkbeck College, London. He embarked on a career as an office boy for James Spratt, an enterprising immigrant from Canada who in 1860 had established his own firm, Spratt's Patent Ltd, in order to manufacture and market his own Meal Fibrine dog cakes. Spratt was immediately impressed with Cruft's enthusiasm and enterprise; he liked to relate how at the initial interview Cruft exhibited the confidence and prescience which was to become his hallmark in later life. Cruft quickly persuaded his employer to allow him to go out soliciting orders from

Charles Alfred
Cruft (1852–1938),
by unknown
photographer, 1931

shooting estates. Spratt's firm prospered and moved to new premises at 28 High Holborn, London, with Cruft by the age of twenty-six managing the office and sales department. He became instrumental in promoting the foundation of canine societies, by which Spratts benefited from improved standards of feeding and management.

In 1878 Cruft was placed in charge of the dog section of the Paris Exhibition, which was an overwhelming success. This led to his receiving invitations to act as manager of the livestock sections of the Brussels and Antwerp exhibitions. For several years he was show manager for the Scottish Kennel Club and the poultry section of the Royal Agricultural Society. In 1886 he accepted a suggestion made by the duchess of Newcastle that there was room for another dog show in London. His first show, held on 10 March 1886 at the Old Royal Aquarium in Westminster, was described in the catalogue as 'the first great show of all kinds of terriers' and attracted 570 entries. Its success can be attributed in part to Cruft's use of the aristocratic patronage of General Lord Alfred Paget and Major-General Julius Raines, among others. The popularity of the show led to its relocation to the central hall, Holborn; it came to be commonly known as 'Cruft's Show', even though its organizer continued to use the grander title, the Great Terrier Show. In 1890 it was extended to include several breeds of toy dogs, which had by this time become popular ornaments for the Victorian upper classes, and in the following year Cruft decided to open it to all breeds, with the Royal Agricultural Hall, Islington, as its venue. The number of entries by this time is credited with exceeding 1200. In 1893 the tsar of Russia exhibited a team of eighteen borzois and the show's prestigious reputation led Queen Victoria to exhibit her dogs there on several occasions.

During the early years at the new venue Cruft's annual show was eulogized by the popular press. The reality was, however, rather different. The newly established Kennel Club, with its professional standards of conduct, was uneasy about shows run by private individuals for their own commercial ends. Cruft, an autocratic manager, had, however, surrounded himself with a carefully selected committee, including a number of members of the Kennel Club, who would endorse his wishes. According to specialist dog magazines his show did not command universal respect among the many exhibitors and did not always constitute a top-class exhibition of quality dogs. These criticisms had little influence on Cruft, who sold space to trade stands and advertisements in the dog catalogue to generate personal income. During this period he experimented briefly with a cat show which failed to live up to his commercial expectations. By the outbreak of the First World War, the show was widely regarded as the foremost of its kind in the world, with entries amounting to 4200 in 1914. Its royal patronage continued with George V's exhibiting his first labrador there in 1916. The show was closed in 1917 owing to the requisitioning of the Agricultural Hall by the military and did not open again until 1921 because of the post-war rabies outbreak which imposed restrictions on the public exhibition of dogs; during the inter-war period, the number of entries rose to an all-time peak of 10,650 in the year of its golden jubilee in 1936.

Cruft was a shrewd, independent, and successful businessman, whose name was synonymous with the show. His remarkable flair for attracting publicity for his event led to his being hailed as the 'British Barnum'. Another factor to which the show's success was sometimes attributed was Cruft's ability to forestall attempts by cliques to influence the appointment of judges. Less sympathetic interpretations emphasize how he managed to mobilize public support to his own ends. His negotiations with the owners of the Royal Agricultural Hall were crucial, in that they enabled him to have a monopoly of the facilities as a dog show, precluding the Kennel Club from leasing the most prestigious venue in the capital. According to conventional wisdom, he was very receptive to new ideas and numerous breeds of dogs made their first appearance at his show. In practice, he had a cavalier attitude to the rules, and attracted attention by providing classes for obscure breeds which generated public interest far out of proportion to their actual numbers. It did not matter if classes had few entrants, because the prize money was automatically reduced when the size of a particular class fell below a profitable level. He also manipulated the catalogue numbering system, deleting consecutive numbers between classes in order to inflate the apparent grand total of dogs entered at his shows. For example, in the 1901 catalogue, the number of entries was specified as 2203, whereas the actual number of dogs was 1572, some 28 per cent less. He was an astute salesman who capitalized on events, after the death of George V staging what he hailed as the Great Coronation Show. Nevertheless, he established what became in his lifetime a famous British institution, which continued to prosper long after his death and which retains his name (although the apostrophe in Cruft's was dropped in 1974).

Cruft maintained a discreet veil over his private life. In 1878 he married Charlotte Hutchinson, the daughter of an Islington carpenter; they had four children. Following Charlotte's death, he married, on 4 October 1894, Emma

Isabel Hartshorn (1866/7–1950), daughter of Samuel Hartshorn, law stationer; there were no children of the second marriage. Cruft's hobby was sailing, in which he indulged during the summer months when work on the dog shows was minimal. Although his son Cecil assisted him in running many of the dog shows in the inter-war period, Cruft became estranged from most of his family. He died at his London home, 12 Highbury Grove, Highbury, on 10 September 1938, leaving most of his considerable fortune to his second wife and one of his daughters. He was buried in Highgate cemetery. His unfinished book, *Charles Cruft's Dog Book*, was eventually published in 1952 as a result of the efforts of his brother-in-law's son, who, following the death of Emma Cruft in 1950, had inherited the right to any royalties from sales of the text.   JOHN MARTIN

Sources F. Jackson, *Crufts: the official history* (1990) · *The Times* (12–15 Sept 1938) · E. Cruft, *Mrs Charles Cruft's famous dog book* (1949) · C. Cruft, *Charles Cruft's dog book* (1952) · 'The man who made dogs', *Our Dogs* (16 Sept 1938) · m. cert. · d. cert. · admission records, Ardingly College
Archives Kennel Club, London | FILM BFI NFTVA | SOUND BL NSA
Likenesses photograph, 1931, Kennel Club Library [*see illus.*] · photograph, repro. in Jackson, *Crufts*, 25
Wealth at death £26,226 9s. 3d.: probate, 8 Nov 1938, CGPLA Eng. & Wales

Cruger, Henry (1739–1827), merchant and politician, was born in New York city on 22 November 1739, one of four sons of Henry Cruger (d. 1780), merchant and member of the New York assembly and council, and his wife, Elizabeth Harris. The Cruger family belonged to an Atlantic community of traders, centred in Bristol, England, with commercial links in North America and the West Indies. The first of the family to settle in North America was Cruger's grandfather John Cruger, who reached New York in 1698 and, in what was to become the family pattern, combined a successful merchant career with involvement in local politics. His son John (1710–1791), as mayor of New York between 1756 and 1765, is known for having twice averted conflict in the city over imperial issues, and was a delegate to the Stamp Act congress of 1765. Henry Cruger's eldest brother, John Harris Cruger, followed in his father's footsteps, becoming a member of the governor's council in 1773. Two other brothers, Nicholas and Telemon, were in the West India trade; Nicholas had a counting-house in St Croix. Henry Cruger himself was educated at King's College in New York, whence his father removed him in 1757 and sent him to receive commercial training in the counting-house of Henry Cruger & Co. in Bristol.

Cruger married, in December 1765, Hannah (d. 1767), the daughter of Bristol merchant Samuel Peach. Through his father-in-law he gained connections with the local radical movement. He was a member of the Bristol common council from the year following his marriage until 1790 and he was a sheriff of the city in 1766–7. In 1766 he went to London with a delegation of Bristol merchants to urge repeal of the Stamp Act. After 1768 Peach and Cruger were among the leaders of an independent society that petitioned against the Middlesex election and endorsed the

radical principle of the right of electors to instruct their members of parliament. Cruger's radical connections earned him a reputation as a 'hot Wilkite', in the words of the prime minister, Lord North (Underdown, 16), and probably ensured that his candidature for parliament had been informally agreed upon by his political associates by 1772.

Cruger is best known as one of only three mainland American colonists to be elected a member of parliament during the late colonial period. The election of 1774, which was overshadowed by the growing crisis with America, was also one that saw both Cruger and Edmund Burke standing in opposition to the incumbent pro-ministerial members for Bristol. Burke had been viewed by Cruger's radical supporters in 1774 as an appropriate second because it was felt that he could attract moderate votes. Nevertheless Burke and Cruger were unlikely political associates, who had clear differences both of principle and temperament. Although some co-operation took place between their respective committees and among their supporters the two did not stand together. In the event Cruger was returned as head of the poll, with Burke in second place. Cruger's acceptance speech, in which he affirmed his support for the right of electors to instruct their members, prompted Burke's famous response setting forth his traditional views on the duty of MPs to rely on their own judgement.

Cruger took his seat in parliament in the wake of the Coercive Acts of 1774, which had triggered a renewal of political conflict between Britain and her North American colonies. Cruger's moderate attitude to the American crisis reflects his Anglo-American origins and Atlantic perspective. As a member of parliament he was determined to dispel his image as a radical, writing that 'the whole House shall be undeceived if a moderate and modest speech can affect it' (Van Schaack, *Henry Cruger*, 13). His motive was to win the ears of the ministers in order to influence them to take a more conciliatory approach to the burgeoning conflict with the colonies. In his first speech he struck a middle road, warning that coercion would only serve to alienate the affections of the colonists and suggesting that parliament should adopt a constitutional line that would secure colonial liberties while maintaining the supremacy of the British legislature. In subsequent debate he lost his temper defending the colonists from Colonel Grant's charge of cowardice; once hostilities began, however, he wrote that the colonists would be 'utterly undone' if they did not make immediate concessions (Dartmouth MS D (W) 1778.lii.1144). He was disappointed by the terms of Lord North's conciliatory proposal, and by June 1775 he confessed that he had despaired of influencing the ministry to adopt more moderate measures.

Five months later, through the intervention of Sir William Meredith, Lord North met Cruger to consult on the crisis. North was exploring the prospect of a commission to the colonies in order to forestall prolonged war. The Cruger family was influential in the strategically important colony of New York, and the British government had secretly been monitoring Henry Cruger's correspondence with his family since early 1775. The interview of November comprehended Cruger's father, who in 1775 had left New York to join his son in Bristol. Father and son urged that a delegation of pro-American politicians be sent to the colonies to resolve Anglo-American differences, but nothing came of their suggestion. As hostilities escalated Cruger continued to oppose both the war and American independence. He supported Lord Chatham's policies over those of the Rockinghams. In late 1777 he supported Wilkes's motion for repeal of the Declaratory Act, and the following year he issued handbills reprinting Lord Chatham's speech to the House of Lords of 20 January 1775. It was not until 1780 that he spoke openly in support of American independence as the only means of ending the war.

Cruger failed in his bid for re-election to parliament in 1780, in part because of his persisting rivalry with Edmund Burke. His supporters, however, secured his election as mayor of Bristol in the following year. He stood again as member for Bristol, as a supporter of William Pitt, in 1784, this time successfully. His campaign was assisted by his eldest brother, John Harris Cruger, who by now was living in England as a loyalist exile. Cruger himself was in America during the campaign, attempting to re-establish trade links there; he had experienced difficulties in gathering his American debts in the years before the war and the conflict itself had done irreparable damage to his merchant business. Unable to restore his fortunes, in 1789 he attempted, through Pitt, to obtain an appointment as British consul in the United States.

Cruger's subsequent career reflects the Atlantic character of his connections and outlook, and the ambiguous nature of his loyalties in an era of Anglo-American conflict. His bid for a consular appointment in America having failed, he declared in the following year that he did not intend to stand again as MP for Bristol. In 1790, while still formally a member of parliament, he departed for New York, taking with him his second wife, Elizabeth Blair, who died that same year. There, two years later, he was elected to the New York state senate, despite opposition protests that, as one who had resided in England and taken oaths as a British government official throughout the war, he was not an American citizen. On the American side of his family, however, he could claim an unimpeachable patriot association in the form of his brother Nicholas, who had fought with the American forces during the war and was a friend of George Washington.

Cruger resided in New York city for the remainder of his life. After serving in the senate, he retired from business and lived privately. With his second wife he had had a daughter; in 1799 he married his third wife, Caroline Smith, with whom he had four more children. Samuel Peach Cruger, his only child by his first wife, did not accompany his father to New York; he remained in Bristol and subsequently changed his name to that of his maternal grandfather, Samuel Peach. Henry Cruger died in New York city on 24 April 1827, and was survived by his third wife.   JULIE M. FLAVELL

Sources H. C. Van Schaack, *Henry Cruger: the colleague of Edmund Burke in the British parliament* (1859) · P. T. Underdown, 'Henry Cruger and Edmund Burke: colleagues and rivals at the Bristol election of 1774', *William and Mary Quarterly*, 15 (1958), 14–34 · J. Brooke, 'Cruger, Henry', HoP, *Commons, 1754–90* · Staffs. RO, Dartmouth MSS · PRO, Colonial Office papers, CO5/134 · H. C. Van Schaack, 'Diary and memoranda of Henry Cruger: conversations with Edmund Burke and Lord North, 1775', *Magazine of American History*, 7 (1881), 358–63 · J. M. Flavell, 'Government interception of letters from America and the quest for colonial opinion in 1775', *William and Mary Quarterly*, 58 (2001), 403–30 · K. Morgan, *Bristol and the Atlantic trade in the eighteenth century* (1993) · E. A. Jones, *American members of the inns of court* (1924) · *Proceedings and debates of the British parliaments respecting North America, 1754–1783*, ed. R. C. Simmons and P. D. G. Thomas, 5, June 1774–March 1775 (New York, 1986)
Archives Col. U., Van Schaack family MSS · Harvard U., Palfrey family papers · New England Historical and Genealogical Society, Boston, Hancock collection · New York Historical Society, Horatio Gates MSS · PRO, Colonial Office papers, intercepted letters, CO5/134 · Staffs. RO, Dartmouth MSS

Cruickshank, Andrew John Maxton (1907–1988), actor, was born on 25 December 1907 at 1A Castlehill, Aberdeen, the son of Andrew Cruickshank, a hall porter, and his wife, Ann Morrison Cadger, a stocking knitter. Cruickshank was educated at Aberdeen grammar school, which he left with the intention of becoming a civil engineer. He had been drawn to the theatre, however, and, having found his way into provincial repertory, spent eighteen months there before his London début in 1930, when he had a non-speaking part in the Paul Robeson *Othello*. Thereafter he built a career which encompassed both classical drama and less demanding West End fare. He performed in both Britain and America, notably in *Lysistrata* in 1936 at the Gate in London, and in a Shakespearian season at the Old Vic from 1937 to 1940, where he played a range of parts including Banquo to Laurence Olivier's Macbeth. He was one of the cast that performed John Gielgud's *Hamlet* at Elsinore in Denmark. After a first marriage to Stella Bickerton in 1934, which ended tragically the same year when she died of meningitis while pregnant, on 12 August 1939 Cruickshank married another actress, (Martha) Curigwen Lewis. They had one son and two daughters; one daughter, Marty, followed her father into the acting profession.

During the Second World War Cruickshank served in the Royal Welch Fusiliers, rising to the rank of major. He was appointed MBE in 1945. After the war he played Wolsey, Kent, and Julius Caesar at Stratford in 1950. In London he appeared in a variety of plays including Frederick Knott's *Dial M for Murder* (1952), Jerome Lawrence and Robert E. Lee's *Inherit the Wind* (1960), Felicity Douglas and Henry Cecil's *Alibi for a Judge* (1965), and William Douglas-Home's *Lloyd George Knew my Father* (1973). He straddled with ease the two worlds of commercial theatre and art theatre: as far as the latter was concerned, he had a particular affinity for Ibsen, and performed with distinction in several of his major works, including *The Master Builder* (1963), *When We Dead Awaken* (1975), and *The Wild Duck* (1980). Cruickshank continued to move happily from one sphere to the other until the end of his career: he was at the National Theatre from 1978 to 1980, appeared in a

Andrew John Maxton Cruickshank (1907–1988), by Jon Lyons, 1969

sustained Scottish characterization of his career. It was one which generated an enormous surge of popular affection both in Scotland and beyond. The series was later reprised on radio with the same cast, but to much less effect.

Cruickshank wrote a number of books on philosophical and religious matters, which he felt deserved rather more serious attention than they were given. At the height of his fame as Dr Cameron he appeared on a number of occasions on the airwaves discussing the work of the Danish philosopher Søren Kierkegaard. His autobiography, published posthumously, alternates constantly between accounts of his professional activities, and meditations driven by a desire to apprehend 'the harmony of all things' (Cruickshank, 77). Although latterly he described himself as a 'protestant Anglican', in religion—and in politics—Cruickshank was an individualist and a freethinker rather than an orthodox believer.

DAVID HUTCHISON

Sources *The Times* (30 April 1988) · *Glasgow Herald* (30 April 1988) · *The Scotsman* (30 April 1988) · A. Cruickshank, *Andrew Cruickshank: an autobiography* (1988) · *WWW*, 1981–90 · L. Halliwell and P. Purser, *Halliwell's television companion*, 2nd edn (1982) · d. cert. · I. Herbert, ed., *Who's who in the theatre*, 16th edn (1977) · b. cert. · m. cert. · *CGPLA Eng. & Wales* (1988)
Archives FILM BFI NFTVA, performance footage |SOUND BL NSA, Bow dialogues, 15 Feb 1966 · BL NSA, Bow dialogues, 31 May 1966 · BL NSA, Bow dialogues, 9 May 1967, C 812/17 C1 · BL NSA, performance recordings
Likenesses G. Anthony, photograph, 1938, Hult. Arch. · G. Anthony, photograph, 1938 (with Victoria Turleigh), Hult. Arch. · J. Lyons, photograph, 1969, Rex Features Ltd, London [*see illus.*] · photograph, 1979, Hult. Arch. · R. Hutchings, photograph, 1985, Hult. Arch. · photographs, Mander and Mitchenson collection; repro. in Cruickshank, *Autobiography*
Wealth at death £70,797: probate, 24 Oct 1988, *CGPLA Eng. & Wales*

revival of Sir David Lindsay's (or Lyndsay's) *The Thrie Estatis*, at the Edinburgh Festival in 1984, and in 1987 he was in the West End production of Jeffrey Archer's *Beyond Reasonable Doubt*. Cruickshank was taken ill during the run of this play and died of bronchopneumonia and heart failure on 29 April 1988 in Westminster Hospital, London.

Andrew Cruickshank learned his trade in the English theatre, but observers of his performances were rarely in any doubt as to his Scottishness, which manifested itself in mannerisms, and in the inflections of his voice, which owed not a little to the pulpit. Cruickshank himself commented 'There is a greater toughness in Scottish acting than I could find in my English colleagues' (Cruickshank, 101). However by the time he came to prominence with television audiences, he had acquired a genial, if crusty, benignity that belied a darker side of his professional persona. That could be seen in several of his stage performances, particularly in his Ibsen roles. *Dr Finlay's Casebook* (1962–71), a BBC television series based on stories by A. J. Cronin, teamed Cruickshank as the older and wiser Dr Cameron with the enthusiastic but much brasher Dr Finlay (Bill Simpson). Together, with the help of their housekeeper, Janet (Barbara Mullen), they ministered to the medical—and often non-medical—needs of a pre-Second World War Scottish small town. In the course of over 150 episodes, Cruickshank was able to offer the most

Cruickshank, Helen Burness (1886–1975), poet, was born on 15 May 1886 in a staff house at Sunnyside Mental Hospital, Hillside, Forfarshire, the youngest of the three children of George Cruickshank (1845–1924), a hospital attendant at Sunnyside, and his wife, Sarah (1850–1940), a domestic servant, daughter of Colin Gibb Wood, master plumber, of Montrose. She had a happy country childhood and later attributed her facility for writing in Scots to her upbringing in Forfarshire, the home of a rich and natural dialect. Annual family holidays in Glenesk gave her a taste for walking and climbing that she later pursued on long trips in the highlands and islands.

Cruickshank was educated at Hillside village school, which she entered at the early age of four, and at Montrose Academy, where she won prizes in every subject. Since her father was unable to afford university fees she left school at fifteen, and entered the civil service in 1903. Cruickshank remained a civil servant for over forty years—until her retirement, on medical grounds, at the end of 1944—holding various clerical and administrative posts, first in London and later in Edinburgh, where she was for many years an executive officer for the Department of Health in Scotland. While in London she was active in promoting better pay for women and women's

Helen Burness Cruickshank (1886–1975), by Vincent Butler, 1969

striking if not conventionally beautiful woman, with an 'astringent and sometimes bawdy' sense of humour (Lochhead), she maintained a busy social life in spite of the demands of work and home and, later, health problems. Invited to a cocktail party at a time when retirement had seriously reduced her income, she found a scarlet pram-cover in the village shop, converted it into a stole, and wore it over a slim, black dress. 'I was told it looked smashing' (Cruickshank, 125).

Cruickshank is particularly remembered for her hospitality at Dinnieduff, where she kept open house for the writers of the Scottish literary renaissance movement of the 1920s and 1930s, including such major figures as Hugh MacDiarmid and the novelist Lewis Grassic Gibbon. She has been called 'a catalyst of the Scottish Renaissance' and a 'handmaid of the Scottish muse'. Yet she disliked such patronizing terms, including 'poetess', and they undervalue her contribution to Scottish literature.

After her mother's death Cruickshank lived alone, and in spite of deteriorating health was able to remain in her own home until the age of eighty-eight. On medical advice she moved into an Edinburgh nursing home—Queensberry Lodge, 105 Holyrood Road—in November 1974, and died there on 2 March 1975. A cremation service, which she had herself planned in detail, was held at Warriston, Edinburgh.　MOIRA BURGESS

Sources H. B. Cruickshank, *Octobiography* (1976) · M. Lochhead, *The Scotsman* (4 March 1975) · J. K. A. [J. K. Annand], 'In memoriam HBC', *Lallans*, 5 (1975) · *The Scotsman* (4 March 1975)
Archives NL Scot., corresp. and papers · U. Edin. L., corresp. and papers · University of Stirling, corresp. | NL Scot., corresp. with Duncan Glen · NL Scot., letters to N. M. Gunn · NL Scot., letters to F. M. McNeill · NL Scot., letters to Mrs Ray Mitchell · NL Scot., letters to William Soutar · U. Edin. L., letters to Gordon Wright · U. St Andr. L., letters to M. F. Mitchie
Likenesses photograph, 1934, repro. in Cruickshank, *Octobiography*, 104 · V. Butler, bust, 1969, Scottish Poetry Library, Edinburgh [*see illus.*] · photographs, repro. in Cruickshank, *Octobiography*

suffrage. She moved to Edinburgh in 1912 and began to write poetry about this time. In 1921 she acquired a studio flat, where for a few years she enjoyed a pleasantly bohemian life, beginning to publish her poetry and developing her interest in the arts. She never married but two love affairs (the partners are not named) are cited in her memoirs as the inspiration for two of her best-known poems, 'There was a Sang' and 'Shy Geordie'.

On her father's death, in 1924, it was assumed that Cruickshank, the only daughter of the family, would provide a home for her mother. She bought a semi-detached villa, Dinnieduff, in the village of Corstorphine (later a suburb of Edinburgh), where she lived for the rest of her life. 'I had regained a mother but lost my freedom … On the whole my mother and I achieved a working synthesis of living together' (Cruickshank, 60, 62).

Cruickshank wrote in both Scots and English (she considered her Scots poetry stronger—probably an accurate assessment), often in lyrical or ballad mode but sometimes experimenting with metre and form in a thoughtful examination of experience and identity. Her first collection was published in 1934, and only two further volumes, together with *Collected Poems*, appeared during her lifetime. She regarded herself as a minor poet, and was certainly overshadowed by the male writers of her day, but twenty-five years after her death her work and influence had yet to be fully evaluated.

Cruickshank's interests centred on Scotland, its problems and politics, and especially its culture. Though debarred from political activity during her civil service career, she became a committed Scottish nationalist. She was a founder member and secretary (taking over from the founder, the poet Hugh MacDiarmid) of the Scottish Centre of International PEN (1927), a founder member of the Saltire Society (1936), and an enthusiast for the Edinburgh International Festival from its beginning in 1947. A

Cruickshank, William (*d.* 1810/11), military surgeon and chemist, was possibly born in north-east Scotland in the 1740s or 1750s. There is no record of his family, education, or early life, but he may be the William Cruickshank who graduated MA from King's College, Aberdeen, on 2 April 1765. The first certain detail of his life is that he received the diploma of the Royal College of Surgeons of England on 5 October 1780. In March 1788 he took up a post (at a salary of £30 per year) as assistant to Adair Crawford, the newly appointed lecturer on chemistry at the Royal Military Academy at Woolwich (established in 1741 to educate the officers of the Royal Regiment of Artillery).

At Woolwich, Crawford and Cruickshank began a series of experiments on the nature of a mineral found at Strontian in Scotland. It was thought to be a barium compound, but they showed that, although it had similar physical properties, it was in fact a new species of 'earth', now known as strontium carbonate. This work, published by Crawford in 1790 (*Medical Communications*, vol. 2), was the first to distinguish a strontium compound from those of barium. In the following year the Finnish chemist Johan

Gadolin offered to send specimens of Scandinavian minerals to the Royal Military Academy in exchange for a British set; Cruickshank was given a grant of £50 to undertake the collection of two sets of minerals, one of which was kept for the chemical lecture room at Woolwich.

On 25 July 1794 Cruickshank was appointed surgeon of artillery. In August 1795 he succeeded to the chemical lectureship (at £100 per annum) following Crawford's death, although the latter had recommended another candidate; as a proponent of Lavoisier's new oxygen chemistry (which he hoped to apply to medicine and surgery), Cruickshank found his application opposed by those of his colleagues who adhered to the phlogiston theory. He was at the same time appointed chemist and apothecary to the ordnance, and became librarian and treasurer of the Royal Artillery Hospital's library. His duties included research on explosives (at the royal laboratory), care of patients, and the examination of supplies of medicine before they were dispensed.

In March 1794 John Rollo was appointed surgeon-general at Woolwich. He and Cruickshank collaborated in the design of a new tourniquet, and his book on diabetes (*An Account of Two Cases of the Diabetes Mellitus*, 1797; 2nd edn. 1798) incorporated some of Cruickshank's research on diabetic urine and on sugars (*Nicholson's Journal*, 1797, 1799). They also worked on distinguishing various diseases by urine analysis (*Philosophical Magazine*, 1st ser., 1, 1798), the disinfection of wards by fumigation with chlorine (before Guyton de Morveau, who described Cruickshank's method in 1801), and the application of oxidizing agents in the treatment of syphilis (to avoid the use of mercury).

In 1800 Alessandro Volta's invention of the voltaic pile became known in England, and Cruickshank immediately began a series of experiments on electrolysis which were so well regarded that Humphry Davy later acknowledged their importance. He built a trough battery which became the model for later voltaic batteries, particularly those used at the Royal Institution and the École Polytechnique. He first repeated the work of Nicholson and Carlisle, who had shown that electricity decomposed water to hydrogen and oxygen, and was able to establish the nature and relative proportions of the gases formed. Then, substituting a salt solution for water, he proved that metals are deposited at the same (negative) electrode as hydrogen, while acids (anions) are deposited on the positive pole (*Nicholson's Journal*, 1801, 187, 254). This was the first example of electroplating, which he suggested might be usefully employed in mineral analysis.

Cruickshank's last series of experiments was carried out following the publication in 1800 of a pamphlet by Joseph Priestley, who sought to re-establish the phlogiston theory by pointing out that it could account for the production of an inflammable gas (thought to be a hydrocarbon) when charcoal and alumina were burnt, as well as for the production of carbon dioxide when the gas was burnt. By passing carbon dioxide over red-hot wire Cruickshank was able to prepare carbon monoxide and determine that it was a compound of carbon and oxygen; this proved that it could be accounted for by the principles of Lavoisier's chemistry (*Nicholson's Journal*, 5, 1802, 1, 201; new ser., 2, 1802, 42).

Cruickshank was elected FRS on 24 June 1802, at a time when he was probably the most prominent chemist active in Britain. Numerous references to his work in the journals of the day show that he was well known and highly respected. By March 1803, however, he had become so ill that John Macculloch took over his duties; on 6 July 1804 he was allowed to retire on a pension of 10s. per day. It is likely that his illness arose as a result of his work on carbon monoxide, during which he unwittingly prepared phosgene (carbonyl chloride): both gases interfere with the function of the lungs, and phosgene is now known to cause mental derangement, from which Cruickshank suffered.

Nothing is known of Cruickshank's activities after his retirement, but military records state that he died in Scotland. At the anniversary meeting of the Royal Society held on 30 November 1811 his name was read out among those who had died since the previous anniversary meeting, thus establishing the date of his death as probably between 30 November 1810 and 30 November 1811. Works of reference published in the nineteenth century often confuse Cruickshank with the Scottish surgeon and anatomist William Cumberland Cruikshank (1745–1800).

K. D. WATSON

Sources A. Coutts, 'William Cruickshank of Woolwich', *Annals of Science*, 15 (1959), 121–33 · P. M. Sanderson and F. Kurzer, 'The work of William Cruickshank', *Chemistry and Industry* (13 April 1957), 456–60 · G. H. Neild, 'William Cruickshank (FRS –1802); clinical chemist', *Nephrology, Dialysis, Transplantation*, 11 (1996), 1885–9 · S. Soloveichik, 'Toxicity: killer of great chemists?', *Journal of Chemical Education*, 41 (1964), 282–4 · J. Rollo, *A short account of the Royal Artillery Hospital at Woolwich* (1801) · H. D. Buchanan-Dunlop, ed., *Records of the Royal Military Academy, 1741–1892* (1895) · J. Kane, *List of officers of the royal regiment of artillery from the year 1716 to the year 1899*, rev. W. H. Askwith, 4th edn (1900) · J. R. Partington, 'The early history of strontium', *Annals of Science*, 5 (1941–7), 157–66 · IGI
Archives PRO, minutes of the board of ordnance, WO 47, WO 46 · RS, nomination certificate

Cruikshank, George (1792–1878), graphic artist, was born on 27 September 1792, and baptized on 6 November at St George's, Bloomsbury Way, London, the second son of Isaac *Cruikshank (1764–1811), caricaturist, and his wife, Mary, *née* MacNaughton (1769–1853). At the time the family lived at 27 Duke Street; by 1808 they had removed to 117 Dorset Street, Salisbury Square. In that four-storey terrace house George, 'cradled in caricature' as he later put it (Jerrold, 1.72), and his elder brother, (Isaac) Robert *Cruikshank (1789–1856), often watched their father prepare drawings and etchings in his attic studio. Their younger sister Margaret Eliza, born on 29 August 1807, also inherited the family proclivity for drawing.

Education George Cruikshank's education was otherwise erratic. He attended classes at an academy in Edgware, but probably not for long. Like many of his generation, his 'life school was in the street' (P. Cruikshank, 53) and watching by his father's side. For the religious services which his devout mother insisted he attend at the Scotch

George Cruikshank (1792–1878), by Daniel Maclise, 1833

church in Drury Lane, George had scant sympathy. But he was an ardent disciple of the theatre, whether play-acting with his boyhood chum Edmund Kean or attending plays on every kind of stage, from patent theatres to rowdy music-halls. Another childhood friend, Thomas Joseph Pettigrew, became a distinguished physician and antiquarian who helped both George and Robert Cruikshank to various artistic commissions in later years.

When, on 1 February 1803, Napoleon declared war on Britain, all the Cruikshank males caught 'scarlet fever'. Their father, Isaac, joined a Bloomsbury volunteer troupe while Robert and George drilled alongside with blackened mop handles and toy drums. Shortly thereafter Robert went to sea as a midshipman in the East India service; marooned on St Helena, he was given up for dead by his family until he returned, alive, in January 1806, having heard the fateful news of Trafalgar while on his way home. During Robert's absence, George aspired to replace him as a seaman. But Isaac's health was deteriorating, and he needed his son's assistance. Reluctantly, George agreed to remain in the studio, even hiding out on occasion from press-gangs. He tried, briefly, to study at the Royal Academy; the keeper and professor of painting, Henry Fuseli, told him he might go in, but 'must fight for a seat' (Jerrold, 1.72–3). He may have attended one course of lectures, but, as he confided in old age, the press of work 'was so great that he had no leisure for the lectures or work of an art student' (ibid.).

George Cruikshank was sketching competently as early

as 1799; by 1803 he was supplying simple designs to wood-engravers for children's games and books. His father taught him the rudiments of etching into copperplates; at the age of thirteen he was executing the titles of his father's caricatures, and also putting in backgrounds, furnishings, and dialogue. When Robert returned home in the winter of 1806, George had surpassed him in skill; though the brothers worked side by side, and with their father, the youngest of the trio by virtue of his talent and vigour surpassed his elders. Younger siblings, Margaret Eliza and a boy who died, aged four, in 1810, added to the family's financial strains, so George's and Robert's independently earned income was crucial. Commissions multiplied. Many prints were collaborative efforts; Robert also painted miniature portraits and George produced hundreds of designs for advertisements, twelfth-night characters, drolls, songheads, and frontispieces. Principal patrons were the dealers Robert Laurie and Jemmy Whittle (old friends of Isaac Cruikshank's) and Johnny Fairburn, an easy-going, genial printseller in the City of London. By 1808 George was no longer marking his work with initials; he signed broadside prints with his full patronym: 'G. Cruikshank'.

Early caricatures The images Cruikshank inscribed derived not only from London street culture but also from the vivid pictorialism of the Bible, Aesop's *Fables*, Bunyan's *Pilgrim's Progress*, Defoe's *Robinson Crusoe*, and Swift's *Gulliver's Travels*, and from the design vocabulary of visual satire sharpened and elaborated by such past masters as William Hogarth and contemporaries such as Thomas Rowlandson and James Gillray. This vocabulary ranged from mimetic images through degrees of distortion to symbolic forms and beyond to rebuses, mock coats of arms, and pictorial puzzles. Napoleon, for instance, might be represented realistically in a portrait bust, or as Gulliver appeared to the king of Brobdingnag, or as 'little Boney', or as a cloven-hoofed devil, or concealed among violets. Caricaturists, competing daily for the public's coppers, had to be inventors and plagiarists, taking popular forms and changing them to hit the new day's fancy. George Cruikshank was the most fecund, original, and deft graphic satirist after Gillray. Between 1808 and 1811, as he lampooned such public events as the Peninsular War and private scandals around the court and Covent Garden, Cruikshank perfected a repertoire of types, lines, symbolic figures such as the quintessential Englishman John Bull, and ways of telling a story that catapulted him into the front ranks. By the age of twenty he was celebrated.

In April 1811 Isaac Cruikshank won a drinking match and collapsed comatose. He never recovered. Robert and George had to maintain their family; Robert, hoping to become a well-paid portraitist, eventually went off on his own, leaving George as the principal breadwinner. So far as we know, he housed his sister until her death in August 1825 and his mother until her death on 10 August 1853. All their support came from his drawings and etchings.

Major caricatures From 1811 Cruikshank's inventiveness and superior artistry rapidly propelled him to *primus inter* *pares.* A caricature of state miners (January 1811), executed for a radical printseller, may be his first extensive political design completed without his father's help. Thereafter Cruikshank produced hundreds of prints, for conservative dealers such as Hannah Humphrey (who commissioned him to complete a few of Gillray's designs) and her nephew George Humphrey to radical publishers and, on occasion, to printsellers such as J. J. Stockdale who distributed pornography. Napoleon was a principal target. Cruikshank parodied his dispatches during the Russian campaign of 1812–13 (*Boney Hatching a Bulletin or Snug Winter Quarters!!!,* December 1812), and adapted themes and images from imported Russian caricatures to depict a heroic Cossack extinguishing a Napoleonic flat candle (*Snuffing out Boney!,* May 1814). Cruikshank never tired of inventing new ways to belittle the emperor and render him ridiculous: calling on familiar British folklore, he turned Napoleon into a Corsican toad in the hole, a Tiddy Doll on Elba hawking broken gingerbread kings, and a noble whose coat of arms, supported by devils, commemorates Bonaparte's crimes. When the decimated French army recruited 300,000 new troops to replace the hundreds of thousands lost during the Russian campaign, Cruikshank imagined *French Conscripts for the Years 1820, 21, 22, 23, 24 & 25*: a mutilated veteran musters infants who would rather play at 'Peep bo' or go 'home to my Mamme' (18 March 1813). In such ways Cruikshank, his brother, and the other pictorial satirists of the period kept up the home spirits and bolstered the resolve of foreign allies.

At the same time, many of Cruikshank's caricatures lampooned venal office-holders in Britain and the licentious, corrupt court of the prince regent, memorialized in one image as a huge whale spouting the 'Dew of Favor' onto his favourite ministers (*The Prince of Whales,* May 1812). In another image, Cruikshank castigates the regent's proclivity to fall in love with bosomy wives whose cuckolded husbands were bought off with court sinecures (*An Excursion to R[agley] Hall,* October 1812). He designed forty-one folding plates on marital and martial subjects for the radical publication *The Scourge* (1811–16), thirty-two plates for a rival, *The Meteor* (1813–14), eight for *The Satirist* (1813–14), and numerous individual plates for Samuel Fores, William Tegg, S. Knight, Fairburn, and other printsellers. He depicted boxing matches, disorderly tavern scenes, Cockneys, the great clown Joey Grimaldi, religious zealots, sporting crazes (Lady Hertford rides the regent splayed on a velocipede or 'hobby'; *Royal Hobby's,* 20 April 1819), and excesses of fashion, like dandies in cinching corsets from a series of plates called *Monstrosities* burlesquing fashion, which appeared annually from 1816 to 1825.

Cruikshank often worked from suggestions by amateurs. George Humphrey, Frederick Marryat the novelist, 'Alfred Crowquill', and William Henry Merle provided ideas for many images. From 1815 Cruikshank's principal collaborator was the antiquarian book dealer and radical publisher William Hone. After the government failed to convict Hone of blasphemous libel in three trials during December 1817, publisher and artist collaborated on sixteen parodic pamphlets which Cruikshank illuminated with witty, allusive wood-engravings—'Gunpowder in boxwood', his brother called them (I. R. Cruikshank, *The Revolutionary Association* [print], 1821). As trade slumped and discontented labourers agitated for political and economic reforms, Hone and Cruikshank lampooned the government and attacked repressive laws. The *Bank Restriction Note* of January 1819, a mordant parody of an actual banknote which protests capital punishment for the passing of easily forged pound notes, was, Cruikshank later said, 'the most important design and etching I ever made in my life' (Jerrold, 1.93–4). Cruikshank and Hone continued in the vein of moderate radicalism, supporting freedom of the press but not universal suffrage, invoking Magna Carta, ancient liberties, and the constitution against governmental repression led by the home secretary Lord Sidmouth, and savaging republicanism, atheism, and the libertinism of the regent, the 'Dandy of Sixty'. Among the most powerful of these propaganda pamphlets was *The Political House that Jack Built,* issued in December 1819 and inspiring conservative counterblasts such as *The Real or Constitutional House that Jack Built.*

When, at the death of George III on 29 January 1820, his eldest son became king and the long-estranged princess of Wales came back to England to claim her status as queen, Hone and Cruikshank took up Caroline's cause, along with City merchants, radical MPs, and William Cobbett. The pamphlets and toys Hone and Cruikshank invented, incorporating demotic imagery, children's verses, and radical propaganda, sold as many as 100,000 copies in a few days: *The Queen's Matrimonial Ladder,* an illustrated paperbound pamphlet incorporating 'A National Toy' in the form of a pasteboard ladder tracking the fourteen stages of the regent's 'progress' as persecutor of his wife, went through dozens of printings. The most powerful image, an adaptation of Gillray's *Voluptuary under the Horrors of Digestion* (1792), turns George IV into a gross, fuddled inebriate whose 'Qualification' (title of the plate) for matrimony (in 1795) had been that he was:

In love [with other women than his betrothed], and in drink,
    and o'ertoppled by debt;
With women, with wine, and with duns on the fret.
(W. Hone, [text of] *The Queen's Matrimonial Ladder* [pamphlet], 1820)

To spare himself from such devastating caricatures, in June 1820 the king directed that Cruikshank be paid £100 'not to caricature His Majesty in any immoral situation', and in the following month both George and Robert Cruikshank had their round trips to the royal pavilion at Brighton paid in order to negotiate a further easing of their satiric representations (George, 10.xii). These royal tactics were unavailing. Graphic and verbal satirists continued to assault their king, and George IV did not help matters. His vanity, fear of mob ridicule, and venality made him and his brothers, in the words of the hard-pressed duke of Wellington a few years later, the 'damn'dest millstone about the neck of any Government that can be imagined' (A. Briggs, *The Age of Improvement,*

1783–1867, 1959, 186). (Impressions of all the prints referred to above are held in the British Museum.)

Book illustration But the tempest over the mistreatment of Queen Caroline blew over quickly, leaving Hone and Cruikshank without cause or occupation. Hone withdrew into antiquarian research and Cruikshank commenced a second career, as book illustrator. His first significant venture, with his brother, Robert, and the writer Pierce Egan, was a rollicking account entitled *Life in London* (1820–21). Their knowledge was gained first-hand: Hone warned his friend Childs that unless he foreswore 'late hours, blue ruin [gin], and dollies' he would destroy himself (MS letter, Hone to Childs, 11 Jan 1821, Berg collection, New York Public Library). But George and his brother preferred the company of pugilists, journalists, jolly tars, gamblers, Grub Street hacks, Bacchanalians, and actors; often he would come home with the milk in the morning reeking of tobacco and beer and laugh while his sister-in-law scrubbed his face and his mother belaboured him with her fists.

Other illustrations soon followed, chief among them being those for two volumes translating the brothers Grimm's fairy tales into English (*German Popular Stories*, 1823–6). These delicate copperplate vignettes, so different from the coarser political satires of the preceding decade, evoked a powerful response from John Ruskin, who, remembering them from his nursery days, called the etchings 'the finest things, next to Rembrandt's, that, as far as I know, have been done since etching was invented' (Ruskin, *The Elements of Drawing*, 1857, in *Works*, 15.222). Starting in 1826, Cruikshank issued his own albums, plates independent of letterpress which contained comic depictions of scenes, characters, and fads: *Phrenological Illustrations* (1826) was followed by *Illustrations of Time* (1827), four series of *Scraps and Sketches* (1828–32), and *My Sketch Book*, in nine parts from 1833 to 1836. In 1828 Cruikshank drew for Sebastian Prowett, a Pall Mall publisher with a considerable interest in the fine arts, images of an Italian puppeteer performing the conjugal endearments of one of England's most beloved couples, *Punch and Judy*. It was largely from looking at these comic vignettes and albums that Charles Baudelaire decided Cruikshank's 'distinctive quality' was 'his inexhaustible abundance of grotesque invention'. Baudelaire acknowledged his other strengths, including 'delicacy of expression' and 'understanding of the fantastic', but felt that Cruikshank's characters were sometimes more vital than conscientiously drawn (C. Baudelaire, 'Some foreign caricaturists', in *Selected Writings on Art and Literature*, ed. and trans. P. E. Charvet, 1972, repr. 1992, 23–4). No doubt Baudelaire would have agreed with many other critics on the artist's inability to portray female beauty. Nevertheless, Cruikshank's sketches of street scenes influenced Henry Monnier's albums of the 1820s and 1830s; and in succeeding generations Paul Garvani, Gustave Doré, and the Goncourt brothers disseminated Cruikshankian subjects and designs to French audiences.

Cruikshank married Mary Ann Walker (*b. c.*1807) in her parish of Dunstable in Bedfordshire on 16 October 1827.

The couple was childless, and until she died in 1849 Mary Ann suffered from ill health, possibly tuberculosis. Settled now into domesticity in a Pentonville terrace house, Cruikshank sought more steady income. One of his hopeful ventures was a comic almanac, issued annually, comprising jokes, poems, stories, lampoons, and full-page plates representing monthly events. These publications, like many other of his independent publications, were issued by Charles Tilt who, along with his successor, David Bogue, remained a principal publisher until the 1850s. The first few years of *Cruikshank's Comic Almanack* (1835–53) went well; William Makepeace Thackeray supplied stories in 1839 and 1840 and the pictures were capital. But it became difficult to sustain invention over the decades, and competition from *Punch's Almanack* (beginning December 1844), which many including Charles Dickens saw as an imitation of Cruikshank's, eventually doomed the artist's venture. Another project initiated in 1835 was to provide comic steel-engravings to Fisher & Son's Anglo-French edition of Sir Walter Scott's fiction, the capstone to five years during which George had produced illustrations of classic eighteenth-century novels for the publisher Roscoe's Novelists Library and developed what Frederick Antal called an 'average-European' style (*Hogarth and his Place in European Art*, 1962, 191).

Cruikshank met Charles Dickens through John Macrone, a young Manxman preparing a fourth edition of Harrison Ainsworth's novel *Rookwood* with illustrations by Cruikshank (1836). Macrone had proposed to Dickens that his 'sketches' of London life, then being printed in various periodicals, be collected in several volumes and reissued with illustrations by Cruikshank; Dickens agreed. On 17 November 1835 Dickens called on the artist at his home and studio in Amwell Street, Pentonville. As over the next year they worked together on two series of *Sketches by Boz* (first series, two vols., February 1836; second series, one vol., December 1836), the relationship warmed from wary professionalism to bibulous bonhomie, interrupted by an occasional outburst of temper, of which each collaborator had his share. These volumes were a great success, both on account of Dickens's rising popularity and because Cruikshank's plates introduced deft and spirited graphic commentaries on the text and the town. In December 1836 the publisher Richard Bentley, seizing an opportunity to sign up the most popular urban artists of the day, hired Dickens to edit, and Cruikshank to illustrate, his new magazine, *Bentley's Miscellany*. Into that journal, from January 1837 to November 1843, Cruikshank poured some of his best work, especially in illustrating *Oliver Twist* and Ainsworth's follow-on, *Jack Sheppard*. Both texts were significantly enhanced by the plates, which often served as the armatures upon which the many dramatic renditions of the novels were staged.

Although Dickens's literary adviser, John Forster, objected to the designs for the illustrations to the last instalments of *Oliver Twist*, and Dickens too asked for one of the plates to be redrawn, other contemporaries thought these the summit of the artist's achievement. Richard Ford, writing in the *Quarterly Review*, asked why royal academicians 'have not ere now insisted on breaking through all puny laws' and voted 'this man of undoubted genius his diploma' (64, June 1839, 102). *Fagin in the Condemned Cell* was roundly praised at the time of its publication; Cruikshank often afterwards enacted stories about its creation; and even Dickens used it as a point of reference, telling his last illustrator, Luke Fildes, that the picture of the Rochester cell in which John Jasper would be incarcerated in *Edwin Drood* should be 'as good a drawing' as Cruikshank's (F. G. Kitton, *Dickens and his Illustrators*, 1899, 214).

The decade between 1835 and 1845 was, for many commentators, the high water mark of Cruikshank's artistic life. The intense focus on his few projects with Dickens, and the rancorous disputes that broke out in later decades, have led biographers to imagine that *Oliver Twist* was the climax of the artist's achievement and that his inability to satisfy Dickens commenced his long falling-off. In fact Cruikshank had decades of acclaim behind him, for a variety of images and social campaigns, before he met Dickens, who was dubbed 'the CRUIKSHANK of writers' by the *Spectator* (26 Dec 1836, 1234). And the very fame that book illustration brought to the middle-aged draughtsman had its downside: if his plates were attached to books (and copyrighted in the name of the publisher who issued those books), then when the titles went out of print so too did the illustrations, an arrangement over which the artist had no control. While Cruikshank's extraordinary assemblage of wood-engravings and steel etchings for Ainsworth's historical novels such as *The Tower of London* (1840) and *Windsor Castle* (1842–3, wood-engravings by W. Alfred Delamotte) deserves to rank among his most sustained, original, and brilliantly executed productions, the texts to which they were attached have so fallen from sight that the plates can hardly be found.

It is also the case that in the 1840s Cruikshank's work begins to bifurcate. He continues to etch many light-hearted or melodramatic scenes, but he also begins to insert a more rigorous, less 'devil may care' morality into some of his work. Domestic idyll is threatened not only by scary railroad monsters smashing into the kitchen—a representation of the railway mania that zigzagged the stock exchange in the 1840s—but also by satanic forces unleashed by individuals unable to control their passions. His etchings for W. H. Maxwell's *History of the Irish Rebellion in 1798* (1845) 'strike savagely off the page', as the novelist John Fowles has observed (Fowles, xxvii). Whereas Maxwell tried to maintain impartiality in his narrative, Cruikshank indicts both sides through portrayals that have often been compared to Goya's *Disasters of War*.

The Bottle Two years later this strain of excoriating remonstrance issued forth in the first of Cruikshank's many mid-century diatribes against personal indulgence: *The Bottle* (1847). 'The Follies of youth', he noted in his diary on 27 September 1846, 'punish us in our old age' (Patten, 2.234).

Prompted by a Manchester reformer, Joseph Adshead, Cruikshank arranged to produce a set of complex narrative plates, similar to those Hogarth had issued a century earlier, promoting temperance. The artist chose an experimental medium, glyphography, which reduced the costs of the prints and thus might make them widely available to the working classes. It was, however, a rather crude process, so Cruikshank had to invent designs that did not depend on delicate lines or multiple gradients of black. The decline and fall of a respectable labourer and his family, tracked in eight plates which were issued on various qualities of paper and later in reduced size sometimes accompanied by verses supplied by Charles Mackay, struck many as extraordinarily effective. Matthew Arnold composed a sonnet in tribute and Dickens urged Forster to a complimentary notice. But Dickens, in a disagreement that was eventually to split the former collaborators asunder forever, cautioned that the consumption of beer, wine, and spirits should be understood as originating 'in sorrow, or poverty, or ignorance', not simply in a thoughtless tipple to celebrate the day (Charles Dickens to John Forster, 2 Sept 1847, in *The Letters of Charles Dickens*, ed. M. House and others, 1965–, 5.156–7). For Dickens, a moderationist, social remedies, especially education and a living wage, would eliminate excess drinking; for Cruikshank, who knew from his own family the ravages of alcoholism, drinking was a destructive habit that could only be stopped by will-power. Indeed, once he had completed his graphic series, Cruikshank realized he ought to heed his own lesson and turn teetotal himself. He did, and until his death he lectured, often somewhat intemperately but usually to appreciative audiences throughout the British Isles, on the evil effects of drink and the beneficial results of sobriety. He refused, however, to sign the pledge because 'pledged to the Almighty on the faith and honour of a gentleman' (Whittaker, 233).

The Bottle garnered much acclaim; it became a standard decoration in temperance rooms and a customary prize at teetotal gatherings. But neither it nor its equally potent successor, *The Drunkard's Children* (1848), made money. Cruikshank's supporters could not understand why the artist was poor, after more than a quarter century when his name had been a byword for prodigious invention, humour, and social commentary. Unknown even to some of his closest friends, however, commissions for illustrations came less frequently with each passing year, neither the *Comic Almanack* nor any of the periodicals he initiated in the 1840s including *Omnibus* (1841–2) and *Table Book* (1845) yielded substantial sums, and Mary Ann was dying. While playing in Dickens's amateur theatrical company during the mid-1840s reunited Cruikshank with cronies of earlier days and with the principals of *Punch*, for which he refused to work, he was not really a member of the inner circle. Tolerated more as an eccentric, sometimes unmannerly, Cruikshank was increasingly isolated from the most popular humorists of the day and relegated to second-rate commissions for third-rate projects.

Domestic concerns After Mary Ann's death on 28 May 1849, Cruikshank collapsed. As he explained to his oldest friend, William Henry Merle:

The many years of anxiety, & the desperate struggle that I have had to keep up my position—as a poor Gentleman—the long—years long, illness of my poor wife—and then the crushing blow of her death! was altogether too much for my strength to bear … for the first time in my life—[I] could not work!!   (to Merle, 6 Nov 1849, in Patten, 2.277)

It was not just the loss of his wife that had overwhelmed him. Many of his old collaborators—authors and publishers—were dead; one of the last, Frederick Marryat, had succumbed in August 1848 after learning of the death of his beloved son at sea. The temperance plates yielded scant revenue, and the hoped-for American sales did not materialize. Chartism and the revolutions of 1848 further dampened interest in Cruikshank's art. And he continued the generosity of his youth, lending money whenever he had an extra sovereign and then growing surprised and eventually disappointed when the loans were not returned. Himself often in debt, especially to Merle, Cruikshank had managed his slender resources so thriftlessly that unless he could sell new work—he owned very little of his previous production—he could not eat. He was, to his surprise, bankrupt; alluding to the California gold rush, he commented to Bogue ruefully: 'I [am] … more convinced than ever, that England is not California' (3 Feb 1849, in Patten, 2.269).

Slowly Cruikshank returned to art, this time essaying oil painting, which he had attempted decades earlier. The results were, on the whole, unsatisfactory. His lifetime practice of working on a small scale with delicate instruments was quite wrong for the bolder gestures required by large canvases; 'the etching point feeling was always in his fingers', he conceded, when a 'painter should paint from his shoulder' (Jerrold, 2.146, 139). He sold a few pictures, usually of literary or humorous subjects. An early effort, *The Disturbed Congregation* (oil on panel, 1849; Royal Collection), depicts an outraged beadle (modelled by his nephew Percy Cruikshank) giving a potent look of reprimand to a guilty young lad (Percy's boy, George) who has dropped his peg top in church. The prince consort purchased it for 30 guineas, but royal patronage dried up thereafter. In the 1860s Cruikshank expended years of labour on a gigantic canvas warning against the evils of drink, *The Worship of Bacchus* (1862; Tate Collection), and on the engraving from it that he published along with an explanation of the hundreds of incidents displayed in his 'diagram of drunkenness'. But this project, like almost all the others Cruikshank tried in the last thirty years of his life, failed. The time and effort he expended on graphic temperance sermons exceeded what any of his conservative, middle-class, and working-class teetotal admirers were willing to pay for, either in an outright contribution or to purchase a plate.

Both professional and domestic prospects seemed to brighten around the time of the Great Exhibition. Cruikshank teamed up with Henry Mayhew, as he had for a couple of comic narratives in the late 1840s, to produce an illustrated serial, to be issued monthly during the exhibition, about the misadventures of a Cumberland family who travel down to London on the spur of the moment. *1851, or, The Adventures of Mr. and Mrs. Sandboys*, began bravely enough with a bravura frontispiece showing the whole world going to the exhibition. Unfortunately, neither author nor artist could sustain the story. In the end Mayhew barely cobbled together enough text to fill his pages, and Cruikshank drew plates that sometimes bore no relation to the letterpress. The serial didn't sell, and neither did Cruikshank's plain or coloured etching of the opening of the exhibition, which had to compete with many other single plates and a huge wood-engraving in the *Illustrated London News*. Prince Albert received a copy early in July.

In the preceding year, on 7 March 1850, Cruikshank had remarried. Eliza Widdison (1807–1890), niece of the publisher Charles Baldwyn who had commissioned the first volume of *German Popular Stories* back in the 1820s, was the same age as Mary Ann; she had received a little education and survived on the small annuities paid to her widowed mother and aunt with whom she lived. Although her resources were meagre, she clung to her status as the daughter of a gentleman. The wedding, by licence, took place at Holy Trinity Church, Islington. Cruikshank, Eliza, his mother, her mother and aunt, a married cook, and a maid of all work moved to 48 Mornington Place, renamed 263 Hampstead Road in 1864. The transformation of the hot-headed bohemian of the regency era into a sober householder who even renounced tobacco seemed complete.

But it was not. Eliza was a reliable, kindly woman who adored her husband and believed him to be the champion of the age. She and the ageing relatives, who all died between 1851 and 1853, looked after his every want. But something prompted Cruikshank to stray. Shortly after his mother's death the housemaid, Adelaide Attree (*bap.* 1831, *d.* 1914), confessed that she was pregnant. Eliza was sympathetic but had to let her go. Eliza did not know that her husband was the father, and that he set up Adelaide in a flat nearby that doubled as a studio. And as a nursery. Adelaide gave birth to eleven children, ten surviving infancy: George Robert (*b.* 20 Nov 1854), Annie Adelaide (*b.* 1858), William Henry (*b.* 12 Jan 1860), Albert Edward (*b.* 10 Jan 1863), Alfred Mills (*b.* 1 March 1865), Eliza Jane (*b.* 16 March 1867), Ada Rose (*b.* 22 Sept 1868), Emma Caroline (*b.* 15 Nov 1869), Ellen Maude (*b.* 9 March 1873), and Arthur Attree (*b.* 17 March 1875). The presumption remains that these were all Cruikshank's children. He did what he could to provide for them, sending money surreptitiously through confidential servants or friends. There is evidence that Eliza knew something about the other family, but not perhaps its extent or her husband's full involvement. Sustaining two separate households on slender means, presenting himself to his loving wife as an upright, honest, and thoroughly principled artist, and keeping the second family a secret forced Cruikshank into financial expedients and concealments that often shortened his temper. These strains also impelled him to look for work in any place where it could be found.

Temperance   One activity that consumed huge amounts of time from 1847 to the end of Cruikshank's life was attendance at temperance meetings. He became an eccentric and beloved figure, his own self-caricature, the St George of water drinkers. Dora Montefiore was fascinated by him when as a child she saw him in the 1860s: 'he had a long mesh of iron grey hair which he trained across the top of his head and kept in its place with a piece of elastic, which arrangement was the delight of us young ones' (Montefiore, 29). He accepted scores of invitations to preside over prizegivings, business meetings of charitable societies, fund-raising dinners, and fetes. He travelled everywhere in Britain and the length and breadth of greater London, from Fulham and Kew to Greenwich and from Exeter Hall to Hampstead. These public meetings seemed to confirm Cruikshank's fame and usefulness, and to an age that thought, as Ruskin put it, that 'the muse of art' might be turned into 'a sister of Charity' (*Works*, 19.199–200), his compassionate sermonizing on the platform and on paper and canvas could be understood as a thoroughly artistic endeavour. He also served on the board of charitable organizations, chief among them being the London Temperance League. He came into daily contact with ardent social reformers such as John Cassell, who published his badly cut minstrel-show illustrations to one of the many competing British editions of *Uncle Tom's Cabin* (1852). Cruikshank worked with James Silk Buckingham, MP for Sheffield in the first reform parliament, and came to know a remarkable group of physicians engaged in urban sanitary reform; chief among these was Benjamin Ward Richardson, knighted in 1893 for his service to humanitarian causes, who became Cruikshank's executor. Journalists who appreciated Cruikshank's temperance efforts included Charles Kent and George Augustus Sala, men who also associated on familiar terms with Charles Dickens.

One of the sore points in Cruikshank's life in the 1850s was Dickens's increasingly public and strident opposition to what he saw as the excesses of temperance. When Cruikshank brought out the first in a series of beautifully illustrated fairy tale books (*Hop o' my Thumb*, 1853) to which he appended texts explaining that all the violence and misery in the stories were caused by drink, Dickens protested in the leader of his weekly magazine, *Household Words* (1 October 1853). He objected strongly to the artist's promoting total abstinence by altering 'harmless little books'. Cruikshank rejoined in the second number of yet another of his venturesome, and quickly unsuccessful, periodicals, *George Cruikshank's Magazine* (February 1854). In the form of a letter from Hop, Cruikshank observes, rightly, that fairy tales were constantly being adapted; furthermore, how wholesome is it for children to be told about parents deserting their offspring without accounting for such cruelty in some way? Whatever the merits of the arguments on either side, Dickens's view prevailed, in part because, as usual, Cruikshank's prose—in the stories and in his defences of them—was much less effective than his drawings. Crushing one of his last hopes for public acclaim and making fun of the good cause of temperance were unforgivable; when Dickens died in June 1870, Cruikshank pronounced, 'One of our greatest enemies gone' (*TLS*, 2 May 1935, 288).

In the 1850s and 1860s Cruikshank wrote pamphlets on topics ranging from how to prevent burglaries during the Great Exhibition to spiritualism. None of these pamphlets had anything like the impact of the Hone collaborations thirty years earlier; collectively they furthered the impression that Cruikshank was growing cranky and irrelevant. His notoriety was embellished by the fiasco of the volunteers. Fears of a French invasion in the winter of 1859 led the secretary of state for war to authorize the lord lieutenants of the counties to commission volunteer corps. Some of these were organized according to trades: the 38th Middlesex enrolled Captain Millais and Private Holman Hunt among other artists. Cruikshank enthusiastically supported the movement, issuing a pamphlet, *A Pop-Gun* (1860), that defended the 1803 volunteers in which he and his father and brother had participated against the ridicule of General Napier. He then joined a temperance corps himself, and rose to be its lieutenant-colonel and commanding officer. But the 48th Middlesex was plagued by the same problems affecting other volunteer corps: inadequate funds, slack discipline, flagging motivation, petty rivalries. Baulked even of promotion to honorary colonel, worn out by drilling and equipping and disciplining and financing his troops, and facing revolt from within, Cruikshank retired on 30 September 1868. This, too, was noticed in the papers, some of them running unfavourable accounts of his mismanagement; and so once again what might have been a constructive and rewarding outlet for his devotion to patriotism, a well-ordered military, and the 'dear lads' he wished to reclaim from drink, blew up in his face.

Later years None of the projects initiated during Cruikshank's last decades turned out well. Ruskin, impelled by recollections of the Grimm illustrations, offered both to underwrite Cruikshank's illustrated autobiography and to collaborate with the artist on fairy tales. Cruikshank laboured on his recollections until his death, going over and over the early years of his life and providing some glass etchings, many inconsequential, but the text never got very far. As for fairy tales, at first Ruskin thought he would write, or edit, old ones, and Cruikshank would illustrate them; but when Ruskin saw the laboured drawings Cruikshank submitted he realized that the light touch of the younger man had been lost. The fallback was a reprint of the Grimm tales, but that proved even more vexatious: unable to obtain the original copperplates, the publisher John Camden Hotten had the illustrations copied by a hireling, never telling Cruikshank. Ruskin, though he knew the plates would not be printed from the originals, none the less provided a preface, which Hotten bound with the reprinted text and facsimile vignettes and stamped on the cover with Cruikshank's signature as warrant of authenticity (1868). The whole shabby business perplexed and saddened the artist.

Charles Augustus Howell, Ruskin's factotum during this period and subsequently 'renowned for wit, knavery and brazenness', as Oswald Doughty describes him (*A Victorian Romantic: Dante Gabriel Rossetti*, 1949, 331), initiated the first of several 'testimonials' intended to supply the artist with money, reawaken interest in his art, and, in some instances, obtain his archive for a public collection. None of these efforts by Howell or by others paid off, but they did disseminate the impression that the artist was a spendthrift and a sponge. Eventually enough donations accrued to enable Cruikshank to pay off some debts and assemble an archive purchased by the Royal Aquarium and Summer and Winter Garden Society for £1000, an annuity of £35 for whoever survived the other, Cruikshank or Eliza, and a modest honorarium to pay for his helping to arrange for an exhibition of his work at the society's premises in 1876. The show went up (1876), but it didn't survive long.

Other projects also led to disappointment. Cruikshank believed in 1870 he was commissioned to design a statue commemorating Robert the Bruce and Bannockburn. He trundled a 5 foot high model by John Adams Acton to Windsor Castle on 1 July to show the queen, who signified her gracious approval. But after years of waiting for funds to be raised to cast the statue, Cruikshank learned in late November 1877 that another sculptor, Andrew Currie, had supplied the winning design, one that Cruikshank believed was unhistorical, and that he was accused of copying the work of the successful artist.

The mishaps of fairyland were no more fortunate. Juliana Horatia Ewing campaigned hard to induce the publisher George Bell to hire Cruikshank to illustrate her children's stories about brownies, dwarfs, and other magical creatures; she succeeded, and Cruikshank's drawings met her high expectations. But the books (*The Brownies*, 1871; *Lob Lie-by-the-Fire*, 1874) did not sell well, and when at last a reprint was called for, Randolph Caldecott supplied new illustrations, thinking that his predecessor's work was in his 'worst style'.

Debt, worry about supporting Eliza, Adelaide, and ten children, and frustration sharpened Cruikshank's temper further. Accounts of his life and character had been published regularly since the 1820s; the most flattering and in many ways perceptive were Thackeray's in the *Westminster Review* (April 1840) and John Paget's in *Blackwood's* (August 1863). When Cruikshank received no credit for initiating the characters and plot of Harrison Ainsworth's novel *The Miser's Daughter*, staged by Andrew Halliday in April 1872, he fired off letters to *The Times* claiming 'the title of originator'. Ainsworth flatly denied the assertion. Cruikshank then resorted to pamphleteering; in *The Artist and the Author* (June 1872) he reasserted his claims to be originator of several of Ainsworth's novels (for which considerable evidence now exists) and attached to this controversy an earlier one, commencing after the death of Dickens in June 1870, in which Cruikshank disputed John Forster's repudiation of the artist's having any hand in the origin, plot, and characters of *Oliver Twist*. It was hard for anyone living in the 1870s to imagine that forty years earlier graphic artists might have had co-equal status in developing new fictions; the triumph of literacy had depreciated illustrators to the rank of copyists, trying to be 'faithful' to a pre-existing text.

In the last several years of his life Cruikshank was much in the public eye, celebrated as St George, riding the hobby-horse of temperance (*The Period*, 17 Sept 1870), ridiculed for his dietary monomanias, exaggerated sense of self-importance, and temerity to challenge the originality of Dickens or Ainsworth. After a short illness in January 1878, Cruikshank succumbed on 1 February to acute respiratory infection and died at his home, 263 Hampstead Road. He was temporarily buried in Kensal Green cemetery on 9 February until the crypt of St Paul's, then under repair, could be reopened. There, on 29 November 1878, his English oak casket was lowered into the ground.

The executors of Cruikshank's estate discovered that he was insolvent, that he had many unpaid debts, and that he had left the entirety of his estate to Adelaide. These were awkward conditions. That they were overcome is owing largely to the efforts and forbearance of Eliza, who ferreted out enough prints and drawings for auction to pay off the debts, used her own declining resources to purchase more of Cruikshank's work which she presented to the Victoria and Albert Museum and the British Museum, and never murmured in public about the shock of finding such a flourishing second household a few streets away. She bequeathed money to the Royal Academy to endow a George Cruikshank prize, but at her death in December 1890 she had insufficient funds to meet all the legacies. The academy declined to accept a partial gift.

ROBERT L. PATTEN

Sources R. L. Patten, *George Cruikshank's life, times, and art*, 2 vols. (1992–6) [incl. bibliography] · B. Jerrold, *The life of George Cruikshank*, 2 vols. (1882) · G. Cruikshank, various MS memoranda and MS drafts for an autobiography, Harvard U., Houghton L. · G. Cruikshank, corresp. and papers, Princeton University Libary, CO256 · A. M. Cohn, *George Cruikshank: a catalogue raisonné* (1924) · F. G. Stephens and M. D. George, eds., *Catalogue of political and personal satires preserved … in the British Museum*, 6–11 (1938–54) · P. Cruikshank, 'George Cruikshank, with some account of his brother Robert Cruikshank', unpublished memoir, Princeton University, New Jersey · J. Wardroper, *The caricatures of George Cruikshank* (1977) · J. Fowles, 'Introduction: remembering Cruikshank', *George Cruikshank: a revaluation*, ed. R. L. Patten, rev. edn (Princeton, 1992) · G. S. Layard, *George Cruikshank's portraits of himself* (1897) · *The works of John Ruskin*, ed. E. T. Cook and A. Wedderburn, library edn, 39 vols. (1903–12), vol. 15, p. 222 · C. Fox, *Graphic journalism in England during the 1830s and 1840s* (1988) · parish register, London, St George's, Bloomsbury Way, 6 Nov 1792 [baptism] · T. Whittaker, *Life's battles in temperance armour* (1892) · D. Montefiore, *From a Victorian to a modern* (1927) · *CGPLA Eng. & Wales* (1878)

Archives BM, albums · Harvard U., Houghton L., autobiography, corresp., and papers · Hunt. L., corresp., drawings, literary MSS, and letters · LMA, corresp., drawings, etc., mainly relating to Middlesex Rifle Volunteers · NYPL, Berg collection, corresp., drawings, papers · Princeton University Library, corresp. and papers, Co256 · priv. coll., MS account books · Rice University, Houston, Texas, Fondren Library, corresp., diaries, papers, photographs, prints · U. Reading L., corresp. relating to claims against his estate · University of North Carolina, Chapel Hill, general and literary manuscripts group, papers, 11005 · University of Virginia, Charlottesville, corresp. and drawings · V&A, corresp. | Hunt. L., letters to E. H. Cocker and Frederick Locker-Lampson · U. Newcastle, letters to Sir Walter Trevelyan · U. Reading L., letters to George Bell · University of North Carolina, Chapel Hill, Whitaker papers, Southern historical collection, 3433

Likenesses D. Maclise, lithograph, 1833, BM, NPG [*see illus.*] · oils, 1836, NPG · G. Cruikshank, self-portrait, etching, 1845, repro. in *George Cruikshank's Table Book* (1845) · F. W. Pailthorpe, etching, pubd 1883, BM, NPG · J. Adams, bust, St Paul's Cathedral, London · C. Baugniet, lithograph, BM · W. Behnes, marble bust, Kensal Green cemetery, London; related plaster bust, NPG · G. Cruikshank, self-portraits, BM · C. E. Wagstaff, stipple (after F. Stone), BM, NPG · J. & C. Watkins, photographs, repro. in Patten, *George Cruikshank's life, times, and art*, vol. 2, frontispiece · photographs, NPG · watercolour drawing, NPG

Wealth at death under £1000: probate, 16 April 1878, *CGPLA Eng. & Wales*

Cruikshank [Crookshanks], **Isaac** (1764–1811), caricaturist and painter, born on 5 October 1764 in the Canongate, Edinburgh, and baptized in the parish on 14 October, was the fifth child and third son of Andrew Crookshanks (*c*.1725–*c*.1783) and Elizabeth (*b. c*.1725), daughter of James Davidson, a gardener at Kinnardie. His father had been a customs inspector at the Edinburgh port of Leith; for his part in the Jacobite uprising of 1745—he was wounded at Culloden—he was fired and dispossessed. Befriended by a family of master printers and publishers, the Ruddimans, Andrew Crookshanks and his family moved first to the New North Kirk parish in Edinburgh, and just before Isaac's birth to the Canongate. There Isaac grew up as the youngest child, coddled and pummelled by his siblings. Athletic and musical—he played the flute until he died—Isaac also absorbed something of the discussions about politics and art that reverberated within his parents' home. About 1783 Andrew died, perhaps as a result of his old wound; Isaac informed his mother that he wanted to be a painter. At first she thought he meant a house painter; eventually Isaac studied with a local artist, possibly John Kay (1742–1826), who taught drawing and etching. Late in 1783 master and pupil travelled south to London, where in January 1784 Isaac Cruikshank published some etchings of Edinburgh characters: *Scotch Eloquence* (30 January 1784) is the first caricature he initialled. Surviving prints from 1784 and 1785 (of which impressions are in the British Museum) give his address as 53 Stanhope Street, Clare Market.

Isaac Cruikshank made his way by means of his clever drawings, geniality, and capacity for turning out whatever the market required. His passion for the stage, transmitted to his sons, was shared by a close friend and patron, the publisher John Roach of Vinegar Yard. Their families, and the young Edmund Kean, used to stage amateur theatricals in Roach's kitchen, and for more than a decade after moving to London Isaac supplied watercolours and illustrations to books about the theatre. William Cumberland Cruikshank (no known relation), Samuel Johnson's 'sweet-blooded' surgeon, also became a friend and family physician; it may have been he who secured Cruikshank the commission to execute a frontispiece for a 1791 collection, *Witticisms and Jests of Dr Johnson*. Within a few years Cruikshank met Mary MacNaughton (1769–1853), daughter of a highland naval officer killed at sea, who had moved down to Finchley with her uncle Archibald MacNaughton and his wife, Sarah. In later years Mary told her sons that she had been raised by the countess of Orkney, although this tale has not been verified. Mary and Isaac were married in the parish of St Anne's, Soho, on 14 August 1788. Her strong-willed, hot-tempered, frugal, and

devout temperament counteracted Isaac's boisterous, bibulous energy and—to her—sacrilegious sense of fun.

When their first son, (Isaac) Robert *Cruikshank (1789–1856), was born on 27 September 1789 the Cruikshanks moved to St Martin's Court, and when Robert's brother George *Cruikshank (1792–1878) arrived on the same day in 1792 they moved to Duke Street, near Montagu House. From about 1800 Cruikshank worked at the British Museum preparing illustrations for George Shaw's multivolume *General Zoology* (1800–26), and in 1803, during the French invasion scare, he drilled with the loyal St Giles's and St George's Bloomsbury Volunteers. At some point before 1807, as the family prospered, they moved to a four-storey terrace house at 117 Dorset Street, Salisbury Square. At least three other children were born: Mary, about 1795, who although attended by Dr Cruikshank did not survive infancy; Archibald (named after Mary's uncle), born about 1806, who died from a fall on 10 August 1810; and Margaret Eliza, born 29 August 1807, a sickly, gentle child who was her mother's favourite, inherited her father's artistic inclinations, and sold some of her own drawings and etchings before dying young in August 1825.

In the early years of his marriage Cruikshank's art flourished. He painted in watercolours (two of his drawings formed part of the William Smith gift to the Victoria and Albert Museum). In 1789 he exhibited at the Royal Academy *Return to Lochaber*, a Scottish genre subject; in 1790 his *Visit to the Cottage* was accepted; and in 1792 *The Distress and Triumphs of Virtue*, a subject that sounds more like Mary's theme than Isaac's. For these works, Cruikshank supplied business addresses, perhaps hoping to set himself up as an entrepreneurial artist. Selling a few paintings a year, however, probably did not yield nearly as much income as could be earned by churning out many lottery puffs, songheads, watercolours, and political and social caricatures. At least 345 prints produced between 1793 and 1800 likely to be by Isaac Cruikshank survive in the British Museum collection, and in E. B. Krumbhaar's *Catalogue Raisonné* more than 1350 images are attributed to him.

The best of these were considered at the time to rival prints by James Gillray and Thomas Rowlandson. While Isaac Cruikshank's politics were influenced by his dealers and customers, he was stalwart in lampooning Napoleon, and with Gillray he developed the portrayal of a stout, prosperous John Bull, sometimes yokel, sometimes a 'cit', often puzzled and grumpy, but never mean and rarely fooled for long. Cruikshank was not kind to those with radical tendencies, such as Charles James Fox, depicted in 1792 as divided between French revolutionary and English statesman (*A Right Honora[b]le alias a Sans Culotte*, 20 December 1792). He also caricatured notorious characters—Thomas Powys, MP for Northamptonshire, a leading county member who tried to forge a coalition between Pitt and Fox (18 February 1784), and Albinia Hobart (countess of Buckinghamshire, 1793–1816), who maintained in her home a notoriously profitable—to her—faro table (10 April 1792 and 24 October 1792). (Impressions of all these are in the British Museum.)

After France declared war on Britain in February 1803,

Cruikshank, a 'true Born Briton' (I. Cruikshank [print], BM 11561, 4 June 1810) and as patriotic as his fellow graphic propagandists, heartened the home front by savaging the enemy, excoriating governmental mismanagement and venality, and celebrating Britain's few victories. His repertoire of beasts, bogeys, and the Corsican monkey diversified and became more sophisticated and allusive. *Buonaparte at Rome Giving Audience in State* (12 March 1797), one of the first to depict Napoleon's actual features taken from a French portrait, spends less effort representing Bonaparte realistically than on displaying his shocking contempt for sacred things, marking him as satanic. A decade later Cruikshank's *French Generals Receiving an English Charge* (28 April 1809) lampoons Bonaparte's grotesquely exaggerated bicorn, but mainly directs its charge at the duke of York. In this print, on the plate of which his son George also worked, Isaac Cruikshank shows the French officers enjoying numerous English 'charges' (French for caricatures), four of them by Isaac Cruikshank on the subject of the duke's scandalous affair with Mary Anne Clarke. Thus not only Napoleon but also errant royals are satirized, while at the same time the caricaturist compares the devastating power of graphic squibs to a corps of soldiers charging the enemy.

In full command of his powers, Cruikshank found steady work from the print dealer S. W. Fores, self-proclaimed 'caricaturist to the first consul', and from the always laid-back and genial Johnny Fairburn. Not only did he design and etch hundreds of his own prints, Cruikshank also worked up ideas from others, notably G. M. Woodward, and felt confident enough of his place in the caricature market to borrow, transform, extend, and allude to his own previous images. He still executed lesser works as well. In the early days, living hand to mouth, he designed for Robert Sayer (*d.* 29 June 1794) and his successors Robert Laurie and Jemmy Whittle series of humorous, non-political prints called 'drolls', 'well calculated', according to Laurie's and Whittle's 1795 catalogue, 'for the shop windows of country booksellers and stationers'. He also drew attractive watercolour portraits and scenes, a few book illustrations, and mild send-ups of fashionable types. At no point was Cruikshank as learnedly and cuttingly satirical as Gillray or as easy with the upper classes as Rowlandson. But at his best his inventive anatomical distortions (long-headed statesmen, manikin enemies), anthropomorphized beasts and bugaboos, landscapes, social portraits, and sympathetic portrayals of ordinary unaffected people have a strong appeal. He was an uneven artist; weak drawing, feeble humour, and convoluted political narratives mar some of his productions.

Isaac Cruikshank passed on to his sons both artistic techniques and subject matter. He also inspired them with a love for everything 'manly' and martial. With his son George Cruikshank, he stood on Ludgate Hill to watch Nelson's coffin pass on its way to St Paul's on 9 January 1806; then the two rushed back to the top-floor studio to collaborate on a folding etched frontispiece for *Fairburn's Edition of the Funeral*. From that point forward, George Cruikshank was of increasing help to his father, whose inveterate habit of spending long nights drinking with cronies in various tavern clubs began taking a noticeable toll on his body and spirits. *The Last Grand Ministerial Expedition* (19 April 1810) displays all Isaac Cruikshank's hard-earned skills: a well-grouped and differentiated crowd, a clear attack on the government's abuse of private citizens—in this case the mob preventing the arrest of Sir Francis Burdett—and an energetic frieze-like design staged across the whole broadsheet. But his print production had been declining for some time. The last clearly datable works are two etched illustrations to Elizabeth Hamilton's *Cottagers of Glenburnie* (1798), reissued by Thomas Tegg in September 1810. Early in April of the following year Cruikshank accepted a challenge for a drinking match; acute alcoholic poisoning sent him into a coma from which he never recovered. On 16 April 1811 he was buried in St Bride's, Fleet Street, just a few doors away from his home. It is doubtful whether he left anything other than his artistic genes and his lessons in art to support his family. A collection of Isaac Cruikshank's watercolour drawings is held in the Huntington Library, California.

ROBERT L. PATTEN

Sources F. G. Stephens and M. D. George, eds., *Catalogue of political and personal satires preserved … in the British Museum*, 6–9 (1938–49) • G. Cruikshank, 'House book', MS memoir, Princeton University Libraries • R. L. Patten, *George Cruikshank's life, times, and art*, 2 vols. (1992–6) • E. B. Krumbhaar, *Isaac Cruikshank* (1966) • R. R. Wark, *Isaac Cruikshank's drawings for drolls* (1968) • [E. J. Nygren], *Isaac Cruikshank and the politics of parody* (1994) • B. Jerrold, *The life of George Cruikshank*, 2 vols. (1882) • *DNB* • G. M. Woodward, *Eccentric excursions* (1796) • parish register, Edinburgh, Canongate, 5 Oct 1764 [birth] • parish register, Edinburgh, Canongate, 14 Oct 1764 [baptism] • parish register, London, St Anne's, Soho, 14 Aug 1788 [marriage] • parish register, London, St Bride's, Fleet Street, 16 April 1811, GL [burial]

Likenesses I. Cruikshank, wash and ink drawing (*A dinner in a tavern*), repro. in Krumbhaar, *Isaac Cruikshank*, frontispiece

Cruikshank, (Isaac) Robert (1789–1856), caricaturist and portrait painter, eldest son of Isaac *Cruikshank (1764–1811) and his wife, Mary, *née* MacNaughton (1769–1853), was born on 27 September 1789 in St Martin's Court, London, and baptized on 25 October at St Martin-in-the-Fields. Three years later, around the time of his younger brother George *Cruikshank's birth (27 September 1792), the family moved to 27 Duke Street, near Montagu House, where his father was preparing illustrations for George Shaw's *General Zoology*. Some time before 1807 the family moved into a four-storey terrace house at 117 Dorset Street, Salisbury Square, and in the top-floor studio Robert learned his trade.

Robert Cruikshank's next two younger siblings did not survive childhood, and a last, sickly girl, Margaret Eliza, was born on 29 August 1807, long after Robert had grown up and left home. Consequently his childhood was spent essentially in the company of his father and his brother. He and George went for a brief time to a school in Edgware; according to Robert's son, Cruikshank was 'constantly devouring' *Robinson Crusoe* (Cruikshank). But for the most part the boys received their education in the streets and at their father's drawing table. Isaac would let

Anne Clarke scandal, is the first identified as by Robert Cruikshank; presumably he contributed to many others signed by his father and brother. With a special devotion to town life and skill as a portraitist, Robert may have tried to establish himself as a painter of portraits in miniature. He did not execute many autographed caricatures until 1818–19, when the craze for velocipedes (early bicycles) and dandified dressing by men and women attracted his pencil. Dandies were a particular target: committed to taste above all else, and imitating the exquisite dress of Beau Brummell, Lord Byron, and Lord Gwydyr, they were, according to Thomas Carlyle, men 'whose trade, office and existence consists in the wearing of Clothes' (Carlyle, 272). Robert Cruikshank's unflattering caricatures of the species between 1818 and the mid-1820s exposed their superficiality, their self-proclaimed exclusivity, and their often tawdry stratagems for dressing and living on slender means.

From 1820 to 1827 Cruikshank produced at least 400 images, memorably lampooning the Queen Caroline affair ('much may be said on both sides'; I. R. Cruikshank, *The Revolutionary Association* [print], June–July 1821) even though he accepted £70 in May 1820 to relinquish drawing George IV as a 'dandy of sixty'. One of the most resonant of his broadsheet caricatures is *Reflection: to be, or not to be* (11 February 1820), which Dorothy George reproduced as the frontispiece to volume 10 of the British Museum's *Catalogue of Political and Personal Satires*. The newly proclaimed George IV, trying on his crown before a pier-glass, is startled by the reflection, not of himself, but of his estranged wife, Caroline, crowned, larger than he, and looking down at him with a contemptuous half-smile. (The king was hoping to exclude her from all royal rights.) The quotation from *Hamlet*, the visual conceit of a mirror reflecting one's hated other, and Robert's characteristic 'love of factual detail and skill as a miniaturist and portrait painter' (George, 10.xlii) combine to provide both a realistic and an inventively allusive image.

Robert Cruikshank was allegedly the originator of Pierce Egan's best-seller *Life in London* (1820–21) and the model for the buck of fashion Corinthian Tom; he and his brother drew the illustrations, and he superintended the scenery for the hugely successful Adelphi Theatre production of the book as a play. Thereafter Cruikshank worked with C. M. Westmacott on imitations of Egan's and his brother George Cruikshank's productions; the latter was so irritated by his elder brother's capitalizing on his fame that relations cooled for some time. Westmacott's *English Spy* (published, under the pseudonym of Bernard Blackmantle, in instalments and two volumes, 1825) contained many telling portraits of notables of the day, especially in the first volume. Sometimes Robert got carried away by his needling and had to apologize, as he did to the duchess of St Albans in Egan's *Finish to the Adventures of Tom, Jerry and Logic* (parts, 1828–9; volume, 1830).

On 3 August 1816 Robert Cruikshank married at St Giles, Camberwell, Surrey, Sarah Skyrme (*bap.* 19 June 1800). A son, Percy Robert, was born on 8 May 1817, and a second son, Douglas Sharpe, was born on 12 October 1818. Robert

(Isaac) **Robert Cruikshank** (1789–1856), by E. W. Pailthorpe (after George Cruikshank)

his sons put in little 'bits' of background and taught them the basics of drawing, watercolour painting, and etching. Both boys showed aptitude early. But they were also enthralled by the fairy tales told by their nurse and by the stories of African jungles, wild animals, witchcraft, and daring escapes that Mungo Park related when a lodger in the 1790s. The brothers delighted in theatre, performing in home-made dramas with their friend Edmund Kean and later attending performances on every kind of stage. They liked all sports, including mischief-making. Catching 'scarlet fever', Robert joined the Loyal North Britons and rose to the rank of sergeant when the volunteers turned out in 1803. And during adolescence both brothers attended boxing and fencing matches, cock-fights, and innumerable tavern contests.

Robert Cruikshank's ardent desire to go to war was diverted by his parents into a midshipman's commission in the East India Company's ship *Perseverance*. Returning on his maiden voyage, Midshipman Cruikshank, who did not get on with his captain, was left behind on St Helena. He hid out from press-gangs during the rainy season, was eventually befriended by the governor of the island, and walked into the Dorset Street house one winter's day in early 1806 to the astonishment of his family, in mourning on account of his reported death.

His father's declining health made Robert Cruikshank's assistance in the studio imperative; his brother George's greater talents and extensive training while his elder brother was at sea promoted his independent work. A caricature of April 1809, *Burning by Contract*, about the Mary seems to have moved upward towards the fashionable West End, taking lodgings first in King Street, Holborn, and then in St James's Place. Possessing an oddly divided sensibility, Robert sought after fashionable society one day and savaged it the next. During the Queen Caroline affair he tended to take the popular side, but he was not above etching for the king's supporters as well. While he tended to lampoon fashion rather than ministers, he did some designs for the radical publisher William Hone and unmistakably caricatured the *ton* in his illustrations for Westmacott. *Cruikshank versus the New Police* (1833) attacked Wellington; the pseudonyms identifying his plates in the later 1820s 'express', according to Dorothy George, 'a raffish, reckless personality' (George, 11.1). Yet his design in May 1831 for a large silk handkerchief, *The Glorious Reform in Parliament*, was praised by *The Times* on 9 May for the 'great force and humour' of its design, and the following year he executed a series of watercolour drawings for the duke of Sussex (see George, 11.1). This latter commission probably came via the influence of Thomas J. Pettigrew, a physician and old family friend who then served as the duke's librarian.

In the later 1820s Robert Cruikshank illustrated a number of notable books. Often they were sequels to previous successes to which he and his brother George had contributed: George Cruikshank did *Points of Humour* and Robert Cruikshank *Points of Misery* in 1823; the brothers collaborated on the charming *London Characters* of 1827; and Robert Cruikshank alone followed up on the success of Egan's *Life in London* with designs engraved on wood by W. C. Bonner for George Smeeton's *Doings in London* (1828) and coloured etchings plus wood-engraved vignettes for Egan's *Finish to the Adventures of Tom, Jerry and Logic*.

Beyond 1830 the records of Robert Cruikshank's achievements are scanty. Wood-engravings for a number of little books for minor publishers such as William Kidd were collected and reprinted as *Facetiae* (2 vols., 1831). These run the gamut of familiar subjects—theatre, fashionable life, tourism, witches, and devils. A few were cut by his son Percy, an artist and wood-engraver who in the family tradition received artistic training from his father. Percy married Harriet Calvert on 8 January 1842. Their son George Percy, born on 13 December 1842, was named after his famous great-uncle; in later life, when he tried to sign his drawings 'George Cruikshank' or 'George Cruikshank Junior', his namesake protested vigorously. About 1880 Percy wrote an unpublished memoir of his father and uncle (MS, Princeton University Libraries) which, though ill-composed and inaccurate, contains numerous amusing episodes about the brothers' temperaments and was extensively incorporated in Blanchard Jerrold's biography of George Cruikshank published in 1882. Both brothers inherited a 'pugnacious' streak and liked to goad one another. Robert thought that George, still housing their aged mother, was too tied to the maternal apronstrings: 'never went to sea—as I did—knows nothing of the world'. George thought his elder 'a perfect savage. Give him a sword, and shield, and he is happy'. Robert cheered the French revolution of 1848, expecting the republic to take on Russian despotism and volunteering to lead the troops; George retorted, 'Then by God, I'd head the Russians, and oppose you!' (Cruikshank, 176, 226).

As a boy Robert Cruikshank had injured his head in a riding accident; to that, as well as to whisky toddies, was attributed his marked decline in the later 1840s. His behaviour became more and more erratic: sober and sensible for weeks at a time, he would suddenly burst forth with some freakish prank or all-night carouse. He was still capable of designing plates, especially on antiquarian and theatrical subjects, for his friend and Islington neighbour George Daniel. But his family finances deteriorated. George Cruikshank found work for his nephew Percy but the patronage was not always tactful or appreciated. To the outside world, each of the brothers appeared at times eccentric if not insane; indeed even to their mother their behaviour seemed excessive.

Robert Cruikshank could be whimsical and kindly, even quite thoughtful and mellow. He was an avid reader, a keen archer, a good talker, a generous host, and, like his father, a quick and impulsive humorist. One of his last projects was to design illustrations for a new life of Edmund Kean. He managed to complete one watercolour sketch, of Kean as Bluebeard, in the kitchen of Roach's house in Vinegar Yard, where as boys Robert and George had shared in amateur theatricals (Jerrold, 1.29n.). About the same time, George painted his brother on horseback, looking very much the gentleman (c.1852, University Club, New York). During the winter of 1856 Robert Cruikshank caught bronchitis. Unable to throw off the infection, he died on 13 March in his modest lodgings, 13 Pleasant Row, Pentonville, and was buried in Highgate cemetery. ROBERT L. PATTEN

Sources F. G. Stephens and M. D. George, eds., *Catalogue of political and personal satires preserved … in the British Museum*, 6–11 (1938–54) · R. L. Patten, *George Cruikshank's life, times, and art*, 2 vols. (1992–6) · P. Cruikshank, 'George Cruikshank, with some account of his brother Robert Cruikshank', MS memoir, Princeton University · B. Jerrold, *The life of George Cruikshank*, 2 vols. (1882) · G. Daniel, *Love's last labour not lost* (1863) · *DNB* · *IGI* · d. cert. · W. Bates, *George Cruikshank: the artist, the humourist and the man, with some account of his brother Robert* (1878) · G. Everitt, *English caricaturists and graphic humourists of the nineteenth century* (1886) · T. Carlyle, *Sartor resartus*, ed. C. F. Harrold (New York, 1937) · E. Moers, *The dandy: Brummell to Beerbohm* (1960) · parish register, London, St Martin-in-the-Fields, City Westm. AC, 25 Oct 1789 [baptism] · R. Cruikshank, letter to William Hone, July 1816, NYPL, Humanities and Social Sciences Library, Berg collection

Archives LMA, corresp. and drawings, 534/1–14 | Princeton University, New Jersey, George Cruikshank collection, MSS · Rice University, Houston, Texas, Fondren Library, George Cruikshank collection, MSS · University of North Carolina, Chapel Hill, Southern Historical collection, George Cruikshank papers, no. 11005, General and Literary Manuscripts Group; Whitaker papers no. 3433

Likenesses P. Egan, portrait, 1820–21 (allegedly the model for Corinthian Tom in *Life in London*) · G. Cruikshank, portrait, oil, gouache, and watercolour on paper, c.1852, University Club, New York · E. W. Pailthorpe, engraving (after G. Cruikshank), NPG [*see illus.*] · group portrait, BM; repro. in G. Cruikshank, 'Interior view of the House of God', *The Scourge, or, Monthly Expositor of Imposture and Folly* (Nov 1811)

Cruikshank, Robert James (1898–1956), journalist, the son of Robert James Cruikshank, a coffee-house keeper from Balleer, co. Armagh, Ireland, and his wife, Ellen Batcheldor, from Kent, was born in Kensington, London, on 19 April 1898. Always known as Robin Cruikshank, he had little formal education, but read widely from childhood. He began a journalistic career as a reporter on the *Bournemouth Guardian*. After service in the First World War he was recommended to the news editor of the *Daily News* in London and remained with that organization for the rest of his life. In 1919 he was sent to Prague to report the founding of the Czechoslovak republic. From the quality of his dispatches his potential as a foreign correspondent was quickly recognized, and it was in this field that he made his mark in journalism. By 1924 he had risen to the post of diplomatic correspondent of the *Daily News* and four years later he was sent to represent the paper in New York.

In this position, which he held for the next eight years, Cruikshank made a reputation as one of the top-ranking British correspondents in America, both through his knowledge and sympathetic understanding of America and Americans and by the vividness and dependability of his reporting. Colleagues marvelled at how little of his copy ever needed alteration and described his stories as a 'sparkling run of words' which completely 'outwrote his fellow correspondents' (Glenton and Pattinson, 50). It was once said of him by an American that he 'came to know Americans better than they knew themselves'. His ability to understand and define the essence of a culture was shown in his novel *The Double Quest*, published in 1936, which wittily contrasted and compared British and American society.

When the post of managing editor of *The Star* became vacant in 1936, Cruikshank was invited to return to England to take it up. He was appointed a director of *The Star*, the evening stable companion of the *Daily News* which in the interval had become the *News Chronicle*. In 1939 he married Margaret Adele, who survived him, a journalist and daughter of Dr J. A. Macknight, of California. They had two daughters.

It was not surprising that after the outbreak of the Second World War Cruikshank's wide knowledge of the American press and pressmen, combined with his general journalistic talent and his gift for getting on with all manner of people, should have resulted in his being appointed in 1941 director of the American division at the Ministry of Information. He was absent from the editorial chair of *The Star* for the rest of the war. He was also in 1941–2 deputy director-general of the British Information Services in the United States. This second Anglo-American period, with its combination of journalism and diplomacy, probably marked the peak of his professional achievement. In his wartime posts, he was remembered most vividly for his 'genius' for creating in the office 'a real spirit of cooperation, extending down to the most junior member of staff' (Hamilton, 16). He was appointed CMG in 1945 and, the war over, returned to become, as it were, one of the senior statesmen of the *Daily News* organization, being appointed a director of Daily News Ltd (the parent company), and of the News Chronicle Ltd.

Cruikshank took an active part in the editorial and general direction of both newspapers and seemed destined for the highest positions. It was a natural move, when Gerald Barry resigned from the editorship of the *News Chronicle* at the end of 1947, that Cruikshank should succeed him. It is questionable whether his talent lay chiefly in the direction of editorship—he was happier and more at ease writing himself than directing others to write—and it seemed that the burdens of editorship lay rather heavily upon him. By 1954 his health had begun to show signs of deterioration which affected his grip on day-to-day control and by the end of the year he found it necessary to resign.

Cruikshank had continued to be a prolific writer in the post-war period. His book *Roaring Century*, written in 1946 to mark the centenary of the *News Chronicle*, gave a good example of his rich appreciation of Victorian Britain. Characteristically he waived his royalties in it in favour of the Printers' Pension Fund. Shortly afterwards he wrote *Charles Dickens and Early Victorian England* (1949) and in 1951 *The Moods of London*. Fellow journalists remembered him most for his 'happy disposition and a complete absence of pomposity' (*The Times*, 15 May 1956, 13). His other great loves besides journalism and literature were music and the theatre: from 1947 to 1955 he was a governor of the Old Vic, and at one time he was among the sponsors of the London Philharmonic Orchestra. He was also a delegate to the subcommission on freedom of information of the Human Rights Commission of the United Nations. He died at his home at 198 West Hill, Putney, London, on 14 May 1956, and was buried on 17 May after a funeral at Putney Vale cemetery. GERALD BARRY, *rev.* MARC BRODIE

Sources *The Times* (15–16 May 1956) · M. A. Hamilton, *The Times* (17 May 1956), 16 · G. Glenton and W. Pattinson, *The last chronicle of Bouverie Street* (1963) · *WWW* · S. E. Koss, *The rise and fall of the political press in Britain*, 2 (1984) · *CGPLA Eng. & Wales* (1956)
Likenesses H. Coster, photographs, 1936, NPG · photograph, U. Edin., department of bacteriology
Wealth at death £2212 15s. 3d.: probate, 3 Aug 1956, *CGPLA Eng. & Wales*

Cruikshank, William Cumberland (1745–1800), anatomist, was born in Edinburgh, the son of George Cruikshank, an excise officer. He was educated at Edinburgh and Glasgow universities, and graduated MA at the latter in 1767. Besides taking the divinity course he studied French and Italian to a level at which he was able to teach fellow students, and become a tutor for several notable families. The acquaintance of two medical men, John Moore and George Montgomerie, led Cruikshank to discard theology and become Moore's medical pupil; and when William Hunter had separated from William Hewson in 1770 and wrote to Glasgow for another assistant, Moore used his influence to have Cruikshank nominated by the college. After arriving in London in 1771 Cruikshank devoted himself to anatomy, and soon gave demonstrations, occasionally standing in for Hunter at some lectures. Hunter later made him a partner in the Windmill

1794, 177) and 'Experiments in which, on the third day after impregnation, the ova of rabbits were found in the fallopian tubes' (87, 1797, 197). Other papers were: 'Remarks on the absorption of calomel from the internal surface of the mouth', at first published as a long letter in a pamphlet by the surgeon Peter Clare, and afterwards separately; and 'Experiments upon the insensible perspiration of the human body, showing its affinity to respiration', at first included in the former letter, but reprinted in 1795. These experiments proved that carbonic acid is given off by the skin as well as the lungs. The Royal Medical and Chirurgical Society of London possessed a quarto manuscript entitled *Anatomical Lectures*, by Cruikshank and Matthew Baillie, dated 1787.

Cruikshank married in 1773 and had four daughters, the eldest of whom married Honoratus Leigh Thomas (1769–1846). Cruikshank died at his house in Leicester Square, London, on 27 June 1800.

G. T. BETTANY, *rev.* MICHAEL BEVAN

Sources '"Observables" at the Royal College of Surgeons: William Cumberland Cruikshank. A link with Samuel Johnson', *Annals of the Royal College of Surgeons of England*, 8 (1951), 325–7 · P. J. Wallis and R. V. Wallis, *Eighteenth century medics*, 2nd edn (1988) · S. C. Lawrence, *Charitable knowledge: hospital pupils and practitioners in eighteenth-century London* (1996) · J. Boswell, *Life of Johnson*, ed. R. W. Chapman, rev. J. D. Fleeman, new edn (1970); repr. with introduction by P. Rogers (1980) · *GM*, 1st ser., 70 (1800), 694, 792 · H. L. Thomas, *The Hunterian oration: delivered before the Royal College of Surgeons … 1827* (1827) · T. J. Pettigrew, *Medical portrait gallery: biographical memoirs of the most celebrated physicians, surgeons … who have contributed to the advancement of medical science*, 4 vols. in 2 [1838–40], vol. 3 · W. I. Addison, *A roll of graduates of the University of Glasgow from 31st December 1727 to 31st December 1897* (1898) · *IGI*

Archives RCS Eng. · Wellcome L.

Likenesses plaster medallion, 1795 (after J. Tassie), Scot. NPG · T. Dickinson, stipple, pubd 1801 (after J. Roberts), BM · J. Corner, line engraving, BM; repro. in *European Magazine* (1787) · T. Rowlandson, group portrait, drawing, RCS Eng. · G. Stuart, oils, RCS Eng. [*see illus.*]

William Cumberland Cruikshank (1745–1800), by Gilbert Stuart

Street School, and after Hunter's death in 1783 he carried on in conjunction with Matthew Baillie, Hunter's nephew.

Cruikshank is remembered as a successful teacher of anatomy and for his original work on the absorbent system. The results of his researches, which had been carried on in conjunction with William Hunter, were published in a quarto volume, *The Anatomy of the Absorbing Vessels of the Human Body* (1786). In it he embodied what he had taught for the previous ten years, having traced the lymphatic vessels extensively through the human body as well as in numerous animals. He had a considerable practice as a surgeon, but his rather nervous temperament stopped him becoming a successful operator. Cruikshank attended Dr Johnson in his last illness, and was termed by him, in allusion to his benevolent disposition, 'a sweet-blooded man'. When Cruikshank was lancing the dying man's legs to reduce his dropsy, Johnson called out to him, 'I want life, and you are afraid of giving me pain—deeper, deeper.' Cruikshank enjoyed the company of literary men, but was susceptible to periods of melancholia and intemperance. He received an honorary MD from Glasgow in 1783, and became FRS in 1797.

Besides his main work, which reached a second edition in 1790, and was translated into French, German, and Italian, Cruikshank wrote comparatively little. Several works on yellow fever and on chemical and other subjects have been erroneously attributed to him. Two important papers by him are in *Philosophical Transactions*. These are 'Experiments on the nerves, particularly on their reproduction and on the spinal marrow of living animals' (85,

Cruise, William (1751/2–1824), legal writer, the second son of Patrick Cruise of Rathugh, co. Westmeath, was admitted a member of Lincoln's Inn on 5 November 1773. As a Roman Catholic he was prevented from practising at the bar (under the statute 7 & 8 Will. III, c. 24), and he practised instead as a licensed conveyancer, for which he acquired a considerable reputation. The bar was opened to him after the act for the relief of Roman Catholics of 1791 (31 Geo. II, c. 32), and he was called to the bar on 8 July 1791 at Lincoln's Inn. His practice, however, seems to have remained wholly in conveyancing.

Cruise was the author of numerous works on legal subjects. In 1783 he published *An Essay on the Nature and Operation of Fines and Recoveries*. The plan of this work, which dealt with an intricate subject of great importance, was suggested by Charles Fearne's classic treatise, *Contingent Remainders*. A second edition was published in 1785, and a third in 1794. In 1804 Cruise's *Digest of the Laws of England Respecting Real Property* was published (reaching a fourth edition in 1835). In this work, which became a popular manual for practitioners and students, Cruise embraced

Sir William Jones's theories on the systematic distribution of general principles with detailed abridgements of cases. In 1810 he published *The Origin and Nature of Dignities or Titles of Honour*, and brought out a second edition in 1823. Given that claims to ancient dignities had become very numerous in the early nineteenth century, Cruise had hoped to publish a collection of all the printed cases that had been presented to the House of Lords, adding such information as could be gathered from the minutes of the committee of privileges. The costs of such a venture and the likely small sale forced him to abandon that ambition. However, his work on *Dignities* was well respected, and was much drawn on in the debates in the House of Lords in 1856 in the Wensleydale peerage case.

Cruise does not appear to have married, and seems to have led a rather reclusive life. In 1823 he retired from the profession, and took to his quarters at The Albany, Piccadilly, London, where he died on 5 January 1824 at the age of seventy-two. Michael Lobban

Sources *Annual Register* (1824) · A. W. B. Simpson, ed., *Biographical dictionary of the common law* (1984) · Holdsworth, *Eng. law*, 14.145 · W. P. Baildon, ed., *The records of the Honorable Society of Lincoln's Inn: the black books*, 4 (1902)

Crull, Jodocus (*d.* 1713/14), writer and translator, was a native of Hamburg who studied medicine at Leiden (MD, 1679) and thereafter settled in England. He was admitted MD of Cambridge by incorporation on 7 August 1681 and licentiate of the Royal College of Physicians on 22 December 1692. Although elected a fellow of the Royal Society on 23 and admitted on 30 November 1681, his name was omitted from the annual lists, presumably from inability to pay the fees. Among the Sloane Manuscripts (no. 4041, fol. 288) is a letter from Crull canvassing votes at the election of a navy physician, but he apparently had little success in his profession and turned to translating and compiling for the booksellers. He resided in both London and the country: he is identified on the Royal College of Physicians list as a 'country' member, and his publication *Denmark Vindicated* (1694) is 'sent from a gentleman in the country, to his friend in London'.

Within his primary ambition to produce vendible books, Crull appears carefully conformist in politics and religion: for example, his two-volume compilation *The Antient and Present State of Muscovy* (1698), designed to catch the market on the occasion of Tsar Peter's visit to London in that year, borrows material from the radical Milton's *A Brief History of Moscovia* (1682) but draws political exempla from English and Russian history favourable to the government of the day, and hence also to the precarious career of an emigré. Similarly, Crull joined other conservatives in replying to Molesworth's anti-clerical and whig attack on the Danish government in his *Denmark vindicated: being an answer to a late treatise [by Robert Viscount Molesworth] called An account of Denmark, as it was in the year 1692* (1694). Most of Crull's books were published with his initials only, and many contain dedications seeking patronage or commissions. Crull's translations include an English version from the Latin of Anne Conway (*The Principles of the most Ancient and Modern Philosophy*, 1692; attributed to Crull by Halkett and Laing); Samuel Pufendorf (*An Introduction to the History of the Principal Kingdoms and States of Europe*, 1695, which achieved nine further editions to 1728; and *Of the Nature and Qualification of Religion*, 1698); Dellon (*Voyage to the East-Indies*, 1698); and *The present condition of the Muscovite empire … in two letters … with the life of the present emperour of China, by Father J. Bouvet* (1699), Crull's version of which was translated into Russian in 1787.

Crull's own writings were on a range of medical, historico-political and topographical subjects, and include *Memoirs of Denmark, containing the life and reign of the late K. of Denmark, Norway, &c. Christian V* (1700); *The Complete History of the Affairs of Spain* (1707; 2nd edn, 1708); *The Jewish history … being an abridgment of Sr. Roger l'Estrange's Josephus* [1702]. *With a continuation* (1708); and *The Antiquities of St. Peters, or the Abbey Church of Westminster* (1711). The date of Crull's death is uncertain: the Royal College of Physicians list for 1713 contains his name, but not the list for 1715, indicating that he probably died in 1713 or 1714.

R. D. Bedford

Sources BL cat. · Wing, STC · *Early English books, 1641–1700* (1961–98) [microfilm] · DNB · *A list of the fellows of the Royal Society, 1664–1767* (1940) · Munk, *Roll*, 1.497 · BL, Sloane MS, 4041, fol. 288 · H. Schroeder, *Lexikon der hamburgischen Schriftsteller*, 1 (Hamburg, 1851), 608 · S. Halkett and J. Laing, *A dictionary of anonymous and pseudonymous publications in the English language*, ed. J. Horden, 3rd edn (1980–) · E. Solly, N&Q, 6th ser., 3 (1881), 231 [on Crull's death date] · B. E. McCarthy, 'A seventeenth-century borrowing from Milton's *A Brief history of Moscovia*', N&Q, 213 (1968), 99–101 · R. D. Bedford, 'Jodocus Crull and Milton's *A brief history of Moscovia*', *Review of English Studies*, new ser., 47 (1996), 207–11

Crum, Walter Ewing (1865–1944), Coptic scholar, was born on 22 July 1865 at Capelrig, Renfrewshire, the eldest son of Alexander Crum (1828–1893), manufacturer and Liberal member of parliament for Renfrewshire (1880–85), and his wife, Margaret Stewart (Nina), eldest daughter of Alexander Ewing, bishop of Argyll and the Isles.

Crum was educated at a Brighton preparatory school (from 1873), Eton College (1879–84), and Balliol College, Oxford (1884–8), gaining a second class in modern history. Failure to obtain a first was generally attributed to the amount of time he spent practising the violin; at one time he hoped to take it up professionally, but his instructor advised against this. Instead, he turned his attention to Egyptology, for he had become interested in the Egyptian monuments he saw on family holidays in Paris. On graduating, therefore, he proceeded first to Paris, to study Egyptology under Gaston Maspero and William Groff, and then to Munich. In 1890 he went to Berlin, on the advice of F. Ll. Griffith, to study under Adolf Erman, whose close friend he became, and Georg Steindorff. Steindorff introduced him to Coptic, which soon became his main preoccupation.

Crum remained in Berlin until 1892, when he applied for a post in the department of Egyptian and Assyrian antiquities at the British Museum. He came first in the examination but was rejected on medical grounds. Since his family's wealth was sufficient to support him, he made no further attempt to obtain an official post. The same year saw his first publications on Coptic, including the chapter on Coptic papyri in W. M. Flinders Petrie's *Medum*, and the first of his bibliographies of Coptic studies and Christian Egypt, which were a highly valued feature of the annual *Archaeological Report* of the Egypt Exploration Fund (later Society) until 1909. His first independent volume, *Coptic Manuscripts Brought from the Fayyum*, appeared in 1893. From that year until 1910 he assisted Petrie with the teaching of Ancient Egyptian and Coptic at University College, London; among his pupils was Sir Herbert Thompson (1859–1944), who became his closest friend. During this period Crum came to feel the acute need for a new Coptic dictionary that would take account of the advances made in Coptic studies since the previous dictionary (Peyron's *Lexicon Copticum* of 1835), and especially of the quantities of new texts being found in Egypt at the time, which were mostly unpublished. He was beginning to make systematic preparations for this project when a major upheaval occurred in his domestic affairs.

In 1896 Crum had married Ella, daughter of Sir Edward Henry *Sieveking, physician to Queen Victoria and the prince of Wales, but the marriage was unhappy and they had no children. At University College, however, Crum met Margaret (Madge) Hart-Davis (1876–1953), who was studying Egyptology at the time, and they fell in love. When their relationship became known, in 1910, they were ostracized by the college, but Ella Crum, a Roman Catholic, refused to divorce him. He and Hart-Davis decided to elope abroad, and settled in Austria, first in Graz and later in Vienna. The two remained together for the rest of Crum's life, and she changed her surname to Crum by deed poll, but they could never marry, since Ella Crum outlived her husband.

In Austria the couple devoted themselves to the first stages of work on the dictionary. Crum travelled to museums and libraries all over Europe collecting material, while still finding time to edit the texts from the Theban monastery of Epiphanius brought to him in 1911 by the American Egyptologist H. E. Winlock. When war broke out in 1914 the Crums were still in Austria, but Winlock persuaded the American state department to take up their case, and they were eventually allowed to leave.

During the war Crum gave up half his income to charities and volunteered for work in the War Office. Afterwards he settled in Westbury-on-Trym, near Bristol, moving to Bath in 1927, where he was later joined by Thompson, who came to assist with the dictionary. This was eventually compiled from more than 240,000 slips. An earlier contract with the Berlin Academy having lapsed in the war, Crum reached an agreement with Oxford University Press in 1927 to share the cost of publication. It appeared in six parts (1929–39) and at once took rank as the definitive dictionary of the Coptic language.

This was Crum's *magnum opus*, but by no means his only important work; he was also responsible for editing a huge number of previously unpublished Coptic texts. The two largest of his text editions were the catalogues of the Coptic manuscripts in the British Museum (1905) and in the John Rylands Library, Manchester (1909), both very substantial works. Other notable titles are one volume of the Cairo Museum catalogue, *Coptic Monuments* (1902); *Coptic Ostraca* (1902); and the first volume of *Koptische Rechtsurkunden des achten Jahrhunderts* (1912). He also contributed numerous articles to journals on Coptic and (until 1898) other Egyptological topics. A full bibliography is given in *Coptic Studies in Honor of Walter Ewing Crum* (1950), vii–xi (revised from *Journal of Egyptian Archaeology*, 25, 1939, 134–8). His achievements were recognized by honorary degrees of PhD (Berlin, 1910) and DLitt (Oxford, 1937); he was elected FBA in 1931. He had a flair for languages, speaking and writing French and German with ease, and knowing many other European languages, as well as Syriac, Ethiopic, and Arabic. Crum's approach to his work, despite its quantity, was always methodical and conscientious, resulting in a very high standard of accuracy. It may be noted that when he discovered that the production costs of the dictionary would be less than expected, he voluntarily repaid subventions towards them from academic bodies. He was always ready to give assistance to other scholars, and little was published on the subject without recourse to him. He could be expansive or highly strung, but was always courteous, modest, and kind. His appearance was tall and strikingly handsome, and some of his friends dubbed him 'our Coptic Apollo'.

After the completion of the dictionary, Crum's energy began to fail. He spent much of his last days acting as next of kin for Thompson in the latter's final illness, and died of a sudden heart attack at his home, 19 Bathwick Hill, Bath, on 18 May 1944, shortly after learning that Thompson had no hope of recovery.   R. S. Simpson

Sources *DNB* · B. Gunn and H. I. Bell, 'Walter Ewing Crum, 1865–1944', *PBA*, 34 (1948), 281–91 · *Year Book of the American Philosophical Society* (1944), 354–8 · *Journal of Egyptian Archaeology*, 30 (1944), 65–6 · *The Times* (22 May 1944), 6 · *Chronique d'Égypte*, 20 (1945), 147–51 · 'A bibliography of Walter Ewing Crum', *Bulletin of the Byzantine Institute* [*Coptic studies in honor of Walter Ewing Crum*], 2 (1950), vii–xi · W. R. Dawson and E. P. Uphill, *Who was who in Egyptology*, 3rd edn, rev. M. L. Bierbrier (1995), 110–11 · R. Hart-Davis, *The arms of time* (1979), 147–8 · R. M. Janssen, *The first hundred years: Egyptology at University College London, 1892–1992* (1992), 6, 11 · M. S. Drower, *Flinders Petrie: a life in archaeology* (1985), 223, 312–13 · *WWBMP*, 1.97 · *WWW, 1941–50* · b. cert.

Archives BL, corresp., Add. MSS 45681–45690 · U. Oxf., Griffith Institute, Egyptological notebooks; papers, notebooks, copies, photographs, dictionary slips, and corresp. relating to Coptic interests | BL, corresp. with Idris Bell, Add. MSS 59508–59509 · Bodl. Oxf., corresp. with J. E. A. Fenwick and T. F. Fenwick

Likenesses black and white sketch, repro. in *Journal of Egyptian Archaeology*, 25 (1939), pl. xii · group photograph, repro. in Dawson and Uphill, *Who was who in Egyptology*, 110 · photograph, repro. in Gunn and Bell, 'Walter Ewing Crum', pl. 15 · photograph, repro. in 'A bibliography of Walter Ewing Crum', *Bulletin of the Byzantine Institute*, frontispiece · photographs (with Madge), repro. in Hart-Davis, *Arms of time*, 147

Wealth at death wealthy; left ninety-three books on Coptic to Edwards Library, UCL

Crump, Charles George (1862–1935), archivist, was born at Wyke Regis, near Weymouth, Dorset, on 9 April 1862, the eldest son of Charles Ashbrook Wright Crump, barrister, of the Inner Temple, then an instructor on the training ship HMS *Britannia*, and his wife, Helen Ann Crane. His parents left England with their family in 1872 and lived at San Remo until 1885. Charles, like his brothers Harry and Louis, was educated by his father, who also took private pupils, for the Indian Civil Service, and obtained seventh place in the examination of 1880, whereupon he entered Balliol College, Oxford, as a civilian in training.

After graduating in jurisprudence in 1883 Crump proceeded to India, but after six months at Cawnpore he was invalided home for good; he retired in 1886. On recovering, he aimed at a post in the home civil service, and while waiting to compete worked under Sir J. A. H. Murray on the *Oxford English Dictionary*. In 1890 he married Lucy (d. 1946), younger daughter of the literary scholar George Birkbeck *Hill, sister of Sir (Edward) Maurice Hill, judge, and sister-in-law of the economic historian Sir W. J. Ashley; they had a son and a daughter.

Crump obtained a post as clerk in the secretary's department of the General Post Office in 1887, from which in 1888 he was transferred as a junior clerk to the Public Record Office. Here he remained until his retirement with the rank of senior assistant keeper (which he held from 1916) in 1923. Although early in his career he was reprimanded for spilling ink on two court rolls, he was later trusted to protect Domesday Book from air raids in February 1918, when he personally accompanied its removal to safer storage in Bodmin prison.

Crump's earliest considerable work was an edition of the works of W. S. Landor (1891–3), but the historical and economic interest of his official duties led him away from purely literary tasks. He contributed to Robert Harry Inglis Palgrave's *Dictionary of Political Economy* (1891–9) and to *Social England* (1893–7) by H. D. Traill. With two colleagues he edited in 1902 the *Dialogus de Scaccario* of Richard fitz Nigel (their edition superseded the 1711 text of Thomas Madox) and he was co-editor of the essays entitled *The Legacy of the Middle Ages* (1926). His extremely acute mind and attractive character are reflected in some degree in *The Logic of History* (1919), *History and Historical Research* (1928), and his one novel, a rather ponderous fantasy of academic life, *The Red King Dreams* (1931).

Crump's official work can be found in such publications as the *List of Foreign Accounts* (1900), *Calendar of Charter Rolls* (1903–27), and the *Book of Fees* (1920–31). He was an active member of the advisory committee appointed in 1912 by the master of the rolls to bring the Public Record Office into closer touch with historical scholars. However, his greatest service to history was his insistence on the need for the study of records in their proper setting as products of an administrative machine, and not merely as evidence of isolated facts. In this respect later historians and archivists are indebted to him. Crump was one of the group of eight original assistant keepers who played a significant role in the evolution of the modern Public Record Office. He died at his home, 179 Hampstead Way, Hendon, London, on 11 December 1935.

CHARLES JOHNSON, *rev.* ROBERT BROWN

Sources *The Times* (13 Dec 1935) · private information (1949) · personal knowledge (1949) · *WWW* · J. D. Cantwell, *The Public Record Office, 1838–1958* (1991) · C. Johnson, 'The Public Record Office', *Studies presented to Sir Hilary Jenkinson*, ed. J. C. Davies (1957), 178–95 · *CGPLA Eng. & Wales* (1936)
Wealth at death £646 4s. 4d.: probate, 6 Feb 1936, *CGPLA Eng. & Wales*

Crump [Crumpe], **Henry** (*fl.* c.1376–1401), Cistercian monk and religious controversialist, was of Irish birth, and became a monk in the abbey of Baltinglass, Wicklow. He was probably a native of the diocese of Meath, where one Matthew Crump was archdeacon between 1373 and c.1393. By c.1376 he was in Oxford, where he preached in the church of St Mary the Virgin against the views of John Wyclif (d. 1384) on the subjection of the clergy and of church property to the state. Wyclif replied in the second book of *De civili dominio*, completed by 1377. Crump was DTh by 1380, when he was one of twelve doctors appointed by the chancellor of the university, William Barton, to a commission that condemned Wyclif's views on the eucharist. In 1382 the university climate had become more favourable to Wyclif, who was supported by the new chancellor, Robert Rygge (d. 1410), and two proctors. Crump attended the council convened on 21 May 1382 by Archbishop William Courtenay (d. 1396) at Blackfriars in London, which condemned further opinions of Wyclif and his followers.

In protest against the choice of a young supporter of Wyclif, Philip Repyndon (d. 1424), to preach the prestigious sermon at St Frideswide's on the feast of Corpus Christi (5 June), Courtenay ordered the publication in Oxford of the council's condemnation of Wyclif, and forbade the preaching of dangerous doctrines there. On 12 June 1382 the chancellor, and others who included Crump, signed the decrees of the Blackfriars Council, and on his return to Oxford the chancellor reluctantly, and under pressure, published the condemnation. Hostilities continued, and Crump was suspended from all scholastic acts, accused of disturbing the peace by calling the adherents of Wycliffite views 'Lollards', the first recorded instance of the use of the word in this context. Crump took his case to London before the archbishop and the king's council, and on 14 July obtained a royal writ commanding the chancellor and proctors to reinstate him in his former position.

At a meeting of the southern convocation convened by Courtenay in November 1382, Rygge sought the condemnation of certain theses that were being debated in the schools by Crump, a Carmelite, and a Franciscan, but the charges were dismissed. Soon afterwards Crump returned to Ireland, where he renewed the old controversy waged by Richard Fitzralph (d. 1360) against the friars' right to hear confessions. He was accused of heresy, brought before the Dominican bishop of Meath, William Andrew (d. 1385), and duly condemned on 18 March 1385. Seven of the heretical tenets mentioned attacked the pastoral privileges of the friars, and their role as confessors. The eighth proposition maintained that the body of Christ in the eucharist was only a mirror of the body of Christ in heaven, an indication that Crump had begun to adopt a view similar to that of his former opponent, Wyclif. In spite of the condemnation Crump returned to Oxford, and maintained his ground. The sentence against him was communicated to the university, but no further action was taken. However, the questionable nature of his views soon became clearer, and they were brought to the notice of the king's council early in 1392. A brief of 20 March 1392 ordered that Crump should be suspended from all scholastic acts in the university until he had appeared in person, and cleared himself of the outstanding charges. By 3 May he had left Oxford.

But Crump was clearly an energetic and persistent controversialist, expressing views regarded as dangerous by upholders of religious orthodoxy, and his opinions were soon brought once more to the attention of the authorities. On 28 May 1392 a council sat in Stamford in Lincolnshire under the presidency of Archbishop Courtenay, which was further attended by the archbishops Thomas Arundel of York (d. 1414) and Robert Waldby of Dublin (d. 1397), and by a number of bishops and friars. It condemned ten propositions put forward by Crump concerning the mendicants' right to hear confessions, and their author was compelled to abjure them. The Carmelite John Langton, who preserved an account of the proceedings, reported that a copy of the previous condemnation, which the bishop of Meath had sent to the university, was discovered by accident in Blackfriars in Oxford on 11 June, shortly after his appearance in Stamford, and too late for his accusers to make use of them. Richard II confirmed the condemnation in a royal decree of 20 March 1393.

Thereupon Crump appears to have returned to Ireland, where he once more caused trouble by joining forces with John Colton, archbishop of Armagh (d. 1404), and John Whitehead, the rector of Stabannan, Louth, and preaching against the Dominicans in Drogheda, who had sought and obtained the *Portiuncula* indulgence from Pope Boniface IX. Crump was still being charged rent for a room in University College, Oxford, in 1397–8, and for arrears in 1399–1400. His last recorded appearance occurs on 26 August 1401, when he was forbidden to preach against the indulgence by the same pope, under pain of excommunication. The date of his death is unknown. Of the works ascribed to him by John Bale—*Determinationes scholasticae, Tractatus contra mendicantes, Responsiones ad obiecta*, all without incipits, and *De fundatione monasteriorum in Anglia, Vita S. Edithe, Vita S. Ethelrede*, all with incipits—no identifiable manuscripts have survived. He is further regarded as the author of the *Quaestiones de privilegiis* (dated 1383) in BL, Royal MS 7 E.x, fols. 63–71.   KATHERINE WALSH

Sources Emden, *Oxf.*, 1.524–5 · *CEPR letters*, 4.105, 120, 190, 465; 5.432–3 · R. O'Bri(an) and É. Bro(uette), 'Henri Crump', *Dictionnaire des auteurs cisterciens*, ed. É. Brouette, A. Dimler, and E. Manning (1975–9), col. 349f. · J. I. Catto, 'Wyclif and Wycliffism at Oxford, 1356–1430', *Hist. U. Oxf.* 2: *Late med. Oxf.*, 175–261 · A. Hudson, 'Wycliffism in Oxford, 1381–1411', *Wyclif in his times*, ed. A. Kenny (1986), 67–84, esp. 73 · A. Hudson, 'Wyclif and the English language', *Wyclif in his times*, ed. A. Kenny (1986), 85–103, esp. 86 · H. E. Salter, ed., *Munimenta civitatis Oxonie*, OHS, 71 (1920), 162 · H. E. Salter, W. A. Pantin, and H. G. Richardson, eds., *Formularies which bear on the history of Oxford*, 1, OHS, new ser., 4 (1942), 252–3; 2, Oxford Historical Society, new ser., 5 (1942), 311–12 · Bale, *Cat.*, 2.246 · Bale, *Index*, 161 · D. Wilkins, ed., *Concilia Magnae Britanniae et Hiberniae*, 3 (1737), 170 · Dugdale, *Monasticon*, 2.319 · [T. Netter], *Fasciculi zizaniorum magistri Johannis Wyclif cum tritico*, ed. W. W. Shirley, Rolls Series, 5 (1858), 113, 289, 311–14, 343–59 · J. L. Copeland, 'The authorship of the British Museum, Royal MS 7 E.X, fols. 63–71', *BIHR*, 15 (1937–8), 70–72 · C. H. Talbot, 'A list of Cistercian manuscripts in Great Britain', *Traditio*, 8 (1952), 402–18, esp. 410

Archives BL, Royal MS 7 E.x, fols. 63–71

Crump, Neville Franklin (1910–1997), racehorse trainer, was born on 27 December 1910 at The Knoll, Scotts Avenue, Shortlands, Beckenham, Kent, the son of Charles Price Crump, a provision agent, and his wife, Beatrice Irene, *née* Mansell. His father had emigrated to become a rancher in Australia after his own father had gambled away the family fortune, but, after eight years in the Antipodes, had returned to England when he read of his sister's engagement. Soon after he established a cheese manufactory in Wells, Somerset. He became master of the south Oxfordshire foxhounds and Crump learned to ride and hunt at an early age. Educated at Hazlewood preparatory school, Marlborough College, and Balliol College, Oxford, where he retained his place through his rowing ability and scraped a pass degree, he later claimed (to Edward Heath) not to remember who his Oxford tutor was. From 1931 to 1935 he served with the 4th hussars and rode as an amateur under National Hunt rules. He resigned from the army in the latter year, believing that the role of the cavalry was being undermined by an emphasis on the mechanical. Ironically he served during the Second World War as a tank trainer at Barnard Castle with the Royal Armoured Corps. Prior to that he was in Palestine as a captain in the North Somerset yeomanry.

After paying a premium to be an assistant with J. L. (Sonny) Hall at Russley Park, near Swindon, in 1937 Crump took out a licence to train a small string at Upavon on Salisbury Plain. On 11 October the same year he married Sylvia Diana (Brownie) Bradley (1915/16–1992), daughter of Hermon Bradley, of independent means, and granddaughter of Sir Alfred Bird, the millionaire custard magnate. They had one daughter, Sarah Jane. In 1944 he moved his training establishment to Middleham, near Leyburn, Yorkshire. His first major training success was the Grand National win of the 50 to 1 shot, Sheila's Cottage, in 1948. This win rapidly increased his clientele and very quickly the stable went from six to over sixty horses. In gratitude he renamed his Middleham home after the winning mare.

Crump retired from training in 1989 after a career that brought him champion trainer's titles in 1951–2 and 1956–7, a hat-trick of Whitbread Gold Cups, and ten Grand Nationals (five Scottish, two Welsh, and three at Aintree). His horses won all but one of the major staying steeplechases: only the Cheltenham Gold Cup eluded him. He helped to establish Middleham as a northern National Hunt training centre to rival the southern-based stronghold of Lambourn. In his early training days he also won sixteen races on the flat. Much of his success was attributable to patience, paying meticulous attention to detail, and being completely involved with his horses and staff. In particular he advocated the loose school for teaching horses to jump and give them confidence. To his mind 'training the horse is no problem; the problem is training the owner' (Fitzgeorge-Parker, 101).

A large, bluff, outspoken man with a booming voice, Crump's humour was unsubtle. When asked if a particular elderly member of the aristocracy would be suitable as a racecourse steward, his reply was that 'he would be perfect. He can't hear, he can't see, and he knows fuck all about racing' (Fitzgeorge-Parker, 174). His was a short fuse, as many an unsaddling enclosure as well as his Middleham gallops could testify. Locals could also suffer from his early morning, off-key baritone as he took his string out to the Middleham gallops. Master of the Aldershot draghounds before the war, he loved dogs almost as much as horses and always had one around. He hated wearing jackets and would refuse dinner invitations unless allowed to wear a sweater. He was honest, always insisting that his horses ran on their merits; he never gambled; and he steadfastly refused to train for bookmakers. On the one occasion when he agreed to pull a horse—Teal at Kelso—so that he could retain it in the yard for the Grand National, his jockey did it ostentatiously by bringing the horse to a halt when it was a fence ahead of the field, dismounting and pretending to remove a stone from its foot before remounting and finishing second. His loyalty was unswerving. Over his career he had only six stable jockeys, all of whom stayed with him until their retirement. He allowed one jockey, Gerry Scott, to ride Merryman, fortunately to victory, in the 1960 Grand National only twelve days after breaking his collar bone. Earlier, when Scott was just an apprentice, an owner accused the young rider of stopping his mount. Without hesitation, Crump told the accuser to remove his horses from the yard. The loyalty was reciprocated. Scott visited Crump three times a week when the latter was in the Morris Grange private nursing home, Middleton Tyas, Richmond, Yorkshire. He died there on 18 January 1997 of bronchopneumonia and Alzheimer's disease. He was survived by his daughter, Sarah.

WRAY VAMPLEW

Sources T. Fitzgeorge-Parker, *Ever loyal: the biography of Neville Crump* (1987) • *The Times* (20 Jan 1997) • *Daily Telegraph* (20 Jan 1997) • *The Independent* (21 Jan 1997) • P. Smyly, ed., *Encyclopaedia of steeplechasing* (1979) • b. cert. • m. cert. • d. cert.

Likenesses photograph, repro. in *The Times* • photograph, repro. in *The Independent* • photographs, repro. in Fitzgeorge-Parker, *Ever loyal*

Wealth at death £257,420: probate, 11 April 1997, *CGPLA Eng. & Wales*

Crumpe, Samuel (1766–1796), physician, was born on 15 September 1766, the eldest of the six children of Daniel Crumpe, of Barleymount, near Killarney, co. Kerry, and his wife and cousin, Grace Orpen, also of co. Kerry. He matriculated at the University of Edinburgh in 1785 and graduated MD in 1788. In the same year, his thesis *De vitiis quibus humores corrumpi dicuntur, eorumque remediis*, was published in Edinburgh.

In April 1793 Crumpe submitted an essay to the Royal Irish Academy on the best means of providing employment in Ireland, for which he was awarded a prize of £50 and membership of the academy. This work, which is little more than a curiosity, was heavily influenced by the economist Adam Smith, and the agriculturist and traveller Arthur Young. Crumpe emerges from this essay as opinionated and authoritarian. His characters are stereotypically Irish, particularly the poor and disadvantaged, who are portrayed as idle, shifty, and mendacious, prone to pilfering and drunkenness, alternately servile and riotous. Crumpe also produced two further medical works, a monograph on the nature and properties of opium (1793), which, along with the previous work, was translated into German, and an article on the discharge of uncommon worms from the stomach. The latter was read before the Royal Irish Academy on 6 December 1794 and published posthumously in 1797, in the academy's *Transactions*.

In May 1792, at Kilfentinan church, in the Church of Ireland diocese of Limerick, Crumpe married Susan Ingram, second daughter of the Revd Jaques Ingram. They had two children, a son who died in infancy in 1794, and a daughter. The family lived at 6 Arthur's Quay, Limerick, where, presumably, Crumpe had his medical practice. He succeeded Dr Hassett as physician to St John's Hospital, Limerick, a position he held until his death from 'fever' on 27 January 1796. Crumpe was interred in the churchyard of St Mary's Cathedral, Limerick, in the same grave as his infant son. His tombstone records that he was a man of

> eminent talents, profound judgement and extensive knowledge … integrity of heart, benevolence of disposition and suavity of manners. As a son, a husband, a parent, a friend, his conduct was such as to merit the tenderest love of those with whom he was connected, the warm approbation and esteem of all to whom he was known.

LAURENCE M. GEARY

Sources Royal College of Physicians of Ireland, Kirkpatrick Archive • Burke, *Gen. GB* • U. Edin. L., special collections division, university archives • *Proceedings of the Royal Irish Academy*, 1 (1836–40), 92 • *GM*, 1st ser., 66 (1796), 255

Crusius, (Eberhard) Lewis (1701–1775), Church of England clergyman and classical scholar, was born in London, the son of Irenaeus Crusius, a clerk. He was educated at Charterhouse School and matriculated from St John's College, Cambridge, in 1719. In January 1733 he was admitted as a pensioner at Queens' College, Cambridge, from where he graduated MA in 1737. He was elected headmaster of Charterhouse in 1748 and continued in post until his resignation in 1767. In 1749 the master of Charterhouse, Nicholas Mann, fined him for 'defect in his duties' (Jameson, 67), but Crusius was later vindicated by the governors who increased his salary. In 1748 he was collated to the prebend of Brecknock, the first in a series of ecclesiastical appointments. On 20 December 1751 he was appointed a prebendary of Worcester Cathedral and he succeeded to the rectories of Shobden, Herefordshire, Stoke Prior, Worcestershire (1754–64), and St John, Bredwardine, Worcestershire (1764–75). He was elected a fellow of the Royal Society on 7 March 1754 and also took the degree of DD (Lambeth) that year.

Crusius's sole work was *The Lives of the Roman Poets* (1726, 1732), which he supplemented with an introductory essay on the origin of poetry. The work went through three editions by 1753 and was translated into German (1777, 1778); it was still regarded as authoritative by Brüggemann in 1797. Designed for 'the Improvement of Youth and the Entertainment of others', Crusius's writing is polite and self-consciously Augustan in style. He admires the civilizing effect of Horace's satire during 'the crisis of Roman greatness' above all else.

Crusius, who was married to Ann, died on 23 May 1775 and was buried under the piazza of Charterhouse chapel. A portrait of Crusius in the dress of a Carthusian monk, with the inscription

His face and dress so aptly fit
He surely was a Jesuit

hangs in the Charterhouse Museum, Godalming.

THOMPSON COOPER, *rev.* PATRICK BULLARD

Sources Venn, *Alum. Cant.* · L. W. Brüggemann, *A view of the English editions, translations and illustrations of the ancient Greek and Latin authors* (1797) · A. Quick, *Charterhouse: a history of the school* (1990), 29–33 · J. L. Smith-Dampier, *Carthusian worthies* (1940) · E. M. Jameson, *Charterhouse* (1937), 67 · F. B. Chancellor and H. S. Eeles, *Celebrated Carthusians* (1936), 296–7 · T. Thomson, *History of the Royal Society from its institution to the end of the eighteenth century* (1812), appx, p. 47 · *Fasti Angl.* (Hardy), 3.80 · J. Chambers, *Biographical illustrations of Worcestershire* (1820), 362, 597 · J. P. Malcolm, *Londinium redivivum, or, An antient history and modern description of London*, 4 vols. (1802–7), vol. 1, pp. 422, 427 · *Annual Register* (1770), 209 · PRO, PROB 11/1008, fols. 280–81
Archives BL, corresp. with Thomas Birch, Add. MS 4303 · BL, corresp. with duke of Newcastle, Add. MS 32725 · Bodl. Oxf., corresp. with Thomas Edwards, Bodl. MSS 1007–1012
Likenesses oils, 1765, Charterhouse Museum, Godalming, Surrey

Cruso, John (*fl.* 1595–1655), poet and military writer, was born in Norwich before 1595, the son of John Cruso, a cloth merchant and church elder, and his wife, Jane Verlincke. His parents had fled Hondschote in Flanders during the 1570s or 1580s. As the eldest son, John took over the family business in Norwich some time after 1613, while his brother Aquila, born in 1595, who matriculated at Gonville and Caius College, Cambridge, in 1610, was the author of the comic drama *Euribates* performed at the college in 1615–16 (MS in Emmanuel College, Cambridge), and later became a minister in the Church of England. Another brother, Timotheus, established himself as a merchant in London. John followed in his father's footsteps within the local Dutch community, and was elected an elder of the Dutch church in Norwich during the 1620s, and from 1627 until 1641 he played a prominent part in the church's life, continuing as an elder beyond 1647. He married some time before 1618, when his eldest son, also John Cruso (1618–1681), was born, but nothing is known of his wife.

When Cruso's son John, a future chancellor of the diocese of St David's, matriculated at Gonville and Caius College in 1632, Cruso had already advanced from musketeer to captain of the Dutch/Walloon company of the Norwich trained bands and embarked on his career as a military writer. He very appropriately donated a copy of his first

work, *Militarie Instructions for the Cavallrie* (1632), to the college (it is now in Cambridge University Library). The book drew heavily on the Dutch experience, not to mention recent Dutch military publications, referring to the war in the Netherlands as 'the Academie of warre, where the art militarie … truely flourisheth' (Cruso, *Militarie Instructions*, 33). As can also be seen from his subsequent military works Cruso's contribution in the emerging field of military writing was mainly as an editor and a translator of continental works. Apart from his involvement in the Dutch/Walloon company in the Norwich trained bands from at least 1621 Cruso, however, does not appear to have gained any direct military experience.

By then Cruso had already proved himself in the field of poetry. In 1622 he was among the leading members of the Anglo-Dutch community who contributed poems to the Leiden published elegy, *Klacht-Ghedichten*, for Simon Ruytinck, the minister to the London Dutch community who had died the previous year. Other occasional poetry by Cruso is preserved in manuscript in the Folger Shakespeare Library, Washington: three elegies post-1627 for his recently departed friend, Laurence Howlet, late lecturer at St Andrew's in Norwich. In 1642 Cruso published in Amsterdam his thoughts on the eighth psalm, *Uytbreydinge over den achsten psalm Davids*, which contained an elegy for another recently dead friend, Johannes Elisonius, late minister to the Dutch church in Norwich. Finally a volume of his epigrams was published in Delft in 1655. This is the last we hear of Cruso, who may well have died shortly afterwards.

While John Cruso was a committed Calvinist, as can be seen from his role as an elder within the Dutch community in Norwich, and his friendship with many of the leading Dutch ministers in England at the time—thus he inherited a folio volume in Johannes Elisonius's will and gave an inscribed copy of his first military work to Jonas Proost, then minister to the Dutch community in Colchester (now in Cambridge University Library)—the dedication of most of his works to leading establishment figures in Norfolk who later became royalists makes it difficult to place him in the political and religious divide caused by the civil war. However, his friendship with the presbyterian and leading parliamentarian, Major-General Philip Skippon, to whom he dedicated two of his military publications—*A Short Method* (the second part of *The Art of Warre*, published in 1639) and his work on military camps from 1642—and the fact that he is named as Captain Cruso in a poem from the radical London mercer, Colonel Edmund Harvey, which is included in the second edition of his *Militarie Instructions* from 1644, would indicate that Cruso sided with parliament, even if he had resigned as captain of the Dutch/Walloon company by August 1643. His distaste for radical puritanism, however, is evident from his commonplace book preserved in St John's College, Cambridge, where the number of satirical poems against puritans is matched only by the anti-Catholic or more specifically anti-Jesuitical material.

Cruso's military works were significant only in that they

were the first to make the new continental, primarily Dutch, military literature available to an English-speaking audience. OLE PETER GRELL

Sources GL, MS 7397/7 · John Cruso's commonplace book, St John Cam., MS 548 (U.26) · J. H. Hessels, ed., *Ecclesiae Londino-Batavae archivum*, 1–2 (1887–9) · J. J. van Toorenenbergen, ed., *Acten van de colloquia der Nederlandsche gemeenten in England, 1575–1609* (1872) · J. J. van Toorenenbergen, ed., *Uitreigser uit de volgenbe colloquia, 1627–1706* (1872) · *The visitation of London, anno Domini 1633, 1634, and 1635, made by Sir Henry St George*, 1, ed. J. J. Howard and J. L. Chester, Harleian Society, 15 (1880) · W. J. C. Moens, *The Walloons and their church at Norwich: their history and registers, 1565–1832*, Huguenot Society of London, 1 (1887–8) · O. P. Grell, *Dutch Calvinists in early Stuart London: the Dutch church in Austin Friars, 1603–1642* (1989) · O. P. Grell, *Calvinist exiles in Tudor and Stuart England* (1996) · E. A. Kent, 'Notes on the Blackfriars Hall or Dutch church, Norwich', *Norfolk Archaeology*, 22 (1924–6), 86–108 · W. Woods, 'Poetry of Dutch refugees in Norwich', *Dutch crossing* (1979), 71–3 · J. C. Arens, 'Nederlandse Gedichten van Jan Cruso uit Norwich', *Spiegel der Letteren* (1964–5), 132–40 · A. H. Nelson, ed., *Cambridge*, 2 (1989), 895–6

Archives GL, MS 7397/7 · St John Cam., commonplace book, MS 548 (U.26)

Cruso, Timothy (*bap.* 1657, *d.* 1697), Presbyterian minister, was born on 27 July 1657. He was probably the son of Timothy Cruso of Newington Green, Middlesex, and his wife, Sarah Hatt. From his early teens Cruso was destined for the dissenting ministry and was one of the first students to enter Charles Morton's academy at Newington Green when it opened in 1675. Among his fellow students were the future presbyterian minister John Shower and Daniel Defoe, who immortalized his schoolfellow's surname in *The Life and Strange Surprizing Adventures of Robinson Crusoe* (1719). At Morton's academy Cruso received a broad education including the study of French, Italian, history, geography, mathematics, logic, and natural philosophy as well as divinity, Hebrew, and the classical languages. From Newington Green he proceeded to a Scottish university where he graduated MA (it is not clear which, but the absence of his name from the surviving rolls of Aberdeen, Edinburgh, or Glasgow suggests St Andrews).

Cruso settled in London about 1687 when he became minister to the presbyterian congregation meeting at Crutched Friars, Mark Lane, a position he retained until his death. He succeeded in distancing himself from the acrimonious doctrinal disputes of the early 1690s between Presbyterians and Independents which first threatened and finally brought about the collapse of the Happy Union of London dissenting ministers. When in 1694 Daniel Williams was voted out of the Pinners' Hall lecture and most other Presbyterian ministers felt obliged to resign from their lectureships, Cruso was chosen to fill one of the vacancies. He was one of the very few Presbyterians to continue his association with Pinners' Hall. He never joined the Independents and remained loyal to the Presbyterians: he 'inculcated love and forbearance among Christians of all denominations' (Wilson, 159).

Cruso was the author of a number of religious discourses and treatises. He published two funeral sermons in 1688: *The Duty and Support Believed in Life and Death* and *The Period of Humane Life Determined by the Divine Will*. Other works show his support for the Williamite regime and the reformation of manners: in 1689 he published the sermons which he delivered on 31 January, the day of public thanksgiving for 'the deliverance of the kingdom' (*The Mighty Wonders of a Merciful Providence*), and on 5 June, the fast day to implore God's blessing on the protestant cause (*The Churches Plea for the Divine Presence to Foster Humane Force*). In 1690 he published *The Christian Lover* and the following year a sermon, *On the Duty and Blessing of a Tender Conscience*. Cruso's best-known work, however, was the volume of sermons which he had preached at Pinners' Hall. The first edition appeared shortly before his death in 1697 but the best edition is that edited by the Independent Matthew Meade (or Mead) and published posthumously in 1699.

Cruso had a reputation well into the eighteenth century as an outstanding and inspirational preacher. He presided over a large and flourishing congregation. However, his dedication and incessant labours probably contributed to his early death at the age of forty. According to Meade, he lived 'too fast … as a taper which wastes itself to give light to others' and 'was so fervent in spirit serving the Lord that this made him willing to spend and be spent, till by degrees he wasted and consumed himself' (Mead, 31). Cruso's health began to deteriorate from the mid-1690s, necessitating the appointment of Francis Fuller as his assistant in 1695. His death, hastened by an asthmatic complaint, occurred in London on 26 November 1697. He was buried in Stepney churchyard where a marble tomb with a Latin dedication was erected over his grave. Matthew Meade preached his funeral sermon, from which it appears that his wife and mother, but none of his children, survived him. After his death his congregation by a majority of one chose as his successor the Independent Thomas Shepherd, but this choice was overruled and a Presbyterian, William Harris, was appointed.

M. J. MERCER

Sources A. Gordon, ed., *Freedom after ejection: a review (1690–1692) of presbyterian and congregational nonconformity in England and Wales* (1917), 247 · W. Wilson, *The history and antiquities of the dissenting churches and meeting houses in London, Westminster and Southwark*, 4 vols. (1808–14), vol. 1, pp. 56–62 · Surman, index of nonconformist ministers, DWL · M. Mead, *Comfort in death: a funeral sermon preached upon the death of Mr. Timothy Cruso* (1698) · *Protestant Dissenter's Magazine*, 6 (1799), 467 · T. S. James, *The history of the litigation and legislation respecting Presbyterian chapels and charities* (1867), 22 · M. R. Watts, *The dissents: from the Reformation to the French Revolution* (1978), 289–97 · H. McLachlan, *Education under the Test Acts* (1931), 76–80 · DWL, Wilton Edwin Rix MSS

Archives DWL, corresp. and papers

Likenesses R. White, line engraving (after T. Forster), NPG · engraving, repro. in Mead, *Comfort in death*, title-page · engravings, repro. in Wilson, *History and antiquities of the dissenting churches*, following p. 56

Crutchley, Sir Victor Alexander Charles (1893–1986), naval officer, was born on 2 November 1893 at 28 Lennox Gardens, Chelsea, London, the only son of Percy Edward

Sir Victor Alexander Charles Crutchley (1893–1986), by Walter Stoneman, 1944

Crutchley (1855–1940) of Sunninghill Park, Ascot, Berkshire, and his wife, the Hon. Frederica Louisa Fitzroy (d. 1932), second daughter of the third Baron Southampton. He entered the navy in 1906 as a cadet at the Royal Naval College, Osborne, followed by two years at Dartmouth. During the First World War he was promoted to lieutenant, in September 1915, and served in the dreadnought *Centurion* in the second battle squadron of the Grand Fleet and was present at the battle of Jutland. In June 1916 the future admiral Roger Keyes assumed command of *Centurion* and acquired a high opinion of Crutchley. Consequently it is not surprising that after he became vice-admiral at Dover and began planning the raid on Zeebrugge and Ostend, Crutchley was chosen to participate in the operation. Crutchley served as first lieutenant to Commander A. E. Godsal (a fellow officer from *Centurion*) in the old cruiser *Brilliant*, specially fitted as a blockship. On the night of 22–3 April 1918 *Brilliant*, along with the similarly fitted *Sirius*, attempted to block the entrance to Ostend while Keyes led the major effort against Zeebrugge. Unfortunately the British did not realize that the Germans had altered the position of the Stroom Bank whistle buoy, used as a navigation point, 2400 yards to the eastward. The blockships, under heavy German fire, grounded in the wrong position and the entrance to Ostend remained open. Crutchley was awarded the Distinguished Service Cross for his part in the action.

Godsal and Crutchley promptly volunteered for a second effort in the now battered cruiser *Vindictive*, a survivor of the raid against Zeebrugge. The attempt took place on the night of 9–10 May. Godsal was killed by a shell just after *Vindictive* entered the harbour and the navigating officer was severely wounded. Crutchley took command but the battered ship grounded under heavy fire at the wrong angle, leaving the channel open. Crutchley ordered the scuttling charges to be blown and the ship abandoned and then, after seeing that the wounded had been evacuated to the motor launch alongside, using his electric torch and impervious to the artillery and machine-gun fire concentrated on the ship, calmly searched the bridge and port side to make sure no one had been left behind before lowering himself to the waiting *ML 254*. The craft had, however, been damaged by shell fire and the commanding officer wounded and when the latter collapsed from loss of blood as the launch limped away Crutchley was forced to take command and organize and lead a bailing and pumping party to stem the flood of water pouring in through shell holes in the bow. They were up to their waists in water and *ML 254* was barely afloat when Keyes in the destroyer *Warwick* found them. Crutchley's energetic and courageous conduct earned him the Victoria Cross.

Crutchley spent the final months of the war in the destroyer *Sikh* of the Dover patrol. His post-war service included the mine-sweeper *Petersfield* in South American waters (1920), the royal yacht *Alexandria* (1921), the cadet-training battleship *Thunderer* (1922–4), the royal yacht *Victoria and Albert* (1924), and in the Mediterranean Fleet the flagship *Queen Elizabeth* (1924–6) and light cruiser *Ceres* (1926–8). Keyes was commander-in-chief, Mediterranean (1925–8), and Crutchley was a member of the Centurions, the admiral's polo team. One memorable match in 1927 found him on the same team as Keyes, the duke of York (the future George VI), and Lord Mountbatten. In 1930 Crutchley married Joan Elisabeth Loveday (d. 1980), the younger daughter of William Coryton of Pentillie Castle, Cornwall. They had a son (Keyes was godfather) and a daughter.

Promoted to commander in 1928, Crutchley in August 1930 was loaned to the New Zealand division of the Royal Navy for three years and served as executive officer in the cruiser *Diomede* in Pacific waters, assuming command of the ship when his captain became ill and remaining in command until promoted captain in 1933. He was senior officer, first mine-sweeping flotilla (1935–6), and captain, fishery protection and mine-sweeping flotilla (1936–7). In May 1937 he was plucked from this somewhat obscure command and given a plum job, captain of the battleship *Warspite*, just nearing completion of a major reconstruction and modernization and destined to become the flagship of Admiral Sir Dudley Pound, commander-in-chief, Mediterranean Fleet. *Warspite*'s acceptance trials proved to be long and difficult, particularly because of persistent trouble with her steering and the amount of new equipment that had been fitted. The additional work necessitated curtailment of weekend leave causing a certain amount of discontent and eventually an anonymous letter to the Admiralty followed by leaks in the press about unrest in the ship. This led to an Admiralty inquiry resulting in three officers, including the executive officer, being relieved. Crutchley disagreed with the findings of the inquiry and, failing to receive satisfaction from the commander-in-chief, Portsmouth, used an Admiralty request for a confidential report on the former executive officer to recommend his immediate promotion to captain.

In the Mediterranean Fleet, Crutchley served as flag captain first to Pound, and after the latter left to become first sea lord, to his successor, Admiral Andrew Cunningham—two of Britain's outstanding naval leaders of the Second World War. After the outbreak of war *Warspite* was ordered to join the Home Fleet in the autumn of 1939 and during the Norwegian campaign Crutchley commanded the ship in the second battle of Narvik (13 April 1940), when her 15 inch guns sank eight large German destroyers and her aircraft a submarine.

Crutchley was commodore, royal naval barracks, Devonport, from 1940 to 1942, and then, after being promoted to rear-admiral, was lent to the Royal Australian Navy and assumed command of task force 44 in June 1942. Crutchley commanded a mixed force of Australian and American cruisers and American destroyers that formed the screening force during the American landings on Tulagi and Guadalcanal in August and his dispositions were in effect on the night of the 8th–9th when Japanese cruisers staged a devastating raid in the waters around Savo Island. The heavy cruisers HMAS *Canberra* and USS *Vincennes*, *Quincy*, and *Astoria* were lost in what was probably the worst defeat suffered by the American navy in a surface action. The Japanese escaped unscathed although they did not take advantage of the opportunity to penetrate the vulnerable transport anchorages. Crutchley was not present, having been called away in his flagship, the heavy cruiser HMAS *Australia*, to a conference with the commander of the American amphibious force. A disaster of this magnitude might well have ended a career but the Australian board of inquiry and a subsequent American investigation exonerated Crutchley, whose share of any blame was minor compared to the multitude of egregious errors in what was predominantly an American operation.

Crutchley remained in the south-west Pacific until July 1944, where he was promoted to vice-admiral and subsequently commanded task force 74 and task group 77.2 (part of the American Seventh Fleet) in the Coral Sea, Central Solomons, Admiralty Islands, and waters around New Guinea. The Americans later recognized these services, appointing him to the Legion of Merit in the highest grade, that of chief commander. From 1945 to 1947 Crutchley was flag officer, Gibraltar. He was made CB in 1945, KCB in 1946, and he retired in 1947 as an admiral. He died at Mappercombe Manor, Nettlecombe, Bridport, Dorset, on 24 January 1986 at the age of ninety-two; and was buried at Powerstock church.

Tall and bearded, with the ribbon of the Victoria Cross testifying to his bravery, Crutchley was a truly commanding presence although notably modest and reticent. He had commanded a variety of ships and forces, often under arduous conditions, and typified to many the ideal naval officer.
PAUL G. HALPERN

Sources R. Keyes, *The naval memoirs of Admiral of the Fleet Sir Roger Keyes*, 2 (1935) · B. Loxton, *The shame of Savo: anatomy of a naval disaster* (1994) · private information (2004) [B. Loxton: correspondence re a biography of Crutchley] · S. W. Roskill, *H.M.S. Warspite* (1957) · *WW* (1984–5) · C. Aspinall-Oglander, *Roger Keyes* (1951) · B. Pitt, *Zeebrugge: St George's Day, 1918* (1958) · Burke, *Peerage* · Walford, *County families* (1920) · *Navy List* (1921) · *Navy List* (1928) · *The Times* (28 Jan 1986) · b. cert. · d. cert.
Archives National Archives of Australia, Melbourne · Naval Historical Center, Washington, DC · PRO, ADM (admiralty records), surveying reports, letters of proceedings, etc. | SOUND U. Leeds, Liddle collection, taped interview by Peter Liddle
Likenesses W. Stoneman, photograph, 1944, NPG [*see illus.*] · photograph, priv. coll.; repro. in Loxton, *The shame of Savo* · photographs, Australian War Memorial Canberra
Wealth at death £1,445,170: probate, 2 April 1986, *CGPLA Eng. & Wales*

Cruttwell, Charles Robert Mowbray Fraser (1887–1941), historian, was born on 23 May 1887 at Denton, near Harleston, Norfolk, the eldest of the three sons of the Revd Canon Charles Thomas *Cruttwell (1847–1911), historian of Roman literature, and his wife, Annie Maud (d. 1926), elder daughter of Sir John Robert *Mowbray (1815–1899), first baronet and MP. He was educated at Rugby School, where he won an open scholarship to read classics and history at Queen's College, Oxford, in 1906. After gaining firsts in classical moderations (1908), *literae humaniores* (1910), and modern history (1911), he was elected to a fellowship at All Souls College in 1911, and while in residence there was in 1912 appointed lecturer in modern history at Hertford College. He served valiantly from August 1914 as a second lieutenant in the Royal Berkshire regiment, fighting in France and Belgium during 1915 and 1916 until invalided home, an experience that deeply influenced his later academic work and also permanently damaged his health.

In 1918–19 Cruttwell worked in the military intelligence department of the War Office; he was then, in 1919, elected to an official fellowship in modern history at Hertford College, where he was also dean from 1920 to 1925. He was no less active in university business—serving among other offices as a statutory commissioner (1923), lecturer (1926–30), delegate of the university press, and member of the hebdomadal council. His administrative ability was characterized by a penetrating intelligence, wide-ranging knowledge, firm grasp of detail, decisive judgement, and a good memory. These talents were recognized when, in 1930, he was elected principal of Hertford. As such he supported moves to establish an honour school of geography in Oxford, and was instrumental in securing his college's association with that chair upon its foundation in 1932, when Professor Kenneth Mason was appointed as the first incumbent. Cruttwell's only conspicuous failure in public life came on the occasion of the 1935 general election, when as Conservative candidate for one of the parliamentary seats at Oxford University he was defeated by A. P. Herbert (independent).

Although Cruttwell devoted much of his time to university administration and to his writing, his strongest interest lay in his college, not least in the life of its chapel. While much of the evidence of his way of dealing with others is anecdotal and contradictory, most surviving records testify to his forceful, forthright, and eccentric character, to his interest in the junior members, and to his genuine concern for their welfare. To many who became his close friends Crutters (as he was widely known) was unstintingly hospitable and generous, both in Oxford and at his country house, Vinnicks, at Highclere, near Newbury, Berkshire, and he was remembered with great affection. To others, however, who did not appreciate that his gruff manner disguised a natural shyness, he appeared a rude, harsh-tempered, and unsympathetic man, given to coarse language and cutting personal remarks; but the charge of misogyny so often levelled against him was vehemently denied by those who came to know him well. If a good deal of attention has since focused on his personal rupture with Evelyn Waugh, a scholar in history at Hertford (1922–4), its real significance has no doubt been exaggerated. That their mutual animosity formed early seems clear from reports of Waugh's scurrilous student pranks and from his own writings, yet it is questionable whether his use of the other's name for a variety of unsavoury fictional characters in many of his later works is sufficient evidence of a lasting and bitter feud, on Cruttwell's part at any rate.

Cruttwell's academic reputation rests primarily on his *History of the Great War, 1914–1918* (1934; 2nd edn, 1936), a monumental work of painstaking composition, conceived in minute detail and on a truly global scale, widely acclaimed at the time and still well regarded. Written in a precise, even clinical style, it displayed a shrewd understanding of the strategic issues and a mastery of the sources then available. It remains perhaps most notable for its frank and fearless judgements on those identified as the 'principal actors' (military, naval, and political) in that tragic conflict, and in 1936 it earned Cruttwell the award of the degree of DLitt from Oxford University. A digest of its leading arguments and conclusions appeared in *The Role of British Strategy in the Great War*, the Lees-Knowles lectures he delivered in Cambridge in 1936. In the same year he published a short biography of Wellington, in which the strengths and weaknesses of the commander are nicely balanced. Among his many other writings, he is remembered for two textbooks on modern British and European history (1928, 1929), both models of clarity and cogency, and for *A History of Peaceful Change in the Modern World* (1937). He was also widely regarded as an authority on the political history of the Rhineland.

Cruttwell enjoyed country pursuits, and served as a Hampshire JP. In his youth he had been a man of strong although rather clumsy physique, but a serious leg wound and other painful complications of wartime service left lasting scars, and in later years he was prone to rheumatic fever. He was forced to resign his principalship through ill health in 1939, and after further prolonged distress he died in a nursing home, the Burden Institute, Stapleton,

near Bristol, on 14 March 1941. He was unmarried. In his will he left his historical books and £1000 to Hertford College, which also holds a good portrait by his cousin, Grace Cruttwell.

GEOFFREY ELLIS

Sources DNB · A. Goudie, ed., *Seven hundred years of an Oxford college: Hertford College, 1284–1984*, new edn (1999) · *Hertford College Magazine*, 29 (May 1941) · H. Carpenter, *The Brideshead generation: Evelyn Waugh and his friends* (1989) · S. Hastings, *Evelyn Waugh* (1994) · K. Mason, 'Memoirs', priv. coll. · W. L. Ferrar, 'Recollections, Hertford College, 1925–1964', Hertford College, Oxford, archives · minutes of governing body, Hertford College, Oxford, archives · *WWW*, 1941–50 · *WWW*, 1897–1915 · priv. coll., C. R. M. F. Cruttwell's private papers
Archives Hertford College, Oxford, MSS · priv. coll., MSS
Likenesses W. Stoneman, photograph, 1931, NPG · G. Cruttwell, oils, c.1937, Hertford College, Oxford
Wealth at death £19,814 15s. 2d.: resworn probate, 18 June 1941, CGPLA Eng. & Wales

Cruttwell, Charles Thomas (1847–1911), classical scholar and Church of England clergyman, was born in London on 30 July 1847, the eldest son of Charles James Cruttwell, barrister, of the Inner Temple, and his wife, Elizabeth Anne, daughter of Admiral Thomas Sanders. Educated under J. A. Hessey at Merchant Taylors' School (1861–6), he proceeded with a foundation scholarship to St John's College, Oxford, in 1866. He was in the first class in classical moderations in 1868 and in *literae humaniores* in 1870, graduating BA in 1871 and MA in 1874; he obtained the Pusey and Ellerton Hebrew scholarship in 1869, won the Craven scholarship for classics in 1871, and the Kennicott Hebrew scholarship in 1872. He was president of the Oxford Union Society in 1872. He was a fellow of Merton College from 1870 until 1885, and was tutor there from 1874 to 1877. Ordained deacon by the bishop of Oxford in 1875 and priest in 1876, he was curate of St Giles's, Oxford, from 1875 to 1877.

In 1877 Cruttwell left Oxford for Bradfield College, where he was headmaster until 1880, when he was appointed headmaster of Malvern College. Despite his efficient scholarship he showed little aptitude for public school administration, and resigned in 1885 to become rector of Sutton, Surrey. A few months later he was appointed rector of Denton, Norfolk, and in 1891 he accepted from Merton College the benefice of Kibworth-Beauchamp. In 1901 he was nominated by Lord Salisbury to the crown benefice of Ewelme, near Wallingford, and in 1903 he was collated by the bishop of Peterborough to a residential canonry. Cruttwell was also select preacher to Oxford University in 1896–8, and again in 1903–5. In 1909 he joined the party of bishops and clergy who visited Germany in the cause of international peace.

On 5 August 1884 Cruttwell married Annie Maud (d. 1926), eldest daughter of Sir John Robert *Mowbray, first baronet. They had three sons and one daughter; one son, Charles Robert Mowbray Fraser *Cruttwell (1887–1941), became principal of Hertford College, Oxford. Cruttwell died at Ewelme rectory on 4 April 1911.

Deeply read in ancient and modern literature, Cruttwell published little. The best of his books, *A History of Roman Literature* (1877), was a concise account of the development of Roman literature from the earliest times until the death of Marcus Aurelius. It reached a sixth edition in 1898.   S. E. FRYER, rev. M. C. CURTHOYS

Sources *The Times* (5 April 1911) · *WW* · Crockford (1911) · J. Foster, *Oxford men and their colleges* (1893) · *CGPLA Eng. & Wales* (1911) **Wealth at death** £9050 8s. 6d.: probate, 29 May 1911, *CGPLA Eng. & Wales*

Cruttwell, Clement (1743–1808), compiler of religious works and gazetteers, was born at Wokingham, Berkshire, the son of William Cruttwell. The printers William *Cruttwell and Richard *Cruttwell [*see under* Cruttwell, William] were his brothers. Nothing is known of Cruttwell's early years, though he appears to have been well educated since his first recorded career was as a surgeon and medical writer in Bath during the 1770s. His first work, *Advice to Lying-in Women*, appeared in 1779. In the following year he undertook one of several significant career changes, entering St Mary Hall, Oxford, where, aged thirty-seven, he matriculated on 14 December 1780. He was soon after ordained.

In 1785 Cruttwell published an edition of Bishop Thomas Wilson's Bible with an accompanying biography. His interest in different biblical texts was again evident in his next major project, *A Concordance of the Parallel Texts of Scripture* (1790), which he not only compiled but also proofread and printed at his house in Oxford. According to the fulsome obituary of Cruttwell in *Gentleman's Magazine*, this undertaking was 'sufficient to occupy the life of an ordinary man' and gave some idea of his 'industry and perseverance' (*GM*, 858). Cruttwell's achievement was widely praised, notably by the bishop of Lincoln, but his exertions also resulted in serious illness and a period of convalescence at the baths at St Armand in the Netherlands. The focus of his work changed again on his return to England when he began to compile the first of three collections, *The Gazetteer of France* (1793). This was followed by *The Gazetteer of the Netherlands* (1794) and his most impressive and popular work, *The Universal Gazetteer* (1798), which quickly sold out in first edition. The success of this work prompted him to compile a second edition including 30,000 new articles, which was published shortly before his death, after a sudden illness, on 5 August 1808 at Froxfield, Somerset. Clearly something of a workaholic whose labours probably hastened his death, Cruttwell also found time for a broad circle of friends to whom, being 'warm, generous, and sincere in his private character', he displayed 'the kindest and most benevolent heart' (ibid., 858–9).   PHILIP CARTER

Sources *GM*, 1st ser., 78 (1808), 858 · Foster, *Alum. Oxon.* · *DNB* **Archives** Glos. RO, corresp. relating to the publication of Bishop Wilson's Bible

Cruttwell, Richard (*bap.* 1747, *d.* 1799). *See under* Cruttwell, William (*bap.* 1741, *d.* 1804).

Cruttwell, Richard (1776–1846), financial writer and Church of England clergyman, was educated at Exeter College, Oxford, and took the degree of BCL on 13 June 1803. He was at one period chaplain of HMS *Trident*, and

secretary to Rear-Admiral Sir Alexander J. Ball, and was perpetual curate of Holmfirth, in the parish of Kirkburton, Yorkshire. In 1822 he was presented by Lord Eldon to the rectory of Spexhall, Suffolk, and held it until his death.

Cruttwell persistently brought forward his views on the currency in numerous treatises and pamphlets. He was violently opposed to the return to bullion as the sole basis of the currency, and believed that in 1815 'our paper currency was … as nearly as it well could be in a state of *absolute perfection*' (*The System of Country Banking Defended*, 1828, 9). He was equally opposed to free trade. A stream of pamphlets from 1825 lambasted what Cruttwell saw as the folly of the fiscal policy adopted by Lord Liverpool's liberal tory government. Cruttwell's most substantial work is *A Treatise of the State of the Currency* (1825). His other writings include: *Catholic Emancipation not Calculated to Relieve the Starving Peasantry of Ireland* (1828?), *Two Modes for Accounting for the Church being in Danger* (1837), *Wellingtoniana, or, How to 'Make' a Duke and How to 'Mar' a Duke* (1837), *Reform without revolution: in a strict union between the mercantile …, monied, agricultural, and labouring classes on the principle of a … sound … standard, … by one of no party* [R. C.] (1839), and *The touchstone of England … excessive taxation … proved … the true cause of England's present public distress* (1843). Cruttwell died in London on 12 November 1846.   W. W. WROTH, rev. H. C. G. MATTHEW

Sources *GM*, 2nd ser., 27 (1847), 100 · BL, Add. MS 19169, fol. 283 **Archives** W. Sussex RO, letters to duke of Richmond

Cruttwell, William (*bap.* 1741, *d.* 1804), printer and bookseller, was baptized on 12 May 1741 in Wokingham, Berkshire, the first of the eight children of William Cruttwell (1710–1768), barber, and his wife, Elizabeth (*d.* 1776). It is not known where he was educated but on 5 October 1756 he was apprenticed to Samuel Idle of Reading, printer. On 4 October 1763 he was transferred to James Harrison of Stationers' Court, London, following Idle's death. In July 1763 his great-uncle, Richard Cruttwell, died, leaving William a property in Wokingham, with the residue of the estate to be split between his brother, **Richard Cruttwell** (*bap.* 1747, *d.* 1799), and his father, after various bequests.

On 26 December 1764, in Sherborne Abbey, Cruttwell married Martha (*d.* 1823), daughter of Richard Wickham, esq., of Horsington, near Sherborne; the couple had five children. Through this connection with Sherborne and bolstered by his legacy, he may have been encouraged to establish *Cruttwell's Sherborne Journal* in late 1764 in opposition to the *Sherborne Mercury*, founded in 1737 and since January 1749 printed by Robert Goadby, a man with strong whig sympathies. Cruttwell remained the proprietor until his death in 1804, although not without mishaps. He was finally freed as a member of the Stationers' Company on 2 May 1775, but three years later he apparently suffered financial difficulties, as an auction notice of his household goods, his printing materials, and his shop stock appeared in the *Sherborne Mercury* on 5 October 1778. The advertisement claimed that 1600 copies of the *Sherborne*

Journal were printed weekly and from a later advertisement it is clear that the production of the newspaper continued under the aegis of his brother Richard, in Bath. In June 1779 Cruttwell was declared bankrupt and his landholdings in Sherborne and Lovington, Somerset, totalling nearly 100 acres, were put up for sale.

It is unclear how Cruttwell recovered his financial position, but a fire insurance policy of 1784 mentions two houses, a printing office, and stock-in-trade insured for £12,000 under his name. The printing office was in Duck Street, Sherborne, and one of his houses was located in Half Moon Street. He enjoyed high social standing and respectability in Sherborne, being elected churchwarden in 1777 and 1778 and becoming a governor of the town's grammar school in 1767 and warden of the governors in 1775. His portrait, by William Beach of Bath, shows a contented and prosperous-looking gentleman on whom 'misfortune did not sour a temper naturally good' (Cruttwell, 38). After the vicissitudes of his bankruptcy he 'enjoyed the fruits of his labour in the bosom of a family who adore him and in a society which reveres him' (ibid., 39). He died on 6 December 1804 in Sherborne, where he was also buried, and in his will he left everything to his wife, satisfied that she would make a fair distribution among their 'dear children' (PRO, PROB 11/1422, fol. 11r).

Cruttwell was in many ways typical of successful eighteenth-century printers whose career was based on the ownership of a provincial newspaper and the medium it provided for local advertising. He was able to establish agencies in Dorset, Devon, Somerset, Cornwall, and London and used this distribution network to promote and service his bookselling, printing, and stationery businesses.

Cruttwell's younger brother Richard, a printer, was baptized on 1 January 1747 in Wokingham, Berkshire, the third child of William and Elizabeth Cruttwell. He was apprenticed to John Carnan, printer, of Elliot's Court, Old Bailey, London, on 7 April 1761 but was not freed as a member of the Stationers' Company until 4 October 1774. Like his brother William, Richard had been left property by his great-uncle Richard Cruttwell in 1763 and, following the example of William, Richard moved westwards, settling in 1768 at Bath, where he bought a share in the *Bath Chronicle*, an established weekly newspaper. On 9 November 1772 he married Anne Shuttleworth (1745–1826), the daughter of the Revd Digby Shuttleworth, rector of Oborne and minister of Castleton, both parishes being contiguous with Sherborne.

In 1770 Richard was living at 1 Westgate Buildings, Bath, with Thomas Beach, painter, as next-door neighbour. However, in late 1775, Richard moved his business to a house on the corner of St James's and Weymouth streets and prospered as his printing and publishing business developed. Among the many works issued by him three are of outstanding merit: John Collinson's *History of Somerset* (1791) and two works on Bishop Thomas Wilson edited by Cruttwell's brother Clement *Cruttwell in 1784 and 1785. He was also one of the earliest publishers to issue local guides and, from 1770 to his death in 1799, he issued

annually the *New Bath Guide* and in 1789 a guide to Cheltenham.

Richard Cruttwell died at Cheltenham on 1 June 1799 and was buried in the family vault beneath St James's Church, Bath, on 7 June. An obituary notice in the *Gentleman's Magazine* notes that:

> His friendship was warm, sincere, and active; his heart, tender and affectionate; his religion pure and practical. This, indeed, was a principle which he never lost sight of, amid the hurry of business, or in the quiet of domestic enjoyment.

Another obituary, in the *Bath Chronicle* (7 June 1799), states:

> His bodily affliction, previous to his dissolution, was long and trying; but borne with the most patient resignation and a fine reliance on the Divine acceptance, through that mediation in which he most sincerely believed. (pp. 708–71)

Richard Cruttwell was another in the mould of successful printer–publishers whose prosperity was founded on a provincial newspaper. He also enjoyed a close family connection and friendship with his brother William in Sherborne.   GEORGE TATHAM

Sources H. A. Cruttwell, *The history of Cruttwell family* (1933), 37–43, 64–75 · C. H. Mayo, *Bibliotheca Dorsetiensis* (1805), 74–8 · R. Wells, *Newsplan: report of the pilot project in the south-west*, Library and Information Research Report, 38 (1986), 164–6 · fire insurance policy, GL, Royal Exchange Assurance, policy 90723 · will, PRO, PROB 11/1422, sig. 162 · will, PRO, PROB 11/1678, sig. 678 [will of Martha Cruttwell] · will, PRO, PROB 11/1376, sig. 483 [will of Richard Cruttwell] · D. F. McKenzie, ed., *Stationers' Company apprentices*, [3]: 1701–1800 (1978) · *Sherborne Mercury* (15 May 1780) · *Sherborne Mercury* (6 Sept 1788) · *Sherborne Mercury* (5 Oct 1788) · *Sherborne Mercury* (21 June 1799) · *Sherborne Mercury* (6 Sept 1799) · *GM*, 1st ser., 69 (1799), 531 · *Bath Chronicle* (7 June 1799)
Likenesses W. Beach, oils

Cruz, Miguel de la. *See* Cross, Michael (*fl.* 1633–1660).

Crynes, Nathaniel (1685/6–1745), book collector, was born in Coventry, the son of Jonah Crynes and his wife, Sarah (*d.* in or after 1745). He was educated at King Henry VIII Grammar School, Coventry, and at St John's College, Oxford, whence he matriculated on 27 June 1704, aged eighteen; he had, however, as he later told Richard Rawlinson, entered the college five terms earlier. He was a Coventry scholar from 1704, and a Coventry fellow from 1707; he graduated BA (1708) and MA (1712). On 26 January 1716 he was elected esquire bedell of arts and physic in the university, holding this office until his death in 1745, though he resigned his fellowship on 17 December 1716. Thereafter he lived in Oxford, occasionally visiting Coventry. At the time of his death he was living in Northgate Street. Richard Rawlinson (who matriculated from St John's in 1708) preserved letters from him written over the period 1728–38. All are dated and were sent from Oxford; some contain answers to questions from Rawlinson involving the university archives, but others more importantly relate to the extensive sales of books, manuscripts, and pictures from the library of Rawlinson's brother Thomas which Rawlinson conducted from 1721 to

1734. Crynes's own library contains a priced set of catalogues of this library. Nathaniel Crynes died, probably in Coventry, on 5 August 1745, and was probably also buried there; he left this to be decided by his executrix, his sister Hannah Crynes.

Crynes's will, dated 6 June 1745, left most of his property in and around Coventry to his sister, with a life interest to his mother, Sarah Crynes. Hannah also received a choice of his English books printed after 1660. The Bodleian Library in Oxford was bequeathed first choice of his remaining books. St John's College received second choice of these (about 1500 books, including three Caxtons), and Balliol and Lincoln colleges were to have alternate choice of the remainder.

Crynes's books, as now kept together on the shelves of the Bodleian, number 968, though this total excludes folios, incunabula (of which there were more than twenty), and manuscripts (of which three had already been purchased by the Bodleian in 1723, seven were presented in 1736, and eight more were bequeathed in 1745). The collection of books consists of English and foreign works of a wide range of dates, and, with the exception of the early books, may be described as useful rather than spectacular. Crynes did not normally rebind the books he owned, and he added notes to many about their rarity and interest. Some, though not all, have his name stamped on the title-page or elsewhere.   R. JULIAN ROBERTS

Sources Foster, *Alum. Oxon.* · V. Sillery, *St John's College biographical register, 1660–1775* (1990) · W. C. Costin, *The history of St John's College, Oxford, 1598–1860*, OHS, new ser., 12 (1958) · W. D. Macray, *Annals of the Bodleian Library, Oxford*, 2nd edn (1890) · St John's College, Oxford, archives, Admin. IA6 · G. R. Tashjian, D. R. Tashjian, and B. J. Enright, *Richard Rawlinson: a tercentenary memorial* (1990)
Archives Bodl. Oxf., letters, MSS Rawl. lett. 29 and 114*
Wealth at death see will, PRO, PROB 11/741

Crystall, Thomas (1468–1535), abbot of Kinloss, was born at Culross, Perthshire, of 'decent stock' (*honesto loco*). His parents sent him at an early age, with his elder brother, to the grammar school of Culross Abbey, a Cistercian house, where he was taught by a monk, Thomas Pearson. Then, as he showed great ability, they removed him prematurely (*praepropere*) to have him trained in music, hoping this would procure him an ecclesiastical position. Crystall received the Cistercian habit at Kinloss, Moray, on 6 January 1487, aged eighteen. Exactly a year later he made his vows and some time after was ordained priest. His talents were appreciated by Abbot William Culross, who approached Rome to have Crystall made his successor. No crown nomination is extant, but Crystall was provided by bulls of 13 January 1500 and received the abbatial blessing from the bishop of Brechin.

Crystall at once began to deal vigorously with urgent economic and domestic needs. In a series of disputes over revenues and rights encroached on by other parties, some of them powerful, Crystall instituted proceedings to recover what was lost and, in some cases after a long struggle, won his case or reached a favourable settlement. In a dispute with the abbot of Deer over tithes, the other Scots abbots decided in Crystall's favour. An unsuccessful candidate in 1490–91 for the Kinloss abbacy had received compensation of a pension from monastic revenues; Crystall took action against him in the privy council, appearing in court personally in Edinburgh, and also won a favourable settlement in Rome.

By now the Kinloss revenues had doubled, and Crystall carried out necessary repairs on buildings and undertook new building work, in the monastery's barony of Strathisla, Banffshire, and its appropriated churches of Ellon and Avoch as well as at Kinloss. Church gear and furnishings were improved, not only vestments and altar vessels but larger items such as bells, statues, organ, and choir-screen, while the abbey church itself was substantially restored. Crystall sent a monk to make purchases in France and Flanders at great cost. Household goods and equipment were similarly renewed. Books were bought for the library, and a missal and a gradual in parchment were commissioned from the Culross scriptorium. The standard of living at Kinloss was raised, and Crystall was also a liberal alms-giver.

Such activities seem to represent Crystall rather as a Renaissance prelate than a Cistercian abbot in the traditional mould, but he was undoubtedly an excellent abbot. Increased revenue enabled him to raise the number of monks from fourteen to twenty or more; during his abbacy he professed twenty-one choir monks and a lay brother. He sent two young monks to study with the Dominicans in Aberdeen. He improved monastic observance at Kinloss, winning praise from the historian Hector Boece, and also at its daughter-houses of Culross and Deer, which he had power to do according to the Cistercian system of filiation. In 1507 he was Cistercian visitor of Scotland, and he successfully intervened in a long-standing dispute at Melrose by removing its abbot to Coupar Angus. He declined preferment to larger abbeys and a bishopric.

In 1526 Crystall decided to resign in favour of Robert Reid; his resignation and Reid's provision took place on 4 August 1528, with Crystall retaining the revenues and right of regress and thus able to continue his munificence. He contracted dropsy; treatment proved ineffective and he died at Strathisla on 30 December 1535. He was buried on the following day in Kinloss Abbey church.

Almost everything known about Crystall derives from the life of him written by Giovanni Ferrerio, a humanist scholar who taught at Kinloss from 1532. Ferrerio used documents and was reasonably accurate but the life was intended to be a gift to Crystall, and so had to be a favourable portrait. A greater drawback is that Ferrerio's conscious efforts at Latin literary style, and his refusal to use non-classical language for medieval things, sometimes obscure his meaning. Nevertheless Crystall is revealed as a great abbot, at a time when Scottish monasticism was not noted for fervour.   MARK DILWORTH

Sources W. D. Wilson, ed., *Ferrerii historia abbatum de Kynlos*, Bannatyne Club, 63 (1839) · M. Dilworth, *Scottish monasteries in the late middle ages* (1995) · M. Dilworth, 'Franco-Scottish efforts at monastic reform, 1500–1560', *Records of the Scottish Church History Society*, 25 (1993–5), 204–21 · *CEPR letters*, vol. 17 · J. A. Clyde, ed., *Acta* *dominorum concilii, 1501–1503*, Stair Society, 8 (1943) · W. M. Brady, *The episcopal succession in England, Scotland, and Ireland, AD 1400 to 1875*, 1 (1876)

Cú Chuimne (*d.* 747), canonist and hymn writer, is associated with Columba's monastery of Iona in a colophon found in the Paris manuscript Bibliothèque Nationale, MS Lat. 12021. His date of birth is unknown but his obit is recorded in 747 in the annals of Ulster, where he is called 'the wise (*sapiens*)'. To Cú Chuimne is also attributed a Latin hymn to the Virgin Mary which is considered the best of early Irish Latin hymns, notable for the hymnodist's skill in versification, being marked with alliteration, assonance, and internal rhyme. The hymn, 'Cantemus in omni die', was intended to be sung and testifies to the devotion to the Virgin which was fostered by Adomnán of Iona and developed in the eighth-century Irish church. Two ancient quatrains in Irish are also associated with Cú Chuimne's name. In the annals of Ulster these are attributed to Cú Chuimne's nurse, while in the eleventh-century *Liber hymnorum* the first quatrain is put in the mouth of Adomnán and the response to the first quatrain, given in the second quatrain, is attributed to Cú Chuimne. The quatrains state that Cú Chuimne squandered his resources on nuns but later repented and devoted himself to learning. These peccadilloes may account for the fact that his name is not mentioned in the later martyrologies.

The colophon copied into the Paris manuscript Bibliothèque Nationale, MS Lat. 12021, states that Cú Chuimne collaborated with Ruben of Dair-Inis (Ruben mac Connad) to compile the *Collectio canonum Hibernensis*. This collection of canons was drawn up from biblical, patristic, penitential, and conciliar sources, both native and foreign. The wealth of sources shows the number of books available to the compilers, perhaps in the library of the monastery at Iona. The *Collectio* was a reference book to the enactments of the church, arranged according to subject rather than chronology, and gave instructions on how an eighth-century Christian should live. There are two main recensions of the collection: A, the shorter, in sixty-five books, in which the latest author cited is Theodore of Canterbury (*d.* 690); and B, the longer, in sixty-eight or sixty-nine books, in which the latest author cited is Adomnán of Iona (*d.* 704). The collection contains decrees which had links with native Irish law concerning the family, property, and ecclesiastical organization. There are parallels to the contents in the eighth-century vernacular legal text *Bretha Nemed* composed in Munster. The *Collectio* was a juridical source which covered not only spiritual but also ecclesiastical and social activity. Evidence for the actual implementation of the decrees seems slight. The text hardly ever suggests that penalties are to be enforced if the stipulations are not observed. It has been argued that there was originally a florilegium of extracts in Ireland on which the *Collectio* was based. The compilers often alter their sources and when the authors cited offer conflicting ideas, no attempt is made to reconcile them. Among the sources, two bodies of native synodical decrees are used. Those of the Synodus Hibernensis were propagated by a faction in

the Irish church, which followed older ecclesiastical practices, while those of the *Romani* followed those of Rome. The decrees of the Synodus Hibernensis are believed to show the influence of Cú Chuimne, since he came from Iona, a centre notable for the conservatism of its practices, which was the last to accept the Roman calculation for the date of Easter, in 716. The Synodus Hibernensis passed rulings which were more likely to mention native legal institutions than were those of the *Romani*.

All the surviving manuscripts of the *Collectio* stem from the continent, where it was influential, and much copied, especially in Brittany. No manuscripts of the text survive from Ireland. The text was known to St Boniface, Archbishop Odo of Canterbury, Bishop Arbeo of Freising, Sedulius Scottus, Wulfstan, and, possibly, the Carolingian empress Judith. In the late eighth and ninth centuries the collection was transmitted on the continent particularly in regions with long Celtic traditions or where the 'officially' promulgated Roman texts seem to have been little copied. The Welsh and Anglo-Saxon evidence points to the existence of an insular tradition of the text. The section on marriage influenced later European conciliar collections. It has been proposed that there was a connection between the stipulations of the text on kings, possibly drawn up under the influence of Adomnán of Iona, and a school of thought in the Irish church at that time which was particularly concerned with altering the succession practice, and especially the inauguration ritual, of kingship, and that this influenced the anointing of Pippin III in Francia.

LUNED MAIR DAVIES

Sources *Ann. Ulster*, s.a. 747 · Bibliothèque Nationale, Paris, MS Lat. 12021, colophon · R. Thurneysen, 'Zur irischen Kanonensammlung', *Zeitschrift für Celtische Philologie*, 6 (1907–8), 1–5 · J. F. Kenney, *The sources for the early history of Ireland* (1929); repr. (1979) · K. Hughes, *The church in early Irish society* (1966) · D. R. Howlett, 'Cú Chuimne's hymn "Cantemus in omni die": an exercise in textual reconstruction', *Peritia* [forthcoming]
Archives Archivio dell'Abbazia, Monte Cassino, MS 297 · Badisches Landesbibliothek, Karlsruhe, MS Aug. XVIII · Biblioteca Labronica, Livorno, MS, formerly no. 10 · Biblioteca Vallicelliana, Rome, MS t. XVIII · Bibliothèque Municipale, Orléans, MS 221 (193) · Bibliothèque Nationale, Paris, MS Lat. 3182 · Bibliothèque Nationale, Paris, MS Lat. 12021 · BL, Cotton MS Otho E.xiii · Bodl. Oxf., Hatton MS 42 · CCC Cam., MS 279 · Dombibliothek, Cologne, MS 210 · Stiftsbibliothek, St Gallen, MS 143 · Cambrai, MS 679 (619)

Cuán ua Lothcháin (*d.* 1024), Gaelic poet, is variously designated Ireland's 'chief poet' (*priméices*, in, for example, the annals of Ulster, or *ardfhili*, in the annals of Inisfallen) and 'chief historian' (*prímshenchaid*, in the annals of Tigernach) in his obituary notices. There are no reliable data concerning his background or career: his family name is twice given as 'ua Leocháin', suggesting a connection with the petty kings of Luigne in Meath; but this variant is too isolated to justify preferring it to the standard form. The annals of Clonmacnoise, surviving only in a seventeenth-century English translation, record a tradition that after the lapse of the high-kingship in 1022 Ireland was governed by Cuán together with one Corcán Cléirech, 'like a free state, & not like a monarchy'; whatever the origin of this fantastic doctrine, it can have no historical basis.

Most of the poems plausibly attributed to Cuán deal with the lore of places in the midlands: 'A chóemu críche Cuind chain', on Tailtiu in Meath, 'Atá sund carn uí Chathbath', on Carn Furbaide near Granard, 'Druim Criaich, céte cét cuan', on Drumcree, Westmeath, and 'Síd Nechtain sund forsint shléib', on the River Boyne, have all been edited by E. Gwynn (Gwynn, vols. 3 and 4); 'Temair Breg, baile na fian' and 'Temair, toga na tulach', both on Tara, have been edited by M. Joynt and by E. Gwynn (Gwynn, vol. 1); and a poem on the Shannon, 'Sáerainm Sinna saigid dún', may also be his work (Gwynn, vol. 3). Besides the antiquarian topics with which they purport to be primarily concerned, some of these poems deal with the reign of Máel Sechnaill mac Domnaill (high-king of Ireland 980–1002, 1014–22), evidently Cuán's principal patron. 'Druim Criaich' asserts the principle that the high-kingship should never pass from father to son, in justification of Máel Sechnaill's own succession; while 'A chóemu' praises him for reviving the royal assembly at Tailtiu in 1007, and calls him 'chosen king of Tara … river Euphrates surging aloft, sole warrior of Europe'. Other poems describe the origin of Máel Sechnaill's dynasty ('Temair Breg', where Tara is called 'a second Rome') and the exemplary rule of his legendary ancestor Cormac mac Airt ('Temair, toga'). In the only surviving non-toponymic composition, 'A fhir iadas in tech' (edited by M. Dillon), the poet asks to be admitted to Tara on the strength of his knowledge of the things which are lucky and unlucky for the king. Cuán seems, however, also to have courted the favour of lesser figures: his poem on Drumcree includes a quatrain praising Lachtna mac Taidc, an otherwise forgotten member of the local dynasty of the Uí Gadra of Luigne.

The annals of Ulster, closely followed by most of the other annals which speak of his death, state that Cuán was killed in the region of Tethba, Westmeath: 'in the same hour the company which had killed him putrified; that was a poet's miracle'. A more realistic account is provided by the annals of Inisfallen: 'the man who killed him was killed immediately, i.e. the son of Gilla Ultáin son of Rodub'. If Cuán's murderer was a nephew of the Fiachra, son of Rodub, who killed the lord of Tethba in 995, this would make him a member of the Muinter Maelshinna: this was in fact a Tethba family, occupying the barony of Kilkenny West in Westmeath; and the name Gilla Ultáin occurs elsewhere in its pedigree. The background of the poet's death in 1024 is impossible to recover in detail, but its broader outlines can be surmised: the petty kingdoms of the western midlands were at this time exceptionally violent and chaotic, and there would have been nothing to protect Cuán there after the passing of his great patron and the eclipse of the national monarchy to which he had aspired.

JOHN CAREY

Sources Ann. Ulster · S. Mac Airt, ed. and trans., The annals of Inisfallen (1951) · W. Stokes, ed., 'The annals of Tigernach [8 pts]', Revue Celtique, 16 (1895), 374–419; 17 (1896), 6–33, 119–263, 337–420; 18 (1897), 9–59, 150–97, 267–303, 374–91; pubd sep. (1993) · AFM · D. Murphy, ed., The annals of Clonmacnoise, trans. C. Mageoghagan (1896); facs. edn (1993) · E. Gwynn, ed. and trans., The metrical dindshenchas, 5 vols., Royal Irish Academy: Todd Lecture Series, 8– 12 (1903–35), 1.14–27; 3.26–33, 286–91; 4.30–35, 42–57, 146–63, 387–8, 418–19 · W. M. Hennessy, ed. and trans., Chronicum Scotorum: a chronicle of Irish affairs, Rolls Series, 46 (1866) · T. O'Rahilly and others, Catalogue of Irish manuscripts in the Royal Irish Academy, 30 vols. (Dublin, 1926–70) · T. K. Abbott and E. J. Gwynn, eds., Catalogue of the Irish manuscripts in the library of Trinity College, Dublin (1921) · S. O'Grady, R. Flower, and M. Dillon, eds., Catalogue of Irish manuscripts in the British Library (formerly British Museum), 2 vols. (1926–53); repr. (1992) · M. Joynt, 'Echtra Mac Echdach Mugredóin', Ériu, 4 (1908), 91–111 · M. Dillon, 'The taboos of the kings of Ireland', Proceedings of the Royal Irish Academy, 54C (1951–2), 1–36

Cubbon, Sir Mark (1784–1861), army officer in the East India Company, son of the Revd Thomas Cubbon, belonged to an old Manx family, and arrived in India in 1800 as a cadet for the Madras infantry. He was appointed a lieutenant in the 15th Madras native infantry on 20 July 1801, and was promoted captain on 6 April 1816, soon after which he went on the staff as an assistant commissary-general. He served as such in the Pindari war, and in 1822 became deputy commissary-general for the Madras presidency. He was promoted major on 23 November 1823, and lieutenant-colonel on 22 April 1826.

In 1831 the people of Mysore rose against the Hindu raja, who had been placed upon the throne by Lord Wellesley after the death of Tipu Sultan in 1799. The rising was suppressed, and a commission, consisting of Major-General Hawker, W. Morison, John Macleod, and Cubbon, reported on its causes. The report showed such gross misgovernment by the raja that Lord William Bentinck, the governor-general, decided to take over the direct administration of the kingdom, allowing the raja a palace and an allowance. A board of two commissioners, of which Cubbon—who was promoted colonel by brevet on 18 June 1831—was the junior, was appointed to govern the kingdom; but they quarrelled, and in June 1834 Cubbon was appointed sole commissioner. He held this post for twenty-seven years without intermission, during which Mysore became prosperous.

Cubbon was a first-rate administrator, and though he ruled despotically with minimal control from the Indian government, no complaint was ever made against him. His system was to rule through Indian agents, and to maintain local institutions, and his belief in the Indian people was apparently repaid by their confidence in him. He simplified the revenue and judicial systems, encouraged the introduction of coffee planting, and maintained the Amrit Mahal at Hunsur, which had been established by Haidar Ali to improve the breed of cattle. Cubbon, who never married, was famous for his hospitality at Bangalore, and for his almost paternal kindness to his subordinate officers. He was made colonel of the 15th Madras native infantry in 1839, promoted major-general in 1846 and lieutenant-general in 1852, and made CB in February 1856 and KCB in May 1857. He kept on good terms with the raja, and it was owing to the opposition of both the raja and of Cubbon that the scheme to transfer supervision of the government of Mysore from the supreme government to that of Madras in 1860 fell through.

Popular and respected, in February 1861 Cubbon resigned his post because of ill health, and prepared to return to England after an absence of sixty-one years. He died on the journey, at Suez, on 23 April 1861. An equestrian statue of him was erected at Bangalore.

H. M. STEPHENS, rev. JAMES LUNT

Sources B. L. Rice, *Mysore and Coorg* (1877) · J. J. Higginbotham, *Men whom India has known: biographies of eminent Indian characters*, 2nd edn (1874) · Dodwell [E. Dodwell] and Miles [J. S. Miles], eds., *Alphabetical list of the officers of the Indian army: with the dates of their respective promotion, retirement, resignation, or death … from the year 1760 to the year … 1837* (1838) · *Hart's Army List* · *East-India Register* · P. Moon, *The British conquest and dominion of India* (1989) · S. Wolpert, *A new history of India* (1993) · Boase, *Mod. Eng. biog.*
Archives Manx National Heritage Library, Douglas, corresp. | BL OIOC, letters to Lord Tweeddale, MSS Eur. F 96
Likenesses Martin, watercolour-and-pencil drawing, 1856–61, NPG · F. C. Lewis sen., mezzotint (after Lewis jun., 1845), NPG · statue, Bangalore, India

Cubbon, William (1865–1955), antiquary and museum curator, was born at Orrestal, Rushen, Isle of Man, on 28 May 1865, the son of James Cubbon, fishing boat skipper, and his wife, Margaret Powell. He was educated at the boys' school, Rushen, and began work in the printing trade in 1880 as an apprentice compositor. He subsequently became a journalist, eventually becoming manager and editor of the *Isle of Man Examiner*. From 1900 until 1906 he was joint proprietor and editor of the *Manx Sun*, which was then taken over by the *Isle of Man Times*, on which he worked until 1912.

Cubbon was brought up to believe passionately in Manx culture, and became an avid advocate of Manx nationalism at a time when such opinions were unpopular among many of the Manx and upholders of Manx culture were often mocked and derided. He saw Manx culture as part of a wider Celtic world, and his interests were wide-ranging. In 1912 he was appointed librarian of the Douglas Library, where he remained until 1922 (having served as manager of the local labour exchange during the First World War). In this post Cubbon began to gather together materials for what became the Manx National Archive. In 1922, the long-projected Manx Museum was established, under the directorship of Philip Kermode, and Cubbon was appointed secretary and librarian. The collections of books, manuscripts, photographs, maps, and official records that Cubbon had amassed at Douglas formed the basis of the collection. On Kermode's death in 1932 Cubbon succeeded as director of the museum, remaining in office until 1940. He was married twice: first, to Margaret Jane (Mollie) Quayle (d. 1922), with whom he had two sons, and second, in 1925, to Hortense Mylechraine.

Cubbon was widely recognized as an authority on Manx subjects and he was particularly interested in the island's Norse connections. He was one of the founder members of the Manx Language Society, begun by A. W. Moore in 1899, and was active in other Manx associations, including the antiquarian society and the World Manx Association. He published widely on Manx subjects, both in articles and books: for his works, including the indispensable two-volume *Bibliographical Account of Works Relating to the Isle of Man* (1933–9), he was awarded an honorary MA by the University of Liverpool in 1949. *Island Heritage* (1952), a series

of essays based on earlier papers, was an impassioned call for Manx nationalism. His scholarship was 'of a lofty order' and he wrote with 'a bold and forthright expression of view' (*Mona's Herald*, 4 Jan 1955). In 1933 and 1939 he was offered a Norwegian knighthood of the order of St Olav, but as a civil servant was obliged to refuse for technical reasons; he was finally awarded the honour in 1947.

William Cubbon died in Brentwood, Essex, at the home of his son Harry, on 1 January 1955. The *Isle of Man Examiner* observed, 'He was the greatest unhonoured Manxman of his day' (7 Jan 1955). LESLIE QUILLIAM

Sources *Mona's Herald* (5 Dec 1933) · *Mona's Herald* (4 Jan 1955) · *Isle of Man Examiner* (7 Jan 1955) · *Isle of Man Weekly Times* (7 Jan 1955) · *Isle of Man Weekly Times* (14 Dec 1962) · *Journal of the Manx Museum*, 6/74 (1957), 8 · M. Douglas, 'Passionately and defiantly Manx', *Manx Life* (July–Aug 1980) · *WWW* · S. Harrison, ed., *100 Years of heritage* (1989)

Cubitt, James (1836–1912), architect, was born in Ilford, Essex, on 20 March 1836, the only son and elder surviving child of James Cubitt (1808–1863), Baptist minister, and his wife, Mary (1796/7–1872). These Cubitts were Norfolk Baptists. James's grandfather William (1754–1814) founded Neatishead Baptist church; a great-aunt, Sophia (1778–1855), dominated Ingham Baptist church; an uncle, William (1801–1888), became a Baptist manufacturer in Shoreditch and in Banbury. The Baptist ministry followed naturally for James's father, a conscientious man with a didactic streak and uncertain health: he attended Stepney College, then served pastorates at Ilford, Stratford upon Avon, Bourton on the Water, and Thrapston. At Ilford he married a widow and took pupils, among them a nephew, Mordecai Cubitt Cooke (1825–1914), the mycologist. No record survives of the younger James's schooling but the wide reading, keen historical sense, and fluent, sharp English of his prime reflect this background of literate, articulate, and often quarrelsome provincial congregations on the cusp of prosperity.

It is not clear what turned Cubitt to architecture. The surname helped, but though the contracting—like the engineering—Cubitts came from Norfolk, and there was a marriage connection with the engineer Sir William Cubitt (1785–1861), there was no real link with them. None the less it did no harm to be thought their kinsman, and *Building News* promoted the myth by calling Cubitt 'a member of the family of that name, which furnished a former President and a vice-president to the Institution of Civil Engineers' (16 May 1890).

From 1851 to 1856 Cubitt was articled to Isaac Gilbert of Nottingham and attended classes at the Nottingham School of Art. Assistantships followed, in Malvern with E. W. Elmslie (1856–7) and in London with R. J. Withers and W. W. Pocock (1857–60). Each had a sound line in public, commercial, and ecclesiastical buildings. Gilbert was a Congregationalist, Pocock a Wesleyan, Withers a churchman—an ecclesiologist noted for plain, correct Gothic. They explain Cubitt's subsequent bias, confirmed by visits to Cotswold, midland, and north-eastern churches.

In 1862 Cubitt was in Camberwell. In the previous year

his father had been appointed tutor at the Pastors' College, founded by the Baptist preaching phenomenon C. H. Spurgeon, in the Metropolitan Tabernacle, recently designed by Pocock. Cubitt's early practice was dominated by commissions associated with Spurgeon: chapels at East Hill, Wandsworth (1862), and Rye Hill, Newcastle upon Tyne (1864), and institutional buildings for the Tabernacle itself (1866–9). The chapels were bold Italianate Romanesque; the rest was Ruskinian–Venetian Gothic.

Other influences now worked on Cubitt. He relished the broad severity of J. L. Pearson, James Brooks, and G. F. Bodley, writing about such work and more technical matters in *Building News*. By 1868 he had moved to 26 Finsbury Place, in partnership with Henry Fuller, another of Isaac Gilbert's pupils. Fuller, who had worked for Alfred Waterhouse, had a growing chapel practice and a reputation for technical innovation. Cubitt completed Fuller's finest building, Clapton Park Congregational Church, Hackney (1869–73).

In 1870 Cubitt published *Church Design for Congregations*, a persuasive manual for prospective chapel builders, advocating a truly protestant architecture for 'a real nineteenth-century church, in a masculine and monumental style'. Convinced that the contemporary spirit was best found in the thirteenth century, he celebrated the 'magnificent capabilities' of column-free naves, central crossings, and galleries 'where the architecture meant them to be'. His sources ranged from Pugin to Viollet-le-Duc, his illustrations from Spain to Byzantium.

Fuller died in December 1872. By 1875 Cubitt had moved his practice to 2 Finsbury Pavement, his home to 5 Eaton Villas, Loughton, Essex, and had married Fanny Emma Comely (1851–1875), a farmer's daughter whose family were mainstays of the elder Cubitt's ministry at Bourton. She died in childbirth four days before the stone-laying of the chapel that her husband designed for his father's old congregation. He never remarried.

The 1870s saw two landmarks in Cubitt's church design. Emmanuel Congregational Church, Cambridge (1874; Early English with Early French detail), celebrated nonconformity's new place in that university. Its nave arches of 'unusual span' gave hearers full view of its pulpit. Union Chapel, Islington (1876–89), won by Cubitt using the Ruskinian pseudonym Torcello in an ill-tempered competition adjudicated by Alfred Waterhouse, was a brick chorale of a church, fine for sung and spoken word, seating 1800, costing £50,000, and hailed as among the most notable buildings erected in Britain between 1842 and 1892 (*The Builder*, 1 Jan 1943).

Union Chapel was Cubitt's masterpiece, but the Baptist Church of the Redeemer, Edgbaston (1882), and the Welsh Church, Charing Cross Road, London (1887), were equally massive vindications of *Church Design*. Thereafter Cubitt mellowed. From 1881 he practised from 2 Broad Street Buildings, Liverpool Street, associated in the 1880s with J. M. Brydon, with G. F. Collinson in the 1890s, and with H. J. Manchip from 1905. In 1890 Cubitt was elected FRIBA, with Waterhouse and Brydon as proposers. The crisply

helpful *Popular Handbook of Nonconformist Church Building* followed in 1892.

France now gave way to the Low Countries, and central crossings to broad naves. Osborne Road Baptist Church, Jesmond, Newcastle (1887), was emphatically Norman, but Avenue Congregational Church, Southampton (1898), and Streatham Congregational Church (1901) were parish churches in fifteenth-century Perpendicular Gothic. Most suggestive of all was Cubitt's fascination with Wren, who 'designed from the inside outwards' (*Contemporary Review*, 46, July 1884).

This announced a proto-member of the arts and crafts movement, as suggested in Cubitt's ancillary buildings for Westgate Road Baptist Church, Newcastle (1886), flagged in his secular commissions—board schools, for example, in Loughton, Leytonstone, Lewisham, and Dulwich—and fulfilled in the schoolroom ('seventeenth-century domestic work') for Union Chapel, Loughton (1898), and in some private houses in Loughton. His last major building was a church, Tabernacl, Bangor (1905), at once Norman and Perpendicular—proof of a Victorian mind pressing forward.

Cubitt was an architect's architect—admired by Waterhouse and Brydon, singled out by Hermann Muthesius—linking the ecclesiologists to the nonconformist conscience. He lived modestly in Loughton, Essex, where his brother-in-law William Vivian ministered until financial disgrace and death terminated his ministry. He died, intestate, on 8 August 1912 at his home, Monghyr Cottage, Loughton (which had been named after an Indian Baptist missionary station), and was buried two days later at Loughton cemetery.   CLYDE BINFIELD

Sources C. Binfield, *The contexting of a chapel architect: James Cubitt, 1836–1912*, Chapels Society, Occasional Publications, 2 (2001) • M. P. English, *Mordecai Cubitt Cooke: Victorian naturalist, mycologist, teacher, and scientist* (1987) • C. B. Jewson, *The Baptists in Norfolk* (1957) • W. Rye, 'Collections for a history of the family of Cubitt of Norfolk', *Norfolk Miscellany* (1877) • C. Welch, ed., *London at the opening of the twentieth century: contemporary biographies* (1905) • *Building News* (16 May 1890) • biographical file, RIBA BAL • H. Muthesius, *Die neuere kirchliche Baukunst in England* (Berlin, 1901) • Regent's Park College, Oxford, Bourton on the Water Baptist Church records • census returns for Spaldwick, Huntingdonshire, 1871 • *Baptist Handbook* (1863), 121 • d. cert. [F. E. Cubitt] • d. cert. • census returns, 1881

Archives Essex RO, Chelmsford, Loughton Union Church records, ERO DNB 3 • Regent's Park College, Oxford, Bourton on the Water Baptist Church records, MSS F. P. C. F. • Islington, Union Chapel records

Likenesses Chalkley Gould of Bournemouth, photograph, repro. in Binfield, *Contexting of a chapel architect*, frontispiece

Cubitt, Joseph (1811–1872). *See under* Cubitt, Sir William (1785–1861).

Cubitt, Lewis (1799–1883), architect, was born in September 1799, the third and youngest son of Jonathan Cubitt (1761–1807), a Norfolk carpenter, and Agnes Scarlett. In July 1814 his eldest brother, Thomas *Cubitt (1788–1855), the most respected and successful of the nineteenth-century London builder–developers, became a member of the Carpenters' Company by redemption (that is, payment of a sum of money). In February of the following

Lewis Cubitt (1799–1883), by Sir William Boxall, 1845

year Lewis was bound to him as an apprentice and thus seven years later he also became a member of the company, this time in the traditional manner. By 1822 his eldest brother had already placed him in charge of smaller jobs, such as the construction of two houses in Berkeley Square. He also received some training in the architectural office of Henry Edward *Kendall (1776–1875), a former pupil of Thomas Leverton and John Nash, whose designs for town houses were well regarded. Lewis later married Kendall's daughter Sophia on 23 January 1830 at St Nicholas, Brighton, Sussex. By 1824 all three brothers were in partnership as 'Messrs. T. W. and L. Cubitt', though this union was dissolved in 1827, Lewis first working with Thomas and then with the middle brother, William *Cubitt (1791–1863), whose firm Lewis joined in 1831. Later in the 1830s Lewis established his own architectural practice at 77 Great Russell Street, London. Most of the extensive residential developments built in Bloomsbury and Belgravia by the Cubitts in the 1820s were probably to designs by Lewis. In comparison with his brothers his own speculative developments were minor, for instance the series of Italianate houses on the south side of Lowndes Square which he designed and built in 1837–9.

During the 1840s Cubitt established a substantial and well-deserved reputation as a railway architect, designing the Bricklayers Arms station, Bermondsey (1842–4; dem.), and a building in Colchester originally intended to be the Victoria Hotel, but which was completed as a lunatic asylum (the Royal Counties Institution, 1843). In engineering terms one of his most impressive achievements during this period was the design of the Digswell Viaduct (1848–

50) for the London to Peterborough railway line (now the east coast main line). This structure, built by Thomas Brassey, consisted of forty brick arches, some 100 feet high, which extended 520 yards to cross the valley of the River Mimram.

Cubitt's involvement with the railways culminated at the end of the decade in his best-known work, the terminus at Battle Bridge for the Great Northern Railway known as King's Cross Station. The Great Northern route, the second, eastern, line to the north, had opened with a temporary station to the north of Regent's Canal in 1850 in time to bring hordes of visitors to the Great Exhibition. The permanent station, on the site of the old smallpox hospital where the New (now Euston) Road intersected the Caledonian Road, was completed in 1852 with remarkable speed and economy (it cost less than the budgeted £123,500). Its utilitarian character was in marked contrast to the nearby Euston Station with its Greek revival propylaeum (1837) by Philip Hardwick. At King's Cross the station consisted of two parallel sheds, each 800 feet long and 105 feet wide, with glazed roofs supported by a system of innovative laminated timber arches rising to a height of 71 feet. These timbers were replaced with curved steel girders between 1869 and 1887 without substantially altering the appearance of the interior. The sheds covered two sets of platforms, one set for departure and the other for arrival. This simple arrangement was lucidly expressed in the organization of the façade, which was constructed of London stock brick. It featured two massive glazed arches set in deep stepped reveals which were separated by an Italianate clock tower 120 feet high and buttressed at either end by severe brick pylons. In the contemporary press it was noted approvingly that 'great plainness prevails: the architect depends wholly for effect on the largeness of some of the features, the fitness of the structure for its purpose, and a characteristic expression of that purpose' (*The Builder*, 9/459, 1851, 731). It was precisely these qualities which caused the building to be held in high regard during that part of the twentieth century when Victorian architecture in general was held in disdain for its frivolity of ornament. Cubitt was also responsible for a number of the structures covering the 45 acres of goods yards which stretched to the north of the terminus, including a substantial granary. His Great Northern Station Hotel, to the west of the train sheds, was a curving Italianate block which in its gentility bore little relation to the sublime grandeur of the main station.

Cubitt seems not to have engaged in professional work after 1852, perhaps confirming the family tradition that he was 'the laziest and least satisfactory of the three' brothers (Colvin, *Archs.*, 282). He received a bequest of £10,000 following the death of his brother Thomas in 1855. He died at his home, 5 Lewes Crescent, Brighton, Sussex, on 9 June 1883, leaving three daughters, Ada, Agnes, and Ellen. His son Lewis predeceased him.

RICHARD JOHN

Sources Colvin, *Archs.* · H. R. Hitchcock, *Early Victorian architecture in Britain*, 1 (1954), 555–9 · H. Hobhouse, *Thomas Cubitt: master builder* (1971) · W. H. Godfrey and W. M. Marcham, *The parish of St*

Pancras, ed. J. R. H. Roberts, 4, Survey of London, 24 (1952) · *The Builder*, 9/459 (1851), p. 731 · d. cert. · *CGPLA Eng. & Wales* (1883) · will, probate department of the principal registry of the family division, London · IGI

Likenesses W. Boxall, oils, 1845, NPG [*see illus.*] · portrait, repro. in Hobhouse, *Thomas Cubitt*, pl. 104

Wealth at death £77,900 10s. 10d.: will, 6 July 1883, *CGPLA Eng. & Wales*

Cubitt, Thomas (1788–1855), builder, was born at Buxton, near Norwich, on 25 February 1788, the eldest son of Jonathan Cubitt (1761–1807), a Norfolk carpenter, and his wife, Agnes Scarlett. He had two younger brothers and two sisters. He trained as a carpenter, and took one voyage to India as a ship's carpenter. With the proceeds he set up in business on his own in Holborn. In 1810 his brother William *Cubitt (1791–1863) joined him, and in 1815 they moved to Gray's Inn Road. They carried out the contract for the building of the London Institution in Finsbury Circus, as well as some speculative development. From his experience with this contract, Cubitt developed a system by which, instead of negotiating with other master craftsmen, he employed directly workmen of all the building trades, employing dozens of men, from brickmakers and masons to plasterers and painters. This was an innovation for speculative house building on a large scale, and it was this step that made Cubitt's name in the building industry. His difficulties in dealing with architects made him decide to concentrate on speculative development rather than contracting for buildings for other people. In 1819 he married Mary Anne Warner (d. 1880); they had twelve children, of whom seven predeceased their father and were buried in the family tomb at Norwood cemetery, south London.

Small developments were undertaken by Cubitt in Highbury, Stoke Newington, and Barnsbury, Middlesex, but his first large 'take' as a developer was on the duke of Bedford's estate in Bloomsbury in 1824. He then took on all the available land for some 167 houses, a venture which was not completed until after his death. The following year he agreed with Earl Grosvenor (later first marquess of Westminster) for 19 acres in the Five Fields, on which Belgrave Square and Eaton Square, were to be built. He found other developers to share the risk, in the shape of George and William Haldimand, who took Belgrave Square, employing George Basevi to design the houses, though Cubitt retained Eaton Place, the north side of Eaton Square, and some houses in Belgrave Square. He took the adjacent Lowndes estate, and also developed Albert Gate, where his enormous mansions were nicknamed 'Malta' and 'Gibraltar', because 'they would never be taken'.

Cubitt also built on the Grosvenor land to the south, together with that of three other major landowners, putting together a very large estate which he called South Belgravia but which was nicknamed 'Mr Cubitt's District' and later became known as Pimlico. This he laid out in a grid of more modest squares and streets, controlling development by smaller builders working to specifications and designs provided by his organization. As part of the development he built several hundred yards of the Thames

Thomas Cubitt (1788–1855), by unknown artist

Embankment. Cubitt also took on other land, in Clapham, where he developed Clapham Park, a suburban residential estate of 250 acres intended for large houses, and a major part of Kemp Town, in Brighton. He himself lived in Clapham Park House.

In 1827 the partnership between Cubitt and his brothers William and the much younger Lewis *Cubitt (1799–1883), the designer of King's Cross Station, was dissolved. William retained the Gray's Inn Road works, which became one of the major Victorian contract building firms, while Thomas and Lewis concentrated on speculative development. Lewis re-joined William in 1831. At Thames Bank, between Vauxhall and Chelsea, Cubitt developed an integrated and comprehensive building works where much of the materials used on his developments were produced, not only joinery and steel girders, but also cement and plasterwork. He had a brickworks on the Medway, where the most up-to-date machinery and methods were used, and other building components were bought direct from the manufacturers—Portland stone stairs from Dorset, and slates from Penrhyn in north Wales.

Cubitt had a professional staff of architects and surveyors, and his own legal and letting departments. His success was also linked to his ability to borrow money at competitive rates and to retain the confidence of backers who would be both loyal and deep-pocketed in the slumps which regularly hit the London building trade. These included the first Lord Carrington, the directors of Smith's Bank, and the clients of a number of London solicitors. Work on the developments undertaken in the 1820s occupied his organization for the rest of his life and he left a number of sites unfilled at his death, to be completed by his executors. Many of the houses were erected by sub-developers; some were very modest, but many successful London builders and developers either trained in his office, or started their careers on his developments.

Cubitt was approached by Prince Albert to alter Osborne House, in the Isle of Wight, as Queen Victoria's marine residence, but in the event it was totally rebuilt to the prince's design, a scheme on which Cubitt worked with the prince himself and with Ludwig Gruner, the prince's adviser on art. He not only built the mansion but also the considerable Italianate gardens and terraces which surround it, and set up the royal estate maintenance staff. His collaboration with the prince, an enthusiastic building owner, on this private royal project was so successful that on the latter's insistence he was given the government contract to build the extensions to Buckingham Palace designed by Edward Blore in 1845–50 and by James Pennethorne in 1852–6. He is credited with having first brought the Great Exhibition project to Prince Albert's attention through his contacts at the Society of Arts, the original promoter.

Through his position as 'our Cubitt' to the royal family Cubitt was responsible for a number of small commissions; thus he erected the model dwellings designed by Henry Roberts, exhibited close to the Great Exhibition in Hyde Park in 1851. He also played an important part in negotiations for the purchase and laying out of the South Kensington estate of the Royal Commission for the Exhibition of 1851, of which Prince Albert was president. The connection between his firm and the royal family is symbolized by the fact that the queen asked his erstwhile general foreman, George Dines, to undertake the building of the Royal Mausoleum at Frogmore on the prince's untimely death in 1861.

Cubitt was concerned in a number of improvements in both town-planning schemes and in building practice in contemporary London, including the campaign for smoke abatement. Though his own developments were famously healthy and free of the epidemics which were a scourge of mid-Victorian London, he was concerned with the problems of the London sewerage system—or lack of it—and published a pamphlet on it at his own expense in 1843, advocating views which anticipated the improvements of the next decade. He became a member of the Institution of Civil Engineers in 1839, and published some papers on the strength of materials. He gave evidence to a number of government and parliamentary bodies inquiring into the parlous estate of the metropolis, where his views as a successful developer on whose estates many of his hearers resided carried considerable weight. These inquiries included the select committee on metropolis improvements of 1838 and the royal commission of inquiry into the state of large towns, 1843–4, and resulted in such legislation as the Building Act of 1844 and the Metropolis Management Act of 1855. He was a promoter of the Battersea Park scheme, for converting the marshy Battersea fields into a public park for south London. He also advocated the creation of trunk routes to serve the suburbs in advance of development, and the greater use of the River Thames as a highway in contrast to the dirty and noisy roads.

Cubitt was often addressed as 'architect' but insisted upon being called a builder. His eminence in his own sphere was recognized by the London Builders' Society, who presented him with a subscription portrait on the grounds of 'his general integrity of character, … his constant efforts to raise the Building Act to high standard, by judicious improvements in the construction of buildings, based upon original and costly experiments' (*The Builder*, 11 March 1848).

At the end of his life Cubitt bought Denbies House, near Dorking, which he totally rebuilt. He also restored the grounds extensively and Prince Albert visited him to plant a symbolic tree. His eldest son, George, became MP for Surrey, and was raised to the peerage as Baron Ashcombe. Cubitt died on 20 December 1855 at Denbies House of cancer of the throat, and was buried in Norwood cemetery. He left property in real and personal estate worth over £1 million. In one of the longest wills then on record, he directed that his building works should be wound up within twenty-one years, and his developments concluded.

HERMIONE HOBHOUSE

Sources *GM*, 2nd ser., 45 (1856), 202–5 · *PICE*, 16 (1856–7), 158–62 · *The Builder*, 13 (1855), 629–30 · H. Hobhouse, *Thomas Cubitt: master builder*, rev. edn (1995) · S. Tallents, *Man and boy* (1943) · D. J. Olsen, *Town planning in London: the eighteenth and nineteenth centuries* (1964) · J. Summerson, *Georgian London*, new edn (1988) · Colvin, *Archs.* · Burke, *Peerage*
Archives Bedford estate office, Bloomsbury, London · Cubitt estate office, London · Grosvenor estate office, London · LMA · RSA, diary
Likenesses H. W. Pickersgill, oils, *c.*1849, London Builders' Society · P. Macdowell, marble bust, 1856, Denbies, Dorking, Surrey · W. Fawke, statue, St George's Drive, London · G. R. Ward, mezzotint and engraving (after H. W. Pickersgill), NPG · oils, NPG [see *illus.*]
Wealth at death over £1,000,000: Hobhouse *Thomas Cubitt*

Cubitt, Sir William (1785–1861), civil engineer and millwright, son of Joseph Cubitt of Bacton Wood, near Dilham, Norfolk, miller, and his wife, Hannah, *née* Lubbock, was born at Dilham. He was educated at the village school there, and also had access to the libraries of two local clergymen, the Revd Erasmus Drury, of South Repps, and the Revd J. Humphrey, of Wroxham. His father moved to South Repps, where Cubitt was employed at an early age in the mill, but later apprenticed for four years to James Lyon, a cabinet-maker, at Stalham. He returned to work with his father at Bacton Wood Mills, employing his leisure time to invent a machine for splitting hides, with more ingenuity than success. He then entered into partnership with an agricultural machine maker named Cook, of Swanton, producing horse threshing-machines and other agricultural implements; he became well known for the accuracy and quality of the patterns produced for the iron castings. Cubitt married; he and his wife, Elizabeth Jane, had a son, Joseph.

In 1807 Cubitt settled at Honing as a millwright and invented and patented a self-regulating windmill sail,

Sir William Cubitt (1785–1861), by Samuel Bellin (after Sir William Boxall, exh. RA 1849)

which became universally adopted, being easier to manage than the large sails then in use. He also devised machines for draining the marshes in the immediate vicinity. In 1812 he moved to the firm of Ransomes of Ipswich, makers of agricultural implements, becoming first chief engineer, and then a partner from 1821 until 1826. During this period he invented the treadmill as a method of employing human labour to grind corn, in the same way as animal power was used at the time. This invention was rapidly adopted in the principal gaols of the United Kingdom, the first being erected in Brixton in 1817; later sites included Bridewell Hospital in London. From 1814 he also acted as a civil engineer, particularly in canal engineering, commencing with reports in 1814, 1820, and 1822 on the Norwich navigation. He earned a national reputation for this work, being responsible for the Oxford Canal, and the Birmingham and Liverpool Junction Canal, though not all these ventures were successful commercially. He was responsible for improving the navigation of the Severn, and the Weaver navigation in the 1840s. He made important reports on the Thames, Tyne, Tees, Ouse, Nene, Witham, and Welland, and was also concerned with the commission for the improvement of the Shannon. He advised on the development of docks, particularly the Bute docks at Cardiff, the Middlesbrough docks and coal drops on the Tees, and the Black Sluice drainage at Boston, Lincolnshire. He also devised two large floating landing stages in Liverpool.

In 1826 Cubitt moved to London where he became well known as an expert witness at parliamentary inquiries.

On 1 April 1830 he was elected a fellow of the Royal Society. On the introduction of railways he moved into that field too, one of his first ventures being as a witness for George Stephenson on the feasibility of making a railway line across Chat Moss. In due course he was appointed engineer-in-chief to the South Eastern Railway, where he impressed contemporaries by adopting the bold scheme of using 18,000 lb of gunpowder to blow down the face of the Round Down cliff between Folkestone and Dover. He then ran the railway line along the beach with a tunnel under the Shakespeare cliff. With the extension of the railway to Folkestone, the establishment of a steamer service between that port and Boulogne led Cubitt to find employment in France, where as consulting engineer he co-operated with a French engineer to build a railway from Boulogne to Amiens. Subsequently he advised on the route from Paris to Lyons. Working with his son, Joseph Cubitt, he was consulting engineer to the Great Northern Railway, one of the leading lines of the time, whose terminus was at King's Cross, designed and built by the architect Lewis Cubitt (1799–1883), the cadet brother of the building contractors Thomas and William Cubitt, but confusingly no relation. As both families of Cubitt came from Norfolk, it seems possible that they might have had a remote connection but the relationship was specifically disowned by Thomas Cubitt, and it seems to have been generally accepted by contemporaries that the two sets of Cubitts, Sir William and his son Joseph, and the three brothers Thomas, William, and Lewis, were not related.

Cubitt joined the Institution of Civil Engineers in 1823, becoming a member of the council in 1831 and a vice-president in 1836. In 1850, as president, he was brought to prominence when he was an *ex officio* member of the Royal Commission for the Exhibition of 1851, under the presidency of Prince Albert. He advocated the adoption of Joseph Paxton's design for the building, and, because of its unusual nature, played a very active part in supervision of the Crystal Palace's construction. After the successful conclusion of the Great Exhibition he was knighted at Windsor by the queen, on 23 December 1851. He was then in his late sixties, but did not retire from business until 1858. He died at his home on Clapham Common, on 13 October 1861, and was buried in Norwood cemetery on 18 October. Contemporaries noted that he was one of the last of the 'self-made engineers', and he was a man much admired for his hard work and honesty.

Cubitt's only son, **Joseph Cubitt** (1811–1872), civil engineer, born at Honing, Norfolk on 24 November 1811, was educated at Castle School, Tottenham, and apprenticed to the firm of Fenton, Murray, and Jackson of Leeds, where his uncle Benjamin Cubitt (1795–1848) was managing engineer. He returned to work with his father, on the South Eastern Railway, then set up on his own in 1843. Like his father he was often called upon to give evidence on railway projects, though contemporaries noted that his retiring disposition denied him the prominence he should have enjoyed. He worked on the southern section of the Great Northern Railway.

Joseph was also engineer to the London Necropolis

Company at Woking, and built the Oswestry and Newtown, the Rhymni, and the Colne Valley railways, as well as being involved in a host of other projects, including the London and South Western Railway, and the piers at Weymouth and Yarmouth. He was also consulted on other ventures, not all of which came to fruition. He was engineer-in-chief to the London, Dover, and Chatham Railway, and in that capacity designed the Blackfriars railway bridge, opened in 1869. He was a member of the Institution of Civil Engineers, and vice-president from 1865. He died at his house, 7 Park Street, Westminster, on 7 December 1872. His wife, Ellen, survived him.

HERMIONE HOBHOUSE

Sources *The Builder*, 19 (1861), 751–2 · *PICE*, 21 (1861–2), 1–2, 554–8 · *PICE*, 10 (1850–51) · Boase, *Mod. Eng. biog.* [see also Joseph Cubitt] · F. S. Williams, *On iron roads* (1883) · *CGPLA Eng. & Wales* (1863) · d. cert. · *PICE*, 39 (1874–5), 248–51 [obit. of Joseph Cubitt] · *CGPLA Eng. & Wales* (1873) [Joseph Cubitt] · private information (2004)
Archives Norfolk RO, plans for navigation from Norwich to Lowestoft 1857 | GL, City of London archives, contract and plan for treadmill
Likenesses T. H. Maguire, lithograph, 1851, BM, NPG; repro. in T. H. Maguire, *Portraits of honorary members of the Ipswich Museum* (1852) · S. Bellin, mezzotint (after W. Boxall, exh. RA 1849), NPG [see illus.] · W. Boxall, oils, Inst. CE · G. Clarke, bust · H. W. Philipps, group portrait, oils (*The royal commissioners for the Great Exhibition of 1851*), V&A · H. S. Turner, lithograph (after bust by G. Clarke) · oils, NPG · woodcut (Joseph Cubitt), NPG; repro. in *The Builder* (22 Jan 1870)
Wealth at death £80,000: resworn probate, Feb 1863, *CGPLA Eng. & Wales* (1861) · under £70,000—Joseph Cubitt: probate, 2 Jan 1873, *CGPLA Eng. & Wales*

Cubitt, William (1791–1863), building contractor and politician, was born at Buxton, Coltishall, Norfolk, in April 1791, the son of Jonathan Cubitt (1761–1807), a carpenter, and his wife, Agnes Scarlett. He had two brothers, Thomas *Cubitt, building contractor, and Lewis *Cubitt, an architect, and two sisters, Mary Agnes (1786–1812) and Sarah (b. 1789). After moving with his family to London, Cubitt served four years in the navy, then joined his brother Thomas as a carpenter in 1810. He married in 1814 Elizabeth (d. 1854), second daughter of William Scarlett; they had a son and four daughters.

In 1815 Thomas and William won an important contract for the London Institution and took land for building works and development in the Gray's Inn Road from the Calthorpe family. On this was built the famous Gray's Inn Road works. There followed extensive contracts for development, including leases on the Bedford estate in Bloomsbury, and the Grosvenor estates in Westminster. However, in 1827 the business was divided between the brothers, William keeping the Gray's Inn Road works, and the contracting side of the business, while Thomas continued the developments on the Grosvenor estates and elsewhere. The youngest brother, Lewis, joined first Thomas and then William, before making an independent career as an architect.

W. Cubitt & Co. was one of the best known of London contractors, responsible for many important buildings, including Fishmongers' Hall, Covent Garden market, Hanwell Lunatic Asylum, and Euston Station. They were civil engineering contractors as well, building a graving dock at Southampton, new docks at Shadwell for the London Dock Company, and repairing old Westminster Bridge. The firm was called in to carry out alterations to public buildings such as the Bank of England and the chapel at Buckingham Palace, extensions to the National Gallery and the stock exchange building, and work for the duke of Wellington's funeral, as well as working on important private houses in both London and the country.

Cubitt interested himself also in development, taking an extensive area on the Isle of Dogs, then being developed. He acquired some 35 acres from the Glengall estate under a series of building agreements from 1842 to 1853. This became known as Cubitt Town, and was developed with industrial and commercial buildings on the riverside, which required the raising of the ground level by some 10 feet, and over a mile of embankment. These buildings included a much-admired and extensive building works for the Cubitt firm, where all types of building components from bricks to timber were manufactured; it included a kiln for ceramic ware, joinery works, and a cement factory, and was equipped with the most up-to-date machinery including a Rennie steam engine, mechanical saws, and a planing machine. There was also an extensive area of working-class housing inland, together with a parish church. Cubitt was involved with the West London Railway Company for some years, saving it from ruin, and 'bringing the shareholders into smoother water' (*Builder*, 21 Nov 1863, 819). He was chairman of the royal commission for the Thames Embankment. He lost his only son in 1841, when the latter was at Cambridge, and this may have led him to take partners into the firm in 1844; he finally withdrew from the contracting business in 1851, though he retained his interest in the land on the Isle of Dogs.

In 1847 Cubitt entered parliament as MP for Andover in the Conservative interest. He represented it until 1861, when he misguidedly stood for the City of London, and failed to get in. However, he was almost immediately re-elected for Andover, and was its MP at his death. He played a considerable part in the City of London, where the firm had offices, becoming sheriff in 1847, alderman for Langbourn ward in 1851, and prime warden of the Fishmongers' Company, and serving as governor of St Bartholomew's Hospital. Two of his daughters married the sons of a fellow alderman, Alderman Humphery, and a third became the wife of Sir Joseph Olliffe, an English physician in Paris. In 1860–1 Cubitt was elected lord mayor of London, and was so successful and popular that, very unusually, he was proposed and re-elected for a second term. His mayoralty was distinguished by his generous hospitality, particularly during the international exhibition of 1862, and by his concern for working people. This was manifested by his opening an appeal first for the men injured in the Hartley colliery disaster of 1861, and then acting as treasurer for the Mansion House Lancashire relief committee. This raised £57,000 for operatives thrown out of work by the American Civil War, which had destroyed the cotton trade. The total subscribed to good causes during his mayoralty was over £250,000.

Cubitt was a prime mover in plans to commemorate Prince Albert, and played a significant part on the committee for the national memorial to the prince consort, which advised the queen. He had a country seat at Penton Lodge, Andover, purchased in 1852 (enabling Lord Palmerston to refer to him, at the lord mayor's banquet in 1861, as a Hampshire neighbour). He died at Penton Lodge on 28 October 1863. His role in the various charitable appeals was recognized by the working people of northern England, muffled peals being rung in more than fifty churches in the Bradford and Manchester areas, while the people of Ashton under Lyne held a special service in his memory.

HERMIONE HOBHOUSE

Sources GM, 3rd ser., 16 (1864) · The Builder, 21 (1863), 777 · The Builder, 21 (1863), 818–19 · The Times (30 Oct 1863), 7d · H. Hobhouse, Thomas Cubitt: master builder, rev. edn (1995) · ILN (10 Nov 1860), 435 · ILN (7 Nov 1863), 478 · S. Tallents, Man and boy (1943) · Boase, Mod. Eng. biog. · City Press (31 Oct 1863), 5 · City Press (7 Nov 1863) · J. Summerson, Georgian London, new edn (1988) · Survey of London, [45 vols.] (1900–), esp. vols. 24, 43–4 · d. cert.
Archives Bedford estate office, Bloomsbury, London · City Westm. AC · Grosvenor estate office, London · LMA, lease books
Likenesses T. L. Atkinson, mezzotint (after F. Grant), NPG · F. Grant, portrait · wood-engraving (after photograph by Mayall), NPG; repro. in ILN (1860), 435
Wealth at death under £200,000: probate, 5 Dec 1863, CGPLA Eng. & Wales

Cubitt, William George (1835–1903), army officer, was born in Calcutta on 19 October 1835, the son of Major William Cubitt of the Bengal native infantry, third son of George Cubitt of Catfield, Norfolk. His mother was Harriet Harcourt. His sister Selena Fitzgerald married in 1859 Julian (afterwards Lord) *Pauncefote. Educated privately at Latham, Yorkshire, he entered the Indian army as ensign in the 13th Bengal native infantry on 26 July 1853. He served against the Santal rebels in 1855.

Promoted lieutenant on 23 November 1856, Cubitt was at Lucknow in 1857 when his regiment mutinied. With the volunteer cavalry he was in the action of Chinhat near Lucknow on 30 June 1857, and was awarded the Victoria Cross for having on the retreat from Chinhat saved the lives of three men of the 32nd regiment. He was afterwards present throughout the defence of the residency at Lucknow. His gallant conduct was commended during the capture of the Tehri Koti on 25–6 September and in a successful attack on a barricaded gateway held by the enemy on 12 November 1857, when he was wounded. He was awarded a year's extra service.

Cubitt married at Fort church, Calcutta, on 19 May 1863, Charlotte Isabella, second daughter of James Hills of Nishchintpur, Bengal, and sister of Lieutenant-General Sir James Hills-Johnes VC. She survived him with three sons and two daughters. The third son, Lewis, died of blood poisoning while assistant commissioner in Uganda, on 31 July 1911.

Cubitt, who was promoted captain on 26 July 1865 and major on 26 July 1873, served with the Duffla expedition on the north-west frontier in 1874–5, when he was mentioned in dispatches. Promoted lieutenant-colonel on 26 July 1879, he was with the Khyber line force in the Second Anglo-Afghan War in 1880. He was promoted colonel on 26 July 1883, and was with the Akha expedition in 1883–4, when he was mentioned in dispatches, and served in the continuation of the Third Anglo-Burmese War in 1886–7, when he was awarded the DSO. At the time of his retirement in 1892 he was in command of the 43rd Gurkhas (later the 8th Gurkha rifles).

Accomplished in outdoor games, especially racquets and cricket, Cubitt after retirement resided at Eastfield, Camberley, Surrey, where he died on 25 January 1903.

H. M. VIBART, rev. JAMES LUNT

Sources The Times (27 Jan 1903) · The Times (7 Feb 1903) · Hart's Army List (1886) · Hart's Army List (1887) · G. W. Forrest, ed., Selections from the letters, despatches and other state papers preserved in the military department of the government of India, 1857–1858, 4 vols. (1893–1912), vol. 3 · C. E. Buckland, Dictionary of Indian biography (1906) · H. J. Huxford, History of the 8th Gurkha rifles (1952) · WWW, 1897–1915 · C. Hibbert, The great mutiny, India, 1857 (1978) · B. Robson, The road to Kabul: the Second Afghan War, 1878–1881 (1986) · LondG (17 Feb 1858) · CGPLA Eng. & Wales (1903)
Likenesses C. Desanges, group portrait, oils, NAM
Wealth at death £213 6s. 4d.: probate, 20 June 1903, CGPLA Eng. & Wales

Cuddon, Ambrose (fl. 1822–1828), publisher and journalist, was probably a native of Suffolk; his date of birth and parentage are unknown. He appears originally to have been connected with the Roman Catholic publishing house of Keating and Brown, but he established his own firm at 62 Crown Street, Finsbury Square, London. In November 1822 he moved to 2 Carthusian Street, Charterhouse Square, where in 1823 he established a Catholic circulating library with about 15,000 volumes. He moved his business to 62 Paternoster Row in January 1825. In January 1822 he began to publish the Catholic Miscellany and Monthly Repository of Information, acting as editor until March when William Eusebius Andrews (1773–1837) undertook this task. Between July 1823 and June 1828 Cuddon was again editor, although he ceased to be the journal's publisher in December 1825 and its printer in 1826, both functions being taken over by the firm of Coe and Moore. Cuddon was the proprietor of the journal until June 1826, when T. M. M. McDonnell is believed to have bought it from him. The Catholic Miscellany was discontinued in 1830. Cuddon appears to have published two other serial works during the 1820s: A New Year's Gift, or, Cuddon's Universal Pocket-Book (1824–7) and A Complete Modern British Martyrology (3 pts, 1824–5), although these works cannot be traced. Cuddon's own fate after 1828 is equally obscure.

The Catholic Miscellany, Cuddon's only important publication, was the most enduring of three significant Catholic journals which appeared in the fifteen years after Waterloo. Like the Catholicon (1816–18) and the Catholic Spectator (1823–6), it was intended primarily for an audience of Catholic gentlemen and clergymen. A typical issue included letters from readers, political news of interest to Catholics, reviews of publications, short biographies of Catholic figures, and a monthly calendar which mingled the dates of saints' days and antiquarian details of their festivals with observations on nature. The *Catholic Miscellany* has been seen as reflecting 'typical Old Catholic provincialism and cultural and political introversion' (Acheson, 89), but Cuddon intended it to be not only 'universally acceptable to Roman Catholics', but also not 'destitute of interest' for our 'separated brethren' (that is, protestants): 'we write for *all*', he claimed (*Catholic Miscellany*, 1/1, 1822, 2). Although it was not a polemical publication (unlike other publications with which Andrews was involved, such as the *Orthodox Journal and Catholic Monthly Intelligencer*), the journal on occasion put up a spirited defence of Roman Catholicism. The relative longevity and the exemplary presentation of the *Catholic Miscellany*—some issues included fine illustrations—made it a significant landmark in the growth of Roman Catholic journalism in nineteenth-century Britain.

THOMPSON COOPER, *rev.* ROSEMARY MITCHELL

Sources Gillow, *Lit. biog. hist.* • *DNB* • S. Acheson, 'Catholic journalism in Victorian Catholic society, 1830–70, with special reference to *The Tablet*', MLitt diss., U. Oxf., 1981 • *N&Q*, 3rd ser., 9 (1866), 307 • J. Gillow, 'Early Catholic periodicals', *The Tablet* (5 Feb 1881), 220

Cuddy, MacGiolla. *See* Archdekin, Richard (1619–1693).

Cudlipp, Hubert Kinsman [Hugh], **Baron Cudlipp** (1913–1998), journalist and publishing executive, was born at 118 Lisvane Street, Cardiff, on 28 August 1913, the youngest son in the family of three sons and one daughter of William Christopher Cudlipp, commercial traveller for a provision merchant, and his wife, Bessie Amelia, *née* Kinsman. Named Hubert on his birth certificate, he decided while still a schoolboy that the name Hugh had a better ring to it, and adopted it for life. He was so successful both in choosing and using this sobriquet that very few of his adult friends ever realized that it was not his actual birth name.

Education and early career Along with his two older brothers, Percival *Cudlipp and Reginald, both of whom also became Fleet Street editors, Hugh Cudlipp was educated first at Gladstone elementary school and then at Howard Gardens secondary school, both in Cardiff. Leaving school, with relief, at the age of fourteen, he was fortunate enough to follow Reginald onto a local weekly paper, the *Penarth News*, published in a dormitory seaside suburb of Cardiff. It was not in fact much of a job: the paper was run on a shoestring and the two younger Cudlipp brothers comprised its entire editorial staff. They were officially apprentices serving their indentures but, with no premiums being paid, salaries in any normal sense were not either. For years afterwards Hugh Cudlipp kept in his possession a letter recording the arrangement made with his father that he was to be paid 5*s*. a week for his first year, 7*s*. 6*d*. for his second, and the princely sum of 10*s*. for his third. The paper, however, folded well before even the first proposed modest increase could come into effect. Cudlipp found himself equally thwarted in his next job. After the collapse of the *Penarth News* he secured a junior reporter's post on the second of the two evening papers that Cardiff then boasted, only to see it disappear in a matter of months through a merger with its more prosperous rival. Not yet sixteen, he shrewdly resolved that his journalistic future did not lie in south Wales, and made for Manchester, in those days second only to Fleet Street in terms of newspaper production.

Cudlipp's career prospered in Manchester. He joined Lord Kemsley's *Manchester Evening Chronicle* and particularly enjoyed his time as a district reporter working in Blackpool. (He later wrote that he found the experience of observing the British working class on holiday 'more instructive than a year at a university' Cudlipp, *Walking on the Water*, 45.)) He also benefited from a solid grounding in the sub-editor's trade. But, although only nineteen, he already knew enough to realize that he would never

Hubert Kinsman [Hugh]
Cudlipp, Baron Cudlipp
(1913–1998), by Henri Cartier-Bresson, 1961

achieve his ambitions in journalism unless he went to London. In 1932 he did just that, transferring to Fleet Street and to another Kemsley title, the *Sunday Chronicle*, where he became an astonishingly young features editor. It was in these early days in Fleet Street that he made his first marriage, on 8 April 1936, to Edith Elizabeth Gertrude (Bunny) Parnell, (1912/13–1938), a journalist and daughter of Frederick Robert Parnell, master upholsterer. Ever afterwards he enigmatically referred to her as 'the channel swimmer'. (In truth it was the Bristol, not the English, channel that she had swum—though as a dutiful fiancé he did follow her in a dinghy.) Everything else about this youthful first marriage he tended to keep to himself, perhaps because it failed long before it was formally ended, in 1938, by her death in childbirth (he was not the father of the baby, who also died).

The *Sunday Pictorial* Cudlipp's decisive career break came just three years after he had arrived in London. He noticed—and was encouraged by his eldest brother, Percy (already editor of Lord Beaverbrook's *Evening Standard*), to follow up—a classified advertisement in the *Daily Telegraph* for 'a bright assistant features editor with ideas, able to take charge' (Cudlipp, *Walking on the Water*, 49). No indication was given as to the paper concerned and, when Cudlipp learned that it was the then limping tabloid the *Daily Mirror*, he almost withdrew his application. The reluctance, however, on the part of Lord Kemsley to offer him more than a 10s. a week increase in order to keep him—'I would have been prepared to stay for an extra quid'—made up his mind for him. On 3 August 1935, when not quite twenty-two, he joined the *Daily Mirror*—where, with two gaps, he remained for the rest of his active journalistic career.

Within six months Cudlipp had been promoted to features editor, and two years later, in September 1937, he found himself transferred—this time as editor—to the *Mirror*'s stable companion, the *Sunday Pictorial*. There he formed what was easily the most influential professional association of his life: his alliance with that paper's newly appointed editorial director, Cecil Harmsworth King. It was he who asked Cudlipp to come over from the *Mirror*, thereby earning for both of them the undying enmity of Harry Guy Bartholomew, the *Mirror*'s editorial director. An aloof and taciturn old Wykehamist (who happened, in *Mirror* terms, to be 'founder's kin': he was nephew to both Northcliffe and Rothermere), King was the polar opposite to Cudlipp. Olympian in his judgements and cold in his manner, King prided himself on being a strategist, once remarking: 'I have a greater gift of foresight than anyone I have ever met' (*Daily Telegraph*). For his part Cudlipp, far more of a natural leader with his dynamic diction and raffish good looks, saw himself simply as a communicator. Between them they created a daring, contemporary version of the *Sunday Pictorial* based on a dashing use of pictures, modern American-style typography, and, above all, political nous of an entirely new kind in a popular paper. The paper's always trenchant anti-appeasement articles were written by Cudlipp himself under the pseudonym of

Charles Wilberforce, a device that enabled him to combine his gift for invective with King's knowledge of the workings of the political system.

The editor's chair of the *Sunday Pictorial* proved the only one that Cudlipp ever occupied, and even then his period in it was interrupted by the war years. Through its criticism of Neville Chamberlain the paper had attracted some opprobrium in right-wing circles, and towards the end of 1940 a question was asked in the House of Commons as to why its editor, only twenty-seven, was not already in uniform. This was an unfair aspersion on Cudlipp's patriotism: he had done his best to get his 'reserved occupation' classification lifted, and was only too keen to take part in the war effort. In December 1940 he enlisted in the Royal Sussex regiment, was soon sent to Sandhurst, and, having arrived as a subaltern in Egypt in time for the battle of El Alamein, was from 1943 to 1946 head of the army newspaper unit for the Mediterranean. In this capacity he founded and launched the British forces' paper, *Union Jack*, the title intended as a conscious riposte to the US army's publication, *Stars and Stripes*. On 31 October 1945 he married a former *Mirror* journalist and future *Evening Standard* columnist, Eileen Mary Ascroft (1915–1962), with whom he had been in love since before the war. She was the daughter of Robert William Ascroft, of independent means, and the divorced wife of Alexander Mackindrick. Cudlipp was appointed OBE (military) in 1945, and the following year was demobilized, with the rank of lieutenant-colonel.

Cudlipp and Cecil King Back in Geraldine House, off Fetter Lane, the headquarters both of the *Daily Mirror* and of the *Sunday Pictorial*, Cudlipp once again found himself facing the abiding animosity of his former boss Bartholomew. It seems implausible that his original defection could still have been held against him; more probably what Bartholomew now recognized in Cudlipp was a threat to his own job. Certainly Bartholomew seems to have wanted him out of the way, and in 1949—with Cecil King temporarily absent in Nigeria, looking after the company's interests there—he succeeded in attaining his objective. It was, however, a short-lived triumph: within two years (Cudlipp spent the intervening period none too happily as managing editor of Lord Beaverbrook's *Sunday Express*) King mounted a counter-putsch, and this time it was Bartholomew who was out. The invitation to Cudlipp to return followed at once, although this time no longer merely as editor of the *Sunday Pictorial* but—now that King had moved up to being board chairman—as editorial director of both papers.

For the next seventeen years King and Cudlipp, two very different individuals—as distinct in their backgrounds as they were disparate in their interests—worked harmoniously together. This was partly because King concentrated on extending the company's commercial base, acquiring the Amalgamated Press in 1958, and following that up with the takeover of the Odhams Group in 1962, bringing two further national newspapers (the *Daily Herald* and *The People*) into Mirror ownership. With a typical touch of hauteur the nephew of Lord Northcliffe declared himself, the following year, the first chairman of the International Publishing Corporation (IPC), a title that eventually passed, somewhat inauspiciously, to Cudlipp. There were, of course, occasional policy disagreements. It was no secret, for example, that in 1956 King thought that the *Mirror* should support Sir Anthony Eden in his attempt to recover the Suez Canal from Colonel Nasser. King may on this occasion have had his finger closer on the working-class pulse than did Cudlipp but the latter argued forcefully that to support 'Eden's war' would be to wreck the paper's traditional relationship not merely with the Labour Party but with all progressive opinion.

Next to journalism, politics had always been Cudlipp's consuming passion and, although he recognized that little or nothing could be done for the Labour Party at the general election of 1955—he eventually came up with the clever, if defeatist, headline 'Keep the tories tame' (*Daily Mirror*, 24 May 1955)—he pulled out all the stops on its behalf in 1959. That year's election result, in which the Conservatives under Harold Macmillan increased their majority from 60 to 100, came as a crushing blow to Cudlipp. Feeling that he had misread the nation's mood, he immediately declared 'a holiday from politics', even removing the traditional slogan 'Forward with the people' from the paper's masthead and ending the twice-weekly political column that had been contributed for the previous four years by the Labour MP Richard Crossman. Instead *Mirror* readers in the week immediately following the election were regaled by the sad tale of Ferdinand the Bull, a creature so gentle that he refused even to do the duty expected of him.

It was not Cudlipp's finest hour. But he soon found a new cause. In the long years of argument over British entry into Europe (or the Common Market, as it was then known) the *Mirror* was always stalwart in making the positive case. The freshly re-elected Conservative government had every reason to feel grateful to it; indeed a Conservative cabinet minister at the time of the initial application in 1961 was heard to murmur 'We should be all right with the *Mirror* behind us'—meaning that the support of the *Mirror* ought to enable the government to win the battle of public opinion (Windlesham, 157). Of course this new alignment put some strain on the paper's time-honoured relationship with the Labour Party, made worse when, at the party conference of 1962, its leader Hugh Gaitskell came out strongly against British entry. Gaitskell's premature death three months later, and the emergence of Harold Wilson as his successor served, however, to ease matters, and by 1964 the *Mirror* was back firmly in Labour's corner (though not perhaps quite as vociferously as in 1959). It may nevertheless have been significant that Cudlipp chose to use the election campaign as the background for relaunching the old working-class *Daily Herald* as a paper now called *The Sun*, 'born of the age we live in' (*Daily Telegraph*). It was one of Cudlipp's few flops, and the unlucky broadsheet was never to prosper until it was bought for a song by Rupert Murdoch and turned into a tabloid in 1969 (something that Cudlipp had always felt

inhibited from doing, for fear of creating a rival to the *Daily Mirror*).

Succeeding Cecil King The early 1960s were not easy years for Cudlipp. His second wife, Eileen Ascroft, died of carbitral poisoning in a tragic accident at their home in Strand on the Green, Chiswick, on 29 April 1962. Nevertheless Cudlipp recovered his normal good spirits with his marriage, on 1 March 1963, to the then editor of the *Woman's Mirror*, Joan Latimer (Jodi) Hyland, daughter of David Jones, solicitor's clerk. This proved easily the longest lasting of his three marriages and brought him both calm and contentment. There was not, however, much sign of those qualities in his professional life. He agonized over the failure of *The Sun* (which, the unkind alleged, meant that he had lost his popular touch), he mourned the fact that the Wilson government was not economically more successful, but above all he had to deal with the increasingly alarming megalomaniac tendencies of his own chairman, Cecil King. Unlike Cudlipp, who had never allowed himself to be bowled over by Wilson, King had great expectations of the new prime minister. Like his uncle Northcliffe in his relationship with Lloyd George, these tended to focus on the part that he would find himself playing as the power behind the throne. Things therefore got off to a bad start when, on forming his government in 1964, Wilson offered King merely a life peerage (rather than the hereditary viscountcy that he had expected), together with a rather humdrum post as minister of state at the Board of Trade. King angrily turned both offers down. He allowed his sense of grievance to fester, and his grand office suite in IPC's new headquarters at Holborn Circus became a gathering place for all the malcontents of Wilson's Labour Party.

How far Cudlipp initially went along with King's disillusioned views is difficult to establish but there seems no question that some kind of Rubicon was crossed at a meeting that Cudlipp personally was asked to set up between King and Earl Mountbatten of Burma, the former chief of the defence staff. At this meeting, held on 8 May 1968 at Lord Mountbatten's Westminster home in the presence not only of Cudlipp but also of Sir Solly Zuckerman, scientific adviser to the government, King recklessly made the suggestion that Mountbatten should hold himself in readiness to take charge of the emergency government that would no doubt be needed after the inevitable military overthrow of the Wilson administration. For Cudlipp the sheer lunacy of this proposal (immediately refused by Mountbatten and branded as 'treachery' by Zuckerman) appears to have brought matters to a head. Two days later, with Cudlipp's encouragement, King's notorious, signed, personal assault on the Wilson government, headed 'Enough is enough', appeared on the front page of the *Daily Mirror*. It was always Cudlipp's defence that he thought this course was preferable to the paper officially endorsing its chairman's line, but he also must have realized what the likely consequences would be. They did not take long to materialize. Three weeks later King was deposed by his own colleagues on the IPC board, and Cudlipp was unanimously chosen as chairman in his place.

Cudlipp never felt entirely happy about wearing King's mantle; his natural habitat was the newsroom, not the sumptuous chairman's quarters on the ninth floor of the new Holborn Circus skyscraper. It was King himself who somewhat patronizingly announced on the day of his dismissal that his old subordinate was 'a first violin rather than a conductor' (*Daily Telegraph*)—and there may have been a germ of truth in that gibe. Certainly it was with some relief that, a year later, Cudlipp allowed IPC to merge with, and become a subdivision of, Reed International (which had traditionally supplied it with its newsprint). This meant that he was no longer responsible for the central commercial strategy of the company and could return to what he did best—inspiring other journalists and lending his own flair to the business of producing mass-circulation newspapers. He did not, however, continue to do so for very long. In October 1971 he announced his impending retirement, which took effect on 31 December 1973. Knighted by Edward Heath in 1973, for his services to the European cause, he was created a life peer, as Baron Cudlipp of Aldingbourne, in the county of Sussex, on the nomination of Harold Wilson in the following year.

Retirement In retirement at Chichester, Sussex, Cudlipp scrupulously observed Stanley Baldwin's injunction against speaking to the man at the wheel or spitting on the deck, and made only one tactical error, when he briefly made a return to what was by then called Mirror Group Newspapers, as a 'consultant' to Robert Maxwell, after those papers had passed into his greedy hands in 1984. His salary from Maxwell was a mere £10,000—and Cudlipp, soon realizing his mistake, ended the arrangement after a single year. Otherwise he concentrated his energies on the cultural life of Chichester, taking particular interest in the Festival Theatre there and becoming, in 1975, founder chairman of the city's annual festivities of music, arts, and fun. He also found time to write: both his autobiography, *Walking on the Water* (1976), and his reflections on the newspaper trade, *The Prerogative of the Harlot* (1980), were written in retirement, although two earlier (rumoured to be 'ghosted') works—*At your Peril* (1962) and *Publish and be Damned* (1955)—had appeared in his active, Fleet Street years. He made occasional speeches in the House of Lords, where he began by taking the Labour whip before, in 1981, joining the short-lived Social Democratic Party. A born raconteur, he was for twenty-five years a highly popular member of the Garrick Club. He died at his home, 14 Tollhouse Close, Avenue de Chartres, Chichester, of lung cancer, on 17 May 1998. He was survived by his wife, Jodi. He had no children.

ANTHONY HOWARD

Sources H. Cudlipp, *Walking on the water* (1976) · H. Cudlipp, *The prerogative of the harlot* (1980) · H. Cudlipp, 'Still with us', *The Oldie* (6 March 1992), 15 · Lord Windlesham, *Communications and political power* (1966) · *Daily Telegraph* (18 May 1998) · *The Times* (18 May 1998) · *The Guardian* (18 May 1998) · *The Independent* (18 May 1998) · personal knowledge (2004) · private information (2004) · b. cert. · m. certs. [Edith Parnell; Eileen Mary Ascroft; Joan Latimer Hyland] · d. cert. · *CGPLA Eng. & Wales* (1998)

Archives U. of Wales, Cardiff, Bute Resource Centre, MSS | HLRO, corresp. with Lord Beaverbrook · King's Lond., Liddell Hart C., corresp. with B. H. Liddell Hart | FILM Cardiff University, Bute Research Centre, includes some 8mm amateur film | SOUND Cardiff University, Bute Research Centre, audio tapes of interviews, speeches, etc.
Likenesses photographs, 1960–69, repro. in *The Independent* · H. Cartier-Bresson, bromide print, 1961, NPG [*see illus.*] · photograph, 1968, repro. in *Daily Telegraph* · photograph, 1969, repro. in *The Times* · D. Goodman, portrait, priv. coll. · J. Hamper, portrait, priv. coll. · S. Spaden, portrait, priv. coll. · photograph, repro. in *The Guardian*
Wealth at death £242,497: probate, 8 July 1998, *CGPLA Eng. & Wales*

Cudlipp, Percival Thomas James [Percy] (1905–1962), journalist, was born at 180 Arabella Street, Cardiff, on 10 November 1905, the eldest son of William Christopher Cudlipp, commercial clerk, and his wife, Bessie Amelia Kinsman. Cudlipp's mother, educated at an elementary school, was a woman of strong personality and considerable intelligence, very ambitious for her children. In addition to Percy and a daughter there were two younger sons, both of whom were to become editors of national newspapers. Cudlipp said that his mother chose the names Percival, Hubert, and Reginald for her sons because they would sound well with knighthoods. The story was probably one of Cudlipp's fabrications but it fairly represents his mother's confidence in her sons. Hubert (Hugh) *Cudlipp (1913–1998) was made a life peer in 1974.

Brought up in the Welsh nonconformist tradition the Cudlipp family attended the Wesleyan chapel at Crwys Street, Cardiff, although it seems that for Percy the most powerful magnet there was not religion but the chapel's flourishing dramatic society, for which, having a natural histrionic gift inherited from his mother, he played the part of Shylock in *The Merchant of Venice*. He was educated at Howard Gardens secondary school, which he left at the age of thirteen. His mother paid a fine so that before reaching school-leaving age Percy could begin work in the office of the *South Wales Echo*, where an opening had occurred which he was determined to fill. He had a precocious talent for rhyme and had already contributed a great deal of verse to the paper, which advertised him as the boy poet of Cardiff. His facility for dexterous and witty verse remained with him throughout his career.

After six years of apprenticeship, during which he had assimilated the techniques of the profession and had been assiduous in attendance at the local night school, Cudlipp went in 1924 to Manchester as a reporter on the *Evening Chronicle*. At the same time he was contributing articles and light verse to London newspapers. Cudlipp's next move was predictable, and predictably early. In 1925 he moved to London as drama critic and humorous columnist on the *Sunday News*. That would have been enough for most journalists but it was not enough for Cudlipp. Through a publicity agent he became a purveyor of topical lyrics to the Co-optimists' revue running in a London theatre. Every afternoon he went to the theatre with the latest edition of the evening newspaper, which provided him with the material for a few verses to add to the lyric.

In 1927, when he married Gwendoline May James, the show ran so long that Cudlipp was compelled to cancel his honeymoon in order that the supply of topical rhymes could continue; he needed the money. He and his wife had one son, Michael, who also became a journalist.

By that time it was becoming known in Fleet Street that a brilliant and versatile talent had descended on it. In consequence in 1929, as Percy Cudlipp, he became a special writer on the *Evening Standard*. He had arrived, at the age of twenty-four, where every ambitious young journalist of the time wished to be, not indeed at the top of the tree but within earshot of Lord Beaverbrook. By this time Cudlipp's free-ranging talent was in full flower. One morning he interviewed Noël Coward; in the later editions of the *Evening Standard* that day there appeared a half-page interview with Coward by Cudlipp, in verse, that was a parody of Coward's style and which astonished even Coward himself.

In 1931 Cudlipp was appointed assistant editor of the *Standard*, and two years later editor. He was then twenty-seven, the youngest editor of a British national newspaper. In becoming an editor Cudlipp turned his back on the particular talent that had marked him out among popular journalists: his ability to write smooth and witty English. From then on he was to be an executive journalist, an editor. If this involved the sacrifice of something which he valued Cudlipp never showed it. At the *Evening Standard*, however, he was not completely happy because of a temperamental clash between himself and the manager of the paper, Michael Wardell, who combined a strong personality with highly conservative views about the paper. In 1938 Cudlipp joined the *Daily Herald* as editorial manager. In 1940, when Francis Williams resigned, Cudlipp became editor in defiance of the veto of the *New Statesman*, which thought that the paper should have a socialist editor. In fact Cudlipp had always been a convinced socialist. The change of newspaper disconcerted those of Cudlipp's associates who had not realized how heavy had been the strain of his editorship at the *Standard*. At the *Daily Herald* he found working conditions far more complicated, and demanding of all his very considerable powers of diplomacy.

The trade unions, the Labour Party, Odhams Press—co-proprietors of the newspaper—each had different views about how a Labour newspaper should be run. There were, too, personal rivalries to consider. Cudlipp was on friendly terms with Herbert Morrison and incurred the dislike of Ernest Bevin, who wished to dominate the newspaper. When Cudlipp left the editorship in November 1953 it seemed that his editorial career was ending in something like frustration. Nothing could have been further from the truth. After a period as columnist in the *News Chronicle* he became founder editor in 1956 of the *New Scientist*, a weekly which sought to convey accurate, authoritative scientific information in language which the layman could understand. In inspiring scientists to become comprehensible Cudlipp performed a notable service and made a brilliant success of the journal. His last years were, therefore, years of triumph.

Cudlipp was a gregarious man of great charm, good-natured and lively minded, a master in speech as in writing of precise and elegant English. After journalism, music was the passion of his life. His wit was sharp and exuberant. Beaverbrook once said of him, 'Percy's spear knows no brother'. But in fact his tongue was without malice. His most celebrated remark was made about one of Beaverbrook's lieutenants who, in describing a ride with Beaverbrook over snow-covered terrain in Surrey, said incautiously, 'It was like the retreat from Moscow. Beaverbrook was Napoleon; I was Marshal Ney'. 'You mean Marshal Yea!', said Cudlipp. It was, however, the victim of the remark who spread its fame.

Cudlipp died at his home, 11 Falmouth House, Clarendon Place, London, on 5 November 1962 and was cremated at Golders Green four days later. He was survived by his wife. G. M. THOMSON, *rev.*

Sources *The Times* (6 Nov 1962) · *The Times* (7 Nov 1962) · *The Times* (15 Nov 1962) · H. Cudlipp, *Walking on the water* (1976) · H. Richards, *The bloody circus: the Daily Herald and the left* (1997) · D. Griffiths, *Plant here The Standard* (1996) · S. E. Koss, *The rise and fall of the political press in Britain*, 2 (1984) · A. J. P. Taylor, *Beaverbrook* (1974) · D. Griffiths, ed., *The encyclopedia of the British press, 1422–1992* (1992) · b. cert. · CGPLA Eng. & Wales (1963) · WWW

Archives HLRO, corresp. with Lord Beaverbrook | FILM BFI NFTVA, news footage

Likenesses D. Low, pencil drawing, NPG · photograph, repro. in Cudlipp, *Walking on the water*

Wealth at death £27,488 8s. od.: probate, 4 Jan 1963, CGPLA Eng. & Wales

Cudmore, Richard (1787–1840), instrumentalist and composer, was born in Chichester, Sussex, and showed a talent for music at a very early age. His first teacher was James Forgett, a local organist, who taught him the violin. At the age of nine he played a solo at a concert in Chichester. About 1797 he was placed under Joseph Reinagle in Oxford, and shortly afterwards became a pupil of Johann P. Salomon, with whom he studied the violin for two years. In 1799 he led the band at the Chichester theatre, and in the same year was engaged as a first violin for the Italian Opera band. He returned, however, before long to Chichester, where he remained until 1808. He then went to London, studied the piano under Joseph Woelfl, and appeared as a solo pianist and violinist at the principal concerts. He also became a member of the Philharmonic Society orchestra.

Shortly afterwards Cudmore settled in Manchester, where for many years he led the Gentlemen's Concerts. He often played in Liverpool, and in one concert he performed a violin concerto by Pierre Rode, a piano concerto by Frédéric Kalkbrenner, and a cello concerto by G. B. Cervetto. He composed concertos for both piano and violin. His best work was an oratorio, *The Martyr of Antioch*, a setting of Henry Milman's poem. Selections from this were performed at Birmingham, Manchester, and Liverpool, and the work was published by subscription. Cudmore died at Wilton Street, Oxford Road, Manchester, on 29 December 1840. He left a widow and family.

W. B. SQUIRE, *rev.* ANNE PIMLOTT BAKER

Sources Grove, *Dict. mus.* · [J. S. Sainsbury], ed., *A dictionary of musicians*, 2nd edn, 2 vols. (1827) · Brown & Stratton, *Brit. mus.* · *Manchester Guardian* (2 Jan 1841) · *Musical World* (21 Jan 1841), 46

Cudworth, Cyril Leonard Elwell [Charles] (1908–1977), music librarian and musicologist, was born on 30 October 1908 at 115 Sedgwick Street, Cambridge, the son of David Charles Cudworth, policeman, and his wife, Alice Caroline Camps. He was one of at least two sons; his given name was Cyril but he was always known as Charles. Educated locally, he did not go on to secondary school, but took a job as an assistant in a Cambridge bookshop, spending his one free afternoon a week copying eighteenth-century symphonies and concertos into keyboard scores in Cambridge libraries or the British Museum reading room. He was encouraged in his musical studies by Edward J. Dent, professor of music at Cambridge, and during the 1930s he had jobs in several university libraries and departments. He became assistant librarian of the music section of the Cambridge University Library in 1943.

In 1946 Cudworth was appointed librarian of the Pendlebury Library at the university music school in Cambridge, and in 1957 he became curator, a post he held until his retirement in 1973. During these years he built up the international reputation of the library, increasing its collection; he also had an extensive knowledge of the musical holdings of other libraries in Cambridge, especially that of the Fitzwilliam Museum. He contributed the article 'Libraries and collections' to the fifth edition of Grove's *Dictionary of Music and Musicians* (1954). As librarian he helped generations of undergraduates and scholars, and in 1958 he was awarded an honorary MA degree by the University of Cambridge. A founder member of the International Association of Music Libraries in 1953, he was a member of the executive committee of the UK branch until 1970, and helped to organize the international conference held in Cambridge in 1959.

Cudworth's musicological interests were concentrated mainly on English eighteenth-century music. He wrote many influential articles and he became recognized as an authority on the English symphony and the English keyboard concerto through articles such as 'The English symphonists of the eighteenth century' (*Proceedings of the Royal Musical Association*, 1951-2), 'A thematic index of English eighteenth century overtures and symphonies' (*Proceedings of the Royal Musical Association*, 1953), and 'The English organ concerto' (*The Score*, 1953). He drew attention to various misattributions, most notably in articles in *Music* and the *Musical Times* in 1952–3 which established that the trumpet voluntary popularized by Sir Henry Wood was not by Henry Purcell but by Jeremiah Clarke and had been first printed in 1700 as 'The Prince of Denmark's March' in *A Choice Collection of Ayres for the Harpsichord*. In 'Ye Olde Spuriosity Shoppe' (*Notes*, 12, 1954–5) he collected all the misattributions, forgeries, and hoaxes he had discovered, including the mistaken attribution to Pergolesi of a number of instrumental works. Another important article was 'Baroque, rococo, galant, classic' (*Monthly Musical Record*, 1953), in which he attempted to define the use of these

terms. One of his last publications, in 1972, was a volume on Handel in the series Concertgoers' Companions, a short biography with a survey of books, editions, and recordings. He contributed many articles on eighteenth-century British and European composers to the 1970 edition of the *Encyclopaedia Britannica*, and was a contributor to the *New Grove Dictionary of Music and Musicians* (1980).

Cudworth also wrote plays, including *Mr Bach of London* (1942, mainly written during fire-watching duty during the Second World War), which were performed by local dramatic societies, short stories about life in the fens, poems, and a novel, *The Silken Chord*, about a seventeenth-century musician; all were unpublished. For his close friend Patrick Hadley, professor of music at Cambridge from 1946 to 1952, he wrote the words for the ballads *The Suffolk Lady* (1948) and *The Gate Hangs High* (1960), and the librettos for the cantatas *Fen and Flood* (1955, following the severe flooding of the fens and the Netherlands in January 1953), *Connemara* (1958), and *Cantata for Lent* (1962). He broadcast often, and was a frequent contributor to the Saturday morning BBC radio programme *Record Review*. He was also interested in local history and architecture, and wrote and broadcast on Dutch influence in East Anglia, his articles including 'The Dutch influence in East Anglia' (*Proceedings of the Cambridge Antiquarian Society*, 37, 1935–6 and 'Dutch gables in East Anglia' (*Architectural Review*, 85, 1939). Charles Cudworth died on 26 December 1977 in the Chesterton Hospital, Cambridge. He left a widow.

ANNE PIMLOTT BAKER

Sources C. Hogwood and R. Luckett, eds., *Music in eighteenth-century England: essays in memory of Charles Cudworth* (1983) · *New Grove*, 2nd edn · *Fontes Artis Musicae*, 25 (1978), 107 · *Brio*, 15/1 (spring 1978), 21–30 · *The Times* (30 Dec 1977) · b. cert. · d. cert.
Likenesses photograph, c.1973, University Music School, West Road, Cambridge, Pendlebury Library
Wealth at death £28,261: probate, 6 March 1978, *CGPLA Eng. & Wales*

Cudworth, Ralph (1617–1688), philosopher and theologian, was born in Aller, Somerset, and baptized there on 13 July 1617. His father, Dr Ralph Cudworth (d. 1624), a fellow of Emmanuel College, Cambridge, who had been lecturer of St Andrew's Church there, was rector of a college living at Aller. His father, who was also a chaplain to James I, had edited works by William Perkins and written a supplement to Perkins's commentary on Galatians. His mother, Mary Machell, had been a nurse to Henry, the eldest son of James I. After her husband's death she married Dr Stoughton, who paid considerable attention to his stepson's education.

Education and early publications On 9 May 1630 Cudworth was admitted as a pensioner at Emmanuel College, Cambridge. On 5 July 1632 he matriculated. He came under the influence of Benjamin Whichcote, who was elected fellow of the college in 1633 and a tutor in the following year. Cudworth worked hard at his studies, taking his BA in 1635 (in which year he published a Latin poem in a collection, *Carmen natalitium*, published in Cambridge) and MA in 1639. In the latter year, having gained a considerable

Ralph Cudworth (1617–1688), by unknown artist

reputation as a scholar, he was elected a fellow of his college. His standing was such that at one time as tutor he had twenty-eight pupils in his care, an unusually large number. Having, together with Henry More, played an important part in introducing Descartes's works into Cambridge, he began to question Cartesian thought, particularly because of the way that its radical dualism failed to find a way of linking the *res extensa* with the *res cogitans*.

In 1642 Cudworth published *A Discourse Concerning the True Notion of the Lord's Supper*. He begins this work by affirming that since 'pure falshood is pure Non-entity', it always seeks to camouflage itself by linking itself up with some truth (*Discourse*, 1676 edn, 1). This notion, which expresses a basic theme of much of his work, led him throughout his studies to attempt to sift out what was right and true from the dross in which it was often located. In this tract, maybe influenced by ideas of Joseph Mede (or Mead, a fellow of Christ's College, Cambridge, who died in 1638), he argues with considerable erudition, that the Lord's supper is not, as Roman Catholics hold, itself a sacrifice but an '*EPULUM SACRIFICIALE* or *EPULUM EX OBLATIS*' (ibid., 27)—that is, a feast in which Christians celebrate and share in the sacrifice made once and for all in the death of Christ. Accordingly the place where they eat is not an altar 'but *a Table*' (ibid., 28). The rite is also to be understood as an '*EPULUM FOEDERALE, a Feast of Amity and Friendship* between God and men' in which they reaffirm their 'inviolable league of friendship' (ibid., 34). Later that year he also published a treatise entitled *The Union of Christ and the Church a Shadow* in which he uses various aspects of

the model of marriage to illuminate the relationship of Christ to the church.

Cudworth received the BD degree in 1646 and the DD in 1651. According to Thomas Birch ('Life and writings of Cudworth', prefaced to *True Intellectual System*, 1820, 1.8 ff.), for the former degree Cudworth defended theses about the reasons ('rationes') for good and evil being eternal and indispensable, and about the immortality of incorporeal substances, thereby criticizing Calvinist views and showing his agreement with Benjamin Whichcote's position. Birch's statement, however, is not without problems, since a form of the theses as Latin verses (printed from Cudworth's papers at the end of John Allen's edition of Cudworth's manuscript *Of Freewill*, 1838), is dated 20 June 1651. This raises the question whether these theses might have been those for Cudworth's DD.

Following the ejection by parliamentary visitors of Dr Thomas Paske, master of Clare College, Cambridge, in 1645 Cudworth was appointed in Paske's place but, according to the Clare admission book, he was not admitted as master until 1650. In the meantime his relationship with Clare College was nominal. Also in 1645 he succeeded Dr Metcalf as regius professor of Hebrew and, according to Thomas Birch, thereafter 'abandoned all the functions of a minister, and applied himself only to his academical employments and studies, especially that of the Jewish antiquities' (Birch, 1.9). A letter of John Worthington, dated 12 May 1646, reports that Cudworth was giving weekly lectures on the Temple of Jerusalem.

A sermon on 1 John 2: 3ff. that Cudworth preached before the House of Commons on 31 March 1647 received the thanks of the house and was printed. The 'Dedication' to the Commons found in the first edition was, however, omitted from the second and third editions through tact in changing circumstances, although it was restored in later ones. The sermon itself expresses Cudworth's religious and moral views. Criticizing dogmatic differences, it affirms that authentic Christian faith is not found in assenting '*merely*' to '*a few barren Notions, in a form of certain dry and sapless opinions*' (1676, 43) but in '*keeping of Christ's Commandments*' (52) in virtue, holiness, and love. It is by how people live that they show whether they have grasped the spirit of Christ, not by their 'acquaintance with *Systems* and *Models* of Divinity' (ibid.) nor by their ritual performances, 'as if Religion were nothing else but a *Dancing* up and down' (ibid., 58).

Appointed master of Christ's College, Cambridge, and marries
On 3 October 1650 Cudworth was presented by Emmanuel College as rector of North Cadbury in Somerset, then worth £300 per annum, and he is reported to have considered leaving Cambridge, probably for financial reasons. The income of the mastership of Clare was small, and in any case he was finding it difficult to obtain. He did reside briefly at North Cadbury, but his responsibilities as master of Clare and professor of Hebrew made it necessary for him to be in Cambridge for at least part of each year. His situation changed with the death of Dr Samuel Bolton, the master of Christ's College, Cambridge, on 15 October 1654. On 29 October, maybe in part due to the

influence of Oliver Cromwell, fellows of the college chose Cudworth to succeed him and Cudworth held this position for the rest of his life. In the same year he married Damaris Andrewes, the wealthy widow of Thomas Andrewes of New Fish Street, London. She may have been the daughter of Matthew Cradock, a London merchant. Through her first marriage she had a son, Thomas Andrewes, who was a fellow of Christ's College from 1669 to 1675, and a daughter, Damaris, who married Edward Abney, who was a fellow of the college from 1655 to 1661. Through her marriage to Cudworth she had at least three sons, John, Charles, and Thomas, and a daughter, also called Damaris. John Cudworth (b. 1655/6) became a pensioner of Christ's College in 1672 when he was sixteen years old, graduating BA in 1677 and MA in 1680. In 1678 he became a fellow of Christ's College, but for most of his fellowship he did not play an active part in the college, although he was occasionally resident; he had a pupil in 1680 and in 1692, was lecturer in Greek in 1687 and 1688, and was senior dean in 1690. His fellowship was declared void on 27 January 1698 because of the estates that he had inherited. Thereafter he lived at Southwold, complaining about his situation and his relations; he died on 9 September 1726. Charles Cudworth (d. 1684) is recorded as being in India in August 1683 and as marrying Mary Prickman, a widow, in February 1684. He is presumably the recipient of a letter written to Damaris Masham's brother by John Locke, dated 27 April 1683. Thomas Cudworth received his MA in 1682. Cudworth's most famous child was Damaris *Masham, the second wife of Sir Francis Masham of Oates in Essex. She was a learned lady who inherited her father's papers as well as his interest in scholarship, defended him against critics who included Leibniz, published (anonymously) A Discourse Concerning the Love of God (1696), and became a friend of John Locke, who made her home his permanent residence in his final years and died there.

Commonwealth to Restoration Cudworth's activities during the Commonwealth included advising those who were producing the Biblia sacra polyglotta (6 vols., 1653–7) under the editorship of Brian Walton. He was appointed on 2 September 1654, with Samuel Bolton and John Lightfoot, as visitors for the universities and certain schools and was asked by Cromwell's council to comment upon the proposal to admit Jews into England (15 November 1655). He also served on the committee devising statutes for Cromwell's college at Durham, and was involved in the committee set up by the Commons on 16 January 1657 to consider revising the Authorized Version of the Bible. In 1654 a poem by him in Latin was included in a collection, Oliva pacis, printed in Cambridge in honour of Oliver Cromwell. Two years later Cudworth became minister at Toft, near Cambridge, but he soon resigned this position. John Thurloe sought his views on Cambridge men suitable for various appointments. In 1658 Cudworth took part in the loyal message sent to Richard Cromwell from Cambridge on the death of his father. On 20 January 1659 he wrote to Thurloe about a proposal to publish a defence

of Christianity against Judaism that paid particular attention to the interpretation of Daniel's prophecy of the seventy weeks, asking whether he might dedicate it to Richard Cromwell, 'to whose noble father' he says that he 'was much obliged' (Birch, 15). The work, which was never printed (BL, Add. MSS 4986–4987) but whose contents were presented in lectures at Cambridge, was praised by Henry More in his Grand Mystery of Godliness (1660, xvi).

At the Restoration, Cudworth wrote a Hebrew poem for the volume Academiae Cantabrigiensis Sōstra which was presented to the king. Among royalists, however, there were those who regarded him with suspicion and there was some opposition, especially from Ralph Widdrington, one of the fellows at Christ's, to his retaining the mastership of the college. Although the objections were overcome, possibly with the aid of Gilbert Sheldon, then bishop of London, Cudworth remained an object of resentment in certain quarters. One expression of it was a gratuitous remark included in a decision by the vice-chancellor, dated 10 May 1666, on a matter raised by Cudworth, that stated that it would be appropriate for the master to be submissive and thankful. Writing about this period Gilbert Burnet later commented that Cudworth not only had 'great strength of genius, and a vast compass of learning' but also 'was a man of great conduct and prudence: Upon which his enemies did very falsely accuse him of craft and dissimulation' (Bishop Burnet's History of his Own Time, ed. G. Burnet and T. Burnet, 2 vols., 1724–34, 1.187).

Writings on morality and the true intellectual system On 1 December 1662 Cudworth was presented by Gilbert Sheldon to the vicarage of Ashwell in Hertfordshire. Though at first he may have paid some attention to the duties of this living, his time was increasingly taken up by his duties as master of Christ's College (which included the work of a bursar and which he did efficiently) and by his studies, and in 1686 ecclesiastical visitors complained that he was neglecting the parish (Bodl. Oxf., MS Tanner 30, fol. 45). In 1664 he published a sermon on 1 Corinthians 15: 57 that he had preached at Lincoln's Inn. Correspondence with John Worthington from early 1665 shows that both Cudworth and Henry More were independently writing about moral good and evil. As a result of Cudworth's unhappiness at the news of a possible rival publication, More held back the publication of his Enchiridion ethicum until 1668. Cudworth, however, never published his own projected work, but at his death left manuscripts (BL, Add. MSS 4978–4982) of 'A discourse of moral good and evil', 'Heads of another book of morality', 'A treatise concerning eternal and immutable morality' (the manuscript of which has not survived although the text was published, first in 1731), and three drafts of a work on free will (the shortest of which, A Treatise of Freewill, was first published with notes by John Allen in 1838). The latter two pieces were printed in 1996 in an edition by Sarah Hutton. Although it is widely held that the manuscript of 'Eternal and immutable morality' represents what Cudworth was working on in the mid-1660s, Edward Chandler's preface to the 1731 edition of A Treatise Concerning Eternal and Immutable Morality (pp. x ff.) and John Tulloch (Rational Theology and Christian

Philosophy in England in the Seventeenth Century, 1872, 217 ff.) suggest that this manuscript was written after *The True Intellectual System of the Universe*. If this be the case it is presumably the manuscript of 'Moral good and evil' that Cudworth was working on when he heard of More's plans.

In 1678 Cudworth was installed as a prebendary at Gloucester and, in the same year, his major and massive work, *The true intellectual system of the universe, wherein all the reason and philosophy of atheism is confuted, and its impossibility demonstrated*, was published. It seems to have been ready for some time since it contains an imprimatur dated 29 May 1671. Thomas Birch (Birch, 20) states that when it appeared some courtiers attempted to discredit Cudworth and it may be that some such opposition was the reason for the delay in publishing. Although the work appears to a large extent to be defending and using the views of Plato and Aristotle (treated in a manner typical of Renaissance humanism rather than of later scholarship) to attack the views of Democritus, Strato, and Lucretius, its primary targets are the atheistic materialism of Thomas Hobbes and what Cudworth dubs 'Hylozoick' atheism. Cudworth expects that Baruch Spinoza will soon publish an exposition of this latter position (see 1678 edn, p. A7 obv.) and considers that it needs to be treated seriously, even though he dismisses Spinoza's *Tractatus theologico-politicus* as being in 'every way so Weak, Groundless and Inconsiderable' that it is not worth confuting (ibid., 707). At exhausting length and with enormous erudition Cudworth seeks to counter atheistic arguments, which he gives in some detail, by showing that

> the First *Original* of all things, was neither Stupid and Sensless Matter Fortuitously moved, Nor a *Blind* and *Nescient*, but Orderly and *Methodical Plastick Nature*; Nor a Living *Matter* … without *Animal Sense or Consciousness*; Nor yet did every thing Exist of it self *Necessarily* from Eternity, without a *Cause*. But there is One only *Necessary Existent*, the Cause of all other things; and this is an Absolutely Perfect Being, Infinitely Good, Wise, and Powerful (ibid., 899)

who does not act arbitrarily but is intrinsically and eternally just and good (ibid., see A3v). In contrast to the Cartesian mechanical view of the world and to the denial of free will by both Cartesianism and Calvinism, Cudworth affirms both free will and the continual creative activity of the divine upon what he calls 'a plastic nature' (ibid., 147–51). By this notion Cudworth attempts to avoid both the view that 'all things are produced Fortuitously, or by the Unguided Mechanism of Matter' and the view that God is to be thought to do 'all things Immediately and Miraculously'. Instead he suggests that

> there is a *Plastick Nature* under him [God], which as an Inferior and Subordinate Instrument, doth Drudgingly Execute that Part of his Providence, which consists in the Regular and Orderly Motion of Matter

but at the same time is under the control of 'a Higher Providence … which … doth often supply the Defects of it, and sometimes Over-rule it' (ibid., 150).

The work had a mixed reception. Shaftesbury, for instance, comments in his *Characteristics* (5, pt 2, 3) that while people did not dispute Cudworth's learning and his

'sincerity in the cause of Deity', some accused him of 'giving the upper hand to the atheists' for having presented their reasons 'fairly'. Others criticized as Arian his Trinitarian interpretation of classical Platonic ideas about the divine (see, for example, Robert Nelson, *Life of Bull*, 1714, 339). William Warburton (*Divine Legation of Moses*, preface to books 4, 5, and 6; in 1846 edn 2.107) reports that Cudworth was so disgusted by the charge that his ostensive attack on atheism had in fact a crypto-atheistic intent that 'his ardour slackened' and he never completed the work that he had originally proposed.

In his later years Cudworth was considered to be a somewhat lonely and rather irritable person, even with those few who were his close friends such as John Worthington, Henry More, and George Rust. Having been taken ill while away from Cambridge, he was brought back to the college and he died at Christ's on 26 June 1688. The next day he was buried in the college chapel. A portrait of him, showing him with auburn hair, hangs in the college hall.

DAVID A. PAILIN

Sources J. Peile, *Biographical register of Christ's College, 1505–1905, and of the earlier foundation, God's House, 1448–1505*, ed. [J. A. Venn], 2 vols. (1910–13) • J. Peile, *Christ's College* (1900) • T. Birch, 'Account of the life and writings of R. Cudworth', in R. Cudworth, *True intellectual system of the universe* (1820) [preface] • BL, Add. MSS 4896–4987 • Bodl. Oxf., MSS Tanner • *The diary and correspondence of Dr John Worthington*, ed. J. Crossley and R. C. Christie, 2 vols. in 3, Chetham Society, 13, 36, 114 (1847–86) • Thurloe, *State papers* • J. A. Passmore, *Ralph Cudworth: an interpretation* (1951) • R. Cudworth, *A treatise concerning eternal and immutable morality*, ed. S. Hutton (1996) • L. Gysi, *Platonism and Cartesianism in the philosophy of Ralph Cudworth* (1962) • IGI • DNB

Archives Bodl. Oxf., letters to John Selden • Bodl. Oxf., MSS Tanner • Bodl. Oxf., Thurloe state papers

Likenesses G. Vertue, line engraving, 1684 (after D. Loggan, 1684), BM, NPG; repro. in R. Cudworth, *A treatise concerning eternal and immutable morality* (1731) • oils, Emmanuel College, Cambridge [see illus.] • portrait, Christ's College, Cambridge

Wealth at death see will, PRO, PROB 11/392, sig. 116

Cuff, Henry. *See* Cuffe, Henry (1562/3–1601).

Cuff, James Dodsley (1780–1853), numismatist, was born at Corsley, near Warminster, the son of a yeoman of that place; his mother was the daughter of Isaac Dodsley, brother of the publishers Robert and James Dodsley. For about forty-eight years, from 1805 until his death, Cuff was a clerk in the Bank of England, the last twenty-eight years of which he spent in the bullion office.

Cuff devoted his leisure time to numismatics. He was one of the original members of the Numismatic Society, founded in 1836, and remained a member until his death. In 1839 he was elected a member of the council, and in 1840 honorary treasurer of the society. He was also a fellow of the Society of Antiquaries. He made three contributions to the *Numismatic Chronicle* (old series). When, in 1847, the publisher John Hearne issued a supplement to Ainslie's *Illustrations of the Anglo-French Coinage* (1830), Cuff, in conjunction with Edward Hawkins, supervised the printing of the work, and contributed descriptions of coins, chiefly from his own cabinet.

Cuff was engaged in coin collecting for more than forty years; his collection, which consisted chiefly of Saxon and

English coins, was a remarkable one, containing many pieces of great rarity, including the petition and reddite crowns and the crown of Henry VIII. In accordance with the directions of his will, Cuff's collection was disposed of by public auction, the sale taking place at Sothebys in London over eighteen days in June and July 1854. The sale catalogue filled 193 octavo pages. The coins sold included Greek and Roman, British, Anglo-Saxon, English (from the Norman conquest to Victoria), Anglo-Gallic, Irish, and Scottish. Cuff's numismatic books were also disposed of, the total sale raising £7054. Compared with similar coin sales between 1854 and 1883, the Cuff sale was remarkable for its length and for the large sum that it realized. Probably the nearest to approach it in scale was the Bergne sale, which took place over eleven days and realized £6102 13s., or the Montagu sale, which lasted seven days and realized £8783 16s. Cuff's English medals came into the possession of the Bank of England, and subsequently passed into the British Museum as part of the bank's collection.

Cuff died at Prescott Lodge, his house at Clapham New Park, on 28 September 1853; he was buried in Norwood cemetery. His wife, a daughter of Bartholomew Barry, a Bristol bookseller, survived him. He had no children.

W. W. WROTH, rev. JOANNE POTIER

Sources GM, 2nd ser., 40 (1853), 532–3 · Boase, *Mod. Eng. biog.*, 1.779 · R. A. G. Carson and H. Pagan, *A history of the Royal Numismatic Society, 1836–1986* (1986) · W. S. Thorburn, *A guide to the history and valuation of the coins of Great Britain and Ireland* (1898) · G. R. Ainslie, *Illustrations of the Anglo-French coinage* (1830); suppl. (1847) · *Numismatic Chronicle*, 2 (1839–40), iii

Archives BM, Bank collection, English medals

Likenesses lithograph, 1837, NPG

Cuff, John (1708?–1772?), optician and microscope maker, was the son of Peter Cuff (b. 1676), watchmaker and member of the Broderers' Company. It is possible that his mother was Rebecca, née Crichlow (b. 1675), who married a Peter Cuff, watchmaker, of the parish of St Martin Ludgate, London, at St Benet Paul's Wharf in 1698. Cuff was apprenticed to James Mann, optical instrument maker, in April 1722 and admitted into the freedom of the Spectacle Makers' Company in January 1730. It is from his likely ages on these dates (thirteen and twenty-one respectively) that the year of his birth has been estimated, though it is possible that he served a previous apprenticeship, perhaps with a clock- or watchmaker given his father's profession and the reputation he later gained for microscopes of all-metal construction.

For nearly twenty years from 1738 Cuff occupied a shop under the sign of the Reflecting Microscope and Spectacles on the north side of Fleet Street, London, three doors east of Crane Court, where the Royal Society had met since 1710. There he made and sold, both retail and wholesale, optical instruments, barometers, thermometers, mathematical instruments, and other curiosities. The microscopes he made included the standard models of the day and several innovative designs, including the perfected 'microscope for viewing opake objects' and the solar or camera obscura microscope, both of which were invented by Johannes Lieberkühn and first demonstrated in London in 1739. Cuff's solar microscopes, with their ability to project a magnified image onto a screen, proved popular and were widely used in public lectures of the time.

Cuff was closely associated with Henry Baker FRS, his advocate if not patron, who included descriptions and plates of Cuff's instruments in his works on microscopy, including the highly successful *Microscope Made Easy* (1742). It was for Baker that Cuff made his double reflecting microscope in 1743. This was a great improvement on its predecessors, being made entirely of brass, supported by a single side-pillar of rectangular cross-section, and having a fine-threaded focus: it was widely copied at home and abroad, and had a strong influence on subsequent designs, microscopes with such characteristics now being referred to as 'Cuff-type'. Cuff also made an aquatic microscope, which was used to study the properties of specimens in water—an activity made all the more popular in salons and drawing-rooms of the time after Abraham Trembley's discovery of the amazing regenerative properties of the polypus in 1740. It was this type of microscope that John Ellis used to compile his *Natural History of the Corallines* (1755).

Cuff was a frequent visitor to meetings of the Royal Society, but failed to secure the required number of votes for election when put up in 1743. He had as little success in the commercial sphere, though his excellence as a workman was highly regarded. He was declared bankrupt in 1750, but raised enough money from the sale of his household effects to continue trading. The arrival in 1757 of Benjamin Martin in the shop next door prompted him to flee some time between July and September from the sign of the Reflecting Microscope and Spectacles, and he moved along Fleet Street to the sign of the Double Microscope, Three Pair of Golden Spectacles, and Hadley's Quadrant, opposite Salisbury Court. He was there for little more than a year before being forced to give up shopkeeping and sell his stock-in-trade at auction. However, he continued to make instruments to order and to take on apprentices. In 1764 he was a signatory to the petition against John Dollond's patent for achromatic lenses.

Cuff had a number of trade cards and advertisements printed, along with several pamphlets, many of which were also translated into French (this was unusual for the time, but possibly not unconnected with Henry Baker's enthusiasm for the language), where he appears as 'Jean Cuff, opticien, faiseur de lunettes & de microscope'. The pamphlets are mainly illustrated descriptions of his microscopes, but also include a 'description of a Gregorian telescope' and a poetic piece of 1747 entitled 'Verses Occasion'd by the Sight of a Chamera Obscura'.

Details of Cuff's death are as uncertain as those of his birth. He served as an assistant at the court of the Spectacle Makers' Company from 1749, having served as its master for one year, to 5 October 1770, when he was discharged at his own request. William Cox, his last apprentice, had been with him since 1767, and was turned over to Charles Lincoln in 1771. A John Cuff was a member from December 1768 to March 1772 of masonic lodge 125, which met at the Bishop's Blaze in Shoreditch. In May 1772 letters of administration were issued for a John Cuff of West Dawlish in Somerset, a county in which there were several clockmakers by the name of Cuff.

Signed examples of Cuff's instruments can be found in the principal collections: they include not only microscopes and other optical instruments but also barometers, which he may have made himself or more likely sold on after adding his signature. Cuff has long been identified as one of the sitters in a portrait by Zoffany now in the Royal Collection, Windsor Castle. There is little evidence to support this identification: when first exhibited at the Royal Academy in 1772 the portrait was called *An Optician with his Attendant*; in a rough draft of the inventory of Kew (*c.*1800) it appears as *Mr Cuff*, but in the published inventory as *A Mathematician*; when lent to the Royal Institution in 1827 it was hung as *Two Old Men*; subsequently it has been known as *The Lapidaries*. In 1859 a pencil note was visible on the stretcher reading 'Dollond the Optician in the Strand London'.   GILES HUDSON

Sources private information (2004) [J. Millburn] · Spectacle Makers' court book, 1695–1738, GL, MS 5213/2 · Spectacle Makers' stamps for freedom, 1699–1736, GL, MS 6031/1 · Spectacle Makers' minute book, 1739–84, GL, MS 5213/3 · Broderers' Company register of freedom admissions, 1694–1728, GL, MS 14664 · alphabet of freedoms, 1714–25, CLRO, CF 28/3 · 'Boyd's Inhabitants of London', Society of Genealogists, London, 33636 · *LondG* (24–7 Nov 1750) · *Daily Advertiser* [London] (5 Aug 1757) · *Daily Advertiser* [London] (3 March 1758) · journal books, RS, vols. 28–9 · G. L'E. Turner, 'Henry Baker, FRS, founder of the Bakerian lecture', *Notes and Records of the Royal Society*, 29 (1974–5), 53–79, esp. 63–4 · O. Millar, *The later Georgian pictures in the collection of her majesty the queen*, 1 (1969), 152 · R. S. Clay and T. H. Court, *The history of the microscope* (1932), 136ff. · G. Clifton, *Directory of British scientific instrument makers, 1550–1851*, ed. G. L'E. Turner (1995) · H. R. Calvert, *Scientific trade cards* (1971) · correspondence of H. Baker and W. Arderon, V&A NAL, Forster Library, Forster MS 47, c. 11–c. 14

Cuffay, William (*bap.* 1788, *d.* 1870), Chartist, was born in Chatham and baptized there on 6 July 1788, one of at least three children of Chatham Cuffay and his wife, Juliana. His grandfather was an African sold into slavery; Cuffay (sometimes spelt Cuffey, Cuffy, or Coffey) is the Twi day-name (*Kofi*) for a male child born on a Friday. Cuffay's father, born on the island of St Kitts, became a cook on a British warship. Brought up by his mother, Cuffay had a younger brother, James, and a younger sister, Juliana. As a boy, though his spine and shin bones were deformed, he 'took a great delight in all manly exercises' (Wheeler, 177). After becoming a journeyman tailor in his late teens, he stayed in that trade for the rest of his life and was respected for his hard work, quiet ways, honesty, reliability, and humour. Mild and unassertive, he was in demand at social gatherings as an accomplished singer and musician. One workmate described him as 'a good spirit in a little deformed case' (Thompson, 189).

Though a late convert to trade unionism, Cuffay took part in the disastrous 1834 strike of London tailors for shorter hours: he stayed out until the bitter end and thereby lost his regular job. It was probably this experience which radicalized him. In 1839 he joined the Chartist movement and helped to form the Metropolitan Tailors'

Charter Association. Two years later the Westminster Chartists elected him to the metropolitan delegate council, and in 1842 he chaired a 'Great Public Meeting of the Tailors', at which the national petition was adopted. In the same year, after the arrest of the movement's national leaders, he was appointed president of a five-man interim executive. In 1844 he was on a committee opposing a bill which would have given magistrates power to imprison a worker for two months merely on his employer's oath. A strong supporter of the Chartist land plan, he was one of three London delegates to the 1846 Birmingham land conference and was repeatedly elected joint auditor to the National Land Company. In 1846 he was one of the ten directors of the National Anti-Militia Association and was a member of the Democratic Committee for Poland's Regeneration. In 1847 he was on the central registration and election committee, and in the following year was on the management committee for a metropolitan democratic hall.

Cuffay was frequently attacked in *The Times*, which referred to London's Chartists as 'the Black man and his party' (Wheeler, 177), and was lampooned in *Punch* and in the *Illustrated London News*, which wrote of 'the comic Cuffey' and his 'nigger humour' (22 April 1848). The savage press campaign cost his wife, Mary Ann, her job as a char-woman—whereupon Richard Cobden gave her employment in his household (Holyoake, 2.3).

In 1848 Cuffay was noted for his militancy. At a meeting in March he pointed to a placard reading 'The Republic for France—The Charter for England' and declared: 'Aye; and if they refused us the Charter, we should then begin to think about a republic' (Weisser, 11 and 43 n. 42). In the following month he was one of three London delegates to the Chartists' national convention, where he was criticized for his 'extravagant expressions' (Weisser, 79). However, he was appointed to chair the committee for managing the procession that, on 10 April, was to accompany the Chartist petition to the House of Commons from a mass meeting on Kennington Common. When this procession was banned, and then called off by Feargus O'Connor, who asked the crowd to disperse, Cuffay protested strongly: the national leadership were 'a set of cowardly humbugs' (*Morning Chronicle*, 11 April 1848).

Elected one of the commissioners to promote the campaign for the Charter after parliament had rejected it, Cuffay was a late—and almost certainly a reluctant—member of the 'Ulterior Committee' that was planning an uprising in London. On 15 August eleven 'luminaries', plotting to fire certain buildings as a signal for the rising, were arrested at the Orange Tree tavern, Bloomsbury, and Cuffay was arrested at his lodgings the next day. He had refused to run away, 'lest it should be said that he abandoned his associates in the hour of peril' (Frost, 165). His conviction at the central criminal court, on 30 September, for levying war on the queen, was obtained through the evidence of two police spies. After a defiant final speech Cuffay and two fellow Chartists were sentenced to transportation for life.

After a voyage of 103 days on the prison ship *Adelaide*,

Cuffay arrived in Hobart, Tasmania, on 29 November 1849. He was allowed to work at his trade for wages, which he did until the last year of his life. His wife joined him in April 1853. After his free pardon on 19 May 1856 he continued his radical activities in Tasmania, where he was described as 'a fluent and effective speaker … always popular with the working classes' (Barrows and Mock, 118).

In 1869 Cuffay entered Tasmania's workhouse, Brickfields Asylum, where he died in July 1870. The superintendent described him as 'a quiet man, and an inveterate reader'. He was buried on 2 August 1870 at Trinity burial-ground, Tasmania, and his grave was marked 'in case friendly sympathisers should hereafter desire to place a memorial stone on the spot' (Barrows and Mock, 118).

PETER FRYER

Sources [T. M. Wheeler], 'Mr William Cuffay', *Reynolds's Political Instructor*, 1/23 (13 April 1850), 177 • D. Thompson, *The Chartists: popular politics in the industrial revolution* (1984) • *ILN* (22 April 1848), 261 • G. J. Holyoake, *Sixty years of an agitator's life*, 2 vols. (1892) • H. Weisser, *April 10: challenge and response in England in 1848* (Lanham, Maryland, 1983) • *Morning Chronicle* (11 April 1848), 6 • T. Frost, *Forty years' recollections: literary and political* (1880) • F. D. Barrows and D. B. Mock, *A dictionary of obituaries of modern British radicals* (1989) [repr. obit. from *The Mercury* (Hobart, Australia, 11 Aug 1870), 3] • J. Saville, 'Cuffay, William', *DLB*, vol. 6 • N. J. Gossman, 'William Cuffay: London's black Chartist', *Phylon*, 44/1 (1983), 56–65 • D. Goodway, *London Chartism, 1838–1848* (1982) • A. Briggs, 'Chartists in Tasmania: a note', *Bulletin of the Society for the Study of Labour History*, 3 (1961), 6–7 • I. J. Prothero, 'Cuffay', *BDMBR*, vol. 2 • J. E. P. Wallis, ed., *Reports of state trials: new series*, 1820 (to 1858), 7 (1896), 467–82 • bap. reg. • G. Rudé, *Protest and punishment: the story of the social and political protesters transported to Australia, 1788–1868* (1978), 217

Likenesses engraving, repro. in Wheeler, 'Mr William Cuffay'

Cuffe, Hamilton John Agmondesham, fifth earl of Desart (1848–1934), lawyer and public servant, was born on 30 August 1848, the second son of John Otway O'Connor Cuffe, third earl of Desart (1818–1865), and Lady Elizabeth (1822–1898), third daughter of John Frederick Campbell, first Earl Cawdor, and his wife, Elizabeth Thynne, daughter of the second marquess of Bath. As a boy Cuffe served as a midshipman in the Royal Navy from 1860 to 1863. He was educated at Radley and at Trinity College, Cambridge, graduating BA in 1869. At the age of twenty-four, in 1872, he was called to the bar by the Inner Temple, in due course becoming a bencher in 1905.

On 19 July 1876 Cuffe married Lady Margaret Joan (1853–1927), second daughter of Henry Thynne Lascelles, the fourth earl of Harewood, and Elizabeth Joanna, daughter of the first marquess of Clanricarde. They had two daughters, Joan Elizabeth Mary, who married Sir Harry Lloyd Verney, and Sybil Marjorie, who married William Bayard Cutting, Geoffrey Scott, and Percy Lubbock. Lord Desart succeeded to the peerage (Irish) as fifth earl on the death of his brother, the fourth earl, in 1898.

Desart had a long and distinguished career in the public service. In 1877 he became secretary to the judicature acts commission, which was responsible for implementing the amalgamation of common law and equity in the new Supreme Court of Judicature and the building of the new Royal Courts of Justice in the Strand. In 1878 he was appointed assistant solicitor to the Treasury, and between 1884 and 1894 served as assistant director of public prosecutions. At the age of forty-six he reached the peak of his career, being appointed solicitor to the Treasury (solicitor to the government) and queen's proctor (solicitor on behalf of the crown principally concerned to ensure that there was no abuse of the divorce laws) in 1894. He also succeeded Sir Augustus Stephenson as director of public prosecutions (DPP), the head of the state prosecution department, a post established only a few years previously.

As DPP, Desart kept a low profile, and did not publicly respond to public criticism. *Causes célèbres* for the prosecution of which he was responsible included the Jameson raid (1896); Jabez Balfour and the Liberator frauds (1895); Florence Maybrick (1889); the Moat Farm murder; Neil Cream; the prosecution of Lord Russell for bigamy before the House of Lords (1901); Oscar Wilde (1895); Adolph Beck (1895). He was averse to invoking the criminal law in matters of morals. As Treasury solicitor he conducted an inquiry into the kidnapping of Dr Sun Yatsen by the Chinese legation in London in 1896.

Desart was a cautious public servant, in the civil service tradition. His period of office as DPP was one of relative tranquillity. He refused to discuss individual cases publicly, although for some years until 1905 his annual report did contain details of *causes célèbres*, albeit expressed in rather bland style. He was involved in a dispute with the Law Society over the prosecution of fraudulent solicitors, but he adhered to a quiet but firm line.

The vesting of three such important public offices in one person was seen as acceptable in the nineteenth century, but became unworkable in the early twentieth century. In 1907 the Criminal Appeal Act, which gave a right of appeal and established the court of criminal appeal, created substantially more work for the DPP. Accordingly the Prosecution of Offences Act of 1908 made the DPP the independent head of an independent department, directly answerable to the attorney-general. Charles Matthews became DPP, and Desart remained Treasury solicitor until his retirement in 1909. In the same year, on the recommendation of H. H. Asquith, he was created Baron Desart of Desart, co. Kilkenny, in the peerage of the United Kingdom, in recognition of his considerable public service.

Desart was sceptical about the usefulness of his role as queen's (and subsequently king's) proctor, which involved intervening in divorce cases, taking the view that most divorce cases were in fact by consent, then not permitted. As he told the divorce commission in 1912, he felt he did more harm than good.

Desart was a British member in the North Sea Inquiry in Paris in 1905, investigating how on its way to the Far East the Russian fleet off Dogger Bank fired on British seamen, apparently thinking them to be the Japanese fleet. Following the Hague Convention of 1907, he was British plenipotentiary and president at the International Naval Conference in London in 1908–9, which produced the declaration of London, proposing prize rules for international law. Although never ratified, it was accepted by the great powers, though in the event abandoned in the First World War in 1916. In 1910 Desart became one of the four British members of the International Court of Arbitration at The Hague. He presided over the United Kingdom prize claim committee in 1915.

In the House of Lords, Desart was a moderate Conservative. He voted for the Parliament Bill in 1911, and against the Welsh Church Disestablishment Bill in 1913. He was elected to the Irish senate in 1921. He received many honours and appointments: justice of the peace; CB (1894); KCB (1898); privy councillor (1913); knight of the Order of St Patrick (1919); his majesty's lieutenant for the county of Kilkenny (1920). He was devoted to Ireland, adopting a moderating and conciliatory approach to Irish affairs. 'Why am I a Unionist? Because I am an Irishman.' Recognizing the seeming inevitability of some form of Irish home rule, as a southern unionist he opposed the Government of Ireland Bill of 1912–14 because of the exclusion of Ulster, as he was opposed to the severance of Ireland in any form. He foresaw the danger of civil war in Ireland, but none the less expressed the wish to see Ireland prosper and its parliament succeed.

A man of strong character and great ability, Desart was an experienced statesmanlike figure who knew everybody of significance in public life. A lovable man and a magnificent friend, he had many friends. An Anglican churchman, he was a profoundly religious man. His principal hobby was shooting, and his clubs were the Travellers and the MCC. He lived at 2 Rutland Gardens, Knightsbridge, London; his house in Ireland, Desart Court, was burnt down by Sinn Féiners. He died aged eighty-six on 4 November 1934 at 29 Wimpole Street, London, leaving no male heir, and no heir presumptive, and the peerage thus became extinct.   ALEC SAMUELS

Sources WWW · Venn, *Alum. Cant.* · Burke, *Peerage* · GEC, *Peerage* · *The Times* (5 Nov 1934) · *The Times* (6 Nov 1934) · J. L. J. Edwards, *The law officers of the crown* (1964), 367–402 · *Law Times* (10 Nov 1934), 338 · *Justice of the Peace and Local Government Review*, 98/45 (10 Nov 1934), 741 · S. Lubbock, *Memories of the earl of Desart* (1936) · J. Rozenberg, *Case for the crown* (1987) · private information (2004) · d. cert.
Archives BL, letters to J. H. Bernard, Add. MS 52781 · Plunkett Foundation, Long Hanborough, Oxfordshire, corresp. with Sir Horace Plunkett · PRO, corresp. with Lord Midleton, PRO 30/67
Likenesses photograph, Gov. Art Coll.
Wealth at death £15,189 15s. 3d.: probate, 17 Dec 1934, CGPLA Eng. & Wales

Cuffe [Cuff], **Henry** (1562/3–1601), classical scholar and secretary to the earl of Essex, is believed to have been the youngest son of Robert Cuffe, of Donyatt, Somerset. The senior branch of the family were modest landowners at Creech St Michael, near Taunton. A Hugh Cuffe, perhaps an elder brother of the subject, obtained land in Munster and was a neighbour there to the poet Edmund Spenser in the 1590s. Henry Cuffe was apparently born in, and received his initial education at, Hinton St George, which was dominated by the Paulet family. Thanks to the patronage of Lady Elizabeth Paulet, he was elected a scholar of Trinity College, Oxford, in May 1578, aged fifteen. He soon demonstrated great ability, especially in the study of

Greek texts. He proceeded BA in 1580 and was elected a fellow of his college in May 1583. However, he was uncomfortable at Trinity and he apparently received a letter of rebuke from Lady Paulet, whose first husband had been the college's founder, in May 1582. By then he was already a protégé of the renowned Greek scholar Henry Savile, of Merton College. He was also a friend of Jean Hotman, another client of the Paulet family, who had recently left Oxford to become secretary to Robert Dudley, earl of Leicester. Cuffe unsuccessfully sought help from Hotman and Leicester to move to Merton.

Cuffe remained a fellow of Trinity until about 1586, when he was forced to resign after making allegations that the college's founder, Thomas Pope, had been a habitual thief. By now, Savile had become warden of Merton and he was able to ensure Cuffe's election as a fellow there on 1 August 1586. He subsequently took his MA degree in February 1589 and held a series of college offices. He was appointed regius professor of Greek in April 1590. When Queen Elizabeth visited Oxford University in September 1592 Cuffe delivered a speech of welcome at Carfax and three days later disputed before an audience of privy councillors and courtiers. He was a university proctor between April 1594 and April 1595.

When Cuffe relinquished this office, or soon afterwards, he took extended leave from his college to join the secretariat of Robert Devereux, second earl of Essex, stepson of the late earl of Leicester and already the chief patron of Henry Savile. Essex matched the salary of £40 per annum which Cuffe had received as regius professor, although Cuffe retained the chair until at least 1597. Essex's other secretaries included Edward Reynoldes, William Temple, and Henry Wotton. Anthony and Francis Bacon were also fixtures in the earl's inner circle. In 1596 Cuffe and Wotton accompanied Essex on his expedition to Cadiz. Working from 'his lordship's large instructions', Cuffe drew up 'A true relacion of the action at Cadiz', a partisan account of the victory which was designed for speedy publication in a form which would seem to be unconnected to the earl. Although Cuffe brought the document back to England, its existence was betrayed to the privy council by Sir Anthony Ashley and all publications about Cadiz were banned. Despite this, various versions of Cuffe's text circulated in manuscript within England and abroad.

In 1597 Essex sent Cuffe on a mission to Florence where the earl had important political interests. This trip enabled him to enjoy the sort of continental tour which was becoming *de rigueur* for Elizabethans who laid claim to cultural and intellectual sophistication. He was in Florence by October 1597 and remained there until at least March 1598. He was in Paris in June and July 1598. During his sojourn in Florence he corresponded with Savile and his colleagues at Essex House, bought books for the library at Merton, became a member of the Accademia della Crusca, and assisted Raphael Columbanius with his edition of Longus's *Pastoral of Daphnis and Chloe*. In September 1598 he was sent back to Paris to meet Essex's friend, the earl of Southampton, who had fled the country after the revelation of his secret marriage to Elizabeth Vernon,

Essex's cousin. A strong bond soon grew between Southampton and Cuffe, cemented by Cuffe's endeavours to provide political advice for the earl by analysing classical texts. According to a later report, Cuffe 'redd Aristotle's Polyticks to hym with sutch exposytions as I doubt did hym but lyttle good; afterwards he redd to my lord of Rutlande' (MS Ashmole 1729, fol. 190r).

Shortly afterwards Essex was appointed lord lieutenant of Ireland and Cuffe, Wotton, and Temple accompanied him there in early 1599, leaving Reynoldes in London. Cuffe soon dominated the earl's secretariat in Ireland, compiling a journal of Essex's actions for transmission to England and pocketing healthy sums from importunate military officers. Like the rest of Essex's entourage in Ireland, including Southampton and Rutland, Cuffe believed that Essex's rivals at court were intent on destroying him by failing to support his campaign and misreporting his actions to the queen. At the end of August, Essex sent him back to England to argue his case. Although Cuffe did his best, Elizabeth remained scathing about the earl's efforts. When Essex himself returned to court at the end of September he was arrested and charged with maladministration, provoking a mental and physical collapse. Although Essex retained Cuffe and Reynoldes as secretaries during his confinement, many other servants were dismissed and Cuffe undoubtedly began to fear for his future. By early 1600 Essex's surviving followers were dividing into two groups. Some, like Reynoldes, urged the earl to recoup his fortunes by humbly seeking Elizabeth's forgiveness. Others, like Cuffe, Southampton, and Essex's steward, Sir Gelly Meyrick, argued that Essex must protect his honour—and the prospects of his followers—by forcibly removing his courtly enemies. While the broken Essex vacillated between these two strategies, Cuffe and others pushed forward with plans for armed action which involved support from Scotland and Ireland. Towards the end of 1600 Essex dismissed Cuffe, allegedly after he had criticized the earl as 'low-spirited and faint-hearted' (Camden, 602).

According to the later report of Henry Wotton, who wrote bitterly about his former colleague, Cuffe was shaken to the core by this sudden collapse of his fortunes. However, Southampton intervened on his behalf and Cuffe's access to Essex was soon restored. This sealed the victory of the hard-liners among Essex's followers. Isaac Casaubon claims that Cuffe's exposition of a passage of Lucan finally convinced Essex to take up arms (Casaubon MS 28, fol. 127r; Camden, 626). While some of the earl's adherents urged Essex to raise the City, Cuffe argued for a *coup de main* against the court, although he later claimed he intended no violence. When Essex blundered into action on 8 February 1601 in a half-hearted attempt to win support in the City, Cuffe remained entirely aloof from the disaster, reading books and bewailing his master's precipitate action. After his arrest Cuffe sought to emphasize his innocence in the rising, but evidence of his earlier plotting soon mounted up. In the days before his execution Essex turned on Cuffe and accused him of being 'a

principall instigator to theis vyolent courses' (SP 12/278, fol. 207r).

At his own trial, and in the official propaganda which described the insurrection, Cuffe was cast as an Iago-like figure in Essex's fall, 'the very seducer of the earl' (*State trials*). He was hanged at Tyburn with Sir Gelly Meyrick on 13 March 1601. Cuffe received little sympathy when, on the scaffold, he reiterated his innocence of the act of treason for which he was condemned to death: 'I am here adjudged to die for plotting a plott never acted [and] for acting an act never plotted' (SP 12/279, fol. 36r). In a narrow sense, he may have been correct, but his long-term complicity in plotting meant that his scholarly logic and rhetoric seemed 'but figgleaves' (SP 12/279, fol. 35r).

Cuffe never married and apparently showed no interest in women. In *The Differences of the Ages of Mans Life* (1607), he mentions women only in connection with 'the woman's treacherous seduction by the divel in the serpent' (Cuffe, 7) and their physical inferiority to men. Cuffe describes sex in his book as 'death's best harbinger' (ibid., 105) and approvingly cites Avicenna and Aristotle on the benefits of semen conservation. Although his property was forfeit to the crown, his will optimistically contained bequests totalling over £2000, a sum which was testimony to his ambition and thirst for material advancement. His posthumous reputation as a traitor was counter-pointed by reports of his witty mockery of his prosecutors, especially Edward Coke and Francis Bacon. Cuffe's reputation as a scholar and political analyst was sustained by the attribution to him of political aphorisms which explained Essex's fall in terms of classical history. He also left behind a manuscript which he apparently wrote during 1600, later published as *The Differences of the Ages of Mans Life* (1607). Despite its title, this learned but poorly constructed work is primarily a refutation of the Aristotelian doctrine of the eternity of the world. Cuffe died as a protestant and was described as a 'purytan' by one of his enemies in 1601 (MS Ashmole 1729, fol. 190r).

PAUL E. J. HAMMER

Sources PRO, SP 12, SP 63 · Cecil MSS, Hatfield House, Hertfordshire · Wood, *Ath. Oxon.*, new edn · W. Camden, *The history of the most renowned and victorious Princess Elizabeth*, 4th edn (1688) · Fuller, *Worthies* (1840) · *Francisci et Joannis Hotomanorum ... clarorum virorum ad eos epistolae*, ed. J. W. van Meel (1700) · J. M. Fletcher, ed., *Registrum annalium collegii Mertonensis, 1567–1603*, OHS, new ser., 24 (1976) [for 1973–4] · P. E. J. Hammer, 'The uses of scholarship: the secretariat of Robert Devereux, 2nd earl of Essex, c.1585–1601', *EngHR*, 109 (1994), 26–51 · P. E. J. Hammer, 'Myth-making: politics, propaganda and the capture of Cadiz in 1596', *HJ*, 40 (1997), 621–42 · *State trials*, vol. 1 · Bodl. Oxf., MS Ashmole 1729 · Bodl. Oxf., MS Casaubon 28 · H. Wotton, *A parallel betweene Robert, late earle of Essex, and George, late duke of Buckingham* (1641) · *Letters from Sir Robert Cecil to Sir George Carew*, ed. J. Maclean, CS, old ser., 88 (1864) · PRO, C 66 · Folger, MS Gb4 · BL, Harley MS 1327 · Gon. & Caius Cam., MS 150/200 · *VCH Somerset* · H. Cuffe, *The differences of the ages of mans life* (1607)

Archives Hatfield House, Hertfordshire, Cecil MSS · PRO, SP 12
Wealth at death approx. £2100—moneys owed to him by three named debtors; incl. bequest of £100 to Sir John Peyton, lieutenant of the Tower: will, Cecil MS 84/1

Cugoano, Ottobah [John Stuart] (*b.* **1757**?), slavery abolitionist and writer, was born on the coast of present-day Ghana, in the Fante village of Agimaque (present-day Ajumako). His parents are unknown. In 1770 he was kidnapped by fellow Africans, sold into slavery to Europeans, and transported to Grenada. After travelling around the West Indies for about two years he was taken to England at the end of 1772 by his master, Alexander Campbell. This was probably the same Alexander Campbell who testified in favour of the slave trade before a committee of the House of Commons on 13–18 February 1790. Cugoano was baptized John Stuart—'a Black, aged 16 years'—at St James's Church, Piccadilly, London, on 20 August 1773.

Cugoano was one of the first identifiable Afro-Britons actively engaged in the fight against slavery. In 1786 he joined William Green, another Afro-Briton, in successfully appealing to Granville Sharp to save a black person, Harry Demane, from being forced into West Indian slavery. With Olaudah Equiano and other 'Sons of Africa', he continued the struggle against slavery with public letters to London newspapers. His efforts culminated in his polemical jeremiad, *Thoughts and Sentiments on the Evil and Wicked Traffic of the Slavery and Commerce of the Human Species* (1787), in which he refuted religious and secular pro-slavery arguments and demanded the immediate abolition of the slave trade and emancipation of all slaves. He also called for condign punishments for slave owners, including enslavement by their former slaves. In 1791 Cugoano published a shorter version of his book entitled *Thoughts and Sentiments on the Evil of Slavery* and announced his intention to open a school for Afro-Britons.

From at least 1784 Cugoano had been employed as a servant by the fashionable painters Richard and Maria Cosway in Schomberg House, Pall Mall. Through Richard Cosway, appointed principal painter to the prince of Wales in 1785, Cugoano probably met the artists who subscribed to his 1791 book—Sir Joshua Reynolds and Joseph Nollekens—as well as the public figures to whom he wrote letters—George III, the prince of Wales, Edmund Burke, Sir William Dolben, and Sharp. Visual and verbal representations of Cugoano can be identified in several portrayals of Cosway and his wife, including Richard Cosway's 1784 etching *Mr and Mrs Cosway*; in William Blake's unpublished satire 'An Island in the Moon' (1784?); and as Pompey in *The Royal Academicians: a Farce* (1786) by Anthony Pasquin (John Williams).

In 1791 Cugoano was living at 12 Queen Street, Grosvenor Square, probably still in Cosway's employ. He wrote to Sharp, probably in 1791, asking to be sent to Nova Scotia to recruit settlers for a second attempt to settle free Afro-Britons in Sierra Leone. No record has been found of Cugoano's either having opened a school or having participated in settling Sierra Leone. Henri Grégoire, often unreliable, reports that a Lord Hoth originally brought Cugoano to England, thus contradicting Cugoano's own account, and that he married an Englishwoman (Grégoire, 189). The cause, date, and place of Cugoano's death, and the date and place of his burial are unknown.

VINCENT CARRETTA

Sources O. Cugoano, *Thoughts and sentiments on the evil of slavery and other writings*, ed. V. Carretta (1999) · H. Grégoire, *An enquiry concerning the intellectual and moral faculties and literature of negroes: followed with an account of the life and works of fifteen negroes and mulattoes distinguished in science, literature and the arts*, trans. D. Warden (1810) · K. A. Sandiford, *Measuring the moment: strategies of protest in eighteenth-century Afro-English writing* (1988) · P. Edwards and D. Dabydeen, eds., *Black writers in Britain, 1760–1890* (1991) · P. Edwards and J. Walvin, *Black personalities in the era of the slave trade* (1983) · parish register (baptism), 20 Aug 1773, St James's, Piccadilly, London
Archives Glos. RO, letters, D3549/13/1/356
Likenesses R. Cosway, etching, Whitworth Art Gallery, Manchester

Cuit [Cuitt], **George, the elder** (1743–1818), painter, was born at Moulton, near Richmond in Yorkshire, the son of a builder. Early in life he showed a great taste for drawing and some of his crayon portraits attracted the notice of Sir Thomas Dundas, bt, of Aske, who employed him to take the likeness of some of his children. So much pleased was he with Cuit's performance that in 1769 he sent him to Italy to study painting, in company with the architect Thomas Harrison (1744–1829); there Cuit met many artists of note, and made great progress, especially in landscape painting, to which his style was suited. In 1775 he returned to England and received various commissions from Dundas. In 1776 he exhibited at the Royal Academy *The Infant Jupiter Fed with Goat's Milk and Honey*; in 1777 some views of Guisborough, Yorkshire, and a portrait. He continued to exhibit at the Royal Academy until 1778. He intended to settle in London, but this was frustrated by illness, which compelled him to return to his native town, Richmond. Here he lived in quiet seclusion, receiving many commissions for painting the scenery of the neighbourhood, especially views of the parks and many fine houses around. Lord Mulgrave, of Mulgrave Castle near Whitby, employed him to paint a set of views of all the ports on the Yorkshire coast which Captain Cook had personally visited, and other scenes connected with the great circumnavigator. 'An ingenious artist and very worthy man', as he is styled in his monumental inscription, Cuit was industrious to the end of his life, though he later exhibited only occasionally in public. He died at Richmond on 7 February 1818, and was buried there. His wife Jane was buried on 13 January of the same year.

Their son **George Cuitt the younger** (1779–1854), etcher, was baptized on 13 October 1779 at Richmond, Yorkshire, his birthplace. In the early part of his life he shared his father's profession as a landscape painter. His mind was turned to etching by a fine collection of Piranesi's etchings which his father had brought from Rome. He moved to Chester about 1804 as a drawing-master, and in 1810 and the following years published several series of etchings, including *Six Etchings of Saxon and Gothic Buildings now Remaining in the City of Chester* (1810–11); *Etchings of ancient buildings in the city of Chester, castles in north Wales, and other miscellaneous subjects* (1816); *History of the City of Chester from its Foundation to the Present Time* (1815). At the age of forty, having realized an independence, he returned to Richmond and built himself a house at

Masham close by, where he resided until his death. Here he published several more sets of etchings of Yorkshire abbeys including Fountains (1822), Kirkstall (1823), and Rievaulx (1825). In 1848 he sold the copyright of his etchings to a Mr Nattali, who collected them into one volume with letterpress, published under the title *Wanderings and Pencillings amongst the Ruins of Olden Times* (1855). Cuitt died at Masham on 15 July 1854. His etchings are far from being mere copies of Piranesi's style, and have great vigour and depth of their own. His dramatic rendering of ruined abbeys and churches means that his etchings continue to be of interest to historians of Romantic landscape and the picturesque. The Grosvenor Museum, Chester, holds forty-eight etchings and fifteen drawings by Cuitt.

L. H. CUST, *rev.* RUTH STEWART

Sources J. Ingamells, ed., *A dictionary of British and Irish travellers in Italy, 1701–1800* (1997) · Redgrave, *Artists*, 2nd edn · Graves, *Artists*, 3rd edn · *GM*, 1st ser., 88/2 (1818), 188 · P. J. Broughton, *Picturesque Chester: the city in art* (1998) [exhibition catalogue, Chester Museums, 1997]
Likenesses G. Cuitt junior, etching (posthumous), BM

Cuitt, George, the younger (1779–1854). *See under* Cuit, George, the elder (1743–1818).

Culbertson, Robert (1765–1823), United Secession minister, was born at Morebattle, Roxburghshire, on 21 September 1765, one of the seven children of James Culbertson (1727/8–1826), a tenant farmer and a member of the Secession church, and his wife, Janet. He was educated at Morebattle parish school and Kelso grammar school, before moving on to Edinburgh University in 1782. He was licensed in the Anti-Burgher Secession church (General Associate Synod) on 2 August 1790, and became pastor of the congregation of St Andrew's Street, Leith, on 1 September 1791. In November 1793 he married Elizabeth, second daughter of John Richmond, an Edinburgh seed merchant; they had five sons and four daughters.

Culbertson was an energetic pastor: the Leith congregation grew during his ministry, necessitating the enlargement of his church. He founded and supported societies for prayer and spiritual discussions; his memorialist recalls that his sermons were 'usually short, but singularly clear, and often delivered with much animation' (Duncan, viii). He was one of the founder members of the Edinburgh (later Scottish) Missionary Society, and actively supported the missions of the General Associate Synod to Nova Scotia and the USA. He was largely responsible for the spread of the Secession church in the Orkneys, helping to organize a new congregation at Kirkwall. Culbertson supported the reunion of the Burgher and Anti-Burgher branches of the Secession church; in 1805 he served as clerk of the Associate Presbytery of Edinburgh, and he acted as convener of the committee appointed to negotiate with the Burgher Secession church (Associate Synod) over reunion in 1820.

Culbertson combined writing with his clerical career. He helped to launch the *Evangelical Magazine*, serving as sometime editor and a regular contributor. In 1800 he published *Hints on the Ordinance of the Gospel Ministry*, a condemnation of lay preaching characteristic of a strict Anti-

Robert Culbertson (1765–1823), by John Kay, 1811

Burgher of the 1790s, and a *Vindication of the Principles of Seceders on the Head of Communion* (1800); *The Coolvenanter's Manual, or, A Short Illustration of the Scripture Doctrine of Public Vows* followed in 1808. He also published several sermons, including one on the death of Princess Charlotte and her son (1817). His chief work, however, was his *Lectures Expository and Practical on the Book of Revelation*, published in 1818 (a new edition appeared in 1826 with a memoir of the author): a critic described it as 'rather tedious but always sensible' (Allibone, *Dict.*).

Culbertson was a tall man, whose appearance was 'characterized by ministerial gravity' (Duncan, ix). Long a sufferer from bilious complaints, he died at his home in Leith on 13 December 1823 and was buried in the family vault in South Leith churchyard on 18 December. With the exception of one daughter, all his children survived him.

ROSEMARY MITCHELL

Sources A. Duncan, 'Memoir', in R. Culbertson, *Lectures expository and practical on the Book of Revelation* (1826), i.v–xxi · Allibone, *Dict.* · J. M'Kerrow, *History of the Secession church*, rev. edn (1841), 651–2, 924
Likenesses J. Kay, etching, 1811, NPG [*see illus.*] · J. Horsburgh, engraving, *c.*1818, repro. in Duncan, 'Memoir', frontispiece
Wealth at death £191 2s. 6d.: inventory, 28 Sept 1924, NA Scot., SC 70/1/31, p. 852

Culen [Cuilén mac Illuilb, Cuilén Hringr] (*d.* 971), king in Scotland, was the son of King *Indulf (*d.* 962). He had two brothers: Eochaid (*d.* 971) and Olaf (*d.* 977). Culen became king on the death of *Dubh in 966 at the hands of the men of Moray. He had opposed King Dubh the year before, gaining support from Donnchad, abbot of Dunkeld, and

Dub Donn, earl of Atholl, who were both killed when Culen was defeated by Dubh at the battle of Duncrub, in modern Perthshire (965). He was killed in 971, with his brother Eochaid, by Rhydderch, son of King Donald of Strathclyde, allegedly on account of some wrong he had done to Rhydderch's daughter. The battle in which he was killed may have taken place in Lothian and he is said to have been buried on Iona. He was succeeded by *Kenneth II who belonged to the branch of the royal dynasty descended from Constantine I.

Culen had one son, **Constantine III** [Causantín mac Cuilén] (*d.* 997), king in Scotland, who was called 'the Bald' by late medieval chroniclers and who reigned for one year and six months (995–7) following the assassination of Kenneth II by Finguala (Finella). He was killed at *rath inber Amon* ('the fort at the mouth of the Almond'), probably near Scone in what is now Perthshire, by Kenneth III, who, like the slayer of Culen, was a member of the alternative branch of the royal dynasty. A late (and debatable) source claims that he was buried on Iona. Constantine had no recorded offspring and was the last of the branch of the royal dynasty descended from King Aed (*d.* 878) to hold the kingship.   DAUVIT BROUN

Sources A. O. Anderson, ed. and trans., *Early sources of Scottish history*, AD 500 to 1286, 1 (1922), 475–7, 517–19 · M. O. Anderson, *Kings and kingship in early Scotland*, rev. edn (1980), 249–53, 265–89

Culin, Patrick. *See* O'Cullen, Patrick (*d.* 1534).

Cullen. For this title name *see* individual entries under Cullen; *see also* Grant, Sir Francis, first baronet, Lord Cullen (1658×63–1726).

Cullen [*née* McLoughlin; *other married name* Reynolds], **Alice** (1891–1969), politician, was born probably in Lochwinnoch, Renfrewshire, on 18 March 1891, the daughter of John McLoughlin, railway platelayer, and his wife, Bridget McKay. Throughout her political career she remained reticent about her background and early life, though in a posthumous tribute reference was made to her roots in west of Scotland farming and weaving communities (*Gorbals View*, 10). Lochwinnoch was a textile village specializing in cotton manufacture. The McLoughlin family also had close connections with the Ayrshire textile and mining village of Kilbirnie near Lochwinnoch, where they worshipped at St Bridget's Roman Catholic Church. She attended elementary school in Lochwinnoch and subsequently trained as a French-polisher. In 1914 she settled in Glasgow, where her first and most enduring home base was in the Hutchesontown district of the Gorbals. About this time she married Harry Bartlett, a hotel waiter, with whom she had a daughter.

Alice Bartlett joined the Independent Labour Party (ILP) in 1916. The organization had established particular strength in the Gorbals, with P. G. Stewart returned in 1895 as Glasgow corporation's first ILP councillor and George Barnes becoming one of Scotland's first Labour MPs in 1906. Labour success in the Gorbals relied heavily on support from the Roman Catholic electorate, estimated at 40 to 50 per cent of the total voting population, and which had emerged largely as a result of Irish immigration from the early nineteenth century. Bartlett was closely identified with this section of the community, and she later stated that the question of Ireland had first brought her into politics (*Glasgow Observer*, 3 Feb 1950). Widowed by 1919, she married, on 19 February 1920, a fellow ILP activist, Pearce Cullen (*b.* 1897/8), a warehouse porter, who was the son of Hugh Cullen, a journeyman bricklayer. They had two daughters. Subsequently she built up a reputation as a champion of health and welfare issues. She took a personal approach to the problems of one of Europe's most congested and notorious slum areas, directly intervening on behalf of individuals and families unable to articulate their grievances at rent courts and labour exchange tribunals.

In 1932 George Buchanan, Labour MP for the Gorbals division, supported the disaffiliation of the ILP from the Labour Party and joined the Maxton-led ILP group at Westminster. Despite Buchanan's stance the Cullens remained loyal to the official party in Hutchesontown, and during the 1930s were prominent within the local ward committee. Alice Cullen succeeded her husband as the committee's secretary in 1938, and in November of that year she replaced Sir John Stewart (brother of P. G. Stewart) as civic representative for Hutchesontown, becoming the city's first Catholic woman councillor. During her ten years in the city chambers she served as a bailie (magistrate) and was sub-convener of the health committee. Yet Cullen faced criticism that she had not taken a sufficiently high profile in municipal affairs, and that she lacked public speaking skills. For years thereafter her inhibited platform performance was compared unfavourably with the eloquent and outspoken Buchanan, even though she was acknowledged to be a committed constituency representative.

In 1948 Buchanan, long reconciled with the Labour Party, resigned his parliamentary seat to become chairman of the newly created National Assistance Board. Defeating three other male aspirants, Cullen, having been widowed for a second time about 1940, was selected to represent Labour in the forthcoming by-election. Among her qualities as the Gorbals candidate were her noncontroversial reputation and devout Catholicism. At a time of intense cold war rhetoric, as one Catholic journal put it, 'some uneasiness was felt that a socialist of communist leanings might be put in [Buchanan's] place' (*The Tablet*, 2 Oct 1948). The religious credentials of Labour's nominee were ensured by the threat of a rival candidate from the independent Christian Labour group, a pro-Catholic organization. In the event only three candidates contested the by-election on 1 October 1948. The challenge to Cullen came from the Communists and Unionists; the latter was the designation used by Scottish Conservatives up to 1965. After a heated and highly personalized campaign Gorbals voters returned her with a majority of 6525, but the poll was unusually low at 50 per cent. Her opponents' relatively strong showing obscured the fact that

Cullen could claim yet another electoral achievement for the Gorbals, as Britain's first female Catholic MP.

Although opposed by an Irish anti-partition candidate in the 1950 general election, in a bitter contest where she faced accusations of equivocation over the issue of Irish reunification, Cullen's position in the Gorbals remained secure. Altogether she fought seven elections, the last in 1966, and she was still MP at the time of her death in 1969. By then boundary change and slum clearance had halved the constituency's electorate from 50,000 in 1948. Cullen's parliamentary interests focused almost exclusively on the issues of health, welfare, and housing, and she contributed infrequently to Commons debate, especially towards the end of her career. Yet the transformation of the Gorbals, in one of Britain's most radical urban redevelopment programmes, meant that during her lifetime her name was associated with progressive policies of environmental improvement. In July 1961 Elizabeth II came to Glasgow and opened a mammoth multi-storey residential development in Hutchesontown, designed by Sir Basil Spence. This high-profile event represented the climax of years of Cullen's campaigning on housing. Along with fellow community activists she ensured that the royal party visited surviving 'single-end' tenements, to contrast the dramatic social changes over the decade.

Of stocky build, bespectacled, and with greying hair, Cullen had a strong Scots accent and cultivated a grandmotherly image, deliberately eschewing glamour in order to appear more down-to-earth in comparison with Unionist opponents. Her ability to relate to Gorbalonians, especially women, made her known as a practical, grass-roots politician. After Pearce Cullen's death she married, on 20 December 1950, William Reynolds (d. 1961), a Glasgow headmaster, but she continued to be publicly known as Alice Cullen. Her third husband also predeceased her. She died of a heart attack at her home at 174 Broomfield Road, Springburn, Glasgow, on 30 May 1969, and was buried at St Kentigern's cemetery, Glasgow, on 2 June. William Ross, then secretary of state for Scotland, summed her up as a loyal Labour backbencher, whose interests were firmly fixed on her constituency and who preferred 'quiet action to publicity' (*Gorbals View*, July 1969, 7).   IRENE MAVER

Sources *Daily Record* (31 May 1969) · *Daily Record* (3 June 1969) · *Evening Times* (2 June 1969) · *Glasgow Herald* (31 May 1969) · *Glasgow Herald* (2 June 1969) · *Scotsman* (2 June 1969) · *Scottish Catholic Observer* (6 June 1969) · *Gorbals View*, 28 (28 July 1969), 1–11 · *Daily Record* (8 Sept 1948); (28 Sept 1948); (2 Oct 1948) · *Forward* (25 Sept 1948) · *Glasgow Herald* (1 Oct 1948); (2 Oct 1948) · *Glasgow Observer* (10 Sept 1948); (24 Sept 1948); (8 Oct 1948) · *The Tablet*, 192 (2 Oct 1948), 210–11 · *Hansard 5C* (1948), 459.1555–7 [maiden speech] · *Daily Record* (Feb 1950) · *Glasgow Herald* (6 Feb 1950); (20 Feb 1950); (25 Feb 1950) · *Glasgow Observer* (3 Feb 1950); (17 Feb 1950) · *Glasgow Herald* (2 Oct 1951); (27 Oct 1951); (5 May 1955); (27 May 1955); (9 Oct 1959); (16 Oct 1964); (1 April 1966) · *Glasgow Herald* (2 Nov 1938) · *Glasgow Observer* (4 Nov 1938) · *Glasgow Herald* (1 July 1961) · *The Times* (1 July 1961) · *WWW*, 1961–70 · m. certs. (2) · d. cert. · *WWBMP*, vol. 4 · *Glasgow Herald* (9 Nov 1950); (21 Dec 1950) · *Glasgow Herald* (3 Nov 1961) · *Glasgow Observer* (29 Dec 1950) · *Glasgow Observer* (10 Nov 1961) · J. Cunnison and J. B. S. Gilfillan, eds., *The third statistical account of Scotland: Glasgow* (1958) · P. Lally, *Lazarus only done it once: the story of my lives* (2000) · R. Ferguson, *Geoff: the life of Geoffrey M. Shaw* (1979) · T. Gallagher, *Glasgow, the uneasy peace: religious tension in modern Scotland* (1987)
Likenesses photograph, Mitchell L., Glas.; repro. in *Gorbals View*, 28 (July 1969), cover · photograph, repro. in *Daily Record* (24 Sept 1948) · photograph, repro. in *Glasgow Herald* (20 Jan 1950) · photograph, repro. in *Glasgow Herald* (2 Oct 1951) · photograph, repro. in *Glasgow Herald* (6 Oct 1964) · photograph, repro. in *Scottish Catholic Observer* (6 June 1969) · photograph, repro. in *Glasgow Observer* (21 Feb 1958) · photographs, Mitchell L., Glas.
Wealth at death £8084 2s.: probate, 26 Aug 1969, NA Scot., SC 36/48/1183; Glasgow sheriff court, pp. 348–51 · £742 19s.: additional inventory, 30 Jan 1970, NA Scot., SC 36/48/1148; Glasgow sheriff court, pp. 389–92

Cullen, (Thomas) Gordon (1914–1994), architect and town planner, was born on 9 August 1914 at Trinity Lodge, Calverley, Yorkshire, the son of Thomas Hetherington Cullen, Wesleyan minister, and his wife, Mary Ann Mofatt. His parents were Scottish. The family lived in Runcorn and Sheffield before moving to London in 1930. Gordon, until then educated at Prince Henry's Grammar School, Otley, enrolled at the Central School of Arts and Crafts in London until advised to switch (primarily for financial reasons) to the Regent Street Polytechnic school of architecture. He showed much promise as a draughtsman, despite being blind in one eye.

Cullen started his career in 1933 as an assistant to the architect Raymond McGrath, and then worked for Godfrey Samuel from 1935 to 1936 and the Tecton group from 1936 to 1938. He belonged to the Modern Architectural Research Group and helped Berthold Lubetkin with such modernist buildings as the Finsbury Health Centre (where he designed the entrance hall mural) and the Highpoint II block in Highgate (where he himself rented a flat). After two years as a freelance architectural artist Cullen was rejected for military service in 1940 because of a heart murmur. He designed factories and Ministry of Information exhibitions before going to Barbados with the colonial service in 1944 to plan self-help housing and schools in the British West Indies.

Cullen returned to London in 1946 to become assistant art editor of the monthly *Architectural Review*, run by the enthusiastic (if domineering) Hubert de Cronin Hastings. Highly original graphics and a score of visionary illustrated articles made Cullen's name within the profession over the next decade. In November 1947 he published 'Westminster regained', a pioneering pedestrianization proposal for Parliament Square. Other articles presented designs for a cathedral precinct in Liverpool, a town next to the Thames near Marlow, and the redevelopment of central Birmingham. Raised to art editor in 1953, he drew studies of such picturesque towns as Ludlow, Shrewsbury, Evesham, and Lyme Regis with the ambition of deriving from them compositional rules which might be applied to new urban centres. A trend in the *Architectural Review* towards more formal architectural criticism may have prompted his decision to revert to freelance work in 1956. If need be, he could always find jobs as a perspective artist for other architects. He married in 1955 the Comtesse Jacqueline de Chabaneix du Chambon. Their daughters were Isabelle, Christine, and Claire.

Cullen spent much time in India in 1959 and 1960, where the Ford Foundation employed him as an adviser on the Delhi regional plan. Meanwhile he collected his review pieces and elaborated on them to produce a book entitled *Townscape* (1961). It used photographs and drawings to exemplify such concepts as possession, viscosity, lines of advantage, enclaves, interpenetration, linear vibration, kinetic unity, 'thisness', and 'hereness' in order to convey his distinctive approach to the urban landscape. This viewed a town not as a series of individual buildings but as a single work of art that slowly disclosed itself to the pedestrian who moved around it. A good townscape offered a sequence of pleasing revelations, creating a sense of drama. Cullen loathed self-effacing suburbs devoid of focal points and vistas. *Townscape* was translated into several languages and discussed in architectural schools across the world. Its prose impressed some as lyrical and others as obscure. Critics complained that Cullen concerned himself exclusively with visual impact, judging a town by the criteria of sculpture or a stage set. Admirers hailed him as an 'urban psychologist' who understood that aesthetic factors deeply affected human well-being: a town should be enjoyed by its inhabitants.

Cullen settled in the village of Wraysbury in Buckinghamshire, where he was a parish councillor (1960–89) and district councillor (1963–73). Funded by Alcan Industries (1964–8), he wrote four studies on new possibilities in city planning, setting out proposals for 'linear circular' towns and urban villages. Municipalities invited his appraisal of their townscapes: Tenterden (1967), Llantrisant (1969), Peterborough (1969–71), and Ware (1973–4). His drawings and paintings of urban scenes (especially French ones) were held in high esteem. In 1974 he designed a new town, Maryculter, for a site near Aberdeen. However, in spite of honorary degrees and awards, including his appointment as CBE (1976), Cullen was often dejected. None of his grand projects was realized; only four of his plans were ever built: a school in St Vincent in the 1940s, a village hall in Wraysbury in the 1960s, and latterly two residential schemes for the London docklands (Swedish Quays and Quay West) in 1988. Combining a fiercely independent mind with shyness, he was ill equipped to persuade developers and politicians. Even his impish humour seemed to fail him as his sight deteriorated in the late 1970s, but a successful operation on his hitherto blind eye in 1980 initiated better times.

Though the London Docklands Development Corporation rejected the design study of the Isle of Dogs on which Cullen worked in 1981, the project brought him into contact with younger architects. In 1985 he formed a partnership with David Price (later his son-in-law) which devised innovative schemes for Greenwich, Cardiff Bay, and the Waverley station area of Edinburgh. Cullen's health gave way after a stroke in 1990. He died of bronchopneumonia at Upton Hospital, Slough, Buckinghamshire, on 11 August 1994 and was buried in St Andrew's churchyard, Wraysbury, on 16 August. He was survived by his wife.

Gordon Cullen was credited, at the very least, with originating the practice of defining pedestrian zones in town centres with bollards and cobbles. At the most, he invented a new form of perception for urban planning.

JASON TOMES

Sources D. Gosling, *Gordon Cullen: visions of urban design* (1996) · *Daily Telegraph* (31 Aug 1994) · *The Independent* (17 Aug 1994) · *The Scotsman* (17 Aug 1994) · *The Guardian* (27 Aug 1994) · *The Times* (7 Sept 1994) · G. Cullen, *Townscape* (1961) · D. Gosling, 'An urban iconoclast', *Landscape Design*, 260 (May 1997), 8–11 · D. Gosling, 'Between God and Mammon', *Landscape Design*, 261 (June 1997), 49–52 · K. Worpole, 'Arts and books', *Prospect* (22 March 2001) · b. cert. · d. cert. · WW

Archives priv. coll., archives

Likenesses G. Cullen, self-portrait, 1950?–1959, repro. in Gosling, *Gordon Cullen*, 21

Cullen, John (*c.*1838–1914), Church of England clergyman and poet, born at Newport, co. Tipperary, Ireland, was the son of a farmer from Newport. Possibly educated privately and at St Aiden's, he briefly entered Trinity College, Dublin, in July 1867 but did not proceed to a degree. By this time he was already working within the Church of England, holding curacies, possibly at St George's, Wigan, Lancashire (1865–7), and definitely at Knipton (1867–9) and Bottesford (1869–74), both in Leicestershire. While at Knipton he married, on 3 May 1869, German-born Leontine Eugenie Dorndinger (or Derndinger; *c.*1841–1906), with whom he had three children. In February 1874 he became vicar of Radcliffe-on-Trent in Nottinghamshire, a position he held until his death.

Cullen was to have a considerable impact on his new parish. Between 1875 and 1907 he organized some nine religious missions to stimulate belief and increase church attendance. He masterminded the extension of the church, St Mary's, believing it necessary because of a rapid increase in population in the parish. The medieval nave and tower were replaced and the Victorian chancel modified between 1878 and 1883 to the design of Goddard and Paget of Leicester. The tower's unusual saddleback roof was said to be the idea of Cullen's German wife as a reminder of her homeland. In his general parish work he kept careful records, relaid the churchyard, encouraged Sunday-school teaching, and supervised the work of the local day school. In 1882 he unwittingly put Radcliffe-on-Trent at the centre of a public health inquiry. Distressed by presiding over the frequent burials of children during a scarlet fever epidemic, he wrote to the Local Government Board in London requesting action. The subsequent investigation came to the notice of the *Nottingham Journal* which waged a long-running campaign against the village, making it notorious during the summer of 1882.

Throughout his life Cullen wrote and translated poetry, mainly from the German. *Horae poeticae*, a collection of poems written in his youth, was published in 1869, followed by various poems and idylls from 1882 onwards. In 1886 he received the thanks of Queen Victoria for his work *Queens Regnant*. Originally written for recitation at Baltimore Female College in the United States, it was dedicated 'To all good women in every land', was well received by American reviewers, and allegedly earned him the reputation of being a supporter of women's suffrage. *Songs of Consolation* appeared in 1893, including a poem dedicated to his brother who had died in 1849. *The River Trent: an Idyll* was published in 1899, its eleven poems described in 1941 as 'a curious blend of Gray's *Elegy*, Tennyson's *In Memoriam* and Victorian vicar'. His own *In Memoriam* was dedicated to his wife, who died in 1906. Much of his work, including *Ian and Edric*, a theological discussion in blank verse, was collected into a 359-page volume, *Poems and Idylls*, in 1913.

In 1893 Cullen was awarded an honorary doctorate of divinity by Illinois Wesleyan University. Of 'very strong and pronounced views', he was long remembered as a benevolent, white-bearded figure in a clerical hat, travelling in a wicker-sided trap. He died at the vicarage, Radcliffe-on-Trent, of apoplexy on 6 May 1914 and was buried two days later at Bottesford where he had been curate forty years before.   PAMELA PRIESTLAND

Sources P. Priestland, ed., *Radcliffe-on-Trent, 1837 to 1920: a study of a village during an era of change* (1989), 50–69, 206 · parish records, Notts. Arch., PR 1508, 1510, 2879, 2897–2898, 2900, 20185–20187 · parish register, Newport, co. Tipperary · parish register, Knipton, Leicestershire · parish register, Bottesford, Leicestershire · parish register, Radcliffe-on-Trent · student records, TCD · private information (2004) · Bingham Rural Sanitary Authority minute books, Rushcliffe Borough Council, Nottingham · scrapbook, Nottinghamshire Local Studies Library, x, ii, 98 (Aug 1941) · *Nottingham Journal* (23 May 1882) · *Nottingham Journal* (2 March 1886) · *Nottingham Weekly Express* (23 Aug 1895) · *Nottingham Daily Express* (9 May 1914) · *Nottingham Daily Express* (1 Sept 1887) · d. cert.

Archives Rushcliffe Borough Council, Nottingham, Bingham Rural Sanitary Authority minute books

Likenesses group portrait, photograph, 1903 (with Sunday-school teachers), Nottinghamshire County Council Libraries; repro. in Priestland, ed., *Radcliffe-on-Trent* · photograph, repro. in *Nottingham Trader* (5 Oct 1912)

Wealth at death £1476 18s. 3d.: probate, 7 July 1914, CGPLA Eng. & Wales

Cullen, Paul

Cullen, Paul (1803–1878), Roman Catholic archbishop of Dublin, was born at Prospect, near Ballitore, in co. Kildare, on 29 April 1803.

Background and early education, 1803–1828 Paul was the third son in a family of eight boys and seven girls of Hugh Cullen and his second wife, Mary Maher. The Cullen and Maher extended families were substantial tenant farmers in the counties of Carlow, Kildare, and Meath, and very well off by Irish standards. At the age of ten, Paul Cullen was enrolled as a day scholar in the local Quaker school at Ballitore. Some four years later he entered Carlow College to study for the priesthood. He was apparently a very shy boy, but his early promise attracted the attention of James Doyle, who was then a professor in the college, and when Doyle was promoted to the see of Kildare and Leighlin in 1819 he offered Cullen a free place at St Patrick's College, Maynooth, the national seminary. Cullen's father, however, was persuaded by his brother-in-law, James Maher, who was just completing his studies for the priesthood in Rome, to send Paul to Rome instead of to Maynooth.

The decision to send Cullen to Rome to pursue his studies at the Urban College of the Society for the Propagation of the Faith, or Propaganda Fide, was the crucial turning

Paul Cullen (1803–1878), by Alessandri Brothers

point in his life. He arrived in Rome on 25 November 1820, at the age of seventeen, where he continued to live and work for the next thirty years, until he finally returned to Ireland in May 1850 as the archbishop of Armagh and apostolic delegate of the pope. On successfully completing his first year at the Urban College, Cullen was awarded a free place in the college, which included tuition, clothing, and room and board. His early letters to his family reveal a remarkably precocious young man with a very practical turn of mind, who also possessed very considerable powers of observation. On completing his first two years of study, however, in which he learned Italian, Latin, and some Hebrew, Cullen was disappointed to find that the college did not offer a formal course in philosophy, which normally was the necessary prerequisite for the study of theology. The problem was that the student body of the Urban College, except for four Irish students, was from those churches that practised the Eastern rite and were still in communion with Rome. As Cullen explained to his father in January 1822,

the Orientals generally come here at an advanced age, and exceedingly ignorant; consequently they would then be old before they could finish a regular course of studies. To avoid this they are almost as soon as they know Latin grammar advanced to theology, and on their account they do not maintain a regular set of professors [of philosophy] in this College. (Cullen MSS)

'Do not', Cullen then cautioned his father, 'let anyone see this, as it would not answer to the idea the Irish have in general of Roman Colleges' (ibid.).

In the spring of 1823 a formal course of philosophy was finally offered in the college, and Cullen spent the next two and a half years studying logic, metaphysics, and ethics, and then physics and mathematics as well as Syriac and Chaldaic. His superiors reported him to be 'very talented, exceedingly studious, chaste in habits, most observant, pious, meek, irreproachable, most praiseworthy in everything' (*DNB*). In June 1823 Cullen took first prize in rhetoric, and in October 1826, at the distribution of prizes in the college by Leo XII, he was awarded first prize in both dogmatic and moral theology, as well as in Hebrew and Greek. Two years later, on 10 September 1828, he was selected by his superiors to undertake a public defence of all theology in 224 theses for his doctorate, on the occasion of a visit to the college by Leo XII and his court. 'Few Italians', Cullen proudly explained to his father several months later, 'less of any other nation, can boast of the pope's presence on such an occasion. I believe no Irishman was ever so honoured in this way' (Cullen MSS).

Priest, rector, and Roman agent, 1829–1849 Cullen was ordained priest on Easter Sunday, 19 April 1829, by Pietro, Cardinal Caprano, former secretary of the *propaganda*, in his private chapel, in the presence of Bartolomeo, Cardinal Cappellari, the prefect of the *propaganda*. Shortly after his ordination Cullen's bishop, James Doyle, asked him to request of Cappellari to be allowed to return home to take up a professorship in Carlow College. Cappellari, however, who was obviously determined to keep this gifted young ecclesiastic in Rome, prevaricated, explaining that Cullen's presence in Rome was required just then for the corrections that had to be made in the new Hebrew Bible that the *propaganda* was about to publish. In June of the following year Cappellari further equivocated when he requested Cullen to replace temporarily a professor of theology in the Urban College who had become ill, and finally in the autumn of that year the cardinal-prefect appointed Cullen professor of scripture in the college. When some five months later, on 2 February 1831, Cappellari was elected pope as Gregory XVI, Cullen's prospects at Rome were, to say the least, greatly enhanced. Indeed, a year later, when the rector of the Irish College in Rome was obliged to resign because of his health, Cullen succeeded him, while continuing to teach scripture in the Urban College. Though there was no regular salary attached to the office of rector of the Irish College, both Cullen's financial situation and his status were greatly improved when he was formally appointed the official agent in Rome of the Irish bishops. As agent, he not only received about £100 a year but he also became privy to all Irish ecclesiastical business done at Rome, and soon became the favourite of the authorities at *propaganda*, which was the congregation of the curia administratively responsible for the Irish church.

Cullen proved to be an able rector and an astute and efficient agent. He increased the student body of the Irish College from less than twenty in 1832 to more than forty by 1835. In the meantime, he petitioned the pope for more spacious quarters for his rapidly expanding little community, and during the summer and autumn of 1834 he returned to Ireland, after an absence of some fourteen years, to visit his family and to solicit funds for the Irish College. Cullen apparently hoped to be allowed to return permanently to Ireland, but the pope insisted that he remain in Rome, and in February 1836 Pope Gregory presented him with the handsome convent and magnificent little church of St Agatha of the Goths on the Quirinal Hill. By the early 1840s Cullen was able to increase significantly the number of free places and to expand the number of students to nearly sixty in his new college. About this time Cullen was created a monsignor, or private chamberlain, by the pope. As the agent of the Irish bishops, meanwhile, he also demonstrated great tact and prudence in dealing with the manifold and delicate commissions he was obliged to attend to. In February 1838, however, a quarrel broke out among the Irish bishops that was eventually to result in a raging conflict in the Irish church, and Cullen was very hard-pressed to maintain his neutrality as the agent of all the bishops in this developing struggle for power in the Irish church.

The quarrel had begun over the differences of opinion among the bishops about the national system of primary education in Ireland. The principals on each side were the archbishop of Dublin, Daniel Murray, and the archbishop of Tuam, John MacHale. MacHale had become convinced that the British government intended to subvert the faith of Irish Catholics through the system, and charged that Murray, who was one of the seven commissioners on the board that governed the system, was not sufficiently aware of the danger. Cullen was slowly drawn into the quarrel, which was fought out with great bitterness over the next three years both in the public press in Ireland and in the bishops' correspondence with *propaganda* at Rome. When Cullen then decided to visit Ireland again in the summer and autumn of 1841 on personal and Irish College business, the *propaganda* authorities requested him to report confidentially on the national system. Cullen, who before his visit had become increasingly partial to the views of MacHale and the nine bishops that supported him in an episcopal body of twenty-six, found that the system did not pose the threat perceived by MacHale, and he advised the authorities that a condemnation of the system would not be prudent. Early in 1841, therefore, *propaganda* finally resolved, with the approval of the pope, that each bishop be allowed to deal with the system in his own diocese as he thought best, which proved to be, in effect, a victory for Murray and the fifteen bishops who had supported him on the issue.

In spite of his discreet defection on this issue, however, Cullen proved to be, in the ensuing struggle for power over the next ten years, a strong partisan of the MacHale faction. In the subsequent quarrel that developed over the government's introduction of a Charitable Bequests Bill in 1844, for example, Cullen actually signed the public protest issued by MacHale against the bill, and he was severely criticized both at home and in Rome for his action. In the midst of this bitter controversy, Cullen proceeded to make matters worse by giving credence in his correspondence with Ireland to a false report that the

Holy See was about to establish diplomatic relations with the British government. MacHale and his friends, lay and clerical, then launched a furious attack on Murray and those bishops that supported him as 'castle bishops', who were prepared to betray their church and people at the behest of the hereditary enemy. The pope and the Roman authorities also came in for their share of abuse in this alleged plot, and the pope was very annoyed with Cullen for his part in having precipitated the crisis. In a private audience on 25 January 1845, therefore, Gregory XVI severely admonished Cullen both for his role in the Charitable Bequests controversy and for his responsibility in spreading rumours about a concordat. The pope's reprimand resulted in Cullen's suffering a physical and mental breakdown, which required an extended visit to Ireland in the summer of 1845 to recover his health.

The struggle between archbishops Murray and MacHale, meanwhile, had been resumed when the government introduced a bill to establish three Queen's Colleges in Ireland to provide for the higher education of Catholics and Presbyterians. Cullen again took the side, though much more circumspectly, of MacHale, who could now count on a strong majority among the Irish bishops. After successive appeals to Rome by Murray and the minority among the bishops in favour of the colleges, the new pope, Pius IX, who had succeeded Gregory XVI in June 1846, finally condemned the colleges in a rescript from *propaganda* in October 1848, finding them grievously and intrinsically dangerous to the faith. Within a month of the issuing of the rescript, Pius IX was driven from Rome and a republic was established. Cullen, who remained in Rome, won the undying gratitude and confidence of Pius IX by assuming the presidency of his alma mater, the Urban College, and placing it under the protection of the American consul in Rome, thus preventing its suppression by the republican regime, while at the same time, at considerable personal risk to himself, providing asylum in the Irish College to several priests and cardinals proscribed by the regime. While the pope was in exile at Gaeta, the archbishop of Armagh, William Crolly, a staunch supporter of Murray in all his confrontations with MacHale, died of cholera in early April 1849. The choice of a successor became so bitter and controversial that the pope decided to reserve the appointment to himself, and after a delay of some eight months finally selected Cullen on 19 December 1849 to succeed Crolly. Cullen was consecrated on 24 February 1850 in the church of St Agatha of the Goths by Castruccio, Cardinal Castracane, for whom Cullen had provided asylum in the Irish College the year before.

Archbishop and cardinal, 1850–1866 Cullen returned to Ireland in early May 1850, charged by the pope, as his apostolic delegate, to convene a national synod for the purpose of bringing reform and unity to the distracted Irish church. The synod was convened at Thurles on 22 August 1850, under the presidency of Cullen, and the bishops present proceeded to legislate a comprehensive canonical frame for a thoroughgoing Tridentine reform of the Irish church. Cullen's more immediate and impressive achievement at Thurles, however, was that he also provided for the resolution of the issue which more than any other had destroyed the harmony and unity of the bishops as a body in the previous decade—the education question. At Thurles, the Irish bishops, with Cullen in the vanguard, made the education question their own, and over the next thirty years they created a *de facto* denominational system and control that resulted in the authority of the British state in Irish educational matters becoming increasingly marginal. In less than two years after the Synod of Thurles, on the death of Archbishop Murray, Cullen was translated by Pius IX on 3 May 1852 from Armagh to Dublin, the wealthiest and most important see in the Irish church.

This emergence of Cullen as the leader of the Irish church, however, was bitterly resented by MacHale, who during the decade of the 1850s proceeded to initiate another series of confrontations with Cullen. The immediate occasion for their quarrel was Cullen's attempt to prevent the Catholic Defence Association, which had been founded in August 1851 to protect the civil liberties of Catholics in Britain and Ireland, from being turned into a political vehicle by MacHale and his supporters. Their quarrel was soon extended to who should control the recently launched Catholic University and to the appropriate political role for priests in the recently founded Tenant Right League. MacHale and his supporters carried their quarrels with Cullen to Rome. They protested Cullen's interference not only in the making of episcopal appointments but in the governance of both the national seminary at Maynooth and the Irish College in Paris. There was hardly an issue or an institution in the Irish church that MacHale did not use to confront or contest Cullen's power and influence. Cullen eventually won this struggle for power because of his very great influence at Rome in the making of episcopal appointments. By 1860 he had reduced MacHale's once formidable power base among the bishops to three or four in a body of thirty. The price Cullen had to pay, however, for this containment, proved to be very high. During their struggle for power MacHale had systematically undermined Cullen's public image as a patriot bishop in Ireland, while at the same time considerably enhancing his own as a staunch defender of the rights and privileges of the Irish church against English intrigue. By 1858, in fact, MacHale had succeeded in reducing Cullen in the public mind, as he had Murray in the 1840s, to a 'castle bishop'. By 1858, moreover, the struggle had finally so unnerved Cullen that he believed he was losing the confidence of Rome, and he suffered another and more severe physical and mental breakdown, which required a long and protracted convalescence of some seven months in Rome before he finally recovered his health and balance.

With the final containment of MacHale, Cullen became the dominant figure in the Irish church, and his achievements both in promoting Roman power and influence in that church and in the making and consolidation of a 'devotional revolution' were most impressive. When Pius

IX called on the Catholics of the world in early 1860, for example, to help him defend his temporal power against the encroachments of France and Sardinia, Cullen not only launched a national collection, which realized the enormous sum of £80,000, but recruited and equipped an Irish brigade of more than 1000 men for the pope's service. The initial collection was soon institutionalized by Cullen into an annual 'Peter's Pence' contribution, which over the next half century in Ireland amounted to about £10,000 a year. Cullen was finally rewarded for his steadfast and loyal support of the Holy See by being created a cardinal on 22 June 1866 by Pius IX. He was also nominated to serve on the Roman Congregations of the Index, Sacred Rites, Discipline of Regulars, and most importantly of all, *propaganda*. He was now by right, rather than favour, included in all Irish business done at Rome. When the First Vatican Council was convened in late 1869, therefore, Cullen was prepared to play a very prominent role. He proved to be not only a strong advocate of the definition of papal infallibility but he presented the basic formulation of the dogma that was eventually accepted by the fathers of the council and promulgated by Pius IX as an article of faith.

Achievement and significance Cullen's role in the making and consolidation of the devotional revolution in Ireland between 1850 and 1880, in which the Irish people, as a people, became the pious and practising Catholics they have remained almost down to the present day, was certainly the achievement on which his true greatness rests. Mass attendance on Sundays improved from perhaps about 40 per cent in the 1840s to some 90 per cent by the 1880s. Over that same period the clerical population, priests, nuns, brothers, and seminarians, doubled, and the ratio of clerics to people improved from about 1 in 1400 to 1 in 400. By 1880, moreover, virtually all of the 1000 Irish parishes had been visited and evangelized by missionaries of the regular orders more than once, and some even three or four times, and confraternities and sodalities of both men and women became a permanent part of the religious landscape. Convents of nuns and teaching brothers had also been established in all of the cities and nearly every town in Ireland, and no Irish ecclesiastic was more forward in encouraging and promoting this profound religious transformation in the lives of the Irish people than Paul, Cardinal Cullen. This great burst of Tridentine reform was canonically consolidated at the Second National Synod of Maynooth, over which Cullen again presided as the pope's apostolic delegate, in September 1875.

Cullen's very significant achievements as an ultramontane and a pastoral reformer in the last two decades of his life, however, were much clouded by his alleged antipathy to Irish political and national aspirations. His uncompromising denunciations during the 1860s of the revolutionary Irish Republican (Fenian) Brotherhood, and the securing of its condemnation by the pope in January 1870, had resulted not only in his being vilified in turn by the

Fenian press in Ireland and America but in the crystallization of that image created by MacHale and his supporters during the 1850s of his being a castle bishop. By late 1864 the Fenian menace proved to be so formidable that Cullen and the great majority of the Irish bishops sanctioned the launching of the National Association as a constitutional alternative. The new association, which advocated the disestablishment of the protestant church in Ireland, land reform, and denominational education, and which soon came to be known as Cullen's Association, never prospered politically. In 1868 the association was eclipsed when W. E. Gladstone and his Liberal Party incorporated its three-point programme in a crusade to do justice to Ireland. Cullen was most prominent among the Irish bishops in promoting this Gladstonian Irish–Liberal alliance in the general election of 1868, which resulted in the disestablishment of the protestant church in 1869 and the passing of a Land Act in 1870. The Irish–Liberal alliance, and the bishops' and Cullen's support of it, however, foundered on Gladstone's Irish University Bill in early 1873, when Cullen persuaded a majority of the Irish Liberal members of parliament to vote against it, thereby defeating the bill and obliging Gladstone to resign.

The emergence, meanwhile, of the home-rule movement, led by Isaac Butt, in 1870, resulted in Cullen's political image becoming even more tarnished. Cullen did not approve of the home-rule movement and its leader because he thought the movement was at once too protestant and too Fenian, and that its leader was lacking in moral probity. Cullen refused, therefore, to endorse either the movement or its leader as long as he lived. For this political stand Cullen was then denounced as a 'West Briton' as well as a castle bishop. What Cullen's attitude to the home-rule movement makes clear, however, is that his politics were essentially 'Catholic' rather than 'nationalist', and that for him Catholic politics were really a function of the education question. It was obvious to Cullen, after the defeat of Gladstone in the general election of 1874, and the return of Disraeli with a Conservative majority of fifty over the Liberals and home-rulers combined, that the Home Rule Party in the House of Commons, given the parliamentary equation, could do nothing for Irish education, not to mention home rule. He also understood that if anything tangible were to be achieved, it would have to be negotiated with the existing Conservative government. From Cullen's point of view, then, the Home Rule Party was not only irrelevant as far as Catholic politics were concerned, but positively utopian in regard to nationalist politics. Cullen, therefore, attempted to open negotiations with the Conservative government for a university bill in 1876, which eventually resulted in the passing of an Intermediate Education Act in 1878 and the promise of a university bill in 1879. By that time, however, Cullen was dead, having unexpectedly passed away in his seventy-sixth year on 24 October 1878 at 59 Eccles Street, Dublin. His funeral was celebrated with great ceremony as befitted a prince of the church and Ireland's first cardinal. He was interred on 29 October in the crypt below the high altar in the church of the Holy Cross at Clonliffe College, which he had founded in 1859 to serve as both his diocesan seminary and his memorial.

Any real understanding of Cullen and his achievements must involve the appreciation that he was politically and psychologically a Roman. He was a great ultramontane because he was first and foremost a Roman. His allegiance to Rome, in the person of the pope and his authority, spiritual and temporal, was uncompromising. How Rome stood, or was likely to stand, on any question was always Cullen's point of departure and his measure for taking action, and his vast correspondence with Rome remains both a monument and a witness to that commitment. He was a formidable ecclesiastical politician because he both understood and played the great game of courtier politics at Rome with consummate skill. His loyalty and commitment to Rome, however, was more than political, it was deeply personal. In the thirty years he lived and worked in Rome, it became the focus of his faith and the love of his life. He gloried in Rome's majesty, mystery, and power, and adored its liturgy, music, and architecture. He became, in fact, so psychologically bound up with Rome that he literally became ill whenever he thought he had lost or might lose the confidence accorded him there. On his return to Ireland in 1850, he attempted to replicate the Roman way at every opportunity until the day he died. Indeed, the church of the Holy Cross at Clonliffe, where he is buried, may well serve as the final comment on Cullen's life and work, for he basically modelled that church, though on a somewhat larger scale, on St Agatha of the Goths in Rome.

EMMET LARKIN

Sources E. Larkin, *The making of the Roman Catholic church in Ireland, 1850–1860* (1980) · E. Larkin, *The consolidation of the Roman Catholic church in Ireland, 1860–1870* (1987) · E. Larkin, *The Roman Catholic church and the home rule movement in Ireland, 1870–1874* (1990) · E. Larkin, *The Roman Catholic church and the emergence of the modern Irish political system, 1874–1878* (1996) · P. MacSuibhne, *Paul Cullen and his contemporaries*, 5 vols. (1961–77) · D. A. Kerr, *Peel, priests, and politics: Sir Robert Peel's administration and the Roman Catholic church in Ireland, 1841–1846* (1982) · R. Sherry, *Holy Cross College, Clonliffe, Dublin* [1962] · E. D. Steele, 'Cardinal Cullen and Irish nationality', *Irish Historical Studies*, 19 (1974–5), 239–60 · E. R. Norman, *The Catholic church and Ireland in the age of rebellion, 1859–1873* (1965) · P. J. Corish, 'Cardinal Cullen and the National Association of Ireland', *Reportorium Novum*, 3/1 (1962), 13–61 · P. J. Corish, *Political problems, 1860–1878* (1967), vol. 5/3 of *A history of Irish Catholicism* · J. J. Whyte, *Political problems, 1850–1860* (1967), vol. 5/2 of *A history of Irish Catholicism* · D. Bowen, *Paul Cardinal Cullen and the shaping of modern Irish Catholicism* (1983) · *Freeman's Journal* [Dublin] (25 Oct 1878) · *Freeman's Journal* [Dublin] (30 Oct 1878) · Dublin Diocesan Archives, Cullen MSS

Archives Dublin Diocesan Archives, corresp. and papers · Irish College, Rome · NRA, corresp. and papers as archbishop of Armagh · NRA, papers as rector of Irish College, Rome | Glos. RO, letters to first Earl St Aldwyn · Irish College, Rome, Kirby MSS · NL Ire., corresp. with Lord Emly · NL Ire., letters to Myles O'Reilly [copies] · Sacred Congregation for the Evangelization of the People, Rome, Irish corresp.

Likenesses photograph, *c.*1850, priv. coll. · oils, *c.*1866, St Patrick's Training College, Drumcondra, Dublin · W. F. Doyle, oils, 1867, Holy Cross College, Clonliffe, Dublin · mezzotint, *c.*1870, repro. in *Lives of the cardinals* [n. d.] · T. Farrell, statue, *c.*1880, Pro-Cathedral, Dublin · T. Farrell, statue, 1881, portico, Holy Cross Church, Clonliffe, Dublin · Alessandri Brothers, photograph, NPG

[*see illus.*] · wood-engraving (after photograph by London Stereoscopic Co.), NPG; repro. in *ILN* (2 Nov 1878)

Cullen, Robert, Lord Cullen (1742–1810), judge and essayist, was born on 22 September 1742 and baptized in the parish of Hamilton, Lanarkshire, on 28 September, the eldest son of William *Cullen (1710–1790), physician, and his wife, Anna Johnstone (d. 1786). He was educated at the University of Edinburgh, where he was a member of the Belles Lettres Society, a debating society, many of whose participants were later influential in Scottish literary and political life. He was admitted advocate on 15 December 1764. He held many posts in the Faculty of Advocates, and was a curator of the Advocates' Library from 1770 to 1775. In the late 1770s he became a member of the *Mirror Club, and contributed six essays to *The Mirror* (1779–80) and *The Lounger* (1785–6), including one on the poems of Ossian championing the poet as a man composing from his observation of nature rather than from art, and another on Shakespeare's *Hamlet*, often attributed to Henry Mackenzie. On 8 February 1783 he moved at the Faculty of Advocates that if the Society of Antiquaries received a royal charter, the Advocates' Library and the Public Register Office should remain the approved repositories for manuscripts connected with the law and antiquities of Scotland, and not the antiquaries' proposed museum; his argument was successful both among his colleagues and with the authorities.

Unlike Henry Mackenzie and the majority of contributors to *The Mirror* and *The Lounger*, Cullen was not a close political ally of Henry Dundas and was a devoted supporter of political reform. Henry Cockburn thought Cullen's best political achievement was a bill for the reform of Scottish representation in parliament in 1785, one of several unsuccessful measures in the period that sought to stop the practice by which qualifying landholdings were split among political connections in order to multiply votes. 'His best professional achievement' (Cockburn, *Memorials*, 144) was thought to be his written argument on behalf of Basil William Douglas, Lord Daer, eldest son of Dunbar Douglas, fourth earl of Selkirk, in support of the right of the eldest sons of Scottish peers to sit for Scottish constituencies in the House of Commons. Cockburn's praise for Cullen is thrown into relief by the rejection of Daer's case by the court of session in 1792 and by the House of Lords in 1793.

Cockburn described Cullen as 'a gentlemanlike person in his manner, and learned in his profession, in which however he was too indolent and irregular to attain steady practice' (Cockburn, *Memorials*, 144). His genial nature—George Hay Drummond, in his poem *Town Eclogue* of 1804, described him as 'courteous C[ullen]' (p. 20)—enabled him to establish good relations with his opponents. Cockburn recounted how Cullen and George Fergusson, Lord Hermand, of 'opposite politics and no friends' (Cockburn, *Journal*, 1.267), were 'soldered' by 'good cheer' over supper at Inveraray. According to Dugald Stewart, Cullen was 'the most perfect of all mimics' (Cockburn, *Memorials*, 144) whose impersonations captured the very thoughts and words of his subjects, and were carried out in such good humour that they provoked little or no hostility.

On 18 November 1796 Cullen took his seat as a judge of the court of session, taking the title Lord Cullen, and on 29 June 1799 he succeeded Lord Swinton as a lord of justiciary. Cockburn noted that he and Sir William Macleod Bannatyne, Lord Bannatyne, were the only two lords of session who were not appointees of Henry Dundas, but their political independence was that of 'two shades of immaterial exception' (Cockburn, *Memorials*, 146). He retained his interest in literature, and declared his intention of completing a biography of his father, but this never appeared. According to Hugh Paton's commentaries on John Kay's *Original Portraits*, late in life he married a servant girl named Russel, but they had no children. Cullen died in Edinburgh on 28 November 1810. Paton wrote that Cullen's widow married a landowner from the West Indies, where she died in 1818.

T. F. HENDERSON, *rev.* MATTHEW KILBURN

Sources *Literature and literati: the literary correspondence and notebooks of Henry Mackenzie*, ed. H. W. Drescher, 1: *Letters* (1989) • A. Stewart, ed., *The minute book of the Faculty of Advocates*, 3: 1751–1783, Stair Society, 46 (1999) • *Memorials of his time, by Henry Cockburn* (1856) • H. Cockburn, *Journal of Henry Cockburn, being a continuation of the memorials of his time*, 2 vols. (1864) • J. Dwyer, *Virtuous discourse: sensibility and community in late eighteenth-century Scotland* (1987) • J. Kay, *A series of original portraits and caricature etchings … with biographical sketches and illustrative anecdotes*, ed. [H. Paton and others], new edn [3rd edn], 2 vols. in 4 (1877) • Anderson, *Scot. nat.* • M. Fry, *The Dundas despotism* (1992) • G. Brunton and D. Haig, *An historical account of the senators of the college of justice, from its institution in MDXXXII* (1832) • A. Doig and others, eds., *William Cullen and the eighteenth century medical world* (1993) • bap. reg. Scot.
Archives NL Scot., corresp. with H. Mackenzie
Likenesses J. Kay, engraving, NPG; repro. in Kay, *Original portraits*

Cullen, William (1710–1790), chemist and physician, was born in Hamilton, Lanarkshire, near Glasgow, on 15 April 1710, the second son of William Cullen and his wife, Elizabeth, the daughter of Mr Robertson of Whistleberry. There were seven sons and daughters from the marriage, and after his father's death Cullen's mother had two further children from her second marriage, to a Mr Nasmyth. Cullen's father was an attorney and agent for the duke of Hamilton, and the proprietor of a small estate in Bothwell. William studied at the local grammar school, under Mr Findlater, and then proceeded in 1726 to the University of Glasgow, where his arts subjects included mathematics, under Robert Simson, in 1727.

Establishing a career It is not known why Cullen decided on a career in medicine, but he was briefly apprenticed to John Paisley, a Glasgow surgeon apothecary with an excellent reputation as a teacher. Having moved to London in 1729 to obtain greater practical experience, Cullen quickly obtained the post as surgeon on a ship (captained by a relative) bound for the West Indies. He remained in Porto-Bello for six months, acquiring an interest in medical geography and the role of climate in the causation of disease. Subsequently he spent some months attached to the apothecary's shop of a Mr William [?] Murray in Henrietta Street, London.

William Cullen (1710–1790), by William Cochrane, *c.*1768

Cullen had returned to Scotland by early 1732 to practise medicine and surgery in Shotts, near Hamilton, and to busy himself in the settlement and education of his siblings, his father and elder brother having died. A small legacy gave him the independence to continue his education. He studied literature and philosophy for several months with a dissenting minister in Northumberland, and then spent two winter sessions at the University of Edinburgh (1734–6), where he was a founder member of what became the Royal Medical Society, a student organization that fostered debate and self-improvement. On leaving Edinburgh he established a practice in Hamilton; here the duke of Hamilton quickly became both patient and patron, and Cullen gained the confidence of most of the grand families of the area. He served as a magistrate for two years, and in 1737 acquired as a pupil William *Hunter (1718–1783). Hunter stayed for three years before continuing his studies in London and Paris. Although he had originally intended to return to Hamilton as Cullen's surgical partner, his career became based in London; however, he once entertained the idea that he and Cullen (then in Edinburgh) would together make Glasgow a major medical rival to the Scottish capital.

Cullen disliked the surgical aspects of what was in essence a general practice, and in order to practise solely as a physician he acquired his MD from the University of Glasgow in 1740. In the following year he married Anna Johnstone (*d.* 1786), whose father was the minister in Kilbarchan. She was a highly intelligent, much admired woman who was happy to open their houses in Glasgow and Edinburgh to Cullen's many pupils and friends. They had seven sons, one of whom was Robert *Cullen (1742–

1810), and four daughters. Cullen's practice in Hamilton flourished, and the duke promised him a laboratory and the superintendence of his botanical garden. However, the declining health and premature death of Cullen's patron scotched those expectations, and in 1744 Cullen was induced to move to Glasgow, where the prospects of medical practice were greater and where he could try his hand at teaching.

Becoming a permanent teacher Although Glasgow University had had professors in several medical subjects since early in the eighteenth century, there was nothing which could be called a medical school there. In winter 1746 Cullen offered lectures on the theory and practice of physic; the following year he successfully added materia medica and botany to his repertory, and he and John Carrick were supplied with apparatus so that they might begin a course in chemistry. Carrick almost immediately fell ill, so Cullen was forced to teach the course by himself. During Cullen's Glasgow period, chemistry was his principal scientific preoccupation, his course being taken by many arts students as well as those pursuing medicine. Among his pupils was Joseph Black, who became a friend and shared many of his research interests. Cullen always preferred to lecture in English, although some of his early teaching in botany was in Latin and he corresponded easily in the language. In his botanical lectures he expounded the sexual system of plants that Linnaeus had only recently first elaborated.

Although he continued to teach chemistry, in 1751 Cullen became professor of medicine in Glasgow, only a few days before his lifelong friend Adam Smith was installed in the chair of logic. When Smith transferred shortly afterwards to the chair of moral philosophy, Cullen supported the unsuccessful candidacy of David Hume for Smith's old chair. But Cullen's success as a teacher in Glasgow was not matched with a lucrative private practice, nor did the medical school prosper in comparison to its rival in Edinburgh. For several years influential friends, among them Henry Home (Lord Kames), had urged Cullen to move to Edinburgh. He also secured the patronage of the third duke of Argyll, a major power broker in Edinburgh University politics. Cullen was finally invited by Edinburgh's town council in 1755 to share the chair in chemistry with Andrew Plummer, who had had a stroke and was unable to give his lectures. The appointment raised some controversy, not least because Black had already been asked by Plummer's relatives to do his teaching. In addition Black was more attractive to the Edinburgh medical community, since he had no interest in becoming a rival in private practice. Black deferred to his former teacher, assuring him that it would be impossible for Cullen's course not to be better than Plummer's had been, even though the latter refused to let Cullen use his apparatus. Plummer died in 1756 and Cullen became sole occupant of the chair. Black succeeded Cullen in the chemistry lectureship in Glasgow.

Cullen was always a natural and successful teacher, attendance at his chemistry courses increasing from seventeen students in his first year to fifty-nine the following year, afterwards rising to 145. Within two years of moving to Edinburgh he was also giving clinical lectures at the Edinburgh Royal Infirmary; only John Rutherford, professor of the practice of physic, had previously availed himself of the invitation of the infirmary's managers. Cullen's move induced Robert Whytt and Alexander Monro also to offer clinical lectures there, so beginning a golden age of clinical instruction in the infirmary. In the winter session of 1760–61, following the death of Charles Alston, professor of materia medica, Cullen gave a course of lectures on that subject, at the request of the students. He had already lectured on materia medica in Glasgow. Although Cullen never repeated the course, copies of lecture notes began to circulate, one set of which became the basis of an unauthorized published edition in 1772. Cullen initially sought an injunction to prevent their sale; however, it emerged that a large number of copies of the volume had already been sold, and the physician who supplied the transcript was not financially involved. Consequently, Cullen agreed to a reissue of the lectures, with a supplement correcting some errors and omissions, and in return for a share of the profits. At the end of his life Cullen rewrote the volume, having never been satisfied with the earlier compromise.

Cullen's clinical lectures at the Edinburgh Royal Infirmary were immensely popular; in addition, his private practice was flourishing, so many students favoured him to succeed Rutherford in his chair in the practice of physic. Rutherford resigned in 1766, but his known preference as successor was John Gregory, then professor of medicine in Aberdeen. The appointment of Gregory deeply disappointed Cullen, to the extent that he initially declined to apply for the chair in the theory of medicine that became vacant later that year on the death of Robert Whytt. By accepting the chair he vacated his own in chemistry, to which Joseph Black was appointed; to their credit, Gregory and Cullen agreed to the petitions of both faculty and students and alternated lectures in the theory and in the practice of medicine. Gregory's death in 1773 left Cullen in sole command of the more prestigious chair in the practice of medicine, and he was without doubt for the rest of his life the principal ornament of the increasingly successful medical school in Edinburgh. He continued his lecturing, clinical teaching, and private practice until late 1789, when ill health and advanced years at last forced him to resign his chair, only shortly before his death. In 1778 Cullen acquired his own property at Ormiston Hill, in the parish of Kirknewton, and he spent as much time as possible there during his last years.

The enquiring mind Cullen's success as a teacher was in part due to the freshness he brought to the many subjects he taught. He was a figure integral to the Scottish Enlightenment, committed to the pursuit of science both for its own sake and for the practical consequences that were assumed to flow from it. He came from the improving, landowning stock of southern Scotland, and he never forgot his roots. His chemistry has been properly described as philosophical in its aims, concerned as it was with the classification of substances into different groups (salts, oils, waters, earths, and metals); with the nature and effects of heat and cold on chemical and physical change; with acidity and alkalinity; and with the natural philosophical principles underlying the material world. He was devoted to experimenting and demonstrating experiments to his students.

At the same time Cullen was alive to the economic potential of natural knowledge. He and his most gifted chemistry student, Black, were ever searching for chemical projects with practical potential. His friendship with Lord Kames was cemented by Cullen's interest in agricultural chemistry and botany, in fertilizers, brewing, sugar production, mining, and other 'arts'. He used a family farm as an arena for putting into practice the fruits of his scientific investigations. In addition, he searched systematically for a cheap manufacturing process to supply bleach for the Scottish linen industry. Kames tried unsuccessfully to convince the (Scottish) board of trustees for manufacturers to provide material support for Cullen's researches.

Cullen also brought the same enquiring spirit to materia medica and its close ally, medical botany. He used existing remedies—tartar emetic, James's powders, hyoscyamus (black henbane), cicuta (hemlock)—with care, noting their physiological effects and employing them in ways that rationally related to his theories of the animal oeconomy (physiology) and his physiological notions of disease.

Like many eighteenth-century medical teachers, Cullen was fascinated by the classification of disease (nosology), and his own published works in the field (for which, see below) exerted a major international influence on both medical theory and medical practice of his era and slightly beyond. Cullen constructed his nosological system as a pedagogical device, to assist in his clinical teaching. It was typical of eighteenth-century nosologies in elevating into disease categories what were later called signs and symptoms, such as pain, fever, or haemoptysis (spitting up blood). Cullen also grappled with the difficulties of relating general, holistic manifestations of disease with the local changes or lesions that could be discovered on examining the patient, or conducting a post-mortem in fatal cases. His compromise was to lump local diseases together as one of his four nosological classes, the other three disease classes being the fevers, wasting diseases (cachexias), and the neuroses. He further subdivided these classes into nineteen orders and 132 genera. His system in essence recognized only two grand divisions of disease, those that were local and those that were general.

Cullen devoted much time to the study of the fevers, 'fever' itself being then regarded as a specific but variable disease of the whole body rather than simply as one symptom of other diseases. The major epidemic diseases such as smallpox were included as fevers, but Cullen classified the various fevers according to the sequence and intensity of differing bedside phenomena associated with them, among them pulse rate, headache, chills, or sweats, and whether the symptoms were continuous or intermittent.

He implicated cold in the production of many fevers, only some of which he held to be contagious.

Cullen introduced the term 'neurosis' into medicine, the act for which he is most commonly remembered historically. Although the word has become assimilated into psychiatry (and general culture), for Cullen, a neurosis was any disorder of sense or motion in which there was no fever or local disease. It incorporated eighteenth-century categories of insanity (melancholy, mania, dementia), but also convulsions, apoplexy (stroke), asthma, colic, diarrhoea, diabetes, rabies, and many other disorders. The neuroses were obviously of major concern to him, since he was long convinced that the nervous system played a fundamental role in producing disease and its symptoms. As he famously remarked, 'In a certain view, almost the whole of the diseases of the human body might be called NERVOUS' (W. Cullen, *Works*, ed. J. Thomson, 2 vols., 1828, 2.330).

Cullen was thus at the forefront of a mid-eighteenth-century fascination with the nervous system, in contrast to Hermann Boerhaave's earlier emphasis on the cardiovascular system, or John Hunter's contemporary one on the blood. Boerhaave's system had been taught to him when he had studied at Edinburgh, but he was then already a mature student with several years of medical practice behind him, and maintained his own ideas. Cullen was extraordinarily well read, possessed a fine personal library, and was acutely conscious of the relationship between his own ideas and approaches and those of his predecessors and contemporaries. He invariably began his courses with a historical lecture, so he was well aware that the German physician Friedrich Hoffmann had also placed the nervous system at the centre of his own system of medicine. Cullen developed his own ideas of neuropathology in his Glasgow days, and his teaching in Edinburgh was especially important in spreading the gospel of the nerves throughout the English-speaking world and, through translations of his books, to Europe.

Cullen's neuropathology informed two important aspects of his medical thinking. It was thoroughly integrated into his physiological approach to disease, whereby the carefully observed sequence of signs and symptoms was rendered intelligible. This sequence in turn dictated the specific therapeutic measures he advocated. His therapeutic approach was equally physiological in its goal of combating the patient's symptoms as they appeared. He was admirably realistic about the limits of the therapies available to him and absorbed from his friend David Hume some of the latter's scepticism about the limits of human knowledge. For Cullen, as for Hume, the constant conjunction of events was what human beings experienced as cause. His lectures were littered with caveats such as 'I am inclined to think', or 'I believe'.

Second, Cullen's doctrine of the nervous system was central to his more general beliefs about culture, civilization, improvement, and sensibility. He accepted Enlightenment ideas of progress and of how the 'nerves' of individuals reflected their race, class, gender, or time of life. Thus, Europeans were more sensitive than inhabitants of 'rude' nations, where the differences between men and women were also minimized. He invoked both social and environmental causes to explain such differences—arguing, for instance, that hysteria was more common in southern Europe than in the northern countries, or more common in England than Scotland, primarily because of the colder climate's impact on the nerves of women.

Cullen's beliefs on these matters mirrored more general cultural notions, but he was less doctrinaire than many of his contemporaries. At the same time he repeatedly emphasized the value of system within medicine and science. System gave order and coherence to thinking and the organization of facts and observations, and Cullen held that the history of medicine revealed a series of tensions between empiricists and dogmatists, with the latter being the source of medical progress. Being a dogmatist, or systematist, was not the same as being dogmatic, which attitude he abhorred. This position gave his own system of medicine both a coherence and an intensely personal gloss, attributes that contributed to his outstanding success as a teacher.

A reluctant author Cullen wrote a good deal, but his career as a prolific author began late and was in many ways forced upon him. His first publication, a chemical article on cold and evaporation, did not appear until 1756, when he was forty-six, and his first book, a minor catalogue of materia medica, did not come out until five years later. He did not publish the books for which he is remembered until after the age at which most people retire. Cullen's reluctance to commit himself to print has been attributed to his earning much of his income in both Glasgow and Edinburgh from student fees. He thus lived in a culture where professors were reluctant to publish their lectures lest students would simply buy their books rather than enrol in their courses.

This economic structure within the Scottish universities undoubtedly contributed to Cullen's diffidence, but the simple pressure of time was probably also to blame. There is evidence that he was planning treatises on both agriculture and chemistry in his Glasgow days, and edited translations of two authors that he admired, Gerard van Swieten and Thomas Sydenham, were also mentioned in letters. That none of these works actually appeared suggests that Cullen was shy about committing his ideas to public scrutiny, although teaching and medical practice were also more immediately rewarding financially.

Cullen had been teaching in Edinburgh for more than a decade before he offered to the world at large his nosology (in Latin), *Synopsis nosologiae methodicae* (1769), the organizing principles of his clinical teaching, without its practical details. It was sufficiently successful to go through four editions during his lifetime, the last one (1784) incorporating his final thoughts on the subject. English translations did not appear until after his death.

Cullen's lectures on the theoretical basis of medicine, called the institutes, formed the basis of the 1772 volume *Institutes of Medicine, Part 1, Physiology*. By then, the pirated edition of his lectures on materia medica having just been published, Cullen would have been aware of how many manuscript copies of all of his lectures were circulating. The fact that he called the volume part 1 suggests that he intended to publish companion volumes on the other parts of the institutes, pathology and therapeutics, but these never appeared. Gregory's death in the following year meant that he was then in sole possession of the chair of the practice of medicine, to which his teaching was henceforth exclusively devoted.

This led to the serial publication, over seven years, of the four volumes of Cullen's *magnum opus*, *First Lines of the Practice of Physic* (1777–84). A fifth volume on diseases of women and children was planned but never appeared. The volumes were arranged nosologically, but they discussed in detail the symptoms and treatments of the diseases that he classified. They contained Cullen's mature thoughts on the essence of medical practice, and they were instantly accorded classic status, going through numerous editions and translations into all the major European languages, as well as adaptations by authors anxious to relate their disease constructs and treatments to differing national contexts. The volumes display Cullen at his clinical best, alert to the complexities of disease, concerned to do his best for his patients, and aware of the strengths and weaknesses of what he had to offer. *First Lines* should be seen as both a culmination and the swansong of Enlightenment medicine. It consolidated its systematic, nosological approach based primarily on symptoms, rather than the pathological changes produced by disease. The latter was the basis of the medicine advocated in France and elsewhere from the early nineteenth century. This meant that Cullen's influence began to wane shortly after his death. By the time John Thomson edited Cullen's *Works* in two volumes (1828), it was partly an act of historical piety. That much of Thomson's edition was reconstructed from manuscripts further testifies to the fact that Cullen always considered teaching as the primary vehicle for communicating his ideas.

The established physician Cullen moved from Glasgow to Edinburgh in 1755 partly because the prospects of medical practice were better in the capital. He was never short of private practice in Edinburgh, despite the fact that the established medical community initially looked upon him as an outsider who was sceptical of Boerhaave's system, even though he had spent two years studying in Edinburgh. In addition to face-to-face encounters with patients, Cullen acquired an extensive practice based on postal consultations, especially after the deaths of Robert Whytt and John Gregory left him as the premier physician in Scotland. Cullen's annual postal consultations doubled (from about fifteen to thirty-five) after 1766, and increased dramatically after 1773 to between 150 and 200 per year. These letters came from many parts of the world, including France, Belgium, Italy, Prussia, the United States, and Madeira. Most originated closer by, from many parts of the British Isles, and from aristocrats as well as untitled men and women. One valetudinarian wrote a twenty-eight-page review of his case. Cullen took these consultations seriously (the standard fee was a guinea each), dictating a careful reply to an amanuensis. He advised on lifestyle, constitution, and diet, as well as ordering interventions such as bloodletting or cupping and the usual gamut of medicines. After 1780 copies of Cullen's replies were duplicated on the famous copying machine patented by James Watt.

In addition to his private and epistolary practice, Cullen regularly saw patients in the teaching wards of the Edinburgh Royal Infirmary. Student case notes survive for a number of patients under his ultimate care. Patients were selected for admission to the wards because their diseases were deemed to have important pedagogical value, so they cannot be easily compared to his middle- and upper-class patients and correspondents. Unsurprisingly, Cullen's hospital patients were more likely to be treated more formulaically according to the diagnosis they carried, in contrast to the highly individualized range of advice offered to his private patients. Phlebotomies were rather more vigorous within hospital than outside of it, but in both sets of patients Cullen showed himself to be a caring physician, although one practising entirely within the conventions of his time.

Father figure and friend Cullen was a major figure in the Edinburgh medical school virtually from his arrival there as a teacher, and, with Alexander Monro secundus, a central figure for the last two decades of his life, at a time when the medical school was probably the leading one in the world. His teaching and publications played an important role, but he had other personal qualities that contributed to the affection felt for him among Edinburgh students. His extensive correspondence, much of it still unpublished, shows how he followed the careers of many of his protégés, a number of whom gained positions of influence within the late Enlightenment medical world.

Among his American students, John Morgan, William Shippen jun., and Benjamin Rush took the Edinburgh ethos across the Atlantic and established the medical school at the University of Pennsylvania, in Philadelphia. William Hunter, from Cullen's early days, remained loyal, and pupils from the Edinburgh period spread out across the British Isles and beyond. These include John Haygarth in Chester and Bath, William Withering in Birmingham and the midlands, William Falconer in Bath, James Carmichael Smyth, John Coakley Lettsom, Robert Willan, and Charles Blagden in London, and Thomas Percival in Manchester. At a time when Scottish and Edinburgh-trained medical men dominated the medical services of the various agencies of the British empire, naval men such as Thomas Trotter and Gilbert Blane remained faithful to their principal medical teacher. Many of his pupils had particular reason to be grateful to Cullen, since he was also the usual port of call if they fell ill during their studies in Edinburgh. His home in the Cowgate, Mint Court, South Gray's Close, in a fashionable part of Edinburgh, was familiar to many of his students.

Cullen was not always lucky with his students. One of his favourites, John Brown, whom at one time he had

wished to see in his own chair of the practice of medicine at Edinburgh, took parts of Cullen's neuropathological teaching and developed it into an entire rival system. Brown believed that all diseases were caused by either over- or under-stimulation of the nerves—that is, they were either asthenic or sthenic, and were to be treated by either depletion or stimulation. His ideas (and personality) earned him the enmity of the Edinburgh medical faculty (including Cullen), with the result that he was forced to take his medical doctorate at St Andrews, and eventually set himself up in London. Although Brown's system was sometimes seen as a logical consequence of Cullen's own emphasis on the primacy of the nervous system in disease, it lacked the subtlety of Cullen's teachings. Brunonianism (as it was called) exerted a considerable influence in Europe, but Brown's death in 1788 meant that his possible succession to Cullen's chair was never an issue.

Cullen also moved with easy familiarity among the literati of Enlightenment Edinburgh. Like Cullen, Adam Smith returned to Edinburgh, and the two remained close friends, exchanging an interesting correspondence on the consequences of a *laissez-faire* market place for medical care. Cullen tended Dugald Stewart in an illness when the latter was a teenager and saw David Hume on the philosopher's deathbed. Francis Hutcheson's son was one of his pupils. When Samuel Johnson visited Edinburgh in 1773, Cullen and his eldest son were among five guests invited to dine with Johnson and Boswell.

Cullen was a sociable man, a member of several of the debating and dining clubs that were central to the exchange of ideas and conviviality in Edinburgh. Among these was the Philosophical Society, which in 1783 became the Royal Society of Edinburgh. He was elected to the Royal Society of London in 1777, although he never went south to sign the admission register, and he was active in the Royal College of Physicians of Edinburgh, of which he became a fellow in 1756. He served as president from 1773 to 1775, during which time he was active in revising the *Edinburgh Pharmacopoeia*. John Pringle (then president of the Royal Society of London) also helped in the new edition. Cullen and Pringle carried on a warm correspondence, even if the latter did not share Cullen's reliance on nosology. Cullen worked to liberalize the entrance criteria of the college, so that those with backgrounds in midwifery or practice under an apothecary might be eligible.

The tenor of Cullen's life carried on regularly for years. His eldest son went into the law, but two of his younger ones opted for medicine. Only Henry sought a medical career. He was appointed a physician to the Edinburgh Royal Infirmary, but William Cullen's attempts to secure him an academic post in the medical school failed, and Henry died only a few months after his father. The death of his wife, Anna, in 1786 affected Cullen deeply, although he finished his treatise on materia medica and began his lectures for the academic year 1789–90. He was unable to continue beyond November, when he tendered his resignation. It was not formally accepted, but James Gregory, professor of the institutes of medicine, was co-appointed to

Cullen's chair in the practice of medicine. Cullen died at his house in the Mint, Edinburgh, on 5 February 1790 and was buried in Kirknewton on 10 February.

Afterlife Cullen received the usual round of obituary notices and a short biography, but it was understood that Robert Cullen, the eldest son, was going to prepare a full-scale biography, based on his father's extensive collection of papers as well as on his intimate knowledge. It never appeared, and it was left to John Thomson, professor of pathology in Edinburgh, to take up the task more than a generation after Cullen's death. Twenty-seven years separated the two volumes of Thomson's massive account of Cullen's life, by which time Thomson and his son William, with whom he collaborated, were both dead, the second volume being completed by David Craigie. By then (1859), Cullen's reputation had fallen dramatically, most commentators considering him a doctor more concerned with arrangement and generalization than with discovery.

Cullen was generally condemned along with his whole century by late nineteenth- and early twentieth-century whiggish historians of science and medicine. His thought remains difficult to study since his lectures changed subtly each year, and much of the evidence of his teaching is still in manuscript form, in his own archives or in numerous student notes in scattered libraries. Seen from the present, eighteenth-century medicine is remote and archaic in ways that the medicine of the nineteenth is not, but the historical Cullen was a wise doctor and a man whose status within his own society was thoroughly earned.

W. F. BYNUM

Sources J. Thomson, W. Thomson, and D. Craigie, *An account of the life, lectures and writings of William Cullen, M.D.*, 2 vols. (1859) · A. Doig and others, eds., *William Cullen and the eighteenth century medical world: a biocentenary exhibition and symposium arranged by the Royal College of Physicians of Edinburgh* (1993) · A. L. Donovan, *Philosophical chemistry in the Scottish Enlightenment: the doctrines and discourses of William Cullen and Joseph Black* (1975) · G. B. Risse, *Hospital life in Enlightenment Scotland: care and teaching at the Royal Infirmary of Edinburgh* (1986) · L. Rosner, *Medical education in the age of improvement: Edinburgh students and apprentices, 1760–1820* (1991) · J. B. Morrell, 'The University of Edinburgh in the late eighteenth century: its scientific eminence and academic structure', *Isis*, 62 (1971), 158–71 · W. S. Craig, *History of the Royal College of Physicians of Edinburgh* (1976) · W. F. Bynam and V. Nutton, eds., *Theories of fever from antiquity to the Enlightenment* (1981) · C. Withers, 'William Cullen's agricultural lectures and writings and the development of agricultural science in eighteenth-century Scotland', *Agricultural History Review*, 37 (1989), 144–56 · *DNB* · W. F. Bynum and R. Porter, eds., *Brunonianism in Britain and Europe* (1988) · C. J. Lawrence, 'Ornate physicians and learned artisans: Edinburgh medical men, 1726–1776', *William Hunter and the eighteenth-century medical world*, ed. W. F. Bynum and R. Porter (1985), 153–76 · J. R. R. Christie, 'Historiography of chemistry in the eighteenth century: Hermann Boerhaave and William Cullen', *Ambix*, 41 (1994), 4–19 · L. Jolley, 'A note on the portraiture of William Cullen', *The Bibliotheck*, 1 (1958), 27–36 · J. V. Golinski, 'Utility and audience in eighteenth-century chemistry: case studies of William Cullen and Joseph Priestley', *British Journal for the History of Science*, 21 (1988), 1–31 · I. A. Bowman, *William Cullen (1710–90) and the primacy of the nervous system* (1975) · A. L. Donovan, 'William Cullen and the research tradition of eighteenth-century Scottish chemistry', *The origins and nature of the Scottish Enlightenment: essays*, ed. J. Donald (1982), 98–114 · IGI

Archives Bodl. Oxf., lecture notes · Exeter Cathedral, medical MSS · JRL, lecture notes · National Library of Medicine, Bethesda, Maryland, lecture notes · NL Scot., lecture notes · NL Wales, lecture notes · Northwestern University, Chicago, medical school library, lecture notes · RCP Lond., medical papers · Royal College of Physicians of Edinburgh, corresp. and papers · U. Edin. L., lectures on chemistry and pharmacy · U. Edin. L., medical and lecture notes · U. Glas. L., corresp., lectures, and notes · University of Kansas Medical Center, Laurence, Clendening History of Medicine Library and Museum, lecture notes · Wellcome L., lecture notes
Likenesses W. Cochrane, oils, c.1768, Scot. NPG [*see illus.*] · D. Allan, pencil and watercolour drawing, 1774, Scot. NPG · D. Martin, oils, 1776, Scot. NPG · J. Tassie, paste medallion, 1786, Scot. NPG · J. Kay, caricature, etching, BM, NPG · J. Russell, oils, Wellcome L.

Cullen, William (1867–1948), chemist and metallurgist, was born at Shettleston, Glasgow, on 18 May 1867, the son of William Cullen and his wife, Margaret Johnston, of Uddingston, Glasgow. He came from a family engaged in the woollen industry and was educated in Glasgow at Hutcheson's Grammar School and, from 1883, at Anderson's College. There he studied chemistry under William Dittmar and remained as his assistant (1885–90). Later he took a course in metallurgy and mining at the School of Mines in Freiburg, Germany.

In 1890 Cullen joined the Nobel Explosives Company Ltd, Glasgow, a connection which was maintained throughout his active life. For a time he worked with Kynochs, a rival explosives firm, and spent over two years as technical adviser at its Arklow factory. He returned to Nobels in 1900 and was appointed manager at the firm's Modderfontein factory, which in 1902 became the British South African Explosives Company. The factory was then the largest explosives works in the world and Cullen became its general manager in 1901 and later a director, an office he retained until 1924. Cullen was twice married: first, in 1897, to Jean Crichton Maclachlan (d. 1945), with whom he had three sons and one daughter; second, in 1946, to Agnes Campbell Macmillan, who survived him.

Technically, Cullen's work was mainly concerned with the development of smokeless powders and the design of plant for the convenient manipulation of the plastic mixtures which become the explosive. In 1915 he returned to Britain, where he made his home in London and joined the department of explosives supply of the Ministry of Munitions, where he worked with K. B. Quinan until 1919 on the design and layout of new explosives factories, needed during the First World War. Thereafter Cullen was active in consulting work, mainly connected with explosives and gold mining. He was a director of several public companies, and was involved in the work of various scientific societies.

Cullen arrived in the Transvaal during the Second South African War, and he played a modest part in the settlement of the South African provinces into the Union and empire. He liked to think of himself as a pioneer in the Rhodes tradition, and was extremely proud of his lifelong friendship with J. C. Smuts, whom he greatly admired. He knew every public personage in South Africa over many years. In the Witwatersrand mining conditions were bad and silicosis was a scourge, and he worked to promote good health conditions underground. He had a strong interest in education, and his efforts helped to bring about the foundation of the University of the Witwatersrand, from which he received the honorary degree of LLD in 1924. He was active in the newly formed scientific societies of South Africa and was president for 1905-6 of the Chemical, Metallurgical and Mining Society, and secretary of the South African Association for the Advancement of Science. He was the first chairman of the South African Red Cross Society, which he helped to found and of which his first wife became head in Britain. She was made OBE for her services. He also served in the Johannesburg mounted rifles of which he was for two years second in command, and for eight years he commanded the regiment of Imperial light horse; he reached the rank of colonel, and was at one time invited to command all the mounted troops in the Transvaal.

Cullen belonged to the Institution of Mining and Metallurgy (president, 1929-30), the Royal Institute of Chemistry, the Institution of Chemical Engineers (president, 1937-9), and the Society of Chemical Industry (president, 1941-3, and later an honorary member). He contributed papers to the publications of these societies. For some years he was honorary treasurer of the Universities Bureau of the British Empire, and a member of the advisory council on mineral resources and chairman of the consultative committee on base metals, both at the Imperial Institute. He wrote many papers and gave many addresses on empire matters. His lasting interest in education took varied forms: for many years, up to a few months before his death, he was a member of Surrey education committee and particularly concerned himself with further education. He was president of the Science Masters' Association in 1944.

For many years Cullen suffered from severe depression caused by an internal malady. When it was finally diagnosed and cured, he felt that he could at last live a normal life. He was, despite his illness, a man of buoyant disposition who could be relied upon for guidance, encouragement, and friendship. He died in the Royal Infirmary, Edinburgh, on 14 August 1948.

L. A. JORDAN, rev. K. D. WATSON

Sources *Nature*, 162 (1948), 560–61 · J. Weir, *JCS* (1949), 259–60 · *The Times* (17 Aug 1948), 6 · *The Times* (25 Aug 1948), 7 · *CGPLA Eng. & Wales* (1948)

Wealth at death £75,059 17s.: probate, 6 Nov 1948, *CGPLA Eng. & Wales*

Culley, George (*bap.* 1735, *d.* 1813), agriculturist, was baptized on 16 April 1735 at Denton, co. Durham, the youngest of the four sons of Matthew Culley, farmer. Little is known of his childhood and adolescence, but it is known that in the early 1760s George and his brother Matthew were sent to Leicestershire as pupils of Robert Bakewell (1725–1795).

In 1767, the Culley brothers took the tenancy of a farm at Fenton, near Wooler, north Northumberland, where they began to practise improved agricultural techniques. At some stage, they were joined there by their brother James. Low-lying marshy land in the Till valley was embanked and drained. A variant of the Norfolk four-course rotation was introduced, forming the basis of the sheep-and-turnip system of husbandry for which both the Glendale area and the Culleys themselves became famous. Rams of Bakewell's new Leicester breed were crossed with Teeswater ewes to create a new and successful breed, known at the time as 'the Culley breed' and subsequently as the Border Leicester. The brothers enjoyed more modest success as breeders of cattle.

Both George and Matthew Culley made several agricultural tours in Scotland and England. Their visits to distant farming regions, and their correspondence with each other while on tour and with other agricultural improvers, helped to shape their ideas about farming and its best practice in their area. Much of this correspondence is preserved in the Culley papers. The brothers received many agricultural visitors in their turn, including Arthur Young (1741–1820) and Sir John Sinclair (1754–1835).

George Culley's growing stature as an agricultural improver was assisted by shrewd business judgement and an eye for effective publicity, in both of which he outshone Matthew. The high prices he charged for letting his best tups, 50 guineas a season by the end of the 1780s, intensified interest in the stock. He became a respected agricultural author with the publication in 1786 of *Observations on Livestock*, widely known as 'Culley on livestock'. This was followed in 1794, 1800, and 1805 by the reports to the board of agriculture for Northumberland and Cumberland, co-authored with John Bailey, agent to the Chillingham estate.

As their farming enterprises prospered, so additional tenancies were taken, until by the early 1790s the Culleys were leasing no fewer than seven farms in north Northumberland at a combined annual rental exceeding £5000. Their account for 1801 indicates a clear farming profit in excess of £9000. The years after 1795 witnessed the transition from tenants to landed proprietors as various estates in the Glendale area were bought; this culminated in 1807 in the purchase from Sir Francis Blake of Fowberry Tower for £45,000. George Culley died on 7 May 1813. He was survived by his wife, Hannah, who was to receive £500 per annum according to his will; and the residue of his estates was to go to their son, Matthew.

JOHN R. WALTON

Sources D. J. Rowe, 'The Culleys, Northumberland farmers, 1767–1813', *Agricultural History Review*, 19 (1971), 156–74 · D. J. Rowe, introduction, in J. Bailey and G. Culley, *General view of the agriculture of Northumberland, Cumberland and Westmorland*, facs. of 3rd edn (1972), iii–xxii, 3–22 · S. Macdonald, 'The role of the individual in agricultural change: the example of George Culley of Fenton, Northumberland', *Change in the countryside: essays on rural England, 1500–1900*, ed. H. S. A. Fox and R. A. Butlin (1979), 5–21 · S. Macdonald, 'The role of George Culley of Fenton in the development of Northumberland agriculture', *Archaeologia Aeliana*, 5th ser., 3 (1975), 131–41 · S. Macdonald, 'The diffusion of knowledge among Northumberland farmers, 1780–1815', *Agricultural History Review*, 27 (1979), 30–39 · S. Macdonald, 'Agricultural improvement and the neglected labourer', *Agricultural History Review*, 31 (1983), 81–90 · *GM*, 1st ser., 83/1 (1813), 661 · Denton parish registers (birth), Durham RO · will, 1813, U. Durham L., archives and special collections, Durham probate records · *Matthew and George Culley: travel journals and letters, 1765–798*, ed. A. Orde (2002)

Archives Northumbd RO, corresp. and papers | U. Newcastle, letters from Robert Bakewell

Wealth at death £500 and household goods to wife; £500 p.a. to wife from rent of estate at Denton, co. Durham; £10,000 in trust to grandchildren; £200 in trust to families of William and Ralph Brown; residue of estate to son: will, 1813

Culliford, William (c.early 1640s–1720×23), revenue official, was the younger son of Robert Culliford (1617–1698), of a Dorset gentry family, and his wife, Elizabeth Lawrence. His father, a somewhat tepid royalist in the civil war, was a cousin of Lord Chancellor Clarendon, though whether this was the cause of William's first appointment, as an excise surveyor in 1666, is not known. His promotion to a more responsible post as register of seizures in the customs took place after Clarendon's fall, under the Treasury commissioners at the request of Sir Edward Pooley or Poley, an influential Suffolk royalist of the second rank whose connection with the Cullifords is unclear. Evidently marked out by his zeal in the revenue service, at the beginning of 1682 Culliford was appointed to survey the western ports. He was given this task by the customs commissioners, but the fair copies of his reports were presented to the Treasury commissioners, the senior of whom was his second cousin Lawrence Hyde, shortly to become Lord Rochester. The first report covered all the ports and their branches from Poole, round the coasts of Dorset, Devon, Cornwall, Somerset, Gloucestershire, Monmouthshire, and Glamorgan as far as Swansea; the second, compiled in 1683 but submitted in 1684, extended only as far as Cornwall. The findings of himself and his colleagues or assistants constituted a damning indictment of maladministration. Some of the staff in the various ports were merely neglectful, whether through old age, drunkenness, or sheer idleness; others were positively dishonest, conniving at evasions and infringements of the law on a shocking scale. If these reports are accepted as a true bill, there would have been no need for merchants to smuggle in the conventional sense throughout the south-west of England and south Wales, including such major trading centres as Bristol and Exeter. Numerous dismissals and 'early retirements' followed, while Culliford was rewarded with membership of the recently created Irish revenue commission, which in 1682–3 replaced the successive revenue farms and undertakings which had managed, or mismanaged, the finances of that kingdom since the Restoration. While he was in London prior to taking up this post, which carried the handsome salary of £1000 a year, he was shot in the back by a former official who had lost his job in one of the western ports and wanted a place in Ireland instead. Although the assailant was convicted of attempted murder, the wound cannot have been too serious since Culliford lived for another thirty-five years or more.

Culliford served in Ireland until 1687. While his return then may indicate disapproval of the policies of Lord Tyrconnell (James II's Catholic viceroy), it did not prevent him from accepting appointment as a customs commissioner for England and Wales in 1688. This had scarcely taken effect before the revolution, which led to his reappointment in Ireland. He failed to win a seat in the Convention Parliament of 1689, but was successful at the next election, sitting for Corfe Castle from 1690 to 1699. The sessions of 1692 and 1693 saw a series of severe attacks on him for alleged malpractices in the Irish revenue administration, especially in the leasing of lands which had changed hands once or more times during the upheavals of 1688–91. He was similarly arraigned in the Irish House of Commons. None of these charges was ever pressed to a successful conclusion, although they resulted in his temporary loss of office. After some abortive earlier applications, in 1696 Culliford took up the new post of inspector-general of exports and imports, at a salary of £500 a year, which he held until 1703, although during the years 1696–1700 he was also a contractor supplying sailcloth for the navy, while in 1701 he again became a customs commissioner. Despite renewed attacks on at least two occasions, he held this post until 1712, possibly losing it due to 'the rage of party' in Queen Anne's last years. He was briefly appointed a commissioner for Scotland under the new Hanoverian-whig regime in 1714–15, but was very soon superseded, whether on account of his age or as a southerner. In 1717 he was compensated for the cost of moving his belongings from London to Edinburgh and back.

Culliford married Elenor Brandling, daughter and coheiress of Colonel Robert Brandling and Helen, daughter of Arthur Lindley and widow of Ingram Hopton. A third share of Felton rectory came to Culliford through her, but he sold it to the husband of one of her two sisters. They had eight children baptized at St Olave's, Hart Street, London. Culliford may have remarried since his will refers to an under-age daughter, who would have been unlikely to have been a child of his wife Elenor.

When Culliford made his will on 6 April 1720 he was living in Whitehall; he had evidently already settled on his sons the Dorset properties inherited from his father and his two elder brothers, providing only for his under-age daughter. He died some time before 25 May 1723, when his will was proved. Whether or not he misused his offices for personal profit, the Cullifords did not maintain themselves as Dorset landowners, selling out to the neighbouring Bond and Pitt families. The fine house surviving at Encombe was built for the Pitts in the 1730s. William Culliford exemplifies the new type of functionary, so necessary to the emergence of Britain as what has been called a 'fiscal-military state'; his own career seems to prefigure the fictional character of Rabourdin, the administrative reformer in Balzac's *Les employés*.   G. E. AYLMER

Sources J. Redington, ed., *Calendar of Treasury papers*, 1, PRO (1868) • W. A. Shaw, ed., *Calendar of treasury books*, 1–31, PRO (1904–61) • *CSP dom.* • *JHC*, 10 (1688–93) • *The journals of the House of Commons of the kingdom of Ireland*, 2 (1753) • *The parliamentary diary of Narcissus Luttrell, 1691–1693*, ed. H. Horwitz (1972) • J. Hutchins, *The history and antiquities of the county of Dorset*, 3rd edn, ed. W. Shipp and J. W. Hodson, 1 (1861), 516–17, 714, 718 • *Dorset*, Pevsner (1972), 51, 200–01 • J. P. Ferris, 'Corfe Castle', HoP, *Commons, 1660–90*, 1.214–15 • M. W. Helms and J. P. Ferris, 'Culliford, Robert', HoP, *Commons, 1660–90* • HoP, *Commons, 1690–1715* [draft] • G. E. Aylmer, *The crown's servants: government and civil service under Charles II, 1660–1685* (2002) •

M. A. E. Green, ed., *Calendar of the proceedings of the committee for advance of money, 1642–1656*, 3 vols., PRO (1888), 986–7 [incl. details about his father, Robert, as a side-changer in the civil war] · C. H. Mayo, ed., *The minute books of the Dorset standing committee* (1902), 16 · [E. Bysshe], *The visitation of Dorset, 1677, made by Sir Edward Bysshe*, ed. G. D. Squibb, Harleian Society, 117 (1977), 16 · W. B. Bannerman, ed., *The registers of St Olave, Hart Street, London, 1563–1700*, Harleian Society, register section, 46 (1916), 79–85, 215–16 · *A history of Northumberland*, Northumberland County History Committee, 15 vols. (1893–1940), vol. 7, p. 286 · N. Williams, *Contraband cargoes: seven centuries of smuggling* (1959), 83–6

Archives PRO, reports, T 64/139, 140

Cullimore, Isaac (1791–1852), Egyptologist, was born in Ireland. He was a member of the Numismatic Society and was one of the first orientalists to make use of astronomy and astronomical inquiries to fix important dates in ancient history. Most of his papers were published in the *Proceedings of the Royal Society of Literature*, of which he was a member. They reflect his interest in the deciphering of hieroglyphics. He also published *Pharaoh and his Princes* (1845) for the Syro-Egyptian Society of London. In 1842 he began his issue of oriental cylinders or seals from the collections in the British Museum of which 174 plates had been published in parts without any descriptive text when he died at Clapham on 8 April 1852.

H. M. Stephens, *rev.* Elizabeth Baigent

Sources *GM*, 2nd ser., 38 (1852), 208 · *Numismatic Chronicle*, 15 (1852–3), 22 · Boase, *Mod. Eng. biog.* · W. H. Ward, 'Babylonian seals', *Scribner's Magazine* (Jan 1887) · W. R. Dawson and E. P. Uphill, *Who was who in Egyptology*, 3rd edn, rev. M. L. Bierbrier (1995) · Prince Ibrahim-Hilmy, *The literature of Egypt and the Sudan*, 2 vols. (1886–7)

Archives BL, corresp. with John Lee, Add. MS 47492

Charles James Cullingworth (1841–1908), by Francis Henry Hart

Cullingworth, Charles James (1841–1908), gynaecologist and obstetrician, son of Griffith Cullingworth (*d.* 1860), bookseller, and his wife, Sarah Gledhill, was born on 3 June 1841 at 23 Commercial Street, Leeds. He was educated at Wesley College in Sheffield before joining the family business, but after his father's death he entered the Leeds school of medicine, qualifying as a member of the Royal College of Surgeons in 1865, and licentiate of the Society of Apothecaries in 1866.

After eighteen months in general practice at Bawtry, near Doncaster, Cullingworth joined the Manchester Royal Infirmary in 1867 as resident physician's assistant, and later as resident medical officer. In 1869 he set up in private practice in Manchester. From 1872 to 1882 he also acted as police surgeon; he had always had an interest in legal matters and published a number of papers on medico-legal topics, including 'Methods of judicial administration in the past' (1884) and 'The criminal responsibility of the insane' (1888).

In 1873 Cullingworth was appointed honorary surgeon to St Mary's Hospital for Women and Children, Manchester, and after gaining his MD from Durham University (1881) he specialized in gynaecology. Cullingworth's work was closely linked with the Victoria University in Manchester; he strongly supported the campaign, in 1880, to gain university status for Owens College, and for the right of the Manchester medical school, from 1883, to confer its own medical degrees. He was determined to ensure a high academic standard of clinical medicine within the newly enchartered Victoria University. Cullingworth was lecturer in medical jurisprudence from 1879 but gave this up in 1885, when he was elected by his colleagues at St Mary's to the chair of obstetrics and gynaecology at Owens College. During his professorship he acted as secretary to the board of studies for the medical school, a position that allowed him to monitor the standard of medical degrees. He worked hard for the Manchester Medical Society, first as honorary librarian (1872–8) and later as honorary secretary (1879–84); he devoted much of his time to cataloguing the medical library and to establishing, in 1884, the *Medical Chronicle*, a monthly medical journal which was based in Manchester. On 15 April 1882 Cullingworth married Emily Mary, daughter of Richard Freeman, a London outfitter; they had at least one daughter.

By 1888 Cullingworth's reputation as a surgeon and medical lecturer had grown so much that he was offered the post of obstetric physician at St Thomas's Hospital, London. He found it difficult to leave Manchester but, once established at St Thomas's, his work quickly expanded and he also acted as visiting physician to the General Lying-in Hospital, York Road. After his retirement in 1904 he was made a governor of St Thomas's. Although an accomplished gynaecological surgeon he preferred the title of physician; in 1879 he had become a member of the Royal College of Physicians, and in 1887 he was elected a fellow. In 1902 he was the first physician to read the Bradshawe lecture to the college on an obstetric topic, 'Intraperitoneal haemorrhage incident to ectopic gestation'. Most of his work in London was presented to the Obstetric Society; he played an active role in the society's affairs and was its president in 1897–9.

Cullingworth was a pioneer of gynaecology. His most important work was on the causes of inflammation of the female pelvic organs—pelvic peritonitis and salpingitis, which he demonstrated was not a primary condition, but usually secondary to some gynaecological infection. He argued that such conditions should be treated surgically; although such treatment later became accepted practice his paper to the Obstetric Society in 1892, entitled 'Abdominal section in certain cases of recurrent peritonitis', provoked considerable comment and criticism from many of his colleagues. His views were fully discussed in his *Clinical Illustrations of the Diseases of the Fallopian Tubes and of Tubal Gestation* (1895), a book well known for its beautiful illustrations. His section on pelvic inflammation in the textbook *System of Gynaecology* (edited by Allbutt and Playfair, 1896) was described in *The Lancet* (23 May 1908) as 'one of the best essays on the subject ever written'. He published widely and made numerous contributions to the *Transactions of the Obstetrical Society of London* and to the *Journal of Obstetrics and Gynaecology of the British Empire*, which he had helped to found, in 1903, and which he edited for the last two years of his life.

Although Cullingworth is mainly remembered as a great surgical teacher it is arguable that his work to improve the standard of midwifery and to prevent puerperal fever was of much greater long-term importance for British obstetrics and the health of women. He deplored the ignorance and poor standards of nurses and midwives that he encountered in his early career, and published a number of instruction books for nurses, such as *A Short Manual for Monthly Nurses* (1884), which ran to six editions. He was especially concerned to improve the training of midwives, and was the leader in the movement to secure their legal registration through the Midwives Act (1902); he was chief executive on the Midwives Bill committee, and advised the privy council and the General Medical Council on the drafting of the bill. He represented the Midwives Institute on the Central Midwives' Board, which was set up to ensure the proper training and practice of registered midwives under the act. In recognition of this work he received the honorary degrees of DCL, from Durham in 1893, and LLD, from Aberdeen in 1904.

In later years Cullingworth suffered from angina but he continued working until his death, at 14 Manchester Square, London, on 11 May 1908. He was buried in Marylebone cemetery. His wife and daughter survived him.

PETER D. MOHR

Sources *Journal of Obstetrics and Gynaecology of the British Empire*, 13 (June 1908), 445–9 · *Journal of Obstetrics and Gynaecology of the British Empire*, 14 (July 1908), 39–61 · J. H. Young, *St Mary's hospitals, Manchester, 1790–1963* (1964) · 'Dr Cullingworth—retired', *St Thomas's Hospital Gazette*, 14 (Oct 1904), 161–71 · W. J. Elwood and A. F. Tuxford, eds., *Some Manchester doctors: a biographical collection to mark the 150th anniversary of the Manchester Medical Society, 1834–1984* (1984) · *The Lancet* (23 May 1908) · *BMJ* (23 May 1908), 1269–72 · J. V. Pickstone, *Medicine and industrial society* (1985) · F. E. Keene, ed., *Album of the fellows of the American Gynecological Society, 1876–1930* (1930) · J. Thompson, *The Owens College: its foundation and growth* (1886) · Munk, *Roll*, 4.322–3 · 'Academical honours for Manchester men', *Manchester Guardian* (22 March 1904) · WWW, 1897–1915 · *Medical Directory* (1902) · b. cert. · m. cert. · d. cert.
Archives JRL, Manchester medical collection
Likenesses F. H. Hart, photograph, PRO, 3/196/59 [*see illus.*] · enlarged photograph; formerly in St Thomas's Hospital, London; destroyed in the blitz · photograph, repro. in Young, *St Mary's hospitals*, 49 · photograph, repro. in Keene, ed., *Album of the fellows*, 147 · photograph, St Thomas's Hospital, London
Wealth at death £28,089 16s. 9d.: probate, 30 May 1908, CGPLA Eng. & Wales

Cullis, Winifred Clara (1875–1956), physiologist and educationist, was the younger daughter and the fifth of the six children of Frederick John Cullis (1842–1931), surveyor and civil engineer of the Gloucester Dock Company, and his wife, Louisa, daughter of John Corbett of Coombe Hill. She was born in Stroud Road, South Hamlet, Gloucester, on 2 June 1875. The Cullis family had lived in Gloucestershire for three hundred years, but moved to Birmingham in 1880, as it offered better educational facilities. Winifred, a lively, generous, and considerate child, learned to read so quickly that her elder brother Cuthbert lost half his fee for teaching her. At the King Edward VI High School for Girls she was known for her outstanding academic ability and for her beautiful speaking voice. Extra tuition in science was obtained for Winifred at Mason College, where a demonstrator threatened to leave as he considered that 'it was indecent for a girl to study biology'. She entered Newnham College, Cambridge, as Sidgwick scholar in 1896, taking a second in both parts of the natural sciences tripos (1899 and 1900), and her MA in 1927. She was elected associate of Newnham College (1919–33) and president of the college roll (1952–5). She obtained the DSc of London in 1908, and the LLD *honoris causa* was conferred on her by Vassar College, New York, USA (1919), Goucher College, Maryland, USA (1931), and Birmingham University (1955).

Winifred Cullis's most influential teachers were her headmistress, Miss Creak, who believed that children should be given time 'to browse, read and think', J. N. Langley, and F. G. Hopkins. In 1901 she assisted T. G. Brodie in the research laboratory of the Royal College of Surgeons and of the Royal College of Physicians, London, and also taught as a part-time instructor in elementary science in a private school for girls. Later that year she was appointed demonstrator in physiology at the London School of Medicine for Women, Langley having written of her sound qualifications, hard and judicious work, independent thought, accuracy, and skill. Successively she was appointed co-lecturer with Brodie (1903–8); part-time lecturer and head of department (1908); full-time lecturer and head of department, with conferment of title as university reader in physiology (1912); and professor (1919). She was the first woman professor in a British medical school and the second in the country. In 1926 she became

Winifred Clara Cullis (1875–1956), by Madame Yevonde, 1944

Australia, New Zealand, and the USA. From 1941 to 1943 she directed the women's section of the British information services in New York, and in 1944–5 lectured in the Middle East, mainly to the Royal Air Force.

Speaking commitments curtailed Winifred Cullis's research, but extended her influence on national and international affairs. She believed that the essential need in the social system was to see that every person had an opportunity for making use of the capacities that were in them, and that education should give the ability to exercise ingenuity and 'determine values in the spiritual and moral life of the community'. In her opinion, teaching the applications of science to responsible daily living should begin at school, because they were keys to health and the prevention of disease. Biology teaching 'should not be given to the least busy member of staff', but to trained teachers, and 'it should not end at the waist'. She instituted courses for teachers of physical education and ballet in schools of the London county council. She broadcast on 'Health and common sense', and made educational films as aids, but not substitutes, for teachers.

Winifred Cullis's tact, regard for others, common sense, grasp of essentials, good humour, and wit made her an admirable committee member and chair and a persuasive opponent. Apart from university, medical school, and hospital committees, she served on the clinical management committee of the Institute of Child Psychology, the council of the National Institute of Industrial Psychology, the fatigue research board of the Medical Research Council, and the Home Office committee on the two-shift system for women and young persons. Her concerns also embraced the British Association for the Advancement of Science, the Trades Union Congress committee on scientific planning of industry, the Central Council of Recreative Physical Training, the King Edward VII Hospital Fund, the BBC Council for Adult Education, and the governing bodies of the Royal Academy of Dancing and Chelsea Polytechnic. She was chairman of the British Film Institute's educational panel, and from 1951 until her death, deputy chairman of the English-Speaking Union. She was also a director of *Time and Tide*.

A non-militant feminist, Winifred Cullis was amused by being exiled to galleries of lecture theatres in Cambridge and lecturers who addressed the mixed audience as 'Gentlemen'. She overcame prejudice through firmness, good sense, ability, and integrity. She was one of the first women to be elected to the Physiological Society (1915), the first woman elected to the deputy chairmanship of convocation of London University and the only woman delegate from the British Association to attend the silver jubilee celebrations of the Indian Science Association. She was a co-founder of the British Federation of University Women, and the International Federation of University Women, and was president of each from 1925 to 1929 and from 1929 to 1932 respectively. The IFUW now awards Winifred Cullis grants for research.

Winifred Cullis was handsome, well built, and well dressed. Although lacking classical beauty, her features were noble, and her blue eyes were kindly and shrewd.

the first holder of the Sophia Jex-Blake chair of physiology, retiring as professor emeritus in 1941. When Brodie died (1916), the University of Toronto invited her to be the acting professor of physiology, pending the appointment of a successor. Apart from that year's secondment, she served the School of Medicine for Women throughout her life, even attending an important meeting the day before she died.

Winifred Cullis's original work included investigation of mechanisms of secretion of urine, perfusion of the isolated mammalian heart, and the effects of fatigue on factory workers. Among those with whom she published papers were W. E. Dixon and W. D. Halliburton. Her greatest contributions were to education, the application of science to healthy living, including sport, and the fostering of international goodwill and the emancipation of both sexes through education. She wrote *The Body and its Health* with Muriel Bond (1935), and *Your Body and the Way it Works* (1949).

Winifred Cullis taught with lucidity, robust humour, enthusiasm, and mastery of the subject. Always nervous beforehand, she sounded at ease whether lecturing to students, broadcasting, or addressing an audience in the Albert Hall. Integrity, warmth, charm, simple but accurate explanations, and the ability to set people at ease, made her a memorable teacher. In 1919 she lectured to troops in Gibraltar and Malta for the Colonial Office, and was appointed OBE, being promoted CBE in 1929. In 1940–41 she travelled thousands of miles, lecturing on wartime Britain in China, Japan, Malaya, the Dutch East Indies,

She was serene, warm, and loved life and people. Unfailingly loyal, high-principled, but tolerant, courageous, and apparently tireless, she enjoyed indifferent health and slept little. She read widely and enjoyed the arts and cross stitch. She died on 13 November 1956 at her home, Vincent House, Pembridge Square, London.

R. E. M. BOWDEN, *rev.* RUTH E. M. BOWDEN

Sources Archives of Royal Free Hospital school of medicine · *The Times* (15 Nov 1956) · *BMJ* (24 Nov 1956) · *The Lancet* (24 Nov 1956) · *University Women's Review*, 47 (1957) · *Newsletter of International Federation of University Women*, 13 (1957) · private information (2004) · personal knowledge (2004) · b. cert. · d. cert.
Archives Bodl. Oxf., corresp. relating to the Society for Protection of Science and Learning · International Federation of University Women and British Federation of Women Graduates, Geneva, archives · Royal Free Hospital, London | FILM BBC WAC, educational programmes | SOUND BL NSA, recorded talks
Likenesses H. Coster, group photograph, 1937, NPG; *see illus. in* Field, (Agnes) Mary (1896–1968) · Madame Yevonde, photograph, 1944, NPG [*see illus.*] · A. Beerton, portrait, William Goodenough House, Mecklenburgh Square, London; loaned by British Federation of Women Graduates · A. Burton, portrait, Crosby Hall, London · P. Dodd, portrait, Royal Free Hospital School of Medicine, London · photograph, International Federation of University Women, rue L'Ancien Port, Geneva, Switzerland · photograph, British Federation of Women Graduates, 4 Mandeville Courtyard, 142 Battersea Park Road, London · photographs, Royal Free Hospital School of Medicine, London · portraits, Royal Free Hospital School of Medicine, London
Wealth at death £31,412 19s. 2d.: probate, 1 Jan 1957, *CGPLA Eng. & Wales*

Cullum, Sir Dudley, third baronet (1657–1720), horticultural writer, was born and baptized on 17 September 1657 at Wickhambrook, Suffolk, the eldest in the family of two sons and two daughters of Sir Thomas Cullum, second baronet, and his wife, Dudley, daughter of Sir Henry North, first baronet, of Mildenhall. His grandfather was Sir Thomas *Cullum (1587–1664). He was educated at Bury St Edmunds School, and was admitted to St John's College, Cambridge, in 1675. While at Cambridge he had smallpox. He succeeded his father in 1680, and on 8 September 1681 he married Anne (*d.* 1709), daughter of John *Berkeley, first Baron Berkeley of Stratton.

In his garden at Hawstead, Suffolk, Cullum cultivated most of the exotics then known to English gardeners, and his orange trees were especially successful. He corresponded with John Evelyn, and published a paper in *Philosophical Transactions* in 1694, entitled 'A new invented stove for preserving plants in the green house in winter'. This gave details of the heated greenhouse he had built at Hawstead, which worked on principles published by Evelyn in 1691 for bringing warmed fresh air into the greenhouse. A list of the plants contained in the greenhouse at the time of his death was among papers preserved at his home, Hardwick House.

Cullum served as high sheriff for the county of Suffolk in 1690, and was elected member of parliament for Suffolk in 1702, but was not re-elected in 1705. His wife died in 1709, and on 12 June 1710 Cullum married a relative, Anne, daughter of James and Dorothy Wicks of Bury St Edmunds. Cullum died on 16 September 1720 and was buried at Hawstead. He had no children. His widow married

the Revd John Fulham, archdeacon of Llandaff. She died on 22 January 1737, but was buried with her first husband at Hawstead.

B. D. JACKSON, *rev.* ANNE PIMLOTT BAKER

Sources GEC, *Baronetage* · J. Cullum, *The history and antiquities of Hawsted and Hardwick in the county of Suffolk*, ed. T.-G. Cullum, 2nd edn (1813), 185–90
Likenesses three portraits, formerly Hardwick House, Suffolk

Cullum, Sir John, sixth baronet (1733–1785), antiquary, was the eldest son of Sir John Cullum, fifth baronet (*bap.* 1699, *d.* 1774), landowner, of Hawstead Place and Hardwick House, Suffolk, and his second wife, Susanna Gery (1712/13–1784), daughter of Sir Thomas Gery, master in chancery, of Ealing. He was born at Hawstead Place on 21 June 1733 and baptized in the chapel there on the 18 July following: 'the last sacred office performed in it', as that wing of the house was soon after demolished (J. Cullum, *History and Antiquities of Hawsted*, 2nd edn, 1813, 158). He entered Bury St Edmunds grammar school in July 1740 and proceeded in October 1751 to St Catharine's College, Cambridge, where he first read mathematics (BA 1756) then, with greater distinction, classics. Elected to a fellowship, he narrowly missed election to the mastership, but in 1762 his father presented him to the living of Hawstead (he had been ordained priest in September 1757), and on 11 July 1765 he married Peggy Bisson (*bap.* 1732, *d.* 1810), daughter of Daniel Bisson of West Ham, Essex; they had no children. In 1774 he succeeded his father as sixth baronet, was elected a fellow of the Society of Antiquaries, and was presented to the vicarage of Great Thurlow by his brother-in-law Henry Vernon. The following year he was elected fellow of the Royal Society.

Within his wide circle Cullum's influence was considerable. He toured in search of topographical antiquities with George Ashby, Francis Grose, Michael Tyson, Craven Ord, and Richard Gough. With the last two he perfected a method of taking impressions of monumental brasses by spreading printer's ink on them, wiping the surface clean, and treading damped paper into the engraved lines to pull out the ink. This technique they employed to great effect on visits to the greater Cambridgeshire and Norfolk churches in September 1780. The bulky results, now in the British Library (Add. MSS 32478–32479), are invaluable as the only record of many memorials since lost. Cullum encouraged Gough to compile his great work *Sepulchral Monuments* (1796) using or copying some of their impressions as illustrations.

Having acquired the Suffolk church notes of Thomas Martin on his death in 1771, Cullum made legible and accurate records to supplement them which were continued after his death by his brother Sir Thomas Gery *Cullum, seventh baronet (1741–1831), surgeon and herald. Cullum also worked and corresponded with his fellow antiquaries William Cole, Peter Sandford, Michael Lort, Thomas Pennant, and James Granger. In February 1779 in London he witnessed Garrick's funeral, and, introduced by Mrs Delany, visited the dowager duchess of Portland and her famous collection of curiosities. By chipping fragments off different parts of Stonehenge in August that

Rev.ᵈ Sʳ John Cullum Barᵗ
Died 1785. Aged 53.

Sir John Cullum, sixth baronet (1733–1785), by Angelica
Kauffman, c.1776

year he found various types of stone, and concluded that
the henge 'neither grew nor was made on the spot'
(Cullum MSS, E2/21/1, 77–8). He inherited his forebears'
enthusiasm for horticulture and botany and kept a naturalist's journal for the last fifteen years of his life, but a projected English flora came to nothing. His articles for the
Antiquarian Repertory, *Philosophical Transactions*, and
Gentleman's Magazine were on many subjects including
observations of natural phenomena.

Cullum improved an earlier *Description of Bury St
Edmunds* for an edition of 1771, but his only substantial
publication was *The History and Antiquities of Hawsted* (1784),
which John Nichols included in *Bibliotheca Topographica
Britannica*. In his preface, Cullum hopes 'that the reader...
will... set a proper value on being born in the eighteenth
century, distinguished above all that preceded it by equal
and well-executed laws, by civil and religious liberty, and a
general civilisation and philanthropy'. He preserved local
sayings, described current agricultural methods, and analysed the population of the parish since registers were
kept, deploring the missed opportunity in 1780 for a
national census.

Having contracted consumption soon after the book
appeared, Cullum consulted several London doctors
about a cure, and on one such trip in September 1784 saw
Blanchard's balloon ascent. On 9 October 1785 he died,
aged only fifty-two, at Hardwick House; he was buried six
days later under a large stone at the north door of Hawstead church to flout the prevalent prejudice against
burial on the north side of churches. His brother immediately listed over 500 works in his working library, and fell

out with Cullum's widow over them. She lived on at Hardwick until her death on 2 August 1810, making an entail in
favour of her nephew, later eighth baronet. Unassuming
and unambitious, when Cullum was not on tour he was
content to serve his parishioners, enjoying his studies and
the friendship of fellow scholars. His memorial records
that he 'mingled the researches of the antiquary with the
studies and practice of the divine'. J. M. BLATCHLY

Sources J. Cullum, preface, in J. Cullum, *The history and antiquities
of Hawsted, in the county of Suffolk* (1784), no. 23 [5/2] of *Bibliotheca
topographica Britannica*, ed. J. Nichols (1780–1800) · J. Cullum, *The
history and antiquities of Hawsted and Hardwick in the county of Suffolk*,
ed. T.-G. Cullum, 2nd edn (1813) · G. M. G. Cullum, ed., *Genealogical
notes relating to the family of Cullum* (1928) · V. J. Torr, 'A guide to Craven Ord', *Transactions of the Monumental Brass Society*, 9 (1952–4), 80–
91, 133–45 · T. G. Cullum, catalogue of Sir John Cullum's library
(1482/8), Oct 1785, Suffolk RO, Bury St Edmunds · Suffolk RO, Bury
St Edmunds, Cullum MSS, E2/21/1 (77–8) · *DNB* · memorial inscription, Hawstead churchyard, Suffolk · parish register (baptism), 18
July 1733, Hawstead · *IGI* · *GM*, 1st ser., 55 (1785), 836

Archives BL, papers and corresp., Add. MSS 5821, 5834, 5846,
6401, 19196, 32478–32479, 33977 · Bodl. Oxf., transcriptions of
Cullum's work and corresp. · Suffolk RO, Ipswich, notes relating
to Suffolk churches · Suffolk RO, Bury St Edmunds, naturalist journals and notebooks; Suffolk church notes

Likenesses A. Kauffman, oils, c.1776, Manor House Museum,
Bury St Edmunds, Suffolk [*see illus.*] · J. Basire, line engraving, 1813
(after oil painting by A. Kauffman, 1778), BM, NPG; repro. in
Cullum, *The history and antiquities of Hawsted and Hardwick*, 2nd edn,
frontispiece

Wealth at death £5000 to children; Bury St Edmunds and Hawstead houses to widow; house in Southwark: will, proved 17 March
1774, PRO, PROB 11/995, sig. 85

Cullum, Sir Thomas, first baronet (1587–1664), local politician, was baptized on 28 April 1587 at Stanhill in Thorndon, Suffolk, the second son of John Cullum (1559–1610) of
Thorndon, from a well-to-do yeoman family, and his wife,
Rebecca, daughter of Thomas Smyth of Bacton, Suffolk.
He was bound apprentice in 1607 in the Drapers' Company to John Rainey of Gracechurch Street, in the parish
of All Hallows, Lombard Street. He gained his freedom in
1616, became warden of the yeomanry in 1626, and
entered the livery in 1627. On 18 February 1623 he married
Mary (1602–1637), second daughter of Nicholas Crisp, a
well-connected London merchant, with whom he had two
sons and two daughters, and six other children who died
in infancy.

Cullum set up in business, initially with his former master, as a woollen draper in Gracechurch Street, where with
great prudence he gradually amassed a large fortune as his
still extant account books for the years 1616–64 testify. His
shop employed eleven apprentices in 1624–42; he had one
of the highest London tithe ratings in 1638, and by 1641 his
business was worth about £20,000. This was enough to
give him solid respectability but he remained at some distance below the City's mercantile élite. Commercial concerns would appear to have largely monopolized his attention until the 1640s when he finally added a civic career.
Joining his company's governing body in 1643, he served
as master in 1643–4. By 1643 he had also become a common councillor and served on two of its committees, and

on 3 August of that year he was elected alderman of Cordwainer, a position he held until 1652. He was a London sheriff in 1646–7 and in 1647 became free of the East India Company.

Cullum's wife was a cousin of Sir Nicholas Crisp, a leading London merchant and customs farmer, who also became a premier royalist. Cullum was prepared to lend money to Sir Nicholas, as well as to another royalist relative, Sir George Strode, yet he himself managed to avoid any open commitment or controversy until London's attempted counter-revolution in 1647. In the meantime his financial acumen was recognized by parliament in his appointment as an excise commissioner in 1643–50. A leading political presbyterian and a current London sheriff, he became a member of the presbyterian-dominated City militia committee of May 1647. After the army's advance on London, Cullum and several other leading citizens were questioned about their role in the attempted counter-revolution and he was imprisoned in the Tower from September 1647 to March 1648.

After 1649 Cullum returned to the pursuit of wealth and began investing substantially in real estate in London and Suffolk. He spent over £10,000 on London property and in 1656 paid £18,000 to purchase the estates of Hawstead and Hardwick in Suffolk. The purchase of a coach in 1654 advertised his social arrival. He subsequently retired to live at Hardwick House in Hawstead on an income derived from rents and stocks, including a considerable investment in the Far East. With a rental income in his last years of about £1350 per annum, he enjoyed a most affluent retirement. There are two portraits of him at Hardwick House, one as an alderman and the other as sheriff; the latter is probably by Cornelius Janssen.

Cullum received a baronetcy at the Restoration but a year later fell into disfavour with the crown and was forced to seek a general pardon to cover him for past offences. He and Sir Thomas Foot, as former excise commissioners, had apparently been exposed in an audit as retaining in their own hands £4400 in excise arrears which they were subsequently obliged to repay. Cullum died on 6 April 1664 at Hawstead and was buried there on 9 April. His will, made on 2 May 1662, listed an extensive number of London properties including his main London home in Gracechurch Street. In the year before his death, his capital had risen to almost £47,000 and his two sons, Sir Thomas Cullum (1628–1680) and John Cullum (1635–1711), were given a most prosperous start in life.

KEITH LINDLEY

Sources A. Simpson, 'Thomas Cullum, draper, 1587–1664', *Economic History Review*, 2nd ser., 11 (1958–9), 19–34 · Sir Thomas Cullum's account book, 1616–64, W. Sussex RO · PRO, PROB 11/314/50 · J. Cullum, *The history and antiquities of Hawsted and Hardwick in the county of Suffolk*, ed. T.-G. Cullum, 2nd edn (1813), 70, 72, 179–80, 183–4 · parish register, All Hallows, Lombard Street, GL, MS 17613 [marriage] · journals, CLRO, court of common council, vol. 40, fols. 62–3 · A. B. Beaven, ed., *The aldermen of the City of London, temp. Henry III–*[1912], 2 (1913), 67, 179 · 'Boyd's Inhabitants of London', Society of Genealogists, London, 9294, 5688 · IGI · GEC, *Baronetage* · V. Pearl, *London and the outbreak of the puritan revolution: city government and national politics, 1625–1643* (1961); repr. with corrections (1964), 314–15 · DNB · CSP dom., 1663–4, 222, 242 · *The visitation of London, anno Domini 1633, 1634, and 1635, made by Sir Henry St George*, 1, ed. J. J. Howard and J. L. Chester, Harleian Society, 15 (1880), 210
Archives Suffolk RO, account book, E2/29/1.1
Likenesses J. Basire, line engraving (after C. Janssen?), BM; repro. in Cullum, *History and antiquities of Hawsted and Hardwick* · C. Janssen?, portrait (in sheriff's robes), formerly Hardwick House, Suffolk · portrait (in alderman's gown), formerly Hardwick House, Suffolk
Wealth at death capital almost £47,000 in year before last account; lands, properties, and leases in London and Hawstead, Suffolk: will, PRO, PROB 11/314/50; Simpson, 'Thomas Cullum'; Sir Thomas Cullum's account books, 1664, W. Sussex RO

Cullum, Sir Thomas Gery, seventh baronet (1741–1831), surgeon and herald, was the second son of Sir John Cullum, fifth baronet (*bap.* 1699, *d.* 1774), landowner, of Hawstead Place and Hardwick House, Suffolk, and his second wife, Susanna Gery (1712/13–1784), daughter of Sir Thomas Gery, master in chancery, of Ealing. He was born on 30 November 1741 at Hardwick House and baptized in the chapel there on 5 January 1742. After two years at Bury St Edmunds grammar school he was admitted to Charterhouse School on the nomination of the duke of Grafton in July 1752. In February 1758 he was apprenticed to Richard Hayles, surgeon of Cambridge, and after attending the lectures of William and John Hunter, he practised successfully in Bury St Edmunds, becoming a member of the Company of Surgeons in 1785 and of the College of Surgeons in 1800. In 1772 he performed a post-mortem on the 340-year-old exhumed body of Thomas Beaufort, duke of Exeter, telling the antiquary Michael Tyson that he had 'got the right hand in spirits' (T. G. Cullum to M. Tyson, BL, Add. MS 19108, fol. 155v). He was appointed Bath king of arms in 1771. On 1 September 1774 at St Mary's, Bury St Edmunds, he married Mary Hanson (1745–1830), daughter of Robert Hanson of Normanton, Yorkshire, and Elizabeth, daughter of Edward Jackson, a substantial apothecary and corporation member of Bury. Thomas and Mary, who shared a love for books, enjoyed a happy marriage and raised two sons and a daughter.

In the same year, 1774, Cullum published privately a *Florae Anglicae*, based on the Linnaean system, which was subsequently superseded by his friend Sir J. E. Smith's *English Flora* (1824), dedicated to Cullum; the genus *Cullumia* in the *Hortus Kewensis* marks the love of botany that he shared with his elder brother Sir John *Cullum, sixth baronet (1733–1785). In October 1785 he succeeded his brother as seventh baronet, and gave up the serious practice of medicine, but retained a life interest in medical developments. Three months later he was admitted a nobleman at Trinity College, Cambridge. With his brother's widow living on at Hardwick for another twenty-five years, Thomas was content to live in Bury, where he served as alderman four times between 1780 and 1807. In 1800 he resigned from the office of Bath king of arms but passed it to his second son, John Palmer Cullum. He made substantial additions to his late brother's Suffolk topographical collections and was a fellow of the Royal Society, the Linnean Society, and the Society of Antiquaries. He was also an early member of the Horticultural Society. To Gillingwater's *Description of Bury* of 1804 he contributed an interesting list of plants and their locations. For a second edition of his brother's *History of Hawsted and Hardwick* (1813) he added only footnotes and a few plates.

Mary, Lady Cullum, died on 13 September 1830 and Cullum died on 8 September 1831 at his house in Northgate Street, Bury St Edmunds; he was buried beside his wife at Hawstead on the first anniversary of her death. Their elder son, Revd Thomas Gery Cullum, eighth baronet (1777–1855), succeeded to Hardwick after his aunt's death in 1810 and was also a botanist and antiquary. It was his grandson Gery Milner Gibson-Cullum FSA (1857–1921) who assembled the family archive and gave it and the fine and extensive Cullum library in trust for the county, both now at Bury St Edmunds Record Office. By 1827 all that was left of Hawstead Place was a statue of Hercules and over forty early seventeenth-century painted panels of emblematic scenes and mottoes now in Christchurch Museum at Ipswich. Hardwick House was pulled down about 1927.   G. S. BOULGER, rev. J. M. BLATCHLY

Hannah Cullwick (1833–1909), by unknown photographer, 1857

Sources J. Cullum, *The history and antiquities of Hawsted and Hardwick in the county of Suffolk*, ed. T.-G. Cullum, 2nd edn (1813) [annotated copy in Suffolk RO, Cullum MSS, HD 903/1] · G. M. G. Cullum, ed., *Genealogical notes relating to the family of Cullum* (1928) · J. Gage, *The history and antiquities of Suffolk: Thingoe hundred* (1838) · commonplace books, 1770–1831, Suffolk RO, Bury St Edmunds, Cullum MSS, 317/1 and 1482/18 · *The Oakes diaries: business, politics and the family in Bury St Edmunds, 1778–1827*, ed. J. Fiske, 2 vols., Suffolk RS, 32–3 (1990–91) · B. Marsh and F. A. Crisp, eds., *Alumni Carthusiani: a record of the foundation scholars of Charterhouse, 1614–1872* (1913) · *DNB* · correspondence, BL, Add. MS 19108

Archives Linn. Soc., corresp. and papers · NL Wales, Welsh travel journal · Suffolk RO, Bury St Edmunds, commonplace books, corresp. · W. Sussex RO, corresp. | Bodl. Oxf., corresp. with John Charles Brooke · Linn. Soc., corresp. with Sir James Smith

Likenesses attrib. G. K. Ralph, oils, *c.*1800, Manor House Museum, Bury St Edmunds, Suffolk · Mrs Dawson Turner, pen-and-ink drawing, 1822, V&A · line engraving, priv. coll. · tracing (after line engraving), Suffolk RO, Ips HD480/15, fol. 72

Cullwick, Hannah (1833–1909), diarist, was born in Shifnal, Shropshire, on 26 May 1833. She was a working-class woman from a then still predominantly peasant area of Britain. The daughter of a saddler and a former housemaid, later a lady's maid, she had a large number of siblings, of whom the closest were her older brother James (Jim) and her younger sisters Mary Ann (Polly) and Ellen. Cullwick worked first in Shifnal, then other parts of the country, and later in Shifnal again, as a domestic servant. Her employment included being pot-girl, under-maid, kitchen maid, cook, scullion, housekeeper, and maid of all work, and she worked for most sectors of the Victorian employing classes. However, she preferred being a maid of all work, as this gave most control over work routines and the greatest scope for exercising her considerable talents and energies.

Having led one of the 'lives of the obscure', Hannah Cullwick aroused public interest in 1950 when the Munby collection at Trinity College, Cambridge, was opened. Attention focused initially on her clandestine relationship with and later marriage to the diarist and minor civil servant Arthur Joseph *Munby (1828–1910), but has increasingly centred upon her own diary, which forms part of the Munby collection. It commences in 1854 (before Munby's starts in 1859) and was kept, albeit with some interruptions, until 1873. It provides unparalleled information about the routines and skills of that most typical of Victorian employment, female domestic service, and also of the complex reactions of servants to their exacting and often overbearing employers. The picture provided bears little resemblance to the often romanticized 'upstairs, downstairs' world, but is rather one of hard, dirty, relentless work for sixteen or seventeen hours a day, with minimal time off each month or quarter. It was also work that required difficult transformations at different stages of the day, between performing extremely dirty 'backstairs' work and making neat and clean public presentations for the family and their guests.

Cullwick met Munby in 1854. They had a long and largely clandestine relationship in which the demands of service meant that they met relatively infrequently. They married at St James's, Clerkenwell, on 14 January 1873, for a long period living as 'servant and master' except when they travelled as a 'lady and gentleman' married couple. However, Cullwick increasingly resented her enforced ladyhood, wanting them to live openly as a married upper-class gentleman and lower-class woman. The disagreements engendered led to her departure from London in 1877 followed by a period in which contact was minimal. The relationship later resumed, although Cullwick remained bitter that Munby continued to keep her place in his life secret from his upper-class friends and acquaintances. She died of heart failure at Shifnal on 9 July 1909, and was buried in the parish church there; Munby died six months later.

Cullwick's diary was begun at Munby's request as a means of keeping him in touch with her life and activities as well as satisfying his need to have these represented. Her diary, however, transcends these origins in a number of important ways. It is almost unique in the detailed account it gives of practices and changes in early and mid-Victorian domestic service, in particular regarding its most common example of the maid of all work. It provides equally rare detailed information on the last remnants of peasant England, for example regarding harvesting activities and peasant Shropshire dress. The diary also demonstrates the complexities of supposed 'illiteracy', for Cullwick could read proficiently and became increasingly at her ease as a writer. As well as inscribing the changing course of a cross-class relationship that was by no means as uncommon as Munby supposed, the diary displays Cullwick's increasing ability to influence or shame Munby in directions desired by her, and acts as a fascinating counter-voice to that inscribed in Munby's own diary. Although unlikely to be seen as one of the 'great' Victorian diaries, it provides a fascinating window on these aspects and more, and has become standard reading for researchers interested in working-class women's work and lives over this period. LIZ STANLEY

Sources Trinity Cam., Munby collection · E. Stanley, *The diaries of Hannah Cullwick* (1984) · D. Hudson, *Munby, man of two worlds: the life and diaries of Arthur J. Munby, 1828–1910* (1972) · E. Stanley, 'Biography as microscope or kaleidoscope? The case of "Power" in Hannah Cullwick's relationship with Arthur Munby', *Women's Studies International Forum*, 10 (1987), 19–31 · E. Stanley, 'Hannah Cullwick', *A skirt through history, 1612–1950* (1994) · M. Hiley, *Victorian working women: portraits from life* (1979) · L. Davidoff, 'Class and gender in Victorian England: the diaries of Arthur J. Munby and Hannah Cullwick', *Feminist Studies* (1979), 87–141 · d. cert. · private information (2004)
Archives Trinity Cam., Munby collection
Likenesses photograph, 1857, Trinity Cam. [*see illus.*] · four portraits, Trinity Cam., Wren Library
Wealth at death £644: administration, 14 Aug 1909, CGPLA Eng. & Wales

Culmer, Richard (*c*.1597–1662), Church of England clergyman and iconoclast, was probably born in the Isle of Thanet, east Kent; his parents are unknown. He was educated at the King's School in Canterbury and in 1613 matriculated as a sizar at Magdalene College, Cambridge. He graduated BA in 1618 and proceeded MA in 1621. In September that year he was ordained as deacon and priest in the diocese of Peterborough. Culmer had returned to Kent by 20 July 1624, when he married his first wife, Katherine Johnson, in Harbledown near Canterbury. In the late 1620s Culmer was probably curate in this parish, where some of his children were baptized and buried.

By 1630 Culmer was curate at Goodnestone next Wingham, Kent, and it is here that the first evidence of his nonconformity emerges. In 1634 he was presented to the church authorities for not using the Book of Common Prayer and for refusing to read the Book of Sports to his congregation. By the end of 1634 the church courts reported that Culmer could not satisfy his conscience that the Book of Sports was lawful and in 1635 he was suspended by the consistory court. This case later formed a small part of the evidence used against Archbishop William Laud at his treason trial in 1644.

After three and a half years' suspension, Culmer returned to Harbledown as curate. At the outbreak of the first civil war he obtained letters of support from sixty-five prominent Canterbury citizens, the members of the parliamentarian county committee for Kent, and the earl of Warwick. They endorsed Culmer as 'a man of exemplary life and conversation and an able and diligent preacher of God's word' and commended him as a 'very forward advancer' of the parliamentarian cause (Culmer, *A Parish Looking-Glasse*, 7–9). In 1643 Culmer was considered by parliament as a candidate for the rectory of Chartham, Kent, but lost out to another nominee. In December that year he gained notoriety when he broke images and stained-glass windows in Canterbury Cathedral: he rapidly published an account of the destruction, in which he defended the need for further reform of the church and enthusiastically described himself 'on the top of the citie ladder, neer 60 steps high, with a whole pike in his hand ratling down proud Becket's glassy bones' (Culmer, *Cathedrall Newes*, 22). At the end of 1644 parliament appointed him as one of the six preachers in Canterbury Cathedral and in 1645 he was intruded into the living of Minster in Thanet by order of parliament.

At Goodnestone, Culmer had fallen out with the patron, Mrs Proude, and at both Harbledown and Minster he engaged in a series of disputes with his parishioners which were recorded in a biography by his son Richard, who was then serving in the army. The younger Richard Culmer's *A Parish Looking-Glasse for Persecutors of Ministers* (1657) is a 'warts and all' account which admitted that Culmer had relieved himself in Canterbury Cathedral during the iconoclasm for fear of the crowd outside, which was ready to 'knock out his brains' (*A Parish Looking-Glasse*). The biography also contains much valuable information about his father's ministry. According to his son, Culmer's parishioners were a quarrelsome lot. When Culmer reproved some in Harbledown for drunkenness, and for breaking the sabbath by playing cricket outside his door, they moved the game to a nearby field and threw stones at his sons, who were sent to spy on them.

Culmer's problems continued in Minster, where his refusal to use the Book of Common Prayer provoked complaints from traditionalists. When Culmer refused to preach on Christmas day he was 'reviled … called rogue, and assaulted in the church yard' (Culmer, *A Parish Looking-Glasse*). Culmer's disapproval of traditional festive culture was also expressed in his opposition to the Minster maypole, which elicited the threat that 'there was a bough strong enough to hang him on it'. At Minster, Culmer encountered the dregs of 'merry England', who abused him from the safety of the alehouse window as a 'devilish roundheaded priest', and 'Blew Dick' (apparently because of his blue garb). On one occasion in 1647 seven men dragged Culmer from the pulpit, and 'crushed his body so' with a wooden plank that he 'vomited blood'. Culmer was able to restore order with the aid of what his son described as 'many good people' in the church. In the summer of the next year Culmer used his influence to persuade some of his parishioners not to sign the county petition against parliament, but as the hostilities of the second civil war intensified he briefly left Minster for London.

Culmer believed that he was opposed at Minster both by

local royalists and by religious Independents who did not find him revolutionary enough. Culmer's position was also aggravated by a long-running tithes dispute, as he refused to accept a cash composition, which his predecessors had done. Eventually Culmer sued six tithe refusers and wrote two tracts in justification of tithes, *The Ministers Hue and Cry* (1651) and *Lawles Tythe-Robbers Discovered* (1655). In his will Culmer claimed that 'many summs of mony are due unto me from occupiers of lands' in Minster (Centre for Kentish Studies, PRC 32/53, fols. 377–8).

According to his son Culmer was hot-tempered, but he also had a sense of humour. When the parish vestry at Minster suggested that an illegitimate girl should be his servant, Culmer refused, because there were 'but eight bastards since his coming thither and desired that he might be excused until the tenth fell' (Culmer, *A Parish Looking-Glasse*, 11). Three anonymous pamphlets attacking Culmer were published in his lifetime: *The Razing of the Record* and *Antidotum Culmerianum* were both printed at the royalist headquarters in Oxford in 1644, and *Culmer's Crown Crackt with his Own Looking-Glass* appeared in 1657. They are the source of many myths and unsubstantiated stories about Culmer, and his son noted of them that 'no wise man would believe that, which no man doth avow, or set his name to' (Culmer, *A Parish Looking-Glasse*, 6).

Culmer was ejected from Minster at the Restoration in 1660, when the previous incumbent, Meric Casaubon, was reinstated. Culmer then moved to nearby Monkton, where he died at the parsonage house on 20 March 1662, and was buried on 22 March. His will made provision for his surviving children, Richard, James, Anne, Katherine, and Elizabeth, while his second wife, Margaret, received an annuity of £30 provided she did not try to claim any more from his estate. Nicholas Thoroughgood, the vicar of Monkton, recorded in his diary the death of 'my loving, faithful, friend Old Mr Culmer', but other memories of Culmer were not so benign (*Calamy rev.*, 154). In 1710 John Lewis, the incumbent at Minster, wrote to John Walker that 'no man was ever more hated than he, and to this day spoken of by those who remember him with all the dislike imaginable' (G. B. Tatham, *The Puritans in Power*, 1913, 59).

JACQUELINE EALES

Sources R. Culmer jun., *A parish looking-glasse for persecutors of ministers* (1657) · *Calamy rev.* · R. Culmer, *Cathedrall newes from Canterbury* (1644) · LPL, VG4/22, fol. 107r · will, CKS, PRC 32/53, fols. 377–8 · J. M. Cowper, ed., *The christnynges, weddinges and burynges in the parish of Herballdowne from 1557 to 1800* (1907) · W. Prynne, *Canterburies doome, or, The first part of a compleat history of the commitment, charge, tryall, condemnation, execution of William Laud, late arch-bishop of Canterbury* (1646), 110–14, 146, 199, 488–97, 505–6 · R. L. Greaves, *Saints and rebels: seven nonconformists in Stuart England* (1985), 63–75 · Venn, *Alum. Cant.*

Culmer, William (*bap.* 1743?, *d.* 1802), naval officer, was born either in Bridgwater or Butleigh, Somerset, and was baptized at Lime (Lyme Regis), Dorset; 1743 remains the most probable date of his baptism, though muster books provide a range of birth dates: 1739, 1750, 1751, and 1752. Based on a baptism date of 1743 Culmer was about twelve when he received his first substantive appointment in the *Ramillies*. During the next four decades he served in over

thirty ships and spent fewer than seven years unemployed. For most of his career he was a midshipman with brief spells as a master's mate, able seaman, and, from 12 May 1795, a lieutenant. Apart from a brief period in the *Prince* the last seven years of his career appear to have been spent on half pay, so he never served afloat as a substantive lieutenant. Commander J. A. Gardner, a fellow seaman in the *Barfleur*, described Culmer as:

> about five feet eight or nine, and stooped; hard features marked with the smallpox; blind in one eye, and a wen (cyst) nearly half the size of an egg under his cheek bone. His dress on a Sunday was a mate's uniform coat, with brown velvet waistcoat and breeches; boots with black tops; a gold-laced hat, and a large hanger by his side like the sword of John-a-Gaunt. He was proud of being the oldest midshipman in the navy (for he had been in that capacity with Lord Hood since 1757) and looked upon young captains and lieutenants with contempt. (*Recollections*, 102)

Culmer's fame rests on the various anecdotes that were told about him, though many were not grounded in fact. On one occasion a young lieutenant was sent to bring Culmer aboard after he had outstayed his leave. He was discovered in a local hostelry basting a goose and somehow persuaded the officer to take over while he returned to the ship. Details differ, but certainly the lieutenant became the butt of jokes through the fleet. Many stories also surrounded the occasion when Culmer was finally persuaded to present himself for the examination in seamanship for lieutenant before a board, several of whom had learned these principles from Culmer.

As Gardner's sketch suggests, Culmer was frequently connected with Samuel, first Viscount Hood, who may have been a relative and was certainly Culmer's sponsor. However, Frederick Hoffman's account of a conversation between Culmer and Hood in 1809 (Hoffman, 153) is clearly inaccurate as regards times and dates. Likewise Culmer did not serve in Hood's first command, the *Jamaica*, nor did he disappear from the navy for eight years as stated by Hood (ibid.), but rather for ten months before rejoining the admiral in the *Thunderer*. In addition to these and other anecdotes there are a number of periods for which the details of Culmer's career remain unclear. On 25 December 1779 he is recorded as deserting from the *Sandwich* as an able seaman, the ship having sailed on the previous day. Yet, six months later, he was appointed to the *Terrible* as an acting lieutenant in the West Indies, a rank he then held for less than two years, again disappearing and reappearing in the *Buffalo* as an able seaman after a further six months.

Culmer's popularity in the fleet probably arose from the way in which he successfully flouted many of the more restrictive conventions that were central to the service, adherence to which was essential for advancement. If not quite of Falstaff's proportions, in other respects he bore a close resemblance to Shakespeare's hero: jovial, humorous, dissolute, and irrepressibly impudent, his 'grog-blosson face' (Parsons, 255) exciting amusement rather than disdain:

> The Bill was, moreover, a comical dog
> And, if rightly I stick to my story,

> He would now and then get so aboard of the grog
> That, d'ye see, he was all in his glory.

And to many of his contemporaries 'A glorious fellow he was, too' (Barker, 7). Culmer died, possibly in Portsmouth, on 17 September 1802.   HENRY BAYNHAM

Sources W. E. May, 'William Colmer', *Mariner's Mirror*, 38 (1952), 231–5 · PRO, muster lists, ADM 36/8038, 8246, 8349, 8352, 8669, 8863, 11353 · *Recollections of James Anthony Gardner*, ed. R. V. Hamilton and J. K. Laughton, Navy RS, 31 (1906) · [M. H. Barker], *Greenwich Hospital, a series of naval sketches, by an old sailor* (1826) · F. Hoffman, *A sailor of King George* (1901) [repr. 1999] · G. S. Parsons, *Nelsonian reminiscences* (1843)
Likenesses G. Cruikshank, cartoon, repro. in Barker, *Greenwich Hospital*

Culpeper family (*per. c.*1400–*c.*1540), gentry, had established itself in south-east England as early as the thirteenth century. By the fourteenth century they had acquired Bayhall, Kent (now in Pembury, east of Tunbridge Wells), as one of their principal seats. The family suffered a severe setback late in 1321, when they supported Sir Bartholomew Badlesmere's unsuccessful resistance to the Despensers at Leeds Castle: Sir Thomas Culpeper, the castellan of Leeds, and his younger brother Walter were executed, while their brothers Nicholas and John suffered imprisonment and forfeiture respectively. Recovery ensued in the person of **Sir John** [i] **Culpeper** (*d.* 1414), who in June 1406 was appointed chief justice of common pleas. It was probably this John Culpeper who had been a retainer of John of Gaunt between 1367 and 1382. His first wife, Elizabeth, daughter and coheir of Sir John Hardreshull, brought to the family extensive Warwickshire property, including the manor of Hartshill. Sir John was a Kentish JP, and MP in 1382. In the 1412 tax assessment he figured as one of the wealthiest of Kentish landowners. He died on 30 August 1414, leaving a widow named Katherine, and was buried at West Peckham, where he had been a tenant of the hospitallers.

Sir John [i]'s eldest son, **Sir Thomas Culpeper** (*d.* 1429), was a Kentish JP, sheriff in 1394, and MP in 1382 and 1383. His marriage to Eleanor, daughter of Nicholas Green, brought her father's manors of Exton, Rutland, and Isham, Northamptonshire, to the family. By the time he died he was possessed of property in Lincolnshire, as well as in Warwickshire, Rutland, Northamptonshire, Kent, and Sussex. His will leaves no doubt as to his wealth. He left his body to be buried in Bayham Abbey, on the Sussex side of the border between Sussex and Kent, where an alabaster tomb had been prepared for him (his son Nicholas was also to seek burial there). As well as making a large number of bequests to religious houses, and leaving a total of £440 in cash to his sons, he provided for legacies to members of his household, who included a butler, a cook, a baker, and 'Malyne my little chambermaid', who received 20s. towards her marriage. A reference to another son, Richard, who had been buried at Pontoise in Normandy, suggests that at least one member of the family had served as a soldier in France. Sir Thomas's will also shows that he had married again; his second wife was

Joyce, the widow of John Vyne, and she survived him. Sir Thomas's brother Sir William [i] Culpeper (*d.* 1457) was sheriff of Kent in 1427, and was buried at West Peckham; from him descended the Aylesford branch of the family. Sir Thomas's daughter Eleanor (*d.* 1422) married Sir Reynold Cobham of Sterborough, and their daughter, another Eleanor, married *Humphrey, duke of Gloucester, in 1428. Thereafter Sir Thomas's sons, **Sir John** [ii] **Culpeper** (*d.* in or before 1447), Walter [i] (*d.* 1462), and Nicholas [i] (*d.* 1434), acted as ducal feoffees (Sir John also stood as the duke's mainpernor).

By 1421 Sir Thomas's eldest son, Sir John [ii] Culpeper, had inherited the Northamptonshire and Rutland property after the death of his mother and aunt, and thereafter established himself as one of the leading members of the midlands gentry. During the 1420s and 1430s he was a Rutland JP, sheriff (1426 and 1430), and commissioner, and also served as sheriff of Northamptonshire in 1431–2. He sat for Rutland in the December 1421, 1427, and 1431 parliaments, and was knighted in 1429 or 1430. Defence of his title to Exton involved him in violent quarrels with William, Lord Zouche, and Thomas Mulso. He died before March 1447, by when his widow, Juliana (*d.* after 1449), had married John Braunspath.

Walter [i] Culpeper's marriage in 1424 or 1425 to Agnes (*d.* 1457), daughter of Edmund Roper of Canterbury and widow and heir of John Bedgebury, brought to the Culpepers her former husband's manor of Bedgebury, about 15 miles south-east of Bayhall, and this became one of their principal residences. Their second son, **Sir John** [iii] **Culpeper** (*d.* 1480), had an eventful public and private life. In January 1459, together with his brothers **Richard** [ii] **Culpeper** (*d.* 1516) and Nicholas [ii] (*d.* 1510), he was ordered to be arrested by the sheriffs of London and brought before chancery to answer allegations of riot and other offences; these may have been politically motivated in the dying days of Lancastrian rule. Certainly, Sir John [iii] proved himself a loyal servant of Edward IV. He was knighted by December 1466, and the following November he appeared on the Kentish bench. In October 1468 he was appointed to the commission to muster Lord Scales's retinue at Gravesend, and the following month he was pricked as sheriff of Kent. From October 1469 until April 1470 he appeared on several commissions of array in the southeast, alongside his brother Richard, but during the readeption of Henry VI he was absent from both commissions of array and the county bench. He returned to public life after Edward's victory at Barnet in April 1471, in which month he was once again arraying soldiers in Kent, and in June he reappeared as a JP. The same month one Thomas Miller, a gentleman of Marden, Kent, and perhaps a Lancastrian die-hard, was alleged to have led a rebellious host against him. He went on to serve on numerous commissions throughout the early 1470s.

Some time before 1460 Sir John [iii] married Agnes, widow of Richard Wakehurst and sister of John and William Gainsford. At his request, the wardship and marriage of Margaret (*d.* 1504) and Elizabeth, the two daughters of

Agnes from her previous marriage and coheirs to the Sussex manor of Wakehurst in Ardingly, were conveyed to him, on condition that he would not marry them off without first obtaining the approval of Richard Wakehurst's feoffees, who included Agnes's brothers. But according to the feoffees he led a gang 'arrayed in the maner of warre' (Attree and Booker, 1.59), including his brothers Richard and Nicholas, and Alexander Clifford, their brother-in-law, to Agnes's house in Goudhurst, north of Bedgebury, where they forcibly removed the Wakehurst sisters. Margaret and Elizabeth were then married to Richard and Nicholas. This provoked a flurry of litigation, beginning with a petition to chancery by the Wakehurst feoffees brought between 1457 and 1460. The dispute had been settled by 1516, when in his will Richard provided for prayers to be said for his parents-in-law. Sir John [iii] was involved in another property dispute in 1475, this time with Brian Talbot, son-in-law of Sir John [ii] and Juliana, to whom the younger Sir John had pledged his manors of Manwood, Hartshill, and Ansley in Warwickshire and 'Assheyne' in Northamptonshire as security for a debt of 1000 marks. The matter was settled by arbitration and Sir John [iii] retained the property. He died on 22 December 1480 and was buried at Goudhurst.

Sir John [iii]'s brother Richard, of Goudhurst and Wakehurst, cannot always be distinguished from **Sir Richard [i] Culpeper** (d. 1485), the son of William [ii] Culpeper (d. 1501) [see below], grandson of Sir William [i] Culpeper (d. 1457), of Aylesford. One of them was an annuitant of the Staffords (later dukes of Buckingham) from 1442. In the 1455 parliamentary election a Richard Culpeper was an unsuccessful candidate for one of the Kentish seats, his failure possibly indicating official doubt as to his loyalty. In 1463 one of the two was granted a lifetime annuity of £10 from the royal manor of Huntingfield, Kent. From October 1469 until April 1470 one appeared on Kentish commissions of array, and accounted as sheriff from September 1470 until November 1471, despite the fact that Henry VI appointed Henry Aucher as sheriff in November 1470; thereafter neither held office during the readeption. A Richard was a commissioner once more in March 1472, the same year that he served as sheriff. In August 1478 James Goldwell, bishop of Norwich, was pardoned for allowing the escape of a Richard Culpeper. In March 1483 one of the Richards was appointed to supervise the River Medway from Aylesford to Penshurst, and the following May, Richard Culpeper of Goudhurst served as a commissioner of array. Richard of Aylesford was pardoned in 1483 or 1484, but in August 1485 Richard of Goudhurst was bound in £100 to appear before the king whenever warned and to behave himself as a true liegeman, so both Richards may have been under suspicion. Richard of Goudhurst appeared on Sussex commissions under Henry VII alongside his brother Nicholas. He died with property in Sussex and Surrey. Nicholas Culpeper founded the Wakehurst branch of the family, and his namesake, the seventeenth-century herbalist Nicholas *Culpeper (1616–1654), was one of his descendants. The brass of Nicholas and Elizabeth in Ardingly church, Sussex, depicts their ten sons and eight daughters. He inherited Hartshill, Bayhall, and Wigsell, Sussex.

Sir John [iii] Culpeper's sons, **Sir Alexander Culpeper** (d. 1541) and his brother Walter [ii] (d. 1520), were the progenitors respectively of the Bedgebury and Wigsell Culpepers. Sir Alexander joined the rising of October 1483 against Richard III, and was attainted the following year. His fortunes were restored under Henry VII, during whose reign he served on several commissions, and he was sheriff of Kent in 1500 and 1507. He was knighted in 1529. One of his sons, Thomas *Culpeper (d. 1541) [see under Katherine], became a gentleman of the privy chamber and was executed for his relationship with his cousin, Queen Katherine Howard. Walter [ii] was escheator for Kent and Middlesex in 1488–9, but his main focus of activity was Calais, where he was under-marshal from at least 1506. He married Anne (d. c.1532), daughter of Henry Auger, esquire, of Losenham, Kent, with whom the Culpepers acquired the manors of Losenham and Woods. He made his will in 1516, but died only in 1520, and was buried at Goudhurst.

The grandson of Sir William [i] Culpeper (d. 1457), **William [ii] Culpeper** (d. 1501), of Aylesford, married by 1457 Margaret, daughter of William, fifth Lord Ferrers of Groby (d. 1443). In addition to his Kentish property, he held the manor of Shenfield, or Fitzwalters, in Essex. In 1476 he was involved in a dispute with Edward Neville, Lord Bergavenny (d. 1476), which resulted in the latter's being bound in 4000 marks (£2666 13s. 4d.) personally to appear in chancery, and to forbear from harming William. He, too, seems to have fallen under suspicion during Richard III's reign, and was pardoned in 1483 or 1484. William's son, Sir Richard [i] Culpeper (d. 1485), was the father, by his second marriage, to Isabel, daughter of Otwel Worsley, of Joyce, who married Lord Edmund Howard, the father of Queen Katherine. Sir Richard's son and heir, Thomas (d. 1493), was under age at his father's death, and in May 1485 his wardship was granted to Sir John Savage, one of Richard III's northern servants settled in the south-east. Sir Richard's brother, Sir Edward Culpeper (1471–1533), served as escheator for Kent and Middlesex in 1511. He was buried at Aylesford.　　　　　　　PETER FLEMING

Sources F. W. T. Attree and J. H. L. Booker, 'The Sussex Colepepers', *Sussex Archaeological Collections*, 47 (1904), 47–81; 48 (1905), 65–98 · HoP, *Commons, 1386–1421*, 2.710–11 · HoP, *Commons, 1509–58*, 1.737–8 · VCH Sussex, 7.100, 129, 131; 9.75, 222, 235, 255 · VCH Warwickshire, 4.6, 132 · Chancery records · CIPM, Henry VIII, 1, no. 820 · E. Hasted, *The history and topographical survey of the county of Kent*, 2nd edn, 12 vols. (1797–1801); facs. edn (1972) · L. Baldwin Smith, *A Tudor tragedy: the life and times of Catherine Howard* (1961), 209–13 · R. Hovenden, ed., *The visitation of Kent, taken in the years 1619–1621*, Harleian Society, 42 (1898) · T. Benolt and R. Cooke, *The visitations of Kent taken in the years 1530–1 … and 1574*, ed. W. B. Bannerman, 1, Harleian Society, 74 (1923) · E. F. Jacob, ed., *The register of Henry Chichele, archbishop of Canterbury, 1414–1443*, 2, CYS, 42 (1937), 5–7, 382–6

Likenesses tomb effigy (John Culpeper), West Peckham, Kent · tomb effigy (Nicholas and Elizabeth Culpeper), Ardingly, Sussex · tomb effigy (John [iii] Culpeper), Goudhurst, Kent

Culpeper, Sir Alexander (d. 1541). See under Culpeper family (per. c.1400–c.1540).

Culpeper, Sir Cheney (bap. 1601, d. 1663), advocate of political reform and technological innovation, was born into a respectable family whose seat was at Greenway Court, Hollingbourne, Kent, and baptized at All Saints, Hollingbourne, on 15 April 1601. He was the elder son of Sir Thomas *Culpeper (1577/8–1662) and Elizabeth Cheney (1582–1638). He followed his father to Hart Hall, Oxford, where he matriculated on 6 November 1618 and graduated BA on 7 February 1620, and thereafter, a year later, to the Middle Temple. He left chambers on 10 February 1625 and was knighted by Charles I at Farnham on 8 September 1628. The following year he was sent to Elizabeth of Bohemia at The Hague with the official letter of condolence on the death of her eldest son. He probably remained there until 1631 when he became a gentleman in her service. He may well have been among the young men at the Middle Temple a decade earlier who, to James I's annoyance, swore an oath to live and die in the service of the winter queen when Habsburg forces invaded the Palatinate.

On 24 October 1632 Culpeper married Elizabeth Stede, the granddaughter of William Stede of Harrietsham, Kent, half-brother to his uncle; the couple had five children. At the time of the marriage his father settled the recently purchased house and estate at Leeds Castle on the couple. Cheney's own estimate that he was worth about £500 per annum at about this time is entirely plausible, but from 1641 onwards unexpected events radically reshaped his life. At some point that year he became gravely ill and was not expected to live, and he assigned the control of his estates to his father. He recovered from his illness, but, in the winter of 1641–2, just as his father's royalism was reinforced by the appointment of his son-in-law and distant kinsman, Sir John Colepeper, as Charles I's chancellor of the exchequer and privy councillor, Sir Cheney's support for the Long Parliament became more pronounced and so Sir Thomas refused to relinquish the estates to his son. Thereafter Culpeper tried to recover his property, sequestered because of his father's royalism. He had to fend off family creditors and sue for relief from parliamentary forced loans, levied from him on the basis of estates which he did not possess and whose revenues he did not enjoy. After the civil war he mortgaged his way out of his immediate difficulties, but his financial stability was compromised and his insecure legal title to his properties was exploited by his brother-in-law. Culpeper eventually surrendered his claims to the Leeds Castle estate and died intestate with debts in London; he was buried at the entrance to the north aisle of the Middle Temple Church on 2 April 1663. His widow was still alive in 1674, when her will was drawn up.

The year 1641 was also fundamental in another respect. Culpeper read by chance the published text of John Gawden's fast sermon, preached before the Long Parliament on Sunday 29 November 1640 on Zechariah 8: 19 ('I will turn your fasts into feasts; therefore love the truth and peace'). It contained an enthusiastic endorsement of the singular promoter of educational change, scientific advancement, and social welfare, Samuel Hartlib, and commended the endeavours of the Moravian educationist Jan Amos Comenius (Komenský). According to Hartlib's diary he met Culpeper for the first time on 3 April 1641, the latter contributing the first of many regular payments to support him. Culpeper's surviving correspondence among Hartlib's papers documents his reactions to, and engagement with, Hartlib's diverse plans for a fundamental reformation of state and society ('Letters', ed. Braddick).

Culpeper emerges from this correspondence as an intriguing virtuoso with a fascination for technical change. During the civil war he experimented with leathern guns and supported the development of Edmund Felton's 'engine' (a form of tank). He was interested in pump technology and new mechanica and used convertible husbandry on his Romney Marsh estate, introduced clover, and concentrated on improved methods of sowing corn by means of a mechanical seed drill as well as exploring the possibilities for a mechanical thresher. He described himself as one of those 'whose spirit God hathe raysed out of this mudde of custom' and who must deploy his 'talents towards others' ('Letters', ed. Braddick, 287). He had carefully considered notions for reforming the patents system to allow the wider distribution of innovations and served as one of the fifteen commissioners for the advancing and regulating of trade established by the Rump in August 1650. As his comments on a proposed 'bank of lands', published by Samuel Hartlib as *An Essay upon Master W. Potters Designe* (1653), indicate, Culpeper was well informed on the example for economic prosperity afforded by the Netherlands.

Culpeper had an abiding interest in chemistry, attempted a translation of the first part of Rudolf Glauber's *Furni novi*, and adopted the notions of the natural world of Nuysement and Vigenère. The purpose of natural philosophy was to discover the 'hidden and inwarde motion' represented by the growing forces encouraged by the sun but forever constrained by the grossness in nature. The art of the chemist was to release the latter from the former, without brutalizing nature. He applied these notions in turn to political events, where he emerges as a committed parliamentarian with a radical political agenda. Political instability ('motion'), like chemical change, involved releasing human energies from the 'gross matter' of 'custome' and the 'dark corners of prescription'. Ecclesiastical monopoly, the aristocratic interest, even the tyranny of kings must eventually be cast down in order to release the light of human reason, the way of public good, and the 'slow motion towards the happines of a nation whether in religion or liberty'. Culpeper's letters reveal his eschatological excitement in the later 1640s. In March 1647, for example, he wrote:

I have still a super confidence that God will finally breake those linsy woolsy packinges up of thinges, which our ecclesiasticall & civill Aristocracies must make for their owne defence, & that the stone (now in full motion) will not ly still till it come to the bottome of the hill.   ('Letters', ed. Braddick, 292–3)

Of Culpeper's reactions at the close of the Commonwealth and protectorate very little is known, but it is not surprising to find him among the supporters for Harrington's *Proposition in Order to the Proposing of a Commonwealth or Democracie*. Perhaps anticipating the age of Elias Artista (predicted by Paracelsus as occurring in 1658), Culpeper's Good Old Cause was one to be worked for and waited for with patience, and whose time was only just nigh.

M. Greengrass

Sources *An essay upon Master W. Potters designe: concerning a bank of lands to be erected throughout this Commonwealth* (1653) · 'The letters of Sir Cheney Culpeper, 1641–1657', ed. M. J. Braddick, *Camden miscellany, XXXIII*, CS, 5th ser., 7 (1996), 105–402 · D. A. H. Cleggett, *Hollingbourne and the Culpepers* (privately published, 1988) · S. Clucas, 'The correspondence of a seventeenth-century "Chymicall Gentleman": Sir Cheney Culpeper and the chemical interests of the Hartlib circle', *Ambix*, 40 (1993), 147–70 · M. Greengrass and M. P. Leslie, eds., *Samuel Hartlib: the complete edition* (1995) [CD-ROM] · W. C. Metcalfe, *A book of knights banneret, knights of the Bath and knights bachelor* (1885) · parish register, Hollingbourne, All Saints, CKS [baptism] · PRO, PROB 6/41, fol. 203 · PRO, PROB 6/67, fol. 40 · J. L. Chester and G. J. Armytage, eds., *Allegations for marriage licences issued by the bishop of London*, 2, Harleian Society, 26 (1887), 208 · F. A. Inderwick and R. A. Roberts, eds., *A calendar of the Inner Temple records*, 3 (1901), 445 · Foster, *Alum. Oxon.* · C. H. Hopwood, ed., *Middle Temple records*, 2: *1603–1649* (1904), 96
Archives University of Sheffield, Hartlib MSS
Wealth at death apparently in debt: administrations, PRO, PROB 6/41, fol. 203; PRO, PROB 6/67, fol. 40

Culpeper, Edmund (*c*.1670–1737), scientific instrument maker, was born in Tarrant Gunville, Dorset, the son of Edward Culpeper, rector of that parish, a former servitor at Merton College, Oxford, who took his BA from Merton in 1658. Edmund Culpeper and the herbalist and astrologer Nicholas Culpeper were probably related, being descended from junior branches of the Culpeper (or Colepeper) family, a large, wealthy, landed family in Kent and Sussex.

In 1684 Culpeper was apprenticed in the Grocers' Company to Walter Hayes, engraver and mathematical instrument maker of Moorfields, London. By 1700 he had taken over his master's shop at the Cross Daggers, Middle Moorfields, and this was given as his address in various advertisements from 1707 to 1731, an address emblematically represented on his trade card. In 1710 he was visited by the noted German traveller Conrad von Uffenbach, who sought out the most eminent instrument makers in London. Rather curiously Culpeper did not become a freeman until 1714; he must have decided to do so because he took on an apprentice the day after he was freed. Culpeper was famous for his optical instruments, especially microscopes, but was also known for a wide variety of mathematical instruments in silver, brass, ivory, and wood, although it is difficult to determine at what point he moved from being a maker to a retailer.

Culpeper was a skilled engraver and there is a memorial brass by him, dated 1694, for Dorothy Williams in Pimperne church, Dorset. Other early examples of his work are a woodblock engraving of a trencher design dated 1687, when he was still an apprentice, and a fine gilt-brass horizontal sundial signed 'E. C.', probably made for his sweetheart, as it has engraved underneath an interlaced geometrical pattern inscribed 'Ann Porteman. This is a True Loves Knot for Thou Cans Part it not 1687'.

Culpeper married by licence on 10 January 1705 Judith Gunn, who survived him. Their son Edmund became free, by patrimony, of the Grocers' Company in 1758. Indeed three generations of Culpepers joined this guild, as the younger Edmund's son John Chandler Culpeper in turn became his father's apprentice in the following year. Both Edmunds may also have been members of the Spectaclemakers' Company.

Culpeper achieved fame by giving his name to a certain type of tripod microscope made in the early eighteenth century, but it is not at all clear that he was its inventor. He was making the screw-barrel microscope invented by James Wilson from at least 1700. In 1710 he advertised 'several sorts of new contrived Microscopes … I may boldly say, no one but my self in the Kingdom has the like variety of 'em', but his characteristic works are his engravings of scales, dials, and sectors. By the time of his death, on 14 May 1737 at his house in Moorfields, he was trading 'Near the Royal Exchange'. He was buried in St Paul's Churchyard, as recorded in the parish register of St Faith's under St Paul.   W. D. Hackmann, rev. Anita McConnell

Sources G. L'E. Turner, *The great age of the microscope: the collection of the Royal Microscopical Society through 150 years* (1989) · G. Clifton, *Directory of British scientific instrument makers, 1550–1851*, ed. G. L'E. Turner (1995) · parish register, St Benet Paul's Wharf · parish register, St Faith's under St Paul [burial] · will, PRO, PROB 11/683, sig. 102

Culpeper, Sir John (*d.* 1414). *See under* Culpeper family (*per. c*.1400–*c*.1540).

Culpeper, Sir John (*d.* in or before 1447). *See under* Culpeper family (*per. c*.1400–*c*.1540).

Culpeper, Sir John (*d.* 1480). *See under* Culpeper family (*per. c*.1400–*c*.1540).

Culpeper, John (1644–1691×4), rebel leader in Carolina, first appears in colonial records in Barbados in 1663. Of unknown origin and ancestry, he arrived in Charles Town, South Carolina, with a single black slave in February 1671. His wife, Judith, joined him the following December accompanied by a woman servant. Quickly recognized by provincial officials as 'a very able Artist', Culpeper produced the earliest extant plan of Charles Town and its environs (Cheves, 285); the original map survives in the Public Record Office, London. On 30 December 1671 he received a commission as surveyor-general of South Carolina from the lords proprietors. He held this appointment for only eighteen months, during which time he obtained a grant for a 370 acre plantation and was elected to the provincial assembly.

In June 1673 Culpeper fled Charles Town with other members of the colonial government. While the specific cause of his departure is not clear, it may have been occasioned by financial controversies. By November 1673 he had arrived in the northern Carolina settlement of Albemarle county where he established himself in business as a planter and merchant. Because of this relocation, some historians have confused Culpeper with another of the same name, John Culpeper (*b.* 1633), brother-in-law of Sir William Berkeley, the governor of Virginia. While the Virginia Culpeper does appear in Albemarle court records, he never lived in the county.

Factional political struggles in northern Carolina, at least in part prompted by efforts to enforce the Navigation Acts, quickly drew Culpeper in. In 1677 he participated in an armed conflict challenging the authority of the acting governor, Thomas Miller, and helped seize the government. The rebels kept control of the province for a year and a half until the lords proprietors appointed a new governor more acceptable to local planters. In December 1679, while in England defending the insurgents' cause, Culpeper was arrested and tried for treason by the crown. The proprietors, eager to downplay the significance of the revolt, successfully defended him against all charges. Perhaps because of the trial, or because he authored the original 'remonstrance' calling for revolt, the conflict is known traditionally as Culpeper's rebellion. While he served as secretary of the rebel assembly, evidence does not support the conclusion that he ever acted as the colony's governor. On returning to Albemarle county he seems to have shunned public life. Following the death of his first wife he married Margaret Bird in 1680. Widowed again, he married Sarah Mayo on 23 August 1688. He died some time between November 1691 and February 1694, survived by his third wife and at least two children still minors.   MEAGHAN N. DUFF

Sources L. S. Butler, 'Culpeper, John', *ANB* · M. E. E. Parker, 'Culpeper, John', *Dictionary of North Carolina biography*, ed. W. S. Powell (1979–96) · L. Cheves, ed., *The Shaftesbury papers and other records relating to Carolina* (1897) · A. S. Salley, ed., *Records of the secretary of the province and the register of the province of South Carolina, 1671–1675* (1944) · A. S. Salley Jr, ed., *Warrants for land in South Carolina* (1973) · M. E. E. Parker and others, eds., *North Carolina higher-court records*, 1: *1670–1696* (1968) · W. L. Saunders and W. Clark, eds., *The colonial records of North Carolina*, 30 vols. (1886–1907), vol. 1 · M. E. Sirmans, *Colonial South Carolina: a political history, 1663–1763* (Chapel Hill, NC, 1966) · H. F. Rankin, *Upheaval in Albemarle: the story of Culpeper's rebellion* (1962)

Culpeper, Nicholas (1616–1654), physician and astrologer, the son of Nicholas Culpeper and his wife, Mary Attersole, was born a little after noon on 18 October 1616, probably at Ockley, Surrey, where he was baptized in St Margaret's Church on 24 October. His father, the rector of Ockley, had been buried there only nineteen days earlier. Consequently, his mother was obliged to leave the rectory, and returned with her infant son to the home of her father, William Attersole, the rector of the parish of St Margaret's at Isfield, Sussex.

The *Culpeper family was an eminent one. One branch owned Leeds Castle in Kent; and Wakehurst Place in Sussex was the seat of Nicholas's father's family. Sir John Colepeper (created Baron Colepeper in 1644) was a royalist who accompanied the future Charles II into exile in France, and returned with him in 1660.

In Effigiem Nicholai Culpeper Equitis .
The shaddow of that Body heer you find,
Which serves but as a case to hold his mind,
His Intellectuall part be pleas'd to looke
In lively lines described in the Booke .   *crose sculpsit*

Nicholas Culpeper (1616–1654), by Thomas Cross, pubd 1649

Education and entry into medicine Nicholas, however, was brought up by his mother's family and educated in Sussex. William Attersole was a scholarly Puritan divine, who was keen for his grandson to follow him into the ministry; probably with that in mind, Culpeper's mother paid for him to begin studies at Cambridge in 1632. The signs were already unpromising, however, as from the age of ten the boy had been inclined to 'Astrology and occult Philosophy' (Ryves, C3r).

About the summer of 1634 Culpeper's intended career was thoroughly upset by a personal tragedy (his second, if one counts the premature death of his father). He and a wealthy, well-born, and apparently beautiful young woman from Sussex had fallen in love and intended to elope; but on her way to their meeting place, she was struck dead by lightning. Culpeper was naturally distraught, and left Cambridge.

Perhaps Culpeper already had an interest in medicine, for his grandfather then found him work with a Mr White, an apothecary, near Temple Bar, in London. Just over a year later, his master's business having failed, Culpeper became apprenticed to another apothecary, Francis Drake, in Threadneedle Street, together with Samuel Leadbetter. When Drake died in February 1639 Leadbetter had just become licensed, and took Culpeper, who was now definitely studying physic, into the business with him. In the same year Culpeper's mother died, and a year later, his grandfather. Having been unable to persuade Culpeper to follow him into the ministry, William Attersole left him a derisory legacy of 40s. Culpeper apparently remarked that 'he had courted two mistresses that had cost him very dear, but it was not the wealth of kingdoms should buy them from him' (Ryves, C3r). Those two mistresses were physic and astrology. They were not his only ones, for soon after this, in 1640, he married Alice Field (b. 1625). It seems to have been a happy union, and Alice brought with her a fortune sufficient to pay for a house to be built in their chosen place of residence: Red Lion Street, in poor and unfashionable Spitalfields, just outside the city walls of London. They had seven children, but their daughter Mary, the fourth, was the only one to survive her father.

Conflict with the College of Physicians Culpeper was still working for Leadbetter. Apothecaries at this time, as well as dispensing remedies, frequently diagnosed illnesses and prescribed; these activities brought them into constant conflict with the College of Physicians, which was anxious to protect its statutory monopoly of internal medicine in and within 7 miles of London. The expense of consulting a licensed physician meant, however, that there was a constant demand not only for apothecaries (who were slightly cheaper), but for unknown numbers of quacks, empirics, 'wise women', herbalists, and midwives, whose services, provided they were given free of charge, were recognized and protected by the so-called 'quacks' charter' of 1542.

Any resolution of these conflicts between the physicians and the apothecaries was hampered by the political and social chaos of the 1640s. This is not to say that the issues disappeared, as was shown on 17 December 1642, when Culpeper was apparently tried for witchcraft; he was acquitted. Then, in 1643, Leadbetter received two warnings from the Society of Apothecaries to stop employing his unlicensed assistant. During the same year Culpeper fought on the side of parliament in the civil war. He received a serious chest wound from a musket ball, which probably hastened his death.

Political and religious beliefs By now Culpeper's political, religious, and social values were well formed; and even by the standards of his day, they were radical. As an ardent republican, he hailed the death of Charles I, seeing it as a portent of the millenarian rule by Christ on earth; and he took the risk of remarking in print of Cromwell's ascendancy that the people had merely 'leapt out the frying pan into the fire' (An Ephemeris for 1656, 'published from his notes'). Culpeper was equally antinomian, denouncing 'the monster called Religion' (Catastrophe magnum, 1652, 19), and testifying that 'All the religion I know is Jesus Christ and him crucified, and the indwelling of the spirit of God in me' (Ephemeris for 1651, G3v). Culpeper committed himself wholeheartedly to the service of the sick among the poor, powerless, and uneducated.

Practising in Spitalfields Some time in 1644 Culpeper established his own practice at his home in Spitalfields,

where he remained for the rest of his life. By now he had a considerable number of clients. Culpeper's most significant service, however, on which he worked the hardest and for which he is best remembered, was writing and translating books, enabling the poor to help themselves. As he pledged in 1650, 'My pen (if God permit me life and health) shall never lie still, till I have given them the whole model of Physick in the native language' (A Physical Directory, 1650, 'To the impartial reader').

One of the ways in which the College of Physicians maintained its monopoly was through the Pharmacopoeia, commonly known as the 'London dispensatory'. This was entirely in Latin—difficult even for some apothecaries, and impossible for the barely literate. Culpeper's first project was therefore to take advantage of the collapse of censorship and translate the Pharmacopoeia into English. It appeared, entitled A Physicall Directory, or, A Translation of the London Dispensatory, in 1649. Culpeper also supplied definitions of terms, added information on what the recipes were to be used for, and provided instructions on how to make the medicines where the Pharmacopoeia's own were too short or unclear. These additions were meant to break the monopoly held by the apothecaries as well as that of the physicians.

This was no disinterested or neutral act, as the royalist newsheet Mercurius Pragmaticus for 4–9 September of that year immediately recognized, accusing Culpeper of 'mixing every receipt therein with some scruples, at least, of rebellion or atheisme', and of endeavouring 'to bring into obloquy the famous societies of apothecaries and chyrurgeons'. William Johnson, the college's chemist, asked whether the result was 'fit to wipe ones breeches withall' (L. Fioravanti, Three Exact Pieces, 1652, preface). The next two editions, of 1650 and 1651, included a 'Key to Galen and Hippocrates, their method of physick', while Pharmacopoeia Londinensis, or, A London Dispensatory (1653), his translation of the college's new edition of the Pharmacopoeia, had appended 'An astrologo-physical discourse', thus becoming a more complete handbook of medical self-help. In these editions Culpeper continued to criticize the self-interest of the college physicians, whom he had already classed with priests and lawyers: 'The one deceives men in matters belonging to their soul, the other in matters belonging to their bodies, and the third in matter belonging to their estates' (A Physicall Directory, 1649, 'To the reader'). But he also warned the reader that physic was indeed a serious and difficult matter.

Ephemeris and The English Physitian In 1651 Culpeper's Ephemeris for that year appeared, followed early the next year by Catastrophe magnum, or, The fall of monarchie: a caveat to magistrates, deduced from the eclipse of the sunne, March 29 1652. He foresaw the end of monarchy across Europe, and a fifth monarchy of divine rule; other astrologers, such as William Lilly, similarly predicted great changes. In the event, 'black Monday', the day of the eclipse, turned out much like any other. Culpeper had apparently taken into account such a possibility, arguing in the Catastrophe: 'Imagine what I write be every word false, what harm will it do princes to prepare for the loss of a kingdom, though it never come? Is it not the way to teach them humility?' (*Catastrophe magnatum*, 75).

Culpeper's *Ephemeris for 1653*, his last, appeared amid a steady stream of the medical publications that were his chief concern. His own work included *A Directory for Midwives* (1651), and *Semiotica uranica, or, An Astrological Judgement of Diseases from the Decumbiture of the Sick* (1651). There were also more translations: *Treatise of the Rickets* (1651), from Francis Glisson's *De rachitide sive morbo puerili, qui vulgo 'the rickets' dicitur, tractatus*; *Galen's Art of Physick* (1652), from the *Ars medica*; and *The Anatomy of the Body of Man* (1653), from John Vesling's *Syntagma anatomicum*.

But Culpeper's *magnum opus* was *The English physitian, or, An astrologo-physical discourse on the vulgar herbs of this nation, being a compleat method of physick, whereby a man may preserve his body in health, or cure himself, being sick* (1652). Costing 3*d*., it provided a comprehensive list of native medicinal herbs, indexed to a list of typical illnesses, using an astrological, rather than Galenic, approach (of the kind still flourishing in popular British culture), and set out in a straightforward and frank style. It sold widely at the time, and there have been over one hundred subsequent editions, including fifteen before 1700. (One edition of 1708 was printed in Boston, Massachusetts; it and the translated *Pharmacopoeia*, printed in 1720, were the first medical books published in North America.)

Death and posthumous publications Culpeper's preface to his translation of the revised *Pharmacopoeia*, dated 30 December 1653, complains that he is 'sick, and weak, no way fit for study or writing'. He died of consumption—aggravated by excessive tobacco smoking, and very possibly his war wound—on 10 January 1654, at home in Red Lion Street, Spitalfields, London, aged only thirty-eight. He was buried in the new graveyard of Bethlem Hospital.

New works, mainly translations, continued to pour forth posthumously, mostly issued by Culpeper's usual printer, Peter Cole, and with the blessing of his widow. New books were *Health for Rich and Poor, by Diet, without Physick* (1656) and *Two Treatises* (1663), and the translations included works by Bartholinus, Riolani, Praevotius, Rivierius, Sennertus, Platerus the elder, Fernellus, and Partlicius. The last, entitled *A New Method of Physick* (1654), and completed three years earlier, was an attempt to integrate the doctrines of Galen and Paracelsus.

At the same time, a rival printer, Nathaniel Brook, issued four new books by Culpeper: *Opus astrologicum* (1654); *Culpeper's Last Legacy* (1655), decried by Alice Culpeper as 'an undigested Gallimoffery', that her husband had never intended to publish (*English Physitian*, 1656, C8*v*); *Mr Culpeper's Treatise of Aurum potabile* (1656); and *Culpeper's School of Physick* (1659).

The treatise on *aurum potabile*, including its true authorship, was attended by considerable controversy. At the end of his life Culpeper left this 'Universal Remedy for all diseases' (*Pharmacopoeia Londinensis*, 1654, B4*v*), prepared by a secret recipe from gold, as a contribution to his wife's estate. As a remedy it was Paracelsian in style, but Culpeper's own explication was accompanied by highly critical remarks about contemporary Paracelsian physicians. In 1655 Alice was selling it, to be administered by a nearby physician, from her house next door to the Red Lyon in Spitalfields. But she, and it, were quickly denounced by an anonymous pamphlet, *Culpeper Revived from the Grave* (1655). Her last contribution to the debate was a 'Testimony and approbation of this book' in *Culpeper's School of Physick* (1659), which also included a biographical essay by William Ryves, a nativity by John Gadbury, and various short eulogies. Alice married the astrologer John Heydon in 1656.

Place in seventeenth-century medicine It would be hard to overstate Culpeper's importance for the medical practice and health education (in the widest sense) of his time and place—far greater, according to one authority, than either William Harvey's or Thomas Sydenham's (Poynter, 'Nicholas Culpeper and his books', 152–3). He not only brought a relatively sophisticated and cheap traditional system of remedies—of the kind sometimes now described as 'holistic', with the emphasis on prevention and the gentle treatment of chronic functional disorders—within the reach of the semi-literate majority of the population; he also put the orthodox medicine of his day, alongside the latest thinking (such as Paracelsian 'chymical or spagirical' medicine), into the realm of public discourse.

However, in admitting the extent of Culpeper's efforts and their impact, one would be equally mistaken to try to turn him into a proto-scientist by distinguishing sharply between the 'modern' or 'advanced' elements and the 'superstitious'; they were inseparable. 'If you do but consider the whole universe as one united body', he wrote,

> and man an epitome of this body, it will seem strange to none but madmen and fools that the stars should have influence upon the body of man, considering he, be[ing] an epitome of Creation, must needs have a celestial world within himself. (*Pharmacopoeia Londinensis*, 1654, A3*v*–A4)

(Perhaps this Hermetic world-view explains why Culpeper never accepted Harvey's demonstration of the circulation of the blood; it smacked too much of the old Aristotelian materialism that he disliked almost as much as Catholic and Anglican supernaturalism.)

Culpeper's Hermeticism and astrology were therefore not a kind of supernaturalism, but rather natural magic, which was religious in a way that suffused what we now think of as the merely natural world: 'as the right use of natural things is from God, so the abuse of them is from the devil' (*A Directory of Midwives*, pt 1, bk 3, section 3). As he replied to a clergyman who had argued that eclipses (such as that of 'black Monday') were harmless, because they had a natural cause, 'God help his calf's head! Is not meat and drink natural, and yet doth it not nourish? Is not poison natural, and yet doth it not destroy?' (*An Ephemeris for 1654*, 15).

However, it should also be noted that in the manner of an experienced physician, Culpeper tempered his theories with pragmatism. For example, he certainly used decumbitures (horoscopes) for the moment when a patient either takes to his bed or consults the physician, or when the latter receives a sample of the patient's urine; and the rationale was the Hermetic one just noted. But

Culpeper was no mere 'piss-prophet'; he rejected the practice of proceeding solely on such a basis, writing (in a characteristically forthright manner) that 'Out of question viewing the patient is a better way to find the disease than viewing the piss, though a man should view as much as the Thames will hold' (*A Physicall Directory*, 1649, A2). Furthermore, 'the astrologer is, or at least ought to be, very well versed in every part of natural philosophy' (*Treatise of the aurum potabile*, chap. 2).

Culpeper also stands out in the tradition of astrological medicine. His predecessors include Richard Forster (*c*.1546–1616), Simon Forman (1552–1611), and Richard Napier (1559–1634); his contemporaries and successors, William Lilly (1602–1681), Richard Saunders (1613–1675), and Joseph Blagrave (1610–1682). This tradition has never entirely died out, but the middle years of the seventeenth century were without a doubt its glory days, and Culpeper their epitome.   PATRICK CURRY

Sources [W. Ryves], 'The life of the admired physician and astrologer of our times, Mr. Nicholas Culpeper', in *Culpeper's school of physick* (1659) · G. Tobyn, *Culpeper's medicine* (1996) · O. Thulesius, *Nicholas Culpeper: English physician and astrologer* (1992) · F. N. L. Poynter, 'Nicholas Culpeper and the Paracelsians', *Science, medicine and society in the Renaissance*, 2 vols. (1972), 1.201–20 · F. N. L. Poynter, 'Nicholas Culpeper and his books', *Journal of the History of Medicine and Allied Sciences*, 17 (1962), 152–67
Likenesses T. Cross, line engraving, pubd 1649 (after unknown artist), BM, NPG [*see illus.*] · portrait, repro. in N. Culpeper, *Pharmacopoeia Londinensis* (1649) · portrait, repro. in N. Culpeper, ed. and trans., *Galen's art of physick* (1652)

Culpeper, Sir Richard (*d.* 1485). *See under* Culpeper family (*per. c.*1400–*c.*1540).

Culpeper, Richard (*d.* 1516). *See under* Culpeper family (*per. c.*1400–*c.*1540).

Culpeper, Sir Thomas (*d.* 1429). *See under* Culpeper family (*per. c.*1400–*c.*1540).

Culpeper, Thomas (*c.*1514–1541). *See under* Katherine (1518×24–1542).

Culpeper [Colepeper], **Sir Thomas** (1577/8–1662), writer on usury, was the third son of Francis Culpeper (1537/8–1591) of Greenway Court, near Hollingbourne, Kent, and his wife, Joan (1544/5–1598), daughter of John Pordage of Rodmersham, Kent, and widow of William Stede. Culpeper, having matriculated on 15 October 1591, aged thirteen, entered Hart Hall, Oxford, as a commoner, but left without taking a degree; on 15 May 1594 he was admitted to Middle Temple. He married, in 1600, Elizabeth (1582–1638), daughter of John Cheyney of Guestling, Sussex. They raised a family of three sons, Cheney *Culpeper (*bap.* 1601, *d.* 1663), Francis (*b.* 1608/9), and Thomas (1625/6–1697?) [*see below*], and eight daughters. Culpeper sat as MP for Chippenham in 1614 and was knighted by James I on 23 September 1619. From the money brought by his marriage, Culpeper was eventually able to buy from the heirs of Sir John (Customer) Smythe (*d.* 1622) Leeds Castle, Kent, which he immediately settled on Cheney.

In 1620 Culpeper began writing his *Tract Against the High Rate of Usury*, which he presented to parliament in 1621, at the time when a bill was before the house, and published it in 1623. The subject was of active concern, for it was apparent that with 10 per cent as the legal rate of interest trade was falling off and English specie was migrating overseas. Culpeper shifted the argument against usury from divine law to economic utilitarianism. He identified the damage done by high interest rates, which encouraged merchants to exchange trade for moneylending where the profits were higher; young merchants were ruined; trades where profits were always less than 10 per cent were being abandoned; land prices were depressed because of the high cost of borrowing for improvements. He contrasted the gloomy domestic picture with that in France and the Low Countries where interest was 6 per cent, trade was thriving, and everywhere the land was being drained and improved. The 1621 bill failed but a reduction to 8 per cent came into law in 1624 as 21 Jac. I, c. 17, Against Usury.

Culpeper sat as MP for Tewkesbury in 1628. He was a royalist in the civil war, as was his family generally, apart from Cheney, who supported parliament. Culpeper's treatise was reprinted in 1641 and twice in 1668, first by Sir Joshua Child as an appendix to his *Discourse of Trade*, and secondly by Culpeper's son Thomas. He died in January 1662 and was buried at Hollingbourne church on 25 January.

Sir Thomas Culpeper (1625/6–1697?) the younger matriculated from University College, Oxford, as a commoner on 27 April 1640 aged fourteen, and was created BA on 8 February 1644. About this time he was elected a fellow of All Souls College. Having travelled abroad he was admitted to Middle Temple on 1 December 1647 but he does not seem to have pursued his studies there continuously, for he proceeded MA from University College on 26 May 1653 and was called to the bar only 'of grace' on 22 November 1661. Knighted soon after the Restoration he inherited Greenway Court at his father's death and retired there. Besides editing and writing a preface for his father's tract on usury he published other pamphlets on the subject, repeating his father's arguments. He also published a collection of homilies entitled *Essayes or Moral Discourses on Several Subjects. Written by a Person of Honour* (1655 and 1671). Culpeper's wife may have been Alice, a member of the extended Culpeper family. Several children were born to them: three sons were mentioned in his will, dated March 1695 and proved on 7 December 1697.

ANITA McCONNELL

Sources N. L. Jones, *God and the moneylenders* (1989) · E. Hasted, *The history and topographical survey of the county of Kent*, 2 (1782), 465–6 · Wood, *Ath. Oxon.*, new edn, 3.533; 4.447 · P. Clark, *English provincial society from the Reformation to the revolution: religion, politics and society in Kent, 1500–1640* (1977) · D. A. H. Cleggett, *History of Leeds Castle and its families* (1990) · C. H. Hopwood, ed., *Middle Temple records*, 1–2 (1904) · Foster, *Alum. Oxon.* · W. A. Shaw, *The knights of England*, 2 (1906), 174 · H. A. C. Sturgess, ed., *Register of admissions to the Honourable Society of the Middle Temple, from the fifteenth century to the year 1944*, 3 vols. (1949) · M. Jansson, ed., *Proceedings in parliament, 1614 (House of Commons)* (1988), 36, 377

Culpeper, Sir Thomas (1625/6–1697?). *See under* Culpeper, Sir Thomas (1577/8–1662).

Culpeper, Thomas, second Baron Culpeper (1635–1689), colonial governor, was baptized on 21 March 1635, the son of John Culpeper, first Baron Culpeper of Thoresway (1600–1660), and his wife, Judith (b. 1606), of Hollingbourne, Kent. Sir John, a staunch royalist, fled England following the execution of Charles I, and when Thomas turned sixteen, he went abroad too. He thus rose to manhood among indigent expatriates who comprised the Stuart court-in-waiting, though, luckily for him, he married Margaret van Hesse (1635–1710), a wealthy Dutch heiress, in 1658.

With the Restoration he, his wife, and father returned to England in the entourage of Charles II. When Sir John died shortly thereafter, he left his son the bankrupt barony of Thoresway, the king's unyielding gratefulness to the Culpepers, and an interest in a proprietary land grant on Virginia's Northern Neck (the peninsula between the Rappahannock and Potomac rivers). The young nobleman, armed with those assets, plus his wife's dowry, and a generous dash of personal charm, set about making his fortune. Culpeper could not gain his father's old post as master of the rolls, though he secured rights to several clerical places in the rolls office, each of which had a reputed market worth of £1500. Charles II quickly found Culpeper more visible and lucrative employment, giving him charge of the Isle of Wight and Carisbrooke Castle. That particular appointment augmented Culpeper's wealth greatly, though it did little to enhance his talents for governance or his willingness to hone them. Even so, he continued as a royal favourite. The king subsequently commissioned him an officer of an infantry regiment and named him to the council for foreign plantations. The latter assignment ultimately enabled him to succeed Sir William Berkeley as governor of Virginia.

Culpeper, whom many contemporaries disdained for his covetousness, cared little for governing Virginia. His real interest lay in profiting from his claim to a huge tract of colonial real estate he had gained as part of his inheritance. His father, along with Berkeley's brother John and others, had formed a group that Charles II designated proprietors of the Northern Neck in 1649. Exile kept the grantees from exploiting the would-be king's generosity, though Sir John Berkeley (afterwards Baron Berkeley of Stratton) named his brother, the governor, his land agent, but little came of that. Indeed, none of the patentees tried to develop the grant after the Restoration. One by one they either died or sold out until only Culpeper and Henry Bennet, first earl of Arlington, remained. On the other hand, Governor Berkeley attempted to rid Virginia of proprietors for ever, and towards that goal, he commenced hugely expensive negotiations that dragged on throughout the 1660s. The dealing grew more complicated in 1673, because Charles II assigned all unpatented land in the colony and all of its quitrents to Arlington and Culpeper. Berkeley's raising of taxes to buy them out contributed to Bacon's rebellion in 1676, the outbreak of which ended further bargaining for some time, though Culpeper appointed land agents who issued patents in his name and collected rents for him. Culpeper eventually bought out Arlington and settled with the crown in such a way as to leave him in sole possession of the Northern Neck.

His tenure as governor was stormy. He swore his oaths of office at Twickenham, Middlesex, on 13 July 1677, soon after Sir William Berkeley's burial, but instead of speedily departing for America, he chose to remain in London. Not even the report of the death of his lieutenant-governor, Herbert Jeffreys, hastened him. Curt orders from Charles II finally dislodged Culpeper in 1679, and once in the colony, he took up residence with his cousin Lady Frances Berkeley (née Culpeper). His brief fling with her had lasting political repercussion because it turned her eventual third husband, Philip Ludwell, into an implacable foe of royal intervention in Virginia affairs. Culpeper convened the general assembly, and once he had coaxed it into granting the crown its desired permanent revenue, he blithely disregarded the rest of his instructions, discontinued the assembly, and sailed to England without royal licence to quit his post.

Culpeper enjoyed himself in London while colonists rioted in a desperate attempt to drive up the price of tobacco. Order returned well before he returned to the colony in December 1682 to conduct his own inquiry into the troubles. The episode was fraught with implications that evidenced his failures as governor. Worse was to come when he helped himself to some £9500 out of the provincial treasury and suddenly returned to England, again without the king's leave. An annoyed Charles II summarily dismissed him and replaced him in August 1683 with Francis Howard, fifth Baron Howard of Effingham.

Culpeper lived another six years with his mistress, Susannah Willis, with whom he had two daughters. He died on 27 January 1689 in the London town house that he maintained with his second family. Mrs Willis buried him swiftly and so privately that his burial site remains unknown. His estate became the object of contentious litigation that dragged through parliament and the high court of chancery for years. Ultimately Mrs Willis succeeded in keeping the portion Culpeper willed to her. His wife got the bulk of the estate, including the Northern Neck proprietary, which passed to her daughter Catherine and into the Fairfax family after Catherine married Thomas Fairfax, fifth Baron Fairfax, in 1690.

Governor Culpeper was not remembered fondly by his contemporaries, least of all the Virginians. Historians have been no kinder to him. Almost without exception they have treated him as a venal politician whose mark on Virginia was very faint indeed. How fairly that reading depicts the man is open to question, if for no other reason than no one has yet undertaken a full, systematic examination of his career.

WARREN M. BILLINGS

Sources F. Harrison, *Proprietors of the Northern Neck* (1925) • D. A. H. Cleggett, *History of Leeds Castle and its families* (1990) • W. M. Billings, J. E. Selby, and T. W. Tate, *Colonial Virginia: a history* (1986) • W. M. Billings, *Councils, assemblies, and courts of judicature: the general assembly of Virginia, 1619–1700* [forthcoming] • D. S. Freeman, *George Washington: a biography* (1949–54), appx. I-I: 'The Northern Neck proprietary' • S. S. Webb, *The governors-general: the English army and* *the definition of the empire, 1569–1681* (1979) · T. J. Wertenbaker, *Virginia under the Stuarts* (1914) · Chancery bills and answers before 1714, HLRO, PRO and House of Lords papers, 1689–1690, file Hamilton, 2, bundle 671

Archives CKS, papers

Likenesses oils (after portrait in Leeds Castle), Virginia Historical Society, Richmond

Wealth at death contents of Leeds Castle valued at £245 6s. 2d.; the greater part of estate became object of widow's suit brought to establish her claim as Culpeper's singular and rightful heir: Chancery bills and answers before 1714, HLRO, PRO and House of Lords, papers, 1689–1690, file Hamilton, 2, bundle 671

Culpeper, William (d. 1501). *See under* Culpeper family (*per.* c.1400–c.1540).

Culpin, Millais (1874–1952), psychologist, was born on 6 January 1874 in Baldock Street, Ware, Hertfordshire, the second of six children of Millice Culpin (1844–1942), a leather seller, and his wife, Hannah Louisa Munsey (c.1850–1937). The family moved to Stoke Newington, in north London. Millais attended the Grocers' Company's School, Hackney, and became one of a group of young entomologists, the North London Natural History Society (later part of the London Natural History Society). This hobby remained a lifelong interest. In 1891 Millice Culpin, now a qualified doctor, and his family emigrated to Brisbane, Queensland. Young Millais spent four formative years as a 'bush schoolmaster' in north Queensland; the lively letters he wrote from there to his former schoolmates were published, edited by his daughter, as *Letters from Laura* (University of Townsville, 1987) and show a gift for scientific and human observation and his lasting affection for the country.

Millais returned in 1897 to enter the London Hospital, where, after winning various prizes and qualifying in 1902, he graduated FRCS in 1907. He held various appointments there before taking up a practice in Shanghai; there he met, and married in 1913, Ethel Maude Bennett (1874–1966) of Trowbridge, Wiltshire, a London Hospital trained nursing sister who had come to take up the post of matron of the Shanghai-Nanking (Nanjing) Railway Hospital, the chief British hospital. Both experienced, in their professional roles, the revolution of 1911, and both retained a warm interest in the Chinese people. Culpin's two sojourns in the tropics were to lead to an interesting paper, 'Neurasthenia in the tropics' (*The Practitioner*, August 1935).

After a visit to his family in Australia, where the only child of the marriage, a daughter, Frances, was born, they returned to England in 1914, just as war broke out. Culpin joined the Royal Army Medical Corps as a surgeon, but soon his obstinate truth seeking led him to question the diagnoses of his seniors in recognizing and treating hysterical/psychosomatic disorders (shell-shock). He worked as a surgeon in the Queen Alexandra Hospital, Portsmouth. Culpin was in France in 1916, but meanwhile in 1915 he and Dr E. G. Fearnsides wrote one of the first articles on the war neuroses (*BMJ*, 9 January 1916). Finally Colonel Aldren Turner, a neurologist, sent Culpin to Maghull

for training under, among others, T. H. Pear and Bernard Hart, only for Culpin to find fresh hostility to the psychoanalytical view when he moved to Moneyhull, Birmingham. Later, at Ewell Military Hospital, he met with understanding and co-operation, and the support of Colonel C. S. Myers. In these struggles Culpin must often have felt isolated and despairing: it is a tribute to him and his fellow workers in the field that their findings were accepted and acted upon in the Second World War.

Culpin was demobilized in 1919. He took a London MD and never practised surgery again. His thesis, published in 1920 as *The Psychoneuroses of War and Peace*, was followed by *Spiritualism and the New Psychology* (1920), and *The Nervous Patient* (1924). He had by now thrown in his lot with the practitioners of psychological medicine. Just after the First World War he was appointed lecturer in psychoneuroses at the London Hospital, the first post of its kind, which he held until 1939, and he began private practice as a psychotherapist in Queen Anne Street, London. This he continued through the Second World War, and later practised in Guildford and St Albans. The family had been for some time settled in Loughton, Essex, near Epping Forest, the scene of his early 'bug-hunting' cycle rides from Stoke Newington and where friends from his student days were already living. In 1932 the family moved to Park Village East, on Regent's Park Canal in north London, until they were bombed out ten years later.

In the early 1920s Culpin was called on to work for the Industrial Health Research Board (*A Study of Telegraphists' Cramp*, by May Smith, Culpin, and Eric Farmer, 1927). He himself valued most his work for the Medical Research Council on miner's nystagmus ('The occupational neuroses (including miner's nystagmus)', *Proceedings of the Royal Society of Medicine*, 1933). While chairman of the industrial section of the British Psychological Society he investigated the bus drivers under treatment for gastric disorders at Manor House, the trade union hospital, revealing psychosomatic symptoms in a stressful job. This type of research became the basis of many job selection procedures in business and industry.

In 1931 Culpin became professor of medical industrial psychology at the School of Hygiene and Tropical Medicine at London University. He enjoyed his work there, the research, the students, and appreciated his colleagues, but remained unimpressed by the trappings of prestige or position. In 1944 he was elected president of the British Psychological Association; he never forgot his debt to Freud's theory of the unconscious which, he told a young colleague years later, he was reminded of every day of his working life, and he enjoyed a friendship with the German analyst Georg Groddeck, whom he visited several times at Baden-Baden. Culpin's chief publications were *Medicine: and the Man* (1927), *The Nervous Temperament* (1930), *Recent Advances in the Study of the Psychoneuroses* (1931), and *Mental Abnormality: Facts and Theories* (1948).

During the years just before the Second World War, Culpin was active in the China medical aid committee and the Academic Assistance Fund (aiding professionals from

Nazi Germany) and during the war he followed with interest the development of the provision of care and treatment for the psychiatric casualties of war through his son-in-law, Lieutenant-Colonel Stephen MacKeith RAMC.

Culpin's father was a stern rationalist, but Millais described himself as a 'cheerful agnostic'. Physically he was tall, dark, regular featured, and mild mannered. He never owned a car, walked with a swift stride, and remained in good health until his death on 14 September 1952 at his home in Hatfield Road, St Albans, of a pulmonary embolism. His ashes were scattered at Wicken Fen, Cambridgeshire, haunt of his favourite swallowtail butterfly. Culpin's nature was as gentle as his mind was keen, and he led a quiet, fairly abstemious life, enjoying until the end a good game of bridge, the *Times* crossword, the company of his family, and the first brimstone butterfly of spring.   FRANCES MILLAIS MACKEITH

Sources M. Culpin, 'An autobiography', *Occupational Psychology* (July 1947) • personal knowledge (2004) • *BMJ* (27 Sept 1952), 727–8 • *The Lancet* (27 Sept 1952) • b. cert. • d. cert. **Wealth at death** £8208 3s. 2d.: administration, 9 Jan 1953, CGPLA Eng. & Wales

Culshaw, John Royds (1924–1980), record producer and television executive, was born on 28 May 1924 at 47 Lethbridge Road, Southport, Lancashire, one of at least two children of Percy Ellis Culshaw, banker's clerk, and his wife, Dorothy Royds. He attended first the Merchant Taylors' School in Crosby and then the King George V Grammar School in Southport, and at the age of sixteen followed his father as a clerk with the Midland Bank. He studied the piano from an early age, but became increasingly dissatisfied with his own musical abilities, and, with encouragement from his mother, developed a deep interest in concert performance and opera.

Culshaw began his war service in 1942 joining the Fleet Air Arm as a volunteer and serving in Trinidad and Europe. While still in the services he attended a concert given by the great Russian composer Sergey Rakhmaninov, and this helped forge the direction of his subsequent career. In November 1946, after his discharge from the services, Culshaw joined the Decca Record Company's publicity department, writing sleeve notes for classical music records. The following year he began work on a biography of Rakhmaninov (published in 1949). In the same year his book on Brahms appeared, as well as a popular introduction to the concerto, and a guide to the main developments of contemporary music.

The failure of his period as editor of the Decca house magazine *Music*, however, convinced Culshaw that his real talents lay elsewhere, and by the end of 1947 he had completed his first recording sessions at Decca as a record producer. During these early years as a Decca producer he made several notable recordings, such as Richard Strauss's *Arabella* and Charles Gounod's *Romeo and Juliet*. Culshaw left Decca in 1954 and went to work for the Hollywood-based Capitol Records, then expanding its classical recording programme. There he made several important records including one of the then comparatively unknown Hungarian conductor George Solti conducting a performance of the Brahms Requiem. He also undertook a series of remarkable recordings of performances by Eduard van Beinum and the Concertgebouw Orchestra of Amsterdam. Culshaw's greatest contribution to recorded culture, however, was to take up the best part of the decade after 1957.

In 1956 Culshaw returned to Decca as manager of the classical record department, having persuaded a reluctant Maurice Rosengarten, then executive manager of the Decca record business, to allow him to produce the first complete stereo recording of Richard Wagner's *Ring* cycle, with George Solti conducting. The first of the four operas, *Rheingold*, was released in 1958, and, according to Culshaw, in the following year it sold more copies than Elvis Presley LPs. Making this mammoth series Culshaw called on the latest recording technology, including stereophonic sound. The recording, 'with its brilliant use of sound effects and aural perspectives, heralded a new era' (*The Times*, 29 April 1980). Culshaw later documented the hilarious details of this momentous event in a book entitled *Ring Resounding: the Recording in Stereo of Der Ring des Nibelungen* (1967).

By the time the project was complete, Culshaw had established himself as one of the world's great record producers. For this work, he was made an OBE in 1966. He subsequently recorded most of the major operas in the repertoire. In addition he received numerous other awards including several prestigious grand prix de disques from the French industry. Moreover, the *Ring* recordings proved to a sceptical music industry that classical music could be successfully encapsulated on disc: a factor that helped ensure the proliferation of a broad range of classical music available on record.

In 1967, after completing his *Ring* cycle, Culshaw moved into the medium of television, becoming head of music at BBC television, thus combining his twin passions for music and visual media. While at the BBC he forged an important working relationship with Benjamin Britten. He persuaded Britten to conduct a television performance of his opera *Peter Grimes* and further he commissioned Britten to write a new opera, *Owen Wingrave*, for the BBC. Culshaw was invited to Snape in Suffolk and reported positively to Britten on the possibilities of transforming The Maltings into a concert-hall, writing that:

> there was a feeling about the place, about its setting by the river with the view of Iken church through the reeds and across the marshes that made it right. If Ben was to have a concert hall on his doorstep, this was it.   (Carpenter, 456)

Culshaw later initiated the Benson and Hedges music festival at Snape (and was planning the fourth season at the time of his death).

During his time with the BBC, Culshaw did much to broaden the availability and the appreciation of classical music on television. In 1975 Culshaw left the BBC and the same year was elected to the Arts Council of Great Britain. He pursued a writing and lecturing career, and in 1977 became a senior fellow in the creative arts at the University of Western Australia. He also took on the responsibility for the annual United Nations concert in New York, and acted as a music consultant to the Australian Broadcasting Commission.

Throughout his life John Culshaw combined personal ambition with a love of recorded music, but he was not without his critics. Donald Mitchell commented unfavourably on the way in which Culshaw courted Britten's favour:

> The manipulative side of it was all too transparent. John certainly made an innovative and influential contribution to the record industry, and we must all be indebted to him for his historic series of Britten recordings. But at the BBC he seemed to me to be out of his depth. (Carpenter, 504)

Nevertheless, he had an ingenuity and a persuasive personality which mostly won him the friendship and respect of colleagues and artistes alike. He made a lasting contribution to the record industry and television, and left a priceless heritage for the listening public.

Culshaw died of cirrhosis and hepatitis on 27 April 1980 at the Royal Free Hospital, London. He never married. His autobiography, which was in the final stage of completion when he died, contains much of interest about the man and the industries he dominated. It was published under the title of *Putting the Record Straight*. The work provides a remarkable insight into the difficulties encountered when highly creative individuals are forced to work together to produce a commercial product. In a glowing obituary *The Times* noted that 'The immense proliferation of classical recordings now available to all, at comparatively low cost, can be directly attributed to Culshaw's pioneering and imaginative work' (*The Times*, 29 April 1980). PETER MARTLAND

Sources J. Culshaw, *Putting the record straight* (1981) · J. Culshaw, *Ring resounding: the recording in stereo of Der Ring des Nibelungen* (1967) · b. cert. · d. cert. · H. Carpenter, *Benjamin Britten: a biography* (1992) · *The Times* (29 April 1980) · J. Culshaw, '"Ben" – a tribute to Benjamin Britten', *The Britten companion*, ed. C. Palmer (1984), 62–7 **Archives** BBC WAC | FILM BFI NFTVA, Culshaw recording the Ring cycle **Wealth at death** £114,659: probate, 7 Aug 1980, *CGPLA Eng. & Wales*

Culverwell family (*per. c.*1545–*c.*1640), merchants and religious radicals, descended from William Culverwell of Wells, Somerset, and his wife (*née* Berney), who produced a remarkable family during the reign of Henry VIII. It included five surviving sons, three of whom gravitated to London and became citizens in the legal sense—that is, by virtue of being 'made free' of one of the livery companies.

The founding brother Nicholas Culverwell (*d.* 1569), the first to achieve success if not demonstrably the eldest, served an apprenticeship under George *Barne (*c.*1500–1558), later lord mayor of London and probably his mother's brother, and was made free of the Haberdashers in July 1549. He immediately married Elizabeth Joyce: their eldest child, Elizabeth, was baptized at St James Garlickhythe in September 1550. Six other children are known to have been born before 1563.

By 1553 Nicholas Culverwell had settled his family in the parish of St Martin Vintry. A convinced protestant probably from his prentice days he may, like his friends George and Thomas Heton, have been one the 'sustainers' of the secret protestant congregation in Marian London, while in 1559 he entertained John Jewel (1522–1571) following his return from exile. Rated that year in the high assessment for subsidy at £90 he was thus officially counted amongst London's 500 richest citizens. His prosperity appears to have been based initially on the Gascon wine trade, but during 1559–60 he attempted, with the aid of Lord Robert Dudley, to establish a government-sponsored company to regulate a new wool staple on the continent, on the grounds that the loss of Calais in 1558 had cancelled the ancient privileges of the Merchant Staplers. The latter, however, retaliated, negotiating a new government charter in early 1561 and transferring their activities to Bruges. The patent granted to Dudley was accordingly surrendered.

In October 1561 Culverwell bought from George Heton a large estate in Stratford-Bow and Bromley by Bow, Middlesex, and in 1566 contributed £3 6s. 8d. for the building of Sir Thomas Gresham's New Exchange, a sum which placed him within the top fifth of the 732 London merchants involved in the scheme. In 1568 he was one of a consortium which, partly under cover of a government contract for the importation of wine and salt, was responsible for providing help for the Huguenot cause in France. Accorded quasi-diplomatic status, Nicholas was sent to negotiate with Cardinal Châtillon, the mayor of La Rochelle, and Jeanne d'Albret, queen of Navarre. A letter mentioning his activities, found on the body of the prince de Condé after the battle of Jarnac (13 March 1569), survives in the Bibliothèque Nationale de France.

Although clearly destined for a spectacular mercantile career Nicholas Culverwell died on 26 October 1569, probably in his early forties. His will, made four days earlier, contains generous bequests and set up two trusts under the auspices of the Haberdashers. A stock of £100 was to provide five young freemen with £20 each for five years, tax-free. A trust fund of £200 was to be established in order to pay £5 per annum to two poor divinity students, one at Christ's College, Cambridge, and the other at Magdalen College, Oxford, 'they to be called for ever by the names of the preachers of Nicholas Culverwell'. The Haberdashers administers the trust to this day. Elizabeth was named sole executrix. Nicholas's four overseers were his brother Richard; the Marian exile John Bodley (father of Sir Thomas), with whom the family had established a lasting friendship; Thomas Heton; and Thomas Sampson, who had been deprived of the deanery of Christ Church for nonconformity in 1565. First to witness the will was the young John Field, on the brink of his career as London's most energetic and determined religious reformer.

Alliances in marriage and faith Nicholas Culverwell's profound impact on London's godly community was spectacularly reflected in the marriage alliances of the next generation. His daughter Elizabeth became the mother of the Church of England clergyman and author William

*Gouge. His eldest son, **Samuel Culverwell** (1551?–1613), graduated BA from Christ's College, Cambridge, in early 1572, matriculated at Heidelberg in October that year (possibly as a disciple of Thomas Cartwright), and in 1578 married Jane, one of the two recorded daughters of Thomas Sampson. He sold the major portion of the Stratford estate and died as rector of Cherry Burton, Yorkshire, and a noted preacher. Of Nicholas's two surviving younger daughters Cecilia (d. c.1630) married Laurence Chaderton, first master of Emmanuel College, Cambridge, while Susan (d. c.1587) was married first to Cuthbert Fuller (d. 1579), brother of Nicholas Fuller, and then to William Whitaker, master of St John's College, Cambridge.

Of Nicholas Culverwell's 'London' brothers, **Laurence Culverwell** (d. 1562) became free of the Coopers by redemption (a money payment) in 1560. **Richard Culverwell** (d. 1586), apprenticed to John Elliott, factor to Sir Thomas Gresham during Mary's reign, became free of the Mercers in 1559, also settling in St Martin Vintry. He took over Nicholas's role within the London godly community and evidently became the mainstay of the politico-religious campaigns of John Field, while himself maintaining an extremely low profile. Despite his diligence in investigating 'the precisians' Richard Bancroft discovered little in the early 1580s beyond the fact that they collected money 'for their brethren that travell for them beyond the Seas' which was 'commonlye delivered to one Field a Preacher in the Citie, and one Culverwell in Tamyse streete' (Peel, *Tracts*, 12). Richard himself probably travelled widely on behalf of the Calvinist cause, bequeathing to his daughter a gold chain given to him by the queen of Navarre 'for the furtherance and defence of the gospel and such as sincerely profess the same' (PRO, PROB 11/69). In 1583 he negotiated the land transactions necessary to establish the site of Emmanuel College, Cambridge, formally founded in 1584. Counted as one of Emmanuel's original benefactors, he bestowed upon it £200 and many books, several of which survive in the college library.

Richard Culverwell died in February 1586, his will suggesting the extent to which he had been responsible for co-ordinating and financing godly stratagems since the death of Nicholas. There were bequests of £2 or £3 to nine leading London preachers, including Field, Robert Crowley, William Charke, Walter Travers, and Thomas Crooke, and the huge sum of £350 was left in trust for distribution to the deserving godly, clerical or lay.

For a variety of reasons Richard Culverwell's death probably ended St Martin Vintry's influence over the affairs of the London godly. He himself had no son to succeed him. He and his wife, Anne (née Hopkins; d. in or before January 1598), had an only daughter, Judith, who in 1585 married the future Sir Thomas Smythe (c.1558–1625) but died within days of her father. Laurence's only son, **Anthony Culverwell** (c.1559–1612) married Sybil, daughter of John *Bodley (c.1520–1591), in 1582 as his first wife but was not regarded by Richard as the heir to his business interests and received only £30 in Richard's will. Following Sybil's death, some time after 1584, he married Sarah Willis, who survived him. The days of organized radical

protestantism were numbered by now. The death of John Field in 1588 and the appearance of the Martin Marprelate tracts thereafter prompted the relentless campaign which amongst much else destroyed the conference movement that Field had founded and guided for twenty years.

Their widows all long outlived the three Culverwell brothers. Alice, wife of Laurence, continued to run his business under the auspices of the Coopers and as Alice Luntley was remembered in Richard's will. Elizabeth, wife of Nicholas, died in 1589 or early in January 1590, appointing John Bodley sole executor and making bequests to Chaderton, Whitaker, and other leading Cambridge divines. Anne, wife of Richard, remained a widow ten years before marrying William Neale (d. 1600), auditor of the exchequer and a close friend of Walter Mildmay.

If Anthony did not inherit the mantle of Nicholas and Richard, the Culverwell genius was dispersed unto the third and fourth generations in the careers of William Gouge, Nathaniel Culverwell (*bap.* 1619, d. 1651), a Culverwell by double descent, and Alexander Whitaker, 'the Apostle of Virginia'. Nathaniel's father, another **Richard Culverwell** (1581/2–1644), was probably a grandson of either John or William Culverwell, the two brothers of Nicholas, Laurence, and Richard who never left Somerset. He matriculated at Exeter College, Oxford, in April 1598 aged sixteen, as 'plebeian' of Somerset. Graduating BA in 1602, he proceeded MA in 1607 and BD in 1617. He married Margaret Horton, daughter of the London merchant Thomas Horton and his wife, Margaret, daughter of Laurence Culverwell and sister of Anthony. Instituted on the crown's presentation to the rectory of St Margaret Moyses, Friday Street, on 30 March 1618 he was buried there on 12 April 1644. Of Nathaniel's siblings, the third Richard Culverwell (1621–1688), was baptized at St Margaret Moyses on 21 April 1621 and died as rector of Grundisburgh, Suffolk.

A pillar of godliness There remains the outstanding figure of **Ezekiel Culverwell** (c.1554–1631), second son of Nicholas Culverwell, who graduated BA at Oxford in 1573, proceeding MA in June 1577. The Oxford records do not mention his college, but since his father endowed a preachership there in 1569 there can be little doubt that Ezekiel was sent to Magdalen, where Laurence Humphrey (whose biography of Jewel is the source for Nicholas's patronage of him) was president. He was ordained deacon and priest at Lincoln in 1585, before arriving in Essex as household chaplain at Leighs Priory, principal seat of Robert, third Lord Rich, in late 1586 or early 1587. Establishing a strong friendship with Richard Rogers, lecturer of Wethersfield, he joined the conference of nonconformist ministers around Braintree which had first met in 1582. He also persuaded his sister Elizabeth and her husband, Thomas Gouge, to send their son William to Felsted School, where the young Gouge was 'trained up three years under the public ministry of his uncle' (Gouge, 'A narrative', sig. A1) before departing for Eton in 1589. Culverwell's activities soon engaged Aylmer's attention: as 'preacher of Felsted' he was amongst those who, some time in 1587, are recorded as having been suspended 'in his last visitation and since for the surplice' (Peel, *Seconde Parte*, 2.260).

Culverwell's position as Rich's chaplain could not protect him from the attentions of Aylmer's officials in the visitation of 1589. In a series of twenty-one articles, probably written by Thomas Rust, vicar of Felsted, his nonconformist practices were comprehensively scrutinized. Subsequent court hearings were admirably handled by Edward Stanhope, Aylmer's vicar-general, who refused to turn the case into a witch-hunt and ostensibly reconciled Culverwell and Rust (and their wives). Culverwell continued to preach at Felsted and a son, Ezekiel (*d. c.*1606), was baptized in the parish church in March 1591. On 23 December 1592 Aylmer instituted Culverwell, on the presentation of Robert Lawson, to the Essex rectory of Great Stambridge. Nothing is known of his first wife but in 1598 he married Winifred (*née* Hildersham), widow of Edward Barefoot, a friend of his brother Samuel's from Cambridge and Heidelberg days, and possibly the sister of Arthur Hildersham.

Following the death of Arthur Dent, Culverwell saw through the press his treatise on the apocalypse, *The Ruine of Rome* (1603), adding a dedicatory epistle to Lord Rich. His reference to his 'near conjunction' with his 'late brother' (sig. 1*v*) led to the erroneous assumption that Dent had married a Culverwell daughter. In April 1605 Culverwell solemnized at Great Stambridge the marriage of Mary Forth to John Winthrop, future governor of Massachusetts. Winthrop later recorded that it was Culverwell who had converted him to godliness and the two men continued to correspond long after Mary's death. Two of Culverwell's three surviving letters are preserved amongst the Winthrop papers.

After the Hampton Court conference in 1604 nonconformity again came under siege as James I pressed his bishops to demand subscription to the prayer book ceremonies as the badge of inclusion within the Church of England. Although undisturbed during Richard Vaughan's episcopate (1604–7) Culverwell could not parry the demands of his successor, Thomas Ravis. On 20 March 1609 he was one of four Essex incumbents deprived by the high commission.

Culverwell apparently spent the rest of his life in London. In 1623 he published *A Treatise of Faith*, a comprehensive attempt to anatomize the scriptural basis of Calvinist belief and practice, which reached an eighth edition in 1648 and prompted a small spate of similar guides to godliness. Alexander Leighton accused Culverwell of Arminian errors in *A Friendly Triall of the 'Treatise of Faith'* (1624). Scorning to name either Leighton or the title of his book, Culverwell penned *A Briefe Answere to Certain Objections Against the 'Treatise of Faith'* (1626). Several shorter works were published after his death.

Culverwell lived out his last years as a widower. Winifred was buried at All Hallows Barkingside in November 1613 and all his children but one—Sarah Barefoot, his executrix—were dead when he made his will in July 1630. He was buried in the parish of St Antholin on 14 April 1631.

C. H. Garrett's *The Marian Exiles* (1938) has been castigated for suggesting that protestant activities abroad between 1553 and 1558 were in some sense an organized withdrawal and planning of a New Jerusalem, the experience of which led directly to the American colonial experiment three generations later. A career such as Ezekiel Culverwell's, which exactly spans the vital eighty years involved, nevertheless gives pause for thought. The child who was dandled on John Jewel's knee just after the death of Mary I lived on to inspire William Gouge, John Winthrop, and also Ezekiel Cheever (1616?–1708)—presumably a godson—to whom he bequeathed £10 and one third of his Latin books. New England's most celebrated schoolmaster, Cheever died in harness more than a decade after the death of Mary II: Ezekiel Culverwell's was thus a vital handshake in the dispersal of the nonconformist protestant tradition. BRETT USHER

Sources B. Usher, 'The silent community: early puritans and the patronage of the arts', *The church and the arts*, ed. D. Wood, SCH, 28 (1992), 287–302 · B. Usher, *The Culverwells: the rise and influence of a Tudor family* [forthcoming] · L. Humphrey, *Joannis Juelli Angli, episcopi Sarisburiensis vita et mors* (1573) · BL, Lansdowne MS 113/20 · GL, MS 15, 857, vol. 1 · GL, MS 2859 · will, GL, MS 9171/26, fols. 147v–148r [Ezekiel Culverwell] · GL, MS 9535/2, fol. 4v · I. W. Archer, *The history of the Haberdashers' Company* (1991) · Mercers' Hall, London, Mercers' Company papers · *Calendar of the manuscripts of the most hon. the marquis of Salisbury*, 1, HMC, 9 (1883); 13 (1915) · T. Gouge, 'A narrative of the life and death of Dr William Gouge', in W. Gouge, *A learned and very useful commentary on the whole epistle to the Hebrewes*, ed. T. Gouge (1655) · A. Peel, ed., *Tracts ascribed to Richard Bancroft* (1953) · A. Peel, ed., *The seconde parte of a register*, 2 vols. (1915) · P. Lake, *Moderate puritans and the Elizabethan church* (1982) · R. G. Usher, ed., *The presbyterian movement in the reign of Queen Elizabeth, as illustrated by the minute book of the Dedham classis, 1582–1589*, CS, 3rd ser., 8 (1905) · D. Trim, 'Sir Thomas Bodley and the international protestant cause', *Bodleian Library Record*, 16 (1997–9), 314–40 · *Two Elizabethan puritan diaries, by Richard Rogers and Samuel Ward*, ed. M. M. Knappen, SCH, 2 [1933] · LMA, DL/C/618, pp. 97–100 · will of Nicholas Culverwell, PRO, PROB 11/52 · will of Richard Culverwell, PRO, PROB 11/69 · will of Elizabeth Culverwell, PRO, PROB 11/75 · V. Lake, 'Richard Culverwell: *Res tuas age*', MS, Emmanuel College, Cambridge, box. COL.9.3 · S. Bush and C. J. Rasmussen, *The library of Emmanuel College, Cambridge, 1584–1637* (1986) · S. B. Babbage, *Puritanism and Richard Bancroft* (1962) · *The Winthrop papers*, ed. W. C. Ford and others, 1 (1929) · S. Foster, *Notes from the Caroline underground: Alexander Leighton, the puritan triumvirate, and the Laudian reaction to nonconformity* (1978) · S. Adams, *Household accounts and disbursement books of Robert Dudley, earl of Leicester, 1558–1561, 1584–1586*, CS, 6 (1995) · *Extracts from the records of the City of London and the books of the joint committee of the City of London and Mercers' Company, upon Gresham affairs … respecting the Royal Exchange and the Gresham Trust, 1564–1825* [1839] · S. Bendall, C. Brooke, and P. Collinson, *A history of Emmanuel College, Cambridge* (1999) · J. L. Chester and G. J. Armytage, eds., *Allegations for marriage licences issued by the bishop of London*, 1, Harleian Society, 25 (1887) · A. R. Maddison, ed., *Lincolnshire pedigrees*, 1, Harleian Society, 50 (1902), 285 · G. Toepke, ed., *Die Matrikel der Universität Heidelberg*, 7 vols. (Heidelberg, 1884–1916)

Archives BL, Egerton MSS, letter of Ezekiel Culverwell · Millersville University, Pennsylvania, Winthrop papers, two letters of Ezekiel Culverwell

Wealth at death possibly £900 in liquid assets, as reflected by bequests; approx. £3000 in moveables and city property, plus estate in Middlesex; Nicholas Culverwell: will, PRO, PROB 11/52, 1569 · comparatively modest; small property in Leicestershire; Laurence Culverwell: will, 1562 · immensely wealthy; over £400 in trusts, £1000 to son-in-law, remainder to widow and daughter;

more than £200 to Emmanuel College, Cambridge; approx. £30 to deserving godly preachers; lease in parish of St Martin Vintry; also widow's jewellery; Richard Culverwell: will, PRO, PROB 11/69, 1586 · £350 in monetary bequests; plus many books; probably no property or other assets; Ezekiel Culverwell: will, 1630

Culverwell, Anthony (c.1559–1612). *See under* Culverwell family (*per. c.*1545–c.1640).

Culverwell, Ezekiel (c.1554–1631). *See under* Culverwell family (*per. c.*1545–c.1640).

Culverwell, Laurence (d. 1562). *See under* Culverwell family (*per. c.*1545–c.1640).

Culverwell, Nathaniel [Nathanael Culverwel] (*bap.* **1619**, *d.* **1651**), philosopher and theologian, was baptized on 13 January 1619 at St Margaret Moyses, Friday Street, in the City of London. He was the eldest of five children of Richard *Culverwell (1581/2–1644) [*see under* Culverwell family (*per. c.*1545–c.1640)], the minister there, and his wife, Margaret. Nathaniel attended St Paul's School during the mastership of Alexander Gill the elder (1565–1635), teacher of John Milton. From 1632 to 1642 he was in receipt of an exhibition worth £10 annually from St Paul's. In 1633 he was admitted pensioner to Emmanuel College, Cambridge, which his great-great-uncle, the wealthy merchant Richard Culverwell, had helped to found in 1584. After graduating BA in 1636, he proceeded MA in 1640 and was elected a fellow of Emmanuel in 1642. There is no record of his having been ordained, or that he became DD. At the time of his election, the luminaries of the Emmanuel fellowship included most of the remarkable cluster of scholars who have come to be known as Cambridge Platonists: Benjamin Whichcote, Ralph Cudworth, Peter Sterry, John Smith, and John Worthington. His Emmanuel contemporaries also included the mathematician John Wallis, and the future archbishop of Canterbury William Sancroft. Very little is known of Culverwell's activities before his premature death in early 1651 (his mother took out letters of administration for his estate on 2 June). He contributed verses on various public occasions: to *EUNODIA, sive, Musarum Cantabrigensis concentus et congratulatio* in 1637 (on the birth of Princess Mary) and to *Irenodia Cantabrigensis* in 1641 (on Charles I's return from Scotland). He also wrote a verse on the death of Richard Holden, possibly a student of his. He was unmarried.

Culverwell's claim to fame rests with his posthumously published book, *An Elegant and Learned Discourse of the Light of Nature* (1652). Based on a set of academic exercises dating from 1646, this was prepared for publication by his younger brother, Richard Culverwell, rector of Grundisburgh, Suffolk, who was assisted by William Dillingham, who had been elected fellow of Emmanuel at the same time as Nathaniel Culverwell. Although Culverwell did not achieve his full promise as a thinker, he deserves on the strength of this book to be considered one of the Cambridge Platonists, whose optimistic and liberal protestant theology he shared. Although the book is dedicated to the stern Calvinist Anthony Tuckney, then master of Emmanuel, it resonates with the humanist spirit and the liberal theological outlook of Benjamin Whichcote. Like the other Cambridge Platonists, Culverwell held that reason and faith are compatible. And like theirs, Culverwell's was a voice of moderation at a time of acute religious discord: according to Dillingham, Culverwell aimed 'to vindicate the use of Reason in matters of Religion, from the passions and prejudices of some weaker ones in these times' (Culverwell, 7). Culverwell was the only member of the Cambridge Platonists to invoke natural law theory as the foundation of his rational ethics. His founding of the legal authority of moral law in the will of God and in the cognitive capacities of human beings has resulted in his being considered a precursor of Locke, major differences between them notwithstanding.

The 'light of nature' of the book's title is human reason, the 'intellectual lamp' placed by God in the human soul to enable mankind to understand the law of nature. According to Culverwell the 'law of nature' is the imprint of divine law in rational beings. While he acknowledged the limitations of postlapsarian human reason, he was optimistic about human capacities, emphasizing reason and free will as preconditions for knowledge of the moral law and the obligation to obey it. For this purpose, all human minds are furnished with 'clear and indelible' principles of reason and morality. He conceived of God as an intellectual being who communicates with man through reason. Like Whichcote, he argued that men become more like God through the exercise of their reason. In coming to a knowledge of God and the eternal law, our reason is aided by experience of the external world which manifests God's wisdom in the fixed order of divine providence. Culverwell also shared with Whichcote the view that many pagan philosophers had led better lives than many Christians, although they were not among the elect of God. He was highly critical of some aspects of Platonism, especially Plato's doctrine of the pre-existence of the soul, but he none the less had a high regard for Plato and attacked Aristotelian dogmatism. He was also aware of the challenge of scepticism, against which he argued that reason offers certainty. In addition to referring to classical sources, his book shows his familiarity with both scholastic theology and contemporary philosophy: indeed, Culverwell stands out among the Cambridge Platonists for his overt use of the scholastic theologians Aquinas and Suarez, from whom he derives his preferred definitions of eternal law and natural law. He also cites John Selden, Grotius, Lord Herbert of Cherbury, and Francis Bacon and demonstrates an awareness of the philosophy of Descartes. In his use of a broad range of sources Culverwell treats the legacy of European philosophy as a single, integrated body of wisdom constituting a perennial philosophy. His model for this was probably Agostino Steucho's *De perenni philosophia* (1540), which he cites.

Culverwell also wrote a number of short theological pieces, including *The White Stone* (1654) and *Spirituall Opticks* (1651), which were added to editions of *An Elegant and Learned Discourse* and reprinted with it in 1654, 1661, and 1669.   SARAH HUTTON

Sources N. Culverwell, *An elegant and learned discourse of the light of nature, with several other treatises* (1652) · R. A. Greene and H. MacCallum, introduction, in N. Culverwell, *An elegant and learned discourse of the light of nature*, ed. R. A. Greene and H. MacCallum (1971) · J. Lagrée, 'Lumière naturelle et notions communes: Herbert de Cherbury et Culverwell', *'Mind senior to the world': stoicismo e origenismo nella filosofia platonica del Seicento inglese*, ed. M. Baldi (Milan, 1996), 35–54 · S. Darwall, *The British moralists and the internal 'ought', 1640–1700* (1995) · S. Bendall, C. Brooke, and P. Collinson, *A history of Emmanuel College, Cambridge* (1999) · Venn, *Alum. Cant.* · DNB · administration act book, 1651, PRO, PROB 6/26, fol. 79
Archives Bodl. Oxf., Rawl. MS Poetical 147

Culverwell, Nicholas (*d.* 1569). *See under* Culverwell family (*per. c.*1545–*c.*1640).

Culverwell, Richard (*d.* 1586). *See under* Culverwell family (*per. c.*1545–*c.*1640).

Culverwell, Richard (1581/2–1644). *See under* Culverwell family (*per. c.*1545–*c.*1640).

Culverwell, Samuel (1551?–1613). *See under* Culverwell family (*per. c.*1545–*c.*1640).

Culy, David (*d. c.*1725), Independent minister, was the son of John and Anne Culy, a Huguenot couple living in Guyhirn, in the Isle of Ely. In 1687 he underwent a religious conversion at March through hearing Francis Holcroft (1628/29?–1692), who had established a number of dissenting congregations in Cambridgeshire. In 1688 Culy recorded: 'the lord sent me out to preach the gospel of his son, whose voice I obeyed. I began first at my owne sisters house at Guihorn, being a widdow.'

Culy and his followers failed to find a spiritual home with the Cambridge Independents and he suffered a period of depression. This was relieved when Richard Davis (1658–1714), minister of the Independent congregation at Rothwell, Northamptonshire, visited Guyhirn in 1691. Two groups from Guyhirn joined the Rothwell church in August and David Culy preached there. By the end of 1692 forty had become members, nine of them called Culy. On 10 November 1693 Culy was made pastor of a separate church at Guyhirn, which met mainly at Isleham, with a branch at Soham.

It is probable that Culy married Anne Delahoi (*d.* 1697), whose daughter, Anne, was born on 11 November 1695 and baptized on the 16th. In 1699 Culy was expelled from Soham for fornication with Ann Scott, and on 9 October 1705 he married Elizabeth Evans. They must have had at least one son, as Abraham Culy, who died about 1850, claimed direct descent.

In his church Culy baptized infants and defended the practice against Thomas Swinton. Contrary to the law, he certified common-law marriages and criticized those who preferred the legality of the parish church for ceremonies. According to an early nineteenth-century source his followers called him 'the Bishop of Guyhorne' (Stevenson, 44). He was clearly a charismatic and effective preacher. There is only one hint of official opposition, when he was prosecuted and acquitted at Wisbech assizes, then pressed into the navy. He was released because he made a nuisance of himself singing hymns.

Culy's doctrines were questioned by the Rothwell church meeting. On 10 February 1696 a letter was read from 'the Church assembling at Guyhorn and Soham' defending Culy against five charges of heresy; the most serious was 'That Christ was not the son of God when upon the Crosse'. Culy's answer was eirenic and he was cleared, but later he was expelled, on 30 May 1702. The Guyhirn congregation remained faithful, and Culy extended his work to Lincolnshire, where he founded a new church at Billinghay, which was licensed in 1720. He recorded a dispute in 1719 with the vicar there, Robert Blaxley, who called him a vagabond and denied the validity of his ordination. Culy died and was buried at Billinghay about 1725.

Two congregations survived until 1850. Guyhirn's doctrines were recorded as 'nearly the same as those of the disciples of Mr. Whitfield' (Lysons, 2.291), which suggests that Calvinist Huguenot teaching remained central. The term Culimite persisted to describe dissenters in Lincolnshire until 1860, though there is no evidence that Culy set out to found a sect.

No writings survive from Culy's lifetime, and it is only possible to date his correspondence with Blaxley. A collected edition of his works was published in London in 1726. The first part, *The glory of the two crown's heads, Adam & Christ unveil'd, or, The mystery of the New Testament opened*, defended the role of Adam in divine grace and modified the most rigorous Calvinism. The second section is a collection of correspondence, entitled *Letters and Answers to and from Several Ministers of Divers Persuasions, on Various Subjects*, mainly containing vigorous polemic. The final part was *Above Forty Hymns Compos'd on Weighty Subjects*, which consisted of half the hymns written by Culy between 1692 and 1694. They mainly stress the themes of divine love, melancholy, and Old Testament typology, but were also used to attack the tenets of Culy's theological opponents. Most of the second collected edition published at Boston in 1787 was pulped. *The Glory of the Two Crown'd Heads* was republished in Plymouth in 1800 with an extensive commentary by the Revd Samuel Reece. The text alone was reprinted at Spilsby, Lincolnshire, in 1820.   DAVID KEEP

Sources K. A. C. Parsons, ed., *The church book of the Independent church Isleham, 1693–1805* (1984) · T. A. Bevis, *David Culy and the Culimites* (1975) · D. Lysons and S. Lysons, *Magna Britannia: being a concise topographical account of the several counties of Great Britain*, 2 (1808), 291 · *N&Q*, 2nd ser., 10 (1860), 407 · R. Brown, 'The religious life and thought of the Cambridgeshire Baptists', BD diss., U. Cam., 1980 · F. J. Gardiner, *History of Wisbech and neighbourhood during the last fifty years* (1898) · W. Stevenson, *A supplement to the first edition of Mr Bentham's history and antiquities of the cathedral and conventual church of Ely* (1817) · N. Walker and T. Craddock, *The history of Wisbech and the fens* (1849) · H. G. Tibbutt, 'The old church book of Rothwell Congregational, 1655–1708', typescript, DWL · E. S. Leedham-Green, ed., *Religious dissent in East Anglia* [Norwich 1991] (1991) · DNB · *The works of Mr David Culy* (1726), 142
Archives DWL

Cumberland. For this title name *see* Clifford, Henry, first earl of Cumberland (*c.*1493–1542); Clifford, Henry, second earl of Cumberland (1517–1570); Clifford, George, third earl of Cumberland (1558–1605); Clifford, Francis, fourth earl of Cumberland (1559–1641); Clifford, Margaret, countess of Cumberland (1560–1616); Clifford, Henry, fifth earl of Cumberland (1592–1643); Rupert, prince and count palatine of the Rhine and duke of Cumberland (1619–1682); George, prince of Denmark and duke of Cumberland (1653–1708); William Augustus, Prince, duke of Cumberland (1721–1765).

Cumberland, George (1754–1848), writer on art and watercolour painter, was born in London on 27 November 1754, the younger son of the four children of George Cumberland (d. 1771) and his wife, Elizabeth Balchen. In 1769 he became a clerk in the Royal Exchange Assurance Company in London, a post he grudgingly endured until the beginning of 1785. He attended the Royal Academy Schools as an honorary student in 1772 and he was an honorary exhibitor at the Royal Academy in 1782 and 1783. In exhibition reviews for the *Morning Chronicle* from 1780 to 1784 he became a passionate advocate of radical neo-classicism, the art of ancient Greece, and especially of the sculptor Thomas Banks (1735–1805). In 1784 he applied for associate membership of the Royal Academy and was unsuccessful—perhaps because he had been highly critical of the institution. In the same year he received a modest inheritance of £300 per year and by March 1785 he was in Paris. In 1785 and 1786 Cumberland visited Italy, staying in Florence and Rome. He was in Switzerland with Charles Long in August 1786. In 1787 Cumberland eloped with Mrs Elizabeth Cooper, *née* Price (1758/9–1837), the wife of his London landlord, and until 1790 they lived in Italy, chiefly in Rome. Elizabeth was known as Mrs Cumberland until her death in Bristol on 2 February 1837 at the age of seventy-nine; it is possible that she and Cumberland never married.

Between 1793 and 1798 while living at Bishopsgate, Egham, Cumberland published seven works, including earlier works of poetry, *A Plan for the Improvement of the Arts in England* (1793), which included proposals for a national gallery of sculpture in Green Park; *An Attempt to Describe Hafod … an Ancient Seat Belonging to Thomas Johnes Esq.* (1796), of which the map was engraved by the artist and poet William Blake; a fable of utopia, *The Captive of the Castle of Senaar* (1798); and the neo-classical treatise *Thoughts on Outline* (1796), eight of whose twenty-four plates were engraved by Blake. Cumberland had been a friend of Blake's since 1784. Blake's last engraved work was to be Cumberland's book-plate. Cumberland bought many of Blake's publications, pressed booksellers to take them, and found work for the artist. They shared an interest in experimental painting techniques, and Cumberland may well have influenced Blake's illuminated printing processes.

In 1803 Cumberland moved to Weston-super-Mare, Somerset, before settling at 1 Culver Street, Bristol, in 1807, where he lived until his death. He was elected an honorary member of the Geological Society in 1810, formed a substantial collection of fossils, contributed to the society's journal, and in 1826 published *Reliquiae conservatae … Descriptions … of some Remarkable Fossil Encrinites*. In Bristol he soon became close friends with the Revd John Eagles (1783–1855), Dr John King (1766–1846), and Francis Gold (1779–1832), all amateur artists with a wide range of sophisticated interests, knowledge, and contacts which were vital to the emergence of the Bristol school of artists and, in particular, to the success of Francis Danby. Patronage by purchase was largely beyond Cumberland's means, but he took much trouble helping Bristol artists with introductions to friends in London, particularly Sir Thomas Lawrence, president of the Royal Academy, the artist Thomas Stothard, and Sir Charles Long, later Lord Farnborough.

Cumberland's own watercolours are almost all small landscape studies which, in their direct and determinedly unpicturesque observations of nature, come impressively close to John Linnell's small sketchbook studies of c.1814. It is significant that it was to be Cumberland who, from Bristol, engineered the crucial introduction of John Linnell to William Blake in 1818, through his son George Cumberland junior. Much of the correspondence in the sixteen volumes of Cumberland's letters, now in the British Library, was with his elder brother—Richard Dennison Cumberland (1752–1825), vicar of Driffield, Gloucestershire—and with his own two sons, George and Sydney. The letters have already been a vital source of information for students of William Blake. They remain a rich source for the study of neo-classicism in the 1780s and 1790s and for the understanding of the evolution of the Bristol school of artists in the second and third decades of the nineteenth century.

Cumberland died at his home, 1 Culver Street, Bristol, on 8 August 1848 and was buried at St Augustine-the-Less, Bristol, on 14 August. His tombstone is now in the churchyard of St George's Chapel, Brandon Hill, Bristol. Some of Cumberland's watercolours are in Bristol Museum and Art Gallery.   FRANCIS GREENACRE

Sources G. E. Bentley, *A bibliography of George Cumberland, 1754–1848* (1975) · G. Keynes, 'Some uncollected authors, 44: George Cumberland, 1754–1848', *Book Collector*, 19 (1970), 31–65 · *The Cumberland papers*, ed. C. Black (1902) · F. J. Milner, 'George Cumberland: a radical neo-classicist', MA diss., U. Birm., 1977 · H. T. de la Beche, 'Anniversary address of the president', *Quarterly Journal of the Geological Society*, 5 (1849), 10–11 · E. Adams, *Francis Danby: varieties of poetic landscape* (1973) · F. Greenacre, *Francis Danby, 1793–1861* (1988) [exhibition catalogue, City of Bristol Museum and Art Gallery and Tate Gallery, London, 1988] · D. Bindman, introduction, in W. Drummond, *George Cumberland … watercolour drawings … 1815–1828* (1977) [exhibition catalogue, Covent Garden Gallery, London, 9 March–6 Apr 1977] · Graves, *RA exhibitors* · *Bristol Mirror* (12 Aug 1848), 8 · W. T. Whitley, *Artists and their friends in England, 1700–1799*, 2 vols. (1928) · George Cumberland's occasional correspondence with newspapers, 1769–1849, 3 volumes of cuttings, Bristol Reference Library, B2659 · J. Ingamells, ed., *A dictionary of British and Irish travellers in Italy, 1701–1800* (1997) · tombstone, St George's Chapel, Brandon Hill, Bristol

Archives BL, MSS | Bristol Reference Library, corresp. with newspapers

Likenesses E. V. Rippingille, oils, 1822, Bristol City Museum and Art Gallery · T. Woolnoth, stipple, 1827 (after N. C. Branwhite), BM, NPG; repro. in G. Cumberland, *An essay on the utility of collecting the best works of the ancient engravers of the Italian school, accompanied by a*

critical catalogue (1827) · E. Bird, pencil drawing, Bristol City Museum and Art Gallery · N. C. Branwhite, pencil drawing, Bristol City Museum and Art Gallery · G. Cumberland junior, pen-and-ink drawing, Bristol City Museum and Art Gallery · enamel miniature, NPG

Cumberland, Richard (1632–1718), bishop of Peterborough, was born on 15 July 1632 in the parish of St Anne, Aldersgate, London. He was the third of five children of Richard Cumberland (*d.* 1661?), a Fleet Street tailor, and his wife (Mary, Margaret, or Marjorie). Cumberland was educated at St Paul's School. In June 1649 he was admitted to Magdalene College, Cambridge, as a pensioner, matriculating the following year. At Cambridge his acquaintances included Hezekiah Burton, the inventor Sir Samuel Moreland, and the diarist Samuel Pepys. Cumberland appears a number of times in Pepys's *Diary*. In 1650 he won a college scholarship and in 1653 he graduated bachelor of arts. In April of the same year he was elected to the John Smith fellowship. He took his MA in 1656, incorporating his degree at Oxford in 1657. At Cambridge he became interested in natural philosophy, particularly mathematics and physics. During his time at Magdalene he is credited by some sources as the inventor of the first mechanical planetary model, or orrery. After scrutiny by three approved 'triers' Cumberland became rector of Brampton Ash in Northamptonshire in December 1658, a living in the gift of Sir John Norwich, baronet and member of the Rump Parliament. Cumberland conformed at the Restoration, and in 1661 he was appointed to be one of the twelve preachers to the University of Cambridge. In 1663 he took his BD. In 1667 he became a domestic chaplain to the distinguished lawyer Orlando Bridgeman, lord keeper of the great seal. In 1670 Bridgeman's patronage secured Cumberland the vicarage of All Saints, Stamford, Lincolnshire, which he held together with the rectory of St Peter's in the same town. He also held a lectureship that obliged him to preach three times a week. On 22 September 1670 he married Anne Quinsey (*d.* 1684), from Aslackby, Lincolnshire, at St Paul's, Covent Garden, in London. Before her death in 1684 Anne had given birth to eight children, of whom four survived to adulthood.

Cumberland's new posts and his augmented income gave him the chance to complete his magisterial treatise on natural law, *De legibus naturae disquisitio philosophica*, which received its imprimatur in July 1671, and which was advertised for sale in February 1672, dedicated to Bridgeman; an 'alloquium ad lectorem' by Cumberland's friend and editor Hezekiah Burton is prefixed. Cumberland was elected to convocation in 1675. In 1680 he proceeded to a doctorate. His thesis maintained (against Roman Catholics) that St Peter had no jurisdiction over the other apostles, and (against nonconformists) that separation from the English church was schismatic. He defended these theses as respondent at the public commencement, an office regarded as unusual for a country clergyman. The 1680s saw him produce two works: the first was a pamphlet dedicated to Pepys, entitled *An Essay towards the Recovery of Jewish Measures and Weights* (1686). The *Essay*, originally designed as an appendix to a new edition of the Bible,

Richard Cumberland (1632–1718), by Thomas Murray, 1706

attempted to translate biblical forms of mensuration into modern equivalents and was presented to the Royal Society, of which Pepys was now president. It became one of Cumberland's best-selling and most widely respected works. He also produced the manuscript for *Sanchoniatho's Phoenician History*, the first English translation of this controversial fragment of Phoenician ancient history, which is recorded in the work of Eusebius; it appeared together with a detailed commentary that sought to reconcile Sanchoniatho's history with the Bible. Sanchoniatho's account revealed the means by which the Phoenicians had corrupted sacred history to deify their own versions of biblical individuals. Cumberland traced the resulting polytheism and idolatry to its most recent manifestation in the Roman Catholic church. On the eve of the revolution of 1688 Cumberland's publisher thought the work too controversial to publish.

In the wake of the revolution, Cumberland was called upon to replace the nonjuring bishop of Peterborough, Thomas White. Cumberland's preferment came on the recommendation of John Tillotson, who described him in a memorandum to the king as 'the most worthy and learned minister in that diocese and always a moderate man' (PRO, SP 8/10/116). Cumberland was astonished to read the first news of his appointment in a newspaper. He was consecrated on 5 July 1691 and enthroned on 12 September. From this time until his death he administered his diocese diligently but with declining efficacy as old age took its toll. He regularly attended the House of Lords until February 1716, when he was finally excused on account of his age. Records of his activity reveal his consistent support for the whigs. He also conspicuously aided

Archbishop Tenison in his struggles in convocation, and in 1701 he carried the archbishop's message proroguing the meeting of the lower house. Intellectually, Cumberland busied himself with studies of ancient chronology. He died in Peterborough on 9 October 1718 and was buried in his cathedral three days later. *Sanchoniatho's Phoenician History* was published posthumously in 1720 with a biographical memoir by Cumberland's son-in-law and domestic chaplain, Squire Payne. His *Origines gentium antiquissimae*, further essays on ancient chronology, were published in 1724. His sole surviving sermon, 'The motives to liberality considered', was published in *The English Preacher* (1774).

Cumberland's interest as a thinker lies mainly in his treatise on natural law, which confirms him as one of the leading natural jurisprudential writers of the seventeenth century. The *De legibus naturae* is a scholarly but complex work, its abstruse Latinity complicated by printing errors that marred the first edition of the book. Cumberland's central thesis is deceptively simple. He argues that natural law directs man to promote the good of the whole system of rational agents, in which his own good is contained as a part. In furthering the common good, man fulfils his individual good and the two are inseparable. This natural law is binding because there are natural rewards attached to its observation and natural punishments attached to its dereliction. Cumberland's discussion appears to be distinctively 'modern' because he arrives at his conclusions without discussion of scripture, and he generates ethical norms without a discussion of the afterlife. He also deployed recent scientific discoveries to back up his ethical claims and discussed morality in mathematical terms. The thesis of the *De legibus naturae* has encouraged some commentators to see Cumberland as a forerunner, if not the founder, of English utilitarianism. However, Cumberland's modernity or his secularism should not be overstated. The *De legibus naturae* sought to demonstrate that moral obligation proceeded from the will of God. Recent work has emphasized the fact that the *De legibus naturae* was conceived as a critical response to the work of Thomas Hobbes. The Restoration period saw much clerical anxiety over the influence of Hobbes's doctrines. The secular modernity of Cumberland's thesis may owe much to his unusual attempt to engage with Hobbes on his own terms. As a churchman of latitudinarian sympathies Cumberland wished to show that science and reason could support the notion of a divinely ordained natural law, rather than subverting it as the work of Hobbes appeared to suggest. This argument proved to be influential at home and abroad: Samuel Pufendorf made extensive use of the *De legibus* in the second edition of his *De jure naturae* (1684); Samuel Parker used sections of the work in his *Demonstration of the Divine Authority of the Law of Nature* (1681); and James Tyrrell produced an English adaptation of the book in his *Brief Disquisition of the Law of Nature* (1692), juxtaposing Cumberland with Locke. Two Latin editions were published on the continent. The eighteenth century saw a further Latin edition, two new English editions, and one French translation.   JON PARKIN

Sources S. Payne, 'Brief account of the life, character and writings of the author', in R. Cumberland, *Sanchoniatho's Phoenician history* (1720) • L. Kirk, 'Richard Cumberland (1632–1718) and his political theory', PhD diss., U. Lond., 1976 • J. Parkin, *Science, religion and politics in Restoration England: Richard Cumberland's De legibus naturae* (1999) • R. Cumberland, *Memoirs of Richard Cumberland written by himself*, 2 vols. (1806–7), vol. 1, pp. 3–6 • *Fasti Angl.* (Hardy), 2.536 • B. Willis, *A survey of the cathedrals of Lincoln, Ely, Oxford and Peterborough* (1730), 510 • L. Kirk, *Richard Cumberland and natural law: secularisation of thought in seventeenth-century England* (1987)
Archives BL, corresp. with Atkinson, Sloane MS 4274, fol. 80 • Bodl. Oxf., corresp. with Thomas Gale, MS A170, fol. 11 • Bodl. Oxf., corresp. with Isaac Laughton, Tanner MS 305, fol. 69
Likenesses T. Murray, oils, 1706, bishop's palace, Peterborough [*see illus.*] • J. Smith, mezzotint (after T. Murray), BM, NPG • oils, Magd. Cam.
Wealth at death lands in Northamptonshire (Burneham, Sibbertoft, and Widdrington), and houses in Westminster, all providing rent; also income from possessions as bishop of Peterborough; great-grandson, Richard Cumberland the dramatist, records that at the end of every year he gave all surplus revenue to the poor, reserving only £25 to pay for his funeral; land passed on to eldest son; household goods divided between his three daughters: will, PRO, PROB 11/566, sig. 222; Cumberland, *Memoirs*, vol. 1, p. 4

Cumberland, Richard (1732–1811), playwright and novelist, was born in the master's lodge of Trinity College, Cambridge, on 19 February 1732, the son of Denison Cumberland (1705/6–1774), a Church of England clergyman, and his wife, Joanna (d. c.1775), daughter of Richard *Bentley, master of Trinity College, Cambridge. His great-grandfather was Richard *Cumberland, bishop of Peterborough, whose only son, another Richard, became archdeacon of Northampton.

Early life and career The child Richard Cumberland was much in the master's lodge, but when six years old was sent to Bury St Edmunds to study under the Revd Mr Kinsman, a Trinity graduate and a friend of Bentley's. Richard described his schoolmaster as 'kind, cordial, openhearted, and an impartial administrator of punishments and praises, as they were respectively deserved' (Cumberland, *Memoirs*, 25). While at Bury St Edmunds he displayed precocity in versification and was head boy of his class. At twelve he was sent to Westminster School, numbering among his classmates William Cowper, George Colman, Charles Churchill, Robert Lloyd, and Warren Hastings.

Cumberland was admitted to Trinity College, Cambridge, as a pensioner on 15 June 1747, matriculated in 1748, and graduated BA in 1751. He became a lay fellow of the college in 1752, with the degree of MA following two years later. Probably because he had been given some of Richard Bentley's books and papers after the master's death in 1742, Cumberland became interested in Greek comedy. He wrote at some considerable length on the subject in the third volume of his periodical paper *The Observer* (1785). After receiving his MA he went to Stanwick, Northamptonshire, where his father had been presented to the living. There Cumberland contemplated writing a universal history, and wrote a play upon Caractacus, which was neither acted nor published. Through his father's connection with George Montagu Dunk, second earl of Halifax, another Trinity man, Cumberland was taken on as Halifax's private secretary in the Board of

Richard Cumberland (1732–1811), by George Romney, c.1771–76

Trade. The position required almost no effort on Cumberland's part, and he took occasion to continue his study of history and his writing, the latter resulting in an epic poem. In 1757 his father changed his living and went to Fulham in Middlesex; Cumberland, visiting him there, became acquainted with George Bubb Dodington, whose villa was but a short mile from the parsonage. Richard became a messenger between Dodington and Halifax when the latter was conducting an intrigue of some sort with the opposition in early 1757.

Cumberland married Elizabeth (d. 1801), daughter of George Ridge of Kelmiston, Hampshire, on 19 February 1759, about the same year in which he wrote his first play intended for the stage, *The Banishment of Cicero*, after recently reading Conyers Middleton's biography of Cicero (1741). The manuscript of the play, in the conventional five acts, was seen by Lord Halifax who recommended it to David Garrick for representation. Garrick politely declined the honour, and although the play was published in 1761 it was never staged. At the time of his marriage Richard became crown agent to Nova Scotia, Halifax being instrumental in getting him that appointment. When Halifax became lord lieutenant of Ireland on 6 October 1761, he made Cumberland his Ulster secretary. But when Halifax became secretary of state in October 1762 Cumberland, who had hoped to be appointed his under-secretary, was passed over. He, however, reconciled himself to the lesser office of clerk of reports with an annual salary of £200.

Prose works Although Cumberland will largely be remembered as a playwright, he was more than merely a man of letters. His novel *Arundel* (1789), written in epistolary form, begs comparison with Samuel Richardson's *Sir Charles Grandison*. *Henry* (1795) is an attempt to emulate Henry Fielding, while *John de Lancaster* (1809), published two years before Cumberland's death, is best left undescribed. Among Cumberland's more notable prose works is the *Anecdotes of Eminent Painters in Spain during the Sixteenth and Seventeenth Centuries*, a product of a visit to Spain. When George Germaine (later Lord Sackville) became colonial secretary at the end of 1775, he made Cumberland secretary to the Board of Trade. Five years later Cumberland was sent to Spain to enter into secret negotiations with the intent to procure a separate treaty with England. After a stay of several months he returned to England without the desired results and discovered that he had spent some £4500 which was never repaid. With the abolition of the Board of Trade soon after his return, and with but half his salary as compensation, he retired to Tunbridge Wells where he remained until his death. His next prose work was in a more familiar genre, a periodical paper called *The Observer* which appeared in five volumes between 1786 and 1790 and contains 152 essays. The essays range from the usual fare of literary criticism (on Shakespeare, Ben Jonson, Milton, Rowe, and others), to general subjects ('Love of praise'), little tales (often running to three or more numbers), historical essays, and a variety of other sub-genres. Of special interest is no. 27, 'Remarks upon novels; particularly of Richardson's *Clarissa*', in which he also invokes Fielding. Unlike other periodical papers, there are thirty-eight consecutive essays (nos. 114–52) on Greek history and literature, with a number of his translations of Greek poetry.

Cumberland's best-known prose work is the *Memoirs of Richard Cumberland, Written by Himself*, published in 1806 with additions in 1807 (2 vols.). It is a social document of considerable interest, especially in the portrayal of several important people: Richard Bentley, Lord Halifax, Bubb Dodington, Lord Sackville, Garrick, and Goldsmith, as well as some actors and actresses. Not of least interest is Cumberland's statement of what he set out to do in his dramatic efforts:

> I perceive that I had fallen upon a time when great eccentricity of character was pretty nearly gone by, but still I fancy there was an opening for some originality, and an opportunity for showing at least my good-will to mankind, if I introduced the characters of persons who had been usually exhibited on the stage, as the butt for ridicule and abuse, and endeavoured to present them in such lights as might tend to reconcile the world to them, and them to the world. (Cumberland, *Memoirs*, 141–2)

This is his rationale for the introduction of a West Indian, an Irishman, and a Jew into his stage works.

The poet Cumberland will not be remembered for his non-dramatic verse, although he wrote in a number of poetic genres, beginning when still a schoolboy. At Westminster School he translated into blank verse Virgil's description of the plague among the cattle from the third *Georgic*, thinking well enough of it to reprint it in its entirety in the *Memoirs* (pp. 49–51). He tried his hand at epic poetry, blank verse, odes, elegies, songs, and pastorals, a number of which were published in his *Miscellaneous Poems* (1778). The most ambitious of his poetic efforts were *Calvary, or, The Death of Christ*, a religious epic (1792), and *Retrospection*, an autobiographical poem (1811), both in blank verse. Nathan Drake, essayist and physician, devoted four essays, nos. 18–21, of his *Literary Hours*, to a discussion of *Calvary*, which he described as 'a work imbued with the genuine spirit of Milton, and destined therefore, most probably, to immortality' (2nd edn, 1800, 1.381–2). He quoted and compared passages from *Calvary* to *Paradise Lost*, commenting on their various merits. Drake concluded, citing a number of other works by Cumberland, 'that to no author of the eighteenth century in polite literature are we under greater obligations' (ibid., 1.455). Drake's praise of the poem was responsible for the publication of seven editions of it between 1800 and 1811. More interest, however, attaches to the poem published shortly before Cumberland's death in 1811. *Retrospection*, 1340 lines in length, may be described as an apologia, a review of his life, with remarks on a number of his contemporaries. There is also much about his parents and children. As a personal document it may be considered more important for understanding Cumberland the man than the two volumes of his *Memoirs*. It was extensively reviewed and greatly praised in the *European Magazine* for May 1811 (pp. 351–4).

The dramatist Cumberland's entry upon the stage began with the somewhat successful musical drama *The Summer's Tale*, produced at Covent Garden on 6 November 1765. This was followed by the very successful sentimental comedy *The Brothers*, also produced at Covent Garden, four years later, on 2 December 1769. His most successful plays are of the sentimental school, but the majority of his dramas, the number of which varies with definitions of drama, are not of it. His next play, *The West Indian*, produced at Drury Lane under the direction of David Garrick on 19 January 1771, was phenomenally successful, with a run of twenty-eight nights. Cumberland sold the copyright for £150 and claimed that 12,000 copies were sold. Several editions of the play were reprinted in Philadelphia during the 1770s, it was performed by students at Yale University some time between January 1771 and 1773, and it appeared on stages in New York, Boston, Philadelphia, and Richmond, as well as in other cities in the United States right up to the end of the nineteenth century. Possibly because of the success of *The West Indian*, in that same year Cumberland received the honorary degree of doctor of civil law from the University of Dublin. Prominent among his many other plays, not wholly in terms of their relative merits, are *Timon of Athens* (1771), *The Fashionable Lover* (1772), *The Choleric Man* (1774), the tragedy *The Battle of Hastings* (1778), *The Walloons* (1782), *The Jew* (1794), and *The Wheel of Fortune* (1795).

The Walloons, performed on 20 April 1782, grew out of Cumberland's experiences in Spain and owed what success it had to the actor John Henderson, for whom the part of the principal character, Father Sullivan, was created. The public was unenthusiastic, and Cumberland, hoping to benefit financially, was disappointed. He was more successful, however, with *The Jew* and *The Wheel of Fortune*; both were performed at Drury Lane, the first on 8 May 1794, the second on 28 February 1795. Not only were they dramatic successes, they also brought him more financial security. The success of *The Jew* stemmed almost entirely from its depiction of the Jew Sheva, reversing the tradition of the Jew as villain. The play was performed in America and Germany, and was translated and published in German, Hebrew, and Yiddish. It surpassed *The West Indian* in popularity, being revived well into the nineteenth century. Cumberland wrote both prologue and epilogue for *The Wheel of Fortune*, another success largely because of the magnificent performance by John Philip Kemble as Penruddock, the principal character.

Perhaps the most widely known description of Cumberland the man is Garrick's, who termed him a man without a skin because of his inability to accept criticism. Equally well known is his portrayal as Sir Fretful Plagiary in Sheridan's *The Critic* (1779), despite Sheridan's having produced *The Battle of Hastings* at Drury Lane in 1778. Cumberland's unacknowledged borrowing from other playwrights was widely known and commented upon, hence Sir Fretful Plagiary. A suspect anecdote has it that Sheridan, in *The Critic*, was retaliating against Cumberland's alleged scolding of his children for laughing at Sheridan's *The School for Scandal*, which supposedly caused Sheridan to remark that 'He ought to have laughed at my comedy, for I laughed heavily at his tragedy' (*DNB*). Garrick himself remained at arms-length courtesy as far as Cumberland was concerned, declining to employ John Henderson, championed by Cumberland, as an actor in his company. Cumberland was much in London literary circles, on terms of some intimacy with Goldsmith, among others. Boswell states that 'Mr. Cumberland assures me that he was always treated with great courtesy by Dr. Johnson', and notes that Johnson, in a letter to Mrs Thrale, wrote that 'The want of company is an inconvenience: but Mr. Cumberland is a million' (Boswell, *Life*, 4.384, n. 2), an ambiguous compliment. Cumberland makes much of his supposed friendship with Johnson in his *Memoirs*, the pertinent passages being reprinted in *Johnsonian Miscellanies*, edited by G. B. Hill, who dismisses Cumberland's anecdotes about Johnson as highly suspect (Johnson, 2.72–8). Hill quotes Sir Walter Scott to the effect that Cumberland 'carried poetic jealousy and irritability farther than any man I ever saw. He was a great flatterer, too.' But Sir Walter also wrote that:

> In the little pettish sub-acidity of temper which Cumberland sometimes exhibited there was more of humorous sadness than ill-will, either to his critics or to his contemporaries … These imperfections detract nothing from the character of the man of worth, the scholar and the gentleman. (ibid., 2.73)

Cumberland and Sir Walter, it should be added, were both honorary members of the Literary Club and Sir Walter included an account of Cumberland in volume 1 of his *Biographical Memoirs*, volume 3 of his *Miscellaneous Prose Works*.

The general opinion of Cumberland the man was negative, with but few of his contemporaries expressing any great affection for him.

Last years At Tunbridge Wells, Cumberland found himself the neighbour of Lord Sackville, upon whose death in 1785 he wrote a pamphlet, *The Character of the Late Viscount Sackville* (1785), in which he defended his friend against the charges that he had not conducted himself properly in American affairs and that he had not led British cavalry in pursuit of the French at Minden, for which he was court-martialled. Cumberland could be loyal to his friends; Sackville's own spoken regard for him is quoted in the *Memoirs* (p. 207). It was at Tunbridge Wells that his *Anecdotes* of Spanish painters was published in 1782, and it was here that he continued to write plays, the novels, *The Observer*, and other pieces. Here, too, two years before his death, he edited a new periodical, the *London Review*, two volumes of which were published, February–May and August–November 1809. His radical idea, which met with very little favour, was that each review should be signed by the reviewer.

The *Gentleman's Magazine* for June 1811 recorded Cumberland's death on 7 May 1811: 'At Mr. Henry Fry's in Bedford-place, Russell-square … a character of long and very distinguished celebrity in the republick of letters' (*GM*). The *London Chronicle* for 9 May 1811 expressed regret at the loss of 'a profound scholar as well as an able writer in various departments of literature and a poet of no inferior class.' Cumberland was survived by four sons and three daughters, yet despite the extent of his paternity, one of his contemporaries had doubts about his sexual orientation. Mrs Thrale, as early as 1777, noted in her diary: 'I have a Notion (Dieu me pardonne) that Cumberland is a — he is so over-attentive, so apparently afraid of his Wife' (*Thraliana*, 135, n. 2). Some twenty years later she confided to her diary: 'something always did whisper in my heart that Cumberland liked the *Masculine* Gender best', adding in a note that 'Cumberland dwells upon the *personal Charms* of his Heroes always with a luscious fondness exceedingly particular, as if he were in Love with them himself' (ibid., 969, and n. 2). Mrs Thrale was not, however, the kindliest of creatures, nor were her suspicions shared by others. On 14 May, Cumberland's body was taken to the collegiate church of St Peter, Westminster, and buried in Westminster Abbey. His friend and schoolfellow, Dr Vincent, dean of Westminster, spoke the funeral oration, saying, among other things, that Cumberland's 'writings were chiefly for the stage, but of strict moral tendency; they were not without faults, but they were not gross, abounding with oaths and libidinous expressions' (Williams, 298). Others were not of the dean's opinion, especially as concerned his novels. Cumberland left his literary remains to his friends Samuel Rogers, Richard 'Conversation' Sharp, and Sir James Bland Burges, with the last of whom he had collaborated in the epic poem *Exodiad* (1808). ARTHUR SHERBO

Sources R. Cumberland, *Memoirs of Richard Cumberland written by himself*, ed. H. Flanders (1856) · *The letters of Richard Cumberland*, ed. R. J. Dircks [n.d., c.1988] · *Unpublished plays of Richard Cumberland*, ed. R. J. Dircks, 2 vols. (1991) · S. T. Williams, *Richard Cumberland, his life and works* (1917) · *Thraliana: the diary of Mrs. Hester Lynch Thrale (later Mrs. Piozzi)*, 1776–1809, ed. K. C. Balderston, 2 vols. (1951) · *GM*, 1st ser., 81/1 (1811) · *London Chronicle* (9 May 1811) · Boswell, *Life* · [S. Johnson], *Johnsonian miscellanies*, ed. G. B. Hill, 2 vols. (1897) · *DNB*

Archives BL, corresp., Add. MS 28851 | BL, letters to George Cumberland, Add. MSS 34691–37060 · Bodl. Oxf., letters to Sir James Bland Burges · Harvard U., Houghton L., MS Le Herr · U. Mich., Clements L., corresp. with Lord George Sackville relating to Spanish affairs · V&A, MS Le Herr · V&A NAL, corresp. with David Garrick

Likenesses V. Green, mezzotint, pubd 1771 (after G. Romney), BM · V. Green, mezzotint, pubd 1771 (after oils by G. Romney), NG Ire. · G. Romney, oils, c.1771–1776, NPG [*see illus.*] · J. Clover, engraving, repro. in Cumberland, *Memoirs* · J. Clover, oils, Tunbridge Wells Council · W. Ridley, stipple (after W. Lane), BM, NPG; repro. in *European Magazine* (1809) · G. Romney, oils, Pollok House, Glasgow · E. Scriven, stipple (after oils by J. Clover), BM, NPG; repro. in *Contemporary portraits* (1814) · oils, in the style of Romney, Tate collection · stipple, BM; repro. in *Register of the times* (1795)

Wealth at death approx. £450: Williams, *Richard Cumberland*

Cumberland, Richard Francis George (1792–1870), army officer, grandson of Richard *Cumberland (1732–1811), was the son of Richard Cumberland, once an officer in the 3rd foot guards, who died on the island of Tobago when awaiting a civil appointment there, and his wife, Lady Albinia Hobart (d. 1853), daughter of George *Hobart, the third earl of Buckinghamshire. Through his mother, one of the ladies of Queen Charlotte's suite, he became a page of honour, and on 27 January 1809 was appointed to an ensigncy in the 3rd foot guards, in which he became lieutenant and captain in 1814. He served as aide-de-camp to the duke of Wellington, of whose personal staff he was one of the last survivors, in the principal actions in the Peninsular War in 1812–14, and was wounded at the repulse of the French sortie from Bayonne. In 1825 he sold out from the army. He was married and had at least one daughter, Mary Frances. He died at his residence, 4 Royal Mint, Aldgate, London, on 9 March 1870.
H. M. CHICHESTER, rev. JAMES LUNT

Sources J. Foster, *The royal lineage of our noble and gentle families* (1883) · R. Cumberland, *Memoirs of Richard Cumberland written by himself*, 2 vols. (1806–7) · *The Times* (14 March 1870) · Boase, *Mod. Eng. biog.* · *CGPLA Eng. & Wales* (1870)

Wealth at death under £800: probate, 26 March 1870, *CGPLA Eng. & Wales*

Cumberland and Strathearn. For this title name *see* Anne, duchess of Cumberland and Strathearn (1743–1808) [*see under* Henry Frederick, Prince, duke of Cumberland and Strathearn (1745–1790)]; Henry Frederick, Prince, duke of Cumberland and Strathearn (1745–1790).

Cumberlege, Geoffrey Fenwick Jocelyn (1891–1979), publisher, was born on 18 April 1891 at Walsted Place, Lindfield, Sussex, the third son and youngest of five children of Henry Mordaunt Cumberlege, landowner, and Blanche Pacquita Genevra Fenwick. He was educated at Charterhouse School and Worcester College, Oxford.

On graduating from Oxford (BA, 1913), Cumberlege was commissioned in the Oxford and Buckinghamshire light infantry and he served with great distinction throughout the First World War, in France (1915–18) and Italy (1918–19).

He was promoted substantive captain in October 1917. He received the Military Cross and was appointed to the DSO. He was mentioned in dispatches three times and was awarded the *croce di guerra*.

On demobilization in 1919 Cumberlege abandoned his plans for joining the Egyptian civil service and joined the Oxford University Press under Humphrey Milford at Amen Corner in London. He was immediately dispatched, with minimum training in publishing, to succeed E. V. Rieu as manager of the Indian branch of the press in Bombay. It was Cumberlege's fate throughout his career to have to deal with exceptional circumstances and conditions of unusual difficulty. In India he found a very small business which had barely survived the war. His predecessor was ill and had to leave for England immediately. London was remote and communication slow, so effectively he was entirely his own master. His task was to publish textbooks for Indian primary and secondary schools, which could afford only the lowest possible prices. However, he worked enormously long hours, established suitable offices in Bombay and branch offices in Calcutta and Madras, and left a branch which continued to thrive.

On 30 November 1927 Cumberlege married Vera Gladys (b. 1908/9), daughter of Major Sir Alexander Doran Gibbons, seventh baronet, landowner of Stanwell Place, Middlesex. They had one daughter and three sons and were happily married. In the same year Cumberlege was recalled from India and appointed vice-president of Oxford University Press, Inc., in New York, where he remained until 1934. In New York, Cumberlege found a disorganized business losing money and then had to return it to profitability in the very adverse conditions of the depression. He set about this task by cutting everyone's salary, including of course his own, and he also saved overheads by temporarily amalgamating the office with Longmans. Most significantly he embarked on a very successful and enterprising publishing programme. He initiated a distinguished list of American children's books, which were also successful in England, and, among many other long-lasting books, he published a translation, *The Odyssey of Homer* (1932), by T. E. Shaw (T. E. Lawrence) and *The Growth of the American Republic* by S. E. Morison and H. S. Commager (1930).

Leaving a reorganized American branch well set for its subsequent successful development, Cumberlege returned to London and four years of peaceful publishing and administration as Milford's principal assistant and potential successor. It was at this time that he published Arthur Upham Pope's monumental *Survey of Persian Art* (1938) but then war came in 1939 and he had to organize the complete evacuation of the London business to Oxford. At the end of the Second World War he faced the daunting task of re-establishing the press in London, rebuilding the staff, reorganizing the Canadian and Australian branches for which as publisher he was responsible, and laying the foundations of the great post-war expansion of the press outside Oxford. In 1945 Cumberlege succeeded Milford as publisher to the University of Oxford, and from then until his final retirement in 1956

all books published by the London business of the press bore his name in the imprint (it was then the practice to distinguish in this way the scholarly publications of the Clarendon Press in Oxford from all others). Cumberlege encouraged the development of books for teaching English as a second language which caused profitable branches to be established in Africa and Asia. He changed the children's book list radically and greatly improved it.

Perhaps Cumberlege's most significant publishing achievement was jointly with the Cambridge University Press to organize and produce the *New English Bible*. This gave him great pleasure, as he was a loyal Anglican churchman. He played his part in the book trade as a member of the council of the Publishers' Association but he refused to become president, because he had too little time remaining.

In 1956 Cumberlege retired only to be immediately recalled as trouble-shooter to New York at a difficult period. During retirement proper he became director and then chairman of the English Hymnal Company. He was also governor of Bishop Otter College, the Church of England college of education at Chichester.

Cumberlege had been a distinguished soldier, and to all the critical problems of his publishing career he brought the military virtues of leadership, quick decision, and positive action, but these were cloaked and modified by great charm of manner. He entirely disregarded his own interests and he inspired lasting loyalty—much helped by his extraordinary powers of mimicry—in his staff, his authors, and his friends, who universally knew him as Jock. He had patrician qualities, and was an amateur in the eighteenth-century definition of the word. Never an intellectual by academic standards, his instinctive publishing judgement was sound in the difficult field that lies between works of academic rigour and the popular trade book.

In appearance Cumberlege was tall and thin with aquiline features and very expressive hands. Among his private interests was collecting early English watercolours, and he was a keen gardener. He was awarded an honorary degree of DCL by Durham University in 1953 and elected an honorary fellow of Worcester College, Oxford (1952). Cumberlege died at his home, Idlehurst, Birch Grove, Horsted Keynes, Sussex, on 29 July 1979, of a heart condition.

JOHN BROWN, *rev.* CLARE L. TAYLOR

Sources P. Sutcliffe, *The Oxford University Press: an informal history* (1978) · *The Bookseller* (11 Aug 1979) · *The Times* (16 Aug 1979) · b. cert. · m. cert. · d. cert. · personal knowledge (1986)
Archives Bodl. Oxf., corresp. with Nevill Coghill · Bodl. Oxf., corresp. with L. G. Curtis
Wealth at death £52,877: probate, 23 Oct 1979, *CGPLA Eng. & Wales*

Cumin [Comyn], **John** (d. 1212), archbishop of Dublin and royal servant, may have come from a minor Somerset family. Certainly it is in connection with this county that his name first appears in the official records: in 1158 and 1159 John Cumin was pardoned debts in Somerset and excused from payments to the sheriffs of Somerset and Worcester.

Royal service, 1163–1181 In 1163 Cumin was present at the Council of Woodstock and witnessed a royal confirmation to the prior and convent of Burton Priory. It seems likely that by this date he had already been in the king's service for a number of years, as at the end of 1163 he represented Henry II at the court of Frederick Barbarossa, a task that would only have been performed by a skilled and trusted official.

Cumin's services were frequently used during the dispute between the king and the archbishop of Canterbury, Thomas Becket. In 1166 he was sent to Rome to request that papal legates be dispatched to England with powers to resolve the dispute. Later this same year he was rewarded with the archdeaconry of Bath, which Pope Alexander III ordered him to resign, as he had obtained the office through lay authority. However, he continued to hold the archdeaconry until at least 1174 and perhaps until 1182 when Peter of Blois was granted the office. The pipe rolls for 1169–73 show that Cumin was active as an itinerant justice in the west country and also that he was custodian of the temporalities of Hereford from 1166 to 1172.

Towards the end of 1170 Cumin was sent to Rome with the task of obtaining absolution from the pope for the archbishop of York and the bishops of London and Salisbury, who had been excommunicated by Thomas Becket. Cumin himself appears on a list of those excommunicated by Becket at about the same time. He was in the middle of negotiations when news of Becket's murder was brought to Italy. Cumin returned quickly to the king's side and was with Henry in Normandy in July 1171. Later in the same year he resumed his activities as an itinerant justice in England. During the following years Henry II continued to send him on diplomatic missions to France and Spain. At the Council of Windsor in 1179 he was appointed as a judge for northern England. In the years 1179–81 he is frequently mentioned as being responsible for the transportation of the king's treasure, usually in the company of the chamberlain, although on one occasion he is himself called chamberlain.

Archbishop of Dublin, 1181–1196 John Cumin held the prebend of Hoxton in St Paul's, London, but apart from this and the archdeaconry of Bath he does not seem to have achieved that accumulation of ecclesiastical benefices so characteristic of royal clerks of the time. He possessed only deacon's orders, and on the face of it his election to the archbishopric of Dublin in the abbey of Evesham in September 1181 was a spectacular promotion. It must be seen as primarily an affirmation of Henry II's belief in his abilities and trust in his loyalty. A key element in Cumin's preferment over other, possibly better qualified, candidates was his loyalty to the king during the Becket dispute. It was vital for the crown's policy in Ireland that the vacancy in the strategically important see of Dublin be filled by a trusted servant.

According to Gerald of Wales the representatives of the Dublin clergy who elected John Cumin at Evesham were 'reasonably united in their choice' (*Expugnatio*, 198–9). The election did however take place in the presence of the king who clearly made his preference known. Cumin's movements immediately after the election are not known. As Pope Alexander III had died shortly before the Evesham election, it is likely that the archbishop-elect remained with the king in England until the election of Pope Lucius III was confirmed. Cumin then made his way to the new pope's court at Velletri, where he arrived in February 1182. He was ordained to the priesthood on 13 March and a week later was consecrated archbishop of Dublin by the pope.

Pope Lucius sent the new archbishop a very comprehensive confirmation of his lands and dignities. The document also included a detailed prohibition of certain abuses concerning the holding of ecclesiastical benefices and chaplaincies which were then apparently prevalent in the Dublin diocese. This prohibition indicates that Cumin had familiarized himself with practices in his new diocese, but it is not known if he obtained the information through a personal visit in the months after his election or through discussion with a well-informed source.

Cumin then returned to England and spent some time following the peregrinations of the royal court. His first securely recorded visit to his diocese came some years after his appointment, when in the autumn of 1184 he was dispatched to Ireland to prepare the way for John's forthcoming visit. He was present at Waterford in April 1185 to welcome John and it was in Waterford that the archbishop received his first grant of land from the prince. During the period in which he acted as John's adviser Cumin lost no opportunity to consolidate and extend the temporal possessions of his new diocese, which he appears to have considered rather small and poor. When John arrived in Dublin he granted to the archbishop the lands and possessions of the bishopric of Glendalough, on account of the smallness and poverty of the Dublin church.

Reform and embellishment of his archdiocese Cumin remained in Ireland after John's return and seriously began the work of administering his diocese and province. One of his first acts was to call a provincial council which opened in Christ Church, Dublin, on 30 March 1186. It was attended by the suffragan bishops and major religious superiors of the province and the opening sermon, on the church's sacraments, was given by the archbishop himself. The canons of the council are preserved in a confirmation of Pope Urban III dated 5 March 1187. Although they show many similarities with English statutes of the same period, they have a definite Irish tone and frequently refer to the Irish church and its special problems. The papal confirmation mentions the archbishop's concern that the people whom he was sent to govern were badly instructed in divine law, and it seems likely that the canons were for the most part Cumin's own work and reflect his pastoral concerns.

The archbishop did not, however, regard his presence in the diocese as essential for bringing about reform. Cumin left Dublin some time in 1186 and remained in England until 1190 when he attended the coronation of Richard I at Winchester. During this time he showed the same concern with augmenting the possessions and privileges of his see and received a series of charters and grants from John. Following the death of his patron Henry II the archbishop lessened his involvement with the royal court, and when he returned to his see in 1190 he devoted his energy to ecclesiastical administration.

In 1191 Cumin issued a charter concerning the elevation of the parish church of St Patrick to collegiate status. This church was situated on land that had been granted to him by John and it was here that the archbishop also began the building of the archiepiscopal palace of St Sepulchre. The consecration ceremony of St Patrick's took place on 17 March 1192 and was attended by the archbishops of Armagh and Cashel, as well as many other ecclesiastics. By founding a secular college Cumin provided Dublin with a convenient resource for the rewarding of royal clerics like himself, although some credence must also be given to his stated aim of desiring to improve the educational standards of the people of his diocese. It is not clear whether the archbishop intended that St Patrick's be elevated to cathedral status; his later, enforced absence from Dublin makes it difficult to reconstruct his motives. There is no evidence that he discriminated against the regular cathedral chapter of Holy Trinity, rather, in all ways he treated it as the cathedral church of his diocese. Furthermore he sponsored the extensive rebuilding of the cathedral which was carried out between 1186 and 1200, perhaps bringing over stone and workers from his native Somerset.

Most of the important acts of Cumin's episcopate can be dated to the years 1191–6 when he maintained more or less constant residence in his diocese. Many of his activities were concerned with extending the temporal boundaries of his see or with ensuring that no other jurisdiction infringed upon it. Thus he took measures to lessen the control exercised by the bishop of Clogher over the Augustinian house of All Hallows, Dublin. He also cut the ties between the Augustinian convent of Grâce Dieu and its mother house of Clonard in the diocese of Meath by moving it to a new residence in Lusk and generously re-endowing it. During these years the archbishop also took further steps towards the unification of the dioceses of Dublin and Glendalough.

Exile and restoration, 1197–1206 In 1197 the career of this loyal servant of the crown took an unexpected turn when he became embroiled in a serious dispute with Hamo de Valognes (d. 1202/3), the Irish justiciar, which resulted in his exile from Dublin for a period of nine years. The initial cause of the dispute is unclear, but it appears that dissension first arose over the question of royal forest rights in lands newly acquired by the archbishop. The agreement that was finally brokered in 1205 certainly refers to this issue. However, the dispute quickly escalated into a full-scale confrontation between the archbishop and the justiciar. Cumin threatened Valognes with ecclesiastical censure and he replied by confiscating some of the temporal

possessions of the diocese. The archbishop then excommunicated Valognes and several of his officials and left for England having placed Dublin under interdict.

Cumin spent the next few years following the movements of the royal court, seeking unsuccessfully to have his grievances redressed. The situation worsened after the accession of King John in 1199, with the temporalities of Dublin being taken into the king's hand and the archbishop banned from the entire realm. Cumin then turned to Rome and found in Innocent III a determined champion of his rights. However it was not until 1205 that King John, faced with the threat of papal excommunication and interdict, gave way and agreed to restore to the archbishop his full liberties and temporal possessions. During his prolonged exile Cumin appears to have spent some time in Paris where Gerald of Wales recalls meeting him. Innocent III paints a colourful though perhaps exaggerated picture of the exile as a feeble old man forced to beg for his needs.

Death and assessment Given that John Cumin's career as a royal official can be traced from the 1150s he must have been fairly advanced in years when he returned to Dublin in 1206. The remaining six years of his episcopate passed without incident and he died in October 1212 'senex et plenus dierum' (Gilbert, 2.279). He was buried in the church of Holy Trinity, whose monks had supported him in his battle with the crown. An early thirteenth-century effigy of an archbishop in St Lawrence's Chapel has been tentatively identified as that of John Cumin.

Gerald of Wales writes that John Cumin would have made outstanding improvements in the condition of the Irish church 'if his spiritual sword had not been continuously checked by the sword of the temporal power' (*Expugnatio*, 198–9). There is a certain irony in the fact that a man who had so effectively advanced his career prospects by remaining faithful to the king during the Becket dispute should find himself, like Becket, exiled from his church and appealing to Rome for help, even if the liberties that Cumin so resolutely defended were related to the lands of his diocese rather than to the dignity of his episcopal office.

While Cumin's episcopate was certainly troubled and greatly occupied with temporal affairs, he did demonstrate a genuine concern for the spiritual well-being of his flock. The canons of the provincial council of 1186 display an awareness of and willingness to address the particular problems of the church in Ireland which had exercised the native reform party. He played a large part in the introduction of the complex machinery of Anglo-Norman ecclesiastical administration into the Dublin province, a process that was to be completed by his successors.

Margaret Murphy

Sources M. Murphy, 'Balancing the concerns of church and state: the archbishops of Dublin, 1181–1228', *Colony and frontier in medieval Ireland: essays presented to J. F. Lydon*, ed. T. B. Barry and others (1995), 41–56 · M. Murphy, 'The archbishops and administration of the diocese and province of Dublin, 1181–1298', PhD diss., TCD, 1987 · A. Gwynn, 'Archbishop John Cumin', *Reportorium novum*, 1 (1955–6), 285–310 · A. Gwynn, ed., 'Provincial and diocesan decrees of the diocese of Dublin during the Anglo-Norman period', *Archivium*

Hibernicum, 11 (1944), 31–117 • M. Murphy, 'Ecclesiastical censures: an aspect of their use in thirteenth century Dublin', *Archivium Hibernicum*, 44 (1989), 89–97 • Giraldus Cambrensis, *Expugnatio Hibernica / The conquest of Ireland*, ed. and trans. A. B. Scott and F. X. Martin (1978) • M. P. Sheehy, ed., *Pontificia Hibernica: medieval papal chancery documents concerning Ireland, 640–1261*, 2 vols. (1962–5) • J. T. Gilbert, ed., *Chartularies of St Mary's Abbey, Dublin: with the register of its house at Dunbrody and annals of Ireland*, 2 vols., Rolls Series, 80 (1884–6) • J. Hunt, *Medieval Irish figure sculpture, 1200–1600* (1974), cat. 26, pl. 62
Likenesses effigy, early 13th cent. (of Cumin?), Christ Church, Dublin, St Lawrence's Chapel

Cumin [Comin], **Robert** [Robert de Cuminis], **earl of Northumbria** (d. **1069**), magnate, was, according to Orderic Vitalis, granted the *comitatus* ('county') of Durham by William I, in the third year of his reign. However, the *Historia regum Anglorum* (attributed, with little certainty, to Symeon of Durham) says that Earl Robert was appointed to govern the area to the north of the Tyne, and this has been seen as one of a number of measures adopted by William in his attempt to bring the area under his control. Orderic may have specified Durham as the seat of Cumin's power as this was where the earl met his death, but it is unlikely that he was using the word *comitatus* in the later sense of earldom. A later source, Gaimar, identifies Earl Robert as the leader of a band of Flemings which suggests that his cognomen, de Cuminis, used by Orderic, may refer to Comines near Lille in Flanders. The earl's relationship to William Cumin, chancellor of David I of Scotland, unsuccessful usurper of the bishopric of Durham in 1141–4, and progenitor of the Scots clan Comyn, is uncertain. Robert Cumin succeeded to the earldom abandoned by Gospatric of Bamburgh. As he is described as being one of those men who paid the wages of their followers by allowing them to pillage and murder, it seems that he was at the head of a company of mercenary soldiers.

Earl Robert came to Durham late in December 1068 with a body of knights (their number varies from 500 to 900 in the sources), but all except two of them were slaughtered on 28 or 31 January 1069. According to Symeon of Durham's tract on the church of Durham (*Libellus de exordio*), the Northumbrians had heard of Cumin's imminent arrival and prepared themselves for flight, but a violent snowstorm prevented their escape. As a result they decided to murder Earl Robert or die in the attempt. As he made his way north, Cumin was met by Æthelwine, bishop of Durham (1056–71), who warned him of the plot against him. Refusing to heed the warning, the earl encamped in the city of Durham where his men committed acts of violence against the men of St Cuthbert. During the night the Northumbrians, who were those living to the north of the Tyne rather than the citizens of Durham, marched south and burst through the city gates slaughtering any Normans they came across. They attacked the earl, who was lodged in the bishop's house, but were beaten off. The Northumbrians therefore decided to set fire to the episcopal residence and when Earl Robert fled the flames he was killed. Sparks from the burning building threatened to ignite the west tower of the cathedral but prayers by the clergy and townsfolk to St Cuthbert proved efficacious and a contrary wind drove back the fire. On hearing of the massacre William I dispatched an army to the north of England but on reaching Allerton in Yorkshire it was engulfed in a black mist. Learning that the local people had a saint who would allow none to persecute them, the punitive expedition turned back. William of Jumièges describes a general conspiracy against William centred on a stronghold called Durham erected in Cumberland (*sic*), but his account of the rising in the north of England is confused and he does not record Cumin's death. Robert Cumin seems to have been succeeded by the native Northumbrian Gospatric who was reinstated in his earldom. Earl Robert's ill-fated attempt to subdue the Northumbrians living to the north of the Tyne illustrates the tenuous hold which William I had on the region for most of his reign.

WILLIAM M. AIRD

Sources Symeon of Durham, *Opera*, vol. 2 • Symeon of Durham, *Libellus de exordio atque procursu istius, hoc est Dunhelmensis, ecclesie / Tract on the origins and progress of this the church of Durham*, ed. and trans. D. W. Rollason, OMT (2000) • *ASC*, s.a. 1068 [texts D, E] • Ordericus Vitalis, *Eccl. hist.*, vol. 2 • *The Gesta Normannorum ducum of William of Jumièges, Orderic Vitalis, and Robert of Torigni*, ed. and trans. E. M. C. van Houts, 2, OMT (1995) • A. Williams, *The English and the Norman conquest* (1995) • W. M. Aird, 'St Cuthbert, the Scots and the Normans', *Anglo-Norman Studies*, 16 (1993), 1–20 • A. Young, *William Cumin: border politics and the bishopric of Durham, 1141–1144*, Borthwick Papers, 54 (1979)

Cumin [Comyn], **William** (d. c.**1160**), ecclesiastic and administrator, was notable for his infamous attempt to usurp the bishopric of Durham between 1141 and 1144. His family origins, possibly from Bosc-Bernard-Commin near Rouen, are obscure. There were several families of Norman clerks in England with connections to cathedral towns such as Bayeux and Rouen, and the Cumin family seems to have been one of them. Several Cumins appear in the chanceries of Henry I and Henry II and in a clerical or ecclesiastical context in Rouen and Bayeux. A John Cumin, probably of the same family, was an administrator prominent in the service of Henry II before becoming archbishop of Dublin in 1182.

The earliest reference to William Cumin occurs c.1121, when he appears as a witness to a gift by Ranulf, chancellor of England, to Bernard the Scribe. He was a pupil and protégé of Geoffrey Rufus, who became chancellor of England in 1123 and in 1133 bishop of Durham, and Cumin's career advanced with that of his patron. Shortly after 1125 Cumin had become archdeacon of Worcester, and it seems probable that Geoffrey Rufus took his protégé with him when he became bishop of Durham. At Durham it appears that Cumin came into contact with David I of Scotland (r. 1124–53), who made him chancellor of Scotland by 1136. William Cumin was thus another prominent member of the Norman occupation of the Scottish royal household so much encouraged by David I after his accession in 1124. Two of Cumin's nephews, William and Osbert, took advantage of the family's breakthrough in Scotland. Symeon of Durham's chronicle describes nephew William as an accomplished young knight trained in the art of warfare and administration, while Osbert was in the service of David's son, Henry, earl of Northumberland.

As chancellor, William Cumin became actively involved in David's policies of absorbing the English northern counties into his kingdom and of supporting Empress Matilda and the Angevin cause against King Stephen in the English civil war. Captured when King David and his army were defeated at the battle of the Standard, near Northallerton in the North Riding of Yorkshire, on 22 August 1138, he was set free in September on the instructions of Alberic, the papal legate. Cumin's ambitious attempt to become bishop of Durham in 1141 fitted in well with the Scottish king's policy in northern England.

In late 1140 or early 1141 Cumin was the guest at Durham of his former patron, Geoffrey Rufus. Realizing that Rufus was near death, Cumin decided to try to secure the see for himself, but Rufus died before William had won all the support necessary for his successful candidature. Nevertheless, buoyed by the Scottish king's support, Cumin took over the administration of the see; but Roger Conyers, the constable, refused to pay homage to him and the prior and one of the archdeacons insisted on a canonical election. Cumin's position was briefly strengthened by Empress Matilda's approval of his candidature, but the papal legate excommunicated him. By 1142 King David appears to have distanced himself from Cumin, and so from 1142 to 1144 William acted as an independent adventurer striving, according to the chronicle of Melrose, 'with blind ambition' to be made bishop. He used violence, and even attempted deceit through a forged letter from the pope purporting to support his candidature.

Cumin's intimidatory tactics could not prevent a canonical election taking place at York in 1143, when William de Ste Barbe, dean of York, was chosen bishop of Durham. It was not for another year that Cumin surrendered his claim to the bishopric, by which time two of his nephews, William, his favourite, and Osbert, had died in the conflict; William de Ste Barbe had also won the crucial support of David's son Henry. In return for renouncing his claims to the bishopric, Cumin secured the secular fortunes of his family through another nephew, Richard, who was given the castle and honour of Richmond. William Cumin himself, after imprisonment and cruel treatment by Richard de Luvetot, sought to revive his career in the south, where he received the support of Gilbert Foliot, then abbot of Gloucester. By 1146 William was in favour with Theobald, archbishop of Canterbury, who pressed his case for absolution before the pope c.1152. Thanks to favour from the Angevin party, Cumin began to regain his benefices in England. He appears prominently in witness lists to Henry of Anjou's charters of c.1153, and again in 1154 and 1156, after Henry had become king of England. By 1156–7 Cumin had recovered his archdeaconry of Worcester. But he was no longer archdeacon by 1161, and it seems probable that he died c.1160. By this time the secular fortunes of his family had a firm foundation, first in

Tynedale, Northumberland, and then in southern Scotland, through the favour given by the Scottish royal family to Cumin's nephew Richard. William Cumin's dramatic but unsuccessful attempt to become bishop of Durham should not obscure his part in the foundation of what was to become the most powerful baronial family in thirteenth-century Scotland.   ALAN YOUNG

Sources A. Young, *William Cumin: border politics and the bishopric of Durham, 1141–1144*, Borthwick Papers, 54 (1979) · A. Young, 'The bishopric of Durham in Stephen's reign', *Anglo-Norman Durham*, ed. D. Rollason, M. Harvey, and M. Prestwich (1994), 353–68 · *Dialogi Laurentii Dunelmensis monachi ac prioris*, ed. J. Raine, SurtS, 70 (1880) · Symeon of Durham, *Opera* · J. H. Round, 'The origins of the Comyns', *The Ancestor*, 10 (1904), 104–19 · *Reg. RAN*, vols. 2–3 · J. H. Round, ed., *Calendar of documents preserved in France, illustrative of the history of Great Britain and Ireland* (1899) · *Fasti Angl., 1066–1300*, [Monastic cathedrals] · *Letters and charters of Gilbert Foliot*, ed. A. Morey and others (1967)

Cumine Ailbhe. *See* Cumméne Albus (*d.* 669) *under* Iona, abbots of (*act.* 563–927).

Cuming, Sir Alexander, second baronet (1691–1775), traveller in America, was born, according to his manuscript autobiography, at Edinburgh on 18 December 1691, the only son of Sir Alexander Cuming, first baronet (*c.*1670–1725), politician, of Culter, Aberdeenshire, and his first wife, Elizabeth (*d.* 1709), second daughter of Sir Alexander Swinton, a Scottish judge styled Lord Mersington. Between 1709 and 1710 he served with the British army in Flanders and, like his father, studied Roman law at Leiden from 1711. Cuming was called to the Scottish bar in 1714, at which time he also held a commission in the Russian army. The award of a pension of £300 p.a. in December 1718 induced him to quit the legal profession. The pension, made either in reward for former services by his family against Jacobitism or in anticipation of Cuming's future support, was stopped in late 1721. Cuming attributed the discontinuation to Sir Robert Walpole's revenge against his father's recent opposition to the ministry. About this time Cuming married Amy (*d.* 1743), daughter of Lancelot Whitehall, a Scottish customs commissioner; they had two children. In 1725, on the death of his father, he became second baronet, of Culter.

On 13 September 1729 Cuming embarked on an extraordinary journey, apparently inspired by Lady Cuming's dream, to the Cherokee mountains on the borders of South Carolina and Virginia. He arrived at Charles Town on 5 December and in early March 1730 he began his journey to the Cherokee Indian country. A fellow of the Royal Society since 1720, *en route* Cuming undertook a survey of the region's geology and plant life. On 3 April he was made 'by the unanimous consent of the people' the 'lawgiver, commander, leader, and chief' of the Cherokees, then a numerous people inhabiting land from the Savannah River to the Tennessee River valley. Cuming returned to Charles Town that month and soon after sailed for Britain with seven Cherokees, including their future leader Attakullakulla.

A meeting with George II at Windsor aroused great public interest and resulted in September in a treaty by which the Cherokees accepted Britain as sovereign and sole trading nation, in return for supplies of guns and powder. Whatever the motive behind Cuming's journey to America, the delegation followed the practice established during previous visits by Mohawk leaders to London and by Indians from the Illinois country to the French court. Cuming's decision to return to Britain with a party of Cherokees may well have been influenced by these encounters. Extracts from his diary, written during his journey, were printed in the *Daily Journal* for 8 October. By this date, however, Cuming was marginalized from the supervision of the Cherokee delegation, whom the government now entrusted to the new governor of South Carolina, Robert Johnson. It was Johnson who accompanied the delegation back to America in October 1730. Cuming's exclusion from the signing and conveying of the treaty may have been due in part to recent allegations of his corrupt business practices in Charles Town, which were printed in the *Edinburgh Weekly Journal* for 16 September.

Cuming's subsequent career was a story of failed colonial schemes and poverty. His proposal to settle up to 300,000 Jewish families on Cherokee land was rejected, as were plans for fiscal reform in the colonies. Rising debts led him to dabble in alchemy and resulted in his incarceration as a debtor in London's Fleet prison in 1737. His wife died during his imprisonment and was buried on 22 October 1743, and he was expelled from the Royal Society in June 1757 for failure to pay his subscription. Cuming was finally released from the Fleet in 1765, when on 30 December he became a pensioner at the Charterhouse on the recommendation of Archbishop Secker. It was here nearly ten years later he died, and he was buried at East Barnet church on 28 August 1775. His title then passed to his only son, Alexander (b. c.1737, d. before 1796), an army officer, whose poor mental health reduced him to an indigent lifestyle at his final home in Red Lion Street, Whitechapel, London.   GORDON GOODWIN, *rev.* PHILIP CARTER

Sources D. D. Martin, 'Cuming, Sir Alexander', *ANB* · S. C. Williams, ed., *Early travels in the Tennessee country, 1540–1800* (1928) · J. Mooney, *Historical sketch of the Cherokee* (1975) [partial repr. of *Myths of the Cherokee* (1900)] · autobiographical notes, BL, Add. MS 39855 · D. Hayton, 'Cuming, Sir Alexander, first baronet', HoP, *Commons, 1690–1715*

Archives BL, autobiographical notes, Add. MS 39855 · NL Scot., letters and memorials [copies] | PRO, SP 36/19, 36/42–5

Cuming, Hugh (1791–1865), conchologist and collector of natural history specimens, was born in the village of Washbrook, near Kingsbridge, south Devon, on 14 February 1791, one of three children born to Richard and Mary Cuming. He may have acquired an interest in conchology from George Montagu, author of several works on British natural history, who had retired to Kingsbridge. Cuming was apprenticed to a sail maker and left England in 1819 to settle at Valparaiso, Chile, to practise the sail-making trade. His mistress, Maria de los Santos, gave birth to a daughter, Clara Valentina, in 1825 and to a son, Hugh Valentine, in 1830. Cuming retired in 1826, a comparatively young, self-made man, and devoted the rest of his life to

Hugh Cuming (1791–1865), by Maull & Polyblank, c.1855

travelling in search of molluscan shells and other natural objects, and to augmenting his large and scientifically significant shell collection.

On 28 October 1827 Cuming set out in the schooner *Discoverer* on a voyage to the Polynesian islands, his vessel being one of the first designed expressly for storing natural history objects. He returned to Valparaiso on 28 June 1828, having made extensive collections of shells and plants. Towards the end of 1828 he was off in the *Discoverer* again in search of shells and plants, his itinerary taking him along the coast of South America as far as Conchagua in the Bay of Fonseca in Central America. This time he often used a dredge of his own design to search for shells almost unobtainable by other means. He returned to Valparaiso about the end of 1829, having amassed abundant and comprehensive collections of plants and zoological specimens, especially shells.

Cuming left Valparaiso for good in May 1831 and sailed for England. There he sold his plants and unwanted zoological specimens and settled at Gower Street in London. On 15 January 1836 he embarked for the Philippines, collected there unremittingly and with great success for four years, and set up in business as a dealer soon after his return to London on 5 June 1840.

Cuming's collections were often praised by contemporary naturalists and he was elected a fellow of the Linnean Society. However, due to his humble origins, dubious marital status, and activities as a dealer, a number of his contemporaries did not hold him in high regard privately, and tried to take advantage of him when they could.

In later life Cuming was stout and of ruddy complexion,

with scanty, white, curly hair. He died of chronic bronchitis, asthma, and dropsy, on 10 August 1865. The following year his shell collection, which provided the basic materials for L. A. Reeve's monumental *Conchologia iconica* (1843–78) and the *Thesaurus conchyliorum* (1842–87) of G. B. Sowerby (father, son, and grandson of the name), was purchased for the nation for £6000.   S. PETER DANCE

Sources S. P. Dance, 'Hugh Cuming (1791–1865), prince of collectors', *Journal of the Society of the Bibliography of Natural History*, 9 (1978–80), 477–501 · S. P. Dance, *A history of shell collecting*, rev. edn (1986) · J. C. Melvill, 'An epitome of the life of the late Hugh Cuming', *Journal of Conchology*, 8 (1895), 59–70 · E. D. Merrill, 'Hugh Cuming's letters to Sir William J. Hooker', *Philippine Journal of Science*, 30 (1926), 153–84 · E. L. Layard, 'Some personal reminiscences of the late Hugh Cuming', *Journal of Conchology*, 8 (1895), 71–5 · H. St John, 'Itinerary of Hugh Cuming in Polynesia', *Occasional Papers Bernice P. Bishop Museum*, 16 (1940), 81–90 · J. T. Howell, 'Hugh Cuming's visit to the Galapagos islands', *Lloydia*, 4 (1941), 291 · W. J. Clench, 'Some notes on the life and explorations of Hugh Cuming', *Occasional Papers on Mollusks*, 1 (1945), 17–28 · parish register (death), North St Giles, 11 Aug 1865 · cemetery register, Kensal Green, 14 Aug 1865

Archives American Philosophical Society, Philadelphia, corresp. · NHM, zoological specimens · RBG Kew, botanical specimens | RCS Eng., London, corresp. with Richard Owen

Likenesses Hawkins, lithograph, 1850, repro. in Dance, 'Hugh Cuming (1791–1865), prince of collectors', 479 · Maull & Polyblank, albumen print, c.1855, NPG [*see illus.*] · photograph, c.1861, repro. in Dance, *History of shell collecting*, pl. 25 · F. P. Orchard, photograph, 1865, repro. in Clench, 'Some notes on the life and explorations of Hugh Cuming', 19 · Sidebotham, autotype photograph, c.1865, repro. in Melvill, 'An epitome of the life of the late Hugh Cuming' · E. Edwards, photograph, NPG; repro. in L. Reeve, ed., *Men of eminence*, 2 (1864)

Wealth at death under £10,000: probate, 23 Oct 1865, *CGPLA Eng. & Wales*

Cuming, Patrick, of Relugas (*bap.* 1695, *d.* 1776), Church of Scotland minister and ecclesiastical agent, was baptized at Inverness on 18 November 1695. He was the elder son of Robert, laird of Relugas (Morayshire), and Magdallan (*d.* 1727), daughter of Finlay Fraser of Inverness. After graduating MA from Edinburgh University on 4 May 1716 he became chaplain to the family of James Erskine, Lord Grange. Licensed by the presbytery of Dalkeith on 5 January 1720, he was ordained to the parish of Kirkmahoe, Dumfriesshire, on 18 August. On 13 March 1725 he was translated to Lochmaben. Soon afterwards he published a sermon calling for restraint within the church, especially regarding lay patronage, which had been causing mounting unrest, locally and nationally, since its restoration in 1712. Although no enthusiast for patronage, Cuming saw obedience to the law as essential if the church's privileges were to be secured. Widely circulated, the sermon prompted his inclusion in the team of ecclesiastical advisers to the earl of Ilay, later third duke of Argyll, and his Edinburgh agent, Andrew Fletcher, Lord Milton, who had recently come to power. Eventually Cuming was brought to Edinburgh and admitted to the second charge of the Old Kirk on 20 January 1732. Eleven months later on 26 November, he married Jean (*d.* 1769), daughter of David Lauder of Huntlywood, advocate, with whom he had six children.

After the death of James Smith in 1736 Cuming became the Argyll interest's chief lieutenant in church affairs. On 7 December of the following year he was appointed professor of ecclesiastical history at Edinburgh University through Ilay's influence. As a result of careful attention to each presentation and preferment, he managed the church and its higher courts with such success that in 1747 he boasted that he could get anyone he wanted elected moderator of the general assembly. In his handling of contested settlements he preferred conciliation to heavy-handed assertion of church authority, and where this proved fruitless he resorted to such expedients as 'riding committees' (which inducted the patron's choice when a presbytery refused) and 'calls', which often were merely sham. Although only palliatives, these practices demonstrated that Cuming was not heedless of those with sensitive consciences. Except when under pressure—as in the Inverkeithing case of 1752—he avoided coercion if diplomacy could suffice. Indeed, notwithstanding his political loyalties, winning respect for the church after the divisions of the past and raising the social standing of its ministers remained his chief goals. His interest in the latter aim was the most likely reason for his support of the scheme to augment stipends in 1749.

In later years Cuming's tendency to let his judgement be affected by personal animosities damaged his reputation. Thus, possibly jealous of the growing influence of William Robertson and his circle, he attempted, in 1756, to discredit them by joining his political and ecclesiastical adversaries in condemning John Home's play, *Douglas*, and in pursuing Alexander Carlyle for attending it. These manoeuvres failed, earning him wide discredit and the nickname Dr Turnstile. Seeking revenge, he again lost ground, in 1758, through a clumsy intervention in Robertson's plans for settling two allies in Edinburgh. Although partially successful, it led to a disastrous split with his able deputy, John Hyndman, who then joined Robertson. Finally, Ilay (now duke of Argyll) died in 1761, and since Cuming's authority was wholly derived from his patron, his leadership passed to Robertson. When the latter was appointed principal of Edinburgh University in the following year Cuming resigned his chair in favour of his son, Robert. A further attempt to embarrass Robertson with the schism overture was made in 1765–6, but its failure showed conclusively that Cuming was now a spent force.

Cuming was elected moderator of the general assembly of the Church of Scotland in 1749, 1752, and 1756, and his university awarded him a DD degree on 13 March 1759. His speeches and lectures were supposedly monotonous, yet Lord Milton considered him 'one of the best preachers' (NL Scot., Saltoun MS 16545, 6.2.1731). On 28 April 1773 he sold his Morayshire estates to his son George for £1500 sterling. He died at Edinburgh of the gravel on 1 April 1776, and was buried two days later in the Lauders of Fountainhall ground, New Kirk.   LAURENCE A. B. WHITLEY

Sources *Fasti Scot.*, new edn, 1.76 · Presbytery registers: Dalkeith, Dumfries, Edinburgh, NA Scot., CH2/424/11; CH2/1284/5M; CH2/121/12 · old parish records, NA Scot., 089/2, 685/47, 685/97

N. M. [N. Morren], *Annals of the general assembly of the Church of Scotland*, 2 vols. (1838–40) · H. Sefton, 'Lord Ilay and Patrick Cuming: a study in eighteenth-century ecclesiastical management', *Records of the Scottish Church History Society*, 19 (1975–7), 203–16 · *The autobiography of Dr Alexander Carlyle of Inveresk, 1722–1805*, ed. J. H. Burton (1910) · *Scotland and Scotsmen in the eighteenth century: from the MSS of John Ramsay, esq., of Ochtertyre*, ed. A. Allardyce, 1 (1888), 250–54 · R. B. Sher, *Church and university in the Scottish Enlightenment: the moderate literati of Edinburgh* (1985) · NL Scot., Gordon-Cuming MSS, dep. 175, boxes 72–5 · G. Bannatine, *The admonition* (1757) · D. Laing, ed., *A catalogue of the graduates … of the University of Edinburgh*, Bannatyne Club, 106 (1858)

Archives NL Scot., Gordon-Cuming MSS, dep. 175, boxes 72–5

Wealth at death Morayshire properties sold to son George for £1500 (28 April 1773): register of deeds, NA Scot., RD4/219

Cuming, William (1769–1852),

portrait painter, was the fourth and youngest son of William Cuming and his wife (*née* Hamilton). He entered the Dublin Society Schools in 1785, and there won a silver medal for figure drawing in 1790. After his studies, and initially residing in Crow Street, Dublin, he quickly established himself as a portraitist and was commissioned in 1792 by the corporation of Dublin to paint Alderman Henry Gore Sankey, the late lord mayor (City Hall, Dublin; badly damaged in the 1908 fire). It is also probably during these early years that he completed Tilly Kettle's portrait (now at the National Gallery of Ireland, Dublin) of their mutual friend, the architect James Gandon (1743–1823). Kettle had not had the time to finish the portrait and so the sitter had entrusted the completion of the gloves, balustrade, walking-stick, and architectural background to Cuming.

Cuming was an integral part of the artists' movement in Dublin to establish annual exhibitions. The first such exhibition to take place for two decades was held in 1800 at 32 Dame Street. Cuming contributed no fewer than eleven portraits. Among these was perhaps one of his most notable works, a portrait (at the National Gallery of Ireland, Dublin) of Vincent Waldré (1742–1814). He continued to contribute to the annual exhibitions until about 1813, being particularly admired for his female portraits.

Following the long-awaited establishment of the Royal Hibernian Academy, Cuming was elected, along with William Ashford and Thomas Sautelle Roberts, to appoint eleven others to form the fourteen academicians. From 1826 to 1832 Cuming exhibited eighteen works at the academy. He was very much involved in its administration, having been elected as president in 1829; he remained president until 1832 when he resigned both from this post and from his profession. He remained active, though, and was appointed as the academy's treasurer in 1835. He finally resigned his membership in 1837.

Cuming's output throughout his career was by no means prolific. Worked with a loose brush and colourful palette, his portraits were considered accomplished but not exceptional, his handling of the head superior to the often weak and flat remainder. Official portraits of Dublin notables made up a good proportion of his work. There are six portraits, including a self-portrait, by Cuming in the National Gallery of Ireland, Dublin. A few of his portraits were engraved in mezzotint by John Raphael Smith and W. Ward. His painting *Christ and Zebedee's Children* was engraved by James Holloway for T. Macklin's Bible and published in 1798.

Cuming was an ardent repealist and an active, sociable man who enjoyed artistic and literary company. He frequently travelled abroad; in 1832, he visited his brother Josiah, who owned sugar plantations in the West Indies. Cuming was never married. He lived at various addresses in Dublin. He had moved in 1795 to 34 Anglesea Street, the house of his brother Hugh. His sister Elizabeth kept house for him at 15 Clare Street, where he had moved in 1808, and subsequently in 20 Lower Abbey Street, where he had moved in 1836. In 1844 he moved to 31 Lower Abbey Street and it is there he died, after a few days of illness, on 5 April 1852. He was buried on 9 April on Mount Jerome.

L. H. CUST, *rev.* JILL SPRINGALL

Sources W. G. Strickland, *A dictionary of Irish artists*, 2 vols. (1913) · J. Turner, ed., *The dictionary of art*, 34 vols. (1996) · A. M. Stewart and C. de Courcy, eds., *Royal Hibernian Academy of Arts: index of exhibitors and their works, 1826–1979*, 1 (1985) · *National Gallery of Ireland: illustrated summary catalogue of paintings* (1981) · B. Stewart and M. Cutten, *The dictionary of portrait painters in Britain up to 1920* (1997) · M. Wynne, 'Tilly Kettle's last painting?', *Burlington Magazine*, 109 (1967), 532–3 · *Engraved Brit. ports.*

Likenesses T. Kirk, bust, exh. 1832, Royal Hibernian Academy · W. Cuming, self-portrait, oils, NG Ire. · E. D. Leahy, oils, Royal Hibernian Academy, Dublin, Ireland

Wealth at death left to the Royal Hibernian Academy one half of his prints and books of prints, and also whatever books might be in his collection on the subject of the fine arts: Strickland, *Dictionary*, vol. 1, p. 244

Cumméne Albus (d. 669).

See under Iona, abbots of (*act.* 563–927).

Cumméne Fota (c.591–662).

See under Connacht, saints of (*act. c.*400–*c.*800).

Cumming. *See also* Cuming.

Cumming, Alexander (1731/2–1814),

watchmaker and mechanician, is said by most sources to have been born in Edinburgh, although there is no trace of his baptism in the parish registers. However, according to the first Scottish *Statistical Account* (vol. 21, 1799), discovered by Mary Cosh, he was a son of James Cumming of the parish of Duthil, Inverness-shire, for which no registers survive for the relevant period. A precocious mechanical skill apparently brought Cumming to the attention of Lord Milton, who took him into his service. According to some authorities he was apprenticed to a watchmaker in Edinburgh, but supporting evidence is lacking. However, he did become a member of the Philosophical Society of Edinburgh. By 1752 he was working in Inveraray, Argyll, as a watchmaker and enrolled as a burgess. Lord Milton was chief Scottish political agent to Archibald Campbell, third duke of Argyll, and he probably recommended Cumming to his patron, since by 1757 Alexander and his brother John were employed by the duke in making an organ for his new castle at Inveraray. Alexander also made a longcase clock for the castle. The duke of Argyll was the uncle of John Stuart, third earl of Bute, tutor and later prime minister to George III. After Argyll's death in 1761 Cumming probably applied to Bute for patronage, for by 1763 he was established in New Bond Street, London, and had acquired a sufficient reputation to be appointed a member of the commission set up in that year to adjudicate on John Harrison's 'timekeeper for discovering the longitude at sea', the name then given to what was to prove the first successful marine chronometer. Cumming was one of those who insisted that a second timekeeper must be made according to Harrison's principles in order to prove both that he had fully disclosed his methods, as required by the act of parliament that created the commission, and that he had invented a reliable means of checking longitude. Cumming's *Elements of Clock and Watch Work Adapted to Practice* (1766), seems to have stemmed partly from an essay he wrote when appointed to the commission on Harrison's timekeeper. He deposited the essay, in which he outlined his ideas about clockwork, with the Philosophical Society of Edinburgh in order to protect himself against the possibility of charges of plagiarism after he had heard Harrison's explanation. The book included one of the earliest designs for a gravity escapement.

Cumming made clocks and watches for a number of eminent contemporaries, including two gold stopwatches for Sir William Hamilton at Naples and in 1769 a watch for Dr Charles Blagden, for whom he also ordered an electrifying machine from the instrument maker Jesse Ramsden. It was at this stage in his career that Cumming married Elizabeth Oswald (*c*.1744–1815) at St Anne's, Soho, London, on 13 May 1769. There were four children of the marriage, including a son, James *Cumming, who became a senior official at the India Office, and a daughter, Ann.

Cumming was especially interested in the measurement of air pressure and became involved in developing the ideas first outlined by Robert Hooke for recording barometer readings. In 1765 he made a special clock for George III that recorded on a chart the variations in barometer readings over the course of a year, and was paid £150 annually to maintain it. This is usually claimed to be the first effective recording barograph. In the following year Cumming made a slightly altered version of the barograph clock for his own use. After his death it was bought by Luke Howard, who used it for the observations that formed the basis of his pioneering work *The Climate of London* (1820). It is now preserved at the Science Museum, London. Between 1770 and 1773 Cumming made experiments designed to investigate the effects of changes in temperature on the barometer and to examine its use for determining height above sea level. Some of these investigations were carried out at Luton Hoo Park, the home of the third earl of Bute, a fellow Scot, who took up an interest in botany and other scientific matters when he retired from politics.

While his principal occupation was making clocks and watches, Cumming also developed a number of mechanical devices. According to J. Hill in *The Construction of Timber from its Early Growth* (1770), Cumming invented the microtome, a device for cutting very thin samples for examination under a microscope, an example of which is preserved in the George III collection at the Science Museum.

The first example of this device was made for Bute, and several were among the effects sold after the earl's death in 1792. In 1781 Cumming's achievements were recognized when he was made an honorary freeman of the Clockmakers' Company of the City of London, and he was elected a fellow of the Royal Society of Edinburgh in 1783. In that year, on the orders of the king, he was involved in experiments at Windsor on a new hydraulic machine for raising water. Again, the first trials of the machine had been carried out at Bute's estate near Luton.

In the early 1790s Cumming retired to Penton Place in Pentonville, then a suburb of London, where he wrote a number of essays on mechanical questions. These included *Observations on the effects which carriage wheels, with rims of different shapes, have on the roads* (London, 1797) and *A Dissertation on the Influence of Gravitation Considered as a Mechanic Power* (Edinburgh, 1803). In 1779 he had invested in land leased from Henry Penton MP and, with his brother John, contributed significantly to the development of the district, and became a magistrate. He was asked to act as an arbitrator in a dispute in 1812 over the price of a clock made by William Hardie for the Royal Greenwich Observatory. Cumming died at Penton Place on 8 March 1814, aged eighty-two, and was buried on 15 March at St James's Chapel, Pentonville Road, Finsbury, London, an offshoot that he had helped to found of the parish of St James's, Clerkenwell.

In an obituary in the *Gentleman's Magazine* Cumming was described as 'eminent for his genius and knowledge in the mechanical sciences'. Other commentators, both among his contemporaries and later, while acknowledging his talents, have been more critical. William Ludlam challenged some of the interpretations of mechanical theory given in *The Elements of Clock and Watch Work* in a letter to the *Gentleman's Magazine* (1st ser., 57, 1787, 300–02), and in the mid-twentieth century G. H. Baillie commented of the same work that 'the reasoning throughout is turgid and frequently wrong' (p. 270). Also, Cumming failed to appreciate the significance of some of the improvements Harrison had incorporated in his marine timekeeper. However, criticisms of Cumming's theoretical knowledge do not detract from the excellence of many of his timepieces and his contributions to scientific enquiry and mechanical invention.

GLORIA CLIFTON

Sources F. J. Britten, *Old clocks and watches and their makers*, ed. G. H. Baillie, C. Ilbert, and C. Clutton, 9th edn (1982) · G. H. Baillie, *Clocks and watches: an historical bibliography* (1951) · [J. Watkins and F. Shoberl], *A biographical dictionary of the living authors of Great Britain and Ireland* (1816) · Watt, *Bibl. Brit.* · H. A. Lloyd, 'Horology and meteorology', NMM, Foulkes MSS · parish register (marriage), St Anne, Soho, London, 1769 · parish register (burial), St James, Pentonville Road, Finsbury, London, 15 March 1814 · J. Hill, *The construction of timber from its early growth* · *Antiques Trade Gazette* (13 March 1982) · A. Q. Morton and J. A. Wess, *Public and private science: the King George III collection* (1993) · W. J. H. Andrewes, 'Even Newton could be wrong: the story of Harrison's first three sea clocks', *The quest for longitude*, ed. W. J. H. Andrewes (1996), 189–234 · *GM*, 1st ser., 84/1 (1814), 414 · M. Cosh, 'Clockmaker extraordinary: the career of Alexander Cumming', *Country Life* (12 June 1969), 1528–35

Archives GL, Clockmakers' Company MSS, 3964, 3973 · RS

Cumming, (Felicity) Anne (1917–1993), writer and sexual
adventurer, was born on 14 December 1917, at Thames
Cottage, Thames Street, Walton-on-Thames, Surrey, the
daughter of Howard Cumming (1885–1957), captain in the
Royal Flying Corps, timber merchant, and later a company director, and his wife, (Eileen) Norah, *née* Groves
(later Rabeneck; 1895–1938). She had at least two brothers.
Her grandfather was Sir Grimble Groves, brewery owner
and Conservative MP for South Salford. She claimed descent from the medieval Scottish magnate Red Comyn. She
spent her childhood on her father's farm in South Africa
before boarding at Horsely Towers School in Kent after her
parents' divorce. She came out as a débutante in 1935, during which year she lost her virginity on a park bench
under the Eiffel Tower. She studied dance with a friend of
Isadora Duncan in Paris and then drama at Dartington
Hall with Mikhail Chekhov, the nephew of the playwright
(who died in the arms of her Russian stepfather Lieve
Rabeneck). Cumming also studied foreign languages in
France and Germany. On 10 September 1938 she married
Henry Landall Lyon Young (*b.* 1909), who had been
brought up in Valparaiso, Chile, and was an aspirant playwright. He was supposedly a distant cousin of Elizabeth,
later the queen mother, and author of *Baroque Tales of Chile*
(1963) and *Regent of Paraguay* (1966). They had two daughters. Cumming, Young, and Chekhov travelled to the
United States, where they hoped to set up a theatrical
company, but Chekhov's death and the outbreak of the
Second World War frustrated these plans. Cumming and
Young continued to live in New York, where she modelled
for *Vogue* and *Harper's Bazaar*. After wartime employment
with British intelligence Cumming returned in 1944 to
London.

In 1948 Cumming eloped across Europe in an army surplus jeep with Richard Mason (*b.* 1919), whom she married
later that year after divorcing Young. Mason, who had
recently published his first novel, *The Wind cannot Read*
(1947), became celebrated as the author of *The World of
Suzie Wong* (1957). While working as a translator, interpreter, and courier for the British Council, Cumming
befriended the writer Francis King in Greece. He found
her 'an exhilarating companion, totally uninhibited in
her talk and her behaviour', who joined him picking up
'eager sailors, soldiers and airmen' (King, 137). The atmosphere of expatriate male homosexuality was congenial to
her. In 1952, while her husband was visiting the South
Seas, she set off by herself for Marrakesh where she met
the Swiss-Canadian painter, writer, and restaurateur
Brion Gysin, who became her lifelong friend. She also
knew William Burroughs and Paul and Jane Bowles. An
intrepid and gleeful traveller, she had numerous sexual
encounters with young Arab men while on a bus tour of
the Sahara. She returned to her husband in Chelsea, but

(Felicity) Anne Cumming (1917–1993), by Denzil McNeelance,
1989

when in 1953 he left on a long Oriental business journey
she decamped to Iran, where she had further amorous
adventures.

In 1955 Cumming separated amicably from Mason (they
were later divorced); he and her first husband liked one
another and were close friends. She settled in Rome,
teaching English in the British Institute, and began a relationship with Beni Montresor (1926–2001), eight years her
junior, who became a successful set and costume designer
for films and opera. (In her memoirs he is referred to as
Rudi or the Baron.) Montresor was the author of several
books, including *Cinderella: from the Opera* (1967) and *Bed-
time!* (1978). When Montresor abandoned Cumming in
1960 he gave her a gold ring inscribed 'Always and Never';
they remained devoted. In 1960 she left the British Institute to earn her living in Rome as a dialogue coach and
publicist for film companies. Thereafter she used men as
divertissements rather than as *raisons d'être*. She was a
woman of tireless physical curiosity, for whom sexual acts
were both agreeably stupefying and emotionally absorbing: 'Copulation is communication; and I want to be
wanted' (Cumming, *Love Habit*, 18).

After Montresor, Cumming had an intermittent twenty-
year relationship with an Italian long-distance lorry
driver, who provided problem-free sex, and with other
men and boys of all classes, some of whom were primarily
interested in other men. She also resumed her sexual
'tourism', and was gang-raped in Cairo in 1963. In 1965 she
lived in Paris for a few months to write a novel, 'Beyond
this Limit', about 'a homosexual who cannot love the men

he sleeps with but who desperately loves a woman' (Cumming, *Love Quest*, 154). It was never finished. From 1968 she regularly visited New York where she ran a series of Chekhov theatrical workshops. She was also an occasional actress, appearing in *The Girl who Couldn't Say No* as George Segal's mother in 1969. A publishing friend persuaded her to write a zestfully licentious account of her love life covering the decade after her fiftieth birthday. This was published as *The Love Habit* (1977). A sequel, *The Love Quest* (1991), describes her sexual tourism from 1952 until the early 1960s. The two books are often cheerfully raffish, but sometimes descend into gruesome particularity about men's bodies and desires. There are droll passages, but also wearying phases in both books. To publicize *The Love Quest* Cumming was photographed topless in the *Sunday Sport*, which in turn elicited an invitation to appear as a dancer in Las Vegas. In the year of her death she appeared on television wearing only a pearl necklace, earrings, and hat in the world's first nude chat show. She revelled in colour, vulgarity, and vitality.

In 1986 Cumming learned that she was HIV-positive and settled in London so as to benefit from the National Health Service. She preferred to keep her status confidential and she continued with her travels until her death. At her flat in Lisson Street she held a regular salon in which she sought to introduce young writers, actors, and designers to useful contacts. As a member of the *nouveaux pauvres* she offered Marks and Spencer food on chipped porcelain bought in nearby Church Street market. Drunkenness bored her, so she served only tea poured from an enormous stained pot. She died of bronchopneumonia on 28 August 1993 at the London Lighthouse, a care centre for people with HIV and AIDS at 111–17 Lancaster Road, Kensington, London.   RICHARD DAVENPORT-HINES

Sources A. Cumming, *The love habit* (1977) • A. Cumming, *The love quest: a sexual odyssey* (1991) • F. King, *Yesterday came suddenly* (1993) • *The Times* (2 Sept 1993) • *The Times* (6 Sept 1993) • *The Times* (24 Oct 1992) • *CGPLA Eng. & Wales* (1938) • *CGPLA Eng. & Wales* (1957) • A. C. Fox-Davies, *Armorial families*, 1 (1929) • *Daily Telegraph* (1 Sept 1993) • J. W. Moir, ed., *Harrow School Register, 1885–1949* (1951) • L. J. Verney, ed., *Harrow School Register, 1986* (1987)
Likenesses P. Hujar, photograph, *c.*1977, repro. in Cumming, *The love habit*, end cover • D. McNeelance, photograph, 1989, News International Syndication, London [*see illus.*]

Cumming, Sir Arthur (1817–1893), naval officer, son of General Sir Henry Cumming (1772–1856), was born at Nancy in France on 6 May 1817. He entered the Royal Naval College at Portsmouth in January 1831, and having passed the course went, on 8 August 1832, to the sloop *Rover* in the Mediterranean. He afterwards served on the Lisbon and the North American stations. He passed his examination in 1837, and in 1840 was a mate of the steamer *Cyclops* on the coast of Syria, where he repeatedly distinguished himself, especially at the storming of Sidon on 26 September; his promotion to lieutenant was dated on the 28th. He was shortly after appointed to the brig *Frolic* on the coast of South America, and in September 1843 was cruising to the southward of Rio de Janeiro in command of the *Frolic*'s pinnace, when, on the 6th, off Santos, he and seven men

boldly captured the piratical slaver *Vincedora*, a large brigantine with a crew of thirty. Two other slavers in company with the *Vincedora* might have put Cumming in a dangerous position, but they fled. Considering the very exceptional nature of the action, and how easily, without great daring and coolness, it might have ended in disaster, Cumming always felt aggrieved at its being reported to the Admiralty as the commonplace capture of a slaver with a cargo of slaves. He had hoped for promotion; his only reward was a severe attack of smallpox, which was raging on the prize, and for which he was invalided. Hobart Pasha, who was at that time in the *Dolphin*, recounted the capture of the *Vincedora* in *Sketches of my Life* (1887) and attributed the success of the adventure to himself [*see* Hampden, Augustus Charles Hobart-].

Cumming was promoted commander on 9 November 1846, and from 1849 to 1851 commanded the *Rattler* on the west coast of Africa. In 1853 he married Marie Adelaide, daughter of Charles Stuart; they had at least one child. On 19 April 1854 he was promoted captain of the *Conflict*, in which he rendered good service in the Baltic, especially at Libau and Riga. In spring 1855 he was appointed to the floating battery *Glatton*, which he took out to the Black Sea and brought home again in spring 1856. From 1859 to 1863 he commanded the *Emerald* in the Channel Fleet. He was nominated a CB on 13 May 1867. On 27 February 1870 he was promoted rear-admiral, and from 1872 to 1875 was commander-in-chief in the East Indies. He was made vice-admiral on 22 March 1876, admiral on 9 January 1880, and was put on the retired list on 6 May 1882. He was created a KCB at Queen Victoria's jubilee on 21 June 1887. After his retirement he lived mostly at his seat, Foston Hall, near Derby. He died at 17 Seymour Street, London, on 17 February 1893 and was buried in the family vault at Brookwood cemetery, Woking, Surrey. His wife survived him.

J. K. LAUGHTON, rev. ANDREW LAMBERT

Sources J. W. D. Dundas and C. Napier, *Russian war, 1854, Baltic and Black Sea: official correspondence*, ed. D. Bonner-Smith and A. C. Dewar, Navy RS, 83 (1943) • O'Byrne, *Naval biog. dict.* • *Annual Register* (1893) • *Army and Navy Gazette* (18 Dec 1886) • *Army and Navy Gazette* (25 Feb 1893) • private information (1901) • Boase, *Mod. Eng. biog.* • Kelly, *Handbk* • *CGPLA Eng. & Wales* (1893)
Likenesses portrait, repro. in *ILN* (25 Feb 1893), 234
Wealth at death £4479 17s. 8d.: probate, 6 May 1893, *CGPLA Eng. & Wales*

Cumming, Barbara Theresa [*name in religion* Hildelith Cumming] (1909–1991), nun, printer, and musician, was born on 15 December 1909 at 61 Thurleigh Road, Battersea, the third daughter of Frederick Mann Cumming (*d.* 1931), a civil engineer's assistant, and his wife, Emma Georgiana Love (1868–1935). Barbara was effectively an only child, as both her sisters died before she was born. She was educated at the county secondary school, Clapham (1920–27) and at the Royal Academy of Music (1927–31). A prize-winning student who gained diplomas and teaching qualifications in piano and elocution, she was appointed sub-professor for piano at the academy in September 1932. She relinquished this post in January

1933, on becoming resident music mistress at the Collegiate School for Girls, Wentworth, Bournemouth, a position that she retained until 1941.

Barbara Cumming first came into contact with the Oxford Group (later Moral Re-Armament) about 1930, and by 1932 was a fully committed member. She fell in love with another member but the leader of the group refused them permission to marry. Her first professional engagement as a pianist was in London, at the Wigmore Hall in April 1939. Beethoven and Brahms were her great loves, and she became well-known as a player of Brahms. In 1940 her school was evacuated to Llangollen; a Christmas spent at Le Bon Sauveur Convent, Holyhead, led to her conversion to Roman Catholicism. She entered Stanbrook Abbey, near Worcester, an enclosed community of Benedictine nuns, on 18 December 1941, at the age of thirty-two, and remained there until her death. She was named Hildelith after the second abbess of Barking.

Dame Hildelith became a full member of the community on 15 August 1946. Many of her monastic duties drew on her musical abilities. She was assistant organist from 1943 to 1979, and director of the choir and director of music from 1969 to 1982. She was cellarer from 1951 to 1955, with responsibility for the business side of the abbey and its properties, at a time of financial crisis for the community. To raise money she recommended the closure of the printing press, founded in 1876. Instead the abbess, Dame Elizabeth Sumner, appointed her printer, in November 1955, a post that she held with great distinction for thirty-five years.

The Stanbrook Abbey Press under Dame Hildelith quickly became one of the leading private presses, renowned for the quality of its book design and press work. She initially sought advice from printers and typographers, notably Jan van Krimpen, whose types were used in the majority of fine books from 1958 onwards. The combination of handmade papers and distinguished types, with the calligraphy and decorations of Margaret Adams, characterized much of Stanbrook's output. The press produced some eighty titles between 1956 and 1988, including Siegfried Sassoon's *The Path to Peace* (1960), the *Rituale abbatum* (1963), and Russell Flint's *The Lisping Goddess* (1968). Dame Hildelith herself wrote *The Stanbrook Abbey Press: Ninety-Two Years of its History*, which was published in 1970.

Dame Hildelith made a significant contribution musically at a time of transition to the vernacular liturgy. She was a founder member of the Panel of Monastic Musicians and edited several books, notably *The Stanbrook Abbey Hymnal* (1974). Appointed an associate of the Royal Academy of Music in 1984, she influenced the establishment of its pioneering postgraduate course in church music studies. It was her friendship with the musicologist, writer, and broadcaster Alec Robertson that led her to set up a memorial fund that provided a church-music scholarship at the Royal Academy of Music in 1988. She unified the apparently divergent worlds of typography and music: 'There is a strange affinity in their respective spheres between plainsong and typography, so that the deep study of one

may enrich the understanding of the other' (Cumming, *Stanbrook Abbey Press*, 145–6). To her, typography was 'silent song'.

Dame Hildelith was a warm-hearted and generous person who made time for people and their requests; her enthusiasm and good humour are apparent in the spirit of joy that infused her work. Her gift for friendship brought her a wide range of contacts outside the community. She suffered a heart attack in 1982, and deteriorating health made large-scale printing projects impossible for the last eight years of her life. She died in Evesham Community Hospital on 19 April 1991, and was buried at Stanbrook on 23 April. She was a fine musician and a first-rate private press printer, but these achievements were expressions of her Benedictine vocation, to which she devoted the major part of her life.   DAVID BUTCHER

Sources Stanbrook Abbey, Worcestershire, archive, Hildelith Cumming MSS · J. Jamieson, 'Dame Hildelith Cumming', Stanbrook Abbey community conference, 6 May 1991, Stanbrook Abbey · [H. Cumming], *The Stanbrook Abbey Press: ninety-two years of its history* (1970) · D. Butcher, *The Stanbrook Abbey Press, 1956–1990* (1992) · *The Times* (8 May 1991) · M. Truran, 'Dame Hildelith Cumming', *Bulletin of the Panel of Monastic Musicians* (1991), 27–8 · b. cert. · d. cert.

Archives Stanbrook Abbey, Worcestershire, archive | Bodl. Oxf., Stanbrook Abbey Press archive

Likenesses S. Harrison, photograph, c.1975, repro. in Butcher, *Stanbrook Abbey Press*

Cumming, Constance Frederica Gordon- (1837–1924), travel writer, was born on 26 May 1837 at Altyre, Morayshire, twelfth child and youngest daughter of Sir William Gordon Gordon-Cumming of Altyre and Gordonstown, second baronet (1787–1854), and his first wife, Eliza Maria (d. 1842), eldest daughter of John Campbell the younger of Shawfield and Islay. In addition to her eleven siblings (one of them the lion hunter Roualeyn Gordon-*Cumming) Constance had three half-siblings from her father's second marriage. She was educated at home and at school in Fulham, Middlesex. In 1867 she was invited to spend a year with a married sister in India and this proved the start of twelve years of travel and a longer period of travel writing. She was well off and well connected, and 'her globe trotting took on the air of a series of rather far-flung social calls' (Robinson, 94). After a year in India with her sister and brother-in-law she spent *Two Happy Years in Ceylon* (2 vols., 1892), where she knew the bishop of Colombo. She then found herself *At Home in Fiji* (2 vols., 1881), the guest of its first governor. In Fiji she met and accepted the invitation of the bishop of Samoa to join him on his rounds, much enjoying *A Lady's Cruise in a French Man-of-War* in the South Seas (2 vols., 1882). A visit to the *Granite Crags* of California (1884) was followed by *Wanderings in China* (2 vols., 1886). After a brief return to Britain in 1879 she set off again for California at the invitation of General and Mrs Ulysses Grant, later finding herself among the *Fire Fountains* of Hawaii (2 vols., 1883).

In later years Gordon-Cumming settled in Scotland, where she spent some time arranging for exhibition the numerous watercolours she had produced in her travels

Constance Frederica Gordon-Cumming (1837–1924), by Barraud, pubd 1893

and working on travel books and articles which have been described as 'almost unreadable, so informative are they' (Middleton, 5). However, her time and her pen were increasingly taken up with furthering the development of numeral type for blind and sighted Chinese in Mandarin-speaking areas of China, for she had been inspired by her visit to William Hill Murray's mission to blind people on her visit to China. She died in Crieff, Perthshire, on 4 September 1924.

Gordon-Cumming's reputation as a traveller has sunk somewhat and she is not now regarded as being on a par with her acquaintance Isabella Bird. Nor are her competent watercolours the equal of the paintings of her friend Marianne North. Her style of writing is so turgid that her works are generally left out of travel anthologies. None the less, the distances she travelled, the exotic locations she reached, and the sheer quantity of her output gain her a place in the history of travel. ELIZABETH BAIGENT

Sources WWW · Burke, *Peerage* · J. Robinson, ed., *Wayward women: a guide to women travellers* (1990) · C. F. Gordon-Cumming, *Memories* (1904) · D. Middleton, *Victorian lady travellers* (1965) · *CCI* (1924)
Archives NL Scot., Fiji diary
Likenesses Barraud, photograph, pubd 1893, NPG [*see illus.*]
Wealth at death £1703 13s. od.: confirmation, 6 Oct 1924, *CCI* · £805: eik additional estate, 29 Nov 1924, *CCI*

Cumming, Hildelith. *See* Cumming, Barbara Theresa (1909–1991).

Cumming, James (*d.* 1827), civil servant, son of Alexander *Cumming (1731/2–1814), watchmaker, of Bond Street, and his wife, Elizabeth Oswald (*c.*1744–1815), joined the Board of Control in 1793 as a clerk. In 1807 he was made head of the revenue and judicial departments, which encompassed all of the internal administration of British India. A bachelor and singularly devoted to the India Office, he spent the next sixteen years compiling an enormous archive on all aspects of the East India Company's government in India: land tenures, revenue administration, customary law, judicial procedures, civil appointments, regulations, and so forth. The board's members changed frequently and it was Cumming who provided stability from one administration to the next, absorbing the information sent from India and advising the board of the appropriate reaction. In 1814 the House of Commons voted him £500 for his assistance in drafting the select committee's fifth report on the government of the Madras territories. Cumming was a great supporter of Thomas Munro's experiments with ryotwari settlement in south India and he had structured the fifth report so as to favour Munro's doctrine at the expense of those who supported permanent settlement. He did the same with subsequent papers; two superficially objective volumes of revenue and judicial papers which he compiled in 1820 were designed to consolidate Munro's political and philosophical victories over his opponents in London.

In 1823, when probably only in his forties, the strain of overwork forced him to retire. Effusive testimonies to the merit of his services from George Canning, John Sullivan, and lords Teignmouth and Binning failed to secure him a pension equal to his closing salary of £1000. In 1824, however, Lord Liverpool granted his sister and long-time companion, Ann, a pension of £200 to prevent her destitution should her brother predecease her and, on Cumming producing a pamphlet recapitulating his services, the court of directors finally allowed him a small additional pension. He died at Lovell Hill Cottage, Berkshire, on 23 January 1827, encumbering his sister with debts accumulated during his final illness. These she liquidated by selling his papers to the company for £400.

Cumming appears to have had little time in his life for anything but the India Office; nevertheless, he is almost certainly the James Cumming FSA who in 1806 published an edition of Owen Felltham's *Resolves*, dedicated to the duke of Gloucester.

H. M. STEPHENS, *rev.* KATHERINE PRIOR

Sources Brief notice of the services of Mr Cumming, 1807 · *GM*, 1st ser., 97/1 (1827), 187 · BL OIOC, Cumming MSS, Home misc. · BL OIOC, board of control MSS · B. Stein, *Thomas Munro: the origins of the colonial state and his vision of empire* (1989)
Archives BL OIOC, Munro MSS · BL OIOC, Home Misc. series, papers
Likenesses J. Thomson, stipple, pubd 1827, NPG
Wealth at death died in debt: BL OIOC, Cumming MSS

Cumming, James (1777–1861), chemist, was born on 26 October 1777 in the parish of St James Piccadilly, London, the son of James Cumming and his wife, Alice Atherton. His grandfather and father were descended from the

Scottish family of Cumming of Altyre, near Forres. In 1797 Cumming entered Trinity College, Cambridge, and in 1801 graduated BA as tenth wrangler. He was elected a fellow of his college in 1803, and proceeded MA the following year. In 1818 he was appointed a university proctor. While a student he had studied natural philosophy, and in 1801–3 assisted Wollaston in demonstrating his physical lectures. In 1815 he succeeded Smithson Tennant as professor of chemistry at the university. Adam Sedgwick the geologist and William Whewell became his friends and colleagues.

In 1816 Cumming was elected a fellow of the Royal Society and to fellowship of the Geological Society. In 1819 he was appointed rector of All Saints, North Runcton, Norfolk, a post he held until death. This preferment enabled him on 17 February 1820 to marry Sarah (1798–1872), eldest daughter of Charles Humfry, a gentleman of Cambridge. Their family eventually consisted of a son, James John Cumming who became rector of East Carlton, Norfolk, and two daughters, Isabella and Harriet.

Cumming's career was significant because of his important example of research-led teaching in a period when laboratories were being developed and discussed. The university provided no apparatus, so by his own skill he constructed or adapted many of the sensitive instruments required for research and lecture demonstrations, and made important modifications and simplifications of electrical methods. Cumming was a founder member of the Cambridge Philosophical Society in 1819 and served as its president in 1825–7. After he repeated Oersted's famous experiments his papers on the application of magnetism as a measure of electricity, expounding the principle of the galvanometer and its sensitivity, appeared in the society's *Transactions* (1821–2).

Cumming's paper on the development of electromagnetism by heat (*Transactions of the Cambridge Philosophical Society*, 1823), re-examined Seebeck's experiments demonstrating the thermoelectric effect by which increasing temperature can alter the position of substances in the thermoelectric series. Cumming repeated the experiments using several different metals and tabulated the results—observations that were important and stimulating at the time. Some specially constructed apparatus enabled him also to test small quantities of substances, and tabulate the relative negativity and sensitivity of each.

Three more papers on thermoelectricity were published in *Annals of Philosophy* in 1823. The first again covered the thermoelectric effect, using metal bars. The second, 'A list of substances arranged according to their thermoelectric relations, with a description of instruments for exhibiting rotation by thermoelectricity', was followed by 'On some anomalous appearances occurring in the thermoelectric series'. This important paper described the effect of gradually heating a metal wire joined to an iron wire, causing the deflection of a galvanometer needle to rise to a maximum as the heat increased, and then reducing and reversing at red heat, thereby producing several changes of order in the thermoelectric series.

Although this work on heat and electricity was anticipated by others, by then Cumming had begun to address the need to modernize the Cambridge medical curriculum for those students who had already graduated BA, and his research enabled him to offer stimulating examples. 'In 1825 he published a detailed syllabus' which to the basics of the science added 'electro-chemistry, the chemistry of bodily fluids, the detection of poisons, and the analysis of mineral waters' (Searby, 223). An excellent lecturer, Cumming was well respected at Cambridge for this instruction so useful to doctors, and because his chemistry lectures included important demonstrations of electromagnetism and thermoelectricity during a period when these were not topics within mathematical lectures. Despite attending to his rectory, and being aged seventy-four in 1851 when the natural science tripos was introduced, he kept his lectures up to date in the next decade.

In 1827 Cumming published *A Manual of Electro Dynamics*, translated from the *Manuel d'électricité dynamique* of J. F. Demonferrand, but with many improvements, an additional section on the construction and application of apparatus for detecting and measuring electrodynamic action, and another on thermoelectricity. There was an appended section on the connection between chemical and electrical action, and one on the order and relative powers of different metals in conducting electricity. The book contained many extra notes and included diagrams and illustrations of apparatus used in the experiments. Some of Cumming's later papers appeared in the British Association for the Advancement of Science *Reports*. He studied other scientific topics such as calculus (stone) in humans and animals, the formation of plumbago on iron, and Dobereiner's experiments using hydrogen upon platinum.

A photograph of Cumming in old age shows that he was well built and clean shaven and had thick white hair, but was partially bald. He was a kind, honest man with a genial nature. Clear thinking and well read, he had the ability to grasp the essentials of any problem, and an aptitude for quotation. He liked to discuss all manner of topics, and he and his wife sometimes invited friends to a soirée, when a singer would provide entertainment.

Although he made no outstanding discoveries, Cumming made his mark with an early description of the galvanometer, and his work on electromagnetism and thermoelectricity. A committed researcher, he worked and lectured until 1860 and suggested various optical experiments even as his health deteriorated shortly before his death on 10 November 1861 at his rectory. He was buried in All Saints' churchyard, North Runcton, on 14 November.   CHRISTOPHER F. LINDSEY

Sources *Lynn Advertiser and West Norfolk Herald* (23 Nov 1861) • A. C. Ramsay, *Quarterly Journal of the Geological Society*, 19 (1863), xxxi • J. W. Clark, 'The foundation and early years of the society', *Proceedings of the Cambridge Philosophical Society*, 7 (1889–92) • memorial plaque, All Saints' Church, North Runcton, Norfolk • P. G. Tait, 'Thermo-electricity', *Nature*, 8 (1873), 86–8 • *DNB* • A. R. Hall, *The Cambridge Philosophical Society: a history, 1819–1969* (1969) • *Romilly's Cambridge diary, 1842–47: selected passages from the diary of the Rev. Joseph Romilly*, ed. M. E. Bury and J. D. Pickles, Cambridgeshire RS, 10

(1994) · parish register (baptism), 21 Nov 1777, London, St James, Piccadilly · H. Hamilton, ed., *The third statistical account of Scotland*, 17: *The counties of Moray and Nairn* (1965), 335 · Venn, *Alum. Cant.* · *GM*, 1st ser., 90/1 (1820), 272 · P. Searby, *A history of the University of Cambridge*, 3: *1750–1870*, ed. C. N. L. Brooke and others (1997), 222–4 · C. Knight, ed., *The English cyclopaedia: biography*, 3 (1856)

Archives CUL, non-scientific papers etc. · Norfolk RO, lawsuit MSS · RS, scientific reports and invitation acceptance · Trinity Cam., letters

Likenesses photograph, Trinity Cam.; repro. in Hall, *Cambridge Philosophical Society*

Wealth at death £7000: probate, 28 March 1862, *CGPLA Eng. & Wales*

Cumming, John (1807–1881), minister of the Presbyterian Church of England, was born at Fintray, Aberdeenshire, on 10 November 1807. He was educated at Aberdeen grammar school and, from 1822, at the University of Aberdeen, where he studied under Professor Duncan Mearns, who inspired his strong allegiance to the established church. He graduated MA in 1827, and continued his studies at the Divinity Hall. During this time he spent his vacations working as a tutor. From 1826 he had a post with a family in Kensington, and attended the Regent Square Presbyterian Church, where Edward Irving, the minister, was then at the height of his preaching fame. Cumming was called one Sunday to preach to the small congregation of a sister church, Crown Court at Covent Garden. Here he so impressed his hearers that in August 1832 they invited him to become their pastor. He was duly ordained and inducted to the church to which he devoted all his working years. His attachment to it was further confirmed in 1833, when he married Elizabeth, the daughter of James Nicholson, one of the elders of Crown Court. They had seven sons and four daughters.

During his ministry Cumming transformed Crown Court. The church was redecorated in 1834, extended in 1841, and finally rebuilt in 1847, at a cost of £1500. He established Sunday schools and ragged schools for local children, which were reputedly attended by over 16,000 children. For the initial conversion of a neighbouring stable into a school, opened in 1836, he raised £146. He also established an elders' prayer meeting, and set up a library for children.

Cumming continued to place much faith in established churches, and participated in a movement among the Scottish churches in England to form an English presbyterian synod of the Church of Scotland. The general assembly rejected their motion, and advised them to form an autonomous synod, which they did between 1836 and 1842. Cumming, however, retained his attachment to his native established church, and during the Disruption controversy was consistently opposed to the formation of the Free Church. In 1837 he published *An Apology for the Church of Scotland*, which won the approval of the archbishop of Canterbury and the bishop of London, and he met the events of 1843 with a plethora of pamphlets. In 1865 he attended the general assembly in Scotland in order to plead for inclusion in the Church of Scotland, but he was once again unsuccessful; this amalgamation did not take place until 1934.

John Cumming (1807–1881), by Mason & Co., *c*.1860

Cumming's enthusiasm for established forms of worship led him to reform the liturgy of his own church. He regarded most contemporary Scottish services as uninspiring, and undertook the republication of 'Knox's liturgy', the Book of Common Order, of 1561. He appointed a singing clerk and prepared a collection of hymns for the use of his congregation. His theology, too, lacked the strict Calvinism of some of his fellow Presbyterians: he was much influenced by John McLeod Campbell's interpretation of the atonement, and held a profound sacramental belief.

Cumming was, however, a keen opponent of both Tractarians and Roman Catholics, as his *Lectures for the Times, or, An Exposition of Tridentine and Tractarian Popery* (1844) showed. In 1838 he engaged in a public debate on doctrine with the Roman Catholic lawyer, Daniel French; both sides claimed the victory, and the published report of the event went through several editions. To mark it Cumming was presented with a polyglot Bible by admirers from Hammersmith. He was also active during the Maynooth controversy of 1845: he lectured for the Protestant Reformation Society, of which he was a prominent supporter. He appeared at meetings to protest at the 'papal aggression' of 1850, and pursued a correspondence with Cardinal Wiseman on the subject of the 'persecuting clause' of the archiepiscopal oath. In 1868 he requested permission to attend the ecumenical council summoned by Pius IX, which was inevitably denied.

Preaching, however, was the central feature of Cumming's ministry. His performances in the pulpit soon started to attract a large congregation—on average, about 500 people—to his church, and he was popularly viewed as the inheritor of Irving's mantle. In 1847, while Crown Court was being rebuilt, the church moved to Exeter Hall. Here his services were attended by up to 4000 people, and the police had to be employed to control the crowds as they left the hall. His appearance in the pulpit was imposing: a contemporary commented that his figure was 'tall and well-formed', with a high forehead swept by 'a flow of dark hair'; 'the whole head is a type of intelligence, from which shine a pair of dark, flashing eyes' (*Penny Pulpit*, 2, 1858). His congregation included many figures from the peerage and social élite, who no doubt appreciated his attachment to the established churches of England and Scotland. In 1862 George Granville Sutherland-Leveson-Gower, second duke of Sutherland, and his wife invited Cumming to their Scottish residence to preach, and in 1866 he gave a sermon at Dornoch Cathedral in the presence of the prince and princess of Wales.

While the Sutherlands patronized him, and Lord Frederick Hamilton described his preaching admiringly as 'one long chain of reasoned argument' (quoted in Cameron), Cumming found much less favour in intellectual circles. Tennyson, whose mother held Cumming's books as her favourite reading, thought him a mountebank, and satirized him in the poem 'Sea Dreams'. Thackeray believed him to be 'a bigot, a blasphemer ... the world would be horrible if he and his could have his way' (Ray, 3.439). But the most remarkable critique of Cumming and his works came from George Eliot, who published a withering article in the *Westminster Review* of October 1855. In it she condemned the 'bigoted narrowness', 'unscrupulosity of statement', and 'lack of charity' towards his religious opponents which Cumming exhibited in his literary works. She wisely avoided attributing these characteristics to him in his private life, as his endeavours among the poor of his parish were extensive.

Cumming rested from his labours during brief holidays and weekly trips to a cottage near Tunbridge Wells, where he occupied himself with bee keeping. Lord Frederick Hamilton recalled Cumming visiting his mother, the duchess, rather imprudently carrying in his pockets the bees which he intended to exhibit to her. Letters which he had published in *The Times* under the pen name Beemaster were the basis of his *Bee-Keeping* (1864).

Both Cumming's preaching and his written works became increasingly dominated by his prophetic interpretations. Much impressed by what he saw as human progress, both mechanical and moral, and deeply interested by geological and scientific discoveries, which he interpreted in the apologetic vein of P. H. Gosse, Cumming turned to study of the books of Genesis and Daniel. The result of his research was the prediction that the second coming would take place in 1867. This theory was expounded in works such as *Signs of the Times, or, Present, Past and Future* (1854) and *The Great Tribulation, or, Things Coming on the Earth* (1859), the latter of which was satirized in *Punch*. The passing of 1867 was attended by no greater tribulation than the Reform Act, and this, combined with the alleged discovery that within two months of his predicted date for the end of the world Cumming was negotiating an extension of the lease on his house for a further twenty-one years, lowered the preacher's reputation considerably. Undeterred, Cumming continued to pursue the prophetic vein in later publications, including *The Seventh Vial, or, The Time of Trouble Begun* (1870).

By now Cumming's ministry and church were experiencing a considerable decline. His congregation shrank to an average attendance of fifty, and from 1876 Cumming himself suffered some ill health. He was much affected by his wife's death in September 1879, and in the July of that year he resigned. On retirement he received an annuity of £500. He died on 5 July 1881 at the Manor House, Chiswick, and was buried at Kensal Green cemetery. He was noted for his preaching and prophetic fervour by both admirers and critics, and though typical in many ways of the evangelical clergyman of his generation, he was exceptional in the breadth of his involvement in contemporary religious activities and enthusiasms.   ROSEMARY MITCHELL

Sources R. B. Knox, 'Dr John Cumming and the Crown Court Church, London', *Records of the Scottish Church History Society*, 22 (1984–6), 57–84 • G. G. Cameron, *The Scots kirk in London* (1979), 131–46 • *Fasti Scot.*, 7.468–9 • *In memoriam: the Rev. John Cumming* (privately printed, London, [n.d., 1881?]) • G. Eliot, 'Evangelical teaching: Dr Cumming', *Westminster Review*, 64 (1855), 436–62 • *The letters and private papers of William Makepeace Thackeray*, ed. G. N. Ray, 3 (1946), 439

Archives Edinburgh PRO, Hope Letters

Likenesses Mason & Co., photograph, c.1860, NPG [*see illus.*] • J. & C. Watkins, carte-de-visite, c.1860, NPG • W. & D. Downey, two cartes-de-visite, NPG • Elliott & Fry, carte-de-visite, NPG • D. J. Pound, stipple and line engraving (after photograph by J. Eastham), NPG • J. Thomson, stipple (after W. Booth), BM • caricature, chromolithograph, NPG; repro. in *VF* (13 April 1872) • portrait, BL; repro. in *Penny Pulpit*, 2 (1858) • prints, BM

Wealth at death £9770 12s. 3d.: resworn probate, Feb 1882, *CGPLA Eng. & Wales*

Cumming, Joseph George (1812–1868), geologist and Church of England clergyman, was born on 15 February 1812 at Matlock, Derbyshire, the son of Joseph Notsall Cumming of Matlock. He was educated at Oakham grammar school, where he was remarkable for his grave earnestness, scarcely ever indulging in games. He was, however, fond of wrestling, and was a great walker, especially visiting Derbyshire and collecting fossil remains. He gained exhibitions at Oakham and in 1830 proceeded to Emmanuel College, Cambridge, where he was senior optime in 1834, graduating BA in 1834 and MA in 1838. He was ordained in 1835 to the curacy of his uncle, James *Cumming, professor of chemistry at Cambridge, and rector of North Runcton, Norfolk. In 1838 he was appointed classical master of the West Riding proprietary school, and in 1841 he became vice-principal of King William's College in the Isle of Man. Cumming remained in the Isle of Man for fifteen years, and studied the geology and antiquarian remains of the district with great care. In 1848 he published *The Isle of Man: its History, Physical, Ecclesiastical, Civil, and Legendary*. In this volume he dealt largely with the mythical tales, succinctly recording the history of the island and carefully examining all the interesting geological phenomena. The lithological character of the island and the disturbances which have produced the subsidence of some geological formations, and the emergence of others, are carefully and accurately described. It remains a work of value.

Cumming was appointed in 1856 to the mastership of King Edward's Grammar School, Lichfield. In 1858 he became warden and professor of classical literature and geology in Queen's College, Birmingham. In 1862 he was presented by the lord chancellor to the rectory of Mellis, Suffolk, which he exchanged in 1867 for the vicarage of St John's, Bethnal Green.

Cumming married in 1838 Agnes Cooper Peckham, with whom he had a family of four sons and two daughters, who, with his wife, survived him. He became a fellow of the Geological Society of London in 1846, and published some papers in the journal of that society. He also published *A Chronology of Ancient, Sacred and Profane History* (1853) and *The Great Stanley, or, James, VIIth Earl of Derby* (1867). He died quite suddenly on 21 September 1868 at St John's vicarage, Bethnal Green, London.

ROBERT HUNT, *rev.* H. C. G. MATTHEW

Sources J. G. Cumming, 'On the tertiary deposits of the Moray Firth and the great Caledonian Valley', *Quarterly Journal of the Geological Society*, 6 (1850), 10–17 · Venn, *Alum. Cant.* · *New Philosophical Magazine* (1869) · Crockford (1868) · *CGPLA Eng. & Wales* (1869) · H. B. Woodward, *The history of the Geological Society of London* (1907)
Archives Bodl. Oxf., rubbings of runic and other remains on the Isle of Man
Wealth at death under £200: administration, 9 Jan 1869, *CGPLA Eng. & Wales*

Cumming, Sir Mansfield George Smith (1859–1923), intelligence officer, was born Mansfield George Smith on 1 April 1859 in India, the youngest in the family of five sons and eight daughters of Colonel John Thomas Smith (1805–1882) of the Royal Engineers, of Föellalt House, Kent, and his wife, Maria Sarah Tyser. After entering the Royal Naval College, Dartmouth, at the age of thirteen, he began his career afloat as acting sub-lieutenant on HMS *Bellerophon*. He served in operations against Malay pirates during 1875–6 and in Egypt in 1883. He suffered, however, from severe seasickness and in 1885 he was placed on the retired list.

Cumming (he changed his name in 1889 after marriage) spent the early 1890s largely as a country gentleman on his second wife's Moray estate. In 1898, while still on the Royal Navy retired list, he was posted to Nelson's old flagship *Victory* 'for special service at Southampton'. The 'special service' included occasional intelligence work abroad, but his main work for the next decade was the construction and command of the Southampton boom defences.

In 1909 Cumming was appointed head of what became

Sir Mansfield George Smith Cumming (1859–1923), by unknown photographer

the foreign section of the secret service bureau (the forerunner of the Secret Intelligence Service, better known as SIS or MI6). He described pre-1914 espionage as 'capital sport', but was given few resources with which to pursue it. His early operations were directed almost entirely against Germany. Between 1909 and 1914 he recruited part-time 'casual agents' in the shipping and arms business to keep track of naval construction in German shipyards and acquire other technical intelligence. He also had agents collecting German intelligence in Brussels, Rotterdam, and St Petersburg.

With the outbreak of the First World War, Cumming's control of strategic intelligence gathering as head of the wartime MI1c was challenged by two rival networks run by general headquarters. Cumming eventually outperformed his rivals. His most important wartime network, 'La Dame Blanche', had by January 1918 over 400 agents reporting on German troop movements from occupied Belgium and northern France. Cumming was less successful in post-revolutionary Russia. Despite a series of colourful exploits, his agents obtained little Russian intelligence of value.

Like the rest of the British intelligence community, the post-war SIS was drastically cut back. Cumming succeeded, however, in gaining a monopoly of espionage and counter-intelligence outside Britain and the empire. He also established a network of SIS station commanders operating overseas under diplomatic cover. To the end of his life Cumming retained an infectious, if sometimes eccentric, enthusiasm for the tradecraft and mystification of espionage, experimenting personally with disguises, mechanical gadgets, and secret inks in his own laboratory. His practice of writing exclusively in a distinctive green ink was continued by his successors. He was appointed CB in 1914 and KCMG in 1919.

Cumming had a fascination with most forms of transport, driving his Rolls at high speed around the streets of London. In his early fifties he took up flying, gaining both French aviators' and Royal Aero Club certificates. But his main passion was boating in Southampton Water and other waters calmer than those which had ended his active service career. In addition to owning 'any number' of yachts, Cumming acquired six motor boats. In 1905 he became one of the founders and first rear-commodore of the Royal Motor Yacht Club.

In 1885 Cumming married Dora, daughter of Henry Cloete of Great Constantia, Cape Colony. After her death he married, on 13 March 1889, a Scottish heiress, Leslie Marian (May), daughter of Captain Lockhart Muir Valiant (afterwards Cumming), of the 1st Bombay lancers and Logie, Moray. As part of the marriage settlement he changed his surname to Smith-Cumming, later becoming known as Cumming. Their only son, Alastair, a dangerous driver like his father, was killed in October 1914, driving Cumming's Rolls in France. Cumming himself lost the lower part of his right leg in the same accident. He died suddenly at his home, 1 Melbury Road, Kensington, London, on 14 June 1923, shortly before he was due to retire.

CHRISTOPHER ANDREW, rev.

Sources C. Andrew, *Secret service: the making of the British intelligence community* (1985) · N. Hiley, 'The failure of British espionage against Germany, 1907–1914', *HJ*, 26 (1983), 867–89 · private information (1993) · *CGPLA Eng. & Wales* (1924) · m. cert. [L. M. V. Cumming] · d. cert.
Likenesses photograph, IWM [*see illus.*]
Wealth at death £39,276 19s. 0d.: probate, 4 March 1924, *CGPLA Eng. & Wales*

Cumming, Roualeyn George Gordon- (1820–1866), lion hunter, the second son of Sir William Gordon Gordon-Cumming, second baronet (1787–1854), and his first wife, Eliza Maria (d. 1842), the daughter of John Campbell and a granddaughter of the duke of Argyll, was born at Altyre, Scotland, on 15 March 1820. The travel writer Constance Gordon-*Cumming was his sister. He was educated at Eton College, but even in his boyhood was distinguished more for his love of sport, especially salmon fishing and deerstalking, than for anything else. He entered the East India Company's service as a cornet in the 4th Madras cavalry in 1838, and on his way to India had his first experience of hunting in South Africa; but the Indian climate did not agree with him, and in 1840 he resigned his commission.

Gordon-Cumming returned to Scotland and devoted himself to deerstalking; but in his own words he found 'the life of the wild hunter so far preferable to that of the mere sportsman' that he obtained an ensigncy in the royal veteran Newfoundland companies. Not finding the opportunities for hunting in North America which he expected, he exchanged in 1843 into the Cape mounted rifles, and once more found himself in Africa. Unsuited to military life, he resigned his commission at the end of the year, and after purchasing a wagon and collecting a few followers he spent the next five years hunting, travelling widely, and exploring the interior of South Africa. In 1848 he returned to Britain, and in 1850 he published his *Five Years of a Hunter's Life in the Far Interior of South Africa*, a book which had immense success and was published in many editions; it made him the lion of the season. In 1851 Gordon-Cumming exhibited his trophies at the Great Exhibition. He then went about the country lecturing and exhibiting his lion skins for some years, and under the sobriquet the Lion Hunter he obtained great popularity and made a good deal of money. In 1856 he published a condensed edition of his book as *The Lion Hunter of South Africa*, and in 1858 he established himself at Fort Augustus on the Caledonian Canal, where his museum was a great attraction to all tourists. He was a man of great height and physical strength. He seems to have had a premonition of death, for he ordered his coffin and made his will just before he died, unmarried, from heart disease, at Fort Augustus on 24 March 1866; provision was made in his will for two illegitimate daughters.

H. M. STEPHENS, rev. LYNN MILNE

Sources R. Gordon-Cumming, *Five years of a hunter's life in the far interior of South Africa*, 2 vols. (1850) · F. C. Metrowich, 'Cumming, Roualeyn George Gordon', *DSAB* · *GM*, 4th ser., 1 (1866), 758–9 · d. cert. · private information (1888)
Likenesses H. Watkins, albumen print, 1855–9, NPG · S. G. Hodgson, coloured lithograph, Africana Museum, Johannesburg, South Africa · C. Norton, watercolour · portrait, repro. in *ILN* (12 June 1852) · portrait, album of South Library, Cape Town, South Africa
Wealth at death £237 6s. 4d.: confirmation, 1866, Scotland · £1427 12s. 6d.: additional inventory, 1866, Scotland

Cumming, Thomas [*nicknamed* the Fighting Quaker] (d. 1774), merchant, is of unknown birth and parentage. He was a private merchant engaged in the African trade. During a business voyage he made the acquaintance of King Amir of Legibelli (South Barbary), whom he found well disposed to British enterprise, and who, being exasperated with the French, had actually begun a war against them. The king requested the British to protect his trade, and on condition of receiving the sole trading rights Cumming agreed to exert his influence with the British government. After ascertaining the strength of the French positions on the coast he returned to England and, having formed a plan for an expedition, presented it to the Board of Trade, by whom it was approved after a critical examination. Many obstacles were placed in his way by the government but at length the ministry granted a military and naval force, as part of the assault on Senegal and Goree, which set sail in March 1757.

Ostensibly under the command of military officers the force was effectively led by Cumming; his local knowledge enabled him to guide it in such a manner that it proved entirely successful. Cumming had hoped, as he explained to the Society of Friends, that bloodshed might be avoided, and avowed that otherwise he would not have urged it. This hope, however, was fruitless, and he then took the entire blame on himself. There is no reason, however, to suppose that Cumming was disowned by the Friends. He died on 29 May 1774 at Tottenham.

A. C. BICKLEY, rev. PHILIP CARTER

Sources *The history of England … by Hume and Smollett: with the continuation from the accession of George III to the accession of Queen Victoria*, ed. T. S. Hughes, new edn, 18 vols. (1854–5), vol. 10, pp. 96–8 · *GM*, 1st ser., 44 (1774), 287

Cumming, William. *See* Cuming, William (1769–1852).

Cumming, William (1821/2–1855), ophthalmologist, was a son of William Spink Cumming, surgeon, and his wife, Ann, *née* Stewart. Nothing is known of his education or medical training, except that he qualified as a member of the Royal College of Surgeons and as a licentiate of the Society of Apothecaries.

Cumming lived in London and by 1846 was in practice with his father and brother at Limehouse; he was also a surgeon at the Royal Ophthalmic Hospital, Moorfields. In June 1846 he sent a paper, 'On a luminous appearance of the human eye', to the Medico-Chirurgical Society of London, detailing his discovery of a way to illuminate the interior of the eye, though he never obtained a view of the tissue and vessels of the retina. A similar technique had been described by J. E. Purkinje at Breslau in 1823, but Cumming was not aware of this work. The ophthalmoscope, which enabled the back of the eye to be examined, was developed from a polarizing apparatus described by Hermann von Helmholtz in 1851.

Cumming was a singularly modest and retiring man, a thoughtful and accurate observer; and had his life been prolonged he would no doubt have further developed his important discovery. By the end of 1854 he was suffering from kidney disease, and after six months he died at 2 Vittoria Place, Limehouse, on 5 June 1855.

JAMES DIXON, *rev.* ANITA McCONNELL

Sources E. T. Collins, *The history and traditions of the Moorfields Eye Hospital: one hundred years of ophthalmic discovery and development* (1929) · D. M. Albert and D. D. Edwards, eds., *The history of ophthalmology* (1996) · personal knowledge (1888) · *Boase, Mod. Eng. biog.* · PRO, PROB 11/2226, sig. 92 · *Association Medical Journal*, 3 (1855), 574 · d. cert. · *The Post Office London directory* [annuals]

Wealth at death under £300: will, PRO, PROB 11/2226, sig. 92

Cummings, Arthur John (1882–1957), journalist and author, was born at Barnstaple, Devon, on 22 May 1882, the third child and eldest of the three sons of John Cummings, journalist, north Devon representative of the *Devon and Exeter Gazette*, and his wife, Maria Elizabeth Richards. Bruce *Cummings was his youngest brother. He attended Rock Park School, Barnstaple, excelling at his studies. A key influence at the school in the development both of his ethical views and of his appreciation of literature was Philip Ernest Richards, then an Oxford undergraduate, later a Unitarian minister before becoming a professor of English in Lahore.

Cummings hoped to study law at Oxford, but had to abandon this ambition when his father became seriously ill. He joined the *Devon and Exeter Gazette*, quickly being given responsibility for writing pieces on a wide sweep of subjects, from musical notices to leading articles and even stock market reports. From Devon he moved successively to the *Rochdale Observer*, the *Sheffield Telegraph*, and, just before the outbreak of the First World War in 1914, the *Yorkshire Post*. He served with the Territorial 4th West Riding (howitzer) brigade, Royal Fleet Auxiliary, seeing action on the western front and being promoted captain. In 1908 he married Lilian, daughter of John Boreham, of Sheffield.

Arthur John Cummings (1882–1957), by Elliott & Fry

She died seven months later of peritonitis. In 1915 he married an artist, Nora, daughter of Arthur Suddards, bank inspector, of Leeds. They had a son, Michael *Cummings (1919–1997), a political cartoonist, and a daughter, Jean, a journalist.

After the war Cummings became an assistant editor on the *Yorkshire Post*. But the paper was generally Conservative in alignment, and politics had become increasingly important to Cummings, as he had developed into, and remained, 'an ardent Liberal' of the distinctly older, nonconformist, style. He eagerly accepted an invitation in 1920 to become an assistant editor of the *Daily News* (later the *News Chronicle*) and remained with that paper for thirty-five years. He became deputy editor and then political editor. He reported on the economic conference at Ottawa in 1932 and was scathing of the government for the agreements reached there. In 1933 he wrote brilliantly on both the Reichstag fire trial and the trial of British engineers in Moscow, with each report showing his deep hatred of totalitarianism and injustice. For his foreign correspondence of that year he was given a Selfridge award.

Of Cummings between the wars it has been said that he was 'the unsparing critic of Conservative governments … No other journalist did as much … to keep the spirit of Liberalism alive in the country during this unhappy period' (Cruikshank). By the late thirties he was perhaps the political commentator with the largest readership in Britain, through his twice-weekly 'Spotlight on politics'. Although remaining a committed Liberal, Cummings 'fraternized' with Labour—something for which he was occasionally criticized—particularly in order to develop a broad left opposition to appeasement with Hitler. In mid-1939 he advocated a Liberal constituency agreement with Labour to 'avoid splitting the anti-appeasement vote' (Koss, 591).

Politics and ethics were the key to Cummings's life. As the 'Liberal conscience of Fleet Street' (Abel), he also earned his description as 'a cheerful Puritan'. Robin Cruikshank said that he could 'well imagine him in Oliver Cromwell's army', fighting as a 'Radical patriot' (Cruikshank). The Institute of Journalists elected him president for 1952–3. In his presidential address he declared his support for the recently established Press Council to monitor standards and ethics in the press. But he also condemned the threat from an over-indulgent use of parliamentary privilege to raise 'pompous or frivolous claims', as a way of reducing 'necessary or legitimate criticism' (*The Times*, 6 July 1957, 10).

Cummings's books included *The Moscow Trial* (1933), *The Press and a Changing Civilisation* (1936), and *This England* (1945). He retired from the *News Chronicle* in 1955, and died at 6 Heather Gardens, Golders Green, Middlesex, on 4 July 1957. He was buried six days later. His wife survived him.

LINTON ANDREWS, *rev.* MARC BRODIE

Sources *The Times* (6 July 1957) · *The Times* (8 July 1957) · *News Chronicle* (6 July 1957) · personal knowledge (1971) · private information (1971) · L. Andrews, *The Times* (15 July 1957), 14 · *Journal of the Institute of Journalists*, 45 (1957), 69 · R. Cruikshank, 'The new president', *Journal of the Institute of Journalists*, 40 (1952), 128 · D. Abel, *The Times* (12 July 1957), 13 · S. E. Koss, *The rise and fall of the political press in Britain*, 2 (1984) · WWW

Archives BLPES, corresp. with Sir Gerald Barry · HLRO, corresp. with Lord Beaverbrook · HLRO, letters to David Lloyd George · King's Lond., Liddell Hart C., corresp. with Sir B. H. Liddell Hart | FILM BFI NFTVA, news footage

Likenesses Elliott & Fry, photograph, NPG [*see illus.*] · photograph, repro. in *Journal of the Institute of Journalists*, 69

Wealth at death £3082 4s. 0d.: probate, 8 Nov 1957, CGPLA Eng. & Wales

Cummings, Bruce Frederick [*pseud.* W. N. P. Barbellion] (1889–1919), zoologist and diarist, was born at Barnstaple, Devon, on 7 September 1889, the youngest of the six children of John Cummings, a journalist, and his wife, Maria Elizabeth Richards. He was educated at a private school in Barnstaple and after leaving school at the age of sixteen was apprenticed until 1910 as a journalist on the *Devon and Exeter Gazette*. Well before leaving school Cummings had developed a strong interest in natural history, especially ornithology. He rejected the prospect of a career in local journalism and aimed to gain a position in natural history at the end of his apprenticeship. In pursuit of this ambition he undertook a strenuous programme of self-education; his diary entry for 10 March 1908 includes, in addition to shorthand and typewriting, 'German, chemistry classes, electricity lectures, zoology (including dissections), and field work' (Barbellion, *Journal*, 13).

Cummings published specialized papers in natural history from as early as 1906. In 1912 he took up an appointment at the Natural History Museum in South Kensington as one of the five new permanent staff appointed to the insect room, soon to be renamed the department of entomology. These positions carried considerable research and curatorial responsibility; his appointment was a remarkable achievement for one who had no formal training in the subject.

The first decade of the twentieth century saw a rapid expansion in the entomological collections of the British Museum (Natural History), as it was formally known, and each of the assistants was assigned particular orders for which he was sole curator and researcher: Cummings was in charge of the Neuroptera, Isoptera, Mallophaga, and Auroplura. The atmosphere in the entomology department in those years was one of mutual isolation, darkened rooms, and stiff formality. According to one of his colleagues, the despair characteristic of Cummings's most famous literary work was the product of this environment (Riley, 2). He was not especially active in the day-to-day responsibilities of his post, and the collections for which he was responsible were still in considerable disorder after his departure. However, one part of the corner of entomology for which he was professionally responsible saw much activity during his tenure, as conditions in the trenches during the First World War led to official demands for information on the behaviour of lice. His diary in these years shows him grappling with the emotional challenge posed by these creatures, expressions of disgust being combined with satisfied remarks on the privilege of scientific detachment.

Cummings's period of employment at the museum coincided with his gradually deteriorating health. He suffered from a degenerative disease of the central nervous system described as 'disseminated sclerosis', but this diagnosis was kept from him for a long time. He married Winifred Eleanor Benger, a fashion designer, on 15 September 1915, and they had a daughter in the following year. In July 1917 Cummings resigned from the museum. Bedridden and in considerable distress he occupied himself with preparing extracts from his voluminous diaries for publication. These were published in the spring of 1919 as *The Journal of a Disappointed Man* under the pseudonym W. N. P. Barbellion. The book was introduced by H. G. Wells, whom some reviewers took to be the author. Wells also organized a trust fund for the maintenance of Cummings and his family.

Sometimes described as a minor classic, *The Journal of a Disappointed Man* was reissued in 1984. Made up of reflective vignettes from the daily life of its author, its interest lies not least in his descriptions of the effects of physical pain and disability, where he combines the precision of a natural historian with the passionate subjectivity of the sufferer. This was not Cummings's first foray into general writing, as he had earlier published a number of essays bearing on the relations between natural history and general culture. Following the success of *The Journal of a Disappointed Man* some of these were republished under his pseudonym with the title *Enjoying Life and other Literary Remains* (1919). The most notable essay is a critique of the ethic of collecting and conservation which first appeared as 'The art of perpetuation' in *Science Progress* (1917) under the name Bruce Cummings.

Cummings died shortly after his thirtieth birthday, on

22 October 1919, at his home, Camden Cottage, Gerrards Cross. *A Last Diary*, whose entries cover the period from 21 March 1918 to 3 June 1919, was published posthumously in 1920. However in contrast to *The Journal of a Disappointed Man*, this diary was written for publication and its quality is unremarkable.   JOSEPH GROSS

Sources W. N. P. Barbellion [B. F. Cummings], *The journal of a disappointed man* (1919) · *A last diary, by W. N. P. Barbellion*, ed. A. F. Cummings (1920) · N. D. Riley, *The department of entomology of the British Museum (Natural History), 1904–1964: a brief historical sketch* (1964) · P. Dombey, 'Books in general', *New Statesman and Nation* (21 July 1945), 43–4 · W. T. Stearn, *The Natural History Museum at South Kensington: a history of the British Museum (Natural History), 1753–1980* (1981) · CGPLA Eng. & Wales (1920) · d. cert.
Wealth at death £132 5s. 5d.: administration with will, 24 July 1920, CGPLA Eng. & Wales

Cummings, (Arthur Stuart) Michael (1919–1997), cartoonist, was born on 1 June 1919 at 99 Spencer Place, Leeds, the only son of Arthur John *Cummings (1882–1957), political editor of the *News Chronicle*, and his wife, Nora Suddards, an artist. Following education at The Hall, Hampstead, London, and Gresham's School, Holt, Norfolk, he studied at Chelsea School of Art, London, where he was taught by Graham Sutherland and specialized in etching. It was there that in 1939 he drew his first cartoon for the left-wing journal *The Tribune*, edited by the future Labour leader Michael Foot. Cummings's studies were then interrupted by the Second World War. He was called up for service in the Royal Air Force and posted to the Air Ministry, where he put his artistic ability to good use as a draughtsman, drawing aeroplane parts for the duration. On discharge he resumed his arts studies at Chelsea and also his contributions to *The Tribune*, with Foot giving him regular work as an illustrator for the book-review page.

In 1948 Cummings had just secured a post as art teacher at St Albans Grammar School for Girls, Hertfordshire, when his father suggested he apply for a cartooning position on the *Daily Express*, where he had learned that the regular cartoonist, Giles, was seeking relief from his demanding schedule. The proprietor, Lord Beaverbrook, a lover of cartoons, could see Cummings's potential, and he was taken on for a trial period by the paper's editor, Arthur Christiansen, who appointed him to alternate with Giles and as political cartoonist in place of the popular Strube, whom Christiansen had sacked the previous year after a disagreement. This could have served as an omen for Cummings, who was himself dismissed at the end of his three months' probation after finding it difficult to maintain a consistent level of originality. But Beaverbrook intervened and Cummings was reinstated.

Apart from his responsibility as political cartoonist, the arrangement was that Cummings and Giles should share the regular production of editorial cartoons. They drew three cartoons a week each, with Cummings producing an additional one for the *Sunday Express* from 1958. He also worked for *Punch*, originally signing himself A. S. M. Cummings but later simply Cummings; he took over its 'Essence of parliament' illustrations from A. W. Lloyd in 1953. That same year, while working in France, he met his future wife, Anne-Marie Monique Pittier, *née* Lethel (b.

1928/9), the daughter of Michel Henri Lethel, director of the French Red Cross. They were married at Kensington register office, London, on 23 March 1956, and made their home at 8 Falkland House, Marloes Road, west London.

Cummings had at first adopted a delicate style in his work for *The Tribune*, but on the *Express* progressed to a bolder technique, with an abundance of solid black areas. He roughed out his cartoons in pencil on A3 paper, producing usually six drawings from which the editor chose one, and used a dip pen and brush with Pelikan black ink on Daler board for the finished work. Like Stanley McMurtry ('Mac'), he often concealed an image of his wife in his cartoons.

Cummings spared no one in his choice of political subjects, and though his Conservatism and patriotism led him to treat Winston Churchill and Margaret Thatcher with respect, others were less fortunate and were portrayed in a style that sometimes descended into crude caricature. Cummings was Churchill's favourite cartoonist, and claimed to be the only political cartoonist to have drawn every British prime minister from Churchill to Tony Blair. A distinctive feature of his drawings were the explanatory labels that he added, with hand-drawn speech and thought bubbles in the manner of Gillray and other eighteenth-century caricaturists. Some of his depictions were controversial. A 1960s cartoon showing a cargoload of golliwogs arriving in Britain caused complaints, and print unions prevented publication of the Scottish edition of the *Express* containing a drawing of President Brezhnev dressed as a Roman Catholic priest with a consignment of tanks marked 'IRA'.

A long-standing member of the Garrick Club, Cummings was a founder member of the British Cartoonists' Association in 1966. He was appointed OBE in 1983. He died of cancer at the Chelsea and Westminster Hospital, London, on 9 October 1997. He was survived by his wife Anne-Marie, and a stepson, Jean-Marc.

ADRIAN ROOM

Sources *The Guardian* (11 Oct 1997) · *The Independent* (11 Oct 1997) · *The Times* (11 Oct 1997) · *The Express* (10 Oct 1997) · M. Bryant, *Dictionary of twentieth-century British cartoonists and caricaturists* (2000) · b. cert. · m. cert. · d. cert.
Archives Beaverbrook Foundation, London · University of Kent, Canterbury, Centre for the Study of Cartoons and Caricature
Wealth at death £696,561: probate, 20 Jan 1998, CGPLA Eng. & Wales

Cummings, William Hayman (1831–1915), singer and musical antiquary, was born on 22 August 1831 at Sidbury, Devon, the son of Edward Manly Cummings and his wife, Julia. The family moved to London and he became a chorister at St Paul's Cathedral. Because William Hawes conducted practices with the help of a riding crop, Cummings's father was compelled to petition the court of chancery in 1842 for the boy's release from such harsh discipline. Cummings then joined the Temple Church choir and secured from E. J. Hopkins, the organist and choirmaster, an excellent musical grounding, including organ lessons. Hopkins later encouraged him to apply, successfully, for the position of organist of Waltham Abbey. Here it was that in 1855 Cummings made his most enduring mark. His generation venerated Mendelssohn; certainly Cummings's own choral compositions owe him much. In any event, he was sufficiently familiar with Mendelssohn's *Festgesang*, an occasional cantata in celebration of the 1840 Gutenberg festival, to unite the music of its second number with Charles Wesley's hymn 'Hark! the herald angels sing'. Cummings left Waltham Abbey to take up a long and distinguished career as a lyric tenor 'of singular sweetness and purity', particularly in the field of oratorio. His only instructor was J. W. Hobbs, a lay clerk at Westminster Abbey, whose daughter Clara he later married. For his 'wonted skill and good taste' and reliable musicianship he was much sought after for London concerts and provincial festivals. At Norwich in 1866, for example, he had to sing everything, some pieces at a moment's notice, when Sims Reeves, the other principal tenor, fell ill. From November 1871, Cummings made the first of two tours of the United States with a small vocal ensemble supporting the baritone Charles Santley.

In London, Cummings taught singing at the Royal Normal School and the School for the Blind. He was appointed a professor at the Royal Academy of Music in 1879, but resigned in 1896 to become principal of a sister institution, the Guildhall School of Music. In the fourteen years before his retirement, he modernized the curriculum. Cummings enjoyed scholarly pursuits. From the age of nineteen he visited auction rooms and successfully bid for important manuscripts and rarities as diverse as autograph scores of Purcell and Beethoven and one of Handel's lace ruffles. His superb library of some 4500 pieces, the last of the great Victorian collections, was undoubtedly the catalyst for Cummings's editions for the Purcell Society (1878, 1889, and 1891) and his monographs on the national anthem (1902), John Blow (1909), and Thomas Arne (1912), which remained useful sources for more than a century. Upon his death the library was sold at auction and, unfortunately, dispersed as far afield as America and Japan. Thus was sadly fulfilled the prophecy that Cummings himself had made in a paper about national collections (1871) to the (Royal) Musical Association, a body of which he was a founding member. Although contemporaries noted in him a certain inflexibility towards others' opinions, his integrity of purpose and devotion to English music was never in question. For such efforts he was made a fellow of the Society of Antiquaries (1884), Doctor of Music (h.c.) of Trinity College, Dublin (1900), and honorary treasurer of the Royal Society of Musicians. Cummings died at his home, Sydcote, Rosendale Road, Dulwich, London, on 6 June 1915; the funeral service took place on 10 June in the church of St John the Evangelist, Dulwich, and he was interred at Norwood cemetery.

HUGH J. McLEAN

Sources MT, 39 (1898), 81–5 · MT, 56 (1915), 394–6 · 'The death of the president', *Proceedings of the Musical Association*, 41 (1914–15), 141–3 · *Catalogue of the famous musical library … of the late W. H. Cummings* (1917) [sale catalogue, Sotheby, Wilkinson & Hodge, London, 17 May 1917] · A. H. King, *Some British collectors of music, c.1600–1960* (1963) · H. J. McLean, 'Blow and Purcell in Japan', MT, 104 (1963), 702–5 · 'Cummings, William Hayman', *New Grove*

Archives NL Scot., corresp. · Ohki collection, Tokyo
Likenesses photograph, repro. in MT (Feb 1898)
Wealth at death £3680 8s. 3d.: probate, 15 July 1915, CGPLA Eng. & Wales

Cummings, William Jeffrey [*formerly* William Jeffery] (1858–1919), runner, was born William Jeffery at Paisley, Renfrewshire, on 10 June 1858, the son of John Jeffery, shoemaker, and his wife, Janet Cummings. His claim to fame comes mainly as a result of a series of races against Walter George which involved both men in controversy over the relative merits of amateur and professional sport. He adopted his mother's maiden name of Cummings as his professional name because 'his parents objected to his appearing on the track' (*Paisley and Renfrewshire Gazette*, 3 Oct 1885).

Cummings came into prominence as a runner when a youth, winning a professional mile race in Glasgow in December 1872. He was then only fourteen. His first major triumph was in 1878 when invited to take part in a mile race at the Lilliebridge grounds, West Brompton, London. He won in a time of 4 minutes 28 seconds, becoming champion of England over the distance. Later in the same year he recorded one of the fastest mile times of the period—4 minutes 18.25 seconds.

Cummings's claim to be the premier distance runner in Britain was soon challenged by George, the leading amateur of the time. To enable him to meet Cummings in a series of races, George was forced to give up his amateur status. This came after a four-year battle with the sport's authorities. The contest between Cummings and George took place over the late summer and early autumn of 1885 and attracted enormous interest. A mile race, at Lilliebridge in front of some 25,000 to 30,000 spectators on 31 August, was won easily by George. Such were the crowds for this event that the gates had to be closed two hours in advance. The second challenge, over 4 miles at Powderhall near Edinburgh on 9 September, ended in victory for Cummings with George actually giving up before the end. The final race, over 10 miles at Lilliebridge a fortnight later, saw Cummings victorious by a clear lap in a record time of 51 minutes 6.6 seconds. The two athletes met again on at least seven occasions but these meetings were generally regarded as 'anticlimatic' (MacGregor, 305). Cummings was the more successful in the longer runs but tended to fail over the popular mile distance.

Cummings enjoyed a long and successful career, racing all over the British Isles and being once described as 'one of the prettiest runners who ever put on a running pump' (Jamieson, 55). Despite one or two minor controversies, 'he was immensely popular with the athletic public of the day' (*Preston Guardian*, 18 July 1919). He was small and slight, weighing only 7 or 8 stones.

Cummings married Esther Turner, and had at least one son. Little else is known of his private life, although he appears to have spent much of his adult life in Lancashire. He ran beershops in Preston, later moved to Blackpool, and eventually returned to Scotland where, after some years of residence, he died at the Royal Cancer Hospital,

Glasgow, on 13 July 1919, his wife having predeceased him. He had still been actively involved in his beloved sport one year before his death. KEITH GREGSON

Sources D. A. Jamieson, *Powderhall and pedestrianism* (1943) · R. L. Quercetani, *A world history of track and field athletics, 1864–1964* (1964) · P. Lovesey, *The official centenary history of the Amateur Athletics Association* (1979) · F. MacGregor, *Famous Scots: the pride of a small nation* (1984) · P. Matthews, *Guinness book of athletics facts and feats* (1982) · *Sunderland Daily Echo* (1 Sept 1885) · *Sunderland Daily Echo* (14 Sept 1885) · *Sunderland Daily Echo* (29 Sept 1885) · *Paisley and Renfrewshire Gazette* (5 Sept 1885) · *Paisley and Renfrewshire Gazette* (14 Sept 1885) · *Paisley and Renfrewshire Gazette* (3 Oct 1885) · *Preston Guardian* (18 July 1919) · b. cert. · d. cert.
Likenesses photograph, repro. in Jamieson, *Powderhall and pedestrianism*, 49

Cummins, Anne Emily (1869–1936), social worker, was born on 12 October 1869 at Wildcroft, Buckland, Reigate, Surrey, the fourth of seven children of Henry Irwin Cummins, Church of England clergyman, and his wife, Mary Anne, *née* Barnard. Her father was a charming Irishman from co. Cork who held livings in the East End of London and at Sion College. He died in the early 1880s, leaving his widow (whose mother, a Lyon, was related to the aristocratic Scottish family) with very little money to bring up the family. Despite the austere and frugal lifestyle there remained strong bonds of affection.

On leaving Kensington high school, which she and her two younger sisters attended, Anne Cummins took a post as governess and went with her employers to Switzerland. On her return she took a temporary teaching post at what later became the Francis Holland School, but soon her thoughts turned to the idea of social work as a career. A friend of her father, Charles Loch, secretary of the Charity Organization Society (COS), suggested she should do the COS training. As part of this she went to St George's Hospital under Edith Mudd, one of the pioneer almoners, and in 1905, at thirty-five, she was appointed the first almoner at St Thomas's Hospital, London.

Elegant and distinguished looking, Cummins also possessed some of the most valuable characteristics for a social worker—a quick intuitive and sympathetic interest in people, and the ability to listen and understand. Conscious of the problems in establishing the role of almoner, which she had witnessed at St George's, she went about her tasks humbly and unobtrusively, working hard to win the respect of medical and nursing colleagues. She prepared regular reports with statistics, showing not only what had been done but also what could be done with an additional almoner. In this way she expanded the hospital department to become the largest in the country.

As almoner at St Thomas's, Cummins pioneered home visits to maternity patients in conjunction with the Southwark Health Society, to improve material conditions and to educate the expectant family. She waged a crusade against the deplorable conditions of homes, poverty, dirt, and ignorance, which she saw as negating the benefits of medical care. She and her helpers urged parents to clean and whitewash their homes and to substitute milk for the fried fish and pickles often given to babies as young as three months. This work became a model for the first local government maternity and child welfare scheme.

In 1909 came an opportunity to expand the almoner's department and to provide some of the services which Cummins had dreamed of. Stafford Northcote and Dr A. B. Howitt, in visiting Dr Richard Cabot of Massachusetts General Hospital, had been surprised to be told that social work there was very similar to that practised for the past four years by Miss Cummins in the almoner's department at St Thomas's. Northcote established a trust in memory of his sister Cicely, which provided funds to expand the hospital social service to in-patients and to assist out-patients attending the obstetric department and phthisical out-patients and their families. Hitherto social work for tubercular patients had been sporadic. Sanatorium treatment was in its infancy. The Northcote almoner and her voluntary helpers visited intensively when necessary, advising on health precautions and on budgeting. There was real respect for patients as people, and help was given with understanding, knowledge, and friendliness. Cummins took great interest in the convalescent home for tubercular men and boys and in the evening clinic for men, which were established through the trust. During and after the First World War she continued to innovate and adapt the service to the needs of the time.

Throughout her career Cummins gave her attention, imagination, and knowledge to solving problems put before her. She was an admirable teacher, inspiring generations of social workers as well as doctors and nurses. In 1907 she became a member of the newly established Hospital Almoners Council, whose objects, as set out in its report for 1907–8, were:

1 To select suitable candidates and arrange for their training.
2 To recommend fully-trained almoners for any vacant post.
3 Generally to promote the appointment of competent Hospital Almoners.

Until her retirement she remained a member of the executive committee of the council (which became the Institute of Hospital Almoners in 1922). In an address, 'The work of hospital almoners', given at the London School of Economics in 1923, she recognized both the changes that had taken place since she started work and how it was bound to alter and enlarge. 'Nothing short of taking an integral part in the new constructive measures for re-establishing the health of the nation would satisfy' (p. 16).

Cummins was much in demand as a speaker. In 1924 she addressed the American Association of Social Workers in Toronto, where great interest was shown in the high standard of training set by the institute. In 1929 she inspired Agnes MacIntyre, one of her staff, to go to Melbourne to set up the first hospital almoner service in Australia and to help plan the social studies diploma course. The report of the medical superintendent of the Royal Melbourne Hospital in 1930 stated that her work was 'of extraordinary service to the hospital and inestimable service to the community' (*Yearbook of Hospital Almoners' Association*).

Cummins retired from St Thomas's in 1929. By then the

hospital which she had served with such great distinction had an almoner's department built on secure foundations, and the profession, through her leadership, had developed a unified system of training. Public recognition came with her appointment as OBE. In the next seven years she continued to take an interest in professional matters and to give papers such as that to the first International Conference on Social Work in Frankfurt in 1932. She died, unmarried, at Quorn Cottage, Broughton, Hampshire, on 8 February 1936, of myocardial degeneration. Her inspiration as a teacher was recognized with the establishment of a scholarship in her name to assist the training of almoners.

The plaudits showered on Anne Cummins on her retirement and after her death indicate that not only was she a visionary with an outstanding ability to empathize with all those with whom she came in contact, but she also had a great sense of fun. Sir Alfred Howitt, chairman of the Northcote Trust, writing in its 1936 annual report, said that without her there would have been no Northcote Trust.

> The trust enabled her to start a form of hospital social work which had never been undertaken before and to make at St Thomas' the most complete almoner service which had ever existed. This could not have been achieved by the mere expenditure of money; it was the genius of Miss Cummins that made the work so successful … Anne Cummins was a joyous inspiration to all who worked for her.   (Morris, 31)

JOAN BARACLOUGH

Sources C. Morris, *The Northcote Trust, 1909–1959* (privately printed, [n.d.]) • *Yearbook of Hospital Almoners' Association* (1927–36) • E. Moberly Bell, *The story of hospital almoners* (1964) • J. Baraclough, preface, *Social Workers' Educational Trust prize winning essays* (1996) • b. cert. • d. cert.
Archives U. Warwick Mod. RC, Hospital Almoners' Association yearbooks and papers relating to Institute of Hospital Almoners | FILM BFI NFTVA, '100 years of health related social work', Kay Richards (producer), A. D. Marriott (director), 1995, British Association of Social Workers [vignette about her work and photograph of her at work]
Likenesses E. Gabain, oils, 1929?, British Association of Social Workers, Birmingham

Cummins, Geraldine Dorothy (1890–1969), writer and medium, was born on 24 January 1890 at 17 St Patrick's Place, Cork city, the fifth of eleven children of Dr (William E.) Ashley Cummins, physician, and his wife, Jane Constable, *née* Hall (d. 1944). She was educated by a governess. She became active in the suffrage movement, and was appointed honorary treasurer of the Munster Women's Franchise League in 1911. She made a number of public speeches in favour of the cause, and through the league became a friend of the writer Edith Somerville. She recalled of this period: 'My advocacy of "Votes for Women" led to my being stoned through the streets of my native city by [the] sweated factory workers whose cause I so ardently espoused' (Cummins, 18).

Cummins pursued a literary career along with her suffrage activities. With her friend Susanne Rouviere Day she wrote two plays for the Abbey Theatre, *Broken Faith* (1914) and the comedy *Fox and Geese* (1917). W. B. Yeats attended the rehearsals of *Broken Faith*, and Cummins treasured his comment 'When I read your tragedy I thought it was written by two men, and am astonished to find that it was written by two women. It has a strength and directness that are masculine qualities' (Cummins, 88). She published two novels, *The Land they Loved* (1919) and *Fires of Beltane* (1936), both of which displayed her continuing concern with women's roles. Her short stories appeared in *Pall Mall*, and in 1959 she published a volume of them as *Variety Show*. Her biography of Edith Somerville (1952) is of little literary merit; her own autobiography, *Unseen Adventures*, appeared in 1951. Cummins's estimation of her literary talents was low, and she described herself as 'slow of speech', and as a 'dull uninformed conversationalist' (Cummins, 48–9). She had a love affair with the poet Austin *Clarke (1896–1974), and married him on 31 December 1920, but the marriage ended, unconsummated, ten days later. Clarke's action for divorce failed, however.

Cummins's principal interest, however, was in psychic phenomena. In June 1914 she had visited Paris with Susanne Day, where they met the psychic Hester Dowden and joined in a ouija board session. On returning to Ireland, Cummins left Cork for Dublin, where she took a job at the National Library of Ireland and became a paying guest in Mrs Dowden's house. Dowden apparently trained her in mediumship, and Cummins became less active in the suffrage cause; at this time she 'abandoned the idea of becoming a politician, it has not seemed to my mind at any time since, as humanly constructive an occupation as that of medium' (Cummins, 11). In 1923 she met Edith Beatrice Gibbes, who became her patron, and Cummins moved to Chelsea to live with Gibbes, returning to Cork each summer to visit her mother. After her arrival in London she began to produce a series of scripts through automatic writing which were later published. One series, apparently from the time of Jesus, was dictated by an early Christian called Cleophas, while a second series, begun in 1935 and finished in 1951, described the fate of Colonel Percy Harrison Fawcett, who had disappeared in South America in 1925. During the Second World War, she received while in a trance a message for President Roosevelt, which she sent to the American embassy.

Beatrice Gibbes died in December 1951, leaving her house in Chelsea to Cummins, who continued to live there but spent increasing amounts of time in Ireland. Cummins died of cancer at Lindville Hospital, Cork, on 25 August 1969, and was buried in St Lappan's churchyard on Little Island in Cork.   MARIA LUDDY

Sources G. Cummins, *Unseen adventures* (1951) • C. Fryer, *Geraldine Cummins: an appreciation* (1990) • *CGPLA Ire.* (1970) • R. Welch, ed., *The Oxford companion to Irish literature* (1996) • R. Hogan, ed., *Dictionary of Irish literature*, rev. edn, 2 vols. (1996)
Archives Cork Archives Institute, Cork, papers | TCD, corresp. with Thomas McGreevy
Likenesses photograph, repro. in Cummins, *Unseen adventures*
Wealth at death £21,970: probate, 26 March 1970, *CGPLA Ire.*

Cunard, Nancy Clara (1896–1965), poet and political activist, was born at Nevill Holt in Leicestershire on 10 March 1896, the only child of Sir Bache Cunard, third baronet

Nancy Clara Cunard (1896–1965), by Sir Cecil Beaton, late 1920s

(1851–1925), grandson of the founder of the Cunard steamship line, and the American heiress Maud Alice (later known as Emerald) Burke (1872–1948) of San Francisco, whose Irish-American father, James Burke, claimed descent from the Irish patriot Robert Emmet. Lady Cunard left her husband when Nancy was in her teens, and went on to preside over the brightest political and artistic salon in London. The prince of Wales, later Edward VIII, was a regular guest, and she afforded notable social promotion to Wallis Simpson; her pre-eminence as a social hostess was therefore dealt a serious blow by the abdication crisis. A legend persists that the Irish writer George Moore (1852–1933), Lady Cunard's faithful friend from before her marriage, was actually Nancy's father (see A. Frazier, *George Moore*, 2000). There is much to be said against this notion, though he always encouraged Nancy's writing and she later wrote a memoir of him.

Education and early career Educated at home in languages, literature, and history; at Miss Woolf's school in London; in Munich for music and German in 1912, and in Paris at a school run by the Misses Ozanne, Nancy also travelled extensively, sharing her mother's passion for art museums and galleries, and for opera and concerts in London and abroad. Her early diaries show a remarkable range of reading, a ready command of languages, and a deep familiarity with the history of European art, music, literature, and dance. She later trained herself as an expert on the arts of Africa. Among her unpublished papers are a monograph on African ivories, notes for a book of images of Africans in European art, and extensive notes on the history of slavery.

A glamorous and wild society girl among the artists at the Eiffel Tower restaurant in London and a member of a group who called themselves the Corrupt Coterie, the aspiring poet rented a studio to write in with her friend the poet, journalist, and actress Iris Tree. Cunard married an Australian, Sydney Fairbourne of the Royal Buckinghamshire hussars, who was wounded at Gallipoli in 1916. The marriage lasted twenty months, ending in divorce on 15 November 1916. In that year she organized with Edith Sitwell the first of a series of fresh and innovative anthologies which appeared annually until 1921, called *Wheels* after Cunard's signature poem, in which war poems by Wilfred Owen appeared next to avant-garde verse by Aldous Huxley and the Sitwell brothers. Cunard's first volume of poetry was *Outlaws* (1921), followed by *Sublunary* (1923), and *Poems (Two), 1925* (1930). Her most important early poem, *Parallax*, was published by Leonard and Virginia Woolf at the Hogarth Press in 1925. Reviews claimed that it plagiarized T. S. Eliot's *The Waste Land*, which was published by Hogarth in the same series and written as a parallax or slanted view of the London of Eliot's poem. It is now known that one anonymous critic was the left-wing poet Edgell Rickword; it was he, ironically, who later arranged for the publication of Cunard's later works, *Negro* and *Authors Take Sides*. Driven from England by this hostile barrage, she began an expatriate life in Paris and a long career as an activist intellectual by joining the surrealists. In the company of, among others, Dali, Breton, and especially the surrealist communist Louis Aragon, with whom she had two passionate affairs, she sharpened her political beliefs, rejected her class background, and embraced American jazz and the music and culture of Africa. A few brilliant columns for *Vogue* in the mid-1920s show what she might have done in society and arts journalism had she followed the path of her close friend Janet Flanner, who wrote a Paris letter for the *New Yorker*.

In Paris, Cunard kept a flat on the rue le Regrattier on Île St Louis, and set up the Hours Press (1928–31), whose history she later documented in *These were the Hours* (1969). Based initially at a shop on the rue Guenegaud, from where she also sold African art objects, and later at Le Puits Carré, her home in La Chapelle-Réanville, Normandy, the press published works by, among others, Robert Graves, Laura Riding, George Augustus Moore, Ezra Pound (*XXX Cantos*), and Louis Aragon (his French translation of Lewis Carroll's *The Hunting of the Snark*). She also discovered Samuel Beckett and published his *Whoroscope* (1930). The rare volume *Henry-Music* is a collection of jazz piano tunes by her lover, the African-American musician Henry Crowder, settings for poems by Cunard, Beckett, Walter Lowenfels, and other modernist poets, the best of them a blues song by Nancy herself.

Icon Nancy Cunard's extraordinary good looks and her reputation for excess in love affairs, dancing to jazz, drinking, and drugs made her the icon of the new woman, the boyish vamp of the twenties. She was famously photographed by Man Ray, wearing African ivory bracelets (1920), and by Curtis Moffat for *Vogue*, wearing a feathered head-dress and looking savage, with her then lover, Louis

Aragon. Her image was also captured in photos and paintings by Cecil Beaton, to whom she resembled 'a robot woman in a German film' (Williams, 131), Wyndham Lewis, Barbara Ker-Seymer, and others, as well as in Constantin Brancusi's elegant abstract sculptures.

Michael Arlen's (1895–1956) roman à clef *The green hat* (1924) and others among his popular novels established Nancy Cunard's reputation as the archetype of the sexually free 'woman of honour'. Staged in London with Talullah Bankhead and in New York with Katherine Cornell playing the Nancy Cunard figure, the play followed the sensational text of the novel, but the silent film with Greta Garbo, *A Woman of Affairs* (1928), was censored beyond recognition. Cunard was generally recognized as Myra Viveash in Aldous Huxley's *Antic Hay*, Lucy Tantamount in his *Point Counter Point*, and as the subject of other unsavoury literary portraits by Wyndham Lewis and Richard Aldington. The most disturbing contemporary portrait of Nancy Cunard is the Fresca section of T. S. Eliot's *The Waste Land*, with her mother parodied as Lady Kleinwurm, and wisely edited out of Ezra Pound's final draft of the poem (*Facsimile Drafts of The Waste Land*, ed. V. Eliot, 1971; L. Gordon, *Eliot's Early Years*, 1977; Chisholm, appx 1).

Political activist In 1931 Cunard brought to London and privately screened a print of the Bunuel-Dali film *L'âge d'or* after it had been attacked by right-wing, Catholic, and antisemitic groups in Paris. She was helped in this venture by Sir Thomas Beecham, her mother's lover. Lady Cunard—in spite of Beecham's defence of Nancy—had disinherited her daughter because of the 'blasphemous and immoral film' and her public appearances in London society with Henry Crowder. As the mother–daughter battle escalated Nancy wrote an attack called *Black Man and White Ladyship*, published it in W. E. B. DuBois's Afro-American journal *The Crisis* in September 1931, and sent it as a privately printed pamphlet at Christmas to Lady Cunard's friends—effectively a printed version of the slap in the mother's face featured in *L'âge d'or*. 'How come, white man, the rest of the world is to be re-formed in your dreary and decadent image?' the pamphlet asks. This personalizing of the politics of imperialism forever marked her as an outcast in England, and staked out her place on the world's stage as a public intellectual. She had broken all the taboos of loyalty to country, class, and family. Hate mail hounded her efforts on behalf of blacks at the time and untoward comments about her sexuality have since compromised her reputation as a radical activist for black arts and liberation.

Negro Having thus broken with her past, Cunard set to work on an enormous encyclopaedia of black history, culture, and politics, at first entitled *Colour*, and later *Negro* (first published in London by Wishart in 1934, after rejections from Cape and Gollancz, among others). Inspired by Crowder, she researched for the work in ethnographic museums with African collections in Europe, most notably the Musée du Congo at Tervueren, outside Brussels, where her assistants Raymond Michelet and Raoul Ubac respectively drew and photographed hundreds of objects. Work on *Negro* took her to the US twice, and to the West Indies; her efforts to get to Africa were frustrated by her not being allowed to travel with a black man (later, she was able to go to north Africa to report on the condition of the Moors during the Spanish Civil War). She enlisted the contributions of many black intellectuals and leaders, among them Langston Hughes (1902–1967), the activist poet, who became a lifelong friend, the novelist Claude Mackay, and the activists George Padmore (1901–1959) and Marcus Garvey. Among other contributors were Africanists and anthropologists, including an early article by Melville Herskovits (1895–1963); the Belgian Robert Goffin wrote a brilliant piece on jazz; nineteen essays were translated from the French by Samuel Beckett, while Rene Crevel's 'The negress in the brothel' was censored in Britain (Cunard boasted of having surreptitiously re-inserted the offending pages at the bindery). They were joined by Ezra Pound on Frobenius, a manifesto by the surrealist group, studies of African culture in Central and South America, and sections on artists, entertainers (including Josephine Baker), boxers, and Harlem. A piece by Kenneth MacPherson called for a negro film union, and she published several major essays in folklore by Zora Neale Hurston. Musical scores and political manifestos from many different groups were represented, with special emphasis given to black candidates for office in the American Communist Party.

As editor of *Negro*, Cunard reprimanded W. E. B. DuBois, another of her contributors, for the timidity of his organization, the National Association for the Advancement of Colored People (NAACP). At issue was the cause of the Scottsboro Boys, the nine young black men, almost lynched, and then sentenced to the death penalty in Alabama for the supposed rape of two young women on a freight train. Cunard and others contributed essays on the Scottsboro Boys to *Negro*. She organized many demonstrations in London and Liverpool and raised money on their behalf. Cunard's pro-black activities were under surveillance by British authorities and the FBI; she was later detained at Ellis Island. But as the communists had ceased to regard the black struggle as the vanguard of the revolution by the time *Negro* appeared in 1934, and as the book was too radical for a mainstream audience, it has never found the wide audience it deserves. Banned in British colonies in Africa and the West Indies, it provoked a furious review in the *Nation* by Jamaica's former governor, Lord Olivier. African and West Indian activists who sought Cunard out in London and Paris told her often of the experience of having read her book while it was banned. Hugh Ford's abridged version of *Negro* (1970; repr. 1996) reprints over half the essays but includes images of Cunard herself, in defiance of her own prefatory declaration that all of the book's illustrations were of black people and African objects. She called herself the 'maker' of the book, which she saw as an international collective effort to recognize the black Atlantic as a global source of African cultures, rather than merely a part of the vogue for black art among white Europeans of the 1920s.

Journalism; the Spanish Civil War In 1935 Cunard wrote to the head of the Chicago-based international wire service, the Associated Negro Press (ANP), for credentials to cover the Abyssinian crisis and Hailie Selassie's visit to the United Nations in Geneva. It was the beginning of three decades' work as a reporter—almost exclusively on race issues—to an international audience of mostly black newspaper readers in the US, Africa, Latin America, and the Caribbean. She also wrote for Sylvia Pankhurst's *New Times*, the General News Service (British colonies, India, and the Far East) and Charles Duff's publications on the Spanish Civil War. For some of her radical journalism she used the pseudonym Ray Holt. George Padmore saw her off on the train for Barcelona on 10 August 1936, and she devoted herself intensively to the cause of Republican Spain for the next three years. Her articles urged Britain, France, and the US to stop their policy of non-intervention in the light of Germany and Italy's support for Franco. In Madrid, at Pablo Neruda's Casa de las Flores, Cunard joined other left intellectuals in collecting poems for Spain, later handset at home on her old printing press at Le Puits Carré as six pamphlets, *Les poètes du monde défendent le peuple espagnol*. These were produced in English, French, and Spanish, and included her own 'F.A.S.C.I.S.M.E' as well as poems by Neruda, Aragon, Garcia Lorca, Langston Hughes, and most famously W. H. Auden's 'Spain'.

In 1937 Cunard translated Pablo Neruda's 'To the Mothers of the Dead Militia' and 'Almeria', for the *Left Review* and wrote an article on Langston Hughes, Jacques Roumain, and Nicolas Guillen called 'Three negro poets'. Her own poems on Spain, including 'To Eat Today' and a translation of Roumain's 'Madrid', were published in 1938. Her *Authors Take Sides on the Spanish War* appeared as a special issue of *Left Review* in 1937. This resulted from a call to British writers; of the replies, 126 were for the republic, five were for Franco and six were neutral. Cunard has not been given credit for originating this brilliant political strategy which, in organizing intellectuals to speak out on a political cause, was entirely in the spirit of the *Negro* anthology. The idea has been widely used since. *Authors Take Sides* included the signatures of black intellectuals Marcus Garvey, George Padmore, and C. L. R. James, an early and largely unrecognized instance of racial solidarity by the British left. The most effective part of her work for Spain was a series of articles in the *Manchester Guardian* in 1938 and 1939 on the condition of the Spanish refugees in French concentration camps after the war. She managed to help a great many of them and was greeted as a heroine when she went to Chile in 1940. But her courageous efforts on their behalf in collecting money, clothing, and supplies were not appreciated by the French authorities, who stopped her from taking refugees from Perpignan back to her house in Normandy.

Second World War; final years During the Second World War, Cunard worked as a translator for the BBC and the ministry of information. Here she encountered the pro-fascist broadcasts of her old friend, Ezra Pound, with which she expressed as much mystification as outrage.

Much of her time in London was spent at the West African Students' Union and she continued to write race-related war stories for the ANP. Her most important work of the time was a collaboration with George Padmore called *The White Man's Duty* (1942). She also published another collective volume, *Poems for France* (1942; in French translation, 1947).

Returning to France after the war Cunard found that the Germans quartered in her house had destroyed her Hours Press books, most of her letters, her collections of modern paintings and African art, and her ivories. She eventually settled in an old stone house in LaMothe Fenelon in the Dordogne. Here she wrote her history of the Hours Press and her memoirs of Norman Douglas (1954) and George Moore (1956). In the outlaw status of both these men she found a source for imagining her own place as an eccentric rebel among minor characters in British cultural history; these memoirs contain all that there is of her autobiographical writing and have been extensively used by her biographers. She kept up her friendships with the left poets Sylvia Townsend Warner and Valentine Ackland, as well as with Janet Flanner and Solita Solano in Paris. But her behaviour became increasingly erratic, and she sought refuge in alcohol. Shortly after coming to London in 1960 she was committed to an asylum; having recovered somewhat, she persuaded Louis Aragon to secure her release, and returned to France. She died on 16 March 1965 in the Hôpital Cochin, Paris, weighing only 26 kilos, but still working on her epic poem against all wars. She was cremated at Père Lachaise cemetery on 25 March. George Sadoul wrote a tribute to her as the epitome of the jazz age: 'Around her shade float Afro-American blues and spirituals, Spanish Republican ballads and the immortal rhythms of French poetry', praising her 'great heart', 'brilliant intelligence', and 'strong character' (*Les lettres Françaises*). Nancy Cunard was an outlaw, as she had envisaged in her poems, a serious political activist, who lived an intense and lonely life dedicated to her causes. She was also a minor English modernist poet. But she was also that rare creature on the world stage, the woman public intellectual. Her name is important in the history of surrealism and *le tumulte noir* in Paris, the struggle against Franco and fascism in the Spanish Civil War, and the twentieth-century global struggle for the recognition of African culture and the fight for racial justice.   JANE MARCUS

Sources A. Chisholm, *Nancy Cunard* (1979) • H. Ford, *Nancy Cunard: brave poet, indomitable rebel* (1968) • N. Cunard, *These were the Hours* (1969) • N. Cunard, *Grand man: memories of Norman Douglas* (1954) • N. Cunard, *GM: memories of George Moore* (1956) • J. Marcus, 'Bonding and bondage: Nancy Cunard and the making of the *Negro* anthology', *Borders, boundaries and frames*, ed. M. G. Henderson (1995) • S. Stanford Friedman, *Nancy Cunard*, in B. K. Scott, *The gender of modernism* (1990) • P. Clements, 'Transmuting Nancy Cunard', *Dalhousie Review*, 60/1/2 (1986), 188–214 • *As wonderful as all that?* (California, 1987) • N. Cunard and H. Speck, *Henry Crowder* (1987) • A. S. Williams, *Ladies of influence* (2000) • *CGPLA Eng. & Wales* (1966)

Archives Ransom HRC, corresp. and literary papers • Southern Illinois University, Carbondale, Illinois, Morris Library, corresp. and papers • State University of New York, Buffalo, E. H. Butler Library, papers | Bodl. Oxf., letters to E. J. Thompson and poems •

JRL, letters to *Manchester Guardian* • Tate collection, corresp. with John Banting
Likenesses M. Ray, photograph, 1920, Man Ray archive • group photograph, *c.*1926, Hult. Arch. • C. Beaton, photograph, 1926–9, NPG [*see illus.*] • A. Wysard, watercolour drawing, 1928, NPG, D289 • H. Cartier-Bresson, bromide print, 1956, NPG • J. Banting, portrait, repro. in Chisholm, *Nancy Cunard* • C. Beaton, photographs, repro. in Chisholm, *Nancy Cunard* • C. Brancusi, sculptures, Man Ray archive • A. Guerara, portrait, repro. in Chisholm, *Nancy Cunard* • O. Kokoschka, portrait, repro. in Chisholm, *Nancy Cunard* • W. Lewis, portrait, repro. in Chisholm, *Nancy Cunard* • E. McCawn, portrait, repro. in Chisholm, *Nancy Cunard* • C. Moffat and B. Ker-Seymer, solarized photographs, Ransom HRC
Wealth at death £14,943—in England: administration, 17 Feb 1966, *CGPLA Eng. & Wales*

Cunard, Sir Samuel, first baronet (1787–1865), shipowner, was born on 21 November 1787 at Halifax, Nova Scotia, the son of Abraham Cunard, merchant, of Philadelphia, and his wife, Margaret Murphy. Both parents came from Loyalist families whose fathers were in shipping before they fled to Canada following the American War of Independence. They had nine children—seven sons and two daughters; Samuel was the second child, but first son. He spent a few years at the only school in Halifax, Halifax grammar. Then, having spent three years in Boston working with shipbrokers, Samuel returned to Halifax, went into partnership with his father as Cunard & Son, and bought their first small vessel. After the death of his father in 1823, he traded as S. Cunard & Co. with the West Indies and South America, making contacts during his frequent visits to London, Liverpool, and Glasgow, and acting as colonial agent for several British concerns. By the early 1830s, Cunard had stakes in coal, timber, China tea (of which he was the sole distributor in North America), whaling, and banking (he set up the first bank in Nova Scotia), and a fleet of forty vessels.

A train ride in 1831 from Liverpool to Manchester opened Cunard's eyes to the possibilities of sea transport by steam, for during the 1830s developments in marine technology enabled steamships for the first time to make long voyages. In 1838 Brunel's *Great Western* from Bristol and *Sirius* from Cork confirmed this advance, and Cunard determined to build a steam fleet of his own. He failed to find investors in Boston and Halifax, but on seeing an advertisement in *The Times*, inviting tenders for a mail contract for North America, he went back to Britain. A friend in the Admiralty liked his proposals and advised him to talk to Robert *Napier, the eminent marine engineer in Glasgow, who not only agreed to build ships but introduced him to the partners of a thriving coastal trading concern, George *Burns in Glasgow and David MacIver in Liverpool. With capital provided by them and their friends, the British and North American Royal Steam Packet Company (later Cunard) was formed; and Cunard, in private negotiation with the government, was granted the mail contract. Every one of these important transactions bore the stamp of Cunard's acumen and determination. *Britannia*, with Cunard aboard on its maiden voyage, was greeted in 1840 in Boston with great excitement, one newspaper calling it the most significant event since the arrival of the Pilgrims.

Sir Samuel Cunard, first baronet (1787–1865), by A. G. Holt, 1849

For a decade Cunard had a monopoly of steam on the Atlantic, but in 1850 the Collins line, with a subsidy from the American government, began to compete strongly. Rather than waste money on a rate war, Cunard made a secret agreement with Collins that lasted until 1855. Collins went bankrupt three years later but by that time, with the appearance of several new British and continental companies, competition had come to stay.

In 1851, looking for new opportunities, Cunard joined the successful enterprise in the Mediterranean and the Levant set up by MacIver in 1849, and became a partner with MacIver and Burns in the British and Foreign Steam Navigation Company in 1855. This new concern had Cunard's management and capital but there was a marked difference between the two companies. British and Foreign built modern ships with screw propulsion, while Cunard stubbornly refused to discard wooden hulls and paddle-driven ships on the north Atlantic. A dynamic man in many ways, it is surprising that he should have shown such deep conservatism. Competitors who kept abreast of new technology had bigger and faster ships that were worked more economically. Moreover, these vessels attracted more passenger traffic because they had more space for luxurious accommodation, good food, and other enticements. Cunard, however, would not change the spartan regime in the mailships, of cramped cabins, candle lighting, poor food, and no public rooms. Nevertheless, safety and regularity sustained Cunard's lead, for the line carried most of the overseas mails in North America. Cunard's first iron hull appeared in 1852, and entry into the steerage business in 1860 made screw propulsion imperative: the last paddle-engined steamer joined the Atlantic fleet in 1862.

After the upheaval of the Crimean War, in which several of Cunard's vessels were taken up by the government, Cunard believed that if he got a footing in Australia by the overland route, he would be able to break into the eastern trades. This was highly speculative. Monopolized by the Peninsular and Oriental Steam Navigation Company (P. & O.), the India and China lines were closely guarded. His announcement of a 'junction' with the European and Australian Royal Mail Company at the end of 1856 turned out to be a damp squib; and when in 1858 he devised a prospectus for a new company for Australia, India, and China, it went no further than P. & O.'s boardroom; there was no place for a second steam company in the East at that time. Yet Cunard did not quite give up his ambition. In 1860, Frederick Hill, secretary to the postmaster-general, was under pressure to find a likely company to compete with or replace P. & O. on the Australian line. In private conversations with Hill, Cunard asserted that a person of established reputation—himself, perhaps?—could easily raise £4 million in the market, and Messrs Napier would quickly build the number of ships needed. P. & O., however, was not for sale.

Cunard was made a baronet in 1859 for his work in linking North America to Britain. He also became a fellow of the Royal Geographical Society for his interest in the regular exchange of plants between Kew Gardens in London and the Boston Botanical Gardens. Small, slight, alert, and active, Cunard had no interest in outdoor pursuits on land; his great love was the sea. Always called 'Sam', he was courteous, formal, a skilful diplomat, a 'doer, not a talker', and an autocrat in his business life. Privately, he had many friends in high society on both sides of the water and spent several months in Britain each year. He particularly enjoyed parties and concerts, had a box at the opera (when in London), and liked to be in the company of literary people. A rich and generous man, he supported the poor in Halifax, as well as the public library and the Mechanical Institute; and he was appointed commissioner of lighthouses. Cunard could have become a member of the Nova Scotian legislative assembly if he had wanted to, although he was not a good public speaker; but his seat on the crown council—a small select group that could silence the 'popular voice' if necessary—suited him perfectly.

Cunard married Susan, daughter of William Duffus, a prosperous Halifax merchant, on 4 February 1815. They had nine children, but his wife died on 23 January 1828, ten days after the last infant's birth. An affectionate father, he took special care of the children after his wife's death. He was fortunate to have close members of his and his wife's extended families ready to help. When his brother, Joseph, fell into debt, he bailed him out; and he supported his father-in-law when he had financial difficulties. Cunard's eldest son, Edward, was groomed to take his place in the shipping business when he retired in 1863, at the age of seventy-six, after a minor heart attack. He died of heart failure on 28 April 1865 at 26 Princes Gardens, Kensington, London.

Cunard's death coincided with the end of the pioneer stage of the transatlantic steamer. The decade following his death, with the appearance of other steamship lines, saw the Cunard Line in the doldrums. The launch of the Cunard Steam-Ship Company as a publicly owned company in 1880, however, saw its re-establishment as the premier transatlantic service. It owned only four ships of 8200 tons in 1840, but by 1880 the fleet had grown to twenty-eight ships of 136,493 tons displacement.

FREDA HARCOURT

Sources H. K. Grant, *Samuel Cunard: pioneer of the Atlantic steamship* (1967) · F. E. Hyde, *Cunard and the north Atlantic, 1840–1973: a history of shipping and financial management* (1975) · J. H. Maber, *North Star to Southern Cross* (1967), chap. 11 · E. W. Sloan, 'Private enterprise and mixed enterprise', *Frontiers of entrepreneurship research: proceedings of the Babson College Research Conference* [Wellesley, MA 1981], ed. K. H. Vesper [1981] · *The Times* (6 Dec 1956), 10d · NMM, P. & O. archive, P. & O. /1/104, 1856–8 · China, Conversations, PRO, POST 29/105, 3, 6 Dec 1960 · 'Select committee on contract packet service', *Parl. papers* (1849), 12.132–6, no. 571 · 'Select committee to inquire into contracts … with steam packet companies', *Parl. papers* (1860), 14.321–2, no. 328 [mail and telegraphic communications] · *DNB* · McIver correspondence, 1847–59, U. Lpool, Cunard Archive, D.138/4, PR4.3/4, PR3.1/16 · *CGPLA Eng. & Wales* (1865) · d. cert.

Archives Public Archives of Nova Scotia, Halifax, corresp. and papers · Public Archives of Nova Scotia, Halifax · U. Lpool, Cunard Archive | U. Lpool, letters to C. MacIver

Likenesses A. G. Holt, portrait, 1849, unknown collection; copyprint, NPG [*see illus.*]

Wealth at death under £350,000: probate, 13 May 1865, *CGPLA Eng. & Wales*

Cundy, James (1793–1826). *See under* Cundy, Thomas, the elder (1765–1825).

Cundy, Joseph (1795–1875). *See under* Cundy, Thomas, the elder (1765–1825).

Cundy, Nicholas Wilcocks (1778–*c*.1837). *See under* Cundy, Thomas, the elder (1765–1825).

Cundy, Samuel (1816–1867). *See under* Cundy, Thomas, the elder (1765–1825).

Cundy, Thomas, the elder (1765–1825), architect, the eldest son of Peter Cundy of Restowrick House, St Dennis, Cornwall, and Thomasine Wilcocks, his wife, was born at Restowrick House and baptized at St Dennis on 18 February 1765. He belonged to an ancient family, of which the main branch was long seated at Sandwich in Kent. Following a disagreement with his father, Cundy left home early, and after being apprenticed to a builder at Plymouth, at the age of twenty-one decided to move to London to seek his fortune. In 1795 he exhibited at the Royal Academy 'a design for a hippodrome and stables', when his address was given as 'at Mr Gardner's, Temple Lane' (RA exhibition catalogue, 1795). In 1797 he took over one of the premises of George Shakespear, master builder, around the site of the present Grosvenor Gardens, and it has been suggested by a later historian that he may have purchased an interest in Shakespear's business (Saint, 1474). He continued to exhibit at the Royal Academy until 1816, when he sent a design for 'a mansion on the banks of the Severn', by which time he had successfully established himself as an architect and builder in Ranelagh Street, Pimlico.

In 1789 Cundy married, at St Martin-in-the-Fields, Mary Hubert of Abingdon Street, Westminster, with whom he had seven sons, the eldest of whom, Thomas *Cundy the younger (1790–1867), accompanied his father to Rome in 1816, and eventually succeeded him in his practice. At the age of twenty-eight the elder Cundy was employed as clerk of the works at Normanton Park, Rutland, under S. P. Cockerell, upon whose retirement he was retained by Sir Gilbert Heathcote to complete the alterations in progress. His tower and portico to Normanton church (1826) are noted for their 'spectacularly Baroque' design (Colvin, *Archs.*). He then went into practice independently as an architect and builder, and received commissions from important patrons; in 1821 he was appointed surveyor to Earl Grosvenor's London estates. The until recently overlooked importance of the Cundy family in the early development of the Grosvenor estates was drawn to the attention of readers of *Country Life* in an article by Andrew Saint, who stated that, 'if one name is to be linked with Belgravia's general conception and appearance, it is that of Cundy, not of Cubitt' (Saint, 1474). Among the important buildings which Cundy either built or made extensive alterations to were Middleton Park and Osterley House for the earl of Jersey, Tottenham Park, Hawarden Castle, Burton Constable, Sion House, Northumberland House, Wytham Abbey, Oxfordshire, and many others. A statement of bills due to Cundy at his death in 1825 includes many aristocratic names including that of the fifth duke of Marlborough, for whom he had surveyed Blenheim in the previous year, perhaps with a view to alterations. Cundy designed in both the Gothic and the neo-classical styles, and a manuscript record book of his work is now in the collection of the Royal Institute of British Architects (RIBA). Cundy died in his sixty-first year on 28 December 1825 at his home in Ranelagh Street, Pimlico, and was buried in the churchyard at Richmond in Surrey, where there is a tomb to his memory. A manuscript account of the family, written by Osbert F. Cundy FRCS in 1874, formerly in the possession of T. J. Cundy of Brant Broughton, Lincolnshire, is now in the RIBA collection. **James Cundy** (1793–1826), his second son, entered the Royal Academy Schools as a sculptor in 1812, at the age of nineteen. In 1817 he exhibited at the British Institution a group of *Eve Supplicating Adam*, in 1818 *The Judgment of Paris*, and in 1823 *Andromeda*. From 1817 to 1823 he exhibited at the British Institution and in 1825 he exhibited at the Society (later Royal Society) of British Artists a work entitled *Musidora*. He was employed as a designer and modeller by Rundell and Bridge, silversmiths. He executed several memorial tablets, one of which, to Dr Benjamin Tate (1823), in Magdalen College chapel, Oxford, was illustrated in the *Gentleman's Magazine* (*GM*, 1st ser., 93/1, 1823, 133). In May 1826 he was killed in a carriage accident in Waterloo Place, leaving Mary, *née* Tansley, his wife, and son, **Samuel Cundy** (1816–

1867), a statuary mason who ran a marble works in Pimlico and was employed on the restorations at Westminster Abbey, and by Sir Giles Gilbert Scott on St Albans Abbey and elsewhere. **Joseph Cundy** (1795–1875), born in London, the third son of Thomas Cundy the elder, was also well known as a speculative architect and builder in Belgravia, and was the father of Thomas Syson Cundy, surveyor to the Fountaine-Wilson-Montagu estates in the north of England, a position in which he was succeeded by his son and grandson. **Nicholas Wilcocks Cundy** (1778–c.1837), architect and engineer, was a younger brother of Thomas Cundy the elder. After moving to London, he was articled to an architect for whom he worked for nine years. His best-known work was the reconstruction of the Pantheon, Oxford Street, as a theatre (1811–12). He was the projector of a ship canal from Portsmouth to London and one of the four competing schemes for the London and Brighton Railway. His publications included: *Reports on the Grand Ship Canal from London to Arundel Bay and Portsmouth* (1825); *Imperial Ship Canal from London to Portsmouth* (1828); and *Inland Transit: the Practicability, Utility and Benefit of Railroads* (1834). He married Miss Stafford-Cooke, and unsuccessfully contested the borough of Sandwich, where his family had historical links.

L. H. CUST, rev. ANNETTE PEACH

Sources Colvin, *Archs.* · *Catalogue of the drawings collection of the Royal Institute of British Architects*, Royal Institute of British Architects, 20 vols. (1969–89) · Graves, *RA exhibitors* · *The Builder*, 25 (1867), 464, 607 · *IGI* · A. Saint, 'The Grosvenor estate, 2: the Cundy era', *Country Life*, 162 (1977), 1474–7 · Inst. CE [Nicholas Wilcocks Cundy] · R. Gunnis, *Dictionary of British sculptors, 1660–1851* (1953) · O. F. Cundy, MS account of the Cundy family, 1874, RIBA BAL
Archives RIBA BAL, record book of work | Croome Estate Trust, Worcestershire, vouchers and papers relating to Lord Coventry's London house · Eaton Hall, Cheshire, collection of drawings relating to Earl Grosvenor's estates · RIBA BAL, MS account of the Cundy family by O. F. Cundy, 1874
Likenesses portrait, priv. coll.; formerly in possession of the late T. J. Cundy of Brant Broughton, Lincs.
Wealth at death under £1500—Joseph Cundy: administration, 31 May 1875, *CGPLA Eng. & Wales*

Cundy, Thomas, the younger (1790–1867), architect, was the eldest of the seven sons of Thomas *Cundy the elder (1765–1825) and his wife, Mary Hubert. He joined his father in architectural practice at an early age, exhibiting drawings of their work at the Royal Academy from 1807. The closeness of their partnership was such that their separate contributions are difficult to disentangle, and in 1816 they visited Rome together. On his father's death in 1825 he succeeded to his practice and also to his position as surveyor to the Grosvenor estate in London. He held this position for forty-one years, during which period the speculative developments of Thomas Cubitt transformed Belgravia and Pimlico. Cundy's most important residential projects included alterations to Tottenham Park, Wiltshire (c.1823–6), for the first marquess of Ailesbury, and the remodelling of Moor Park, Hertfordshire (c.1830), for the first marquess of Westminster, for whom he also enlarged Grosvenor House, Upper Grosvenor Street, London (dem. 1927), with an extension to the gallery (1825–7) and the addition of a Doric entrance screen (1842–3). His extensive list of ecclesiastical commissions began with Normanton church, Leicestershire (1826–9), in a vigorous baroque idiom with a circular tower inspired by Thomas Archer's St John's, Smith Square. His later churches were predominantly Gothic and increasingly found favour with the ecclesiologists. These include St Paul's, Knightsbridge (1840–43), Holy Trinity, Paddington (1844–6; dem. 1984), St Michael's, Chester Square (1844), St Mark's, Hamilton Terrace (1846–7), St Barnabas, Pimlico (1847–50), St Gabriel's, Warwick Square (1851–3), and St Saviour's, Pimlico (1864). He married Arabella, daughter of John Fishlake of Salisbury, with whom he had three sons and one daughter. They lived at 13 Chester Square, Pimlico. His third son, Thomas Cundy (b. 1820), joined him in practice and eventually succeeded him. Cundy retired to Bromley in Kent, where he died on 15 July 1867, aged seventy-seven.

L. H. CUST, rev. RICHARD JOHN

Sources Colvin, *Archs.* · *The Builder*, 25 (1867), 607 · *Building News* (30 Aug 1867), 598 · d. cert. · *CGPLA Eng. & Wales* (1867)
Archives City Westm. AC, papers
Wealth at death under £3000: probate, 6 Aug 1867, CGPLA Eng. & Wales

Cunedda (*supp. fl.* late 4th–mid-5th cent.), ruler in north Wales, is said to have led the migration of a section of his north British people from Manau in Gododdin, the area around the headwaters of the Forth still commemorated in Clackmannan, to north Wales, where he expelled the Irish settlers and founded the dynasty that ruled Gwynedd until the early ninth century. The purported date of these events was either the end of the fourth century or the middle of the fifth. Such is the story told by the *Historia Brittonum* (sometimes ascribed to Nennius), which was written, probably in north Wales, in 829 or 830. The corpus of British genealogies (the Harleian) assembled in the mid-tenth century, makes Cunedda son of Œtern (possibly Eternus), grandson of Padarn Pesrut (Peternus of the Red Cloak), and great-grandson of Tegid (Tacitus). He is himself father of eight (or nine) sons, each the eponym of a subdivision of the early medieval kingdom of Gwynedd (for example, Meirion for Meirionydd, Rhufon for Rhufoniog, and so on), and is therefore progenitor not only of the main dynasty of Gwynedd, but also of the lines of sub-kings ruling its constituent elements.

This sparse information is almost certainly an aetiological myth, which had three principal functions. First, it provided a model for the intervention of a new and alien dynasty at a time when the house of Cunedda had made way for that of Merfyn. It also linked Gwynedd with the north British area where a 'heroic age' had played itself out in the sixth century, to the accompaniment of formative poetry ascribed to the bards Aneirin and Taliesin: their renown is recorded in the immediately preceding sentence of the *Historia Brittonum*.

Finally, it firmly cemented into the history of the main kingdom those parts which might otherwise have been aspiring to separate destinies. Thus it can be suggested that Ceredig became Cunedda's ninth 'son' when Ceredigion was incorporated into Gwynedd in 872. Cunedda's Roman-sounding ancestors are of the type often used to lend grandeur to the remoter reaches of Welsh genealogies: the most popular choices are Constantine himself and Magnus Maximus, both of whom began their bids for power at the head of the army in Britain. The dating of Cunedda's life given by the *Historia* or implied by the genealogies is correspondingly artificial. The *Historia's* '146 years before Maelgwn, *magnus rex apud Brittones*' ('great king of the Britons') (534?–547?) means 388, in other words the death of Magnus Maximus, one of early medieval British tradition's few 'historical horizons'; adjustment in the genealogies to make Cunedda not Maelgwn's *atavus* (great-great-great-grandfather), as in the *Historia*, but merely *proavus* (great-grandfather) serves to transfer his activity to the period when, on the evidence of Gildas and Bede, the Britons' struggle with the 'Picts and Scots' was at its height.

These observations show that Cunedda is essentially a figure of the ninth and tenth centuries. His historical role was to legitimize a particular perception of the past and present in the Gwynedd of that period. Whether he had a historical existence in his own right is impossible to say, but is perhaps rather more likely than not. If so, he should surely be envisaged as the leader of a warband from the very fringes of the British world, who contrived to make an effective intervention far from his home base, in much the same way as warriors from Gwynedd are celebrated by Aneirin among the participants in the battle fought by the Gododdin themselves against the Northumbrians at Catterick. That his presence in Gwynedd was part of a master-plan by the authorities in sub-Roman Britain to regain control of the situation is no more (or less) than agreeable fantasy.

PATRICK WORMALD

Sources T. Mommsen, ed., 'Historia Brittonum', *Chronica minora saec. IV. V. VI. VII.*, 3, MGH Auctores Antiquissimi, 13 (Berlin, 1898), 111–222 · 'Harleian genealogies', *Early Welsh genealogical tracts*, ed. P. C. Bartrum (1966), nos. 1–3, 17–18, 26, 32–3, pp. 9–13 · D. N. Dumville, 'Sub-Roman Britain: history and legend', *History*, new ser., 62 (1977), 173–92, esp. 181–3 · M. Miller, 'The foundation-legend of Gwynedd', *BBCS*, 27 (1976–8), 515–32 · M. Miller, *The saints of Gwynedd* (1979), 1–3 · K. H. Jackson, *The 'Gododdin': the oldest Scottish poem* (1969), 69–75
Archives BL, Harleian MS 3859

Cuneo, Terence Tenison (1907–1996), painter, was born on 1 November 1907 at 215 Uxbridge Road, Hammersmith, London, the only child of Cyrus Cincinato Cuneo (*d.* 1916/17), artist, and his wife, Nellie Marion (Nell), *née* Tenison, also an artist and a relative of the poet Tennyson. His father was born in the United States, of Italian descent, and was related to Garibaldi; he studied under Whistler and was a successful magazine illustrator in London until his death, from blood poisoning, when Terence Cuneo was nine.

Cuneo was educated at St Michael's College, Dawlish, and at Sutton Valence School, Kent. He then studied at Chelsea Polytechnic and the Slade School of Fine Art before following in his father's footsteps as a commercial illustrator, working for magazines such as the *Boy's Own Paper*, *The Magnet*, and the *Christian Herald*. In 1931 he joined the London Sketch Club, at one of whose meetings he met his future wife, Catherine Mayfield Monro (1908/9–1979), younger daughter of Edwin George Monro, army major and company director. They married on 28 September 1934 and had two daughters, Linda (*b.* 1937) and Carole (*b.* 1941).

During the Second World War, Cuneo was war artist for the *Illustrated London News* in France in 1940, served briefly with the Royal Engineers, portraying underground activities in occupied Europe (the subject of a one-man exhibition) in 1941, and then served as an official war artist, producing propaganda paintings for the Ministry of Information, the political intelligence department of the Foreign Office, and the War Artists' Advisory Committee. He also illustrated the book *How to Draw Tanks*.

After the war the publicity manager of the London and North Eastern Railway commissioned Cuneo's first poster design, *Giants Refreshed*, showing locomotives in Doncaster railway works. This was the beginning of a railway poster career that lasted for the next half century. Cuneo designed the set of stamps commemorating the 150th anniversary of the Great Western Railway in 1985, and had a train named after him in 1990. His largest painting (20 ft x 10 ft), commissioned by the Science Museum in 1967, was of the concourse of Waterloo Station.

Cuneo was official artist at Elizabeth II's coronation in 1953, and his painting, *The Coronation of Queen Elizabeth II in Westminster Abbey*, was presented to the queen by her lords lieutenant in 1955. His paintings covering numerous other state and royal functions range from *King George VI and Queen Elizabeth at the Middle Temple Banquet* (1950) to *The Commonwealth Prime Ministers' Banquet, Guildhall* (1969). Cuneo was a renowned portrait painter also. Among his subjects were Edward Heath (1971), Field Marshal Viscount Montgomery of Alamein (1972), King Hussein of Jordan (1980), and Colonel H. Jones VC (1984). He painted the queen on numerous occasions; his portraits *H. M. the Queen as Colonel-in-Chief, Grenadier Guards* (1963) and *H. M. the Queen as Patron of the Kennel Club* (1975) were particularly admired. He held one-man exhibitions at RWS Galleries, London, in 1954 and 1958, at the Sladmore Gallery, London, in 1971, 1972, and 1974, and at the Mall Galleries, London, in 1988. He was appointed OBE in 1987 and CVO in 1994, and was president of the Industrial Painters Group and the Society of Equestrian Artists.

Cuneo 'was immensely conservative as an artist, to a point that would make Sir Alfred Munnings look like some mad revolutionary tearaway' (*The Times*); nevertheless his works were enduringly popular. He was renowned for putting a mouse in his paintings; this first appeared in 1953 and subsequently in most of his paintings. His autobiography was entitled *The Mouse and his Master* (1977). He was an insatiable traveller and had a mischievous sense of humour. He painted almost until his death; his last, unfinished, painting was of the channel tunnel. He died, a millionaire, at Arbrook House, Copsem Lane, Esher, Surrey, on 3 January 1996, of bronchopneumonia and heart failure, and was cremated in Leatherhead on 17 January. A memorial service was held at St Martin-in-the-Fields on 17 April. He was survived by his daughter Carole, his wife,

Catherine, and daughter Linda having predeceased him. A retrospective exhibition of his railway art was held at the National Railway Museum in York in January 1997.

BEVERLEY COLE

Sources T. Cuneo, *The mouse and his master* (1977) · N. Chakra, *Terence Cuneo: railway painter of the century* (1990) · N. Harris, *Railway paintings by Cuneo: a retrospective* (1997) · *The Times* (5 Jan 1996) · *The Independent* (8 Jan 1996) · *WWW* [forthcoming] · b. cert. · m. cert. · d. cert. · C. Cuneo, www.terencecuneo.co.uk/htm/about_tc.htm, 4 Dec 2002
Archives National Railway Museum, York, MSS
Likenesses photograph, 1948, repro. in *The Independent* · photograph, repro. in *The Times* · photograph, Hult. Arch. · self-portrait, oils, repro. in www.terencecuneo.co.uk/htm/about_tc.htm
Wealth at death £1,470,953: probate, 11 April 1996, *CGPLA Eng. & Wales*

Cungar. *See* Cyngar (*supp. fl.* early 8th cent.).

Cuningham, James MacNabb (1829–1905), military surgeon and medical administrator, was born at the Cape of Good Hope on 2 June 1829, the son of Major William Cunningham of the 54th Bengal infantry. Cuningham, who altered the spelling of his surname, read medicine at Edinburgh University and graduated MD in 1851, receiving a commendation for his thesis on diseases of the aorta. Soon after joining the Bengal medical service in November 1851 he was appointed superintendent of Bareilly prison; later he occupied a similar position at Meerut. At the latter station he was also engaged in non-medical duties, as the superintendent of the government press for the North-Western Provinces. Cuningham was twice married: first, on 2 March 1854, to Mary, only daughter of James McRae, and second, after her death, to Georgina Euphemia, daughter of Robert Reid Macredie, on 11 April 1889.

Cuningham's aptitude for administrative work led to his appointment in 1866 as secretary to the new Indian sanitary commission. In the same year he was made professor of hygiene at the Calcutta Medical College, and in 1869 he was appointed to the new post of sanitary commissioner to the government of Bengal. He also became the first sanitary commissioner to the government of India, a post which he held from 1875 until his retirement in 1885. In addition to these considerable duties, Cuningham was made head of the Bengal medical department in 1880 and promoted to the rank of surgeon-general.

Cuningham made few original contributions to medical science and achieved renown chiefly on account of his administrative work. He eschewed laboratory work in favour of epidemiological investigation. As one obituarist put it, 'he was apt to throw cold water on strivings towards the truth by local enquiry and clinical and pathological investigation' (*BMJ*, 164). He sought to exclude from official reports all theoretical speculations on the nature and spread of diseases such as cholera, especially those which seemed to imply the need for government intervention or the outlay of public money. The official view of cholera, which Cuningham defended with great vigour, was that it was not a contagious disease and that the quarantines imposed against vessels sailing from India were unnecessary. According to Cuningham cholera could be prevented only by general sanitation and education of the public in hygiene, a view which he expounded in his most important publication, *Cholera: what the State can do to Prevent it*, in 1884 (translated into German in 1895).

Cuningham maintained this position despite mounting criticism until he retired from the Indian Medical Service. In India he became embroiled in bitter conflicts with A. C. De Renzy and W. R. Cornish, the sanitary commissioners of the Punjab and Madras respectively, who held the fashionable view that cholera was a water-borne disease. De Renzy's persistent refusal to toe the official line eventually led to his dismissal and transfer to a remote station in Assam. But while Cuningham's insistence that cholera was not a contagious disease won him the admiration of Indian officials, it was eventually to cost him his scientific reputation. His position was attacked and even ridiculed in the British medical press, while the endeavours of his Indian opponents were held up as models of scientific enquiry. However, Cuningham was generally held in high esteem as an administrator and his pivotal role in building a sanitary infrastructure in British India was widely acknowledged.

Cuningham left India in April 1885 and in June the following year was made a companion in the Order of the Star of India. He was appointed honorary surgeon to Queen Victoria in 1888, and served on the army sanitary committee from 1891 to 1896. In 1892 he was made an honorary LLD of Edinburgh. He died at his home in Buckingham Palace Mansions, Grosvenor Gardens, London, from a stroke, on 26 June 1905, survived by two sons and a daughter from his first marriage.   MARK HARRISON

Sources *BMJ* (15 July 1905), 164–5 · *The Lancet* (1–8 July 1905), 42, 48, 122 · D. G. Crawford, ed., *Roll of the Indian Medical Service, 1615–1930* (1930) · M. Harrison, *Public health in British India: Anglo-Indian preventive medicine, 1859–1914* (1994)
Archives BL OIOC, govt. of India (sanitary) proceedings
Wealth at death £7616 19s. 8d.: probate, 22 July 1905, *CGPLA Eng. & Wales*

Cuningham, Vera Irene Walpole Martin (1897–1955). *See under* Smith, Sir Matthew Arnold Bracy (1879–1959).

Cuningham, William (*c.*1531–1586), physician and cartographer, was probably born in Norfolk. He was admitted pensioner at Corpus Christi College, Cambridge, in 1548, matriculated three years later, and graduated MB in 1557. Cuningham also travelled on the continent, possibly in connection with Mary Tudor's accession to the throne, and probably visited Antwerp, Cologne, and Strasbourg. He graduated MD from Heidelberg in 1559; his portrait in *The Cosmographical Glasse* of that year shows him in doctoral robes. Cuningham describes Heidelberg thus:

> a florishing Universitie ... ther florished 1559 in Phisicke, D. John Langius, the Princes Phisician, Jacob Curio, Thomas Erastus, Petrus Lotichius Secundus, all Doctors in Physick: And D. Balduinus the Reader of the Civill Lector, with divers others, of whom I was very gentely interteined at the time of my Commensment. (Cuningham, 181)

From 1556 to 1559 Cuningham lived and practised in Norwich, and from 1558 to 1566 he published a series of almanacs in connection with his astrological studies. He is best remembered, however, for *The Cosmographical Glasse*, a geographical study produced in the form of a dialogue between student and teacher and dedicated to 'Robert Duddeley', Queen Elizabeth's favourite, who had become a privy councillor and knight of the Order of the Garter four months previously. It is clear that this represented the thin edge of an academic wedge as a hopeful Cuningham promised, in return for Dudley's anticipated patronage, to present him with a further seven works, along 'With divers others, whose names I omit for sondry causes' (Cuningham, preface). These have not survived but *The Cosmographical Glasse* contains several of the astrologer's own engravings, including a realistic map of Norwich, as well as some semi-autobiographical commentary. It is difficult not to detect Cuningham's own experiences in his arguments in favour of reading his work 'in a pleasaunte house or warme study':

> [F]rom this peregrination, thy wife with sheadinge salte teares, thy children with lamentations, nor thy frendes with wordes shal dehort & perswade the. In travailing, thou shalt not be molested with the inclemencye of th'Aere, boysterus windes, stormy shoures, haile, Ise, & snow. Comming to thy lodginge, thou shalt not have a churlish & unknown hoste, which shall mynister meate twise sodden, stinking fish, or watered wine. Going to rest, thou shalt not feare lowsy beddes, or filthy sheates. In Somer, the sone with his fierye beames, shall not vexe thee: nor yet in winter, stormye Saturnus shal make thy beard frosen. In sayling, thou shalt not dread Pirates, feare Peries and greate windes, or have a sicke stromacke though unholsome smelles.   (ibid., preface)

Many of the book's examples feature Norwich, including the lunar eclipses of 1556 and 1558; Cuningham adds, 'touching this my booke of Longitudes and Latitudes, I have for the chief places of Englande used bothe my frendes travailes, and also mine owne observations' (ibid., 169). His descriptions rely in part upon classical sources and show much of the prejudice of the time; the Irish are thus 'savage, wilde & beastly, they are given to sorcerie, superstition, & witchcraft' (ibid., 172), Africans are 'blacke, Savage, Monstrous, & rude' (ibid., 186), while the Indians of the Americas 'be filty at meate, & in all secrete actes of nature, comparable to brute beastes. Their bread is rotes, & theyr meate mans fleshe, for all theyr enemies, which they overcome, they with great banketyng devoure' (ibid., 201). A projected cosmography dealing specifically with England appears not to have been produced.

In 1563 Cuningham was appointed public lecturer at Surgeons' Hall, London, and from at least 1565 he lived at Coleman Street. In that year he wrote an 'Address to the professors of Chirurgerie', prefixed to Hall's translation of *Cirurgia parva*, and penned an epistle to his approved friend Thomas Gale, prefixed to Gale's *Works of Chirurgerie* (1586). Cuningham also wrote 'De definitione, causis, signis, symptomatibus, et curatione chameliantiaseos, sive, Morbi Gallici'. His religious sympathies appear to have been anti-Catholic. His 1564 almanac predicted a plague sent by God in response to Mary Tudor's burnings:

'O the blood, the blood of God's martyrs shed in London and through England for the testimonies of Christ, crieth for vengeance' (Capp, 157). Cuningham died in 1586. His will mentions a wife, Joyce.

SAMUEL PYEATT MENEFEE

Sources W. Cuningham, *The cosmographical glasse* (1559) · C. H. Cooper and T. Cooper, 'William Cuningham (or Kenningham)', *N&Q*, 3rd ser., 4 (1863), 305 · B. S. Capp, *Astrology and the popular press: English almanacs, 1500–1800* (1979) · J. Pound, *Tudor and Stuart Norwich* (1988) · Venn, *Alum. Cant.* · PCC wills, 1558–1604, GL, MS 9171/18ff. 3071–3074
Archives Bodl. Oxf., MS 14
Likenesses portrait, repro. in Cuningham, *Cosmographical glasse* · portrait, University of Illinois, Urbana-Champaign; repro. in W. Cuningham, *A newe almanac and prognosticator for 1558* · woodcut, BM; repro. in Cuningham, *Cosmographical glasse*

Cuninghame [Cunningham], **James** (*fl.* 1698–1709), trader and naturalist, was probably born in Scotland. He trained as a surgeon, and in London became familiar with the botanists Samuel Doody, Charles Dubois, and Robert Uvedale. In 1698 he sailed to China as a surgeon in the East India Company. In January, the ship was impounded by the Spanish on La Palma, Canary Islands, and the crew was imprisoned. Cuninghame contrived to collect plant specimens, as he did in June when the ship reached Batavia on the way to the station at Amoy (Xiamen) in the Taiwan Strait, and in Malacca (February 1699), the Cape, Ascension Island (May), and St Helena on the return voyage. In 1700 he sailed on the *Eaton* via the Cape to the settlement at Chusan (Zhoushan), south-east of Shanghai, on which island he remained two years. During his stay he turned his scientific knowledge to good account, and made large botanical and other collections.

Cuninghame was the first European to have successfully returned botanical collections from China, and he sent to other botanists, including Dubois, Plukenet, and Petiver, many new plants including flowering and fruiting specimens of tea, for which he was repeatedly thanked in their works. Cuninghame collected about 600 different species in China and they are labelled with full descriptions, localities, uses, and local names in beautiful handwriting, though, like later collectors, he was very restricted in the areas he was permitted to botanize. Plukenet published many of his findings and reproduced, in the third volume of his *Phytographia*, drawings of the specimens then in the hands of John Woodward (now in Sherard's herbarium at Oxford). Petiver described about 200 of Cuninghame's plants in his *Museii Petiveriani*; the plants now form part of the Sloane herbarium in the Natural History Museum, with 789 Chinese plant drawings Cuninghame had collected. From Ascension, Cuninghame forwarded to Petiver the first account to be published of plants and shells observed there, and his observations of Chusan agriculture, including the first description of the cultivation of tea, were printed in the *Philosophical Transactions of the Royal Society*.

In February 1703 the post in Chusan was abandoned and Cuninghame was sent to the company's station at Pulo

Condor to try to open up trade with Cochin-China, in competition with the Chinese. Although he continued to collect plants, perhaps to the neglect of his duties, the venture was otherwise a failure and, in 1705, the Macassar servants rebelled, fired the fort in the night, and massacred almost all the Europeans: all the survivors save Cuninghame were murdered by the Cochin-Chinese who went to aid the company but turned to looting instead. Cuninghame was wounded and imprisoned in Barrea for nearly two years, the company having failed to give appropriate tribute to the local king in the first place.

After his release in 1707 Cuninghame sailed to Batavia, and thence to Banjarmasin in southern Borneo, to take charge of that settlement for the company. Ten days after his arrival, the local people, incited by the Chinese, destroyed the post, which was abandoned. Soon after this Cuninghame embarked for England. His last letters, from Calcutta, addressed to Sloane and Petiver, were dated 4 January 1709, but he probably died at sea. An undated inventory of his goods, taken on the *Greyhound* by Captain Jones, comprised his clothes and various personal and trade items.

Cuninghame was elected a fellow of the Royal Society in 1699, but his publications were few. However, the specimens he collected were more significant, being distributed to the experts of his day and comprising the first major contribution to European knowledge of oriental plants. Robert Brown commemorated Cuninghame in the Latin name of the Chinese fir, *Cunninghamia*, now extended to the fossil plants *Cunninghamites* and *Cunninghamiostrobos*.

GORDON GOODWIN, rev. D. J. MABBERLEY

Sources J. Britten and J. E. Dandy, eds., *The Sloane herbarium* (1958) · E. Bretschneider, *History of European botanical discoveries in China*, 2 vols. (1898) · M. J. van Steenis-Kruseman, 'Cunningham (or Cuninghame), James', *Flora Malesiana*, 1/1 (1950), 123 · M. J. van Steenis-Kruseman, 'Cunningham (or Cuninghame), James', *Flora Malesiana*, 1/5 (1958), cclxx · H. M. Clokie, *An account of the herbaria of the department of botany in the University of Oxford* (1964) · A. M. Coats, *The plant hunters* (1969) · R. Desmond, *The European discovery of the Indian flora* (1992) · will and inventory, PRO, PROB 11/524, sig. 253
Archives NHM, Sloane MSS, letters · NHM, Sloane herbarium, specimens · U. Oxf., department of plant sciences, Sherard and Du Bois herbaria, specimens

Cuninghame, William (*c.*1775–1849), writer on prophecy, was born at Bridgehouse, Ayrshire, the only son of William Cuninghame (*d.* 1804) of Bridgehouse (who in 1779 purchased the estate of Lainshaw, near Stewarton, Ayrshire) and his second wife, Elizabeth, daughter of James Campbell, merchant, of Glasgow. He was educated in Kensington, London, later studying at Utrecht University before taking up an appointment in the Bengal civil service. While in India he came under the spiritual influence of the Baptist missionary William Carey. In 1804, upon the death of his father, Cuninghame inherited the Lainshaw estate and returned to Scotland. In 1818 he established a sabbath school in nearby Stewarton, subsequently seceding from the Church of Scotland after his views on grace and the atonement were criticized, his reasons being given in a pamphlet, *Narration of the Formation of a Congregational Church at Stewarton* (*c.*1822). He criticized the kirk session's decision of 1826 to prohibit Wesleyan ministers (teachers at his school) from receiving communion in the church. Between 1827 and 1843 he served as minister of a Congregational church in Stewarton, providing funds for the construction of a large meeting-house and comfortable manse, and a suitable endowment. As patron, in 1839 Cuninghame led the successful protest against the proposed division of the parish of Stewarton by the presbytery of Irving, sparking off the celebrated Stewarton case (1839–43); this in turn made the Scottish Disruption almost inevitable.

Cuninghame spent much of his time on his Lainshaw estate, where he developed an interest in scientific agriculture. Unmarried, his increasing deafness caused him to withdraw from much of outside life and to concentrate instead on the writing of over twenty books on prophecy and biblical chronology. He also published widely in a number of religious journals, especially the *Christian Observer*, sometimes under the pseudonym Talib or Sophron. Most influential of Cuninghame's numerous publications were his *Dissertation on the Seals and Trumpets of the Apocalypse* (1813; rev. edn, 1817), which argued for a wholly literal interpretation of the prophecies, especially those of the second coming, and his *Letters and Essays … on … Israel* (1822), which established that the Messiah would reign on earth at Jerusalem over the restored Jews, and that their restoration to Palestine would be a critical step in the 'end times'. Always interested in missions, he was an active supporter of the London Society for Promoting Christianity amongst the Jews and the Continental Society. His *Letter … on … Jewish Colonisation* (1849) urged the formation of a society to promote the agricultural settlement of believing Jews in Palestine. A complete list of his works can be found at the end of his *The Fulfilling of the Times of the Gentiles, a Conspicuous Sign of the End* (1847).

When Cuninghame was tempted away from Lainshaw it was usually to attend some gathering connected with the burgeoning prophetic movement, such as the first of the celebrated Albury conferences (1826) organized by another wealthy Scot, Henry Drummond. Here and elsewhere Cuninghame advanced the 'historicist' view of prophecy, dominant in protestant theology, which asserted the progressive and continuous fulfilment of prophecy from the time of Daniel, the Old Testament prophet, through to that of John, author of the Revelation (as opposed to the 'futurist' view advanced by John Nelson Darby and the Plymouth Brethren, which claimed that the larger part of the Apocalypse was still to be fulfilled at some future date). His writings were deeply pessimistic: he believed the world to be 'in the midst of the last great earthquake which precedes the second Advent' (*Christian Observer*, 1814, 759). Despite his opposition to the futurist position, Cuninghame came to accept the notion of the 'rapture', or the coming of Jesus in the air to take away his church prior to the commencement of the great earthly tribulation, albeit not the 'secret rapture' advanced by many of his prophetic rivals. The '2300 year' question was at the centre of his polemical contribution to contemporary prophetical debate. In offering an interpretation of Daniel 8:14 he claimed that the number 2300 (which in the text refers to days, but is understood as years) is correct, as opposed to Jerome's claim in favour of 2200 and the later Septuagint's claim in favour of 2400. His determined views on the minutiae of prophetic speculation, however, brought him into sharp conflict with several leading prophetic scholars, including George Stanley Faber, James Hatley Frere, Edward Irving, and the historian Samuel R. Maitland. His correspondence with the prominent evangelical Edward Bickersteth led to the latter's conversion to premillennialism (*Christian Observer*, 1850, 284). Cuninghame died at Lainshaw on 6 November 1849 and was buried there. With Faber and Frere, he ranks at the forefront of prophetic scholarship during the first half of the nineteenth century. GRAYSON CARTER

Sources W. H. Oliver, *Prophets and millennialists: the uses of biblical prophecy in England from the 1790s to the 1840s* (1978) • D. F. Wright, 'Cuninghame, William', *DSCHT* • L. R. G. Froom, *The prophetic faith of our fathers*, 4 vols. (1946–54) • Anderson, *Scot. nat.*, 1.747–8 • *Christian Observer*, 6 (1807), 701–5, 774–7 • *Christian Observer*, 7 (1808), 209–13, 345–8 • *Christian Observer*, 9 (1810), 16–17, 195–6 • *Christian Observer*, 13 (1814), 163–80, 752–60 • *Christian Observer* (1850), 284 • *GM*, 2nd ser., 32 (1849), 670 • J. Paterson, *History of the county of Ayr: with a genealogical account of the families of Ayrshire*, 2 (1852), 455–6 • D. Bank and A. Esposito, eds., *British biographical index*, 4 vols. (1990) • Allibone, *Dict.* • J. W. Brooks, *Dictionary of writers on the prophecies* (1835), lxxi • Irving, *Scots.*, 87 • W. Orme, *Bibliotheca biblica* (1824), 134–5 • Watt, *Bibl. Brit.*, 1.227 • [J. Watkins and F. Shoberl], *A biographical dictionary of the living authors of Great Britain and Ireland* (1816)

Archives NRA Scotland, family and estate MSS

Likenesses marble bust, Congregational church, Stewarton, Ayrshire • portrait, Presbyterian church, Lainshaw, Ayrshire

Cunliffe, Marcus Falkner (1922–1990), Americanist, was born on 5 July 1922 at the Municipal Maternity and Infants' Hospital, Castleton, near Rochdale, the second son of Harold Cunliffe (1888–1970), farmer, and his wife, Kathleen Eleanor Falkner (1897–1972), who was from Monmouthshire; her father had served in the Royal Artillery before taking up an administrative post with a south Wales steel company. The family lived at Diggle, on the edge of the Pennines, before Harold Cunliffe abandoned the land and began a profitable laundry business in Manchester, to which he drove daily. When Marcus was eight, the family and its business moved to Newcastle upon Tyne. Marcus first attended an elementary school in Jesmond, and then the Royal Grammar School, Newcastle, from 1932 to 1940. At the latter he was heavily influenced by two masters: Samuel Middlebrook, a historian; and the poet Michael Roberts (*d.* 1948), editor of the *Faber Book of English Verse*, as well as by Roberts's wife, Janet Adam Smith (*d.* 1999), who worked on the editorial staff of the *New Statesman*. In 1939 the school was evacuated to Penrith, Cumberland.

In October of the following year, Cunliffe gained an open scholarship to Oriel College, Oxford. He remained for five terms before attending officer cadet training courses at Perham Down, Wiltshire, and Sandhurst. In 1942 he was commissioned into the Royal Tank regiment. From June 1944 until May 1945 Cunliffe served (mainly as an intelligence officer) with 144 regiment, Royal Armoured Corps, 33 armoured brigade, seeing action in north-west France, Belgium (including the Ardennes counter-offensive), the Netherlands, and Germany. Towards the end of the war, 144 regiment was renamed 4th Royal Tank regiment. In August 1945 Cunliffe was given a privileged attachment to the military history team at the headquarters of the British army of the Rhine. He worked on an account of the Twenty-First Army group's campaigns that was later published (with co-author Hugh Darby) as *A Short Story of 21 Army Group* (1947).

In January 1946 Cunliffe returned to Oxford to read for the abbreviated 'wartime' BA degree in modern history, and in October 1947 he gained first-class honours. As his degree course was one year shorter than conventional degrees, he was permitted to spend the remaining money from his scholarship on postgraduate research. He completed a BLitt thesis entitled 'The British army as a social institution, 1815–60'. Cunliffe began by specializing in British history, and his serious interest in United States history was really a development after his time at Oriel. He had been impressed by the American contribution to the allied victory in 1945, had been absorbed by American literature since his schooldays, and was captivated by American culture, style, and the movies. He recalled that he had been 'cheered by the easy abundance of post-war America'. Indeed, he had been 'taken' by America (Cunliffe, 'Backward glances', 85, 86–7). As a result, he spent the years 1947 to 1949 as a Commonwealth fellow at Yale University, where he studied under David Potter and Ralph Gabriel.

In 1949 Cunliffe was appointed to the first lectureship in American studies in Britain at the University of Manchester. He proved a true pioneer in developing an American studies degree in a British university. He developed in his teaching interdisciplinary approaches that brought together perspectives derived from the combination of history and literature. His task was not easy, as British university life in the 1950s was insular and conservative. Cunliffe zealously built up the American collection in the university library ('All that American rubbish' was the unguarded opinion of the senior staff (private information)). Appointed head of department, he recruited a group of distinguished colleagues, including (among others) Dennis Welland, Maldwyn A. Jones, and Howard Temperley. 1954 was a year of achievement: he spent most of it as a Commonwealth (now called Harkness) fellow at the University of Chicago and was promoted to senior lecturer, and his first major book on an American theme, *The Literature of the United States*, was published. Cunliffe's approach was historical, and successfully blended 'biographical and socio-cultural information with stylistic and aesthetic observations' (4th edn, 10). *The Literature of the United States* remained the standard work for decades, and went through three further editions; the fourth edition (1986) included two new chapters on women writers and southern literature. The interdisciplinary direction that Cunliffe imparted to the subject was reinforced by his devotion to the British Association for American Studies,

founded in 1955. He served as its first secretary and then as chairman from 1962 to 1965.

Cunliffe devoted much of the early 1950s to writing British regimental history. *The Royal Irish Fusiliers, 1793–1945* (1952) and *History of the Royal Warwickshire Regiment, 1919–1955* (1956) are clearly the successful discharging of past obligations. Yet they played an important part in Cunliffe's future development because he began to demonstrate a skill at combining telling detail with the broad overview. This combination is evident in two of his mature books published at the end of the decade. *George Washington: Man and Monument* (1958) is a subtle short biography linked to an analysis of Washington as a national symbol. *The Nation Takes Shape, 1789–1837* (1959) offers a cogent, synoptic account of the period. Producing two books simultaneously was made possible by a fellowship held in 1957–8 at the Center for Advanced Study in the Behavioural Sciences, Palo Alto, California.

In 1949 Cunliffe married Mitzi Solomon, a sculptor, and daughter of a wealthy Jewish New York manufacturer of glass products. They had three children: Antonia, Shay, and Jason. The Cunliffes were an extraordinarily colourful couple. Their house in Didsbury, Maldwyn Jones recalled, 'became an acknowledged centre, not only for University colleagues, but also for the varied intellectuals whom the press dubbed the "Didsbury set"'. Cunliffe was generous, relaxed, charming, urbane, vivacious, witty, playful, and attractive to women. He was also a man of paradoxes and contradictions. His appearance changed over time from the well-groomed and clipped air of the ex-officer in tweed suits to a more flamboyant and modish look with longish hair and beard. An undergraduate at Manchester recalled that 'I was as impressed by his sartorial splendour (those *ties*) and glimpses of a lifestyle I had associated with film stars and actors, as with his seemingly inexhaustible knowledge of American history, literature … and popular culture' (White). But the showman, whether masquerading as bohemian or high society figure, concealed a deceptive capacity for hard work.

From 1959 to 1960 Cunliffe spent a year as visiting professor at Harvard, where he cemented a growing friendship with Arthur M. Schlesinger junior. Although given the chair of American history and institutions in 1959, Cunliffe had grown bored with Manchester, and in 1965 was appointed professor of American studies at the University of Sussex. He played a major part in establishing that university's exciting reputation during its first hectic decade. American studies at Sussex was at the forefront of new developments, as the subject embraced the social sciences and eventually topics such as women's history. Cunliffe moved easily and without self-consciousness in the circles inhabited by the most distinguished of American historians. His interest in historiography was demonstrated by the work he edited with Robin W. Winks, *Pastmasters: some Essays on American Historians* (1969). In 1972 Cunliffe's love affair with Sussex and his dedication to liberal values were badly bruised by the 'Huntington affair'. An invitation issued by a colleague to Samuel P. Huntington, an adviser to the Johnson administration during the

Vietnam war, distinguished political scientist, and author of *The Soldier and the State* (1957), to lecture at Sussex, provoked outrage and denunciation. Cunliffe supported the case for freedom of speech. This upheaval in his professional life coincided with personal storms and the formal end of his first marriage in 1971. The academic year 1969–70 had been spent at the graduate centre of the City University of New York. While living in New York he met and then in November 1971 married the journalist Lesley Hume (1945–1997).

Cunliffe's interests from the 1960s onwards revolved around the history of the presidency, military history, and aspects of American national identity. The last two themes tended to coalesce and resulted in Cunliffe's most important, original, and influential contribution to scholarship: *Soldiers and Civilians: the Martial Spirit in America, 1775–1865* (1968). This book is a study of national character and values that places the American military experience within a social context. Cunliffe was ahead of his time in developing a sophisticated concept of military history. The subject was deeply unfashionable at the time of the book's publication in the USA, when as a result of disillusion with the Vietnam war all things military were decried. *Soldiers and Civilians* did not receive the attention or praise that it deserved. Also in 1968 Cunliffe published *The Presidency* (producing books in pairs was characteristic of him). An enlarged edition appeared in Britain under the title *American Presidents and the Presidency* in 1972. Although a work of synthesis, this remains (in its third edition) one of Cunliffe's most enjoyable and sparkling books.

In 1973–4 Cunliffe spent another year in the USA, this time as visiting professor at the University of Michigan. He edited volumes 7 and 8, on American literature, for the *Sphere History of Literature in the English Language*. A year later he collaborated with his wife in producing *Burke's Presidential Families of the USA* (1975), voted 'Reference book of the year' by the *US Library Journal*. Cunliffe was also swept up by the ferment of debate over slavery and race relations provoked by Robert W. Fogel and Stanley L. Engerman's *Time on the Cross* (2 vols., 1974). His contribution was *Chattel Slavery and Wage Slavery: the Anglo-American Context, 1830–1860* (1979), a provocative study of American resentment over British criticisms of slavery. It had originally started life as the Lamar memorial lectures delivered in April 1978 at Mercer University, Macon, Georgia. Thereafter he produced no major work on American history: for several years he found the subject too restricting, and turned to world history, editing *The Times History of our Times* (1971) and writing *The Age of Expansion, 1848–1917* (1974).

The late 1970s were a period of some frustration and disenchantment. Cunliffe sought solace on the American academic scene: in 1976 he was awarded an honorary doctorate by the University of Pennsylvania; 1977–8 was spent as a fellow of the Woodrow Wilson International Center for Scholars, Washington, DC; he delivered the 1978 Jefferson memorial lectures at Berkeley, although these remained unpublished. The failure of his application for the Rhodes chair in American history at Oxford was a disappointment. Cunliffe had personal reasons for contemplating a permanent move across the Atlantic. In 1978 he met the American historian Phyllis Marynick Palmer (*b.* 1944), whom he married in 1984, his second marriage having ended in divorce in 1979.

Consequently, in 1980 Cunliffe left Sussex and moved to the George Washington University, Washington, DC, as university professor. He was only the second person in the history of that university to hold the title. The last decade of his life was spent keeping his older works in print and producing a volume of his essays, published posthumously as *In Search of America: Transatlantic Essays, 1951–1990* (1991). He admitted, 'I feel I have spent too much time in recent years putting coats of paint on old structures instead of completing new ones …' (private information).

Cunliffe was essentially a very modest man, but he tended to underestimate the esteem with which he was held. He certainly had not run out of ideas. In 1989 he signed a contract to write a collective biography of all the Roosevelts. He was acknowledged as the most fertile, creative, original, and adventurous British Americanist of his generation. He was an inspired (and inspiring) teacher, with a clutch of distinguished pupils: Sir Malcolm Bradbury (1931–2000), Michael J. Heale, and Michael C. C. Adams, among many others. He worked ceaselessly for the United States Information Agency, lecturing in India, Japan, Kenya, and much of Europe on their behalf. As a historian, he was happiest dealing with the period from 1775 to 1865, but he was more than just a historian, and his range was formidable. His purview swept every aspect of American culture and ideas, including art (the pictorial images in his books are more than just decorative), music, culture, mythology, literature, and thought, although his literary writings tend to treat thought as a branch of the history of ideas. Cunliffe had always turned his back on specialization; he was a polymath who was influenced by the social sciences, for his writings reveal a surprising attachment to 'models' as a method of explanation and means of comparison. It was emblematic of his paradoxical nature that his swirling visual and literary sense was complemented by a preference for typologies. All his writings are adorned with a graceful and evocative prose style. Cunliffe as a commentator on America stands comparison with Lord Bryce and Sir Denis Brogan.

Although an academic by training and inclination, Cunliffe had no patience with theoretical disputes. He had much in common with the pre-war man of letters, for example Leonard Woolf, who ignored disciplinary boundaries and scorned narrow specialization. Cunliffe, an indefatigable correspondent, cultivated a glamour and sage-like manner consistent with this kind of public figure. The true significance of his writings can be found in his dissection of ideas of American distinctiveness and the quest for American national identity. Cunliffe argued that the USA was not as exceptional as many American writers claimed. He always stressed the European (and especially British) threads in the fabric of American culture. In the 1960s he had been very critical of assumptions that the south was a distinct American section. The interconnections between Western cultures were a prominent theme in Cunliffe's corpus (he was a talented linguist, spoke French fluently, and had good German and also some Italian). In the mid-1980s, perhaps as a reaction to the chauvinism of the Reagan years, he embarked on an uncompleted, ambitious project on the emergence of the great popular author, a comparison of Walter Scott, Charles Dickens, Mark Twain, and Victor Hugo. He died of leukaemia in the George Washington University Memorial Hospital, Washington, DC, on Sunday 2 September 1990 and was cremated.   BRIAN HOLDEN REID

Sources B. Holden Reid and J. White, eds., 'Marcus Cunliffe: a pastmaster', *American studies: essays in honour of Marcus Cunliffe*, ed. B. Holden Reid and J. White (1991), 1–19 · M. Cunliffe, 'Cunliffe's early years', typescript, priv. coll. [B. Holden Reid] · M. Cunliffe, 'Backward glances', *Journal of American Studies*, 14 (1980), 83–102 · B. Holden Reid, foreword, in M. Cunliffe, *Soldiers and civilians: the martial spirit in America, 1775–1865*, 3rd edn (1993), ix–xv · M. A. Jones, 'Marcus Cunliffe: the Manchester years', *British Association for American Studies Newsletter*, 64 (July 1991), 19–20 · J. White, 'Marcus Cunliffe: an appreciation', *British Association for American Studies Newsletter*, 64 (July 1991), 7–8 · WWW · personal knowledge (2004) · private information (2004) [Keith Cunliffe; Dr Phyllis Palmer; Dr John White; Professor Vivien Hart; Professor Rupert Wilkinson; Professor Peter J. Parish] · b. cert. · *The Times* (4–5 Sept 1990) · *The Guardian* (4 Sept 1990) · *New York Times* (5 Sept 1990) · ANB

Archives George Washington University Library, Washington, DC

Cunliffe, Sir Robert Alfred, fifth baronet (1839–1905),

politician, was born on 17 January 1839, the eldest son of Robert Ellis Cunliffe (1808–1855) of the Bengal civil service, and his wife, Charlotte (d. 1856), eldest daughter of Iltid Howell. He was educated at Eton College, and in 1852 was appointed an ensign and lieutenant in the Scots Fusilier Guards.

Cunliffe succeeded to his grandfather's baronetcy and the family estates in Denbighshire in 1859, and retired from the guards three years later with the rank of captain. Thereafter, Cunliffe devoted himself to the public life of north Wales. He was a magistrate and deputy lieutenant of Denbighshire, and served as high sheriff in 1868. His political career began when he was returned for the Flint boroughs at a by-election in 1872 as a Liberal—an unusual affiliation for a member of the Welsh aristocracy at this time—but he was unable to hold the seat at the general election of 1874. He remained out of parliament until 1880, when he won the Denbigh boroughs by just fifteen votes for the Liberals, recommending himself to the electorate as a strong supporter of Gladstone's financial prowess: 'the exchequer of the country would never be right until it was under the management of Mr. Gladstone', he told an audience in Wrexham (*North Wales Guardian*, 20 March 1880).

On his return to parliament Cunliffe's career was chiefly notable for his speech in 1884 seconding Stuart Rendel's motion that government give the college at Aberystwyth a grant. He was spoken of as a possible candidate for office when a 'small berth' (as a groom-in-waiting) became

vacant in 1882, but was not appointed, perhaps because it was not certain he could hold his seat in the consequent by-election. At all events, he lost his seat at the general election of 1885.

The year 1886 witnessed the crisis of Cunliffe's political career. Strong supporter and neighbour of the premier though he was, Cunliffe professed himself unwilling to 'follow Gladstone blindly' over home rule, and after 1886 he was to be counted among the ranks of the Liberal Unionists. In 1892 he fought the Flintshire seat for the Unionists, adding a refusal to offer anything more than neutrality on the disestablishment of the church in Wales to his existing opposition to home rule. He was—perhaps inevitably—defeated. He ended his life as the chairman of the East Denbighshire Unionist Association.

Of his life outside politics, Cunliffe's obituarist noted that he 'never devoted much time to pleasurable pursuits'. Instead, he seems to have revelled in his role of active local leadership. His chief interest was the militia. In 1872 he was appointed lieutenant-colonel-commandant of the Denbighshire militia, and retired with the rank of honorary colonel in 1886. He was a staunch churchman, and was closely associated with the £10,000 renovation of the parish church in Wrexham, of which he was a churchwarden. His other interests were numerous. He became a county councillor in 1889, and was also a governor of the county school, a member of the Denbigh education authority, and a proponent of the university extension lectures at Wrexham. He served as president of both the Wrexham Area Literary Society and the local branches of the societies for the prevention of cruelty to children and animals. He was a trustee of the Wrexham Working Men's Hall Fund and chairman of the local directors of the Alliance Assurance Company.

Cunliffe married twice. His first wife, Eleanor Sophia Egerton Leigh, whom he married on 5 August 1869, was the only daughter of Colonel Egerton Leigh of Chester, and died in 1898 having had five children. His second wife, whom he married on 5 January 1901, was the Hon. Cecilie Victoria, daughter of Colonel the Hon. William Sackville-West and sister of the third Baron Sackville. Cunliffe died on 19 June 1905 at 17 Basil Mansions, Sloane Street, London, of pneumonia, aged sixty-six, and was buried in Wrexham cemetery on the 21st. He was succeeded by his elder son, Foster Hugh Egerton Cunliffe, who was killed in action on the Somme in 1916.   MATTHEW CRAGOE

Sources *North Wales Chronicle* (23 June 1905), 2 · *Dod's Parliamentary Companion* (1880) · Burke, *Peerage* · *The diary of Sir Edward Walter Hamilton, 1880–1885*, ed. D. W. R. Bahlman, 2 vols. (1972)

Archives U. Wales, Bangor, Yale MSS

Likenesses photograph, repro. in *North Wales Chronicle*

Wealth at death £63,088 15s. 8d.: probate, 3 Aug 1905, CGPLA Eng. & Wales

Cunliffe, Walter, first Baron Cunliffe (1855–1920),

merchant banker and governor of the Bank of England, was born on 3 December 1855 at 29 Kensington Gate, London, the eldest of the four sons and second of the six children of Roger Cunliffe (d. 1895), of Tyrrell's Wood, Leatherhead, merchant banker, and his wife, Anne Edge. He was educated at Harrow School, where he was in the shooting eleven, and at Trinity College, Cambridge, where he won the inter-university mile race in 1877—he earned a half-blue for running—and took a second-class ordinary degree in 1878. He then spent two years travelling widely and working as a stockman in Queensland, Australia, before returning to England and taking up a career in the City. In 1890 he and his two brothers Arthur and Leonard founded the merchant bank Cunliffe Brothers, with offices in Cornhill. On his father's death in 1895 he came into a substantial fortune and his estate in Surrey; indeed, the City believed him to be a millionaire. This fortune should have increased both his ability to do business and the stature of his house. Nevertheless, Cunliffe Bros. was never a front-rank firm, and on 1 January 1920—five days before his death—it was absorbed by the merchant bank Frühling and Goschen, which became the new house of Goschen and Cunliffe (which failed in December 1939).

Cunliffe's enduring reputation rests on his activities as governor of the Bank of England, on his chairmanship of the eponymous Cunliffe committee of 1918, and on his membership of the reparations commission of the British delegation to the Versailles peace conference in 1919. He became a director of the bank in 1895, deputy governor in 1911, and succeeded as governor in 1913. There were two decisive occasions during his period in office, one of which made his reputation and authority, the other of which badly damaged both. The first was after the outbreak of the First World War in August 1914, when the clearing banks refused or rationed gold sovereigns to their customers; the stock exchange was in turmoil, and bankruptcy threatened the merchant banks because their acceptance credits could not be repaid. Cunliffe successfully argued against the suspension of gold payments; he agreed that the bank would discount all outstanding bills of exchange (with the government standing the financial risk), which calmed the money market; and he placed guards at the doors of enemy banks to prevent removal of foreign securities. Cunliffe thereby gained great authority as governor of the bank, and he was asked to stay on beyond the normal two-year term, to retire only in March 1918.

But this authority increased the autocratic and aggressive, even bullying, tendencies of Cunliffe's character, and hubris brought nemesis. The bank traditionally controlled policy on exchange rates, but the Treasury's greatly increased spending overseas had encouraged an increasing interest in maintaining the rate of the pound. The bank and the Treasury were agreed on this, but Cunliffe, who had great contempt for Treasury officials, grew suspicious of the means by which the Treasury was financing its overseas purchases. In July 1917, during a period of turmoil in British financing abroad, he cabled the Bank of Canada in Ottawa, where some of the British reserves were held, ignoring the instructions of the Treasury. The chancellor, Andrew Bonar Law, was incandescent, and Cunliffe's friendship with the prime minister, David Lloyd

George, did not prevent his being forced to put his resignation into the chancellor's hands. His imminent retirement was announced in November 1917.

In 1918 Cunliffe nevertheless chaired the commission on currency and foreign exchanges, the first report of which dealt with the means whereby the gold standard could be maintained. His influence on the commission on the reparation of damage at the Versailles conference was irresponsible: he spoke of German payments of $120 billion, while J. M. Keynes of the Treasury put the German capacity to pay at $10 billion. Cunliffe knew little of Germany and admitted that his figure 'was little more than a shot in the dark as he had been pressed to arrive at it between a Saturday and a Monday' (DNB). He ultimately insisted on a lower but still astronomical figure (leading him and his British colleague on the commission, Lord Sumner, to be dubbed 'the heavenly twins'). This was his final public service.

Cunliffe was twice married: first in 1890 to Mary Agnes (d. 1893), younger daughter of Robert Henderson, a merchant, of Randalls Park, Leatherhead; and second in 1896, to Edith Cunningham, fifth daughter of Colonel Robert Tod Boothby of St Andrews. There were three sons and three daughters of the second marriage. Cunliffe was created baron in 1914 and GBE in 1917, and he received several foreign orders.

'Over six feet tall, of broad physique and rolling gait, with imposing features and a walrus moustache' (DNB), Cunliffe could appear a rock when reassurance of strength was needed, as in July–August 1914. His pleasures were traditional: he hunted and fished, shot game large and small, and farmed as a gentleman should; he was also a connoisseur of silver and antiques. No one called him clever: he frequently reacted by emotion and intuition rather than after thought and 'had the advantage of knowing his own mind, perhaps not a very difficult one to know' (Sayers, 66). Usually laconic, gruff with most, he could be jovial with friends. He was a director of the North-Eastern Railway from 1905 and of the P. & O. Line from November 1919. Cunliffe died of septicaemia after ten days' illness at his home, Headley Court, Epsom, Surrey, on 6 January 1920. He was succeeded, as second baron, by his son Rolf (1899–1963). KATHLEEN BURK

Sources R. S. Sayers, *The Bank of England, 1891–1944*, 1 (1976) • *The collected writings of John Maynard Keynes*, ed. D. Moggridge and E. Johnson, 16 (1971) • K. Burk, *Britain, America and the sinews of war, 1914–1918*, new edn (1985) • R. P. T. Davenport-Hines, 'Cunliffe, Walter', *DBB* • A. Lentin, 'Lord Cunliffe, Lloyd George, reparations and reputations at the Paris peace conference, 1919', *Diplomacy and Statecraft*, 10/1 (1999), 50–86 • *DNB* • *CGPLA Eng. & Wales* (1920) • A. Lentin, *Lloyd George and the lost peace: from Versailles to Hitler, 1919–1940* (2001)

Archives Bank of England Archive, London | BL OIOC, letters to Lord Reading, Eur. MSS E 238, F 118 • HLRO, Bonar Law MSS • HLRO, letters to David Lloyd George

Likenesses A. John, portrait, 1919, Bank of England, London • F. Dodds, portrait?, Bank of England, London

Wealth at death £650,000: probate, 3 Feb 1920, *CGPLA Eng. & Wales* • £905,192: Davenport-Hines, 'Cunliffe, Walter'

Cunningham family (*per. c.*1340–1631), nobility, was probably descended from vassals of the Moreville family, which in the twelfth century held extensive estates in Cunningham in north Ayrshire. Cunningham became a Stewart lordship under King Robert I. The first prominent member of the Cunningham family was **Sir William Cunningham** (d. 1396x9), whose father was a cousin of Robert I (the precise relationship is not clear), and who was himself twice addressed by David II in charters as *consanguineus*. Sir William's earliest recorded appearance is on a list of cautioners appointed in parliament in 1344 to ensure that the kindred of the late Alexander Ramsay would not harm his killer, Sir William Douglas of Liddesdale. In 1351 Cunningham was sheriff of Lanark, and his eldest son, Robert (who predeceased him), became a hostage for the ransom of David II in 1357. About 1361, possibly as compensation for this, or in recognition of some obscure hereditary claim, or as a counterbalance to Stewart power in the south-west, Sir William received a royal grant of the lands of the earldom of Carrick. Subsequently he was known as lord, rather than earl, of Carrick, and held the lands until 1368, when the earldom was granted to the king's nephew John Stewart (later King Robert III), on his marriage to Annabella Drummond. Sir William's principal estate was Kilmaurs, north-west of Kilmarnock, in Cunningham, and he also held the nearby lands of Lambroughton, Kilbride, and Skelmorlie, as well as Ranfurly in mid-Renfrewshire and Polquhairn in Kyle. He was also sheriff of Ayr, and the family was thus well placed to take advantage of the power vacuum left when the Stewarts ascended the throne of Scotland in 1371. All that is known of his wife, Margaret, is her forename.

On Sir William's death he was succeeded by his second son, **Sir William Cunningham of Kilmaurs** (d. 1413x15). He too was sheriff of Ayr. In 1384 (by which time he had been knighted) he and his retinue helped to defeat an English force which had landed at South Queensferry, on the southern shore of the Forth. Through his marriage to Margaret, one of the coheirs of the Renfrewshire family of Danielston of that ilk, the younger Sir William acquired further lands in Cunningham and elsewhere in Scotland, notably in Glencairn in western Dumfriesshire, from which the family was later to take its peerage title as earls of Glencairn. Sir William may also have been married later to Mary Stewart, daughter of *Robert III and widow of James Kennedy of Dunure in Carrick.

Sir William died between August 1413 and December 1415, and was succeeded by his eldest son, **Sir Robert Cunningham of Kilmaurs** (d. 1430/31), who was one of the Scottish lords who met King James I at Durham as hostage for his deliverance from English captivity in 1424. Robert was knighted at the king's coronation later that year, and was a member of the assize which convicted Murdoch Stewart, duke of Albany, and others of his family of treason at Stirling in May 1425. He was also one of four lords subsequently commissioned to lead a force to crush a rebellion led by James Stewart, a younger son of Duke Murdoch. Another leader was Sir John Montgomery of Eaglesham, whose daughter, Anne, Robert Cunningham contracted to marry on 6 June 1425. With his brother-in-law, Sir Alexander *Montgomery of Ardrossan [see under

Montgomery family], Sir Robert was in 1430 appointed joint keeper of Kintyre and Knapdale in Argyll, with custody of castles Sween and Skipness, as part of a campaign to assert royal control over the territories of the lordship of the Isles. But he seems to have been dead by 4 February 1431, and was succeeded by his son **Alexander Cunningham**, first earl of Glencairn (1426?–1488), who must have been still only a child.

Following Sir Robert's death, the office of bailie of Cunningham, which he had been given for life under the terms of the 1425 marriage contract, reverted to Sir Alexander Montgomery. However, when in 1449 James II granted the office heritably to Montgomery's son Alexander, this gave rise to an often murderous feud which was not finally settled until 1609. But arbitration in 1454–5 led to an agreement that Alexander Cunningham of Kilmaurs would act as bailie until Lord Montgomery's grandson, now his heir, reached his majority, and since Cunningham accounted at the exchequer in 1457 and 1458, this had obviously taken effect. He was in favour with James II, having supported him against the ninth earl of Douglas in 1455 (the Montgomerys, by contrast, were very probably Douglas supporters), and became a lord of parliament between 8 February 1463 and 13 January 1464 as Lord Kilmaurs, sitting in every parliament between then and 1488. He married Margaret, daughter of Adam Hepburn, second Lord Hailes. In 1464 he had to defend himself against a—surprising—charge of rendering assistance to the exiled Douglases. His defence, for which he offered to undergo three alternative modes of proof (an assize, compurgation, or combat), was successful. In 1466 he was confronted with the service of Alexander Montgomery as heir to his father in the office of bailie of Cunningham; it seems clear from the fact that the service occurred before sheriffs *in hac parte* at Linlithgow, rather than in Cunningham, that Kilmaurs was hostile to any reversion of the office to the Montgomerys. There is no evidence to show how the office was exercised between 1466 and 1470 (when Lord Montgomery died, having been predeceased by his grandson who left yet another minor heir, Hugh), or indeed in the 1470s. In 1481, however, the office was being exercised by John Ross of Montgreenan, king's advocate and a favourite of King James III; so it would seem that Kilmaurs had lost control of it.

Nevertheless, when Prince James rose against his father in 1488 Kilmaurs took the side of the king, perhaps stimulated by the presence in the prince's forces of Hugh, second Lord Montgomery. For assistance rendered to the king at Blackness Castle, Kilmaurs was on 28 May 1488 created earl of Glencairn. However, at the battle of Sauchieburn on 11 June 1488 the new earl was killed, possibly by Lord Montgomery. In October there was passed a parliamentary act rescinding all grants of new dignities by James III since 2 February 1488. The bailie of Cunningham was granted back to the Montgomery family by James IV in 1488 and was confirmed again in 1498. On 17 October 1488 the grant of the earldom was annulled by act of parliament, making all creations since 2 February 1488 void. Glencairn's eldest son, Robert Cunningham, second Lord

Kilmaurs (d. 1489) held only the lordship of parliament, not the earldom, and sat in parliament in 1489 as such. He had married, some time before 19 July 1476, Christian (d. 1491x6), daughter of John *Lindsay, first Lord Lindsay of the Byres (d. 1482) [see under Lindsay family of the Byres (per. 1367–1526)]. On his death, also at the hands of Lord Montgomery late in 1489, Robert was succeeded by his only son, **Cuthbert Cunningham**, second earl of Glencairn (c.1470–1540/41). When he was of age Cuthbert married, about 24 June 1492, Marion Douglas (d. in or after 1511), daughter of Archibald *Douglas, fifth earl of Angus (c.1449–1513), and his first wife, Elizabeth. The marriage helped to secure his family's position and the earldom of Glencairn was revived in his favour on 15 August 1503, on the occasion of James's marriage to Margaret Tudor. Cuthbert aided the attempt of John Stewart, twelfth earl of Lennox, to liberate James V from the Douglases and was wounded fighting in this cause at Linlithgow on 4 September 1526, when Lennox was killed. For most of Glencairn's lifetime the Cunninghams were at feud with the Montgomerys, vying for jurisdictional control of the Cunningham bailiary. Cuthbert's son, William *Cunningham, master and later third earl of Glencairn (d. 1548), burnt Eglinton Castle, the principal seat of the Montgomerys, in 1528, but the feud was eventually, if only temporarily, pacified in 1536. Cuthbert had died by May 1541.

William Cunningham, the third earl, married before 1509 Katherine (d. 1528x36), second daughter of William Borthwick, third Lord Borthwick. He was briefly treasurer in 1526 and after January 1536 he married Elizabeth, daughter of John Campbell of West Loudon. He was taken prisoner at the battle of Solway Moss in 1542. Ransomed shortly afterwards, he supported the English during the 'rough wooing' until defeated by James Hamilton, second earl of Arran, outside Glasgow in May 1544. His son Alexander *Cunningham, fourth earl of Glencairn (d. 1574/5), was in matters of religion a prominent reformer and a supporter of the king's party during the Marian civil war. Although the Cunninghams broadly shared their chief's enthusiasm for protestant reform, they were less inclined to support his political activities. Only the laird of Cunninghamhead joined Glencairn in the so-called chaseabout raid of 1565, directed against Queen Mary's marriage to Henry Stewart, Lord Darnley, while John Cunningham of Drumquhassill with other kinsmen held Dumbarton for the queen in 1568. Alexander was married first, about 1526, to Janet (Jane), daughter of James Hamilton, first earl of Arran, and then, after their divorce in 1545, to Jane (d. in or after 1575), daughter of Sir John Cunningham of Caprington.

Tensions between the Cunninghams and the Montgomerys resurfaced in 1571, when the fourth earl's son of his second marriage, Alexander Cunningham of Montgreenan, was appointed commendator of Kilwinning Abbey and contested the right of Hugh Montgomery, third earl of Eglinton, to act as bailie of the abbey's regality. However, **William Cunningham**, fifth earl of Glencairn (b. c.1526, d. in or before 1580), who was probably of age by 1547, showed little interest in his half-brother's dispute. He first attended the privy council in 1569, having married Janet (d. 1596), daughter of John Gordon of Lochinvar and his wife, Margaret, about 20 August 1547. He had died by 24 February 1580. In 1577 the Cunninghams were described as composed of 'men of fayre landes and of greate power of their owne surname' (Rodgers, 10) Their cadet branches included the lairds of Glengarnock, Cunninghamhead, Robertland, Aiket, Auchenharvie, Montgreenan, and Caprington, all in Ayrshire, although the earls of Glencairn also held lands in Renfrewshire, where their main seat at Finlaystone Castle lay near the River Clyde, and in Dumfriesshire and Dunbartonshire. The fifth earl's son, **James Cunningham**, sixth earl of Glencairn (c.1552–1630), participated in the Ruthven raid in 1582, but soon lost confidence in the new government and after its demise was reconciled to the king. In 1585, however, a Cunningham died in an attack on a Montgomery church, and shortly afterwards James signed a band with other kinsmen agreeing to protect whomever would assassinate Hugh Montgomery, fourth earl of Eglinton. The young earl, riding from Langshaw Tower, was ambushed and killed by Cunningham horsemen on either 18 or 20 April 1586. The Montgomerys retaliated by raiding Cunningham lands in the Irvine valley. Of the known murderers the laird of Clonbeith and the heir of Corsehill were killed within two years, while Robertland fled to Denmark to escape retribution; the laird of Aiket was finally shot in 1602. Kilwinning, who was implicated in the conspiracy, was shot outside his house in 1591, precipitating further violence between the kindreds, though support for the feud among the Cunninghams was never universal.

The crown made repeated attempts to reconcile the families between 1595 and 1604. Then on 1 July 1606, while parliament was sitting in Perth, the earl of Glencairn and Sir Alexander Seton, master of Eglinton, passed on the high street in the evening and fighting broke out between their retinues, at the end of which one of Glencairn's servants lay dead. Following this disturbance the king renewed his efforts to end the feud and the parties finally submitted to a decreet arbitral of 16 March 1609. At its height the feud had undoubtedly caused real privation for some of the families of the participants, but any adverse consequences for the Cunningham kindred do not appear to have been lasting. Indeed the laird of Robertland's self-imposed exile proved prosperous, for in 1590 he returned to Scotland in the entourage of Anne of Denmark, to a knighthood and to the office of master stabler to the new queen. Glencairn himself was an active member of the privy council and acted as one of the commissioners in 1604 for the proposed union with England. He married, first, on 5 September 1574, Mariot or Margaret (d. 1610), daughter of Colin Campbell of Glenorchy and mother of the seventh earl, and second, before 14 July 1612, Agnes, daughter of Sir James Hay of Kingask; she was formerly married to someone called Preston. Glencairn died after May 1630 and was briefly succeeded by his son **William Cunningham**, seventh earl of Glencairn (b. in or after 1575, d. 1631). William had married about 1609 Janet, daughter of Mark Kerr, first earl of Lothian, and mother of

William *Cunningham, eighth earl of Glencairn (1610/11–1664). He died in October 1631 and was buried with his ancestors in Kilmaurs parish church. His wife was still alive in 1647.

HECTOR L. MACQUEEN and JOHN SIMMONS

Sources NA Scot., Glencairn muniments, GD 39 · J. M. Thomson and others, eds., *Registrum magni sigilli regum Scotorum | The register of the great seal of Scotland*, 11 vols. (1882–1914), vols. 1–2 · G. Burnett and others, eds., *The exchequer rolls of Scotland*, 2–11 (1878–88) · W. Fraser, *Memorials of the Montgomeries, earls of Eglinton*, 2 vols. (1859), vol. 2 · *APS*, 1124–1567 · G. W. S. Barrow and others, eds., *Regesta regum Scottorum*, 5–6, ed. A. A. M. Duncan and B. Webster (1982–8) · S. I. Boardman, 'Politics and the feud in late medieval Scotland', PhD diss., U. St Andr., 1989, 171–8 · H. Boece, *Scotorum historiae a prima gentis origine*, ed. G. Ferrerio, 2nd edn (Paris, 1574), appx, fol. 400v · *Scots peerage* · Acta dominorum concilii, NA Scot., CS 5/19, fol. 132r · [T. Thomson], ed., *The acts of the lords auditors of causes and complaints, AD 1466–AD 1494*, RC, 40 (1839) · W. H. Bliss, ed., *Calendar of entries in the papal registers relating to Great Britain and Ireland: petitions to the pope* (1896) · *CDS*, vol. 3, nos. 1551, 1576, p. 434; vol. 4 · *Report on the Laing manuscripts*, 2 vols., HMC, 72 (1914–25) · J. M. Thomson, 'A roll of the Scottish parliament, 1344', *SHR*, 9 (1911–12), 235–40 · R. K. Hannay, ed., *Acts of the lords of council in public affairs, 1501–1554* (1932) · *GEC, Peerage* · *Reg. PCS*, 1st ser. · C. Rodgers, ed., *Estimate of the Scottish nobility during the minority of James the Sixth* (1873) · [T. Thomson], ed., *The historie and life of King James the Sext*, Bannatyne Club, 13 (1825) · military report on Ayrshire, BL, Cotton MS Titus cxii, fols. 88–9 · K. M. Brown, *Bloodfeud in Scotland, 1573–1625* (1986) · N. Macdougall, *James IV* (1989) · J. Paterson, *History of the county of Ayr: with a genealogical account of the families of Ayrshire*, 1 (1847) · D. M'Naught, *Kilmaurs parish and burgh* (1912) · R. Close, *Ayrshire and Arran* (1992)

Archives NA Scot., Glencairn muniments, GD 39

Cunningham, Sir Alan Gordon (1887–1983), army officer, was born in Edinburgh on 1 May 1887, the youngest child in the family of three sons and two daughters of Daniel John *Cunningham (1850–1909), professor of anatomy, of Dublin and Edinburgh universities, and his wife, Elizabeth Cumming Browne. His elder brother, Andrew Browne *Cunningham (1883–1963), became an admiral and Viscount Cunningham of Hyndhope. Alan Cunningham was educated at Cheltenham College and the Royal Military Academy, Woolwich.

Commissioned into the Royal Artillery in 1906, Cunningham served throughout the First World War on the western front with the Royal Horse Artillery and on the staff; he was decorated with the MC (1915) and DSO (1918) and was five times mentioned in dispatches. Cunningham served in the Straits Settlements in 1919–21, then passed Naval Staff College, instructed at the Small Arms School, Netheravon, and in 1937 as lieutenant-colonel attended the Imperial Defence College. In the same year he became commander Royal Artillery, 1st division, and in 1938 was promoted major-general to command 5th anti-aircraft division. Early in the Second World War he commanded several infantry divisions, and then in 1940 was selected as general officer commanding east Africa for the campaign to reconquer Abyssinia led by Sir A. P. Wavell.

Here Cunningham—a slight, fine looking, charming but sometimes choleric man—showed himself a brilliant, daring leader, moving with astonishing speed and achieving startling results. The campaign started late in January

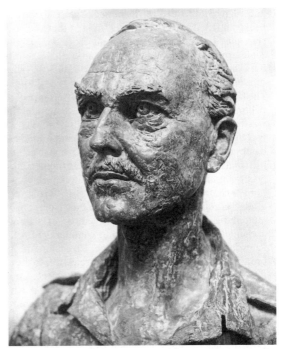

Sir Alan Gordon Cunningham (1887–1983), by Sir Jacob Epstein, 1943

1941. The forces of General Sir William Platt advanced from Sudan; Cunningham's—consisting of four brigades mainly of south, east, and west African troops—advanced from Kenya. Thrusting into Somaliland, Cunningham captured Mogadishu on 25 February, and by using seaports as supply bases, reached Harar a month later, having advanced 1000 miles. He then turned on Addis Ababa, which fell on 5 April. In two months he and his men had covered 1700 miles, liberated nearly 400,000 square miles of country, and taken 50,000 prisoners, all at the cost of 500 casualties. The last stages of the campaign saw Platt and Cunningham converging on Amba Alagi where the duke of Aosta surrendered on 16 May. Italian east Africa had been conquered in four months. Cunningham was appointed both CB and KCB in the same year (1941).

In June 1941 Wavell, commander-in-chief, Middle East, was replaced by Sir Claude Auchinleck, who chose Cunningham to command what was now called the Eighth Army. So Cunningham found himself running a mobile, fluctuating battle against Rommel in Auchinleck's winter offensive, operation Crusader in the western desert. He planned two separate actions—one, an armoured thrust with 30th corps which would outflank the frontier defences and concentrate at Sidi Rezegh, so drawing Rommel's armour to its destruction; second, a mainly infantry operation with 13th corps and the Tobruk garrison to overcome frontier defences. It turned out otherwise. The British armoured brigades were dispersed, outfought by Rommel's superior tactics and tanks. After a week's fighting Rommel led the Afrika Korps on a raid to the rear of Cunningham's forces. This move, together with his tank losses, greatly disconcerted Cunningham and he recommended to Auchinleck that the battle be broken off. Auchinleck correctly insisted that the offensive must continue, forcing Rommel back for essential replenishment, and, because he believed that Cunningham was now 'thinking defensively', he decided to relieve him of his command and replace him with Neil Ritchie. The fact was that Cunningham, with no experience of the pell-mell style of desert fighting practised by Rommel, was unable to control such fast-moving operations. Nor was his health up to the strain of command under such conditions. He accepted his dismissal with staunch dignity, and after hospital treatment returned to England.

Cunningham then held a series of appointments at home—commandant Staff College (rare for a non-graduate) and general officer commanding Northern Ireland and eastern command. In November 1945 he was appointed high commissioner and commander-in-chief Palestine and high commissioner Transjordan. He brought his customary courage and shrewdness to the difficult problem of attempting to mediate between Arabs and Jews, holding the appointment until May 1948 when the British left Palestine. Caught in 'a bitter contest between Jews and Arabs, each fearing domination by the other' (Cunningham, 490), he nevertheless 'enabled the British to depart from Palestine with a modest amount of dignity and, in their own eyes, self-respect' (Louis, 144). Indeed, Cunningham has been described by one authority as 'a remarkable proconsul' (ibid.).

In 1951 Cunningham, who had been appointed GCMG in 1948, married Margery Agnes, widow of Sir Harold Edward Snagge KBE, and daughter of Henry Slater, of the Indian Civil Service. After leaving Palestine he lived in Hampshire, becoming deputy lieutenant, and was able to enjoy his favourite pastimes of gardening and fishing. He was also colonel commandant, Royal Artillery, from 1944 to 1954, and president of the council of Cheltenham College from 1951 to 1963. He lived until he was ninety-five, and died at the Clarence Nursing Home in Tunbridge Wells on 30 January 1983. JOHN STRAWSON, *rev.*

Sources *The Times* (1 Feb 1983) · I. S. O. Playfair, *The Mediterranean and the Middle East*, 1–2 (1954–6) · *CGPLA Eng. & Wales* (1983) · W. R. Louis, 'Sir Alan Cunningham and the end of British rule in Palestine', *Journal of Imperial and Commonwealth History*, 16/3 (1987–8), 128–47 [special issue] · WWW · A. Cunningham, 'Palestine: the last days of the mandate', *International Affairs*, 24/3 (July 1948), 481–90
Archives NAM, corresp. and MSS · St Ant. Oxf., Middle East Centre, MSS; MSS as high commissioner for Palestine | Bodl. RH, letters to Arthur Creech Jones | FILM BFI NFTVA, documentary footage · BFI NFTVA, news footage · BFI NFTVA, propaganda film footage (Ministry of Information) · IWM FVA, news footage | SOUND BL NSA, news recordings
Likenesses J. Epstein, bronze sculpture, 1943, IWM [*see illus.*]
Wealth at death £57,835: probate, 11 April 1983, *CGPLA Eng. & Wales*

Cunningham, Alexander, first earl of Glencairn (1426?–1488). *See under* Cunningham family (*per. c.*1340–1631).

Cunningham, Alexander, fourth earl of Glencairn (d. 1574/5), nobleman, was the eldest son of William *Cunningham, third earl of Glencairn (d. 1548), and Katherine Borthwick, daughter of William, third Lord Borthwick.

Family background and early career With his father, Alexander was from his earliest active years an adherent of the party that favoured closer alliance with England, and at the same time became a prominent leader of the movement for religious reform. He spent some time in England as a hostage for his father, who was among those Scots prisoners taken at the rout of Solway Moss in November 1542 and later released on promising to further Henry VIII's dynastic plans in Scotland. In the 1540s both the third earl and his eldest son were in receipt of English pensions. In the spring of 1543 the English ambassador, Sir Ralph Sadler, in conveying to Henry VIII Glencairn's desire to have Alexander, then a hostage, released, declared:

> for such a man as his son is may not be spared out of so wild a country. I have talked with the man ... and in my poor opinion there be few such Scottish in Scotland, both for his wisdom and learning and well dedicate to the truth of Christ's word and doctrine. So that I think that if he were at home he would ... do much good here in the country where now the gospel is set forth in English and open proclamations made. (Sanderson, 59)

Sadler's last allusion was to the act of the Scottish parliament of March 1543 permitting the use of the New Testament in the vernacular, a measure favoured by the Cunninghams, father and sons.

Alexander was committed to the radical reform of the church, doctrinal as well as institutional. His satirical verse in the form of 'Ane epistle direct fra the holy armite of Allarit [Loretto, near Musselburgh, Edinburghshire] to his bretharen the Gray Freires' was included by John Knox in his *History of the Reformation in Scotland*. The poem not only ridiculed what Cunningham saw as the fraudulent miracles which the hermit of Loretto, Thomas Doughty, performed at this popular shrine, but it also put into the friar's mouth the faults which 'thir Lutherians' were said to have found in him and his brethren: their hypocrisy in pretending to be poor when they were not, their corruption of the creed, their false doctrines, and their dependence on their vows and religious way of life to 'bring you to salvation' which 'quite excludes Christ his Passion' (*Knox's History*, 2.334). Alexander's younger brother Andrew was tried for heresy in 1539, but was acquitted on making a formal recantation. These brushes with the ecclesiastical establishment did not deflect the Cunninghams from their adherence to protestantism.

During his father's lifetime Alexander was also groomed to inherit a position of leadership in the politics and society of south-west Scotland. His family's power rested on its possession of widespread lands in nine sheriffdoms, especially the lordships and baronies of Glencairn (Dumfriesshire), Kilmaurs (Ayrshire), Kilmaronock (Dunbartonshire), and Finlaystone (Renfrewshire). This territorial interest brought the Cunninghams into conflict with the Montgomery earls of Eglinton in Ayrshire and the Campbell earls of Argyll in the highland border-country, at the same time making them allies of the Stewart earls of Lennox, who also inclined towards alliance with England. Territorial possessions did not in themselves guarantee wealth. The handing over to Alexander by his father in 1545 of a chest containing 103 documents relating to their wadset (mortgaged) lands indicates an estate burdened with debts. Alexander himself borrowed heavily from Edinburgh moneylenders over the next decade. However, his military and social prestige remained undiminished. An English report in 1558 included the earl of Glencairn among the most powerful Scottish nobles.

Public leadership in the 1540s and 1550s The English invasions of 1544–5, launched in retribution for the breaking of the Anglo-Scottish royal marriage treaty of June 1543, severely tested the Cunninghams' support for Henry VIII's cause in Scotland and provoked English allegations of treachery against them. Yet Alexander, who succeeded his father as earl of Glencairn in 1548, while he tempered his pro-English efforts to take account of political developments at home, remained committed to Anglo-Scottish rapprochement and to religious reform. He was present at the trial for heresy in 1550 of fellow Ayrshireman Adam Wallace and publicly dissociated himself from the judgment. When Wallace declared that he foresaw his own condemnation at the hands of his judges, Glencairn turned to the prelates nearest to him and said, 'Tak you yon [the responsibility] my lords of the clergy; for here I protest for my part that I consent not to his death' (*Knox's History*, 1.115). His known attachment to the Anglophile party caused the queen dowager, Mary of Guise, to include him with a group of potential trouble-makers whom she took with her on a prolonged visit to France in 1550. He also received a French government pension, which he diverted to the use of one of his creditors in 1557. At the same time he was one of those who in the early 1550s were prepared to co-operate with Mary when she chose to conciliate rather than confront the Anglophile reformist party, and when the church itself tried to forestall trouble by holding a reform-orientated provincial council at her request.

Like others in his party, Glencairn may have hoped to achieve a *modus vivendi* with the political and religious establishments in which a gradual and peaceful reform of faith and practice might proceed. At Easter 1556, during John Knox's visit to Scotland, Glencairn invited the reformer to preach and dispense the protestant communion to a gathering of his household and friends at Finlaystone Castle, Renfrewshire. Afterwards, having followed Knox eastwards, he and the Earl Marischal persuaded Knox to invite Mary of Guise, now regent, to the preaching in Edinburgh, but she declined the role of patron of reform offered to her. From 1557 until the reformation crisis of 1560 Glencairn was a prominent member of the group known as the lords of the congregation, the political leaders of the protestant community. In March 1557 he and others sent Knox an invitation (soon withdrawn) to return to Scotland, and he was a signatory to the first band (or bond) of the congregation, drawn up in December 1557, by which the leaders of reform bound themselves to protect protestant practice and their chosen preachers. After Mary of Guise issued a proclamation against unlicensed preachers at Easter 1559 Glencairn and another Ayrshire leader, Sir Hugh Campbell of Loudoun,

sheriff of Ayr, warned her of serious trouble if she tried to enforce the prohibition. In that same season, when the former Dominican John Willock preached in the burgh church at Ayr, Glencairn was prepared to support him in his proposed disputation with the Catholic apologist Quintin Kennedy, abbot of Crossraguel.

Glencairn dominated a gathering of the congregation of Ayrshire which met at Craigie kirk towards the end of May 1559 to debate whether or not to join the mustering of protestant companies in their impending confrontation with the regent and her French-backed forces at Perth. Glencairn spoke out in favour of solidarity with national rather than local concerns at this important juncture:

> let every man serve his conscience. I will by God's grace see my brethren at St Johnston [Perth]; yea, albeit never man should accompany me, I will go, and if it were but with a pike upon my shoulder; for I had rather die with that company than live after them. (*Knox's History*, 1.171)

Having persuaded them to follow him, he then led the armed company of some 2500 to Perth. He subscribed the band drawn up by the congregation there on 31 May 1559 and acted as its delegate in meetings with the regent and her representatives in July. As the likelihood of military confrontation increased, he was one of those who wrote to Cecil in July 1559 explaining the congregation's avowed reasons for resisting the regent's government, maintaining that its prime concern was with the survival of the reformed faith, but pointing out the threat posed by France to Scottish sovereignty and English security, and asking for English support in the crisis. From the autumn of 1559 to the spring of 1560 Glencairn was closely involved in the actions of the congregation against Mary of Guise and for an English alliance. He subscribed the treaty of Berwick of 27 February 1560, under which the congregation was to receive English military help, and was among the Scottish leaders who met the English army when it entered Scotland at the end of March. In August he sat in the Reformation Parliament which adopted the reformed confession of faith and abolished the mass and papal jurisdiction.

Post-Reformation career Glencairn was sent to England as ambassador in October 1560, among other things to propose a marriage between Queen Elizabeth and the third earl of Arran. He was one of the nobles who subscribed the Book of Discipline, the blueprint for the organization and provision of the reformed church, in January 1561. He afterwards went to the west of Scotland, where, with the earls of Arran and Argyll, he helped to dismantle the apparatus of Catholic worship in former monastic churches. After Queen Mary's return to Scotland from France in August 1561 Glencairn became a member of the privy council. He led the seventy-seven individuals who subscribed the band of Ayr on 4 September 1562 in defence of the reformed religion. He attended the general assembly of the church in June 1564, when he and other politicians caused discord by sitting and deliberating apart from the ministers. In June 1565 the protestant nobles agreed to Mary's plans to marry Henry Stewart, Lord Darnley, only on condition that the reformed faith be established in parliament and the mass abolished. The celebration of mass in the queen's chapel was seen by them as compromising the 1560 religious settlement, although this had not been formally ratified by the queen. Glencairn's objections to the Darnley marriage probably arose from the fear that an heir would be brought up a Roman Catholic on Mary's initiative since Darnley was thought by some to be indifferent in religion and, more immediately, that the match would put an end to the hope of accommodation with Queen Elizabeth, who professed to disapprove of it.

Moved by these concerns, Glencairn joined the earl of Moray and other protestant lords at Ayr in August 1565 in preparation for their short-lived uprising against the queen's marriage, which became known as the chaseabout raid; since the marriage had by then taken place, committed protestants such as Glencairn may still have seen armed resistance as a means of putting pressure on Mary to ratify the religious settlement. On 31 August he was among those lords who marched on Edinburgh; in September they were put to the horn as rebels. From Dumfries that same month he and other rebel lords wrote at different times to Randolph, Cecil, Bedford, and even Queen Elizabeth herself asking for support for their stance and in defence of their heritages, which they alleged Queen Mary threatened. They requested arms for this purpose and vowed that all they sought was the establishment of the religion they professed and that the country should not be governed by strangers. On 1 October Elizabeth assured them that she would work for their reconciliation with Mary, but did nothing more to help them. On 6 October Glencairn was one of the Scottish nobles reported to have crossed the border and entered Carlisle, where they asked for asylum.

According to Knox, Glencairn returned to Scotland early in 1566. Although not personally implicated in the murder of Riccio on 9 March, he had been summoned to parliament with the other rebel lords to answer a charge of treason, but was acquitted with them on 12 March; he is said to have left Edinburgh on 17 March while the queen still threatened retribution on the Riccio conspirators. By 29 April, however, he was back on the privy council. On 1 May 1567, three months after Darnley's murder and shortly before Mary's marriage to Bothwell, he subscribed a band at Stirling in defence of the young Prince James, and he was among the leaders of the confederate lords who confronted the forces of Mary and Bothwell at Carberry, Edinburghshire, on 15 June, and to whom Mary surrendered. Following the queen's imprisonment in Lochleven Castle and her deposition on 24 July, Glencairn and his servants destroyed the altars and furnishings of the royal chapel at Holyrood; it annoyed some that he undertook this on his own initiative.

Glencairn was a firm supporter of the king's party and of the earl of Moray's regency. In one of the writs signed by Mary at Lochleven he was appointed joint regent with the earl of Morton until Moray's return to Scotland, or to act with Moray if he declined to be sole regent. At the coronation of James VI on 29 July he carried the sword of state, and he was one of only four earls to attend the convention of estates held in July–August. After Mary's escape from Lochleven Castle on 2 May 1568 he commanded a division of the king's forces at the battle of Langside, near Glasgow, on 13 May. He attended the convention of estates held by Moray in July 1569. In August that year he and Lord Semple were commanded to lay siege to Dumbarton Castle, the last stronghold of Mary's supporters. On the death of the regent, Mar, in October 1572 Glencairn was suggested as a successor, but the convention which met in November elected Morton. He remained a friend of John Knox and visited him in his last illness.

Family   Glencairn's first wife, whom he married about 1526, was Janet (Jane) Hamilton, daughter of James, first earl of Arran; they were divorced in 1545. They had three sons, William *Cunningham, fifth earl of Glencairn [see under Cunningham family], Andrew of the Syde, and James, prior of Lesmahagow, and a daughter, Margaret, who married first John Wallace of Craigie and second (as his second wife) Andrew, second Lord Ochiltree. In 1550 Glencairn married Jane Cunningham, daughter of Sir John Cunningham of Caprington, who survived him. They had a son, Alexander, commendator of Kilwinning, and a daughter, Janet (Jean, Jane), who married first (as his second wife), in 1573, Archibald, fifth earl of Argyll, and second, in 1583, Sir Humphrey Colquhoun of Luss. Glencairn made his will at Kilmaronock Castle, Dunbartonshire, on 9 April 1574. He was alive on 2 December that year, when he gave consent to a charter by his son Alexander, but had died by 8 March 1575, when that charter was confirmed by the crown. The date of his death given by the *Diurnal of Remarkable Occurrents* as 23 November 1574 may be an error for 23 December.

MARGARET H. B. SANDERSON

Sources NA Scot., GD 39 · LP Henry VIII · CSP Scot., 1547–63 · John Knox's History of the Reformation in Scotland, ed. W. C. Dickinson, 2 vols. (1949) · Scots peerage, 4.239–41 · M. H. B. Sanderson, Ayrshire and the Reformation (1997) · Edinburgh commissary court, registers of testaments, NA Scot., CC8/8/3, fol. 256 · J. M. Thomson and others, eds., Registrum magni sigilli regum Scotorum / The register of the great seal of Scotland, 11 vols. (1882–1914), vol. 4 · CSP for., 1564–5 · T. Thomson, ed., A diurnal of remarkable occurrents that have passed within the country of Scotland, Bannatyne Club, 43 (1833) · J. Spottiswood, The history of the Church of Scotland, ed. M. Napier and M. Russell, 2, Bannatyne Club, 93 (1850)
Archives NA Scot., Glencairn muniments
Wealth at death debts exceeded goods: NA Scot., CC8/8/3, fol. 256

Cunningham, Alexander, of Block (1650x60–1730), jurist and scholar, was the eldest of the six children of John Cunningham (d. 1668), minister of Cumnock, Ayrshire, from 1647, and Elizabeth Cunningham (d. 1677). His father, proprietor of the small estate of Block in Ayrshire, was a younger son of Alexander Cunningham of Collellan. Refusing to conform to episcopacy in the kirk, in 1662 he was confined to his parish, while his brother William, minister of Kilbride, was deprived of his. Cunningham probably graduated from the University of Edinburgh in 1676 before moving to that of Utrecht, where between about 1677 and 1680 he studied Roman law with Johannes

Voet, who later described him as his 'former pupil, beloved as one of the best' (J. Voet, *Commentarius ad Pandectas*, Leiden, 1698–1704, 48, xix, 2). He probably also studied with the classicist, historian, and bibliographer J. G. Graevius. By 1678 the 'discreet and intelligent' Cunningham was acting for British collectors at book auctions in the Netherlands (NL Scot., Yester MS 14407, fols. 53–4). He became a good friend of James and Robert Wodrow (the latter the apologist for Presbyterian resistance to the restored Stewart episcopal regime), although he was always happy to associate with supporters of the regime and was accused by one Presbyterian in 1686 of having grown 'lax and extravagant in his principles' (*Journal of the Hon. John Erskine of Carnock, 1683–1687*, 1893, 218).

In 1686 Cunningham was appointed tutor to Lord George Douglas, youngest son of the first duke of Queensberry. Cunningham was to ensure that Douglas, an intended diplomat, became skilled in Roman law, classics, and ancient history. The two travelled first to Utrecht, where Douglas studied Roman law under Cunningham's guidance, before in 1687 pursuing further study in Heidelberg, Strasbourg, and Basel. Cunningham also instructed Douglas in bibliography, guiding his collection of an important library of law, classics, numismatics, history, and modern—especially Italian—literature. Autumn 1689 saw them in Italy, where they stayed until 1692, when they moved to the German lands, Poland, and Denmark. They returned to London in late 1692 and reached Scotland in January 1693, having met many notables, including G. W. Leibniz.

Cunningham had contemplated a study of Anglo-Saxon (he later bought the Anglo-Saxon manuscript known as the Moore Bede, now in Cambridge University Library, before selling it to Bishop John Moore) but he now determined on a project to rationalize the Roman law. Lord George Douglas died in 1693; Queensberry decided to donate his books to the Advocates' Library in Edinburgh. Cunningham handed them over in 1695 while also donating a copy of the Spanish heretic Servetus's *Christianismi restitutio* (1553) to Edinburgh University Library in memory of his pupil.

In 1694 Cunningham was chosen as tutor to John Campbell, Lord Lorne, son of the earl (later first duke) of Argyll. The two did not go abroad until the spring of 1697, Cunningham spending much of the intervening period in London. There he moved in circles that included John Locke and Joseph Addison, while Francis Gastrell, Boyle lecturer in 1697, introduced him to Christopher Codrington, on whose behalf he collected books for the library bequeathed to All Souls in Oxford. He also acted as an intellectual intermediary between Locke and Leibniz. Famous as 'the best chess-player in Europe' (R. Wodrow, *Life of James Wodrow, A.M.*, 1828, 174), he came to the attention of Charles Spencer, the chess-playing bibliophile and third earl of Sunderland, with whom he remained close until the latter's death in 1722. Acting with his nephew James Logan in supplying books, Cunningham's knowledge and taste shaped Sunderland's great library.

Between 1697 and 1700 Cunningham travelled abroad with Lorne, visiting the Low Countries and (twice) Italy, collecting books. He projected 'a scheme for proving the divine original of the Christian religion' (R. H. Story, *William Carstares: a Character and Career of the Revolutionary Epoch (1649–1715)*, 1874, 257–8). This excited the interest of Locke, Leibniz, Pierre Allix, and others, including William Carstares and James Wodrow. However, though demonstrating a mastery of Hebrew, the early Christian fathers, and biblical and Judaic studies, Cunningham never carried out this work. He also proposed a new edition of Justinian's *Corpus juris civilis*, improving the transmitted texts of the Roman law through critical and historical scholarship while also aiding the student with rational and systematic commentaries. Travel permitted him access to important manuscripts and opportunities to buy books. In 1698 the Scottish parliament awarded him £150 per annum for five years (renewed in 1704) to support this work.

Between 1700 and 1703 Cunningham visited France, Italy, the Netherlands, and possibly Spain before in 1703 settling at The Hague, where, apart from a visit to London from 1716 to 1719, he lived until his death. He worked on the Roman legal texts, perhaps with undue optimism, thinking his edition near completion by 1705. His failure to collate the most important manuscript of the *Digest*, the *Littera Florentina*, was a major problem; after 1709 he had a competitor in Henrik Brenkman, a young Dutchman who made such a collation. Cunningham's character is revealed by his loan of rare books to Brenkman. He never entirely lost interest in his own project.

Disagreement with Richard Bentley's 1711 edition of Horace stimulated Cunningham to edit the poet. Cunningham formulated rules for editing ancient texts, reflecting his work on the *Corpus juris civilis*, and stressing the significance of the study of manuscripts and early editions. Eventually *Q. Horatii Flacci poemata, ex antiquis codd. & certis observationibus emendavit, variasque scriptorum & impressorum lectiones adjecit Alexander Cuningamius* and *Alexandri Cuningamii animadversiones, in Richardi Bentleii notas et emendationes ad Q. Horatium Flaccum* were published at The Hague in 1721. Cunningham thereafter worked on full notes for his text of Horace while producing editions of Virgil and Phaedrus, posthumously published in Edinburgh in 1743 and 1757 respectively. The first arose out of his work on Horace, the second was a response to Bentley's edition of 1726.

After 1720 Cunningham remained occupied with the antiquarian book trade, especially on behalf of Sunderland. He had assisted and advised his close friend Andrew Fletcher of Saltoun on the acquisition of law books for his major library. Cunningham supplied books to the Advocates' Library and bought at auctions in the Netherlands for Scottish collectors. Cunningham was a familiar figure at The Hague, visited by statesmen and scholars. J. G. Reinerding, son of the librarian at Wolfenbüttel, described him to Leibniz as 'an extremely friendly man' (Niedersächsische Landesbibliothek, LBr. 765, fols. 8–9, 27 Sept 1715). Generally good-natured, Cunningham was generous with advice and assistance to others—both scholars, such as Brenkman and J. P. D'Orville, and young law students. The most notable of the latter was Andrew Fletcher, Lord Milton, nephew of Cunningham's friend.

In January 1730 Cunningham suffered a stroke; he died, unmarried, at The Hague, probably some time before September 1730, with his nephew and heir George Logan, minister of Dunbar, in attendance. His literary remains were taken to Scotland, while his personal library was auctioned in Leiden between 20 and 28 November of the same year. His lasting legacy is probably the impact that he had on major libraries, such as the Advocates' Library, the Codrington Library, and Cambridge University Library (through Bishop Moore's collection), and on now dispersed collections, such as those of Sunderland and of Andrew Fletcher of Saltoun. He has often been confused with his relative Alexander Cunningham (1654–1737), the historian, who became British resident in Venice.

JOHN W. CAIRNS

Sources J. W. Cairns, 'Alexander Cunningham's proposed edition of the Digest', *Tijdschrift voor Rechtsgeschiedenis*, 69 (2001) · registers of deeds and testaments, NA Scot. · BL, Blenheim MSS · Leibniz-Archiv, Niedersächsische Landesbibliothek, Hannover · NL Scot., Saltoun MSS; Yester MSS; Delvine MSS · Universiteitsbibliotheek Leiden, Burman letters · Universiteitsbibliotheek Utrecht, van Eck corresp. · Bodl. Oxf., D'Orville MSS · Universitätsbibliothek München, Gronovius corresp. · W. A. Kelly, *Library of Lord George Douglas* (1997) · A. K. Swift, 'The formation of the library of Charles Spencer', DPhil diss., U. Oxf., 1986 · B. H. Stolte, *Henrik Brenkman* (1981) · *Bibliotheca Cuningamia* (Leiden, 1730)

Archives BL, Blenheim MSS · Bodl. Oxf., D'Orville MSS · Niedersächsische Landesbibliothek, Hannover, Leibniz-Archiv · NL Scot., annotated copies of Justinian's *Institutiones* and Best's *Ratio emendandi leges* · NL Scot., Saltoun MSS

Cunningham, Alexander (1654–1737), historian and diplomat, has often been confused with the critic and jurist of the same name (c.1650–1730), especially as they in some ways had parallel lives, and knew the same people. His parentage is uncertain: Alexander was a favourite Christian name among several branches of the house of Cunningham. He was clearly not the son of the minister of Ettrick, as was long asserted, but he seems to have been linked closely to the Glencairn family; he was a relation of General Henry Cunningham, governor of Jamaica, a Glencairn descendant. Virtually nothing is known for certain about his youth: he may have been forced to go to Ireland in the aftermath of the Rye House plot of 1683; later in the 1680s he was possibly part of the Scottish expatriate community in the United Provinces, where he also seems to have made friends with English refugees, and he may have travelled to England with William of Orange in 1688.

From 1692 to 1695 Cunningham was travelling tutor to James Carmichael, later earl of Hyndford, and his brother, William, future solicitor-general of Scotland; they spent two winters at Utrecht and Franeker. He later observed that there were so many Cunninghams tutoring in Europe at this time 'that it was believed in Germany that "Cunningham" was English for a travelling governor' (Cunningham, *History*, 1.xxxviii). He spent much of the period from 1697 to 1700 in Italy; in June 1699 he was in Florence,

corresponding with Antonio Magliabechi, the renowned scholar and bibliophile, who was librarian to Grand Duke Cosimo III. In 1701 Cunningham was dispatched on an important mission to Paris. This was nominally connected with a projected commercial treaty between Scotland and France, on which he had conferences with the marquis de Torcy, but it also involved him in spying on French military preparations. In December 1701 he returned to Rome with Nicholas Leake and William Moncrief, and was still there in April 1702.

Under Queen Anne, Cunningham continued to be an active agent of the whig party. 1703 saw him visiting Hanover with Addison, exchanging letters with Leibniz, and aiding the reconciliation of Somers and Harley. Between 1703 and 1705 he corresponded with the Dutch humanist Gisbert Cuper, burgomeester of Deventer, mainly on numismatics; he acted as intermediary in Cuper's sale of medals to the earl of Pembroke. He was well acquainted with, and often consulted by, the framers of the Anglo-Scottish Union of 1707. After spending time in the Netherlands and Italy in 1706 and 1707, he was back in London by July 1707, probably bringing the government news of the failure of the assault on Toulon. Over the following year he had a lengthy political correspondence with the duke of Montrose, especially over the current election, and he influenced the passage of the whig bill to restrain the power of cathedral deans. Towards the end of 1710, on the fall of the whig ministry, Cunningham returned to tutoring, accompanying Lord Lonsdale to Germany and Italy. He remained in Italy until March 1712.

The Hanoverian succession brought him his reward: on 15 August 1715 he was appointed British ambassador to Venice. From there he kept a watchful eye on Jacobite machinations, while attempting to stop their credit; he prevented British soldiers from being taken into Venetian service; and he aided George I's efforts at mediation between Venice and the Ottoman Turks. He contested his recall in June 1719 and eventually left Venice on 5 November. Returning on a pension to England by January or February 1720, Cunningham seems to have qualified as a barrister and—although there is no evidence he ever practised in the courts—to have been much in demand as a chamber counsel.

During his retirement Cunningham worked on his *History of Great Britain from the Revolution in 1688 to the Accession of George the First*. After his death the *History* came into the possession of Thomas Hollingbery, archdeacon of Chichester, who, unsure if there was a market for the lengthy work in its original Latin, had it translated into English, with a suitable introduction, by William Thomson, the continuator of Robert Watson's *Philip III*, who contributed to the confusion about Cunningham's identity. The *History* was published in two quarto volumes in 1787. Cunningham was clearly a man of strong views—the earl of Buchan called him 'ultimus Scotorum' (Horn, 'Scottish Writers', 17)—and he particularly blamed the Scottish nobility for subjecting almost every aspect of Scottish government to English direction in the century prior to the

Union. The *History* is largely a detailed narrative of military campaigns, allied to lengthy treatment of domestic political matters, including reflections on the characters and actions of leading politicians, with most of whom he was acquainted.

Stylistically William Thomson found Cunningham 'like Erasmus, master of the whole compass of latinity' (Cunningham, *History*, 1.lxviii–lxix). At times his pithy brevity rivalled that of Tacitus; at others it became 'bold and ardent' (ibid., 1.lxxiii), as when at the siege of Lille (1708) the allies 'ascended the enemy's works … as if they had been storming the flaming vault of heaven' (ibid., 1.lxxiv). Overall Cunningham drew his characters with discriminating impartiality. Alongside Somers, Godolphin, and Harley he praised the tory Rochester just as highly. He compared Peterborough favourably with Marlborough, the whig hero. And he had much to say in favour of James II before his accession. His hero was William III: 'in his common conversation … courteous and affable; in matters of importance, grave and reserved … so mild and merciful that he would have pardoned his worst enemies' (ibid., 1.255). Bishop Burnet, 'by nature double-minded' (ibid., 1.60), was his *bête noire*. Collectively, his main scorn was reserved for Scottish highlanders, women, and priests. Highlanders 'in time of peace … live by rapine', in battle they target the enemy's baggage, and 'if that once falls into their hands, disregarding all discipline and oaths … home they run' (ibid., 1.122). Although individuals like Queen Mary and the electress Sophia gained his respect, Cunningham approved of the Salic law, which in France 'declared women to be adapted only to spinning and other domestic employments, but no way fit to treat of public affairs' (ibid., 2.143). He described the tories as 'indeed no wiser than women' (ibid.). Women also tended to fall under the malign influence of priests. He extolled such bishops as Compton and Tillotson, 'the grace and ornament of his order' (ibid., 1.131), directing his ire towards high-church clerics, especially Sacheverell—'a man of uncommon impudence' (ibid., 2.275)—but, above all, towards the sophistical Jesuits: 'what society of men … has been more inhumanly cruel, or … in so many instances betrayed the abominable principles of a Nero?' (ibid., 2.421).

Cunningham died on 15 May 1737 in London, and was buried the same day in the chancel of St Martin-in-the-Fields. Apparently unmarried, he left most of his wealth to a nephew. Had his *History* been published soon after his death, it might have had considerable influence, but by 1787 historians had access to a variety of official sources and family papers, and Cunningham's work is usually acknowledged only in the odd footnote.

BASIL MORGAN

Sources D. B. Horn, 'Some Scottish writers of history in the 18th century', *SHR*, 40 (1961), 1–18 · J. W. Cairns, 'Alexander Cunningham's proposed edition of the Digest: an episode in the history of the Dutch elegant school of Roman law (part 1)', *Tijdschrift voor Rechtsgeschiedenis* (2001) · *DNB* · Chambers, *Scots.* (1835) · D. B. Horn, *The British diplomatic service, 1689–1789* (1961) · G. Holmes, *The trial of Doctor Sacheverell* (1973) · J. Ingamells, ed., *A dictionary of British and Irish travellers in Italy, 1701–1800* (1997) · D. Irving, *Lives of Scotish writers*, 1 (1839), 234–8 · Crito, 'On the supposed identity of Cunningham the critic and Cunningham the historian', *Scots Magazine and Edinburgh Literary Miscellany*, 66 (1804), 731–3 · 'A friend to accuracy', *GM*, 1st ser., 88/2 (1818), 100–02 · *The letters of Joseph Addison*, ed. W. Graham (1941) · P. Smithers, *The life of Joseph Addison*, 2nd edn (1968) · will, PRO, PROB 11/683, sig. 102 · parish register, St Martin-in-the-Fields, City Westm. AC, 15 May 1737 [burial] · *Jean Le Clerc: epistolario*, ed. M. G. Sina and M. Sina, 2 (Florence, 1991), 44–5 · *Correspondence of George Baillie of Jerviswood, 1702–1708*, ed. G. E. M. Kynynmond (1842) · 'Letters of Andrew Fletcher of Saltoun and his family, 1715–1716', ed. I. J. Murray, *Miscellany … X*, Scottish History Society, 4th ser., 2 (1965), 143–73

Archives Biblioteca Nazionale Centrale, Florence, letters to Antonio Magliabechi, Magl. VIII 1160, nos. 46, 47 · BL, corresp. with Lord Townshend and Horace Walpole concerning Lord Lonsdale and politics, both British and international, Add. MS 38501 · BL, letters to H. Worsley concerning his business as ambassador at Venice, Add. MS 15936 · CUL, letters to Sir Isaac Newton, Add. MS 4007, fols. 569–571.A.C · Koninklijke Bibliotheek, The Hague, corresp. with Gisbert Cuper, burgomeester of Deventer, primarily on numismatics, 72 H 21 · NA Scot., Montrose muniments, letters to duke of Montrose concerning political matters, especially the election, GD 220/5/127/1–14 · NA Scot., Stair muniments, letters to earl of Stair concerning politics and international affairs, GD 135/141/3a, 6: 10 · NA Scot., Stair muniments, letters to Stair concerning international affairs, GD 135/141/10, 14, 21, 24 · Niedersächsische Landesbibliothek, Hannover, Leibniz archive, letters to G. W. Leibniz, LBr.186, fols. 4–13 · Universiteitsbibliotheek Leiden, letters to P. Burman concerning literary matters and numismatics, MS Burm. Q.23.1–2

Wealth at death over £12,000: Crito, 'On the supposed identity', 733; will, NA Scot., CC 8/8/101, fols. 223v–227v; will, PRO, PROB 11/683, sig. 102

Cunningham, Sir Alexander (1814–1893), army officer in the East India Company and archaeologist, was born at John Street, Westminster, on 23 January 1814, the second son of Allan *Cunningham (1784–1842), Scottish poet and author, and his wife, Jean, *née* Walker (1791–1864), and brother of Joseph Davey *Cunningham (1812–1851), Peter *Cunningham (1816–1869), and Francis *Cunningham (1820–1875). With his brother Joseph he was educated at Christ's Hospital, and both brothers were given Indian cadetships through the influence of Sir Walter Scott. Alexander attended Addiscombe College from 1829 to 1831, and was commissioned second lieutenant in the Bengal Engineers on 9 June 1831. After the usual technical training at Chatham, he reached India on 9 June 1833. His first three years were passed with the sappers at Delhi and in other ordinary duties. Lord Auckland, on his arrival in India in 1836, appointed him an aide-de-camp. For four years he served on the staff, and his identity can be detected under his initials in Emily Eden's *Up the Country*. During this period he first visited Kashmir, then almost *terra incognita* to the British.

On his marriage in 1840 to Alice, daughter of Martin Whish, of the Bengal civil service, Cunningham accepted the appointment of executive engineer to the king of Oudh. While laying out the new road from Lucknow to Cawnpore, he was called away in 1842 to active service, to assist in suppressing an uprising in Bundelkhand headed by the raja of Jaipur. He was next appointed to the new military station of Nowgong in central India. In December

1843 he was present at the battle of Panniar, fought against the rebellious troops of Gwalior, where he succeeded in turning the enemy's guns against themselves. He received six months' *batta* (extra pay), and the promise of brevet rank. During the next two years (1844 and 1845) he acted as executive engineer at Gwalior, where he built a ten-arched stone bridge over the Morar River. In February 1846 he was summoned to join the army of the Sutlej, just before the battle of Sobraon. He constructed two bridges of boats across the Beas River, and so he established his reputation as a field engineer.

After the First Anglo-Sikh War the territory between the Sutlej and Beas rivers was annexed and placed under John Lawrence, who appointed Cunningham to occupy the hill tracts of Kangra and Kulu. As reward for his success in this he was chosen to demarcate the frontier between the Kashmir province of Ladakh and Tibet. At first he had to return, but ultimately he accomplished the task with Sir Richard Strachey. He also settled the boundary between the states of Bikaner and Bahawalpur.

In the Second Anglo-Sikh War (1848–9) Cunningham again served as field engineer, in command of the pontoon train. He was present at the battles of Chilianwala and Gujrat, was mentioned in dispatches, and received a brevet majority. At the peace he returned to Gwalior, and explored the Buddhist monuments of central India. In 1853 he was transferred to Multan, where he designed the monument to P. A. V. Agnew and W. A. Anderson, whose murder had formed the prelude to the Second Anglo-Sikh War. In 1856, now lieutenant-colonel, he was promoted chief engineer in Burma, then newly annexed. Within two years he had extricated the accounts from confusion and organized a public works department. He also visited every out-station in the province from Toungoo to Tavoy. He was thus absent from India during the uprising of 1857. After its suppression he was appointed in November 1858 chief engineer in the North-Western Provinces, where he implemented similar reorganization. He retired with the rank of major-general on 30 June 1861.

In 1861 Cunningham began a new career by which he became better known than as a soldier or administrator, when Lord Canning appointed him to the new post of archaeological surveyor to the government of India. In his early days Cunningham had formed the acquaintance of James Prinsep, the founder of the scientific study of Indian coins and inscriptions. The first of his many contributions to the *Journal of the Bengal Asiatic Society* was an appendix to Prinsep's 1834 paper on the relics discovered in the Manikyala Tope. In 1837 he excavated on his own responsibility—as was then usual—the Buddhist ruins near Benares known as Sarnath, and made careful drawings of the sculptures. His visits to Kashmir and his work on the boundary commission resulted in two monographs, published in 1848 and 1854. The results of his exploration in central India with his friend Colonel Maisey, *The Bhilsa Topes* (1854), was the first serious attempt to reconstruct the history of Buddhism from its architectural remains. At the time of his appointment to his new archaeological post, Cunningham therefore had accumulated both knowledge and data which enabled him to produce four valuable reports within as many years. In 1865, for economic reasons, his department was abolished, and he returned to Britain. He wrote *The Ancient Geography of India, Part I: the Buddhist Period* (1871), which he intended to follow by another volume (never written) on the Muslim period.

In 1870 Lord Mayo re-established the archaeological survey, and appointed Cunningham its director-general. Every cold season he minutely explored some portion of the immense ruin-strewn plain of northern India, from Taxila on the west to Gaur on the east. Of twenty-four annual reports, thirteen embodied the results of his own discoveries, while the remainder were written under his supervision. During this period he published the first volume of the *Corpus inscriptionum Indicarum* (Calcutta, 1877), containing the first collected edition of the edicts of Asoka, *The Stupa of Bharhut* (1879), and *The Book of Indian Eras* (1883), with tables for calculating dates. In September 1885 he finally retired.

After his return to Britain, Cunningham continued his studies to the very last. In 1892 he brought out a magnificently illustrated volume entitled *Mahabodhi*, on the great Buddhist temple near Gaya in Bengal. But the chief interest of his last years was numismatics. In India he had formed an unequalled collection of coins, which he used as historical evidence. An example was the paper he contributed to the 1892 Oriental Congress, entitled 'The Ephthalites or White Huns', in which he first collected the literary evidence, and then illuminated the subject from his numismatic learning. In *Coins of Ancient India* (1891) he proposed original views on the origin of money, and maintained that coined money was known to the Indians before Alexander's invasion. This was followed by the posthumously published *Coins of Medieval India* (1894), and by a series of papers in the *Numismatic Chronicle* on the coins of the Indo-Scythians.

Much of Cunningham's collection, chiefly copper coins, together with his papers and notebooks, was lost in the steamship *Indus*, which foundered off the coast of Ceylon in November 1884. The gold and silver pieces escaped, having previously been shipped to England. During his lifetime Cunningham allowed the British Museum to buy all those needed for its collection, virtually at the price they had cost him. After his death those which he had more recently acquired were similarly sold. He was appointed CSI when the Order of the Star of India was enlarged in 1871, CIE in 1878, and KCIE in 1887. Cunningham died on 28 November 1893 at his residence, 2 Cranley Mansions, Gloucester Road, South Kensington, London, after a lingering illness; he was buried in the family vault in Kensal Green cemetery, London. His wife had predeceased him. He was survived by two sons: Lieutenant-Colonel Allan J. C. Cunningham (1842–1928) served in the Bengal and Royal Engineers, and Sir Alexander F. D. Cunningham (1852–1935) in the Indian Civil Service.

J. S. COTTON, *rev.* JAMES LUNT

Sources *Royal Engineers Journal* (1 March 1894) · *Hart's Army List* · M. Edwardes, *British India* (1967) · H. M. Vibart, *Addiscombe: its heroes and men of note* (1894) · E. W. C. Sandes, *The military engineer in India*, 1 (1933) · P. Moon, *The British conquest and dominion of India* (1989) · T. A. Heathcote, *The military in British India: the development of British land forces in south Asia, 1600–1947* (1995) · E. Miller, *That noble cabinet: a history of the British Museum* (1974) · Boase, *Mod. Eng. biog.* · CGPLA Eng. & Wales (1894)

Wealth at death £26,040 17s. 10d.: probate, 21 Feb 1894, CGPLA Eng. & Wales

Cunningham, Allan [*pseud.* Hidallan] (1784–1842), poet and songwriter, was born in a cottage near Blackwood House in the parish of Keir, Dumfriesshire, on 7 December 1784. His father, John Cunningham (1743–1800), was descended from an Ayrshire family, and in 1784 was factor to a Mr Copeland of Blackwood. John Cunningham married Elizabeth Harley, daughter of a Dumfries merchant, and they had five sons and four daughters. James, the eldest son (1765–1832), became a builder and contributed to magazines. Thomas Mounsey *Cunningham (1776–1834) became managing clerk to Sir John Rennie, the engineer; he wrote songs and poetry and contributed articles to the *Edinburgh Magazine*. John, the third son, died young. Peter Miller *Cunningham (1789–1864), the fifth son, became a naval surgeon.

When Allan Cunningham, the fourth son, was two years old, his father became factor to Patrick Miller of Dalswinton, and was a friend and neighbour of Burns during the poet's Ellisland period. The young Allan was educated at a dame-school at Quarrelwood, and before completing his eleventh year was apprenticed to his brother James, then a stonemason in Dalswinton village. In leisure moments he read all the books he could procure, picked up popular poetry, was a welcome guest at village merrymakings, and fond of practical jokes. During the fears of an invasion he joined another lad in alarming the whole countryside by putting mysterious marks on the houses by night, which were attributed to French agents. They escaped detection. He heard Burns recite 'Tam O'Shanter', and later walked in the poet's funeral procession. When about eighteen he went with his brother James to pay a visit of homage to James Hogg, who became a warm friend of both brothers. He paid 24s. for a copy of Scott's *Lay of the Last Minstrel* on its publication in 1805, and when *Marmion* came out walked to Edinburgh and back to catch a glimpse of the author. A letter to the minister of Dalswinton, John Wightman (April 1806), shows that he was then reading widely and writing poetry. Some poems by him, signed Hidallan (a hero of Ossian's), were published in *Literary Recreations* (1807), edited by Eugenius Roche. His employer offered him a partnership, which he declined. While working on the mansion of Arbigland he fell in love with Jean Walker (1791–1864), a servant in the farm where he lodged, and wrote the song 'The Lass of Preston Mill' for her.

In 1809 R. H. Cromek was travelling in Scotland to collect songs. He brought an introduction to Cunningham from Mrs Fletcher, well known in Edinburgh circles. Cunningham produced his poems, which Cromek thought poor imitations of Burns. Cunningham then hit upon the plan of disguising them as old songs. Cromek was impressed and probably taken in. He accepted them readily, stating 'give me more' (Hogg, 51). Cunningham continued to forward ballads to Cromek in London, and Cromek persuaded him to go to London himself and try the literary life. Cunningham consented, reaching London on 9 April 1810. The collection *Remains of Nithsdale and Galloway Song* appeared the following December, of which Cunningham says that 'every article but two little scraps was contributed by me' (ibid., 79), a fact not discernible from Cromek's acknowledgement in the introduction of Cunningham's services in drawing 'many pieces from obscurity'. The book, which contains interesting accounts in prose of the Scottish border peasantry, obviously by Cunningham, was favourably received, and the mystification as to the origin of the ballads was always transparent to some, especially Scott and Hogg. An article on this volume by Professor John Wilson in *Blackwood's Magazine* (December 1819) first drew public attention to Cunningham's poetical merits. Cromek paid Cunningham with a bound volume and a promise of 'something handsome' on a new edition. He also received Cunningham in his house, and gave him an introduction to the sculptor Francis Chantrey, who was just rising into notice.

Cunningham obtained employment from a sculptor named Bubb at 26s. a week. He applied to Eugenius Roche, now editing *The Day*, who allowed him 1 guinea a week for poetry, and employed him as a parliamentary reporter. He describes his performance in this capacity ('pretty severe work') in a letter to his brother, dated 29 December 1810 (Hogg, 87), where he announces another collection of songs. Jean Walker now went to London, and they were married at St Saviour's, Southwark, on 1 July 1811. He obtained employment from his countryman William Jerdan, editor of the *Literary Gazette*, and in 1813 published a volume of *Songs, Chiefly in the Rural Language of Scotland*. In 1814 he was engaged by Chantrey as superintendent of his establishment, and gave up writing for newspapers. He lived afterwards at 27 Lower Belgrave Place, Pimlico. He acted as Chantrey's secretary, conducted his correspondence, represented him during his absence, and occasionally offered artistic assistance. He became a favourite of Chantrey's sitters and visitors. This employment lasted until Chantrey's death in 1841 when Cunningham was left an annuity of £100.

Cunningham worked hard to provide for a growing family. He 'rose at six and worked till six' in Chantrey's studio, and wrote in the evening. He contributed a series of humorous stories of Scottish social and religious life called 'Recollections of Mark Macrabin, the Cameronian', to *Blackwood's Magazine* (1819–21). He gave up *Blackwood's* for the *London Magazine*. In 1820 he submitted a drama called *Sir Marmaduke Maxwell* to Sir Walter Scott, whose personal acquaintance he had made when Scott was sitting to Chantrey. Scott thought it unfit for the stage, but praised its poetry in the preface to *The Fortunes of Nigel*. It was published in 1822 with some other pieces. In 1822 also appeared two volumes of *Traditional Tales of the English and Scottish Peasantry*, and in 1825 four volumes of *The Songs of Scotland, Ancient and Modern*, which was favourably received. This includes 'A Wet Sheet and a Flowing Sea', which though written by a landsman became one of the best-known sea songs, 'The Wee, Wee German Lairdie', which represents Scottish feeling about the Hanoverians, and 'It's Hame, and it's Hame', which was praised by Scott as 'equal to Burns' (preface to *The Fortunes of Nigel*). In the following years he tried romances such as *Paul Jones* (1826), *Sir Michael Scott* (1828), *The Maid of Elvar*, a poem in twelve parts (1833), and *Lord Roldan* (1836). He adopted a fashion of the day by bringing out the *Anniversary* for 1829, an annual with contributions from Southey, Lockhart, Hogg, and others. From 1829 to 1833 appeared his six-volume *Lives of the most Eminent British Painters, Sculptors, and Architects*, forming part of Murray's Family Library. It is more simply written than his usual prolix style, and had a large sale. His personal knowledge of contemporary artists added to its value. An edition in three volumes, edited by Mrs Charles Heaton, appeared in Bohn's Standard Library in 1879. Further edited versions were published in 1893 and 1908. From 1830 to 1834 he contributed a series of articles to *The Athenaeum*, 'Biographical and critical history of the literature of the last fifty years'. *The Works and Life of Burns*, in eight volumes, which appeared in 1834, was the last work of importance during his life. He corrected the last proofs of a life of Sir David Wilkie just before his death, and it appeared posthumously, edited by his son Peter.

Cunningham's domestic life was happy. His letters to his mother show an enduring filial affection. A poem to his wife, printed in Alaric Watts's *Literary Souvenir* for 1824, gives a pleasing and obviously sincere account of his life-long devotion. They had five sons and a daughter. Scott in 1828 obtained cadetships for two sons, Alexander *Cunningham and Joseph Davey *Cunningham, in the Indian service. Peter *Cunningham became clerk in the Audit Office, and was a well-known antiquary. Francis *Cunningham also entered the Indian army. In 1831 Allan Cunningham visited Nithsdale, was presented with the freedom of Dumfries, and entertained at a public dinner, at which Carlyle made a cordial speech in his honour. Carlyle afterwards met Cunningham in London. He admired the 'stalwart healthy figure and ways' of the 'solid Dumfries stonemason' (Carlyle, *Reminiscences*, 2.211), and exempted him, as a pleasant *Naturmensch*, from his general condemnation of London scribblers. His early opinion of Cunningham remained unchanged: 'Allan Cunningham I love; he retains the honest tones of his native Nithsdale true as ever; he has a heart and a mind simple as a child's but with touches of a genius singularly wild and original' (*Collected Letters*, 3.139).

Cunningham had already suffered a paralytic attack in 1839 (presumably some kind of stroke), and he died at his home, 27 Lower Belgrave Place, on 29 October 1842, the day after a second attack. He was buried at Kensal Green on 4 November.

LESLIE STEPHEN, *rev.* HAMISH WHYTE

Sources P. Cunningham, introduction, in A. Cunningham, *Poems and songs* (1847) • D. Hogg, *The life of Allan Cunningham* (1875) • C. Rogers, *The modern Scottish minstrel, or, The songs of Scotland of the past half-century*, 3 (1856), 1–8 • J. G. Wilson, ed., *The poets and poetry of*

Scotland, 2 (1877), 61–4 • S. C. Hall, *A book of memories of great men and women of the age* (1871), 422–30 • C. Rogers, *A century of Scottish life* (1871), 210–11 • Chambers, *Scots.*, rev. T. Thomson (1875) • *The Times* (31 Oct 1842), 5 • J. Holland, *Memorials of Sir Francis Chantrey* [1851], 263 • F. Miller, *The poets of Dumfriesshire* (1910), 192–6 • T. Carlyle, *Reminiscences*, ed. J. A. Froude, 2 vols. (1881) • G. E. H. Hughes, 'The life and works of Allan Cunningham', PhD diss., U. Cam., 1975 • *The collected letters of Thomas and Jane Welsh Carlyle*, ed. C. R. Sanders and K. J. Fielding, 3 (1970)

Archives Hornel Library, Broughton House, Kirkcudbright, letters and poems • Liverpool Central Library, notes and letters • Mitchell L., Glas., letters and *The mariner's song* • NL Scot., letters; lives of painters and related corresp. • U. Edin. L., special collections division, misc. corresp. and poems • V&A NAL, notes and additions to his *Lives of Wilson and Gainsborough* | Mitchell L., Glas., letters • NL Scot., letters to William Blackwood & Sons • NL Scot., letters to Charles Gray and MS poem • NL Scot., letters to James Hogg • NL Scot., corresp. with J. G. Lockhart • NL Scot., letters, mostly to John McCrone relating to his edition of Burns • NL Scot., letters to Oliver and Boyd • NL Scot., corresp. with Sir Walter Scott • NL Scot., letters to Robert Southey • U. Edin. L., special collections division, letters to David Laing and Nodwell and Martin • Yale U., Beinecke L., letters to Joseph Bordwine • Yale U., Beinecke L., letters to John Macrone

Likenesses F. Chantrey, drawing, 1822, repro. in Cunningham, 'Introduction' • W. Brockedon, pencil-and-chalk drawing, 1832, NPG • H. Room, oils, *c.*1840, NPG • H. Weekes, marble bust, 1842, Scot. NPG • F. Chantrey, plaster bust, Scot. NPG • J. Jenkins, stipple (after J. Moore), BM, NPG; repro. in W. Jerdan, *National portrait gallery* (1832) • D. Maclise, lithograph, BM, NPG; repro. in *Fraser's Magazine* (1832) • D. Maclise, pencil study (for his lithograph), V&A • A. C. McBryde, engraving, repro. in Hogg, *Life of Allan Cunningham* • J. J. Penstone, wash drawing, Scot. NPG • H. W. Pickersgill, oils, Scot. NPG • F. W. Wilkin, lithograph, BM

Wealth at death left annuity of £100 by Chantrey which would revert at death to Cunningham's wife

Cunningham, Allan (1791–1839), botanist and explorer, was born on 13 July 1791, at Wimbledon, Surrey, first of two sons of Allan Cunningham (d. 1828), head gardener at Wimbledon House, and Sarah Juson, *née* Dicken, who died when he was a child. His younger brother was Richard *Cunningham (1793–1835). After schooling at the Revd John Adams's academy, Putney, and employment in a conveyancer's office, from 1808 he assisted W. T. Aiton with the second edition of *Hortus Kewensis*. He thus met Robert Brown and Joseph Banks, and subsequently applied to Banks for a position as a paid botanical collector. Cunningham first collected in Brazil with James Bowie, from December 1814 until September 1816, when Cunningham was transferred to New South Wales.

As botanist with John Oxley's expedition, Cunningham explored the westward-flowing Lachlan River for five months in 1817. Between December 1817 and 1822 he sailed five times as botanist to Phillip Parker King's hydrographical surveys of the north and north-western coasts of Australia, also visiting Timor, Van Diemen's Land, and Mauritius. He later contributed the botanical appendix to King's *Narrative of a Survey of the Intertropical and Western Coasts of Australia* (1827). From 1822, despite remaining employed by the Royal Botanic Gardens at Kew his major motivation became exploration, although he regularly collected around Sydney, Bathurst, and in the Illawarra district, 'his favourite botanising ground' (Heward, 62). In 1823, accompanied as on subsequent journeys by a small number of assigned convicts, he explored north of Bathurst—discovering a stock route to the Liverpool plains. However, this discovery proved insignificant compared with his finding, in 1827, the Darling downs, a rich agricultural area of southern Queensland, which he opened the following year to the new Moreton Bay settlements via the pass subsequently named Cunningham's Gap. A final exploration in 1829 eliminated the possibility that the western rivers might drain via the Brisbane River, convincing him that there must be somewhere a large, north-flowing, continental river. In 1826–7 he visited New Zealand; in 1830 he spent five months on Norfolk Island.

At his own request Cunningham returned to England in 1831, where he arranged some of his collections, while living on accumulated means at Strand on the Green, across the Thames from Kew. For his election as a fellow of the Linnean Society of London in January 1832 he was nominated by ten very distinguished supporters including W. J. Hooker, George Bentham, and John Lindley; he was held in such esteem that the council in February refunded his life membership fees.

Cunningham had advised the Australian Agricultural Company during his residence in Sydney, and in London he commented, unfavourably, on the South Australian Land Company's plan for a settlement at the mouth of the Murray River. Although sometimes interpreted as a consequence of disagreement with Charles Sturt over the relationship of the Murray and Darling rivers, his advice was probably based on genuine doubts, given the style of settlement proposed.

After his brother, Richard, died in 1835 Cunningham, although in ill health, applied successfully for the post of colonial botanist thus vacated. He arrived again in Sydney in March 1837 but soon became disenchanted with the tasks expected of him. Although it is unlikely to have been the sole reason for his resignation, the inappropriateness of his being a 'cultivator of official cabbages and turnips' ('The botanical, alias the kitchen garden', Sydney Herald, 29 Jan 1838), preyed upon him. In April 1838 he sailed for New Zealand, returning to Sydney, seriously ill, in October of that year. He died in Sydney on 27 June 1839 and was buried on 2 July at the Scottish church. In 1901 his remains were reinterred in the monument erected in the Sydney Botanic Gardens soon after his death. Cunningham was unmarried and left bequests from his estate of over £3000 to Robert Heward, his botanical friend and first biographer, and others, and provided for his own memorial tablet to be placed alongside one he had supplied to commemorate his brother in St Andrew's Presbyterian Church, Sydney. His well-written journals were not published and he has a short bibliography. However, he named about a hundred and thirty Australian plants and in such regard were his 'most continuous and extensive' botanical travels held (J. D. Hooker, cxvi), that almost as many species are named after him.

Politically conservative, Cunningham favoured the 'exclusive' faction in New South Wales debates over its political development, and argued to the parliamentary committee on secondary punishment (1832) that the convict regime was not too harsh. In his personal relationships he lacked self-confidence, and this was reflected also in concern for excessive detail which occasionally became 'useless punctilio' (McMinn, 121), but, despite Governor Macquarie's describing him in a letter to Banks as an 'unbred illiterate man' (McMinn, 31), his friendships crossed social barriers.

                           A. M. LUCAS

Sources R. Heward, 'Biographical sketch of the late Allan Cunningham', *Journal of Botany*, 4 (1842), 231–320 · W. G. McMinn, *Allan Cunningham: botanist and explorer* (1970) · C. Finney, *Paradise revealed: natural history in nineteenth-century Australia* (1993), 26–31 · Linnean Society election certificates, Linn. Soc. · minute books, Linn. Soc. · 'Kew collectors', RBG Kew, 4to ser. 1, fol. ser. 5–7 · D. J. Carr and S. G. M. Carr, eds., *People and plants in Australia* (1981), 236–44 · A. D. Chapman, *Australian plant name index*, 4 vols. (Canberra, 1991) · J. D. Hooker, introduction, *The botany of the Antarctic voyage of H. M. discovery ships Erebus and Terror*, 3 (1860), cxvi · PRO, George Yard Chapel, RG 4/3595, no. 29 [birth and baptism] · W. J. Hooker, 'A brief biographical sketch of the late Richard Cunningham', *Companion to the Botanical Magazine*, 2 (1836), 210–21 · parish register, London, St Marylebone, 20 Aug 1790, LMA, X23/49 [marriages], (10.187, no. 5593)
Archives Linn. Soc. · Mitchell L., NSW, diary · NHM, journals, corresp., and papers · NL Scot., corresp. · RBG Kew, corresp. and papers | Linn. Soc., Mackay collection · RBG Kew, 'Kew collectors'
Likenesses oil on wood panel, c.1835 · A. Picken, lithograph, BM · A. Picken, lithograph, Mitchell L., NSW · J. E. H. Robinson, watercolour, Linn. Soc. · lithograph (after drawing by D. Macnee), RBG Kew
Wealth at death over £3000: McMinn, *Allan Cunningham*, 102

Cunningham, Andrew Browne, Viscount Cunningham of Hyndhope

(1883–1963), naval officer, was born at 42 Grosvenor Square, Rathmines, Dublin, on 7 January 1883, the third of the five children of Daniel John *Cunningham (1850–1909), then a professor of anatomy at Trinity College, Dublin, and his wife, Elizabeth Cumming (d. 1926), daughter of the Revd Andrew Browne of Beith, Ayrshire. A brother was General Sir Alan Gordon *Cunningham (1887–1983). Cunningham's ancestry was wholly Scottish and he always thought of himself as a Scot, though he spent but little time there, even after his father had taken up the chair of anatomy in Edinburgh. After early schooling in Dublin he was at Edinburgh Academy, aged ten, when his father asked him if he would like to join the navy. 'Yes,' he replied, 'I should like to be an admiral', though he had no more than a vague interest in ships and the sea (Cunningham, 13). After three years at Stubbington House, Hampshire, which specialized in preparing boys for the Royal Navy, he entered the training ship *Britannia* in January 1897, passing out tenth of sixty-five cadets in May 1898, with first-class passes in mathematics and seamanship.

Apprenticeship to high command, 1898–1939 Cunningham, who had an early reputation for belligerence and boldness, sought and obtained a posting to the Cape station and shortly after his arrival contrived to join a naval artillery brigade in the Second South African War. He saw little action but learned much about self-reliance, leadership, and initiative. Following promotion to sub-lieutenant in 1903 he was appointed to the destroyer *Locust*, and began a

Andrew Browne Cunningham, Viscount Cunningham of Hyndhope (1883–1963), by Yousuf Karsh, 1943

thirty-year association with destroyers. Promoted lieutenant in 1904, he secured his first command, torpedo boat no. 14, in 1908 but his reputation as a first-class ship handler and man of action was made in the destroyer *Scorpion*, to which he was appointed in 1911 and in which he served until 1918. Destroyer commands offered great scope for individual flair and responsibility and demanded determination and vigour.

Cunningham, who spent more than a third of his career in the Mediterranean, served with distinction in the Dardanelles campaign, being promoted commander in 1915 and appointed DSO in 1916. His judgement, fearlessness, resolution, and devotion to exacting standards were noted by his seniors, who remarked on his unquenchable zeal. He was audacious and successful in his support of the forces ashore and learned much about both combined operations and the nature of the eastern Mediterranean. His quest for action took him to the Dover patrol early in 1918, in command of *Termagant*, though he had few opportunities to close with the enemy. Nevertheless, he earned a bar to his DSO and in March 1920 a second bar for his service in the Baltic under Rear-Admiral Walter Cowan, an aggressive and extremely demanding flag officer whom Cunningham regarded as a mentor. Cunningham in *Seafire* led a division of destroyers helping to uphold the newly won independence of the Baltic republics and in tense and dangerous situations exhibited his characteristic decisiveness, courage, and matchless energy. Shortly after his return he was promoted captain at the age of thirty-seven. As a captain (D), he refined the torpedo and anti-submarine tactics of his flotillas. When Cowan was

appointed commander-in-chief, North America and West Indies, in 1926, he requested Cunningham as his flag captain and chief of staff; Cunningham commanded successively the light cruisers *Calcutta* and *Despatch*.

In 1929 Cunningham was sent to the Imperial Defence College. Profiting from the broadening of his education in diplomacy, current affairs, and inter-service co-operation, he regarded it as an excellent preparation for high command. Appointed to the new battleship *Rodney* in command in December 1929, he married, on the 21st of that month, Nona Christine Byatt (1889–1978), a daughter of Horace Byatt, a headmaster of Midhurst, Sussex; the marriage was extremely happy but there were no children. After serving as commodore of Chatham barracks, Cunningham was promoted rear-admiral in September 1932 and, following two more senior officers' courses, achieved his heart's desire—appointment as rear-admiral (D) in the Mediterranean Fleet (January 1934–April 1936). He was also appointed CB in 1934.

The commander-in-chief, Mediterranean, was the redoubtable Admiral Sir William Fisher, an officer of great intellect, tireless dedication, and outstanding ability as a fleet commander. Cunningham's own distinguished tenure of the same command owed much to Fisher's brilliant example. Cunningham drove the flotillas extremely hard, developing night fighting skills, precision in ship handling, independent initiative and judgement, and the most exacting standards. Though a severe and eagle-eyed taskmaster, he endeared himself to his captains, who had absolute confidence in his leadership, born of unparalleled experience in destroyers and in the Mediterranean. His relief was his *Britannia* term-mate, Rear-Admiral James Somerville, but Cunningham was soon serving in the Mediterranean again. Promoted vice-admiral in July 1936, a year later he was called upon to succeed Vice-Admiral Sir Geoffrey Blake, who had become ill, as vice-admiral commanding, battle-cruiser squadron, and second-in-command, Mediterranean Fleet, to Admiral Sir Dudley Pound.

In October 1938 Cunningham began his first spell of duty in the Admiralty, as deputy chief of naval staff, charged with feverish preparations for war. He deputized on occasion for the terminally ill first sea lord, Admiral Sir Roger Backhouse, whose retirement in spring 1939 brought Pound to the Admiralty, leading to Cunningham's appointment in command of the Mediterranean Fleet. Appointed KCB in January 1939, he was promoted acting admiral on 1 June 1939, when he assumed command.

Commander-in-chief, Mediterranean, 1939–1942 Long recognized as an outstanding officer, Cunningham possessed abundant self-confidence, apparently inexhaustible energy, the ability to grasp situations quickly and to issue prompt, unequivocal orders, and the capacity to inspire unquestioning loyalty and unstinting effort. ABC, as he was known, was a difficult man to serve, his fierce blue eyes heralding a man of moderate height with a ruddy complexion, with a fearsome roar, at times irascible and impatient, always exacting in his standards and demanding service from his staff to the point of exhaustion. Like many such martinets and hard-driving leaders, he respected those who stood up to him. Cunningham drove himself as hard as he did his subordinates and rewarded their loyalty and service with firm support and sound advice in their future careers. Many became longstanding friends and recalled that the apparently forbidding and formidable ABC was quick to forgive and that the belligerent, even bullying, demeanour would often vanish in a twinkle of his eyes, to be replaced by a bawdy humour and a teasing manner.

Cunningham was deeply solicitous of the welfare of those who served under him and not infrequently tender and sympathetic to the point of soft-heartedness. Though he was almost as disparaging of staff officers as he was of gunnery specialists, he was rare among admirals of his day in delegating responsibility to his staff, sometimes to a frightening extent. Cunningham did not enjoy the intellectual capacity of Sir William Fisher, and he was not a student of war as was the commander-in-chief, Middle East, General Wavell, nor did he possess the many-sided technical genius of Somerville or Mountbatten. He did not indulge in introspection, though he was not unreflective, and he never wasted words, though when he spoke he did so with vigour, cogency, and conciseness. He had undoubtedly gained much of practical value from his several senior officers' courses, even more from serving under Cowan and Fisher, and he had a clear appreciation of strategic realities and priorities, as well as a genuine commitment to close co-operation with the army and air force.

Cunningham's fitness for high command was derived in part from his shrewd distillation of an exceptional amount of sea time, most of it in independent commands imposing an almost constant exposure to problem solving, and the examples set by distinguished superiors, together with an instinctive genius for the handling of ships, both singly and in the mass, and for the conduct of war at sea. By 1939 he possessed exceptional skill as a fleet commander, a sublime tactical acumen, a clinical precision in the exercise of command, and an unrivalled knowledge of the Mediterranean in all its moods and quarters. Cunningham was not a noted student of naval history but he was fully alive to his Nelsonian inheritance as Britain's naval commander in the middle sea. His prescription for the exercise of sea power was exactly the same as that of the victor of Trafalgar: the primary function of a fleet was to seek out and destroy its enemy, and the bolder the methods the better. Like Nelson he believed in keeping war at sea simple and direct; he encouraged, indeed expected, his captains to exercise their own initiative within the strategic canvas which he embroidered with clear, easily comprehended broad principles.

When Cunningham took command of the Mediterranean station it did not enjoy a high priority in the provision of resources, as the probable immediate threats appeared to come from Germany and Japan; the government hoped to appease Mussolini and hold Italy to a firm if surly neutrality. Though there were tangible if limited arrangements for co-operation with the French navy, Cunningham felt grave concern at the neglected state of naval defences in the Mediterranean. The historic base, Malta, was regarded as indefensible in the face of Italian bombing and in wartime the fleet would have to fall back on Alexandria, equally bereft of air defences and vulnerable to Italian attacks from Libya; moreover, Alexandria lacked adequate dockyard resources. The fleet could expect little assistance from the RAF, as it was grossly over-stretched and could supply little in the way of fighter cover or reconnaissance. As the army was equally weak, the fleet offered the only means of offensive action. However, the Fleet Air Arm was short of carriers and aircraft, none of which were up to date, and offered limited scouting strength, no fighter cover, and a puny strike force capable only of slowing enemy heavy ships—if it could hit them. When Mussolini began to make obvious preparations to join the war in spring 1940 Cunningham's fleet was reinforced and he devised a strategy that was aggressive without being reckless. Confident of holding the eastern Mediterranean and hoping that the French would protect the western basin, he proposed sweeps in the central portion to test the Italian fleet's readiness to fight and the capacity of Mussolini's air force to deny the traditional exercise of sea power. Pound displayed absolute confidence in Cunningham and the two developed a full and frank correspondence.

Italy's entrance into the war on 10 June 1940 was accompanied by the collapse of France. Churchill's decision to commit Britain (and the Commonwealth) to a full-scale war in the Mediterranean led to an ultimatum to the French navy to align itself with the Royal Navy or suffer effective demilitarization. A French squadron at Alexandria, under Vice-Admiral Godfroy, was persuaded to disarm its vessels but only after delicate negotiations carried on in a rapidly changing context which threatened to bring about a gunfight in the harbour. Cunningham conducted the talks with Godfroy in a firm but skilful manner, displaying a patience rarely ascribed to him, as well as a diplomatic finesse of consummate subtlety. In the light of tragic confrontations with the French elsewhere Cunningham's achievement was outstanding.

Cunningham continued to challenge the Italian fleet to a duel and on 9 July, while each fleet was covering convoys in the central Mediterranean, they exchanged fire off Calabria. Enjoying good reconnaissance and splendid intelligence, Cunningham attempted to cut off the Italians from their bases, using the carrier *Eagle*'s Swordfish to slow down his faster opponents. No torpedoes struck home and the clash between the heavy ships was brief and conducted at long range. After Cunningham's flagship, the *Warspite*, hit the Italian flagship, *Giulio Cesare*, at a distance of 13 miles, the enemy turned for home, making smoke and launching heavy land-based bombing attacks on the British forces, though without result. The Italians outpaced Cunningham, who declined to fall into a submarine and mine trap and returned to base. The British claimed a lasting moral ascendancy over the Italian navy but the enemy, who lacked a comparable battle squadron at that time, made a sensible decision to retire.

Over the next six months Cunningham and Vice-Admiral Sir James Somerville, commanding force H at Gibraltar, steadily restored British control of the Mediterranean, allowing reinforcements of ships and aircraft to reach the eastern Mediterranean and Malta and permitting the running of convoys to the Middle East. Apart from the bold and capable exercise of sea power by the two outstanding British admirals, the poor state of Italian equipment and training, and Italy's shortage of oil and other resources, the British supremacy was made possible by the presence of modern carriers equipped with fighters, *Ark Royal*, with force H, and *Illustrious*, which joined Cunningham in September 1940. Fleet fighters eliminated enemy shadowers and nullified Italian high level bombing attacks.

It was by the exercise of carrier striking power, however, that the Mediterranean Fleet gained its principal victory in this period. The concept of a carrier air strike against the Italian fleet at Taranto had originated in 1935, at the time of the Abyssinian crisis. On 11 November 1940 *Illustrious* launched twenty-one Swordfish at night and 160 miles from Taranto. The attack, planned meticulously and executed bravely, disabled three of Italy's six battleships for the loss of two aircraft. It represented the Fleet Air Arm's greatest ever triumph and enabled Cunningham to carry the war to the enemy fleet, which would not come to him. The operation was one of several carried out in the same voyage; convoys were escorted and a successful raid conducted on shipping in the Adriatic. Cunningham, always conscious of the severe pressure on his slender resources, was adept at making optimum use of his forces.

Wavell's spectacularly successful desert offensive of December 1940, aided by Air Chief Marshal Sir Arthur Longmore's carefully directed air support and a naval inshore squadron, gave the British crucial airfields on the southern flank of the convoy route to Malta, though it imposed on the navy the crippling burden of maintaining Tobruk throughout an eight-month siege. These triumphs exhibited the interdependence of the military, air, and naval campaigns in the Mediterranean, a fact of which the three commanders-in-chief were well aware; Cunningham, Longmore, and Wavell drove the chariot of war in complete harmony. In January 1941 Cunningham was confirmed in the rank of admiral and in March appointed GCB.

The days of triumph were short-lived, for Italy's early disasters prompted German intervention, initially with a *Luftwaffe* force specializing in anti-ship operations. On 10–11 January 1941 Cunningham's forces, escorting a convoy from the west to Malta, were surprised by dive-bombers which sank the cruiser *Southampton* and crippled *Illustrious*. For the remainder of the war German air power was to be the Royal Navy's most formidable opponent in the middle sea. The co-ordination of the enemy's air forces and Italian naval forces was far from perfect, however, and when the Italian fleet sortied against British convoys to

Greece in March 1941 it failed to receive adequate air reconnaissance and fighter cover. The British had also broken enemy codes and the resulting Ultra information enabled Cunningham to intercept the enemy off Cape Matapan on 28–9 March. Air strikes from the new carrier, *Formidable*, first saved Cunningham's scouting cruisers from annihilation and then severely damaged the Italian flagship, *Vittorio Veneto*. She was able to regain enough speed to escape but a third torpedo strike crippled the heavy cruiser *Pola*. Cunningham boldly decided to risk a fleet encounter at night, relying on British skill at night fighting, honed in the Mediterranean in the 1930s, supported by radar and the confidence engendered by previous skirmishes with Italian ships. His battle squadron came upon *Pola*'s sisters, *Zara* and *Fiume*, sent to escort the cripple home, guns trained innocently fore and aft, and in a few minutes blew them out of the water; *Pola* and two destroyers were dispatched by light forces. The victory was literally a signal success for the British, thanks to their intelligence breakthrough, but it owed much to the persistence of the Fleet Air Arm, the high level of training of the surface forces, and pre-eminently to the qualities of leadership exhibited by the commander-in-chief. Cunningham, who displayed an intuitive grasp of the developing situation, coolly weighed the odds for and against a night action, with its evident hazards and uncertain rewards. He conveyed his aggressive, determined, and confident manner to his subordinates, handled his fleet with decisiveness and, for the most part, gave orders of admirable brevity and precision. Matapan confirmed his reputation as the outstanding seaman of the war and effectively scuttled Italian fleet operations of any substance and seriousness.

Once again, however, the victor's laurels were turned quickly into wreaths of another kind. In April 1941 allied forces evacuated Greece in the face of the *Luftwaffe* and the Panzers, enduring severe bombing on their return to Egypt. Less than a month later Cunningham was compelled to rescue allied forces from Crete. These two evacuations were carried out by allied warships and merchantmen in the face of overwhelming axis air power, to which the RAF and Fleet Air Arm could make virtually no reply. Though the bulk of the troops were carried safely to Egypt, warships and troopships suffered severe losses and damage, with several thousand seamen and soldiers killed. Cunningham remained at Alexandria to co-ordinate the operations of his scattered forces, their ships' companies exhausted by continuous voyaging from the beginning of the year, the hazards of negotiating strange harbours at night and the incessant air attacks. He yearned to be at sea with them, sharing their dangers and discomforts, and was well aware that the strain was becoming unendurable—yet he was determined that the navy should not let the army down, uttering his most famous remark, generally reported as 'It takes the Navy three years to build a ship but three hundred years to build a tradition' (Pack, 177). After the evacuation of Crete at the end of May 1941 Cunningham's fleet was reduced by a half. Crucially, it lacked a carrier, as *Formidable* had been sent, foolishly, to attack airfields on Rhodes with scarcely a handful of planes and had been put out of action for eight months. The absence of a carrier and the limited support available from shore-based aircraft led Cunningham to demand and obtain an RAF naval co-operation group, analogous to Coastal Command. After Crete, Cunningham was forced on to the defensive, save for an effective contribution to the army's conquest of Vichy Syria and Lebanon. The loss of Libya to Rommel, coupled with the expulsion from Crete, made the supply of Malta a major headache.

The catalogue of naval disasters in the Mediterranean continued to the end of 1941 with the sinking of *Ark Royal* and one of Cunningham's battleships, *Barham*, by newly arrived German U-boats and, finally and decisively for the Mediterranean Fleet's line-of-battle, the crippling in December of *Queen Elizabeth* and *Valiant* by Italian human torpedoes, which attacked the battleships in Alexandria harbour. Cunningham himself acknowledged a measure of the responsibility for this last catastrophe; he was essentially a seagoing admiral and, while vocal about the air defence deficiencies of Alexandria, he seems to have neglected defence against this form of attack, despite the Italians' deserved reputation for skill and bravery in this field. As the war against Japan had opened disastrously with the loss of *Prince of Wales* and *Repulse*, Cunningham was left to struggle on with a handful of small cruisers and overworked destroyers. He was fortunate in acquiring another doughty and resourceful Nelsonian admiral, Philip Vian, who in December 1941 and again in March 1942 fought off superior Italian forces while conducting convoys to Malta. The island's future hung in the balance as the axis air attacks redoubled in an effort to neutralize the base and terminate its air, surface, and submarine threats to the Libyan convoys. Cunningham could only pray for the island's safe deliverance for on 3 April 1942 he hauled down his flag prior to taking up the headship of the British Admiralty delegation in Washington. Cunningham, who became a baronet in January that year, had been the outstanding British commander of the war thus far, a fearless leader whose presence with the fleet inspired and reassured his men; in harbour he constantly visited ships, hospitals, and shore stations. His departure was kept secret—a testimony to his reputation among his enemies and an acknowledgement that there was no adequate replacement.

The British Admiralty delegation, Washington, 1942 The United States' entry into the war in December 1941 made a detailed joint strategy, the exchange of technical data, and the assurance of a steady supply of American equipment matters of urgency. A combined chiefs of staff had been established and Admiral Ernest J. King, who had a reputation for being awkward to almost everyone, had become the United States chief of naval operations. Pound felt that Cunningham, who was as tough and determined as King, was the right man to head the British Admiralty delegation (BAD) at that critical stage of the war. Though Cunningham arrived home early in April, it was not until late June that he reached Washington,

Churchill having made persistent attempts to appoint him to the Home Fleet. In Washington there was precious little for him to do: the vast BAD organization was already running smoothly and was concerned chiefly with routine matters. Cunningham was there to bring his broadside to bear on King should the latter fail to co-operate as wholeheartedly as the British wished. King was somewhat uncommunicative, often a reluctant co-operator, and frequently extremely rude; given Cunningham's redoubtable reputation for standing no nonsense, some heated confrontations were inevitable. It says much for Cunningham's patience, skill, and robust character that he generally gained what was required from King. More important, he impressed American civilian and military leaders as a man of integrity, resolution, clarity of thought, and keen strategic insight, with the capacity for thinking and commanding on a grand scale.

Allied amphibious operations in the Mediterranean, 1942–1943 Cunningham, a confirmed advocate of dealing with the Mediterranean situation first, was influential in swinging the opinion of the American high command behind operation Torch, the Anglo-American landings in French north Africa. His evident willingness to co-operate with the Americans, his great prestige as a Mediterranean commander, and the trust he engendered led to an American proposal to appoint him naval commander under General Eisenhower, the allied supreme commander. Cunningham, though not seeking the post, was nevertheless delighted to return to the front line; liaison and administrative work in Washington and the endless socializing quickly made him fret for life at sea. Torch was an ambitious, difficult, and highly uncertain operation. It was the first major allied offensive, it had to be launched from main bases thousands of miles away, it required vast forces of merchantmen, landing craft, and escorting warships and aircraft, and it was likely to meet opposition from the Vichy French. Many thousands of sailors and soldiers had to be trained hastily in landing operations and the planning had to be compressed into a few weeks in summer 1942.

When the operation was launched in November 1942 it proved highly successful, despite fierce resistance by the French and inevitable shortcomings in the co-ordination and training of the various services. In part, the triumph was due to good fortune in the shape of fine weather and a baffled and unusually sluggish enemy, and it owed much to Eisenhower's determination to make Anglo-American co-operation work all down the line, as well as to the painstaking planning of Vice-Admiral Sir Bertram Ramsay and his team. Nevertheless, Cunningham played a key role, for he acted as Eisenhower's *alter ego*, imparting to the untried American staff officer his own robust confidence and formidable will and setting an example to other subordinates of utter loyalty to the commander-in-chief. Cunningham kept a firm grip on naval operations from Casablanca to Tunis and though he regretted the failure to land as close to Tunis as possible, he urged his forces forward to capture more ports and to harry enemy shipping, finally ensuring that few of the considerable axis army in Tunisia escaped. To his distaste, much of his time was occupied in political discussions with French leaders. Initial Vichy hostility was halted by Admiral Darlan, who effectively switched sides from collaboration with the axis to intimate co-operation with the allies. Darlan's deal with Eisenhower, which brought about an early cease-fire, was unpopular with allied public opinion but the arrangement was stoutly supported by Cunningham as a crucial measure enabling the allies to turn their attention to the axis.

The north African campaign took far longer than had been envisaged, due chiefly to the allies' failure to accept Cunningham's advice to land as far east as Bizerte. However, in late January 1943 Churchill, Roosevelt, and their staffs met at Casablanca to plan the next western offensive. There being no realistic prospect of invading northwestern Europe in 1943, it was decided to invade Sicily, as it would enable the Mediterranean route to the East to be reopened and would provide airfields from which southern Germany could be bombed; the conquest of Sicily might also bring about the fall of Mussolini. Planning operation Husky, however, proved to be a nightmare, as the senior commanders could not agree on landing places. Once again, plans had to be redrafted at a very late stage, though Cunningham himself was convinced that any one of the plans would have been successful. He had a somewhat fraught relationship with Ramsay, who was once again the chief planner; it is possible that Cunningham, who had become commander-in-chief, Mediterranean, for a second time in January 1943, and also an admiral of the fleet, felt jealous at having such an able, senior and semi-independent admiral in his bailiwick. He was suspicious of Ramsay's good relations with generals Alexander and Montgomery, for Cunningham disparaged Alexander and disliked Montgomery's arrogance and mischief-making. However, Cunningham's long Mediterranean experience paid good dividends.

Setting up his headquarters in Malta, Cunningham took charge of an armada of 3000 vessels, the largest to date. Rough seas presented a late hazard but also a bonus in that they lulled the defenders into believing that the operation could not take place on the night of 10 July. Once again, Cunningham's nerve held firm and his subordinates derived confidence from the knowledge that the master was at the helm. Calmer weather, meticulous organization, and better trained and more experienced crews enabled the landing to take place against minimal opposition. Once Sicily was cleared of the enemy in late August, it seemed logical to seize the opportunity of Mussolini's fall and Italian overtures for an armistice to invade the mainland to seize further airfields in the toe of Italy and incite Italians to rise up against their German occupiers. Landings near Reggio and at Taranto were virtually trouble-free but the major assault at Salerno, south of Naples, almost ended in disaster as a fierce German riposte pushed the allied troops back to the beaches; the

situation was saved by lavish use of air power and by Cunningham's prompt provision of capital ships for bombardment, with telling effect. Cunningham took justifiable pleasure in watching the Italian battle fleet drop anchor at Malta, making his most famous signal: 'Be pleased to inform Their Lordships that the Italian Battle Fleet lies at anchor under the guns of the fortress of Malta' (Cunningham, 565). It was, fittingly, almost the last act of his seagoing career.

First sea lord, 1943–1946 In October 1943 Cunningham succeeded the dying Pound but his succession was by no means automatic. Churchill, with whom Cunningham had frequently crossed swords, foresaw exasperating conflicts. He believed Cunningham was unsuited to staff work and was also less receptive to modern technology than the premier's choice, Admiral Sir Bruce Fraser, commander-in-chief, Home Fleet. Indeed, Fraser was offered the post but, recognizing that Cunningham enjoyed the navy's support, declined. Cunningham's appointment satisfied public opinion and also the Americans, among whom he commanded considerable respect. Cunningham approached his new post with some trepidation. Not only was he congenitally unfitted for shorebound administration, he also doubted his ability to hold his own intellectually with the other chiefs of staff, Field Marshal Sir Alan Brooke and Marshal of the RAF Sir Charles Portal. Fortunately they welcomed him warmly and the trio constituted an effective and generally harmonious team, united in their stand against the prime minister's frequently madcap strategy. Moreover, Cunningham was an effective and experienced delegator and avoided the clogging detail which had often ensnared his predecessor. He was already well known to the American joint chiefs of staff so that in meetings of the combined chiefs of staff he knew how to conduct his business, even with the prickly King. He and the American chief of naval operations had a somewhat strained relationship, despite their mutual respect. Cunningham displayed a fisherman's cunning in playing the prime minister, exhibiting a patience and tactical skill largely unglimpsed in previous appointments, and resisted Churchillian attempts to interfere in the direction of operations and flag appointments. Cunningham was fortunate also that the worst of the war at sea was over.

Nevertheless, there were still major decisions to be made, principally on the deployment of a British fleet against Japan, which led to a running battle between the prime minister and the chiefs of staff lasting almost a year. Churchill wanted to recover lost colonies but Cunningham, supported by Brooke and Portal, pointed out that the way to end the Far Eastern conflict speedily and economically was to attack Japan's homeland. This direct strategy, fighting alongside America's great task forces, was designed to give Britain a more substantial voice in the Pacific peace settlement and post-war oriental commerce. Cunningham triumphed through persistence and Fraser led the British Pacific Fleet in the final assault on Japan in the spring and summer of 1945. Cunningham had also to ensure destruction of Germany's remaining major surface units and to devise emergency measures to cope with a recrudescence of the U-boat threat in early 1945. He stood firmly behind Ramsay as the latter planned the landings in Normandy in June 1944. Perhaps the most serious problem facing the navy at this time was the acute shortage of manpower, just when it had to find thousands of landing craft and air crews, man new construction, provide personnel for the Pacific Fleet, and maintain long-running commitments in the Atlantic and the Mediterranean. Cunningham acted vigorously to prune older ships and shore stations but the problem remained intractable.

For the most part Cunningham enjoyed good relations with station commanders, some of whom (A. U. Willis in the Mediterranean, Arthur Power in the East Indies, Bernard Rawlings and Philip Vian in the Pacific) were his protégés, but he encountered difficulties with Fraser both in the Home Fleet and in the Pacific. Fraser upheld the autonomy of a fleet commander, while Cunningham asserted the Admiralty's right to direct maritime strategy; both could be obstinate. Mountbatten, at that time supreme allied commander, south-east Asia, also irritated Cunningham by his intrigue, pretensions, and attempts to purloin ships destined for the Pacific. Cunningham also supported his commander-in-chief, Eastern Fleet, Admiral Sir James Somerville, in a dispute with Mountbatten over control of the Eastern Fleet. Cunningham turned to Somerville in autumn 1944, when it seemed necessary to send to Washington as head of BAD an admiral experienced in sea and air warfare (especially in the East), with high technical skills, a warm personality, shrewd judgement, and resolution. King had become more unbearable and less co-operative but Somerville, the most effective head of BAD, skilfully employed a blend of bluntness, salty humour, and an engaging manner to extract the required resources.

After Japan surrendered in August 1945 Cunningham faced an unpalatable end to his naval career. He had become first sea lord just as Columbia wrested Neptune's trident from Britannia and any prospect of restoring parity was shattered by the nation's virtual bankruptcy. However, like most British leaders Cunningham believed that Britain should continue to play a great power role and he also hoped, somewhat naïvely, for an integrated imperial defence policy. He was quick, too, to sense a growing threat from the Soviet Union. Cunningham was little interested in technology and was unable to fathom the full significance of electronic developments but he did ensure that captured German scientists and their equipment formed part of a strong Admiralty research and development programme. He was conservative in terms of ship design and conditions on board ship but he yielded to post-war social and economic pressures by agreeing to the reform of officer entry and service pay. Moreover, the years of struggle against axis air power in the Mediterranean and Fleet Air Arm triumphs at Taranto and Matapan had made him a vigorous advocate of naval aviation and he did much to raise the Fleet Air Arm's profile within the navy, especially within the Admiralty itself. The Admiralty was persuaded to retain the Women's Royal Naval Service after the war. A firm advocate of inter-service co-operation, he insisted on a strong amphibious capability and sought to make the Royal Marines the core of future combined operations.

However, running down the navy to a shadow of its wartime self was hardly a congenial occupation for one who had entered the mighty Victorian navy. In June 1946, following heart trouble, he stepped down in favour of his chosen successor, Admiral Sir John Cunningham (no relation), then commander-in-chief, Mediterranean. Andrew Cunningham had adapted quickly and effectively to the demands of Whitehall life, revealing unsuspected patience and a talent for handling awkward personalities with subtlety and firmness. He gave free rein to subordinates, leaving himself clear to deal with the major strategic and policy issues. His term of office was less fraught and demanding than that of Pound but he employed his considerable authority, unparalleled seagoing experience, high standing with the Americans, shrewd judgement, crisp decision making and clear strategic insight to maintain the Royal Navy's interests in a war increasingly dominated by other arms and the new superpowers.

A great seaman: epilogue and epitaph, 1946–1963 Cunningham, created Baron Cunningham of Hyndhope in 1945 and Viscount Cunningham of Hyndhope in 1946, refused the governor-generalship of Australia on health grounds. He continued to speak for the navy in public and, occasionally, in the House of Lords. He was prevailed upon to write his autobiography, *A Sailor's Odyssey* (1951). He had proudly renewed his Scottish connections by becoming a knight of the Thistle in 1945, and served as lord high commissioner to the Church of Scotland in 1950 and 1952. Otherwise raising geese and gardening at his home at Bishop's Waltham in Hampshire and fishing in Scottish rivers were his principal activities. He remained vigorous and active to the end, dying suddenly, on the way to St Thomas's Hospital, on 12 June 1963, aged eighty, after attending the House of Lords. He was buried at sea off Portsmouth six days later and his most visible monument is a bust in Trafalgar Square, London.

By common consent Cunningham ranks with the greatest of British admirals and there are many parallels between his approach to high command and that of Nelson. Both had an intuitive grasp of the significance of sea power for the British Empire and made much of the Royal Navy's traditions of invincibility, unmatched seamanship, and burning desire to engage the enemy more closely. Like Nelson, Cunningham set down a spare, simple doctrine of sea warfare based on calculated aggressiveness. ABC was a relatively modest man and considerably more able intellectually than he affected to be. His undoubted greatness lay in his single-minded dedication to professional excellence, an early exposure to the problems and possibilities of independent command, a clear mind, a strong nerve, and formidable physical courage. He possessed the priceless capacity for instantly sizing up a situation and issuing crisply concise, unambiguous orders which displayed a profound, intuitive grasp of a problem and its solution. He distilled with shrewdness his experience of courses and commands and the examples set by his seniors but his principal asset was an immense instinctive gift for war at sea.   MICHAEL SIMPSON

Sources BL, papers of Admiral of the Fleet Viscount Cunningham of Hyndhope · NMM, Papers of Admiral of the Fleet Viscount Cunningham of Hyndhope · CAC Cam., papers of Admiral of the Fleet Viscount Cunningham of Hyndhope · PRO, Admiralty records · cadet records, Britannia Royal Naval College, Dartmouth · PRO, war cabinet (chiefs of staff) records · A. Cunningham [first Viscount Cunningham], *A sailor's odyssey: the autobiography of admiral of the fleet, Viscount Cunningham of Hyndhope* (1951) · S. W. C. Pack, *Cunningham the commander* (1974) · *CGPLA Eng. & Wales* (1963) · m. cert. · d. cert. · *DNB* · J. Winton, *Cunningham* (1998) · O. Warner, *Cunningham of Hyndhope: admiral of the fleet* (1967)
Archives BL, corresp. and papers, Add. MSS 52557–52584 · CAC Cam., papers and letters · NMM, papers · PRO, admiralty and war cabinet papers | CAC Cam., corresp. with Sir James Somerville · IWM, letters to Sir Gerald Dickens · King's Lond., corresp. with Sir Gerald Dickens; corresp. with Sir B. H. Liddell Hart · NL Scot., letters to Principal George and Professor Douglas Duncan | FILM BFI NFTVA, current affairs footage · BFI NFTVA, documentary footage · BFI NFTVA, news footage · BFI NFTVA, record footage · IWM FVA, actuality footage · IWM FVA, current affairs footage · IWM FVA, news footage | SOUND IWM SA, oral history interview
Likenesses W. Stoneman, photograph, 1932, NPG · R. Langmaid, oils, 1942, NMM · photograph, 1942, Hult. Arch. · British Official Photograph, group portraits, photographs, 1943, Hult. Arch. · H. Carr, oils, 1943, IWM · Y. Karsh, photograph, 1943, NPG [*see illus.*] · D. S. Ewart, oils, *c*.1944, Gov. Art Coll. · M. Bone, group portrait, chalk drawing, 1945 (*Presenting White Ensign to Dean at St Giles Cathedral*), IWM · J. Esten, photograph, 1945, Hult. Arch. · W. Stoneman, photograph, 1945, NPG · J. Worsley, oils?, 1945, IWM · group portrait, photograph, 1945, Hult. Arch. · O. Birley, oils, 1947, Royal Naval College, Greenwich · O. Birley, oils, 1947, Britannia Royal Naval College, Dartmouth · O. Birley, oils, 1947, IWM · F. Belsky, bust, Trafalgar Square, London · photographs, IWM
Wealth at death £15,310 16s.: probate, 7 Oct 1963, *CGPLA Eng. & Wales*

Cunningham, Anna [Anne], **marchioness of Hamilton** (*d.* **1647**), noblewoman, was the fourth daughter of three sons and six daughters born to James *Cunningham, sixth earl of Glencairn (*c*.1552–1630) [*see under* Cunningham family] and his first wife, Mariot or Margaret (*d.* 1610), daughter of Colin Campbell of Glenorchy and his second wife, Catherine Ruthven. Margaret *Cunningham (*d.* 1622?), who married Sir James Hamilton, master of Evandale, was her sister. Anna's date of birth is unknown, but on 30 January 1603 she was contracted to marry the fourteen-year-old Lord James *Hamilton (1589–1625), eldest son of John *Hamilton, first marquess of Hamilton (1539/40–1604), bringing with her a dowry of 40,000 merks Scots (£2222 sterling). The following year her husband inherited his father's titles and James VI and I subsequently made him a gentleman of the bedchamber, a privy councillor, and steward of the royal household. He spent much of his time at court, leaving his plain but capable wife to bring up their family of at least eight children, including William *Hamilton, later second duke of Hamilton, and run his vast estates.

This the marchioness did, with energy and decision. She rode constantly round their lands, which stretched from Arran in the west of Scotland to Kinneil in the east, and oversaw all the expenditure. She did not learn to write until adult life, but the accounts bear her signature of authorization and some of them are entirely in her bold, italic hand, her calculations done in an alarming mixture of arabic and roman numerals. She initiated building work, employed the well-known decorative painter Valentine Jenkin to embellish ceilings and walls both at Hamilton Palace, the principal family seat, and at Kinneil, re-stocked the palace deer park, and undertook extensive planting. In the 1630s, thanking her relative Sir Colin Campbell of Glenorchy for fir seeds, she told him:

> Belive me, I think moir of them nor ye can imagin, for I love them moir nor I dou all the frout tris in the wordil. I have alrady ane four or fayf houndir of my awin planting that is pratti treis. (Breadalbane muniments, GD112/860b)

As is evident from her will, the marchioness also supervised industrial activities. She left to her eldest son the rights to her coalworks at Kinneil. In the past, she said, this enterprise had cost her much money and her servants had reaped the rewards, but she believed that the works were now in such a good state that they would bring him substantial benefit. Likewise she left him all her salt pans, 'for the profit wil be greit give [if] God send piece' (Hamilton archives, RH98/29/3).

After her husband's sudden death in London in 1625, Anna continued to run the estates for their eldest son, James *Hamilton, third marquess and later first duke of Hamilton (1606–1649). He was Charles I's principal Scottish adviser, and the outbreak of the first bishops' war in 1639 brought mother and son into conflict. As a convinced covenanter who was said to have attended conventicles in person, and who participated in the Shotts revival about 1630, the marchioness was bitterly opposed to Charles's ecclesiastical innovations, and when her son was appointed to command a royalist fleet sent north in June 1638 to crush the king's opponents she raised a troop of cavalry for the covenanting cause. According to contemporary reports, she rode at its head by day and by night, with her pistols and carbine at her side, threatening to shoot her son with a silver bullet should he set foot in Scotland.

The marchioness none the less continued to look after her son's estates, and three years later he sent his elder daughter, Anne [*see* Hamilton, Anne (1632–1716)], to be brought up by her. He himself returned to Hamilton in 1646 and sent for his younger daughter, Susanna. The girls were deeply upset when the marchioness fell seriously ill the following autumn during a visit to Edinburgh. Their father declined to take them to see her, however, telling them, 'Your sorrows would be increased, to be an eyewitness of her weak condition' (Marshall, *Duchess Anne*, 23). She died soon afterwards and was buried on 16 September 1647 at Hamilton parish church as she had wished, 'in the tombe of Hamilton, besayd my deir lord' (Hamilton archives, RH98/29/3).   ROSALIND K. MARSHALL

Sources R. K. Marshall, *The days of Duchess Anne* (1973) · R. K. Marshall, 'The house of Hamilton in its Anglo-Scottish setting in the seventeenth century', PhD diss., U. Edin., 1970 [incl. a

5-vol. calendar of the duke of Hamilton's archives] · R. K. Marshall, 'The plenishings of Hamilton Palace in the seventeenth century', *ROSC: review of Scottish culture*, ed. A. Fenton, H. Cheape, and R. K. Marshall (1987) · *Scots peerage*, vol. 4 · Lennoxlove, East Lothian, Hamilton archives, MS RH98/29/3 · NA Scot., Hamilton muniments, GD406 · GEC, *Peerage* · NA Scot., Breadalbane muniments, GD 112/860b

Archives NA Scot., Hamilton muniments, corresp., GD406 · Lennoxlove, East Lothian, Hamilton archives, account books, invoices, land transactions, etc.

Likenesses D. Mytens, oils, 1625, Lennoxlove, East Lothian, Hamilton collection · E. Harding, engraving (after G. Jamesone), Scot. NPG · G. Jamesone, oils (as a widow), priv. coll.

Cunningham, Sir Charles (1755–1834), naval officer, was born at Eye in Suffolk; details of his parents are unknown. He entered the navy from the merchant service in 1775, as a midshipman of the frigate *Aeolus*. In 1776 the *Aeolus* went to the West Indies, where Cunningham was transferred to the *Bristol*, carrying the flag of Sir Peter Parker. In June 1779 he received an acting order as lieutenant, and towards the end of the year he was for a short time first lieutenant of the *Hinchingbroke* with Captain Horatio Nelson. Continuing on the same station he was, in September 1782, appointed to command the brig *Admiral Barrington*, and sent by Sir Joshua Rowley to cruise for the protection of Turk's Island, to the north of St Domingo. During the brig's absence at Jamaica for provisions the French occupied Turk's Island, and repelled an attempt to regain it, made by Nelson in the *Albemarle*. The *Admiral Barrington* was paid off at Jamaica in May 1783, and Cunningham returned to England in the *Tremendous*.

In 1788 Cunningham went to the East Indies in the *Crown* with Commodore William Cornwallis, who would have been very familiar with his service in the West Indies between 1779 and 1782. Cornwallis promoted him commander into the sloop *Ariel* on 28 October 1790. On the declaration of war with France in February 1793 Cunningham, then in command of the brig *Speedy*, went out to the Mediterranean with dispatches; he remained attached to the Mediterranean Fleet and on 12 October, having assisted in the capture of the frigates *Modeste* and *Impérieuse*, was made post into the latter, renamed the *Unité*. He exchanged into the *Lowestoft* in April 1794 and in the summer assisted at the siege of Calvi, a service for which he, together with the other frigate captains, was specially mentioned in Lord Hood's dispatch, which he carried home overland, leaving Calvi on 11 August and reaching London on 1 September. In April 1796 he was appointed to the frigate *Clyde*, in the North Sea, and in May 1797 he was refitting at the Nore when the mutiny broke out. Cunningham, a popular captain, was, however, not absolutely dispossessed of the command, and succeeded, after seventeen days, in bringing his men back to their duty. During the night of 29 May the *Clyde* slipped her cables, and before morning was safe in Sheerness harbour. Her defection was the signal to many other ships to do likewise, and within a week the fleet had returned to its allegiance.

Continuing in the *Clyde* in the North Sea and in the channel, Cunningham had the good fortune to meet the French frigate *Vestale* in the Bay of Biscay, which he captured without serious difficulty; for though of nominally the same number of guns, the *Vestale* mounted only 12-pounders on her main deck, compared to the *Clyde*'s 18-pounders. Furthermore the *Vestale*'s crew was smaller, and ravaged by yellow fever; she was not purchased for the navy. The capture, which was creditable enough to Cunningham, and not discreditable to the French captain, was commended by Lord Keith, with absurd exaggeration, as 'one of the most brilliant transactions which have occurred during the course of the war'. George III was in the theatre at Weymouth when he received the news, and commanded it to be communicated to the audience, on which the audience offered an enthusiastic rendition of 'Rule Britannia'. After a very active and successful commission over more than six years, and which included taking the Spanish ship *Veloz* in August 1800, the *Clyde* was paid off in June 1802. In May 1803 Cunningham was appointed to the *Prince of Orange*, and for a few months he commanded a squadron keeping watch on the Dutch in the Texel; but in September he was rewarded for his zealous and effective service, being nominated a commissioner of the victualling board. Such shore appointments were suitable rewards for relatively elderly captains (he was then forty-eight) who could not expect a flag appointment.

In 1806 Cunningham was appointed commissioner of the dockyards at Deptford and Woolwich. He held this post until April 1823, when he became superintendent of the dockyard at Chatham; and in May 1829 he retired with the rank of rear-admiral. On 24 October 1832 he was created knight commander of the Royal Guelphic Order by William IV, another veteran of the West Indies theatre (1779–82). After a late entry into the service, and lacking any powerful interest, Cunningham had secured his promotion through professional skill, zeal, and initiative. The connection with Nelson and William Cornwallis is striking, as was his conduct during the Nore mutiny. Ashore he was efficient and a credit to his profession; a fine officer in all respects.

Cunningham was twice married; details of his wives are unknown, though it is known that he had been left a widower for some years, living latterly with his daughters in the neighbourhood of Eye. He died there on 11 March 1834. J. K. LAUGHTON, *rev.* ANDREW LAMBERT

Sources *The dispatches and letters of Vice-Admiral Lord Viscount Nelson*, ed. N. H. Nicolas, 7 vols. (1844–6), vol. 1 · D. Syrett and R. L. DiNardo, *The commissioned sea officers of the Royal Navy, 1660–1815*, rev. edn, Occasional Publications of the Navy RS, 1 (1994) · W. L. Clowes, *The Royal Navy: a history from the earliest times to the present*, 7 vols. (1897–1903) · G. E. Manwaring and B. Dobrée, *The floating republic: an account of the mutinies at Spithead and the Nore in 1797* (1935)

Archives NMM, log book and corresp.

Likenesses H. Wyatt, oils, *c.*1833–1834, NMM

Cunningham, Sir Charles Craik (1906–1998), civil servant, was born on 7 May 1906 in Dundee, the only child of Richard Yule Cunningham of Abergeldie, Kirriemuir, Forfarshire, a stationer and bookseller, and his wife, Isabella Adam, *née* Craik. He had a brilliant academic career at the

Sir Charles Craik Cunningham (1906–1998), by unknown photographer

Harris Academy, Dundee, and St Andrews University, where he read English, German, and Humanity, graduating with a first-class degree in 1928 and BLitt in 1929. (He later received an honorary LLD from St Andrews, in 1960.) He joined the administrative civil service in 1929. He was posted to the small Scottish Office in Whitehall, and was soon spotted as a high flyer. From 1933 to 1934 he was private secretary to the parliamentary under-secretary of state for Scotland, and from 1935 to 1938 he was private secretary to three successive secretaries of state. He married, on 10 July 1934, Edith Louisa (1910–1990), daughter of Frank Coutts Webster. It was a long and happy marriage. They had two daughters, Edith Isobel (b. 1935) and Margaret (b. 1937).

In 1939 Cunningham was due to go to Edinburgh as an assistant secretary in the newly created Scottish home department, but the outbreak of the Second World War kept him in London for some fifteen months, acting as a liaison officer between the new department and the Whitehall ministries. When he eventually moved to Edinburgh, he rose steadily up the hierarchy and in 1948 was appointed secretary of the department, a post he held for nine years. He remained throughout firmly in charge. Later in life he looked back nostalgically to the time when James Stuart was his political superior, as secretary of state (from 1951 to 1957); Stuart concentrated on major governmental policies, and gave his senior officials a fairly free hand. The Scottish home department's role was

at this period expanding in a wide spectrum of activity, including penal reform, police and fire service training, child care, hydroelectricity, roads, tourism, and the fishing industry. Cunningham felt that his department had a real contribution to make in promoting Scotland's economic development. He was knighted KBE in 1952, having been appointed CVO in 1941 and CB in 1946.

Cunningham, as a stout defender of Scottish interests, became well known in Whitehall, and in 1957 the home secretary R. A. (Rab) Butler agreed to his appointment as permanent under-secretary of state at the Home Office. The responsibilities of the Home Office in the field of criminal justice were familiar enough to Cunningham from his Scottish experience, although the scale was greater. He lost no time in setting up for the first time a professional research unit, and encouraged the creation of the Cambridge Institute of Criminology. The year 1959 saw the publication of Butler's white paper *Penal Practice in a Changing Society*, the first general discussion on penal methods since the Gladstone report of 1895. In 1960 a royal commission on the police was appointed. In 1963 Cunningham merged the work of the Prison Commission into that of the Home Office, to improve co-operation between all the divisions dealing with offenders. When he left office, he had brought to an advanced state proposals for appointing a Parole Board.

Cunningham was assiduous in coping with the various other activities of the Home Office, which included relations with the Channel Islands and the Isle of Man, and running the state management scheme for the public houses and breweries of the Carlisle and Gretna Green districts. He used to travel and meet those concerned on the ground. He also found himself facing a new problem: immigration from the Commonwealth. He was involved in the anxious discussions which led to the Commonwealth Immigration Act, 1962, which for the first time imposed restrictions on entry to the UK from the Commonwealth. In 1965 he accompanied Lord Mountbatten on a mission to various Commonwealth countries to try to persuade them to set up controls and health checks at source. In Pakistan it fell to him to conduct the negotiations.

Cunningham (who was promoted KCB in 1961) brought with him to the Home Office the personal style he had evolved in Scotland, a style made possible only by his prodigious capacity for work. On important policy issues he liked to present to ministers only his own submission, setting out his account of the facts and arguments, and his recommendations. The staff found it somewhat frustrating that their efforts were not seen by ministers, but Butler, although he found the procedure rather odd compared with his experience in the Foreign Office, did not disturb it. Nor did Henry Brooke, who succeeded Butler in 1962 and achieved unpopularity in liberal circles for what was thought to be insensitive handling of some immigration and deportation cases. Sir Frank Soskice, who followed Brooke in 1964 (and, like him, failed to improve his reputation while at the Home Office), also accepted what was on offer. But Roy Jenkins, who succeeded Soskice towards the end of 1965, found the procedure unacceptable. He wanted to know all about the background and to see what others had said so that he could make up his own mind. He began with a confrontation with Cunningham over some staff appointments, but the main battle took place over submissions. Cunningham in the end had to give way. Jenkins respected his great ability, but would not agree to a further extension of his appointment, and he retired in the summer of 1966.

Cunningham was almost immediately appointed to the board of the Atomic Energy Authority, and in October 1966 he became its deputy chairman. During his five years in the post he devoted his skill and energy to furthering the authority's interests. He tried hard to resist proposals for breaking up the authority, and encouraged diversification into non-nuclear work. From 1971 to 1974 he chaired the newly formed Radiochemical Centre Ltd, and he was a founder member of the National Radiological Protection Board. He also chaired selection boards for the civil service commission. In 1972 he chaired the Ugandan Resettlement Board, which tackled with energy and considerable success the formidable problem of resettling some 28,500 Ugandan Asians expelled by Idi Amin. He was promoted GCB in 1974.

Cunningham was a small, wiry individual, with extraordinary stamina. He was always punctilious in attending functions where he thought his department should be represented, and would then work at home far into the night. He was polite and courteous, albeit with touches of impatience; in private conversation he exercised a highly entertaining, if somewhat mordant, wit; and he was a fluent public speaker. He was essentially a liberal and humane man, but tended sometimes to be a little rigid in his approach. He was not a dominant figure in Whitehall, but was much respected as an effective departmental head. A man of formidable intellect and complete integrity, a prodigious and conscientious worker, an expert in so many fields, in possession of an outstanding analytical ability, he was a public servant of great distinction.

Lady Cunningham died in 1990, and in the following year Cunningham moved back to Edinburgh. He continued to live an active life, although troubled by failing sight, but a few months before his death he went into the Strachan House Nursing Home, Edinburgh. He died there on 7 July 1998, of cancer. He was survived by his two daughters. ALLEN OF ABBEYDALE

Sources The Times (10 July 1998) · The Independent (10 July 1998) · The Guardian (13 July 1998) · The Scotsman (13 July 1998) · Daily Telegraph (15 July 1998) · R. Jenkins, A life at the centre (1991) · Baron Butler of Saffron Walden [R. A. Butler], The art of the possible: the memoirs of Lord Butler (1971) · P. Ziegler, Mountbatten: the official biography (1985) · WWW · Burke, Peerage · private information (2004) · personal knowledge (2004)

Likenesses photograph, 1972, repro. in Daily Telegraph · photograph, repro. in The Times [see illus.] · photograph, repro. in The Independent · photograph, repro. in The Guardian

Wealth at death £573,482.86: confirmation, 2 Dec 1998, CCI

Cunningham, Cuthbert, second earl of Glencairn (c.1470–1540/41). See under Cunningham family (per. c.1340–1631).

Cunningham, Daniel John (1850–1909), anatomist, born at the manse of Crieff, in Strathearn, on 15 April 1850, was the youngest son in a family of three sons and four daughters of John *Cunningham (1819–1893) and his wife, Susan Porteous (d. 1902), daughter of William Murray, a banker in Crieff and his wife, Susan Porteous, a relative of Captain John Porteous. After education at Crieff Academy Cunningham spent some three years working in a large mercantile business in Glasgow. But his inclination was for medical study, and in 1870 he entered the University of Edinburgh as a medical student whence he graduated in 1874 with the highest honours. For a few months he practised in Glasgow, but he returned in 1876 to become demonstrator of anatomy in the University of Edinburgh, and for a time held, with this post, the chair of physiology in the Edinburgh Veterinary College. In 1882 he became professor of anatomy in the school of the Royal College of Surgeons in Ireland, and the next year was appointed professor of anatomy in Trinity College, Dublin. Here, for twenty years, he was the most popular teacher in the university. In 1903 he succeeded Sir William Turner as professor of anatomy in the University of Edinburgh where he worked with enthusiasm and success until his death. He married, in 1878, Elizabeth Cumming, eldest daughter of Andrew Browne, minister of the parish of Beith in Ayrshire; they had two daughters and three sons, the latter including Andrew Browne *Cunningham, Viscount Cunningham of Hyndhope (1883–1963), and Sir Alan Gordon *Cunningham (1887–1983).

As a lecturer Cunningham had the talent of illuminating scientific subjects by illustrations drawn from every field of science. His enthusiasm and perseverance were contagious, and roused the latent powers of both colleagues and pupils. He published original research in human and comparative anatomy, as well as in anthropology. In addition to numerous papers in the Journal of Anatomy and Physiology, of which he was the acting editor, and in other scientific publications, he issued Report on the Marsupialia Brought Home by H.M.S. Challenger (1878) and The Dissector's Guide for Students (1879), which subsequently developed into his Manual of Practical Anatomy (2 vols., 1893–4). The Cunningham Fund, founded in memory of Timothy Cunningham, for the publication of work of special merit connected with the Royal Irish Academy, issued two papers by Cunningham: On the Lumbar Curve in Man and the Apes (1886) and On the Surface Anatomy of the Cerebral Hemispheres (1892). To the Transactions of the same academy he contributed a 'Memoir on Cornelius Magrath, the Irish giant: a research into the connection which exists between giantism and acromegaly' (1891); and to the Transactions of the Royal Dublin Society a 'Memoir on the microcephalic idiot' (1895). He delivered before the Anthropological Institute in 1902 the third Huxley memorial lecture, on 'Right-handedness and left-brainedness', for which he was awarded a memorial medal. In conjunction with Edward Hallaran Bennett he wrote The Sectional Anatomy of Congenital Caecal Hernia (1888). Of the Textbook of Anatomy, published in 1902 by the pupils of Sir William Turner, he acted as editor and joint author.

In administrative affairs Cunningham exercised great influence in the councils of the universities and of the learned societies with which he was connected, and he played a significant part in the establishment of postgraduate instruction at Edinburgh. He was a member of the commission to inquire into the management of the sick and wounded in the Second South African War, of the War Office committee on the standard of candidates and recruits for the army, and of the vice-regal commission on the inland fisheries of Ireland. He was largely responsible for inaugurating the medical department of the Territorial Army in Scotland. Cunningham received many honorary degrees—MD and ScD, Dublin, LLD, St Andrews and Glasgow, and DCL, Oxford, in 1892, on the celebration of the tercentenary of Trinity College, Dublin. He was elected FRS on 4 June 1891, and was president of the Royal Zoological Society of Ireland, and vice-president of the Royal Dublin Society.

Cunningham became ill towards the end of 1908 and journeyed to Egypt, and then the Riviera, in the hope of regaining his health. He died at his home, 18 Grosvenor Crescent, Edinburgh, on 23 June 1909. His funeral service was held at St Cuthbert's parish church before his body was interred in Dean cemetery, Edinburgh, on 26 June. A memorial service was held in St Giles's Cathedral on 27 June. He was survived by his wife and children. A memorial bronze bas-relief was placed, in duplicate, on the walls of the anatomical departments of the University of Edinburgh and of the University of Dublin.

G. A. GIBSON, rev. MICHAEL BEVAN

Sources BMJ (3 July 1909), 53–7 · The Lancet (3 July 1909), 54–5 · CGPLA Eng. & Wales (1909) · WWW
Archives U. Edin., corresp. and working papers · Wellcome L., papers
Likenesses O. Sheppard, bronze panel, TCD; replica, U. Edin.
Wealth at death see sealed, 10 Sept 1909, CGPLA Eng. & Wales

Cunningham, David (c.1540–1600), bishop of Aberdeen, is of uncertain parentage—his father may have been William Cunningham of Cunninghamhead. Although the identification cannot be taken as certain, he was probably the David Cunningham who was incorporated in St Leonard's College, St Andrews, by 25 March 1557, and who graduated MA between 23 November 1560 and 6 November 1562—most probably in 1561. These dates suggest that he was born about 1540. There is no doubt that he studied in France, first in Paris, and then at Bourges, where he read civil law. He clearly found no difficulty in accepting protestantism, for by 1562 he had become minister of Lanark. Under a contract of 20 December 1569 he married Katherine Wallace. In November 1570 he was transferred to the parish of Lesmahagow, and two years later to that of Cadder. In 1573 he was mentioned as minister of Monkland, and in 1574 he was also in charge of Lenzie.

In 1573 the general assembly elected Cunningham to the committee that formulated instructions for the assembly's commissioners in their forthcoming negotiations with the regent and the privy council concerning the remuneration of ministers. Two years later the assembly nominated Cunningham and three others to review the election of George Douglas as bishop of Moray, and in 1576 he was appointed to a committee to investigate the state of the kirk in Ayrshire, Clydesdale, and Lennox. The committee's report was drafted by Cunningham, who in that same year was also elected to a committee chosen to prepare the assembly's answers to questions from the government. In the meantime Cunningham was also one of several ministers who helped Andrew Melville with preparing the second Book of Discipline. Melville had introduced reforms at Glasgow University from 1574, and probably facilitated Cunningham's translation to Glasgow, where in 1576 he was dean of the faculty of arts and subdean in the cathedral. The government appointed him in 1584 to perform the principal's duties, until the position was filled by Patrick Sharp at the beginning of 1586.

In 1576 Patrick Adamson, minister of Paisley and Regent Morton's chaplain, accepted the archiepiscopal see of St Andrews. Cunningham succeeded him as chaplain to Morton's household, but did not keep that position for long, since on 5 October 1577 he was appointed to the see of Aberdeen; he was consecrated on 11 November. In the same year he became chancellor of King's College, Aberdeen, a post which he held until his death. As well as his bishopric he had the charge of Aberdeen East parish, which in 1596 he exchanged for St Nicholas's parish; this too he held until he died. His acceptance of Aberdeen did not at first estrange Cunningham from a general assembly that was becoming increasingly hostile to bishops, possibly because it hoped to use him as a means of access to the regent. But Morton's fall in 1580 and his execution in 1581 saw Cunningham reduced to hiding in the west in abject poverty, a fate which Andrew Melville's nephew James saw as God's punishment of Cunningham's apostasy from the 'guid cause' by becoming a bishop.

Cunningham's relations with the general assembly were commonly strained thereafter. The assembly increasingly saw itself as the supreme authority in the kirk, and could not therefore accept the appointment of bishops by the government. It raised the issue in 1580, 1582, and 1583, though without conclusion. Then in 1586 it accused Cunningham of adultery with one Elizabeth Sutherland. The loss of the assembly's records makes it impossible to know whether the charge was politically inspired, but in the following year James VI (though not the assembly itself) found that he had been sufficiently cleared of the slander. In 1585 Cunningham founded a grammar school at Banff, but his effectiveness as bishop was probably limited by the poverty to which his predecessor had reduced his see. He became a trusted servant of King James, however, and baptized Prince Henry at Stirling on 30 August 1594. In the winter of 1596–7 he took part in the negotiations which eventually led to the reconciliation of the Catholic earl of Huntly with the government, and in 1598 he was sent with Peter Young on an embassy to Denmark and northern Germany in order to gain support for James VI's claim to the English throne.

Cunningham died in Aberdeen on 3 August 1600, leaving assets valued at £3052 Scots. He had no children. He was survived by his wife, who two years later married Robert Udny of Tillicortrie, second son of William Udny of that ilk.   THOMAS RIIS

Sources P. J. Anderson, ed., *Officers and graduates of University and King's College, Aberdeen, MVD–MDCCCLX*, New Spalding Club, 11 (1893) • D. Calderwood, *The history of the Kirk of Scotland*, ed. T. Thomson and D. Laing, 8 vols., Wodrow Society, 7 (1842–9), vols. 3–5 • C. Innes, ed., *Munimenta alme Universitatis Glasguensis / Records of the University of Glasgow from its foundation till 1727*, 4 vols., Maitland Club, 72 (1854) • R. Lippe, ed., *Selections from Wodrow's biographical collections: divines of the north-east of Scotland*, New Spalding Club, 5 (1890) • J. M. Anderson, ed., *Early records of the University of St Andrews*, Scottish History Society, 3rd ser., 8 (1926) • *Aberdeen Journal notes and queries*, 6 (1913) • T. Riis, *Should auld acquaintance be forgot … Scottish–Danish relations, c.1450–1707*, 2 vols. (1988) • *Fasti Scot.*, new edn, vols. 3, 6–8 • J. Durhan and J. Kirk, *The University of Glasgow, 1451–1577* (1977) • D. G. Mullan, *Episcopacy in Scotland: the history of an idea, 1560–1608* (1986) • J. Kirk, *Patterns of reform: continuity and change in the Reformation kirk* (1989)
Wealth at death £3052 Scots: Mullan, *Episcopacy in Scotland*, 128

Cunningham [Calze], **Edward Francis** (*c*.1741–1793?), portrait painter, is thought to have been born in Kelso, the son of a Scottish gentleman with Jacobite leanings. His peripatetic career is the subject of much hearsay and misapprehension. It is thought that his father, having been involved in the Jacobite rising, fled Scotland following the defeat of Charles Edward Stuart in 1745 and settled in Bologna. Cunningham, who accompanied him, was apparently raised under the name Calze or Calza, probably in reference to his Scottish place of birth. He trained first as an artist in Parma and from 1757 in Rome, in the studio of Anton Raphael Mengs, one of six Scottish artists introduced by the Jacobite advocate Andrew Lumisden. In 1762 he was in Parma, where he studied under Giuseppe Baldrighi (1723–1803) and at the Accademia di Belle Arti. (A dated nude study by him still survives there.) Cunningham is also supposed to have studied in Naples, in the studio of Francesco de Mura, and in Venice. It was presumably after this that he visited Paris, where he painted a portrait of the king of Denmark, which apparently attracted further commissions. Among these were two pastels, signed Calze and dated 1768, of Louis Adrien Thiery and his wife, Catherine Thérèse Auguste (ex Christies, London, 4 July 1984, lot 147).

Cunningham was subsequently invited to England by his patron, the second Lord Lyttleton. At this time he inherited his father's estate and apparently resumed using his Scottish family name. For a while he is said to have given up painting, although he exhibited at the Royal Academy between 1770 and 1773, mainly in pastels, under the name E. F. Calze. Horace Walpole referred to him in his exhibition catalogue as an Italian. He was possibly also the self-styled 'F. Calza, il Bolognese' who exhibited at the Royal Academy between 1777 and 1781. Cunningham's academy exhibits included portraits of the Danish minister Baron Diedeu (1770) and Monsieur Nolken, the Sardinian envoy (1772), and *A Hunting Piece* (1773). In 1770 he was living in London in Pall Mall, opposite St James's Square, although his subsequent addresses included Gerrard Street, Soho, Great Marlborough Street, and latterly Mount Street, Grosvenor Square, at a Mr Pasquier's. In England Cunningham is reputed to have lived lavishly, resulting in his bankruptcy. According to Edwards, Cunningham's 'profligacy and want of principle obliged him to leave England, but not before he had ill-treated his patron, who compelled him to atone for his improper conduct in one of the courts of Westminster Hall' (Edwards, 42–3).

It was after this event, some time after 1773, that Cunningham left England for St Petersburg in the train of the duchess of Kingston. He was subsequently employed by Catherine the Great, before moving to Berlin, apparently in 1784, where he was patronized by the Prussian court. Portraits painted there include *Frederick the Great returning to Sans Souci after the manoeuvres at Potsdam, accompanied by his generals*. A number of his court portraits still exist in Berlin: Sir Ellis Waterhouse describes them as 'peculiar in colour and coarse in execution' (Waterhouse, *18c painters*, 96). His portrait of the queen of Prussia belongs to the British Royal Collection. A number of Cunningham's portraits, including Prussian and British subjects, were engraved by Cunego, Haas, Townley, and Valentine Green, who engraved a portrait of Catherine Clarke dated 1771. His portrait of Admiral Sir Samuel Hood was engraved by Albanesi in 1782. Among his latest known works is a portrait of Elena Toregiani seated at the piano, signed and dated 'Calze fece l'anno 1793' (ex Phillips, London, 27 October 1987, lot 28). Cunningham is reported to have died in Berlin on 28 April 1793, although it has also been claimed that he returned once more to England, succeeding commercially, before dying in poverty in 1795.

L. H. CUST, *rev.* MARTIN POSTLE

Sources Thieme & Becker, *Allgemeines Lexikon*, 8.199–200 • Redgrave, *Artists*, 2nd edn, 110 • J. Ingamells, ed., *A dictionary of British and Irish travellers in Italy, 1701–1800* (1997), 262 • E. Edwards, *Anecdotes of painters* (1808); facs. edn (1970) • Waterhouse, *18c painters*, 96

Cunningham, Francis (1820–1875), army officer and literary editor, was the youngest son of Allan *Cunningham (1784–1842), Scottish poet and songwriter, and his wife, Jean Walker (1791–1864). He inherited from his father a love of literature also seen in the life of his brother Peter *Cunningham (1816–1869), author and literary editor. Francis Cunningham's other brothers were equally influential on his life, however, in the conduct of their military careers: Sir Alexander *Cunningham (1814–1893), was a general of the British forces in India and an archaeologist; Joseph Davey *Cunningham (1812–1851), was also a soldier in India, and a historian of the Sikhs.

In 1838 Francis Cunningham joined the 23rd light infantry of the Madras army as an ensign. In the next year he was appointed to the 'Shah's Sappers', which was to escort into Kabul, according to Lord Auckland's proclamation, Shah Shuja, the British choice for the legitimate monarch of the Afghans. In the disaster that followed in 1841–2, as the Afghan tribes revolted and the British troops retreated toward India, the young officer and field engineer won distinction, especially at the defence of Jalalabad. There he

Francis Cunningham (1820–1875), by Sir Francis Legatt Chantrey

was recognized by his comrades in the Madras army as showing 'by his fertility of resource, his gallant bearing, and unextinguishable vivacity … the life and soul of that memorable defence' (*Athenaeum*). Immediately on the withdrawal of his army into India, Cunningham was placed by Lord Ellenborough in the Mysore commission. During the remainder of his military career, in which he rose to the rank of lieutenant-colonel, Cunningham held a special position in the British establishment that ruled from Bangalore this part of central India (which remained peaceful even during the time of the mutiny). Visitors remembered not only his 'fine presence and delightful companionship' but his superb private library open to all, 'a perfect marvel for an Indian station' (ibid.) in mid-century.

By 1861 Cunningham's health had begun to break under the stress and intensity of his service. He retired to London to a little house on Clarendon Road, Kensington, where 'hall, staircase, and every room … were crowded with curious books, rare engravings, and a few valuable old pictures' (*Athenaeum*), especially four 1798 pencil drawings of Charles Lamb, S. T. Coleridge, Robert Southey, and William Wordsworth. Among his books (later given to the British Library) were Lamb's copy of the 1616 folio of Ben Jonson, with marginal notes by Lamb and Coleridge, and Lamb's copy of Beaumont and Fletcher. This house became the centre of the bachelor and semi-invalid's last fourteen years. A frequent contributor to the *Saturday Review*, he produced a new (if not always accurate) text of Christopher Marlowe in 1870 and a new text of Philip Massinger in 1871. Whatever their limitations (he was always the enlightened amateur), both texts produced useful and original notes and perceptive emendations. After he published a new edition of Ben Jonson in three volumes in 1871, Cunningham revised and reissued in 1875 William Gifford's 1816 text of Ben Jonson. He fully intended to use these early works as the basis for the first modern authoritative and complete edition of Jonson, but he died at his home, 18 Clarendon Road, London, on 3 December 1875, before he could complete the task. His friend A. H. Bullen, who wrote Cunningham's obituary in *The Athenaeum* fifteen days after his death, praised his 'many qualifications for the task' of producing this edition of Jonson and 'his intention to edit Ben Jonson elaborately' (*Athenaeum*).

When the twentieth-century editors C. H. Herford and Percy and Evelyn Simpson made their definitive edition of Jonson in eleven volumes, they turned to Cunningham, pointing out his failures. He had, for instance, made the proper corrections of Jonson's texts in his 1871 edition, but simply reprinted Gifford's own incorrect text in 1875, then adding a list of corrections and supplementary notes—a method Swinburne disparaged. In his revision of Gifford's text of Jonson's *English Grammar*, Cunningham also revealed his lack of reading of the manuscript evidence of Jonson's texts and their proper order. Yet the twentieth-century editors also praised Cunningham's abilities, noting that he had been the first to edit and print the full version of William Drummond's *Conversations with Ben Jonson*, to add to the canon a number of poems, and to find new biographical documents and evidence.

W. A. SESSIONS

Sources *The Athenaeum* (18 Dec 1875), 830–31 · Boase, *Mod. Eng. biog.* · DNB
Likenesses F. L. Chantrey, marble bust, Scot. NPG [*see illus.*]
Wealth at death under £2000: administration, 17 June 1876, CGPLA Eng. & Wales

Cunningham, Sir George (1888–1963), administrator in India, was born on 23 March 1888 at Broughty Ferry, on Tayside, Forfarshire. He was the third son of a jute merchant, James Cunningham. His mother, Anna, *née* Sandeman, died in 1892 when he was just four, and the family afterwards moved to St Andrews. He was educated at Fettes College and at Magdalen College, Oxford. He successively captained the Oxford and Scottish rugby teams, and won eight international caps in all before his entry into the Indian Civil Service and departure for the subcontinent in 1911. He served initially as an assistant commissioner in the Punjab, but most of his professional career was devoted to the north-west frontier, where he established his reputation as this volatile region's most distinguished officer since Herbert Edwardes in the mutiny period. Cunningham served his apprenticeship (1914–17) as assistant to the chief commissioner, Sir George Roos-Keppel. This experience was further widened with a spell as political agent (1922–3) in the tribal territories of North Waziristan. During this first period of Cunningham's career, the north-west frontier was rocked by the 1919 disturbances and the hostilities with Afghanistan, and he acquired the expertise in dealing with the delicate intertribal relations and defence issues which were to be the distinguishing features of his career. After a brief spell in

Sir George Cunningham (1888–1963), by Bassano, 1947

1925–6 as counsellor at the British legation in Kabul, Cunningham was transferred to New Delhi where he spent five years as private secretary to the viceroy, Lord Irwin.

Serious unrest resurfaced in the north-west frontier with rioting in Peshawar on 23 April 1930. The agitation was connected with the All-India National Congress civil disobedience movement, although it had a strong local dimension and was orchestrated by the Pakhtun nationalist Khudai Khidmatgars ('Servants of God'). The Khudai Khidmatgar movement had been formed by Abdul Ghaffar Khan, and its members wore uniforms dyed by red brick dust and were dubbed the Red Shirts by the colonial authorities. The British repression of the disturbances was accompanied by the introduction of representative institutions with the establishment of a new legislative council in April 1932. Cunningham returned to the frontier to serve as home member. He was acting governor from November 1932 to May 1933, and later served as governor for the period 1937–46.

The hallmark of this period was Cunningham's tact in his dealings with the Khudai Khidmatgars, who were allied with the Congress from 1931 onwards. In the later stages of the Pakistan movement, the Red Shirts' ties with the 'Hindu' Congress in the overwhelmingly Muslim frontier appeared increasingly anomalous. They sowed the seeds for the tensions between a Pakhtun and Pakistani identity which were to surface after 1947. Cunningham initially encouraged the United Muslim Nationalists rather than the Khudai Khidmatgars, when he invited their leader, Sir Abdul Qaiyum, to form a ministry in March 1937. It survived until September, when Dr Khan

Sahib formed a Congress ministry. Cunningham established a good working relationship with his ministers until their resignation in November 1939. It was his accurate reading of the decline in the frontier Congress's fortunes, however, which lay behind his restrained response to the 1942 Quit India movement. Despite the misgivings expressed in New Delhi, Cunningham's approach avoided the confrontations of the 1919–20 and 1930–32 periods. General Sir Claude Auchinleck indeed remarked that Cunningham's masterly handling of the Quit India campaign was worth two army corps. Cunningham however had to bow to the desire of the viceroy, Lord Linlithgow, for the encouragement of a non-Congress government. Again he perceptively observed that Aurangzeb Khan's Muslim League government, which came to power in May 1943, was likely to be short-lived and beset with corruption and factionalism. Its poor performance contributed to the Muslim League's patchy results in the 1946 elections.

Cunningham retired to Britain in the spring of that year. His distinguished career had seen him successively appointed CIE (1925), CSI (1931), KCIE (1935), KCSI (1937), and finally, in 1946, GCIE. The following April he was installed as rector of St Andrews University, from which he had already received an honorary LLD. Within three months, however, he was back in Peshawar as governor of the frontier which had now become part of Pakistan, at the request of M. A. Jinnah, the governor-general. There could have been no greater testament to the high regard in which Cunningham's knowledge of the frontier was held. He soon found himself plunged into a political maelstrom.

The Muslim League had few historic roots in the frontier, but within a week of independence Dr Khan Sahib's Congress ministry had been dismissed. Abdul Ghaffar Khan's continuing championing of the Pakhtunistan demand at a time of tension with both neighbouring India and Afghanistan presented Cunningham with a major problem. He became seriously ill in the spring of 1948 and retired home on the advice of his doctors.

Cunningham was elected an honorary fellow of his old Oxford college in 1948. His retirement was spent at St Andrews with his devoted Irish wife, Kathleen Mary (née Adair), whom he had married on 2 January 1929. He was elected captain of the Royal and Ancient Golf Club, and in keeping with the sporting prowess of his youth was still able to break eighty on its demanding greens when over the age of seventy. Cunningham died suddenly, on 8 December 1963, at the Teddington home of Lady Halifax, while he was on his annual pilgrimage to the Oxford–Cambridge rugby match at nearby Twickenham.

Sir George Cunningham was held in great respect by his colleagues, not just because of his immense knowledge and expertise, but because of his tact, imperturbability, and tolerance. He was the outstanding official of his generation in a region which was of crucial strategic importance to the Indian empire. IAN TALBOT

Sources N. Mitchell, *Sir George Cunningham: a memoir* (1968) · E. Jansson, *India, Pakistan or Pakhtunistan? the nationalist movements in the North-West Frontier Province, 1937–47* (1981) · O. Caroe, *The Pathans,*

550 BC–AD 1957 (1973) • J. W. Spain, *The way of the Pathans* (1975) • A. H. Swinson, *North-west frontier: people and events, 1839–1947* (1967) • A. K. Gupta, *NWFP legislature and freedom struggle, 1932–47* (1976) • A. Vaiyum, *Gold and guns on the Pathan frontier* (1945) • G. L. Zutshi, *Frontier Gandhi* (1970) • G. Cunningham, 'Reforms in the North-West Frontier Province of India', *Journal of the Royal Central Asian Society*, 24 (1937), 90–101 • J. Bright, *Frontier and its Gandhi* (1944) • *DNB*

Archives BL OIOC, corresp. and papers, Eur. MS D 670 • CAC Cam., papers | BL OIOC, Caroe MSS • BL OIOC, corresp. with Sir T. H. Keyes, Eur. MS F 131 • BL OIOC, corresp. with Lord Linlithgow, Eur. MS F 125 • BL OIOC, Mudie MSS • BL OIOC, North-West Front-ier Province governor and chief commissioner fortnightly reports • Bodl. Oxf., corresp. with Sir Aurel Stein | SOUND BL NSA, current affairs recording • IWM SA, oral history interview **Likenesses** Bassano, photograph, 1947, NPG [*see illus.*] **Wealth at death** £172,428 2s. 3d.: confirmation, 20 Jan 1964, CCI

Cunningham, Sir Henry Stewart (1832–1920), lawyer and novelist, was born at the vicarage, Harrow, Middlesex, on 30 June 1832, the fifth son and penultimate child of the fourteen children of the Revd John William *Cunning-ham (1780–1861); Henry was the third of the four children from his father's second marriage, to Mary Calvert (1800–1849), a general's daughter and the sister of Sir Harry Verney, model Christian landowner. The vicarage was a stronghold of educated evangelicalism. Henry's mother intended him for the church, and he was sent to Mr Ren-aud's evangelical school at Bayford, Hertfordshire, before attending Harrow School (1845–51), where his father had been a governor since 1818. At Harrow he won the Peel medal. He then spent four months as a private tutor in Norwich before matriculating at Trinity College, Oxford, in 1851, where he took a second class in Greats (1856) and won the chancellor's prize for the English essay.

On 10 June 1859 Cunningham was called to the bar of the Inner Temple, London. He supplemented his earnings by writing: in the summer of 1860 he was in Italy report-ing on Garibaldi's successes, and in 1861 his first novel, *Wheat and Tares*, was published. His paternal uncle Francis Cunningham, vicar of Lowestoft, Suffolk, and his wife, the former Richenda Gurney, were recognized as the model for the clerical household in this—not unkind—satirical account of the evangelical milieu of a fashionable watering-place. Five other novels followed, all of which demonstrate a fondness for Latin tags and a tendency for the comedy of manners to sit uneasily with a romantic plot in which a serious illness, or tragic death, effects a morally educative lesson.

On his father's death in 1861, Cunningham and his younger sister, Emily, moved to 6 Craven Hill, Hyde Park, London, but the household had to be dismantled in 1866 when his partner in a tea firm, in which he had invested his own and other relatives' money, absconded, leaving him bankrupt. Later that year he became government advocate and legal adviser to the Punjab. He was joined first by Emily and then by his brother-in-law, Sir James Fitzjames Stephen, in whose task of codifying Indian law he became involved in 1871. After a break in Simla, he served as advocate-general in Madras from 1872 (possibly

1873) to 1877: appointed a member of the famine commis-sion, he drew upon the expertise of another family con-nection, Florence Nightingale. On furlough, he married, on 28 July 1877, the Hon. Harriett Emily Lawrence (*d.* 1918), daughter of John Laird *Lawrence, first Baron Lawrence, who had been viceroy of India when Cunningham first arrived. The couple returned to Calcutta, where he became a high court judge (1877–87). In 1881 the famine commission made its report, and he published *British India and its Rulers* (1881), a conservative appraisal of Britain's imperial rule. Two of his novels, *The Chronicles of Dustypore* (1875) and *The Coeruleans: a Vacation Idyll* (1887), offer shrewd portraits of Anglo-Indian society. In 1887 he and his wife returned to England, accompanied by their son Lawrence (*b.* 1878) and daughter (*b.* 1887).

Cunningham was created KCIE in January 1889, assumed several financial directorships, and campaigned on public health issues both in India and in London. His penultimate novel, *The Heriots* (1890), a tale of the upper-class English society in which he and his family now lived, and who divided their time between London and Brighton, was much fêted by his contemporaries. He died on 3 September 1920 at his home, 83 Eaton Place, London, and was buried on the 7th in the churchyard at Banstead, Surrey.

ELISABETH JAY

Sources M. M. Verney, *Sir Henry Stewart Cunningham, KCIE* (1923) • *WWW* • J. Foster, *Men-at-the-bar: a biographical hand-list of the mem-bers of the various inns of court*, 2nd edn (1885) • E. Stock, *My recollec-tions* (1909) • Foster, *Alum. Oxon.* • d. cert. • *DNB* **Likenesses** W. E. Miller, portrait, 1877, repro. in Verney, *Sir Henry Stewart Cunningham*, frontispiece • Elliott & Fry, photograph, 1916, repro. in Verney, *Sir Henry Stewart Cunningham*, facing p. 114 **Wealth at death** £35,871 5s. 9d.: probate, 22 Oct 1920, CGPLA Eng. & Wales

Cunningham, Sir Hugh (1642/3–1710), local politician and merchant, was apparently a descendant of one of the Ayrshire Cunninghams. However, since there are no refer-ences to his birth, and because contemporary sources and his coat of arms as recorded in the Lyon court allude to both the Craigend and the Cunninghamhead families, it has not been possible to identify his lineage. Cunningham was known in the city of Edinburgh from at least 1674, when, upon payment of 'fourscore ten pund Scots' (Edin-burgh Guild register, 1675), he became an Edinburgh dean of guild. Burgess Hugh Cunningham quickly established himself as a successful Edinburgh merchant who, in mid-dle age, embarked upon what was to become a notable political career, culminating in his service as lord provost. It is plain from the numerous documents recorded in the registers of deeds that Hugh or Hew Cunningham, mer-chant—not to be confused with his Edinburgh contem-porary and associate Hugh Cunningham, lawyer (witness to the subject's son Alexander's baptism in 1685)—was already a relatively wealthy man when he settled in the city. From the evidence of personal bonds issued to not-ables such as Sir David Dunbar, Sir Godfrey McIntosh, and Sir John Ramsay, from numerous transactions relating to the import, processing, and sale of tobacco, his interest in a Leith comb manufactory, and references to his partnership with Sir James and William Dick of Braid, woollen merchants, it is plain that Cunningham prospered during the last years of pre-union Scotland.

Edinburgh merchants were the most influential local political figures in the community and it is hardly surprising that at the same time Cunningham was developing his business portfolio he also nurtured a political career. In November 1689 he was elected as one of the masters of Paul's Work (by this time the erstwhile pre-Reformation charitable institute had become a linen manufactory). In 1692 he was selected as one of two merchant councillors. By September of the following year he was not only a bailie of the city but also master of the Company of Merchants of the city of Edinburgh. A water bailie of Leith in 1694, his influential civic positions also involved him in perennial matters such as the appointment of two 'toune officers weekly for keeping the streits free from beggars' (Edinburgh town council minutes, 1 Nov 1693, Armet, *Extracts … 1689–1701*). During this period the city's finances were none too healthy and to pay creditors the authority borrowed money from some of its more affluent citizens, Hugh Cunningham offering a bond of £4000 (Edinburgh town council minutes, 16 May 1694, Armet, *Extracts … 1689–1701*). It was in this same year that the Canongate recorded his free entry as one of its burgesses 'for most generous and good deeds'. By 1698 he had risen to the significant position of first bailie of Edinburgh and, following his second year (1701) as master of the Merchant Company, he achieved the pinnacle of his political career when he became lord provost of Edinburgh on 6 October 1702.

The period of his tenure as lord provost was not a momentous one for the city, then a 'dull deflated capital, burdened with debts and poor' (Armet, *Extracts … 1701–1718*, vii). However, his term did see several turbulent events. The successful resolution of a dispute with the professors of Edinburgh University was contrasted by riots in 1703 and again in 1704. The latter tumult arose from the legal decision to release the crew of the English vessel the *Worcester* (convicted of piracy upon a Scottish ship), and resulted in the mob lynching of the ship's captain and his two mates. Although Scotland and Edinburgh were shortly to embark upon the adventure of the Act of Union and then the Jacobite rising of 1715, there is nothing to indicate that Cunningham was other than a loyal Scottish merchant, keen to exploit commercial opportunity and happy to serve his fellow citizens. To that end, in addition to his public offices which also included service as baron of Easter and Wester Portsburgh and commissioner to the general assembly of the Church of Scotland, he acted as treasurer to the Scottish Society for the Propagation of Christian Knowledge, was credited with the foundation of the Merchant Maiden Hospital which opened in 1707, and endowed the Kilmaurs parish school in Ayrshire with a tenement of land.

On 15 December 1681 Cunningham married Anna Moncrieff (*c*.1660–1734) in Edinburgh. By 1697 the couple had five children (Alexander, Helen, Catherine, Hew, and Mathew). By the same year he had subscribed £500 to the ill-fated Darien scheme and was on his way to establishing the financial base that a decade later allowed him to purchase a six-room house in Lothians Land, off Edinburgh's High Street, and lend Edinburgh town council £24,000 Scots to service the authority's debt. In the light of these achievements it is little wonder that he received a knighthood, in 1702; the only curiosity is that he was installed as 'of Milcraig and Livingstone', was freely referred to as 'of Craigend', yet lived his last year or so and was finally interred as Sir Hugh Cunningham of Bonniton.

In October 1704 Sir Hugh petitioned the town council 'ernestlie', desiring that he be the first to be granted a burial plot in a newly established section of Greyfriars burial-ground now known as the Covenanters' Prison. Upon his death at the age of sixty-seven on 16 December 1710, he was interred in the desired ground. The man and his passing are marked by a suitably ornate and substantial 30-foot stone monument that dominates the avenue and southern wall of the kirkyard.

RICHARD IAN HUNTER

Sources M. Wood and T. B. Whitson, *The lord provosts of Edinburgh, 1296 to 1932* (1932) · Edinburgh old parish register extracts, 1681–97 · H. Armet, ed., *Extracts from the records of the burgh of Edinburgh, 1689–1701*, [13] (1962) · H. Armet, ed., *Extracts from the records of the burgh of Edinburgh, 1701–1718*, [14] (1967) · registers of the deeds of Scotland, 1678–1715, NA Scot. · J. Brown, *The epitaphs and monumental inscriptions in Greyfriars churchyard, Edinburgh* (1867) · Edinburgh Guild register, 1669–76, Edinburgh City Archives, SL 141/1/4, (24 Feb 1675) · A. Heron, *The rise and progress of the Company of Merchants of the city of Edinburgh, 1681–1902* (1903) · D. McNaught, *Kilmaurs parish & burgh* (1912) · Register of burgesses of the burgh of the Canongate, 1622–1733 · W. P. Anderson, *Silences that speak* (1931) · Moses bundle 134, Edinburgh City Archives, document 5294 (29 July 1709) and 1694 poll tax

Likenesses J. Medina, oils

Wealth at death wealthy; property acquisitions and extensive financial dealings

Cunningham, James. *See* Cuninghame, James (*fl.* 1698–1709).

Cunningham, James, sixth earl of Glencairn (*c*.1552–1630). *See under* Cunningham family (*per. c*.1340–1631).

Cunningham, James, thirteenth earl of Glencairn (1749–1791), literary patron, was born on 1 June 1749 at Finlaystone, the second son of William Cunningham, twelfth earl of Glencairn, and the eldest daughter of Hugh McGuire, a violinist from Ayr. Through the death of his elder brother in 1768 he succeeded to the earldom on his father's death in 1775. He served as a captain in the West fencible regiment, and was one of the sixteen representative Scots peers in the House of Lords from 1780 to 1784, during this time supporting Fox's India Bill.

Glencairn became acquainted with Burns soon after the publication of the Kilmarnock edition of the *Poems*, and through him Burns was introduced to the publisher William Creech, who had been Glencairn's tutor, Creech subsequently agreeing to publish the new edition of the *Poems*. In his patronage of Burns, Glencairn managed to be genuinely useful, without injuring the poet's pride. Burns wrote 'Verse to be Written below a Noble Earl's Picture' for him, and said of his assistance in 1787: 'The noble Earl of Glencairn, to whom I owe more than to any man on earth, does me the honor [sic] of giving me his strictures: his hints, with respect to impropriety or indelicacy, I follow implicitly' (*Letters*, 1.100). Throughout the letters and the commonplace book there is much evidence of Burns's genuine respect and admiration for his patron, and it was through Glencairn that Burns obtained a situation in the excise.

Glencairn never married, and in 1786 he disposed of the estate of Kilmaurs to the marchioness of Titchfield. In 1790, owing to declining health, he was advised to spend the winter in Lisbon, but the change failed to effect any benefit. Having decided to return, he died on 30 January 1791, soon after landing at Falmouth, and was buried in the church there. He was succeeded by his brother John, on whose death, in 1796, without issue, the title became dormant. Burns was deeply affected by his death, as he expressed in a letter to Alexander Dalziel, in which he asked for permission to attend the funeral: 'God knows what I have suffered, at the loss of my best Friend, my first my dearest Patron & Benefactor; the man to whom I owe all that I am & have!' (*Letters*, 2.439). He also composed 'Lament for James, Earl of Glencairn', perhaps the best of his elegies, and named his fourth son James Glencairn (*b.* 1794) in his memory.

T. F. HENDERSON, rev. DOUGLAS BROWN

Sources R. Douglas, *The peerage of Scotland*, 2nd edn, ed. J. P. Wood, 2 vols. (1813) · *GM*, 1st ser., 61 (1791), 186 · M. Lindsay, *The Burns encyclopedia*, 2nd edn (1970) · *The letters of Robert Burns*, ed. J. de Lancey Ferguson, 2nd edn, ed. G. Ross Roy, 2 vols. (1985)
Likenesses H. Robinson, stipple (after K. Macleay), NPG

Cunningham, John (*d.* 1591). *See under* North Berwick witches (*act.* 1590–1592).

Cunningham, John (*c.*1575–1651), naval officer in the Danish service, was born at Barns, near Crail, Fife, the second son of Alexander Cunningham, laird of West Barns and Gallowside, and his wife, Christiane Wood. Cunningham's early years remain obscure. Before reaching Denmark he is supposed to have travelled throughout Europe and gained experience at sea. He was probably enlisted by the Danes for his knowledge of the Arctic waters. James VI of Scotland recommended Cunningham to his brother-in-law Christian IV (1577–1648), and from 1603 Cunningham was active as a sea captain in the Danish–Norwegian navy. During the next fifteen years he played an important part in the implementation of Christian's foreign policy.

In May 1605 Christian IV dispatched three ships, commanded by Cunningham, to re-establish links with Greenland and to recover the lost Scandinavian colonies. Cunningham returned to Copenhagen in August 1605 with valuable cartographical data and minerals. He and his men kidnapped some Greenland Inuit, whom they brought back to Denmark as samples of the native population; they were put on display in Copenhagen as exotic creatures from the far north. The expedition was regarded as a success and it has ever since been looked upon as the rediscovery of Greenland. A larger expedition, with Cunningham as captain of the *Lion*, was sent to Greenland in 1606 in the hope of finding silver ore. Cunningham and his crew were also instructed to map the coast of Greenland and investigate opportunities for trade. This expedition approached the shore of Labrador and sailed almost to the mouth of Cumberland Sound before returning to Denmark in October.

On 9 March 1607, in Helsingør (Elsinore), Cunningham married a Danish woman, of whom no details are known. He married again, at Bodøgaard, Nordland, Norway, on 4 September 1625; his second wife was the widowed Danish peer, Ellen Clausdatter Hundermark (*d.* 1633). There were no children from either marriage but with his mistress, a woman from Bergen who died in 1674, Cunningham had a son, Jakob Hansen Cunningham (1619–1686), and a daughter, Kirsten Hansdatter (*c.*1620–1699). In his capacity as commander he participated in a number of expeditions to the northern regions; their aim was to ensure Christian IV's dominion of the northern seas and to discourage pirates, buccaneers, and others from trespassing illegally on the king's seas. During the Kalmar War between Denmark–Norway and Sweden (1611–13) Cunningham engaged in sorties against Swedish strongholds in the Baltic Sea. Jon Olafsson, an Icelandic sailor and a rifleman who sailed with Cunningham in 1616, described him as a strange and peculiar kind of person, especially when intoxicated.

For his outstanding naval service in coastal waters Cunningham was granted a post as district governor of Vardøhus and Finnmark. With its unprotected eastern borders facing Russia and Sweden, Finnmark was the northernmost outpost of the dual monarchy. Here Cunningham ruled for thirty-two years, an unusually long tenure for a local official. His efforts are all the more remarkable in that his period as district governor coincided with great hardships and reports of famine among the populace. His paternalistic care for his subordinates and his true concern for them was resented by the merchants, whose complaints to the king changed nothing.

The rapidly expanding integration into the Danish–Norwegian realm of the native Sami people led to enormous challenges to rule in Finnmark. The struggle to obtain fishing privileges in the bounteous salmon rivers at Tana and Alta was also a part of this picture. Cunningham managed these concessions and, as a result, clashed with the common laws of the Sami when he began leasing the same concessions to Danish, Dutch, and Norwegian trading companies in 1629. Legal persecutions and severe sentences were used against rebellious Sami during the 1630s. Another of Cunningham's tasks was to ensure that ships from the British Isles, the Netherlands, and other seafaring nations did not venture into the king's waters without permission in their desire to take part in the lucrative trade with north-west Russia and the northern whale fishery, which were expanding rapidly during the first half of the seventeenth century.

Cunningham was sometimes present during the court

proceedings of Finnmark's many brutal witch trials. Some fifty-two cases have been documented from his period as district governor, most of which were raised against alleged witches who were sentenced to death at the stake. Although there were suggestions that witchcraft had been used against Cunningham on one occasion and against his servants he does not appear to have been a driving force in these persecutions, and he was present at few of the trials. Cunningham died at Gerdrup, an estate in Danish Sjaelland, and was buried at Eggeslevmagle church on 9 December 1651.   RUNE HAGEN

Sources M. Conway, *No man's land: a history of Spitsbergen from its discovery in 1596 to the beginning of the scientific exploration of the country* (1906) • S. Dalgård, *Dansk–Norsk hvalfangst, 1615–1660: en studie over Danmark–Norges stilling i europeisk merkantil expansion* (1962) • C. C. A. Gosch, ed., *Danish Arctic expeditions, 1605 to 1620*, 1, Hakluyt Society, 1st ser., 96 (1897) • *Grönlands historiske Mindesmærker*, tredie Bind (1845) • R. Hagen, 'The witch-hunt in early modern Finnmark', *Acta Borealia*, 1 (1999), 43–62 • *The royal correspondence of King James I of England (VI of Scotland) to his royal brother-in-law, King Christian IV of Denmark, 1603–1625*, ed. and trans. R. M. Meldrum (1977) • *Norske Rigs-registranter* (1865–87) • J. Olafsson, *Oplevelser som bøsseskytter under Christian IV*, ed. J. Clausen and P. Fr. Rist, trans. S. Blöndal (1905) • T. Riis, *Should auld acquaintance be forgot … Scottish–Danish relations, c.1450–1707*, 2 vols. (1988) • H. Sandvik and H. Winge, eds., *Tingbok for Finnmark, 1620–1633* (1987) • *Thingbog offuer Wardøehuuss lehn, 1648–1654*, National Archive of Tromsø • W. Wood, *The East Neuk of Fife: its history and antiquities* (1862)

Cunningham, Sir John, first baronet (d. 1684), lawyer, was the eldest son of John Cunningham of Brownhill, Tarbolton, Ayrshire, and his second wife, Elizabeth, daughter of Sir John Sinclair of Ratter. He was admitted an advocate on 25 January 1656 and readmitted on 5 June 1661. On 31 January 1661 he was appointed to plead the case of the marquess of Argyll on trial for high treason. With George Mackenzie he was named one of the justices-depute on 10 May 1661. Soon after 1663 he purchased the estate of Lambrughton, possibly in connection with his marriage to Margaret, daughter of John Murray of Touchadam and Polmaise, for the first of their eight children (five boys, three girls) was baptized on 7 February 1664. He was elected a commissioner to the convention of estates for Ayrshire in 1665. He sold the family estate at Brownhill in 1667. About this time Gilbert Burnet referred to Cunningham's religious beliefs as being 'episcopal beyond most men in Scotland', episcopacy being 'a divine right, settled by Christ', and to his legal ability, he being 'very learned in the civil and canon law, and in the philosophical learning' (*Bishop Burnet's History*, 1.336–7). On 21 September 1669 he was created a Scottish baronet. In 1670 he was empowered as patron to repair the churches of Kilmaurs and Dreghorn out of vacant stipends.

In 1674 Cunningham was embroiled in controversy between some advocates and the lords of session for his adherence to the opinion that an appeal could be made from the court of sessions to parliament. Charles II declared such appeals illegal, and when Cunningham persisted in his opinion he was debarred from practising his profession. He was restored in the following year after petitioning for readmission and disclaiming the right of appeal. He was elected to parliament in 1678, but his election was declared void on a technicality. In 1679 Cunningham played a key role in the attacks on the duke of Lauderdale, travelling to London to put their case. For Burnet at this time he was 'a learned and judicious man, and had the most universal, and indeed the most deserved reputation for integrity and virtue of any man, not only of his own profession, but of the whole nation' (*Bishop Burnet's History*, 2.230). Cunningham was elected to represent Ayrshire in parliament in 1681. In 1682 he was engaged in the controversy over the duke of York sitting in the Scottish council without taking the oaths, but in effect he backed the duke's right to sit, as 'a commission to represent the king's person fell not under the notion of an office' (ibid., 2.303–4). In 1683 he purchased the ancient family seat of Caprington from the eighth earl of Glencairn. He died on 17 November 1684 and was buried three days later. His son William succeeded as second baronet.

     STUART HANDLEY

Sources GEC, *Baronetage* • M. D. Young, ed., *The parliaments of Scotland: burgh and shire commissioners*, 1 (1992), 167–8 • *Bishop Burnet's History*, 1.436–7; 2.230, 303–4 • J. Paterson, *History of the county of Ayr: with a genealogical account of the families of Ayrshire*, 2 (1852), 410–11 • *Historical notices of Scotish affairs, selected from the manuscripts of Sir John Lauder of Fountainhall*, ed. D. Laing, 2, Bannatyne Club, 87 (1848), 570 • G. Mackenzie, *Memoirs of the affairs of Scotland* (1821), 34, 268–77 • J. Willcock, *A Scots earl in covenanting times: being life and times of Archibald, 9th earl of Argyll (1629–1685)* (1907), 193–4 • *Report of the Laing manuscripts*, 1, HMC, 72 (1914), 401–2

Cunningham, John (1729?–1773), poet, born in Dublin, was the younger son of a wine cooper in Dublin of Scottish extraction, who after winning a lottery prize of £1200 set up as a wine merchant and eventually became a bankrupt. His mother's maiden name was Fleming. Cunningham was educated at Drogheda and began writing when he was only twelve years old, publishing several minor poems in the Dublin papers, and in 1746 he wrote a farce, *Love in a Mist* (1747), which was said to have provided David Garrick with hints for his *The Lying Valet*. Presented successfully on the Dublin stage, *Love in a Mist* gained its author the acquaintance of the players. He soon left Dublin for England and the life of a strolling player. Unfortunately Cunningham had little acting talent: his only moderately successful performances came in the roles of mock-French characters.

Cunningham became aware of his insufficiencies as an actor, but his pride prevented him from returning to Dublin. After experiencing some difficulties in the north of England, he became in 1761 an actor on the Edinburgh stage under the direction of James Love (Dance). At this time Cunningham began to write more seriously and produced a number of prologues and epilogues that would later appear in his *Poetical Works* (1781).

In 1761 in London Cunningham published his *An Elegy on a Pile of Ruins*, a poem of 144 lines that combined the growing interest in England's medieval past with the poet's skill in depicting landscape. Presumably encouraged by the success of the poem, in 1762 Cunningham left Edinburgh for London where he hoped to succeed in the world of letters. He was discouraged, however, by the bankruptcy of one of the key publishers who had been interested in his work and by the politics and scandal of the literary world. Knowing himself best suited to a more retired life, Cunningham quickly left London and returned to Edinburgh where West Digges had replaced Love as the manager of the theatre. Digges became something of a patron to Cunningham, and Cunningham furnished Digges with prologues and epilogues, as he had done for Love.

Cunningham's delicacy of conversation and rectitude of conduct earned him a good deal of respect in Edinburgh; yet when Digges ceased to manage the theatre, Cunningham returned to Newcastle upon Tyne where he had spent some years prior to his first appearance in Edinburgh. In a letter to Philip Lewis of the Theatre Royal at Covent Garden, dated 3 November 1764 from Scarborough, Cunningham discussed his failed 1762 trip to London and his preference for a retired life. But he also said he was willing to undertake some translations from the French for Mr Davies, presumably Thomas Davies, the publisher and future biographer of Garrick. There is other evidence that Cunningham may have been more active in the London literary world than his biographical notices were later to suggest, for several of his poems were published after 1762 in Hugh Kelly's *Court Magazine* (1762–5).

Shortly before 1766 Cunningham collected his various poetical pieces in order to prepare them for publication. According to a memoir of Cunningham published in William Woodfall's *Morning Chronicle* (14 October 1773), David Garrick was among the foremost of those who supported the publication. Love, then employed at Drury Lane, informed his old friend of Garrick's enthusiasm, whereupon the poet produced an elegant dedication to Garrick. But when presented with the dedication copy, Garrick sent Cunningham the meagre sum of 2 guineas. Instead of complaining publicly, Cunningham sent the money back to London, directing that it be applied to the newly established trust for needy actors.

The publication of Cunningham's *Poems, Chiefly Pastoral* at Newcastle in 1766 was followed by a reissue in London the same year; the poems established Cunningham as a poet of some talent. But he quickly relapsed into a life of retired indolence and produced only one more volume before his death. This was a second edition of his poems with a few new pieces that was published by his friend Thomas Slack at Newcastle in 1771. It was Slack who took Cunningham into his home in Newcastle during the poet's final months. Cunningham died aged forty-four from the debilitating effects of a nervous disorder on 18 September 1773, and was buried in the churchyard of St John's, Newcastle.

Cunningham's achievement was modest. His best efforts were in the poetry of landscape, and here he was influenced by current interests in the Gothic and the picturesque. In these respects Cunningham owes something to both the landscape poets and the graveyard school. His handling of rhyme and rhythm demonstrates his good ear, and in general his poetry, in reflecting popular taste, is clear and accessible.   ROBERT R. BATAILLE

Sources 'Memoirs of the late Mr John Cunningham', *London Magazine*, 42 (1773), 495–7 · 'Memoirs of the late Mr John Cunningham', *Morning Chronicle* (14 Oct 1773) · 'Life of John Cunningham', *The poetical works of Jo. Cunningham*, Bell's Edition: the Poets of Great Britain, 106 (1797), v–xi · *DNB*
Archives BL, papers, Add. MS 50249
Likenesses P. Audinet, line engraving, BM, NPG; repro. in *Biographical Magazine* (1794) · W. H. Worthington, line engraving (after T. Bewick), BM, NPG; repro. in B. W. Procter, *Effigies poeticae, or, The portraits of the British poets* (1824)

Cunningham, John (1819–1893), Church of Scotland minister and ecclesiastical historian, the son of Daniel Cunningham, an ironmonger, was born at Paisley on 9 May 1819. Educated at two preparatory schools and the grammar school in Paisley, he matriculated at Glasgow University in 1836. In 1840 he became a student at Edinburgh University under Sir William Hamilton and John Wilson (1785–1854). He was gold medallist in both classes, and also won Wilson's prize for his poem 'The hearth and the altar'. After studying divinity at Edinburgh Cunningham was licensed to preach by the presbytery of Paisley in the spring of 1845. After a short assistantship at Lanark he was ordained in August 1845 as parish minister of Crieff, Perthshire. Shortly after, on 23 December 1846, he married Susan Porteous (d. 1902), only daughter of William Murray, a banker in Crieff, and his wife, Susan Porteous; the couple had three sons and four daughters. Their son Daniel John *Cunningham (1850–1909) became a professor of anatomy.

Cunningham remained at Crieff for forty-one years, during which he was prominent in promoting an act of parliament opening Church of Scotland appointments to members of all Scottish presbyterian bodies; he also helped to secure the act which modified the Westminster confession of faith. He was a pioneer among Scottish theologians in advocating the introduction of instrumental music into church, and the 'Crieff organ case' in the church courts of 1867 stirred up much controversy, although Cunningham was ultimately victorious.

In 1859 Cunningham published a two-volume *Church History of Scotland*, concluding with the events of 1831. In a second revised edition, published in 1882, he described the Disruption in an unusually impartial narrative. In 1869 he published *The Quakers, an International History*, and he contributed several articles on philosophy and history to the *Westminster Review*, the *Edinburgh Review*, and other periodicals. In 1874 Cunningham published an unsatisfactory treatise—which, however, he thought his best book—entitled *New Theory of Knowing and Known*. He was the author of two numbers in the well-known *Scotch Sermons* of 1880. In his Croall lectures, published in 1886 as *The Growth of the Church*, he discussed the nature of ecclesiastical organization and authority.

Crieff, meanwhile, was becoming a fashionable health resort: the handsome church of St Michael's, with a new organ, was substituted for the old parish church, and an assistant was appointed to work with Cunningham.

Active for the welfare of his parish, Cunningham was chaplain of the local Volunteers from 1859 to 1888, and for forty-two years he was a trustee and governor of Taylor's Educational Institution, Crieff. In 1886 he was chosen moderator of the general assembly of the Church of Scotland, and in the same year he was appointed principal of St Mary's College, St Andrews. He received the degree of DD from Edinburgh University (1860), an LLD from Glasgow (1886), and an honorary LLD from Trinity College, Dublin (1887). He died at St Andrews on 1 September 1893, and was buried in the cathedral burying-ground.

T. W. BAYNE, rev. ROSEMARY MITCHELL

Sources *The Scotsman* (2 Sept 1893) · personal knowledge (1901) · private information (1901) · *Fasti Scot.*, 7.425–6 · A. L. Drummond and J. Bulloch, *The church in Victorian Scotland, 1843–1874* (1975), 303 · *The Athenaeum* (9 Sept 1893), 359 · *Wellesley index*
Likenesses oils, U. St Andr., St Mary's College
Wealth at death £2834 18s. 7d.: corrective inventory, 30 April 1894, *CCI* (1893) · £213 8s. 2d.: additional estate, 3 July 1896, *CCI*

Cunningham, Sir John Henry Dacres (1885–1962), naval officer, was born on 13 April 1885 at Demerara, British Guiana, the son of Henry Hutt Cunningham QC (*b.* 1851), the stipendiary magistrate in the British colony, and his wife, Elizabeth (Bessie) Harriet (or Mary; *b.* 1855), the daughter of the Revd John Park. Cunningham was only a teenager when he and his younger sister, Barbara, were orphaned as a result of a seafaring accident that claimed the lives of both of their parents. Brought back to England in the wake of this double tragedy, the two children were brought up by their mother's relatives in Ulverston, on the fringes of the Lake District.

John Cunningham's scholastic talents were quickly in evidence at Stubbington House School and shone through his time as a cadet in HMS *Britannia* (1900–01), where he was regarded as possessing one of the finest intellects seen in the training ship in recent years. Unfortunately, his social skills left much to be desired. Apart from doing nothing to cultivate popularity he was generally seen as being a rather morose, impatient, and disdainful individual who rarely praised anyone and was often withering in his criticism of those whose work did not measure up to the highest standards he set for them. An aloof and introverted figure known for his biting sarcasm, Cunningham made few friends either at school or within the service. But if being a loner discomforted him he showed little sign of it at any stage of his life or during his career. Self-assured to the point of arrogance and immensely hardworking, Cunningham was highly competitive and relished pitting himself against even the most difficult of challenges. A shrewd and complex personality, he managed to gain the respect but not the devotion of his peers and subordinates.

After passing out of *Britannia* in 1901 he was posted as a midshipman to the cruiser HMS *Gibraltar*, the flagship on the Cape of Good Hope station, at the time of the Second South African War. Awarded the queen's medal, Cunningham returned home in 1904 as a sub-lieutenant to take the qualifying examinations for promotion to lieutenant. Achieving a first-class certificate in all five subjects (a

Sir John Henry Dacres Cunningham (1885–1962), by Walter Stoneman, 1941

so-called 'five-oner'), he was promoted in October 1905. Opting to eschew gunnery for the less glamorous field of navigation as his specialization, he duly qualified at the navigation school and was thereafter appointed as assistant navigator in the cruiser HMS *Illustrious*. During the next three years he graduated to the role of navigator of the gunboat *Hebe*, the cruiser *Indefatigable* in the West Indies, and the minelayer *Iphigenia* in home waters. He was little inconvenienced by the rigours of the first-class ship course in 1910 and was rewarded with an instructor's position at the navigation school. In the same year, on 8 March, he married his first cousin Dorothy May (*d.* 1959), daughter of C. K. Hannay. Cunningham had spent some of his early adolescence in Ulverston with Dorothy after his parents had perished at sea. They were married for forty-nine years and had two sons, John and Richard; John became a fire brigade chief and Richard a lieutenant in the Submarine Service, killed in action on board *P33* in August 1941.

Cunningham went back to sea in 1914 as navigator in the cruiser *Berwick* on the West Indies station and in the following year was transferred to the ill-fated battleship *Russell* in the Mediterranean. Surviving her sinking by a mine in Maltese waters in April 1916, Cunningham was appointed navigator in the battle cruiser *Renown*. While serving in the Mediterranean he was promoted commander in 1917, and in the final year of the war became navigator of the *Lion* in the Grand Fleet. Further preferment came his way when he was appointed to serve as navigator in the newly commissioned battle cruiser *Hood* in 1920 and as squadron navigator for the entire battle-cruiser squadron commanded at the time by Sir Roger Keyes. He returned ashore in 1922 to serve as commander of the navigation school and followed this a year later by appointment as master of the fleet in the *Queen Elizabeth*, the flagship of Admiral Sir John de Robeck. Promoted captain in 1924 he served for a time on the staff of the Royal Naval College at Greenwich before becoming deputy director of plans at Admiralty House. After commanding the cruiser–minelayer *Adventure* (1928–9), he returned to Whitehall as director of plans (1930–32) at a time of economic crisis for the entire country. Emerging from a torrid period for the Royal Navy, Cunningham was glad to go back to sea and take command of the battleship *Resolution* while becoming flag captain to Admiral Sir William Fisher, the commander-in-chief of the Mediterranean Fleet. After being appointed aide-de-camp to the king in 1935 Cunningham reached flag rank in 1936 at the age of fifty-one. Later in the year he was offered the post of assistant chief of naval staff. This brought him into close contact with the influential figure of Admiral Sir Ernle Chatfield, the first sea lord. Cunningham's workload increased substantially in 1937 when he assumed responsibility for administering the Fleet Air Arm upon its transfer from the Air Ministry to the Admiralty. His new role initially brought with it a slight change of designation, but the importance of his duties was reflected in the elevation of the office in 1938 to that of fifth sea lord and chief of naval air services with a seat on the Board of Admiralty. He was made MVO in 1924 and CB in 1937.

As Europe began gearing up for war in the early summer of 1939 Cunningham was promoted vice-admiral and was ordered to take command of the 1st cruiser squadron in the Mediterranean, flying his flag in the *Devonshire*. Shortly after war broke out in September, Cunningham's cruiser squadron returned to reinforce the Home Fleet under Admiral Sir Charles Forbes. Assigned to the Norwegian campaign from the outset, Cunningham made the best of a desperately poor job. His finest hour came, ironically, in the wake of the allied defeat when he was asked to lead a mixed force of three cruisers, nine destroyers, and three French transports to the port of Namsos, to the north of Trondheim, in order to evacuate the roughly 5700 allied troops of 'Mauriceforce' that had congregated there. Arriving off Namsos during the night of 1 May, Cunningham postponed the evacuation by twenty-four hours in the hope that the beautifully clear weather would deteriorate and help to conceal the mass evacuation. On the evening of 2 May a bank of fog obligingly descended, shrouding the evacuation operation from the German Luftwaffe and allowing the entire 'Mauriceforce' to be spirited away from Namsos in a single heroic night's work. Although badly mauled by bombing and strafing the next day, Cunningham's diminished task force returned with its human cargo safely to Scapa Flow a few days later.

Cunningham's next major assignment took him back across the North Sea and well into the Arctic circle to the port of Tromsø on 7 June in order to rescue King Haakon VII, Crown Prince Olaf, and other members of the Norwegian royal family, along with government ministers and the country's gold reserve. Under strict instructions not to break radio silence, Cunningham in the *Devonshire* had picked up his evacuees and was on his return leg to the United Kingdom when his ship received a garbled distress call from the British carrier HMS *Glorious*—only some 70 miles away—which was being engaged by vastly superior enemy forces. Whether a narrow sense of duty or mere callous self-preservation dictated his total lack of response one will never know, but his inaction effectively left the crew of the *Glorious* and her two screening destroyers—HMS *Acasta* and HMS *Ardent*—to fend for themselves against overwhelming odds. Despite taking the fight courageously to the German pocket battleships *Scharnhorst* and *Gneisenau*, the unequal contest was soon over and all three British warships were sunk with the loss of 1519 officers and men. Only forty-six survived their freezing ordeal in the North Sea. In recent years criticism of Cunningham's role in this tragedy has surfaced. Throughout his life Cunningham claimed not to have received any information about the distress call from *Glorious*. This view was sharply contested in a British television documentary on the subject aired in 1997, featuring a prominent member of the wireless telegraphy staff on board the *Devonshire* who could remember receiving the message and entering it into the wireless telegraphy log at the time. It is further alleged that Cunningham either personally doctored the ship's log to eliminate any mention of the SOS call or ordered that any evidence of it be struck from the record. Until the Admiralty opens all the files relating to this incident in 2015, and perhaps not even then, this matter will remain unresolved.

Cunningham's burgeoning career prospects were not arrested by this incident, however, and he continued to take on new assignments. He confronted his trickiest task yet in September 1940 when he was appointed joint commander with Major-General N. M. S. Irwin of operation Menace—an effort to land a mixed force of 6670 British and Free French soldiers at Dakar in Senegal in a bid to provide a base for General de Gaulle's Free French movement in west Africa. This expedition turned out to be an ignoble failure, undermined by a lack of secrecy and co-ordination on the one hand and compromised by resolute Vichy French hostility and defensive firepower on the other. Once again Cunningham somehow emerged unscathed from this latest débâcle and the Admiralty was content to support him in his seemingly unstoppable drive to get to the top of his profession.

Knighted in the new year's honours, Cunningham was recalled to Admiralty House in the early months of 1941 and appointed fourth sea lord and chief of supplies and transport. This proved to be a very demanding administrative position, but Cunningham was ideally suited to deal with the complexities of the job and revelled in the myriad aspects of it. He remained at the helm for more than two years before being sent in June 1943 to the eastern Mediterranean as commander-in-chief, Levant, with the acting rank of admiral. Promotion to admiral followed in August and when the two Mediterranean commands were merged later in the year he was confirmed as the commander-in-chief and assumed the responsibility for all allied warships in the same theatre. Admittedly, by this time the naval situation in the Mediterranean had improved significantly, but there were still important amphibious operations to launch at Anzio and in the south of France, both of which he oversaw.

Cunningham remained in the Mediterranean until he was brought home to relieve Admiral Viscount Cunningham of Hyndhope as first sea lord in May 1946. While he could be satisfied that he was the first navigating officer ever to have made it to the pinnacle of his profession, Cunningham was under no illusions about the problems he had inherited from his namesake. Substantial budget cuts and disarmament had already taken place and more of the same were in the pipeline. To make matters worse the sharp divisions that existed within the chiefs of staff committee made Cunningham's task of defending the integrity of the Royal Navy even more complicated. Undermined by personal wrangling and animosity, the committee proved to be utterly ineffectual, both collectively and individually, in resisting the Labour government's radical plans for the armed services over the next two years. Presiding over an almost skeletal navy was not particularly edifying for a person of Cunningham's nature, so when the opportunity to retire from the service presented itself in September 1948 he grasped it with some alacrity. By then he had been made a GCB in 1946, a freeman of the City of London in the following year, and had been promoted to admiral of the fleet in January 1948. He had also received a set of distinguished orders and decorations from France, Greece, Norway, and the United States for his work on their behalf in the recent war. After leaving the navy Cunningham spent the next ten years as chairman of the Iraq Petroleum Company before retiring finally in 1958 at the age of seventy-three. He survived his wife by three years and died in the Middlesex Hospital on 13 December 1962.

Vain and egotistical, as well as being a strict disciplinarian who insisted on precision and hated any slack attitude and inattention to detail from those who worked for him, Cunningham was known to be a formidable character. Astute and experienced in driving both ships and men, there is no doubt that he accomplished much in his life, but the nagging doubt remains as to the soundness of his judgement under all circumstances, particularly at sea.

MALCOLM H. MURFETT

Sources J. Winton, *Carrier 'Glorious': the life and death of an aircraft carrier* (1999) • M. H. Murfett, ed., *The first sea lords: from Fisher to Mountbatten* (1995) • C. Barnett, *Engage the enemy more closely: the Royal Navy in the Second World War* (1991) • S. W. Roskill, *The war at sea, 1939–1945*, 1 (1954) • V. W. Howland, 'The loss of HMS *Glorious*', *Warship International*, 1 (1994), 47–62 • private information (2004) • *DNB* • *CGPLA Eng. & Wales* (1963)
Archives PRO, DEFE/CAB files • PRO, first sea lords MSS, ADM 205 | BL, corresp. with Viscount Cunningham, Add. MS 52562 | FILM BFI NFTVA, news footage • IWM FVA, actuality footage | SOUND IWM SA, oral history interview
Likenesses W. Stoneman, photograph, 1941, NPG [*see illus.*] • J. Worsley, oils, 1945, IWM • O. Birley, oils, *c.*1945–1948, Royal Naval College, Greenwich • W. Stoneman, photograph, 1946, NPG • Wayland, photograph, NPG
Wealth at death £25,514 5*s.* 0*d.*: probate, 8 April 1963, *CGPLA Eng. & Wales*

Cunningham, John William (1780–1861), Church of England clergyman, was born in Middlesex on 3 January 1780, most probably the son of John and Ann Cunningham. He was educated privately before he entered St John's College, Cambridge, and was admitted as Duckett scholar in November 1798. He graduated BA (fifth wrangler) in 1802 and MA in 1805. He was briefly a fellow of St John's College before his marriage in 1805 to Sophia Williams (1780–1821), the youngest daughter of the banker Robert Williams of Rickmansworth. They had a family of ten children. Cunningham married for a second time on 24 July 1827. His new wife was Mary Calvert (1800–1849), daughter of General Sir Harry *Calvert and his wife, Caroline Hammersley; they had a family of four children, including Sir Henry Stewart *Cunningham, lawyer and novelist.

Cunningham was ordained deacon in May 1803 and priest in December 1803, and served as the curate of the Surrey parishes of Send and Ripley (1803–4) and of Oakham (1804–8). In January 1809 he became curate to John Venn at Clapham parish church and became a popular preacher. Venn appeared as Berkely in Cunningham's book *The Velvet Cushion* (1814; 10th edn, 1816), a novel subtitled 'an historical account of divisions within the Church of England since the Reformation'. This work earned Cunningham the sobriquet Velvet Cunningham. In April 1811 he became the vicar of Harrow on the Hill, the presentation having been purchased by his father-in-law. In his parish he erected churches and schools, and promoted public health and sabbath observance. From 1818 he was an active governor of Harrow School and the pupils attended his church, continuing to do so even after a chapel was opened at the school in 1839. Cunningham had a strained relationship with the headmaster, Christopher Wordsworth, but he was widely respected and his counsel was widely sought. Frances Trollope, who was a local resident, expressed her dislike of evangelicalism in general and Cunningham in particular in her scurrilous novel *The Vicar of Wrexhall* (1837), in which the hypocritical Revd William Jacob Cartwright abuses his position in order to gain power. The book was condemned by Samuel Wilberforce as 'a most abominable personal attack' upon Cunningham (A. R. Ashwell and R. G. Wilberforce, *The Life of the Right Rev Samuel Wilberforce*, 1, 1880–82, 114).

Cunningham was one of the leaders of the evangelical movement in the mid-nineteenth century: he was a strong supporter of the Church Missionary Society, being one of the most frequent speakers at its annual meetings, and often addressing other meetings in the Exeter Hall. His interest in mission had begun in Cambridge where he had won an essay prize provided by wealthy East India Company chaplain, Claudius Buchanan. He attended the

Islington clerical meeting and between 1834 and 1859 frequently took the chair. Many of his sermons were published. A minor literary figure who wrote poetry and hymns, he was also editor of the *Christian Observer* from 1850 to 1858. Cunningham died at Harrow on the Hill on 30 September 1861 and was interred in the parish church.

A. F. MUNDEN

Sources Venn, *Alum. Cant.* · J. Julian, ed., *A dictionary of hymnology*, rev. edn (1907); repr. in 2 vols. (1915), 273 · R. F. Scott, ed., *Admissions to the College of St John the Evangelist in the University of Cambridge*, 4: *July 1767 – July 1802* (1931), 215–16 · E. Stock, *The history of the Church Missionary Society: its environment, its men and its work*, 1–3 (1899) · E. Jay, *The religion of the heart* (1979)
Archives Herts. ALS | BL, letters to Lord Aberdeen and others · Bodl. Oxf., corresp. with Lord and Lady Byron · Devon RO, Acland MSS, letters to Sir Thomas Dyke · Dorset RO, letters and diaries · Norfolk RO, Upcher MSS · Sandon Hall, Staffordshire, Harrowby Manuscript Trust, letters to Lord Harrowby
Wealth at death £12,000: probate, 30 Oct 1861, *CGPLA Eng. & Wales*

Cunningham, Joseph Davey (1812–1851), army officer in the East India Company and historian, was born in Lambeth on 9 June 1812, the eldest son of Allan *Cunningham (1784–1842), Scottish poet and author, and his wife, Jean, *née* Walker (1791–1864). Among his brothers were Sir Alexander *Cunningham (1814–1893), Peter *Cunningham (1816–1869), and Francis *Cunningham (1820–1875). He was educated at private schools in London, and showed such mathematical ability that his father was strongly advised to send him to Cambridge. But the boy wished to be a soldier; and, at his father's request, Sir Walter Scott procured him a cadetship in the East India Company's army. He went to Addiscombe College (1829–30), from which he passed out first, with the first prize for mathematics, the sword for good conduct, and the first nomination to the Bengal Engineers in 1831. He attended the usual Chatham engineering course, gaining high praise from his instructors, Colonel Pasley and Colonel Jebb. He sailed for India in February 1834 with strong letters of introduction to the many Scots then filling high posts in India. On reaching India he was appointed to the staff of General Macleod, chief engineer in the Bengal presidency, and in 1837 he was selected, entirely without solicitation from himself, by Lord Auckland to join Colonel Claud Wade, political agent on the Sikh frontier, as assistant, with the special duty of fortifying Ferozepore, the agent's headquarters. This appointment brought him into close connection with the Sikhs; he spent the next eight years of his life in political posts in that part of India, and so was able to obtain the thorough knowledge of Sikh manners and customs which made his *History of the Sikhs* such a valuable book. In 1838 he was present at the interview between Lord Auckland and Ranjit Singh; in 1839 he accompanied Wade when he forced the Khyber Pass, and was promoted first lieutenant on 20 May in that year; in 1840 he was placed in charge of Ludhiana, under G. Russell Clerk, Wade's successor, and as political officer accompanied Brigadier-General Shelton and his army through the Sikh territory to Peshawar on his way to Kabul, and then accompanied Colonel Wheeler and Dost Muhammad, the deposed amir of Afghanistan, back to British territory; in 1841 he was sent on a special mission to the principality of Jammu; in 1842 he was present at the interview between Lord Ellenborough and Dost Muhammad and the Sikhs; in 1843 he was assistant to Colonel Richmond, Clerk's successor; and in 1844 and 1845 he was British agent to the princely state of Bahawalpur.

These numerous appointments had made Cunningham familiar with Sikh character, and when the First Anglo-Sikh War broke out he was attached first to the headquarters of Sir Charles Napier in Sind, and then to that of Sir Hugh Gough, the general commanding the army in the field. On 16 January 1846 Gough detached Cunningham to act as political officer with the division under the command of Sir Harry Smith. With Smith, Cunningham was present at the skirmish of Badiwal and at the battle of Aliwal. When Smith joined the main army Cunningham was attached to the staff of Sir Henry Hardinge, to whom he acted as additional aide-de-camp at the battle of Sobraon. He was promoted captain by brevet on 10 December 1845, and was on the conclusion of the war appointed by Hardinge to the lucrative appointment of political agent at Bhopal. He was thus singularly fortunate for so young an officer; and, having then relative leisure, he devoted himself to historical research. His earliest works were chiefly on archaeological and antiquarian studies—in connection with which his brother Major-General Sir Alexander Cunningham became famous—but he soon settled down, at his father's recommendation, to write his great work, the *History of the Sikhs*. He spent four years on it, and on publication in 1849 it was much praised by the British press, a verdict later writers confirmed, for it has been recognized as a very important authority on the subject.

Although this history made Cunningham's name as a historian, it brought him disgrace with his superiors. In his last chapter, on the First Anglo-Sikh War, he used information obtained while acting as political agent with the army in the field, and alleged that two Sikh generals, Lal Singh and Tej Singh, were bought. Both Hardinge and Colonel Henry Lawrence, who had acted as political agent after the death of Major Broadfoot, claimed that there had been no secret negotiations with any Sikh leader; but the confidential position which Cunningham had held, and still more his disgrace which followed, were strong arguments that such negotiations did occur, in which other individuals than the two named were involved. It was surmised at the time that Frederick Currie, created a baronet for his political services at the conclusion of the Anglo-Sikh War, knew more of the matter than Hardinge or Lawrence, but the truth or falsity of Cunningham's statements has yet to be proved. Their truth seems probable from the prompt disgrace of the author, for in 1850 Cunningham was removed from his agency and ordered to regimental duty. This meant a reduction of his income to about one-fourth, besides the certainty of never being again employed in the political service, and the nominal cause of his disgrace was the disclosure of documents only known to him in his confidential, political capacity.

The disgrace apparently broke his heart, though he made no open or public complaint of his treatment. He had been promoted captain in the Bengal Engineers on 13 November 1849, and he had just been appointed to the Meerut division of public works when he died suddenly near Ambala on 28 February 1851, before attaining his fortieth year.   H. M. STEPHENS, *rev.* JAMES LUNT

Sources J. D. Cunningham, *A history of the Sikhs* (1849) [1853, 1966] · H. C. B. Cook, *The Sikh wars: the British army in the Punjab, 1845–1849* (1975) · *The letters of the first Viscount Hardinge of Lahore … 1844–1847*, ed. B. S. Singh, CS, 4th ser., 32 (1986) · *GM*, 2nd ser., 35 (1851) · J. J. Higginbotham, *Men whom India has known: biographies of eminent Indian characters*, 2nd edn (1874) · M. Edwardes, *British India* (1967) · H. M. Vibart, *Addiscombe: its heroes and men of note* (1894)

Archives BL OIOC, corresp. with Henry Lawrence, MSS Eur. F 85

Cunningham, Laurence Paul [Laurie] (1956–1989), footballer, was born in the St Mary's wing of Whittington Hospital, Islington, London, on 8 March 1956, the second son of Elias Cunningham, a paint sprayer, and his wife, Mavis Iona, *née* Trout. Both his parents were from the West Indies. Having represented Haringey schools and south-east counties' schools, Cunningham joined Arsenal Football Club aged fifteen as an apprentice but failed to impress. He moved to Leyton Orient in August 1972, and made his professional début in 1974 in a Texaco cup match against West Ham United. In March 1977 he was sold to West Bromwich Albion for £110,000 plus two players in part-exchange. At this point it was thought that Cunningham would become the first black player to gain full England honours, such were his prodigious talents. In fact, Vivian Anderson of Nottingham Forest beat him to that honour by a few months in 1979. Laurie Cunningham did, however, become the first black player to represent England, when he was selected by manager Ron Greenwood for the under-21 side against Scotland in April 1977. Cunningham marked the event by scoring a goal.

After eighty-six appearances and twenty-one goals for West Bromwich Albion, where he formed a close friendship with two other black players, Cyrille Regis and Brendon Batson, in a successful side managed by Ron Atkinson, Cunningham moved to Real Madrid of Spain for £995,000 in June 1979. Once again he scored on his début, this time in front of 100,000 fans at the Bernabeu Stadium, Madrid. In March 1983 he moved on loan to Manchester United but made just five appearances. His career was now blighted by injury, and for the next six years he moved between several clubs without managing to re-establish himself. Olympique Marseille (France), Leicester City, Sporting Gijón (Spain), Charleroi (Belgium), and Wimbledon all preceded a final move to Rayo Vallecano of Madrid, a Spanish second-division side. Here his career seemed to settle down. He married and had a child (Sergio) and helped the club gain promotion. However, in the early hours of 15 July 1989 he was killed in a car crash in Madrid.

Cunningham was a wing-forward, who usually played on the left side. At his peak he was tremendously popular with deft footwork, speed, and poise. He was a slow developer, however, and according to his first manager, George Petchey of Leyton Orient, 'There was a time when Peter Angell and myself wondered if we could win him over. He turned up for training when he liked' (Kaufman and Ravenhill, 116). In the last match of the 1974–5 football season, against Southampton, Cunningham turned up late for the pre-match talk. Petchey told him that, unless he scored a goal, he would be heavily fined. He netted a tremendous goal. In Madrid he was idolized and was dubbed El Negrito and, in his first season with the club he scored fifteen goals and helped the side to a league and cup double. His career began to fall away after he had gained the last of his six full England caps in 1981, and he preferred spending his time as a male model, fashion designer, and boutique owner rather than training to play football. At thirty-two, however, he was brought on as a substitute in Wimbledon's FA cup win over Liverpool in 1988. He once said:

> I don't think I've ever fulfilled my potential. Coaches and managers, except for George Petchey and Peter Angell at Leyton Orient, have not always appreciated how much I can do. Even at Real Madrid I couldn't express myself fully, because they treated me as an orthodox winger—and I am capable of much more than that. (ibid.)

JOHN HARDING

Sources *The Times* (17 July 1989), 35 · N. Kaufman and A. Ravenhill, *Leyton Orient: a complete record, 1881–1990* (1990) · D. Lamming, 'The English football internationalists', in D. Lamming, *The English football internationalists who's who* (1990) · A. Hamilton, *Black pearls of soccer* (1982) · T. Matthews, *The A–Z of West Bromwich Albion* (1996) · G. Willmore, *The Hawthorns encyclopaedia: an A–Z of West Bromwich Albion FC* (1996) · b. cert.

Cunningham, Lady Margaret (*d.* 1622?), autobiographer, was one of the six daughters of James Cunningham, sixth earl of Glencairn (*d.* 1631), and his first wife, Mariot or Margaret (*d.* 1610), daughter of Colin Campbell of Glenorchy. Despite her high birth she was distinguished principally by misfortune, and by the fact that she wrote a detailed account of the cruelty she suffered at the hands of her first husband; the account provides evidence of the acute vulnerability of wives and the inability of law, custom, and even powerful kinsmen to guarantee protection from brutal husbands. On 24 January 1598 Margaret married Sir James Hamilton (*d.* in or after 1608), master of Evandale, who was from a wealthy and well-connected family. For the next three years she continued to reside with her parents at Finlaystone in Renfrewshire and it is not clear when the marriage was consummated. When she visited Evandale between February and May 1601 Sir James and his parents did not receive her in the family house at Crawford-John, but directed her to a nearby inn. Her first child, James, was born at her father's house on 4 July 1601. In February 1602 she returned to Evandale and was once more accommodated at the inn; an appeal to her parents-in-law for help in paying the bill yielded only 40 merks and eight sacks of farm meal.

A pattern set in of alternate neglect and abuse by Sir James and his parents. Repeated attempts by Lady Margaret to take up residence with her husband were rebuffed, and the small amounts of money the Hamiltons reluctantly supplied from time to time proved insufficient to cover the costs of the lodgings to which she was forced to resort. Efforts at mediation, most notably by the Hamiltons' successive clan chiefs John Hamilton, first marquess of Hamilton (1532–1604), and his son James Hamilton, second marquess, who in 1603 married Lady Margaret's sister Lady Anne *Cunningham (d. 1647), had little success. At different times Lady Margaret took refuge with her parents and with Lady Anne. Temporary reconciliations between the couple led to the birth of four more children, John (12 October 1603), Jean (March 1605), Christian (November 1606), and Thomas (April 1608), but Sir James oscillated between absence (including periodic visits to France), infidelity, repentance, silence, and violence. When in 1604 he took a dislike to Lady Margaret's gentlewoman, Abigail Hamilton, he and two menservants turned both women out of the house at Evandale at night, threatening them with a sword and not allowing them to put on any clothes whatsoever. Lady Margaret records that the night was 'foul' and that she was both sick and pregnant at the time. Naked, they had to seek shelter in the minister's house and they went on to accept charity for nine weeks from the family of a servant.

This was only one of several sudden evictions, and Lady Margaret was always short of money. In 1605 she was given the rent from a mill, but from this had to provide for herself, the children, her husband, and all his household. When his father died in March 1606 Sir James increased the number of his retainers, but gave her nothing from the inheritance. That September he attempted to sell the barony of Carstairs, but when Glencairn intervened legally, presumably because this property and title had been settled by nuptial contract on his daughter's children, Sir James cut off Lady Margaret's meagre allowance. Persistent mediation in her favour by Alexander Lindsay of Dunrood made no headway, so in January 1607 she brought a lawsuit for maintenance, assisted by her father, her brother-in-law Hamilton, and the earl of Abercorn (another Hamilton kinsman). She spent £100 in legal expenses, but without conclusion. However, through the influence of Hamilton and the laird of Benhaith, she obtained a small allowance.

That summer saw final attempts at reconciliation. In May Lady Margaret wrote a long letter to Sir James in France, addressing him as 'dear heart', full of devout exhortation and hopeful wishes for his future salvation. She enclosed a poem of her own composition on the same theme in irregularly rhyming pentameters and a book, The Resolved Christian. When he returned in June Margaret was initially so frightened of him that she refused to share his bed, but his promises of reformation brought from her forgiveness and a diamond ring as a token. Yet soon afterwards his behaviour relapsed into harshness and negligence. Following the death of his mother that September, Sir James sent Margaret and their children to live in Libertoun, with very inadequate provision. Having at first refused to visit her for five weeks after the birth of their fifth child in April 1608, Sir James arrived not with money to meet their debts but with an expectation of resuming connubial relations. Lady Margaret, knowing that he was now excommunicated for manslaughter and was living in adultery with a certain Jennat Campbell, finally and irrevocably refused him. In August he retaliated by again throwing his wife and children out of the house. Once more her kinsmen tried to intervene, but when she wrote her testimony on 29 September Lady Margaret described herself as surviving in Libertoun still destitute.

At this point, under Scottish law Lady Margaret would have been entitled to divorce with a right of remarriage, and at costs less than elsewhere in Europe. However, within a few years Sir James conveniently died. In her will Lady Margaret stated her hope that he had been redeemed before death: she had long ago fully forgiven him. It was thus as a widow that she married Sir James Maxwell of Calderwood, becoming his third wife. Her later letters reveal a happy marriage, which produced two sons, John and Alexander, and four daughters, Susanna, Anne, Margaret, and Catherine. Her daughter Jean Hamilton married Maxwell's son, another Sir James. Left a widow again in 1622, and with two of her sons dead, Margaret wrote from Malsly to her sister the marchioness of Hamilton imploring her and the marquess to take care of her surviving children, several of whom were still young and needed tuition. She enclosed a will dated 2 October 1622, written as if she were sick and dying, asking for her son Thomas to be taken in as a follower of the Hamiltons' eldest son, the earl of Arran, and reminding her sister of a promise made to Glencairn to help her other children; those from her first marriage were not entitled to her small income after her death, while those from the second were dependent on payment by the heir of Calderwood of 6000 merks to be shared between them all. Lady Margaret died at Malsly, probably soon afterwards. JULIA GASPER

Sources C. K. Sharpe, ed., A pairt of the life of Lady Margaret Cuninghame … written with her own hand (1827) • GEC, Peerage • DNB • W. Grant and D. D. Murison, eds., The Scottish national dictionary, 9 (1974) • H. Prater, Cases illustrative of the conflict between the laws of England and Scotland regarding divorce (1835)
Wealth at death died poor: Sharpe, ed., Pairt of the life

Cunningham, Peter (d. 1805), Church of England clergyman and poet, was the son of a naval officer. He did not have a university education but became a priest and was ordained by Dr Drummond, archbishop of York, in 1772. He first served the curacy of Almondbury, near Huddersfield, and in 1775 he became curate to the Revd T. Seward, father of Anna Seward, at Eyam, near the Peak. He was very popular there, and is mentioned in Anna Seward's correspondence. While at Eyam he published two poems, 'Britannia's naval triumph' and the 'Russian prophecy'. It is not certain when Cunningham left Eyam: it is possible he stayed there until the Revd Seward's death in 1790. In a letter to the Revd T. Wilson in 1788 he described himself as 'reconciled to obscurity' (N&Q), and he refused both Lord Rodney's offer of an introduction to the duke of Rutland, then lord lieutenant of Ireland, and the chaplaincy at Smyrna. In 1789 he published a poem, 'Leith Hill', in imitation of Denham's 'Cooper's Hill', which shows detailed knowledge of the neighbourhood, and in 1800 he published his best-known descriptive poem, 'St Anne's Hill', set in Chertsey, the place of his last curacy. In July 1805 he died suddenly at the annual dinner of the Chertsey Friendly Society, to which he preached a sermon every year.   H. M. STEPHENS, *rev.* S. C. BUSHELL

Sources Nichols, *Illustrations*, 6.47–67 · *N&Q*, 2nd ser., 8 (1859), 259 · *GM*, 1st ser., 55 (1785), 212 · *Letters of Anna Seward: written between the years 1784 and 1807*, ed. A. Constable, 1 (1811), 291–2
Archives Bodl. Oxf., letter-book

Cunningham, Peter (1816–1869), author and literary critic, the third of five sons of the Scottish poet and song-writer Allan *Cunningham (1784–1842) and his wife, Jean Walker (1791–1864), was born at Pimlico on 1 April 1816. His brothers included Sir Alexander *Cunningham, Joseph Davey *Cunningham, and Francis *Cunningham. He was educated at Christ's Hospital, London, and in 1834, through Sir Robert Peel, obtained a position in the Audit Office, in which he rose to be chief clerk. On 14 September 1842 he married Zenobia, daughter of the painter John *Martin, at St George's, Hanover Square, London.

Cunningham is chiefly remembered as a writer, particularly for his *Handbook of London* (2 vols., 1849), which contained considerable original information about places of interest in London, illustrated by quotations from authors associated with them. Many later works on London were indebted to Cunningham's *Handbook* and to his numerous other topographical and antiquarian works on the city, some in Murray's guidebook series. For his antiquarian work he was elected fellow of the Society of Antiquaries. In addition he wrote several works of biography and literary criticism. For the Shakespeare Society, of which he was treasurer, he edited *Extracts from the Accounts of the Revels at Court in the Reigns of Elizabeth and James I* (1842), and wrote a life of Inigo Jones (1848). His edition of Horace Walpole's *Letters* (1857) was a valuable work in its day. He was a contributor to several periodicals, including *Gentleman's Magazine*. Cunningham retired from the Audit Office in 1860, and died at London Road, St Peter's, St Albans, on 18 May 1869.

T. F. HENDERSON, *rev.* ELIZABETH BAIGENT

Sources *Men of the time* (1868) · *The Athenaeum* (29 May 1869), 736 · M. L. Pendered, *John Martin, painter* (1923) · BL, Add. MS 28509 · BL, Egerton MS 1787 · m. cert. · d. cert.
Archives BL, letters · U. Edin. L., corresp. · Yale U., Farmington, Lewis Walpole Library, letters from him | BL, letters to Richard Bentley, with related items, Add. MSS 46617, 46651–46652 · Bodl. Oxf., letters to Isaac Disraeli · U. Edin. L., letters to James Halliwell-Phillipps · U. Edin. L., letters to David Laing
Likenesses C. Martin, chalk drawing, c.1859, NPG · wood-engraving (after photograph by Cundall), NPG; repro. in *ILN* (23 Feb 1856)

Cunningham, Peter Miller (1789–1864), naval surgeon and pioneer in Australia, fifth and youngest son of John Cunningham (1743–1800) of Dalswinton, near Dumfries, land steward and farmer, and his wife, Elizabeth, *née* Harley, the daughter of a Dumfries merchant, was born at Dalswinton in November 1789. He was brother of Thomas Mounsey *Cunningham (1776–1834) and of Allan *Cunningham (1784–1842). He attended local schools, then studied medicine at Edinburgh University; on 10 December 1810 he entered the navy as an assistant surgeon, and

served on the coast of Spain. From August 1812 until promoted to the rank of surgeon (28 January 1814) he was employed on the *Marlborough* (74 guns), on the coast of North America. In 1816 he served in the *Confiance* (32 guns), on Lake Erie, where he became the close friend of the traveller Hugh Clapperton. Between 1819 and 1828 he made five voyages to New South Wales as surgeon-superintendent of convict ships, in which 747 convicts were transported with only three deaths. However, his failure to report whooping cough among the soldiers' children on board during his last voyage led to a serious epidemic in Sydney.

Cunningham came to regard Australia as his adopted country. In 1825 he was granted 1200 acres on the Upper Hunter River, and in 1830 a further 1340 acres, previously leased; he used convict labour and claimed to have spent much on stock and improvements. Liberal and humane, he prided himself on providing education and recreation for the convicts under his charge. In 1827 he published his two-volume *Two years in New South Wales … its peculiar advantages to emigrants; of its topography, natural history, etc.* This became very popular and was translated into German; it remains a valuable historical source. With his savings and the profits from the book he hoped to establish himself as a settler on his property. However he failed, partly because of a severe drought, and in May 1830 he returned to England.

Cunningham's well-earned reputation at the Admiralty soon gained him naval employment again, and on 22 October 1830 he was appointed to the *Tyne* (28 guns), in which he served on the South American station until January 1834, and had opportunities of observing the effects of tropical climates on European constitutions. He joined the *Asia* (84 guns) in 1836, and was present at the blockade of Alexandria in 1840. He left the sea and went on half pay in May 1841, was classed unfit for further service in 1850, and retired in 1860. As a result of his experiences he published two further works: *On the motions of the earth, and on the conception, growth, and decay of man and causes of his diseases as referable to galvanic action* (1834) and *Hints for Australian Emigrants, with Descriptions of the Water-Raising Wheels in Egypt* (1841), advocating irrigation. He also contributed an account of a visit to the Falkland Islands to *The Athenaeum*, and was a frequent contributor elsewhere. He was amiable and conciliatory in character, a man of remarkable powers of observation, greatly attached to his brother Allan, and very popular among his friends. He died, unmarried, at his home, 11 Lovegrove Place, Greenwich, London, on 6 March 1864.

G. C. BOASE, *rev.* ANDREW LAMBERT

Sources L. F. Fitzhardinge, 'Cunningham, Peter Miller', *AusDB*, vol. 1 · *GM*, 3rd ser., 16 (1864), 799 · O'Byrne, *Naval biog. dict.* · Boase, *Mod. Eng. biog.* · D. Hogg, *The life of Allan Cunningham* (1875) · *CGPLA Eng. & Wales* (1864)
Wealth at death under £50: administration with will, 9 Dec 1864, *CGPLA Eng. & Wales*

Cunningham, Richard (1793–1835), botanist, was born on 12 February 1793 at Wimbledon, Surrey, the second son of Allan Cunningham (d. 1828), head gardener at Wimbledon House, and his wife, Sarah (formerly Juson, née Dicken). His older brother was Allan *Cunningham (1791–1839). After schooling at the Revd John Adams's Putney Academy, he joined his older brother working with W. T. Aiton on *Hortus Kewensis*. From 1816 Allan Cunningham was botanizing in Australia: during the 1820s he became concerned that he was not receiving credit for new plants sent from Australia, most of which lay undescribed in London, a worry Richard Cunningham shared. To protect Allan's interests, Cunningham conspired against Aiton (for whom he was still working as amanuensis at Kew) and Robert Brown (1773–1858), who each had claims to Allan's plants. With the knowledge of William Hooker, then professor of botany at Glasgow, he engaged in an ethically suspect 'clandestine movement' (Cunningham to Hooker, 5 Feb 1825), to arrange publication of Allan's descriptions in Barron Field's *Geographical Memoirs of New South Wales* (1825) and in P. P. King's *Narrative of a Survey of the Intertropical and Western Coasts of Australia* (1827).

In August 1832 Cunningham embarked for Sydney to take up the position of colonial botanist and superintendent of the Botanic Garden, a post for which he had been recommended by his brother and approved by Brown. After a period collecting in New Zealand he joined, as botanist, Major Thomas Mitchell's 1835 expedition to trace the Darling River in western New South Wales. He was not a skilled bushman, and on April 17 he was missing when the party encamped for the night near the Bogan River. Only his dead horse and some personal artefacts were found by the expedition. A later search-party contacted tribesmen, and were told that he had been killed by Aborigines (with whom he had camped) after his strange behaviour at night had alarmed them. His remains are buried near Dandaloo station, about 35 miles west of Narromine in New South Wales.

Cunningham was primarily a herbarium assistant and even as colonial botanist in Sydney, aiding others such as Johan Lhotsky (b. 1800) to work up collections, he himself published little. He died before he could establish a major independent reputation and is remembered more for his official position and relationship to his brother Allan than for major contributions to botany, although his important New Zealand collections were included in his brother's 'Florae insularum Novae Zelandiae' (published serially in *Annals and Magazine of Natural History*, 1–4, 1836–9).

A. M. LUCAS

Sources [W. J. Hooker], 'A brief biographical sketch of the late Richard Cunningham, colonial botanist in New South Wales', *Companion to the Botanical Magazine*, 2 (1836), 210–21 · RBG Kew, directors' corresp., vol. 72, nos. 73–5, 87 · NSW corresp., misc. A–G, 1832, PRO, CO 201/229, fols. 278–9 · Cunningham to Hay (7 May 1832) and related corresp., 1832, PRO, CO 201/229, fols. 280–97 · NSW dispatches, 1835, PRO, CO 201/248, fols. 261–5 · C. Finney, *Paradise revealed: natural history in nineteenth-century Australia* (1993) · W. G. McMinn, *Allan Cunningham: botanist and explorer* (1970) · register of births and baptisms, George Yard Chapel, no.42, PRO, RG 4/3595 · parish register, London, Marylebone Road, St Mary, 20 Aug 1790 [marriage]

Archives RBG Kew, directors' corresp.

Likenesses pencil, c.1830, RBG Kew; repro. in Hooker, 'A brief biographical sketch', facing p. 210; version, Mitchell L., NSW; repr. in D. J. Carr and S. G. M. Carr, eds., *People and plants in Australia* (1981), 245

Cunningham, Sir Robert, of Kilmaurs (d. 1430/31). *See under* Cunningham family (*per.* c.1340–1631).

Cunningham, Thomas Mounsey (1776–1834), poet, was born at Culfaud, Kirkcudbrightshire, on 25 June 1776, second of the nine children of John Cunningham (1743–1800), farm steward, and Elizabeth Harley, daughter of a Dumfries merchant. He was an elder brother of Allan *Cunningham (1784–1842), poet and biographer of Burns, and of Peter Miller *Cunningham (1789–1864), a naval surgeon. His early education was at a dame-school and the village school of Kellieston, after which he attended Dumfries Academy and studied bookkeeping, mathematics, French, and Latin.

At sixteen Cunningham became clerk to John Maxwell of Terraughty, but remained with him only a short time. He then contemplated taking up a clerical post in South Carolina, but was dissuaded by his father's employer and was instead apprenticed to a millwright at Dalswinton. On the conclusion of his apprenticeship in 1797 he found employment at Rotherham, until his employer became bankrupt and he went to London. He then considered emigrating to the West Indies, but when he learned that his employer had set up in business at Lynn in Norfolk, he rejoined him there.

Cunningham had begun to compose songs and poetry at an early age and in 1798 'The Har'st Kirn' ('harvest home') was published in Brash and Reid's *Poetry, Original and Selected*. About 1800 he moved to Wiltshire, and soon afterwards to Cambridgeshire, where he wrote 'The Hills o' Gallowa', one of his most popular songs, which has been attributed by some to Burns. At about this time he also wrote 'The Cambridgeshire Garland' and 'The Unco Grave'.

In 1805 Cunningham was in Dover, and proceeded to London, where he found work in the employ of Sir John Rennie the engineer. After this he was for some time foreman superintendent of Fowler's chain cable manufactory, before rejoining Rennie's establishment in 1812 as a well-paid clerk, and later as chief clerk, assisted by his eldest son. In 1805 he began to contribute poetry to the *Scots Magazine*, attracting the notice of James Hogg, who addressed an epistle to him (*Scots Magazine*, 1805, 621–2) and called him 'Nithsdale's lost and darling Cunningham'. He was a major contributor to Hogg's *Forest Minstrel* (1810). After the establishment of the *Edinburgh Magazine* in 1817, he contributed poems and songs, and, under the title of 'Literary legacy', several prose sketches on modern and antiquarian subjects.

Cunningham appears to have been sensitive to criticism and as a consequence did not publish for long periods, including the last years of his life, during which he destroyed many of his writings. Hogg wrote of him 'I always marvel how he could possibly put his poetical vein under lock and key, as he did all at once; for he certainly then bade fair to be the first of Scottish bards' (*Memoir*, 72). Cunningham died from an attack of cholera on 28 October 1834 in Princes Street, Blackfriars Road, London. Although no marriage has been traced, he left a son and daughter.

T. F. HENDERSON, *rev.* SARAH COUPER

Sources Chambers, *Scots.* (1868–70) · C. Rogers, *The modern Scottish minstrel, or, The songs of Scotland of the past half-century*, 2 (1856), 223–8 · Anderson, *Scot. nat.* · J. Hogg, 'Memoir of the author's life' and 'Familiar anecdotes of Sir Walter Scott', ed. D. S. Mack (1972), 72 · J. G. Wilson, ed., *The poets and poetry of Scotland*, 1 (1876), 537–8 · D. Hogg, *The life of Allan Cunningham* (1875) · *Scots Magazine and Edinburgh Literary Miscellany*, 67 (1805), 621–2 · *Scots Magazine and Edinburgh Literary Miscellany*, 68 (1806), 206–8 · J. Hogg, *The forest minstrel* (1810)

Cunningham, Timothy (*d.* **1789**), barrister and antiquary, was a member of the Middle Temple, and lived in chambers at Gray's Inn for over thirty years. He was probably a native of Ireland. In 1759 he sought employment as copyist at the British Museum from the antiquary Dr John Burton (1696–1771). His terms, however, of 2*d.* a sheet for foreign languages, with some small extra allowance for preliminary researches, seem to have been thought too high. His circumstances seem to have improved later, as he was the author or compiler of numerous legal and antiquarian books, many of which ran to several editions. These included *The Law of Bills of Exchange, Promissory Notes, Bank-Notes, and Insurances* (1760; 6th edn, 1778), *A New Treatise on the Laws Concerning Tithes* (1765; 4th edn, 1777), and *A New and Complete Law Dictionary* (2 vols., 1764–5; 3rd edn, 1783).

Cunningham was elected a fellow of the Society of Antiquaries on 29 January 1761, but although a testimonial for his admission to the Royal Society was signed in the same year by the bishop of Ossory, by Dr Charles Morton, and others, he did not became a fellow of the Royal Society. He died at Gray's Inn in April 1789, leaving a legacy of £1000 to the Royal Irish Academy for the encouragement of learning in Ireland by awarding prizes for literary or scientific works of distinction. The council made every effort to secure a portrait or bust of their benefactor, but none existed.

A. M. CLERKE, *rev.* J. A. MARCHAND

Sources *GM*, 1st ser., 59 (1789), 574 · *European Magazine and London Review*, 40 (1801) · *Monthly Review*, 27 (1762), 153–4 · *Monthly Review*, 37 (1767), 233 · *Monthly Review*, 68 (1783), 89–90 · Watt, *Bibl. Brit.*

Cunningham, Waddell (**1729–1797**), merchant and politician, was born in Ballymacilmoyle, in the parish of Killead, co. Antrim, Ireland, the youngest son of John Cunningham, sometime ship's captain and a small farmer, and his wife, Jane Ross Waddell, of Islandderry, in the parish of Dromore, co. Down. The various Cunninghams and Waddells of counties Antrim and Down made up a large and well-established family network with involvements in farming, linen manufacture, and overseas trade. Some time around 1750 Waddell Cunningham was sent to provincial New York to assist a kinsman, probably the Belfast merchant James Ross (*d.* 1765), in his annual flaxseed trade to Ireland. For a young man of intelligence and ambition, the availability of credit, access to good quality Irish linens, and links to the Irish market for North American flaxseed provided a sufficient opening.

By 1752 Cunningham was operating a store in New York

Waddell Cunningham (1729–1797), by Robert Home, *c.*1786

city, and a year later he purchased his first share in an ocean-going vessel. His trade benefited from competitive pricing, careful management of debt, and friends in high places, particularly the customs service. Smuggling operations in Long Island Sound through correspondents in Amsterdam, Rotterdam, and Hamburg were part of a commerce that was energetic and far-ranging. Cunningham quickly rose to prominence and became a central figure in New York's influential Irish merchant community.

Partnership with Thomas Greg (*d.* 1796), twelve years his senior and one of the most successful merchants in Belfast, coincided with the formal declaration of war against France in May 1756. Cunningham was adept at seizing wartime opportunities and, by 1763, held shares in at least ten privateer warships, all the while supplying the French islands with desperately needed provisions and 'warlike stores'. Although prosecuted and fined for trading with the enemy, and arrested and briefly jailed in 1759 for inciting a mob to harass a customs informer, Cunningham made a fortune during the war, investing his profits in frontier land, real estate in New York city, and a sugar plantation in the West Indies.

In July 1763 Cunningham became involved in a violent altercation outside the Merchants' Coffee House in New York city that led to the brutal wounding of a fellow merchant, Thomas Forsey. 'My Conduct was imputable to Heat, not Malice', Cunningham later wrote, 'to a Want of Self-Possession' (*New-York Gazette*, 13 Oct 1763). The affair took on larger significance in October 1764 after a jury brought in damages of £1550 in a civil proceeding. When the court refused an appeal based on the size of the award, Governor Cadwallader Colden created a constitutional crisis by attempting to force an appeal, thus threatening the sanctity of jury verdicts. The storm of protest associated with *Forsey* v. *Cunningham*, which came as a prelude to the Stamp Act crisis, abated only after the privy council sided with the legal community in New York.

On the eve of his trial Cunningham returned to Ireland, leaving junior partners to manage the firm until its dissolution in 1775. On 9 November 1765 he married Margaret (Peggy; *d.* 1808), the daughter of Samuel Hyde (*d.* 1744), a wealthy Belfast merchant. The couple, who remained childless, established themselves in a large home on Hercules Lane in Belfast, which also served as the centre of Cunningham's business operations. In addition to commercial, financial, and industrial activities (sugar refining, glass making, flour milling, the manufacture of oil of vitriol, and development of the Donegal herring fishery), he became a middleman on the estate of Lord Donegal. Cunningham's involvement in the evictions of 1769 and 1770 has been exaggerated, but he held leases on 520 acres of the earl's land, 370 acres of which lay in the town land of Ballypalliday, co. Antrim, the origin of the Hearts of Steel, an agrarian society founded to protect tenants and occupiers. Sporadic violence, mostly the burning of buildings and maiming of cattle, rendered large areas of the north of Ireland ungovernable. On 19 December 1770, outraged by the timidity of local authorities, Cunningham 'did in Person support and aid a Constable in apprehending [the] notorious ringleader of the Hearts of Steel' (*Journals of the House of Commons ... Ireland*, 8.428). Four days later a band of about 1200 well-armed and determined 'Steelboys' marched on Belfast to free their leader from the barracks. At first unsuccessful, part of the mob then attacked and set fire to Cunningham's home. With five agitators dead outside the barracks and the Steelboys threatening destruction of the town, officials released the prisoner.

During the American War of Independence Cunningham smuggled guns and ammunition, linens and woollens, and salted provisions to the American forces as he carried on an intermittent trade with loyalist correspondents in New York city. Meanwhile he was elected lieutenant of the Belfast first volunteer company, established in March 1778 in response to the threat of French invasion. With Ireland stripped of regular British troops, he periodically took his men into the countryside to maintain order and protect property. In May 1780 Captain Cunningham presided over a convention of volunteer companies at Belfast that petitioned Henry Grattan on Irish rights, and he was one of the Belfast delegates to the Dungannon Convention two years later.

Participation in the volunteer movement inexorably drew Cunningham into politics. In 1783, the year he retired from trade, Lord Donegal rejected a petition asking that he be offered one of Belfast's two seats in the forthcoming Irish parliamentary session. At nearby Carrickfergus, a freeman borough with a large electorate, Cunningham easily defeated Joseph Hewitt, the son of Baron Lifford, lord chancellor of Ireland. Elected on a platform of parliamentary and commercial reform, Cunningham earned both the praise of members, who welcomed

'his fund of mercantile knowledge into this house', and the enmity of vested interests, who saw him as unpredictable and dangerous. But when 'the honest and victorious merchant' took his seat in March 1784, the legality of his election was challenged (Millin, 38). The defeated candidate complained that Belfast men wearing cockades reading 'freedom of election' had brought undue influence on the electorate (McDowell, 295). Cunningham stood again at Carrickfergus a year later, but his enemies were fully arrayed. 'The matter has been carry'd on in so avowd & scandalous a manner', wrote one observer, 'that even W. C. enemies wish him success' (PRO NIre., T 765/2/1/135). He lost in a close contest.

Cunningham now threw his considerable energy into public service: as a founder of the White Linen Hall in Belfast; as a charter member of the Belfast Harbour Corporation; as a trustee of the Second Presbyterian Congregation; and as a promoter of the Belfast Academy, the Linen Hall Library, and the Belfast Charitable Society. He was, as well, the first president of the Belfast chamber of commerce. In 1785 he opened the Belfast discount office to facilitate transactions at the new Linen Hall, and two years later he founded a bank. In 1784 Cunningham was also instrumental in raising funds to build a Roman Catholic chapel in Belfast, into which he marched his volunteer company and its regimental band in honour of the first celebration of mass. 'I would shudder if WC's interest, ambition, and therefore inclination and abilities were combined against me', wrote a woman who knew him in the 1780s (PRO NIre., T 765/2/2/249).

A man of strong republican instincts, Cunningham was an ardent supporter of the French Revolution. His Belfast first volunteer company, wearing green cockades to honour Irish nationalism, was at the centre of Bastille day celebrations in Belfast in the early 1790s. But Cunningham was a moderate who sought reform at a measured pace, particularly the granting of political rights to Roman Catholics. In 1792 he angrily confronted Theobald Wolf Tone on this question and, although remaining active in the cause of parliamentary reform, distanced himself from the extremism of the United Irishmen infecting the middle class in Belfast.

Cunningham stood firm against the rising tide of revolution. He declared for the king and joined the yeomanry early in 1797, serving as captain of the 4th company of Belfast yeoman infantry. But he was neither a reactionary nor a pawn of the aristocratic élite, whom he despised. The compassion he showed as a magistrate may have grown out of his experience as an impetuous upstart in colonial New York. In the popular mind, Cunningham was the embodiment of what could be achieved by those of modest means with an abundance of ability. His death, at his home in Hercules Lane, on 15 December 1797, during a period of harsh repression in the north of Ireland, brought an outpouring of affection. 'The poor man and the industrious mechanic may long regret his decease', wrote one observer. His funeral on 17 December 1797 at the parish church at Newtownbreda (Knockbreda) on the outskirts of Belfast was attended by 'a great concourse' of citizens (*Belfast News-Letter*, 18 Dec 1797). His estate, excluding his sugar plantation on Dominica, was valued at £60,000.   THOMAS M. TRUXES

Sources *Belfast News-Letter* (1754–97) · *New York Mercury* (1752–65) · *New-York Gazette, or, The Weekly Post-Boy* (1752–65) · *Northern Star* (1792–5) · G. Chambers, *Faces of change: the Belfast and Northern Ireland Chambers of Commerce and Industry, 1783–1983* (c.1984) · T. M. Truxes, *Irish–American trade, 1660–1783* (1988) · A. T. Q. Stewart, *A deeper silence: the hidden roots of the United Irish movement* (1993); repr. as *A deeper silence: the hidden origins of the United Irishmen* (1998) · T. M. Truxes, ed., *Letterbook of Greg & Cunningham, 1756–57: merchants of New York and Belfast* (2001) · letter-books of Greg and Cunningham, merchants of New York and Belfast, 1764–5, New-York Historical Society, New York · G. Benn, *A history of the town of Belfast from the earliest times to the close of the eighteenth century*, 2 vols. (1877–80) · S. S. Millin, *Sidelights on Belfast history* (1932) · last will and testament, 13 Dec 1797, PRO NIre., CR 4/9B/13 · pedigree of the Waddell family of Islandderry, PRO NIre., T 2197/3 · W. A. Maguire, 'Lord Donegall and the Hearts of Steel', *Irish Historical Studies*, 21 (1978–9), 351–76 · H. A. Johnson, 'George Harison's protest: new light on Forsey versus Cunningham', *New York History*, 50 (1969), 61–82 · letters, PRO NIre., Drennan MSS, T 765 · V. D. Harrington, *The New York merchant on the eve of the revolution* (1935) · *The journals of the House of Commons of the kingdom of Ireland*, 19 vols. (1796–1800) · R. B. McDowell, *Ireland in the age of imperialism and revolution, 1760–1801* (1979) · N. E. Gamble, 'The business community and trade of Belfast, 1767–1800', PhD diss., TCD, 1978
Archives PRO NIre., Drennan deeds | New York Historical Society, Greg and Cunningham letter-books · PRO NIre., Drennan letters
Likenesses R. Home, oils, c.1786, Ulster Museum, Belfast [*see illus.*] · portrait, repro. in Chambers, *Faces of change*, 36
Wealth at death approx. £60,000; plus plantation on island of Dominica: will, PRO NIre., CR 4/9B/13

Cunningham, Sir William (d. 1396x9). *See under* Cunningham family (*per. c.*1340–1631).

Cunningham, Sir William, of Kilmaurs (d. 1413x15). *See under* Cunningham family (*per. c.*1340–1631).

Cunningham, William, third earl of Glencairn (d. 1548), magnate, was the only son of Cuthbert *Cunningham, third Lord Kilmaurs and second earl of Glencairn (c.1470–1540/41) [*see under* Cunningham family], and his wife, Marion Douglas (d. in or after 1511), daughter of Archibald, fifth earl of Angus. He was twice married: first (before 10 July 1509) to Katherine, daughter of William, third Lord Borthwick; and second (after January 1536) to Elizabeth, daughter and heir of John Campbell of West Loudoun (widow successively of William Wallace of Craigie and Robert, fourth Lord Crichton of Sanquhar). When his father died, some time between May 1540 and May 1541, Cunningham inherited a huge reservoir of territorial and military power through the possession of lands in nine sheriffdoms, of which the most important were the lordships and baronies of Glencairn (Dumfriesshire), Kilmaurs (Ayrshire), Finlaystone (Renfrewshire), and Kilmaronock (Dunbartonshire). As a landholder on the highland border he had uneasy relations with the powerful earl of Argyll, but he was an ally of the earls of Lennox, dynastic rivals of the Hamiltons, who saw their political future in alliance with England.

The Cunningham chiefs enjoyed a remarkably strong line of succession in the first half of the sixteenth century.

As master of Kilmaurs (or Glencairn) William Cunningham acted in partnership with his father for all but the last six or seven years of his own adult life, and from the early 1530s his own sons were politically active. During the early years of James V's minority he identified with the Anglophile party led by Archibald Douglas, sixth earl of Angus, who in 1514 married the previous king's widow, Margaret Tudor, and John Stewart, twelfth earl of Lennox, in opposition to the French-born regent, John Stewart, second duke of Albany. As early as 1516 the English border officials regarded the master of Kilmaurs as a useful agent. In July 1524, with Lennox and other Scottish lords, he made a 'profession of obedience' to Henry VIII, and he signed a covenant to that effect in the following August (*LP Henry VIII* 4/1 no. 540). He received an English pension. In June 1526 he was made treasurer of Scotland. However, Angus's refusal that same month to hand over custody of the king to the next guardians on an agreed rota caused Kilmaurs and his father to support Lennox in his attempts to break the power of the Douglases and to rescue the king from them. Kilmaurs took part in an abortive rescue attempt in Edinburgh on 1 September 1526; four days later his father was wounded at the battle of Linlithgow where another attack on the Douglases failed and Lennox was killed. Having fallen foul of Angus, Kilmaurs was deprived of the treasurership on 29 October.

After James V assumed the government in 1528 on the fall of Angus, William Cunningham was given responsibilities which included forming part of Mary of Guise's escort when she came to Scotland in 1538, and acting as vice-admiral under Lord Maxwell during James V's expedition to the northern and western isles in 1541. Cunningham was an important royal agent in the isles in the last year of James's reign. He was among those prisoners taken after the Scottish defeat at Solway Moss on 24 November 1542, who were released on 'assuring' themselves to advance English interests in Scotland. Glencairn, as he now was, was ransomed for £1000 and later sent three sons to England as hostages. After the death of James V on 14 December 1542 the Anglophile party promoted plans for a peace treaty with England and a marriage between Prince Edward and the infant Queen Mary. Glencairn was a prominent member of this group, and in March 1543 he was among the commissioners appointed by parliament to negotiate the royal marriage and peace treaties. The treaty was concluded in London in June and officially proclaimed in Edinburgh on 26 July, when Glencairn was among those who witnessed the proclamation. While in London he and other Scots lords privately signed an undertaking to put Scotland in Henry's hands should Mary die without children.

Like other magnates Glencairn exploited the system of church appointments to his family's advantage: through patronage of his family's foundation of Kilmaurs collegiate church, through his son Robert's office of minister or prior of the Trinitarian house at Fail in Kyle, and through his youngest son William's appointment to the bishopric of Argyll in 1539, later exchanged for the deanery of Brechin. At the same time he and his sons were among those who saw the progress of church reform in England as an important ideological reason for closer union between England and Scotland. Glencairn supported both the act of the Scottish parliament of March 1543 which permitted the possession and reading of the vernacular New Testament, and the appointment of protestant preachers at court that same year by the governor Arran. Glencairn's second son, Andrew, was accused of heresy in 1539, but although he formally recanted and was reprieved, he and his older brother Alexander *Cunningham remained committed to the cause of reform. Glencairn himself gave public support to the protestant reformer George Wishart when he preached in Ayr in 1545.

Glencairn was prominent in the broadly based alliance which gathered around Angus (who returned to Scotland in 1543) and Matthew Stewart, thirteenth earl of Lennox, in opposition to the governor after his capitulation to the pro-French Cardinal Beaton in September 1543. Glencairn and other lords refused to attend the queen's coronation that month unless the treaties with England were ratified, but a parliament in December 1543, which was dominated by Beaton, cancelled the treaties and re-enacted the anti-heresy laws. There was a failed attempt at reconciliation between the parties in January 1544. The opposition led by Glencairn was defeated the following May in a military confrontation with the governor's forces near Glasgow, when Glencairn's son Andrew was killed.

The English invasions of 1544 and 1545, Henry's retribution for the breaking of the treaties, had the effect of drawing all Scottish parties together in self-defence and modified Glencairn's adherence to the English king. He was among those who offered support to Mary of Guise in 1544 while she tried to form her own party in opposition to Arran. When Lennox, who had earlier retreated to England leaving Glencairn in charge of Dumbarton Castle, returned in the autumn of 1544 to harry the west, he found Glencairn and others reluctant to help him. Henry became suspicious of the real motives of Glencairn and his heir, Alexander. Glencairn continued to protest his loyalty to Henry privately to English agents, and redeemed himself somewhat in English eyes when in December 1544 he and Angus put up a noticeably half-hearted resistance to an English attack at Coldingham in Berwickshire. But at the Scottish parliament that same month he and Angus were absolved from all treasonable actions, and they took part in the Scottish victory over the English at Ancrum Moor on 27 February 1545.

Contact was maintained between Glencairn, his son, and English agents throughout 1545, but trust between them weakened. After the murder of Beaton on 29 May 1546 and the ending of political reprisals against the Anglophiles from that quarter, Glencairn appears to have renewed his support for English intervention in Scottish affairs, while his personal relations with English agents on the borders improved. Writing to Wharton on 11 April 1547 he apologized for his failure to keep a meeting at his own Dumfriesshire castle of Glencairn, due to illness, saying that he had also missed the convention at Edinburgh.

He put pressure on the English agent by promising to be at Glencairn by the end of the month provided his son Alexander (still a hostage in England) was brought to Carlisle. In July he sent 'overtures' to Somerset which included details of his promised support for an English army should it enter Scotland by the west march. He was able, he assured Somerset, to conduct an army from Carlisle to Glasgow without challenge, to raise 2000 of his friends and allies in Ayrshire and Renfrewshire, and to offer the English fleet 'one of the best havens in Christendom' at Ardmore on the Clyde opposite his own castle of Finlaystone (*CSP Scot.*, 1547–63, 1.26), a demonstration of the extent of his territorial power in the west of Scotland.

Glencairn died in March 1548. He had five sons: Alexander, who succeeded him as fourth earl; Andrew, killed in 1544; Hugh of Watterston; Robert of Montgreenan, minister of Fail; and William, successively bishop of Argyll and dean of Brechin; and two daughters, Elizabeth, who married Sir John Cunningham of Caprington, and Jane (Jean), who married Robert Fergusson of Craigdarroch.

MARGARET H. B. SANDERSON

Sources NA Scot., Glencairn muniments, GD 39 · *LP Henry VIII* · *CSP Scot.*, 1547–63 · *John Knox's History of the Reformation in Scotland*, ed. W. C. Dickinson, 2 vols. (1949) · *Scots peerage*, 4.235–9 · M. H. B. Sanderson, *Ayrshire and the Reformation* (1997) · J. Cameron, *James V: the personal rule, 1528–1542*, ed. N. Macdougall (1998)
Archives NA Scot., Glencairn muniments

Cunningham, William, fifth earl of Glencairn (*b. c.*1526, *d.* in or before **1580**). *See under* Cunningham family (*per. c.*1340–1631).

Cunningham, William, seventh earl of Glencairn (*b.* in or after **1575**, *d.* **1631**). *See under* Cunningham family (*per. c.*1340–1631).

Cunningham, William, eighth earl of Glencairn (**1610/11–1664**), royalist army officer, was the son of William *Cunningham, seventh earl of Glencairn (*d.* 1631) [*see under* Cunningham family], and Janet Kerr, daughter of Mark Kerr, first earl of Lothian. In March 1630 he matriculated at Glasgow University, and he inherited his title on his father's death in October the following year. He married Anne Ogilvy (*d.* 1661), daughter of Lord Deskford, the contract being dated 5 April 1637.

In the early stages of the Scottish revolt against Charles I Glencairn avoided publicly committing himself, but in 1639 as civil war approached he 'deserted his country' (*Letters and Journals of Robert Baillie*, 1.201) by joining the king in England. In May he and other Scottish royalists sailed from Newcastle in the hope of obtaining military help from the marquess of Hamilton, whose fleet was in the Firth of Forth, and then leading a royalist rising in the north. However, Hamilton was unable to give significant help, and when the royalists landed at Aberdeen on 6 June Glencairn 'depairted home' (J. Spalding, *Memorials*, 2 vols., 1844–5, 1.204). When a settlement was reached between king and covenanters in November 1641 Glencairn was made a member of the Scottish privy council and of the committees which took effective control of the country in the following two years. The king's trust in him was

William Cunningham, eighth earl of Glencairn (1610/11–1664), by John Michael Wright, *c.*1661

shown by the fact that he was the only colonel whom Charles chose to nominate when a Scottish army was sent to Ireland early in 1642. In the debate in 1642–3 over whether or not the covenanters should intervene in the English civil war, which culminated in the signing of the solemn league and covenant in September 1643 and the invasion of England in January 1644 in support of the English parliament, Glencairn took a neutral stance, arguing against intervention on either side. This was enough, however, to earn him a letter from the king in December 1643 thanking him for how 'affectionately and resolutely' he had served him (NL Scot., MS 773, fol. 74), and the following month he was granted a pension of £300 sterling a year. By April 1644 Glencairn had agreed to be colonel of a regiment of the covenanters' army in England, though (as with his regiment in Ireland) he showed little interest in leading it in the field. None the less his regiment's service against the king in England and against the marquess of Montrose in Scotland are clear indications that he had committed himself to the covenanting cause. After the battle of Kilsyth (15 August 1645), at which his regiment was destroyed, the covenanting regime temporarily collapsed, and Glencairn fled to Ulster and negotiated with the Scots army there to persuade it to send help to Scotland.

With the defeat of Charles I in the English civil war, however, Glencairn was one of those who moved towards believing that it was now necessary to help the king against the English parliament to achieve a satisfactory settlement, and in June 1646 he urged Charles to sign the solemn league and covenant to make this possible. The king appointed him justice general of Scotland on 13 November 1646, and he supported the engagement treaty with the king, being appointed a colonel in the army the engagers raised in 1648. After the army was dispersed by Cromwell at the battle of Preston, Glencairn was active in the negotiations with the kirk party that led to the disbanding of engager forces, and he was subsequently deprived of all public offices. This was the common fate of engagers, but the kirk party showed itself unusually vindictive in Glencairn's case, annulling (2 March 1649) the 1488 patent that had created his earldom.

However, Glencairn benefited from the swing back towards royalism provoked by Cromwell's invasion in 1650, and by May 1651 he had given full satisfaction to the church for his role in the engagement. When Charles II undertook his despairing invasion of England (to try to divert the English from Scotland) Glencairn was one of the nobles ordered to remain in Scotland and lead continued resistance to the English. He was soon forced to submit, but early in 1653 he offered to raise men and give leadership to the disorganized bands of royalists still opposing the English in the highlands. The exiled Charles II commissioned him commander-in-chief (4 March 1653) until Lieutenant-General John Middleton could be sent from the Netherlands to take over command, though to avoid raising jealousies it was arranged that the highlanders should be manoeuvred into taking the decision themselves to appoint Glencairn as their leader. This was done at a meeting in Lochaber in July 1653. At first Glencairn had considerable success, with a policy of not confronting English forces but making small-scale raids deep into the lowlands to raise men and seize horses and supplies, but from the first there were deep personal rivalries and divisions as to policy and among royalist leaders, and opposition to his leadership forced him to reveal his secret commission from the king.

Though Glencairn had accepted that Middleton would supersede him, he made it clear that he expected to be next in command to him, but when Middleton arrived early in 1654 he brought Sir George Monro as his second in command. Glencairn felt not only personally insulted but believed that there was a plot by professional soldiers 'to suppresse the nobilitie' (J. Turner, *Memoirs*, 1829, 115), and in April he fought a duel with Monro. Various stories circulated as to its immediate cause, but with Glencairn furious at being supplanted and Monro a man notorious for bad temper, a clash between the two was almost inevitable. Monro was badly wounded, and shortly after the duel Glencairn withdrew his forces from Middleton. He continued to resist the English, but the royalist effort was now hopelessly divided. By the summer Glencairn was ill, 'bedfast' with 'a languishing sickness', and demoralized (Firth, *Scotland and the Protectorate*, 64, 168). He negotiated to surrender on good terms to the English commander-in-chief, George Monck, and he and about 300 men handed in their arms at Dumbarton on 7 September. In justification of his conduct Glencairn argued that 'wee are not the first who hes capitulated', and complained of having 'long wrestled with divers mens discontented humors'. Most of his men had deserted and this had combined with 'my owne greate sickness' (Firth, *Scotland and the Commonwealth*, 164, 169) to make continued resistance impracticable.

Glencairn was, however, subject to much criticism: in Edinburgh 'the only time hee shewd his head, hee was cald publikely rogue and Traytor, one who engaged Gentlemen in a busyness, and then sold them and left them in the end' (*Nicholas Papers*, ed. G. F. Warner, 2, 1892, 168); and 'Glencairne ledd the way to the rest, as of going out, so of coming in, for which much blame lyes on him' (*Letters and Journals of Robert Baillie*, 3.288). Glencairn re-opened communications with the king, but these were intercepted by the English and he was imprisoned in Edinburgh Castle, where he had been for some time by September 1656. He was free by August 1659, when he signed a bond not to act against the Commonwealth, and in October, when Monck summoned a meeting which undertook to maintain the peace in Scotland while he imposed a political settlement in England, Glencairn presided over the shire representatives. With the restoration of monarchy in 1660 Glencairn's past failings were forgotten and his resistance to the English rewarded. In August 1660 he returned to Scotland (after a visit to court) as lord chancellor, and in January 1661 he was elected president of the Scottish parliament. He supported the re-establishment of episcopacy in Scotland, but is said to have come to regret it—not least because his dispute with the archbishop of St Andrews over precedence ended in victory for the latter. Politically his influence waned after he joined Middleton (now the king's commissioner to parliament) in a failed plot to have their rival, the earl of Lauderdale (the king's Scottish secretary), declared incapable of public office in 1662. His first wife having died of measles in January 1661, Glencairn married Lady Margaret Montgomery (1617–1665), daughter of Alexander *Montgomery, sixth earl of Eglinton, and widow of John Hay, first earl of Tweeddale. He died 'of a purpie fever' in his house at Bolton, Haddingtonshire, on 29 May 1664 (*Diary of Mr John Lamont*, 170), and was given an elaborate state funeral at St Giles's, Edinburgh, where he was buried, on 28 July.

DAVID STEVENSON

Sources DNB · GEC, *Peerage* · *Scots peerage* · *Calendar of the Clarendon state papers preserved in the Bodleian Library*, ed. O. Ogle and others, 5 vols. (1869–1970) · *The letters and journals of Robert Baillie*, ed. D. Laing, 3 vols., Bannatyne Club, 73 (1841–2) · C. H. Firth, ed., *Scotland and the Commonwealth: letters and papers relating to the military government of Scotland, from August 1651 to December 1653*, Scottish History Society, 18 (1895) · C. H. Firth, ed., *Scotland and the protectorate: letters and papers relating to the military government of Scotland from January 1654 to June 1659*, Scottish History Society, 31 (1899) · *The life of Mr Robert Blair ... containing his autobiography*, ed. T. M'Crie, Wodrow Society, 11 (1848) · *The memoirs of Henry Guthry, late bishop*, 2nd edn (1747) · *APS* · F. D. Dow, *Cromwellian Scotland, 1651–1660* (1979) · E. M. Furgol, *A regimental history of the covenanting armies, 1639–1651* (1990) · *The Clarke Papers*, ed. C. H. Firth, 4, CS, new ser., 62 (1901) · *The diary of Mr John Lamont of Newton, 1649–1671*, ed. G. R. Kinloch, Maitland Club, 7 (1830) · C. Innes, ed., *Munimenta alme Universitatis Glasguensis / Records of the University of Glasgow from its foundation till 1727*, 4 vols., Maitland Club, 72 (1854) · NA Scot., Glencairn muniments, GD39 · NA Scot., Hamilton muniments, GD406

Archives NA Scot., muniments · NL Scot., corresp., MS 3139 | BL, letters to Lord Lauderdale and Charles II, Add. MSS 23114–23120 · Buckminster Park, Grantham, corresp. with second earl of Lauderdale

Likenesses J. M. Wright, oils, c.1661, Scot. NPG [*see illus.*]

Cunningham, William (1805–1861), Free Church of Scotland minister and theologian, was born at Hamilton, Lanarkshire, on 2 October 1805, the eldest of three sons of Charles Cunningham (d. 1811), merchant, and his wife, Helen (d. 1860). His father died prematurely from injuries sustained in a fall from a horse, and the family went to live with his grandfather at Drafane Farm in the parish of Lesmahagow. Eventually they settled in Dunse (later Duns), Berwickshire, where his mother had family. This was fortunate for William as the local school had an excellent classics teacher who detected his ability and prepared him for entry to Edinburgh University in 1820. At Edinburgh he befriended an even more accomplished classicist, John Brown Patterson. While still a divinity student Cunningham opined that controversy would probably be his life's work, and this proved a prescient remark. At this time he was a moderate in church politics and an admirer of John Inglis (1763–1834), but in time he came to be more influenced by the preaching of Robert Gordon (1786–1853), and became a member of the evangelical party.

Licensed by the presbytery of Duns in December 1828, Cunningham was appointed assistant to Dr John Scott of the Middle Parish Church, Greenock, in January 1830, and in October of that year was ordained as his colleague and successor. Cunningham's four years at Greenock were highly successful, and he distinguished himself as a champion of doctrinal orthodoxy at a time when events on the other side of the Clyde, in the parish of Row, led to the deposition of the minister there, John McLeod Campbell, in whose case Cunningham himself gave evidence to establish the charge of heresy. In Greenock, too, he met Janet Denniston (d. 1888), and married her there on 15 July 1834. They had five daughters and six sons.

In January 1834 Cunningham moved to Trinity College Church, Edinburgh. He had made his mark a year earlier with a powerful speech at the general assembly, yet his ministry in Edinburgh was not deemed a success. Scotland's ecclesiastical capital was a place where any minister was liable to suffer by comparison, and Cunningham became convinced that he did not have it in him to be a popular preacher. His efforts in the pulpit compared poorly with his speeches in church courts and on public platforms, but it was increasingly the latter that he was required to make as the events unfolded which culminated in the Disruption of 1843. From the outset Cunningham was at the heart of the controversy, one in which his intellectual power, skill in debate, and apparent relish of conflict marked him as a principal combatant. Nor was this the sole controversy in which he was embroiled, for he found time to rebut the arguments of voluntaries and to attack the pretensions of Roman Catholics. He went too far in the latter instance when, in 1836, he charged the editors of *Encyclopaedia Britannica* with making changes to appease Catholic opinion, and was forced to make a public retraction.

In the summer of 1838 a bout of typhus brought Cunningham close to death, but he returned to robust health to take a full part in the non-intrusion crisis. He proved an effective contributor to the pamphlet literature of the time, crossing swords with John Hope (1794–1858), the dean of the Faculty of Advocates, and James Robertson (1803–1860) of Ellon, the emerging champion of the moderate party. The degree of DD was conferred on him by Princeton in 1842, an honour unlikely to have been awarded him by any Scottish university at that time. It was his sole degree, as he had not graduated from Edinburgh. Following the Disruption, Cunningham was appointed as junior professor of theology at the Free Church's New College in Edinburgh. Before he took up his duties, he travelled to the United States to promote his church's cause. On his return he was attacked by critics of the Free Church's links with churches in the slave-holding states of America, and the clamour for the return of 'tainted money' only gradually subsided.

The death of David Welsh in 1845 brought Cunningham to the church history chair and he became principal of New College after the death of Thomas Chalmers in 1847. This promotion drew him unwittingly into fresh controversy over the issue of theological training for the Free Church ministry. Cunningham was anxious that New College should be allowed to establish itself on a sound basis before any extension of provision was made for institutions in Aberdeen and Glasgow. The debate continued for years and engendered bad feeling out of all proportion to the issue at stake. In 1855, when the extensionists finally triumphed, Cunningham withdrew from the church courts, feeling thoroughly alienated from former colleagues, not least Robert Smith Candlish. Between 1855 and 1860 he was editor of the *British and Foreign Evangelical Review*.

In 1858 the loss of sight in his right eye occasioned a wave of sympathy for Cunningham, and the breach with colleagues was swiftly healed. In the circumstances, his nomination to be moderator of the general assembly of 1859 was felt to be highly appropriate, especially as it was the first to be held in the Free Church's new Assembly Hall. A public subscription for him raised £7061. Although his energies were diminished, his status within the Free Church remained unchallenged, and his speech in the 1861 assembly debate in favour of the union of Presbyterian churches in Australia was decisive. It was his last such intervention. He died at his home, 17 Salisbury Road, Edinburgh, on 14 December 1861, and was buried next to his mother in the Grange cemetery four days later.

In his lifetime Cunningham was unable to publish the main body of his work, though he produced an edition of Edward Stillingfleet's *The Doctrines and Practices of the Church of Rome Truly Represented* (1837) with extensive notes and edited *Sermons by the Rev Robert Bruce* (1843) for the Wodrow Society. Several works, edited by his literary executors, appeared posthumously in 1863: *The Reformers: the*

Theology of the Reformation and *Discussions on Church Principles*, which included his reviews and pamphlets. *Historical Theology*, which was published at the same time, comprised an outline of his church history lectures, and would surely have benefited from the revision and expansion that only Cunningham could have provided. His *Sermons from 1828 to 1860* (1872) were edited by J. J. Bonar.

Cunningham's formidable presence was due in part to his remarkable appearance. He was 6 feet tall and of a powerful physique, but it was his head that, as the missionary Alexander Duff put it, 'left an indelible impression on the mind' (Rainy and Mackenzie, 40). This was topped by hair that, one observer stated, 'more resembles a mass of blacky-brown cotton or wool, and what course the cranium pursues through it, or whether it extends to the height of six or twelve inches above eyes and ears, is all conjecture' (Smith, 80). An obituary vividly recalled his unmistakable appearance 'with his stout build, his unbuttoned greatcoat, his rolling gait, like a big schoolboy—his open, artless face—his huge stick, with its free circulation on its axis—and his sturdy uprightness and downrightness of act and speech' (*The Scotsman*, 16 Dec 1861). A keen snuff-taker, the effects of the habit were latterly evident in his voice. In private Cunningham was quite at odds with his public image, being warm and approachable. He was without the guile of an intriguer and the disputes which told most greatly on him were those within the Free Church itself. After his death his church lacked a commanding figure who combined orthodoxy with authority, a lacuna that was keenly felt as it struggled to come to terms with the influence of biblical criticism.

LIONEL ALEXANDER RITCHIE

Sources R. Rainy and J. Mackenzie, *Life of William Cunningham, DD* (1871) · *Fasti Scot.* · J. A. Wylie, *Disruption worthies: a memorial of 1843*, ed. J. B. Gillies, new edn (1881), 193–200 · *British and Foreign Evangelical Review* (1871), 752–92 · J. Smith, *Our Scottish clergy*, 3rd ser. (1851), 75–82 · J. Macleod, *Scottish theology in relation to church history since the Reformation*, [3rd edn] (1974) · *The Scotsman* (16 Dec 1861) · H. Watt, *New College, Edinburgh: a centenary history* (1946) · A. Whyte, *Former principals of the New College, Edinburgh* (1909) · A. L. Drummond and J. Bulloch, *The church in Victorian Scotland, 1843–1874* (1975), 17–19 · *DSCHT* · *DNB*

Archives U. Edin., New Coll. L., lecture notes and papers | NL Scot., letters to J. J. Bonar · U. Edin., New Coll. L., letters to Thomas Chalmers

Likenesses photograph, 1859, repro. in Rainy and Mackenzie, *Life of William Cunningham, DD*, facing p. 61 · W. Bonnar, oils, Scot. NPG · L. Ghémar, lithograph, BM · J. Watson-Gordon, oils, Scot. NPG · lithograph, repro. in Wylie, *Disruption worthies*, facing p. 193 · oils (posthumous), U. Edin., New Coll

Wealth at death £1195 13s. 4d.: confirmation, 23 Dec 1862, NA Scot., SC 70/1/114/588

Cunningham, William (1849–1919), economic historian and Church of England clergyman, was born on 29 December 1849 at 50 Queen Street, Edinburgh, the second of three children born to James Cunningham, a lawyer, and his second wife, Elizabeth Boyle Dunlop, youngest daughter of Alexander Dunlop of Keppoch, Dunbartonshire. Religion was an important part of family life: William's father moved from the Episcopal church to founding a branch of the Church of England in Edinburgh, and

William Cunningham (1849–1919), by William Strang, 1908

later to the Free Church of Scotland. His mother came from a strong Presbyterian background, and her brother took a leading part in the Free Church.

Cunningham suffered from asthma and was educated at home by an English tutor. From the age of twelve he intermittently attended Edinburgh Institution (1861–4), before proceeding to the Edinburgh Academy (1864–5). In 1865 he entered the arts course at Edinburgh University, where he received his MA in 1869. In the summer of 1868 he studied German at the University of Tübingen, and entered Gonville and Caius College, Cambridge, in 1869. In 1872 he won a scholarship at Trinity College and was listed first with Frederick William Maitland for the moral science tripos.

Having resolved his religious doubts by embracing the personal theology and social views of F. D. Maurice, Cunningham hoped to combine a clerical and academic career. He was ordained in 1873 and served as a curate at Horningsea, near Cambridge (1873–4), as chaplain at Trinity College (1880–91), curate of Great St Mary's, Cambridge (1879–83), of which he was subsequently vicar (1887–1908), and as archdeacon of Ely (1907–19). Cunningham took both his pastoral and administrative duties seriously throughout his career and in later years was active in convocation.

Cunningham was attracted to both Hegelian and Comtist philosophy but his failure to win a fellowship threatened his academic prospects. He wrote a dissertation, *The Influence of Descartes on Metaphysical Speculation in England*,

which was published in 1876 and took a doctorate in mental science from Edinburgh in the same year. He became a DD at Cambridge in 1889 with a dissertation on Augustine of Hippo. Although he was deputy to the Knightbridge professor of moral philosophy in 1879, a Hulsean lecturer in 1885, a Birkbeck lecturer in ecclesiastical history in 1886–90 and 1908–10, and wrote dozens of papers and pamphlets on church subjects, he failed in his applications for a permanent university teaching position in philosophy or theology.

Instead Cunningham launched his academic career through the new university extension scheme, serving as an extension lecturer (1874–8) in Leeds, Bradford, and Liverpool, and teaching as many as 600 students per term. On 1 June 1876 he married his cousin Adèle Rebecca Dunlop, daughter of Andrew Anderson Dunlop, a merchant of Dublin. The couple had two children: James Michael, who died as an officer in France in 1918, and Audrey, a historian and biographer of her father. In 1878 Cunningham was named an examiner for the new history tripos at Cambridge. His duties included lecturing on economic history. He had attended Alfred Marshall's lectures in economics and had developed a strong interest in social questions. Realizing that a textbook was needed in economic history, he seized the opportunity. *The Growth of English Industry and Commerce* (1882) was an immediate success and laid the foundation for the study of economic history at Cambridge. It went through six editions and expanded to fill two large volumes.

Cunningham was an early supporter of the education of women at Cambridge and his subsequent volumes owed much to the assistance of the first generation of women economic historians, including L. C. A. Tomn, who, as L. C. A. Knowles, occupied the first chair in economic history in England at London. From 1884 to 1888 Cunningham served as a university lecturer in history and from 1888 to 1906 he was a lecturer at Trinity College. From 1891 to 1897 he was the Tooke professor of economics and statistics at King's College, London. In 1891 he was elected a fellow of Trinity College. In 1899 he taught at Harvard and in 1914 he gave the Lowell lectures in Boston. Cunningham was a founding fellow of the British Academy, president of the economic section of the British Association (1891, 1905), and president of the Royal Historical Society (1911). He received honorary degrees from Edinburgh and Brown universities. In 1880–81 he travelled widely in India, and in later years also visited South Africa and Palestine.

Cunningham's reputation rests largely on his economic history, which has been called neo-mercantilist, and as an apologist for British imperialism. He explained that Britain's economic success was not rooted in *laissez-faire*, but in a tradition of national economic regulation from the medieval through the mercantilist periods. Indeed, he put forward the view that Victorian free trade policy had been the imperialism of free trade. Cunningham's support for an inductive economics placed him in opposition to Alfred Marshall's efforts to lay a more deductive and theoretical foundation for political economy in Britain. These differences, aggravated by personal and academic competition, broke into an open controversy with Cunningham's paper of 1892, 'The perversion of economic history'. The English *Methodenstreit*, the conflict between inductive and deductive economics, was further inflamed when Cunningham and most of the economic historians supported protection during the Edwardian tariff reform agitation, while Marshall and most economic theorists defended free trade. In his numerous writings on tariff reform, Cunningham insisted on the proposition that economics must be seen in relation to a particular time and place.

Cunningham expounded his imperial views in numerous articles, speeches, and books, such as his two-volume *An Essay on Western Civilization in its Economic Aspects* (1898–1900). His vision consisted of a combination of British nationalism, an established religion with a social gospel, an evolutionary view of society, and a belief that economic history and political economy should be an applied subject in the service of Western civilization, the British empire, and conservative social reform. His views were an important component of a social imperialism which supplanted a tradition of liberal individualism in Britain. After several years of ill health he died on 10 June 1919 in Cambridge. The funeral was held at Great St Mary's on June 13 and he was buried in the cemetery at Wilburton, halfway between Cambridge and Ely. His wife survived him.   GERARD M. KOOT

Sources A. Cunningham, *William Cunningham: teacher and priest* (1950) [incl. bibliography] · W. R. Scott, 'William Cunningham, 1849–1919', *PBA*, [9] (1919–20), 465–74 · H. S. Foxwell, 'Archdeacon Cunningham', *Economic Journal*, 29 (1919), 382–90 · L. Knowles, 'Archdeacon Cunningham', *Economic Journal*, 29 (1919), 390–93 · G. M. Koot, *English historical economics, 1870–1926* (1987) · B. Semmel, 'William Cunningham: national economist', in B. Semmel, *Imperialism and social reform: English social-imperial thought, 1895–1914* (1960) · R. N. Soffer, *Discipline and power: the university, history and the making of an English elite, 1870–1930* (1994) · m. cert.
Archives CUL | BLPES, Cannan collection · BLPES, Knowles MSS · CUL, letters to Lord Acton · Harvard U., Baker Library, H. S. Foxwell MSS · King's AC Cam., letters to Oscar Browning · U. Cam., Marshall Library of Economics, J. N. Keynes MSS · U. Cam., Marshall Library of Economics, Marshall MSS · University of Sheffield Library, Hewins MSS
Likenesses E. H. Kennington, oils, 1908, NPG; related portrait, Trinity Cam. · W. Strang, chalk and watercolour drawing, 1908, Scot. NPG [*see illus.*] · photograph, repro. in Cunningham, *William Cunningham*, frontispiece
Wealth at death £28,508 15s. 1d.: administration with will, 2 Sept 1919, *CGPLA Eng. & Wales*

Cunnington [*née* Pegge], **Maud Edith** (1869–1951), archaeologist, was born on 24 September 1869 at Vernon House, Briton Ferry, Glamorgan, one of the seven children of Charles Pegge, formerly Pigg (*b.* 1834), surgeon, and his wife, Catherine Milton Leach (*b.* 1837), fifth of the fourteen daughters of Robert Valentine Leach of Devizes, Wiltshire. When Robert Leach's business as a corn merchant failed, he established a private asylum at Briton Ferry where his future son-in-law was a doctor. By the time Catherine married, her father had been able to return to Devizes, where he bought and restored Devizes Castle.

Maud was educated briefly at Cheltenham Ladies' College. On 9 July 1889 she married (Edward) Benjamin Howard Cunnington (1861–1950), the son of Henry Cunnington, a wine merchant. Benjamin, who had been a journalist before joining his father's business, was the fourth generation of his family to record and preserve the antiquities of Wiltshire and was for sixty years the honorary curator of Devizes Museum. Maud's involvement with archaeology is said to have developed through the interest of their only child, Edward, whose death in the First World War was a grief from which she never recovered.

In 1897 the Cunningtons settled at 33 Long Street, Devizes, where Maud spent each winter writing articles and excavation reports and sorting and mending pottery, at which she was expert. To the chagrin of later archaeologists she left no original notes, but her detailed articles in the *Wiltshire Archaeological Magazine*, 1909–42, provide a good overview of her work. In the early days she recorded the destruction of barrows for such purposes as a golf course near Warminster, providing stone for a cowshed floor, and levelling the 'flying course of the new Aviation School on the downs above Upavon' (*Wiltshire Archaeological Magazine*, 37, 1912, 603).

Maud Cunnington's most important contribution was not in rescue work but in original excavations. Most notable of these were the first known Neolithic causewayed camp at Knap Hill, Alton Priors, 1908–9; a village site of the Hallstatt period at All Cannings Cross, 1911 and 1920–22; West Kennet Long Barrow, 1925; Woodhenge, which was named by the Cunningtons, 1926–8; and the Sanctuary on Overton Hill, 1930. She rediscovered the Sanctuary, lost since the eighteenth century, by standing at Stukeley's viewpoint and counting the telegraph poles to a distant glimpse of the site. Woodhenge was first identified from the air since nothing of the former timber structure was visible on the ground. Both Woodhenge and the Sanctuary are the subject of books by her (1923 and 1929). The sites were purchased by the Cunningtons and presented to the nation.

The Second World War brought excavations to a close, but Maud Cunnington and her husband continued their long-standing involvement with Devizes Museum and with the Wiltshire Archaeological Society, of which she had been elected president in 1931. Their finds were deposited in the museum, and Maud was co-author of the museum catalogue (1934). She is known to have had disagreements with other notable archaeologists; but she was respected for her dedication and integrity and she earned the gratitude of many.

In recognition of her pioneering work Maud Cunnington was made an honorary life member of the Cambrian Archaeological Association and of the Society of Antiquaries, Scotland. In 1948 she was made CBE for services to archaeology, the first woman to be so honoured; but she probably never knew this. Bedridden since 1947, she suffered from Alzheimer's disease. She and her husband, who predeceased her by three months, were nursed at home by a family friend. She died at her home, 33 Long Street, Devizes, on 28 February 1951, and was cremated on

3 March at Arnos Vale, Bristol. She left almost all her property (£14,000) to Devizes Museum, so enabling a professional curator to be appointed according to her wishes.

PENELOPE RUNDLE

Sources 'In memoriam Maud Edith Cunnington', *Wiltshire Archaeological and Natural History Magazine*, 54 (1951–2), 104–6 · notes on the Cunnington family [Richard Emery Sandell, Hon. Librarian, Wiltshire Archaeological Society, c.1960], Wiltshire Archaeological Society, Devizes, Box 336, MS 2773 · R. H. Cunnington, 'The Cunningtons of Wiltshire', *Wiltshire Archaeological and Natural History Magazine*, 55 (1953–4), 211–36, esp. 224–32 · 'In memoriam Benjamin Howard Cunnington', *Wiltshire Archaeological and Natural History Magazine*, 53 (1949–50), 498–500 · C. T. Barker, 'Ben and Maud Cunnington: the Gower connection', *Wiltshire Archaeological and Natural History Magazine*, 80 (1986), 232–4 · annual report, Wiltshire Archaeological Society, *Wiltshire Archaeological and Natural History Magazine*, 54 (1951–2), 464 · R. A. M. Green, *A bibliography of printed works relating to Wiltshire, 1920–1960* (1975) · diary of W. E. V. Young, 1951, Wiltshire Archaeological Society Library, Devizes · private information (2004) [Paul Robinson, curator of WANHS Museum, Devizes; archivist at Cheltenham Ladies' College] · b. cert. · m. certs. [subject and parents] · d. cert. · census returns for Glamorgan, 1861 · parish register, St Clement's, Briton Ferry, Glamorgan RO · *Kelly's directory of Wiltshire* (1889–1951) [annual directories] · *Wiltshire Gazette* (8 March 1951)
Likenesses group portrait, photograph, 1896–9 (with family), repro. in Barker, 'Ben and Maud Cunnington' · photograph, 1926, repro. in Cunnington, 'The Cunningtons of Wiltshire'
Wealth at death £14,009 10s. 9d.: probate, 9 May 1951, CGPLA Eng. & Wales

Cunnington, William (1754–1810), antiquary, was born near Gretton, Northamptonshire, the second of five children of John Cunnington (c.1730–1812), a draper or clothier, and his wife, Elizabeth Cooper (1732–c.1820), both natives of Gretton. Having been apprenticed by his father to a draper or clothier in or near Warminster, Wiltshire, Cunnington settled in or about 1775 at Heytesbury, Wiltshire, where he built up a successful business as a wool merchant, mercer, and draper. In 1787 he married Mary Meares (1757–1812), daughter of Robert Meares, whom he had probably met at the Congregational chapel where they both worshipped. They had three daughters, who from their teenage years assisted their father as his amanuenses.

Cunnington suffered through much of the last twenty years of his life from severe headaches, for which his doctor suggested he ride out in the countryside. During these journeys on the Wiltshire downs he became interested in the barrow graves which are abundant in that region. A man of active mind and acute observation, he was assisted in his developing antiquarian interests by the writer John Britton. From 1800 Cunnington began digging open the Wiltshire barrows, with the assistance of H. P. Wyndham, MP for the county, and the Revd William Coxe of Bemerton. Among those that they excavated were the Golden Barrow in the parish of Upton Lovel and the barrows of Normanton Down and Bush Barrow, near Stonehenge. Coxe also introduced Cunnington in 1801 to the learned antiquarian the Revd Thomas Leman of Bath. Though Leman had observed that Cunnington was 'certainly a very clever man, but without the advantages of a learned education …' (Cunnington, 19), he gave him helpful advice and encouragement in the early part of his archaeological career, and commented upon his manuscripts. In 1801 Cunnington was elected a fellow of the Society of Antiquaries of London, and its journal contains his 'Account of tumuli opened in Wiltshire, in three letters from Mr William Cunnington to Aylmer Bourke Lambert' and his 'Further account of tumuli opened in Wiltshire' (*Archaeologia*, 15.122–9, 338–46). Lambert was himself a renowned antiquary, botanist, and geologist, and a lifelong friend of Cunnington.

From 1803 Cunnington was assisted in his excavation work by Sir Richard Colt Hoare, the wealthy owner of Stourhead, Wiltshire, with whom he opened more than 450 barrows. Hoare described Cunnington's methods of excavating as being much more thorough than those of his predecessors, and dedicated to him the first part of his *Ancient History of Wiltshire* (1812) on the ground that the existence of the book was mainly due to Cunnington's pioneering work and his extensive collection of antiquities. Hoare purchased this collection after Cunnington's death, and it is now in the Devizes Museum, Wiltshire. Cunnington also collected fossils and minerals, corresponding with the geologist William Smith, for whom he procured a fine series of samples. Though their methods would be criticized in comparison to twentieth-century standards, Cunnington and Hoare made an important contribution to early archaeological excavation in Britain, refining their methods, and attempting at least some form of recording and categorization. However, their greatest achievement was in the collection of evidence rather than the advancement of historical theory, which in their period continued to be hampered by the short historical chronology dictated by biblical authority.

Cunnington died at Heytesbury on 31 December 1810 from what was identified in his 1975 biography as probably being acromegaly, a rare and slowly debilitating disease caused by a benign pituitary tumour. This causes a slow lengthening of the features, including face and fingers, apparently confirmed by a portrait of 1808. He was buried in Heytesbury church on 4 January 1811.

DAVID BOYD HAYCOCK

Sources R. H. Cunnington, *From antiquary to archaeologist: a biography of William Cunnington*, ed. J. Dyer (1975) · *GM*, 1st ser., 80 (1810), 670 · *GM*, 1st ser., 81/1 (1811), 185–6 · R. Hayman, *Riddles in stone: myths, archaeology and the ancient Britons* (1997), chap. 10 · DNB
Archives Devizes Museum, Wiltshire Archaeological and Natural History Society, corresp. and papers; further corresp. and papers · S. Antiquaries, Lond., account of Wiltshire excavations
Likenesses S. Woodford, oils, 1808, Wiltshire Archaeological and Natural History Society, Devizes, Wiltshire · J. Basire, line engraving (after S. Woodford, 1808), BM, NPG; repro. in R. C. Hoare, *The ancient history of south (north) Wiltshire*, 2 vols. (1812–21)

Cunny, Joan (c.1508/9–1589). *See under* Essex witches (*act.* 1566–1589).

Cunobelinus [Cymbeline] (d. c.AD 40), king in southern Britain, is the Cymbeline of Holinshed's *Chronicles* (1578) and of Shakespeare's play. The father and predecessor of Cunobelinus, **Tasciovanus** (d. c.AD 10), had greatly extended the tribal kingdom of the Catuvellauni from its heartland north of the lower Thames eastward into what is now Essex and Suffolk and northward into modern Northamptonshire, thereby creating the largest of the Iron Age kingdoms in Britain. This expansion was chiefly at the expense of the Trinovantes of present-day Essex. On some of his coins Tasciovanus boasted the title *rigonos*, probably Celtic for *rex* ('king'), thus possibly indicating a will to exercise a power independent of Roman direction. On the death of Tasciovanus about AD 10, Cunobelinus succeeded him. The time was one in which Roman diplomatic and commercial influence in southern Britain was increasing. The area occupied by the Catuvellauni was well placed for the exploitation of new opportunities. It was surrounded by lesser powers and had access to the trade routes which led to and from Roman Gaul. The tribal territory also commanded vital raw materials, especially iron, and contained rich farmlands.

There are hints in the contemporary coinage of a power struggle among the rulers of south-eastern Britain early in the first century AD. Cunobelinus emerged as the principal victor and he subsequently held sway for three decades as the dominant king of the southern British. Nothing is recorded of his personality, nor of the detailed events of his long reign. It is known that he had at least three sons, two of whom were to play the leading part in opposing the Roman invasion of Britain in AD 43. For the rest, his reign can only be reconstructed in outline from the evidence of coinage and archaeology. From his base in the Catuvellaunian heartland Cunobelinus appears first to have consolidated his hold over the Trinovantes. Shortly after AD 10 he was issuing coins bearing the mint mark CAM, for Camulodunum (Colchester), the principal centre of the Trinovantes. It is therefore clear that he had successfully annexed that people by then. He next turned his attention to the area south of the Thames. By AD 25 he had seized control of much of Cantium (Kent), while his brother Epaticcus extended his power over the Atrebates of the middle Thames valley. To the north, Cunobelinus pushed the bounds of his kingdom to the fenland margins, either directly or with the aid of sub-kings, so that his authority was effectively unchallenged in south-eastern Britain. Not inappropriately, the second-century Roman writer Suetonius referred to him as *Britannorum rex* ('king of the Britons') and not merely as the ruler of a single tribe. Cunobelinus inscribed the title *rex* on some of his coins, possibly after recognition by the emperor Tiberius as an allied ruler of Rome. For a time he struck coins bearing designs which closely copy those of Roman issues. Some of these coins may well have been struck from dies engraved by Roman craftsmen who came to Cunobelinus's kingdom under a diplomatic arrangement.

During Cunobelinus's long reign of some thirty years relations between southern Britain and the Roman world were stable, probably reflecting mutually agreed arrangements designed to preserve the status quo. Tiberius had no desire to extend Roman dominion into Britain. Cunobelinus had nothing to gain by disturbing the peace. There

was indeed much to lose, for Roman trade links with Britain developed strongly early in the first century AD. Luxury imports of wine, fine metalwork, pottery, and other Roman goods were exchanged for a wide range of British products: corn, cattle, gold, silver, iron, slaves, and hounds, according to Strabo, writing about AD 17. The prestige which this trade generated, allied with material benefits to British nobles, would not have gone unregarded by Cunobelinus. A clear sign of the British king's acceptance of a stable relationship with Rome is provided by the return to Gaul of several shiploads of Roman troops after they had been driven on to the British coast in AD 16. The native centre of Camulodunum was greatly extended under Cunobelinus's rule, until a vast complex of about 7 square miles was bounded by massive earthen dykes. Elsewhere in the kingdom other centres began to assume urban form, as at Verulamium (St Albans) and Durovernum (Canterbury). In several respects Cunobelinus brought southern Britain close to the world of Rome. When he died, about AD 40, his mantle passed to two of his sons, *Caratacus and *Togodumnus [*see under* Roman Britain, British leaders in (*act.* 55 BC–AD 84)], who were to adopt different policies towards the great power across the channel.

MALCOLM TODD

Sources Suetonius, 'Vita Gaii', *The twelve caesars*, trans. R. Graves (1957), 44 · *Dio's Roman history*, ed. and trans. E. Cary, 7 (1924), lx.19 · Strabo, *Geography*, ed. and trans. H. L. Jones (1917–33), ii.5, 8; iv.5, 1–3 · S. S. Frere, *Britannia: a history of Roman Britain*, 3rd edn (1987) · P. Salway, *Roman Britain* (1981) · R. D. Van Arsdell, *Celtic coinage of Britain* (1989) · C. F. C. Hawkes and M. R. Hull, *Camulodunum* (1947)

Cunynghame, Sir Arthur Augustus Thurlow (1812–1884), army officer, was born on 12 August 1812, the fifth son of Colonel Sir David Cunynghame, fifth baronet (1769–1854), of Milncraig, Argyll, and his first wife, Maria (*d.* 21 Feb 1816), illegitimate daughter of Edward *Thurlow, the lord chancellor. He was commissioned second lieutenant, by purchase, in the 60th Royal Rifles on 2 November 1830, and was promoted first lieutenant on 22 May 1835. After serving with his battalion in the Mediterranean he became aide-de-camp to Lord Saltoun in China in 1841, and was present at the capture of Chinkiang (Zhenjiang) and at the siege of Nanking (Nanjing). He got his company in the 3rd foot (the Buffs) in 1841, became major in that regiment in 1845, and lieutenant-colonel 13th light infantry in 1846, exchanging as captain and lieutenant-colonel to the Grenadier Guards on 1 December 1846, then as junior lieutenant-colonel to the 20th foot in America on 27 April 1849. He next exchanged to the 27th Inniskillings, which he commanded for a short time in Ireland, and retired on half pay in 1853.

Cunynghame married, on 18 September 1845, the Hon. Frances Elizabeth, daughter of Field Marshal Viscount Hardinge; they had two sons and three daughters. In 1854, in the Crimean War, Cunynghame, who became a brevet colonel on 20 June 1854, accompanied the army to the east as assistant quartermaster-general of the 1st division. He was present at the landing in the Crimea, at the battles of the Alma, the Chernaya, Balaklava, and Inkerman—where he was with the guards in the Sandbag Battery and led into action a party of his old corps, the 20th—and at the siege of Sevastopol up to March 1855. In that month he became a local major-general, and in May took command of a division of the Turkish contingent, and for his services received the thanks of the sultan and the Turkish rank of lieutenant-general. In October 1855 he sailed with 10,000 Turks to occupy Kerch and held that fortress during the second winter of the Crimean occupation. He was made CB in July 1855, an officer of the Légion d'honneur, and received the Mejidiye. Cunynghame became major-general in the British army in 1861, and in 1863, when on the Bengal staff, was at Lahore in command of the reserve of the army employed in the Sitana campaign. In April 1869, when in command of the northern district of Ireland, he twice received the thanks of the Irish executive during the Fenian rising. In June 1869 he was made KCB. He commanded the forces in South Africa from 1874 to 1878, including the period of the Cape Frontier War, and was lieutenant-governor of Cape Colony from 5 March 1877 to 1878. In 1876 he was transferred as colonel-commandant to the Royal Rifles from the 36th, of which he had been appointed colonel in 1868. He became general in 1877, was made GCB in June 1878, and retired in 1879, residing at Hurlingham Lodge, Fulham.

Cunynghame was an extensive traveller and the author of several books based on his military services and travels in China, America, the Caucasus, and South Africa. His hastily compiled *My Command in South Africa in 1874-8* (1879) contains valuable information on South Africa during the controversial government of Sir Bartle Frere at the Cape. Cunynghame died on board ship at Aden on 1 April 1884, returning from a pleasure trip to India. He was survived by his wife.   H. M. CHICHESTER, *rev.* JAMES LUNT

Sources Burke, *Peerage* (1959) · *Hart's Army List* · A. W. Kinglake, *The invasion of the Crimea*, [new edn], 9 vols. (1877–88) · 'Copy of a letter from Commissary-General Filder', *Parl. papers* (1856), 40.341, no. 2042 [duties of the commissariat department] · *ILN* (29 Nov 1884) [will] · *The letters of the first Viscount Hardinge of Lahore ... 1844–1847*, ed. B. S. Singh, CS, 4th ser., 32 (1986) · A. Cunynghame, *Recollections of service in China* (1844) · A. Cunynghame, *My command in South Africa in 1874-8* (1879) · Boase, *Mod. Eng. biog.* · *CGPLA Eng. & Wales* (1884)
Archives NAM, corresp. and papers [microfilm] | BL, corresp. with Lord Carnarvon, Add. MS 60800
Likenesses wood-engraving, 1878 (after photograph by W. Hermann), NPG; repro. in *ILN* (23 March 1878)
Wealth at death £16,079 5 *s.*: administration with will, 29 Oct 1884, *CGPLA Eng. & Wales*

Cure family (*per. c.*1540–*c.*1620), masons and sculptors, worked in London. **William Cure the elder** (1514/15–1579) was born in Holland and was brought over to England in 1541 or 1542 to work on Nonsuch Palace for Henry VIII. He became an English citizen in 1552, married an Englishwoman, Anne, and by 1571 had six children, all born in his adopted country. In 1549 he is recorded as living in London north of the Thames but by 1559 he had moved south of the river to the parish of St Thomas the Apostle, Southwark, where he apparently remained for the rest of his life. Returns of aliens for November 1571 state that he was fifty-six at that time. Details of Cure's work are few and far

between. In September 1552 he was paid for unspecified tasks on one of the buildings owned by Edward, duke of Somerset. He made a terracotta mould for casting in wax an image of an Inuit who had been brought back to England on Sir Martin Frobisher's voyage of 1576 and he may have been the 'Cure' who made a fountain for Sir Nicholas Bacon's garden at Redgrave in Suffolk in 1568. He died in 1579; his wife survived him.

Cornelius Cure (d. 1608/9) was the son of William Cure the elder. By 1587 he had entered the service of the lord treasurer, Lord Burghley, and in 1596 Burghley recommended him for the post of master mason of the royal works, describing him as 'honest, erect and full of invention' and as having 'sen much worke in forrein places' (MS letter to Mr Killagrewe, 26 May 1596, CUL, Ee.3.56.94). Cure was duly appointed in the same year. He had, in fact, already been active in the royal office of works, having worked on fountains in the Privy Gardens at Greenwich Palace and Hampton Court in 1595–6. It is also likely that he had designed the great fountain in Conduit Court at Hampton Court *c.*1584 and he may have been the 'Cure' who, ten years previously, had drawn plans and elevations for an unexecuted monument to Henry VIII. Once in office, his most significant work was to undertake the memorial to Mary, queen of Scots, in Westminster Abbey (1606). A number of important church monuments dating from the 1560s onwards can be attributed to his workshop, notably the homogeneous group which includes those of Sir Philip and Sir Thomas Hoby at Bisham, Berkshire (*c.*1566), and Dean Nicholas Wotton (d. 1567) in Canterbury Cathedral. Lord Burghley's tomb is also likely to be his (*c.*1590; St Martin's, Stamford, Lincolnshire) and so is the memorial that Burghley erected at about the same time to his wife, Mildred, and his daughter Anne, countess of Oxford, in Westminster Abbey. In 1595–6 Cornelius is known to have had a house and workshop in Southwark. He probably spent his life there. A payment is recorded to him in 1608; he is known to have died by December the following year.

William Cure the younger (d. 1632) was the son of Cornelius Cure and maintained the family tradition of living in Southwark, being recorded in his grandfather's parish of St Thomas the Apostle at the time of his death.

From 1605 onwards Cure shared the office of master mason of the king's works with his father and he succeeded him on Cornelius's death. It fell to him to continue work on Mary, queen of Scots' tomb which he did not complete until 1613. This long delay looks like an early sign of the dilatoriness that was to blight Cure's career, causing him in 1619 to lose the work of building the Whitehall Banqueting House to Nicholas Stone the elder. In that same year Francis, Lord Russell of Thornhaugh (later fourth earl of Bedford), had recourse to law to make Cure complete three family tombs which he had ordered: one commemorating himself and his family; a second his paternal grandparents, Francis Russell, second earl of Bedford, and Margaret, his wife; and a third his aunt, Anne, countess of Warwick. They were eventually erected in the family chapel at Chenies, Buckinghamshire, *c.*1620.

Two further tombs are documented as the sculptor's work, those of Sir Roger Aston and his family at St Dunstan's, Cranford, Middlesex (1612–13), and James Montague, bishop of Winchester, in Bath Abbey (1618–19). The latter was executed in collaboration with Nicholas Johnson.

Like his father, Cure worked on the fountains at Hampton Court. He also made one for Nonsuch Palace in 1615–16 and a large chimneypiece with no overmantel for a third royal residence, Somerset House, in 1613–14. None of this work survives but it is to be hoped that it was of better quality than his three authenticated architectural sculptures, the statues of Henry VIII, Anne of Denmark, and Charles, prince of Wales (later Charles I) on the great gate of Trinity College, Cambridge (1613–14). He died in 1632 leaving a widow named Joanna, with whom he had three children who were minors at that time. He was buried on 4 August at St Thomas the Apostle, Southwark.

ADAM WHITE

Sources A. White, 'A biographical dictionary of London tomb sculptors, c.1560–c.1660', *Walpole Society*, 61 (1999), 1–162, esp. 36–48 · H. M. Colvin and others, eds., *The history of the king's works*, 3–4 (1975–82) · M. Whinney, *Sculpture in Britain, 1530 to 1830*, rev. J. Physick, 2nd edn (1988), 51–5 · K. A. Esdaile, 'William Cure II and his work at Trinity College, Cambridge', *Burlington Magazine*, 80 (1942), 21–2

Cure, Cornelius (d. **1608/9**). *See under* Cure family (*per. c.1540–c.1620*).

Cure, William, the elder (**1514/15–1579**). *See under* Cure family (*per. c.1540–c.1620*).

Cure, William, the younger (d. **1632**). *See under* Cure family (*per. c.1540–c.1620*).

Cureton, Sir Charles (**1826–1891**). *See under* Cureton, Charles Robert (**1789–1848**).

Cureton, Charles Robert (1789–1848), army officer, son of a Shropshire gentleman, was born in 1789. He obtained an ensigncy in the Shropshire militia on 21 April 1806, and was soon promoted lieutenant. Extravagance led to debts, and he fled from his creditors. Disguising himself as a sailor, and leaving his uniform on the beach, he embarked for London, where he enlisted as Charles Roberts in the 14th light dragoons in 1808. His friends concluded that he was drowned while bathing.

In 1809 Cureton was sent to join regimental headquarters at Portalegre in Portugal, with recommendations from the officers at home. His merits and bravery in action gained him promotion to sergeant. He served with the 14th in the battles of Talavera (27 July 1809) and Busaco (27 September 1810). On 1 October he was wounded in the right leg by a bullet when crossing the Mondego, near Coimbra. At the battles of Fuentes d'Oñoro (3 and 5 May 1811) he received on the 5th a sabre cut which fractured his skull, and another on his bridle hand. In March and April 1812 he took part with his regiment in the third siege and capture on 6 April of Badajoz, in the battle of Salamanca (22 July), the capture of Madrid (14 August), and the battle of Vitoria (21 June 1813).

Having been sent on duty to St Jean de Luz in that year, he was recognized by an officer on Wellington's staff from the Shropshire militia. Wellington made him sergeant of the post of the army headquarters, and on 24 February 1814, in recognition of his services, he was gazetted, in his proper name, ensign without purchase in the 40th foot. He served with them at the battles of Orthez (27 February 1814), Tarbes (20 March), and Toulouse (10 April).

On 20 October 1814 Cureton exchanged into the 20th light dragoons, was promoted lieutenant, and appointed adjutant on 27 June 1816; when the regiment was disbanded on 25 December 1818, on the withdrawal of the troops from the occupation of France, he was placed on half pay, but was brought into the 16th lancers as lieutenant and adjutant on 7 January 1819. His further commissions were: captain (12 November 1825), major (6 December 1833), brevet lieutenant-colonel (23 July 1839), regimental lieutenant-colonel (21 August 1839), and brevet colonel (3 April 1846).

Cureton went to India with the 16th in 1822, when he resigned the adjutancy and served at the second siege of Bharatpur under Viscount Combermere from December 1825 to its capture on 18 January 1826.

In 1839 Cureton accompanied the 16th to Afghanistan in the army of the Indus under Sir John Keane. He was appointed assistant adjutant-general of cavalry, was selected to command the advanced column through the Bolan Pass, marched to Kandahar, and was at the capture of Ghazni on 23 July. He commanded an advanced force, which seized the enemy's guns and secured possession of the Kabul citadel in August 1839. He was mentioned in dispatches, received the Afghan order of the Durani empire (third class), and was promoted brevet lieutenant-colonel.

In the Gwalior campaign Cureton commanded a cavalry brigade at the battle of Maharajpur (29 December 1843), was mentioned in dispatches, and on 2 May 1844 was made a CB, military division. In the Sutlej campaign he commanded the cavalry in the force under Sir Harry George Wakelyn Smith, and took part in the capture of Dharm-Kote on 18 January 1846, in the advance towards Ludhiana, and in the action near Badiwal on the 22nd, when it was due to the cavalry's efforts that Smith only lost a large portion of his baggage.

Cureton commanded the cavalry at the battle of Aliwal (28 January), when he smashed a large body of the celebrated Ayin troop trained by General Paolo di Bartolomeo Avitabile (a Neapolitan mercenary in Ranjit Singh's service), and routed the Sikh right, the 16th lancers breaking a well-formed infantry square of Avitabile's regiment, and, despite the enemy's steadiness, reforming and charging back repeatedly. Sir Harry Smith signally defeated the Sikhs, and in his dispatch of 30 January said, 'In Brigadier Cureton Her Majesty has one of those officers rarely met with; the cool experience of the veteran soldier is combined with youthful activity; his knowledge of outpost duty and the able manner he handles his cavalry under the heaviest fire rank him among the first cavalry officers of the age' (*GM*, 318); while Sir Henry Hardinge, the governor-general, observed: 'This officer's whole life has been spent in the most meritorious exertions in Europe and Asia, and on this occasion the skill and intrepidity with which the cavalry force was handled obtained the admiration of the army which witnessed their movements.' Cureton commanded a cavalry brigade at the battle of Sobraon (10 February) and was again mentioned in dispatches. He received the thanks of parliament, and was made an aide-de-camp to the queen, and colonel in the army, on 3 April.

On 7 April 1846 Cureton was appointed adjutant-general of the queen's forces in the East Indies. In the Punjab or Second Anglo-Sikh War, Cureton commanded the cavalry division and three troops of horse artillery at the action at Ramnagar on 23 November 1848, and was killed when leading the 14th light dragoons to the support of the 5th light cavalry. He was buried in the Punjab with military honours. He was a strict disciplinarian, but reportedly a most genial and popular officer with all ranks.

Several of his sons survived him, and two were distinguished soldiers. His eldest son, **Edward Burgoyne Cureton** (1822–1894), army officer, born on 25 May 1822, became an ensign in the 13th foot on 21 June 1839. He was promoted lieutenant (19 December 1843), captain (31 January 1851), major (26 December 1856), brevet colonel (28 December 1868), major-general (29 September 1878), lieutenant-general (1 July 1881), colonel of the 3rd hussars (19 April 1891), of the 7th dragoon guards (23 September 1891), and of the 12th lancers (30 April 1892). He exchanged from the 13th foot into the 3rd light dragoons in March 1840; served with the 16th lancers at the battle of Maharajpur on 29 December 1843; and served with his own regiment at Mudki on 18 December 1845, when he was severely wounded, and at Sobraon on 10 February 1846. Having exchanged with the 12th lancers, he served with them in the Cape Frontier War of 1851–3, and was thanked in general orders. He served through the Crimean campaign from 31 July 1855, took part in the battle of the Chernaya, in the siege and capture of Sevastopol, and in the operations around Eupatoria, was mentioned in dispatches, and received a brevet majority. He married in 1856 a daughter of Captain John Swindley, and, in 1860, Mary Anne, daughter of T. Hesslewood: she survived her husband. He was assistant quartermaster-general, Dublin district, in April 1862 to November 1864; assistant commandant, cavalry depot, from July 1866; commandant from February 1868; and was placed on half pay in July 1874. He retired from the active list in October 1881. He died at home, Hillbrook House, Kearsney, near Dover, Kent, on 9 February 1894.

Sir Charles Cureton (1826–1891), army officer, born on 25 November 1826, was commissioned ensign in the East India Company's army on 22 February 1843; ensign, 38th Bengal Native Infantry, on 22 September 1843; captain on 25 May 1857, major on 20 July 1858. He became brevet colonel on 14 February 1868, lieutenant-colonel on 22 February 1869, major-general on 22 February 1870, lieutenant-general on 1 October 1877, and general on 1 December 1888. He arrived in India on 24 June 1843 and he was

appointed adjutant of the 12th regiment of irregular cavalry on 14 January 1846. He served in the Sutlej campaign, and was at the battle of Aliwal (28 January 1846). In the Punjab campaign he was aide-de-camp to his father until the latter's death at the battle of Ramnagar (23 November 1848), where he was himself slightly wounded. He took part in the passage of the Chenab on 2 and 3 December, in the battle of Gujrat (21 February 1849), and in the pursuit, under Sir Walter Gilbert, of the Sikh army, the capture of Attock, and the occupation of Peshawar.

Cureton served in the north-west frontier campaign of 1849 to 1852, including the expedition to the Usafzai in 1849, and the operations against the Mohmands in 1851 and 1852. On 4 May 1852 he was appointed second in command of the 2nd irregular cavalry. He took part in the suppression of the Santal rebellion in 1856, and of the Indian mutiny in 1857. He served against the Sialkot mutineers, and took part in the action of Trimu Ghat, also against the Gogaira rebels. He raised and commanded Cureton's Multani cavalry, and continued to command it after it became the 15th Bengal cavalry, from December 1859 to March 1866. He served with it, and had charge of the intelligence department, throughout the campaigns in Rohilkhand and Oudh in 1858 and 1859, and was present at the actions of Bhagwala, Nagina, Bareilly, Shahjahanpur, Banai, Shahabad, Bankegaon, Mahidipur, Rasalpur, Mitaoli, and Biswan, was eleven times mentioned in dispatches published in general orders, and received brevets of major and lieutenant-colonel. He distinguished himself as a cavalry leader, and performed many acts of great personal bravery. He served in the north-west frontier campaign of 1860, and on 2 June 1869 was made a CB, military division.

Cureton commanded the Oudh division of the Bengal army from October 1879 to October 1884. He was promoted KCB, military division, on 30 May 1891. He married Margaret S. Holmes, daughter of the Revd Dr W. A. Holmes of Templemore, co. Tipperary, and they had three sons, two of whom entered the army. He died at his home, Lynmead, Carlisle Road, Eastbourne, Sussex, on 11 July 1891.

R. H. VETCH, rev. ROGER T. STEARN

Sources BL OIOC · dispatches, *LondG* · *The Times* (24 Jan 1849) · *The Times* (14 July 1891) · *The Times* (13 Feb 1894) · *GM*, 2nd ser., 31 (1849) · *Colburn's United Service Magazine*, 1 (1849), 477–8 · R. Cannon, ed., *Historical record of the twelfth, or the prince of Wales's royal regiment of lancers* (1842) · W. F. P. Napier, *History of the war in the Peninsula and in the south of France*, 6 vols. (1828–40) · J. W. Kaye, *History of the war in Afghanistan*, 2 vols. (1851) · J. W. Kaye, *A history of the Sepoy War in India, 1857–1858*, 9th edn, 3 vols. (1880) · G. B. Malleson, *History of the Indian mutiny, 1857–1858: commencing from the close of the second volume of Sir John Kaye's History of the Sepoy War*, 3 vols. (1878–80) · E. J. Thackwell, *Narrative of the Second Seikh War, in 1848–49* (1851) · J. H. Lawrence-Archer, *Commentaries on the Punjab campaign, 1848–49* (1878) · C. Gough and A. D. Innes, *The Sikhs and the Sikh wars* (1897) · *Annual Register* · *Hart's Army List* (1854) · *Hart's Army List* (1891) · Kelly, *Handbk* (1891) · Boase, *Mod. Eng. biog.* · R. Muir, *Britain and the defeat of Napoleon, 1807–1815* (1996) · J. A. Norris, *The First Afghan War, 1838–1842* (1967) · P. Macrory, *Signal catastrophe: the story of a disastrous retreat from Kabul, 1842* (1966); repr. as *Kabul catastrophe* (1986) · C. Hibbert, *The great mutiny, India, 1857* (1978); repr. (1980) · T. A. Heathcote, *The military in British India: the development of British land* *forces in south Asia, 1600–1947* (1995) · B. Bond, ed., *Victorian military campaigns* (1967) · *CGPLA Eng. & Wales* (1894)

Likenesses oils, *c.*1844, Royal United Services Institute, London

Wealth at death £22,092 15s. 11d.; Charles Cureton: resworn probate, June 1893; *CGPLA Eng. & Wales* (1891) · £15,549 17s. 2d. Edward Burgoyne Cureton: probate, 14 March 1894, *CGPLA Eng. & Wales*

Cureton, Edward Burgoyne (1822–1894). *See under* Cureton, Charles Robert (1789–1848).

Cureton, William (1808–1864), Syriac scholar, was born in Westbury, Shropshire, the son of William Cureton and his wife (of whom little is known). He was educated at Newport grammar school. Owing to the death of his father family resources were scarce, and William took a Careswell exhibition from his school to enable him to study at Christ Church, Oxford, where he matriculated as a servitor on 19 October 1826. He graduated BA in 1831 and MA in 1832. He immediately took deacon's orders upon graduating in 1831 and was ordained priest in 1832. His first curacy was at Oddington in Oxfordshire. Dean Gaisford later appointed him as one of the chaplains of Christ Church. In 1840 he was made select preacher to the university. Cureton became a chaplain-in-ordinary to Queen Victoria in 1847 and he delivered sermons at the Chapel Royal, St James, and at St Margaret's, Westminster; and finally Lord John Russell presented him in 1849 to a canonry at Westminster, which he held, together with the adjoining rectory of St Margaret's, until his death in 1864.

Cureton began his study of Arabic soon after he graduated from Christ Church, and in 1840 published his *Short account of the first volume of the autograph MS of Ibn Khallikan's biographical dictionary*. His subsequent appointment to the post of sub-librarian at the Bodleian Library in Oxford enabled him to continue this study. He was at the Bodleian Library from 1834 to 1837, and then moved to the British Museum in London, where he became assistant keeper of manuscripts, in succession to Sir Frederic Madden.

As the only oriental scholar in his department at the British Museum, Cureton's first task was to catalogue its holdings of Arabic manuscripts. The first part of this catalogue, which detailed the museum's Arabic and Christian writings as well as its Islamic theological, legal, and historical texts, was published in Latin in 1846, and work was begun for the next volume. In the meantime Cureton had published the Sunni text, *Abd Allah b. Ahmad, Pillar Creed of the Sunnites* (1843), and an edition of Esh-Shahrastani's *Kitab el-milal wa-n-nahal* or *History of Mohammedan Sects* (2 vols., 1842 and 1846). When he first joined the British Museum the number of Syriac manuscripts was relatively small, comprising about eighty documents. But in 1841 and 1843 a large number (nearly 600) of important new acquisitions were made from the Nitrian monasteries by Dr Tattam, and Cureton's life's work was cut out for him. Entirely ignorant of Syriac, he took on the job of learning the language in order to be able to classify the new documents. While drawing up an outline catalogue, he discovered many interesting manuscripts, of which he gave an account in 1845 in *Quarterly Review*, together with a narrative of how they had been discovered and purchased.

The most exciting discoveries which Cureton made while cataloguing the Syriac manuscripts in the Nitrian collection were the versions of the epistles of St Ignatius to Polycarp, to the Ephesians, and to the Romans; these were argued to have been the only genuine ones (a position no longer held). Cureton published *Epistles of St Ignatius* in 1845, launching a controversy among biblical scholars over the authenticity and centrality of the manuscripts. Some eminent theologians (including Christopher Wordsworth, Lee, and Bunsen) supported Cureton's claim to the originality of the manuscripts, while others opposed him (including Baur and Jacobson). Cureton supported his claims in his *Vindiciae Ignatiane* of 1846, and his view was subsequently confirmed by Justus Lipsius, though afterwards doubted by Joseph Barber Lightfoot, bishop of Durham, and eventually overturned by twentieth-century biblical scholarship.

Cureton's second important find in the British Museum manuscripts comprised some fragments of a Syriac version of the gospels which differed markedly from the well-known Peshitta, or official biblical text of Syriac Christians of the fifth century, and which he argued was much more faithful to the original Hebrew text of St Matthew's gospel. These 'Curetonian gospels' were an important contribution to the attempt to reconstruct the earliest Christian texts, though later superseded by the discovery of seemingly earlier manuscripts. Further Syriac sources were edited and published by the Oriental Text Society as *The Festal Letters of Athanasius* (1848), which was later included (in English translation) in E. B. Pusey's *Library of the Fathers* and published in German at about the same time. Less renowned discoveries included *Ilias: Fragments of the Iliad from a Syriac Palimpsest, Found among the Nitrian Manuscripts*, and published by the trustees in 1851, and *Remains of a Very Ancient Recension of the Gospels in Syriac* (1858).

After his retirement to Westminster, Cureton continued to publish Syriac extracts from the British Museum collection and to suggest their importance for contemporary biblical scholarship. The *Ecclesiastical History of John of Ephesus* was published by Oxford University Press in 1853, and translated into English by Payne Smith (afterwards dean of Canterbury) in 1860. In 1855 Cureton brought out *Spicilegium Syriacum*, which was thought to shed light on Bardesanes, Melito of Sardes, Ambrose, and Mara bar Serapion, but whose authenticity was afterwards contested by Merx and H. G. A. Ewald. Eusebius's *History of the Martyrs in Palestine* was brought out in 1861, and *Ancient Syriac documents relative to the earliest establishment of Christianity in Edessa and the neighbouring countries* was published posthumously in 1864.

Cureton was an active member of the Society for the Publication of Oriental Texts, a member of the Royal Society and of other societies, and an honorary DD of Halle. In 1855 he was elected a correspondent of the Institute of France and in 1860 he was made a member of the Académie des Inscriptions et Belles-lettres. He became BD and DD in 1858. He was also crown trustee of the British Museum. As a clergyman he was noted for his educational work in Westminster, and volumes of his sermons as royal chaplain were published in 1848 and 1858.

After an illness brought on by a railway accident in 1863, Cureton died on 17 June 1864 at his home, Brook House, Westbury, Shropshire. He was survived by his wife, Harriet, to whom the late subject's portrait was given by his parishioners on the day of his funeral.

STANLEY LANE-POOLE, rev. SINÉAD AGNEW

Sources The Times (30 June 1864), 12 • Boase, Mod. Eng. biog. • Allibone, Dict. • Foster, Alum. Oxon. • Ward, Men of the reign, 237–8 • S. Maunder, The biographical treasury, another edn, rev. W. L. R. Cates, [8 vols.] (1882), 166 • Oxford University Calendar (1829), 323 • 'Royal commission to inquire into … the British Museum', Parl. papers (1850), vol. 24, no. 1170 • F. L. Cross, ed., The Oxford dictionary of the Christian church, 2nd edn, ed. A. E. Livingstone (1974); repr. (1983)

Archives BL, letters to Philip Bliss, Add. MSS 34572–34582 • BL, letters to W. E. Gladstone, Add. MSS 44358–44400

Likenesses portrait, 1859, Church of England photographic portrait gallery • G. Richmond, chalk drawing, 1861, NPG • portrait, repro. in GM, 17 (1864), 520–23 • wood-engraving (after daguerreotype by Beard), NPG; repro. in ILN (29 April 1854)

Wealth at death under £16,000: probate, 27 July 1864, CGPLA Eng. & Wales

Curle, Hippolitus (1595–1638), Jesuit, was born at Antwerp on 31 December 1595, the younger son of Gilbert Curle (d. 1601x13), former secretary of Mary, queen of Scots, and his wife, Barbara Mowbray (d. 1613x18), former lady-in-waiting to Mary. He is said to have studied humanities at the Scots College in Douai but is not recorded in its register. Having graduated in universal philosophy, perhaps at Douai, he entered the Jesuit noviciate at Tournai on 20 September 1618. After the two-year noviciate he studied theology at Douai 1620–24 and was ordained priest on 14 September 1623. Minister and procurator in the Scots College, Douai, in 1625, he was at Cambrai as a tertian (third-year probationer) in 1627 and confessor in 1628, then returned to his former duties at Douai. He was professed of the three vows in November 1632. When the Douai rector died in March 1633, Curle took over as vice-rector until a new rector was appointed in 1634.

In May 1613 Curle's widowed mother made her will in his favour, as his elder brother had already become a Jesuit. His mother presumably having died, Curle made a donation of his property to the Douai college on 1 September 1618, shortly before he entered the noviciate, to take effect when he made his first vows in 1620 or if he died. His father's unmarried sister, Elizabeth Curle, who had been maid-of-honour to Mary, queen of Scots, was his executor. She made her will shortly before her death on 29 May 1620 in terms very similar to Curle's donation. In 1624 Curle was given leave by his superior to dispose of his possessions and in September 1626 he made over everything to the Scots College in Douai. He continued to live at Douai until his death there on 21 October 1638, and is regarded as the college's second founder.

MARK DILWORTH

Sources biographical compilations, Jesuit Archives, London • H. Foley, ed., Records of the English province of the Society of Jesus, 7/1 (1882), 189 • J. F. S. Gordon, ed., The Catholic church in Scotland (1874), 539 • Scottish Catholic Archives, CA 2/2 [Scots College, Douai] • Dodd's Church history of England, ed. M. A. Tierney, 5 vols. (1839–43),

vol. 4, pp. 127, ccxlvii–cclii • P. J. Anderson, ed., Records of the Scots colleges at Douai, Rome, Madrid, Valladolid and Ratisbon, New Spalding Club, 30 (1906) • CSP Scot., 1571–88; 1585–6, 135; 1597–1603, 847

Curling, Henry (1802/3–1864), novelist, was an infantry officer in the period following the Napoleonic wars. He went on half pay in 1834 and retired in 1854. He was a frequent contributor to periodicals and also published over twenty novels, including The Soldier of Fortune (1843; repr. 1852 and 1854), John of England: an Historical Romance (1846), Shakspeare: the Poet, the Lover, the Actor, the Man (1848), Frank Beresford, or, Life in the Army (1858; 2nd edn, 1862), The Miser Lord: a Sequel to 'Frank Beresford' (1859), and Self-Divorced, or, The School for Wives (1861). As the titles indicate, most of his fiction was of a military or historical character. He also published a variety of other works, including a pamphlet calling for the formation of a volunteer rifle corps (1852), another pamphlet entitled A lashing for the lashers: an exposition of the cruelties practised upon the cab and omnibus horses of London (1851), The Merry Wags of Warwickshire: a Drama (1854), and Recollections of the Mess-Table and the Stage (1855). Henry Curling died at his home, Weardale Villa, Earls Court Road, Kensington, London, on 10 February 1864.

[ANON.], rev. REBECCA MILLS

Sources GM, 3rd ser., 16 (1864), 405 • T. Cooper, A new biographical dictionary: containing concise notices of eminent persons of all ages and countries (1873), 471 • Allibone, Dict. • J. Sutherland, The Longman companion to Victorian fiction (1988) • Boase, Mod. Eng. biog. • d. cert.

Archives NL Scot., letters to William Blackwood & Sons

Curll, Edmund (d. 1747), bookseller, was born probably in the west of England and is of unknown parentage; in later life he said he was the son of a tradesman. In an addendum to his will of 1742 Curll says he is just entering his sixtieth year, which suggests that he was born in July of 1683, but newspaper obituaries written at his death listed him as aged seventy-two—which would mean that he was born in 1674 or 1675. Nothing is known of his youth, but his later familiarity with Greek and Latin indicates that he was given a traditional classical education. In 1698 or 1699 he was apprenticed to a London bookseller named R. Smith—probably the Richard Smith who had just set up his business in 1698, and who underwent bankruptcy in 1706. If Curll stayed with Smith for the traditional seven-year apprenticeship, he would have been ready to start his own business by 1705, and indeed in January 1706 he was involved in buying book collections and selling them by auction; an early catalogue refers to his shop on the Strand at the sign of the Peacock near St Clement's Church. Since Curll published a second edition of a book (Caesar's Commentaries of his Wars in Gaul, translated by Martin Bladen) published by Smith, he probably took over Smith's business at the time of the latter's bankruptcy. Curll was an appraiser of Smith's stock in 1706 when Smith himself was in hiding from his creditors. In 1708 Smith charged that Curll and two others had conspired to defraud him, knowingly undervaluing the stock. Among the stock were the sheets for Caesar's Commentaries, sheets which Curll then took over to print as his own. Curll's reply, and the outcome of the case, remains unknown, so it is of course possible that Curll had not acted improperly; but he was often accused of a great deal of impropriety later.

Early publications Curll continued to work in loose partnerships with a number of other small publishers, including the same Richard Smith, John Baker, Benjamin Bragge, Robert Halsey, and Charles Smith. Indeed, the title-page for the edition of *Caesar's Commentaries* says the book was 'printed for R. Smith, sold by Cha. Smith and E. Curll'. Such partnerships were normal practice in the era, especially among the less successful publishers, and Curll entered into similar ones continually throughout his career. Some of these partnerships were highly opportunistic: for example, in 1712 during the witchcraft trial of Jane Wenham, Bragge wrote and published several pamphlets arguing for her innocence, while Baker wrote and published three arguing for her guilt; Curll's and Baker's names both appear on the various pamphlets' title-pages, and all three men probably thought up the scheme together. Meanwhile, Curll remained involved in the auction business, but his main interest was in publishing. He was, especially in the early years, nothing if not eclectic as a publisher. One of the earliest titles to bear his imprint was a combination volume of John Dunton's *Athenian Spy* and an anonymous work, *The Way of a Man with a Maid*; the latter was probably pornography, a field in which Curll continued to work. But 1707 also saw him put out religious titles: *The Devout Christian's Companion* by Robert Warren, *Sermons on Several Subjects* by the Revd Mr Conant, and *Exposition of the Church Catechism* by Joseph Harrison.

January 1707 also saw Curll's first involvement with the works of contemporary poets. He advertised that he would soon print a collection of Matthew Prior's poems. The copyright to Prior's work was owned by the powerful bookseller Jacob Tonson, who quickly sent a letter to the *Daily Courant* (24 January) affirming that he had sole rights to Prior's work, and therefore that whatever Curll printed must be spurious. Curll ignored Tonson, and published Prior's *Poems on Several Occasions* (which were in fact genuine) that week; the title-page shows Curll in partnership with Richard Burrough and John Baker. Tonson appears to have pursued the matter no further, and he collaborated with Curll in 1709 on an edition of Thomas Hill's Latin poems; in 1709 Curll produced the seventh volume of Tonson's edition of Shakespeare, and in 1714 he did the ninth volume for a new edition. The Prior book of 1707 illustrates Curll's courage, and also the shadowy nature of copyright in the era: if Tonson had felt fully secure in his ownership of Prior's works, one assumes that he would have brought a legal complaint against Curll. Curll went on to print a new collection of Prior in 1716 (*A Second Collection of Poems on Various Occasions*), and this time the poet himself took out an advertisement objecting to the book. Curll printed a counter-advertisement, averring that the first advertisement had been written by an impostor, and he went ahead and published the book.

Another controversy in these early years involved the patent medicines that Curll also sold at his shop, and a book he published entitled *The Charitable Surgeon* (1708), whose author was listed only as 'T. C., Surgeon'. The book concerned cures for the pox—noting that the best cures were to be purchased at Curll's shop—and it attacked another writer on the same subject, John Spinke, claiming that Spinke's cure, involving mercury, was ineffective. Spinke replied in a series of angry pamphlets, and Curll replied in a newspaper, the *Post Boy*, scoffing at Spinke and his learning; he said he would give Spinke 5 guineas if he could translate any five Latin lines. Spinke immediately went to Curll's shop and translated five lines of Virgil on the spot. Spinke eventually had T. C.'s pills analysed, and found that they were themselves mercury. But Curll continued to publish *The Charitable Surgeon*, along with titles such as *A new method of curing, without internal medicines, that degree of the venereal disease, called a gonorrhea, or clap* (1709); as late as 1736, he published a version of Fracastoro's epic *Syphilis*.

In 1710 Curll moved to the sign of the Dial and Bible on Fleet Street, and in 1712 he opened a branch shop in Tunbridge Wells; his business was thriving despite—or because of—the controversies. He now entered into new partnerships with a series of more established publishers, notably John Morphew, with whom he worked closely between 1710 and 1713. Morphew had connections in the tory government, and he and Curll produced a number of pamphlets—some written by Curll himself, apparently his first venture into authorship—concerning the Sacheverell controversy. Curll attacked Bishop Burnet for his role in the affair, and he argued that Sacheverell was being abused by whig partisans. Two pamphlets known to have been written by Curll were *Some Considerations Humbly Offer'd to the Right Reverend the Lord Bishop of Salisbury*, and *A Search after Principles* (both 1710, both saying 'printed for J. Morphew' on the title-pages). A writer named George Sewell, in Morphew's employ, also wrote on the issue; when Curll and Morphew eventually parted, Sewell stayed on and wrote for Curll, producing many tracts as well as some collections of poetry.

Relations with authors At this same period Curll began to produce material related to Jonathan Swift—without Swift's permission. In 1710 he published an unauthorized version of *Meditations upon a Broomstick*, following it up with an explanatory 'key' to this and other works by Swift, including *A Tale of a Tub* (the key was printed in 1713). In these keys Curll revealed Swift's authorship of the *Tale* and some other satirical works that Swift had hoped to keep anonymous; probably Swift's authorship was a relatively open secret, but the Curll publications made it quite public. Swift had, of course, little legal recourse under the laws of the time. In 1726 Curll published a key to *Gulliver's Travels*, which again identified Swift as the author. The key was supposedly written by 'signor Corolini, a noble Venetian now residing in London', Corolini being an Italianate version of *curl*. While these keys are disappointing in terms of both their style and their critical acumen, they remain none the less of interest in showing how a contemporary might have read Swift: Gulliver, for example, is said to be in fact Swift's friend, Robert Harley, earl of

Oxford. Swift himself spoke of Curll with contempt, though he also saw him as a convenient target of satire on the venality of the publishing world: in a 1716 letter to Pope he referred to Curll as one of the 'tools in my opinion as necessary for a good writer, as pen, ink, and paper' (*Correspondence of Alexander Pope*, 359). The fullest expression of Swift's view of Curll comes only in his *Verses on the Death of Dr. Swift* (1731), where he speculates on how the world will react to the news of his death:

> Now *Curl* his Shop from Rubbish drains;
> Three genuine Tomes of *Swift's* Remains.
> And then, to make them pass the glibber,
> Revis'd by *Tibbalds, Moore and Cibber*.
> He'll treat me as he does my Betters.
> Publish my Will, my Life, my Letters.
> Revive the Libels born to dye;
> Which POPE must bear, as well as I.
> (*Poems*, 560–61)

The lines reveal Swift's contempt for Curll and his output, and they turned out to be quite prophetic, as Curll pirated an edition of Swift's letters much later, a piracy that led to a major court decision.

Another author Curll antagonized in these years was the poet Edward Young, but in this case Curll was clearly the one being abused. Young sent Curll in May 1717 a poem by a friend, Thomas Newcomb, together with a letter urging its publication. Curll did publish it that August under the title *An Ode Sacred to the Memory of the Countess of Berkeley*, prefaced by Young's letter. But then Young announced in the *London Evening-Post* that the letter was a forgery and not his. Curll immediately replied in the same paper, and soon Young had to admit that Curll was telling the truth. Young printed an apology, explaining his disavowal of the letter on the ground that he had not wanted to seem to be dictating what the public should think of Newcomb's poem. But we now know that Young's motives were strictly political: government power had shifted over the summer of 1717, and Young now did not want to be associated with the policies of the earl of Berkeley. Young and Curll made up later, and Young even wrote to Curll in 1739, 'Be assur'd I bear You no Illwill'; Curll published Young's poems in 1740 (*Correspondence of Edward Young*, 76). But the incident of 1717 is instructive with regard to Curll's reputation. Clearly, Young assumed that his disavowal would be believed over anything Curll might say. Moreover, he assumed he could in effect use Curll for his own political ends. Young was wrong on both counts; but a similar pattern emerged in the long relationship between Curll and Alexander Pope.

Encounters with Pope In 1716 Curll acquired—how and where have never been ascertained—the manuscript of three poems, one each by Pope, John Gay, and Lady Mary Wortley Montagu. Curll was evidently unaware of exactly who the three authors were, and he advertised it as a forthcoming volume 'by a Lady of Quality', adding that one of the poems sounded like 'the laudable Translator of Homer' (Straus, 51). Pope contacted Curll, warning him not to publish the poems; Curll ignored him, and Pope's attempted intervention served only to demonstrate that he was in fact one of the authors. The volume came out in

March under the title *Court Poems*. Pope might—like Prior before him—have simply accepted Curll's acts, but he chose to make a firmer statement. He and his publisher, Barnaby Bernard Lintot, invited Curll to meet them at the Swan tavern in Fleet Street on 28 March. At the meeting Pope appeared resigned but conciliatory, his only concern being that the volume might do some harm to Gay's prospects at court. But in the meanwhile he had laced Curll's drink with a powerful emetic, and when Curll returned home, he was violently ill. The incident might have ended there, but Pope went much further: he quickly published two pamphlets describing what had happened, with the added satiric barb of reporting sadly that the 'poison' had killed Curll (declaring one's adversary dead was a device Swift had used in 1709 in his *Bickerstaff Papers*). The first pamphlet, which appeared within two days of the meeting at the Swan, was entitled *A full and true account of a horrid and barbarous revenge by poison, on the body of Mr. Edmund Curll, bookseller; with a faithful copy of his last will and testament*. The narrative opens by stating that Curll 'was Yesterday poison'd by Mr. *Pope*, after having liv'd many years an Instance of the mild Temper of the *British* Nation' (*Prose Works*, 259). Pope planned the attack quite well, for the childish and vicious nature of the emetic trick was palliated by the wit of the pamphlets, and Curll appeared not as a victim but as a most deserving villain.

The punishment meted out to Curll, and the publicity that followed, were so out of balance with the offence of publishing *Court Poems* that modern scholars now believe Pope had come to see Curll as one of the 'tools' Swift described. Pope was in the process of stabilizing and extending his image as the dominant sage of the era, and the Curll episode was meant to reveal the poet as a powerful and proud figure who would not stand for the ruthless exploitation that people of Curll's sort would attempt. Pope may have guessed that he was creating a lifelong enemy in Curll, but if so he would have seen this too as a valuable situation, one that would generate continuous publicity and contribute to his status as the exemplary man of letters under constant assault from the tenth-rate denizens of Grub Street. And Curll, no stranger to the idea of valuable publicity, may have also seen great advantage in being cast as Pope's highly visible enemy. He played the role with relish. He quickly (31 May 1716) advertised a poem by John Oldmixon, *The Catholick Poet*, along with a piece by the critic John Dennis entitled *The True Character of Mr. Pope and his Writings*. Both pieces emphasized Pope's religion, highly damning in the aftermath of the Jacobite rising of 1715. A number of Jacobite sympathizers were being tried, and some executed, during 1716, and these attacks depicted Pope as a traitor—as well as impugning his morality and sneering at his hunchbacked physique. Curll went even further in attacking Pope's self-created image as guardian of public morality, for he acquired—again, where or how is unclear—an unpublished manuscript of a poem Pope had written some time earlier, a bawdy version of the first psalm. In late June 1716 Curll brought the poem out in full folio format, entitled *Version of the First Psalm*; the luxurious folio seemed to mock the juvenile, indecent—and to some, blasphemous—humour of the poem. In Curll's advertisements for the poem he also announced that he would henceforth be the publisher of all Pope's works.

Curll attracted more adverse publicity in April 1716 when he and his printer, Daniel Bridge, were arrested for printing an unauthorized account of the recent trial of the earl of Wintoun. They were both released on 10 May, having successfully petitioned for their release on the ground that their incarceration put their families in jeopardy. They were given official reprimands by the lord chancellor. A further indignity came on 2 August, when Curll accepted an invitation to Westminster School. The head of the school, John Barber, had delivered a funeral oration in July for the respected scholar Dr Robert South. Curll was planning to produce a biography of South, and he acquired a copy of Barber's oration without Barber's permission. When Curll arrived at the school, apparently hoping to be honoured for the biography, he was surrounded by the students, forced down on his knees, and made to beg forgiveness; they proceeded to whip him and toss him in a blanket. The affair is reminiscent of the emetic given by Pope, and the fact that the Westminster master and boys copied it indicates Pope's success in depicting Curll as worthy of nothing but such treatment. As in the Pope affair, a pamphlet was soon produced, this one written by Samuel Wesley (John Wesley's elder brother) in the form of a mock-heroic poem. It alludes directly to the Pope emetic in describing Curll being tossed in the blanket:

This sure might seem enough for once, Oh!
This tossing up, and tumbling down so;
And well thy Stomach might incline
To spue without Emetick Wine.
(Straus, 73–4)

Business success While Curll might have been made a laughing-stock, his business none the less seems to have thrived, and it seems likely that he played the role of disreputable publisher even more heartily as a result, growing bolder as he went along. He published, for example, a poem by 'J. Gay' entitled *The Petticoat* in June 1716. The poem was written by one of his hired authors, Francis Chute, and Curll explained that Chute was using a pseudonym—Joseph Gay. Of course, the intent was to make the poem appear to be by John Gay, and Curll went on to use the J. Gay name twice more, for works that were actually written by J. D. Breval.

The biography of Dr South was one of many biographies that Curll produced, having observed the growing taste among the public for short biographies of recently deceased public figures. His method was, however, quite improvisational: whenever a celebrated person died, Curll would advertise that a biography was being produced, asking readers to contribute any bits of information, letters, or the like that could help ensure the biography would be complete. Often these bits were all Curll had to work with, so he would add in whatever he could gather from the obituaries and bind it together with the letters or anecdotes readers had contributed, thus getting

his life to market before the competition could. Often he would include previously published works or speeches by the deceased. When a given life sold well, he would follow it up with second or third editions—some of which contained new material, and some of which did not. Despite the humiliation at Westminster School, he published the life of Dr South just a few months afterwards, and in 1717 he produced lives of Dr Daniel Williams, Bishop Gilbert Burnet, and Elias Ashmole. Some of the lives he published contained little more than the deceased's last will and testament, but some included interesting information; though Curll's lives are often crude at best, they are none the less historically significant as early examples of modern biography, and they often sold well. But their wholly unauthorized nature and the sheer randomness of what might appear in such a biography moved Dr John Arbuthnot to declare that Curll had added a new terror to death.

Curll continued to publish an extraordinarily wide range of texts; translations, poetry, fiction, divinity, medicine, and antiquarian material came from his press, usually in cheaply produced editions, almost always priced at 1s. or 2s. There is no complete bibliography of works published by Curll, either alone or in one of his numerous joint ventures, and the cheapness of the books' production unfortunately ensured that relatively few survived. But it would not be an exaggeration to see Curll as catering for, and perhaps helping to create, a new lower end for the book market. In the absence of such a bibliography, one can only speculate, but it would appear that Curll's 'scandalous' publications must have been greatly outnumbered by his respectable ones—though it is the former for which he is chiefly remembered. He sometimes encountered trouble over these lives, notably in 1721, when he advertised a forthcoming biography of the duke of Buckingham, together with his will. The House of Lords summoned Curll, and after questioning him passed a standing order (31 January 1721) making it a crime to publish anything by or about a lord without permission—an order that remained in force until 1845.

One of Curll's more salacious titles was the anonymous volume *Eunuchism Display'd* (1718)—though, like many of his similar books, the title suggests a more prurient book than the contents deliver. But in the *Weekly Journal* for 5 April 1718 Daniel Defoe attacked the book as a piece of pornography, coining a new term for the production of such books: curlicism. Curll, far from being offended, seemed to take some pride in the term, and he rapidly produced a pamphlet in his defence entitled *Curlicism Display'd* (May 1718), in the text of which he made enough references to his various titles that he could hope the reader's interest would be aroused.

Clashes with authority In 1723 Curll moved from his Fleet Street shop to Catherine Street off the Strand. During his three years at this new location he again found himself in serious trouble over two titles. The first, *A Treatise of the Use of Flogging in Venereal Affairs* (1718), was a translation by George Sewell of a Latin text that had been around since at least 1639. The book was intended to be—or seemed to be—for the instruction of physicians. Curll added a sexually orientated frontispiece, and ensured that the title-page would clarify for the reader what the book's genre was: 'Printed for E. Curll, in Fleet-Street, … where may be had, The Cases of Impotency; and Eunuchism and Onanism Display'd'. In 1724 he published another translation of an old, widely circulated pornographic text, giving it the English title *The Nun in her Smock*. The book is, as usual, less explicit than the reader might have expected, but it does include the theme that healthy sexual exploration—such as that of the titular nun—was never forbidden by Christ, only by Christian institutions. Early in 1725 an anonymous complaint was lodged against Curll, naming these two titles.

As was his custom, Curll defended himself against this complaint by quickly producing a pamphlet, *The Humble Representation of Edmund Curll*; and, as was his custom, he took advantage of the publicity by issuing a second edition of *The Nun in her Smock*. But this time the authorities moved against him: on 2 March 1725 he was arrested, and was held until July. There was currently no law against publishing pornography as such; the most recent obscenity case had been in 1707 (concerning a non-Curll title, *The Fifteen Plagues of a Maidenhead*), and then the court determined that obscenity cases were the province of the ecclesiastical courts. The government now indicated that it would prosecute Curll under the libel law—which would, clearly, have been stretching the definition of libel. Curll tried to weaken any sentiment there was against him by printing a public apology, together with a promise to leave publishing altogether. His apology appeared in the newspapers on 3 December 1725, reading more like an advertisement than an apology:

> I hereby most humbly ask Pardon for these Offences; but being resolved never more to offend in the like Manner, I give this Notice, that so soon as two Books, now in the Press, are finish'd, (viz. 1. The Miscellaneous Works of the Memorable Patriot *Andrew Marvel* esq.; in Prose and Verse. 2. The *Case of Seduction*; being the late Proceedings at Paris against the Rev. Abbé des Rues, for committing Rapes upon 133 Virgins. Written by himself) I am resolved to retire from all Publick Business.   (Straus, 106)

The apology clearly did not satisfy the prosecutors; Curll's shop was raided, nine more books were seized, and Curll was re-arrested, this time remaining in prison until July 1726. While there, he continued writing and publishing, producing an anonymous pamphlet about prison abuses (*The Prisoner's Advocate*). While he was imprisoned, he entered upon another enterprise that led to further trouble. He met a very old, dying prisoner named John Ker, who showed him his memoirs. The memoirs contained what might be interpreted as state secrets from the preceding generation, so Curll exercised great caution, agreeing to publish them only after they had been read and approved by the office of the prime minister, Robert Walpole. Walpole did not reply, and Curll assumed—incautiously—that this meant that the memoirs were approved. When he was released, he published the memoirs in three volumes between July and November 1726.

Curll was still anxious about the text, and he first printed a notice in the *Evening Post* for 5 July stating that he was not the publisher of Ker's *Memoirs*; he could say, accurately enough, that the book was printed 'for the author'. He also repeated his pledge to give up publishing. But Ker died on 8 July—Curll, again incautiously, decided to go ahead and publish the rest of the *Memoirs*, this time under the imprint of his son, Henry Curll. Virtually nothing is known about Curll's son, or about Curll's wife Elizabeth, mentioned only in his will as his second wife. We only know that Henry died before 1742, leaving no children, and that he was in some ways involved with his father's business, as in the case of the Ker memoirs; he also did some publishing under his own name. Shortly after the final volume of Ker's *Memoirs* was published, Curll and his son were both arrested; though Henry was quickly released, Curll stayed in prison from November 1726 to 12 February 1728. At that point he was fined 25 marks apiece for the publication of *The Nun in her Smock* and the treatise on flogging and, more ominously, he was sentenced to an hour in the pillory for the Ker *Memoirs*. Such a sentence often resulted in the prisoner's death, as the public was encouraged to abuse the prisoner in whatever manner they wished. But on his pillory day, which was 13 February, he arranged to have a broadside printed and distributed to the crowd stating that his punishment was due to his having displayed his loyalty to the much beloved Queen Anne; when his hour was up, the crowd carried him off on their shoulders.

More trouble with Pope Curll's running battle with Pope began to reheat when, in 1726, he purchased some of the poet's letters and printed them, without permission, of course. When Pope published the first version of his *Dunciad* (1728), Curll figured prominently among the 'dunces'. Curll fought back on several fronts: he published a pirated version of the poem, a series of 'keys' explicating its allusions, and a series of poems in reply—*The Popiad* (which Lady Mary Wortley Montagu, Pope's erstwhile friend, evidently wrote, at least in part), *The Female Dunciad*, and *The Twickenham Hotch-Potch*, all in 1728. Such public quarrels were good business for both men. In 1729 Pope published his own new, annotated version, *The Dunciad Variorum*, in which Pope said Curll deserved to be in the poem because 'if ever [Pope] ow'd two verses to any other, he ow'd Mr. Curl some thousands' (*Poems*, 104). Curll replied with a pamphlet titled *The Curliad: a Hypercritic upon the Dunciad Variorum* (1729), a document which, like many of Curll's biographies, is both highly interesting and highly frustrating. It amounts to a sort of public defence of his actions with regard to both Pope and the charges of obscenity recently made against him, and as such is valuable autobiographically, but it is fragmentary and clearly a hurried production. He sums up the infamous emetic affair briefly, saying: 'I then despised the Action, and have since, in another manner, sufficiently *Purged* the Author of it' (p. 21). In defence of his two obscene titles he includes a testimonial by a Dr. Rose, 'a very learned and worthy Member of the College of Physicians', who argues that *The Nun in her Smock* is of value in showing the abuses and perversions to which Catholicism is liable (the attack on Pope is implicit), and the book on flagellation is justified as it details a manner of sexual arousal that might help men overcome impotence (p. 14). Curll returns to his own narration, describing his actions in the Ker affair, insisting on his blamelessness, and saying that his hour in the pillory was no cause for shame: 'I have always been of Opinion, that, it is the *Crime*, not the *Punishment*, or the *Shape* of a Man, which stamps his *Ignominy*' (p. 19).

Curll moved to a new location in 1729, to Bow Street in Covent Garden. When that year he printed a volume of work by and about William Congreve—much of it without permission—Dr Arbuthnot complained of it. Curll, in defiance, announced that his shop would henceforth be known as the Congreve's Head, and he set up a portrait of Congreve over his door. Curll moved again, in 1731, this time to nearby Burleigh Street. The battle with Pope continued, as Curll printed a notice (March 1733) of a life of Pope that he was planning, and he now called for any contributions readers could make. His advertisement notes that the biography will be nearly complete: 'Nothing shall be wanting but his (universally desired) Death. Any Memoirs, &c. worthy of his Deserts, if sent to Mr. Curll, will be faithfully inserted' (Straus, 156). A mysterious person, known only as P. T., contacted Curll, offering a number of letters from Pope; Curll wanted to know whether the letters were genuine, even going so far as to write to Pope about them, but getting no satisfaction. There were clandestine meetings with a man named Smythe, P. T.'s agent, and eventually Curll printed the letters. It is now known that Pope himself engineered the entire affair, goading and tricking Curll into printing his letters so that Pope would now be forced to publish a 'correct' edition. The stratagem effectively drew attention away from the sheer effrontery of a living poet printing his own letters, which had never been done before. Pope also wanted Curll to appear particularly disreputable at this juncture (1735) when London booksellers were campaigning for a new copyright extension that would greatly favour them; Curll's presence on the scene as a seedy thief of private letters would be good rhetoric against the booksellers' proposal—and indeed the proposal was defeated.

Final years and death In 1735 Curll moved again, to Rose Street in Covent Garden, and this time he set up shop under the sign of the Pope's Head. By 1737 he had published five volumes of Pope's correspondence. In 1741 Pope brought an action against Curll regarding his publication of Swift's letters: noting that the book contained letters both to and from Pope, Pope claimed that he had copyright in those letters. The court ruled that Pope did have rights to those letters he had written, but not to those written to him. This decision has been hailed as a landmark victory for authors' rights to their own letters, and even as marking the end of the old patronage system of literature, finally ushering in the new system based on authors' commercial rights.

In his last years Curll's publishing output was as varied and prolific as ever, ranging from pornography (a series of books about Merryland) to a highly respected twenty-volume set of county histories, *Anglia illustra*, by Richard Rawlinson. On 14 July 1742 he added a codicil to his will—in rhyming couplets, Pope's medium:

> I have no relatives, my Son is dead,
> He left no issue and his Wife's re-wed;
> Therefore no legacies at all I leave,
> But all I've got to my dear Wife bequeathe.
> (PRO, PROB 11/763, fol. 160r)

The codicil tells all that is known about his family, save that in the will itself his wife's name, Elizabeth, is given. Curll died on 11 December 1747.

Curll's significance in the history of publishing lies in his having helped to create the modern literary marketplace. Pope's depiction of him as a loathsome dunce and crook has been powerful—leading not least to his becoming known as the Unspeakable Curll, a nickname popularized by his biographer Ralph Straus—but scholars more recently have begun to question that image. While Curll often acted in ways that Pope and others considered unscrupulous, he was also inventive, energetic, and always alive to the value of publicity and the need to create a market for one's product.

RAYMOND N. MacKENZIE

Sources N. Ault, *New light on Pope* (1949); repr. (1967) · W. Ayre [E. Curll], *Memoirs of the life and writings of Alexander Pope* (1745) · A. Boehm, 'The poetics of literary commerce: popular and patrician bookselling and the rise of publishing, 1700–1825', PhD diss., Indiana University, 1992 · E. Curll, *The Curliad: a hypercritic upon the Dunciad variorum* (1729); repr. (1975) · D. Foxon, *Libertine literature in England, 1660–1745* (New York, 1965) · D. Foxon, *Pope and the early eighteenth-century book trade* (1991) · J. V. Guerinot, *Pamphlet attacks on Alexander Pope, 1711–1744* (1969) · R. L. Haig, '"The Unspeakable Curll": prolegomena', *Studies in Bibliography*, 13 (1960), 220–23 · P. M. Hill, *Two Augustan booksellers: John Dunton and Edmund Curll* (Lawrence, KS, 1958) · C. Ingrassia, 'Dissecting the authorial body: Pope, Curll, and the portrait of a "Hack Writer"', *'More solid learning': new perspectives on Alexander Pope's 'Dunciad'*, ed. C. Ingrassia and C. N. Thomas (Lewisburg, PA, 2000), 147–65 · H. Leek, 'The Edward Young–Edmund Curll quarrel: a review', *Papers of the Bibliographical Society of America*, 62 (1968), 321–35 · M. Mack, *Alexander Pope: a life* (1985) · J. McLaverty, 'The first printing and publication of Pope's letters', *The Library*, 6th ser., 2 (1980), 264–80 · D. F. Passman, 'William Symson, *Gulliver's travels* and "Curllicism" at its best', *Études Anglaises*, 40/3 (1987), 300–12 · *The correspondence of Edward Young, 1683–1765*, ed. H. Pettit (1971) · W. Raleigh, 'Early lives of the poets', *Six essays on Johnson* (1910), 98–127 · H. Ransom, 'The personal letter as literary property', *Studies in English*, 30 (1951), 116–31 · P. Rogers, 'The case of Pope v. Curll', *The Library*, 5th ser., 27 (1972), 326–31 · P. Rogers, *Hacks and dunces: Pope, Swift and Grub Street* (1980) · M. Rose, 'The author in court: Pope v. Curll 1741', *The construction of authorship: textual appropriation in law and literature*, ed. M. Woodmansee and P. Jaszi (Durham, NC, 1994), 211–29 · E. L. Ruhe, 'Edmund Curll and his early associates', *English writers of the eighteenth century*, ed. J. H. Middendorf (New York, 1971), 69–89 · D. Saunders and I. Hunter, 'Lessons from the 'Literatory': how to historicise authorship', *Critical Inquiry*, 17 (1991), 479–509 · L. Schachterle, 'The first key to *Gulliver's travels*', *Revue des Langues Vivantes*, 38 (1972), 37–45 · R. Straus, *The Unspeakable Curll* (1927) · W. J. Thoms, *Curll papers: stray notes on the life and publications of Edmund Curll* (privately printed, London, 1879) · R. Thompson, *Unfit for modest ears: a study of pornographic, obscene and bawdy works written or published in England in the second half of the seventeenth century* (1979) · P. Wagner, *Eros revived: erotica of the Enlightenment in England and America* (1988) · *A window in the bosom: the letters of Alexander Pope*, ed. J. A. Winn (Hampden, CT, 1977) · PRO, PROB 11/763, sig. 209 · *The correspondence of Alexander Pope*, ed. G. Sherburn, 1 (1956) · *The poems of Jonathan Swift*, ed. H. Williams, 2 (1958) · *The prose works of*

Alexander Pope, 1, ed. N. Ault (1936) • A. Pope, *The Dunciad*, ed. J. Sutherland, rev. edn (1953), vol. 5 of *The Twickenham edition of the poems of Alexander Pope*, ed. J. Butt • *DNB* • *GM*, 1st ser., 17 (1747), 592
Archives Bodl. Oxf., letters and papers • University of Kansas, Lawrence, Kenneth Spencer Research Library
Likenesses W. Hogarth, engraving, 1736 • prints, repro. in Straus, *Unspeakable Curll*

Curll, Walter (1575–1647), bishop of Winchester, son of William Curll (d. 1617), auditor of the court of wards, was born at Hatfield, Hertfordshire. He matriculated at Christ's College, Cambridge, about 1592 before going to Peterhouse, where he graduated BA, probably in 1595, and proceeded MA in 1598. That year he was elected fellow of his college, perhaps through the influence of Archbishop Whitgift, but travelled before furthering his studies. On his return he was ordained on 20 February 1603 and was licensed as a preacher of the University of Cambridge in 1607. He received the degrees of BD in 1606 and DD in 1612. Four years later he relinquished his fellowship but in gratitude for his service 'the College gave him a years profit' (Foster, *Alum. Oxon.*, 1.313).

After incumbencies at Little St Mary's, Cambridge, from 1605 to 1606, Plumstead from 1608 to 1609, and Little Moneghan in Kent (1610–12), Curll acquired through the patronage of the third earl of Pembroke the Wiltshire livings of Wilton St Mary with Bulbridge (1611), Ditchampton (1612), Mildenhall (1619), and Fugglestone St Peter and Bemerton (1620). In 1615 he was appointed to the prebend of Lyme and Halstock in Salisbury Cathedral, and on 8 March 1622 was appointed dean of Lichfield Cathedral. Before the latter appointment Curll had also become a chaplain-in-ordinary to James I. He first appeared on the court's Lenten roster in 1616, and then in the years 1617 and 1618 and from 1622 to 1625. On Low Sunday 1622 he preached a sermon (later published) reflecting James's policies at that time, if at odds with the stance of his patron, Pembroke. With its theme of peace and holiness it censured those protestant hawks who wanted to pursue a holy war in Europe and those who caused dissension in the Church in England. He continued to appear as a Lenten preacher during Charles I's time, preaching at least in the years from 1628 to 1631. While dean he was also elected prolocutor of the lower house of the convocation of Canterbury in 1628.

Curll was appointed bishop of Rochester on 14 July 1628 and consecrated on 7 September. He was given dispensation to keep the incumbencies of Mildenhall, and Fugglestone, and the Salisbury prebend. William, the only surviving child of Curll and his wife, Elizabeth, was baptized on 26 December 1628 at Bromley in Kent. After only fifteen months at Rochester, on 4 December 1629, Curll was enthroned as the bishop of Bath and Wells. Very little is known about his time there, except that, unlike his two predecessors, Mawe and Laud, he resided in Wells. After he left his successor, William Piers, sued him in the court of arches for the dilapidation of the episcopal residence and alleged deprivation of fines for leases. The case came before Laud on 12 May 1636, and as a result Curll had to pay

Walter Curll (1575–1647), by unknown artist, 1635

Piers £240. After three years at Wells, when Bishop Richard Neile of Winchester was translated to York, Curll was elected in his place—probably through the influence of Laud; he was enthroned on 16 November 1632. Through Laud he was appointed in 1637 prelate of the Garter and lord high almoner to Charles I. He was also a benefactor of the new chapel for Peterhouse, consecrated on 17 March 1632, and he even contributed towards the cost of compiling the polyglot Bible, published from 1653 to 1657.

During the 1630s Curll supported the Caroline–Laudian programme for the beautification of churches and worshipping God in the beauty of holiness, in his diocese of Winchester and as visitor to New, Corpus, Trinity, St John's, and Magdalen colleges at Oxford. At the last of these he praised its president, Dr Frewen, for the renovations made to the chapel but urged that the ante-chapel also be decorated. The result was the great western window, a copy of Schwartz's *Last Judgment*, as well as another eight windows in 'best Normandy glasse' of the saints, mostly of the early church (Magdalen College, MS CS/36/3/1–6).

Curll complied too with Laud's *Instructions of 1629*, reissued in 1633, with its restriction on lecturing and the replacing of the Sunday afternoon sermon with catechizing. With the reissue of the Book of Sports, also in 1633, Curll immediately suspended or excommunicated *ab officio et a beneficio* some ministers who did not read it. Yet he was not as ruthless in pursuing conformity in all the Laudian policies as some other Caroline bishops, such as Wren and Montagu, as is evident from his visitation articles for Bath and Wells in 1630 and Winchester in 1633 and 1636. Later, when the Long Parliament began its attack on bishops, Curll was identified not with pro-

Laudian bishops but, as his appointment in 1640 and 1641 to committees to consider religious innovations reveals, with Calvinist moderates such as bishops Joseph Hall, Thomas Morton, and John Williams. There is little direct evidence of Curll's doctrinal beliefs. One sermon on Luke 15: 10 survives from his time as bishop of Winchester, in which he urged his congregation to repentance and contrition as the only way to experience joy in this life and to make the angels rejoice in heaven (CUL, Dd 5.31). In similar vein, at the public fast at St Mary's, Oxford, on 10 May 1644, he preached again the sermon delivered in 1622 in which he had pleaded for peace and holiness in living.

During the civil war Curll supported the royalists and helped to defend Winchester against parliament. In 1645 when Cromwell captured the city and they were forced to surrender, Curll found himself almost destitute. He was deprived not only of his episcopal home and income but also his private property. Many years later, the publisher Edmund Curll wrote, 'In these common Calamities, he suffer'd much for the King's and his own Cause' (E. Curll, vii). With his wife Elizabeth and son William, Curll retired to his sister's home in Soberton, Hampshire. Despite his own sufferings he did what he could to relieve the hardships of his fellow clergy and royalists. John Walker declared that he 'was a man of very great charity to the poor, and expended large sums in the repairs of churches' (Walker, 76). According to Curll's will drawn up on 15 March, 31 March, and 4 April 1647, he bequeathed 20 marks to his native town of Hatfield and 20 nobles to the poor of Soberton. Although it was later claimed that he was then 'in narrow circumstances', he was still able to leave numerous bequests to his relatives of goods and money, including an annuity to his sister Dorothie Keene charged on the manor of Soberton. Within a few months he had died, in London, his will being proved by his son on 10 November 1647. He was buried privately in the chapel in Soberton parish church. By 1712, all that remained of his tomb was 'a flat grey free-stone', as the 'Brass containing the Inscription, are broke off by sacrilegious Hands' (E. Curll, viii).   M. DORMAN

Sources E. Curll, *Some account of the life of Rt. Rev'd father in God, D'r. Walter Curl, bishop of Winchester* (1712) · Foster, *Alum. Oxon.* · W. Curll, *A sermon preach'd at White-Hall on the 28. of April, 1622 by Walter Curll, D. D. & dean of Lichfield* (1622) · Venn, *Alum. Cant.* · J. Walker, *An attempt towards recovering an account of the numbers and sufferings of the clergy of the Church of England*, 2 pts in 1 (1714), 76 · S. H. Cassan, *The lives of the bishops of Winchester*, 2 (1827), 133–7 · PRO, SP 14/120/11, 16/110/7, 16/111/18, 16/117/65, 16/152/19, 16/225/88 · PRO, PROB 11/202, fols. 144–5 · K. Fincham, ed., *Visitation articles and injunctions of the early Stuart church*, 1 (1994), 186; 2 (1998), 276 · J. Milner, *The history civil and ecclesiastical and survey of the antiquities of Winchester* (1801), 400–13 · J. Davies, *The Caroline captivity of the church: Charles I and the remoulding of Anglicanism, 1625–1641* (1992) · P. E. McCullough, *Sermons at court: politics and religion in Elizabethan and Jacobean preaching* (1998), 138, 140, 212 [incl. CD-ROM] · B. Willis, *A survey of the cathedrals*, 3 vols. (1742), vol. 1, p. 400 · *Fasti Angl.* (Hardy) · E. Hasted, *The history and topographical survey of the county of Kent*, 2 (1782), 43–4 · H. Chauncy, *The historical antiquities of Hertfordshire* (1700), 313

Archives PRO, SP 14/120/11, 16/110/7, 16/110/48, 16/111/18, 16/117/65, 16/152/19, 16/225/88

Likenesses oils, 1635, Winchester College, Hampshire · portrait, 1635, bishop's palace, Wells [*see illus.*] · T. Cecill, line engraving, BM, NPG · oils, Peterhouse, Cambridge

Wealth at death bequests of money, goods, and annuity on manor of Soberton, Hampshire: PRO, PROB 11/202, fols. 144–5

Curr, Edward (1798–1850), politician and entrepreneur in Australia, was born on 1 July 1798 at Sheffield, England, the son of John Curr, who managed the duke of Norfolk's estate and coalmines. He was educated at Sedgley Park School and Ushaw College, and resisted parental pressure to enter a profession or move into business. His marriage to Elizabeth Micklethwait(e), daughter of Benjamin (1762–1798) and Mary Micklethwaite of Ardsley, was accompanied by a generous financial settlement and this, together with a guarantee from his father, seems to have decided him on a commercial career in Van Diemen's Land. Edward and Elizabeth Curr arrived in Hobart in 1820. The patronage of Lieutenant-Governor William Sorell compensated for early business reversals and Curr was active in the foundation of Roman Catholic communities on the island. After the death of his father in 1823 he returned to England with his wife and children and completed a promotional publication, his *Account of the Colony of Van Diemen's Land* (1824). Sorell, also visiting England, helped to arrange Curr's appointment as chief agent of the Van Diemen's Land Company, and from his return in 1826 until 1842 Curr tried to secure the interests of the company in its tract of 350,000 acres in the north-west of the island.

The task required the co-ordination of practical exploration, the development of appropriate livestock breeding programmes, and the cultivation of influential contacts in a small community which resented the company's monopolistic claims. Curr's associates chastised him for his management performance and for his haughty demeanour towards local officials, and in 1839 the company's directors gave him a year's notice. He then took his family to the mainland, where he established his own pastoral business in the Port Phillip district of New South Wales. Leaving the affairs of his up-country properties to his sons, he became prominent in the political life of Melbourne. He was the first candidate to be nominated for Melbourne in the inaugural election for the New South Wales legislative council in 1843, but his adherence to Roman Catholicism stirred up fierce sectarianism and, narrowly defeated, he chose to identify more closely with Irish immigrant groups; ironically, he was later criticized for a marked want of deference to the predominantly Irish clergy. Towards the mid-1840s Curr, motivated by an apparent threat from radical Orangemen and other Port Phillip militants, was attracted by the demand that Port Phillip district be separated from New South Wales and made a distinct colony. He chaired the Separation League and lobbied vigorously in England and in the colonial press. In 1845 he was elected to the legislative council, but resigned after nine months because of the difficulty of attending its sittings in Sydney.

Curr was tall, powerfully built, resolute and resourceful, and was frequently embroiled in controversial disputes.

He did not flinch from opposing the highest colonial authorities, and his commanding presence and clear statements of opinion were welcomed in many quarters. Occasionally his forceful personality diverted attention from his adoption of contradictory positions: for example, ignoring the views of urban supporters, he campaigned for the importation of convict labour to assist the pioneer pastoralists. He died on 16 November 1850, five days after the arrival of the news that parliament had passed the act separating the Port Phillip district, to form Victoria, and was buried in Melbourne general cemetery on the 19th. He left his wife and the surviving eleven of their fourteen children financially secure.

Edward Micklethwaite Curr (1820–1889), pastoralist and author, was born on 25 December 1820 in Hobart, the eldest child of Edward and Elizabeth Curr. After an education at Stonyhurst College, Lancashire (1829–37), and a year in France, he assisted his brother William in managing the family's properties in the Port Phillip district. In 1852–4 he travelled in Europe and the Middle East, finishing in Ireland where on 31 January 1854 he married Margaret Vaughan (1830/31–1886) from co. Kildare, who bore him five sons and three daughters. After returning to Victoria in that year, he worked in New Zealand and Queensland, before settling in Victoria again in 1862, when he was employed as an inspector of stock by the Victorian government; here his innovative contributions to the formulation and implementation of stock management policies proved critical in the consolidation of the pastoral frontier. His practical and scholarly interests were represented in *Pure Saddle Horses* (1863), *An Essay on Scab in Sheep* (1865), *Recollections of Squatting in Victoria* (1883), and a four-volume work, *The Australian Race: its Origins, Languages, Customs* (1886–7). His later works are highly valued for their atypically sympathetic approach to the indigenous peoples. Far less active in colonial politics than his father, he died in Melbourne on 3 August 1889 and was buried in the Roman Catholic section of the St Kilda general cemetery, Melbourne. He had often complained that his father had invested too much of the family wealth in the cause of separation; more importantly, his published reflections on the impact of European occupation suggest that the son is the larger historical figure. J. M. POWELL

Sources P. de Serville, *Port Phillip gentlemen and good society in Melbourne before the gold rushes* (1980) · J. West, *The history of Tasmania*, ed. A. G. L. Shaw, [new edn] (1971) · S. Morgan, *Land settlement in early Tasmania* (1992) · A. Sutherland, *Victoria and its metropolis* (1888) · J. Keaney, 'Early education in Victoria', *Footprints: Journal of the Melbourne Diocese Historical Commission* (March 1992), 12–19 · H. G. Turner, *A history of the colony of Victoria*, 2 vols. (1904) · A. L. Meston, *The Van Diemen's Land Company, 1825–42* (1958) · AusDB · *The Argus* [Melbourne] (20 Nov 1850) · *The Australasian* (10 Aug 1889) [Edward Micklethwaite Curr]

Archives Tasmanian State Archives, Hobart, Van Diemen's Land Company records

Likenesses sketch (Edward Micklethwaite Curr), repro. in Sutherland, *Victoria and its metropolis*, vol. 1, p. 282

Curr, Edward Micklethwaite (1820–1889). *See under* Curr, Edward (1798–1850).

Curran, Amelia (1775–1847), painter, was born in the city of Cork, the eldest of nine children of the Irish reformer John Philpot *Curran (1750–1817), and his wife, Sarah, *née* Creagh (*c*.1755–1844). Her early years were divided between Dublin, where her father practised as a barrister, and the family's cottage at Priory Glen, outside Newmarket, co. Cork, where her maternal grandfather practised as a physician. With her father she was a visitor at the home, in Somers Town, Middlesex, of the philosopher and novelist William Godwin, and in winter 1811 she saw much of the Presbyterian minister and teacher Aaron Burr, also a regular visitor to the Godwins. Burr described her in 1812, the year in which she first met the poet Shelley, as having 'all the genius and eloquence of her father, and the vivacity, the ingenuousness, and the sensibility of her sex and her country' (*Journals of Claire Clairmont*, 108). Shelley's first wife, Harriet, thought differently:

> I have seen Miss Curran: she resides in England. What I saw of her I did not like … She is not half such an Irishwoman as myself, and that is why I did not feel disposed to like her. Besides, she is a coquette, the most abominable thing in the world. I met her at Godwin's house also. (to Mrs Nugent, 16 Jan [1813]; *Letters of Percy Bysshe Shelley*, 1.349)

The diarist Henry Crabb Robinson met Amelia Curran at dinner at the Godwins on 10 January 1813 and noted that 'she is very plain, and did not say anything absolutely good or new, but seemed alive to perceive anything in any way worthy of notice' (Reiman, 6.498). A year later, in March 1814, he met her there again, noting that 'she was free and sometimes graceful in her freedom' (ibid.). When she left in 1814 to study painting in Italy, Godwin wrote her a letter of introduction to his close friend Maria Gisborne. In 1818 she was again in England, and at the invitation of Godwin attended on 30 March one of William Hazlitt's 'Lectures on the English poets' at the Crown and Anchor tavern. On his death, in 1817, her father had left her an annuity of £50; in addition to the provision that he had already made for her this enabled her to abandon a lukewarm plan to become a lady-in-waiting to a member of the royal family and to return to Italy, where she settled in Rome to establish herself as a portrait painter.

On 23 April 1819 Claire Clairmont (daughter of Godwin's second wife, Mary Jane Clairmont), who had accompanied the Shelleys to Italy and was the mother of Byron's natural daughter, Allegra, noted in her diary: 'Drive in the Borghese [Gardens, Rome]—We think we see Miss Curran' (*Journals of Claire Clairmont*, 108). This sighting marks the beginning of three months' intensive association between Amelia Curran and the Shelley household, who commissioned her to make portraits of themselves. Having postponed their journey to Naples in order to give her further sittings, on 7 May 1819 the Shelleys moved to 65 via Sistina, next door to Amelia, who lived at no. 64. There she painted the portraits of Shelley (NPG), Mary Shelley (formerly in the possession of E. J. Trelawny), their four-year-old son, William (Carl H. Pforzheimer Library, New York; reproduced in K. N. Cameron and D. H. Reiman, eds., *Shelley and his Circle*, 1961, frontispiece), and Claire

Clairmont (City of Nottingham Museums, Newstead Abbey collections). Following William's death, from malaria, on 7 June the Shelleys and Claire left Rome. Amelia also succumbed to malaria, but recovered. In February 1820 Lady Sidney Morgan met her in Rome and found her 'full of talent and intellect, pleasant, interesting, and original; and she paints like an artist' (*Journals of Claire Clairmont*, 108n.). In 1821–2 she lived at Naples, where she became a Roman Catholic. Her letters to Mary Shelley in 1822 record her address in Paris, to which she may have gone following the breakdown of a relationship. (Jane Williams, widow of Shelley's friend Edward, with whom he had drowned, had informed Mary that Amelia Curran had been married for two years.) By 1824 she was living at her former address in Rome, where she remained for the rest of her life.

As one of very few *ad vivum* portraits of Shelley, Amelia Curran's painting, described by Edward Dowden as 'the hasty work of an imperfectly trained amateur'—is important as 'that by which the face of Shelley is most widely known' (Dowden, 2.265). During the time that he was sitting to her Shelley was writing *The Cenci* (1819); a copy of a portrait identified at the time as that of Beatrice Cenci and attributed to Guido Reni, the original of which Shelley had seen in the Palazzo Colonna, he 'kept on the wall of his room in the via Sestina' (Holmes, 516). In his biography of the poet, Richard Holmes observes that 'there is a most striking resemblance between the Reni portrait of La Cenci and the Curran portrait of Shelley … Both are oddly androgynous creations' (ibid.). In his preface to *The Cenci* (p. viii) Shelley included a detailed description of the 'Beatrice Cenci' portrait, in which he contemplates the 'fixed and pale composure of the features'— 'the lips have that permanent meaning of imagination and sensibility which suffering has not repressed'—and reveals in a mirror-like image his identification with the subject, whom he described as 'one of those rare persons in whom energy and gentleness dwell together without destroying one another: her nature was simple and profound'. The psychological qualities that he attributes to La Cenci, transparently a reflection of his own, suggest that his interpretation of the portrait engendered in him an intense moment of self-awareness (of a kind that was fundamental to his vision as a Romantic poet) that makes his identification with the heroine of his drama a conscious act. His absorption was clearly evident to Amelia Curran, whose Romantic portrait of him, while different in pose, is heavily influenced by that believed at that time to represent Beatrice Cenci. In September 1819 he commissioned her to make a copy of 'the Cenci portrait' (whereabouts unknown), from which an etching was made by William Bell Scott; this was reproduced as the frontispiece to *The Cenci* (1819). The etching includes a monogram that intertwines the letters P, B, S, and C (the initials of Percy Bysshe Shelley and Beatrice Cenci).

Copies by Alfred Clint (NPG) and Malcolm Stewart (1900; Bodl. Oxf.) and numerous engravings, including that by William Finden reproduced in William and Edward Finden's *Illustrations to the Life of Byron* (3 vols., 1833) and as the frontispiece to Shelley's *Poetical Works* (ed. M. Shelley, 4 vols., 1839), have contributed to the enduring predominance of Amelia Curran's portrait of Shelley. The portrait also forms the basis of a painting by Joseph Severn, *Shelley at the Baths of Caracalla* (1845; priv. coll.), commissioned by Shelley's son Percy Florence, in which the poet is shown composing *Prometheus Unbound*. Severn, who knew Amelia Curran in Rome, made a copy of his imaginative painting, which his son Arthur Severn gave to the Keats–Shelley Memorial House, Rome.

Mary Shelley's letter to Amelia Curran of 20 June 1820 indicates that Claire Clairmont did not like her own portrait, though in a subsequent letter dated 25 September 1820 Mary sent a message to Miss Curran that Claire would 'be obliged to you if you let her have her picture' (*Letters of Mary Wollstonecraft Shelley*, 1.114). Like her portrait of Shelley, Amelia Curran's much-reproduced portrait of Claire Clairmont, whose letters and journals are an important source for Shelley and Byron scholars as well as independent literary works of the Romantic period, is the image by which Claire is known. Between 23 April and 2 June 1819 Claire's journal records frequent visits between the Shelley household and Amelia, portrait sittings, and visits with Amelia to exhibitions and to Tivoli. On 14 May her journal records a visit to Amelia's to see 'Will's portrait' and 'A discussion concerning jealousy' (*Journals of Claire Clairmont*, 111). Claire later 'told [Edward Augustus] Silsbee that since Shelley could not abide Miss Curran he "had a lackadaisical look" when he sat in Rome for his portrait by her' (*Clairmont Correspondence*, 2.375, n. 6). She 'recalled the artist as a "witty *epigrammatic vulgar* bitter old maid"' (ibid.).

This view, which may have been the outcome of the 'discussion concerning jealousy', is tempered by entries in Mary Shelley's journal, which also records the family's sittings to Amelia Curran and visits with her around Rome and its environs. Following Shelley's death, in 1822, Mary wrote to her in Rome, asking if she could have the (then unfinished) portrait of Shelley. Amelia received only Mary's second letter asking for the portrait (forwarded to her address in the faubourg St Germain, Paris), and replied:

> Your picture and Claire's I left … at Rome … The one you now write for I thought was not to be inquired for; it was so ill done, and I was on the point of burning it with others before I left Italy; I luckily saved it just as the fire was scorching it, and it is packed up with my other pictures at Rome. (6 Oct 1822; *Letters of Mary Wollstonecraft Shelley*, 1.241)

The portraits of Mary and Claire were collected by the Cornish adventurer Edward Trelawny, who had been a member of the Shelley and Byron circle in Pisa. After corresponding with Amelia about Shelley's portrait for some years Mary eventually received it in London, and wrote in her journal: 'Thy picture is come, my only One—thine— those speaking eyes—that mild yet animated look— Unlike aught earthly wert thou ever & art now' (7 Sept 1826 [1825?]; *Journals of Mary Shelley*, 2.496). Her own portrait by Amelia remains untraced.

Amelia Curran died in Rome in 1847, and was buried in

the church of St Isidore; J. H. Newman, afterwards Cardinal Newman, gave her funeral oration. A few years later a former admirer, Valentine, Lord Cloncurry, who recalled her as 'the most witty and agreeable woman I ever knew, full of talent and kindness—a musician, a painter and a writer', commissioned a memorial plaque that was subsequently placed in the church (*Clairmont Correspondence*, 2.375, n. 6). He also presented to the church of St John the Baptist in Blackrock, co. Dublin, a copy by her of a Madonna after Murillo. Administration of the goods, chattels, and credit of 'Amelia Curran late of the City of Rome Spinster' was granted to her brother William Henry Curran, residing in the city of Dublin on 3 May 1848 (will).

ANNETTE PEACH

Sources D. F. Moore, 'John Philpot Curran and his family', *Dublin Historical Record*, 15/1 (1958–60), 50–61 · *The Clairmont correspondence: letters of Claire Clairmont, Charles Clairmont, and Fanny Imlay Godwin*, ed. M. K. Stocking, 2 vols. (1995) · J. Shelley, ed., *Shelley and Mary*, 4 vols. (privately printed, 1882) [journals and letters; annotated copy, Bodl. Oxf.] · *The journals of Mary Shelley*, ed. D. R. Feldman and D. Scott-Kilvert, 2 vols. (1987) · *The letters of Mary Wollstonecraft Shelley*, ed. B. T. Bennett, 3 vols. (1980–88) · *The journals of Claire Clairmont*, ed. M. K. Stocking and D. M. Stocking (1968) · N. I. White, *Shelley*, 2 vols. (1947) · K. N. Cameron and D. H. Reiman, eds., *Shelley and his circle, 1773–1822*, 5–6, ed. D. H. Reiman (1973) · E. Dowden, *The life of Percy Shelley*, 2 vols. (1886) · *The letters of Percy Bysshe Shelley*, ed. F. L. Jones, 2 vols. (1964) · will, PRO, PROB 6/224, fol. 38r · R. Walker, *National Portrait Gallery: Regency portraits*, 2 vols. (1985) · [W. Finden and E. Finden], *Finden's illustrations to the life and works of Byron*, 3 vols. (1833) · notes and photographs, NPG, Heinz Archive and Library · corresp. and notes, City of Nottingham Museums, Newstead Abbey collections · D. Piper, *The image of the poet* (1982), 162–3 · R. Holmes, *Shelley: the pursuit* (1974); repr. (1987) · P. B. Shelley, *The Cenci* (1819)

Wealth at death probably £20: will, PRO, PROB 6/224, fol. 38r

Curran, Sir Charles John (1921–1980), broadcasting administrator, was born in Dublin on 13 October 1921, the only son and eldest of the four children of Felix Curran, an army schoolmaster, and his wife, Alicia Isabella Bruce, from Aberdeen. Curran referred later to his 'Irish birth without an Irish upbringing', because after three weeks he left Dublin for Aberdeen, his mother's native home. He had no Scots upbringing either, since in 1924 his family moved to the West Riding of Yorkshire, where he studied at the local elementary school and at Wath-on-Dearne grammar school before entering Magdalene College, Cambridge, in 1939. He obtained a first class in part 1 of the history tripos in 1941.

Familiar with army ways, Curran served in the Indian army in India, Cyprus, and Italy from 1941 to 1945 before completing his degree in history in 1946 with a first class in part 2 and joining the British Broadcasting Corporation as a talks producer in 1947. In 1949 he married Silvia, daughter of John Meyer, restaurateur. They had one daughter. After only three years with the BBC Curran left the corporation and the country to become for one year assistant director (1950–51) of the Canadian commercial journal *Fishing News*. His father's mother had been born in Nova Scotia, and he himself retained an active interest in Canada. He had also shown a gift for learning languages,

Sir Charles John Curran (1921–1980), by Godfrey Argent, 1970

first in India, and when in August 1951 he returned to the BBC it was to join its monitoring service at Caversham as a report writer.

In September 1953 Curran became the BBC's first internally selected administrative trainee, visiting or working for a time in different departments of the BBC in and out of London and assisting in the preparation of the BBC's first personnel manual. His subsequent progress inside the corporation was rapid and distinctive—from the external services in Bush House to Canada again, this time as BBC representative from 1956 to 1959; back to Bush House as head of external broadcasting administration; on to Broadcasting House as the BBC's secretary (1963–6), a post of varying status and influence at different times in the history of the BBC, but during the regime of the director-general Sir Hugh Greene, who had personally selected Curran for the job, a key post drawing him into discussions of policy, often highly controversial policy, as well as of administration; back again to Bush House as director of external services (1967–9), which brought him into close touch with government; and on Greene's retirement becoming, to his considerable surprise, director-general himself in April 1969. He was knighted in 1974 and had honorary degrees from the City University (DLitt, 1977) and the Open University (DUniv, 1978).

In his autobiographical study, *The Seamless Robe*, Curran's only book, published in 1979, he made much of the complementarity and underlying unity of his experiences before 1969. The title (and contents) reflected even more strongly, however, his deep, but never flaunted, religious conviction. He was the first Roman Catholic director-general of the BBC, taking over at a difficult time, when the Ulster issue was posing serious dilemmas for broadcasters as well as for politicians. His religion did not prove a handicap, although his scrupulous conscience never made life easy for him, and his philosophy of broadcasting, set out neatly in thoughtful lectures, was very different from that of Greene or of Baron Hill of Luton, his first chairman. Curran, never immune from criticism, thought of himself as 'a broadcasting manager'. Yet he was not content with management. He insisted on quality of output, stressing its dependence not on committees but on individual producers operating in freedom.

Under Curran's regime the BBC survived intact as an institution, although the Annan committee on broadcasting, which reported in 1977, the year of Curran's departure from the BBC, revealed most of the stresses, financial as well as political and social, which Curran had experienced personally but had never been able to eliminate institutionally. He remained until 1978 president of the European Broadcasting Union, a post to which he had been elected in 1973 and which he greatly treasured. He was also from 1978 managing director of the television news agency Visnews. Curran died on 9 January 1980 at Barnet General Hospital following a heart attack.

ASA BRIGGS

Sources C. Curran, *The seamless robe* (1979) · private information (1993) · personal knowledge (2004) · *The Times* (10 Jan 1980) · *CGPLA Eng. & Wales* (1980)
Archives SOUND BL NSA, documentary recording
Likenesses G. Argent, photograph, 1970, NPG [*see illus.*] · photograph, Hult. Arch.
Wealth at death £169,116: probate, 6 March 1980, *CGPLA Eng. & Wales*

Curran, Joan Elizabeth, Lady Curran (1916–1999). *See under* Curran, Sir Samuel Crowe (1912–1998).

Curran, John Philpot (1750–1817), politician and lawyer, was born on 24 July 1750 at Newmarket, co. Cork, the first of five children of James Curran and Sarah Philpot (*c.*1727–1807). Though it was claimed by an early biographer that he rose to eminence 'from the humblest state of friendless obscurity' (Ryan, 1.298), his background was neither as lowly nor as unconnected as some have pronounced. Descended from a Cromwellian soldier named Curwen who came to Ireland from the north of England but who was not among the major beneficiaries of the land settlement effected at that time, his father James was sufficiently well educated to cite the classics in conversation, to debate the metaphysical doctrines of Locke, and to secure the position of steward to the manorial court at Newmarket. Because his income from this source and from farming, which he also pursued, was modest, Curran reputedly stated that 'the only inheritance that I could boast of from my poor father, was the very scanty one of an unattractive face and person like his own' (Curran, *Life*, 3). He was certainly closer to his mother. She was descended from 'respectable stock' and it was from her that he supposedly inherited his loquacity and 'native genius' (Ryan, 1.298).

Education His talents notwithstanding, Curran might not have received an opportunity to make something of them but for the intervention of Nathaniel Boyse, the rector at Newmarket, who taught him 'grammar and classical rudiments' (Ryan, 1.301). Boyse and Mrs Curran shared the expectation that Curran would enter the church, and with financial support from Elizabeth Aldworth, the wife of the local landowner, and Boyse, Curran was enrolled in Midleton Free School. It was there, under the direction of Dr Carey, that he received 'the first stimulus of effective

John Philpot Curran (1750–1817), by Hugh Douglas Hamilton, *c.*1798–9

advancement' (ibid.) and he repaid those who had placed their confidence in him by securing second place in the sizarship entrance examination which gained him admittance to Trinity College, Dublin, on 16 June 1767. Claims that Curran was not an attentive student are belied by the fact that he won a college scholarship in 1770. At the same time, he revelled in the freedom student life allowed him; Trinity was, he later confided, 'the scene of many boyish follies and many happy hours'. Curran's eagerness to sample the distractions offered by the city of Dublin and his cavalier attitude towards authority got him into several scrapes with college officers and others, but his willingness later to forgive 'even the fellows' (Curran, *Life*, 18), whom he actively disliked while an undergraduate, illustrates that it was not an unrewarding period in his life. His was, at the same time, not the conduct of one who aspired to religious orders and, concluding that the church was not for him, he determined, to his mother's regret, in his second year to opt instead for the law. Graduating from Trinity College with a BA in the summer of 1771, he made what he himself termed the 'transition from dependence to liberty' (ibid.) when he proceeded to London and to the Middle Temple in the summer of 1773.

Curran did not much enjoy his time in London. Lonely and impecunious, he determined 'to apply to reading' as 'the only means of making solitude supportable' and so he could 'attend the Courts … with more advantage'. He was 'for the first five months … almost totally a recluse'. Rising daily at 4.30 a.m., he spent ten hours a day reading—'seven at law, and three at history or the general principles of politics' (Curran, *Life*, 21, 25, 28). Aware that his success in the law depended on his ability as a public speaker, he sought to overcome the impediment that had led to his being denominated 'stuttering Jack Curran' at school, and that prompted friends to advise him to concentrate on becoming 'an eminent chamber counsel' because 'nature never intended you for an orator' (ibid., 29). He did not find it easy, but through regular attendance at the debating societies frequented by law students and continuous practice he acquired the necessary confidence. Curran honed his skills, thereby moderating his shrill timbre and provincial accent, by reading aloud, by debating propositions with himself, and by joining in the proceedings of the Robin Hood and other well-known debating societies where his readiness to advocate the cause of Catholic relief earned him the nickname 'the little Jesuit from St Omers'.

Marriage and early legal career Having satisfied the requirements of the Middle Temple, Curran returned to Ireland and, in 1774, married his sweetheart Sarah Creagh (c.1755–1844), whose father, Richard, a physician based at Newmarket, was a member of a respected Cork family. Curran and Richard Creagh shared the same whig patriot outlook, as Curran's poetry from this time testifies, but making a living took precedence over politics. Sarah Creagh's small portion kept the couple in funds for a time, but the birth of their first child, Amelia *Curran, in 1775 underlined the urgency of his securing remunerative employment. Curran contemplated seeking his fortune in America but, having determined to remain in Ireland, he sought a call to the Irish bar and was successful in Michaelmas term 1775. His legal career got off to an inauspicious start. Curran's first case was in the court of chancery, but he was so overcome by nervousness that he had to be rescued by his fellow counsel. Since he had had a similar experience when he first sought to debate while a law student at the Inner Temple, Curran had no reason to despair. His fee income for his first year's practice was a modest 82 guineas, but the rises registered during the late 1770s indicate steady if unspectacular progress. It was not enough to enable him and his growing family to live well, but as his income improved so too did their domestic circumstances and by 1782 he was sufficiently well off to take up residence in the more elegant surrounds of Ely Place. As this implies, by this date Curran had emerged as one of the most skilful advocates at the Irish bar. Like many barristers, then and since, he was helped by friends like Arthur Wolfe (afterwards Lord Kilwarden), who put the Sligo election case of *Ormsby* v. *Wynne* his way. But his rising reputation derived primarily from his ability as a pleader and his refusal to yield to the egregious and, occasionally, bullying conduct of senior judges. His celebrated exchange with Judge Christopher Robinson, who was well known for his authoritarian political as well as legal views, in which he turned the tables on the judge by citing his penchant for publishing his 'absurd' (Curran, *Life*, 70) sentiments anonymously, might have resulted in his being deprived of the right to practise had the judge pursued his threatened complaint. Instead, it enhanced his reputation, and his repute was increased further in 1780

when he successfully represented a Catholic priest in a case of assault brought against the protestant peer Lord Doneraile at Cork assizes. Curran's success in persuading the court to award his client 30 guineas in damages derived in no small part from the ingenious manner in which he discredited one of the defendant's main witnesses, and his triumph was augmented when he responded to the same witness's challenge to a duel by declining to return fire when the two men met. It was with good reason therefore that he was made a king's counsel in 1782.

Politics, 1779–1789 Curran's rising stature in the law was complemented by an emerging social and political profile. This is most clearly demonstrated by his membership of the celebrated patriotic and convivial society the Monks of the Order of St Patrick. Better known by its colloquial name, the Monks of the Screw, it was the brainchild of the barrister and patriot MP Barry Yelverton, with whom Curran had become friendly in the mid-1770s. Curran was a founder member with sundry other lawyers and politicians in 1779, and he was sufficiently well thought of by them to become an officer of the society. It is not clear precisely what form their gatherings took, but they provided Curran with an excellent opportunity to rub shoulders with and to get to know some of the most influential patriot politicians and rising barristers of the moment. His involvement also suggests that Curran was disposed to favour the assertive patriot line currently being advanced by Henry Grattan, Denis Daly, John Forbes, and Edward Newenham who were also members of the society.

Curran's own political ambitions at this time are difficult to establish. It can reasonably be assumed that he was as eager as most members of the Monks that legislative independence should be achieved but he did not participate in the campaign to bring it about. Politics was a career that only the wealthy could easily sustain and he did not have the disposable income. Like Grattan and Yelverton, he needed a patron, and he appeared to have found one when the wealthy Cork landowner Richard Longfield offered in 1783 to purchase a seat for him in the Irish parliament for the borough of Kilbeggan. Longfield's expectation was that Curran would prove a valuable member of the parliamentary interest he sought to establish, and he lobbied Dublin Castle for 'high preferment in the law' (Johnston, 'Members', 178) for him, but Curran was temperamentally unsuited to taking direction from others. The problem was that whereas Longfield's object was self-advancement, Curran's was to advance popular reforms. This did not pose a serious difficulty so long as Longfield deemed it in his political interest to take the popular reformist line on fiscal and political issues favoured by Curran, who made his first significant political speech in support of Henry Flood's motion for parliamentary reform on 29 November 1783. Not surprisingly, given the general hostility to the idea, Curran's advice to the house 'not to make a public declaration' (*Speeches*, 38) critical of the volunteer convention out of which the Reform Bill had arisen was ignored by those present. More consequently, the general assessment by the end of the session was that he 'had not yet made much progress' (Johnston, 'Members', 178). This may explain the reluctance of the Irish administration to respond positively to Longfield's request for legal preferment for him, but of equal relevance was his disposition to take the popular line on issues. Inevitably, given their contrasting outlooks and aspirations, the relationship between Longfield and Curran was not destined to endure, and, while the precise circumstances remain unclear, Curran bought himself the freedom of action he desired by paying Longfield £1500 (£1000 of which was borrowed) to release him from his parliamentary connection.

Once he had extricated himself from his relationship with Longfield, Curran was free to pursue the independent patriot line he desired. As he had demonstrated in 1783, he was largely content during the mid-1780s to take the lead from Henry Flood. So he joined with Laurence Parsons and William Brownlow on the commencement of the 1785 session in supporting a motion proposed by Flood on 14 February advocating fiscal retrenchment. More dramatically, his defence of the volunteers against official criticism on the same day set him on a collision course with John Fitzgibbon, the attorney-general, and the die was cast for a relationship that was to be characterized by strong mutual animus ten days later when the Commons came to discuss the controversial issue of the use of attachments by the courts, a form of criminal proceeding that precluded resort to jury trial. To patriots like Curran, the application by the attorney-general to the court of king's bench for the attachment of the sheriff of Dublin in 1784 (*R. v. Reily*), because he had convened a meeting of freeholders to nominate representatives to a congressional assembly on parliamentary reform, was 'subversive of the trial by jury and … of liberty'. Fitzgibbon disagreed so violently with this analysis that he dismissed Curran as a 'puny babbler'. This was ground enough for a challenge though, contrary to what has been claimed by several of Curran's biographers, no duel ensued. The outcome was different six months later when Curran and Fitzgibbon clashed once more. The occasion was the crucial debate on William Pitt's plan to bind the kingdoms of Great Britain and Ireland in a commercial union. Like most patriots, Curran only slowly reached the conclusion that the proposed 'commercial arrangement' involved the 'surrender of that constitution which has been established by the virtue of the nation' in 1782 (*Speeches*, 50), but having arrived at this determination he made some of the strongest speeches against it. His assertion on 12 August that if approved it must lead 'to a schism between the two nations that must terminate in a civil war, or in a union at best' (ibid., 54) was rhetorically effective; it was also logically problematic, and it clearly rankled the attorney-general who strongly favoured the measure. Surviving accounts of the exchange are incomplete, but it is clear that the two men had a heated verbal exchange in the course of which the irascible Fitzgibbon asserted that 'Curran was no lawyer and that the monstrous nonsense that came from him was fit only for Sadler's Wells' (Kelly,

Duelling, 138). A duel ensued in which neither party was injured, but the deliberation with which Fitzgibbon took aim after Curran had fired first and missed bore ample witness to the fact that the antipathy the two men bore each other was as much personal as it was political.

Curran's preparedness on 15 August 1785 to support Henry Flood's motion calling on MPs 'not to enter into any engagement to give up the sole and exclusive right of the parliament of Ireland to legislate for Ireland' (*Speeches*, 54) was the last occasion when he took his lead from Flood in the House of Commons as the latter concentrated on Westminster politics thereafter. The absence of Flood combined with Henry Grattan's reluctance to sunder his links with the castle meant there was space on the opposition benches for a leading spokesman who was prepared to take on the administration. Curran's particular 'currancy [*sic*] of eloquence, … keen and malignant' (Agnew, 307) gave him a natural advantage over those with a less coruscating turn of phrase and less skilled in *ad hominem* argument, but his legal career took precedence. As a result, he made relatively few speeches in the Commons in the late 1780s compared with other prominent opposition figures. His sentiments on the occasions that he did venture forward, on the Portugal trade and on pensions on 11 and 13 March 1786 for instance, were ostentatiously learned and aggressively liberal, but he seldom took up and ran with an issue. Even during the 1787 session when he was more than usually active, his spirited stand against coercion when the Commons debated how it should respond to the campaign against tithes orchestrated by the Rightboy agrarian movement was essentially reactive. He had by then reached the point in his political career when he was not quite living up to expectations. He possessed, as his speeches amply demonstrate, an enviable capacity to reach for 'luminous phrases, poetical allusions and the liveliest turns of fancy'; he could be witty, logical, and convincing, 'shrewd, sarcastic and severe' when necessary; and he was 'unrivalled' in the facility with which he could resort to 'satire' to embarrass his opponents and to advance his arguments (Scott, 19–20). Yet, as William Drennan's description of him, during a particularly eventful trial, as 'the fiercest imp of the pandemonium' (Agnew, 307) suggests, his parliamentary reputation derived from his ability as a critic rather than as a promoter of policy or legislation. This reflected the fact that he was a defence counsel first and a politician second. Significantly, he was earning enough from the law by the late 1780s to be able to travel and to purchase a suitable residence for himself and his eight surviving children. He visited France in 1787 and Holland in 1788, and in 1790 purchased Holly Park, a house on 35 acres, at Rathfarnham, near Dublin, which he renamed The Priory and which was his main residence for the rest of his life.

Radical politician, 1789–1797 The years 1789–90 represent something of a turning point in Curran's life as a politician and advocate, as he allied himself more closely with those interests that sought to reform and reshape Irish politics. The first hint of this was provided during the regency crisis when Curran played a prominent part in the attempt by a combination of Irish whigs and patriots to offer George, prince of Wales, an unlimited regency as a result of the incapacity of George III. The king's recovery ensured this came to naught, but the episode brought Curran significantly closer to Henry Grattan, John Forbes, and other leading Irish whigs and patriots, and he threw in his lot with them on the foundation of the Irish Whig Club in 1789. This gave the parliamentary opposition greater coherence and resulted in Curran's playing a more active role in the House of Commons. As in the 1780s, his contributions were mainly supportive; in 1789 and 1790 he was to be heard endorsing proposals to disfranchise excise officers, criticizing the manner in which Dublin Castle distributed positions in the controversial Dublin police, and supporting John Forbes's motion for a place bill and Henry Grattan's request for an inquiry into the sale of peerages. Curran's rhetoric on these occasions was frequently polemical and sarcastic. But it was his pungent condemnation on 4 February 1790 of 'the sluices of corruption' (*Speeches*, 98), his claim that 'in this administration a place may be found for every bad man', and his condemnation of the venal manner in which stamp officers were appointed that prompted the most threatening response. Infuriated by Curran's remarks, which he deemed personally slighting, the conservative controversialist John Giffard, who was in the pay of Dublin Castle, shook his stick at Curran 'in a manner which ... was too plain to be misunderstood' (Curran, *Life*, 151) when the two men encountered each other on the street. Unwilling to let the insult pass and thereby expose every gentleman 'to personal violence from the ruffians of your administration' (ibid.), Curran demanded of the chief secretary Robert Hobart that he dismiss Giffard, and, when he refused, challenged him to a duel. Nobody was injured in the encounter that followed, but the episode reflected badly on Curran who had set a useful precedent the previous year when he had inaugurated the prosecution of a witness who had challenged him following an aspersive cross-examination.

Curran's assertive behaviour during his dispute with Hobart arose out of his conviction that the 'liberty' of the subject was under serious threat as a result of government corruption. This impression was reinforced by his positive perception of events in France where, he informed MPs on 4 February 1790, 'twenty-four millions of people ... have burst their chains, and, on the altar erected by despotism to public slavery, they have enthroned the image of public liberty' (*Speeches*, 99). Enthused by this, he renewed his attack on 'corruption' on 12 February 1791 with the argument that it must 'ultimately effect the destruction of ... society' if not 'punished and prevented' (ibid., 132). However, his request for parliamentary approval for an investigation into the 'corrupt' manner that patronage and preferment were dispensed was denied. Now regarded in castle circles as 'virulent in opposition' (Johnston, 'Commons', 24), Curran consolidated his emerging reputation

as one of the few truly radical voices in the House of Commons by vigorously advocating the cause of Catholic relief over that of 'Protestant ascendancy' in February 1792 on the grounds that 'an increase of the democratic power can scarcely ever be dangerous' (*Speeches*, 142). Eleven months later, at the beginning of the 1793 session, he pronounced 'strongly in favour of ... the most unlimited admission [of Catholics] to the constitution' (Minto MSS, MS 12927, fol. 47) and he underlined his commitment to radical constitutional reform by warning MPs on 8 February that 'a fair representation of the landed and commercial property of the nation ought to be accomplished ... within this session' or else 'we shall become odious and contemptible to the nation, and they will look to themselves' (*Speeches*, 152–3). Curran's stance on the question of Catholic emancipation and on the only slightly less contentious subject of war with France was palpably more radical than that taken by mainstream whigs like Henry Grattan and George Ponsonby. However, unlike Lawrence Parsons with whom he co-operated on occasions, he was unwilling 'to separate or even differ' (Rosse MSS, F/19) with them in the House of Commons. One consequence of this was that during the 1794 session, he joined with Grattan and other moderate whigs in urging, with 'much fancy and elegant diction', motions and causes that the less tolerant Parsons dismissed as 'trash' (ibid.).

Given the weakness of the opposition as a result of defection and absenteeism, this was not an inappropriate strategy, and it appeared it might prove personally advantageous to Curran when it emerged in autumn 1794 that Earl Fitzwilliam was to become lord lieutenant of Ireland. Unlike Grattan and George Ponsonby, Curran was not party to the behind the scenes discussions that formed the backdrop to Fitzwilliam's brief term in Ireland, but he sat with them on the Treasury benches when parliament opened on 22 January 1795. Given that Fitzwilliam was known to favour Catholic emancipation and that his name was mentioned in connection with the solicitor-generalship, Curran had good reason to be there. However, before his appointment could be advanced Fitzwilliam was recalled, and Curran was thrust into opposition once more. He made a lengthy speech on 15 May 1795 in support of his call for an address to the crown that drew attention to abuses in fiscal administration, to the failure to relieve Catholics, and to the 'notorious traffic in honours' in the hope that steps would be taken 'in order to allay the fever of the public mind' (*Speeches*, 240, 242). His request was denied, but unwilling to admit defeat he joined with Grattan, Ponsonby, and a handful of others in 1796 in a futile rearguard stand against the increasingly coercive response of the conservative majority in parliament to the revolutionary unrest gripping the country. Curran was more active in 1796 than he had been for several years in the supporting role he clearly found congenial, but neither his condemnation of the Insurrection Bill in February as a 'law for the rich ... against the poor', nor his strong endorsement on 13 October of Grattan's motion to extend 'the blessings and privileges of the constitution' to all 'without any distinction of religion' was heeded (ibid., 248, 249). He continued to articulate a liberal, reformist viewpoint in the face of proposals to suspend *habeas corpus*, and the reality of the military disarming of Ulster, but his criticism of the draconian security policy being pursued fell on deaf ears. He was convinced that policies committed to the 'union' of the people would prove more efficacious, but having made this point on 15 May 1797 in support of George Ponsonby's motion calling for parliamentary reform and Catholic emancipation he withdrew in protest, with the handful of whigs still active in the House of Commons, and did not seek re-election in the general election held that year.

Radical lawyer Parallel with his efforts in the 1790s to promote a political agenda that was at once reforming and inclusive, Curran expanded and enhanced his reputation as a defence attorney by acting in a series of high-profile court cases. These may be said to have begun in 1790 when he was retained to represent the common council of Dublin corporation in their lengthy dispute with the aldermen arising out of their refusal to accept a placeman nominated by the aldermen as lord mayor of the city. Because differences of this nature came within the jurisdiction of the privy council, which was chaired when such matters were at issue by the lord chancellor, Curran found himself pleading before John Fitzgibbon who had been elevated to that eminent position in 1789 and whose antipathy effectively put an end to his lucrative chancery practice. Influenced by this and by the realization that precedent was on the side of William James, the nominee of the aldermen, Curran controversially chose not to argue the case on a point of law but to arraign the tenor of government in general and Fitzgibbon personally as 'a mean, *illiberal* and unprincipled minion of authority' (Kavanaugh, 226) when the matter came before the privy council for a third time in June 1790. Predictably, the verdict handed down was not to Curran's liking, but the judgement of liberal activists was kinder for when the authorities moved against the Dublin Society of United Irishmen, Curran was their counsel of choice. His first client was Hamilton Rowan whose trial for inciting the public to take up arms 'to overturn the established constitution' (*Speeches*, 160) took place on 29 January 1794. Curran was unable to secure Rowan's acquittal but his nuanced deconstruction of the charge against him was a masterpiece of forensic pleading as well as contextual extenuation for which he was rightly applauded. As a result, Curran was soon in heavy demand, and his success in securing the acquittal of seven defenders at Drogheda in April 1794 on the charge of 'raising … insurrection' (ibid., 191), of the proprietor of the *Northern Star* on a charge of libel in May, and of William Drennan in June on the charge of seditious libel, confirmed that he was the leading counsel in political cases then practising at the Irish bar. He was unable to prevent the handing down of a capital sentence when the Revd William Jackson was tried for treason in April 1795, but it was not for want of effort and his cross-examination of the chief prosecution witness John Cockayne was widely regarded as masterly. Other celebrated cases followed over the following years. The most notable was that of William Orr, the young Presbyterian farmer, who was tried and found guilty in the autumn of 1797 of administering the oath of the United Irishmen to a soldier; but he also defended Peter Finnerty, the publisher of the radical newspaper *The Press*, in December 1797 for a libel arising out of the Orr trial, and Patrick Finney for high treason in January 1798.

Inevitably, given his record, Curran was the main counsel of the leaders of the rising of 1798 when they were brought for trial from July 1798. The first to be tried were the Sheares brothers, but Curran's eloquent defence was insufficient to prevent a capital verdict. Similar judgments followed in other cases, yet, despite these verdicts and the hostile atmosphere in which the trials were conducted, Curran displayed considerable courage and great resolve. He pleaded at the bar of the house against the act of attainder of Lord Edward Fitzgerald on 20 August and before the court of king's bench on 12 November against the conviction of Wolfe Tone by a military court, though in neither instance did his justified interventions produce the outcome he desired. Despite this, it was widely assumed within the loyalist community that Curran's representation of suspected rebels could only be explained by his membership of the United Irishmen. This was not so. It may be that he 'knew everything that was going on, and [that] his whole heart was in the cause' (Madden, 3.241) as W. J. McNeven claimed later, and that he merely tactfully 'avoided committing himself to the councils of the United Irishmen' (Tone, 879), as Tone opined, but both are to be believed when they state that he was never a member of that organization. At the same time, Tone's admission that 'had the project of liberating Ireland succeeded, he would have been amongst the foremost to hail and join her independence' (ibid.) suggests that his sympathies were with the United Irish leadership from the mid-1790s.

Later career Following the rising of 1798, Curran re-entered the Irish House of Commons in May 1800 for the constituency of Banagher with the intention of opposing the proposed Act of Union, but it was already too late. One does not have to agree with the judgement of his friend Valentine Lawless that 'the sun of Curran's career set with the Act of Union' (Cloncurry, 143) to accept that the final seventeen years of his life were an anticlimax to what had gone before. He continued to practise law, and he was retained in some of the most celebrated cases of the early years of the new century. This involved his prosecuting Sir Henry Brown Hayes for abduction in 1801, the infamous Dublin town-major John Sirr for assault and false imprisonment in 1802, the marquess of Headfort for criminal conversation in 1804, and defending Owen Kirwan against a charge of treason in 1803 and Judge Robert Johnson against libel in 1805. However, domestic difficulties conspired to cast an increasing shadow over his professional life. Curran's troubled domestic life had first come to the public's notice in 1795 when he had instituted proceedings against the Revd Abraham Sandys for criminal conversation with his wife. He was awarded damages, but their modest size indicated that as far as the jury was concerned he had to accept some of the blame for his wife's infidelity. Potentially more serious was his daughter Sarah's involvement with Robert Emmet since this resulted in his house being searched in July 1803 and, following the discovery of some of Emmet's letters to Sarah, in Curran being brought before the Irish privy council. He had nothing to fear, but the whole episode was more than merely embarrassing. It contributed to the erosion of his liberal sympathies, and ensured that when the Fox–Grenville administration was formed in 1806 it was unwilling to deliver on the compact Curran and George Ponsonby had entered into in 1795 that in the event of Ponsonby's becoming lord chancellor Curran would become attorney-general. He was offered the mastership of the rolls instead, but the matter was so badly handled that Curran only accepted it 'at the urgent insistence of his family' (Cloncurry, 144). He was made an Irish privy councillor at the same time.

Curran was never at ease in his new situation. He was not at home on the judicial bench, and he was not comfortable either with the conservative-minded politicians in charge in Ireland. It was not surprising therefore that he accepted the invitation of the electors of Newry to stand for that constituency for the Westminster parliament in 1812. He was soundly defeated, and two years later he signalled his withdrawal from public life when he resigned the rolls for an annual pension of £2700. He did some travelling thereafter, but both his faculties and his physical health were in decline, and following a fit of apoplexy he died on 14 October 1817 at his London residence, 8 Amelia Place, Brompton, and was buried on 4 November at Paddington cemetery.

In a letter to his friend Leonard McNally written in 1810, Curran confessed that he wished 'for posthumous reputation' (Fitzpatrick, 203). His efforts on behalf of newspaper proprietors facing government prosecution helped secure him an enduring reputation as a champion of press freedom. The judgement of the *Annual Register* that 'as a lawyer he was not particularly distinguished by the depth of his knowledge, or the depth of his researches, but there was scarcely any on the Irish bench who equalled him in addressing a jury' (*Annual Register*, 1817, 148) was not uncomplimentary, but it was equivocal compared with the generous assessment of Wolfe Tone that his 'legal exertions' represented 'an imperishable monument to his own and to his country's fame' (Tone, 879). The latter, indeed, was the assessment that found greatest favour in nineteenth- and early twentieth-century Ireland when a steady flow of memoirs, biographies, recollections, and editions of his speeches served to ensure that the prevailing image of his life and deeds was overwhelmingly positive. This was emphasized in 1835 when a Dublin committee oversaw the transfer of his body from London for placement in 1837 beneath an imposing Irish granite sarcophagus modelled on that of Scipio Barbatus in Rome in the recently opened Catholic cemetery at Glasnevin. It was not an inappropriate final resting place for a man who throughout his life had advocated Catholic relief, but it

symbolized at the same time that the memory of John Philpot Curran that endured was that of counsel to the United Irishmen rather than that of liberal politician.

JAMES KELLY

Sources W. H. Curran, *The life of the right honourable John Philpot Curran* (1882) [with additions and notes by R. S. Mackenzie] · *The speeches of the right honourable John Philpot Curran*, ed. T. Davis, 2nd edn (1855) · R. Ryan, *Biographica Hibernica: a biographical dictionary of the worthies of Ireland* (1819–21) · C. Phillips, *Recollections of Curran and some of his contemporaries*, 2nd edn (1822) · W. O'Regan, *Memoirs of the legal, literary and political life of … John Philpot Curran* (1817) · W. J. Fitzpatrick, *Secret service under Pitt* (1892) · L. Hale, *John Philpot Curran: his life and times* (1958) · [J. Scott], *A review of the principal characters of the Irish House of Commons* (1789) · E. M. Johnston, 'Members of the Irish parliament, 1784–7', *Proceedings of the Royal Irish Academy*, 71C (1971), 139–246 · E. M. Johnston, 'The state of the Irish House of Commons in 1791', *Proceedings of the Royal Irish Academy*, 59C (1957–9), 1–56 · D. F. Moore, 'John Philpot Curran and his family', *Dublin Historical Record*, 15/1 (1958–60), 50–61 · *The Drennan-McTier letters*, ed. J. Agnew, 1 (1998) · V. B. L. Cloncurry, *Personal recollections of the life and times: with extracts from the correspondence of Valentine, Lord Cloncurry* (1849) · R. R. Madden, *The United Irishmen: their lives and times*, 2nd edn, 4 vols. (1857–60) · W. T. W. Tone, *Life of Theobald Wolfe Tone*, ed. T. Bartlett (1998) · J. Kelly, *That damn'd thing called honour: duelling in Ireland, 1570–1860* (1995) · J. Kelly, *Henry Flood: patriots and politics in eighteenth-century Ireland* (1998) · NL Scot., Minto MS 12927 · Birr Castle, Birr, Offaly, Rosse MSS · A. C. Kavanaugh, *John Fitzgibbon, earl of Clare* (1997) · M. Elliott, *Wolfe Tone: prophet of Irish independence* (1989) · F. E. Ball, *The judges in Ireland, 1221–1921*, 2 vols. (1926)

Archives Royal Irish Acad., fee book

Likenesses H. D. Hamilton, oils, *c.*1798–1799, NG Ire. [*see illus.*] · T. Lawrence, oils, exh. RA 1800, NG Ire. · J. R. Smith, mezzotint, pubd 1801 (after oil painting by T. Lawrence, 1799–1800), NG Ire. · oils, 1807, NPG · J. Heath, stipple, 1809 (after J. Comerford), BM, NPG; repro. in J. Barrington, *Historic memoirs* (1809) · attrib. H. D. Hamilton, oils, *c.*1810, King's Inns Library, Dublin · F. Chantrey, bust, *c.*1812, AM Oxf. · S. Freeman, engraving, 1815 (after oil painting attrib. H. D. Hamilton) · plaster death mask, *c.*1817, NG Ire. · T. Wageman, stipple, pubd 1818 (after J. Saxon), BM · H. H. Meyer, stipple, pubd 1819 (after oil painting by T. Lawrence, 1799–1800), NG Ire. · J. Doyle, lithograph, pubd 1830 (after his portrait), NG Ire. · E. McInnes, mezzotint, pubd 1842 (after T. Lawrence), BM, NPG · S. Freeman, stipple, BM; repro. in *British gallery of contemporary portraits* (1815) · S. Freeman, stipple (after unknown portrait), NG Ire.; repro. in T. Cadell and W. Davies, *British gallery of contemporary portraits*, 2 vols. (1822) · S. Freeman, stipple (after oil painting by T. Lawrence, 1799–1800), NG Ire. · H. H. Houston, stipple (after H. Hopson), NG Ire.; repro. in *Universal Magazine* (1791) · C. E. Wagstaff, stipple (after oil painting by T. Lawrence, 1799–1800), NG Ire.; repro. in W. Jordan, *National portrait gallery of illustrious and eminent personages*, 5 vols. (1830–34) · oils (in youth), King's Inns Library, Dublin · print (after unknown portrait), NG Ire. · two oil paintings, NG Ire.

Wealth at death £10,000–£12,000 in Irish funds; plus freehold house and lands at Rathfarnham, co. Dublin; also unknown sum in US funds: will, 19 Sept 1816, O'Regan, *Memoirs*, 300–01

Curran [*née* Barry], **Marian** [*known as* Mrs Pete Curran] (*fl.* 1890–1910), trade unionist and tailoress, was of Irish extraction but nothing is known of her early life. By the 1890s she was living in London at 12 Charles Square, Hoxton. She married Peter Francis (Pete) *Curran (1860–1910), leader of the Gasworkers' Union, who was also of Irish extraction but born in Glasgow. Her husband successfully stood as Labour Party parliamentary candidate for Jarrow (1907), and served as its MP until 1910. They had two daughters and two sons, and were living at Walthamstow by 1910.

Marian Barry worked to give voice to the low-paid, casual 'sweated' worker, starting her career in the labour movement (1895) by representing the east London tailoresses, a body which later affiliated to the Women's Trade Union League. She became assistant secretary to the league (1896); her first meeting was at a Gloucester vinegar and pickle factory where she formed a union of two hundred girls. In May 1896 Marian Barry spoke at a meeting of laundresses, held under the auspices of the Gasworkers' Union, where she possibly met her future husband; that year she attended the Trades Union Congress as a league observer. Her work for the league included a punishing schedule of meetings. Nominated by the London Trades Council, she was elected to the technical education board of the London county council (1897). From 1898 until 1905 Marian Barry was less politically active; when she then attended the funeral of league president Emilia, Lady Dilke, it was as Mrs Pete Curran, the name she always used thereafter. As league organizer (1906) she continued her meetings in Britain and Ireland and helped in the *Daily News* Sweated Industries exhibition.

This organizing work continued during Pete Curran's election campaign, when, with other Labour women, Marian Curran founded the Jarrow branch of the Women's Labour League, calling the Labour Party 'the men's party'. She apologized in her report to the Women's Trade Union League (October 1907) that: 'owing to the suddenness with which we were thrown into the by-election at Jarrow, I was unable to send in my notes for the last quarter' (*Women's Trade Union Review*, October 1907, 35). It is possible that the couple faced some financial hardship as MPs were then unpaid.

The campaign for school meals, organized at local level by the Women's Labour League, was one of Marian Curran's concerns, on which she lobbied Jarrow local authority; she also formed part of the organizing committee for the Women's Labour Day exhibition (1909). Pete Curran made sweated work the focus of some of his parliamentary questions and was also a supporter of women's suffrage. Marian Curran was elected in 1908 to the Women's Labour League executive committee, which stood in silent respect on the death of her husband, shortly after his defeat in the January 1910 election. Thereafter, she confined her trade union organizing to occasional support for new staff, but was active on Hackney labour exchange.

In the other great movement of her time, the women's suffrage campaign, there is little evidence of Marian Curran's activity. This is probably due more to the paucity of the record than to her disengagement from the struggle for women's enfranchisement. 'Woman Suffrage' was listed among the aims of the Jarrow Women's Labour League and the Women's Labour League executive moved definitely, if slowly, behind the campaign. Marian Curran spent her energy organizing working women, industrially and in local politics. In common with other Women's Labour League members, she worked to proclaim the rights of women and saw the burgeoning labour movement as a means for their fulfilment.

Although an important figure in the group of women working with female labour in London at the beginning of the twentieth century, Marian Curran had a much lower profile than others, such as Margaret Macdonald. The reports of the Women's Trade Union League curiously did not herald her entry into organizing work in the same laudatory tones used, for instance, of Mrs Marland Brodie, who worked over much the same period, and were also silent on her activities after Pete Curran's death. This neglect may have been caused by her personality or, more probably, her class, as Marian's background as a tailoress differed from that of the middle-class, educated women who were prominent in socialist politics. The date of her death is not known.

CHRISTINE COLLETTE

Sources Women's Labour League secretarial correspondence and related papers, People's History Museum, Manchester · Women's Labour League, report of Jarrow branch, 5 July 1907, National Museum of Labour, Manchester, WLL/64 · *Annual Reports* [Women's Trade Union League] (1899–1910) · G. Tuckwell, ed., *Women's Trade Union Review* (1896–1910) · Trades Union Congress Library, London, Gertrude Tuckwell collection, 1890–1920 [microfilm] · 'Infancy of the Labour party', BLPES, coll. misc. 0196 · Ruskin College, Oxford, Pete Curran by-election MSS · Ruskin College, Oxford, James Middleton and Lucy Middleton MSS · C. Collette, *For labour and for women: the Women's Labour League, 1906–1918* (1989) · B. Nield, 'Curran, Peter (Pete) Francis', *DLB*, vol. 4 · d. cert. [Peter Curran]

Archives BLPES, Margaret MacDonald MSS, infancy of the labour party · People's History Museum, Manchester, Women's Labour League secretarial corresp. and related papers · Ruskin College, Oxford, Pete Curran by-election MSS · Ruskin College, Oxford, James Middleton and Lucy Middleton MSS · Trades Union Congress Library, London, Gertrude Tuckwell collection

Curran, Peter Francis [*formerly* Patrick Francis] (1860–1910), trade unionist and politician, was born in Glasgow on 28 March 1860, the son of George Curran, a causey layer, and his wife, Bridget, *née* McGinty. He was named Patrick by his parents who were Irish Catholics, but became known as Pete. After a national school education, he began work in the blacksmith's shop of a steelworks. He assisted the hammer-driver, later rising to that job himself. He was initially active in the Irish Land League, but, influenced by the ideas of Henry George, joined the Scottish Land Restoration League. Not long after he again shifted his allegiances, becoming a member of the Social Democratic Federation. In 1881 he married Mary, daughter of Peter McIntyre, an egg dealer.

In the late 1880s Curran left Glasgow for London where he found work at the Royal Arsenal, Woolwich. He soon began to appear on socialist platforms and took a full part in the upsurge of the 'new unionism' of 1889, so much so that, having worked with Will Thorne and others to establish the National Union of Gasworkers and General Labourers, by September 1889 he had become a full-time official, the secretary of the union's west of England district. There he gained some notoriety when with two other union leaders he was convicted of intimidation at Plymouth and ordered to pay a fine. The case, *Curran v. Treleaven*, became a landmark when in 1891 it reached the

Peter Francis Curran (1860–1910), by A. Weston

Court of Appeal and the earlier verdict was overturned. In 1891 Curran returned to London as the national organizer of the gasworkers. At about this time, he joined the Fabian Society in which he took an active part until 1900 when he resigned because of the society's failure to denounce the Second South African War. At meetings of the Trades Union Congress he was associated with the younger socialist delegates who called for a collectivist programme and greater political action. In 1893 he supported James Macdonald in a successful amendment requiring the parliamentary committee of the TUC to give financial aid to candidates accepting the principle of collective ownership; and at the 1894 TUC he was among the delegates who secured the replacement of Charles Fenwick (described by Curran as a round peg in a square hole) as secretary of the parliamentary committee.

By the early 1890s Curran was politically close to those socialists involved in the creation of the Independent Labour Party (ILP). In 1893 he attended the founding conference of the ILP and sat on its national administrative council until 1898. At the general election of 1895 he was the ILP candidate at Barrow, where he was a poor third in the poll. In the autumn of 1897 he again represented the ILP, at a by-election in the Barnsley constituency notable for the way in which the leaders of the Yorkshire Miners' Association, particularly Ben Pickard, supported the Liberal candidate and denounced the socialists. Curran was again at the bottom of the poll, his campaign not helped by rumours that he had deserted his wife. Whatever the truth of these, in 1897 or 1898 he married his second wife, Marian Barry. He took a leading role in the General Federation of Trade Unions, which formally came into being in 1899, and became its chairman, a post he held until his death.

Curran worked with Keir Hardie and Ramsay MacDonald in preparing the ground for what was to be the inaugural conference of the Labour Representation Committee (LRC) in February 1900. At the conference he spoke in favour of an independent party of labour and was elected to the executive committee of the LRC. Three years later he moved the resolution requiring officials and organizations affiliated to the LRC strictly to abstain from identifying themselves with or promoting the interests of any section of the Liberal or Conservative parties. For three or four years before the general election of 1906 he nursed the Jarrow constituency, but he was defeated in a straight fight with the Liberal candidate, Sir Charles Palmer. The death of Palmer caused a by-election in July 1907 when Curran again contested the seat, along with Liberal, Conservative, and Irish nationalist candidates. Though accused of playing down his socialism, Curran was able to gain Jarrow for Labour. He had taken an active part in the 'right to work' agitation of the National Unemployed Committee, which was formed in 1903, and made the question of unemployment one in which he specialized in the House of Commons. As well as a 'right to work' bill and the eight-hour day, he advocated a system of state insurance.

All who knew Curran acknowledged the genial and convivial side of his personality. In February 1909 he suffered the embarrassment of an appearance in court, where he was fined 10s. for being drunk and incapable in the street. By the general election of January 1910 his health was ruined, a factor which probably contributed to his narrow defeat, by sixty-seven votes, at Jarrow. On 14 February 1910 he died at his home, 1 Pretoria Avenue, Walthamstow; the principal cause of death was certified as cirrhosis of the liver. He was survived by his wife, Marian *Curran, also a trade unionist, and by his two sons and two daughters.

Pete Curran's funeral took place on the afternoon of Saturday 19 February 1910 and was made the occasion of a great demonstration of mourning. According to *The Times* report (21 February 1910), thousands followed the hearse to Leytonstone Roman Catholic cemetery, a journey of 2 miles through 'thick lines of sympathising spectators'. The procession was led by the Stepney gasworkers' brass band and as well as his widow and four children the mourners included several Labour MPs and trade union officials. One of those present, Ben Tillett, writing in *Justice* (26 February 1910) described Curran as a man of 'courage, mingled with ambition, and some egotism; virile and eager with an Irishman's rollicking humour and optimism and notable for the sturdy frame, the square determined jaw, the small alert eyes of the man of action'.

D. E. MARTIN

Sources H. Pelling, 'Two by-elections: Jarrow and Colne Valley, 1907', in H. Pelling, *Popular politics and society in late Victorian Britain* (1979) · D. Rubinstein, 'The independent labour party and the Yorkshire miners: the Barnsley by-election of 1897', *International Review of Social History*, 23 (1978), 102–34 · W. Thorne, *My life's battles* (1925) · H. A. Clegg, A. Fox, and A. F. Thompson, *A history of British trade unions since 1889*, 1 (1964) · B. C. Roberts, *The Trades Union Congress, 1868–1921* (1958) · F. Bealey and H. Pelling, *Labour and politics, 1900–1906: a history of the Labour Representation Committee* (1958) · L. Barrow and I. Bullock, *Democratic ideas and the British labour movement, 1880–1914* (1996) · *The Times* (16 Feb 1910) · *The Times* (21 Feb 1910) · *Justice* (26 Feb 1910) · *Labour Leader* (4 March 1910) · DLB · WWBMP, vol. 1 · CGPLA Eng. & Wales (1910) · m. cert. · d. cert.

Archives JRL, Labour History Archive and Study Centre, papers · Ruskin College, Oxford, by-election papers | BLPES, corresp. with the independent labour party
Likenesses photograph, 1893, repro. in H. Pelling, *The origins of the Labour Party, 1880–1900* (1965), facing p. 176 · A. Weston, photograph, People's History Museum, Manchester [*see illus.*] · photograph, repro. in *Labour Annual* (1898), 102 · photograph, repro. in Rubinstein, 'The independent labour party and the Yorkshire miners', 125
Wealth at death £119: administration with will, 23 March 1910, *CGPLA Eng. & Wales*

Curran, Sir Samuel Crowe [Sam] (1912–1998), physicist and university administrator, was born in Ballymena, co. Antrim, on 23 May 1912, the second of four sons of John Curran (1885–1959), a steelworks foreman, and his wife, Sarah Owens, *née* Crowe (1886–1968). His mother had gone to her ancestral home a few weeks before his birth so that he could be born in Northern Ireland. Soon afterwards she returned with him to her husband and family in Wishaw, Lanarkshire, where Sam spent the remainder of his childhood and youth. He was essentially, in both speech and outlook, a west of Scotland man.

In 1929, after attending Wishaw high school, Curran entered Glasgow University, where he gained first class honours in mathematics and natural philosophy. He joined the physics department as a PhD research student in 1934, proposing to work on the diffraction of beta rays of radium. He found that he had to modify and reconstruct Geiger counters which had long lain idle, and he showed how versatile Geiger counters were when associated with a good pulse amplifier. It was in this field that he later made a major impact. After completing his Glasgow thesis, 'Diffraction of beta rays by thin films', in 1937, he moved to St John's College, Cambridge, to study for a further PhD. At the Cavendish Laboratory (where there was a new 1 million volt particle accelerator) he introduced his improved Geiger counters, and also explored new methods of proportional counting. One of his assistants, studying for her PhD in physics, was his future wife, Joan Strothers [**Joan Elizabeth Curran**, Lady Curran (1916–1999)], daughter of Charles William Strothers, an optician, and his wife, Margaret Beatrice, *née* Millington. Joan was born in Swansea on 26 February 1916, and was educated at Swansea Girls' High School before entering Newnham College, Cambridge, with an open scholarship in 1934. Encouraged by her Newnham tutor A. C. Davies, she joined the Cavendish Laboratory after graduation in 1937. It was said of her that 'she had the scientific equivalent of gardening green fingers', and 'had the reputation of extreme dexterity and being outstandingly neat and skilful in the deployment of equipment' (*Independent*, 19 Feb 1999).

On 1 September 1939 Curran's and Strothers's supervisor, Philip Dee, took his team to spend a month at the Royal Aircraft Establishment, Farnborough. Two days later war with Germany was declared. They never returned to the Cavendish; instead, they moved to Exeter, where Curran and Strothers joined a small team developing the proximity fuse, based on transport-receive miniature radio. This was later an important weapon in destroying enemy planes, and was largely responsible for the destruction of over ninety per cent of the V1 rockets launched against southern England in 1944. From Exeter Curran and Strothers—who married on 7 December 1940—moved to join Dee, Bernard Lovell, Alan Hodgkin, Herbert Skinner, Bill Burcham, and others at the Telecommunications Research Establishment at Leeson House, Langton Matravers, in the development of centimetre radar for installation in aircraft. Curran had worked on

Sir Samuel Crowe Curran (1912–1998), by unknown photographer, 1969

pulse amplifiers before the war and with the development of a spark plug modulator devised by him, he was soon handling 50 kilowatts of pulse power at repetition rates of over 2000 per second. Curran (with Hodgkin and Burcham) was responsible for the detailed contacts with firms manufacturing the radar system. Soon all aircraft were being fitted with it. It was used in night fighters; it enabled bombers to carry out precision targeting; and it became a vital factor in enhancing the ability of planes to protect merchant shipping from U-boat attack, and thus played a large part in winning the battle of the Atlantic. Meanwhile Joan Curran, as part of the countermeasures group in an adjoining laboratory, was cutting up strips of tinfoil and developing the idea which led to operation Window, the scattering of clouds of these strips as a way of misleading enemy radar. From 1942, Bomber Command regularly employed this deception in order to provide the equivalent of radar smoke screens. Perhaps its greatest success came on D-day, 6 June 1944, when clouds of foil dropped by bombers of 617 squadron simulated an invasion force of ships heading towards the Pas de Calais, and persuaded the Germans to concentrate vital forces there rather than in Normandy.

Early in 1944 Curran, accompanied by his wife, was transferred to the University of California, Berkeley, to work under the direction of Ernest Lawrence on the separation of isotopes of uranium as an important part of the Manhattan project (the development of the atomic bomb). While there, in his spare time, Curran invented the scintillation counter for the detection and counting of radiation sources. This was later used in almost every scientific laboratory in the world, though Curran made no monetary gain from it. It was during their stay at Berkeley that the Currans' eldest child and only daughter, Sheena, was born, severely mentally handicapped. They also had three sons, each of whom went on to complete a PhD.

After the war, Curran joined the staff of Glasgow University, where Philip Dee was now professor of natural philosophy. During this period he invented a proportional counter to measure a number of different radiations. He was elected a fellow of the Royal Society in 1953. In March 1955 he was invited to join Sir William Penney at the Atomic Weapons Research Establishment, Aldermaston, to help develop a hydrogen bomb for Britain, a project completed by 1957. In all, Curran spent four and a half very successful years at Aldermaston, and represented the UK Atomic Energy Authority in highly technical visits to Berkeley, Livermore, Los Angeles, Oak Ridge, and other major US and European centres.

In 1959 Curran was invited to become principal of the prestigious Royal College of Science and Technology (RCST) in Glasgow, and to steer it through to university status. He readily accepted. He was keen to continue and expand the college's tradition of useful learning, and in the process to create a completely new kind of university. He pointed out to Sir Keith Murray (chairman of the University Grants Committee) that in 1960 the RCST was producing more than ten per cent of all the graduates with university-level technology qualifications in the United Kingdom, and more graduates in technology than all four Scottish universities put together. In the spring of 1961 Murray informed Curran that his committee had reached the unanimous conclusion that they should recommend to government that the RCST should merge with the Scottish College of Commerce to become a university. In March 1962 a statement was made to this effect in the House of Commons, and Murray agreed to Curran's suggestion that the new university should be named Strathclyde, after the ancient Scottish kingdom. Thus the University of Strathclyde, with Curran as its first principal and vice-chancellor, the first new university in Scotland for 381 years and the first technological university in Britain, came into being. Lord Todd of Trumpington, a distinguished scientist and Nobel laureate, and himself a native of Glasgow, was appointed chancellor.

In order to maintain a suitable balance, Curran resolved that the ratio of science and technology students to arts and business students should be maintained at two to one. He blamed much of the industrial and manufacturing decay in the UK on the failure of governments and universities to recognize the importance of technological education at the highest level. He was adamant about the role that his university should play: it would be, as John Anderson, the founder of the college, had envisaged some 170 years previously, 'a place of useful learning'. Curran also insisted that it should be located, as the Royal College had been, in the heart of industrial Glasgow. Expansion on a massive scale was necessary. By the time Curran retired in 1980, more than twenty major buildings, including accommodation for 1220 students out of a total student population of 6700, had been erected on about 24 acres of the city centre. Student playing fields covering about 270 acres were laid out a few miles from the city, and a staff recreational centre of 50 acres was established, including Ross Priory, a magnificent house on the banks of Loch Lomond. Its walled garden was named in Joan Curran's honour and a summer house was later erected in her memory.

Remembering his wartime days, Curran set in train co-operation with industry at a time when it was not fashionable for universities to do so. He encouraged departments to appoint visiting professors from industry and he appointed top industrialists (as well as academics and students) to the university court. With the help of Anthony Wedgwood Benn, the energy minister, he built, in 1966, a Centre for Industrial Innovation, a forerunner of science parks, where academics and industrialists could co-operate in fruitful research. He encouraged members of staff to accept consultancies in industry, and he also encouraged departments to appoint promising members of staff to personal professorships. Only later did such things become commonplace.

Curran could also be outward-looking. With the increasing interest in teaching and research in the nuclear field, he chaired a committee of the Scottish universities which persuaded the Department of Scientific and Industrial Research to provide a 100 kW reactor (later upgraded to

300 kW) at the national engineering laboratory, East Kilbride, together with associated staff, buildings, equipment, and running costs for the first five years. This facility was available to all the Scottish universities (and later Queen's University of Belfast was also included). In 1966 he established a close academic link between Strathclyde and the technical University of Łódź, Poland. This was at a time when Poland was part of the Soviet bloc and communication between the people of Poland and of the UK was difficult. The initiative was enormously successful, leading to a two-way exchange of students and staff, to shared degrees, and to close and lasting friendships. Curran was appointed commander of the order of Polonia Restituta by the Polish government in 1976.

Two things especially angered Curran: the very low salaries paid to scientists by comparison with businessmen, and the failure to recognize how science and technology had helped to win the Second World War. As he pointed out, there were no scientists in the parades to mark the fiftieth anniversaries of VE-day and VJ-day, yet it was the discoveries and developments by scientists and engineers—radar, the proximity fuse, operation Window, and the atomic and hydrogen bombs, to mention only a few—that made victory possible.

Curran served on innumerable government, public, and private bodies influencing science policy throughout the country, chaired the advisory committee on medical research (1962–75), and was chief scientific adviser to the secretary of state for Scotland (1967–77). He was knighted in 1970. He received many honorary degrees—including, on his retirement, the first fellowship of the university that he had founded. Joan Curran also received an honorary doctorate of laws from the university in her own right, in 1987. The Curran building, housing various departments of the University of Strathclyde, was named after them. Curran's main recreations were clock making (he had a number of patents) and golf. He was very proud of having published an article on 'The physics of the golf swing' in *Business Scotland*.

After the birth of their daughter Sheena, the Currans threw themselves into work for the disabled, and continued to do so until their deaths. In 1954 they helped to organize the public meeting which led to the foundation of the Scottish Association of Parents of Handicapped Children (later the Scottish Society for the Mentally Handicapped, and later still ENABLE), which by the time of their deaths had more than 5000 members and over seventy branches across Scotland. Curran served as president of the organization from 1954 until 1991. In 1964 the Glasgow branch named its office and leisure facilities Curran House in his honour.

Sam Curran died of cardiorespiratory arrest at the Nuffield McAlpine Hospital, Glasgow, on 25 February 1998, a few days after a prostate operation. His wife Joan died in Glasgow of cancer on 10 February 1999. They were both cremated at Daldowie crematorium, Glasgow, and were survived by their daughter and three sons.

W. W. FLETCHER

Sources W. W. Fletcher, 'Samuel Crowe Curran', *Memoirs FRS*, 45 (1999), 95–109 · S. C. Curran, *Recollections and reflections* (privately printed, Glasgow, 1986) · *The Scotsman* (28 Feb 1998) · *The Scotsman* (4 March 1998) · *The Herald* (28 Feb 1998) · *The Independent* (3 March 1998) · *The Times* (19 March 1998) · *The Guardian* (30 March 1998) · *The Herald* (16 Feb 1999) [Lady Curran] · *The Independent* (19 Feb 1999) [Lady Curran] · *The Scotsman* (24 Feb 1999) [Lady Curran] · *WWW* · personal knowledge (2004) · private information (2004) · b. cert. · m. cert. · d. cert.
Archives University of Strathclyde, Glasgow, research papers, talks, articles, and MSS relating to university developments | SOUND University of Strathclyde
Likenesses photograph, 1969, repro. in *The Times* [see illus.] · double portrait, photograph, 1979 (with Lady Curran), repro. in *The Independent* (19 Feb 1999) · photograph, 1980, repro. in *The Scotsman* (28 Feb 1998) · oils, University of Strathclyde · photograph, repro. in *The Herald* (28 Feb 1998) · photograph, repro. in *The Guardian* · photograph, repro. in Fletcher, 'Samuel Crowe Curran', *Memoirs FRS*, 94 · photograph (Lady Curran), repro. in *The Herald* (16 Feb 1999)
Wealth at death £113,239.81: confirmation, 1998, *CCI* · £246,449.74—Lady Curran: confirmation, 1999, *CCI* · £149,898.37—Lady Curran: eik additional inventory, 2000, *CCI*

Currer, Frances Mary Richardson (1785–1861), book collector, was born on 3 March 1785 at Eshton Hall, near Gargrave, in the West Riding of Yorkshire. She was the posthumous daughter and sole heir of the Revd Henry Richardson (1758–1784) who, shortly before his death, took the name of Currer on succeeding to the estates of Sarah Currer. Her mother was Margaret Clive Wilson, the only surviving child and heir of Matthew Wilson of Eshton Hall; she was a niece of Clive of India.

'She is', wrote Mrs Dorothy Richardson in 1815:

> in possession of both the Richardson and Currer estates and inherits all the taste of the former family, having collected a very large and valuable library, and also possessing a fine collection of prints, shells, and fossils, in addition to what were collected by her great grandfather and great-uncle. (Nichols, 252)

T. F. Dibdin considered that Currer's collection placed her 'at the head of all female collectors in Europe' (*Reminiscences*, 2.949) and that her country house library was, in its day, surpassed only by those of Earl Spencer, the duke of Devonshire, and the duke of Buckingham. Seymour De Ricci wrote that she was 'England's earliest female bibliophile' (De Ricci, 141).

Dibdin relates that the library had substantial holdings in natural science, topography, antiquities, and history, together with a collection of the classics. There were rarities, some early printed books, a collection of Bibles, and a fine gathering of illustrated books. Although 'collected with a view to utility … The books individually are in the finest condition, and not a few of them in the richest and most tasteful bindings' (Stewart). The manuscripts included the correspondence (1523–4) of Lord Dacre, warden of the Anglo-Scottish marches, the Richardson correspondence, and the Hopkinson papers. John Hopkinson (1610–1680) was secretary to Dugdale during his Yorkshire visitation. Dibdin first estimated the number of volumes at 15,000 and, later, 18,000. In 1852, Sir J. B. Burke put the number at 20,000 (Burke, 1.127).

In 1820 Robert Triphook compiled *A catalogue of the library of Miss Currer at Eshton Hall, in the deanery of Craven and county of York*, of which fifty copies were printed. In 1833 a second catalogue was prepared by C. J. Stewart, on a modified system devised by Hartwell Horne for the British Museum (although not used) in an edition of 100 copies; it had an excellent index. In 1835 Currer had printed for private circulation *Extracts from the literary and scientific correspondence of Richard Richardson, MD of Brierley, Yorkshire*, edited by Dawson Turner.

Currer has been described as extremely accomplished and amiable. In a letter to Dawson Turner in 1837 Dibdin wrote: 'She has a heart as big as St Paul's Dome and as warm as Volcanic lava, but this is acted upon strangely and capriciously at times'; he went on: 'she can show an indifference or niggardliness of feeling, which is utterly unaccountable' (Dawson Turner MSS). Currer had been a generous patron of Dibdin from early days, and his expectations may have risen too high at times.

Frances Currer was shy, and her deafness, which increased with age, explains her somewhat secluded life at Eshton Hall. But she was not a recluse, being 'renowned for her generosity to all kinds of charities' (Barker, 105), which included the Keighley Mechanics' Institution and the new school at Cowan Bridge, attended by the Brontë sisters. It is probable that she was the 'wealthy lady in the West Riding of Yorkshire' who gave £50 in 1821 to help pay the debts of the newly widowed Patrick Brontë (Barker, 105). Charlotte Brontë used her surname for her pseudonym, Currer Bell.

Currer never married, although relations with Richard Heber (1774–1833) were close. He shared her interest in books, and also owned property in Yorkshire; she made loans to him when his financial difficulties were pressing. There were rumours of a closer alliance and, after his death, her defence of his reputation from (well-founded) allegations of homosexuality suggests some lingering affection.

Frances Currer died at Eshton Hall on 28 April 1861 and was buried beside her mother at St Andrew's Church, Gargrave, on 6 May. In 1800 her mother had married Matthew Wilson, a cousin; Eshton Hall was inherited by their descendants. Currer had hoped that her library would remain at Eshton Hall but her half-brother sold the major part at Sothebys in 1862; it realized nearly £6000, but the manuscripts were retained. A second sale in 1916 raised more than £3700; the Hopkinson manuscripts were bought by Bradford Public Library, and the Richardson correspondence was bought by Quaritch and then dispersed. The remaining books were sold in 1979 and in 1994.

COLIN LEE

Sources Nichols, *Illustrations*, 1.225–52 · A. Lister, 'The lady of Eshton Hall', *Antiquarian Book Monthly Review*, 12 (1985), 382–9 · T. F. Dibdin, *Reminiscences of a literary life*, 2 vols. (1836), 949–57 · R. Myers and M. Harris, eds., *Antiquaries, book collectors and the circles of learning* (1996), 112 n. 80 · J. Barker, *The Brontës* (1994), 105, 119, 480, 928 (n. 5) · *GM*, 3rd ser., 11 (1861), 89–90 · T. F. Dibdin, *Bibliographical tour* (1838), 1081–90 · J. Martin, *Bibliographical catalogue of books privately printed*, 2nd edn (1854), 257, 445, 459 · S. De Ricci, *English collectors of books and manuscripts* (1930); repr. (New York, 1969), 141–3 · J. B. Burke, *A visitation of the seats and arms of the noblemen and gentlemen of Great Britain* (1852), 1.127 · C. J. Stewart, *A catalogue of the library of Miss Richardson Currer at Eshton Hall* (1833) · Trinity Cam., Dawson Turner MSS

Archives Bodl. Oxf., Currer–Dibdin corresp., MS Eng. misc. d 85–6 · Bodl. Oxf., Phillipps–Robinson MSS, corresp. with Sir Thomas Phillipps · Trinity Cam., Dawson Turner MSS

Likenesses Masquerier, portrait, 1807, priv. coll.; repro. in Lister, 'The lady of Eshton Hall'

Wealth at death £3000: probate, 26 July 1861, CGPLA Eng. & Wales

Currer, William (*c*.1617–1668), iatrochemical physician, came from Yorkshire; details of his early life are unknown. On 27 May 1641, 'aged twenty-four', he was admitted at Leiden University. Less than two years later, on 9 May 1643, that university conferred upon him the degree of doctor of medicine. Thereafter Currer appears to have served as a physician to the army in Ireland, for in April 1646 the committee of lords and commons for Ireland issued a warrant to pay him £150. In early November 1646, having successfully defended his thesis on kidney disease, he was incorporated MD at Oxford University. On 6 November Currer appeared before the College of Physicians of London and promised to obey the college in all matters. Currer did not remain long in England and was soon back in Ireland as physician to Lord Inchiquin's army in Munster. While in Ireland he was said to have 'collected a number of Irish Medecins as also much of the Natural History of that Country especially about Mines'. This collection of manuscripts, however, together with 'some other Dutch books', fell into the hands of Dr Harding, a minister and commissioner at Cork, from whom Currer was unable to retrieve them (Hartlib, 'Ephemerides', 1651).

At 6.00 p.m. on 31 August 1650 the antiquary Elias Ashmole recorded that he 'first saw Dr. Currer'. The timing proved to be propitious and as the two became acquainted so Ashmole began to regard Currer's 'skill in transmutation of metal', making notes in cipher of 'Dr: Currers way' (Josten, 2.542, 551; 'Alchemical method'). Another of Currer's contacts was the widely travelled physician Robert Child, with whom he shared interests in herbal medicines, chemistry, and mining. Writing on 2 February 1653 to Samuel Hartlib, Child praised Currer as a man 'reall & honest to his freind', adding that he thought him 'a very good Chymist' (Sheffield University Library, Hartlib papers, HP 15/5/18B). Child also suggested that Currer would make a suitable companion for a young Bermudan iatrochemist in his circle, George Starkey. It was to prove a poor recommendation.

On 2 April 1652 Currer was summoned before the College of Physicians and gently advised that if he wished to continue practising medicine in London he should submit himself to an examination and abide by the statutes of the realm. Even unlicensed, Currer's reputation as a physician remained untarnished within certain circles, for Child informed Hartlib from Ireland that he was glad to hear that Currer thrived in London. Starkey, moreover, was careful to exempt 'Dr. Currar' as one of several 'Chymically given' physicians in his Helmontian attack on Galenic medical practice (Starkey, *Natures Explication*, sig. A5r). The volatile Starkey, however, was soon portraying himself as the innocent victim of Currer's underhand tactics in a legal dispute. Even so, Starkey conceded that his 'perverse, wretched Adversary' was a man 'of no contemptible parts', wanting

> neither *Wit as a Man*, nor *Learning as a Scholar*, nor *Discretion as a Theorical Dissenter* from the *Galenical* way; nor *Acuteness as a Chymical Pretender*, but if he want something in Nature to make him a compleat upright Man, much more in Grace to make him a true Christian. (Starkey, *Pyrotechny Asserted*, 162-3)

This period also marked Currer's involvement in the compilation of two works of philology that profited from both the scholarly and financial resources of Elias Ashmole and his associates.

In July 1660, on the recommendation of the marquess of Ormond, Currer was granted the post of physician-general to Charles II's army in Ireland. His allowance was to be 10s. a day. Currer continued in the post for several years. Such was his standing that his name appeared on the patent granted to the College of Physicians of Dublin on 8 August 1667. Not all though, were so enamoured of Currer's medical skill. Writing to the earl of Dorset, Lady Broghill recounted the death of Lady Kildare 'by some fisik she took off Doctor Currar, itt was soe voyelent that she lived 1 hower after she took itt. Thanks be to God, my uncle had a fare scape off the docter' (*Seventh Report*, HMC, appx, 249). William Currer, 'Chemicall Phisitian' and 'most intire freind' of Elias Ashmole, died on 16 September 1668 and was buried in the chancel of St Clement Danes, Westminster, on 1 October 1668 (Josten, 3.1129). William Floyd preached the funeral sermon. To his loving friend, Nathaniel Hinshaw, Currer bequeathed 'All my Bookes medicines and Glasses which I use for Kymicall preparations' (PRO, PROB 11/328, fol. 79v).

ARIEL HESSAYON

Sources annals, RCP Lond., 3.232r; 4.41r · S. Hartlib, 'Ephemerides', 1651, Sheffield University, HP 28/2/11B–12A · Sheffield University, Hartlib papers, HP 15/5/18B · Bodl. Oxf., MS Ashmole 374, fol. 62r · 'The alchemical method of William Currer', Bodl. Oxf., MS Ashmole 1417, fols. 64r, 93r · *Elias Ashmole (1617–1692): his autobiographical and historical notes*, ed. C. H. Josten, 5 vols. (1966 [i.e. 1967]), vol. 2, pp. 542–3, 551, 642, 654, 730, 753; vol. 3, p. 1129 · P. C. Molhuysen, ed., *Bronnen tot de geschiedenis der Leidsche Universiteit*, 2 (The Hague, 1916), 272 · G. Starkey, *Natures explication and Helmont's vindication* (1657), sig. A5r · G. Starkey, *Pyrotechny asserted and illustrated* (1658), 162–3 · A. Hessayon, 'Gold tried in the fire': the prophet Theaurau John Tany and the puritan revolution [forthcoming] · *Seventh report*, HMC, 6 (1879) · will, PRO, PROB 11/328, fol. 79v · *The correspondence of Robert Boyle*, ed. M. Hunter, A. Clericuzio, and L. Principe, 6 vols. (2001), vol. 1, p. 167, vol. 2, p. 93, vol. 4, p. 213 · J. D. H. Widdess, *A history of the Royal College of Physicians of Ireland, 1654–1963* (1963), 14 · R. S. Wilkinson, 'The Hartlib papers and seventeenth-century chemistry [pt 2]', *Ambix*, 17 (1970), 85–110, esp. 101, 108

Currey, Frederick (1819–1881), mycologist, was born on 19 August 1819, probably at Norwood in Surrey, the son of Benjamin Currey, clerk of parliaments. He was educated at Eton College and at Trinity College, Cambridge, where he took his BA in 1841. He studied law at Lincoln's Inn, being called to the bar in 1844. He died at 2 Vanbrugh Park

Road, Blackheath, on 8 September 1881 from an 'affection of the liver' and was buried at Weybridge, where his wife had been previously interred. Currey was elected a fellow of the Linnean Society in 1856 and of the Royal Society in 1858. In 1860 he was elected secretary of the Linnean Society, which office he held until 1880 when he became vice-president and treasurer. His writings consist of several papers on fungi and a work on local botany, together with translations of W. F. B. Hofmeister's *Vergleichende Untersuchungen der … höherer Kryptogamen* (*Germination, Development and Fructification of the Higher Cryptogamia*, 1862) and of H. Schacht's *Microscope and its Applications to Vegetable Anatomy* (1853). He also edited the second edition of Charles David Badham's *Esculent Funguses of England*. The genus of fungi *Curreya* was named after him. His collection of fungi later formed part of the Kew herbarium.

B. D. JACKSON, *rev.* GILES HUDSON

Sources B. Dayden Jackson, *Journal of Botany, British and Foreign*, 19 (1881), 310–12 · *Gardeners' Chronicle*, new ser., 16 (1881), 412 · Venn, *Alum. Cant.* · CGPLA Eng. & Wales (1881)
Archives Linn. Soc., drawings, notebooks, papers · NHM · RBG Kew
Likenesses crayon, Linn. Soc.
Wealth at death £8054 5s. 6d.: probate, 21 Oct 1881, CGPLA Eng. & Wales

Currie [*formerly* Curry], **Sir Arthur William** (1875–1933), army officer, was born in Adelaide township, near Strathroy, Ontario, Canada, on 5 December 1875, the son of William Garner Curry (1845–1891), and his wife, Jane Patterson (1847–1924). Both his parents were Canadian born, their families having originally migrated from Scotland and Ulster. Curry was raised on his father's farm, and educated at Strathroy Collegiate Institute (from 1889) and Strathroy model school.

In 1894 Curry moved to Victoria, British Columbia, and shortly thereafter he became a schoolmaster in Sydney. He moved back to Victoria in 1896 where he continued teaching until 1900, when he began working as an insurance salesman. Soon after arrival in Victoria he joined the militia (1897) as a gunner and changed the spelling of his name to Currie. In 1900 Currie was offered a commission as a 2nd lieutenant. He rose rapidly in rank and by 1909 was commanding officer of the 5th regiment, BC brigade garrison artillery. On 14 August 1901 he married Lucy Sophia (1875–1969), youngest daughter of William Chaworth-Muster of Nottingham, England, and Comax, British Columbia. Currie then went into business for himself; he and his wife had two children, Marjorie (b. 1902) and Garner (b. 1911). In 1904 Currie took over the insurance agency for which he had been working. In 1908 he entered a real estate partnership and began selling and speculating on property. In 1913 he ended his term as commanding officer of the 5th regiment, just as the speculative bubble in west-coast real estate burst. Also in that year he was asked to take command of a newly formed militia unit, the 50th regiment. Deeply in debt when war broke out in 1914, he was not able to accept command of the British Columbia military district. When subsequently offered a brigade in the Canadian expeditionary force he borrowed money, paid off most of his debts, and left to take command of the 2nd Canadian infantry brigade. With this brigade he withstood the onslaught of superior forces at St Julien in 1915 and in the same year was promoted successively colonel and brigadier-general. When the Canadian corps was formed in September 1915 Currie was given command of the 1st Canadian division, and with the rank of major-general led his men on the Somme and at Vimy Ridge. In 1917 when General Byng was promoted to army commander, Currie became the first Canadian to become commander of the Canadian corps. Concerned at the time that his pre-war debts would become an impediment, he took steps to eliminate them. His promotion was approved with the endorsement of Sir Douglas Haig and the Canadian government. Currie's subsequent career was extraordinarily successful. He planned and carried through the battle of Hill 70 (August 1917) and led his corps at Passchendaele (October). Perhaps his and the Canadian corps' greatest achievement was during the fighting from the battle of Amiens (August 1918) through to the Armistice on 11 November, known as the Last Hundred Days. This fighting was the greatest sustained advance for the British forces during the entire war. Currie and the Canadian corps greatly distinguished themselves, but criticism of the campaign was launched in the Canadian parliament, by Sir Sam Hughes, which resulted in postwar controversy and a libel action in 1928 which totally vindicated Currie. He was mentioned in dispatches nine times, was appointed CB in 1915, KCMG in 1917, KCB in 1918, and GCMG in 1919. He received many foreign decorations.

After the armistice Currie remained for a time in command of the Canadian forces on the Rhine and upon his return to Canada he was promoted general, and made inspector-general, and military counsellor to the militia forces of Canada (1919). In 1920 he became principal and vice-chancellor of McGill University. While at McGill he gave his services unsparingly to the Canadian Legion of British Empire Service League, of which he was honorary president; to the Canadian Institute of International Affairs; to the Carnegie Foundation for the Advancement of Teaching, of which he was a trustee; to the governorship of the Montreal General and Royal Victoria hospitals; and to the Bank of Montreal. Throughout his tenure at McGill, he was a tireless advocate of veterans' rights and benefits. Eighteen universities in Great Britain, Canada, and the United States of America conferred honorary degrees upon him.

Currie was a courageous and resourceful commander possessed of great initiative and an instinctive grasp of tactics. Lloyd George called him a brilliant commander and his own prime minister, Robert Borden, thought him the most able corps commander in the British army. He died of pneumonia in Montreal on 30 November 1933, and was buried in that city. Controversy over Currie's place in Canadian military history has resulted largely from the vicious accusations of Sam Hughes and the ensuing libel action. Legal vindication, however, did not stop subsequent journalistic speculation about the Canadian corps commander. Although not a charismatic individual, he had outstanding tactical skill and organizational abilities. Posthumous discovery that Currie had used government funds issued to his militia unit in 1914 to pay private debts and that he had not replaced them until 1917 contributed to the controversy. His accomplishments as brigade, division, and corps commander during the First World War place him among Canada's most outstanding military leaders.

A. M. J. HYATT

Sources H. M. Urquhart, *Arthur Currie: the biography of a great Canadian* (1950) · A. M. J. Hyatt, *General Sir Arthur Currie: a military biography* (1987) · R. J. Sharpe, *The last day the last hour: the Currie libel trial* (1988) · D. G. Dancocks, *Sir Arthur Currie: a biography* (1985) · *The Times* (1 Dec 1933) · *The Times* (5 Dec 1933) · G. W. L. Nicholson, *Canadian expeditionary force, 1914–1919: official history of the Canadian army in the First World War* (1962) · R. H. Michel, 'The general portrayed: Sir Arthur Currie and his painters', *Fontanus: from the collections of McGill University*, 7 (1994), 73–102 · J. E. Edmonds, ed., *Military operations, France and Belgium*, 14 vols., History of the Great War (1922–48)
Archives McGill University, Montreal, MSS · NA Canada, MSS
Likenesses R. Jack, oils, 1917, McGill University, Montreal, Canada · W. Orpen, oils, 1919, Canadian War Museum, Ottawa, Canada · J. De Camp, oils, 1920, Smithsonian Institution, Washington, DC · J. S. Sargent, group portrait, oils, 1922 (*General officers of World War I*), NPG
Wealth at death C$800 p.a. for widow: Sharpe, *Last day*, 246

Currie, Bertram Wodehouse (1827–1896), banker, was born on 25 November 1827, at Harley Street, Marylebone, Middlesex, the second son of Raikes *Currie (1801–1881), banker and MP for Northampton (1835–57), and his wife, the Hon. Laura Sophia (d. 1869), daughter of the second Baron Wodehouse. John Wodehouse, first earl of Kimberley, was his cousin. He had three brothers (of whom the youngest, Philip Henry Wodehouse *Currie, was created Baron Currie in 1899) and two sisters. He was educated at Cheam under the progressive Dr Mayo, who taught him with such terrifying realism about the 'last trump' that he would jump out of his skin when someone blew a cornet in the street. Afterwards he was at Eton College (1840–45) and he also studied at Weimar, in Germany, where he became proficient in foreign languages.

After returning to London, Currie entered his father's banking business at 29 Cornhill, in the City, in 1847. He was not his father's favourite son, and his acute business sense was not fully appreciated until at his instigation the bank amalgamated with Glyn, Mills to become Glyn, Mills, Currie, in 1864. He married on 31 October 1860 Caroline Louisa (1836/7–1902), daughter of Sir William Lawrence Young, fourth baronet, Conservative MP for Buckinghamshire from 1835 to 1842. They had two sons.

After the Overend Gurney crisis of 1866 Currie emerged as the dominant partner in the bank, and he soon secured his reputation as one of the most intelligent leaders of the banking community. The first chairman of Glyn, Mills, Currie was George Glyn, afterwards first Baron Wolverton; Currie's reservations about him reveal his own epicureanism and his admiration for versatility, erudition, and vision:

If he had not been so engrossed in the details of business, and if his domestic environment had been a little more intellectual and aesthetic, his natural talent for conversation and society would … have been developed … but the puritanical and philistine element which prevailed in his days in the banking and mercantile world checked his flight, and made his private life somewhat colourless. (*Recollections*, 1.95)

Currie's ambitions for himself were cut in the opposite pattern to Wolverton's. He took broad views, and had wide interests outside the bank parlour, but never compromised his dedication to private banking by accepting other commercial responsibilities. It was at Currie's prompting that Glyn, Mills, Currie became a joint-stock company in 1885. Currie was instrumental in financing the Manchester Ship Canal in the late 1880s. He had a lifelong friendship with Edward Baring, first Baron Revelstoke, and together with William Lidderdale of the Bank of England he was crucial during the Baring crisis of 1890 in averting a collapse in financial confidence. On 11 February 1891 E. W. Hamilton of the Treasury called him 'the ablest of all City authorities' (BL, Add. MS 48655, fol. 27).

In the City, Currie was not a representative figure. He advocated reformation of the corporation of London:

The perpetual guzzling of Aldermen and Common Councillors, the jobbing in City lands, in which some of them were notoriously engaged, their want of public spirit, the cadging for subscriptions on every possible occasion, the thirst of Mayors and Recorders for titles and orders—all these excited my bile. (*Recollections*, 1.83–4)

Currie was chairman of the City of London Liberal Association at a time when most City leaders had abandoned Liberalism. The 'boredom and banality' of parliamentary life, however, deterred him from a candidacy (*Recollections*, 1.82–3). He advised W. E. Gladstone on financial topics, lent his Whitehall house to the Gladstones when they left Downing Street in 1885, and also put at their disposal his Surrey house, where the Grand Old Man once held a meeting of ministers. Gladstone much appreciated Currie's 'unbounded kindness' on these occasions (Gladstone, *Diaries*, 11.129). Currie supported Gladstone's Irish policy, and in 1892 he mediated on his behalf with Henry Labouchere when the latter pressed his claim to office in the incoming Liberal administration.

To have known Mr Gladstone, and to have enjoyed his friendship, is among the most interesting events of my life … I have never conversed with any man whose intellectual superiority I was so ready to acknowledge, or who … was so free from the demon of commonplace. (*Recollections*, 1.84)

Currie was not a democrat, but exclusive and invidious in his judgements; he supported Robert Lowe's arguments against extending the franchise in 1866 and he mistrusted Rosebery's admiration of Bismarck. He described himself as having an 'anxious and apprehensive temperament' (*Recollections*, 1.53).

Currie's opinions were valued by Sir Reginald Welby and other Treasury officials. As financial member of the Council of India from 1880 to 1895, he steadily gained in authority and expertise. He also testified to the gold and silver commission in 1887, was a delegate at the Brussels International Monetary Conference of 1892, where he was a ruthless, sarcastic opponent of bimetallism, and served on the Indian currency committee, in 1893, and on the Irish finance committee. As a monometallist he contributed to the *National Review* in June 1895 and promoted the Gold Standard Defence Association in that year (he was chairman in 1895–6).

Currie bought a suburban villa, Coombe Warren, near Kingston upon Thames in Surrey, which had been built in 1868 by the father of John Galsworthy and which was immortalized in *The Forsyte Saga*. There and at Minley Manor on Bagshot Heath in Hampshire, which he inherited from his father, he indulged his 'mania for building and making gardens' (*Recollections*, 1.58). In both counties he was a magistrate; he was also high sheriff of London in 1892, and high steward of Kingston upon Thames in 1893. He despised the mediocrity of his suburban neighbours:

Nothing can be so utterly banal and uninspiring for the young as the associations of the modern suburban villa. Villadom has already given its name to a school of politicians distinguished for the absence of ideas, for the glorification of chauvinism, for faith in such patriots as that precious pair of knights, Sir Ashmead Bartlett and Sir Howard Vincent. (*Recollections*, 1.37)

Such fastidious scorn explains the description of him by Constance Smith (mother of Vivian Smith, first Baron Bicester): 'extremely clever, intellectual and agreeable … an avowed and mocking Atheist, extremely satirical and cynical, and I have never dined there without hearing him pass bitter and ironical remarks upon people' (Kynaston, 1.295). Currie visited Brazil in 1849 and the USA in 1850, and travelled extensively in Europe, but latterly railed against the effects of mass tourism.

In December 1895 Currie underwent an operation for cancer of the tongue; after cancer reappeared in his neck glands he was told in August 1896 by Henry Butlin that his case was hopeless. He retired immediately from business. Two months later he was received into the Roman Catholic church to the high gratification of his wife (who had converted in 1862). Although Hamilton believed Currie's conversion was chiefly intended 'to please his wife before his death' (BL, Add. MS 48670, fol. 89), the religious testimony which he wrote at this time has the hallmark of sincerity. He died on 29 December 1896, at 1 Richmond Terrace, Whitehall, London, survived by his wife.

RICHARD DAVENPORT-HINES

Sources *Bertram Wodehouse Currie, 1827–1896: recollections, letters, and journals*, ed. [C. L. Currie], 2 vols. (1901) · C. L. Currie, *Bertram Wodehouse Currie: a memorial* (1897) · D. Kynaston, *The City of London*, 4 vols. (1994–2001) · R. Fulford, *Glyn's, 1753–1953: six generations in Lombard Street* (1953) · J. Powell, 'Testimony in high places: the conversion of Bertram Wodehouse Currie', *Recusant History*, 19 (1988–9), 198–207 · Lord Kilbracken [J. A. Godley], *Reminiscences of Lord Kilbracken* (1931) · BL, diaries of E. W. Hamilton · BL, Gladstone MSS · Gladstone, *Diaries* · *The journal of John Wodehouse, first earl of Kimberley, for 1862–1902*, ed. A. Hawkins and J. Powell, CS, 5th ser., 9 (1997) · *CGPLA Eng. & Wales* (1897) · *The Times* (30 Dec 1896) · A. C. Fox-Davies, ed., *Armorial families: a directory of gentlemen of coat-armour*, 7th edn, 1 (1929), 481–2

Archives BL, memoranda and corresp. with W. E. Gladstone, Add. MSS 44491–44789 · Norfolk RO, Kimberley MSS

Likenesses E. W. Eddis, oils, 1836, repro. in *Bertram Wodehouse Currie, 1827–1896*, vol. 1, facing p. 5 · Le Jeune, photograph, 1872, repro. in *Bertram Wodehouse Currie, 1827–1896*, vol. 2, facing p. 72 · photograph, *c*.1880, repro. in Fulford, *Glyn's, 1753–1953*, facing p. 208 · Byrne, photograph, 1896, repro. in *Bertram Wodehouse Currie, 1827–1896*, vol. 2, frontispiece

Wealth at death £696,244 1*s*. 3*d*.: resworn probate, Nov 1897, *CGPLA Eng. & Wales*

Currie, Sir Donald (1825–1909), shipowner, was born on 17 September 1825 at Greenock, the third son of James Currie (1797–1851), a barber, and Elizabeth (1798–1839), daughter of Donald Martin. The family moved from Greenock to Belfast in 1826, where they belonged to the conservative Presbyterian congregation in Fisherwick Place.

Education, marriage and early career Currie was educated at the Belfast Academy and the Royal Belfast Academical Institution from 1832 to 1839. In 1840 he returned to Greenock, working in the shipping office of his uncle John Martin of Hoyle Martin & Co., and four years later, like so many Scots, went south to Liverpool, joining Charles MacIver, family friend and manager of Samuel Cunard's British and North American Royal Mail Steam Packet Company. It was not long before he settled into Liverpool life. As a member of the Presbyterian congregation at the new Free Church in Canning Street, he played his part in setting up the Young Men's Evangelical Association, and in 1851 married Margaret, daughter of another Scot, John Miller, senior partner in the general merchants Miller, Houghton & Co. Currie and his wife had three daughters. Appointed head of the cargo department, he travelled on the continent between 1849 and 1854 to establish new agencies at Le Havre, Paris, Antwerp, and Bremen, and took much of the responsibility for MacIver's Mediterranean interests as far afield as the Levant and the Black Sea. By 1859 he was a well-regarded figure in local shipping circles, becoming treasurer of the powerful Liverpool Steam Ship Owners' Association.

Opening the Castle Line Currie left Cunard in 1862 to run his own sailing ships as the Castle Line from Liverpool and London in the India trade. At first he concentrated on Calcutta, exploiting the novelty of a regularly timetabled service, but soon began to diversify his activities, chartering vessels to other Asian ports and exploring the possibilities of the Calcutta–New York connection. From 1863 he also moved into the regular Baltic trade. An elder brother, James, was manager of the Leith, Hull, and Hamburg Steam Packet Company; Donald became one of its principal shareholders, and in 1866 with other partners also set up his own Liverpool and Hamburg Steam Ship Company.

The opening of the Suez Canal in 1869, rapid growth in the size of ships, and the introduction of steam shipping on the routes to the East, created a new and very difficult set of conditions. While other important competitors moved quickly, Currie's already extended operations and relatively limited resources made him hesitant, both in building new steamers and in committing them to India. His loss of a new ship on its maiden voyage in 1872, and a developing connection with the London shipbroker G. H.

Sir Donald Currie (1825–1909), by Walter William Ouless, 1908

Payne who chartered some of Currie's boats for a new service to the Cape of Good Hope, were decisive. Currie switched to the much smaller and less lucrative Cape trade in competition with the existing holder of the imperial government's mail contract, the Union Steam Ship Company. Using his position in the Leith, Hull and Hamburg to buy or charter several of their vessels, in addition to his new purchases, he wooed the Cape merchants and in 1874 won a colonial government subsidy to help his newly formed Castle Packets Company survive the next two years. Officials and merchants, dissatisfied with the Union Company's service and hoping for miracles from a breath of competition, were happy to see the mail contract divided with Currie when it was renegotiated in 1876.

Currie seized the opportunity of an upturn in trade and a measure of security to expand his company rapidly, more than doubling the Castle Company's tonnage to 48,000 by 1881. The company itself was also reorganized, first in 1877 with an expanded capital, Currie himself as the largest shareholder, and his family enterprise of Donald Currie & Co. as its managers. Then, in 1881, the new Castle Mail Packets Company Limited was floated publicly, with a subscribed capital of £720,000 and further resources of nearly £0.5 million; Currie was made manager in perpetuity, in return for which he enjoyed the highly favourable remuneration of 5 per cent per annum of the company's gross earnings.

Public relations were quite as essential as financial preoccupations to Currie's style of management in the 1870s and to the initial establishment of Castle Mail. Joining the Royal Colonial Institute in 1874, he carefully cultivated prominent public figures both in Britain and in South Africa, including Sir John Molteno, the Cape's prime minister, whose son Percy later married Currie's daughter Elizabeth, and Sir Robert Herbert, permanent under-secretary at the Colonial Office. He was very active among shipowners in shaping the mercantile marine safety legislation of 1876, and received the Royal Society of Arts Fothergill gold medal for his contributions to safety in shipbuilding. He mediated between President Brand of the Orange Free State and British officials in their dispute over the diamondiferous territory of Griqualand West, and supported the Boer delegation to London in 1877 protesting against the Transvaal's annexation; he scored a lucky coup by both bringing to Britain news of the devastating defeat at Isandlwana and speedily taking back the military instructions which averted further disasters; and he subsequently gave evidence to the Carnarvon commission on Britain's naval defences.

Politics and the development of Castle Mail Frequenting corridors of power, he also entered national politics, unsuccessfully contesting the Greenock election of 1876 and becoming Liberal MP for Perthshire in 1880. Currie, however, never had strong political ambitions. His political involvement, like his contacts with influential officials and public figures, remained limited to areas likely to serve his business interests, by providing him with contacts or information and building up his reputation for respectability. It was a successful strategy, symbolized first by his appointment as a CMG in 1877; and then by a knighthood in 1881. On his ships, as later on the neighbouring Perthshire estates of Garth and Glen Lyon which he purchased in 1880 and 1885, he enjoyed entertaining the influential and the journalists who might record the events. In 1880 and 1881 Gladstone was prominent among those entertained in a style which prompted *Vanity Fair's* Spy to caricature Currie on the occasion of his elevation to a KCMG, as 'Knight of the Cruise of Mr. Gladstone' (21 June 1884). Currie's orchestration of personal publicity and public flotation in the summer of 1881 was brilliant, with *The Times* noticing Castle Mail's prospectus and Currie's new title on the same day (20 July 1881). Not a week later, on 25 July, Currie entertained a large gathering of British and colonial MPs, shipping representatives, and minor British and Prussian royalty on board his new and largest steamship at the opening of Leith's new docks.

Amid the accumulated pomp and circumstance which impressed most onlookers as intended, Currie's shaping of the new Castle Mail company represented a most striking business coup. With competition on the Cape route stiffening, with a serious downturn in commercial conditions upon him as the diamond share boom broke and imperial military spending in southern Africa sharply declined, Currie not only obtained an astonishingly high price for his old company, but transferred to the new shareholders a significant proportion of the costs of its recent expansion. Moreover, the structure of Castle Mail left Currie virtually free to indulge his enjoyment of display and personal prominence at the company's expense, and unhampered by any effective control by shareholders

over his management. The 'council' which oversaw the company's affairs sounded impressive but lacked power, for it was composed almost entirely of Currie's friends and nominees; useful for their social standing or government connections in colonial affairs, at the Admiralty, and in telegraph construction, they did not possess the working knowledge of company matters which might have benefited shareholders.

In Castle Mail, Currie had created perhaps the grandest example of a phenomenon common at the time, that of the shipping company in which shareholders' losses financed managerial self-indulgence and extravagance, and where, despite mounting criticism from newspapers and a few investors, no effective opposition emerged. Throughout its life Castle Mail's declared and distributed profits frequently compared unfavourably with other major companies'. Returns were kept within the firm, details of earnings and managers' commissions remained confidential; to finance its further operations and expansion, Currie very cleverly deployed the significant reserves created at flotation together with generous annual allowances for depreciation and successive bank loans, rather than risk his authority by trying to raise further ordinary share capital against the company's persistently discounted shares. This position he was able to sustain for almost twenty years.

The South African shipping conference, 1883 Currie's further distinction as a shipowner in the 1880s lay in his role as architect of the South African shipping conference. Against the background of severe economic depression, he brought the several southern African lines together in 1883 to defend their common interest in avoiding a rate-cutting war and possible bankruptcy. Agreed rates, pooled cargo, controlled voyage schedules, and a system of deferred rebates to compel merchants' loyalty to particular lines, became the order of the day. Not surprisingly the conference provoked vociferous criticism, but the inability of the several governments in South Africa to organize a common response left Currie in charge of the field. His combination of energy, administrative skill, and negotiating talent was such as to win over the German lines and other new challengers in the 1890s and beyond, with the result that the conference repulsed all attackers during his lifetime.

Diversification beyond shipping: diamonds and southern Africa The pursuit of happiness for Donald Currie lay in business competition and diversification. Not only the cut-throat world of steam shipping but the speculative condition of southern Africa's mineral discoveries and urban expansion offered him almost limitless opportunity. One natural extension of his interests lay in linking ship to shore; difficult anchorages and limited port facilities for larger ships led him to set up local landing and boating companies at Port Elizabeth, Durban, and Beira. African Lands and Hotels, established in 1897, was responsible for Cape Town's famous Mount Nelson Hotel. His first venture beyond shipping occurred in 1881, when he acquired some 75 per cent or £19,000 worth of shares in the newly formed Namaqua Copper Company. This gave him a lasting interest in the future of South-West Africa, but his major concerns, like those of so many after 1880, lay in the gold, diamonds and real estate of the Transvaal and northern Cape. Investments in these crucial sectors not only held out the possibility of personal gain; at least as important were the contacts and commercial information they generated, providing Currie with current business and insights into the future development of the passenger and freight trades so vital to his shipping line.

Currie's route into diamonds opened up early in 1886 when, having set up the African Mining Corporation, he used it to make strategic investments in the Kimberley mine, while also investing independently on his own account there, and in the nearby Bultfontein mines. This was a time when the future of diamond mining was seen to lie in the amalgamation of the numerous existing companies, so that production and marketing could be controlled in pursuit of stable, high prices. Currie naturally recognized the principle involved, so akin to that of his shipping conference. He tried but was unable to outmanoeuvre larger or more unscrupulous players, such as Cecil Rhodes and Barney Barnato; however, by a mixture of shrewdness and luck, his shareholdings were such that he emerged in November 1888 as chairman of the London board of the new De Beers Consolidated Mines. He held that position for three years, and remained for many years a director, while also enjoying the huge dividends which De Beers regularly paid in the 1890s.

The attraction of diamonds was rivalled only by the lure of gold. Early in 1887, and working this time through contacts in Natal which handled so much of the Transvaal trade rather than his Cape Town agents, Currie followed a similar approach. He established the African Investment Corporation, again under the control of family and very close friends, and bought up claims. Some were of little worth, but by the mid-1890s his Durban-Roodepoort Gold Mining Company was one of the most productive of all, regularly offering its shareholders dividends between 40 and 80 per cent.

Currie also made investments of a more speculative kind, for instance in exploration companies and Rhodes's British South Africa Company. They seem to have reflected less material conviction than his need to keep in touch with local developments and to nurture political connections. Rhodes in particular, much as Currie disliked him and refused to join the South Africa Company's board, was too powerful to be ignored. In a similar way, Currie was drawn into activities associated with the wider partition of Africa. The prospect of rival shipping firms, French, German, Portuguese, or British, invading his sphere from the north on both coasts, as well as foreign annexations, was ever-present after 1880. To prevent this on the west, Currie devoted much energy to supporting both the territorial claims of the Cape government to South-West Africa, and those of the trader Robert Lewis to copper-mining concessions at Otavi. On the east he dabbled with William Mackinnon in schemes to develop the Portuguese territory of Mozambique. On both sides of the continent, he negotiated constantly for mail contracts and government subventions which would help Castle Mail steamers nose northwards, towards Zanzibar, Mauritius, or Luanda. He displayed boundless persistence and ingenuity in devising arguments—about the need for defence, the necessity of stimulating legitimate trade and thwarting foreign ambitions—capable of winning Admiralty or Foreign Office support, and of mortifying the Treasury.

An ambivalent reputation Currie's reputation was consequently a mixed one. Respected for his business acumen and held up as a contemporary model for emulation, he was simultaneously distrusted by many who had dealings with him; warmly appreciated for his genial hospitality, he was also found unctuous and self-centred. He was described by a director of De Beers as 'the Scotch Fox' (Rothschild archives, B17 Rh), and such epithets, as well as cynical comment about his vanity and social climbing, sat uneasily alongside his always dignified, bearded and increasingly patriarchal appearance. The unscrupulousness which in the 1890s led to a series of libellous but uncontested pamphlets by one former employee stands in marked contrast to the finer feelings of a considerate landlord, consistent churchgoer, and discerning collector of J. M. W. Turner's paintings.

In the 1890s, Currie's relations with public figures in London and South Africa steadily cooled. Personally secure, he had less need to cultivate them, and his cruises carrying the great and the good ceased after Gladstone's last outing to Kiel in 1895. His claims to have the public interest at heart were more than ever regarded as exaggerated and insincere; increasingly, not only merchants but politicians and industrialists found his management of the shipping conference intolerable and his readiness to make terms with German lines a betrayal of British interests. The Cape government's serious attempt to deprive the Castle and Union companies of the mail contract in 1899 was as worrying for Currie as its failure to find an alternative contractor was comforting. He was reaching the limits of his ability to sustain Castle Mail under its existing organization, given the need for extensive rebuilding to meet renewed challenges from his main competitors.

Creation of Union Castle Company His response late in 1899 was to go for a merger of Castle Mail and the Union Company. In an agreement marked by his characteristic blend of ingenuity and effrontery, Currie in effect paid the shareholders of the Union Company to allow him to take them over. Early in 1900, on a tide of heady expectations as to its prospects in a prosperous post-war and perhaps federated South Africa, Currie attended the birth of the new Union Castle Company, to be managed like its predecessor by Donald Currie & Co. It was a masterly if flawed achievement, reflecting no particular talent for innovation but demonstrating most tellingly the potential for survival of the small family firm in the face of all the pressures for enlargement of scale in the form of public limited companies.

Its operations Currie now left increasingly to his three sons-in-law whom he had brought into the management agreement in 1896. In the 1890s he had established the London shipping exchange, taken an active interest in the London chamber of commerce, and supported the inclusion of seamen within the Workmen's Compensation Act of 1897; but in 1900 he retired from parliament and withdrew from any major part in London's shipping world. The one exception to this was his appearance in 1908 before the royal commission investigating shipping rings, where to the last he maintained his uncompromising rejection of all the criticisms levelled at them. It was Currie's last and this time essentially fruitless stand, for the report issued shortly after his death rejected his arguments. Only months later in 1910, the government of the new Union of South Africa, which embodied the federation Donald Currie had always favoured as the region's natural political system, took steps to bring the shipping ring to heel and precipitated the sale of Castle Mail by his heirs.

Honours and death After 1900, Currie spent much more time aboard his steam yacht, cruising with his family among the Scottish isles and in the Mediterranean. He realized some investments, and made several substantial donations, notably to University College Hospital, London, the universities of Edinburgh and Queen's, Belfast, and his old schools. Edinburgh reciprocated with its LLD, the City of Belfast with conferment of its freedom. Strangely, and notwithstanding his visits there in 1887–8 and 1893, there was nothing for South Africa, the source of much of his wealth, either at this time or later in his will. One of the richest men of his day, he died from chronic cystitis and cardiac failure in a nursing home, the Manor House, at Sidmouth, in Devon, on 13 April 1909, survived by his wife and all three daughters. His widow received the king's condolences, his family shared his estate of almost £2.5 million, and he was buried in the churchyard of Fortingal between Garth and Glen Lyon, Perthshire.

ANDREW PORTER

Sources A. N. Porter, *Victorian shipping, business, and imperial policy: Donald Currie, the Castle line and southern Africa*, Royal Historical Society Studies in History, 49 (1986) · F. S. Phillipson Stow to C. J. Rhodes, 8 Sept 1887, Rothschild archives, London, B17 Rh · Gladstone, *Diaries* · *CGPLA Eng. & Wales* (1909)
Archives priv. coll., family MSS · Rothschild archives, New Court, London | Bank of Scotland, Edinburgh, Union Bank of Scotland archive · BL, letters to W. E. Gladstone, Add. MSS 44454–45787 · Bodl. Oxf., corresp. with Lord Kimberley · British and Commonwealth Shipping, Castle Mail and Union Castle minute books, St Mary Axe, London · National Archives of South Africa, Cape Town, colonial secretary MSS; prime minister MSS · PRO, Colonial Office MSS; Foreign Office MSS; Treasury MSS; Board of Trade MSS
Likenesses W. W. Ouless, oils, 1908, Scot. NPG [see illus.] · Ape [C. Pellegrini], caricature, watercolour study, NPG; repro. in *VF* (21 June 1884) · W. W. Ouless, oils, University College Medical School, London · photograph, priv. coll.; repro. in Porter, *Victorian shipping*, frontispiece

Wealth at death £2,377,052 7s. 5d.: probate, 21 May 1909, *CGPLA Eng. & Wales*

Currie, (William) Finlay (1878–1968), actor, was born on 20 January 1878, at 35 Cumberland Street, Edinburgh, son of Annie Currie, Post Office clerk (his birth certificate states he was illegitimate and names no father). He completed his education at George Watson's College, Edinburgh, and began his adult working life as an organist and choirmaster. However, he was attracted to the theatre and he began what turned out to be a successful career on the variety stage with an inauspicious appearance as a courtier in W. H. Murray's *Cromond Brig* at the Pavilion, Edinburgh, in 1898. He then joined Adeler and Sutton's Pierrots, touring Scotland in concert parties. With his own act sufficiently developed Currie made his independent London début in June 1902 at the South London Music-Hall, billed as 'Harry Colvo, the double-voiced vocalist'. By 1906 he was well enough established on the variety stage to undertake an American tour that included New York, where he played at Tony Pastor's renowned Vaudeville theatre on 14th Street. This success was followed by a period of over ten years working in Australia as the principal comedian in the company managed by Sir Benjamin Fuller. Finlay Currie's variety career is reported to have been encouraged by Harry Lauder. Currie returned to London in 1930 and pursued a career on the legitimate stage which tended to be overshadowed by his subsequent relatively high film profile. He appeared in more than twenty West End plays between 1930 and 1950, including Edgar Wallace's *The Case of the Frightened Lady* at Wyndham's Theatre in 1931; *Magnolia Street* by Golding and Rawlinson at the Adelphi in 1934; *Duet in Floodlight* by J. B. Priestley at the Apollo in 1935; Ivor Novello's *Crest of the Wave* at Drury Lane in 1937; and Arthur Miller's *Death of a Salesman* at the Phoenix in 1949. During this time he acted with various companies such as the Venturers, the Repertory Players, and the Stage Society. It was, however, on screen that Finlay Currie was destined to gain wide and lasting recognition as a talented and thoroughly professional character actor. In the film world he enjoyed the reputation of being willing to work in the most exacting circumstances, often travelling far to fulfil an engagement. His first film, *The Case of the Frightened Lady* (1932), marked the beginning of a long and successful career. Halliwell's *Filmgoer's Companion* (1977) described him as 'a welcome screen face well into his eighties'. In fact, increasing age, a portly physique, and craggy features framed by a mane of white hair made him a much sought after actor in biblical and historical epics, including *Quo Vadis* (1951), *Ivanhoe* (1952), *Rob Roy* (1953), *Ben Hur* (1959), and *The Fall of the Roman Empire* (1964). He was instantly recognizable on screen, with the soft Scottish accent that he never completely disguised. His film credits, impressive in their diversity, include also *Rome Express* (1932), *The Edge of the World* (1938), *The Brothers* (1946), *The History of Mr Polly* (1949), *Billy Liar* (1963), and *Bunny Lake is Missing* (1965). While the nature of character acting often confines the actor to supporting roles, it does not inhibit the possibility of fine performances, and in

1951 Currie's portrayal of Queen Victoria's highland servant John Brown in *The Mudlark* earned him high praise. But he gave possibly his most memorable performance as the convict Magwitch in the David Lean version of *Great Expectations* in 1946.

Currie continued to accept stage and television roles regardless of advancing years. The year 1965 saw him celebrating his eighty-seventh birthday by opening in a play in Connecticut in the USA, and at eighty-nine he played the bishop in the BBC television version of *Les misérables*, confirming his stamina and enduring appeal. A quiet man, in his private life he took his recreation in book collecting; maintaining his Scottish connections, he particularly favoured the work of Robert Burns. Finlay Currie was married to the American variety actress Maud Courtney (1884–1959), who first appeared on the London stage in 1901. She was the original performer of the song 'The Honeysuckle and the Bee'. They worked together for a time with Currie billed as 'Mr C' in *Sketches at the Piano*. They had two children, George and Marion. Finlay Currie died from kidney and heart failure on 10 May 1968, at Chalfont and Gerrards Cross Hospital in Buckinghamshire. P. S. BARLOW

Sources J. Parker, ed., *Who's who in the theatre*, 15th edn (1972) · L. Halliwell, *Halliwell's filmgoer's companion* (1977) · private information (2004) [family] · *The Times* (11 May 1968) · *Daily Telegraph* (11 May 1968) · *Variety* (15 May 1968) · b. cert. · d. cert.

Wealth at death £1588: probate, 12 Aug 1968, *CGPLA Eng. & Wales*

Currie, Sir Frederick, first baronet (1799–1875), administrator in India, third son of Mark Currie (1759–1835), a distiller of Duke Street, Bloomsbury, and his wife, Elizabeth (d. 1856), daughter of John Close of Easby, Yorkshire, was born on 3 February 1799. He was educated at Charterhouse School and the East India Company's college at Haileybury and, after arriving in Bengal in 1818, filled a variety of judicial and revenue posts in Gorakhpur district. In 1835 he became commissioner of Benares division and in May 1840 was appointed a judge of the *sadr diwani* and *nizamat adalat* at Allahabad. In 1844 he was appointed foreign secretary to the government of India.

As foreign secretary Currie accompanied the governor-general, Sir Henry Hardinge, throughout the First Anglo-Sikh War (1845–6) and was deputed by him to negotiate the treaties of Lahore and Bhyrowal. Currie did not determine the content of either treaty, but his diplomatic skills so impressed Hardinge that he urged the home authorities to reward him with a baronetcy, a request which was granted in January 1847.

In 1847 Currie joined the supreme council but was subsequently dispatched to Lahore as resident when Henry Lawrence became ill. Historians have judged Currie's residency harshly, saying that he was too steeped in the regulation government of Bengal to adapt to the Punjab 'experiment' of John and Henry Lawrence. The real difference, however, was that Currie went to Lahore hoping to make the regency work and unlike the Lawrences did not intend to rule the Sikhs as though they were already British subjects. In April 1848, within days of assuming office, Currie was lamenting John Lawrence's overbearing

interference in the Punjab's internal affairs, but in spite of such insights he did not foresee the revolt which erupted in the summer of 1848 and ended with the Punjab's annexation.

In March 1849 Currie took up his seat again in the supreme council, an office he held until 1853, when he returned to England. He was elected a director of the East India Company in 1854 and chairman in 1858. In the aftermath of the uprising of 1857 he advised the government on the transfer of power from company to crown and became vice-president of the first council of the secretary of state for India, a post which he held until 1860. He was made an honorary DCL by the University of Oxford in 1866.

Currie was married three times: first, on 7 August 1820 to Susannah (d. 1832), daughter of John Pascal Larkins of the Bengal civil service; secondly, on 3 September 1834 to Lucy Elizabeth (d. 1835), daughter of Robert Merttins *Bird of the Bengal civil service; and thirdly, on 10 February 1841 to Katherine Maria (d. 1909), daughter of George Powney Thompson also of the Bengal civil service. He had children from all three marriages, totalling eight sons and four daughters. Currie died on 10 September 1875 at St Leonards, and was succeeded by his eldest son.

H. M. STEPHENS, *rev.* KATHERINE PRIOR

Sources *East-India Register and Directory* (1843–50) · H. T. Prinsep and R. Doss, eds., *A general register of the Hon'ble East India Company's civil servants of the Bengal establishment from 1790 to 1842* (1844) · BL OIOC, Haileybury MSS · S. S. Thorburn, *The Punjab in war and peace* (1904) · Lord Hardinge's correspondence, BL OIOC, Broughton MSS · Burke, *Peerage* (1939) · *DNB* · R. L. Arrowsmith, ed., *Charterhouse register, 1769–1872* (1974) · F. C. Danvers and others, *Memorials of old Haileybury College* (1894) · H. H. Dodwell, *Cambridge history of India*, 5 (1968) · N. M. Khilnani, *British power in the Punjab, 1839–1858* (1972) · F. P. Gibbon, *The Lawrences of the Punjab* (1908)

Archives BL, corresp. with Major G. Broadfoot, Add. MSS 40127–40129 · NA Scot., corresp. with Dalhousie · PRO, corresp. with Lord Ellenborough, PRO 30/12

Likenesses wood-engraving, repro. in *ILN* (9 Oct 1858)

Wealth at death £18,000: probate, 14 Oct 1875, *CGPLA Eng. & Wales*

Currie, James (1756–1805), physician and author, was born in Kirkpatrick Fleming, Dumfriesshire, on 31 May 1756, the second of at least nine children and the first and only surviving son of James Currie (1716–1773), minister of the Church of Scotland, and his wife, Jean Boyd (d. 1769). Currie's youngest sister was the mother of William Henry *Duncan (1805–1863), medical officer of health for Liverpool. In 1762 his father transferred to nearby Middlebie, where Currie received his early education from his father and at the parish school. Later, he attended the excellent Dumfries grammar school, where he shared a room with William Charles Wells (1757–1817).

In 1771 Currie's father, then fatally ill, apprenticed him to a factor in an American store operated by the Glasgow firm of William Cunninghame & Co. in Cabin Point, Virginia. Currie's years there were filled with troubles. Later he recalled 'hard usage and numberless mortifications ... and the misfortune I had of living with a man from whom nothing could be learned that belonged to either the man of business or the gentleman' (Shapiro, 212). Currie became gravely ill with an 'endemic fever', probably malaria, and suffered repeated bouts of the disease. On his father's death, he gave his share of the estate to his sisters.

Currie's life became impossible as political unrest increased. He wrote a defence of the Scottish merchants, which appeared anonymously in Pinckney's *Virginia Gazette* of 23 March 1775, his first published work. Finally he sought refuge with his cousin, James Currie, the principal physician of Richmond, Virginia. Although Currie sympathized with the Americans he remained a loyalist, and petitioned for permission to leave the state for medical training at Edinburgh. This was given, and he boarded ship in the spring of 1776. Unfortunately, another Virginia ship seized them and all the passengers were turned out on shore without their goods. Currie returned to Virginia and was soon drafted into the colonial army. He found a substitute, only to be drafted for a second time. He again boarded a ship which was also seized, and he sailed for 150 miles in an open boat to appeal against the seizure. He sailed at last in September 1776, on an American vessel, to St Martin's, one of the Leeward Islands. During the voyage the ship was pounded by three autumn gales; three times it was pursued and fired upon by British or French ships, and twice American privateers boarded the ship.

Hoping to recoup his losses Currie traded between Antigua and St Eustatius, but his employer failed and he lost everything. Exhausted and despairing he suffered yet another attack of fever and became paralysed. As he was convalescing on Antigua he was commissioned to convey to Britain a letter complaining of Admiral Young. Even this voyage proved stormy and dangerous, but after two near shipwrecks he landed at Deptford on 2 May 1777.

Currie then joined his aunt and sisters in Edinburgh. In December he enrolled in the medical school, and he soon became a favourite of William Cullen, who probably inspired his lifelong interest in the effects of heat and cold. He took courses in the liberal arts as well as in medicine and renewed his acquaintanceship with old friends from Dumfries. He joined at least three Edinburgh clubs including the Medical Society of Edinburgh. Currie held responsible posts in the society, including membership of the printing committee, along with John Aikin and Thomas Percival. He was also an active member of the Speculative Society. However, that spring he fell seriously ill with rheumatic fever, which damaged his heart; his lungs were already weak.

In his final year at Edinburgh, Currie hoped to be named physician to an army expedition to Jamaica. Because the expedition was to sail before he could become MD at Edinburgh, he obtained his degree from Glasgow University, on 30 March 1780. However, on reaching London he found that the post had gone to another physician. Delayed in the capital he witnessed the Gordon riots and composed letters on the subject for a London newspaper. Two of these letters, signed Caius, were published in the *Public Advertiser*: they defended the Scots against the bigotry that had been stirred up by opponents of Lord Bute. Currie at last decided to stay in England and open a practice. With

the encouragement of Matthew Dobson, who intended to retire, he finally chose Liverpool, and arrived there in October 1780.

In the first few months Currie continued to struggle. Discouraged he wrote to George Bell: 'I get a little practice, but my patients seem to die out of spite' (Thornton, 122). However, he soon established himself in Liverpool where he was liked and respected. Soon after his arrival he became a physician to the dispensary, which he served until 1784. He became an intimate friend of William Roscoe, with whom he founded the Liverpool Literary Society (this was forced to disband in 1793 because of suspicions that it was Jacobin). He became an honorary member of the Manchester Literary and Philosophical Society in 1781.

On 9 January 1783 Currie married Lucy (d. 1836), the daughter of William Wallace, a very wealthy Liverpool merchant of Irish descent. It appears to have been a very happy marriage, and Lucy's wealth at last enabled Currie to assist his sisters. The couple had nine children, three of whom died young. In 1784 he again fell ill. Three of his sisters died that year of consumption. In January he left his sickbed to consult with Thomas Percival about George Bell, who was dying of typhus, and returned home expecting to die himself. Two days later, on 5 February, his first son, William Wallace, was born. In April he travelled to Bristol to repair his health on the advice of Erasmus Darwin, who included Currie's case in his *Zoonomia*. Although he recovered, he suffered from consumption for the rest of his life.

In 1786 Currie became physician to the Liverpool Infirmary. In the same year, in accord with his lifelong interest in mental illness, he began working to establish a lunatic asylum. John Howard supported him, and the asylum opened in 1792. In 1788 he became a member of the London Medical Society; in 1791 FRCPE; and in 1792 FRS. He helped to found numerous civic institutions including the Liverpool Athenaeum and the Liverpool Botanic Garden. About 1796 he began campaigning for a fever hospital like that in Manchester, persisting despite strong opposition. This institution, the House of Recovery, opened after his death in 1806.

Currie always loved his native land. As he grew successful, Scots of every description found a welcome in his house, and he helped many young men including Henry Duncan, the founder of the Savings Bank, and Thomas Campbell, the poet. During much of his life Currie delighted in literary and philosophical activities. He reviewed books in both the *Analytical Review* and the *Critical Review*. He often discussed biography with Roscoe, himself a distinguished biographer, and he planned works of his own. He wrote several sketches for Liverpool newspapers signed the Recluse and composed a biographical sketch of his friend George Bell.

Following the death of Robert Burns in 1796, Currie, who had met Burns only once but had many ties to Burns's circle, volunteered to prepare an edition of Burns's work, accompanied by a biography. Currie had expected that he would receive an organized selection of Burns's most important papers; instead he was horrified to find a 'huge and shapeless mass … the complete sweepings of his drawers' (Thornton, 358). Nevertheless he persisted, to the detriment of his own health. The result was his four-volume edition of *The works of Robert Burns: with an account of his life, and a criticism on his writings, to which are prefixed, some observations on the character and condition of the Scottish peasantry*, first published in 1800, with many subsequent editions. Currie's goal was to raise funds for the support of Burns's widow and family, and in this he succeeded. The edition was praised by reviewers, and by Burns's brother Gilbert. However, many later admirers of Burns's poetry were angered by Currie's suggestion that he drank to excess. Their adulation of Burns led to unfounded claims about Currie's own character and conduct. Robert Thornton's biography, *James Currie, the Entire Stranger, and Robert Burns* (1963) demonstrated the injustice of such aspersions.

Currie's most important medical work was *Medical reports, on the effects of water, cold and warm, as a remedy in fever and other diseases … To which are added, observations on the nature of fever* (1797). This edition sold out rapidly, and three more revised and enlarged editions appeared in 1798, 1804, and 1805. Currie worked on the final edition up to the day of his death. He borrowed the idea of treating fevers with cool baths from William Wright, but supported it with many clinical experiments and observations, including simultaneous observations of the pulse rate and temperature of fever patients.

Currie's early life had made him hate bigotry, captivity, and slavery. In Liverpool he worked behind the scenes for abolition of the slave trade. With Roscoe he wrote a poem entitled *The African*, and for years he corresponded with William Wilberforce, supplying him with devastating information about the slave trade. Currie and his family attended the Paradise Street presbyterian chapel and endorsed the abolitionist sermons of John Yates. He drew up the Liverpool resolution for repeal of the Test Act in 1790. He also favoured universal religious toleration, supported the United Irishmen, and sympathized with the French revolutionaries; he considered Pitt a traitor to the values he had once championed. His views were well known in Liverpool.

In 1793 Currie borrowed money to enable him to emigrate and then wrote *A letter, commercial and political, addressed to the Rt Hon. William Pitt … by Jasper Wilson*. The pamphlet, dated 6 June 1793, was printed secretly in Liverpool and distributed in London, probably through Wilberforce, and it attempted to persuade the prime minister not to declare war with France. It sold out instantly, and two more editions also sold out within two months. It was widely reprinted throughout England, Europe, and America. By 1794 Currie's authorship of the work was well known, though he never admitted it publicly. To his surprise he retained the trust of Liverpudlians and his practice did not suffer. When a French invasion threatened Liverpool in 1797 Currie not only subscribed for its defence but was appointed to a committee to oversee the preparations. In 1802 he was awarded the freedom of Liverpool,

and in 1803 he was asked to command the Liverpool fusiliers, but declined. To the very end of his life he insisted that he was a loyal monarchist.

In 1799 two doctors charged with the care of the French prisoners of war in Liverpool borough gaol asked Currie for help in improving the deplorable conditions, because he was the only person they trusted. Finding the prisoners naked, sick, and starving, Currie sought to help them, using Maxwell Garthshore, a London physician, as an intermediary. Currie's interference was deeply resented by the government, and by Joseph Banks and Gilbert Blane, chief of the government medical inspectors. However, Currie's extremely well-researched charges resulted in the dispatch of a commission to Liverpool which, despite its effort to discredit him as a Jacobin, conceded that conditions must be improved and that the prisoners needed more food and clothing. Currie's efforts were honoured in 1926 by Alfred de Curzon, the French consul.

In the winter of 1800–01 Currie caught pneumonia. Although he continued to work after recovering, he suffered from an incessant cough and feared he was fatally ill. In May 1804 he paid a last visit to Scotland to set his affairs in order. He returned to Liverpool, worked through the summer, and attended the deathbed of Thomas Percival in Manchester before he himself was prostrated. In November 1804 he travelled to Clifton. That winter he moved between Clifton and Bath, as he alternated between despair and partial recovery. In March 1805 he resigned from the Liverpool Infirmary and decided to remain in Bath. By midsummer he was very weak and he decided to travel along the south coast. He sent for his wife and his eldest son, William Wallace. After a week of intense suffering he died of heart failure at Sidmouth in Devon, on 31 August 1805, and was buried in the parish church there. Lucy Currie lived until 1836.

William Wallace Currie recalled his father as tall, well-built, and dignified, with piercing, dark blue eyes. Although he could be playful he was also melancholy. He loved Scottish songs. William summed up his father's character as one of 'ardent humanity' (Thornton, 379).

MARGARET DELACY

Sources R. D. Thornton, *James Currie, the entire stranger, and Robert Burns* (1963) · R. W. Shapiro, 'James Currie—the physician and the quest', *Medical History*, 7 (1963), 212–31 · W. W. Currie, ed., *Memoir of the life, writings and correspondence of James Currie*, 2 vols. (1831) · I. Sellers, 'William Roscoe, the Roscoe circle, and radical politics in Liverpool, 1787–1807', *Lancashire and Cheshire Hist. Society*, 120 (1968), 45–62 · T. H. Bickerton and R. M. B. MacKenna, *A medical history of Liverpool from the earliest days to the year 1920*, ed. H. R. Bickerton (1936) · F. L. Pleadwell, 'That remarkable philosopher and physician, Wells of Charleston', *Annals of Medical History*, new ser., 6 (1934), 128–42 · J. W. Estes, 'Quantitative observations of fever and its treatment before the advent of short clinical thermometers', *Medical History*, 35 (1991), 189–216 · H. Douglas, *Robert Burns, a life* (1976) · *DNB* · A. de Curzon, *Dr James Currie and the French prisoners of war in Liverpool, 1800–1801* (1926) · *GM*, 1st ser., 75 (1805), 885

Archives Lpool RO, corresp. and journal, 920CUR · Lpool RO, corresp. relating to the slave trade and treatment of French POWs · Mitchell L., Glas., corresp. | NL Scot., corresp. with W. Cadell and Davies, MSS 1653–1655

Likenesses R. H. Cromek, line engraving, pubd 1807 (after H. Hone), BM, NPG · R. H. Cromek, stipple, 1807 (after H. Hone),

Wellcome L. • W. T. Fry, coloured stipple, 1816 (after T. Hargreaves), Wellcome L. • T. A. Dean, engraving, 1830 (after W. Williamson, 1791), Wellcome L. • stipple, 1839 (after T. Hargreaves), Wellcome L. • J. Brain, stipple (after T. Hargreaves), Wellcome L. • T. A. Dean, engraving (aged thirty-five; after Williamson), Liverpool Athenaeum; repro. in Thornton, *James Currie*, facing p. 145 • W. T. Fry, stipple (after T. Hargreaves), BM, NPG; repro. in *The British gallery of contemporary portraits* (1816) • Stothard?, crayon drawing, U. Edin. • portrait, Liverpool Central Library; repro. in Bickerton and others, *Medical history of Liverpool*, facing p. 52 • stipple, NPG

Wealth at death   £4000 agreed in marriage settlement; approx. £955 in specific bequests; plus trust fund; property: Thornton, *James Currie*, 372

Currie, Sir James (1868–1937), educationist, was born in Edinburgh on 31 May 1868, the eldest son of the Revd James Currie, principal of the Church of Scotland Training College, Edinburgh, and his wife, Jane Lyall, daughter of George Key, of St Vigeans, Forfarshire. He was educated at Fettes College, at Edinburgh University, and at Lincoln College, Oxford, to which he gained a classical scholarship in 1888; he graduated in 1892.

Currie returned to Edinburgh where he taught for a number of years in one of the Scottish education board's schools, which gave him valuable practical experience. In 1899 he joined the Egyptian education department and in 1900 was selected by Lord Cromer to be the first director of education in Anglo-Egyptian Sudan. He had two main educational objectives. The first was to develop basic education in Western-style (but Arabic-language) elementary schools (*kuttabs*), not least in order to counteract the influence of the traditional Koranic schools (*khalwas*), officially regarded as centres of superstition and fanaticism. Consequently *kuttab* education was encouraged by the institution of a 'voluntary education tax', which originated as a bargain between Currie and the distinguished Sudanese educationist Babikr Bedri, and was later extended to most of the riverine northern Sudan.

Currie's second main objective was to train a small number of Sudanese for minor government posts. They were educated in so-called 'primary' schools, where some English was taught. Unlike *kuttab* education, primary education was limited to the anticipated vacancies for its leavers. Between 1906 and 1914 primary enrolment was virtually static at about 770 pupils, while *kuttab* enrolment expanded from 1280 to over 3600. In the early 1900s Gordon Memorial College at Khartoum, of which Currie was *ex officio* principal, was a model primary school, upon which was superimposed a number of vocational courses. Several research institutes, including the Wellcome medical laboratories and a geological survey, were more or less loosely affiliated to the college.

Currie was determined to support only those types of education which served the economic needs of the Sudan. Consequently he denied even the most modest financial assistance to southern Sudanese education, and later refused to support educational ventures in the south in the absence of a comprehensive southern educational policy based on extensive anthropological and sociological research. He nevertheless did not oppose girls' education, which in the early 1900s was believed to serve no economic or administrative purpose. When in 1907 Babikr Bedri demonstrated that a girls' school could function without provoking unmanageable local opposition, Currie supported the school both financially and otherwise.

Before 1914 Currie was one of a small minority of civilians in an administration dominated by British officers seconded from the Egyptian army. He was not always *persona grata* to his military colleagues: some of them thought his ideas 'too dogmatic', even 'socialistic'. He was moreover an outspoken supporter of the gradually growing civilian element in the administration. In 1911 he became a member of the governor-general's council. By 1912 educational expenditure had risen to 4 per cent of the Sudan government's revenue—a figure which declined significantly under his successors, falling as low as 1.9 per cent in 1926. But by 1913 he felt that the administration was failing adequately to support the academic development of Gordon College. In 1914 he resigned.

Currie married in 1913 Hilda Beatrice, only daughter of Sir Thomas Hanbury, a merchant and botanist, of La Mortola, Ventimiglia, Italy; they had a daughter who died in childhood. On his return to Britain he settled in Wiltshire, where he farmed. He soon became involved in important war work. In 1916 he was appointed director of a new labour supply department, which trained unskilled labour for semi-skilled tasks in the manufacture of munitions. In 1918 he became controller of the Ministry of Labour's training department, which was particularly successful in the rehabilitation of disabled former servicemen. These voluntary services were recognized when he was made a KBE in 1920. He stood unsuccessfully for parliament in the Devizes constituency as an Asquithian Liberal in the 1918 general election.

In 1922 Currie became the first director of the Empire Cotton Growing Corporation and in 1923 a member of the government's advisory committee on native education in tropical Africa. Between the wars he served, often as chairman, on the governing bodies of several institutions, including the Imperial College of Tropical Agriculture, Trinidad. He was a governor of the Imperial College of Science and Technology, South Kensington. As chairman of the governors of Dauntsey's School, Devizes, he modernized and greatly enlarged a small local grammar school and gained for it a national reputation. In 1933 he was created KCMG.

Currie's links with the Sudan did not cease in 1914. In 1921–2 he was one of the Sudan's representatives in the difficult but ultimately successful negotiations with the Treasury for the refinancing of the Sennar Dam construction works. He revisited the Sudan in 1926 and 1932. He was unhappy at the lack of educational progress, and especially at the negative effects upon education of the policy of indirect rule, which he sharply criticized in the *Journal of the African Society* (vols. 33, 1934, and 34, 1935). He was an outspoken, even combative man, and this public criticism was unwelcome in Khartoum. One senior official attributed it to Currie's 'failing powers'. Certain other comments were even less charitable. In 1936 he suggested the secondment of Christopher Cox to serve as director of education in the Sudan. He also prompted Sir Stuart Symes to invite the De La Warr commission, set up in 1936 to report on education in British East Africa, to extend its work to the Sudan. The commission's report, published in 1937, compared the Sudan's educational progress unfavourably with that of British East Africa, a conclusion which, had he lived to read it, would have neither surprised nor displeased him. Currie died at Corpus Christi College, Cambridge, on 17 March 1937. Until 1956 a bronze bust of him stood in the original Gordon College building of the University of Khartoum.   G. N. SANDERSON

Sources U. Durham L., department of palaeography and diplomatic, Sudan archive, Wingate MSS • M. W. Daly, *Empire on the Nile* (1986) • B. Bedri, *Memoirs*, trans. Y. Bedri and P. Hogg, 2 (1980) [with introduction by G. N. Sanderson] • *DNB* • L. M. Passmore Sanderson and G. N. Sanderson, *Education, religion and politics in southern Sudan, 1899–1964* (1981) • Sudan government, annual reports of the education department, 1901–14, National Record Office, Khartoum • Sudan government, annual reports of the Gordon Memorial College, 1904–14, National Record Office, Khartoum • M. O. Beshir, *Educational development in the Sudan, 1898–1956* (1969) • M. W. Daly, *Imperial Sudan* (1991) • Sudan government, report of Lord De La Warr's education commission, 1937, National Record Office, Khartoum • *CGPLA Eng. & Wales* (1937)

Archives Ministry of Education, Khartoum, archives | Bodl. RH, corresp. with Lord Lugard • U. Durham L., department of palaeography and diplomatic, Sudan archive, corresp. with Sir Reginald Wingate

Likenesses W. G. John, bust, *c*.1918; formerly at University of Khartoum, Sudan, *c*.1956

Wealth at death £60,819 0s. 5d.: probate, 6 July 1937, *CGPLA Eng. & Wales*

Currie [*née* Lamb], **Mary Montgomerie**, **Lady Currie** [*pseud.* Violet Fane] (1843–1905), poet and writer, was born on 24 February 1843 at Littlehampton, Sussex, the eldest among the four children of Charles James Savile Montgomerie Lamb (1816–1856) and (Anna) Charlotte, *née* Gray (*bap.* 1824, *d.* 1880), eldest daughter of Arthur Hopwood Gray, draper and, allegedly, smuggler, of Bersted, Sussex. Mary Lamb's grandfather was Sir Charles Montolieu Lamb, second baronet, of Beauport, Sussex, who married Mary, daughter and heir of Archibald Montgomerie, eleventh earl of Eglinton; her great-grandfather was Sir James Bland Burges, afterwards Lamb. At sixteen Charles Lamb eloped with Anna Charlotte, then nineteen. A few weeks after her birth, Mary was sent to her grandparents at Beauport, near Battle, accompanied by a letter from her father confessing his secret marriage. Sir Charles and Lady Mary Lamb had the infant baptized on the billiard table and adopted her. Her father immediately departed with his wife on a tour of Europe and the East, and returned to England a year and a half later a devotee of 'the Oriental life', a proponent of European revolution, and an avowed agnostic.

Mary Lamb's upbringing at Beauport thereafter was, by her own account, unorthodox in the extreme. She wore Turkish dress, as did both her parents, 'went barefoot, had no bed, wore no nightgown, and was summoned by the clapping of hands'. She acquired her father's opposition to established religion and his vegetarianism, and

throughout her life encouraged romantic tales of her mother's 'gipsy blood'. She also absorbed the influence of her father's many literary friends and acquaintants, including Edward Bulwer-Lytton, George Borrow, and Edward Fitzgerald. Charles Lamb died in 1856, blind and deserted by his wife, without succeeding to the baronetcy. Lady Sophia Eglinton, wife of the fourteenth earl, took over Mary Lamb's education and brought her out in London society, where she soon met with considerable success. She etched the illustrations for a reprint of Tennyson's *Mariana* (Worthing, 1863) and began to pursue a literary career.

On 27 February 1864 Mary Lamb married Henry Sydenham Singleton (1818/19–1893) of Mell, co. Louth, and Hazeley, Hampshire, an Irish landowner. Her first book-length publication, a volume of passionate love poetry entitled *From Dawn to Noon*, appeared in 1872 under the pseudonym Violet Fane. The name was taken from a character in Disraeli's *Vivian Grey* (she later claimed to have forgotten the source) and remained her primary *nom de plume*, though for newspaper and magazine publication she sometimes preferred anonymity, the single initial 'V', or, on occasion, Pamela, Kajin, or Vera. *From Dawn to Noon* rapidly became a *succès de scandale*. The poems were widely understood to be addressed to Clare Vyner, a wealthy Yorkshire squire with whom Mary Lamb had fallen in love in the early 1860s and whose refusal to marry her had precipitated her into the match with the much older Singleton. Several more volumes followed: *Denzil Place: a Story in Verse* (1875), published in America as *Constance's Fate* (savaged by the press for its sympathetic portrayal of an adulterous woman), a more sentimental verse narrative, *The Queen of the Fairies* (1876), and a drama in prose and verse, *Anthony Babington* (1877). Her *Collected Verses* was published in 1880.

A beautiful and charming woman, with a reputation for original and witty conversation, Violet Fane was a well-known figure in London society of the 1870s and 1880s. W. H. Mallock dedicated his satire *The New Republic* (1877) to her, and represented her as the unhappily married and captivating Mrs Sinclair 'who has published a volume of poems, and is a sort of fashionable London Sappho' (p. 27). Oscar Wilde frequented her house in Grosvenor Place and solicited two poems from her for the *Woman's World* magazine. Other members of her coterie included Robert Browning, Algernon Swinburne, A. W. Kinglake, Alfred Austin, the duchess of Argyll (Princess Louise), James McNeil Whistler, and Lily Langtry. Mrs Singleton's love affairs grew ever more complicated, and a source of much gossip in the scandal sheets of the day. In the early 1870s she exchanged illicit vows with Philip Henry Wodehouse Currie of the Foreign Office (see below). Their liaison rapidly became an open secret, and she acted as his hostess at entertainments for foreign dignitaries. Her involvement with Vyner nevertheless continued for several years, and in 1880 she also had a more discreet affair with Currie's cousin, the poet and traveller Wilfrid Scawen Blunt, whose diaries provide the most detailed account of her life beside her own (incomplete and unpublished) memoirs.

Mary Singleton's love life provided the inspiration for most of her verse and prose. In 1877–8 she wrote a series of sketches for Edmund Yates's magazine, *The World*, collected as the *Edwin and Angelina Papers* (1878). The barely disguised account of her acrimonious relationship with her husband (the morose 'Edwin'), and her affair with Currie ('D'Arcy') made it her most scandalous publication to date. Three novels followed: *Sophy, or, The Adventures of a Savage* (1881), which drew heavily on memories of her childhood at Beauport and proved her most popular work, going through three editions in its first year; *Thro' Love and War* (1886), in which the heroine shamelessly pursues a military man she meets in a railway carriage; and her study of modern womanhood, *The Story of Helen Davenant* (1889). She returned to poetry with *Autumn Songs* (1889), and in 1892 her poems were again collected, this time handsomely bound in two volumes in a limited edition of 365 copies. In the same year she published her sole work of translation, *Memoirs of Marguerite de Valois, Queen of Navarre*.

Henry Singleton, with whom Mary had two sons (Harry and John) and two daughters (Clara and Sophy), died on 16 March 1893, and on 24 January 1894 Mary Singleton married Sir Philip Henry Wodehouse *Currie (1834–1906), later Baron Currie of Hawley and newly appointed British ambassador to Constantinople. She followed him to Pera, where they lived until 1898, then on a second ambassadorial posting to Rome. During her time abroad she published regularly in English magazines, principally the *Pall Mall Magazine* and *Ladies' Realm*, and produced two volumes of poetry: *Under Cross and Crescent* (1896) and *Betwixt Two Seas: Poems and Ballads Written at Constantinople and Therapia* (1900). To the amusement of the British press, Sultan Abdul Hamid II, seeking favour with the British embassy, ordered a translation of her poems into Turkish. In her last years she contributed to a number of periodicals, using her own name. Her prose essays were reprinted in *Two Moods of a Man* (1901) and *Collected Essays* (1902). The Curries retired to Hawley, Hampshire, in 1903, accompanied by Clara's daughter Pera, whose upbringing they had taken over. Lady Currie died of heart failure on 13 October 1905 while staying at the Grand Hotel, Harrogate. She was buried in the family vault at Mattingley church, Hawley, near Winchfield, Hampshire, on 18 October.

During her lifetime several of Violet Fane's poems were set to music, notably 'For Ever and For Ever' by Sir Paolo Tosti. Lily Langtry's memoirs capture the predominant response of contemporaries to her work, recalling her as a writer of 'ardent love poems, which in those hypocritical days were considered highly improper'. Regarded, in her own time, as a late-Victorian Laetitia Landon, she is now more likely to find attention as a writer of (in Wilfrid Scawen Blunt's words) 'very superior society verse'.

HELEN SMALL

Sources literary correspondence, unpubd memoirs (covering her family history and early childhood), diaries, family papers,

photographs, and newspaper cuttings relating to her career, U. Reading L., Violet Fane archive · M. Singleton, letters to Wilfrid Scawen Blunt, FM Cam., Blunt papers [64 letters] · W. S. Blunt, autograph diaries, and MS of *Alms to oblivion*, FM Cam., Blunt papers [esp. pt. 6, chap. 5, 'Angelina'] · *The Times* (16 Oct 1905) · *Westminster Gazette* (16 Oct 1905) · *The Times* (14 May 1906) [obit. of Lord Currie] · *The Times* (25 Jan 1894), 10a · *The Queen* (3 Feb 1894), 186 · Burke, *Peerage* (1905) · Burke, *Peerage* (1910) · *WW* (1904) · biographical preface, V. Fane, *Poems* (1892) · 'Lady artists of the day: Lady Currie (Violet Fane)', *The Lady* (29 Dec 1904), 1069 · A. T. C. Pratt, ed., *People of the period: being a collection of the biographies of upwards of six thousand living celebrities*, 1 (1897), 284 · *Men and women of the time* (1899) · W. H. Mallock, *The new republic* (1877) · W. H. Mallock, *The new republic* (1877); repr. with introduction by J. Lucas (1975) · W. H. Mallock, *Memoirs of life and literature* (1920) · *The letters of Oscar Wilde*, ed. R. Hart-Davis (1962) · *More letters of Oscar Wilde*, ed. R. Hart-Davis (1985) · *Oscar Wilde on vegetarianism: an unpublished letter to Violet Fane* (1991) · L. Langtry, *The days I knew* [n.d.] · M. Baring, *The puppet show of memory* (1922) · F. Hays, *Women of the day: a biographical dictionary of notable contemporaries* (1885) · Allibone, *Dict.* · 'review of *Denzil Place*', *Saturday Review*, 40 (24 July 1875), 120 · W. Scawen Blunt, *My diaries: being a personal narrative of events, 1888–1914*, 2 vols. (1921) · M. Montgomerie Currie, 'Are remarkable people remarkable-looking?', *Nineteenth Century and After* (Oct 1904), 622–42 · E. Longford [E. H. Pakenham, countess of Longford], *A pilgrimage of passion: the life of Wilfrid Scawen Blunt* (1979) · *Wilfrid Scawen Blunt: a memoir by his grandson the earl of Lytton* (1961) · I. Anstruther, *The knight and the umbrella: an account of the Eglinton tournament, 1839* (1963) · *Wellesley index* · *Readers' guide to periodical literature, 1900–1904* · J. Sutherland, *The Longman companion to Victorian fiction* (1988)

Archives U. Reading L., literary corresp. and family papers | FM Cam., letters to Wilfrid Scawen Blunt · Sheff. Arch., letters to earl of Wharncliffe

Likenesses A. Bassano, photograph, repro. in *The Queen* · Sebah and Zoallier, photograph, repro. in 'Lady artists of the day', *The Lady* · engraving (after photograph by A. Bassano), repro. in Fane, *Poems* · photographs, U. Reading L., Violet Fane archive, MS 2608/6

Wealth at death £31,784 0s. 10d.: probate, 17 Feb 1906, *CGPLA Eng. & Wales*

Currie, Philip Henry Wodehouse, Baron Currie (1834–1906), diplomatist, born in London on 13 October 1834, was the fourth son of Raikes *Currie (1801–1881) of Bush Hill, Middlesex, and Minley Manor, Hampshire, MP for Northampton (1837–57), and his wife, Laura Sophia (d. 1869), eldest daughter of John Wodehouse, second Baron Wodehouse. He was educated at Eton College and entered the Foreign Office at the age of twenty. He served in that department for forty years, moving up the various grades of political staff to become assistant under-secretary of state for foreign affairs in 1882 and permanent under-secretary of state, the highest permanent post in the Foreign Office, in 1888. He was précis writer to the earl of Clarendon during the latter's tenure as foreign secretary and was temporarily attached to the British legation at St Petersburg in 1856 and 1857, during Lord Wodehouse's special mission to the Russian capital on the conclusion of the Crimean War. He assisted Julian Fane in his duties as protocolist to the conferences on the affairs of Luxembourg in May 1867.

When Lord Salisbury was sent to Constantinople in 1876 to act as British plenipotentiary to the conference on the

Philip Henry Wodehouse Currie, Baron Currie (1834–1906), by Cyril Flower, Baron Battersea

Eastern question, Currie was appointed secretary to his special mission. Salisbury formed a high opinion of Currie's abilities; it was to be the beginning of a friendship and close professional relationship between the two men. On Salisbury's accession to the foreign secretaryship in April 1878, Currie became his private secretary and when Lord Beaconsfield and Lord Salisbury attended the Congress of Berlin the following June, Currie and Montague Corry (later Lord Rowton) accompanied them as joint secretaries to the special mission. Currie received the CB in recognition of his services. On his return to Britain in addition to his work as private secretary, Currie was entrusted by Salisbury with the correspondence respecting Cyprus, which had been leased from the sultan under the convention of 4 June 1878.

When Earl Granville succeeded Salisbury as foreign secretary, Currie resumed his work in the Foreign Office as senior clerk in charge of the Eastern department. He was attached as secretary to the special mission sent to invest King Alfonso XII of Spain with the Garter in 1881 and was appointed assistant under-secretary in October 1882. From June to August 1884 Currie acted as joint protocolist to the conferences held in London on the finances of Egypt. In 1885 he was created KCB and in December 1888 was promoted permanent under-secretary of state in succession to Lord Pauncefote, who became British ambassador at Washington.

Currie again worked very closely with Salisbury when the latter returned to the foreign secretaryship between 1885 and 1886 and again from 1887 until 1892. The permanent under-secretary not only had the full confidence of his chief but seemed to understand what was in Salisbury's mind without being given explicit instructions. In 1885, for instance, Currie, who had been taking the waters at the fashionable spa at Bad Homburg, secured an invitation to spend three days alone with Bismarck, the German chancellor, at Friedrichsrühe, during which they discussed a whole range of questions. Without written instructions from Salisbury, Currie was able to express the foreign secretary's views and to put out feelers which he knew Salisbury was anxious to follow up.

In fact it was often Currie, as permanent under-secretary, who expanded on official instructions to ambassadors and ministers through private letters sent regularly to posts abroad. Salisbury disliked giving precise orders; he would sketch out his position and then let Currie fill in what was left unsaid. He sometimes even left to Currie the task of receiving ambassadors before they went out to their missions in order to explain what general lines the foreign secretary intended them to follow. Salisbury refused to see either Sir Robert Morier or Sir Nicolas O'Conor, for example, when they left in 1885 and 1886 for their respective posts in St Petersburg and Constantinople; nevertheless, his short note to Currie explaining that he did not wish to see O'Conor or to give him any instructions provided the permanent under-secretary with all the guidance he needed for his conversation with the ambassador.

Currie served for five years as permanent under-secretary, during which he was made GCB in 1892. He was then appointed by Lord Rosebery in December 1893 as British ambassador at Constantinople and, following precedent, was sworn of the privy council. He held this embassy for four and a half very difficult years when relations between Britain and Turkey were exceedingly tense. During 1895 and 1896, in response to the repeated Turkish massacres of the Armenians, representatives of the great powers intervened to demand reforms and the investigation and punishment of the perpetrators. Lord Kimberley in 1895 and then Lord Salisbury (1895–1901) took the lead in trying to secure the co-operation of the other powers, especially Russia, to bring pressure on the sultan to rein in the Muslim fanatics and to grant concessions. These efforts met with little success, in part because the tsar refused to sanction any coercive measures against the sultan. There was a moment, in August 1896, after a bloody massacre of Armenians in Constantinople by Muslim mobs armed by the Turkish authorities, when it appeared that Britain might intervene despite the risks involved. These were eventually judged to be too high and the idea was dropped, but Currie was instructed to press the sultan to keep Muslim fanaticism in check. A further incident embittered relations between Britain and the sultan when Sa'id Pasha, a former grand vizier imprisoned when he refused to resume his office at the sultan's command, escaped and took refuge in the British embassy. It took five days of negotiations before the sultan promised Currie that the recalcitrant ex-minister would not be molested in any way. The sultan made no secret of his wish to have Currie replaced, but Salisbury turned a deaf ear to these intimations.

In 1897 the troubles of Asia Minor were succeeded by the revolt of Crete, which was followed by Greek army support for the Cretans, the outbreak of war between Greece and Turkey, and the disastrous defeat of the Greek army. The great powers acting in concert intervened to secure favourable terms for Greece and the autonomy of Crete under Turkish suzerainty, but the physical strain on Currie during this period was considerable and his health gave way. The situation in Constantinople would have taxed any British representative, but Currie lacked the patience, infinite tact, and indirectness of approach needed in the Ottoman capital. He was therefore more than happy to succeed Sir Clare Ford at the embassy at Rome in July 1898, his last post before he was retired on pension on 17 January 1903.

Unfortunately, what should have been a peaceful sojourn was marked by tension. This arose from the feeling in Rome that Italian interests with regard to Tripoli had been ignored during the course of Britain's negotiations with France, which led to the Anglo-French agreement of March 1899 concerning the Sudan and Nile basin. The British Foreign Office was in fact not sympathetically inclined towards supporting Italian interests in Africa, which were the main subjects of discussion during Currie's time in Rome. Neither in Constantinople nor in Rome therefore did the ambassador enjoy the kind of success that his great ability and social advantages merited. Indeed Currie's efficiency, clarity of judgement, and familiarity with the details of foreign policy were more appropriate to service in the Foreign Office in London than to the conduct of diplomacy abroad.

Currie, who belonged to a well-known banking family, was a man of considerable wealth and he entertained as befitted a 'grand seigneur'. He was more at ease among a small circle of friends and acquaintances who shared his refined tastes and enjoyed his incisive powers of conversation and good-natured irony than in the wider diplomatic circle in which he had to move. On 24 January 1894 he married Mrs Mary Montgomerie Singleton, née Lamb (1843–1905), a well-known author and poet under the *nom de plume* of Violet Fane [see Currie, Mary Montgomerie]. There were no children. Currie was raised to the peerage in 1899 as Baron Currie of Hawley. He died on 12 May 1906 at Hawley, Hampshire, and was buried three days later at St Andrew's Church, Minley, near Fleet, Hampshire.

ZARA STEINER

Sources The Times (14 May 1906) · A. Ramm, 'Lord Salisbury and the Foreign Office', The Foreign Office, 1782–1982, ed. R. Bullen (1984) · R. Jones, The nineteenth-century foreign office: an administrative history (1971) · Z. S. Steiner, The foreign office and foreign policy, 1898–1914 (1969) · DNB · The Times (16 May 1906) · The Times (7 July 1906) **Archives** PRO, corresp. and papers, FO 800/114 | BL, corresp. mainly with Lord D'Abernon, Add. MSS 47685, 48922b, 48938–48939 · BL, corresp. with Sir Austen Layard, Add. MSS 39012–39139 · Bodl. Oxf., corresp. with Lord Kimberley · CUL, letters to Lord Hardinge · PRO, corresp. with Lord Cromer, FO 633 · PRO, corresp. with Sir Arthur Nicolson, PRO 30/81

Likenesses C. Flower, Baron Battersea, photograph, NPG [see illus.]
Wealth at death £141, 468 3s. 10d.: probate, 24 June 1906, CGPLA Eng. & Wales

Currie, Raikes (1801–1881), banker and politician, was born on 15 April 1801, the second son of Isaac Currie (1760–1843), a banker of Bush Hill, Enfield, Middlesex, and his wife, Mary Anne (d. 1834), daughter of William Raikes, a prominent East India merchant. The Curries were an old Scottish family from Berwickshire. Migrating to London in the mid-eighteenth century, they established themselves as distillers, and it was out of this business that the banking firm was born. The Raikes were also connected with banking and it was the growing professional links and friendship between the two families which brought Currie's parents together. Their marriage in 1789, two years after Mary Anne's brother, Robert Raikes, joined Curries & Co., further improved the prospects of Isaac Currie's banking firm. Mary Anne's uncle, Thomas Raikes, was governor of the Bank of England from 1797 to 1799, and her cousin, George Raikes, followed her brother and joined Curries in 1806, marrying her daughter, Marianne, in 1814.

Currie was educated at Eton College, in preparation for joining his father's bank at 29 Cornhill, London. At the age of eighteen he was greatly influenced by his reading and analysis of John Locke's *Essay Concerning Human Understanding*. Believing the study of metaphysics to be of supreme importance, he was particularly impressed with the work of David Hartley, Thomas Brown, Thomas Reid, and Dugald Stewart. From this study, in part, he developed a radical commitment to independence of thought and private judgement, yet believed that life was a 'dreary, cheerless thing without the belief of immortality, and an entire trust in an all-wise and all-beneficent Creator' (*Currie, 1827–1896*, 1.195). On 28 June 1825 he married Laura Sophia (d. 1869), daughter of the second Baron Wodehouse of Kimberley, Norfolk; they had four sons and two daughters. In the following year, on the death of George Raikes, Currie became a partner in Curries & Co.

As Isaac Currie actively directed the business, his son devoted substantial time to politics and philanthropy. He established a mechanics' institute, assisted in the formation of a literary and scientific institution, and established and maintained at his own expense a school for the education of eighty children. Currie served as magistrate and deputy lieutenant for Middlesex, and as magistrate for Buckinghamshire, Essex, Hampshire, and Kent. In the wake of the abortive Hungarian revolution of 1848, Currie offered considerable assistance to prominent émigrés, including Lajos Kossuth and Paul Strzelecki.

With the death of his father in 1843, effective management of the bank fell to Raikes Currie, who eventually brought his two eldest sons, George and Bertram Wodehouse *Currie, into the business. Bertram was taken in as partner in 1852, and almost immediately became the guiding force of Curries & Co., allowing his father more time for travelling and parliamentary affairs. In 1864 Curries &

Co. merged with Glyn, Mills & Co. to become Glyn, Mills, Currie & Co., moving business to 67 Lombard Street.

In September 1836 Currie accepted an offer to stand as Liberal candidate for Northampton borough on the platform of repeal of the Septennial Act, support for the ballot, strict economy in government, removal of all civil disabilities, abolition of tithes and pluralities, and a 'moderate fixed duty on corn … with a view to a gradual return to the sound principle of free-trade in the great staple of man's subsistence' (*Northampton Mercury*, 10 Sept 1836). A committed Benthamite throughout his career, he readily paraded to the electors the 'hackneyed phrase' which stood as his guiding political principle—'the greatest happiness of the greatest number'. Surprising most observers, he was elected on 27 July 1837, ahead of the sitting Conservative, and held the seat until March 1857. Though wealthy, he was neither vain of his wealth nor parsimonious. He appealed to 'the operative classes' through frankness and a genuine flattery, finding them to be 'as a body, beyond all comparison, the most honest politicians'. Currie admitted that the working classes were justifiably suspicious of 'all professions' from 'pretended friends', and argued that the progress of the people depended principally upon their circumstances, modified by laws and institutions (*Northampton Mercury*, 3 Dec 1836).

Energetic, but not ambitious for fame, Currie often worked behind the scenes with friends, including George Grote, Lord Overstone, George Warde Norman, and Charles Buller, to promote an advanced Liberal social agenda, and the economic reforms recommended by philosophic radicalism. In 1837–8 he served on the House of Commons' committee which adopted Rowland Hill's proposal for twopenny postage. He voted in the small minority favouring Charles Villiers's annual motion for the abolition of the corn laws, and for George Grote's annual motion for the adoption of the ballot. During the 1840s Currie became intimately involved in forwarding the various banking and trade reforms which culminated in the Bank Charter Act of 1844 and Sir Robert Peel's repeal of the corn laws in 1846. In 1841 he joined Overstone, Norman, Samuel Gurney, and Lionel Rothschild in supporting Lord John Russell's nomination for the City of London, as the 'Minister of Free Commerce' (O'Brien, 1.26–7). Though an avowed radical, Currie as early as 1841 became convinced that Peel would repeal the corn laws, and deeply regretted the Conservative prime minister's death, exclaiming that he would not 'have given him for a whole wilderness of Whigs!' (*Currie, 1827–1896*, 1.382). He supported Peel's financial policy in parliament against his own party.

In 1849, and again in 1857, Currie proposed Lionel Rothschild as parliamentary candidate for the City of London, pleading the cause of civil and religious liberty, and the loyalty of 2000 Jewish voters in the constituency. At the meeting of the parliamentary committee of the Liberal Registration Association on 10 March 1857, Currie himself was suddenly proposed along with Rothschild, in the wake of Lord John Russell's premature announcement that he would not contest the seat at the general election called following the defeat of Palmerston's administration in a parliamentary division on the government's China policy. Russell reconsidered his decision, entered the race without the support of the registration association, and proceeded to come third in the poll, leading to Currie's defeat. Currie then retired from politics, and largely from public life.

Currie had a 'happy, easy disposition', according to his son, and 'never allowed the cares of life to depress his spirits'. He took great pleasure in his extended family, and was especially instrumental in promoting the career of his nephew John *Wodehouse, later first earl of Kimberley. Largely independent of others for his enjoyment, however, he was seldom disappointed, reading much and amusing himself 'with the ordinary pleasures of the country' (*Currie, 1827–1896*, 1.57–8). He died at his country residence, Minley Manor, near Farnborough, Hampshire, on 16 October 1881, and was buried five days later. His fourth son, Philip Henry Wodehouse *Currie, a diplomat, was created Baron Currie. JOHN POWELL

Sources Bertram Wodehouse Currie, *1827–1896: recollections, letters, and journals*, ed. [C. L. Currie], 2 vols. (1901) • 'Curries & Co. in the nineteenth century', *Three Banks Review*, 62 (1964), 42–54 • *The correspondence of Lord Overstone*, ed. D. P. O'Brien, 3 vols. (1971) • *The journal of John Wodehouse, first earl of Kimberley, for 1862–1902*, ed. A. Hawkins and J. Powell, CS, 5th ser., 9 (1997) • Burke, *Gen. GB* • Kimberley journal, Bodl. Oxf., MSS Kimberley • d. cert.

Archives BL, Rowland Hill MSS, Add. MS 31978, fol. 25 • Bodl. Oxf., MSS Kimberley • Hants. RO, Currie and Wodehouse MSS, 109M72 • LUL, corresp. with Edwin Chadwick • Norfolk RO, letters to Lord Wodehouse • Royal Bank of Scotland, London, group archives, Curries Bank papers

Likenesses G. Richmond, portrait, 1835, repro. in *Bertram Wodehouse Currie, 1827–1896* • panel portrait, priv. coll.

Wealth at death £284,595 4s.: resworn probate, April 1882, CGPLA Eng. & Wales (1881)

Currie, Sir William Crawford

Currie, Sir William Crawford (1884–1961), shipowner, was born in Calcutta on 4 May 1884, the elder son of William Currie, East India merchant of Glasgow and Calcutta, and his wife, Jessie, also of Scotland. Currie's father was senior partner in Mackinnon Mackenzie & Co., managing agents of the British India Steam Navigation Company (BISN), and kinsman of its founder, William Mackinnon.

Currie was educated at the Glasgow Academy, Fettes College in Edinburgh, and Trinity College, Cambridge, where he gained a rugby blue and a certificate from the Royal Humane Society (1904) for saving a child from drowning. After graduating in history (1905), he gained qualification as an accountant in Glasgow and left for Calcutta (1910) to join his father in Mackinnons. In 1914 Currie married Ruth Forrest, daughter of C. S. Dods of Edinburgh. They had two sons; the elder was killed in action in Burma in 1944.

A partner in 1918, Currie took his father's place as senior partner in 1922 and began to take a prominent part in public life in India. Sheriff of Calcutta in 1921–2, he sat on the Bengal legislative council (1921–5) and in 1924 was elected president of both the Bengal chamber of commerce and the Associated Chambers of Commerce of India, Burma, and Ceylon. In 1925, during his last year in the east, he was appointed a member of the council of state for India and received a knighthood for his services.

Currie returned to London to become a partner of Gray Dawes & Co., agents of BISN, and was soon immersed in shipping affairs. He was appointed to the Imperial Shipping Committee (1926–30) and elected president of the chamber of shipping of the United Kingdom (1929–30).

In 1932 Alexander Shaw (later Lord Craigmyle), who had become chairman of the Peninsular and Oriental Steam Navigation Company (P. & O.) and BISN because of the serious illness of James Lyle Mackay, first earl of Inchcape, invited Currie to join P. & O. as deputy chairman and managing director; in 1938 he was elected chairman in succession to Craigmyle.

While keeping in close touch with the affairs of the P. & O. group in the Second World War, Currie was a member of the advisory council of the Ministry of War Transport throughout the war and became director of the liner division at the ministry (1942–5). He was also on the executive committee of the Red Cross Society and order of St John (1942–7), and a member of the Red Cross Prisoners-of-War committee (1943–6). His war service was recognized by a GBE (1947) and by France with the Légion d'honneur (1953).

After the war Currie had the major task, under very difficult conditions, of repairing damage and replacing losses sustained by the P. & O. group's fleets. His quick success in this mammoth undertaking showed the measure of his power and determination. Currie also had to deal with revolutionary changes in the structure of the P. & O. group brought about by the transfer of power in India; and as a trustee and partner in Mackinnons, he had to make new arrangements for the agency: it was reorganized as Inchcape & Co. Ltd with himself as a director.

During these crowded and anxious years, Currie found time to become president of the Institute of Marine Engineers (1945–6), chairman of the British Liner committee (1946–8), prime warden of the Worshipful Company of Shipwrights (1949), and a member of the Commonwealth Shipping Committee. Among a multitude of business interests he was deputy chairman of the Williams Deacon's Bank, extraordinary director of the Royal Bank of Scotland, chairman of the Marine and General Mutual Life Assurance Society, and director of the Suez Finance Company and the Southern Railway. Other activities included a year as high sheriff of Buckinghamshire (1947), president of the Seafarers' Education Service, chairman of the committee of management of the training ship *Worcester*, a trustee of the National Maritime Museum at Greenwich, member of the council of King George's Fund for Sailors, an honorary member of the Company of Master Mariners, and honorary captain, Royal Naval Reserve.

Currie had none of the arrogance of a 'City tycoon'. Short and stocky, he was a man of great modesty, winning charm, and innate kindliness. He led by persuasion and example and made friends everywhere. In the P. & O. company, he had the respect, devotion, and affection of all grades of employees on land and at sea, British and Indian; in return he knew them by name, and wrote notes of thanks or appreciation in his own hand. Called Sir Willy, he was genuinely loved in the company and esteemed in the shipping industry at large. In his seventies he found it hard to keep up with the momentum of change. He belonged to the pre-war world, and his retirement in 1960 was not before time.

A keen sportsman in his younger days, he continued to hunt and shoot whenever he had the time. His home was Dinton Hall in Aylesbury. Currie died on 3 July 1961 at Aylesbury. He was survived by his wife.

FREDA HARCOURT

Sources The Times (4 July 1961) · 'Historical notes', 4 Aug 1981, P. & O. head office, 79 Pall Mall, London · WWW
Archives NMM, P. & O. archives · P. & O., London, archives
Likenesses W. Stoneman, photograph, 1942, NPG · R. J. Swan, oils, c.1960 (after E. I. Halliday), P&O head office, 79 Pall Mall, London · oils, Chamber of Shipping, 12 Carthusian Street, London · photographs, P. & O. head office, 79 Pall Mall, London
Wealth at death £159,344 16s. 2d.: confirmation, 29 Sept 1961, CCI

Curriehill. For this title name see Marshall, John, Lord Curriehill (1794–1868).

Curry, John (1702/3–1780), historian and religious activist, was born in Dublin. According to the short memoir prepared by Charles O'Conor, which is the only source of information on Curry's background and early life, he was descended from the O'Corra family, most of whose properties in co. Cavan were forfeited during the Cromwellian land confiscation. His grandfather, who fought in the Jacobite army of James II, died, it is claimed, at the battle of Aughrim in 1691; as a result the remainder of the family's landholdings also were forfeited. This obliged John Curry's father to take up 'mercantile business' and he was sufficiently successful to be able to send his son to study medicine in Paris. Having secured 'a diploma for the practice of physic at Rheims', Curry returned to Dublin and set up a practice in Cow Lane. He achieved some repute as a physician, and in 1743 he published *An Essay on Ordinary Fevers*; thirty-one years later he returned to this subject with a work entitled *Some Thoughts on the Nature of Fevers* (1774).

Curry was a man of energy and ability, eager to improve the society in which he lived. He deemed the penal laws against Catholics to be both personally and socially regressive. The anti-Catholic animus fostered within the Irish protestant establishment by sermons commemorating the 'massacres' perpetrated during the 1641 rising induced him to publish *A brief account from the most authentic protestant writers of the causes, motives and mischiefs of the Irish rebellion on 23rd day of October 1641* (1747; 2nd edn, 1752). There, among other things, he maintained that Catholics had been prompted to rebel by oppression and claimed that dissenters posed a greater threat to the state than Catholics. A hostile response came from Walter Harris, entitled *Fiction Unmasked, or, An Answer to a Dialogue Lately Published* (1752; 2nd edn, 1757), to which Curry responded in turn in 1758. Significantly, Curry's *Historical Memoirs of the Irish Rebellion in the Year 1641* (1758) was fuller and better researched than its predecessor; it was still constructed, however, with the primary purpose of undermining the convictions of Irish protestants, born out of their strongly held understanding of what had happened in 1641, that Catholics were conspiring to extirpate them.

Coming from the pen of the first eighteenth-century historian to describe the critical events of the seventeenth century from a Catholic perspective, Curry's accounts of the 1641 rising reflected the emerging confidence of middle-class Catholics. His writings also highlighted their growing conviction that neither their past behaviour nor their current conduct justified their continuing social and economic marginalization and that Ireland, as well as Irish Catholics, would profit and prosper if Catholics were allowed to participate more fully in the life of the kingdom. Curry's thinking on this subject was greatly influenced by Charles O'Conor, a fast friend by the mid-1750s. Both men were encouraged by the apparent softening of the protestant determination to uphold the penal laws and they decided to establish a Catholic organization to promote their cause that would clearly delineate an alternative to the 'Jacobite politics' (Leighton, 109) still adhered to by most Irish Catholics. The first such body, an association of Dublin Catholics established on Curry's initiative in July 1756, was geographically and socially too limited to prosper. Undeterred, Curry continued to promote the cause. Taking advantage of the favourable climate created by the Seven Years' War he produced further pamphlets, notably three 'appeals … in vindication of the political principles of Roman Catholics', between 1757 and 1760. He also helped to prepare an address of loyalty signed by 400 Catholics in 1759, despite the reservations of some bishops and gentry. He saw that enhanced rights would follow if Catholics were seen to disprove the imputation of disloyalty inherent in their attachment to the Jacobite cause. He therefore joined Charles O'Conor and Thomas Wyse of Waterford to form in 1760 a Catholic Committee whose membership included the elected representatives of nine Dublin parishes. This did not satisfy a number of Catholic gentry, who seceded in protest at the suggestion that the committee should present a loyal address to George III on his accession to the throne. Despite this set-back Curry and O'Conor soldiered on. Curry acted as the point of contact between the committee and Lord Taaffe, who was the effective Catholic leader during the early 1760s, but little was achieved and the committee ceased to function in 1763.

Curry continued to promote the Catholic cause in print. Among the steady stream of publications that flowed from his pen between the mid-1760s and early 1770s were further instalments of his revision of seventeenth-century Irish history in the form of *An Essay towards a New History of the Gunpowder Treason* (1765), *A Parallel between the Pretended Plot in 1762 and the Forgery of Titus Oates in 1679* (1767), and *Occasional remarks on certain passages in Dr Leland's 'History of Ireland' relative to the Irish rebellion in 1641* (1773). He also published *A Candid Enquiry into the Causes and Motives of the Late Riots in the Province of Munster* (1766), in which he sought to exonerate Catholics from the charge of responsibility for agrarian disorder. With Charles O'Conor he published *Observations on the Popery Laws* in 1771. The warm reception accorded this last work demonstrated the effectiveness of Curry's strategy to promote the cause of Catholic relief, though his own relations with some elements of Catholic opinion were not always close. His promotion of addresses to lords Townshend and Harcourt and, in particular, an oath of allegiance upset many clergy and gentry, and he played little if any part in the quarterage dispute that dominated the concerns of the merchant dominated committee for nearly a decade following its reanimation in 1767. He was in the main content to support the line taken by the aristocracy because it offered the best prospect of the legal changes that he desired. The critical first step was to enact an oath of allegiance, and Curry was a member of the sub-committee that prepared a text closely resembling that which passed into law in 1774. He subscribed publicly on 28 June 1775. He subsequently acted as intermediary between the general committee and Lord Trimleston, who emerged as the leader of Catholic opinion in the mid-1770s. He also prepared the address presented to the earl of Buckinghamshire in 1777, and in 1778 he lobbied Edmund Burke to intervene with the prime minister, Lord North, to advance the major measure of relief that allowed Catholics to acquire property on virtually the same terms as protestants. He remained an active member of the committee until his death on 17 March 1780, in his seventy-eighth year, at his residence at Summerhill, Dublin. He was buried in St Kevin's churchyard. His wife, Mary (1710–1784), with whom he had three sons, survived him by four years.

Though overshadowed in historical memory by Charles O'Conor, Curry has an equal claim to fame. Although he was not as learned as O'Conor, his fluid and ready pen contributed more towards disseminating the idea that Catholics were loyal subjects and towards building up a Catholic interpretation of seventeenth-century Irish history. His major statement on this subject, *Historical Review of the Civil Wars in Ireland*, was prepared for posthumous publication by O'Conor in 1786. A large, two-volume work, it testifies to the important contribution made by this gifted, committed, and generous man to the cause of Catholic relief and to the elaboration of a distinctively Catholic historical and political vision.

JAMES KELLY

Sources M. McGeehin, 'The activities and personnel of the general committee of the Catholics of Ireland, 1767–84', MA diss., University College Dublin, 1952 • *The letters of Charles O'Conor of Belanagare*, ed. C. C. Ward and R. E. Ward, 2 vols. (1980) • C. O'Conor, 'An account of the author', in J. Curry, *Historical review of the civil wars in Ireland* (1810) • E. Magennis, 'A "beleaguered protestant"? Walter Harris and the writing of *Fiction unmasked*', *Eighteenth-Century Ireland*, 13 (1998), 86–111 • M. Wall, *Catholic Ireland in the eighteenth century* (1989) • J. Brady, *Catholics and Catholicism in the eighteenth-century press* (1965) • P. Fagan, *Catholics in a protestant country: the papist constituency in eighteenth-century Dublin* (1998) • T. Bartlett, *The fall and rise of the Irish nation: the Catholic question, 1690–1830* (1992) • C. D. A. Leighton, *Catholicism in a protestant kingdom: a study of the Irish ancien régime* (1994) • *DNB* • *The correspondence of Edmund Burke*, 4, ed. J. A. Woods (1963) • *Dublin Evening Post* (18 March 1780) • *Dublin Evening Post* (19 Oct 1784)

Archives Dublin Public Library, O'Conor MSS • Royal Irish Acad., O'Conor MSS • Sheff. Arch., corresp. with Edmund Burke

Curry, John (*b.* 1873/4, *d.* in or after **1936**). *See under* Knock, visionaries of (*act.* 1879).

Curry, John Anthony (1949–1994), ice skater, was born at 284 Chester Road, Birmingham, on 9 September 1949, the third son of Joseph Henry Curry, office equipment salesman, and his wife, Rita Agnes Hancock, *née* Richards. At his local primary school and later at Solihull School he was good at physical training and athletics, though not at the team games. He was captivated by the theatre the first time he was taken to see a musical, and wanted to become a dancer, but his parents thought it an unsuitable occupation for a boy. He saw an ice show on television when he was seven, and asked to go skating: he never understood why skating was acceptable to his parents while dancing was not. His mother took him to the nearby Summerhill ice rink for a series of fifteen-minute lessons costing 3*s*. each. It was clear from the start that he had talent, and his teacher, Ken Vickers, ably provided him with both the basics of skating and a sense of style. He won his first competition at the age of eight, and soon passed the proficiency tests of the National Skating Association, but did not begin serious training and competitive skating until he was thirteen.

His father's tuberculosis and death when Curry was sixteen made these years difficult, especially as his family could not see how he could make a living from a largely amateur sport and professional entertainment of limited popularity. But Curry was ambitious and determined, and his unusual talent, especially in the free skating, brought him the Rank trophy at Southampton in 1965. After six months under the tutelage of Armand Perrier at Solihull ice rink he went to London to train with Arnold Gerschweiler at the more sophisticated rink at Richmond. Always short of money, he paid for his lessons by working in a supermarket and as a receptionist.

The regime at Richmond was tough. He rose at five in the morning and trained until noon, when he went to his paying job. His school figures (the weakest part of his competition performance) improved, but he was demoralized by a winter trip to Davos and by his financial position; he was tempted to give up competitive skating and join a show called *Holiday on Ice*. He came ninth in his first overseas competition, the Prague Golden Skate, in 1966. On borrowed money he went to the United States to take lessons from Peter Dunfield, but they did not get on: Dunfield told him he was too old to learn, and after three months Curry returned to Britain. A less single-minded man would have accepted Dunfield's verdict. Curry won the British junior championship in 1967 and the Jennings trophy for free skating at Nottingham ice stadium in 1968 but this was not enough to break into the top class of the sport. He once more shook off his depression and returned to Richmond, this time with a new coach, Alison Smith, a specialist in musical interpretation. With her help he won the British men's championship for the first time in 1970 (he had been runner-up in 1968 and 1969). He

John Anthony Curry (1949–1994), by Robert Mapplethorpe, 1982

won it four more times between 1972 and 1975. His progress was underlined by fourth place in the world championships of 1972 and third in the European competition in 1974. His financial worries were ended in 1973, when an American enthusiast, Ed Mosler, offered him sponsorship. He went into the world championship at Munich that year looking for more improvement, but came only seventh. Once more he was on the verge of giving up.

Instead, Curry returned to America, where he trained first with Gustave Lussi at Lake Placid, and then with Carlo and Christa Fassi in Colorado. The 76-year-old Lussi had been the inventor of modern jumping, and he had Curry jumping in a confined space from a standing start, with the aim of achieving height not simply through momentum but by muscular co-ordination. He fell over a lot, and it was not only his body that was bruised. With the Fassis he had intensive coaching on his figures. The attention to detail and hours of practice paid off and brought Curry a bronze medal at the world championships in 1975. There was almost an upset at the British championships in December, however, when Curry, aiming to peak for the European and world championships in the new year, scraped to victory over the rising star Robin Cousins. The European competition pointed up the difficulties facing Curry. Judging skating is bedevilled by subjectivity, the judges tend to cling to tradition, and in 1976 the cold war was still being vigorously waged in sport. Curry was a modernizer, introducing costumes akin to those of male dancers, allowing full freedom of movement and in striking colour schemes. He favoured balletic arm movements, and in practice sessions introduced a big spread eagle to precede the double axel. The Russians informed the judges that this was an illegal element which must be penalized; Curry was tipped off, and while he retained the move in practice, he dropped it from his competition performance. Even so, it was a close-run thing; Curry won gold, with the Czechoslovakian judge voting for Curry, the first time an Eastern European judge had supported a Western skater. Curry had learned not to fight the judges but to adapt his programme to their requirements. He had also helped to control his nerves by taking a positive thinking course.

It was a great boost for Curry to go to the winter Olympics at Innsbruck in February 1976 as European champion, and he was further encouraged by being selected as flag-bearer for the British team at the opening ceremony. Curry was confident that his schedule had brought him to a peak, technically, physically, and mentally. He was second after the compulsory figures, and went into first place after the short programme. His free skating programme, to Leon Minkus's *Don Quixote* ballet music, was a triumph of controlled athleticism and musical interpretation. He performed three immaculate triple jumps, but they were part of a seamlessly choreographed routine, not mere technical exercises surrounded by connective tissue. Two of the nine judges voted against him, the Soviet and the Canadian, but they were both suspended for national bias (having voted for their own compatriots), and Curry's gold was thus effectively unanimous: his score of 105.9 out of 108 remained the highest in the history of the competition. Against the advice of his coach Curry then entered the world championships in Göteborg and won gold, giving him a clean sweep of the men's titles for 1976. He was appointed OBE in the 1976 summer honours list, and was voted BBC sports personality of the year. He retired from competition after the Göteborg competition.

Curry formed his own professional skating company, the John Curry Theatre of Skating. He wanted to move professional skating away from the 'tinsel and feathers', end-of-the-pier show, and to explore the possibilities of skating as a form of dance, borrowing ideas from ballet. They performed at the Cambridge Theatre, the London Palladium, and the Royal Albert Hall, using a wide range of musical styles and ballet choreographers, including Kenneth Macmillan. He diversified his interests, appearing as an actor at a number of provincial theatres, and, in America, as a dancer in *Brigadoon*. He held master classes for young skaters, and settled in New York. He had publicly acknowledged his homosexuality just before the Olympics in 1976: it was a courageous act, as he knew it could prejudice some of the judges still further against his style of skating. In 1987 he was diagnosed HIV positive, and in the following year he partnered the American Olympic champion Jo-Jo Starbuck in the *Skating for Life* show in New York to raise money for AIDS research. When he developed full-blown AIDS himself in 1991 he returned to Britain to live with his widowed mother. 'New York when you are ill is no place to be', he said (*The Times*, 16 April 1994). He was elected to the World Figure Skating Hall of Fame in 1991. He died from an AIDS-related illness at Arrow Leys, Binton, Stratford upon Avon, on 15 April 1994.

John Curry's calmness on ice (despite his intense nervousness before a performance), his technical brilliance, and unrivalled elegance of style made him a unique figure in ice skating, the first British man to excel at the sport. A bronze statue of Curry, by Stanley Taub, was unveiled at the National Ice Centre in Nottingham in 2001.

TONY MASON

Sources *The Independent* (16 April 1994) · *The Times* (16 April 1994) · E. Oglanby, *Black ice: the life and death of John Curry* (1995) · K. Money and J. Curry, *John Curry* (1978) · www.worldskatingmuseum.org [World Figure Skating Hall of Fame profile] · www.olympic.org/uk/athletes/index_uk.asp [Olympic Movement] · b. cert. · d. cert. · WWW
Likenesses photographs, 1971–80, Hult. Arch. · R. Mapplethorpe, photograph, 1982, NPG [*see illus.*] · S. Taub, bronze statue, *c.*1999, National Ice Centre, Nottingham · photograph, repro. in *The Times* · photograph, repro. in *The Independent* · photographs, repro. in Money and Curry, *John Curry*

Cursiter, Stanley (1887–1976), painter, museum director, and cartographer, was born on 29 April 1887 at Kirkwall, Orkney, the fourth of four children of John Scott Cursiter (1850–1896), baker and spirit merchant, and his wife, Mary Johan, daughter of John Thomson of Newark in Sanday. Educated at Kirkwall grammar school (1893–1904), at the age of thirteen Cursiter gained a certificate in advanced building construction.

Cursiter moved to Edinburgh in 1904, where, unable to afford training as an architect, he undertook a five-year apprenticeship with McLagen and Cumming, chromolithographers. Encouraged by the firm to attend classes at Edinburgh School of Art, Cursiter also received tuition from the Scottish designer W. S. Black in 1904, and, during a brief period at the Royal College of Art, London, from the printmaker W. R. Lethaby in 1908. After 1909 he worked successfully as a designer and began to paint. He was elected a member of the Society of Scottish Artists (SSA) while still a student; his early paintings were of models dressed in costumes he had made for them, for example *Woman in White* (Fleming-Wyfold Art Foundation, London), or nude, which found a ready market.

In 1914 Cursiter joined the 1st battalion of the Scottish Rifles (Cameronians). On 14 October 1916 he married a fellow Orcadian, the violinist Phyllis Eda Hourston (1888–1975); they had one daughter, Margaret. A week later he was in the front line on the Somme. Ill health prevailed and he was eventually transferred to the field survey battalion to print maps. There Cursiter developed a revolutionary way of transferring vital information from aerial photographs of enemy troop movements to maps, cutting crucial production time from six weeks to twenty-four hours. He subsequently designed a portable printing press to run from a lorry motor. Demobilized in 1919, he left the army with two mentions in dispatches and was made a military OBE.

Cursiter continued to paint, dividing his time between Edinburgh and Orkney. In 1920, on account of continuing poor health, he moved to Cassis in the south of France for six months, producing a fine series of landscapes. His love of geology and antiquities, his passion for architecture, combined with his extensive knowledge and experience of printing techniques and cartography, bestowed a unique textural, structural quality to his work such as in *Red Lacquer* (1922; Pier Arts Centre, Stromness, Orkney).

In 1925 Cursiter became keeper of the Scottish National Portrait Gallery, under the directorship of Sir James Caw. He continued to paint, and was elected associate of the Royal Scottish Academy in 1927 and member in 1937. As ever, Cursiter's keen intellect, commitment, and problem-solving skills had far-reaching results. Picture conservation became an early preoccupation. He completely redesigned heating, humidity control, hanging space, and lighting to minimize the risk of fire in the very awkward Victorian Gothic building. As director of the National Gallery of Scotland from 1930, his collaboration with restorer Martin de Wild of Haarlem and the Rijksmuseum, Amsterdam, led to the development of a significant new and advanced method of wax relining technique. Cursiter also established a restoration department, redesigned lighting, and designed interior pillars modelled on the famed ancient Greek monument of Lysicrates. He made a working scale-model of the galleries, including scale copies of every picture, and designed and made sliding metal screens for easy storage and retrieval of pictures. In short, he revolutionized the traditional time-consuming way of rehanging a collection.

In 1938 Cursiter drew up plans for a new art centre, incorporating a gallery for modern and contemporary art, craft, industrial design, and a historical collection of Scottish art. He also envisaged that this centre would, had it been built, include facilities for film, performance, and sound, with a travelling exhibitions department. During the Second World War he first secured the dispersal of the national collection and for a short time returned to military cartography as a trainer at the Ordnance Survey, Southampton. The deterioration of the national collection in storage hastened his return to Edinburgh. For the remainder of the war he organized over eighty groundbreaking exhibitions in the empty galleries: 'Art of the Allies'; the Scottish colourists, S. J. Peploe and F. C. B. Cadell; 'Women's Work', which showed peacetime paintings and embroideries alongside their wartime activities; and over twenty exhibitions of children's art which raised the profile of art teaching in Scotland.

In 1948 Cursiter resigned as director and from his various committees and returned to painting. He received many honours that year, including appointment as CBE. On the strength of one portrait commission, *Robert Wilson, Chairman of Heriot Watt College* (1948; Heriot Watt University), Cursiter found himself launched on a successful portrait career. As royal painter and limner in Scotland (1948) he subsequently painted *The Queen Receiving the Honours of Scotland in St Giles Cathedral* and a portrait of the queen mother. An art historian, he wrote two notable books: in 1947, a tribute to Samuel John Peploe (1871–1935), *An Intimate Memoir of an Artist and of his Work*, and in 1949 *Scottish Art at the Close of the Nineteenth Century*. An autobiography, *Looking back: a Book of Reminiscences*, was published privately in 1974.

An intelligent, articulate, well-read but modest man, Cursiter viewed his achievements as a series of fortuitous coincidences of whom he met and of opportunities presented. In 1911 Cursiter visited Roger Fry's first, controversial post-impressionist exhibition at the Grafton Galleries; he recalled, 'I got the shock of my life. Here was painting and colour as I had never imagined it' (Cursiter, 44). Returning the next day, Cursiter was introduced to Roger Fry and Clive Bell, and promptly arranged to borrow some twenty pictures for the next SSA exhibition in Edinburgh. The exhibition was a cultural landmark, bringing the work of Cézanne, Van Gogh, and Gauguin to Scotland for the first time. The effect of these works on Cursiter was decisive. He painted a series of seven radically modern paintings of which *The Sensation of Crossing the Street—the West End, Edinburgh* (1913; priv. coll.) is the most far-reaching. Close in style to Italian futurism, Cursiter comments only that the paintings 'were not modelled on the work of any individual artist, but just grew out of the search for new methods of expression prompted by contact with the new form of art' (*Stanley Cursiter: Centenary Exhibition*, 11).

Orkney, its people and culture, played a deep and influential part throughout Cursiter's life, immortalized in his paintings such as in *Linklater and Greig* (1930; Stromness Museum, Orkney), and enriched by his lifelong friendships with Orcadians, the writers Neil Gunn and Eric Linklater, the poet Edwin Muir, and the playwright James Bridie (O. H. Mavor). Retired in Orkney, by 1975 he could no longer paint. Typically his energies went into the preservation of St Magnus's Cathedral and latterly, in collaboration with sculptor Reynold Eunson, the new development of St Rognvald's Chapel. He died of bronchopneumonia on 22 April 1976 at his home, 70 Victoria Street, Stromness, Orkney. JILL C. MACKENZIE

Sources S. Cursiter, *Looking back: a book of reminiscences* (privately printed, Edinburgh, 1974) · *Stanley Cursiter: centenary exhibition* (1987) [exhibition catalogue, Pier Arts Centre, Stromness, Orkney] · *The Scotsman* (23 April 1976) · A. Eddington, 'The paintings and lithographs of Stanley Cursiter', *The Studio*, 82 (1921), 340 · W. Hardie, *Scottish painting, 1837 to the present* (1990) · b. cert. · m. cert. · d. cert.

Archives NL Scot., corresp. and papers · Orkney Archives, Kirkwall, corresp. and papers | NL Scot., letters to WRH, corresp. relating to futurist pictures · NL Scot., letters to Neil Gunn · Orkney Archives, Kirkwall, corresp. with E. W. Marwick · TCD, corresp. with Thomas Bodkin

Likenesses S. Cursiter, self-portrait, oils, Scot. NPG · photograph, repro. in *Stanley Cursiter: centenary exhibition*

Curson, Robert. *See* Courson, Robert de (*d*. 1219).

Curson, Sir Robert, styled Lord Curson, and Baron Curson in the nobility of the Holy Roman empire (*c.*1460–1534/5), soldier and courtier, was of Blaxhall, near Saxmundham, Suffolk, and may have been the son of the Robert Curson who was escheator for Suffolk in 1472–3. There is heraldic evidence for his mother being a Delves of Stafford. Little is known of Curson before he was knighted in 1489, but he was one of the king's champions, wearing the red dragon of Wales and the queen's favour on his helmet in tournaments at Sheen and Westminster in 1494 on the creation of Prince Henry as duke of York. The motto on his 'imprese' was 'There to we be redy'. He was sheriff of Norfolk and Suffolk in 1496–7. In 1498 he married Anne (*née* Southill), widow of Sir George Hopton, and on 21 March forcibly entered the Hopton manor of Westleton, claiming that it was Anne's for life, depriving her stepson Arthur, the heir. Curson was joined in this enterprise by several other Cursons: Thomas, Robert, John, and Nicholas must have been relations.

In 1499 Curson became captain of Hampnes Castle in the Calais marches on his own security of 800 marks. On 29 August he obtained a licence to leave his post in order to fight the Turks under the aegis of the emperor Maximilian I, calling first on the earl of Suffolk at Guînes Castle and then on the emperor himself. Suffolk's steward Thomas Killingworth reported to his master that Curson had conversed with Maximilian about Henry's murders and tyrannies, and obtained an assurance that the emperor would assist a Yorkist attempt on the English crown. On 21 October 1501 Curson was publicly proclaimed a traitor from the pulpit at Paul's Cross with five others including Edmund de la Pole, earl of Suffolk. Sir James Tyrrell and Sir John Wyndham were eventually beheaded, and Suffolk and Sir William Courtenay were sent to the Tower. Surprisingly Curson was not punished, but was soon after made a baron of the Holy Roman empire. His name appeared on the pardon roll of 5 May 1504 as a member of the royal household, and again on that of 10 April 1505. Historians from Polydore Vergil onwards have debated the reason for his pardons. The latest theory is that for a time, shaken by the judicial murder of the harmless earl of Warwick in November 1499, Curson sided with Suffolk, only to realize by mid-1502 that the Yorkist cause was hopeless, after which his loyalty to Henry was total.

A fortnight into Henry VIII's reign Curson was again pardoned for treason, presumably because his services were required. From 3 June 1509 his annual fee was set at £400 and so it remained until 1520, when he (or his son Robert) attended the Field of Cloth of Gold. Although he never became an English peer, his title Lord Curson seems to have been recognized at court from about 1513 when as master of the ordnance in the rearward he served under Brandon in the French campaigns. From 1515 to 1534 he served as a Suffolk JP, and it is likely that Robert (Norfolk JP, 1531–47) and John (Norfolk JP, 1555, *d.* 1581) were his son and grandson. Staunchly conservative in religious matters, he cut down boughs to stoke the fire under the Lollard Peke at Ipswich in 1515. Later that year he witnessed amazing scenes at Gracechurch, the chapel of Our Lady in St Matthew's parish. The twelve-year-old Jane Wentworth, daughter of Sir Roger Wentworth of Gosfield, Essex, suffered violent fits which only visits to Gracechurch and the image there would cure. After the last visit she retired for the night only to summon the bailiffs and other worthies to her chamber for a two-hour sermon, after which she fell into another fit. Curson promptly cured her by thrusting his own cross decorated with a *pietà* into her hands, but that was not the end of the story. He wrote a full account of this Ipswich miracle for the king, which brought first Katherine of Aragon in 1517, then the king

on 8 October 1522, to stay at his Ipswich mansion overnight in order to visit the chapel. In his *Dialogue Concerning Heresies* of 1529 Thomas More described it as the best example of a modern miracle in England.

In 1522 Curson took part in the Morlaix raid. His first wife having died, by 1523 he had married again, and he and his new wife, Margaret, were joint executors of the will of his kinsman William Curson, a gentleman of Blaxhall. As a reward for entertaining his sovereign he received a gilt cup as a new year gift in 1524; in 1532 his gift to the king was twelve swans. His Ipswich property in St Peter's parish covered nearly 2 acres, with a tower porch under which horsemen could ride. The plaster decorations on the ceiling of the best chamber included the badges of Henry and Katherine, and Charles Brandon and Mary Tudor alongside his own. There were two courtyards, a chapel, large gardens, and ample stabling. Because the property abutted the college Wolsey founded in 1528, the cardinal planned to retire there after the manner of the provost of Eton. Curson had acceded to Wolsey's demand, but was saved from losing his property by the cardinal's death in 1530. His last recorded task was to take the Suffolk JPs' oaths to the Act of Succession (implying loyalty to the Boleyn marriage), a mark of royal trust at a fraught time. By his will of 31 October 1534 (proved 12 March 1535), Curson left bequests to Hoxne and Blaxhall churches and lands at Blaxhall, Kelsale, Tunstall, and Dunningworth, and requested burial in the church of the Ipswich Greyfriars. The dissolution inventory of 1538 included 'a feyn herse clothe that ley upon the lorde Cursons herse' (Wodderspoon), implying a latten cradle over the stone tomb for which Curson had left £10. His mansion became the residence of Thomas Manning, dispossessed prior of Butley, whom Cranmer consecrated in 1536 the first and only suffragan bishop of Ipswich. Thereafter it was used by bishops of Norwich when visiting the southern and most troublesome parts of their diocese. Curson's young widow married Sir Edward Green of Halstead, Essex, and survived him also. Her will shows that the monument covering Curson and his first wife had been moved to St Peter's Church in Ipswich; here she joined them in 1577 at a cost to her executors of over £10. No Curson traces remain in the church today.

J. M. BLATCHLY

Sources D. MacCulloch, *Suffolk and the Tudors: politics and religion in an English county, 1500–1600* (1986) • W. Busch, *England under the Tudors: King Henry VII* (1895) • A. Hanham, 'Edmund de la Pole and the spies, 1499–1506', *Parergon Bulletin of Australian and New Zealand Association for Medieval and Renaissance Studies*, new ser., 6 (1988), 103–20 • BL, AUG. MS 1, vol. 2, no. 48 • BL, Stowe MS 881 • S. Pegge, *Sylloge* (1787), 93–4 • J. G. Webb, 'Sir Robert Curson', *Newsletter of the Suffolk Institute of Archaeology and History*, 31 (spring 1991), 9–10 • 'The booke of certaine triumphes', BL, Harley MS 69, fols. 3B and 6 • J. Wodderspoon, 'Notes on the Grey and White Friars, Ipswich', *Original Papers of the Suffolk Archaeological Association*, pt 3 (Nov 1848), 16 • will of Dame Margaret Green, formerly Lady Curson, PRO, PROB 11/59, sig. 42 [dated 1577] • will, Norfolk RO, NCC 287 Attmere

Archives BL, narrative of the Ipswich miracle in the hand of W. H., Harley MS 651, fols. 194v–196v

Wealth at death estates and property in Ipswich, Blaxhall, Tunstall, Dunningworth, and Kelsale: will, Norfolk RO, NCC 287 Attmere

Curteys, Richard (1532?–1582), bishop of Chichester, was born in Lincolnshire to unknown parents. He entered St John's College, Cambridge, on a Lady Margaret scholarship in the autumn of 1550, graduated BA in 1553, and was incorporated MA in 1556; he proceeded BTh in 1565 and DTh in 1569. He was elected fellow of St John's in 1553 and senior fellow in 1559. Although he kept a low profile during the reign of Mary I, his subsequent academic career was marked by theological controversy and factionalism. During the height of the vestiarian controversy of the mid-1560s, when St John's became a seat of clerical puritanism, Curteys, with the backing of the university chancellor, Sir William Cecil, led an attempted reformation of nonconformist irregularities of clerical dress and mishandling of college properties during the temporary absence of the master of the college, Richard Longworth. This reforming effort failed, and the more extreme puritan faction, led by William Fulke, prevailed. Longworth pretended to amend his ways and, because Cecil failed to back him, Curteys was driven out of Cambridge in 1566.

Curteys's academic career now ended, in 1567 Cecil secured the deanery of Chichester for him with Archbishop Parker's approval. He was installed on 5 March. Long regarded as an eloquent preacher, Curteys also became chaplain to the queen and to the archbishop at about the same time. Sermons which he delivered before the queen at Greenwich, Richmond, and Westminster were subsequently published. After taking up residence in Chichester, he began reforming the cathedral chapter with the same tactlessness he had displayed at Cambridge. The members of the chapter—who neglected preaching, practised irregular leasing policies, and, in at least one case, continued Catholic practices—may have needed reforming, but Curteys quickly alienated the treasurer, the equally contentious William Overton, who was the son-in-law of the bishop of Chichester, William Barlow. The latter's death on 13 August 1568 caused Overton to begin scheming to obtain the bishopric for himself. Archbishop Parker, while admitting that the choice of candidates did not inspire confidence, indicated to Cecil his preference for Curteys. Curteys had to wait nearly two years for royal approval and consecration while the crown collected the temporalities of the diocese at the rate of £676 per annum. Licence to elect was given on 30 March 1570, and he was consecrated on 21 May following. He was then said to be aged forty-eight, but thirty-eight seems more likely. Curteys's efforts to reform the cathedral chapter continued after his appointment as bishop, and he was particularly strict in enforcing cathedral statutes concerning residence in the cathedral close and preaching duties in rural parishes where chapter prebendaries owned impropriated rectories. But he also further alienated the prebendaries by his attempts to pack the chapter with his supporters.

Because of its relative isolation, lack of learned preachers, and lingering religious conservatism, Sussex, which was coterminous with the diocese of Chichester, had experienced only a limited reception of protestant ideas before Curteys became bishop. He brought with him nearly forty Cambridge graduates, who joined him in an energetic campaign of preaching across the entire diocese, conducting visitations and depriving conservative or unlearned parochial clergy. He also began enforcing uniformity of worship among the Sussex gentry and the citizens of Chichester in a manner that did not distinguish between incorrigible recusants and outwardly conforming crypto-Catholics. An attempt to confront some thirty-five of these individuals, nearly all of them members of the gentry, at a consistory held in the cathedral church on 2 March 1577, rather than pursuing the more usual course of individual and private conferences, brought numerous complaints to the privy council. Curteys's assertion that Catholic gentry continued to serve as justices of the peace was correct, but most did so at the price of occasional conformity. Moreover, the government recognized that the prestige of local office holding constituted an incentive to conform to the religious settlement, but Curteys was not content with outward conformity, and those summoned complained of his inquisitorial methods. His enemies, led by Sir Thomas Palmer of Parham, Thomas Lewkenor of Selsey, and Richard Ernley, also complained that his methods of inquiry discredited them in the eyes of the commonalty. The council listened sympathetically, and their letter to Curteys, now lost, clearly left him much chastened.

The struggle between Curteys and the Sussex gentry went beyond the enforcement of religious uniformity. He was active as a justice of the peace in thwarting smuggling, trading with pirates, and the illegal export of grain—all of which touched his enemies' economic interests. They fought back by accusing the bishop of bribery, extortion, simony, gambling, drunkenness, adultery, and the like. Pressure from the privy council led Curteys to forbear exercising his powers as a magistrate. The campaign to destroy Curteys continued at the Lewes quarter sessions, where in 1578 his opponents obtained an indictment against his brother, Edmund, vicar of Cuckfield, for barratry (selling ecclesiastical preferments) and sought to have him deprived by the court of high commission. Without waiting for that body to complete its proceedings, Sir Francis Walsingham, on behalf of the privy council, wrote to Curteys demanding that he remove Edmund from his benefice. This the bishop avoided doing, and the deprivation was therefore carried out in 1581 by the court of high commission. Later, in 1585, when Walsingham realized that his hasty judgment of Edmund Curteys had been coloured by prejudiced witnesses, he tried to make amends by having Edmund reinstated in his old prebend of Thorney. Curteys's failure immediately to comply with the privy council order to deprive his brother probably contributed to a further humiliation. Some time in 1578 the council suspended him from the exercise of his episcopal duties, a suspension never more than partially lifted. The case is reminiscent of the suspension of his friend and colleague Archbishop Edmund Grindal in 1577.

Curteys's attempt rigorously to enforce religious uniformity faltered because he behaved too much like a medieval prelate and neglected to seek the co-operation of the Sussex gentry. However, he was able in 1576 to arrange for Richard Fletcher, the town preacher of Rye, to exercise spiritual jurisdiction within that town, where he co-operated thereafter with the magistrates of that staunchly protestant community in the maintenance of moral order. Curteys also bequeathed the legacy of a strong clerical puritan movement founded upon exercise conferences, which he had introduced to his diocese from 1570 onwards in an attempt to enhance preaching qualifications among the parish clergy. These prophesyings survived in Chichester diocese because of the disruption of episcopal administration caused by Curteys's suspension, and the conferences came to rest upon co-operation between magistrates and clergy. Clerical nonconformity went virtually unpunished until 1605, when Archbishop Bancroft deprived ten Sussex clerics who had subscribed the millenarian petition presented to King James I at the beginning of his reign.

Richard Curteys died on 30 August 1582 and was buried in Chichester Cathedral on the following day. He left a widow, whose name is unrecorded, and it is known that a sister had resided with him before she married a resident of Aldingbourne. He kept open hospitality, although the revenues of the bishopric were much diminished, and, consequently, died deeply in debt. His will, which does not survive, was administered in February 1583. A collection of ten sermons on Psalm 25 which Curteys had preached at Tewkesbury was published in 1600 under the title *The Care of a Christian Conscience*. He was also the translator of a commentary on St Paul's epistle to the Romans, attributed to the twelfth-century exegete Hugh of St Victor, which appeared in 1577 (STC 13923).   ROGER B. MANNING

Sources PRO, SP 12/25/14, 38/11, 39/19, 96/p. 175, 112/13, 20, 24, 31, 32, 113/34, 37, 43, 44, 49, 50, 129/16, 123/27, 131/26, 130/22, 188/58, 137/31, 158/42 · PRO, C 202/144 · PRO, SP 13/25/14 · BL, Add. MSS 6246, fol. 45, 29546, fols. 50v–51v, 39355, fol. 168v, 39454, fols. 42–43v; Egerton MS 1693, fol. 128; Harley MS 703, fols. 89–95, 2143, fol. 31v · W. Sussex RO, ep. I/15, box A2(1); ep. II/24/1 · M. Bateson, ed., 'A collection of original letters from the bishops to the privy council, 1564', *Camden miscellany, IX*, CS, new ser., 53 (1893), 8–11 · *The manuscripts of Rye and Hereford corporations*, HMC, 31 (1892), 45–6, 52 · F. G. Bennett, ed., *Statutes and constitutions of the Cathedral Church of Chichester* (1904), 22–8 · R. Cortesse, *The truth of Christes naturall body* (1577), preface · *Correspondence of Matthew Parker*, ed. J. Bruce and T. T. Perowne, Parker Society, 42 (1853), 290, 331, 350 · W. D. Peckham, ed., *The acts of the dean and chapter of the cathedral church of Chichester, 1545–1642*, Sussex RS, 58 (1959), nos. 668, 730, 734–9, 777, 861, 751, 645, 657, 671, 819, 861, 867, 865, 950, 982, 692 · R. B. Manning, *Religion and society in Elizabethan Sussex* (1969), 63–125 · H. C. Porter, *Reformation and reaction in Tudor Cambridge* (1958), 108–35 · *Fasti Angl.*, *1541–1857*, [Chichester] · administrations, PRO, PROB 6/63, fols. 49r, 61r · Cooper, *Ath. Cantab.*, 1.455–9

Archives PRO, SP 12, 13; STAC 5/C43/10 · W. Sussex RO, ep. I, II | BL, Add. MSS, Egerton MSS, Harley MSS

Wealth at death impoverished: PRO, PROB 6/63, fols. 49r, 61r

Curteys, William (*d.* 1446), abbot of Bury St Edmunds, was the last great ruler of that house. His reputation was well established by 1422 when he was one of three senior Bury monks to sit on a committee of thirteen appointed by the general chapter of the English Benedictines: its purpose was to suggest modifications of the reforms that Henry V sought to impose on the order. By *c.*1417 Curteys was cellarer and in 1423 became prior. He was elected abbot on 14 February 1429, after the death of Abbot William Exeter. Henry VI granted him his temporalities on 18 February, he was blessed by Philip, bishop of Ely, in the Dominican church in Cambridge on 6 March, and he was installed at St Edmunds on 8 March. The beginning of Curteys's abbatiate was inauspicious. William Exeter had left such heavy debts that Curteys had to sell the valuables and utensils belonging to the abbatial household. In addition, he had immediately to defend the abbey's spiritual exemption against encroachments by William Alnwick, bishop of Norwich. The main problem was Alnwick's papal commission to suppress heresy. In 1428 Curteys, as prior, had allowed the bishop to hold an inquiry in Bury St Edmunds to discover any Lollards lurking in the town. But when abbot he obtained papal confirmation of his house's spiritual exemption in Bury, to include right of jurisdiction over heresy cases. He himself then instituted proceedings against heretics in Bury in 1431 and again in 1438.

Shortly after Curteys's succession a disaster overtook the fabric of the abbey church: on 18 December 1430 the south side of the great west tower suddenly collapsed, and on 30 December 1431 the east side fell. The north side was taken down early the next year and the task of rebuilding began. To help meet the estimated cost of 60,000 ducats (about £10,000), Curteys obtained a papal indulgence for all persons contributing towards the expense. Bequests in wills of many fifteenth-century Bury townsmen show that work continued at least until *c.*1500.

Nevertheless, Curteys's abbatiate marked the abbey's last period of splendour. Most spectacular was the visit of Henry VI, then aged twelve, with household and attendant magnates, which lasted from 1 November 1433 until 23 April 1434. Curteys was on his manor of Elmswell when informed of the intended royal visit, and hurried back to Bury St Edmunds to put his palace in repair, a task completed by eighty craftsmen and workmen within a month. He also arranged for a magnificent procession of 500 Bury townsmen, all mounted, to meet the king on Newmarket Heath and conduct him to the abbey. There Henry was met by Bishop Alnwick and Abbot Curteys, both in full pontificals, attended by the monks in their 'most precious copes'. After due ceremony in the church the king repaired to the abbot's palace, the beautiful furnishings of which excited great admiration. Henry remained there for the Christmas festivities and for Epiphany, receiving rich gifts from Curteys. He then moved to the prior's lodgings because of its proximity to 'the sweet stream [of the River Lark] and pure air, and the delightful scent of the vineyard' (Dugdale, *Monasticon*, 3.113). From there the king went hunting and hawking, but on 23 January he moved to the abbot's manor of Elmswell for more sport. Before the royal party finally departed on 23 April, Curteys received King Henry, Duke Humphrey of Gloucester, and the other magnates into confraternity in chapter.

To celebrate this visit Curteys commissioned John Lydgate, Bury monk and court poet, to write the 'Lives of Saints Edmund and Fremund'. An illuminated copy of the poem, now BL, Harley MS 2278, was made for presentation to the king, an event that took place c.1438. The illumination is distinctive in style and of exceptionally high quality, and was almost certainly executed in Bury itself. Indeed, in Curteys's day a school of illuminators flourished in the town. Curteys was one of its patrons, and after his death there was a marked decline in the quality of its work. Moreover, under Curteys, St Edmunds had a high reputation for scholarship. John Whethamstede, abbot of St Albans, wrote to Curteys, c.1435, urging him to send one of his monk–scholars, 'by whom you are especially well supported', to the Council of Basel to defend the monastic order against its enemies (Arnold, 3.254). Curteys's patronage of learning was already apparent during his priorate, when he financed the construction at Gloucester College, Oxford, of the exceptionally generous accommodation for Bury monk–scholars. Significantly, the library of Gloucester College formed part of St Edmunds' block. Curteys, when abbot, built a library in the abbey for the monks' book collection: other religious houses built libraries in the later middle ages, but in Bury's case it was quite possibly the Gloucester College Library that provided both incentive and model.

Probably because of the new library, Curteys included two clauses concerning the monks' books in the reforming constitutions he issued in 1441. One clause stipulated that the monks should produce before the abbot all communal books in their possession within fifteen days, on pain of suspension; the other imposed even heavier penalties on monks, including those studying in Oxford, who lost such books by lending, pledging, or selling them. Inscriptions in surviving Bury books show considerable activity in Curteys's time in their care: class-marks, ex-libris and other inscriptions, contents lists, and indexes were added variously to a number of volumes. Curteys himself gave the monks' collection at least two of the extant books; the little twelfth-century copy of Virgil's *Aeneid*, now Cambridge, Trinity College, MS 623, and the thirteenth-century copy of Isidor's *Etymologiae*, now Durham University Library, MS Cosin V.iii.20. After his death, there is little sign of care being taken of the book collection.

Curteys's period of power also marked a 'high-point of archival activity and expertise' at St Edmunds (Thomson, 34). When cellarer, Curteys produced the massive, two-volume register of the cellary's archives, now CUL, MSS Gg.iv.4, and Additional 4220, and, when prior, a register, now lost, for that office. Simultaneously, no doubt under Curteys's influence, the obediences produced registers: the five surviving examples are remarkably similar in their excellent arrangement and substantial size. When abbot, Curteys supervised the production of the most impressive register of all, the giant and strikingly handsome two-volume register of his abbatiate, now BL, Add. MSS 14848 (pt 1) and 7096 (pt 2). It is an invaluable historical source. Besides copies of documents concerning Curteys's abbatial administration and public life (such as of Henry's circular letters requesting aid for his French war), it includes, for example, a copy of his constitutions of 1441 and a graphic account of Henry's visit in 1433–4. After Curteys's time the regular practice of compiling registers was abandoned at Bury.

On 6 November 1442 Eugenius IV granted Curteys an indulgence for admission as a brother of the hospital of St Anthony in London, and he died early in 1446. Little is known about him personally. He had a sister, Joanna, married to one of the abbey's officials, a William Monke: on 10 August 1432 Curteys granted Joanna and William a minor corrody in St Saviour's Hospital in Bury. A description of Curteys's now lost crozier survives in his agreement with the London goldsmith John Horwell, who was to make it 'as skilfully and beautifully as he could' in silver and gold gilt (BL, Add. MS 14848, fols. 79, 79v).

ANTONIA GRANSDEN

Sources BL, Curteys's register, pt 1, Add. MS 14848 · BL, Curteys's register, pt 2, Add. MS 7096 · Dugdale, *Monasticon*, vol. 3 · R. M. Thomson, *The archives of the abbey of Bury St Edmunds*, Suffolk RS, 21 (1980), 34–40, 135–9 (nos. 1289–90), 146–7 (no. 1295), 150–52 (nos. 1299–1300), 153–4 (no. 1304), 155–61 (nos. 1306–15) · V. H. Galbraith, ed., 'Some new documents about Gloucester College', in *Snappe's formulary and other records*, ed. H. E. Salter, OHS, 80 (1924), 337–86, esp. 340–41, 351–3, 383–5 · M. R. James, *On the abbey of St Edmund at Bury*, Cambridge Antiquarian RS, 28 (1895), 41, 82, 108–11 · A. B. Whittingham, 'Bury St Edmunds Abbey: the plan, design and development of the church and monastic buildings', *Archaeological Journal*, 108 (1951), 168–88, esp. 175, 180 · R. C. E. Hayes, 'William Alnwick, bishop of Norwich (1426–1437) and Lincoln (1437–1449)', PhD diss., University of Bristol, 1989 · N. J. Rogers, 'Fitzwilliam Museum MS 3-1979: a Bury St Edmunds book of hours and the origins of the Bury style', *England in the fifteenth century* [Harlaxton 1986], ed. D. Williams (1987), 229–43 · W. F. Schirmer, *John Lydgate: a study in the culture of the XVth century*, trans. A. E. Keep (1961) · J. A. F. Thomson, 'A Lollard rising in Kent: 1431 or 1438?', *BIHR*, 37 (1964), 100–02 · J. Gage, 'Historical notices of the great bell tower of the abbey church of St Edmundsbury', *Archaeologia*, 23 (1831), 327–33 · J. Gage, 'Letters from King Henry VI to the abbot of St Edmundsbury, and to the alderman and bailiffs of the town, for the suppression of the Lollards', *Archaeologia*, 23 (1831), 339–43 · W. A. Pantin, ed., *Documents illustrating the activities of … the English black monks, 1215–1540*, 3 vols., CS, 3rd ser., 45, 47, 54 (1931–7), vol. 2, p. 121; vol. 3 · T. Arnold, ed., *Memorials of St Edmund's Abbey*, 3, Rolls Series, 96 (1896), xxix–xxxiii, 242–79 · *CPR, 1429–46* · C. Harper-Bill, ed., *Charters of the medieval hospitals of Bury St Edmunds*, Suffolk RS, Suffolk Charters, 14 (1994), p. 149, nos. 239, 241 · BL, Cotton MS Claudius A.xii, fol. 118v

Archives BL, register, Add. MSS 7096, 14848 | CUL, MS Gg.iv.4, Add. MS 4220

Curtin, John (1885–1945), prime minister of Australia, was born in Creswick, Victoria, on 8 January 1885, the eldest of the four children of John Curtin (1854–1919), a policeman, and his wife, Catherine Bourke (1859–1938). Both parents were Irish-born. Curtin's father was invalided out of the police force in 1890 and spent the next eight years as a hotel manager in Melbourne and several towns in rural

John Curtin (1885–1945), by unknown photographer, c.1941–5

Victoria before settling, poor and unemployed, in the Melbourne suburb of Brunswick. Educated at a succession of schools, young John had to leave to become the family breadwinner. He was a printer's devil, page-boy, office boy, and labourer, then in 1903 became an estimates clerk for an iron manufacturer. As he later recalled, the last was a 'school of profound computations' in which:

> for seven years, I calculated, measured, and otherwise evolved the precise cost to a gentleman profiteer of importing iron from Germany, running it through an abominable noisy machine, and passing it on to a nicely organized trust, preparatory to its consumption by the building contractors of Australia. (Ross, 9)

Early political career Jack Curtin joined the Brunswick Political Labor Council and the Victorian Socialist Party, under the respective tutelage of two gifted English immigrant agitators, Frank Anstey and Tom Mann, and soon gained a reputation as a boy orator on the Yarra Bank and on Melbourne street corners and as a contributor to the weekly *Socialist*. He also found time to play amateur cricket and football. In 1908 he moved the resolution to change the name of the Political Labor Council to the Australian Labor Party and, despite his affiliations with the Victorian Socialist Party, also moved that the party should never ally itself with others. He described himself as a utopian revolutionary socialist and criticized those Labor

men, Anstey included, who joined that 'upholstered gasworks' (Day, 158) known as parliament rather than working in the industrial movement.

In 1911 Curtin accepted a full-time post as secretary of the Victorian Timberworkers' Union and was soon very active recruiting members, founding and editing a newspaper, and campaigning for the Workers' Compensation Act (1914). In the federal elections of 1914 his ambition overruled his ideology and he stood unsuccessfully for the seat of Balaclava—'a first-rate fighter with the mild appearance of a curate' (Ross, 33), wrote the Sydney *Bulletin*. Violently against the war, disillusioned by union routine and corruption, and drinking far too hard, Curtin resigned his post in November 1915 to work on a short-term project for the politically and industrially powerful Australian Workers' Union, but he had to enter a private hospital in mid-1916 to dry out. Though Curtin later abstained for long periods, he never fully overcame his drink problem and smoked forty cigarettes a day until his last months.

Curtin was back into the political fray in August 1916, when he was appointed secretary to the national executive of the Australian trade union anti-conscription campaign. He agreed with the Hardie–Vaillant resolution of the Socialist International of 1910 in favour of a general strike to prevent war, and argued that socialism would conquer both war and poverty. He addressed many meetings, including one of 50,000 on the Yarra Bank, wrote pamphlets, and worked 'with the energy of a tornado' (Ross, 50). Conscription was defeated in two plebiscites, but at the cost of splitting the Labor Party and losing government. In the aftermath of the first vote Curtin, who had refused a call-up for local military service, was gaoled for three days. During the second campaign he was fined for preaching revolution.

In February 1917, with a salary rise, Curtin was appointed editor of the *Westralian Worker*, which was supported by the Australian Workers' Union, in Perth, Western Australia, and on 21 April he married Elsie (1890–1975), daughter of Abraham Needham, a Tasmanian fellow socialist, in a local register office—she being a Methodist and Curtin a lapsed Catholic. A daughter was born in late 1917 and a son in 1921. Curtin began remaking himself as a moderate and respectable journalist, and in due course bought his first house in the fashionable beachside suburb of Cottesloe, a train ride from his downtown office.

Enters parliament Curtin tried again to enter the federal parliament in 1919, standing unsuccessfully for Perth. In 1921 he supported the insertion of the socialization objective into the Labor platform, but he was an implacable opponent of the communists, earning their lasting enmity when he opposed the Fremantle seamen's strike of 1924. During the 1920s he was a moving spirit in the Western Australia branch of the Australian Journalists' Association and instrumental in introducing a journalism diploma at the university. In 1924 he travelled to Geneva as an Australian delegate to a meeting of the International Labour Organization, and in 1927–8 he served on a federal royal commission into child endowment, filing a minority report in favour. He failed to win the federal seat of Fremantle in 1925 but finally won it in November 1928. Barring an interlude from 1931 to 1934, he held Fremantle for the rest of his life.

In Canberra, Curtin quickly became a back-bencher to watch, though he narrowly missed election to the front bench when Labor formed government at the end of 1929. His major preoccupation was with financial reform to alleviate unemployment—the expansion of credit via changes in the reserve bank rules. Instead, the government adopted the deflationary premiers' plan in 1931, and the party split again, as it had over conscription. Curtin was unheeded when he argued for maintaining party unity at the expense of office and allowing the conservatives to implement the draconian plan. In the subsequent election he lost his seat.

Curtin returned to Perth and made his living as a freelance journalist, though early in 1933 he was appointed full-time paid chairman of the advisory council to prepare Western Australia's case for the Commonwealth Grants Commission. Secession was in the air in Western Australia, and Curtin demonstrated how the state's industries suffered under the federal arrangements. In September 1934 he regained the seat of Fremantle.

James Scullin stepped down as Labor leader in October 1935 and Curtin, after pledging privately to abstain from alcohol, was elected by one vote as his successor. Curtin inherited a party in disarray. In New South Wales, J. T. Lang's dominant faction had been expelled from the party in 1931 and was still estranged. A unity conference brought some of the Langites into federal caucus in 1936, but these 'cannibals' (Day, 323) were to cause Curtin problems for years to come. As leader Curtin chose his policy ground well: avoiding the divisive financial questions, he concentrated on national defence. While the conservative Lyons government relied on imperial defence and appeasement of the dictators, Curtin stressed continental defence (army and air force over navy) and non-intervention in Abyssinia and Spain. This also masked the rift in his party between right-wing Catholics and the international socialists. Domestically, he now stood for 'the maximum of Socialistic benefits within the capitalist system' (ibid., 353). Curtin lost his first federal elections as leader in 1937, but made modest gains.

When war broke out in Europe in 1939 Labor opposed the reintroduction of compulsory military training and the dispatch of Australian forces overseas, arguing that the best contribution Australia could make to the war effort was to see to its own defences. However, when Germany invaded France and the Low Countries, Labor agreed to send reinforcements: 'The men are there and we will not abandon them' (Ross, 186). At the federal elections in September 1940 Labor came within a whisker of government, and the prime minister, Robert Menzies, offered Labor places in a national government. Fearing another split in his fragile party, Curtin refused, though he promised full co-operation in the war effort and agreed to join an advisory war council. Curtin's patience was rewarded a

year later when, in quick succession, Menzies was overthrown and Arthur Fadden's new government lasted only forty days before two independents crossed the floor to put Labor into power.

Prime minister, 1941–1945 Curtin became prime minister on 7 October 1941. Shrewdly, he kept the best conservative appointees in place, among them S. M. Bruce, the former prime minister, as high commissioner in London, General Sir Thomas Blamey as commander of the 2nd Australian Imperial Force, Frederick Shedden as cabinet secretary, and Essington Lewis, the chief executive of the mining giant Broken Hill Proprietary, as munitions supremo. Curtin made his main rival, H. V. Evatt, foreign minister, and placed one of the leading Langites, E. J. Ward, in charge of the vexed area of labour and national service. He told one of his senior public servants to 'Carry out Menzies' policy. There's nothing wrong with his policy—only see that it is carried out!' (Ross, 223).

No sooner was Labor in government than Australia's war changed utterly when Japan attacked Pearl Harbor, Singapore, Hong Kong, and Manila, simultaneously bringing the United States into the conflict and threatening the invasion of Australia. Curtin broadcast a defiant message next day: 'We shall hold this country and keep it as a citadel for the British-speaking race and as a place where civilization will persist' (Serle, 554). His new year's message put the situation more starkly: 'Australia looks to America, free of any pangs as to our traditional links or kinship with the United Kingdom ... we know ... that Australia can go and Britain still hold on' (Ross, 247). It then went on to demand an all-in effort.

Churchill smarted at Curtin's 'harsh tones' (Day, 439), and Roosevelt thought the message 'tasted of panic and disloyalty' (Ross, 247), but the United States was already determined to use Australia as a main base, and Curtin as national leader was simply trying to establish publicly some semblance of control. Curtin gratefully accepted Churchill's offer to send the bulk of Australia's forces back to defend their home soil, but was dumbfounded when, in the light of the fall of Singapore on 15 February 1942, Churchill further suggested that the 7th division be diverted to Rangoon. Losing the Singapore base, and with it the Australian 8th division, was, in Curtin's words, an 'inexcusable betrayal' (Ross, 258), and he refused to sacrifice another. Curtin won the 'cable fight' (Day, 440), though the troops had to continue their way across the Indian Ocean without naval escort. It is much less well known that Curtin consented to Australia's 9th division's remaining in the Middle East until 1943 and to other elements of the 6th division being diverted to Ceylon.

Curtin welcomed the United States general Douglas MacArthur as the allied commander for the south-west Pacific area in March and placed Australia's forces at his disposal. 'You take care of the rear and I will handle the front' (Day, 463), MacArthur said. Curtin set about his task with great thoroughness. By means of radio and the press he 'made friends with the nation' (Ross, 269), coaxing and chiding them into maximum effort. With his principal lieutenant, J. B. Chifley, the treasurer, he defied party dogma to introduce industrial conscription ('the man-power'). There followed rationing of all kinds, fully feder-alized income taxes, pay-as-you-earn taxation, and the mobilization of huge numbers of women. At its peak in 1943 Labor had more than doubled the numbers in the armed forces and war work. Australia achieved 71.4 per cent engagement of its workforce in direct war activities to the United Kingdom's 75.1 per cent. Manufacturing boomed. War loans were oversubscribed. Strikes, though not eliminated, were kept under control: 'putting miners in gaol would not produce coal' (Day, 520). Unemploy-ment benefits were made available and child endowment increased. The 'total war economy' not only helped win the war but also made life in general better for the nation.

In November 1942 Australian volunteers and thousands of American conscripts were fighting in the islands above Australia, while Australian conscripts were restricted by their terms of enlistment to national territory. In these circumstances Curtin felt he must risk some form of con-scription for overseas military service. Given his and his party's history, the decision was most difficult. Unlike W. M. Hughes in 1916, Curtin used the mechanisms of the party, carefully persuading sufficient members of the state and federal executive committees to accept a com-promise: the conscripts would fight only beneath the equator in and about New Guinea, effectively in an extended defence of the mainland. Curtin carried his party, and the bill became law in February 1943.

In the federal elections of September 1943 Curtin and Labor were rewarded with substantial majorities in both houses, though a referendum a year later failed to secure the continuation of federal war powers into the looming peace in order to facilitate reconstruction. In January 1944 Australia and New Zealand signed a regional pact engin-eered by Evatt to stake British Commonwealth claims in the region after the war. This considerably annoyed the Americans, and Curtin distanced himself adroitly from Evatt's excesses when he visited Washington in April. In London for the Commonwealth prime ministers' confer-ence mid-year, Curtin floated the idea of pooling sover-eignty in a permanent Commonwealth secretariat and council, the better to integrate and co-ordinate British and dominion activities post-war, but found no interest from the Canadians, South Africans, and British. He wished to use the Commonwealth to bolster Australia's position as 'the bastion of British institutions … in the Southern World' (Day, 543) and act as a counterpoise to American influence there.

Curtin had had heart trouble for some years and suf-fered a serious attack in November 1944. While he returned to work briefly in the new year, he was again hos-pitalized in March, and he died at the prime minister's lodge in Canberra on 5 July 1945, a month before the end of the Pacific war. Though a long-time rationalist, he was buried on 8 July with Presbyterian rites in Perth's Karra-katta cemetery.

Achievement Curtin stood 5 feet 11 inches tall and weighed about 12 stone. Bespectacled and soberly dressed,

he might have been a suburban bank manager. A cast in his left eye had to be hidden by his image makers. Often withdrawn and of a nervous disposition, he steeled him-self for his public work, but his sincerity, superb orator-ical and literary skills, mastery of his brief, consummate powers of conciliation, and sound political sense made him an exceptional war leader. His great achievement was to keep the Labor Party united and effective in govern-ment through Australia's darkest hour. To do so, he had the wisdom to abandon some of his and his party's earlier principles, and Australia was the better for it.

CARL BRIDGE

Sources D. Day, *John Curtin: a life* (Sydney, 1999) • L. Ross, *John Cur-tin: a biography* (Melbourne, 1977) • G. Serle, 'Curtin, John', *AusDB*, vol. 8 • *In his own words: John Curtin's speeches and writings*, ed. D. Black (1995) • C. Lloyd and R. Hall, eds., *Backroom briefings: John Curtin's war* (1997) • A. Chester, *John Curtin* (1943) • P. Hasluck, *The government and the people*, 2 vols. (1952–70) • D. Horner, *High command* (1982) • D. Horner, *Inside the war cabinet* (1996) • N. Lee, *John Curtin: saviour of Australia* (1983) • D. Langmore, *Prime ministers' wives* (Melbourne, 1992)
Archives John Curtin Prime Ministerial Library, Perth • National Archives of Australia, Canberra, corresp. | National Archives of Australia, Canberra, F. Shedden papers • NL Aus., Lloyd Ross papers | FILM Australian War Memorial, Canberra • BFI NFTVA, documentary footage; news footage • National Film and Sound Archive, Canberra, Screen Sound Australia • Screensound Arch-ive, Canberra | SOUND Australian War Memorial, Canberra • John Curtin Prime Ministerial Library, Perth, Western Australia
Likenesses photograph, c.1941–1945, NL Aus. [*see illus.*] • D. Rubo, oils, Parliament House, Canberra

Curtis, Dunstan Michael Carr (1910–1983), lawyer and civil servant in Europe, was born on 26 August 1910 at 6 Cheyne Gardens, Chelsea, London, the only child of Arthur Cecil Curtis, a civil servant, and his wife, Elizabeth, a teacher and painter, the daughter of Austin Cooper Carr, of Broxton Lower Hall, Cheshire. In 1923 he went to Eton College, where he reached the sixth form, was in Pop, and excelled at rugby football, which he abandoned in favour of sailing, his lifelong passion after he went up to Trinity College, Oxford, in 1929. He gained a third-class honours degree in philosophy, politics, and economics in 1933. In 1932 he spent the long vacation learning French with Pro-fessor Martin at Wimereux, near Boulogne, with a group of friends, one of whom was Terence Rattigan, who wrote his play *French without Tears* based on this occasion.

After qualifying as a solicitor in 1937, Curtis became legal adviser and business manager to Michel Saint-Denis, the French theatrical director at the Old Vic drama school. When Saint-Denis was broadcasting to occupied France as Jacques Duchesne, Curtis broadcast for him in French after the St Nazaire raid. War found Curtis with a Royal Naval Volunteer Reserve commission, commanding a motor torpedo boat with coastal forces engaged in land-ing allied agents in France. In the St Nazaire raid of March 1942 he commanded the motor gunboat from which Com-mander R. E. D. Ryder, leading the naval forces, directed operations. The purpose was to destroy the dry dock and deny its use to the battleship *Tirpitz*. Once the former American destroyer *Campbeltown* had successfully rammed the all-important lock gate with her cargo of explosives, Curtis put his motor gunboat alongside the old mole and landed the ground forces. He remained until ordered by Ryder to withdraw with survivors. He was awarded the DSC in 1942.

Later he commanded the naval wing of no. 30 assault unit in north Africa, Sicily, and north-west Europe where his knowledge of German helped him to receive the surrender of Kiel, after a spirited telephone conversation with Admiral Dönitz, the German naval commander-in-chief. Curtis was promoted commander and received a bar to his DSC and the croix de guerre.

When the war was over he was a tireless advocate for peace. In 1947 he became deputy secretary-general of the European Movement. When the consultative assembly of the Council of Europe met in August 1949 at Strasbourg University, he helped in drafting their proposals, including the European convention on human rights, the council's outstanding achievement. In spring 1950 he joined the council secretariat as counsellor in charge of assembly committees. In this key post, efficiency and a delightful personality made him the trusted adviser of all parties.

In 1954 the assembly elected him deputy secretary-general. The deaths of both the secretary-general and the clerk of the assembly left Curtis in sole charge of all council branches pending new appointments to those posts. Everything worked admirably. Curtis should have been appointed secretary-general in 1960 but the assembly decided in favour of a politician.

Two of Curtis's projects stand out. From 1955 a chance occurred to merge the Council of Europe and the Organization for European Economic Co-operation (OEEC). Although Curtis won support for this from both organizations, he failed because of the abortive British plan to create an enlarged European free trade area, which was opposed by the six countries of the OEEC. When Britain first sought membership of the European Economic Community (EEC) in 1960, Curtis undertook two secretariat studies: on future links between the community and Commonwealth, and between the six countries of the OEEC and the seven-power EFTA. When Britain joined the EEC in 1972 both of Curtis's reports were put into practice.

Curtis left the Council of Europe in 1962. From 1964 to 1973 he was a senior partner in the Paris office of the law firm Herbert Smith & Co. When Britain entered the EEC Curtis enjoyed an Indian summer as secretary-general to the conservative (later democrat) group in the European parliament, a post from which he retired in 1976. He was appointed CBE in 1963.

In 1939 Curtis married Monica, daughter of James Grant Forbes, lawyer, of Boston, Massachusetts. They had a son and a daughter. After a divorce he married in 1950 Patricia (Tony) Elton, sociologist and daughter of George Elton Mayo, an industrial sociologist at Harvard University. Curtis was good-looking—his fair hair was an oriflamme. His personality radiated fun, his courage, especially in final ill health, was profound, and he had a great sense of humour. He died on 9 September 1983 in Montgomery.

COSMO RUSSELL, *rev.*

Sources *The Times* (13 Sept 1983) · personal knowledge (1990) · private information (1990) · *CGPLA Eng. & Wales* (1983)
Wealth at death £37,000: probate, 22 Nov 1983, *CGPLA Eng. & Wales*

Curtis, Edmund (1881–1943), historian, was born on 25 March 1881 in Bury, Lancashire, the fifth of the six children of Francis Curtis, an architectural draughtsman (*d.* 1918), of Rathmullen, co. Donegal, and his wife, Elizabeth Elliott of Belfast. At fifteen he was working in a rubber factory at Silvertown, east London, and voicing his melancholy in verses which found their way into the weekly press. The resulting publicity brought him two benefactors, through whose generosity he was sent to Allhallows School, Honiton, where one of them, Cecil Grant, was an assistant master. Curtis proved a rewarding pupil. When Grant, in 1898, became headmaster of a new co-educational boarding-school in Keswick, he took Curtis with him as head boy. In 1900 Curtis went to Keble College, Oxford, as a commoner, and gained a first class in modern history four years later.

As a lecturer in history at Sheffield (1905–14) Curtis published *Roger of Sicily* (1912) and became recognized as a medieval scholar. He had frequently visited Ireland, and had acquired a working knowledge of Irish, when in 1914 he was appointed professor of modern history at Trinity College, Dublin. Here for the rest of his career he left an abiding impression on his pupils, earning the affection of many whose backgrounds and views were very different from his own. No politician, he 'drifted helplessly in the cross-currents of Trinity academic life' (Lyons, 8). He was never elected to a fellowship, and so remained outside the college's governing circle. Characteristically, he left the residue of his estate as a fund for the benefit of college servants. In 1918 he married Margaret Louise, daughter of Richard Barrington, of the Royal Irish Constabulary. The marriage was dissolved in London in 1925, as a result of his wife's affair with the novelist Liam O'Flaherty. There were no children.

Combining erudition with independence of judgement, appreciative alike of Gaelic and Anglo-Norman civilization, Gaelic-nationalist in sympathy but proud of his protestant and 'planter' ancestry, and an admirer of English character and institutions, Curtis had an unusual blend of qualities for an Irish historian. However, he worked too much in isolation, taking little account of changing academic fashion or current research. He remained true to the Stubbsian constitutionalism he had absorbed at Oxford, harnessing it to medieval and modern Irish themes, including what he dubbed, revealingly, 'aristocratic Home Rule'. His writing, though warmed by a strong historical imagination, was structurally weak and not always accurate in detail. His editing of documents had technical deficiencies. But he had the merits of a pioneer, and he was a courageous opponent of the narrow sectarianism that marked much that passed for history in Ireland at that time. His *History of Medieval Ireland* (1923; 2nd edn, 1938) was unusual for the equal attention it paid to Gaelic and settler society. His outline *History of Ireland* (1936) held the field for several decades. His *Calendar of*

Ormond Deeds (6 vols., 1932–43) unlocked the treasures of the largest medieval archive in Ireland.

Although pensive and solitary, Curtis was well endowed with social gifts and was a memorable talker. One of his pupils has left a sketch of him on a late visit to Donegal: bounding into the saddle of an ancient bicycle; sleeping in a nightcap and nightgown, under which he wore a black silk cravat; carrying raw liver sandwiches in his pockets to ward off the pernicious anaemia that eventually killed him; endlessly curious about local history, dialects, and folklore.

Curtis died at the Elpis Nursing Home, Mount Street, Dublin, on his sixty-second birthday, 25 March 1943, and was buried in the protestant churchyard at Malahide. His work continues to earn respect for the breadth of its sympathies and has found advocates among those who regard an eirenic 'present-centredness' as a legitimate part of the Irish historian's calling.

T. W. MOODY, *rev.* ROBIN FRAME

Sources T. W. Moody, 'The writings of Edmund Curtis', *Irish Historical Studies*, 3 (1942–3), 393–400 · T. W. Moody, 'Edmund Curtis', *Hermathena*, 63 (1944), 69–78 · J. F. Lydon, 'Historical revisit: Edmund Curtis' *A history of medieval Ireland* (1923, 1938)', *Irish Historical Studies*, 31 (1998–9), 535–48 · R. J. H. Corbett, 'A personal reminiscence of Edmund Curtis, sometime professor of modern history in the University of Dublin', *Search: A Church of Ireland Journal*, 19/2 (winter 1996), 127–31 · F. S. L. Lyons, 'T. W. M.', *Ireland under the union, varieties of tension: essays in honour of T. W. Moody*, ed. F. S. Lyons and R. A. J. Hawkins (1988), 1–33 · C. Brady, ed., *Interpreting Irish history: the debate on historical revisionism, 1938–1994* (1994) · A. J. Otway-Ruthven, *A history of medieval Ireland* (1968), foreword · R. B. McDowell and D. A. Webb, *Trinity College, Dublin, 1592–1952: an academic history* (1982)

Archives TCD, papers and corresp. · TCD, papers, incl. notes relating to Kilkenny Castle muniment room and notes relating to conversations with George Moore · University College, Dublin, notes relating to Poyning's statutes

Wealth at death £1938 16s. 2d.: probate, 25 Aug 1943, *CGPLA Eng. & Wales*

Curtis, Ian Kevin (1956–1980), musician, was the only son and eldest child of Kevin Curtis, a detective officer in the Transport Commission police, and his wife, Doreen, *née* Hughes. He was born on 15 July 1956 in the Memorial Hospital, Old Trafford, Manchester. The family lived in Hurdsfield, on the outskirts of Macclesfield, and Curtis attended Trinity Square primary school, Macclesfield, Hurdsfield junior school, and, from 1967, the King's School, Macclesfield. When he was sixteen he met Deborah Woodruffe. They married at St Thomas's Church, Henbury, on 23 August 1975; their daughter, Natalie, was born on 16 April 1979.

Curtis early formed an ambition to make a career in music. In 1973 his family moved to New Moston, Manchester, and he soon ceased to attend the local college, preferring to work in a record shop and to attempt, unsuccessfully, to run his own second-hand record stall. In need of money, however, he began employment at a local office of the Ministry of Defence, transferring after a few months to the Manpower Services Commission and in 1977 to the

Ian Kevin Curtis (1956–1980), by Kevin Cummins, 1979

employment exchange in Macclesfield. After a period living in Oldham, Curtis and his wife returned to Macclesfield, to 77 Barton Street, in May 1977.

Having never abandoned his ambition, in the spring of 1976 Curtis met Peter Hook, Bernard Sumner, and Terry Mason, three friends who allowed Curtis to join their incipient band as the singer. Although still learning to play their instruments, the band gave their first performance, under the name Warsaw, on 29 May 1977 at the Electric Circus, Manchester. Stephen Morris became their drummer that summer. Their first appearance on vinyl followed that October, a single track on *Short Circuit*, a 10-inch compilation of upcoming Manchester bands. Now renamed Joy Division, the band cut their first record—an EP called *An Ideal for Living*—in December 1977. The new name, a reference to the group of female prisoners used by the Nazis as prostitutes for the army, raised eyebrows in the media throughout their career. Joy Division owed their first television appearance, performing 'Shadowplay' on Granada Television's *Granada Reports* in September 1978, to its presenter, Tony Wilson. When Wilson started his influential Factory record label, the group contributed two tracks to its first offering, the EP *A Factory Sample*, released in January 1979.

On 27 December 1978 Curtis had his first recognizable epileptic fit, at a time when Joy Division's profile was rapidly rising, with their début London performance. At the end of January 1979 they recorded the first of their two sessions for the BBC Radio 1 disc jockey John Peel. Their first album, *Unknown Pleasures*, appeared in June 1979, a happy collaboration with producer Martin Hannett (1950–1991), who helped to establish Joy Division's trademark sound, giving prominence to Hook's lead guitar style of bass-playing, introducing then innovative effects on the drums, and making spare but effective use of new technology in the form of synthesizers and syndrums. Coupled with Curtis's low, sonorous voice, Joy Division's music evolved into one of intense, portentous rhythms and melodies that were, at their best, haunting. At the end of August 1979 Curtis left his civil service job, as Joy Division embarked on a national tour supporting the Buzzcocks. The single 'Transmission' was released that October.

Epilepsy, continual performing, and drugs combined to exacerbate Curtis's volatile, often depressive, temperament. Guilt and emotional confusion may also have played a part. He had begun an affair with Annik Honoré, a Belgian he seems to have met first while performing in Brussels, and increasingly shunned his wife. Joy Division toured Europe in January 1980 and began preparations for an American tour later in the year. In March 1980 the band recorded their second album, *Closer*, and their most successful single, 'Love Will Tear Us Apart'. By this time, some of Curtis's lyrics, plangent cries of depression and desperation, suggested a deepening blackness of mood. The pressures of performing were provoking more frequent epileptic fits. As Curtis continued his relationship with Annik Honoré, his wife began divorce proceedings. Returning briefly to the house that he had shared with her, 77 Barton Street, Macclesfield, in the early hours of Sunday 18 May 1980 Ian Curtis hanged himself. The previous evening he had watched Werner Herzog's *Stroszek*, a film about a man who kills himself rather than choose between two women. He was cremated at Macclesfield crematorium on 23 May 1980. His memorial stone, erected by his widow, bears the words 'Love Will Tear Us Apart'.

Curtis's desire for the limelight was confessional. His stage performances displayed the contrasts in a character that was generally quiet and polite, yet capable of bouts of depression or anger. His manic dancing—perhaps unwittingly parodizing his epileptic fits—counterpointed his melancholic lyrics. Curtis helped Joy Division to capture a *Zeitgeist*. The group's presentation of itself was as brooding and enigmatic as their singer's own persona: their reluctance to give interviews suggested sullenness as often as it deepened their mystique; they deliberately omitted the names of their songs from the outside of their album covers, Peter Saville's monochrome designs for which spawned a thousand T-shirts; and their use of images of 1940s totalitarianism kicked against the comfortable, middle-class background from which Curtis, at least, had sprung. At the heart of the group's success, though, was a music that, while often dour, immediately appealed. While the remaining members of Joy Division gained continued if not greater success under their apt new name, New Order, Curtis's death triggered a long succession of cover versions of the group's songs: 'Love Will Tear Us Apart' had been recorded by at least seventeen different artists by the end of the century, including P. J. Proby and Paul Young. More subtle, yet more profound, was an influence on many features—from musicianship to style and demeanour—of a host of groups that sprang up in the aftermath of the punk rock transformation of popular music. While Curtis's suicide, when on the brink of commercial success, seemed to mirror the deaths of other cult figures of late twentieth-century youth, such as Jim Morrison and Janis Joplin, the story of his life, uncovered in the biography *Touching from a Distance* by his widow, Deborah, tells of a deeply personal struggle of a timeless and tragic kind.   MARIOS COSTAMBEYS

Sources D. Curtis, *Touching from a distance: Ian Curtis and 'Joy Division'* (1995) · J. W. Davis, 'Joy Division', home.adelphia. net/~joedavis/docs/jd/joy.htm [New Order and Factory images], 21 Dec 1999 · C. Warren, 'Joy Division Shadowplay', www.lwtua.free-online.co.uk/shadowplay/joyd.html, 21 Dec 1999
Archives FILM BFI NFTVA, documentary footage | SOUND BL NSA, documentary recordings · BL NSA, performance recordings
Likenesses A. Corbijn, photograph, 1979, repro. in A. Corbijn, *Famouz: photographs, 1975–88*, new edn (1997) · K. Cummins, photograph, 1979, NPG [see illus.] · K. Cummins, photographs, 1979–80, Kevin Cummins, London; repro. in Curtis, *Touching from a distance*
Wealth at death £6746: administration, 10 July 1980, *CGPLA Eng. & Wales*

Curtis, John (*fl.* **1790–1797**), landscape painter, was a pupil of the landscape painter William Marlow with whom he and his wife lodged at Twickenham. In 1790 he exhibited at the Royal Academy *A View of Netley Abbey*, and was an occasional exhibitor in the following years. In 1797 he departed from his usual style, exhibiting a naval encounter showing the *Indefatigable* and *Amazon* frigates under Sir Edward Pellew engaging a French ship, *Les Droits de l'Homme*. His watercolour *The Thames at Twickenham* was sold at Sothebys in 1980 and his oil painting of Green Park is at Anglesey Abbey. Nothing is known of his subsequent career. Some of his views have been engraved.

L. H. CUST, rev. R. J. LAMBERT

Sources Waterhouse, *18c painters* · Bryan, *Painters* · M. H. Grant, *A dictionary of British landscape painters, from the 16th century to the early 20th century* (1952)
Archives Courtauld Inst., Witt Library

Curtis, John (1791–1862), entomologist, was born at Norwich on 3 September 1791, the son of Charles Morgan Curtis (d. 1796), a stone-engraver and sign-painter, and Frances (d. 1822?), who became a flower cultivator following Charles's death. In childhood, through his mother's influence, Curtis became interested in natural history, in particular the study of insect life. He studied the botany and entomology of the ponds and marshes in the neighbourhood of Norwich with Richard Walker (1791–1870), a local naturalist. It is believed that Curtis contracted 'rheumatic fever' (probably malaria) through his exertions while working with Walker; upon his recovery he was sent to school in Norwich by his mother.

When Curtis was sixteen he was placed in a Norwich lawyer's office as a writing clerk, a position he did not enjoy. He soon made the acquaintance of Simon Wilkin (1790–1862), who invited Curtis to live with him at Costessey (Cossey), near Norwich. Having moved to Costessey in 1811, Curtis met many naturalists, such as the revds William Kirby (1759–1850) and William Spence (1783–1860). During this period Curtis was placed for a time with a Mr Edwards of Bungay to learn engraving. Here he became acquainted with the works of Pierre-André Latreille (1762–1833), and began to dissect, draw, and describe insects systematically, and to engrave them on copper. His first published work was on the plates for Kirby's joint work with Spence, *An Introduction to Entomology* (1815–26).

At some point between 1817 and 1819 Curtis went to London, visiting William Kirby at Barham, near Ipswich, *en route*. Here Curtis made the acquaintance of the entomologist Alexander Macleay (1767–1848), secretary of the Linnean Society until 1825, when he departed for Australia. Curtis subsequently assisted Kirby in bringing out descriptions of Australian insects, which were published in the *Transactions* of the Linnean Society, and in other work. In London, Curtis took lodgings from Miss Dorothy Western, 12 Charles Street, Berkeley Square. He was presented to the naturalist Sir Joseph Banks (1743–1820), president of the Royal Society (1788–1820), who granted Curtis free use of his library and introduced him to William Elford Leach (1790–1836), assistant keeper of the natural history department in the British Museum, with whom Curtis studied shells. It was at Leach's house that he met the entomologist James Charles Dale (1791–1872), of Glanvilles Wotton, Sherborne, who became his lifelong friend and patron. In 1819 or 1820 Curtis married Lydia, probably from Middlesex, with whom he had a son and a daughter. When his son, Edward John, was born, the Curtis family was residing most probably at 4 Grove Place, Lisson Grove, London.

After settling in London, Curtis worked as a writer and 'commissioned entomological agent for wealthy patrons' (Clark, 204), such as Dale. During his early days in the capital, Curtis executed much botanical drawing and engraving for the Horticultural and Linnean societies. He became a fellow of the Linnean Society in 1822, and, after meeting Georges Cuvier (1769–1832) and Latreille, began his great work *British Entomology* (1824–39). The work (partly financed by Dale) extended to sixteen volumes, appearing in 193 parts with 770 plates. The plates were exquisitely drawn, with the figures of the rarer and more beautiful species being coloured, and in many instances included the plants upon which the specimens were found. Dale's name appeared on almost every page, and it was from his collection that Curtis derived a vast portion of the material from which his elaborate work was drawn up. Their names came to be considered synonyms. Cuvier pronounced *British Entomology* to be 'the paragon of perfection', but its success was much hindered by the attacks of James Francis Stephens (1792–1852) in his *Illustrations of British Entomology* (1827–37) and elsewhere. Incidentally, Stephens had employed Curtis's younger brother, Charles Morgan, as his first artist in the earlier volumes of his *Illustrations*. Curtis's work was defended by Dale in Loudon's

Magazine of Natural History. However, Curtis, like Stephens, sustained considerable financial loss on the publication of his work, which left him impoverished and bitter.

In July 1825 Curtis and Dale made an expedition to Scotland, where they met the novelist and poet Sir Walter Scott. After a tour that included some of the western islands, they returned to Edinburgh on 20 August 1825, having added more than thirty new species to the list of British insects. In 1830 Curtis visited France, via Jersey, and collected insects from Bordeaux to Fréjus with great results. The tour included an investigation of the quarries of Aix-en-Provence, where Lyell and Murchison obtained fossil insects. Curtis was elected a fellow of the Oxford Natural History Society in 1833; in the same year he suffered an attack of dysentery. At about this time he was living at 57 Charlotte Street, London. In 1835 he visited Ireland. Two years later, owing to difficult circumstances, he moved to 11 Robert Street, near Regent's Park, London. He managed visits to Italy in 1843, 1850, and 1851.

For many years Curtis made a special study of the habits and economy of the various species of insect pests. The results of his investigations were communicated to the *Gardener's Chronicle* (1841–55), under the signature 'Ruricola', and to the *Journal of the Royal Agricultural Society* (which series ran until 1857). These articles culminated in his *Farm insects: being the natural history and economy of the insects injurious to the field crops of Great Britain and Ireland, and also those which infest barns and granaries. With suggestions for their destruction. Illustrated with numerous engravings* (1860).

In the early 1840s, having failed to obtain a position at the British Museum, Curtis was awarded a civil-list pension of £100. This was increased by £50 in April 1861, when his eyesight failed through the strain of his microscopical investigations and engravings. He was president of the Entomological Society in 1855 (from which post he resigned in 1857), and was an honorary member of the Société Entomologique de France and of various other learned societies in Europe and America.

At some point, possibly before 1855, Curtis was widowed. On 27 June 1860 he married Matilda (*b.* 1828?), daughter of Samuel Bliss, a law stationer of 12 Stanmore Street, Islington, London; the couple had two sons. Curtis died on 6 October 1862, at his home, 18 Belitha Villas, Barnsbury Park, Islington. A post-mortem revealed that his death was a result of stomach cancer. He was survived by Matilda and his children. His insect collections were sold by auction to Sir Frederick McCoy (1823–1899), the founder of the National Museum of Natural History and Geology, Melbourne.

James Hooper, rev. Yolanda Foote

Sources [J. Chambers], introduction, in [J. Chambers], *A general history of the county of Norfolk*, 1 (1829), 50 · J. Freeman, *Life of the Rev. William Kirby* (1852), 426 · *The Athenaeum* (11 Oct 1862), 462 · J. O. Westwood, 'Notice sur John Curtis', *Annales de la Société Entomologique de France*, 4th ser., 3 (1863) · C. Knight, ed., *The English cyclopaedia: biography*, 6 vols. (1856–8) · Boase, *Mod. Eng. biog.* · G. Ordish, *John Curtis and the pioneering of pest control* (1974) · A. T. Gage and W. T. Stearn, *A bicentenary history of the Linnean Society of*

London (1988) • J. F. M. Clark, 'Science, secularization, and social change: the metamorphosis of entomology in nineteenth-century England', DPhil diss., U. Oxf., 1994 • C. Mackechnie Jarvis, 'A history of the British Coleoptera', *Proceedings and Transactions of the British Entomological and Natural History Society*, 8/4 (1976), 91–112 **Archives** NHM, watercolour drawings • Oxf. U. Mus. NH, Hope Library, notes, drawings, and papers • Royal Entomological Society of London, diary and letters | BL, corresp. with Sir Robert Peel, Add. MSS 40464, 40534, 40562, 40573, 40584 • Oxf. U. Mus. NH, Hope Library, letters to J. C. Dale **Likenesses** T. H. Maguire, lithograph, 1851, BM, NPG; repro. in T. H. Maguire, *Portraits of honorary members of the Ipswich Museum* (1852) **Wealth at death** under £2000: probate, 23 Oct 1862, *CGPLA Eng. & Wales*

Curtis, John Harrison (1778–1860), otologist, was the first child of Thomas Curtis (*b.* 1749) and his wife, Susannah, *née* Simmons. Nothing is known about his early life or education. He was said to be insignificant and short in stature but he was self-reliant and naturally shrewd.

In the early nineteenth century the management of aural conditions not infrequently fell into the hands of certain practitioners who were neither interested in diagnosis nor concerned with the indications for their treatment. Curtis was the most notorious of these; he had been a dispenser in the navy, but had no medical qualifications. His ideas and practice were a mixture of charlatan and of applied common sense. They were published in 1817 in his book *Treatise on the Physiology and Diseases of the Ear*, which ran to four editions. Although this book owed much to the work of John Cunningham Saunders, whose classification of ear diseases Curtis used, it received heavy contemporary criticism; nevertheless, it did have some value as it made medical practitioners aware of the need to treat ear disease. At the time physicians generally hesitated to treat the discharging ear, believing that nature should be allowed to take its course.

Curtis wrote in a popular style (it is believed often with the aid of a ghost-writer), which appealed to a prejudiced public and created a favourable climate for active treatment. He recommended astringent agents for all kinds of ear discharge, and paracentesis in cases of Eustachian tube obstruction. His *Treatise* is distinguished by the frontispiece, which illustrates a collection of French and Spanish artificial ears. For some patients Curtis recommended that 'German silver ears were better than any!' His comments on the development of ear trumpets were reasonable and he was responsible for the design of a collapsing speaking tube and one of the early 'acoustic chairs'. Curtis's second book was *Cases Illustrative of Treatment of the Diseases of the Ear, both Local and Constitutional* (1818). His method of examination was to carry out a superficial visual inspection and to palpate the tympanic membrane with a blunt probe to determine whether it was intact or perforated. His favourite treatment was to syringe the ear with a huge instrument not unlike a garden syringe. This instrument was once used on Mr (later Sir) Robert Peel, who dared to enquire of Curtis what he was hoping to achieve. Never a man to be put off, Curtis aimed the tip of

John Harrison Curtis (1778–1860), by R. Cooper, pubd 1819 (after J. Shand)

the syringe directly at the ear canal and gave it a little dig, saying 'Mr Peel, if you don't hold your tongue, I shall certainly do you a mischief' (Clarke). The patient remained quiet! A later publication, *An Essay on the Deaf and Dumb* (1829), showed the necessity for treatment in early infancy and contained some observations on congenital deafness. Curtis also wrote *Observations on the Preservation of Sight* (1834), and *Observations of the Preservation of Health in Infancy, Youth, Manhood and Age* (1837).

Curtis married a protégée of a Mrs James, who had considerable landed property in Kent. He established himself in London in an imposing home in Soho Square, which was then a fashionable area, and soon gained a large and aristocratic practice; later it included George IV and the duke and duchess of Gloucester. In order to advertise and further his claims as an aurist, in 1816 he founded at 20 Carlisle Street the Dispensary for Diseases of the Ear. This was the first specialist ear hospital in Britain. It filled such an urgent need that in 1820 it was necessary to seek larger premises, at 10 Dean Street, at which time the king gave his patronage to the dispensary. (A further move to Frith Street took place in 1876, and in 1904, when new buildings were opened again in Dean Street, the title of the dispensary was changed to the Royal Ear Hospital.)

In 1838, at the peak of his career, Curtis wrote a letter to *The Lancet* which showed great ignorance. In it he claimed that a deficiency of cerumen (earwax) was one of the commonest causes of deafness and that the effective treatment was painting the meatus with creosote. This prompted Joseph Toynbee strongly to refute this and other statements and strengthened Toynbee's own drive to rescue the care of ear disease from the hands of quacks. Thus Curtis provided not only Britain's first ear dispensary (which was purchased from his executors and revitalized by William Harvey), but also the stimulus for the new dedicated otologists, among whom were Toynbee, James Yearsley, William Wilde, George Pilcher, and James Hinton.

Curtis was very wealthy for a time but he squandered his fortune, fell into debt, and fled to the Isle of Man, where he subsequently died in an asylum in 1860.

NEIL WEIR

Sources N. Weir, *Otolaryngology: an illustrated history* (1990) · J. F. Clarke, *Autobiographical recollections of the medical profession* (1874) · W. R. Merrington, *University College Hospital and its medical school: a history* (1976) · A. Politzer, *History of otology*, trans. S. Milstein, C. Portnoff, and A. Coleman (1981) [Ger. orig. (1907)] · J. H. Curtis, 'Letters to the editor', *The Lancet* (24 Nov 1838), 328 · J. H. Curtis, 'Letters to the editor', *The Lancet* (29 Dec 1838), 534 · J. T. [J. Toynbee], 'Letter to the editor', *The Lancet* (8 Dec 1838), 422
Likenesses W. S. Letherbridge, oils, exh. RA 1814 · R. Cooper, stipple, pubd 1819 (after J. Shand), NPG, Wellcome L. [*see illus.*] · A. R. Freebairn, line engraving, 1839 (after E. W. Wyon; after Sarti), Wellcome L. · T. H. Maguire, lithograph, 1850, Wellcome L. · Sarti, engraving (after medal bust), NPG, Wellcome L.

Curtis, Lionel George (1872–1955), writer and public servant, was born at The Outwoods, near Derby, on 7 March 1872, the youngest of four children of the Revd George James Curtis (d. 1904), rector of Coddington church, Ledbury, Herefordshire, and his wife, Frances (d. 1913), daughter of the Revd John Edmund Carr, of The Outwoods. His early years were spent at Coddington rectory with his siblings Mary, Charles, and Arthur; family wealth ensured a comfortable upbringing. His parents were evangelical Christians, followers of Pearsall Smith and 'the Way of Holiness'. In later life Curtis came to question the literalness of their biblical beliefs, but he inherited their evangelical fervour and their conviction that 'the distinctions … between religion and politics … are false' (May, 62).

Curtis was educated at the Wells House, Malvern Wells, and Haileybury College. He was not noted as a particularly gifted student. In 1891 he entered New College, Oxford; he obtained third classes in classical honour moderations in 1892 and in *literae humaniores* in 1894. He left Oxford with little idea of what career he wished to follow, but with a circle of friends who were to remain devoted to him for the rest of their lives.

While an undergraduate, Curtis had developed an interest in the 'social question', reading F. D. Maurice and spending two vacations trudging the roads disguised as a tramp in order to gain firsthand experience of the working of the poor law. On leaving Oxford, he worked for three years for the Haileybury Guild, managing a boy's club in the East End. Through this work he met and was much influenced by Octavia Hill and Canon Barnett. A recommendation from the latter secured Curtis's appointment in 1897 as part-time secretary to Leonard Courtney. Curtis combined devilling for Courtney with studying law. He was eventually called to the bar by the Inner Temple in 1902. Meanwhile, on Courtney's recommendation,

Lionel George Curtis (1872–1955), by Ramsey & Muspratt, *c*.1935–40

he gained brief but valuable experience in municipal affairs as private secretary to Lord Welby, vice-chairman of the London county council, in 1899.

South Africa, 1899–1909 On the outbreak of the Second South African War in October 1899, Curtis's brother Arthur, a captain in the Royal Artillery, was among those who were swiftly besieged at Ladysmith. Curtis himself enlisted in December 1899, with his friends Max Balfour and Lionel Hichens, in the cyclists' section of the City Imperial Volunteers. For the next six months the three companions performed a variety of tasks, from carrying dispatches to commandeering cattle, but only once came under enemy fire. Curtis's letters home—published in 1951 as *With Milner in South Africa*—testify to his boyish sense of adventure, but also to his respect for his Boer opponents. He was discharged following the capture of Pretoria, in June 1900, and returned home to administer the estate of his brother Arthur, who had died of typhoid three days after the relief of Ladysmith.

Curtis returned to South Africa in October 1900, determined to play a part in the reconstruction of the war-torn colonies. Through a combination of perseverance, luck, and Oxford connections, he obtained an interview with Sir Alfred Milner, who agreed to take him on his staff as assistant imperial secretary. One of his tasks was to draw up a plan for the new Johannesburg municipality, and in April 1901 he was appointed acting town clerk. The appointment of someone so young and inexperienced was widely criticized, but over the next two years Curtis's hard work and organizing ability won him the admiration of many former critics. The apprehension that he would serve the interests of the wealthy mine owners was soon confounded: indeed, it was largely through Curtis's persistence that the boundaries of the new municipality were drawn to include the mines. Nevertheless, Curtis's self-assurance often created friction. At one point the *Transvaal Critic* described him as 'a malapert young gentleman sitting on the necks of the Town Council as he dictates to the universe' (Lavin, *From Empire to International Commonwealth*, 52).

Curtis was promoted assistant colonial secretary of the Transvaal, with responsibility for municipal affairs, in February 1903. As in Johannesburg, he had to create a system of municipal government more or less from scratch. Again, his efficiency won him many admirers, while his abrasive personality caused problems. In October 1905 he was given responsibility also for 'Asiatic' affairs. Convinced that unlimited Indian immigration would mean the end of a 'white' South Africa, he pressed for a system of registration and fingerprinting designed to exclude further immigrants. Curtis's proposals brought him into conflict with the Indian community, led by Mahatma Gandhi, but they were largely embodied in the elected Transvaal assembly's first piece of legislation, the Asiatic amendment ordinance of 1907. By then, however, he was no longer a member of the Transvaal civil service, having resigned in September 1906 in anticipation of self-government, and following a dispute over departmental responsibilities.

Curtis was only one of a number of young Oxford graduates whom Milner had recruited to work in the administration of the new colonies. Sir William Marriott described them, caustically, as 'Milner's Kindergarten'. The name stuck, and was adopted by the members of the group themselves. The Kindergarten became an unusually tightly knit group of friends, drawn together by background and education, and united by shared values and a common veneration for Lord Milner. In South Africa they lived and holidayed together, and many evenings were spent in earnest discussion of political and social problems. Besides Curtis, the Kindergarten included his New College friends—for whom he had found employment with the Johannesburg town council—John Dove, Richard Feetham, and Lionel Hichens; other members included Robert Brand, George Craik, Patrick Duncan, William Marris, J. F. (Peter) Perry, Geoffrey Robinson (later Dawson), and Hugh Wyndham. After 1905 they were joined by Philip Kerr and, following Milner's replacement by Lord Selborne, Dougal Malcolm. The Kindergarten bond was a powerful one, and endured long after the majority of the group had left South Africa.

Milner's long-term aim in South Africa was to unite the various colonies as a loyal dominion under the British flag. The failure of his schemes to attract British settlers, and what he saw as the premature grant of self-government to the former republics, led him to be pessimistic after his retirement. The Kindergarten, by contrast, saw the unification of South Africa as the key to economic prosperity

(and therefore British immigration), but also to that reconciliation between British and Afrikaners which was essential for future imperial loyalty. 'I have always told you that I am much more of a pro-Boer than you', Curtis wrote to Milner (Lavin, *From Empire to International Commonwealth*, 77). Milner was persuaded to secure funds for the Kindergarten from the Rhodes Trust (set up under the terms of Cecil Rhodes's will), and Curtis—by now acknowledged as 'the Prophet' of the group—was set to work on a memorandum setting out the case for unification. With minor amendments by Selborne, and after a wrangle between the latter and the Colonial Office, the memorandum was published on Selborne's authority (and supposedly in response to a request from the Cape government, orchestrated by Curtis) in July 1907.

The publication of the Selborne memorandum was the trigger for a rapid movement towards the unification of South Africa. The Kindergarten helped the movement in a variety of ways. Curtis, now a nominated member of the Transvaal upper house, organized closer union societies throughout the four colonies, and engaged in dextrous backroom persuasion. Kerr edited *The State*, the organ of the movement. Brand and Duncan advised the Transvaal delegation to the National Convention. By June 1909 a constitution had been agreed, and Curtis returned to England to lobby for its passage unamended through the British parliament. In August parliament passed the South Africa Act, and on 31 May 1910 the Union of South Africa was established. Selborne wrote to Curtis that 'the main credit for this work must always be yours' (May, 35). Ignoring the largely independent role of local politicians, Curtis also believed that the unification of South Africa was the direct outcome of the persuasive power of the Selborne memorandum, reinforced by the activities of the closer union societies.

The Round Table, 1909–1916 As early as 1907, Curtis wrote to Selborne that South Africa was a 'microcosm' of the British empire and that, once unification was accomplished, the Kindergarten might 'begin some work of the same kind in respect of Imperial Relations' (Lavin, 'Lionel Curtis and the idea of the commonwealth', 99). During the summer of 1909 Milner organized a series of meetings for Curtis with potential sponsors and collaborators, and sufficient agreement was reached to hold the first meeting of the Round Table at Plas Newydd, Lord Anglesey's estate in Anglesey, over the weekend of 4–5 September 1909. Among those present, besides Milner and the available Kindergarten, were lords Howick, Lovat, and Wolmer, and F. S. Oliver. The Round Table was soon joined by Leo Amery, Lord Robert Cecil, Reginald Coupland, Edward Grigg, and Alfred Zimmern, but the core of the group remained, until the Second World War, the Kindergarten.

The aim of the Round Table was deceptively simple: to ensure the permanence of the British empire by reconstructing it as a federation representative of all its self-governing parts. Curtis depicted this as the logical outcome of the movement towards self-government in the dominions, and the only alternative to disruption and independence. The Plas Newydd meeting endorsed Curtis's strategy for achieving the aim (based on the Kindergarten's experience in South Africa) and agreed to appoint him general secretary of the Round Table and Philip Kerr editor of its eponymous journal, at salaries of £1000 each. Curtis was in fact to remain employed by the Round Table, except for a brief period when he was employed by the Colonial Office, until 1931, when he came into a substantial inheritance from his mother's side.

The two Round Table employees, together with William Marris, set out on a tour of Canada immediately, in September 1909. They returned with similar impressions, but radically different conclusions: Kerr believed that any attempt to stampede Canada into imperial federation would be counter-productive, whereas Curtis believed that time was of the essence. This was only the first of numerous disagreements within the Round Table, during which Curtis's colleagues attempted to restrain his ardour. Undeterred, he set out on a tour of the dominions—South Africa, New Zealand, Australia, then back via Canada—writing up his arguments as the first of a series of Round Table Studies, and forming branches in all the major centres of population. Through high-level contacts and his own remarkable persuasive skills, Curtis was able to recruit members from among the leading figures in each dominion. Nevertheless, his activities aroused considerable suspicion, which was not helped by his habit of masquerading as a South African, and his lack of candour concerning the extent to which the branches were intended to be propaganda, and not merely study, groups. The movement suffered an early setback at the Imperial Conference of 1911, when, having read Curtis's memorandum, the prime minister of New Zealand, Sir Joseph Ward, made an impassioned but confused plea for imperial reconstruction, only to be savaged by his prime ministerial colleagues.

Curtis's Round Table Studies failed to convince many of his fellow Round Tablers either in the dominions or in the London group. Particular sticking points were his insistence that any imperial government should have the power of direct taxation, and that India and the dependencies should come under the control of the dominions as well as of Britain. His elaboration of the 'principle of the Commonwealth'—the idea that the empire existed in order to promote self-government, in the dependencies as well as the dominions—only made matters worse. Various of his colleagues described the principle as illogical, unhistorical, dangerous, and irrelevant to the movement's fundamental aim.

Curtis's reaction to such criticism was not to modify his ideas, but to embark on an even more ambitious programme of 'studies'. His year as Beit lecturer in colonial history at Oxford, in 1912–13—which prompted the Beit professor, H. E. Egerton, to complain that he felt like a country rector with the prophet Isaiah as his curate—gave Curtis the opportunity to add academic substance to his arguments. Thereafter, he set to work on a three-volume study of the imperial problem, tackling, respectively, its history, its contemporary manifestations, and its possible solutions; he also worked on a shorter volume, designed for popular consumption.

By the outbreak of the First World War, Curtis had still to finish any of his projected volumes. The arguments within the Round Table remained unresolved, and were exacerbated by the circumstances of the war. Many believed that the dominions' war efforts made a reconstruction of the empire unnecessary; Curtis, by contrast, argued that unity would have prevented—and, without institutional change, was unlikely to survive—the war. The original plan was for Curtis to publish his volumes on behalf of all the Round Table groups, and as the fruit of their collective research. This proved impossible, but Curtis was authorized to publish, under his own name, *The Commonwealth of Nations, Part One* (his historical examination of the empire and of the principle of self-government) and *The Problem of the Commonwealth* (the one-volume argument for a federation of the empire), both in 1916.

The publication of Curtis's books aroused considerable interest in the press. Few public figures were willing to endorse his conclusions, but many admitted the force and cogency of his arguments. Curtis immediately set out on a tour of the dominions, to arrange for local publication and stimulate debate. His hopes that the Round Table groups would convert themselves into propagandist organs were soon disappointed: the groups (particularly in Canada) showed themselves anxious to distance themselves from his views. Even in England, the majority of his colleagues tempered sympathy with scepticism. Eventually they committed what for Curtis was the heresy of admitting co-operation to be a more fruitful line of advance than federation, at the time of the 1917 imperial war cabinet and conference. By then, however, Curtis's interest had shifted elsewhere.

Empire to Commonwealth Curtis arrived in India in November 1916 to promote his books and attempt to form Round Table groups there. He ended up staying until February 1918, unable to resist embroiling himself in the debate on the constitutional future of the country. His interest in India had first been aroused by Marris, and in 1912 and 1915 he had taken part in discussions with a group of experts collected by the Round Table, to find ways of meeting Indian demands for self-government and equality of status within the empire without endangering stability or British interests. In 1915 he suggested the system which he later called 'diarchy', whereby responsibility for a range of subjects could gradually be transferred from a British-controlled provincial administration to a parallel, Indian-controlled one—or, if necessary, back again. He persuaded Indian civil servant Sir Frederick William Duke to draw up a scheme for Bengal, and sent copies to the viceroy and the India Office. When he arrived in India, therefore, he came already armed with a constitutional blueprint.

Curtis expounded the case for 'diarchy' in a series of *Letters to the People of India* and *Indian Studies* in 1917, and scored a notable success by persuading a group of Europeans and Indians from Bengal to sign a widely publicized

Joint Address. Following Edwin Montagu's declaration of August 1917 and his arrival in India in November, Curtis met the secretary of state on numerous occasions, and lobbied vigorously for the adoption of his scheme, with considerable success. Back home, he brought his influence to bear on the joint select committee charged with examining Montagu's report, driving its chairman, Lord Selborne, at times to distraction. The resultant Government of India Act of 1919 (the Montagu–Chelmsford reforms) differed in several respects from Curtis's original proposal but incorporated the most important element of his scheme. Lord Ampthill commented in the House of Lords that, 'but for the chance visit to India of a globe-trotting doctrinaire with a positive mania for constitution-mongering, nobody in the world would ever have thought of so peculiar a notion as that of "Dyarchy"' (Lavin, *From Empire to International Commonwealth*, 135).

Curtis's interest in the question of trusteeship led him to publish an influential article in the *Round Table* of December 1918, setting out the case for a system of mandates under a League of Nations, and advocating Anglo-American co-operation as the basis for post-war international stability. On the strength of this he was appointed a member of Cecil's League of Nations section at the Paris peace conference. His contribution to the conference at an official level was perhaps less significant than his unofficial work promoting the idea of an Anglo-American institute of international relations, to guide official thinking after the war. This resulted, in 1919, in the founding of the Institute (later the Royal Institute) of International Affairs in London and, slightly later, of the Council on Foreign Relations in New York. Curtis was acknowledged as the 'father' of the British Institute (Gathorne-Hardy, 1): it was he who organized the first meetings, secured funds from Sir Abe Bailey and others, and persuaded Colonel R. W. Leonard to purchase 10 St James's Square (Chatham House) as its permanent home. He resigned as secretary of the institute in 1930, to prevent it being seen as a 'one-man show' (May, 241), but he remained a councillor and a member of the endowment committee. In 1944 he was honoured by being made a president of the institute.

In June 1921 the *Round Table* published another influential article, written by Curtis and John Dove after a visit to Dublin, which advocated ending the Anglo-Irish conflict by giving the fullest measure of dominion self-government to the south. This resulted in Curtis's appointment as second secretary (and in effect constitutional adviser) to the British delegation at the Anglo-Irish treaty talks of October to December 1921, and as adviser to the colonial secretary on Irish affairs until October 1924. In the latter capacity he worked to ensure the observance of the treaty obligations on both sides, and was instrumental in securing the appointment of an Irish boundary commission, in accordance with the terms of the treaty, and with his friend Richard Feetham as chairman, in May 1924.

Meanwhile, on 16 April 1920 Curtis had married his former secretary, Gladys Edna (*d.* 1965), known as 'Pat', the youngest of ten daughters of Prebendary Percy Richard Scott, of Tiverton. In June 1924 she lost a child in late pregnancy, in circumstances which left her unable to conceive again. She was a devoted wife, who endured with fortitude Curtis's alternations of enthusiasm and neglect.

Prophet of federalism In May 1921 Curtis was elected to a fellowship at All Souls College, Oxford, where he joined many Kindergarten and Round Table colleagues, and was one of few fellows to earn the friendship of T. E. Lawrence. He and Pat moved to Hales Croft, Kidlington, a house converted for them by Herbert Baker, which was to be their home until his death. After resigning from the Colonial Office, he engaged with enthusiasm in university politics and fund-raising. He was largely responsible for the founding of the Oxford Society in 1930, and for securing the gift of the Wytham Abbey estate to the university. He was also involved, with Reginald Coupland, Kerr, and others, in unsuccessful attempts to found an Oxford school of government or of African studies. His interest in environmental questions found expression in short-lived but intense campaigns against sky-writing and ribbon development.

Through Chatham House, Curtis was closely involved with the organization of a series of unofficial Commonwealth relations conferences, and with the Institute of Pacific Relations. His interest in the Far East (which he regarded as the most probable storm centre of future conflict, and therefore the testing ground of international and imperial co-operation) resulted in his acting as adviser to the municipal council of the Shanghai international settlement in 1929–30, and publishing *The Capital Question of China* in 1932. In 1935 he unsuccessfully attempted to persuade the British government to hand over control of its South African protectorates to South Africa, arguing that only by having responsibility for all the consequences of their 'native' policy would South Africans come round to a more liberal view. He published a longer version of his controversy with Margery Perham in *The Times* as *The Protectorates of South Africa* (1935), gallantly allowing Perham the last word. His interest in Africa also resulted in his securing funds from the Carnegie Foundation for an *African Survey*, which he persuaded Lord Hailey (now a member of the Round Table) to write.

Curtis's main work between the wars was writing a new series of Round Table studies, eventually published as *Civitas Dei* (3 vols., 1934–7). This was a long and at times rambling discourse on the idea of commonwealth from the time of Aristotle onwards. His assertion that he saw the hand of God in the British empire was derided by his more sceptical colleagues (who once again refused Curtis's work the Round Table imprimatur), but it was well received, especially in liberal Anglican circles.

Curtis's empire federalism remained undimmed after its decisive rejection by the Imperial Conference in 1921, but it gradually became submerged in a vision of an international commonwealth, based on a union of the Western democracies and their empires. With the failure of appeasement (which he warily criticized), federalism regained its currency, and Curtis once again engaged in federalist activism, promoting Clarence Streit's book *Union now* and joining Lord Beveridge and others in sponsoring federal union. His attempts to convert the latter from what he considered its excessively Eurocentric orientation led to frequent internal conflict, and eventually to Curtis's leaving the group.

Curtis spent the majority of the Second World War in Oxford, co-ordinating the work of Chatham House's foreign research and press service (at Balliol College), and organizing servicemen's league groups. Ostensibly as the outcome of the latter, he published a series of pamphlets advocating immediate federation between the British Commonwealth, the United States, and the surviving Western democracies. The Round Table's rejection of his creed embittered him, but with funding from Sir Malcolm Stewart and others he maintained his output of pamphlets after the war. Notably in *The Master-Key to Peace* (1947) and *The Open Road to Freedom* (1950), he argued that atomic power and the cold war had brought a federation of the Western democracies within the realm of practicable possibilities. He joined the executive committee of United Europe in 1947, and attended the Hague conference in 1948, where he argued for a wider framework of federation which would include the British Commonwealth and the United States. His work for international peace was recognized by his nomination for the Nobel peace prize in 1947; in 1949, the thirtieth anniversary of the founding of Chatham House, he was made a Companion of Honour.

Curtis died at his home in Kidlington on 24 November 1955, and was buried in the chapel of All Souls College on 26 November. Tributes from around the world testified to the enormous range of his influence. He was not an original thinker, but he was a persuasive writer and even more persuasive in person. As Lord Salter later recalled, 'neither I nor others … often succeeded' in 'resisting what Lionel Curtis wished [us] to do' (Salter, 239). His influence was at its height in the years before, during, and immediately after the First World War, largely as a result of his contacts through the Kindergarten and Round Table. In later years he ploughed a more lonely furrow, and came almost to relish his image as a prophet scorned.

ALEX MAY

Sources DNB · *The Times* (25 Nov 1955) · *The Times* (26 Nov 1955) · *The Times* (1 Dec 1955) · *The Times* (7 Dec 1955) · [D. Malcolm], 'Lionel Curtis', *The Round Table*, 46 (1956), 103–10 · D. Lavin, *From empire to international commonwealth: a biography of Lionel Curtis* (1995) · A. Salter, *Memoirs of a public servant* (1961) · G. M. Gathorne-Hardy, *Lionel Curtis, CH, 1872–1955* (1955) · A. J. Toynbee, *Acquaintances* (1967) · A. L. Rowse, 'Lionel Curtis', *Glimpses of the great* (1985) · J. W. Shepardson, 'Lionel Curtis', honours diss., Harvard U., 1949 · K. A. Schiller, 'Lionel Curtis, the man', *Freedom and Union* (Oct 1949), 7–8 · H. V. Hodson, 'Preface', in L. Curtis, *World war, its cause and cure*, rev. edn (1992) · D. Lavin, 'History, morals and the politics of the empire: Lionel Curtis and the Round Table', *Essays presented to Michael Roberts*, ed. J. Bossy and P. Jupp (1976), 117–32 · D. Lavin, 'Lionel Curtis and the idea of the commonwealth', *Oxford and the idea of the commonwealth: essays presented to Sir Edgar Williams*, ed. F. Madden and D. K. Fieldhouse (1982), 97–121 · J. McColgan, 'Implementing the 1921 treaty: Lionel Curtis and constitutional procedure', *Irish Historical Studies*, 20 (1976–7), 312–33 · R. Pryor, 'A bibliography of the works of Lionel George Curtis', DipLib diss., U. Lond., 1955 · J. E. Kendle, *The Round Table movement and imperial union* (1975) · W. Nimocks, *Milner's young men: the kindergarten in Edwardian imperial affairs* (1968) · H. V. Hodson, 'The Round Table, 1910–81', *Round Table*, 71 (1981), 308–33 · A. C. May, 'The Round Table, 1910–1966', DPhil diss., U. Oxf., 1995 · R. Symonds, *Oxford and empire: the last lost cause?* (1986) · Janitor [J. G. Lockhart and M. Lyttelton], *The feet of the young men: some candid comments on the rising generation*, 2nd edn (1929) · D. Lavin, 'Lionel Curtis and Indian dyarchy', *The federal idea*, ed. A. Bosco, 1 (1991), 193–209 · D. Lavin, 'Lionel Curtis and the founding of Chatham House', *Chatham House and British foreign policy, 1919–45*, ed. A. Bosco and C. Navari (1994), 61–71 · L. Curtis, *With Milner in South Africa* (1951) · P. B. Rich, *Race and empire in British politics* (1986) · CGPLA Eng. & Wales (1956)

Archives Bodl. Oxf., corresp. and papers | BL, corresp. with Albert Mansbridge, Add. MS 65260 · BL OIOC, corresp. with J. S. Meston, MS Eur. F 136 · BLPES, corresp. with Violet Markham · BLPES, letters to E. D. Morel · Bodl. Oxf., letters to Geoffrey Dawson · Bodl. Oxf., Lionel Hichens MSS · Bodl. Oxf., Viscount Milner MSS · Bodl. Oxf., corresp. with Gilbert Murray · Bodl. Oxf., letters to Maud, Countess Selborne · Bodl. Oxf., corresp. with second Earl Selborne · Bodl. Oxf., corresp. with Sir Alfred Zimmern · Bodl. RH, Baron Brand MSS · Bodl. RH, corresp. with Lord Lugard · Bodl. RH, corresp. with J. H. Oldham, MS Afr. s 1829 · Bodl. RH, Margery Perham MSS · King's Lond., Liddell Hart C., corresp. with Sir B. H. Liddell Hart · NA Canada, Sir Robert Borden MSS · NA Scot., corresp. with eleventh marquess of Lothian · NL Aus., corresp. with Alfred Deakin, 3296A · NL Scot., F. S. Oliver MSS · NL Wales, corresp. with Thomas Jones · Queen's University, Kingston, Ontario, Edward Grigg MSS · U. Birm. L., special collections department, letters to Francis Brett Young · U. Lond., Institute of Commonwealth Studies, corresp. with Richard Jebb · U. Reading L., corresp. with Nancy Astor · University of Cape Town Library, corresp. with Patrick Duncan, BC 294

Likenesses photograph, c.1922, repro. in Lavin, *From empire to international commonwealth*; priv. coll. · O. Birley, oils, 1932, Royal Institute of International Affairs, Chatham House, London · A. John, drawing, 1933, repro. in Lavin, *From empire to international commonwealth* · Ramsey & Muspratt, photograph, c.1935–1940, NPG [see illus.] · K. Wojnarowski, bronze bust, 1954, Royal Institute of International Affairs, Chatham House, London · photograph, 1955, repro. in *The Times* (25 Nov 1955) · M. Greiffenhagen, portrait, Prior Croft, Camberley, Surrey

Wealth at death £19,908 7s. 8d.: probate, 13 Feb 1956, CGPLA Eng. & Wales

Curtis, Dame Myra (1886–1971), civil servant and college head, was born on 2 October 1886 at 11 Belle Vue Road, Sunderland, co. Durham, one of three daughters of George Curtis, a telegraphist in the Post Office, and his wife, Annie Johnson, an elementary school teacher. Her forebears were north-country working-class, and she was brought up in a hard-working, close-knit family, which valued education. As a young girl she attended Dame Allan's endowed school at Newcastle upon Tyne until the family moved to Winchester, where she attended Winchester School for Girls. In 1904, with the assistance of a Charlotte Yonge scholarship from her school and a county scholarship, she entered Newnham College, Cambridge. At Newnham she formed enduring friendships and found the college 'a place of liberation and intellectual stimulus' (M. E. G., 54). She read for the classical tripos, being ranked in the first division of the second class in 1907. After leaving Cambridge she spent seven years as an assistant editor

Dame Myra Curtis (1886–1971), by Charles Hewitt, 1948

for the Victoria History of the Counties of England and also undertook private teaching.

In 1915 Curtis became a temporary civil servant in the war trade intelligence department, moving in 1917 to the Ministry of Food, where she remained until 1922. She attained permanent status in 1923 after completing the necessary special examination for the administrative class and worked in the Ministry of Pensions. From 1928 to 1937 she was superintendent at the savings bank department of the Post Office, where she introduced a machine accounting system to remove the drudgery of compiling the manuscript ledgers used for bookkeeping since the savings bank had been instituted in 1861. Although she had no business training—she endorsed the generalist ethos of the British civil service that 'if you can do one thing you can do anything' (M. E. G., 54)—her system was regarded as a model of its kind. In 1937 she moved to the Treasury as assistant secretary and director of women's establishments, where she was known as a 'firm disciplinarian' (ibid.).

Following her retirement from the civil service in 1941 Curtis, who had retained her links with Cambridge as a member of the university's women's appointments board (from 1938), was elected principal of Newnham College, taking office in January 1942. She continued to undertake public work as commissioner in the War Damage Commission (1943–50), a member of the Central Land Board (1947–59), and a member of the General Medical Council (1955–66).

In November 1944 Curtis was appointed by Herbert Morrison, the home secretary, a member of a committee chaired by Sir Godfrey Russell Vick to investigate conditions in remand homes administered by the London county council, following critical comments by John Watson, a juvenile court magistrate. The inquiry began her interest in addressing the needs of the nation's problem children. Although the report on remand homes (published in February 1945) was regarded by some critics as a whitewash, she was appointed in March 1945, also at Morrison's recommendation, to head an interdepartmental committee to inquire into the care of deprived children. The setting up of the Curtis committee reflected an acknowledgement by the government of shortcomings in its treatment of orphans and other children in need of state care. Government departments were already considering the problem of children left homeless when wartime evacuation schemes were wound up, and were aware that the abolition of the poor law recommended by the Beveridge report in 1942 required new arrangements for the thousands of children currently looked after by public assistance authorities. But the decisive intervention was made by Lady Allen of Hurtwood (Marjory Allen), who had investigated the plight of children in local authority homes and found that there was no single government department with responsibility for the care of such children. Allen's letter to *The Times*, published on 15 July 1944, exposing the isolation, neglect, and lack of affection suffered by children in care, caused a sensation and public opinion forced the government to institute an inquiry. The decision was reinforced by the outcry following the death in January 1945 of Dennis O'Neill, a twelve-year-old boy in local authority care, from abuse and beatings by his foster parents.

The Curtis committee undertook 'the first enquiry in this country directed specifically to the care of children deprived of a normal home life, and covering all groups of such children' ('Report of the care of children committee', *Parl. papers*, 1945–6, 10.5, Cmd 6922). When it published its final report, in September 1946, the committee had heard over 200 witnesses and visited more than 400 institutions, bringing to light the extent of 'the physical, emotional and intellectual deprivation suffered by some of the children in public care' (Cretney, 218). Its inquiries showed that the existing divided responsibilities assumed by several government agencies were not working to the benefit of the children in the state's care. The Curtis committee insisted on the need to establish personal links in the care of children, and recommended the appointment by local authorities of children's officers: qualified women who would specialize in childcare and take a personal interest in each individual child. A single central department would have responsibility for maintaining standards in homes run by both local authorities and voluntary organizations. The latter issue gave rise to an exchange of letters in *The Times*, in October and November 1946, between Lady Allen and Curtis. Allen complained that the committee had insufficiently addressed the shortcomings of the voluntary sector, which she disliked as carrying the stigma of charity. While there was an ideological basis to the exchange, since Allen preferred centralized state control of childcare, it also stemmed from her resentment at not being invited to chair the inquiry which her campaigning had brought about.

The recommendations of the Curtis committee were embodied in the path-breaking Children's Act of 1948, which vested in the Home Office responsibility for overseeing the care of homeless or deprived children, though provision of care and inspection of homes rested with local authorities. Its provisions for trained professionals to staff institutions and to ensure that children received the most appropriate care were important in opening and securing the status of a new vocation for educated women. In recognition of her work on the inquiry, Curtis, who had been made CBE in 1942, was appointed DBE in 1949.

As principal of Newnham, Curtis enabled the college to carry on in the face of wartime and immediate post-war restrictions, and 'injected business efficiency into the academic habits of *laissez-faire*, not without some passive resistance' (M. E. G., 55). She continued, however, to be frustrated and at times exasperated by what she regarded as the 'indecisiveness' of academic administration. Nevertheless, at the request of the fellows, she postponed her retirement for two years, until 1954. She played an important part in the negotiations on behalf of the women's colleges which resulted in women being admitted as full members of Cambridge University in 1948. In 1952 she was the first woman elected to the council of the senate at Cambridge, and she chaired the women's appointments board. She also chaired a committee which promoted a third foundation (in addition to Newnham and Girton) to accommodate the growing number of women at Cambridge; New Hall was granted recognition by the university and opened in October 1954.

Curtis's outlook was primarily that of an administrator, with an overwhelming urge 'to get things done and to jog the inefficient' (M. E. G., 57). Her 'impelling impetus was ethical, not religious', avoiding sentimentality (*The Times*, 29 June 1971). She enjoyed cookery and gardening. In retirement she lived in Cranbrook, Kent, sharing her home for a short period with her friend the Irish historian Constantia Maxwell, and latterly at Chichester, Sussex. Curtis died in a nursing home at Bognor Regis, Sussex, on 27 June 1971. MARY ALVEY THOMAS

Sources M. E. G., *Newnham College Roll Letter* (1972), 53–7 · J. S. Boys Smith, 'Dame Myra Curtis and New Hall', *Newnham College Roll Letter* (1972), 57–9 · *The Times* (29 June 1971) · *WWW*, 1971–80 · M. A. Thomas, 'The politics of childhood in post-war Britain', PhD diss., Boston College, 1994 · S. M. Cretney, 'The state as a parent: the Children Act 1948 in retrospect', in S. M. Cretney, *Law, law reform, and the family* (1998), chap. 9 · J. Packman, *The child's generation: child care policy from Curtis to Houghton* (1975) · R. A. Parker, 'The gestation of reform: the Children Act 1948', *Approaches to welfare*, ed. P. Bean and S. MacPherson (1983) · H. Hendrick, *Child welfare: England, 1872–1989* (1994) · H. Glennerster, *British social policy since 1945* (1995) · b. cert. · *CGPLA Eng. & Wales* (1971) · d. cert.

Likenesses C. Hewitt, photograph, 1948, Hult. Arch. [*see illus.*] · K. Hutton, double portrait, photograph, 1948 (with Jeanne Heal), Hult. Arch. · K. Hutton, group portrait, photograph, 1948, Hult. Arch. · W. Stoneman, photograph, 1957, NPG · photographs, Newnham College archives

Wealth at death £17,016: probate, 27 July 1971, *CGPLA Eng. & Wales*

Curtis, Patrick (*d.* 1832), Roman Catholic archbishop of Armagh, was born in Stamullen, co. Meath, Ireland. Little is known of his early life; indeed the year of his birth was a mystery even to his contemporaries. Having completed his studies at the Irish College, Salamanca, he was ordained to the priesthood for the diocese of Dublin. While serving as chaplain to a Spanish man-of-war during the Anglo-Spanish hostilities he was captured by an English frigate and taken to London, where he ministered to Spanish prisoners. This distinguished service was brought to the attention of Charles III of Spain, who nominated him rector of the Irish College at Salamanca in March 1780. He completed a doctorate in divinity in 1789 and was subsequently appointed regius professor of astronomy and natural history at the University of Salamanca.

Although Curtis remained rector until 1817 his administration was troubled. Throughout the period he suffered ill health, while the severity of his regime brought criticism from a variety of quarters. In 1789 the four archbishops of Ireland objected to some of his regulations. In 1803, in consequence of complaints from students and the bishop of Salamanca, he was called before the royal *camara* to give an account of his administration of the temporalities of the college; he also faced opposition from his own students and the rector of the Irish College at Alcalá when he was charged to amalgamate the two colleges. These difficulties paled into insignificance when compared to the disruption caused by the Peninsular War, during which Curtis was driven from Salamanca on three occasions. Indeed in 1811 he was arrested by the French as a spy, and his life was saved only by the timely entry of the British into the city. It was at this time that he met Arthur Wellesley, the future duke of Wellington, to whom he supplied intelligence; the nature of this information is unclear but its value can be gauged from Wellington's frequent mentions and high recommendations of Curtis to the Spanish authorities in response to appeals from him. Significantly, too, the Irish students left Salamanca in 1811 to serve as interpreters in the army of General Sir John Moore, who was distinguished for his humanity in suppressing the Irish rising of 1798.

Curtis resigned the rectorship of Salamanca in 1817 and returned to Dublin, where he lived quietly on a pension granted him by the government for his service in the Peninsular War. Yet in spite of his advanced years he was immediately mentioned once the archdiocese of Armagh became vacant in 1818, on the death of Richard O'Reilly. This was not altogether surprising, since six of the Irish episcopate were graduates of Salamanca and one of their number, Daniel Murray of Dublin, had described his former rector as 'un veritable trésor' in an earlier letter to *propaganda fide* recommending him for promotion to the episcopate (Macauley, 333). There was, however, significant opposition to Curtis from the clergy of the province of Armagh; two parish priests appealing to Rome on behalf of a rival candidate warned the sacred congregation that he was 'a man of a turbulent character, and tyranick disposition; a man at least 74 years old, and consequently incapable of discharging the laborious duties of a bishop in Ireland' (ibid., 338).

Curtis nevertheless was the choice of the establishment; he was formally recommended to the Holy See by the archbishops of Ireland, while the popular press carried reports that the aged cleric had canvassed government support for his candidacy. Curtis shrewdly contradicted these allegations in a series of letters to Wellington. He denied any ambition for Armagh and pleaded that he had initiated the correspondence in order that the government might assert its influence to preclude himself or an objectionable candidate from an appointment where 'much good or evil might eventually be the consequence' (*Despatches, Correspondence*, 1.24–5).

Curtis had effectively conceded a veto to the government, a prize sought by successive administrations since 1782. Wellington was not slow to appreciate the import of this concession and enthusiastically recommended Curtis to Castlereagh and Lord Sidmouth, minister of home affairs, as an 'honest, loyal man, who behaved well throughout the war' (*Despatches, Correspondence*, 1.28). These sentiments were in turn relayed to Lord Talbot, lord lieutenant of Ireland, but perhaps more importantly they were communicated to the Vatican, where the secretary of state, Cardinal Consalvi, a personal friend of Castlereagh, owed a debt of gratitude for Britain's efforts in securing the return of the Papal States to Pius VII at the Congress of Vienna.

The pope confirmed Curtis's appointment as archbishop of Armagh in August 1819. Thereafter Curtis's pastoral efforts were overshadowed by the vigour of the younger prelates of the age but his attitude towards the British government, and his opposition to Daniel O'Connell and the agitation of the Catholic Association, are noteworthy. While he was an ardent supporter of Catholic emancipation he remained convinced of the propriety of a government veto on episcopal appointments, a point upon which he wrote to Wellington in December 1828. This correspondence initiated an extraordinary train of events. Wellington replied, promising eventual relief, but urged Catholics to bury their grievances in oblivion for a time. A copy was sent to the viceroy, the marquess of Anglesey, who wrote a remarkable letter to Curtis in which he rejected the duke's position, arguing that 'every constitutional means should be adopted to force on the measure' (*Despatches, Correspondence*, 5.308–9). This difference precipitated Anglesey's recall from Ireland, while the breach of confidence resulted in a cooling of relations between Wellington and Curtis.

Curtis died of cholera at Drogheda on 24 July 1832. According to W. J. Fitzpatrick 'the voluminous papers of the late distinguished Primate, Dr Curtis, were found in the year 1841, scattered around the hayloft of a premises belonging to a grocer in Drogheda' (*The Life, Times, and Correspondence of Dr Doyle, Bishop of Kildare*, new edn, 2 vols., 1880, 2.45). Curtis is largely forgotten in the historiography of the period, which was perhaps unwilling to accommodate a prelate whose character was so much at odds with the confident sentiments of the age of O'Connell.   H. M. STEPHENS, *rev.* DÁIRE KEOGH

Sources A. Macauley, 'The appointments of Patrick Curtis and Thomas Kelly as archbishop and coadjutor archbishop of Armagh', *Seanchas Ardmhacha*, 10/2 (1982), 331–65 • D. J. O'Doherty,

'Students of the Irish College, Salamanca', *Archivium Hibernicum*, 6 (1917), 1–26 • W. J. Fitzpatrick, *The secret service under Pitt* (1892) • *The dispatches of … the duke of Wellington … from 1799 to 1818*, ed. J. Gurwood, 13 vols. in 12 (1834–9) • A. R. Wellesley, second duke of Wellington, *Despatches, correspondence, and memoranda of Field Marshal Arthur, duke of Wellington, K.G.: in continuation of the former series*, 8 vols. (1867–80) • *Supplementary despatches (correspondence) and memoranda of Field Marshal Arthur, duke of Wellington*, ed. A. R. Wellesley, second duke of Wellington, 15 vols. (1858–72)

Archives Armagh Roman Catholic Diocesan Archives, episcopal corresp. and papers • NRA, corresp. and papers | NRA, priv. coll., corresp. with Lord Gormanston and James Logan

Curtis, Philip Kenneth Edward (1926–1951), army officer, was born on 7 July 1926 at 43 Pembroke Street, Devonport, Devon, the only child of John Curtis, a general labourer, and his wife, Florence Richards. As a teenager during the Blitz, he served as a volunteer ARP warden in Plymouth. Desperately keen to join the services before the war ended, he tried to enlist in the RAF, but was rejected because of his age. In 1944, however, he was accepted by the army but not sent overseas. In May 1946 he received a regular army emergency commission in the Duke of Cornwall's light infantry, though he never served in any battalion of that regiment. On 4 May 1946, while still in the army, he married Joan Doreen Hayes, a local Devonport girl, and they had a daughter, Philippa Susan. He was demobilized in 1948 and placed on the reserve of officers.

Curtis secured a job with Roneo, the duplicator firm, but found life exceedingly dull. Then, just as he had settled into family life, disaster struck. His young wife died suddenly, leaving a grieving husband with a tiny child to bring up. Not long after this the Korean War broke out. The British government had quickly to resort to recalling reservists to fill depleted ranks, particularly in the infantry. Curtis received his recall papers. As a widower with responsibility for a small child he could have claimed exemption, but when his wife's mother, Mrs Beatrice Hayes, undertook to look after his daughter, Curtis was persuaded he could follow his orders. He joined A company, the Gloucestershire regiment (popularly known as the Glosters), in Korea in March 1951.

Late in April 1951 A company were given the task of defending Castle Hill, a feature south of a river over which the Chinese were expected to attack, but somewhat isolated from the rest of the battalion. Curtis commanded no. 1 platoon and was positioned on the reverse slope of the hill in reserve. On the night of 22–3 April the Chinese attacked *en masse*.

For almost six hours the attacks continued and the two forward platoons, particularly no. 2 platoon on the right, suffered severely but held on. The company commander, Major Angier, ordered Curtis to counter-attack at dawn. Initially successful, the platoon reached the forward slope of the hill without loss. Suddenly hundreds of Chinese sprang up and charged. Within minutes they had secured a bunker on Curtis's right and began firing a machine-gun at point-blank range. Gathering a group of men, Curtis worked his way under intense fire to a fold in the ground only 20 metres from the bunker. The machine-gun and the gunners were clearly visible through the apertures. Curtis began to hurl at the bunker grenades which were passed to him by his men. The Chinese returned heavy fire forcing the group back, except for Curtis, who remained exposed and continued to throw grenades. He was hit in the head and was dragged back under cover. He was roughly bandaged but struggled to get up and had to be held down by his men, one soldier sitting on his chest to restrain him. Despite this, he broke free to resume his solo assault. Still hurling grenades, he staggered to within a few metres of the bunker. As a grenade left his hand he was hit in the stomach and fell, mortally wounded. The last grenade he threw destroyed the machine-gun.

As the Chinese eventually overran the Glosters—and those captured spent many months in prison camps—it was not until after the war that Curtis was recommended for the Victoria Cross. The investiture took place on 6 July 1954. Attending to receive the cross were his mother, his seven-year-old daughter Susan, and his wife's mother, Beatrice Hayes. Curtis was buried in the Commonwealth War Graves cemetery, Korea. MARK ADKIN

Sources M. Adkin, *The last eleven?* (1991) · C. N. Barclay, *The first commonwealth division* (1954) · T. Carew, *The Korean War* (1988) · E. Linklater, *Our men in Korea* (1954) · T. Carew, *The glorious Glosters* (1970) · b. cert. · m. cert. · d. cert. · A. Farrar-Hockley, *The British part in the Korean War*, 2 vols. (1990–95) · *The register of the Victoria cross*, 3rd edn (1997)

Curtis, Sir Roger, first baronet (1746–1816), naval officer, was born on 4 June 1746, the son of Roger Curtis, farmer. He came from Downton, Wiltshire, and entered the navy in 1762 on the *Royal Sovereign* (100 guns). After the peace of Paris he went in the *Assistance* (50 guns) to the west coast of Africa, served in the guardship *Augusta* (64 guns) at Portsmouth, and went in the *Gibraltar* (20 guns) to Newfoundland. In 1769 he served in the *Venus* (36 guns) with Samuel Barrington, with whom he transferred to the *Albion* (74 guns) in the Channel Fleet at the time of the Falkland Islands mobilization. He was made lieutenant on 19 January 1771, going to Newfoundland in the sloop *Otter*, where Molyneux Shuldham was governor and commander-in-chief. Curtis moved from Newfoundland with Shuldham, who in 1775 was appointed commander-in-chief of the North American station; he was made second lieutenant of the flagship *Chatham* (50 guns). On 11 July 1776 Shuldham promoted Curtis to the command of the sloop *Senegal*. In this ship Curtis caught the eye of the next commander-in-chief, Lord Howe, who on 30 April 1777 appointed him flag captain of the *Eagle* (64 guns), and in doing so started a long professional relationship. Curtis returned to England with Howe, reaching St Helens on 25 October 1778.

Curtis's refusal to take the *Eagle* to the Far East earned him a black mark from Lord Sandwich. This may account for his not having an active command until he took the *Brilliant* (36 guns) to the Mediterranean. He sailed for Gibraltar in late 1780, but was forced on to Minorca by two Spanish frigates and a xebec, escaping narrowly in light winds. He arrived at Minorca on 31 December 1780 and was blockaded there by French frigates, a state of affairs about which his lieutenant, Colin Campbell, protested,

both verbally and later in print. However, on 15 April 1781 Curtis escorted twenty-five storeships to Gibraltar, bringing them in safely on 27 April. He stayed in Gibraltar for the next eighteen months, playing a big part in the successful defence and earning General George Eliott's praise, though Curtis himself remained unconvinced of Gibraltar's value to the British, describing it as a 'Golden Image of English Idolatry' (S. Conn, *Gibraltar in British Diplomacy in the Eighteenth Century*, 1942, 258). Thereafter he commanded a thousand seamen as the marine brigade, for which Eliott appointed him a brigadier-general. The climax of this gruelling siege was the assault of the Spanish floating batteries on 13–14 September 1782, which failed dramatically. Curtis distinguished himself when he went off in ships' boats to cut the gunboats off, but instead rescued several hundred burnt and drowning Spaniards, at great risk to himself and the crew of his boat. Eliott wrote: 'For some time I felt the utmost anguish, seeing his pinnace close to one of the largest ships at the moment she blew up, and spread her wreck to a vast extent around' ('Biographical Memoirs', 6.270). His coxswain was killed and several others wounded. It was a grisly scene and Curtis's bravery was much celebrated in prints. He returned to England when Howe relieved the garrison, whereupon he was knighted. It was at this point, according to Sir John Barrow, that Curtis made his only political gesture when he offered to serve on Howe's Board of Admiralty (Barrow, 164). Instead Curtis was sent to Morocco, with Captain John Blankett, to renew the Anglo-Moroccan treaty of friendship. In March 1783 he returned to Gibraltar, at Eliott's request, now as a commodore, accepted the flag of truce from the Spaniards on 3 October, and returned to England at the end of the year. The *Brilliant* was paid off in January 1784.

In May of that year until December 1787 Curtis commanded the guardship *Ganges* (74 guns) at Portsmouth. For the next two years he was on half pay, though Ralfe claims that in 1789 he was sent on a two-month secret mission to Sweden, Denmark, and Russia (Ralfe, 2.43). Curtis's partnership with Howe was revived when he was flag captain of the *Queen Charlotte* (100 guns) in May 1790 during the mobilization, but in December of that year he went to the guardship *Brunswick* (74 guns), and he continued in her until early 1793. On this ship he dealt with 'a putrid and highly infectious fever', which he described in a twenty-four page pamphlet, *The means used to eradicate a malignant fever, which raged on board his majesty's ship Brunswick, at Spithead, in the spring of the year 1791* (1795?).

Curtis again joined Howe as captain of the *Queen Charlotte* and was thus present at the battle of 1 June 1794. He was widely held to be responsible for urging caution on Howe, when ships were called back from pursuing the retreating French at the end of the four-day battle. Yet he was also held responsible for the ungenerous and partial tone of Howe's official dispatch, being described by Cuthbert Collingwood (one of those overlooked) as 'an artful, sneeking creature, whose fawning insinuating manners creeps into the confidence of whoever he attacks and whose rapacity wou'd grasp all honours and all profits that come within his view' (Hughes, 50). For his part in the battle Curtis received a baronetcy, a gold chain from the king, and a colonelcy of marines. He was also promoted rear-admiral on 4 July 1794. Shortly afterwards Curtis had the unpleasant job of prosecutor at the court martial of Molloy of the *Caesar* (74 guns), whose conduct during the battle had earned Howe's intense displeasure. From the autumn of 1795 Curtis flew his flag in a number of ships for short periods, as they worked up after refits. The first was the *Canada* (74 guns), in which he struck his flag on 18 September 1795; next were the *Powerful* (74 guns) and *Invincible* (74 guns) until 31 March the following year, and then the *Formidable* (74 guns) in the channel. From early 1797 he commanded a detached squadron off the coast of Ireland, countering the French invasion threat, flying his flag in the *Prince* (98 guns), a notoriously bad sailer. In May 1798, amid the greatest secrecy, his ships joined Lord St Vincent in the blockade off Cadiz. He was promoted vice-admiral on 14 February 1798 and came ashore on 13 March 1799.

In May 1800 Curtis was appointed commander-in-chief at the Cape of Good Hope station, which by that time was a routine post. He flew his flag in the *Lancaster* (64 guns) from 8 June 1801 to 24 February 1803. In a letter to Nelson Curtis described it as 'an abominable station' (NMM, Croker collection, CRK/3, 12 Nov 1803) and he returned in ill health, which necessitated an operation, and with rheumatism.

Promoted admiral on 23 April 1804, he now had a long period on half pay, during which he fretted; nor was he to have an active commission again. With the change of ministry in January 1805 he was appointed to the 'Commission for revising the civil affairs of His Majesty's navy', upon which considerable task he was engaged until the end of 1807. After a further period of inactivity he was appointed commander-in-chief at Portsmouth in early 1809, in which he continued until April 1812. During this command he was president of the court martial of Admiral Lord Gambier, in the dispute with Lord Cochrane.

Curtis has appeared to later commentators as overcautious, but his professionalism was admired by his colleagues, and Nelson was a good friend; he described Curtis as 'an able officer and conciliating man' (*Dispatches and Letters*, 6.135). He is also remembered by the Sir Roger Curtis Islands, or Curtis Group, in the Bass Strait, of which the most prominent is called the Devil's Tower, or Fortification Isle, after part of the Gibraltar fortifications. Curtis married Sarah (*d.* 1817), the youngest daughter of Mattich Brady, of Gatcombe House, Portsea. They had a daughter and two sons, of whom the elder son, Roger, died as a post captain on 12 July 1802 and the other, Lucius, became an admiral of the fleet, dying in 1869. Curtis himself died on 14 November 1816 and was survived by his wife, who died on 10 April of the following year.   ROGER KNIGHT

Sources DNB · J. Ralfe, *The naval biography of Great Britain*, 2 (1828), 32–44 · 'Biographical memoirs of Sir Roger Curtis', *Naval Chronicle*, 6 (1801), 261–76 · J. Drinkwater, *A history of the late siege of Gibraltar*, 4th edn (1790) · *Steel's Original and Correct List of the Royal Navy* (1800–16) · NMM lieutenants' logs, PRO, ADM/L/L/17 (*Lancaster*); ADM/L/C/29 (*Canada*) · R. Curtis, letters to Nelson, 1803–5, NMM, Croker collection, CRK/3 · R. Morriss, *The royal dockyards during the revolutionary and Napoleonic wars* (1983) · T. H. McGuffie, *The siege of Gibraltar* (1965) · *The dispatches and letters of Vice-Admiral Lord Viscount Nelson*, ed. N. H. Nicolas, 7 vols. (1844–6); repr. (1997–8), vol. 6 · J. Barrow, *The life of Richard, Earl Howe* (1838) · J. Horsburgh, *India directory, or, Directions for sailing to and from the East Indies* (1809–16) · *GM*, 1st ser., 87/1 (1817), 381 · *The private correspondence of Admiral Lord Collingwood*, ed. E. Hughes, Navy RS, 98 (1957)

Archives Brenthurst Library, Johannesburg, South Africa, journal · NMM, journal of embassy to Morocco | BL, Wellesley papers, corresp. with Curtis, Cape of Good Hope · BL, letters and orders to Lord Bridport, Add. MSS 35194–35198 · Boston PL, letters to Croker · Hunt. L., Howe papers

Likenesses Miller, drawing, 1782, repro. in *European Magazine* (1 Jan 1783) · J. Caldwell, line engraving, 1783 (after W. Hamilton), BM, NPG · W. Hamilton, engraving, pubd 1783 · M. Brown, oils, 1794, NMM · caricature, pubd 1795 · oils, *c.*1800, NMM · Bartolozzi, Landseer, Ryder, and Stow, group portrait, line engraving, pubd 1803 (*Commemoration of the victory of June 1st 1794*; after R. Smirke), BM, NPG · W. Reynolds, 10 Dec 1817 (after M. Brown) · M. Brown, group portrait, oils (*The glorious first of June*) · R. Grignion, engraving (*The gallant captain nobly exerting himself in saving the lives of the drowning Spaniards … on the memorable 13 September 1782*; after Metz), repro. in G. F. Raymond, *A new, universal and impartial history of England* [n.d., 1785?] · W. Ridley, stipple (after Rivers), BM, NPG; repro. in *Naval Chronicle* (1801) · J. Trumbull, group portrait, oils (*Gibraltar: the sortie of the night of 26–27 November 1781*), Cincinnati Art Museum

Wealth at death see will, PRO, PROB 11/1586

Curtis, Samuel (1779–1860), nurseryman and magazine editor, was born on 29 August 1779 at Walworth in Surrey. Nothing is known of his early life or education. In 1800 he acquired Walworth nursery which he held until about 1825. In 1801 he married Sarah, the only daughter of William *Curtis (1746–1799), author of *Flora Londinensis*, and founder of the *Botanical Magazine*, thereby succeeding to its proprietorship. Not long after he moved to Glazenwood, near Coggeshall, Essex, where he established a nursery. In 1827 Curtis's wife died, leaving their many children motherless. About 1846 he sold his rights in the magazine, just when lithography was about to supersede the slow and costly plate-printing. He retired to an estate he bought, La Chaire–Rozel in Jersey, where he died on 6 January 1860. Curtis's works included a monograph on *Camellia* (1817) and *Beauties of Flora* (1806–20). He was made a fellow of the Linnean Society in 1810.

B. D. JACKSON, rev. ALEXANDER GOLDBLOOM

Sources Desmond, *Botanists*, rev. edn, 187 · M. Hadfield, R. Harling, and L. Highton, *British gardeners: a biographical dictionary* (1980), 80–87 · *Curtis's Botanical Magazine*, 3rd ser., 16 (1860) [extra leaf issued with volume]

Archives Curtis Museum, Alton, Hampshire, account of family

Likenesses portrait, NHM

Curtis, Thomas (*d.* 1712), Quaker schismatic, was probably born in Reading, and was the son of Arthur Curtis. He served as a captain in the New Model Army and was appointed a sub-commissioner for sequestrations in Berkshire in January 1652. In 1651 he married Anne (1631–c.1703), daughter of Robert Yeamans, sheriff of Bristol, who had been hanged in 1643 for supporting Charles I. Curtis, a wealthy woollen draper at Reading, and his wife owned part of the manor of Sanderville and Bray, South Moreton, Berkshire. He became a Quaker in 1654 through the work of John Audland and John Camm at Bristol, and the following year published *A Copie of a Letter* addressed to the presbyterian minister Samuel Wells of Banbury, an assistant to the Oxfordshire commission. When George Fox went to Reading on 30 June 1655 he stayed with the Curtises, as did Alexander Parker and George Bishop. According to Parker, the Curtises 'formerly Lived very high, and very rich in Apparell, but are stripped of all, he hath ripped his gold buttons of[f]; & his wife hath stript of[f] all her Jewells, and rich attire' (Caton MS 3.292). For disrupting a church service at Reading, the Curtises were incarcerated in 1656. The same year they visited Fox in Launceston gaol, after which Curtis preached at Liskeard and Falmouth, Cornwall. With William Simpson, he was instrumental in converting Mary Penington. He was at Lyme Regis and Bridport, Dorset, in early 1657 with Fox and Josiah Coale; he was imprisoned briefly at Bridport and for over five months at Exeter that same year. In 1658 Curtis preached in Oxfordshire and Gloucestershire, and he was a signatory of the Quaker declaration presented to parliament on 6 April 1659 offering to take the place of imprisoned Friends.

When parliament requested recommendations of Friends with estates who could serve as JPs in 1659, Curtis suggested George Lamboll and Andrew Knight, noting that neither would take an oath. He accepted an appointment as militia commissioner for Berkshire in July, a decision that disappointed Fox. Yet he respected the Quaker leader, referring to him on 5 January 1659 in messianic language as 'the father of all the faithfull … who was ded and is alive & for ever lives' (Swarthmore MS 3.87). Commencing in late August 1659 Fox spent ten weeks at the Curtises' home, recovering from illness and working on his *Great Mistery of the Great Whore Unfolded* (1659). In October Curtis and nineteen other Quakers petitioned Richard Cromwell and his council for legal reform. After visiting the south-west in February 1660, Fox and Curtis went to Swarthmore, Lancashire, in the spring. With Margaret Fell, Anne Curtis met with Charles II in July on behalf of Fox and other incarcerated Friends. As conditions worsened for Friends, Curtis was physically abused and arrested at Steventon, Berkshire, in October. When Quakers continued to meet in Curtis's house, further imprisonments followed in the 1660s for both Thomas and Anne. On 19 June 1666 officials seized books, papers, and £150 from his prison chamber, and in August 1670 magistrates distrained his possessions and padlocked his house. With other Quakers he was released by Charles II in 1672.

When John Story and John Wilkinson divided the Quaker movement by objecting to the centralization of authority and other matters, the Curtises supported them, and were present when Wilkinson and Story met with Fox at Worcester Castle in January 1675. The break was not complete, for Curtis accompanied Fox to Bristol in March 1676, and one of two letters Fox wrote to the Curtises in December was conciliatory. Unswayed by the London meeting's condemnation of Story and Wilkinson in June 1677, the Curtises led a splinter group at Reading that sometimes met separately from those who supported Fox.

Curtis opposed women's meetings because they subverted natural order and taught women to preach, and likened the yearly meeting to a Cromwellian cabal that hatched and disseminated plots.

Curtis attracted supporters in Berkshire, Bristol, Buckinghamshire, and Hertfordshire. Fox, George Whitehead, and William Welch visited him at Caversham in January 1678, presumably to discuss the breach, while the conciliatory efforts of Isaac Penington and Anthony Sharp, who had married the Curtises' daughter, Esther, on 27 March 1663, were likewise unsuccessful. When Curtis travelled in Ireland in 1678, in part with Sharp, his enemies asserted that he had accused Fox of attempting to establish popery in England. Following Story's death in 1681, Curtis and others published testimonials in 1683, and in the same year he contributed a testimonial to the Cornish Friend Loveday Hambly. The dispute at Reading worsened in 1684 when Curtis's group closed the meeting-house and worshipped elsewhere, complaining that Fox's supporters had refused to remove their hats when members of the Curtis faction prayed. The dispute was publicly aired when Lambol published *Something in Answer to Thomas Curtis and B[enjamin] C[ole]'s Reasons* [1686]. Curtis's group unsuccessfully sought a reconciliation in 1693. In October 1696 he became embroiled in further controversy when William Clarke of the King's Heath meeting accused him of propagating false doctrine by contending that he knew of no Christ but the one within himself.

Following Anne's death about 1703, Curtis remarried. Another attempt to heal the division was made in November 1706, when William Penn, whose wife, Gulielma, had been friends of the Curtises, urged him not to desert the Quakers, but to return, childlike. The breach in the movement was not healed until May 1716, some four years after Curtis's death at Reading on 14 November 1712. Because of the lengthy rift, Curtis's role as an early Quaker leader was minimized in Fox's journal.   RICHARD L. GREAVES

Sources *The journal of George Fox*, ed. N. Penney, 2 vols. (1911) • RS Friends, Lond., Swarthmore MSS 1.168, 169, 361; 3.87, 88, 137, 149 • RS Friends, Lond., Penington MS 4.130, 141–7 • RS Friends, Lond., Barclay MS 86 • RS Friends, Lond., Caton MS 3.292 • *CSP dom.*, 1657–8, 156–7; 1658–9, 351; 1663–4, 647 • N. Penney, ed., 'The first publishers of truth': being early records, now first printed, of the introduction of Quakerism into the counties of England and Wales* (1907) • J. Besse, *A collection of the sufferings of the people called Quakers*, 1 (1753), 11–15, 19, 24–7, 29 • W. C. Braithwaite, *The beginnings of Quakerism*, ed. H. J. Cadbury, 2nd edn (1955) • R. L. Greaves, *Dublin's merchant–Quaker: Anthony Sharp and the community of Friends, 1643–1707* (1998) • P. Mack, *Visionary women: ecstatic prophecy in seventeenth-century England* (1992) • M. A. E. Green, ed., *Calendar of the proceedings of the committee for compounding … 1643–1660*, 1, PRO (1889), 526 • *VCH Berkshire*, 3.500 • 'Dictionary of Quaker biography', RS Friends, Lond. [card index] • C. H. Firth and R. S. Rait, eds., *Acts and ordinances of the interregnum, 1642–1660*, 3 vols. (1911) • private information (2004) [M. Brod] • H. Barbour and A. O. Roberts, eds., *Early Quaker writings, 1650–1700* (1973)

Archives RS Friends, Lond., Barclay MSS • RS Friends, Lond., Penington MSS • RS Friends, Lond., Swarthmore MSS

Curtis, William (1746–1799), botanist and entomologist, was born on 11 January 1746 in Lenton Street, Alton, Hampshire, into a Quaker family; his father, John Curtis, was a tanner in fairly comfortable circumstances. He was educated at Eggar's Free Grammar School from 1755, and at fourteen years old was apprenticed to his grandfather, John Curtis, an apothecary. He appears to have acquired his botanical tastes from Thomas Legg, an ostler who had studied some of the popular herbals of the time. When he was twenty Curtis moved to London as apprentice to George Vaux, apothecary, in Pudding Lane. He later associated himself with Thomas Talwin, licentiate of the Apothecaries' Company, under whom he qualified, and to whose practice at 51 Gracechurch Street he succeeded. He also acted as a demonstrator in botany while studying at St Thomas's Hospital.

Curtis soon established a reputation as a botanist which led to his appointment as demonstrator of plants and *praefectus horti* of the Society of Apothecaries (1772–7) at the Chelsea Physic Garden. He established a botanical garden for the cultivation and study of native British plants at Bermondsey in 1773, though later, in 1779, he cultivated the more extensive London Botanic Garden at Lambeth Marsh. In 1789, because of smoke pollution, he moved the plants to a still larger garden in Brompton.

Curtis combined the study of insect metamorphoses with botany, his first published work being *Instructions for Collecting and Preserving Insects* (1771), and in 1772 he translated Linnaeus's *Fundamenta entomologiae*. These publications secured him notice and in 1775 he commenced his *Flora Londinensis*, which established his reputation. This work extended to six fasciculi of seventy-two plates each, which remain the finest illustrations of British plants ever published. In 1781 he undertook the long-running *Botanical Magazine*, which supplemented his income. In 1782 much alarm was created by the appearance in vast numbers of the brown-tail moth (*Phalaena* (*Bombyx*) *chrysorrhoea*) and large rewards were offered for their destruction. Curtis carefully studied the natural history of this caterpillar which defoliates fruit- and other trees, and wrote *A Short History of the Brown-Tail Moth* (1782).

Curtis printed occasional catalogues of his garden, and his *Lectures on Botany* were published in 1803 after his death, with beautiful coloured plates. His *British Grasses*, also posthumous (1802), was immensely valuable to farmers. Curtis was one of the original fellows of the Linnean Society, and his entomological papers appeared in its transactions, including 'Silpha grisca and Curculio lapathi' (1791) and another, posthumously (1799), showing that aphids produce 'honeydew' on plants.

Curtis was described as short, well built, and neat, with a full and ruddy face, a pleasant companion, of good humour, a faithful husband and tender father, a kind and generous friend. For the last year of his life Curtis suffered a heart condition which he bore with resignation. He died on 7 July 1799, leaving a wife, Mary, *née* Winter, and a daughter, Sarah. A large circle of scientific friends followed his remains to their resting place in Battersea church.   ROBERT HUNT, *rev.* K. G. V. SMITH

Sources W. H. Curtis, *William Curtis, 1746–1799, fellow of the Linnean Society, botanist and entomologist* (1941) · W. T. Stearn, 'William Curtis, 1746–99', in W. Curtis, *A short history of the brown-tail moth*

(1967) · J. E. Lousley, 'William Curtis, 1746–1799', *London Naturalist*, 25 (1945), 3–12 · R. J. Thornton, 'Sketch of the life and writings of the late Mr William Curtis, London', in W. Curtis, *Lectures on botany* (1803) · *Exhibition in commemoration of the bicentenary of the birth of William Curtis FLS, 1746–1799* (1946) [exhibition catalogue, Curtis Museum, Alton, Hampshire] · S. Savage, 'William Curtis and the Linnean Society: with three of his unpublished papers', *Proceedings of the Linnean Society of London*, 158th session (1947), 13–20 · J. S. L. Gilmour, 'A "Catalogue of London plants" attributed to William Curtis', *Journal of the Society of the Bibliography of Natural History*, 2 (1943–52), 181–2 · J. Ardagh, 'Curtis's botanic gardens', *Chronica Botanica*, 9 (1945), 75 · F. D. Drewitt, *The romance of the apothecaries' garden at Chelsea*, 3rd edn (1928) · J. W. Hunkin, 'William Curtis, founder of the *Botanical Magazine*', *Endeavour*, 5 (1946), 13–17 · *GM*, 1st ser., 69 (1799), 628–9, 635–8 · will, PRO, PROB 11/1332, sig. 766

Archives Curtis Museum, Alton, Hampshire, corresp. and papers · Linn. Soc., notes and unpublished entomological papers · Royal Horticultural Society, London

Likenesses stipple, pubd 1800, BM · W. Evans, stipple, BM, NPG; repro. in R. J. Thornton, *New illustration of the sexual system of Carolus von Linnaeus*, 2 vols. (c.1807) · A. Kauffmann, miniature · attrib. J. Wright, oils, Royal Horticultural Society, London · attrib. Zoffany, oils, probably India · oils on copper, Curtis Museum, Alton, Hampshire · portrait, repro. in Savage, 'William Curtis and the Linnean Society', following p. 14 · silhouette, repro. in *Botanical Magazine* (1799)

Curtis, Sir William, first baronet (1752–1829), banker and politician, was born on 25 January 1752, in London, the third of five sons of Joseph Curtis, manufacturer of ship's biscuit at Wapping, who died in 1771, aged fifty-six, and of his wife, Mary, daughter of Timothy Tennant of Wapping. Curtis and his elder brother Timothy carried on the business after their father's death. In 1776 he married Anne (*d.* 1833), daughter and coheir of Edward Constable of London. Curtis's popularity in Wapping led, in 1783, to membership of the Drapers' Company and to his election as alderman for Tower ward. He had already made some successful ventures in the Greenland whale fishery and he now established the bank known as Robarts, Curtis, Were & Co. He served as sheriff (1788–9) and lord mayor (1795–6). During the French wars he commanded the 9th regiment of London Volunteers and was later president of the Honourable Artillery Company. Among other civic activities he was director of the West and East India Dock companies and president of Christ's Hospital. After 1804 he was also a conspicuous and influential figure at Ramsgate, where he built Cliff House and kept a luxurious private yacht.

Curtis's election as MP for the City of London in 1790, after several attempts elsewhere, fulfilled his ambition for a wider sphere. In an age when ministers attached great value to opinion in the City, Curtis was prominent as a supporter both of Pitt's financial and war policies and of those of his successor, Addington, by whom he was rewarded with a baronetcy in 1802. He displayed more independence during the confused political alignments of the 1804–9 period but resumed his role of customary government supporter from 1810 onwards. Since after 1808 the Common Hall of Liverymen was increasingly dominated by the radical party led by Waithman, the readiness of Pittite City MPs like Curtis, Charles Price, and James

Shaw to stand up to popular pressure in their constituency was of considerable assistance to the Perceval and Liverpool administrations. Curtis consciously risked his seat in 1809, for example, by voting to acquit the duke of York of charges of corruption.

On the other hand, Curtis tenaciously defended the privileges of the corporation of London and the interests of the mercantile community, and even after 1810 he was prepared to go against the government on issues of importance where his own views and those of his constituents coincided. He voted against the unpopular new corn law of 1815 and (more successfully) against the controversial proposal to renew the income tax in 1816. However, he lost his seat in 1818, mainly because, as a member of the Commons' 'secret committee' of 1817, he approved the suspension of habeas corpus. Refusing a peerage, he was eventually brought in for the pocket borough of Bletchingley in 1819. He regained his City seat in 1820, but abandoned it at the general election of 1826 and was returned instead for Hastings, retiring through ill health within a year.

A robust, jovial, coarse-featured, self-confident man of convivial habits and flamboyant tastes, Curtis was a constant target of whig and radical cartoonists. Though his speeches in the Commons lacked polish, it was probably his plebeian accents and mannerisms that enabled his opponents to depict him as an illiterate buffoon. He lent himself to further ridicule by such exploits as sailing his yacht, bedecked with patriotic flags, to the Downs in 1809 carrying refreshments for the officers of the Walcheren expeditionary fleet, and appearing, like his royal master, in full highland costume at George IV's levee at Holyrood in 1822. Yet he was honest, generous, and public-spirited, entertained leading cabinet ministers, was a personal friend of Lord Sidmouth, and a favourite with George IV, who stayed at his Ramsgate house on his way to Hanover in 1821, and commissioned Sir Thomas Lawrence to paint his portrait in 1823. Mrs Arbuthnot, who met him in 1824 in the company of the Bank of England director William Ward, described them as 'clever intelligent men & full of anecdote & conversation'. He died at his house in Ramsgate on 18 January 1829 and was buried at Wanstead, Essex. He left Cliff House and an annuity of £2000 to his wife, Anne. There were five surviving children, three sons and two daughters. NORMAN GASH

Sources HoP, *Commons* · GM, 1st ser., 99/1 (1829) · *Annual Register* (1793–1829) · *The Farington diary*, ed. J. Greig, 8 vols. (1922–8) · Burke, *Peerage* · J. Foster, *The peerage, baronetage, and knightage of the British empire for 1883*, 2 [1883] · DNB · *The journal of Mrs Arbuthnot, 1820–1832*, ed. F. Bamford and the duke of Wellington [G. Wellesley], 2 vols. (1950) · *Dyott's diary, 1781–1845*, ed. R. W. Jeffery, 2 vols. (1907) · *The diary of Henry Hobhouse, 1820–1827*, ed. A. Aspinall (1947) · J. G. Lockhart, *Memoirs of Sir Walter Scott*, 5 vols. (1900) · *The letters of King George IV, 1812–1830*, ed. A. Aspinall, 3 vols. (1938) · P. Boyd, ed., *Roll of the Drapers' Company of London* (1934)

Likenesses S. Drummond, portrait, c.1799 · J. Clover, portrait, exh. RA 1807 · T. Lawrence, portrait, 1812, priv. coll. · W. Sharp, line engraving, pubd 1814 (after T. Lawrence), BM, NPG · R. Dighton, coloured etching, 1820, NPG, V&A · T. L. Busby, coloured line engraving, pubd 1822, BM · G. Cruikshank, coloured etching, pubd 1822, NPG · T. Lawrence, oils, 1823, Royal Collection · F. Chantrey, pencil drawing, 1827, NPG · F. Chantrey, marble bust, 1828, AM Oxf. · H. Hopper, monument, 1829; formerly in Ramsgate · W. Bromley, line engraving (after S. Drummond), BM, NPG; repro. in *European Magazine* (1799) · P. Pindar, cartoon, repro. in P. Pindar, *The fat knight and the petition* (1815) · cartoons and caricatures, repro. in F. G. Stephens and M. D. George, 'Catalogue of prints and drawings in the British Museum', 11 vols. (1870–1954) · cartoons and caricatures, GL

Wealth at death £300,000; executors declared his personal property to be under £140,000: *GM*

Curtis, William Edward (1889–1969), experimental physicist, was born on 23 October 1889 at Islington, London, the younger child and only son of Charles Curtis, a gilder, originally of Horsham in Sussex, and his wife, Emily Sarah Haward, from Ipswich. He was outstanding at school (Owen's, Islington), and at Imperial College, London, where he graduated with a first-class degree in physics in 1910. He was awarded the governor's scholarship in 1908 and 1909 and shared the Tyndall prize in 1908. Later he became the first student ever to take the new London University honours degree in astronomy, obtaining a first. He was appointed to a college demonstratorship at Imperial and his research was supervised by Alfred Fowler.

Fowler introduced Curtis to some of the major problems in spectroscopy, particularly to the observation that certain stellar spectra have lines with wavelengths close to some of the Balmer lines of hydrogen and yet are apparently emitted by helium. Niels Bohr solved this problem in 1913 as an extension to his theory of the hydrogen atom, when he showed that these lines are due to ionized helium; contemporaneous experimental work by Fowler and Curtis proved that the lines are definitely due to helium and not to a new form of hydrogen as certain scientists had assumed. In the course of this work Curtis discovered a unique band spectrum, emitted by excited helium, which was to become his main research interest, though temporarily interrupted by the First World War.

At the outbreak of war Curtis was in Riga waiting to go to Kiev to observe a solar eclipse. The expedition was called off and Curtis returned to England by a devious route and enlisted as a sapper in the Royal Naval division. After initial training he was sent to Gallipoli where he served during the whole campaign, being twice mentioned in dispatches. For the rest of the war he was an instructor in the wireless training centre at Malvern.

In 1918 Curtis married (Adeline Mary) Grace, the only daughter of Charles Mitchell, of the War Office; they had two children, a son, who became a physicist, and a daughter, who became a doctor and the wife of Professor R. L. Plackett. On demobilization Curtis returned to Imperial College and to his study of spectra. From the college he moved in 1919 to a lectureship at the University of Sheffield, then to a readership at King's College, London, and finally to a professorship at Armstrong College at Newcastle upon Tyne in the University of Durham. In each of these posts he made his mark, gradually blossoming on the research side into a world specialist on band spectra and on the teaching side into a gifted lecturer noted for his skill in demonstration. He published many scientific papers but perhaps the most important were those in the decade 1922–32 on the band spectrum of the helium molecule, for which accurate wavelength measurements could be made and the theoretical predictions of the new quantum mechanics tested with great precision. For his contributions to spectroscopy he was elected a fellow of the Royal Society in 1934.

Curtis took up his professorship at Newcastle upon Tyne in 1926 and for more than forty years took a leading part in the educational life of Armstrong College, the university, and the city. As the head of the physics department he built up strong research schools in spectroscopy and acoustics. Later a school of theoretical physics was created. In 1931 a serious constitutional upheaval began involving Armstrong College and the Medical College and Curtis, as a senior science professor, reluctantly, but inevitably, became much involved. The outcome was a royal commission and the creation of one large college named King's College under a rector.

Curtis's contributions to the Second World War were varied. After chairmanship of the Durham University recruiting board he moved in 1940 to Leamington Spa as director of camouflage and decoy, and when air attacks diminished became successively a scientific adviser at the Ministry of Home Security, with Solly Zuckerman and J. D. Bernal, and then, in 1943, superintendent of applied explosives at Fort Halstead.

On returning to Newcastle, Curtis became more and more involved in college and public affairs. He was sub-rector of King's for three years (1947–50), president of the Institute of Physics (1950–52), and senior adviser in civil defence for the north-eastern region. For his work for civil defence he was appointed CBE in 1967, and in 1969 the University of Newcastle named its largest theatre the Curtis Auditorium.

Curtis retired in 1955 but continued to be very active, especially in lectures whose purpose was to stimulate interest in science in young people by showing demonstrations for which school facilities were inadequate. They succeeded admirably and drew huge audiences for many years. Outside his professional life he was impressive as a man of many parts. He had boundless physical energy and played many games well, especially cricket. He liked music and was a modest performer. He died at Newcastle upon Tyne on 6 May 1969.

G. D. ROCHESTER, rev.

Sources G. D. Rochester, *Memoirs FRS*, 16 (1970), 63–76 · *CGPLA Eng. & Wales* (1969) · personal knowledge (1981)
Likenesses photograph, repro. in Rochester, *Memoirs FRS*, facing p. 63
Wealth at death £16,506: probate, 22 July 1969, *CGPLA Eng. & Wales*

Curwen family (*per. c.*1500–*c.*1725), gentry, was already long established in Cumberland by the end of the fifteenth century. They had by then become pre-eminent among the gentry families of the west of the county, where the principal aristocratic estate was the Percy family's honour of Cockermouth. The Curwens of Workington always constituted the chief lineage, though there was also a cadet branch at Camerton.

Securing a position Sir Thomas Curwen (*c.*1493–1543) was said in the seventeenth century to have been brought up at court with the future Henry VIII. Although this tradition has proved impossible to substantiate it remains an appropriate one, since the family was notable for the extent to which it progressed through an alliance with the crown. Thomas Curwen became forester of Galtres, Yorkshire, in 1529, an esquire of the body in 1530, and steward of the royal estates at Sheriff Hutton, Yorkshire, in 1531. These offices allowed him independence of his father, Sir Christopher Curwen, who lived until 1535, at least seven years after Thomas had married as his first wife, Agnes (*d.* 1537/8), daughter of Sir Walter Strickland of Sizergh and his wife, Elizabeth Pennington of Muncaster, with whom he had two sons and two daughters. Under Sir Thomas the Curwen inheritance included the manors of Workington and Drigg, probably the manor of Stainburne, other lands, for example at Gilcrux and at Winscale, and the manor of Thornthwaite in north Westmorland. He does not appear to have purchased more land outright but his leases, of the site and demesne of Furness Abbey in 1540 worth some hundreds of pounds a year, and of property at Sheriff Hutton, boosted his means. Although his income must have been reduced by the dower estate of his mother, who outlived him, provision for his younger sons does not seem to have involved alienation of lands.

Sir Thomas served as a JP and sheriff of Cumberland. In the 1530s he became the ally of Sir Thomas *Wharton (*c.*1495–1568), from 1544 Baron Wharton, who although at first a retainer of the Percys owed his subsequent advancement even more than Curwen himself to crown patronage. Wharton's daughter was married to Curwen's heir in October 1534, while Curwen had himself married Wharton's sister Florence by 7 November 1538; they had a son and a daughter. Wharton was an executor of his brother-in-law's will, and also had the wardship of the latter's eldest son, after Sir Thomas died at Workington in 1543, probably in November.

Sir Henry Curwen (*c.*1528–1596) was nearly sixteen at his father's death. He was a JP for Cumberland from 1554 and sheriff four times under Elizabeth, and a JP for Westmorland from about 1584. Sir Henry was a member of parliament for Cumberland in the reigns of each of Henry VIII's children, initially following the Wharton interest, but was not elected after 1563. Notwithstanding different opinions by early Elizabethan bishops concerning his religious inclinations, he was loyal to all the regimes. He may have been fortunate to have been elsewhere when Mary, queen of Scots, landed at Workington in 1568, but he supported the crown in the northern rising of 1569, was knighted in 1570, recommended to Burghley in 1572, and was commissioned to take the oaths of other justices in 1592. Sir Henry's estate management afforded important purchases, in 1556 the manor of Harrington, in 1564 the advowsons of Harrington and Workington, the manor of Rottington in 1579, and an estate at Sella Park in 1594. He established a market at Workington in 1573 and encouraged the use of the town as a port, not least by the copper works at Keswick with which he traded and invested; he also mined coal around Workington.

Matrimonial complications At his death on 25 December 1596 Sir Henry Curwen left behind complex matrimonial arrangements which had long-term effects on the family's fortune. After his marriage at the age of about six in 1534 to Agnes Wharton, Sir Henry's marital circumstances were never simple. Lord Wharton made his first adult marriage for him, in 1548, with the widowed Mary Anne, daughter of Sir Nicholas Fairfax of Gilling, Yorkshire, and Jane Palmes. The validity of this marriage was challenged in 1556 and again in 1566 on the grounds of his having been married as a minor. Mary, Lady Curwen was probably alive in 1570, but no later than 1584 Sir Henry began a relationship with his servant Janet Crosby, which seems to have produced an illegitimate son and daughter before the birth in 1590 of Thomas, their first legitimate child, on whom Curwen settled the Sella Park estate, thus establishing a new cadet branch. He bequeathed leases and significant annuities to Janet (who may have been still alive in 1626) and all their children, one of whom, Bridget, drew her annuity until 1682. A long-lived father delayed independence for an eldest son, but Curwen seems to have avoided such tensions by building a house for the heir, **Sir Nicholas Curwen** (1550–1605), on the north Westmorland manor of Thornthwaite about 1576. Nicholas's first wife, Anne, daughter of Sir Simon Musgrave of Hartley, Westmorland, and his wife, Julian Ellerker, died in the early 1580s. By 1585 he had married Elizabeth, daughter of Thomas Carus of Kirkby Lonsdale and Anne Preston of Over Levens, Westmorland. She brought land into the marriage which enhanced Sir Nicholas's income and independence, which no doubt helped him in 1588 to renounce claims to his father's personal estate, intended for the children born to his father and Janet Crosby. Although Elizabeth, Lady Curwen enjoyed her dower estate until her death in 1611, it was her lands, rather than Curwen patrimony or purchases, which afterwards provided for the surviving daughters of her marriage. Nevertheless, Sir Nicholas sold the manor of Drigg in 1597.

As a teenager Sir Nicholas Curwen was involved in serious rioting in Carlisle in 1568 but avoided the 1569 rising. Towards the end of his father's life he became a JP for Cumberland about 1592 and was MP in 1593; he was pricked sheriff in 1600. He continued his father's involvement in border affairs, and he was one of Lord Warden Scrope's first choices to take over the government of the west marches in his absence in 1601. Nicholas Curwen was knighted in 1603, and in the same year he formed a connection with the ninth earl of Northumberland by joining with other gentry in petitioning him to press the privy council to lift taxes on the region and to allow the gentry to defend their lands by suppressing border thieves. In 1604 Curwen and the earl's chief officer in Cumberland, Sir Wilfrid Lawson of Isel, joined the king's border commission. Lawson was a new and rising star among the west Cumberland gentry, but the Curwens still retained their old-established pre-eminence in that region.

Sir Nicholas Curwen died on 16 January 1605, when his only son, **Sir Henry Curwen** (c.1581–1623), was about twenty-four. On 1 January 1601 Sir Henry had married Catherine (1580–c.1605), daughter of Sir John Dalston of Dalston and Anna, daughter of Thomas Tyrell of Tudebroke, Essex, with whom he had two sons. He was the first head of the family to have been to university, having matriculated at Pembroke College, Cambridge, in 1595. By 1606 he had been knighted. Sir Henry continued to exploit coal on the estate, some of which was used to boil seawater for salt; and iron ore mines at Harrington were developed. Overall he seems to have maintained the family wealth, and in his will probably indicated prosperity when he directed a relaxed attitude to foreclosure of his mortgages of other gentry's lands, though, like his father, Henry sold off distant property under the strain of long-lived dowagers and annuitants. Young Curwen's independence and enterprise led him into conflict with two of the county's aristocratic landowners, Lord William Howard and, especially, the earl of Northumberland. Sir Henry refused to pay his feudal relief to the earl in 1608 and built a new fishgarth on the Derwent at Workington without Northumberland's permission. In a struggle which occupied much of the following decade, the earl instructed his officers to pull the fishgarth down as many times as Curwen built it. When in 1619 Sir Henry wrote to the earl professing, like his ancestors before him, 'faithfull affection to that famous house [of Northumberland]', and offered service, his words are better seen as healing a dispute than as evidence of socially conservative loyalties among the northern gentry (Alnwick Castle MSS, X.II.3, bundle 10c). In return, the earl responded to complaints about the damage done by his deer and sent Curwen a warrant for a stag and hind, in time for Christmas 1619. Curwen was sheriff of Cumberland that year, MP in 1621, a deputy lieutenant, and, by 1617, a JP.

Religious and political difficulties Sir Henry Curwen's omission from the bench before 1617 may be explained by allegations of recusancy. In 1607 a report for Cecil on the religious affiliations of the Northumberland gentry also mentioned Sir Henry and his mother as papists. Historians have amplified the accusation by pointing to Curwen connections with the Catholic Fairfaxes of Yorkshire, but this evidence says more about the Fairfaxes than the Curwens. The informant's genealogy was not very impressive, for Sir Henry's mother was long dead. The reference must be to his stepmother, Elizabeth, Lady Curwen, the daughter of a Catholic family. Sir Henry, the report continued, had just married the widow of Christopher Wright, a gunpowder plotter. Certainly Sir Henry was married no later than May 1609 to Margaret, daughter of Thomas Buskell of Heversham, Westmorland, and Frances Cholmley of Middlesex, and in 1626 Sir John Lowther of Lowther explicitly noted her as the plotter's widow. But corroboration of the links made in 1607 and 1626 between Sir Henry and the aftermath of the 1605 plot has proved elusive, while elsewhere Wright's wife has been identified as Margaret Ward. At all events Margaret, Lady Curwen was convicted as a recusant in 1630, and remained one until her death in

1656. Their eldest son, Eldred, was not regarded as a recusant until the civil war, but was known as a Catholic thereafter. No proof of recusancy was ever established against Sir Henry. However, the status of his stepmother and the accusation against his second marriage may have damaged his position, while his settlement of the manor of Rottington on his new wife and their eldest son, ancestor of the Curwens of Rottington, cost the Workington family more land.

Sir Henry died suddenly in 1623, and was succeeded by his eldest son, **Sir Patricius Curwen**, baronet (c.1602–1664), who was made a baronet on 12 March 1627. He matriculated at Queens' College, Cambridge, in 1620, and had married on 28 February that year Isabel (d. 1667), daughter of Sir George Selby of Whitehouses in Durham and Margaret Selby. Their only child, born in 1621, died in 1636. Isabel's portion was not immediately spent on buying out the annuities created by his great-grandfather and father, or on buying extra land. In 1640 his purchase of half of the manor of Beckenham in Kent seems to have been involved in capitalizing the annuities for Lady Curwen of Rottington. Money was spent improving the Workington estate, houses, and mineral works. In competition with other coal owners so fierce that the privy council had to mediate disputes, Curwen sold considerable quantities of coal, and additionally traded in iron ore, salt, and fish, and operated at least one sea-going barque around the Irish Sea littoral. Cattle grazing was also important on his demesne lands.

Sir Patricius Curwen was a determined follower of the established church. He also played a prominent role in county government, sitting for Cumberland in all Charles I's parliaments, serving as deputy lieutenant, JP, and sheriff, and generally supporting the central government. Buckingham obtained him his baronetcy, and Curwen was a commissioner for the forced loan and an effective, if early and unchallenged, collector of ship money as sheriff. In the Long Parliament he supported Strafford, and went on to be a royalist in 1642, though not an especially effective one. He did actively support the royalist cause again in 1648, and was thus twice heavily fined, in all about £3100. Although Sir Patricius refused office under republic and protectorate, Thomas Curwen of Sella Park kept the Curwens in local government office in the 1640s and early 1650s. Apparently without any previous personal connection with the Percys, before 1655 Sir Patricius aligned with the earl of Northumberland as lieutenant of Northumberland's honour of Cockermouth, and worked effectively as the earl's officer until his death. He returned to his normal position in county politics and administration at the Restoration, and is judged in the 1661 parliament to have been a moderate cavalier.

Decline, eclipse, and recovery By the time of the Restoration the supremacy of the Curwens in west Cumberland was coming under threat, even though two more cadet branches of the family had by now been established, at Sella Park and Rottington. The principal challenge came from the Lowther family of Whitehaven, baronets from 1642. Coal, iron ore, salt, and cattle traded through that rival port in the 1640s and 1650s. Curwen's attempt in the 1660s to strike at the Whitehaven trade through control of the customs failed, but the initiative suggests he recognized and feared the potential of Whitehaven. Sir Patricius had secured for Workington by 1650 a new trade in lead from the earl of Northumberland's estates mined by a London-based consortium, which he joined. He had also acquired some useful leases from Northumberland and from the church. But the Curwen mines at Workington had done badly during the war, and iron ore production seems to have ceased. If the more entrepreneurial side of Curwen's estate management was in difficulty, his effective land management had, compared with his father's rentals of 1617, produced increases in the income expected for 1660 for individual properties of between 30 per cent and 122 per cent.

Sir Patricius Curwen died on 15 December 1664. His heir was his brother Thomas Curwen (1605–1673), a protestant who died unmarried on 24 February 1673, to be succeeded by his recusant half-brother Eldred Curwen of Rottington (c.1615–1673), who himself died on 25 April following and was followed by his young son, Henry Curwen (1661–1725). Edmund Sandford's observation in 1675, that the port of Workington was not the haven of resort that it had been as the collieries were decayed, does not surprise after such rapid inheritances, though comments by another local observer in 1687 on the improving estate management of the Curwens at Rottington show that all was not lost. Henry Curwen, who did not marry, served as a JP for Cumberland when James II appointed Catholics to the bench, was made sheriff in 1687, and fled abroad with his king. The nadir for the Curwens was reached in 1696 when the protestant Darcy Curwen of Sella Park tried unsuccessfully to claim his Workington kinsman's estate on the grounds that the absent Henry must be dead. This was enough to draw Henry home from France but it did not yet bring the Curwens back from eclipse. That did not fully happen until after Henry Curwen's death in 1725. Then the Sella Park line inherited the settled family estates, including Workington, but Henry's will alienated the extensive unsettled properties, some of which later passed to the Lowthers of Whitehaven. Nevertheless, the protestant family line returned the Curwens of Workington to county politics, eventually as knights of the shire and in rivalry with the Lowthers. Economically too, the Curwens again competed well as coal owners and shippers, before the male line once more failed in 1778. The heiress, Isabella, daughter of Henry Curwen of Workington, married a cousin, who in 1790 took the family name as John Christian *Curwen (1756–1828).

C. B. PHILLIPS

Sources Cumbria AS, Whitehaven, Curwen of Workington Hall papers, D/Cu · Cumbria AS, Carlisle, Lonsdale papers (Lowther and Whitehaven estates), D/Lons · Leconfield papers, 1500–1700, Cumbria AS, Carlisle · Alnwick Castle, duke of Northumberland's MSS, 1590–1700 · BL, duke of Northumberland's letters and warrants [microfiche] · J. F. Curwen, *A history of the ancient house of Curwen* (1928) · C. B. Phillips, 'The gentry in Cumberland and Westmorland, 1600–1665', PhD diss., University of Lancaster, 1973 · HoP, *Commons, 1509–58* · HoP, *Commons, 1558–1603* · HoP, *Commons, 1660–*

90 • Keeler, *Long Parliament* • *LP Henry VIII*, vols. 1–21 • *CPR, 1494–1578* • M. E. James, *Society, politics and culture: studies in early modern England* (1986) • J. Nicolson and R. Burn, *History and antiquities of Westmorland and Cumberland*, 2 vols. (1777) • W. Farrer, *Records relating to the barony of Kendale*, ed. J. F. Curwen, 3 vols., Cumberland and Westmorland Antiquarian and Archaeological Society, record ser., 4–6 (1923–6)

Archives Cumbria AS, Whitehaven, account book • Cumbria AS, Whitehaven, deeds, manorial and estate records, legal papers, family and personal papers • Cumbria AS, Whitehaven, letters and petitions for royalist compositions [Sir Patricius Curwen] • Cumbria AS, Carlisle, account book [Sir Patricius Curwen] | Cumbria AS, Carlisle, earl of Lonsdale's MSS

Likenesses group portrait, *c*.1928, Workington Hall; repro. in Curwen, *History of the ancient house of Curwen*

Curwen, Alice (*c*.1619–1679). *See under* Curwen, Thomas (*c*.1610–1680).

Curwen, Sir Henry (*c*.1528–1596). *See under* Curwen family (*per. c*.1500–*c*.1725).

Curwen, Sir Henry (*c*.1581–1623). *See under* Curwen family (*per. c*.1500–*c*.1725).

Curwen, Henry (1845–1892), journalist and author, born at Workington Hall, Cumberland, was descended from the Curwens of Workington Hall, a well-known family in the county. He was the son of Henry Curwen, rector of Workington, and grandson of Henry Curwen (1783–1860) of Workington; his mother was Dora, the daughter of General Goldie. He was educated at Rossall School, Fleetwood, Lancashire, and afterwards settled for a time in London, where he worked for the publisher John Camden Hotten. He had the chief hand in compiling several books which bore only the publisher's name on the title-page, among them the *Golden Treasury of Thought*. His first literary effort under his own name was *Echoes from French Poets*, a volume of translations of French poetry, published by Hotten in August 1870. It contained verse translations from Alfred de Musset, Alphonse de Lamartine, Charles Baudelaire, and others. He was attracted to the writings of Edgar Allan Poe, and in 1872 he translated from the French Baudelaire's *Study of the Life and Writings of Poe*. He also contributed a very sympathetic account of Poe's career to the *Westminster Review*, in which he also wrote some elaborate articles on other writers who had suffered, such as Henri Murger, Novalis, Sándor Petőfi, Honoré de Balzac, and André Chenier. These articles, which appeared between 1871 and 1873, were published collectively in two volumes in December 1874 under the title of *Sorrow and Song: Studies of Literary Struggle*. In 1873 he published a readable account of English booksellers and publishers, under the title of *A History of Booksellers: the New and the Old*. He followed this in 1876 with *Within Bohemia, or, Love in London*, a volume of short stories which was the first of many.

In 1876 Curwen left England for India, which became his home. General Nassau Lees, who had then recently acquired the *Times of India*, an Anglo-Indian paper published in Bombay, selected Curwen as assistant editor, under the editorship of Grattan Geary. Soon after his arrival, he described in the paper a tour through the districts stricken by the great famine of 1876–7.

Though immersed in journalism, Curwen found time to continue his other literary work. In August 1879 he published *Plodding on, or, The Jog Trot to Fame and Fortune*, the last volume that appeared under his name. *Zit and Xoe*, a short anonymous novel which was an imaginative description of the earliest condition of mankind from the Darwinian point of view, was reprinted from *Blackwood's Edinburgh Magazine* in 1886. It was followed in 1888 by a longer story in two volumes, *Lady Bluebeard*, a story of modern society. His last effort in fiction appeared in 1891 under the title of *Dr Hermione*. It was marked by the same characteristics as the two previous works—slightness of plot, picturesque description of scenery, and insight into character.

Meanwhile, in 1880 Curwen became chief editor of the *Times of India*. He conducted the paper in a scrupulous spirit of fairness and raised it to a high rank among Anglo-Indian journals. General Lees, the paper's proprietor, who died in 1889, offered Curwen by will the first refusal of the whole concern. This he accepted, and he thus became proprietor with his manager, Charles Kane. Soon afterwards his health failed. He died, unmarried, on 22 February 1892 on the P. & O. steamship *Ravenna*, three days after leaving Bombay, and was buried at sea. A brass mural tablet was placed in St Thomas's Cathedral, Bombay, by his friends.

R. P. KARKARIA, *rev.* NILANJANA BANERJI

Sources obituaries in the Indian press (privately printed, *Times of India* press, 1892) • M. Macmillan, *Calcutta Review*, 97 (1893); repr. in M. Macmillan, *Globe-trotter in India and other essays* (1895) • personal knowledge (1901)

Archives NL Scot., letters to William Blackwood & Sons

Curwen [Coren], Hugh (*c*.1500–1568), archbishop of Dublin, was born at High Knipe, Bampton, Westmorland. He had at least two brothers, James and Christopher. James was the father of Mary Bancroft, mother of Richard, the future archbishop of Canterbury. Curwen was educated at Oxford, possibly at Brasenose College. On 18 February 1528 he took the degree of bachelor of canon law; on 5 July 1532 he became a doctor of canon law. In 1530 he is recorded as being a canon and notary at Cardinal College. Previous accounts of Curwen's life record that he attended Cambridge almost twenty years earlier, becoming vicar of Buckden in 1514, but these details relate to a different man. Earlier histories, including the *Dictionary of National Biography*, have also stated that Hugh Curwen was the chaplain who in 1532 and 1533 preached before Henry VIII, supporting the royal supremacy and the king's divorce. However, state records make clear that the chaplain in question was Dr Richard Coren or Curwen, who was also the king's almoner and one of the members of the king's council who administered interrogatories to Bishop John Fisher and Sir Thomas More. It is certain also that it was Richard Coren and not Hugh Curwen who was one of the commissioners sent to Calais by the king in the spring of 1540.

Recorded as a proctor in the chancellor's court in 1528, Curwen was appointed on 18 June 1533 as rector of Ferriby, Lincolnshire. On 3 October 1535 he became vicar-general to Bishop Fox of Hereford and on 19 September

1536 was entrusted with the delicate task of carrying out a visitation at Wigmore Abbey, where the abbot had been accused of serious sexual and financial irregularities. On 29 January 1538 Curwen was appointed prebendary of Hunderton in the diocese of Hereford. The see of Hereford was shortly after vacated by the death of Fox and on 8 May 1538 Curwen was appointed by Archbishop Cranmer as keeper of the spiritualities, empowered to visit the church and diocese, instruct the clergy, and arrange for use of the scriptures in the vernacular. On 1 September 1538 Curwen received the living of Great Mongeham, Kent, and by April 1542 he had been appointed as one of the king's chaplains. On 7 April 1542 he was made prebendary of Alveley in the collegiate church of Bridgnorth, Shropshire.

On 1 June 1541 Curwen became dean of Hereford and on the death of Bishop Skip in 1552 was again keeper of spiritualities. In 1552 he became rector of Eaton Bishop, and in 1553 of Lugwardine, both in Herefordshire. On the accession of Queen Mary, he conformed to Catholicism and became chaplain to the queen. On 18 February 1555 Mary wrote to direct his appointment to the archbishopric of Dublin, where he would replace the reforming Archbishop Browne, deposed early in 1554. The pallium was granted by the pope on 23 August 1555 and Curwen was consecrated on 8 September 1555 at St Paul's Cathedral. On 13 September Curwen also became lord chancellor of Ireland, and he arrived in that country on 20 October 1555. He resumed the deanery of Hereford which he had recently resigned and continued to hold it until 1558. On 5 December 1557 Curwen was also appointed Irish lord justice jointly with Sir Henry Sidney.

During his Marian tenure Curwen worked assiduously on behalf of the Catholic church, preaching his first sermon in Advent 1555 at Christ Church, Dublin, where he also reinstated a marble statue of Christ taken down by Archbishop Browne. In 1556 he convoked a provincial synod aimed at restoration of the old rites of divine worship. Before the Irish parliament, summoned in Dublin on 1 June 1557, he read out a bull from Pope Paul IV 'upon his knees, in open parliament, deliberately and distinctly, in a high voice' (Ronan, *Dublin*, 447). He was assigned by Queen Mary to a number of commissions considering matters of religion and law and order. On Queen Elizabeth's accession in 1558, Curwen was at once appointed keeper of the great seal, and was soon afterwards confirmed as lord chancellor of Ireland. He accepted the Acts of Supremacy and Uniformity and although he has been accused of being the only Irish bishop to change religious allegiance, this is not the case. Several others accepted both acts, and two the Supremacy only.

In 1559 the statue restored in Christ Church by Archbishop Curwen generated considerable excitement when it was seen to bleed from the head during a Sunday service. Curwen, 'being displeased', bade a sexton investigate and a bloodsoaked sponge was found concealed amid the crown of thorns. The fraudsters, led by Father Richard Leigh, were punished by being obliged to stand for three Sundays before the pulpit with their hands and legs tied.

On the first of these Sundays, Archbishop Curwen preached on St Paul's second letter to the Thessalonians, focusing upon the verse: 'God shall send them strong delusions that they should believe a lie.' According to Strype, this converted more than a hundred persons 'who swore they would never attend mass more' (Strype, *Parker*, 1.90). More significantly Curwen, who at once had the statue removed, wrote an account of these events to Archbishop Parker. It appears that Parker used the letter to persuade Queen Elizabeth to consent, albeit reluctantly, to the removal of religious images from churches.

Curwen's archbishopric and office of lord chancellor made him an important member of the queen's council at Dublin but there is evidence that, after Elizabeth's accession, he may not always have been a vigorous member of that body. Although his name appears on council documents, examination of the state papers suggests that Curwen was not a frequent correspondent with the queen's secretary or privy council, and that letters to Curwen from London were not especially numerous and were largely concerned with routine business. On 12 July 1559 the queen wrote to Curwen that certain patents could be sealed by the lord deputy alone. By 1560 Lord Deputy Sussex was already appealing on Curwen's behalf that he be translated to the see of Hereford to 'comfort him in his old years' (PRO, SP 63/2/41), and in 1563 the queen was proposing that he be relieved of his offices and granted a pension. However, the plan was not acted upon.

In church matters too, Curwen appears to have been dilatory. It may be that he had found the Henrician approach to reform more appealing than the Elizabethan. He displayed marked generosity towards his great-nephew Richard Bancroft, paying for his education at Christ's College, Cambridge, and appointing him prebendary at St Patrick's Cathedral in Dublin. He also made offers of preferment to a nephew, Philip Curwen, a Franciscan who had remained faithful to Catholicism; these were rejected, however. Despite his concern with family links, Curwen did not marry and this could suggest an attachment to older religious forms. Protestant episcopal colleagues expressed exasperation at his inertia, adding regular recommendations that he be recalled to England. Bishop Brady of Meath viewed him as an 'unprofitable workman' and in October 1564 complained that he only 'preacheth now and then' (PRO, SP 63/10/30; 63/13/74). Loftus decried him as a man unwilling to further 'our business' who ought to be 'provided for at home' (PRO, SP 63/15/12). Schemes for the turning of buildings at St Patrick's Cathedral into a university were opposed by Curwen in 1564 and by January 1565 Bishop Brady was openly doubting Curwen's commitment to reform, declaring both the archbishop and the prebendaries of St Patrick's to be 'living enemies of the truth' and 'disguised dissemblers' (PRO, SP 63/12/7). In October 1566 Archbishop Loftus of Armagh was even more forceful in urging Curwen's removal. Accusing him of swearing 'terribly' in open court, he added: 'Is it not time and more than time that such a one be removed?' (PRO, SP 63/19/19).

In poor health, with his abilities and faith thus questioned, Curwen could do little but hope for escape. In March 1566 the queen indicated her intention to translate him to Oxford. Curwen had developed palsy in 1564, and in May 1566 he begged the queen to recall him soon as he 'suffered extremely' during the Irish winter (PRO, SP 63/17/63). A year's prevarication followed, and by 20 April 1567 Lord Deputy Sidney was describing Curwen as being speechless and senseless. It was not until 10 June 1567 that the queen finally allowed his translation to the see of Oxford. On 11 August Curwen took ship from Ireland. Clearly unfit for the duties of his new diocese, he settled at a house in Swinbrook, Oxfordshire. In February 1568 he travelled north for a last visit to his native Bampton. He returned to Oxford, died at Swinbrook in October 1568, and on 1 November was buried at Burford church. In his will, which he had made in 1564, he bequeathed his estate to his brother Christopher.   HELEN COBURN WALSHE

Sources *LP Henry VIII, addenda*, 1 · PRO, state papers Ireland, SP 60, SP 62, SP 63 · *CSP Ire., 1509–1625* · *CSP dom., 1547–1603* · J. Morrin, ed., *Calendar of the patent and close rolls of chancery in Ireland for the reigns of Henry VIII, Edward VI, Mary, and Elizabeth*, 2 vols. (1861–2) · *State papers published under ... Henry VIII*, 11 vols. (1830–52) · M. V. Ronan, *The Reformation in Ireland under Elizabeth, 1558–1580* (1930) · M. Ronan, *The Reformation in Dublin, 1536–58* (1926) · E. P. Shirley, ed., *Original letters and papers in illustration of the history of the church in Ireland during the reigns of Edward VI, Mary and Elizabeth* (1851) · J. Murray, 'The Tudor diocese of Dublin: episcopal government, ecclesiastical politics and the enforcement of the reformation, c.1534–1590', PhD diss., TCD, 1997 · Emden, *Oxf.*, 4.137–8 · J. Strype, *The life and acts of Matthew Parker*, new edn, 3 vols. (1821) · J. Strype, *Memorials of the most reverend father in God, Thomas Cranmer* (1694) · W. A. Phillips, ed., *History of the Church of Ireland*, 2 (1934), chaps. 4–6 · Foster, *Alum. Oxon.*, 1715–1886 · Cooper, *Ath. Cantab.*, vol. 1 · Venn, *Alum. Cant.*, 1/1 · Wood, *Ath. Oxon.*, new edn · H. Cotton, *Fasti ecclesiae Hibernicae*, 6 vols. (1845–78) · *The whole works of Sir James Ware concerning Ireland*, ed. and trans. W. Harris, 2 vols. in 3 (1739–45, [1746]) · L. F. Renehan, *Collections on Irish church history*, ed. D. McCarthy, 1 (1861) · S. B. Babbage, *Puritanism and Richard Bancroft* (1962) · S. G. Ellis, *Tudor Ireland: crown, community, and the conflict of cultures, 1470–1603* (1985) · DNB

Curwen, John (1816–1880), music educationist, was born on 14 November 1816 at Hurst House, Heckmondwike, Yorkshire, the eldest son of Spedding Curwen, an Independent minister of an old Cumberland family, and his wife, Mary, daughter of John Jubb of Leeds. Curwen's boyhood was spent principally at Hackney, Middlesex, and (after 1828) at Frome, Somerset. His schooling was mostly at Ham, Surrey, and at Frome, but at the age of sixteen he entered Wymondley College in Hertfordshire to prepare for the Independent (Congregational) ministry. A few months later the college was moved to London, and renamed Coward College. The students attended University College. In 1838 Curwen was appointed assistant minister at Basingstoke, where he also kept a small school; in 1841 he held a similar post at Stowmarket, but ill health caused him to resign after eighteen months and he went to live with his father at Reading for a year. In May 1844 he was given charge of the Congregational chapel at Plaistow, London, where he remained until 1864.

At an early stage in his ministerial career Curwen showed great interest in teaching. He studied the writings of Pestalozzi, David Stow, and others, and throughout his life displayed great insight into educational psychology and methodology. His attention was soon drawn to the educational and moral value of music, and his own lack of knowledge of the subject and inability to read musical notation led him to explore various teaching systems. About 1840 he was given a copy of *A Scheme to Render Psalmody Congregational* (1835). Published anonymously, it was the work of Sarah Anna Glover (1786–1876), who had employed a very successful system of musical instruction in the Norwich school where she taught. Already in demand as a lecturer on educational matters, Curwen was at a conference of Sunday-school teachers at Hull in the autumn of 1841, when he was requested to recommend the best and simplest way of teaching music. This led to an examination of Glover's book, and a visit to her school. A modified adoption of her system was then embodied in a series of articles in the *Independent Magazine* for 1842, in which the 'tonic sol-fa' system, as Curwen called it, was first advocated. In the same year he became engaged to Mary (d. 1880), daughter of Joseph Thompson, a Manchester merchant, whom he married in May 1845. They had three children, Mary Eleanor (b. 1846), John Spencer (1847–1916) and Joseph Spedding (1849–1919). In June 1843 Curwen's *Singing for Schools and Congregations* appeared (rev. edn as *A Grammar of Vocal Music*, 1848), and from this time the adoption of the system spread rapidly. This was despite its having no official recognition; a rival system advocated by John Hullah was sanctioned for use in teacher-training institutions. Its growth was aided by a series of articles by Curwen which appeared from 1852 in Cassell's *Popular Educator*, which enjoyed a vast circulation. In 1853 it was estimated that two thousand persons were engaged in learning the tonic sol-fa method; ten years later the number had increased in Britain to 186,000 and was also spreading overseas. In 1853 he started the *Tonic Sol-Fa Reporter*, and in 1855 visited Scotland, lecturing on the new system.

In April 1856 Curwen was compelled by a breakdown to leave England for seven months, which he spent in Germany and Switzerland. His letters from there were afterwards published as *Sketches in Nassau, Baden, and Switzerland* (1857). On resuming his duties he raised £3000 for a new church at Plaistow, which opened in 1860. On the outbreak of the American Civil War he sided ardently with the North, publishing various tracts on the subject, and organizing the first Freed Slaves' Aid Society in England. He had long borne the financial risk of publishing his works, but to facilitate their printing he established in 1863 a press at Plaistow, at first known as the Tonic Sol-fa Agency, and from 1874 as John Curwen & Sons. This initiated larger-scale production of music in tonic sol-fa notation, and led Curwen to believe, mistakenly, that his system could be self-sufficient rather than, as hitherto, a useful initial stage on the way to reading staff notation. He even tried applying it unsuccessfully to instrumental music.

In 1864 Curwen resigned his ministry and devoted himself entirely to music. He continued to modify and improve his system, and to lecture throughout the kingdom. In the winter of 1866–7 he was appointed Euing lecturer at Anderson's University, Glasgow, and in August 1873 he acted as one of the judges at the Welsh national eisteddfod at Mold. In the wake of continuing opposition from the official institutions influenced by Hullah, Curwen founded in 1869 the Tonic Sol-fa College, an examining body which was to ensure that a certain standard of efficiency was attained by the teachers of the system. In 1875 he summed up all his pedagogical experience in *The Art of Teaching as Applied to Music*. Although some professional musicians continued to scorn tonic sol-fa, its proven practical value in schools eventually led to official recognition by the education authorities, and its predominance lasted until the general decline in teaching sight-singing in the middle of the twentieth century. In modified forms (particularly that made by Zoltan Kodály) it is still found useful worldwide.

On 17 January 1880 Curwen sustained a great blow in the death of his wife. In May he went to Manchester to visit a sick brother-in-law. He stayed at Heaton House, Heaton Mersey, Lancashire, and here he was suddenly taken ill, and a few days later died, on 26 May. He was buried at City of London cemetery, Ilford, on 3 June.

W. B. Squire, rev. Peter Ward Jones

Sources J. S. Curwen, *Memorials of John Curwen* (1882) · B. Rainbow, *John Curwen: a short critical biography* (1980) · H. W. Shaw, 'The musical teaching of John Curwen', *Proceedings of the Royal Musical Association*, 77 (1950–51), 17–26 · m. cert.

Archives BL, notebook, Add. MS 50752

Likenesses W. Gush, oils, 1874, NPG · photograph, *c*.1880, repro. in Curwen, *Memorials of John Curwen* · G. H. Swinstead, oils, NMG Wales

Wealth at death under £25,000: probate, 20 Sept 1880, *CGPLA Eng. & Wales*

Curwen, John Christian (1756–1828), agriculturist and politician, was born on 12 July 1756 at Ewanrigg, Dearham, Cumberland, the eldest to survive infancy of the sons of John Christian of Ewanrigg, and his wife, Jane, eldest daughter of Eldred Curwen of Workington Hall, Cumberland. He was educated at Peterhouse, Cambridge; he left the university without a degree about 1774. On 10 September 1775 he married Margaret, daughter of John Taubman of Castletown, Isle of Man. She died in 1778, leaving a son, also John Christian. He remarried on 5 October 1782 at Edinburgh; his second wife was his cousin Isabella, daughter of his uncle and guardian, Henry Curwen of Workington. She brought him £5000 p.a. and her family's support in the career in Cumberland politics which he subsequently began. They had five sons and three daughters. He took on the surname Curwen in 1790 [*see* Curwen family (*per. c*.1500–*c*.1725)].

A whig in politics, Curwen was returned to the House of Commons for Carlisle in 1786, was defeated for that constituency in 1790, regained it in 1791, held it until 1812, and held it again from 1816 to 1820. He then represented Cumberland from 1820 until his death. He was an active parliamentarian who supported Catholic emancipation, parliamentary reform, and the repeal of the corn laws. To emphasize his concern for his constituents he once

John Christian Curwen (1756–1828), by Charles Turner, pubd 1809 (after John James Halls)

appeared in the House of Commons dressed like a Cumberland labourer and carrying a loaf and a cheese under his arms. In 1796 he made an ineffectual bid to reform and virtually abolish the game laws. Politically, he is best known for Curwen's Act, which was passed in 1809. The act was one of the very few significant reforms of the pre-1832 system; it attempted to reduce the sale of seats and the number of government placemen in the Commons, but was less successful than contemporaries initially feared.

Curwen's interest in agriculture probably dated from a long journey through Europe following the death of his first wife in 1778. He was a friend of Arthur Young and knew the leaders of progressive agricultural opinion in Scotland. In Cumberland he embarked on an improvement programme on his estates at Workington Hall. In 1805 he inaugurated the Workington Agricultural Society, which had a profound impact on local agriculture in the first half of the nineteenth century. In 1807 he received the gold medal of the Society of Arts, Commerce, and Manufactures, for his agricultural innovations. Many of his ideas were published in *Hints on Agricultural Subjects* (1809), and his views on Ireland, where he spent time between 1813 and 1816, appeared in *Observations on the state of Ireland, principally directed to its agriculture and rural population* (1818). Part, at least, of his motive in studying agriculture was to improve the lot of the labouring poor. To the latter end he was also responsible for establishing a savings bank at Workington, and for various friendly societies.

Curwen's estates lay on the west Cumberland coalfield, and he took a particular interest in the collieries inherited from his father and his second wife, as well as in others which he purchased and leased in the area. However, he was hit by the trade depression after the Napoleonic Wars, and by the 1820s Workington colliery was in decline. Increasing costs and declining profits forced him to borrow, and from 1819 until 1827 Curwen owed more than £120,000. Consequently he was not able to invest in improved mining techniques in the later years of his life.

Curwen was sheriff of Cumberland in 1784–5 and was active in the militia. He died at Workington Hall on 11 December 1828.   J. V. BECKETT, rev.

Sources H. Lonsdale, *The worthies of Cumberland*, 1 (1867) • HoP, *Commons* • O. Wood, *West Cumberland coal, 1600–1982/3* (1988) • *GM*, 1st ser., 99/1 (1829), 178–9 • C. Maycock, *A passionate poet: Susan Blamire, 1747–94* (2003)
Archives Cumbria AS, Whitehaven, papers
Likenesses C. Turner, engraving, pubd 1809 (after John James Halls), NPG [*see illus.*] • A. Plimer, enamel miniature, priv. coll.

Curwen, Sir Nicholas (1550–1605). *See under* Curwen family (*per. c.*1500–*c.*1725).

Curwen, Sir Patricius, baronet (*c.*1602–1664). *See under* Curwen family (*per. c.*1500–*c.*1725).

Curwen, Sir Thomas (*c.*1493–1543). *See under* Curwen family (*per. c.*1500–*c.*1725).

Curwen, Thomas (*c.*1610–1680), Quaker missionary, was born in Baycliff in the parish of Aldingham, near Ulverston in Furness, Lancashire; his parents' names are not known. About 1641 he married 'a strict religious professor' (Backhouse and others, 200); the maiden name and parentage of his wife **Alice Curwen** (*c.*1619–1679), Quaker missionary, remain unknown. The Curwens were converted to Quakerism about 1652 during George Fox's mission in Furness. In 1654–6 Curwen was numbered with twenty-six other Friends from Furness and elsewhere in Lancashire who were 'several times committed for speaking to priests and people in their public assemblies' (Nightingale, 35); in 1659 he was assessed for unpaid parish tithes at 12*s.*—though he had goods distrained to the value of £2 10*s.*—and was rounded up with co-religionists, 'Taken from their homes or from the market or their employment by a party of horsemen and sent to Lancaster Castle without any warrant' (Nightingale, 32). By 1663 Curwen was free but headed a presentment list of thirteen Quakers in Aldingham township. A further imprisonment in 1665 led to his involvement with other Friends within Lancaster Castle prison in a debate against the Baptist–Fifth Monarchist prisoner John Wiggan, and issuing in a published form (with an appendix by Margaret Fell) the Quaker riposte to a work widely distributed in north Wales and the north-west by Wiggan.

From as early as 1660 Alice Curwen, who had by now emerged as a Quaker preacher, had felt a deep concern for Friends in the American colonies and the persecutions they underwent and, with their family grown, between 1676 and 1678 she and her husband undertook a mission to both Quakers and non-Quakers in Rhode Island, New England (in a critical period of Native American raids), and New Jersey. The Curwens were gaoled in Boston under Massachusetts law and publicly flogged, but went on to evangelize in Barbados among both the European and Afro-Caribbean populations. In one letter Alice reproved a plantation-owner for 'preventing thy Servants, whom thou callest thy Slaves' from attending a Quaker meeting:

> for I am perswaded, that if they whom thou call'st thy Slaves, be Upright-hearted to God, the Lord God Almighty will set them Free in a way that thou knowest not; for there is none set free but in Christ Jesus, for all other Freedom will prove but a Bondage.   (*A Relation*, 18)

Following their return to England the Curwens continued their preaching work in London, the south-east, and the east midlands, though retaining their links with Furness and especially with Swarthmoor. In the winter of 1677–8, when they were active in Huntingdonshire, Alice still gave their home as Baycliff and wrote a letter addressed to the Swarthmoor meeting.

Though 'she seemed not very aged and but a few days before appeared a healthy strong woman' (R. T., 'A testimony concerning Alice Curwen', in *A Relation*, unpag.), Alice Curwen died in London 'on the 7th Day of the 6th Moneth' 1679, aged about sixty. Thomas Curwen contributed an entry in the obituary compilation in her memory, *A relation of the labour, travail and suffering of that faithful servant of the Lord Alice Curwen*, recalling her as 'a dread and a terror to the wicked where-ever she came … her children … were convinced by her wise walking before them' (Mack, 382). One of these children, Thomas, a Quaker London glover, maintained close business links with the Fells of Swarthmoor. Thomas Curwen died at Blackfriars, London, aged about seventy, on 1 August 1680, and was buried there. *A Relation*, which put together letters between the Curwens and colonial Friends, along with Thomas Curwen's 'Account of the suffgs. of Friends and breaking up a meeting in New England by warrant' and 'The sufferings of Thomas Curwen which he hath suffered for conscience sake towards God', as well as a record by the Quaker writer Rebecca Travers of Alice Curwen's peaceable demise, provided a retrospect over the heroic work of this early north Lancashire Quaker couple of modest farming folk, propelled into a transatlantic mission.

MICHAEL MULLETT

Sources J. Smith, ed., *A descriptive catalogue of Friends' books*, 1 (1867) • B. Nightingale, *Early stages of the Quaker movement in Lancashire* [n.d., *c.*1921] • E. Backhouse, T. J. Backhouse, and T. Mounsey, *Biographical memoirs … of the … Society of Friends* (1854) • P. Mack, *Visionary women: ecstatic prophecy in seventeenth-century England* (1992) • *The household account book of Sarah Fell of Swarthmoor Hall*, ed. N. Penney (1920) • *The short journal and itinerary journals of George Fox*, ed. N. Penney (1925) • *A relation of the labour, travail and suffering of that faithful servant of the Lord Alice Curwen* (1680) • 'Dictionary of Quaker biography', RS Friends, Lond. [card index]

Curzon, Sir Clifford Michael (1907–1982), pianist, was born on 18 May 1907 in London, the younger son and second of three children of Michael Curzon, antique dealer, and his wife, Constance Mary Young, an accomplished amateur singer. His uncle, the composer Albert Ketèlbey, tried out his latest compositions on the family piano and gave the boy his first abiding musical memories. Curzon's

Sir Clifford Michael Curzon (1907–1982), by Karl Pollak

first studies were on the violin. At the unusually early age of fourteen he was admitted to the senior school of the Royal Academy of Music, where his professor was Charles Reddie, through whose own teacher, Bernhard Stavenhagen, Curzon could claim to be a great-grand-pupil of Liszt. Curzon's pianistic ability to learn new repertory at speed impressed Sir Henry J. Wood, then conductor of the Royal Academy of Music first orchestra. Wood gave Curzon his first Promenade Concert appearance in 1922 as one of the soloists in a Bach triple-keyboard concerto and took him as his concerto pianist on concert tours of Britain. Curzon left the academy with the McFarren gold medal and other prizes. At this time his repertory centred on Romantic and post-Romantic virtuoso piano works which better-known pianists did not play—for example, pieces by D'Indy and Frederick Delius. He also gave the first performance of Germaine Tailleferre's *Ballade*. Although later Curzon regretted his 'neglect of music of the first quality' this was a suitable repertory for an ambitious pianist whose seniors might well have found him too immature for great classic masterpieces. Nevertheless the young Curzon was specially praised for his account of Schubert's 'Wanderer' fantasia in Liszt's then more popular transcription for piano and orchestra.

It was through his familiarity with Delius's piano concerto that Curzon gained his entrée to the repertory which was to become his speciality. The pianist Katharine Goodson wished to rehearse this work with another pianist taking the orchestral part; Reddie recommended her to Curzon, who subsequently accompanied her at home in

numerous of the great piano concertos which he had hitherto neglected, an experience of value when he came to learn the solo parts himself. In 1926 his father had to abandon his business through illness: the son took a sub-professorship at the Royal Academy of Music to support his family by teaching the piano, while still undertaking concert engagements. An unexpected legacy enabled him to spend two years in Berlin as a pupil of Artur Schnabel. It was from him that Curzon inherited the intellectual seriousness and perfectionism of technique and style which subsequently established his international reputation as an interpreter *par excellence* of the Viennese classics and German Romantics. Among these were Liszt, whose B minor sonata Curzon included in the Berlin recital which he gave before leaving Schnabel's tutelage, together with Beethoven's 'Les adieux' sonata, Schubert's *Moments musicaux*, and a recent work by Ernst Lothar von Knorr, a Berlin pedagogue—Curzon always preferred his recitals to include a contemporary work.

Curzon then went to Paris, where he studied the harpsichord with Wanda Landowska and attended the classes of Nadia Boulanger. These two great musicians undoubtedly supplemented Schnabel's Teutonic practical and intellectual tuition. In Paris he also met and married in 1931 the American harpsichordist Lucille Wallace (*d.* 1977), daughter of Edward Wallace, a Chicago businessman. Her acute sense of style in performance came to match his own. They adopted the two sons of the soprano Maria Cebotari after her and her husband's untimely deaths in 1949.

Curzon returned to England in 1932 to build a new international career in the classic repertory, though his programmes still included more recent music. He was the best exponent of the piano concerto of John Ireland and was a witty and poetic first soloist in the second piano concerto of Alan Rawsthorne during the Festival of Britain in 1951. In 1946 he introduced Lennox Berkeley's piano sonata, which is dedicated to him. A wartime friendship with Benjamin Britten found them giving concerts as a two-piano team for which Britten composed the *Scottish Ballad*, premièred by them at the Proms in 1944. Later, at Britten's Aldeburgh festival, Curzon was often a visiting soloist.

In America, which he visited for the first time in 1938, Curzon continued regularly to play a large repertory. His concert schedule was calculated to allow for lengthy preparation with frequent intervals for sabbatical study. In Britain in 1945 he concentrated increasingly on that 'music of the first quality' which he had ignored in his youth—Mozart, Beethoven, Schubert, Brahms. It had been Schnabel's repertory; Curzon played, not in Schnabel's way, which was sometimes uncommunicative, but frankly, generously, yet with the utmost attention to every note and its relative weight in context. The virtues which he applied to Mozart's piano concertos—he regarded them as the most perfect music ever composed—included line-drawing that colours itself and a control of structure through harmony and feeling for ensemble, which was overwhelming when the conductor was sympathetic. He achieved them with Britten often, and also with Daniel Barenboim and Sir Colin Davis. In chamber music he gave unforgettable readings of Schubert's 'Trout' quintet, Dvořák's and Elgar's piano quintets, and the Mozart and Schumann concerted works with piano. Curzon seldom played chamber music at public concerts, but it was evident that chamber music was a necessary element of his art. He was an ideal host, a lively raconteur, a keen connoisseur of painting and literature, and appreciative of other countries and their cultures, food, drink, and language. On the concert platform he appeared nervous in his middle years (he always played from score) but latterly learned to calculate every note for perfect effect, and when he was clearly no longer physically powerful his mastery of the piano seemed even more magical and potent.

Curzon was awarded many honours, notably honorary doctorates in music at Leeds (1970) and Sussex (1973) and the gold medal of the Royal Philharmonic Society in 1980. He was appointed CBE in 1958 and knighted (a rare honour for a pianist) in 1977. He died in London on 1 September 1982. WILLIAM MANN, rev.

Sources *The Times* (3 Sept 1982) · M. Loppert, 'Curzon, Sir Clifford (Michael)', *New Grove* · A. Blyth, 'Clifford Curzon', *Gramophone*, 48 (1971), 1794 · private information (1990) [K. Loveland] · *CGPLA Eng. & Wales* (1982)

Archives BL, annotated scores, music notes, student compositions, and other papers, Add. MSS 64966–65087 | FILM BFI NFTVA, home footage | SOUND BL NSA, documentary recordings · BL NSA, oral history recording · BL NSA, performance recordings · BL NSA, *Talking about music*, 162, 1LP0200417 S2 BD2 · BL NSA, *Talking about music*, 199, 1LP0201886 S1 BD1 · BL NSA, *Vintage years*, BBC Radio 3, 18 Oct 1997

Likenesses photographs, 1949, Hult. Arch. · E. Auerbach, photograph, 1961, Hult. Arch. · E. Auerbach, photograph, 1963 (with A. Bliss), Hult. Arch. · K. Pollak, photograph, NPG [*see illus.*]

Wealth at death £1,622,638: probate, 1 Oct 1982, *CGPLA Eng. & Wales*

Curzon, Lady Cynthia Blanche. *See* Mosley, Lady Cynthia Blanche (1898–1933).

Curzon, George Nathaniel, Marquess Curzon of Kedleston (1859–1925), politician, traveller, and viceroy of India, was born on 11 January 1859 at Kedleston Hall, Derbyshire, the second of the eleven children of the Revd Alfred Nathaniel Holden Curzon, fourth Baron Scarsdale (1831–1916), rector of Kedleston, and his wife, Blanche (1837–1875), daughter of Joseph Pocklington Senhouse of Netherhall in Cumberland. His family was of Norman ancestry and had lived on the same site since the twelfth century. In 1759 Sir Nathaniel Curzon, later first Baron Scarsdale, demolished the existing house at Kedleston and commissioned Robert Adam to build him a great country house in the Palladian style. His descendant, George Nathaniel, was always conscious, however, that the family home was more distinguished than the family which inhabited it, and from an early age he was determined to prove himself a fitting master for Kedleston. In the closing words of the epitaph he composed for himself, 'he sought to serve his country and add honour to an ancient name'.

Curzon's mother, worn out by childbirth, died in 1875 at the age of thirty-seven; her husband survived her for

George Nathaniel Curzon, Marquess Curzon of Kedleston (1859–1925), by John Singer Sargent, 1914

forty-one years. Neither parent, however, exerted a major influence on the life of George Nathaniel. Scarsdale was an austere and unindulgent father who believed in the long-held family tradition that landowners should stay on their land and not go 'roaming about all over the world'. He thus had little sympathy for those travels across Asia between 1887 and 1895 which made his son the most travelled man who ever sat in a British cabinet. A more decisive presence in Curzon's childhood was that of his brutal governess, Ellen Mary Paraman, whose tyranny in the nursery stimulated his combative qualities and encouraged the obsessional side of his nature.

Curzon was a good-looking and talented child. Unlike his siblings, who had inherited their father's long narrow face, he had a large and spherical head, while his pink cheeks, high forehead, and hazel eyes gave him an almost cherubic appearance. At the age of ten he was removed from the daily influence of his governess and sent to Wixenford, a preparatory school in Wokingham, where he embarked on a period of prize-winning academic achievement that lasted for fifteen years. This competitiveness, which was alien to the traditions of his family and which he retained all his life, was stimulated by the assistant master, Archibald Dunbar, who like Miss Paraman was both a good teacher and a savage disciplinarian. There can be little doubt that the two of them exercised a powerful influence for good and bad on the character of their charge.

Eton and Oxford At Eton College, where he was a pupil from 1872 to 1878, Curzon was a controversial figure who was liked and disliked with equal intensity by large numbers of masters and other boys. This strange talent for both attraction and repulsion stayed with him all his life: few people ever felt neutral about him. His housemaster at Eton, the Revd C. Wolley Dod, was a poor and unimaginative teacher who frequently complained to Lord Scarsdale about his pupil's stubbornness and insubordination. His principal grievance was Curzon's attachment to another housemaster, Oscar Browning, an opponent of the school's sporting ethos who helped to foster the intellectual interests of the brightest pupils. Regarding Curzon as 'one of the most brilliantly gifted boys' he had ever come across, Browning was responsible for encouraging his passion for art and history. His was the third and most beneficial of the major educational influences on the boy's life.

The young Curzon was motivated by a 'passionate resolve to be at the head of the class' and at Eton he achieved almost as much as a non-athlete is capable of achieving. He won a great many academic prizes and was awarded a record number of distinctions for outstanding work. He was also captain of the Oppidans, a member of Pop, and president of the literary society, which had been founded by Browning. At 'Speeches' on 4 June and at the meetings of the literary society, he acquired that love of rhetoric, that fondness for sonorous and elaborate language which he never lost.

In October 1878 Curzon went up to Oxford to read for a classical degree at Balliol College, which, under the dynamic mastership of Benjamin Jowett, was enjoying its first period as a kindergarten for aspiring politicians and diplomats. Shortly beforehand he suffered acute pains for the first time from that curvature of the spine which tormented him for the rest of his life. Although his doctor allowed him to go to university only on condition he rested and wore a steel appliance to support his spine, Curzon went to Oxford in a confident mood, intent on 'laying the foundations and preparing for the superstructure of his career'. He soon became the leading tory undergraduate of his day, his views reflecting Disraeli's creed of paternalism with social reform, national honour with the mandatory vision of empire. But then, as later, he was less interested in political ideas than in forms of oratory, in statesmanship, and in the practice of government.

As president of the Oxford Union and secretary of the Canning Club, Curzon struck his Oxford contemporaries as a man destined for a major political career. Most people were impressed by his wit, his eloquence, and his hard work, but others, including Jowett, found him too verbose and self-assured. Many friends of both sexes considered him the best of company, but more distant acquaintances discerned an air of superiority that inspired those lines which journalists quoted against him for the rest of his life:

My name is George Nathaniel Curzon,
I am a most superior person.
My cheek is pink, my hair is sleek,
I dine at Blenheim once a week.

Curzon believed the first couplet, published in the *Masque*

of Balliol, to have been written by his friend Cecil Spring-Rice, though the real author seems to have been J. W. Mackail; the second couplet probably was by Spring-Rice.

At the end of his fourth year Curzon narrowly failed to add a first in Greats to the first he had achieved in moderations two years earlier. He was humiliated by the result and allegedly threatened to devote the rest of his life 'to showing the examiners that they had made a mistake'. Travelling with friends to the eastern Mediterranean in the winter of 1882–3, he spent his spare time writing an essay on the emperor Justinian which won the Lothian history prize at Oxford. On his return he studied hard for a prize fellowship at All Souls College, which he gained in November 1883, and the following year he won the Arnold essay prize with a long work on Sir Thomas More.

Politics and travel For a short period after Oxford, Curzon managed to give the impression he was leading the life of a handsome dilettante, embarking on a series of risky love affairs (most notably with Lady Grosvenor) and enjoying a rich social life in London and the great country houses. Like most of his close friends, he belonged to that mildly exotic aristocratic circle later known as the Souls; he was also an assiduous and talented member of Wilfrid Scawen Blunt's Crabbet Club, where he once won the annual poetry competition. But his passionate and romantic nature did not prevent him from serving his political apprenticeship, first in the erratic shadow of Lord Randolph Churchill and then under the more stable aegis of the marquess of Salisbury, for whom he briefly worked as an unpaid private secretary during the Conservative government of 1885–6. At the same time he was looking for a suitable parliamentary constituency. In 1885 he stood for South Derbyshire, a county which in the past had automatically sent his undistinguished ancestors to Westminster, and was easily defeated. But the following year he was selected for Southport, which was narrowly held by the Liberals, and at the general election of June 1886 he gained it with a majority of 461.

Curzon's maiden speech, which was chiefly an attack on home rule and Irish nationalism, was regarded in much the same way as his oratory at the Oxford Union: brilliant and eloquent but also presumptuous and rather too self-assured. Subsequent performances in the Commons, often dealing with Ireland or reform of the House of Lords (which he supported), received similar verdicts; despite his oratorical talents, he showed early on that he did not have a good parliamentary manner. Although commentators compared him to Lord Randolph Churchill, Curzon chose to make his name not as a firebrand orator from the back benches but as an expert on Asia, a continent that had fascinated him since hearing a lecture by Sir James Stephen at Eton, which had infected him with a passion for the mystery of the East and for Britain's dominion of India.

The period of Curzon's great travels began in August 1887 with a journey round the world followed by a visit to Russia and central Asia in 1888–9, a long tour of Persia in

1889–90, an expedition to the Far East in 1892, and a daring foray through the Pamir to Afghanistan in 1894. A bold and compulsive traveller, fascinated by oriental life and geography, he was awarded the gold medal of the Royal Geographical Society for his exploration of the source of the Oxus. Yet the main purpose of his journeys was political: they formed part of a vast and comprehensive project to study the problems of Asia and their implications for British India. At the same time they reinforced his pride in his nation and her imperial mission.

During his travels Curzon sent home articles for *The Times* and other newspapers, and on his return he wrote *Russia in Central Asia in 1889* (1889), the two massive volumes of *Persia and the Persian Question* (1892), and *Problems of the Far East* (1894). Each of these was highly regarded and contributed to his reputation as the country's most knowledgeable politician on Asiatic affairs. In November 1891 the prime minister recognized the fact by appointing him under-secretary for India, a fitting post for a young man who was about to dedicate his Persian book to 'the officials, civil and military in India, whose hands uphold the noblest fabric yet reared by the genius of a conquering nation'. Although Curzon held the post only until the following July, when the Conservatives left office, his reputation was enhanced by his handling of the India Councils Bill (1892). Critics might agree with Henry Labouchere, the Liberal MP, who compared Curzon's performance at the dispatch box to that of 'a divinity addressing black beetles', but the young under-secretary was widely regarded as 'the coming man' on the Conservative benches, a worthy antagonist of those Balliol-schooled Liberals, H. H. Asquith and Sir Edward Grey.

On his return from Afghanistan at the beginning of 1895, Curzon announced his engagement to Mary Victoria (1870–1906) [see Curzon, Mary Victoria], daughter of Levi Zeigler Leiter, a Chicago millionaire and philanthropist. A musical girl of much charm and beauty, she had met the young English politician in 1890 and had quickly fallen in love with him. Curzon's response had been more lukewarm, probably because he was involved with other women at the time. But in March 1893, at the end of a journey round the world, he proposed to her in Paris; on her acceptance he insisted on keeping their engagement secret for two years while he completed his 'scheme of Asiatic travel' by means of a perilous excursion into Afghanistan and the Pamir. Throughout his courtship Curzon's behaviour was uncharacteristically cold and unromantic, and his engagement was probably an act of impetuosity. Nevertheless, the marriage (on 23 April 1895) turned out to be a firm and happy one which produced three daughters, (Mary) Irene *Curzon (1896–1966), Cynthia [see Mosley, Cynthia Blanche (1898–1933)], and Alexandra Naldera.

When the Conservatives returned to office in June 1895, Curzon was appointed a privy councillor and under-secretary of state at the Foreign Office. As Salisbury, who became foreign secretary as well as prime minister, was in the House of Lords, Curzon became the government's chief foreign policy spokesman in the Commons. In spite of his chief's secretive ways and reluctance to discuss matters with his deputy, he was successful in the role of presenting and defending the government's position. And although he chafed at his inability to influence policy towards Africa and the French empire, he sometimes had the satisfaction of seeing his views prevail in Asia. Convinced that withdrawal from Chitral on India's north-west frontier would lead to a Russian occupation of the area, in 1895 he managed to persuade the government to retain a British force there. He was equally successful three years later in convincing a reluctant cabinet that, following the German and Russian occupation of two Chinese ports, Britain's interests required acceptance of a Chinese offer to lease a third port in the area, Weihaiwei.

Viceroy of India Although Curzon could have expected to join the cabinet at the next reshuffle, he had decided several years earlier that, before aiming for the highest offices of state at home, he wanted to be viceroy of India. Accordingly, he wrote lengthy letters to Salisbury pointing out that he had been preparing himself for the post for many years and arguing that the Indian climate and conditions of work required a youthful and vigorous viceroy. The prime minister kept him waiting for a year but in 1898 recommended him to Queen Victoria as Lord Elgin's successor. A recurrence of his back troubles made it doubtful whether he could take up the post, but a specialist's over-optimistic forecast persuaded Salisbury to allow the appointment to stand. In September Curzon visited the queen at Balmoral and shortly afterwards (11 November 1898) received the title of Baron Curzon in the peerage of Ireland, a device which left him the option of returning to the House of Commons after his term of office. He and his family left Britain before Christmas and on 6 January 1899, a few days before his fortieth birthday, he was proclaimed viceroy in Calcutta's Government House, a magnificent building based on the plan of Kedleston.

The viceroy's constitutional superior was Lord George Hamilton, the wise and gentle secretary of state for India, who was responsible to the cabinet and to parliament for the actions of the Indian government. But Curzon was as impatient of control from London as he was of inefficiency among his subordinates in India. He believed his duty was to be head not only of his council and the government but of all the departments as well. Bent on reforming every aspect of British rule in India, he began with the secretariats and the provincial governments, slashing his way through bureaucratic procedures and rapidly increasing the turnover of business. 'Efficiency of administration', he proclaimed, was 'a synonym for the contentment of the governed' (L. G. Fraser, *India under Curzon and After*, 1911, 214). In his pursuit of reform he acquired a reputation for trampling on the feelings of officials. But Hamilton, confronted with conflicting evidence about the viceroy's popularity, understood the cause: 'the strong, self-reliant men' recognized in Curzon a 'master mind', but the mediocrities feared and disliked him (Hamilton to Godley, 30 Aug 1901, BL OIOC, Kilbracken MS 102/6b).

On his arrival in Bombay, Curzon announced that he had come to India 'to hold the scales even' between the different races and religions of the country, and later he could claim accurately that he had 'never wavered in a strict and inflexible justice between the two races'. He also insisted privately that his first duty was to the people of India and that he would rather resign than sacrifice their interests. But justice and good government for the people did not mean in Curzon's view that they should be allowed to participate at a senior level in either process. Like many of his predecessors, he believed that their interests were best served by their traditional rulers, the British and the native princes. He failed to see that the Indian National Congress, founded in 1885, was producing a new nationalist élite, and he dismissed it as a small, noisy, middle-class movement, which he refused to consider as a future partner in the administration of India.

Although Congress resented Curzon's refusal to take it seriously, its leaders praised both his early reforms and his insistence on equal justice. They particularly applauded his tough stand on indiscipline in the army. After incidents resulting in both cases in the death of an Indian, he insisted on collective punishment for two regiments, the west Kent and the 9th lancers, which had tried to hush up the crimes of their soldiers. This action was strongly resented by the army and its supporters in Britain. As the foreign editor of *The Times*, Valentine Chirol, observed to a later viceroy, 'no one had ever challenged unpopularity among his own people so fearlessly as [Curzon] did in his endeavours … to secure even justice for Indians against Europeans' (Chirol to Hardinge, 12 May 1915, CUL, Hardinge MSS).

Curzon's first year and a half in India were overshadowed by famine and plague. He twice visited the stricken areas of western India and handled the crisis with an energy and efficiency that greatly reduced the degree of suffering. By the spring of 1900, 5 million people were receiving relief, but the mortality rate had only marginally increased. The crisis stimulated the viceroy's determination to extend the irrigated area of the subcontinent, which he did, especially in the semi-desert wastelands of the Punjab. Among his notable agricultural reforms were the Co-operative Credit Societies Act (1904), which was the first attempt to solve the problem of peasant indebtedness, and the Punjab Land Alienation Act (1905), which prevented moneylenders from taking a holding in settlement of debt.

The viceroy's reforms encompassed every aspect of Indian life from the police and the railways to education and conservation. After presiding over an educational conference in Simla in 1901, he set up a commission to visit the universities of India and produce a report that would form the basis of new legislation. The conclusions of the report were incorporated in the Universities Act of 1904, a measure much criticized by Indian nationalists at the time but one which was later recognized as an important reform of the university system. The same year saw the passing of the Ancient Monuments Bill, perhaps the most far-sighted of Curzon's reforms. He created a directorate-general of archaeology, multiplied the restoration budget by a factor of eight, and personally oversaw repairs to monuments all over India. His restoration of the Taj Mahal and the other monuments of Agra gave him much satisfaction. 'If I had done nothing else in India', he told his wife, 'I have written my name here, and the letters are a living joy' (4 April 1905, Lady Alexandra Metcalfe MSS, priv. coll.).

The viceroy's administrative reforms included the creation of the North-West Frontier province, which was detached from the Punjab, a satisfactory settlement of the Berar question with the nizam of Hyderabad, and the controversial partition of Bengal, a measure that was revoked, to Curzon's fury, by the British government in 1911. In foreign affairs he was assertive, urging the establishment of a British protectorate of Kuwait and successfully preventing the growth of French influence in Muscat. But the home government, perturbed by these ambitions, resisted his demands for a more vigorous Persian policy. It was not until 1902 that the foreign secretary, Lord Lansdowne, accepted Curzon's advice by warning Russia not to interfere in southern Persia. The following year Lansdowne further pleased the viceroy by declaring that Britain would resist the establishment of a naval base by any foreign power in the Persian Gulf. But Curzon was less successful in his efforts to persuade London to take a firmer line with the amir of Afghanistan and the Dalai Lama in Tibet.

In January 1903 a vast durbar was held in Delhi to celebrate the accession of King Edward VII. Planned entirely by the viceroy, this splendiferous occasion has often been seen as the apogee of the British empire in India. It was also something of a turning point in the viceroyalty. Despite occasional arguments, the relationship between viceroy and secretary of state had been a successful one for over four years; indeed, Curzon recognized that Hamilton had been a wise counsellor and an important ally in the programme of reforms. But in September 1903 Arthur Balfour, who had succeeded Lord Salisbury as prime minister, replaced Hamilton with St John Brodrick, the viceroy's oldest friend. This change, together with the appointment of Lord Kitchener as commander-in-chief in India, proved disastrous for Curzon. Had he returned to England at the end of his five-year term, neither would have caused him much trouble. But he was tempted to stay on and see his reforms in action. His wife and friends repeatedly urged him to return after five years and prepare to lead the Conservatives after Balfour's retirement. But adamant that his duty lay in India, he persuaded the prime minister to grant him a second shorter term from 1904. Balfour later regarded his assent as one of the greatest mistakes of his premiership.

In January 1904 Lady Curzon, who was expecting their third child, sailed with her daughters to England. But her husband decided to remain in India for the legislative season in Calcutta. One of his principal occupations was the study of the Bengal question. The successful settlement of the Berar problem had prompted him to examine the issue of provincial boundaries, and he had concluded that Bengal, with a population almost double that of Britain, would be governed more efficiently if it was divided in two. The scheme was finally sanctioned by Brodrick in June 1905, and the new province of East Bengal and Assam, which had a Muslim majority, was inaugurated. This policy, which Bengali Hindus regarded as an attempt to weaken Congress, lost the viceroy his popularity with that nationalist élite that had hitherto applauded his reforms and his stand on equality of justice between the races.

Curzon sailed for England at the end of April, leaving Lord Ampthill as viceroy until his return. He was appointed lord warden of the Cinque Ports, an honorary post, and on arrival embarked with enthusiasm on the restoration of Walmer Castle, which came with the position. This enthusiasm was quickly dissipated by his wife's long and desperate illness at the end of the summer; for several weeks she hovered between life and death before eventually beginning a slow recovery. Meanwhile the home government had at last sanctioned Francis Younghusband's mission to Tibet, which Curzon had advocated as the only way of forcing the Tibetans to honour past agreements. But when Younghusband extracted a favourable treaty from the Tibetans, he was repudiated by Brodrick on the grounds that he had exceeded his instructions, an action which exacerbated the deteriorating relations between Curzon and his old friend. Their friendship soon foundered altogether over the future of the military department in India.

The struggle with Kitchener The Indian army was administered by the commander-in-chief, who was its executive head, and the military member, a major-general on the viceroy's council responsible for transport, supplies, and other administrative matters. This division of responsibility had been accepted by Lord Roberts and all previous commanders-in-chief, who had recognized that the task of running the army required the labours of the two men and their respective departments. They had realized, moreover, that if the commander took the field in wartime, it was vital for the viceroy to have a second military adviser at hand.

On taking over as commander-in-chief at the end of 1902, Kitchener told Curzon he wished to abolish the post of military member and add its responsibilities to his own. It was intolerable, he argued, that a subordinate military authority should be in a position either to criticize or to recommend the commander's proposals. After the viceroy expressed his opposition to the scheme, Kitchener embarked on a long and surreptitious campaign to win the support of influential circles in Britain. Through contacts in the press, secret telegrams, and a network of correspondents, he managed to convert many crucial figures—notably the prime minister and the secretary of state for India—to his view that the military department should disappear. Although suspicious that Kitchener was plotting behind his back, the viceroy remained unaware of the extent of the intrigue.

While Curzon was on leave in England in 1904, Kitchener managed to induce the government in London to transfer the control of supply and transport from the military department to himself. Shortly afterwards he decided

to resign on the grounds that even the reduced power of the department made his position 'impossible'. Although he was persuaded temporarily to withdraw his resignation, the home government was alarmed by the threat and anxious to accede to his demands. Weak and unpopular, the cabinet therefore warned Curzon through Brodrick that Kitchener's resignation 'would be regarded more anxiously at this moment than any other'.

Although his wife remained ill in London, Curzon returned to India in December 1904 and took over from Ampthill. He brought with him an advance copy of a dispatch from London asking the Indian government to examine the issue of the military department. In March 1905 the viceroy's council decided unanimously—with the exception of Kitchener—that the department should be preserved, and dispatched its reply to London. Several weeks earlier, however, the commander-in-chief had secretly sent his own reply to his supporters in England who had distributed it to the prime minister, the India Office, and various sections of the press. In April Brodrick formed a committee, consisting almost entirely of Kitchener's partisans, to settle the matter, and the following month he sent the government's verdict to India. Although the secretary of state backed Kitchener's case for abolition, all the experts invited to testify before the committee were opposed, and Brodrick's dispatch announced a compromise whereby the military department was replaced by a much weaker military supply department.

On reading the government's dispatch in mid-June, Curzon's first instinct was to resign. But he was persuaded by his colleagues on the council to try to induce Kitchener to agree to modifications of the dispatch. To the astonishment of his supporters in Britain, the commander-in-chief accepted modifications that would have virtually restored the military member to his former position. The viceroy therefore decided not to resign, a decision he later deeply regretted. In the following weeks Kitchener, encouraged by Brodrick, gradually reneged on his agreement, and Curzon became convinced that the home government was trying to force his resignation. When the secretary of state refused to accept the viceroy's nominee, General Barrow, as the new military supply member, Curzon concluded that he did not have the confidence of the government and telegraphed his resignation. The prime minister accepted it on 16 August 1905 and announced the appointment of Lord Minto as his successor. Staying on to welcome the prince of Wales to Bombay in early November, Curzon finally left India, an angry and embittered man, on 18 November. But in his farewell speech at Bombay's Byculla Club, he delivered a notable example of his particular brand of oratory and of his view of the imperial mission.

To fight for the right, to abhor the imperfect, the unjust, or the mean, to swerve neither to the right hand nor to the left, to care nothing for flattery or applause or odium or abuse—it is so easy to have any of them in India—never to let your enthusiasm be soured or your courage grow dim, but to remember that the Almighty has placed your hand on the greatest of His ploughs, in whose furrow the nations of the future are germinating and taking shape, to drive the blade a little forward in your time, and to feel that somewhere among these millions you have left a little justice or happiness or prosperity, a sense of manliness or moral dignity, a spring of patriotism, a dawn of intellectual enlightenment, or a stirring of duty, where it did not before exist—that is enough, that is the Englishman's justification in India. It is good enough for his watchword while he is here, for his epitaph when he is gone. I have worked for no other aim. Let India be my judge. (T. Raleigh, ed., *Lord Curzon in India*, 1906, 589–90)

The viceroy's resignation has subsequently been attributed to personal antagonism between Kitchener and himself, between two masterful men each determined to have his own way. British India's judgement at the time remains more valid. There the conflict was seen as essentially between civilian and military control of the army, a conflict which ended in victory for the military because of a prolonged intrigue which drew in the two crucial figures in the cabinet. Curzon lost because, unlike his opponent, he had refused to become a conspirator.

Bereavement and opposition Despite the support of King Edward VII, the fallen viceroy received no public recognition for his remarkable services in India. Balfour's refusal to recommend an earldom was repeated by Sir Henry Campbell-Bannerman, the Liberal leader asked to form a government on the day after Curzon's return to England. In deference to the wishes of the king and the advice of his doctors, Curzon did not stand in the general election of 1906 and thus found himself excluded from public life for the first time in twenty years. It was at this time, the nadir of his career, that he suffered the greatest personal loss of his life. Mary Curzon had never fully recovered from her nearly fatal illness and in July 1906 she fell ill again, deteriorated quickly, and died in her husband's arms. She was buried in the church at Kedleston, where Curzon designed his memorial for her, a lovely Gothic chapel added to the north side of the nave. Although he was neither a devout nor a conventional churchman, Curzon retained a naïve religious faith; in later years he sometimes said that he was not afraid of death because it would enable him to join Mary in heaven.

As Lord Scarsdale still occupied Kedleston, his eldest son set up house with his three daughters at Hackwood near Basingstoke and lived there and at 1 Carlton House Terrace, a London mansion he had bought with his father-in-law's money before going to India. In March 1907 he defeated Lord Rosebery in a contest for the chancellorship of Oxford University and threw himself so energetically into the cause of university reform that critics complained he was ruling Oxford like an Indian province. On a visit to South Africa in 1909, where he was supposed to be convalescing after a motor accident, he wrote a memorandum of book length called *Principles and Methods of University Reform*. Although his ideas were considered too radical by Oxford's governing body, most of them were endorsed by a royal commission after the First World War and were subsequently enacted.

In January 1908 Curzon finally entered the House of Lords with the help of Lord Lansdowne, who persuaded a sufficient number of Irish lords to elect him as one of their representative peers. He grew to like the Lords, where his stately oratory was perhaps more appropriate than in the Commons, but he remained a strong advocate of its reform and persistently urged a reduction in its hereditary membership. Still bitter about his treatment in India, he stayed aloof from his Unionist colleagues and for eighteen months seldom spoke except in debates on Asian subjects; two of his most powerful speeches were attacks on the Anglo-Russian convention of 1907 and the system of Indian military administration set up to please Lord Kitchener. Domestic politics failed to interest him—he remained an agnostic on the issue of tariff reform—until Lloyd George delivered his radical budget of 1909. Then he supported the stance of his party leaders and spoke in favour of Lansdowne's motion to reject it in the Lords. The success of the motion led to the dissolution of parliament and to the two inconclusive elections of 1910.

In the absence of Balfour, who was ill, the first Unionist campaign was dominated by Curzon, who was fighting his first election since 1895 and who relished a highly publicized speech-making tour of Lancashire. After the elections he scoffed at the Liberal government's threat to restrict the House of Lords' veto on legislation to two years and unwisely advised his party both 'to fight in the last ditch' and to dare Asquith to create new peers in order to carry the Parliament Bill through the upper house. As soon as he realized, however, that Asquith was not bluffing, he changed his mind and attempted to persuade his colleagues that it was preferable to retain the house with a limited veto than to provoke its virtual destruction. Throwing himself with characteristic energy into battle against the 'Diehards', who were determined to defeat the Liberals in the Lords, he persuaded enough Unionists to support the bill or abstain for the government to carry the day. This action, which ended the constitutional crisis, earned him the lasting enmity of the Unionist right.

Curzon, who was finally made an earl in the coronation honours of 1911, was always an administrator rather than a parliamentarian. Opposition politics left him restless and searching for causes he could pursue. In addition to his work at Oxford, he became president of the National League for Opposing Women's Suffrage, but most of his causes were geographical, artistic, or conservationist. In 1911 he became president of the Royal Geographical Society and raised enough funds to buy it new premises in South Kensington. In the same year he became a trustee of the National Gallery and devised a far-sighted scheme, which was unfortunately not adopted for many years, to exempt owners from death duties on their houses and paintings if they undertook to keep their collections intact and opened them to the public. He also became a prominent figure in the Royal Society for the Protection of Birds and one of the most enlightened conservationists in the country. In 1911 he bought Tattershall Castle in Lincolnshire, which he restored and bequeathed to the nation; a few years later he did the same on a grander scale with Bodiam Castle in Sussex. His subsequent restoration of both Kedleston and Montacute House in Somerset makes him a unique figure in the history of the National Trust, which by 1990 owned all four properties.

The First World War In May 1915 Curzon was one of the Unionist politicians invited to join a coalition cabinet under Asquith. Although he was given the title of lord privy seal, he was effectively a minister without portfolio, a position which he found extremely frustrating. As a member of the Dardanelles committee, he urged the cabinet to introduce compulsory military service, he opposed the evacuation of the Gallipoli peninsula, and he advised against the Indian army's ill-fated advance on Baghdad during which the shortcomings of Kitchener's system were tragically demonstrated. (In 1917 a royal commission's report on the Mesopotamian campaign condemned the system and vindicated Curzon's stance of twelve years earlier.) At the beginning of 1916 he became a knight of the Garter and was appointed chairman of the Shipping Control Board, a committee which allocated shipping resources between the competing demands of the navy, the army, and the merchant marine. But he hankered after more demanding and imaginative work and hoped that Asquith would create an Air Ministry with himself at its head. Although the prime minister believed that such a ministry would increase friction between the Admiralty and the War Office, which jealously protected their own spheres of aerial activity, he did make Curzon president of a new Air Board in May 1916. Much of the rest of the year was spent trying to overcome the obstructiveness of the Admiralty, now headed by his old friend and adversary Balfour, but his views were eventually adopted and an Air Ministry was established in 1918.

By the end of 1916 all the Unionist ministers, including Curzon, had come to the conclusion that Asquith was too indecisive a prime minister to win the war. At a meeting on 3 December they decided that their leader, Andrew Bonar Law, should urge him to resign and inform him that, if he refused, all the Unionist ministers would resign themselves. Their private papers make it clear that at the time they expected Asquith to go and that Lloyd George would succeed him. But this was not made immediately obvious to the prime minister, who for two days believed he could carry on; only when he understood the decision taken on 3 December did he decide to surrender his office. The incident was subsequently misrepresented by Lord Beaverbrook and later historians who claimed that the Unionists had resigned in order to strengthen Asquith's hand against Lloyd George. After Curzon's death, Beaverbrook alleged that the former viceroy had seen Asquith on 4 December and assured him he would never serve under Lloyd George. This charge, which has done much damage to Curzon's reputation, is unfounded; a study of the documents reveals that there was no meeting between the two on 4 December and that Curzon could not have given the assurance.

In December 1916 Curzon became a member of Lloyd George's war cabinet. Three weeks later, on 2 January 1917, following a long love affair with the novelist Elinor *Glyn, he married the much younger Grace Elvina Trilla Duggan (1877–1958), daughter of Joseph Monroe Hinds, at

one time United States minister in Brazil, and widow of Alfred Duggan of Buenos Aires. But his second marriage was much less happy than his first. Grace was a fashionable society woman who loved horse-racing, and the couple's lack of common interests, together with their failure to produce an heir, led to a tempestuous relationship.

Curzon's work under Lloyd George was the most sustained, vital, and concentrated he had been required to do since leaving India. As lord president of the council, he was leader of the House of Lords, and as one of five members of the war cabinet, he was a key figure in the team meeting day after day to discuss and direct the main areas of the war effort. He was also Lloyd George's usual choice as chairman of innumerable subcommittees dealing with matters as diverse as timber, import restrictions, and a settlement for Ireland. Although he and the prime minister were never on close terms, he was the only man who remained in the cabinet throughout Lloyd George's premiership.

The war cabinet spent much of the summer of 1917 discussing military strategy and allowed itself to be persuaded by the military to sanction General Haig's disastrous autumn offensive which culminated in the slaughter at Passchendaele. It also had to deal with a number of Asian questions. Curzon was strongly opposed to Zionist aims in Palestine and argued that Jewish immigrants would not be able to establish a homeland there without expelling the indigenous Arabs. Although he managed to include a commitment to the 'non-Jewish communities' in the Balfour Declaration, he remained convinced that the policy was mistaken, 'the worst' of Britain's Middle East commitments and 'a striking contradiction of our publicly declared principles' (Curzon to Bonar Law, 14 Dec 1922, HLRO, Bonar Law MS 111/22/46). He was also anxious about any change of policy that might loosen the bonds between Britain and India. But he realized that the wartime atmosphere, stirred by the Russian Revolution and by what he called 'the free talk about liberty, democracy, nationality, and self-government which have become the common shibboleths of the Allies', meant that substantial concessions had to be made. Thus he did not dissent from the cabinet view that self-government within the British empire should be stated as their aim for India so long as it was made clear that it was 'under British guidance that this end must be pursued, and alone can be achieved', and that the essential safeguards of British justice and power were not weakened (Curzon's memoranda to imperial war cabinet, 17 June 1917, and war cabinet, 2 July 1917, BL OIOC, Curzon MS 112/164).

In August 1917 the government declared its aim to be 'the gradual development of self-governing institutions in India under the aegis of the Crown'. Curzon did not interpret this to mean a handover of power within the foreseeable future but a developing process that would take generations or even centuries. He was thus horrified when Edwin Montagu, the secretary of state for India, quickly produced a scheme, later known as the diarchy, whereby in each province elected native ministers would run matters such as health, education, and agriculture, while the local British governor would retain control over finance, the police, and other 'reserved' matters. Believing that the plan would 'lead by stages of increasing speed to the ultimate disruption of the Empire' (Curzon to Montagu, 25 July 1918, Cambridge, Trinity College, Montagu MS AS 3/2/15), Curzon refused to serve on the cabinet committee appointed to prepare legislation. When the bill came up for its second reading in December 1919, he told the Lords it was a 'daring experiment' which was unlikely to lead to better government, but he accepted it as necessary in that era when people preferred to govern themselves badly than be 'even superbly governed by another race' (*Hansard 5L*, 37, 12 Dec 1919, 1048–9).

After the conclusion of the armistice in November 1918, Curzon rose in the House of Lords to make an eloquent appraisal of Britain's role in the war. He declared:

> The British flag never flew over a more powerful or a more united Empire than now; Britons never had better cause to look the world in the face; never did our voice count for more in the councils of the nations, or in determining the future destinies of mankind.   (*Hansard 5L*, 32, 18 Nov 1918, 162)

Curzon's experience of ceremonies made him a natural choice as an organizer of events and memorials to celebrate victory and commemorate the dead. He organized the peace celebrations in the summer of 1919, he supervised the erection of the cenotaph in Whitehall, he designed its unveiling ceremony—a restrained and moving ritual centred on a two-minute silence and the haunting lament of the 'Last Post'—and he planned another ceremony for the burial of an unknown soldier in Westminster Abbey. These events aroused such strong feelings that popular opinion demanded an annual service at the Cenotaph, and Curzon was asked to devise the remembrance day service, one of his finest and most lasting achievements.

The Foreign Office In January 1919, in addition to his other duties, Curzon was asked to take charge of the Foreign Office while Lloyd George and Balfour (who remained foreign secretary) were pursuing a peace treaty in Paris. The division of responsibility between Curzon and Balfour was unclear, and an unsatisfactory situation was further complicated by Lloyd George's insistence on dealing with areas of the world which interested him. When the prime minister formed a larger cabinet in October 1919, Curzon and Balfour exchanged posts, but the new foreign secretary remained leader of the House of Lords. Lloyd George, who had negotiated the treaty of Versailles, largely retained control of affairs in Europe and Russia, while Curzon dealt with the rest of the world. This division of labour between a prime minister who had achieved the status of international statesman and a foreign secretary with unparalleled Asian experience was, in the hectic post-war years, not unreasonable. The partnership broke down, however, when they disagreed on the most crucial Euro-Asian issue, the peace settlement with Turkey.

Curzon personally directed negotiations which led to the Anglo-Persian agreement in August 1919 and was delighted with an outcome that seemed to cement British influence in Tehran. He was thus disgusted when the Persian government, although heavily bribed by the British, failed to ratify the agreement which was subsequently discarded by Reza Khan after his *coup d'état* in February 1921. In the Middle East he favoured a policy of setting up independent Arab states under British tutelage, as happened in Iraq. But he acquiesced with great reluctance in the decisions of the San Remo conference to award the Palestine mandate to Britain and the Syrian mandate to France. In Egypt he was surprised by the strength of local nationalism but soon realized that the government had no option but to accept the conclusion of the Milner commission, which recommended the abolition of Britain's protectorate and the establishment of an independent constitutional monarchy. Against the fierce opposition of both Lloyd George and Churchill, his views eventually prevailed, and in March 1922 Egypt was recognized as an independent monarchy under her sultan, henceforth known as King Fuad I.

Early in 1919 Curzon circulated three memoranda to the cabinet outlining his views on a settlement with Turkey. They contained two principal arguments: that a peace treaty must be negotiated swiftly and that, as a result of its defeat, Turkey should lose its European territory but be left in possession of its Anatolian heartland. He was opposed to landing European troops in Asian Turkey and was particularly scornful of the suggestion to install the Greeks in Smyrna. Lloyd George, however, was passionately pro-Greek and even encouraged the Smyrna occupation. Again the prime minister's policy prevailed at San Remo where the conference decided on a settlement— later embodied in the treaty of Sèvres—that turned the straits into a neutral zone and gave Greece eastern Thrace, various islands in the Aegean, and control of the Smyrna area for five years, after which the local population would decide its future. As Curzon predicted, this solution was completely unacceptable to Turkish public opinion which soon coalesced behind the nationalist rebellion of Mustapha Kemal, the future Atatürk.

In 1921, during which he received a marquessate, the foreign secretary spent much of his time trying to persuade the Greeks that the occupation of Smyrna was a blunder that would end in their military defeat. In March 1922 he was laid low by a combination of phlebitis, thrombosis, and lymphangitis which kept him out of action for five months. He returned to his office in August just in time for the long-predicted débâcle in Asia Minor when the Turkish nationalists overwhelmed the Greek army, sacked Smyrna, and advanced northwards to threaten allied forces occupying Chanak in the neutral zone on the Asiatic shore of the straits. At a cabinet meeting on Friday 15 September, Curzon warned against trying to stop the Turkish advance by military means. But the following day, while he was at Hackwood, Lloyd George and Churchill issued a communiqué to the press warning of war if the 'violent and hostile Turkish aggression' succeeded in seizing control of the straits. The effect of this bellicose statement was to persuade France and Italy to withdraw their forces from the threatened areas of the neutral zone and leave the way open for a Turkish confrontation with the much smaller British force under the control of General Sir Charles Harington. Furious with his colleagues' 'flamboyant manifesto', which he first saw in the newspapers, Curzon insisted on going alone to Paris to restore a united allied position with the French premier, M. Raymond Poincaré. After a long and bad-tempered meeting, Curzon and Poincaré agreed on terms to offer Kemal, including the statements that they 'viewed with favour' Turkey's claim to eastern Thrace and that they would remove their troops from Constantinople after a peace settlement.

But Curzon's success was undone by news of a revolution in Greece, which encouraged the anti-Turkish faction in the cabinet, led by Lloyd George, Churchill, and Lord Birkenhead, to make another belligerent gesture. Outraged by Kemal's refusal to respect the neutral zone, they persuaded the cabinet on 29 September to send an ultimatum threatening to open fire on the Turks unless they left the zone. War was averted largely by the good sense of Harington, who did not deliver the ultimatum, and by the vigour of the foreign secretary, who finally convinced his colleagues that the problem could be solved by diplomacy. Negotiations between the allies and the Turks opened at Mudanya, and the crisis appeared to have passed when a combination of fresh Turkish demands and French acquiescence again threatened conflict. Among other things, the Turks now insisted on occupying eastern Thrace immediately, in advance of a peace treaty and without guarantees for the minorities. As the French commander on the spot was prepared to concede on all issues, Curzon again crossed the channel to patch up a united position with Poincaré. After another heated meeting, allied unity was largely restored on the basis of the British formula. On 11 October the Turks signed the Mudanya convention by which they agreed to withdraw from the neutral zone until after a peace treaty, and accepted the proposal that eastern Thrace should be administered by the allies for a month before the Turks returned.

On 10 October the Conservative leader, Austen Chamberlain, summoned his ministerial colleagues to a meeting to reaffirm their decision to fight a general election under Lloyd George. Curzon was one of a small minority who opposed the scheme, arguing that such a move made before the party's meeting of the National Union of Conservative Associations (which was known to be hostile to the continuation of the coalition) would be regarded as a transparent trick; he was also worried that an election would dislocate foreign policy on the eve of a crucial conference on the Near East. The election talk came at a time when the foreign secretary was feeling increasingly disenchanted with his association with Lloyd George. For four years he had submitted to the prime minister's meddling in foreign affairs and the humiliations that these had sometimes entailed. On 14 October 1922, just after the Chanak crisis, Lloyd George made a violent speech in Manchester denouncing the barbarity of the Turks, and on the same day Curzon discovered that he had been secretly intriguing with an Italian emissary. The foreign secretary

decided he had had enough. Three days later he placed his resignation in Lloyd George's hands and the following day he was one of several Conservatives who urged their former leader, Andrew Bonar Law, to come out of retirement and fight the election at the head of the anti-coalitionist faction. On 19 October Law easily defeated Chamberlain in a vote at a meeting of MPs at the Carlton Club and forced the government's resignation. In the ensuing week he became Conservative leader, formed his cabinet (with Curzon still at the Foreign Office), and dissolved parliament. A comfortable Conservative victory in November allowed the foreign secretary to set off for Lausanne in search of a peace with Turkey.

The conference of Lausanne was Curzon's finest moment as foreign secretary. Through diplomatic skill and force of personality, he dominated the eleven weeks of the proceedings, dealing with his allies, France and Italy, as shrewdly as he managed the Turks. His achievements were embodied in the treaty of Lausanne of 1923 which secured the freedom of the straits, achieved a relatively high level of regional stability, and, by restoring Turkish sovereignty to the Turkish heartland, enabled the new country to make the transition from enfeebled empire to nation state. It was the most successful and the most lasting of the post-war treaties.

In May 1923 it was diagnosed that the prime minister was suffering from cancer of the throat, and on Whit Sunday he resigned. Curzon, who earlier had been appointed to act as deputy prime minister in Law's absence, confidently expected to be his successor. Law, who also thought he would be succeeded by his foreign secretary, gave no advice to the king, but two members of his entourage misrepresented his views and gave the king's private secretary, Lord Stamfordham, the impression that he favoured the chancellor of the exchequer, Stanley Baldwin. Balfour advised the monarch that it was essential for the prime minister to be in the House of Commons, but in private admitted that he was prejudiced against Curzon. George V, who shared this prejudice, was grateful for the advice and authorized Stamfordham to summon the foreign secretary to London and inform him that Baldwin would be chosen. Believing that he was being summoned to form a government, Curzon was devastated by the news. His first instinct was to retire from public life, but he was persuaded to stay on as foreign secretary and a few days later he proposed Baldwin's election as leader of the Conservative Party.

For the rest of the year the new prime minister allowed Curzon to form his foreign policy virtually unhindered. Most of the issues that needed to be dealt with were European. He scored one minor success in forcing the Soviet government to remove certain of its agents from Asian capitals and another in helping to end the Italian occupation of Corfu. But the most critical issues were the questions of French security and the reparation payments the allies had imposed on Germany four years earlier at Versailles. Although the government strove to be neutral between the two countries, Curzon considered Poincaré's stance to be unreasonable and helped defeat his various schemes for weakening Germany, notably the attempt to set up separatist states in the Rhineland and the Palatinate. He also did much towards solving the reparations issue by urging the formation of a committee with United States participation to study the question: this led the following year to the Dawes plan and French withdrawal from the Ruhr, and in 1925 to the Locarno pact.

In November 1923 Curzon opposed Baldwin's decision to call an election on the issue of protection and correctly forecast an electoral reverse. The first Labour government was formed in January 1924, and Curzon vacated the Foreign Office after a tenure which, including those first nine months under Balfour, had lasted for almost exactly five years. After nearly nine years of continuous service in the cabinet, Curzon embarked on new duties as leader of the opposition peers. But he was able to devote much of 1924 to his other interests, restoring Kedleston and replanting the garden, serving as chairman of the trustees of the National Gallery, and completing one of his finest books, a study of Calcutta and the viceroys which was posthumously published under the confusing title *British Government in India*. In the previous year he had published *Tales of Travel*, a charming collection of memoirs and essays which attracted good reviews and successful sales. A similar volume, *Leaves from a Viceroy's Notebook*, was brought out after his death.

After his electoral victory in November 1924, Baldwin formed his second government and decided that the state of Anglo-French relations would be improved by a change at the Foreign Office. Curzon reacted indignantly to the news that the new foreign secretary would be Austen Chamberlain, but he suppressed his initial desire to retire from politics and agreed to serve as lord president of the council and leader of the House of Lords. In March 1925, while staying the night at Cambridge, he suffered a severe haemorrhage of the bladder. He was taken to London the next day, and on 9 March an operation was performed. But he knew it was the end, that the suffering and overburdened body, which he had pushed so hard for so long, was giving up. He died at 1 Carlton House Terrace, London, on 20 March 1925 at the age of sixty-six. His coffin, made from the same tree at Kedleston that had encased Mary, was taken to Westminster Abbey and from there to his ancestral home, where he was interred beside Mary in the family vault on 26 March. In the parliamentary tributes Asquith encapsulated essential truths when he described Curzon as 'a great and unselfish servant of the state … always ready in that service to "scorn delights and live laborious days", a man who pursued high ambitions by none but worthy means' (*Hansard 5L*, 60, 23 March 1925, 614).

Assessment Few statesmen have experienced such vicissitudes of fortune in both their public and their personal lives. Curzon's career was an almost unparalleled blend of triumph and disappointment. Although he was the last and in many ways the greatest of Victorian viceroys, his term of office ended in resignation, empty of recognition and barren of reward. After ten years in the political wilderness, he returned to government yet, in spite of his knowledge and experience of the world, he was unable to assert himself fully as foreign secretary until the last weeks of Lloyd George's premiership. And finally, after he had restored his reputation at Lausanne, his last ambition was thwarted by George V.

Curzon was one of the outstanding political intellects of his generation, yet his influence in later life seldom matched his ability. This was partly caused by his failure to solve the problem that marred both his life and his career—the problem of human relations, of how to manage other people. It was also caused by the general perception of him as an anachronism, a Victorian viceroy at a time when political rights for Indians became an issue, an Edwardian foreign secretary at a time when foreign policy was no longer a matter of stately rejoinders between the chancelleries of Europe but a hectic round of conferences trying to solve the problems thrown up by the First World War, dismantling empires, creating new nations, redrawing dozens of frontiers in Europe, Asia, and Africa.

But history can be kinder to Curzon than his contemporaries were. His viceregal administration needs no apology: if he was blinkered about Indian nationalism, he was ahead of his time on matters of conservation and education, and the disasters of the Mesopotamian campaign vindicated his opposition to Kitchener's scheme. As foreign secretary, he revealed a similar blend of foresight and antiquated ideas, but again the final verdict must be positive. His contemporaries might jeer at certain policies, but he was the only minister far-sighted enough to see that the Balfour Declaration would lead to decades of Arab–Jewish conflict, that Lloyd George's pro-Greek policy would lead to a bloodbath in Anatolia, and that the Montagu–Chelmsford reforms would lead to the rapid breakup of the British empire. As with his later European policies, he did not of course receive praise for prophecies fulfilled while he was out of office or after his death. But they should be placed to the credit of a man too often assumed to have been gazing permanently and despondently into the past. DAVID GILMOUR

Sources D. Gilmour, *Curzon* (1994) · K. Rose, *Curzon: a most superior person* (1969) · D. Dilks, *Curzon in India*, 2 vols. (1969–70) · Earl of Ronaldshay [L. J. L. Dundas], *The life of Lord Curzon*, 3 vols. (1928) · H. Nicolson, *Curzon: the last phase* (1934) · N. Nicolson, *Mary Curzon* (1977) · G. Curzon, *Reminiscences* (1955) · *Lady Curzon's India*, ed. J. Bradley (1985) · P. King, *The viceroy's fall* (1986) · W. Lawrence, *The India we served* (1928) · *CGPLA Eng. & Wales* (1925)

Archives BL OIOC, corresp. and papers · Duke U., corresp. relating to Victoria Memorial Hall, Calcutta · Lincs. Arch., corresp. and papers relating to Tattershall Castle · PRO, corresp., FO 800/28 147–158 · University of Alberta, corresp. and papers relating to Victoria Memorial Hall, Calcutta | All Souls Oxf., letters to Sir William Anson · BL, corresp. with Arthur James Balfour, Add. MSS 49732–49734 · BL, corresp. with Lord Cecil, Add. MS 51077 · BL, corresp. with Lord D'Abernon, Add. MSS 48923–48933 · BL, corresp. with Sir Charles Dilke, Add. MS 43893 · BL, letters to W. E. Gladstone, Add. MSS 44456–44526 · BL, letters to Sir Edward Hamilton, Add. MSS 48626–48627 · BL, corresp. with Macmillans, Add. MS 55245 · BL, corresp. with Lord Midleton, Add. MSS 50072–50077 · BL, corresp. with Lord Northcliffe, Add. MS 62153 · BL, corresp. with Society of Authors, Add. MSS 56685 · BL OIOC, corresp. with Lord Ampthill, MS Eur. E 233 · BL OIOC, letters to Sir Edmund Barrow, MS Eur. E 420 · BL OIOC, Cotlan MSS · BL OIOC, corresp. with Sir

Henry Cotton, MS Eur. D 1202 · BL OIOC, letters to Sir William Foster, MS Eur. E 242 · BL OIOC, corresp. with Sir Frederic Fryer, MS Eur. E 355 · BL OIOC, letters to Arthur Godley, MS Eur. F 102 · BL OIOC, corresp. with Lord George Hamilton, MSS Eur. C 125–126, D 508–510, F 123 · BL OIOC, corresp. with Sir Terence Keyes, MS Eur. F 131 · BL OIOC, corresp. with Lord Kitchener, MS Eur. D 686 · BL OIOC, letters to Sir Walter Lawrence, MS Eur. F 143 · BL OIOC, corresp. with Lord Morley, MS Eur. D 573 · BL OIOC, corresp. with Sir Henry Richards, MS Eur. F 122 · BL OIOC, corresp. with Sir Herbert White · BL OIOC, corresp. with Sir Francis Younghusband, MS Eur. F 197 · Bodl. Oxf., letters to Herbert Asquith · Bodl. Oxf., corresp. with Geoffrey Dawson · Bodl. Oxf., letters to George William Forrest · Bodl. Oxf., corresp. with H. A. Gwynne · Bodl. Oxf., letters to Sir Henry Miers · Bodl. Oxf., corresp. with Lord Milner · Bodl. Oxf., corresp. with Sir Horace Rumbold · Bodl. Oxf., corresp. with Lord Selborne · CAC Cam., corresp. with Lord Randolph Churchill · CAC Cam., corresp. with Lord Esher · CAC Cam., corresp. with Alfred Lyttelton · CAC Cam., corresp. with Sir Cecil Spring-Rice · Carlisle Castle, Howard of Penrith MSS · CKS, letters to Aretas Akers-Douglas · CUL, corresp. with Lord Hardinge · CUL, letters to Sir Samuel Hoare · CUL, Lyttelton MSS · Cumbria AS, Carlisle, letters to Lord Howard of Penrith · Duke U., Perkins L., letters to Sir Albert Schindler · Glos. RO, letters to Sir Michael Hicks Beach · Hatfield, Salisbury MSS · Herts. ALS, letters to Lady Desborough · HLRO, corresp. with J. C. C. Davidson and Andrew Bonar Law · HLRO, corresp. with David Lloyd George · HLRO, letters to Herbert Samuel · HLRO, corresp. with John St Loe Strachey · IWM, corresp. with Sir Henry Wilson · King's AC Cam., letters to Oscar Browning · Lincs. Arch., letters to F. M. Yglesias relating to purchase of Tattershall Castle · Lpool RO, corresp. with earl of Derby · NA Scot., corresp. with Philip Kerr · NAM, letters to Lord Roberts · NL Scot., corresp. with Lord Minto · NL Scot., corresp. mainly with Lord Rosebery · NRA, priv. coll., letters to Sir Edward Clarke · Nuffield Oxf., corresp. with Lord Emmott · priv. coll., Lady Alexandra Metcalfe MSS · PRO, corresp. with Lord Midleton, PRO 30/67 · PRO, corresp. with Lord Kitchener, PRO 30/57, W0159 · RGS, corresp. with Royal Geographical Society · Scott Polar RI, letters to Robert and Kathleen Scott · SOAS, letters to Sir Henry Durand · U. Birm. L., corresp. with Austen Chamberlain · U. Leeds, Brotherton L., letters to Sir Edmund Gosse · U. Reading, corresp. with Lady Astor · Wellcome L., letters to Sir Thomas Barlow · Wilts. & Swindon RO, corresp. with Sir Michael Herbert · Wilts. & Swindon RO, corresp. with Lord Pembroke | FILM BFI NFTVA, news footage

Likenesses B. Stone, photograph, 1898, NPG · M. Prior, two pencil drawings, c.1903, BL OIOC · M. Beerbohm, caricature, 1908, AM Oxf. · M. Beerbohm, caricature, 1909, All Souls Oxf. · F. W. Pomery, statue, c.1912, Calcutta, India · P. de Laszlo, oils, 1913, All Souls Oxf. · P. de Laszlo, portrait, 1913, priv. coll. · G. Reid, oils, 1913, Government House, Calcutta, India · print, pubd 1913 (after unknown photograph), NPG · J. Cooke, oils, 1914 (after J. S. Sargent), NPG · H. von Herkomer, oils, 1914, Examination Schools, Oxford · J. S. Sargent, oils, 1914, RGS [see illus.] · W. H. Thornycroft, bronze statue, 1918, Victoria Memorial Hall, Calcutta, India · H. Furniss, pen-and-ink sketch, NPG · F. C. Gould, ink and watercolour sketch, V&A · London Stereoscopic Co., photograph, NPG · B. Mackennal, bronze statue, Carlton Gardens, London · B. Partridge, cartoon, NPG; repro. in *Punch* (8 Feb 1922) · B. Partridge, cartoon, NPG; repro. in *Punch* (16 May 1923) · Russell & Sons, photograph, NPG; repro. in *Our conservative and unionist statesmen*, vol. 4 · Spy [L. Ward], chromolithograph caricature, NPG; repro. in *VF* (18 June 1892) · Spy [L. Ward], drawing, NPG

Wealth at death £354,894 1s. 10d.: probate, 22 July 1925, CGPLA Eng. & Wales

Curzon, (Mary) Irene, *suo jure* Baroness Ravensdale, and Baroness Ravensdale of Kedleston (1896–1966), welfare worker, was born on 20 January 1896 at 4 Carlton House Gardens, London, the eldest of the three daughters of George Nathaniel *Curzon (1859–1925), and his first wife,

Mary Victoria Leiter (1870–1906) [see Curzon, Mary Victoria]. When Curzon was appointed viceroy of India in 1898—and created Baron Curzon of Kedleston—Irene, her four-month-old sister, Cynthia Blanche [see Mosley, Cynthia Blanche], and their mother sailed to India and Government House in Calcutta, where 600 servants awaited them. She returned in 1904 to England, where the youngest Curzon daughter, Alexandra Naldera, was born. In the family Irene was known as Ne-ne, Cynthia as Cimmie, and Alexandra as Baba.

When Curzon resigned as viceroy in 1905 he returned home and leased Hackwood, the huge house near Basingstoke that became the nearest thing to a family home his daughters knew. After their mother's early death in 1906 Irene and her younger sisters were brought up largely by a devoted nanny and educated by governesses. In 1911 Curzon was created Earl Curzon of Kedleston and Baron Ravensdale (with reversion to his daughters as well as heirs male) in the coronation honours. In the following year Irene was sent to be 'finished' in Dresden, then noted for its music, architecture, and general culture; it was here that her lifelong passion for music developed. In 1917 she began what was to be a lifetime of voluntary work when she first went to talk and sing to the boys of the Broad Street Club in the East End of London, to whom she gave a billiard table, and whom she visited weekly for the next forty years except when abroad.

Irene Curzon's coming-of-age party was in January 1917; with it came the right to the income from the money left in trust for her by her mother. By now she was passionate about fox-hunting and wished to take a hunting box at Melton Mowbray, a cause of arguments with her father, who did not wish to hand over her income to her. In July 1918 she escaped the difficulties of home life by going to France to do war work for the YMCA. On her return the financial disputes with her father began almost at once. After repeated attempts to come to an arrangement, she finally needed to have recourse to the law to obtain what was rightfully hers, resulting in an immediate and permanent breach with her father, whom from the age of twenty-five she never saw again.

Soon afterwards, in 1922, Irene Curzon began one of the journeys that punctuated her life, this time round the Middle East, where the orientalist Ronald Storrs, then governor of Jerusalem and Judea, proposed to her. Her dark good looks were of the sort that would have been admirably appropriate for the consort of an ambassador or a minister, although in contrast to her somewhat formidable exterior she was warm-hearted, loving, and emotional. She established herself at Melton Mowbray, at the heart of the glittering hunting set that surrounded the prince of Wales during the 1920s. During the season she went to London, and in spring and autumn she frequently travelled. In 1925, on the death of her father, she inherited the barony of Ravensdale.

In London Irene Ravensdale's passion for music and the theatre brought her many friends, from Arthur Rubinstein to Beatrice Lillie. She was president of the Melton

Mowbray Amateur Dramatic Society and the Leicester Symphony Orchestra (conducted by the young Malcolm Sargent). She was also chairman and fund-raiser for the British Women's Symphony Orchestra and became treasurer of the Musicians' Benevolent Fund. In 1929 she helped her sister Lady Cynthia Mosley in her successful election campaign for the parliamentary seat of Stoke-on-Trent. Throughout all these activities her voluntary work continued; and she often took parties of the boys and girls on holiday, sometimes in the British Isles, sometimes abroad. She was a strong supporter of the World Congress of Faiths, founded by Sir Francis Younghusband in 1936, and took a prominent part in the early congresses before 1939, when the religious leaders of the world were brought together. She was herself a pious Anglican, but during her travels she had been impressed by Eastern religions and philosophies.

Irene Ravensdale received many proposals of marriage—her suitors including Nevile Henderson, when he was head of the mission in Belgrade, and Victor Cazalet MP—but she remained single. When Lady Cynthia died in 1933 she gave up her hunting life to become a surrogate mother to the three Mosley children; she was their official guardian when Sir Oswald Mosley was detained (under regulation 18B) in 1940, and devoted much of her income to maintaining the family home at Denham. During the Second World War, with the Mosley children largely grown up, she worked in London shelters, broadcast, and travelled the country speaking at youth rallies and clubs on behalf of the Church of England. 'She inherited something of her father's oratorical powers,' said *The Times* in its obituary, 'and what she lacked was balanced by her manifest intensity of feeling and conviction.'

Irene Ravensdale was a long-standing campaigner for the right of peeresses in their own right to sit in the House of Lords but it was not until the Life Peerages Act of 1958 that she was able to take her own seat there, when she was created one of the first four women life peers in recognition of her work as chairman of the Highway clubs, vice-president of girls' clubs and mixed clubs, and joint president of the London Union of Youth Clubs. She took as her title Baroness Ravensdale of Kedleston.

Baroness Ravensdale's voluntary work with young people informed her contributions to the House of Lords. In her maiden speech (4 February 1959), on the funding of youth services, she cited her experience of over forty years and spoke of a growing need for grant aid now that there was no longer a large leisure class to run the clubs voluntarily. She subsequently (18 May 1960) applauded the countess of Albemarle's report on local authority provision for youth services. She strongly criticized (5 May 1959) the government's Street Offences Bill for its sexual double standard, penalizing prostitutes while leaving their clients unpunished. In a debate (1 June 1960) on magistrates' powers to control clubs, she alleged that the act had the effect of pushing prostitution under the carpet, driving the women into drinking dens and clubs run by criminals. Her real moment of glory in the House of Lords came in

that debate when, speaking of the prostitutes who frequented the East End that she knew so well from her charity work, she told her fellow peers authoritatively, 'They will charge a "fiver" (your Lordships will forgive me for being so sordid and vulgar) for a long spell and £1 for a "quick bash"' (*Hansard 5L*, 224.244). Her deliberately strong language caught the attention of the male peers and made headlines in the press.

In her later years she was an active president of the World Congress of Faiths and in great demand as a church speaker. In 1953 she published an autobiography, *In Many Rhythms*. She died on 9 February 1966.

ANNE DE COURCY

Sources *The Times* (10 Feb 1966) · *The Times* (14 Feb 1966) · A. de Courcy, *The viceroy's daughters: the lives of the Curzon sisters* (2000) · N. Nicolson, *Mary Curzon* (1977) · D. Gilmour, *Curzon* (1994) · Curzon MSS, BL · Irene Ravensdale's diaries and letters, priv. coll.
Archives BL, MSS
Likenesses photograph, 1930, repro. in de Courcy, *The viceroy's daughters*, pl. 28 · photograph, 1958, repro. in de Courcy, *The viceroy's daughters*, pl. 56
Wealth at death £129,555: probate, 28 April 1966, CGPLA Eng. & Wales

Curzon [*née* Leiter], **Mary Victoria**, Lady Curzon of Kedleston (1870–1906), vicereine of India, was born on 27 May 1870 at 924 Indiana Avenue, Chicago, the second of the four children of Levi Ziegler Leiter (1834–1904), merchant and millionaire, and his wife, Mary Theresa (1845–1913), daughter of Benjamin Carver and his wife, Nancy. Her parents were American; her father was neither Jewish nor a Dutch Calvinist as has sometimes been claimed, but was from Swiss Mennonite stock. She had an elder brother, Joseph, and two sisters, Nancy (Nannie), and Marguerite (Daisy). In 1881 the Leiters moved to Washington, and during her formative years Mary accompanied her family to London several times. Her beauty was fêted on both sides of the Atlantic, especially after her formal launching into American society during the 1888 season.

In 1890, while the guest of Lady Brownlow at Ashridge, Hertfordshire, Mary Leiter was introduced to George Curzon and fell in love with him. The ambitious George Nathaniel *Curzon (1859–1925), eldest son of Lord Scarsdale and heir to Kedleston Hall, Derbyshire, was thirty-one years old. Their subsequent meetings and letters were intermittent, for his preoccupation was with affairs of state rather than of the heart. However, they were secretly engaged in March 1893. The engagement was formalized six weeks before the wedding, which took place on 22 April 1895, in Washington. The couple then returned to England; she never set foot on American soil again.

The first three years of marriage were very difficult. Curzon, by now under-secretary of state at the Foreign Office, was dedicated to his work, and Mary saw little of him. She soon found that living in London was quite different from being a visitor, especially after the birth of her first child, Mary Irene, on 20 January 1896. The vibrant social life of her earlier visits gave way to domestic routine. She mixed uneasily with her husband's friends, particularly the social circle known as the Souls (of which her

Mary Victoria Curzon, Lady Curzon of Kedleston (1870–1906), by Underwood & Underwood, 1903

husband was a prominent member) who resented her presence.

Curzon offered himself for the viceroyalty of India in 1898 when Lord Elgin's term expired, and after some hesitation Lord Salisbury agreed. The appointment was formally announced on 11 August 1898. On 28 August Mary gave birth to their second daughter, Cynthia Blanche (who eventually married Sir Oswald Mosley). The new viceroy was created Baron Curzon of Kedleston in the Irish peerage, and in December 1898 the Curzons and their children left for India.

As vicereine Mary Curzon flowered. Some had doubted—unnecessarily—whether an American could fulfil such an exacting role. Her natural beauty and elegance were enhanced by great charm. She was the perfect counterpoise to Curzon, whose aloof manner often disguised extreme physical discomfort from a back injury. Soon the Curzons were thrown into the routine of entertaining in Calcutta and Simla, dictated by complex rules of imperial protocol. Part of the year was spent 'on tour' where life was more relaxed, but still subject to considerable formality, especially when visiting the princely states. The Indian climate soon took its toll of Mary's health, which was never strong; she now suffered serious migraines. Government House in Calcutta, modelled on Kedleston, and the viceregal lodge at Simla were both built on a grand scale, but were highly inconvenient as residences, although Curzon effected some improvements.

The high point of Curzon's viceroyalty was the 1902 coronation durbar at Delhi. Every detail of the vast two-week extravaganza was planned by Curzon himself, and while some used the occasion to criticize his diplomacy, the vicereine's grace and elegance won universal acclaim. The climax of the celebrations was the state ball in the Mughal Palace at which nearly 4000 guests, including fifty Indian princes, were received by the Curzons. But the memory which remained long after the festivities was of Lady Curzon wearing the spectacular dress in cloth of gold, designed by Worth and embroidered with peacock feathers and emeralds, a reminder of the peacock throne of the Mughal rulers.

Failing health, exacerbated by the Indian climate, darkened the last years of Mary Curzon's life. She returned to London in January 1904 and her third daughter, Alexandra Naldera, was born there on 20 March. Curzon returned in May before taking the unprecedented step of a second term as viceroy, but during his time in England Mary became very seriously ill at Walmer Castle. Torn between his two loves, his work and his wife, Curzon did not return to India until she was out of danger. Mary was determined to join him, and on 9 February 1905 left for India. She remained with him during the stormy months of office which culminated in Curzon's resignation and subsequent return to England in December 1905. By then she was seriously ill. She died in Curzon's arms, in their London home in Carlton House Terrace, from a heart attack on 18 July 1906. Her body was taken to Kedleston, where she was buried on 23 July after a private funeral service. If their courtship had been cool, it was recompensed by the deepening of their mutual love, particularly during the Indian years. Although Curzon later remarried, he was buried beside Mary in the memorial chapel he had built and embellished at Kedleston after her death.

VALERIE BONHAM

Sources N. Nicholson, *Mary Curzon* (1977) · D. Gilmour, *Curzon* (1994) · M. Fowler, *Below the peacock fan: first ladies of the raj* (1987) · *Lady Curzon's India*, ed. J. Bradley (1985) · M. Bence-Jones, *The viceroys of India* (1982) · *The Times* (19 July 1906) · J. Abdy and C. Gere, *The Souls* (1984)

Archives BL OIOC, corresp., MS Eur F 111–112, MSS Eur F 306 · priv. coll. | FILM BFI NFTVA, news footage

Likenesses Underwood & Underwood, photograph, 1903, NPG [*see illus.*] · photographs, repro. in *Lady Curzon's India*, ed. Bradley · photographs, repro. in Abdy and Gere, *The Souls* · portraits, photographs, priv. coll.

Wealth at death £11,875 16s.: probate, 4 Aug 1906, *CGPLA Eng. & Wales*

Curzon, Nathaniel, first Baron Scarsdale (1726–1804), art collector, was born on 23 December 1726 at Queen Square, Bloomsbury, London, the elder of the two surviving sons of Sir Nathaniel Curzon, fourth baronet (1675–1758), MP and barrister of the Inner Temple, and his wife, Mary (d. 1776), the daughter of Sir Ralph Assheton, second baronet. He was educated at Westminster School, and while there, in 1742, led three other friends into carving their names on the back of the coronation chair. In 1745 he went up to Christ Church, Oxford, and in 1749 he was made DCL. He served as MP for Clitheroe from 1748 to 1754, when he replaced his father as MP for Derbyshire, a seat he retained until 1761. Following Oxford he made a brief tour through northern France and the Low Countries, but he does not seem to have visited Italy. In 1750 he married

Lady Caroline (d. 1812), the eldest daughter of Charles Colyear, second earl of Portmore. They had five sons, three of whom predeceased their father, and two daughters. At Newmarket in 1751 Curzon and Lord March (William Douglas, later the notorious fourth duke of Queensberry) rode their horses, Silver Leg and Chance, against wagers of £50 and £100, of which Curzon won the second encounter.

It is for the splendid house and the surrounding park at Kedleston in Derbyshire, where there had been Curzons since the reign of Henry I, that Curzon will be especially remembered. When he succeeded as fifth baronet in 1758 he was already planning to demolish the existing Queen Anne house and build a great Palladian mansion, in which he brought together important features of a number of great buildings he had seen and admired. He wanted to follow the basic plan of Holkham Hall in Norfolk, which was based on Palladio's unbuilt Villa Mocenigo, illustrated in *Quattro libri*, and in December 1758 he invited Matthew Brettingham, the builder of Holkham, to make drawings. Work began in 1759, but in 1761 Robert Adam was appointed surveyor of the building, and it was he who designed the south front in 1765. The magnificent hall, lined with Corinthian columns, and the saloon, with a dome and central skylight imitating the Pantheon in Rome, which housed his sculpture collection, were the inspiration of Curzon himself. Adam did much of the interior decoration, including the mosaic ceiling in the library. Curzon built up a large art collection: some paintings he inherited, others he acquired—among them twenty-nine pictures bought for him in Italy—and he also commissioned new works from artists such as Nathaniel Hone. In the park he removed the formal rides, canals, and ponds of the 1720s and created a natural landscape. For the pleasure grounds Adam designed a magnificent bridge and several buildings, notably a gothic temple.

Curzon was elevated to the peerage as first Baron Scarsdale on 9 April 1761. Through John Leveson-Gower, first Earl Gower, he was appointed chairman of committees in the House of Lords, which took up much time between 1775 and 1789 but provided a regular income to help in completing the house.

Curzon died at Kedleston on 6 December 1804 and was succeeded in the barony by his eldest son, Nathaniel.

LESLIE HARRIS, *rev.* ANNE PIMLOTT BAKER

Sources L. Harris, 'The picture collection at Kedleston Hall', *The Connoisseur* (July 1978), 208–17 · J. Hardy, 'Robert Adam and the furnishing of Kedleston Hall', *The Connoisseur* (July 1978), 196–207 · L. Harris, *Robert Adam and Kedleston: the making of a neo-classical masterpiece*, ed. G. Jackson-Stops (c.1987) · *Derbyshire*, Pevsner (1953) · Burke, *Peerage* · Foster, *Alum. Oxon.* · *Old Westminsters* · archives, Kedleston Hall, Derbyshire · T. H. Taunton, *Portraits of celebrated racehorses*, 1 (1887) · J. C. Sainty, 'Origin of chairmen of committees in the House of Lords', *House of Lords Record Office Memorandum*, 52 (1974)

Archives priv coll., archives

Likenesses A. Devis, double portrait, 1754 (with Caroline Curzon), Kedleston Hall, Derbyshire; repro. in *Connoisseur* (July 1978) · N. Hone, double portrait, 1761 (with Caroline Curzon), repro. in Harris, *Robert Adam and Kedleston*

Curzon, Robert, fourteenth Baron Zouche of Harringworth (1810–1873), traveller and collector of manuscripts, elder son of Harriet Anne Bishopp, *suo jure* Baroness Zouche of Harringworth (1787–1870), and the Hon. Robert Curzon (1774–1863), son of Assheton, first Viscount Curzon, was born at 58 Welbeck Street, London, on 16 March 1810. He was educated at Charterhouse (1821–5) and entered Christ Church, Oxford, in 1829, but, having failed responsions and shown no aptitude for study, left without taking his degree in 1831, when he was returned by Clitheroe to the House of Commons. The borough was disfranchised in 1832, and Curzon never sat for another. In 1833 he began those travels which have made his name renowned. Setting out with his close friend Walter Sneyd, Curzon travelled through Europe before visiting, with George Joseph Palmer, Egypt and the Holy Land in 1833–4, on a tour of research among the monastery libraries, gathering many valuable manuscripts. He returned to England in 1834, before setting out on a second tour in 1837–8, when he visited Mount Athos and bought five manuscripts from several monasteries there, before making further purchases in Egypt. His experiences are recorded in his *Visit to the Monasteries in the Levant* (1849). It immediately gained popularity, running to six editions by 1881. From a scientific point of view, also, these revelations of monastic treasures were of great importance, and it was Curzon's experience that set others on the track which led to the acquisition of the magnificent collection of Nitrian manuscripts by the British Museum. Curzon has subsequently been criticized for removing the manuscripts to Britain, but it seems certain that many owe their preservation to the removal.

In October 1841 Curzon was appointed attaché at the embassy at Constantinople and private secretary to Sir Stratford Canning, where he spent his leisure exploring the city and particularly the manuscripts there. In January 1843 he was appointed a commissioner, with Lieutenant-Colonel W. Fenwick Williams, for defining the boundaries between Turkey and Persia, and he remained, at Erzurum for the most part, engaged in this task until January 1844, when he returned to England. In recognition of his services he received decorations from both the shah and sultan. The diplomatic service was, however, not to his taste, and he returned to England in 1844, publishing an account of his stay in Armenia (1854). On 27 August 1850 he fulfilled a long-held wish to find a wife when he married Emily Julia (1831/2–1866), daughter of Sir Robert Wilmot-Horton. Their children were Robert, the fifteenth Baron Zouche (1851–1914), and a daughter, Darea, the sixteenth baroness (1860–1917). His later travels in Italy were devoted partly to the discovery of manuscripts; and the Philobiblon Society published in 1854 his *Account of the Most Celebrated Libraries of Italy*. His interest in manuscripts, however, was at least as much excited by the actual writing as by the contents. He was a student of the history of handwriting, and his valuable collection of manuscripts had been gathered with a view to a treatise on the subject, which he never completed, although in 1849 he printed fifty copies of his *Catalogue of Materials for Writing*, which

Robert Curzon, fourteenth Baron Zouche of Harringworth (1810–1873), by William Holl (after George Richmond, 1859)

comprises examples in Syriac, Arabic, Turkish, Uigar, Persian, Armenian, Greek, and Coptic. These manuscripts were deposited by his son in the British Museum and left permanently to the museum by his daughter. On 15 May 1870 he succeeded his mother in the barony, as fourteenth Baron Zouche (or de la Zouche) of Harringworth, inheriting properties very greatly encumbered by his parents, particularly his father, who spent money too freely and managed family affairs ineptly. There was, however, enough money for him to undertake some rebuilding at Parham. Lord Zouche was deputy lieutenant of Sussex and Staffordshire, where his estates of Parham and Ravenhill were situated. He died at Parham on 2 August 1873 and was buried in the family vault beside his wife.

STANLEY LANE-POOLE, *rev.* ELIZABETH BAIGENT

Sources I. H. C. Fraser, *The heir of Parham* (1986) · A. N. L. Mumby, *Phillipps Studies no. 3* (1954) · A. N. L. Munby, *Connoisseurs and medieval miniatures, 1750–1850* (1972) · C. Hussey, *Parham Park, Sussex* (1990) [reprint from *Country Life*, 1, 8, 15 (June 1951)] · W. R. Dawson and E. P. Uphill, *Who was who in Egyptology*, 3rd edn, rev. M. L. Bierbrier (1995) · *The Times* (7 Aug 1873) · J. J. Norwich and R. Sitwell, *Mount Athos* (1966)

Archives BL, notes and collections relating to antiquarian interests, MSS 39583–39671, 8729–8855 | Bodl. Oxf., corresp. with Sir Thomas Phillipps · Ches. & Chester ALSS, letters to Lord de Tabley; letters to John Leicester Warren · Keele University, letters to Walter Sneyd · NRA, priv. coll., journal, corresp. with Stratford Canning · Trinity Cam., letters to Lord Houghton

Likenesses studio of R. Beard, daguerreotype photograph, *c.*1845, NPG · W. Holl, engraving, *c.*1858, repro. in Fraser, *Heir of Parham*, frontispiece · G. Richmond, portrait, 1859, Killerton, Devon · C. Pilvey, photograph, 1861?, repro. in Fraser, *Heir of Parham*, following p. 190 · W. Holl, stipple (after G. Richmond, 1859), BM, NPG [*see illus.*]

Wealth at death under £40,000: probate, 9 Oct 1873, CGPLA Eng. & Wales

Cusack, Cyril James (1910–1993), actor, was born on 26 November 1910 in Durban, South Africa, the son of James Cusack, an Irish officer with the Natal mounted police, and his wife, Alice, *née* Cole, a Cockney music-hall dancer. After the break-up of his parents' marriage in 1916 Cusack spent a peripatetic childhood, initially in Ireland, touring with his mother and her actor-lover, Brefni O'Rourke. Having made his stage début in Tipperary as Little Willie in *East Lynne* (1916) he went on to play countless juvenile roles in melodramas staged in 'fit-ups' such as barns and pubs. He even portrayed a girl in *Shot at Dawn* and the cat in *Dick Whittington*. During a performance of the latter his tail became entangled in a roller curtain and he was 'left suspended in the air and had to be rescued by the second comedian' (*The Times*, 28 July 1990). By this time he had already begun what turned out to be the longest screen career of any British-based performer. However, his début in Fred O'Donovan's *Knocknagow, or, The Homes of Tipperary* (1918) was hardly a model of realism, as the rudely healthy Cyril was cast as an evicted waif left desolate by the roadside.

Yet, this 'glorious adventure' (*The Times*, 8 Oct 1993) seriously disrupted Cusack's education, as he recalled in 'Every week in a different school', an essay in *A paler shade of green: a unique study of the dominant expatriates of the world Irish arts scene* (1972). Speaking in a mixture of his mother's Cockney accent and O'Rourke's brogue, Cusack (who was also fluent in Gaelic) eventually settled into a council school on the Caledonian Road in north London, where he told his classmates 'how wonderful Ireland was, how there were Red Indians in Wicklow and how I had seen a lion near the mountains. I almost believed the stories myself. It was my incipient nationalism coming out' (*The Times*, 28 July 1990). After returning to Ireland in the early 1920s he enrolled in the Dominican College at Newbridge, co. Kildare, and from there entered University College, Dublin, to read politics, modern history, and Roman law, with the intention of applying for the bar. However, his extra-curricular activities soon took precedence, as he published a volume of poetry and appeared in such plays as W. B. Yeats's *The Pot of Broth*.

It was clear, therefore, that acting was in Cusack's blood, as he recalled towards the end of his life: 'It always was. I could never get away from it. Sometimes I think acting is my *first* nature, not my second' (*The Times*, 28 July 1990). So he joined his mother and O'Rourke on their summer excursions to Norwich and Windsor, before making his London bow with a last-act cameo in Arnold Bennett's *Milestones*. However, it was in Ireland that he found his feet, as he appeared frequently with his mother's company at the Queen's Theatre and toured with Jimmy O'Brien's troupe. His big break came with his début at the Abbey Theatre, Dublin, in 1932. He played two small parts in A. P. Fanning's one-act piece *Vigil*, but the director listed him twice in the programme, as Cyril Cusack and Cyril O'Rourke.

Over the next thirteen years, Cusack performed in sixty-five productions at the Abbey, although he also spent two seasons at the Gate Theatre, particularly impressing as Paris opposite Micheál Mac Liammóir in *Romeo and Juliet*.

Cyril James Cusack (1910–1993), by Fred Daniels, 1948

His stock was also rising in London, with his efforts in *Ah, Wilderness* (1936) and *Thunder Rock* (1941) drawing critical acclaim. Yet it was with Irish drama that he was most closely associated. He excelled as Covey in Sean O'Casey's *The Plough and the Stars* (1939), and rejected an offer of Hamlet in order to play Christy Mahon in J. M. Synge's *The Playboy of the Western World* (1938). But it was his St Patrick's day performance as Dudebat, opposite Vivien Leigh in George Bernard Shaw's *The Doctor's Dilemma*, at the Haymarket in 1942, that made the most headlines. Having spent lunchtime sampling illicit whiskey with his stand-in, Cusack already felt unwell as the play began. By the scene in the artist's studio, he started misquoting his lines and was forced to improvise. Eventually he dried altogether and began delivering dialogue from *The Playboy of the Western World*. The curtain was brought down and the stage manager sent out the equally inconvenienced understudy to complete the show. Next day, both Dudebats were fired by the formidable impresario Binkie Beaumont, and Cusack entered a twenty-year West End exile.

In 1945 Cusack married the actress Maureen Margaret Kiely (d. 1977); they had three daughters, Sinead, Sorcha, and Niamh, and two sons, Paul and Padraig. In the same year as his marriage Cusack severed his links with the Abbey, following a row over his insistence that a national theatre had a duty to tour the provinces. He had a spell managing the Gaiety Theatre, during which he premiered Synge's *The Bishop's Bonfire* (1955). He also formed his own production company, and began appearing regularly in films to finance roving programmes of classical and Irish dramas. Lamenting the scarcity of Irish pictures, he mostly worked in England in such diverse projects as *Odd*

Man Out (1947), *The Elusive Pimpernel* (1950), *The Man who Never Was* (1956), and *The Waltz of the Toreadors* (1962). 'In my film parts,' he said, 'I have concentrated on veracity of characterisation. In the last few years, I think my work in films has improved in some ways; it is more solid, less intuitive and perhaps technically better than it used to be' (Cusack, 30). Invariably cast in supporting roles, he effortlessly stole scenes with his customary economy and ease. François Truffaut, who directed him in *Fahrenheit 451* (1966), wrote of him:

> Cyril Cusack is the most restless actor I have known. He is a man of good nature and mildness. He can play his scenes in so many styles; he can be baroque, malicious, lyrical, but he can never be terrifying. (Cusack, 24)

Perhaps the most telling description of his method came in a review of his performance in a 1988 Abbey production of Gorky's *The Lower Depths*—'His touch is light like a feather, but it has the impact of an electric volt' (*The Times*, 8 Oct 1993).

The 1960s proved something of a golden age, which Cusack labelled his 'second apprenticeship' (*The Times*, 8 Oct 1993). In 1961 he not only won the International Critics' Award as the best actor of the season in *Arms and the Man* and *Krapp's Last Tape* (both 1960), but also premiered *The Temptation of Mr O* (1961), a play based on Kafka's *The Trial*, which he wrote in rhythmical prose and Dublinese. Two years later he returned to the London stage as Mobius in the Royal Shakespeare Company's Aldwych production of Dürrenmatt's *The Physicists* (1963), and helped restore Boucicault's *The Shaughraun* to the international repertory with his 1968 performance as Conn. Whether on film in *The Taming of the Shrew* (1967), *Galileo* (1968), *The Day of the Jackal* (1973), and *My Left Foot* (1989), or on stage as Fluther Good in *The Plough and the Stars* (1977), and The Inquisitor in *Saint Joan* (1984), he continued to garner acclaim. Particularly admired was his Chebutykin in Chekhov's *The Three Sisters* (1990), which co-starred his daughters Sinead, Sorcha, and Niamh. His wife Maureen having died in 1977, in 1979 he married Mary Rose, with whom he had a daughter, Catherine.

Despite plans to concentrate on writing, Cusack persisted in acting almost to the end of his life, appearing with his grandson Sam in *Danny, the Champion of the World* (1991). He died of motor neurone disease at 41 Burlington Lane, Chiswick, London, on 7 October 1993. He was survived by his second wife, Mary, and by his six children. A memorial mass was concelebrated at the Church of Corpus Christi, Covent Garden, on 4 November 1993.

DAVID PARKINSON

Sources C. Cusack, 'Every week in a different school', *A paler shade of green: a unique study of the dominant expatriates of the world Irish arts scene*, ed. D. Hickey and G. Smith (1972) • C. Lyon, ed., *The international dictionary of films and filmmakers: actors and actresses* (1991) • *The Times* (8 Oct 1993) • *The Guardian* (8 Oct 1993) • *The Independent* (8 Oct 1993) • *Daily Mail* (8 Oct 1993) • P. Burt, 'A childhood', *The Times* (28 July 1990) • L. A. Passow, *Daily Mail* (29 May 1999) [interview] • d. cert. • *The Times* (15 Nov 1993) [interview with Lesley Aird Passow] • *Daily Mail* (29 May 1999) [interview with Lesley Aird Passow]

Archives Boston University, letters and poems to Lesley Aird Passow

Likenesses F. W. Daniels, bromide print, 1948, NPG [*see illus.*] · group photograph, 1990, repro. in *The Independent* [from *Irish Times*] · photograph, repro. in *The Times* (8 Oct 1993) · photograph, repro. in *The Guardian* · photograph, repro. in *Daily Mail* (8 Oct 1993) · photographs, Hult. Arch.

Wealth at death £281,905: administration, 7 July 1994, *CGPLA Eng. & Wales*

Cusack, Margaret Anne [*name in religion* Mary Francis Clare; *called* the Nun of Kenmare] (1829–1899), founder of the Sisters of St Joseph of Peace and writer, was born on 6 May 1829 in York Street, Dublin, the elder of two children of Dr Samuel Cusack, a dispensary doctor, and his wife, Sarah, *née* Stoney. Both parents came from a long tradition of Irish protestantism, the Cusacks claiming descent from Sir Thomas Cusack, one of Henry VIII's reformers influential in establishing the Church of Ireland. Sarah Stoney was of zealous evangelical settler stock, from Oakley Park, near Birr, King's county. Baptized into the Church of Ireland, Margaret Anne's early years were spent in borrowed splendour in a mansion near Coolock, even as the family fortunes dwindled. She developed a rebellious, imperious temperament in her efforts to compete with her younger brother, Samuel, for her mother's affection, and the isolation of her childhood led her to religious enthusiasm. From the age of nine she began to attend revivalist meetings at the home of her cousin, the Hon. Catherine Massy. When her parents separated, Cusack, aged fourteen, went with her brother to live with her Great-Aunt Baker in Exeter, Devon, and joined the Plymouth Brethren.

On the death of her fiancé, Charles Holmes, Cusack enrolled in the Anglican Sellonite sisterhood of Dr Pusey. Uncomfortable with the volatile Oxford Movement and sceptical of the motives of her religious superior, Priscilla Sellon, Cusack converted to Roman Catholicism and was received into the Catholic church on 2 July 1858 with the minimum of instruction. Aged thirty, she entered a Staffordshire convent of the Sisters of Penance but, dissatisfied, withdrew and returned to Ireland, where she immediately entered the Poor Clare Convent in Newry, co. Down, on 2 July 1859. For some years she enjoyed peace and fame, writing and publishing on a variety of subjects. She published in quick succession lives of St Francis, St Clare, and St Patrick, two volumes of Irish history, local histories of the counties of Cork and Kerry, a study of Daniel O'Connell, and a series of publications on the plight of poor girls. In all, she wrote about fifty books and pamphlets during her life.

Cusack was among those chosen to make a new foundation of Poor Clare nuns in Kenmare, co. Kerry, in October 1871. In 1879 famine devastated the west of Ireland and Cusack used her pen to raise funds and to expose the landlord system that created the famine, for which she also held the government responsible. Her particular target was the administration of the Lansdowne estate. Cusack's writings on the land question created many enemies, including Archdeacon Higgins, the Roman Catholic parish priest of Kenmare, who succeeded in isolating her from her religious sisters and having her transferred back to Newry in 1881.

Margaret Anne Cusack [the Nun of Kenmare] (1829–1899), by unknown photographer, pubd 1889

An even stormier phase of Cusack's life now began. Impelled by her concern for the better training of female domestic servants, she launched her campaign to found a convent at Knock, co. Mayo, where she claimed that Archdeacon Cavanagh, the parish priest of Knock, had invited her to make a foundation. The difficulties she encountered in this project included not only canonical obstacles and misunderstanding about her mission, but also her own imperious temperament. She claimed visions and revelations, which seemed to exploit the local Knock apparition, so much so that the Catholic archbishop of Tuam, Dr McEvilly, considered her visions 'all bosh' [*see* Knock, visionaries of (*act.* 1879)]. He gave grudging permission for a foundation, but on 19 October 1883 withdrew that consent and ordered her to found a Poor Clare convent instead. Cusack insisted that she was making a new foundation, the Sisters of Peace. Deadlock ensued, and on the advice of her friend Cardinal Manning, after further humiliations she moved to England, where she made her foundation in Nottingham in the diocese of Bishop Bagshawe in 1884. She left behind her in Knock an impressive group of buildings, a convent, and two schools.

In February 1884 Cusack went to Rome to apply for a dispensation from her vows as a Poor Clare. The investigation of her case carried out by Roman authorities reflected the varied perceptions of those who met her. To some she was an excellent religious; to others her actions were incomprehensible and her fitness to found an order suspect. Two years later she went to the United States, instructed by Bishop Bagshawe to raise funds and open houses of the order of the Sisters of St Joseph of Peace. Only one bishop, Dr Wigger of Newark, New Jersey, welcomed her to his diocese. There she opened a holiday house for working girls, trained them, and placed them in service. In 1889 her first autobiography, *The Nun of Kenmare*, appeared. Convinced that her order would not prosper while she was the object of ecclesiastical disapproval, she left her religious community, resigning as leader in 1888. She also seceded from the Roman Catholic church. She strove to make her living by lecturing on her experiences to mainly protestant audiences. Her final conversion, in 1895, was to Methodism, and her last writings, for instance *Revolution and War: the Secret Conspiracy of the Jesuits in Britain* (1910), reflected her anti-clerical hostility towards the Church of Rome. She returned to England and died at 21 Lansdowne Crescent, Leamington Spa, Warwickshire, the home of protestant evangelical friends, on 5 June 1899. Eccentric and wilful, she never abandoned her pursuit of justice for the poor. In 1974 she was officially recognized by Rome as the founder of the Sisters of St Joseph of Peace but remains a controversial figure.

MARGARET MAC CURTAIN

Sources M. F. Cusack, *The Nun of Kenmare, an autobiography* (1889) · M. A. Cusack, *The story of my life* (1891) · I. ffrench Eagar, *Margaret Anna Cusack*, 2nd edn (1979) · C. Clear, *Nuns in nineteenth-century Ireland* (1987) · d. cert.
Archives Archivio Vaticano, Vatican City, Archives of Propaganda Fide, Scritture riferite nei congressi; udienze di Nostro Signore · Elizabeth Seton College, New Jersey, Wigger MSS · Irish College, Rome, Kirby MSS
Likenesses photograph, pubd 1889, NPG [*see illus.*] · lithograph, repro. in Cusack, *Nun of Kenmare*, frontispiece
Wealth at death £478 4s. 5d.: probate, 17 June 1899, CGPLA Eng. & Wales

Cusack, Michael [Mícheál Cíosóg] (1847–1906), schoolmaster and a founder of the Gaelic Athletic Association, was born on 20 September 1847 at Carron parish, Burren, co. Clare, Ireland, second son of Matthew Cusack (d. 1868), a herdsman, and his wife, Bridget Flannery (d. 1864), both of co. Clare. He was educated locally at two parish schools and, after a two-year course at a teacher-training institution in Enniscorthy, co. Wexford, and at the Central Model School in Dublin, qualified in 1866 as an officially recognized primary-level 'national teacher'. Between 1866 and 1874 Cusack taught in counties Clare, Galway, and Down, joining the staff of Blackrock College near Dublin in 1874. Blackrock was to become famous as the cradle of Irish rugby football, a game which later in the 1870s Cusack played in Dublin with some success. By 1871 he had acquired a further qualification enabling him to teach at secondary level. On 16 June 1876 he married, at Dromore Catholic church, Margaret Woods (1854?–1890). In 1877 Cusack opened his own Civil Service Academy (popularly called Cusack's academy) in Dublin, where with considerable success he prepared candidates for entry to the professions, the army, police, and civil service.

From boyhood Cusack had participated in the traditional athletics of rural Ireland—running, jumping, lifting, and throwing weights. However, at twenty-seven he was getting too old for athletics, so instead he threw himself enthusiastically into its management on his arrival at Blackrock in 1874, and for the next ten years served on several club committees as well as officiating at many meetings. There was, he believed, an urgent need to reform Irish athletics. Dominated by a non-nationalist class-conscious élite which kept out artisans, soldiers, police, and others, it allowed results to be rigged and tolerated widespread betting at meetings. However, Cusack's abrasive personality and his strong nationalist views did not make for harmony, and when he found his efforts continually thwarted he first extended his arguments to the columns of national and sporting newspapers, and then began to advocate the formation of a separate body for nationalist athletes and others excluded by existing bodies.

In 1882 Cusack discovered that a form of hurling ('hurley') was being played by undergraduates of Trinity College, Dublin, among them a law student named Edward Carson. This ancient Celtic ball game played with a curved stick had become almost extinct after the famines of the 1840s. An attempt by Cusack and some hurley players to fuse their version with the more robust game he had known in co. Clare failed, and by 1884 he was planning a new sports body, with the dual aim of taking over athletics for nationalists and reviving hurling. That summer he won influential backing for this idea from Maurice Davin, a Tipperary athlete who had achieved international fame. At a poorly attended meeting, called by Davin and Cusack and held in the co. Tipperary town of Thurles on 1 November 1884, the Gaelic Athletic Association (GAA) was founded, with Davin as president and Cusack as joint secretary. Despite an unpromising start, it transpired that Cusack had successfully laid the necessary preparatory organizational foundations, and the new body rapidly established itself throughout Ireland. Once again, however, his quarrelsome personality led to serious rifts on the executive. Eventually in July 1886 Cusack lost his post as secretary at a turbulent meeting, from which Davin inexplicably absented himself. For the remaining twenty years of his life Cusack was only on the fringe of the GAA, loyal to it in his own abrasive fashion but never again holding office at national level. For a year (1888) he edited his own weekly *Celtic Times*, using it to attack the GAA executive during a critical year for the association. In 1893 he was briefly secretary of a feud-riven Dublin board, and as late as 1901 he ran a younger rival close in the annual election of GAA secretary. His private school having closed, he subsisted precariously on private tutoring and journalism, but after his wife's death in 1890 his family of six (two daughters and four sons) was scattered and he himself fell into ill health. Cusack died, penniless, in Dublin on 28 November 1906, and was buried beside his wife in Glasnevin cemetery, Dublin.

It was in the late 1890s that James Joyce met Cusack, who became the model for the Citizen (a nickname

Cusack had given himself), the main actor in the famous Cyclops episode in Joyce's *Ulysses*. While Joyce's character is in many respects a caricature of Cusack, the little that has survived about Cusack's lifestyle at the time suggests that there is at least a core of truth in Joyce's portrayal of the eccentric, boastful, antisemitic figure, who with his dog Garryowen dominates the boisterous gathering in Kiernan's pub beside Dublin's historic Green Street court house. In appearance Michael Cusack was of medium height, but very broad-shouldered. From the time he settled in Dublin he had a beard, which grew longer as he aged. Instead of trousers, he invariably wore knee-breeches, and a wide-rimmed hat (of the type then associated with members of the revolutionary Fenian movement), and carried a heavy blackthorn stick. Whether as founder of what became the biggest Irish sports body (and the earliest in the Irish cultural revival of the late nineteenth century), or as the model for a prominent character in Joyce's seminal novel, or simply as the only founder of an influential Irish socio-political organization in modern times to have been dismissed within twenty months, Michael Cusack carved out his own personal niche in Irish history. MARCUS BOURKE

Sources M. de Burca, *Michael Cusack and the GAA* (1989) · L. P. Ó Caithnia, *Micheál Cíosóg* (Dublin, 1982) · M. de Burca, *The GAA: a history* (1980) · T. F. O'Sullivan, *Story of the GAA* (1916) · *Celtic Times* (1888) · R. Ellmann, *James Joyce*, rev. edn (1982) · Cusack family prayer book, priv. coll. · d. cert.

Archives county library, Ennis, co. Clare, *Celtic Times* · NL Ire., letter, MS 18560

Likenesses photograph, *c.*1880–1900, repro. in de Burca, *Michael Cusack and the GAA*; priv. coll. · photograph, *c.*1900, repro. in de Burca, *Michael Cusack and the GAA*; priv. coll.

Cusack, Sir Thomas (1505?–1571), lawyer and administrator, was the eldest son of John Cusack, landowner, and his wife, Alison Wellesley. He was born into a long-established and wealthy pale family in Cushingstown, co. Meath. After entering the Inner Temple in 1522, he was by 1530 a senior member of the inn.

Cusack attached himself to Thomas Cromwell by 1530 and was appointed chancellor of the exchequer in Ireland in 1532 as part of Cromwell's attempts to reform the Dublin administration. Throughout the 1530s Cusack reported regularly to Cromwell on Irish affairs. Unwaveringly loyal during the Kildare rebellion (1534–5), he was appointed second justice of the common pleas in 1535, a post he held only briefly, and was employed on several tasks, offering advice and service to a royal commission sent by Cromwell to investigate the government of Lord Leonard Grey, lord deputy, in 1538. He divorced his first wife, Joan Hussey, with whom he had a son and two daughters, in 1537 on the grounds of consanguinity. On Cromwell's fall in 1540, Cusack quickly switched allegiance to Grey's successor as lord deputy, Sir Anthony St Leger, to whom he became a close adviser and ally. Appointed to the commission for the suppression of Irish religious houses in 1540, he acquired substantial pieces of monastic property, often at considerable discounts, the most important of which was the Augustinian nunnery of Lismullen, co. Meath, where his sister had been abbess.

Knighted by St Leger in 1541, he acted as speaker of the House of Commons in the parliament of 1541–3, where he has been credited by some historians as being the principal influence behind the statute establishing Ireland as a kingdom. Made master of the rolls in 1542, Cusack was centrally involved throughout the early 1540s in the extensive series of diplomatic and dynastic agreements concluded with Gaelic and Old English lords, labelled collectively by later historians as the policy of surrender and regrant.

Appointed lord chancellor in 1546, replacing the disgraced John Alen, Cusack remained in favour under Edward VI, being reconfirmed in the chancellorship in August 1550 and made lord justice (jointly with Gerald Aylmer) in December 1552. During this time Cusack energetically sustained his diplomatic efforts in relation to the Irish lordships, conveyed in his reports a highly optimistic evaluation of the state of Ireland, and was an ardent advocate of the establishment of provincial councils. He retained the chancellorship under Mary I, but was discredited in 1556 by revelations concerning his part in the scandalous financial dealings of the St Leger regime and his role in the suppression of St Patrick's Cathedral, Dublin. Dismissed from office and imprisoned briefly, Cusack gradually returned to favour in the early years of Elizabeth I's reign, serving under Thomas Radcliffe, third earl of Sussex, lord lieutenant, on several commissions in Munster and Connaught and on circuit in the English pale. His perceived sympathy for Gerald fitz James Fitzgerald, fourteenth earl of Desmond, and the Geraldine faction in general aroused Sussex's suspicion; and his support for complaints in the pale against the abuses of the English garrison coupled with his advocacy of conciliation with Shane O'Neill widened the breach. Patronized by Sussex's chief English critics, Robert Dudley, earl of Leicester, and Sir Henry Sidney, Cusack enjoyed a brief period of high favour at court in 1565, being personally received by Elizabeth and promised reappointment as chancellor. Changes in the currents of court politics, the decision to make war on O'Neill, and the rising influence of the anti-Geraldine Thomas Butler, eleventh earl of Ormond, all contributed to Cusack's eclipse. Refused office, he retained his position on the Irish privy council and served Sidney as a commissioner in Munster and in the pale. His influence waned in the later 1560s; Cusack complained of lack of countenance and reward and gradually withdrew from public life.

Cusack died on 1 April 1571 and was interred in Trevet, co. Meath, in a highly decorated tomb, now broken. His second wife was Matilda or Maud Darcy (*d.* before 1559), with whom he had three sons and eight daughters, and his third was Genet Sarsfield (*d.* in or after 1571), with whom he had no known children. His will, dated 31 March 1571, makes elaborate provisions for his children and reveals serious concern about impending inheritance disputes. It reveals also Cusack's characteristic ambivalence in regard to religion. Orthodox under every regime, an enthusiastic participant in the confiscation of church lands, and a member of the powerful commission for ecclesiastical causes established in the early 1560s to enforce conformity to the Elizabethan settlement, he also attempted to protect George Dowdall, Catholic archbishop of Armagh, in the Edwardian years and retained thereafter close contacts with leading recusant figures in the pale, and his will, at once affirming his obedience to the royal supremacy, also bequeathed a yearly sum to be paid to a priest to say mass and pray for his soul in the manner of a traditional chantry chapel. Cusack's political views were equally balanced. Though generally a proponent of diplomacy rather than force in the Tudor government's dealings with the Irish lordships, he could occasionally, as in the case of Ulster in the 1550s, advocate violent military action, and frequently professed his belief in the severe administration of the law. Unusual among the pale gentry in forwarding a policy of conciliation toward and assimilation with the old Irish enemies, he may be seen as a figure who most clearly foresaw the need for the palesmen to take leadership in the process of the English revival in Ireland, before newer arrivals displaced them.

Ciaran Brady

Sources C. Brady, *The chief governors: the rise and fall of reform government in Tudor Ireland, 1536–1588* (1994) · J. S. Brewer and W. Bullen, eds., *Calendar of the Carew manuscripts*, 6 vols., PRO (1867–73) · *CSP Ire., 1509–74* · F. E. Ball, *The judges in Ireland, 1221–1921*, 1 (1926), 200–02 · H. Gallwey, 'The Cusack family of counties Meath and Dublin', *The Irish Genealogist*, 5 (1971–5), 591–613

Archives PRO, state papers Ireland, Edward VI, 'Book' on the state of Ireland, 1552, SP 61/4/43, fols. 132r–145v | PRO, state papers Ireland, Henry VIII, SP 60 · PRO, state papers Ireland, Edward VI, SP 61 · PRO, state papers Ireland, Mary I, SP 62 · PRO, state papers Ireland, Elizabeth, SP 63

Cusance, William (*d.* 1360), administrator, came of a Burgundian family, several of whose members established themselves in England in the early fourteenth century. He began his career as a clerk of Hugh Despenser the younger (*d.* 1326), who secured Cusance's promotion into Edward II's government as keeper of the great wardrobe on 11 September 1320. The baronial opposition to the Despensers, and a general antagonism demonstrated towards aliens, forced him out of office on 20 December 1321, but after Edward II's political recovery in 1322 he was quickly returned to favour and was appointed keeper of the wardrobe of Prince Edward on 23 June 1323. This close association with the heir to the throne protected Cusance from the political reaction against the associates of Edward II and the Despensers in the winter of 1326–7, and by 1332 he had re-emerged as keeper of the wardrobe to Edward III's brother, John of Eltham, earl of Cornwall. He served as keeper of the king's wardrobe from 27 May 1340 to 25 November 1341 and spent much of this time in the Low Countries, where he witnessed the battle of Sluys and helped to organize the siege of Tournai. His close association with the king during a time of considerable political turmoil brought him further rewards and he was appointed treasurer of the exchequer on 28 October 1341, remaining in this position until 12 April 1344, when he was replaced by William Edington.

Before 1349, Cusance's ecclesiastical preferment was fairly modest: he secured the prebend of Wenlocksbarn in St Paul's Cathedral, London, in 1335, and was made prebendary of Lafford in Lincoln Cathedral in 1340. After retiring into relative obscurity in 1344, however, he made an unexpected and notable comeback in 1349–50. He was appointed dean of the royal free chapel of St Martin's-le-Grand, London, in June 1349 and a few weeks later, on 5 July, was reappointed keeper of the wardrobe. It was highly unusual for those who had served as treasurer to return to the wardrobe. Cusance seems to have returned to government service specifically to implement a new financial policy, whereby the large numbers of estates falling into the king's hands as a result of the deaths of tenants-in-chief during the plague of 1348–9 were used to support the domestic expenditure of the royal household. Having set this system in motion, he quickly renounced office again on 14 February 1350; on the following day the king granted him the archdeaconry of Cornwall and a prebend in Exeter Cathedral as rewards for service. This preferment brought him little satisfaction, however, for he found his appointment challenged by a nominee of the pope, and the resulting legal contest continued intermittently for seven years. The deanery of St Martin's-le-Grand must also have proved something of a disappointment. Cusance had been brought in specifically to ensure that the fabric of the royal chapel was restored; after his death, however, it was disclosed that the buildings had suffered considerable further neglect. He died in 1360, on or before 5 May; his property was confiscated by the crown to cover debts remaining from his time at the wardrobe.

W. M. Ormrod

Sources Tout, *Admin. hist.* · W. M. Ormrod, 'Edward III's government of England, c.1346–1356', DPhil diss., U. Oxf., 1984 · *Chancery records*

Cushendun. For this title name *see* McNeill, Ronald John, Baron Cushendun (1861–1934).

Cushing, Peter Wilton (1913–1994), actor, was born at Normandy, Goldstone Road, Kenley, Surrey, on 26 May 1913, the second son of George Edward Cushing (1881–c.1959), quantity surveyor, and his wife, Nellie Maria, *née* King (1880–c.1964). His grandfather Henry Cushing had been a member of Sir Henry Irving's stock company, while his aunt Maude Ashton was also in the theatre. She later confided to her nephew that she feared his mother's distress at not having a daughter might have driven him to 'become another Oscar Wilde—perhaps not in the poetic sense, but most certainly in the other, treated as you were—from the cradle—as a gel' (Cushing, 14). However, any disquiet aroused by his stage début, at a Dulwich kindergarten, as an elf was soon allayed by a ready talent for rugby that emerged at Shoreham grammar school, Sussex, and Purley county secondary school. This athleticism also manifested itself in the garden stunts he performed in imitation of screen stars Tom Mix and Pearl White, and his comic-book hero Tom Merry, whose code of honour would long be Cushing's byword.

Exploiting his gift for art, Cushing joined the surveyor's department of Coulsdon and Purley urban district council in the summer of 1933. However, much of his time was

Peter Wilton Cushing (1913–1994), by Anthony Buckley, 1953

spent writing to repertory companies, often under the name of Mr Ling. Only after an abortive suicide trip to Exmouth did he consider formal training, and he began evening classes at the Guildhall School of Music and Drama in 1935. He made his professional bow at the Connaught Theatre in June 1936, with a walk-on part in J. B. Priestley's *Cornelius*, only to receive a lecture from producer Bill Fraser for attempting to steal the scene with an improvised piece of business involving chewing gum. Having taken his first villainous role as King Rat in *Dick Whittington* (1936) at Southampton's Grand Theatre, he spent the next three years touring the north and midlands with the William Brookfield Players and Harry Hanson's Court Players.

In January 1939 Cushing decided to try his luck in Hollywood. He made his screen début as a royal messenger who skirmishes with the Three Musketeers in James Whale's *The Man in the Iron Mask* (1939). He also served as Louis Hayward's double during the split-screen filming that enabled the star to appear as twins. Further bit parts followed, including a career-favourite slot in Laurel and Hardy's *A Chump at Oxford* (1940), before his performance in *Vigil in the Night* (1940) prompted the *Daily News* to compare his acting to Spencer Tracy's. However, his only headline part in this period was as Clive of India in *Your Hidden Master* (1940), an instantly forgotten episode in MGM's shorts series, *The Passing Parade*.

Ranked 4c on volunteering for war service, Cushing spent fifteen months working his passage across the United States in order to get home. During this time he parked cars at Coney Island, assisted a vaudeville magician, provided radio voice-overs, and spent a season in summer stock at the Green Mansions holiday camp in the Adirondacks. In Canada he found employment as a cinema usher and a clerk at the Montreal YMCA, in addition to appearing in the propaganda short *We All Help* (1942). He also made Nazi and Japanese flags for Michael Powell and Emeric Pressburger's location-shot war adventure, *49th Parallel* (1941), only to be arrested after a prying neighbour reported him as a spy. On returning to Britain in March 1942, he enlisted in the Entertainments National Service Association (ENSA) and fell in love with (Violet) Helen Beck (1905–1971), his co-star in a touring production of Noël Coward's *Private Lives*. They married at Kensington register office on 13 April 1943. There were no children of the marriage.

Despite his Hollywood credentials, Cushing's career stalled following his West End début in *War and Peace* (1943), and he was reduced to handpainting silk scarves for a textile company. The post-war period saw only occasional bookings at the BBC and the Kew Theatre, until he was cast as Osric in Laurence Olivier's Oscar-winning adaptation of *Hamlet* (1948), which earned him a berth on the Old Vic's ensuing tour of Australia. However, work remained in short supply and, finally, he suffered a nervous breakdown during rehearsals for Bridget Boland's *The Damascus Blade* (1950).

In 1951, at his wife's suggestion, Cushing decided to try the relatively new and still somewhat disreputable medium of live television. On 2 December he starred as Charles Appleby in J. B. Priestley's *Eden's End*, and was soon appearing so frequently that one comedian defined television as 'Peter Cushing with knobs on' (Cushing, 103). Having surprised many as Mr D'Arcy in a six-part version of *Pride and Prejudice* (1952), he demonstrated such versatility in productions such as *Tovarich*, *Beau Brummel*, and *1984* (all 1954) that he earned the nickname the 'BBC's maid-of-all-work'. Accolades including the *Daily Mail* readers' award for the best television actor of 1953 also boosted his film prospects. However, his ability to shift from the scheming (Sir Palamides in *The Black Knight*, 1953) and the imposing (Memnon in *Alexander the Great*, 1955) to the unassuming (Henry Miles in *The End of the Affair*, 1955) was rapidly forgotten once he played the meddlesome baron in Hammer Films' all-colour shocker *The Curse of Frankenstein* (1957).

It mattered not that he was about to exhibit his watercolours at the Fine Art Society in Bond Street, nor that his television career was about to hit new heights as 221B Baker Street's legendary resident in *Sir Arthur Conan Doyle's Sherlock Holmes* (1958–9), for overnight Cushing, who was terrified of the dark, became synonymous with horror. He assumed the role of Mary Shelley's misguided scientist on four more occasions and five times pursued Christopher Lee's Count Dracula, in the guise of vampire hunter *extraordinaire* Professor Van Helsing. In addition to Hammer, Amicus and Tyburn also kept him busy with a string of ghoulish adventures, which Cushing approached with equal professionalism, in spite of their decreasing quality and originality. Following his wife's death in 1971, he sought solace in work, completing thirty-two pictures in eleven years.

In his second volume of autobiography, *Past Forgetting* (1988), Cushing recalled with some pleasure his various methods of demise—being impaled by a harpoon in *Fury at Smuggler's Bay* (1961); plunging with a hatchet in his back in *Twins of Evil* (1971); succumbing to a tankful of spiders in *Madhouse* (1973); and being mauled by moggies in *The Uncanny* (1976). Yet he was still capable of surprises, twice playing Dr Who—in *Dr Who and the Daleks* (1965) and *Daleks: Invasion Earth AD 2150* (1966)—and delivering a disturbing performance as a former SS commandant in the underrated *Shock Waves* (1975). He even reached a new audience as Grand Moff Tarkin in *Star Wars* (1977), a part he played primarily in carpet slippers, as his boots were too small.

Cushing survived a prostate cancer scare in 1982, and bowed out of films with *Biggles* in 1985; he was appointed OBE three years later. However, he remained active in his Whitstable retirement, playing a wartime pilot in BBC Radio Kent's *Human Conflict* (1990) and co-narrating *Flesh and Blood: the Hammer Heritage of Horror* (1994) with Christopher Lee for American television. He also wrote articles on cigarette cards for the *Card Times* and contributed the rap segment for the single 'No White Peaks' in 1991. In 1994 he published privately *The Bois Saga*, a phonetic history of Britain written during his convalescence in the early 1950s. He died from a recurrence of his cancer at the Pilgrim's Hospice, Canterbury, on 11 August 1994. He was cremated, and a memorial service was held at St Paul's, Covent Garden, on 12 January 1995.   DAVID PARKINSON

Sources P. Cushing, *An autobiography and past forgetting* (1999) [originally published in two volumes, as *Peter Cushing: an autobiography* (1986) and *Past forgetting—memoirs of the Hammer years* (1988)] · D. Miller, *The Peter Cushing companion* (2000) · H. Maxford, *Hammer, house of horror* (1996) · M. Hearn and A. Barnes, *The Hammer story* (1997) · *The Times* (12 Aug 1994) · *The Times* (13 Jan 1995) · *The Independent* (12–22 Aug 1994)
Likenesses photographs, 1948–75, Hult. Arch. · A. Buckley, photograph, 1953, NPG [*see illus.*] · photograph, repro. in *The Times* (12 Aug 1994) · photograph, repro. in *The Independent* (12 Aug 1994) · photographs, Kobal collection · photographs, Ronald Grant archive · photographs, Huntley archives
Wealth at death £282,163: probate, 20 Dec 1994, *CGPLA Eng. & Wales*

Cushing, Thomas (1725–1788), merchant and politician, was born on 24 March 1725 in Boston, Massachusetts, the son of Thomas Cushing (b. 1694), leading merchant and public official, and Mary Bromfield (b. 1696). Little is known of Thomas's early life, but he was probably brought up in the expectation that he would one day take over the family business from his father. He attended Harvard College, graduating with a BA in 1744 and an MA in 1747. In 1747 he returned to Boston to pursue a merchant career, specializing in importing woollen goods. On 1 October that year he married Deborah Fletcher (b. c.1727), with whom he had two children.

Typical of leading Bostonian merchant families of the day, the Cushings had a tradition of active service to the town and colony in appointed and elected offices. Thomas held several minor offices before becoming justice of the peace in 1760. In 1761 he began fourteen years of service in the Massachusetts legislature, the general court. In 1766 he was elected speaker, a position to which he was annually re-elected until 1774. He was a member of the popular party, which opposed the British-backed faction of Thomas Hutchinson and Andrew Oliver, and the increasing influence of royal authority. Nevertheless Cushing can only be described as a moderate in the radical Boston politics that produced such men as Samuel Adams, John Hancock, and James Otis jun. Throughout the crisis over authority and taxation that plagued Anglo-American relations in the 1760s, Cushing favoured moderate responses. He did not support motions for the non-importation of British manufactured goods until 1770, fearing that radical supporters of such actions truly sought independence rather than reform. Through his political and mercantile associations he maintained a regular correspondence with several American and English radicals in London. However, he was wary of becoming too closely associated with the growing radicalism, regularly begging his correspondents not to have his letters reprinted or distributed. The Americans in London were known for such uses of the press, most infamously using the tactic to topple the Hutchinson–Oliver faction in 1773. Cushing was also always keen to portray Boston as orderly, and was wary of British depictions of New Englanders as riotous and Boston as in chaos. In the wake of the trouble over the Townshend duties (1767), one of several parliamentary attempts to impose taxation without representation on the American colonists in the decades leading to the American War of Independence, Townshend declared to Dennys DeBerdt in London that 'I am persuaded the commanders of the troops and men-of-war [sent to Boston] are not a little surprised at the errand they were sent upon; they will find themselves placed among an orderly peaceable and well-behaved people' ('Letters', 353).

In 1773 Cushing became more supportive of American patriotism when faced with the 'Intolerable Acts', which were passed by parliament in response to the patriots' dumping of East India Company tea into Boston's harbour. One of the measures included the closure of Boston's port, which Cushing as a merchant adamantly opposed. In 1774 and 1775 he was part of the Massachusetts delegation to the first and second continental congresses. There Cushing once again found himself to be a moderate, favouring economic measures rather than force. Like many other moderates, he was shed from Congress's ranks, as that body became increasingly radical and bent on a war of independence. After being replaced in December 1775 he served briefly as an agent for the navy before returning to Massachusetts political life. His reputation as a moderate evidently did not hinder his office-holding in the revolutionary government of Massachusetts, in which he was judge of probate, chief justice of the court of common pleas for Suffolk county (which included Boston), and justice of the superior court. He also became a founder of the American Academy of Arts and Sciences in Boston in 1780.

By the early 1780s any animosity between Cushing and the leading radical of the pre-revolutionary era had evaporated. He joined Samuel Adams in an unsuccessful bid to create an all-powerful single legislature in the state constitutional convention of 1780. Cushing was elected the first lieutenant-governor under the new constitution alongside the first governor, John Hancock. The two were repeatedly re-elected until Hancock, conveniently pleading poor health, unexpectedly resigned in December 1785, probably in an effort to avoid accountability for an economic depression and a nearly bankrupt government. Cushing then ran for the governorship with Hancock's support, but was defeated narrowly by Hancock's outspoken critic James Boudoin. By election of the legislature, Cushing kept his position as lieutenant-governor. The Hancock–Cushing ticket was reinstated the following year when Hancock was re-elected governor. Cushing kept his office until his death at Boston of lung fever on 28 February 1788.　　　　　　　　　TROY O. BICKHAM

Sources 'Letters of Thomas Cushing, from 1767–1775', *Collections of the Massachusetts Historical Society*, 4th ser., 4 (1858), 347–66 · C. E. Kershaw, 'Cushing, Thomas', *ANB* · C. K. Shipton, *Sibley's Harvard graduates: biographical sketches of those who attended Harvard College*, 11 (1960), 377–95
Archives L. Cong., Dennys DeBerdt letter-book

Cushing [*née* May; *other married name* Williams], **Winifred Emma** [*pseud.* Patience Strong] (**1907–1990**), author and poet, was born on 4 June 1907 in Catford, London, the younger daughter and second of three children of Alfred William May, postal worker at Mount Pleasant, London, and his wife, Nell Mason. She played the piano by ear at the age of four and began composing verses when very young. She was educated at the local school in Catford and then at Cusack's College, where she learned shorthand and typing. She worked in a patent agency and subsequently in a music publisher's office, which stimulated her interest in writing lyrics for popular music. She was nurtured by Lawrence Wright, an influential music publisher of the time, and among the lyrics she subsequently wrote were those for the well-known tango 'Jealousy', and the ballad 'The Dream of Olwen'.

In August 1935, spurred by the success of the prose poem writer Wilhelmina Stitch, who wrote regularly for the *Daily Sketch*, she decided to try to perform a similar service for the rival *Daily Mirror* and, 'with a poem in my pocket'—the subsequent title of her autobiography—she visited the paper's features editor with her proposal. He was impressed and invited her to return the following day with eighteen further poems, and a suitable pseudonym for a regular column. That evening a friend visited her with the gift of a book by an American author, Adeline D. T. Whitney, with the title *Patience Strong* (1870). The next day she presented the editor with the further poems—and her new name.

Patience Strong continued to write a daily poem for the *Daily Mirror*, without interruption, from then onwards and throughout the Second World War, under the heading 'The Quiet Corner', which became synonymous with her work. Some critics derided her verse for its sentimentality, but readers responded warmly to her poems and to her philosophy, feeling that they knew her personally and could confide in her; she replied to each correspondent,

Winifred Emma Cushing [Patience Strong] (1907–1990), by Howard Coster, 1936

and her office at her home became something of an adjunct to the local post office, when servicemen and women, and those left at home, wrote to thank her for her poems and support, explaining that she had been able, through her verses, to speak for them. An example of her work is:

> Give me a window with a view that flows to meet the sky.
> Give me a garden where the trees can feel the winds blow by …
> Give me good days and sleep-blessed nights when I have closed the door
> —and anyone can have the world. I'll never ask for more.
> (P. Strong, *Give me a Quiet Corner*, 1972)

In the late 1940s Strong transferred from the *Daily Mirror* to its sister Sunday newspaper, *The Pictorial* (subsequently the *Sunday Mirror*), and she also began contributing her poems to the weekly magazine *Woman's Own*. Her sojourn with each was over forty years. Latterly her poems appeared in the quarterly journal *This England*.

In the late 1930s Strong's books of prose poems began publication, with *Every Common Bush* (1937), and many titles followed, published by Frederick Muller, under which imprint her books appeared until her death, when posthumous compilations were issued. Her books, which numbered more than seventy, include *Quiet Corner Reflections* (1938), *A Christmas Garland* (1948), *The Patience Strong Bedside Book* (1953), *The Blessings of the Years* (1963), *Come Happy Day* (1966), *A Joy Forever* (1973), *Poems from the Fighting Forties* (1982), and *Fifty Golden Years* (1985, to commemorate her fiftieth anniversary as Patience Strong). She also wrote many booklets with a specifically religious basis for the Henry E. Walter Company. Her posthumous publications included *Tapestries of Time* (1991) and many of her early titles were reissued by Grace Publishers. Patience Strong's poems appeared on calendars and greetings cards and similar publications for more than fifty years, and also continued to be published. Two gramophone records of the author reciting favourite poems were issued: 'The Quiet Hour' (1963) and 'The Quiet Corner' (1978).

Patience Strong was attractive in personality and appearance, and her beauty could not better have complemented the nature of her work. She was a devout Christian who explored many churches—Baptist, Methodist, Church of England, Christian Science, and, in later years, the British Israel movement. Her faith in God governed her life. She had a great gift for communication, and regarded this as her mission in life. She was a countrywoman, who found her inspiration in the changing seasons of the English countryside, in all its moods, as shown in her verse:

> This is what he dreamed about beneath the desert sky:
> brown earth breaking on the plough and white gulls
>   wheeling by ...
> This is what he fought for on a beach in Normandy:
> parish church and village green, his English legacy.
> These things did he know and love. He lived and died for
>   them ...
> Speak no word. The evening thrush will sing his requiem.
> (P. Strong, *Magic Casements*, 1950)

In 1931 Strong married the son of a master builder who was an alderman of the city of Liverpool, Frederick Arnold (Paddy) Williams, architect. He died in 1965, and in 1967 she married Guy Cushing, buyer, who had retired from the John Lewis Partnership, the son of William Isaac Cushing, draper, and his wife, Amanda, the great friend of the author who had given her the book *Patience Strong* many years before. He predeceased her in 1979. There were no children of either marriage. Patience Strong was made a freeman of the City of London in 1970. She died on 28 August 1990 at her home, Sunnyside, The Street, Sedlescombe, Sussex.   DOREEN MONTGOMERY, *rev.*

Sources P. Strong, *With a poem in my pocket* (1981) · personal knowledge (1996) · *The Independent* (1 Sept 1990) · *The Times* (31 Aug 1990) · **Likenesses** H. Coster, photograph, 1936, NPG [*see illus.*] · **Wealth at death** £231,873: probate, 18 Dec 1990, *CGPLA Eng. & Wales*

Cushny, Arthur Robertson (1866–1926), pharmacologist, was born at Speymouth, Morayshire, on 6 March 1866, the fourth son of the Revd John Cushny, minister of the established church successively at Fochabers, Speymouth, and Huntly, and his wife, Catherine Ogilvie, daughter of Alexander Brown, procurator fiscal of Elgin. He was educated at Fochabers Academy and Aberdeen University, where he graduated MA in 1886 and MB, CM in 1889. At Aberdeen John Theodore Cash, regius professor of materia medica, aroused his interest in pharmacology. As holder of the George Thompson fellowship Cushny worked for a year at Bern under Hugo Kronecker, and later at Strasbourg under Oswald Schmiedeberg, then the most distinguished pharmacologist in Europe. From 1892 to 1893 he acted as Schmiedeberg's assistant, and in the latter year, on the recommendation of the American pharmacologist

Arthur Robertson Cushny (1866–1926), by John Moffat

John Abel, was appointed, at the age of twenty-seven, to the chair of pharmacology in the University of Michigan at Ann Arbor. In 1896 he married Sarah Firbank, an Englishwoman whom he had met in Strasbourg. She was the daughter of Ralph Firbank, a railway engineer. They had one daughter.

In 1905 Cushny returned to England in order to become the first professor of pharmacology in University College, London. The chair was the first of its kind in England, designed to ensure emphasis on experimental pharmacology. In 1918 he succeeded Sir Thomas Fraser as professor of materia medica and pharmacology at Edinburgh University.

While at Ann Arbor, Cushny continued researches, begun at Strasbourg, on the action of the digitalis glucosides, which involved also an investigation of the physiology of the mammalian heart—subjects on which he wrote many papers, culminating in an exhaustive monograph, *The Action and Uses in Medicine of Digitalis and its Allies* (1925). In the course of these studies he incidentally suggested that the clinical condition known as *delirium cordis* might be identical with auricular fibrillation, a heterodox prediction which was verified ten years later as the result of the application of electrocardiographic methods to humans. The condition now known as auricular fibrillation has proved to be one of the most important diseases of the heart.

While in the United States, Cushny also began to study

experimentally the functions of the kidneys and the action of diuretics. To this subject he made many valuable contributions, and published *The Secretion of Urine* (1st edn, 1917; 2nd edn, 1926), in which he co-ordinated the mass of contradictory evidence which had accumulated since Carl Ludwig's day, for which purpose, as he says in the preface, 'it was necessary to sift thoroughly this mass of printed matter of over 6,000 pages'. His account of kidney secretion was accepted not only as the most authoritative critical review of past work, it also put forward a novel view of the functions of the kidney which was to serve as a foundation for further research, and is specially associated with Cushny's name.

In 1903 Cushny published his first study of the pharmacological actions of optical isomers, in which he showed that *l*-hyoxyamine is about twenty times as active as the *d*-isomer, and about twice as active as the *dl*-compound (atropine). Later he made similar quantitative studies of other optical isomers, which proved, as is now accepted, that two substances, identical in chemical composition and structure apart from their optical activity, may differ widely in pharmacological activity. He went on to demonstrate how complex the pharmacological action of optical isomers could be. Cushny summarized his own and other investigations on this subject in the Dohme lectures delivered at the Johns Hopkins University at Baltimore in 1925, published as *Biological Relations of Optically Isomeric Substances* in 1926.

These three subjects formed, perhaps, Cushny's chief scientific interests, and his contributions to them constitute his main claim to a permanent position in the history of his science. In addition he published a long and valuable series of monographs covering a wide field of pharmacological inquiry. In 1899 appeared the first edition of his *Textbook of Pharmacology and Therapeutics*, which went through eight editions in his lifetime. It was the first authoritative textbook to be written in English by an experimental pharmacologist, and it played an important part in guiding teaching and research during a period in which therapeutics was emerging from the mists of tradition and empiricism.

The originality of his researches, the authority of his writings, and his international friendships made Cushny one of the leading pharmacologists of his generation. He was a man large of mind, heart, and stature, outwardly austere, inwardly kindly, generous in helping others. He served on many commissions and international conferences, notably the royal commission on whisky and other potable spirits (1908). He received honorary degrees from the universities of Aberdeen and Michigan and was elected FRS in 1907 and to the Royal Society of Edinburgh in 1919. Cushny died suddenly of a cerebral haemorrhage at his home, Peffermill House, Edinburgh, on 25 February 1926. His wife and daughter survived him.

J. A. GUNN, rev. M. P. EARLES

Sources DSB, 15.99–104 · WWW, 1916–28 · *Journal of Pharmacology and Experimental Therapeutics*, 27 (1926), 265–86 · H. H. D. [H. H. Dale], PRS, 100B (1926), xix–xxvii · *The Lancet* (6 March 1926), 519–20 · BMJ (6 March 1926), 455–7 · H. Holmstedt and G. Liljestrand,

Readings in pharmacology (1963), 261–8 · J. Parascandola, *The development of American pharmacology* (1992) · private information (1937) · personal knowledge (1937) · *CGPLA Eng. & Wales* (1926)

Archives U. Edin. L., special collections division, lectures and laboratory notes · Wellcome L., corresp., notebook, papers

Likenesses photograph, 1925–6, U. Edin. · J. Moffat, photograph, Wellcome L. [*see illus.*] · photograph, repro. in *Journal of Pharmacology and Experimental Therapeutics* · photograph, repro. in PRS · photograph, repro. in BMJ · photograph, repro. in *The Lancet* · photograph, repro. in Holmstedt and Liljestrand, *Readings in pharmacology*

Wealth at death £22,140: probate, 28 March 1926, *CGPLA Eng. & Wales*

Cusins, Sir William George (1833–1893), pianist and conductor, was born in London on 14 October 1833. As a child he sang in the Chapel Royal, then entered the Brussels conservatory where for two years he studied composition, piano, and violin under François-Joseph Fétis and others. In December 1847 he won a king's scholarship to the Royal Academy of Music, to which he was re-elected in 1849; here his teachers were Cipriani Potter, Charles Lucas, Sterndale Bennett, and Prosper Sainton. In the same year he was appointed organist of Queen Victoria's private chapel at Windsor and became a violinist at the Royal Italian Opera under Costa. In 1851 he was made an assistant professor at the Royal Academy, later professor. From 1867 to 1883 he conducted the concerts of the Philharmonic Society, giving in all 134 concerts, including the first English performance of Schubert's 'Great' C major symphony (1871) and Brahms's *German Requiem* (2 April 1873). In 1870 he was appointed master of the queen's music in succession to his uncle George Frederick Anderson. In 1883 he became an honorary member of the Accademia di Santa Cecilia. He conducted the London Select Choir in 1885, when he was also appointed professor of piano at the Guildhall School of Music. He was knighted in 1892, and awarded the cross of the Spanish order of Isabella the Catholic in 1893.

Cusins performed as a pianist at the Gewandhaus, Leipzig, in 1856, and in Rome (1883) and Berlin, as well as at many London concerts. He gave his own annual series in London from 1885. As a conductor he was praised for his 'steadiness and decision of purpose' and his 'care and earnestness'. Eduard Hanslick, visiting England in 1886, described him as 'a pedantic gentleman, with grey whiskers, black coat, and white tie … He looks exactly like an English clergyman, and conducts also very piously'. His compositions include a *Royal Wedding Serenata* (1863), two concert overtures, *Les travailleurs de la mer* (1869) and *Love's Labour's Lost* (1875), an oratorio, *Gideon* (Gloucester, 1871), a trio in C minor (1882), Te Deum (1882), a jubilee cantata, *Grant the Queen a Long Life* (1887), a septet for wind and bass (1891), a symphony in C (1892), a violin sonata in A minor (1893), and an unpublished piano concerto in A minor and a violin concerto, as well as many anthems, Masonic prayers, songs, and piano pieces. He also edited a collection of settings of Tennyson (1880) and some of Schumann's piano music. His publications include *Handel's 'Messiah': an Examination of the Original and some Contemporary MSS* (1874), described by the Handel scholar William

C. Smith as 'an important foundation pamphlet', and a long article on Agostino Steffani, which appeared in the earlier editions of *Grove's Dictionary of Music and Musicians* and which, though now superseded by modern research, continues to be cited as a pioneering piece of work. In 1862 he married Louisa Mary, daughter of G. H. Ladbury. He died suddenly from influenza at the Hôtel de la Grotte in Remouchamps, Ardennes, Belgium, on 31 August 1893, survived by his widow and children. He was buried temporarily at Spa in Belgium, and reinterred at Kensal Green cemetery on 30 October 1894.

F. G. EDWARDS, rev. JOHN WARRACK

Sources Grove, *Dict. mus.* · *New Grove* · Brown & Stratton, *Brit. mus.* · *Musical Herald* (Dec 1892), 355–7 · private information (1901) · M. B. Foster, *History of the Philharmonic Society of London: 1813–1912* (1912) · 'Dr Hanslick on music in England', *MT*, 27 (1886), 518–20 [orig. in *Neue Freie Presse*] · *The Magazine of Music*, 10/7 (July 1893) · Burke, *Peerage*
Likenesses Barraud, photograph, repro. in *Musical Herald*, 355
Wealth at death £3741 8s. 8d.: probate, 25 Oct 1893, *CGPLA Eng. & Wales*

Cussans, John Edwin (1837–1899), antiquary, was born on 30 October 1837 at Gloster Place, Plymouth, Devon, the second son (of eleven children) of Thomas Cussans (b. 1797?) and Matilda Ann, *née* Southwood (d. 1870). His father and grandfather had been army officers, and the family had connections with Jamaica. Educated at the South Devon collegiate school in Plymouth from 1848 to 1852, Cussans became a mercantile clerk in London in 1853. He went to America in 1858, possibly as a photographer and draughtsman, and by 1861 was correspondent of the *Morning Chronicle*. His dispatches, favourable to the Confederacy, required a speedy departure from New York. He immediately went to Russia as a photographer, but returned in 1863 to London, where he resided for the rest of his life.

Cussans's commitment was henceforth to writing on genealogy and heraldry, and, above all, to the preparation of his *History of Hertfordshire*. Where he obtained his profound historical and heraldic knowledge is unknown. His *Handbook of Heraldry* (1869) went to many editions and became a standard work. It was during the 1860s that he prepared his *History of Hertfordshire* (3 vols., 1870–81), for which he is now chiefly known. This massive undertaking, of which he commented 'I loved my work too well to get rid of it in a perfunctory manner' (Johnson, 'Introduction', x), contained complex genealogies as well as engravings. It covered not only the gentry but also more humble folk, with an emphasis on the Church of England and its clergy. He financed the volumes by subscription, but eventually admitted that he lost £3000 on the venture. Financial necessity forced him in 1881 to enter the service of the Anglo-Californian Bank, of which he became secretary; gout necessitated his retirement in 1897. The *History* is a tour de force, based firmly on his travels in Hertfordshire, and his corrections of Robert Clutterbuck's earlier history of 1827. It is an accurate account containing numerous personal anecdotes, many of them humorous. Cussans's annotated copy (now in the collection of Hertfordshire Archives and Local Studies) reveals his prejudices, and provides an intriguing picture of nineteenth-century Hertfordshire life. He records, for example, that Colonel Clinton of Cockenhatch, Barkway, 'was never seen there except on Sundays, when Sheriffs' writs could not be served' (Johnson, 'Introduction', xi). Robert Kennard of Theobalds enlarged his fortune by supplying stores to the government during the Crimean War: 'If rumour may be believed (and in this case I think it can), suffice it to say that the official examination of stores was very lax' (ibid.). The *History* was reissued in 1972, and extracts from Cussans's grangerized version appeared in 1987, under the title *A Professional Hertfordshire Tramp*. His wit and gaiety led William Branch Johnson to call Cussans the 'laughing historian'.

Cussans married Emma Prior Ward (b. in or after 1841), daughter of John Prior Ward and his wife, Sarah, *née* Hunt, on 10 March 1863. She survived him, and of their ten children eight were alive when Cussans died of acute gout on 11 September 1899 at his home, 46 St John's Park, Upper Holloway, London. He was buried at Highgate cemetery.

ALAN RUSTON

Sources W. B. Johnson, introduction, in J. E. Cussans, *History of Hertfordshire*, 1 (1972), v–xiv · *Hertfordshire Mercury* (23 Sept 1899) · A. de C. Cussans, 'John Edwin Cussans: herald and historian', *Hertfordshire Countryside*, 12/48 (1958), 136–7 · W. B. Johnson, 'Laughing historian: John Edwin Cussans, 1837–1899', *Hertfordshire Past and Present*, no. 11 (1971), 35–42 · [J. E. Cussans], *A professional Hertfordshire tramp*, ed. A. Deacon and P. Walne, Hertfordshire Record Society, 3 (1987) · W. B. Johnson, 'John Edwin Cussans—his annotated history', *Hertfordshire Countryside*, 13/52 (1959), 162–3 · W. B. Johnson, 'John Edwin Cussans—his annotated history', *Hertfordshire Countryside*, 13/54 (1959), 64–5 · b. cert. · m. cert. · d. cert.
Archives Cheshunt Public Library · Herts. ALS, Hertfordshire collections, corresp. and papers | Herts. ALS, corresp. with J. W. Carlile
Likenesses photograph or engraving, Herts. ALS
Wealth at death £2194 15s. 9d.: probate, 6 Oct 1899, *CGPLA Eng. & Wales*

Cust, Aleen Isabel (1868–1937), veterinary surgeon, was born on 7 February 1868 at Cordangan Manor, co. Tipperary, Ireland, the fourth of six children of Sir Leopold Cust, baronet (1832–1878), land agent, and his wife, Charlotte Sobieske Isabel (1835–1914), daughter of Vice-Admiral Charles Orlando Bridgeman. Aleen was the granddaughter of Sir Edward *Cust (1794–1878). On the death of her father in 1878, her mother and Major Shallcross Fitzherbert Widdrington of Newton Hall, Northumberland, became her joint guardians. Aleen became a close friend of the Widdringtons, who recognized her independent spirit and gave her the moral support that she did not receive from her family. After a private education Aleen began training as a nurse at the London Hospital, but she gave it up and decided to become a veterinary surgeon. Her family disapproved, but she had a modest private income and in 1894, at the age of twenty-six, she proceeded to Edinburgh, adopted the surname Custance to avoid further embarrassment to her family, and for the next five years had a frugal existence as a student. Having spent the first year in gaining qualifications for entry, she was admitted to the New Veterinary College, Edinburgh (the school founded by William Williams in 1873, not to be confused with the New Edinburgh Veterinary College which John Gamgee founded in 1858 or the Edinburgh Veterinary College founded by William Dick in 1823). She eventually went on to qualify as Britain's first woman veterinary surgeon.

Aleen was a distinguished student, first in her classes and a gold medal winner in her first year. In May 1897 she was due to sit the first of her professional examinations but on receiving an application from Miss Custance the examinations committee of the Royal College of Veterinary Surgeons decided they did not have the power to admit women to their examinations. The council of the college was divided on the matter and when the minutes of the meeting were published in the *Veterinary Record* of 24 April 1897 the profession at large took up the debate. The college took counsel's opinion; they were advised not to admit the lady and to invite her to issue a writ of *mandamus*. Aleen wanted the proceedings to be held in Scotland but the college refused and she took it no further. She completed her training in 1900, and although she could not call herself a veterinary surgeon Professor Williams gave her a testimonial and recommended her for a post as an assistant to William Augustine Byrne (1865–1910), who was in practice in co. Roscommon, Ireland. Byrne had qualified the previous year at the Royal Veterinary College, London, and on inheriting Castlestrange, a castle in Athleague, he set up in practice there. He was an engaging personality, handsome, witty, and popular both socially and professionally. The arrival of Miss Cust as his assistant caused consternation and scandalized the priesthood, but her competence and poise won her respect. There is reason to believe that they lived as man and wife and that she had two daughters, born in Scotland, who were later adopted. Aleen never married, though in 1904 she was engaged to Bertram Widdrington, son of her guardian.

As Aleen's reputation grew she became more widely accepted by the profession, but in 1905 she was again in conflict with the Royal College of Veterinary Surgeons. She had been appointed by Galway county council to the part-time, official post of veterinary inspector under the Diseases of Animals Act. The college opposed the appointment because she was not a member, and the Irish department of agriculture would not approve it. The post had to be re-advertised, but when the county council again appointed Miss Cust the department agreed to a provisional arrangement whereby she was designated an 'inspector', but not a 'veterinary inspector'. At that time she was living in Ballygar, several miles from Athleague, presumably in practice on her own account. When Byrne died in 1910 she took over his practice, which she ran from Fort Lyster, a house in Athleague. She made her visits riding side-saddle on an Arab stallion, or driving one of her several horses in a gig. When the day's work was done she would dress formally for dinner, and be waited on by her servants.

In 1915 Aleen left Ireland to offer her services during the First World War. She drove her own car to Abbeville in France and attached herself to an establishment of the Young Men's Christian Association. The probable reason for her going there was because it was close to the headquarters of the army veterinary and remount services. The hard-pressed veterinary corps was handling tens of thousands of horses in transit to and from the front, and it may be surmised that Aleen was keen to volunteer her considerable veterinary experience with horses, albeit unofficially. The records of her war service are sparse but there is one reference to Miss Cust in the war diary of Brigadier-General Garrat and another in the diary of Major-General Sir John Moore, the director of veterinary services in France. War Office records show that she was in the Queen Mary's Army Auxiliary Corps from 14 January 1918 to 10 November 1918.

With the passing of the Sex Disqualification (Removal) Act of 1919, which forbade the exclusion of women from the professions, the Royal College of Veterinary Surgeons could no longer refuse to consider Aleen Cust for membership. On receiving her application the examinations committee had the courtesy to require that she attend only the oral part of the final examination. She was awarded her diploma of membership on 21 December 1922, twenty-two years after completing her training in Edinburgh. Aleen had returned to Athleague after the war but was no longer welcomed in what became the Irish Free State, and in 1924 she retired to Plaitford in the New Forest. In the autumn of 1936, when her health was failing, she planned to spend the winter with friends in Jamaica. She arrived on 5 January 1937 but died on Kingston Island, probably of a heart attack, on the 29th, and was buried there.

SHERWIN A. HALL

Sources C. Ford, *Aleen Cust, veterinary surgeon: Britain's first woman vet* (1990) · *CGPLA Eng. & Wales* (1937) · private information (1997) · Burke, *Peerage*
Likenesses charcoal drawing, 1965 (after photograph repro. in *Veterinary Record*), Royal College of Veterinary Surgeons · photograph, repro. in *Veterinary Record* (7 April 1934)
Wealth at death £29,915 11s. 8d.: probate, 14 April 1937, *CGPLA Eng. & Wales*

Cust, Sir Edward, baronet (1794–1878), army officer, historian, and politician, sixth son of Brownlow Cust, first Baron Brownlow (1744–1807), and his second wife, Frances (1756–1847), *née* Bankes, and brother of John Cust, first Earl Brownlow, was born at 30 Hill Street, Berkeley Square, London, on 17 March 1794. He was educated at Eton College (1805–8) and Sandhurst, gazetted a cornet in the 16th light dragoons on 15 March 1810, and was present at the battle of Fuentes de Oñoro. He was promoted lieutenant into the 14th light dragoons on 27 December 1810, and served with them at the sieges of Ciudad Rodrigo and Badajoz, and in the battles of Salamanca, Vitoria, the Pyrenees, the Nivelle, and the Nive, and left the army in the field only on promotion to the rank of captain in the 16th light dragoons in December 1813. He was placed on half pay in 1814, recalled to service in 1815 in the 5th dragoon guards, and did not see active service again. He became major in 1821, and was promoted lieutenant-colonel in 1826, colonel in 1841, major-general in 1851, lieutenant-general in 1859, colonel of the 16th light dragoons in 1859, and general in 1866.

In 1816 Prince Leopold of Saxe-Coburg-Saalfeld appointed Cust as his equerry. This post he held for many years, and became master of the household to the king, retaining a position of confidence until the king's death. In 1831, when Leopold was made king of the Belgians, Cust was made KCH.

Cust was tory MP for Grantham from 1818 until 1826, when he was elected for Lostwithiel, which he represented until its suppression by the 1832 Reform Act. He criticized the public architectural works of the time, and succeeded in securing a system of competition for public buildings, under which he was named a commissioner for rebuilding the houses of parliament and for selecting the design of the Wellington monument.

In 1845 Cust was appointed assistant master of the ceremonies to the queen, and in 1847 master of the ceremonies. He enjoyed her personal friendship for many years, and resigned his post only because of ill health in February 1876, when he was created a baronet. He dabbled in literature, and wrote military histories, which were at one time valued: *Annals of the Wars of the Eighteenth Century* (5 vols., 1857) and *Lives of the Warriors of the Thirty Years' War* (2 vols., 1865). For these he received in 1869 the gold medal of the Austrian empire from the emperor. He also wrote *Noctes dominicae, or, Sunday Night Readings* (1848) and *Family Readings: the New Testament Harmonised and Explained* (1850). For these an honorary DCL was conferred on him in 1853 by the University of Oxford. He was for many years senior magistrate for the hundred of Wirral.

Cust married on 11 January 1821, at Marylebone church, Mary Anne, only child of Lewis William Boode, of Amsterdam and Peover Hall, Cheshire, and heir of her mother, Margaret Dannett, of Leasowe Castle, Birkenhead, daughter of the Revd Thomas Dannett, rector of Liverpool. Mary Cust was a lady of the bedchamber to the duchess of Kent, mother of Queen Victoria. A cat fancier, she wrote *The Cat: its History and Diseases* (1856). Sir Edward died at 84 Jermyn Street, St James's, on 14 January 1878, in his eighty-fourth year, one of the last surviving Peninsular officers, and was buried at Belton, near Grantham. Lady Cust died on 19 July 1882, aged eighty-two. She and Sir Edward left one son, Leopold, who succeeded his father, and four daughters.

[Anon.], rev. James Lunt

Sources Hart's Army List · The Times (17 Jan 1878) · H. Graham, *History of the sixteenth, the queen's, light dragoons (lancers), 1759–1912* (privately printed, Devizes, 1912) · Boase, *Mod. Eng. biog.* · GEC, *Peerage* · HoP, *Commons* · Burke, *Peerage*
Archives Flintshire RO, Hawarden, corresp. and papers · NRA, priv. coll., corresp. and papers | BL, corresp. with Sir Robert Peel, Add. MSS 40395–40583 · Flintshire RO, Hawarden, Erddig MSS
Wealth at death under £18,000: probate, 2 July 1878, *CGPLA Eng. & Wales*

Cust, Henry John Cockayne [Harry] (**1861–1917**), politician and journalist, was born on 10 October 1861 in London, the elder son of Henry Francis Cockayne Cust (1819–1884), Conservative MP for Grantham (1874–80) and a major in the north Salopian yeomanry cavalry, and his wife, Sarah Jane (d. 1867), daughter of Isaac Cookson, of Meldon Park, Northumberland, and widow of Major Sidney Streatfeild. He went to Eton College in 1874, where he was captain of the Oppidans, and in 1881 entered Trinity College, Cambridge. At Cambridge he was a member of the boat club and of the Magpie and Stump (a light-hearted debating society) and was elected to the Apostles, the exclusive literary society, in 1883. He was elected to a scholarship at Trinity in that year and graduated BA with second-class honours in the classical tripos in 1884. He was admitted to the Inner Temple on 17 August 1888 but was not called. He obtained the *baccalauréat en droit* in Paris but did not practise. Instead, he decided to forgo a legal career and entered parliament in 1890 as Conservative MP for Stamford, Lincolnshire.

Cust was a socialite and a member of the Crabbet Club (1888–94), founded by Wilfrid Scawen Blunt, whose members included George Curzon and George Wyndham. He was also a member of the intellectual and aristocratic coterie called the Souls. The group included some of the most wealthy and powerful men and women of the day, among whom were George Curzon, Margot Tennant (later Lady Asquith), and the politicians Arthur Balfour and George Wyndham. Cust, as a handsome young man, was popular among the set and had numerous affairs, one of which was with Violet *Manners (1856–1937), wife of Lord Granby. Despite the knowledge of the affair among the Souls, the birth of their daughter Lady Diana Manners (later Lady Diana *Cooper) in 1892 was not acknowledged until well into the twentieth century. Cust left Violet for an affair with Pamela Wyndham, sister of George Wyndham, but she was sent to India to get over Cust. Cust then seduced Emmeline Mary Elizabeth (Nina) Welby-Gregory (1867–1955), daughter of Sir William Earle Welby-Gregory, fourth baronet. Under pressure from Balfour, he was forced to marry her on 11 October 1893, when it was thought that she was pregnant by him. Nina adored her husband but this affection was not returned and she lived a childless and lonely marriage.

In 1895 Cust retired from parliament. He had been denounced by the feminist Millicent Fawcett, as a scoundrel unfit for public office. He devoted himself to journalism. In October 1892 he met the American millionaire William Waldorf Astor, who, at their first meeting, invited Cust to edit the *Pall Mall Gazette*. He accepted at once, despite lacking any working knowledge of such a position. During his editorship he made the paper the best evening paper of the day. Among his contributors were H. G. Wells, Alice Meynell, and Rudyard Kipling. His journalism was active in that he did not flinch from saying what he thought needed to be said. This strong trait, together with political disagreements and the rejection of Astor's own written contributions, finally forced Astor to dismiss him in February 1896. Such was the loyalty of his staff that they had to be persuaded by him not to resign. His short period as an editor was the high point of his professional career.

Cust continued his social life in London and found time to write the introduction to Machiavelli's *The Art of War* and *Florentine History* in the Tudor Translations series, edited by his friend W. E. Henley. During his time at the *Pall Mall Gazette* Cust contributed many poems and these were collected by his widow and his nephew Ronald Storrs and published in 1918 as *Occasional Poems*. As a poet his sole claim to fame was as author of 'Non nobis domine', though his authorship was not recognized until the second edition of the *Oxford Book of English Verse* (1939). In 1900 he re-entered parliament as member for Bermondsey; he remained there until 1906. In August 1914 he founded and became chairman of the fund-raising central committee for national patriotic organizations. He served as a JP for Lincolnshire and also Bedfordshire.

Cust was of average height and an assiduous dresser, as is shown to good effect in the Spy cartoon of 1894. Lady Diana Cooper thought him 'Very beautiful with noble hands and impeccable filbert-shaped nails. He wore a coat such as I never saw another wear—dark blue cloth, flaring, full, with a flat sable Eton collar. It was like Holbein's *Ambassadors*' (Abdy and Gere, 69). He was one of the greatest conversationalists of his time, and Curzon aptly sums him up in the obituary in *The Times*: 'He was the unchallenged leader of the dinner-table. Quip, retort, repartee, quotation, allusion, epigram, jest—all flashed with lightning-speed from that active workshop, his brain' (*The Times*, 3 March 1917). One succinct and brash parliamentary quotation illustrates this: 'My position is quite clear, I have nailed my colours to the fence' (Abdy and Gere, 70). He was the cousin of the third and last Earl Brownlow (1844–1921) and spent his life vainly waiting to inherit the barony of Brownlow. Cust died of heart failure at his home, 17 Hyde Park Gate, London, on 2 March 1917 and after cremation at Golders Green on 5 March was buried at Belton church, Lincolnshire, on 7 March. Nina Cust survived him by thirty-eight years.   DAMIAN ATKINSON

Sources DNB · A. Lambert, *Unquiet Souls: the Indian summer of the British aristocracy, 1880–1918* (1984) · J. Abdy and C. Gere, *The Souls* (1984) · Burke, *Peerage* · Burke, *Gen. GB* · J. W. Robertson Scott, *The life and death of a newspaper* (1952) · R. Storrs, *Orientations* (1937) · Lord Lytton, *Wilfrid Scawen Blunt* (1961) · *The letters of Arthur Balfour and Lady Elcho, 1885–1917*, ed. J. Ridley and C. Percy (1992) · A. Davies, *Dictionary of British portraiture*, 4 (1981), 26 · WWBMP · A. Tinniswood, *Belton House, Lincolnshire* (1992) · D. Griffiths, ed., *The encyclopedia of the British press, 1422–1992* (1992) · Venn, *Alum. Cant.* · WWW · *The Times* (3 March 1917) · *The Times* (6 March 1917)

Archives Lincs. Arch., letters and papers · Princeton University Library · priv. colls. | Bodl. Oxf., corresp. with Margot Asquith · Trinity Cam., letters to Sir Henry Babington Smith

Likenesses photograph, *c.*1890, repro. in Abdy and Gere, *Souls* (1984) · V. Granby, drawing, 1892, repro. in V. Granby, *Portraits of men and women* (1900) · lithograph, 1892, NPG · Spy [L. Ward], cartoon, 1894, NPG; repro. in *VF* (15 Feb 1894) · V. Granby, drawing, 1898, repro. in Lambert, *Unquiet Souls* · N. Cust, tomb effigy, 1920–29, Belton church, Lincolnshire; repro. in Abdy and Gere, *Souls* · N. Cust, bust, Belton House, Lincolnshire; repro. in Tinniswood, *Belton House* · London Stereoscope Co., photograph, repro. in C. Lewis Hind, *Naphtali* (1926) · London Stereoscope Co., postcard, NPG

Wealth at death £16,395 14s. 3d.: administration with will, 31 July 1917, CGPLA Eng. & Wales

Cust, Sir Herbert Edward Purey- (1857–1938), naval officer and hydrographer, was born on 26 February 1857, the second son of Arthur Perceval Purey-Cust (1828–1916), dean of York (1880–1916), and his wife, Lady Emma Bligh, younger daughter of the fifth earl of Darnley. He entered the Royal Navy in 1870, was promoted to midshipman in 1872, and to sub-lieutenant in 1876. He served in the steam frigate *Newcastle* in China, and then in the sloop *Squirrel* at Devonport, where he was promoted to lieutenant. After a time in HMS *Valiant* in the channel squadron, he specialized in hydrographic surveying from 1881. He was appointed to HMS *Fawn* and worked for two years in the Red Sea and on the east coast of Africa. After taking a course in 1884 at the Royal Naval College, Greenwich, where he gained the first prize for general proficiency, he joined the surveying sloop *Rambler*. On passage out to China she was involved in military operations in the Sudan, based on Suakin, for which Purey-Cust was awarded the Egyptian medal and the khedive's bronze star. In China Purey-Cust surveyed the south channel of the Yangtze (Yangzi) River from the imperial Chinese customs cruiser *Kua-Hsing*. His four years in the *Rambler* were followed by three in HMS *Egeria* in the Pacific and the eastern archipelago.

Purey-Cust obtained his first command, the converted yacht *Dart*, in 1892, and spent three and a half years surveying on the east coast of Australia, in Tasmania, and in the New Hebrides (now Vanuatu). Working off the island of Ambrym, *Dart*'s surveys were interrupted by a volcanic eruption, which threw molten lava into the sea near the ship. Steam and dust clouds put a stop to surveying, and the ship's company gave help to the inhabitants of the island before resuming work. Purey-Cust was promoted to commander in 1894, and before leaving Australia in 1895 married Alice Ella (d. 1945), daughter of George Stuart Hepburn of Smeaton. In England Purey-Cust joined the hydrographic department as a naval assistant until, in November 1897, he was sent back to the *Rambler* in command. In three years in this ship he ranged widely, from the Strait of Belle Isle and the West Indies to east and west Africa and the Red Sea. His work included surveys of the South African coast in 1900, for which he successfully applied for the South African medal for himself and his ship's company. He was promoted to captain in 1900, and left the *Rambler* in Malta in 1901. His final sea command was the paddle surveying vessel *Triton* from 1902 to 1905, working in home waters. He was commended by the hydrographer for his ingenuity in devising a transparent plastic protractor, which remained in use until automatic plotting devices were introduced in the 1970s.

In April 1907 Purey-Cust was appointed assistant hydrographer, and two years later became hydrographer of the navy. As the storm clouds gathered over Europe he was much concerned with preparing the hydrographic service for war. He ordered new surveys of the southern North Sea. He also prepared the systems required for promulgating navigational information to warships and friendly merchant vessels under the constraints of wartime secrecy. He relinquished office on 31 August 1914, shortly after war broke out. He had been promoted to rear-admiral in 1910, and made CB in 1911. Not content to idle in retirement, during the war Purey-Cust was commissioned as a captain RNR in November 1914, and appointed in command of the fleet auxiliary *Zaria*; initially employed as a store ship, from 1915 *Zaria* was a depot ship for auxiliary patrol craft, with Purey-Cust holding an appointment as commodore RNR. *Zaria* was paid off early in 1919, when Purey-Cust reverted to the retired list. He had been promoted to vice-admiral on the retired list in 1915, and to admiral in 1919, in which year he was made KBE.

Herbert and Alice Purey-Cust had two children, a son, Arthur John, born in 1897, who followed his father into the Royal Navy and was killed in action in HMS *Strongbow* in October 1917, and a daughter, Marjorie, born in 1905, who survived them both. Sir Herbert died in Highgate on 11 November 1938; he was buried in Highgate cemetery on the 15th.   R. O. MORRIS

Sources A. Day, *The admiralty hydrographic service, 1795–1919* (1967) · *Report by the Hydrographer of the Navy* (1885–1914) · *The Times* (12 Nov 1938) · *The Times* (16 Nov 1938) · Burke, *Peerage*
Likenesses photograph, 1910, Taunton hydrographic office
Wealth at death £29,993 2s. 0d.: probate, 13 Jan 1939, *CGPLA Eng. & Wales*

Cust, Sir John, third baronet (1718–1770), speaker of the House of Commons, was born on 29 August 1718, eldest son of Sir Richard Cust, second baronet (*bap.* 1680, *d.* 1734), landowner, of Leasingham, Lincolnshire, and Anne (*d.* 1779), daughter of Sir William Brownlow, fourth baronet, of Belton, Lincolnshire. He was educated at Grantham grammar school, and from 1731 at Eton College. He was still at school when he succeeded his father in title and estate on 25 July 1734. In 1735 he went to Corpus Christi College, Cambridge, and graduated MA in 1739. He also in 1735 enrolled at the Middle Temple, and was called to the bar in 1742: it is not known whether he ever practised. Cust entered parliament on 18 April 1743, having been returned at a by-election for Grantham by his mother's brother John, who had obtained an Irish peerage as Viscount Tyrconnel in 1718. The Belton estate, which controlled one seat in that borough, was bequeathed to Cust's mother when Lord Tyrconnel died on 27 February 1754, and Cust continued to represent Grantham until his death. Shortly after entering parliament he married, on 8 December 1743, Etheldred (1719/20–1775), daughter of Thomas Payne of Hough, Lincolnshire, and Elizabeth Folkes; they had two sons and two daughters.

In parliament Cust voted with government until 1746, being a whig supporter of Henry Pelham and the duke of Newcastle. But in 1747 he went over to the new Leicester House opposition of Frederick, prince of Wales, and was appointed a clerk in his household, with the task of supervising the bill of fare. He was put down for a post in the Treasury when the prince should become king. After the prince died in 1751 Cust was appointed a clerk in the household of his widow and son, and, since the princess dowager of Wales sided with the Pelham ministry, again voted with government until Leicester House reverted to opposition in 1755. Cust resented the growing ascendancy of Lord Bute at the court of the young prince of Wales, and

resigned his post there in 1756. During the Seven Years' War he spent much time with the Lincolnshire militia, being colonel of its southern battalion from 1758 to 1761, and he had made little impact on the House of Commons before his elevation to the speaker's chair in 1761.

Cust was not one of those first thought of on the retirement of Arthur Onslow, the speaker throughout George II's reign. But after difficulty arose in filling the vacancy, Cust's friends and family pushed his candidature, especially with the Commons leader George Grenville. Cust's pleasant character had made him no enemies, and Lord Bute, George III's favourite, did not hold his previous conduct against him. The head of the ministry, the duke of Newcastle, wrote to the duke of Bedford on 20 October, 'They have … determined to have Sir John Cust. I doubt not a very bright one, but a sort of plodding orderly man' (*Correspondence*, 3.62). He admitted private misgivings to an old friend, John White. 'He is not of my recommendation, and consequently I am not answerable for his fitness for his office' (BL, Add. MS 32929, fol. 409). The success of Arthur Onslow had led contemporaries to underestimate the task of being speaker. Horace Walpole, who has misled historians by stating that Cust was a tory nominated by Lord Bute, and later proved a severe critic of Cust as speaker, did not at the time foresee any problem. 'Bating his nose, the Chair seems well filled' (*Letters of Horace Walpole*, 5.140). Cust was chosen speaker on 3 November 1761 without opposition, and revived the old but lapsed tradition of professed modesty, of both a 'disabling speech' and token resistance on the way to the chair. The charade was to prove all too true. Cust was a squire, with little aptitude for the post. He did possess considerable knowledge of parliamentary history, rather than procedure, and assisted in the ongoing compilation of an index to the Commons journals. But he lacked the forceful personality needed for the stormy debates of the 1760s.

The speaker's chair was not yet above politics, but Cust's mother, to assure his financial independence of government, on his election to the chair made over to him the main Brownlow estate of Belton. Cust did not need or receive an office while he was speaker, but he regarded it as part of his duty to give advice and assistance to government. He attended various meetings of leading ministerial members summoned to discuss forthcoming parliamentary business: and the continuing contemporary view of the chair as an adjunct of government was reflected in an abortive opposition plan to challenge his reappointment in the new parliament of 1768. The speaker could not debate from the chair, or allow his opinions to bias his conduct there. Only once is Cust known to have incurred criticism in that respect, over the Cumberland election case of 1768, and his intervention then was excused as an opinion on a point of procedure. Convention allowed Cust to speak in committee. Sir John did so on America in 1766, opposing the Rockingham ministry by his support of Grenville's coercive approach to the colonies. In 1769 the controversial Middlesex election case was never debated in committee, but Cust personally intervened to frustrate an opposition move to send a petition from Lincoln on that subject, even using his status as speaker to explain and defend the Commons resolution.

It was not Cust's political bias that led to criticism of him as a speaker, but his general incompetence in respect of both procedural knowledge and the maintenance of order. There is abundant evidence that many of Cust's procedural opinions from the chair were not in accordance with previous parliamentary practice. Sometimes they were ignored, and sometimes overruled, as on the use of the king's name in debate on 11 December 1761, and on his opinion of 10 February 1764 that a committee was necessary before any tax could be repealed. A speaker so often wrong could not command respect. But it was Cust's failure to maintain order in debate that made his spell in the chair notorious. He never carried out his threats of 'naming' disorderly members, and his resorts to general reproofs were unavailing. Contemporary comments confirm the impression of his weakness that is conveyed by the direct evidence of the debates, as when parliamentary diarists often wrote 'noise'. On his resignation in 1770 Horace Walpole wrote, 'In no light was Sir John Cust a loss. His want of parts and spirit had been very prejudicial. He had no authority' (Walpole, *Memoirs*, 4.33). Lord North, in a eulogy of Cust at the election of his successor, stressed his amiable character, a positive disadvantage for the post. The lesson had been learnt, for the next speaker, Sir Fletcher Norton, possessed a formidably abrasive personality. The reputation Cust left behind him is shown by this comment of Nathaniel Wraxall, who did not enter the Commons until 1780. 'The Chair of the House of Commons, during the whole course of the eighteenth century, was never filled with less dignity or energy, than by Sir John Cust' (Wraxall, 1.374).

The irony is that Cust literally gave his life in the service of the house. Lengthy debates on John Wilkes hastened his death. The session of 1763–4 dominated by the *North Briton* case was twice interrupted by adjournments caused by the speaker's ill health, which thereafter was a matter of concern to his family and friends. His fate was sealed by the long debates of 1769 on the Middlesex election. He collapsed in the chair on 12 January 1770, resigned it on 17 January, and died on 24 January at St Margaret's, Westminster. He was buried at Belton on 8 February 1770. His widow died on 22 January 1775. Family tradition that his death was caused by ailments brought on by long periods of confinement in the chair is confirmed by a newspaper report of 27 January 1770 that the House of Commons had just introduced a 'rule for the Speaker to depart the Chair whenever the usual calls of nature should require his absence … The want of so provident a regulation is thought to have hastened the death of the last Speaker' (*London Evening-Post*, 27 Jan 1770). On his deathbed Sir John was assured that if he lived he would have a peerage, and if not his son should be made a peer. This promise was fulfilled when the next peerage creations took place, on 20 May 1776. His heir Sir Brownlow Cust was created Baron Brownlow of Belton, in recognition of his father's service

in the chair. Onslow's heir was made a peer at the same time, and so began the tradition that the speakership should be rewarded by a peerage.

PETER D. G. THOMAS

Sources L. Cust, ed., *Records of the Cust family*, 3 (1927) • P. D. G. Thomas, *The House of Commons in the eighteenth century* (1971) • L. B. Namier, 'Cust, Sir John', HoP, *Commons, 1754–90* • A. I. Dasent, *The speakers of the House of Commons* (1911) • M. MacDonagh, *The speaker of the house* (1914) • *The letters of Horace Walpole, fourth earl of Orford*, ed. P. Toynbee, 16 vols. (1903–5) • H. Walpole, *Memoirs of the reign of King George the Third*, ed. G. F. R. Barker, 4 vols. (1894) • N. W. Wraxall, *Historical memoirs of his own time*, new edn, 4 vols. (1836) • N. W. Wraxall, *Posthumous memoirs of his own time*, 2nd edn, 3 vols. (1836) • *Correspondence of John, fourth duke of Bedford*, ed. J. Russell, 3 vols. (1842–6) • *DNB* • GEC, *Baronetage*
Archives Lincs. Arch., parliamentary papers, personal accounts | BL, letters to Lord Egmont, Add. MS 47014
Likenesses E. Seeman, group portrait, oils, *c*.1743, Belton House, Lincolnshire • J. Reynolds, oils, 1761, Belton House, Lincolnshire • portrait, CCC Cam. • portrait, Palace of Westminster, London, Speaker's House; repro. in Dasent, *Speakers of the House of Commons*

Cust, Sir Lionel Henry

Cust, Sir Lionel Henry (1859–1929), art historian, was born at 13 Eccleston Square, London, on 25 January 1859, the only son of Sir Reginald John Cust (*d.* 1913), barrister, and his wife, Lady Elizabeth Caroline (*d.* 1914), elder daughter of Edward Bligh, fifth earl of Darnley. He was a first cousin of Henry John Cockayne Cust, the politician and journalist. He was educated at Eton College, and matriculated at Trinity College, Cambridge, in 1877. He was elected a scholar of the college in 1880, and obtained a first class in the classical tripos of 1881.

In 1882 Cust entered the civil service, obtaining a post in the War Office, but the work was not congenial to him, and at the suggestion of Sidney Colvin he was transferred in 1884 to the department of prints and drawings at the British Museum, of which Colvin had recently become keeper. Here Cust's real interests were engaged. He had a good eye and an extremely retentive memory; his knowledge of pictures and prints had been enlarged by study on the continent; he was methodical, conscientious, and enjoyed research. His *Index* to the Dutch, Flemish, and German artists represented in the print room (1893), followed by an *Index* to the French artists (1896), was of great service to students, and the preparation of it made him familiar not only with major masters but also with innumerable minor artists. Writers on art in Britain had hitherto mostly been attracted to the Italian schools; Cust's predilection was for the schools of northern Europe. Of Van Dyck and also of Dürer he made a special study.

In 1895 Cust was appointed director of the National Portrait Gallery in succession to Sir George Scharf. His first task was the moving of the collection from its temporary home at Bethnal Green to the new gallery in St Martin's Place, followed by the compilation of catalogues of the holdings (1896, 1901–2). The study of portraiture in Britain appealed to his love of history and genealogy and to his interest in established families, including his own. The obituary notice in *The Times* described Cust as 'a walking genealogy' to the extent that 'he may be said to have slept with Burke at his bedside'. Cust also had a wide knowledge

Sir Lionel Henry Cust (1859–1929), by Sir John Lavery, 1912

of the collections in the great country houses. The biographies of artists, notable for their accuracy and painstaking research, contributed to the *Dictionary of National Biography* made a fresh beginning in the study of British art, as did his exhibition catalogues of portraiture organized for the Oxford Historical Society (1904, 1905, 1906). At the same time Cust maintained his former interests. An authoritative study of Dürer's paintings and prints was published in 1897, followed in 1898 by a monograph on an early German engraver, *The Master 'E.S.' and the 'Ars moriendi'*. His *History of the Society of Dilettanti* appeared in 1898, and his *History of Eton College* in the following year. As a writer Cust lacked the graces of style, but he was always a master of facts. In 1900 he published his most important single book, a large and exhaustive work on Van Dyck. Two small monographs on the same master appeared in 1903 and 1906, and a further study in 1911.

In 1901 Cust was offered the post of surveyor of the king's pictures, and with the consent of the trustees was allowed to combine this with his directorship of the National Portrait Gallery. He resigned the directorship in 1909, but continued to hold the office of surveyor until 1927. In 1901 he was also appointed gentleman usher to the court. Cust's duties as surveyor involved the supervision of all the collections in the various royal palaces; and he was responsible for a good deal of rearrangement and rehanging of the pictures, which had become rather static during the reign of Queen Victoria. His office brought him

into close personal contact with Edward VII. He published a work on the collection entitled *The Royal Collection of Paintings: Buckingham Palace* (1905), *Windsor Castle* (1906). *Notes on the Authentic Portraits of Mary, Queen of Scots* and a large illustrated work, *The Bridgewater House Gallery*, had appeared in 1903.

From 1909 to 1919 Cust was joint editor with Roger Fry of the *Burlington Magazine*. Among his own numerous contributions to the magazine was a series of notes on pictures in the royal collections, published in book form in 1911. In the long-neglected field of early portraiture in Britain his work was particularly valuable. He set himself the task of clearing away the myths and discovering the facts, his most notable service being the rehabilitation of the sixteenth-century painter H. E. (Hans Eworth), long erroneously identified with Lucas d'Heere. His study of Eworth, which contains a full catalogue of the painter's works, was published in the Walpole Society's *Annual* (vol. 2, 1913). Studies of other foreign artists working in Britain at a similarly early date were also undertaken. Cust was keenly interested in the movement for introducing good pictures into schools, and for many years, until its dissolution, was chairman of the Art for Schools Association, founded in 1883.

Cust's personal appearance hardly suggested his zest for scholarly research and his capacity for hard and rapid work. Inclined to plumpness, and given to shyness, he none the less gave the impression of one who enjoyed life to the full in the Edwardian style. He had a great love of music as well as of painting, and a gift for simple pleasures. A volume of his poetry, *Ludibrium ventia*, was published privately in 1904. The extraordinary accuracy of his memory enabled him to dispense with notebooks. He married in 1895 Sybil, sixth daughter of George William Lyttelton, fourth Baron Lyttelton, and half-sister of Bishop Arthur Temple Lyttelton and of the statesman Alfred Lyttelton. They had one son. His wife contributed a memoir of Cust to his posthumously published volume *King Edward VII and his Court* (1930). Cust was created KCVO in 1927. He also received the degree of LittD at the University of Cambridge, and was made FSA, a chevalier of the Belgian order of Leopold, an honorary member of the Royal Academy of Antwerp, and a knight of grace of the order of St John of Jerusalem. He died on 12 October 1929 at Datchet House, Datchet, Buckinghamshire, where his later married life was spent.

LAURENCE BINYON, *rev.* CHRISTOPHER LLOYD

Sources *The Times* (14 Oct 1929), 19 · *Burlington Magazine*, 55 (1929), 251 · S. Cust, 'Memoir', in L. Cust, *King Edward VII and his court: some reminiscences* (1930), v–xxiii · O. Millar, *The queen's pictures* (1977), 200–203 · private information (1937)

Archives NPG, corresp. · NPG, research notes

Likenesses photograph, 1905, NPG · J. Lavery, oils, 1912, NPG [*see illus.*] · photograph, repro. in Cust, *King Edward VII and his court*

Wealth at death £7212 19s. 1d.: probate, 28 Dec 1929, CGPLA Eng. & Wales

Cust, Maria Eleanor Vere (1862/3–1958), first woman fellow of the Royal Geographical Society, was the second

Maria Eleanor Vere Cust (1862/3–1958), by Maull & Fox, 1917

daughter of Robert Needham *Cust (1821–1909), orientalist, and his first wife, Maria Adelaide Hobart (d. 1864), daughter of Henry Lewis Hobart, dean of Windsor. Miss Cust acted for many years as her father's secretary, materially aiding his studies, and also worked for many years as a medical missionary in India. Her father, an active fellow of the Royal Geographical Society, keenly advocated the admission of women as fellows. The society's desire for pre-eminence in sponsoring exploration sat ill with its inability to elect eminent women travellers to its numbers, and its decision to award medals to Lady Franklin and Mary Somerville served only to emphasize how untenable was its more general exclusion of women. After deciding in 1847 that it was 'not deemed expedient at present' (Mill, 57) to consider a suggestion that women be admitted as members, and in 1860 that women should not be admitted as honorary members, the council of the society agreed on 4 July 1892 to the election of women to the fellowship on the same footing as men. On 28 November 1892 fifteen 'well qualified ladies' (Mill, 107) were elected after the approval of a motion by Robert Cust that 'this meeting desires to associate itself with the gracious act of the Council in recognising the right of ladies to the fellowship of the Royal Geographical Society' (GJ, 1893). The women were to be presented to the president in alphabetical order and, in the absence of Isabella Bird Bishop who

was in Tibet, the ceremonial welcome was received by Miss Cust. Opponents ensured that the 1892 election was followed by a long period in which no women were elected and the issue was finally settled only in 1913, since when women have been elected on the same basis as men. Maria Cust's pride in her fellowship was shown by her including it on the title-page of her only published work, *Lucem sequor* (1906), a collection of her own indifferent verse—which shows the influence of her religion and the East—and of her passable translations of Heine, von Eichendorff, Hugo, and others. Miss Cust died at The Hydro, Stansboroughs, Watford, Hertfordshire, on 2 January 1958 at the age of ninety-five, a few days after breaking her leg. Her obituarist wrote: 'knowledgeable and well travelled, she retained to the end of her life … friends of all ages who regarded her as a pioneer of women's activity in a sphere wider than the domestic one' (GJ, 1958, 146). This is a kind interpretation and she is remembered now chiefly as a symbol of the recognition of women's fitness to engage in public life on the same terms as men.

ELIZABETH BAIGENT

Sources H. R. Mill, *The record of the Royal Geographical Society, 1830–1930* (1930) · *GJ*, 1 (1893), 77–80 · *GJ*, 124 (1958), 145–6 · *Proceedings* [Royal Geographical Society], new ser., 14 (1892), 553 · *The Times* (6 Jan 1958) · M. Bell and C. McEwan, 'The admission of women fellows to the Royal Geographical Society, 1892–1914: the controversy and the outcome', *GJ*, 162 (1996), 295–312
Likenesses Maull & Fox, photograph, 1917, RGS [*see illus.*]
Wealth at death £9463 10s. 2d.: probate, 5 March 1958, CGPLA Eng. & Wales

Cust, Sir Richard, first baronet (*bap.* 1622, *d.* 1700), politician, was baptized on 23 June 1622 at Dowsby, Lincolnshire, the eldest son of Samuel Cust (*bap.* 1594, *d.* 1663) of Pinchbeck in the same county, and Ann (*c.*1600–1655), daughter of Richard Burrell of London and Dowsby. He was educated at Trinity College, Cambridge, from 1638 and the Inner Temple, London, which he entered on 18 February 1641. He was called to the bar on 5 February 1650. On 29 August 1644 he married Beatrice (*c.*1624–1715), daughter and heir of William Pury of Kirton, Lincolnshire.

The Custs had been settled at Pinchbeck since the fourteenth century, but it was only in James I's reign that they joined the ranks of the local gentry, after Richard's father, Samuel, a Lincoln's Inn lawyer, acquired the estate at Dowsby through marrying Ann Burrell. Richard added an estate at Kirton through his own marriage and then in 1654 purchased the Blackfriars in Stamford which became his principal residence.

Such evidence as survives about his religious beliefs suggests that Cust was a zealous puritan. His marriage to Beatrice Pury brought the family into alliance with Humphrey Walcott (whose stepdaughter she was), one of the most prominent godly gentlemen from the puritan stronghold of Boston. Cust's commitment to godly causes is demonstrated by his correspondence with Sir Henry Vane the younger, who became a close friend after he settled in Lincolnshire in 1651. Vane refers to their shared enthusiasm for messianic speculation and Cust's devotion to 'seeking God and wayting only upon him for such births of his Providence as may carry on the good of the nation' (E. C. Cust, 217). The Custs were also committed parliamentarians. During the civil war Samuel served alongside Walcott on the county committee and Richard was commissioned as captain of the horse in the Holland militia in December 1642. There is no evidence that he was involved in the fighting, but thereafter he was known as Captain Cust. From 1649 onwards he was an active justice on the Holland bench and in 1653 he was elected to represent the shire in the Barebones Parliament, probably on the recommendation of his father-in-law, Walcott, who was also elected. He played only a minor role in the parliament and in 1656 he was one of a slate of radical candidates in Lincolnshire, led by Vane, which was defeated in the elections to the second protectorate parliament. However, he remained active in various local commissions throughout the 1650s and in summer 1659, with the return of the Rump Parliament, he was reappointed to his captaincy in the Lincolnshire militia and entrusted by the council of state with the task of rounding up suspected royalists.

Given his radical connections Cust survived the Restoration remarkably unscathed. He was removed from the commission of the peace in 1660, but was able to sue out a pardon for his earlier actions, probably through the good offices of his kinsman, the secretary of state, Sir Edward Nicholas. He also befriended the earl of Lindsey and his brothers, Charles and Peregrine Bertie, the leading royalist connection in the shire. It was with the assistance of Charles, secretary to the Treasury, that he purchased his baronetcy in 1677, having been knighted at an earlier but unknown date. Restored to the commission of the peace in 1670, in 1678 Cust used his by now considerable influence in Stamford to help secure Charles Bertie's return in a by-election. With the Popish Plot and exclusion crisis, however, the pattern of local politics was transformed and old puritans and parliamentarians like Cust found themselves back in favour.

During the March 1679 election in Stamford, Cust was still co-operating with the Berties, but having been persuaded to stand himself, by the will of the local electors, as he claimed, he severed his ties with them. At the start of the parliament he was still classified as doubtful in a list of Shaftesbury's supporters, but he soon showed himself a reliable ally of the exclusionists, speaking in favour of measures to counteract the popish threat. He was elected again for the second and third Exclusion Parliaments, by which time his radical enthusiasm of the 1650s had resurfaced. In April 1681 he was said by a council informant to have attended a meeting with Shaftesbury and other whig leaders at which he declared in favour of 'a free state and no other government' (*CSP dom.*, 1680–81, 232). In the reaction which followed he was dismissed from the commission of the peace and had his house searched for arms by Lindsey, who described him as one of the leaders of the 'disaffected' in the county (*CSP dom., July–Sept 1683*, 180). By 1685, however, he was apparently on good terms with the Berties once again and, although he was listed among the opposition in 1687, he does not appear to have been active during the revolution.

Sir Richard's career provides a good example of how a radical puritan of the 1650s could come to terms with the Restoration and then re-emerge as a whig in the 1680s. He died in 1700 and was buried at St George's Church, Stamford, on 5 September. His wife survived him, as did their four daughters, but their three sons all predeceased him. His estate and title passed to his grandson, another Richard.   RICHARD CUST

Sources E. C. Cust, *Records of the Cust family, 1469–1700* (1898), chap. 9 • C. Cust, *Some account of the Cust family* (1923) • D. Scott, 'Cust, Richard', HoP, *Commons, 1640–60* [draft] • P. Watson, 'Cust, Sir Richard', HoP, *Commons, 1660–90*, 2.182–3 • C. Holmes, *Seventeenth century Lincolnshire* (1980) • A. Woolrych, *Commonwealth to protectorate* (1982) • *CSP dom., 1680–83* • C. H. Cooper and T. Cooper, 'Sir Richard Cust', *N&Q*, 3rd ser., 3 (1863), 437–8 • W. A. Shaw, *The knights of England*, 2 vols. (1906) • IGI • Venn, *Alum. Cant.*
Archives Belton House, Lincolnshire, family papers
Likenesses P. Lely, portrait; at Belton House, Lincolnshire, in 1898
Wealth at death approx. £1000 p.a.: *CSP dom., July–Sept 1683*, 180; Cust, *Records*, 250

Cust, Robert Needham (1821–1909), East India Company servant and orientalist, was born at Cockayne Hatley, Bedfordshire, on 24 February 1821, the second son of Henry Cockayne Cust (1780–1861), canon of Windsor, and his wife, Lady Anna Maria Elizabeth (d. 1866), eldest daughter of Francis Needham, first earl of Kilmorey. His father was the second son of Brownlow Cust, first Baron Brownlow (1744–1807).

Cust was educated at the Revd H. Burn's school in Mitcham, Surrey (1830–33), Eton College (1834–40), and the East India Company's college at Haileybury (1840–42), where he distinguished himself in Sanskrit, Persian, Arabic, and Hindustani. In 1844 he was posted to Ambala as assistant to the governor-general's agent for the north-western frontier, Major George Broadfoot, and temporarily took charge as agent when Broadfoot was killed in action at Ferozeshahr in December 1845. In 1846 he was appointed deputy commissioner of Hoshiarpur and under the guidance of John Lawrence enthusiastically implemented the paternalistic, 'non-regulation' style of government that became the hallmark of the Punjab administration. In November 1849 he was transferred back to his old district of Ambala.

In May 1852, after eighteen months' furlough, Cust was appointed officiating joint magistrate of Benares and three months later became officiating magistrate of Banda. In March 1855 he returned to England to study for the bar and while there married, on 10 May 1856, Maria Adelaide (d. 1864), second daughter of Henry Lewis Hobart, dean of Windsor, with whom he had two sons and three daughters. He was called to the bar at Lincoln's Inn in August 1857 and returned to India in February 1858, whereupon he was appointed commissioner of Lahore. Subsequently he acted as financial commissioner of the Punjab and in 1861 as judicial commissioner. At Lahore he was remembered by his subordinate officers as a stickler for the rules and a great talker, but gloomy and prone to moralizing.

On 17 January 1864 Maria died, seven days after giving birth to their third daughter. Cust, who was devastated by her death, went home to England to settle the children, and upon his return in October became acting home secretary to the government of India (1864–5). On 28 December 1865 he married Emma, eldest daughter of Edward Carlyon, rector of Debden, Hampshire, and shortly afterwards took up a seat on the board of revenue in the North-Western Provinces. Unhappily, in August 1867 Emma too died in childbirth, whereupon Cust quit India immediately, just nine months short of qualifying for his pension.

Back in England he recovered his energy and spirit, and on 11 November 1868 he married Elizabeth Dewar (d. 1910), only daughter of J. Mathews. In 1867–8, at the prompting of his old boss John Lawrence, now viceroy, he drafted a code of revenue law for northern India, but this was his last official undertaking. Independently wealthy, he devoted his remaining years to oriental philology and religion, travelling throughout Europe, north Africa, and Asia and attending numerous international congresses. He was a prominent member of many literary societies and of the Royal Geographical Society, and from 1878 until 1899 served as honorary secretary of the Royal Asiatic Society. Inexhaustibly prolific, between 1870 and 1909 he published more than sixty volumes, all of which he financed himself, and hundreds of articles and reviews. Chief among his works are *Modern Languages of the East Indies* (1878), *Modern Languages of Africa* (1883), *Oceania* (1887), *The Caucasian Group* (1887), and a seven-part series, Linguistic and Oriental Essays (1880–1904). Even at the time, however, Cust's scholarship was regarded as intelligent rather than profound and it is actually his diaries and letters, with their unique portrayal of Victorian sensibility in India, which have proved to be the most durable of his writings.

Cust was a devout, evangelizing Christian, but he rejected literal interpretations of the Old Testament and prided himself on a scientific understanding of the development of different religions. He served on the committees of the Church Missionary Society and the Society for the Propagation of the Gospel, as well as supporting numerous philanthropic ventures. In 1899 he published his autobiography, *Life Memoir, 1821–1899*. He died on 28 October 1909 at his residence, 49 Campden Hill Road, Kensington, and was buried at Putney Vale. His wife, Elizabeth, died six months later. He was survived by their only child, Anna Maria Elizabeth (b. 1870), and three children of his first marriage: Albinia Lucy (1857–1929), Robert Henry Hobart (1861–1940), a Renaissance art specialist, and Maria Eleanor Vere *Cust (1862/3–1958), a geographer.

KATHERINE PRIOR

Sources Cust's diaries, 17 vols., 1842–1905, BL · Burke, *Peerage* (1949) · ecclesiastical records, BL OIOC · *DNB* [see also similar memoir in the *Journal of the Royal Asiatic Society*, 1 (1910), 255] · R. N. Cust, *Life memoir, 1821–1899* (1899) · G. R. Elsmie, *Thirty-five years in the Punjab, 1858–1893* (1908) · *CGPLA Eng. & Wales* (1909)

Archives BL, diaries, Add. MSS 45390–45406 · BL OIOC, MS Eur. E 182 · CUL, civil, criminal, and revenue judgment books; corresp., notes, and essays | BL, Broadfoot MSS, Add. MSS 40127–40131
Likenesses M. Carpenter, oils, c.1840, Eton · photographs, 1867–96, BL, pasted into Cust's diaries
Wealth at death £47,606 0s. 1d.: probate, 12 Nov 1909, *CGPLA Eng. & Wales*

Custance, Henry (1842–1908), jockey, born at Peterborough on 27 February 1842, was the son of Samuel Custance, a postboy, and his wife, Elizabeth Carpenter. Devoted from childhood to horses and to riding, he rode at thirteen in a pony race at Ramsey in Huntingdonshire. After vainly seeking employment at Newmarket, he spent three years at Epsom, where, in his own words, he had 'a jolly, though rough, time' in the employment of Edward (Ned) Smith of South Hatch, who was associated with the sporting journal *Bell's Life*, and raced his horses in the name of Mellish.

Custance's first important victory was gained on Rocket in 1858 in the Cesarewitch, which he won again in 1861 on Audrey. In 1860 he was attached to the Russley stable, then under the management of Matthew Dawson, and that season he rode over forty winners, including Thormanby in the Derby. This victory earned him a present of £100 from the owner, Mr Merry, the only gift he received in three years of riding for the Glasgow ironmaster. In 1863 he became stable jockey at East Ilsley for James Dover, who trained the 1866 triple crown winner Lord Lyon. Unfortunately Custance missed the Two Thousand Guineas ride because of a fall at the Epsom spring meeting. He won a third Derby in 1874 on the vile-tempered George Frederick. By this time Custance was having to waste heavily just to make 8 stone 10 lb, and in 1879 he retired. His last winning mount was Lollypop in the All-Aged Stakes at the Newmarket Houghton meeting.

As a jockey Custance was bold and resolute, had good hands, and was a fine judge of pace. After his retirement from the saddle he long remained a familiar figure on the racecourse. He held for many years a licence as deputy starter to the Jockey Club, and was also official starter to the Belgian Jockey Club. In 1885 he officiated at the Derby, thus becoming the first person to both win and start that race. Living at Oakham, where he was proprietor of The George inn, he regularly hunted with the Quorn and Cottesmore packs. He was always a cheerful and amusing companion, and published *Riding Recollections and Turf Stories* in 1894. He died of a paralytic seizure at his home, 53 New Walk, Leicester, on 19 April 1908, leaving a widow, Mary. Laid out in 1906, New Walk led to Leicester's Victoria Park, site of the city's original racecourse.

EDWARD MOORHOUSE, rev. WRAY VAMPLEW

Sources R. Mortimer, R. Onslow, and P. Willett, *Biographical encyclopedia of British flat racing* (1978) · H. Custance, *Riding recollections and turf stories* (1894) · *Sporting Life* (20 April 1908) · *The Times* (20 April 1908) · J. Simmons, *Leicester past and present*, 2 vols. (1974) · *CGPLA Eng. & Wales* (1908)
Wealth at death £8081 6s. 2d.: probate, 14 May 1908, *CGPLA Eng. & Wales*

Custance, Olive Eleanor (1874–1944). *See under* Douglas, Lord Alfred Bruce (1870–1945).

Custance, Sir Reginald Neville [*pseud.* Barfleur] (1847–1935), naval officer and author, was born in Belfast on 20 September 1847, the eldest son of General William Neville Custance and his second wife, Mary, eldest daughter of Thomas Meggison of Walton, Northumberland. He entered the navy in September 1860 aboard the training ship *Britannia*. He then served in the frigate *Euryalus* and was present at the bombardment of the Japanese clan forts at Kagoshima in 1863, and Shimonoseki in 1864. He was promoted lieutenant on 6 February 1868, a year in which he received the Royal Humane Society silver medal for life-saving. He served in the West Indies between 1868 and 1872, before joining the instructing staff of the gunnery training ship HMS *Excellent* in 1873. He remained aboard the *Excellent*, as a senior staff lieutenant, from 1875 to 1878. He was promoted commander on 31 March 1878, and spent the following year at the Royal Naval College, Greenwich. Between November 1880 and early 1884 he commanded the sloop *Flamingo* in the West Indies. His promotion to the substantive rank of captain followed on 31 December 1885.

In October 1886 Custance was ordered to the Admiralty, to prepare a scheme for mobilization. He was subsequently appointed assistant director of naval intelligence on the formation of the naval intelligence department, and served under Captain W. H. Hall until 1889 and then under Captain Sir Cyprian Bridge. Bridge, along with Admiral Philip Colomb, became a major influence on his intellectual development. While at the Admiralty, Custance had a good working relationship with Captain John *Fisher, the director of naval ordnance; both supported the battleship against the French torpedo boat challenge. In January 1890 he took command of the cruiser *Phaeton* in the Mediterranean. Between September 1893 and January 1895 he served as naval attaché at Washington and Paris. In February 1895 he took command of the new second-class battleship *Barfleur*, serving in the Mediterranean and from early 1898 the China station. He later took her name as his pen-name, a reflection of his preference for small battleships, based on the views of Bridge and Sir John Laughton.

Between March 1899 and November 1902 Custance, who had been promoted rear-admiral on 1 August 1899, was director of naval intelligence. The appointment reflected the high opinion of his abilities held at the Admiralty. A well-informed student of strategy, Custance used his position to promote the study of history as the basis for the development of modern doctrine. He also established the defence and trade divisions of the department. He forced the intelligence department into the heart of Admiralty policy-making, by a combination of will-power and intellect. At this stage he was considered among the most brilliant officers in the service; yet his subsequent career was ruined by a clash of wills that warped his judgement. His relationship with Fisher deteriorated when Fisher went to the Mediterranean, largely as a result of Fisher's constant criticism of Admiralty policy, both in official correspondence and carefully handled newspaper leaks. The two

men became bitter enemies after the Admiralty visit to Malta in 1901. Fisher had argued that more destroyers should be attached to his fleet, and persuaded the board to ignore Custance's advice that these were unnecessary. Custance knew that Fisher was exaggerating the threat to serve his own ambitions, and used the German navy as a counter-argument for keeping forces at home. This was considered premature, but it rapidly became policy when Fisher returned to the Admiralty in late 1904.

Between November 1902 and November 1904 Custance served as second in command of the Mediterranean Fleet. In early 1903 the Admiralty set up two committees to investigate the possibilities of long-range firing. Custance presided over the Mediterranean committee, and firings were carried out by his flagship, the *Venerable*. In view of the limited possibilities for combining range and observation with control of the guns, he initially deprecated long-range fire. After the first series of firings additional equipment was installed aboard the ship, and the results improved significantly. Custance's methodical work, reflecting six years at *Excellent*, laid the groundwork for the development of more sophisticated equipment and control systems that permitted accurate fire at hitherto unimagined distances. His report was highly commended by the Admiralty. Custance's interest in fire control led him to clash with Fisher over the merits of Arthur Pollen's promising designs.

In 1904 Custance was made KCMG and on 20 October that year he was promoted vice-admiral. He spent the next two years ashore, publishing under his pen-name, Barfleur, historically based criticisms of contemporary naval policy, collected in the volume *Naval Policy: a Plea for the Study of War* (1907). In February 1907 Fisher appointed him second in command of the Channel Fleet, under Lord Charles Beresford, because the two men disliked one another. Fisher's divide-and-rule tactics backfired. Discovering that a shared hatred overrode other misunderstandings, they formed the core of the 'syndicate of discontent' ably supported by Rear-Admiral Doveton Sturdee, Beresford's chief of staff, and a galaxy of retired admirals. While Beresford was the figure-head, Custance provided the brains. His personal animus drove the syndicate, and reduced the last three years of Fisher's term at the Admiralty to one long rearguard action. Whatever the merits of either case, the real beneficiary was the army, which exploited Beresford to assume the leading position in national strategy. In this Custance revealed the worst side of his character, allowing personal antipathies to colour his judgement, to the detriment of the service and the state.

Promoted full admiral in May 1908, Custance hauled down his flag for the last time in July, an occasion marked by the customary KCB. He lingered on the active list until 1912, and was created GCB the following year, and an honorary DCL from the University of Oxford. He continued to be consulted, notably by Churchill, but the bitter hostility of Fisher ensured that he had no influence. His chances for fleet command, or service at the Admiralty, for which he was well suited, were destroyed by his role in the 'syndicate'. He was too clearly identified with the quarrel to be employed by those seeking to heal the breach.

The remainder of Custance's life was devoted to the study of war, and the promotion of his thesis that the naval mind had become divided into two schools, the *matériel* and the historical, and that the dominance of the *matériel* school resulted in warships designed on entirely incorrect principles. The generalization was erroneous and simplistic, as his own career demonstrated. The pamphlets *The Fighting Power of the Capital Ship* (1909) and *The Military Growth of the Capital Ship* (1910) were stimulating and intelligent critiques of Fisher's policy; in them Custance argued that speed had been important throughout the nineteenth century because the enemy would be running away, and that this was no longer the case because the relative naval balance had shifted away from the Royal Navy. Consequently, as both sides wanted to fight, firepower would decide the contest.

During the First World War Custance publicly criticized the influence of Sir Julian Corbett on the doctrine of the navy. He considered that Corbett had deprecated the importance of seeking decisive battle. Subsequently he contributed to the *Naval Review*, the closed-circulation professional journal, and published three more books: *The Ship of the Line in Battle* (1912), *War at Sea: Modern Theory and Ancient Practice* (1919), and *A Study of War* (1924). The last two were peculiarly wrong-headed, arguing that sound strategy required a concentration on the military aim of destroying enemy armed forces before attempting to secure political aims. As Donald Schurman observed, Custance's work adds 'to our knowledge of naval controversy, but not to the growth of naval history' (Schurman, *Education*, 14). Custance died at his home, Beaumont Broad, Broadclyst in Devon on 30 August 1935.

Custance was part of a small but professionally significant group of officers who made a serious study of war in the last quarter of the nineteenth century. This group, linked to Professor Sir John Knox Laughton, included Cyprian Bridge, Philip Colomb, Doveton Sturdee, Gerard Noel, and Prince Louis of Battenberg. All were members of the council of the Navy Records Society, which used history as the basis from which to develop a modern naval doctrine. However, Custance saw history as a source of support for his case, not an all-embracing approach to the comprehension of major issues. Although possessed of a powerful mind and great knowledge of the service, he had little influence on policy. His narrow, dogmatic, and inflexible opinions were delivered with an uncommon degree of venom, especially when dealing with Fisher. He lacked the mental flexibility to benefit from debate.

Custance set high standards for his subordinates, both as officers and gentlemen. He kept a generous table as an admiral, and was interested in the views of junior officers. However, he lacked the personal warmth to inspire unthinking devotion, while his suspicious nature made him a difficult superior. A confirmed bachelor, his arrogant and unbending approach deprived his work of lasting value, and his life of close society. The one friend of his

last years was Admiral Sir Herbert Richmond, another cold intellectual naval outsider. It was through Richmond, and personal correspondence, that Custance's notion of a service divided between the historical and the *matériel* schools came to influence the work of the American historian Arthur J. Marder. Marder considered that Custance combined 'a nasty temperament devoid of generosity' with 'the cleverness of a monkey' (Marder, *From the Dreadnought*, 1.91). Custance's quarrel with Fisher warped his judgement, and deprived the navy of the services of a highly competent and learned officer. The sad irony was that the two men agreed on so many of the key issues concerned with the modernization of the Royal Navy.

ANDREW LAMBERT

Sources M. Allen, 'Rear Admiral Reginald Custance: director of naval intelligence, 1899–1902', *Mariner's Mirror*, 78 (1992), 61–76 · B. D. Hunt, *Sailor-scholar: Admiral Sir Herbert Richmond, 1871–1946* (1982) · A. J. Marder, *Portrait of an admiral: the life and papers of Sir Herbert Richmond* (1952) · A. J. Marder, *The anatomy of British sea power*, American edn (1940) · A. J. Marder, *From the Dreadnought to Scapa Flow: the Royal Navy in the Fisher era, 1904–1919*, 5 vols. (1961–70), vol. 1 · D. M. Schurman, *Julian S. Corbett, 1854–1922: historian of British maritime policy from Drake to Jellicoe*, Royal Historical Society Studies in History, 26 (1981) · D. M. Schurman, *The education of a navy: the development of British naval strategic thought, 1867–1914* (1965) · R. F. MacKay, *Fisher of Kilverstone* (1973) · R. S. Churchill, *Winston S. Churchill*, 2: *Young statesman, 1901–1914* (1967) · R. S. Churchill, ed., *Winston S. Churchill*, companion vol. 2/3 (1969) · G. M. Bennett, *Charlie B: a biography of Admiral Lord Beresford of Metemmeh and Curraghmore* (1968) · R. A. Burt, *British battleships, 1889–1904* (1988) · B. M. Ranft, *Technical change and British naval policy, 1860–1939* (1977) · J. T. Sumida, *In defence of naval supremacy: finance, technology and British naval policy, 1889–1914* (1989) · H. W. W. H., 'Admiral Sir Reginald Custance: an appreciation', *Naval Review* (1935), 681–5 · R. N. Custance, *War at sea: modern theory and ancient practice* (1919) · DNB · CGPLA Eng. & Wales (1935)

Archives NMM, logbooks and papers, MS 77/145 | Bodl. Oxf., corresp. with Lord Selborne · CAC Cam., corresp. with A. H. Pollen · NAM, letters to Spenser Wilkinson · NMM, Bridge MSS · NMM, corresp. with Sir Julian S. Corbett · NMM, Noel MSS · NMM, Richmond MSS

Wealth at death £11,347 14s. 11d.: probate, 6 Nov 1935, CGPLA Eng. & Wales

Cutcliffe, John. *See* Roquetaillade, Jean de (*d.* 1362).

Cutforth, Reynolds [René] (1909–1984), broadcaster and writer, was born on 6 February 1909 at 89 Woodville Road, Swadlincote, Derbyshire, the son of Edwin Henry Cutforth, manager of an earthenware manufacturing business, and his wife, Cecily King. Educated at Nevill Holt School, Leicestershire, and also at Uppingham preparatory school (c.1918–22), he then attended Denstone College, Staffordshire (1922–9). Tersely described by a tutor as 'certainly not a worker', the young Cutforth found fossil hunting far more interesting than tedious scholarship. After leaving school he used a small inheritance to travel extensively abroad.

Over the course of the next decade Cutforth spent time in a number of countries in Europe and the Balkans, but also went as far afield as Abyssinia, India, Burma, and China. He held a variety of jobs as schoolmaster, secretary, and guide. A facility for languages was put to good use and

Reynolds [René] **Cutforth** (1909–1984), by Fay Godwin, 1969

Cutforth later claimed, on joining the BBC, to have a smattering of Russian, Urdu, Arabic, and Amharic. He joined the army in 1940, 'because it seemed that was where the reality of war could make its greatest impact' (*The Times*, 2 April 1984) and early in 1941 was commissioned lieutenant with the Sherwood Foresters. Seconded to the Ministry of Information he covered the war in the western desert of north Africa. Wounded and captured, he was subsequently a prisoner of war in Italy and Germany. By then Cutforth had married Violet Mary Dewar Robson; and by late 1946 they had a child. This marriage came to an end, and he subsequently remarried.

In December 1946 Cutforth became a sub-editor with BBC news. It became clear, however, that reporting was his real métier and in 1949 he became a general BBC reporter. Cutforth blossomed in this new role, swiftly and smoothly developing his own inimitable natural broadcasting technique. He had an unemotional, vivid, and accurate literary style, reporting what he saw, in voice and through the written word, with directness, calm, and clarity. Following the outbreak of the Korean War, Cutforth served as a war correspondent there, a role in which he excelled: 'his ear for detail, for the spontaneous remark or outburst of feeling lent his despatches from such desperate scenes as the stand of the Gloucesters at Imjin River such memorable vividness' (*The Times*, 2 April 1984). Cutforth used the experience to write his first book, *Korean Reporter*, published in 1952. The work was a typically readable, if unadorned, account of the courage of soldiers and the agony of existence for refugee civilians, which also

revealed some of the corruption of the civil administration.

Cutforth sought more freedom to develop his own writing interests, and became a freelance correspondent after Korea. This was not the end of his BBC career, however, as he continued to work for the corporation. In a burnished career in radio he reported for the BBC from at least seventy-four countries and on a variety of dramatic events, from the arrival of the Dalai Lama in India after fleeing from Tibet, to a depiction of the devastation caused by the Agadir earthquake. Yet, as he revealed in his book *René Cutforth Reporting* (1955), nothing gave him greater pleasure than compiling what became his métier: thirty-minute reports on subjects as diverse as cheeses, fairs, old cars, and odd characters.

During the 1950s and 1960s Cutforth's name and voice became familiar to many listeners to the Home Service. He contributed reports to such major radio series as *From our Own Correspondent* (1959–60) and *The Way We Live Now* (1960–65), and personally presented *René Cutforth with Something to Say* (1961) and *René Cutforth: his Life and Times* (1967). The impact of the 1930s on him were revealed in another book, *Later than We Thought* (1976). This was a highly personal account of W. H. Auden's 'mean and sordid decade' which opened in depression and ended in war. In it Cutforth embraced major events and personalities, but did not attempt a formal historical narrative.

In another work, *Order to View* (1969), Cutforth wrote in the foreword that 'I should be sorry if anybody mistook this book for an autobiography: it's a report of my life and times, and reporting is an event in extraversion'. The book was a characteristically fluent and entertaining revelation of a life thoroughly enjoyed, sometimes in rather eccentric and irascible fashion, but always with vigour and good humour. He displayed a similar brio in his enthusiastic response to the blandishments of television, especially his *European Journey* series for Granada TV. Cutforth died from chronic bronchitis and emphysema on 1 April 1984 at Hosdens Farm, Great Maplestead, Essex. He was survived by his wife, Sheila Marjorie Cutforth.

ALAN H. PROTHEROE

Sources private information (2004) · personal knowledge (2004) · R. Cutforth, *Order to view* (1969) · staff files, BBC WAC, L 1/110 · *The Times* (2 April 1984) · b. cert. · d. cert.
Archives BBC WAC | FILM BFI NFTVA, performance footage | SOUND BL NSA, 'Clever old fox: Rene Cutforth, foreign correspondent', BBC Radio 4, 5 April 1984 · BL NSA, performance recordings · IWM SA, oral history interview · IWM SA, performance recording
Likenesses F. Godwin, photograph, 1969, NPG [*see illus.*]
Wealth at death £13,227: administration, 1984, *CGPLA Eng. & Wales*

Cuthbert [St Cuthbert] (*c*.635–687), bishop of Lindisfarne, was born in Northumbria of unknown parentage about the year 635.

Sources In some respects Cuthbert is an extremely well-documented figure, since his life and posthumous miracles were described in no fewer than four works written within a short time of his death: a prose life written in Latin by an anonymous monk of Cuthbert's own church of Lindisfarne some time between 699 and 705; a life in Latin verse written by Bede between 705 and 716, probably very soon after 705; a second prose life in Latin by Bede, written before 721; and finally an extended treatment of the saint in no fewer than six chapters of Bede's *Historia ecclesiastica* written by 731. As a member of the religious community of Lindisfarne, the anonymous monk was naturally in a very good position to obtain authentic information and genuine traditions about Cuthbert, and in particular to draw on the testimony of witnesses who had known him. Although writing a little later and at Monkwearmouth and Jarrow rather than Lindisfarne, Bede was also in a position to be well informed, for he was able to draw on the anonymous work and to confirm and amplify it through close contacts with the Lindisfarne community, notably the abbot of Lindisfarne, Herefrith, who had been present at Cuthbert's death. In the case of his prose life, he states that his work had been read to the senior members of that community for their approval and suggestions. It is important to emphasize, however, that all these compositions were fundamentally hagiographical in nature. In other words, they were more concerned to present Cuthbert as a saint than as a historical figure, more preoccupied with his miracles and feats of asceticism than with his role in the society and the political structures of his day. It is therefore by no means easy to derive from them a picture of the historical Cuthbert as opposed to the contemporary image of Cuthbert as a saint.

Chronology of Cuthbert's career The first fixed point in Cuthbert's career is his entry into the monastery of Melrose. That this occurred in 651 is indicated by the fact that his decision to become a monk was believed to have been precipitated by a vision of the ascent to heaven of the soul of Áedán, bishop of Lindisfarne, who died in that year. Since Bede states that Cuthbert was at this time at the beginning of his adolescence, a stage of life said by Isidore of Seville to have begun at fifteen, this makes possible the deduction that Cuthbert was born c.635. After a period at Melrose, Cuthbert went with his abbot, Eata (d. 685/6), to establish a new monastery at Ripon, and there he was made guest master. The donor of the monastery's land, King Aldfrith, fell under the influence of Wilfrid (d. 709) and, disapproving of the Irish method of calculating the date of Easter in use at Ripon (as at Melrose, Lindisfarne, and elsewhere), he expelled the community of Ripon, which returned to Melrose. This was presumably before the Synod of Whitby of 664, which decided against the Irish method. Assertions that Cuthbert became prior of Lindisfarne in 664 are founded only on the twelfth-century Easter table annals known as the *Annals of Lindisfarne*. They are certainly incorrect in view of the statements of Bede's prose life to the effect that both Cuthbert and Boisil, prior of Melrose, contracted the plague which afflicted England in 664, and that when Boisil died of it but Cuthbert survived, the latter became prior of Melrose in Boisil's place and remained in that office for an unspecified number of years. After this, Eata summoned Cuthbert to Lindisfarne, where he remained as prior until he left to

establish himself as a hermit on the small rocky island of Inner Farne, just to the south. The dates of these movements are obscure. The *Annals of Lindisfarne* state that he left for the Inner Farne in 676 and was there for nine years, on which latter point they are supported by what is probably an early eleventh-century Durham text, the *Historia de sancto Cuthberto*, but there is no way of evaluating the veracity of this tradition. Following the expulsion of Bishop Tondbehrt from the see of Hexham in 684, Cuthbert was at first elected to that see, but was at once assigned instead to the see of Lindisfarne, of which he was consecrated bishop on 26 March 685. He was at Lindisfarne at Christmas 686, but he then returned to his hermitage on the Inner Farne and died there on 20 March 687.

Origins No reliable information is extant about Cuthbert's family, though information given in the accounts of his miracles suggests that he may have come from the area known as Lothian, between the Tweed and the Forth. In one such account, Cuthbert as a boy is guarding sheep near the River Leader, which flows into the Tweed near Melrose; it was of course at Melrose itself that he became a monk. In another account of his boyhood, Cuthbert prays for some monks who are in danger of being shipwrecked on the River Tyne, and, although it has often been assumed that the principal river of this name is meant, it is possible that the river in question was the Tyne which flows into the North Sea at Tyninghame, a little way north of Dunbar. Finally, another miracle story is set in the context of a visit paid by Cuthbert to his foster mother at a place called 'Hruringaham', which is unidentified but would appear to have been in the region of Melrose. By the time of Bede, the kingdom of Northumbria was bounded on the north by the Firth of Forth, and there is reason to suppose that Edinburgh had fallen into Northumbrian hands as early as 638. The area of Melrose, although a border region in later centuries, would in Cuthbert's time have been close to the heartland of Northumbrian power, with its political centres at places such as Bamburgh, Dunbar, and Yeavering in the fringes of the Cheviots. Cuthbert's name suggests that he was of Anglo-Saxon rather than British origin, but it is less clear from what social class he derived. The story of how he saw a vision of the soul of Áedán being taken to heaven is set at a time when Cuthbert was guarding sheep on behalf of their (or perhaps his) lords, and this has been taken to show that he was of humble, perhaps even peasant, origin. The story, however, has strong biblical connotations of the annunciation to the shepherds, so that religious symbolism may here have overridden factual accuracy; and even if the story is accurate it may be that Cuthbert's guardianship of the sheep was more a form of aristocratic military service against rustlers than the occupation of a humble peasant boy. The fact that Cuthbert had a foster mother suggests, moreover, that he was of aristocratic extraction, as also does the account of his arrival at Melrose armed with a spear, mounted on a horse, and accompanied by a servant. In addition, the anonymous life makes a brief allusion to a period of his career before he became a monk when he was 'dwelling in camp with the army, in the face of the enemy', and there is reason to suppose that warfare would have been a predominantly aristocratic activity.

Social and political context Whatever his origins, Cuthbert was on intimate terms throughout his career with the highest ranks of Northumbrian society. Ripon was a royal foundation, and Lindisfarne was not only royally founded but was located only a few miles by sea from the royal fortress of Bamburgh and was regularly visited by the king. The Inner Farne itself lies only 2 miles from Bamburgh. While prior of Melrose he was invited to visit Coldingham by the abbess, Æbbe (d. 683), sister of King Oswiu; and later, while a hermit on Farne, he was closely associated with another royal abbess, Ælfflæd (d. 714), sister of King Ecgfrith. She is supposed to have been cured by the miraculous power of his girdle; and on another occasion she is said to have met him on Coquet Island, where he prophesied the imminent death of her brother the king and gave her to understand that he would be succeeded by her illegitimate half-brother Aldfrith, who was then on the island of Iona. This prophecy was fulfilled, and Cuthbert was in company with Ecgfrith's queen at Carlisle when he is supposed to have perceived from afar that the king had been defeated and killed by the Picts at the battle of 'Nechtanesmere' (685), and to have been instrumental in moving the queen to safety. Whatever the truth of these stories they indicate that Cuthbert was regarded as intimately associated with the royal house, almost indeed as a royal holy man. This impression is strengthened by the prominence in Cuthbert's miracle-stories of men of the high rank of 'count' (*comes*), almost certainly important royal officials. The Northumbrian church of Cuthbert's time, and Lindisfarne in particular, was a very wealthy and aristocratic institution and Cuthbert was unquestionably closely involved in it. He is found banqueting with the princess Ælfflæd, abbess of Whitby, and being offered beer and wine by an abbess called Verca, who also gave him a *sindo*, possibly a silk garment, which he would not wear while alive but wished to be wrapped in when in his coffin. It seems likely, however, that he wore in his lifetime the gold and garnet cross preserved in Durham Cathedral treasury, and it is certain that his tomb was adorned with sumptuous treasures shortly after his death.

Religious context Cuthbert's career spanned a formative period in the history of the Northumbrian church, which had been permanently established with the foundation of the church of Lindisfarne, possibly in the year of Cuthbert's birth, by Áedán, who came from the Irish monastery of Iona at the invitation of King Oswald of Northumbria. Following this, Lindisfarne became the principal church and only episcopal see of Northumbria, subject to Iona which supplied its bishops, and apparently following Irish practices, notably in the calculation of the date of Easter. In 664, however, the Synod of Whitby ruled against these practices in favour of those of the church of Rome, and effectively ended the dependence of the Northumbrian church on Iona. The bishop's see for Northumbria

was then located at York, and after 678 Northumbria was divided into more manageable dioceses, of which Lindisfarne was one. Cuthbert must therefore have begun his career under Irish influence, but, unlike some Irish and Irish-trained churchmen who left Northumbria after 664, he seems to have been prepared to transfer his allegiances; and it is said that he experienced hostility from the monks of Lindisfarne to whom he tried to introduce a new rule, possibly that of St Benedict which entered Northumbria at that time in the wake of Roman and continental influence. It may be that Cuthbert's credentials as a supporter of the Roman party enabled him to be promoted posthumously as a major saint in a way which was not possible for earlier bishops such as Áedán who were of course of the Irish party. Indeed, the anonymous life tried to play down Cuthbert's own Irish associations by claiming that he accepted the Roman ('Petrine') tonsure at Ripon, which it purported to regard as already under Roman influence. On all counts, this was a historical distortion, and what was certainly the true position, that Cuthbert accepted the tonsure under Irish influence at Melrose, was set out by Bede, perhaps writing at a time when the subject had become less inflammatory. Bede too, however, may have been guilty of distortion in his handling of Cuthbert's relations with the Picts, who also followed Irish practices in Cuthbert's time. According to Bede, a visit which Cuthbert made to the land of the Picts was not intended to be of long duration but was prolonged by a storm, so that Cuthbert and his party were only able to eat when a dolphin was miraculously washed up for them. The anonymous life, however, represents the storm as interrupting a voyage Cuthbert and his companions were making to Pictland, and implies that they continued that voyage after the storm had subsided. The indications in the texts are that they were intending to spend Epiphany in Pictish company.

How far Cuthbert's own religious and devotional activity was the product of Irish influence is less easy to ascertain. Accounts of his ascetic practice of praying up to his neck in the cold sea, and his close association with birds and animals, have sometimes been regarded as characteristically Irish, but are in fact common to accounts of hermits and holy men in other milieux. On the other hand, his withdrawal to the Inner Farne, although in some respects reminiscent of the withdrawal into the desert of Egyptian hermits such as Anthony, is characteristically Irish insofar as it involves an island, and Cuthbert was associated with at least one other hermit who lived on an island, Herbert of Derwent Water (Hereberht; d. 687). Moreover, Cuthbert's hermitage was comparable to Irish hermitages, such as that at Inishbofin, not only in its location but also in its construction. As Bede describes it, it was 'almost round in plan, measuring about four or five poles from wall to wall; the wall itself on the outside is higher than a man standing upright; but inside he made it much higher by cutting away the living rock, so that the pious inhabitant could see nothing except the sky from his dwelling' (*Two Lives*, ed. Colgrave, 216–17). It may be also that Cuthbert's practice, while on Lindisfarne, of retreating to enjoy solitude on a nearby island, certainly to be identified with the small tidal island known as St Cuthbert's Island just off the southern tip of the main island, was the result of Irish influence. It should be emphasized, however, that Irish influence was also present on the continent where it mingled with that of the Frankish and Roman churches, so that Cuthbert's debt to the Irish church, and Iona in particular, may not be so great or so direct as appears at first sight. Moreover, the image of Cuthbert presented by the hagiographical texts, which are the only sources, may be misleading. Unquestionably he was a devout and ascetic holy man; but, in view of the intimate involvement of the church with the Northumbrian royal family and aristocracy, and in view of the scale and importance of the diocese of Lindisfarne, it seems likely that in reality Cuthbert was more worldly, more akin to his contemporary Wilfrid, than the anonymous monk of Lindisfarne and Bede wished their readers to believe.

Equally problematic is Cuthbert's role as a pastor. According to the lives, he was actively involved in evangelization of the country people while at Melrose and also during his time at Lindisfarne. This concern with pastoral work even while bishop of a major royal church has also been associated with the influence of the Irish church, in which bishoprics were very small and bishops were therefore in a position to conduct evangelization in their dioceses. It is not clear, however, how far the accounts of Cuthbert's preaching can be taken as historical fact, for in Bede's case in particular they seem closely to reflect that author's complaints that the bishops of his own day did not undertake such preaching; so that Bede's picture of Cuthbert as preacher may be more idealized than real.

The cult of Cuthbert at Lindisfarne After his death on the Inner Farne, Cuthbert's body was taken back to Lindisfarne the same day and buried in a stone sarcophagus on the right side of the altar in St Peter's Church. Eleven years later, however, Bishop Eadberht of Lindisfarne (d. 698) gave the monks permission to open the grave and put the remains in a more elevated place to facilitate veneration of them. On opening the grave, the monks found the body undecayed and the clothing still fresh. In the words of the anonymous monk, 'the skin had not decayed nor grown old, nor the sinews become dry, making the body tautly stretched and stiff; but the limbs lay at rest with all the appearance of life and were still moveable at the joints' (*Two Lives*, ed. Colgrave, 130–33). Investigations of the saint's remains in 1899 suggested the possibility that this report was correct and that the body really had been preserved. Possibly some form of embalming had been involved, or natural processes had arrested decay. At all events, it appears that the process by which a saint's body was raised up and found to be undecayed was a form of recognition of his or her sanctity, a sort of canonization. Cuthbert's body was placed in a wooden chest (*theca*), generally identified with the coffin inscribed with images of Christ and the evangelist symbols, the archangels, the apostles, and the Virgin and Child, now preserved in the treasury of Durham Cathedral. This coffin was placed on the floor of the sanctuary, and a series of miracles was believed to have been worked there, some through the agency of the shoes, clothing, and hair of the saint, which had been retained as secondary relics. Bishop Eadberht was buried in Cuthbert's original grave as a mark of his devotion to the saint; and his successor, Eadfrith, bishop of Lindisfarne (r. 698–c.721), did much to promote the saint's cult. He appears as the dedicatee of both prose lives, of which that by Bede must have done much to spread Cuthbert's fame in view of the reputation of the writer. According to a tenth-century colophon in the Lindisfarne gospels, Eadfrith was also responsible for the production of that magnificently illuminated book 'for God and for St Cuthbert'. It is possible that it was intended for display purposes, to add to the splendour of the saint's tomb, and it may have been Eadfrith who began the collection of treasures associated with Cuthbert, which came to include a wooden portable altar, subsequently encased in silver, the gold and garnet cross referred to above, a liturgical comb, and silks, among them a dalmatic of *c.*800. The small copy of St John's gospel, which is now at Stonyhurst College, complete with its original binding, seems also to have been with the saint's body. Further, it is tempting to connect Eadberht's re-roofing of the church of Lindisfarne in lead with his desire to provide an appropriate setting for Cuthbert's cult. It would appear that the Inner Farne was also developed as a centre of pilgrimage, with a resident hermit (Cuthbert's immediate successor was called Felgild), and with holy sites associated with Cuthbert. Cuthbert's posthumous importance may have extended beyond the area of Lindisfarne, however, for there are indications, especially in Bede's verse life, that he was being regarded as a patron saint of Northumbria. When the vikings sacked Lindisfarne in 793, Alcuin certainly seems to have regarded this calamity as pertinent to the whole of Britain: 'What assurance is there for the churches of Britain, if St Cuthbert … defends not his own?' (E. Dümmler, ed., *Epistolae Karolini Aevi* II, no. 20). The evidence of surviving manuscripts points to the popularity of both prose lives on the continent, and by the ninth century Cuthbert was being venerated at Fulda in Hesse, and he appeared in the martyrologies of Florus of Lyons, of Wandalbert, of Hrabanus Maurus, of Ado of Vienne, of Usuard, of Notker, and in the Codex Epternacensis of the Hieronymian martyrology.

The cult of St Cuthbert in ninth- and tenth-century England The principal source for this period is the anonymous *Historia de sancto Cuthberto*, which has been claimed as a mid-tenth-century work from Chester-le-Street but seems more likely to be a product of Durham in the second quarter of the eleventh century. A number of other Durham works are dependent on it, namely: the so-called *Chronicle of the Monastery of Durham*, reconstructed from later medieval texts but apparently originally a chronicle written in the Book of the High Altar in Durham Cathedral in 1072–3; the so-called *Capitula de miraculis et translationibus sancti Cuthberti*, of which the oldest component dates from 1083–1104; and the *Libellus de exordio atque procursu istius, hoc est*

Dunhelmensis, ecclesie ('Tract on the origins and progress of this the church of Durham'; sometimes known as *Historia Dunelmensis ecclesiae*) written by Symeon of Durham between 1104 and 1109. These texts seem to indicate that, although the viking attack of 793 did not destroy the church of Lindisfarne, Cuthbert's body and the religious community of Lindisfarne were moved to Norham on the River Tweed in the time of Bishop Ecgred (r. 830–45). It is unclear whether the body was returned to Lindisfarne, but according to these Durham texts the religious community, now best termed the Community of St Cuthbert, spent a period of either seven or nine years from 875 in a series of peregrinations across northern England with the body of St Cuthbert, which took it as far afield as the mouth of the River Derwent, Whithorn in Galloway, and Crayke just to the north of York. The texts represent this period as one of flight before the vikings, but the fact that the Community of St Cuthbert retained many of its early lands and treasures might suggest that the moves were of a more calculated nature, but presented to us in the hagiographical manner as reminiscent of the Israelites in the wilderness. The *Historia de sancto Cuthberto* documents extensive land grants in the area of co. Durham made to the community in the course of the earlier ninth century, so there may have been good practical reasons for moving southward from Lindisfarne.

In 883 (or 885) the community settled at Chester-le-Street, where the Danish Christian King Guthfrith (in association with King Alfred as certain of the texts claim) endowed it with extensive lands between the rivers Tyne and Wear. There the community, the see, and the shrine of St Cuthbert were fixed for a century or more. In addition to lands, the kings mentioned above are said to have defined the rights of sanctuary to be accorded to those fleeing to the saint's body. These became an important feature of the cult as it developed at Durham in the course of the middle ages. They may in fact have originated as early as the eighth century, for in his prose life Bede puts into the mouth of the dying saint the wish that his body should not be buried on Lindisfarne 'on account of the influx of fugitives and guilty men of every sort, who will perhaps flee to my body, ... and you will be compelled very frequently to intercede with the powers of this world on behalf of such men' (*Two Lives*, ed. Colgrave, 278–9).

There is evidence to suggest strong southern English interest in the cult of Cuthbert in the tenth century. The shrine is said to have been visited by King Æthelstan and King Edmund, both of whom made rich gifts, perhaps represented by the stole and maniple from Winchester and the ninth-century Byzantine silk (the 'nature goddess silk') found in the tomb, and including also land. The tenth-century copy of Bede's lives of the saint (now Cambridge, Corpus Christi College, MS 183), also contains liturgical material for the saint's cult and a painting of a king with the saint. It has usually been regarded as a gift of Æthelstan to the shrine, but in fact it is not certain that it belonged to the Community of St Cuthbert before the late eleventh century, and it may have been a devotional book belonging to Æthelstan himself. At all events, it was a product of southern England and, taken together with other evidence, it shows clearly the veneration accorded Cuthbert there.

The cult of St Cuthbert at Durham According to the Durham sources, a further viking threat led the community to move to Ripon with the body of St Cuthbert in 995. As they were returning in the same year, the body became too heavy to move and the saint informed one of their number in a vision that he wished to be moved to the seemingly uninhabited peninsula at Durham, and this was duly done, the body being established first in a wooden church, then in a stone church called the White Church, then finally in the new cathedral. Further land-grants were made to the community, including one by Cnut who came to Durham as a pilgrim. The extent to which Cuthbert was assigned a posthumous role as the recipient and guardian of lands is striking. The *Historia de sancto Cuthberto* credits him with having been given the original endowment of Lindisfarne on either side of the River Tweed, which is historically improbable, and then catalogues a number of other grants as having been made to him in life and in death, so that the text often reads more like a cartulary than a saint's life.

To judge from Cuthbert's prominence in liturgical calendars, the cult was popular in later Anglo-Saxon England and its popularity spanned the Norman conquest. Although the last Anglo-Saxon bishop of Durham, Æthelwine (r. 1056–71), fled for a time to Lindisfarne with Cuthbert's body to escape William the Conqueror's devastations, and himself ended his life in a royal prison, the saint's position seems to have continued unchanged. In 1083, William of St Calais, bishop of Durham, expelled the canons of the Community of St Cuthbert and replaced them with Benedictine monks, but, to judge from the work of their historian Symeon, and of the *Capitula de miraculis*, Cuthbert's cult established itself among them, so that in 1104 his remains were inspected, confirmed to be undecayed, and translated into the east end of the new Norman cathedral, where they remained in an imposing shrine until their desecration by Henry VIII's commissioners in 1542. The cult was certainly important in the twelfth century and later, and was given impetus not only by Symeon's work but also by the major collection of miracle stories, the *Libellus de admirandis beati Cuthberti virtutibus quae novellis patratae sunt temporibus* written in the third quarter of the twelfth century by Reginald of Durham, who claimed Cuthbert as the most popular saint of the day, competing successfully with Edmund of Bury and Æthelthryth of Ely. Either a contemporary of Reginald or Reginald himself wrote another work, the *Libellus de ortu sancti Cuthberti*, which provided Cuthbert with a spurious Irish royal ancestry. The cult's development must have been restricted, however, by the exclusion of women from any but the westernmost parts of Durham Cathedral, and at some periods even from the churchyard. This exclusion, which was perhaps motivated by the concerns of a celibate Benedictine cathedral community, was seemingly justified on the grounds of Cuthbert's alleged misogyny. In fact this finds no mention in the early lives, which, on the contrary, emphasize his contacts with women. Although the shrine occupied the usual position behind the high altar of the church, it is striking that when the east end was enlarged in the thirteenth century to create the chapel of the nine altars no special provision was made to increase access to Cuthbert's shrine, which was evidently not a major priority. Nevertheless, the cult was already well established in northern England and in southern Scotland, as evidenced by churches dedicated to the saint and by place names embodying his name.

Rivalled, but not eclipsed, by Thomas Becket, Cuthbert continued to be one of Britain's most popular saints for the rest of the middle ages. A visit to his shrine was a more or less obligatory part of any progress through northern England, as by the future Pope Pius II in 1436, Henry VI in 1448, Richard III in 1483, and Margaret Tudor in 1503. The presence of the so-called 'corsaint' within Durham Cathedral provided that church with the most extensive and respected sanctuary privileges in northern England; and the custody of his shrine was entrusted to the monastic feretrar and his staff. The latter's most important source of income derived from the offerings regularly made by pilgrims at the pyx or box of St Cuthbert; and although these had declined to less than £20 per annum by the mid-fifteenth century, the many valuable gifts of plate and jewels to the shrine included such fabulous items as the mysterious 'great emerald', valued at over £3330 in 1401. Above all, Cuthbert remained an essentially northern saint, still capable of perpetuating the myth of a unique body of 'Cuthbert folk', whose loyalties to their great spiritual patron were always liable to become stronger than those to their bishop or their king. For obvious reasons, such intense devotion was exploited rather than resisted by the rulers of the late medieval north, most notably on the many occasions between the 1290s and the battle of Flodden in 1513 when the saint's famous banner was carried across the Tweed on (usually victorious) English expeditions against the Scots.

Whether popular enthusiasm for Cuthbert's cult had undergone any significant decline before the last Benedictine monks of Durham finally surrendered their monastery to the crown (31 December 1539) is difficult to determine. Although the last of his recorded medieval miracles, the healing of Richard Poell, one of Henry VII's retainers, occurred in 1503, a generation later the affection of northerners for their saint was still alleged to be the biggest obstacle to the progress of the Reformation north of the Tees. According to the late sixteenth-century *Rites of Durham*, Cuthbert was still being remembered as the cathedral's most beneficent patron long after the ruthless desecration of his remains by Henry VIII's commissioners in 1542. The saint's body was thereafter reburied in its original coffin and remained undisturbed until the grave was opened by Canon James Raine (1791–1858) and others in 1827 with the polemical intention of proving that Cuthbert's body was by no means miraculously incorrupt. Although one of the most remarkable archaeological investigations of its age, this reopening of the saint's coffin is explicable only in terms of sectarian tension in the years before Catholic emancipation in 1829 and of the consecration of a new Catholic church of St Cuthbert at Durham. The canons of Durham were also anxious to dispel the local belief that the real remains of St Cuthbert were not in their cathedral at all but had fallen into Roman Catholic hands from the sixteenth century onwards. Although not entirely successful in that intention, many of the objects (including the coffin) found with the saint in 1827 undoubtedly did date from an early period in the history of his cult: they were removed before Cuthbert's own bones were returned to his grave behind the cathedral's high altar. The latter have only been disturbed once again, during the medical examination of 1899, referred to above. During the twentieth century, as was particularly obvious in the widespread celebrations which marked the 1300th anniversary of his death in 1987, Cuthbert steadily enhanced his posthumous reputation as the most benevolently charismatic of all British saints.

DAVID ROLLASON and R. B. DOBSON

Sources *Two lives of St Cuthbert: a life by an anonymous monk of Lindisfarne and Bede's prose life*, ed. and trans. B. Colgrave (1940) · *Bedas metrische 'Vita sancti Cuthberti'*, ed. W. Jaager (Leipzig, 1935) · Bede, *Hist. eccl.* · Symeon of Durham, *Opera* · Symeon of Durham, *Libellus de exordio atque procursu istius, hoc est Dunhelmensis, ecclesie / Tract on the origins and progress of this the church of Durham*, ed. and trans. D. W. Rollason, OMT (2000) · *Reginaldi monachi Dunelmensis libellus de admirandis beati Cuthberti virtutibus*, ed. [J. Raine], SurtS, 1 (1835) · G. Bonner, D. Rollason, and C. Stancliffe, eds., *St Cuthbert, his cult and his community to AD 1200* (1989) · F. Battiscombe, ed., *The relics of St Cuthbert* (1956) · D. Rollason, *Saints and relics in Anglo-Saxon England* (1989) · E. Craster, 'The patrimony of St Cuthbert', *EngHR*, 69 (1954), 177–99 · E. Craster, 'The Red Book of Durham', *EngHR*, 40 (1925), 504–32 · B. Colgrave, 'The post-Bedan miracles and translations of St Cuthbert', *The early cultures of north-west Europe* (H. M. Chadwick Memorial Studies), ed. C. Fox and B. Dickins (1950), 305–32 · M. Aird, 'The making of a medieval miracle collection: the liber de translationibus et miraculis sancti Cuthberti', *Northern History*, 28 (1992), 1–24 · V. Tudor, 'The misogyny of St Cuthbert', *Archaeologia Aeliana*, 5th ser., 12 (1984), 157–67 · D. Rollason, M. Harvey, and M. Prestwich, eds., *Anglo-Norman Durham, 1093–1193* (1994) · J. Raine, *St Cuthbert, with an account of the state in which his remains were found upon the opening of his tomb in Durham Cathedral, in the year 1827* (1828)

Likenesses manuscript illumination, CCC Cam., MS 183, fol. 1v; *see illus. in* Æthelstan (893/4–939)

Cuthbert (d. 760), archbishop of Canterbury, succeeded to the archbishopric in 740. If he was the same Cuthbert who became bishop of the Magonsæte in 736, he was probably (like his predecessors Tatwine and Nothhelm) of Mercian origin. In favour of the identification is the interest shown by both men in Latin verse: two epigrams survive from the pen of Cuthbert of the Magonsæte, and the archbishop was perhaps the intended recipient of a collection of Latin verses made by Milred, bishop of Worcester. Milred certainly lent the archbishop a copy of the poems of Optatianus Porfyrius, court poet to Constantine the Great, for in a letter to Lul, archbishop of Mainz, he complains that Cuthbert has not returned it.

In Cuthbert's time, southern England was dominated by Æthelbald of Mercia (r. 716–57). In 746 or 747, Boniface, archbishop of Mainz, complained to Æthelbald of the king's abuse of church privileges, and a contemporaneous letter to Cuthbert alleges that the king's officers had compelled monks to labour on the building of royal residences and other public works. In the same letter, Boniface deplored the general state of the English church, complaining of drunkenness, 'foolish superstitions in dress', the immoral behaviour of female pilgrims to Rome, and family monasteries controlled by their lay founders; concern over the latter had been voiced a decade earlier by Bede. Boniface reported the decrees of Frankish synods on similar topics, with the implicit suggestion that Cuthbert should institute such reforms in England, and later in the same year the archbishop convened a synod of the Southumbrian province at 'Clofesho'. The site, which is as yet unidentified, was appointed by the Synod of Hertford in 672 as the annual meeting-place for general synods, though the 747 council is the first known to have been held there. It probably lay in Mercia, perhaps in Middle Anglia. The site was certainly under the control of the Mercian kings, for King Æthelbald and his nobles were present at the meeting of 747, and later synods at 'Clofesho' were attended by his successors.

The acts of the council in 747 are preserved in a manuscript put together in the late eighth century. Although it was damaged in the Cottonian fire of 1731, enough survives to be checked against earlier transcripts. The collection of texts which it contains appears to represent 'a concerted programme of reform undertaken by Archbishop Cuthbert and King Æthelbald in direct response to the criticisms levelled at them by Archbishop Boniface' (Keynes, *Councils*, 6). The collection includes an abridgement of Gregory the Great's *Regula pastoralis* ('Pastoral care', on the duties of bishops), Boniface's letter to Cuthbert, and Æthelbald's grant of privileges to the church, issued at Gumley in 749; it may once have included Boniface's letter of reproof to Æthelbald himself.

Several chapters of the 747 *acta* reflect Frankish legislation reported by Boniface. In the matter of lay monasteries, however, the English synod took a more pragmatic view than that of Boniface. He had recommended excommunication for offenders, but the synod at 'Clofesho', while deploring the existence of such houses, confined itself to insisting (chapter 5) that provision should at least be made for the ministry of a priest. This softly-softly approach seems to have borne fruit; in the diocese of Worcester (the only one for which adequate evidence survives), the figure of the thegn-abbot, the lay lord of the monastery, vanished in the later eighth century. This may not be entirely the result of episcopal application of the 747 canons. One of the motives behind the founding of family monasteries was to acquire bookland (land granted in perpetuity by a royal diploma), which originated as an ecclesiastical tenure, but from the second half of the eighth century royal grants of bookland began to be made to laymen for purely lay purposes, removing the need for such stratagems. Many lay foundations did come into episcopal hands in the late eighth and early ninth centuries, and Æthelbald himself gave the minster of Cookham, in

what is now Berkshire, to Christ Church, Canterbury, in Cuthbert's time. Whether this was an improvement is debatable. Although the more austere churchmen, Frankish and English, might take a dim view of family monasteries and minsters, they clearly enjoyed popular support and it is by no means certain that all (or any) were the sinks of iniquity portrayed by Bede and Boniface.

Little is known of Cuthbert's later years. He remained in touch with Boniface, sending letters and gifts by the hand of his deacon Cyneberht. When Boniface was martyred in 754, Cuthbert wrote a letter of condolence to his successor Lul, reporting that Boniface, with Gregory the Great and Augustine, had been adopted as a special patron of the English church. The murder of Æthelbald of Mercia in 757 and the ensuing civil war in Mercia diminished Mercian influence on Kent and it may have been under the auspices of Cynewulf of Wessex rather than Æthelbald's eventual successor, Offa, that Cuthbert held a second synod in 758, known only from a grant made on the occasion by Cynewulf to Bath Minster.

In Canterbury itself, Cuthbert was remembered as the builder of the church of St John the Baptist, immediately to the east of the main cathedral. Little is known of its form. Eadmer, who saw it before it was burnt down with the rest of the complex in 1067, describes it simply as an *ecclesia*, and in the Christ Church cartulary it is called a basilica. As the dedication suggests, it was intended as a baptistery, though it may have had other uses as well; certainly by 1066 it was used for judicial ordeals and for the keeping of the cathedral archives. It was also, from the first, intended as a mortuary chapel for the archbishops of Canterbury, breaking with the earlier tradition of interring the archbishops at the monastery of St Peter and St Paul (later St Augustine's) outside the city walls. Such interments were in line with the late Roman requirement of extramural burial, but even at Rome itself this practice had largely ceased. In later traditions Cuthbert is said to have observed the change when he went to Rome for his pallium, and to have obtained the permission of Pope Gregory III to institute the same practice at Canterbury. It is far from certain, however, that Cuthbert ever visited Rome, for archbishops began to fetch their pallia from the pope only in the tenth century; in the earlier period, the popes dispatched pallia to the archbishops. Most of the post-conquest explanations of Cuthbert's innovation are clearly polemical, reflecting the later dissension between Christ Church and St Augustine's, one of whose chroniclers calls the removal of burial rights from his house 'foul, snake-like and matricidal'. It was presumably in opposition to the complaints from St Augustine's that the post-conquest cartularist of Christ Church concocted the story that when Cuthbert felt himself close to death, he forbade his clergy to toll for him, and commanded them to keep his death concealed until after they had buried him. Not until the third day after his demise did the bells toll, but when Abbot Ealdhun and his monks came to fetch his corpse to St Augustine's they found it safely interred in his own church. All that can really be said of the change in burial practice is that it happened, and that, following his death on 26 October 760, Cuthbert was the first of the archbishops to be buried in his new church.

ANN WILLIAMS

Sources N. Brooks, *The early history of the church of Canterbury: Christ Church from 597 to 1066* (1984) • P. Sims-Williams, *Religion and literature in western England, 600–800* (1990) • S. Keynes, *The councils of Clofesho* (1994) • A. W. Haddan and W. Stubbs, eds., *Councils and ecclesiastical documents relating to Great Britain and Ireland*, 3 (1871) • S. Keynes, 'The reconstruction of a burnt Cottonian manuscript: the case of Cotton MS Otho A I', *British Library Journal*, 22 (1996), 113–60 • C. Cubitt, 'Pastoral care and conciliar councils: the provisions of the 747 Council of Clofesho', *Pastoral care before the parish*, ed. J. Blair and R. Sharpe (1992), 193–211 • *English historical documents*, 1, ed. D. Whitelock (1955) • C. Cubitt, *Anglo-Saxon church councils, c.650– c.850* (1995) • R. Fleming, 'Christ Church's Anglo-Norman cartulary', *Anglo-Norman political culture*, ed. C. W. Hollister (1997), 83– 155 • M. Tangl, ed., *Die Briefe des heiligen Bonifatius und Lullus*, MGH Epistolae Selectae, 1 (Berlin, 1916) • W. Stubbs, ed., *Memorials of St Dunstan, archbishop of Canterbury*, Rolls Series, 63 (1874) • *William Thorne's chronicle of St Augustine's Abbey, Canterbury*, trans. A. H. Davis (1934)

Cuthbert, Gwendoline Emily. *See* Meacham, Gwendoline Emily (1892–1981).

Cuthbertson, Sir David Paton (1900–1989), medical researcher and nutritionist, was born on 9 May 1900 in Kilmarnock, Ayrshire, the only child of John Cuthbertson MBE FRSE, secretary of the West of Scotland Agricultural College, and his wife, Lilias Ann Bowman, formerly matron of Kilmarnock Infirmary. He was educated at Kilmarnock Academy. After army service (1918–19), first as a cadet, later as second lieutenant (temporary) in the Royal Scots Fusiliers, he entered Glasgow University, from which he graduated BSc in 1921, with chemistry as the principal subject. He won the Dobie-Smith gold medal and was awarded a scholarship by the Scottish board of agriculture to undertake research in chemistry. He decided, however, that his interest in research required a medical degree and he graduated MB, ChB from the University of Glasgow in 1926, having obtained the Hunter medal in physiology and the Strang-Steel scholarship for research, which enabled him to carry out the work during vacations for his first scientific publication, in the *Biochemical Journal*, in 1925.

Cuthbertson's first appointment (1926) was as lecturer in pathological biochemistry in the University of Glasgow and clinical biochemist to Glasgow Royal Infirmary. It was while holding this joint appointment that he carried out the initial studies on the changes in metabolism in surgical patients which led, later, to worldwide recognition. In the eight years he held this post, before being appointed to the Grieve lectureship in physiological chemistry in the University of Glasgow in 1934, he published twenty-seven papers, mainly on the effects of immobility, bed rest, infection, or injury, on metabolism in surgical patients. In 1934 he studied with Professor Karl Thomas in Leipzig University.

Cuthbertson's nutritional investigations at this time included studies on the interactions of carbohydrate and fat with the metabolism of protein, some of which were carried out in collaboration with colleagues, of whom one, Hamish N. Munro, was to gain a considerable international reputation for his work in nutrition about thirty years later. In 1937 his MD was awarded with honours and he gained the Bellahouston medal of the University of Glasgow. Undoubtedly, however, it was the publication of his Arris and Gale lecture of the Royal College of Surgeons of England in *The Lancet* (1942, 1, 433–7), entitled 'Post-shock metabolic response', which gained for him his greatest and enduring international recognition. Textbooks throughout the world came to refer to his general classification of the changes in metabolism which follow serious injury as the 'ebb' and 'flow' phases, the ebb phase corresponding to the period of clinical shock, and the flow phase to the subsequent period of increased energy consumption, which gradually returns towards normal with healing and recovery.

During the later years of the Second World War business travel (to research or scientific committee meetings) became part of Cuthbertson's life and continued until his death. His secondment to the Medical Research Council (MRC) in London in 1943 required frequent travel between Glasgow and London until 1945. In that year he became director of the Rowett Research Institute, Bucksburn, Aberdeen, a post which he held until his retirement in 1965 with a knighthood; he had been appointed CBE in 1957. Under his direction the institute expanded with new buildings and facilities, such that in 1951 there were nine sections, and in its jubilee year in 1963 the number of staff had increased fourfold. There were laboratories for studies with trace elements, radioactive isotopes, and a large animal calorimeter. The Rowett became internationally renowned in nutrition research.

On retirement Cuthbertson returned to full-time research on the changes in metabolism following injury, with support from the MRC and Glasgow Royal Infirmary. He continued to publish scientific papers and review articles, and travel widely to scientific meetings, being particularly welcome in the USA. Two of his notable attributes were his ability to obtain support for research and to encourage others. His eminence was recognized by honorary degrees from Rutgers (1958), Glasgow (1960), and Aberdeen (1972), and honorary fellowship or membership of royal colleges and societies.

Cuthbertson was 6 feet tall, and had a pleasant personality and a gently positive approach. He found time for art— watercolours and engraving—and many of his colleagues received personally engraved Christmas cards. Another activity was golf—he played in Scottish inter-university matches, and for many years participated in the matches between the senates of the ancient Scottish universities. In 1928 he married Jean Prentice (*d.* 1987), a nursing sister in Glasgow Royal Infirmary and daughter of the Revd Alexander Prentice Telfer, of Tarbet, Dunbartonshire. Cuthbertson died at home in Troon on 15 April 1989, having played golf in the morning. He is commemorated in the annual Cuthbertson lecture of the European Society for Parenteral and Enteral Nutrition, and by a plaque in Glasgow Royal Infirmary.

ADAM FLECK, *rev.*

Sources personal records, Royal Society of Edinburgh · *The Times* (21 April 1989) · personal knowledge (1996)
Archives Rowett Research Institute, corresp. and papers relating to Rowett Research Institute [mainly copies] · Royal Society of Edinburgh · U. Glas., Archives and Business Records Centre, autobiographical essays | Trinity Cam., corresp. with R. L. M. Synge
Wealth at death £348,113.14: confirmation, 5 July 1989, *CCI*

Cuthbertson, John (*bap.* 1743, *d.* 1821), instrument maker, was baptized at Dearham, Cumberland, on 1 July 1743. He was the second of four children (the eldest of whom predeceased him) and elder son of Jonathan Cuthbertson, an innkeeper and yeoman, and his second wife, Mary Fisher. He has been confused with his younger brother, Jonathan, also born in Dearham, and baptized on 11 September 1744, who followed the same profession; their publications have been listed in several prominent works under John's name alone. Jonathan died in 1806.

Nothing is known about the brothers' formal education or early apprenticeships. In 1761 John Cuthbertson was apprenticed to the instrument maker James Champneys and moved with him to Amsterdam in 1768. Champneys was one of a number of prominent London instrument makers who brought a petition against Peter Dollond in 1764 to annul (unsuccessfully, as it turned out) the achromatic lens patent which had been granted to Dollond's father in 1758. In 1766 Champneys had to pay a heavy fine for infringing Dollond's patent, and he was made bankrupt in that year. This may have been one of the reasons for his move to the Netherlands with his apprentice. Cuthbertson followed the fairly common practice of marrying his master's daughter; he and Jane Champneys were married on 1 September 1768, and it must have been shortly afterwards that the move to the Netherlands took place, as Cuthbertson appears in the Amsterdam *poorterboek* on 29 December 1768. Only John took the poorter's oath necessary for those who wanted to establish a business; from this we may surmise that James Champneys lived with the newly married couple, and that the business was solely in Cuthbertson's name. Cuthbertson and his wife had four children in Amsterdam, but only their sole daughter, Jane, survived.

Cuthbertson became noted for his glass-plate frictional electrical machines, a technology which he took with him from London but which he developed to a high state of perfection in the Netherlands. Some of the improvements may have originated from his brother, Jonathan, who had set up a flourishing instrument-making business in Rotterdam. Cuthbertson also advanced the subject of electricity, writing books, giving public lectures, and assisting some of the foremost Dutch scientists with their experiments. In 1783 he constructed a very large twin-plate electrical machine for one of these scientists, Martinus van Marum, the director of the experimental cabinet of the Teyler's Foundation in Haarlem. This frictional generator, the largest of its type, produced 24 inch discharges, equivalent to about 300,000 volts.

Cuthbertson returned to London some time between 1793 and 1796, perhaps because of the worsening political situation in the Dutch Republic. His brother decided to remain behind and died in Rotterdam. John settled at Poland Street in London. It cannot have been easy for a man in his fifties to start afresh as an instrument maker there. In 1799 he invented an electrometer named after him and produced a simplified version of his plate electrical machine, which became the most popular type in England. He also designed several air-pumps. In 1810 he wrote his last scientific papers. He was buried on 18 July 1821 in his parish church, St James's, Piccadilly. He probably died intestate.

W. D. HACKMANN, *rev.*

Sources W. D. Hackmann, *John and Jonathan Cuthbertson* (1973) · W. D. Hackmann, *Electricity from glass: the history of the frictional electrical machine, 1600–1850* (1978), 154–64

Cuthburh [St Cuthburh, Cuthburga] (*fl. c.*700–718), supposed abbess of Wimborne, was the daughter of Coenred (*d. c.*694), a minor king of Wessex, and sister of the powerful King *Ine. She married King *Aldfrith of Northumbria (*d.* 704/5), a godson of Aldhelm, abbot of Malmesbury, and the marriage should be seen in the context of other alliances between the West Saxon and Northumbrian royal houses. Aldfrith's children included *Osred I, king of the Northumbrians, and it is thought that Cuthburh was his mother. According to the Anglo-Saxon Chronicle for 718, Aldfrith and Cuthburh separated during their lifetimes (that is, before 704/5, when Aldfrith died) and Cuthburh founded the monastery of Wimborne. Presumably, like other widowed or separated queens, she held the position of abbess in her community, though that is not specifically stated in contemporary sources. It is often assumed that before she founded Wimborne, Cuthburh entered the monastery of Barking, since a Cuthburga appears among the nuns of Barking to whom Aldhelm dedicated his *De virginitate*; but there is no evidence to confirm this identification with the ex-queen. Cuthburh may have been joined at Wimborne by her sister Cwenburh, as both are known to have been venerated at Wimborne from the late Saxon period. The year of Cuthburh's death is not known, but 31 August was the day of her *depositio* in medieval calendars. She was buried in Wimborne Minster. The assumption which has sometimes been made, that she was still living in the second quarter of the eighth century and was the abbess Tetta who had charge of Leoba, is unlikely to be correct, especially as Leoba's biographer states that other abbesses had ruled between the foundation of the monastery and the appointment of Tetta.

BARBARA YORKE

Sources *ASC*, s.a. 718 [text A] · *Aldhelm: the prose works*, trans. M. Lapidge and M. Herren (1979) · [Rudolf of Fulda], 'Vita Leobae abbatissae Biscofesheimensis auctore Rudolfo Fuldensi', [*Supplementa tomorum I–XII, pars III*], ed. G. Waitz, MGH Scriptores [folio], 15/1 (Stuttgart, 1887), 118–31 · D. W. Rollason, 'Lists of saints' resting-places in Anglo-Saxon England', *Anglo-Saxon England*, 7 (1978), 61–93 · J. M. J. Fletcher, 'The marriage of St Cuthburga, who was afterwards foundress of the monastery at Wimborne', *Dorset Natural History and Antiquarian Field Club*, 34 (1931), 167–85 · P. H. Coulstock, *The collegiate church of Wimborne Minster* (1993) · B. Yorke, *Nunneries and the Anglo-Saxon royal houses* (2003)

Cuthred (*d.* 756), king of the West Saxons, succeeded to the kingship on the death of Æthelheard in 740. In a charter of the previous year, Cuthred's name appears in the witness list directly after that of Æthelheard and before Queen Frithugyth, and this special position suggests that he was Æthelheard's designated successor, presumably a close relative and possibly his son. No succession dispute in 740 is recorded, but the Anglo-Saxon Chronicle mentions that a West Saxon atheling named Cynric was killed in 748, and that Cuthred fought the arrogant ealdorman Æthelhun in 750, and both these incidents may relate to unsuccessful attempts to overthrow Cuthred and seize the kingship.

King Æthelbald of Mercia almost certainly exercised some power in Wessex at the time of Cuthred's accession, although the nature and extent of this power are far from clear. The Anglo-Saxon Chronicle records that Cuthred and Æthelbald fought the Britons in 743: probably Cuthred was assisting the Mercians against the Welsh in accordance with some subjection to, or alliance with, Mercia. In 744 Æthelbald authorized the sale of land in what is now Somerset to the monastery at Glastonbury in a charter which Cuthred attests, and Æthelbald is also recorded as a direct benefactor of the house, granting lands, which are unidentified but may have lain in the same area, in the 740s.

However, Cuthred retained his independent royal title and frequently acted without any reference to Mercia. He was a benefactor of monasteries, granting estates in what are now Dorset and Somerset to Sherborne. He gave Wdetun (probably Wootton Bassett in Wiltshire) to Malmesbury in 745 and the unidentified 'Thruhham' to Winchester in 749. About 745 he confirmed the grants of all previous kings, including Æthelbald, to Glastonbury. It may be that Wessex was effectively independent, though subject to Æthelbald's influence when he chose to exert it there.

Later in the reign, probably about 750, Cuthred rebelled against Æthelbald. There was a battle at 'Beorhford' which Cuthred is said to have won, and there is no evidence for any further Mercian power in Wessex during Cuthred's lifetime. The Anglo-Saxon Chronicle, summing up the reign, says that Cuthred fought stoutly against King Æthelbald, which implies that he enjoyed some success. The evidence is far from conclusive, but it seems likely that during the 750s Cuthred was able to free Wessex from Mercian influence.

In 753 Cuthred turned his attention to fighting the Cornish. In 756 he died and was succeeded by *Sigeberht, who may have been his son. HEATHER EDWARDS

Sources ASC, s.a. 740, 741, 743, 748, 750, 752, 753, 756 [texts A, E] • AS chart., S 255, 256, 257, 258, 259, 1410, 1678–9 • Bede, Hist. eccl., 5.23 • F. M. Stenton, 'The supremacy of the Mercian kings', Preparatory to 'Anglo-Saxon England': being the collected papers of Frank Merry Stenton, ed. D. M. Stenton (1970), 48–66 • F. M. Stenton, Anglo-Saxon England, 3rd edn (1971) • P. Wormald, 'Bede, the "Bretwaldas" and the origins of the "gens Anglorum"', Ideal and reality in Frankish and Anglo-Saxon society, ed. P. Wormald, D. Bullough, and R. Collins (1983), 99–129 • H. Edwards, The charters of the early West Saxon kingdom (1988)

Cutler, Ann (1759–1794), hand-loom weaver and Methodist evangelist, was born in Thornley, near Longridge, in the parish of Chipping, Lancashire; nothing is known of her parents. After living a strict, moral life she was converted in 1785 by the revivalist Wesleyan William Bramwell, and in the same year received the gift of 'entire sanctification' taught by John Wesley, whom she later met at Preston in 1790. She soon began to obtain converts by praying in public meetings. Nicknamed 'Praying Nanny', she customarily rose at midnight for prayer, slept until 4 a.m., prayed until 5 or 6 a.m., then studied the Bible and prayed again. When weaving she prayed briefly twelve or fourteen times daily. Her public prayers, though brief, were generally in a loud voice. She searched the New Testament 'to know what blessings were promised to her; and if she could satisfy herself ... of what the promise contained, she instantly believed that the Lord would give it' (Bramwell, 1796, 9). Her greatest gift was not in argument or exhortation but in her powerful praying and her insight into individual spiritual conditions. Like other Methodist women of this period she had the unusual mystical experience of visions of the Trinity perceived in the three separate persons: 'I have union with the Trinity thus. I see the Son through the Spirit, I find the Father through the Son, and God is my all in all' (ibid., 19).

Ann's early evangelism was in the Lancashire Fylde district, where she was sometimes accompanied by Martha Thompson (1733–1820), reputed to be the first Methodist in Preston. Martha exhorted and sang, Ann prayed and directed people to conversion. Eventually Martha's father, fearing for his daughter's health, warned her not to continue: 'Nanny Cutler will soon kill thee. She is as strong as a horse, and thou hast no business to try to work with her' (Taylor, 131). Ann's greatest successes were in the Yorkshire revival of 1792–4, when she worked with William Bramwell to stir up revivals, notably in Dewsbury, Birstall, and the Bradford and Otley areas, and possibly also in Leeds. She provoked many conversions and claims to entire sanctification, a doctrine she often emphasized. During 1794 she helped to stimulate revivals in Lancashire (notably Oldham and Manchester), Cheshire, Staffordshire, and Derby. Though probably influenced by worsening social conditions and the troubled state of Methodism following Wesley's death in 1791, these revivals owed much to the charisma of Bramwell and Cutler.

By strict self-discipline and self-denial—she apparently lived chiefly on milk and herb tea—Ann Cutler, despite her humble origins, became a powerful evangelist. In appearance she was 'of medium height and build, of comely appearance, plain and neat in her dress and of a very modest, retiring disposition' (Taylor, 60). She never married and apparently, unlike most Methodists, had covenanted with God to live a single life. Anxious to avoid any appearance of impropriety, she rejected any escort from young men, even when working late in the evening. She died in Macclesfield, of a chest infection, on 29 December 1794 and was buried there in the churchyard of Christ Church, whose minister was the Revd David Simpson, a friend of John Wesley. HENRY D. RACK

Sources W. Bramwell, A short account of the life and death of Ann Cutler (1796) • J. Baxter, 'The great Yorkshire revival, 1792–96', Sociological Yearbook of Religion, ed. M. Hill, 7 (1974), 46–76, esp. 49, 54, 57,

59 · P. W. Chilcote, *John Wesley and the women preachers of early Methodism* (1991), 94–5, 102, 223–4, 259–60 · W. Bramwell, *A short account of the life and death of Ann Cutler*, new edn (1827) [additional material of Z. Taft] · Z. Taft, *Biographical sketches of the lives … of various holy women*, 2 vols. in 1 (1825–8); facs. edn (1992), 301–24 · J. Taylor, *The apostles of Fylde Methodism* (1885), 33, 57–61, 131 · W. F. Richardson, *Preston Methodism: two hundred fascinating years, 1779–1996* (1978), 9–12 · R. Allen, *History of Methodism in Preston and its vicinity* (1866), 37–8 · J. R. Robinson, *Notes on early Methodism in Dewsbury* (1900), 80 · V. Ward, *A memoir of the late Rev. John Nelson the Second*, 2nd edn (1838), 27–8 · *The letters of the Rev. John Wesley*, ed. J. Telford, 8 vols. (1931), vol. 8, pp. 214–15

Cutler, Sir Horace Walter (1912–1997), local politician, was born on 28 July 1912 at 14 Wargrave Avenue, Tottenham, Middlesex, the fourth of seven children of Albert Benjamin Cutler (1871–1934), joiner, and his wife, Mary Ann, *née* Rice. He attended the local council elementary school before winning a scholarship to Tottenham grammar school. From there he transferred to Harrow grammar school and subsequently to Hereford Cathedral school. Having abandoned hopes of a legal career he worked for his father—now a master builder—'typing, making tea and licking stamps' (*Evening Standard*, 7 April 1970). His father was one of the men who built outer London between the wars, covering the virgin lands of South Harrow and Pinner with 7000 'Cutler houses', built to a model which included leaded windows designed by Horace Cutler himself. His circumstances changed dramatically during 1934, first with his marriage on 17 February to Betty Gladys Martin (*b.* 1914), daughter of Michael Henry Martin, barrister, and then with the death of his father in a road accident three months later. Cutler took over the family business with his older brother Benjamin, becoming secretary and *de facto* manager until he joined the Royal Naval Volunteer Reserve as a lieutenant during the Second World War.

After the war Cutler returned to the family firm, but he found himself increasingly disenchanted both with the tighter building controls of the 1940s and with the *étatisme* of the post-war world, crystallized in a conflict with the Inland Revenue over tax arrears that led to the firm of B. H. Cutler's being wound up. Cutler was 'bitter, furious and wronged' (*Daily Telegraph*); the episode reinforced his hostility to state socialism. His Conservatism was already well established: he had joined the Junior Imperial League in 1932. He later claimed: 'I didn't join for the politics, I joined for the girls' (ibid.), but by 1947 he had assumed the unromantic role of treasurer of the Harrow West Conservative Association. Eager to vent his views in local politics, he decided to work night and day until he was financially independent, concentrating upon building up an insurance business and a chain of coin-operated launderettes, and speculating in development land. In 1954 he and his wife were divorced, and on 13 July 1957 he married Christiane Gabriele Muthesius (*b.* 1935), a ground stewardess for Trans-World Airlines at Frankfurt and daughter of Dr Klaus Muthesius.

Financial security enabled Cutler to develop a public career, which began with his election to Harrow urban district council in 1952. With his building background he devoted himself largely to housing and planning issues. As chairman of the housing committee during 1955–8 he made Harrow (which had become a borough in 1954) one of the few local authorities to sell some of its housing stock, under legislation of 1952. He served as mayor of Harrow in 1958–9, and led the council from 1962 to 1965. He was also deputy leader (1962) and leader (1963–5) of Middlesex county council, to which he was first elected in 1955.

The absorption of Middlesex into the new Greater London council (GLC) in 1965 provided Cutler with a national platform. Though Labour won the first election, Cutler and his colleagues brought a fresh 'Middlesex style' to County Hall (*The Times*, 29 May 1967), and when the Conservatives won the second election in 1967 substantial policy innovations were anticipated. Most of them emanated from Cutler, who, having narrowly lost the leadership of

Sir Horace Walter Cutler (1912–1997), by Brian Harris, 1981

the tory group to Desmond Plummer, became deputy leader and chairman of the housing committee.

Cutler's views on housing were epitomized in a television interview of 1969 in which he suggested that 'local authorities ought to get out of housing … because they don't know how to run it' (Young and Kramer, 68). GLC policy was four pronged: the reduction of rent subsidies to eliminate a housing deficit of £4.75 million, the introduction of a rebate scheme to help poorer tenants, the encouragement of housing associations, and the sale of council houses to their occupiers. The rent increases brought rent strikes and other protests, including a march on Cutler's Ibiza villa by GLC tenants, but Cutler's sense that the GLC's 'two-car tenants' aspired to home ownership proved accurate, and 16,000 houses had been sold by the time the Conservatives left office in 1973. Cutler himself moved on from the housing committee to chair the new policy and resources committee in 1970. His brief there was to strengthen the council's public transport role, following hostile reaction to its urban motorway proposals of 1969 and its assumption of overall responsibility for London Transport in 1970. One of the committee's first reports advocated the extension of the Piccadilly Line of the London Underground to serve Heathrow and of the projected Fleet Line into south-east London.

Cutler's departure from the housing committee was not unwelcome to a national tory leadership nervous about the public impact of his policies in an election year. Cutler was certainly never close to Edward Heath, even in his 'Selsdon' phase. He belonged to the Monday Club, and he developed during these years a populist political style which was not to Heath's taste. In the general election of 1970, when he fought and lost Willesden East in what would be his only parliamentary contest, he called for a complete ban on immigration for ten years and for legislation to make criminals compensate their victims.

When Labour regained power on the GLC in 1973, and nationally in 1974, Cutler gained the freedom of opposition. Elected leader of the GLC tory group in 1974, he capitalized on Labour's difficulties as the government struggled with the effects of the oil shock in 1973, and substantial rate increases were forced upon the GLC by the consequent cuts in government support. His suggestion that ratepayers withhold part of their rate payments in protest was denounced as 'preaching anarchy' by the Labour minister Robert Mellish. There was, though, a more constructive side to Cutler's thought. Recognizing that the 85 per cent rate rises were prompted by the wish to maintain social services in the face of the OPEC crisis's devastating effect upon London's manufacturing sector, he called for a shift in policy from welfarism to urban regeneration, criticized Whitehall for curbs on industrial development in London, and called for greater investment in public transport—'in other words, applied commonsense' (*The Times*, 13 March 1978). His advocacy of a strategic investment role for the GLC was consistent with the view formed while he chaired the council's policy and resources committee in the early 1970s, that the GLC

'must be recognized for what it clearly is—regional government' (GLC press release, 23 Feb 1971, LMA, GLC/DG/PRB/35/013, no. 72). By the mid-1970s, though, a still more radical view had developed among some London Conservative MPs and in parts of the press: that the GLC's 'profligacy' required more of a root and branch solution—the abolition of what they saw as a redundant authority. In the 1977 GLC election Cutler was forced to promise an inquiry into the structure and functions of the council.

The Conservatives recaptured the GLC in 1977 in one of the first electoral triumphs for the 'new right'. Cutler became GLC leader. His party's success owed much, though, to the failings of the Labour administration; its policy remained only partially shaped. A policy group on housing had deliberated since 1975, but its results differed little from Cutler's 1967 initiatives, with the emphasis on transfers to the boroughs and council house sales. The most striking innovation was the homesteading scheme, a form of institutionalized squatting by which London families would be assigned derelict houses rent free for three years on condition that they repaired them, and then allowed to purchase them at pre-renovation value on a 100 per cent GLC mortgage. The chance to secure a sizeable capital asset in return for three years' work was enticing, and 11,000 applicants had to be reduced to 200 by ballot, but the first winners received their keys, a pot of paint, and a set of brushes from the Conservatives' national leader, Margaret Thatcher, in April 1978.

While homesteads were eye-catching, it was urban regeneration which mattered most to Cutler. The promised inquiry into the GLC's purpose, conducted by Sir Frank Marshall, produced a report largely congenial to Cutler, emphasizing the GLC's strategic role. Cutler himself was particularly interested in the future of the Docklands area in east London. He envisaged 'a thriving, vigorous new heartland for our city', proposing for the area at various points a garden city, a free port, 'twenty-first-century shopping centres', a Tivoli Garden, film studios, a heliport, and the channel tunnel terminus, to create 'a quality of life unparalleled in the world' (GLC press releases, 2 June 1977, 27 Feb 1978, 9 Nov 1978, 13 Dec 1979, LMA, GLC/DG/PRB/35, and Cutler to L. Drinkwater, 28 Feb 1980, GLC/TO/PM/SEC/1/001(2)). It was decided to divert the extension of the Fleet (Jubilee) tube line from south-east London to Docklands. Most ostentatiously Cutler proposed that London host the 1988 Olympic Games, with the Olympic village located in Docklands. This battery of ideas betrayed an impulsive, if creative, eclecticism. It was only in the autumn of 1979, with a tour of urban centres in the United States, that Cutler began to devise a more comprehensive strategy for urban revival, based upon American precedents, involving local commerce and finance in public–private regeneration projects.

Ironically, Cutler's grip on power began to loosen after Thatcher became prime minister in 1979. He had expected—and received—little support from the Labour government during his first two years as council leader. He met the most dispiriting Whitehall snub of this period, the denial of central support for the Jubilee Line extension, with a quixotic pledge to build the line unaided, but in reality he was counting upon a tory election victory to realize his aims. He revered Thatcher. Though Thatcher secured Cutler a knighthood in 1979 her attitude towards him was ambiguous. She tended to prefer the concept of the self-made man to the reality, and he failed, in the words of one obituarist, 'to gain entry into her metropolitan court' (*The Guardian*, 4 March 1997). She admired his housing work, which formed the basis of national policy after 1979, but if she had any faith in large-scale urban regeneration she did not wish to entrust it to local government. The creation in 1979 of a quango—the London Docklands Development Corporation—to play the role in revitalizing the area that Cutler had envisaged for the GLC was received by him very guardedly. He openly criticized the Thatcher government's restrictions upon local authorities and the tilting of the rate support grant towards the shires. With council elections approaching he also feared that the GLC tories would be tarred by Thatcher's unpopularity. A sense of powerlessness is evident in his ever more shrill warnings that 'Old MacDonald's Marxist farm' would be established in London if the GLC fell to Labour's new left. His warnings failed to prevent the Labour victory in May 1981 which effectively signalled the end of his political career; he stepped down as leader of the tory opposition at County Hall in 1982. He was subsequently sidelined as the decision was taken to include a pledge to abolish the GLC in the Conservatives' general election manifesto of 1983. Learning of the commitment only from the press he vented his frustration in an explosive private row with Thatcher which ended their relationship.

Cutler was an idiosyncratic local politician who made a virtue of going against the grain, often to the discomfort of those around him. Among the GLC tories what he acknowledged as 'my rather autocratic style' (*Harrow Observer*, 30 April 1982) caused disquiet. His relationship with the GLC staff was worse. He made no secret of his contempt for 'the little Hitlers' who needed 'a Ph.D. in incompetence before they can get the sack' (Cutler, *Cutler Files*, 46–7, 55). With both party and bureaucracy he got things done by working closely with a small number of trusted subordinates. His unconventional methods could none the less cause problems even for his intimates. Cutler nurtured a conspicuous public image during his GLC years: what had been a full naval beard when he entered public life became a trimmed and pointed one, and he was seldom seen in public without his 'uniform' of blue suit, blue shirt, spotted bow tie, and blue buttonhole. Showmanship was part of his style: 'I have never scorned publicity', he wrote with some understatement in 1982 (Cutler, *Cutler Files*, 80). He courted the charge of clownishness, but he was also a talented and creative politician. Many features of late twentieth-century London—the tube extensions, the gentrified Covent Garden, the rejuvenated Docklands, and even the London marathon (a spin-off from the Olympic Games proposal)—had their roots in his work. More generally the London of the early twenty-first century—characterized by 60 per cent owner occupation

and prospering on the basis of services, new industries, and tourism—was largely the London that Cutler envisaged emerging from the 1970s recession, even if he was frequently thwarted in trying to bring it about.

Cutler spent much of his retirement in his Ibiza villa, but died at the Austenwood Nursing Home, 29 North Park, Gerrards Cross, Buckinghamshire, on 2 March 1997 following a series of strokes. He was buried at Fulmer parish church ten days later. His two wives survived him, as did the son from his first marriage, and the son and three daughters from his second.   JOHN DAVIS

Sources H. Cutler, *The Cutler files* (1982) · H. Cutler, *Rents: chaos or common sense?*, Monday Club pamphlet (1970) · H. Cutler, 'The future of the GLC', *London Town* (March 1978) · H. Brack, 'The truth about London's council housing', *Evening Standard* (7 April 1970) · Greater London council press releases, 1971–2, 1977–81, and other GLC papers, LMA · *The Times* (1967–82) · *Harrow Observer* (1952–82) · *Downtown America*, Greater London council (1979) · *A new housing policy of London: Inner London must live*, Greater London council (1978) · *Daily Telegraph* (3 March 1997) · *The Times* (3 March 1997) · *The Independent* (4 March 1997) · *The Guardian* (4 March 1997) · O. Cock, *The Villager: News and Views of Pinner* (July 1997) · K. Young and J. Kramer, *Strategy and conflict in metropolitan housing* (1978) · WWW · b. cert. · m. certs. · d. cert. · *Evening Standard* (7 April 1970) · *CGPLA Eng. & Wales* (1997) · divorce cert.

Archives Harrow Local Studies Centre, papers, incl. some personal papers · LMA, file of papers as leader and four files of secretariat | LMA, GLC housing committee files

Likenesses R. Harwood, oils, 1959 · photograph, 1970, repro. in *The Independent* · photograph, 1970, repro. in *Willesden East manifesto* · photograph, 1977 (with M. Thatcher), repro. in *The Times* (7 May 1977) · B. Harris, photograph, 1981, News International Syndication, London [*see illus.*] · photograph, repro. in *The Times* (30 March 1982) · photograph, repro. in *Harrow Observer* (15 May 1952) · photograph, repro. in Cutler, *Rents* · photographs, Hult. Arch.

Wealth at death £299,913: probate, 29 Oct 1997, *CGPLA Eng. & Wales*

Cutler, Sir John (1607/8–1693), merchant and financier, was the son of Thomas Cutler, a member of the Grocers' Company. Early in his career he abandoned commerce for finance and specialized in lending money to impoverished landowners on the security of their estates. In this way he made a fortune and amassed considerable landed property during the interregnum, while discreetly avoiding any serious involvement in politics. In 1657 he acquired the Harewood estate in Yorkshire from one of his largest creditors, the second Lord Strafford, and for a while resided there, at Gawthorpe Hall, in miserly seclusion. But a narrow escape, when he was nearly seized by the highwayman John Nevison, induced him to leave the hall and take a cottage in Gawthorpe village, where, attended by his servant, a man of similar habits to his own, he was secure from the fear of being attacked.

At the Restoration, Cutler advanced £5000 to the new regime and also promoted the subscriptions raised by the City of London, thereby earning himself a baronetcy and a lucrative share in the office of receiver-general of Derbyshire and Nottinghamshire. His election as treasurer of St Paul's in 1663 characteristically combined personal gain with public philanthropy: according to his friend Samuel Pepys:

Sir John Cutler (1607/8–1693), by Arnold Quellin, c.1683

it seems he did give £1500 upon condition that he might be treasurer for the work, which, they say, will be worth three times as much money, and talk as if his being chosen to the office will make people backward to give. (Pepys, 4.430)

The following year he founded a lectureship at Gresham College with a salary of £50 a year, settling it on Robert Hooke for life, under the auspices of the Royal Society, to which he was promptly elected as an honorary fellow.

An influential member of the Grocers' Company for many years, Cutler offered in 1668 to pay for the rebuilding of the company's parlour and dining-room, destroyed in the great fire. He seems indeed to have borne the lion's share of the expense, and after the completion of the work in 1669 it was resolved that his statue and picture should be placed in the upper and lower rooms of his buildings, 'to remain as a lasting monument of his unexampled kindness'. He again contributed liberally to the restoration of the company's hall in 1681, and an inscription was placed there recounting his various benefactions. For the Royal College of Physicians he provided an anatomical lecture theatre, entirely at his own expense. Opened in 1679, this was named the Cutlerian Theatre. In a niche on the outside of the building was a full-length statue of Cutler, set up in obedience to a vote of the college. However, after his death his executors made a demand on the college of £7000, comprising the money actually spent, which had been set down as a loan in Cutler's books, together with interest. Eventually they were prevailed on to accept a settlement of £2000. The college then obliterated the inscription, *Omnis Cutleri cedat labor Amphitheatro*, which in gratitude it had placed beneath the figure. Indeed, Cutler's avarice, notorious to his contemporaries, was immortalized by Pope (*Works of Alexander Pope*, 3.54–6). One of Cutler's last public benefactions was to rebuild in 1682 the north gallery in his own parish church of St Margaret, Westminster, for the benefit of the poor. He also gave an annual sum of £37 to the parish for poor relief. As a landlord, however, he may not entirely have deserved Pope's censure. Another acquaintance, the antiquary Ralph Thoresby, recalled that on his Yorkshire estates Cutler had indulged his tenants during poor harvests, so much so that rents were £5000 in arrears at his death.

Hitherto almost apolitical, Cutler stood for parliament for the first time in September 1679, on the court interest. He was rejected by his neighbours in the Westminster constituency, but was returned, probably on the recommendation of his son-in-law Sir William Portman, at Taunton. In June 1680 he served as foreman of the grand jury that acquitted Lord Castlemaine from involvement in the Popish Plot, but otherwise seems to have played little part in the Exclusion Parliaments; he gave up his seat in October 1680 when he admitted that his own re-election at Taunton had been invalid. Nevertheless, he seems to have prospered in the tory reaction after 1681, and at the beginning of James II's reign was at the peak of his fortunes: he was chosen master warden of his company for the second time in 1685, and the following year purchased the impressive Cambridgeshire estate of Wimpole. But when the king sought to pursue a policy of indulgence to Catholics and dissenters Cutler havered, and in consequence lost the various offices he held in local government. He responded in silence to the revolution of 1688, though he was elected to the Convention Parliament, for a pocket borough, Bodmin, controlled by his second son-in-law, Lord Radnor. Though he is not known to have committed himself on any party issue, he did make one notable speech, arguing for parsimony in public affairs by reducing the salaries paid to customs commissioners.

Cutler's first wife, whom he married on 11 August 1642, was Elizabeth (d. 1650), the daughter and coheir of Sir Thomas Foote, bt, lord mayor of London in 1650. Their only child was a daughter, named Elizabeth, who became the wife of Sir William Portman bt, KB, of Orchard Portman, Somerset, taking with her a fortune of £30,000. She predeceased her father, leaving no children. He married, second, on 27 July 1669, Alicia (d. 1685), the daughter of Sir Thomas Tipping, of Wheatfield, Oxfordshire. Their only daughter, also named Elizabeth, married Charles Bodvile Robartes, second earl of Radnor, and died, without children, on 13 January 1697. She had married without her father's consent, but two days before his death he sent for her and her husband and 'told them he freely forgave them and had settled his estate to their satisfaction'. Cutler died, after a long illness, at his home in Tothill Street, Westminster, on 15 April 1693, aged eighty-five, and was buried in St Margaret's, Westminster, on 28 April. His fortune was popularly reckoned at about £600,000 in cash, together with some £6000 a year in landed property. The land went to his surviving daughter, with a remainder to a nephew, Edmund Boulter; the money, after various charitable bequests, including a substantial endowment to the Royal Naval Hospital, Greenwich, and sums given to poor relatives, was divided between Boulter and the Radnors.

D. W. HAYTON

Sources E. Cruickshanks, 'Cutler, Sir John', HoP, *Commons* · J. B. Heath, *Some account of the Worshipful Company of Grocers of the city of London*, 3rd edn (privately printed, London, 1869), 298–307 · GEC, *Baronetage* · T. Pennant, *Some account of London*, 2nd edn (1791), 418–19 · Munk, *Roll* · *The works of Alexander Pope*, ed. W. Elwin and W. J. Courthope, 10 vols. (1871–89), vol. 3, pp. 154–6 · Pepys, *Diary*, 4.430 · D. Lysons, *The environs of London*, 3 (1795), 454 · N. Luttrell, *A brief historical relation of state affairs from September 1678 to April 1714*, 3 (1857), 76–87 · *The diary of Ralph Thoresby*, ed. J. Hunter, 1 (1830), 233–4 · DNB · will, PRO, PROB 11/413, sig. 42 · sentence, PRO, PROB 11/416, sig. 172

Likenesses bust, c.1670, Grocers' Hall, London; destroyed 1965 · oils, c.1670, Grocers' Hall, London; destroyed 1965 · A. Quellin, marble statue, 1681–2, Grocers' Hall, London · A. Quellin, statue, c.1683, Guildhall Museum, London [*see illus.*] · stipple, pubd 1815 (after oil painting), NPG

Wealth at death £600,000 in cash; plus approx. £6000 p.a. landed property (estates in Yorkshire, Cambridgeshire, etc.): Luttrell, *Brief historical relation*, vol. 3, p. 81

Cutler [*married names* Greenleaf, Dudley Ward], **Kate Ellen Louisa** (1864–1955), actress, was born on 14 August 1864 at 28 Queen's Road, Marylebone, London, the daughter of Henry Cutler, an artist and singer, and his wife, Mary Ann, *née* Tims. She is reported to have studied voice 'at the conservatoire in Watford' and made her first known appearance on the stage with Horace Lingard's touring comic opera company in 1888, taking over, in turn, the principal *soubrette* part of Pepita (in Manchester) and then the *ingénue* role of Inez (for London), the two girls who are candidates for the real princess in Charles Lecocq's *La princesse des Canaries*. She next appeared with the Carl Rosa Light Opera Company in the supporting role of Malaguena in Robert Planquette's *Paul Jones* (1889) before joining the company of George Edwardes's *In Town* and beginning a steady rise that would result in a career as the ultimate *ingénue* of the Victorian and Edwardian musical theatre.

Kate Cutler was cast in *In Town* as a take-over to the small *ingénue* role of Lady Gwendoline, but covered and deputized latterly for the show's star, Florence St John, and she fulfilled the same function in *A Gaiety Girl*, moving up from the small part of Lady Edytha Aldwyn to replace Decima Moore in the juvenile lead of the piece. She succeeded Ada Reeve, when that lady departed, soon after the opening night, in the title role of the Gaiety's highly successful *The Shop Girl* (1894) and then left the Edwardes organization to take over from Isa Bowman as Connie, the juvenile lady of *All Abroad* (1895).

In 1895 Kate Cutler created her own first good musical-comedy role, as Mabel Kavanagh, the *ingénue* heroine—alongside the rather more prominent *soubrette*, Kitty Loftus—of the show starring Arthur Roberts, *Gentleman Joe*, and, in the wake of the craze awakened by Beerbohm Tree's production of *Trilby*, went on to play a burlesque Trilby in Nellie Farren's production of *A Model Trilby*. She returned to Edwardes's management the following year to create the juvenile lead, May Mildreth, in *The Clergyman's Daughter* out of town. When the piece was brought into the Gaiety, as *My Girl*, the role was given to Ellaline Terriss, and instead Miss Cutler appeared in town as Dorothy Travers in the less successful *Monte Carlo* (1896). She came into her own, however, when she was cast, for the piece's London showing, in the title role of Suzette in *The French Maid* (1897), created in the provinces by the genuinely French Andrée Corday. Just how much she had risen in status was shown when she finally left the long-running show and was replaced by the same Kitty Loftus to whom she had played second fiddle in *Gentleman Joe*. She went on to score another big success in 1898 as Elsie Crockett in *Little Miss Nobody*. The following year she played Catarina in the operetta taken from the French *L'amour mouillé* and then found her most successful role of all as the *ingénue*, Angela, in the original production of *Florodora*, in which she introduced 'The Fellow who Might'.

Kate Cutler took on the unenviable task in 1900 of starring as Victoria Chaffers opposite the unpredictable, often inebriated Arthur Roberts in a London season of his touring show *HMS Irresponsible*—this time ousting Kitty Loftus, who sued the producer and star (and lost)—and took over the soprano role of Princess Soo-Soo in the record-breaking *A Chinese Honeymoon* (1901) when that piece, once its success became evident, began to be cast with star performers. In 1902 she created one of her most appealing roles, as Nora, the befuddled young bride of the classy musical comedy *The Girl from Kay's* (where she sang 'Papa'), opposite the star comic Willie Edouin. *The Lovebirds* (1904, in which she played Grace Rockingham) gave her a rare experience of failure, but this was quickly remedied by a delightful star part as the Baroness Papouche in Edwardes's Gaiety Theatre musical *The Spring Chicken* (1905). By now over forty (though she claimed to have been born in 1870), she abandoned musicals and turned instead to the straight stage and to performing playlets and sketches in the music halls.

Over the next decade Kate Cutler was seen regularly in the West End in featured roles in plays, appearing with Tree in revivals of *The Red Lamp* (1907, Felise) and *A Woman of No Importance* (1907, Lady Stutfield), as the feather-headed little milliner, Madame Henriette, to the *Bellamy the Magnificent* of Charles Wyndham (1908), the seduced servant girl to *The Real Woman* of Evelyn Millard, and the pretty widow, Marion Nairn, alongside Charles Hawtrey in Somerset Maugham's *The Noble Spaniard* (1909). She played the would-be social Mrs Dallas-Baker, alongside Marie Löhr and Robert Loraine, in Somerset Maugham's *Smith* (1909) and Lydia Languish in Sheridan's *The Rivals*

(1910) with Lewis Waller, took over from Ethel Irving in the leading role of *The Witness for the Defence* (1911), and performed in *The Ogre* (1911) and *The Fire Screen* (1912), then took a turn into the music halls, where she appeared alongside George Alexander in Max Beerbohm's *A Social Success* and in several other short plays.

Thereafter Kate Cutler moved towards playing mostly aristocratic and charming character roles and made brief returns to the musical stage as gracious older ladies such as Helen in *That's a Good Girl* (1928), Mrs Gerard in *Dear Love* (1929), and the Queen of Vassau in *Command Performance* (1933). In the 1930s she was still finding good parts in the London theatre: in 1936 she was seen as Old Lady Squeamish, alongside Michael Redgrave and Edith Evans, in *The Country Wife* at the Old Vic, and in 1938, half a century after her début, with another graduate of the musical-comedy stage, Marie Tempest, as Belle Schlessinger in *Dear Octopus*. She also appeared in several films, including the screen versions of *That's a Good Girl* (1933) and *Pygmalion* (1938).

Unfailingly graceful, ladylike, and charming ('she always looks as if she has a sprig of lilac under her nose', reported her contemporary Emily Soldene), and the possessor of a pretty light soprano voice, the young Miss Cutler was, as a genuine and durable *ingénue*, the ideal partner for some of the more rumbustious comedy actors of her time. As an older actress, although she rarely found new roles as important as those she had created on the musical stage, she kept up a full career with very few bald spots, thanks to her always-winning stage presence and demeanour. She married, on 12 April 1900, the director and choreographer Sidney Ellison (whose real name was George Greenleaf), the stager of *Florodora*, but they had separated before his death in 1930, and she subsequently married Major Charles Dudley Ward, who also predeceased her. She died at her home, 41 Onslow Square, London, on 14 May 1955, and was cremated at Putney Vale crematorium.

KURT GÄNZL

Sources K. Gänzl, *The encyclopedia of the musical theatre*, 2 vols. (1994) · K. Gänzl, *The British musical theatre*, 2 vols. (1986) · *The Era* (1886–1919) · J. Parker, ed., *Who's who in the theatre*, 6th edn (1930) · b. cert. · m. cert. · d. cert. · *The Times* (18 May 1955)
Likenesses Bassano, photographs, 1895, NPG · Johnston & Hoffmann, photograph, *c.*1905, NPG · photograph, repro. in Gänzl, *Encyclopedia of the musical theatre*
Wealth at death £6194 10s. 11d.: probate, 26 July 1955, CGPLA Eng. & Wales

Cutler, Timothy (1684–1765), college head and Church of England clergyman, was born on 31 May 1684 in Charlestown, Massachusetts, fifth child of Martha Wiswall and Major John Cutler, an anchorsmith, member of the Massachusetts assembly, and Jacobite supporter. Having been raised a Congregationalist, Cutler graduated from Harvard in 1701 and in 1709 became pastor of the Congregational church of Stratford, Connecticut, where he was ordained on 11 January 1710.

Cutler, who would later support episcopacy, ironically had been sent to Stratford to counteract the local Anglican influence of the Society for the Propagation of the Gospel

in Foreign Parts (SPG). On 1 February 1711 he married Elizabeth Andrew, whose father was then acting rector of Yale College; the couple had eight children, born between 1711 and 1722. This family connection no doubt assisted Cutler in becoming the college's new rector, or president, in 1719. His student Jonathan Edwards described Cutler as 'extraordinarily courteous ... loved and respected by all who are under him' (Woolverton, 127). A capable college administrator, he experienced few problems with undergraduate discipline, except a food strike in 1721. Although he was respected for his learning and linguistic skills, many described him as haughty and domineering. Ezra Stiles noted he was a man 'of an high, lofty, & despotic mien' (Shipton, 85).

At Yale in 1722 Cutler concluded graduation ceremonies with the surprising Episcopalian expression 'And let all the people say, Amen'. Since coming to Yale, he had met with other Congregationalist ministers to discuss the holdings of Yale's library, including donated works written by liberal Anglicans who expressed latitudinarianism, rationalism, and Arminianism. Through such unorthodox readings they had come to doubt the validity of their ordination, as Cutler declared in a formal statement before the college trustees. This shocking defection to the Church of England involved not only the rector but the college's tutor Daniel Brown, former tutor Samuel Johnson, and four ministers from neighbouring parishes. Governor Saltonstall of Connecticut arranged a debate in the college library, but the trustees proved no match for those who had already weighed carefully Congregational and Anglican arguments. Three of the seven agreed to return to their meeting-houses, but Cutler, Johnson, Brown, and James Wetmore remained convinced of the invalidity of their ordination. Consequently Cutler was 'excused' from further service at Yale, and henceforth college officers had to subscribe to the Saybrook platform and explicitly confirm their opposition to Arminianism and prelates.

The Revd Henry Caner later claimed, in delivering Cutler's funeral sermon, that only his conscience could have caused him to abandon his means of support, given the demands of his large family. Yet Cutler himself admitted that he had long held opinions favouring episcopacy. He may have been waiting for a superior opportunity before declaring himself. Subscribers at Christ Church, Boston, made such an offer by paying for the passage of Cutler, Johnson, and Brown to London for episcopal ordination. Their visit to London entailed considerable touring, business, and hardship. Cutler contracted smallpox, but had recovered by March 1723 to be baptized, confirmed, and then ordained as deacon. On 31 March 1723 he and his two companions were ordained priests, and in June the bishop of London licensed Cutler as an SPG missionary for Boston and Johnson for Stratford; Brown had died in April from smallpox. Both Cutler and Johnson also received honorary degrees from Oxford and Cambridge universities. No doubt they were seen as intriguing converts, but also as symbols of the anticipated Anglican growth in New England. Cutler preached on the last Sunday in December

1723 as rector of the newly constructed Christ Church, a position he retained until his death forty-two years later.

A supporter of high-church and tory views, Cutler vigorously defended colonial Anglicanism. His strong opinions favouring ties with England, an Anglican establishment, and separation from dissenters generated criticism both from dissenters and latitudinarian Anglicans who considered his views intolerant. The assistant rector of King's Chapel, Boston, Henry Harris, who had opposed Cutler's appointment as rector, labelled his behaviour 'imprudent' and his principles 'uncharitable' (Shipton, 91). His former career had not made Cutler tolerant of dissenting opinions or institutions: he wished instead that Harvard College be turned into an Anglican institution. A thorn in the side of the Congregational establishment in Massachusetts, he attempted in 1725 to prevent a synod of ministers on the grounds that it would be prejudicial towards the Church of England; royal attorneys-at-law agreed that such a synod would violate the king's prerogative. Cutler had won a startling victory, but then lost his attempt to gain admission to the board of overseers of Harvard College. He fought a long battle to free his parishioners from mandatory taxation for the Congregational church, and for decades he unsuccessfully urged English ecclesiastical officials about the need for colonial bishops. Cutler was a fierce critic of revivalist George Whitefield in the 1740s, and considered religious enthusiasm a serious threat to Anglicanism.

Having been incapacitated by a stroke in April 1756, Cutler died on 17 August 1765 in Boston. He left four published sermons. His 1722 conversion had shaken Yale College and proved that the Church of England could pose a real threat to Congregationalism. Cutler's defection encouraged colonial Anglicans to hope for an expansion beyond its minority status in New England, but it also helped to strengthen New Englanders' convictions about the religious and political dangers of episcopacy. The uncompromising zeal of defectors like Cutler served to heighten dissenter–Anglican tensions.   NANCY L. RHODEN

Sources *Papers of the Society for the Propagation of the Gospel in Foreign Parts* [microfilm] · W. S. Perry, ed., *Historical collections relating to the American colonial church*, 5 vols. in 4 (1870–78), vol. 3 · C. K. Shipton, *New England life in the eighteenth century: representative biographies from Sibley's Harvard graduates* (1963), 79–101 · A. C. Guelzo, 'Cutler, Timothy', *ANB* · J. F. Woolverton, *Colonial Anglicanism in North America* (1984) · M. K. D. Babcock, 'Difficulties and dangers of prerevolutionary ordinations', *Historical Magazine of the Protestant Episcopal Church*, 12 (1943), 225–41 · R. Warch, *School of the prophets: Yale College, 1701–1740* (1973) · 'Cutler, Timothy', *Dictionary of American religious biography*, ed. H. W. Bowden, 2nd edn (1993), 136–7 · C. Bridenbaugh, *Mitre and sceptre: transatlantic faiths, ideas, personalities, and politics, 1689–1775* (1962) · Nichols, *Illustrations*, vol. 4 · H. E. Starr, 'Cutler, Timothy', *DAB*, 5.14–15 · G. Weaver, 'Anglican–Congregationalist tensions in pre-revolutionary Connecticut', *Historical Magazine of the Protestant Episcopal Church*, 26 (1957), 269–85 · *Who was who in America: historical volume, 1607–1896* (1963), 132

Archives Mass. Hist. Soc., Bright family papers · Ohio Historical Society, Columbus, Winthrop Sargent papers · Society for the Propagation of the Gospel in Foreign Parts, papers [microfilm]

Likenesses H. Willard, Yale U. Art Gallery; repro. in Shipton, *New England life* · portrait (after P. Pelham, 1750), Christ Church, Boston

Wealth at death £210, one third of which was library of 1130 volumes: Shipton, *New England life*, 101

Cutler, William Henry (*b.* **1792**, *d.* in or after **1824**), organist and music teacher, was born on 14 January 1792 in London. He was taught music by his father at an early age and was educated as a chorister at St Paul's Cathedral. He appears to have been a prodigy on the violin (it is reported that he owned an Amati which had belonged to William Crotch) and played a concerto by Giornovichi at the age of five. He also had some lessons on the spinet from J. H. Little and on the piano from G. E. Griffin. From about 1799 he was taught singing and thoroughbass by Samuel Arnold, and in 1800 he made his début, at a concert at the Haymarket Theatre, playing a piano concerto by Viotti. In 1801 he studied at Cambridge for a short time under Busby, but in 1803 was placed in the choir of St Paul's Cathedral. After leaving there he studied the theory of music under William Russell and received some advice in composition from Clementi. He also sang at the Vocal Concerts, the Concerts of Ancient Music, and the Glee Club. In 1812 Cutler took the degree of BMus at Oxford, submitting an anthem, 'O praise the Lord', which was performed there on 1 December and subsequently published by subscription. About 1818 he was appointed organist of St Helen's, Bishopsgate, London, and shortly afterwards adopted the Logierian system of teaching music. He opened an academy for this purpose in his house in Broad Street Buildings, but the venture was unsuccessful and came to an end after a few years, although he continued to teach using Logier's system. In 1821 Cutler sang at the Drury Lane oratorios, but was unsuccessful, apparently due to nervousness. In 1823 he resigned his post at St Helen's, and became organist of the Quebec Chapel, Portman Square. About this time he may have taught in Yarmouth and Norwich as well as in London. His last public appearance took place in London on 5 June 1824, when he directed a grand concert at the Opera House. John Braham and Giuditta Pasta both sang, but in spite of this the affair appears to have been a failure. Afterwards Cutler published a manifesto, explaining that he had hoped to gain both fame and money by this venture, but the critics declared that 'his exposé is even more curious than his oratorio, and he has condescended to prove that however bad his music may be, his logic and his English are even worse'. After this Cutler's activities are a mystery, and the date of his death is unknown. It is reported that in 1824 he had residences in London at 2 Paul's Chair, St Paul's Churchyard, and 69 Cornhill. A printed list of his compositions was issued in 1823, containing items published by Clementi, Preston, Chappell, Paine and Hopkins, and Betts. His works include a string quartet and some church music. In 1824 he wrote to R. M. Bacon, the editor of the *Quarterly Musical Magazine and Review*, on the subject of the metronome, reproducing a table of figures devised by Clementi.

W. B. SQUIRE, *rev.* DAVID J. GOLBY

Sources J. C. Kassler, *The science of music in Britain, 1714–1830: a catalogue of writings, lectures, and inventions*, 1 (1979), 247–8 · W. H. Cutler, 'Metronome', *Quarterly Musical Magazine and Review*, 6 (1824), 31–3 [letter to the editor] · *The Harmonicon*, 2 (1824), 146 · [J. S. Sains-bury], ed., *A dictionary of musicians*, 2 vols. (1824) · *London Magazine*, 10 (1824), 87–8 · Grove, *Dict. mus.* (1954)

Cutner, Solomon [*performing name* Solomon] (1902–1988), pianist, was born on 9 August 1902 at 39 Fournier Street, in the East End of London, the youngest in the family of four sons and three daughters of Harris Cutner (formerly Schneiderman), master tailor, the grandson of a Polish émigré from Cutnow, and his wife, Rose Piser. Showing exceptional musical talent from early childhood, at the age of seven he came to the attention of Mathilde Verne, a fashionable London piano teacher and former pupil of Clara Schumann. She persuaded Solomon's parents to sign a contract, relinquishing him into her care for five years, and within a year she had launched him success-fully as a child prodigy, with a début at the Queen's Hall in June 1911, playing Mozart's 'Little B♭' concerto, the slow movement of Tchaikovsky's first piano concerto, and a polacca by Alice Verne. The concert was conducted by Theodor Müller-Reuter, another of Clara Schumann's pupils. Billed from the outset as Solomon, sometimes wearing a sailor suit, sometimes in velvet knickerbockers and a lace collar, he captivated his audiences. He was invited to play at Buckingham Palace in 1912, and he made his Proms début in 1914 playing Beethoven's second piano concerto.

After Solomon had spent five miserable years with Mat-hilde Verne, forced to practise for many hours a day in a locked room, his parents refused to sign another contract, and for a year he gave concerts throughout England chap-eroned by one of his brothers. In 1916 he decided to give up all public performances, and, after a farewell recital at the Wigmore Hall shortly before his fourteenth birthday, he began studying with Dr Simon Rumschisky in London, while attending King Alfred School in the North End Road in the mornings. His studies were financed through a fund set up by an American, Mrs Colson. He spent three years with Rumschisky, a medical doctor who had studied the physiological aspects of playing the piano. Solomon later claimed that he was one of the greatest teachers in the world, and had taught him all his technique. In 1919, financed by Mrs Colson, Solomon went to Paris, where his teachers included Lazare Lévy, Marcel Dupré, and Alfred Cortot.

Still only nineteen, Solomon returned to the concert platform with a Wigmore Hall recital in 1921. The 1920s were difficult years for him, for English audiences then preferred foreign pianists such as Artur Schnabel. Although he toured the USA in 1926 he remained rela-tively unknown outside England. Thanks to Sir Henry Wood he performed regularly at the Queen's Hall Promen-ade Concerts. Sir Arthur Bliss wrote his viola sonata (1933) for Solomon and Lionel Tertis, and when Solomon was asked by the British Council to represent Great Britain at the New York World Fair in 1939 he commissioned Bliss to write a piano concerto. During the Second World War Solomon joined the Entertainments National Service Association and gave many concerts, both for troops abroad and in army camps and hospitals at home, making

Solomon Cutner (1902–1988), by unknown photographer

many converts to classical music. Through his concerts on the wards at St Mary's Hospital, Paddington, he came into contact with Sir Alexander Fleming, and was successfully treated for a septic thumb through the inhalation of peni-cillin in the very early days of its development as an antibi-otic.

After the war Solomon became an international celeb-rity, following an enthusiastic reception in the USA on his tour in 1949. He spent the next few years touring and recording, before a stroke ended his career in 1956. He was left with an active brain, but a speech impediment. Though he struggled to express himself, his playing days were over. In the remaining years of his life he could take no interest in his career, achievements, or recordings.

Solomon was one of the three greatest English pianists of the twentieth century, with Dame Myra Hess and Sir Clifford Curzon, and possibly the greatest twentieth-century British interpreter of Schumann. During his early career he was best known for his performances of Chopin, but he later concentrated on Mozart, Beethoven, Schu-mann, and Brahms. Critics commented on the elegance and purity of his playing, its clarity and accuracy, and the controlled nature of his performances. Famous record-ings from the early 1950s include those of the Brahms *Vari-ations and Fugue on a Theme by Handel*, Beethoven's 'Moon-light' sonata, the two Brahms piano concertos, and Schumann's *Carnaval*. He also played chamber music, recording the Beethoven cello sonatas with Gregor

Piatigorsky, and he formed a trio with Zino Francescatti and Pierre Fournier for the 1955 Edinburgh festival.

Solomon was short and stocky, almost completely bald from an early age, with short, thick fingers. He displayed none of the temperamental behaviour usually associated with great artists, and despite his years of adulation as a child prodigy he developed into a charming and modest person, nicknamed Solo by Walter Legge, manager for artists and repertory at the Gramophone Company. He had a passion for betting and gambling, possibly originating in his trips to the races with the elderly mother of his landlady while he was studying in Paris, and he loved to visit the casinos in Cannes and Monte Carlo. He enjoyed bridge and golf, and for years played tennis daily with his old friend Gerald Moore.

Solomon was appointed CBE in 1946 for his wartime work. He had honorary degrees from Cambridge (MusD, 1974) and St Andrews (LLD, 1960). On 15 October 1970 he married, after a long relationship begun in 1927, a former pupil, Gwendoline Harriet (b. 1905/6), daughter of Patrick Byrne, an Irish doctor and surgeon. They had not married earlier because Solomon was an Orthodox Jew and Gwendoline a gentile. They had no children. Solomon died on 22 February 1988 in London. ANNE PIMLOTT BAKER, rev.

Sources *The Independent* (25 Feb 1988) · *The Times* (24 Feb 1988) · M. Verne, *Chords of remembrance* (1936) · G. Moore, *Am I too loud?* (1962) · D. Dubal, *The art of the piano: an encyclopedia of performers, literature and recordings* (1990) · R. Pound, *Sir Henry Wood* (1969) · B. Crimp, *Solo* (1995) · private information (1993) [G. H. Cutner] · b. cert. · m. cert. · *CGPLA Eng. & Wales* (1988)
Archives SOUND BBC Sound Recordings archive
Likenesses E. Auerbach, photographs, 1958 (with Benno Moiseiwitsch), Hult. Arch. · photograph, repro. in *The Independent* · photograph, NPG [*see illus.*]
Wealth at death under £70,000: probate, 15 June 1988, *CGPLA Eng. & Wales*

Cutpurse, Moll. *See* Frith, Mary (1584x9–1659).

Cutt, John (*bap.* 1613, *d.* 1681), merchant and politician, was baptized in Bath, the second of six children of John Cutt (1563–1625), a merchant, and his second wife, Bridget, the daughter of Arthur Baker of Aust in Gloucestershire. Almost nothing is known regarding the first thirty years of his life. His younger brother Richard (1615–1676) was apprenticed to a Bristol merchant in 1626. The family appears to have been puritan in sympathy and relatively close-knit, for in the mid-1640s the four Cutt brothers (Baker, John, Richard, and Robert) and their sister, Ann, arrived in New England, first at the Isles of Shoals fishing grounds off the New Hampshire coast, then at Boston with letters of credit in 1646. Shortly thereafter, Baker returned to England, Robert obtained land in Kittery on the north side of the Piscataqua River, Ann married John Shipway, and Richard and John (while owning property on the Isles of Shoals) settled in Portsmouth on the south side of the Piscataqua, later to be part of the province of New Hampshire.

With capital gained in the fishing trade, both John Cutt and Richard acquired large amounts of property in and around Portsmouth. In 1658 he received a sawmill and timberland grant from the town and expanded his commercial activities into the overseas mast and lumber trade. While Richard Cutt concentrated on the fish trade, by the early 1660s John had become the richest merchant in Portsmouth, and, according to the town tax lists, he remained so for the rest of his life. His economic success in the lumber and fishing trades served as a model to other new enterprisers and attested to the abundant economic opportunities in mid-seventeenth-century northern New England.

When the two Cutt brothers settled in Portsmouth, they found the town under the legal jurisdiction of puritan Massachusetts as part of its Norfolk county. Both men strongly supported this political and religious alliance and became involved in Massachusetts's politics, serving as deputies to its assembly and judges in its county courts. Richard was elected a deputy from Portsmouth six times between 1665 and 1675 and John once in 1676; Richard was elected an associate of the county court annually from 1653 to 1675, and John was elected from 1665 to 1679. Both strongly supported the presence of puritan clergy in Portsmouth and were founders of its first Congregational church under the ministry of Joshua Moodey in 1671. In 1662 John married Hannah Starr (1632–1674), the daughter of Dr Comfort Starr of Boston; they had four surviving children. After Hannah's death he married Ursula (d. 1694) in 1677. He was probably the wealthiest man in the Piscataqua region.

However, by the late 1670s his business, family, town, and church seemed threatened by Robert Tufton Mason, a proprietary claimant to all the lands between the Piscataqua and Merrimack rivers, and by King Charles II's anger towards Massachusetts's imperialism which led him and his officials to consider creating a separate colony of New Hampshire in the region where Cutt lived. Although Cutt had, from 1665, consistently opposed both the proprietary claims and the idea of a separate colony, in 1679 the crown created the royal province of New Hampshire and sent over a commission naming him as its president (executive) with a nine-member council (six of which were named and drawn from the elected leadership of the local towns and empowered to choose the other three) and an assembly elected from the four local towns. Moreover, the commission, while not explicitly recognizing Mason as proprietor, promised him ownership of all the unimproved lands in the province and required that all owners of improved property would have to pay him one-fortieth of the yearly value of their property in order to obtain title to their lands. But the commission also required the president and council to arbitrate in any dispute regarding his claims.

Cutt and the councillors found themselves in a difficult dilemma. They wanted nothing to do with Mason or royal government, but refusing to accept their appointments might mean the loss of their lands and local authority. Most of the council wanted to resist by not participating in the new government, but Cutt accepted his commission; and in a compromise with the opponents of this action, he agreed to have their leader, Major Richard Waldron, as his deputy and head of the militia, whereupon they all accepted their offices. In spring 1680 this new government, under the leadership of Cutt and Waldron, appointed puritan allies as judges and militia officers; determined who qualified to vote for assemblymen in the four towns; and, with the newly elected assembly, enacted a number of civil and criminal laws which became known as the Cutt code. The code generally followed the laws and practices of puritan Massachusetts and Plymouth, and it confirmed all land titles to the towns and the individuals concerned and stated that any controversies over land titles would be determined by juries of twelve men elected by town freemen, thus defying both Mason and the crown's commission.

By summer 1680 Cutt had become ill and began missing council meetings. He did, however, sign two extraordinary documents in May and June. The first was a council letter to the government of Massachusetts, thanking it for its past protection and explaining that the New Hampshire people neither sought nor desired to be separate from it. The second was a letter from the council to the crown opposing separation from Massachusetts because New Hampshire was too small and militarily weak, and opposing the Masonian proprietary claims as only 'pretensions'.

During the autumn and winter of 1680 Cutt's illness grew worse. In March 1681 the council and assembly declared 17 March as a day of public fasting and prayer in recognition of his grave condition. He died at Portsmouth on 27 March 1681 and was buried at the Bank. He could die content that he and other New Hampshire leaders had done all they could to conserve the political, social, and religious values they held so dear. His pragmatic acceptance of royal government for New Hampshire eased local tensions and showed how local leaders could use royal institutions for their own ends, initiating an approach that would come to dominate New Hampshire politics for the next century. Finally, through marriages of the daughters of both John and Richard into the Waldron and Vaughan families, New Hampshire's first political dynasty was born, a dynasty that would dominate the colony's politics for the next thirty-five years.

DAVID E. VAN DEVENTER

Sources Portsmouth town records, New Hampshire State Library, Concord, New Hampshire · N. Bouton and others, eds., *Provincial and state papers: documents and records relating to the province of New Hampshire*, 40 vols. (1867–1943), vols. 1, 17, 31 · S. Noyes, C. T. Libby, and W. G. Davis, *Genealogical dictionary of Maine and New Hampshire*, 5 vols. (Portland, ME, 1928–39) · D. E. Van Deventer, *The emergence of provincial New Hampshire, 1623–1741* (1976) · J. R. Daniell, *Colonial New Hampshire: a history* (1981) · *Collections of the New Hampshire Historical Society*, 8 (1866) · W. Crompton, 'Cutt, John', *ANB* · J. Farmer, *Genealogical register of the first settlers of New England* (1829)
Archives New Hampshire State Library, Concord, New Hampshire, Portsmouth town records
Wealth at death £9723 9s. 7d.: inventory, Farmer, *Genealogical register*, 75

Cuttance, Sir Roger (*b.* 1608/9, *d.* in or after 1678), naval officer, came from a prominent merchant family of Weymouth, with trading links to Virginia and New England in the 1630s. Henry Cuttance and Edward Cuttance, one of whom was almost certainly his father, served as mayor of the borough in 1632–3 and 1641–2 respectively and Roger Cuttance himself served two terms in the same office, in 1658–9 and 1666–7. He is said to have learned his seafaring skills in the Newfoundland fishery, and in 1636 a Roger Cuttance, aged twenty-seven, of Weymouth, is reported to have lately served as master's mate of the *Hopewell* of Weymouth, on a voyage to Newfoundland. In 1647 he stated that he had 'faithfully served the parliament at sea from the beginning of the unhappy differences in this kingdom' (Mayo, 262). In June 1651 he became captain of the *Pearl*, in which he took part in the capture of Jersey. On the outbreak of the First Anglo-Dutch War in May 1652 he was transferred to the *Sussex* of 40 guns, and commanded her until the peace, taking part in the battles of the Kentish Knock (28 September 1652), Portland (18 February 1653), and off the Texel (2–3 June and 31 July 1653). In 1654 he commanded the *Langport*, with Robert Blake, in the Mediterranean, and assisted in the reduction of Porto Farina on 4 April 1655. In October 1655 he accompanied the general to England, returning with him to the coast of Spain in the following spring, but came home again with Edward Mountagu and Richard Stayner in October 1656. In May 1657 he was appointed to the *Naseby*, in which ship he continued for the next four years, for the greater part of the time as Mountagu's flag captain, and especially when, in May 1660, the *Naseby* had her name changed to *Royal Charles*, and brought the king to England. In April 1660 he had written to the mayor of Weymouth advocating the selection of Mountagu as an MP for Weymouth and Melcombe Regis, Mountagu being duly returned. In 1661 he moved, with Mountagu, then earl of Sandwich, to the *Royal James*, and in 1665 to the *Prince*, in which Sandwich hoisted his flag as admiral of the Blue squadron. In the Second Anglo-Dutch War his decisive conduct in the battle of Lowestoft on 3 June contributed to the defeat and rout of the Dutch. After the battle he was offered the position of rear-admiral of the White squadron, but declined it out of loyalty to Sandwich, with whom he continued to serve as flag captain. He was knighted by the king on 1 July 1665, and served on the Tangier and fishery committees. However, the naval careers of both Sandwich and Cuttance were blighted by the irregular distribution of prize goods from Dutch East Indiamen captured in September, and many, including Pepys, believed that Cuttance was the really guilty person. He was not employed at sea again after the 1665 campaign, but in 1673 he worked for the Navy Board at Weymouth, shipping stores from there to Portsmouth. He made his will on 6 April 1678, at which time he owned a house in Weymouth and a farm at Bradnam.

Cuttance's son Henry (*d.* 1690) served as a lieutenant at Porto Farina and Santa Cruz, being captured by the Spanish in 1658 when commanding a Bordeaux convoy. He was held prisoner in San Sebastian until exchanged for the royalist Captain Richard Beach in 1659. He held three commands after the Restoration but was dismissed after the Four Days Battle of 1666 and later commanded merchant ships in the Mediterranean trade. Sir Roger's will also mentions two other sons, Joseph, a lieutenant of the *Royal Prince* in 1665–6, and Roger.

J. K. LAUGHTON, rev. J. D. DAVIES

Sources Pepys, *Diary* · *The journal of Edward Mountagu, first earl of Sandwich, admiral and general at sea, 1659–1665*, ed. R. C. Anderson, Navy RS, 64 (1929) · M. Weinstock, ed., *Weymouth and Melcombe Regis minute book, 1625–60*, Dorset RS (1964) · 'An enquiry into the causes of our naval miscarriages', *The Harleian miscellany*, ed. W. Oldys and T. Park, 12 vols. (1808–11), vol. 1, p. 571 · PRO, PROB 11/359, fol. 345 · C. H. Mayo, ed., *The minute books of the Dorset standing committee* (1902) · *CSP dom.*, 1673 · PRO, HCA 13/52, fol. 337v · Bodl. Oxf., MSS Carte 73, fols. 384, 395; 74, fol. 445 · W. A. Shaw, *The knights of England*, 2 vols. (1906) · *Le Neve's Pedigrees of the knights*, ed. G. W. Marshall, Harleian Society, 8 (1873)

Wealth at death farm at Bradnam divided equally between sons Henry and Joseph; £200 to son Roger: will, PRO, PROB 11/359, fol. 345

Cutting [Cuttinge], **Francis** (*c*.1550–1595/6), lutenist and composer, was probably born in East Anglia, where his future patrons, the Howards, held extensive estates on which Cuttings had long been tenants. Nothing is known of his family background, though he may have been related to the John Cutting who was a lay clerk of the choir of King's College, Cambridge, from 1574 to 1580. Francis was probably employed as a musician in the Howard household, for from March 1582 the names of eight of his ten children appear in the registers of St Clement Danes, Westminster, in which parish Arundel House, the Howards' London residence, was situated. He rented a tenement on this site for 40s. per annum, and on 23 February 1583 Philip, earl of Arundel, granted him a lease in reversion on the property for twenty-one years, the term to begin when the previous lease expired in 1592.

Cutting is among the earliest English lute composers whose names are known. Some forty works survive, eleven of which appeared posthumously in William Barley's *A New Booke of Tabliture* (1596). They comprise variations, arrangements (including reworkings of pieces by William Byrd and Thomas Morley), and dance movements. Some of the latter bear titles suggestive of the aristocratic circles in which he moved, for example 'Sir Walter Raleigh's Galliard' and 'Sir Fulke Greville's Pavan'. Cutting's music is characterized by extensive use of sequence, occasional flashes of harmonic daring, and a textural variety that ranges from the simple homophony of his 'Toy', to the complex interplay between chordal and imitative writing seen in 'Mrs Anne Markham's Pavan and Galliard'.

Cutting was buried at St Clement Danes on 7 January 1596. Letters of administration were granted to his widow, Elizabeth, a week later, but in August 1607 a further grant in respect of goods unadministered was made to their eldest daughter, Margaret, and her husband, John Courtman. In her will, made at St Bartholomew-the-Great on 1 September 1597, Elizabeth Cutting expressed a wish to be buried beside her husband and recorded that Lord Thomas

Howard owed £20 to her estate. Her bequests included 'my seale Ringe of the lute' which significantly she left to their son Thomas, who later had a distinguished career as a lutenist.

DAVID MATEER

Sources administration for Francis Cutting, PRO, PROB 6/5, fol. 154v · PRO, E164/45; E164/46 · will, GL, MS 9051/5 (archdeaconry court of London), fols. 102–3 [Elizabeth Cutting] · parish of St Clement Danes, vol. 1, 1558–1638/9; surveyors' accounts, 1581–1604, City Westm. AC, MS B1 · M. Spring, *The lute in Britain: a history of the instrument and its music*, 2nd edn (2001) · R. Spencer, 'Cutting, Francis', *New Grove*, 2nd edn · L. Hulse, 'Francis and Thomas Cutting: father and son?', *The Lute: the Journal of the Lute Society*, 26/2 (1986), 73–4 · C. L. Kingsford, 'Bath Inn or Arundel House', *Archaeologia*, 72 (1922), 243–77 · W. W. Newcomb, *Lute music of Shakespeare's time* (Pennsylvania, 1966) · M. Fitch, ed., *Index to administrations in the prerogative court of Canterbury*, 4: 1596–1608, British RS, 81 (1964) · M. Long, ed., *Francis Cutting: selected works for lute* (1968) · D. Lumsden, 'The sources of English lute music', PhD diss., U. Cam., 1957

Cutts, Edward Lewes (1824–1901), antiquary, was born on 2 March 1824 at Sheffield, the son of John Priston Cutts, optician, and his wife, Mary, daughter of Robert Waterhouse. He was educated at Sheffield collegiate school, graduated BA at Queens' College, Cambridge, in 1848, and was ordained in the same year. On 23 April 1846 he married Marian, daughter of Robert Knight of Nottingham; they had ten children, seven of whom survived their father. Two sons, John E. K. Cutts and John Priston Cutts, worked together as ecclesiastical architects. Marian Cutts died in 1889. Cutts was curate successively of Ide Hill, Kent, until 1850, of Coggeshall, Essex, until 1857, and of Kelvedon, Essex, until 1859, and was perpetual curate of Billericay, also in Essex, until 1865. He then became general secretary of the Additional Curates Society, resigning in 1871 to become vicar of Holy Trinity, Haverstock Hill, London.

Cutts's first publications were in medieval archaeology. *A Manual for the Study of the Sepulchral Slabs and Crosses of the Middle Ages* appeared in 1849. A series of articles in the *Art Journal*, beginning in 1856, was collected and published as *Scenes and Characters of the Middle Ages* (1872; 4th edn 1922). From 1852 to 1866 Cutts was honorary secretary of the Essex Archaeological Society and editor of its *Transactions*.

Most of Cutts's subsequent writings were published by the Society for Promoting Christian Knowledge. They include works on many ecclesiastical subjects, devotional books, and children's historical fiction. *Turning Points of English Church History* (1874), *Turning Points of General Church History* (1877), and *Parish Priests and their People in the Middle Ages* (1898) were among his books that had more than one edition. *Some Chief Truths of Religion* (1875) was translated into Swahili and printed at the Universities Mission Press at Zanzibar in 1895. Cutts contributed the volumes on Jerome (1878) and Augustine (1881) to the series The Fathers for English Readers. *A Handy Book of the Church of England* under his editorship went through eight editions (1892–1901). Cutts's ecclesiastical writings are solid and establishmentarian, exhibiting their author's high-church temperament but treating other parties with sympathy.

He was awarded an honorary DD by the University of the South in Sewanee, Tennessee, in 1876.

Cutts broke the routine of a parish clergyman and writer in 1876 when he visited the Assyrian Church of the East as the representative of Archbishop Tait of Canterbury. Accompanied by his son William, he travelled to Turkish Kurdistan and Persia, met the patriarch and bishops, and brought back a scheme for an educational mission. From this journey came his official report *The Assyrian Christians* (circulated privately), *Christians under the Crescent in Asia*, describing his mission and recording a census of the church, and a fine children's book, *Amina: a Tale of the Nestorians* (all 1877). These and his other efforts in keeping the proposed mission before the church public during the next four years led to the establishment of the archbishop of Canterbury's Assyrian mission. Cutts died at Holy Trinity vicarage, 70 Haverstock Hill, on 2 September 1901, and was buried at Brookwood cemetery, Woking. R. E. GRAVES, *rev.* J. F. COAKLEY

Sources BL cat. · *The Times* (4 Sept 1901) · *The Times* (6 Sept 1901) · *The Athenaeum* (7 Sept 1901) · *The Guardian* (11 Sept 1901) · private information (1912) · J. F. Coakley, *The church of the East and the Church of England: a history of the archbishop of Canterbury's Assyrian mission* (1992) · LPL, Tait MSS · B. F. L. Clarke, *Church builders of the nineteenth century* (1938) · *CGPLA Eng. & Wales* (1901)

Archives LPL, letters to A. C. Tait

Likenesses photograph, priv. coll.

Wealth at death £2213 16s. od.: probate, 15 Nov 1901, *CGPLA Eng. & Wales*

Cutts, John, Baron Cutts of Gowran (1660/61–1707), army officer and politician, was born at Woodhall, Arkesden, Essex, the second son of Richard Cutte or Cuttes (*d. c.*1669) of Woodhall, a squire of an old family owning property at Arkesden and Matching in that county, and his wife, Joan, the daughter of Sir Richard Everard, baronet, of Much Waltham, Essex. He entered St Catharine's College, Cambridge, as a fellow-commoner on 20 February 1677, but his name does not appear among the graduates until the date of his honorary degree in 1690. He was admitted to the Middle Temple on 14 July 1678.

Early career Following their father's death about 1669, John's elder brother, Richard Cutts, inherited the estate at Arkesden and, in the succeeding year, the Cambridgeshire estates of his father's collateral relative Sir John Cutts, baronet, of Childerley, Cambridgeshire. About 1685 Richard died unmarried, and the family estates, which were then worth £2000 a year, passed to John. Some time before this Cutts had joined the service of William, prince of Orange, at The Hague; he was with him in 1685, when he was also associated with the retinue of James Scott, duke of Monmouth. In a letter to William III in March 1699 asking for assistance with financial difficulties, Cutts would remind the king of the events of 1685 and:

> how earnestly you desir'd me (by the Duke of Monmouth) to break my match with Mrs [Elizabeth] Villiers and what a promise you made me upon it; I consider'd how often you have, Sr, renew'd your promise of favour; I consider'd what you have done since for her, and for her Relations. (King, 40)

John Cutts, Baron Cutts of Gowran (1660/61–1707), by Nicholas Dixon, *c.*1690

Later in the same year Cutts, who had scholarly tastes and wrote flowing and not ungraceful verses, made his first appearance in print, in England, in 'La muse de cavalier, or, An apology for such gentlemen as make poetry their diversion not their business, in a letter by a scholar of Mars to one of Apollo' (10 November 1685). The letter, which is in rhyme, alludes to some anonymous critic who had objected to soldiers wielding the pen, and accused Cutts of 'railing against the stage and court', and to whom there is an indecent rejoinder appended.

Some historians have suggested that Cutts sympathized with Monmouth in the June 1685 rebellion, but no clear evidence survives to prove it. At any rate, Cutts did not accompany him to England. On Monmouth's defeat and death Cutts was one of many to volunteer to join the imperial general Duke Charles of Lorraine in fighting the Turks. Through his connections with William III he found favour in the imperial army, and he greatly distinguished himself by his heroism at the siege and capture of Buda in July 1686, for which he received the appointment of adjutant-general to the duke of Lorraine, apparently the first military commission he ever held. A passage in Joseph Addison's *Musae Anglicanae* (1699) is said to refer to Cutts having been the first to plant the imperialist flag on the walls of Buda. In addition he served as an aide to the duke at the battle of Mohacs (12 April 1687). Cutts appears to have left imperial service in February 1688, when he probably briefly returned to London. There, in March 1688, he published his *Poetical Exercises, Written on Several Occasions*, with a dedication to Mary, princess of Orange (later Mary II). It also contains a piece dedicated to Anne

Scott, duchess of Monmouth, who had asked Cutts's opinion of Boileau's poems, and a few songs 'set by His Majesty's Servants, Mr. Abel and Mr. King'.

Service with William III in the Netherlands and Ireland
Unsympathetic to James II, Cutts sought military service in the Dutch republic. On 17 April 1688 Thomas Herbert, eighth earl of Pembroke, was succeeded by Henry Sidney as colonel of the English regiment on Zeeland pay. On the same day Cutts received his commission from the stadholder as colonel-commandant of that regiment, along with an additional commission from the *raad van state* as lieutenant-colonel of the same regiment. A small portrait of Cutts, painted by the court painter Wissing somewhere about this time, shows a handsome young fellow with dark hazel eyes and features less aquiline than in later likenesses, in silvered corslet, lace neckcloth, and dark wig. General Hugh Mackay of the Dutch service, who knew Cutts well, described him a year or two later as 'pretty tall, lusty and well shaped, an agreable companion, with abundance of wit, affable and familiar, but too much seized with vanity and self-conceit' (*DNB*) which was, no doubt, a truthful epitome of his character.

Cutts was one of 'the gentlemen of most orthodox principles in church and state' who sailed to England with William of Orange at the revolution of 1688, and he remained in England with the regiment. By June 1689 he had become colonel of this regiment—which was not one of the six so-called Holland regiments, and was disbanded later—but his name has not been found in the War Office (Home Office) military entry books of the period. In January 1690 he was ordered to complete his regiment to a hundred men per company, and in March proceeded with it to Ireland. Before leaving, Cutts presented a petition to inquire into Catholic lands liable to forfeiture, and shortly thereafter 'the king made him a grant of lands belonging to the jesuits in certain counties' (Luttrell, 2.24). He served through the campaign of that year and distinguished himself at the battle of the Boyne on 1 July 1690. Macaulay, in *The History of England*, states that at the Boyne Cutts was at the head of his regiment, since famous as the 5th fusiliers. There is no proof that Cutts was ever in that regiment, and the regiment known then and after as Cutts's Foot, as stated above, was one of those afterwards disbanded. On 27 August Cutts was with the grenadiers, when he was wounded during the repulse of the attack on Limerick. By letters patent, dated 12 December 1690, King William 'was pleased to confer a mark of favour on Colonel John Cutts' by creating him Baron Cutts of Gowran, co. Kilkenny, in the kingdom of Ireland. About the same time the University of Cambridge conferred on him the honorary degree of LLD.

On 18 December 1690 Cutts married his first wife, a widow with a large jointure. She was Elizabeth (1659/60–1693), the daughter of George Clark, a merchant of London, and had been twice married before, first to John Morley of Glynde, Sussex, and secondly to John Trevor, the son and namesake of the secretary of state to Charles II. The special licence is extant, and describes Cutts as a bachelor, aged twenty-nine, and the lady a widow, aged thirty. Cutts

returned to the army in Ireland in July 1691, and succeeded to the command of the prince of Hesse-Darmstadt's brigade when the prince was disabled by wounds at Aughrim. Limerick surrendered to Cutts, and he was at the head of the troops that took possession of the city.

Foreign and domestic service, 1693–1695
In March 1692 Cutts embarked for Flanders, where he was wounded at the battle of Engheim on 23 June. At the battle of Steenkerke on 3 August his regiment was one of those cut to pieces in Mackay's division, and he was grievously wounded in the foot. He returned to England on crutches, and soon after his recovery lost his wife, who died on 19 February 1693, her jointure of £2500 a year passing away to the next heir. On 22 March 1693 he was promoted brigadier-general of foot. In July the same year he was reported by Narcissus Luttrell to be engaged to one of the queen's maids of honour, a sister of the notorious duellist Charles, Baron Mohun, but the match never took place.

In April the same year Cutts was appointed governor of the Isle of Wight, an appointment he held until his death. Through this position he acquired considerable political influence. As he wrote, 'the king may (if he please) be master always of six voices in Parliament' (*Frankland-Russell-Astley MSS*, 77). A series of thirty-two letters, addressed by Cutts to his lieutenant-governor, Colonel John Dudley, afterwards governor of Massachusetts, extend over a period of ten years and afford some insight into his ways as governor. Dissimilar as they were in many respects—for Dudley had been bred to the ministry and had much of the puritan about him—both men were eager place-hunters, and conscious that they were necessary to each other. Cutts is constantly stimulating Dudley's zeal by promises of preferment, and exacting in return all manner of services, not only in managing the municipal and electoral constituencies of the island, but in paying his bills, pacifying his creditors, who appear to have never been wanting, and even bottling his wine. Now and then Dudley is taken to task with some vivacity, but the coolness never endured long. Unfortunately the lieutenant-governor's replies are not forthcoming.

In December 1693 Cutts was elected on his own interest as MP for Cambridgeshire. The following year an anonymous pamphleteer identified him as a whig member of the influential Rose Club. In the subsequent elections of 1695, 1698, and 1701 he was elected as MP in his own interest as knight of the shire for Cambridgeshire and in the government's interest for the Isle of Wight, but in all those instances he preferred to sit for Cambridgeshire.

Cutts was one of the brigadiers in the disastrous Brest expedition of 1694 under John, third Baron Berkeley of Stratton, and Lieutenant-General Thomas Talmash which was designed to reduce French attacks on English shipping in the channel and the western approaches. Cutts accompanied Carmarthen in his daring reconnaissance, in a small galley, of the French position in Camaret Bay. He was overruled when he advised caution should major French forces appear to defend the landing area. On 8 June he was ordered to command the nine companies of grenadiers which formed the vanguard of the landing. Approaching what Talmash had assumed would be an undefended beach in Camaret Bay, Cutts hesitated to land when French regular troops opened heavy fire. Talmash ordered him to persist, but Cutts was eventually wounded in the third attempt at landing and withdrew his grenadiers with 2000 casualties. When General Talmash died of his wounds, Cutts succeeded him as colonel of the Coldstream Guards (3 October 1694). Cutts accompanied William III on the continent in August and returned to England by November. On the death of Queen Mary in December, Cutts, who appears to have indulged his poetic tastes amid all the distractions of court and camp, wrote a monody, a rather stilted effusion, which appears in *State Poems*.

In spring 1695 Cutts was sent to Flanders as one of the commissioners for settling the bank of Antwerp, and in the summer he was engaged at the siege of Namur, where his splendid courage throughout was evident from the opening assault on the heights of Bouge above Namur on 18 July. The final assault, on 30 August, gained him the honourable nickname of the Salamander. Reminiscent of the mythical animal capable of enduring fire without harm, Cutts crossed a large open ground with his foot soldiers to reach a breach in the demi-bastion on the right flank of Terra Nova. Although slightly wounded, he returned to action with a bandaged head to lead three battalions back into attack, before being repulsed; 1349 men were killed or wounded.

Companion to William III and diplomat, 1695–1698 Cutts returned to England the popular hero of the siege. He was in constant attendance on the king's person when not employed on military duty. Besides William Bentinck, earl of Portland, he was the only witness of William's interview with the conspirator Sir Thomas Prendergast, and his devotion to the king in defeating Sir George Barclay's assassination plot was recompensed by the gift of the forfeited manor of Dumford, said to be worth £2000 a year. It had belonged to John Caryll, Mary of Modena's former secretary, and Cutts afterwards sold it to Caryll's brother for £8000. In 1696 Cutts was appointed captain of the bodyguard, and in January 1697 he married his second wife, Elizabeth (1678/9–1697), the only daughter of Sir Henry Pickering, baronet, of Whaddon, Cambridgeshire. Luttrell claimed that she possessed £1400 a year.

In 1696 Cutts's name first appears on a list in the correspondence between William III and the earl of Portland as one of the members of parliament who spoke French fluently and who were suitable for possible employment as a diplomatic negotiator. In the summer of 1697 he was engaged in the informal negotiations which led to the treaty of Ryswick, during which he was dispatched without credentials on a mission to Vienna. He brought home the welcome tidings of peace. A few weeks later he had the misfortune to lose his young wife, who died on 23 November 1697, after giving birth to a dead child. She was only eighteen, and is described by Francis Atterbury, who preached her funeral sermon, as a young person of great piety. Nahum Tate addressed to Cutts 'a consolatory poem … on the death of his most accomplished lady', and John Hopkins published an elegy at the same time (1698).

On 4 January 1698 the palace at Whitehall was burned down, on which occasion Cutts, combating the flames with the wretched appliances then available, at the head of his Coldstreamers, was as conspicuous as he had been in the breach at Namur.

Debtor and parliamentarian, 1699–1702 In 1699 Cutts faced bankruptcy and debtor's prison. Estimating his debts at £17,500, he privately appealed to William III for relief, reminding the king of many promises, and begging that his confidence may be respected, as he had never betrayed his majesty's secrets. In 1700 he was engaged in a dispute with the burgesses of Newport, Isle of Wight, in respect of their having returned a certain mayor after another person had been appointed to the office by Cutts. The case was tried at *nisi prius* before Lord Chief Justice Holt on 7 May 1700, when the jury found a special verdict. A little later Richard Steele, who was Cutts's private secretary from 1695 to about 1705, and who was indebted to him for his company in Lord Lucas's fusiliers, dedicated to Cutts his 'Christian hero'. Steele subsequently published in the fifth volume of *The Tatler* some of Cutts's verses, as the productions of Honest Cynthio.

In April 1701 Cutts made his most well-known act as an MP when he proposed an amendment to the address to the king on the partition treaty, stating that the Commons did not regard France's renewal of the treaty of Ryswick as a sufficient guarantee. Seconded by William Cavendish, marquess of Hartington, it appeared that the amendment would pass by forty votes, but Secretary of State Sir Charles Hedges reminded members of the need for unanimity on an issue that was tantamount to a declaration of war. Despite the king's personal preference for the amendment, it was not passed. At about the same time Cutts absented himself from the vote to impeach Charles Montagu, Baron Halifax, later claiming that he had acted with Robert Harley and the tories and recalling that he 'made such steps … that I was become obnoxious to the ministry then reigning' (*Diary of Sir Richard Cocks*, 95n). As brigadier-general, Cutts accompanied Marlborough to the Netherlands in 1701.

The War of the Spanish Succession, 1702–1707 In March 1702, with the accession of Anne to the throne, Cutts's appointment as governor of the Isle of Wight was renewed, but, over Cutts's objection, the queen reserved the right to approve of the deputy he appointed. In addition he became a major-general on the English establishment and was placed in command of English troops serving in the Dutch republic. After a brief visit to England in the spring of 1702 he returned to the Netherlands bearing the tidings of the combined declaration of hostilities, which formally opened the War of the Spanish Succession. In July 1702 was offered the appointment as governor of Jamaica and general of the forces in the West Indies, but declined, wanting to participate in the action in the Low Countries.

He took an active part in the ensuing operations, and won fresh fame by the capture of Fort St Michael, a detached bastion and the principal defence on the western side of the important fortress of Venloo in Gelderland, by a sudden assault on 18 September 1702. The achievement was variously regarded. Cutts's enemies, and they were many, viewed it as a vainglorious act of one who, in the words of Swift, was 'brave and brainless as the sword he wears'. Nor was this idea altogether scouted in the army, where Cutts's romantic courage rendered him popular. Captain Robert Parker of the Royal Irish, who was one of the storming party, after describing the onrush of the assailants 'like madmen without fear or wit', wound up by saying:

> Thus were the unaccountable orders of my Lord Cutts as unaccountably executed, to the great surprize of the whole army, and even of ourselves, when we came to reflect upon what we had done. However, had not several unforeseen accidents concurred, not a man of us could have escaped. (R. Parker, *Memoirs of the most Remarkable Military Transactions*, 1747, 85–6)

Cutts, the hero of many assaults, had probably measured the chances more truly than his critics. In any case the enterprise succeeded, and the subsequent surrender of Venloo allowed the allies to move against Stevenswert and Ruremond, clearing the French from the Meuse as far as Maastricht. It was, as Cutts suggests, in a modest and soldierlike letter to Daniel Finch, second earl of Nottingham, the first real blow struck at the enemy. Cutts's persistent detractor, Swift, who wrote of him as 'about fifty, and the vainest old fool alive', seized the occasion for a scurrilous lampoon entitled 'Ode to a Salamander', which gave deep offence to Cutts's friends.

In the first parliament summoned after the accession of Queen Anne, Cutts was again elected for Cambridgeshire, but preferred to represent the borough of Newport, Isle of Wight, for which he sat up to the time of his death.

Having been promoted lieutenant-general, Cutts remained in command of the English troops when Marlborough went home in the winter of 1702–3. In February 1703 he was given credentials to negotiate a cartel with the French for the exchange of prisoners, and subsequently he made the campaign of 1703. When the troops again went into winter quarters he returned home. Marlborough had intended him to leave with the army, but changed his mind when it appeared that he might easily get into a dispute with the Dutch army. In March 1704 Queen Anne gave him a present of £1000 out of her privy purse, apparently to compensate him for being passed over when Marlborough's brother Charles Churchill became general of foot. In any case, Cutts remained notoriously in debt. Marlborough revealed further difficulties when, in preparing for the Blenheim campaign in May, he warned Godolphin not to let Cutts know that he intended to march beyond the Mosel, 'for he is not capable of keeping a secret' (*Marlborough–Godolphin Correspondence*, 1.291). After a long wait for favourable weather at Harwich, Cutts and several other officers carrying money for

the army joined Marlborough in the camp at Burgheim on 15 July, after the battle of the Schellenberg.

On 13 August 1703 the allied army, commanded by Prince Eugene and Marlborough, marched westwards to meet the French in eight large columns. After passing through a narrow area Marlborough created a ninth column on the extreme left, with twenty battalions and fifteen squadrons under Cutts. In this position Cutts crossed the River Nebel and commanded the army's southern flank facing the village of Blenheim, the stronghold of Tallard's right flank along the Danube. Cutts's forces, including Rowe's and Ferguson's brigades as well as Huben's Hanoverians, gave him a force of about 11,000 men. He made repeated assaults on the village and met stiff resistance from the twenty French battalions there. Seeing that Cutts's repeated assaults attracted additional French reinforcements from the surrounding area, Marlborough ordered him to cease the attacks and to concentrate on holding the French from sending reinforcements from Blenheim to support the main French army. In the final stages of the battle Cutts was joined by the earl of Orkney and General Charles Churchill in encircling the village and preventing the 10,000 French troops from breaking out of Blenheim, eventually forcing them to surrender. On the return march in October Cutts captured the town of Trier for the army's winter quarters, and shortly thereafter he returned to England. In the distribution list of the queen's bounty after the victory Cutts's name appears as senior of the four lieutenant-generals with the army who received £240 each as such.

Blenheim was Cutts's last fight. On 23 March 1705 he was appointed commander-in-chief in Ireland under James Butler, second duke of Ormond, a post considered to be worth £6000 a year. He was cordially received by Ormond, and was sworn in one of the lords justices. However, his health was much broken, and he appears to have been aggrieved at his removal from more active scenes. According to an account published in the first volume of the *Monthly Miscellany* (1707) he contracted a third marriage, but of this there are no particulars. He died in Dublin, rather suddenly, on 26 January 1707, leaving, so his detractors said, not enough money for his burial. He was interred in Christ Church Cathedral, but no monument was erected to him. George Montagu, a friend of Horace Walpole and a grandson of the first Lady Cutts by a former husband, wanted to erect a monument to Lord Cutts, for which Walpole wrote an epitaph in 1762, but the design was never carried further.

Cutts had no children. Besides his elder brother, who predeceased him, he had three sisters: Anne, who married John Withers of the Middle Temple, and died young; Margaret, who married John Acton of Basingstoke; and Joanna, who remained unmarried. Cutts left his entire estate to his widowed cousin Mrs Dorothy Pickering, of Lincoln's Inn Fields, and to his sister Joanna, executor of his will. Joanna Cutts remonstrated with Swift on account of his persistent abuse of her brother, and her name appears in the *Calendar of Treasury Papers* (1708–14) as her late brother's representative in respect of certain outstanding claims for sums expended on Carisbrooke Castle during his governorship of the Isle of Wight.

H. M. CHICHESTER, rev. JOHN B. HATTENDORF

Sources S. S. Swartley, *The life and poetry of John Cutts* (1917) · J. C. R. Childs, *The British army of William III, 1689–1702* (1987) · H. Horwitz, *Parliament, policy and politics in the reign of William III* (1977) · H. W. King, 'The descent of the manor of Horham and of the family of Cutts', *Transactions of the Essex Archaeological Society*, 4 (1869), 25–42 · B. Burke, *A genealogical history of the dormant, abeyant, forfeited and extinct peerages of the British empire*, new edn (1866) · will, PRO, PROB 11/492, fols. 215v–216 · F. J. G. ten Raa, ed., *Het staatsche leger, 1568–1795*, 6 (Breda, 1940), 255–6 · *The Marlborough–Godolphin correspondence*, ed. H. L. Snyder, 3 vols. (1975) · P. Verney, *The battle of Blenheim* (1976) · Venn, *Alum. Cant.* · *Report on the manuscripts of Mrs Frankland-Russell-Astley of Chequers Court, Bucks.*, HMC, 52 (1900) · *The parliamentary diary of Sir Richard Cocks, 1698–1702*, ed. D. W. Hayton (1996), 95, 219 · N. Luttrell, *A brief historical relation of state affairs from September 1678 to April 1714*, 6 vols. (1857) · P. Osborne, *A journal of the Brest expedition* (1694) · *N&Q*, 5th ser., 10 (1878), 498 · F. Atterbury, *Sermons and discourses*, 5th edn, 4 vols. (1740–45), 1.203
Archives BL, corresp. and papers, Add. MSS 69379–69380 | BL, letters to John Ellis, Add. MSS 28880, 28900, 28901, 28911, 28913–28914, 28926 · BL, corresp. with duke of Marlborough, Add. MSS 61162, 61285, 69379 · BL, letters to Lord Middleton, Add. MS 41842 · BL, Nottingham MSS, Add. MSS 29588–29589 · BL, Rochester MSS, Add. MS 15896 · BL, corresp. with Sir Richard Steele and papers relating to Cutts collected by Steele, Add. MS 61686 · NL Ire., corresp. with duke of Ormond
Likenesses R. Williams, mezzotint, c.1685 (after W. Wissing), BM, NPG · studio of W. Wissing, oils, c.1685, NPG · N. Dixon, miniature on vellum, c.1690, NPG [*see illus.*] · attrib. T. Murray, oils, St Catharine's College, Cambridge · J. Simon, mezzotint (after G. Kneller), BM, NPG
Wealth at death owed and was owed significant sums: sister's correspondence, *Report on the manuscripts*; will, PRO, PROB 11/492, fols. 215v–216

Cutwode, Thomas. *See* Dymoke, Tailboys (*bap.* 1561, *d.* 1602/3).

Cuyler [*married name* Rice], **Margaret** (1758–1814), actress and courtesan, was allegedly the daughter of an army officer who rose to the rank of lieutenant-colonel in an Irish regiment and died in 1790, leaving his fortune to his mistress. For this information, and for details about her early life which may have owed more to John Cleland's *Fanny Hill* than to any respect for the truth, the only sources are the 1790 and 1792 editions of *The Secret History of the Green Rooms*. According to the narrative provided there, Margaret Cuyler was abandoned by her father (who, like the child's mother, goes unnamed), brought up as a playmate of George III's daughters by their deputy governess, procured by the notorious Mother Kelly, and rescued by Captain Cuyler of the 46th foot, whose common-law wife she became and whose child she bore and nursed during its few weeks of life. She was again abandoned when Captain Cuyler was dispatched to America, lived for three years with a Major Metcalf and then briefly with an unnamed young lord until the earl, his father, broke the match, and was then kept successively by an auctioneer and, in turn, the managers of London's two patent theatres, Richard Brinsley Sheridan of Drury Lane and Thomas Harris of Covent Garden.

It seems a circuitous way of explaining how a courtesan came to work in the theatre, but it was certainly at Drury Lane that Cuyler made her début on 4 January 1777, as Miranda in *The Tempest*, and it is possible that Sheridan was her partisan patron. Then, and throughout an undistinguished career on the stage, it was her appearance rather than her acting that attracted the admiration of reviewers. George Colman the younger, who was her manager for most of her summer seasons at the Haymarket, thought her 'a fine woman: a full-grown Irish Venus, without the Graces; and, though an indifferent actress, good enough for the indifferent part of Miss Mortimer' in Harriet Lee's *The Chapter of Accidents* (Peake, 2.51). It is a sober footnote in R. B. Peake's *Memoirs of the Colman Family* that shows that Margaret Cuyler married Dominic Rice of Gray's Inn on 21 February 1778. Nothing more is known of the marriage, and contemporary gossip continued to regard Cuyler as more consistently a courtesan ('Cyprian' was the term in currency) than a wife. Acting was, perhaps, her way of keeping up appearances. Although she continued to perform intermittently at Drury Lane and regularly at the Haymarket during the summer closure of the patent theatres until the spring of 1809, she was limited to supporting roles in comedy and farce. Her starring roles were reserved for routs and masquerades. On 24 May 1783, for example, the *Morning Herald* described the impression she made at a masquerade staged to give a French aristocrat a taste of English fashion: 'The lovely Mrs C—r appeared in the circle with peculiar éclat ... the beautiful simplicity of her dress proved the delicacy of her taste in that important article, and exhibited her gracefully elegant form to the utmost advantage'.

Like many Cyprians, Cuyler lived richly so long as her protectors kept faith by her. She is known to have been living in elegance in St Albans Street in 1784 during a period of four years' absence from the Drury Lane company, but by 1808 she was needy enough to call on help from the Drury Lane Actors' Fund. She was living seedily in Lambeth by then, and in Walworth when she died there on 14 March 1814. It was presumably her old theatrical companions who rallied round to arrange for her burial on 22 March in the actors' church of St Paul's, Covent Garden.

PETER THOMSON

Sources Highfill, Burnim & Langhans, *BDA* · R. B. Peake, *Memoirs of the Colman family*, 2 vols. (1841) · D. E. Baker, *Biographia dramatica, or, A companion to the playhouse*, rev. I. Reed, new edn, rev. S. Jones, 3 vols. in 4 (1812) · [J. Haslewood], *The secret history of the green rooms: containing authentic and entertaining memoirs of the actors and actresses in the three theatres royal*, 2 vols. (1790) · [J. Haslewood], *The secret history of the green rooms: containing authentic and entertaining memoirs of the actors and actresses in the three theatres royal*, 2nd edn, 2 vols. (1792)
Likenesses Thornthwaite, engraving, 1785 (after E. F. Butney) · E. F. Butney, drawing (as Cressida)

Cuzzoni [*married name* Sandoni], **Francesca** (1696–1778), singer, was born in Parma on 2 April 1696, the daughter of Angelo Cuzzoni, a professional violinist, and Marina Castelli. She was taught by Francesco Lanzi and made her

Francesca Cuzzoni (1696–1778), by Philip Mercier, 1723–5

operatic début at Parma in 1714. She sang in Bologna in 1716–17 before becoming *virtuosa di camera* to Grand Princess Violante of Tuscany and performing in opera at Florence, Siena, Mantua, Genoa, and Reggio. In Venice in 1718 and 1719 she sang with Faustina Bordoni, who was to be her great rival in London. Cuzzoni appeared in other major Italian operatic centres before, in autumn 1722, the directors of the Royal Academy of Music engaged her as the leading soprano of their opera company. They sent the composer and singing teacher Pietro Sandoni (1685–1748), who had been working in London, to take her to England. The *London Journal* of 27 October 1722 reported that 'Mrs. Cotsona, an extraordinary Italian Lady' was expected daily from Italy, but she arrived more than two months later. It was rumoured that she had married Sandoni on the journey.

Cuzzoni made a triumphant début at the King's Theatre on 12 January 1723 as Teofane in Handel's *Ottone*. She is said to have disliked her first aria, 'Falsa imagine', and angered Handel in a rehearsal by refusing to sing it.

> 'Oh! Madame, (said he) je sçais bien que Vous êtes une veritable Diablesse; mais je Vous ferai sçavoir, moi, que je suis Beelzebub le *Chéf* des Diables'. With this he took her up by the waist, and, if she made any more words, swore that he would fling her out of the window. (Mainwaring, 110–11)

Her performance of this aria 'fixed her reputation as an expressive and pathetic singer' (Burney, 4.287). Immediately, half-guinea opera tickets were reported to be selling at up to 4 guineas and at her benefit in March it was believed that noblemen were giving her 50 guineas a ticket. During the next five years she sang in operas by

Attilio Ariosti and Giovanni Bononcini, but most importantly was given a series of leading operatic roles by Handel, with the castrato Senesino as leading man. She created Emilia in Handel's *Flavio* (14 May 1723), Cleopatra in *Giulio Cesare* (20 February 1724), Asteria in *Tamerlano* (31 October 1724), the title role in *Rodelinda* (13 February 1725), and Berenice in *Scipione* (12 March 1726). In summer 1724 she visited Paris, where her singing much impressed Louis XV. Cuzzoni was 'short and squat, with a doughy cross face, but fine complexion; was not a good actress; dressed ill; and was silly and fantastical' (Burney, 4.299), but the brown silk dress trimmed with silver which she wore as Rodelinda became 'a national uniform for youth and beauty' (ibid.). Although on 11 January 1725 the *Daily Journal* reported that Cuzzoni was to marry 'San-Antonio Ferre' the next day, it appears that she was regularizing her union with Sandoni, for on 22 August Mrs Pendarves wrote: 'Mrs. Sandoni (who was Cuzzoni), is brought to bed of a daughter: it is a mighty mortification it was not a son' (*Autobiography … Mrs Delany*, 1.117). She continued to perform as Cuzzoni.

In spring 1726 the attractive and brilliant Faustina Bordoni joined the company. Cuzzoni and Faustina had equal salaries and Handel wrote equally important parts for them both. They sang together in his *Alessandro* (5 May 1726) and in the following season in new operas by Ariosti and Bononcini, and in Handel's *Admeto* (31 January 1727). They quickly acquired rival groups of supporters, whose partisanship grew increasingly rowdy. The climax came on 6 June 1727 when, in the presence of Princess Caroline, 'Hissing on one Side, and Clapping on the other' led to 'Catcalls, and other great Indecencies' (*British Journal*, 10 June 1727). The opera, Bononcini's *Astinatte*, was abandoned and there were no more performances that season. The satirical pamphlets *The Devil to Pay at St. James's* and *The Contre Temps* show the rival ladies caught up in the fracas, exchanging insults and pulling each other's headdresses. Gay parodied their rivalry in the Polly–Lucy scenes of *The Beggar's Opera*, premièred at Lincoln's Inn Fields Theatre on 29 January 1728. However, the two sopranos appeared together throughout the 1727–8 season, when Cuzzoni created three more Handel roles, Constanza in *Riccardo Primo* (11 November 1727), Laodice in *Siroe* (17 February 1728), and Seleuce in *Tolomeo* (30 April 1728). Her voice and technique were exceptional. Years later Charles Burney was to echo the praise of her contemporaries:

> It was difficult for the hearers to determine whether she most excelled in slow or rapid airs … Her high notes were unrivalled in clearness and sweetness; and her intonations were so just and fixed, that it seemed as if it was not in her power to sing out of tune. (Burney, 4.307)

Her ornaments 'took possession of the soul of every auditor, by her tender and touching expression' (ibid., 4.318–19).

The opera company expenses were ridiculously high (Senesino, Cuzzoni, and Faustina were each receiving about 1500 guineas a year) and the Royal Academy collapsed in summer 1728. After giving birth to a child that July, Cuzzoni travelled with Sandoni via Paris and Munich to Vienna, where her singing was admired, but the opera company could not afford her salary demands. During the next few years she sang in opera at Modena, Venice, Piacenza, Naples, Bologna, and Florence before working with her husband in Genoa, where she sang in his *Olimpiade* and *Adriano in Siria*. They returned to London in April 1734 to join Senesino in the Opera of the Nobility, which had been set up in opposition to Handel's company and had Porpora as its principal composer. Mrs Pendarves found her singing as well as ever, but it was the great castrato Farinelli, who joined in October 1734, who was the centre of attention. Cuzzoni left the company in summer 1736 and sang in Florence and Turin, where she was paid the huge sum of 8000 lire. Her last operatic appearances seem to have been at Hamburg in 1740. The *London Daily Post* for 17 September 1741 reported from Italy that she was to be beheaded for poisoning her husband, but although he seems to have been in poor health, he did not die until 1748. Cuzzoni sang in concerts in Amsterdam in 1742 and worked in Stuttgart as a court singer from December 1745. By this time Sandoni had returned to Bologna, where he died on 16 August 1748. That autumn Cuzzoni absconded to Bologna, leaving debts behind her in Stuttgart. She was in London in 1750 and had a benefit concert in May, when Burney heard her singing in 'a thin cracked voice' (Burney, 4.522). On 2 August Horace Walpole wrote to Horace Mann that 'old Cuzzoni' (Walpole, *Corr.*, 20.169) had been arrested for a £30 debt and bailed by Frederick, prince of Wales. She sang at a concert for the Decayed Musicians Fund on 16 April 1751 and at a benefit concert arranged for her by Gaetano Guadagni on 27 April. On 20 May she made a newspaper appeal to the nobility and gentry to support her in one final performance so that she could pay her creditors. In these last concerts she sang Handel arias, including her first success, 'Falsa imagine'. She returned to the continent and about 1770 was living 'in a very mean condition, subsisting by the making of buttons' (Hawkins, 5.313). There are no reports of her children, who may not have survived beyond infancy. Cuzzoni died in poverty in Bologna on 19 June 1778.

OLIVE BALDWIN and THELMA WILSON

Sources W. Van Lennep and others, eds., *The London stage, 1660–1800*, pts 2–3 (1960–61) · *British Journal* (29 Dec 1722) · *British Journal* (10 June 1727) · *Daily Journal* (11 Jan 1725) · *Daily Post* [London] (11 July 1728) · *General Advertiser* (18 May 1750) · *General Advertiser* (15 April 1751) · *General Advertiser* (27 April 1751) · *General Advertiser* (20–21 May 1751) · *General Advertiser* (23 May 1751) · *London Daily Post and General Advertiser* (17 Sept 1741) · *London Journal* (27 Oct 1722) · *London Journal* (22 Dec 1722) · *London Journal* (5 Jan 1723) · *London Journal* (19 Jan 1723) · *London Journal* (30 March 1723) · C. Sartori, *I libretti italiani a stampa dalle origini al 1800*, 7 vols. (Cuneo, 1990–94) · Burney, *Hist. mus.*, vol. 4 · J. Hawkins, *A general history of the science and practice of music*, 5 (1776) · O. E. Deutsch, *Dokumente zu Leben und Schaffen*, vol. 4 of (1985) *Händel-Handbuch*, ed. W. Eisel and M. Eisel (1978–85) · J. Milhous and R. D. Hume, eds., *A register of English theatrical documents, 1660–1737*, 2 (1991) · *The autobiography and correspondence of Mary Granville, Mrs Delany*, ed. Lady Llanover, 1st ser., 1 (1861) · Walpole, *Corr.*, vol. 20 · J. Mainwaring, *Memoirs of the life of the late George Frederic Handel* (1760) · P. F. Tosi, *Observations on the florid song*, trans. J. E. Galliard (1742) · *The contre temps, or, Rival queans* (1727) · *The devil*

to pay at St. James's* (1727) · J. Milhous and R. D. Hume, 'Opera salaries in eighteenth-century London', *Journal of the American Musicological Society*, 46 (1993), 26–83 · W. Dean and J. M. Knapp, *Handel's operas, 1704–1726* (1987) · L. Lindgren, 'Parisian patronage of performers from the Royal Academy of Musick (1719–28)', *Music and Letters*, 58 (1977), 4–28 · W. Dean and C. Vitali, 'Cuzzoni, Francesca', *New Grove*, 2nd edn, 6 · L. Lindgren, 'Sandoni, Pietro Giuseppe', *The new Grove dictionary of opera*, ed. S. Sadie, 4 (1992)
Likenesses J. Vanderbank, line engraving, 1723 (after J. Vanderbank), BM, *Harvard TC* · P. Mercier, chalk drawing, 1723–5, BM [*see illus.*] · W. Hogarth, line engraving, 1724 (*Masquerades and Operas*), BM; repro. in R. Paulson, ed., *Hogarth's graphic works*, rev. edn (1970) · J. Goupy, etching, c.1730 (after M. Ricci), BM, *Harvard TC*; repro. in A. Blunt and E. Croft-Murray, *Venetian drawings of the XVII and XVIII centuries in the collection of her majesty the queen at Windsor Castle* (1957) · J. Caldwell, line engraving (after E. Seeman), repro. in Hawkins, *General history* · J. Caldwell, line engraving (after E. Seeman), BM, *Harvard TC* · M. Ricci, drawings, Royal Collection; repro. in A. Blunt and E. Croft-Murray, *Venetian drawings of the XVII and XVIII centuries in the collection of her majesty the queen at Windsor Castle* (1957) · A. M. Zanetti, two caricatures, Biblioteca e Istituto della Fondazione Giorgio Cini, Venice
Wealth at death died in poverty: Burney, *Hist. mus.*

Cwenthryth (*fl.* **811–c.827**), abbess, was the daughter of *Cenwulf, king of the Mercians (d. 821), and abbess of Winchcombe Minster in the west of Mercia and of Minster in Thanet in Kent. In 811 she witnessed one of her father's diplomas as 'the king's daughter' (*AS chart.*, S 165), which probably indicates that at that date she had not yet entered religion. She may first have been established as abbess of the Winchcombe house, which seems to have had an existing connection with her kindred: it was the burial place of her brother *Cynehelm who probably died c.811 and who is reputed, according to a much later and definitely disreputable tradition, to have been murdered at her instigation. Cynehelm's *passio* (account of martyrdom) relates that the body of the murdered boy was brought to Winchcombe for burial. Watching the procession from a window, Cwenthryth cursed her brother by reciting the psalter backwards, whereupon both her eyes fell out onto the page. The blood-stained psalter was later displayed at Winchcombe. Cenwulf himself was also buried there in 821.

Along with Winchcombe, Cwenthryth inherited from her father the wealthy Kentish houses of Minster in Thanet and Reculver, which had been acquired by Cenwulf and treated as hereditary family property; it is not clear whether she had an association with these minsters before her father's death. She also inherited a longstanding and acrimonious dispute with Wulfred, archbishop of Canterbury. As a result of an agreement reached with Cenwulf in 821, Wulfred expected to gain control over Minster in Thanet and Reculver: but Cwenthryth continued to deny him his rents and due 'obedience'. In 825 he initiated a lawsuit to force her to submit to him and provide massive compensation for his losses. Cwenthryth, who could no longer count on support from the Mercian ruler, was eventually forced to concede, although her stubbornness kept the litigation in hand until about 827. By this time she may have retreated from Kent back to Winchcombe; certainly by 826 Archbishop Wulfred was in a position to dispose of Minster in Thanet property without explicit reference to her consent. Cwenthryth's subsequent history is unknown.   S. E. KELLY

Sources AS chart., S 165, 1267, 1434, 1436 • D. W. Rollason, 'The cults of murdered royal saints in Anglo-Saxon England', *Anglo-Saxon England*, 11 (1983), 1–22 • S. Bassett, 'A probable Mercian royal mausoleum at Winchcombe, Gloucestershire', *Antiquaries Journal*, 65 (1985), 82–100 • W. Levison, 'Winchcombe Abbey and its earliest charters', *England and the continent in the eighth century* (1946), 249–59 • N. Brooks, *The early history of the church of Canterbury: Christ Church from 597 to 1066* (1984)

Cwichelm (*d.* **636**), king of the Gewisse, was the son of King *Cynegils (*d.* 642) and seems to have ruled the Gewisse (or West Saxons, as they subsequently become known) with his father, perhaps from 611 and probably as a junior partner, until his death in 636. Battles involving Cynegils and Cwichelm are recorded in the Anglo-Saxon Chronicle for 614 against Britons at the unidentified 'Beandun' and for 628 at Cirencester, where their principal opponent was Penda of Mercia. Bede records how in 626 Cwichelm sent Eomer to assassinate King Eadwine of Northumbria in his hall on the River Derwent on Easter day. Eomer gained access to the king on the pretext of having a message to deliver from Cwichelm, but when he attempted to attack Eadwine with his sword, Lilla, one of the king's thegns, interposed his own body and was slain instead. Eadwine was wounded in the attack, and when he recovered led an army to Wessex to take revenge. Although the perpetrators of the crime are said to have been punished, and the E text of the chronicle claims that five kings were killed, Cwichelm was not among them, as his death is not recorded until 636. The reasons for the attempted assassination are not given, but are presumably connected with the wide-ranging overlordship which Eadwine is said to have exercised over the other Anglo-Saxon kingdoms. In the year in which he died Cwichelm was baptized by Bishop Birinus, who had converted his father in the previous year. Cwichelm left a son, Cuthred, who was baptized in 639 and in 648 was granted control of an area based on Ashdown by his uncle, King *Cenwalh.

BARBARA YORKE

Sources ASC, s.a. 614, 626, 628, 636 • Bede, *Hist. eccl.*, 2.9 • B. A. E. Yorke, *Kings and kingdoms of early Anglo-Saxon England* (1990)

Cybi [St Cybi, Kebi, Mo Chop] (*fl.* **6th cent.**), founder of churches, was the patron saint of Caergybi, Holyhead. His father is given in the two, closely related, versions of his life as Salomon son of Erbin son of Gereint, but in the thirteenth-century genealogical tract on the saints, *Bonedd y saint* as Selyf (Salomon) son of Gereint son of Erbin, thus agreeing with the tale entitled *Gereint vab Erbin*, one of 'the three romances', as well as with other Welsh texts. For *Bonedd y saint*, Cybi belonged to the royal line of Cornwall, descended from Custennin (if he were the Constantine of Dumnonia denounced by Gildas, the chronology of the lives would be seriously askew). Although the lives do not derive Cybi from Custennin, preferring instead Lludd, they make him a native of eastern Cornwall, the strip of land between the Tamar and Lynher, where his father, Salomon, was *princeps militie*, by which

was probably intended the *penteulu*, the head of the household troop of a king, an office held, according to the Welsh laws, by a close agnatic kinsman of the king.

The lives took Cybi first to 'the schools', then to Jerusalem and back to St Hilaire at Poitiers, where he was said to have lived for fifty years, finally being consecrated bishop. He returned briefly to Cornwall, where he refused the kingship, and travelled onwards to Edeligion in south Wales, between the Rhymni and the Usk. There King Edelic attempted to eject the saint, fell down blinded, repented, and gave the saint two churches, Llangybi and *Lanauer Guir*. From there he went by way of St David's to Ireland, where he sought out St Énda of Aran. Eventually his disciples quarrelled with Cruimther Fintan (Fintan the Priest). Before Fintan's wrath Cybi was obliged to retire, first to Meath, where he built the *ecclesia magna* Mochop (Cell Mór Mo Chop), then to Brega, and finally back to Wales, where he settled at Holyhead, the later *caer* ('fortress') of Cybi. There he stayed until his death, on 8 November in an unspecified year, and there he was buried. His shrine is said to have been rifled by pirates in the fifteenth century.

Mo Chop is an Irish hypocoristic form of the name Cybi and reasonable evidence for the existence at some period of Cybi's cult in the Irish midlands. The life of St Énda reports a story in which a principal part is taken by a St Pupeus (perhaps a form of the name Pompeius). There may be some connection between Pupeus and Cybi, although there are philological objections to a direct identification of the two names. Among his disciples were Caffo of Llangaffo, Llibio of Llanllibio, Maelog of Llanfaelog, and Peulan of Llanbeulan—all Anglesey churches, and all, except Llangaffo, close to Caergybi. The final episodes of the lives narrate conflicts with Maelgwn, king of Gwynedd. It is implied that Caergybi was originally a royal fortress, used as a hunting-lodge by Maelgwn. By extending claims of sanctuary even to wild animals pursued by the royal hounds Cybi steered the king into granting him the entire ridge of land where the royal fort was situated. The lives thus offer a narrative connecting most of the churches named after Cybi, whether in Ireland, Gwent, or Anglesey, asserting his status as the principal saint of western Anglesey and confirming Caergybi's rights of sanctuary.   T. M. CHARLES-EDWARDS

Sources P. C. Bartrum, ed., *Early Welsh genealogical tracts* (1966) • 'Vita I sancti Kebii', *Vitae sanctorum Britanniae et genealogiae*, ed. and trans. A. W. Wade-Evans (1944) • 'Vita II sancti Kebii', *Vitae sanctorum Britanniae et genealogiae*, ed. and trans. A. W. Wade-Evans (1944) • C. Plummer, ed., 'Vita sancti Endei abbatis de Arann', *Vitae sanctorum Hiberniae*, 2 (1910), 60–75, esp. 68–71 • S. Baring-Gould and J. Fisher, *The lives of the British saints*, Honourable Society of Cymmrodorion, Cymmrodorion Record Series, 2 (1908), 202–15 • E. R. Henken, *Traditions of the Welsh saints* (1987), no. 30 • E. R. Henken, *The Welsh saints: a study in patterned lives* (1991) • M. Richards, *Welsh administrative and territorial units* (1969) • O. Padel, *A popular dictionary of Cornish place-names* (1988), 80 [on Cornish dedication: Duloe]

Cyfeilliog (*d.* **927**), bishop of Ergyng, appears in two guises. In the main version (texts A, B, C, and D) of the Anglo-Saxon Chronicle he is named in the annal for 914: he was captured by a viking fleet operating in the Irish Sea and ransomed by Edward the Elder for 40 pounds. He was there described as bishop of Ircingafeld namely Ergyng (Archenfield). It is significant that it was Edward the Elder who came to the bishop's aid: his father, Alfred, had been sought as a lord by Brochfael ap Meurig and Ffernfael ap Meurig, kings of Gwent, for fear of the Mercians and their lord, Æthelred, Alfred's son-in-law. It appears that Edward the Elder was continuing Alfred's role as patron of the southern Welsh.

Cyfeilliog is also one of the supposed bishops of Llandaff. His death is given in a note in the Book of Llandaff and he appears as the beneficiary of a series of grants which can be approximately dated to the last decade of the ninth century and the first two decades of the tenth. All the identified places in these grants, however, were situated within Gwent Is Coed rather than Ergyng. The main grantor is named as Brochfael, probably the king of Gwent named by Asser as submitting to Alfred in the 880s. It may be supposed that Ergyng was at this period linked with Gwent, but it is still striking that the identified places are all in Gwent Is Coed rather than Gwent Uwch Coed, adjacent to Ergyng. Not even in the charters in the Book of Llandaff does it appear that Cyfeilliog had any connection with Glamorgan or Llandaff. His title in the chronicle is thus one of the pieces of evidence showing how the Book of Llandaff was assembled from the archives of local churches in south-eastern Wales. His obit of 927 is given in the Book of Llandaff at the end of the collection of charters attributed to his episcopate.

T. M. CHARLES-EDWARDS

Sources ASC, s.a. 914 [texts A, B, C, and D] · J. G. Evans and J. Rhys, eds., *The text of the Book of Llan Dâv reproduced from the Gwysaney manuscript* (1893), 231–7 · W. Davies, *An early Welsh microcosm: studies in the Llandaff charters* (1978), 182–4 · M. Richards, *Welsh administrative and territorial units* (1969)

Cymbeline. *See* Cunobelinus (*d. c.*AD 40).

Cynan ap Maredudd (*fl.* 1277–1297). *See under* Gruffudd ap Rhys (*d.* 1201).

Cynan Garwyn (*fl. c.*550–*c.*600), king of Powys, was son of *Brochfael Ysgithrog of Powys. Cynan ruled the kingdom of Powys in north-east and east Wales in the late sixth century. His epithet Garwyn or possibly Carwyn means either 'of the White Thigh' or 'of the White Chariot'. Regarded by the later genealogists as one of the royal descendants of Cadell Ddyrnllug, little reliable information is known of Cynan's reign. He may have been 'Aurelius Caninus', one of the Welsh kings chastised by Gildas in the mid-sixth century, though his kinsman Cynin ap Millo has also been suggested as a candidate. According to a poem addressed to Cynan (and probably erroneously attributed to the famous Taliesin), he was a great war-leader who fought widely throughout Wales: on the Wye, against the men of Gwent, on Anglesey, in Dyfed (possibly against Aergul Lawhir ap Tryffin), in Brycheiniog, and even in Cornwall. Gildas, it might be noted, drew attention to 'the thirst for civil war and constant plunder' of Aurelius Caninus. In the life of St Cadog, Cynan Garwyn is said to have been discouraged

from such a raid against Glamorgan through the saint's intercession. He is there called king of Rheinwg, situated either in Dyfed or, more likely, on the Herefordshire–Brecknockshire border. The Welsh life of St Beuno claims that Cynan granted land at Gwyddelwern (in Edeirnion) to Beuno, demonstrating that he was capable of non-violent acts, but such hagiographical notices are notoriously unreliable. The sources give no indication that Cynan Garwyn fought against the English, in which regard he was more fortunate than his son and probable successor *Selyf Sarffgadau. His other sons include Eiludd (sometimes conflated with Selyf) and, in unreliable sources, also Maredudd and Dinogad.   DAVID E. THORNTON

Sources *The poems of Taliesin*, ed. I. Williams, trans. J. E. Caerwyn-Williams (1968) [Welsh orig. *Canu Taliesin* (1960)] · R. Bromwich, ed. and trans., *Trioedd ynys Prydein: the Welsh triads*, 2nd edn (1978) · *Gildas: 'The ruin of Britain', and other works*, ed. and trans. M. Winterbottom (1978) · P. C. Bartrum, ed., *Early Welsh genealogical tracts* (1966) · D. P. Kirby, 'The bards and the Welsh border', *Mercian studies*, ed. A. Dornier (1977), 31–42

Cynddelw. *See* Ellis, Robert (1812–1875).

Cynddelw Brydydd Mawr (*fl. c.*1155–*c.*1195), court poet, was the most notable of the early *gogynfeirdd. The epithet Brydydd Mawr (great poet), applied to him, may originally have referred to his physical stature, but inevitably became associated in people's minds with his unequalled mastery of his art. During the earlier part of his career he probably lived near the royal court of Powys at Mathrafal in Caereinion and this may indeed have been his principal home all his life. In mid-career, however, he spent much time in Gwynedd and was apparently granted lands in the township of Maenan in Rhos uwch Dulas by his patron Owain Gwynedd. During the final phase of his career he also visited Deheubarth. He is known to have had at least one son, Dygynnelw, in whose memory he composed a moving short elegy.

As a professional poet, Cynddelw must have served a thorough apprenticeship at the feet of a master poet, but of this nothing is known. There is a tradition, unfortunately preserved only in a series of *englynion* which has many doubtful features, that Cynddelw defeated his fellow poet Seisyll Bryffwrch in a contest for the role of *pencerdd* of Madog ap Maredudd, king of Powys; success in poetic contest conferred the right to teach fledgeling poets, and this Cynddelw certainly did.

After his death Cynddelw became an exemplar to other members of the fraternity of Welsh professional poets, as is made clear by Dafydd Benfras in the thirteenth century, and by Iorwerth Beli, Gwilym Ddu o Arfon, Gruffudd ap Tudur Goch, Dafydd ap Gwilym, and Gruffudd Gryg in the fourteenth. This high reputation was well deserved. Of his verse some 3852 lines have been preserved, rather more than thirty per cent of all the work of the twelfth- and thirteenth-century *gogynfeirdd*. It occurs in four medieval manuscripts—NL Wales, Peniarth MS 1, the Black Book of Carmarthen; NL Wales, Peniarth MS 3; NL Wales, MS 6680B, the Hendregadredd manuscript; and Jesus College, Oxford, MS 111, the Red Book of Hergest—as well as in NL

Wales, MS 4973B, of c.1631, and again this relative profusion of sources cannot be matched by any other of his fellow professional poets. Cynddelw's surviving corpus consists of some forty-eight poems, of which twenty are in *awdl* metres and the remainder are *englynion* or quasi-*englynion*; judged by line-count, however, he is seen to be overwhelmingly the poet of the *awdl* rather than the *englyn* (the ratio is about three to one). The matter of his verse displays a similar imbalance: of his forty-eight poems, all but eight are in praise of royal or noble patrons, living and dead (if his elegies for Dygynnelw and his fellow poet Bleddyn Fardd are included). The remainder consist of religious poems, two love poems, and three poems on miscellaneous subjects.

Cynddelw began his career as a panegyrist in the court of Madog ap Maredudd, king of Powys (d. 1160), and he composed eulogies, and on occasion elegies, not only for Madog himself but also for many of his descendants, for the sub-kings Cadwallon ap Madog and Hywel ab Ieuaf, and for such magnates as Rhirid Flaidd; notable too are the two poems 'Gwelygorddau Powys' ('The lineages of Powys') and 'Breintiau gwŷr Powys' ('The privileges of the men of Powys'), probably composed soon after Madog's death to uphold the privileges of his retinue, then under threat. The lofty poem for St Tysilio and his church of Meifod may have been similarly motivated. When Madog died it was apparent to Cynddelw that the focus of power in Wales henceforth lay in Gwynedd, in the court of Owain Gwynedd (Owain ap Gruffudd), and he emigrated there, celebrating his new patron's prowess in a series of eulogies and a remarkable elegy, as well as praising his retinue, his heir designate Hywel ab Owain, and (in death) a member of his personal retinue Ithael ap Cedifor Wyddel. At the very end of his career Cynddelw may have hailed the rising star of Owain Gwynedd's grandson Llywelyn ab Iorwerth, but this is far from certain. When Owain Gwynedd died in 1170, Rhys ap Gruffudd of Deheubarth was for nearly a generation a dominant force in Welsh politics, and Cynddelw clearly saw in his court an opportunity for patronage, though his three surviving poems for Rhys—of which two appear designed to pacify the patron following some slight offered him by the poet—must be dated c.1190, when the careers of both patron and poet were drawing to a close. In all his panegyric verse Cynddelw upholds, often with profound emotional commitment and irresistible rhetorical force, the traditional heroic virtues of courage, generosity, political and military sagacity, and high lineage. The tone, even in the poems in which he seeks to placate his royal patrons, is never less than supremely self-confident.

In contrast, in the two love poems he composed, Cynddelw plays to perfection the role of the anguished lover: there are features in these poems that echo contemporary continental love poetry and foreshadow later developments in Welsh poetry. In his religious poems, however, the note of self-confidence is again apparent, even in the moving *marwysgafn*, or death-bed poem, which he presumably composed in old age. He was not without a sense of humour: apart from his self-mocking love poetry he composed a mock-heroic elegy for a cherished cockerel. Equally striking is the *englyn* in which he rebuked a monk from the Cistercian abbey of Strata Marcella for refusing his request to be buried in the abbey: if this incident really happened, Strata Marcella missed an opportunity to honour the bones of one of Wales's greatest medieval poets.

R. GERAINT GRUFFYDD

Sources *Gwaith Cynddelw Brydydd Mawr*, ed. N. A. Jones and A. P. Owen, 2 vols. (1991–5) · A. P. Owen, '"A mi, feirdd, i mewn a chwi allan": Cynddelw Brydydd Mawr a'i grefft', *Beirdd a thywysogion: barddoniaeth llys yng Nghymru, Iwerddon a'r Alban, cyflwynedig i R. Geraint Gruffydd*, ed. M. E. Owen and B. F. Roberts (1996), 143–65 **Archives** Jesus College, Oxford, MS 111 · NL Wales, MS 4973B · NL Wales, MS 6680B · NL Wales, Peniarth MSS 1, 3

Cynddylan ap Cyndrwyn (*fl. c.*616–*c.*641), king in Wales, was son of Cyndrwyn of Powys. He seems to have been an important ruler in the southern part of the kingdom of Powys during the middle decades of the seventh century. Knowledge of him and his dynasty is restricted almost exclusively to a series of elegiac poems composed perhaps no earlier than the ninth century, one of which takes the form of a eulogy by his sister Heledd on his death at English hands. Cynddylan's territory encompassed parts of western Shropshire and south-east Montgomeryshire into which Powys still extended at the start of this period. His seat of power was called 'Pengwern', which some have identified as Shrewsbury. Furthermore, in one poem he is termed the lord of Dogfeiling: this was an area outside Cynddylan's traditional territories but it may have come under the control of his dynasty if the power of the kings of northern Powys declined following the killing of Selyf Sarffgadau at Chester between 613 and 616. Cynddylan's father, Cyndrwyn, is credited with a large progeny (the extant lists of which omit Cynddylan himself), and it is possible that the dynasty was (or claimed to be) Cadelling, that is, descendants of the Powysian dynastic founder Cadell Ddyrnllug.

The activities of Cynddylan's dynasty and its chronology are sketchy to say the least. Cynddylan may at least once have raided Anglesey, if reference to his presence at Menai on that island is reliable. His brother Gwion is said to have been one of the allies of Selyf Sarffgadau against Æthelfrith of Northumbria at Chester between 613 and 616. Cynddylan himself may have fought against the Northumbrian king Oswald as an ally of Penda of Mercia at the battle of Maserfelth, near Oswestry, in 641. The location of this battle would certainly have been of interest to Cynddylan, and Penda was not averse to forging alliances with Welsh kings. However, whether Cynddylan was among Penda's Welsh allies at the battle of 'Winwaed' in 655 is impossible to determine. The putative alliance with Mercia did collapse at some point because Cynddylan is said to have launched a raid beyond the River Tern into Lichfield. If this attack was directed against the Mercians, it possibly caused them to counter-attack by striking against Cynddylan at his home at 'Pengwern'. Here he and many of his kinsmen were slain, leaving only Heledd to bemoan the deaths and the consequent collapse of the dynasty. The date of these attacks on Lichfield and 'Pengwern' are difficult to determine, though some would date the second to a point after the restoration of Mercian power under Wulfhere in 659.   DAVID E. THORNTON

Sources I. Williams, ed., *Canu Llywarch Hen* (1935); pbk edn (1978) · P. C. Bartrum, ed., *Early Welsh genealogical tracts* (1966) · D. P. Kirby, 'The bards and the Welsh border', *Mercian studies*, ed. A. Dornier (1977), 31–42

Cynegils (*d.* 642), king of the Gewisse, was the first of the Gewissan kings to be converted to Christianity. He was probably the son of King *Ceol (*d.* 597), as recorded in the West Saxon genealogical regnal list, but individuals of the same name appear with a different descent in genealogies in the Anglo-Saxon Chronicle. Cynegils came to power in 611 and for the greater part of his reign seems to have ruled in association with his son *Cwichelm (*d.* 636). The two of them are recorded as killing the peculiarly precise number of 2045 Britons at the unidentified 'Beandun' in 614, and as fighting with *Penda of Mercia at Cirencester in 628, after which they came to terms, which may have included the marriage of Cynegils's son *Cenwalh to a daughter of Penda. The latter battle is generally regarded as deciding that the Cirencester area in the province of the Hwicce, where there had been Saxon as well as Anglian settlement, would owe allegiance to Mercia rather than to Wessex. It may have been part of the process which encouraged the West Saxons (or the Gewisse, as they seem to have been known in the early seventh century) to concentrate on expansion further south. It must also have been in Cynegils's reign, some time after 616, that a battle took place between the Gewisse and the East Saxons in which the three sons of Sæberht were killed.

A mutual enmity towards Penda of Mercia may explain the alliance between Cynegils and *Oswald of Bernicia, king of all Northumbria, which was sealed by Oswald's marriage to a daughter of Cynegils some time after 635. The two houses were also united by an antipathy towards the Deiran royal house; Cynegils's son Cwichelm had attempted the assassination of King Eadwine of Deira, who had ruled all Northumbria before Oswald and had forced him into exile. Oswald, as a powerful overlord, was probably the senior partner in the relationship and his standing as godfather to Cynegils at the latter's baptism in 635 could support such an interpretation. However, it cannot necessarily be inferred that Oswald used his position to compel Cynegils to become a Christian. Northumbrian missionaries do not seem to have been involved in Cynegils's conversion, as he was baptized by Bishop Birinus who had received an independent commission from Pope Honorius to work in a pagan region in England. Bede says that Cynegils and Oswald together gave Dorchester-on-Thames to Birinus for his episcopal see, but though Oswald may have been present at the ceremony, it is unlikely that he had any authority to bestow land in Cynegils's kingdom. Dorchester was formerly a small Roman town which had been a focus for the earliest Saxon settlement in the upper Thames valley, out of which the

kingdom of the Gewisse is presumed to have arisen. Cynegils died in 642 and was succeeded by Cenwalh. He was also thought to have been the father of *Centwine, king of Gewisse.   BARBARA YORKE

Sources *ASC*, s.a. 611, 614, 628, 633, 635, 641 · D. N. Dumville, 'The West Saxon genealogical regnal list and the chronology of early Wessex', *Peritia*, 4 (1985), 21–66 · Bede, *Hist. eccl.*, 3.7 · S. C. Hawkes, 'The early Saxon period', *The archeology of the Oxford region*, ed. G. Briggs, J. Cook, and T. Rowley (1986), 64–108 · B. Yorke, *Wessex in the early middle ages* (1995)

Cynehelm [St Cynehelm, Kenelm] (*supp. fl.* 803×11), martyr, is the subject of an elaborate *passio* (account of martyrdom) which can be dated on internal evidence to the years 1045–75, although purportedly drawing on English songs and writings. According to this *passio*, he was the son of King *Cenwulf of Mercia (*d.* 821), to whose throne he succeeded as a boy of seven years. His sister *Cwenthryth instigated his tutor Æscberht to kill him. While hunting with the child in a wood on 17 July, Æscberht beheaded and buried him at Clent (in what is now Worcestershire). Cwenthryth acceded to the kingdom; but a dove miraculously delivered to Pope Leo III (*r.* 795–816) a parchment inscribed in English to the effect that Cynehelm was buried decapitated under a thorn tree at Clent. The pope accordingly sent legates to Wulfred, archbishop of Canterbury, and the other English bishops to have Cynehelm's body recovered and enshrined. In the event, the body was taken to Winchcombe and, as the procession bearing it approached that church, Cwenthryth stood at a window reciting the psalter backwards by way of a curse, for which she was punished by having both eyes drop out on to the page, the blood-stained psalter being later displayed at Winchcombe.

This *passio*, although interesting as a work of hagiography, is factually unreliable. There was indeed a person called Cynehelm who appears in the witness lists of a number of reliable early charters, one granted by King Cuthred of Kent, the remainder by King Cenwulf of Mercia. If the Cynehelm of these charters in any way inspired the legend of the child-martyr, the details of his life must have diverged radically from those imputed to him in the *passio*. The documents, which designate Cynehelm *princeps* or *dux*, date from 803 to 811 and so make it impossible that he could have succeeded Cenwulf at the age of seven. (William of Malmesbury translated into Latin a document purporting to be an English translation of a papal confirmation in 798 of the monastery of Glastonbury to 'King Kinelm', but it is very doubtful if this is a correct record.) Moreover, the Anglo-Saxon Chronicle makes it clear that Cenwulf was immediately succeeded by Ceolwulf, making no mention of Cynehelm. Further, it gives the date of Cenwulf's death as 819 (821 is in fact correct) and this date is found also in the *passio*, suggesting that the author of that work was using the chronicle to provide a plausible context for his narrative.

That Cynehelm was indeed venerated as a saint by the early eleventh century is shown by an entry in the later section of the list of saints' resting places, *Secgan be þam godes sanctum þe on Engla lande ærost reston* ('Concerning

God's saints who formerly rested in England'), which dates from that period. The entry states that Kenelm, referred to as 'royal child' (*cynebearn*), rests at Winchcombe, Gloucestershire, a monastery founded by the Mercian kings in the late eleventh century (Liebermann, 19). Winchcombe was restored as a Benedictine monastery by Oswald, bishop of Worcester (961–92), and it is likely that he was responsible for promoting Cynehelm's cult there. Certainly the martyr's feast day on 17 July appears in calendars from the third quarter of the tenth century, and in the sacramentary of Fleury (Orléans, Bibliothèque Municipale, MS 127 (105)), which was probably written at Winchcombe at about the same time, he has proper prayers and mass and is prominent among the martyrs. As noted above, the saint's *passio* was in existence by the mid-eleventh century, and a series of versions is found in later manuscripts and compilations as well as in the works of twelfth-century historical writers such as William of Malmesbury and John of Worcester. From that time onwards, Cynehelm became a widely known saint, commemorated at various ecclesiastical centres, and more popularly by an Old English couplet relating to his place of burial: 'In Clent Cow-valley, Kenelm king's son lies under a thorn-bush deprived of his head' (Love, 67). By the fourteenth century, his cult was sufficiently familiar to be alluded to in Chaucer's *Canterbury Tales*.

DAVID ROLLASON

Sources R. Von Antropoff, 'Die Entwicklung der Kenelm-Legende', diss., Friedrich-Wilhelms-Universität, Bonn, 1965 · W. Levison, *England and the continent in the eighth century* (1946) · F. Liebermann, *Die Heiligen Englands* (1889) · S. R. Bassett, 'A probable Mercian royal mausoleum at Winchcombe, Gloucestershire', *Antiquaries Journal*, 65 (1985), 82–100 · D. W. Rollason, 'Lists of saints' resting-places in Anglo-Saxon England', *Anglo-Saxon England*, 7 (1978), 61–93 · R. C. Love, ed. and trans., *Three eleventh-century Anglo-Latin saints' lives: Vita s. Birini, Vita et miracula s. Kenelmi, and Vita s. Rumwoldi*, OMT (1996)

Cynesige [St Cynesige, Kynsige] (*d.* 1060), archbishop of York, seems to have come from the eastern Danelaw, perhaps from Rutland where he inherited the manor of Tinwell. He is said to have been born by caesarean section, but the story was probably invented to supply a miraculous start to the life of a man who was later honoured as a saint at Peterborough. John of Worcester and Symeon of Durham describe him as a royal clerk at the time of his appointment to York, but Peterborough tradition maintained that he had been a monk of that house. If he was a royal priest he may have been the Cynesige *presbyter* who witnessed three Abingdon charters of 1050, but it seems unlikely that he was the Cynesige *presbyter* who witnessed a Devon charter of 1026. Whatever his background, his promotion to York in 1051 implies that he was at least acceptable to the faction opposed to Earl Godwine, and that may account for the fact that although his pontificate coincided with the first part of that of the simoniacal Stigand at Canterbury, Cynesige apparently did not play as large a part in the political life of the country as did his successor Ealdred. In 1059, however, he and Earl Tostig and Bishop Æthelwine of Durham, the chief men of Northumbria, conducted Malcolm of Scotland to his meeting with Edward the Confessor. Cynesige was presumably present at that meeting, and at others at which he witnessed four of the five known royal charters from the period of his archiepiscopate.

In 1056 Cynesige presided over a council in London at which he consecrated Herewald bishop of Llandaff in the presence of Edward the Confessor. In May 1060 he apparently consecrated Earl Harold's minister at Waltham, Essex. He is also said to have consecrated two bishops of Glasgow, Magsue and John, but it is doubtful whether they ever resided in that diocese. They were probably titular bishops of Glasgow, working as suffragans in the York diocese.

In his own diocese Cynesige continued the work of his predecessor Ælfric at the houses of secular canons (there were no monasteries in the diocese). At Beverley he carried on the work on the dormitory and refectory, and built a stone tower, probably at the west end of the church. He gave bells to Beverley, and to Stow, Lincolnshire, and Southwell, Nottinghamshire, and he also gave books and ornaments to Beverley. Peterborough tradition recorded that, unlike his household, he lived an ascetic life, eating simple food and travelling on foot to preach in the towns and villages of his diocese in Lent.

Cynesige died on 22 December 1060 at York, and was buried, in accordance with his wishes, at Peterborough Abbey, to which he gave with his body the estate at Tinwell and £300 worth of ornaments, which were later taken by the Confessor's queen, Edith. The abbey seems to have attempted to promote a cult of Cynesige, who was called by its twelfth-century chronicler *sanctus*. Cynesige was certainly not a martyr, so there must have been some aspect of his character, probably an element of asceticism, which encouraged the attempt at canonization. If he was unable to enforce similar standards on his household, he may have lacked authority. Later in the middle ages, Cynesige's bones, like those of his predecessor Ælfric, were placed in a chest and built into the north wall of the chancel, near the high altar of the abbey church. They were rediscovered when the altar was destroyed in 1643.

JANET COOPER

Sources J. M. Cooper, *The last four Anglo-Saxon archbishops of York*, Borthwick Papers, 38 (1970) · F. Barlow, *The English church, 1000–1066: a history of the later Anglo-Saxon church*, 2nd edn (1979) · R. K. Morris and E. Cambridge, 'Beverley Minster before the early 13th century', *Medieval art and architecture in the East Riding of Yorkshire*, ed. C. Wilson, British Archaeological Association Conference Transactions, 9 (1989) · W. Davies, 'The consecration of the bishops of Llandaff in the tenth and eleventh centuries', *BBCS*, 26 (1974–6), 53–73 · S. Gunton, *The history of the church of Peterburgh*, ed. S. Patrick (1686) · *ASC*, s.a. 1060 [text D]

Cynethryth (*fl. c.*770–798), queen of the Mercians and abbess of Cookham, was the wife of King *Offa and the mother of his son and successor, *Ecgfrith [see under Offa]. Her origins are unknown, as is the date of her marriage. She attested her husband's charters on a regular basis from *c.*770 until his death in 796, and is the only Anglo-Saxon queen in whose name coins are known to have been issued. The surviving examples are versions of Offa's coins, with her name substituted for his and some adjustment made to the image; they are thought to have been inspired ultimately by coins in the name of the Byzantine empress Irene (*d.* 802). Offa seems to have ensured that his wife enjoyed an unusually high status, perhaps in order to strengthen his son's claim to inherit the kingdom. Cynethryth's prominent position was remembered by later generations, with disastrous consequences for her reputation; post-conquest sources connected with the cult of St Æthelberht of Hereford claim that it was she and not Offa who was responsible for the murder of that East Anglian king in 794.

Cynethryth probably remained a significant figure during the brief reign of her son Ecgfrith, for she attests two of his diplomas as queen, but when he died shortly after his father she appears to have entered religion. Offa had founded and acquired a large number of religious houses, which he had converted into the hereditary property of his family; his project was confirmed by a papal privilege, naming Cynethryth and her offspring as heirs. One of these minsters was Cookham, in what is now Berkshire, where Cynethryth established herself as abbess. In 798 she was forced to come to an agreement with the archbishop of Canterbury, whose church had an ancient claim to Cookham: in exchange for ceding another monastery at 'Bedeford' and the huge estates in Kent which Offa had attached to it, she was allowed to retain Cookham and was also given in compensation a third minster at 'Pectanege'. As one of Offa's principal heirs, Cynethryth probably played a major role in the management of an extensive network of family monasteries and their landed endowments; these seem to have included Glastonbury Abbey, which she may have been forced to cede to the new rulers of Mercia, and Fladbury in modern Worcestershire, where her daughter Æthelburh was abbess. Apart from Ecgfrith and Æthelburh, her offspring included *Eadburh, who married *Beorhtric, king of the West Saxons, and Ælfflæd, wife of *Æthelred I, king of Northumbria [*see under* Oswulf].

S. E. KELLY

Sources P. Grierson and M. Blackburn, *Medieval European coinage: with a catalogue of the coins in the Fitzwilliam Museum, Cambridge*, 1: *The early middle ages (5th–10th centuries)* (1986), 279–80 · M. R. James, 'Two lives of St Ethelbert, king and martyr', *EngHR*, 32 (1917), 214–44 · D. W. Rollason, 'The cults of murdered royal saints in Anglo-Saxon England', *Anglo-Saxon England*, 11 (1983), 1–22 · *AS chart.*, S 152, 1258 · P. Stafford, *Queens, concubines and dowagers: the king's wife in the early middle ages* (1983) · W. Levison, *England and the continent in the eighth century* (1946), 29–30
Likenesses coins, repro. in Grierson and Blackburn, *Medieval European coinage*

Cynewulf (*d.* 786), king of the West Saxons, was the hero of the Anglo-Saxon Chronicle's long and detailed annal for 757. He became king in that year, having gained the support of most of the leading men of Wessex and driven out his predecessor, Sigeberht. Like many West Saxon kings, he is said to have been descended in the paternal line from Cerdic. This may have been true, but it is not advisable to take such statements on trust, since this descent was apparently considered to confer a legal title to rule in Wessex, and would therefore have been claimed whether it

was true or false. In fact, Cynewulf is one of five kings in the period from 726 to 802 who do not feature in the extant genealogies of the West Saxon kings.

During the first year of the reign a meeting was held between Cynewulf and King Æthelbald of Mercia, with their leading lay and clerical supporters, at which Æthelbald gave some land in what is now Wiltshire to the West Saxon monastery at Malmesbury. What other business was transacted at this meeting is unknown. It is possible that Cynewulf accepted some sort of subjection to Mercia, but perhaps more likely that Æthelbald recognized Cynewulf as the new rightful king of the West Saxons. Whatever relationship existed between them was terminated later the same year by Æthelbald's assassination, and there is little doubt that Cynewulf then enjoyed over twenty years of independent rule, free from any outside influence.

Cynewulf was a benefactor of the church, granting lands in modern Somerset, Dorset, and Wiltshire to monasteries, but there is also an instance of his retaining for himself estates claimed by the church. He fought against the Cornish on a number of occasions, and at least one grant of land near the western border was intended to support these wars, presumably through the prayers of the monks. He corresponded with Boniface's successor, Lul, and he appears to have had some amicable contact with King Offa of Mercia. He was present in 772 at a remarkable meeting, held in Sussex and attended also by the kings of Mercia and Kent, the leaders of the South Saxons, and numerous other persons, lay and clerical. The subject of this meeting was probably the fate of the South Saxons, who at this time were losing their independence and entering a phase of Mercian domination.

In 779, however, Offa fought against Cynewulf at Benson in the upper Thames valley. Offa captured the town and also seized Cookham and many other places in the area previously controlled by Cynewulf. In 781, following the settlement of a dispute with the see of Worcester, Offa gained control of the monastery at Bath, including various lands which lay on the border between Mercia and Wessex and were of strategic importance, giving him, among other things, command of both sides of the River Avon. Cynewulf at this time certainly lost to Mercia various areas which had formerly been West Saxon, but there is no indication that he was in any other respect subject to Mercian power. He probably continued as the wholly independent king of a slightly reduced kingdom. These recent conflicts did not prevent Cynewulf and Offa from attending a joint council in 786 on the occasion of the visit to England of Pope Hadrian's legates.

Later that year Cyneheard, brother of Cynewulf's defeated predecessor, Sigeberht, emerged as a contender for the West Saxon kingship. The Anglo-Saxon Chronicle recounts how Cynewulf and Cyneheard fought at the house of Cynewulf's mistress at 'Meretun', each supported by the unswerving loyalty of their followers. Both died. Cynewulf was buried at Winchester, and Beorhtric became king.

HEATHER EDWARDS

Sources *ASC*, s.a. 757, 779, 786 [texts A, E] · *AS chart.*, S 96, 260–65, 269, 1256, 1258, 1681–90 · F. M. Stenton, 'The supremacy of the Mercian kings', *Preparatory to 'Anglo-Saxon England': being the collected papers of Frank Merry Stenton*, ed. D. M. Stenton (1970), 48–66 · F. M. Stenton, *Anglo-Saxon England*, 3rd edn (1971) · P. Wormald, 'Bede, the "Bretwaldas" and the origins of the "gens Anglorum"', *Ideal and reality in Frankish and Anglo-Saxon society*, ed. P. Wormald, D. Bullough, and R. Collins (1983), 99–129 · H. Edwards, *The charters of the early West Saxon kingdom* (1988) · D. N. Dumville, 'Kingship, genealogies and regnal lists', *Early medieval kingship*, ed. P. H. Sawyer and I. N. Wood (1977), 72–104 · S. Keynes, 'England, 700–900', *The new Cambridge medieval history*, 2, ed. R. McKitterick (1995), 18–42

Cynewulf [Cynwulf, Kynewulf] (*fl.* **9th cent.**), poet, concealed his name in runes near the end of four (or perhaps only three) poems, preserved in Exeter Cathedral Library, MS 3501 (the Exeter book), and in Vercelli, in the Biblioteca Capitolare, MS CXVII (the Vercelli book), both of *c.*1000. Nothing is known of him other than what he says of himself. In the nineteenth century some scholars identified the poet with other Anglo-Saxons of that (not uncommon) name, most often with Cynewulf (*c.*740–779), a bishop of Lindisfarne. The Northumbrian bishop's authorship would accord with the poet's probable dialect which was Northumbrian or Mercian, but has nothing else to commend it. That his verses are preserved in later West Saxon manuscripts is not relevant for localizing the originator, as the same is true of almost all Old English poetry. Dates of composition of Old English verse are not usually ascertainable; the ninth century is likely but undemonstrable. The fact that the first element of the name is *Cyne-* and not *Cyni-* makes a date of composition earlier than the beginning of the ninth century unlikely, though a date in the last quarter of the eighth century cannot be ruled out. It seems that the poet used two forms for his name, with and without *e* at the end of *Cyn(e)-*. Forms of *Cyn(e)-* without *e* are rare and early, and, though the philological evidence is not conclusive, it may indicate Mercia rather than Northumbria. (The form Kynewulf, used in the *Dictionary of National Biography*, derives from a different transliteration of the first rune.)

The poems (with titles as given by modern scholars) in which Cynewulf's runic 'signature' occurs are: certainly, 'Christ II' and 'Juliana' in the Exeter book and 'Elene' and (though not certainly) 'The fates of the apostles' in the Vercelli book. In all of his poems Cynewulf makes free use of Latin sources, patristic, biblical, and hagiographic, never confining himself strictly to a single source. 'Christ II' opens with Christ on earth and then dwells on the ascension to teach the way to salvation at the last judgment. 'Juliana' is a versified life of a virgin martyr who prefers maidenhood to marriage even when honourably intended for her, and perseveres in virginity in spite of threats and torture to make her submissive to worldly authority. 'Elene' relates St Helena's search for and miraculous finding of the true cross; it opens with a battle in which the Emperor Constantine, Helena's son, achieves victory in the sign of the cross. 'The fates of the apostles', much shorter than the other poems, is a versified martyrology of the twelve apostles. In each of these poems Cynewulf's name is hidden in a passage near the end, where at the thought of death and the last judgment the poet invites prayer. The runes were read first as CYN(E-)WULF by J. M. Kemble in 1840; and, for 'The fates of the apostles', less conclusively, by A. S. Napier in 1888. The 'signatures' fall into two classes: first, the runes stand for letters which combine to form the name, as in 'Juliana', lines 704–8; second, the runes themselves form the name, and, furthermore, the traditional rune names (or perhaps near homonyms) are used as nouns within the sentences in which the runes spell the poet's name. The order of the runes in all but 'The fates of the apostles' corresponds to the order of letters in name.

'Juliana', lines 703b–709a, may be translated:

> C, Y, N will go their way troubled: the King, the Dispenser of glories, will be severe when stained with sins E, W, U await in awe what He will adjudge them according to their deeds, in requital of life. L, F will tremble, will lie sorrowfully. (trans. E. G. Stanley, from Chambers, Förster, and Flower, fol. 76*a*)

The self-referential passage begins with the second half of line 695, and leads up to a request that whoever recites 'Juliana' should pray for Cynewulf. Structurally, this ending seems integral with the original versified life of Juliana, and not a later addition.

The passage in 'Christ II' with the 'signature' (lines 789b–807a) is obscure and its interpretation involves departing from the known sense of the rune names. It may be translated (with, in brackets, the meaning of the rune name, followed, where necessary, by a contextual sense):

> Truly, I expect and also fear a judgement the more severe, when the Prince of angels returns, because I did not keep well what my Saviour commanded me in the Scriptures; for that I must see the terror of requital for sin, as I know to be true, where many will be led into the assembly before the countenance of the eternal Judge, when *cen* ['the torch', perhaps for *cene*, 'the bold one'] flickers [or 'trembles'], hears the King, the Ruler of the heavens, pronounce, speak stern words to those who had obeyed him feebly in the world, while *yr* ['bow', perhaps for *yrmþu*, 'misery'] and *ned* ['need'] could find help most readily. There, in that place, must many a one, afraid and weary, await what harsh punishments He will adjudge him according to his deeds. *Wynn* ['joy'] of earthly treasures will have gone. *Ur* ['aurochs', perhaps for 'our(s)'] was for a long time, encompassed by the floods of *lagu* ['water'], a share of the joys of life, *feoh* ['riches'] in the world. (trans. E. G. Stanley, from Chambers, Förster, and Flower, fol. 19*b*)

The self-referential passage begins at line 779 with the first word, NE, large as for a new section. The lines immediately preceding it seem to close 'Christ II', so that Cynewulf, if not the author of 'Christ II', may have appended the section.

In 'Elene' the self-referential section, the 'epilogue', begins at line 1236 with the first word, þUS, large. The preceding section had been brought to a close with *Finit*, so that it looks as if Cynewulf appended the 'epilogue'. In it, lines 1236–50 rhyme (not always exactly, even when translated back into Northumbrian or Mercian). Rhyming sequences are rare in Old English verse. He describes himself as old and moribund. As in the other self-referential passages he grieves at his sinful state, and, after the passage with runes, he meditates on the mutability of the world and on the last judgment. The passage with the runes, lines 1256b–1270, may be translated:

> The man was always till then oppressed by surging cares, *cen* ['the torch', perhaps for *cene*, 'the bold one'] becomes weak though he received treasures, embossed gold. *Yr* ['the bow'], comrade in *ned* ['need'], grieved, endured constringent care, a cruel mystery, where formerly the proud *eoh* ['steed'] adorned with filigree work galloped, traversed the miles of track. With the passing of years, *wynn* ['joy'] and sport have become weak, youth and ancient pomp have changed. *Ur* ['aurochs', perhaps for 'ours'] was in former times the radiance of youth: now the days of old have gone forth in accord with the span of years, the joy of life has departed as *lagu* ['water'] flows away, the dissipated floods. *Feoh* ['possessions'] shall be mutable for everyone beneath the sky.   (trans. E. G. Stanley, from C. Sisam, fols. 132v–133r)

The runic passage of 'The fates of the apostles', lines 96–106, is obscure and occurs on a badly damaged page of the Vercelli book (fol. 54r). The beginning may mean, 'Here someone sagacious in wisdom, who enjoys poetical recitation can discover who composed this section'; the end may mean, 'Now you may be able to know who in these words was annunciative to men'. Not all the runes can be read, and the order of those that can be read does not spell CYN(E)WULF.

Most scholars agree that Cynewulf wrote the four poems, 'Christ II', 'Juliana', 'Elene', and 'The fates of the apostles'. All four passages with his 'signatures' are sufficiently similar in style and content for it to be likely that one poet composed them. The poems to which they are appended are, however, stylistically different, and differ in the treatment of their subjects: it could be argued that Cynewulf is the author of 'Juliana' and perhaps of 'The fates of the apostles', but only appended his epilogues to 'Christ II' and 'Elene'.

In nineteenth- and early twentieth-century Anglo-Saxon scholarship Cynewulf was, for various reasons and with varying degrees of probability, thought to be the author of all or most of the poems in the Exeter and Vercelli books, as well as perhaps of parts of *Beowulf*, or it was thought that, if the 'unsigned' poems were not by Cynewulf himself, they were products of 'the school of Cynewulf', a school invented to accommodate that view, and since discredited.   E. G. STANLEY

Sources R. W. Chambers, M. Förster, and R. Flower, eds., *The Exeter book of Old English poetry* (1933) · C. Sisam, ed., *The Vercelli book* (Copenhagen, 1976) · K. Sisam, 'Cynewulf and his poetry', *Studies in the history of Old English literature* (1953), 1–28 · J. M. Kemble, 'On Anglo-Saxon runes', *Archaeologia*, 28 (1840), 327–72 · A. S. Napier, 'The Old English poem "The fates of the apostles"', *The Academy* (8 Sept 1888), 153 · R. I. Page, *An introduction to English runes* (1973), 205–12 · R. Derolez, 'Runica Manuscripta', *Werken Uitgegeven door de Faculteit van de Wijsbegeerte en Letteren* [Rijksuniversiteit, Ghent], 118 (1954), 391–6 · G. P. Krapp, ed., *The Vercelli book* (1932) · G. P. Krapp and E. V. K. Dobbie, eds., *The Exeter Book*, Anglo-Saxon Poetic Records, 3 (1936) · K. Jansen, *Die Cynewulf-Forschung*, Bonner Beiträge zur Anglistik, 24 (1908)

Archives Biblioteca Capitolare, Vercelli, MS CXVII · Exeter Cathedral Library, MS 3501

Cyngar [St Cyngar, Cungar, Congar, Cungarus] (*supp. fl.* **early 8th cent.**), holy man, appears to have given his name to Congresbury, Somerset. As is often the case with

saints attested only in sources of a much later date than their supposed lives, it is necessary to disentangle the slender indications of the early existence of Cyngar as a cult figure from the elaborations of later hagiographers, who probably had no more concrete evidence for their subject than exists today.

The hagiographical material begins in the twelfth century, with a life of Cyngar surviving on a fragment in a late twelfth-century hand (now Wells Cathedral Library, Series IV/24a). It claims that Cyngar, or Cungarus, the son of an emperor of Constantinople and a woman named Luceria, fled from his inheritance and came, via Italy and Gaul, to Britain, where he founded an oratory at Congresbury, which was granted to him by Ine, king of the West Saxons (*d.* 726), before moving to Wales and making a similar foundation. He was eventually buried at Congresbury. The life also says that King Edgar's death in 975 was prompted by his violation of this site during a hunt. The broad outline of this account also appears in a marginal note in a fifteenth-century copy of Ranulf Higden's *Polychronicon*, given by the writer and bibliophile John Blacman to Witham Charterhouse, Somerset, probably in 1474. There is also a collect for Cyngar in another fifteenth-century Wells manuscript. In the later fifteenth century the life of Cyngar was augmented and subsequently included in Wynkyn de Worde's *Nova legenda Angliae* of 1516. Unlike most of this book, it was not taken from the mid-fourteenth-century *Sanctilogium* of John Tynemouth, and its immediate source has vanished. It adds to the earlier account the information that Cyngar was also known as 'Docuuinus', because, it says, this means 'teacher' in the 'British' language. This may be an attempt to associate Cyngar with St Docco, the original eponym of St Kew, Cornwall. The life in its twelfth-century form appears to consist of the bare outlines of an earlier account, giving Cyngar's origins and attaching him emphatically to Congresbury, which is embellished by chapters establishing a connection with Wales and illustrating the dangers of violating the saint's sanctuary. Nearly all the life's motifs appear in contemporary lives of Welsh saints, especially the life of Illtud and the second lives of Cadog and Gildas, all of which have been attributed to Caradog of Llancarfan (*fl.* 1136–1138) or to his school. The life of Illtud tells a similar story of the death of King Edgar. This heavy-footed warning to kings not to trespass on ecclesiastical rights suggests a context for the composition of the life of Cyngar: the efforts of the diocese of Wells to secure possession of Congresbury from the king.

This motive is also apparent in the earlier evidence for Cyngar. The earliest dateable reference to him appears in an Old English list of saints' resting-places, known as the *Secgan*, deriving from Wessex and written in or after 1013, in which he is already associated with Congresbury. An account of the saint, followed in Blacman's manuscript, forms part of a treatise purportedly by Giso, bishop of Wells from 1061 to 1088, and embodied in the twelfth-century short history (*Historiola*) of the see. It credits Cyngar with instituting a college of canons at Congresbury, which King Ine transferred to Wells, thus providing the foundation of the bishopric (Wells was actually founded c.909). It also relates that Cyngar founded a similar college in Wales. A calendar attributed to Giso (now BL, Cotton MS Vitellius A. xviii) gives the feast of 'Congar' on 27 November.

Congresbury itself was already the site of a minster by 886, when, as his life of Alfred avers, Asser received it and another Somerset minster, Banwell, from the king. There is no record of a minster at Congresbury after Asser's time, and the later fate of the estate there is uncertain. Banwell was back in royal hands later in the tenth century, and Giso's account claims that Cnut gave Congresbury to Duduc, who transferred it to Wells while he was bishop there, from 1033 to 1060. But, according to Giso, it was subsequently seized by Earl Harold Godwineson, and Domesday Book confirms that Harold held it in 1066, though the king had recovered it by 1086. Wells finally acquired it from King John.

While no written evidence attests Congresbury before 886, archaeological excavations conducted on the hilltop of Cadbury–Congresbury between 1968 and 1973 elaborate the picture of Congresbury as a religious centre. A shrine that formed part of the last phase of settlement on the hilltop site in the sixth century, though more likely to have been pagan, may have been Christian. The cult of Cyngar may just possibly have begun on Cadbury–Congresbury but, since there are no signs of habitation on the hilltop between the sixth century and the twelfth, its focus must have shifted quickly to the settlement at the foot of the hill. The church there, however, is now dedicated to St Andrew, the patron of Wells Cathedral. It is just as possible that the figure of Cyngar was invented to explain the hybrid British–English place name Congresbury, as it is that the English name of the place was derived from the British name of the saint (-bury, originally -byrig in Old English, means a fortification, or even a monastic settlement). Since the cult is attested in the *Secgan* earlier than the efforts of the bishopric of Wells to lay claim to Congresbury, its creation cannot be ascribed to the latter. Rather, the bishops of Wells appropriated a saint whose origins were then, and remain, deeply obscure.

The cult of Cyngar seems to have spread to Wales, where it is indicated in the place names of Llanwnda, Pembrokeshire, Ynys Gyngar, near Criccieth in Caernarvonshire, and Llangyngar, now Hope, Flintshire, and in a dedication at Llangefni, Anglesey. The twelfth-century life of Dyfrig (Dubricius) in the Book of Llandaff names 'Congur' as one of Dyfrig's disciples, and a charter in the same source refers to a monastery in the Gower called 'Lann Connur'. It is possible that this Welsh evidence attests a different saint, since the name appears (usually as Congar) in Welsh calendars of the fifteenth and sixteenth centuries under 7 November, whereas calendars of the thirteenth and fourteenth centuries from Somerset give 27 November. Such a dislocation is not conclusive, however, and the twelfth-century hagiographical evidence gives good grounds for linking the Somerset Cyngar with Wales. He can also be associated with Cornwall: a late Welsh genealogy makes Cyngar the great-great-grandson of an otherwise unknown Cornish king named Constantine. This may simply be a mistake based on the life's claim of his origin at Constantinople, but his name is paralleled by the obscure St Ingonger commemorated at Lanivet, Cornwall. The latter has been identified with the Breton saint Congar, attested in such place names as St Congard, Roscongar, and Lescongar, whose feasts are kept on 13 February and 12 May. While these differences from the Somerset evidence may indicate two or more saints, they can equally be explained by the dissemination of a single cult which was adapted to fit local devotional calendars.

MARIOS COSTAMBEYS

Sources G. H. Doble, 'St Congar', *Antiquity*, 19 (1945), 32–43 • D. W. Rollason, 'Lists of saints' resting-places in Anglo-Saxon England', *Anglo-Saxon England*, 7 (1978), 61–93 • *Bibliotheca hagiographica latina antiquae et mediae aetatis*, 2 vols. (Brussels, 1898–1901) [suppls., 1911 and 1986, 2013] • J. P. Armitage-Robinson, 'A fragment of the life of St Cungar', *Journal of Theological Studies*, 20 (1918–19), 97–108 • J. P. Armitage-Robinson, 'The lives of St Cungar and St Gildas', *Journal of Theological Studies*, 23 (1921–2), 15–22 • J. P. Armitage-Robinson, 'St Cungar and St Decuman', *Journal of Theological Studies*, 29 (1927–8), 137–40 • P. Grosjean, 'Cyngar Sant', *Analecta Bollandiana*, 42 (1924), 100–20 • 'A brief history of the bishoprick of Somerset from its foundation to the year 1174', *Ecclesiastical documents*, CS, 8 (1840) • F. Wormald, ed., *English kalendars before AD 1100*, 1, HBS, 72 (1934) • P. Rahtz and others, *Cadbury Congresbury, 1968–73: a late/post-Roman hilltop settlement in Somerset* (1992) • *Alfred the Great: Asser's Life of King Alfred and other contemporary sources*, ed. and trans. S. Keynes and M. Lapidge (1983) • C. N. L. Brooke, 'The archbishops of St David's, Llandaff and Caerleon-on-Usk', *The church and the Welsh border in the central middle ages* (1986), 16–49 • C. N. L. Brooke, 'St Peter of Gloucester and St Cadog of Llancarfan', *The church and the Welsh border in the central middle ages* (1986), 50–94 • S. M. Pearce, 'The dating of some Celtic dedications and the hagiographical traditions of south-western Britain', *Report and Transactions of the Devonshire Association*, 105 (1973), 95–120 • C. W. Lewis, 'The literary tradition of Morgannwg down to the middle of the sixteenth century', *Glamorgan county history*, ed. G. Williams, 3: *The middle ages*, ed. T. B. Pugh (1971), 449–554 • private information (2004) • J. G. Evans and J. Rhys, eds., *Liber Landavensis* (1893)

Cyngen ap Cadell (d. 854/5), king of Powys, was the son of Cadell ap Brochfael (d. 808) of Powys. Cyngen ruled the kingdom of Powys in north-east and east Wales from 808, when his father died, until his own death in 854 or 855, or shortly before that date. He is the last known king of the Cadelling dynasty of Powys, descended from Cadell Ddyrnllug of the fifth century, and his reign was characterized by constant military pressure from England, especially the rulers of Mercia, and possibly also from the neighbouring kings in Gwynedd. However, not all relations with Gwynedd were necessarily hostile: the later genealogies represented Cyngen's sister Nest as wife of the king of Gwynedd, Merfyn Frych (less correctly of Merfyn's son Rhodri Mawr), and the so-called 'Bamberg cryptogram' of Dubthach deciphers as a short greeting to Cyngen from his brother-in-law Merfyn. Cyngen's own wife is unknown but two of his sons appear to have been involved in a fraternal struggle in 814 when one Gruffudd (or Griffri) ap Cyngen was slain by his brother Elise. The reason for this struggle and its implications for Cyngen's position are impossible to determine. His other sons were called Aeddan and Ieuaf.

It was the pressure from the English that probably caused the demise of Cyngen's line and may have compelled him to journey to Rome, where he was to die in 854 or 855. Though not all English raids into Wales are specifically said to have involved Powys, that kingdom's easterly location must have meant it felt the brunt of their force. In 816 the English, probably Cenwulf, king of Mercia, raided north Wales, as far as Snowdonia and Rhufoniog, which would only have been accessible by passing through Powys. Two years later Cenwulf attacked Dyfed in south Wales, but he had no doubt returned his attention to Powys in 821 when he died at Basingwerk (according to the twelfth-century historian Geoffrey Gaimar). This proved to be no reprieve for Cyngen, for in 822 the English, probably under Cenwulf's successor, Ceolwulf, are said to have destroyed the fortress at Deganwy and taken Powys into their power. The implications of these events for Cyngen are not clear, though he may have been subjected to Mercian overlordship. In 828 Ecgberht, king of Wessex, the dominant English ruler at that time, marched into Wales and compelled all the Welsh kings (presumably including the unfortunate Cyngen) to submit to him. Finally, in 853 the combined forces of Burgred of Mercia and Æthelwulf of Wessex invaded Wales, again exacting the submission of the Welsh kings. It was perhaps this that drove Cyngen, if he was still in Wales by this date, to undertake his pilgrimage to Rome, though not all early medieval Welsh kings who made that pilgrimage did so as a result of political pressure and at least one later returned to Wales.

This pressure from the English, so characteristic of the reign of Cyngen ap Cadell, is reflected in Powysian literary output of the time. For example, the so-called 'pillar of Elise' (or Eliseg) which Cyngen commissioned from the mason Cynfarch, bears an inscription commemorating the victories of Cyngen's ancestor Elise ap Gwylog against the English in the previous century. In a more pessimistic vein scholars have dated to this period in Powysian history the composition of a cycle of poems attributed to Llywarch Hen concerning the defeat of Cynddylan ap Cyndrwyn of southern Powys in the mid-seventh century. The fortunes of the kingdom on Cyngen's death are difficult to determine: he did have sons, but it is not known whether they succeeded on Cyngen's death or whether Rhodri Mawr annexed what was left of Powys on account of his mother's connection with the kingdom.

DAVID E. THORNTON

Sources J. Williams ab Ithel, ed., *Annales Cambriae*, Rolls Series, 20 (1860) · T. Jones, ed. and trans., *Brenhinedd y Saesson, or, The kings of the Saxons* (1971) [another version of *Brut y tywysogyon*] · T. Jones, ed. and trans., *Brut y tywysogyon, or, The chronicle of the princes: Peniarth MS 20* (1952) · T. Jones, ed. and trans., *Brut y tywysogyon, or, The chronicle of the princes: Red Book of Hergest* (1955) · P. C. Bartrum, ed., *Early Welsh genealogical tracts* (1966) · *ASC*, s.a. 828, 852, 853 [texts A, E] · R. Derolez, 'Dubthach's cryptogram', *L'Antiquité Classique*, 21 (1952), 359–75 · *L'estoire des Engleis by Geffrei Gaimar*, ed. A. Bell, Anglo-Norman Texts, 14–16 (1960) · J. E. Lloyd, *A history of Wales from the earliest times to the Edwardian conquest*, 3rd edn, 2 vols. (1939); repr.

(1988) · N. K. Chadwick, 'Early culture and learning in north Wales', in N. K. Chadwick and others, *Studies in the early British church* (1958), 29–120

Cynidr [St Cynidr, Chenedre, Cinitr] (*fl.* **6th cent.**), founder of churches, is not the subject of any surviving life. He was, however, one of the principal saints of south-east Wales and thus appears in the series of texts claiming kinship between important saints and heroes and the eponymous king of Brycheiniog, Brychan; Cynidr is the patron saint of Glasbury, and his feast day is 8 December in Welsh calendars. An important document about Glasbury, perhaps of the twelfth century, survives in a fifteenth-century manuscript, Douai, MS 322. His churches were all in the same area: Glasbury (Y Glas ar Ŵy, 'the community on the Wye'); Kenderchurch in Archenfield (Lann Cinitr in the Book of Llandaff, not to be confused with Kentchurch); and Llangynidr in Brycheiniog (on the Usk just below its juncture with the Crawnon). Glasbury was clearly the principal church. First, Cynidr is said to be from Maelienydd, which, with Elfael and Ceri, forms the march between the Wye and the Severn. Glasbury, however, is at the far southern end of Elfael, suggesting that it was the main church of both Maelienydd and Elfael. Second, the document in the Douai manuscript begins with a list of the names of thirteen bishops of 'clas Chenedre' before 'they departed to Hereford'. That is to say, at a period before, probably, the twelfth century, the community (*clas*) of Cynidr included bishops. Since Glasbury is 'Y Glas ar Ŵy', 'the community on the Wye', the 'clas Cynidr' is likely to have been based at Glasbury. The list, it may be noted, includes one certain and two other probable English names.

Cynidr was sufficiently important to be worth importing into regional kinship links. According to the *Generatio sancti Egwini*, Cynidr was a brother of Egwine, the saint of Llanigon across the Wye to the east, and of *Cadog of Llancarfan; their father was *Gwynllyw, the eponymous king, and saint, of Gwynllŵg, with his church at St Woolloos, Newport. In the life of Cadog by Lifris, Cynidr appears as a witness for Cadog to guarantee the sanctuary obtained from King Arthur, Maelgwn, Rhun, and Rhain. According to *De situ Brecheniauc*, however, Cynidr's mother was Keingayr (Kehingayr, elsewhere Reingar) daughter of *Brychan, eponymous founder of Brycheiniog. These claims may reflect the situation of Cynidr's other churches, Llangynidr ('church of Cynidr') in Brycheiniog and Llangynidr (Kenderchurch) in Archenfield (Ergyng), the latter being close to Cadog's churches in Gwent Uwch Coed.

T. M. CHARLES-EDWARDS

Sources L. Fleuriot, 'Les évêques de la "Clas Kenedyr", évêché disparu de la région de Hereford', *Études Celtiques*, 15 (1976–7), 225–6 · *ASC*, s.a. 1055 [texts C, D] · J. Earle, ed., *Two of the Saxon chronicles parallel: with supplementary extracts from the others*, rev. C. Plummer, 1 (1892), 186 · P. C. Bartrum, ed., *Early Welsh genealogical tracts* (1966) · W. H. Hart, ed., *Historia et cartularium monasterii Sancti Petri Gloucestriae*, 1, Rolls Series, 33 (1863), 314–16 · R. W. Banks, ed., 'Cartularium prioratus s. Johannis evang. de Brecon', *Archaeologia Cambrensis*, 4th ser., 14 (1883), 221–36, esp. 227 · Lifris, 'Vita sancti Cadoci', *Vitae sanctorum Britanniae et genealogiae*, ed. and trans. A. M. Wade-Evans (1944), 24–141 · S. Baring-Gould and J. Fisher, *The lives of* the *British saints*, 4 vols., Honourable Society of Cymmrodorion, Cymmrodorion Record Series (1907–13) · M. Richards, *Welsh administrative and territorial units* (1969) · P. Sims-Williams, *Journal of Ecclesiastical History* · J. Williams, 'Some particulars concerning the parish of Glasbury', *Archaeologia Cambrensis*, 4th ser., 1 (1870), 306–23

Cynric (*fl.* **6th cent.**), king of the Gewisse, was one of the founders of the royal house of the Gewisse (later known as the West Saxons) and their second recorded king. In the Anglo-Saxon Chronicle he is presented as the son of *Cerdic (*fl.* 6th cent.), and is said to have arrived with him in 495 and to have shared in his early successes against the British. However, in certain genealogies Cynric appears as the grandson of Cerdic, via a son called Creoda who does not feature in the annals at all. In the chronicle Cynric is said to have succeeded to the throne with Cerdic in 519, but his regnal years were counted from 534, said to be the year of Cerdic's death. He is reported to have ruled for twenty-six or twenty-seven years. His successor, his son *Ceawlin, seems to have been given too long a reign in the chronicle, however, and Cynric's dates need to be brought forward, though they cannot be established with any certainty. Following Cerdic's death, Cynric is represented as extending West Saxon control into what is now Wiltshire. In 552 he is recorded as defeating Britons at Old Sarum, and in 556, with the assistance of Ceawlin, as fighting them at Barbury Castle; both are sites of Iron Age hill forts. It is quite possible that these areas of what is now Wiltshire came under the control of Cynric's family in the second half of the sixth century, but it was not necessarily the case that those who opposed them would have been 'British', for there had been Anglo-Saxon settlement in the Salisbury area since the fifth century.

BARBARA YORKE

Sources *ASC*, s.a. 495, 508, 519, 527, 530, 534, 552, 556 · D. N. Dumville, 'The West Saxon genealogical regnal list and the chronology of early Wessex', *Peritia*, 4 (1985), 21–66 · B. Eagles, 'The archaeological evidence for settlement in the fifth to seventh centuries AD', *The medieval landscape of Wessex*, ed. M. Aston and C. Lewis (1994), 13–32 · B. Yorke, *Wessex in the early middle ages* (1995)

Cynwal, Wiliam (d. **1587/8**), Welsh-language poet, the eldest son of John ap Dafydd ap Hywel and his wife, Lowri, daughter of John ap Robert Palcws. He lived at Ysbyty Ifan, Denbighshire, where he combined farming with his profession as a bard; his home in 1567 was Cerrigellgwm. Cynwal married Margred, daughter of Robert Wyn; they had four daughters. Cynwal also had an illegitimate son, Thomas. He was a disciple of Gruffudd Hiraethog, the foremost Welsh bardic teacher of the day; like other of Hiraethog's disciples he inherited some of his manuscripts. Cynwal was awarded the second-highest bardic degree of *disgybl pencerddaidd* at the Caerwys eisteddfod of 1567; his claim that he was later awarded the premier degree of *pencerdd* at a nuptial feast accords with known bardic practice. Cynwal's earliest extant work—an example of the short *englyn* metre—is dated to 1561, but a *cywydd* composed in 1564, described by him as his first ever, marks the beginning of his bardic career proper.

Cynwal's manuscripts—containing not only his own poems, but also genealogical and heraldic matter, a bardic grammar, and bruts—display his familiarity with the main branches of bardic learning; like his teacher, Gruffudd Hiraethog, he possessed particular expertise in genealogy. In addition to over 230 longer poems (*cywyddau* and *awdlau*), some 500 of his *englynion* are extant, many of them combined in lengthy sequences. (Manuscripts containing copies of his poems are held by the National Library of Wales, University of Wales, Bangor, Cardiff Central Library, the British Library, and Christ Church, Oxford.) Cynwal was a competent but intensely traditional poet whose work testifies to the stagnation prevalent in contemporary bardism. The bulk of his output consisted of eulogies and elegies addressed almost exclusively to gentry and clergy in north Wales; he also composed request poems, amatory verse, and poems on religious and moral subjects (many of his *englynion* being in this vein). Among his more interesting poems were two composed in defence of women in response to attacks on the fair sex by other poets; one of these is in the 'free' (accentual) metres, one of only two poems in these metres by Cynwal.

Cynwal is chiefly renowned as the adversary of Edmwnd Prys, archdeacon of Merioneth, in the longest bardic debate (*ymryson*) extant in Welsh. The debate, dated *c.*1581–7, amounted to fifty-four *cywyddau*, of which Cynwal contributed nineteen [see Cywyddwyr (*act. c.*1330–*c.*1650)]. It started with a poem by Prys requesting the gift of a bow from Cynwal for a mutual acquaintance, but the Cambridge-educated archdeacon soon digressed to canvass more important matters. He castigated poets like Cynwal for their mendacious praise poems and for peddling false pedigrees, urging them to displace eulogy with divine poems based on scripture and learned poems based on the arts and sciences. Cynwal's rather limited response to this humanist critique illustrates his conservatism: he deplored Prys's resort to satire, urged him to confine himself to divine matters, decried his lack of a bardic teacher and formal bardic qualifications, and charged him with ignorance of bardic etiquette.

The debate was ended by Cynwal's death, Prys concluding it by diplomatically composing an elegy praising his adversary's bardic learning. Cynwal's will, dated 22 November 1587, was proved on 16 January 1588. He was buried at the parish church of Ysbyty Ifan.

GRUFFYDD ALED WILLIAMS

Sources E. Roberts, 'Wiliam Cynwal', *Transactions of the Denbighshire Historical Society*, 12 (1963), 51–85 · R. Williams, 'Wiliam Cynwal', *Llên Cymru*, 8 (1964–5), 197–213 · G. P. Jones and R. L. Jones, 'Wiliam Cynwal', *Llên Cymru*, 11 (1970–71), 176–204 · S. R. Williams, 'Testun beirniadol o gasgliad llawysgrif Mostyn 111 o waith Wiliam Cynwal ynghyd â rhagymadrodd, nodiadau a geirfa', MA diss., U. Wales, 1965 · G. P. Jones, 'Astudiaeth destunol o ganu Wiliam Cynwal yn llawysgrif (Bangor) Mostyn 4', MA diss., U. Wales, 1969 · R. L. Jones, 'Astudiaeth destunol o awdlau, cywyddau ac englynion gan Wiliam Cynwal', MA diss., U. Wales, 1969 · G. A. Williams, *Ymryson Edmwnd Prys a Wiliam Cynwal* (1986) · *Heraldic visitations of Wales and part of the marches … by Lewys Dwnn*, ed. S. R. Meyrick, 2 vols. (1846) · will dated 22 Nov 1587, proved, 16 Jan 1588, NL Wales,

St Asaph diocese, probate records, copies of wills, 1584–8, fols. 515v–516v

Wealth at death monetary bequests totalling £35 9s. 4d., plus bequests of land, beasts, and moveable goods of unspecified value: St Asaph diocese, probate records, copies of wills, 1584–8, fols. 515v–516v, NL Wales

Cyples, William (1831–1882), philosopher and poet, was born on 31 August 1831 at Longton in Staffordshire. He was the second child of George Cyples and his wife, Ann, *née* Steward. Both parents worked in the potteries. He was largely self-educated but he owed his initial education to his mother, a strong-minded woman. He became a journalist, edited several provincial newspapers, and contributed to many leading periodicals, as well as publishing some anonymous novels, a book of verse—*Pottery Poems*—and an epic poem, *Satan Restored* (1859). This Miltonic epic already testifies to Cyples's philosophical bent; the plot of the redemption of Satan is used to dramatize the theological argument that

> Justice and law are but the lesser forms
> Which love sometimes assumes to hide his face.

Cyples's poetic premise, that even Satan cannot be irretrievably damned since God's justice must be subordinate to his love, is related to the more liberal theological trends of the mid-nineteenth century. The culmination of Cyples's philosophical interests, which were encouraged by J. S. Mill and G. H. Lewes, came with the publication of *An Inquiry into the Process of Human Experience* in 1880, three years after he had moved to London from Nottingham, where he had long been based. The book, couched in a rather ponderous scientific vocabulary, is a response to the physiologically based psychology of Alexander Bain, G. H. Lewes, and Herbert Spencer. Cyples argues against the naïve determinism of their materialist psychology. Making use of some of the strategies of Humean scepticism, he denies that physiology furnishes any evidence for the determination of consciousness by the material world. He proposes instead a model in which what he terms 'the Actualisation of the Ego' (W. Cyples, *An Inquiry into the Process of Human Experience*, 1880, 18 ff), the sense both of self and of a material world, is produced by more or less complex associations internal to the nervous system; for Cyples these associations are the product of habit and are potentially under the control of the will. From this basis of a physiological psychology divested of physical determinism, Cyples goes on to elaborate an account of ethical conduct, and of aesthetic judgement, as a process of progressive self-actualization. The development of physical science is itself an expression of this process, which will finally culminate in the restoration of a mystical religious faith. Cyples's emphasis on self-actualization as the central feature of all forms of knowledge, and his insistence that mysticism was the culmination of science, anticipated the late nineteenth-century revival of interest in occultism. His philosophy was given a critical reception, which focused chiefly on his somewhat clumsy pseudo-scientific vocabulary. He replied to

this in *Mind* (5.390). He died of heart disease at Hammersmith on 24 August 1882. A novel, *Hearts of Gold*, was published posthumously in 1883.   GAVIN BUDGE

Sources DNB · J. Sully, review, *Mind*, 5 (1880), 273–80

Cyprianus, Abraham (*bap.* 1656, *d.* 1718), surgeon and physician, was baptized on 7 January 1656 in the Oudekerk of Amsterdam, the son of a surgeon, Allardus Cyprianus, and Sarah Beijerlant. Cyprianus studied philosophy at the Amsterdam Athenaeum, and in 1678, presumably intending to practise medicine, visited the famous Paris hospitals with Pieter Guenellon the younger. On returning, Cyprianus became a member of the Amsterdam surgeons' guild (23 June 1680), and also took an MD at Utrecht with a thesis, 'De carie ossis' (22 November 1680). He and Hillegonde Sara Aernouts published their banns on 25 February 1683 and were married shortly thereafter. In his practice, like his father before him, Cyprianus gained a reputation for being particularly good at the surgical removal of bladder stones and in 1684 earned the office of Amsterdam city surgeon and lithotomist. He also joined the city's Collegium Medicum and became an active member of the important, if informal, scientific academy known as the Collegium Privatum Amstelodamense. It is probably through this later group that he met John Locke during Locke's period of exile in the Netherlands.

In February 1689, after the coup d'état of William of Orange, Locke returned to England, and, soon after, Cyprianus followed him. He returned to the Netherlands in the autumn, and then sailed back to London in March 1690. From Locke's correspondence it appears that Cyprianus returned to Amsterdam before April 1692, when he was preparing to pay a visit to England once more; apparently he travelled freely back and forth between England and the Netherlands. The regents of the Dutch University of Franeker offered Cyprianus the post of medical, anatomical, and surgical professor on 6 May 1693, with the large salary of 1600 gulders per annum, and on 22 June 1693 he took up the post with an oration *De chirurgia encomiastica* (which was published). The University of Leiden offered him a professorship of theoretical medicine and chemistry in April 1694, but he declined it. In 1696 Cyprianus successfully performed a lithotomy on the influential Sir Thomas Millington, which was later described in *Epistola historiam exhibens … ad Th. Millington* (1700). Millington is known to have later extravagantly praised Cyprianus's abilities. That same summer of 1696, part of a letter of Cyprianus's to a Dr Sylvestre was published in the *Philosophical Transactions*, reporting on a new-born child born with 'a large wound in the breast, supposed to proceed from the force of [maternal] imagination' (*PTRS*, 19/221, 1696, 221, 291–2). Cyprianus continued to travel: he is recorded as obtaining a royal pass to sail to the Netherlands in July 1697, but he was back in London again by December 1697, prepared to testify in a malpractice trial against an older, rival Dutch lithotomist, Joannes Groenevelt.

Cyprianus became a licentiate of the Royal College of Physicians on 30 September 1699. Hans Sloane nominated him for a Royal Society fellowship on 30 November 1700; he is recorded among the 'persons of other nations' on the society's rolls until 1713 (after which he is listed as British). His book on Millington's operation appeared in 1700, as did his work describing the extraction of a foetus of twenty-one months (the result of an extra-uterine pregnancy), *Epistola historiam exhibens foetus humani post XXI. menses ex uteri tuba*. In October 1701 he agreed to instruct two surgeons of St Thomas's Hospital in lithotomy. He was known to other European surgeons as very skilled and knowledgeable, although the English translator of Boerhaave's *Aphorisms* mentions in 1742 that Cyprianus's attempts to discover a lithontriptic medicine were in vain, since he worked from Van Helmont's theory that stones were due to an increase in the spirituous and volatile parts of the blood. While there is no record of his having joined the Dutch church at Austin Friars, London, it was there that he was buried on 2 May 1718, in Heer Decker's grave, near the consistory, a place of honour.

HAROLD J. COOK

Sources annals, RCP Lond. · 'Register of baptisms, 1602–1874, marriages ... and burials, 1671–1853, of the Dutch church, Austin Friars', GL, MS 7382 · Gemeentearchief, Amsterdam · *CSP dom.*, 1697 · J. H. Hessels, ed., *Register of the attestations or certificates of membership, confessions of guilt, certificates of marriages, betrothals, publications of banns etc. preserved in the Dutch Reformed Church, Austin Friars, London, 1568 to 1872* (1892) · F. N. L. Poynter, *The journal of James Yonge* (1963) · *The correspondence of John Locke*, ed. E. S. De Beer, 8 vols. (1976–89) · *Œuvres complètes de Christiaan Huygens*, ed. Société Hollandaise des Sciences, 22 vols. (1888–1950), vol. 8 · *Boerhaave's aphorisms: concerning the knowledge and cure of diseases* (1742) · G. A. Lindeboom, *Dutch medical biography* (1984) · M. Hunter, *The Royal Society and its fellows, 1660–1700: the morphology of an early scientific institution*, 2nd edn (1994) · H. J. Cook, *Trials of an ordinary doctor: Joannes Groenevelt in 17th-century London* (1994) · F. G. Parsons, *The history of St Thomas's Hospital*, 3 vols. (1932–6)

Likenesses portrait, Rijksprentenkabinet, Amsterdam

Cyriax, James Henry [*formerly* Hendrik Edgar] (1904–1985), orthopaedic physician, was born on 27 October 1904 at 71 Oakley Street, Chelsea, London, the son of Edgar Ferdinand Cyriax and his wife, Annjuta, formerly Kellgren. Both parents were medical doctors with a practice in London devoted to the treatment of musculoskeletal disorders by exercise and manipulation. His paternal grandfather, Julius Friedrich Theodor Cyriax, was a manufacturing chemist who had emigrated from Germany as a young man bearing a licence to manufacture and sell salicylates—later to become an important drug in musculoskeletal disorders; he had been a patient of Cyriax's maternal grandfather, Jonas Henrik Kellgren, a Swedish army officer who had migrated to England and established a school of Swedish gymnastics and a private hospital in London. Cyriax was educated at University College School, London, Gonville and Caius College, Cambridge, where he rowed, and at St Thomas's Hospital medical school. He qualified MRCS LRCP in 1929 and graduated MD in 1938, the title of his dissertation being 'The pathology and treatment of chronic sprain of the elbow'. A subsequent essay on the subject won him the Heberden prize in 1943. He was admitted MRCP by examination in 1954, but curiously for a man of his distinction he was never elected

a fellow, possibly because of the rivalry he provoked within his peer group. It seems that one faction containing some of his colleagues at St Thomas's championed his cause, but other fellows opposed his election on the grounds of his failure to establish a scientific validation of his methods.

After qualification Cyriax became house surgeon to the department of orthopaedic surgery at St Thomas's and rapidly saw the need for an equivalent medical department. The department and school of massage and medical gymnastics had been established by James Mennell and Minnie Randall SRN after the First World War; Mennell retired in 1936, and two years later Rowley Bristow, an orthopaedic surgeon, was put in overall charge of the department. Beneath him Phillip Bauwens ran the electrical department and Cyriax the massage department. Cyriax was appointed assistant medical officer in 1937. To maintain parity between the two departments patients always received treatment from both sections regardless of their needs. However, after the Second World War the orthopaedic department relinquished overall control and the two coalesced into the single department of physical medicine.

Cyriax's early publications concerned tennis elbow and carpal tunnel syndrome. His work on the cervical and lumbar spine was truly pioneering and together with his contribution to the shoulder fully recognized the new concept of referred pain. He was largely responsible for propagating the idea that sciatica was due to a 'slipped disc' and that the pain could be averted by epidural injections of local anaesthetic. Not all his ideas were novel, but the doggedness with which he pursued them was sometimes provocative. Cyriax married first Leonora Rosina Anna (Mono) Capello, Italy's first female barrister. A son, George (b. 1935), and a daughter, Camilla (b. 1939), were born before their parents' divorce. In 1947 Cyriax married Patricia Jane McClintock (b. 1919), a physiotherapist. They had two sons, Peter and Oliver.

Cyriax was a wonderful clinician with a powerful sense of logic. His persuasive arguments were based on a very strong self-belief and his enthusiasm for work was insatiable. He wrote and spoke fluently. Besides over thirty lesser publications, his main contribution is his two-volume *Textbook of Orthopaedic Medicine*. Volume 1, *The Diagnosis of Soft Tissue Lesions* (1947), went into eight editions. It expounded his systematic method for diagnosis by the meticulous taking of the history, and by physical examination in the whole range of soft tissue disorders. This was a major contribution as the investigative technology of the time could not contribute, blood tests and X-rays being largely irrelevant. Volume 2, *The Treatment of Soft Tissue Disorders by Massage and Injection* (1944), went into ten editions. It was a manual to guide doctors injecting local anaesthetics and corticosteroids and for physiotherapists giving treatment by massage and friction. Cyriax was a publisher's nightmare: after publication his daily notes for additions and amendments to his main textbook usually led to a new edition being available long before its predecessor had sold out.

Cyriax thrived on hard work: never an evening or week-end passed without his enhancing his *magnum opus*. His reputation spread as an arch-manipulator. He was often perceived as the flamboyant practitioner, sleeves rolled up, tugging or twisting at some part of the spine, a drama which produced relief, often with the accompaniment of a clunk or a click of the heel. However, for the *cognoscenti* and his many disciples his main contributions lay in history-taking and clinical examination. Cyriax despised and had no time for those who did not accept his logic, and went out of his way to irritate the 'old buffers'. His contact with orthopaedic medicine—a term he coined—and St Thomas's Hospital were virtually unbroken until his retirement from the National Health Service. He allegedly worked until the last moment permitted under the regulations of the time—midnight, 31 December of the year in which his sixty-fifth birthday occurred.

In Britain Cyriax was somewhat outside the main stream of medicine. In the late 1960s he co-founded with colleagues the Institute of Orthopaedic Medicine. This gradually fell away and in 1979 he founded the Society of Orthopaedic Medicine, which included physiotherapists. In addition to teaching doctors, its function was to raise the professional status of physiotherapists, in recognition of which he was made a fellow of the Chartered Society of Physiotherapy. When the British Association of Manual Medicine was founded as a forum to bring osteopaths and chiropractors together with doctors, Cyriax sat uneasily as its first president. The association changed its name to the British Institute of Musculoskeletal Medicine and sponsored a diploma through the Society of Apothecaries. Rather more recognition came from abroad. Cyriax was honorary president of the French Society of Orthopaedic Medicine and visiting professor at the University of Rochester, New York.

An ebullient character, Cyriax devoted his life to his work and to his physiotherapists. His regular parties for physiotherapists and junior doctors were legendary. He was frequently seen dressed totally in green with the initials JHC on the brogue toecaps of his shoes. His consulting room was filled with green malachite. He did much to propagate and sustain the principles of soft tissue medicine among rheumatologists and physiotherapists and still has a large following in the UK and abroad. An example of his logic could be seen as he walked backwards along Lambeth Palace Road and onto Westminster Bridge 'so as to see the arrival of the bus'. He died at University College Hospital, Camden, London, on 17 June 1985 and was buried at Hampstead cemetery.

JOHN A. MATHEWS

Sources personal knowledge (2004) · private information (2004) [Royal College of Physicians, Addenbrooke's Hospital, British Society of Rheumatology] · *The Times* (25 Jan 1985) · *BMJ* (6 July 1985), 61 · *Physiotherapy*, 71/7 (1985), 325 · *Physiotherapy*, 71/8 (1985), 364 [letter] · b. cert. · m. cert. [Patricia Jane McClintock] · d. cert. · *WW*
Likenesses photograph, repro. in *Physiotherapy*, 71/7 (1985), 325
Wealth at death £228,089: probate, 27 Sept 1985, *CGPLA Eng. & Wales*

Cywyddwyr (*act. c.*1330–*c.*1650), Welsh-language poets, active from the late middle ages, are distinguished by their use of the *cywydd* as their principal metrical form.

Origin The origins of the *cywydd* metre are uncertain, but it seems likely that it belonged to the domain of popular song before it was adopted by bardic poets in the second quarter of the fourteenth century, when it was given its strict form of couplets consisting of seven-syllable lines rhyming on stressed and unstressed syllables alternately, each line containing one of the elaborate harmonies of *cynghanedd*. The development of the *cywydd* was an essential part of the tendency to enliven and popularize the traditional court poetry in the period following the loss of political independence in the late thirteenth century [*see* Gogynfeirdd (*act. c.*1080–1285)]. The new metre coincided with an increased receptivity to continental literary fashions, which did much to invigorate Welsh poetry in the fourteenth century. The first poet to realize the potential of the *cywydd* was *Dafydd ap Gwilym, probably in the 1330s. Its use was confined initially to light love poetry, but Dafydd also took the very significant step of employing it in a small group of highly personal eulogies to his patron, *Ifor ap Llywelyn (Ifor Hael). The *awdl* remained the appropriate form for traditional praise poetry until Dafydd's younger contemporary *Iolo Goch began to employ the *cywydd* for that purpose about the middle of the fourteenth century. By the end of the century the new metre was firmly established as the main medium for all poetic functions, and it was to remain so for over 200 years. Several thousand poems have survived from these three centuries, the work of some 400 poets.

The older *awdl* metres continued to be used quite extensively by the *cywyddwyr* throughout the later middle ages, as did the more succinct *englyn* form. The poets of this period are therefore sometimes distinguished by the social status of their patrons, rather than by their preferred metrical form, as *beirdd yr uchelwyr* ('the poets of the gentry'). After the demise of the independent princes the *uchelwyr* class formed the aristocracy that provided patronage for the poets. As landowners who played a prominent role in local government, the *uchelwyr* mostly supported the new order imposed by the English in Wales, but nevertheless they remained loyal to their native language and culture. By the later fifteenth century a number of families of English descent had become prominent patrons of the poets, such as the Salesburys of Denbighshire.

The praise of the poets was valuable to the *uchelwyr* in confirming their status as leaders of Welsh society, and in addition the new lightness of style made the poetry popular entertainment in noble houses. The fact that the poets were often of noble birth themselves (such as Llywelyn Goch ap Meurig Hen of the Nannau family in Merioneth) made for a closer relationship between poet and patron than in the age of the princes. Many of the patrons seem to have taken a keen interest in the poetic craft, and a few actually attained high standing as poets on an amateur basis. The most notable example of the gentleman poet is *Dafydd ab Edmwnd; less well known, but probably more representative, is Ieuan Gethin of Glamorgan (*fl.* 1437–1490), whose bold disregard for convention clearly reflects his amateur status.

Organization and performance These amateurs were very much exceptions to the rule, however, and the bardic order was primarily a professional body with strict rules governing the training and qualification of apprentices, not dissimilar to other craft guilds of the middle ages. Statutes purporting to have been drawn up by Gruffudd ap Cynan, king of Gwynedd in the twelfth century, cannot in fact be traced back beyond their sixteenth-century manuscript copies, but nevertheless they probably do reflect bardic practice over the preceding two centuries. A master poet (*pencerdd*) would be responsible for the training of one or more pupils, which would no doubt have consisted mainly of study and imitation of the classics of the bardic tradition extending back to Taliesin and Aneirin. A notable example of a bardic teacher in the sixteenth century is *Gruffudd Hiraethog, whose pupils were the outstanding poets of the Elizabethan period, such as *Wiliam Llŷn, Siôn Tudur, and Simwnt Fychan, all of whom graduated at the second Caerwys eisteddfod of 1567. There are instances of the poetic craft being passed on over several generations within a family, but it does not seem to have been confined to bardic families to the extent that it was in medieval Ireland.

One of the major changes consequent on the loss of the royal courts was that even poets of the highest standing were forced to become itinerant to a much greater degree than ever before. Whereas the *pencerdd* formerly held an established position in a prince's court, in the age of the *uchelwyr* he did not belong to any household in particular, but travelled from one noble house to another. The poets were especially welcome at the major religious festivals and on local saints' days, as well as on the occasion of weddings, funerals, and other noteworthy events such as the completion of a new house. They would undertake extensive circuits covering the length and breadth of Wales, and thus fostered the development of a common literary language and even a sense of Welsh national identity.

Very little is known about the actual performance of the poetry. It seems that poems would normally have been recited before an audience assembled in a nobleman's hall. The recitation was sometimes by the poet himself, or alternatively by a professional reciter (*datgeiniad*). Reference is sometimes made to harp accompaniment, but virtually nothing is known about the relationship between words and music. Poems would usually have been composed without recourse to writing, and although copies of praise poems may have been kept by recipients in a family manuscript, there was a very strong tradition of oral transmission extending well into the sixteenth century. From about the middle of the fifteenth century it became common for poets to keep copies of their own work; the most striking holograph manuscripts are those of Lewys Glyn Cothi.

Repertory The poetry of the *cywyddwyr* can be divided into several clearly defined genres according to topic. Most

common, and no doubt fundamental to the poets' livelihood, was eulogy. Bardic praise projected an idealized image of the nobleman based on the twin poles of ferocity as a warrior and courteous civility as head of a household. This standard pattern was tailored to fit the individual by the addition of such details as genealogical references (sometimes, especially in the later period, at considerable length), heraldic devices, offices held, and descriptions of the household. This information can be useful to the historian, but in view of the element of exaggeration and idealization it must be treated with caution. At their worst praise poems were mere mechanical flattery. At their best, in the work of masters such as *Guto'r Glyn and *Tudur Aled (*c.*1465-1525x7), as well as lesser-known practitioners such as Tudur Penllyn (*c.*1420–*c.*1485) and Lewys Môn (*fl.* 1485–1527), they were witty and inventive compositions in which particular details took on a wider social significance. Nor did subservience prevent poets from proffering advice to their patrons and even criticizing their behaviour, as when Dafydd ab Edmwnd urged an Anglesey nobleman not to marry an Englishwoman, or when Tudur Aled sought to bring a family feud to an end for the good of the community.

An important subcategory of eulogy was the elegy. The commemoration of the dead had been one of the poet's primary functions since the beginnings of the bardic tradition, and by the later middle ages it had developed into an elaborate convention in which the poet's expression of his personal grief represented the loss suffered by the community as a whole. Elegies would be performed on a specified day some time after the funeral, and would also serve as prayers for the soul of the departed and declarations of the continuity of the family. Another mode of praise which was developed extensively in the work of the *cywyddwyr* was the *cywydd gofyn*, a request poem soliciting a gift either for the poet himself or on behalf of a patron. The gifts requested ranged from harps to millstones, but the most common types were horses, clothing, and weapons, all representing the nobility of the giver. The chief interest of these poems lies in the imaginative descriptions of the gifts using the technique of serial metaphors known as *dyfalu*. Tudur Aled was an outstanding exponent of the *cywydd gofyn*, and his request for a horse from the abbot of the Cistercian house of Aberconwy Abbey is justly famous for its vivid description.

Almost all of the *cywyddwyr* composed some devotional poetry, which often consisted of imprecations to the saints or even versifications of saints' lives. Some poets seem to have been particularly devout, such as *Lewys Glyn Cothi (*fl.* 1447–1489), the moralist *Siôn Cent, and Maredudd ap Rhys (*fl.* 1440–1483). Another genre which is represented in the work of most poets is the love lyric. Again, some appear to have specialized in this type of poem, most notably the great Dafydd ap Gwilym, whose influence is apparent in the work of his fifteenth-century successors such as *Bedo Brwynllys and Ieuan Deulwyn. The conventions of courtly love dominated the love poetry of the period, but that is not to say that it had no basis in personal experience. Evidence from court proceedings has now shown that poems by Ieuan Dyfi (*fl. c*.1500) complaining about his unfaithful mistress, Anni Goch, do indeed reflect real events.

Another important item in the poets' repertory was satire. The Celtic bard was traditionally believed to have the power to cause harm and even death by reciting a cursing poem. Such a belief was still current in late medieval Wales, as shown by a number of truly malignant satires on noblemen who were foolish enough to shut their doors on the bards. But satire also had a more benign function in mock flytings, in which one poet would be set up as a *cyff clêr* to be verbally abused by others as ribald entertainment at feast-day gatherings. Exchanges of a more sober nature took place in the form of debates (*ymrysonau*) on the principles of the poetic art, such as *Gruffudd Gryg's attack on the exaggerations of Dafydd ap Gwilym's love poetry at the beginning of the *cywydd* period, and the lengthy *ymryson* between the professional bard Wiliam *Cynwal and the Renaissance humanist Edmwnd *Prys in the 1580s.

Popular beliefs concerning the supernatural powers of the bard also came into play in the highly specialized genre of vaticinatory poetry, the *cywydd brud*, prophesying an ultimate Welsh victory over the Saxons and the regaining of their rightful sovereignty over the island of Britain. The tradition can be traced back at least as far as the tenth century, but it flourished especially during the Wars of the Roses, when both Lancastrians and Yorkists were able to lay claim to the prophesied deliverer. Bardic support weighed most heavily on the side of the Tudor family, and the whole prophetic tradition virtually came to an end when the Welshman Henry Tudor attained the throne in 1485. Pre-eminent among exponents of the *cywydd brud* was *Dafydd Llwyd o Fathafarn; other notable specialists in this field in the fifteenth century were Dafydd Gorlech and Robin Ddu of Anglesey.

The system of training for the professional bardic order seems to have excluded women entirely. However, a few women did learn and practise the poetic craft as amateurs. The only woman by whom a substantial body of strict-metre poetry has survived is Gwerful Mechain (*fl.* 1460–1500), who was associated with a circle of poets in Powys that included Dafydd Llwyd o Fathafarn and Ieuan Dyfi. Gwerful composed a defence of women in response to a virulent misogynist attack by Ieuan, and was involved in more than one bawdy exchange. She has become infamous for her erotic verse, including a poem in praise of the female sexual organs, but in fact this is only one of a wide range of topics in her work.

Decline A number of factors contributed to the decline of the medieval bardic order in the sixteenth century, but the one decisive cause was the increasing Anglicization of the Welsh gentry consequent on the closer ties between England and Wales in the Tudor period. As a result of its innate conservatism the bardic order was unable to adapt to either the new social order or the print culture of the Renaissance, and fell into terminal decline as it lost both

patronage and social standing. This was of course a gradual process, and the tradition continued longer in some areas than others. Wiliam Llŷn (1534/5–1580) is generally regarded as the last of the master poets of the middle ages, but the Phylip family of Ardudwy maintained bardic practices in Merioneth well into the seventeenth century. By that time it was becoming increasingly difficult to make a living from poetry alone, and as poets fell back on other trades the professional bardic order came to an end. The old tradition did not die out altogether, but was continued in rudimentary form by folk poets, who also preserved the social function of poetry within their communities.

Even before the end of the bardic tradition the work of the *cywyddwyr* had become the subject of study by Renaissance humanists such as John Davies of Mallwyd, who referred to them as 'guardians of the old language' (much of which he preserved in his Welsh–Latin dictionary of 1632). The medieval poetic art was revived by the neo-classical movement of the eighteenth century, and passed on into modern times by the institution of the eisteddfod. The preparation of reliable editions of the works of the *cywyddwyr* has been one of the principal tasks of modern Welsh scholarship, and it is a task by no means yet complete. Saunders Lewis has done more than any other critic to illuminate the aesthetics and social philosophy of medieval Welsh poetry, and to inspire veneration for the period of the *cywyddwyr* as the golden age of Welsh literature, when poetry of the highest artistry was fully integrated into the society that produced it.

DAFYDD JOHNSTON

Sources T. Parry, *Hanes llenyddiaeth Gymraeg hyd 1900* (1944) · A. O. H. Jarman and G. R. Hughes, eds., *A guide to Welsh literature*, 2: *1282–c.1550* (1979)

Czaplicka, Marya Antonina [Marie Antoinette] (1884–1921), anthropologist, was born on 25 October 1884 in Warsaw, daughter of Felix Lubicz Czaplicki and Sophie Zawisza. Educated and trained as a geography teacher in Warsaw and Libau (now Liepaja, Latvia) between 1894 and 1905, from 1906 to 1909 she studied natural history in the Warsaw Museum, giving private tuition and acting as a secretary to pay her way. Aged twenty-six endowed with 'a considerable amount of personal charm' (Czaplicka MSS), the first woman to obtain a Mianowski fellowship, she studied ethnology at the London School of Economics in 1910, and met the American anthropologist Henry Usher Hall. At Somerville College, Oxford (1911–12), she obtained a diploma in anthropology. R. Marett, reader in anthropology, eager to combine her scientific and linguistic qualifications (she knew German, Russian, English, Ukrainian, and her native Polish and was to learn Uralic and Tungusic languages), thought she 'might profitably devote herself to a synthesis of recent Russian work on the tribes of the Far North' (Czaplicka MSS). He somewhat lightheartedly suggested a monograph; she enthusiastically agreed, being 'keen almost to a fault' (Czaplicka MSS). Grants from Somerville and Bedford colleges enabled the impoverished scholar to complete *Aboriginal Siberia* (1914).

Little fieldwork had been done in north-central Siberia, the vanishing lifestyle of whose peoples involved 'magico-

Marya Antonina Czaplicka (1884–1921), by F. A. Swaine, pubd 1916

protect its fledgeling democracy against Bolshevism. Strongly opposed to militarism, she fulminated against the 'unscientific' German-fomented pan-Turkism. Such views coupled with rare expertise led to work in the Foreign Office, the Admiralty, and the war trade intelligence department, where she merited official Polish appreciation for 'devotion to her country'. Her political views appear in *Turks of Central Asia* (1918), 'The Siberian colonist or Sibiriak' in (W. Stephens, *The Soul of Russia*, 1916), 'A plea for Siberia' (*New Europe*, 28 March 1918), and 'Poland' (*Geographical Journal*, 53, 1919).

In 1920 the Royal Geographical Society's Murchison grant recognized Czaplicka's 'ethnographical and geographical work in northern Siberia'. A fellow of the Royal Geographical Society and the Royal Anthropological Institution, she lectured in anthropology at Bristol University from 1920, becoming 'quite the life' of the university speleological society and the Clifton Ladies' Debating Society. Her sudden death in Bristol on 27 May 1921 was a great shock. The official explanation, heart failure, concealed suicide by poison. A Polish Catholic, Marya Czaplicka must have been desperate. Why should a 36-year-old woman with a substantial academic record and promising future take her own life? Failure to obtain a cherished permanent university post 'was understandably a great blow, for she was taking out letters of naturalization in order to be qualified for it' (Czaplicka MSS). She may have concluded that a foreigner and woman could never achieve acceptance. A contributory reason may have been debts of over £200. Marett wrote: 'she struck fire out of whatever she touched … Too late her many friends realised that she was living on her organic capital' (Marett, 106). Unmarried, Czaplicka left no descendants. She was buried in Bristol. In her work she had broken new ground: reclassifying the Siberian peoples, treating shamanism in a novel way, and presenting the first systematic account of arctic hysteria (Czaplicka, *Aboriginal Siberia*, vi). She provided substantial contributions to the *Encyclopaedia of Religion and Ethics* (ed. J. Hastings, 1916–21), investigated Cossack communities (*Journal of the Central Asian Society*, 5, 1918), and links between environment and religion ('Influence of environment upon the religious ideas and practices of the Aborigines of northern Asia', *Folklore*, 25, 1914). Had she lived she might have left a scientific legacy similar to that of her contemporary and correspondent Bronislaw Malinowski (Collins and Urry, 188–20).

The Marya Antonina Czaplicka Fund was established in 1971 in her memory by a bequest from the anthropologist Mrs Barbara Aitken (Barbara Freire-Marreco) to assist members of Somerville College studying the ancient world, anthropology, or the natural sciences to attend conferences and meetings abroad.

DAVID N. COLLINS

Sources M. Czaplicka, *My Siberian year* (1916) • M. Czaplicka, *Aboriginal Siberia* (1914) • R. Haviland, *A summer on the Yenesei* (1915) • R. Marett, *Man*, 21 (1921), 105–6 • *The Times* (30 May 1921) • H. Hall, 'The Siberian expedition', *Museum Journal* [University of Pittsburgh], 6 (1916), 27–45 • D. Curtis, 'When ignorance was bliss', *Nineteenth Century and After*, 78 (1915), 609–30 • M. Czaplicka, 'Siberia and some Siberians', *Journal of the Manchester Geographical Society*,

religious institutions … of a very special and psychologically curious type' (Czaplicka MSS). To fill the gap this young woman became one of few Poles to volunteer for a year's exile in Siberia: 'the outcome of my own eager desire and interest' (Czaplicka, *Siberian Year*, 4). A Mary Ewart scholarship at Somerville in 1914 enabled her to visit the northern Yenisey tundra with Henry Hall of the Philadelphia University Museum and two female companions. Czaplicka and Hall wintered with the nomads. In 1915 they returned via wartime Petrograd and Warsaw. Her books and letters ignore illness, seasickness bad enough to cause vomiting of blood, lack of money, inadequate supplies, rare correspondence, harsh temperatures, lack of sanitary facilities, glutinous mud in spring, mosquitoes and dust in summer. Rare glimpses of dry humour and a lyrical joy at tundra flowers and the northern lights betray little about her emotions or relationships. One Siberian companion mentioned her 'tireless energy and a most winning address [which], even apart from her intellectual gifts and knowledge of the world, marked Miss Czaplicka's striking personality' (Haviland, 3). The other companion, Dora Curtis, tartly remarked that she would walk for 35 kilometres up to the knees in tundra moss 'with only a piece of bread and appear unsatisfied in the end … she can accomplish these feats because she has great spirit but afterwards she pays for them dearly' (Czaplicka MSS). Relevant publications include *My Siberian Year* (1915), 'On the track of the Tungus' (*Scottish Geographical Magazine*, 33, 1917), and 'Siberia and some Siberians' (*Journal of the Manchester Geographical Society*, 32, 1916, 27–42).

Subsequently (1916–19) Mary Ewart lecturer in ethnology at Oxford, Czaplicka was a member of Lady Margaret Hall, where she 'instituted a most enterprising Folk-Lore Club' (Marett, 105) and lectured in Britain and the USA. Politically she favoured an independent, democratic Poland, and advocated allied intervention in Siberia to

32 (1916), 27–42 · *Somerville Students' Association Report* (1911–13) · Somerville College, Oxford, Czaplicka MSS · D. Collins, 'Letters from Siberia by M. A. Czaplicka, 1914', *Sibirica*, 1 (1995), 61–84 · D. Collins and J. Urry, 'A flame too intense for mortal body to support', *Anthropology Today*, 13 (1997), 18–20 · D. Collins, introduction, *Collected works of M. A. Czaplicka*, ed. D. Collins, 1 (1999), ix–xxxviii **Archives** Pitt-Rivers Museum, Oxford · Somerville College, Oxford | University of Pennsylvania Museum, Pittsburgh, Henry Hall/Czaplicka MSS · University of Pennsylvania Museum, Pittsburgh, Henry Hall MSS **Likenesses** F. A. Swaine, photograph, repro. in Czaplicka, *My Siberian year*, frontispiece [*see illus.*] · double portrait, photograph (with H. Hall), Pitt-Rivers Museum, Oxford **Wealth at death** debts of over £200: *The Times*, 30 May 1921

Czarnikow, (Julius) Caesar (1838–1909), sugar broker, was born at Sondershausen, Germany, the third son in a family of seven sons and two daughters of Moritz Czarnikow (*b.* 1795), agent and commissioner of commerce to the prince of Sondershausen, and of his wife, Johanne Bar (*b.* 1812), who had married in 1828. The family origins were probably Polish-Jewish, and Johanne was certainly Jewish.

Little is known of Czarnikow before 1854, when he joined a London sugar broker as a clerk. Early on he was especially connected with the broker firm of Weber and Biddulph, which provided him with useful introductions to the Biddulph and Martin banking families. In 1861 he took British nationality and became a 'sworn broker' by licence of the corporation of London; both were essential preliminaries to establishing in March 1861 his own business of Czarnikow & Co., colonial brokers. In 1863 he married Louisa, daughter of the late Revd Spencer Ashlin, a Scottish nonconformist minister; they had a son, Horace, later of Cranford Hall, Northampton, and a daughter, Ada Louisa, later the wife of Colonel Charles Jenkinson. His wife, for long an invalid following a carriage accident, died in 1911.

Czarnikow specialized in the raw sugar trade when sugar consumption was rising rapidly and when beet sugar was replacing cane. He dealt in beet sugar from when it was first exported from Germany and in this presumably enjoyed a competitive advantage, though his rivals reckoned that 'an almost uncanny' ability to 'foreshadow market movements' was the real secret of his success (Janes and Sayers, 53).

In 1871 and 1881 Czarnikow established agencies in the major refining centres of Glasgow (Czarnikow and Boog) and Liverpool (Czarnikow and Cox), and in 1891 he opened a New York business (Czarnikow, MacDougall & Co.). His firm became especially known for its weekly market circular, known generally as 'Czarnikow's Circular', first published in 1863. 'Probably everyone in the European and TransAtlantic sugar trade would agree that in many respects the Circular is second to none', reckoned one observer (Hutcheson, 127). By then Czarnikow had emerged as a major figure in the international sugar trade and he enjoyed excellent contacts in the City, especially with German houses such as Schroders and Kleinworts. His firm maintained a distinctive German character: two English employees named Smith were differentiated as

'Grosser Smith' and 'Kleiner Smith', and his partners at the time of his death were all continental migrants to the City of London.

In 1888, in an attempt to win back to London trade lost to new continental futures exchanges and in the face of fierce opposition from London's established brokers, Czarnikow was the leader in forming the London Produce Clearing House, the forerunner of the International Commodities Clearing House and the City's first futures market. He was its deputy chairman (1888–1907) and later its chairman (1907–9). He also chaired Sena Sugar Factory Ltd, formed in 1906 and owner of sugar estates in Mozambique. He opposed sugar bounties and favoured empire preference.

Caesar Czarnikow was short and stocky, had unflagging energy, and smoked large cigars. His leadership was autocratic and he was impulsive and short-tempered; he was capable of sacking and re-employing the same person on the same day. He was also penny-pinching, but his generosity was referred to and his most noted charitable act appears as a £1000 donation to the Zoological Society of London for the construction of an aviary at London Zoo. Possessing a passion for flowers and animals, Czarnikow once owned, *inter alia*, monkeys, emus, eagles, and, briefly, a bear.

In 1901 Czarnikow acquired a country estate at Effingham Hill, Surrey, and he lived at 103 Eaton Square, London, where he died suddenly from a heart attack on 17 April 1909; he had done a full day's work the day before. He was buried at Effingham on 21 April 1909. His leadership in the international sugar trade was then without dispute. His obituary in *The Times* described his business as 'the largest of its kind in the world'; three years earlier a leading City banker had observed that 'he seems to be known as a sort of king of the sugar market … & to be the best judge of the sugar market going' (Kynaston, 337). His son never joined the Czarnikow partnership and his family's connection with the firm ended soon after his death.   JOHN ORBELL

Sources A. Kidner, 'Czarnikow, Julius Caesar', *DBB* · H. H. Janes and H. J. Sayers, *The story of Czarnikow* (1963) · J. M. Hutcheson, *Notes on the sugar industry* (1901) · D. Kynaston, *The City of London*, 2 (1995) · *The Times* (19 April 1909), 11d · J. Wake, *Kleinwort Benson: a history of two families in banking* (1997) · CGPLA Eng. & Wales (1909) · *The Times* (22 April 1909) **Likenesses** H. von Herkomer, oils, *c.*1901, repro. in Janes and Sayers, *Story of Czarnikow*; known to be at Czarnikow & Co. in 1963 **Wealth at death** £701,117 11s. 10d.: probate, 29 May 1909, CGPLA Eng. & Wales

Da. For names including this prefix *see under* the substantive element of the name; for example, for Duarte da Silva *see* Silva, Duarte da.

D'Abernon. For this title name *see* Vincent, Edgar, Viscount D'Abernon (1857–1941).

Daborne, Robert (*c.*1580–1628), playwright, was the son of Robert Daborne sen. (1551–1612), haberdasher, originally of Guildford, Surrey, and Susan Travis (*bap.* 1561, *d.* 1626). The family recorded their pedigree and arms in the visitation of Surrey in 1621. Daborne's father owned the keepership of Castle Garden in Guildford, held by patent from the crown, and leases to twenty plots of land and gardens, with 5 acres of land in the Blackfriars, London (which Robert later attempted to claim). The family held other properties in Norfolk, Surrey, and Hertfordshire. In 1589 Daborne's father was assessed on an income of £50 in Tower ward, London: his investments with other London merchants in two ships reconfirm that he enjoyed a tidy income. However, about 1604 he was forced to borrow £400 from friends to cover his debts; the lenders included the dramatist Sir Cornelius Fermedo, author of *The Governour*. Chiefly responsible for his straitened circumstances was his profligate son Robert, the dramatist, who was notably absent from his father's will.

Robert Daborne's birth date can be estimated at about 1580, based on his matriculation at King's College, Cambridge in 1598. On admission he donated two books to the library, both of them by John Hus, the protestant reformer. There is no evidence to show that Daborne was awarded a degree, but he was later referred to as 'Master of Arts' on the title-page of *The Poor Man's Comfort*. The first part of Daborne's life seems to have been blighted by self-induced poverty and familial conflict. In 1602 he married Anne Younger of Burlingham, Norfolk, daughter of Robert Younger, an attorney of the common pleas. On 20 August 1609 Daborne asked his father-in-law whether he and his family could move temporarily into the Youngers' home in Shoreditch. The couple were virtually homeless, and Daborne could not provide for his family. Shortly after the couple moved in, however, both of Anne's parents died and the situation ended in an acrimonious lawsuit. Three years later, following his father's death, Daborne's mother and a group of creditors sued Daborne, claiming that he tried to hinder the sale of the Blackfriars properties, and that he was indebted to his father for no less than £600.

Daborne was active in the theatrical scene from 1610 when he was a patentee for the Children of the Queen's Revels at the Whitefriars Playhouse. He probably wrote for this company as well, and he continued as a dramatist when they amalgamated with Lady Elizabeth's Men in 1613. In the next several years he collaborated with Cyril Tourneur, Nathan Field, Philip Massinger, and John Fletcher, writing plays at breakneck speed, as did other professional dramatists. Today Daborne is remembered not for his compositions but for his letters written to Philip Henslowe, the theatrical entrepreneur who backed Lady Elizabeth's Men financially (Greg, 67–85). Daborne's missives illustrate important literary and financial aspects of the Jacobean theatre, yet they also demonstrate the sadder aspects of Daborne's life. He seems to have been continually in debt and frantic with work. In 1616 Daborne's second wife, Frances, asked Henslowe, then on his deathbed, to release her husband of his debts. Despite his many collaborations only two of Daborne's single-authored tragedies were published. The first was *A Christian Turned Turk* (1612); the other, *The Poor Man's Comfort* (1655), of which there is a manuscript copy at the British Library (MS Egerton 1994, fols. 268–93). Additionally, commendatory verses by Daborne preface Christopher Brook's (C. B.'s) *Ghost of Richard the Third* (1615).

By 1617 Daborne had left the stage and taken up holy orders. In this profession he seems to have built a much more successful life: he published a sermon at Waterford, Ireland, in 1618, became chancellor there in 1619, then prebendary of Lismore in 1620, and finally dean of Lismore in 1621. He died at Lismore on 23 March 1628. Four years later William Heming, son of the eminent actor John Heming, drew attention to Daborne's dramatic life transition, remarking that he died 'amphibious by the ministry' (Bentley, 3.190).   S. P. CERASANO

Sources D. S. Lawless, 'Robert Daborne, senior', *N&Q*, 222 (1977), 514–16 · M. Eccles, *Brief lives: Tudor and Stuart authors* (1982), 28–36 · W. W. Greg, *Henslowe papers: being documents supplementary to Henslowe's diary* (1907) · D. S. Lawless, 'Some new light on Robert Daborne', *N&Q*, 224 (1979), 142–3 · P. Holloway, 'Robert Daborne: some new information', *N&Q*, 221 (1976), 222 · *DNB* · E. K. Chambers, *The Elizabethan stage*, 4 vols. (1923) · G. E. Bentley, *The Jacobean and Caroline stage*, 7 vols. (1941–68) · W. H. G. Flood, 'Fennor and Daborne at Youghal', *Modern Language Review*, 20 (1925), 321–2 · 'The poor man's comfort', BL, MS Egerton 1994, fols. 268–93 · D. S. Lawless, 'Philip Kingman: some new information', *N&Q*, 224 (1979), 141–2 · B. Maxwell, 'Notes on Robert Daborne's extant plays', *Philological Quarterly*, 50 (1971), 85–98 · W. H. Phelps, 'The early life of Robert Daborne', *Philological Quarterly*, 59 (1980), 1–10
Archives Dulwich College, London, letters to Philip Henslowe

Dacre. For this title name *see* individual entries under Dacre; *see also* Fiennes, Thomas, ninth Baron Dacre (*b.* in or before 1516, *d.* 1541); Fiennes, Gregory, tenth Baron Dacre (1539–1594); Fiennes, Anne, Lady Dacre (*d.* 1595); Lennard, Francis, fourteenth Baron Dacre (1619–1662); Brand, Barbarina, Lady Dacre (1768–1854).

Dacre family (*per. 1542–1716*), gentry, of Lanercost, owed its position in Cumberland to the efforts of Henry VIII and his ministers to extend royal power in north-west England from the 1530s onwards, and particularly at the expense of the Barons Dacre of Gilsland.

The founding father The founder of the Lanercost family, **Sir Thomas Dacre** (*d.* 1565), was the illegitimate son of Thomas *Dacre (1467–1525), the second baron, and an unknown mother, and was first recorded in 1529 as the apparently loyal servant of his half-brother William *Dacre (1500–1563), the second baron's successor. For Thomas Dacre as for others, disillusion with the Gilsland Dacres seems to have followed William's trial for treason in 1534, the more so, perhaps, because he himself appears to have been arrested as a suspected accessory to Lord Dacre's cross-border machinations. By 1535 he was serving as a soldier in Ireland, subsequently returning to Cumberland as an associate of Sir Thomas Wharton, whom the crown was promoting in the north-west as a counterbalance to the Dacres of Gilsland and the Cliffords. Thomas Dacre's abilities were appreciated, but he lacked the resources for office: in September 1537 the third duke of Norfolk, considering possible keepers for Tynedale, described Dacre as 'a quick, sharp man, brought up in practices of such wild people … but he is too poor to serve in that office' (*LP Henry VIII*, 12/2, no. 696).

The decisive change in Thomas Dacre's fortunes came in 1542. On 24 November he fought at Solway Moss, just two days after he was granted in tail male the house and site of the dissolved Augustinian priory of Lanercost, a few miles south of Naworth, the principal residence of Lord Dacre. Thomas was thus ensconced as an agent of royal authority in the Gilsland Dacres' backyard. In December 1545 he was granted a pension of £20, and in either that year or 1547 he was knighted, while by 1552 he was deputy warden of the west march. Perhaps he still lacked the means to enable him to wield authority effectively, for in June that year he successfully petitioned for the churches and estates formerly held by the canons of Lanercost. Concentrated in Gilsland, but with outliers in the west and centre of Cumberland, they had an estimated gross value of just over £70; this may not have constituted riches, but the grant still made Sir Thomas an important landowner.

The preamble to his first will, dated 9 May 1552, suggests that Sir Thomas Dacre was protestant in religion, unlike his staunchly Catholic kinsmen at Naworth. Not surprisingly he lost ground at the accession of Queen Mary, but equally predictably he recovered it under Elizabeth, for in 1559–60 he was sheriff of Cumberland. Moreover, he clearly hoped for the backing of central government as he and his sons engaged in a series of fierce quarrels with the Dacres of Naworth. In October 1559 Sir Ralph Sadler wrote to Sir William Cecil in support of Sir Thomas's elder son, Christopher, allegedly persecuted by Lord Dacre with 'som malyce and great extremyte' in a dispute over hunting rights (BL, Add. MS 33591, fols. 198–9). A year later a hunting party from Naworth rampaged over the Lanercost demesnes, and when Christopher remonstrated Lord Dacre's second son, Leonard, allegedly told him, 'Thou arte a varlett and a knave and I shall breake the payte' (PRO, STAC5/D35/21). The rivalries of the two families were probably exacerbated by the ostentatious building works which Sir Thomas undertook at Lanercost (datable to 1559 from a stained glass window now in the parish church). The west range of the monastic complex became the centre of an imposing residence, with a great hall on its first floor and a four-storey tower at its west end. Lit by large new windows, the hall was decorated within by high-quality wall-paintings, dominated by a huge representation of the Dacre arms.

This show of independence notwithstanding, as long as Lord Dacre was warden of the west march (1549–63) he was probably too strong for Sir Thomas Dacre of Lanercost, who on 19 June 1561 was appointed marshal of the garrison at Berwick. His sojourn there was unhappy, however, and he complained bitterly of arrears of payment. Described as 'old and weak' in June 1563 (CSP for., 1563, 403), he was probably glad to be replaced on 26 February 1564. Lord Dacre was no longer warden now, and later that year Sir Thomas was again appointed sheriff of Cumberland. He probably died on 17 July 1565, since on that day his son Christopher succeeded him as sheriff, holding office until 16 November following. Bishop John Best had thought Sir Thomas suspect in religion, but that may only reflect Best's ardent evangelicalism, for the preamble to

Sir Thomas's second will, made on 7 July, in which he required burial 'in my parish Churche of Lanercoste', was impeccably protestant (Cumbria AS, Carlisle, MS DMh.10/7/5, 401). He had married three times. The identity of his first wife is unrecorded, and of his second it can only be said that her forename was Elinor and that she was dead by 1565. He left two sons, Christopher and William, and a daughter, Anne, and also an illegitimate son, John, who served with him at Berwick. Despite Sir Thomas's earlier claims of poverty, his son William claimed in 1566 that his father had died possessed of goods and chattels worth £1800.

Husbands, wives, and rivals William Dacre's opponent was his presumed stepmother, **Jane Dacre** [née Carlisle], Lady Dacre (d. 1575), and it is possible that the money claimed was in fact her own, for she was a wealthy woman in her own right. Born into a leading Carlisle family, she inherited the Whitehall property on the city's Abbey Street, and also benefited from a liaison with Sir John Lowther (d. 1553), constable of Carlisle Castle in the 1540s; they had a daughter, Mabel. In his will, drawn up on 3 February 1553, Lowther made Jane his joint executor and residuary legatee, and it seems likely that at least some of her valuables were given her by him. But the 'great Chyne of Gold', valued at £65 5s., probably came from a more exalted source, for early in 1564 she visited Scotland for the marriage of her nephew John, the legitimated son of her sister Elizabeth and the third Lord Sempill, and was there presented with a chain worth £60 by Mary, queen of Scots. In the inventory of Jane Dacre's will, drawn up on 7 January 1575 and proved on 24 March following, her goods (excluding debts) were valued at £394 2s. 10d., to which money, jewellery, and plate contributed just over £200. Her house was amply, even richly, furnished, with two well-equipped kitchens. The presence of 'a byble in Englissh' may indicate that she shared her husband's religious position (Jones, 147). Judging by Sir Thomas's reference to her in his own will, referring to 'the naturall love & good will I bear & intend towards hir better advanciment & maintenance of hir lyvinge hearafter durynge her lyffe naturall, justly & well at my hands desarved' (Cumbria AS, Carlisle, MS DMh.10/7/5, 401), his marriage to her had been a happy one. But perhaps because of William Dacre's lawsuit she made no mention of her husband's family in her will, and requested burial not at Lanercost, but in St Mary's parish church in Carlisle.

Sir Thomas's heir was his elder son, **Christopher Dacre** (d. 1593). His father had secured his marriage into the Cumbrian gentry, in August 1563 asking for six weeks' leave from Berwick in order to attend Christopher's wedding to Alice, daughter of Sir Henry Knyvett of Scaleby. Like his father, Christopher served the crown on the borders. He was at the siege of Leith in 1560, and in the 1580s made interesting proposals for a line of earthwork defences against Scottish raids, modelled on Hadrian's Wall. Sheriff of Cumberland again in 1581–2, he was described as an enemy to thieves in 1584. But allegedly as a result of his 'unkynde and hard dealing … towards his wyfe' (PRO, STAC5/D13/25), he fell out with the Knyvetts and the Musgraves, and from the early 1570s onwards was constantly engaged in litigation, especially over Scaleby Castle. Since he also spent money on the family mansion (a fireplace bears his initials and the date 1586), his finances may have been under pressure—in 1588 Edward Musgrave claimed that Dacre had been outlawed for debt. As disorder grew on the borders in the last decades of Elizabeth's reign, Dacre became increasingly incapable of dealing with it, and was later remembered as 'a very weak man' who had been unable to protect his tenants (Bain, 2.144). But although he may have sold a few properties, his estate was substantially intact when he died on 16 June 1593.

Christopher Dacre's son and heir **Henry Dacre** (1576/7–1623) was sixteen when his father died, and entered on his lands in February 1599. Probably in the same year he married Mary, daughter of Thomas Salkeld of Corby, and settled lands and tithes upon her jointly with himself. In 1602 he also settled £20 per annum on his sister Dorothy, who married Richard Neile, later bishop of Durham. Probably the most important development of his father's life had been the disappearance in 1569–70 of the Dacres of Naworth. Henceforward the crown no longer needed to promote or protect the Lanercost Dacres in order to control the latter's kinsmen, and Henry Dacre found himself without influential patrons when he fell out with the new lord of Naworth, Lord William Howard, who had married a Dacre heiress, and who from 1603 played a leading role in the final pacification of the borders. Quarrelsome and litigious, Lord William soon fell out with Henry Dacre. In 1610 the two men were at odds over a watermill at Walton, a few miles west of Lanercost, while in 1615 or 1616 Howard had Dacre summoned before Star Chamber on a charge of poaching the king's deer and fined £100. Dacre resisted as best he could, but Lord William's superior resources enabled him to maintain the pressure, and a demand for suit of court seems finally to have brought Henry Dacre to heel. On 7 August 1621 he admitted owing suit and gave no further trouble.

The impact of civil war Henry Dacre died on 6 October 1623, and like his own father left a minor as his heir. **Sir Thomas Dacre** (b. 1606, d. before 1674) was nearly seventeen at his father's death, having been born on 4 November 1606. His wardship and marriage were granted to his mother in 1625, for a payment of 500 marks, and he had livery of his lands on 29 June 1629. By 1630 he had married Dorothy Brathwaite of Warcop, and by December 1633 (the year in which he was knighted) he was the father of a son. In 1637–8 he was sheriff of Cumberland. Sir Thomas proved staunchly royalist in the crisis that broke in 1639, raising men for that year's campaign against Scotland and preparing to resist a Scottish counter-attack in 1640; when civil war broke out in England he became colonel of a royalist regiment in the north-west. The results of his commitment, however, were disastrous for himself and his family. His military contribution to the king's cause (according to himself he raised 400 horse) was vitiated by his quarrels with his fellow officers, which eventually prompted a petition from the gentry of Cumberland that

he be removed from the county. Nevertheless he served in Carlisle during the year-long Scottish siege of 1644–5, and then joined the king when the city fell. On 23 September 1645 he fought for Charles I at Rowton Heath, where 'Hee was in many parte of his body wounded 30 peeces of his scull taken out of his head'; meanwhile his estate in Cumberland had been sequestered, 'his woods cutt downe, and his Howses plundred & Defaced to the value of 10000 li & upwardes' (PRO, SP 29/9, fol. 217).

In November 1645 Sir Thomas Dacre submitted to parliament, and he petitioned to compound for his estates in 1647. But when civil war broke out again in 1648 he joined the royalist army and was in Appleby Castle when it fell to parliamentary forces on 9 October. Though required to go overseas (it may have been now that he went to Ireland and the Netherlands, as he later claimed), he again tried to compound in 1650, but was presumably regarded as irreconcilable, for his lands were declared forfeit on 18 November 1652. In fact he did not lose everything. Parts of his inheritance were protected by settlements, particularly tithe revenues which formed part of his mother's dower (Mary Dacre lived until at least 1653), while Lanercost itself was sold to Thomas Wharton, who was probably acting as Sir Thomas's own agent. In 1656 Dacre was able to contribute £10 to the decimation tax, though according to himself he continued to work for a Stuart restoration—'he Adventured into England purposely to promote your Maties service wch hee hath to his utmost done to the often hazard of his life' (PRO, SP 29/9 fol. 217). But at the Restoration his petition for reward met with no response.

Dying fall The civil wars were crucial for the fortunes of the Dacres of Lanercost. After 1660 they still held their core estates, but though they continued to enjoy respect, thenceforward they never seem to have been free of debt. Financial embarrassment caused sales of property, particularly at Haresceugh and Lazonby, and may also have prompted quarrels between Sir Thomas Dacre and his eldest surviving son and heir, **Henry Dacre** (b. in or before 1633, d. 1696). The latter's marriage to Mary Sibson had brought him property in Dalston and the suburbs of Carlisle, which, however, Sir Thomas persuaded him to sell in 1669, presumably to help disencumber his future patrimony. Perhaps this caused the dispute between father and son which was settled in autumn 1670 by Sir Daniel Fleming of Rydal. Sir Thomas's last years are obscure, and it is not known exactly when he died. But it is clear that by 1674 Henry Dacre had inherited an impoverished estate. A JP and captain of militia, his sobriquet, Squire Dacre, reflects a residual standing in his home county, but this hardly helped him in a lifelong struggle with debts, only temporarily alleviated by sales and leases. Between January 1675 and June 1680 he was outlawed eight times, on five occasions for debt, and an assignment of part of his estate in 1690 was specifically made 'for the payment of debts' (Cumbria AS, Carlisle, MS DX/218/2, fol. 30).

Henry Dacre's wife Mary had died by 9 April 1674, when

her husband was recorded as contracted to marry Margaret, daughter of William Charlton of Longlee, Northumberland. From his first marriage he had a son, Thomas, who predeceased his father, and a daughter, Dorothy, who married Joseph Appleby of Kirklinton; two sons, William and James, were born of his second marriage, and each in turn inherited the Lanercost estate. In 1688 their father was one of the few Cumberland JPs to accept James II's proposed suspension of the penal laws against Catholics. Both his surviving sons were said to be papists, though it is possible that in fact they were nonjurors, heirs to the royalism of their father and grandfather. **William Dacre** (d. 1704/5) was reputed a papist in June 1705, but by then he had been dead for at least three months. He had married a daughter (her first name is unknown) of Sir John Swinburn of Capheaton, Northumberland, and they had a daughter who died young. William's will, drawn up on 3 November 1704 and proved on 2 March following, shows that his wife and child were provided for by settlements; realizing that this could be detrimental to his brother James, who was not then twenty-one, William left him a Northumberland estate. Their mother, who outlived both her sons, was named sole executor. **James Dacre** (1685/6–1716) was likewise in 1708 and 1715 reputed a papist and a man whose loyalty to the protestant succession could not be trusted, and he failed to take the oaths of abjuration and allegiance. In 1715 he was even said to have promised to raise forty men for James Stuart, the Old Pretender, 'but he was taken with a fortunate fever, which hindered him of his Design, and preserved him and his Family from Ruin' (Jarvis, 36). His health certainly seems to have been poor, for he died aged thirty, unmarried, on 16 July 1716, shortly after making a brief will, and was buried at Lanercost three days later. The annual rental of his estates was just under £200, his recorded debts some £1800.

James Dacre was the last male descendant of the first Sir Thomas. His heir for most of his estate was his half-nephew Joseph, the son of Joseph Appleby and Dorothy Dacre, who later took the name Dacre-Appleby. But under the grant of 1542 Lanercost reverted to the crown, and in 1718 Charles Howard, third earl of Carlisle, obtained a lease of it. The earl could not immediately take possession, however. The whimper with which the Dacres had ended was immediately followed by a hollow bang, as a Henry Dacre took possession of the Lanercost estate, claiming to be a descendant of Sir Thomas through his son William, and proceeded to establish himself by terrorizing his neighbours. A member of an Unthank family of Dacres, Henry was in fact an impostor, as he eventually admitted, but fear and force, compounded by the sheer difficulty of establishing his identity, enabled him, his brother George, and their mother (who Henry said had put them up to it) to maintain a precarious occupation for several years. Not until 1724 were these fraudulent Dacres finally dislodged. It was an unexpectedly melodramatic end to the story of a family which had previously been in unspectacular decline for some seventy years.

HENRY SUMMERSON

Sources H. Summerson and S. Harrison, *Lanercost Priory, Cumbria: a survey and documentary history*, Cumberland and Westmorland Antiquarian and Archaeological Society, research ser., 10 (2000) · C. R. Hudleston and R. S. Boumphrey, *Cumberland families and heraldry*, Cumberland and Westmorland Antiquarian and Archaeological Society, extra ser., 23 (1978) · wills, Cumbria AS, Carlisle, MSS DMh. 10/7/5; DX/218/2 [William Dacre, 1704; James Dacre, 1716] · Castle Howard, North Yorkshire, MS F1/41 · BL, Add. MS 33591 · U. Durham L., Howard of Naworth MSS, C 115/2, 23, 25, 31, 63; C 172/28 · chancery, inquisitions post mortem series II, PRO, C 142/234, no. 62; C 142/399, no. 148 · state papers domestic, Charles II, PRO, SP 29/9 · star chamber proceedings, Elizabeth I, PRO, STAC 5/D13/25, 32; D16/6; D20/19; D28/25; D35/21; D36/19 · star chamber proceedings, James I, PRO, STAC 8/15/1; 179/17 · J. Bain, ed., *The border papers: calendar of letters and papers relating to the affairs of the borders of England and Scotland*, 2 vols. (1894–6) · *LP Henry VIII*, vols. 6–21 · *VCH Cumberland*, vol. 2 · *CSP for.*, 1558–65 · *CSP Scot.*, 1547–69 · W. A. Shaw, *The knights of England*, 2 (1906) · A. Hughes, *List of sheriffs for England and Wales: from the earliest times to AD 1831*, PRO (1898); repr. (New York, 1963) · state papers, interregnum, committee for compounding with delinquents, PRO, SP 23/80 · T. W. Willis, ed., *The register of the parish of Lanercost, Cumberland, 1666–1730* (1908) · J. Raine, ed., *Wills and inventories from the registry of the archdeaconry of Richmond*, SurtS, 26 (1853) · P. R. Newman, *Royalist officers in England and Wales, 1642–1660: a biographical dictionary* (1981) · G. B. Brown, H. Whitehead, and J. Wilson, 'The monuments in the choir and transepts of Lanercost Abbey', *Transactions of the Cumberland and Westmorland Antiquarian and Archaeological Society*, 1st ser., 12 (1893), 312–43 · B. L. Thompson, 'Dean Barwick and his will', *Transactions of the Cumberland and Westmorland Antiquarian and Archaeological Society*, 2nd ser., 65 (1965), 240–83 · B. C. Jones, 'Before Tullie House', *Transactions of the Cumberland and Westmorland Antiquarian and Archaeological Society*, 2nd ser., 88 (1988), 125–48 · M. H. Merriman, '"The epystle to the queen's majestie" and its "Platte"', *Architectural History*, 27 (1984), 25–32 · J. Nicolson and R. Burn, *The history and antiquities of the counties of Westmorland and Cumberland*, 2 vols. (1777); repr. (1976) · R. C. Jarvis, *The Jacobite risings of 1715 and 1745*, Cumberland county council record ser., 1 (1954)

Dacre, Charlotte. *See* Byrne, Charlotte (1782?–1825).

Dacre, Christopher (d. 1593). *See under* Dacre family (*per.* 1542–1716).

Dacre, Henry (1576/7–1623). *See under* Dacre family (*per.* 1542–1716).

Dacre, Henry (b. in or before 1633, d. 1696). *See under* Dacre family (*per.* 1542–1716).

Dacre, James (1685/6–1716). *See under* Dacre family (*per.* 1542–1716).

Dacre, Jane, Lady Dacre (d. 1575). *See under* Dacre family (*per.* 1542–1716).

Dacre, Leonard (d. 1573), rebel, was the second of four sons of William *Dacre, third Baron Dacre of Gilsland and seventh Baron Greystoke, and his wife, Elizabeth Talbot. On the evidence of a letter to Francis Russell, second earl of Bedford, referring to 'my education in your house', Leonard Dacre spent at least part of his youth in the household of the Russells (*CSP dom.*, addenda, 1566–79, 201). He suffered from a physical disability, perhaps curvature of the spine—Mary, queen of Scots, is reported as referring to him as 'Dacres with the croked Bake' (Haynes, 446)—but this did not prevent his being active in his family's traditional sphere of influence in Cumberland and the Anglo-

Scottish borders. He served against the Scots in the late 1550s, and was returned to parliament as a knight of the shire for Cumberland in 1558, 1559, and 1563. His father provided for him by acquiring estates for him in Yorkshire and Derbyshire, later valued at just over £200 per annum. However, Lord Dacre's plans to secure the future of his family had other and less beneficial effects. In 1557 he devised an entail securing the descent of his lands to his son, Sir Thomas Dacre, with successive remainders to Leonard and to his younger brothers, Edward and Francis, in each case with a specific limitation to their heirs male. The reservation was bitterly resented by Thomas Dacre's second wife, Elizabeth Leyburne, who was the mother of three daughters as well as a son, and set her at odds with her brothers-in-law. For his part Leonard Dacre took exception to the jointure Thomas Dacre had settled upon his wife, describing it as greater 'than ever anye the wyves of the auncestors of the said Lorde Dacre had' (PRO, STAC5/D37/16).

The rift thus created in the Dacre family would do much to destroy it. Thomas Dacre, who succeeded his father as fourth Baron Dacre in 1563, died on 1 July 1566, leaving an infant heir, George, who became fifth baron. On 29 January 1567 his widow married Thomas Howard, fourth duke of Norfolk. At this time Leonard Dacre was primarily concerned with the descent of his own Yorkshire estates; he was contemplating matrimony, and on 7 May 1567 conveyed parts of his manor of Mountgrace to trustees 'to the use and behofe of suche wief as he the said Leonard shall espouse and marye' (BL, Harley MS Ch. 77. E 56). But there is no evidence that he did marry, or even that he had a particular wife in mind, and the accidental death of George, killed by falling from a vaulting horse on 17 May 1569, turned his attention elsewhere. Dacre now claimed the barony of Gilsland under Edward IV's award of 1473 entailing it on Humphrey Dacre and his heirs male, but his right was challenged by Norfolk in the interest of his three stepdaughters, George's sisters. The case was heard in the earl marshal's court between 12 and 19 June 1569. For Dacre the vital evidence was Edward IV's award, but his quarrel with the fourth Lord Dacre and his wife meant that he did not have access to the muniments of his own family, which had been carried off by his sister-in-law when she married Norfolk, and were later variously reported to be at Kenninghall, Norfolk, and the London Charterhouse, both Howard mansions. Dacre requested and received permission to search the records in the Tower of London, but those did not include the parliament rolls, which were stored in the Rolls Chapel and Rolls House, and at the end of a week he could produce only an irrelevant writ of 15 Henry III. Consequently the court ruled against him, finding that the Dacre barony had lapsed and that in other respects George's heirs were his sisters Anne, Mary, and Elizabeth. On 25 July their wardship was granted to Norfolk, who swiftly married them to three of his sons.

The failure of his bid for the barony led Dacre into treason. His family was conservative in religion, but his overriding purpose in turning to conspiracy and rebellion was less the restoration of Catholicism than the maintenance of the Dacres in their traditional greatness, with himself as their head. In this he was at one with the traditional values of the border society in which he had been raised, as given vivid expression in the 'Advice' which he received at precisely this time from Richard Atkinson, a dependent of his family's: 'The poor people … favour you and your house, and cry and call for you and your blood to rule them all' (James, 276). The support which Dacre now gave to Mary, queen of Scots, and her English allies was primarily directed to achieving this end. His first move was surprising, to promote Mary's marriage to his own enemy Norfolk, a widower since the death of the former Elizabeth Dacre on 4 September 1567. The proposed match formed part of a widely discussed plan to secure Mary's restoration to Scotland with English assistance, and Dacre doubtless hoped that a friendly regime north of the border would give him leverage south of it. He tried to secure Mary's escape from Wingfield Manor in Derbyshire, probably in August 1569, and was even reported to have talked with her on the roof. But Norfolk, who distrusted Dacre, advised against the scheme, and no action followed. On 8 October the duke was sent to the Tower.

The Scottish queen's cause was now taken up by militant Catholics in the north of England, where in November the earls of Northumberland, and Westmorland rebelled in the name of their traditional faith. They certainly looked to Dacre for support, but he drew the correct conclusions as to the northern rising's chances of success, and calculated that he still had more to gain by remaining loyal to Elizabeth I—in a visit to the court at Windsor Castle, Berkshire, he promised his service against the rebel earls, and gave it so convincingly that on 26 December he was among those recommended for the queen's 'commendation'. Between 17 and 20 November his brothers had forcibly taken possession in his name of Naworth, Greystoke, and Kirkoswald castles and most of the other former Dacre possessions in Cumberland, but when Northumberland and Westmorland tried to take refuge at Naworth on 20 December, their supposed ally sent them on their way over the border. The abject failure of the rising left Dacre in a quandary, however. His chances of retaining the family estates against a legal challenge were slight, while with the queen's forces in control of northern England, and the Scottish borders held in check by James Stewart, earl of Moray, armed resistance was hardly an option.

In the first weeks of 1570 Dacre was regarded with growing suspicion by the English government, giving rise to much discussion as to how he could be dislodged from Naworth. Nothing was done, however, until the assassination of Moray on 23 January brought a new urgency into the situation. English dissidents could now hope for Scottish backing, especially from Marian loyalists, in a second northern uprising which might become the launching pad for Mary's restoration to her Scottish throne, or even her installation on the English one. In such a rising Dacre's role was likely to be pivotal, ensconced as he was within a few miles of the border, with numerous and powerful allies in Scotland, and surrounded by loyal and warlike tenants. In the words of Baron Scrope, the warden of the west march, 'the whole country, as well the gentry as others, are so addicted to a Dacre, as although I find no fault with them in any other service, they are not to be credited in this' (*CSP dom., addenda, 1566–79*, 204). Scrope attempted to persuade Dacre to meet him in Carlisle, but Dacre blandly pleaded an injured leg and declined to move. The queen and her advisers appreciated that a frontal attack might simply drive Dacre into the arms of his allies, yet to leave him undisturbed was to allow their enemies to gather strength. Amid mounting tension it was resolved that Henry Carey, first Baron Hunsdon, the warden of the east march, should bring his forces with speed and secrecy over the Pennines and join forces with Scrope, bringing guns from Carlisle, 'in the Wastes, so as to be at Naworth before day and beset the house' (ibid., 230–31).

Hunsdon left Berwick on 15 February, and was at Hexham by the 18th. But Dacre had learned of his coming, and although he knew that reinforcements from Scotland were on their way, he resolved to intercept him. Gathering a company estimated at 3000 men, which 'came on everie hill shootenge [shouting] and crienge after hym', he confronted Hunsdon's force, only 1500 strong, on 20 February 'in a verie streighte place nighe unto the River of Gelte', south of Brampton (BL, Cotton MS Caligula C. I, fol. 522*v*). The Dacre tenantry rose splendidly to the occasion on behalf of their ancestral lords, giving what Hunsdon himself described as 'the proudest charge upon my shot that ever I saw' (*CSP dom., addenda, 1566–79*, 241), but they were outmanoeuvred and outgunned. Hunsdon gave ground in order to fight where he could not be outflanked by superior numbers, and with the 'shot' of 500 musketeers from the Berwick garrison overwhelmed his enemies, whose foot soldiers were mostly archers. A cavalry charge led by Hunsdon completed the rout. As many as 400 of the Gilsland men may have been killed. Dacre was momentarily captured, and though he was rescued by a group of Scots he left his red bull banner behind him as he fled over the border. He was proclaimed a traitor next day, and when Hunsdon took possession of Gilsland in the queen's name he reported that:

> I never heard any man so cried out upon and cursed, both by men, women and children as Leonard Dacre; all affirm that he persuaded them it was only for the maintenance of his title, and to keep the possession, which otherwise would be taken from him by force. (ibid., 244)

Dacre never returned to England. At first he lingered in Scotland among his allies, whose harbouring of him served to justify a series of devastating cross-border raids by the earl of Sussex later in the year. But by January 1571 he was at Antwerp, and thereafter formed part of the group of exiles who frequented the court of the duke of Alva, eking out an impoverished living on a Spanish pension, amid compatriots many of whom distrusted him for his earlier double-dealing. In England he continued to be perceived as a dangerous man, and agents of William Cecil, first Baron Burghley, several times reported that he

planned to sail to Scotland, to stir up further trouble on the borders. But if those schemes had any basis in reality they were ended when Dacre died of fever at Brussels on 12 August 1573, still unmarried, and was buried there in the church of St Nicolas. His tombstone epitaph, now lost, styled him Baron Dacre, and described him—with some generosity—as having preferred to die in the Catholic faith rather than live in schism in England.

Dacre was survived by his two brothers. Edward, who fled from England with him, died near Antwerp in 1584, but Francis, who had avoided involvement in his brothers' treasons, stayed in England and struggled doggedly to establish his claim to the family lands. But although he was returned to parliament for Westmorland in 1588, his mounting debts eventually caused him to leave the country about 1591, whereupon he was attainted. He briefly entered the service of the Spanish crown, but by about 1597 was in Scotland. After 1603 he appealed to James I for a pension, and obtained one in 1609 after renouncing all his rights, but it was only intermittently paid—in 1626 he petitioned Charles I for its restoration. Francis died on 19 February 1633, when his heir was his only son, Randal. The latter died in London on 10 December 1634 and was buried at Greystoke on the 27th at the expense of his cousin, Thomas Howard, fourteenth earl of Arundel. His petition to Charles earlier in the year, for bounty 'towards the restoration of a ruinated howse' (Essex RO, D/DL/F11), provides an apt comment on the disaster which misfortune and treason had brought upon his once great family.

HENRY SUMMERSON

Sources PRO, star chamber proceedings, Elizabeth I, STAC 5/D37/16; PRO, star chamber miscellanea, STAC 10/8/1/736; PRO, chancery, six clerks office, pleadings series I, C2/Eliz I/A9/28 · BL, Cotton MS, Calig. C. I · BL, Harley MS, Ch. 77. E 56 · Cumbria AS, Carlisle, DMH/10/6/17 · Essex RO, Chelmsford, D/DL/F11, L5, L7/1, T9, Z24 · GEC, *Peerage*, 4.21–6 · *CSP dom., 1547–80; addenda, 1566–79* · *CSP for., 1569–71*, 72–4 · *CSP Scot., 1569–74; 1581–3; 1586–93* · APC, 1558–70 · CPR, 1566–72 · *A collection of state papers ... left by William Cecill, Lord Burghley*, ed. S. Haynes, 1 (1740) · C. G. Young, 'Additions to Dugdale's *Baronage*: Dacre of Gillesland', *Collectanea Topographica et Genealogica*, 5 (1838), 317–28 · C. Jamison, G. R. Batho, and E. G. W. Bill, eds., *A calendar of the Shrewsbury and Talbot papers in the Lambeth Palace Library and the College of Arms*, HMC, JP 7 (1971) · C. Sharp, ed., *Memorials of the rebellion of 1569* (1840) · [G. Ornsby], ed., *Selections of the household books of the Lord William Howard of Naworth Castle*, SurtS, 68 (1878) · F. Collins, ed., *Yorkshire fines, I*, Yorkshire Archaeological Society, record series, 2 (1887) · *Correspondance diplomatique de Bertrand de Salignac de la Mothe Fénélon*, ed. A. Teulet, 3, Bannatyne Club, 67 (1840) · T. F. Knox, ed., *Records of the English Catholics under the penal laws*, 1 (1878) · HoP, *Commons, 1558–1603*, 2.1–4 · G. M. Fraser, *The steel bonnets: the story of the Anglo-Scottish reivers* (1971) · M. James, *Society, politics and culture: studies in early modern England* (1986)

Wealth at death lands valued at £207 13s. 9¾d. p.a.: CPR, 1569–72, no. 1828 · occupied more valuable lands at forfeiture, but his claim to them rejected in court

Dacre, Thomas, second Baron Dacre of Gilsland (1467–1525), magnate and soldier, was born on 25 November 1467, the eldest son of Humphrey Dacre, first Baron Dacre (d. 1485), and his wife, Mabel Parr (d. 1508). Still a minor when his father died, Thomas's wardship was granted to his mother. He was already active in northern affairs, however, and was said to have 'raysed the north contrye' for Richard III in 1485 (Summerson, 'Carlisle and the English west march', 103). He quickly made his peace with Henry Tudor, who on 3 March 1486 gave him custody of the English west march, a position earlier held by his father. Dacre would hold it continuously, either as lieutenant or, from 1504, as warden, until a few months before his death. The wardenship was vital to his interests, since his principal possessions were the exposed border baronies of Burgh by Sands and Gilsland; their proximity to Scotland probably explains why Dacre was prepared to discharge the office's heavy military and administrative duties for a yearly salary of only 200 marks. In view of the region's solidly Yorkist sympathies, however, Henry VII also took care to divide authority in the north-west, appointing separate keepers for the city and castle of Carlisle (generally Sir Richard Salkeld), the lordship of Penrith (Sir Christopher Moresby), and Bewcastle (Sir John Musgrave). It was said of Dacre and Moresby that 'the kinges strength within the counte of Cumberland dependith in effect oonly betwixt thaym twoo' (PRO, STAC2/26/11), but the result was a struggle for power. Only following an improvement in relations with Scotland did the king's grip relax. Dacre was successively allowed to farm the shrievalty of Cumberland, Penrith (after Moresby's death in 1499), and in 1501 given charge of Carlisle.

The gradual reduction in royal subventions which these changes entailed threw the marchers back on their own resources. Yet initially Dacre was in no position to meet the challenge. His battle-hardened tenantry constituted a significant military resource, but his ancestral possessions were scarcely worth £300 a year, even in peacetime, and Dacre's two baronies were acutely vulnerable to Scottish raids. In the long term Dacre's marriage in 1487 to Elizabeth Greystoke (1471–1516), granddaughter of Ralph *Greystoke, fifth Baron Greystoke (d. 1487) [see under Greystoke family], offered a solution. Greystoke was a much wealthier barony than Gilsland, and Elizabeth was heir to estates throughout the north worth some £850 annually, thereby not only providing a much more certain income but also transforming Dacre's standing from impoverished border baron to regional magnate. Dacre had abducted Elizabeth, a royal ward, from the Clifford castle of Brougham, Westmorland, but later suggested that there had been a pre-contract between them. The Greystoke inheritance was also claimed by Lord Greystoke's second son, Sir John Greystoke, as heir male. The resulting succession dispute was exploited by Henry VII as a means of controlling his turbulent warden. At first he allowed both parties to secure some estates, and although the unexpected deaths of Sir John and his son in 1501 and 1508 respectively made Elizabeth sole heir, the king still extracted substantial fines for livery from Dacre in 1501, and subsequently forced him to give no less than twelve recognizances, including one in 1506 for 'his goode aberinge' (PRO, SP 1/1 fol. 71v). Dacre was also subjected to a *quo warranto* challenge to his rights and franchises in Gilsland.

In spite of occasional clashes Henry VII, and Henry VIII likewise in the first years of his reign, was anxious to keep the peace with Scotland. Dacre was much involved in the diplomacy to which this policy gave rise, usually through agents but sometimes in person, most strikingly when in 1504 he collaborated with James IV when the latter led a force against thieves in Eskdale; the two men played cards as well as co-operating to hang border bandits. Dacre visited the Scottish court as late as 1513 in an attempt to prevent the outbreak of war, but the failure of this pacific policy gave him much greater scope for his particular talents. Henry VIII's military ambitions were chiefly directed against France, but Scotland's 'auld alliance' with that country automatically entailed war for England on two fronts. Dacre's wardenship of the west march had been renewed in July 1509. In 1511, with Berwick under threat, he became warden-general of all three marches, at the remarkably ungenerous salary of £433 6s. 8d. He distinguished himself at Flodden, leading a cavalry charge to repel a dangerous Scottish onslaught early in the battle, and as he himself later wrote, earning the hatred of the Scots afterwards 'by reason that I found the body of the King of Scots slain in the field' (*LP Henry VIII*, 2/1 no. 2913). Thereafter Dacre's unrivalled knowledge of leading Scottish officials and borderers was constantly employed to keep the marches in uproar; in 1518 he was elected to the Order of the Garter for his services.

Except when a lieutenant and army royal came north for major campaigns, Dacre remained in charge of the English borders until 1525. He had been warden of the middle marches before (1502–6), but he had no lands in the east marches, and although he was given custody of the archbishopric of York's liberty of Hexham and the Tailboys liberty of Redesdale, neither those lordships nor his own modest territorial base round Morpeth proved a match for the extensive Percy interest and connection in Northumberland. But the fifth earl of Northumberland could not win the king's trust and was excluded from border office. The more substantial gentry families, accustomed to Percy leadership, increasingly resented Dacre as an intruder, forcing him to develop closer ties with the more lawless upland squires and even with the barely controllable border clans or 'surnames'. On the west march, by contrast, where he was the obvious choice as warden, Dacre improved his holdings and extended his *manred* by buying and retenanting strategic wastelands. He also built or strengthened key castles like Naworth, Askerton, Kirkoswald, Rockcliffe, and Drumburgh. In 1523, when he raised 4000 men for a Scottish campaign, the earl of Surrey reported that Dacre could 'bringe out of his contre 2 or 3000 men' to strengthen the east marches and may 'at all tymes with litle charge have 4 or 5000 men off his owne' to resist invasion, 'and so can noone other man doo' (*State Papers, Henry VIII*, 4.12, 29, 51, 54). Yet despite this emphasis on military service rather than rents from his tenantry, Dacre's estates still yielded over £1500 per annum, making him the eighth most wealthy English peer.

Dacre was still active on the borders in the early 1520s.

In September 1522 he kept his nerve when a substantial Scottish army under the duke of Albany threatened to attack Cumberland, playing for time at first by claiming to be unable to read Albany's letters, which were written in French, and eventually persuading the Scots to withdraw. Wolsey, aware of the weaknesses of Carlisle's defences, saw their retreat as a miracle. A year later there was another invasion scare, and Dacre mustered the men of the west march, but in the end the Scots attacked in the east. By 1524, however, Dacre was pleading to be discharged from his increasingly unwelcome duties in Northumberland, on account of age, debility, gout, and a sore leg. But his suggestions that Henry, Lord Percy, the fifth earl's son, should succeed him were unavailing, and despairing of release he relaxed his grip on the 'surnames'. As the marches collapsed in disorder, Dacre was summoned before the council in Star Chamber in January 1525, charged with 'bearinge of theaves' (BL, Lansdowne MS 1, fol. 43). He was imprisoned, fined £1000, and dismissed. Released in September, he died on the borders on 24 October 1525, killed by a fall from his horse. He was buried in his family's mausoleum in Lanercost Priory.

Surrey wrote of Dacre that 'there is no hardier or better knight' (*LP Henry VIII*, 3/2, no. 3364). Yet to say that Dacre's disgrace in 1525 'marked the end of the age of the medieval robber baron' is misleading (Guy, 123), even though Tudor monarchs were henceforth distrustful of Dacre's style of marcher lordship. He was a cultured noble, with 'good wit and good fortune' (GEC, *Peerage*, 4.20 n. e), who served the Tudors loyally and well for forty years. When he received Queen Margaret at Morpeth in 1515, a courtier reported that he had 'not sene myche a better trymmed howse of a barons house in my lyfe', and he commented enthusiastically on the plate and 'the hangynges of the hall and chambyrs with the newest devyse of tappestry' (PRO, SP 49/1, fols. 58–9). Dacre was also a conscientious patron of Lanercost Priory. He contributed towards works there—his arms appear on the church facade—and in 1524 wrote to the convent expressing fears that the house's religious life might suffer because the prior was devoting so much time to building. Elizabeth Greystoke died in 1516, and two years later Dacre was hoping to marry the widow of Sir Christopher Pickering, but nothing came of this. His heir was his son William *Dacre, whom he matched with the fourth earl of Shrewsbury's daughter Elizabeth, and who also came to rule the west march, though without achieving the wider ascendancy that his father had enjoyed. The other children of his marriage were Humphrey, Mary (who married Shrewsbury's heir Francis Talbot), Mabel (who married Henry, seventh Lord Scrope of Bolton), and Joan. He also had an illegitimate son Thomas, founder of the *Dacre family.

STEVEN G. ELLIS

Sources H. Summerson, *Medieval Carlisle: the city and the borders from the late eleventh to the mid-sixteenth century*, 2 vols., Cumberland and Westmorland Antiquarian and Archaeological Society, extra ser., 25 (1993) • S. G. Ellis, *Tudor frontiers and noble power: the making of the British state* (1995) • H. Summerson, 'Carlisle and the English west march in the later middle ages', *The north of England in the age of Richard III*, ed. A. J. Pollard (1996), 89–113 • R. Robson, *The rise and fall of the English highland clans: Tudor responses to a medieval problem* (1989) • GEC, *Peerage*, 4.18–21; 6.197–200 • State papers published under ... Henry VIII, 11 vols. (1830–52) • M. James, *Society, politics, and culture: studies in early modern England* (1986) • J. Hodgson, *A history of Northumberland*, 3 pts in 7 vols. (1820–58) • [G. Ornsby], ed., *Selections of the household books of the Lord William Howard of Naworth Castle*, SurtS, 68 (1878) • G. W. Bernard, *The power of the early Tudor nobility: a study of the fourth and fifth earls of Shrewsbury* (1985) • H. Miller, *Henry VIII and the English nobility* (1986) • J. A. Guy, *The cardinal's court: the impact of Thomas Wolsey in star chamber* (1977) • chancery close rolls, PRO, C 54/394 • *LP Henry VIII*, vols. 1–4 • BL, Lansdowne MS 1 • court of star chamber, proceedings, Henry VIII, PRO, STAC2/26/11 • state papers, general series, Henry VIII, PRO, SP1/1 • state papers, Scotland series I, Henry VIII, PRO, SP49/1 • H. Summerson and S. Harrison, *Lanercost Priory, Cumbria: a survey and documentary history*, Cumberland and Westmorland Antiquarian and Archaeological Society, research ser., 10 (2000)

Archives BL, letter-book, Add. MS 24965 | Castle Howard archives, Castle Howard, Yorkshire • Cumbria AS, Carlisle, Howard of Greystoke archive, D/HG • U. Durham L., department of palaeography and diplomatic, Howard of Naworth MSS, C/201

Wealth at death £1535 p.a. (incl. Durham lands); excl. Dacre lands in the palatinate of Durham worth c.£1000 a year: PRO, C54/394

Dacre, Sir Thomas (*d.* 1565). *See under* Dacre family (*per.* 1542–1716).

Dacre, Sir Thomas (*b.* 1606, *d.* before 1674). *See under* Dacre family (*per.* 1542–1716).

Dacre, William, third Baron Dacre of Gilsland and seventh Baron Greystoke (1500–1563), magnate, was the eldest son and heir of Elizabeth Greystoke, Baroness Greystoke (1471–1516), and Thomas *Dacre, second Baron Dacre of Gilsland (1467–1525), her husband. Born on 29 April 1500, he succeeded to the barony of Greystoke on his mother's death in August 1516, and to the barony of Gilsland on his father's death in October 1525. He married Elizabeth Talbot (*d.* c.1559), the fourth earl of Shrewsbury's daughter, probably about 1520. Towards the end of his father's long rule of the borders, Lord Greystoke served successively as his captain of Norham and Carlisle and deputy warden of the west marches. Yet the king's decision in mid-1525 to promote as earl of Cumberland a relative outsider to the county, Lord Clifford, and then to appoint the new earl as deputy warden, was hardly likely to commend him to the Dacres. Trouble ensued after Lord William refused to surrender Carlisle Castle or to relinquish farms of land traditionally associated with the wardenry. Cumberland found it impossible to rule without Dacre's co-operation: in 1527 the king finally agreed to appoint Dacre as warden, but further trouble followed over custody of Carlisle, which Cumberland retained until 1529. And whereas the earl of Northumberland, as incoming warden across the Pennines, received an enhanced salary and fee'd retainers to help him restore order, Dacre's salary remained the now traditional early Tudor £153 6s. 8d. a year, far less than fifteenth-century wardens.

Anglo-Scottish hostilities recommenced in 1532–3, but the English military effort was concentrated on the opposite march—even though the *casus belli* was possession of the 'debateable land', north of Carlisle—so leaving Dacre to shift for himself. When peace was finally concluded in May 1534, Dacre was suddenly arrested while in London to attend parliament. Concurrently, royal commissioners seized his property and vainly searched his residences for incriminating papers. None the less, Dacre was charged with treason for holding secret meetings and making private treaties with Scottish enemies in wartime for mutual indemnity from raids and invasions. These charges reflected the world of cross-border connections in which a conscientious warden necessarily moved so as to discharge his office. Dacre, for instance, generally enjoyed good relations with his Scottish counterpart and distant kinsman, Lord Maxwell. Yet in the process he risked accusations of getting too close to the king's enemies. Lady Dacre, who had come to London to plead for her husband, was ordered by the king to cease her intercessions until after his trial, on 9 July. There Dacre defended himself for seven hours and was eventually found not guilty. A great cheer went up in Westminster Hall when the verdict was announced. Apparently, the lords triers dismissed as proceeding from malice the evidence of the chief witness, Sir William Musgrave, formerly Dacre's household servant. Dacre was the only nobleman to be so acquitted during Henry VIII's reign, but the king none the less tried to cripple his influence in the west march. Dacre's subsequent pardon for misprision of treason cost £10,000: he paid 7000 marks of it within three months (the plate and ready money seized by the commissioners), the rest in instalments by 1541. He had also to surrender all letters patent and leases and live near London (later at Henderskelf, near the northern council's seat at Sheriff Hutton). Cumberland replaced him as warden, thereby further exacerbating the tensions between them arising out of the circumstances of Dacre's arrest, and Dacre was left to try to rebuild his credit by studious loyalty for the remainder of the reign.

After recovering most of his property—disputes with Cumberland, Musgrave, and Sir Thomas Wharton dragged on into the 1550s—Dacre instituted a survey in 1536 of his Cumberland estates. Despite his pressing need for money, military service remained a priority: he ordered his officials not to take more than three years' rent for gressum (entry fine), and to let any vacant tenement to 'a good archer ... and rather to him for lesse gryssome then to ane oder being none archer' (University of Durham, Howard of Naworth MS C/201/5, fols. 4r–4v). When the Pilgrimage of Grace began in October 1536, the rebels approached Dacre to lead them, but he rode instead to Naworth to stay the country. Only after his departure in early November did his Cumberland tenants join the pilgrimage. Finally, the following February, he hurried northwards again upon news of the siege of Carlisle, but his uncle, Sir Christopher, had already dispersed the rebels before his arrival.

Dacre's loyalty was rewarded by appointment to the king's council in the north, but the king ignored the duke of Norfolk's recommendation concerning the wardenries, noting that Dacre's reappointment would stoke the feud with Cumberland. Instead, he appointed Wharton as deputy warden, supported by crown pensioners. Unsurprisingly, Dacre declined the lesser post as keeper of turbulent Tynedale: 'he had rather loose one fynger of every hande then to medle therwith' (State Papers, Henry VIII, 5.108). The king also pointedly withheld Lanercost Priory, the traditional Dacre burial place, after its dissolution, granting it in 1542 to Dacre's illegitimate half-brother, Sir Thomas Dacre, a crown pensioner and follower of Wharton in the Dacre heartland and later a staunch protestant. The quarrelsome Wharton soon realized the difficulties of ruling without Dacre's co-operation. Even after Wharton's extensive landed acquisitions, Dacre's Cumberland estates (worth approximately £750 annually c.1537–47 in a total rental of about £2500 per annum) were still worth more than Wharton's entire holdings, and Wharton's modest Cumberland possessions (former Percy estates around Cockermouth) were also in the strategically less important west of the county. Effectively, therefore, Wharton's suggestion in 1543 that the king exchange Dacre's three baronies of Burgh, Gilsland, and Greystoke for lands elsewhere was an admission of failure; but it was only after the old king's death that Protector Somerset had Dacre reappointed warden, on 17 April 1549.

Dacre had commanded the rearguard in Somerset's Scottish expedition of 1547, but Somerset's Scottish adventures held fewer attractions for the succeeding Dudley regime, which distrusted both Dacre's regional dominance and also his religious conservatism. Dacre was ousted again in February 1551 and imprisoned in London for his feud with the Musgraves. He was finally reconciled with the Cliffords through the mediation of his brother-in-law, Shrewsbury: in 1554 Dacre's daughter Anne married Henry Clifford, second earl of Cumberland. Queen Mary reappointed him on 2 January 1554 (also briefly, as warden of the middle marches to May 1555), a reward for loyalty against Lady Jane Grey. Thereafter he served continuously, despite increasing age, infirmity, and complaints of misrule by local rivals, until April 1563. Elizabeth's distrust of Catholic nobles in sensitive posts was probably the main reason for his removal and replacement by the protestant Lord Scrope. His religious conservatism was well known: he had denounced the Book of Common Prayer in the Lords during Edward VI's reign. In November he fell ill just before Sunday dinner at Kirkoswald and retired to the great chamber, saying: 'Thomas [his heir], take my place, for I am sick.' After lingering for three days he died about 4 or 5 a.m. on Thursday 18 November 1563, and following procession and funeral—kept as traditional as possible—he was buried in Carlisle Cathedral on 14 December. He had four sons, as well as his daughters, Anne and Magdalen [see Browne, Magdalen, Viscountess Montagu]: Thomas, fourth Baron Dacre, whom Dacre matched with the earl of Westmorland's daughter; and Edward, Francis, and Leonard *Dacre.

Dacre's chequered career epitomized the difficulty encountered by Tudor marcher lords in trying both to meet the crown's increased expectations about what constituted acceptable conduct, and concurrently to preserve their estates and regional connection at a time when Tudor policy and economic pressures were steadily undermining traditional methods of border defence. In the face of Tudor notions of an ordered society, a more traditional aristocratic concept of order, focused on loyalty to the family lineage, pervaded the Dacre household. Dacre's son noted his father's concern 'for the continuance of his house in honour' and also 'his great foresight of the stay of his name' on the borders (Summerson, 2.519). Yet, without the steady royal backing his father had enjoyed as warden, Dacre's rule of the borders was undistinguished. His lifestyle was appropriately lavish: Naworth Castle was sumptuously furnished with large quantities of gold and silver plate, numerous carpets, cushions, and hangings, including eight 'large peaces of hanginges of the story of Julius Caesar', and others in red 'set with my lordes armes and cognysaunce' (PRO, SP 1/84, p. 6). In 1541/2 Dacre bought 104 yards of 'London tawny' red cloth for the livery of his servants. His table was similarly supplied with all manner of fish, meat, and wine: in 1529/30 Dacre purchased pepper, sugar, currants, green ginger, 's>ketts', biscuits, 'marmulet', comfits, and nutmegs in London, and his household accounts for 1541/2 also list prunes, almonds, cinnamon, and liquorice. No wonder, then, that Bishop Best of Carlisle could describe him as 'something too mighty in this country and as it were a prince' (Bouch, 200–01).   STEVEN G. ELLIS

Sources S. G. Ellis, *Tudor frontiers and noble power: the making of the British state* (1995) · H. Summerson, *Medieval Carlisle: the city and the borders from the late eleventh to the mid-sixteenth century*, 2 vols., Cumberland and Westmorland Antiquarian and Archaeological Society, extra ser., 25 (1993) · H. Miller, *Henry VIII and the English nobility* (1986) · R. W. Hoyle, ed., 'Letters of the Cliffords, lords Clifford and earls of Cumberland, *c.*1500–1565', *Camden miscellany, XXXI*, CS, 4th ser., 44 (1993), 1–189 · GEC, *Peerage* · *State papers published under … Henry VIII*, 11 vols. (1830–52) · *LP Henry VIII* · M. James, *Society, politics, and culture: studies in early modern England* (1986) · M. L. Bush, 'The problem of the far north: a study of the crisis of 1537 and its consequences', *Northern History*, 6 (1971), 40–63 · G. W. Bernard, *The power of the early Tudor nobility: a study of the fourth and fifth earls of Shrewsbury* (1985) · S. E. Taylor, 'The crown and the north of England, 1559–70: a study of the rebellion of the northern earls, 1569–70, and its causes', PhD diss., University of Manchester, 1981 · C. M. L. Bouch, *Prelates and people of the lake counties: a history of the diocese of Carlisle, 1133–1933* (1948), 200–01 · U. Durham L., archives and special collections, Howard of Naworth MSS, C/201/3, C/201/5
Archives Bodl. Oxf., household accounts | Castle Howard, North Yorkshire · Cumbria AS, Howard of Greystoke archive, D/HG · U. Durham L., department of palaeography and diplomatic, Howard of Naworth MSS, C/201
Wealth at death probably about £3000 p.a.: U. Durham, Howard of Naworth MS C/201/3

Dacre, William (*d.* 1704/5). *See under* Dacre family (*per.* 1542–1716).

Dacres, Arthur (*bap.* 1624, *d.* 1678), physician, was the sixth son of Sir Thomas Dacres (1587–1668), MP for Hertfordshire and Higham Ferrers, of Cheshunt, Hertfordshire, and Martha, daughter of Thomas Elmes of Lilford, Northamptonshire; he was born in Cheshunt, where he was baptized on 18 April 1624. He entered Magdalene College, Cambridge, in December 1642, and graduated BA in 1646. He was elected a fellow of his college on 22 July 1646, and took the degree of MD on 28 July 1654. He settled in London, where he was elected a fellow of the College of Physicians on 26 June 1665, and assistant physician to Sir John Micklethwaite at St Bartholomew's Hospital on 24 March 1669, on the resignation of Christopher Terne. On 20 May 1664 he was appointed professor of geometry at Gresham College, but held office for only ten months, resigning on 20 March 1665, to be succeeded by Robert Hooke, whom he had originally defeated in the competition for the post (Ward, 167–9). Dacres was censor at the College of Physicians in 1672, and died in September 1678, being still assistant physician at St Bartholomew's. He was buried at St Bartholomew-the-Less, London.

NORMAN MOORE, *rev.* PATRICK WALLIS

Sources Venn, *Alum. Cant.* · Munk, *Roll* · J. Ward, *The lives of the professors of Gresham College* (1740) · V. C. Medvei and J. L. Thornton, eds., *The royal hospital of Saint Bartholomew, 1123–1973* (1974) · HoP, *Commons*

Dacres, James Richard (1749–1810), naval officer, was the son of Richard Dacres, one-time secretary to the garrison at Gibraltar, and his wife, Mary (*née* Bateman). He entered the navy in 1762 on the frigate *Active*, commanded by Captain Herbert Sawyer. On 21 May 1762 the *Active*, in company with the sloop *Favourite* cruising off the Algarve, captured the Spanish register ship *Hermione*, which had sailed from the Caribbean before Britain had declared war on Spain and was thus unaware of the state of hostilities. The *Hermione* was carrying an enormously rich cargo of dollars, gold coin, ingots of gold and silver, cocoa, and blocks of tin, to the total of £519,705 10s. 0d. This was sufficient to make every man on the two British ships relatively wealthy, and even the able seamen received the equivalent of approximately thirty-five years' pay. On arrival at Portsmouth the treasure was conveyed to London in twenty wagons, each decorated with flags and accompanied by a party of sailors.

From the frigate *Active* Dacres was transferred to the frigate *Aeolus*, commanded by Captain William Hotham. Cruising in the channel, the *Aeolus* captured a number of privateers and other enemy vessels. The *Aeolus* also recaptured a British merchantman from Jamaica which was said to be of considerable value. Subsequently Dacres served in the frigate *Thames*, commanded by Captain John Eliot and, after 1766, the *Jersey* (60 guns), carrying the pendant of Commodore Sir Richard Spry, commander-in-chief in the Mediterranean. Shortly afterwards Spry appointed Dacres lieutenant of the frigate *Montreal* (32 guns), commanded by Captain Phillips Cosby. He continued in the *Montreal* until 1774, when Cosby returned to England.

At the commencement of the American War of Independence Dacres was appointed second lieutenant of the frigate *Blonde*, commanded by Captain Philemon Pownoll. The *Blonde* was ordered to escort troop transports carrying General Burgoyne's army to Canada. Upon arrival in Quebec in June 1776 Pownoll received a request from Commodore Douglas, commanding British naval forces on the Great Lakes, for the loan of officers and men to assist with the fitting out and manning of ships for service there. Dacres appears to have been selected to lead this party, and upon arrival was given command of the schooner *Carleton* armed with twelve 6-pounder guns.

Dacres distinguished himself in two actions against American naval forces on Lake Champlain. Of these, the more notable was an attack on 11 October 1776 commanded by Captain Pringle on an American force drawn up to defend the passage between the island of Valicour and the mainland. Because the enemy were to windward only the *Carleton* and twenty gunboats were able to engage them, which they did for several hours, destroying the largest American schooner and a gondola. At nightfall Pringle recalled the *Carleton* and the gunboats, and during the hours of darkness the American force withdrew. On the following morning Pringle set off in pursuit and at noon on 13 October he came up with the American force near Crown Point.

After an engagement lasting two hours the American force broke up in disarray. The galley *Washington*, with General Waterburgh on board, was captured and several other vessels destroyed. Dacres was sent home with dispatches and a recommendation for promotion. Upon arrival he was promoted commander (25 November 1776) and given the sloop *Sylph* (14 guns). Soon after he was given command of the slightly larger sloop *Ceres*, serving on the Leeward Islands station. On 1 August 1777 he married Eleanor Blandford Pearce at Totnes, Devon. In March 1778 the *Ceres*, accompanied by the *Ariadne* (20 guns), chased two American frigates off Barbados, catching one, the *Alfred*, on 9 March.

At the end of 1778 the *Ceres* was captured by the French frigate *Iphigenie* (36 guns), after a chase of 48 hours, during which Dacres successfully drew the enemy frigate away from the convoy of troop transports which he was escorting. Dacres's commander-in-chief wrote to the Admiralty: 'I cannot help regretting the loss of this sloop, not only as she sailed remarkably well, but as Captain Dacres is an officer of infinite merit' (*Naval Chronicle*, 26.273). On his being exchanged by the French, Dacres was appointed briefly acting captain of the *Sultan* (74 guns) before being given command of the frigate *Maidstone* (28 guns). His promotion to post captain does not seem to have been confirmed by the Admiralty until November 1780 when he was given the frigate *Perseus* stationed at the Downs. Towards the end of the war he commanded the frigates *Orpheus* and *Aurora* before being paid off in 1783.

At the outbreak of war against revolutionary France in 1793 Dacres was given command of the *Sceptre* (64 guns) and, as part of Admiral Howe's fleet, was employed blockading Brest and the Bay of Biscay. In July the fleet was sent to engage a French force under the command of Vice-Admiral Morard de Galles off Belle Île; however, owing to unreliable winds, the French ships successfully avoided an action.

In the following year the *Sceptre* was sent to join Commodore Ford's squadron in the West Indies and on 1 June was actively involved in the bombardment and capture of Fort Bizothen at Port-au-Prince. In the West Indies the crew of the *Sceptre* suffered heavily from yellow fever and the ship was subsequently ordered home as escort to a convoy. On his return to England Dacres was transferred to command of the *Barfleur* (98 guns) attached to Lord Bridport's fleet in the channel, and he was present when Bridport defeated a French fleet off the southern coast of Brittany in June 1795, though the *Barfleur* was not involved in the action. At the end of the year the *Barfleur* became the flagship of Vice-Admiral Waldegrave and was sent to the Mediterranean. In spring 1796 Waldegrave was sent with five sail of the line to recover the British frigate *Nemesis* which had been captured by the French and was being held at Tunis. On the night of 9 March the boats of the squadron successfully cut out the *Nemesis* and one of her captors, the French corvette *Sardine*. The *Barfleur* was present at the battle of Cape St Vincent in February 1797, where she suffered relatively few casualties, before in April Dacres returned to England in the frigate *Flora*. He was next given command of the new *Foudroyant* (80 guns) which he retained until February 1799 when he was promoted rear-admiral of the blue.

During the peace of Amiens, Dacres served as commander-in-chief at Plymouth and, on the resumption of war in 1803 he hoisted his flag in the frigate *Franchise*. He then became second-in-command of the Jamaica station, under Sir John Duckworth, which proved a very lucrative position as some eighty vessels were taken as prizes during this period.

On 23 April 1804 Dacres was raised to rear-admiral of the red, and a year later he succeeded Duckworth as commander-in-chief at Jamaica. He remained at Jamaica until 1809 when, his health having deteriorated, he asked to be recalled. He returned to England, where he died on 6 January 1810.   TOM WAREHAM

Sources *Naval Chronicle*, 26 (1811), 265–77 · J. Marshall, *Royal naval biography*, 4 vols. (1823–35) [with 4 suppls.] · O'Byrne, *Naval biog. dict.* · W. James, *The naval history of Great Britain, from the declaration of war by France in 1793 to the accession of George IV*, [8th edn], 6 vols. (1902) · G. W. Allen, *A naval history of the American revolution*, 2 vols. (1913) · D. Syrett and R. L. DiNardo, *The commissioned sea officers of the Royal Navy, 1660–1815*, rev. edn, Occasional Publications of the Navy RS, 1 (1994)

Likenesses R. Page, engraving, pubd 1811 (after R. Bowyer), NMM, NPG

Dacres, Sir Richard James (1799–1886), army officer, was the elder son of Vice-Admiral Sir Richard Dacres (1761–1837) and his wife, Martha, the daughter of John Phillips Milligan. He received a nomination to the Royal Military Academy, Woolwich, in 1815, and, after his instruction there, was gazetted second lieutenant in the Royal Artillery on 15 December 1817. He was promoted first lieutenant on 29 August 1825 and captain on 18 December 1837, and was in 1843 transferred to the Royal Horse Artillery, commanding the 2nd, or Black, troop for many years in different parts of the world, but without any combat service. In 1840 he married Frances (Fanny) Brooking, daughter of H. Phillips Thomas of Mottingham, Kent; she survived her husband.

He was promoted brevet major on 11 November 1851, lieutenant-colonel on 23 February 1852, and in 1854 was appointed to command the three troops of Royal Horse Artillery accompanying the army sent to Turkey. They were attached to the cavalry division under Lieutenant-General the earl of Lucan, and Dacres commanded them in the descent on the Crimea and at the battle of the Alma. This force headed the advance on Sevastopol, and was engaged at Bulganek and Mackenzie's farm, and at the battle of Balaklava. In the repulse of the Russian sortie of 26 October Dacres commanded all the artillery engaged. At the battle of Inkerman (5 November) Dacres was present with the headquarters staff, and had his horse killed under him. On the death of Brigadier-General Fox-Strangways in that battle Dacres took command of all the artillery in the Crimea, and continued in that post until the end of the war. He was promoted brevet colonel on 23 February 1855 and major-general on 29 June 1855, and was made a KCB in June 1855 for his services. At the end of the war he was made a commander of the Légion d'honneur, a commander of the first class of the order of Savoy, and a knight of the second class of the Mejidiye.

In 1856 Dacres was appointed commander of artillery in Ireland before becoming commandant of Woolwich garrison from 1859 to 1864. He was made colonel-commandant of the Royal Horse Artillery on 28 July 1864, being promoted lieutenant-general on 18 December 1864 and general on 2 February 1868; he was made a GCB in 1869, and was placed on the retired list in 1877. He was appointed constable of the Tower of London and lieutenant and *custos rotulorum* of the Tower Hamlets on 27 July 1881, and became master gunner of England, as senior officer of the Royal Artillery, in 1882. The same year his brother, Admiral Sir Sidney Colpoys *Dacres, who had also taken part in the bombardment of Sevastopol, was appointed visitor and governor of Greenwich Hospital. In July 1886 Dacres was made a field marshal, but he did not long survive this last promotion, and died at his residence, 28 Palmeira Square, Hove, Brighton, aged eighty-seven, on 6 December 1886.

H. M. STEPHENS, *rev.* CHRISTINE J. KELLY

Sources J. Kane, *List of officers of the royal regiment of artillery from 1716*, rev. edn (1869) • *Men of the time* (1884) • *The Times* (10 March 1884) • *The Times* (7 Dec 1886) • R. Fenton, *Fenton's Crimean photographs*, 2 (1856), no. 129 • Boase, *Mod. Eng. biog.* • Kelly, *Handbk* • Burke, *Peerage*

Archives NAM, corresp. with Sir William Codrington

Likenesses R. Fenton, photograph, 1855, repro. in *Fenton's Crimean photographs* • engraving, repro. in *ILN*, 79 (1881), 181

Wealth at death £568 1s. 6d.: probate, 21 Jan 1887, CGPLA Eng. & Wales

Dacres, Sir Sidney Colpoys (c.1805–1884), naval officer, was son of Vice-Admiral Sir Richard Dacres (1761–1837) and his wife, Martha Phillips, *née* Milligan, and brother of General Sir Richard James *Dacres. He entered the navy in 1817, becoming lieutenant in 1827. In 1828, while lieutenant of the frigate *Blonde*, he landed in command of a party of seamen to assist in the capture of Kastro Morea (30 October) in the Peloponnese, for which he received the grand cross of the Légion d'honneur and the cross of the Holy Redeemer of Greece. In 1834 he was promoted commander, and from 1836 to 1839 commanded the steamer *Salamander*, being employed during part of the time on the north coast of Spain against the Carlist rebels. On 1 August 1840 he was advanced to post rank, and, after several years on half pay, commanded the *St Vincent* from 1847 to 1849 as flag captain to Sir Charles Napier in the channel. From 1849 to 1852 he commanded the frigate *Leander* also in the channel. On 3 June 1852 he was appointed to the *Sans Pareil*, the first steam battleship, in which he went to the Mediterranean and took part in the operations before Sevastopol, including the bombardment of 17 October 1854, where he supported Rear-Admiral Lyons's attack on Fort Constantine: for this he received the CB. From July 1855 until he attained his flag on 25 June 1858 he was captain-superintendent of Haslar Royal Naval Hospital and the Royal Clarence victualling yard at Gosport. In August 1859 he was appointed captain of the fleet in the Mediterranean, under Vice-Admiral Fanshawe, and afterwards with Sir William Martin. In December 1861 he moved to the *Edgar*, as second in command in the Mediterranean; and in April 1863, still in the *Edgar*, was appointed commander-in-chief in the channel, where he remained until promoted vice-admiral on 17 November 1865, having been made KCB on 28 March of the same year. In the following July he accepted a seat at the Admiralty under Sir John Pakington. When Hugh Childers formed a new board in December 1868, Dacres became first naval lord, and continued so until November 1872.

Dacres was not a noteworthy naval lord, and his term as first naval lord was particularly unfortunate. His appointment as a Liberal under the Conservatives indicated merely the increasingly apolitical nature of the naval members of the board; his only significance lay in being the first senior officer to press for the abolition of masts, and a partisan of Coles and the turret system, supporting the epochal *Devastation* battleship design of 1869. He did nothing to resist the measures introduced by Childers, notably much reduced estimates and the effective destruction of the board. The end of board meetings and the elevation of the controller, Sir Spencer Robinson, to a seat on the board reduced Dacres's role and exposed his limitations. Unable to control Robinson or restrain Childers, despite several public 'rows', he was forced to watch as a series of disasters (culminating in the loss of the *Captain*), unfolded, and destroyed a profoundly unhappy and ineffective board. When Childers resigned, Dacres only waited for a suitable opportunity to leave his post for the dignified retirement of Greenwich. He had neither the talent nor the energy to rebuild the Admiralty board, leaving the task to Sir Alexander Milne, a far abler man. Dacres became full admiral in 1870, and GCB on 20 May 1871; on his retirement he was appointed visitor and governor of Greenwich Hospital.

On 1 October 1840 Dacres married Emma, daughter of Mr D. Lambert of Tavistock Square, London; they had several children, including Seymour Henry Pelham Dacres, a captain in the navy, who died in Japan on 28 May 1887, aged forty. Dacres died on 8 March 1884 at his home, 47 Brunswick Square, Brighton, his wife surviving him. He was a solid professional sea officer, brought up in the sailing navy, the high point of whose career came on 17 October 1854 before Sevastopol. He lacked the administrative or political talents for a successful first naval lord; Childers probably recognized this and appointed him for this very reason, because Childers wished to rule alone.

J. K. LAUGHTON, *rev.* ANDREW LAMBERT

Sources S. M. Eardley-Wilmot, *Life of Vice-Admiral Edmund, Lord Lyons* (1898) · J. H. Briggs, *Naval administrations, 1827 to 1892: the experience of 65 years*, ed. Lady Briggs (1898) · S. Sandler, *The emergence of the modern capital ship* (1979) · O'Byrne, *Naval biog. dict.* · A. W. Kinglake, *The invasion of the Crimea*, [new edn], 3 (1877) · A. D. Lambert, *The Crimean War: British grand strategy, 1853–56* (1990) · *The Times* (10 March 1884) · *CGPLA Eng. & Wales* (1884) · *Navy List*
Archives BL, letters to Sir Charles Napier, Add. MSS 40023, 40042–40045 · NMM, corresp. with Sir Alexander Milne · Royal Commonwealth Institute, London, Childers MSS · W. Sussex RO, Lyons MSS
Likenesses Lock & Whitfield, woodburytype photograph, NPG; repro. in T. Cooper, *Men of mark: a gallery of contemporary portraits*, 7 (1883), 15 · wood-engraving (after photograph by J. Watkins), NPG; repro. in *ILN*, 62 (5 April 1873), 321
Wealth at death £4494 12s. 5d.: probate, 23 June 1884, *CGPLA Eng. & Wales*

Dadabhoy, Sir Maneckji Byramji (1865–1953), industrialist and politician in India, was born in Bombay on 30 July 1865. He came of a much respected Parsi family, the second son of Khan Bahadur Byramji Dadabhoy JP, registrar of joint stock companies and assurances. He was educated in Bombay at the well-known Fort and Proprietary High School, and then at St Xavier's College. In 1884 he married Bai Jerbanoo, second daughter of Khan Bahadur Dadabhoy Pallonji, with whom he had two daughters. In the same year he went to England, was admitted to the Middle Temple, and in 1887 called to the bar. On his return to India he began to practise at the Bombay high court and at an unusually early age was elected a member of the Bombay municipal corporation. In 1888 he was made a justice of the peace. In 1890 he moved to Nagpur and enrolled as an advocate at the court of the judicial commissioner of the Central Provinces. He was appointed manager of Raja Bahadur Laxman Rao Bhonsla's estate in Nagpur, and negotiated the partition of that estate between the Raja Bahadur and his brother. For this he received a record fee, and the case brought him prominence in his profession. He was elected to the Nagpur municipal corporation and served that body for forty years (1890–1930). In 1896 he was appointed government advocate. He found time to write commentaries on the Central Provinces Tenancy Acts of 1888 and 1898 which became standard works. He was retained by the Great Indian Peninsula Railway in connection with the development of its communications in the Central Provinces, and was also associated with the activities of a wealthy Marwari business house in Ahmadabad.

Dadabhoy increasingly moved into the industrial and public life of his province. Through partnership in a mining syndicate, he had a share in the development of the considerable mineral resources of the Central Provinces.

He was director of a number of textile mills, founded and was managing director of the Nagpur Electric Light and Power Company, and was managing proprietor of several collieries and other industrial concerns. His interests and ability brought him leadership in the Indian industrial community as a whole. In 1907 he presided at the Central Provinces and Berar industrial conference, and in 1911 he was elected president of the All-India industrial conference in Calcutta. Throughout his public career he took a keen practical and urgent interest in the industrialization of India. He was recognized as an authority on the economic life of the country, and served on a number of commissions dealing with finance and economics, including the Indian fiscal commission (1921–2) and the royal commission on Indian currency and finance (1925–6). From 1920 to 1932 he was a governor of the Imperial Bank of India.

Dadabhoy's long experience of municipal politics served him well when he entered the wider parliamentary field in 1908, as a nominated, and then an elected member of the governor-general's legislative council. He soon established a prominent position as a forceful, independent, and constructive critic of the government of India. In 1921 he was elected to the council of state, to which he was subsequently nominated in 1926, 1931, and 1937. He became its president in 1932. He filled this post with distinction and general acceptance until 1946, when the constituent assembly was established to draw up a constitution for the independent India which was to come into being in 1947.

Dadabhoy was short of stature, and this often left the members of the council of state in some doubt whether their president was standing up or sitting down—a dilemma which gave him much amusement. If short, he was sturdy and robust, and gave the impression of great physical strength. He had an agile mind, shrewd judgement, great tact, and a rare capacity for making friends. His politics were liberal: a friend of John Gorst and a member of the council of the liberal East India Association, he was a committed but moderate nationalist. He was not a supporter of the radicalism of the Gandhian Congress. Although a frequent and candid critic of the government, he was a profound believer in the value of Indo-British partnership and friendship to the Commonwealth and to the world. This conviction was the keynote of his public and parliamentary career and the theme of his outspoken and constructive contribution as a delegate to the second session of the round-table conference in London in 1931. It was also the basis of his conduct during his years as president of the council of state. Throughout some of the stormiest periods in India's political history, he succeeded in exercising his authority and influence with the general support of all parties in the house.

Dadabhoy was gregarious, cosmopolitan, and hospitable. In the United Kingdom he entertained lavishly at Kingsnympton Hall, on Kingston Hill, Surrey. He was a generous host at his spacious house in Nagpur, and at the many social clubs of which he was a member, in Bombay,

Delhi, Simla, and Calcutta. For his services in India Dadabhoy was appointed CIE (1911) and knighted in 1921. He was subsequently made KCIE (1925) and KCSI (1936). He died in Nagpur on 14 December 1953.

FREDERICK JAMES, rev. A.-M. MISRA

Sources *The Times* (15 Dec 1953) · *Times of India* (15 Dec 1953) · *WWW*, 1951–60 · *Who's who in India, 1911* (1911), 4.33–4 · *Hitavada of Nagpur* (16 Dec 1953) · private information (1971) · personal knowledge (1971)

Dadd, Richard (1817–1886), painter, was born on 1 August 1817 at 293 High Street, Chatham, Kent, the fourth of the seven children of Robert Dadd (1788/9–1843), chemist, and his wife, Mary Ann (1790–1824), the eldest daughter of Richard Martin, shipwright, and his wife, Sarah. He was the third of the four sons of this marriage, and had two half-brothers by his father's second marriage, to Sophia Oakes Munk (*d.* 1830).

Education and early career Dadd attended the cathedral grammar school at Rochester from 1827 to 1831, receiving a thorough grounding in Latin. He began to draw seriously when he was about thirteen. The Kent countryside, the River Medway, and the royal naval dockyard (where many of his family worked), inspired a lifelong love of landscape and shipping subjects. It is unclear whether he received formal teaching at this stage, but his earliest surviving watercolours demonstrate a familiarity with techniques used in miniature painting, and the scale and meticulous detail of his later work suggest that he was truly a miniaturist at heart.

In 1834 the family moved to London, living at 15 Suffolk Street, Charing Cross, where Robert Dadd ran a gilding and ormolu manufacturing business which he had acquired from André Picnot, his first wife's brother-in-law. Richard Dadd entered the Royal Academy Schools in 1837, after a period spent drawing at the British Museum. He won medals for drawing and painting, and was considered an outstanding student in a group which included a number of the future most celebrated painters of the Victorian era—William Powell Frith, Augustus Egg, and John 'Spanish' Phillip (his future brother-in-law). He was a charming and lively companion, noted for his good humour and kindness as well as his diligence. The author of a somewhat premature obituary (*Art Union*, 5/58) wrote that 'all who knew him speak of the exceeding gentleness and sweetness of his nature, which, though sensitive, was anything but irritable; he was satisfied with small praise for himself, but ready and lavish of his praise of others'.

Dadd's first exhibited works, *Portrait of a Dog* and *Head of a Soldier of the 17th Century*, were displayed at the Suffolk Street Galleries of the Society of British Artists in 1837. He continued to exhibit regularly, there and at the British Institution, and from 1839 at the Royal Academy. His output soon included scenes from history and literature, subjects that were almost essential for a young artist wishing to make his way. A watercolour of *Don Quixote Resolving to Sally out as a Knight-Errant* (exh. Society of British Artists, 1839) was the first painting Dadd sold. Other early works include *Alfred the Great in Disguise of a Peasant, reflecting on the Misfortunes of his Country* (exh. RA, 1840) and *Elgiva the*

Richard Dadd (1817–1886), by Henry Hering, *c.*1856 [painting *Contradiction: Oberon and Titania* in Bethlem Hospital]

Queen of Edwy in Banishment (exh. Royal Manchester Institution, 1840). In the late 1830s he also painted many small informal watercolour portraits of family and friends, typified by the *Portraits of Thomas and Elizabeth Carter* (Bethlem Royal Hospital Museum).

Fairy paintings of the 1840s In 1841 Dadd established his reputation as a fairy painter with two scenes from Shakespeare's *A Midsummer Night's Dream*, *Titania Sleeping* (exh. RA; Louvre, Paris) and *Puck* (exh. Society of British Artists, 1841; priv. coll.), attracting critical acclaim for his poetic imagination and his accomplished portrayal of the nude figure. These were followed by other fairy subjects including *Fairies Assembling at Sunset to Hold their Revels* (exh. Royal Manchester Institution, 1841), which won the opinion that 'Mr Dadd is emphatically the poet among painters' (*Art Union*, 3, Oct 1841, 171) and *Come unto these Yellow Sands* (exh. RA, 1842; priv. coll.), which approached 'more nearly to the essence of the poet [presumably Shakespeare] than any other illustrations we have seen' (*Art Union*, 4, July 1842, 161). Dadd's fairy paintings from this period can be seen as lyrical evocations of the world of nature, though they were essentially theatrical in concept, with brilliant dramatic lighting and carefully choreographed figures. His principal work at this time, however, was a series of paintings, said to number more than a hundred, to decorate 26 Grosvenor Square (now dem.), the London house of Henry, sixth Baron Foley. The subjects, chosen by Dadd himself, were scenes from Byron's dramatic and demon-haunted poem 'Manfred', and from 'Jerusalem Delivered', a romance of the crusades by the sixteenth-century Italian poet Torquato Tasso. His skill as an illustrator appears in another commissioned work, the wood-engravings for 'Robin Goodfellow' in *The Book of British Ballads*, ed. S. C. Hall, 1842, for which he drew directly onto the wood blocks.

Travels and the beginnings of mental breakdown

In 1842, on the recommendation of David Roberts, Dadd was employed to accompany Sir Thomas Phillips, the Welsh lawyer and former mayor of Newport, as artist and travelling companion on a tour of Europe and the Near and Middle East. He left England with Phillips on 16 July 1842 on a journey which was to last ten months and take them through Switzerland, north Italy, Greece, Turkey, Syria, Palestine, Egypt, Malta, and back through Italy from the south. In the course of it Dadd was to experience the beginnings of a catastrophic mental breakdown, from which he never fully recovered. Most of the drawings which he made during the journey were pencil sketches, the incessant travelling leaving little time for more finished work. A surviving sketchbook, now in the Victoria and Albert Museum, crammed with tiny figures, heads, trees, buildings, boats, camels, scraps of landscape, fragments of sculpture, and architectural details, shows the quality of his meticulous draughtsmanship which, despite the difficulties, was always sharp, precise, and vivid. Two more substantial watercolours also survive, a small full-length *Portrait of Sir Thomas Phillips in Arab Dress* (Bethlem Royal Hospital Museum, Kent) which was probably made during the relative leisure of a trip on the Nile, and a companion portrait of Phillips in Turkish costume.

During the latter part of the journey Dadd started to show signs of mental disturbance. In Rome, in April 1843, he was beginning to grow irrationally excited and quarrelsome on religious subjects, causing some concern to Phillips, but then seemed to recover his self-control. In fact he was already experiencing outright delusions, believing that he was persecuted by the devil who appeared in different disguises including that of Phillips himself. He later confessed to having felt an impulse to attack the pope in a public place, an impulse which he resisted because the pope was too well protected. After a stay in Rome the journey continued, but his mental state deteriorated again and he left Phillips in France at the end of May and alone hurried home to England, where word soon spread that he had returned insane.

To those who knew him, Dadd's character appeared to have changed. He had become watchful, suspicious, and unpredictable, concealing the fact that he was receiving messages and instructions from unknown sources (probably in the form of voices), but occasionally dropping hints that he was pursued by evil spirits, and was himself searching for the devil. Eventually he came to believe that the Egyptian god Osiris was the supreme being controlling all his actions, and the source of his 'secret admonitions'. However, for much of the time Dadd still behaved normally. He had resumed work immediately on his return, submitting a hastily drawn cartoon of *St George and the Dragon* to the competition to decorate the new Palace of Westminster. He also completed one major painting based on his travels in Syria, a carefully composed and tranquil *Caravan Halted by the Sea Shore* (exh. Liverpool Academy, 1843; priv. coll.).

Life in Bethlem and Broadmoor

After a period of apparent recovery Dadd's condition worsened again, and on 28 August 1843 he persuaded his father to accompany him to Cobham Park in Kent, near to his childhood home of Chatham, where he stabbed him to death with a knife bought specifically for the purpose. Dadd later explained that he had killed the devil in disguise, and seems to have retained this belief throughout his life, talking objectively about the murder as an event for which he held no personal responsibility. He made his way to France, but was arrested after trying to cut the throat of a stranger who was travelling with him in a carriage. Dadd was confined in a French asylum for ten months, and extradited in July 1844 to appear before the magistrates at Rochester. Though formally committed for trial, he was certified insane and was admitted on 22 August to the state criminal lunatic asylum attached to Bethlem Hospital at St George's Fields in Southwark, south London. He was never to know freedom again.

The 'government wing', where Dadd was first confined, had been built in 1816 to house patients sent by the courts and later through other legal channels. It was a prison-like block with heavily barred windows at the back of the main building, largely untouched by reforms which were taking place in the rest of the hospital. The internal environment was dark, cramped, and dismal, the outer world restricted to a bleak, high-walled exercise yard, and many of his companions were hardened criminals who had become insane while in prison. Dadd's living conditions were much improved in 1857, when he and some of the 'better class' of criminal patients were moved to a specially converted ward in the main hospital, but far greater improvements occurred in 1864, when all the criminal patients were transferred from Bethlem to the new state asylum of Broadmoor in Berkshire. Built like a small village at the top of a hill, its terraced gardens had views over the surrounding countryside, and there were many more facilities for recreation and employment.

Later works: travel paintings and water-colours

For some years Dadd was considered a dangerous patient, being unpredictable and sometimes violent, his conversation being rambling and incoherent when touching on the subject of his delusions. However, he soon began to work again in Bethlem, and effectively maintained his career as a painter for the rest of his life, though his pictures were rarely seen outside the asylums. A visitor in 1845 wrote of some recent drawings that they

> exhibit all the power, fancy, and judgment for which his works were eminent previous to his insanity. They are absolutely wonderful in delicate finish. They consist principally of landscapes—memories of eastern scenes, or wrought from a small sketchbook in his possession. (*Art Union*, 7)

These drawings almost certainly included the spectacular

moonlight scene *Artist's Halt in the Desert* (exh. 'Art Treasures of the United Kingdom', Manchester, 1857; British Museum, London), recalling an episode in the Holy Land when he and his party had paused at night by the shore of the Dead Sea. Another was probably *View in the Island of Rhodes* (V&A), a bare rocky landscape depicted with almost photographic exactitude. He continued to paint landscapes and seascapes throughout his years of confinement, working both from sketches and from his remarkable visual memory, and never losing the sense of space and immediacy.

Of Dadd's watercolours from the 1850s many were imaginative figure compositions, comprising scenes from literature, history, the Bible, and everyday life, and included a series of over thirty 'Sketches to Illustrate the Passions': examples are held by Bethlem Royal Hospital Museum, Kent, and the Victoria and Albert Museum and the British Museum, London. For these he used washes of low-key colour and strongly drawn outline, but in his most characteristic and personal style he developed a highly refined version of the miniaturist's technique of stippling with the point of the brush, achieving extreme delicacy of texture and colour and a haunting, dreamlike quality. This technique was used in *Port Stragglin* (1861; British Museum, London), an almost hallucinatory view of an imaginary seaport; two eastern scenes, *Fantasie égyptienne* (1865; Bethlem Royal Hospital Museum, Kent) and *Fantasie de l'hareme égyptienne* (1865; Ashmolean Museum, Oxford); *A Wayside Inn* (1871; Bethlem Royal Hospital Museum, Kent); and *Tlos in Lycia* (1883; Leeds City Art Galleries, Leeds), a landscape painted three years before his death, but still recalling his travels of forty years earlier.

Later works in oils The same subject matter inspired Dadd's oil paintings, which include *The Flight out of Egypt* (1849–50; Tate collection); *Mercy: David Spareth Saul's Life* (1854; J. Paul Getty Museum, Malibu); *Mother and Child* (1860; priv. coll.); two seascapes, *The Diadonus* (1861; priv. coll.) and *Sailing Ships* (1861; priv. coll.); *Atalanta's Race* (c.1877; priv. coll.); and *Italian Wandering Musicians* (c.1878; priv. coll.; also replicated in watercolour). He also painted two highly original portraits, *Portrait of Sir Alexander Morison* (1852; Scottish National Portrait Gallery, Edinburgh), one of the Bethlem physicians, and *Portrait of a Young Man* (1853; Tate collection), and a more conventional *Portrait of Dr William Orange* (1875; Broadmoor Hospital, Berkshire). His two acknowledged masterpieces mark his only return to fairy painting. Small paintings, each of which took many years to complete, they are prodigious feats both of imagination and of design, filled with microscopic detail and teeming with myriads of tiny figures amid tapestries of natural plant forms. *Contradiction: Oberon and Titania* (1854–8; priv. coll.) was painted for the Bethlem physician superintendent Dr Charles Hood, and *The Fairy Feller's Master-Stroke* ('quasi 1855–64'; Tate collection) for the steward George Henry Haydon (it was later owned by the poet Siegfried Sassoon).

Last years and death In Broadmoor Dadd's talents found additional outlets, in painting scenery and a drop curtain for the theatre (now des.), as well as murals, furniture, and other decorative items, and in more ephemeral activities such as the production of comic cartoon figures at Christmas, and diagrams and illustrations for lectures and entertainments. Interviewed at the age of sixty, he appeared by this time to have accepted his fate, but still considered it unjust, feeling that society did not understand him. Dark and handsome in his youth, with expressive features, in later years he gave the impression of a scholarly recluse, with a snow-white beard and mild blue eyes gazing benignly from behind spectacles. Throughout the desolate circumstances of his later life he had clung to his identity as an artist, and although his personality was radically changed, insanity had not destroyed his intellect. He retained the delusion that he was subject to the will of Osiris, but after three decades in an asylum he still talked with intelligent interest about painting and the art world, read the *Satires* of Juvenal, and played the violin. He died in Broadmoor from consumption on 8 January 1886, and was buried in the cemetery within the hospital grounds.

Conclusion Dadd's work, most of which had been given away in his lifetime and remained in private hands, was largely forgotten until the 1960s. *The Fairy Feller's Master-Stroke* was his first painting to become widely known, but the full range of his work did not begin to be appreciated until a retrospective exhibition, 'The Late Richard Dadd', was shown at the Tate Gallery, London, in 1974, and subsequently in Hull, Wolverhampton, and Bristol. A substantial number of his works are in the Bethlem Royal Hospital Museum, Kent, the Tate collection, the Victoria and Albert Museum and British Museum, London, and the Ashmolean Museum, Oxford.

PATRICIA H. ALLDERIDGE

Sources P. Allderidge, *The late Richard Dadd* (1974) [exhibition catalogue, Tate Gallery, London, 19 June–18 Aug 1974] · *Art Union*, 5 (1843), 267–71 · '"Her majesty's pleasure": the parricide's story', *The World* (26 Dec 1877), 13–14 · *Kentish Independent* (2 Sept 1843) · *Kentish Independent* (3 Aug 1844) · *Maidstone Journal and Kentish Advertiser* (5 Sept 1843) · *Rochester, Chatham and Strood Gazette* (6 Aug 1844) · *Art Union*, 7 (1845), 137 · W. Wood, *Remarks on the plea of insanity, and on the management of criminal lunatics* (1851) · parish registers, St Mary's Church, Chatham [baptism and marriage], St Mary's Church, Gillingham [burial], Medway Archives and Local Studies Centre, Rochester, Kent · J. Martineau, *Victorian fairy painting* (1997) [exhibition catalogue, RA] · T. Phillips, letters to his brother, 1842–3, priv. coll. · Bethlem Royal Hospital, Beckenham, Kent · Broadmoor Hospital, Crowthorne, Berkshire · *The exhibition of the Royal Academy* (1839–42) [exhibition catalogues] · *Catalogue of the works of British artists in the gallery of the British Institution* (1838–41) [exhibition catalogues]

Archives Bethlem Royal Hospital, Beckenham, Kent, Archives and Museum, book containing sketches and notes | Bethlem Royal Hospital, Beckenham, Kent, Archives and Museum, hospital case notes, poem, letters from or concerning him to David Roberts · Broadmoor Hospital, Crowthorne, Berkshire, archives

Likenesses R. Dadd, self-portrait, etching, 1841, Bethlem Royal Hospital, Beckenham, Kent · R. Dadd, self-portrait, watercolour, c.1841, repro. in Allderidge, *The late Richard Dadd*; priv. coll. ·

H. Hering, photograph, *c.*1856, Bethlem Royal Hospital, Beckenham, Kent [*see illus.*]

Dade, William (*bap.* 1741, *d.* 1790), antiquary, was baptized on 26 January 1741 at Burton Agnes in the East Riding of Yorkshire, the son of Thomas Dade (*c.*1700–1759), vicar of Burton Agnes, and his wife, Mary Norton. His grandfather had also been a Yorkshire incumbent and among his ancestors were the brothers John and Christopher Wright of Holderness, who were involved in the Gunpowder Plot. After being educated locally, by Mr Cotes of Shipton and Mr Bowness of Holderness, Dade was sent to Hackney, where he was taught by Mr Newcombe, before being admitted to St John's College, Cambridge, on 12 April 1759. He matriculated in Michaelmas 1762, but there is no evidence of his having taken a degree. He was ordained deacon at York in 1763 when he served the curacy of St Martin-cum-Gregory in the city. He was priested in 1765 and after further curacies in the city he was instituted as vicar of St Olave, Marygate, in York in 1771; he added two further York livings, those of St Mary, Castlegate, and St Michael, Spurriergate, in 1773. By this date Dade had begun his genealogical and antiquarian researches, in the process of which he experimented with new and fuller forms of registration for baptisms and burials, introducing these to his parishes. His scholarly reputation and his influence with Archbishop William Markham led to his recommended form of registration being required throughout the diocese after the visitation of 1777, and printed registers were devised and used with a varying degree of completeness in several parishes in the diocese of York and elsewhere until another form was adopted nationally in 1812.

In 1776 Dade was appointed to the livings of Barmston and Ulrome in Holderness, which he held in plurality with his York livings until his death. He moved to Barmston and, under the patronage of William Constable of Burton Constable, embarked on a history of Holderness which was to be illustrated with engravings. The volume reached proof in 1784 and some fragments survive in the British Library, but ill health prevented completion of the project. His working manuscripts for the history, and for a proposed history of Beverley, were sold after his death and deposited in the library at Burton Constable, where George Poulson used them as the basis of the history of Holderness which he published in 1840–41. A series of seventeen engravings designed for the original history was published in 1835. These papers are now held at the library of the Yorkshire Archaeological Society, Claremont, Leeds. In 1783 Dade was elected FSA and corresponded with another Yorkshire antiquary, John Charles Brooke, Somerset herald; these letters are among Brooke's manuscripts in the Bodleian Library. Dade died after a short illness at Barmston on 2 August 1790 and was buried there.   WILLIAM JOSEPH SHEILS

Sources G. Poulson, preface, *The history and antiquities of the seigniory of Holderness*, 1 (1840) · W. J. Sheils, 'Mobility and registration in the north in the late 18th century', *Local Population Studies*, 23 (1979), 41–4 · Venn, *Alum. Cant.* · ordination papers, 1763, Borth.

Inst. [clergy index] · *DNB* · *GM*, 1st ser., 60 (1790), 767, 1196–7 · parish registers, York · parish registers, Barmston, Yorkshire · monument, Barmston, Yorkshire

Archives BL, partial set of proof sheets with his MS corrections of *History and antiquities of Holderness* · Chetham's Library, Manchester, Yorkshire monumental inscriptions | Bodl. Oxf., letters to John Charles Brooke · East Riding of Yorkshire Archives Service, Beverley, letters to Thomas Grimston · W. Yorks. AS, Leeds, Yorkshire, Yorkshire Archaeological Society, genealogical collections and papers for a history of Beverley, MSS 80–83

Daer. For this title name *see* Douglas, Basil William, Lord Daer (1763–1794) [*see under* London Corresponding Society (*act.* 1792–1799)].

D'Aeth, Frederic George (1875–1940), social administrator and lecturer in social work, was born on 1 July 1875 at 4 Hydeside Terrace, Edmonton, Middlesex, the fourth of seven children of Alfred D'Aeth, a clerk in the Bank of England, and his wife, Elizabeth Gosling. The family were of Huguenot stock, originally from Ath, on the Franco-Belgian border. Educated at the Mercers' School, Holborn, he began working life as a clerk with the Northern Assurance Company. After attending classes at King's College, London, he went to Oxford in 1896 to study theology as a non-collegiate student at St Stephen's House. He graduated BA in 1899, his first curacy being at St Matthew's, Habergham Eaves, in Burnley, Lancashire, then a thriving industrial town whose sturdy community life was a lasting inspiration to him. In 1902 he became a curate at St Margaret's, Leytonstone, Essex, where the apathy of the residents was in painful contrast to that of Burnley.

Disillusioned by the attitude of the church to the problems of poverty, and believing that the poor were more sinned against than sinning, D'Aeth abandoned his career as a clergyman, though not his deeply felt moral values, and became a lecturer in the embryonic school of social work at Liverpool University. The unique combination of moral principle with sound commercial practice exemplified in Liverpool provided a context within which D'Aeth at last found peace of mind. His brief was to bring together the study of social problems and the training of social workers. To that end he secured the recognition of sociology by the university as an academic discipline, and of the diploma in social work as an approved professional qualification. The content of what was taught he left to the academics, an early indication of his grasp of the distinction between policy making and administration. His consequent association with Eleanor Rathbone, Liverpool's first woman city councillor, and Elizabeth Macadam, warden of the Victoria Women's Settlement, constituted an unparalleled apprenticeship in the investigation of social problems and the preparation of reports. On 6 July 1908 he married Margaret Seville (*d.* 1960), the daughter of a cotton merchant and herself a worker at the Victoria settlement; they had two sons and settled permanently on Merseyside.

Experience of the confusion of charitable effort, then a major agency in the relief of poverty, convinced D'Aeth of the need for machinery for the co-ordination of the medley of charitable agencies as a prerequisite of social advance. Accordingly he was instrumental in setting up the Liverpool Council for Voluntary Aid in 1909, following the recommendation of the royal commission on the poor laws that every city should provide a mechanism for the co-ordination of the voluntary sector. As its director of reports he achieved a national reputation as one of the founders of the National Council of Social Service (now the National Council for Voluntary Organisations), and established Liverpool as the flagship of the movement for the management of social change.

D'Aeth was committed to a single basic principle: the moral right of the individual to share in the responsibility for the way in which the community as a whole managed its affairs. He wanted to emancipate the poor from whatever obstructed their exercise of that right. He modestly perceived his own contribution as being the devising of a system of management specifically designed to facilitate the new relationship between government and governed which that entailed. D'Aeth achieved remarkable success in persuading a host of voluntary agencies to co-ordinate their efforts.

Sprightly and energetic, D'Aeth possessed what colleagues described as a 'well-nigh irresistable charm'. Yet, in spite of the fact that he became a public figure, D'Aeth remains a singularly elusive character. He only once broke his self-imposed silence regarding his experiences as a clergyman and never gave formal expression to the principles and practice of social responsibility to which he was committed. This anonymity was due less to false modesty than to an instinctive grasp of what was appropriate to the role of a social administrator. It was for that reason that he refused the offer of an OBE for his services during the First World War, the only honour he ever accepted being that of vice-president of the Liverpool Council of Social Service in 1932.

D'Aeth's career was halted in 1924 when he was a victim of the post-war epidemic of 'sleeping sickness', or encephalitis. D'Aeth struggled to continue to work but finally retired in 1931. He died on 4 February 1940 at his house, Linderfield, College Avenue, Freshfield, Lancashire, a largely forgotten man. However, there is now a new appreciation of his pioneering role in the creation of a welfare society—in which the welfare state would be the servant and not the master. He was survived by his wife.

MARGARET SIMEY

Sources H. R. Poole, *Liverpool council of social service, 1909–59* (1960) · M. Simey, *Principles and practice* [forthcoming] · M. Simey, *The disinherited society* (1996) · E. Macadam, *The new philanthropy* (1934) · J. MacCunn, *Ethics of citizenship* (1921) · W. Eager, *Making men* (1954) · M. Brasnett, *Voluntary social action: a history of the National Council of Social Service, 1919–1969* (1969) · Earl of Woolton, *Memoirs of the earl of Woolton* (1959) · Jones and Muirhead, *Life and philosophy of Edward Craig* (1921) · J. B. Lancelot, *Chavasse* (1929) · E. P. Hair, ed., *Arts, letters, society: a miscellany* (1996) · T. Kelly, *For advancement of learning: the University of Liverpool, 1881–1981* (1981) · *Thomas Hancock Nunn: the life and work of a social reformer ... by his friends* (1942) · CGPLA Eng. & Wales (1940) · private information (2004) [Cathy Hawkes] · b. cert. · m. cert. · d. cert.

Wealth at death £1930 14s. 0d.: probate, 5 April 1940, CGPLA Eng. & Wales

Dafforne, James (1803/4–1880), writer on art, joined the staff of the *Art Union* (later the *Art Journal*) in 1845, and contributed to its pages for thirty-five years, until his death. His many books are mainly collections of articles which first appeared in the journal, containing pictures and a biographical sketch of the painter. The first to be published was *Pictures by Charles Robert Leslie* (1872); this was followed by similar books on Sir Edwin Landseer, J. M. W. Turner, and various popular early Victorian painters. He also compiled the *Pictorial Table-Book* (2 vols., 1873), and in 1877 published *The Albert Memorial, Hyde Park: its History and Description*. His last book, *The Life and Works of Edward Matthew Ward, R.A.*, appeared in 1879. In 1870 he published *The Arts of the Middle Ages*, a translation of Paul Lacroix's *Les arts au moyen âge et à l'époque de la Renaissance* (1869). Dafforne died on 8 June 1880, aged seventy-six, at Delce Cottage, the house of his son-in-law, the Revd C. E. Casher, in Brodrick Road, Upper Tooting, London.

ERNEST RADFORD, *rev.* ANNE PIMLOTT BAKER

Sources *Art Journal*, 42 (1880), 248 · *The Athenaeum* (19 June 1880), 799 · Boase, *Mod. Eng. biog.* · Allibone, *Dict.* · d. cert.

Daffy, Thomas (1616/17–1680), inventor of the 'elixir salutis', was probably the son of Giles Daffy (d. 1643?), of Abingdon, Berkshire, though the Abingdon registers contain no entries for the family. Among the administrations in the parish of St Clement, Eastcheap, London, in 1643, was one for a Giles Daffy. Thomas Daffy matriculated at Pembroke College, Oxford, in 1635, at the age of eighteen, and took his BA in 1639 and MA in 1642. He was curate at Teddington, Middlesex, in 1646, and in 1647 he was presented by John Manners, eighth earl of Rutland, to the living of Harby in Leicestershire. Probably in the same year he married, his wife's name being Katherine.

In 1648 Daffy was ejected from his living by the parliamentary visitors, and no successor was appointed until 1659. Daffy's high-church views apparently offended his patron's wife, the countess of Rutland, who inclined towards puritanism. Although he could claim a fifth of his former income to support his family, this was quite inadequate, and Daffy moved to Leicester where his four children, Thomas, Daniel, Margaret, and Katherine, were baptized between 1649 and 1654. If his father had died in 1643, as seems possible, he could not have looked for financial support from that direction, and Daffy may have devised his elixir in order to make some money. The medicine was a soothing syrup for colds and fevers; according to the later medical writer James Makittrick Adair, a principal ingredient was the laxative tincture of senna.

Daffy became rector of Pluckley, Kent, in 1657, and in December 1660 he was appointed rector of Redmile, Leicestershire, a poorer living than Harby despite being close to Belvoir Castle. Even so, he was well enough off—doubtless thanks to the elixir—to educate his son Thomas at Melton Mowbray School and to enter him in 1666 as a pensioner (receiving no college scholarship) at St John's College, Cambridge. The son, sometimes confused with his father (for example, in *GM*, vol. 85, part 2, 1815, 493), graduated and in 1673 became headmaster of his old school; he remained there until he died in 1716.

By 1673 the elixir's reputation was such that George Booth, first Baron Delamere, used several bottles of the elixir for treating Elizabeth, daughter of the Presbyterian minister Adam Martindale, who was ill with a severe cold and cough. Elizabeth died, but her father was convinced that her life could have been saved if she had been able to take enough of the elixir sooner and had better looked after herself. Daffy died at Redmile in 1680. He was buried on 28 September 1680. No will is to be found in the prerogative court of Canterbury or in the archdeaconry court of Leicester.

Daffy's appearance is quite unknown, and given the obscurity of his life he must have been of a retiring disposition; how he came to know the Cheshire-based Lord Delamere can only be guessed at. It appears to have been members of the Daffy family who made the elixir famous. Daffy's son Daniel, an apothecary in Nottingham, marketed it for some years, after which Daniel's sister Catherine (as she now called herself) offered it for sale at the Hand and Pen, Maiden Lane, London. However, their father had divulged the secret formula to a relative, Anthony Daffy of London, and it was probably his son Anthony (*d.* 1750) and his wife (*d.* 1732) who sold their variety at 2*s.* 6*d.* for half a pint, from Salisbury Court, London, as a sovereign remedy against internal obstructions. The elder Anthony's son Elias (*b. c.*1663), a doctor and MB from Cambridge, may have been responsible for conveying on the label the approbation of Charles II's physician, Sir Edmund King, and of Dr John Radcliffe (1650–1714). In 1748 yet another version was being sold in Ipswich at 1*s.* a bottle as a drink to help most distempers. In 1812 so many different varieties were on sale that a schedule to that year's Patent Medicine Act referred to 'Daffy's elixir, by whomever made'. Its popularity persisted well into the twentieth century.   T. A. B. CORLEY

Sources *DNB* · J. Nichols, *The history and antiquities of the county of Leicester*, 2/1 (1795); 3 (1800–04) · Foster, *Alum. Oxon.* · Venn, *Alum. Cant.* · *GM*, 1st ser., 85/2 (1815), 493 · *The life of Adam Martindale*, ed. R. Parkinson, Chetham Society, 4 (1845), 209 · J. H. Pruett, *The parish clergy under the later Stuarts: the Leicestershire experience* (1978), 13 · R. Porter, *Health for sale: quackery in England, 1660–1850* (1989) · Walker rev. · *IGI*

Dafoe, John Wesley (1866–1944), journalist in Canada, was born near Combermere in the Ottawa valley, Upper Canada, on 8 March 1866, the eldest son of a pioneer farmer, Calvin Dafoe, and his wife, Mary Ann, daughter of John Elcome, farmer, of nearby Bangor. After attending local schools until the age of fifteen, he became a teacher in one of them. Three years later he was in Montreal learning his way as a reporter for the *Montreal Star*, then edited by Hugh Graham (later Lord Atholstan) who tutored him well. As parliamentary correspondent he began to acquire a reputation as political observer and commentator. It gained for him, briefly and perhaps prematurely, the editorship of the fledgeling *Ottawa Journal*. He was not a success. He then moved west and for six years he honed his skills with the *Manitoba Free Press*. He married Alice Parmelee, daughter of William G. Parmelee, the deputy minister of customs and excise, in Ottawa in 1890. They raised a large family of four daughters and three sons. Dafoe subsequently returned to Montreal in 1892 and edited the *Montreal Herald* for three years and then rejoined the editorial staff of the *Montreal Star*.

By this time Dafoe was a vigorous champion of the Liberal Party and attracted the notice of Clifford Sifton, minister of the interior in the Liberal cabinet of Sir Wilfrid Laurier. Sifton had acquired control of the *Manitoba Free Press* and in 1901 he appointed Dafoe editor. It was the beginning of a long, successful, but occasionally difficult relationship. Sifton was not often in Winnipeg and their full and frequent correspondence is a rich mine of information on Canadian public life. Within a short time the *Free Press* was the most influential (and prosperous) newspaper in western Canada, whose interests Dafoe championed with the federal Liberals. Increasingly, he came to see himself as a friendly but not uncritical adviser to government. It led to some odd situations.

As minister of the interior, Sifton initiated a vigorous immigration policy seeking out the peasantry of eastern Europe who, he was convinced, would make the vast Canadian prairies a great breadbasket. Dafoe approved of the economic thrust of the policy but, unlike Sifton, deplored its social consequences. For years he editorialized about the danger of 'Balkanizing' Canada and demanded a unilingual school system to neutralize the presumed threat. Similarly, when Sifton campaigned against the proposed reciprocity treaty between Canada and the United States in 1911, Dafoe gave it vigorous support. He was first and always a free-trader, but he had little choice if the *Free Press* was to maintain its influence (and income) in western Canada, which Sifton was forced to acknowledge.

Publisher and editor stood firmly together during the First World war. However, when in 1917 Laurier, now leader of the opposition, opposed conscription for overseas service, Dafoe broke with the Liberals and ranged the *Free Press* behind a union government pledged to compulsory service. It would be ten years before Dafoe returned to the Liberal fold. In the interval, he gave editorial blessing to the post-war Progressive Party, which represented predominantly western agrarian interests. When the majority of them were absorbed by the Liberals in 1926, Dafoe also returned. But he remained an independent Liberal counsellor, turning down a cabinet post among other offers. He did accept an appointment to the Rowell–Sirois royal commission of 1937–40 which fundamentally reshaped the Canadian confederation.

Dafoe's greatest preoccupation during the 1930s was the worsening situation in Europe. Here he seemed torn. His nationalism drew him more and more to see Canada as a North American country, best free of European (and especially British) entanglements. At the same time, he was perhaps the most vocal exponent in the country of the principle of collective security and the League of Nations. But the ambivalence disappeared when war began in

1939, and the *Free Press* gave solid support to the government's war effort. Dafoe remained at his editorial desk until he died after a brief illness, at Winnipeg, on 9 January 1944.

J. W. Dafoe never wished to be anything but a journalist, and he was, arguably, Canada's best. His prose was vigorous and direct rather than elegant; designed to explain and persuade rather than to charm. Secure in his abilities, he surrounded himself with the best young people he could find and for three decades the *Free Press* was the most influential newspaper in the country. He cared little for public honours, rejecting a knighthood among others. But he did accept several honorary degrees and served devotedly as chancellor of the University of Manitoba from 1934 until his death. Somehow he found time for private writing; his books included *Over the Canadian Battlefields* (1919), *Laurier: a Study in Canadian Politics* (1922), *Clifford Sifton in Relation to his Times* (1931), and *Canada: an American Nation* (1935), and he edited *Canada Fights* (1941).

J. E. REA

Sources University of Manitoba Archives · NA Canada, Dafoe MSS, Sifton MSS · G. V. Ferguson, *Life of Dafoe* (1948) · G. R. Cook, *The politics of John W. Dafoe and the Free Press* (1963) · *The Dafoe–Sifton correspondence, 1919–1927*, ed. R. Cook (1966) · M. S. Donnelly, *Dafoe of the 'Free Press'* (1968) · W. L. Morton, ed., *The voice of Dafoe* (1945) · J. E. Rea, *T. A. Crerar: a political life* (1997) · D. J. Hall, *Clifford Sifton*, 2 vols. (1981–5)
Archives NA Canada · University of Manitoba, Winnipeg, archives | NA Canada, Sifton MSS · Queen's University Archives, Kingston, Ontario, Crerar MSS
Likenesses E. W. Grier, portrait, office of *Free Press*, Winnipeg, Canada

Daft, Richard (1835–1900), cricketer, was born at Nottingham on 2 November 1835, the son of John Daft (*c*.1790–*c*.1876), a cavalryman who served in the Peninsular war, and his wife (*née* Wood). He learned cricket as a boy from George Butler (1810–1887), the Nottinghamshire player and Trent Bridge groundsman. He began his career as an amateur in 1857, and played for the Gentlemen against the Players in 1858. In the following year he became a professional for Nottinghamshire (whom he continued to play for until 1881), and first represented the Players against the Gentlemen in 1860. He was probably at his best between 1861 and 1876, and in the 1870s he had no superior as a batsman except W. G. Grace, to whom he was second in the national averages on four occasions. Among outstanding performances were his 118 for the North against the South at Lord's in 1862 on a difficult wicket, 111 at Old Trafford in 1867 for the All England eleven against the United All England eleven, and 161 for Nottinghamshire against Yorkshire at Trent Bridge in June 1873. He captained Nottinghamshire (1871–80) after the retirement of George Parr, and his side won the county championship on six occasions.

In 1879 Daft took a team composed of some of the best Yorkshire and Nottinghamshire professionals to Canada and the United States. They returned unbeaten having made a substantial profit. He had already shown his business acumen in opening (1873) a sports emporium in Nottingham. At a dinner in his honour in 1877 the county

showed the high regard in which he was held 'both on the cricket field and in social life' (*Wisden*, 1878) by presenting him with gifts of solid silver, including a tea and a coffee set, and a cheque for £500. After relinquishing first-class cricket he worked as landlord of the Trent Bridge inn in Nottingham from 1881 to 1883. However, he often made large scores as an amateur in club matches and, in 1891, he was persuaded once more to represent Nottinghamshire at the Oval. He showed much of his 'old grace' (*Wisden*, 1882).

As a batsman, Daft was distinguished by his elegance and style. He played the ball using his height in what came to be seen as the classical model of batting, quick on his feet and ready to drive. *Bell's Life* (1864), the leading sports newspaper of its time, wrote that to 'have witnessed Daft play an innings was to know cricket'. His *Kings of Cricket* was published in 1893 and is an interesting commentary upon many of the players of his day and a valued analysis of the development of the game from the travelling England elevens to the establishment of the county championship.

Daft was the outstanding member of a cricketing family, four of whom played for Nottinghamshire. He married about 1862 Mary (1842–1918), daughter of Butler Parr. Their son Harry (1866–1945) played with his father at the Oval in 1891 and also played association football for England. At the end of his cricketing career Daft retired to the native place of his old captain, George Parr, at Radcliffe-on-Trent, where he kept a small brewery. There he died on 18 July 1900; his wife and two sons survived him.

GERALD M. D. HOWAT

Sources A. Haygarth, *Arthur Haygarth's cricket scores and biographies*, 6 (1876) · *Wisden* (1901) · *The Times* (19 July 1900) · *Cricket* (26 July 1900) · R. S. Holmes, *Cricket* (24 Sept 1891) · W. Caffyn, *Seventy one not out* (1899) · F. Gale, *Echoes from old cricket fields* (1871) · F. S. Ashley-Cooper, *Nottinghamshire cricket and cricketers* (1923) · R. Daft, *A cricketer's yarns*, ed. F. S. Ashley-Cooper (1926) · H. S. Altham, *A history of cricket* (1926) · P. Bailey, P. Thorn, and P. Wynne-Thomas, *Who's who of cricketers*, rev. edn (1993)
Likenesses Mayall, photograph, *c*.1860, repro. in Daft, *Cricketer's yarns* · photograph, *c*.1860, Marylebone Cricket Club, London · Phillips, photograph, *c*.1870, repro. in *Cricket* (26 July 1900) · sketch, *c*.1870, repro. in Holmes, *Cricket* (24 Aug 1891)

Dafydd ab Edmwnd (*fl.* 1450–1497), poet, belonged on his father's side to a branch of the Hanmer family of Maelor in Flintshire, descendants of Thomas of Macclesfield, one of Edward I's officers in north-east Wales. He possessed considerable lands in Maelor, including the principal estate of the Hanmers, yr Owredd, but he lived on his mother's inheritance at Pwll Gwepra in the parish of Northop (Llaneurgain), by the bank of the River Dee on the site of the modern Connah's Quay. He was a bardic pupil of Maredudd ap Rhys, and in his turn he was teacher to two of the finest poets of the later fifteenth century, Gutun Owain and Tudur Aled, both of whom composed elegies on his death acknowledging their debt to him. Tudur Aled's reference to Dafydd as his 'uncle by blood' has not been satisfactorily explained, but it may be that both were connected to the Coedymynydd family.

Dafydd ab Edmwnd first came to prominence when he

won the silver chair for poetry at the eisteddfod held under the auspices of Gruffudd ap Nicolas at Carmarthen about 1451. The most substantial surviving account of that eisteddfod, written in 1636, attributes a variety of poetic feats to Dafydd, demonstrating his superiority over all the other bards of Wales; but it should be borne in mind that the author was also a Flintshire man. It is certain, however, that Dafydd was responsible for revising the rules of Welsh poetics at that eisteddfod by virtue of the status which his victory conferred on him. He deleted two simple kinds of *englyn* from the 24 metres, and to replace them he devised two arguably unnecessarily complex new metres, *gorchest y beirdd* (literally 'the poets' feat'—a title which reveals a great deal about Dafydd's attitude towards the craft of poetry) and *cadwynfyr*. Other metres were tightened up, making full use of *cynghanedd* obligatory and the rules of *cynghanedd* itself were made more strict by proscribing former laxities. It is also likely that it was Dafydd who translated the new Latin grammar into Welsh, a translation which from that time on became part of the Welsh bardic grammars. These changes were embodied in the copy of the bardic grammar made by his pupil Gutun Owain, who was with him at the Carmarthen eisteddfod. They reflect the new virtuosity at the beginning of the golden age of classical Welsh poetry, and were no doubt intended to make it more difficult for unqualified minstrels to encroach upon the domain of the highly trained bards.

Since Dafydd ab Edmwnd was a gentleman poet, he did not depend on patronage for his livelihood, and was therefore able to indulge his delight in love poetry in the tradition of Dafydd ap Gwilym, though, as Saunders Lewis observes, these poems suggest that his true love was the *cywydd* metre, not the girl. Love poems comprise the majority of the seventy-seven items in the only available collection of his work. Dafydd also delighted in elaborate bardic flytings, which would have been undertaken for the amusement of audiences and as a test of his poetic skill. Two such poetic exchanges have survived between Dafydd and Guto'r Glyn (who refers to him familiarly as Deio), one of which consists of grotesque descriptions of each other's genitalia. The few poems that Dafydd did address to noblemen are free of any obligation to pander to their interests, and display great independence of mind, such as that urging Rhys Wyn of Anglesey not to marry an Englishwoman, and in particular his best-known poem, an elegy on the death of the harpist Siôn Eos, which is a protest against the barbaric practice of capital punishment for murder under the newly established English law, as opposed to the custom of compensation under the old Welsh law. Dafydd's latest poem can be dated no earlier than 1497, since it contains a reference to Sir Thomas Salesbury, who was knighted for his part in the battle of Blackheath in that year. According to Gutun Owain's elegy on Dafydd's death, he was buried in St Chad's church at Hanmer.   DAFYDD JOHNSTON

Sources T. Roberts, ed., *Gwaith Dafydd ab Edmwnd* (1914) · D. J. Bowen, 'Dafydd ab Edmwnt ac Eisteddfod Caerfyrddin', *Barn*, 133–55 (1973–5), 441–8

Dafydd ab Owain Gwynedd (*d.* 1203). *See under* Hywel ab Owain Gwynedd (*d.* 1170).

Dafydd ap Gruffudd (*d.* 1283), prince of Gwynedd, was the third of four sons of *Gruffudd ap Llywelyn (*d.* 1244) and his wife, Senana, and grandson of *Llywelyn ab Iorwerth (*d.* 1240).

Early career Dafydd first appears in the historical record on 12 August 1241 when he and his younger brother Rhodri, both still under age, were placed in the custody of Henry III. They were given as sureties for their mother's good faith in an agreement with the king by which she endeavoured to secure the release of her husband from imprisonment by his half-brother, *Dafydd ap Llywelyn (*d.* 1246). After his elder brothers Owain and *Llywelyn ap Gruffudd (*d.* 1282) shared the patrimony of Gwynedd in 1246, and secured the king's endorsement of their position a year later, Dafydd may have associated himself with Llywelyn, whose charter to the priory of Penmon in 1247 he witnessed. The Welsh chronicle *Cronica de Wallia* states, however, that he became captain of the household troops (*dux familie*) in Owain's service, and by 1252 he is found exercising lordship over the commote of Cymydmaen in the cantref of Llŷn. The cantref formed part of Owain's portion of Gwynedd and he may have ceded the commote in response to his younger brother's demands for a share of the patrimony. Dafydd pressed his claims upon the king and in September 1253 Henry took his fealty for whatever portion of Gwynedd he could secure for himself. The two elder brothers were required to provide the portion due to Dafydd 'according to the custom of Wales' (*Close Rolls*, 7.419), but, although Owain may have been prepared to accommodate him, Llywelyn was resolutely opposed to any further partition of Gwynedd. The proposals put to the king 'concerning Llywelyn's brothers' (ibid., 10.104) may have urged that Dafydd be given an estate in Perfeddwlad or the Four Cantrefs, the land east of the River Conwy then in the king's possession. Negotiations were of no avail, and in June 1255 Owain and Dafydd brought an army against Llywelyn to resolve the issue by force. They were defeated at Bryn Derwin on the borders of the commotes of Arfon Uwch Gwyrfai and Eifionydd and imprisoned, but whereas Owain was held for twenty-two years Dafydd was released before Llywelyn advanced into Perfeddwlad in November 1256. The lands given him by Llywelyn were mainly located in that area.

Dafydd is found in Llywelyn's service in the next years, participating in a campaign in south-west Wales in 1258 when he is described as 'a young man most splendid in arms' (*Annales Cambriae*, 96). In the same year he appears second to Llywelyn in a record of an agreement between the princes of Wales and a group of Scottish magnates, and in 1260 he and Llywelyn put their seals to an agreement for the prolongation of the truce with Henry III. Dafydd may have been formally recognized as second to Llywelyn in the prince's councils. When, in the summer of 1262, Henry III heard a rumour that Llywelyn was dead he was anxious to ensure that Dafydd, who in the king's estimation was no 'true heir to Wales' (*Close Rolls*, 12.142–3), should not succeed to the supremacy that Llywelyn had by then established in Wales.

Relations with his brother Llywelyn to 1278 Henry evidently made an attempt to entice Dafydd from Llywelyn's allegiance shortly before he set out from Chester on his Welsh campaign in 1257, holding forth a prospect that upon the defeat of Llywelyn the king would retain Anglesey and Perfeddwlad and divide the remainder of Gwynedd between Owain and Dafydd. Henry's efforts were of no avail, but the Lord Edward, in the course of his intervention in the march of Wales in April 1263, received Dafydd into his allegiance. Although he was in no position to make his will effective, Edward granted him the cantref of Dyffryn Clwyd and the commote of Ceinmeirch, a provision extended three months later so as to convey the cantrefs of Dyffryn Clwyd and Rhufoniog. The grants were made until such time as Dafydd, by his efforts and Edward's aid, could secure his inheritance in Gwynedd Uwch Conwy, that is in the land west of the Conwy centred on Snowdonia. This was to remain Dafydd's principal ambition throughout his life, and dissatisfaction with the territorial provision made for him by his brother was probably an important reason for his defection. Under the terms of the treaty of Montgomery in September 1267 it was 'specially ordained' that he be given the lands which he held before his departure. If Dafydd were not satisfied, further provision should be made by five named members of the prince's council and, if he were still not content, justice would be done to him according to the law and custom of Wales in the presence of two persons who would inform the king of the decision. The matter was required to be resolved by Christmas but agreement is not known to have been reached before 1269, when a compact was made that gave Dafydd no more than he possessed upon his secession to the king. Dafydd was married, after 1265, to Elizabeth, sister of Robert Ferrers, earl of Derby (d. 1279), and widow of William Marshal (d. 1265). Through his wife he held the manor of Folesham, Norfolk, then exchanged with John Marshal for the manor of Norton, Northamptonshire.

Although Dafydd served in Llywelyn's forces in Glamorgan in 1271 and is mentioned as one of his councillors two years later, relations between the brothers remained difficult. The surviving evidence indicates that in 1274 Dafydd ap Gruffudd and Gruffudd ap Gwenwynwyn (d. 1286) conspired to kill Llywelyn. At a session of the prince's council in April 1274 Gruffudd and his son Owain were convicted of infidelity, but action against Dafydd was taken only later in the year following a confession by Owain ap Gruffudd, who was held in custody as a surety for his father's good faith. Dafydd was summoned to appear before the prince's council at Rhuddlan to answer charges against him. Told to appear again at Llanfor in Penllyn, Dafydd fled to England with an armed following. Gruffudd ap Gwenwynwyn did likewise and Edward I received them into his realm. Dafydd asked for Edward's guidance as to how he could do most to damage Llywelyn, and sought the king's aid in doing so. Refusing to do homage to Edward at Chester in August 1275, Llywelyn gave as his main reason

the king's decision to receive the two vassals who had conspired to kill him.

In the war of 1277 Dafydd served alongside William Beauchamp, earl of Warwick, in a force based at Chester which advanced into Powys Fadog. Reporting during April that Dafydd was making demands concerning the payment of his men and insisting that he retain booty taken by them, Warwick feared that he might withdraw from the king's service. Dafydd was also said to be angry that certain men, probably magnates engaged in the campaign, were asking the king for land in Wales. Dafydd's continued concern for his interests, and perhaps anxiety over his continued fidelity, may have prompted Edward's charter of 23 August, which indicated that, upon securing Gwynedd Uwch Conwy, he would divide the land between Dafydd ap Gruffudd, Owain ap Gruffudd, and himself. The two Welsh lords would be summoned to the king's parliaments in England like the other earls and barons of the realm. Dafydd was also granted the lordship of Hope, where, with Edward's help, he began to build the castle of Caergwrle. By the autumn Edward had other intentions. On 10 October he issued a charter granting Dafydd the two cantrefs of Dyffryn Clwyd and Rhufoniog in Perfeddwlad, thereby affirming the grant which he had made upon Dafydd's defection in 1263. Once more the grant was made so as to provide for Dafydd until he could secure his share of the patrimony in Gwynedd Uwch Conwy, but on this occasion Edward was able to put his will into effect immediately. Edward may have been reluctant to see Dafydd established in Snowdonia, and a negotiated settlement with Llywelyn was secured by the treaty of Aberconwy on 9 November. A week earlier, in a document which points to a key issue in the negotiations, Edward granted Llywelyn a life-interest in Gwynedd Uwch Conwy in return for his acknowledgement of Dafydd's hereditary right there. The substance of this agreement was then embodied in a treaty which, creating only a life-interest for Dafydd in Dyffryn Clwyd and Rhufoniog, and leaving his aspiration for a share of Snowdonia still unrequited, provided no permanent solution to the problems that Dafydd had posed.

The war of 1282–1283 Dafydd was at Rhuddlan in September 1278 when, in Edward's presence, Llywelyn agreed to fulfil the terms of an earlier financial settlement with Rhodri ap Gruffudd. Dafydd gave a security that the money pledged by Llywelyn to Rhodri could be raised on his English estates. At the same time the king issued to Dafydd a grant for life of the manor of Frodsham, Cheshire, previously held at will. There is no certain evidence of discord between Dafydd and the crown until late 1281. He had previously been summoned to the county court of Chester to answer a claim by William de Venables to lands in Hope and, according to Dafydd's account, an inquisition had shown that the lands in question were in Wales and were subject to Welsh, not English, law. The decision appears to have been reversed following Reynold de Grey's appointment as justice of Chester in November 1281. Dafydd went to court and, in a loud voice, declared that the land was in Wales and that he had no need to answer in the county court. He pleaded that the laws of Wales be respected like the laws of other nations. He subsequently complained of interference by royal officers in his lordships of Dyffryn Clwyd and Rhufoniog, and he was particularly aggrieved at the actions of Reynold de Grey. He shared his aversion to Grey with the communities under the justice's authority in Rhos and Tegeingl and this common experience was a major cause of renewed conflict in 1282 when Dafydd played the main initiating role. On Palm Sunday (22 March) 1282 Dafydd launched an attack on the castle of Hawarden, capturing its custodian, Roger Clifford (d. 1285), and Rhuddlan was put under siege. Dafydd was probably the inspiration behind the almost simultaneous rising on the part of several of the princes of south-west Wales. Llywelyn may have tarried before committing himself to war, and Dafydd was certainly the main object of Edward's anger during the conflict.

Dafydd's castle of Caergwrle fell to forces advancing from Chester on 16 June, three months after hostilities began. The main royal advance began in early August and Grey was able to reach Ruthin, the centre of Dafydd's lordship of Dyffryn Clwyd, by the third week of the month. There is, however, no indication that the king's army reached the vicinity of Denbigh until mid-October, and this suggests that strong resistance was encountered in Dafydd's lordship of Rhufoniog. Along with Rhos, Rhufoniog was granted to Henry de Lacy, earl of Lincoln, on 16 October, and Dyffryn Clwyd was conveyed to Grey on 23 October.

Conflict was stayed upon intervention by John Pecham (d. 1292), archbishop of Canterbury. Dafydd's grievances were included among the materials sent to Pecham before he entered Snowdonia for discussions with Llywelyn and probably with Dafydd. Upon his return to Rhuddlan, finding the king still bent upon the princes' unconditional surrender, Pecham secured the magnates' consent to proposals that they would be prepared to recommend to the king if Llywelyn and Dafydd were to submit. Llywelyn was offered sanctuary in England, Dafydd was given only an opportunity to leave for the Holy Land, never to return unless recalled by the king. In a trenchant reply Dafydd said that, when he went to the Holy Land, he would do so of his free will, for God and not for man. He, and others with him, had gone to war to defend their patrimony and their liberties. He insisted that he was fighting a just war, and that he was prepared to answer before God for what he had done in the name of justice.

When Llywelyn subsequently departed for the march Dafydd was left to defend Gwynedd Uwch Conwy and, after his brother's death on 11 December 1282, assuming the style 'prince of Wales and lord of Snowdon', he maintained resistance for several months. However, the English assault forced Dafydd's withdrawal to his innermost fastnesses. Castell y Bere fell on 25 April and thereafter Dafydd was a fugitive, searches being made for him by contingents of soldiers far and wide in Snowdonia and further afield. The Hagnaby chronicle states that he sent his wife and Roger Clifford to the king to plead for mercy but to no avail. Dafydd was captured on 22 June 1283 and six days later Edward announced that he had been taken by men of his own nation. He was imprisoned at Rhuddlan. The magnates of the realm and representatives of the shires were summoned to Shrewsbury by the morrow of Michaelmas for the trial of 'the last survivor of a family of traitors' (*Calendar of Various Chancery Rolls, 1277–1326*, 281). Edward expressed his anger at the perfidy of one whom the king had received as an exile, nourished as an orphan, and endowed with lands and placed among the great ones at court. Dafydd was tried and sentenced to death for treason. He was dragged to the scaffold as a traitor, he was hanged for homicide and, because he had committed the murders during the Lord's passion, he was disembowelled and his entrails burnt. For plotting the king's death his body was quartered and sent to four English cities. Geoffrey of Shrewsbury was paid 20s. for executing the judgment on Saturday 2 October. Dafydd's head was placed beside that of his brother at the Tower of London.

Dafydd had two sons, Llywelyn and Owain, who, after their capture, were taken under escort through Acton Burnell to Bristol Castle. Llywelyn died there in 1287 and was buried in the Dominican church; Owain was still at Bristol in 1325. Dafydd was said to have had seven daughters, one of whom was named Gwladus (d. 1328); they were sent to the Gilbertine house of Sixle, Lincolnshire, and other nunneries. The poet Bleddyn Fardd composed Dafydd's elegy and another poem to commemorate Owain, Llywelyn, and Dafydd together.   J. B. Smith

Sources *Chancery records* · *Close rolls of the reign of Henry III*, 14 vols., PRO (1902–38) · *Calendar of various chancery rolls … 1277–1326*, PRO (1912) · J. E. Lloyd, *A history of Wales from the earliest times to the Edwardian conquest*, 3rd edn, 2 vols. (1939); repr. (1988) · J. B. Smith, *Llywelyn ap Gruffudd, prince of Wales* (1998) · R. R. Davies, *Conquest, coexistence, and change: Wales, 1063–1415*, History of Wales, 2 (1987) · *Littere Wallie*, ed. J. G. Edwards (1940) · F. M. Powicke, *King Henry III and the Lord Edward: the community of the realm in the thirteenth century*, 2 vols. (1947) · D. Stephenson, *The governance of Gwynedd* (1984) · *Gwaith Bleddyn Fardd ac eraill o feirdd ail hanner y drydedd ganrif ar ddeg*, ed. R. Andrews and others (1996) · *Registrum epistolarum fratris Johannis Peckham, archiepiscopi Cantuariensis*, ed. C. T. Martin, 3 vols., Rolls Series, 77 (1882–5) · J. Williams ab Ithel, ed., *Annales Cambriae*, Rolls Series, 20 (1860) · T. Jones, ed., 'Cronica de Wallia and other documents from Exeter Cathedral Library, MS 3514', *BBCS*, 12 (1946–8), 27–44

Dafydd ap Gwilym (*fl.* 1330–1350), poet, was born perhaps *c.*1315 at Brogynin, an estate located partly in the parish of Llanfihangel Genau'r-glyn and partly in the parish of Llanbadarn Fawr in northern Cardiganshire, some 5 miles inland from the castle and borough of Aberystwyth. He may have died *c.*1350, possibly as the result of the black death, and was probably buried at the Cistercian abbey of Strata Florida (although the Premonstratensian abbey of Talyllychau also lays claim to his bones). Place-name evidence in his poems confirms overwhelmingly his attachment to his place of birth in northern Cardiganshire, although it also shows that he wandered freely over much of Wales as it then was. It should be stressed that the dates of birth and death given above are conjectural (many scholars would prefer a somewhat later floruit), and an element of uncertainty surrounds his family history also.

Parentage and early writings He was the son of Gwilym Gam (Crooked William) ap Gwilym ab Einion of the line of Gwynfardd Dyfed, who lived in northern Pembrokeshire during the latter part of the eleventh century and whose descendants collaborated consistently and profitably with the Anglo-Norman conquerors. According to genealogies, Gwilym married Ardudful, daughter of Gwilym ap Rhys of the line of *Ednyfed Fychan [see under Tudor family, forebears of (per. c.1215–1404)]; she was thus the sister of Llywelyn ap Gwilym ap Rhys, a substantial landowner in the parishes of Pen-boyr and Nevern in south-west Wales, deputy constable of Newcastle Emlyn in 1343 and deputy justiciar of south Wales (under Sir Gilbert Talbot) in 1344–5. On both his mother's side and (more distantly) his father's, Dafydd ap Gwilym was related to Sir Rhys ap Gruffudd, by far the most powerful Welsh magnate in the southern principality during the first half of the fourteenth century. As far as is known, Dafydd had no brothers or sisters, nor did he *sensu stricto* ever marry, in spite of the fact that his attachment to women provided the matter of the greater part of his verse.

As might be expected from his relatively high birth, and as the meagre evidence on the topic in his own verse suggests, Dafydd ap Gwilym was not left without means by his parents. The presumption is that he inherited lands that he was able to let and thus live on the income; but this income he certainly supplemented with the earnings he received from declaiming his verse (perhaps to his own musical accompaniment) in gentry households throughout Wales: judging by the surviving corpus, his love songs attracted such earnings no less than formal panegyric. Crucial to his formation as a poet was the fact that he was partly brought up at Newcastle Emlyn by his uncle Llywelyn ap Gwilym who apparently taught him the art of Welsh verse as well as more mundane accomplishments, which might have included a knowledge of French and English. It has been argued that he also spent some time at Strata Florida Abbey, where he would have learned a certain amount of Latin as well as liturgical singing. At that time important manuscripts were still being produced in the scriptorium at Strata Florida; the gentry household of Ieuan Llwyd at Parcrhydderch some 10 miles to the southwest was a focus of patronage for professional poets; and somewhere in the vicinity Einion Offeiriad (Einion the Priest) was preparing his manual on Welsh poetic art at the behest of Sir Rhys ap Gruffudd. Dafydd's innate poetic gifts were thus expanded and developed by an educative process which left him endowed not only with complete mastery of the traditional forms of Welsh versecraft but also with a sensitivity to external influence and a readiness to experiment which proved fundamental to his later career as a poet.

Verse compositions Dafydd ap Gwilym's verse, in its most recent critical edition, consists of 150 poems, comprising in all rather more than 7000 lines; since 1952 a further 3 poems have been added to the canon (others are under discussion). Of these 153 poems it may be said that 27 are traditional in theme—panegyric, satire, poetic debate, and religious devotion—while the remaining 126 celebrate

love, often but not always in a woodland setting; the line count of these love poems amounts to almost 6000. An analysis of the corpus by metrical form is equally revealing: 8 of Dafydd's poems are *awdlau*, 5 are sequences of *englynion*, and the remaining 140 are *cywyddau*. These figures define Dafydd as overwhelmingly a love poet employing the *cywydd* metre. This is in stark contrast to the situation obtaining in the previous century (and even, in some circles, in his own century as well), when the Welsh professional poet was typically a court official praising the king and the occasional nobleman in *awdl* metres, although *englynion* were also sometimes used. Dafydd thus represents a decisive break with tradition in both metrics and matter. He may indeed have invented the *cywydd* metre by embellishing and regularizing the humble *traethodl* hitherto used exclusively (as far as can be judged) by lower-grade poets, and he certainly popularized the *cywydd* to the extent that it remained the staple of Welsh professional poetry for a further 300 years [see Cywyddwyr (act. c.1330–c.1650)]. The break with tradition as regards matter is more difficult to assess: Dafydd certainly had his forerunners as love poet, but the scale and preponderance of love poetry in Dafydd's verse is entirely new. While it is clear that there was a shift in taste from panegyric to love poetry among the class that increasingly assumed the role of patron, that is the landowning, office-holding *uchelwyr* (literally 'men of high birth'), it has been argued that Dafydd's love poetry may be disguised panegyric, designed to uphold the ideals and morale of the Welsh élite in the face of the Norman advance. Nevertheless, it is likely that Dafydd is chiefly a love poet because that is the role that best suited both his personality and his experience of life.

Before describing Dafydd ap Gwilym's love poetry in more detail, however, it may be as well to glance briefly at his more traditional verse. His five conventional but skilful and sincere religious poems include a metrical version of the liturgical prayer *Anima Christi*, which had only recently become popular. Of his praise poems, seven are addressed to Ifor ap Llywelyn (Ifor Hael), and it is noteworthy that four of the seven are *cywyddau*, probably the first praise *cywyddau* ever composed. Other recipients of his praise, whether in life or death, include his uncle Llywelyn ap Gwilym, his neighbour Ieuan Llwyd of Genau'r-glyn, Hywel ap Goronwy, dean (and later bishop) of Bangor, and Angharad, wife of Ieuan Llwyd of Parcrhydderch. There is also a group of four mock elegies for his friend and patron Rhydderch, the son of Ieuan Llwyd, and for his fellow poets Gruffudd ab Adda ap Dafydd, Madog Benfras, and Gruffudd Gryg. Dafydd's satiric *awdl* for Rhys Meigen, which is supposed to have caused Rhys's death, is clumsy invective like so many of its kind. His acrimonious poetic debate with Gruffudd Gryg, however, has as its core one question of substance: the validity or otherwise of the self-abasement typical of the new love poetry that Dafydd personified.

Love poetry Of the 126 love poems now attributed to Dafydd ap Gwilym, nearly two-thirds are anonymous, in the sense that the object of the poet's love is not named in any of them. In 35 poems, however, she is named as Morfudd, in 9 as Dyddgu, and in 3 as Efa, Elen, and Luned respectively. It is a striking fact that the husbands of both Morfudd and Elen can be identified in records and that the father of Dyddgu can be traced—albeit tentatively—in pedigrees; furthermore, Luned is linked with Hugh Tyrrel, a royal official who died in Brittany in 1343, and Efa may just possibly be the second wife of Ifor ap Llywelyn. That is, Dafydd ap Gwilym's loves were indeed creatures of flesh and blood, and not figments of his imagination as was once thought. The figures given above show clearly Morfudd's pre-eminence among them, and a case can be made for assuming that the greater part of Dafydd's 'anonymous' love poems were also addressed to her. If this assumption is made, the story of their relationship becomes somewhat clearer. The daughter of a Merioneth *uchelwr*, Morfudd first met Dafydd while both were living in north-west Wales. They fell in love, and Dafydd began to compose *cywyddau* in praise of her, probably the first *cywyddau* ever composed: these became hugely popular. Dafydd and Morfudd may even have entered into a loose form of marriage contract with each other. Later, however, Morfudd was married formally to a man known as Y Bwa Bychan (the Little Hunchback), who was a neighbour of Dafydd's in north Cardiganshire and who henceforth (as Y Bwa Bach) was to play the role of the Jealous Husband in Dafydd's verse. Dafydd continued to pursue Morfudd, however, and was sometimes accepted and sometimes rejected. Eventually Y Bwa Bychan appears to have secured Dafydd's banishment from his house and lands in north Cardiganshire, and this may have been the occasion of his sojourn with Ifor ap Llywelyn in south-east Wales (another theory is that he may have gone to Ifor ap Llywelyn following the murder of his uncle Llywelyn ap Gwilym, which may have been connected with the granting of the castle of Emlyn to Sir Richard de la Bere in 1346). Finally Dafydd was forced to acknowledge defeat and to renounce Morfudd. It should be stressed that this outline depends entirely on the internal evidence of the poems and on later tradition—both highly problematic sources—but it does offer a framework into which many of Dafydd's love *cywyddau* can provisionally be fitted.

Such a bare outline, however, does scant justice to the rich texture of Dafydd ap Gwilym's verse and the complexity of the emotions expressed in it. As already mentioned, much of this verse has a woodland setting and Dafydd celebrates lovingly not only his beloved's beauty but also the glory of wild nature and the creatures which inhabit it. Birds are especially favoured, and are also prominent among the agents chosen by him to act as his messengers of love: some of his most dazzling passages of *dyfalu* (a descriptive technique involving the accumulation of juxtaposed metaphors) are devoted to such. Sometimes the scene shifts to the beloved's house, but Dafydd is often ill at ease in such a setting, where hindrances to his assignations abound (although nature, too, can produce such hindrances). One memorable poem is set in Dafydd's parish church of Llanbadarn Fawr, where his devotion to the young women in the congregation rather than to the

Blessed Sacrament might be thought to give point to the admonitions levelled at him from time to time by the friars (admonitions which, except towards the end of his life, he scornfully rejects). Although in a sense an Aberystwyth man, his experience of boroughs elsewhere in Wales is not uniformly happy, since these provide the setting for his most *fabliau*-like escapades in which he is invariably worsted. Mention of *fabliaux* serves to underline the point that Dafydd was seemingly well aware of the fashions and conventions of love poetry in Europe in his time, and that he makes considerable, if highly individualistic, use of such fashions and conventions. How he came to know of these fashions and conventions is a matter still under discussion: some of them may have reached him through sub-literary channels, others by personal contact within the mixed society of which he was a member. Moreover, it has been pointed out that there are possible direct borrowings in his work from the *Amores* of Ovid, from *Le roman de la rose*, and from the poetry of Jean de Condé. It is not as a confusing blend of influences that Dafydd's verse impresses, however, but as the product of the unified vision of a man who was able to respond to the full to the joys and sorrows of life—for which the joys and sorrows of love provided a far from inadequate metaphor—and to express his response in poetry of consummate craftsmanship, unflagging invention, and haunting verbal music.

R. GERAINT GRUFFYDD

Sources *Gwaith Dafydd ap Gwilym*, ed. T. Parry, 1952, 2nd edn (1963) · D. Johnston, '"Cywydd y gal" by Dafydd ap Gwilym', *Cambridge Medieval Celtic Studies*, 9 (1985), 71–89 · R. G. Gruffydd, '"Englynion y cusan" by Dafydd ap Gwilym', *Cambridge Medieval Celtic Studies*, 23 (1992), 1–6 · A. J. Owen and D. F. Evans, eds., *Gwaith Llywelyn Brydydd Hoddnant, Dafydd ap Gwilym, Hillyn ac craill* (1996), 49–92 · *Dafydd ap Gwilym: the poems*, ed. and trans. R. M. Loomis (Binghampton, NY, 1982) · R. Bromwich, *Aspects of the poetry of Dafydd ap Gwilym* (1986) · H. Fulton, *Dafydd ap Gwilym and the European context* (1989) · *Selections from the Dafydd ap Gwilym Apocrypha*, ed. H. Fulton (1996) · H. M. Edwards, *Dafydd ap Gwilym: influences and analogues* (1996) · R. G. Gruffydd, 'Dafydd ap Gwilym: an outline biography', *Celtic languages and Celtic peoples*, ed. C. J. Byrne and others (1992), 425–42 · NL Wales, Peniarth MSS 53, 87

Archives NL Wales, Peniarth MSS 53, 87

Dafydd ap Llywelyn (*c.*1215–1246), prince of Gwynedd, was the son of *Llywelyn ab Iorwerth (d. 1240) and *Joan (d. 1237), illegitimate daughter of King *John. Llywelyn was promised Joan's hand in 1204 and the marriage probably took place the next year. Dafydd had not been born in August 1211 when Llywelyn submitted to King John and was forced to concede that, if he were to have no son with Joan, his lands would be ceded to the king who would provide for Llywelyn's bastard son *Gruffudd ap Llywelyn (d. 1244) as he wished.

Early career Dafydd may have been born *c.*1215. He is first mentioned in May 1220 when, at a meeting at Shrewsbury with the justiciar, Hubert de Burgh, Archbishop Stephen Langton, and the papal legate, Pandulf, royal approval was given to Llywelyn's decision that he should be succeeded by Dafydd rather than by Gruffudd. Two years later Llywelyn secured papal approval for an ordinance declaring his wish to set aside the custom of his country by which, he said, in words with a clear reference to Galatians 4: 30, 'the son of the handmaiden should be heir with the son of a freewoman and illegitimate sons possess the inheritance like the legitimate' (*CEPR letters*, 1.87). He provided that Dafydd, his son with his wedded wife, should succeed him by hereditary right. He secured the consent of the magnates of Wales in 1226, a year in which Dafydd and his parents met the king at Shrewsbury. Llywelyn had had no success in his efforts to secure royal recognition of the supremacy over Powys and Deheubarth that he had established during the conflicts of the reign of John, but he evidently hoped that his son would be able to succeed not only to Gwynedd but to his wider dominion. When, however, Dafydd did homage to the king in 1229 (possibly upon his coming of age at fourteen years), he did so for the 'rights and privileges' to which he would succeed upon his father's death (*CPR, 1225–32*, 269). This was a form of words which would be interpreted in accordance with the king's wishes in due course. During William (V) de Briouze's imprisonment following his capture in 1228 Llywelyn secured a promise of the marcher lord's daughter, Isabella, as Dafydd's wife, with the lordship of Builth as her marriage portion. In May 1230, following his affair with Joan, Briouze was hanged by Llywelyn, but the prince immediately wrote to the marcher's widow, Eva, conveying his wish that the marriage should still take place. Dafydd and Isabella were probably married before the end of 1232 when arrangements were made for the assignment of a portion of the Briouze inheritance. Llywelyn had already secured possession of the lordship of Builth.

Struggle with half-brother Gruffudd From 1231 onwards, sometimes in association with his mother or his father's seneschal Ednyfed Fychan (*d.* 1246), Dafydd was engaged on diplomatic missions to the king. Adversely affected by Llywelyn's offensives in the march between 1231 and 1234, undertaken on the prince's sole initiative or in association with Richard Marshal, earl of Pembroke, Henry III repeatedly intimated his readiness to discuss not only a truce but the treaty of peace by which Llywelyn sought formal acknowledgement of his broad supremacy. Successive attempts at negotiation produced no more than a truce and by 1237, when Llywelyn endured a paralytic stroke, Dafydd's role in the quest for a permanent settlement was greatly enhanced. There is probably some substance in Matthew Paris's account, that the two princes' search for a permanent peace was made urgent by the recalcitrance shown by Gruffudd ap Llywelyn. Gruffudd had suffered two periods of imprisonment but was now at liberty and represented a challenge to his brother's succession. Anxieties in Gwynedd may explain Llywelyn's decision early in 1238 to summon the princes of Wales to an assembly at which they would do homage to Dafydd. Henry III reacted with a firm order to Llywelyn and Dafydd, and to the princes of Powys and Deheubarth, forbidding the homages. The marchers were alerted and summoned to a meeting at Oxford. No more was heard of the issue of homage and the Welsh chronicle *Brut y tywysogyon* is probably correct in recording that, at a gathering at the Cistercian abbey of Strata Florida in the autumn of 1238, the Welsh princes swore fealty to Dafydd, making no mention of homage.

Succession and submission to Henry III The chronicle states that in 1239, before the death of Llywelyn, Dafydd ap Llywelyn seized Gruffudd and his eldest son, Owain, and imprisoned them in the castle of Cricieth. Matthew Paris, however, in an informed account of the course of events following the death of Llywelyn on 11 April 1240, offers a different interpretation according to which Gruffudd was at liberty at that time. Acting swiftly Dafydd came to Henry at Gloucester on 15 May and did homage for his right in Gwynedd. Lands which other barons claimed against him were made subject to arbitration and it was clearly stated that the homages of all the princes of Wales should remain with the king of England. The Tewkesbury chronicler, who states that Dafydd came before Henry wearing the coronet of Gwynedd and that he was knighted by the king, conveys that Dafydd was allowed to do homage only for the lands that Llywelyn had held by right (*de jure*), revealing the humiliating extent to which he had surrendered to the king. Fortified none the less by Henry's endorsement of his succession to Gwynedd, Dafydd was able to return to his patrimony to confront the challenge presented by his half-brother. Gruffudd was probably seized, as Paris indicates, in the early autumn of 1240. The capture was alleged to have been accomplished by treachery and on this account, possibly among others, Dafydd incurred the unrelenting wrath of Richard, bishop of Bangor. Dafydd's support in lay society in Gwynedd was less than complete, but, with the adherence of Ednyfed Fychan and a number of key lineages, he strengthened his position in the patrimony. A new confidence came to be reflected during the following months in a marked intransigence in his relations with the crown over the arbitration procedures to which he was bound by the treaty of Gloucester.

By the summer of 1241 Henry was resolved upon a military campaign as a means of imposing discipline upon the prince of Gwynedd. Dafydd was already bereft of adherents among the Welsh princes who, promptly upon Llywelyn's death, had done as they were bidden and returned to the king's fealty. His position was undermined by Henry's decision, contrary to his endorsement of Dafydd's succession in 1240, to take up the cause of Gruffudd. Prompted by an initiative on the part of Gruffudd's wife, Senana, who sought his release from imprisonment, Henry undertook to secure his release and make a judgment of his court, according to Welsh law, concerning the portion of his father's patrimony which belonged to him but which Dafydd denied him. The list of Welsh princes and marcher lords who pledged the agreement between Henry and Senana on 12 August provides a graphic indication of the powerful influences that converged to bring Dafydd to submission. Confronting the king's army in the four cantrefs of Perfeddwlad (the lands between the Conwy and the Dee) Dafydd could not offer effective resistance and found withdrawal beyond the Conwy to Snowdonia impossible. On 29 August, at Gwerneigron on the banks of the Elwy near St Asaph, he accepted terms that reflected his dire plight. He was required to hand over Gruffudd to the king and agree to accept the judgment of the king's court concerning the portion of the patrimony due to Gruffudd. The agreement raised the prospect that Gwynedd would be divided into two parts, to be held by the two brothers as tenants-in-chief of the crown. Dafydd yielded Englefield (north-east Wales from the River Clwyd to the Dee) and accepted that the lands that Llywelyn had possessed by might, and that should have been subject to arbitration, be restored to their lords. It was emphasized again that the homage of the Welsh lords of Wales ought by right to belong to King Henry. At Rhuddlan two days later he agreed to place himself under ecclesiastical jurisdiction if he were ever to renounce his fealty to the crown and acknowledged that breach of faith would incur the forfeiture of his entire inheritance. In another document executed in London in the autumn, when the essential features of his submission were rehearsed once more, he made a further concession that if he were to die without heir his patrimony would be ceded to the king.

Resistance to English power, and death Gruffudd was transferred to the Tower of London in September 1241 but Henry made no attempt to divide the patrimony. In 1243–4 the brothers brought actions in the king's court alleging breach of the king's peace but Dafydd did not appear, excusing himself because he suffered an illness that caused him to lose the hair of his head and the nails of his toes and fingers. The issue of Gruffudd's share of the inheritance is not known to have been broached in legal action. While Gruffudd remained in his custody Henry had the means of keeping Dafydd under restraint. The king may also have been prepared to tolerate the fact that Gruffudd's second son, *Llywelyn ap Gruffudd (d. 1282), had established lordship in Dyffryn Clwyd, one of the three of the four cantrefs which formed part of Dafydd's dominion. However, Gruffudd's death on 1 March 1244, in an attempt to escape from captivity, released Dafydd from the constraints placed upon him. Presenting himself as the avenger of his brother, Dafydd quickly summoned the princes of Wales to a new alliance in resistance to the English king and won a good measure of support. Henry sent Gruffudd's eldest son, Owain ap Gruffudd, to Chester with a view to releasing him so that he could draw support away from Dafydd when opportunity arose. But, though he won complete freedom before the end of 1244, Owain did not enter Gwynedd while Dafydd lived. By then Llywelyn ap Gruffudd, setting aside the animosities that had riven the lineage, had joined forces with Dafydd. Henry was confronted with a broad Welsh alliance founded upon a new-found unity in Gwynedd.

During this period of armed resistance Dafydd endeavoured to break free from his subjection to Henry III by making an appeal to Innocent IV. The enterprise was designed to enable Dafydd to hold his dominion as a papal fief. Innocent's first response shows that Dafydd had argued that his parents had given him as a ward (*alumnus*) to the Church of Rome, and that on this account he sought to be absolved from the pledges exacted from him upon his submission to King Henry. The pope's letter raised the prospect that the king of England would be summoned to Caerwys and examined on the prince's behalf by the abbots of Aberconwy and Cymer. Nine months later, reflecting both Henry's rebuttal and his alacrity in meeting his financial obligations to the Holy See, Innocent repudiated his previous response and accepted that Dafydd's ancestors had long been vassals of the king.

It appears that during the period when he negotiated with the papal court, excommunicated by the archbishop of Canterbury and his land under interdict, Dafydd styled himself 'prince of Wales'. His decision to use the style reflected the broad, though not universal, support that he won among the princes of Wales. After prolonged delay an army was summoned to Chester for a campaign on which the king embarked in August 1245. He advanced to the Conwy and encamped for two months in the fortifications of Deganwy. A force from Ireland ravaged Anglesey, but the king was unable to breach the defences of Snowdonia. The soldiers at Deganwy suffered deprivation and by early October, conceding the need to make a truce with Dafydd, Henry withdrew. Before conflict was renewed Dafydd was dead. He died at Aber on 25 February 1246 and was buried at the abbey of Aberconwy. There were already signs of fissure among the prince's adherents in Deheubarth but it was only after his death that the alliance fell apart.

Historians' judgements upon the prince who failed to maintain the supremacy established by his father have tended to be somewhat harsh. Dafydd had come to an unenviable inheritance, his patrimonial dominion wracked by Gruffudd ap Llywelyn's challenge for the succession and his father's broader supremacy necessarily impermanent in the absence of recognition by the crown in a formal peace treaty. Dafydd's strenuous and sustained resistance in 1244–6 undoubtedly won him respect in his time. Two years before he died the poet Dafydd Benfras had commemorated Gruffudd ap Llywelyn in vibrant terms which suggest firm adherence, but in his elegy to Dafydd, in which he proclaimed him to be the rightful ruler of Gwynedd, he composed a deeply moving tribute to a steadfast defender of his land who yielded nothing to the crown of London. He was deemed to be one who had proved entirely worthy of his lineage.

According to the terms of his submission in 1241 Gwynedd would now fall to the king for either of two reasons: Dafydd had rebelled against the crown and he had died without heir. Even so, royal appropriation of Snowdonia was not politically feasible. After the two eldest sons of Gruffudd ap Llywelyn, Owain and Llywelyn, had agreed to share the patrimony between them, Henry, by the treaty of Woodstock in April 1247, endorsed the arrangement, but he confined the brothers to the land west of the Conwy. A year later Henry allowed Owain and Llywelyn to remove the body of their father, Gruffudd ap Llywelyn, from London to Aberconwy to be laid beside Llywelyn ab Iorwerth and Dafydd ap Llywelyn. Dafydd Benfras composed an elegy which, commemorating the three princes together, accorded each one a place of honour in the annals of their dynasty.

J. B. SMITH

Sources *Chancery records* · J. E. Lloyd, *A history of Wales from the earliest times to the Edwardian conquest*, 2 vols. (1911) · J. B. Smith, *Llywelyn ap Gruffudd, prince of Wales* (1998) · R. R. Davies, *Conquest, coexistence, and change: Wales, 1063–1415*, History of Wales, 2 (1987) · G. A. Williams, 'The succession to Gwynedd, 1238–47', *BBCS*, 20 (1962–4), 393–413 · M. Richter, 'David ap Llywelyn, the first prince of Wales', *Welsh History Review / Cylchgrawn Hanes Cymru*, 5 (1970–71), 205–19 · J. B. Smith, 'Dynastic succession in medieval Wales', *BBCS*, 33 (1986), 199–232 · *Littere Wallie*, ed. J. G. Edwards (1940) · F. M. Powicke, *King Henry III and the Lord Edward: the community of the realm in the thirteenth century*, 2 vols. (1947) · R. F. Walker, 'Hubert de Burgh and Wales, 1218–32', *EngHR*, 87 (1972), 465–94 · *Gwaith Dafydd Benfras ac eraill o feirdd hanner cyntaf y drydedd ganrif ar ddeg*, ed. Y Chwaer Bosco and others (1994) · *Paris, Chron.* · T. Jones, ed. and trans., *Brut y tywysogyon, or, The chronicle of the princes: Red Book of Hergest* (1955) · *Curia regis rolls preserved in the Public Record Office* (1922–) · *CEPR letters*
Likenesses M. Paris, manuscript drawing, in or before 1259, CCC Cam., MS 16, fol. 132*r*

Dafydd Benfras (*c*.1195–1258/9). *See under* Gogynfeirdd (*act. c*.1080–1285).

Dafydd Ddu Eryri. *See* Thomas, David (1759–1822).

Dafydd Ddu o Hiraddug (*d*. in or before **1371**), grammarian and poet, was presumably a native of the township of Hiraddug in the parish of Cwm, which was part of the commote of Rhuddlan in the hundred of Tegeingl in north-east Wales. He may have been the boy 'David Duy' who was a member of the household of Llywelyn ab Ynyr, bishop of St Asaph, in 1311. It is perhaps less likely that he was the 'Magister David de Rhuddallt' who obtained preferment in the diocese of Bangor between 1318 and 1328, although there is a village named Rhu(dd)allt in the commote of Rhuddlan. The fact that he is styled 'Athro' (*magister*) in his grammar book and elsewhere suggests that he was a university graduate, probably of Oxford. He may indeed have been at one time chancellor of the cathedral church of St Asaph. In 1357 'Magister David de Englefield', a canon of St Asaph, was Archbishop Islip's vicar-general during a vacancy in the see. The vacancy was filled when Archdeacon Llywelyn ap Madog ab Elis was made bishop, and Dafydd Ddu may have succeeded him as archdeacon, residing at Diserth. By 1371 Ithel ap Robert was archdeacon and Dafydd Ddu was probably dead. Edward Lhwyd records a tradition that he was buried at Diserth, and this is to be preferred to the slightly later tradition that his remains lie at Tremeirchion. Folk-tales about him proliferated, and in the Renaissance he was confused with Roger Bacon.

Dafydd Ddu (his epithet means 'Black') is best known as the reviser of Einion Offeiriad's grammar book or poets' manual. An early copy of his revision is extant in Aberystwyth, National Library of Wales, MS Peniarth 20, of *c*.1330, probably written at the Cistercian abbey of Valle Crucis. Dafydd preserves the basic arrangement and much of the material of Einion's grammar but relocates some of the material, amplifies it somewhat, and occasionally adds to it (he rarely omits or curtails). He has forty-seven examples of metres and metrical faults compared to Einion's thirty-nine. Whereas Einion's grammar credits Einion with the invention of three 'new' metres, Dafydd's

revision credits these to Dafydd. Both versions have one metrical example that is Dafydd's own work, which may point to some collaboration from the beginning.

Dafydd Ddu is also the author of three skilful religiodidactic poems: on the history of the world from Adam to Christ (largely based on *L'Enfant sage*), on the ten commandments (combined with the two evangelical precepts, as in Mark 12: 29–30), and on the evanescence of life. *Gwasanaeth Mair* ('Mary's service'), a metrical translation of *Horae beatae Mariae virginis*, has been ascribed to him. The case for his authorship of the mystical treatise *Ymborth yr enaid* ('Food for the soul') is more precarious.

R. GERAINT GRUFFYDD

Sources R. G. Gruffydd, 'Wales's second grammarian: Dafydd Ddu of Hiraddug', *PBA*, 90 (1996), 1–29 · G. J. Williams and E. J. Jones, eds., *Gramadegau'r penceirddiaid* (1934) · *Gwaith Einion Offeiriad a Dafydd Ddu o Hiraddug*, ed. R. G. Gruffydd and R. Ifans (1997) · *Gwassanaeth Meir*, ed. B. F. Roberts (1961) · R. Iestyn Daniel, ed., *Ymborth yr enaid* (1995) · *Parochialia … by Edward Lhwyd*, ed. R. H. Morris (1909–11)
Archives BL, Add. MSS · NL Wales, various collections | Bodl. Oxf., Jesus College MSS · Cardiff Central Library, foundation collection · U. Wales, Bangor, Gwyneddon collection · U. Wales, Bangor, Mostyn collection

Dafydd [David] **Gam** (*d*. **1415**), warrior, was descended lineally from the native Welsh rulers of Brycheiniog; his own pedigree, which can be documentarily established from the mid-thirteenth century, runs as follows: Dafydd Gam ap Llywelyn ap Hywel Fychan ap Hywel ab Einion Sais. Every one of his forebears from Einion Sais (*fl*. 1270) down to Dafydd's father, Llywelyn, had given distinguished service to the Bohun earls of Hereford as lords of Brecon. They had held some of the major offices in the lordship, notably those of sheriff, constable, and master-sergeant; they had stood loyally by the Bohun family during the political crises of 1297 and 1322; and they in turn had been well rewarded with leases, annuities, and gifts. They were clearly the premier and wealthiest Welsh family of the lordship and are a striking example of a native family that flourished under the rule of an English aristocratic family.

When the Bohun family failed in the male line in 1373, the lordship of Brecon eventually came into the possession of Henry Bolingbroke, earl of Derby, by his marriage to Mary, one of the two daughters and coheirs of the last Bohun earl of Hereford. Dafydd Gam—the nickname Gam probably refers to a squint or other sight defect—probably entered Bolingbroke's service in the 1380s, thus continuing his family's long tradition of service to the lords of Brecon. In 1399 he was already in receipt of a substantial annuity of 40 marks; with his lord's accession to the throne in September 1399 he could have looked forward to wider avenues of service and even greater rewards. He, his son Morgan, and his brother Gwilym (or William) were all described as king's esquires early in the new reign. Instead his career was to be dominated for the next twelve years by the revolt of Owain Glyn Dŵr. In life and in legend Dafydd Gam became one of Owain's most die-hard opponents. He and his family received grants of lands confiscated from the Welsh rebels in Cardiganshire and in the lordship of Brecon, and the Scottish chronicler Walter Bower assigns a prominent place to Dafydd in the crushing defeat of Glyn Dŵr at the battle of Pwll Melyn near Usk on 5 May 1405. The story that he was seized at the parliament held by Owain Glyn Dŵr at Machynlleth in 1404 after plotting Glyn Dŵr's death first appears in antiquarian writings in the seventeenth century; but it is clear that Dafydd's reputation as a mortal enemy of Glyn Dŵr was established much earlier. He may indeed, as has been suggested, be the model for Shakespeare's Fluellen, the archetypal Welshman.

What is beyond doubt is that Dafydd Gam and his family paid heavily for its opposition to Glyn Dŵr. In 1403–4 his father, Llywelyn ap Hywel, was given an annuity of £20 for his services and as a compensation for the losses he had suffered at the hands of Welsh rebels. The hounding of the family continued after the revolt began to wane. Llywelyn was given a comprehensive pardon in May 1411 in order to thwart the legal snares that his Welsh enemies were deliberately setting for him. But the greatest blow came in 1412 when Dafydd Gam himself was captured by the Welsh and ransomed for a sum variously estimated at 200 and 700 marks. He was given permission to raise a personal subsidy from the duchy of Lancaster estates in Wales in order to meet the ransom demand.

Dafydd Gam served with three foot archers at the battle of Agincourt (25 October 1415), where he was slain. By the sixteenth century legends of his bravado at the battle and claims that he was knighted there for his valour were circulating; but though his death is recorded in several chronicles, there is no contemporary substantiation in them, or in any other source, for the legends.

Dafydd is alleged by the genealogies to have married Gwladys, daughter of Gwilym ap Hywel Crach (who was certainly bailiff of Pencelli in the lordship of Brecon, 1374–6). His descendants in the male line eventually adopted the Anglicized surname Games. They were among the most prominent patrons of Welsh poets in the fifteenth century. Gwladys, Dafydd Gam's daughter, married successively Sir Roger *Fychan (Vaughan) of Tretower [see under Vaughan family] and Sir William ap Thomas of Raglan. Her son by the latter marriage was William, the first Herbert earl of Pembroke.

T. F. TOUT, rev. R. R. DAVIES

Sources R. R. Davies, *Lordship and society in the march of Wales, 1284–1400* (1978) · R. R. Davies, *The revolt of Owain Glyn Dŵr* (1995) · J. E. Lloyd, *Owen Glendower* (1931) · *Chancery records* · W. Bower, *Scotichronicon*, ed. D. E. R. Watt and others, new edn, 9 vols. (1987–98), vol. 8 · T. Walsingham, *The St Albans chronicle, 1406–1420*, ed. V. H. Galbraith (1937) · T. Pennant, *Tours in Wales*, ed. J. Rhys, 3 vols. (1883) · N. H. Nicolas, *History of the battle of Agincourt*, 3rd edn (1833) · PRO, SC 6 · PRO, DL

Dafydd Llwyd o Fathafarn (*fl. c.*1400–*c.*1490), poet, was the son of Llywelyn ap Gruffudd ab Ieuan Llwyd and his wife Goleubryd ferch Madog. He was of gentry stock, his residence being Mathafarn in the parish of Llanwrin in western Powys. His wife was Margred ferch Gwilym ap Llywelyn Fychan. According to genealogical sources they had six children, four sons and two daughters.

Together with Robin Ddu of Anglesey, Dafydd Llwyd was the most prolific exponent of Welsh vaticinal poetry, the *cywydd brud*, during the fifteenth century [see also Cywyddwyr (*act. c.*1330–*c.*1650)]. This poetry, which enjoyed a new vogue during the Wars of the Roses, expressed the ancient desire for the restoration of Welsh sovereignty over the island of Britain, usually focusing hope on a *mab darogan* ('son of prophecy') who would achieve this aim by military conquest. Over forty of Dafydd's extant canon of some eighty poems are composed in this vein. Many of these poems are deliberately obscure and vague and not easily associated with contemporary events, being essentially a reworking of old material, much of it derived from Geoffrey of Monmouth. Others, however, are more specific, referring to identifiable contemporary figures, though often in bird or animal guise. Although Dafydd addressed a poem to Edward IV and enjoyed the patronage of his prominent supporter William Herbert, earl of Pembroke (*d.* 1469), he was primarily a partisan of the Lancastrian Tudors. Having initially hailed Jasper Tudor as deliverer of the Welsh, his hopes eventually centred on Henry Tudor. A number of his poems anticipated Henry's landing in Pembrokeshire in 1485, in particular a majestic ode to St David, which invokes the protection of the patron saint for Henry's cause. According to a tradition generally accepted by historians, Henry enjoyed Dafydd's hospitality at Mathafarn *en route* through Wales to Bosworth and consulted the elderly poet as to his fate. After Henry's victory at Bosworth, Dafydd hailed him in an exultant poem, rejoicing that there was now 'a golden crown on our kinsman'. He also vilified the dead Richard III, deriding his physical shortcomings ('a feeble leg instead of a mighty thigh', 'a little ape') and cataloguing his crimes, in particular his murder of the princes in the Tower ('a slavish boar tortured the sons of Edward in his prison'). After 1485 Dafydd addressed further vaticinal poems to Henry, to his son Arthur, and to his leading Welsh supporter Sir Rhys ap Thomas. Despite his undoubted devotion to the king, there are hints of unease in these later poems at Henry's dependence on English counsellors.

Apart from his vaticinal poetry Dafydd addressed eulogies to prominent patrons such as William Herbert, earl of Pembroke, Walter Devereux (Lord Ferrers), and Sir Rhys ap Thomas. Of his elegies the most notable are a poem on the death of Sir Gruffudd Fychan, who was executed by Henry Grey, count of Tankerville, at Powis Castle in 1447, an elegy to William Herbert following his execution after the battle of Banbury in 1469, and an elegy to an unnamed girl who died of bubonic plague, in which the symptoms of the disease are graphically described. Dafydd participated in poetic disputes with Llywelyn ap Gutun (involving the poetess Gwerful Mechain) and the cleric 'Sir' Rhys of Carno. Also worthy of note among his occasional poems are the sexually explicit verses he exchanged with Gwerful Mechain, and a poem recalling an encounter with a girl at Ludlow from whom he had contracted venereal disease.

Dafydd died in extreme old age. Elegies were composed

in his honour by Dafydd ap Hywel and Hywel Dafydd Llwyd ab y Gof, the latter poet indicating that all his sons had predeceased him.   GRUFFYDD ALED WILLIAMS

Sources W. L. Richards, *Gwaith Dafydd Llwyd o Fathafarn* (1964) • W. L. Richards, 'Cywyddau brud Dafydd Llwyd ap Llywelyn ap Gruffudd o Fathafarn', *Llên Cymru*, 2 (1952–3), 244–54 • W. L. Richards, 'Cywyddau ymryson a dychan Dafydd Llwyd o Fathafarn', *Llên Cymru*, 3 (1954–5), 215–28 • E. Roberts, *Dafydd Llwyd o Fathafarn* (1981) • P. C. Bartrum, ed., *Welsh genealogies, AD 300–1400*, 8 vols. (1974) • P. C. Bartrum, ed., *Welsh genealogies, AD 1400–1500*, 18 vols. (1983) • G. A. Williams, 'The bardic road to Bosworth: a Welsh view of Henry Tudor', *Transactions of the Honourable Society of Cymmrodorion* (1986), 7–31 • R. W. Evans, 'Prophetic poetry', *A guide to Welsh literature*, ed. A. O. H. Jarman and G. R. Hughes, 2: *1282–c.1550* (1979), 278–97 • E. I. Rowlands, 'Dilid y Broffwydoliaeth', *Trivium*, 2 (1967), 37–46

Dafydd y Garreg Wen. *See* Owen, David (1711/12–1741).

Dafydd, Marged. *See* Davies, Margaret (c.1700–1785?).

D'Agar, Charles (1669–1723), portrait painter, was probably born in Paris, the only surviving son of **Jacques** [Jacob] **D'Agar** (1642–1715), portrait painter, and his wife, Marie Picard, whom he had married c.1669. Jacques D'Agar had been born in Paris of unknown parents. He may have studied under Jacob Ferdinand Voet, although this remains uncertain. The work of father and son is often confused, the father's reputation as a portraitist at the English court erroneously surpassing that of his son. As protestants the Agar family emigrated to London at some time between 1678 and 1681, by which time they had been made denizens; on 31 January 1682 Jacques D'Agar was officially expelled from the French academy on religious grounds. He was active in England until 1684, but only one of his works from this period is known: a full-length portrait of Charles II's French mistress, Louise de Kéroualle, duchess of Portsmouth (c.1682; Det Nationalhistoriske Museum på Ferderksborg, Denmark). This work was among a group of paintings listed as having been brought with him from England to Denmark that he eventually sold to the king of Denmark in 1702 (letter, NPG); it is the only work securely attributed to him that was likely to have been painted while he was in England. He and his family left England in 1684 for Copenhagen, where, as gentleman of the court and painter in ordinary to the king, he worked at the courts of Christian V and Frederick IV until his death there on 16 November 1715. His self-portrait, painted in 1693 and sent by Christian V to Cosimo III, is now in the Uffizi Galleries, Florence.

Although his *œuvre* was clearly of more consequence to English art than that of his father, Charles D'Agar has largely been consigned to his father's shadow. Municipal records show that he was living with his father in Copenhagen between 1686 and 1689, but Charles D'Agar had returned to London by 1691, after which time he enjoyed success as a court portraitist. He painted in the style of Michael Dahl; his few known works are mannered and competent, the most notable of which is *Lord George Douglas* (c.1700) at Drumlanrig Castle, Dumfriesshire. Many of his portraits were engraved in mezzotint during his lifetime by George White, John Simon, Francis Cornaro, John Smith, and John Faber jun., although these have been erroneously catalogued as by Jacopo D'Agar. After the painter's death in Leicester Fields, London, in May 1723, George Vertue attended the sale of his collection of prints and drawings and reported that Agar had been 'a good curteous Man. [who] came into good business & reputation among the court Ladyes by his pleasant manner of painting, affability & ... for several years before he died he was much employ'd ... but [he was] afflicted violently with the Gout & Stone' (Vertue, *Note books*, 3.15). Horace Walpole later sharply honed Vertue's observations, noting that Agar 'rose to great business, though upon a very slender stock of merit' (Walpole, 4.11). Charles D'Agar left a widow, Susannah.   JULIA MARCIARI ALEXANDER

Sources Vertue, *Note books*, 1.83, 166, 126–7; 3.4, 15 • J. C. Smith, *British mezzotinto portraits*, 1 (1878), 325, 406; 3 (1880), 1076, 1104, 1117, 1119, 1155, 1213, 1254; 4 (1882–4), 1581–2 • P. Lespinasse, 'Jacques d'Agar, portraitiste des rois de Danemark', *Gazette des Beaux-Arts*, 5th ser., 15 (1927), 241–9 • H. Walpole, *Anecdotes of painting in England: with some account of the principal artists*, ed. R. N. Wornum, new edn, 3 vols. (1849); repr. (1876); repr. in 4 vols. (New York, 1969), vol. 2, p. 269; vol. 4, p. 11 • C. Hardouin, 'Jacques ou Jacob d'Agar', *Visages du grand siècle: le portrait français sous le règne de Louis XIV, 1660–1715*, ed. E. Coquery (1997), 198 • E. K. Waterhouse, *The dictionary of British 16th and 17th century painters* (1988), 65 • Thieme & Becker, *Allgemeines Lexikon*, 1.112 • Bénézit, *Dict.* • D. Brême, 'Agar, Jacques d'', *The dictionary of art*, ed. J. Turner (1996) • L. Dussieux, *Les artistes français à l'étranger*, 3rd edn (Paris, 1876), 72, 275–6, 348 • Bryan, *Painters* (1903–5), 1.8 • 'Jacques d'Agar', *Cyclopedia of painters and paintings*, ed. J. D. Champlin and C. C. Perkins (1888), 15 • T. Cooper, *A new biographical dictionary: containing concise notices of eminent persons of all ages and countries* (1873), 473 • Redgrave, *Artists* • will, PRO, PROB 11/591, fol. 1v
Likenesses J. D'Agar, self-portrait, oils, 1693, Uffizi Galleries, Florence, Italy

D'Agar, Jacques (1642–1715). *See under* D'Agar, Charles (1669–1723).

Dagley, Richard (d. 1841), genre painter and engraver, was an orphan and was educated at Christ's Hospital, London. Having an interest in art, and being delicate, he was apprenticed to Thomas Cousens, a jeweller, watchmaker, and sometime painter of ornaments and miniatures, whose daughter Elizabeth (b. 1755) he married on 2 November 1785 at St James's, Westminster. The couple had two sons, Edward (b. 1790) and Richard (b. 1791). Dagley was a friend of Henry Bone, with whom he worked enamelling views on the backs of watches and mythological compositions on bracelets, and painting eyes for rings and brooches, as was then the fashion. He exhibited irregularly at the Royal Academy from 1785 until 1833, mostly genre pictures. His career was similarly erratic. He made several medals and took to watercolour drawing. About 1805 he was working as a drawing-master in a lady's school in Doncaster, but was back in London from 1815. In 1818 he published *A Compendium of the Theory and Practice of Drawing and Painting*. Dagley reviewed books on art and, after the publication of his first book, *Gems Selected from the Antique* in 1804, with plates designed and engraved by him, he worked as an illustrator, most notably on *Flim-Flams*, a collection of anecdotes by Isaac D'Israeli, and for *Takings*, a humorous poem by Thomas Gaspey (1821). He also published books of his own engravings 'illustrated' in poetry or prose by others; his second volume on gems (1822) had poetry by Dr G. Croly and *Death's Doings* (1826) was a meditation on the arrival of death. Dagley's engraved work is often slight. As explained in the preface to *Death's Doings*: 'I have endeavoured to show the way a certain class of writing may be embellished without incurring the expense of those laboured and highly finished engravings which make a work prohibitively expensive'. Dagley died in 1841.　　　　　　　　　L. A. FAGAN, rev. KATHERINE COOMBS

Sources *Art Union*, 3 (1841), 86–7 · *GM*, 2nd ser., 15 (1841), 664–5 · Redgrave, *Artists* · IGI

Dagnall, Charles (d. 1774?), colliery owner and ivory comb maker, is a figure about whom biographical details are sparse. He lived at Eccleston on the edge of what became the industrial town of St Helens in Lancashire. Many people with the name of Dagnall made hair combs throughout the eighteenth century both in Liverpool and inland around Prescot, first using horn and then ivory imported from Africa. The comb maker Samuel Dagnall was often registered in St Helens chapelry, as were his sons James and Thomas, and Henry Dagnall, a contemporary of Samuel. The only entries at St Helens for Charles Dagnall, ivory comb maker, record the births of his daughters Ann and Margaret in 1736 and 1737. Marriages of Charles Dagnall to Hannah Tickle, registered in Huyton parish in 1724, and to Alice Hill, registered in Liverpool in 1735, were both within the area of the comb-making trade, and may refer to the same person; but his birth and death, the birth of his daughter Rachel, and the birth and death of his son James (who died in 1772 after inheriting £350 from John Tickle) went unregistered. Knowledge of Dagnall depends largely on ten letters written between 1 June 1754 and 9 May 1763, which give a vignette of the vicissitudes and personality of an irascible early modern manufacturer.

In 1746 Dagnall leased the coal beneath land owned by George Rice, Henry Seddon, and Basil Thomas Eccleston, from whom he also leased a 23 acre pastoral holding with a comb shop. The lease provided full rights to enter farm tenants' land in the furtherance of mining (but not, as in later leases, with specified recompense for or restitution after damage). The first recorded steam engine in what was to become St Helens was installed by Dagnall, and things went smoothly until 1753, when he sought to renew the lease. A higher rent was asked, which Dagnall refused. He continued mining at the old rent, but raised the price of his coal from 2*d.* to 3*d.* per hundredweight. The colliery's water problems increased costs, took power from the miller, who 'plagued' Dagnall in consequence, and flooded and spoiled farmland; the tenants responded by filling pits and interfering with colliery drainage works when damages were refused.

A new lease was drawn up at the higher rent in 1755, but Dagnall still did not sign, and in 1757 he stopped all payment, though he continued to mine and neglected to fill abandoned pits. In his letters Dagnall protested against 'ill youmered' third parties, the state of the comb trade and water problems, and blustered that it was unwise to pursue claims against him. Although he had 'often wondered that God suffers them so long' that opposed him, he pointed out that Richard Farrar 'never dode well after' meddling with his drainage works, and that 'God took away his life in a little time after'; John Willcock had 'not prospered very well since [abusing me] for he had liked a suffer death'; and of both Mr Chaddock and Mr Deane, who made the same error, Dagnall noted that 'death was his End' (Wrightington MSS, D/D Wr 2755).

Basil Eccleston's initial tolerance of Dagnall may have been because they were both Roman Catholic non-jurors. Attempts to arrange meetings were frustrated, and proposed arbitrators (prominent Roman Catholics among them) refused to act, perhaps because they already knew something about Dagnall. He demurred at one such suggestion because 'as to chuseing atorneys I think the writeings between you & me mentions onest men to chuse [and] I heard Late Mr. Geo. Potter say he thought it was nex to imposable for a torney to be onest' (ibid.). Dagnall did not pay the £185 for which Eccleston sued him in the palatinate court in 1760, disagreed with the £154 13*s.* fixed by further arbitration in 1762, and was offered a settlement at £125 15*s.* 6*d.* in 1763 (PRO, PL 6/82/27). It is unlikely that Dagnall paid the debt.

By 1759 Dagnall had opened two other collieries, one with a steam engine, but they both failed. By 1766 his affairs were in the hands of assignees, and he was declared bankrupt with debts of £2000 in 1770. Dagnall's death probably occurred at Eccleston in 1774, the year in which a law suit was brought against his heirs by his bankruptcy trustees, from whom Dagnall had withheld his late son's inheritance.　　　　　　　　　　　　　　　JOHN LANGTON

Sources T. C. Barker and J. R. Harris, *A Merseyside town in the industrial revolution: St Helens, 1750–1900* (1954) · J. Langton, *Geographical change and industrial revolution: coalmining in south west Lancashire, 1590–1799* (1979) · Wigan Archives Service, Leigh, Wrightington papers, D/D Wr 2755, D/D Wr 1078 · palatinate of Lancaster bills, 14 Feb 1774, PRO, PL 6/86/32

Archives PRO, palatinate of Lancaster bills · Wigan Archives Service, Leigh, Wrightington papers, D/D Wr 2755, D/D Wr 1078

Dagoe, Hannah (d. 1763), thief, was born in Ireland and went to London when very young. She began her working life as a milliner but was a basket-woman in Covent Garden at the time of her condemnation. She married a Spanish seaman named Diego (or Dago) while in Whitechapel gaol for debt, and on his death or his abandonment of her she married William Connor, keeper of that gaol, whom she survived. The *Gentleman's Magazine* records that Dagoe was condemned to death at the Old Bailey sessions on 15 April 1763 for the theft (on 17 March) of household goods belonging to Eleanor Hussey, a widow of Dagoe's acquaintance and 'being all the poor woman had in the world'. According to the *Complete Newgate Calendar*, Dagoe 'broke into Hussey's room and stripped it of every article which it contained' including some 'creditable household furniture'. Described as 'a strong masculine woman', Dagoe was 'the terror of her fellow-prisoners' during her short confinement in Newgate gaol (Rayner, 4.16–17). The *Select Trials* asserts that she stabbed a person in Whitechapel gaol and a Ralph Wayne on a previous confinement in Newgate because she resented the fact that he had turned evidence against his two accomplices.

On 3 May, the day before her execution, Dagoe, in company with two other felons who were to die with her—the forger John Rice and highwayman Paul Lewis—was observed by James Boswell as they made their way to chapel. Boswell had intended walking to the Tower of London to watch John Wilkes being taken to the court of common pleas to face charges of seditious libel over his attack on George III and Lord Bute in the *North Briton* (no. 45, 23 April 1763). Boswell had arrived too late but, being determined to see prisoners of some sort, had made a detour to Newgate on his way back to Westminster. Dagoe made no impression on Boswell: she was, according to him, a 'big unconcerned being'. Rather, it was the handsome and youthful Paul Lewis who styled himself after John Gay's highwayman hero Captain MacHeath that captured Boswell's imagination. It was Lewis who compelled Boswell to go to Tyburn 'with horrid eagerness' the following day in order to observe his last behaviour. The executions of Dagoe, Rice, and Lewis were the first that the 23-year-old Boswell had seen at Tyburn and the first of many described in his journal.

On 4 May Rice, Lewis, and Dagoe travelled the 3 miles from Newgate to Tyburn in two carts because Rice, whose request to travel in a mourning coach had been denied, was permitted to travel in a cart by himself. There was 'a most prestigious crowd of spectators' including Boswell and his friend William Temple who were close enough to the scaffold to 'clearly see all the dismal scene' (*Boswell's London Journal*, 252). According to the *Select Trials*, Dagoe maintained 'a resolute firmness in her look' while the *Complete Newgate Calendar* records how, during the journey, Dagoe appeared unconcerned at the prospect of her fate and ignored the ministrations of the Roman Catholic priest who accompanied her. When the cart drew up under the gallows, however, Dagoe's behaviour changed dramatically and the scene that ensued was 'extraordinary and unprecedented' because of the contempt it demonstrated for the conventions and ceremonials of the scaffold.

Dagoe struggled to get her pinioned arms free and immediately attacked her executioner, Thomas Turlis, daring him to hang her and punching him so violently in the chest that she almost knocked him down. She then threw her hat, cloak, and other articles of clothing into the crowd in order to cheat Turlis of the hangman's right to dispose of the possessions of the condemned. Eventually Dagoe was overpowered and Turlis got the rope around her neck. However, before the signal was given for the carts to move off and the condemned to be 'launched into eternity', Dagoe bound a handkerchief around her head and over her face and threw herself out of the cart with such violence that she broke her neck and died instantly. The executions shocked James Boswell so much that he was thrown into a 'deep melancholy' and was unable to sleep alone for several nights (*Boswell's London Journal*, 252). However, his thoughts were with the genteel Paul Lewis, not Dagoe, whose actions passed without comment in the journal—an indication that the late eighteenth-century vogue for sentimental spectatorship at the gallows seldom extended beyond the dignified gentleman to plebeian criminals such as Hannah Dagoe.

BARBARA WHITE

Sources J. L. Rayner and G. T. Crook, eds., *The complete Newgate calendar*, 4 (privately printed, London, 1926), 16–17 · *GM*, 1st ser., 33 (1763), 199, 207–11, 254 · *Boswell's London journal, 1762–63*, ed. F. A. Pottle (1950), vol. 1 of *The Yale editions of the private papers of James Boswell*, trade edn (1950–89), 250–52 · F. A. Pottle, *James Boswell: the earlier years, 1740–1769* (1966); repr. (1984), 111–12 · *Select trials … at the sessions house in the Old Bailey … from the year 1741 to the present year*, 1764, 4 (1764), 280–3 · L. Benson, ed., *The book of remarkable trials and notorious characters, from 'Half Hanged Smith', 1700, to Oxford who shot at the queen*, 1840 (c.1871), 181 · H. W. Bleackley, *The hangmen of England* (1929) · V. A. C. Gatrell, *The hanging tree: execution and the English people, 1770–1868* (1994); repr. (1996) · *A genuine account of the … life and transactions of J. Rice, braker, for forgery; P. Lewis, a highwayman; and Hannah Dagoe, for stealing goods out of a dwelling house* (1763)

D'Aguilar, Sir George Charles (1784–1855), army officer, second son of Joseph D'Aguilar, formerly a captain in the 2nd dragoon guards (Queen's Bays), and later of Liverpool, was born at Winchester in January 1784. He entered the army as an ensign in the 86th regiment on 24 September 1799, and joined his regiment in India, where he remained for eight years. He was promoted lieutenant on 1 December 1802, and acted as adjutant to his regiment from 1803 to 1806, and as brigade major from 1806 to 1808. During these years he saw much service, principally against the Marathas, and was present at the capture of Baroach in 1803, of Powindar in 1804, and Ujjain in 1805. In 1806 he served in the siege of Bharatpur by Lord Lake, and was severely wounded in the last unsuccessful assault; in 1808 he was promoted captain into the 81st regiment, which he joined in England in May 1809. In the same month he married Eliza, second daughter of Peter Drinkwater of Irwell House, Manchester; they had several children, including General Sir Charles Lawrence D'Aguilar KCB, an officer distinguished in the Crimean War.

In June 1809 D'Aguilar accompanied Brigadier-General the Hon. Stephen Mahon (later Lord Hartland), in command of the 2nd cavalry brigade, in the Walcheren expedition as aide-de-camp, and on his return he was sent as assistant adjutant-general to Sicily. There he attracted the favourable notice of Lord William Bentinck, the general commanding in the Mediterranean, and was sent by him on a special military mission to Ali Pasha, the famous pasha of Yanina, and to Constantinople. He was then selected by Major-General William Clinton to accompany him to the east coast of Spain as military secretary, and acted in the same capacity to Sir John Murray when he superseded Clinton. He carried home the dispatches announcing the victory of Castalla over Marshal Suchet on 13 April 1813 and, as he had luckily been promoted major on 1 April 1813, he received the additional step to the rank of lieutenant-colonel as reward for his news on 20 May 1813. He was also made a substantive major in the

Greek light infantry raised by Richard Church, and remained with that corps until its reduction in 1815. He then joined the duke of Wellington in Flanders, just too late for the battle of Waterloo, and was gazetted major in the rifle brigade on 6 March 1817.

In 1823 D'Aguilar went on the staff again as assistant adjutant-general at the Horse Guards, and was afterwards made deputy adjutant-general at Dublin, a post which he held for eleven years. While there he published his *Practice and Forms of District and Regimental Courts-Martial*, which passed through numerous editions and remained the official authority until 1878. He also published in 1831 *The Officers' Manual*, a translation of the '*Military Maxims of Napoleon*'. He was made a CB in July 1838 and major-general on 23 November 1841, when he left Dublin, and was appointed to command the northern district in Ireland at Belfast, which he held until 1843. In that year he was selected to command the troops in China, and went to Hong Kong to take command of the division left there on its annexation, and of the troops at Chusan (Zhoushan) and Amoy (Xiamen).

The situation of the British in China was at that time critical owing to the ill feeling raised by the war, and on 1 April 1847 D'Aguilar was informed by Sir John Davis, the British commissioner, that in consequence of the ill treatment of the English residents by the Chinese of Canton (Guangzhou) an expedition must be sent out to punish that city. D'Aguilar accordingly started the next day with the 18th regiment (Royal Irish) and the 42nd Madras native infantry, accompanied by the commissioner. He went to the Bogue (Humen), and in two days his force captured all the forts and batteries on the Canton River, spiking 879 guns. He prepared to attack Canton, but an assault was avoided by the prompt submission of the Chinese authorities. Lord Palmerston approved the vigour of these operations. D'Aguilar returned to England in 1848. He was appointed colonel of the 58th regiment in 1848 and transferred to the 23rd regiment in 1851, in which year he became a lieutenant-general; in 1852 he was made KCB. He held the command of the southern district at Portsmouth 1851–2, and died in Lower Brook Street, London, on 21 May 1855.   H. M. Stephens, *rev.* James Lunt

Sources J. Philippart, ed., *The royal military calendar*, 3rd edn, 5 vols. (1820) · *GM*, 2nd ser., 44 (1855) · *Colburn's United Service Magazine*, 2 (1847), 622–7 · private information (1888) · Boase, *Mod. Eng. biog.*

Archives CUL, corresp. and press cuttings | Herts. ALS, letters to E. B. Lytton · NL Scot., letters to Sir Thomas Cochrane · NL Scot., corresp. with Admiral Charles Graham and Lord Rutherford · PRO, letters to Henry Pottinger, FO 705

Dahl, Michael (1659–1743), portrait painter, was born on 29 September 1659 in Stockholm, Sweden. Nothing of his father is known. His mother, Catarina, had a lengthy widowhood in difficult circumstances, as is recorded in a letter from Dahl, written in Rome and dated 6 October 1687, in which he also refers to a sister. George Vertue—who knew Dahl during his English career—was told by the painter's pupil Hans Hysing that Dahl was the pupil in

Michael Dahl (1659–1743), self-portrait, 1691

Stockholm of drawing-master Martin Hannibal (*c.*1674–*c.*1676) and then of the painter David Klöker Ehrenstrahl.

On 30 July 1682 Dahl was issued with a passport and he travelled to England, probably in anticipation of filling the vacuum created by the death of the dominant English portrait painter, Peter Lely. Vertue claimed that Dahl was 'brought from Stockholm to England by Mr. Souters', information that he was given by 'J. Sowter of Exeter'; Vertue added that 'Mr. White [Robert White (1645–1703) the engraver] had 30 pounds of this Gentleman for the King of Swedens plate' (Vertue, *Note books*, 1.33). Sowter was probably Swedish in origin (Soter), and possibly a relation of Dahl's.

Dahl's earliest identifiable work is a portrait of a noted English divine, Samuel Clarke (1599–1683). The painting is lost, and even the mezzotint after it by an unknown engraver has been said to be a copy after an engraving by White. But the bold, rugged simplicity of Dahl's portrait shows through, reflecting the influence of Ehrenstrahl, and is distinct from White's elegant reticence. It was perhaps through White that Dahl met Godfrey Kneller, London's most important portraitist, after whose works the engraver had made many prints. In 1684 Dahl travelled to Paris with Henry Tilson, a pupil and assistant of Lely's who may also have worked for Kneller. Indeed Dahl and Tilson may have accompanied Kneller, who was sent to France by Charles II to paint Louis XIV in late 1684. Dahl's presence in Paris in the spring of 1685 is confirmed in a letter by the Swedish ambassador, Count Lillieroot.

From Paris, Dahl and Tilson journeyed to Rome. Here Dahl converted from Lutheranism to Roman Catholicism, which gained him access to the exiled Queen Kristina, whose portrait he painted (Grimsthorpe Castle, Lincolnshire). The queen secured him an introduction to Pope Clement XI, who presented the painter with a gold medal. Dahl also painted a portrait of Pietro Garoli (1638–1716), professor of perspective at the Accademia di S. Luca, who later taught James Gibbs. Despite these Roman successes, Dahl told his mother in October 1687 that he had:

> no great desire to stay any longer … for here portraits are not of much account, only historical pictures being valued, and for this reason I wish to go to some other place and seek to win back what I have spent here on my studies …
> (Nisser, 12)

Accordingly, Dahl seems to have left Rome with Henry Tilson on 29 October 1687.

Dahl reached England in March 1689. He may have been hoping for patronage from the Catholic James II, but in the preceding November the king had been deposed and the protestant regime of William and Mary had been established. Kneller and John Riley became, jointly, principal painter to the new sovereigns; with Riley's death in 1691 Kneller reigned supreme. Nevertheless, Dahl flourished: as Vertue put it, 'the Great Business and high carriage of Kneller gave a lustre to the actions or works of Mr. Dahl—a man of great modesty and few words' (Vertue, Note books, 3.118). Yet their rivalry should not be exaggerated; Kneller may actually have passed patronage to Dahl. Soon after his return from Italy, for instance, Dahl painted a bust of the duke of Schomberg (d. 1690) (priv. coll.), of whom Kneller had painted a grand equestrian portrait for William III.

Like Kneller, Dahl had been introduced to England by a merchant. Yet court patronage was still crucial for the careers of both painters. Dahl does not seem to have worked for William and Mary; instead, Prince George of Denmark, a fellow Scandinavian who had married Princess Anne in 1683, became the painter's 'Royal Patron—and great promoter of his fortune' (Vertue, Note books, 3.118). An instance of this promotion is Dahl's patronage by the prince's groom of the stole and first gentleman of the bedchamber, John, third Lord Berkeley of Stratton, rear-admiral of the blue, of whom Dahl painted a bold, armoured three-quarter length about 1693 (priv. coll.). The head—doubtless based on a large drawing, a practice Dahl learned in Kneller's studio—is identical to that employed in Dahl's large-scale conversation piece (Chiswick House, London) showing Lord Berkeley at a table, drinking, with the duke of Kingston and Charles, earl of Burlington. This richly dressed, sombre group recalls the design and something of the psychological drama of William Dobson's *Prince Rupert, and Colonels William Murray and John Russell*.

Berkeley's wife was Jane Temple, afterwards countess of Portland (1672–1751), whose portrait formed one of a series of eight full-length 'Beauties' (Petworth House, Sussex) which Dahl painted for the duke of Somerset about 1696, after the duke had quarrelled with John Closterman. They were painted in emulation of Kneller's 1690–91 Hampton Court 'Beauties', whose format and numbers they share. They also contain painted reliefs and sculpture which appear to have Neo-Platonic allusions. In 1826 the Dahl series were reduced to three-quarter lengths by rolling them up, rather than by cutting, as was long believed to be the case. It is stated that 'They must have been painted after the fire of 1714 gutted this part of [Petworth]' (Rowell, 19). But this date is very unlikely since the ladies are too young in appearance and Margaret Sawyer, countess of Pembroke, died in 1706. In 1722 Vertue rhapsodized that the Petworth 'Beauties' 'shew the great skill of Mr. Dahl in Art, beauty, of grace, genteel artfull draperies finely painted & well dispos'd' and pronounced them his 'best work' (Vertue, Note books, 3.43; 2.81). Dahl had a fine way with adolescent sitters, as in the joint portrait *Allen (Later Earl) Bathurst and Peter Bathurst, in Roman Dress* (c.1695; priv. coll.) of the sons of Sir Benjamin Bathurst, treasurer of the household to Princess Anne. Another enchanting example, from about 1700, is a portrait of an unknown boy as an archer (ex Sothebys, New York, 3 June 1988). This was inscribed as by Lely, and was attributed in 1988 to Kneller, an instance of the confusion that still surrounds the identification of Dahl's work.

With the accession of Anne as queen in 1702, Dahl received increased patronage. A set of fourteen admirals (emulating Lely's for the duke of York) was split between Kneller and Dahl, instead of going to the former, who remained principal painter alone. Dahl's heads, especially that of Admiral Hopson, are finely characterized, but the designs generally lack the martial spirit of the Knellers. In 1704 Dahl painted a grand equestrian portrait of Prince George for the queen's guard-chamber at Windsor Castle. With Queen Anne as his patron, he inevitably painted many tories, including the second earl of Oxford and his circle of artists and virtuosi. But one must not politically pigeon-hole Dahl (or indeed Kneller, although the latter painted the whig Kit-Cat Club). The two artists shared many patrons, including the Marlboroughs (a portrait of about 1695 of the duchess at Althorp, supposedly with 'cut' hair and long believed to be by Kneller, was in fact by Dahl and depicts her with her hair let down); Alexander Pope; and the first duke of Chandos.

Dahl's portraits ranged from busts to groups. His finest bust was of the aged first earl of Bradford (priv. coll.). His three-quarter length of three unknown men in a library (ex Sothebys, London, 23 July 1952) of about 1720 is a masterpiece, and includes an exceptionally sensitive head, for which there exists a fine drawing (ex Sothebys, London, 11 July 1991). A handsome full-length is his portrait of Henrietta, Countess Ashburnham (1717; Walker Art Gallery, Liverpool). Perhaps Dahl's finest full-length group, once given to Kneller, is the *Popham Family* (c.1710), formerly at Littlecote, Wiltshire (ex Sothebys, London, 2 November 1985). A proto-rococo portrait, it shows Alexander Popham, his wife, and small daughter and dog on a terrace. The expressions are tender, the forms and composition lively; and the colour a subtle harmony of cool blue, green, grey, and pale yellow against warm pink and brown.

In 1723 Dahl might have succeeded Kneller as principal painter but for his refusal to paint the baby duke of Cumberland. Much earlier, Dahl had also turned down an offer to succeed Ehrenstrahl as court painter. His 1723 decision may also have been due to age: he was then sixty-four years old. In 1725 he moved from Leicester Fields, where he had occupied a studio since 1696, to Beak Street, Golden Square. He had married an Englishwoman about 1707, but nothing further is known of his wife. His will was made in 1735; its shaky signature suggests that he may have already retired. He died on 20 October 1743 in London, and was buried at St James's Piccadilly on 27 October. He had willed all his 'prints Books & Drawings and all other things which belong to my Business of painting' to his son Michael, 'a hopeful young painter. dyd two or three years before him' (Vertue, *Note books*, 3.118). No works by Michael Dahl the younger are known, however.

Dahl's daughters sold much of their father's collections, including his own works, in a:

> two days sale 147. lots … many curious & valuable Italian paintings besides those of his own paintings … some history peeces as big as the life … the large piece, the Holy Family. the Virgin and Child St. Joseph & St. John. &c. Diana & Endymion-Venus & Cupid St. John. standing a lamb by him. Venus—laying on a Couch.   (Vertue, *Note books*, 3.121)

The sale fetched £700. The large 'Holy Family' seen by Vertue was probably an oblong composition (136 cm × 165 cm) showing an angel, the Madonna, the Christ child and a lamb (St John), and St Joseph, which appeared at Finarte auction house, Rome, 27 October 1981 (lot) 91, wrongly as by 'Gottfried Kneller', with a false Kneller 'signature'. The *Venus and Cupid* was with the dealer Larby in Stockholm in 1935. Venus's pose derives from the antique sculpture *Nymph 'alla spina'* (Uffizi, Florence), in Dahl's time in the Palazzo Caffarelli, Rome. At York Art Gallery there is a *Magdalen* by Dahl and at Stockholm there is a signed and dated 1691 *Holy Family with St Dorothy* which recalls Van Dyck's *Ages of Man*, formerly at Mantua in the collection of the duke where Dahl must have seen it during his Italian journey. A 1722 mezzotint by John Faber after Dahl's *Susanna in the Bath* is recorded, but untraced.

Likenesses of Dahl are uncommon, although Vertue recorded an early portrait of him by Kneller, a bust by Michael Rysbrack, and several self-portraits. Of the self-portraits two are known, a bust in a cap of about 1700 (Gripsholm Castle, Sweden) and a signed and dated 1691 three-quarter length in the National Portrait Gallery, London. The latter shows the painter in his own, short hair (presumably in imitation of ancient Roman style) gesturing deferentially towards a bust of the Medici *Venus* as an emblem of beauty, below which rest his palette and brushes.

Dahl's importance for English painting rests on the alternative variant of the baroque style that he offered during the period of Sir Godfrey Kneller's ascendancy (1690–1723): while lacking Kneller's power and structure, his style was generally lighter, and often more charming, at least in portraits of women. Dahl's most significant pupil was his fellow Swede Hans Hysing, who moved to London about 1700, and with whom Alan Ramsay worked briefly in 1734.   J. DOUGLAS STEWART

Sources Vertue, *Note books* · W. Nisser, *Michael Dahl and the contemporary Swedish school of painting in England* (1927) · E. Waterhouse, *Painting in Britain, 1530–1790*, 4th edn (1978) · J. D. Stewart, 'Some portrait drawings by Michael Dahl and Sir James Thornhill', *Master Drawings*, 11 (1973), 34–44; pls. 26–42 · D. Piper, *Catalogue of seventeenth-century portraits in the National Portrait Gallery, 1625–1714* (1963) · M. Whinney and O. Millar, *English art, 1625–1714* (1957) · L. Stainton and C. White, *Drawing in England from Hilliard to Hogarth* (1987) [exhibition catalogue, BM] · J. D. Stewart, *Sir Godfrey Kneller and the English baroque portrait* (1983) · C. H. C. Baker, 'Michael Dahl, pioneer portrait painter', *Country Life*, 124 (1958), 1164–5 · C. H. C. Baker, *Lely and the Stuart portrait painters: a study of English portraiture before and after van Dyck*, 2 vols. (1912) · Waterhouse, *18c painters* · will, PRO, PROB 10/1959 · C. Rowell, *Petworth House, West Sussex* (1997)

Likenesses G. Kneller, oils, 1684–5 · M. Dahl, self-portrait, 1686 · M. Dahl, self-portrait, oils, 1691, NPG [*see illus.*] · M. Dahl, self-portrait, oils, *c.*1700, Gripsholm Castle, Sweden · C. Richter, miniature, 1709; Sothebys, 18 Dec 1986 · J. Thornhill, drawing, 1714–19 (*The connoisseurs and Sir James Thornhill*), Art Institute of Chicago · M. Rysbrack, bust, 1723–32 · G. Hamilton, group portrait, oils, 1735 (*A conversation of virtuosi … at the Kings Armes*), NPG · T. Chambars, line engraving (after M. Dahl), BM; repro. in H. Walpole, *Anecdotes of painting in England … collected by the late George Vertue, and now digested and published*, 2 (1762)

Dahl, Roald (1916–1990), writer of fiction, was born on 13 September 1916 at Villa Marie, Fairwater Road, Llandaff, Glamorgan, the son of Harald Dahl, shipbroker, and his second wife, Sofie Magdalene, daughter of Olaf Hesselberg, meteorologist and classical scholar. His parents were prosperous Norwegians. His father had given up farming near Oslo, and settled with his wife and two small children (a son and a daughter) in Wales, where he made a fortune as a shipbroker. When his first wife died suddenly, he married Sofie Hesselberg. She took on the existing family, and had four children of her own. Roald, her only son, was her third child, later nicknamed the Apple. One of his older sisters married the microbiologist Sir Ashley Miles.

Early life When Dahl was only three another beloved, older sister and his father died within two months of one another. This was the first in a series of catastrophes and mortal disasters that dogged his life, and, he claimed, gave his work a black savagery. His mother, a devoted matriarch, ran the family. In the summers she took them to Norway, where her family fostered Dahl's interest in insects and birds, Nordic trolls, and witches. She gave Dahl his passion for reading—in particular Galsworthy, Kipling, and Hugh Walpole—all best-sellers of the day. She was immortalized as the grandmother in *The Witches* (1983).

Dahl was an undistinguished rebel at Llandaff Cathedral school, St Peter's in Weston-super-Mare, and Repton School. Those few of his contemporaries who remembered him remarked only on his bullying humour and competitive spirit, and his hatred of authority. His proudest achievement was to invent a mousetrap that plunged its victims into a bowl of water, with the Dahlian logo, 'catch as cats can't'. In his account of his childhood, *Boy* (1984), he revealed the cruel flogging pleasurably inflicted by Repton's headmaster, G. F. Fisher (later archbishop of

Roald Dahl (1916–1990), by Dumant, 1971

Canterbury). Dahl claimed that the hypocrisy of his headmaster's brutal beatings followed by pious sermons in Repton chapel cured him of any inclination towards Christianity. Dahl described his ferocious beatings in clinical detail in his story 'Lucky Break'.

War service Resisting the attractions of a university education, at eighteen Dahl joined the Public Schools Exploring Society's expedition to Newfoundland. He joined Shell in 1934, and was sent to Dar es Salaam, Tanganyika. When the Second World War broke out in 1939, he drove to Nairobi, Kenya, to volunteer for the Royal Air Force. Learning to fly over the Kenyan highlands was a master experience, and provided aerial images both magical and nightmarish for his subsequent writing. He served with 80 fighter squadron in the western desert in 1940, and was severely wounded when his Gloucester Gladiator biplane ran out of petrol and crash-landed in the Libyan desert. His injuries never left him, and he later converted the pain and frustration of his crash and seven months in hospital into fantasies in the style of Biggles. He declined convalescent leave in Britain, and fought in the hopeless air defences over Athens and then the Peloponnese. Invalided home to London, he was posted to Washington as assistant air attaché (1942–3) and worked in security (1943–5). He was appointed flight lieutenant in 1943—not wing commander, as he claimed in *Who's Who*. While Dahl was in Washington, C. S. Forester—creator of Captain Hornblower and author of many popular novels—asked him for RAF anecdotes to be used as propaganda. He sent Dahl's romanticized version of his plane crash to the *Saturday Evening Post*, where it appeared in 1942 under the misleading title 'Shot down over Libya: an RAF pilot's factual account'. In it Dahl informed his readers that his Hurricane had been brought down in flames by a burst of machine-gun fire while strafing a column of trucks. His stories in the *Saturday Evening Post* marked the beginning of Dahl's accidental but prodigious career as a writer.

Disney tried to make a film of one of Dahl's stories called 'The Gremlins' (1943), which concerned a tribe of goblins who were blamed by the RAF for everything that went wrong with an aircraft. Gremlin stories were rife in the RAF at the time, and several other books about them

had already appeared, but Dahl was happy to boast that he had invented them. 'The Gremlins' was such a success that the self-dramatizing RAF hero became a frequent guest of Eleanor and Franklin D. Roosevelt at the White House and their weekend retreat, Hyde Park. This entrée was exploited by the British intelligence services, who made him a spy—on the Americans. Or so Dahl later claimed.

Tales of the Unexpected Dahl's short stories, published in such distinguished notice-boards of the genre as the *New Yorker* and *Harper's Magazine*, tiptoed along the tightrope between the macabre and the comic in a manner reminiscent of Hector Hugh Munro (Saki). They were horrific, fantastic, and unbelievable. Lapsed vegetarians do not commonly find themselves being slit up for sausage-meat in a homely abattoir, nor do babies fed on royal jelly turn into bees. In a typical Dahl story a woman clubs her husband to death with a frozen leg of lamb and then feeds it to the detectives who have come to search for the murder weapon, or a rich woman goes on a cruise, leaving her husband to perish in an elevator stuck between two floors in an empty house. When the stories were published as collections, *Someone Like You* (1953, revised 1961) and *Kiss, Kiss* (1960), Dahl broke through into the best-seller lists and became a celebrity. His popular fame was augmented by the translation of his ripping yarns to the small screen in *Alfred Hitchcock Presents* from 1965 onwards, and then in *Roald Dahl's Tales of the Unexpected*, which ran on television around the world for many years from 1979 onwards. Preoccupied as they are with greed, revenge, cruelty, and the rest of the dark side of human nature, his stories were both bizarre examples and also trendsetters of the fashionable 1960s genre of black comedy. Not a few critics denounced his work as sadistic, antisocial, and misogynist. But Saki would have recognized his combination of the macabre with fantasy and wit.

On 2 July 1953 Dahl married the film star Patricia Neal (b. 1926), who was on the rebound from her long affair with Gary Cooper). She was the daughter of William Burdett Neal, manager of the Southern Coal and Coke Company, of Packard, Kentucky. They had one son and four daughters. Their son Theo was brain-damaged at the age of four months when he was tipped out of his pram in New York and fell under a cab. His skull was smashed and he was not expected to live. But working with his consultant and a friend who was an aircraft designer of hydraulic pumps, Dahl pioneered the Wade-Dahl-Till Valve. This non-blocking valve drains fluid from the brain, and has since been used to treat thousands of children with brain injuries. Ultimately, after years of desperate illness, Theo did recover. Meanwhile his older sister Olivia contracted a rare form of measles aged seven and died of encephalitis.

Children's fiction Dahl now turned to writing books for children—claiming, implausibly, that he had run out of plots for adult Gothic horror. *James and the Giant Peach* (1967) was spotted as an instant new planet in the sky of children's fiction. The story begins with James's parents being eaten by a runaway rhino on a crowded shopping street, an opening that Evelyn Waugh would have cheered. The story tells how the orphan James escapes the guardianship of two monstrous aunts, the wicked Aunt Spiker and the dastardly Aunt Sponge. One day 'this disgusting beast', 'this filthy nuisance' (the aunts never call James by his real name) spills a bag of magic worms ('Miserable creature!') near the roots of a peach tree. A peach swells to enormous proportions and James goes to live inside it. With a set of lovable and resourceful insects as crew, James and the giant peach roll, float, and fly from darkest rural England over the Atlantic to a ticker-tape reception in New York, squashing the aunts as flat as pancakes en route. It is rude, naughty, anti-adult, creepy, and sometimes cruel. *The Giant Peach* had a successful run as an opera at Covent Garden.

James and the Giant Peach was followed in the same year by *Charlie and the Chocolate Factory* (filmed in 1971 as *Willy Wonka and the Chocolate Factory*), the most popular children's book yet. This established the tricks of Dahl's magic trade and attraction. Its hero, Charlie Bucket, is the poorest boy imaginable (one bar of chocolate a year and two helpings of cabbage as a special treat on Sundays). His four grandparents, all over ninety, 'as shrivelled as prunes and as bony as skeletons', lie huddled and hungry in their one bed, 'two at either end dozing away the time with nothing to do'. But Charlie's visit to the mysterious Wonka chocolate factory, a children's utopia of mint grass and chocolate rivers, changes the Bucket family fortunes. Mr Willy Wonka, the imperious chocolate wizard, is looking for a protégé he can trust. He disposes of Charlie's rivals (greedy Augustus Gloop, disobedient Violet Beauregarde, spoilt Veruca Salt, brash Mike Teevee) and chooses skinny, wide-eyed Charlie as the heir to his secret recipes—which include sugar-coated pencils for sucking, luminous lollies for eating in bed, and stickjaw for talkative parents. So the underdog triumphs, as usual with Dahl. His dialogue smacks of Carroll, and his verses of Belloc. A stock topic of Dahl's was to pick on human weaknesses and vices, such as gluttony, bossiness, or untidiness, and invite his young readers to rejoice in the sticky end to which their possessors come. These first children's books also flaunt the cheeky vocabulary, the zany pathos, the funniness, and the undisciplined plotting that were the penprints of Dahl. An eminent American critic called *Charlie and the Chocolate Factory* 'cheap, tasteless, ugly, sadistic, and for all these reasons, harmful' (Treglown, 188); and an English headmaster doing research into children's reading charged Dahl with 'incipient fascism' (as opposed to the 'paternalist feudalism' of Enid Blyton). Even Margaret Meek, the distinguished authority on children's books, commented primly: 'I do not trust Dahl as implicitly as his young readers do, because I find his view of life seriously flawed by a particular kind of intolerance.'

Dahl claimed that the secret of his success as a writer for children was that he appealed to their baser instincts:

When you are born you are a savage, an uncivilised little grub, and if you are going to go into our society by the age of ten, then you have to have good manners and know all the do's and don'ts—don't eat with your fingers and don't piss on the floor. All that stuff has to be hammered into the savage, who resents it deeply. So subconsciously in the child's mind these giants become the enemy. That goes particularly for parents and teachers. (*The Times*, 30 Nov 1990)

Not all teachers, parents, and librarians were as keen as their children on Dahl, especially in the United States. He was accused of violent exaggerations of language and grotesque characterizations. To his detractors Dahl was capricious (most adults are portrayed as cruel monsters); racist (the Oompa-Loompas in *Charlie and the Chocolate Factory* were black pygmy slaves before Dahl gave them long hair and rosy skin in a prudently revised edition); rude (a whole chapter in *The BFG* [Big Friendly Giant] is devoted to the joys of farting); and misogynist (James's aunts, Sponge and Spiker, are 'ghastly hags'; Matilda's headmistress, Miss Agatha Trunchbull, treats her pupils with extreme violence and grievous bodily harm). 'Real witches dress in ordinary clothes and look very much like ordinary women. In fact, they look just like your schoolteacher or respectable aunt. But secretly they are bald, their spit is as blue as bilberry, and to them little boys smell of dogs' droppings, FRESH dogs' droppings.' *The Witches* (1983) was placed on the restricted list in many American schools, after parents complained that it either frightened their children or encouraged them to take an interest in the occult. Beneath Dahl's robust caricature, simple morality, and rich comic invention, critics detected an undercurrent of vengeful sadism and black misanthropy.

In spite of high-minded disapproval, Dahl's books were hugely popular with children. They were inventive, rich, imaginative, surprising, funny, and full of the bizarre words that please children. Throughout the 1980s and 1990s, several of them continually topped the best-seller lists both in the UK and abroad. When the first edition of *Charlie and the Chocolate Factory* was published in China, it had a print run of two million, the biggest print run of any book to date. By the end of the twentieth century the sales of his eighteen children's titles totalled well over 35 million books. They included *Fantastic Mr Fox* (1970), *Charlie and the Great Glass Elevator* (1973), *Danny, the Champion of the World* (1975), *The Enormous Crocodile* (1978), *The Twits* (1980), *George's Marvellous Medicine* (1981), *Revolting Rhymes* (1982), and *The Witches* (1983), and *The BFG* (a Big Friendly Giant who kidnaps a girl from an orphanage and deposits her in the queen's bedroom, 'with the Queen herself asleep in there behind the curtain not more than five yards away'), *The Vicar of Nibbleswicke*, and *The Minpins*, all published posthumously (1991).

Family, character, and assessment While pregnant with their fifth child, Patricia Neal suffered a series of massive strokes. Again Dahl refused to accept the grim prognosis. He set about bringing her back into the world with a determination that shocked onlookers by its brutality and ruthlessness. She was helped through her long recovery by Dahl until she was well enough to resume acting. Some said that he humiliated her by treating her like a child, and bullied her back into health with force and even sadism. Dahl not only recreated his wife. He ran his household, adored his children, planned the garden, wrote screenplays (unsuccessfully), and continued to produce stories. Dahl then divorced Neal in 1983 and on 15 December the same year married her best friend and his longtime mistress, Felicity Ann Crosland, former wife of Charles Reginald Hugh Crosland, businessman and farmer, and daughter of Alphonsus Liguori d'Abreu, thoracic surgeon, of Birmingham. They lived with their eight children of previous marriages at Gipsy House, Great Missenden, Buckinghamshire. There Dahl wrote, always in pencil, in a hut in the garden.

Dahl published two volumes of autobiography, *Boy: Tales of Childhood* (1984) and *Going Solo* (1986). He wrote several scripts for films, among them the James Bond adventure *You Only Live Twice* (1967) and *Chitty Chitty Bang Bang* (1968). He was as scornful of the men in suits who run Hollywood studios as Scott Fitzgerald and P. G. Wodehouse. He was a publisher's nightmare. The president of Alfred Knopf described his manner as 'unmatched in my experience for overbearingness and utter lack of civility' (Treglown, 215). He refused a request from his editor to tone down *The Witches* on the grounds that he was 'not as frightened of offending women as you are' (ibid., 225). He denounced Salman Rushdie under sentence of death by the Islamic fatwa as 'a dangerous opportunist' (*The Times*, 28 Feb 1989). And he accused the Jews of cowardice in the Second World War for not doing more to resist the Nazis. He told a reporter in 1983 that 'there is a streak in the Jewish character that does provoke animosity' (Treglown, 237), and declared that even a miserable man such as Hitler did not single them out for nothing. Invited to review *God Cried*, an account of the Israeli invasion of Lebanon, he launched a headlong attack on all Israelis, and to many it appeared an attack on Jews.

By the end of his life Dahl was bitter at not receiving the knighthood that he felt he deserved, and he became increasingly self-important, ordering a Rolls-Royce from his publisher's to collect manuscripts from his home. He was 6 feet 6 inches tall, a chain-smoker, a lover of fine wine, a collector of contemporary painting, a grower of roses and orchids, a picture restorer, and a gambler on horses. He looked after 100 budgerigars that flew wild around his garden. He was a chocaholic. In the garden hut where he wrote he kept a huge silver ball made by packing together the silver paper from all the chocolate bars he ate. He also kept there as a trophy to show visitors one of his arthritic hip bones which had been replaced.

Dahl's public statements were often intemperate. Some of his stories about himself were as tall as he was, and as fantastical as his fictions. But he had a magical touch for the macabre and the surrealist. The pied piper and lord of misrule of topsy-turvydom was the most popular children's writer of his or any age. Generations of children grew up with Dahl's books, and were able to *enjoy* reading them to their own children. They were translated into innumerable languages, filmed, and televised. Their saturnine author replied in rhyme to schoolchildren's fan mail:

> Oh wondrous children miles away
> Your letters brightened up my day.
> (Treglown, 294)

He adored children, and they loved the grotesque worlds he created for them. His attachment to his family was the one consistency in a life of contradictions. His first wife remarked cynically that 'he had an enormous appreciation for anything he generated'. His personal tale of the unexpected was that his story-telling talent sprang from tragedy and bile. Shortly before he died, he said: 'I don't think you find many chaps or women in their mid-seventies who think like I do, and joke and fart around. They usually grow pompous, and pomposity is the enemy of children's writing' (*The Times*, 30 Nov 1990). The key to his success, he frequently said, was to conspire with children against adults. He died of leukaemia on 23 November 1990 at the John Radcliffe Hospital, Oxford, and was buried on 29 November at Great Missenden parish church. He was survived by his wife Felicity, his former wife Patricia Neal, and four of his children. PHILIP HOWARD

Sources R. Dahl, *Boy* (1984) · R. Dahl, *Going solo* (1986) · R. Dahl, *A sweet mystery of life* (1989) · B. Farrell, *Pat and Roald* (1970) · J. Treglown, *Roald Dahl: a biography* (1994) · WWW · personal knowledge (2004) · private information (2004) · b. cert. · m. cert. [Felicity Ann Crosland] · d. cert.
Likenesses Dumant, photograph, 1971, Hult. Arch. [see illus.] · S. Karadia, photograph, repro. in *The Times* (24 Nov 1990) · S. Karadia, photograph, repro. in *The Times* (30 Nov 1990) · oils, priv. coll. · photograph, repro. in *The Times* (24 Nov 1990)
Wealth at death £2,843,217: probate, 13 Feb 1991, *CGPLA Eng. & Wales*

Daiches, Salis (1880–1945), rabbi and author, was born on 10 March 1880 in Vilna, Lithuania (once part of Poland, but then under Russian rule), the second son of Israel Hirsch Daiches (d. 1937) and his wife, Bela Bielitsky. His father, a distinguished rabbi and scholar (latterly principal rabbi of the Orthodox congregations in Leeds until his death), was descended from a long line of rabbis going back some 500 years. Salis Daiches's early childhood was spent in Neustadt-Sherwindt near the German–Lithuanian border, where he remembered studying the Talmud by the light of rush candles stuck into the wall; his schooldays were spent at the *Gymnasium* in Königsberg, Germany.

Daiches's higher education was spent studying philosophy at Berlin University, as well as taking courses in rabbinical studies at Hildesheimer seminary. Subsequently he graduated AM, PhD in Leipzig, his doctoral thesis being on the relation of David Hume's philosophy to history. Although his native language was Yiddish, he abandoned it for Hebrew which he saw as the language of Jewish culture. In 1907 he settled in England, furthering his research on Kant and Judaism by reading at the British Museum. On 4 August 1909 he married Flora (*b*. 1889/90), daughter of Barnett Levin, a cabinet-maker. They had two sons and two daughters. Rabbi Samuel Daiches, his elder brother, became a professor of Jews College, London, and was a scholar with an international reputation.

After working in Hull, Hammersmith, and Sunderland, Daiches went to Edinburgh in March 1919 to succeed the Revd Jacob Furst, whose ministry in the city had lasted for some forty-four years. Ministering at the Graham Street Synagogue, Edinburgh, Dr Daiches was one of the few in Britain to hold a full rabbinic diploma which allowed him to perform all religious functions and to legislate on Jewish law and ritual. In Edinburgh Daiches found that the local Hebrew community was divided into a number of factions who held their services in three different places of worship. Unlike England, Scotland had never passed punitive legislation against its Jewish immigrants, although it was not until the end of the seventeenth century that the first Jewish resident arrived in Scotland. The earliest Jewish families in Scotland came predominantly to Edinburgh from Holland; later from Russia, Poland, Germany, and the Baltic ports. In the early years of the nineteenth century they formed the first *Kehillah* (congregation of Jews) in Edinburgh. After many difficulties and successes (including the uniting of the Edinburgh Jewish factions into one Hebrew community), Daiches presided over the construction and opening of the Salisbury Road Synagogue in 1932.

By this time Daiches had become the unofficial spiritual leader of the Jews in Scotland, and took an active part in founding the Conference of Scottish Churches and Scottish Jews; he was also the joint convener of the Jewish Christian Fellowship and a prominent freemason, chaplain to Lodge Solomon. A man of learning and wide culture, his literary style was clear and forceful. Daiches became widely known in Edinburgh, often appearing on the public platform, where he impressed his listeners with the eloquence of his preaching. He was the author of a volume of essays about Judaism (1928), and also published a Hebrew grammar for beginners (1939, with Duncan Cameron). In private life, he was a connoisseur of Havana cigars, later taking up pipe smoking—always with Balkan Sobranie tobacco.

Early in 1945 Daiches was injured in a road accident; having practically recovered from his injury, he was admitted in April to a nursing home at 12 Randolph Crescent, Edinburgh, where he died on 2 May 1945. He was buried at Piershill cemetery, Edinburgh. His wife survived him. Chief Rabbi Israel Brodie said of Dr Daiches: 'He was a persuasive advocate of the Jewish viewpoint on questions of general moment. He pleaded with passion and manliness for justice for the persecuted and downtrodden of his people. With prophetic fire he sang the hopes of a people once more restored to its land' (*Scotsman*, 26 Nov 1952). His elder son, David Daiches (*b.* 1912), became a distinguished professor and scholar of English and Scottish literature; his other son, Lionel Daiches (1911–1999), was a notable Scottish solicitor and QC. In a memoir, first published in 1957, David Daiches wrote evocatively of the 'two worlds' of his Edinburgh Jewish childhood, and movingly portrayed his father.   MICHAEL T. R. B. TURNBULL

Sources The Scotsman (3 May 1945) • 'Late Edinburgh rabbi', The Scotsman (26 Nov 1952) • D. Daiches, WAS: a pastime from time past (1975) • D. Daiches, Two worlds: an Edinburgh Jewish childhood; promised lands: a portrait of my father (1997) • L. Daiches, Russians at law (1960) • A. Phillips, A history of the origins of the first Jewish community in Scotland: Edinburgh, 1816 (1979) • m. cert. • d. cert. • private information (2004) [Jenni Daiches, granddaughter]

Archives NL Scot., letters and sermons

Likenesses portrait, repro. in D. Daiches, *Two worlds*, new edn, cover

Wealth at death £388 13s. 5d.: confirmation, Scotland, 1947, CCI

Daig mac Cairill (*d.* 587). *See under* Ulster, saints of (*act. c.*400–*c.*650).

Dain, Sir (Harry) Guy (1870–1966), general practitioner, was born in Birmingham on 5 November 1870, the eldest of six children of Major Dain, draper, and his wife, Diana Weaver. He was educated at King Edward's Grammar School (1883–7) and at Mason College, to which in 1892 the medical department of Queen's College, Birmingham, was transferred. He qualified MRCS LRCP in 1893 and took the MB BS (Lond.) in the following year.

Dain spent his entire career in his native city of Birmingham. After holding appointments as resident medical officer at the Children's Hospital and assistant house-surgeon at the General Hospital, he settled in general practice. Later he became head of a large partnership in Selly Oak. Dain was married twice: on 17 July 1897 to Flora Elizabeth Lewis, a nurse, who died in 1934; and on 1 February 1939 to Alice Muriel Hague, a dispenser, who survived him. There were two daughters and two sons of the first marriage, of whom one son was killed in the Second World War. One daughter and one son entered the medical profession.

On the introduction of national health insurance Dain began to develop a long-lasting interest in medical politics. In Birmingham he was a member of the first insurance committee and of the first panel committee. Very soon he became its chairman, and in 1917 he became a member of the insurance acts committee in London. For six years he presided over the annual conference of local medical and panel committees (1919–24) and for twelve years (1924–36) he was chairman of the insurance acts committee itself. During this period it was said that his name was suggested for every sub-committee or deputation to the government. Though no orator Dain had the gift of clear and persuasive speech, and an enviable ability to disentangle complicated matters. While everyone was afforded a full part in decision making, it was made easier by the way in which Dain presented the essential facts and drew attention to the root of a problem. In 1936 the Dain Testimonial Fund was established to mark his work on behalf of insurance practitioners. At his request the fund was used to help finance the education of the children of medical practitioners who had fallen on hard times.

In 1934 Dain was elected to the General Medical Council as a direct representative of GPs in England and Wales. He remained a member until his resignation in 1961. This was the longest period of service of any medical practitioner. Dain joined the British Medical Association (BMA) in 1896. Between 1937 and 1942 he was chairman of the association's representative body, his membership of which spanned the period 1919–57. He was a member of the BMA council from 1921 to 1960, serving as chairman in the period 1943–9. The 1940s were testing years for the medical profession, owing to the planning and introduction of the National Health Service (NHS). By virtue of his position in the BMA, Dain became one of the chief spokesmen for the profession. In some ways he was an unlikely leader. Well into his seventies, he was 'an unspectacular, competent family doctor … better known as a steady negotiator than a forceful leader' (*The Times*, 1 March 1966). However, whether he was negotiating at the ministry, or in the chair of council, or at mass meetings of the profession, or holding press conferences, he was steadfast, persuasive, honest, and patient, never departing from the principles he held to be essential. It was his great achievement to keep the profession united in the face of the most severe pressures.

Dain's attitude towards the proposed NHS was conditioned by his experiences as a panel practitioner and as a medical politician. These had bred in him a deep suspicion of government involvement with medicine and throughout the negotiations over the new service he fought against the prospect, real or imagined, of state control of the medical profession. He was particularly fearful that doctors would become salaried civil servants and that patients would lose their right to choose their own doctors. At the time of his election as chairman of the BMA's council (in 1943) he remained opposed to the creation of a comprehensive service, preferring instead an extension of the national health insurance scheme with the preservation of private practice on a large scale. While the wartime coalition remained in power, with Henry Willink as minister of health, Dain remained satisfied with the direction of negotiations. Indeed, in March 1945 he informed a group of Nottingham doctors that discussions with the minister comprised 'a constructive attempt to implement the entirely admirable preamble of the [February 1944] White Paper, *A National Health Service*' (*BMJ*, Supplement, 7 April 1945, 52).

The advent of a Labour government with Aneurin Bevan as minister of health changed all of this, even though Dain had great personal admiration for Bevan's qualities as a politician, regarding him as knowledgeable, decisive, and determined. When the National Health Service Act received royal assent in November 1946 Dain's assessment was hostile. 'The Act', he told a BMA meeting in Exeter, 'is part of the nationalization programme which is being steadily pursued by the Government. What the Minister appears to have done is to have taken the Bill which we had partly fashioned and to have inserted into it the Socialist principles of State ownership of hospitals, direction of doctors, basic salary for doctors, and abolition of buying and selling of practices' (*BMJ*, 16 Nov 1946, 747). Dain maintained this intransigent attitude throughout 1947 and well into 1948, notwithstanding Bevan's commitment that he would never introduce full-time salaried service. In a speech at Shrewsbury, delivered in April 1948, Dain urged the profession to refuse service under the act. But when the BMA's plebiscite went against this advice

Dain, democrat that he was, accepted the decision without demur. In a letter to *The Times* on 18 June 1948, he pledged that the profession would 'do its utmost to make the new Service a resounding success'.

In recognition of his service to his profession Dain received the honorary degrees of LLD from Aberdeen in 1939, and MD from Birmingham in 1944. As a member of more than twenty years' standing he was elected FRCS in 1945, having served for some years on the council. He was awarded the gold medal of the BMA in 1936. It was with special pleasure that in 1957 he became the first recipient of the Claire Wand award for outstanding services to general practice. He was knighted in 1961, a year after he retired, aged ninety.

Dain's interests in medicine were wide, and throughout his association with the BMA he continued to devote much of his time to his busy practice in Birmingham, where he was popular with patients. His leisure interests included gardening and playing bridge. In appearance Dain was short, dapper, and smart. He had blue eyes, a kindly face, and a briskness of manner. Mentally alert and physically fit into his nineties, he died at Highmead, Aberdyfi, Merioneth, on 26 February 1966. A memorial service was held at St Pancras Church, London, on 23 March.

DEREK STEVENSON, *rev.* P. W. J. BARTRIP

Sources *BMJ* (5 March 1966); (12 March 1966); (2 April 1966) · *The Lancet* (12 March 1966) · *The Times* (1 March 1966) · *The Times* (24 March 1966) · *Annals of the Royal College of Surgeons of England*, 38 (1966) · A. Cox, *Among the doctors* (1950) · *WW* (1962) · *WWW*, 1961–70 · J. P. Ross and W. R. Le Fanu, *Lives of the fellows of the Royal College of Surgeons of England, 1965–1973* (1981) · M. Foot, *Aneurin Bevan: a biography, 1945–1960* (1973), vol. 2 of *Aneurin Bevan: a biography* · personal knowledge (1981) · private information (1981) · m. cert. [Flora Elizabeth Lewis] · m. cert. [Alice Muriel Hague]
Archives British Medical Association
Likenesses D. Jagger, oils, *c.*1952, British Medical Association House, London · W. Bird, photograph, 1961, NPG · photographs, British Medical Association House, London, BMA Archives
Wealth at death £98,869: probate, 25 Aug 1966, *CGPLA Eng. & Wales*

Dainov, Zvi Hirsch (1831/2–1877), rabbi, was born in Slutsk, near Minsk, Belorussia (then part of the Russian empire), the son of Ze'ev Dainov. In Russia from 1867 Dainov developed a reputation as an exponent of the *haskalah* or Jewish enlightenment, but rejected the secularism that characterized the majority of the *maskilim* (Jewish enlightenment thinkers). He wrote polemics in Hebrew and Yiddish in the periodical literature of the period, especially in *HaShahar* ('The Dawn'), the leading Hebrew journal published in Vienna. Like the *maskilim* he advocated reform of the Jewish educational system, abolition of the *heder* (private Jewish schoolroom), and the entry of Jews into government schools, where they could acquire secular knowledge and practical skills. This was against the background of the reforming policy of the 'Tsar Liberator' Alexander II in the 1860s. Optimism was engendered among the Jews that Russia would follow the path of Western liberal development. He was active in the Society for the Promotion of Culture Among the Jews of

Russia and corresponded with its one time director, his contemporary the *maskil* Judah Leib Gordon (1830–1892).

Dainov was dubbed the *Slutsker maggid* ('Preacher of Slutsk') because he travelled throughout the Jewish pale of settlement, from Vilna in the north to Odessa in the south, disseminating his views and raising funds for the cause of the *haskalah*. Despite his personal religious conservatism, Dainov's views on education aroused the ire of traditionalists, whose suspicions were not allayed by the fact that he discarded the traditional garb of the rabbi. In 1869 he published a sermon in Hebrew entitled 'Kevod melekh' ('Honour of the king') on the theme of loyalty to the tsar. A Russian translation soon appeared. However, his hoped-for appointment to a government post did not materialize.

In 1874 Dainov left Russia for London, where he continued to preach to the Russian Jewish immigrants in the East End, being most closely associated with the Hevrat Ein Ya'akov ('Well of Jacob congregation'). He was treated with suspicion by Chief Rabbi Nathan Adler. Nevertheless, the oratorical skills of the 'Russian *maggid*' were deployed by the Anglo-Jewish establishment against the Hebrew Socialist Union, founded in 1876 by fellow Russian émigré Aaron *Lieberman.

Aged just forty-six, Dainov died of pleurisy at the London Hospital on 6 March 1877 and was buried two days later at the West Ham Jewish cemetery.

SHARMAN KADISH

Sources *Jewish Chronicle* (9 March 1877) · C. Roth, ed., *Encyclopaedia Judaica*, 16 vols. (Jerusalem, 1971–2) · *Jewish Encyclopedia* (1903) · L. P. Gartner, *The Jewish immigrant in England, 1870–1914* (1960), 105 · E. Lederhendler, *The road to modern Jewish politics* (1989), 122, 204 n. 54

Dainton, Frederick Sydney, Baron Dainton (1914–1997), chemist and public servant, was born on 11 November 1914 at 66 Ranby Road, Sheffield, the youngest of the four children of George Whalley Dainton (1857–1930), stonemason, and his second wife, Mary Jane (1873–1943), a domestic servant, daughter of John Bottrill. George Dainton's first wife was Sarah Bottrill, who died after the birth of their fifth child; he subsequently married her younger sister, Mary Jane.

Early years and education Dainton's father was a master stonemason who, although able to draw up plans for stonework, was nevertheless able to read only with difficulty. Fred (as he was known to friends and family) therefore acquired familiarity with libraries at an early age, as he was expected to find books to take home and read to his father, who insisted, after every few paragraphs, on analysing what had gone before and discussing it with him. Perhaps this was the grounding for what became his formidable analytical skills and attention to detail.

Academic ability was soon recognized and Dainton was able to move quickly through his school education—at Hunter's Bar infant school, Greystones elementary school, and the Central Secondary School for Boys, all in Sheffield—with the aid of real sacrifices by his parents and with various scholarships. His father died of cancer while he was still at the Central Secondary School, and at the age of sixteen he left school to work as a bank clerk, to help his mother. Fortunately, the school made it possible for him to return to education after a very short time by providing a small sum from a charitable fund. In December 1932 he went to Oxford to take the science scholarship examinations. He was offered an open exhibition at St John's College to read chemistry, and this, together with a modest grant and loan from Sheffield city council, made it just possible for him to accept the offer to start in 1933.

Dainton's tutor was H. W. (Tommy) Thompson, who disconcerted Dainton in his first tutorial by criticizing severely his first essay, and requiring him to do it again the following week. But the effect was to ensure that he made up his mind that this would never happen again. Thompson's qualities as a tutor impressed Dainton very much, however, and he particularly admired the synoptic view Thompson took of the whole subject. He had to live very frugally in college, and he was surprised one day to be called to see the senior tutor (Dr Lane Poole), who asked him why his battels were so low. The senior tutor and St John's treated him with great sensitivity, steering him towards various modest sources of funds which he could earn as prizes and scholarships to help him through his studies; a scholarship from the Goldsmiths' Company was one of these, and was the beginning of a long relationship with that institution. In 1937 he was awarded a first-class degree, having worked with Thompson for his part two on gas phase kinetics.

Cambridge, Chalk River, and Leeds Instead of remaining in Oxford, Dainton decided that he would like a change. He therefore went to Cambridge to work with R. G. W. Norrish. While he was working for his PhD there his promise was recognized, and in 1939 he was awarded a Goldsmiths' Company senior studentship. In 1944 he was appointed a university demonstrator in chemistry, with the busy timetable of an Oxbridge don of the time, juggling an intensive schedule of lecturing, demonstrating, and supervision of students studying for parts one and two of the natural sciences tripos, coping with ARP responsibilities, and at the same time remaining involved in a lot of extra mural research for the Ministry of Supply, the Ministry of Aircraft Production, and other bodies. He had some excellent students at Cambridge, who did very well in the tripos examinations, and he believed that their good performance was responsible for his election in 1945 to a fellowship at St Catharine's College. One of these very early students recalled his first tutorial with Dainton, during which the latter tore apart an essay entitled 'The kinetics of the hydrogen chlorine reaction' and made him write it again.

It was at Cambridge that Dainton met a fellow research student, Barbara Hazlitt Wright (*b.* 1917), zoologist, daughter of Dr W. B. Wright of Manchester. They were married on 27 August 1942, the hottest day of the year; it was the beginning of a wonderful partnership which was to last for fifty-five years. They had a son and two daughters.

In 1946 Dainton received an invitation to go to the Chalk River laboratories in Canada for three summer months, and his experience in this short period was the beginning of many years of important work on radiation chemistry, the study of the chemical processes which are initiated when high energy radiation passes through matter.

After five productive years as a Cambridge don focused on teaching and research, Dainton was invited to go to Leeds as professor of physical chemistry, and in the summer of 1950 he, Barbara, and two small children moved to Leeds. There the major preoccupation of his research became to gain a better understanding of the underlying mechanisms of the movements of the atoms or electrons in molecules which are undergoing relatively simple reactions brought about by the absorption of heat, light, or ionizing radiation; for example, the conditions defining whether certain common plastics can be made, and their stability to heat and light ensured; or the basic physico-chemical processes underlying the susceptibility of humans to benefit from nuclear radiation or to be damaged by it. The outstanding work done at Leeds led to his election as a fellow of the Royal Society in 1957. He spent fifteen years at Leeds, and he remembered them as scientifically the most productive and happy of his life. The work he did there with his collaborators, and with Dr Ken Ivin, gave him immense satisfaction.

The University of Nottingham When an invitation to become vice-chancellor of the University of Nottingham arrived in 1964, Dainton's initial reaction was to reject it; but when he visited the chairman of the council, he was intrigued to discover that Nottingham was at the very early stage of planning a new medical school. From his experience at Cambridge, he had long believed that the medical curriculum needed reform, and in particular needed to integrate the pre-clinical and clinical parts of the course. He had found at Leeds that there were strong forces against reform in the medical establishment, and thought that to found a new medical school successfully would be the best way of spreading new ideas. He was therefore tempted to accept the invitation, particularly when it was agreed that he could at the same time remain honorary director of the Cookridge Laboratory, where the sources of radiation used for his research were situated. He took up his post in 1965.

In the year of his move to Nottingham, Dainton was asked to become a member of the Council for Scientific Policy, an important national committee on which he served for some fifteen years, including a period as chairman from 1969 to 1972. An active member of the council, he became a passionate supporter of the 'dual support' system for universities which arose from the Science and Technologies Act of 1965. One of his first tasks was to chair a subcommittee to look into the 'swing away from science' in schools, and a major report was published in 1968. The committee recommended universal teaching of mathematics and more broadly based A level courses at school, both on general educational grounds, and so as to defer premature specialization; it also recommended a change in university entrance requirements and courses. He greatly regretted that successive governments failed to grasp the nettle and, in his opinion, consistently fudged the issue on this matter. During his time at Nottingham he

also served as president of the Faraday Society, from 1965 to 1967.

In the late 1960s the government became concerned about the effectiveness and interrelationships of the large libraries funded directly or indirectly by central government, and it was felt that the whole problem required thorough investigation; in 1967 Dainton was invited to tackle it. After initial hesitation, he agreed to chair a small, high-powered committee, the national libraries committee, which began work in 1968 and reported in 1969. The committee thought that unifying these diverse libraries into a National Library under a board of management was absolutely essential for good services to be given right across the field of knowledge. Furthermore, the committee emphasized the absolute need to house the vast and valuable national collections in accommodation which was purpose-built and environmentally satisfactory. The hope was that, at the very least, this would break the log jam which had developed over the proposed new building for the British Museum Library.

Both Dainton and his wife, Barbara, devoted an important part of their lives to teaching the young, and treated their pupils with characteristically unstuffy kindness (Dainton reserved his more formidable manner for grown-ups), which was normally reciprocated with warmth and affection. So it came as a great shock to them late in 1968, for the first time in their lives, to find that there were students banded together in various groups who without knowing anything about Dainton regarded him as their natural enemy. This was a very unhappy time for a vice-chancellor who firmly believed that problems should be solved by clear thinking and calm reasoned argument. Nevertheless, he

> quietly steered Nottingham University through the years of student unrest, creating meeting grounds for the representatives of the 'Free University of Nottingham' and leaving them wondering how they could treat such a responsive and understanding man as a symbol of repressive authority. (*The Guardian*)

By this time Dainton had demonstrated formidable analytical powers, and in almost any subject with which he was concerned he always displayed a remarkable mastery of detail. He was therefore often confident that his analysis of a problem was correct, and he could on occasion deal devastatingly with those with whom he disagreed. These qualities were no doubt among those which led government to appoint him a member of some of its most demanding committees—including, besides the national libraries committee and the Council for Scientific Policy, the Central Advisory Council for Science and Technology, and the advisory committee on scientific and technical information (of which he was chairman, from 1966 to 1970).

Oxford, and the Council for Scientific Policy In 1969 the electors to the Dr Lee's professorship of chemistry invited Dainton to Oxford. He had shortly before been made chairman of the Council for Scientific Policy and was realizing the heavy burden this represented on top of the rigid timetable of a vice-chancellor. One of his greatest delights after moving to Oxford was when his wife, Barbara, was invited to demonstrate and to give lectures on molluscs for the department of zoology. Later, a vacancy for a lectureship arose at St Hilda's College, and she was appointed, later still being made a supernumerary fellow and a member of the governing body.

The three years following Dainton's taking up the Dr Lee's chair proved to be extremely active ones with the Council for Scientific Policy. Dainton chaired a working group to review the research council structure in 1970. The following year the Central Policy Review Staff, the government 'think tank', was established with Victor Rothschild (third Baron Rothschild) as its first director-general, and Rothschild produced a report advocating the abolition of the Council for Scientific Policy and the distribution of government funds for research on the basis of the customer/contractor principle. This ran counter to the proposals of the Council for Scientific Policy, and the government called for a wide public debate on the matter. The two reports were published in November 1971 as appendices to a green paper, 'Framework for government research and development' (*Parl. papers*, 1971–2, 35, Cmnd 4814). After much argument, the Council for Scientific Policy succeeded in moderating the more extreme components of the Rothschild report; the government established the Advisory Board for the Research Councils in place of the former Council for Scientific Policy. Dainton was its first chairman, from 1972 to 1973.

It was also at this time (1972–5) that Dainton was president of the Chemical Society; this was a particularly demanding time because the amalgamation of the society with the Faraday Society and the Royal Institute of Chemistry, to form what became the Royal Society of Chemistry, was under negotiation.

The University Grants Committee In 1973 Dainton resigned his professorship at Oxford and became chairman of the University Grants Committee (UGC), a position he held for five difficult years. On the second day in his new office he was told of draconian measures arising from the oil crisis, the first of which was that all university building work must cease; his first task was to persuade ministers to exempt the building of halls of residence from this rule, and the second was to make sure that no university became bankrupt. This was a period which saw 30 per cent inflation and great financial stringency; it is a tribute to Dainton's political skills that the universities suffered no more seriously than they did.

Dainton very much admired the mode of operation which had evolved for the University Grants Committee, and was dismayed when by 1974 it became clear that the quinquennial system was defunct. In the words of John Carswell, secretary of the UGC, 'Once the State had plucked up the courage to reach for the tap controlling the money supply, it was found to lie remarkably near to hand, and it became addicted to its use' (Dainton). Dainton and his colleagues fought powerful rearguard actions to save universities from the worst effects of financial stringency, many no doubt behind closed doors, and all

the universities had reason to be grateful for the work which Dainton did.

Retirement In 1978, when he retired from the University Grants Committee, Dainton was invited to become chancellor of the University of Sheffield. This gave him an opportunity to renew his connections with his native city, and repay some of the debt which he felt he owed; he took enormous pleasure in his visits to Sheffield, and was remembered at the university with warmth and affection. By this time his sight was failing, but he soldiered on without complaint, with the help of his wife, Barbara.

After his formal retirement, Dainton also became chairman of the National Radiological Protection Board (NRPB), from 1977 to 1985. There he deployed his scientific knowledge and experience of affairs to great effect, ensured good relations with government departments, and established the NRPB as an authoritative and independent body. He was also chairman of the British Library board (1978–85), when the problem was to persuade government of the urgent need for a completely new library. This plan implied that the reading-room at the British Museum would no longer be used by the library, and there was vigorous opposition from a group of academics. Dainton found that of the thirty-three strong defenders of the round reading-room, only fourteen had readers' tickets. The new library was subsequently built and, although its construction was marked by deep controversy, it soon settled down with an excellent reader service and proper environmental control to preserve its contents as well as was possible. The very existence of this great library at St Pancras was in no small measure due to the efforts of Dainton, and it gave him great satisfaction.

Dainton became a non-trade freeman of the Goldsmiths' Company in 1972, and progressed through the various strata of membership to be prime warden in 1982–3. His duties for the company, particularly in its many educational and charitable activities, gave him great pleasure, not least because of the help the company had twice given him as a student.

Dainton had wondered whether he would find final retirement tedious, but there were numerous other invitations to deploy his skills. One was the invitation, in 1979, to join the council of the Royal Postgraduate Medical School, of which he became chairman in 1980, and president from 1990 to 1997; he took great pleasure in maintaining his long interest in medical education in this way. He was also on the council of the London School of Economics, and chairman of its libraries board during an extensive redevelopment. He was asked to advise on matters relating to higher education to many countries overseas, and he and his wife made excursions all over the world; some people approaching the age of eighty would find such travel rather a burden, but Dainton revelled in it. He was also a trustee of the Natural History Museum (1974–84) and of the Wolfson Foundation (1978–88), and a member of the Crafts Council (1984–8), the Museums and Galleries Commission (1985–92), and the Foundation for Science and Technology (1987–97).

A new outlet for Dainton's energies was opened with his elevation to a life peerage in 1986, as Baron Dainton of Hallam Moors, in the county of south Yorkshire. He was soon recognized for his clear and lucid contributions to debates, but it was his work in the select committee on science and technology, as well as his chairmanship of the house library and computers sub-committee and membership of the offices committee, which was remembered with respect, even with awe, by some.

Dainton died following coronary failure on 5 December 1997 at the John Radcliffe Hospital, Oxford. He was cremated at the Oxford crematorium on 12 December, and his ashes were scattered on Hallam Moors. He was survived by his wife and three children.

Assessment Dainton devoted his whole life to scientific research, to the welfare of education, most particularly higher education, and to fostering the right environment in which intellectual life, scholarship, and research could prosper. Some found him an intimidating and formidable opponent in the cut and thrust of an argument, and so he often was, because of his remarkably clear memory, quick mind, and incisive ability to see to the root of a problem, all combined with the direct manner reputedly common among Yorkshiremen. But he was a very kind and generous man, especially with the young, with a delightful sense of humour and a great fund of amusing anecdotes for almost any occasion.

Dainton's influence on the affairs of scholarship, research, and education was enormous; the chairmanship of the Council for Scientific Policy and later the Advisory Board for the Research Councils, of the University Grants Committee, of the National Radiological Protection Board, and of the British Library board, all came at critical periods, and his contribution affected the subsequent history of these institutions. He received numerous national and international honours, including twenty-five honorary degrees, the Davy medal of the Royal Society (1969), the Faraday medal of the Royal Society of Chemistry (1974), and the Crookshank medal of the Royal College of Radiologists (1981). He was the author of *Chain Reactions* (1956), *Choosing a British University* (1981), and *Universities and the National Health Service* (1983), as well as of numerous papers in scientific journals. REX RICHARDS

Sources F. Dainton, *Doubts and certainties: a personal memoir of the twentieth century* (2001) · P. Gray and K. J. Ivin, *Memoirs FRS*, 46 (2000), 87–124 · video interview with Lord Walton, Oxford Brookes University [also at Royal College of Physicians] · *The Times* (8 Dec 1997) · *The Independent* (8 Dec 1997) · *The Independent* (22 Dec 1997) · *The Guardian* (8 Dec 1997) · *Daily Telegraph* (10 Dec 1997) · personal knowledge (2004) · private information (2004) [Lady Dainton] · b. cert.
Archives University of Sheffield, papers | FILM Oxford Brookes University, interview with Lord Walton, May 1991 · priv. coll., recorded talk | SOUND BL NSA, National Life Story Collection, 'City lives', 1989, C409/028/01–06 · BL NSA, oral history interview · BL NSA, performance recordings
Likenesses J. Mendoza, portrait, Goldsmiths' Hall, London · W. Narraway, portrait, U. Nott. · T. Stubley, portrait, University of Sheffield · T. Stubley, portrait, BL · photograph, repro. in *The Times* · photograph, repro. in *The Independent* (8 Dec 1997) · photograph, repro. in *The Guardian* · photograph, repro. in *Daily Telegraph* · photographs, National Radiological Protection Board, Chilton, Oxfordshire
Wealth at death £214,499: administration with will, 4 June 1998, CGPLA Eng. & Wales

Daintree, Richard (1832–1878), geologist and photographer, was born at Hemingford Abbots, Huntingdonshire, on 13 December 1832, the son of Richard Daintree, a prosperous farmer, and his wife, Elizabeth. He was educated at Bedford grammar school and in 1851–2 at Christ's College, Cambridge, but left without completing a degree to seek a warmer climate for his health, and in 1852 emigrated to Victoria. After eighteen months prospecting for gold he was appointed in February 1854 to the Victorian geological survey under Alfred Selwyn (1824–1902). Much of his work comprised routine mapping and a prolonged but unsuccessful search for coal deposits. He earned a reputation as being amiable and warm-hearted, and a competent geologist. For six months in 1856–7 he studied assaying under John Percy (1817–1889) at the Royal School of Mines, London. He also learned photography and on his return to Victoria pioneered its use in geological exploration. In 1857 he published, together with Antoine Fauchery, a volume of photographs entitled *Australia*. In the same year, on 1 December, he married Lettice Agnes (1838–1915), daughter of Henry Foot, surveyor and land speculator; they were to have six daughters and two sons.

Unsatisfied in his work, in 1863 Daintree entered into partnership with the Hann family in establishing a group of pastoral properties in the newly opened Burdekin River district of northern Queensland. He moved there with his family in 1864, resigning from the geological survey in January 1865. Daintree spent much of his time in north Queensland searching for minerals. In 1867, together with William Hann, he developed the Lynd copper mine on the Einasleigh River, but high freight costs soon doomed the project. For the same reason, the coal deposits which he identified at the Bowen River were not developed until the 1920s. However, his mineral discoveries at Cape River (1867), the Gilbert (1869), and the Etheridge (1869–70) provoked immediate gold rushes, and later led to the establishment of more permanent goldfields. The Queensland government recognized his work by creating a geological survey in 1868 and appointing him government geologist for northern Queensland, based in Townsville. This appointment led to his withdrawal from his pastoral ventures—by then deep in debt.

Against many difficulties Daintree continued his photography. His uncommonly skilful studies of Aborigines, pastoral life, and mining camps now provide a valuable historical record. When Queensland was invited to participate in the London Exhibition of Art and Industry in 1871 Daintree urged the merits of photography and mineral specimens as publicity, and was appointed special commissioner. He was shipwrecked *en route* for London, but salvaged enough material to make a creditable display and in March 1872 was appointed Queensland's agent-general in London. Using his photography innovatively to stimulate interest in Queensland he oversaw a marked increase in emigration; however, complaints arose about the character of the migrants, and an investigation in 1875 by the Queensland premier, Arthur Macalister, revealed corruption among Daintree's subordinates. Although personally untainted, Daintree resigned in broken health in 1876, at which time he was appointed CMG. Following retirement he wintered twice in Menton, France, hoping to regain his health. However, he died on 20 June 1878 at Beckenham in Kent.   GEOFFREY BOLTON

Sources G. C. Bolton, *Richard Daintree: a photographic memoir* (1965) · P. Quartermaine, 'International exhibitions and emigration: the photographic enterprise of Richard Daintree, agent-general for Queensland, 1872–76', *Journal of Australian Studies*, 13 (1983), 40–55 · E. J. Dunn and D. J. Mahony, 'Biographical sketches of the founders of the geological survey of Victoria', *Bulletin of the Geological Survey of Victoria*, 23 (1910), 18 · A. Mozley, 'Richard Daintree, first government geologist of northern Queensland', *Queensland Heritage*, 1/2 (1965), 11–16 · I. G. Sander, *Queensland in the 1860s: the photography of Richard Daintree* (1977) · J. McKay, '"A good show": colonial Queensland at international exhibitions', PhD diss., University of Queensland, 1996 · J. Black, *North Queensland pioneers* (1931) · A. Fauchery and R. Daintree, *Australia* (1857) · *Votes and proceedings*, Queensland Legislative Assembly (1868–76) · R. Etheridge, 'Richard Daintree', *Geological Magazine*, new ser., 2nd decade, 5 (1878), 429–32 · 'Richard Daintree', *Bulletin of the Cairns Historical Society*, 34 (1961) · private information (2004) · Christ's College, Cambridge, admission records · parish register (baptism), Hemingford Abbots, 1833 · *AusDB*

Archives priv. coll. · Royal Historical Society of Queensland, Brisbane · South Brisbane, John Oxley Library | James Cook University, Townsville, Queensland, Maryvale MSS · Mitchell L., NSW, W. B. Clarke MSS

Likenesses photograph, repro. in *Australasian Sketches* (17 May 1873), 17 · photograph, repro. in Bolton, *Richard Daintree*

Wealth at death under £3000: probate, 21 Aug 1878, *CGPLA Eng. & Wales*

Daintrey, Adrian Maurice (1902–1988), artist and art critic, was born on 23 June 1902 at Foulsa Road, Balham, London, the youngest of the three children of Ernest Daintrey, solicitor, and his wife, Lucy Mary Blagdon. His talent for drawing was the only distinction to emerge from his schooldays at Charterhouse, but this was sufficient for his father to encourage him to enter the Slade School of Fine Art, London, in 1920. Daintrey blossomed with the companionship of other students such as Allan Gwynne-Jones and Rex Whistler, and on the strength of one of his paintings, he was awarded a scholarship. However, he smarted under the stern academic regime imposed on the Slade by Henry Tonks (much preferring Philip Wilson Steer). Seeking encouragement in a less rigid approach to art, he introduced himself to Augustus John, and a thirty-five-year relationship began. He frequently joined the circle gathered round John at La Tour Eiffel restaurant in Percy Street, and he visited John's home, Fryern Court, in Hampshire, where he and his fellow painter George Lambourn sometimes helped John's painting speed and concentration by working with him in the studio. Another lifelong friendship established at this time was with Anthony Powell, whom Daintrey met through his neighbour, the artist Nina Hamnett.

Daintrey sought to break out of the strictures of the Slade by copying old masters. He often made use of the National Gallery's copying-days for students, in common with Duncan Grant and Vanessa Bell. He found them convivial company and shared an enthusiasm for European art. In pursuit of wider horizons he enrolled at the Académie de la Grande Chaumière in Paris when he had finished at the Slade in 1924. During his stay in Paris he became friends with the painter Matthew Smith, who shared his enthusiasm for impromptu outings. He continued his copying activities at the Louvre but an unhappy love affair and money difficulties made him decide to return to England, and he took up a post of art-master at Dean Close School in Cheltenham, Gloucestershire. (Daintrey loved women, from prostitutes to high-society ladies, and he devoted time and attention to their pursuit, often at the expense of his painting.) He was rescued from the spiritual discomforts of teaching by an introduction to Dorothy Warren, who ran a gallery which attracted an affluent and aristocratic clientele. On the strength of the exhibition she offered him, he handed in his notice at Dean Close and his career began in earnest. His first show in 1928 was shared with Paul Nash and included a portrait of Augustus John. Among his purchasers from this exhibition was Sir Augustus Daniel, then director of the National Gallery. Through an introduction by John, he met Lord Alington and began his lifelong association with landed and aristocratic patrons from whom he gained many commissions (among the many houses he painted were Chatsworth, Derbyshire; Cliveden, Buckinghamshire; Mereworth Castle, Kent; and Crichel House, Dorset), though he was never entirely free from money worries.

Daintrey had an unfussed painting style reminiscent of the French painter Albert Marquet. Although his portraits were successful, it is for his paintings and distinctive pen-and-wash drawings of landscape and architecture, especially London streets, that he is remembered. His loose yet rhythmic line gave a vitality and deceptive casualness to his draughtsmanship which ensured that it was never laboured or dull. In 1935 he moved to Oakley Street, Chelsea, London. Donald MacLean had a flat at the same address and they quickly developed a sympathetic companionship as 'last-minute men', frequently playing golf (a passion of Daintrey's) together at one of the unfashionable clubs on the outskirts of London. MacLean's extreme political views puzzled Daintrey but he interpreted these attitudes as wild rather than sinister and they were rarely discussed. Certainly MacLean remained on sufficiently intimate terms to act as best man at Daintrey's brief wartime marriage to Pamela Mary Hardy (*b*. 1919), a Red Cross nurse, on 27 September 1941. (The couple divorced in 1949.)

With the declaration of war, Daintrey joined the air-raid precautions (ARP) and then in June 1940 enlisted in the army as a driver. As an untidy though debonair man, he coped inadequately with the trials of kit-inspections and parades, but was rescued from the increasing nightmare by a commission into the camouflage organization. After training at Farnham, he was posted to the Middle East.

Egypt was a revelation to him visually and brought back the desire to paint and draw. He was then moved to Italy for which he developed a lasting passion, returning often after the war, on occasion for specific commissions (such as a set of drawings of Siena for Aubrey Baring).

At the beginning of the 1950s Daintrey found himself out of step as far as London galleries were concerned. He resolved the situation by holding exhibitions of paintings and drawings in his studio, and with the support of his pre-war clientele these provided him with a fairly constant source of income. Sir David Eccles, then minister of works, began buying drawings in series for distribution to British embassies and government houses around the world. In the 1960s there was a revival of a more general, public interest, and he mounted eleven one-man exhibitions between 1964 and 1988. During this period Daintrey did not neglect his literary talents, writing for *Punch* as their art critic from 1953 to 1961, and in 1963 publishing a volume of reminiscences, *I must Say*, with Chatto and Windus. From the late 1960s he returned to teaching at the City and Guilds (of London) Art School, where he took a highly successful Sunday class for part-time students. Having moved on to become librarian there, he retired finally in the late 1970s, but nevertheless continued to keep up a prodigious output of paintings and drawings from his studio in Little Venice, London, and his trips abroad.

In 1984 Daintrey moved into sheltered accommodation at the old Charterhouse School in London. On 11 October 1988 he died in his sleep at Sutton's Hospital there after a series of small strokes. He was buried at Christ Church, Chelsea, London, on 31 October. His former wife survived him. The British Museum, the Imperial War Museum, St Thomas's Hospital, London, and the Government Art Collection have examples of his work. SALLY HUNTER

Sources A. Daintrey, *I must say* (1963) · *The Independent* (15 Oct 1988) · *Daily Telegraph* (13 Oct 1988) · *The Times* (13 Oct 1988) · *The Guardian* (15 Oct 1988) · introduction, A. Daintrey, *Adrian Daintrey* (1988) [exhibition catalogue, Sally Hunter Fine Art, London, 3–26 Feb 1988] · *CGPLA Eng. & Wales* (1989) · private information (2004)
Likenesses A. John, two oil portraits, *c*.1924, repro. in *A voyage around Adrian Daintrey* (1997) [exhibition catalogue, Sally Hunter Fine Art, London, 17 July–8 Aug 1997] · A. Daintrey, self-portrait, oils, 1946, priv. coll.; repro. in *A voyage around Adrian Daintrey* (1997) [exhibition catalogue, Sally Hunter Fine Art, London, 17 July –8 Aug 1997]
Wealth at death under £70,000: probate, 6 June 1989, *CGPLA Eng. & Wales* · £56,248.72: private information

Daircell. *See* Mo Ling (*d.* 697).

Dakar, André de. *See* Evans, Rudolph Bayfield (1897–1987).

Dakin, Henry Drysdale (1880–1952), biochemist, was born at 60 Fitzjohn's Avenue, Hampstead, London, on 12 March 1880, the youngest of a family of five sons and three daughters of Thomas Burns Dakin and his wife, Sophia, formerly Stevens. His father was then the owner of a sugar refinery in London, but later acquired an iron and steel business in Leeds, and moved there with his family in 1893. Dakin, after a brief period at the Merchant Taylors' School, London, therefore transferred at the age of thirteen to the Leeds modern school. On leaving school he was apprenticed to the Leeds city analyst, T. Fairley, before he entered, in 1898, the Yorkshire College, Leeds. In later years he recalled this early and strict scientific discipline of an analyst's laboratory as valuable training for his lifelong devotion to the then newly emergent science of biochemistry.

Dakin's course for the BSc brought him at once into contact with Julius B. Cohen, then the lecturer in organic chemistry at the Yorkshire College. It was with Cohen that Dakin began to acquire his lasting interest in the optical activity of organic compounds, its influence on their biological activities, or on their acceptability as nutrients. His specially vivid interest in the selective action of a natural enzyme on one component of a racemic compound led Cohen to give him the nickname Zyme, which his friends were to use as a familiar mode of address for the rest of his life.

After obtaining his BSc in 1901 from the University of Manchester, and spending a further year with Cohen as his personal assistant and demonstrator, Dakin was awarded a research exhibition by the 1851 Commissioners, and worked with it at the Jenner (later the Lister) Institute under S. G. Hedin; at Heidelberg, with A. Kossel; and for a final period again at the Lister Institute. These researches covered enzymatic actions on proteins and, selectively, on racemic esters of mandelic acid; on arginase and protamines; and on the synthesis of the hormone adrenaline and related active bases.

At that juncture the physician and biochemist Christian A. Herter (1865–1910) of New York was enquiring in London for somebody with suitable scientific and personal qualifications for an appointment with him in a private laboratory for biochemical researches which he had installed, and fully equipped, on two upper floors of his Madison Avenue mansion. Dakin accepted this unusual opportunity, for which, indeed, he had unique qualifications; and, in the event, he was to spend the rest of his working life in developing its special possibilities. Its conditions accentuated in him an inborn shrinking from any kind of publicity, which prevented him from taking part in any open meeting, discussion, or ceremony. He was elected FRS in 1917 but an invitation to deliver the Croonian lecture was met by a penitent refusal; and the award to him of its Davy medal (1941) was accepted only because, in wartime conditions, it could be presented in his own library. Congenial colleagues, however, were always welcomed to free and lively discussions of researches in private. Dakin had, indeed, a genius for quietly intimate friendships. Meanwhile publications of his own important researches in biochemistry were issuing in a steady stream from the Herter Laboratory.

After Herter died in 1910 his widow, Susan Dows Herter (*d.* 1951), was eager to maintain the laboratory, with Dakin thenceforward in sole charge of its uses. In 1916 their personal devotion was confirmed by their marriage. Dakin, though chronically unfit for active service, had hastened to Britain to offer his services for any national purpose. He eventually found opportunity for researches on the antiseptic treatment of wounds, and became an active advocate and exponent of the use of a buffered hypochlorite solution. This he used to great purpose in the *Aquitania* (then serving as a hospital ship for the Dardanelles) after having arranged for the installation of an electrolytic tank, with which an unlimited supply of the hypochlorite solution—Dakin's solution—could be made from sea water.

The Dakins moved later from Madison Avenue to a house and estate at Scarborough-on-Hudson, some 30 miles upriver from New York. There the laboratory was reinstated in a special building, and Dakin continued his researches, with their characteristic, unhurried perfection, almost until his death, on 10 February 1952, a year after that of his wife. They had no children. He had received honorary doctorates from Leeds, Yale, and Heidelberg. Dakin was cremated and his ashes buried, as he had requested, in his wife's grave.　　　H. H. DALE, *rev.*

Sources P. Hartley, *Obits. FRS*, 8 (1952–3), 129–48 · private information (1971) · personal knowledge (1971) · *The Times* (22 Feb 1952), 8e · *BMJ* (23 Feb 1952), 441 · *The Lancet* (23 Feb 1952), 426 · *New York Times* (11 Feb 1952), 25 · L. Baguenier-Desormeaux, 'Henry Drysdale Dakin à Compiègne, en 1915', *Revue d'Histoire de la Pharmacie*, 28 (1981), 79–88 · R. M. Hawthorne, 'Henry Drysdale Dakin, biochemist (1880–1952), the option of obscurity', *Perspectives in Biology and Medicine*, 26 (1983), 553–66 · P. Hartley, *Nature*, 169 (1952), 481–2 · H. T. Clarke, *JCS* (1952), 3319–24 · J. Cattell, ed., *American men of science*, 8th edn (1949), 556 · *Journal of Biological Chemistry*, 198 (1952), 491–4
Likenesses photograph, 1915, repro. in Baguenier-Desormeaux, 'Henry Drysdale Dakin à Compiègne' · G. D. Acker, photograph, Wellcome L.

Dakins, William (1568/9–1607), biblical scholar and Church of England clergyman, was probably the son of William Dakyns (d. 1598), vicar of Ashwell, Hertfordshire. Recorded as attending Westminster School on 2 July 1582, then aged thirteen, in 1586 he was offered a scholarship at Trinity College, Cambridge, where he graduated BA in 1591. He was elected a minor fellow on 3 October 1593 and major fellow on 16 March following; in 1594 he also proceeded MA. Dakins was appointed lecturer in Greek at Trinity on 2 October 1602. From 1603 to 1605 he was vicar of Trumpington. On 6 July 1604 the lord mayor and aldermen of London received a letter from James I, who following representations from 'divers of the Council' asked that Dakins, an 'ancient divine', be 'preferred before any other' to the professorship of divinity at Gresham College in London (Ward, 45). Dakins also had the support of John Cowell, vice-chancellor of Cambridge University, of Dr Robert Some, and of other eminent figures. He was installed as professor on the 14th. Soon afterwards he became one of the group of scholars who met at Westminster to prepare the translation of St Paul's epistles for what would become the Authorized Version of the Bible. Dakins did not live to see the task completed. He was appointed junior dean of Trinity on 2 October 1606, but died on 18 February following.　　　STEPHEN WRIGHT

Sources J. Ward, *The lives of the professors of Gresham College* (1740) · Venn, *Alum. Cant.*, 1/2.3 · R. Chartres and D. Vermont, *A brief history of Gresham College* (1998) · *Old Westminsters* · C. W. Foster, ed., *The state of the church in the reigns of Elizabeth and James I*, Lincoln RS, 23 (1926)

Dakyns [née Pattinson], **Winifred** (1875–1960), naval officer, was born on 16 September 1875 at Bensham Lodge, Gateshead, co. Durham, the youngest daughter of John Pattinson, analytical chemist, and his wife, Mary Jane, née Swan. She was educated at Gateshead high school and Newnham College, Cambridge, where she met, and married on 21 June 1902, Henry Graham Dakyns (1873/4–1937), a mechanical engineer.

During the First World War Winifred Dakyns (and to a lesser extent her husband) was involved with the voluntary aid detachment (VAD), run jointly by the British Red Cross and the order of St John. She worked closely with the director, Katharine Furse, and when Furse left in 1917 following a disagreement over the organization and employment of VAD nurses, Dakyns was one of a number of senior members who also left.

Shortly thereafter, in November 1917, Furse was appointed as the first director of the newly re-created Women's Royal Naval Service (WRNS) and looked to her former VAD colleagues to form the nucleus of the officer corps. In December Dakyns was appointed one of two assistant directors, working closely with Furse and with her deputy, Edith Crowdy, to draw up the terms and conditions of service for the WRNS. As the service grew, two more assistant directors were appointed and Dakyns assumed the title of assistant director (administration) with particular responsibility for the smooth running of the rapidly expanding service. She held this post until 1919, when the WRNS demobilized. Along with the other officers she was appointed CBE (military) 'for valuable services in connection with the war' (*London Gazette*, 9 May 1919), and, in respect of her service with the VAD, made an honorary serving sister of the order of St John of Jerusalem.

After the war Dakyns became honorary secretary of the University Women's Club and was actively concerned in its running for thirty years. Known as a woman whose firmness of character was overlain by a kind and gentle manner, she was living at Wickham Farmhouse, College Lane, Hurstpierpoint, Sussex, at the time of her death at Cuckfield Hospital, Cuckfield, Sussex, on 22 January 1960.　　　LESLEY THOMAS

Sources K. Furse, *Hearts and pomegranates* (1940) · U. S. Mason, *Britannia's daughters: the story of the WRNS* (1992) · *The Wren* (Feb 1960), 34 · b. cert. · m. cert. · d. cert. · *CGPLA Eng. & Wales* (1960)
Wealth at death £53,659 19s. 4d.: probate, 3 May 1960, *CGPLA Eng. & Wales*

D'Albert, Eugen Francis Charles (1864–1932), pianist and composer, was born on 10 April 1864 at 9 Newton Terrace, Glasgow, the son of Charles Louis Napoléon D'Albert (1809–1886) and his wife, Annie Rowell. His father, though born in Germany, was a musician of mixed Italian and French descent who had established himself as a dancing-master and composer first in London, then in Newcastle, where he met and married a local girl, Annie Rowell, and then in Glasgow, where their son was born and brought up.

At the age of ten D'Albert attended the New Music School in London, whose director was Arthur Sullivan, and he became the pupil of John Stainer and Ebenezer Prout. His talents as a pianist were soon noticed: at sixteen he played Schumann's piano concerto at the Crystal Palace, and a year later he played a concerto of his own composition in London under Hans Richter. Richter agreed to take him to Vienna, where he came to the notice of Brahms, Eduard Hanslick, and, through Richter's introduction, Liszt. His career henceforth was based entirely in Germany, where his fame as a pianist grew. Liszt referred to him as the 'young Tausig', and he toured widely, notably to the United States in 1904–5. In 1895 he was appointed conductor at Weimar but resigned immediately when he found that the position was shared by two others. He changed his first name from Eugène to Eugen and identified wholly with German culture. He took Swiss citizenship in 1914 and resided mostly thereafter in Zürich. His private life, like his concert career, was restless, for he was married six times and had eight children. Louise Salingré was his first wife. The second was the Venezuelan pianist, singer, and conductor Teresa Carreño, who had played to Abraham Lincoln in the White House before D'Albert was born. Little is known about his later wives, who were Hermine Finck, Ida Fulda, Fritzi Jauner, and Hilde Fels, or his final partner Virginia Zanetti.

As a composer D'Albert was immensely prolific. He had considerable success with his piano and chamber music, and he gave a lot of attention to the stage, composing altogether twenty-one operas, all of which were staged in German theatres. His style derived from German Romantic music, especially that of Schumann and Brahms, with later modern touches in the manner of Richard Strauss and Hans Pfitzner, both of whom were his friends. He also formed close relationships with Engelbert Humperdinck and the dramatist Gerhart Hauptmann. His cello concerto (1899) is an appealing work in a compressed one-movement form modelled on Weber and Liszt. The seventh of his operas, *Tiefland*, first performed in Prague in 1903, was a worldwide success and has still not entirely disappeared from the repertory. *Flauto solo*, a comic opera first performed in 1905, was successful also. His last complete opera, *Die schwarze Orchidee* (Leipzig, 1928), betrayed signs of a more playful modernism, but his debt to German traditions was strong. *Tiefland* is based on a drama by the Catalan playwright Angel Guimerá, with a story of violent sexual passion set in the foothills of the Pyrenees. It provides a link between Italian *verismo* and German expressionist opera, although the orchestral textures recall a more Wagnerian language. D'Albert was also a prolific composer of lieder.

D'Albert's fame as a pianist was based on a formidable virtuoso technique, sometimes compared to that of Busoni. He was not a teacher, but he imparted the spirit of his playing in his editions of Bach's preludes and fugues and of Beethoven's sonatas. He also transcribed Bach's organ works for the piano and composed a cadenza for Beethoven's piano concerto no. 4. His work as a composer, especially for the theatre, drew him gradually away from the concert stage, so that he never came to be recognized as truly the equal of Busoni, Paderewski, and the many other keyboard giants who emerged at the beginning of the century. D'Albert died in Riga, Latvia, on 3 March 1932, and was buried in Morcote, near Lugano, Switzerland.

HUGH MACDONALD

Sources W. Raupp, *Eugen d'Albert: ein Künstler- und Menschen-Schicksal* (Leipzig, 1930) • *New Grove*, 1.208–9 • C. Pangels, *Eugen d'Albert: Wunderpianist und Komponist* (Zürich, 1981); Eng. trans. *Eugen d'Albert* (1999) • S. Sadie, ed., *The new Grove dictionary of opera*, 4 vols. (1992) • L. Fincher, ed., *Die Musik in Geschichte und Gegenwart: Personenteil*, 2nd edn, 1 (Kassel, 1999)

Dalbiac, Sir James Charles (1776–1847), army officer, was the eldest son of Charles Dalbiac, of Hungerford Park, Berkshire. He entered the army as a cornet in the 4th light dragoons on 4 July 1793, and passed the whole of his military life in that regiment. He was promoted lieutenant on 24 February 1794, captain on 11 October 1798, major on 15 October 1801, and lieutenant-colonel on 25 April 1808. In 1805 he married Susanna Isabella, eldest daughter of Lieutenant-Colonel John Dalton, of Sleningford Hall, Ripon, Yorkshire; they had one daughter, Susanna Stephania (1814–1895), who married in 1836 James Henry Robert Innes-Ker, sixth duke of Roxburghe. In 1806 Dalbiac published *A military catechism for the use of young officers and non-commissioned officers of the cavalry*.

Dalbiac saw no service until his regiment was ordered to Portugal in April 1809. He landed as second lieutenant-colonel to Lord Edward Somerset, and in July 1809 led the left wing of his regiment in the famous charge at Talavera. He served throughout the Peninsular campaigns of 1810, 1811, and 1812, and commanded the 4th light dragoons, in the absence of Lord Edward Somerset, in the cavalry actions of Campo Mayor on 25 March, and of Los Santos on 16 April 1811, and also in Cotton's spirited attack on Soult's rearguard at Llerena on 11 April 1812. At the battle of Salamanca, on 22 July 1812, the 4th light dragoons was brigaded with the 5th dragoon guards and 3rd light dragoons under the command of Major-General Le Marchant, and took its part in the famous charge in which the general was killed. Napier commemorated not only this charge, but the conduct of Mrs Dalbiac at the battle:

> an English lady of a gentle disposition, and possessing a very delicate frame, had braved the dangers and endured the privations of two campaigns … In this battle, forgetful of everything but the strong affection which had so long supported her, she rode deep amidst the enemy's fire, trembling, yet irresistibly impelled forwards by feelings more imperious than terror, more piercing than the fear of death. (Napier, bk 18, chap. 3)

After Salamanca, Dalbiac returned to England, and never again went on active service. He was promoted colonel on 4 June 1814, was brigadier-general commanding the Gujarat district of the Bombay army from 1822 to 1824, and was promoted major-general on 27 May 1825. He was prosecutor of the court martial on Colonel Brereton and Captain Warrington, who were at Bristol during the riots of 1831, and for his services was knighted (1831) by William IV. He unsuccessfully contested Ripon in 1832, and was Conservative MP for Ripon from 1835 until he retired in 1837. He showed his tory opinions in his pamphlet of 1841, *A Few Words on the Corn Laws*. He was promoted lieutenant-general on 28 January 1838, and made colonel of the 3rd dragoon guards in January 1839, from which he was transferred to the colonelcy of his old regiment, the 4th light dragoons, on 24 September 1842. According to the *Gentleman's Magazine*, he was 'an ardent disciple of Izaak Walton' (*GM*, 308). He died at his chambers in the Albany, London, on 8 December 1847.

H. M. STEPHENS, *rev.* ROGER T. STEARN

Sources *GM*, 2nd ser., 29 (1848), 308 · J. Philippart, ed., *The royal military calendar*, 3 vols. (1815–16) · W. F. P. Napier, *History of the war in the Peninsula and in the south of France*, 6 vols. (1828–40) · Fortescue, *Brit. army*, vol. 8 · D. Gates, *The Spanish ulcer: a history of the Peninsular War* (1986) · A. J. Guy, ed., *The road to Waterloo: the British army and the struggle against revolutionary and Napoleonic France, 1793–1815* (1990) · R. Muir, *Britain and the defeat of Napoleon, 1807–1815* (1996) · WWBMP

Archives NRA, priv. coll., papers incl. diaries and family correspondence relating to Peninsular War | BL OIOC, letters to Lord Tweeddale, MSS Eur F 96 · East Riding of Yorkshire Archives Service, Beverley, Howard–Vyse MSS · East Riding of Yorkshire Archives Service, Beverley, letters to Thomas Northcliffe and wife · priv. coll., Russell MSS · Woburn Abbey, letters to Lord George William Russell

Likenesses Miss Sharples, double portrait, drawing, 1832, NPG · F. R. Say, oils (posthumous; after A. Morton?, 1837), probably Floors Castle, Borders region · R. Sharples, group portrait, oils (*The trial of Colonel Brereton—after the Bristol riots, 1831*), Bristol City Art Gallery · wood-engraving, NPG; repro. in *ILN* (1847–8)

Dalbier, John (*d.* 1648), army officer, is of unknown origin. He was said by Sir Thomas Roe to have been a felt dresser in Strasbourg, although this could have been a disparaging comment, and it was also said that he had a wife in Strasbourg. Roe was also the source for the story that Dalbier left his wife in Strasbourg when he embarked on his military career. He was commonly referred to as being German, and by 1622 was described as a merchant. He was then serving as paymaster to Count Ernst von Mansfeld, a post which he held until the latter's death. Dalbier handled negotiations for Mansfeld in Amsterdam and Paris and in November 1624 joined him in London to help raise the army that left Dover in the following January. He may have accompanied Mansfeld on his journey of 1626 into the Balkans, where the count was killed; he was one of three men who arrived at Venice to arrange for the funeral and settle Mansfeld's affairs.

Dalbier was said to have been disappointed not to have secured employment with the Venetian republic and in May 1627 was in England, where he entered the service of the duke of Buckingham as commissary of the musters. He was sent to the Low Countries in connection with the king of Denmark's operations and later in the year accompanied Buckingham on the expedition to the Île de Ré, taking a leading role in advising the duke on military matters and thus arousing the professional jealousy of the other officers. Dalbier went back to England to expedite reinforcements and supplies, returning to Ré before the army's withdrawal. In January 1628 he and Sir William Balfour were commissioned by the king to raise a force of 1000 cavalry in Germany. Dalbier's instructions related to

the relief of Stade, which was being defended by Sir Charles Morgan's troops, but when the force was maintained after the garrison surrendered in April there was apprehension that it might be employed to intimidate parliament. Such fears, together with animosity towards Buckingham, prompted a sharp attack on Dalbier in the House of Commons in June 1628, during which he was described as untrustworthy, disloyal, incompetent as a military engineer, and a papist, although his financial abilities were acknowledged. Sir Thomas Jermyn responded by relating an incident that occurred while Dalbier was one of the elector palatine's four companions on a journey towards the Palatinate. When they encountered a party of imperial troops his quick thinking and persuasive manner saved the day, demonstrating his loyalty, for he could have received a large reward for betraying the elector.

Dalbier's reputation was such that in 1629 he was mentioned by the duke of Savoy as a possible negotiator with the Swiss cantons. He subsequently entered the Swedish service and was taken prisoner by Tilly at the capture of Neu-Brandenburg in 1631. Charles I solicited his release, through Philip Burlemachi, who was apprehensive that he would enter the service of the emperor. Dalbier was released and returned to England in December 1632 with news of the death of Gustavus Adolphus at Lützen. In 1635 he was living in the parish of St Martin-in-the-Fields and was described as a German and a servant to the king.

By 1642 Dalbier was detained in the king's bench prison for debt, but on the instance of the earl of Essex was released to serve in the parliamentary armies. He served under Essex and Sir William Waller as quartermaster-general and colonel of a regiment of horse. He was given command of fourteen troops of horse sent to relieve Gainsborough in July 1643, was wounded at the battle of Cheriton in March 1644, and took part in the Lostwithiel campaign. He continued to serve with Essex's army until summoned to London in October 1644 as a witness in the examination of Colonel John Butler for the latter's part in the surrender of Essex's infantry. Dalbier was under some suspicion himself and was still held for questioning in February 1645. Essex highly valued his services as quartermaster-general and pressed for his return, claiming that because of his absence 500 men had left the army. Although released Dalbier was not appointed to the New Model Army and his regiment was sent to serve under Edward Massey. He was, however, entrusted with the siege of Basing House, which was stormed in October 1645, following the arrival of Oliver Cromwell with a detachment of the New Model. Dalbier was then given command at the siege of Donnington Castle in Berkshire. The destruction of the village deprived his troops of adequate quarters nearby and he complained of the shortage of money to pay them, which led to unrest. The difficulties prevented him from forcing a surrender before the winter but the governor, Sir John Boys, capitulated on 1 April 1646. Dalbier then took part in the siege of Wallingford Castle, which surrendered in July.

Dalbier was among the predominantly presbyterian

officers in the cortège at the earl of Essex's funeral in October 1646. He was also in the forefront of the attempt to raise a force to defend London against the New Model Army in July 1647, and was implicated in the attempted coup and attack on parliament on 26 July. By April 1648 articles had been prepared against him. He joined the royalist troops which the earls of Holland and Buckingham raised in Surrey in July 1648 and was with the detachment that moved northwards, arriving at St Neots in Huntingdonshire on 9 July. It was surprised there the next morning and Dalbier was cut down by the soldiers; according to Edmund Ludlow, they 'hewed him in pieces' because they resented his treachery, though according to John Rushworth's account he died of his wounds on the following day, 11 July (E. Ludlow, *The Memoirs of Edmund Ludlow*, ed. C. H. Firth, 2 vols., 1894, 1.198).

STEPHEN PORTER

Sources [T. Birch and R. F. Williams], eds., *The court and times of Charles the First*, 1 (1848), 266–7, 313, 321; 2 (1848), 205–6, 210–11 · *CSP Venice, 1621–3*, 478, 507; 1623–5, 45, 473, 483; 1625–6, 73, 78; 1626–8, 138, 218, 390, 406, 471, 544, 576, 585, 598, 601; 1628–9, 2, 5, 96–7, 132, 241, 267; 1629–32, 139–40 · *CSP dom.*, 1627–8, 273, 310, 313, 361, 372, 496, 499, 514, 533, 537; 1628–9, 129, 183, 253, 341; 1629–31, 44, 181, 311; 1631–3, 34, 61, 122, 424–5; 1634–5, 298, 579; 1635, 457, 562; 1637, 327; 1644, 69, 530; 1644–5, 13, 15–16, 36, 57, 104, 106, 408, 497; 1645–7, 60, 128, 202, 204–5, 209, 399, 402, 418, 419 · R. C. Johnson and others, eds., *Proceedings in parliament, 1628*, 4: *Commons debates, 1628* (1978), 180, 184, 186, 188–9, 192, 243, 246–7, 259–60, 276 · PRO, SP 75/9/47 · BL, Egerton MS 2647, fol. 97 · J. Adair, *Cheriton, 1644: the campaign and the battle* (1973), 113–14, 180 · *The manuscripts of his grace the duke of Portland*, 10 vols., HMC, 29 (1891–1931), vol. 1, p. 334 · *DNB* · R. Ashton, *Counter-revolution: the second civil war and its origins, 1646–8* (1994), 354, 409 n. 154 · I. Gentles, 'Political funerals during the English revolution', *London and the civil war*, ed. S. Porter (1996), 213 · *JHC*, 3 (1642–4), 544; 4 (1644–6), 48 · *JHL*, 4 (1628–42), 681, 716; 6 (1643–4), 44, 47

Dalby, Isaac (1744–1824), mathematician and surveyor, was born in Gloucestershire, possibly in the Stroud area, into a family in modest circumstances. He was one of at least three boys. He attended a local grammar school and was destined to be a clothworker but, having taught himself mathematics, was appointed assistant master in a country school where he remained for three years before opening his own school in another part of the country. When this failed to prosper he went to London in 1772. There he was appointed assistant mathematics master at Archbishop Tenison's Grammar School, Charing Cross. While there he came to know many men of science and, after about a year, was appointed by the Hon. Topham Beauclerk to make astronomical observations, act as librarian of Beauclerk's 30,000 books, and undertake chemical experiments in his specially designed laboratory at Highgate. After Beauclerk's death in 1780 and the dismantling of his establishment in 1781 Dalby was engaged to catalogue Lord Beauchamps's library. In 1782 he was appointed mathematics master of a naval school at Chelsea, but this failed and in 1787 Jesse Ramsden, whose great theodolite was crucial to the success of the enterprise, recommended Dalby to William Roy to help with the triangulation through Kent and part of Sussex to the channel coast in connection with the linking of the Greenwich and Paris meridians. Dalby was employed on

this triangulation from 1787 to 1789. Roy was in very poor health by the time the fieldwork was finished and commissioned Dalby to correct his account of the work while he went to Lisbon to recruit his health. Roy later worked on calculations to prepare field measurements for publication and to do this he applied a theorem ascribed to Albert Girard to compute the excess of the three angles of a spherical triangle above 180 degrees. He further demonstrated that this excess was the same whether the figure of the earth was a sphere or a spheroid (both papers were published in the *Philosophical Transactions* for 1790). Roy died in 1790 but the project of national survey which he had promoted and initiated was taken up by the duke of Richmond as master-general of the ordnance. Dalby was the first person to be appointed to the staff of what was to become the Ordnance Survey and was thus an important link between the two earliest phases of survey work, namely the Paris–Greenwich triangulation and the Ordnance Survey proper. In 1791 Dalby was involved in the remeasurement of Roy's base on Hounslow Heath and during Dalby's time on the survey triangulation was extended over the southern counties of England as far as Land's End. Dalby's accounts of the work appeared in the *Philosophical Transactions* and the *Account of the operations carried out for accomplishing a trigonometrical survey of England and Wales* (with William Mudge, 3 vols., 1784–96).

In 1799 Dalby was appointed first professor of mathematics in the senior department of the Royal Military College, High Wycombe, and later, when the department moved to Sandhurst, went to live at Farnham, Surrey. He was an assiduous teacher, publishing for his students a *Course in Mathematics* (2 vols., 1805) which went to six editions. He was a founder member of the Linnean Society and also contributed often to the *Ladies' Diary*. He died, unmarried, at his home at Farnham on 3 February 1824.

ELIZABETH BAIGENT

Sources W. A. Seymour, ed., *A history of the Ordnance Survey* (1980) · C. Close, *The early years of the ordnance survey* (1926); repr. with introduction by J. B. Harley (1969) · Y. O'Donoghue, *William Roy, 1726–1790* (1977) · S. Widmalm, *Mellan kartan och verkligheten: geodesi och kartläggning, 1695–1860* (Uppsala, 1990) · J. B. Harley and Y. O'Donoghue, introduction, in *The old series ordnance survey maps of England and Wales*, Ordnance Survey, 1: *Kent, Essex, East Sussex and South Suffolk* (1975) · F. W. Steer and others, *Dictionary of land surveyors and local map-makers of Great Britain and Ireland, 1530–1850*, ed. P. Eden, 2nd edn, ed. S. Bendall, 2 vols. (1997) · E. G. R. Taylor, *The mathematical practitioners of Hanoverian England, 1714–1840* (1966) · T. Leybourn, *The mathematical questions proposed in the 'Ladies' Diary', and their original answers*, 4 vols. (1817) · will, PRO, PROB 11/1699 sig. 254

Likenesses J. J. Halls, oils, exh. RA 1817, Staff College, Camberley, Surrey · J. Thomson, stipple, pubd 1827 (after W. Derby), BM, NPG

Dalby, Robert (d. 1589), Roman Catholic priest, came from Hemingbrough in the East Riding of Yorkshire. He was a Church of England clergyman before his conversion to Roman Catholicism. He arrived at the English College, then at Rheims, on 30 September 1586, was ordained priest at Châlons on 16 April 1588, and was sent to England on 25 August that year. He landed at Scarborough, was arrested soon afterwards, and imprisoned in York Castle.

After his trial he and another priest, John Amias, were executed as traitors in York on 15 or 16 March 1589. They appear to have succeeded in converting the thief who shared their scaffold.   J. T. RHODES

Sources G. Anstruther, *The seminary priests*, 1 (1969) · H. Foley, ed., *Records of the English province of the Society of Jesus*, 3 (1878), 739 · R. Challoner, *Memoirs of missionary priests*, ed. J. H. Pollen, rev. edn (1924) · J. H. Pollen, ed., *Unpublished documents relating to the English martyrs*, 1, Catholic RS, 5 (1908) · J. H. Pollen, ed., *Acts of English martyrs* (1891) · Gillow, *Lit. biog. hist.* · *DNB* · M. C. Questier, *Conversion, politics and religion in England, 1580–1625* (1996)

Dalderby, John (*d.* 1320), bishop of Lincoln, came from a family holding property in the village of Dalderby, 2 miles south of Horncastle in Lincolnshire. He studied at the University of Oxford, proceeding to the degree of master of arts before 1269, and subsequently incepting as doctor of theology. He also studied and lectured in the faculty of medicine. He was remembered by John Schalby as a distinguished scholar, 'a bright gem of knowledge' (*Book of John de Schalby*, 16). His career at the university was supported by a series of ecclesiastical benefices: the family living of Dalderby (1269), the rectory of Heather in Leicestershire (1271), and the archdeaconry of Carmarthen (1283). He had become chancellor of Lincoln by 1291.

Following the death of Oliver Sutton in 1299, Dalderby was elected bishop of Lincoln on 15 January 1300. He was consecrated at Canterbury on 12 June. During the first year of his episcopate, parliament met at Lincoln, Edward I staying at the bishop's manor of Nettleham. Dalderby nevertheless opposed the king's demand for a subsidy on ecclesiastical property, on the grounds that papal consent had not been obtained. In 1315, however, possibly because the defence of the realm was in question, Dalderby supported royal taxation, writing to the collectors of a tenth to urge haste because of 'the dire perversity of the Scots'.

Dalderby played little part in national affairs, considering that his role lay rather in his diocese, as the shepherd of his flock. He was concerned that the cure of souls in the parishes should be properly provided, and he acted against abuses such as unlicensed non-residence and pluralities, and the incapacity of incumbents through deficiency of orders, illness, or old age. He laid stress on the provision of an educated clergy, refusing to admit to benefices clerks of insufficient learning, and granting leave of absence to incumbents for study. He offered indulgences to those hearing the sermons of certain preachers. He fostered his cathedral church at Lincoln; he granted an indulgence in 1307 to all who contributed to the building of the great central tower, augmented the endowment of the priest-vicars, and resolved a dispute between Dean Roger Martival and the chapter.

The diocese of Lincoln contained many religious houses over which the bishop had powers of visitation and correction. Dalderby mediated in disputes at the abbeys of Peterborough and Bardney. His attempts to enforce strict enclosure on the nunneries of the diocese, under the papal bull *Periculoso*, met with a hostile reception. At Markyate in 1300, as he was leaving, some of the nuns threw their copy of the statute after him, announcing that they

had no intention of observing it. Between 1308 and 1311 Dalderby acted in the proceedings against the knights templar in England; his pleas of pressure of business and ill health suggest that he brought little enthusiasm to the task.

From 1315 Dalderby became increasingly infirm, and was assisted in his duties by a coadjutor. But in 1319 he found a compromise for his see with the archbishop of Canterbury in a long-running dispute over probate jurisdiction. He died at his Lincolnshire manor of Stow Park on 12 January 1320 and was buried in the south transept of the cathedral. His former registrar, John Schalby, remembered him as 'an eloquent man, given to meditation and most devout; an excellent preacher of the word of God; not covetous; like a second Nicholas showing amiability to clerks, open-handed, munificent; and like a second Joseph prospering in all things' (*Book of John de Schalby*, 16–17). After his death, widespread reports of miracles wrought through his intercession prompted attempts in 1327 and 1328 to secure his canonization. These were unsuccessful but, like Bishop Robert Grosseteste (*d.* 1253) before him, Dalderby was venerated in Lincoln as a saint. As early as 1321 an indulgence was granted to those coming to worship God at his tomb. From the offerings made, a costly shrine was erected over his burial place. This was destroyed at the Reformation; some small fragments remain. The office composed for use on his feast day survives among the archives of the dean and chapter.

NICHOLAS BENNETT

Sources C. Clubley, 'John de Dalderby, bishop of Lincoln, 1300–1320', PhD diss., U. Hull, 1965 · *The book of John de Schalby: canon of Lincoln, 1299–1333, concerning the bishops of Lincoln and their acts*, trans. J. H. Srawley, another edn (1966) · R. E. G. Cole, 'Proceedings relative to the canonization of John de Dalderby, bishop of Lincoln', *Associated Architectural Societies' Reports and Papers*, 33 (1916), 243–76 · Emden, *Oxf.*, 1.536 · *Fasti Angl., 1066–1300*, [Lincoln] · J. H. Denton, *Robert Winchelsey and the crown, 1294–1313: a study in the defence of ecclesiastical liberty*, Cambridge Studies in Medieval Life and Thought, 3rd ser., 14 (1980) · C. W. Foster and K. Major, eds., *The registrum antiquissimum of the cathedral church of Lincoln*, 2, Lincoln RS, 28 (1933), 134

Archives Lincs. Arch., Lincoln diocesan records, registers 2–3

Dale, Benjamin James (1885–1943), composer, was born on 17 July 1885 at 7 Hill Side, Upper Holloway, London, a son of Charles James Dale (*b.* 1842), potter, and his wife, Frances Anne Hallett. His father was an amateur musician who conducted the Finsbury Choral Association. Sir Henry Hallett *Dale, the physiologist and pharmacologist, was his brother.

Dale attended the Stationers' Company's School, Hornsey, and Oakfield School, Crouch End. The fourteen-year-old made his début as a composer with the performance of his orchestral overture *Horatius*. At the Royal Academy of Music, where he enrolled in 1900 on the same day as Arnold Bax, he studied the piano and organ. Here Dale won several prizes, including the Sir Michael Costa composition prize and the Charles Mortimer prize in 1902, the Charles Lucas medal in 1903, and the Royal Academy of Music club prize and the Dove medal in 1905.

The piano sonata in D minor, one of Dale's most significant works, was begun in 1902 while he was still a student. Completed in 1905, it was an ambitious and virtuosic piece consisting of four substantial movements, lasting in total about forty-five minutes and covering sixty-two pages of printed music. As well as following a Lisztian model, it demonstrated the influences of Richard Wagner, Richard Strauss, and the Russian nationalists, composers to whom Frederick Corder, his teacher at the academy, introduced his pupils.

The Russian pianist Mark Hambourg had established an annual competition for a new piano work at the Royal Academy of Music. At the last minute Dale decided to submit his piano sonata, which was chosen in 1906 as the winner from sixty entries. Hambourg played only the variations, and his interpretation was not faithful to Dale's score. Dale refused to join him on stage, despite the rapturous reception, and he subsequently returned the prize. Dale's fellow students York Bowen (to whom he dedicated the sonata), Myra Hess, and Irene Scharrer subsequently performed the sonata in public recitals. The technical demands of Dale's sonata and its colossal length prevented it from getting firmly established in the repertory. The movements were sometimes performed separately, but the issue of the sonata on pianola roll in 1910, and its subsequent reissue in 1924, helped to bring the work to a wider public.

Dale is remembered also for his compositions for viola. Inspired by Lionel Tertis, he wrote his suite for viola and piano in 1906. The final two movements were orchestrated, with the 'Romance' becoming one of the most frequently played pieces in Tertis's repertory because of its wonderful and memorable melodic line. Dale also wrote a *Phantasy* for viola and piano, and an *Introduction and Andante* for six violas for Tertis's pupils. In 1913 he completed a choral setting of Christina Rossetti's Christmas hymn 'Before the paling of the stars'.

Before the First World War, Dale held several posts as organist in London, and he was appointed professor of harmony at the Royal Academy of Music in 1909. He was devoted to German and Norwegian culture, and admired the music of Grieg. A frequent visitor to Germany, he was on his way to the Bayreuth Festival in 1914 when war broke out. Along with many other musicians, Dale was interned in Ruhleben, Germany, where he continued to write music, now for camp entertainments. Towards the end of the war he broke his arm and was moved to the Netherlands.

Dale returned to England in 1918, but his health had suffered during internment, and he composed little until his return from an examining tour of Australia and New Zealand in 1919–20. This tour prompted him to write a violin sonata in 1921–2 and the festival anthem 'A Song of Praise' in 1923. His last work, *The Flowing Tide*, was sketched in 1924, although not completed until 1943. Dale married former composition student Kathleen Richards (1895–1984) in October 1921. A composer and musicologist, she was also a pianist, who broadcast frequently from 1927 to 1931. Following their divorce Dale married (Frieda Emma Auguste) Margit Kaspar of Munich in December 1936.

In later years Dale worked as a professor of composition and harmony at the Royal Academy of Music, and was appointed warden there in 1936. He continued to examine for the Associated Board of the Royal Schools of Music, and was one of the three musicians on the BBC's music advisory panel from 1936. His administrative and teaching roles left him little time to compose, and this, coupled with his hypercritical approach, meant that he produced few works. He had a precocious talent, and it is remarkable that a young student composer should have developed his own style so quickly, but the activity burnt him out. Dale wrote demanding and lengthy works, which were infrequently played. His musical style was an extension of the Romantic aesthetic, which fell out of favour after the First World War; he was strongly opposed to advanced contemporary trends.

During rehearsals in London on 30 July 1943 for *The Flowing Tide*, Dale collapsed with a heart attack, and he died on the way to St Mary Abbots Hospital, Kensington. Sixty years after his death he was still remembered as an understanding and inspiring teacher with a great sense of humour.

LISA HARDY

Sources *WWW*, 1941–50 · L. Foreman, 'Dale, Benjamin James', *New Grove*, 2nd edn · H. F. Redlich, 'Dale, Benjamin James', *Die Musik in Geschichte und Gegenwart*, ed. F. Blume (Kassel, Bärenreiter-Verlag, 1949–86) · L. Foreman, disc notes to Peter Jacobs's recording of B. Dale, piano sonata, Continuum CCD 1044, 1992 · L. Hardy, *The British piano sonata, 1870–1945* (2001) · F. Corder, 'Benjamin Dale's pianoforte sonata', *MT*, 59 (1918), 164–7 · E. Evans, 'Modern British composers, III: Benjamin Dale', *MT*, 60 (1919), 201–5 · E. Evans, 'Benjamin Dale', *Cobbett's cyclopedic survey of chamber music* (1929) · C. Foreman, 'The music of Benjamin Dale (1885–1943)', *RAM Magazine*, 238 (1985), 2–11 · F. Dawes, 'Dale, Kathleen', *New Grove*, 2nd edn · b. cert. · d. cert. · *CGPLA Eng. & Wales* (1943)

Archives Royal Academy of Music, London, MSS

Likenesses photographs, repro. in Foreman, disc notes

Wealth at death £2690 11s. 5d.: probate, 18 Oct 1943, *CGPLA Eng. & Wales*

Dale, David (1739–1806), merchant and cottonmaster, was born on 6 January 1739 at Stewarton, Ayrshire, the son of William Dale (1708–1796), a grocer and general dealer, and his second wife, Martha Dunlop (1719–1796). Dale was a local herdboy, and then in the 1750s an apprentice weaver in Paisley, a major centre for fine weaving. After working as a journeyman in Hamilton and Cambuslang, near Glasgow, he became clerk to a Glasgow silk mercer before setting up in 1763 as a linen yarn dealer in rented premises in Hopkirk's Land in Glasgow; his rent was £5 per annum and he sublet half of his premises to a watchmaker.

Gradually, Dale developed a substantial trade in partnership with Archibald Paterson, a wealthy candlemaker and fellow nonconformist, as a yarn importer and broker; but after 1769 he diversified into a number of partnerships and trades, including the Glasgow inkle factory and weaving. That year he became a burgher of Glasgow and a member of the Merchant Guild and Trades House. In 1777 Dale married Ann Caroline (d. before 1800), daughter of John Campbell of the Citadel, and a director of the Royal

David Dale (1739–1806), by John Henning, 1803

chamber of commerce; he was one of its first directors and was twice elected chairman. Also a member of the town council, he was twice a magistrate. After seceding from the Church of Scotland in the late 1760s, Dale became pastor of the Old Scotch Independents; this commitment motivated him to learn Hebrew and Greek so that he could read early editions of the Bible. His philanthropy was formed by his religion: diverse causes such as the British and Foreign Bible Society, the Town Hospital, the Royal Infirmary, Bridewell prisoners, Calton charity school, the Andersonian Institution, and the Humane Society attracted his support. In years of dearth he assisted in financing purchases of meal and American grain to keep down local prices. In all, during his life he gave about £52,000 to various charities. Despite his initial unpopularity, incurred by leaving the established church, Dale became widely respected for his business ability, and his temperament. Short and stout, he was highly gregarious with a notable sense of humour; a fine singer, he loved traditional Scottish ballads.

Dale was prepared to take profits on capital assets, especially in anticipation of financial crises, but apart from Stanley Mills, where he was probably unduly influenced by Robert Owen, his withdrawal from business was conditioned by his health, which deteriorated gradually from the late 1790s. He sold New Lanark in 1799 to Owen and his partners, and then disposed of other businesses. The Royal Bank's Glasgow management passed to Scott Moncreiff in 1800, although Dale retained his shares and gave advice.

Dale purchased ground in Charlotte Street, Glasgow, and employed Robert Adam to build his house in 1783 at a cost of £6000. This magnificent residence included an octagonal room, which Dale used as his study, and possessed ceilings and fireplaces of the type which made Adam's reputation. There in 1799 Robert Owen married Dale's eldest daughter, Ann Caroline. In 1800 Dale purchased Rosebank, Cambuslang, near Glasgow, where he died on 7 March 1806; he was buried in the Ramshorn (St David's) churchyard, Glasgow. His will (10 November 1804) established trustees to care for the interests of his five surviving daughters; this trust remained active for many years after Dale's death.   JOHN BUTT

Bank; of their seven children, one daughter and the only son died young.

In 1784 Dale founded New Lanark, initially with Richard Arkwright as his partner, and was also involved in cotton mills at Catrine (1786), Blantyre (1787), Kilmore (*c*.1791), Spinningdale (1791), Newton Stewart (*c*.1795), and Stanley (1802). All these ventures were managed by professional managers. Dale was also involved in a disastrous coalmining venture at Barrowfield, and with George Macintosh and P. J. Papillon established at Dalmarnock the first turkey-red dyeworks in Britain in 1785. In 1783 he was appointed, along with Robert Scott Moncreiff, the first Glasgow agent of the Royal Bank of Scotland; by 1800 discounts of bills of exchange at this branch had reached about £1 million. By 1804 Dale also held an extensive shareholding in the Forth and Clyde Canal Company. His business empire was administered from warehouses in St Andrew's Square.

New Lanark made Dale famous, for it was a highly profitable but humanely managed enterprise. Its visitors' book opens in 1795, revealing that the village was well-known to tourists—the book contains about 750 signatures per year in the late 1790s—before the arrival of Robert Owen. Dale provided very good living conditions, sensible clothing, and nutritious food for the large number of pauper apprentices, which he took from the Glasgow and Edinburgh poorhouses. He also provided schooling, and supported the healthy exercise of country dancing, establishing the policies which later brought fame to Owen.

In 1783 Dale became a founder member of the Glasgow

Sources D. J. McLaren, *David Dale of New Lanark* (1983) · W. G. Black, *David Dale's house* (1908) · I. Donnachie and G. Hewitt, *Historic New Lanark: the Dale and Owen industrial community since 1785* (1993) · A. Liddell, *Memoir of David Dale esq.* (1854) · J. Butt, ed., *Robert Owen, prince of cotton spinners: a symposium* (1971) · J. Butt and I. F. Clarke, eds., *The Victorians and social protest* (1973), chap. 1 · S. G. Checkland, *Scottish banking: a history, 1695–1973* (1975) · R. Owen, *The life of Robert Owen written by himself*, 2 vols. (1857–8); facs. edn with introduction by J. Butt (1971) · Chambers, *Scots.*, rev. T. Thomson (1875) · D. R. [D. Robertson], rev., *Glasgow, past and present: illustrated in dean of guild court reports and in the reminiscences and communications of Senex, Aliquis, J.B., &c*, 3 vols. (1884) · J. Sinclair, *Statistical account of Scotland*, 15 (1795) · G. Stewart, *Curiosities of Glasgow citizenship* (1881) · A. J. Cooke, 'Robert Owen and the Stanley mills', *Business History*, 21 (1979), 107–11 · A. J. Cooke, 'Cotton and the Scottish highland clearances: Spinningdale, 1791–1806', *Textile History*, 26 (1995), 89–94 · will, Lanarkshire commissary court, 10 Nov 1804, NA Scot.

Archives Mitchell L., Glas., letters to Claude Alexander of Ballochmyle · NL Scot., Dale–Moncrieff letters · U. Glas., Archives and Business Records Centre, New Lanark visitors' book | NA Scot., Campbell of Jura MSS
Likenesses J. Tassie, paste medallion, 1791, Scot. NPG · cartoon, 1793, Mitchell L., Glas.; repro. in Kay, *The morning walk* · J. Henning, glass paste medallion, 1803, NPG [*see illus.*] · H. Thomson, stipple, pubd 1822 (after medallion by J. Henning), BM, NPG · oils, Glasgow Art Collections · portrait, Glasgow corporation
Wealth at death £10,000–£12,000—liquid assets: Lanarkshire commissary court, NA Scot., 1804–1806

Dale, Sir David, first baronet (1829–1906), industrialist, was born on 11 December 1829 at Murshidabad, Bengal. He was the younger son of David Dale, an employee of the East India Company and judge of the city court there, and his wife, Ann Elizabeth, daughter of the Revd George Douglas of Aberdeen. Dale's great-uncle was David Dale, the Glasgow banker and philanthropist, whose daughter married the socialist Robert Owen and was mother of Robert Dale Owen. His elder brother, James Douglas (1820–1865), joined the Indian army on the Madras establishment, and became lieutenant-colonel. Dale's father died on board the *Providence* on 23 June 1830, during the voyage home with his wife and children. Mrs Dale, while travelling with her children to New Lanark to visit her family, was detained at Darlington by an accident to the mail coach, and received such kindness from Quakers of that town that she returned and made Darlington her home. She became a member of the Society of Friends in 1841, and died in 1879.

Dale was educated privately at Edinburgh, Durham, and Stockton. Brought up among Quakers, Dale remained a member of the Society of Friends until the late 1880s.

Dale's adult career began in the office of the Stockton and Darlington Railway Company, and in 1852, at the age of twenty-three, he was appointed secretary to the Middlesbrough and Guisborough section of the line. On 27 January 1853 he married a widow, Annie Backhouse Whitwell, *née* Robson (d. 1886), who already had two children; another son and daughter were born to them.

In 1858 Dale entered into partnership with William Bouch and became lessee of the Shildon locomotive works; the partnership ended in the early 1870s. Henceforth his activities rapidly expanded. He was concerned with the formation of the Consett Iron Company, of which he was appointed inspector in 1858, subsequently becoming managing director in 1869 and chairman in 1884. In 1866 he embarked on extensive shipbuilding enterprises in co-operation with the firms of Richardson, Denton, and Duck of Stockton, Denton and Grey of Hartlepool, and Thomas Richardson & Sons of Hartlepool, who combined together with a view to amalgamation. Dale became vice-chairman of this ambitious undertaking, but the union was not successful, and the companies reverted shortly afterwards to their former independent positions. Dale retained an interest in the two first-named concerns. He was also managing partner of Pease & Partners Ltd, and chairman of companies working iron ore mines near Bilbao in Spain. In 1881 he became a director of the North Eastern Railway Company, having previously served as director of the Stockton and Darlington Railway, and on the formation of the Sunderland Iron Ore Company in 1902 he was appointed chairman. He was an active member of the Durham Coal Owners' Association and of the Cleveland Mine Owners' Association.

Dale owes his main distinction to his pioneer application of the principle of arbitration to industrial disputes. The first board of arbitration was formed in connection with the iron trade of the north of England in March 1869, and Dale was its first president. The experiment was successful, serving to stabilize the industry's previously disorganized and volatile industrial relations. In recognition of Dale's services to the Iron Trades Conciliation Board he was publicly presented in 1881 with an address and a portrait painted by W. W. Ouless. Dale's important position within industry led to his appointment on several royal commissions, among which were those on trade depression (1885–6); on mining royalties (1889–93); and on labour (1891–4). At the Berlin labour conference of 1890, convened by the German emperor, he was one of the representatives of Great Britain, and during the sittings he received marked attention from the emperor and Bismarck. He helped to found the Iron and Steel Institute in 1869, and acted as honorary treasurer from that date until 1895, when he was elected president. His first wife having died in 1886, on 2 August 1888 he married Alice Frederica, elder daughter of Sir Frederick Milbank, of Barningham Hall, Yorkshire. She died in 1902.

In politics Dale was a Liberal, though his attention to business interests prevented him from standing for parliament. He became high sheriff for Durham in 1888, and the University of Durham made him an honorary DCL in 1895. He was created a baronet in the same year.

Active to the end, Dale died at York on 28 April 1906, and was buried in his home town of Darlington. In his honour a Sir David Dale chair of economics was instituted in 1909 at Armstrong College, Newcastle upon Tyne, then part of Durham University. A memorial lectureship on labour problems was also initiated at Darlington, the first lecture being delivered by Sir Edward Grey on 28 October 1910.

L. P. SIDNEY, rev. IAN ST JOHN

Sources E. Grey, *Sir David Dale: inaugural address delivered for the Dale Memorial Trust; to which is prefixed a memoir by Howard Pease* (1911) · *The Times* (30 April 1906) · J. S. Jeans, *Pioneers of the Cleveland iron trade* (1875) · *Journal of the Iron and Steel Institute*, 69 (1906), 2, 270-β · *Biographical Magazine* (June 1886) · A. Christie and C. Shaw, 'Dale, Sir David', *DBB*
Likenesses W. W. Ouless, portrait, 1881; priv. coll., 1912 · Barraud Ltd, photograph, repro. in *Journal of the Iron and Steel Institute*, facing p. 272 · photograph, repro. in Grey, *Sir David Dale*
Wealth at death £121,831 18s. 5d.: probate, 1 June 1906, CGPLA Eng. & Wales

Dale, Harold Edward (1875–1954), civil servant and author, was born at 24 Shadwell Road, Islington, London, on 5 December 1875, the son of Henry James Dale, a 'manufacturing electrician', and his wife, Caroline Harrison. After attending St Paul's School he went to Balliol College, Oxford, in 1894, following his elder brother Frank Harry Busbridge Dale (1871–1918) who became chief inspector of elementary schools. At Balliol he gained firsts in both classical moderations (1896) and *literae humaniores* (1898), and won several prestigious university prizes. In 1898 he was elected to a fellowship at New College which continued until 1905. Meanwhile he had also come first in the civil service examination and in 1898 joined the Colonial Office. As a Colonial Office official he undertook varied assignments—a mission to British Honduras in 1903–4, one of the British representatives at the Anglo-French conference on the New Hebrides in 1906, assistant secretary to the Imperial Conference of 1909, and Colonial Office representative at the north Atlantic fishing arbitration at The Hague in 1910. On 4 March 1911 Dale married Isabel Woodrow, (1885/6–1950), daughter of Samuel George Warner, actuary, at Balham Congregational Church.

A change of direction came in 1910 when Dale became secretary to the Development Commission, a body set up in 1909 to encourage rural development, including agricultural research and advisory services. This appointment meant that he eventually transferred to the Board of Agriculture and Fisheries, where he became in 1917 an acting assistant secretary. In 1919 he received a permanent appointment and was made CB. After moving to agriculture Dale undertook tasks which again took him abroad, in 1920 to Fiji to initiate a reorganization of the civil service in that area, and in 1923–4 to Jamaica as financial commissioner. In 1927 he was promoted to principal assistant secretary in the Ministry of Agriculture and Fisheries, from which he retired in 1935. A few years later he left London to live in Blewbury, Berkshire. Shortly before the death in 1950 of his wife he moved to Oxford, living at Norham End, Norham Gardens. He died, at the Radcliffe Infirmary, Oxford, on 30 July 1954.

Dale was a man of outstanding intellectual ability and highly regarded in the civil service. That he did not reach the highest levels may in part have been due both to his lifelong dedication to varied scholarly interests and to his natural shyness. He regularly published reviews and articles on classical subjects, and only a year before he died a fourth edition of Jowett's translation of the *Dialogues* of Plato came out, jointly edited by Dale and D. J. Allan, a fellow of Balliol. Dale also wrote on agricultural topics, but is best remembered for what he wrote on the civil service after retirement. *The Higher Civil Service of Great Britain* was written as the Second World War approached and published by Oxford University Press in 1941. It contains a detailed and well-informed account of the small group to which he had belonged, and which in those days occupied a predominant position in the immediate support of ministers in the formulation of policy, the preparation of legislation, and the general administration of the country. His calm and thorough treatment of his subject is enlivened by shrewd judgements on men and affairs, and by a certain dry wit sharpened by his own official experiences. The text is generously adorned with quotations in Latin and Greek, with no translations offered.

In 1943 Dale gave the Sidney Ball lecture in Oxford, published in the same year as a Barnett House paper under the title *The Personnel and Problems of the Higher Civil Service*.

Essentially this offers a summary of some features of the earlier book. He also contributed a chapter on parliament and the civil service to a book entitled *Parliament: a Survey*, published in 1952. His work stands at the beginning of a lively tradition of descriptive and critical writing about the civil service and its place in the British parliamentary system. He provided a model for subsequent academic scholars and for one or two from the service itself, notably C. H. Sisson. But within two decades of his death the scholar–administrator so impressively exemplified by Dale had become virtually extinct. NEVIL JOHNSON

Sources WW · WWW · *The Times* (2 Aug 1954) · *The Times* (5 Aug 1954) · I. Elliott, ed., *The Balliol College register, 1900–1950*, 3rd edn (privately printed, Oxford, 1953) · b. cert. · m. cert.
Archives U. Reading, Rural History Centre, corresp. relating to biography of Sir Alfred Daniel Hall
Wealth at death £4126 2s. 10d.: probate, 15 Sept 1954, *CGPLA Eng. & Wales*

Dale, Sir Henry Hallett (1875–1968), physiologist and pharmacologist, was born at 5 Devonshire Street, Islington, London on 9 June 1875, the third son and third of the seven children of Charles James Dale (*b*. 1842), manager of a pottery manufacturing firm, and his wife, Frances Anne, daughter of Frederick Hallett, a furniture-maker in Clerkenwell. Dale's younger brother, Benjamin James *Dale, who died in 1943, was a composer of some distinction and warden of the Royal Academy of Music. At several stages of his education Dale faced financial problems. Seemingly destined for a commercial career, at sixteen he won a scholarship to the Leys School, Cambridge. Three years later he entered Trinity College, Cambridge, on a minor scholarship and a sub-sizarship in natural sciences; he was soon awarded a sizarship and then won a major foundation scholarship in 1896. In his natural sciences tripos, parts one (1896) and two (1898), he was placed in the first class.

Dale stayed in J. N. Langley's department of physiology for a further two years. His college scholarship of £100 per annum was not sufficient to keep him, and when he failed to obtain a Coutts–Trotter studentship at Trinity, which went to Ernest Rutherford, Dale collected whatever demonstratorships and private coaching he could. When, shortly afterwards, Rutherford was appointed as professor at McGill University, the studentship fell vacant, and Trinity College divided it between Dale and R. J. Strutt (later fourth Baron Rayleigh), and allowed them to retain their scholarships as well. When Dale presented his thesis for a college fellowship, he did so again in competition with Strutt. This time he was unsuccessful, though the thesis was highly commended. Dale was financially unable to remain in Cambridge. He devoted a few weeks to 'shameless cramming' of descriptive anatomy and then sat for a Schuster scholarship at St Bartholomew's Hospital, London—awarded on examination in anatomy and physiology—and was elected. While at Bart's, Dale lived with his parents for reasons of economy. A few months before he qualified BCh, Cambridge, in 1902, he was awarded the George Henry Lewes studentship, founded by George Eliot, and made arrangements with professors

Sir Henry Hallett Dale (1875–1968), by Yousuf Karsh, 1949

E. H. Starling and W. Bayliss to work in the department at University College, London. During the tenure of this studentship, in October 1903, he also spent four months in Frankfurt-am-Main working under Paul Ehrlich. On returning to London, Dale applied for the Sharpey studentship in physiology at University College, London, and was appointed in March 1904.

Dale married that year his first cousin Ellen Harriet (d. 1967), daughter of F. W. Hallett. They had three children, all of whom studied either physiology or medicine. Their elder daughter, Alison Sarah, married Alexander Robertus Todd FRS, professor of organic chemistry at Cambridge. Their second daughter, Eleanor Mary, married Robert Edgar Hope Simpson, a medical practitioner. Their third child, a son, Robert Henry (d. 1957), became a plastic surgeon in Saskatoon, Canada.

Later in 1904 Dale accepted a research post in physiology at the Wellcome Physiological Research Laboratories offered to him by Henry S. Wellcome. Dale spent ten extremely fruitful years there, the first eighteen months as their pharmacologist and the remainder of the time as director. Here he met George Barger and engaged a number of young men who started their scientific career with him, including Arthur Ewins, Alexander Glenny, P. P. Laidlaw, and J. H. Burn. In 1914 Dale became director of the department of biochemistry and pharmacology of the projected Central Institute for Medical Research, which in 1920 became the National Institute for Medical Research at Hampstead. In 1923 Dale was made chairman of the committee of departmental directors and, in 1928, the first director of the institute, a position he held until his retirement in 1942, when he accepted the directorship of

the Royal Institution, becoming at the same time Fullerian professor of chemistry. He retired from this position in 1946.

In 1936, when Sir Henry Wellcome died, Dale was nominated as one of the founding trustees of the Wellcome Trust. He was its chairman from 1938 to 1960, and continued as scientific adviser until 1968, giving advice until a week before he died at the age of ninety-three. To commemorate his unique services as chairman, the trust in 1961 endowed a Royal Society professorship, the Henry Dale research professorship.

Dale was secretary of the Royal Society from 1925 to 1935 and its wartime president from 1940 to 1945, which brought special responsibilities. During his secretaryship obituary notices of the fellows of the society, previously published in the society's *Proceedings*, were for the first time published collectively in a single volume each year. He also inaugurated the system whereby fellows were encouraged to write and deposit personal records, for the benefit of future obituarists. During his presidency a meeting of the society was held outside Britain for the first time, in India; the number of fellows to be elected each year was increased from twenty to twenty-five and women were admitted to the fellowship for the first time in 1945. Dale set up the British Commonwealth Science Committee, to foster scientific co-operation, which led to the Royal Society Empire Scientific Conference in 1946. His presidency brought him secret duties; in 1942 he chaired a small, highly confidential, scientific advisory committee to the war cabinet, and later he advised the post-war cabinet until 1947.

Dale's last two years as director of the National Institute for Medical Research were devoted to the detailed planning of a building at Mill Hill. After his retirement Dale became a member of the Medical Research Council (1942–6), chairman of its post-war committee on the medical and biological application of nuclear physics (1945–9), member of the advisory committee on atomic energy (1945–7), chairman of the radioactive substances advisory committee (1949–52), of the governing body of the Lister Institute, and of the scientific committee of the British Council. He was president of the Royal Society of Medicine (1948–50) and of the British Council (1950–55), and in 1947 presided over the British Association at its Dundee meeting and over the seventeenth International Physiological Congress at Oxford. He was a trustee of the National Central Library (later part of the British Library lending division) and a member of the Standing Commission on Museums and Galleries.

A substantial part of Dale's research career, on chemical mediators in the functioning of the body, came from work on a fungus, ergot of rye. In 1906 he provided the first example of an adrenergic blocking agent by showing that an extract of ergot, called ergotoxine, reversed the raising effect on the blood pressure of both sympathetic nerve stimulation, and of the application of adrenaline. Some of this work was done in collaboration with T. R. Elliott, although the two men never published together, and they were some of the earliest experiments to suggest mechanisms of chemical neurotransmission, for which Dale was ultimately to share the Nobel prize. In 1907 he discovered histamine in an extract of ergot, and with Barger determined its chemical structure and physiological actions, and in 1909 he discovered an extract from the posterior pituitary gland which had the property of contracting the uterus. The following year Dale and Barger, after an extensive chemical and physiological study of over fifty structurally related substances, introduced the useful term 'sympathomimetic', now in general use, for chemicals that imitated the effects of the sympathetic nervous system. In 1913 Dale made a fundamental discovery that anaphylactic contractions of smooth muscle resulted from the formation of cell-fixed antibodies, which changed prevailing views about the mechanisms of anaphylaxis, allergy, and immunity. In 1914, in collaboration with Arthur Ewins, Dale discovered a naturally occurring source in ergot of a vasoactive substance, acetylcholine. He characterized its physiological effects, and showed that it acted on smooth muscles, gland cells, and the heart; and in a different fashion, on the cells of autonomic ganglia and the adrenal medulla. Later work revealed a similar action at motor end-plates in the peripheral nervous system. This distinction allowed Dale, over twenty years later, to suggest, and to establish with several co-workers, the physiological role of acetylcholine at several sites in the autonomic nervous system and at the neuromuscular junction.

During the First World War, employed by the Medical Research Committee, Dale directed his energies to war work, studying amoebic dysentery, gas gangrene, and wound shock, organizing alternative British supplies of the anti-syphilitic, Salvarsan, produced in Germany. Immediately after the war he returned to the study of histamine, and with Laidlaw made a beautiful analysis of its vascular effects and the mechanism of histamine shock. In 1929, with Harold Dudley he first isolated acetylcholine and histamine from an animal source, a discovery that greatly stimulated his own, and others', research into acetylcholine. In 1934 he coined the terms 'cholinergic' and 'adrenergic' to distinguish nerve fibres by the chemical neurotransmitter they might use. For his work on the role of acetylcholine in chemical neurotransmission he was awarded the Nobel prize in physiology or medicine in 1936, shared with the Austrian pharmacologist Otto Loewi. A somewhat different, but immense contribution that Dale also made to therapeutics throughout the world was his experimental and administrative work, from the 1920s onwards, in establishing international standards for hormones, vitamins, and various other drugs; he himself provided the first international standard for insulin.

Dale published numerous scientific articles and two books, one of which, *Adventures in Physiology*, is an annotated collection of his most important papers. He also contributed several notices to the *Dictionary of National Biography*.

Dale's work was recognized by his appointment as a fellow of the Royal Society (1914); CBE (1919); knight (1932); GBE (1943); and by his admission to the OM (1944). Dale shared the unique position of being holder of two orders of merit—the second one being the order of merit of the German Bundesrepublik (1955)—with only one other person in Britain, T. S. Eliot. In 1949 Dale received Belgium's grand croix of the order of the Crown. In 1900 Dale won the Gedge prize, Cambridge University; in 1909 the Raymond Horton Smith prize; in 1926 the Cameron prize, University of Edinburgh. A research professorship of the Royal Society bears his name and in 1959 a Dale medal was struck in his honour by the Society of Endocrinology. It is awarded annually and the recipient delivers the Sir Henry Dale lecture. Dale was an honorary fellow of Trinity College, Cambridge, of University College, London, and of the Chemical Society. He received honorary degrees from twenty-five universities, including eleven in Britain; he was the recipient of seventeen medals, an honorary member of the Physiological Society, British Pharmacological Society, Pharmaceutical Society, Royal Society of Medicine, and the Royal Society of Edinburgh, and the Royal Society of New Zealand, an honorary associate of the Royal College of Veterinary Surgeons, and an honorary, foreign, corresponding, or associate member of thirty-seven foreign scientific societies. Dale died in the Evelyn Nursing Home, Cambridge, on 23 July 1968.

W. FELDBERG, rev. E. M. TANSEY

Sources W. S. Feldberg, *Memoirs FRS*, 16 (1970), 77–174 · E. M. Tansey, 'The early scientific career of Sir Henry Dale FRS (1875–1968)', PhD diss., U. Lond., 1990 · H. H. Dale, *Adventures in physiology*, repr. 1965 (1953) · personal knowledge (1981) · private information (1981) · *BMJ* (3 Aug 1968), 318–21 · *The Times* (24 July 1968) · *Chemistry in Britain*, 5 (1969), 276–7 · *International Journal of Neuropharmacology*, 8 (1969), 83–4 · W. S. Feldberg, 'The early history of synaptic and neuromuscular transmission by acetylcholine: reminiscences of an eye witness', *The pursuit of nature* (1979), 65–83 · W. S. Feldberg, 'On the distribution of cholinergic neurons: personal reminiscences of the thirties', *Cellular and molecular basis of cholinergic function*, ed. M. J. Dowdall and J. N. Hawthorne (1987), 1–10 · W. S. Feldberg, *Fifty years on: looking back on some developments in neurohumoral physiology* (1982) · E. M. Tansey, 'Illustrations from the Wellcome Institute Library: Sir Henry Dale's laboratory notebooks, 1914–1919', *Medical History*, 34 (1990), 199–209 · H. H. Dale, 'Autobiographical sketch', *Perspectives on Biological Medicine*, 1 (1958), 125–37 · E. M. Tansey, 'What's in a name? Henry Dale and adrenaline, 1906', *Medical History*, 39 (1995), 459–76 · J. H. Gaddum, *Vasodilator substances of the tissues*, ed. and trans. F. C. MacIntosh (1986) [Ger. orig. *Gefässerweiternde Stoff der Gewebe*, Leipzig (1936)] · E. M. Tansey, 'An F4-vescent episode: Sir Henry Dale's laboratory, 1919–1942; the first W. D. M. Paton memorial lecture', *British Journal of Pharmacology*, 115 (1995), 1339–45 · A. S. V. Burgen, 'Dale and Dudley's discovery of acetylcholine in mammals', *Trends in Neurosciences*, 2 (1979), xii · H. H. Dale, *An autumn gleaning* (1954) · E. M. Tansey, 'Chemical neurotransmission in the autonomic nervous system: Sir Henry Dale and the discovery of acetylcholine', *Clinical Autonomic Research*, 1 (1991), 63–72 · E. M. Tansey, 'Barts at the turn of the century: Henry Dale's experience', *Barts Journal*, 18 (1995), 23–24 · W. F. Bynum, 'Dale, Henry Hallett', *DSB* · J. C. Eccles, 'The development of ideas on the synapse', *The historical development of physiological thought*, ed. C. M. Brooks and P. F. Cranefield (1959), 39–6 · A. R. Hall and B. A. Bembridge, *Physic and philanthropy: a history of the Wellcome Trust, 1936–1986* (1986) · E. M. Tansey, 'Henry Dale and the microcirculation', *International Journal of Microcirculation—Clinical and Experimental*, 14/1–2 (1994), 95–103 · E. M. Tansey, 'Sir Henry

Dale and autopharmacology: the role of acetylcholine in neuro-transmission', *Essays in the history of the physiological sciences*, ed. C. Debru (1995), 180–93 · F. Lembeck and W. Giere, *Otto Loewi: Ein Lebensbild in Dokumenten* (1968)

Archives PRO, papers relating to scientific advisory committee, CAB 127/213-238 · Royal Institution of Great Britain, London, corresp. and papers · RS, papers · Wellcome L., notebooks and papers | Bodl. Oxf., corresp. relating to Society for the Protection of Science and Learning · CAC Cam., corresp. with A. V. Hill · CUL, corresp. with Sir Frank Young · Rice University, Houston, Texas, Woodson Research Center, corresp. with Julian Huxley · U. Glas., corresp. with Edward Hindle · Wellcome L., corresp. with A. V. Hill · Wellcome L., corresp. with Sir Thomas Lewis | FILM BFI NFTVA, news footage | SOUND BL NSA, recorded talk

Likenesses H. Coster, photographs, *c.*1930, NPG · W. Stoneman, photographs, 1931–52, NPG · F. Dodd, oils, 1944, National Institute for Medical Research, London · J. Gunn, oils, 1945, RS · Y. Karsh, photograph, 1949, NPG [*see illus.*] · A. R. Middleton Todd, oils, 1952, Salters' Company, London · M. Gill, portrait, Royal Society of Medicine, London · C. Lovatt Evans, Wellcome L. · T. C. Turner, photograph, Wellcome L. · J. Ward, portrait, Leys School, Cambridge · group photograph (with Niels Bohr and M. Penin) · portrait, NPG

Wealth at death £67,863: probate, 11 Feb 1969, *CGPLA Eng. & Wales*

Dale, Joseph (1749/50–1821), music publisher and composer, is of obscure origins, although it is possible given his later interests that he was Scottish. He is first identified as the organist of St Antholin, Budge Row, Watling Street, London, in February 1777, a post he held until only a few months before his death. Dale's publishing business commenced at his home, 19 Chancery Lane, London, in 1783, and gradually increased in size throughout his life. In 1786 he took over the circulating music library formerly belonging to Samuel Babb, and about the same time he also acquired plates, copyrights, and books from William Napier and Charles Bennett, whose collection had formerly belonged to John Welcker. His most significant publications include a number of first editions of works such as William Shield's operas *Rosina* and *The Flitch of Bacon*. Other works published by his firm include a plethora of sheet music and country dances, several collections of English and Scottish songs, piano music by Muzio Clementi, Jan Ladislav Dussek, Jean-Baptiste Krumpholtz, and Daniel Steibelt, and theoretical treatises such as those by A. F. C. Kollmann. Dale became a freeman of the Merchant Taylors' Company on 7 October 1789, and a liveryman on 6 July 1791.

Not noted for his compositional skill, Dale was, however, the composer of large quantities of concertos, sonatas, and arrangements for harpsichord or piano of vocal works and the works of other composers. The letters of George Thomson, editor and publisher of the most noted Scottish song collection of the era, make it clear that Dale was prone to utilizing the works of others, and even publishing works under the names of composers such as Ignace Joseph Pleyel and Leopold Kozeluch, entirely without their consent or knowledge. Beginning with three 'Pleyel' sonatas published in 1794 and later utilizing the same trick with works by 'Kozeluch' and possibly others, Dale set out to capitalize on the established market for works incorporating Scots airs. (Resulting publications included *Dale's Twelve Grand Sonatas … by Ignace Pleyel op. 14*, books 1–4 probably published between 1794 and 1796, and [*Three*] *Grand Scotch Sonata[s]*, published about 1799.) Many of Dale's other extant publications would suggest similar appropriation, demonstrating how demand arose for the introduction of copyright laws at the beginning of the nineteenth century.

About 1780 Dale married Caroline, with whom he had twelve children, including at least four who followed him into the music business—James, Joseph, Christopher, and William. His son Joseph Dale (*bap.* 1783, *d.* in or after 1821) was apprenticed to him in 1797, and with his father was responsible for the invention of a new tambourine on which a patent (no. 2295) was taken out in February 1799. Dale then took his son William Dale (*b. c.*1780x85, *d.* 1827?) into partnership between about 1805 and 1809, after which William set up his own business as a publisher, music seller, and instrument dealer (*c.*1809–27). William's business was continued by Elspeth Dale, presumably his widow, until about 1832, when it was succeeded by Dale, Cockerill & Co. In his *Six Sonatas for Harpsichord or Piano-Forte* (1783), William described himself as assistant organist at the Chapel Royal, but there is no other evidence that he held this post. Together with his father, William Dale is also listed as 'Piano Forte Maker (by Appointment) to his Royal Highness the Prince of Wales' in the *17th Book of 12 Songs* (*c.*1810). James Dale (*bap.* 1781) composed, printed, and published some piano sonatas and other sheet music for piano from Kennington. Christopher Dale (*bap.* 1787) was a music and musical instrument seller in Chelsea. Given the entry for Joseph Dale in Doane's 1794 *Directory* as 'Music-Seller & Circulating Library', the J. Dale listed as an organist, composer, and viola player at the Academy of Ancient Music is most likely to have been one of his sons Joseph junior and James. A further Dale who is listed by Doane as a violinist at the Covent Garden Theatre may have been any one of Dale's five other sons.

Dale was described as resident in Edinburgh when his son Joseph married Anne Esther Bishop at the British embassy chapel, Paris, on 13 July 1821. It is unknown when he moved there. He died in Edinburgh, aged seventy-one, on 21 August 1821, at which time he was described by the *Gentleman's Magazine* as 'long known in the musical world as a teacher of the piano-forte'. Although there is no indication that he had taught before this time, it may be that he turned to teaching after the decline of his publishing business in the closing years of his life. Neither cause of death nor place of burial is known. His wife survived him.

CLAIRE M. NELSON

Sources J. D. Brown, *Biographical dictionary of musicians: with a bibliography of English writings on music* (1886); repr. (1970) · Burney, *Hist. mus.*, new edn · D. Dawe, *Organists of the City of London, 1666–1850* (1983) · J. Doane, ed., *A musical directory for the year 1794* [1794]; facs. edn (1993) · C. Humphries and W. C. Smith, *Music publishing in the British Isles, from the beginning until the middle of the nineteenth century: a dictionary of engravers, printers, publishers, and music sellers*, 2nd edn (1970) · J. C. Kassler, *The science of music in Britain, 1714–1830*, 2 vols. (1979) · R. R. Kidd, 'The sonata for keyboard with violin accompaniment in England (1750–1790)', PhD diss., Yale U., 1967 · D. W. Krummel and S. Sadie, eds., *Music printing and publishing*, rev. edn (1990) ·

B. Matthews, ed., *The Royal Society of Musicians of Great Britain: list of members, 1738–1984* (1985) · C. Nelson, 'The influence of Scotland in London's musical life in the 18th century', DMus diss., Royal College of Music, London · M. Pincherle, 'L'edition musicale au dix-huitième siècle: une lettre de Thomson à Ignace Pleyel', *Musique*, 1 (1928), 493–8 · Z. E. Pixley, 'The keyboard concerto in London society, 1760–1790', PhD diss., U. Mich., 1986 · W. S. Newman, *The sonata in the baroque era*, 4th edn (1983) · H. W. Shaw, *The succession of organists of the Chapel Royal and the cathedrals of England and Wales from c.1538* (1991) · *GM*, 1st ser., 91/2 (1821), 284 · W. C. Smith and P. W. Jones, 'Dale', *New Grove*, 2nd edn · C. B. Hogan, ed., *The London stage, 1660–1800*, pt 5: *1776–1800* (1968) · Highfill, Burnim & Langhans, *BDA* · *Répertoire international des sources musicales*, ser. A/I, 9 vols. (Munich and Duisburg, 1971–81); addenda and corrigenda, 4 vols. (1986–99) · E. B. Schnapper, ed., *The British union-catalogue of early music printed before the year 1801*, 2 vols. (1957) · L. Baillie and R. Balchin, eds., *The catalogue of printed music in the British Library to 1980*, 62 vols. (1981–7)

Archives GL, trade card

Wealth at death relatively large estate, incl. business and contents of the business, such as musical instruments: will, PRO, PROB 11/1649, sig. 599

Dale, Robert William (1829–1895), Congregational minister, was born on 1 December 1829 at Hawkesbury Grove in the parish of St Mary Newington, London. He was the elder surviving son of Robert Dale (*d.* 1869), a hat-trimmer, and his wife, Elizabeth (*d.* 1854). There were six children, but only Robert and Thomas (*b.* 1839) survived. Thomas Dale, fellow of Trinity College, Cambridge, died after a short illness in 1883. The parents were poor. They were members of Tabernacle, Moorfields, where Dr John Campbell ministered. Dale's early education was perfunctory. He had a good word for Wilby's 'Pestalozzian Academy', but hated the school he attended afterwards at Rayleigh, Essex. More to his liking was John T. Willey's school near his home. His literary ambitions were aroused early, and his first article appeared in *Youth's Magazine* in 1842. In January 1844 he became an assistant teacher at Ebenezer White's school at Andover, but found teaching uncongenial. He experienced an acute spiritual crisis at this time which led to his being admitted a member at the East Street Congregational Church, Andover. It was there that he began to preach in April 1845, but left the town in June 1845. He wished to enter the ministry but Dr John Campbell declined to support his request. He returned to teaching, first at Brixton and then at Leamington Spa. Members of the Spencer Street Church there offered to provide him with the money to go to college. He entered Spring Hill College, Birmingham, in autumn 1847 and was there until the summer of 1853. His intellectual brilliance was displayed when he took a London BA with first-class honours and later an MA which brought him the gold medal in philosophy. Of his teachers the one that most impressed him was Henry Rogers.

Dale first preached at Carr's Lane Church, Birmingham, in September 1849, and in September 1852 he began to take services there once a month. He was thus brought into close contact with the minister, John Angell James, and although he was initially critical of the older man's staid evangelicalism, he gradually became an admirer and eventually was the author of his biography. On 1 July 1853 Dale was elected assistant preacher by the church and in

Robert William Dale (1829–1895), by Henry John Whitlock

July 1854 co-pastor with James. When James died, on 1 October 1859, Dale succeeded him and remained the minister of Carr's Lane until his death.

The beginning of Dale's ministry coincided with a more militant phase in the history of Birmingham nonconformity. He was responsible over the years for establishing new churches at Edgbaston, Moseley, Yardley, and Acock's Green. From 1860 he began to pay special attention to young people but was never a success as a children's preacher, although he arranged classes to educate them. As a preacher he was a formidable presence both in the pulpit and on the public platform, due mainly to the intellectual power and the ethical relevance of his sermons and speeches. He caused some mutterings among the older members by smoking a pipe and refusing to wear the traditional black coat and white tie of the dissenting minister. He declined to use the title 'Reverend', but consented to be addressed as 'Doctor' after the University of Glasgow had bestowed the honorary degree of doctor of laws upon him in 1883. These idiosyncrasies stemmed from his objections to symbols that put ministers in a sacerdotal class apart from lay people.

Dale was to become one of the most prominent representatives of nonconformity in England. By 1864 he was asserting that participation in politics was a 'positive and imperative duty' for Christians and those who decline to discharge it were 'guilty of treachery both to God and man' (Dale, 250). Nonconformist leaders before his day were usually genteel whigs; Dale represented a newer Liberalism. Towards the end of the 1860s, under the inspiration of the 'municipal gospel' preached by George Dawson and Dr H. W. Crosskey (1826–1893), the geologist and Unitarian divine, the movement to use the power of the town council to improve the administration, education, and social conditions of Birmingham was under way. Although the practical political implementation of the ideals was in the hands of Joseph Chamberlain, the moral support of nonconformists was ensured by Dale's ceaseless energy in addressing ward meetings and securing suitable candidates for municipal elections. There was hardly an aspect of municipal life that was not influenced by Dale.

Dale was an English nationalist who believed that the nation was a divine institution, a conviction that suggests German influences. Hence his enthusiasm for the celebrations to mark the wedding of the prince of Wales in 1863. He was not a pacifist and believed that the power of the armed forces could be used in defence of freedom. He supported the Crimean War, sided with the north in the American Civil War, and sympathized with Garibaldi in his campaign to unite Italy. On the other hand he was opposed to granting any kind of self-government to India.

It was the controversy over elementary education that brought Dale to national prominence. Most Congregationalists in the 1860s still believed that education should be provided by voluntary effort. Dale by 1866 was advocating the establishment of a national state system of education that would be compulsory, and free for those who could not pay the fees. When W. E. Forster introduced his Education Bill on 17 February 1870, Dale became one of its most vociferous critics because he felt that the provisions which it made for some denominational teaching in schools violated the principle of religious equality. So began the 'nonconformist revolt'. Dale's position was that the schools should be secular and that any religious instruction should be voluntary. He became notorious as the man who would 'banish the Bible from the schools'. He found considerable support among Baptists and Congregationalists, and was himself largely responsible for gathering 1885 representatives to a conference in Manchester in January 1872 which enthusiastically supported his views. The result was such widespread opposition to Gladstone's ministry that it contributed substantially to its defeat at the 1874 election. It was ironic that nonconformists had deployed their forces with such effect that they struck a serious blow at their own political influence. The inevitable result over the next years was that they had to accept compromises. But the government saw fit to make use of Dale's expert knowledge of education by appointing him to the royal commission into the working of the Education Acts in 1885.

Dale was a determined advocate of the disestablishment of the Church of England. He joined the Liberation Society in 1860 but its contentious spirit was not to his taste. He did not secede from it, but in 1875 and 1876 he conducted an independent disestablishment campaign assisted by James Guinness Rogers. They addressed fourteen large meetings at the main centres of population, but the impetus was lost as public attention turned to other matters in 1877.

In April 1886 Gladstone introduced his Irish Home Rule Bill, which produced such bitter wrangling among Congregationalists that Dale felt compelled in 1888 to withdraw from the activities of the Congregational Union (of which he had been chairman in 1869) because he feared that his own brand of Unionism, strongly hostile to home rule, would serve only to exacerbate the bitterness. Nevertheless he performed one more signal service to his denomination by agreeing to become chairman of the first International Congregational Council, which met at London in 1891.

In fact, 1886 marked the beginning of Dale's gradual retirement from public controversy. He had come to feel that he had devoted too much time to public affairs, and liberal politics especially, and now wished to concentrate on theological and historical study. Ever since his student days Dale had taken a keen interest in Spring Hill College. He was chairman of its educational board from 1859 and played a large part in the arrangements to move the college to Oxford, where it was opened in 1889 as Mansfield College. He served as the chairman of its council until 1894.

Dale thought of himself as an exponent of evangelical theology. In 1878, for example, he supported the declaration made by the Congregational Union in defence of its evangelical faith. His book, *Christian Doctrine* (1894), confirms his adherence to the classical doctrines of the trinity, the incarnation, and the resurrection. In ecclesiology he combined warm loyalty to the Congregational pattern of church government with a high doctrine of the church as a divine institution, and believed that one of the weaknesses of the evangelical revival was that its individualism had eroded this conviction, a topic which he discussed in *The Evangelical Revival* (1880) and in his sermon *The Old Evangelicalism and the New* (1889). He was critical of Calvinism, especially its teaching about total depravity and double predestination. His popular book *The Atonement* (1875) also modified the traditional evangelical teaching by substituting for it the juridical view that Christ's death was a voluntary sacrifice of his life to vindicate God's eternal law of righteousness. Even more dramatic at the time was his commitment to the doctrine of conditional immortality, that is, the belief that immortality is God's gift to believers and that the unrepentant will be annihilated. His thinking represents the gradual erosion of evangelical theology in the interest of making it more ethical, more socially relevant, and more sensitive to the implications of the belief in God's love.

On 21 February 1855, at Andover, Dale married Elizabeth, the second daughter of William Dowling of Over Wallop, Hampshire. They had three children. Alice died on 24 June 1865, aged six, and Claire died on 6 June 1884.

Their only son, Alfred, became Sir Alfred William Winter-slow Dale (1855–1921). After a brilliant academic career he became principal of Liverpool University College in 1899 and vice-chancellor of Liverpool University from 1903 to 1919. He edited and completed his father's massive *History of English Congregationalism* (1907) and wrote his biography, *Life of R. W. Dale* (1899), an impressive scholarly work.

Throughout his life Dale had suffered from occasional bouts of physical prostration, but in 1891 it was discovered that he was afflicted with a serious heart condition, which hastened his death. He preached for the last time on 10 February 1895, and died on 13 March at his home, Winter-slow House, 115 Bristol Road, Birmingham, survived by his wife. He was buried at Key Hill cemetery on 18 March 1895.

Dale was one of the most impressive figures in Victorian nonconformity. His preaching, although lacking the imagination of a Spurgeon or the histrionics of a Joseph Parker, appealed to large audiences. He was one of the group of leaders who taught nonconformists to realize and exercise their social and political influence, and that led, for good or ill, to the politicizing of nonconformity. His public activities as an educationist and politician brought him into close contact with a surprising number of the most distinguished people in the kingdom. Through his travels in France, Switzerland, Australia, and the United States he established an international reputation. Dale was a prolific author, publishing numerous tracts and sermons, in all some sixty-four titles. He also contributed articles from time to time to the periodical press, and edited *The Congregationalist* from 1871 to 1878.

R. TUDUR JONES

Sources A. W. W. Dale, *Life of R. W. Dale* (1899) · A. Peel, *These hundred years: a history of the Congregational Union of England and Wales, 1831–1931* (1931) · J. H. Muirhead, ed., *Nine famous Birmingham men* (1909) · H. Davies, *Worship and theology in England*, 4 (1962), 197, 322–33 · D. W. Bebbington, *The nonconformist conscience: chapel and politics, 1870–1914* (1982), chap. 7 · J. Charles, 'Safle Ddiwinyddol Dr Dale', *Dysgedydd* (1895), 145–9 · *Congregational Year Book* (1896) · E. P. Hennock, *Fit and proper persons: ideal and reality in nineteenth-century urban government* (1973)

Archives Birm. CA, letters and papers · U. Birm., letters received | U. Birm., corresp. with Joseph Chamberlain

Likenesses E. O. Ford, statue, Birmingham Museums and Art Gallery · H. J. Whitlock, carte-de-visite, NPG [*see illus.*] · photograph, repro. in Dale, *Life of R. W. Dale* · photograph, repro. in *Evangelical Magazine* (March 1871) · wood-engraving (after H. Furniss), NPG

Wealth at death £5937 16s. 5d.: resworn probate, Sept 1895, CGPLA Eng. & Wales

Dale, Samuel (*bap.* 1659, *d.* 1739), apothecary and physician, son of North Dale (*bap.* 1618), silk-thrower, and his wife, Christian, was baptized on 15 August 1659 at St Olave's, Hart Street, London. Dale was apprenticed for eight years to Thomas Wells, a London apothecary, on 5 May 1674. He was in Braintree, Essex when he received a licence to practise medicine, on 3 April 1682, from Lambeth. As he did not intend to practise in London he did not claim his freedom of the Society of Apothecaries.

Samuel Dale (*bap.* 1659, *d.* 1739), by George Vertue, 1737

Dale at first lived at Bocking End, Braintree; later he moved to the Old House in Bradford Street, at the invitation of his cousin John Ruggles, who owned the property. Dale became a close friend of John Ray who lived at nearby Black Notley. Both in the *Historia* and in the two editions of the *Synopsis stirpium Britannicarum*, Ray acknowledged the valuable assistance he had received from Dale's critical knowledge of plants, and it is from Dale's letters to Sir Hans Sloane that we learn many details of the last hours of Ray, whose executor Dale was. Dale's own chief work was the *Pharmacologia*, which first appeared in 1693; a supplement was published in 1705, a second edition in 1710, a third in 1737, and others after Dale's death. *Pharmacologia* was the first systematic work of importance on the subject. Dale's nine contributions to the *Philosophical Transactions*, between 1692 and 1736, deal with a variety of subjects, biological and professional, the most important, perhaps, being the first published account of the fossil shells of Harwich cliff. In 1730 Dale published the second great work of his life, *The History and Antiquities of Harwich and Dovercourt*, by Silas Taylor (alias Domville), his own appendix to which exceeds in bulk the main work and provides a complete account of the natural history of the district. This book reached a second edition in 1732. Like his father-in-law, Joshua Draper MB, Dale was a member of Braintree's governing body, the 'Council of 24'. Dale died on 6 June 1739 and was buried in the dissenters' burial-ground at Bocking. His books on botany and his herbarium he bequeathed to the Society of Apothecaries; the herbarium was moved to the British Museum (South Kensington), and the neat and elaborate tickets to the plants, many of which he obtained from the Chelsea garden and from numerous correspondents, show Dale to have been an accomplished botanist. In spite of his contributions to the *Philosophical Transactions*, and unlike his friend Joseph Andrews, apothecary of Sudbury, he was not a fellow of the Royal Society. Linnaeus commemorated Dale's services to botany in the leguminous genus *Dalea*.

G. S. BOULGER, *rev.* JUANITA BURNBY

Sources The Society of Apothecaries of London, court minutes, MS 8200/2, fol. 183v · IGI · P. J. Wallis and R. V. Wallis, *Eighteenth century medics*, 2nd edn (1988) · E. Szlichcinska, 'A brief life of John Ray', *John Ray, naturalist, 1627–1705* (1977) · W. Ashwell, 'The excellent Mr Ray', *John Ray, naturalist, 1627–1705* (1977) · G. S. Boulger, 'Samuel Dale', *Journal of Botany, British and Foreign*, 21 (1883), 193–7, 225–31 · G. S. Boulger and J. Britten, 'Joseph Andrews', *Journal of Botany, British and Foreign*, 56 (1918), 257–8 · J. H. Bloom and R. R. James, *Medical practitioners in the diocese of London … annotated list, 1529–1725* (1935)
Archives BM, herbarium · Bodl. Oxf., life of John Ray · CUL, department of manuscripts and university archives, journal of journeys between Braintree and Cambridge · NHM, papers | BL, letters to Thomas Birch, Add. MS 4304 · BL, Sloane MSS, letters to James Petiver · BL, Sloane MSS, letters to Sir Hans Sloane · Essex RO, Chelmsford, letters to William Holman
Likenesses G. Vertue, line engraving, 1737, BM, NPG, Wellcome L. [*see illus.*] · Rivers, line engraving, 1812, Wellcome L. · oils (Samuel Dale?), Apothecaries' Hall, London

Dale, Sir Thomas (*d.* 1619), soldier and administrator, is of unknown parentage. Given his letter to the states general (1618) which boasted of thirty years' employment in the Dutch cause, he was probably a common soldier in the earl of Leicester's expedition to the Low Countries (1588). In the early 1590s he may have been a member of Prince Henry's household. A captain with the English forces in Ireland in 1594, he returned there in 1598–9 under the earl of Essex after a period in French service. In February 1599 Dale was in Dieppe delivering an Essex missive to the governor; in April he was recruiting in England for the Irish army. His part in the Essex rebellion is obscure, but for some reason he lost his command and in 1601 he was arrested for duelling. By August 1603, on the recommendation of Henri IV of France, Dale was a garrison captain in the Dutch town of Terthol, and enjoyed the patronage of Sir Francis Vere, commander of the English troops in the Netherlands.

Dale also attracted the attention of James I. Writing to Ralph Winwood, the English envoy to the states general, in March 1604 Sir Robert Cecil said that the king wished him to 'take notice of his gracious opinion of the merit of Captain Dale both for having been a valiant and long servitor, and having for the most part rendred them upon his (own) charges' (Neill, 73). Dale was knighted in June 1606, and soon after was at Oudewater, with Sir Thomas Gates, a patentee of the Virginia Company. By 1610 Dale had come to the notice of the company, especially the earl of Southampton (its future treasurer), whom Dale had first met in Paris in 1598, and in February he was named lord marshal; the title of deputy governor was added later. In February 1611 Dale was given a three-year leave of absence from his Dutch service to enable him to help retrieve the fortunes of the company's unprofitable settlement in Virginia. Shortly before he left England (March 1611) Dale married Elizabeth Throckmorton (*d.* 1640?), granddaughter of Sir Thomas Throckmorton, and a distant relation of Vere; they had no children.

Bringing long-unused armour from the Tower as a defence against native arrows, Dale arrived in Virginia on 10 May 1611. Within a couple of days he grabbed Captain Newport by the beard, threatening to hang him for exaggerating the colony's prosperity. As third in command of the colony after Thomas, Lord De La Warr, and Gates, he was acting governor during their absence (June to August). Dale helped codify the colony's laws and regulations, published in England (1612) as the *Lawes Divine, Morall and Martiall*. These were once attributed to Dale's sole authorship, even being referred to as Dale's laws; but he 'merely took the system he found in operation, formalized it and enforced it strictly' (Rutman, *Virginia Company*, 12). Only the 'Instructions of the marshal' were Dale's alone—a section defining the duties of various military ranks, based on his experience of military codes used in the Netherlands. Once formalized, the legal code was at first enforced with draconian strictness, in parallel labour and defence structures, on colonists who were largely the idle and insubordinate products of English gaols and brothels. Dale himself had no high opinion of the settlers he had brought with him, describing them in a letter to the earl of Salisbury (17 August 1611) as 'disordered … prophane … riotous, so full of Mutenie and treasonable Intendments' (Brown, 506–7). Some who stole from the stores he bound to trees and starved to death. This harshness was gradually mitigated.

In September 1611 Dale led 300 settlers to form a second township at 'Henrico (polis)', about 55 miles up the James River from the insalubrious Jamestown; it had the first hospital in English America. He later established a fishing settlement on the eastern shore, known as 'Dale's Gift'. In a search for exotic staples Dale began the first of many experiments in winemaking, using a native grape. His overall aim was to fortify and firmly control the peninsula between the James and York rivers, from the neighbourhood of modern Richmond to Chesapeake Bay. This involved almost constant skirmishes with the American Indians. In the spring of 1614 (when Dale was again acting governor), after a number of raids on Indian villages along the Pamunkey River, he invested the former residence of Powhatan, the local paramount chief, whose daughter, Pocahontas, had been captured by the colonists the previous year. Dale then made peace (which lasted until 1622), cemented by the marriage of Pocahontas (in whom Dale took a fatherly interest) to the Englishman John Rolfe. In the same year, the Chickahominy tribe, Powhatan's rivals, asked to become English subjects, and they contracted to supply the English with corn and archers for use against the Spaniards. On 19 August 1614 James I applied to the states general for an extension of Dale's leave of absence 'in order that he may complete the work so well begun' (Neill, 76). Later that year Dale attempted to further seal the peace by offering to marry Powhatan's eleven-year-old youngest daughter, a suit rejected by her father.

In April 1616 Dale sailed home on the *Treasurer*, bringing with him Rolfe and Pocahontas, as well as samples of experimental tobacco, sassafras, pitch, potash, sturgeon, and caviar—the aim being to give Virginia the revived public interest it badly needed. He arrived in England in June, and then prosecuted a suit against the states general for the pay arrears due to him while in Virginia. He was in the Netherlands when in November 1617 he was given command of an East India Company fleet, at a salary of £480 per annum, for an expedition against the Dutch viceroy, Jan Pieterszoon Coen, in the East Indies. In February 1618, having secured full pay arrears (£1000) from the Dutch, he sailed for the East. Dale almost drowned at the Cape, when a small skiff capsized, and his flagship, the *Sun*, was later wrecked on the island of Engano, near Java, with the loss of all his possessions. In revenge Dale captured a richly laden Dutch ship; Coen retaliated by burning the English factory at Jakarta. Dale, reinforced by ships from Bantam, then confronted Coen's inferior fleet off Jakarta (30 December 1618). He should have easily won the day-long battle that began on 2 January 1619: but his fleet was hesitant and defensive, largely because it incorporated three separate ventures, each with its own commander, reluctant to risk his own ships for the common good. Although reinforced from Bantam, when the Dutch retreated towards the Banda Islands, Dale failed to follow, opting instead for a bungled seizure of the Dutch headquarters at Jakarta. He then ordered the fleet to sail to the Coromandel coast of India, where he died of the flux at Masulipatam on 9 August 1619. He was buried there.

Dale was posthumously lauded by Sir Edwin Sandys, leader of the liberal element within the Virginia Company, as the man who, 'with great and constant severity, reclaymed almost miraculously those idle and disordered people and reduced them to labour and an honest fashion of life' (Kingsbury, 1.267). His quasi-military approach, allied to a dogmatic religious conviction, did help to ensure Virginia's continuance as a colony; yet, at his exit, it exhibited 'the quiet primness of a corpse' (Prince, 362) and was some years away from its ensuing tobacco-based affluence. During his short time in the East Indies he was feared rather than loved by his subordinates, he allowed his rapacity and hot temper to override his judgement, and he was ill-matched against the composed detachment of Coen.

BASIL MORGAN

Sources D. B. Rutman, 'The Virginia Company and its military regime', *The old dominions: essays for Thomas Perkins Abernethy*, ed. D. B. Rutman (1964), 1–20 · *CSP col.*, vol. 3 · G. Milton, *Nathaniel's nutmeg* (1999) · D. B. Rutman, 'The historian and the marshal—a note on the background of Sir Thomas Dale', *Virginia Magazine of Natural History and Biography*, 68 (1960), 280–94 · D. B. Rutman, 'Sir Thomas Dale', *American dictionary of biography* · W. F. Prince, 'The first criminal code of Virginia', *American Historical Association Annual Report, 1898*, 1 (1899), 311–63 · P. L. Barbour, *Pocahontas and her world* (1971) · E. D. Neill, *History of the Virginia Company of London* (1869) · N. Canny, 'England's New World and the Old, 1480s–1630s', *The origins of empire*, ed. N. Canny (1998), vol. 1 of *The Oxford history of the British empire*, 148–69 · P. A. Bruce, *The Virginia Plutarch* (1929), 43–56 · S. M. Kingsbury, *Records of the Virginia Company of London*, 4 vols. (1906–

35) · A. Brown, *The genesis of the United States* (1891) · A. Calder, *Revolutionary empire: the rise of the English-speaking empires from the 15th century to the 1780s* (1981) · D. B. Quinn and A. N. Ryan, *England's sea empire, 1550–1642* (1983)

Likenesses Brueckner, engraving, repro. in Bruce, *Virginia Plutarch*

Dale, Thomas (1748/9–1816), physician, was the son of Thomas Dale (*d.* 1750), of Charlestown, South Carolina, and his third wife, Hannah Simons. His father, a physician, justice of the peace, and member of the upper house of assembly, was the son of Francis Dale, an apothecary in Hoxton, Middlesex, and the nephew of Samuel Dale of Braintree. Dale was born in Charlestown, but came to England and entered St Paul's School on 10 February 1757. On 7 June 1763 he was apprenticed to Joseph Partington, a London apothecary, for eight years at a premium of £63. He gained his freedom of the Society of Apothecaries on 2 July 1771. Proceeding to the University of Edinburgh, he took the degree of MD on 12 June 1775, and wrote his dissertation on erysipelas. He became a licentiate of the College of Physicians in 1786, and subsequently practised in the City of London, working as physician to the London Association for Assurances on Lives and from 1806 as consulting physician to the City Dispensary.

A good linguist and classical scholar, Dale was one of the originators of the Literary Fund, which was founded in 1788 by the Revd David Williams to help authors in distress, and from 1790 until 1806 he served as registrar to the society. He died at his house in Devonshire Square, Bishopsgate, London, on 21 February 1816, aged sixty-seven; he was buried in Bunhill Fields, London.

G. S. BOULGER, rev. KAYE BAGSHAW

Sources Munk, *Roll* · *GM*, 1st ser., 86/1 (1816), 275 · N. Cross, *The Royal Literary Fund, 1790–1918: an introduction … with an index of applicants* (1984)

Likenesses stipple, BM, NPG

Dale, Thomas (1797–1870), Church of England clergyman and university teacher, was born on 22 August 1797 at Pentonville, London, the only son of four children of William Dale, who on his wife's death in 1800 remarried and departed for the West Indies to conduct a weekly newspaper, dying soon after his arrival. Dale was given an evangelical upbringing by his maternal grandmother, a Mrs Smith, a relation securing a nomination to Christ's Hospital, London, in 1805. An apparently unhappy school career ended when Dale went up to Corpus Christi College, Cambridge, in 1817, having already published *The Widow of Nain and other Poems*, which was favourably reviewed by *Blackwood's Edinburgh Magazine* and went through six editions. Together with *The Outlaw of Taurus* (1818) and other poems, this publication both financed his university career and generated employment as a tutor. One pupil was a son of the East India agent, stockbroker, and publisher James Malcott Richardson of 23 Cornhill, London, whose daughter Emily Jane (1803–1849) Dale married on 22 November 1819, when she was only sixteen. The eldest son of the couple's large family (at least seven sons and five daughters) was the ritualist Thomas Pelham *Dale (1821–

1892); another was James Murray Dale (1822–1877), author of *The Clergyman's Legal Handbook* (1858).

At university Dale mostly associated with evangelicals, including Charles Simeon. In 1822 he took deacon's orders, in 1823 both graduating BA and being ordained priest. For some three years he served as curate at St Michael, Cornhill, London, where his preaching greatly increased attendances; he then proceeded to an assistant preachership at St Bride's, Fleet Street (1826–30) and an evening lectureship at St Sepulchre's, Snow Hill (1828–30).

Dale's literary reputation advanced with the appearance of his translation of Sophocles in 1824, T. S. Hughes praising its 'natural and colloquial air' (*QR*, 31, 1824–5, 203). His tutoring prospered, and before he took his MA in 1826 he had moved from a house adjoining Greenwich Park to Lady Byron's former abode in Beckenham, Kent. From 1828 to 1830 Dale was professor of English language and literature (the first in England) at University College, London. His lectures emphasized moral considerations in the appraisal of literature; seeking to counteract the secularity of the 'godless' college, he joined with John Williams and Dionysius Lardner in attempting to purchase an episcopal chapel in Gower Street in 1828, opening a 'theological institution' in 1829, and establishing a divinity lectureship, to which Dale was appointed. Dale resigned in 1830 and was elected incumbent of St Matthew's, Denmark Hill. He established a school in Grove Lane, Camberwell, where his pupils included Joseph Henry Dart, Alexander Penrose Forbes (future bishop of Brechin), and John Ruskin. Ruskin later described Dale as 'my severest and chiefly antagonist master' (J. Ruskin, *Praeterita*, vol. 2, chap. 9), and challenging Dale's views on literature certainly helped forge his own. Surviving correspondence, however, exhibits a surprising warmth and intimacy; Ruskin also went frequently to hear Dale preach.

In January 1835 Sir Robert Peel, desiring 'a resident clergyman of high character, and eminent as a preacher' (BL, Add. MS 40409, fol. 105), appointed Dale vicar of St Bride's, Fleet Street, London. Here he consolidated his reputation as one of the most popular preachers in the capital—the *Presbyterian Review* (September 1836) noting the 'overwhelming effect' of his sermons—despite being 'a queer-looking man, who bent low over his manuscript, and read rapidly for more than an hour without once looking up' (Balleine, 155). In the same year Dale was appointed professor of English literature and history at King's College, London (Robert Southey having refused the position), a post he held until 1840. In February 1841 he took on the post of Golden lecturer at St Margaret's, Lothbury, resigning in 1849 only once he had ended its dependence on income derived from a notorious public house. Bishop Blomfield recognized the success of Dale's ministry at St Bride's by promoting him in March 1843 to a prebend of St Paul's (vacated 1846), and, in the following October, Peel, who often worshipped at St Bride's, gave him a canonry in the same cathedral.

Dale's most significant preferment came in July 1846, when the dean and chapter presented him to the vicarage of St Pancras, the most populous parish in London. Here Dale, with the enthusiastic support of Blomfield, initiated an ambitious programme of church extension in 1847, raising over £700 in one day, and over £2500 in the first year. By 1849 the parish was divided into sixteen districts, each with its own clergyman and place of worship. Despite repeated reassurances, his efforts encountered resistance from parishioners fearing the reimposition of compulsory church rates, and Dale consequently was unable to resort to legislation and relied greatly on voluntary financial support, including his own considerable contributions. These efforts took their toll, and in 1859 Dale announced his intention of resigning, which he did in March 1861, accepting the rural rectory of Therfield, Hertfordshire, from the dean and chapter. After his resignation the parish of St Pancras was divided into twenty incumbencies.

Short, with a fair complexion and blue eyes, Dale had a quiet, dignified and somewhat stern manner. He was a prolific author (of more than seventy publications); his later writings were almost exclusively on religious subjects, save his edition of William Cowper's poems (1859). Described in 1844 as a 'very-decided evangelical' (Bodl. Oxf., MS Add. C.290), Dale supported many evangelical causes. He was sometimes characterized as a 'high-church evangelical' on account of his advocacy of frequent communion—'the sole outward pledge of sound churchmanship and vital Christianity' (Dale, *Companion for the Altar*, 1836, 6). In 1860 he introduced evening communions at St Pancras.

In 1869 Dale refused Gladstone's offer of the deanery of Ely, but the following year accepted that of Rochester. On 14 May 1870, shortly after his appointment, Dale died suddenly at his son's residence, 2 Amen Court, St Paul's, London. He was buried in Highgate cemetery.

ARTHUR BURNS

Sources *The life and letters of Thomas Pelham Dale*, ed. H. P. Dale, 2 vols. (1894) · draft biographical notice of Dale corrected by him, BL, Add. MS 28509, fols. 392–3 · H. H. Bellot, *University College, London, 1826–1926* (1929) · F. J. C. Hearnshaw, *The centenary history of King's College, London, 1828–1928* (1929) · D. J. Palmer, *The rise of English studies: an account of the study of English from its origins to the making of the Oxford English School* (1965) · C. E. Lee, *St Pancras Church and parish* (1955) · S. Palmer, *St Pancras: being antiquarian, topographical and biographical memoranda relating to the extensive metropolitan parish of St Pancras, Middlesex* (1870) · T. Hilton, *John Ruskin: the early years* (1985) · G. R. Balleine, *A history of the evangelical party in the Church of England*, new edn (1951) · review, *QR*, 31 (1824–5), 198–210, esp. 203 · T. Dale, *Five years of church extension in St Pancras* (1852) · Allibone, *Dict.* · BL, Peel MSS · J. F. Waller, ed., *The imperial dictionary of universal biography*, 3 vols. (1857–63) · 'The principal clergy of London classified according to their opinions on the great church questions of the day', 1844, Bodl. Oxf., MS Add. C. 290

Archives BL, Add. MS 28509 · UCL, letters | BL, Peel MSS · BL, Ruskin MSS, Add. MS 37725, fols.11–16 · LPL, Blomfield MSS · LPL, letters to Archbishop Tait

Likenesses H. Cousins, mezzotint, pubd 1836 (after J. Lonsdale), NPG · W. O. Geller, mezzotint, *c.*1842 (after J. Lucas), NPG · D. J. Pound, stipple and line engraving (after photograph by Mayall), BM, NPG; repro. in *Illustrated News of the World* · pastel drawing (as a child), repro. in Dale, *Life and letters of Thomas Pelham Dale*, facing p. 28 · photograph (after bust by E. Boehm), repro. in Dale, *Life and* *letters of Thomas Pelham Dale*, frontispiece · portrait, repro. in *Drawing-room portrait gallery of eminent personages*, 4th ser. (1860) · wood-engraving (after photograph by J. Watkins), NPG; repro. in *ILN* (31 Dec 1859)

Wealth at death under £14,000: resworn probate, Dec 1870, CGPLA Eng. & Wales

Dale, Thomas Pelham (1821–1892), Church of England clergyman, born at Greenwich on 3 April 1821, was brought up in Beckenham, Kent. He was the eldest son of Thomas *Dale (1797–1870), rector of St Pancras, canon of St Paul's, and dean of Rochester, and his wife, Emily Jane (1803–1849), daughter of J. M. Richardson, publisher, stockbroker, and East India agent, of Cornhill, London. After education among his father's pupils at King's College, London, and a short abortive engineering apprenticeship, in 1841 Dale went up to Sidney Sussex College, Cambridge (BA 1845, twenty-fifth wrangler). His set in college was composed of 'reading men' (*Life and Letters*, 1.56), and his mathematics tutor was the Revd John William Colenso (1814–1883), later the controversial bishop of Natal. He was elected fellow of his college, and proceeded MA in 1848.

Bishop Sumner of Winchester ordained Dale deacon (1845) and priest (1846), to be assistant curate at the Camden Chapel, Camberwell, Surrey. In 1847 he became rector of St Vedast, Foster Lane—a Wren church with Grinling Gibbons carving—with St Michael-le-Querne in the City of London. In 1848 he married Mary, eldest daughter of William Francis of Reigate: they had four children, two of whom were later ordained, and Mary survived her husband. From 1856 to 1859 Dale took resident pupils, 'hobbledehoys … the only work he found positively distasteful' (*Life and Letters*, 1.64). After Guilford Street and Torrington Square the couple moved in 1859 to 5 Woburn Square, London, to enable Mary Dale to look after her mother. In 1866 the Dales moved to 6 Ladbroke Gardens, Notting Hill.

Dale was almost 6 feet tall, thin, with a slight stoop. He had light brown hair, a broad forehead, deep-set blue eyes, and a fair complexion. As a young man he wore whiskers, but later a beard. He suffered from a delicate throat and dyspepsia: the latter 'made him dislike any but the plainest food, and of that he ate sparingly' (*Life and Letters*, 1.57). He especially enjoyed reading Dickens, and liked quoting Sam Weller and Mrs Gamp.

A considerable scholar, Dale was librarian of Sion College in the City of London from 1851 to 1858, and reorganized its catalogue and borrowing system. From this time he conducted scientific experiments with Dr John Hall Gladstone (1827–1902) on the relationship between temperature and refraction in materials. Dale supplied mathematical and conceptual aspects of work that could be regarded as an early precursor of mass spectrometry.

The deaconess order had been revived on the continent, and in England Anglican sisterhoods, associated with the Oxford Movement, had been founded. Dale wanted to form a residential society of ladies for charitable parish work for the poor, including nursing and servant-training, which would be different from and more flexible than the

sisterhoods, and would entail no vows. He and others founded the North London Deaconesses' Institution, housed at 50 Burton Crescent, King's Cross. Approved by Archibald Campbell Tait, bishop of London, it was formally opened in November 1861, with Dale its secretary and chaplain. Its head sister was his relation by marriage, the forceful Elizabeth Catherine Ferard (1825–1883), who in July 1862 became the first deaconess in the Church of England. She and others who joined wanted a community closer to a sisterhood than Dale had envisaged, while he 'made strenuous efforts to keep to his original designs' (*Life and Letters*, 1.74). Miss Ferard and Dale, who 'saw his cherished scheme fading away' (ibid., 1.75), disagreed, and in 1868 he, greatly disappointed, resigned, and the institution developed on Miss Ferard's lines.

At St Vedast's Dale worked diligently to build up his small congregation. He founded a young women's Bible class, in spite of opposition from non-resident ratepayers. Originally an evangelical, Dale came to believe that advanced ritual was the logical outcome of evangelical theology, asserting primitive and supernatural reality against modern scepticism. He began to use eucharistic vestments at Christmas 1873.

Dale's relations with churchwardens and other ratepayers were stormy. He objected to a £30 annual audit dinner and one churchwarden's use of his personal bank account for parochial funds. In 1873–5 there were disputes about faculties for the removal of box pews and other furnishings. Opposition to Dale crystallized around his 'ritualism', especially after he offered six weeks' hospitality in 1875 to the congregation of St Alban the Martyr, Holborn, during the Revd Alexander Heriot Mackonochie's suspension. In 1876 Dale's churchwardens complained against him under the Public Worship Regulation Act (1874). This first such London case became a *cause célèbre*. Dale was supported by the English Church Union in his prosecution by the Church Association. An inhibition was obtained against Dale in the court of arches (November 1875) and Bishop Jackson sent another clergyman to conduct services at St Vedast's. The case was referred to Archbishop Tait, who could not act in the matter because he was patron of St Michael-le-Querne. In 1876 Dale joined the Society of the Holy Cross. In December 1878 he recommended all his former practices. J. C. Serjeant, his churchwarden, obtained a fresh judgment from Lord Penzance in the court of arches on 28 October 1880. Two days later Dale was arrested at home in Notting Hill on a writ of *significavit* and imprisoned in Holloway prison. To his high-church supporters Dale was the victim of persecution, 'a prisoner for conscience-sake' (*Life and Letters*, 1.307). In prison he was treated well. The staff were 'most kind and attentive' (ibid., 1.284), and he had two rooms and was allowed to make tea and boil eggs. Nevertheless his health suffered from the strain and suspense.

Dale's incarceration drew great sympathy from all but his most die-hard opponents. After a flurry of correspondence and memorials, the English Church Union obtained Dale's bail and release on Christmas eve 1880. Lord Justice James opined that the technical flaw in the writ leading to

Dale's release was no less trifling than the ritual irregularities for which he had originally been cited. The imprisonment of Dale and other clergymen did more than anything else to turn public opinion against Disraeli's attempt to put down ritualism by law.

Soon after his release Dale was presented to the rectory of Sausthorpe-cum-Aswardby, near Spilsby, Lincolnshire, by the patron, the Revd Charles Trollope Swan, and was inducted on 21 April 1881. There he became known as a diligent, kindly pastor. He took up his Hebrew again, painted watercolours, and conducted research in optics, electricity, and magnetism. Dale's publications included papers on chemistry with John Hall Gladstone (1853, 1861, 1863), a *Commentary on Ecclesiastes* (1873), a work of ecclesiastical biography, *A Life's Motto* (1869), and controversial pamphlets including *The St. Vedast Case: a Remonstrance Addressed to All True Evangelicals* (1881). Following a chill, he died of heart failure at the rectory, Sausthorpe, Lincolnshire, on 19 April 1892 and was buried in Sausthorpe churchyard on 25 April. His daughter Helen Pelham Dale published the two-volume *Life and Letters of Thomas Pelham Dale* (1898).

ALAN WILSON

Sources *The life and letters of Thomas Pelham Dale*, ed. H. P. Dale, 2 vols. (1894) · *Law reports: queen's bench division*, 2 (1877), 558–69; 6 (1881), 376–475 · *DNB* · *Church Times* (22 April 1892) · *The Guardian* (12 Feb 1879) · *The Guardian* (3 Nov 1880) · *The Guardian* (10 Nov 1880) · R. M. Grier, *The imprisonment of the Revd T. P. Dale* (1880) · T. P. Dale and J. H. Gladstone, 'Researches on the refraction, dispersion and sensitiveness of liquids', *PTRS*, 153 (1863), 317–43 · T. P. Dale and J. H. Gladstone, 'On the influence of temperature on the refraction of light', *PTRS*, 148 (1858), 887–94 · N. Yates, *Anglican ritualism in Victorian Britain, 1830–1910* (1999), 256–9 · J. Bentley, *Ritualism and politics in Victorian Britain: the attempt to legislate for belief* (1978), 101–3 · Venn, *Alum. Cant.* · Boase, *Mod. Eng. biog.* · J. S. Reed, *Glorious battle: the cultural politics of Victorian Anglo-Catholicism* (1996) · O. Chadwick, *The Victorian church*, 2nd edn, 2 (1972)

Archives CKS

Likenesses photographs, repro. in *Life and letters*, ed. Dale · wood-engraving (after photograph by Fradelle), NPG; repro. in *ILN* (20 Nov 1880) · wood-engraving, NPG; repro. in *ILN* (20 Nov 1880)

Wealth at death £5602 11s. 8d.: probate, 13 June 1892, *CGPLA Eng. & Wales*

Dale, Valentine (*c.*1520–1589), civil lawyer and diplomat, was born about 1520, the only son of John Dale (*c.*1500–1552), landowner, and his wife, Joan (*d.* in or after 1552). The family was a cadet branch of the Dales of South Tidworth and Fyfield, Hampshire. He was educated at King's School, Worcester, whence he was in receipt of an exhibition in 1543–4, and was at the University of Oxford from about 1538 to 1552, where he supplicated for BA in 1541, proceeded to study canon and civil law, and graduated BCL in 1545. He was literate in Greek as well as Latin: a supplication to William Cecil, principal secretary, was in both languages and much later, in 1580, George Edrich dedicated to him a manuscript translation into Greek of Cicero's *De amicitia*. Dale was fellow of All Souls from 1542 until at least 1550, when, although never ordained, he apparently contemplated an ecclesiastical career.

John Dale may have been the lawyer of Gray's Inn and MP for Guildford in 1529. Evidently ill-endowed and often embarrassed by debt, he certainly dealt in wheat and trafficked in leases, at various times on the sites of Cleeve Abbey and Cleeve rectory in Somerset, Llandysul rectory in Wales, and Sarson manor in Abbots Ann, Hampshire. He died intestate before 12 October 1552, after which his widow, Joan, remitted her rights to their son, who engaged in a series of chancery suits for possession. He was probably unsuccessful, since several leases appear to have already expired or been assigned by his father. He was, however, JP for Hampshire in 1553. He leased Devynock rectory in Brecknockshire from the crown in 1563–76. Dale inherited Fyfield as male heir from his cousin William Dale in 1566. Local connections are also suggested by his election, first for the town of Taunton in 1558, and later for the borough of Hindon, Wiltshire, in 1584, although on this second occasion he declined the seat.

Dale already had important connections. He sought help from Cecil in becoming official to the archdeacon of York, presumably unsuccessfully, and was collated in 1550 by Thomas Cranmer, archbishop of Canterbury, to the vicarage of Winterbourne Earls, Wiltshire, which he resigned in 1553–4 for Llandysul rectory, Cardiganshire. Instead he embarked on a career in civil law—an avenue with few direct applications in England, except diplomacy. Having apparently supplicated unsuccessfully on several occasions for the doctorate of civil law at Oxford, he graduated as such about 1550 at Orléans and hence was incorporated at Oxford in 1552, where he was still resident, and at Cambridge in 1562. He was admitted to the College of Advocates in 1553 and to Gray's Inn and henceforth practised in the court of arches and other civilian courts.

If Cecil initially found no use for Dale's legal or French language skills, his fellow principal secretary Sir William Petre, also a civilian and Oxford graduate, did. By June 1553 he was employing Dale to settle mercantile disputes with France, perhaps as secretary under the leadership of Dr Nicholas Wotton, whose report from France in 1554 was laudatory about Dale: 'I believe he will prove one of the meetest men you have at home to do the Queen's highness service abroad' (HoP, *Commons, 1509–58*, 5). The comment presaged a highly distinguished future in foreign relations. There was nevertheless a ten-year hiatus in Dale's ambassadorial activities, while he established the legal foundations that underpinned his diplomatic credentials and in particular his expertise in maritime and international law. Already by 1557 he was a surrogate (deputy judge) of the admiralty. It was as one of three civil lawyers returned to the boroughs under the patronage of John White, bishop of Winchester, that Dale was MP for Taunton in 1558.

At this early stage Dale's career may have been financed by a fortunate marriage. The evidence for this is somewhat indirect. His public and private lives intertwine with those of a fellow civilian, Dr Robert Forth (*d.* 1595), of London and Streatham, Surrey, who appears from his graduation dates to have been about ten years Dale's junior. Although it cannot be proved, the Elizabeth Forth (*d.* 1590) whom Dale married in the late 1550s was most probably

Forth's stepmother rather than his sister or daughter: she named him and his sons as her executors in her own will. If Elizabeth had children from a previous marriage she may have been older than Dale, perhaps explaining why they had only one child, Dorothy (1560–1618). He may have been assisted in his career by her inheritance and in turn may have helped his younger friend, Forth.

Following the decision by Margaret, duchess of Parma, regent of the Low Countries, to place an embargo on English cloth, Dale was sent there in 1563 on embassy; however, he failed to have the ban lifted. He returned in 1564 to refute allegations of English attacks against Flemish and Dutch shipping. Between 1569 and 1571 he advised Cecil on maritime law and in 1571 was commissioned to inquire into the seizure of Spanish treasure two years earlier. The following year he was instrumental in securing the pardon of a group of Sussex mariners convicted of piracy in 1569. When consulted by the government, he urged that the Spanish ambassador, Guerau de Spes, should be punished for threatening the security of the realm, urging the same treatment against John Lesley, bishop of Ross, in 1571. He was sufficiently valuable to the government for Lord Burghley (Cecil), lord treasurer, in his capacity as steward of the lands of the bishopric of Chichester, to have him returned in 1572 to parliament for the city of Chichester.

Dale's French language skills, which had been used again in negotiations with the French ambassador Bertrand de Salignac de la Motte-Fénélon in 1569, also fitted him for the key post of resident ambassador in Paris in succession to Sir Francis Walsingham, who was embarrassed financially and extremely anxious to be relieved. Although apparently the third choice, Dale was backed by both Walsingham and Burghley, but the queen had qualms about his inexperience. He had actually bought horses and engaged servants when his appointment was put on hold. Appointed in November 1572, Dale eventually took up office about 15 April 1573 in Paris, where he was well-received by the papal nuncio as not such an 'obstinate Huguenot' as his predecessor (*CSP Rome*, 1572–8, 102). Thomas Wilkes, probationary fellow of All Souls College at Oxford, served as his secretary. Dale's surviving reports reveal him to have been assiduous and reliable. He remained in Paris until recalled in October 1576. He seems to have escaped the financial difficulties of his predecessor, but left at least one debt unpaid for the rest of his life. In reward for his new responsibilities, he was appointed at the queen's instance (and at no cost to herself) first as archdeacon of Surrey on 13 February 1573, Sir Walter Mildmay interceding with Burghley on his behalf, and then on 8 January 1574 as dean of Wells and canon residentiary, with a share of the common fund; although an absentee, married, and a layman, it was not right, so the crown asserted, that he should be financially disadvantaged by his services to the state. He had, however, to ensure the customary sermons were preached. Dale held both the deanery and canonry until his death in 1589, adding, in 1585, the mastership of Sherburn Hospital in co. Durham, for which he received a dispensation and following which

he was also appointed to the commission of the peace and the quorum for co. Durham.

On his return from Paris, Dale resumed his legal career. Perhaps already a master of requests by 1564 and certainly by 1576, he was a judge of the court of admiralty in 1565 and became commissary-general from 30 January 1585, jointly with Sir Julius Caesar, in the absence of a lord high admiral. He held this last post until his death. He was frequently delegated to hear particular cases of piracy and patents were issued to implement his decisions. In 1577 he was granted a £100 annuity for counselling and attending on the queen. By 1579 he was a master in chancery, and in 1581 he was appointed a commissioner in ecclesiastical causes. In 1579 Dale was among those deputed to implement the treaty of Bristol. He was consulted by the government on many other matters, such as marriage negotiations between the queen and François Valois, duc d'Anjou, in 1581, and enjoyed the confidence of not only Burghley but also of Elizabeth herself. He officiated at a string of treason trials, serving as commissioner for those of Philip Howard, first earl of Arundel, on 18 April 1580, of Dr William Parry on 20 January 1585, of Anthony Babington on 5 September 1586, and finally, in October 1586, at that of Mary, queen of Scots. Immediately afterwards, at Burghley's request, he wrote a memorandum justifying Mary's execution for Elizabeth, to salve her conscience. He was appointed JP and of the quorum for Hampshire by 1583. Although Dale was never a privy councillor, Burghley arranged his return to parliament repeatedly for Chichester, in 1584, 1586, and 1589; also elected for Thomas Cooper, bishop of Winchester's, borough of Hindon, Wiltshire, in 1584, he declined to serve. The privy council rebuffed an attempt to make him resign his seat in 1586. He served on many Commons committees, relating to legal, mercantile, security, and international matters in those parliaments and also in 1581, when his seat is not known. He is also reported to have often advised Sir Christopher Hatton, lord chancellor, the 'good lord' whom he appointed overseer of his will (PRO, PROB 11/74, sig. 92).

Although 'old and stout' and indeed unwell, the veteran Dale was commissioned in July 1587 to lead lengthy negotiations for peace with Philip II. Dispatched in February 1588 to Alessandro Farnese, duke of Parma, Philip's commander in the Low Countries, he failed in this impossible objective, but took great pains, more he claimed than on the previous embassy, and wrote most of the reports himself. While abroad he noted preparations for the Spanish Armada, which he faithfully reported. Among his entourage was the young Robert Cecil, whom he praised to Burghley: he was 'assured he loveth and liketh me and he is assured I love and like him' (HoP, *Commons*, 1558–1603, 6).

Dale resided in the parish of St Gregory by Paul's in London from at least 1560 until his death. It was there on 5 August 1560 that Dorothy was baptized and there also that she was married on 13 November 1581 to Lord John North, eldest son and heir of Roger North, second Baron North, and his wife, Winifred. Dale died on 17 November 1589 in his home parish. His will was proved next day and he was buried in his parish church on 2 December. He still had other residences at Fyfield and, from 1585, at Sherburn Hospital. He appears to have held little other land, but was certainly very comfortably off, as Dorothy's marriage into the peerage demonstrates. In 1589 he was assessed for the subsidy at £100, which compares favourably with Forth's rating of only £70. Dale's income may have derived in part from his legal practice, but was drawn principally from his ample rewards from the crown. These took the form of annuities—£100 from the crown from 1577 and £40 from the bishopric of Ely from 1583; of the valuable livings that he treated as sinecures, without any obligations to reside or officiate; and of the leases of the rectories of Devynoke, Brecknockshire, and Thanet, Kent, which he was granted in 1583. He left a life interest only in all his leases and moveables to his widow, perhaps because she had children of her own, with the reversion to his daughter, and £100 towards the marriage of his granddaughter Elizabeth North. His widow died in October 1590: her Forth kinsmen, whom she named as executors, declined to act and administration was granted to Sir John North.

MICHAEL HICKS

Sources DNB · Emden, *Oxf.* · HoP, *Commons, 1558–1603* · HoP, *Commons, 1509–58* · will, PRO, PROB 11/74, sig. 92 · *VCH Hampshire and the Isle of Wight*, vol. 4 · *Fasti Angl., 1541–1857*, [Salisbury] · *Fasti Angl., 1541–1857*, [Ely] · *CPR, 1560–63* · *CSP dom.*, 1547–80 · *CSP for.*, 1547–53; 1553–58; 1563–65; 1569–77; 1579–80; 1588 · PRO, C 142/152/142 · PRO, C 142/39/18 · PRO, C 1/499/67; C 1/781/25; C 1/1345/4; C 1/1347/8; C 1/1422/5–6 · GEC, *Peerage* · Bodl. Oxf., North MSS · IGI
Archives Bodl. Oxf., diplomatic and family papers | BL, Cotton MSS · BL, Cotton MSS, corresp. and papers
Wealth at death £100 p.a. in 1589: *Visitation of London 1568*, Harleian Soc. 109–10 (1957–8)

Dale, Sir William Leonard (1906–2000), lawyer and civil servant, was born on 17 June 1906 at The Rectory, Preston in Holderness, in the East Riding of Yorkshire, the elder son and eldest of the three children of the Revd William Dale (1852–1934), Church of England clergyman, and his wife, Rose (1870–1963), daughter of Herbert Leonard, farmer, of Marfleet, Yorkshire. His rural vicarage upbringing was characterized by plainness and duty. From his mother, however, he inherited a love of music and natural talent as a keyboard player, taking over her role as parish organist from the age of ten.

After Hymers College, Hull, Dale entered into articles with solicitors in the city. But that was not enough to contain his energies and, after an external London University LLB, he boldly took himself off to read for the bar, supporting himself on a Gray's Inn scholarship and occasional appointments as a suburban church organist. Call in 1931 was followed by a London pupillage, practice briefly on the north-eastern circuit, and a return to chambers in the Temple. Times were thin, and on the spur of the moment he joined an English solicitor practising in Jaffa. The randomness and oddity of life under the British mandate appealed to him, but the strain told, and in 1935, again on the spur of the moment, he applied for a legal post in the Colonial Office. On 12 September 1936 he married his second cousin, Emma Patricia Goulton (Biddy) Leonard (b.

1910/11), daughter of Thomas Goulton Leonard, stockbroker, but she was soon diagnosed as having multiple sclerosis and the marriage ended in divorce in 1943. On 30 November 1948 he married Elizabeth Elwyn, an American architect, but that marriage, too, was childless, and they were divorced in 1953.

By then Dale's civil-service career had taken further twists. He moved to an administrative position in the wartime Ministry of Supply in 1940, returning to the Colonial Office after VJ-day to the legal complexities of Raja Brooke's cession of Sarawak to the British crown. He was made CMG in 1951, in which year he fielded a request to identify a legal adviser for the newly minted kingdom of Libya by promptly volunteering himself. He returned in 1953, despite the Libyan government's entreaties to stay on as a supreme court judge, described in a grateful Foreign Office letter as 'the highest tribute ... to [his] wisdom and single-mindedness' (private information).

A move to the Ministry of Education in 1954 produced a rewarding change of work. But Lord Hailsham's arrival as minister in 1957 led to clashes, to which Dale characteristically responded by declaring himself semi-redundant, and taking up work for half the day at the Foreign Office. In 1961 he became the legal adviser to the Commonwealth Relations Office (CRO), and in the following year he was seconded to the central Africa office to help deal with the break up of the Central African Federation. He was promoted KCMG in 1965, and retired a year later, a period which spanned the CRO's amalgamation with his old department, but not the final merger into a single Foreign and Commonwealth Office. In London on 17 June 1966, his last day in service, he married, to his lasting happiness, Gloria Finn (b. 1922), textile designer, of Washington, DC, daughter of Charles Spellman, stockbroker. They had one daughter, Rosemary.

Although thoroughly disinclined to fade away, Dale can hardly have imagined that a further thirty years' active work lay ahead. A spell in the law officers' department (1967–8) was followed by another lightning decision to move to Beirut as general counsel to the United Nations Relief and Works Agency for Palestinian refugees. Return home in 1973 opened the most productive and creative phase of Dale's legal life, and a working partnership with Kutlu Fuad, head of the legal division in the Commonwealth Secretariat, which had been founded in Dale's CRO days. First came a study of how to provide competent Commonwealth draftsmen, commuted into a fuller investigation into what legislative *style* would best meet the needs of newly independent countries, and unlocking Dale's abiding interest in simpler approaches to writing statutes. Then came the call to take over the government legal advisers course (another Dale–CRO creation), through which over the next quarter-century Dale cajoled a galaxy of eminent British figures into nurturing the practical skills of generations of overseas lawyers. The final flowering came in the decision of London University's Institute of Advanced Legal Studies to found a centre for legislative studies in Dale's honour on his ninetieth birthday. The mark of his continuing vigour and determination lay in his becoming its founding director and establishing a firm base for its activity before stepping down shortly before his death.

Dale published in 1994 an entertaining (if somewhat romanticized) autobiography under the title *Time Past, Time Present*, which told among other things how his most enduring published work (*The Law of the Parish Church*, 7th edn, 1998) first came to birth as the winner of a Gray's Inn essay prize in 1931. In 1983 came *The Modern Commonwealth*, a sound guide to that subject. But he was proudest of all of his *Legislative Drafting, a New Approach* (1977), which, though less a new recipe than a justified critique of the stuffiness of the English parliamentary drafting style, was well received. He died of prostatic cancer on 8 February 2000 at Compton Lodge, 7 Harley Road, Camden, London, and was buried at St Pancras Church, Finchley, London. He was survived by his wife and their daughter.

F. D. BERMAN

Sources W. Dale, *Time past, time present* (1994) • W. Dale, 'The government legal advisers course and the IALS', *Commonwealth Law Bulletin*, 23 (1997), 1275–82 • F. D. Berman, 'Sir William Leonard Dale, 1906–2000: an appreciation', *Amicus Curiae*, 27 (2000), 20–23 • *Daily Telegraph* (14 March 2000) • *The Independent* (12 April 2000) • Burke, *Peerage* • *WW* • *WWW* • personal knowledge (2004) • private information (2004) [Lady Dale] • b. cert. • m. cert. [Emma Patricia Goutlon Leonard] • m. cert. [Gloria Finn] • d. cert.
Likenesses K. Brennan, photograph, 1994, repro. in Dale, *Time past*, frontispiece • photograph, 1994, repro. in *Daily Telegraph* • A. Adams, charcoal and chalk drawing, U. Lond., Institute of Advanced Legal Studies • photograph, repro. in *The Independent*
Wealth at death £238,423—gross; £236,129—net: probate, 23 March 2000, CGPLA Eng. & Wales

Daley, Sir (William) Allen (1887–1969), medical officer of health, was born at Bootle, Lancashire, on 19 February 1887, the elder son of William Daley (d. 1911), medical officer of health of Bootle, and his wife, Mary Allen. He was educated at Merchant Taylors' School, Crosby, and at the University of Liverpool. He graduated BSc (London) in chemistry in 1906, then MB, ChB (Liverpool), in 1909, with first-class honours, and MB, BS (London), in 1910, with distinction in medicine. He obtained the Cambridge diploma in public health in 1911 with distinction, and his London MD degree in 1912. After holding resident posts in Liverpool he became resident medical officer at the London Fever Hospital in 1911. In May that year his father was drowned at the age of forty-seven in a yachting accident and Daley was recalled to Bootle to succeed him as medical officer of health at the early age of twenty-four.

For the next forty-one years Daley held posts of increasing responsibility and importance in the field of preventive medicine. The early work at Bootle showed energy and promise leading to similar appointments successively in Blackburn (1920–25) and Hull (1925–9). Daley was appointed in 1928 to serve on a departmental committee of the Ministry of Health on the recruitment and training of midwives and his work there was noticed by the medical officer of health of the London county council, Frederick Menzies. In 1929 Daley was appointed a principal medical officer of the London county council and in 1938 he became deputy to Menzies. In the nine years before the outbreak of war in 1939 the hospitals of the Metropolitan Asylums Board and the metropolitan boards of guardians were being integrated into a single service by the London county council. Menzies had chosen well: Daley's apparently unlimited energy and industry had found an appropriate task. Within a short time he had a complete grasp of the complexities of the service down to the smallest detail. He recorded and reported on all his activities and copies were distributed widely so that staff were made aware of progress or delay in all projects. It was commonplace to hear from staff that at no other time or place in their careers were they so well informed about their work. Daley chaired many departmental committees dealing with such diverse subjects as pathological services, hospital standards and staffing, the district medical service, the ambulance service, and the tuberculosis scheme. He was demonstrably a master of the committee method: well informed, affable, and urbane.

In 1939 Daley succeeded Menzies as county medical officer; in the same year he was elected FRCP. During the Second World War he had the difficult task of guiding the hospital service during a time when it acquired a reputation of never refusing a casualty a bed, though many buildings were badly damaged. His work was recognized by a knighthood in 1944 and, in 1947, by an honorary physicianship to George VI. Daley took a special pride in his election to the council of the Royal College of Physicians while a practising medical officer of health, a rare honour. In 1943 he published with Reginald Coleman a paper entitled 'The development of the hospital services with particular reference to the municipal hospital system of London', in *Proceedings of the Royal Society of Medicine* (35, 1941–2, 45–56).

The National Health Service Act of 1946 led to a further period of great activity during which the London county council hospitals were transferred to the newly formed regional hospital boards, and simultaneously steps were taken to absorb the personal health services previously in the care of the metropolitan boroughs which made up the county council area. This was accomplished with Daley's accustomed skill in 1948, even though he regretted the loss of the responsibility of local authorities for hospitals, and four years later he reached the official retiring age. This had no perceptible effect on his activities; he transferred his personal files to his home and continued to serve on the many committees to which he had been appointed in a personal capacity.

Daley was president of the Central Council for Health Education, having been a founder member and the author of a paper in the 1920s which played a considerable part in the thinking which led to the formation of the council. In 1927 he published *Population Education in Public Health* (with Hester Viney) and an interview with him on the topic of health education was published in the *Health Education Journal* (1, 1943, 19–23). He was chairman of the Chadwick trustees and president of the National Association for Maternal and Child Welfare. These were appointments which he continued to the end of his life, but in addition he held appointments on boards of governors of hospitals and other bodies concerned with health. Age limits removed him from many of these, but to the end he retained the vice-chairmanship of the academic board of the Royal Postgraduate Hospital at Hammersmith in west London.

At the time of his retirement from his official post, Daley had written or spoken on 250 occasions, varying from addresses for learned societies to speeches at prize-givings. Some fifteen years later this had been increased to more than 450. He delivered the Croonian lectures to the Royal College of Physicians, the De Lamar lecture at Johns Hopkins School of Hygiene and Public Health, Baltimore, and a report to the World Health Organization and Rockefeller Foundation on health and social workers in England and France. After his retirement he visited Australia on behalf of the Nuffield Foundation, lecturing on the British National Health Service, and he lectured also in North America, where for several months he was associate health officer of the city of Baltimore.

In 1913 Daley married Mary (Marie; d. 1962), daughter of Edward Toomey, of Liverpool; they had a daughter who became a consultant obstetrician and gynaecologist in London and a son who became a consultant physician also in the capital at St Thomas's Hospital. Although in the last five years of Daley's life physical afflictions slowed him down, there was no lack of mental power and he continued by correspondence and conversation to be one of the best-informed, as well as one of the best-known, figures in public health circles. He died on 21 February 1969 at Tenerife during a winter holiday.

A. B. STEWART, rev. MICHAEL BEVAN

Sources *The Times* (24 Feb 1969) · *BMJ* (1 March 1969) · *The Lancet* (8 March 1969) · private information (1981) · personal knowledge (1981) · *WWW* · Munk, *Roll* · *CGPLA Eng. & Wales* (1969)
Archives Wellcome L., papers
Likenesses W. Gibbons, oils, 1967, priv. coll.
Wealth at death £47,657: probate, 26 June 1969, *CGPLA Eng. & Wales*

Daley, Harry (1901–1971), police officer and author, was born at 49 Stevens Street, Lowestoft, Suffolk, on 14 November 1901, the second son and fourth of the five children of Joseph Daley (d. 1911), skipper of a fishing smack, and his wife, Emily Firman, a former parlourmaid. He was educated from the age of three at the local school and, despite considerable financial hardship and the long absences at sea of his bawdy, easy-going, and adored father, his childhood was exceptionally happy. In the great 'September gale' of 1911, however, Joseph Daley was one of the many fishermen lost at sea. Instead of going on to secondary school, Harry gave up his education to become a telegram boy. During the First World War, Zeppelin raids and rumours of a German invasion decided Daley's mother to move the family to the relative safety of Dorking, Surrey, where her eldest daughter was living. Here Daley got a job with a grocer, driving a pony and trap round the countryside collecting orders for goods.

Daley was avid for culture and began buying the sort of eclectic volumes sold cheaply from the boxes that stood

Harry Daley (1901–1971), by Duncan Grant, 1931

outside booksellers' shops. Weekends were spent visiting London to explore theatres, cinemas, galleries, and concert halls. At the age of twenty-four he decided, almost on a whim, to join the Metropolitan Police force. He was not the most likely recruit, since he was inclined to plumpness and described himself as 'well below average plain common sense; sexually both innocent and deplorable; honourable if not exactly honest; trusting; truthful; romantic and sentimental to the point of sloppiness' (Daley, *This Small Cloud*, 78). The selection committee nevertheless judged him 'a good type of chap—just what we want', and he began training at Peel House in March 1925 (ibid., 77). Having passed his examinations, he was posted to 'T' division, based in Hammersmith, west London. His first beat was in Chiswick, but after a few months he was transferred to Hammersmith itself, a lively part of the capital where the police lived in comparative harmony with petty criminals, their relationship eased by small bribes. Daley, who was homosexual, and took no great pains to hide the fact, found himself attracted to the sharply dressed and cheeky young crooks who thronged the streets, and soon numbered several of them among his friends and lovers. When he was obliged to make arrests, most of these young men philosophically accepted it as a 'fair cop' and struck dramatic poses when their captor, a keen amateur photographer, snapped them as they were loaded into Black Marias.

It was while on his Hammersmith beat in 1925 that Daley met J. R. Ackerley, a local resident whose pioneering play about homosexuality, *The Prisoners of War*, then running in London, had impressed him. The two men struck up a conversation, probably had a brief sexual relationship, and became lifelong friends. Ackerley introduced Daley to E. M. Forster, with whom he embarked on an important but troubled love affair. Although Forster was delighted to accompany Daley on his beat and be introduced to his working-class associates, he was appalled by the policeman's recklessness and constitutional lack of discretion—Daley described 'safety first' as a 'contemptible slogan' (Daley, *This Small Cloud*, 6). The relationship foundered in 1932, but it had given Daley an entrée into the literary world, where he was painted by Duncan Grant and entertained people with his stories. Recognizing a skilled raconteur, Ackerley, then working as an assistant talks producer at the BBC, persuaded Daley to make some radio broadcasts about his life. 'Not a happy one?' was broadcast on the Home Service on 25 March 1929 and subsequently published in *The Listener*, as were several other talks on the police, his Lowestoft childhood, and other subjects. Daley sometimes spoke as an official representative of the Metropolitan Police, but it was thought politic for other talks, such as an enthusiastic account of criminal activity at London street markets, to be broadcast and published under the pseudonyms of Joe Daley and Harry Firman.

In 1935 Daley was transferred to Vine Street, but he preferred the suburbs to Soho, and was much happier when he was sent to Wandsworth early in the Second World War. 'Wandsworth was full of lively, good-looking people who thought nothing of telling a policeman to get stuffed', he recalled. 'It was a marvellous place and I couldn't see myself making many arrests' (Daley, *This Small Cloud*, 183). After the war he reluctantly took a temporary staff job, running a police recruitment centre in Beak Street, but he longed to get back to the streets. On 21 May 1950 he left the police to join the merchant navy as a master-at-arms. He was forty-nine. His new career was cut short by the onset of diabetes, which led to periods of depression. In 1957 he retired to Dorking, living at 78 Pixham Lane with his younger brother David.

During the 1940s Daley had tried writing short stories, and submitted them to Ackerley, who had become the literary editor of *The Listener*. None was ever published, partly because they were, characteristically, 'rather near the knuckle' (*Letters*, 63). After his retirement, on Ackerley's advice, Daley began writing a book of reminiscences. This was partly a therapeutic exercise: he had always been quick to take offence, even when none was intended, but as he wrote the book, he realized that he had in fact had a generally happy and fortunate life. *This Small Cloud*—the title refers to his homosexuality—was highly indiscreet about his own life and work, but he did not mention any of the famous people with whom he had been involved. This remarkable book is not only funny, touching, and self-deprecatory, but is an important social document. It was published posthumously in 1987, with an afterword by Clive Emsley, historian of the police. It was the only piece of writing that Daley did not destroy before his death, which occurred at Dorking General Hospital on 12 March 1971 as a result of his diabetes. Following cremation at Surrey and Sussex crematorium, Worth, his ashes were scattered at Box Hill, Surrey.

PETER PARKER

Sources H. Daley, *This small cloud* (1987) · P. Parker, *Ackerley* (1989) · P. N. Furbank, *E. M. Forster: a life*, 2 vols. (1977–8) · *The letters of J. R. Ackerley*, ed. N. Braybrooke (1975) · letters from Harry Daley to P. N. Furbank, priv. coll. · private information (2004) · b. cert. · d. cert. **Likenesses** D. Grant, oils, 1931, Guildhall Art Gallery, London [*see illus.*] · photographs, repro. in Daley, *This small cloud*; priv. colls. **Wealth at death** £803: probate, 7 April 1971, *CGPLA Eng. & Wales*

Dalgairns, John Dobrée [*name in religion* Bernard] (1818–1876), Roman Catholic priest and scholar, was born on Guernsey on 21 October 1818, the eldest of the six children (three boys and three girls) of William Dalgairns (*b. c*.1790), an officer in the Scots 7th fusiliers in the Peninsular War, and his wife, Caroline, *née* Dobrée (*b.* 1797), a landowning member of an old Guernsey family. He was baptized (6 November 1818) an Anglican in the town church of St Peter Port and grew up bilingual in French and English like his fellow Catholic convert Peter le Page Renouf, also born on Guernsey. He was educated at Elizabeth College, Guernsey (1826–35), where he won several prizes, and matriculated at Exeter College, Oxford, on 4 February 1836. He graduated BA with a second-class degree in 1839, when he befriended John Henry Newman and became associated with the radical wing of the Oxford Movement, which aimed to renew the high-church tradition within the Church of England. Through an anonymous letter, signed 'A Young Member of the University of Oxford', which appealed to French Catholics for their prayers for the movement and was published in the French Catholic newspaper *L'Univers* in 1841, he came into contact with the Passionist priest Father Dominic Barberi, who replied to his letter in the same publication, and with the Abbé Hilaire Lorain, superior of the seminary in Langres, who visited him in Oxford. In 1841 Newman began to pay him scholarship money from 'The Fund' he had created for young scholars (*Letters and Diaries of John Henry Newman*, 7.517).

Under protestant attack as a crypto-Roman Catholic for writing Tract 90 in 1841, Newman withdrew from Oxford to the village of Littlemore. On 22 March 1842 Dalgairns was the first to reside there with him, translating the volume on St Matthew in Newman's edition of Aquinas's *Catena aurea* of patristic quotations from scripture (St Matthew, 1842; the series, 4 vols., 1841–5). He also wrote two reviews (October 1841 and October 1842) on French themes for the extreme Anglo-Catholic journal the *British Critic*, then edited by Newman's brother-in-law Thomas Mozley, and a number of biographies in Newman's collection *The Lives of the English Saints* (1843–5). The short biographies which he contributed were: St Stephen Harding (translated into French in 1848 and German in 1865), St

John Dobrée Dalgairns (1818–1876), by unknown photographer

Ailred, St Robert of Newminster, and St Waltheof (all Cistercians), as well as the verse portion and some paragraphs for Newman's life of St Bettelin. He also wrote the lives of St Helier and St Bartholomew the Hermit, and completed William Lockhart's life of St Gilbert in the same series. In 1842 he unsuccessfully tried to deter Renouf from writing to the Catholic bishop Nicholas Wiseman without the knowledge of the high-church leader Edward Bouverie Pusey, but was himself received into the Catholic church on 29 September 1845 by Father Barberi at Aston Hall, Staffordshire. In October of the same year he went to Langres to lodge with Canon Lorain and to study for the priesthood, being ordained priest on 19 December 1846.

Dalgairns was attracted by the example of the famous French Dominican Henri Dominique Lacordaire to become a Dominican himself, but when Newman and his companions decided to become Oratorians he joined Newman's noviciate at Santa Croce in Rome in 1847, and was one of the original Oratorian community established by Newman and F. W. Faber at Maryvale, St Wilfrid's, Cotton, and Birmingham. He adopted the name in religion of Bernard, after the greatest of the Cistercians, in part to distinguish himself from Newman by Christian name (*Letters and Diaries of John Henry Newman*, 12.134). He was arguably the community's finest scholar, and was, after Newman, 'the intellectual giant of the congregation' (Kerr, 2.14). Newman could ill afford to lose him, but in 1849 he

followed Faber to establish the new oratory in London, Newman reflecting in melancholy manner, with reference to Dalgairns's arrival in Littlemore in 1842, that seven years was 'the term of *Contubernium* [tent companionship] with my friends' (Chapman, 212).

Another friend from Langres, the Abbé Félix Philpin de Rivière (1814–1907), afterwards himself an Oratorian, sent the religious order he had founded, the Congregation of Calvary, to work with the Oratory in London; Dalgairns helped these nuns to establish themselves under their new name of the Sisters of Compassion. His study of the founder of the Roman Oratorians, St Philip Neri, appeared in five parts in the liberal Catholic journal *The Rambler* (1849–50), and his work *The Devotion to the Heart of Jesus, with an Introduction on the History of Jansenism* (1853) was translated into French, German, and Italian. In 1858 he attacked Sir John Acton's defence of the proposition that St Augustine was 'the father of Jansenism' in *The Rambler*; the ultramontane Dalgairns disliked Acton's derivation of the seventeenth-century anti-papal heresy of Jansenism from a canonized saint like Augustine. His later work *The Holy Communion, its Philosophy, Theology, and Practice* (1861) also opposed the austere Jansenist hostility to frequent communion. Dalgairns's abiding interest in medieval mysticism recurred in 'The German mystics of the fourteenth century', mostly on the Blessed Henry Suso, which he wrote for the *Dublin Review* (44, 1858, 31–99; separately published, 1858), and in his essay on the medieval spiritual life prefixed to the 1870 edition of *The Scale of Perfection* by Walter Hylton (or Hilton). Dalgairns's treatise 'The spiritual life of the first six centuries' was prefixed to a translation of Countess Hahn-Hahn's *Lives of the Fathers of the Desert* (2 vols., 1867).

Dalgairns was highly critical of Faber's autocratic rule in London, and he returned to Birmingham in October 1853, where he befriended Mother Margaret Hallahan, the founder of the English Dominican nuns at Stone in Staffordshire. In August 1856, during the quarrel between the two oratories over London's right to relax the rule forbidding oratories to hear nuns' confessions, Dalgairns took the side of the London house, acknowledging to Newman his 'settled intellectual conviction that the idea of the London House was more like the historical Philippine idea [after St Philip Neri] than was that of the Birmingham house' (*Letters and Diaries of John Henry Newman*, 17.351). Dalgairns lost contact with Newman, and in 1864 wrote to the English bishops opposing Newman's plan for an oratory in Oxford. In 1870, in a letter to the French newspaper *Le Monde*, he deplored Newman's published letter of the same year to his bishop, William Bernard Ullathorne, which criticized the opportuneness of the definition of papal infallibility, declaring that 'To differ from Father Newman is the one great sorrow of my life' (ibid., 25.121–2). Newman then told bishop David Moriarty (8 May 1870) that the 'great intimacy' which had existed between himself and Dalgairns from 1842 to 1845 had ceased when they became Catholics, adding that since Dalgairns had 'left his status pupillaris he has shown an ingrained self conceit and arrogance which I think I never found in such a degree in any one else' (ibid., 25.122). This arrogance is not recorded by others. Dalgairns lived at the London Oratory in Kensington from August 1856 until his final illness.

In 1863 Dalgairns succeeded Faber as the second superior of the London Oratory, and wrote in defence of the Oratorians against the lawsuit and claims by Alfred Smee, the brother-in-law of the deceased Oratorian Father William Antony Hutchison, that the community had squandered Hutchison's private wealth and buried him under his assumed religious name of Antony. Smee replied in *The private and secret burial ground of the Oratory. Rejoinder to the manifesto of Dr Dalgairns* (1864). Dalgairns's health broke down in 1865, when he was succeeded as superior by Father Francis Knox. He was a member from 1869 of James Knowles's Metaphysical Society; four of his papers on metaphysical subjects were published in Knowles's *Contemporary Review* (1870–74): 'On the theory of the human soul'; 'The bearing of infallibility on religious truth'; 'Is God unknowable?', and 'The personality of God'. Dalgairns remarked of the Metaphysical Society that 'We have not converted each other, but we certainly think better of each other' (Ward, 309). A member of the society, the editor of *The Spectator*, R. H. Hutton, described Dalgairns as 'a man of singular sweetness and openness of character, with something of a French type of playfulness of expression' (Day, 26). William Thomson, archbishop of York, and the Unitarian James Martineau thought Dalgairns the best of the society's metaphysicians, and Martineau wrote that 'if I had gained nothing from the Metaphysical Society but the impression of Father Dalgairns's personality, I should have been for ever grateful to it' (Ward, 310). Dalgairns himself wrote 'On the relation of scholasticism to modern philosophy: Mr Hutton and Mr Martineau' (*Dublin Review*, 20, 1873, 281–325). Preaching at the dedication in 1873 of the great new church of St Philip Neri in Arundel, built by the fifteenth duke of Norfolk, Dalgairns described the building as a 'protest against the spirit of the age' (Robinson, 60). He prepared the first marquess of Ripon for his reception into the Catholic church at the Brompton Oratory in September 1874; his part remained secret, as Disraeli was unable to discover for Queen Victoria who had 'cooked' the conversion (Rossi, 63). During the last year of his life, he suffered from mental illness. He died at the St George's Retreat, conducted by the Sisters of St Augustine, at Burgess Hill, near Brighton, on 6 April 1876, and was buried at the London Oratorians' private cemetery at Sydenham.   Sheridan Gilley

Sources correspondence, 1842–72, London Oratory, Oratory MS collection · R. Kerr, 'The Oratory in London', 2 vols., London Oratory, Oratory MS collection · *The letters and diaries of John Henry Newman*, ed. C. S. Dessain and others, [31 vols.] (1961–) · R. Chapman, *Father Faber* (1961) · W. Ward, *William George Ward and the Catholic revival* (1893) · E. H. Day, ed., 'Letters from Oxford and Littlemore: an unpublished correspondence on the Oxford Movement', *The Treasury* (Oct 1911) · J. M. Robinson, 'The dukes of Norfolk and the London Oratory', *The London Oratory centenary, 1884–1984*, ed. M. Napier and A. Laing (1984) · J. P. Rossi, 'Lord Ripon's resumption of political activity', *Recusant History*, 11 (1971–2), 61–74 · d. cert.

Archives Keble College, Oxford, letters · London Oratory, corresp. | Birmingham Oratory, letters to J. H. Newman · BL, letters to Lord Ripon, Add. MS 43625
Likenesses photograph, London Oratory [*see illus.*] · portrait, London Oratory; repro. in Napier and Laing, eds., *London Oratory*, 59 · portrait, repro. in A. W. Hutton, ed., *The lives of the English saints*, 5 (1901), facing p. 55
Wealth at death under £1500: probate, 24 May 1876, *CGPLA Eng. & Wales*

Dalgarno, George (*c*.1616–1687), writer on language, was 'borne at Old Aberdeen, and bred in the university at New Aberdeen', according to Wood (Wood, *Ath. Oxon.*, 506). No primary documentary evidence has survived concerning his family background. His date of birth, usually given as about 1626 on the basis of Wood's estimate that at his death he was 'aged sixty or more' (ibid.), must be placed at least ten years earlier, taking into account his matriculation at Marischal College, Aberdeen, in 1631. However, if he subsequently graduated, there is no record of his having done so. Dalgarno's arms are said by Wood to be 'gules, three otter's heads, erased argent' (*Life and Times of Anthony Wood*, 3.225), but neither college of arms holds any surviving evidence.

It is not known what Dalgarno was doing in the period between his leaving Aberdeen and his first appearance in Oxford, where he 'taught a private grammar school with good success for about thirty years together, in the parishes of St. Michael and St. Mary Mag[dalen]' (Wood, *Ath. Oxon.*, 506). He was evidently known to be adept at shorthand, and in early 1657 he was asked by friends to evaluate one of the systems of brachygraphy that had recently been published. His modification of this scheme was brought to the notice of Samuel Hartlib, who encouraged its further development into a 'real character', a universal notational system designed for scientific and pansophic purposes. Dalgarno's first such scheme was published as a broadsheet at the end of the same year. Responses from contemporary scholars to which it was sent for comment, together with Dalgarno's covering letters and samples of his notational system, are preserved in the British Library (Sloane MS 4377, fols. 139–46) and in the Hartlib papers at the University of Sheffield.

Dalgarno's efforts brought him into contact with a circle of thinkers in the University of Oxford who were later to form the nucleus of the Royal Society. Notable among these were John Wallis and Seth Ward, whom Hartlib records in his diary to be aiding Dalgarno in his improvement of the shorthand system in 1657, and John Wilkins, who embarked on a collaborative venture with Dalgarno with a view to further developing the 'real character' into a philosophical language based on rational principles. As work progressed, however, it emerged that Dalgarno and Wilkins had irreconcilable differences of opinion about the basis of the philosophical language, and their association ceased. Dalgarno, fearing that his ideas would be pre-empted, rushed a revised scheme into print in 1661 in an unassuming octavo volume with the title *Ars signorum*, to which was prefixed a letter from the newly restored Charles II, royal support having been petitioned by John Wilkins, John Wallis, and Seth Ward. Wilkins in the meantime solicited help elsewhere in elaborating his own scheme, published under the auspices of the Royal Society in 1668 in a lavishly produced folio volume entitled *An Essay towards a Real Character and a Philosophical Language*. Wilkins's *Epistle to the Reader* indicated that the work's origins lay in the assistance he had given to 'another person' in the framing of a 'real character', but this person remained unnamed. Contemporaries felt that Dalgarno's work had been outdone and overshadowed by this new scheme. However, Dalgarno's own autobiographical account (Christ Church MS 162; printed in Cram and Maat) reveals that he believed the two schemes to be radically different in nature, and that the logical excellence of his own had failed to be understood.

After the Restoration, Dalgarno was appointed master of Queen Elizabeth College, Guernsey, but by 1662 he was back in Oxford. In the meantime he had married a fellow Aberdonian, Margaret Johnston. The Guernsey and Oxford parish records show that he had nine children in the following years, not all of whom survived infancy. In 1670 Dalgarno undertook again the mastership of Queen Elizabeth College, but he resigned in 1672 on grounds of ill health. Over the intervening years the link with the island had been maintained; the poll-tax returns for the parish of St Mary Magdalen, Oxford, in 1667 reveal that the pupils at his school were for the most part from Guernsey (Cram, 814–17). In 1669 Dalgarno moved his school to the parish of St Mary the Virgin, relinquishing his lease on the university-owned Little Print House. In this conveyance he is for the first time styled MA of the University of Oxford, a degree for which no details have been traced.

Dalgarno remained intellectually active in the latter part of his life. In 1680 he published *Didascalocophus, or, The Deaf and Dumb Man's Tutor*, which is of particular interest for his situating of the language of the deaf in a general scheme of the theory of signs—or 'sematology' in Dalgarno's terms—and for an appendix which offers a pioneering treatise on phonotactics, the analysis of consonant clusters. In 1685 Dalgarno submitted a paper to the Oxford Philosophical Society concerning the implementation of a philosophical language; the minutes recorded that he had laid aside this study and was ready to hand on his papers on the subject to any worthy undertaker (Gunther, 4.133). Dalgarno died of fever on 28 August 1687, having made his will a few days earlier on 25 August. He was buried on 30 August in the parish of Mary Magdalen, Oxford, 'in the north side of the church' (Wood, *Ath. Oxon.*, 506).   DAVID CRAM

Sources BL, Sloane MS 4377, fols. 139–46 · University of Sheffield, Hartlib papers · Christ Church Oxf., MS 162 · D. F. Cram and J. Maat, *George Dalgarno on universal language: 'The art of signs', 'The deaf and dumb man's tutor', and the unpublished papers* (2001) · Wood, *Ath. Oxon.*, 1st edn · *The life and times of Anthony Wood*, ed. A. Clark, 5 vols., OHS, 19, 21, 26, 30, 40 (1891–1900) · P. J. Anderson and J. F. K. Johnstone, eds., *Fasti academiae Mariscallanae Aberdonensis: selections from the records of the Marischal College and University, MDXCIII–MDCCCLX*, 3 vols., New Spalding Club, 4, 18–19 (1889–98) · D. F. Cram, 'George Dalgarno and Guernsey', *Reports and Transactions*

[Société Guernesiaise], 22 (1986–90), 808–26 · R. Plot, *The natural history of Oxfordshire, being an essay toward the natural history of England* (1676) · J. Wallis, *A defence of the Royal Society and the Philosophical Transactions* (1670) · J. Wilkins, *An essay towards a real character and a philosophical language* (1668) · R. T. Gunther, *Early science in Oxford*, 4: *The Philosophical Society* (1925) · V. Salmon, 'The evolution of Dalgarno's Ars signorum', *Studies in honour of Margaret Schlauch*, ed. M. Brahmer and others (1966), 353–71 · *DNB* · Oxford City Archives, P5.9 · Bodl. Oxf., wills Oxon 92 · U. Oxf., archives, SEP/x/19

Archives Christ Church Oxf., treatises, MS 162 | BL, Sloane MS 4377, fols. 139–46 · University of Sheffield, Hartlib MSS

Wealth at death see will, Bodl. Oxf.

Dalgety, Frederick Gonnerman (1817–1894), wool merchant and sheep farmer, was born on 3 December 1817 in Canada, where his father was a lieutenant in the Irish fusiliers; he had at least two younger half-brothers. Nothing is known of his education or early career before his arrival in Australia at Sydney on 2 June 1834.

Early career Dalgety became a clerk in the merchant house of T. C. Breillat & Co., before moving to Melbourne in December 1842 as manager of the new office of Griffiths, Borrodaile & Co., a firm hitherto based in both Sydney and Launceston and which specialized in importing goods for 'squatters' and purchasing their goods for export. In 1845 Griffiths withdrew and set up a separate concern in Sydney; Dalgety became a partner in Dalgety, Borrodaile, and Gore, of Melbourne and Geelong. Problems arose when Borrodaile then withdrew and demanded repayment of his capital at a time of falling wool prices, when growers were in debt to the firm. John Gore, the London merchant on whom the firm relied, had second thoughts about providing capital for his son Harry's partnership, and he was restricting Dalgety's credit in London.

The firm narrowly escaped failure in 1848 as a result of the strict line that Dalgety took with his debtors, but he had suffered 'the greatest anxiety which I would not again undergo to secure a fortune' (Dalgety to John Gore, 7 Feb 1849, Dalgety archives, N8/19). It was clear that he needed better access to the financial resources of London, and a solution appeared in 1849 when John Gore proposed that they should form a partnership. Dalgety set out for London to complete the agreement, but Gore unfortunately died. Dalgety traded in London in association with Gore's sons, but by 1852 he was back in Melbourne with his finance still unresolved. He returned, however, to a very different situation: Victoria was experiencing a gold rush, and Melbourne was in a phase of explosive development. Dalgety's fortunes were to be transformed.

Initially Dalgety continued in his partnership with Harry Gore, whose brothers provided the crucial connection with London. Dalgety made perhaps £150,000 by 1855 from the firm, as well as a considerable profit from property he had purchased at Melbourne in 1846—he sold it in 1853, for building, at a profit of 4000 per cent. But his new wealth was little compensation for the discomforts of Melbourne. Life was 'infernally dull' in the absence of a 'smiling female face', and he could 'only hope my moral resolve will be sufficiently strong, to enable me to resist the temptation of taking one … on the doubtful capacity of housekeeper'; his will would, he felt, hold out 'for I have paid the penalty too frequently to incur the risk again' (Dalgety to Tobias, 25 June 1852, Dalgety archives, N8/20). His initial thoughts were to retire to England and give up business, for he was 'naturally of an excitable and anxious temperament' (Dalgety to F. and E. Gore, 1 Aug 1853, Dalgety archives, N8/20); however, a further bout of self-analysis led him to conclude that 'I am not cut out for a life of idleness or a life of gaiety' (Dalgety to J. Gore, 7 June 1853, Dalgety archives, N8/20). Moreover, as so often in his career, family responsibilities played their role, for he had two younger brothers 'to push forward in the world' (Dalgety to his doctor, 13 July 1852, Dalgety archives, N8/20). The impression is of a man who had acquired wealth through fortunate timing, but who lacked confidence and flexibility, preferring to keep to what he knew—commodity trade with settlers.

Partnership with Du Croz Continuation in business required a base in London, and Dalgety decided that the best resolution of his difficulties was to sever all ties with the Gores, to settle in London where he would run the business in person, and to find others to operate the business in the colonies. He formed a partnership with Frederick Du Croz (1821–1897), a merchant in Van Diemen's Land, to create Dalgety & Co., and they settled in London in 1854. The Geelong business was run by Charles Ibbotson, and in 1857 Dalgety returned to Australia to make James Blackwood the managing partner in Melbourne. The basic structure of the firm was set for the next twenty years, and Dalgety firmly held to the view that merchant firms should be based on close personal ties and family involvement, in order to create trust for the transaction of business over long distances.

In 1855, soon after Dalgety moved to London, he married Blanche Trosse Allen (1836–1883), the niece of his uncle's wife. Their first child was born in 1860, after his return from Australia in 1859, and Dalgety became impressed by the need to provide for a large and young family: Blanche died in 1883 in childbirth, and five sons and five daughters survived to adulthood. The firm prospered in the 1860s, opening further branches in Australia and New Zealand, and it moved away from its earlier role as a general merchant to specialize in selling wool on consignment and in lending to pastoralists. Dalgety was the largest importer of wool in London in the 1860s, at a time when about 80 per cent of the Australian wool clip was consigned for sale in London. The firm's capital grew from £75,000 in 1852 to £348,000 in 1861, of which Dalgety held £200,000; by 1879 the capital was £934,000, of which Dalgety held £300,000.

By the late 1870s Dalgety & Co. was starting to falter as its original partners became older, and Dalgety failed to adapt to the new circumstances of the wool trade. The capital of the firm had grown through retaining profits, which was no longer adequate by the mid-1870s to provide settlers with funds for fencing their properties and acquiring freeholds. Dalgety was facing increasing competition in London from colonial banks such as the Bank of New South Wales and from finance houses such as the Australian Mercantile Land and Finance Company. They had access to larger sums of money from their depositors and from the sale of debentures to *rentiers* in England and Scotland; and they were able to offer mortgages to settlers, and to move (in the contrary direction to Dalgety) from pastoral finance to handling consignments of wool. The next stage, towards the end of the nineteenth century, was to sell wool at auctions within Australia rather than in London. These changes posed a threat to Dalgety's continued prosperity.

Dalgety proved incapable of adapting to the new realities, being essentially a simple-minded colonial merchant who was not able to move from the world of visible trade in wool to more abstruse dealings in finance. In the early 1870s he came under attack from growers in the colonies, who suspected that they were being exploited by London merchants; above all he came into bitter conflict with Sir Daniel Cooper of the Bank of New South Wales, who could pose as the protector of the growers. Dalgety's loathing of this 'little Sydney blaguard [*sic*]' and his 'ignorant and vulgar aspersions' knew no bounds (Dalgety to C. Nichols, 10 Aug 1871, Dalgety archives, N39/42), and by 1873 he was 'really tired of occupying the position of a muzzled Badger placed under a Trough, for every Cur to snap at' (Dalgety to J. Blackwood, 17 April 1873, Dalgety archives, N39/42). The serious point behind Dalgety's bluster was that he was failing to adapt, for the increasing need for finance was making the firm more and more dependent on bankers for loans.

Although Dalgety admitted that 'we must be strong in capital' (Dalgety to Blackwood, 22 Dec 1875, Dalgety archives, N39/42), the problem was that the firm was—like all partnerships—susceptible to reduction of capital when partners opted to take their undistributed profits from the firm, or to retire. Dalgety was putting large sums into the acquisition of a landed estate and the construction of Lockerley Hall, at East Lytherly, Hampshire, from 1868, and he also made large purchases of sheep stations in New Zealand. His aim was not to achieve 'immediate and high returns' (Dalgety to C. Ibbotson, 26 Nov 1875, Dalgety archives, N39/42). Although he complained constantly at the low return and the difficulties of control, his strategy was clear from his will made in 1893: the New Zealand properties were to be held by his trustees 'with a view to their being ultimately taken over by my sons rather than to be sold' (will, proved 11 April 1894, London). His response to the attacks of Cooper, and to the changing world of the City, was to retreat into the world he knew best: sheep, which increasingly dominated his letters as he advised his station managers on minute details of breeding and washing wool. In the early 1870s Dalgety had about 100,000 sheep in New Zealand, and the stations offered a solution to his mounting concern over his young family.

'I have five young sons growing up', he remarked in 1879, 'and I should like in these difficult times for providing for sons, to form a future house for some of them in New Zealand' (Dalgety to W. Burnett, 22 May 1879, Dalgety archives, N8/21). None of his sons, he ruefully admitted, was capable of holding a job in the City; they were constantly failing their examinations at Cambridge and in the navy and army. The eldest son, Freddy, was kind and considerate, 'not quick or clever with books but fond of outdoor sports, a capital rider, good shot, plays cricket and lawn tennis well, and fond of animals' (Dalgety to A. Blackwood, 10 July 1884, Dalgety archives, N39/45). Charles, the only one who entered the firm, soon left and begged to be sent to New Zealand. 'He is gentlemanly and has no vices', commented his father, 'so I hope he will make a good colonist' (Dalgety to W. Burnett, 3 Sept 1891, Dalgety archives, N39/46). He was also plagued by his drunken half-brother, his incompetent brother-in-law, and his feckless cousin: New Zealand was the solution for all. 'Verily one's relatives are a source of humiliation and anxiety', he concluded (Dalgety to A. Blackwood, 20 Jan 1876, Dalgety archives, N39/43).

The Doxat years Perhaps it was this need to provide for his children which made Dalgety reluctant to change the basis of the firm into a merchant bank. However, it also reflected his own inadequate grasp of financial issues. He dealt with a single commodity on the frontier of the world economy, without connections in European financial centres. During the 1870s he retreated into his estate activities and left the active management of the firm to others. In 1878 Du Croz announced his wish to retire from the London house; Blackwood and Ibbotson's health was failing; and in 1879 Blackwood's son Arthur was taken into partnership in Melbourne, despite Dalgety's justified doubts about his abilities. Dalgety's response was to seek the injection of more capital by the traditional means of recruiting an additional partner. His choice was inspired, for it fell on E. T. Doxat, a partner in the wool brokers Edenborough and Doxat, valued at about £250,000. Edenborough, it was reported, was a 'half imbecile'; Doxat was 'very clever but not scrupulous, one must exercise utmost caution in dealing with him' (Kleinwort Information Book 1, fol. 88). Doxat was to rescue the firm from the increasingly inept Dalgety.

Doxat took over the running of the business with great dynamism and soon obtained ascendancy over the elderly partners. He was energetic, capable, indispensable, perceptive, and unscrupulous: Dalgety stood no chance. Doxat soon discovered that the firm was less secure than he had assumed and was furious that he had been misled into taking a drop in income. He was concerned from the start at the reliance on bankers and brokers for credit, which would be fatal if wool prices fell. Clearly the firm was not able to compete in the business of consigning wool when banks and finance houses were able to offer loans and mortgages to pastoralists. Access to cheap funds was crucial. A bitter battle started for control of the firm. Dalgety preferred to continue in the old way, simply replacing retiring partners. 'I cannot see why', he wrote to Arthur Blackwood, 'we could not work on as we are comfortably and independently, if we are only content to work within our capital, and our legitimate credit' (Dalgety to A. Blackwood, 23 Aug 1883, Dalgety archives, N39/45).

Accordingly, Dalgety made a further trip to Australia and New Zealand in 1881 in a search for new blood. He was repeating the strategy of the 1850s, which Doxat felt was no solution. No sooner had he arrived in the colonies than Doxat and the London partners put forward a plan they had vainly proposed before his departure: conversion to a joint-stock company. Dalgety was horrified and continued with his negotiations to bring in new partners; to his disgust, the London partners refused to agree. Dalgety returned home to do battle, urging that the firm was making an adequate profit, and that conversion would simply alienate its 'staunch and valuable connection' (Dalgety to A. Blackwood, 6 April 1882, Dalgety archives, N39/44).

Doxat, however, was perfectly correct to see that the capital of the firm was inadequate to compete with banks and finance houses. 'I cannot understand myself', Doxat informed Arthur Blackwood, 'how Dalgety who is so chary of bills and financing thinks the business is to be worked' (Doxat to A. Blackwood, 9 June 1881, Dalgety archives, N8/23). The matter was eventually resolved after the death of Dalgety's wife in 1883, which gave him 'sole anxious care' of a large and young family, and made him disinclined to face 'constant worrying and bullying' (Dalgety to C. Ibbotson, 6 Sept 1883, Dalgety archives, N39/45), and the conversion of the company by Arthur Blackwood. The partnership became a limited company in 1884. The business was now able to secure cheap funds through the issue of debentures, which amounted to £2m by 1888. The firm was also able to shift from consignments to London, which remained stable, to local sales in Australia, where Dalgety's was one of the three dominant firms before the First World War.

Dalgety himself retreated from the business and became increasingly involved in his activities as a major landowner in Hampshire and New Zealand; he also became deputy lieutenant for Hampshire. The net value of his estate in 1893 was £779,993; he also had £66,852 in investments other than land and the firm. These investments were misjudged, however, for the New Zealand estates were not a success and he had bought land in England shortly before the long-term fall in property prices. Dalgety died from cancer, at Lockerley Hall on 20 March 1894, and was buried at the church of St John the Evangelist, Lockerley, which he had rebuilt. His memorial window, appropriately enough, portrayed Christ the good shepherd, with a sheep across his shoulders.

MARTIN DAUNTON

Sources M. J. Daunton, 'Firm and family in the City of London in the nineteenth century: the case of F. G. Dalgety', *Historical Research*, 62 (1989), 154–77 · R. M. Hartwell, 'Dalgety, F. G.', *AusDB*, vol. 4 · A. McMurchy, 'F. G. Dalgety and the making of an Australian pastoral house', PhD diss. University of Queensland, 1984 [referred] · R. M. Hartwell, 'Dalgety and Co. Ltd: a history', Australian National University, Canberra, Archives of Business and Labour · *Appendix to the journals of the house of representatives of New Zealand* (1892), 1.B–20A · G. Davison, ed., *Melbourne on foot* (1980), 122–3 · L. G. D. Acland, *The early Canterbury runs* (1951) · Australian National University, Canberra, Archives of Business and Labour, Dalgety archives, deposit N8, N39 · 'Kleinwort information book 1, UK, 1675–1907', GL, MS 22,030, fol. 88 · d. cert. · *CGPLA Eng. & Wales* (1894)

Archives Australian National University, Canberra, Archives of Business and Labour, deposit N8, N39
Wealth at death £380,386 8s. 2d.: resworn probate, Aug 1894, *CGPLA Eng. & Wales* • £779,993—including New Zealand property: 1893, Australian National University, Archives of business and labour, Dalgety deposit, personal ledgers, N39/51

Dalgliesh, William (1733–1807), Church of Scotland minister and writer on theology, was born in Galloway. It is not certain who his parents were. He was educated at the University of Edinburgh and was ordained to the ministry of the Church of Scotland in Peebles in 1761, where he remained until his death. He married Jean Gibson (1748–1819) on 7 July 1773.

In 1776 Dalgliesh published anonymously *The True Sonship of Christ Investigated*, in which he argued that Christ, although he had always existed as God, only became the son of God at the moment of his incarnation, when he became fully man as well as fully God. The more orthodox position, that Christ was the eternal son of God, was argued in reply in several pamphlets, including two written by the Revd Adam Gib, a leading Secession minister, and Revd Michael Arthur, the Secession minister in Peebles. Dalgliesh wrote *The Self-Existence and Supreme Deity of Christ Defended* in 1777 in reply to Gib. Although he explicitly rejected Arianism, his opponents believed that his writings approached that heresy. Dalgliesh also published a four-volume collection of sermons (1799–1807), six single sermons, a study on the excellence of the British constitution (1793), and an account of his parish in Sir John Sinclair's *Statistical Account of Scotland*. He received the degree of DD from the University of Edinburgh in 1786.

In Peebles, Dalgliesh fought doggedly to ensure his clerical entitlement to pasture, and he also secured the right to build a new manse in 1770. He took great interest in the affairs of the community as well, however, overseeing the building of a new church building (St Andrew's, opened in 1784) to replace the old Cross Kirk, serving as chaplain to the Peeblesshire regiment of volunteers, and giving generously to charitable causes. Dalgliesh died at home at the manse, Peebles, on 20 September 1807; he was buried in Peebles four days later. He was survived by his wife, who died on 7 September 1819.

W. G. Blaikie, *rev.* Emma Vincent Macleod

Sources *Fasti Scot.*, new edn, 1.288 • C. B. Gunn, *The ministry of the presbytery of Peebles, AD 296–1910* (1910) • C. B. Gunn, *The book of the Cross Kirk, Peebles, AD 1690–1784: settled presbyterianism* (1914) • C. B. Gunn, *The book of the parish church of Peebles, AD 1784–1885: Presbyterianism* (1917) • *Caledonian Mercury* (28 Sept 1807) • S. Scott, *Peebles during the Napoleonic wars* (1980) • m. reg. Scot

Dalhousie. For this title name *see* Ramsay, William, first earl of Dalhousie (d. 1672); Ramsay, George, ninth earl of Dalhousie (1770–1838); Ramsay, Christian, countess of Dalhousie (1786–1839); Maule, Fox, second Baron Panmure and eleventh earl of Dalhousie (1801–1874); Ramsay, George, twelfth earl of Dalhousie (1806–1880); Ramsay, James Andrew Broun, first marquess of Dalhousie (1812–1860); Ramsay, John William Maule, thirteenth earl of Dalhousie (1847–1887) [*see under* Ramsay, George, twelfth earl of Dalhousie (1806–1880)].

Dalison, William (d. 1559), judge and law reporter, was the second son of William Dalison (d. 1546) of Laughton, Lincolnshire, and Anne, daughter of George Wastneys. Although he has been claimed as a member of Cambridge University, this is probably a result of confusion with the William Dalison who was at the King's Hall from 1532 to 1543. The future judge followed his father to Gray's Inn in 1534, and rose rapidly in the legal profession. He is said to have been called to the bar as early as 1537, and he became a reader in 1548. His second reading (on 32 Hen. VIII c. 33, concerning wrongful disseisins) was given as a serjeant-elect in 1552, when he was still probably under the age of forty. Dalison became a serjeant-at-law on 17 October 1552. He was to remember Gray's Inn in his will, with a bequest of £5 towards the repairs of the hall and another 20s. towards the commons.

Dalison married Elizabeth, daughter of Robert Dighton of Little Stourton, at an unknown date; they had four sons and five daughters. After practising as a serjeant for a mere three years, during which time he served as member of parliament for Lincolnshire, he was appointed one of the justices of the queen's bench on 2 November 1555. On the death of Mary I he was reappointed, but died after serving only one term into the new reign. During his last five years he sat as an assize judge on the northern circuit, and in that capacity served also as second justice of the county palatine of Lancaster. He was a member of Serjeants' Inn, Chancery Lane, to which he bequeathed 40s. towards commons and repairs.

Dalison was a law reporter of some importance, though his best work remains unpublished. Eleven cases attributed to 'Justice Dalison', with others taken from Bendlowes's reports, were printed in appendices to Ashe's *Epieikeia* (1609) and to the 1633 edition of Keilwey. A more substantial volume appeared in 1689, again also containing reports from Bendlowes, as *Les reports des divers special cases … colliegees par Gulielme Dalison*. Since most of the contents of both editions date from after the judge's death, these attributions must be generally false, though it seems probable that the earlier cases are by Dalison. In the manuscripts, as in the printed editions, the texts begin in 1546 but are often mixed with reports by Richard *Harpur which extend into the 1570s, and as a result the authorship of the cases between 1546 and 1558 has not yet been precisely established. The best of the manuscripts associated with Dalison (BL, Harley MS 5141) was clearly written by a serjeant or judge of the early 1550s, a fact which eliminates Harpur, and is doubtless correctly attributed. It includes the largest surviving collection of cases argued at closed sessions in Serjeants' Inn, several of which are landmarks in the history of criminal law. Dalison left all his books, including 'my bookes of the lawes of this realme' to his eldest son, William, a member of Gray's Inn, but only one of them (a medieval register of writs) has been traced.

Dalison died on 18 January 1559. He had settled in the city of Lincoln, and until the civil war there was a stone altar tomb in Lincoln Cathedral, with a brass figure, following his testamentary instructions for a tomb with 'my pycture with my justice robeis and coyf even as I sytt in jugement'. The executors of his will renounced, and the administration was committed to his widow, Elizabeth.

J. H. BAKER

Sources HoP, Commons, 1509–58, 2.5–6 · L. W. Abbott, *Law reporting in England, 1485–1585* (1973), 113–41 · Sainty, *Judges*, 29 · will, PRO, PROB 11/42B, sig. 9 · PRO, C 142/118/94 · F. Peck, ed., *Desiderata curiosa*, new edn, 2 vols. in 1 (1779), 297 · BL, Loan MS 38, fol. 112 [drawing of monument and inscription] · J. H. Baker and J. S. Ringrose, *A catalogue of English legal manuscripts in Cambridge University Library* (1996), 310
Archives CKS, family and personal papers
Likenesses brass effigy on monument, c.1559, BL, Dugdale, Loan MS 38, fol. 112; repro. in Abbott, *Law reporting*

Dalkeith. For this title name *see* Townshend, Caroline, *suo jure* Baroness Greenwich [Caroline Scott, countess of Dalkeith] (1717–1794).

Dall, Nicholas Thomas (d. **1776**), decorative artist and scene-painter, was of Scandinavian origin. Nothing is known of his parentage or early life; however, he probably studied in Bologna in the 1740s under one of the masters of architectural capriccios for which the city was renowned. While there he may have received the commission from Thomas Anson for a number of capriccios to adorn the drawing room of Shugborough Hall, Staffordshire, which were in place by 1748. Philip Yorke, later second earl of Hardwicke, who visited the house in August that year, saw 'a fine room … with large pictures of Architecture, Painted at Bologna' (Croft-Murray, 24). Painted in distemper on canvas, these large paintings of ruins (four large oblongs, two upright panels, and two overdoors) are methodologically and stylistically in keeping with Bolognese works of the 1720s.

It is likely that Dall came to England at Anson's behest; a signed drawing in the British Museum testifies that he was certainly in London by November 1756. He continued to enjoy the patronage of the Anson family as witnesses a landscape shown at the Royal Academy in 1773, a view of Great Haywood, Staffordshire, belonging to Mrs Hannah Anson. From 1757 until his death Dall was a scene-painter at Covent Garden; the first payment was made to him on 16 September of that year for a salary of £1 10s. a week. His salary of 12s. a day (£100 a year) was stopped in February 1760, as he was making scenes for oratorios, and in December of that year he received an additional payment 'for a Model & Making a Crown Intended for the King's Box' (Rosenfeld and Croft-Murray, 49). His salary continued to rise, and for the season of 1773–4 he received £250 per annum. The scenery he painted and productions on which he worked after 1768 are fairly well documented: a prompt book of *Measure for Measure* (New York Public Library) lists 'Dall's Hall' and 'Dall's Town' as stock pieces (ibid., 50) and the productions for which he painted specific scenery included *Rape of Prosperine*, *Cymbeline*, and *Sylphs*. In 1771–2, with Giovanni Battista Cipriani and John Inigo Richards (with whom he had worked at Covent Garden from 1765, and who succeeded him as principal scene-painter), he painted scenery for Dr Arne's *Fairy Prince with the Installation of the Knights of the Garter*. In the following year Dall also produced scenery for the private theatres of William Hanbury at Kelmarsh, Northamptonshire, and Tate Wilkinson at Hull.

Although he worked principally as a scene-painter, Dall continued as a decorative painter: in the library at Harewood House, Yorkshire (designed by Robert Adam for Edwin Lascelles) he painted four inset landscape paintings; and at Moor Park, Hertfordshire, where he was paid £18 18s. in 1769 for 'repainting part of a ceiling' (Croft-Murray, 197). He exhibited at the Society of Artists between 1761 and 1770 and at the Royal Academy from the year of his election as ARA in 1771 to 1776, giving his address as Great Newport Street, London. He showed landscapes and views of ruins, often of Yorkshire where he evidently continued to enjoy patronage; for example, in 1774 he exhibited four landscapes including a view of Harewood Castle belonging to Edwin Lascelles. Title and dedication cartouches depicting Fountains Abbey and Middleham Castle by Dall ornament a map of Yorkshire produced by Thomas Jeffrys in 1772.

Dall died intestate at his home in Great Newport Street, London, on 10 December 1776 but his estate was granted to his widow, Ann, who supplied the theatre as a linen draper. A benefit held for her at Covent Garden on 3 May 1777 raised just over £91. Their daughter made her début as a singer at Covent Garden in February 1790. There are two drawings by Dall in the British Museum and two further works are in the Tate collection.

DEBORAH GRAHAM-VERNON

Sources E. Croft-Murray, *Decorative painting in England, 1537–1837*, 2 (1970) · S. Rosenfeld and E. Croft-Murray, 'A checklist of scene painters working in Great Britain and Ireland in the 18th century [pt 2]', *Theatre Notebook*, 19 (1964–5), 49–64 · Graves, *RA exhibitors* · Waterhouse, *18c painters*

Dallam, George (d. **1684**), organ builder, was probably born in Brittany, a son of Robert *Dallam (c.1602–1665), whom he may have accompanied to England in 1660. His mother was possibly named Isabella Turpin. In a letter to New College, Oxford, Robert Dallam refers to his sons George and Ralph *Dallam (d. 1673) in connection with work at St George's Chapel, Windsor. During the 1660s George Dallam lived in London in the parish of St Andrew by the Wardrobe, but by 1670 he was living with his wife, Jane, in Bradshawe's Rents, Porpool (Purple) Lane, Hatton Garden. Two children, Elizabeth and Robert, were baptized in St Andrew's, Holborn, on 26 May 1670 and 12 May 1672 respectively. In 1672 Playford referred to him as 'that excellent organ-maker [dwelling] now in Purple Lane, next door to the Crooked Billet, where such as desire to have new organs, or old mended, be well accomodated'.

Dallam built organs for the cathedrals of Durham (1662) and Norwich (1664) and for Dulwich College (1669). He was among the last English organ builders to continue the pre-Commonwealth style of instrument (one with a tonal structure of octaves and fifths, and without pedals, reeds, or mixtures), which by the end of his life was being eclipsed by the new styles of Bernard Smith and Renatus Harris. Dallam died in December 1684. After proving his will, his wife continued to administer the business until

1694, collecting quarterly tuning fees from St Martin-in-the-Fields and overseeing the completion of work on the chaire organ at Hereford Cathedral (1686).

CHRISTOPHER KENT

Sources B. Matthews, 'The Dallams and the Harrises', *Journal of the British Institute of Organ Studies*, 8 (1984), 59–68 · B. B. Edmonds, 'The Dallam family', *Journal of the British Institute of Organ Studies*, 3 (1979), 137–9 · M. Cocheril, 'The Dallams in Brittany', *Journal of the British Institute of Organ Studies*, 6 (1982), 63–77 · D. E. Dallam, *The Dallam family* (1929)

Dallam, Ralph (d. **1673**), organ builder, was probably born in Brittany, one of the sons of Robert *Dallam (c.1602–1665). His mother was possibly Isabella Turpin. He may have travelled to England with his father in 1660, since in a letter to New College, Oxford, Robert Dallam refers to his sons George *Dallam and Ralph in connection with work at St George's Chapel, Windsor. Ralph completed his father's instrument for New College, Oxford (1665), and built new organs at Norton by Galby, Leicestershire (1664), St Augustine's, Hackney (1665), the case of which was moved to East Claydon, and Lyme Regis. His organs followed the pre-Commonwealth style established by his father. His larger instruments were double organs of two manuals with flue pipes of metal and wood, without pedals or reeds. Their tonal structures comprised diapason choruses of octaves and fifths without mixtures.

In February 1672 Dallam began making an organ at St Alfege, Greenwich, but he was fatally wounded when hit by a piece of falling masonry there, and died in London in 1673. He was buried at the church on 8 August 1673. An epitaph was erected by his partner, James White, described in Dallam's will of 2 August (from the parish of St Katharine Coleman) as a citizen and virginal maker in London. White also completed the organ.

CHRISTOPHER KENT

Sources B. Matthews, 'The Dallams and the Harrises', *Journal of the British Institute of Organ Studies*, 8 (1984), 59–68 · B. B. Edmonds, 'The Dallam family', *Journal of the British Institute of Organ Studies*, 3 (1979), 137–9 · M. Cocheril, 'The Dallams in Brittany', *Journal of the British Institute of Organ Studies*, 6 (1982), 63–77 · D. E. Dallam, *The Dallam family* (1929) · BL, Lansdowne MS 938

Dallam, Robert (c.**1602–1665**), organ builder, was probably born in London, one of the six children of Thomas *Dallam (bap. 1575, d. in or after 1630). He had completed an apprenticeship as a member of the Blacksmiths' Company by about 1623. Some time during the 1620s he married his first wife, whose name is unknown, and travelled in France: their son Thomas was born in Brittany about 1630. After working with his father at Bristol Cathedral in 1630, over the next decade Dallam fulfilled an unbroken succession of independent commissions, including Magdalen College, Oxford (1631, main case now at Tewkesbury Abbey), York Minster (1634), St John's College, Cambridge (1635–6), repairs to Archbishop Laud's organ at Lambeth (paid on 12 November 1635), Jesus College, Cambridge (1635), Lichfield Cathedral (1636), Queen Henrietta Maria's private chapel at Somerset House (1640), and Gloucester Cathedral (1640–41). The accounts of the construction of his instrument of two manuals and fourteen stops for

York Minster are unusually detailed; the work cost a total of £610, with £307 being for the organ and the remainder for its case and gallery. His English organs follow the style established by his father: instruments (without pedals) of one or two manuals (double organs) with flue pipes of metal and wood. The tonal structure comprised a diapason chorus sounding in octaves and fifths without mixtures or reeds.

In 1643 Dallam, a Catholic recusant, left for Brittany with his family. His first wife died that year, and it is not clear whether Dallam's sons Ralph *Dallam (d. 1673) and George *Dallam (d. 1684) were from this marriage or from his second, to Isabella Turpin. Robert became organist of Quimper Cathedral in 1646 and built three instruments there between 1643 and 1648 at a cost of £5300. Before his return to England at the Restoration he built organs in St Jean-du-Doigt (1652), Plestin-les-Grèves (1653), Brélevenz, near Lannion (1654), Notre Dame, Lesneven (1654), St Houardon, Landernau (repairs, 1656), and Notre Dame du Mûr, Morlaix (1656). After completing work at Lesneven and St Pol in January and May 1660 he returned to England by the autumn to sign a contract for an organ at St George's Chapel, Windsor.

Dallam's last work was for New College, Oxford, where, after re-erecting his two-manual instrument of 1631 (moved to Hampton Court between 1654 and 1660), he proposed a new organ of two manuals and twenty-four stops in the French style with mixtures, reeds, and mutations. However, he was prevailed upon to continue the native pre-Commonwealth style. While completing this organ he died on 31 May 1665, aged sixty-three or in his sixty-third year, and was buried outside the north-west door of the chapel. His tombstone, engraved in Latin (with the family arms, ermine, two flanches, each charged with a doe passant), celebrated his enrichment of 'numerous districts in Europe by means of the art in which he peculiarly excelled'.

Dallam's son Thomas (c.1630–1720), known as the 'Sieur de la Tour', worked extensively in Brittany as an organ builder. Thomas's two sons, Toussaint (b. c.1659) and Mark Anthony (1673–1730), worked in both Brittany and England, particularly the latter, who died in York after working at Leicester (1716), New College, Oxford (1714), Prestbury (1723), Ripon (1719), and at Southwell Minster and Whitchurch (1730).

CHRISTOPHER KENT

Sources B. Matthews, 'The Dallams and the Harrises', *Journal of the British Institute of Organ Studies*, 8 (1984), 59–68 · M. Cocheril, 'The Dallams in Brittany', *Journal of the British Institute of Organ Studies*, 6 (1982), 63–77 · M. Sayer, 'Robert Dallam's organ in York Minster, 1634', *Journal of the British Institute of Organ Studies*, 1 (1977), 60–68 · J. Harper, 'The Dallam organ in Magdalen College, Oxford: a new account of the Milton organ', *Journal of the British Institute of Organ Studies*, 9 (1985), 51–65 · gravestone, New College, Oxford

Dallam, Thomas (bap. **1575**, d. in or after **1630**), organ builder and diarist, was baptized at Flixton, Lancashire, on 1 May 1575, probably the son of Thomas Dalham, who was an itinerant blacksmith but who was reputedly from an old and socially elevated Catholic family that seems to have had two branches in north-west England, one from the village of Dallam near Warrington, Lancashire, and the other from Haverbrack Hall, near Kendal. Between about 1589 and about 1596 he served an apprenticeship in organ building under the aegis of the Blacksmiths' Company of London. He then became a liveryman.

Dallam's first recorded work, in collaboration with Randolph Bull, was a commission from Queen Elizabeth to make and deliver a mechanical organ and clock to the sultan of Turkey in Constantinople. The party which left London on 9 February 1599 included Michael Watson, Dallam's joiner, and his friend Ned Hale. For the fourteen months they were away Dallam kept a diary which, although it at times expresses disgust at the 'rude and barbarus doged Turks' (Dallam, 39), acknowledges the warm welcome the travellers received in many quarters, displays a lively curiosity about unfamiliar sights and customs, and provides evidence of the reactions of a non-seafaring Englishman to Mediterranean travel at this period. He was impressed by the buildings, trees, and rich clothing, and on visiting 'som monimentes in Troy' (ibid., 47) broke off a piece of a white marble pillar and took it away with him. Once at his destination, his lengthy demonstration of the workings of the clock and organ earned him forty-five gold pieces and much respect; he was even granted a surreptitious (and dangerous) view of the grand signor's concubines. Fearing that he would be prevented from leaving, he took advantage of an illness to return home covertly, and arrived back in London in April 1600.

Unmarried at the time of his voyage—he wrote that he lied about this, inventing a wife and children in an effort to evade persuasion to stay in Turkey—Dallam married soon after his return; his wife's name is unknown. They had four sons, of whom Robert *Dallam became an organ builder, and two daughters, including Katherine, who married Thomas Harris or Harrison and became the mother of Renatus *Harris. Robert's sons George *Dallam and Ralph *Dallam also became organ builders.

Between 22 June 1605 and 7 August 1606 Dallam built an organ for King's College chapel, Cambridge, at a cost of £371 17s. 1d., although his first name does not appear in the accounts. In the years 1607 to 1609 he tuned and repaired instruments for Robert Cecil, earl of Salisbury, and built a new organ for Norwich Cathedral. This instrument was built partly in London, then shipped along the coast to Norfolk and ferried to a wharf behind the cathedral. Extensive extant details of the project include the procurements of materials and payments to workers and artisans. Work at St George's Chapel, Windsor, in 1609 comprised repairs and alterations to enable the choir organ to be played from its own keyboard in the back of its case. The instrument built for Bishop Henry Parry and Dean Arthur Lake at Worcester Cathedral in 1613 is described by Thomas Habington (1560–1647) as 'a most fair and excellent organ, adorned with imperial crowns, red roses, including the white fleur-de-lys, pomegranates, being all royal badges' (Habington). An inscription commemorated both the generosity of the bishop and dean and the 'meditation and mediation' of the organist,

Thomas Tomkins. Exact tonal details of this organ are contained in a letter of prebendary Nathaniel Tomkins, written on 22 May 1665 after repairs. A double organ of identical specification was built for St John's College, Oxford, and similar instruments were constructed for Eton College (1613–14) and the Scottish Chapel Royal (1616), the latter within a case by Inigo Jones and at a cost of £300.

On 29 September 1626 Dallam was appointed a steward for the annual feast of lord mayor's day by the court of the Blacksmiths' Company, but he was fined £10 on 12 October for refusing the office, probably on account of his preoccupation with repairs to his instrument at Norwich Cathedral. A year later he appeared in person, requesting exemption from the stewardship, and agreed to pay his fine in instalments so as to retain his place in the livery. In his last commission for making 'the greate Double Organ and Cheir Organ' (Freeman, 66) for Bristol Cathedral in 1630 he was assisted by his son Robert and paid £258 2s. 7d.

The date and place of Dallam's death are unknown. His achievement was the consolidation of the two-manual 'double organ' with twelve to fourteen flue stops (without reeds, mixtures, or pedals) as the norm for English cathedrals and for larger collegiate churches during the pre-civil war period.   CHRISTOPHER KENT

Sources G. Sumner, 'The origins of the Dallams in Lancashire', *Journal of the British Institute of Organ Studies*, 8 (1984), 51–7 · B. Matthews, 'The Dallams and the Harrises', *Journal of the British Institute of Organ Studies*, 8 (1984), 59–68 · B. Matthews, 'Thomas Dallam at Norwich Cathedral', *Journal of the British Institute of Organ Studies*, 10 (1986), 102–11 · B. Edmonds, 'The chayre organ, an episode', *Journal of the British Institute of Organ Studies*, 4 (1980), 19–34 · S. Mayes, *An organ for the sultan* (1956) · D. Stevens, *Thomas Tomkins: three hitherto unpublished voluntaries* (1959) [preface to] · T. Dallam, 'The diary of Master Thomas Dallam, 1599–1600', *Early voyages and travels in the Levant*, ed. J. T. Bent, Hakluyt Society, 87 (1893), 1–98 · T. Habington, *A survey of Worcestershire*, ed. J. Amphlett, 2 vols., Worcestershire Historical Society (1895–9) · A. Freeman, 'The organs of Bristol Cathedral', *The Organ*, 2 (1922–3), 66

Dallán Forgaill [Dallan] (*fl.* **597**), poet, mourned the death of St Columba (Colum Cille), founder of the monastic community of Iona, in one of the earliest surviving poems in Irish, the *Amra Choluim Chille* ('The wonders of Colum Cille'). The patron for whom the poem was composed was probably Áed mac Ainmuirech, high-king of Ireland and a cousin of Columba. Dallán Forgaill means 'blind one of superior testimony' (blind poets have not been uncommon in Ireland, as elsewhere); this is most unlikely to have been his original name, but any reliable information about either his name or his family background does not exist. The sources for the poet's career are twofold: first, the poem itself; second, eleventh- or twelfth-century texts, principally the preface added in 1007–8 to a reissue of the poem on behalf of the high-king Máel Sechnaill mac Domnaill. At the time, the long-enduring power of the Uí Néill was threatened by the upstart Brian Bóruma, king of Munster, who now claimed to be king of Ireland. Máel Sechnaill required his scholars to publicize the claims of the Uí Néill to power; one such claim was the sanctity of their principal saint, Columba. Another was that the privileged status of the poets stemmed from an agreement said to have been brokered by Columba between Dallán and the principal kings of the northern half of Ireland: poets owed their rank and their allegiance to the Uí Néill and their northern allies, not to any king of Munster; and since poets were the major publicists of eleventh-century Ireland, Máel Sechnaill could hope for serious assistance from this association. The immediate context of the reissue of the *Amra* with its accompanying prefatory and glossarial matter was probably another act of renewal, in 1007, of a major assembly, with attendant horse-races and other entertainments, the fair of Tailtiu; at this assembly, Ferdomnach, a scholar associated with the reissue, was installed as 'heir of Colum Cille', namely abbot of Kells, a monastery closely associated since its foundation with Máel Sechnaill's ancestors.

According to the preface, Dallán Forgaill came from a minor people, the Masraige of Mag Slecht (in what is now co. Cavan). This is contradicted by the genealogies of the saints, of similar date, which attribute Dallán to the branch of the Airgialla situated in the Foyle basin and thus neighbours of Columba's kindred, Cenél Conaill. The genealogies, however, show evident signs of uncertainty as to where they should place someone whose saintly status was, in any case, of recent date (perhaps a result of the publicity given to the *Amra* in 1007–8). There is no way of knowing whether the scholars who came to Máel Sechnaill's aid in 1007 had any reliable information about Dallán. Admittedly the reference to the Masraige of Mag Slecht looks specific enough, but the effect was to associate Dallán with Bréifne, where the Uí Ruairc dynasty was increasing in power.

More reliable evidence is offered by the poem itself—not that it provides any biographical detail, but it does at least indicate what sort of poet he was. The poem is emphatically learned: it employs a vocabulary far removed from that of ordinary speech, including a deliberately extensive Latin element, and it celebrates the learning as well as the asceticism of the saint. The text added in 1007 says that Dallán Forgaill was a leading scholar in Latin scriptural learning as well as chief poet, enjoying a rank that would entitle him to celebrate the greatest men of his time. These assertions may stem from an interpretation of the poem itself, including its reference to Áed mac Ainmuirech: although the glosses make serious mistakes in the interpretation of the text, they testify to serious study of a poem that they admit to be exceptionally difficult. As the eleventh-century scholars recognized, the poem exhibits a rapprochement between vernacular and Latin scriptural learning; whether that was achieved through the expertise of Dallán himself or through his collaboration with others is unknown.

T. M. CHARLES-EDWARDS

Sources W. Stokes, ed. and trans., 'The Bodleian *Amra Choluimb Chille*', *Revue Celtique*, 20 (1899), 31–55, 132–83, 248–87, 400–37 · *Amra Choluimb Chille, Iona: the earliest poetry of a Celtic monastery*, ed. T. O. Clancy and G. Márkus (1995), 96–128 · *Ann. Ulster* · P. Ó Riain, ed., *Corpus genealogiarum sanctorum Hiberniae* (Dublin, 1985), p. 64, no. 426; p. 77, no. 633 · M. A. O'Brien, ed., *Corpus genealogiarum Hiberniae* (Dublin, 1962), 407 · *Félire Óengusso Céli Dé / The martyrology of Oengus the Culdee*, ed. and trans. W. Stokes, HBS, 29 (1905) · D. Ó hÓgáin, *Myth, legend and romance: an encyclopaedia of the Irish folk tradition* (1990), 148–50 · M. Herbert, 'The preface to *Amra Coluim Cille*', *Sages, saints and storytellers: Celtic studies in honour of Professor James Carney*, ed. D. Ó. Corráin and others (1989), 67–75

Dallas, Alexander Robert Charles (1791–1869), Church of England clergyman, was born on 29 March 1791 at Colchester, the penultimate of the seven children of Robert Charles *Dallas (1754–1824), barrister and man of letters. His mother, Sarah, was the daughter of Benjamin Harding of Hacton House, near Hornchurch, Essex. Of Scottish origin, the elder Dallas had lived in Jamaica but returned to England because of his opposition to slavery, abandoning an estate that had been built up by his wealthy physician father. The family was a cultivated one in literature and music, and Alexander was educated informally within the family circle until at the age of eleven he was sent to a school in Kennington, London, for three years. A handsome, intelligent, sturdily built boy, from an early age he showed considerable strength of character. His way was helped by his family's social position: two great-uncles were generals, an uncle was the American secretary of the Treasury, a cousin was the American ambassador to the British court, and another was Lord Byron, the poet. (Shortly after the death of his father in 1824 Dallas was to publish correspondence and recollections of Byron, which brought him literary notoriety.)

Through his father's influence Dallas was appointed a clerk in the Treasury in 1805, and then gained a commission as deputy assistant commissary-general with the British force that was sent to garrison Cadiz in 1810. He spent two years there, developing the scrupulous concern for detail that was to characterize his later work in the Church of England and his management of the Irish Church Missions to the Roman Catholics (ICM). He took part in several engagements in the Peninsular War (1812–13), and in 1815 he was at Quatre Bras and was with the 3rd division at Waterloo. By the end of the Napoleonic conflicts he was a socially popular figure in London, Le Havre, and Paris, composing literary and musical pieces dealing with the Peninsular campaign. On 4 May 1818 he married at Morden, Surrey, Mary Anne Edge (*d.* 1847), the widow of a solicitor and daughter of Robert Ferguson. She brought a considerable dowry to the marriage, which produced four sons and two daughters.

Dallas attempted to study law, then abruptly moved to Oxford in 1819 to study divinity as a gentleman commoner of Worcester College. There he encountered evangelicalism, and to escape the worldly life of the university community he left without taking a degree. He was ordained in 1821 and became curate of Radley, and was then successively curate at Highclere (1821–4), Wooburn, and Burford (the latter two in 1824–7), and was presented with the living of Yardley in 1827. He had met Charles Sumner, the strongly evangelical bishop of Winchester and brother of the archbishop of Canterbury, and in 1828 Sumner obtained for Dallas the remunerative rectory of Wonston, only 7 miles from Winchester. He remained there as a zealous evangelical clergyman until his death. He acted as

Alexander Robert Charles Dallas (1791–1869), by Richard James Lane (after Louisa Brock, 1852)

chaplain to the bishop of Winchester, and the archbishop of Canterbury conferred on him the degree of master of arts.

Never was a parish more dutifully attended to pastorally than Wonston during the incumbency of Dallas. It was then that he used his commissariat skills to compile a massive statistical survey of his parish to aid in his control of every aspect of parish life. His pastoral zeal was tempered by a grievous domestic crisis which occupied him from 1841 until the death of his wife. His marriage was not a happy one, with many pecuniary embarrassments, which caused him much stress, contributing to a nervous breakdown shortly before his wife's death at Boulogne in 1847.

During these years of trial, Dallas developed a passionate interest in opposing the Tractarian movement, and in affairs in Ireland, which he was able to indulge thanks to the support of Bishop Sumner. He also immersed himself in the millenarian speculations which fascinated many evangelical leaders. From 1839 he made visits to Dublin on behalf of the Jews' Society, and became an important speaker at evangelical missionary meetings.

As a boy Dallas had been acquainted with the horrors associated with the Wexford rising in 1798, and a sermon he preached on behalf of the starving Irish during the famine of 1822, as well as his interest in the 1834 relief work of the evangelical archbishop of Tuam, Power le Poer Trench, showed that his concern for Ireland was of long standing. He had no difficulty in agreeing with those evangelical leaders who chose to view the Tractarians as agents of the papacy. By 1845 he had identified himself

with the wealthy and influential protestant zealots who wanted to launch a missionary counter-offensive against the papacy in Ireland, and he offered to organize such a campaign.

Dallas began by using the penny post to deluge 'respectable' Roman Catholics in Ireland with an evangelical pamphlet, *The Voice of Heaven to Ireland*, in 1846. He then began to organize mission stations from where agents of the ICM could move out among the people in a major proselytizing movement. The first of these stations was at Castelkerke, and this brought upon the ICM agents the wrath of the Roman Catholic archbishop of Tuam, John MacHale. Charges of bribery by the agents were made, confrontations took place, and this resulted in more protestant financial aid being raised in places like Exeter Hall in London. For over a decade, after the end of the famine, the ICM enjoyed considerable success, making thousands of converts, most of whom were forced to migrate in the face of sectarian pressure. Then, from about 1867, the work of the ICM faltered, as Dallas's health declined. He died at 4 Church Terrace, Lee, Kent, on 12 December 1869, aged seventy-eight, and was buried at Wonston on the 17th. By the time of Dallas's death the ICM had erected twenty-one churches, forty-nine schoolhouses, twelve parsonages, and four orphanages. Dallas was strongly supported in his work by his passionately evangelical second wife, Ann Biscoe Tyndale (*d.* 1877), whom he married on 18 December 1849. The ICM continues to maintain a nominal existence in Ireland.   DESMOND BOWEN

Sources A. R. C. Dallas, *Story of the Irish Church Missions*, pt 1 (1867) · [A. B. Dallas], *Incidents in the life and ministry of the Rev. Alexander R. C. Dallas, A. M., by his widow* (1871) · *Correspondence of Lord Byron with a friend, including his letters to his mother, written ... in 1809, 1810 and 1811*, ed. A. R. C. Dallas, 3 vols. (1825) · A. R. C. Dallas, *Ministerial responsibility* (1837) · A. R. C. Dallas, *Pastoral superintendence: its motive, its detail and its support* (1841) · A. R. C. Dallas, *Pastor's assistant: intended to facilitate the discharge of the pastoral office in the Church of England*, 3 vols. (1842) · A. R. C. Dallas, *Real Romanism as stated in the creed of Pope Pius IV* (1845) · A. R. C. Dallas, *Present spiritual efforts for Ireland: a letter to a friend in Dublin on some recent remarks with reference to the special fund for the spiritual exigencies of Ireland* (1847) · A. R. C. Dallas, *Castelkerke* (1849) · A. R. C. Dallas, *Proselytism in Ireland: the Catholic Defence Association against the Irish Church Missions on the charge of bribery and intimidation* (1852) · D. Bowen, *Souperism: myth or reality? A study of Catholics and Protestants during the great Irish famine* (1970) · D. Bowen, 'Alexander R. C. Dallas: the warrior saint', *The view from the pulpit: Victorian ministers and society*, ed. P. T. Phillips (1978), 17–44 · *CGPLA Eng. & Wales* (1870)
Archives Irish Church Missions Library, London · Wonston, Hampshire
Likenesses R. J. Lane, drawing on stone, 1835 · R. J. Lane, lithograph (after L. Brock, 1852), NPG [*see illus.*] · W. H. Mote, portrait
Wealth at death under £4000: probate, 27 Jan 1870, *CGPLA Eng. & Wales*

Dallas, Elmslie William (1809–1879), painter and mathematician, the second son of William Dallas and his wife, Sarah Day, and a descendant of Alexander Dallas of Cantray, Inverness-shire was born in London on 27 June 1809. He became a student at the Royal Academy Schools in 1831, and in 1834 won a gold medal and a travelling studentship. His first pictures, studies of a Roman convent, were hung at the academy in 1838. In 1840 he assisted

L. Grüner in decorating the garden pavilion at Buckingham Palace, with a series of views of Melrose, Abbotsford, Loch Awe, Aros Castle, and Lake Windermere, to illustrate the writings of Sir Walter Scott. From 1841 to 1858 he exhibited at the Royal Scottish Academy. As his works were well received in Edinburgh, he chose to settle there permanently and moved to the city in 1842. He principally painted highly studied interiors and medieval subjects, though several landscapes, notably of the Roman campagna, were also successful. He also practised photography. For some years he was a teacher in the Edinburgh School of Design, retiring in 1858 when the school merged with the science and art department. In 1855 he published *The Elements of Plain Practical Geometry*, which was highly commended by the mathematician Professor Philip Kelland in his report to the board of trustees for manufactures, though it was regarded as too elaborate to be used in the design schools. In 1851 Dallas was elected a fellow of the Royal Society of Edinburgh, to whom he presented papers on the structure of the algae and of diatomacea, on crystallogenesis, and on the optical mathematics of lenses. On 16 June 1859 he married Jane Fordyce Rose (*b.* 1830/31), daughter of James Rose, writer to the signet, of Dean Bank, Edinburgh. Elmslie William Dallas died in Edinburgh on 26 January 1879; he was survived by his wife.   James Dallas, *rev.* Suzanne Fagence Cooper

Sources *Proceedings of the Royal Society of Edinburgh*, 10 (1878–80), 340 · Graves, *Brit. Inst.* · J. Johnson, ed., *Works exhibited at the Royal Society of British Artists, 1824–1893, and the New English Art Club, 1888–1917*, 2 vols. (1975) · J. Halsby and P. Harris, *The dictionary of Scottish painters, 1600–1960* (1990), 44 · m. cert., Scotland · *CCI* (1879)
Wealth at death £766 12s. 4d.: confirmation, 6 May 1879, *CCI*

Dallas, Eneas Sweetland (1828–1879), journalist and author, elder son of John Dallas of Jamaica, a physician and planter of Scottish parentage, and his wife, Elizabeth Baillie, daughter of the Revd Angus McIntosh of Tain, and sister of the Revd Caldor McIntosh, was born in Jamaica. He was brought to England at the age of four, and educated at Edinburgh University, where he studied philosophy under Sir William Hamilton, and acquired the habit of applying notions derived from eclectic psychology to the analysis of aesthetic effects in poetry, rhetoric, and the fine arts. His first publication on this was *Poetics: an Essay on Poetry* (1852), published when he had taken up residence in London. In December 1853 he married, according to Scottish law, Miss Isabella *Glyn (1823–1889), widow of Edward Wills, an actress well known for her Shakespearian readings; on 12 July 1855 he was again married to her at St George's, Hanover Square, London. They separated not long after, and his wife divorced him on 10 May 1874. He was considered handsome and charming and his conversation bright and courteous.

Dallas made his career mainly in anonymous journalism. He first made his mark in London by sending an article to *The Times*, a critique which by its vigour and profundity secured immediate attention. From about 1855, for many years Dallas was on John T. Delane's staff. He wrote, in careful, graceful English, obituaries—including those of Palmerston, Aberdeen, Derby, Metternich,

Thackeray, Hood, Macaulay, Prince Albert, and Leopold I of Belgium, book reviews, and political articles. 'Not without prejudice' (Morison, 2.470), in his reviews he expressed his hostility and contempt for, among others, the Napiers and English travellers, especially mountaineers, and for sport, especially fox-hunting. He also attacked J. A. Froude's *History of England*. He also contributed to the *Daily News*, *Saturday Review*, *Pall Mall Gazette*, and *The World*, and for a time in 1868 edited *Once a Week*.

Dallas became well known in London literary and theatrical circles. He published *The Gay Science* (2 vols., 1866), a title borrowed from the Provençal troubadours, which attempted to discover the source in the constitution of the human mind of the pleasure of poetry. The subject was too abstruse for the general reader, and the book did not meet with the attention which some considered it deserved. He was a correspondent for *The Times* at the 1867 Paris Exhibition and during the siege of Paris in 1870. In 1868 he edited an abridgement of Richardson's *Clarissa Harlowe*. Dallas was knowledgeable about cooking, and his encyclopaedic *Kettner's book of the table: a manual of cookery: practical, theoretical, historical* (1877) incorporated recipes supplied by his friend Auguste Kettner, former chef to Napoleon III. He began a new edition of La Rochefoucauld's *Maxims*, and wrote an elaborate article on it, which was unpublished at his death.

Dallas died suddenly at his home, 88 Newman Street, Oxford Street, London, on 17 January 1879, and was buried at Kensal Green cemetery, London, on 24 January.

G. C. Boase, *rev.* Roger T. Stearn

Sources *The Times* (11 May 1874), 13 · *The Times* (18 Jan 1879), 9 · *ILN* (8 Feb 1879), 78, 129, 131 · *Pall Mall Gazette* (21 Jan 1879), 8 · *The World* (22 Jan 1879), 10 · *The Athenaeum* (25 Jan 1879), 122 · *The Athenaeum* (1 Feb 1879), 152 · *The Academy* (25 Jan 1879), 74 · *The Era* (2 July 1876), 4 · *Law Journal Reports*, new ser., 46/1 (1876), 51–3 · [S. Morison and others], *The history of The Times*, 2 (1939) · Boase, *Mod. Eng. biog.* · Ward, *Men of the reign* · H. R. Fox Bourne, *English newspapers: chapters in the history of journalism*, 2 (1887) · E. S. Dallas, *Kettner's book of the table*, preface by D. Hudson, repr. (1968)
Archives News Int. RO, papers | Herts. ALS, letters to Lord Lytton · NL Scot., corresp. with Blackwoods · U. Edin. L., letters to David Ramsey Hay
Likenesses engraving, repro. in *ILN* · wood-engraving, repro. in Morison, ed., *History of The Times*, 470

Dallas, George, of St Martins (*c.*1636–1701), lawyer, was a younger son of William Dallas of Budyett, Nairnshire, by his first marriage. He was apprenticed to John Bayne of Pitcairly, writer to the signet, described by Dallas as 'a great penman in his age, and so known' (G. Dallas, preface), and was admitted a writer to the signet on 16 July 1661. He served as a commissioner to the convention of estates in 1665, 1667, and 1678, and a commissioner to parliament in 1669–74, 1681, and 1685–6 (all for the county of Cromarty, where he lived at St Martins in the parish of Cillicudden). He was also a commissioner of supply in 1667, 1678, 1685, 1689, and 1690. He was deputy keeper of the privy seal in 1681 and keeper in 1690. He was admitted gratis a burgess of Edinburgh in 1687.

Dallas is chiefly remembered as the author of *A system of stiles, as now practicable within the kingdom of Scotland: and reduced to a clear method, not heretofore*, written between 1666 and 1688 and published in 1697. This volume of 904 small folio pages, divided into six parts, remained for many years an indispensable part of the library of every Scottish conveyancer. Walter Ross referred to the 'vast opake body' of the work, and described how the hearts of apprentices *'failed within them*, when presented, in the Writing-office, with such a frightful volume of arid, naked, unintelligible Forms' (Ross, 1.x–xi). This is an exaggeration: a later commentator, Lord Macmillan, noted that Dallas's *Stiles*, by using original documents, preserves much of historical as well as legal interest. The *Stiles* is referred to by Sir Walter Scott: thus, in *Waverley*, Bailie Macwheeble 'whipped down "Dallas of St Martin's Styles" from a shelf, where that venerable work roosted with Stair's "Institutions", Dirleton's "Doubts", Balfour's "Practiques", and a parcel of old account books'. A new edition in two volumes appeared in 1774.

Dallas's nephew William Dallas of Budyett (1664–1713), the son of his brother Hugh, was apprenticed to his uncle, and admitted a writer to the signet in 1687. George Dallas married, on 3 July 1660, Margaret, daughter of James Abercromby of Pittencrieff and Janet Dowling or Daillin. They had two daughters and four sons, including James of St Martins, George of Parkley, and John, writer in Edinburgh. Margaret was buried in Greyfriars Church, Edinburgh, on 16 October 1697. George Dallas was buried there also, on 13 April 1701.

Dallas was the great-grandfather of Lieutenant-General **Sir Thomas Dallas** (*bap.* 1758, *d.* 1839) of the 1st Madras cavalry. Thomas married Mary Elliot (1767–1814) and they had one son and three daughters. He distinguished himself as a cavalry officer in the Carnatic, at the siege of Seringapatam and, under Arthur Wellesley, in the Anglo-Maratha wars. He was appointed KCB in 1815 and GCB in 1833. He died at Bath on 12 August 1839. George Dallas was also ancestor of the writer Robert Charles *Dallas, the clergyman Alexander Robert Charles *Dallas, and of Alexander James Dallas (1759–1817), secretary of the United States treasury, and his son George Mifflin Dallas (1792–1864), vice-president of the United States and minister to Great Britain.   W. D. H. SELLAR

Sources G. Dallas, *A system of stiles, as now practicable within the kingdom of Scotland: and reduced to a clear method, not heretofore* (1697); 2nd edn, 2 vols. (1774) · J. Dallas, *The history of the family of Dallas* (1921) · M. D. Young, ed., *The parliaments of Scotland: burgh and shire commissioners*, 2 vols. (1992–3) · *The Society of Writers to His Majesty's Signet with a list of the members* (1936) · W. Ross, *Lectures on the history and practice of the law of Scotland, relative to conveyancing and legal diligence*, 2nd edn, 2 vols. (1822)
Archives NL Scot., letters to Sir Ludovick Gordon
Likenesses oils, Signet Library, Edinburgh

Dallas, Sir George, first baronet (1758–1833), political writer, was born in London on 6 April 1758 and baptized on 23 April 1758 at Founders' Hall, London, the younger son of Robert Dallas (*d.* 1797), insurance broker, of 2 Cooper's Court, St Michael, Cornhill, and his wife, Elizabeth, daughter of the Revd James Smith, minister of Kilbirnie, Ayrshire. He was educated at Geneva with his brother, Sir Robert *Dallas (1756–1824), who went on to become lord

chief justice of the common pleas. At the age of eighteen George Dallas went to Bengal as a writer in the East India Company's service, and soon after his arrival published at Calcutta a clever poem, entitled *The India Guide*, in which he described the incidents of a voyage to India, and the first impressions on the mind of a European of Indian life. It was dedicated to Anstie, the author of the *Bath Guide*, and is said to have been the first publication which was issued from the Indian press. This attracted the attention of Warren Hastings to his abilities, and Dallas was appointed superintendent of the collections at Rajeshahi. After filling this post for a few years, failing health compelled him to resign. Before leaving India he spoke at the meeting held at Calcutta on 25 July 1785 against Pitt's East India Bill, and was deputed by the inhabitants of that city to present a petition on their behalf to the House of Commons against the bill. During his residence in Bengal he acquired an extensive knowledge of Indian affairs, and the suave and sagacious manner in which he exercised his functions procured him the respect of the native people and Europeans alike. Not long after his return to England, on 12 June 1788 he married Catherine Margaret (*d.* 1846), fourth daughter of Sir John Blackwood, baronet, and his wife, Dorcas, afterwards Baroness Dufferin and Claneboye; they had four sons and three daughters. In 1789 Dallas published a pamphlet in vindication of Warren Hastings, and in 1793 his *Thoughts upon our Present Situation, with Remarks upon the Policy of a War with France*. This pamphlet, which was directed against the principles of the French Revolution, went through several editions, and at Pitt's suggestion was reprinted for general distribution.

In 1797, while on a visit to a relative in the north of Ireland, Dallas wrote several tracts, addressed to the inhabitants of Ulster, the first of which was entitled *Observations upon the Oath of Allegiance, as Prescribed by the Enrolling Act*. This was followed by a *Letter from a Father to his Son, a United Irishman*, in which he argued with great force against unlawful confederacies in general. At the close of the same year his three *Letters to Lord Moira on the Political and Commercial State of Ireland* appeared in the third, fourth, and fifth numbers of the *Anti-Jacobin*, under the signature of Civis. These letters were afterwards republished at Pitt's request in a separate form. In 1798 he issued an *Address to the People of Ireland on the Present Situation of Public Affairs*. On 31 July 1798 he was created a baronet. In 1799 he published *Considerations on the impolicy of treating for peace with the present regicide government of France*. At a by-election in May 1800 he was returned to the House of Commons as the member for Newport in the Isle of Wight.

While in parliament Dallas published a work entitled *Letter to Sir William Pulteney, bart., member for Shrewsbury, on the subject of the trade between India and Europe*. In this letter he advocated the cause of the free merchants, and recommended a more liberal system of commercial intercourse between Britain and its Asiatic dependencies. He retired from parliamentary life at the dissolution in June 1802, and resided for some years in Devon for the benefit of his health. In 1806 he published his *Vindication of the justice and policy of the late wars carried on in Hindostan and the Dekkan by*

Marquis Wellesley, and in 1813 he wrote an anonymous tract on the religious conversion of Hindus, under the title of *A Letter from a Field Officer at Madras*. His last work was the *Biographical memoir of the late Sir Peter Parker, bart., captain of H. M. ship Menelaus, &c.*, which was published anonymously in 1815. Dallas frequently took part in the debates at India House, where, owing to his intimate acquaintance with eastern affairs, his opinion had great influence. He died at Brighton on 14 January 1833, in the seventy-fifth year of his life, and was buried in St Andrew's Church, Waterloo Street, Brighton, where there is a monument to his memory. His wife survived him many years, and died at Henrietta Street, Cavendish Square, London, on 5 April 1846. His youngest son, Robert Charles Dallas, succeeded him in the baronetcy.   G. F. R. BARKER, *rev.* REBECCA MILLS

Sources *Annual Register* (1834), 198 · *Annual Biography and Obituary*, 18 (1834), 30–40 · *IGI* · *GM*, 1st ser., 103/1 (1833), 270–71 · Watt, *Bibl. Brit.*, vol. 1 · *N&Q*, 7th ser., 2 (1886), 187, 435 · C. J. Pary, *Index of baronetage creations* (1967), 44 · Burke, *Peerage* · will, PRO, PROB 11/1811, sig. 74
Archives Bodl. Oxf., corresp. and papers, incl. poems | Redbridge Central Library, Ilford, letters to Long and Wellesley families
Wealth at death see will, PRO, PROB 11/1811, fols. 194–6

Dallas, George (1878–1961), trade unionist and politician, was born in Glasgow on 6 August 1878, the son of George Dallas, a shoemaker, and Mary Hay. He grew up in Kilmaurs, Ayrshire, and worked at a coalmine after leaving elementary school before resuming his formal education at the Glasgow and West of Scotland Technical College and, later, at the London School of Economics. His interest in politics began early, and he joined the Socialist League in Glasgow when he was sixteen. He worked briefly in London as a clerk for a coal merchant, and participated in pro-Boer demonstrations. On returning to Glasgow he became involved in the trade union movement, as district secretary for the shop assistants' union. For a time he ran his own men's outfitting shop in Motherwell. He stood as a socialist candidate in the municipal elections of 1907, and was organizing secretary for the Independent Labour Party in Scotland from 1908 to 1912. He was prominent in early attempts to organize factory girls in Scotland, in particular through exposing appalling working conditions in the dyeing industry and through his involvement in the strikes by thread-workers at Neilston in Renfrewshire in 1910. One of the strikers at Neilston, Agnes Brown (1888?–1916), went on to become a trade union official and organizer for the Women's Labour League; she and Dallas were married in 1913.

Dallas left Scotland in 1912 to become chief organizer for the National Federation of Women Workers in London, but in the following year he went to work for the Workers' Union as organizer in London and the home counties. He assisted in a rapid expansion of membership before and during the First World War, being associated particularly with the union's organization of agricultural workers. He was appointed to the Agricultural Wages Board established under the legislation of 1917 and acted as secretary for the workers' representatives. His first wife

died in 1916, and he married her younger sister, Mary (*d.* 1973), in 1920; they had two sons, Kenneth and Roland. Dallas was one of the first residents of Welwyn Garden City, where he moved in 1922, and he became a JP for Hertfordshire. He stood unsuccessfully for parliament as the Labour candidate for Maldon in 1918 and 1922, and for Roxborough and Selkirk in 1923. He was elected as MP for Wellingborough in 1929, but lost the seat in 1931 and never sat in parliament again; he narrowly failed to regain the Wellingborough seat in 1935 and was later selected as Labour's prospective candidate for Belper, but he gave it up before the general election of 1945.

Dallas had an active role within the Labour Party at a national level, notably in the party's rural campaigning in the 1920s and 1930s, and in developing its agricultural policy. He chaired Labour's advisory committee on agricultural and rural problems, and was one of the party's chief spokesmen on rural issues. He gained wide respect as an expert on the agricultural industry and served on the executive committee of the Agricultural Economics Society (1930–37). He was a member of the 1919 royal commission on agriculture and signatory of the resulting minority report, and sat on the council of agriculture for England, which he chaired in 1933. In 1930 he was one of the major figures involved in non-party demonstrations to publicize the crisis in arable farming. He was a member of the national executive committee of the Labour Party from 1930 to 1944, vice-chairman in 1936–7, and chairman in 1937–9. He sat on the party's international subcommittee from 1931 (as chairman from 1940), and travelled abroad to attend conferences organized by European socialist parties in the 1930s.

Dallas settled in Northamptonshire in 1929 and was involved in local public life, helping to found the county's rural community council, chairing his local parish council at Great Doddington and sitting as a JP (from 1938). He was chairman of the River Nene catchment board throughout its existence (1930–51), which contemporaries regarded as one of his most important contributions. During the Second World War he chaired the timber control board, overseeing the expansion of domestic timber production. He was appointed CBE in 1946. He was staunchly anti-communist, and in 1956 helped to found the Friends of Free China Association, of which he became president. He spent his last years in Bishop's Stortford, where he died in hospital on 4 January 1961; he was cremated three days later in Cambridge.   C. V. J. GRIFFITHS

Sources K. Dallas, 'Dallas, George', *DLB*, vol. 4 · *The Labour who's who* (1924) · *Report of the 60th Annual Conference of the Labour Party* (1961) [notice of death] · *The Times* (5 Jan 1960) · *Journal of Proceedings of the Agricultural Economics Society* · *TGWU Record* (Feb 1961) · minutes of the national executive committee of the labour party, People's History Museum, Manchester
Likenesses photograph, repro. in *The Times*
Wealth at death £863 14s. 9d.: probate, 8 Feb 1961, CGPLA Eng. & Wales

Dallas, Sir Robert (1756–1824), judge, was born on 16 October 1756, the eldest son of Robert Dallas (*d.* 1797), insurance broker, of 2 Cooper's Court, St Michael, Cornhill, and

Kensington, and his wife, Elizabeth, daughter of the Revd James Smith, minister of Kilbirnie, Ayrshire. His father's family originally came from Cantray in Inverness-shire. He was educated at Dr Elphinstone's school in Kensington and subsequently at Geneva, alongside his younger brother, the future political writer Sir George *Dallas, under the tutorship of the distinguished Swiss pastor Chauvet. He entered Lincoln's Inn as a student on 4 November 1777.

Dallas practised his public speaking before the debating society in Coachmaker's Hall, where he 'adorned the debates with his general knowledge, and conciliated all by his perfect politeness' (E. Henderson, *Recollections of John Adolphus*, 1871, 102–3). His experiences in Coachmaker's Hall provided an invaluable preparation for his career as an advocate.

Dallas was called to the bar on 6 November 1782. Being 'both a good lawyer and an accomplished speaker' (Holdsworth, *Eng. law*, 13.542) he soon acquired a considerable practice in London and on the western circuit. He came to specialize in parliamentary and privy council work, and was engaged in many notable cases. The first of these occurred in 1783, when he was retained as junior counsel by the East India Company to challenge Charles James Fox's East India Bill. On 16 December Dallas made a long and effective speech urging the company's case at the bar of the House of Lords.

In 1787 Dallas was briefed as junior counsel for the defence of Warren Hastings whose impeachment, instigated and managed mainly by Edmund Burke and Fox, was to last for seven years. Dallas, together with Thomas Plomer (later master of the rolls), was led by Edward Law (later first Baron Ellenborough), and this triumvirate proved a powerful and effective legal team. Their ability to work in unison in frustrating Burke and his co-prosecutors was exemplified by the poet John Bell, who likened the impeachment proceedings to a game of chess:

> When Burke his game forward endeavours to bring,
> Lawe [sic] advances a pawn, and gives check to his King;
> Burke covers his King, Plomer instantly sees
> An advantage—and, lo! Edmund's Queen is en prise.
> Burke rallies his men, and prepares for the fight,
> Dallas whispers a move, and Burke loses a knight.
> (J. Bell, *Letters from Simpkin the Second, to his Dear Brother in Wales*, 1789, letter xxiii)

Dallas's performances in defence of Hastings have been widely and justly lauded. Among those impressed by 'his exertions and ... his polished addresses' (Foss, *Judges*, 15) was Frances Burney, who wrote in June 1792, 'Mr Dallas closed his answer to the first Charge, with great spirit and effect, and seemed to make numerous prosylites for Mr Hastings' (*The Journals and Letters of Fanny Burney*, ed. J. Hemlow, C. D. Cecil and A. Douglas, 1972, 1.192). Hastings was fully exonerated in 1795 and Dallas, having 'greatly distinguished' himself (Holdsworth, *Eng. law*, 13.542), took silk on 2 March of that year. He was elected a bencher of Lincoln's Inn on 23 April, going on to become treasurer in 1806.

Dallas's practice continued to thrive following his appointment as king's counsel. He received numerous briefs as counsel to parliamentary committees investigating contested elections, but he also participated in more high-profile cases. Between 1806 and 1808 he led for the defence of General Thomas Picton, the former governor of Trinidad, who was accused of unlawfully authorizing the use of torture on a young girl thought to have been involved in a theft on the island. Dallas's masterly defence in Picton's first trial was unsuccessful, but he successfully argued for a retrial and secured a special verdict for the former governor although in the event no action was ever taken against Picton. In 1807 Dallas was briefed by the Jamaican merchants and planters to challenge Lord Grenville's bill to abolish the slave trade. On 20 February Dallas presented his clients' case at some length before the bar of the House of Commons, but the bill was subsequently passed in March 1807. Dallas was a first-rate barrister, well versed in substantive law and commanding tremendous powers of advocacy. James Scarlett, first Baron Abinger, considered him, along with such names as Spencer Perceval, Samuel Romilly, and Thomas Erskine, to be 'amongst the élite of the profession in the Common Law' (Scarlett, 83), and adjudged him 'a man of excellent understanding, and an elegant and graceful speaker' (ibid., 88).

Dallas also enjoyed a brief political career. In the 1802 general election he became MP for the Cornish borough of Mitchell, resigning in February 1805, when he was appointed chief justice of Chester. He became MP for Dysart burghs in Scotland in March 1805, but served only until 1806. He was not particularly active in the Commons, but his contributions were effective, and he was a useful supporter of Addington. On 6 May 1813, on Lord Chancellor Eldon's recommendation, Dallas was appointed solicitor-general in the earl of Liverpool's administration. He was knighted on 19 May. He held the post for only six months, before being raised to the bench, and his tenure of the office was fairly unremarkable.

Dallas had a long judicial career, both part-time and full-time. The chief-justiceship of Chester was the foremost Welsh judgeship. The Welsh judgeships were then part-time posts, often held by English barristers—at the time of Dallas's appointment, Chester was recognized 'as a sure stepping-stone for promotion to the English Bench' (Williams, 29). The office carried an annual salary of £730, and Dallas was assisted by the second justice of Chester, Judge Francis Burton. While at Chester, Dallas acquired a reputation for clemency and humanity which was not enjoyed by many judges of the time—he sought to prevent executions where possible; and when they were inevitable, he forbore from subjecting the condemned to moralizing tirades from the bench.

Dallas told Henry Addington, first Viscount Sidmouth, who had helped him secure the appointment, that the chief-justiceship was 'a source of very considerable present satisfaction' (Thorne, 560), although he was prepared to resign in July 1806, if offered a post as assessor to the courts of prize appeals and plantation causes. In the event, no such offer was made, and Dallas remained chief justice of Chester until his resignation in 1813.

Following his brief tenure of the solicitor-generalship, Dallas was appointed a puisne justice of the court of common pleas on 18 November 1813, succeeding Sir Vicary Gibbs. Just before this appointment, in accordance with tradition, he was made a serjeant-at-law, giving rings with the motto *mos et lex*. In October 1817, he sat as one of four judges forming the special commission which tried the Derbyshire Luddites for high treason. On 21 October he 'most ably' (Foss, *Judges*, 16) summed up in the trial of William Turner who was convicted and, with Jeremiah Brandreth and Isaac Ludlam the elder, hanged and decapitated on 7 November.

In November 1818, again succeeding Sir Vicary Gibbs, Dallas was appointed lord chief justice of the common pleas and was sworn of the privy council on 19 November. In March 1820 he and Lord Chief Justice Charles Abbott headed the special commission which was set up to try the Cato Street conspirators for high treason. On 21 and 22 April 1820 Dallas presided and summed up at the trial of the 'highly neurotic' (J. Stanhope, *The Cato Street Conspiracy*, 1962, 86) James Ings who had planned to take the heads of Sidmouth and Robert Stewart, Viscount Castlereagh, as trophies of the revolution. His summing-up was, according to Foss, 'remarkable for [its] fairness and perspicuity' (Foss, *Judges*, 16). Ings was convicted and, with four others, hanged and decapitated on 1 May 1820, the last traitors to suffer the ignomy of decapitation after execution.

Also in 1820 Dallas and Abbott headed the judges who attended the 'trial' of Queen Caroline, the wayward consort of the wayward King George IV. The 'trial', which was in fact the consideration of the bill of pains and penalties introduced to obtain a royal divorce, was presided over by Lord Chancellor Eldon. Dallas and his colleagues were present only to advise the Lords on points of law. This was not always a dry task—one of the earliest points requiring judicial deliberation was whether the queen, if consenting to 'violation' by someone owing no allegiance to the crown, thereby committed high treason. The bill finally came to nothing, but it promulgated yet another *cause célèbre* in which Dallas played a significant role.

An excellent barrister, Dallas 'lost none of his reputation' on the bench (Scarlett, 88). He was 'much liked on account of his gentlemanly manners' (Thorne, 560), interrupting counsel only rarely and not reticent in praising an effective performance by an advocate who appeared before him. As Foss notes, he executed his judicial office 'with acknowledged ability and universal respect' (Foss, *Judges*, 16).

But Dallas the judge was much more than a mere adornment of the bench, and a trier of infamous causes. He was a 'very good lawyer', with 'a remarkable grasp of legal principle, and a power of stating clearly the essential facts of a case' (Holdsworth, *Eng. law*, 13.543). This is well demonstrated by the continued authority of a number of his judgments, despite their great age. So, for instance, his ruling on the law of fixtures in *Buckland* v. *Butterfield* (1820) is still good law, while the substance of his ruling in *Leigh* v. *Paterson* (1818), concerning the measure of damages for a

repudiation of a contract for the future sale of goods, was codified in section 51(3) of the Sale of Goods Act, 1979.

Dallas's urbanity and humanity have already been referred to. His love of the law, meanwhile, and his industry, are well exemplified by Sir John Patteson's recollection of a time when Dallas and Patteson were both guests at a country house, Dallas passing the wet vacation afternoon by reading Serjeant Williams's 'Note on executory devises' (E. Manson, *The Builders of our Law during the Reign of Queen Victoria*, 1895, 203). In spite of this strong work ethic, however, Dallas also enjoyed a rather puckish sense of humour. After his death, his widow published privately a collection of his *Poetical Trifles*, many of which are delightfully whimsical and amusing. They include his famous epigram composed during Warren Hastings's impeachment, and directed at Edmund Burke, who Hastings's counsel believed to have orchestrated the whole affair predominantly to 'gratify his malignity and his vanity' (Lord Campbell, *Lives of the Chief Justices*, 1857, 3.132):

Oft have I wonder'd why on Irish ground
No poisonous reptile ever yet was found;
Reveal'd the secret stands of Nature's work,—
She saved her venom to create a Burke.

Dallas was twice married. His first wife, whom he married on 11 August 1788, was Charlotte Jardine, daughter of Lieutenant-Colonel Alexander Jardine, sometime consul-general at Corunna, Spain; they had one son and one daughter. Charlotte Dallas died on 17 October 1792 and on 10 September 1802 Dallas married his second wife, Giustina, daughter of Henry Davidson of Tulloch Castle, with whom he had five daughters.

Having held the chief justiceship of the common pleas for five years, Dallas was forced by ill health to retire at the end of 1823. He died in London on Christmas day 1824.

NATHAN WELLS

Sources R. G. Thorne, 'Dallas, Robert', HoP, *Commons, 1790–1820* · Holdsworth, *Eng. law*, vol. 13 · Foss, *Judges*, vol. 9 · W. R. Williams, *The history of the great sessions in Wales, 1542–1830* (privately printed, Brecon, 1899) · *Hansard 1* (1807); (1815) · *State trials*, vols. 32–3 · R. Fulford, *The trial of Queen Caroline* (1967) · P. Scarlett, *A memoir of the Rt Hon James, first Lord Abinger* (1877) · R. Dallas, *Poetical trifles* (1825) · Sainty, *King's counsel* · Sainty, *Judges* · W. P. Baildon, ed., *The records of the Honorable Society of Lincoln's Inn: the black books*, 4 (1902) · *GM*, 1st ser., 95/1 (1825), 82–3
Likenesses W. Holl, print, stipple, pubd 1824 (after bust by R. W. Sievier), BM, NPG · G. Hayter, group portrait, oils (*The trial of Queen Caroline, 1820*), NPG

Dallas, Robert Charles (1754–1824), writer, was born in Kingston, Jamaica, the son of Robert Dallas MD, physician, and his wife, a daughter of Colonel Cormack. He was educated at Musselburgh, Scotland, and under James Elphinston at Kensington. He trained as a barrister at the Inner Temple, and on coming of age went to Jamaica to take possession of Dallas Castle, the estate which he had inherited upon his father's death. Dallas was appointed to 'a lucrative office' (*GM*, 642) in Jamaica. After three years there, he visited England, and married Sarah, daughter of Benjamin Harding of Hacton House, near Hornchurch, Essex; among their children was the Church of England clergyman Alexander Robert Charles *Dallas. He returned with his wife to Jamaica, but resigned his position and left the West Indies for good after finding that her health was badly affected by the climate. Dallas spent several years in France, until forced to flee by the French Revolution, and subsequently moved to America, where his brother went on to become a prominent lawyer. Dallas's nephew George Mifflin Dallas was subsequently to become vice-president of the United States, and to have the city of Dallas, Texas, named after him. Robert Charles Dallas, however, was less enamoured of life in America, and, 'disappointed … in the idea which he had formed of it', returned to England (*GM*, 642).

Dallas became a prolific author, in a variety of genres, dedicating all of his work to 'the defence of society and reason against Jacobinism and confusion' (R. C. Dallas, *Miscellaneous Works*, 1.xvi). Dallas's works of fiction include three long and moralistic novels, set mainly in contemporary Britain, which centred on virtuous male heroes: *Percival, or, Nature Vindicated* (1801), *Aubrey* (1804), and *Sir Francis Darrell, or, The Vortex* (1820). He also wrote two collections of tales, *The Morlands: Tales Illustrative of the Simple and Surprising* (1805) and *The Knights: Tales Illustrative of the Marvellous* (1808), as well as tragedies, a farce, and numerous poems. Dallas's extensive non-fictional writings likewise sought to counter the threat posed by the 'constitution reformers of the day' (R. C. Dallas, *Letter to Charles Butler*, 4). Although an Anglican himself, he wrote *The New Conspiracy Against the Jesuits Detected* (1815) to protect the reputation of the order in the name of a united loyalist front against the forces of revolution. He also translated several works by the French author Bertrand de Moleville, defending the record of Louis XVI. Despite 'an ardent tendency in my heart to disapprove the slave-trade' (*History of the Maroons*, 1803, 2.392), Dallas's *History of the Maroons* offered a qualified acceptance of the institution of slavery in a fallen world, and addressed criticisms of planters' behaviour and the government's conduct against the rebellious Jamaican maroons.

Dallas remains best-known, however, as a result of his connection with Lord Byron; his sister, Henrietta Charlotte, was married to George Anson Byron, uncle of the poet. Dallas initiated a period of correspondence with Byron, after writing to praise his work *Hours of Idleness*. Byron in response told Dallas how he was flattered by such 'a tribute from a man of acknowledged genius' (R. C. Dallas, *Correspondence of Lord Byron*, 23), and the pair wrote to each other frequently between 1808 and 1811. Dallas assumed a role as an editor of Byron's early poetry, suggesting alterations to his work, and attempting to persuade him to remove any hint of religious scepticism. Dallas later professed 'some pride in the part I took in combating his errors' (A. R. C. Dallas, 3.2); Byron, according to a contemporary, 'grew weary of such lecturing … dropped his intimacy with Mr. Dallas, and fell into other hands' (*GM*, 531). In recognition of Dallas's assistance, however, Byron gave him the copyrights to the first two cantos of *Childe Harold's Pilgrimage* and 'The Corsair', in addition to a series of letters written to his mother during his eastern travels. Dallas later prepared these letters for publication,

prefaced by his own recollections of the poet, with a view to issuing a memoir of Byron's life between the years 1808 and 1814, ready to appear after the poet's death. Although Dallas claimed that the letters had been personally gifted to him, Byron's executors, Hobhouse and Hanson, intervened to obtain an injunction from Lord Eldon, which prevented the publication of the correspondence. Dallas died shortly afterwards, either on 21 October 1824 or on 20 November 1824, at Ste Adresse in Normandy, bled to death following 'an inflammatory fever' (A. R. C. Dallas, 3.90). He was buried at Le Havre in the presence 'of the British consul and many of the respectable inhabitants' (*GM*, 643). Dallas's book on Byron was published in Paris in 1825, edited by his son, A. R. C. Dallas, and prefaced by an account of the legal dispute, vindicating the conduct of Dallas.   JAMES WATT

Sources *GM*, 1st ser., 94/2 (1824), 642–3 • Allibone, *Dict.* • R. C. Dallas, *The miscellaneous works and novels of R. C. Dallas*, 7 vols. (1813) • *Correspondence of Lord Byron with a friend*, ed. R. C. Dallas, 3 vols. (1824) [copy of suppressed edn of Byron's correspondence, without title page (in BL)] • *Correspondence of Lord Byron with a friend, including his letters to his mother, written … in 1809, 1810 and 1811*, ed. A. R. C. Dallas, 3 vols. (1825) • *DNB* • R. C. Dallas, *A letter to Charles Butler, esq. relative to the new conspiracy against the Jesuits* (1817)

Dallas, Sir Thomas (*bap.* 1758, *d.* 1839). *See under* Dallas, George, of St Martins (*c.*1636–1701).

Dallaway, James (1763–1834), antiquary, was born on 20 February 1763 in the parish of Sts Philip and James, Bristol, the son of James Dallaway (1730–1787) of Stroud, Gloucestershire, a banker, and his wife, Martha (1739–1783), the daughter of Richard Hopton of Worcester; only he and his younger sister survived childhood. He was educated at Cirencester grammar school, matriculated from Trinity College, Oxford, in June 1778, and graduated BA in 1782 and MA in 1784. His failure to be elected a fellow was attributed to his satirical verses on a senior member of the college. Having been ordained deacon in late 1785 by the bishop of Gloucester he became curate at Rodmarton, Gloucestershire, to Samuel Lysons (father of the antiquaries Daniel and Samuel), and then at Rodborough. He was engaged to assist Richard Bigland in editing his father's papers; before they parted acrimoniously in early 1794 he completed the first twenty-two parts of Ralph Bigland's *Historical, Monumental, and Genealogical Collections, Relative to the County of Gloucester* (1786–94) and gained a valuable introduction to the College of Arms. His *Inquiries into the Origin and Progress of the Science of Heraldry in England* (1793) was dedicated to the earl marshal. He was elected a fellow of the Society of Antiquaries in 1789.

In October 1793 Dallaway was ordained priest in Gloucester; in the same year he returned to Oxford to attend the Radcliffe Infirmary and gained the degree of MB in December. He made a special study of 'the plague', for, through the fourth earl of Bute's influence, Robert Liston had chosen him as physician and chaplain for his embassy to the Ottoman empire. The party left in March 1794 and travelled overland to Constantinople. Dallaway's *Itinerary*, published in 1805, was one of the period's most detailed reports of the Balkans. After leaving for home in

October 1795, Dallaway travelled via the Greek islands and Italy. Loss of most of his notes in transit precluded his planned continuation of Gibbon's *Decline and Fall*, but his *Constantinople, ancient and modern, with excursions to the shores and islands of the archipelago and to the Troad* (1797) was well regarded in its time, helped to awaken interest in the ancient manuscripts to be found there, and contributed to the debate on the location of ancient Troy. The papers of an earlier ambassador's wife had passed to Lord Bute, her grandson. When he reluctantly agreed to an authorized edition, he commissioned Dallaway to prepare *The Works of … Lady Mary Wortley Montagu* (5 vols., 1803), which a later editor described as 'shockingly incompetent' (Halsband, 290). Dallaway also reviewed books on Turkish topics for the *Monthly Review*.

Back in England, Dallaway was appointed by the earl marshal, the eleventh duke of Norfolk, to be his secretary from 1 January 1797; he served in this post for the rest of his life, being reappointed by the deputy for the twelfth duke (1815–24) and then by the twelfth duke himself. The College of Arms became his regular place of work. Two years later the duke presented him to the rectory of South Stoke, adjoining Arundel Park, Sussex. This he resigned in 1803 on collation to the nearby vicarage of Slinfold, but he remained in residence as curate until in 1804 he was presented to the vicarage of Leatherhead, Surrey, where he resided from 1805. On 26 June 1800 he had married Harriet Anne (*d.* 1867), the second daughter of John Jefferis, alderman of Gloucester. Their only child, a daughter, was born in 1816. His wife shared his interests—she wrote *A Manual of Heraldry for Amateurs* (1828)—and was a competent artist; in 1821 she published etchings of the vicarage, to which Dallaway provided text. In 1811 he was given the prebend of Hova Ecclesia in Chichester Cathedral, which he exchanged for that of Ferring in 1816; the latter he resigned in 1826. At least between 1820 and 1822 he undertook tutoring.

Dallaway's parochial duties and his office as earl marshal's secretary left ample leisure for antiquarian studies. His journey through Italy had strengthened his interest in art history, and he published *Anecdotes of the arts in England, or, Comparative observations on architecture, sculpture, & painting, chiefly illustrated by specimens at Oxford* (1800); *Observations on English Architecture, Military, Ecclesiastical, and Civil* (1806; enlarged edition 1833, as *A Series of Discourses upon Architecture in England*); *Of statuary and sculpture among the ancients, with some account of specimens preserved in England* (1816); *Account of all the pictures exhibited in the rooms of the British Institution from 1813 to 1823, belonging to the nobility and gentry of England* (1824); and an edition with considerable additions of Horace Walpole's *Anecdotes of Painting* (5 vols., 1826–8). He was a valuable continuer of Walpole's work, especially on Gothic architecture and medieval architects, while his attempt to divide the Gothic style into periods and to produce lists of contemporary buildings in each style deserves some of the credit commonly given to Thomas Rickman.

In April 1811 Dallaway agreed with the duke of Norfolk to compile and prepare for the press a two-volume *History of the Western Division of Sussex*. A volume containing 'preliminary observations' and covering the city and rape of Chichester appeared in 1815, and that for Arundel rape followed in 1819 (though all but twenty copies were destroyed by fire). These were criticized on publication (and by later historians) for their numerous errors, and revision of Arundel rape and writing of Bramber rape were left to Edmund Cartwright (1773–1833) for publication in 1830. Dallaway's later historical work comprised several short pieces on Bristol and Leatherhead.

In 1830 Joseph Hunter (1783–1861) found Dallaway 'a fine hearty-looking gentleman, full of conversation' (BL, Add. MS 36527), a description well reflected in the only known likeness, by his wife in 1821 (watercolour miniature, Plymouth Museum and Art Gallery). Dallaway died on 6 June 1834 and was buried with Richard Duppa (1770–1831) in Leatherhead churchyard. With property bequeathed by Duppa, Dallaway's estate was worth at least £10,000.

JOHN H. FARRANT

Sources F. W. Steer, 'Memoir and letters of James Dallaway, 1763–1834', *Sussex Archaeological Collections*, 103 (1965), 1–48 · F. W. Steer, 'Memoir and letters of James Dallaway, 1763–1834 … a postscript', *Sussex Archaeological Collections*, 105 (1967), 62–9 · *GM*, 2nd ser., 2 (1834), 318–20 · T. J. Hope, 'The travels of the Rev. James Dallaway in the Ottoman empire: some unpublished correspondence with Robert Liston', *Sussex Archaeological Collections*, 112 (1974), 9–14 · T. J. Hope, 'John Sibthorp's last expedition to the Balkans: the accounts of Sibthorp and Dallaway about their travels in 1794', *Revue des Études Sud-East Européennes*, 12 (1974), 87–102 · B. Frith, introduction, in R. Bigland, *Historical, monumental and genealogical collections, relative to the county of Gloucester*, ed. B. Frith, 4 (1995) · J. H. Harvey and F. B. Benger, 'James Dallaway, antiquary, vicar of Leatherhead, 1804–1834', *Proceedings of the Leatherhead and District Local History Society*, 2 (1957–66), 214–19 · R. Halsband, *The life of Lady Mary Wortley Montagu* (1956) · family genealogy, *c.*1870, W. Sussex RO, Add. MS 20232 · bishop's transcripts for South Stoke, W. Sussex RO, Ep I/24/111 · Foster, *Alum. Oxon.*

Archives W. Sussex RO, personal and family corresp. and papers, Add. MSS 20186–20259

Likenesses H. A. Dallaway, watercolour, 1821, Plymouth Museum and Art Gallery; repro. in Steer, *Memoir*, facing p. 1

Wealth at death approx. £10,000: will, 1834, PRO

Dalley, William Bede (1831–1888), politician in Australia, born in George Street, Sydney, on 5 July 1831, was the son of convict parents. His father, John Dalley, was born in Dorset, England; his mother, Catherine Spillane, was born in Cork, Ireland. He was educated at various preparatory schools—including Fort Street School—and at the old Sydney College. In 1842 he entered St Mary's Seminary as a day pupil, and came under the tuition of the Roman Catholic archbishop John Bede Polding; with him he contracted a friendship which endured until Polding's death in 1877. In 1856 he was called to the bar, and in 1877 was nominated a queen's counsel. In 1856 he was elected as a member for the city of Sydney and took his place in the first parliament in New South Wales under responsible government. In 1858 he would have been returned a second time; but, finding that his election was likely to exclude Charles Cowper, with whose party he had identified himself, he drove to the polling booths and asked electors to vote for his colleague. He was immediately afterwards returned for Cumberland Boroughs. In

November, more to suit his colleagues' convenience than to satisfy his own ambition, he became solicitor-general. He early distinguished himself in parliament by his eloquence, while his popularity was enhanced by his being a native of the colony. In February 1859 Cowper's ministry resigned office.

In 1860 Dalley went overseas for the first time, visiting England, Ireland, and Europe. In the following year, he accepted a commission to return to England with Henry Parkes to continue the work begun by John Dunmore Lang of persuading working-class people with skills to emigrate to the colony. They lectured in most of the large towns of Great Britain, but met with little success. Dalley returned to Sydney in June 1862. Between October 1862 and November 1864 he represented Carcoar, but this was the last time he either stood for or took a seat in the legislative assembly. He did not take politics seriously again for many years, preferring instead to concentrate on his lucrative law practice and to devote himself to reading the classics of English literature and penning articles and reviews for such journals as the Sydney *Punch*. In 1864 he unsuccessfully defended the bushranger Frank Gardiner, whom he had known as a boy; in 1868 he helped defend (again unsuccessfully) Henry O'Farrell, the man who had attempted to assassinate the duke of Edinburgh at Clontarf during the latter's visit to Australia in 1867-8. In 1865 he became editor and part proprietor of the *Freeman's Journal*, the colony's principal independent Catholic newspaper.

In February 1875, Dalley was reappointed to the legislative council (he had first been offered appointment to the upper house in May 1861 but declined it in favour of accepting the post as emigration commissioner) and served in it until April 1880. Drawn back to politics by his friend John Robertson—he served as attorney-general in Robertson's third ministry (February 1875–March 1877) and again in his fourth (August–December 1877). During his two and a half years in the cabinet he worked so hard that his legal opinions filled five volumes published by the government printing office. Wanting to reward Dalley, Robertson offered him a supreme court judgeship in 1876, which he declined; and then the title of queen's counsel (1877), which he accepted. At the end of 1877 he effectively retired from public life, although in 1879 he vigorously opposed Parkes's Public Instruction Bill, which abolished government aid to denominational schools.

In January 1881 Dalley received a severe blow when his wife, Eleanor Jane (the daughter of a wealthy Sydney wine merchant, William Long, whom he had married on 15 June 1872), succumbed to typhoid fever and died. Grief-stricken he left Clairvaux, the mansion overlooking Sydney harbour which he had built for her at Rose Bay, and never set foot in it again. After living in several places he eventually settled at Marinella, a small castle which he had designed and built at Manly on the north shore. In 1881-2 he was little involved in either politics or the law but, after being briefed by prominent Chinese, he was given leave to speak against the Chinese Restriction Bill from the floor of the legislative council, after which the

council modified its most objectionable clauses. At the close of 1882 the Parkes ministry was defeated, and in January 1883 Dalley reluctantly accepted the request of his friend Alexander Stuart that he be reappointed to the legislative council and become attorney-general for the third (and last) time. In October 1884 Stuart became ill and his duties as prime minister and colonial secretary fell upon Dalley, and gave the latter an opportunity of attaining fame. In February 1885 the news of the fall of Khartoum and the death of General Gordon at the hands of Mahdist rebels in the Sudan awakened enormous sympathy in the Australian colonies, and in New South Wales a keen desire to assist the imperial government by the dispatch of troops. The idea originated with Edward Strickland, a former British army officer living in retirement in Sydney, but it was Dalley who did more than anyone else to carry out the project. On 12 February he telegraphed the home government offering two batteries of artillery and a battalion of infantry, five hundred strong, to serve in the Sudan. The offer was accepted with some modifications, and occasioned considerable enthusiasm in England and Australia. In New South Wales Parkes, who had temporarily retired from politics, vehemently condemned Dalley's action, but despite this a patriotic fund to provide for the dependants of any soldiers who might be killed or wounded in the Sudan raised about £26,000 in less than a month. On 3 March a contingent of some 770 volunteers sailed for Suakin, on the Red Sea, under the command of Colonel Richardson, a veteran of the Crimean War.

The ministry resigned office early in October 1885 and in the following year Dalley refused a knighthood and also the succession to the chief-justiceship on the death of his brother-in-law, James Martin. But he accepted appointment to the privy council, the first Australian to receive that honour. He died at his home, Annerley, Darling Point, Sydney, on 28 October 1888, and was buried in the cemetery at Waverley, Sydney, on 30 October. He left three sons and two daughters.

Dalley spent more than thirty years in the forefront of public life in Australia's premier colony. He was universally loved, admired, and respected. His death occasioned widespread sorrow and the largest funeral seen in Sydney to that time. Yet he left no permanent mark on Australia. In the short term the Sudan expedition had a profound effect on the imperial authorities in London, but by the late twentieth century most Australian historians regarded it as having been of little importance; Dalley's legal opinions were rarely consulted and his many writings (which were sketchy and ephemeral) were of little interest. Nevertheless he has been remembered in Australia, especially by Catholics, as one of the most able and eloquent statesmen of the colonial era.

MALCOLM JAMES SAUNDERS

Sources B. T. Dowd, 'William Bede Dalley: scholar, orator, patriot and statesman, 1831–1888', *Royal Australian Historical Society Journal and Proceedings*, 31 (1945), 201–48 · *Sydney Morning Herald* (29 Oct 1888), 6–7, 8 · B. Nairn and M. Rutledge, 'Dalley, William Bede', *AusDB*, vol. 4 · B. Doyle, 'Noted statesman was son of early convict parents', *Catholic Weekly* (9 Jan 1958), 11, 14 · JTD, 'William Bede Dalley: a sketch', *Austral Light*, 6/8 (Aug 1897), 433–46 · Major-

General Antill, 'Dallying with Dalley', *Sunday Sun* (5 Jan 1930) · T. Heney, 'William Bede Dalley', *Sydney Quarterly Magazine*, 5/4 (Dec 1888), 296–301 · J. F. Byrne, 'William Bede Dalley: an appreciation', *Manly*, 2/3 (Oct 1924), 109–17 · *Freeman's Journal* [Dublin] (3 Nov 1888), 8–10, 15 · J. A. Froude, *Oceana, or, England and her colonies* (1886), 161–77, 195–7, 207–13 · J. P. McGuanne, 'Men of the days long past: William Bede Dalley', *Austral-Briton* (11 March 1916), 10–12 · H. F. M., 'William Bede Dalley', *New Triad* (1 June 1928), 17 · K. S. Inglis, *The rehearsal: Australians at war in the Sudan* (1985) · M. J. Saunders, *Britain, the Australian colonies, and the Sudan campaigns of 1884–5* (1985) · *Sydney Morning Herald* (31 Oct 1888), 7, 9, 18 · C. N. Connolly, *Biographical register of the New South Wales parliament, 1856–1901* (1983), 74

Archives Mitchell L., NSW, Parkes MSS

Likenesses C. A. Simonetti, marble bust, *c*.1886, Legislative Council of New South Wales, Macquarie Street, Sydney, Australia · bronze statue, *c*.1897, Hyde Park, Sydney, Australia · J. E. Boehm, medallion, St Paul's Cathedral, London · wood-engraving, NPG; repro. in *ILN* (23 Oct 1886)

Wealth at death £6851—in Australia

Dalling and Bulwer. For this title name *see* Bulwer, (William) Henry Lytton Earle, Baron Dalling and Bulwer (1801–1872).

Dalling, Sir John, first baronet (*c*.1731–1798), army officer and colonial governor, was born at Earsham Street, Bungay, Suffolk, the son of John Dalling (*d*. 1744), who owned the staithe and navigation of Bungay and the nearby manor of Bardolph, and Anne, daughter of Colonel William Windham of Earsham Hall, near Bungay. His mother's elder brother, William Windham, who inherited Earsham Hall, was comptroller of the household to William Augustus, duke of Cumberland, when Cumberland was commander-in-chief in Flanders, and it is likely that Windham used his influence to secure for Dalling an ensign's commission in the army (dated 24 February 1747). He was promoted captain in the 4th King's Own regiment of foot on 21 January 1753, and then major in the 28th foot on 2 February 1757. In March 1757 he sailed with the 28th foot for North America to join the campaign against the French. Again, his path had been eased by his uncle's connections, in this case his friendship with Sir Jeffrey Amherst, commander of the British forces in North America. Dalling's regiment was part of the failed expedition against Louisbourg, led by John Campbell, fourth earl of Loudoun, and in October 1757 joined the garrison at Fort Cumberland.

Early in 1758 Dalling took part in the successful expedition against Louisbourg under Amherst. After the capitulation of the town, on 27 July 1758, he was sent by Amherst with 300 troops to reduce French fishing settlements along the coast of Prince Edward Island, returning to camp on 20 August with a large quantity of materials to build winter quarters. Still a major, though now second in command of his regiment, Dalling took part in James Wolfe's expedition to capture Quebec in 1759 and was given command of a body of light infantry. During the stalemate of July fighting patrols were sent out to scour and ravage the countryside. Dalling's raiding party of 25 July was one of the more successful, returning with 250 prisoners and some 500 horses, sheep, and cows.

Following the capture of Quebec in September, Dalling joined the garrison, where his light infantry were employed in the petty warfare of the winter months, skirmishing with forces sent by the French commander, de Levis, to capture British outposts. In February, during a sharp exchange in the snow near the settlement of Church at Point Levi, Dalling was injured in the foot, a troublesome wound which required several operations. However, on 27 February 1760, before returning to England to convalesce with his uncle at the house of the duke of Cumberland, he was made lieutenant colonel of the 43rd foot, and on 28 April 1760, at the battle of St Foy, he commanded the light infantry stationed on Lieutenant-Colonel James Murray's right flank. The arrival of British naval forces in May forced the French to retreat.

Dalling took command of the 43rd foot in 1761, while it was encamped on Staten Island in readiness for the descent on the French West Indies. He led his regiment in the capture of Martinique, Grenada, St Lucia, and St Vincent and its dependencies in late 1761 and early 1762. From garrison duty on Martinique, in May 1762, his regiment was ordered to join the expedition against Havana, Cuba; the siege lasted until mid-August. Afterwards Dalling was ordered with his regiment to Jamaica, where, apart from visits to England, he remained for the next twenty years. About 1767 he married Grace (1746/1747–1768), the eldest daughter of Philip Pinnock (1720–1778), speaker in the Jamaican assembly in 1768–9 and from 1775 to 1778. The Pinnocks, a wealthy and influential family, assisted Dalling's social and professional rise in the colony. On 4 December 1767 Dalling transferred his lieutenant-colonelcy to the 36th regiment, which had replaced the 43rd foot on garrison duty, and about 1768 he was made governor of Fort Charles and lieutenant-governor of the island. However, his wife died on 6 July 1768, aged twenty-one, leaving an infant daughter, Elizabeth Windham Dalling—who in turn died at sea on 1 November 1768. In or possibly before 1770 Dalling married, secondly, Louisa (*d*. 1824), the daughter of Excelles Lawford, of Burwood, Surrey.

Dalling was promoted to the brevet rank of colonel on 25 May 1772 and on 14 August 1772 transferred his lieutenant-colonel's commission to the 50th foot, that regiment having succeeded the 36th foot on garrison duty. Upon the death of Sir William Trelawny in December 1772, Dalling acted as governor until the arrival of Sir Basil Keith in January 1774. During this brief interlude Dalling took an interest in the small British settlement on the Mosquito Coast. He imposed a new constitution on the settlers which strengthened the position of the superintendent, Thomas Hodgson. When in November 1773 Dalling, at the superintendent's request, dissolved the local council, alarm was raised in London, where the government, mindful of the weakness of British claims to the Mosquito Coast, recalled Hodgson. When Keith arrived in Jamaica, he annulled Dalling's policy and entered into new negotiations with the settlers. Dalling later renewed his interest in Central America with disastrous consequences.

Upon the arrival of the 3rd battalion of the 60th (Royal

American) regiment Dalling was made its colonel commandant (16 January 1776). Following the death of Keith in 1777, on 29 August 1777 Dalling was promoted to the rank of major-general and on 1 September 1777 was confirmed as governor of Jamaica. He was expected by the British government to prepare the island's defences for the possibility of French attack, should France intervene in the War of American Independence.

Dalling often seemed a reluctant governor. He reported somewhat prophetically to Lord George Germain, secretary of state for the colonies, in 1779 that:

> through his wound, gout and the effect of the climate on his nerves, he will soon find himself not equal to the charge … and would therefore wish to be considered an old woman at home than to prove himself so in office abroad. (*Stopford-Sackville MSS*, 95a)

The threat of French invasion in 1778 was averted temporarily by the arrival of reinforcements. When Spain entered the war in June 1779, Dalling was instructed to consider offensive action against the coast of Central America. However, the Spanish moved more quickly, destroying the British settlement of St Georges Key in the Bay of Honduras in mid-September. A small force sent by Dalling under the command of Major William Dalrymple was unable to recapture the key, but took instead the Spanish port of Omoa in the Bay of Honduras and with it 3 million dollars of Guatemalan gold.

Although lacking experience of independent command, Dalling was now emboldened to carry out a grandiose scheme to capture Fort St Juan, which guarded the entrance to Lake Nicaragua, and then to establish a series of forts across the isthmus of Central America. He sent a force of 400 soldiers, which sailed on 3 February 1780 on the *Hinchingbrook*, under the naval command of Captain Horatio Nelson. However, owing to constant delays and a lack of knowledge of the terrain, the fort was not captured until 29 April and the onset of the rainy season. Sickness and disease began to deplete the force, which was forced to return to the coast, leaving behind a small garrison.

Dalling refused to believe that the expedition was effectively ruined and continued to send reinforcements to the coast during the summer. In total, some 1400 men were sent, of whom just 320 survived. In November Dalling finally gave the order to blow up the fort and evacuate the remaining troops. His position was now precarious in the extreme. Military failure and the renewed threat of invasion were compounded by a series of natural disasters in the colony. On 2 October 1780 a tidal wave destroyed the town of Savanna La Mar, and this was followed by a hurricane and an earthquake. In 1781 there was another hurricane and a catastrophic fire in Kingston. A financial crisis caused by a lack of specie in the colony only worsened the economic distress of wartime. Moreover the death of his father-in-law, Philip Pinnock, in 1778 had removed an important source of support in the assembly, with whom relations had rapidly deteriorated following Dalling's imposition of martial law in 1779.

With an all too evident want of judgement, Dalling became embroiled in a quarrel with Admiral Sir Peter Parker over the division of the spoils from the raid on Omoa. This escalated to the point where he ignored a direct order from the government and was removed from office. When Dalling dismissed the attorney-general, Thomas Harrison, for refusing his request to prosecute Parker for trespassing on the crown's possessions, Harrison took the matter to the lords of the Admiralty. Their report of 5 April 1780 ordering Harrison's reinstatement (as advocate-general) was ignored by Dalling, who then suspended members of the local judiciary after they also supported Harrison. A Board of Trade inquiry later criticized Dalling's abuse of power and ordered the reinstatement of the judges.

Growing doubts over Dalling's conduct as governor were heightened by the fall of Mobile in March 1780 and Pensacola in May 1781, though delays in sending reinforcements were due partly to a lack of transports. Thus in March 1781 Germain was ready to yield to Dalling's earlier request to return home. Perversely, however, Dalling had changed his mind, having conceived a desperate plan to conquer the Dutch possession of Curaçao. Germain sent two further orders in June and December recalling him to Britain. Dalling left before receiving the second, handing over his commission as governor to Lieutenant-Governor Archibald Campbell and boarding ship on 24 November 1781. Notwithstanding evident failings, Dalling was promoted (under the rule of strict seniority) to the rank of lieutenant-general on 20 November 1782. He was made a baronet on 11 March 1783. On 1 November 1783 he transferred to the colonelcy of the 37th regiment, a commission he held until his death. He was never given an active military command after his Central American adventure, though between 1784 and 1786 he was commander-in-chief at Madras and a member of the council. Upon his recall he was granted an annuity of £1000 for life. On 3 May 1796 he was promoted to the rank of general.

Dalling died on 16 January 1798 at Clifton, near Bristol. His fifth but eldest surviving son and heir from his second marriage, William Windham Dalling (1774–1864), who inherited the Windham estate at Earsham, succeeded him as second and last baronet. His other children included John Windham Dalling, his youngest son, who served as a midshipman on the *Defence* at Trafalgar in 1805, and Anne Louise (d. 1853), who married General Robert Meade; their son John eventually inherited Earsham.

JONATHAN SPAIN

Sources GEC, *Baronetage*, vol. 5 · *Cassell's biographical dictionary of the American War of Independence, 1769–1783*, ed. M. M. Boatner (1973) · Burke, *Gen. GB* (1952) · *Army List* (1757–98) · *GM*, 1st ser., 68 (1798), 88 · Boase, *Mod. Eng. biog.* · O'Byrne, *Naval biog. dict.* · E. Mann, *Old Bungay* (1934) · *N&Q*, 147 (1924), 138 [E. E. West, Pinnock family] · W. J. Gardner, *History of Jamaica*, 3rd edn (1971) · Fortescue, *Brit. army*, vols. 2–3 · G. Metcalf, *Royal government and political conflict in Jamaica, 1729–1783* (1965) · F. Parkman, *Montcalm and Wolfe* (1964) · *Historical records of the 43rd (Monmouthshire light infantry) regiment*, ed. R. G. A. Levinge (1868) · *Report on the Palk manuscripts*, HMC, 74 (1922) · D. S. Daniell [A. S. Daniell], *Cap of honour: the story of the Gloucestershire regiment* (1951) · *Ninth report*, 3, HMC, 8 (1884), 94–95a · *Report on the manuscripts of Mrs Stopford-Sackville*, 2, HMC, 49 (1910), vol. 2

Archives BL, observations, as governor of Jamaica, on attack upon island of Trinidad, Add. MS 36806 · BL, operation against Grenada, Add. MS 34990 · Norfolk RO, official corresp. and papers | BL, letters to Haldimand, Add. MSS 21731, 21733 · PRO, Germain corresp., CO 137/73 · U. Mich., Clements L., letters to George Germain
Likenesses engraving, NPG; repro. in A. J. O'Shaughnessy, *An empire divided: the American Revolution and the British Caribbean* (2000), 190
Wealth at death granted £1000 annuity upon recall from India, 1796: obituary, *GM*; will, 1798, GEC, *Baronetage*

Dallinger, William Henry (1842–1909), Wesleyan Methodist minister and biologist, was born in Devonport on 5 July 1842, the son of Joseph Stephen Dallinger, artist, etcher, and engraver. He was educated privately and showed an early inclination towards natural history. His religious instinct led him to qualify for the Wesleyan ministry in 1861. After serving Wesleyan churches in Faversham, Cardiff, and Bristol, he passed to Liverpool, where he remained for twelve years (1868–80). On 18 December 1866, while in Cardiff, he married Emma Jane (*b.* 1842), daughter of David Goldsmith, an ironmonger from Bury St Edmunds. The couple had one son.

In 1870, in Liverpool, Dallinger began microscopic researches, which he pursued for ten years, into minute septic organisms. In 1880 he was appointed governor and principal of Wesley College, Sheffield. After eight years, the Wesleyan conference, recognizing his scientific attainments, allowed him to retire from the position while retaining the status and privilege of a Wesleyan minister but without pastoral charge. In addition to his work as minister and governor, Dallinger was a successful public lecturer on microscopical subjects, and for thirty years he lectured for the Gilchrist Educational Trust.

Dallinger's contributions to science were of two kinds— his classical investigations into the life history of certain micro-organisms, and his improvements in microscopical technique. In collaboration with John James Drysdale of Liverpool he concentrated his research on protozoa, in particular on flagellates, about which little was then known. In addition Dallinger and his colleague contributed valuable evidence regarding the then controversial question of abiogenesis (the apparent spontaneous generation of life). They were able to show that flagellates subjected to increasingly high temperatures could be forced to exist in temperatures ordinarily lethal to unacclimatized specimens. Further research showed that the spores of such organisms were also resistant to very high temperatures. These discoveries led to the realization that the ordinary precautions (such as boiling) by which organic solutions were sterilized were insufficient. More importantly, however, his contemporaries believed that these results explained the origin of life in experiments where spontaneous generation had been supposed to occur.

As an expert microscopist, Dallinger enjoyed the highest reputation. His earliest biological researches were rewarded by an unsought grant of £100 from the Royal Society, and he was elected FRS in 1880. He occupied the post of president of the Royal Microscopical Society four times (1884–7) and that of the Quekett Club (1890–92). He

was requested to present his principal results at the British Association meeting in Montreal in 1884, and while there he was awarded an honorary degree of LLD from Victoria University. In 1892, at the celebration of the tercentenary of Trinity College, Dublin, he received his DSc degree, and four years later Durham University created him a DCL in recognition of his contributions to science.

In 1879 Dallinger delivered the Rede lecture at Cambridge, 'The origin of life', which he illustrated with the life histories of simple organisms. His chief papers were published in the *Monthly Microscopical Journal* (1873–6). He edited and rewrote William Benjamin Carpenter's book *The Microscope and its Revelations* (1890; new edn, 1901), and was author of a theologico-scientific work, *The Creator and what we may Know of the Method of Creation* (1887). He died at his home, Ingleside, New Stead Road, Lee, Kent, on 7 November 1909. He was survived by his wife.

F. W. GAMBLE, *rev.* YOLANDA FOOTE

Sources *Nature*, 82 (1909–10), 71 · A. E. S., *PRS*, 82B (1909–10), iv-vi · personal knowledge (1912) · L. C. Sanders, *Celebrities of the century: being a dictionary of men and women of the nineteenth century* (1887) · *WWW* · *Men and women of the time* (1899) · *CGPLA Eng. & Wales* (1909)
Archives CUL, letters to Sir George Stokes
Likenesses H. C. Balding, stipple (after photograph by J. Hawke), NPG · Maull & Fox, photograph, RS · attrib. E. Thomas, oils, Wellcome L. · portrait, repro. in *Journal of the Royal Microscopical Society* (1909)
Wealth at death £7270 3s. 11d.: probate, 22 Nov 1909, *CGPLA Eng. & Wales*

Dallingridge, Sir Edward (*c.*1346–1393), administrator and soldier, was the son and heir of Roger Dallingridge (*c.*1315–1380) and his wife, Alice (*d.* 1360x64), daughter and eventual heir of Sir John Radingden. Dallingridge's early career as a soldier owed much to the influence of his father's association with the leading landowner in Sussex, Richard (II) Fitzalan, earl of Arundel (*d.* 1376). His first experience of campaigning, which he was to recall in 1386 when giving evidence in the *Scrope v. Grosvenor* case, was as a member of the earl's company in the royal army which camped outside Paris in the winter of 1359–60. Much later, in May 1387, he also took part in an expedition at sea under Arundel's son Richard (III). His experience of soldiering, however, was not confined to service with the Fitzalans. In 1373 he joined John of Gaunt, duke of Lancaster, on his great *chevauchée* across France from Calais to Bordeaux, while in 1374 and 1375 he served in naval expeditions under Edward, Lord Despenser. A number of the attachments that he forged as a result of military service formed the basis of more enduring peacetime ties. Edward Despenser retained him for an annual fee of £40 and granted him the office of master forester at Rotherfield, Sussex, while also making him an executor of his will. Other lords with Sussex interests took him into their service. The most notable of these was John de Montfort, duke of Brittany, who was lord of the rape of Hastings. The duke, like Despenser, granted him a handsome annuity of £40 assigned on his Sussex lands. Dallingridge's portfolio of annuities represented a substantial addition to his income.

On the death of his father in 1380 Dallingridge inherited the family estates, which comprised a messuage at Dalling Ridge near East Grinstead, the manors of Bolebrook and Sheffield, Sussex, and other lands in Pevensey rape. The bulk of these lands fell within Ashdown Forest, where the Dallingridges had long wielded considerable influence as hereditary foresters. In the early 1380s Dallingridge championed the cause of his fellow gentry in a bitter dispute with the duke of Lancaster, to whom Edward III had granted the lordship of the rape (and thus of Ashdown) in 1372. Lancaster, an exacting lord, had vigorously asserted his franchisal rights, and Dallingridge and his associates had retaliated by attacking ducal officials and disrupting sessions of the hundredal courts. In June 1384 Dallingridge was attached at Lancaster's suit to answer charges against him and, treating the case as a matter of honour, answered them boldly with a wager of battle. The jury found in Lancaster's favour, and Dallingridge was placed in confinement until 26 July when Arundel, his patron, taking advantage of the duke's absence, interceded on his behalf while the king was his guest at Arundel Castle. Lancaster had his adversary rearrested in October, with the result that he was unable to attend the parliament to which he had recently been elected, but he was released in the following January, and his political standing suffered little harm.

Dallingridge's long association with Arundel meant that he almost certainly supported the earl in the political crisis of 1387–8 in which Richard's opponents, the appellants, of whom Arundel was one, took up arms against the king and 'appealed' (that is, prosecuted) his favourites. Dallingridge was elected to represent Sussex in the Merciless Parliament in which the appeal was heard, and on its dissolution he was appointed to take oaths in the county pledging support for the appellants' regime. However, in the year after the Merciless Parliament his career took a new turn. In or shortly before July 1389 he was retained as a king's knight. Two months previously Richard had dismissed the appellant ministers. Arundel's vigorous retainer, however, had evidently made an impression on the king, and the latter took Dallingridge into his pay. In a matter of weeks he became one of the leading figures in the royal administration. From the early summer of 1389 he is found serving as a member of the king's council, and in the period covered by John Prophete's minute book (1392–3) he was one of the most regular attenders of that body. Richard's confidence in his ability is reflected in his appointment as warden of the city of London when the king confiscated the city's liberties in 1392.

The most eloquent witness to Dallingridge's greatness in Sussex is the castle which he built at Bodiam in the later 1380s. Dallingridge had acquired the manor of Bodiam by his marriage to Elizabeth, daughter and heir of the wealthy knight Sir John Wardieu. The Wardieus' manor house had stood on an elevated site at the northern end of the village. Dallingridge, abandoning this, laid out a new site lower down by the River Rother. The castle, a symmetrical lake fortress, formed the centrepiece of a series of works—an enlarged village where a market and fair were held, new watercourses and millponds. Although he obtained a licence to crenellate, Dallingridge's new castle at Bodiam was hardly intended to fulfil a serious defensive function. Rather it was a splendid lordship seat, an expression of its owner's self-confidence.

Sir Edward Dallingridge died in July or August 1393 and was buried in Robertsbridge Abbey near Bodiam. His heir was his son John, another active figure locally.

NIGEL SAUL

Sources HoP, Commons, 1386–1421, 2.738–42 • N. E. Saul, 'Bodiam Castle', History Today, 45/1 (1995), 16–21 • S. Walker, 'Lancaster v. Dallingridge: a franchisal dispute in fourteenth-century Sussex', Sussex Archaeological Collections, 121 (1983), 87–94 • Chancery records
Wealth at death approx. £500

Dallington, Sir Robert (1561–1636x8), author and courtier, was born at Geddington, Northamptonshire. From about 1575 to about 1580 he was at Corpus Christi College, Cambridge; there is no record of his graduation, but in 1601 he was incorporated at Oxford as MA of Cambridge. While at Corpus he became known to the Buttes family of Norfolk, who were his first patrons, and for a time he was a schoolmaster in Norfolk, probably at Thornage or Great Ryburgh where the Buttes family had houses. On the death of Sir William Buttes in 1583 Dallington put together a Booke of Epitaphes, containing his own verses and those of twenty-seven others, many of them Corpus men. He addressed Sir William's son Thomas as his 'Maecenas' for sustaining his studies. These next bore fruit when in 1592 he published The Strife of Love, a partial translation of the Hypnerotomachia Poliphili (1499) attributed to Francesco Colonna. This was dedicated to the memory of Sir Philip Sidney, to Sidney's surviving friends, and to his successor as Renaissance role model, the earl of Essex; it was thus angling for patronage on the large scale. The book celebrated an artistic and architectural culture which Dallington had not yet seen; but he was not the only Elizabethan Englishman to write about Italy in expectation rather than from experience. The sensual delights evoked in the Hypnerotomachia would have shocked many of Dallington's countrymen, not least the strait-laced gentry of Norfolk, and indeed his association with the Buttes family ended by or at this time. However, he had secured a much grander patron in the fifth earl of Rutland, with whom he at last saw Italy (as also France and Germany) while attending the earl as tutor and man of business in 1595–7. In the same capacity he went with the earl's brother Francis Manners on another grand tour between 1598 and 1600; the party, which included Inigo Jones, was received by Emperor Maximilian II.

Along with Rutland and his brothers, Dallington was involved in Essex's rebellion in 1601. On 8 February he was committed to the king's bench prison, and on 15 May was called before the council in Star Chamber and fined £100, subsequently remitted. He remained in the service of the family. In 1604 his View of France was first published, and in 1605 his Survey of … Tuscany. Both were written for private circulation, and were printed without the author's permission, but they established his reputation as a cicerone. His Italophilia was particularly influential in rekindling affections stifled in England by the Reformation.

In 1605 Rutland had introduced Dallington to Prince Henry, whom he would serve for four years without reward. In December 1609 Rutland, in writing to Salisbury, renewed his recommendation of Dallington for the prince's service. At the same time Dallington presented Henry with a manuscript translation, 'Aphorismes civill and militarie', selected from the Italian historian Guicciardini. These moves were successful, and from 1610 to 1612 Dallington was fee'd as a gentleman-in-ordinary of the prince's chamber, joining the distinguished group of scholars who attended James I's high-minded heir. Following the prince's death in 1612 Dallington reworked his *Aphorismes*, which were published in 1613 with a new dedication to Prince Charles. Improbably the ruse worked a second time, and Dallington became one of the few members of Prince Henry's household to be retained by the new heir. It has even been suggested that Charles may have derived his unfortunate persuasion that duplicity was a princely virtue from reading Dallington's Guicciardini.

On 9 July 1624 the prince obtained for Dallington the mastership of the Charterhouse, against the wishes of the ecclesiastical hierarchy, who wanted an appointment from their own profession. Dallington was nevertheless obliged to take deacon's orders. On 30 December that year he was knighted. When Dallington drew up his will on 25 April 1636 he was in good health, but he died within two years, and was buried at the Charterhouse. By the will, proved on 1 March 1638, he left £300 to the poor of Geddington to perpetuate a dole he had already established there. His nephews John and Thomas Ayre are the only family mentioned in his will.   C. S. KNIGHTON

Sources Wood, *Ath. Oxon.: Fasti* (1815), 292–3 • Foster, *Alum. Oxon.* • Venn, *Alum. Cant.*, 1/2.4 • *The manuscripts of his grace the duke of Rutland*, 4 vols., HMC, 24 (1888–1905), vol. 4, pp. 411, 448–9, 451, 453 • *Calendar of the manuscripts of the most hon. the marquess of Salisbury*, 21, HMC, 9 (1970), 170–71 • *CSP dom.*, 1598–1601, p. 412; 1623–5, p. 292; 1627–8, p. 49; 1631–3, p. 183 • *APC*, 1600–01, 160, 356, 484, 488 • K. J. Höltgen, 'Sir Robert Dallington (1561–1637): author, traveler, and pioneer of taste', *Huntington Library Quarterly*, 47 (1984), 147–77 • R. C. Strong, *Henry, prince of Wales, and England's lost Renaissance* (1986), 30–31, 210 • Fuller, *Worthies* (1662), 2.288 • J. Bridges, *The history and antiquities of Northamptonshire*, ed. P. Whalley, 2 (1791), 311 • PRO, PROB 11/176, fols. 188r–189r

Archives Northants. RO, Finch-Hatton MSS

Wealth at death £387 16s. 8d.—in cash bequests, incl. £47 16s. 8d. to inmates and servants of the Charterhouse, and £300 to poor of Geddington: PRO, PROB 11/176, fols. 188r–189r

Dallmeyer, John Henry [*formerly* Johann Heinrich] (1830–1883), optician, was born Johann Heinrich Dallmeyer on 6 September 1830, at Loxten, near Versmold, in the department of Minden, Westphalia, the second son of William Dallmeyer, a farmer with scientific interests, and his wife, Catherine Wilhelmina, *née* Meyer, of Hengelaye, Loxten. Dallmeyer studied at the village school until the age of fourteen, when his manifest intelligence and assiduity led his parents to send him to a higher school, and in 1845 he moved to Osnabrück, where a kindly childless relative, Westmann Meyer, sent him to a school conducted by a notable teacher, a Mr Schuren. He remained there for two years, studying geometry and mathematics. His scientific ability was now so evident that on leaving school he was at once apprenticed for three years to an optician at Osnabrück named Aklund. There he quickly progressed as a workman, so that by the end of his apprenticeship he had far surpassed his master. From an early age Dallmeyer appears to have intended moving to England, and by working as a commercial correspondent in his spare time he earned enough to pay for English lessons.

Dallmeyer moved to London about 1850. For a few weeks he suffered great hardship, but was helped by an old Osnabrück schoolfriend. After five weeks he found employment in the workshop of an optician, W. Hewitt, who had learned his trade under Andrew Ross, and who shortly afterwards returned to Ross's employment, placing Dallmeyer in an unpleasant position in Ross's workshop. From his quiet and retiring ways he was dubbed 'the gentleman', while his still poor English placed him at a great disadvantage. Unhappy with his position he sought other employment, and acted for a year as French and German correspondent to a firm of coffee importers. On the bankruptcy of this firm he was invited by Ross's foreman to return to the workshop, but he refused to do so as a workman. Eventually Dallmeyer was appointed scientific adviser to the great optician's firm, and entrusted with the testing and finishing of the finest optical apparatus. Ross's approval of Dallmeyer's character and ability extended to allowing him to marry his second daughter, Hannah, in 1854. In 1859 Andrew Ross died; he left Dallmeyer a third of his large fortune, estimated at £20,000, and the telescope-making section of his business.

About this time Dallmeyer's name was first publicized by Sir John Herschel in the article on telescopes in the eighth edition of the *Encyclopaedia Britannica*, where he listed the most important refracting telescopes then known, adding as to several that 'Mr. Dallmeyer laid claim to the personal execution, and the computation of their curvatures'. The largest object-glass for a telescope made by Dallmeyer did not exceed 8 inches in diameter (his preferred size was 4⅛ inches), but all contemporary observers who used his instruments praised highly their exquisite definition. This was partly due to Dallmeyer's method of polishing glass underwater, thereby obtaining a 'black' polish seldom met with. Several of Dallmeyer's telescopes were used in government expeditions to observe eclipses of the sun and the transits of Venus, and they continued to be so used long after his death. In 1861 Dallmeyer was elected a fellow of the Royal Astronomical Society, and he served for several years on its council. At the exhibition of 1862 Dallmeyer appeared as a manufacturer of photographic, and more especially, portrait lenses; the greater part of his fame and fortune from this time rested on the admirable instruments which he supplied to photographers in all parts of the world, and of which more than 30,000 had been sold up to the time of his death. His 'triple achromatic lens', designed in 1861, was described by the jurors as 'free from distortion, with chemical and visual foci coincident'. This lens worked at f/10 and was popular for copying, and architectural work, but was replaced by his Rapid Rectilinear in 1866. Dallmeyer's Patent Portrait lenses were constructed on the Petzval principle, but with one modification: the relative positions of the flint and crown glass in the posterior combination were reversed, so as to render it possible, by slightly unscrewing them, to introduce spherical aberration at will and thus secure that 'soft focus' preferred by some nineteenth-century artists. In 1864 Dallmeyer patented a single-element wide-angle lens which was largely used for photographing landscapes. It consisted of two pieces of crown and one of flint glass worked to the proper curves and cemented together so as to form a meniscus of rather deep curvature.

Dallmeyer was for many years a prominent member of the Royal Microscopical Society, and his work in the construction of object-glasses for the microscope is well known and appreciated. His last important improvement was in the condenser used in the 'magic lantern' (which Dallmeyer preferred to call the optical lantern). This was effected at the request of an old friend and veteran photographer, the Revd T. F. Hardwich. The new condenser consisted of a plano-convex combined with a double convex lens, one surface of the latter being nearly flat. This principle is used in slide projectors to this day. Dallmeyer constructed a photoheliograph for the Vilna observatory of the Russian government in 1863, for taking 4 inch pictures of the sun. This instrument was a complete success, and Harvard College observatory was supplied with a similar one in the following year. In 1873 orders for five photoheliographs for the transit of Venus expeditions were executed for the British government. These gave 4 inch images of the sun. They were later fitted with new magnifiers so as to give a solar image 8 inches in diameter, and were for many years used for solar photography. At the various exhibitions at Dublin and Berlin (1865), Paris (1867 and 1878), and Philadelphia (1876), Dallmeyer's lenses received the highest awards. The French government bestowed on him the cross of the Légion d'honneur, while Russia appointed him to the order of St Stanislaus. The surveying departments of British and foreign governments left the optical work of the instruments they ordered entirely in Dallmeyer's hands. Every instrument was tested by him personally before it left his establishment. Dallmeyer contributed several papers–chiefly on photographic optics—to various periodicals; his pamphlet on the choice and use of photographic lenses, passed through six editions. For many years he served on the council of the Royal Photographic Society.

After Hannah's death Dallmeyer married again, in 1862; his second wife was Elizabeth Mary, eldest daughter of T. R. Williams of Seller's Hall, Finchley. He left five children; his eldest son, Thomas Rudolphus Dallmeyer (b. 1859), continued the business, and in 1891 was one of the independent inventors of a telephoto lens. About 1880 Dallmeyer was forced to cease active work, and during the

next few years he undertook several long journeys in search of health. He lived in a mansion that he had built, Sunnyfield, at Hampstead Heath. He died while on a cruise off the coast of New Zealand, being lost overboard, presumed drowned, on 30 December 1883. His wife survived him. W. J. HARRISON, rev. P. D. HINGLEY

Sources private information (1888) · Monthly Notices of the Royal Astronomical Society, 45 (1884–5), 190–91 · British Journal of Photography (18 Jan 1884), 37 · R. Kingslake, A history of the photographic lens (1989), 9, 29, 30, 40, 64, 133–7, 221 · M. Holbrook, R. G. W. Anderson, and D. J. Bryden, Science preserved: a directory of scientific instruments in collections in the United Kingdom and Eire (1992), 82, 223 · D. Howse, Greenwich observatory, 3: The buildings and instruments (1675–1975) (1975), 13, 55, 93–4, 96, 118, 120 · d. cert. · m. cert. · CGPLA Eng. & Wales (1884)

Likenesses photograph, repro. in Kingslake, History, 220

Wealth at death £78,257 3s. 8d.: probate, 13 Feb 1884, CGPLA Eng. & Wales

D'Almeida, João (c.1572–1653), Jesuit missionary in Brazil, was born in London of English Catholic parents, his original name being probably John Mead or Meade. At the age of ten he was taken to Viana do Castelo, in Portugal, by a merchant named Bento da Rocha, in whose family he was brought up, and to whom he was apprenticed. He later wrote of this as follows: 'I was withdrawn from England, from the city of London, a very nest of heresies, at a time when they were most rampant', and was henceforth known by the Portuguese version of his name (Foley, 7/2.1322). In 1588 he accompanied da Rocha to Pernambuco, in Brazil, where he attended a Jesuit school at Olinda for four years (1588–92). He entered the Society of Jesus at Bahia on 1 November 1592, and the following year, on completion of his noviciate, joined the community at Vitoria, in the captaincy of Espirito Santo. Its rector, José de Anchieta, renowned as the 'apostle of Brazil', an ascetic and thaumaturge, was to have a formative influence on d'Almeida's character.

After ordination at Bahia in 1602 d'Almeida spent many years in southern Brazil, undertaking arduous missionary journeys on foot to the remote regions between São Paulo and the River Plate. These included two expeditions across the Serra do Mar to evangelize the Carijó peoples in the vicinity of the Lago dos Patos. In 1616 he and a companion established settlements for the protection of Carijó from the island of Santa Catarina. From 1639 until his death he lived at the Jesuit college in Rio de Janeiro, where he was much in demand as a confessor and counsellor, and was venerated for his extreme austerity. His advice was sought by, among others, Salvador Correia de Sá, the governor of Rio and admiral of the Brazilian fleet. It was as a result of d'Almeida's augury of divine favour that de Sá ventured in 1648 on his naval expedition to Angola which ended successfully, against all odds, with the recapture of Luanda from the Dutch. This event, which confirmed d'Almeida's reputation as an oracle, ensured the very survival of the Portuguese empire by recovering control of the African slave trade upon which the production of Brazilian sugar and tobacco depended.

D'Almeida died at the Jesuit college in Rio on 24 September 1653 and was interred in its chapel. The hagiographical *Vida do P. Joam d'Almeida* written by his friend and fellow Jesuit Simão de Vasconcellos, dedicated to Salvador de Sá and published at Lisbon in 1658, extended d'Almeida's fame as a seer, healer, spiritual athlete, and miracle worker. The first book to be published about the work of the Society of Jesus in Brazil, it was reissued in a Latin version by Antonio de Macedo at Venice in 1669, and at Rome in 1671. The substantial extracts included by Henry More in his *Historia provinciae Anglicanae S.J.* (1660) first brought d'Almeida to the attention of his fellow English Catholics.   G. MARTIN MURPHY

Sources S. de Vasconcellos, *Vida do P. Joam d'Almeida* (Lisbon, 1658) · C. R. Boxer, *Salvador de Sá and the struggle for Brazil and Angola, 1602–1686* (1952) · H. More, *Historia missionis Anglicanae Societatis Iesu* (St Omer, 1660), 503–18 · C. R. Boxer, 'Salvador Correia de Sá e Benevides and the reconquest of Angola in 1648', *Hispanic American Historical Review*, 28 (1948), 483–513 · H. Foley, ed., *Records of the English province of the Society of Jesus*, 7/2 (1883), 1321–9 · J. Hemming, *Red gold: the conquest of the Brazilian Indians* (1978), 264, 595 · A. de Backer and others, *Bibliothèque de la Compagnie de Jésus*, new edn, 8, ed. C. Sommervogel (Brussels, 1898), 485 · S. Leite, *Historia da Companhia de Jesus no Brasil*, 6 (Lisbon, 1945); 8 (Lisbon, 1949)
Archives Archivum Romanum Societatis Iesu, Rome, Bras. 8.110–113, 261–263v
Likenesses R. Collin, engraving, repro. in de Vasconcellos, *Vida*

Dál Riata [Dalriada], **kings of** (*act. c.*500–*c.*850), rulers in Scotland, were the lords of a realm whose name was also given to an ancient small kingdom, situated in the northeast corner of Antrim, northern Ireland, and named from the *dál* ('division', primarily in the sense of people rather than territory) of Réte—a mythical ancestor.

Origins to 609 Traditionally a colony of the Dál Riata settled in Britain, probably before 500, and during several generations the two territories, though separated by 13 miles of sea, formed a single kingdom with its centre of power in Britain. The link was dissolved, perhaps in the time of *Domnall Brecc (d. 642/3), but *c.*700 the Dál Riata in Britain were still, to *Adomnán, 'the Irish [Latin *Scoti*] of Britain', and long afterwards their kings were counted among the overkings of Irish provinces. The eastern limit of their British realm, separating the Scots from the Picts, was 'the mountains of the spine of Britain' (*Life of Columba*, 2.46), that is, Drumalban. The northern and southern limits cannot be defined so clearly, but the popular equation of Dál Riata with Argyll is probably not far wrong. The historical kings of the Dál Riata were derived by genealogists from two brothers, Fergus and Loarn (or Lorne), the sons of Erc. Most were descended from Fergus's grandsons, Comgall and Gabrán, and ruled territories which included Cowal and Kintyre. The descendants of Lorne (*cenél Loairn*) further north had a territory larger than modern Lorne; for some forty years, before and after 700, their kings successfully disputed the overkingship.

A regnal list, versions of which are still extant, began with **Fergus** [Fergus II; *called* Fergus Mór] (*d.* 501), reputedly a contemporary of St Patrick. Such a list seems to have been used retrospectively by an annalist to enter the deaths of kings at the appropriate places, counting the reign lengths back as far as Comgall and Gabrán. Their father, Domangart, and Fergus himself, were added later in different annal compilations.

Comgall mac Domangart [Congallus I] (*d. c.*538) died 'in the thirty-fifth year of his reign' (Anderson, *Early Sources*, 1.10). His family gave their name to Cowal, the district to the south of Loch Fyne. He was succeeded by his brother **Gabrán** [Goranus] (*d. c.*558), who reigned for about twenty years. Later stories seem to connect Gabrán with the southern Pictish country and the River Forth, but all that can be learned from the annals is that he died in the same year (*c.*558) in which the Pictish king Brude mac Maelchon caused a flight, or withdrawal, of Scots. This event, unexplained, was clearly a Scottish disaster. It is unclear whether Gabrán's death was connected with it, but the words used of his death do not suggest that he died in battle or by violence.

Gabrán was succeeded by his nephew **Conall mac Comgall** [Congallus II] (*d.* 574). In 563 Conall was visited in Britain by St Columba (*d.* 597), who had recently arrived from Ireland to begin his life of 'pilgrimage'. There were two traditions about the foundation of Columba's monastery in Iona. Pictish tradition was the probable source of Bede's statement that the island was given to Columba by Picts. But an entry attached to the notice of King Conall's death in the Irish annals says that Conall was the donor. There may have been truth in both traditions. In 568 Conall joined with the king of Meath in an expedition in 'Iardoman', probably the Inner Hebrides. He died in 574 and was succeeded by his cousin *Aedán (or Áedan) mac Gabrán. The choice of Conall's successor seems to have lain between Aedán and his brother Eoganán, and it was the latter who at first had the powerful support of Columba. But, prompted by angelic visions, according to Iona tradition, the saint changed his mind and gave Aedán his blessing.

Aedán was remembered partly for the concord he reached with the northern Uí Néill relating to the status of the Irish part of Aedán's kingdom. In a famous meeting at Druim Cete (or Druim Cett) in Derry, it was agreed (or so it appears) that military service from the Dál Riata in Ireland should be paid to Áed, son of Ainmire, and his successors, their taxes and tribute to Aedán and his successors. This implicitly ruled out any rights claimed by kings of the Ulaid over the Irish Dál Riata. The annals date the meeting in the year after Aedán's accession, that is in 575, but there are difficulties in the dating, and it has been plausibly argued that the true date may have been *c.*590.

There was a tradition that Aedán had fought against the Picts during thirteen years, seemingly before he became king. It is doubtful whether any of his later battles, noticed in the annals, involved hostility between him and the Picts. His last battle, which Bede dated in 603, was fought at 'Degsastan', perhaps near the present English–Scottish border. It was a brave attempt to halt the northward spread of the Angles of Northumbria, but Aedán's army was heavily defeated and, says Bede, from that time until the present day (*c.*731) no king of Scots in Britain had dared to engage in battle against the Angles.

Aedán died a few years later. Figures in lists and annals (none very dependable at this period) suggest that he may have died in 609, but had ceased to reign in 608. The date 609 is slightly confirmed by separate sources (the martyrology of Tallaght and the eleventh-century prophecy of Berchan) which would fix the day of his death as 17 April, a Thursday. Berchan says that he died in Kintyre, Fordun that he was buried at Kilkerran (Campbeltown).

Eochaid Buide and his sons, 609–c.660 Aedán had a number of sons, of whom at least four died in battle in their father's lifetime. His successor, **Eochaid Buide** [Eugenius IV] (d. c.629), was one of the younger ones (his epithet means 'yellow') [see also Eugenius I–VIII (act. c.350–763)]. It was not usual for a king to be followed immediately by his son, and perhaps that was why it was told of Eochaid that when he was a child Columba prophesied that he would be king after Aedán.

The entry of Eochaid's death (c.629) in the annals of Ulster reads: 'Death of Eochaid Buide, king of the Picts, son of Aedán. So I have found in the Book of Cuanu' (Anderson, *Early Sources*, 1.151). It is not clear how much of the entry came from Cuanu's book (a version of the annals, of uncertain date, known only from the Ulster annalist's quotations from it, of which this is the last). Eochaid's kingship 'of the Picts' has not been satisfactorily explained.

Eochaid Buide's death was followed by the brief reign of **Connad Cerr** (d. c.629), whose epithet means 'crooked' or 'left-handed'. On the evidence of the Irish synchronisms, Connad Cerr is usually thought to have been Eochaid Buide's son. A genealogical section in the *Míniugud senchasa fher nAlban* ('Explanation of the genealogy of the men of Scotland') names Connad Cerr in a list of Eochaid's sons. This text, however, is not to be depended on; in the same sentence Domnall Dond, Eochaid's grandson who died c.696, is included among Eochaid's sons. In the Latin lists Connad Cerr is a 'son of Conal', and it would appear that in the synchronisms the phrase 'his son' (a mac) has been displaced. A difficulty in accepting the reading of the Latin lists was pointed out by Bannerman: the only possible known Conal is Comgall's son, the king who died in 574, and a son of his would seem too old to be made king about 629.

Connad Cerr died in the same year in which he became king, in a battle at Fid Eóin in Ireland, an internal quarrel of the Dál nAraidi, southern neighbours of the Irish Dál Riata. His successor was Domnall Brecc, Eochaid Buide's son. Domnall had an unlucky reign. In 637 he chose to side with Congal Cáech, overking of the Ulaid, against Domnall, Áed's son, head of the Cenél Conaill branch of the northern Uí Néill. (Legend said that Congal was a nephew of Domnall Brecc.) Domnall's connection with the battle of Moira (in Down), in which Congal lost his life, is known, not from the annals, but from Cumméne, the seventh abbot of Iona, author of a work on Columba. A passage from the book, copied into an early manuscript of Adomnán's life of the saint, quotes a prophecy of the evil consequences to any of King Aedán's descendants who

shall fail in loyalty to the Cenél Conaill, Columba's kindred. Cumméne (who died in 669) adds that the prophecy had been fulfilled 'in our time' in the battle of Moira, when Domnall Brecc without provocation wasted the province of Domnall, son of Áed. Domnall Brecc is not said to have been present in the battle.

No more is heard of Domnall Brecc in Ireland. It may be that the Irish Dál Riata no longer acknowledged his kingship. A severance of the two Dál Riatas would account for the warning attributed to Columba, that Aedán's descendants might 'lose the sceptre of this kingdom from their hands' (Anderson, *Early Sources*, 1.160). There was a second sense in which Domnall might be said to have lost the sceptre. He was still apparently king in 642 or 643, at his death in battle against Owen, king of the Strathclyde Britons; but it seems that he no longer reigned alone. Reign lengths suggest that from 637 until his death the kingship was shared between him and **Ferchar** [Fearchair I, Ferchardus I] (d. c.651), a son of Connad Cerr. The evidence, however, is ambiguous. In the lists Ferchar stands before Domnall Brecc. And the only mention of Ferchar in the annals is a notice of his death, peculiar to the annals of Ulster, in 693. The year is improbably late, though not quite impossible; it has been conjectured that the entry belonged to a group of badly misdated entries (including one of the death of Domnall Brecc), and that Ferchar really died c.651.

The period of Northumbrian domination, c.660–685 If the Latin lists are right in making Connad Cerr a son of Conal, and if Conal was the Conall Comgall's son who reigned from c.558 to 574, then Ferchar was, as far as can be ascertained, the last member of the house of Comgall to be a king of Dál Riata. After him the kingship seems to have been divided again, this time between **Conall Crandomna** [Congallus III] (d. 660), who was a brother of Domnall Brecc, and, until Conall's death, a 'Dúnchad son of Dubán'. This Dúnchad has not been identified satisfactorily, but there is a distinct possibility that he was the grandfather of a later king, Fiannamail. Conall Crandomna and Dúnchad are said to have reigned together for ten years (651?–660). After Conall's death **Domangart** (d. 673), a son of Domnall Brecc, became sole king. It was perhaps towards the end of the joint reign that Scots in Britain, as well as Picts, became tributary to Oswiu, king of Northumbria (d. 670). When Cumméne, writing in his own person, says that since the day of the battle of Moira the descendants of Aedán have been held down by *extranei* ('strangers' or 'outsiders'), he is probably referring to, and lamenting, their subjection to Northumbria, which was to continue long after Cumméne's death.

Domangart died in 673 by violence of some kind (*jugulatio*). He was one of the very few kings to whom contemporary annalists attached the label 'king of Dál Riata'. He was followed by two sons of his uncle Conall Crandomna, who reigned in succession: Maelduin (or Mael Dúin), who died peacefully in 688 or 689, and Domnall Dond, who met a violent death, perhaps in 696. In 685, towards the end of Maelduin's life, Scots as well as Picts were freed from Northumbrian dominion by the Pictish victory at Dunnichen and the death of King Ecgfrith.

Ferchar Fota and his rivals, 685–700 It may be that the violent deaths of Domangart (673) and Domnall Dond (696?) reflect antagonism between the two branches of Eochaid Buide's descendants through his sons Domnall Brecc and Conall Crandomna, but nothing is known of the circumstances. The king-lists at this period are corrupt and defective. One piece of list evidence that cannot be ignored is the twenty-one-year reign of **Ferchar Fota** [Fearchair II, Ferchardus II] (*d.* 697), immediately before that of Eochaid, son of Domangart. The annals twice mention Ferchar Fota (his epithet means 'the Tall'): in 678 when he lost many of the tribe of Lorne in a battle against Britons, and in 697 when he died. Sons and grandsons of his became overkings of the Dál Riata, but the annal evidence affords no room for Ferchar himself as overking. It can only be guessed that he exercised kingship somewhere outside his own kingdom of Lorne, the northernmost of the kingdoms of the Dál Riata. Genealogists derived its kings from a brother of Fergus, son of Erc, two centuries earlier.

Domnall Dond's successor was a younger cousin, **Eochaid** [Eugenius V] (*d.* 697), the son of Domangart, son of Domnall Brecc. The lists give Eochaid a strange epithet, Rianamhail and the like. In one text (list E) it was understood to mean 'crooked nosed' and translated into Latin as *habens curvum nasum*. He was killed in 697, the year in which Ferchar Fota died. He left at least one son, another Eochaid, who does not appear in the annals until 726, and may have been very young when his father was killed.

Ainfcellach (*d.* 719), a son of Ferchar Fota, followed Eochaid in the overkingship, but in the next year was driven out and carried, a prisoner, to Ireland. His successor, presumably his captor, was **Fiannamail** (*d.* 700), Dúnchad's grandson, described as 'king of Dál Riata' at his death. It is supposed that his grandfather was the Dúnchad, Dubán's son, who had held part of the overkingship in the 650s. Fiannamail's ability to remove his predecessor to Ireland prompts the question whether he belonged to a royal family of Irish Dál Riata. But the available evidence is unsatisfactory. That the guarantors of Adomnán's law (697) include both Fiannamail 'grandson of Dúnchad', with no title, and 'Eochu grandson of Domnall' (that is, Eochaid, son of Domangart), with the title rí, 'king', tells very little about Fiannamail's status. A 'king of Kintyre' called Dúnchad Becc is noticed by the annals in 721; his name suggests that he may have been of the same family as Fiannamail. The absence of Fiannamail from the genealogical section of the *Míniugud senchasa fher nAlban* is not relevant; this text brings its lists in general no further down than Aedán's grandsons. But though Fiannamail is not in the king-lists of the Dál Riata, there is a strong possibility that he was present in the original list. If, owing to a scribal dislocation, his name, mistaken for an epithet, was attached to the name of Eochaid, son of Domangart, that would account both for Fiannamail's apparent absence and for Eochaid's unexplained epithet Rianamhail.

The rule of Selbach, 700–730 Fiannamail himself was killed in 700, and **Selbach** [Selvach] (*d.* 730), a son of Ferchar Fota, began a twenty-three-year reign as overking. His brother Ainfcellach, Fiannamail's victim, is not heard of again until 719. After four violent ends to reigns in as many years, Selbach's reign seems like a period of stability; nevertheless, the annals record several armed conflicts, against members of the old royal family or against kinsmen of his own. In 701 he destroyed the Lorne fortress of Dunolly, and in 714 he rebuilt it. In 712 he besieged a place in the south of Kintyre, perhaps Dunaverty. In the autumn of 719 he fought against his brother Ainfcellach, last heard of in 698, who was killed in the battle. Soon after, in a battle at sea, Selbach was beaten by Dúnchad Becc and the Cenél nGabráin. There were also battles against the Britons in 704, 711, and 717, in which Selbach is not actually named.

In 723 Selbach adopted the clerical habit, and the overkingship of the Dál Riata, together with the kingship of Lorne, evidently passed to his son **Dúngal** (*d. c.*736). In 726, when Dúngal was thrown *de regno*, the overkingship returned to the old ruling family in the person of Eochaid, son of Eochaid (son of Domangart, son of Domnall Brecc). In the next year Selbach came out of retirement to fight a battle with adversaries who are described as the *familia* of Eochaid, grandson of Domnall. No doubt Eochaid, son of Eochaid, was involved, but it is not recorded that he was actually present in the battle. Selbach died in 730.

Wars to west and east, 730–778 In 733 Eochaid, son of Eochaid, died. It is not known whether he was still alive when *Flaithbertach, a great-grandson of Domnall, son of Áed, and the last of the Cenél Conaill to be counted as a high-king of Ireland, brought a fleet of the Dál Riata to Ireland to assist him against his rivals. The campaign was a failure; in the following year Flaithbertach was forced to abdicate.

In 733 also Dúngal of Lorne was active off the north Irish coast, and he profaned the monastery in Tory Island by forcibly removing Brude, son of the Pictish king *Oengus mac Forgusso (Onuist son of Uurguist), who had taken sanctuary there. The origin of the enmity that certainly existed from this time between Dúngal and Oengus is obscure. In this same year Dúngal's cousin **Muredach** (*d.* 771), son of Ainfcellach, 'assumed the kingship of the tribe of Lorne'. In the next year Dúngal was overtaken by Oengus's avenging anger. Dúngal's fortress was destroyed, and he was wounded and fled to Ireland.

After the death of Eochaid the overkingship was perhaps divided between Muredach of Lorne and an Alpin whom the Irish synchronisms, not very dependably, call a 'son of Eochaid'. If that is true, he was most likely a half-brother of the king who had just died. It has been suggested that Alpin was the man of that name (not very common among the Scots) who had made himself overking of the Picts from 726 to 728 and had then been forced into flight by Oengus.

In 736 Oengus made a determined incursion into territory of the Dál Riata, accompanied by his brother Talorgan. He took Dunadd, and his brother routed an opposing army led by Muredach. Dúngal and his brother Feradach were captured, and Dúngal is not heard of again. It is pleasant to conjecture that Feradach became the father of the Pictish king Ciniod, son of Uuredech, who reigned from 763 to 768.

Little is known about relations of the Dál Riata with the Picts following Oengus's conquest. Iona ceases to be a source of contemporary annal information about 740. The conquest should probably be seen as a chiefly personal one, a matter of tribute and hostages. There is nothing in writing to suggest that Oengus himself assumed the status of a king of the Dál Riata, though some evidence may yet be extracted from rock carvings on Dunadd. There is no record of Muredach, son of Ainfcellach, after 736 until his death in 771, noticed in the seventeenth-century annals of the four masters. Alpin is not mentioned in annals at all, either before or after 736. The first king after Muredach in the original list of the Dál Riata was **Aed** [Áed] **Find** (d. 778), said when he died to have reigned for thirty years, so his reign was counted from 748. Before Aed the Latin lists insert a **Ewen** [Eogan] (d. 763), Muredach's son; perhaps a genuine king of Lorne, he was styled Eugenius VIII by Fordun, who gives 763 as the year of his death. In 750 there is a (probably late) entry in the annals of Ulster which has been variously translated: 'Ebbing of the sovereignty of [Oengus]' (Anderson, *Early Sources*, 1.240) or 'End of the reign of [Oengus]' (*Ann. Ulster*, 204–5). It is uncertain how far it relates to the Dál Riata. Welsh sources record a heavy defeat of Picts by Britons in the same year.

Aed was almost certainly a son of the King Eochaid who died in 733. Some texts of the pedigree are corrupt, but the one in the Poppleton manuscript can be accepted as true: 'Aed Find son of Eochaid son of Echu son of Domangart son of Domnall Brecc' (Anderson, *Kings and Kingship*, 189). He may have been very young when his father died. In 768 there was a battle in Fortriu 'between Aed and Cinaed', that is, Aed Find and Ciniod, son of Uuredech (Feradach), king of Picts. Presumably Aed had invaded Fortriu. He was remembered, however, for more than military success. He had an epithet (in the older version of the Irish synchronisms) Airectech, from *airecht*, 'a public assembly'. Nearly a century after his death a body of law, adopted by an assembly of Scots for a united Pictish–Scottish kingdom, was named after him: 'laws of Aed son of Eochaid'.

The union of the Dál Raita with the Picts Aed was succeeded in 778 by his brother Fergus who died in 781. Each brother is 'king of Dál Riata' in the annals. Defects in the sources over the next sixty years make it difficult to establish the sequence of kings with certainty. The following list, especially the dates, should be treated with caution (for further details *see* *Picts, kings of the).

r. 781–*c.*805, Domnall. He is not mentioned in the annals. The later synchronisms call him 'Constantine's son', which is probably an editorial fiction.

r. 805–7, Conall, son of Tadg. King of Picts until 789, when he was routed by Constantine, son of Fergus, a Pictish rival, he was king of Dál Riata from 805. He was killed in 807 by Conall, son of Aedán, in Kintyre.

r. 807–11, Conall, son of Aedán. He killed Conall, son of Tadg, in 807. His death does not occur in the annals.

r. 811–20, *Constantine (or Causantin) [see under Picts, kings of the], son of Fergus (who was son of Eochaid and brother of Aed Find). King of Picts from 789 when he routed Conall, son of Tadg, and king of Dál Riata also from 811, he died in 820, a 'king of Fortriu'.

r. 820–832 or 834, *Oengus [*see under* Picts, kings of the], also a son of Fergus and also styled 'king of Fortriu'. He died in 834, but may have abdicated in 832.

r. 832?–836, Aed, son of Boanta. He was killed in 839, supporting Eoganán, son of Oengus, in battle against 'pagans' (perhaps Danes).

r. 836–9, *Eoganán, son of Oengus, king of Picts [*see under* Picts, kings of the]. He died in 839 with many men of Fortriu, in the conflict with the 'pagans'.

In addition Donncorci (Brown Oats). He died in 791 as 'king of Dál Riata', but is otherwise unexplained.

Constantine was said to have built the church of Dunkeld, and Oengus to have built the church of Kilrymont (St Andrews). Constantine and Eoganán, and perhaps Oengus also, are commemorated in a Northumbrian *Liber vitae*.

Constantine, his brother Oengus, and his nephew Eoganán are the first certainly to have held both kingships simultaneously. They may have owed their Pictish kingships to dynastic intermarriages. After Eoganán's death in 839 the two kingships apparently separated again. His successor as king of the Dál Riata was his possible cousin **Alpin** (d. 840), son of Eochaid, son of Aed Find. Alpin is not mentioned in the annals, except later as father of Kenneth (or Cinaed) I, but he has a place in the genealogy of kings of the Scots and the Irish synchronisms.

Alpin has been confused with the eighth-century king of the same name. For medieval users of the Latin lists the confusion was easy. The original Latin list virtually ended at Fergus (d. 781). Its three latest kings (Muredach, Aed Find, and Fergus) became displaced so that they stood before Selbach instead of after; and all the kings after Fergus were dropped. So the list came to end at Alpin son of Eochaid, with a reign of three years (733–6), understood by a later editor or copyist to be Kenneth's father, after whose death 'the kingdom of Scots was transferred to the kingdom of Picts' (Anderson, *Early Sources*, 1.270).

Kenneth's father seems in fact to have reigned for only one year (839–40). He was said to have been killed in warfare against the Picts, and this may well have been true. The late thirteenth-century chronicle of Huntingdon dates his death exactly on 13 Kal. Aug. (20 July), possibly copied from an early source; but the year, 834, was almost certainly arrived at by counting back reign lengths in a faulty regnal list.

*Kenneth I, the son of Alpin, is said by the Scottish chronicle to have become king of the Dál Riata two years before he 'came to Pictavia'. It was perhaps in these two years (840–42) that he arranged to borrow reinforcements from the Airgialla, as noted by the annals of the four masters. Their date, 835, may have been arrived at by the same method as the chronicle of Huntingdon's date for the death of Alpin. Kenneth was king for sixteen years in the east (842–58) and died in Forteviot, in modern Perthshire. For the first six years he was perhaps occupied in eliminating a remnant Pictish kingdom. In 848 or 849 he brought relics of St Columba to Dunkeld.

The name Dál Riata, for land or people, continued in occasional use, but the title king of Dál Riata is not used in the annals of Ulster after the 790s. Kenneth and his brother and sons are each described at their deaths as *rex Pictorum*.   MARJORIE O. ANDERSON

Sources A. Boyle, trans., *Irish synchronisms* ('Fland's synchronisms'), in 'The Edinburgh synchronisms of Irish kings', *Celtica*, 9 (1971), 169–79 · A. O. Anderson, ed. and trans., *Early sources of Scottish history, AD 500 to 1286*, 2 vols. (1922); repr. with corrections (1990), esp. vol. 1, pp. cxlii–cxlix · K. H. Jackson, ed. and trans., *Duan Albanach*, *SHR*, 36 (1957), 125–37 · M. O. Anderson, *Kings and kingship in early Scotland* (1973); rev. edn (1980) · *Ann. Ulster* · Bede, *Hist. eccl.* · J. Bannerman, *Studies in the history of Dalriada* (1974), 47–9 · *Adomnán's 'Life of Columba'*, ed. and trans. A. O. Anderson and M. O. Anderson (1963); new edn (1993) · *Adomnán's 'Life of Columba'*, trans. R. Sharpe (1995) · M. Ní Dhonnchadha, 'The guarantor list of *Cáin Adomnáin*', *Peritia*, 1 (1982), 178–215 · F. Palgrave, ed., *Documents and records illustrating the history of Scotland* (1837) [incl. Chronicle of Huntingdon] · D. N. Dumville, 'Ireland and North Britain in the earlier middle ages: contexts for *Míniugud senchasa fher nAlban*', *Rannsachadh na Gàidhlig 2000*, ed. C. Ó. Baoill and N. R. McGuire (2002), 185–211

Dalrymple, Sir Adolphus John, second baronet (1784–1866), army officer and politician, was born on 3 February 1784, probably at his parents' house, 29 Somerset Street, St Marylebone, Middlesex. He was the first child and eldest son of Sir Hew Whitefoord *Dalrymple (1750–1830), army officer, and his wife, Frances, Lady Dalrymple (1753–1835), daughter of Lieutenant-General Francis Leighton (1696–1773) and his wife, Renea, *née* Pinfold. At the time of his birth Dalrymple's father was a captain and lieutenant-colonel in the 1st regiment of foot guards. Adolphus was christened in March 1784 in the parish church of St Mary in Marylebone High Street, and was educated at Harrow School from September 1796 until the spring of 1799.

Dalrymple was connected by birth to both military and political society in southern Scotland. His father procured his first commission and his first promotion, and a family friend provided a safe and decorative posting. When his military career faltered, his father-in-law set him on a parliamentary career, one furthered by his family connections in East Lothian. Once out of parliament, sheer longevity secured him a steady progress to the rank of general.

On 25 October 1799 Dalrymple was gazetted ensign in the 55th (Westmorland) regiment of foot, the regiment having its headquarters on Guernsey, of which Sir Hew Dalrymple was lieutenant-governor. On 12 June 1800 he was promoted lieutenant in the 37th (North Hampshire) regiment of foot, of which Sir Hew was colonel. He served as aide-de-camp to his father, then a lieutenant-general, on Guernsey from being first commissioned until 5 February 1801, when he exchanged to the 1st (King's) dragoon guards.

Dalrymple served with the 1st dragoon guards in England until being appointed, in July 1802, aide-de-camp to Lieutenant-General Sir James Craig (1748–1812), who was then commanding the eastern district of England. He obtained his captaincy in the 18th (light) dragoons on 7 January 1803 and served with that regiment in England until being reappointed aide-de-camp to Craig on 24 July 1803. On 19 May 1803 he and his younger brother, Leighton Cathcart Dalrymple—a lieutenant in the 15th (King's) regiment of (light) dragoons—served as esquires to Craig at his installation as a knight companion in the Order of the Bath. Dalrymple remained Craig's aide-de-camp until May 1806, serving with him in Malta, Sicily, and Naples as part of the force sent under Craig's command to reinforce the kingdom of Naples against France. In June 1806 he was appointed military secretary to his father, who had been ordered to Gibraltar as lieutenant-governor. He served with Sir Hew as military secretary on Gibraltar and in Portugal in 1808 when Sir Hew was appointed to command the British expeditionary force there. Following the armistice, or convention, agreed at Cintra at the end of August 1808, Dalrymple brought home his father's dispatches announcing the news to government. He obtained a majority in the 3rd (East Kent) regiment of foot (the Buffs) on 15 September 1808 and exchanged to the 19th (light) dragoons on 17 November 1808. He may have been stigmatized by his association with the convention of Cintra, and his father's subsequent disgrace, because he never saw active service again.

On 23 June 1812 he married Anne (1782–1858), only daughter of Sir James Graham, bt, MP, of Kirkstall, Yorkshire (1753–1825); they had no children. On 1 June 1814 he obtained a lieutenant-colonelcy in the 60th (Royal American) regiment of foot, soon afterwards transferring to the half-pay list of the 2nd garrison battalion; he remained on the half-pay list until 1841.

On 14 February 1817 Dalrymple began his parliamentary career, coming temporarily into parliament for Weymouth and Melcombe Regis with the assistance of his father-in-law. He lost his seat at the general election of 1818 but returned to the Commons on 5 April 1819 as member for Appleby, a borough of which his father-in-law was recorder. He represented Appleby until 1826, when he was elected to the Haddington burghs, a seat previously represented by his kinsman Sir Hew Hamilton Dalrymple (later Dalrymple Hamilton), bt (1774–1834); he remained MP for Haddington until 1832. On 9 April 1830 he succeeded his father as second baronet of High Mark, Wigtownshire, a property which Sir Hew had inherited in 1753 from his father, Captain John Dalrymple (1692–1753), late 6th dragoons. On 22 July 1830 he was promoted colonel and appointed aide-de-camp to William IV. Losing his seat in 1832, he was elected to represent Brighton in 1837 and appointed aide-de-camp to Queen Victoria, an appointment and seat which he retained until 1841. He left parliament in 1841 and was promoted major-general on 23 November 1841. On 11 November 1851 he was promoted lieutenant-general, and on 11 April 1860 general. As well as Delrow House and High Mark, which he inherited from his father, Dalrymple owned or occupied houses at 129 Park Street, Grosvenor Square, London, and in Brunswick Terrace, Brighton. He was also a founder member of the

United Services Club. He died at Delrow House, Aldenham, Hertfordshire, on 3 March 1866, and was buried in the family vault in the churchyard of the church of St John the Baptist, Aldenham. STEPHEN WOOD

Sources Army List (1799–1866) · Hart's Army List (1840–66) · R. G. Thorne, 'Dalrymple, Sir Adolphus John', HoP, Commons · Return of members of parliament, 1696–1876, part II (1878) · N. H. Nicolas, History of the orders of knighthood of the British empire, 4 vols. (1842) · R. Douglas, The peerage of Scotland, 2nd edn, ed. J. P. Wood, 2 vols. (1813) · Burke, Peerage · W. T. J. Gun, ed., The Harrow School register, 1571–1800 (1934) · parish register (baptism), church of St Mary, St Marylebone, London, March 1784 · memorial tablet, church of St John the Baptist, Aldenham
Archives BL, Add. MSS 38242, 40407, 40410, 40485, 40515, 45880 · PRO, War Office papers | NAM, Sir Hew Dalrymple MSS
Likenesses A. Stewart, watercolour on ivory miniature, c.1805, Scot. NPG · A. Stewart, watercolour on ivory miniature, c.1808, 15th/19th The King's Royal Hussars, Newcastle-upon-Tyne, Regimental Museum · Dickinson & Co., lithograph (after an unknown portrait), NPG
Wealth at death under £30,000: probate, 7 April 1866, CGPLA Eng. & Wales

Dalrymple, Alexander (1737–1808), hydrographer, was born on 24 July 1737 at Newhailes, near Edinburgh, eleventh of the fifteen children of Sir James Dalrymple, second baronet (1692–1751), of Hailes in the county of Haddington, and Christian Hamilton (c.1703–1770), youngest daughter of Thomas, sixth earl of Haddington. His father was member of parliament for Haddington burghs and an auditor to the exchequer of Scotland. His childhood was spent at the family home at Newhailes and at school in Haddington. After his father's death in 1751, and the succession of his eldest brother, David *Dalrymple (later Lord Hailes), to the baronetcy, Alexander embarked on an East India Company career. Through the acquaintance of Lieutenant-General James St Clair (Dalrymple's father's sister's second husband) with William Baker, chairman of the East India Company, Dalrymple was appointed a writer on 1 November 1752, and posted to Madras where he arrived in May 1753.

Early career Under the protection of George Pigot, governor of Madras, through a connection between the governor's brother, Admiral Hugh Pigot, and General St Clair, Dalrymple rose to sub-secretary and enjoyed the use of Robert Orme's library for research into the company's earlier trade to Burma, Indo-China, and Borneo. In February 1759 Pigot freighted the Cuddalore (Captain George Baker) for Dalrymple 'to attempt to discover a new route to China through the Molucca Islands and New Guinea'. Dalrymple made three voyages between 1759 and 1764 to the Philippines, Borneo, and Sulu. In the first, based at Canton (Guangzhou), he reconnoitred Borneo, the Philippines, and the coast of Cochin-China. For the second, in the London in 1762, he had James Rennell as companion for a voyage to Sulu and Balambangan, where he had obtained for the company a grant of land. In Madras in 1763 he went through the formality of resignation, confident of reinstatement, to return to London to promote a trading settlement at Balambangan. En route to Canton for passage to England he became provisional deputy governor at Manila for a short period in April 1764, in the aftermath of the treaty of Paris, and he arrived in London in the summer of 1765.

Dalrymple continued in London the research he had begun in India into the 'counterpoise' theory of a great southern continent, which led to the publication of An Historical Collection of the Several Voyages and Discoveries in the South Pacific Ocean in 1769–71. He proposed himself to William Pitt and the earl of Shelburne to undertake a voyage of exploration, and, after summarizing his research in 1767 in An Account of the Discoveries Made in the South Pacifick Ocean Previous to 1764, he became the Royal Society's candidate to lead the transit of Venus expedition. After a misunderstanding between the Royal Society and the Admiralty in April 1768 over the command of the chosen ship, Dalrymple declined to take second place in the expedition under a sea officer, and James Cook was subsequently appointed both commander and Royal Society observer. In two pamphlets in 1773 Dalrymple was the most uncompromising of many critics of John Hawkesworth's literary edition of the account of the voyage: the consequent public misperception that Dalrymple was an implacable opponent of Cook after his supposed supersession in the voyage is only now being rectified.

Between 1769 and 1771 Dalrymple published charts and navigational memoirs, chiefly from his 1760s voyages, to support his plan for a trading settlement at Balambangan, but he was dismissed in March 1771 from the East India Company's planned expedition after a disagreement over its composition. In the same month he was elected a fellow of the Royal Society, with Benjamin Franklin and Nevil Maskelyne among his supporters. He maintained a technical correspondence with the French hydrographer Jean Baptiste Nicolas Denis d'Après de Mannevillette through the 1770s, and began to publish in 1774 a series of Plans of Ports in the East Indies with sailing directions.

Return to the East India Company Dalrymple successfully applied for reinstatement in the East India Company in 1775 to serve as a member of the Madras council in Pigot's second term as governor, sailing with him in the Grenville in April. In Madras in 1776 he was embroiled in the controversy which Pigot had been appointed to resolve. A group of council members and others had loaned the nawab of Arcot large sums of money against the revenue of lands then in his possession, but disputed with the raja of Tanjore. To restore Tanjore, as Pigot was instructed, would have rendered Arcot incapable of paying his debts, and in turn would have bankrupted his creditors on the Madras council. Pigot was driven to the limits of constitutionality to assert his authority, and was summarily arrested in October 1776 by the opposing faction. Dalrymple returned overland to London to represent Pigot's case, arriving in April 1777, and was obliged to remain while all Madras council members were recalled for an investigation of their conduct.

His use of Pigot's John Arnold chronometer in the Grenville had shown Dalrymple the value of accumulating coherent series of longitude observations at sea for recommending best tracks to follow at different seasons, and for constructing accurate charts. In April 1779 he proposed himself, and was appointed by the company at £500 a year, to examine the ships' journals which had accumulated in East India House and to publish charts and nautical instructions, a responsibility he was to hold, on retainer, for the rest of his life. He advocated, first privately and then officially, a complex form of chronometer log-keeping with tables of the gradations of wind and weather. The wind scale he derived from John Smeaton's calibration of windmill sails, and he later transmitted it to the young Francis Beaufort, who adopted it and by whose name it is now known. Dalrymple continued a publicist for, and proponent of, the use of Arnold's chronometers by ships' captains and for survey. This culminated in his 1806 pamphlet *Longitude* defending Arnold's memory against the claims of Thomas Earnshaw.

Dalrymple proposed in 1779 a scheme of coastal charts for the East Indies navigation, from the Mozambique Channel to China. His investigative work in subsequent years was directed towards that scheme, and he continued to publish plans of ports and sets of coastal views each year for eventual incorporation. The impossibility of reconciling observations in past dead-reckoning journals and the slowness of delivery of new chronometer journals inhibited his main progress. Despite recommending and preparing schemes for surveys of both the Coromandel and Malabar coasts of India in the 1780s, the latter under John McCluer, whose *Account of the Navigation between India and the Gulph of Persia* Dalrymple had published in 1786, he found his attempts to draw reliable charts of the Indian Ocean brought to a standstill for the lack of reliable longitude data. Instead, during the fifteen years between his appointment in 1779 and the emigration of his chief engraver William Harrison to Philadelphia in 1794, Dalrymple published almost 550 plans of ports and small-scale charts of parts of the East Indies navigation, with forty-five plates of coastal views, and between fifty and sixty books and pamphlets of nautical instructions, many of them in two or three editions, as his *General Collection of Nautical Publications*. His reputation was based on these publications, whose spare style contrasted with the ornateness of commercial chart atlases.

Dalrymple kept alive his theoretical claim to return to the council at Madras until it was extinguished by a provision of Pitt's India Act of 1784 which prohibited those long absent from India from resuming their seniority. He advanced his case again in 1790, when the East India Company was reported to be considering resuming the appointment of civilian governors, but the award of an annuity of £500 a year in April 1791 marked the end of his Madras pretensions. Dalrymple by now had an established position in London: a close friend of Sir Joseph Banks and a regular member of the influential Royal Society club dining weekly under Banks's chairmanship, he became involved in the geographical aspects of many questions of science and government. Among a close-knit group which included Philip Stephens, Evan Nepean, James Rennell, and William Marsden he provided plans and topographical information for Vancouver's voyage,

advised the Colonial Office on routes to supply Nootka Sound after the Spanish controversy in 1790, furnished sailing directions to Cathcart's abortive embassy to China in 1788, advised Banks on the privy council examination of Meares, and advised on ports of refuge in South America for the southern whale fishery. In other fields Dalrymple corresponded with Charles Pierre Claret (later comte de Fleurieu), his counterpart at the Depot des cartes et plans de la marine in Paris, over exploration questions, and provided, through his own research and his connection with Samuel Wegg of the Hudson's Bay Company, the geographical basis for a scheme to unite the activities of the Hudson's Bay and East India companies through the shipping of otter pelts from the north-west coast of America to China.

Hydrographer to the Admiralty Dalrymple was appointed hydrographer to the Admiralty on 13 August 1795, the order in council which created the post having been approved the previous day. The post was created for Dalrymple, probably at the instance of Sir Philip Stephens, ostensibly to organize a growing collection of charts and plans, but also clearly to give official status to the geographical and navigational information he was increasingly asked to provide. Dalrymple consulted the East India Company two months before his appointment, and held the new post, at £500 a year, in parallel with his East India Company responsibility and his annuity. For the Admiralty Dalrymple had to run a hydrographical office with a subordinate staff, and was occupied for five years, successively with Aaron Arrowsmith and John Walker as his assistant, in sorting, classifying, and arranging the charts and then evaluating them to select and compile information for the use of ships.

In 1800 Dalrymple was allowed to hire engravers and obtain a Matthew Boulton rolling-press. He had no authority to commission surveys, only to engrave charts from materials supplied by ships' officers, supplemented by manuscripts in the hydrographical office and by foreign printed charts. He began proofing his own charts in November 1800, the first a plan of Houat Island in Quiberon Bay: proof impressions from over 150 plates are known from Dalrymple's Admiralty operations. He established two series of charts, from the surveys of Murdoch Mackenzie and Graeme Spence, to cover the south coast of England from the Thames to the Lizard, but he never had either the budget or the responsibility to publish charts in quantity. Dalrymple continued to produce charts and plans for the East India Company after 1795, and arranged in 1804 for the Admiralty to take 100 impressions from his East India Company plates, which by then numbered 817. Later he reprinted for the Admiralty many of his nautical instructions to accompany the charts.

In 1806 Dalrymple published sets of his East India Company charts and nautical directions together grouped geographically as volumes in the *Collection of Nautical Memoirs and Journals*. Although few examples survive they represent the culmination of his idea for publishing geographical information.

Dalrymple continued to co-operate with other hydrographers: he took into the Admiralty in 1795 the charts and journals of the voyage of Joseph Antoine Bruny d'Entrecasteaux, brought to St Helena by Elisabeth-Paul Edouard, chevalier de Rossel, when the expedition broke up in Batavia, and employed Rossel, then in exile, to compute the results of the voyage observations. He encouraged James Horsburgh, who succeeded him as hydrographer to the East India Company, to publish the charts and sailing directions he had established as a ship captain between India and China, and in 1805 he furnished Francis Beaufort with a full set of his East India Company charts and sailing directions. In the 1806 fourth edition of his *Essay on Nautical Surveying* he published much of the information assembled for his unfinished manual 'Practical navigation' in the 1780s.

As a fellow of the Society of Antiquaries Dalrymple was active in oriental antiquarianism: between 1791 and 1808 he published for subscribers two volumes of *Oriental Repertory*, a part work embracing the history, culture, and topography of the East Indies, including much of his own research, among this his early work on the Madras records.

The controversy which marred Dalrymple's last years, and which led to his dismissal from the Admiralty and death in 1808, arose partly from changes in the Admiralty's expectations for the function of his office, and partly from his own intransigence in deflecting them. He fulfilled a request in May 1807 to purchase and arrange 'a compleat set of all Charts published in England', but declined to supply an evaluation of them because, as commercially published charts, they generally lacked memoirs of authorities, and because he was unfamiliar with the coasts they covered. He suggested to the Admiralty that a committee of naval officers should advise on charts for fleet use, and a chart committee of Home Popham, E. H. Columbine, and Thomas Hurd duly began work in November 1807. The committee suggested greater direction of Dalrymple's activities, particularly the prioritization of charts for engraving.

The issue chosen to ease Dalrymple into retirement was that of the security copies he had made in 1795 of the charts of d'Entrecasteaux's voyage before returning them to France. Treating these as confidential until the information they contained should be published in France, Dalrymple consistently refused to supply them to the chart committee, and was dismissed by the Board of Admiralty on 28 May 1808. His intense anger at the mode of his removal manifested itself in vituperative letters, including one to Viscount Melville, and in the hastily compiled pamphlet *Case of Alexander Dalrymple*. He died three weeks later, on 19 June 1808, at 57 High Street, Marylebone, Middlesex, at the age of seventy-one, probably of a heart attack induced by his fierce reaction to his dismissal. He was buried at St Marylebone parish church. The hydrographic office was immediately reconstituted, also as a chart supply office, under Thomas Hurd as his successor.

Dalrymple lived alone in London from 1781, first at 72 Titchfield Street, and after 1789 at various addresses in High Street, Marylebone, where he had constructed a freestanding library. He outlived all his siblings, his sister Rachel dying in 1801, and he was survived by his niece Christian and great-nephew Sir John Pringle Dalrymple. He suffered increasingly from erysipelas, and developed a gastric condition for which he spent time each summer at Cheltenham taking the waters. He latterly formed a friendship in Cheltenham with a young woman, Mary Selby, whom he made his residuary legatee, jointly with his great-nephew, by a codicil to his will in 1805.

Dalrymple's library of geographical works, his nautical papers, and the copper plates of his charts and plans were his most tangible legacy. The voyages and travels, atlases, charts, maps, and nautical papers were bequeathed to the Admiralty at a valuation, and went to form the core of the Admiralty library and of the hydrographic office collections. His copper plates and copyright of his nautical publications were declined by the East India Company. Later almost 400 of his copper plates were bought by the Admiralty, reputedly as scrap metal, and many were re-issued by Hurd as Admiralty charts. William Marsden received Dalrymple's oriental language books, and the remaining collections were sold at auction by King and Lochee in 1809 and 1810.

ANDREW S. COOK

Sources A. S. Cook, 'Alexander Dalrymple (1737–1808), hydrographer to the East India Company and to the admiralty, as publisher', PhD diss., U. St Andr., 1992 • H. T. Fry, *Alexander Dalrymple ... and the expansion of British trade* (1970) • 'Memoirs of Alexander Dalrymple', *European Magazine and London Review*, 42 (1802), 323–8, *321–7, 421–4 • R. T. Gould, 'A history of the hydrographic department of the admiralty', c.1925, UK Hydrographic Office archives, Taunton

Archives BL, extracts of voyages, Add. MSS 19293–19294 • BL, geographical collections, Add. MS 33765 • BL OIOC, Home misc. series, corresp. relating to India • NL Scot., family corresp. and memoirs | Hunt. L., letters to Sir Francis Beaufort • NA Scot., corresp. with Henry Dundas • NL Scot., memoirs and corresp. with Henry Dundas • NL Scot., Newhailes papers, family letters, MS 25286 • PRO, Admiralty papers, Hydrographer's corresp., ADM 1/3522–3523

Likenesses J. T. Seton, oils, 1765, repro. in G. Williams, 'The Endeavour voyage', *Science and exploration in the Pacific*, ed. M. Lincoln (1998); priv. coll. • line engraving, 1794 (after J. Brown), BM • W. Daniell, soft-ground etching, pubd 1809 (after profile by G. Dance), BM, NL Aus., NPG; repro. in Cook, 'Alexander Dalrymple' • Ridley, engraving (after portrait by J. Brown, 1794), repro. in A. Arrowsmith, *Map of the world* (1794), 1802

Dalrymple, Sir David, first baronet (c.1665–1721), politician, was the fifth son of James *Dalrymple, first Viscount Stair (1619–1695), politician and lawyer, and Margaret (d. 1692), eldest daughter of James Ross of Balniel, Wigtownshire, and widow of Fergus Kennedy of Knockdaw. His elder brothers included John *Dalrymple, first earl of Stair, Sir James *Dalrymple, antiquary, and Sir Hew *Dalrymple, lawyer. He was educated at Edinburgh (1677) and the University of Utrecht (c.1685).

On 3 November 1688 Dalrymple became a member of the Faculty of Advocates. On 4 April 1691 he married Janet Murray, daughter of Sir James Rochead of Inverleith, Edinburgh, and widow of Alexander Murray of Melgund, Forfar; they had three sons and four daughters. He was made a baronet on 8 May 1700, represented Culross in the

Scottish parliament from 1698 to 1707, and was solicitor-general to Anne. Having been in 1706 a commissioner to arrange the treaty of union, he was elected to the first British parliament in February 1707, and represented the Haddington burghs from 1708 until his death.

Dalrymple was appointed lord advocate in Scotland in 1709 at a salary of £1000 a year. As the descendant of a prominent whig family he was dismissed from this office during the tory ministry of 1710–14, and was then reappointed in 1714. During the whig split he sided with the government on issues such as the Septennial Act, but later criticized the ministry for its plan to sell estates confiscated after the Jacobite rising of 1715. In 1720 he became auditor of the Scottish exchequer. He died the following year on 3 December, and was succeeded by his son James; his second son, Hugh, inherited the Melgund estates and the name of Murray of Kynnymond.

Janet Sorensen

Sources J. M. Simpson, 'Dalrymple, Hon. Sir David', HoP, Commons · GEC, Peerage, new edn

Archives Hunt. L. · NL Scot., MSS and corresp. · NRA Scotland, priv. coll.

Dalrymple, Sir David, third baronet, Lord Hailes (1726–1792), judge and historian, was born on 26 October 1726 in Edinburgh, the eldest of the sixteen children of Sir James Dalrymple, second baronet (1692–1751), and Christian (c.1703–1770), daughter of Thomas *Hamilton, sixth earl of Haddington, and his countess, Helen *Hope. One of his younger brothers was the hydrographer Alexander *Dalrymple.

He was brought up in Edinburgh, where his father was auditor of exchequer, and at Newhailes, the family house near Musselburgh, 5 miles east of the city. His family was whig and Hanoverian, and he was sent to Eton College, an experience which he enjoyed and during which he developed a taste for classical literature and English manners. He was at Eton in 1742, but must have left in that year, for he was admitted to the Middle Temple on 8 August. From the Middle Temple he went to Utrecht, where he spent eighteen months studying Roman law. His experience at Utrecht was a happy one, and he later wrote a defence of Dutch women against the attack by Mark Akenside in his 'Ode upon Leaving Holland'. He returned to Scotland in 1746, and without attending a Scottish university was admitted advocate on 23 February 1748, presenting a thesis, 'De condictione furtivae'.

Dalrymple as advocate Dalrymple was not a great court advocate, but on his father's death he inherited both an estate encumbered by debt and responsibility for fifteen younger siblings. A paid profession was necessary. However, much of the court argument of the period was conducted in the form of written pleadings, and in these he excelled. His clarity of thought and simple style lent themselves to this form of debate, and promotion followed. On 1 April 1755 he recorded, 'I began my office of Advocate Depute [crown prosecutor] at Stirling. A ridiculous day of the year. At that time I was very ignorant of criminal law, but good intentions have, I hope, atoned for my defects' (NL Scot., Newhailes MS 25426, fol. 6). His legal

Sir David Dalrymple, third baronet, Lord Hailes (1726–1792), by Allan Ramsay, c.1766–7

knowledge however seems to have passed unquestioned, and it was a hesitancy of manner and a natural tendency to see both sides of a question that made him unsuitable for argument in open court. On his appointment as a judge he remarked, 'The altercation of the bar was not agreeable to me. I might add that the being *of a side* was disagreeable' (NL Scot., Minto MS 11017, fol. 70).

Nevertheless Dalrymple undertook all the usual duties of the young advocate. He was examinator for new entrants in 1752–3, and again in 1759 and 1765. In January 1752 he became a curator of the library of the Faculty of Advocates. He was always interested in books: in October 1751 he had spent several days helping to catalogue the books at Tyninghame (the home of his mother's family). He opposed the appointment of David Hume as keeper of the Advocates' Library in February 1752, no doubt on the grounds, as Hume put it, of his 'profane and irreligious principles' (Hillyard, 103). None the less in May 1753 Hume asked Dalrymple to comment on his *Enquiry Concerning the Principles of Morals* (1751) when a new edition was in prospect. In the following year Dalrymple was one of the advocates who insisted on the removal of certain objectionable books that Hume had bought. 'He was so excessively holy,' according to Hume, 'that nothing could bring him over to the opposite party' (ibid., 108). Nevertheless on 3 April 1754 Hume asked Dalrymple to lend him James Heath's *Flagellum, or, The Life and Death … of O. Cromwell* (1679) citing Julian the Apostate, who approved of charity by Christians to non-Christians. Dalrymple, who did not like to be teased, replied sourly that he would have lent it anyway. They continued to meet, for example at the Select

Society, where Dalrymple was a member from July 1754—in Hume's words, 'Monboddo's oddities divert—Sir David's zeal entertains' (*Letters*, 1.220)—but they were never on intimate terms. Dalrymple demitted office as senior curator of the library in January 1757, but was curator again in 1771.

While still an advocate Dalrymple regularly went to plays and concerts, played golf at Musselburgh, and participated in the club life of Edinburgh. In November 1751 he attended the newly founded Revolution Club (the name referred to the revolution of 1689–90) in the company of William Robertson the historian, then minister of Gladsmuir. In February 1755 he was instrumental in setting up the Edinburgh Society for the Encouragement of Arts and Manufactures, an offshoot of the Select Society, something he considered one of his important public achievements. In 1756 he 'had the honour of setting an example for the establishment of presbyterial libraries in Scotland' (NL Scot., Newhailes MS 25426, fol. 140) in Dalkeith and Haddington, to which he personally gifted a number of books. In 1759 he collected subscriptions (including that of James Boswell) towards the publication of James Macpherson's *Fragments of Ancient Poetry*.

Characteristic of one of Dalrymple's interests was his appointment from 1753 to 1755 as advocate for the poor, and from July 1756 until he became a judge (though with a brief gap in 1757) he was one of the representatives of the Faculty of Advocates on the board of management of the Edinburgh workhouse. Among his many other 'endeavours to serve the public' (NL Scot., Newhailes MS 25426, fol. 140) of which he was proud was his *Proposals for Carrying on a Certain Public Work in the City of Edinburgh*, published anonymously in 1761; although this has been regarded as a satire on proposals made by Sir Gilbert Elliot, Lord Minto, for the construction of public lavatories in Edinburgh, Dalrymple seems to have meant his contribution to the debate on the public hygiene of Edinburgh to be taken seriously. From August 1761 he was a trustee for the annexed estates, forfeited to the crown after the Jacobite rising of 1745. He had 'two great objects … that of making the people happy & of discountenancing jobs' (NL Scot., Minto MS 11016, fol. 55). He took a particular interest in the settlement of retired soldiers and sailors, the former with some success, the latter—'brave thoughtless fellows who could no more settle than their element does' (NL Scot., Minto MS 11017, fol. 12)—with less.

Dalrymple could be shocked by crime. On 16 October 1761 two ships were wrecked in a storm off the coast of East Lothian. Though there were survivors, the coast dwellers considered any goods washed ashore as theirs by right. Dalrymple, furious, published for free distribution what he called *A Sermon which might have been Preached in East Lothian on the 25th of October 1761*, in which he attacked those 'hell taught casuists' who argued that this was anything other than common theft. Much apparently was returned.

Dalrymple married later than many of his contemporaries. There was a lady with whom he was deeply in love in 1753 and 1754, but she turned him down, and it was not until 12 November 1763 that he married Anne, daughter of George Brown of Coalstoun, a judge as Lord Coalstoun. They had one surviving daughter, Christian (1765–1838); Anne died in childbirth on 18 May 1768, after giving birth to twins, and Dalrymple wrote a Latin epitaph in her memory. His second marriage, on 20 March 1770, was to Helen (b. 16 May 1741), daughter of Sir James *Fergusson of Kilkerran, second baronet, and a judge as Lord Kilkerran; they had one daughter, Jean (1778–1803), who married her cousin Sir James Fergusson of Kilkerran, fourth baronet, in 1799.

In the court of session The 1760s also saw professional advancement for Dalrymple. He was a member of the council of the Faculty of Advocates from 1764, but gave this up when, on 6 March 1766, he became a judge, with the title Lord Hailes. In his new position he found further means to express his interests. The provision of the means of support for the poor continued to be near to his heart. In August 1767, in a case brought by the parish of Roxburgh to have a beggar returned to Crailing, his place of birth, Hailes argued successfully for the responsibility of the parish of residence. He broadened the argument:

> Glasgow is supplied with inhabitants principally from the West Highlands … It would be hard were all the industrious poor to be remanded back to their place of nativity as soon as their place of residence can no longer profit by their industry. The consequences are dreadful. (Brown, 1.198)

Though perhaps not remarkable as a lawyer, Hailes was one of the first people to focus proper scholarly attention on the legal history of Scotland. His *Examination … of the Regiam majestatem* of 1769 is characteristic of his historical work—painstaking and dispassionate. The work rejected the convention by which the origins of Scots feudal law were traced back to the eleventh-century kings Malcolm II and Malcolm III, Hailes emphasizing instead the Anglo-Norman influences during and following the reign of David I. His most well-known judgments related to disputed successions to estates and titles. His judgment in the Douglas cause given in July 1766 is a point-by-point demolition of the credibility of Lady Jean Douglas. 'When it suits her conveniency she did not hesitate to assert what I wish I could find a gentler name for than falsehoods' (NL Scot., MS 5355). His finding for the Hamiltons was overturned by the House of Lords on appeal in 1769, when a mob, possibly including James Boswell, threw stones at his windows. His *Additional Case of Elisabeth … Countess of Sutherland* of 1771 secured him a lasting reputation as a peerage lawyer.

Hailes's approach to history was forensic rather than literary. He examined important events in the light of contemporary documents, and endeavoured to remove the myths surrounding them. His *Memorials and Letters Relating to the History of Britain in the Reign of James I* (1762) was followed in 1766 by a similar volume for the reign of Charles I, and his *Remarks on the History of Scotland* (1773) established his reputation for writing history in a completely new way. In the James I volume, he remarks of a letter of Thomas Hamilton, first earl of Haddington (an ancestor of his), 'This letter gives a more lively idea of those times than an hundred Chronicles can do' (Dalrymple, *Memorials and Letters*, 4).

Hailes's reputation as a historian is based on his *Annals of Scotland*, published in two volumes in 1776 and 1779. He had been pressed to write such a work. Robert Urie, the Glasgow publisher, recorded a conversation on the subject at which the need for a good history of Scotland had been discussed. One of the participants 'named your Lordship as the only person he knew to be equal to the undertaking' (NL Scot., Newhailes MS 25301, fol. 83).

The work was already well under way in June 1774 when Hailes sent Sir Adam Fergusson of Kilkerran the section covering the first half of the wars of independence. By October 1775 John Murray was chosen as a publisher, partly because only a London publisher could guarantee sales in England and partly because, in the words of Gilbert Stuart, he was 'intelligent beyond what I could have expected from a bookseller' (NL Scot., Newhailes MS 25302, fol. 96). The first volume was published in a handsome quarto. 'Nelly [Helen Fergusson, his second wife] in particular was a great ennemy of the small octavo. She could not bring herself to suppose that such a size was consistent with the dignity of history' (ibid., fol. 65). 150 copies were sold in the first fortnight of publication, and although Murray felt that the prospect of a second volume had held some people back (and the price had made others hesitate) sales were good. The *Annals* was also received with approval by Samuel Johnson, to whom the work had been submitted for his literary opinion. Johnson, in a letter to Boswell of 27 August 1775, called them 'a new mode of history which tells all that is wanted … without laboured splendour of language, or affected subtilty of conjecture' (Boswell, *Life*, 2.383). It remains Hailes's greatest work, modelled on the written court pleadings of which he had composed so many, and marks the point at which almost for the first time Scottish history was studied in a scientific manner. He was pressed by Hugh Blair and others to continue beyond 1370, but refused to do so, perhaps for fear of arousing controversy.

Hailes also took an interest in early Scottish poets. Apart from his possibly misplaced enthusiasm for James Macpherson, he published in 1770 a collection entitled *Ancient Scottish Poems*, taken from the Bannatyne manuscript.

Hailes's other writing related mainly to the classics, to early church history, and to the history of the Church of England. *The Private Correspondence of Dr Francis Atterbury* (1768) and his *Remains of Christian Antiquity* (1776–80) remain of some value. His *Enquiry into the Secondary Causes … for the Rapid Growth of Christianity* (1786), in which he attacked Gibbon over his account of the effect of Christianity on the decline of the Roman empire, caused a stir at the time, but was really a minor skirmish in the ongoing controversy between theological traditionalists such as Hailes and more liberal thinkers led by David Hume.

Man of letters Hailes's place within the Scottish Enlightenment is important for his own scholarship, for the friendships he maintained, and for the help he was able to provide. In addition to his difficult relationship with David Hume, Hailes knew Henry Home, Lord Kames, of whom he said, 'I knew Lord Kaims long & at the bar & on the bench *sine jurgio* [without quarrel] tho' I was as fond of *my* way as he was of *his*' (NL Scot., Newhailes MS 25429, fol. 49).

Hailes knew James Boswell through Boswell's father, Alexander Boswell, Lord Auchinleck. They were together at least as early as a northern circuit in 1758. In 1763 Boswell asked Hailes to serve as an intermediary between him and his father, and his was one of the names Boswell was able to use in developing his relationship with Johnson. Hailes had a high opinion of Johnson. He had been a regular subscriber to *The Rambler* at least since 1751, and had read *Rasselas*. When Johnson and Boswell were in Scotland in 1773, the three of them dined together on 17 August, along with Sir Alexander Dick, John Maclaurin, Dr James Gregory, and Dr John Boswell. According to Boswell, 'all was literature and taste, without any interruption' (Boswell, *Life*, 5.48). Hailes, Johnson, and Boswell met again in November when the travellers returned to Edinburgh. It is not clear whether the 'most agreeable day' (ibid., 5.398) they spent together was at Newhailes or in Edinburgh. Boswell, writing to Hailes the following year, remarked that Johnson:

> said it was a pity you was a Whig. I know not if your worship will approve of the apology that I made for you. I said, 'You must excuse him. He has all the good principles which compose a Tory but has early imbibed a kind of prejudice against the family of Stuart. Dryden says,
>
> We grant an o'ergrown whig no grace can mend
> But most are Babes that know not they offend
>
> Our friend Lord Hailes is a babe in that particular.' (NL Scot., Newhailes MS 25295, fol. 35)

Hailes was not especially amused, even though Boswell sums up his political position accurately enough. Both men remained in touch with Hailes, but always by letter. Indeed, in a general way after he became a judge Hailes dropped the clubs and the personal contacts he had built up in favour of maintaining friendship by correspondence.

Hailes was widely esteemed as a literary critic. Boswell, Robertson, and James Beattie all submitted texts for his approval. Adam Smith, Gilbert Stuart, Hugo Arnot, and Sir Gilbert Elliot were among his correspondents. He was in touch with most of the English bishops, most notably Thomas Percy, bishop of Dromore, and Richard Hurd, bishop of Worcester, as well as with Thomas Balguy, archdeacon of Winchester. He corresponded with Horace Walpole, and with Edmund Burke, whom he did not meet until 1791. Burke described him as 'the pleasantest, the most good humoured, the most unaffected, & the most communicative man of letters I ever conversed with' (NL Scot., Newhailes MS 25305, fol. 86). He was a reader of wide-ranging interests, and added to the fine library inherited from his father and grandfather, which survives largely intact. The list of non-legal books he had read in one year in the early 1750s went from Montesquieu and Voltaire to William King's *Art of Cookery*, published in 1708. He was always happy to lend his books. Hume benefited from this generosity, as has been mentioned, but so did Robertson, and Gilbert Stuart, who was a near neighbour at Fisherrow, felt it necessary in 1776 to write, 'I am quite ashamed of having recourse so often to your library' (NL Scot., Newhailes MS 25302, fol. 169). Hailes also sent some books to the Royal College of Physicians of Edinburgh in 1791 when he discovered that he owned suitable books which did not appear in the college's library catalogue.

A full list of works by Hailes would be very difficult to build; the best, perhaps surprisingly, is in John Kay's *Portraits*. The task is made more complicated by the substantial number of pamphlets and contributions to magazines that Hailes made anonymously. Unlike many of his contemporaries Hailes did not keep a list of the essays and notices he submitted to periodicals: he probably 'regarded his magazine articles as being ephemeral productions, unworthy of collection' (Carnie, 234). His appearance was amiable and plump (indeed, early personal accounts suggest a high expenditure on sweetmeats), and his habits, latterly at least, were sedentary. Hailes spent as much time as he could at Newhailes, the beautiful house he had inherited. Although he is rightly associated with the place, it is clear that he enjoyed rather than embellished it. When in Edinburgh he lived first of all in the Old Mint House at the foot of Todrick's Wynd, and then from about 1760 at 23 New Street.

Last years Hailes remained an active judge until his final illness. He continued to be noted for his compassion: Alexander (Jupiter) Carlyle, his parish minister, described in the funeral sermon he preached 'his abhorrence of crimes; his tenderness for the criminals' (Carlyle, 12). One example was the case of William Malcolm, who in 1789 was convicted at a court in Perth, where Hailes was the circuit judge, of stealing a horse. He received the conventional punishment of a whipping and transportation, but between the two Hailes personally paid for him to be completely reclothed. The Perth lawyer charged with seeing to this business wrote, 'You observe, with great propriety, that want of cleanliness in our Prisons often occasions the Jail-distemper which is sometimes attended with very fatal consequences' (NL Scot., Newhailes MS 25305, fol. 25). Malcolm had been in the artillery, but had been discharged after six years as not being able to 'learn his exercise' (NA Scot., JC 11/21), and there was more than a suggestion that he was not really of sound mind. The jury, however, found him guilty, and Hailes had to give the appropriate punishment. He may have felt that justice had not really been done. Hailes also retained his concern for the interests of the poor, and in 1790 published a play, *The Little Freeholder*, in which he holds up to criticism a landowner who wants to demolish a cottage in order to improve the view from his great house.

Hailes died at Newhailes on 29 November 1792. He was on the bench until three days before his death when a stroke, followed by a second one shortly afterwards, carried him off. He was buried at Morham in East Lothian. He was survived by his second wife (who died on 10 November 1810) and his two daughters. He left no will, but on 3 March 1781 had drawn up a deed, not registered until 4 December 1792, within a week of his death, by which he arranged that 'the right of primogeniture shall always take place among females and their descendants' (NA Scot., Register of deeds, 1792, vol. 292, fol. 1190). This unusual arrangement is specified three times in the document, and it was his daughter Christian who inherited Newhailes and lands in West Lothian and Kirkcudbrightshire. PATRICK CADELL

Sources NL Scot., Newhailes MSS · NL Scot., Minto MSS · Justiciary Court Records, NA Scot. · Annexed Estate Records, NA Scot. · minute books, NL Scot., Faculty of Advocates MSS · Boswell, *Life* · R. H. Carnie, 'Lord Hailes's contributions to contemporary magazines', *Studies in Bibliography*, 9 (1957), 233–44 · B. Hillyard, 'The keepership of David Hume', *For the encouragement of learning: Scotland's National Library, 1689–1989*, ed. P. Cadell and A. Matheson (1989), 103–9 · A. Carlyle, *Sermon on the death of Sir David Dalrymple, bart., Lord Hailes* (1792) · M. P. Brown, ed., *Decisions of the lords of council and session, from 1766 to 1791*, 2 vols. (1826) · D. Dalrymple, *A sermon which might have been preached in East Lothian on the 25th of October 1761* (1761) · D. Dalrymple, *Memorials and letters relating to the history of Britain in the reign of James I* (1762) · *The letters of David Hume*, ed. J. Y. T. Greig, 2 vols. (1932) · J. Kay, *A series of original portraits and caricature etchings*, ed. H. Paton, 2 vols. (1827), 1.367–70 [list of works by Hailes] · *Scots peerage* · R. A. Austen-Leigh, ed., *The Eton College register, 1698–1752* (1927) · J. Hutchinson, ed., *A catalogue of notable Middle Templars: with brief biographical notices* (1902) · J. Grant, *Cassell's old and new Edinburgh*, 3 vols. [1880–83]

Archives NL Scot., corresp., legal and historical papers | BL, letters to T. Birch, Add. MS 4304 · BL, letters to Lord Hardwicke and Charles Yorke, Add. MSS 35606–35639, *passim* · BL, corresp. with Bishop Percy, Add. MS 32331 · NL Scot., letters to John Mackenzie · NL Scot., Newhailes MSS · NL Scot., corresp. with George Paton · NRA, priv. coll., corresp. with William Creech · U. Edin., letters to earl of Buchan · U. Edin., letters to John Davidson and Hugh Warrender · Yale U., corresp. with J. Boswell · Yale U., Beinecke L., letters to Thomas Balguy

Likenesses A. Ramsay, portrait, *c*.1766–1767, Newhailes, East Lothian [*see illus.*] · J. Kay, caricature, engraving, 1793, NPG; repro. in J. Kay, *Edinburgh portraits: a series of original portraits and caricature etchings*, 1 (1837), pl. 147 · J. T. Seton, oils, Newhailes, East Lothian · oils (after J. T. Seton), Dunrobin Castle, Highland

Wealth at death owned fine house and some very rich land in East Lothian (Newhailes, Overhailes, Morham, Traprain) as well as land at Kirknewton (West Lothian) and Drysdale and Caruthers in Kirkcudbrightshire

Dalrymple [*née* Campbell; *other married name* Primrose], **Eleanor, countess of Stair** (*d*. 1759), victim of marital abuse, was the seventh and youngest child of James Campbell, second earl of Loudoun (*d*. 1684), landowner, and his wife, Lady Margaret Montgomerie, daughter of Hugh, seventh earl of Eglinton. After being educated at home she married, in June 1697, Sir James Primrose (*c*.1680–1706), MP and landowner, of Carrington, who was created Viscount Primrose in 1703; they had three sons and a daughter. Primrose, however, was cruel as well as dissolute and Eleanor was afraid of him. One morning, as she was dressing in their Edinburgh lodgings, she happened to glance at her window and saw him reflected there, coming towards her with his drawn sword in his hand and a murderous expression on his face. Terrified, she managed to scramble out of the window and, still only half clad, ran to his mother's house for protection.

Eleanor refused to go back to Primrose and soon afterwards he went abroad. For months she heard nothing of him until eventually a foreign fortune-teller came to Edinburgh and one of her female friends persuaded her to visit him. They went together to his lodgings in the Canongate, their servants' tartan plaids pulled over their heads to conceal their faces. Eleanor recorded how the fortune-teller spoke to her and led her over to a mirror where, to her amazement, she saw the interior of a church gradually appear before her with a bridal party standing near the altar. As she gazed in disbelief she realized that the bridegroom was her husband. Suddenly a man entered the church and she recognized him as one of her brothers. He rushed up to Primrose, threatened him, and then the image dissolved, leaving Eleanor deeply shaken. When she went home she wrote down a detailed account of what she had seen and locked it in a drawer.

Some time later Eleanor's brother returned from a trip to the Netherlands. He was strangely reticent about his visit but he finally admitted that he had news of Lord Primrose. During his stay the brother had made friends with a wealthy Dutch merchant, whose only daughter was about to marry. He was invited to the wedding and when he arrived at the church he was aghast to discover that the bridegroom was none other than Lord Primrose. He said at once that this was his sister's husband and the marriage was stopped. Eleanor was so shocked at her brother's story that she fainted but when she had recovered she went to the drawer and took out her description of her visit to the fortune-teller. It had taken place on the very day of her husband's attempted second marriage. Scott used this colourful tale as the basis for 'My Aunt Margaret's Mirror', one of his *Chronicles of the Canongate*.

Primrose returned to Scotland and died on 13 June 1706. Not long afterwards John *Dalrymple, second earl of Stair (1673–1747), a distinguished soldier and diplomat, fell deeply in love with Eleanor. She told him that, after her past experiences, she could never take another husband and she remained deaf to all his persuasions. In the end he decided to take matters into his own hands. He knew that every day Eleanor prayed at a particular window overlooking a busy street. One evening he bribed her servants to let him into her house and hid himself in a small room. Next morning he went half-dressed to the window and made sure that the passers-by saw him. To save her reputation Eleanor was forced to marry him and their wedding took place on 7 March 1708, at the church of St Peter Cornhill, London.

Eleanor's health had been badly affected by the stress of her first marriage and she and Stair had no children but her letters to him show a deep affection for him. His heavy drinking was a problem during their early years together; often violent when drunk he hit her in the face one night and woke next day to find her weeping and covered in blood. Overcome with remorse he promised to change his ways and after that she always sat beside him at social events and restricted the amount of wine that he took.

During Stair's prolonged absences his mother, Elizabeth Dundas of Newliston, dowager countess of Stair, managed the family estates while Eleanor became a prominent society figure in London, Bath, and Edinburgh. Her visits to Moffat, Dumfriesshire, to take the waters helped to turn it into a successful spa. She made many useful contacts, kept her husband informed of all the latest news, and in the mid-1740s supervised William Adam's second phase of alterations at Newliston, which had become her principal home after her mother-in-law's death. Lord Stair died at Queensberry House in Edinburgh on 9 May 1747. Eleanor survived him for a further twelve years and three days after her death on 21 November 1759, she was buried beside him at Kirkliston. ROSALIND K. MARSHALL

Sources NA Scot., Stair Muniments, Eleanor, countess of Stair, letters to her husband, 1711–45, GD135/143 · R. Chambers, *Traditions of Edinburgh*, new edn (1868), 76–82 · *DNB* · *Scots peerage*, 5.508; 7.110; 8.152–4 · R. Douglas, *The peerage of Scotland*, 2nd edn, ed. J. P. Wood, 2 (1813), 532 · *Edinburgh Chronicle* (Nov 1759) · J. Gifford, *William Adam, 1689–1748* (1989), 76 · GEC, *Peerage*
Archives NA Scot., letters to her husband, GD135/143
Likenesses G. Kneller, oils, priv. coll.; photograph, Scot. NPG · oils (after Kneller), priv. coll.; photograph, Scot. NPG · oils, priv. coll.

Dalrymple, Grace. *See* Eliot, Grace (1754?–1823).

Dalrymple, Sir Hew, first baronet, Lord North Berwick (1652–1737), judge and politician, was the third son of James *Dalrymple, first Viscount Stair (1619–1695), and Margaret (d. 1692), daughter of James Ross of Balneil and widow of Fergus Kennedy of Knockdaw. Like his father and elder brothers Sir John *Dalrymple (1648–1707) and Sir James *Dalrymple (1650–1719), he made his fortune at the Scottish bar. After graduating from the University of Edinburgh in 1671 he went abroad, as many prospective advocates did, to study the civil law at the University of Leiden. On returning to Scotland from the Netherlands he gave proof of his learning on 10 February and was admitted into practice on 23 February 1677.

Within a fortnight Dalrymple obtained the first of several public offices through the influence of his father. In pursuit of a new alliance with the Dutch against the French, Charles II instructed his privy council to appoint a governor-general over designated seaports with authority to issue passes to friendly vessels. The council, of which Dalrymple's father was a member as president of the session, decided that the novice advocate was suited to the job. More plausibly, it was decided not long afterwards that he was suited to the task of sitting as a judge in the commissary court of Edinburgh. It was common enough for young advocates to be appointed as commissaries, particularly those with a good reputation for learning, and Dalrymple had barely been admitted to the bar before he was assigned the task by the Faculty of Advocates of examining the learning of other candidates for admission. However, in this instance the office of commissary was resigned in favour of the new judge by his elder brother,

Sir Hew Dalrymple, first baronet, Lord North Berwick (1652–1737), by William Aikman

Sir James Dalrymple of Borthwick, and it soon transpired that he was not entirely suited to the role. While receiving evidence in a divorce case he became irritated with the interruptions of one of the advocates. The debate grew heated, the advocate accused the judge of partiality, and instead of sending him to cool his heels in the cells, as he might have done, Dalrymple challenged him to a duel. The privy council intervened and sent both parties to prison for a while, but the dispute was soon resolved and forgotten.

By the time this incident occurred, in early February 1684, Dalrymple had lost the support of his father, who had been driven into exile in the Netherlands in 1682—in fact he spent his time at the University of Leiden—following his opposition to the Test Act. Dalrymple accompanied his father on at least part of his journey abroad, but he seems to have remained in practice in Edinburgh as an advocate at the bar of the session and other courts and as a judge in the commissary court throughout the 1680s. These were difficult times for his family, yet despite the indictment of their father for treason both he and his two elder brothers, and eventually his younger brother Sir David *Dalrymple of Hailes (c.1665–1721), were able to flourish professionally. By the close of the decade his eldest brother, Sir John Dalrymple, then master and later first earl of Stair, had attained to office as king's advocate, a privy councillor, a lord of exchequer, justice clerk, and an ordinary lord of session. When Dalrymple's father was restored to the presidency of the session in 1689 the stage was set for his final rise to eminence. He had served a solid apprenticeship for high judicial office by pleading at the bar of the session, privy council, and justiciary court for

over a decade and by adjudicating on matrimonial and testamentary matters in the commissary court. His father had once again become the dominant figure in the session, where his elder brother was soon to become a principal clerk, and although his eldest brother's career had suffered a temporary setback on the arrival of William and Mary, he had been restored as king's advocate in 1690 and had become joint secretary of state in 1691. With a younger brother making his way at the bar and another, Thomas, on his way to becoming physician to the king, Dalrymple had a powerful family to promote his ambitions, though belonging to a powerful family also meant that he had many enemies. Hostility towards the Dalrymples was particularly intense at the time of the revolution.

In 1690 Dalrymple was elected to represent the burgh of New Galloway, in the region where his father and eldest brother were building up estates, in parliament. His father was elected to represent Ayrshire, where the original family home was situated, and his eldest brother was influential behind the scenes in shaping the programme of legislation they both supported. On his return to office the master of Stair focused his attentions on politics and left others to fulfil the legal duties of the king's advocate. In late 1690 Dalrymple appeared in court to act as his brother's substitute in prosecuting crimes. In early 1691 a more formal arrangement was made. Sir William Lockhart of Carstairs was appointed their majesties' solicitor with power to prosecute the crimes normally dealt with by the king's advocate. Dalrymple was appointed one of his two assistants and remained busily engaged in fulfilling the duties of the king's advocate for the next few years. After Lockhart's death in 1694, and with the master of Stair in difficulty again, Sir James Stewart of Goodtrees was appointed king's advocate and Dalrymple was elected in his place as dean of the Faculty of Advocates. Later in 1695 he was forced to apologize to parliament for publishing a work entitled *Information for the Master of Stair*, defending his eldest brother's role in the events leading up to the massacre of Glencoe. As it was clear that his brother was to be blamed for the affair and removed from office, Dalrymple disowned his remarks as mistaken. The setback to his brother's career was again only temporary, and the affair seems to have had no long-term effect on his own prospects. He was re-elected as dean of the Faculty of Advocates in 1696, 1697, and 1698, and during these years was prominently engaged in the expansion of the recently established Advocates' Library (the basis of the later National Library of Scotland) and in an eventually successful endeavour to restore law teaching to the Scottish universities.

In November 1695, four months after his eldest brother lost office as secretary of state, Dalrymple's father died. He was not replaced immediately as president of the session and the search for a new president became the focus of a struggle for power between the magnates who were gradually recovering their traditional dominance of Scottish politics. The earl of Tullibardine obtained from the king a letter in favour of Sir William Hamilton of

Whitelaw, an ordinary lord of session since 1693 and an able jurist who had written a treatise on criminal procedure, had circulated some notes on the *Institutions of the Law of Scotland* written by Dalrymple's father, and was editing for publication a collection entitled *Doubts and Questions in the Law* composed by Sir John Nisbet of Dirleton. Hamilton had a strong claim to office, and enjoyed support among the other lords of session, but his appointment was successfully blocked by the second duke of Queensberry, the lord privy seal, who meant to thwart the earl of Tullibardine and to promote an alliance with the Dalrymples and the earl of Argyll. The lords of session responded to the production of a new letter from the king in favour of Sir Hew Dalrymple of North Berwick, as he then became, by insisting that they would have to examine his fitness for office before he joined the court. After a three-day trial he was finally admitted to the presidency on 7 June 1698, taking his title from the extensive estates he had been building up in and around North Berwick. He at once began to compile a collection of reports of the decisions of the court, similar to those compiled by his father in the 1660s and 1670s. Like his father he maintained his collection for twenty years, from the time of his appointment in 1698 until 1718. The volume was published posthumously in 1758, but has not been particularly highly valued either by lawyers or historians.

According to a contemporary, Dalrymple was 'believed to be one of the best presidents that ever was in that chair, and one of the compleatest lawyers in Scotland' (*Memoirs of the Secret Services*, 211). He was 'a very eloquent orator, smooth and slow of expression, with a clear understanding, but grave in his manner', and he was also 'a man of inimpeached integrity, and of great private worth and amiable manners'. Appointed both as a privy councillor and as a commissioner of exchequer in 1698, he sat for the burgh of North Berwick in the last Scottish parliament before the Union of 1707. He was an enthusiastic supporter of the Union, as were his brothers and the duke of Queensberry, the royal commissioner to the parliament.

After 1707 Dalrymple was able to devote more time to the session, of which he remained president until his death. He had tried to escape from office a decade earlier, after the earl of Seafield took to exercising his theoretical right as chancellor to attend and preside over the court, but his demand for a pension equal to his salary had been too much for the London administration. More successful was his attempt at the same time to have one of his sons appointed as an ordinary lord of session. **Hew Dalrymple of Drummore**, Lord Drummore (1690–1755), the third son of Dalrymple and his first wife, Marion, daughter of Sir Robert Hamilton of Presmannen, another lord of session, had been admitted to the bar when just under twenty years of age in 1710. He became an ordinary lord of session just sixteen years later, on 29 December 1726. He became a lord of justiciary on 13 June 1735, and died at Drummore, close to North Berwick, on 18 June 1755, at the age of sixty-four. On 26 February 1711 he had married Anne (*d.* 1731), daughter of John Horn of that ilk, a fellow advocate, and

they had a son who became an ordinary lord of session in 1777 as David Dalrymple of Westhall.

Sir Hew Dalrymple of North Berwick had eleven other children with his first wife, whom he had married on 12 March 1682. Their first son, James, died young, but the baronetcy passed in 1737 to their second son, Sir Robert Dalrymple of Castleton, also an advocate. Two further sons, John and William, served in the army, of which their cousin, the second earl of Stair, became commander-in-chief. Little is known of two remaining sons, Alexander and another James. The eighth child and eldest daughter, Margaret, married Sir John Shaw of Greenock. Little is known of the next daughter, Marion, but her younger sister Anne married Sir James Stewart of Goodtrees, the son and heir of the king's advocate appointed in 1694. Elizabeth, the eleventh child, was married to Sir James Suttie of Balgonie, and Eleanor, the twelfth, was married to Sir Thomas Hay of Alderston. On 6 April 1711 Dalrymple was married for a second time, to Elizabeth, daughter of John Hamilton of Bangour and widow of John Hamilton of Hedderwick, and with her he had two more daughters, Marion, who married Ludovic Colquhoun of Luss, and Johanna. Dalrymple died on 1 February 1737. In 1718 he wrote to his eldest brother asking him to look after the interests of his children, complaining that he had 'no favours to buy off' and lamenting that he had never been 'able to do anything' for his kin (Graham, 2.384). In truth, the family had done pretty well by each other.

J. D. FORD

Sources GEC, *Baronetage* · F. J. Grant, ed., *The Faculty of Advocates in Scotland, 1532–1943*, Scottish RS, 145 (1944) · J. M. Pinkerton, ed., *The minute book of the Faculty of Advocates*, 2 vols., Stair Society, 29 (1976), Stair Society, 32 (1980) · G. Brunton and D. Haig, *An historical account of the senators of the college of justice, from its institution in MDXXXII* (1832) · *Reg. PCS*, 3rd ser. · P. W. J. Riley, *King William and the Scottish politicians* (1979) · *Annals and correspondence of the viscount and the first and second earls of Stair*, ed. J. M. Graham, 2 vols. (1875) · M. D. Young, ed., *The parliaments of Scotland: burgh and shire commissioners*, 2 vols. (1992–3) · *Memoirs of the secret services of John Macky*, ed. A. R. (1733) · G. W. T. Omond, *The lord advocates of Scotland*, 2 vols. (1883) · *Historical notices of Scotish affairs, selected from the manuscripts of Sir John Lauder of Fountainhall*, ed. D. Laing, 2 vols., Bannatyne Club, 87 (1848) · 'General inventory of the writs and evidents of the lands, barony and estate of North Berwick', 1707, U. Edin. L., MS La. III. 330

Archives Mount Stuart Trust Archive, Rothesay, corresp. · NA Scot., corresp. and papers | Hunt. L., letters to earl of London · NA Scot., letters to duke of Montrose

Likenesses W. Aikman, oils, Parliament Hall, Edinburgh [*see illus.*] · attrib. J. B. de Medina, oils, Scot. NPG

Wealth at death extensive estates and income in 1707

Dalrymple, Hew, of Drummore, Lord Drummore (1690–1755). *See under* Dalrymple, Sir Hew, first baronet, Lord North Berwick (1652–1737).

Dalrymple, Sir Hew Whitefoord, first baronet (1750–1830), army officer, was born in Ayr on 3 December 1750, the only son of Captain John Dalrymple (1692–1753) of the 6th dragoons and his second wife, Mary, *née* Ross (*c.*1719–1793), the daughter of Alexander Ross of Balkail, Wigtownshire. Widowed in 1753, his mother married Lieutenant-Colonel James Adolphus Dickenson *Oughton (*bap.* 1719, *d.* 1780) in 1755. In 1763 Dalrymple became an ensign in his stepfather's regiment, the 31st. A lieutenancy followed in 1766, but in neither rank did Dalrymple serve with the regiment. In 1767 Oughton became deputy commander-in-chief, north Britain, and Dalrymple attended Edinburgh University (1767–8). In 1768 he obtained a captaincy in the 1st (or Royal) regiment, of which Oughton's superior, Lord Lorne, was colonel. With the royals, Dalrymple served in Minorca. His stepfather being an assiduous freemason, Dalrymple embraced the craft in 1768—although he was never as active as Oughton. Peacetime soldiering allowed him to travel—he visited Dresden and Vienna in 1777—and honed his administrative skills.

Dalrymple was abroad at the time of Burgoyne's surrender at Saratoga in October 1777. Returning hastily in the hope of preferment, he found that Oughton had already exerted influence in Scotland for him. Although denied a lieutenant-colonelcy because of his youth, later that year he became major in the 77th (or Atholl) highlanders being raised by Oughton's fellow freemason, the duke of Atholl. Appointment of the regiment's lieutenant-colonel took a year, so Dalrymple exercised executive command of the 77th until 1779, stationed near Cork with the troops protecting Ireland from invasion. In 1779 he stood proxy for Oughton at an installation of knights of the Bath. As was customary, he was knighted beforehand—the last act of patronage that Oughton, who died in 1780, bestowed on him.

By 1780 Dalrymple was seeking a lieutenant-colonelcy. Having obtained that of the 68th regiment in 1781, he exchanged it for a company in the 1st foot guards in 1782. On 16 May 1783 he married an heiress, Frances Leighton (1753–1835), the youngest daughter of General Francis Leighton, and settled in Marylebone, where the couple had two sons and three daughters. He was promoted colonel in 1790. War in 1793 brought him active service with the first detachment of officers in the guards brigade formed for service in Flanders. As his letters to his wife revealed, he found this first experience of war horrifying. Having seen action, Dalrymple returned in 1794 to command the recruiting depot at Chatham and was promoted major general in October.

Dalrymple was posted to the northern district in 1795 and appointed lieutenant-governor of Guernsey in March 1796, receiving the local rank of lieutenant-general in November 1799. The absentee governor was Jeffrey Amherst, Baron Amherst (1717–1797), a friend and contemporary of Oughton's. During his five years on Guernsey, Dalrymple was in frequent contact with French royalists, *chouans*, whose intelligence he relayed to London regularly. He obtained ensigncies for his two sons, Adolphus and Leighton, in the 55th regiment—which had been stationed on Guernsey during his posting there: both served him as aides-de-camp, as Dalrymple had served Oughton. In 1797 he obtained the colonelcy of the 81st regiment, and the following year he transferred to that of the 37th—in which Oughton had served.

Promoted lieutenant-general in January 1801, Dalrymple commanded the northern district from 1802 until May 1806, when he was appointed lieutenant-governor of Gibraltar; he became governor in November 1806. He soon received overtures from influential Spaniards who were unhappy about Spain's alliance with France: he encouraged these, reported them to London, and helped establish a network of British agents in Spain. Following the uprising of *Dos Mayo* 1808, Dalrymple established formal links with several Spanish generals and fed British funds to Spain.

The subsequent French invasion of Spain threatened Britain's ally Portugal, and an expedition was prepared, commanded by Lieutenant-General Sir Arthur Wellesley, who held the cabinet post of chief secretary for Ireland. Since military failure in Portugal could destabilize the government, it was decided that Wellesley should be superseded by two senior lieutenant-generals, Sir Harry Burrard (1755–1813) and Dalrymple.

Dalrymple arrived in Portugal on 22 August 1808, the day after Burrard, and countermanded Wellesley's orders for a pursuit of the French following the latter's victory over the French under General Andoche Junot at Vimeiro (21 August). Dalrymple had been given secret carte blanche by Castlereagh to act upon his own initiative to expel the French from Portugal. There the British were victorious and, reinforced by the arrival of Sir John Moore's corps, in a very strong position relative to the French; there was little danger of the British being defeated. Nevertheless Dalrymple lacked confidence in Wellesley, considered him rash, and did not approve his conduct of the campaign. Wellesley pressed for immediate advance, but Dalrymple refused. The French had lost heavily at Vimeiro and Junot believed they could not fight another battle. So on 22 August he sent General François Christophe Kellerman under flag of truce. He proposed an armistice and evacuation of the French troops, but with terms presumptuously favourable to the defeated French—terms they believed were the best they could hope to gain. Dalrymple negotiated and, presumably from lack of confidence and intelligence, accepted the French terms and agreed to the convention of Cintra (30 August 1808), by which the French army—with its arms, equipment, and loot from the Portuguese—was repatriated in British ships. Wellesley called this 'a very extraordinary paper', and Michael Glover has written that 'on Dalrymple's side it was a masterpiece of ineptitude … never has a victorious army with every advantage in its hands signed an agreement which gave so much to its defeated enemies with so little to itself' (Glover, 138–9). Dalrymple delayed reporting it to London.

The Portuguese protested. Beresford wrote from Lisbon to Wellesley that 'people here of every class are enraged … this treaty has lowered us much in their estimation' (Glover, 154). Wellesley and Moore agreed Dalrymple was unfit to command, and both wrote disloyal letters home, Wellesley especially, traducing Dalrymple and distancing himself from the convention (which he had signed) in an effort to protect himself. In Britain victory was expected in Portugal and there was jubilation at the news of Vimeiro. News of the 'disgraceful convention' (Muir, 54) aroused hostile opinion in Britain, where it was denounced by the king, the press, politicians, and the public, and also by Cobbett, Wordsworth, and Byron. The government disliked it but considered themselves bound by it, though Canning wanted it broken. Dalrymple was ineffective in commanding the army in Portugal, which became demoralized and faction-ridden, and because of Cintra he was recalled to England. In November the government appointed a board of inquiry composed of generals, the majority of whom were determined not to blame Dalrymple and Burrard. Appearing before them, Dalrymple, although he had been the commanding officer and so responsible, blamed Wellesley, alleging he had acted on Wellesley's advice and with his consent. As Glover has written, Dalrymple's attempt 'to shuffle responsibility on to his subordinate was discreditable in the extreme' (Glover, 193). The board produced an unconvincing 'whitewash' report (December 1808) exonerating all. Yet, according to Rory Muir, 'both armistice and convention contained concessions which no British general should ever have been willing to grant', and Dalrymple's 'subsequent disgrace was not unmerited' (Muir, 52.3). Dalrymple, who had promised Castlereagh before the inquiry convened not to reveal his secret carte blanche in order to protect the government, was reprimanded by the king and never received another command. He transferred from the colonelcy of the 37th regiment to that of the 19th in 1810 and to that of the 57th in 1811. Promoted general in 1812, he received a baronetcy in May 1815 and was appointed governor of Blackness Castle in 1818.

The ending of the war in 1815 inspired the publication of memoirs and campaign histories. In 1818 Dalrymple wrote a memoir of the Peninsular War, but it was not published until 1830, by his son. By this time the marquess of Londonderry, Castlereagh's half-brother, had published his own campaign history (in 1828), which criticized Dalrymple and the convention of Cintra. Some later historians were to be more favourable to Dalrymple—indeed, he helped both Robert Southey and Sir William Napier with their histories of the Peninsular War—but the stigma of Cintra remains attached to his name. This stigma added to the sadness of his last years. His younger son, Leighton Cathcart, died in 1820 of wounds received while commanding the 15th hussars at Waterloo, and Lady Dalrymple became unstable during the 1820s. Dalrymple died at his London house, 23 Upper Wimpole Street, on 9 April 1830 and was buried in his family's vault in the churchyard of St John the Baptist, Aldenham, Hertfordshire, near his country home, Delrow House. He was succeeded as baronet by his elder son, Adolphus John *Dalrymple (1784-1866), Conservative MP successively for Weymouth (1817-18), Appleby (1819-26), Haddington Burghs (1826-30, 1831-2), and Brighton (1837-41), at whose death on 3 March 1866 the baronetcy became extinct.

Most twentieth-century historians of the Peninsular War were unfavourable to Dalrymple's role in the convention of Cintra. An exception was Richard Schneer's revisionist interpretation (1980) attempting to exonerate Dalrymple, which argued that he successfully implemented government policy to gain control of Portugal but was made a scapegoat, and which blamed the government and Wellesley. STEPHEN WOOD

Sources NL Scot., MS 9716 · National Museums of Scotland, MS M1990.660.2 · NAM, MSS 9403.129.2-49 · BL, Add. MSS 35510-35542, *passim* · Blair Castle, Perthshire, Atholl MSS 334-342, 345-350 · W. F. P. Napier, *War in the Peninsula and south of France, 1807-14*, 6 vols. (1834-40) · *DNB* · *GM*, 1st ser., 100/1 (1830), 558 · Boase, *Mod. Eng. biog.* · *WWBMP*, vol. 1 · R. Muir, *Britain and the defeat of Napoleon, 1807-1815* (1996) · M. Glover, *Britannia sickens: the convention of Cintra* (1970) · E. Longford [E. H. Pakenham, countess of Longford], *Wellington*, 1: *The years of the sword* (1969) · R. M. Schneer, 'Arthur Wellesley and the Cintra convention: a new look at an old puzzle', *Journal of British Studies*, 19/2 (1980), 93-119 · C. D. Hall, *British strategy in the Napoleonic war, 1803-15* (1992) · P. W. Schroeder, *The transformation of European politics, 1763-1848* (1996)

Archives NAM, papers relating to Middlesex regiment, 9403.129.2-49 · National War Museum of Scotland, Edinburgh, corresp. and papers · NL Scot., corresp. and papers relating to Peninsular War · NRA, priv. coll., papers | BL, corresp. with Sir James Willoughby Gordon, Add. MSS 49483-49484 · BL, letters to Sir Robert Keith, Add. MSS 35510-35542, *passim* · PRO NIre., corresp. with Lord Castlereagh

Likenesses D. Martin, oils, *c*.1768, National Museums of Scotland, Edinburgh · C. Williams, caricature, 1808 (with Junot), Scot. NPG · stipple, pubd 1808, NPG · O. Carbonnier, engraving, pubd 1824 (after drawing by H. Edridge, 1794), NAM · C. Turner, mezzotint, pubd 1831 (after J. Jackson, *c*.1825), BM, NAM; please see comments below · J. Jackson, portrait, priv. coll. · attrib. J. B. de Medina, oils, Scot. NPG · A. Stewart, miniature, NG Scot.

Wealth at death see will, PRO, PROB 11/1771

Dalrymple, Ian Murray (1903-1989), film producer and writer, was born on 26 August 1903 in Johannesburg, Transvaal Colony, one of the three sons of Sir William Dalrymple (1864-1941), a mining company director, and his wife, Isabel Rayner (d. 1938). He was educated at Rugby School and at Trinity College, Cambridge (where he edited *The Granta*, 1924-5). Having entered the film industry in a job with Adrian Brunel, he was a film editor from 1927 to 1935, editing a number of fine films of the early 1930s, particularly at the Gainsborough studio—*Sunshine Susie* and *The Ghost Train* (both 1931), *Jack's the Boy* (1933), *Evergreen* (1934)—and then became head of the editing department at Gaumont-British under Michael Balcon. He wrote for films as early as 1929 (*Taxi for Two*), and by the late 1930s scriptwriting came to predominate in his career. Among numerous successes as co-scriptwriter, often for the director Victor Saville or the producer Alexander Korda, were *Storm in a Teacup* (1937), which he also co-directed with Saville, *South Riding*, *Pygmalion*, uncredited but for which he received an Academy award for best adapted screenplay, and *The Citadel*, for which he was again nominated (all 1938), *Q Planes*, *The Lion has Wings* (story), and *French without Tears* (all 1939) and *Pimpernel Smith* (1941). He also co-wrote and directed *Old Bill and Son* (1940). On 21 September 1927 he married Muriel Stewart Connochie (b. 1903/4), with whom he had a son and a daughter. Following their divorce, on 3 June 1939 he married (Joan) Margaret Craig (*b*. 1915/16), with whom he had two sons.

Dalrymple (often simply called Dal) had also worked occasionally on the production side of film-making, and in 1940 he became executive producer at the Crown Film Unit. It succeeded the General Post Office film unit, spearhead of the British documentary movement of the 1930s; now, as part of the Ministry of Information, it led British wartime propaganda. The documentaries or semi-documentaries produced, including *London Can Take It* (1940), *Target for Tonight* (1941), *Malta GC* and *Coastal Command* (both 1942), and *Western Approaches* (1944), were almost as popular with audiences as feature films, and 'served their purpose admirably and even movingly, that purpose being to boost morale ... [and they] left us with a unique and poignantly living record of the period' (*The Independent*, 1 May 1989, 14). In addition, two he made with the director Humphrey Jennings, *Listen to Britain* (1942) and *Fires were Started* (1943), were not only invaluable and evocative war records but also minor classics of film poetry.

After briefly working again with Korda on *Perfect Strangers* (1945), Dalrymple formed Wessex Film Productions, so called because he hoped to film the novels of Thomas Hardy. It operated as part of Independent Producers, based at Pinewood Studios. Results were generally good from its first offering, the 'refreshingly original' *The Woman in the Hall* (1947). *Esther Waters* (1948), though, which Dalrymple also co-directed, was a 'dreary drama', and dissuaded him from his plans for the Hardy films. *Once a Jolly Swagman* (1948) was good, *Raising a Riot* (1955) an engagingly fresh comedy, and *A Hill in Korea* (1956), though it did poorly at the box office when released in the week of the Suez invasion, was a flawed but gritty war film. Dalrymple's biggest success was *The Wooden Horse* (1950), an exciting version of a famous wartime prison camp escape. Also in 1950 he produced the last film directed by Humphrey Jennings before his death, *A Family Portrait*, a documentary made for the Festival of Britain. Wessex's films were 'typical of the solidly crafted British output of the time' (*The Times*, 2 May 1989). But although Dalrymple had added a realist approach to features, he had often put his own resources into films which did not pay him back, and he certainly suffered financially.

Dirk Bogarde recalled Dalrymple as 'modest, cautious, calm, and in every way a gentle man' (*The Independent*, 1 May 1989, 14). He was known for encouraging young talent, from editors when at Gaumont-British, to actors (including Bogarde and Stanley Baker) and directors (Jack Lee and Wendy Toye) at Wessex. Michael Powell called him 'one of the great men of the British cinema' (*Halliwell*, 106). Several Wessex films were co-productions with Korda's London Films, and for them Dalrymple co-wrote and produced *The Heart of the Matter* (1953), from Graham Greene's novel. Later in the decade he produced a good version of *The Admirable Crichton* (1957), from J. M. Barrie's play, and the excellent *A Cry from the Streets* (1958). Dalrymple's film ventures in the 1960s were fewer and less notable, but included scripting *Mix me a Person* (1962), a

straight vehicle for the singer Adam Faith, and producing such family fare as *Hunted in Holland* (1961) and *Calamity the Cow* (1967). Dalrymple was a fellow of the Royal Society of Arts and in 1957–8 was the highly respected chairman of the British Film Academy. In the early 1950s he had been a director of the Argo Record Company for several years; in the late 1960s he supervised film projects for Argo and was film adviser to its parent company, Decca Limited. Dalrymple died, in Queen Mary's University Hospital, Roehampton, on 28 April 1989, survived by his wife.

ROBERT SHARP

Sources www.uk.imdb.com, 28 Sept 2001 · *The Times* (2 May 1989), 18f · *The Independent* (1–2 May 1989) · *WW* · D. Gifford, *The illustrated who's who in British films*, 13th edn (1978) · *Halliwell's who's who in the movies*, 13th edn (1999) · m. certs. · d. cert.

Likenesses photograph, *c*.1960–1965, repro. in www.britmovie.co.uk, 12 Nov 2001

Dalrymple, James, first Viscount Stair (1619–1695), lawyer and politician, was born in May 1619 at Drummurchie in Ayrshire, the only child of James Dalrymple of Drummurchie (*d*. 1625) and of Janet (*d*. 1664), daughter of Fergus Kennedy of Knockdaw. His father was the second son of James Dalrymple, laird of Stair, a small estate on the River Ayr, situated midway between Ayr and Catrine. The estate, acquired by the family through marriage in the fifteenth century, had passed on the death of the future first viscount's grandfather to his elder son, John Dalrymple, whose only child was also called James. In 1620 this James Dalrymple transferred the estate to his uncle, the first viscount's father, and it was in the house of Stair, still standing, that the first viscount spent his early years. After his father's death in 1625 he was raised by his mother, who was said to have inherited from her ancestors a firm commitment to the reformed faith. On his father's side he also had ancestors who were known to have played leading roles in the history of the Scottish Reformation. His grandfather had openly supported John Knox in the 1560s, his great-grandfather had fought with the earl of Glencairn in the 1540s, and his great-grandfather's own grandmother was one of the fifteenth-century dissidents referred to by Knox as the 'Lollards of Kyle' (*John Knox's History of the Reformation in Scotland*, ed W. C. Dickinson, 2 vols., 1949, 1.8 and 2.56).

Education, 1628–1637 According to Dalrymple's sons he was educated at the parish school of Mauchline, about 5 miles from his home. When the surviving records of the local kirk session opened in 1669, the school had been meeting for some years in the converted chancel of the medieval church, the remainder of which had been restructured, with a pulpit as its focus and no fixed communion table. In 1642, when the surviving records of the local presbytery opened, the master of the school had for some years been the reader of the church, responsible for the religious education of young and old alike. As a schoolmaster his ultimate aim would have been to prepare his abler pupils for entry into the nearest university, where teaching and all other activities were conducted entirely in Latin, and where the ministers and readers of the local parishes had almost all received their training. Whether

James Dalrymple, first Viscount Stair (1619–1695), by Sir John Baptiste de Medina

or not Dalrymple did attend the parish school at Mauchline, by 1633 he had somewhere made himself sufficiently proficient in Latin to enter the University of Glasgow at the usual age of fourteen.

At the university emphasis continued to be placed on religious instruction, through a continuing routine of prayer, catechizing, and sermons, and the liberal arts were generally taught by graduates who were in the course of preparing for the ministry. In his first year Dalrymple was taught by James Forsyth, who had graduated in 1625, had been appointed as regent of the fourth class or *linguae Graecae professor* in 1631, and was to become minister at Old Kilpatrick in 1635. In both his second and third years he was taught by William Wilkie, who had graduated in 1627, had been appointed as a regent a year later, was promoted from regent of the third class or *logicae professor* to regent of the second class or *moralis philosophiae professor* in 1635, and was to become minister at Govan in 1640. In his last year he was taught by John Rae, who had graduated in 1618, had been appointed as a regent in 1623, was promoted to regent of the first class or *physiologiae professor* in 1635, and was to fail to enter the ministry after supporting the 'Canterburian' regime in 1638.

The designations of the regents give a fair impression of the curriculum in the 1630s, moving from further study of the humanities through a grounding in logic to the study of philosophy, except that some elements of metaphysics and mathematics were also studied in the later years. The philosophical texts were predominantly Aristotelian, and the methods of teaching—mostly by 'dictate' and disputation—were indicative of a scholastic revival. At regular intervals the students were given the opportunity to rehearse their philosophical learning in formal disputations, and at the end of their course, about the middle of the July of their final year, those who had been found fit to graduate participated in a public disputation at which they sought to impress an audience of ministers, burgesses, and local dignitaries. In 1637 Dalrymple was presented to an audience as the most able student in his class.

Army and academy, 1637–1647 Three months after Dalrymple received his degree, two new regents were appointed in the university, and two years later another position went to the student who had been placed only sixth in his class. Given that Dalrymple was appointed to a regency in 1641, he was presumably unwilling to return to the university at this stage, though what he was doing is not entirely clear. He was said by William Forbes—writing in his *Journal of the Session* in 1714 with advice from Dalrymple's sons—to have been present in Edinburgh in 1638 when the national covenant was subscribed. By his own account—prefaced to a set of academic *Theses* he published in 1646—he had responded to the constitutional crisis and to the disruption of ordinary academic life by joining the army raised to confront the king in the first bishops' war. After the war ended in June 1639, he was appointed tutor to Archibald Campbell, Lord Lorne, son and heir of the eighth earl of Argyll. But on the outbreak of the second bishops' war in the summer of 1640 he had rejoined the army, 'indignant at scholastic effeminacy when the Ark and Israel were in the open air'. He indicated that he had been with the army that marched into England in August 1640 and that he had been involved in fighting that cost many lives, possibly at Newburn. Forbes maintained that he had been given charge of 'a Company of Foot in the Regiment commanded by William, E. of Glencairn, afterwards Chancellor', but this cannot have been correct. Glencairn was not commissioned to raise a regiment until 1642, and during the bishops' wars he had conducted himself, in Robert Baillie's phrase, 'otherways than his forbears' (*Letters and Journals of Robert Baillie*, 1.205–6). It would seem more likely that Dalrymple had served in the regiment raised by John Campbell, earl of Loudoun, who was made chancellor of Scotland in September 1641. A near kinsman of Argyll and a landowner in the Mauchline area, Loudoun had raised from Ayrshire and Lanarkshire one of the two regiments of foot that advanced on the English positions at Newburn.

Dalrymple claimed in 1646 that he had endured hardship as a soldier, though in Baillie's opinion 'none of our gentlemen was any thing worse of lying some weekes together in their cloake and boots on the ground, or standing all night in armes in the greatest storme' (*Letters and Journals of Robert Baillie*, 1.212–13). Baillie, who had accompanied the western regiments as a chaplain along with other former regents at Glasgow, such as Robert Blair and David Dickson, praised these soldiers for their 'pietie and militar discipline'. According to Forbes, when Dalrymple appeared to be examined for the post of regent in 1641 he was still clothed in the buff and scarlet of an army officer, and he was himself quick to stress that he had been permitted to take up the post without surrendering his military command, which he presumably retained until the army was disbanded about six months later. It was Forbes's understanding that he had been persuaded to return to Glasgow by some of his former teachers, though the only one who remained was John Rae. Dalrymple's own impression, that Argyll had engineered his recall to Glasgow so that he would be available to teach Lord Lorne 'in hac Academia', seems rather implausible, though not impossible. The need for a new regent in the university had arisen suddenly on 26 February when William Hamilton, one of the regents appointed in October 1637, had resigned from office. Dalrymple was appointed barely a week later, on 4 March.

Since Dalrymple's departure in July 1637 there had been changes in the staffing of the university. A regent had been appointed to teach the humanities to new students and another had been promoted to teach medicine to advanced students, prompting the principal of the university to petition the general assembly of the church to take steps to secure the teaching of theology, hitherto the only higher discipline that had been taught. A commission including Argyll and Loudoun as elders, and Baillie and Dickson as ministers, had been established to visit the university, and a year later it had submitted a report, written by George Young, a former regent and minister at Mauchline, which proposed the appointment of Dickson as professor of theology. Two years later another report proposed the appointment of Baillie as a second professor of theology, together with the suppression of the chair of medicine. It thus remained in essence a religious seminary that Dalrymple returned to in 1641, where he was now expected as a regent 'to try what conscience each Scholler makes of secret devotions, morning and evening', to have his students subscribe the national covenant, and to ensure first that they could understand its significance (Innes, 2.455–6).

By the time the new academic year opened in the autumn of 1641, Rae had left the university and William Semple had been selected for appointment as regent of the humanity class. Dalrymple was duly promoted to be regent of the fourth class, with responsibility for the teaching of Greek and dialectic. In September 1642, however, the church commissioners recommended that the older system of regenting, in which each class would be taken right through the curriculum by the same teacher, be revived. In October 1643 Dalrymple therefore carried on teaching the same class, which he took through to graduation in July 1646. As Baillie later recalled, this 'considerable class' had among its number 'divers worthy youths, some of our prime nobility and gentry', including the lords Lorne, Cathcart and Torphichen, the future regent and minister Hugh Binning, the future benefactor of the university John Snell, and the future lord of session Sir Thomas Wallace of Craigie (W. I. Addison, *The Snell Exhibitions*, 1901, 11). Since 1645 the students had been residing in Irvine, Dickson's former parish, having moved

there to avoid a visitation of the plague, but it was apparently in the hall of the university that they defended the *Theses logicae, metaphysicae, physicae, mathematicae et ethicae* that were sent to the press by Dalrymple in 1646. Dedicated to Lorne, who like most noblemen had left without finishing his course, these were the first theses published by a Glasgow regent and give some indication of what he had been teaching.

At his admission as a regent Dalrymple had sworn to remain in office for at least six years and to give at least three months' notice before he left, a commitment he honoured, for he gave notice of his intention to leave in April 1647. He had also promised that he would resign immediately if he decided to marry, which he had done in 1643 (by contract dated 20 September), when he had sworn an amended oath in which he gave no undertaking to remain celibate. His wife was Margaret Ross (d. 1692), daughter of James Ross of Balneil in Wigtownshire and widow of Fergus Kennedy of Knockdaw, who brought to the marriage a valuable estate near Glenluce. By the time of her death the couple had ten children. Their eldest son, John *Dalrymple, was born in 1648 and later became a king's advocate, a lord of session, secretary of state for Scotland, and the first earl of Stair. Three other sons also became successful advocates. Sir James *Dalrymple of Borthwick, born in 1650, became a clerk of session and is better remembered as a historian. Sir Hew *Dalrymple of North Berwick, born in 1652, achieved the eminence of president of the session in succession to his father. Sir David *Dalrymple of Hailes, born in 1665 or thereabouts, followed in his eldest brother's footsteps as a principal law officer of the crown. A fifth son, Thomas Dalrymple, born in 1663, became eminent in another profession and was appointed physician to the queen. There were also five daughters who mostly made successful marriages, except for one whose marriage became the stuff of legend and provided Sir Walter Scott with the inspiration for his *Bride of Lammermoor*. Another daughter was reputed to be possessed of an evil spirit, as was her mother, but no serious charge of witchcraft was ever brought.

Bar and bench, 1647–1661 The family's formal connection with the legal profession began on 17 February 1648, when Dalrymple was admitted as an advocate in the college of justice, though he may have been related to Andrew Dalrymple, a notary public in Mauchline, who appears in several records as 'servitor' to the earl of Loudoun and who was sufficiently prosperous to act as guarantor for the payment of Loudoun's debts. In 1624 Dalrymple's patrimonial estate had been mortgaged to Andrew Dalrymple, and one of the first things he did on being admitted to the bar was to redeem the mortgage on 1 March 1648. A Glasgow graduate himself, Andrew Dalrymple sent one of his sons to the university in 1643, and it is possible that his success as a lawyer had some influence on James Dalrymple's decision to enter the legal profession. Another possible source of influence was the example of James Roberton, who also sent a son to the university in the 1640s and who was installed as its rector in 1646, the year in which

Dalrymple finished his first run through the undergraduate course and faced the prospect of starting again with a class of novices. Roberton had departed from the career pattern of regents appointed before 1633 by seeking employment outside the church and the schools. While still a regent he had become a judge in a local commissary court, and when he left the university in 1626 it was to prepare for admission as an advocate. By 1646 he had established a flourishing practice and gained a further judicial appointment in the justiciary court. Dalrymple came close to following Roberton's career pattern, for in 1646 he almost secured appointment as commissary of Glasgow, losing out to another future rector (NA Scot., GD 135/2724, and CC 9/1/17, fol. 105r).

Before his admission to the bar Dalrymple persuaded the lords of session that he was qualified for legal practice by delivering a short oration on a text from the *Libri feudorum*. One judge, Sir John Scot of Scotstarvet, believed the speech worth preserving, and later appended a copy to his 'Trew relation of the principal affaires concerning the state'. It seems likely that Scot was more impressed with the political relevance of the speech, which dealt with a topical issue, than with its demonstration of legal learning. Unlike Roberton and most other prospective advocates, Dalrymple had not gone abroad to study at a continental law school, and his familiarity with the civil, canon, and feudal laws could only have been acquired by private and undirected study during his time as a regent. Forbes certainly believed that this had been his preoccupation at Glasgow, and Dalrymple did himself indicate that he had been studying law since the early 1640s. A collection of legal materials was built up at Glasgow during the seventeenth century, and it is possible that his ambition in 1641 was to follow the recent example of Robert Mayne, the regent of philosophy who was appointed to teach medicine as an advanced discipline, by becoming in due course the first professor of law in the university. If so, his hopes would have been dashed by the report of the church commissioners a year later. As Dalrymple had to pursue his interest in law in an environment dominated by the study of theology, it is scarcely surprising that in the speech he delivered in 1648 he strayed into the domain of the moral theologians, drew on his knowledge of Aristotelian philosophy, and reminded the judges of the difficulties faced by those who had been left to wander in the byways of the civil law without a guide.

In the months between leaving Glasgow and being admitted to the bar Dalrymple had been observing the practice of the session, of which, it turned out, he was to see little more from the perspective of an advocate. The sittings of the court had been disrupted throughout the preceding decade, and remained intermittent between February 1648 and the last sitting for a decade in February 1650. By the time the court assembled for its first session since his admission in June 1649—with its meetings confined to weekday mornings during June and July—its membership had been purged of 'malignants' by the radical regime formed under Argyll's leadership after the Whiggamore raid. At the core of the army that had marched on Edinburgh from the south-west in 1648 had been a body of men raised by Loudoun, with Dickson as their chaplain, and while there is no direct evidence that Dalrymple participated in the military manoeuvres, he benefited from their outcome. In March 1649 he had been appointed to a parliamentary commission, chaired by Loudoun and consisting mostly of prominent lawyers and politicians, which was supposed to revise the laws of Scotland. In the same month he departed for The Hague as secretary to the parliamentary commission sent to negotiate with Charles II, and he remained out of Scotland until the middle of June. He was in Scotland between November 1649 and February 1650 when the session met for the last time, and he was back in the Netherlands between March and May 1650, when he again served as secretary to the parliamentary commission sent to negotiate with the king. Suspicions among some ministers that he had been keen to dilute the demands made of the king might have led to difficulty in the further purge of the session called for at the end of May, but in fact he managed to preserve a reputation for radicalism during this period. He was commonly believed to have drafted the western remonstrance, issued in October 1650, which criticized the deal struck with the king and called for a more stringent cleansing of all judicatories.

After May 1652 Dalrymple was at last able to gain some extended experience at the bar. In that month seven commissioners for the administration of justice in Scotland were appointed from London, and although Dalrymple, together with most other advocates, withdrew from practice for a few months in 1654 rather than swear an oath of allegiance to the Commonwealth, he was otherwise to remain in continuous practice until July 1657, when he was appointed to the bench on the recommendation of George Monck. The new judges, most of whom were drawn from the English bar, had been instructed to bring the law of Scotland into line with the law of England, though it was recognized that in the absence of English clerks and attorneys the local procedure would need to be followed. The result was a sustained and largely successful struggle by the local lawyers against the Anglicization of their legal system, a struggle that continued until April 1659 when the judges stopped sitting. Despite repeated efforts to revive the English court, it was not until June 1661 that the administration of justice was restored in Scotland through the appointment of lords of session on the old model. According to Forbes, who claimed to have seen documentary evidence in the hands of Dalrymple of Borthwick, James Dalrymple had been approached for advice by Monck before he departed with the army of occupation for England in 1659. He had urged Monck to call a full and free parliament and to find some way of 'setting the Course of Justice a going'.

During the two-year period of enforced leisure that preceded the restoration of the session, Stair wrote the first draft of the treatise on which his reputation was later to rest. Eventually printed as *The Institutions of the Law of Scotland*, the treatise drew together the major sources of Scots law from the first half of the century. The reports of the decisions of the lords of session compiled by earlier judges and advocates were most frequently cited, along with references to acts of the Scottish parliaments and to other treatises on the customary and statutory law. These local sources were connected with the texts of the learned laws and with discussion of the laws of nature and nations, usually in the form of a preface to discussion of the local sources. Systematic arrangement was one of the more distinctive features of the treatise, for no previous writer on the 'practick' of Scotland had thought so hard about the fundamental structure of the law. Dalrymple maintained that his concern was with the rights people could enjoy. He dealt first with the ways in which different rights could be created, then with the ways in which they could be transferred from one person to another, and eventually with the ways in which they could be asserted or defended in legal proceedings. The third part was not in fact completed until much later, when a few other changes were made and references were added to later decisions and statutes, but it was against the background of Dalrymple's experience as an advocate and judge in the English court that the treatise first took shape. Although awareness of English law is evident, it was on the local and learned sources that attention was focused.

Forbes later suggested that Dalrymple had done so much to clarify the foundations of the law and to reduce it 'into a sound and solid Body' that if it were ever lost it could be retrieved and reconstituted from his book (Forbes, xl). Forbes concluded that he ought to be regarded as 'a Founder and Restorer of our Law', as he commonly has been during the last two centuries, when he has been credited with saving Scots law from eclipse in the parliamentary union of 1707. Dalrymple has been acclaimed as the father of the modern law of Scotland, and his treatise has been accorded the status of a formally binding source, equivalent in authority to the decisions of the higher courts. Rather exaggerated claims have even been made to the effect that his book lies open on the desk of every practising lawyer in the country, which seems unlikely, notwithstanding the appearance of a sixth printed edition in 1981. Since 1981 historians have pointed out that Forbes's view was not widely endorsed until the nineteenth century, and it has been suggested that Dalrymple should be viewed as only one among many jurists who wrote about Scots law in the seventeenth and eighteenth centuries. It may perhaps be anticipated that when the current revisionist fervour subsides his historical importance will be measured by the degree to which he managed to produce a distinctive response to the conditions outlined in the preceding paragraphs of this memoir. If he is unlikely ever to be hailed again as 'that oracle of the law of Scotland' (Lord President Blair, *Faculty Collection*, 1812, 588), it seems equally unlikely that any history of the law of Scotland will ever be regarded as complete without an account of his work.

Court and council, 1661–1681 When the session was revived in June 1661 the judges were almost all elevated from the bar—they were men such as James Roberton who had refused to serve in the administration of 'the usurper'.

Dalrymple, who assumed the courtesy title of Lord Stair, was the solitary exception of a judge translated from the English court. Later he explained that his appointment was a mark of personal favour from a monarch with whom he had become familiar a decade earlier, adding that he was to receive a further mark of royal favour in 1664, when he failed to make a declaration against the national covenant, lost his place in the court, but was permitted to return after making his own version of the declaration (*Apology*, 4). Summoned to London by the king, he took the opportunity to visit France with his eldest son before resuming his place at the court's next sitting. In January 1671, after six more years as an ordinary lord of session, he was made president of the court by royal decree, contrary to the wishes of his colleagues on the bench but with support from the ninth earl of Argyll, his former pupil, and the earl of Lauderdale. As president he remained in the session for a further ten years, impressing contemporary observers with two rather ambiguous qualities. In the first place, some remarked on the range of his learning in philosophy and theology, while others complained about his tendency to address the advocates who appeared before him as if they were his students. All were struck by his scholastic bearing on the bench. In the second place, some observers praised his equable temperament as the ideal disposition for a judge, while others accused him of concealing strong prejudices behind a veneer of impartiality. The miniature of Stair by Sir John Medina—of which an enlarged copy now hangs in the Parliament Hall in Edinburgh—certainly reveals little more of the character behind his impassive if faintly amused features than it does of the twisted neck concealed behind his full-bottomed wig.

Stair was out of office for six months at the start of 1664, and spent a further two months in London in the autumn of 1670 as a parliamentary commissioner to treat for union. The sittings of the whole court were disrupted for two months in the same year by a dispute between the judges and advocates, and for over a year about 1674 by a more serious dispute, and in 1679 Stair was summoned to London once again to advise the king, and stayed there for at least two months. With the exception of these interludes, however, he devoted a considerable part of his time during these decades to judicial business, afterwards boasting in the *Decisions* he published of his assiduous attendance in the court. His typical day while the court was sitting—from November until March (with a break at Christmas) and throughout June and July—involved the perusal of papers submitted by parties, the hearing of oral arguments at the bar, and the compiling of a personal record of the court's decisions, as well as an invariable routine of religious devotions. As president he chaired the plenary sessions of the fifteen lords of session and took responsibility for the preparation of acts of sederunt, a type of subordinate legislation, though he was no longer required to take his turn in supervising the early stages of litigation or in gathering and assessing evidence. During the six months of each year when the court was not sitting he made a point of staying away from Edinburgh, instead throwing himself into the active management of the estates that he was gradually accumulating around Stair and Glenluce.

Forbes understandably described Stair as a man who was 'indefatigable in Business' and who 'knew not what it was to be idle', for he was also involved during these decades in affairs of state. As well as serving on the commission appointed to treat for union with England, which had insisted on the continuing independence of the Scottish legal system, Stair had served on the parliamentary commissions of supply and for the plantation of kirks in the early 1660s, and in 1669 he had been appointed to a commission set up to examine and reform the procedures of the supreme courts. In January 1671, when he became president of the session, he also became a member of the privy council and embarked on a period of close involvement in the government of Scotland, dominated at the time by the duke of Lauderdale, with whom Stair remained on good terms. As member of parliament for Wigtownshire between 1672 and 1674, and again as a member of the convention of estates in 1678, he promoted the interests of the government, particularly by presenting constitutional arguments that helped to limit the opportunity for open discussion of government policy. As a member of the parliament of 1681, on the other hand, he adopted a role in opposition to the new regime of James, duke of York. The Lauderdale regime had formally come to an end in September 1680, when its leader had resigned from office as the secretary of state for Scotland, but it had in reality been moribund since the summer of 1679, when Stair and others had been required to defend its record before the king. Although Stair had concentrated then on defending the session, and had apparently succeeded in persuading the king that the judges could be trusted, his legal career had become too closely connected with his political career for it to continue much longer.

There were three principal charges made against the Lauderdale regime in 1679 that had threatened to undermine Stair's personal position. The first was of corruption, in the session as elsewhere. Stair contested the charge so far as the court was concerned, and later made much of the fact that despite rigorous investigation no evidence had ever been found to substantiate the rumours of malversation on his part. The second charge was of despotism, not only in the general suppression of dissent to government policy but also in the particular opposition to parliamentary involvement in the appointment of judges and the review of the session's decisions. Stair consistently asserted the supremacy of the session as a royal court of law, but he also laid claim to a lifelong belief in preserving a balance between the prerogatives of the prince and the liberties of the people, and he denied that he had been personally responsible for the harsh treatment of the advocates in 1674 after an attempt was made to take a case on appeal to parliament from the session. The third charge was of tyranny, not so much in the session, though it was alleged that the rulings of the court

deprived people of any security, as in the oppression of Presbyterian nonconformists by the privy council. Stair argued that the council of the 1670s had tried to repair the damage done by Lauderdale's predecessors, that it had been driven to adopt harsher measures by the unjust aspersions of Lauderdale's opponents, and that he had himself attempted to limit the severity of the measures adopted. While he had repudiated the radicalism of his earlier years, earning condemnation in some quarters as 'an unfriend to honest people' (W. Row, *Life of Mr. Robert Blair*, 1848, 469), he had never abandoned his commitment to the reformed faith, and he had managed both to retain the trust of the more moderate ministers and to earn the distrust of the bishops as 'a false and cunning man' (Burnet, 2.45).

Retirement and reinstatement, 1681–1695 Although Stair often claimed that he had planned to retire in 1681, at the age of sixty-two, his departure from the court and council was actually precipitated by political events. Faced with the prospect of rule by a Catholic prince, he tried in parliament to have an act passed securing the protestant religion as defined in the Westminster confession, and when that failed he succeeded in having a reference to the Scots confession of 1560 inserted into another act which then required all holders of public office both to promise obedience to the king and to promise assistance to each other in the defence of the true faith. Argyll, who took the oath under the act 'so far as consistent with itself', was prosecuted for treason, convicted, and sentenced to death, though he escaped into exile in the Netherlands. Stair declined to take the oath. He travelled to London, but was prevented from seeing the king. He asked friends to intercede with the duke of York on his behalf, but to no avail. When new commissions for the court and council were issued in the autumn his name was omitted from them. He retired to his estates but found it difficult to avoid confrontation with the troops who were harassing his Presbyterian tenants. Advised by the king's advocate that his safety could not be guaranteed, he followed Argyll into exile and arrived in the Netherlands in the autumn of 1682, without his wife, who joined him in the following summer, though accompanied by at least one of his sons.

Before leaving Scotland Stair had used his time in retirement to prepare an edition of his *Institutions* for the press, bringing the draft he had written twenty years earlier up to date by inserting citations of more recent cases. In the Netherlands he prepared for the press two volumes of the case reports he had been working on during the sittings of the session, which appeared in 1683 and 1687 as *The Decisions of the Lords of Council and Session*, the first case reports printed in Scotland. In 1686 he sent through a Dutch press a treatise on physics entitled *Physiologia nova experimentalis*, a Latin translation of a work he had written some time earlier in English. Presented to the Royal Society in the same year as Newton's *Principia*, it was regarded at the time as an able synthesis of the old science. It is possible that Stair also spent time in the Netherlands working on the second edition of his *Institutions*, which was eventually published in 1693, and on a theological treatise entitled *A Vindication of the Divine Perfections*, which was eventually published in 1695, though there is no clear evidence, internal or external, that he did so. Nevertheless, what is clear is that he returned during his years of exile to the life of a scholar. Shortly after arriving in the Netherlands he matriculated as a member of the University of Leiden, where his son Hew had studied law in the 1670s, and he became acquainted with the professors of law both there and at Utrecht. As the years passed he travelled beyond Leiden, at first in the Netherlands and then in Germany, often visiting other Scots exiles. It was reported by the Presbyterian ministers that 'he frequently mett with them for prayer, and ordinary once a week, and sometimes oftner, kept a private fast in his family' (R. Wodrow, *Analecta*, 4 vols., 1842–3, 1.304).

Stair's travels brought him into close contact with exiles who were plotting the overthrow of the Scottish government. Attempts to have him implicated in a variety of plots and to bring him home to stand trial for treason failed before 1684, and the charges of treason brought against him *in absentia* at the end of that year were eventually abandoned in March 1687, after his eldest son became king's advocate to James VII. While there is no conclusive proof of Stair's involvement in any conspiracy before the end of 1684, by 1687 he was certainly plotting against the king. He had contributed financially to the cost of Argyll's abortive rising in May 1685, and he had been drawn into the circle of William of Orange by the spring of 1687. In November 1688 he sailed back to Britain in William's flagship, and for much of 1689 he served as William's principal adviser on Scottish affairs in London, liaising between the prince and the earl of Melville, the secretary of state for Scotland. In October 1689 he was restored to the presidency of the session after a disgruntled litigant shot Sir George Lockhart of Carnwath, the current incumbent, outside the court. Stair made less during the next six years of his purported plan to retire in 1681, instead insisting that he had at last been reinstated in an office of which he had been wrongfully deprived. His reappointment by the king and queen had been strongly opposed in the parliament of 1689, but not surprisingly the other lords of session, who had mostly been recommended for appointment by Stair, had expressed their support for his return to office. Already knighted on his initial appointment as a lord of session in 1661, and created a baronet of Nova Scotia on his return to the court in 1664, he was raised to the peerage on 1 May 1690 as the first Viscount Stair, Lord Glenluce and Stranraer.

Having returned in the early 1680s to the life of a scholar, Stair returned in the early 1690s to the life of a judge and statesman. His past was immediately dredged up in a pamphlet published by Robert Ferguson in *Vindication of the Late Proceedings and Votes of the Parliament of Scotland*. Stair defended his past record and his recent reappointment in an *Apology* published in 1690, but rumours of corruption began to circulate again, and in 1693 a formal complaint was raised against him in parliament. Although the charge was not sustained, several statutes were enacted by the parliament to change the procedure of the court and expose the decision-making process to external scrutiny, all of which were subjected to criticism by Stair. Now entitled to a seat in parliament as a peer of the realm, Stair had served on the important commissions established in 1690 for the settlement of the church and the visitation of the universities, and he had become a prominent figure in the faction known as 'the courtiers'. His eldest son had been appointed joint secretary of state with Melville in January 1691 and had been left as sole secretary by the end of that year. As a member of the privy council in 1691 Stair had supported the raising of militia to defend the country against Jacobite incursions, and had been party to the proclamation requiring highland chiefs to take an oath of allegiance to the crown before the end of the year. There is some evidence that Stair was among the councillors who argued against acceptance of the late submission by Alasdair Macdonald of Glencoe. His son was certainly a prime mover in the business, and after a report from a royal commission of inquiry into the massacre of 1692 was laid before parliament in June 1695 he was dismissed from office. By the autumn of that year Stair was seriously ill. He died in Edinburgh on 25 November, at the age of seventy-six, and was buried in St Giles's, adjacent to the Parliament House where he had passed so much of his time as a lawyer and statesman. No monument was raised to his memory in the church before the twentieth century, when he was honoured as the author of the treatise that had laid the foundations of the modern Scottish legal system.

J. D. FORD

Sources A. J. G. Mackay, *Memoir of Sir James Dalrymple, first Viscount Stair* (1873) · *Annals and correspondence of the viscount and the first and second earls of Stair*, ed. J. M. Graham, 2 vols. (1875) · D. M. Walker, ed., *Stair tercentenary studies* (1981) · G. M. Hutton, 'The public career of Sir James Dalrymple, first Viscount Stair', 1981, U. Glas., MS Gen. 1514 · W. Forbes, *A journal of the session* (1714), xxix–xl · C. Innes, ed., *Munimenta alme Universitatis Glasguensis / Records of the University of Glasgow from its foundation till 1727*, 4 vols., Maitland Club, 72 (1854) · *The letters and journals of Robert Baillie*, ed. D. Laing, 3 vols. (1841–2) · J. Kirkton, *A history of the Church of Scotland, 1660–1679*, ed. R. Stewart (1992) · *Bishop Burnet's History* · 'An impartial account of some of the transactions in Scotland', *A collection of scarce and valuable tracts … Lord Somers*, ed. W. Scott, 2nd edn, 11 (1814), 547 · *Historical notices of Scotish affairs, selected from the manuscripts of Sir John Lauder of Fountainhall*, ed. D. Laing, 2 vols., Bannatyne Club, 87 (1848) · G. Mackenzie of Rosehaugh, *Memoirs of the affairs of Scotland from the Restoration of King Charles II*, ed. T. Thomson (1821) · J. Maidment, ed., *A book of Scotish pasquils, 1568–1715* (1868) · J. Nicoll, *A diary of public transactions and other occurrences, chiefly in Scotland, from January 1650 to June 1667*, ed. D. Laing, Bannatyne Club, 52 (1836) · *Information for Mr Duncan Robertson and his spouse, against the viscount of Stair* (1695) · J. Dalrymple, Viscount Stair, dedicatory epistle, *Theses logicae, metaphysicae, physicae, mathematicae et ethicae* (1646) · J. Dalrymple, Viscount Stair, dedicatory epistle, *Decisions of the lords of council and session*, 2 vols. (1683–7) · *An apology for Sir James Dalrymple of Stair, president of the session, by himself* (1690) · NA Scot., Stair papers, GD135/310

Archives NA Scot., muniments, GD135 [copies] | BL, letters to duke of Lauderdale and Charles II, Add. MSS 23126–23138, 23242–23247, *passim* · Buckminster Park, Grantham, corresp. with duke of Lauderdale • NA Scot., corresp. with Lord Melville • U. Edin. L., letters to earl of Lauderdale

Likenesses J. B. de Medina, portrait, Newhailes, East Lothian [see illus.] • engraving, repro. in H. Walpole, *A catalogue of royal and noble authors of England, Scotland and Ireland*, ed. T. Park, 5 vols. (1806), vol. 5, p. 126 • oils (after miniature by J. B. de Medina), Parliament Hall, Edinburgh

Dalrymple, Sir James, of Borthwick, first baronet (1650–1719), antiquary, was the second son of Sir James *Dalrymple, baronet, of Stair, later first Viscount Stair (1619–1695), the celebrated jurist, and his wife, Margaret (d. 1692), daughter of James Ross of Balniel and widow of Fergus Kennedy of Knockdaw. His elder brother was John *Dalrymple, first earl of Stair, lord president of the court of session. His younger brothers included Sir Hew *Dalrymple and Sir David *Dalrymple. Born into one of late seventeenth-century Scotland's leading political dynasties, whose ubiquitous influence rested on formidable legal prowess, Dalrymple was predictable in his vocational inclination. Unfortunately no record survives of his education. He was admitted a member of the Faculty of Advocates on 25 June 1675 and appointed one of the commissaries of Edinburgh. Like his supremely adaptable kinsmen, he comfortably rode out the public turmoil following the revolution of 1688–9 in Scotland. He became a principal clerk of the court of session on 30 November 1693 and a baronet of Nova Scotia on 28 April 1698, taking the style Dalrymple of Borthwick from his seat in Edinburghshire.

Dalrymple's lasting significance, just like his father's fame, derives chiefly from one major scholarly production. The immediate context of the *Collections Concerning the Scottish History* (1705) was a specific controversy enlivened by the claim of the English lawyer William Atwood that the Scottish church was historically subject to the jurisdiction of the archdiocese of York. Correctly interpreted by Scottish readers as a slur on their nation's sovereign independence, Atwood's insinuations, though built on a longer tradition of aggressive English scholarship, were especially unwelcome amid the continuing debates over Anglo-Scottish relations that shortly afterwards were to culminate in parliamentary union. Encouraged by patriotic scholars like David Crawford, James Anderson, and Sir Robert Sibbald to place in the public domain the fruits of his own historical research, Dalrymple sought to dispatch some of the more extravagant English distortions of Scottish history which, left unchallenged, might well have thrown into question Scotland's right to maintain the distinctive church settlement re-established as recently as 1690.

Dalrymple's contribution to the controversy—shaped by his family's pro-union whig politics and moderate Presbyterian commitments—was as problematical as it was subtle. It exposed the more tendentious aspects of Atwood's reasoning. It issued its own eloquent counter-argument, suggesting that Scotland was itself the true home of protestant virtue. Indeed, its treatment of early medieval history amply demonstrated how England had in fact been less resistant to Roman practices than those

parts of Britain later incorporated into the kingdom of the Scots. Yet Dalrymple's case also included some questionable interpretations of Scotland's past, precisely formulated so as to underline the historical particularism of reformed Scottish protestantism without lending dangerous credence to the democratic and covenanting theories invoked by more radical Presbyterians to justify the post-1690 settlement. For example, though reliant on the dubious treatment of fragmentary and conflicting historical evidence, Dalrymple gave much coverage to the claim, then fashionable among moderate Presbyterians, that the early Celtic church had been organized on properly presbyterian lines. Not surprisingly, the acute topicality of these historical perspectives to contemporary Anglo-Scottish relations, as well as to internal Scottish debates over church government, ensured that Dalrymple's research, and his subsequent *Vindication of the Ecclesiastical Part of Sir James Dalrymple's Historical Collections* (1714), issued in response to detailed criticism from Atwood and John Gillane, would attract intense scrutiny from other scholars for much of the eighteenth century.

Dalrymple's first wife, whom he married on 2 January 1679, was Catherine (d. 1689), daughter of Sir James Dundas of Arniston; their son Sir John Dalrymple, second baronet (1682–1743), was a lawyer and agricultural improver. Dalrymple remarried twice: on 15 September 1691 he married Esther Cunninghame (d. 1700) of Enterkine, widow of William Fletcher of New Cranston, and on 7 September 1701 Jean Halket (d. 1734), widow of Sir Adam Gordon of Dolphally; she survived him. Dalrymple died in May 1719 at Borthwick Castle, and was buried in the church nearby.   DAVID ALLAN

Sources Scots peerage • GEC, *Baronetage*, 4.379–80 • F. J. Grant, ed., *The Faculty of Advocates in Scotland, 1532–1943*, Scottish RS, 145 (1944), 50 • F. J. Grant, ed., *The commissariot record of Edinburgh: register of testaments*, 3, Scottish RS, old ser., 3 (1899), 68 • W. Atwood, *The superiority and direct dominion of the imperial crown of England over the crown and kingdom of Scotland* (1704) • W. Ferguson, 'Imperial crowns: a neglected facet of the background to the treaty of Union of 1707', *SHR*, 53 (1974), 22–44 • A. S. Bell, ed., *The Scottish antiquarian tradition* (1981) • C. Kidd, *Subverting Scotland's past: Scottish whig historians and the creation of an Anglo-British identity, 1689–c.1830* (1993)

Archives NL Scot., Adv. MSS 29.1.2; 29.3.4 • NL Scot., index to *Collections concerning Scottish history*, Adv. MS 34.6.9 • NL Scot., notes on *Collections concerning Scottish history*, Adv. MS 49.7.12

Wealth at death silver plate and medals: testament proved in Edinburgh Commissariot, 8 Sept 1720

Dalrymple, James (1859–1934), tramway manager, was born on 15 September 1859 at 3 Gaskill Street, Charlton upon Medlock, Lancashire, the son of James Dalrymple, a draper, and his wife, Margaret, *née* Adams. His family was Scottish and in 1864 moved to Gatehouse of Fleet, Kirkcudbrightshire, where Dalrymple attended school until the age of fourteen and afterwards worked at the Union Bank. In 1880 he was transferred to its Glasgow office, where in 1881 he entered municipal service. Having qualified as a chartered accountant, he became accountant to the newly formed municipal tramways department in 1894, rising in 1902 to deputy general manager and in 1904 to manager.

In his obituary in the *Glasgow Herald* (2 July 1934) Dalrymple is described as an 'energetic and competent organiser' under whose leadership the tramways reached 'a high state of perfection' and 'spread farther and farther into the countryside'. He controlled the second largest tramway undertaking in the UK with well over 8000 employees and a book value of about £7 million; remarkably for a municipal concern, the entire capital debt was paid off by 1917 despite a policy of low fares. The undertaking was a progressive one, with well-built trams fitted with the latest features, such as windscreens and upholstered seats. In 1923 he persuaded the corporation of Glasgow to take over the neighbouring company-operated lines in Airdrie and Paisley, but Dalrymple's expansionist dictum of 'we've still a long way to go' was not accepted without controversy, and for his part he did not always approve of voter-driven pressure for ever lower fares, though in the event increased passenger numbers more than compensated for these.

Dalrymple's organizing ability was shown to supreme effect in the First World War when he recruited a total of 10,000 men from the city within fourteen months, including a battalion raised from tramway men in September 1914 within a record twenty-four hours. Advertisements and military bands were carried on the trams and collections made for war schemes, though in the latter case Dalrymple had to be reprimanded for selling tickets involving lottery prizes. The tramway workshops were used for war work, including building aircraft bodies, and in 1920 Dalrymple was made a CBE for his contribution to the war effort. His own military experience was confined to a volunteer rifle brigade. Over 3000 tramway men joined up, so pre-war plans for employing women as conductors were put into effect in March 1915, followed in November by what were probably the first ever women drivers in the UK, a development which aroused much interest from other hard-pressed tramway managers.

Dalrymple served on two committees of the Board of Trade (the department then responsible for tramways) and was a member of the council and president (1910–11) of the Municipal Tramways Association (MTA), in whose journal he published a number of professional papers. He was consultant to tramways in Bombay, Chicago, Johannesburg, and São Paulo; the last two of these were after his retirement in 1926, which resulted directly from his handling of labour relations, but was also the consequence of a long history of conflict between a strong-minded manager and the elected tramways committee. After the general strike he dismissed 316 men and refused to reinstate them, despite a decision by the committee to do so. Although supported on a close vote in the full council, he did not withdraw his resignation. Described variously by councillors as a sympathetic manager and as arbitrary and unreasonable, Dalrymple was clearly something of a martinet whose approach was becoming outdated as the political balance changed on the council. J. Beckett of the MTA nevertheless described him on 9 December 1926 as having had 'one of the greatest careers in the tramways service of this country. Among English-speaking peoples no man is better known in the tramway world' (*Tramway and Railway World*, 60.338). As well as being a JP, his outside interests included charitable and Scottish societies. A stocky, bearded man who appears in numerous official photographs, Dalrymple was married to Elizabeth Gardner McGowan (who survived him), and they had a daughter and a son. In June 1934 he had a cerebral haemorrhage and died a few days later, on 1 July, in a nursing home at 3 Claremont Terrace, Glasgow. After a funeral service at Lansdowne church, Glasgow, on 4 July, he was buried at Gatehouse of Fleet.   RICHARD J. BUCKLEY

Sources R. W. Brash, *Glasgow in the tramway age* (1971) · C. A. Oakley, *The last tram* (1962) · *Electrical Review*, 115 (1934) · *Glasgow Herald* (2 July 1934) · *Transport World*, 76 (1934), 57 · *Tramway and Railway World*, 39 (1916), 356 · *Tramway and Railway World*, 41 (1917), 234 · *Tramway and Railway World*, 43 (1918), 31 · *Tramway and Railway World*, 62 (1927), 41 · *Tramway and Railway World*, 60 (1926), 338–9 · *Journal of the Municipal Tramways and Transport Association (Incorporated)*, 13 (1934), 249–51, 396 · *50 years of municipal transport, 1894–1944* (1944) · J. Barrie, *Memories of Glasgow's tramways, 1927–1962* (1971) · *Galloway Advertiser and Wigtownshire Free Press* (20 Feb 1896) · *Galloway Advertiser and Wigtownshire Free Press* (3 Feb 1916) · *Galloway Advertiser and Wigtownshire Free Press* (2 May 1918) · *Glasgow Herald* (6 Nov 1915) · *Glasgow Herald* (2 Dec 1919) · *Glasgow Herald* (31 March 1920) · *Glasgow Herald* (26 Nov 1926) · *Glasgow Herald* (2 Dec 1926) · *Glasgow Herald* (10 Dec 1926) · *Glasgow Herald* (17 Dec 1926) · *Glasgow Herald* (24 Dec 1926) · *Glasgow Herald* (31 Dec 1926) · *Glasgow Herald* (4 July 1934) · *Glasgow Herald* (5 July 1934) · I. L. Cormack, *Glasgow tramways* [1973] · *Light Railway and Tramway World*, 12 (1906), 367 · *Jubilee of the Glasgow tramways* (1922) · CGPLA Eng. & Wales (1934) · d. cert. · b. cert. · R. J. S. Wiseman, 'The tramways of Bombay, 2', *Tramway Review*, 158 (1994), 224–7

Likenesses sketch, 1915, The Baillie · J. R. Middleton, oils?, 1919 · cartoon, repro. in Oakley, *The last tram* · photograph, repro. in *Jubilee of the Glasgow tramways*, facing pp. 78 and 104 · photograph, repro. in *Glasgow Herald* (31 Dec 1926)

Wealth at death £11,432: *Journal of the Municipal Tramways*, 396

Dalrymple, John, first earl of Stair (1648–1707), politician and lord advocate, was the eldest son of James *Dalrymple, first Viscount Stair (1619–1695), and Margaret Ross (d. 1692), widow of Fergus Kennedy of Knockdaw, and daughter of James Ross of Balneil. Among his brothers were Sir James *Dalrymple (1650–1719), Sir Hew *Dalrymple (1652–1737), and Sir David *Dalrymple (c.1665–1721).

Early career and marriage Little is known of Dalrymple's early life. In 1667, while travelling in England with his friend and companion Sir Andrew Ramsay of Abbotshall, he was introduced to Charles II in London by John Maitland, first duke of Lauderdale. Arriving at Chatham just as the Dutch fleet sailed up the Medway Dalrymple is said to have assisted in preventing an English man-of-war from being blown up, and as a result, or possibly as a mark of respect to his father, he was knighted by the king that year as Sir John Dalrymple of Stair.

On 3 September 1668 Dalrymple was appointed as a commissioner for levying the militia in Renfrewshire and Ayrshire. By contract dated 17 and 19 January 1669 he married Elizabeth (d. 1731), daughter and heir of Sir John Dundas of Newliston. Two years earlier Elizabeth appears to have been forcibly abducted and possibly raped by one William Dundas, an advocate, and soldiers, including an officer in the earl of Linlithgow's regiment. This was the

John Dalrymple, first earl of Stair (1648–1707), by Sir John
Baptiste de Medina

subject of a privy council investigation, but 'no further
proceedings of consequence were taken in the affair' and
Elizabeth 'proved herself in after-years an excellent wife
to Sir John Dalrymple, distinguished alike for her good
management at home and knowledge of country matters,
and for her strict profession of religion' (*Annals of Stair*,
118). The couple had six sons and four daughters.

Appointed as an excise commissioner and a justice of
the peace for Linlithgowshire on 11 July 1671 Sir John was
admitted as an advocate to the Scottish bar on 27 February
1672. He appears to have been a gifted lawyer and he
gained a reputation for 'giving no quarter to his adversaries,—a quality in his speaking which continued with him
throughout life' (*Annals of Stair*, 119). In January 1675 he
acted for the defence against Sir John Nisbet of Dirleton,
the current king's advocate, in a dispute over a disorderly
election concerning Rutherglen burgh council. In November 1678 Dalrymple was a spokesman for the College of
Justice in a dispute with Edinburgh town council over the
payment of annuities, while on 10 August 1680 he was
recorded as the convener of the excise commissioners in
the stewartry of Kirkcudbright.

Dalrymple gained particular notice in 1681 as junior
counsel to the king's advocate, Sir George Lockhart, in the
defence of Archibald Campbell, ninth earl of Argyll, over
his opposition to the controversial Test Act, recently
passed by the Scottish parliament. Sir John acquitted himself well, despite the fact that Argyll was found guilty of
treason and sentenced to death. Dalrymple's pleading
'displayed great logical ability and power of argument;

and his whole conduct in the defence … marked him in
the eyes of his countrymen and of the Government to be
possessed of abundant talent and resource' (*Annals of Stair*,
120). Sir John himself had subscribed the Test Act by 4
November 1681, when his name was included on lists of
those who had signed.

Conflict with Claverhouse Sir John's fortunes changed for
the worse in 1682 when he was subjected to harassment
by the Scottish administration of James, duke of York.
That year his father, Lord Stair, president of the court of
session, had been deprived of his judgeship following his
refusal to take the test oath and had gone into exile in the
Netherlands. On 27 January John Graham of Claverhouse,
as a captain of dragoons in the king's forces, was issued
with an official warrant to quarter his forces at Dalrymple's house, as well as at the house of one Sir Robert
Maxwell at Kirkcudbright. Claverhouse's instructions and
orders were part of a military operation in Galloway
against covenanting rebels and activities, but a dispute
quickly arose between Claverhouse and the Dalrymple
family interest. On 31 August Sir John supplicated the
privy council in the name of himself and his father on
behalf of some of their tenants in the regality of Glenluce
who had been fined and imprisoned by Claverhouse for
non-attendance at church and involvement in conventicles, having already been judged and fined for those
offences by Sir John, as baillie of the regality. Indeed, he
argued that they were 'all persones who doe actually goe
to church and live regularly and are willing to enact themselves so to doe' (*Reg. PCS*, 7.546). Observing that Sir John
had prevented Claverhouse from exercising his jurisdiction, the privy council none the less ordered that Dalrymple's tenants were to be set at liberty, as long as they first
paid the fines imposed by Claverhouse. According to Sir
John Lauder of Fountainhall, Dalrymple was given 'a chek
and reprimande, that heritable Bailzies or Shireffs, who
are negligent themselfes in putting the laws to execution,
should not offer to compete with the Shireffs commis-
sionat and put in by the Privy Counsell, who executed vigorously the King's laws' (*Historical Notices*, 1.374).

The authority of Claverhouse appears to have been
upheld, but the issue continued to rumble on throughout
the winter of 1682–3. On 6 January 1683 the privy council
refused to allow Dalrymple to examine witnesses over the
free quartering of Claverhouse's soldiers.

On 12 February, following complaints and counter-
complaints of obstruction, it found Dalrymple guilty on
six specific counts. First he had employed Alexander Baillie and John Dunbar to be his clerks and baillies of Glenluce regality when they had been formerly convened
before Claverhouse and had confessed to 'their convers-
ing with and resetting of rebels and traitoures and guilty
of disorderly withdrawing from the church and of disorderly baptizing of their children' (*Reg. PCS*, 8.53). Second
he had imposed inadequate fines on those guilty of disorders, failed to exact the fines, and obstructed
Claverhouse in his commission. Third he had prohibited
people within his regality from appearing before
Claverhouse, despite the fact that the latter was sheriff of

Galloway, with a privy council commission for dealing with delinquents cited to his court. Fourth Dalrymple had employed one of his servants, one Samuel McAdam, to enter into 'a most tumultuary and seditious instrument or manifesto in his oune name and in name of the gentlemen of the shyre' against Claverhouse's soldiers for alleged exaction and oppression, despite the fact that no complaint had been made to either Claverhouse or his officers, in order to 'breid private dislike and animosity betuixt the countery people and the Kings sojours and these intrusted to serve him' (ibid.). Fifth Dalrymple had misrepresented Claverhouse to the privy council as guilty of several acts of exaction and oppression; he had in fact proceeded legally. Finally Dalrymple had 'murmured' against Claverhouse as sheriff of Galloway and misrepresented his judicial proceedings.

As a result Sir John was formally deprived of the jurisdiction and office as baillie of Glenluce regality, fined £500 sterling (£6000 Scots), ordered to pay the expenses of witnesses, and was subjected to imprisonment at the privy council's pleasure. Claverhouse, on the other hand, was instructed to fulfil his commission and continue uplifting fines in Galloway. Imprisoned in Edinburgh Castle Dalrymple was released on 20 February, following payment of his fine.

From prisoner to lord advocate On 11 September 1684 Fountainhall noted that Dalrymple had been arrested during the night at his house at Newliston and his papers seized and examined. He was taken 'like a malefactor' from Holyrood Abbey by a 'greit guard of souldiers' in broad daylight and was imprisoned in Edinburgh tolbooth; his brothers Hew and James were put under bail to answer when called. No incriminating information was found in Sir John's papers, but the lord treasurer was 'incensed' that Sir John refused to provide any information regarding the late chancellor, the earl of Aberdeen, then under suspicion, and that through his father's exile Dalrymple 'had secured his estate from ther grips' (Historical Notices, 2.558). He remained imprisoned for almost three months. On 13 September the privy council granted permission to his wife, Dame Elizabeth Dundas, to visit him in prison with her maidservant, although the keepers of the tolbooth were specifically instructed that they were to 'suffer no other person to see, speak or converse with him, till further order' (Reg. PCS, 9.172). He was liberated on 11 December but was cautioned to present himself whenever called for under the pain of £5000 sterling (£60,000 Scots) and confined to Edinburgh. At the time of the death of Charles II in February 1685 Sir John was still more or less a state prisoner, although on 2 March 1685 Fountainhall records that his liberty was extended to a 10-mile radius around Edinburgh. On 30 November James VII authorized his release on condition that the Scottish privy council found that he had not been in correspondence with people involved in the 1685 Argyll rebellion, but according to Fountainhall his confinement was not fully taken off until 29 January 1686.

Yet by the end of that year Dalrymple's position was dramatically transformed. In December he departed for London and in February 1687 returned to Scotland as lord advocate. Warrants issued from Whitehall on 21 January, 2 February, and 5 February respectively appointed him at a salary of £400 sterling (£4800 Scots), awarded £200 sterling (£2400 Scots) to cover his expenses in London, absolved him from a requirement to subscribe to the Test Act, and added Sir John to a Scottish privy council committee for auditing Treasury accounts. Additionally he received a comprehensive pardon for his father's family, including his mother, brother, and sisters. He was formally admitted as lord advocate at a privy council meeting on 17 February at which the king's suspension of the Test Act was announced. As lord advocate Sir John was at the forefront of the prosecution early in May 1687 of participants in the 1679 covenanting rebellion at Bothwell Bridge, and on 20 May he was included on the new privy council. His financial position was further improved when, on 15 August, a royal warrant authorized the discharge of the outstanding sum (£166 13s. 4d. Scots) of the fine of £500 sterling (£6000 Scots) which had been previously imposed by Charles II's privy council. Following the death, on 19 January 1688, of Sir James Foulis of Colingtoun, Dalrymple replaced him as justice clerk, with a salary of £400 sterling (£4800 Scots), increased on 29 February to £600 sterling (£7200 Scots). This probably helped his purchase that year of Castle Kennedy. As the political crisis escalated, on 18 October he was added to the secret committee of the privy council.

The revolution of 1689–1690 It has been argued that 'from the very beginning of the revolution, if not before' Sir John and his father were 'planning the re-establishment and expansion of the family's interest'. Sir John's tenure of office as lord advocate under King James had associated him 'with some of the administration's more dubious measures' and thus had not endeared him to 'the new men of the revolution', but as 'an able lawyer and administrator' and a pragmatic political operator Sir John was 'prepared to serve the new court as he had done the previous one as long as the rewards were forthcoming' (Riley, King William, 16).

Sir John sat as MP for the burgh of Stranraer in the 1689 convention, and played an important role in its political business and committees. He subscribed the legislation of 16 March which stated that the meeting of the estates was free and lawful. On 20 March he was added to the committee which dealt with issues of strategic security. On 21 March Dalrymple was among those deputed to continue negotiations with the Catholic George Gordon, first duke of Gordon, who was still in control of Edinburgh Castle. Dalrymple was a member of the crucial committee for settling the government established on 27 March, and of its subcommittee which was instructed to 'draw the Reasons of Vacancy' (Balfour-Melville, 1.24) of the Scottish crown and which drew up the two leading constitutional documents of the Scottish settlement, namely the claim of right and the articles of grievance.

On 30 March Dalrymple was named as part of the militia

in Wigtownshire, and on 27 April as a commissioner of supply there and in Ayrshire. On 16 April he was among those appointed to draw up a letter from the estates to be presented to William with the offer of the Scottish crown. On 23 April Dalrymple was appointed as a commissioner for the burghs in the negotiations for union with England and as one of three envoys to London to attend William and Mary with the offer of the Scottish crown; their formal instructions were issued on 25 April. However, Dalrymple's behaviour at the coronation ceremony at the Banqueting House in Whitehall on 11 May caused controversy in parliament in July. William Johnston, fourth earl of Annandale, accused Dalrymple of subverting the wishes of the Convention by ensuring that the Scottish coronation oath was tendered and accepted by William and Mary *before* they accepted the claim of right and the articles of grievance. Sir James Stewart of Goodtrees, writing to William Denholm of Westshields in London on 13 July, noted that the 'designe' of a vote the previous day 'was clearly to reatch the Kings Advocat' (*Leven and Melville Papers*, 168); 'the Parliament yesterday was more hott than ever' observed the parliamentary high commissioner, William Douglas, third duke of Hamilton, to Melville (ibid., 170). Hamilton had intervened to defend Dalrymple, 'his Majesties only Officer of State here' (ibid.), and had adjourned parliament to a later date. Had he not done so, Hamilton informed Melville, 'I believe they had votted him to prisone' (ibid.).

Prior to the meeting of the first session of the Williamite parliament on 5 June 1689 Sir John, who received the most royal favour of the three commissioners who had offered the Scottish crown to William and Mary, was reappointed as lord advocate. The marquess of Argyll and Sir James Montgomerie of Skelmorlie had to be satisfied with places on the privy council. As lord advocate Dalrymple was 'virtually the sole spokesman for the court' (Riley, *King William*, 23) in parliament due to the absence of the secretary of state, Melville, in London and the political ineffectiveness of its president, William Lindsay, eighteenth earl of Crawford. Due to his association with the court and the unpopularity of his family, throughout the session Sir John was 'under violent and incessant attack' from 'the club', the constitutional reform group which sought to restrict the royal prerogative (ibid., 22). Sir Patrick Hume of Polwarth informed Melville on 29 June that 'there is great disgust against Sir John Dalrymple, because he is brought in office' (*Leven and Melville Papers*, 106). None the less, he continued as a leading spokesman for the court in the 1690 parliamentary session.

As lord advocate Dalrymple was actively involved, by autumn 1689, in the deprivation of ministers who refused to accept the presbyterian settlement of the Church of Scotland and declined to pray for King William and Queen Mary or publicly supported the cause of the forfeited King James. On 15 August 1689 Dalrymple appeared personally before the privy council to present the crown's case against Patrick Trent, a minister in Linlithgow, for such behaviour. A privy councillor himself since 27 May, he

played an important role in its affairs throughout 1690. Already an exchequer commissioner, on 21 January 1690 Dalrymple was appointed to a committee to investigate inmates and conditions in the several prisons of Edinburgh and the Canongate, while on 28 January he became a regulator of the printing and reprinting of pamphlets throughout the kingdom. On 8 February he was among those commissioned to invite King William to come to Scotland to convene parliament.

Dalrymple was also closely involved in monitoring Jacobite activity. On 18 February the privy council appointed Dalrymple, Archibald Campbell, tenth earl of Argyll, and Sir James Montgomerie of Skelmorlie to examine one Alexander Strachan, brought as a prisoner from Glasgow and promised his life and freedom from torture as long as he gave a full confession of his knowledge of the activities of the forfeited King James or any of his party in Ireland who were in contact with any person in Scotland or England. Two days later Dalrymple was appointed to a committee for the security of the country, on 28 February to a similar committee preparing for a military campaign against Jacobite activity in Scotland, and by 11 April he had joined a committee dealing with the escape of prisoners from the Canongate tolbooth in Edinburgh. It was in this month that Sir John became master of Stair, following his father's elevation to the peerage.

Stair's prominence brought him into danger. On 4 August the privy council ordered that several prisoners, including one Henry Neville Payne, previously described as 'a traffequing papist' (*Reg. PCS*, 15.358), be tortured for their involvement in a 'treasonable and hellish plot' (ibid., 356) against King William and Queen Mary in Scotland and England. Two days later a letter in 'ane unknowen hand' dropped at Stair's door held him responsible for the decision to torture this 'English Gentleman of considerable Quality' and threatened that if the procedure went ahead the lord advocate should be 'pistolled' (Balfour-Melville, 2.252–3). Privy council records indicate that Payne was eventually tortured on 10 and 11 December, and on 30 December confined as a close prisoner in Edinburgh Castle.

Stair and the 1692 massacre of Glencoe Stair's rising political ascendancy was further recognized by his appointment as joint secretary of state for Scotland with Lord Melville on 10 January 1691. He accompanied King William to continental Europe that year and he wrote letters to Scottish politicians from The Hague, Brussels, and other places in the Low Countries between February and August. Throughout this period he kept in close touch with the government's highland policy in the aftermath of the first Jacobite rising. In a letter from William's camp at 'Gerpines' on 23 July Stair instructed Sir Thomas Livingston, commander-in-chief of his majesty's forces in Scotland, that 'non under your command doe commit any acts of hostilitie against the Highlanders' (*Leven and Melville Papers*, 631). However, while prepared to pardon those who submitted the Williamite government adopted a hardline stance in a proclamation of 27 August 1691, which 'threatened the utmost extremity of the law against chiefs who did not take the oath of allegiance' by 1 January 1692 (Donaldson, 220). Writing on 2 December to John Campbell, first earl of Breadalbane, Stair expressed the view that 'the clan Donell must be rooted out' (ibid., 221), and he played a key role in planning their destruction. The next day he wrote to Lieutenant-Colonel James Hamilton, deputy governor of the garrison of Fort William, asking 'whether you think that this is the proper season to maul them in the cold long nights, and what force will be necessary' (ibid.). Stair was overjoyed to hear from Archibald Campbell, earl of Argyll, that the chief of the MacDonalds had failed, in technical terms, to take the oath of allegiance by the required date and wrote on 11 January 1692 to Sir Thomas Livingston that 'it's a great work of charity to be exact in rooting out that damnable sect, the worst in all the Highlands' (ibid., 222). A further letter of 30 January expressed their shared conviction that 'it were a great advantage to the nation that thieving tribe were rooted out' (*Carstares State Papers*, 250).

The massacre of MacDonalds at Glencoe which took place on 13 February 1692 following instructions issued by William and Stair in January caused political outrage. In the following year a formal commission of inquiry exonerated the king, pointing the finger of blame primarily at Stair, who thereby became prey to attacks by his opponents. Glencoe was the main topic of business in the parliamentary session of 1695 (9 May–17 July) and on 24 June the Scottish parliament voted that 'the Execution & Slaughter of the Glencoe men' was a 'murder' (*APS*, 9.377). On 10 July a parliamentary address to King William, which again absolved him of blame for the massacre, formally attacked Stair, who was absent from proceedings. The estates found that Stair's correspondence had 'exceeded' the king's instructions 'towards the killing and destruction of the Glencoe men' (ibid., 424). An analysis of Stair's letters had revealed that he had 'absolutely and positively ordered' the Glencoe men 'to be destroyed' and had viewed the failure of MacDonald to take the oath on time as 'a happy incident since it afforded an opportunity to destroy them' (ibid.). Furthermore he had urged it 'with a great deal of zeal as a thing acceptable and of public use' (ibid.). They concluded that 'the Master of Stairs excess in his Letters against the Glencoe men has been the Original cause of this unhappy business' (ibid., 425). However, the estates referred to the king action 'for vindication of your Government' (ibid.), and the latter chose to support his servant. Stair lost his position as secretary of state, but following the death of his father on 25 November, succeeded as second Viscount Stair. Towards the end of the year, William issued him with a formal scroll of discharge, freeing him from the consequences of his role in the Glencoe massacre on the grounds that at the time of the massacre Stair was in London as secretary of state and 'being ... many hundreds of miles distant, he could have no knowledge of, nor accession to, the method of execution' (MacDonald, 180–81, appx 13). Accordingly he was pardoned for 'any excess of zeal, or going beyond his instructions' (ibid.).

Stair's political career after Glencoe Despite royal rehabilitation Stair remained unpopular and he attended neither the 1696 nor 1698 parliamentary sessions. He first took his seat as a peer in the parliamentary session of 21–7 May 1700 and attended the ninth session, from 29 October 1700 to 1 February 1701, in which the crisis of the Darien project was an explosive political issue. On 5 November Stair was included on the important committee for the security of the kingdom and in the controversial vote of 16 January 1701 supported the presentation to the king of a relatively conciliatory parliamentary address, as opposed to a more critical act.

In the aftermath of William's death and the accession of Queen Anne, Stair attended the parliamentary session of 9–30 June 1702. As before he served on the committee for the security of the kingdom and was confirmed as a privy councillor. He was also a Scottish commissioner in the abortive union negotiations of 1702–3 and he attended all the sessions of the union parliament of 1703–7. By a patent dated 8 April 1703 and read in parliament on 6 July 1704 he was created by Queen Anne earl of Stair, Viscount Dalrymple, Lord Newliston, Glenluce, and Stranraer. Appointed on 22 August 1703 to the committee for examining public accounts, as earl of Stair he became a commissioner of supply for Wigtownshire on 5 August 1704 and a member of the important council of trade on 14 August 1705. A month later parliament passed an act in his favour for holding fairs twice a year at the burgh of barony of Glenluce. According to the Jacobite George Lockhart, in the winter of 1706 Stair, who was again serving as a commissioner for the treaty of union, Hugh Campbell, third earl of Loudoun, and David Boyle, first earl of Glasgow, used their collective influence in Ayrshire to prevent the gentlemen of that shire from presenting an address to parliament opposing the union. According to Bishop Gilbert Burnet, Stair played an important role for the court during the 'great and long debates' of the 1707 parliamentary session, managing the debates 'on the side of the union' with the chancellor, James Ogilvy, Viscount Seafield (*Bishop Burnet's History*, 163). Stair's last political act was a contribution to the heated debate over article 22 of the treaty of union, which was concerned with future Scottish representation within the new British parliament. After it had been finally approved on 7 January 1707 Stair retired to his lodgings. He died suddenly in bed during the early hours of 8 January, 'his spirits being quite exhausted by the length and vehemence of the debate' (ibid., 166). Hume of Crossrigg attributed Stair's death to apoplexy (Hume, 194). Stair was buried at Kirkliston, Linlithgowshire, three days later, on 11 January 1707. He was survived by his wife, who died on 25 May 1731, and was succeeded as second earl by his son John *Dalrymple (1673–1747).   JOHN R. YOUNG

Sources *Annals and correspondence of the viscount and the first and second earls of Stair*, ed. J. M. Graham, 2 vols. (1875) · *Reg. PCS*, 3rd ser. · *APS, 1670–1707* · *Scots peerage* · E. W. M. Balfour-Melville, ed., *An account of the proceedings of the estates in Scotland, 1689–1690*, 2 vols., Scottish History Society, 3rd ser., 46–7 (1954–5) · W. H. L. Melville, ed., *Leven and Melville papers: letters and state papers chiefly addressed to George, earl of Melville ... 1689–1691*, Bannatyne Club, 77 (1843) · *State* papers and letters addressed to William Carstares, ed. J. M'Cormick (1774) • Historical notices of Scotish affairs, selected from the manuscripts of Sir John Lauder of Fountainhall, ed. D. Laing, 2 vols., Bannatyne Club, 87 (1848) • G. Donaldson, ed., A source book of Scottish history, 3: 1567–1707 (1961) • D. Szechi, ed., 'Scotland's Ruine': Lockhart of Carnwath's memoirs of the union (1995) • Bishop Burnet's History • D. J. MacDonald, Slaughter under trust: Glencoe-1692 (1965) • P. W. J. Riley, King William and the Scottish politicians (1979) • P. W. J. Riley, The union of England and Scotland (1978) • P. Hopkins, Glencoe and the end of the highland war (1998) • GEC, Peerage • D. Hume, A diary of the proceedings in parliament and the privy council of Scotland, May 21, 1700 – March 7, 1707, Bannatyne Club, 27 (1828)

Archives Hunt. L., letters to earl of Loudoun • Leics. RO, corresp. with earl of Nottingham • NA Scot., corresp. with Sir John Clerk • NL Scot., corresp. with the first and second marquesses of Tweeddale • U. Nott. L., letters to William III and Lord Portland

Likenesses J. B. de Medina, portrait, Newhailes, East Lothian [see illus.]

Dalrymple, John, second earl of Stair (1673–1747),

diplomat and army officer, was born at Edinburgh on 20 July 1673, second son of John *Dalrymple, second viscount and first earl of Stair (1648–1707), and his wife, Elizabeth (d. 1731), daughter and heir of Sir John Dundas of Newliston.

Early career When only eight years old, in April 1682, Dalrymple accidentally shot his elder brother dead at the family seat in Wigtownshire. He received a pardon from Charles II, but his parents reportedly could not bear to see his face, and after three years at a tutor's he was sent over to his grandfather, Sir James *Dalrymple (1619–1695), who was then in exile in the Netherlands. The boy studied at Leiden University, where he attracted the attention of William III, prince of Orange. When the latter became king of Scotland he reinstated Sir James Dalrymple as lord president, created him Viscount Stair, and gave him and his son dominant places in the Scottish administration.

Dalrymple's early career was characterized by military service. He joined the campaign of 1692 as a volunteer with the Angus regiment (afterwards the Cameronians), was present at the battle of Steenkerke, and served in various subordinate grades throughout the Nine Years' War. He became master of Stair when his father succeeded to the viscountcy in 1695 and gained his first diplomatic experience as part of the embassy to Vienna in 1700 of Robert Sutton, second Baron Lexington. He then travelled on the continent for a year, and on his return was, on 12 May 1702, appointed second lieutenant-colonel in the Scots foot guards, the commission being antedated to the first day of Anne's reign. In 1703, in which year he became Viscount Dalrymple on his father being created earl of Stair, he joined the army in Flanders as aide-de-camp to John Churchill, first duke of Marlborough, who became his patron and mentor. He distinguished himself at the taking of Peer and at Venlo, where he saved the life of Prince Frederick of Hesse-Cassel, afterwards king of Sweden. He was probably present at the battle of Blenheim in 1704, and in 1705 he was made colonel of a regiment in the Dutch service. His career in the Dutch army was brief: on 1 January 1706 he was made colonel of his old regiment, the Cameronians. He commanded a brigade of infantry at the battle of Ramillies (23 May 1706); as a reward for his services he was appointed brigadier-general on the English

John Dalrymple, second earl of Stair (1673–1747), by Allan Ramsay, c.1744

establishment on 1 June, and succeeded Lord John Hay as colonel of the 2nd dragoons (later the Scots Greys) on 15 August. He thereafter commanded a cavalry brigade, consisting of his own regiment and the Royal Irish Dragoons.

In January 1707 Dalrymple succeeded his father as earl of Stair. Like his father he was a staunch supporter of the union with England, and he was chosen by the outgoing Scots parliament as one of the original sixteen representative peers to the first parliament of Great Britain. However, he failed to be re-elected the following year and resumed his military career in the Low Countries. He greatly distinguished himself at the battle of Oudenarde in 1708, when he exposed himself to the fire of two of the allied battalions in order to save them from inflicting loss on each other, and was given the honour of presenting the dispatches at court. Stair was promoted major-general on 1 January 1709, and later that year commanded his brigade at the siege of Lille and the battle of Malplaquet, after which he unsuccessfully proposed making a dash at Paris with his horsemen. Stair was sent on a special mission to Augustus II, elector of Saxony and king of Poland, the following winter, when he showed his ability as an ambassador, and won the confidence of Augustus, who had a special medal struck in his honour. He rejoined the army in time to cover the siege of Douai. He was promoted lieutenant-general on 1 January 1710, and also made a knight of the Thistle. He also covered the siege of Bouchain in 1711. In the same year Marlborough used him as an agent in an attempt to come to an understanding with Lord Oxford's administration. Stair was unsuccessful, and both he and Marlborough were subsequently recalled. Promoted general on 1 January 1712, Stair was compelled to sell his regiment to David Colyear, first earl of Portmore, in 1714. He retired to Edinburgh, where he became associated with the squadrone faction in Scottish politics and was involved in preparations to secure the accession of George, elector of Hanover, whom he had known on the continent.

Stair had earlier (7 March 1708) clandestinely married Eleanor, Viscountess Primrose [see Dalrymple, Eleanor, countess of Stair (d. 1759)] daughter of James Campbell, second earl of Loudoun, and widow of James, first Viscount Primrose. This lady, known for her beauty and strong will, had been abused by her first husband, and had been left a widow in 1706. Her experience inspired Sir Walter Scott's short story 'My Aunt Margaret's Mirror', and gave rise to the oft told but apocryphal story that after Primrose's death she declared she would never marry again. Stair, however, declared that he would win her, and to get over her reluctance he concealed himself in her house, and by appearing at her bedroom window compelled her to marry him, to save her reputation.

Ambassador to Paris On the accession of George I, Stair returned to favour. He was again elected a representative peer, was made a lord of the bedchamber, appointed colonel of the Inniskilling dragoons, sworn of the privy council, and appointed minister-plenipotentiary at Paris. In January 1715 he reached Paris and commenced his famous mission by compelling his predecessor, Matthew Prior, to give up the secret correspondence with the tory ministers on which were based most of the charges made in the impeachment of Robert Harley, earl of Oxford, and Henry St John, Viscount Bolingbroke. During the few months which elapsed before the death of Louis XIV, Stair occupied himself in preparing for the new reign, and took care to make friends with Philippe, duke of Orléans, the future regent. The era of peace which followed the wars of Louis XIV was really initiated by James Stanhope and Orléans, and it was Stair's duty to maintain the compact at Paris and to watch over the policy of Orléans.

Though suspicious of French aims and convinced that the French court looked on the British as 'their natural and their necessary enemys' (Black, 204), Stair worked hard to implement the French alliance. Stair himself never wavered from the view he had formed under Marlborough that alliance with Austria should be the cornerstone of British foreign policy. Despite a lack of tact, Stair effectively represented British interests. He went out of his way to maintain the dignity of his position as British representative to the French court, staging a lavish official entry into Paris in 1719, when his rank was raised from minister-plenipotentiary to ambassador. His punctiliousness and habit of outspokenness periodically provoked arguments with French ministers.

Stair's greatest service came in his efforts to combat the threat of Jacobitism. He continually insisted that the French abide by the terms of the treaty of Utrecht in this and other regards. He put together an effective (if expensive) intelligence service that was able to keep his government—and the French court—informed of Jacobite intrigues. He provided timely warning of the Jacobite rising of 1715, though his agents were unable to intercept

James Stuart and prevent his belated departure for Scotland. Pressure from Stair limited covert French assistance and ultimately led to the Jacobite court's removal to Italy. Part of Stair's knowledge was gained first hand. He cultivated Lord Bolingbroke, the Jacobite secretary of state, and after the rising corresponded with the earl of Mar. He later helped to bring to light the intrigues of Cardinal Alberoni of Spain.

Stair's recall from Paris in 1720 resulted from his inability to get along with his fellow Scot and comptroller of French finances, John Law. Ironically, several years earlier Stair had unsuccessfully tried to find employment for Law in the British government and had introduced him in Paris to the Abbé Dubois. Though their worsening relationship was attributed by some to Stair's jealousy of Law, it was based at least in part on Stair's belief that Law's financial policies were aimed ultimately at undermining the British economy.

Stair gained considerable fame from his embassy—Sir Winston Churchill later described him as 'one of the most capable ambassadors … ever sent to Paris' (Churchill, 4.882)—but his rewards were largely the intangible ones of reputation. He returned from France with his modest fortune damaged by his lavish lifestyle there.

The Walpole era During the 1720s Stair partially retired from politics as he occupied himself in repairing his shaky finances. Though he continued to attend the House of Lords, he lived mostly on his estates in Scotland, either at the Stair family seat of Castle Kennedy in Wigtownshire, or at Newliston in Linlithgowshire, which he had inherited from his mother. An active agricultural reformer, he was a founding member of the Society of Improvers in the Knowledge of Agriculture in 1723. He introduced many improvements on his farms, and was among the first in Scotland to plant turnips and cabbages on a large scale. He also attempted, without great success, to exploit mineral resources on his estates, as well as establishing a woollen mill. It was also alleged that he laid out Newliston in imitation of the military positions at the battle of Blenheim. Lady Stair became a leader of society in Scotland, among other things helping to popularize Moffat as a spa.

Though Stair successfully solicited the sinecure of vice-admiral of Scotland from Sir Robert Walpole in 1729, the two were never close. While some attributed this to Stair's perception that he was unjustly neglected by Walpole and to his resentment at the domination of Scottish patronage by Sir Robert's ally Archibald Campbell, earl of Ilay, Stair genuinely disagreed with the administration's pro-French foreign policy and held the country whig view that Walpole and Ilay were corrupting influences whose power threatened British liberties. By 1732 Stair was clearly moving towards opposition. This became evident during the political crisis that broke over Walpole's Excise Bill in 1733. Stair made a famous if unsuccessful attempt to win over Queen Caroline and spoke frequently against the ministry in the House of Lords. He was first dismissed from his sinecure for his pains (April 1733) and a year later, after he had supported an opposition measure intended to make it more difficult to dismiss military officers for their parliamentary conduct, he lost his regiment, George II remarking that he 'would never let a man keep anything by favour who had endeavoured to keep it by force' (Hervey, 1.288). Stair found a particular focus for his efforts in the opposition's challenge to ministerial control of the elections of the representative Scottish peers and led, with Charles Douglas, third duke of Queensberry, and Alexander Campbell, second earl of Marchmont, a co-ordinated campaign to elect an opposition slate of peers at the 1734 general election. The strength of Ilay, whom Stair sometimes referred to as 'congé de lire' (Graham, 2.274), and the ministry were too much, however. The 'King's List' was elected handily; Stair and six other opposition peers lost their seats. Stair joined in a petition alleging irregularities in the election that was rejected by the House of Lords in 1735. Thereafter Stair took no part in peers' elections until he was returned to the sixteen in 1744 after Walpole's fall. He remained an active supporter of the opposition, however, an interest he shared with Sarah Churchill, dowager duchess of Marlborough, who for several years lent Stair £1000 annually to make up for his loss of income (and who cancelled Stair's debt in her will).

War of the Austrian Succession After Walpole's fall Stair was rapidly rehabilitated. He was appointed field marshal on 28 March 1742, and made (non-resident) governor of Minorca. Though he had not seen active service for thirty years, he was appointed to command the pragmatic army sent to act with Hanoverian and Austrian forces in support of Maria Theresa. He was also appointed ambassador-extraordinary to the states general with the goal of gaining active Dutch participation in the upcoming campaign. The Dutch declined to send a contingent, though they did agree to garrison the Netherlands barrier forts, releasing 6000 Hessians for service with the pragmatic army. Having argued unsuccessfully for an invasion of France, in the spring of 1743 Stair followed the example of his patron Marlborough and moved rapidly into Germany. He was, however, outmanoeuvred by the French general, Noailles, and also found himself subordinate to George II when the latter came to Germany in person to take command of the army. At the ensuing battle of Dettingen (27 June 1743), Stair showed his usual bravery and exercised much of the tactical direction on the allied side under the overall command of the king. The allies were able to take advantage of French mistakes to win the day. Stair pressed the king to follow up the victory with a vigorous pursuit; his advice, however, was rejected by George II. Feeling he was ignored in favour of the king's Hanoverian counsellors, Stair resigned. In a strongly worded memorandum he reminded the king of the importance of the Austrian alliance and asked 'leave to return to my plough without any mark of your displeasure'. George II, who in April 1743 had reappointed Stair colonel of the Inniskilling dragoons, accepted the resignation. A year later George II was lamenting Stair's departure, writing to the duke of Cumberland, 'I wish my Lord Stair was in Flanders' (Charteris, 156). Later in 1744, when a Jacobite rising was expected,

Stair offered his services to the king once more, and was made commander-in-chief of all the forces in south Britain; he was also elected a representative Scottish peer. In 1745 he was again made colonel of his old regiment, the Scots Greys.

As commander of the forces in England, Stair was slow to appreciate the seriousness of the Jacobite rising in 1745 and largely occupied himself in assembling forces for others to command. His most novel piece of advice—that the Jacobite army in Scotland be distracted by allowing loyal Scottish aristocrats to raise their own regiments (as was being done in England)—was not taken. After Culloden he unsuccessfully advised a generous policy towards former rebels. In 1746 he received his last appointment as general of the marines, and on 9 May 1747 he died at Queensberry House, Edinburgh, and was buried on 23 May 1747 in the family vault at Kirkliston, Linlithgowshire. His countess survived him twelve years, and remained until the day of her death, on 21 November 1759, a prominent figure in Edinburgh society.

Stair was well respected by his contemporaries, though he was not always easy to get along with. Lord Hervey, a political opponent, while acknowledging his reputation for 'honour and integrity' and the 'skill and credit' with which he had conducted the Paris embassy, also noted that he was 'of a warm, prompt temper, and when he was angry did not hesitate to express his being so in very strong and irritating terms' (Hervey, 1.136-7). One of the more visible of the generation of Scottish aristocrats that made the transition to service of the British state under the union, Stair's fame as a soldier and a diplomat helped to mark paths that others would follow.

H. M. STEPHENS, rev. WILLIAM C. LOWE

Sources Annals and correspondence of the viscount and the first and second earls of Stair, ed. J. M. Graham, 2 vols. (1875) · J. Black, Natural and necessary enemies (1986) · R. Harding, 'Lord Cathcart, the earl of Stair and the Scottish opposition to Walpole, 1732-1735', Parliamentary History, 11 (1992), 192-217 · M. Orr, Dettingen, 1743 (1972) · W. Robertson, Proceedings relating to the peerage of Scotland, from January 16, 1707 to April 29, 1788 (1790) · E. Charteris, William Augustus duke of Cumberland (1913) · W. S. Churchill, Marlborough: his life and times, 4 (1938), vol. 4 · John, Lord Hervey, Some materials towards memoirs of the reign of King George II, ed. R. Sedgwick, 3 vols. (1931) · J. Baynes, The Jacobite rising of 1715 (1970) · B. Lenman, An economic history of modern Scotland (1977) · Scots peerage, vol. 8 · GEC, Peerage, vol. 12/1

Archives BL, corresp., Add. MSS 35452-35460 · BL, order book, Add. MS 20005 · Mount Stuart Trust, Isle of Bute, corresp. and accounts · NL Scot., diaries · NYPL, corresp. and diary · Yale U., Beinecke L., letters and papers | BL, letters to George Bubb, Egerton MSS 2170-2175 · BL, corresp. with Lord Carteret, Add. MSS 22532, 22537-22538 · BL, letters to James Craggs, Stowe MSS 246-247 · BL, corresp. with Jean Robethon, Stowe MSS 223-231, passim · BL, letters to Thomas Robinson, Add. MSS 23810-23815 · BL, corresp. with Yorke family, Add. MSS 35452-35460 · CKS, corresp. with Lord Stanhope, U1590/0145 · Hunt. L., letters to earl of Loudon · NA Scot., corresp. with earl of Mar · NA Scot., letters to duke of Montrose · NRA, priv. coll., letters to duke of Douglas · priv. coll., letters to Lord Cathcart

Likenesses J. Faber, mezzotint, 1703 (after A. Ramsay), BM, NPG · W. Aikman, oils, c.1727, Art Gallery and Museum, Glasgow · A. Ramsay, portrait, c.1744, priv. coll. [see illus.] · G. Kneller, portrait, repro. in Graham, ed., Annals, vol. 1, p. 221; formerly in possession of the earl of Stair, Oxenfoord Castle, 1875 • oils, Scot. NPG • water-colour on ivory miniature, Scot. NPG

Dalrymple, John, fifth earl of Stair (1720–1789), politician and writer, was the son and heir of George Dalrymple of Dalmahoy (d. 1745), Edinburghshire, a baron of the court of exchequer, and his wife, Eupheme, daughter of Sir Andrew Myreton, bt, of Gogar. On 8 December 1741 he was admitted to the Scottish bar as an advocate but later entered the army where he attained the rank of captain.

In May 1747 Dalrymple inherited the family's estates following the death of his uncle, John *Dalrymple, second earl of Stair. Dalrymple had been a favourite of his uncle who also intended him to inherit the earldom. This he briefly did and in August 1747 voted at the election of the Scottish representative peers. However, in the following year the House of Lords denied his right to the title which passed to his cousin James. Though John retained the family's estates he did not assume the earldom until the death of the fourth earl, William, younger brother of James, third earl, on 27 July 1768. Chosen as a representative peer in 1771 Stair voted with the whigs and was critical of Lord North's treatment of the American colonies which led to revolution. In 1774 he presented a petition to the government on behalf of Massachusetts for which he received the thanks of the colony. His prescience in American affairs earned the title of the 'Cassandra of the state' from Horace Walpole who later described him as 'an honest Scot, enthusiastic in the cause of America' (*Last Journals of Horace Walpole*, 1.530; *Catalogue of the Royal and Noble Authors*, 5.166).

Having failed to be returned as a representative peer in 1774, Stair dedicated himself to writing on political and fiscal matters. His *The State of the National Debt, Income and Expenditure* was published two years later and was followed by, among others, *Considerations preliminary to the fixing of supplies ... for 1781: an attempt to balance the income and expenditure of the state*, *State of Public Debts* (both 1783), and *On the Proper Limits of Government's Interference with the Affairs of the East India Company* (1784).

Stair married Margaret (d. 1798), daughter of George *Middleton, a London banker; the couple had one son, John *Dalrymple, who later inherited the earldom and achieved prominence in the diplomatic service. The fifth earl died at Culhorn in Wigton on 13 October 1789; he was survived by his wife, who died on 3 February 1798.

PHILIP CARTER

Sources GEC, *Peerage* • *The last journals of Horace Walpole*, ed. Dr Doran, rev. A. F. Steuart, 2 vols. (1910) • *A catalogue of the royal and noble authors of England, Scotland and Ireland ... by the late Horatio Walpole*, ed. T. Park, 5 vols. (1806)
Archives Hunt. L., letters to earl of Loudon

Dalrymple, Sir John, of Cousland [later Sir John Hamilton-Macgill-Dalrymple], **fourth baronet** (1726–1810), lawyer and historian, was the eldest son of Sir William Dalrymple of Cousland, third baronet (1704–1771), advocate, and his first wife, Agnes (d. 1755), daughter of William Crawford of Glasgow. Great-grandson of the great Scottish jurist James, Viscount Stair, and a prominent member of a large,

influential legal dynasty, he was educated at Edinburgh University and Trinity Hall, Cambridge, for the Scottish bar and entered the Faculty of Advocates in 1748. On 7 October 1760 he married his cousin Elizabeth Hamilton-Macgill, daughter of Thomas Hamilton-Macgill (formerly Hamilton) and Elizabeth Dalrymple, 'without her father's consent'. She was an heiress with a substantial fortune. They had thirteen children, eight of whom predeceased him. In 1771 he succeeded his father as fourth baronet.

A protégé of the duke of Argyll and his *sous-ministre* Lord Milton, Dalrymple was appointed solicitor to the board of excise in May 1759 and depute lord advocate in March 1760. He had his eye on a seat in parliament but was checked by the rising star of Scottish politics, Henry Dundas, Milton's deadly enemy. In reply to a request for Dundas's electoral support in 1760, Dalrymple was given a blunt refusal and was told: 'I would now feel that I had formed my attachments erroneously in Scotland' (NL Scot., MS 16714, fol. 201). His subsequent attachment to Lord North (after whom he named one of his sons) probably accounted for his promotion to the bench of the court of exchequer in Scotland in 1776—a place he held until 1807. After North's death in 1792, he made up his quarrel with Dundas somewhat obsequiously, telling him, 'I transfer my attachment from Lord North to you' (NL Scot., MS 1051, fol. 101). Henceforth he was to rely on Dundas for advancing his family and his many projects and chemical inventions. These included a recipe for making soap out of herrings, and one for making beer at sea out of 'cold water, or even putrid water'. It was, he told Dundas, 'not only good but delicious' (ibid., fols. 117–18). His leading political project was a proposal for a measure of Roman Catholic relief between 1775 and 1778. This, he told North, would encourage Catholics to 'support the funds, hunt out privateers and help him at elections' and would also boost Catholic recruitment for the American war (NA Scot., Stair MSS, GD 135/149). His negotiations with leading Catholics in England, Scotland, and Ireland seem to have gone beyond the brief North had given him but laid the foundations for the limited relief granted in England and Ireland in 1778. Plans for similar measures for Scotland were proposed and aborted in the wake of the anti-popery riots of that year.

Dalrymple was an active, well-liked if sometimes irritating member of the Edinburgh literati, and a prominent member of important societies such as the Select Society, the *Poker Club, and the Glasgow Literary Society. He was an early protégé of Lord Kames and a member of a circle which included David Hume and Adam Smith and was interested in placing the study of law and legal institutions on new philosophical and historical foundations. Like these, he was an early reader of Montesquieu's *De l'esprit des lois* and he published a substantial *Essay towards a General History of Feudal Property in Great Britain* (1757) which Montesquieu (who was notoriously generous with his time and encouragement when dealing with young scholars) seems to have read in draft and to whom it was posthumously dedicated. The *Essay* was generally well received, Hume commenting: 'I think it really deserves it' (*Letters*, 1.266). Dalrymple valued Montesquieu as much for his belief in the importance of a nobility in curbing despotism as for his methodological insights into the study of law. His own views were developed in 1764 in his highly public opposition to a proposal to curb the right of landowners to entail their property, a practice which Smith and most of the literati regarded as an abomination and an obstruction to free commerce in land. For Dalrymple, however, 'a solid and lasting nobility and gentry are the best barriers against the invasion of the crown and the false popularity of particular men and the insolence of the rabble', and it was this 'which has kept the Scots a respectable people, from the most distant periods of their history' (J. Dalrymple, *Considerations upon the Policy of Entails in Great Britain*, 1764, 41, 62).

Contemporaries knew Dalrymple best for his *Memoirs of Great Britain and Ireland from the dissolution of the last parliament of Charles II until the sea battle of La Hogue* (1771). It was dedicated to the lord chancellor—a close friend—and acknowledged the criticisms of Hume, Smith, and Blair. In fact the *Memoirs* took little account of the new 'philosophical' approach to the study of history that Hume and Smith were making their own. Dalrymple's was pretty much a traditional whig attempt to unlock the hidden secrets of the revolution of 1688 with new documentation. Dalrymple put it around that he had been given £2000 for the text: Strahan thought it overvalued at £750. Hume wished his friend's book well and thought that 'the ranting bouncing Style … may perhaps take with the Multitude. This however I am certain of, that there is not one new Circumstance of the least Importance from the beginning to the End of the Work' (*Letters*, 2.238 and n.). To tease Hume, Strahan suggested that Dalrymple—or even 'Ossian' MacPherson—might be the man to bring his *History of England* up to date.

Dalrymple was an interesting but minor member of the Scottish literati. Alexander Carlyle, who knew him as a student at Edinburgh, thought 'the blossom promised better fruit' (*The Autobiography of Dr. Alexander Carlyle of Inveresk, 1722–1805*, ed. J. Hill Burton, 1910, 35). His *Essay* is worthy but pales beside the profound analyses of feudal civilization provided by Hume, Smith, Robertson, and Kames. The *Memoirs* irritated some but, as Hume noted, proved to be a damp squib. His projects are the work of a well-meaning, well-connected, and opinionated amateur projector. Boswell got him right: 'Though Sir John Dalrymple's style is not regularly formed in any respect, and one cannot help smiling sometimes at his affected *grandiloquence*, there is in his writing a pointed vivacity, and much of a gentlemanly spirit' (Boswell, *Life*, 508). So did Henry Dundas: 'My volatile countryman', he told Pitt in 1799, 'always mixes nonsense of various kinds into all his productions, but there [are] some clever ideas inter[s]persed' (PRO, 30/8/157, fols. 268–9).

Towards the end of his life Dalrymple inherited several estates through his marriage and as a consequence added the name Hamilton-Macgill to his surname. He died, aged eighty-four, on 26 February 1810 and was survived by his wife. Their fourth but eldest surviving son, John Hamilton Macgill *Dalrymple, succeeded as fifth baronet.

NICHOLAS PHILLIPSON

Sources *Scots peerage*, vol. 7 [Stair, Earls] · NL Scot., MSS 1051, 11016, 16714, 16733, 16687, 16695, 16733 · NA Scot., Stair MSS, GD 135/149 · PRO, 30/8/157, fols. 268–9 · R. K. Donovan, 'The military origins of the Roman Catholic relief programme of 1778', *HJ*, 28 (1985), 79–102 · R. K. Donovan, 'Sir John Dalrymple and the origins of Roman Catholic relief, 1775–1778', *Recusant History*, 17 (1984–5), 188–96 · N. T. Phillipson, 'Lawyers, landowners and the civil leadership of post-Union Scotland', *Juridical Review*, new ser., 21 (1976), 97–120 · *The letters of David Hume*, ed. J. Y. T. Greig, 2 vols. (1932) · E. Haden-Guest, 'Edinburghshire (Midlothian)', HoP, *Commons, 1754–90*, 1.478–9 · A. Murdoch, 'The people above': politics and administration in mid-eighteenth-century Scotland (1980) · R. B. Sher, *Church and university in the Scottish Enlightenment: the moderate literati of Edinburgh* (1985) · J. Robertson, *The Scottish Enlightenment and the militia question* (1985) · J. Boswell, *Life of Johnson*, ed. R. W. Chapman, rev. J. D. Fleeman, new edn (1970); repr. with introduction by P. Rogers (1980) · GEC, *Baronetage* · *DNB*

Archives NL Scot., corresp. and papers | Birm. CA, letters to Matthew Boulton · BL, corresp. with C. Yorke, second earl of Hardwicke, and third earl of Hardwicke, Add. MSS 35609–35728, *passim* · Sheff. Arch., corresp. with Edmund Burke · U. Edin. L., corresp. with James Cumming

Likenesses J. Brown, pencil drawing, *c*.1780, Scot. NPG

Dalrymple, John, sixth earl of Stair (1749–1821), diplomatist, was born in Edinburgh on 24 September 1749, the only son of John *Dalrymple, fifth earl of Stair (1720–1789), landowner and politician, and his wife, Margaret (*d*. 1798), a daughter of George *Middleton, a London banker, and Mary Campbell. He was educated at Eton College (1762–6) and at Edinburgh University where he took classes in logic and metaphysics. Styled Viscount Dalrymple from 1768, he went on the grand tour; he met Voltaire in December 1771, who described him as 'philosophe comme Spinoza' (Ingamells, 267), and travelled to Naples, Rome, and Venice in 1776–7. Given the temporary role of captain in the newly raised 87th foot on 10 October 1779, he served during the revolutionary war in America and was present at the successful attack on New London and Fort Griswold in September 1781 led by Brigadier-General Benedict Arnold. After being sent to England with the dispatches by Sir Henry Clinton, Dalrymple was appointed minister-plenipotentiary to Poland, with instructions to discover whether there was any design in the courts of Europe to dismember the Ottoman empire. The severity of the climate in Poland affected his health and he returned to England in 1784. Following his appointment as envoy and minister-plenipotentiary to the court of Berlin on 5 August 1785 he reported on the mood of the country at the accession of the new king of Prussia in the autumn of 1786 and was commissioner to confer the Garter on the landgrave of Hesse-Cassel. He sought leave to return to England in 1787 and declined a mission to Russia because of the climate and expense. After succeeding his father as sixth earl on 13 October 1789, he managed his extensive estate in Galloway and continued his interest in politics; he sat as a Scottish representative peer from 1790 to 1807 and from 1820 until his death. He died, unmarried, at his house in Spring Gardens, London, on 1 June 1821 and was buried in the vault at Inch, Wigtownshire.

D. M. ABBOTT

Sources Scots peerage · Stair muniments, NA Scot. · NL Scot., Liston MSS · The Scots Revised Reports, House of Lords Series, 4 (1821–7), 906, 966 · GEC, Peerage · DNB · J. Ingamells, ed., A dictionary of British and Irish travellers in Italy, 1701–1800 (1997)
Archives NA Scot., corresp. and papers · NA Scot., Stair muniments · PRO, letter-book and corresp., FO 353 | BL, letters to Sir Robert Keith, Add. MSS 35515–35539, passim · BL, letters to duke of Leeds, Add. MSS 28061–28067 · U. Durham L., letters to second Earl Grey · U. Nott. L., letters to Lord William Bentinck
Wealth at death £31,465 7s. 9d.: NA Scot, 3 Dec 1824, CC 8/8/150, fol. 266

Dalrymple, John (1803–1852), ophthalmic surgeon, was born at Norwich, the eldest son of William *Dalrymple (1772–1847) and his wife, Marianne, formerly Bertram. He studied under his father, a surgeon at the Norwich and Norfolk Hospital, and in London at the united medical school at Borough Hospital, Southwark; he became a member of the Royal College of Surgeons in 1827. He established a practice at 8 New Broad Street, in the City of London, and afterwards moved to the West End, first to 6 Holles Street and then to 60 Lower Grosvenor Street, where his abilities brought him many patients. Dalrymple specialized in surgery of the eye; in 1832 he was elected assistant surgeon to the Royal London Eye Hospital, working as a demonstrator at the hospital's Saunderian Institution, and in 1843 full surgeon. He was elected fellow of the Royal Society in 1848, and in 1851 he became a member of the council of the Royal College of Surgeons.

Dalrymple's Anatomy of the human eye, being an account of the history, progress, and present state of knowledge of the organ of vision in man (1834) was the first book of its kind in English. It was, however, marred by a reliance on the outdated works of Johann Gottfried Zinn, by errors of translation from the Latin excerpts, and by careless quotation. For many years Dalrymple collected watercolour paintings of the eye, and from these he selected thirty-six plates and other illustrations for his major book, The Pathology of the Human Eye (1852). None of the illustrations relied on the microscope as Dalrymple felt that the diminution of the image brought with it a loss of detail, though he himself was an experienced and capable microscopist. Preparation of his atlas began before the publication of Hermann von Helmholtz's description of the ophthalmoscope in 1851, and was supervised by Dalrymple and his colleague John Scott.

Dalrymple published medical and scientific papers on various topics in natural history. His interest in chemistry led him to be an enthusiastic promoter of the Royal College of Chemistry, founded in 1845. He suffered for several years from bronchitis and pneumonia, and in 1849 he resigned from his position as surgeon to the Royal London Hospital, though he was persuaded to remain as consultant surgeon. He died at 60 Lower Grosvenor Street on 2 May 1852.

G. T. BETTANY, rev. ANITA McCONNELL

Sources D. M. Albert and D. D. Edwards, eds., The history of ophthalmology (1996) · The Times (6 May 1852) · W. W. C., Medical Times and Gazette (8 May 1852), 471 · Abstracts of the Papers Communicated to the Royal Society of London, 6 (1850–54), 250–51 · Boase, Mod. Eng. biog. · The Lancet (8 May 1852), 452 · d. cert.

Dalrymple, John Hamilton Macgill, eighth earl of Stair (1771–1853), army officer, fourth but eldest surviving son of Sir John *Dalrymple of Cousland, fourth baronet (1726–1810), author of Memoirs of Great Britain, and his wife and cousin, Elizabeth, only child and heir of Thomas Hamilton-Macgill of Fala and Oxenfoord, was born in Edinburgh on 15 June 1771. He entered the army on 28 July 1790 as an ensign in the 100th foot, and served as captain in Flanders in 1794 and 1795. As lieutenant-colonel he accompanied the expedition to Hanover in October 1805, and in 1807 he went to Zealand and was present at the siege of Copenhagen. He succeeded to the baronetcy on the death of his father on 26 February 1810. While captain in the guards he sought a substitute for corporal punishment in the army, and explained his scheme to the duke of Wellington. He was colonel of the 92nd foot from 1831 to 1843, and of the 46th foot from 1843 until his death. In 1838 he attained the rank of general.

On retiring from active connection with the army Dalrymple took a strong interest in politics, and in 1812 and 1818 contested Midlothian unsuccessfully as a whig. After the 1832 Reform Act, of which he was 'one of the most zealous and influential of the supporters in Scotland' (GM, 307), he was returned by a majority of sixty-nine over Sir George Clerk, an event which, according to Lord Cockburn, 'struck a blow at the very heart of Scottish toryism' (Memorials ... by Henry Cockburn, 42). However, Dalrymple, who favoured the immediate abolition of slavery, retired in 1835, and at the 1835 election Clerk recovered the seat.

Dalrymple was twice married, first on 23 June 1795 to Harriet (d. 16 Oct 1823), eldest daughter of the Revd Robert Augustus Johnson of Kenilworth, Warwickshire, and second, on 8 June 1825, to Adamina (d. 1 Aug 1857), daughter of Adam *Duncan, first Viscount Duncan (1731–1804); but by neither marriage had he any children. He succeeded to the earldom of Stair on the death of his kinsman, John William Henry Dalrymple, seventh earl, on 22 March 1840. From April 1840 to September 1841 and from August 1846 to August 1852 he was keeper of the great seal of Scotland. On 11 August 1841 he was created a peer of the United Kingdom, as Baron Oxenfoord, and in July 1847 a knight of the Thistle. In his later years he was much concerned with improving his estates in Midlothian and Galloway. He died on 10 January 1853, at his seat, Oxenfoord Castle, Midlothian, and was buried at Cranston. The estates and earldom of Stair devolved on his brother, North Hamilton Dalrymple (1776–1864), while his United Kingdom peerage became extinct.

T. F. HENDERSON, rev. ROGER T. STEARN

Sources GM, 2nd ser., 39 (1853), 307–8 · Burke, Peerage · GEC, Peerage · T. C. W. Blanning, The French revolutionary wars, 1787–1802 (1996) · A. J. Guy, ed., The road to Waterloo: the British army and the struggle against revolutionary and Napoleonic France, 1793–1815 (1990) · Memorials of his time, by Henry Cockburn (1856) · WWBMP
Archives NA Scot., corresp. and papers · NL Scot., corresp. | BL, corresp. with Lord Holland, Add. MS 51593 · Glos. RO, letters to H. W. Rooke · Heriot-Watt University, Edinburgh, Gibson-Craig

MSS · NA Scot., corresp. with Lord Lothian · NRA, priv. coll., letters to Henry Duncan · UCL, letters to James Brougham
Likenesses G. Hayter, group portrait, oils (*The House of Commons, 1833*), NPG

Dalrymple, William (1723–1814), Church of Scotland minister and author, was born in Ayr on 29 August 1723, a younger son of James Dalrymple, sheriff-clerk of Ayr. Educated at Glasgow University (MA, 1740), he was licensed to preach on 2 May 1745 and ordained minister of the second charge at Ayr on 18 December 1746, becoming senior minister on 10 June 1756. On 21 August 1749 he married Susannah, *née* Hunter (d. 1809), daughter of his predecessor as minister of Ayr, with whom he had nine children. He received the DD degree from St Andrews on 7 May 1779 and became moderator of the general assembly of the Church of Scotland two years later (24 May 1781). During his ministry he tempered his Calvinism with an emphasis on common sense and good works.

Dalrymple had private means; his small estate, Mount Charles, lay 'not far to the west of Alloway' (Mackay, 28), which may explain why he was present to baptize the future poet, Robert Burns, on 26 January 1759, within a day of the birth. Dalrymple's nephew Robert Aiken (1739–1807), an Ayr attorney, later became a patron of Burns. In two of the poet's satires Dalrymple is cast as a beleaguered hero in tandem with the more controversial William McGill (1732–1807), minister of the second charge in Ayr from 1760. In Burns's 'The kirk of Scotland's garland, or, The kirk's alarm' (1789), the 'Orthodox, who believe in John Knox' are ironically warned of the 'heretic blast' emanating from the Ayr pulpit: the poem first mentions McGill and then Dalrymple (the prosaic name elided to fit the anapaestic metre):

> D'rymple mild, D'rymple mild, tho' your heart's like a child,
> And your life like the new-driven snaw;
> Yet that winna save ye, auld Satan maun have ye,
> For preaching that three's ane and twa
> (*Poems and Songs*, 1.479)

In 'The Holy Tulzie' (1784–5) both ministers are again named as foes of the evangelicals:

> There's D'rymple has been lang our fae;
> M'gill has wrought us mickle wae
> (ibid., 1.72)

Burns's father had much admired both ministers; indeed, Dalrymple was generally beloved for charity and kindness displayed over the sixty-eight years of his ministry. One who disliked him was John Murdoch (1747–1824), once Burns's schoolmaster, who was dismissed from his teaching post in Ayr after publicly accusing Dalrymple of being 'revengeful as Hell, and as false as the devil; and a damned liar' (Lindsay, 250). Burns's brother Gilbert explained that Murdoch was drunk at the time, but the reason for his enmity is not now known.

Between 1766 and 1803 Dalrymple published eleven works on religious topics, many of which, including *Family Worship Explained and Recommended*, *A History of Christ* (both 1787), and *The Acts of the Apostles Made Easy* (1792), took the form of accessible biblical commentary. Dalrymple died in Ayr on 28 January 1814. Among the offspring of his four adult daughters were William Dalrymple Maclagan (1826–1910), archbishop of York, and Sir Douglas Maclagan (1812–1900), professor of medical jurisprudence at Edinburgh University.   CAROL McGUIRK

Sources *Fasti Scot.*, new edn · *The poems and songs of Robert Burns*, ed. J. Kinsley, 3 vols. (1968) · M. Lindsay, *The Burns encyclopedia*, 3rd edn (1980) · J. A. Mackay, *R. B.: a biography of Robert Burns* (1992) · DNB

Dalrymple, William (1772–1847), surgeon, the son of John Dalrymple and his wife, Anne, was born at Norwich, where his father, a native of Dumfriesshire, had settled, and was baptized on 27 September 1772 at the local Presbyterian church. He was educated at Aylsham grammar school before attending Norwich School. After an apprenticeship in London with Devaynes and Hingeston, court apothecaries, and studying under Henry Cline and Astley Cooper, he returned to Norwich in 1793 and opened a surgery in his father's house. In 1799 he married Marianne Bertram, and they had six sons (including John *Dalrymple) and three daughters.

Dalrymple's ardent advocacy of radical opinions retarded his progress for some years, and it was not until 1812 that he became assistant surgeon of the Norfolk and Norwich Hospital; he was elected a full surgeon in 1814. He held this position until 1839, when he retired because of ill health. In 1813 he attracted great attention through the successful performance of the then rare operation of tying the common carotid artery. He attained great success as an operator, especially in lithotomy. Dalrymple also formed a valuable collection of anatomical and pathological preparations, which he gave to the Norfolk and Norwich Hospital on his retirement from practice in 1844. His last years were passed in London, where he died on 5 December 1847. He was buried in Highgate cemetery on 11 December.

Dalrymple's many operative successes were achieved despite poor health. An advocate of civil and religious liberty, his sense of responsibility and honour were high, his character and conversation were elevated, and his teaching was judicious. His publications consisted of a few papers in medical journals.

G. T. BETTANY, *rev.* MICHAEL BEVAN

Sources GM, 2nd ser., 29 (1848), 314–16 · IGI

Dalton, (Edward) Hugh Neale, Baron Dalton (1887–1962), politician, was born at The Gnoll, near Neath, Glamorgan, on 26 August 1887, the eldest child of Canon John Neale *Dalton KCVO CMG (1839–1931) and his wife, Catherine Alicia Evan-Thomas (1863–1944). The descendant of Welsh landowners on his mother's side and Anglican clergy on his father's, Hugh Dalton was not obviously destined for a career as a socialist politician. Yet he became one of the best known Labour leaders of the inter-war and early post-Second World War period, and one of the most influential intellectuals in politics of his generation.

Upbringing, Cambridge friendships, and Fabianism Key to Dalton's early development was a childhood in The Cloisters at Windsor Castle, where his father was a member of the St George's Chapel chapter, having spent much of his

(Edward) Hugh Neale Dalton, Baron Dalton (1887–1962), by Roper, 1945

adult life as tutor and companion to the two sons of the prince of Wales, Eddie and George (later George V). Hugh's adult radicalism can be seen, at least in part, as a rebellion against a childhood environment of aristocratic snobbery and monarchical opulence. His education was conventional. In 1895 Hugh entered St George's choir school at Windsor, which his father had helped to set up. In 1898 he was sent to Summer Fields, a boarding preparatory school in Oxford and crammer for the most famous public schools, and thence, in 1901, to Luxmoore's House at Eton College, where (by his own description) he was 'rather bored and indifferent' and acquired the political views of a 'Joe Chamberlainite, a Tory Democrat, a self-confessed Imperialist' (Pimlott, 29). In 1906 he entered King's College, Cambridge, with a closed exhibition, to read mathematics. Here he became a close friend of Rupert Brooke, who started at King's the same term. Both were part of a glittering circle of undergraduates and younger dons that included Arthur Schloss (later Arthur Waley, the Sinologist), Ben Keeling, Francis Birrell, Gerald Shove, Maynard Keynes, and Goldsworthy Lowes Dickinson.

Dalton's association with Brooke coloured the rest of his life. 'No Cambridge friendship of mine meant more to me than this', Dalton wrote later, 'and the radiance of his memory still lights my path' (Call Back Yesterday, 38). Brooke died in 1915. Dalton felt his loss and that of other Cambridge contemporaries during the First World War very deeply. His political commitment to preventing war, and his generous habit of befriending much younger men and giving them encouragement, were consciously linked

to memories of this phase in his life. Meanwhile he had been attracted to socialism as an undergraduate. Following the election of a reforming Liberal administration early in 1906, advanced political theories were in the air. Infected by the mood, Dalton exchanged Chamberlain for Keir Hardie and Sidney Webb: at the end of his first term, he and Brooke joined the Fabian Society, an intellectual discussion and pressure group set up in 1884 that had already profoundly influenced progressive opinion. From the start Dalton took the society's activities and preoccupations seriously, acquiring a Fabian outlook that characterized his future career. A keen participant in the society's activities, he quickly came to the attention of Beatrice Webb, who perceptively described the 21-year-old undergraduate in 1908 as 'one of the most astute and thoughtful of our younger members—by nature an ecclesiastic—a sort of lay Jesuit—preparing for political life' (Pimlott, 50).

Marriage, war service, and academic economics At Cambridge Dalton abandoned mathematics, and in 1910 he was awarded an upper second-class degree in the new discipline of economics. Although he moved to London the same autumn to read for the bar at the Middle Temple, he had little interest in the law, and in the following year began work on a doctorate, supervised by Professor Edwin Cannan at the London School of Economics (LSE), on the inequality of incomes. In May 1914 he was called to the bar. Later the same month he married Ruth Fox (1890–1966) [see Dalton, (Florence) Ruth, Lady Dalton], a fellow Fabian and former student at the LSE. When the First World War broke out in August, he joined up and was placed in the Army Service Corps. Sent to France, he witnessed—at a safe distance—the battle of the Somme. At his own request he transferred to the Royal Artillery, and in 1917 he was sent to the Italian front, where he commanded a 6 inch howitzer, and was decorated by the Italian government (medaglio al valore militare) for his part in the retreat following the battle of Caporetto. His experiences during the rapid withdrawal to the River Tagliamento provided material for his first book, *With British Guns in Italy*, published in 1919.

Dalton's experience of war spurred him politically. By the time of his return to England following the armistice, he had a firm ambition to enter parliament as a Labour MP. Other jobs and activities were seen as stepping-stones. It took six years to achieve his aim. Meanwhile he built a career as an academic economist. After a brief experience working at the Ministry of Labour and as a teaching assistant, he was appointed Sir Ernest Cassel reader in economics at the LSE in 1920. The same year he published *Some Aspects of the Inequality of Incomes in Modern Communities*, based on his doctoral thesis. This was a theoretical work with a practical purpose, and developed the ideas of A. C. Pigou and Edwin Cannan, offering an intellectual justification for economic socialism. The case against large inequalities of income, he argued, 'is that the less urgent needs of the rich are satisfied, while the more urgent needs of the poor are left unsatisfied'. Dalton wrote other books on economics, including a celebrated textbook,

Principles of Public Finance (1922), which was translated into many languages and continued to be prescribed reading for economics students until the 1960s. He also published a polemical call for a wealth tax, *The Capital Levy Explained* (1923).

However, the bases of Dalton's economic thinking and of his political outlook on economic questions are to be found in *Inequality of Incomes*, a book that has had a wide influence and has been described by the economist Amartya Sen as 'a classic contribution' (Pimlott, 138). It was his first, and effectively his last, such contribution. Dalton scarcely remained at the forefront of his discipline, and a personal coolness between him and his friend and former tutor, Maynard Keynes, reduced the interest he might have shown in new doctrines. After the early 1920s, and especially after he entered parliament, Dalton regarded academic economics as a second string. Indeed, his self-image was that of a man of action: he tended to pour scorn on other academic socialists who wrote and campaigned from the security of the ivory tower. Instead of cultivating economists, he sought the attention of leading figures in the Labour world—especially Arthur Henderson—and he made himself available to the emerging Labour Party as a policy expert.

Labour MP Although Labour increased its parliamentary representation rapidly in the early 1920s, Dalton at first found it hard to get a seat. Public frustration was compounded by private tragedy. In 1922 the Daltons' only child, Helen, died at the age of four. The impact of this catastrophe never left them. In the short run it seems to have encouraged Hugh to pursue his career with heightened ferocity. In 1924, following four unsuccessful contests in different constituencies, he was elected MP for Camberwell (Peckham division). However, a dispute with the local party led him to switch seats during his first parliamentary term. After a period of uncertainty he was adopted as candidate for the Bishop Auckland division, a mining constituency in co. Durham, which he represented from 1929 to 1931 and from 1935 to 1959.

In parliament, as one of the few Labour MPs with a solid professional or academic background, Dalton quickly made his mark, building an almost unassailable position as a member of the Labour establishment. In 1925 he was elected to Labour's parliamentary executive (shadow cabinet), a position he retained until his voluntary retirement from it thirty years later. The following year trade union backing ensured his election to the Labour Party national executive committee (NEC). Although he was defeated in the NEC election the following year, he regained his place the year after. A busy political life did not interrupt his writing. Increasingly his interests had moved from economics to foreign policy. In 1928 he published another book, *Towards the Peace of Nations*. In this he advocated a 'strong' League of Nations policy, and—in notable contrast to other radical writers on war and peace at the time—called for a league equipped with the economic and military weapons necessary to police the world and punish transgressors. Following the election of a second minority Labour government in 1929, Dalton was given the post of under-secretary at the Foreign Office. The job appealed to him, even if his bombastic style did not entirely appeal to Foreign Office officials, who found him difficult to handle. Nevertheless, as deputy to the foreign secretary, Arthur Henderson, he played an important part in negotiations aimed at providing an international disarmament treaty.

Labour's programme: practical socialism The episode was short-lived: when the government collapsed in 1931 and Ramsay MacDonald formed the National Government, Dalton forfeited his office and joined most of his Labour colleagues on the opposition benches. At first his position within the Labour Party was strengthened by defections which made him one of the leading figures on the NEC. The moment did not last. In the general election of October 1931 he lost his seat, and for a time seemed politically marginalized. Fortunately he was able to return to a full-time post at the LSE. There followed a period of reflection and travel. Since, however, most of the other Labour leaders had also been defeated, he was not out of the limelight for long. His position on the NEC, together with his academic income and Ruth's private means, provided a solid base—which many other former ministers lacked—for a political recovery. There were obstacles. The much-reduced Parliamentary Labour Party, under the leadership of George Lansbury, had responded to the 1931 electoral disaster by moving sharply to the left. Dalton had to deal with a party in the Commons that supported near-pacifism in foreign affairs, and advocated the 'socialization' of the banks at home. Over the next few years Dalton's mission was to restore reason to Labour's counsels. He became the party's most articulate and persuasive voice in favour of policies that took account of the world as it really was, and which sought to secure Labour's re-election.

In 1935 Dalton published his own bold assessment of a future Labour government's policy options, *Practical Socialism for Britain*. If *Inequality of Incomes* was intellectually Dalton's most ambitious work, *Practical Socialism*—later described by Roy Jenkins as 'the first swallow' of the post-1935 summer' of socialist reformism—was politically the most influential. In it Dalton revived and updated nuts-and-bolts Fabianism, a doctrine that in the 1920s had sunk in a sea of sentimental rhetoric, and in the early 1930s had been dismissed by impatient communists and fellow-travellers. Dalton's message was defiantly pragmatic: 'if our concern is with practical politics', the author declared, 'we do better to decide the direction of advance than to debate the detail of Utopia' (Pimlott, 217). The essence of 'practical politics' was practical planning. Much of the book was devoted to this topic, linking Labour Party ideas to those of non-Labour planning enthusiasts, and providing what eventually became a virtual blueprint for the first post-war Labour administration. Dalton did not write the book in a vacuum: many of the key ideas came out of discussions with a group of younger political aspirants with economic interests, including Douglas Jay, Hugh Gaitskell, and Evan Durbin. Over the next few years the same group refined Dalton's political approach, and married it to a Keynesian economic one.

Rejection of appeasement and Churchill's coalition Domestic policy was one of Dalton's main concerns in the 1930s. The other was the threat of continental fascism. A visit to Germany in April 1933 brought home to him the danger of Nazism. 'Germany is horrible', he wrote privately on his return, at a time when Labour's official policy favoured unilateral disarmament. 'A European war must be counted now among the probabilities of the next ten years' (Pimlott, 227). After regaining his Bishop Auckland seat in the 1935 election, he was appointed Labour foreign affairs spokesman, and set about changing the party's international policy. In 1936–7 he served as chairman of the Labour NEC, and made maximum possible use of a hitherto largely titular office. By the end of 1937, with help from sympathetic trade union leaders, Dalton had moved the party from semi-pacifism to a policy of armed deterrence and rejection of appeasement. This change had an important effect in the months before the declaration of war in September 1939, making it possible for Labour—though still in opposition—to stiffen the dithering National Government in its post-Munich resolve to stand up to Hitler. It also facilitated the cross-party alliance that succeeded in bringing down Neville Chamberlain in May 1940.

Dalton was still writing. During the so-called 'phoney war', he published *Hitler's War: before and after*, a short tract in which he looked ahead to the end of hostilities, once again stressing the need for a strong system of collective security, and advocating a post-war federal union of European states, including post-Nazi Germany. In the meantime he urged a 'warmonger' policy, and favoured taking the war onto the enemy's home ground at the earliest possible moment. When Winston Churchill became prime minister at the head of a wide-ranging war coalition, Dalton was appointed minister of economic warfare, with responsibility for depriving the enemy of supplies. Churchill also placed him in command of the Special Operations Executive (SOE)—a secret organization charged with carrying out clandestine warfare.

At first, the importance of SOE seemed small. When Churchill asked Dalton in July 1940 to 'set Europe ablaze' with anti-German partisan and terrorist activity (Pimlott, 298), the words sounded almost ironic, and may have been intended to be so. With the threat of Nazi invasion of Britain imminent, Europe did not seem the most likely place for a conflagration. However, Dalton threw himself into the secret aspect of his new duties with characteristic energy. With the diplomatist Gladwyn Jebb as his chief executive officer, Dr Dynamo—as he was nicknamed—succeeded in turning SOE into the co-ordinator of resistance activity across the occupied territories of the continent. There is still disagreement over the precise extent of SOE's impact. During Dalton's period as responsible minister, however, it could claim several successful operations. Thus it seems to have played a key part in engineering a *coup d'état* in Yugoslavia, and it also helped to bring about a temporary blocking of the Danube.

In February 1942, as part of a ministerial reshuffle, Dalton was shifted from the Ministry of Economic Warfare to the Board of Trade, where he was placed in charge of a wide empire that included consumer rationing and other wartime controls, with an increasing responsibility—as the end of the war approached—for post-war planning and reconstruction. A major legislative landmark was Dalton's 1945 Distribution of Industry Act, inspired by the minister's own experience of poverty in his north-east constituency. This particular measure set the pattern for subsequent post-war regional policies, aimed at mopping up pockets of unemployment.

Socialist chancellor of the exchequer Like most of his contemporaries Dalton did not expect Labour to win the July 1945 general election. However—just in case it did—he made a point of telling Clement Attlee that he would like to be foreign secretary in any possible Labour administration. Attlee did not commit himself. However, following Labour's landslide victory the incoming prime minister told his colleague that he would 'almost certainly' get the Foreign Office, and even encouraged him to pack his bags for the journey to Potsdam. Dalton's excitement at this prospect was short-lived. Within hours Attlee—possibly influenced by an audience with the king, who urged him to think again—had changed his mind, and appointed Ernest Bevin foreign secretary, sending Dalton to the Treasury instead. 'When told that I was not to be foreign secretary, but chancellor of the exchequer, I was not unhappy, or disappointed, for more than half an hour', Dalton later recalled. 'I swallowed my fate in one gulp' (*High Tide*, 4). The decision had profound implications, both for Britain and for the world. It also determined what was to be the climax—and crisis—of Dalton's career.

Dalton's period at the Treasury was greatly affected, for good and ill, by his own background as an expert in economics and public finance. The new chancellor brought enthusiasm, socialist commitment, and expert knowledge to his post, which had been reduced in authority by the heavy wartime emphasis on physical planning, but which now rapidly acquired a vital strategic importance, partly because of the political status of its holder. Over the next couple of years Dalton was able to play a vital role as one of the government's 'big five', together with Attlee, Bevin, Herbert Morrison (lord president), and Sir Stafford Cripps (Board of Trade), who provided a directive inner core to the administration during its most energetic and radical phase.

Later Dalton wrote that he faced six urgent problems at the Treasury when he arrived there: the re-conversion of industry, manpower, and expenditure to peaceful purposes; a smooth transition from war to peace, avoiding unemployment, industrial unrest, and inflation; honouring Labour's pledge to extend the social services; altering taxation so as to cut the total, while reducing the gap between rich and poor; the carrying out of nationalization pledges; and, finally, finding a way to pay for the imports needed to maintain employment and prevent starvation. Dalton's first challenge was to tackle the consequences of the announcement in Washington of an abrupt end to the wartime lend-lease arrangement with the United States, on which Britain had depended heavily. Dalton sent his former tutor, Maynard (now Lord) Keynes, to the American capital to negotiate a large North American loan. The success of these negotiations bought time for domestic reform, though at high risk. At home the new chancellor set the pace for the new administration, dominating parliament with his oratory and intellectual power. 'He bestrode the world', Lord Callaghan later recalled. At the time Michael Foot—who became a fierce left-wing critic—wrote that the chancellor's stature 'was increased by every speech he made' (Pimlott, 441). This was Dalton's zenith. Physically he was imposing. 'He curves his towering, six-foot-three inch frame far over the Dispatch Box', one newspaper reported in March 1947, 'screws his bald domed head sideways and upwards and, from time to time, rolls his pale blue eyes so that the whites blaze and flash with an almost Mephistophelian effect' (ibid., 442).

Dalton introduced four budgets—in October 1945, April 1946, April 1947, and November 1947. The measures these contained justify describing him as the most socialist—or at any rate, the most levelling—chancellor ever to have held office. In some ways he was old-fashioned. In particular he did not follow the new practice of relating budget proposals to a detailed survey of the whole economy. His budgetary approach was described by observers as 'Gladstonian' in style. Though he accepted the principle that fiscal policy could be used as a long-run full-employment weapon, he can be described as Keynesian only in a broad sense. At the same time he did not forget his own sermons in *Inequality of Incomes*. The redistributive aim of his budgets was to some extent disguised because of the need to reduce the total of tax compared with high wartime levels. Nevertheless tax cuts in his budgets were heavily in favour of the worst off. As his future protégé Anthony Crosland put it later, Dalton 'maintained, and even extended, the great advance towards income-equality that was made during the war' (Pimlott, 454).

One of Dalton's most creative schemes was the setting up of a special National Land Fund, to be used to reimburse the Inland Revenue for land offered by executors to meet the obligations of deceased owners. As a result of this measure many important houses and lands passed to the National Trust. Dalton also provided money for development areas. In the City he became the most detested chancellor since Lloyd George, especially when he spoke—too gleefully—of fulfilling the pledge to banish unemployment, and of his own determination to 'find, with a song in my heart, all the money necessary for sound constructive schemes' (Pimlott, 457). The phrase 'with a song in my heart' became a trademark, and when the tide turned against him it was used by cartoonists and tory enemies as evidence of his devil-may-care treatment of the nation's finances.

Financial crisis and resignation It took time, however, for the hostility to crystallize. Dalton's first major enactment as chancellor, nationalizing the Bank of England, aroused remarkably little opposition in the financial world, partly because the act did not in practice provide the degree of control over other banks that had been anticipated in Labour's pre-war proposals. More controversial (though not initially) were Dalton's 'cheap money' policies, designed to speed reconstruction through increased local authority borrowing. At first cheap money seemed to work. However, the floating in January 1947 of a new stock, notoriously known as 'Daltons', turned the tide against him. The undated stock quickly plummeted, taking with it much of the chancellor's reputation. Faced with what has been described as 'a gigantic bear raid' of institutional sellers, Dalton's efforts to find support from public funds failed, and many purchasers suffered severe losses. This set-back was accompanied by a wave of criticism across a wider front, just as the government faced serious difficulties as a result of a fuel shortage triggered by the coldest winter in living memory. Suddenly 'annus mirabilis' had become 'annus horrendus', and Dalton faced a major financial crisis. During the middle months of 1947 a dollar drain became a torrent, forcing the suspension, in August 1947, of the free convertibility of dollars and pounds which had been a key aspect of the North American loan agreement. For the administration this was a turning point, and Dalton was widely blamed.

Worse was to come. On 12 November 1947 the chancellor opened his fourth budget, seen as an emergency measure against inflation. Ironically, this final Dalton budget has come to be regarded as a pioneering initiative, which for the first time fully incorporated Keynesian principles, providing a model for the subsequent 'austerity' budgets of Sir Stafford Cripps. As it turned out, Dalton was not at the Treasury to see the effects of the new approach. Walking through the lobby on his way to deliver the budget speech, he was approached by a reporter on the London evening *Star* who stopped him and asked a question. The chancellor replied precisely, giving details of the main tax changes he was about to announce. The reporter immediately telephoned his editor, and copies of the *Star* containing the information in the stop-press section were on sale before the chancellor had reached the relevant part of his speech. There was no movement on the stock exchange attributable to this leak, which the opposition accepted was no more than a regrettable accident. However, Dalton's position had been weakened over preceding months. Some colleagues had come to regard him as a liability, and he had unwisely become involved in a Cripps-led manoeuvre aimed at persuading the prime minister to stand down. Dalton's offer of resignation was accepted, and his career as a front-line minister came to an end. Cripps became chancellor, and the big five became the big four.

From Dalton's own point of view, the disaster was doubly unlucky. Not only were the circumstances of his resignation humiliating in themselves. The timing—in the aftermath of a financial collapse, when his own reputation was at its lowest point—meant that he got little credit when the economy began to show signs of recovery a few months later. Instead, the myth that the country had been saved by an ascetic chancellor taking over from a profligate one became firmly established.

Brief return to office, retirement, and death Nevertheless, there was a comeback of sorts. In June 1948 Attlee brought the former chancellor back into the cabinet as chancellor of the duchy of Lancaster and effectively minister without portfolio. In November Dalton became head of the British delegation to the Committee of Western European Powers, a new body charged with looking at ways of increasing European unity. Negotiations led eventually to the Statute of the Council of Europe, signed in London in May 1949, following the acceptance of Dalton's own proposal that the new European assembly should be established in Strasbourg, as a symbol of Franco-German amity. After the general election of 1950 Dalton was at first made minister of town and country planning. In February 1951 his responsibilities were extended to include housing, and he became minister of local government and planning. With the retirement of Sir Stafford Cripps through ill health and the death of Bevin, Dalton's star seemed once more to be rising—especially as the new chancellor of the exchequer, Hugh Gaitskell, was a personal friend and protégé. Labour's election defeat at the end of the year, however, ended Dalton's ministerial career, and in 1952 he lost his seat on Labour's national executive.

After the 1955 election Dalton retired from the shadow cabinet and in 1959 he stood down as an MP. In January 1960 he accepted a life peerage. Meanwhile he had caused a stir with the publication of the first two volumes of his autobiography, *Call Back Yesterday* (1953) and *The Fateful Years* (1957), based on private diaries, which set a new fashion for 'confessional' memoirs. A third volume, *High Tide and After*, was published early in February 1962. A week later, on 13 February, Lord Dalton died at St Pancras Hospital in London. His wife survived him by four years. Two volumes of his diaries have been published posthumously (*The Second World War Diary*, 1986, and *The Political Diary*, 1987).

Assessment Hugh Dalton's legacy was diffuse and controversial. Though he had devoted friends, he made many enemies, often in his own party. Renowned for his booming voice and mischievous enjoyment of gossip, he was often seen as an arch-conspirator who (as Harold Wilson once put it) was apt to meet himself coming back. There were other insults: tories called him a class traitor, leftwingers a bully. Critically, his platform style, though powerful, could seem contrived, and did not convey the moral authority and sincerity of purpose that other, equally ambitious, politicians achieved. At times he did not seem to take himself entirely seriously, and even caricatured his own faults and eccentricities. Partly for these reasons, he did not acquire a position in the socialist pantheon. Nevertheless his influence on British political history and Labour Party ideas bears comparison with that of any other Labour politician who did not become prime minister. As an intellectual he was important in developing Fabian thought, and in helping to give it a hard economic edge. As a politician he was both a powerful and determined advocate and a back-room expert, who was personally responsible for many of the key Labour Party documents of the 1930s and war period, setting the scene for the post-war Attlee government. As chancellor of the exchequer his policies helped to facilitate an ambitious domestic reform programme, in the most adverse conditions. Meanwhile, he talent-spotted and nurtured several generations of young political aspirants. The grouping later known as the Gaitskellites emerged from the circle of his younger friends. In addition to Hugh Gaitskell himself, Anthony Crosland, Roy Jenkins, Denis Healey, George Brown, and James Callaghan were among those who learned from him and benefited from his practical help.

Dalton's political beliefs, rooted in early twentieth-century socialist thought and the ethical philosophy of G. E. Moore, were in many ways typical of his generation of left-of-centre intellectuals. He firmly believed in the state as the instrument of social betterment. He also believed in planning as a means to achieve greater economic equality. Yet he was not a doctrinaire. Unlike some contemporaries he was never tempted by the Marxist certainties in vogue in the 1930s; and he was slow to accept the Keynesian ideas which his own group of friends enthusiastically (and sometimes uncritically) endorsed. Some of his opinions were maverick. Though an early advocate of versions of European federalism, he had an emotional dislike of Germans, whom he blamed—somewhat indiscriminately—for the human tragedy of two world wars. On the other hand, he was one of the few British politicians who early on recognized the danger posed by the Nazi dictatorship. More than many political leaders, he was consistent in his thinking. More than most, he took a close, professional interest both in political ideas and in the details of the policies he supported. A member of the second generation of Labour leaders, he played an important part in giving his party the intellectual confidence not only to make it electable, but also to make it effective.

BEN PIMLOTT

Sources B. Pimlott, *Hugh Dalton* (1985) · *The political diary of Hugh Dalton, 1918–1940, 1945–1960*, ed. B. Pimlott (1986) · *The Second World War diary of Hugh Dalton, 1940–1945*, ed. B. Pimlott (1986) · H. Dalton, *Call back yesterday: memoirs, 1887–1931* (1953) · H. Dalton, *The fateful years: memoirs, 1931–1945* (1957) · H. Dalton, *High tide and after: memoirs, 1945–1960* (1962) · CGPLA Eng. & Wales (1962)

Archives BLPES, corresp., diaries, and papers · Nuffield Oxf., papers · People's History Museum, Manchester, letters and notes · PRO, corresp. and papers, CAB 127/204–212 | BLPES, corresp. with Lord Beveridge · BLPES, letters to Edwin Cannan · BLPES, corresp. with J. E. Meade · BLPES, corresp. with first Baron Piercy · Bodl. Oxf., corresp. with Clement Attlee · Bodl. Oxf., corresp. with Lord Ponsonby · HLRO, corresp. with Lord Beaverbrook · HLRO, corresp. with Viscount Davidson · King's Lond., Liddell Hart C., corresp. with Sir B. H. Liddell Hart · NL Wales, letters to Desmond Donnelly · Ruskin College, Oxford, corresp. with James Middleton · St Ant. Oxf., corresp. with H. St. J. B. Philby · U. Hull, letters to Harold Laski | FILM BFI NFTVA, news footage | SOUND IWM FVA, oral history interview · IWM FVA, recorded talk

Likenesses Roper, photograph, 1945, NPG [*see illus.*] · W. Stoneman, photograph, 1945, NPG · G. Davien, plaster bust, 1947, NPG

Wealth at death £26,966 11s. 6d.: probate, 12 July 1962, CGPLA Eng. & Wales

Dalton, James (*bap.* 1700?, *d.* 1730), street robber, was probably born in Cow Cross, London, and may have been the child baptized at St Andrew's, Holborn, on 14 January 1700 whose parents were James and Elizabeth Dalton. It was said that Dalton's father was hanged about 1705 and that he had insisted his son watch the execution. His mother may then have married a butcher about 1711. James had at least one sibling, Edward Dalton. The only description of Dalton is that he was 'a little Man' (Old Bailey sessions paper, January 1730). He attended schools in Cow Lane, St John's Lane, and Fleet Lane, but left home before 1719 after quarrelling with his stepfather. He became a pickpocket in Fleet Street, then joined a gang which committed thefts, street robberies, and burglaries. About this time, according to his own account, he entered an arranged marriage for 2 guineas at St Clement's Church in the Strand with 'a Gentleman's Daughter' (Dalton, *Life and Actions*, 11), who was pregnant by another man and required a husband to restore her respectability.

In 1719 Dalton was arrested for burglary and to avoid prosecution gave evidence at the Old Bailey against two of his colleagues. However, later that year he was convicted at the Old Bailey of stealing linen goods and sentenced to transportation. He was put on board the *Honor* in May 1720, but a mutiny among the prisoners enabled him to escape at Cape Finisterre, Spain, and he was back in London by early 1721. There he married Mary Tomlin, 'a Barrow-Woman' (Dalton, *Life and Actions*, 29) but was soon arrested by Jonathan Wild and sentenced to death in March 1721 at the Old Bailey for returning early from transportation. This sentence was reduced to transportation for fourteen years, and he was put on the *Prince Royal* for Virginia in August 1721. The discovery of a file baked into a gingerbread cake foiled Dalton's escape attempt, and he landed in America in late 1721. He escaped and travelled back to Bristol, but he was arrested by Wild's agents and returned to Virginia. Again he escaped, this time to the West Indies where he stayed for about eighteen months before returning to America. There he married a carpenter's daughter with whom he had a son, although neither can be identified.

Abandoning his family, Dalton sailed for England, but *en route* was pressed into the Royal Navy. By 1728 he was back in London and a member of a ferocious gang of street robbers which operated mainly in the area near his birthplace bordered by St Paul's Cathedral and Smithfield market in the east and Lincoln's Inn in the west. The gang's robbery of Sir Gilbert Heathcote on 28 February 1728 may have prompted the government's decision to offer a reward for the conviction of London street robbers. A fringe member of the gang, Martin Bellamy, was arrested shortly afterwards and, while in prison, confessed to a journalist who had posed as a government official empowered to give immunity from prosecution in exchange for his co-operation. This confession led to the arrest of Dalton, and, as a key member of the gang, his offer to appear for the crown was preferred to that of Bellamy. His evidence helped to convict six colleagues in May 1728. Fearing the wrath of their friends and relatives, he

fled to Virginia, but was back in London in 1729. In January 1730 he was imprisoned for three years for attempting to rob the physician Richard Mead, and then in April he was sentenced to death for robbing John Waller in November 1729. Dalton was outraged at the accusation: while admitting he had 'done many ill Things, and had deserved Death many times', he denied this charge. He also denounced Waller as 'a man of a vile Character' who informed for the reward (Old Bailey sessions paper, April 1730); although Dalton had been paid for his evidence in 1728, he presumably distinguished between informing to avoid being hanged and incidentally getting a reward, and informing solely for the reward. While in Newgate he told his life story to a hack writer employed by Robert Walker, the publisher, and this appeared as *The Life and Actions of James Dalton* (1730).

Dalton was hanged on 12 May 1730. His accusations against Waller resurfaced in 1732 when the latter was convicted of charging an innocent man with robbery for the reward offered. Dalton's infamy had made him an easy target, but friends of those betrayed in 1728 may have prompted Waller: Dalton had feared that they might falsely accuse him and he was assaulted during the Mead trial. Waller was beaten to death in the pillory, for which crime Edward Dalton, James's brother, was hanged.

Dalton's career illustrates a popular view of the professional criminal's life at that time: graduating from sneak thefts to violent robberies, forced abroad through transportation but keen to return to a relatively narrow area of London in spite of the risks. His life confirmed contemporary fears of gang crime and criticisms of the criminal justice system: that it relied on criminals who, having bargained for their freedom, returned to crime, and that transportation was ineffective. An indication of his notoriety, and his most lasting memorial, is the appearance of his 'Wigg Box' above Moll Hackabout's bed in William Hogarth's *The Harlot's Progress* (plate 3).

PHILIP RAWLINGS

Sources *A genuine narrative of all the street robberies committed since October last by James Dalton* (1728) · [J. Dalton], *The life and actions of James Dalton* (1730) · *The life and infamous actions of that perjur'd villain John Waller* (1732) · *The life of Martin Bellamy* (1728) · G. Howson, *Thief-taker general: the rise and fall of Jonathan Wild* (1970) · P. Rawlings, *Drunks, whores and idle apprentices: criminal biographies of the eighteenth century* (1992) · *The proceedings at the sessions of the peace* (1729–30) [Old Bailey sessions papers, 8–10 April 1730] · *IGI*

Dalton, John (*bap.* 1709, *d.* 1763), poet and Church of England clergyman, was baptized in Dean, Cumberland, on 20 September 1709, the son of the Revd John Dalton, rector of Dean (1705–12). He received his school education at Lowther in Westmorland, and when sixteen years old was sent to Queen's College, Oxford, entering the college as batteler on 12 October 1725, being elected tabardar on 2 November 1730, and taking the degree of BA on 20 November 1730. Shortly afterwards he was selected as tutor to Lord Beauchamp, the only son of the earl of Hertford, the seventh duke of Somerset. Horace Walpole asserts that Henrietta *Knight, Lady Luxborough, was in love with Dalton (she was estranged from her husband in 1736), and further implies that both she and her friend the duchess of Somerset had been guilty of improper conduct with him.

At this time Dalton adapted Milton's masque *Comus* for the stage. He retained Milton's text, but added his own verse to create dialogue and to introduce scenes which provided opportunities for acting on a stage and for the best use of music, which was written by Thomas Arne. *Comus* was first produced at Drury Lane Theatre, London, on 4 March 1738 and was repeated successfully. One notable performance, on 5 April 1750, was in the presence of the last surviving relative of John Milton, Mrs Elizabeth Foster. For this performance Dr Samuel Johnson wrote a prologue which was read by the actor David Garrick.

Dalton had proceeded MA on 9 May 1734, and in the following month accepted a living that was being held for a minor. In June 1741 he was elected to a fellowship at Queen's. His pupil, Lord Beauchamp, died in 1744, but by this time Dalton had become a practising Church of England priest (for a time at St James's, Westminster). None the less, he still received patronage from the duke of Somerset and through the duke's influence he was appointed a canon of Worcester Cathedral in 1748, and about the same time obtained the rectory of St Mary-at-Hill in the City of London. On 26 February 1749 he married Mary Gosling, a sister of Sir Francis Gosling, alderman of London. Dalton took the degrees of BD and DD on 4 July 1750. He died at Worcester on 22 July 1763, and was buried at the west end of the south aisle of Worcester Cathedral. His widow eventually inherited his estate on the death of his brother, Richard Dalton, in 1791.

Dalton published sermons and moral epistles as well as the text of his adaptation of *Comus*, which was frequently reprinted throughout the eighteenth century. After his death he continued to be known for poems associated with 'picturesque' descriptions. His *Descriptive poem, addressed to two ladies* [the two Misses Lowther] *at their return from viewing the mines near Whitehaven* (1755), was extracted in Thomas West's *A Guide to the Lakes* (1784) and there was read by William Wordsworth and other poets of the next generation.

W. P. COURTNEY, *rev.* JOHN WYATT

Sources T. West, *A guide to the lakes in Cumberland, Westmorland and Lancashire*, 3rd edn (1784), appx · J. Herbage, ed., *Musica Britannica: a national collection of music*, volume III: '*Comus*', a masque by John Milton adapted by John Dalton with music by Arne (1951), 161 · N. Nicholson, *The Lakers: the adventures of the first tourists* (1955), 27–9, 63 · *IGI* · Walpole, *Corr.*, vols. 11, 32
Archives Queen's College, Oxford, letters to Joseph Smith, provost of Queen's College
Likenesses monumental inscription, Worcester Cathedral

Dalton, John (1726–1811), army officer in the East India Company, was the only child of Captain James Dalton, (*d.* 1742), army officer in the 6th foot; his mother, whose maiden name was Smith, was from Limerick. On his father's side, Dalton was great-great-grandson of Colonel John Dalton, of Caley Hall, near Otley, a royalist officer of an old Yorkshire family. Before his death in the West Indies in 1742, probably in one of the minor descents on Cuba

after the British failure before Carthagena, James Dalton had obtained for his son, then fifteen, a second lieutenancy in the 8th marines, lately raised by Colonel Sir Thomas Hanmer. Young Dalton embarked with a small detachment of that corps in the *Preston* (50 guns), commanded by the sixth earl of Northesk, which sailed from Spithead in May 1744; and after serving off Madagascar and Batavia, arrived in Balasore Roads in September 1745, and was afterwards employed on the Coromandel coast. When the marine regiments were disbanded in 1748, Dalton was appointed first lieutenant of one of the independent marine companies formed on shore at Madras by order of Admiral Edward Boscawen. The following year he transferred his services to the East India Company, becoming captain of a company of European grenadiers, and made the campaigns of the next three years against the French under Governor Joseph Dupleix and their native allies. In June 1752 he was appointed commandant of Trichinopoly by Major Stringer Lawrence. He defended the garrison with great skill and bravery against treachery within and overwhelming numbers of assailants without for several months until it was finally relieved in the autumn of 1753. He resigned his appointment on the ground of ill health on 1 March 1754, and received the thanks of the governor in council for his services. He returned to England in 1754, at the age of twenty-eight, having 'amassed a fortune of £10,000 and a fair share of military fame'. At Ripon, on 7 March 1756, he married the second daughter of Sir John Wray, bt, of Glentworth, Lincolnshire, and Sleningford, Yorkshire. The couple had three sons and three daughters, including Thomas, army officer in the 11th dragoons, who took the name Norcliffe in 1807; John, also an officer in the 4th light dragoons; and James, rector of Croft, Yorkshire, and botanist. After his wife's death in 1787 Dalton resided at Sleningford, which he had purchased from her brother. He died on 11 July 1811.   H. M. CHICHESTER, *rev.* PHILIP CARTER

Sources C. Dalton, *A life of Captain John Dalton* (1885) · [R. Orme], *A history of the military transactions of the British nation in Indostan* (1763) · T. C. Raikes, *Service of the 102nd regiment of foot (royal Madras fusiliers)* (1867)
Archives BL OIOC, corresp., MSS Eur. Orme · East Riding of Yorkshire Archives Service, Beverley, journal of military transactions in the East Indies

Dalton, John (1766–1844), chemist and natural philosopher, was born (by his own account) on 6 September 1766 at Eaglesfield, near Cockermouth in Cumberland, second of the four children and second son of Joseph Dalton, a weaver, and Deborah Greenup. His parents had married in 1755; both were members of the Society of Friends.

Early life and education Dalton went first to a Quaker school at Pardshaw Hall, run by a Mr John Fletcher. The family was not well off (although it had some better-off distant connections) and at the age of ten, to gain a livelihood, he entered the service of Elihu *Robinson (1734–1809). Robinson actively encouraged the young Dalton's aptitude for study, and in 1778 Dalton set up a school on his own account—first in a barn at Eaglesfield and then in

John Dalton (1766–1844), by Thomas Phillips, 1835

the Quakers' meeting-house. He taught children of all ages from toddlers to unruly youths, and took every opportunity to educate himself. (He once copied out a number of the *Ladies' Diary* which came his way, possibly his first acquaintance with any sort of literature of science.)

After two years the school failed and Dalton survived as an agricultural labourer until, at the age of fifteen, he joined his brother Jonathan as assistant in a school at Kendal, run by his cousin George Bewley. On Bewley's retirement, in 1785, they took over the school and ran it themselves, but with only moderate success. In spite of help and encouragement by the Dalton family, the school did not grow. The discipline was stern and Dalton was, by nature, more of a student than a rigorous classroom teacher. However, he was skilled at individual tuition, a fact that was to be much noticed and valued later on in his career.

Dalton also gave, for small fees, lectures on scientific topics; a syllabus issued by him in 1787 offered tuition in mechanics, pneumatics, astronomy, and the use of globes. In this enterprise he was following the example of the many itinerant lecturers of his time, from some of whom he learned a good deal more basic science. He was not, however, just a receptacle for other people's knowledge. He was able to test his own capacity by answering questions in the *Gentleman's Diary* and the *Ladies' Diary*, and so for the first time saw his work in print.

From his earliest days, encouraged and instructed by Elihu Robinson, Dalton was an assiduous observer, in natural history and (most importantly for his eventual fame)

in meteorology. As a member of the Society of Friends Dalton benefited from the interest taken in him by other Quakers of comfortable means, especially John Gough's encouragement and tuition. Gough (1757–1825) was the blind philosopher of Wordsworth's *Excursion*, from whom Dalton learned a little Latin, Greek, and French, and some higher mathematics. Gough also encouraged him to enter his meteorological observations in a journal, which he did to the last day of his life. He had some skill (though not remarkable) with his hands, supplying a fellow enthusiast, Peter Crosthwaite, with a rough and ready barometer and thermometer of his own construction so that simultaneous observations could be made at Kendal and at Keswick. A particular object of these simultaneous observations was the aurora, displays of which he and friends continued to record for many years.

Encouragement of Dalton by fellow Quakers stopped short, however, of urging social advancement. He hoped to improve himself by entering a learned profession, either the law or medicine. Gough was gentle in his discouragement, Dalton's London barrister uncle, Thomas Greenup, harsh but realistic. He said that there was no hope of entry into the superior professions for one of Dalton's social status, though he might have some hope of entering the corresponding occupations of lower status, apothecary or attorney. However, Dalton's opening to a future of fame (and a comfortable living, if not a fortune) came in the 1790s through developments taking place in the rapidly growing industrial town of Manchester.

Arrival in Manchester There had been for some time a concentration of intellectual activity in the north-west: the Warrington Academy had flourished under Joseph Priestley and Manchester itself had been a fertile ground for communities, formal and informal, of men of scientific and literary learnings, or of religious or political persuasion. Some were professional, some were industrialists; all were convinced of the need for extending opportunities for education in their area. These had necessarily to be different from, and alternative to, the traditional centres at the old universities. In Manchester a group of Unitarians had set up Manchester Academy (later renamed New College) in 1786. In addition, a strongly felt need for some alternative to the learned societies of the metropolis led to the founding, in 1781, of the Manchester Literary and Philosophical Society (almost always referred to as the Lit. and Phil.).

In 1793 Dalton was offered (at the suggestion of several leading Manchester citizens and of Gough) a post as professor of mathematics and natural philosophy at Manchester Academy, and thus went to live in a town which had surprised him, when he first got to know it, as being made mostly of brick. As soon as he was settled in his new post he joined the Literary and Philosophical Society, being known already to those members who had been responsible for bringing him to Manchester. He put up with the post for only a few years, because the pay was too little and the conditions uncongenial, and he determined to live the life of a freelance. (The college was eventually moved to York in 1803 and Dalton would, in any case, have preferred to stay in Manchester.) Although he was now a lone worker, the Lit. and Phil. provided Dalton with an institutional base of greater value and distinction than the college, and was to be a central influence in his life (and he in its) for the rest of his days. From it he began to issue the many publications which marked the growth of an influence he could hardly have foreseen.

At first Dalton lived in the Manchester Academy building. Later following an invitation by the wife of an acquaintance (the Revd William Johns), he took lodgings with the family for the next thirty years, eventually staying on in the house in George Street when the family left Manchester in 1830. He lived a modest but not unsociable life, with the company of many friends, acquired for the most part through the Lit. and Phil. All his life these friends saw that he was well cared for, a task made easier by his habit of living a life of strict regularity. It was said that a neighbour could set his watch by observing the moment at which Dalton opened a window to read a thermometer.

Early publications At Kendal Dalton had accumulated a number of papers which appeared in 1793 under the title *Meteorological Reflections and Essays*. This contained not only a record of his unremitting observations but also inferences of the causes of the meteorological phenomena so exposed. These reflections, which inevitably concerned the relation between air, water, and water vapour, played an important part in the evolution of his future theories. They had been set in print while Dalton was living in Kendal however, when he moved they were still only in proof, and were therefore published in Manchester. This (fortuitously) served to identify him as a Manchester man.

The book began with a description of the instruments needed for observation. There followed a series of typical observations and essays on their interpretation. Then a more interesting section on the aurora showed Dalton's breadth of experience with many instruments, even including work with a new design of theodolite. The final section interpreted the findings of the earlier sections, offering theories and speculations, including one of great ingenuity—proposing that the aurora is of electrical or magnetic origin. (This turned out to have been anticipated by Halley, but was none the less an excellent idea.) These essays were interesting but not remarkable enough to make any striking impression. However, with hindsight, they can be seen to contain the germs of many of the ideas which Dalton later developed into striking innovations.

Dalton soon became accepted as a natural philosopher of local consequence by the presentation of some papers at the Lit. and Phil., and by their publication in its new *Memoirs*. The earliest, of 1794 and 1799, consolidated his Manchester reputation: three papers of 1803 gave him a European reputation.

The first paper, of 1794, was on colour vision. Dalton achieved the extraordinary feat of detecting in himself and showing how to detect the fact that some people observed colours with more limited discrimination than others. (The colour vision phenomenon, although now known to be more complex than Dalton supposed, is termed Daltonism in some countries.) Not surprisingly, in following papers, he reverted to the kind of subject which had dominated the *Essays*—the behaviour of air and vapours, the kernel, it may be, of later ideas, but not yet presented in any distinctive way. He took a step forward in March 1799 in a paper which examined the question of the origin of springs. Why did springs continue to run? Where did their water come from? Dalton was able to relate the continuous replenishment of springs to the succession of rainfall, thereby initiating (if crudely) the quantitative study of what is now spoken of as the hydrological cycle. For example, he devised a simple way of estimating the quantity of flow of water in a river. A paper the following month challenged Rumford's assertion of 1798 that heat is transferred in liquids only by convection. This was all good, though not outstanding, work which demonstrated Dalton's ability to find the right quantitative approach to qualitative problems.

Dalton's next papers showed that quality so well and applied it to problems of such importance that they were soon reprinted in other journals in France and in Germany. He became an international figure, at a remarkable speed for the time. Even so, his most striking contribution to scientific thought was yet to come. Over the next decade he made successive contributions to areas already seen to be central to understanding of the physical world and requiring elucidation—the physics of fluids and gases. Although the greatest fame came, almost incidentally, from his theory of the fundamental determinant of chemical composition (an atomic theory), it was his search for an explanation of some physical phenomena that led him to this radical contribution to the whole theory and practice of chemistry.

Dalton's earlier work had followed the eighteenth-century concern for the study of gases and vapours, discoveries being made in the quantitative behaviour of individual gases. The seventeenth-century Boyle's law was already familiar and other relations were discovered. Some prominent problems, however, related to mixtures of gases, and mixtures of gases and vapours. For example, air was shown by Lavoisier to have two components, oxygen and nitrogen: were they mixed or chemically combined? Another subject for investigation was water vapour in the atmosphere: was it dissolved in some way, or chemically combined? Dalton wrote a paper in *Nicholson's Journal* in 1801 and more extensively in the *Memoirs* of the Lit. and Phil. In these papers, published between 1801 and 1803, he held that each gas in a mixture of two gases behaves as if the other were not there: that the pressure of a gas mixture is made up of the sum of the partial pressures of the components. His view was challenged and controverted but it could not be ignored. This law of partial pressures was not his only discovery. He established the law of the thermal expansion of gases but his French contemporaries were quick to point out that it had been put forward by J. A. C. Charles about 1787 and, although not published, had been communicated to Gay-Lussac. However, it took Dalton to see its significance and put it into context.

When Dalton arrived in Manchester in 1793, he became a permanent member of a community he already knew, one well established by some very able people including the Henry family. Thomas Henry (1734–1816) had built up a good business by the application of scientific judgements and knowledge. His son William (1774–1836) carried on a family pattern and did scientific work of lasting value, besides promoting the development of science by writing a good textbook and trading in instruments. William Henry and Dalton worked in parallel and together, but in different styles. Henry was probably the better experimenter, and was able to establish one fact of value to Dalton: he showed that water dissolves the same volume of gas whatever the pressure (Henry's law). Its significance to Dalton was that it supported his overall mechanical view of the thermal and physical properties of gases and vapours.

Atoms and atomic weights It remains uncertain how Dalton arrived at the idea which was to change the philosophy of chemistry: he may have been led to it by reflection on such problems as the difference between the composition of a mixture of oxygen and nitrogen and a compound of oxygen and nitrogen; he must also have been familiar with the results of other investigators' work on the quantitative composition of many other compounds; and it is possible that he was led to it by seeking purely mechanical explanations of the behaviour of gases. The results he produced went beyond all this. The destruction of so much of his remaining papers in an air raid of 1940 may well make it impossible ever to arrive at an entirely satisfactory explanation of his mental processes. Be that as it may, he decided to make a remarkable addition to his paper of 21 October 1803 when it was in proof:

> An enquiry into the relative weights of the ultimate particles of bodies is a subject, as far as I know, entirely new: I have lately been prosecuting this enquiry with remarkable success. The principle cannot be entered upon in this paper, but I shall just subjoin the results, as far as they appear to be ascertained by my experiments.

There follows the first rudimentary table of atomic weights. Dalton did not at first use the word atom in the sense which it acquired soon after and retained until the early twentieth century. His earlier discussion is, like those of Newton and other earlier corpuscular philosophers, in terms of particles. What was original in Dalton was not 'atom' but 'atomic weight'. The atomic constitution of matter was a very old idea, classical in origin: it was not new even to Newton, whose 'solid, hard massy' particles were a restatement of old ideas. Vague and unsatisfactory theories of the constitution of compounds had been put forward, for example by William Higgins, but were of too little use to have gained any currency. Dalton's theory was clear and useful. Arguing from physical properties he identified the origin of chemical distinctness, and showed how the chemical distinctness of compounds could be attributed to a simple natural characteristic: each element is composed of atoms, identical with all the other atoms of that element. A compound of two elements is composed of units each consisting of small whole numbers of atoms. What was then original in Dalton was not that atoms exist, but that each element is distinguished by the characteristic weight of the atoms of which it is composed and that this characteristic proportionate weight can be determined by systematic quantitative analysis.

It took even Dalton himself some time to appreciate the full significance of his own work. The diffusion of the atomic weight theory took some years. He discussed the list of atomic weights appended to his October 1803 paper with Thomas Thomson, who drew attention to Dalton's views in his own publications and eventually became a positive advocate of his theories. Dalton also put them forward in several important lectures, as at the Royal Institution and in Edinburgh and Glasgow.

After some caution Dalton committed himself to a major statement in his own large work, of 1808. He entitled it (with perhaps a touch of conceit in imitation of the title of Newton's masterpiece) *A New System of Chemical Philosophy*. It appeared in several parts, of which the first part of volume one was important, the second part (published in 1810) less so, and the second volume, which appeared in 1827, out of date and out of touch.

In the formal presentation of his ideas there began to appear a rigidity in Dalton's character which, in spite of fame, later prevented him from continuing lifelong leadership in the scientific world. For example, it was necessary to show on paper the composition of substances as determined by analysis, to show how many atoms of one element combined with how many atoms of another element or elements to form a compound. Dalton had a good visual imagination, but he let it tie him down to showing these compositions pictorially: one atom would be shown as a circular symbol, another by another kind of circle, and so on. The constituent particle of a compound would be depicted by a conjunction of two or more of these circles. One justification for this was Dalton's adherence to the belief that heat was a kind of fluid ('caloric') and that the heat in, say, a gas, resided in the atmospheres of caloric surrounding each constituent atom. These symbols were clumsy to produce, to reproduce, and to discuss. The great Swedish chemist Berzelius accepted the best in Dalton's theory and devised a simple letter notation (the H_2O, H_2SO_4 notation) which eventually became almost universally accepted. Dalton rejected this and so disqualified himself from taking as useful a part as he might in the great dialogue on chemical composition which was to be one of the features of nineteenth-century science.

Character Nevertheless, as with many a good man, Dalton's defects did not diminish his personal influence. It was not easy to take to him at first acquaintance, but he was liked, and even cherished. Above middle height, he always wore Quaker clothes, and was severe but neat in appearance. His speech was gruff, but his choice of language clear and, even in discussion of abstruse scientific matters, lucid and intelligible. Many anecdotes survive to illustrate his humanity, such as one relating the astonishment of a French visitor who came to pay respects to the great investigator and found him giving a lesson in elementary arithmetic to a small boy. It is also told, of a student who required a certificate of attendance at a course of Dalton's and had missed one of the lectures, that when he asked Dalton for a certificate Dalton declined but invited him to come back so that Dalton could repeat the lecture to this audience of one and so qualify him.

Dalton never married but was at ease with women, particularly educated women, and they in turn were at ease with him. In the personal reminiscences of many people who met him throughout his life there are tales of his courteous behaviour to women, a concern for their well-being and, towards some, a warm affection that might, in another man of his time, have led observers to predictions of marriage. However, when asked why he did not marry he replied that he had never had time.

As a lecturer Dalton could not match contemporary experts such as Davy and Faraday, but he spoke well enough to be asked back to many of his venues. Among many friends, Peter Ewart, a Scottish engineer settled in Manchester, was close to much of Dalton's experimental effort and helped him with the making of apparatus. One of Ewart's products is of particular importance—a set of small balls fitted with holes and spokes, which Dalton said he used to illustrate his theories of combination. They survive in the Science Museum, South Kensington, compact evidence of a good relationship. They were probably more than toys: twentieth-century chemists have made use of structural models very similar in principle to Dalton's.

Although much of Dalton's material is lost, enough of his correspondence survives, intact or in quotation, to reveal that he was a good correspondent, keeping in touch with friends and colleagues including some of his French acquaintance. His style was Quaker to his Quaker friends, the usual forms of address being used for others. This applied also to his conversation, switching to and from Quaker usage as his sense of courtesy required.

As his reputation grew and he was invited more and more into learned circles Dalton developed good relationships far and wide. The most intimate lay in Manchester and in his old Cumbrian home territory. In London he enjoyed the company of men he could admire. He respected Davy, who returned his respect without accepting all Dalton's theories. His greatest admiration was for William Hyde Wollaston (1766–1828), who came nearest of any of Dalton's immediate contemporaries to seeing what might be the deeper significance of the atomic weight concept and the structural concepts it implied. He did not, however, follow through his arguments about what was essentially crystal structure in his Bakerian lecture of 1812, and a scientific chance was lost.

Further lecturing, later papers, and the Lit. and Phil. Outside his regular basic teaching Dalton presented many lecture courses of the kind which was of particular importance in his day in promoting the scientific education of an influential section of a community going through what is now called the industrial revolution. The lecture content was not the simple science of his schoolmaster days; it was of the kind sought by the group who created the important societies of the day, such as the Lit. and Phil. in Manchester and the Royal Institution in London. At first he had lectured as an employee of a college, but after seeking his freedom he behaved as did other professional lecturers, living on fees. He offered practical demonstrations in his lectures and gradually increased his repertoire by buying apparatus, not only in Manchester but also elsewhere, when his lecturing travels took him to cities which could sustain a scientific instrument trade. Those who saw a need for useful science were prepared to pay for it. Dalton's professional, fee-attracting, lecturing career lasted from his early Manchester days to 1835 when he no longer needed to work hard to gain a livelihood.

Dalton's lectures were not merely reports of other people's work, though he was grateful in his early days for the opportunity for extensive reading offered by Manchester's Chetham's Library, which he greatly admired. He included in many of his lectures his own views, some of which were new ideas based on his own experimental studies, the detail of which were presented for a large part in his papers to the Lit. and Phil. but also in other journals, which were increasing in number. He gave important series in Manchester in 1808, 1811, 1814, and 1820, and became well known and welcome in Leeds, another growing industrial town, as well as in Edinburgh and Glasgow.

Although Glasgow and Edinburgh could each claim a long scientific tradition, and Manchester was creating one of its own, it was still in London that the largest concentration of scientific interest and talent was to be found. There were two main foci, the Royal Society and the Royal Institution. Although the Royal Institution was not unique in its constitution or objectives it was blessed with the presence of genius—Humphry Davy and then his successor, Michael Faraday. In 1804 Dalton was invited to lecture there to an audience which expected excellence, and, although they found Dalton's gruff manner very different from the fluency of Davy, the material presented was good enough for Dalton to be asked back again. Dalton modestly asked Davy to advise him on style and manner, which Davy did with charm and courtesy, and effectively.

Only fragments of the texts of Dalton's lectures survive. Each fragment and syllabus shows that he covered a wide range of topics, sufficient to give the listener a balanced view of the state of physical science of the day. They also dealt with matters which were under continuous scrutiny and experimental study, including those very questions to which Dalton's contributions had brought him his international reputation.

Dalton's eminence in scientific thought did not yet place him at the centre of national scientific policy making, but in Manchester he became part of the local policy establishment. He was secretary of the Lit. and Phil. from 1800 to 1809, when he became vice-president. On the death of Thomas Henry the obvious successor to the presidency was his son William; however, William, who had worked closely with Dalton, advised that it be offered to the latter, who subsequently held the office until his death. During his long membership the Lit. and Phil. was housed in a semi-permanent home in which Dalton was able to keep his papers and apparatus, and to carry on his experimental work for many years, as if it had been a personal domain.

Dalton's attitude to his own publications marks the several elements of his character and his changing attitude to the society in which he lived. The first appearance of his name in a magazine helped Dalton feel he had a toe in the wider world, and gave him practice in self-expression, disciplined by his conversion of his records of meteorological observations into a personal interpretation. He made his move to Manchester while the *Essays*, based on the observations of a young man, were turning into the work of a mature Manchester man. He thought highly of his own work in this field—too highly, it seems, because later in life when he sought to restore a reputation beginning to look old-fashioned he merely republished the work, at a time when everything in it had already been digested into the general body of science and his observational methods looked primitive and out-dated.

As an officer of the Lit. and Phil. Dalton would have been expected to offer papers from time to time, and his record is substantial. Of the more than 130 papers he is recorded as having read, more than thirty were published in the *Memoirs*. They changed little in character, while scientific publication at large was acquiring more and more of the modern style of presentation of results for criticism. Dalton's main contributions to the progress of physical science were concentrated in the years 1800 to 1810. He was a good physicist but his influence was eventually more on chemistry, to overall progress in which he never managed to come to terms.

Travels and honours Dalton enjoyed his Manchester life and appears to have been proud of living in a growing community and not to have minded the pervasive dirt and constant noise. All the same the open country of his youth drew him back regularly, to walk every year on the hills, to climb Helvellyn, and to recover the enjoyment of the natural world which had led him to the life of science in the first place.

In 1822 he was invited to Paris and met many of the great among the French scientific community. At dinner at Arcueil he met Laplace, Berthollet, Biot, Arago, and Fournier. Biot took him to the *Institut*, he met Ampère at his laboratory, and Cuvier at the museum. Some French colleagues had criticized his work, but so had some of his countrymen. Scientific life is like that: criticism and respect go hand in hand, and on only one occasion did Dalton respond sharply to comment, when James Forbes misunderstood his lifelong devotion to daily recording.

Dalton was much and appropriately honoured during his maturity, when the influence of his great work was fully appreciated. Apart from his Manchester community the French were the first to mark him out, with election in 1816 as a corresponding member of the Académie des Sciences; in 1830, after the death of Humphry Davy, they accorded him the great honour of electing him one of its eight foreign associates. He was also elected an honorary member of scientific societies in Berlin, Munich, and Moscow, and in Britain to many provincial societies, for example, in Bristol, Cambridge, Leeds, and Sheffield. He had declined the honour of election to the Royal Society in 1810, perhaps on the grounds of expense, but in 1822 he accepted election to fellowship.

It is an irony that although his relatives thought the higher level of social standing were beyond the young man, the older Dalton was honoured by degrees awarded by two universities, Oxford and Edinburgh. The last thing his relatives would have expected was that he would be presented at court, an event that was engineered by Babbage in 1834 when Dalton visited London to sit for the celebrated sculptor Francis Chantrey, who had been commissioned to portray him. Here a Quaker problem arose: Dalton could not wear court dress, which included a sword, so he abandoned for once his sober black Quaker garb and appeared in the red robe of his Oxford doctorate. Whether, with his colour vision defect, he realized how striking he must have looked remains a conjecture.

In 1826 George IV created the Royal Society's royal medal, of which Dalton was the first recipient. The way in which it was presented illustrates the way in which appreciation of scientific achievement changes as new ideas become absorbed into the body of knowledge. In 1804 Davy had rejected Dalton's mixed gas theories but in 1826, as president of the Royal Society, he spoke of him as having made chemistry amenable to simple arithmetic. This sounds like faint praise but Davy had got it right. Dalton's physical studies had made it possible for chemistry to develop a quantitative self-consistency which it had lacked before Dalton had introduced the concept of atomic weight.

In his home town of Manchester Dalton was already the acknowledged and elected leader of its scientific community, so some other form of honour had to be contrived: a public appeal for contributions was launched which raised the 2000 guineas asked for as a fee by Francis Chantrey. The statue he created was placed in 1838 in the Royal Manchester Institution. A copy in bronze was later placed in front of the Manchester Royal Infirmary. Some critics thought it exaggerated in its noble character—that the man had been a warmer, kindlier one than Chantrey's stern image suggested. Dalton's warmth, his enquiring eye, his dry expression, come out in other portraits and caricature sketches. The most interesting portraits from the point of view of the historian of science are the daguerreotypes that were made, soon after the invention of the process.

The younger Dalton appears to have been a most admirable progressive character; the older Dalton showed a sad inability to recognize that time passes, and that the conduct of science was changing. Dalton's imagination seems to have been visual and pictorial, as is seen in his observer's response to nature, and his representation of atomic arrangements, but there was much in physical science that needed more than the visual to interpret it. The visual came back with stereochemistry, but not until a generation after Dalton's death.

Dalton continued teaching and consultation, not yet having any other considerable source of income to relieve him of the burden of gainful work. One of his pupils was James Joule, but the instruction never reached the point at which it could be said that Dalton had inspired Joule to any of his later brilliant work. The personal impression, however, was considerable, and the fact that there was even a little communication between two such great personalities adds a touch of the romantic to a Manchester tradition.

In 1834 there was at last a change in his fortunes, brought about by the death of Dalton's brother Jonathan, from whom the modest family estate passed to John. He now had the means to set up house on his own after a lifetime of being a boarder. He found a housekeeper, and more importantly a friend, in Peter Clare, a skilled watchmaker and mechanic, who had helped him develop apparatus and now helped him sustain the burdens of a life becoming increasingly difficult. Dalton continued to attend meetings, and, almost to his last days, to read the occasional paper, on the subject he had always cared about more than any other—meteorology. Dalton had been hurt by an attack made on him in 1832 by James Forbes, the young, confident professor of natural philosophy at Edinburgh, who derided the old-fashioned recording of daily data and called for new methods of meteorological study. Forbes spoke of Dalton as if he had always been primarily a chemist and had done a little meteorology as a sideline. Dalton countered, ill-advisedly, by issuing, in 1834, a reprint of his 1793 *Meteorological Essays*. However, in the last paper he ever gave, Dalton showed a characteristic magnanimity by speaking well of Forbes's work. He was bitterly hurt by one event: he submitted a paper on arsenates to the Royal Society which was rejected as being of insufficient quality. He had it printed at his own expense, and added the lament: 'Cavendish, Davy and Wollaston are no more'.

Even though his scientific work could not keep up with new discoveries and methods Dalton was able to go along with changes in the relations between scientists. His progress in scientific esteem had been marked by his successive enrolment into existing scientific circles and societies. In his later years he was prominent in a new creation, the British Association for the Advancement of Science, which had been founded in protest at the alleged inadequacy of a scientific establishment dominated by the Royal Society. Dalton was present at the first meeting of the British Association, held in York in 1831. At this he urged that the association should never meet in London because the future of British science lay in its encouragement in the provinces. The dignity of the association was guaranteed by its meeting in Oxford in 1832, at which meeting the university awarded Dalton an honorary DCL degree.

Dr Dalton, as he now was, continued to keep a contented balance between national dignity and provincial informality. His recreation was walking, and he enjoyed an occasional game of bowls at his favourite inn, the Dog and Partridge. He was not a solitary man; whether walking the hills, working with William Henry, or just enjoying a pipe, he was approachable, and was consulted particularly by industrialists who found him ready to help solve chemical problems that arose in their manufactures. The new gas industry, for example, offered him particular interest.

Pension and final years In 1829 Brewster, Babbage, and others considered Dalton's continued hard work in the classroom, and came to the conclusion that, even though he might choose to labour in this way, he ought to have a basic income to allow him to act freely. Backed up by Brougham and others they therefore petitioned for a civil-list pension for Dalton and in 1833 succeeded in obtaining £150 a year for him. This was increased to £300 in 1836. From then on Dalton could enjoy the certainty of financial comfort, but he had eventually to accept the physical burdens of old age. He continued to attend meetings but needed the helping arm of friends. He suffered a number of strokes but defiantly continued his scientific life, making the last, unfinished entry in his meteorological diary on 27 July 1844, the day of his death. He had expressed a wish that his eyes be examined after his death to see if anything could be discovered about his colour vision defect. This was done but nothing was found that shed light on what remained a mystery.

The Manchester public authorities thought Dalton's passing should be marked by public demonstration. His coffin lay in state in the town hall, as Lyon Playfair wrote, 'like a king' (T. W. Reid, *Memoirs and Correspondence of Lyon Playfair*, 1899, 58). Forty thousand people are reported to have filed past it to pay tribute. On 12 August the funeral cortège numbered a hundred coaches and was a mile long. Dalton was buried in Ardwick cemetery.

In addition to bequests to friends and relatives Dalton's will had made provision for the endowment of a chair at Oxford, but a late codicil provided instead for the Johns family, who had fallen on hard times. His intellectual legacy remains: he was one of the first of the modern type of professional scientist, the man who combines the study of the external world with the duty to instruct and with his own need to gain a livelihood. Without any help from the great universities, the established church, or the wealth of an old-established family, he made, on his own, a career in which he brought about as profound a change in the nature of physical science as any one man has ever done.

FRANK GREENAWAY

Sources E. Patterson, *John Dalton and the atomic theory* (1970) · J. R. Partington, *A history of chemistry*, 3 (1962) · J. R. Partington, *A history of chemistry*, 4 (1964) · H. Lonsdale, *The worthies of Cumberland*, 5 (1874) · F. Greenaway, *John Dalton and the atom* (1966) · D. S. L. Cardwell, ed., *John Dalton and the progress of science* (1968) · A. Thackray, *John Dalton: critical assessments of his life and science* (1972) · A. Thackray, 'Dalton, John', *DSB* · A. Wurtz, *A history of chemical theory from the age of Lavoisier to the present time*, ed. and trans. H. Watts (1869) · A. Thackray, introduction, in H. E. Roscoe and A. Harden, *A new view of the origin of Dalton's atomic theory*, facs. edn (1970)
Archives JRL, corresp. and papers · RBG Kew, herbarium · Sci. Mus., meteorological register

Likenesses J. Lonsdale, oils, 1825, Manchester University · W. Brockedon, chalk drawing, 1834, NPG · F. Chantrey, pencil sketches, 1834, NPG · T. Phillips, oils, 1835, NPG [*see illus.*] · F. Chantrey, marble statue, exh. RA 1837, Royal Institution, Manchester · H. Cardwell, marble bust, *c.*1840, Christie Library, Manchester · C. Jordan, watercolour drawing, *c.*1840, Manchester Medical Society · B. R. Faulkner, oils, *c.*1840–1841, RS · Nicklin, daguerreotypes, 1842, Man. CL · W. Theed junior, statue, 1854, Piccadilly, Manchester · J. Allen, oils, Manchester Literary and Philosophical Society · F. Chantrey, marble statue, Royal Institution, Manchester · F. Chantrey, plaster bust, AM Oxf. · C. Turner, engraving, Man. CL · oils (after J. Allen, 1816), Salford City Art Gallery · watercolour drawing, Scot. NPG

Wealth at death £8000; plus real estate: Patterson, *John Dalton*; Lonsdale, *Worthies of Cumberland*

D'Alton, John (1792–1867), historian, son of William D'Alton, was born at his father's family home, Bessville, co. Westmeath, Ireland, on 29 June 1792. His mother, Elizabeth Leyne, was also descended from an ancient Irish family. D'Alton was sent to the school of the Revd Joseph Hutton, Summerhill, Dublin, and passed the entrance examination of Trinity College, Dublin, in 1806. He became a student in 1808, joined the college historical society, and gained the prize for poetry. Having graduated at Dublin, he was in 1811 admitted a law student of the Middle Temple, London, and King's Inns, Dublin. He was called to the Irish bar in 1813.

D'Alton confined himself chiefly to chamber practice. He published an able treatise on tithes, *The history of tithes, church lands, and other ecclesiastical benefices: with a plan for the abolition of the former, and the better distribution of the latter*, in Dublin in 1832. He attended the Connaught circuit, having married a Miss Phillips, from that province. His reputation as a genealogical researcher won him lucrative employment, and he received many fees in the important Irish causes such as *Malone v. O'Connor, Leamy v. Smith*, and *Jago v. Hungerford*. He wrote a short *Memoir of the Family of French* (1847). With the exception of an appointment in 1834 as commissioner of the loan fund board, he held no official position, but a pension of £50 a year on the civil list, granted in 1856, was some recognition of his literary abilities. His first publication was a metrical poem called *Dermid, or, Erin in the Days of Boru*. It was published in a substantial quarto in twelve cantos in 1814. In 1827 the Royal Irish Academy offered a prize of £80 and the Cunningham gold medal for the best essay on the social and political state of the Irish people from the arrival of Christianity to the twelfth century, based on works of medieval literature, excluding those in Irish or other Celtic languages. Full extracts were to be given and all original authorities consulted. D'Alton obtained the highest prize, with the medal.

D'Alton's 'Essay on the ancient history, religion, learning, arts and government of Ireland from the birth of Christ to the English invasion', which was read on 24 November 1828, was published in volume sixteen of the *Transactions of the Royal Irish Academy*. In 1831 he also gained the prize offered by the Royal Irish Academy for an account of the reign of Henry II in Ireland. He then employed himself in collecting information regarding prehistoric and medieval antiquities, including the ruins

of castles and abbeys. These formed the basis for short pieces on Irish topography contributed to the *Irish Penny Journal*, with drawings by Samuel Lover. In 1838 D'Alton published his valuable *Memoirs of the Archbishops of Dublin*. In the same year he published an exhaustive *History of the County of Dublin*. His next work was a beautifully illustrated book, *The History of Drogheda, with its Environs* (1844), containing an account of the Dublin and Drogheda Railway, with a history of the progress of locomotion in Ireland. Shortly afterwards followed *The history of Ireland from the earliest period to the year 1245, when the annals of Boyle, which are adopted, as the running text authority, terminate* (1845). Lord Lorton, the proprietor of Boyle, contributed £300 towards the publication. In 1855 D'Alton published *Illustrations, Historical and Genealogical of King James's Irish Army List* (1689), which contained the names of most prominent Irish families of distinction, with historical and genealogical illustrations. Subsequent enlarged volumes brought the history of most families up to the date of publication.

In 1864 D'Alton was asked to write the *History of Dundalk*. He had prepared the earlier part of this work, but as his strength was failing, it was entrusted to J. R. O'Flanagan, who wrote the section covering the sixteenth to the nineteenth centuries. D'Alton's starkly factual approach probably impaired the literary success of his books.

In his last years D'Alton's ill health confined him to his house, but he was very hospitable, loved society, and was a talented singer. He occupied himself towards the end of his life in writing an autobiography, which was never published. He died on 20 January 1867 at his home, Summerhill, Dublin. J. R. O'FLANNAGAN, *rev.* MICHAEL HERITY

Sources *Proc. RIA*, 10 (1866–9), 46–50 · *The Post* (21 Jan 1867) · personal knowledge (1888) · *CGPLA Eng. & Wales* (1867) · Burtchaell & Sadleir, *Alum. Dubl.*

Archives Chicago University, Joseph Regenstein Library, corresp. and papers · NL Ire., corresp. and papers · Royal Irish Acad. · TCD, letters to his wife | Bodl. Oxf., corresp. with Sir Thomas Phillipps

Likenesses watercolour, NG Ire.

Wealth at death under £1500: probate, 11 April 1867, *CGPLA Ire.*

Dalton, John (1814?–1874), Roman Catholic priest and writer, was of Irish parentage, and spent his early years at Coventry. After education at Sedgley Park School, near Wolverhampton, he entered St Mary's College, Oscott, in 1830, and was ordained priest there in 1840. He subsequently served on the missions at Northampton, Norwich, and King's Lynn, and became a member of the chapter of the diocese of Northampton. For some years from 1858 he resided at St Alban's College, Valladolid. After his return from Spain he settled at St John's Maddermarket, Norwich, where he spent the remainder of his life, with the exception of a brief interval in 1866, when Archbishop Manning sent him to Spain to collect subscriptions towards the erection in London of a cathedral in memory of Cardinal Wiseman.

Dalton was a man of wide culture who translated many works, mainly on spirituality, from Latin, Spanish, and

German. His publications included translations of Novalis, Bellarmine, Balmez, and St John of the Cross, but he is chiefly distinguished for his translation of six of the works of St Teresa of Avila, published between 1851 and 1856. He also translated C. J. von Hefele's *Life of Cardinal Ximenez* (1860) as well as a version of the manuscript 'Life of St Winifred' in the British Museum (1857). While at King's Lynn he commissioned A. W. Pugin to build a new church there, and published *A Few Remarks on the Revival of Church Architecture* (1843). Dalton died at St John's Maddermarket, Norwich, on 15 February 1874.

THOMPSON COOPER, *rev.* G. MARTIN MURPHY

Sources Gillow, *Lit. biog. hist.* · *Weekly Register and Catholic Standard* (28 Feb 1874) · *Norfolk Chronicle* (21 Feb 1874), 5

Dalton, John Neale (1839–1931), Church of England clergyman and royal tutor, was born on the Isle of Thanet, Kent, on 24 September 1839, the eldest of five sons (among nine children) of John Neale Dalton (1808–1880), a Church of England clergyman, and his wife (and first cousin), Eliza Maria (1807–1895), daughter of William Allies. The herald Lawrence *Dalton was an ancestor. He went from Blackheath proprietary school to Clare College, Cambridge, as a scholar, afterwards taking a first in theology. Bishop Samuel Wilberforce ordained him in 1865, and his first curacy was in his father's parish of Milton Keynes. He was next a curate in Cambridge (1866–9) and then at Whippingham on the Isle of Wight, where he impressed Queen Victoria during her residence at Osborne.

In 1871 Dalton was appointed tutor to Queen Victoria's grandsons Prince Albert Victor (Eddy), duke of Clarence and Avondale, and his younger brother Prince George, duke of York (afterwards George V). He proved more concerned with their moral character than with book learning. Dalton enforced a meticulously strict routine on the princes, and was obsessively concerned to stop errors or infractions. The princes were not, however, deeply or broadly educated. The narrowness of George V's outlook, and his excessive punctilio over formalities, may be attributable to Dalton's influence. As a royal tutor he became accomplished at artifice. By dissuading the queen from sending the older boy to public school, where he might be contaminated by vicious influences, Dalton ensured that he remained the princes' tutor while they were naval cadets on the *Britannia* at Dartmouth (1877–9).

Dalton again proved his aptitude at intrigue by securing the decision—despite opposition in the cabinet and from courtiers—to send the princes (then aged fourteen and fifteen) on a world cruise lasting three years (1879–82). The princes were thus removed from the influence of their family and the court and delivered wholly into the charge of Dalton, who accompanied them on HMS *Bacchante* as their chaplain and tutor. His account of this cruise published in 1886 covers 1518 pages; it is an ill-judged affair, by turns showy, pedantic, and self-glorifying. On the *Bacchante* Dalton was regarded as a martinet whose difficult temper disrupted the wardroom. He became jealous of the senior midshipman's intimacy with the princes, and having denounced 'his almost feminine ways', had him

sent away (Nicolson, 22). Although Prince Eddy became depressed during his long sojourn at sea, Prince George thrived. Dalton's *Sermons to Naval Cadets* was published in 1879.

At the end of the voyage Dalton was made CMG (1882) and governor to Eddy at Trinity College, Cambridge, until 1885. In 1884 he was nominated to a canonry at Windsor, which he held until his death. On 16 January 1886 he married Catherine Alicia (1863–1944), daughter of Charles Evan-Thomas, Glamorgan landowner and colliery proprietor, and sister of Admiral Sir Hugh Evan-*Thomas. They had a daughter and two sons, of whom the elder, (Edward) Hugh Neale *Dalton, became a leading Labour politician and the younger died at birth. Canon Dalton had a romantic interest, doubtless sublimated, in young men. He reorganized the Windsor choir school in 1892, and liked to terrify or charm its choristers.

Dalton caused much unrest during his forty-seven years at Windsor. His love of the buildings and traditions of St George's Chapel was wholehearted; but as the chapel's steward, responsible for managing its finances and protecting its fabric, he made his colleagues miserable. In obtaining his objects he was adamant and unscrupulous. 'Thank heavens there are two things I have never had; nerves or a conscience', he once exclaimed (Bolitho, 111). He was a bully and firebrand who shouted down colleagues who thwarted him. Perhaps, after his importance in the royal family and his years at sea, he was frustrated by the pettiness of cloister life; but certainly he seemed to revel in quarrels. The perversity of Dalton's behaviour was rooted in his social values. He was disrespectful of noblemen and contemptuous of his fellow clergy, but capable of geniality, patience, and humility with servants, poor or knavish youths, and pilfering or unlucky working men. When the poor of Windsor were unwell, he was an energetic and solicitous visitor. Finding the wife of a lodge keeper ill in bed, he got on his knees and scrubbed the kitchen floor for her.

Although the contents of Dalton's sermons were commonplace, no one could doze during them. The range of his voice from high falsetto to thunderous bass was remarkable. He loved the Bible, and his readings of its more dramatic passages ('My father hath chastised you with whips, but I will chastise you with scorpions', for example) were histrionic. He had severe but handsome features and stupendous physical vitality. He was a good Hebrew scholar (though detractors falsely claimed that he published a translation of the Psalms without knowing a word of Hebrew), but curiously ignorant of English literature. On church architecture and antiquarian subjects he could speak authoritatively. His rollicking manners—he was something of an expurgated Falstaff—had an outlet at dinners of the Drapers' Company, of which he was master in 1919–20.

Dalton accompanied Prince George, as prince of Wales, on his voyage to Australia (1901), and retained his pupil's devotion always; among other court appointments, he was domestic chaplain during George V's reign. He was created CVO in 1901 and promoted KCVO in 1911. Having read a lesson at evensong on 28 July 1931, he died of a stomach haemorrhage a few hours later that evening at his house in Windsor Castle cloisters. After cremation at Woking on 30 July, his ashes were interred in the south aisle of St George's Chapel on 31 July.

RICHARD DAVENPORT-HINES

Sources *The Times* (29 July 1931) · *The Times* (31 July 1931) · B. Pimlott, *Hugh Dalton* (1985) · H. Dalton, *Call back yesterday: memoirs, 1887–1931* (1953) · H. Bolitho, *Older people* (1935) · A. V. Baillie, *My first eighty years* (1951) · A. C. Deane, *Time remembered* (1945) · R. Thorndike, *Children of the Garter* (1937) · H. Nicolson, *King George V: his life and reign* (1952) · J. Gore, *King George V* (1941) · *The Athenaeum* (5 June 1886), 739–41 · b. cert. · Burke, *Peerage* · Burke, *Gen. GB* · *The Times* (27 March 1944) · Crockford · *University of Cambridge book of matriculations and degrees, 1851–1900* (1902), 153
Archives BLPES, MSS · LPL letters · Royal Arch. · St George's Chapel, Windsor, corresp. and MSS · Worcester College, Oxford, letters | Devon RO, letters to F. Hingeston-Randolph · King's AC Cam., letters to O. Browning · Trinity Cam., letters to H. Smith
Likenesses photograph, 1882, repro. in Pimlott, *Hugh Dalton*, p. 16
Wealth at death £6941 14s. 9d.: probate, 23 Sept 1931, *CGPLA Eng. & Wales*

Dalton, Lawrence (d. 1561), herald, was one of the thirteen children (eight sons and five daughters) of Roger Dalton (d. in or after 1527), of Bispham, near Croston, Lancashire, and his fourth wife, Jane Jakes of Berkhamsted, Hertfordshire; he also had two half-brothers and a half-sister from his father's first marriage. Not known to have attended a university, Lawrence Dalton was appointed Rouge Croix pursuivant on 15 November 1546, when Sir Christopher Barker, the husband of his aunt Ellen, was Garter king of arms. He was promoted to Richmond herald on 12 April 1547. On 15 January 1549 he offered to pay the other heralds 40s. towards the value of cloth which he had received from the great wardrobe on their behalf and embezzled. In August 1553 he accompanied Norroy in attending upon the army in Scotland. He received a royal pardon on 26 April 1556 for all usuries and taking of gifts from any subject and all consequent actions and bills against him in any court.

Dalton was created Norroy king of arms on 6 September 1557; the creation ceremony did not take place until 9 December 1558, and before then he made no grants of arms. In February 1558 Dalton and Rouge Dragon pursuivant went north to attend the earl of Westmorland on an expedition against the Scots. They remained at Newcastle and Berwick recording pedigrees and arms of prominent men in the north, returning to London in time for Dalton to officiate as Norroy at the funeral of Queen Mary on 12 December 1558. These pedigrees have never been counted at the College of Arms as an official visitation. Further pedigrees made for him in 1560–61 survive in the British Library (Add. MS 12466).

In November 1560 the other heralds accused Dalton of having the French pox and suggested that as a sick man he should have only half the fees of his office. He refused to answer their charges whereupon they resolved that they would neither eat nor drink with him and that he should have no profits of his office. He was reinstated by the earl marshal in early 1561 on the advice of two physicians and

received a commission to make a visitation of his province on 27 June 1561. In 1560 and 1561 he made over forty grants of arms, more than half of them to established families in Lancashire, his county of origin. His death was sudden; having granted a crest to Adam Hulton on 10 December 1561, he drew up his will on the 12th and died early next day. He was buried on the 15th at St Dunstan-in-the-West, London, where a memorial brass was attached to a pillar. Sketches of two different versions of it survive; both show him wearing a tabard and crown. Portraits on letters patent in the year of his death show him with reddish hair and a short beard. A detailed record survives of his funeral, which was attended by four unnamed sisters, two named brothers-in-law, and the whole office of arms. The funeral sermon, preached by Jean Véron, the vicar of St Martin Ludgate, commended him for his upright and just dealing with all men. His wife, Dorothy (d. 1596), daughter of Richard Breame of London, was the executor and sole beneficiary of his will, which was proved on 26 January 1562. Neither his will nor hers mentions any children.

THOMAS WOODCOCK

Sources [F. W. Dendy], ed., *Visitations of the north*, 1, SurtS, 122 (1912) · A. Wagner, *Heralds of England: a history of the office and College of Arms* (1967), 90, 113, 182n. · W. H. Godfrey, A. Wagner, and H. Stanford London, *The College of Arms, Queen Victoria Street* (1963), 110 · Coll. Arms, Old Partition MSS, misc. fols. 143–146b, 151 · Coll. Arms, MS letter, I.13, 32–3 [funeral certificate] · partition book, Coll. Arms, vol. 1, p. 128 · A. R. Wagner, *The records and collections of the College of Arms* (1952), 78–9 · C. B. Norcliffe, ed., *The visitation of Yorkshire in the years 1563 and 1564*, Harleian Society, 16 (1881), 85–8 · M. Noble, *A history of the College of Arms* (1804), 171–2 · will, 20 Dec 1596, PRO, PROB 11/88, sig. 87 [Dorothy Dalton, wife]
Archives BL, pedigrees collected for him as Norroy, Add. MS 12466 · Coll. Arms, collection of his grants of arms, MS 1 or 2 H6
Likenesses effigy (after drawing by unknown artist), repro. in Dendy, ed., *Visitations of the north*, frontispiece · effigy (after his memorial brass), St Dunstan-in-the-West, London; repro. in Dingley, *History from marble*, Camden Society (1868), vol. 2, p. 490/cccclvii · portrait, Coll. Arms, MS, Grant to William Partryche 1561; repro. in J. Dallaway, *Heraldry in England* (1793), pl. 12, facing p. 174

Dalton, Michael (1564–1644), barrister and legal writer, was born on 28 September 1564 at Linton, Cambridgeshire, the eldest son of Thomas Dalton (d. 1602) of Hildersham in the same county and Eleanor Jellebrand (d. 1616/17). Born to a gentry background, he had at least two brothers, Thomas (d. in or before 1619) and George, as well as several sisters. He matriculated from Trinity College, Cambridge, in January 1580 and entered Lincoln's Inn from Furnival's Inn on 25 November 1581. He was called to the bar on 24 November 1589 and in 1597 he served as a JP in the county of Essex. In July 1587 he married Frances (d. 1601), daughter of William Thornton, with whom he had three sons and six daughters. After Frances's death at West Wratting, Cambridgeshire, on 7 July 1601, he married on 27 July 1602 at Carlton in the same county Mary (1565–1647), daughter of Edward Elrington. Together they had two sons and three daughters.

Both the manor of Parys in Cambridgeshire and the improprietorship of the rectory of Little Abington in the same county fell to Dalton at his father's death in 1602. He served as a JP in his native county in 1602 and again in 1603 after the accession of James I. In 1604 he expanded his estates when Thomas Frenche conveyed to him the manor of Hammonds in Cambridgeshire, which was henceforth associated with the manor of Parys. In the same year he became deputy steward of the University of Cambridge.

In 1618 Dalton published a popular legal treatise for local magistrates and JPs entitled *The Countrey Justice*, for which he remains historically significant. The work was part of a larger established genre of English legal writing that included both Fitzherbert's *L'office et auctoritee de justices de peace* (1514, English translation 1538) and William Lambarde's *Eirenarcha* (1610). Practising JPs and other local magistrates used Dalton's book widely during the remainder of the early modern period, and it remains an important source for both local and legal historians of early modern England. A second edition appeared in 1619, a third in 1630, and a fourth edition (posthumously) in 1655, and the work remained in circulation into the eighteenth century, being reprinted in 1666, 1682, 1690, and 1742.

Shortly after the publication of *The Countrey Justice* Dalton's legal career flourished. On 1 August 1622 John Williams, bishop of Lincoln and lord keeper, named him one of the masters in chancery. Although the list of Sir Dufus Hardy does not confirm this appointment, the title-page of the 1655 edition of *The Countrey Justice* describes him as holding that office, and a document in the library of St John's College, Cambridge, gives the exact date of his appointment. Also in 1622 Dalton was associated to the bench of his inn. In 1623 he published an additional legal treatise entitled *Vicecomitum, or, The Office and Authoritie of Sheriffs*, which appeared in an abridged version in 1628 and was reprinted as late as 1700.

In 1631 Dalton was fined £2000 for having permitted his daughter Dorothy to marry her maternal uncle, Sir Giles Elrington of Horseheath, Cambridgeshire. This fine was later remitted. He may have been the Michael Dalton who in 1636 gave an enclosure called 'Hunts' to purchase coats for ten impoverished children. Apparently residing at West Wratting at the time of his death in November 1644, Dalton was buried there on 19 November. He was survived by his wife, Mary, and at least three of his children reached adulthood, Oliver (d. 1619) and Thomas (d. 1639), both of whom predeceased him, and a daughter, Dorothy, from his second marriage. He settled the reversion of the manor of Parys on his grandson Michael (son of Oliver), as well as the rectory of Little Abington upon the latter's marriage to Susan Tyrrell in 1639. A second grandson, also named Michael, was the son of Thomas. One of the grandsons was serving as a commissioner of sequestrations for the county of Cambridgeshire in 1648. D. A. ORR

Sources DNB · W. R. Prest, *The rise of the barristers: a social history of the English bar, 1590–1640* (1986), 354 · St John Cam., MS S. 27 (James 419) · Venn, *Alum. Cant.*, 1/3 · *VCH Cambridgeshire and the Isle of Ely*, vol. 6 · private information (2004) [Society of Genealogists] · M. Dalton, *The countrey justice* (1618)
Archives BL, 'Breviary of state of Roman church and empire', Add. MS 4359 · CUL, Breviary of state of Roman Church till Martin Luther · Inner Temple, London, papers · St John Cam., commonplace book, breviate of controversies, notes on office of JP · Yale U., Beinecke L., 'A breviary of the Roman (or Westerne) church and empire'
Likenesses M. Tyson, etching, 1623 (after C. Neve), BM, NPG · W. Marshall, line engraving, BM; repro. in *A manuall or Analecta*, 6th edn (1648)

Dalton, Ormonde Maddock (1866–1945), classical scholar and medieval archaeologist, was born in Cardiff on 3 January 1866, the second of the three sons of Thomas Masters Dalton, solicitor, and his wife, Emily Mansford. From Harrow School he won an exhibition at New College, Oxford, where he obtained a first class in classical moderations (1886) and in *literae humaniores* (1888). He then travelled in France and Germany, visited a brother's coffee plantation at north Coorg in India, and in 1894 taught at Abbotsholme School in Derbyshire.

In 1895 Dalton entered the department of British and medieval antiquities at the British Museum under Sir Wollaston Franks, and was promoted first class assistant in 1901 and assistant (later called deputy) keeper in 1909. In 1921 he became keeper of British and medieval antiquities when that very heterogeneous collection was separated from ceramics, ethnography, and oriental antiquities. He was conscientious in this role, the administrative side of which took away from his research, but he 'shirked no part of the task, and he was deeply respected for his charmingly courteous and sympathetic treatment of subordinates' (Hill, 14).

In the British Museum Dalton's first duties were ethnographical. He collaborated with Hercules Read in *Antiquities from the City of Benin* (1899) and with Thomas Athol Joyce in the *Handbook to the Ethnographical Collections* (1910). He became a fellow of the Royal Anthropological Institute in 1895, was honorary secretary and editor of its *Journal* from 1896 to 1897, and contributed to its publications. He was also elected a fellow of the Society of Antiquaries in 1899, served four times on its council, in 1900–22, and contributed important articles to *Archaeologia*; he was elected FBA in 1922. But Dalton's interest changed from ethnology to archaeology with his *Catalogue of Early Christian Antiquities* (1901), one of the British Museum's series of departmental catalogues which, because of the wealth of commentary in them, became standard works on the subjects concerned. This was followed by the official *Guide to the Early Christian and Byzantine Antiquities* (1903; 2nd edn, 1921), and his account of the *Treasure of the Oxus* (1905; 2nd edn, 1926) which had been acquired through Franks. He was one of the secretaries (with Robert Weir Schultz) of the Byzantine Research and Publication Fund which produced *The Church of the Nativity at Bethlehem* (1910), *The Church of Saint Eirene at Constantinople* (1913), and *The Church of Our Lady of the Hundred Gates* (1920), by various authors, and collected much still unpublished material.

Dalton's prolific output in the years before the First World War included his *Guide to the Mediaeval Room* (1907; rev. edn, 1924), the *Catalogue of the Ivory Carvings of the Christian Era* (1909), papers on the great Cyprus treasure of silver plate (*Archaeologia*, 57/1, 1900, and 60/1, 1906; *Burlington*

Magazine, March 1907), and the catalogue of the McClean bequest in the Fitzwilliam Museum, Cambridge (1912). They were followed by the *Catalogue of the Engraved Gems of the Post-Classical Periods … in the British Museum* (1915). But his most distinguished work is *Byzantine Art and Archaeology* (1911), an encyclopaedic survey of all fields of craftsmanship except architecture. This omission was repaired in his translation (with Hermann Justus Braunholtz) of Strzygowski's *Origin of Christian Church Art* (1923), and in *East Christian Art: a Survey* (1925). Other interests are represented by a translation (with introduction) of the *Letters of Sidonius* (2 vols., 1915), a translation (with a long introduction) of the *History of the Franks* by Gregory of Tours (2 vols., 1927), and an uncompleted version of the *Dialogues* and *Letters* of Sulpicius Severus.

Inveterate shyness limited Dalton's activities outside the British Museum, but at Bath, where he retired in 1928, he was an assiduous and generous, if sometimes awkward, host. Glimpses of his inner life are afforded by three books published under the pseudonym W. Compton Leith (*Apologia diffidentis*, 1908; *Sirenica*, 1913; and *Domus doloris*, 1919), certainly his, although never fully acknowledged. The third book contemplated the effect of pain in the disciplining of the mind and body, and was written during a period of convalescence after he was knocked down by a motor car and seriously injured. This accident ended his war work for the Admiralty, in which he had been engaged in map making. In official life he was courteous and kindly, a skilful collector and critic, of boundless industry and learning.

In 1940 Dalton moved to his cottage in the Quantocks, where he acquired unspoiled land and transferred it to the National Trust. He died at his home, White Cottage, Holford, Somerset, unmarried, on 2 February 1945, leaving his estate to New College to found a research scholarship.

J. L. MYRES, *rev.* MARK POTTLE

Sources *The Times* (7 Feb 1945) · G. Hill, 'Ormonde Maddock Dalton, 1866–1945', *PBA*, 31 (1945), 357–73 · *CGPLA Eng. & Wales* (1945) **Likenesses** W. Stoneman, photograph, 1925, NPG · photograph, repro. in Hill, 'Ormonde Maddock Dalton' **Wealth at death** £21,935 12s. 5d.: probate, 25 May 1945, *CGPLA Eng. & Wales*

Dalton, Richard (*c*.1715–1791), art dealer and librarian, was the son of the Revd John Dalton of Darlington, co. Durham, and younger brother of the Revd John *Dalton, rector of St Mary-at-Hill, London. Dalton was apparently apprenticed to a coach-painter at Clerkenwell, London, and travelled to Italy in 1739 to continue his studies as a painter, helped by his elder brother's connection with Algernon Seymour, earl of Hertford (later seventh duke of Somerset), working first at Bologna. By 1741 he was studying in Rome under Agostino Masucci. He produced at this time highly finished red chalk drawings after classical statues, of which a series, dated 1741–2, is in the Royal Collection. By July 1741 he was also active as a dealer, especially in prints, and had sold a collection, formed partly from that of the painter Francesco Imperiali, to Lord Lincoln. By May 1743 Dalton informed Horace Mann of a Raphael which was to be sold from the Cybo collection.

Richard Dalton (*c*.1715–1791), by Johan Zoffany, *c*.1765–8 [with his wife, Esther de Heulle, and their niece Mary de Heulle]

Dalton may have had business in Venice, as J. Clephane's letter-book records a letter of 7 August to 'Mr Smith at Venice for Dalton' (NA Scot., Rose of Kilravock MSS, 33/22(28)).

Dalton returned to London later in 1743. In 1747 he went again to Rome, with the artist Thomas Patch. In 1749–50 they were with the sculptors Joseph Wilton and Simon Vierpyl, the engraver James Basire, and the architect Matthew Brettingham the younger in the Palazzo Zuccari. Dalton also came to know the architect Robert Wood and the young Joshua Reynolds in Italy. In 1749 he was taken by Roger Kynaston and John Frederick on their tour of Sicily, where in May they met James Caulfield, first earl of Charlemont. Dalton was invited to join Charlemont's party as travelling draughtsman. The party travelled to Malta, Constantinople, Turkey, and Egypt, returning by way of Greece. The drawings Dalton made include the earliest visual records of a number of monuments. Seventy-nine were published in Dalton's *Musaeum Graeceum et Aegyptiacum* or *Antiquities of Greece and Egypt* (1751), of which there were further printings in 1752, 1781, and 1790: it was reissued in a definitive edition in 1791 as *Antiquities and views in Greece and Egypt … with manners and customs of the inhabitants from drawings made on the spot, A.D. 1749*. Dalton was in England by 1751.

In 1754 Dalton advertised that casts from the antique and prints after Raphael were available at his lodgings in Great Ryder Street, St James's, showing his desire to promote himself as an antiquary and dealer. In 1755 he was appointed librarian to the prince of Wales, later George

III, probably largely through the influence of John Stuart, third earl of Bute. Dalton's third visit to Italy in 1758–9 had the express aim of enriching the prince's collection in medals, drawings, and prints (and that of Bute), as well as to acquire pictures for Sir Richard Grosvenor, seventh baronet. Dalton's activities are detailed in letters to Bute and Grosvenor. He travelled through Germany to Bologna. By 4 July 1758 he had acquired a group of pictures for Grosvenor, including two attributed to Ludovico Carracci, and on 8 July he reported to Grosvenor about sales from the Arnaldi collection at Florence. On behalf of the prince of Wales he examined the Stosch collection of medals. Letters of October and November 1758 to Bute demonstrate that Dalton was buying drawings for both Grosvenor and the prince of Wales, including Guercino drawings from the Casa Gennari and the Baruffaldi collection of miniatures. A letter of 31 March 1759 reports Dalton examining in detail the drawings owned by Cardinal Albani, and in May Dalton referred to drawing collections in Venice, especially those of Joseph Smith (Consul Smith) and Zanetti. He also examined and purchased works by English artists resident in Italy.

With the accession of George III in 1760, Dalton's position as his librarian accordingly became more significant: he played a key role in acquiring works for the Royal Collection. Although the major acquisition, that of Consul Joseph Smith's collection, was arranged by Bute, Dalton was sent to Venice to supervise the negotiations, arriving there on 4 December 1762. Dalton visited Bologna in 1763, having been in Rome and Florence, and secured additional drawings from the Casa Gennari. In connection with the purchase the engraver Francesco Bartolozzi, whom Dalton met at this time, made a number of prints for him after drawings by Guercino. Dalton also attempted unsuccessfully to buy Poussin landscapes owned by the Aldrovandi family to add to those drawings already acquired for the Royal Collection from the Albani collection. Bute's resignation as prime minister in 1763 and withdrawal from public life slowed the pace of acquisitions for the Royal Collection in which Dalton had played such a crucial part. Dalton was also the first to engrave in line etching the series of portrait drawings by Hans Holbein which had been found by Queen Caroline at Kensington Palace. But his etchings were not a success and a more famous set of stipple engravings were later made by Bartolozzi (1792–1800).

On 25 June 1764 Dalton married Esther de Heulle (d. 1782). In 1765 he became treasurer of the newly formed Incorporated Society of Artists and was elected a fellow of the Society of Antiquaries in 1767. He also purchased large premises in Pall Mall for a print warehouse where, in 1767, an academy of arts, with the support of George III, was established. Dalton, with his patronage and support from the king, was involved in the art world politics which led to the foundation of the Royal Academy in 1768, and which also met during its early years at Dalton's Pall Mall premises. Dalton became an honorary Royal Academician and held the post of antiquary to the academy from 1770 to 1784.

Dalton and his wife went to Italy in 1768–9 with a Miss Robinson, visiting Venice and later Rome. In June 1769 they travelled with the painters James Forrester, George Robertson, and others to Caprarola before following the via Flaminia from Narni to Foligno and then crossing the Apennines to Loreto and Ancona, where they left Forrester's party. The Daltons went on to Florence, where Richard was caricatured by Thomas Patch. They then went back to Rome, where Dalton continued to act as a dealer and purchaser of works, particularly drawings. Less is known of his later years. He apparently returned to Italy in 1774–5 and with the death of George Knapton in 1778 was appointed surveyor of the king's pictures. During the 1770s and 1780s Dalton spent much of his time in England, where he was able to organize and catalogue much of the material he had acquired for the Royal Collection, and put many of the drawings into albums. However, the king was now taking less interest in pictures and Dalton's own judgement was questioned. Horace Walpole, writing probably in 1787–8, said that Dalton persuaded the king to extract the heads from a Leonardo manuscript and paste these into two volumes. In 1790 it was thought that Dalton would never advise the king to purchase the important Orléans collection, whose sale was being considered. Dalton, in addition to acting for the king, for Grosvenor, and for Lord Bute, is known to have advised Thomas Hollis and Sir James Lowther about pictures. Dalton died on 7 February 1791 at St James's Palace, where he lived. His own collection was sold at Christies on 9 and 11 April in the same year.

JOHN SUNDERLAND

Sources J. Ingamells, ed., *A dictionary of British and Irish travellers in Italy, 1701–1800* (1997) · F. Russell, 'Dalton, Richard', *Dictionary of art* (1996) · D. Mahon and N. Turner, *Drawings by Guercino in the collection of her majesty the queen at Windsor Castle* (1987) · W. T. Whitley, *Artists and their friends in England, 1700–1799*, 2 vols. (1928); repr. (1968) · S. C. Hutchison, *The history of the Royal Academy, 1768–1986*, 2nd edn (1986) · M. Levey, *The later Italian pictures in the collection of her majesty the queen* (1964)
Archives Mount Stuart Trust Archives, Isle of Bute, Bute MSS
Likenesses J. Zoffany, group portrait, oils, *c.*1765–1768, Tate collection [see illus.]

Dalton [*née* Hamilton Fox], **(Florence) Ruth**, Lady Dalton (**1890–1966**), politician and public servant, was born on 9 March 1890 at Oak House, Farnborough, the only child of Thomas Hamilton Fox, a brewer, and his wife, Elizabeth Valentine (d. 1931), daughter of Captain Stuart Ogilvy, a soldier. She later characterized her childhood as isolated and loveless; she in turn was felt to lack warmth and affection. Although emotionally deprived, her entire life was financially secure, not least because of the generosity of her mother's friend Sir Arthur Paterson. Ruth was educated, as were many middle-class girls of her generation, by a mixture of private tutors and formal schooling; she attended Chantry Mount School, Bishop's Stortford. Between 1909 and 1914 Ruth studied for a BSc(Econ), specializing in the new discipline of sociology, at the London School of Economics, where she belonged to the Fabians, was elected joint secretary of the students' union, and met (Edward) Hugh John Neale *Dalton (1887–1962); on 28 May 1914 they married. On 17 December 1917, when Hugh was away on active service, Ruth gave birth to a daughter, Helen. In 1921 the daughter was sent to a residential home and, although the Daltons saw their daughter, she did not live with them. In June 1922 Helen died of a kidney disease and the two were apparently filled with remorse, blaming themselves for her death.

During the First World War the government temporarily employed large numbers of women. Ruth Dalton translated foreign newspapers in the war trade intelligence department and then from 1918 to 1919 she worked as assistant secretary to the Workers' Educational Association. In the early 1920s Ruth and Hugh lived part-time in Cambridge, where he was prospective parliamentary candidate for the Labour Party and where Ruth worked for the birth-control movement, running Cambridge's first birth-control clinic with Leah Manning.

In 1925 Ruth Dalton was elected to the London county council (LCC) for Peckham. She was a member of the LCC from 1925 to 1931, and an alderman from 1936 to 1942 and 1946 to 1952. She became chair of the parks committee and introduced the practice of holding sculpture exhibitions in London parks. She helped to develop a green-belt policy and was responsible for redecorating and reopening Kenwood House after its transfer to the LCC. Although she was politically active in her own right, many of Ruth Dalton's activities were intertwined with her husband's political career. The most unusual support she gave him came in 1929. He was MP for Peckham but had squabbled with his agent and had decided to fight a different seat at the general election. He was selected for Bishop Auckland, but in December 1928, a few months before the general election was due to be called, the sitting MP, Benjamin Spoor, died. If Hugh had resigned his seat in Peckham it would have created three by-elections (Bishop Auckland, Peckham, and Gateshead, the seat held by John Beckett, who was intending to contest Peckham). Following the recent precedent of Hilda and Walter Runciman at St Ives, a solution was found in Ruth's standing in the by-election for Bishop Auckland on the understanding that she would step aside in her husband's favour when the general election was called. Ruth Dalton won the by-election held in February 1929, took her seat in parliament, asked her first question, and made her maiden speech (which was well received) on 13 March 1929, concerning the appalling poverty created by unemployment in her constituency. Asked by Ramsay MacDonald to consider continuing her political career, she told him that she had never wished to become an MP and preferred her work on the LCC: 'there we *do* things. Here it all seems to be talk' (Brookes, 66). She duly stood aside in May 1929 when the general election was called. She continued to help Hugh at elections, speaking at meetings and dealing with the press. At this time the two were close, but this did not last.

During the Second World War Ruth Dalton was keen to move away from her husband and, in common with many other women, to take up war work. Early in 1941 she joined the Ministry of Supply and became a liaison officer with hostels for women workers in armaments factories

in the north of England. Although she lived in Manchester, a city she detested, and had to travel, which was not easy in wartime, she enjoyed her work. What she really wanted to do, however, was to work in France and in 1944 she managed to secure her release from the Ministry of Supply and to join the United Nations Relief and Rehabilitation Administration. At first she worked in London as the personal assistant to the director of the organization's displaced persons division before moving to France.

On her return to Britain in 1946 Ruth Dalton moved back with her husband, now chancellor of the exchequer, and resumed the role of supportive politician's wife. She also resumed her own public work: from 1946 she was a member of the executive and publicity committees of the National Trust; from 1946 to 1952 she was an LCC alderman again; she sat on the board of the Royal Ballet; and from 1957 to 1962 she was a member of the Arts Council. She embodied the early Labour Party's emphasis on personal improvement and uplifting activities, and always displayed a strong, if dour, sense of public duty. Her pale skin, dark eyes, short hair, and absence of make-up contributed to a stern image. She died four years after her husband, on 15 March 1966, at her home, 185A Ashley Gardens, London, and was cremated at Golders Green on 21 March.

HELEN JONES

Sources B. Pimlott, *Hugh Dalton* (1985) · H. Dalton, *Call back yesterday: memoirs, 1887–1931* (1953) · H. Dalton, *The fateful years: memoirs, 1931–1945* (1957) · H. Dalton, *High tide and after: memoirs, 1945–1960* (1962) · *The Second World War diary of Hugh Dalton, 1940–1945*, ed. B. Pimlott (1986) · *The political diary of Hugh Dalton, 1918–1940, 1945–1960*, ed. B. Pimlott (1986) · *The Times* (17 March 1966) · *The Times* (19 March 1966) · *Register, 1895–1932*, London School of Economics (1934) · P. Brookes, *Women at Westminster: an account of women in the British parliament, 1918–1966* (1967) · b. cert. · m. cert. · d. cert.
Archives BLPES, letters to her husband, condolences on his death, and address book | FILM BFI NFTVA, news footage
Likenesses photographs, BLPES
Wealth at death £30,228: probate, 12 May 1966, *CGPLA Eng. & Wales*

Dalwood, Hubert Cyril (1924–1976), sculptor, was born on 2 June 1924 at 78 Whiteladies Road, Clifton, Bristol, the eldest of two sons and a daughter of Cyril Herbert Dalwood (1889–1961), a commercial traveller, and his wife, Edith Mary, *née* Mitchell (1887–1965). Widely known as Nibs, Dalwood was one of the most charismatic, talented, and innovative British sculptors of his generation. He left school in Bristol at an early age and was apprenticed to the Bristol Aeroplane Company (1940–44), during which time he attended the Bristol School of Art part-time. After two years with the Royal Navy he entered the pioneering Bath Academy of Arts, Corsham Court, Wiltshire (1946–9), where his principal tutor was Kenneth Armitage.

In 1950 Dalwood won a travelling scholarship to Italy, where he worked in a bronze foundry in Milan, becoming familiar with contemporary Italian sculpture and acquiring important technical skills. In Sicily he met Mary Lilian Nicolson (1923–1991), a university lecturer, whom he married in London on 15 December 1951; they had two daughters. He returned to Britain that year and was appointed to the Newport School of Art. His work hitherto had been carved, but he now began to model in clay for casting. Although he cast some works in lead, most remained in plaster and, consequently, few have survived. His sculptures were then largely figurative, some in relief; an example from this period is *Standing Draped Figure* (lead, 1954, Tate collection). Initially realistic, his figures became more distorted as he sought to express physically the subject's phenomenological experience. Influenced by Rodin and Degas as well as by contemporary sculpture, many of these works were of old women and defied the conventional beauty of the nude.

Having shown there since 1949, in 1954 Dalwood had his first one-man exhibition at Gimpel Fils, London, who would remain his dealers. He became a Gregory fellow at the University of Leeds in 1955. There he joined a vibrant group of innovative artists and teachers centred on the Leeds College of Art under the leadership of Harry Thubron. He continued with his figuration until 1957, when the sculptures became more abstract and allusive. He produced a significant body of works which were totemic in nature and this new direction was announced in the title of *Icon* (1958, Leeds City Art Gallery). Several, such as *Double Casket* (1958, priv. coll.), appeared utilitarian and he described them as ritualistic objects. Their cryptic quality was enhanced by their decoration with a range of abstract marks, at times calligraphic and often sexual. Such pieces were complemented by a series of reliefs, the forms of which were equally suggestive. All the works were cast in aluminium and the retention of the immediacy of his handling of the clay became his hallmark. He left Leeds in 1960, his first marriage ended in divorce in April 1963, and on 19 November of that year he married (Phoebe) Caroline Gaunt (*b*. 1932), a research bacteriologist and teacher, with whom he had two sons; they settled at 223A Randolph Avenue in Maida Vale, London.

In terms of critical reputation and, arguably, the quality of the work, 1958 to 1962 was Dalwood's great period. The establishment of his reputation was marked in 1959 by the award of first prize at the John Moore's exhibition in Liverpool for his ovoid *Large Object* (aluminium, 1959, casts in the Tate collection, Museum of Modern Art, New York, and Art Gallery of Ontario, Toronto). He received a number of commissions, including works for the universities of Liverpool, Leeds, Manchester, and Oxford, and his success was capped by his exhibition at the 1962 Venice Biennale at which he won the David Bright prize. For a time, his work acquired an overtly political accent; with *OAS Assassins* (aluminium, 1962, Tate collection), for example, he commented upon contemporary political violence.

Dalwood became an increasingly familiar figure in the art world of London in the 1960s, though his rejection of the constructed formalism of Anthony Caro set him outside the dominant sculptural idiom. He taught part-time at various institutions, including the Royal College of Art and the Hornsey, Leeds, and Maidstone schools of art, and made several prolonged foreign trips. He was invited to international sculpture symposia in Yugoslavia (1963), Canada (1967), and Czechoslovakia (1968). As visiting professor at the University of Illinois, Urbana (1964–5), he was able to see the United States, where he was struck by the sculptors of the west coast, but especially by the Illinois landscape. The flat expanses punctuated by man-made structures such as grain silos stimulated his existing interest in architecture and spatial relations. The effect of this would emerge in a new group of sculptures, partly constructed from prefabricated aluminium parts, in which arrangements of columns mixed with more organic forms. This departure was marked by *Mirage* (1966, destroyed), shown at the 1966 Battersea Park open-air sculpture exhibition. The reflective surfaces of such pieces introduced dialogues between the sculpture, the viewer, and their surroundings. In addition to a range of forms, he experimented with new materials, including plastics, enamelled panels, light boxes, and kinetic elements. A second American sojourn at the University of Wisconsin, Madison (1967–8), was followed by a number of sculptures named after local places, such as *Oconomowoc I* (aluminium, 1969, artist's estate). These aped the terrain and included arrangements of columns and patterns like river-beds. Landscape and gardens would remain Dalwood's predominant concern, though his interest lay in man's intervention in nature rather than the pastoral.

In 1968 Dalwood became head of sculpture at the Hornsey School of Art in north London, and in 1974 he was appointed to the same post at the Central School of Art and Design. As a teacher he encouraged diversity and individualism so that his influence was not reflected in a transfer of style. He acquired a huge studio in Stepney, east London, where he eventually settled with his last partner, the sculptor Rosalind Archer; his second marriage ended in divorce in February 1974. Relatively few sculptures were produced during the 1970s, a reflection of the demands of full-time teaching and the number of large-scale projects he undertook. Two enormous sculptures (both subsequently dismantled) were made for exhibitions. The first, *Arbor* (1972), for the 'British sculpture '72' exhibition at the Royal Academy, where it filled a room, incorporated artificial grass and combined organic forms with an architectural structure. In the second, *Otera*—shown at 'Magic and Strong Medicine' at the Walker Art Gallery, Liverpool, and the Hayward Gallery, London, in 1973—the deep red colouring and such features as fabric scarves revealed Dalwood's growing fascination with Japanese culture. In 1972 he had won a Churchill scholarship to visit India and the Far East, where he had found Japanese gardens to be the greatest achievement in man's interaction with nature. This experience stimulated a series of sculptures—some called *Bonzai Gardens*—which incorporated gravel and even plants.

In his last years Dalwood sought a sculpture which defied scale (a long-held fascination) and worked only on small or monumental pieces. Collaborations with two architects—Tom Hancock and Tony Irving—provided several commissions from the Arab states, some of which involved actual landscaping, and these informed the table-top works too. Thus his last sculptures were imaginary landscapes, some of which included such natural features as stylized clouds, while others carried more architectural structures. The profusion of these suggests that he was aware of his apparently sudden final illness, the rare systemic sclerosis. Dalwood died on 2 November 1976 in St Bartholomew's Hospital, London, and was cremated on 5 November at Finchley. He had continued as an active figure in British sculpture, as a teacher, and as a member of professional bodies. However, by the time of his death interest in his work had waned and a posthumous retrospective in 1979 won a polite rather than enthusiastic critical response.

CHRIS STEPHENS

Sources C. Stephens, *The sculpture of Hubert Dalwood* (1999) · J. Jones, recorded interviews with Hubert Dalwood, priv. coll. · N. Lynton, introduction, *Hubert Dalwood: sculptures and reliefs* (1979) [exhibition catalogue, Hayward Gallery, London, 24 Jan – 4 March 1979] · *CGPLA Eng. & Wales* (1977) · b. cert. · d. cert.
Archives SOUND priv. coll., recorded interviews of Dalwood by John Jones

Wealth at death £23,442: administration, 9 Dec 1977, *CGPLA Eng. & Wales*

PICTURE CREDITS

Cranfield, Lionel, first earl of Middlesex (1575-1645)—private collection. Photograph: Photographic Survey, Courtauld Institute of Art, London

Cranko, John Cyril (1927-1973)—© Cecil Beaton Archive, Sotheby's; collection National Portrait Gallery, London

Cranmer, Thomas (1489-1556)—© National Portrait Gallery, London

Cranstoun, George, Lord Corehouse (d. 1850)—Scottish National Portrait Gallery

Crapper, Thomas (1837-1910)—V&A Images, The Victoria and Albert Museum; photograph National Portrait Gallery, London

Craven, Hawes (1837-1910)—V&A Images, The Victoria and Albert Museum

Craven, Pauline Marie Armande Aglaé (1808-1891)—© National Portrait Gallery, London

Craven, Peter Theodore (1934-1963)—Vintage Speedway Magazine / John Chaplin Collection

Craven, Sir William (c.1545-1618)—Phillips Picture Library

Craven, William, earl of Craven (bap. 1608, d. 1697)—private collection; photograph National Portrait Gallery, London

Crawford, Emily (1831?-1915)—© National Portrait Gallery, London

Crawford, William Sharman (1781-1861)—photograph © Ulster Museum. Photograph reproduced with the kind permission of the Trustees of the National Museums & Galleries of Northern Ireland

Crawley, Aidan Merivale (1908-1993)—© National Portrait Gallery, London

Crawshay, Richard (1739-1810)—© National Museums and Galleries of Wales

Craxton, (Thomas) Harold Hunt (1885-1971)—private collection

Craxton, Janet Helen Rosemary (1929-1981)—private collection

Crazy Gang (act. 1931-1962)—© Cecil Beaton Archive, Sotheby's; collection National Portrait Gallery, London

Creagh, Sir Garrett O'Moore (1848-1923)—© National Portrait Gallery, London

Crealock, John North (1836-1895)—© National Portrait Gallery, London

Creasy, Sir Edward Shepherd (1812-1878)—© National Portrait Gallery, London

Creech, Thomas (1659-1700)—© Bodleian Library, University of Oxford

Creed, Sir Thomas Percival (1897-1969)—© National Portrait Gallery, London

Creevey, Thomas (1768-1838)—private collection

Creighton, Louise Hume (1850-1936)—© Estate of Glyn Philpot

Creighton, Mandell (1843-1901)—© National Portrait Gallery, London

Creighton, Robert (1593-1672)—photograph: The Paul Mellon Centre for Studies in British Art

Cresswell, Madam (d. c.1698)—© National Portrait Gallery, London

Crèvecoeur, J. Hector St John de (1735-1813)—© National Portrait Gallery, London

Crew, Nathaniel, third Baron Crew (1633-1721)—© Bodleian Library, University of Oxford

Crewe, Frances Anne, Lady Crewe (bap. 1748, d. 1818)—private collection. Photograph: Photographic Survey, Courtauld Institute of Art, London

Crewe, Sir Randolph (bap. 1559, d. 1646)—photograph by courtesy Sotheby's Picture Library, London

Cribb, Tom (1781-1848)—unknown collection; photograph Sotheby's Picture Library, London / National Portrait Gallery, London

Crichton, Sir Archibald William (1791-1865)—private collection

Crichton, James [the Admirable Crichton] (1560-1582)—The Royal Collection © 2004 HM Queen Elizabeth II

Crippen, Hawley Harvey (1862-1910)—Getty Images - Hulton Archive

Cripps, Charles Alfred, first Baron Parmoor (1852-1941)—© National Portrait Gallery, London

Cripps, Dame Isobel, Lady Cripps (1891-1979)—© Popperfoto

Cripps, Sir (Richard) Stafford (1889-1952)—© Karsh / Camera Press; collection National Portrait Gallery, London

Crisp, Sir Nicholas, first baronet (c.1599-1666)—private collection; © reserved in the photograph

Crisp, Samuel (1707-1783)—© National Portrait Gallery, London

Critchley, Sir Julian Michael Gordon (1930-2000)—© Jillian Edelstein / Network Photographers; collection National Portrait Gallery, London

Critchley, Macdonald (1900-1997)—© National Portrait Gallery, London

Crockett, Samuel Rutherford (1859-1914)—© National Portrait Gallery, London

Crockford, William (bap. 1776, d. 1844)—© Copyright The British Museum

Croft, Herbert (1603-1691)—Country Life Picture Library

Croft, Sir James (c.1518-1590)—Country Life Picture Library

Croft, William (bap. 1678, d. 1727)—Faculty of Music, University of Oxford

Croke, Sir George (c.1560-1642)—reproduced by permission of the Earl of Verulam. Photograph: Photographic Survey, Courtauld Institute of Art, London

Croke, Sir John (1553x6-1620)—by kind permission of the Earl of Leicester

and the Trustees of the Holkham Estate. Photograph: Photographic Survey, Courtauld Institute of Art, London

Croker, John Wilson (1780-1857)—by courtesy of the National Gallery of Ireland

Croly, George (1780-1860)—© National Portrait Gallery, London

Crome, John (1768-1821)—© National Portrait Gallery, London

Crome, John Berney (1794-1842)—© National Portrait Gallery, London

Crommelin, (Samuel-)Louis (1652-1727)—photograph © Ulster Museum. Photograph reproduced with the kind permission of the Trustees of the National Museums & Galleries of Northern Ireland

Crompton, Robert (1879-1941)—© Copyright The British Museum

Crompton, Samuel (1753-1827)—© National Portrait Gallery, London

Cromwell, Henry (1628-1674)—unknown collection; photograph Sotheby's Picture Library, London / National Portrait Gallery, London

Cromwell, Oliver (1599-1658)—in the collection of the Duke of Buccleuch and Queensberry KT

Cromwell, Richard (1626-1712)—© National Portrait Gallery, London

Cromwell, Thomas, earl of Essex (b. in or before 1485, d. 1540)—© The Frick Collection, New York

Cronin, Archibald Joseph (1896-1981)—© National Portrait Gallery, London

Crookes, Sir William (1832-1919)—© National Portrait Gallery, London

Crooks, William (1852-1921)—© National Portrait Gallery, London

Croone, William (1633-1684)—by permission of the Royal College of Physicians, London

Crosbie, Andrew (1736-1785)—in the collection of the Faculty of Advocates

Crosdill, John (1751/1755-1825)—© National Portrait Gallery, London

Crosland, (Charles) Anthony Raven (1918-1977)—Getty Images - Hulton Archive

Cross, Edward (bap. 1774, d. 1854)—Christie's Images Ltd. (2004)

Cross, John Kynaston (1832-1887)—© National Portrait Gallery, London

Cross, Richard Assheton, first Viscount Cross (1823-1914)—© National Portrait Gallery, London

Cross, Sir (Alfred) Rupert Neale (1912-1980)—photograph reproduced by courtesy of The British Academy

Crosse, Richard (1742-1810)—V&A Images, The Victoria and Albert Museum

Crossman, Richard Howard Stafford (1907-1974)—© National Portrait Gallery, London

Crotch, William (1775-1847)—© National Portrait Gallery, London

Crouch, Frederick Nicholls (1808-1896)—© National Portrait Gallery, London

Crowe, Eyre Evans (1799-1868)—V&A Images, The Victoria and Albert Museum

Crowe, Dame Sylvia (1901-1997)—© News International Newspapers Ltd

Crowther, Geoffrey, Baron Crowther (1907-1972)—© National Portrait Gallery, London

Crowther, Samuel Ajayi (c.1807-1891)—© National Portrait Gallery, London

Croxall, Samuel (1688/9-1752)—© National Portrait Gallery, London

Crozier, Eric John (1914-1994)—© reserved; collection National Portrait Gallery, London

Crozier, Francis Rawdon Moira (1796-1848)—© National Maritime Museum, London

Cruden, Alexander (1699-1770)—© National Portrait Gallery, London

Cruft, Charles Alfred (1852-1938)—© The Kennel Club Picture Library

Cruickshank, Andrew John Maxton (1907-1988)—Jon Lyons / Rex Features

Cruickshank, Helen Burness (1886-1975)—Collection Scottish Poetry Library, Edinburgh; photograph © National Galleries of Scotland

Cruikshank, George (1792-1878)—© National Portrait Gallery, London

Cruikshank, (Isaac) Robert (1789-1856)—© National Portrait Gallery, London

Cruikshank, William Cumberland (1745-1800)—reproduced by kind permission of the President and Council of the Royal College of Surgeons of England. Photograph: Photographic Survey, Courtauld Institute of Art, London

Crutchley, Sir Victor Alexander Charles (1893-1986)—© National Portrait Gallery, London

Cubitt, Lewis (1799-1883)—© National Portrait Gallery, London

Cubitt, Thomas (1788-1855)—© National Portrait Gallery, London

Cubitt, Sir William (1785-1861)—© National Portrait Gallery, London

Cudlipp, Hubert Kinsman [Hugh], Baron Cudlipp (1913-1998)—© Henri Cartier-Bresson / Magnum Photos; collection National Portrait Gallery, London

Cudworth, Ralph (1617-1688)—by permission of the Master, Fellows, and Scholars of Emmanuel College in the University of Cambridge

Culbertson, Robert (1765-1823)—© National Portrait Gallery, London

Cullen, Paul (1803-1878)—© National Portrait Gallery, London

Cullen, William (1710-1790)—Scottish National Portrait Gallery

Cullingworth, Charles James (1841-1908)—© reserved

Cullis, Winifred Clara (1875-1956)—© Yevonde Portrait Archive; collection National Portrait Gallery, London

Cullum, Sir John, sixth baronet (1733–1785)—Manor House Museum, Bury St Edmunds

Cullwick, Hannah (1833–1909)—The Master and Fellows, Trinity College, Cambridge

Culpeper, Nicholas (1616–1654)—© National Portrait Gallery, London

Cumberland, Richard (1632–1718)—reproduced by kind permission of the Bishop of Peterborough / Photograph: The Paul Mellon Centre for Studies in British Art

Cumberland, Richard (1732–1811)—© National Portrait Gallery, London

Cuming, Hugh (1791–1865)—© National Portrait Gallery, London

Cumming, (Felicity) Anne (1917–1993)—© News International Newspapers Ltd

Cumming, Constance Frederica Gordon- (1837–1924)—© National Portrait Gallery, London

Cumming, John (1807–1881)—© National Portrait Gallery, London

Cumming, Sir Mansfield George Smith (1859–1923)—© Imperial War Museum, London

Cummings, Arthur John (1882–1957)—© National Portrait Gallery, London

Cunard, Nancy Clara (1896–1965)—© Cecil Beaton Archive, Sotheby's; collection National Portrait Gallery, London

Cunard, Sir Samuel, first baronet (1787–1865)—© National Portrait Gallery, London

Cunningham, Sir Alan Gordon (1887–1983)—© reserved; The Imperial War Museum, London; photograph National Portrait Gallery, London

Cunningham, Andrew Browne, Viscount Cunningham of Hyndhope (1883–1963)—© Karsh / Camera Press; collection National Portrait Gallery, London

Cunningham, Sir Charles Craik (1906–1998)—© reserved; News International Syndication; photograph National Portrait Gallery, London

Cunningham, Francis (1820–1875)—Scottish National Portrait Gallery

Cunningham, Sir George (1888–1963)—© National Portrait Gallery, London

Cunningham, Sir John Henry Dacres (1885–1962)—© National Portrait Gallery, London

Cunningham, Waddell (1729–1797)—photograph © Ulster Museum. Photograph reproduced with the kind permission of the Trustees of the National Museums & Galleries of Northern Ireland

Cunningham, William, eighth earl of Glencairn (1610/11–1664)—Scottish National Portrait Gallery

Cunningham, William (1849–1919)—Scottish National Portrait Gallery

Curll, Walter (1575–1647)—photograph: The Paul Mellon Centre for Studies in British Art

Curran, Sir Charles John (1921–1980)—© National Portrait Gallery, London

Curran, John Philpot (1750–1817)—National Gallery of Ireland

Curran, Peter Francis (1860–1910)—by permission of the People's History Museum

Curran, Sir Samuel Crowe (1912–1998)—© News International Newspapers Ltd

Currie, Sir Donald (1825–1909)—Scottish National Portrait Gallery

Currie, Philip Henry Wodehouse, Baron Currie (1834–1906)—© National Portrait Gallery, London

Curry, John Anthony (1949–1994)—© The Robert Mapplethorpe Foundation. Courtesy Art + Commerce Anthology; collection National Portrait Gallery, London

Curtin, John (1885–1945)—by permission of the National Library of Australia

Curtis, Ian Kevin (1956–1980)—Photography by Kevin Cummins / IDOLS; collection National Portrait Gallery, London

Curtis, John Harrison (1778–1860)—© National Portrait Gallery, London

Curtis, Lionel George (1872–1955)—© National Portrait Gallery, London

Curtis, Dame Myra (1886–1971)—Getty Images - Charles Hewitt

Curwen, John Christian (1756–1828)—© National Portrait Gallery, London

Curzon, Sir Clifford Michael (1907–1982)—© reserved; collection National Portrait Gallery, London

Curzon, George Nathaniel, Marquess Curzon of Kedleston (1859–1925)—The Royal Geographical Society, London

Curzon, Mary Victoria, Lady Curzon of Kedleston (1870–1906)—© National Portrait Gallery, London

Curzon, Robert, fourteenth Baron Zouche of Harringworth (1810–1873)—© National Portrait Gallery, London

Cusack, Cyril James (1910–1993)—© Estate of Frederick William Daniels; collection National Portrait Gallery, London

Cusack, Margaret Anne [the Nun of Kenmare] (1829–1899)—© National Portrait Gallery, London

Cushing, Peter Wilton (1913–1994)—© Kenneth Hughes / National Portrait Gallery, London

Cushing, Winifred Emma [Patience Strong] (1907–1990)—© National Portrait Gallery, London

Cushny, Arthur Robertson (1866–1926)—Wellcome Library, London

Cust, Sir Lionel Henry (1859–1929)—by courtesy of Felix Rosenstiel's Widow & Son Ltd., London, on behalf of the Estate of Sir John Lavery; collection National Portrait Gallery, London

Cust, Maria Eleanor Vere (1862/3–1958)—The Royal Geographical Society, London

Cutforth, Reynolds [René] (1909–1984)—© Fay Godwin; collection National Portrait Gallery, London

Cutler, Sir Horace Walter (1912–1997)—© News International Newspapers Ltd

Cutler, Sir John (1607/8–1693)—Guildhall Art Gallery, Corporation of London

Cutner, Solomon (1902–1988)—© National Portrait Gallery, London

Cutts, John, Baron Cutts of Gowran (1660/61–1707)—© National Portrait Gallery, London

Cuzzoni, Francesca (1696–1778)—© Copyright The British Museum

Czaplicka, Marya Antonina (1884–1921)—© National Portrait Gallery, London

Dadd, Richard (1817–1886)—© Bethlem Royal Hospital Archives and Museum

Dahl, Michael (1659–1743)—© National Portrait Gallery, London

Dahl, Roald (1916–1990)—Getty Images – Dumant

Dale, David (1739–1806)—© National Portrait Gallery, London

Dale, Sir Henry Hallett (1875–1968)—© Karsh / Camera Press; collection National Portrait Gallery, London

Dale, Robert William (1829–1895)—© National Portrait Gallery, London

Dale, Samuel (bap. 1659, d. 1739)—© National Portrait Gallery, London

Daley, Harry (1901–1971)—© 1978, Estate of Duncan Grant, courtesy of Henrietta Garnett; collection Guildhall Art Gallery; photograph National Portrait Gallery, London

Dalgairns, John Dobrée (1818–1876)—London Oratory; photograph © National Portrait Gallery, London

Dallas, Alexander Robert Charles (1791–1869)—© National Portrait Gallery, London

Dalrymple, Sir David, third baronet, Lord Hailes (1726–1792)—photograph by kind permission of The National Trust for Scotland

Dalrymple, Sir Hew, first baronet, Lord North Berwick (1652–1737)—Sir Hew Hamilton-Dalrymple Bt

Dalrymple, James, first Viscount Stair (1619–1695)—photograph by kind permission of The National Trust for Scotland

Dalrymple, John, first earl of Stair (1648–1707)—photograph by kind permission of The National Trust for Scotland

Dalrymple, John, second earl of Stair (1673–1747)—private collection; photograph National Portrait Gallery, London

Dalton, (Edward) Hugh Neale, Baron Dalton (1887–1962)—© reserved; collection Science & Society Picture Library; photograph National Portrait Gallery, London

Dalton, John (1766–1844)—© National Portrait Gallery, London

Dalton, Richard (c.1715–1791)—© Tate, London, 2004